ASPLOS XX

Twentieth International Conference on Architectural Support for Programming Languages and Operating Systems

March 14–18, 2015
Istanbul, Turkey

Sponsored by:

ACM SIGARCH

ACM SIGOPS

ACM SIGPLAN

Association for Computing Machinery

In co-operation with: ACM SIGBED

With Support from:

Bilkent University, NSF, VMware, Intel, Google, ARM, Oracle, Microsoft Research, Facebook, IBM Research, and HP Labs

Association for Computing Machinery

Advancing Computing as a Science & Profession

The Association for Computing Machinery
2 Penn Plaza, Suite 701
New York, New York 10121-0701

ISBN: 978-1-4503-2835-7

Additional copies may be ordered prepaid from:

ACM Order Department
PO Box 30777
New York, NY 10087-0777, USA

Phone: 1-800-342-6626 (USA and Canada)
+1-212-626-0500 (Global)
Fax: +1-212-944-1318
E-mail: acmhelp@acm.org
Hours of Operation: 8:30 am – 4:30 pm ET

ACM Order #: 415155

Printed in the USA

ASPLOS 2015 General Chairs' Welcome

On behalf of the ASPLOS organizing committee, we are very pleased to welcome you to Istanbul, Turkey, for the 20th International Conference on Architectural Support for Programming Languages and Operating Systems (ASPLOS-XX) on March 14-18, 2015. Istanbul is a jewel of a city, with its unique historical accumulation and splendid natural beauty, blended into a modern metropolis. Each civilization that has made Istanbul its home has left its mark in sublime and splendid ways, and the result is a city that gives one the feeling of universal history at every step from the Roman era to the Byzantine and Ottoman eras.

Visitors will enjoy a wide variety of activities in a city where two continents meet on the blue waters of the Bosphorus to offer an abundance of unique natural, historical, cultural, and culinary experiences. Many of the historical sites including the Blue Mosque, Hagia (St.) Sophia, Hippodrome, Grand Covered Bazaar, Obelisk of Theodosius, Serpentine Column, The Maiden's Tower, Galata, and Basilica Cistern will be explored as part of our social activity. The conference banquet will be held at the Bosphorus, where we will enjoy a view of many historic places in Asia and Europe simultaneously.

ASPLOS has been the best place to share and exchange innovative ideas regarding integrative research comprising computer architecture, programming languages, and operating systems. This year is no different thanks to the organizing committee, reviewers, contributing authors, and particularly the program committee and the chair, Sandhya Dwarkadas. She and the program committee did a great job in selecting an extremely interesting program. Several exciting workshops and tutorials will also be part of the conference. This year, we created a new ASPLOS-ACM Student Research Competition (SRC) sponsored by ACM and Microsoft Research. ASPLOS-ACM SRC is a forum for undergraduates and graduate students to share their research results, exchange ideas, and improve their communication skills while competing for prizes. We would like to thank all members of the organizing committee and steering committee as well as the technical program committee and the external reviewers.

We would also like to thank the corporate supporters of ASPLOS who have provided generous financial support: VMware – our primary supporter this year, Google, ARM, Oracle, Microsoft Research, and IBM Research. Our thanks also go to ACM SIGARCH, ACM SIGOPS, ACM SIGPLAN, and the National Science Foundation for providing funding for the student grants.

We hope you find the program exciting as we have a packed program with 48 technical papers, a panel, banquet, business meeting, two keynotes, a WACI session, and potentially a debate. We hope this provides a stimulating platform and you enjoy staying in Istanbul.

Let us meet where continents meet!

Ozcan Ozturk
ASPLOS 2015 General co-Chair
Bilkent University

Kemal Ebcioglu
ASPLOS 2015 General co-Chair
Global Supercomputing

ASPLOS 2015 Program Chair's Message

It is my pleasure and privilege to serve as program chair for ASPLOS 2015 - the Twentieth International Conference on Architectural Support for Programming Languages and Operating Systems. This year's conference has set new records in terms of the number of submissions, and reinforces ASPLOS's tradition of encouraging work on innovative multidisciplinary research spanning computer architecture and hardware, programming languages and compilers, operating systems and networking, and applications.

The 2015 conference saw a record 287 submissions (compared to 217 in 2014, an increase of 32%), with a total of 1,018 paper authors from 287 institutions spread across at least 22 countries and spanning 5 continents: a clear indication that our community is growing, and that ASPLOS is the premier venue of choice for disseminating high quality interdisciplinary work.

There was a wide diversity in topics, ranging from quantum computing to human computer interaction, with the most popular being scheduling and resource management, memory systems, power/energy/thermal management, and multicore and heterogeneous architectures. 97 papers self-identified as relating to architecture, 72 to parallelism, 70 to operating systems, 51 to programming models and languages, and 34 to compiler optimizations.

Some Notes on the Review Process: All reviewing and discussion, including that at the PC meeting, was double blind. As in past ASPLOS conferences, I used a 2-phase review process, with each paper receiving 3 reviews in round 1, and a minimum of an additional 2 reviews in round 2. In order to improve the quality of review assignment, in conjunction with the paper title and abstract (with sometimes a need to skim the paper directly), I used a combination of topic and interest match with reviewers, and suggestions for reviewers from both the authors and the round 1 reviewers (during the round 2 assignment).

I continued to monitor reviews for papers through both rounds 1 and 2 as they came in for quality, substance, and tone, to correct any expertise mismatch, and to find experts in the multiple areas each paper might span, including experts outside of the program and external review committees, a step that is essential for a conference with the breadth that ASPLOS covers. Reviewer feedback in this process was extremely helpful.

In keeping with ASPLOS'14 and other conferences, not all papers were moved to round 2. In particular, papers with no round 1 reviews advocating acceptance, and with clear consensus (based both on substantive review content and comment exchange) among the reviewers that the paper did not rise above the acceptance bar for the conference, did not move to round 2. Approximately 35% of the papers fell in this category. Each of these decisions involved the active participation of all the reviewers.

After the rebuttal phase, each paper was assigned a discussion lead. The discussion lead's job was to carefully read all reviews, the rebuttal, and prior online comments (several papers had extensive online discussions after both rounds 1 and 2), and then initiate a discussion with the goal of reaching a conclusion on whether papers were to be accepted, rejected, or discussed at the PC meeting. The goal of the discussion lead (and my monitoring) was to ensure that every reviewer participated in the discussion after reading the other reviews and the rebuttal. During this process, if new reviewers were considered required based on the rebuttal content, they were sought.

The program committee meeting was held at the Chicago O'Hare Hilton on November 7th, 2014. All but two PC members were in attendance, both due to medical emergencies. PC members had access to the reviews for all papers for which they had no declared conflict. Paper authors were not revealed during the PC meeting, and since the discussion continued to be blind, PC papers were not singled out for separate discussion. PC members were asked to leave the room for papers for which they were declared as a conflict (which included any papers they were authors on) prior to revealing the paper title and number being discussed.

During the PC meeting, all papers categorized as a preliminary accept (15) were discussed first. The PC also had a chance during and prior to the PC meeting to bring up papers for discussion that were classified as tentatively rejected (i.e., all papers were open for discussion at the PC meeting). The majority of the time during the PC meeting was spent on the papers categorized as needing discussion. The result of the extensive reviewing, online discussion, and PC meeting is now in your hands for your reading pleasure, with 48 accepted papers, 16 of which were shepherded. In addition to the decision process, for every paper where the authors chose to provide a rebuttal, the discussion lead, in collaboration with the other reviewers, provided the authors with a summary outlining the main criteria leading to the decision outcome for the paper (whether or not the rebuttal answered reviewer questions or addressed concerns or shortcomings expressed in the reviews), along with feedback for improvement.

The Program: In addition to the 48 accepted papers, the conference includes two invited keynote speeches. Edward Lee from the University of California at Berkeley will talk about incorporating time into the semantics of programs in support of cyber-physical systems. Guruduth Banavar from IBM will give a talk on the capabilities of and the challenges in realizing cognitive computing. We will maintain the tradition of past ASPLOS conferences in convening a Wild and Crazy Ideas (WACI) session, organized by John Criswell, Arrvindh Shriraman, and Emmett Witchel. Lightning sessions each morning will provide a quick introduction to the key ideas that will be presented in the talks that day. New this year is the ASPLOS-ACM Student Research Competition, which will allow a showcase for student research via poster presentations during the poster session.

Acknowledgements: A big thank you to my 35 program committee members and 68 external review committee members for their hard work and for gracefully handling the extra review load from the unanticipated large increase in the number of papers (up to 23 papers were reviewed by each PC member, and up to 9 papers reviewed by each ERC member, for a total of 1,223 reviews). Thanks also to the 36 outside reviewers who provided additional expert opinions. Andrew Chien handled my conflicts, assigning reviewers to these papers and monitoring both online and PC meeting discussion. John Carter was my double checker in tracking paper outcomes during the PC meeting and allowed me to retain my sanity toward the end of the day. Thanks to Eddie Kohler, HotCRP's author, for the quick follow up to my questions and on fixes for my occasional bug reports; HotCRP and its coloring and tracking features were extremely useful through the review process. Dave Costello, technical staff member here at the University of Rochester, made installing HotCRP a cinch, making himself available at all times to analyze any performance issues and to ensure that the server had no hiccups through the submission and review process. My students Xiaowan Dong and Sharanyan Srikanthan were a tremendous help in tailoring the HotCRP php scripts to my needs. A special thank you to Xiaowan for her attention to detail and her patience in generating summary statistics as I asked for them.

I follow in the footsteps of past PC chairs, with particular thanks to Sarita Adve for establishing a solid review process and for including me in the 2014 ASPLOS program committee so that I was ready and thinking about 2015. The steering committee provided valuable guidance on interpreting and setting policies. The organizing committee and the general chairs, Ozcan Ozturk and Kemal Ebcioglu, deserve special thanks for taking care of all the logistics and allowing me to focus on the technical program, and for bringing us together for the conference at such a spectacular venue.

Last, but not least, thanks to the 1,018 authors of the submitted papers for sending their work in to ASPLOS. I hope you enjoy reading the papers in these proceedings and continue to submit your interdisciplinary work to ASPLOS. The conference provides a unique opportunity for stimulating interaction with experts across a diverse range of subdisciplines and I look forward to seeing many of you at the conference.

Sandhya Dwarkadas
ASPLOS 2015 Program Chair
University of Rochester

Table of Contents

Session 2B: Warehouse Scale Computing I

Session Chair: Lingjia Tang *(University of Michigan, Ann Arbor)*

Session 3A: Memory and Security II

Session Chair: Dan Tsafrir *(Technion – Israel Institute of Technology)*

Session 3B: Warehouse Scale Computing II

Session Chair: Yunji Chen *(Chinese Academy of Sciences)*

Session 4A: Energy

Session Chair: Arrvindh Shriraman *(Simon Fraser University)*

Session 4B: Reliability

Session Chair: Emery Berger *(University of Massachusetts, Amherst)*

Session 5A: I/O and Accelerators

Session Chair: Ganesh Gopalakrishnan *(University of Utah)*

Session 5B: Approximation

Session Chair: Steve Blackburn *(Australian National University)*

Keynote Address II

Session Chair: Kemal Ebcioglu *(Global Supercomputing)*

Session 6A: Parallelism and Compilation

Session Chair: Xipeng Shen *(North Carolina State University)*

Session 6B: Testing and Tainting, Verification and Security

Session Chair: Josep Torrellas *(University of Illinois at Urbana-Champaign)*

Session 7A: Memory Models II

Session Chair: Hans Boehm *(Google)*

Session 7B: GPUs

Session Chair: Ozcan Ozturk *(Bilkent University)*

Session 8A: Scalable Parallelism

Session Chair: Osman Unsal *(Barcelona Supercomputing Center)*

Session 8B: Memory Management

ASPLOS 2015 Conference Organization

General Chairs:	Ozcan Ozturk *(Bilkent University, Turkey)* Kemal Ebcioglu *(Global Supercomputing, USA)*
Program Chair:	Sandhya Dwarkadas *(University of Rochester, USA)*
Publicity Chairs:	Onur Mutlu *(Carnegie Mellon University, USA)* Engin Ipek *(University of Rochester, USA)* Atakan Dogan *(Anadolu University, Turkey)*
Registration Chair:	Suleyman Tosun *(Hacettepe University, Turkey)*
Finance Chair:	Smail Niar *(University of Valenciennes, France)*
Local Arrangements Chair:	Alper Sen *(Bogazici University, Turkey)*
Industry Chairs:	Emre Ozer *(ARM, UK)* Mustafa Ozdal *(Intel, USA)* Bugra Gedik *(Bilkent University, Turkey)*
Tutorial Chairs:	Osman Unsal *(Barcelona Supercomputing Center, Spain)* Serdar Tasiran *(Koc University, Turkey)*
Workshop Chairs:	Alper Buyuktosunoglu *(IBM, USA)* Augusto Vega *(IBM, USA)* Haluk Topcuoglu *(Marmara University, Turkey)*
Travel Grant Chair:	Ulya Karpuzcu *(University of Minnesota, USA)*
Student Advocates:	Gurhan Kucuk *(Yeditepe University, Turkey)* Eren Kursun *(JPM, USA)*
Web Chair:	Oguz Ergin *(TOBB University, Turkey)*
Poster/Lightning Session Chair:	Arrvindh Shriraman *(Simon Fraser University, Canada)*
Submission Chairs:	Xiaowan Dong *(University of Rochester, USA)* Sharanyan Srikanthan *(University of Rochester, USA)*
Steering Committee:	Sarita Adve *(University of Illinois at Urbana-Champaign, USA)* Rajeev Balasubramonian *(University of Utah, USA)* Ras Bodik *(UC Berkeley, USA)* Doug Burger *(Microsoft, USA)* George Candea *(EPFL, Switzerland)* Al Davis *(University of Utah, USA)* Jeremy Gibbons *(Oxford University, UK)* Vivek Sarkar *(Rice University, USA)* David Wood *(University of Wisconsin, USA)*

Program Committee: Rajeev Balasubramonian *(University of Utah / HP Labs, USA)*
Andrew Baumann *(Microsoft, USA)*
Ricardo Bianchini *(Rutgers University / Microsoft, USA)*
Hans-J. Boehm *(Google, USA)*
John Carter *(IBM Research, USA)*
Calin Cascaval *(Qualcomm, USA)*
Yunji Chen *(ICT Chinese Academy of Sciences, China)*
Andrew Chien *(University of Chicago / Argonne, USA)*
Alan L. Cox *(Rice University, USA)*
John Criswell *(University of Rochester, USA)*
Angela Demke Brown *(University of Toronto, USA)*
Peter Druschel *(Max Planck Inst. for Software Systems, Germany)*
Sandhya Dwarkadas *(University of Rochester, USA)* (chair)
Jason Flinn *(University of Michigan, USA)*
Antonio Gonzalez *(UPC Barcelona, Spain)*
R. Govindarajan *(IISc, India)*
Dan Grossman *(University of Washington, USA)*
Boris Grot *(University of Edinburgh, UK)*
Erik Hagersten *(Uppsala University, Sweden)*
Mary Hall *(University of Utah, USA)*
Kim Hazelwood *(Google, USA)*
Gernot Heiser *(NICTA / UNSW, Australia)*
Hillery Hunter *(IBM Research, USA)*
Alvin Lebeck *(Duke University, USA)*
David Meisner *(Facebook, USA)*
Jason Nieh *(Columbia University, USA)*
Mark Oskin *(University of Washington, USA)*
Steve Reinhardt *(AMD, USA)*
Jennifer Sartor *(Ghent University/Vrije University, Belgium)*
Xipeng Shen *(North Carolina State University, USA)*
Tatiana Shpeisman *(Intel, USA)*
Asia Slowinska *(Vrije University, Netherlands)*
Serdar Tasiran *(Koc University, Turkey)*
Dan Tsafrir *(Technion – Israel Institute of Technology, Israel)*
Jeffrey Vetter *(Oak Ridge National Lab / Georgia Tech., USA)*
Yuanyuan Zhou *(UC San Diego, USA)*

External Review Committee:

Vikram Adve *(University of Illinois at Urbana-Champaign, USA)*
Gheorghe Almasi *(IBM T.J. Watson Research Center, USA)*
Jose Nelson Amaral *(University of Alberta, Canada)*
Sorav Bansal *(IIT Delhi, India)*
Emery Berger *(University of Massachusetts Amherst, USA)*
Steve Blackburn *(ANU, Australia)*
Pradip Bose *(IBM T. J. Watson Research Center, USA)*
Edouard Bugnion *(EPFL, Switzerland)*
Mainak Chaudhuri *(IIT Kanpur, India)*
Dilma Da Silva *(Texas A&M University, USA)*
Chen Ding *(University of Rochester, USA)*
Chris Emmons *(ARM, USA)*
Natalie Enright Jerger *(University of Toronto, Canada)*
Michael Ferdman *(Stony Brook University, USA)*
Maria Garzaran *(University of Illinois at Urbana-Champaign, USA)*
Ashvin Goel *(University of Toronto, Canada)*
Ganesh Gopalakrishnan *(University of Utah, USA)*
Haryadi Gunawi *(University of Chicago, USA)*
Rajiv Gupta *(UC Riverside, USA)*
Tim Harris *(Oracle Labs, Cambridge)*
Y. Charlie Hu *(Purdue University, USA)*
Galen Hunt *(Microsoft, USA)*
Engin Ipek *(University of Rochester, USA)*
Stefanos Kaxiras *(Uppsala University, Sweden)*
John Kim *(KAIST, Korea)*
Martha Kim *(Columbia University, USA)*
Steve Ko *(SUNY Buffalo, USA)*
Ulrich Kremer *(Rutgers University, USA)*
Orran Krieger *(Boston University, USA)*
John Kubiatowicz *(UC Berkeley, USA)*
Benjamin Lee *(Duke University, USA)*
Kai Li *(Princeton University, USA)*
Felix Xiaozhu Lin *(Purdue University, USA)*
David Lowenthal *(University of Arizona, USA)*
Brandon Lucia *(Microsoft Research, USA)*
Margaret Martonosi *(Princeton University, USA)*
Kathryn McKinley *(Microsoft/UT Austin, USA)*
Todd Mowry *(Carnegie Mellon University, USA)*
Madanlal Musuvathi *(Microsoft Research, USA)*
Abdullah Muzahid *(UT San Antonio, USA)*
Thu Nguyen *(Rutgers University, USA)*
Keshav Pingali *(UT Austin, USA)*
Gilles A Pokam *(Intel, USA)*
Arun Raghavan *(Oracle Labs, USA)*

External Review Committee (continued):

Ravi Rajwar *(Intel, USA)*
Umakishore Ramachandran *(Georgia Tech. University, USA)*
Parthasarathy Ranganathan *(Google, USA)*
Lawrence Rauchwerger *(Texas A&M University, USA)*
John Regehr *(University of Utah, USA)*
Arrvindh Shriraman *(Simon Fraser University, Canada)*
Kai Shen *(University of Rochester, USA)*
Anand Sivasubramaniam *(Pennsylvania State University, USA)*
NiranjanSoundararajan *(Intel, USA)*
Michael Spear *(Lehigh University, USA)*
Karin Strauss *(Microsoft Research and University of Washington, USA)*
Michael Swift *(University of Wisconsin—Madison, USA)*
Lingjia Tang *(University of Michigan, USA)*
Mohit Tiwari *(UT Austin, USA)*
Josep Torrellas *(University of Illinois at Urbana-Champaign, USA)*
Dean Tullsen *(UC San Diego, USA)*
Robert Watson *(University of Cambridge, UK)*
Hakim Weatherspoon *(Cornell University, USA)*
Emmett Witchel *(UT Austin, USA)*
David Wood *(University of Wisconsin, USA)*
Peng Wu *(Huawei America Labs, USA)*
Lixin Zhang *(ICT/CAS, China)*
Wei Zhang *(IBM T.J. Watson Research Center, USA)*
Xiao Zhang *(Google, USA)*

Additional reviewers:

Tor M. Aamodt
Keith Adams
Erik Altman
James Bornholt
Herbert Bos
David Brooks
Leland Chang
Peter M. Chen
Fred Chong
Alexandra Fedorova
Dirk Grunwald
Rachid Guerraoui
Sudhanva Gurumurthi
William Harris
Michael Huang
Aamer Jaleel
Avinash Kodi
Christos Kozyrakis
Feng Liu
Ji Liu
Shan Lu
Virendra J. Marathe
Jason Mars
John Mellor-Crummey
Naveen Muralimanohar
Pablo Montesinos Ortego
Colin Percival
Daniel Sanchez
Timothy Sherwood
Yan Solihin
Vijayalakshmi Srinivasan
Per Stenstrom
G. Edward Suh
Xi Wang
Gu-Yeon Wei
Willy Zwaenepoel

ASPLOS 2015 Sponsors & Supporters

Sponsors:

In-cooperation with:

Supporters:

Architectural Support for Cyber-Physical Systems

Edward A. Lee
University of California, Berkeley
Berkeley, California, USA
eal@eecs.berkeley.edu

Abstract

Cyber-physical systems are integrations of computation, communication networks, and physical dynamics. Although time plays a central role in the physical world, all widely used software abstractions lack temporal semantics. The notion of correct execution of a program written in every widely-used programming language today does not depend on the temporal behavior of the program. But temporal behavior matters in almost all systems, and most particularly in cyber-physical systems. In this talk, I will argue that time can and must become part of the semantics of programs for a large class of applications. To illustrate that this is both practical and useful, we will describe a recent effort at Berkeley in the design and implementation of timing-centric software systems. Specifically, I will describe PRET machines, which redefine the instruction-set architecture (ISA) of a microprocessor to embrace temporal semantics. Such machines can be used in high-confidence and safety-critical systems, in energy-constrained systems, in mixed-criticality systems, and as a Real-Time Unit (RTU) that cooperates with a general-purpose processor to provide real-time services, in a manner similar to how a GPU provides graphics services.

ACM Classification: C.3 SPECIAL-PURPOSE AND APPLICATION-BASED SYSTEMS, Real-time and embedded systems

Author Keywords: Cyber-Physical Systems; Embedded Systems; Real-Time Systems; Computer Architecture

ASPLOS'15, March 14–18, 2015, Istanbul, Turkey.
ACM 978-1-4503-2835-7/15/03.
http://dx.doi.org/10.1145/2694344.2694375

Biography

Edward A. Lee is the Robert S. Pepper Distinguished Professor in the Electrical Engineering and Computer Sciences (EECS) department at U.C. Berkeley. His research interests center on design, modeling, and analysis of embedded, real-time computational systems. He is the director of the nine-university TerraSwarm Research Center (http://terraswarm.org), a director of Chess, the Berkeley Center for Hybrid and Embedded Software Systems, and the director of the Berkeley Ptolemy project. From 2005-2008, he served as chair of the EE Division and then chair of the EECS Department at UC Berkeley. He is co-author of six books and hundreds of papers. He has led the development of several influential open-source software packages, notably Ptolemy and its various spinoffs. He received the B.S. degree in Computer Science from Yale University, New Haven, CT, in 1979, the S.M. degree in EECS from the Massachusetts Institute of Technology (MIT), Cambridge, in 1981, and the Ph.D. degree in EECS from the University of California Berkeley, Berkeley, in 1986. From 1979 to 1982 he was a member of technical staff at Bell Telephone Laboratories in Holmdel, New Jersey, in the Advanced Data Communications Laboratory. He is a co-founder of BDTI, Inc., where he is currently a Senior Technical Advisor, and has consulted for a number of other companies. He is a Fellow of the IEEE, was an NSF Presidential Young Investigator, and won the 1997 Frederick Emmons Terman Award for Engineering Education.

Mojim: A Reliable and Highly-Available Non-Volatile Memory System

Yiying Zhang Jian Yang Amirsaman Memaripour Steven Swanson

Department of Computer Science and Engineering, University of California, San Diego

{yiyingzhang,jianyang,amemarip,swanson}@cs.ucsd.edu

Abstract

Next-generation non-volatile memories (NVMs) promise DRAM-like performance, persistence, and high density. They can attach directly to processors to form non-volatile main memory (NVMM) and offer the opportunity to build very low-latency storage systems. These high-performance storage systems would be especially useful in large-scale data center environments where reliability and availability are critical. However, providing reliability and availability to NVMM is challenging, since the latency of data replication can overwhelm the low latency that NVMM should provide.

We propose *Mojim*, a system that provides the reliability and availability that large-scale storage systems require, while preserving the performance of NVMM. Mojim achieves these goals by using a two-tier architecture in which the primary tier contains a mirrored pair of nodes and the secondary tier contains one or more secondary backup nodes with weakly consistent copies of data. Mojim uses highly-optimized replication protocols, software, and networking stacks to minimize replication costs and expose as much of NVMM's performance as possible. We evaluate Mojim using raw DRAM as a proxy for NVMM and using an industrial NVMM emulation system. We find that Mojim provides replicated NVMM with similar or even better performance than un-replicated NVMM (reducing latency by 27% to 63% and delivering between 0.4 to 2.7× the throughput). We demonstrate that replacing MongoDB's built-in replication system with Mojim improves MongoDB's performance by 3.4 to 4×.

ASPLOS '15, March 14–18, 2015, Istanbul, Turkey..

ACM 978-1-4503-2835-7/15/03. . . $15.00.
http://dx.doi.org/10.1145/2694344.2694370

Categories and Subject Descriptors D.4.2 [*Storage Management*]: Main memory

Keywords non-volatile memory; distributed storage systems; reliability; availability; data center; storage-class memory

1. Introduction

Fast, non-volatile memory technologies such as phase change memory (PCM), spin-transfer torque magnetic memories (STTMs), and the memristor are poised to radically alter the performance landscape for storage systems. They will blur the line between storage and memory, forcing designers to rethink how volatile and non-volatile data interact and how to manage non-volatile memories as reliable storage.

Attaching NVMs directly to processors will produce non-volatile main memories (NVMMs), exposing the performance, flexibility, and persistence of these memories to applications. However, taking full advantage of NVMMs' potential will require changes in system software [3].

The need for such changes is especially acute in large-scale data center environments where storage systems require more than simple non-volatility. These environments demand reliability and availability in the face of hardware, software, and network failures. Without this reliability and availability, NVMM will only be suitable as a transient data store or as a caching layer—it will not be able to serve as a reliable primary storage medium.

Data centers traditionally provide both reliability and availability by adding redundancy using replication [5, 11, 15, 55, 56] or erasure coding schemes [18, 21]. These approaches rest on the assumption that storage is slow, so the cost of the network and software protocols required to implement replications is acceptable.

NVMM will change this situation completely, since the networking and software overhead of existing replication mechanisms will squander the low latency that NVMM can provide. The interface with NVMM is also different from traditional storage: applications access NVMM directly with fine-grained memory operations.

We propose *Mojim*[1], a system that provides replicated, reliable, and highly-available NVMM as an operating system service. Applications can access data in Mojim using normal load and store instructions while controlling when and how updates propagate to replicas using system calls. Mojim allows applications to build data persistence abstractions ranging from simple log-based systems to complex transactions.

Mojim uses a two-tier architecture that allows flexibility in choosing different levels of reliability, availability, consistency, and monetary cost, while minimizing performance overhead. The primary tier includes one *primary node* and one *mirror node*. Mojim can, depending on the configuration, keep these nodes strongly or weakly consistent. An optional secondary tier provides an additional level of redundancy with one or more *backup node*s that are weakly consistent with the primary tier.

Mojim efficiently replicates fine-grained data from the primary node to the mirror node using an optimized RDMA-based protocol that is simpler than existing replication protocols. The mirror node replicates data to the backup nodes in the background, thus keeping the secondary tier off the performance-critical path. This design offers good performance and two strongly consistent copies of data plus more copies of weakly consistent data. To further improve availability and reliability, Mojim also provides a fast recovery process and atomic semantics that guarantee data integrity.

In building Mojim, we explore the performance and monetary cost impacts of providing availability, reliability, and consistency with NVMM, and we explore trade-offs among replication protocols for NVMM. Interestingly, we find that adding availability, reliability, and consistency does not necessarily impair NVMM performance, as long as the replication protocols and software layers are optimized for NVMM.

We evaluate Mojim using raw DRAM as a proxy for future NVMMs and with an industrial NVMM emulation system. Our evaluation shows that, surprisingly, Mojim reduces the average latency of the un-replicated system by 27% to 63%, even when it provides strongly consistent copies of data. Mojim's performance gain is mainly due to inefficiencies in the current instruction sets the un-replicated system uses to enforce data persistence. Mojim provides 0.4 to 2.7× the throughput of the un-replicated system. We also run several popular applications including a file system [12], the Google Hash Table [16], and MongoDB [40] on Mojim. The MongoDB results are the most striking: Mojim is 3.4 to 4× faster than the MongoDB replication mechanism and 35 to 741× faster than un-replicated MongoDB.

The rest of the paper is organized as follows. Section 2 provides some background on persistent memory and replicated storage systems. We present Mojim and its implementation in Sections 3 and 4. Section 5 describes our experience adapting applications to use Mojim. We then present the evaluation results of Mojim in Section 6. Finally, we discuss related work in Section 7 and conclude in Section 8.

[1] Mojim (魔镜) is the Chinese word for "magic mirror."

2. NVMM in the Data Center

NVMM blurs the line between memory and storage, and it poses new challenges for system designers and architects. Previous research on NVMM has focused on how to use these memories in a single machine [3, 8, 9, 12, 39, 58, 59], while most mission-critical data resides in distributed, replicated storage systems (e.g., in data centers). For NVMM to succeed as a first-class storage technology, it must provide the reliability and availability that these storage systems require [26].

Mojim's goal is to make NVMM a reliable and highly-available storage layer suited to these data center environments. Achieving this goal will require designers to address trade-offs between performance, reliability, monetary cost, and consistency. Below, we introduce NVMM and discuss why it demands new approaches to providing availability, reliability, and consistency in storage systems.

2.1 Next-Generation Non-Volatile Memory

NVM technologies are closing the performance, cost-per-bit, and capacity gap between low-latency, volatile memory technologies and high-capacity, persistent storage technologies [25, 32, 49, 62]. Next-generation NVM technologies (like PCM, the memristor, and STTM) are byte-addressable and projections show that their performance may approach that of DRAM [20, 27, 35, 60]. For example, PCM, the most mature next-generation NVM technology, has access latencies within a small factor of DRAM [33, 34, 38, 48].

Attaching next-generation NVMs to the main memory bus provides a raw storage medium that is orders of magnitude faster than modern disks and SSDs. NVMM presents many new technical challenges and has inspired a host of research projects on topics including OS management of NVMM [3], user-space libraries and programming models [8, 58], specialized NVMM file systems [9, 12, 59], and hybrid main memory and heterogeneous memory allocation [39, 41, 50]. This work focuses on the problems of replicating NVMM content so that NVMM can be applied in a distributed data center context.

2.2 NVMM Availability, Reliability, and Consistency

Although NVMM protects against power failure by making the contents of memory persistent, it does not address the other ways that systems fail, including software, hardware, and networking errors that are common in data centers [14, 42]. Providing availability and reliability in such environments is important to meet client SLAs [55] and application requirements. Strong consistency is also desirable in storage systems, since it makes it easier to reason about system correctness.

Adding redundancy or replication is a common technique for providing reliability and availability [1, 5, 11, 15, 17,

18, 29, 46, 47, 51, 52, 56, 61]. Various protocols exist to provide different consistency levels among redundant copies of data [2, 4, 11, 22, 31, 47]. For traditional storage systems with slow hard disks and SSDs, the performance overhead of replication is small relative to the cost of accessing a hard drive or SSD, even with complex protocols for strong consistency. With NVMMs, however, the networking round trips and software overhead involved in these techniques [4, 22, 31, 56] threaten to outstrip the low-latency benefit of using NVMMs in the first place. Even for systems with weak consistency [11, 47], increasing the rate of reconciliation between inconsistent copies of data can threaten performance [17, 28].

Since NVMM is vastly faster than existing storage technologies, it presents new challenges to data replication. First, NVMM-based systems must deliver high performance to justify their increased cost relative to disks or SSDs. Existing replication mechanisms built for these slower storage media have software and networking performance overhead that would obscure the performance benefits that NVMM could provide.

Second, NVMM is memory, and applications should be able to use it like memory (*i.e.*, via load and store instructions without operating system overheads for most accesses) rather than as a storage device (*i.e.*, via I/O system calls).

3. Mojim Design

Mojim provides an easy-to-use, generic layer of replicated NVMM that ensures reliability, availability, and consistency, while sacrificing as little of NVMM's performance as possible. Mojim uses a two-tier architecture and supports several operating modes to let applications tune Mojim's reliability, availability, and consistency to match their particular needs.

This section discusses Mojim's interfaces and architecture and the different modes Mojim provides.

3.1 Mojim's Interfaces

Mojim is an operating system service that provides reliable and highly-available NVMM. This section describes Mojim's typical usage scenario and the interface it provides.

To use Mojim, a system configuration file specifies a set of *Mojim regions* on the *primary node* to be replicated, along with a *mirror node* and a list of *backup nodes* where the replicas should reside. The primary node supports reads and writes to the replicated data. The mirror node and backup nodes support reads only. Kernel modules can access these regions and use them to build complex, replicated, memory-based services such as a kernel-level persistent key value store, a persistent disk cache, or a file system. The kernel could also make these services available to applications via a `malloc()`-like interface.

While Mojim can serve as the basis for many memory-based services, deploying an NVMM-aware file system to manage the replicated NVMM region would provide the most flexibility in application usage models. The file system would provide familiar file-system-based mechanisms of allocation and naming as well as conventional file-based access for non-performance-critical applications. The key requirement of the file system is that, for an *mmap*'d file, it maps the the NVMM pages corresponding to the file directly into the applications' address spaces rather than paging them in and out of the kernel's buffer cache. In our experiments, we use PMFS [12] for this purpose.

With a file system in place, applications can create files in the Mojim-backed file system and map them into their address space using *mmap*. We call the NVMM area mapped by applications the *data area*. After an *mmap*, applications can perform direct memory accesses to the data area using load and store instructions on the primary node and load instructions on the mirror node.

Mojim provides a mechanism called a *sync point* that allows applications to control when and what updates in the data area propagate to the replicas. At each sync point, Mojim atomically replicates all memory regions specified by an application.

Two APIs allow applications to create sync points: *msync* and *gmsync*.

Mojim leverages the existing *msync* system call to specify a sync point that applies to a single, contiguous address range. The semantics of Mojim's *msync* correspond to conventional *msync*, and applications that use *msync* will work correctly without modification under Mojim. Mojim allows an application to specify a fine-grained memory region in the *msync* API and replicates it atomically, while traditional *msync* flushes page-aligned memory regions to persistent storage and does not provide atomicity guarantees [45].

Mojim's *gmsync* adds the ability to specify multiple memory regions for the sync point to replicate, allowing for more flexibility than *msync*.

Mojim provides a mechanism to allow applications to make their data persistent atomically, but it does not provide primitives for synchronization. It would be possible to add synchronization primitives to Mojim, but this would increase the complexity of the system and require selecting a set of synchronization mechanisms to support. A better approach would be to build synchronization mechanisms that leverage Mojim's mechanisms.

Figure 1 shows a simple example in C of how to use Mojim to manage an append-only log on Mojim. The program first opens and *mmap*s a file in a Mojim region. It then updates the access count of the log and makes this value persistent with the conventional *msync* API. Next, it appends a log entry and updates the size of the log. It makes both these data persistent with an *gmsync* call. The atomicity that *gmsync* provides guarantees that the log size is consistent with the log content on the replica nodes.

```
int fd = open("/mnt/mmapfile", O_CREAT|O_RDWR);                    // open a file in mounted Mojim region
void *base = mmap(NULL, 40960, PROT_WRITE,
                  MAP_SHARED, fd, 0);                              // mmap a 40KB area in the file

unsigned long *access_count_p = base;                             // access count of the log
unsigned long *log_size_p = base + sizeof(unsigned long);         // size of the log
int *log = base + 2*sizeof(unsigned long);                        // the log

*access_count_p = *access_count_p + 1;                            // memory load and store
msync(access_count_p, sizeof(unsigned long), MS_SYNC);            // call conventional msync

int beautiful_num = 24;
unsigned long curr_log_pos = *log_size_p;                         // memory load and store
log[curr_log_pos] = beautiful_num;
*log_size_p = *log_size_p + 1;
struct msync_input { void *address; int length; };
struct msync_input input[2];
input[0].address = &(log[curr_log_pos]);
input[0].length = sizeof(int);
input[1].address = log_size_p;
input[1].length = sizeof(unsigned long);
gmsync(input, 2, MS_MOJIM);                                       // call gmsync to commit the log append
```

Figure 1. Sample code to use Mojim. *Code snippet that implements a simple log append operation with Mojim.*

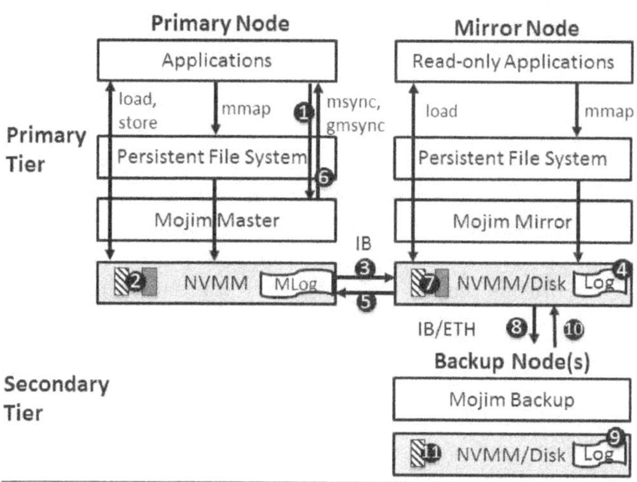

Figure 2. Mojim Architecture. *The numbered circles represent different steps in the Mojim replication process. MLog stands for the metadata log.*

3.2 Architecture

Mojim uses a two-tier architecture. The primary tier contains a primary node and its read-only mirror node; the secondary tier includes one or more backup nodes with weakly consistent, read-only copies of data. Figure 2 depicts the architecture of Mojim.

Mojim's primary tier contains a pair of mirroring nodes: a primary node replicates data to its mirror node at each *sync point* (i.e., call to *msync* or *gmsync*). The application can read and write data on the primary node, but Mojim only allows reads from the mirror node.

The primary tier offers good performance even when guaranteeing strong consistency, since it requires only one networking round trip for each sync point. Existing architectures that allow writes to all replicas (*E-writeall*) [31], or that use one primary and multiple secondary nodes (*E-chain and E-broadcast*) [2, 56], require multiple networking round trips or other performance overhead to guarantee strong consistency. We will discuss how Mojim differs from these existing schemes in more detail in Section 7.

To further improve performance, we connect the primary node and the mirror node with a high-speed Infiniband link and use an efficient software and networking layer to replicate data between them.

To improve reliability, we place the primary node and the mirror node on different racks, since failure bursts often happen within the same rack [14, 42].

The optional secondary tier includes one or more backup nodes to maintain additional copies of data. It provides additional reliability and availability, so that failure bursts will not be catastrophic. The mirror node replicates data to the backup nodes in the background. Thus, data in the backup nodes is not strongly consistent with data in the primary tier. By keeping the replication to the secondary tier in the background and off the performance-critical path, Mojim ensures good application performance.

With both tiers in operation and a total of N nodes, Mojim can tolerate $N-1$ node failures. In most environments, one or a few backup nodes are enough to prevent data loss, since failure bursts are more likely to involve only a small number of nodes [14, 42]. Also, in most failure bursts, the nodes do not all fail at the same time; failures are usually separated by a few seconds. A fast recovery can thus prevent data loss even with few copies of replicated data. We discuss recovery optimizations in Section 4.3.

Scheme	R	A	C	$
S-unreplicated	0	Worst	N/A	Low
M-async	1	Good	Weak	Fair
M-sync	1	Good	Strong	Fair
M-syncdisk	1	OK	Strong	Low
M-syncsec	$N-1$	Best	Strong+Weak	High
M-syncseceth	$N-1$	Good	Strong+Weak	Fair
E-writeall	$N-1$	Best	Strong	High
E-chain	$N-1$	Best	Strong	High
E-broadcast	$N-1$	Best	Strong	High

Table 1. Replication Schemes. *Mojim supports a wide range of reliability, availability, consistency, and monetary cost levels (columns 2-5). The reliability column represents the number of node failures that can be tolerated in a system of N nodes. The last three rows compare Mojim to other existing replication schemes.*

3.3 Mojim Modes and Replication Protocols

Mojim supports several replication modes and protocols that allow users to choose different levels of performance, reliability, consistency, availability, and monetary cost depending on application requirements.

Table 1 summarizes these different modes and their properties, and we discuss them below using the numbered circles in Figure 2 to illustrate the replication process in each mode.

Across all the modes Mojim provides, Mojim achieves most of its performance by adopting a different architecture than most replicated storage systems. Instead of supporting multiple consistent replicas, Mojim only supports strong consistency at a single mirror node. This decision makes our replication protocols much simpler (e.g., there's no need for multi-phase commit or a complex consensus protocol) and, therefore, allows for much higher performance.

Mojim achieves the goal of providing its atomic data persistence interface by ensuring that atomic operations are replicated atomically to the mirror node and the backup nodes, by appending replicated data to logs on the mirror node and the backup nodes.

Un-replicated without Mojim: A single machine without Mojim (*S-unreplicated*) must flush an *msync*'d memory region from the processor's caches to ensure data persistence. S-unreplicated has poor availability and is only as reliable as the NVM devices. Moreover, even if the NVMM is recovered after a crash, data can still be corrupted. For example, if a crash occurs after a pointer is made persistent but before the data it points to becomes persistent, the system will contain corrupted data.

Sync: Mojim's *M-sync* mode guarantees strong consistency between the primary and the mirror node. It provides improved reliability and availability over S-unreplicated, since in the case of a failure the mirror node can take the place of the primary node without losing data.

In M-sync, when an application calls *msync* or *gmsync* (① in Figure 2), Mojim pushes data from the primary node to the mirror node via RDMA (③) and writes the data in the mirror node log (④). The primary node waits for the acknowledgment from the mirror node (⑤), and then returns the *msync* or *gmsync* call (⑥). The mirror node later takes a checkpoint to apply the log contents to the data area (⑦). Mojim stores both the mirror node logs and its data area in NVMM for high performance and fast recovery.

In M-sync, Mojim does not flush data from the primary node's caches (②). Modern RDMA devices are cache-coherent, so they will send the most up-to-date data [24, 30]. Thus, the mirror node always gets the latest data and pushing data to the mirror node is sufficient to ensure persistence. If the primary node crashes, the mirror node has the most up-to-date data. If the mirror node crashes, the primary node has all the data, but it may not be persistent, so the primary node immediately flushes its caches to prevent data loss. This means there is a small "window of vulnerability" after a mirror node failure during which a primary node failure could result in data loss. On our system, this window lasts for 450 μs, the time required to flush the processor caches.

Surprisingly, our evaluation results show that M-sync offers performance comparable to or better than S-unreplicated because flushing CPU caches is often more expensive than pushing the data over RDMA. The current *clflush* instruction is strongly ordered and cannot utilize the parallelism offered in modern processor architecture. Intel recently announced two instructions that are more efficient than *clflush* and that will be available on future systems [23], which should help resolve this problem.

Sync with cache flush: To close the window of vulnerability mentioned above, Mojim can flush data from the primary node's caches (②) before returning to applications' *msync* or *gmsync* calls (⑥). This mode is called *M-syncflush*, and with M-syncflush, all data can survive simultaneous failures of the primary node and the mirror node.

Async: *M-async* provides weaker consistency between the primary node and the mirror node. M-async ensures that data is persistent on the primary node for each sync point (②) and pushes the data to the mirror node (③), but it does not wait for the mirror node's acknowledgment (⑤) to complete the application's *msync* or *gmsync* call (⑥). Thus, data on the mirror node can be out of date relative to the primary node. M-async must flush the primary node CPU caches at each sync point to ensure that the latest data is persistent.

Sync with slow storage: To reduce the monetary cost of M-sync, Mojim supports a mode that stores the log on the mirror node in NVMM, but stores the mirror node's data area on a hard disk or SSD (*M-syncdisk*). M-syncdisk has a slower recovery process than M-sync, since Mojim needs to read data from hard disk or SSD to NVMM before applications can access them.

Sync with the secondary tier: *M-syncsec* adds the secondary tier to M-sync and increases reliability and availability by adding more copies of data. Mojim replicates data from the mirror node to the backup node in the background

(⑧-⑪). M-syncsec provides two strongly-consistent copies of the data at the primary and mirror nodes and one weakly-consistent data copy at each backup node. The amount of inconsistency between the mirror node and backup nodes is tunable and affects the recovery time. Even though the data at each backup node may be out-of-date, it still represents a consistent snapshot of application data because of the atomic semantics Mojim provides. Our evaluation results show that M-syncsec delivers performance similar to M-sync because replication to the backup nodes takes place in the background.

Sync with low-cost secondary tier: M-syncsec requires fast networks between the mirror node and backup nodes, which increases the monetary cost and networking bandwidth consumption of the system. A lower cost option, *M-syncseceth*, uses Ethernet between the mirror node and backup nodes. M-syncseceth has the worst performance of all the Mojim modes, but it still provides the same reliability, availability, and consistency guarantees as M-syncsec.

4. Implementation

This section describes our implementation of Mojim in the Linux kernel. The core of Mojim comprises an optimized network stack and the replication and recovery code.

4.1 Networking

The networking delay of data replication is the most important factor in determining Mojim's overall performance. Mojim uses Infiniband (IB), a high-performance switched network that supports RDMA. RDMA is crucial because it allows the primary node to transfer data directly into the mirror node's NVMM without requiring additional buffering, copying, or cache flushes.

Mojim uses *IB-Verbs*, a set of native IB APIs based on send, receive, and completion queues [37]. IB-Verbs requires the application to post send (receive) requests to send (receive) queues. It uses completion messages in the completion queue to indicate the completion of requests and supports both polling and interrupts to detect completions. IB-Verbs offers native IB performance and outperforms alternative IB protocols such as IPoIB and RDS (see Section 6.2). Existing IB-Verbs implementations are userspace libraries that bypass the kernel. We created a kernel version of IB-Verbs for Mojim.

Mojim uses a thin protocol based on the reliable transportation mode of IB-Verbs. The Mojim protocol directly fetches data from the primary node and writes it to NVMM on the mirror node. For each sync point, the primary node posts a send request on the IB send queue and polls for its completion. The mirror node posts a set of receive requests in advance and polls for the arrival of incoming messages. Our measurements show that polling is more efficient than interrupts.

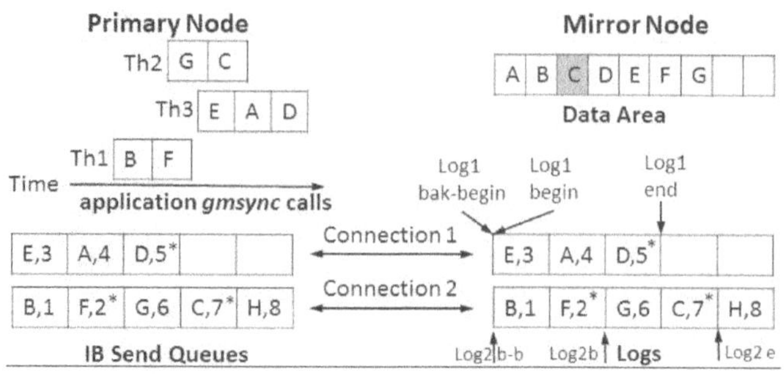

Figure 3. Example of Mojim Replication. *An example of Mojim's replication process. Each cell represents a request. The letter in the cell stands for the memory address and the number in the cell represents its unique ID. The upper-left part shows three threads placing three* gmsync *calls. The upper-right part shows the data area on the mirror node. The * represents the end mark of a* gmsync *operation. The gray cell in the mirror node data area represents the data that is recovered after a crash.*

The protocol does not require explicit acknowledgment messages from the mirror node to the primary node, since we configure the IB link to provide a successful completion notification for the primary node's send request only once the data transfer succeeds. In the event of an error or a timeout, the primary node resends the message to the backup node. After a set number of unsuccessful re-send attempts, Mojim invokes its recovery process.

To sustain high bandwidth, Mojim creates multiple IB connections to handle client requests. For each connection, we assign one thread on the mirror node to poll for incoming messages. On the primary node, we let the application thread perform IB send operations for M-sync and use a background thread to post these operations for M-async.

4.2 Replication

We now describe the Mojim replication process and the techniques that we use to enable reliable, atomic, and consistent data replication.

Primary tier replication: At each sync point, the primary node posts IB send requests containing the target memory regions. Mojim ensures that all requests belonging to the same atomic operation are consecutive and on the same IB connection and marks the last request to let the mirror node know the end of an atomic operation. Since Mojim's reliable IB protocol ensures ordering in each IB connection, these requests will appear in the same order on the mirror node. A unique ID on each send request allows the mirror node to keep updates ordered across IB connections. For recovery purposes, the primary node stores the memory addresses of the most recent requests in a *metadata log*.

For each IB connection, the mirror node maintains a circular log and a thread that polls incoming requests. Mojim places the logs in NVMM for good performance and persistence and pre-allocates fixed-size buffers on the logs for RDMA accesses. With pre-allocated memory slots, Mojim only needs one IB roundtrip to replicate data from the primary node to the mirror node. Because the receive buffer size is fixed, we limit the size of each send request on the primary node and break original memory regions into multiple send requests if needed. Since RDMA writes directly to NVMM, there is no need to flush the cache on the mirror node.

After all the data for a sync point has arrived on the log, the mirror node can write them to their permanent locations in the data area. This checkpointing happens periodically after a configurable number of requests (*CHECKPOINT_THRESH*) have been received, as well as when the system is idle and when a log is full. Mojim maintains global pointers to the beginning and end of each log to indicate data available for checkpointing.

To ensure that read-only applications on the mirror node see a consistent view of their data, Mojim removes the page table entries of the affected memory locations before a checkpointing operation. During the checkpointing, an application reading from those pages will generate a page fault. We changed the page fault handler to wait until Mojim completes the checkpointing and then restore the page table entries and return the application read.

Secondary tier replication: Replication to the secondary backups occurs in the background when there is data on the mirror node's logs. The protocol for replication to the backup node mimics the replication to the mirror node. The mirror node maintains a pointer for each log to indicate the amount of data that has not yet been replicated to the backup node. Mojim uses a threshold (*SECONDARY_TIER_THRESH*) to limit the amount of such unreplicated data on the mirror node and stalls further replication to the mirror node until un-replicated data drops below SECONDARY_TIER_THRESH.

Example: Figure 3 illustrates an example of Mojim's data structures and its replication process. In this example, Mojim uses two IB connections and two mirror node logs. Three application threads post three *gmsync* calls to the two IB send queues. To guarantee atomicity, Mojim serializes thread 2's requests after thread 1's requests on the second send queue. Mojim then sends these requests to the mirror node's logs. The mirror node threads poll for the completion of these writes and update the log-end pointers when they have received all requests belonging to one *gmsync* call. The checkpointing service processes the logs from the log-begin pointer to the log-end pointer. The mirror node replicates the log content between the log-bak-begin pointer and the log-end pointer to the backup node.

4.3 Recovery

Fast recovery is crucial to providing high availability and preventing data loss in the event of a failure. There are three types of failure scenarios: primary, mirror, and backup node failures. Mojim uses heartbeats to detect failures, but other techniques [7, 36] are possible.

When the primary node fails, the mirror node becomes the new primary node and a backup node becomes the new mirror node. The new primary node first sends the un-replicated data in its logs to the new mirror node and checkpoints its log content to its data area after the failure. For M-syncdisk, the new primary node needs to load data from the data file on disk to the NVMM. After these operations, applications can restart on the new primary node. Until these operations complete, the Mojim contents will be unavailable.

One option for activating a new backup node is to wait for the failed node to come back online. Rebooting the machine is often sufficient and more efficient than constructing a new node [14]. When the crashed primary node restarts, it receives the new data accumulated during its down time from the new primary node. When the failed node cannot reboot fast enough, a human operator or a system monitoring service selects a new backup node based on its available NVMM size, its networking topology, and other criteria [6, 53]. The new node receives a complete copy of the memory region and begins processing updates from the new mirror node.

When the mirror node or the backup node fails, the recovery process is similar. If the mirror node fails, the primary node first flushes its CPU caches. It also uses its metadata log to locate un-replicated data and sends them to the backup node. To restart the mirror node or the backup node, Mojim replays the logs and writes only the completed atomic operation content to the data area, with the help of the atomic operation end mark and unique IDs. In the example in Figure 3, the mirror node crashes after Mojim checkpoints G. The recovery process will checkpoint C and discard H. If the failed node cannot restart, a newly chosen node receives replicated data from the primary node as described above.

When both the primary node and the mirror node fail in quick succession, Mojim falls back to the backup node. Now Mojim needs to reconstruct two new nodes that the administrating node selects. This recovery process is more costly than the recovery of a single node failure. We reduce the risk of this situation by placing nodes on different racks and by setting a small SECONDARY_TIER_THRESH, thus speeding up the recovery process of a single node failure.

5. Mojim Applications

We have ported several existing systems to Mojim to illustrate how applications can use Mojim's interface. The applications include the PMFS file system [12], the Google hash table [16], and MongoDB [40].

5.1 PMFS

The Persistent Memory File System [12] (PMFS) provides a conventional file-system-like interface to NVMM, allowing applications to allocate space with file creation, limit access to data via file permissions, and name portions of the

NVMM using file names. The key difference between PMFS and a conventional file system is that its implementation of *mmap* maps the physical pages of NVMM into the applications' address spaces rather than moving them back and forth between the file store and the buffer cache.

PMFS ensures persistence using *sfence* and *clflush* instructions. Mojim invokes its replication when PMFS performs its persistence procedure. Mojim's M-sync also removes *clflush* and only performs *sfence* on the primary node. Mojim's change required modifications to just 20 lines of PMFS source code. Applications can use *mmap* to gain load-/store access to a file's contents and then use *fsync*, *msync*, or *gmsync* to manage replication and data consistency.

5.2 Google hash table

Google hash table [16] is an open source implementation of sparse and dense hash tables. Our Mojim-enabled version of the hash table stores its data in *mmap*'d PMFS files and performs *msync* at each insert and delete operation to let Mojim replicate the data. Porting the Google hash table to Mojim requires changes to just 18 lines of code.

5.3 MongoDB

MongoDB [40] is a popular NoSql database. Several aspects of MongoDB make it a good comparison point for Mojim. First, MongoDB stores its data in memory-mapped files and performs memory loads and stores for data access—a perfect match for Mojim's NVMM interface. Second, MongoDB supports both single node and replication in a set of nodes in several different modes (called "write concerns") that trade off among performance, reliability, and availability. Mojim provides similar functionality with a more general mechanism.

By default, MongoDB logs data in a journal file and checkpoints the data to the memory-mapped data file in a lazy fashion. With the *JOURNALED* write concern, MongoDB blocks a client call until the updated data is written to the journal file. With the *FSYNC_SAFE* write concern, MongoDB flushes all the dirty pages to the data file after each write operation and blocks the client call until this operation completes.

MongoDB supports data replication across a set of machines. A primary node in a MongoDB replica set serves all write requests and pushes *operation logs* to the secondary nodes. Secondary nodes can serve read requests but may return stale data. The MongoDB write concern *REPLICAS_SAFE* returns the client request after at least two secondary nodes have received the corresponding operation log. The REPLICAS_SAFE write concern does not wait for journal writes or checkpointing on the primary node.

Mojim offers another way to provide reliability and availability to MongoDB. With the help of Mojim's *gmsync* API and its reliability guarantees, we can remove journaling from MongoDB and still achieve the same consistency level. To guarantee the same atomicity of client requests as available through MongoDB, we modify the storage engine of MongoDB to keep track of all writes to the data file and group the written memory regions belonging to the same client request into a *gmsync* call. In total, this change requires modifying 117 lines of MongoDB.

An alternative way of using Mojim is to run unmodified MongoDB on Mojim by configuring MongoDB to place both its data file and journal file in Mojim's *mmap*'d data area. When MongoDB commits data to the journal or checkpoints the data to the data file, it performs an *msync* operation, which will trigger Mojim's data replication transparently.

6. Evaluation with DRAM

In this section, we study the performance of Mojim under each of the configurations and applications we described in Sections 3 and 5. Specifically, we first evaluate the performance of different Mojim modes and compare them to existing replication methods. We then evaluate the effects of different application parameters and Mojim configurations, the performance of applications ported to Mojim, and Mojim's recovery costs.

6.1 Test Bed Systems

We use two different systems to evaluate Mojim. The first is an industrial NVMM emulation system from Intel called PMEP [12]. PMEP augments an off-the-shelf, dual-socket server platform with special CPU microcode and custom firmware. It partitions the system's DRAM into emulated NVMM and regular DRAM. PMEP emulates NVMM read latency, read and write bandwidth, and data persistence costs. For read latency and read/write bandwidth, PMEP modifies the CPU and the memory controller. The PMEP platform uses write-back CPU caches and does not emulate NVMM write latency. It uses software to emulate the cost of data persistence: the kernel running on PMEP issues *clflush* instructions followed by an *sfence*, and adds a *write barrier* delay to model the cost of ensuring data persistence in NVMM. In our experiments, we emulate NVMM by setting the read latency to 300 ns, read and write bandwidth to 5 GB/s and 1.6 GB/s (1/8 of DRAM bandwidth), and the write barrier delay to 1 μs, the configuration used in Intel's PMFS project [12].

Each PMEP node has two 2.6 GHz 8-core Intel Xeon processors, 40 MB of aggregate CPU cache, 8 GB of DDR3 DRAM used as normal DRAM, 128 GB of DRAM used as emulated NVMM, and a 7200 RPM 4 TB hard disk. They also have 40 Gbps Mellanox Infiniband NICs and are directly connected to each other via Infiniband without a switch. The platforms run Ubuntu 13.10 and the 3.11.0 Linux kernel.

We have access to only two PMEP machines (located at an Intel facility), so to evaluate Mojim modes that require more than two machines, we use similar machines in our

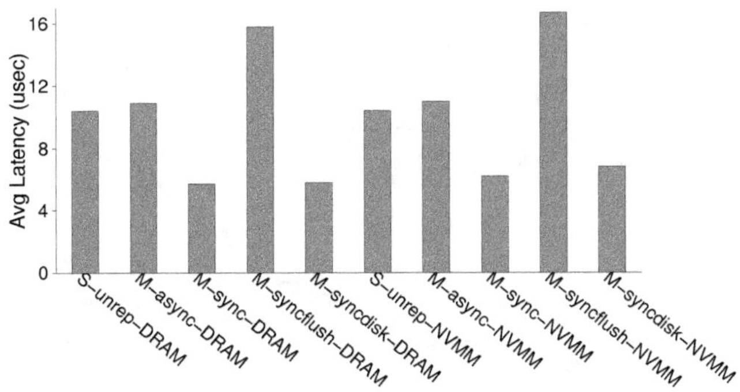

Figure 4. msync Latency with DRAM and NVMM. *The average 4 KB* msync *latency with PMEP's DRAM and NVMM modes.*

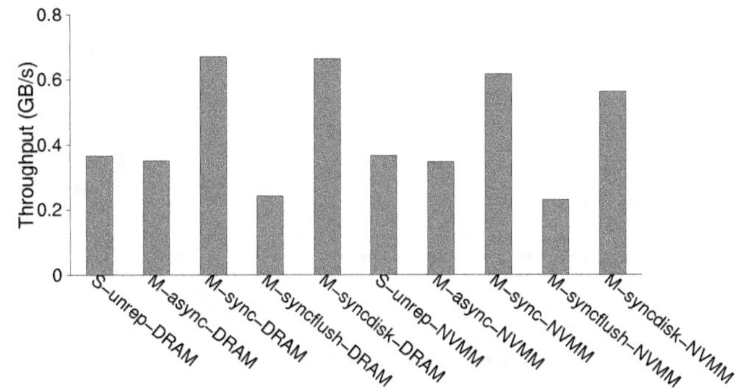

Figure 5. msync Throughput with DRAM and NVMM. *The 4 KB* msync *bandwidth with PMEP's DRAM and NVMM modes.*

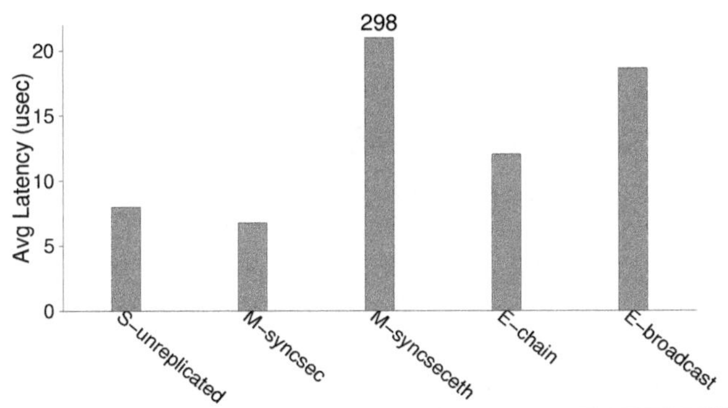

Figure 6. msync Latency with DRAM-based machines. *The average 4 KB* msync *latency with S-unreplicated and Mojim two-tier architecture.*

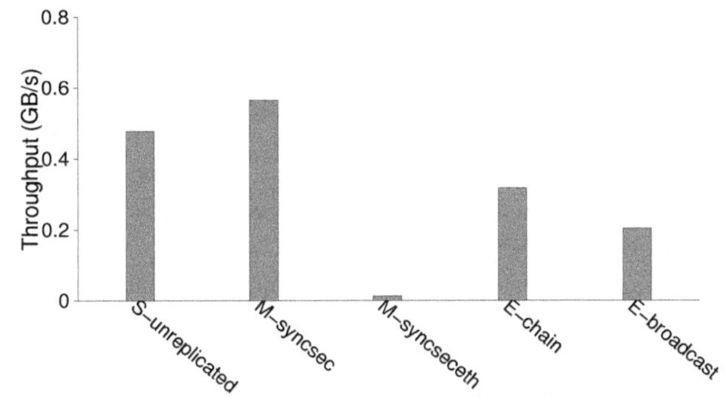

Figure 7. msync Throughput with DRAM-based machines. *The 4 KB* msync *throughput with S-unreplicated and Mojim two-tier architecture.*

lab that do not include PMEP functionality and use ordinary DRAM as a proxy for NVMM. Each of these machines has two Intel Xeon X5647 processors, 48 GB DRAM, one 40 Gbps Mellanox Infiniband NIC, and a 1000 Mbps Ethernet. A QLogic Infiniband Switch connects these machines' IB links. All machines run the CentOS 6.4 distribution and the 3.11.0 Linux kernel.

In all experiments, unless otherwise specified, we set CHECKPOINT_THRESH (the frequency of checkpointing the mirror node logs) to 1 (after each log write) and SECONDARY_TIER_THRESH (the threshold for sending unreplicated data to the backup nodes) to 40 MB.

6.2 Overall Replication Performance

We first compare the microbenchmark performance of Mojim modes that only involve two nodes using the PMEP platforms. To evaluate the impact of NVMM vs. DRAM, we run the same experiments with both PMEP's DRAM mode and its emulated NVMM.

Figures 4 and 5 present the average latency and throughput of *msync* calls with S-unreplicated, M-async, M-sync, M-syncflush, and M-syncdisk. For each experiment, we perform 10000 random 4 KB *msync* calls in a 4 GB *mmap*'d file.

Surprisingly, M-sync outperforms S-unreplicated significantly for both DRAM and emulated NVMM (reducing latency by 45% and 40% respectively). Even though M-sync waits for a networking round trip between the primary node and the mirror node, it still outperforms S-unreplicated because it does not need to flush data from processors' caches, while S-unreplicated must flush data on each *msync*. M-async's performance is similar to S-unreplicated, as it also needs to flush primary node's caches. M-syncflush has higher latency than S-unreplicated, since it performs both cache flushes and networking round trips.

Placing the mirror node data on disk adds only 1% to 10% overhead. However, M-syncdisk does not support read applications on the mirror node and adds an overhead in recovery time (see Section 6.5).

Comparing DRAM and emulated NVMM, the performance with emulated NVMM for all schemes is close to that with DRAM, indicating that the performance degradation of NVMM over DRAM only has a very small effect over application-level performance.

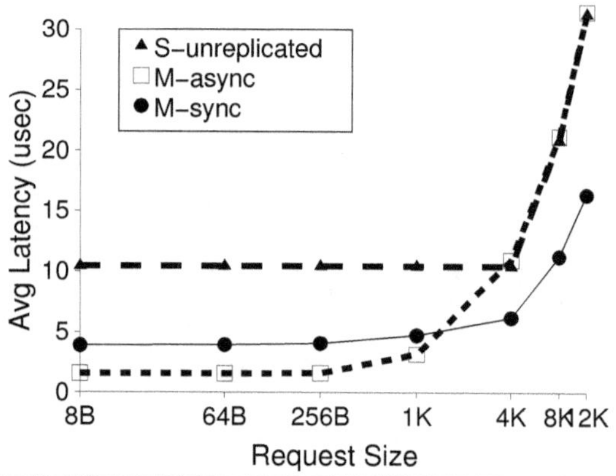

Figure 8. Average *msync* Latency with Different *msync* Sizes on Emulated NVMM. *The average latency of* msync *operation on NVMM with request sizes from 8 bytes to 12 KB.*

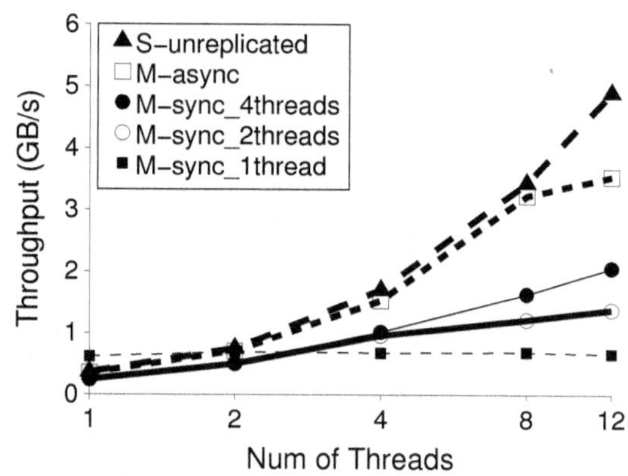

Figure 9. Throughput with Different Application Threads on Emulated NVMM. *The* msync *throughput with 1 to 12 threads performing* msync.

Next, to augment the PMEP results with more machines and to test Mojim's two-tier architecture, we use three DRAM-based machines in our lab to evaluate the performance of Mojim's two-tier modes and two existing schemes that use a one-primary, multiple-secondary architecture (Table 1). One of these existing schemes, *E-chain*, allows writes only at the primary node and propagates data replication from the primary node to the secondary nodes in a serialized order [2, 56]. The other existing scheme, *E-broadcast* [15], is similar to E-chain but broadcasts updates to the secondary nodes. E-chain and E-broadcast use one primary node and two secondary nodes interconnected by IB. They use the same IB protocol that we implemented for Mojim.

Figures 6 and 7 plot the average latency and throughput of using our lab machines to run the experiments shown in Figures 4 and 5. Compared to S-unreplicated, Mojim with the secondary tier does not degrade performance if a fast network connects the backup node. However, the lower-cost Ethernet configuration degrades performance by 37×, because the mirror node cannot drain its circular log fast enough and has to stall the primary tier replication.

Both E-chain and E-broadcast are slower than Mojim, increasing latency by 1.8× and 2.8× respectively, compared to M-syncsec.

Finally, we compare Mojim with two existing IB kernel protocols, RDS and IPoIB. We find that they both have worse performance than Mojim's networking protocol on IB-Verbs, with 4.9× and 31× slowdown.

Overall, Mojim delivers performance similar to or better than no replication while adding reliability and availability. Mojim's good performance is due to its efficient replication protocol, its ability to avoid expensive cache flush operations, and its optimized software and networking stacks.

6.3 Sensitivity Analysis

Both Mojim's configuration parameters and application-level behavior can affect performance. In this section, we measure their impact on Mojim's performance.

6.3.1 *msync* Size

The amount of data per *msync* has a strong impact on performance. Figure 8 plots the average latency of performing *msync* calls to random memory regions of 8 bytes to 12 KB with S-unreplicated, M-async, and M-sync using PMEP's emulated NVMM.

For smaller request sizes, M-async performs much better than S-unreplicated. S-unreplicated underperforms because of the current way *msync* call are implemented in Linux, with the *msync* call handler checking for the range of the *msync* memory and rounding it to memory pages (4 KB page for the default Linux kernel). With Mojim, we modify the *msync* call handler to allow any memory address range and only flush and replicate the application-specified memory regions.

M-sync does not perform *clflush* (since transferring the data to the mirror node guarantees persistence). As a result, its performance is always better than S-unreplicated and is better than M-async when *msync* size is bigger than 1 KB.

6.3.2 Application Threads and Networking Connections

Application thread count and the number of network connections Mojim uses also impact performance. Figure 9 presents the 4 KB *msync* throughput with one to 12 application threads for S-unreplicated, M-async, and M-sync using PMEP's emulated NVMM.

Both M-async and S-unreplicated scale well with the number of application threads, while M-sync with one IB connection (and thus one log) scales poorly. With more con-

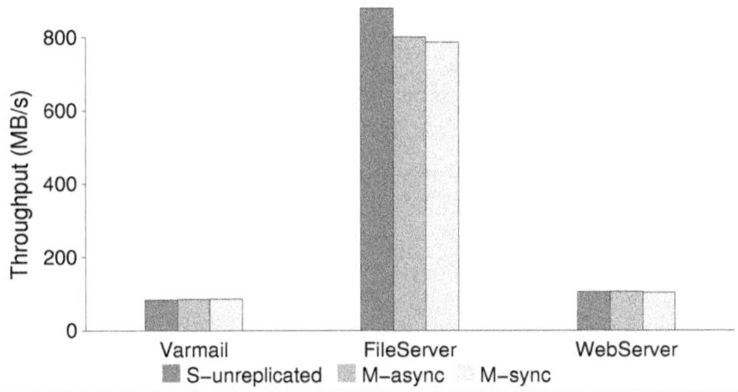

Figure 10. Filebench Throughput with Emulated NVMM. *The throughput of three Filebench workloads with single machine and no replication, the M-async mode, and the M-sync mode.*

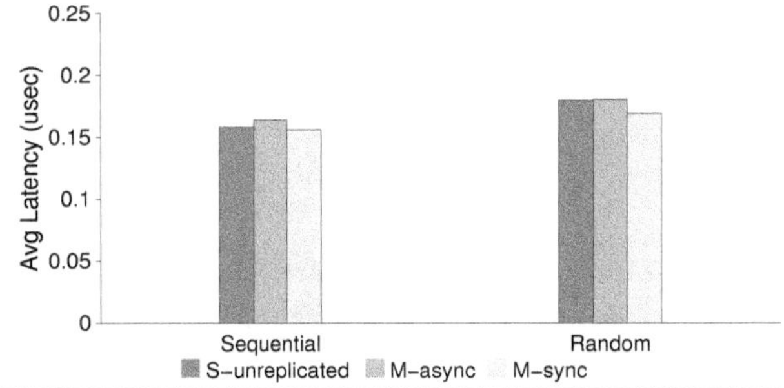

Figure 11. Google Hash Table Average Latency with Emulated NVMM. *The average latency of sequentially and randomly inserting key-value pairs to the Google dense hash table.*

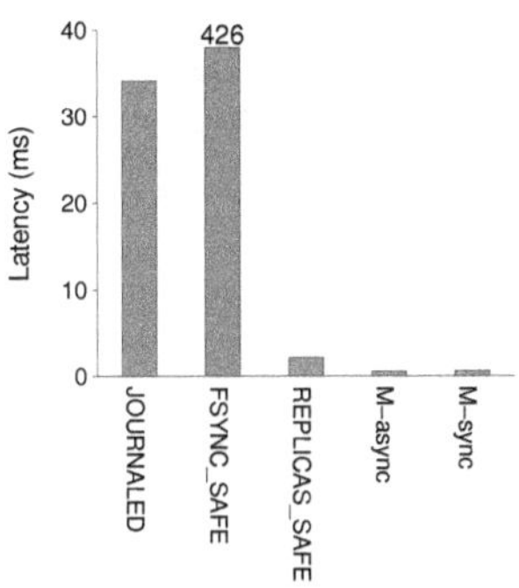

Figure 12. Insert Avg Latency. *Average latency of inserting key-value pairs on emulated NVMM.*

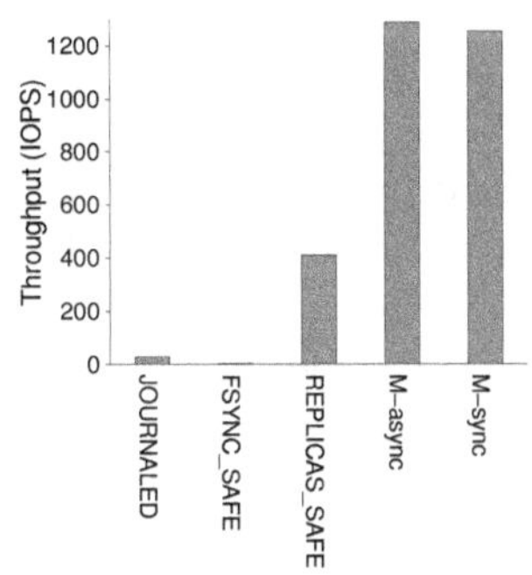

Figure 13. Insert Throughput. *Throughput of inserting key-value pairs on emulated NVMM.*

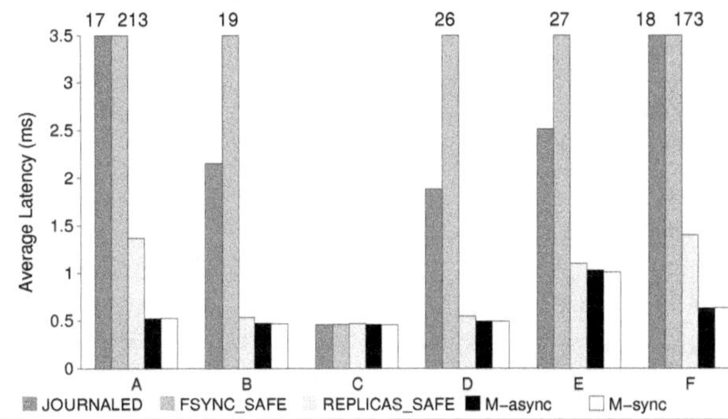

Figure 14. YCSB Average Latency. *Average latency of YCSB workloads on emulated NVMM.*

nections, M-sync's scaling improves. A tradeoff with increasing networking connections is that Mojim uses more threads to poll for receiving messages, consuming more CPU cycles.

6.3.3 Checkpoint and Secondary Tier Replication Thresholds

We change the two thresholds Mojim uses in its configurations: we change CHECKPOINT_THRESH, the frequency of checkpointing the mirror node logs, from 1 to 10000, and we change SECONDARY_TIER_THRESH, the amount of un-replicated data to the backup node, from 40 KB to 400 MB. We find that neither CHECKPOINT_THRESH nor SECONDARY_TIER_THRESH affects the application performance, because both the checkpointing process and the secondary tier replication via IB are fast enough not to block the primary tier replication.

6.4 Application Performance

In this section, we present the evaluation results for three applications: a file system, a hash table, and a NoSql database.

6.4.1 PMFS

We use the FileServer, WebServer, and VarMail workloads in the Filebench suite [54] to evaluate different Mojim modes under PMFS using emulated NVMM. Figure 10 presents the throughput of the three workloads of Filebench. For WebServer and Varmail, both M-async and M-sync yield performance similar to S-unreplicated. For FileServer, M-async and M-sync have slightly worse performance than S-unreplicated.

6.4.2 Google hash table

We perform sequential and random key-value insertion to the Google Dense Hash Table [16]. Each key-value pair contains an integer key and a random integer value. Figure 11 plots the average latency of S-unreplicated, M-async, and M-sync with emulated NVMM. For both workloads, all three schemes have similar performance, showing that Mojim has small performance overhead when it comes to hash table operations.

Workload	Read	Update	Scan	Insert	Read&Update
A	50	50	-	-	-
B	95	5	-	-	-
C	100	-	-	-	-
D	95	-	-	5	-
E	-	-	95	5	-
F	50	-	-	-	50

Table 2. YCSB Workload Properties. *The percentage of different operations in each YCSB workload.*

6.4.3 MongoDB

MongoDB is a natural fit for Mojim. We evaluate how MongoDB and Mojim compare using micro- and macro-benchmarks.

Microbenchmark: Our microbenchmark inserts key-value pairs to MongoDB. Each insert operation contains 10 key-value pairs, with each pair containing 100 bytes of randomly generated data. Figures 12 and 13 present the average latency and throughput of key-value pair insertions with PMEP's emulated NVMM. We set the MongoDB replication method to use two replicas (the primary node and the secondary node) and connect these nodes with IB.

MongoDB with Mojim outperforms the MongoDB replication method REPLICAS_SAFE by 3.7 to 3.9×. This performance gain is due to Mojim's efficient replication protocol and networking stack.

Mojim also outperforms the un-replicated JOURNALED MongoDB by 56 to 59× and the un-replicated FSYNC_SAFE by 701 to 741×. JOURNALED flushes journal content for each client write request. FSYNC_SAFE performs *fsync* of the data file after each write operation to guarantee data reliability without journaling. Both these operations are expensive.

To evaluate Mojim's two-tier architecture with MongoDB, we perform the same set of experiments using three DRAM-based machines in our lab. Similar to the PMEP results, Mojim's M-syncsec outperforms MongoDB's replication method by 3.4 to 4×, the un-replicated JOURNALED MongoDB by 35 to 43×, and the un-replicated FSYNC_SAFE by 238 to 311×, suggesting that Mojim's replication is better than MongoDB replication.

Finally, MongoDB can run unmodified on Mojim by configuring both its journal and data file to be in a *mmap*'d NVMM region. In this case, its performance is similar to JOURNALED, with a performance overhead of 0.2% to 6%. However, Mojim provides better reliability and availability than the un-replicated MongoDB.

Macrobenchmark: YCSB [10] is a benchmark designed to evaluate key-value store systems. YCSB includes six workloads that imitate web applications' data access models. The workloads contain a combination of read, update, scan, and insert operations. Table 2 summarizes the number of these operations in the YCSB workloads. Each workload performs 1000 operations on a database with 1000 1 KB records.

Figure 14 presents the latency of MongoDB and Mojim using the six YCSB workloads on emulated NVMM. For most workloads, both M-async and M-sync outperform the un-replicated and replicated MongoDB schemes. The performance improvement is especially high for write-heavy workloads. We also find similar results with three DRAM-based machines.

6.5 Recovery

Recovery performance is important because it directly affects availability and may impact reliability, since Mojim is vulnerable to additional node failures during some recovery scenarios. To test the robustness of the system, we stop a Mojim node at random and find that the rest of the system can continue serving client requests correctly. We further measure the recovery time in the event of a node failure.

We use a typical recovery scenario to illustrate Mojim's recovery performance. When a mirror node fails with M-syncsec, the recovery process requires sending the remaining, un-replicated data to the backup node, flushing the CPU caches on the primary node, and copying all the data areas to the new mirror node. Mojim performs these operations in parallel. We set SECONDARY_TIER_THRESH to 40 MB and use three machines in our lab to perform the recovery performance evaluation.

Mojim takes 450 μs to flush the 26 MB CPU caches on the primary node. Before the primary node flushes all its caches, if it also fails, there will be data loss. The window of vulnerability also depends on how soon the failure can be detected, thus in practice it will be longer than 450 μs [7]. It takes 14 ms to send 40 MB of data to the backup node and 1.9 seconds to send a 5 GB data area to the new mirror node. The whole recovery process completes in 1.9 seconds for a 5 GB NVMM. Even for a 1 TB NVMM, the recovery process will only take 6.5 minutes. Notice that the vulnerability window depends on how fast primary node detects a failure and flushes its caches, not on NVMM size.

For M-syncdisk, Mojim also needs to read the data file from the disk to the NVMM before applications can access the data. In this case, recovery takes 17 seconds for a 5 GB data file, a much higher cost in availability than when we use NVMM for the data area.

7. Related Work

This section places Mojim in context with other related research projects and systems.

Non-Volatile Main Memory: Recent years have seen increased interest in NVMM. Researchers have focused on NVMM-related problems, such as building NVMM file systems [9, 12, 59], hybrid DRAM/NVMM memory systems [39], memory allocators [41], memory management and paging mechanisms [3], and programming models [8, 58]. While previous research has focused on un-replicated NVMM in a single machine, Mojim focuses on providing reliability, high availability, and redundancy to NVMM in data center environments.

Redundancy and Replication: To provide data reliability and availability, many systems use data redundancy or replication [1, 5, 11, 15, 17, 18, 29, 46, 47, 51, 52, 56, 61]. Several previous systems adopt the architecture of one primary and multiple backups [2, 15, 56]. These systems either use a total ordering of node to serialize data replication [2, 56] or broadcast the replicated data and have the primary wait for all the backups [15] to guarantee strong consistency. Mojim uses a two-tier architecture containing one primary node, one mirror node, and multiple backup nodes. Mojim's replication between the primary node and mirror node and the background replication to the backup nodes is more efficient than replication among one primary and multiple backups.

Other architectures allow writes to all replicas (E-writeall) [11, 29, 47, 55]. Systems that require strong consistency among the replicas use Paxos-like protocols [4, 22, 31]. With such architectures, at least two networking round trips are needed to deliver strong consistency. Moreover, the round trips are necessary at each write (memory store) rather than for the less frequent sync points. In contrast, Mojim only replicates data at sync points. Ensuring strong consistency for the Mojim primary tier is also much simpler and has much smaller performance cost. There are also systems that implement weak consistency protocols for the E-writeall architecture [11, 29, 47]. These systems require a reconciliation process for conflicts, which can increase performance overhead [17]. Mojim does not involve any reconciliation and supports strong consistency in its primary tier.

Mojim's architecture is similar to the two-tier architecture proposed [17], which reduced the locking and reconciliation overhead in mobile, disconnected environments. However, we focus on data center environments where nodes are mostly connected. Moreover, Mojim's primary tier only uses one primary and one mirror node for good performance.

To reduce system downtime, commercial storage systems often maintain a pair of interconnected nodes (called high-availability pairs) [13, 19, 43, 57]. When one node fails, the other member of the pair takes over its duties. Most of these high-availability pair schemes rely on shared storage and do not replicate storage data, whereas Mojim replicates data in NVMM. Moreover, Mojim can also provide additional redundancy with its secondary tier.

Finally, RAMCloud is a low-latency key-value store that keeps all data in DRAM [44]. While Mojim and RAMCloud both provide reliable memory-based storage systems, RAMCloud provides a key-value interface rather than a memory-like interface to applications. The key-value software layer adds significant latency to accesses and obscures much of the performance of the underlying memory. Mojim offers a memory-based interface (*i.e.*, applications access Mojim using memory load and store instructions). Based on the interface it supports and its performance targets, Mojim makes design decisions differently from RAMCloud. Mojim replicates NVMM to NVMM at application sync points, while RAMCloud replicates key-value contents on each put operation to slow storage devices. Mojim does not shard memory, because sharding would result in portions of applications' NVMM being on a remote node, vastly increasing latency. As a result, Mojim uses fail-over to recover from failures instead of RAMCloud's approach that relies on sharded data storage to achieve fast recovery.

8. Conclusions

We have described Mojim, a system for providing reliable and highly-available NVMM. Mojim uses a two-tier architecture and efficiently replicates data in NVMM. Our results demonstrate that Mojim can provide replication with small cost, in many cases even outperforming the un-replicated system. In doing so, Mojim paves the way for deploying NVMM in data centers that wish to take advantage of NVMM's enhanced performance but require strong guarantees about data safety.

Acknowledgments

We thank the anonymous reviewers for their enormously valuable feedback and comments, which have substantially improved the content and presentation of this paper. We also thank Dulloor Subramanya, Jeff Jackson, and the vLab team from Intel Corp. for their help with the PMEP platforms. Finally, we thank the members of the NVSL research group for their insightful comments.

This work was supported in part by the Center for Future Architectures Research (C-FAR), one of six centers of STARnet, a Semiconductor Research Corporation program sponsored by MARCO and DARPA. Any opinions, findings, and conclusions or recommendations expressed in this material are those of the authors and do not necessarily reflect the views of C-FAR or other institutions.

References

[1] Atul Adya, William J. Bolosky, Miguel Castro, Gerald Cermak, Ronnie Chaiken, John R. Douceur, Jon Howell, Jacob R. Lorch, Marvin Theimer, and Roger P. Wattenhofer. FARSITE: Federated, Available, and Reliable Storage for an Incompletely Trusted Environment. In *Proceedings of the 5th Symposium on Operating Systems Design and Implementation (OSDI '02)*, Boston, Massachusetts, December 2002.

[2] Peter A. Alsberg and John D. Day. A principle for resilient sharing of distributed resources. In *Proceedings of the 2nd International Conference on Software Engineering (ICSE '76)*, San Francisco, California, October 1976.

[3] Katelin Bailey, Luis Ceze, Steven D. Gribble, and Henry M. Levy. Operating system implications of fast, cheap, non-volatile memory. In *Proceedings of the 13th USENIX Conference on Hot Topics in Operating Systemsi (HotOS '13)*, Napa, California, May 2011.

[4] Mike Burrows. The chubby lock service for loosely-coupled distributed systems. In *Proceedings of the 7th Symposium on Operating Systems Design and Implementation (OSDI '06)*, Seattle, Washington, November 2006.

[5] Brad Calder, Ju Wang, Aaron Ogus, Niranjan Nilakantan, Arild Skjolsvold, Sam McKelvie, Yikang Xu, Shashwat Srivastav, Jiesheng Wu, Huseyin Simitci, Jaidev Haridas, Chakravarthy Uddaraju, Hemal Khatri, Andrew Edwards, Vaman Bedekar, Shane Mainali, Rafay Abbasi, Arpit Agarwal, Mian Fahim ul Haq, Muhammad Ikram ul Haq, Deepali Bhardwaj, Sowmya Dayanand, Anitha Adusumilli, Marvin McNett, Sriram Sankaran, Kavitha Manivannan, and Leonidas Rigas. Windows azure storage: A highly available cloud storage service with strong consistency. In *Proceedings of the 23rd ACM Symposium on Operating Systems Principles (SOSP '11)*, Cascais, Portugal, October 2011.

[6] Mosharaf Chowdhury, Srikanth Kandula, and Ion Stoica. Leveraging endpoint flexibility in data-intensive clusters. In *Proceedings of the ACM SIGCOMM 2013 Conference on SIGCOMM (SIGCOMM '13)*, Hong Kong, China, August 2013.

[7] Byung-Gon Chun, Frank Dabek, Andreas Haeberlen, Emil Sit, Hakim Weatherspoon, M. Frans Kaashoek, John Kubiatowicz, and Robert Morris. Efficient replica maintenance for distributed storage systems. In *Proceedings of the 3rd Symposium on Networked Systems Design and Implementation (NSDI '06)*, San Jose, California, May 2006.

[8] Joel Coburn, Adrian M. Caulfield, Ameen Akel, Laura M. Grupp, Rajesh K. Gupta, Ranjit Jhala, and Steven Swanson. Nv-heaps: Making persistent objects fast and safe with next-generation, non-volatile memories. In *Proceedings of the Sixteenth International Conference on Architectural Support for Programming Languages and Operating Systems (ASPLOS '11)*, New York, New York, March 2011.

[9] Jeremy Condit, Edmund B. Nightingale, Christopher Frost, Engin Ipek, Doug Burger, Benjamin C. Lee, and Derrick Coetzee. Better i/o through byte-addressable, persistent memory. In *Proceedings of the 22nd ACM Symposium on Operating Systems Principles (SOSP '09)*, Big Sky, Montana, October 2009.

[10] Brian F. Cooper, Adam Silberstein, Erwin Tam, Raghu Ramakrishnan, and Russell Sears. Benchmarking cloud serving systems with ycsb. In *Proceedings of the 1st ACM Symposium on Cloud Computing (SoCC '10)*, New York, New York, June 2010.

[11] Guiseppe DeCandia, Deniz Hastorun, Madan Jampani, Gunavardhan Kakulapati, Avinash Lakshman, Alex Pilchin, Swami Sivasubramanian, Peter Vosshall, and Werner Vogels. Dynamo: Amazon's Highly Available Key-Value Store. In *Proceedings of the 21st ACM Symposium on Operating Systems Principles (SOSP '07)*, Stevenson, Washington, October 2007.

[12] Subramanya R. Dulloor, Sanjay Kumar, Anil Keshavamurthy, Philip Lantz, Dheeraj Reddy, Rajesh Sankaran, and Jeff Jackson. System software for persistent memory. In *Proceedings of the EuroSys Conference (EuroSys '14)*, Amsterdam, The Netherlands, April 2014.

[13] EMC Corporation. EMC VNXe High Availability. `https://www.emc.com/collateral/hardware/white-papers/h8276-emc-vnxe-high-availability-wp.pdf`.

[14] Daniel Ford, François Labelle, Florentina I. Popovici, Murray Stokely, Van-Anh Truong, Luiz Barroso, Carrie Grimes, and Sean Quinlan. Availability in Globally Distributed Storage Systems. In *Proceedings of the 9th Symposium on Operating Systems Design and Implementation (OSDI '10)*, Vancouver, Canada, December 2010.

[15] Sanjay Ghemawat, Howard Gobioff, and Shun-Tak Leung. The Google File System. In *Proceedings of the 19th ACM Symposium on Operating Systems Principles (SOSP '03)*, Bolton Landing, New York, October 2003.

[16] Google Inc. Google Sparse Hash. `http://goog-sparsehash.sourceforge.net`.

[17] Jim Gray, Pat Helland, Patrick O'Neil, and Dennis Shasha. The dangers of replication and a solution. In *Proceedings of the 1996 ACM SIGMOD International Conference on Management of Data (SIGMOD '96)*, New York, New York, June 1996.

[18] Lisa Hellerstein, Garth A. Gibson, Richard M. Karp, Randy H. Katz, and David A. Patterson. Coding Techniques for Handling Failures in Large Disk Arrays. *Algorithmica*, 12(2):182–208, August 1994.

[19] Hewlett Packard. HP NonStop operating system. `http://h17007.www1.hp.com/us/en/enterprise/servers/integrity/nonstop/nonstop-os.aspx`.

[20] M Hosomi, H Yamagishi, T Yamamoto, K Bessho, Y Higo, K Yamane, H Yamada, M Shoji, H Hachino, C Fukumoto, et al. A novel nonvolatile memory with spin torque transfer magnetization switching: Spin-ram. In *Electron Devices Meeting, 2005. IEDM Technical Digest. IEEE International*, pages 459–462, 2005.

[21] Cheng Huang, Huseyin Simitci, Yikang Xu, Aaron Ogus, Brad Calder, Parikshit Gopalan, Jin Li, and Sergey Yekhanin. Erasure coding in windows azure storage. In *Proceedings*

of the USENIX Annual Technical Conference (USENIX '12), Boston, Massachusetts, June 2012.

[22] Patrick Hunt, Mahadev Konar, Flavio P. Junqueira, and Benjamin Reed. Zookeeper: Wait-free coordination for internet-scale systems. In *Proceedings of the USENIX Annual Technical Conference (USENIX '10)*, Boston, Massachusetts, June 2010.

[23] Intel. Add Support for New Persistent Memory Instructions. http://www.lwn.net/Articles/619851.

[24] Intel. Intel 64 and IA-32 Architectures Software Developer's Manual. http://www.intel.com/content/dam/www/public/us/en/documents/manuals/64-ia-32-architectures-software-developer-manual-325462.pdf.

[25] Engin Ipek, Jeremy Condit, Edmund B. Nightingale, Doug Burger, and Thomas Moscibroda. Dynamically replicated memory: Building reliable systems from nanoscale resistive memories. In *Proceedings of the 14th International Conference on Architectural Support for Programming Languages and Operating Systems (ASPLOS XIV)*, Pittsburgh, Pennsylvania, March 2010.

[26] James Pinkerton. The Future of Computing: The Convergence of Memory and Storage through Non-Volatile Memory (NVM). Storage Industry Summit, San Jose, California, Jan 2014.

[27] Brian G Johnson and Charles H Dennison. Phase change memory, September 2004. US Patent 6,791,102.

[28] Brent ByungHoon Kang, Robert Wilensky, and John Kubiatowicz. The hash history approach for reconciling mutual inconsistency. In *Proceedings of the 23rd International Conference on Distributed Computing Systems (ICDCS '03)*, Providence, Rhode Island, May 2003.

[29] John Kubiatowicz, David Bindel, Patrick Eaton, Yan Chen, Dennis Geels, Ramakrishna Gummadi, Sean Rhea, Westley Weimer, Chris Wells, Hakim Weatherspoon, and Ben Zhao. OceanStore: An Architecture for Global-Scale Persistent Storage. In *Proceedings of the 9th International Conference on Architectural Support for Programming Languages and Operating Systems (ASPLOS IX)*, Cambridge, Massachusetts, November 2000.

[30] Amit Kumar and Ram Huggahalli. Impact of cache coherence protocols on the processing of network traffic. In *Proceedings of the 40th Annual IEEE/ACM International Symposium on Microarchitecture (MICRO '07)*, Chicago, Illinois, Dec 2007.

[31] Leslie Lamport. Paxos Made Simple. *ACM SIGACT News*, 32(4):18–25, November 2001.

[32] Benjamin C. Lee, Engin Ipek, Onur Mutlu, and Doug Burger. Architecting phase change memory as a scalable dram alternative. In *Proceedings of the 36th Annual International Symposium on Computer Architecture (ISCA '09)*, Austin, Texas, June 2009.

[33] Benjamin C. Lee, Engin Ipek, Onur Mutlu, and Doug Burger. Phase change memory architecture and the quest for scalability. *Commun. ACM*, 53(7):99–106, 2010.

[34] Benjamin C Lee, Ping Zhou, Jun Yang, Youtao Zhang, Bo Zhao, Engin Ipek, Onur Mutlu, and Doug Burger. Phase-change technology and the future of main memory. *IEEE micro*, 30(1):143, 2010.

[35] Myoung-Jae Lee, Chang Bum Lee, Dongsoo Lee, Seung Ryul Lee, Man Chang, Ji Hyun Hur, Young-Bae Kim, Chang-Jung Kim, David H Seo, Sunae Seo, et al. A fast, high-endurance and scalable non-volatile memory device made from asymmetric ta2o5- x/tao2- x bilayer structures. *Nature materials*, 10(8):625–630, 2011.

[36] Joshua B. Leners, Hao Wu, Wei-Lun Hung, Marcos K. Aguilera, and Michael Walfish. Detecting Failures in Distributed Systems with the Falcon Spy Network. In *Proceedings of the 23rd ACM Symposium on Operating Systems Principles (SOSP '11)*, Cascais, Portugal, October 2011.

[37] Mellanox Technologies. Rdma aware networks programming user manual. http://www.mellanox.com/related-docs/prod_software/RDMA_Aware_Programming_user_manual.pdf.

[38] Micron Technology Inc. P8p parallel phase change memory (pcm). http://www.micron.com/~/media/Documents/Products/Data%20Sheet/PCM/p8p_parallel_pcm_ds.pdf.

[39] Jeffrey C. Mogul, Eduardo Argollo, Mehul Shah, and Paolo Faraboschi. Operating system support for nvm+dram hybrid main memory. In *The Twelfth Workshop on Hot Topics in Operating Systems (HotOS XII)*, Monte Verita, Switzerland, May 2009.

[40] MongoDB Inc. MongoDB. http://www.mongodb.org/.

[41] Iulian Moraru, David G Andersen, Michael Kaminsky, Niraj Tolia, Parthasarathy Ranganathan, and Nathan Binkert. Consistent, durable, and safe memory management for byte-addressable non volatile main memory. In *Conference on Timely Results in Operating Systems (TRIOS '13)*, Farmington, Pennsylvania, November 2013.

[42] Suman Nath, Haifeng Yu, Philip B. Gibbons, and Srinivasan Seshan. Subtleties in tolerating correlated failures in wide-area storage systems. In *Proceedings of the 3rd Symposium on Networked Systems Design and Implementation (NSDI '06)*, San Jose, California, May 2006.

[43] NetApp Inc. NetApp SnapMirror Data Replication. http://www.netapp.com/us/products/protection-software/snapmirror.aspx.

[44] Diego Ongaro, Stephen M. Rumble, Ryan Stutsman, John Ousterhout, and Mendel Rosenblum. Fast Crash Recovery in RAMCloud. In *Proceedings of the 23rd ACM Symposium on Operating Systems Principles (SOSP '11)*, Cascais, Portugal, October 2011.

[45] Stan Park, Terence Kelly, and Kai Shen. Failure-atomic msync (): a simple and efficient mechanism for preserving the integrity of durable data. In *Proceedings of the EuroSys Conference (EuroSys '13)*, Prague, Czech Republic, April 2013.

[46] David Patterson, Garth Gibson, and Randy Katz. A Case for Redundant Arrays of Inexpensive Disks (RAID). In *Proceed-*

ings of the 1988 ACM SIGMOD Conference on the Management of Data (SIGMOD '88), Chicago, Illinois, June 1988.

[47] Karin Petersen, Mike J. Spreitzer, Douglas B. Terry, Marvin M. Theimer, and Alan J. Demers. Flexible Update Propagation for Weakly Consistent Replication. In *Proceedings of the 16th ACM Symposium on Operating Systems Principles (SOSP '97)*, Saint-Malo, France, October 1997.

[48] Moinuddin K Qureshi, Michele M Franceschini, Luis A Lastras-Montaño, and John P Karidis. Morphable memory system: a robust architecture for exploiting multi-level phase change memories. In *Proceedings of the 37th Annual International Symposium on Computer Architecture (ISCA '07)*, June 2010.

[49] Moinuddin K. Qureshi, Vijayalakshmi Srinivasan, and Jude A. Rivers. Scalable high performance main memory system using phase-change memory technology. In *Proceedings of the 36th Annual International Symposium on Computer Architecture (ISCA '09)*, Austin, Texas, June 2009.

[50] Luiz E. Ramos, Eugene Gorbatov, and Ricardo Bianchini. Page placement in hybrid memory systems. In *Proceedings of the International Conference on Supercomputing (ICS '11)*, Tucson, Arizona, 2011.

[51] Sean Rhea, Patrick Eaton, Dennis Geels, Hakim Weatherspoon, Ben Zhao, and John Kubiatowicz. Pond: The oceanstore prototype. In *Proceedings of the 2nd USENIX Symposium on File and Storage Technologies (FAST '03)*, San Francisco, California, April 2003.

[52] Antony Rowstron and Peter Druschel. Storage Management and Caching in PAST, A Large-scale, Persistent Peer-to-peer Storage Utility. In *Proceedings of the 18th ACM Symposium on Operating Systems Principles (SOSP '01)*, Banff, Canada, October 2001.

[53] David Spence, Jon Crowcroft, Steven Hand, and Tim Harris. Location based placement of whole distributed systems. In *Proceedings of the 2005 ACM Conference on Emerging Network Experiment and Technology (CoNEXT '05)*, Toulouse, France, October 2005.

[54] Sun Microsystems. Solaris Internals: FileBench. `http://filebench.sourceforge.net/`.

[55] Douglas B. Terry, Vijayan Prabhakaran, Ramakrishna Kotla, Mahesh Balakrishnan, Marcos K. Aguilera, and Hussam Abu-Libdeh. Consistency-Based Service Level Agreements for Cloud Storage. In *Proceedings of the 24th ACM Symposium on Operating Systems Principles (SOSP '13)*, Farmington, Pennsylvania, November 2013.

[56] Robbert van Renesse and Fred B. Schneider. Chain replication for supporting high throughput and availability. In *Proceedings of the 6th Symposium on Operating Systems Design and Implementation (OSDI '04)*, San Francisco, California, December 2004.

[57] VMWare Inc. VMware High Availability. `http://www.vmware.com/files/pdf/VMware-High-Availability-DS-EN.pdf`.

[58] Haris Volos, Andres Jaan Tack, and Michael M. Swift. Mnemosyne: Lightweight persistent memory. In *Proceedings of the Sixteenth International Conference on Architectural Support for Programming Languages and Operating Systems (ASPLOS '11)*, New York, New York, March 2011.

[59] Xiaojian Wu and A.L.N. Reddy. Scmfs: A file system for storage class memory. In *International Conference for High Performance Computing, Networking, Storage and Analysis (SC '11)*, Nov 2011.

[60] J Joshua Yang, Dmitri B Strukov, and Duncan R Stewart. Memristive devices for computing. *Nature nanotechnology*, 8(1):13–24, 2013.

[61] Ming Zhong, Kai Shen, and Joel Seiferas. Replication degree customization for high availability. In *Proceedings of the EuroSys Conference (EuroSys '08)*, Glasgow, Scotland UK, March 2008.

[62] Ping Zhou, Bo Zhao, Jun Yang, and Youtao Zhang. A durable and energy efficient main memory using phase change memory technology. In *Proceedings of the 36th Annual International Symposium on Computer Architecture (ISCA '09)*, Austin, Texas, June 2009.

SD-PCM: Constructing Reliable Super Dense Phase Change Memory under Write Disturbance

Rujia Wang
University of Pittsburgh
ruw16@pitt.edu

Lei Jiang
University of Pittsburgh
lej16@pitt.edu

Youtao Zhang
University of Pittsburgh
zhangyt@cs.pitt.edu

Jun Yang
University of Pittsburgh
juy9@pitt.edu

Abstract

Phase Change Memory (PCM) has better scalability and smaller cell size comparing to DRAM. However, further scaling PCM cell in deep sub-micron regime results in significant thermal based write disturbance (WD). Naively allocating large inter-cell space increases cell size from $4F^2$ ideal to $12F^2$. While a recent work mitigates WD along word-lines through disturbance resilient data encoding, it is ineffective for WD along bit-lines, which is more severe due to widely adopted μTrench structure in constructing PCM cell arrays. Without mitigating WD along bit-lines, a PCM cell still has $8F^2$, which is 100% larger than the ideal.

In this paper, we propose SD-PCM for achieving reliable write operations in super dense PCM. In particular, we focus on mitigating WD along bit-lines such that we can construct super dense PCM chips with $4F^2$ cell size, i.e., the minimal for diode-switch based PCM. Based on simple verification-n-correction (VnC), we propose LazyCorrection and PreRead to effectively reduce VnC overhead and minimize cascading verification during write. We further propose (n:m)-Alloc for achieving good tradeoff between VnC overhead minimization and memory capacity loss. Our experimental results show that, comparing to a WD-free low density PCM, SD-PCM achieves 80% capacity improvement in cell arrays while incurring around 0-10% performance degradation when using different (n:m) allocators.

ASPLOS '15, March 14–18, 2015, Istanbul, Turkey..

http://dx.doi.org/10.1145/2694344.2694352

Categories and Subject Descriptors C.0 [*Computer Systems Organization*]: GENERAL-Hardware/software interfaces

Keywords Phase Change Memory; Write Disturbance

1. Introduction

Phase Change Memory (PCM) has recently emerged as a promising memory technology that supplements to traditional DRAM technology for future main memory systems. As modern applications increasingly demand for large amount of memory, it is important to construct highly scalable and dense main memory with low power consumption [14, 21]. Unfortunately, DRAM faces both scalability and power consumption challenges — the path to scale DRAM beyond 20nm is unclear, and the refresh power from DRAM chips of large capacity is significant [16]. PCM has better scalability and better cell size — PCM chips can be constructed with 20nm technology and diode-switch based PCM exhibits $4F^2$ cell size [8]. As a non-volatile memory technology, PCM has no leakage power from the cell. In recent studies, PCM has been proposed to replace a significant portion of DRAM main memory for achieving the overall energy effectiveness [14, 21, 35].

A PCM cell takes advantage of phase change material (GST [24]) to record data. By the application of heat generated through electrical pulses, the phase change material inside each PCM cell can be melted (RESET) or crystallized (SET). Scaling PCM in deep sub-micron regime faces non-negligible inter-cell thermal interference during programming, referred to as write disturbance (WD) phenomenon. That is, the heat generated for writing one cell may disseminate beyond this cell and disturb the resistance states of its neighboring cells. WD in PCM was first observed at 54nm [15], and has become more significant at and below 20nm technology [4, 13].

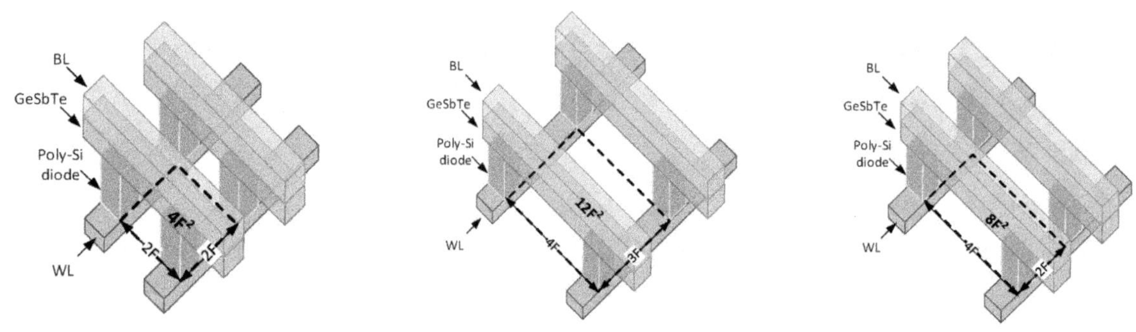

(a) Ideal super dense chip (4F^2/cell) (b) Prototype chip [8] (12F^2/cell) (c) DIN[10]-enhanced chip (8F^2/cell)

Figure 1. Write disturbance (WD) has a large impact on PCM cell density.

The existing solutions for mitigating WD in PCM are ineffective. A simple yet widely adopted solution is to allocate sufficient thermal bands between cells, which results in significantly deviated PCM chip capacity from its theoretical ideal. For example, in recent prototype PCM chips [4, 8], 20nm and 40nm extra inter-cell space was introduced along word-lines and bit-lines, respectively, which results in only 33% memory capacity of the ideal, as shown in Figure 1(b). Naively adopting mitigation techniques developed for other memory technologies (such as NAND Flash), e.g., verify-n-correct (VnC), may lead to cascading verification and large performance overhead.

The work that is most related to our design is *DIN* [10], a recent proposal that addresses WD in PCM through disturbance-aware data encoding, which minimizes data patterns that are more vulnerable to disturbance. However, *DIN* applies only to WD along word-lines. Studies revealed that WD errors along bit-lines are more significant than those along word-lines. This is because PCM cell array widely adopts μTrench structure [18], which connects cells along one bit-line with one GST rail while different bit-lines are isolated by dielectric, e.g., oxide material. Since oxide has better thermal isolation [12] than GST, the disturbance along bit-line is more significant than that along word-line. Without proper WD mitigation along bit-lines, *DIN* achieves 8F^2 cell size, an 33% improvement over the low density design. However, it is still 100% larger than the 4F^2 ideal, , as shown in Figure 1(c).

In this paper, we propose SD-PCM for achieving reliable write operations in super dense PCM. A super dense PCM chip is built by allocating only minimal inter-cell space along both bit-lines and word-lines. We devise a set of techniques to mitigate WD errors with low performance overhead. In particular, we make the following contributions.

- We illustrate that WD along bit-lines translates to disturbance errors with high possibility. A simple adaption of verification and correction (VnC) for WD errors would require VnC on per-write basis and may lead to cascading verification, resulting in large performance degradation. In the paper, we propose LazyCorrection and PreRead that effectively minimize verification and correction overhead, respectively.
- We propose (n:m)-Alloc for achieving good runtime tradeoff between VnC overhead minimization and memory capacity loss. (n:m)-Alloc selectively marks a set of device rows as *no-use*, i.e., not to be allocated to any process. By storing no data in these rows, we effectively reduce the necessity of doing verification on these rows, and thus gain the flexibility to match the VnC overhead to the performance demand of high priority applications.
- We evaluate our proposed schemes and compare them to the state-of-the-art. The experimental results show that our design can achieve 80% capacity improvement in memory cell arrays over the WD-free low density PCM design. SD-PCM incurs around 0-10% performance degradation when adopting different (n:m) allocators.

The rest of this paper is organized as follows. Section 2 introduces PCM and WD background. Section 3 illustrates the challenges of mitigating WD along bit-lines. Section 4 elaborates the design details of our three schemes. Section 5 and Section 6 discuss our experimental methodology and results. Section 7 discusses additional related works. Section 8 concludes the paper.

2. Background

2.1 PCM Basics

Phase Change Memory (PCM) stores data by utilizing phase change material, e.g., $Ge_2Sb_2Te_5$ (GST). A PCM cell uses its fully amorphous state with high resistance and its fully crystalline state with low resistance to represent bit '0' and '1', respectively. PCM switches between two states by heating the cell with current pulses. The RESET operation heats the cell above melting temperature (about 600 °C) and quench quickly; the SET operation requires the temperature above the crystallization temperature (about 300 °C) and below the melting temperature for a relatively long period. In short, SET requires lower temperature but longer time than RESET.

A PCM chip can be built in 2D cell array that is similar to DRAM [6, 24]. As shown in Figure 1(a), a diode-switch based PCM cell can achieve $4F^2$ per cell (where F is the feature size) [4, 8]. The cell that stores one bit is called Single-level-cell (SLC) while the cell that stores multiple bits is called Multiple-level-cell (MLC).

2.2 Write Disturbance in PCM

The write disturbance (WD) in PCM arises from the inter-cell heat dissemination during programming. When resetting a PCM cell, the programming heat may spread to its neighboring cells and corrupt their stored values. Figure 2 exhibits two neighboring PCM cells along one bit-line. Since these two cells belong to different memory lines (word-lines), a write happens on at most one of them. For example, one write only reset the left cell and leave the right cell untouched. The right cell is referred to as an *idle* cell in this paper. Because of the disseminated heat along the bit-line, in the case if the right cell is in fully amorphous state, a part of its amorphous volume may collapse into crystalline fractions, which greatly reduces its resistance and loses the stored bit '0' [4, 13].

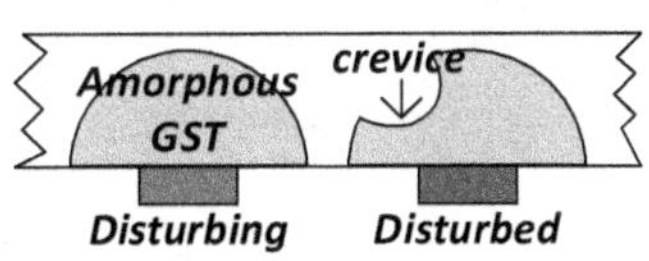

Figure 2. WD along a bit-line.

WD in PCM was first reported at 54nm [15]. However, as fast technology scaling keeps reducing inter-cell distance, the WD in PCM has become a non-negligible reliability issue at 20nm. Recent works [4, 13] demonstrated that WD is a major obstacle for the practical deployment of PCM.

2.2.1 WD Vulnerable Data Pattern

WD in PCM may manifest as an error only in a particular data pattern, i.e., the bit in a PCM cell $Cell_1$ may be disturbed only when its neighboring cell $Cell_0$ is under RESET while $Cell_1$ is idle and in amorphous state. This is because: (i) heat dissemination decays fast horizontally. The temperature that $Cell_1$ can reach (due to $Cell_0$ being RESET) is always below the melting temperature threshold but may be higher than the crystalline temperature threshold. Thus, $Cell_1$ may be crystallized if it stays in RESET state (i.e., amorphous state), but cannot be melt if it is in SET state (i.e., crystalline state) [13]. (ii) since SET current is only about half of RESET current, the temperature increase during SET is four times lower than that during RESET [26]. Thus, the disturbing influence of SET operation can be ignored [27].

Figure 3 illustrates the location of vulnerable PCM cells. For a cell being RESET, its neighbor cell is vulnerable if it stores bit 0 and is idle. Vulnerable cells may appear along a word-line or a bit-line. Vulnerable cells do not always produce disturbance errors. However, in the worst case, one RESET may disturb four neighboring cells and introduces four bit errors.

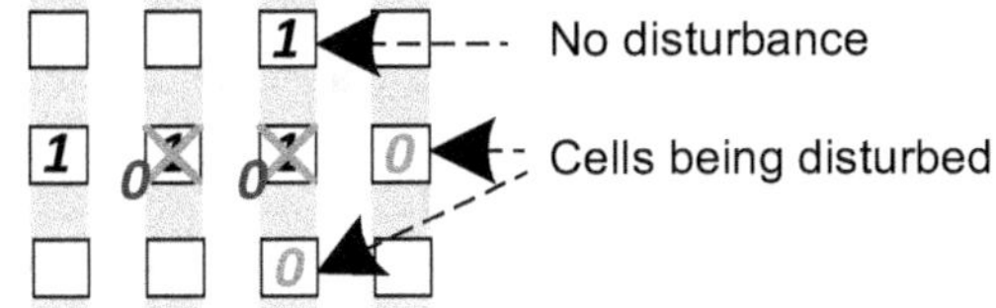

Figure 3. WD-vulnerable data pattern.

2.2.2 Modeling Write Disturbance

We adopted the WD model from [10] that includes a PCM cell thermal model, a PCM cell scaling model, and a PCM thermal disturbance model. The PCM cell thermal model is used to evaluate the interference temperature elevation during one RESET operation for the cells generated using the PCM cell scaling model. By combining the PCM cell thermal model and the PCM cell scaling model, the disturbance temperature increment can be computed for different technology nodes. In this paper, we focus on 20nm technology. We fed the disturbance temperature rise during a RESET operation into the PCM thermal disturbance model to compute WD bit error rate.

Table 1. Disturbance Probability for $4F^2$ cells

Between two cells along	Temp↑	Error rate (SLC)
Word-line	310 °C	9.9%
Bit-line	320 °C	11.5%

Given feature size F (F=20nm in this paper), 2F cell-to-cell space represents the minimal distance, i.e., two cells are placed next to each other. The cell array often adopts the μTrench structure [18], where PCM cells are fabricated on a GST (chalcogenide) bar serving as a bit-line. Two GST strips are separated by oxide material. Since oxide has better thermal isolation [12] than GST, the interference temperature elevation along a word-line for 40nm inter-cell space is 310 °C [10], and along a word-line for 40nm inter-cell space is 320 °C, i.e., 10°C higher [4]. We summarize the thermal disturbance error rates for SLC PCM cells in Table 1. The details of the models are in [10].

2.2.3 Difference from Other PCM Errors

Write disturbance error is different from other types of errors in PCM, such as hard failure error and resistance drift error. The error rate of write disturbance is much higher than the rates of these two types of errors.

The hard failure error in PCM happens when a PCM cell fails to change its state when injecting programming currents. A PCM cell may stuck at high or low resistance state and its value can not be changed any more. In contrast, WD error is a type of soft errors — a disturbed cell can be corrected by rewriting.

The soft error due to resistance drift in PCM [5, 31] reflects the fact that the resistance of a PCM cell increases spontaneously after write operation. It happens when there is no operation accessing the cell. In addition, resistance drift happens even at room temperature [9]. Studies show that MLC PCM cells are vulnerable to resistance drift. Resistance drift is not treated as a major reliability concern in this paper as we consider SLC PCM only. In contrast, WD error happens when an amorphous state cell is idle but its neighboring cell is under RESET. Moreover, it can only occur under a higher disturbing temperature (i.e., above crystallization point). The disturbed cell can be considered as "partially" SET.

3. Motivation

In this section, we discuss the inadequacy of two widely adopted disturbance mitigation techniques. One is to allocate sufficient inter-cell space. The other is to rectify disturbed cells through Verify-n-Correct (VnC).

3.1 Allocating Large Inter-cell Space

WD in PCM heavily depends on the inter-cell distance. The shorter distance between two PCM cells there is, the more significantly WD errors prevail [13, 25]. Therefore, a simple yet widely adopted approach to mitigate write disturbance is to allocate sufficiently large inter-cell space.

Figure 1(b) illustrates a WD-free prototype chip with $12F^2$ cell size [8]. Thermal disturbance decays very fast horizontally. As a result, allocating 3F along bit-line and 4F along word-line effectively eliminates all WD errors. The chip allocates more inter-cell space along bit-lines because WD along bit-lines is more severe than that along word-lines. The major issue of large inter-cell space is memory capacity loss, e.g., the cell array of the prototype chip achieves only 33% of the memory capacity of an ideal cell array ($4F^2$ cell size).

Figure 1(c) illustrates the cell array enhanced with WD-aware data encoding scheme [10]. It shrinks inter-cell space along word-lines but not along bit-lines. As a result, WD may manifest along word-lines only. The DIN scheme [10] performs additional checks and rewrites to ensure write reliability. The DIN-enhanced cell array achieves $8F^2$/cell, or a 33% memory capacity increase from that in the prototype chip. However, comparing to the ideal, its cell size is still 100% bigger, representing 50% capacity loss.

Note, the cell array density improvement often translates to a smaller chip size reduction. For example, PCM cells occupy 46.6% of the total chip area of the prototype chip [8]. The DIN-enhanced scheme achieves 33% cell array density improvement, or 15.4% chip size reduction.

Challenge 1: is it possible to enable the super dense PCM with or close to $4F^2$ cell size?

3.2 VnC: Verify and Correct Disturbance Errors

While WD errors are soft errors, traditional software correction schemes, such as SECDED ECC or strong BCH, are not applicable. This is mainly due to the relatively high WD error rates (as shown in Table 1).

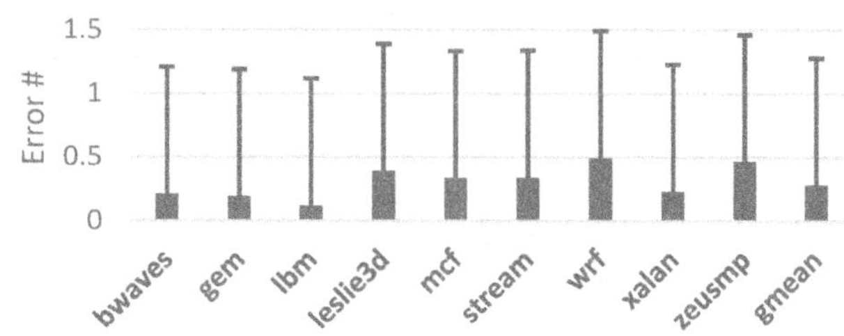

(a) Manifested errors within the same word-line

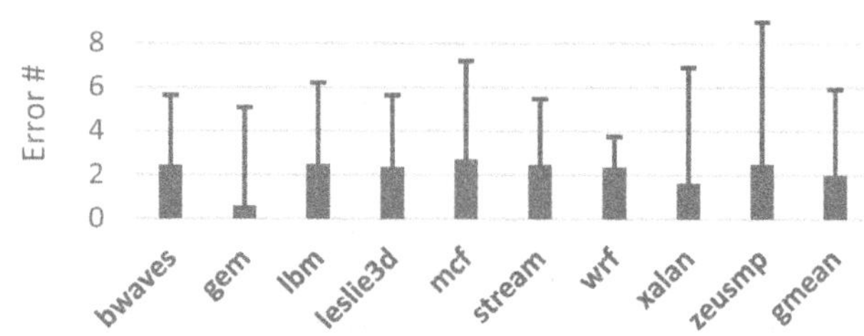

(b) Manifested errors in one adjacent PCM line

Figure 4. WD errors when writing a PCM line in super dense PCM ($4F^2$/cell).

Figure 4 reports the average and maximum WD errors when writing a PCM line.We adopt differential write [35] to minimize the total number of cell writes per write operation, and the DIN scheme [10] to mitigate WD along word-lines. From the figure, the WD errors within the same word-line are well mitigated — on average, there are 0.4 errors. Unfortunately, one write produces up to 9 WD errors in one adjacent line (64B). This requires 82 bits, or 16% space overhead if adopting a strong BCH code [32]. In addition, WD errors accumulate fast. Writing a PCM line ten times may produce 20 WD errors in different bit locations of its adjacent line, defeating a strong ECC protection with reasonable space overhead.

Another widely adopted disturbance mitigation approach is to verify and, if necessary, correct appeared WD errors, this is referred to as VnC in the paper. The issue with WD errors along bit-lines is that these errors are not in the PCM line being written. In order to apply VnC scheme, we need to read the old data of adjacent device lines before writing the current line, read again after write, compare the data from two reads, and correct adjacent lines if WD errors appear. Disturbed cells are in '0' state and require RESET operations

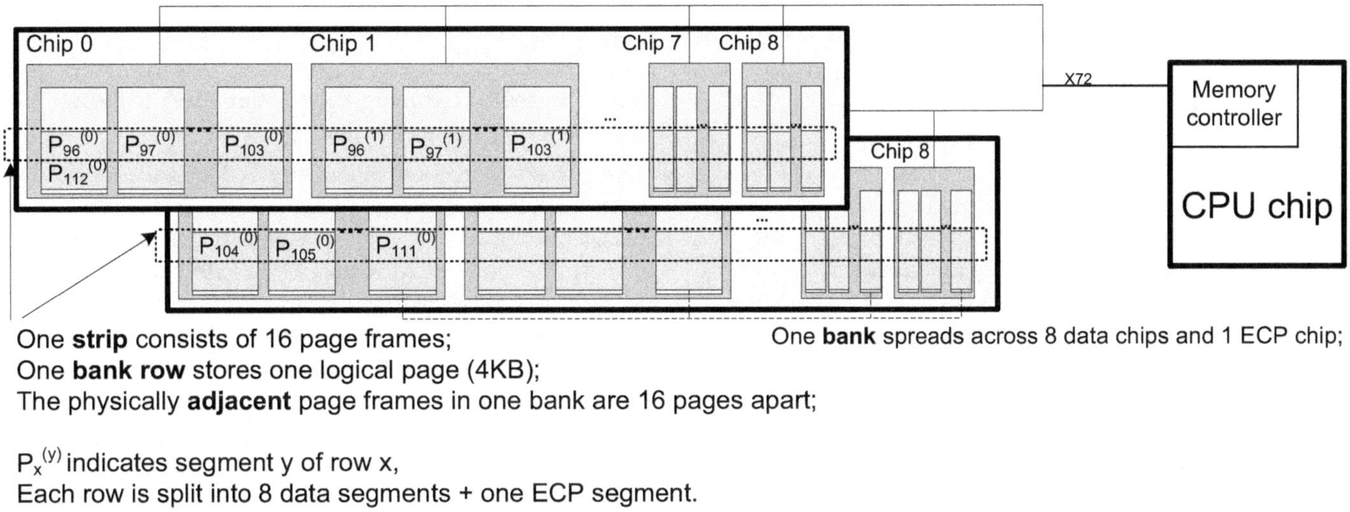

Figure 6. The baseline architecture.

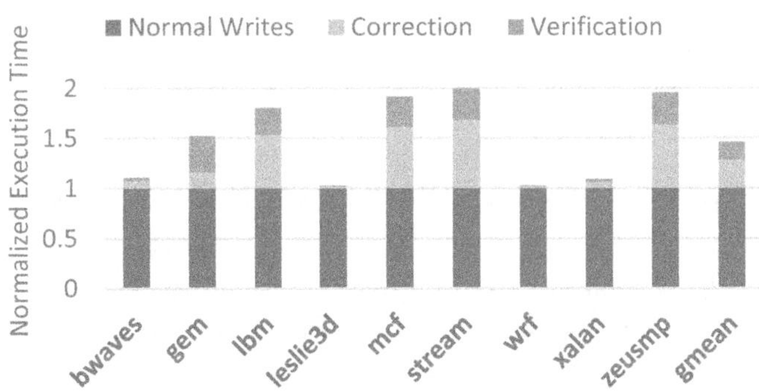

Figure 5. VnC overhead at runtime.

to correct. Thus, writing adjacent lines requires additional VnC processing, resulting in cascading verification and large performance loss.

Figure 5 shows the performance degradation when applying the basic VnC. The experimental setting is in Section 5. From the figure, the overheads for verification and correction are 19% and 28%, respectively. In total, the performance loss is about 47%.

Challenge 2: How to reduce VnC performance impact with low hardware cost?

4. SD-PCM: Enable Reliable Write Operations in Super Dense PCM

4.1 Design Overview

In this paper, we devise SD-PCM to enable reliable writes in super dense PCM (i.e., $4F^2$/cell). In particular, we focus on mitigating WD errors along bit-lines and adopt DIN [10] to minimize WD errors along word-lines. The techniques developed in this paper allow us to choose the densest cell array (Figure 1(a)). As a comparison, the densest cell array of previous PCM designs is shown in Figure 1(c), reflecting 50% memory capacity loss from SD-PCM.

An overview of the baseline architecture of SD-PCM is shown in Figure 6. One DIMM consists of two ranks and each rank has eight banks. At the device level, one bank stores 4096 SLC cells in one row, which spreads across eight PCM data chips. That is, one device row holds the content of one logical page in the OS. There is one additional chip that adopts ECP scheme to defend against hard errors [28].

For discussion simplicity, the rows with the same index from all banks form a *strip*. To maximize parallelism at runtime, a modern OS often maps its physical page frames interleaved across multiple ranks and banks. [17], i.e., one strip consists of 16 consecutive physical pages, and the pages saved in two adjacent rows in one bank are 16 pages apart.

Our design is built on top of the basic Verify and Correct (VnC). Figure 5 illustrates that both verification and correction operations introduce non-negligible performance overhead. Therefore we develop two schemes, LazyCorrection and PreRead, to reduce the overheads, respectively. To further minimize performance impact from VnC and meet the demand of high priority applications, we develop (n:m)-Alloc for achieving good runtime tradeoff between VnC overhead minimization and memory capacity loss.

4.2 LazyCorrection: Reduce Correction Overhead with WD-free ECP

On average, one PCM line write triggers two WD errors in each of its adjacent lines. The hardware cannot start correcting disturbed cells until after the write and the verification steps finish. It is clearly ineffective to prolong the write latency by two RESETs (and further verification) just for a small number of incorrect cells. In this paper, we propose to record error locations and values in the ECP region, and rectify the adjacent lines only if there are more errors than what ECP can handle. In the design, we prioritize the allocation of ECP entries to hard errors, and handle WD errors using unused ECP entries. In the case if hard errors used up all ECP entries of one PCM line, the WD mitigation for this line would rollback to the basic VnC strategy.

Naively writing ECP region faces the same WD issue, which needs expensive VnC process. To prevent cascading verification and correction, we propose to utilize low density ECP chip (i.e., $8F^2$/cell) for storing ECP pointers (as shown in Figure 7). By buffering WD errors in ECP and utilizing low density ECP chips, we effectively reduce per-write correction overhead and greatly minimize the possibility of cascading verification. The is referred to as LazyCorrection.

LazyCorrection is performed after verification and thus never leaves an adjacent line in erroneous state. Assume we use ECP-`N` where `N` represents the maximal number of errors that ECP can protect, and an adjacent line has accumulated `X` errors (WD errors and/or hard errors) before the current line write. Assume the after-write verification step detects `Y` new errors. The correction step may be skipped if (`X`+`Y`$\leq$`N`). Otherwise, the hardware tries to correct all (`X`+`Y`) cells. Some ECP pointers may record hard errors, the correction write can only clear WD errors. The hard errors are still recorded in the ECP region. This correction triggers cascading verification, which reads and verifies its adjacent lines, until no error detected after one verification.

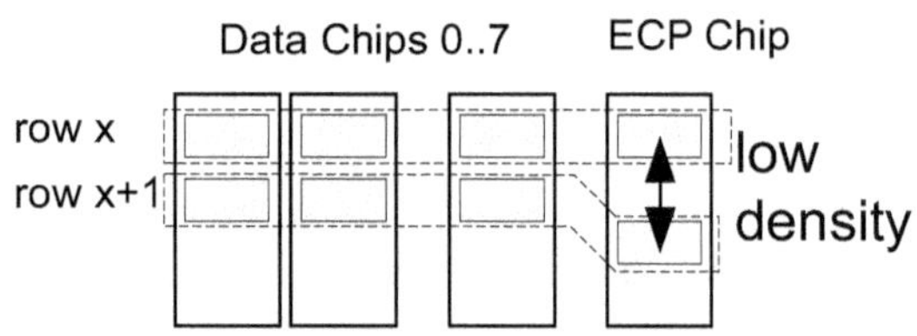

Figure 7. Buffering WD errors in low density ECP region.

When WD errors appear, there is a demand to correct disturbed cells. Without LazyCorrection, each demand is translated to a correction operation. LazyCorrection improves performance by consolidating several correction demands into one correction operation — at the time when there are more WD errors than what ECP can handle. LazyCorrection also consolidates correction demands into normal write. That is, a normal write operation clears the accumulated WD errors in ECP, and thus hides its impact.

A disadvantage using low density ECP chip is that it holds fewer rows comparing to a super dense ECP chip. To ensure ECP protection for every data row, we either need to increase the size of our low density ECP chip, or integrate two ECP chips (of the same size as data chips). In this paper, we adopt the former, which has 100% larger cell array. The latter is also of modest cost. While integrating two ECP chips leads to large cost, it helps to protect 100% more memory capacity. If the memory is built using low capacity data chips, protecting the same memory capacity also requires two ECP chips. In addition, the external data bus is the same (72 bits). For either choice, one memory accesses access only one ECP chip.

4.3 PreRead: Reducing Verification Overhead by Reading Adjacent Lines Early

While LazyCorrection effectively reduces the correction overhead, the performance loss due to verification of adjacent lines is still significant. Comparing to WD-free low density PCM, SD-PCM requires four extra reads operations — two pre-write read operations and two post-write read operations. The former buffers the old data before possible disturbance while the latter checks if the disturbance does happen.

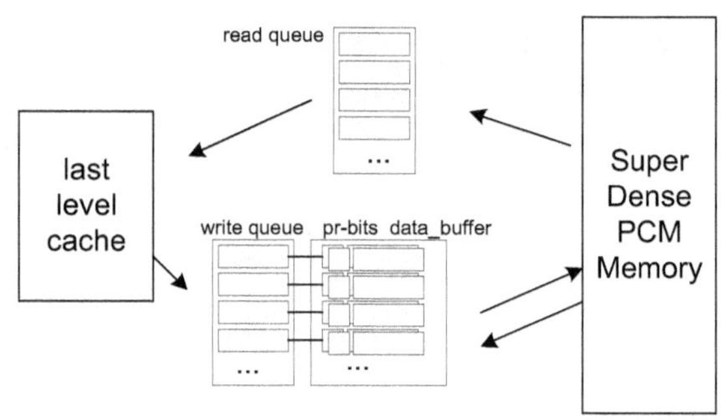

Figure 8. PreRead proactively loads old data of adjacent lines.

To minimize the performance impact of extra read operations, we propose PreRead, which performs the two pre-write reads when the write request is still in the write queue. PreRead is effective because: (i) by default, SD-PCM buffers write requests and flushes those writes when the queue is full, which triggers bursty write. A write request often experiences a long queuing time during which the PreRead operation can be scheduled. (ii) Studies showed that the memory banks in a PCM-based main memory system have a lot of idle periods [23]. Thus, a PreRead operation often has the opportunity to be issued when its associated memory bank is idle, which introduces low performance impact.

Figure 8 shows the hardware enhancement to the write queue to enable PreRead — each entry is enhanced with two PreRead flag bits and two 64B buffers. The flag bits are used to indicate if PreRead operations have been issued for one or both adjacent lines. The return data are buffered in the data buffers for later verification. Note that an adjacent line is 16 physical frames away from the line to be written. Since the hardware uses the physical address directly for PreRead, and may not know its corresponding logical page address, the fetched data is buffered for data verification only. PreRead is not prefetching as the latter needs to forward the fetched data to the upper level caches.

Pre-write reads are not as critical as *real* read requests, i.e., those from the OS or user applications. They have lower priority for scheduling. For example, when combining PreRead and write cancellation [22], a real read request may cancel both write and pre-write read requests. This helps to minimize VnC overhead on application performance.

PreRead needs to handle the case when two consecutive lines reside in the buffer simultaneously. For example, buffering the write to line i needs to PreRead both line i-x and line i+x. Here we assume two adjacent PCM lines are x lines away due to interleaving memory layout. If a new write request modifies line i+x and thus needs to PreRead line i, instead of naively reading the data from the memory, we forward the up-to-date data of line i from the buffer directly. This is necessary because, by the time we write line i+x, line i should have already been updated and the memory holds the new data.

4.4 (N:M)-Alloc: A WD-aware Page Allocator for Flexible VnC Overhead Minimization

SD-PCM effectively reduces the average VnC overhead through LazyCorrection and PreRead. However, it still imposes non-negligible performance degradation on memory write-intensive applications. This could become a concern if these applications have high priority and need to finish within tight time constraints. In this section, we present (n:m)-Alloc ($0<n\leq m$), a WD-aware page allocator for minimizing VnC overhead on write-intensive applications.

(N:M)-Alloc uses n out of m consecutive device strips within a block. It is proposed based on the observation that, when writing a PCM line, it is necessary to verify and correct both of its adjacent lines only if these lines store useful data. If the OS can proactively mark one or both adjacent lines as *no-use*, i.e., not to be allocated to any process, the VnC overhead can be reduced or even eliminated, which greatly speeds up the write operation. For example, since (1:2)-Alloc uses every other device strip, there is no need to perform VnC at runtime. When using (2:3)-Alloc, each PCM line has one adjacent line that stores data, and one that does not. A write operation needs to verify and correct only one adjacent line, incurring less overhead.

The design goal of (N:M)-Alloc is to achieve a trade-off between performance and capacity. While it disables a subset of rows, it gains the flexibility to match the performance demands of various applications.

We mark strips as *no-use* within each 64MB independently. As we will elaborate next, the OS performs (n:m) allocation on blocks whose sizes are $2^i \times$64MB ($i\geq 0$). A (2:3) allocator marks the 2nd strip of each 3-strip group. A 3-strip group may span across a 32MB block boundary, but never across any 64MB block boundary. Given a larger block, e.g., a 128MB block, we treat it as two 64MB blocks in marking strips.

(n:m) page allocation. We integrate (n:m) allocation with the buddy-system based page allocation in modern OS. The OS performs (1:1) allocation by default, i.e., no marking, and (n:m) allocation ($n\neq m$) only if it receives explicit requests from the kernel or user applications. The OS manages the page allocation for each (n:m) allocator independently and maintains a separate free-block-list-array. A new field — (n:m) allocator tag, is added to the page table to indicate from which allocator the page is allocated. This tag is then loaded to the TLB and passed to the memory controller.

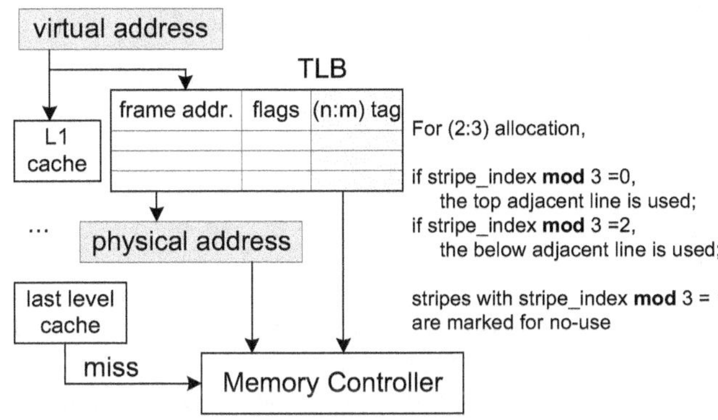

Figure 9. Enhancing TLB with (n:m) allocator tag.

Given a PCM line to be written, the memory controller uses the allocator tag to determine if its adjacent lines are used. Additional verification and correction commands are sent to PCM only if one or both adjacent lines are not marked for *no-use*. Figure 9 illustrates the enhancement to the page table and the TLB entry. After having the physical memory address, the memory controller first computes its strip index within its 64MB block, and then determines which of its adjacent lines need to be verified.

To ensure reliability, if a PCM line belongs to the first strip of its 64MB block, the hardware always verifies its top adjacent line; if a line belongs to the last strip of its 64MB block, its below adjacent line is always verified.

Integrating (n:m)-Alloc with buddy-system based page allocation. In the baseline buddy-system, the OS maintains lists of blocks that are power of two number of pages, e.g., a 2^3-page-sized block list (abbrev. 2^3-list). Given a memory request asking for 16 pages, the OS gets one block from the 2^4-list to service the request. If there is no block on the 2^4-list but one on the 2^5-list. The OS splits the 2^5-page block, returns a 16-page block to the requester, and links the other 16-page block to 2^4-list.

Our WD-aware buddy page allocator maintains one free-block-list-array Free-(n:m) for each (n:m) allocator. (1:1)-Alloc is the same as the baseline allocator as it allocates all strips within a region. Free-(1:1) is the only free list array if no other (n:m) allocator ($n\neq m$) is requested. If there is a request for (n:m) allocation and Free-(n:m) is empty, the OS gets one 64MB block (or a power two number of 64MB block if the requested size is larger) from Free-(1:1) and places it in the appropriate entry in Free-(n:m).

Using (1:2) allocation as an example, we illustrate how to perform page allocation. Assume there is a request asking for 32 pages (128KB). Since it is bigger than a device strip (16 pages), we adjust the requested size and allocate a block

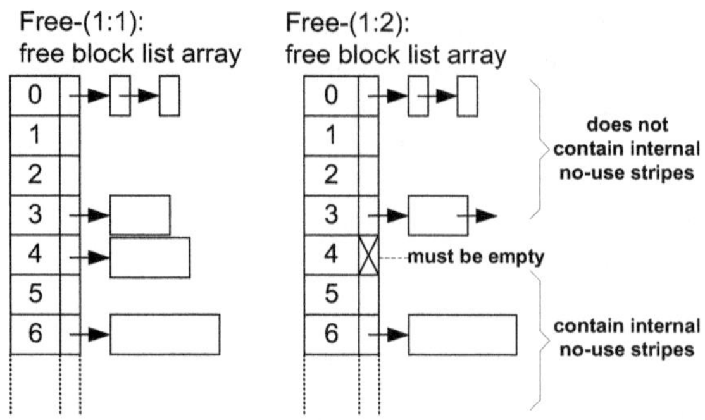

Figure 10. Enabling (n:m)-Alloc in the buddy system for page allocation.

with 64 page frames. The OS will then associate logical pages 0 to 31 to physical frames 0 to 15, and 32 to 47, respectively. The *no-use* strips become *internal fragments*. If there is a request asking for 8 pages (32KB). We service the request directly if there are entries in 2^3-list. If not, we find a block from 2^5-list. All (n:m) allocators with n≠m do not use 2^4-list because requests asking for 16 pages always have their sizes adjusted to 32 pages. When splitting a block that is 16-page or bigger, the OS only uses/links the sub-blocks that are not marked as *no-use*. In the example, the 32-page block is split into two 16-page blocks. The first block is returned to satisfy the 8-page request while the second is marked as *no-use*. The first block is then split to two 8-page blocks with the first one returned to service the original request, and the second linked to 2^3-list. The 16-page *no-use* block becomes *external fragment*.

When freeing a block, the corresponding *no-use* blocks are also reclaimed. In particular, freeing a 16-page block in (1:2)-Alloc automatically forms a 32-page block after reclaiming its *no-use* buddy. An (n:m) allocator (n≠m) can return its 64MB or bigger blocks to (1:1)-Alloc to form larger blocks and reduce fragmentation.

DMA support. While a paging system may freely associate logical pages to physical frames, some operations may demand consecutive page frames, e.g., a DMA operation uses physical addresses to determine the source and target of the moved data, and thus demands for consecutive physical pages. To enable WD-aware DMA operation, we communicate the allocator tag to the DMA controller. For simplicity, we only allow (1:1) or (1:2) allocation choices. For (1:1) allocation, the DMA controller performs the same as the baseline, For (1:2) allocation, the DMA controller skips every other strip automatically.

5. Experimental Methodology

5.1 Baseline Configuration

To evaluate our proposed schemes, we conducted simulation using an 8-core in-order CPU with PCM based main memory. We used an in-house simulator that models the entire memory hierarchy including L1, L2 and DRAM last level cache, PCM based main memory, and memory controller. By default, memory controller buffers incoming write requests and flushes them when write queue is full, which triggers bursty write. Bursty write blocks incoming read requests until it finishes. All timing constraints, memory bank conflict and DDR scheduling constraints are included in simulation as well. Due to the power constraint and the limited number of write drivers, the hardware supports up to 128 SLC cell writes in parallel. The detail of simulation parameters is summarized in Table 2.

CPU	8-core single issue in-order CMP, 4GHz
L1	private, I/D separate, 32KB per core, 64B line
L2	private, 2MB per core, 4-way LRU, 64B line, write back
L3	DRAM cache, private, 32MB per core, 8-way LRU, 64B line, write back, 50ns (200-cycle) hit
Main Memory	8GB, 1 channel, 2 ranks, 8 banks per rank 32-entry write queue per bank
PCM latency	Read: 100ns(400 cycles) Write (SET): 200ns (800 cycles) Write (RESET): 100ns (400 cycles) SLC: 128-bit parallel write [8]

Table 2. Baseline Configuration

5.2 Simulated Workloads

We selected programs from SPEC2006 [2] and STREAM [3] benchmark suites to construct simulated workloads. Table 3 lists the RPKI/WPKI (read/write per thousand instructions) of each program. We used the PIN tool [1] to capture and filter 10 million references to main memory (which normally correspond to several billion instructions of execution time) after skipping application initialization phase and after warming up caches. In the experiment, each core runs one copy of these applications, forming multi-programming workloads running in different virtual address spaces.

Suite	Benchmark	RPKI	WPKI
SPEC2006	bwaves	17.45	0.47
	gemsFDTD	9.62	6.67
	lbm	14.59	7.29
	leslie3d	2.39	0.04
	mcf	22.38	20.47
	wrf	0.14	0.02
	xalan	0.13	0.13
	zeusmp	4.11	3.36
SREAM	copy,scale,add and triad	2.32	2.32

Table 3. Simulated Applications

We adopted the performance metric *Speedup* as

$$Speedup = CPI_{base}/CPI_{tech}$$

from [22] and [10], where CPI_{base} and CPI_{tech} are the cycles of execution from the baseline setting and the setting with different schemes described in 5.3.

5.3 Compared Schemes

We implemented and compared the following schemes.

- `DIN` — This scheme implements DIN-enhanced SLC PCM ($8F^2$/cell, as shown in Figure 1(c)). DIN [10] helps to mitigate WD errors along word-lines. 4F inter-cell space helps to achieve WD-free along bit-lines.
- `baseline` — This scheme implements the basic verify-n-correct (VnC) on super dense PCM ($4F^2$/cell, Figure 1(a)). It often runs into cascading verification due to WD errors along bit-lines.
- `LazyC` — This scheme implements $LazyCorrection$ on top of `baseline`. By default, we used 6 ECP entries for each PCM line (64B).
- `PreRead` — This scheme implements $PreRead$ on top of `baseline` for super dense PCM ($4F^2$).
- `(n:m)-Alloc` — This scheme implements (n:m) allocation on top of `baseline`. For simplicity, we assume one application uses one (n:m)-Alloc for all of its memory demands. In a real system, an application may demand (n:m) allocation (n≠m) only for performance-critical data structures.

6. Results

6.1 PCM Capacity Gain

SD-PCM enables the construction of super dense PCM with $4F^2$/cell while `DIN` uses $8F^2$/cell. The memory capacity improvement for the same sized cell array is 100%. In SD-PCM, `LazyC` needs low density ECP cell array. Therefore, the cell arraies of data chips are of the same size while the cell array of the ECP chip is two times bigger. In `DIN`, both data and ECP cell arrays are of the same size. For fair comparison, we analytically increase the cell array size in `DIN` such that the total sizes of all cell arraies are the same in two settings. This gives 4GB for SD-PCM and 2.22GB for `DIN`, i.e., SD-PCM achieves 80% ($= (4 - 2.22)/2.22$) memory capacity improvement for the cell arrays.

If using chips of the same size, to construct 4GB memory, `DIN` needs 16+2 chips while SD-PCM needs 8+2 chips. This reflects approximately 38% chip size reduction. If using bigger chips for low dense PCM, `DIN` needs 8+1 big chips while SD-PCM need 8 small chips and 1 big chip. The small chip is 23% smaller (as cell array accounts for 46.6% chip area [8]). This reflects approximately 20% ($= (0.77 \times 8 + 1)/(8+1)$) chip size reduction.

6.2 Design Overhead Analysis

SD-PCM introduces low hardware cost. LazyCorrection is integrated with existing ECP design. While it asks for low density ECP chips, the external bus width keeps the same, which incurs low hardware overhead. PreRead needs to add two flag bits and two 64B buffers for each entry in the write queue. This accounts for $(64B + 2b) \times 32 \times 2 = 4KB$ for a 32-entry write queue. Compared to the original write buffer size, 2KB, this increment is moderate. While the associativity of write buffer remains the same, search complexity is almost equal to baseline design. In our experiments, we found that its impact on performance is negligible. (n:m)-Alloc adds one 4-bit flag to support 16 different allocators. This accounts for bigger overhead. However, page table usually has many bits reserved. The overhead is insignificant.

6.3 System Performance

Figure 11 compares the performance of different schemes. The results are normalized to `baseline`, i.e., the basic VnC scheme. From the figure, `baseline` has on average 31% performance degradation from `DIN`. This is because of the extra verification and correction operations performed for each write operation.

`LazyC` achieves 21% performance improvement over `baseline`. This is because `LazyC` effectively reduces the correction overhead. We observed 30% and 31% performance improvement when combining `LazyC` with `PreRead` and (2:3)-Alloc, respectively. For memory intensive benchmarks, such as *lbm*, *mcf*, *zeusmp*, `LazyC+(2:3)-Alloc` achieves more benefits over `LazyC+PreRead`. This is because the memory banks are less idle when running these benchmarks — there is less chance to fetch adjacent lines early. On average, `PreRead` and `(2:3)-Alloc` achieve comparable results, when combining with `LazyC` individually.

Combining `LazyC`, `PreRead` and `(2:3)-Alloc` achieves further improvement. On average, it achieves 37% improvement over `baseline`, which is around 5% degradation from `DIN`. Using the most aggressive allocator `(1:2)-Alloc` can effectively eliminate VnC overhead. It does not need to be combined with `LazyC` or `PreRead` as verification and correction operations are not needed.

6.4 Sensitivity to ECP Entries

`LazyC` buffers WD errors in ECP region. Since WD errors accumulate fast, the more that ECP can protect, the fewer corrections `LazyC` shall trigger. The tradeoff is that storing more ECP pointers need more storage space.

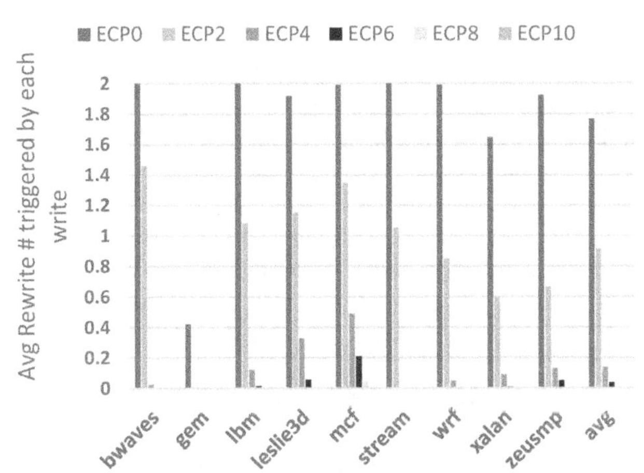

Figure 12. ECP entry number affects correction operations.

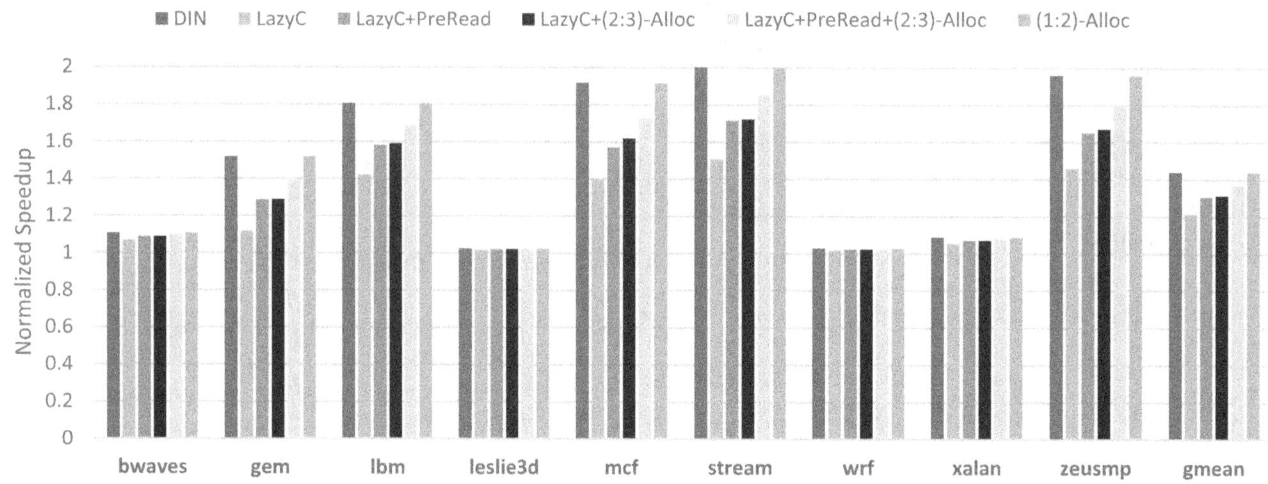

Figure 11. System performance under different schemes (normalized to `baseline`, bigger is better).

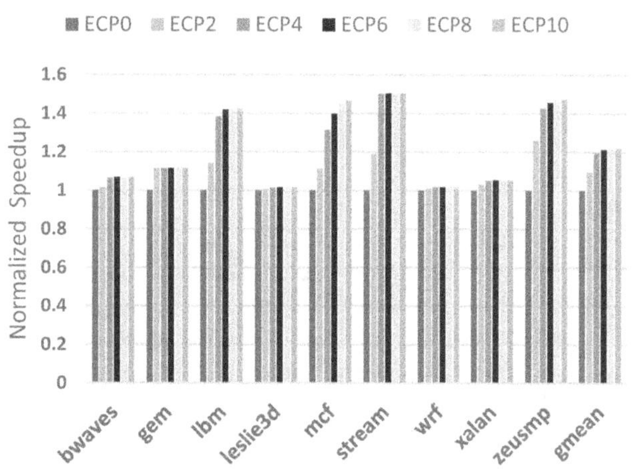

Figure 13. ECP entry number affects system performance.

Figure 12 reports the number of correction operations when having different ECP entries. ECP-0 uses no ECP and thus is the same as `baseline`. From the figure, ECP-0 triggers 1.8 corrections on average, indicating that a write request in `baseline` almost always need to correct both of its adjacent lines. The benchmark $gemsFDTD$ changes less bits per write, leading to fewer WD errors, and fewer correction operations.

When ECP entries grow, the number of correction operations per write decreases significantly. From the figure, ECP-4 triggers on average only 0.14 writes. Only for one highly memory-intensive benchmark *mcf*, ECP-8 shows observable result (0.04 correction per write). For most benchmarks, the default setting ECP-6 is sufficient.

Figure 13 compares performance when having different ECP entries. The results are normalized to `baseline`. Increasing ECP entry number from 0 to 6 helps to achieve 21% improvement. Further increasing the entry number shows negligible improvement.

Lifetime impact. ECP was designed for protecting hard errors. In SD-PCM, `LazyC` uses ECP entries if hard errors do not use up all ECP entries. If there are two hard errors, `LazyC` can only protect up to four WD errors when using ECP-6. Clearly, the number of hard errors increase as ECP chip approaches its lifetime. Figure 14 plots the performance degradation at different times throughout the lifetime of PCM DIMM. Here we ignore the impact of shrinking memory spaces, such as more page faults in the system. From the figure, we observed 0.2% performance degradation when the DIMM is approaching the lifetime limit. Clearly, this is negligible as an aging DIMM has smaller memory capacity, which often has a much larger impact on overall system performance.

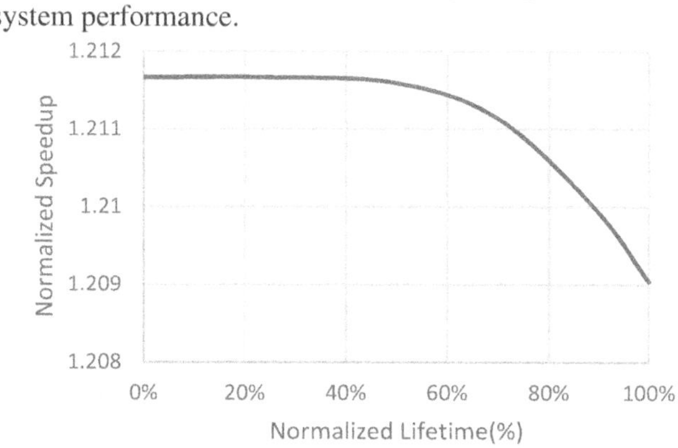

Figure 14. ECP entry number affects system performance.

6.5 Sensitivity to Write Queue Size

In `PreRead`, the memory controller needs to scan the write queue to issue pre-write read operations. Increasing the queue size helps to improve the opportunity of finding an appropriate write whose requested bank is currently idle. Figure 15 summarizes the system performance when having different numbers of entries in the write queue, ranging from 8 to 64.

Increasing the queue size is beneficial only for memory intensive workloads such as *mcf* and *gemsFDTD*. On average, a write queue with 32 entries per bank is sufficient — in LazyC+PreRead, it helps to minimize the performance degradation within 10% from DIN.

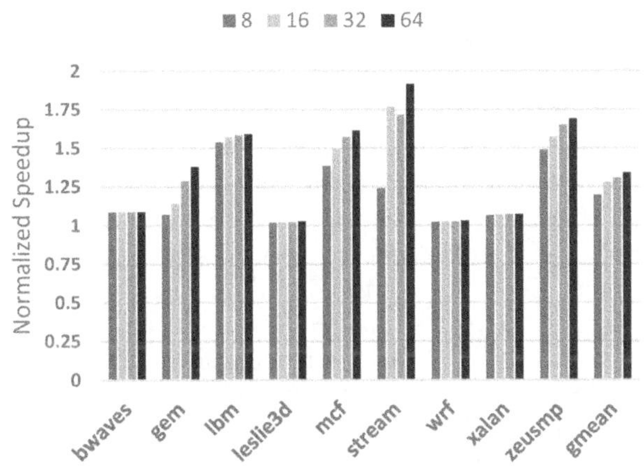

Figure 15. Using different queue sizes in LazyC+PreRead.

6.6 Sensitivity to n:m Ratio in (N:M)-Alloc

Figure 16 plots the performance impact using different (n:m allocators. We ignore the impact due to memory capacit loss in (n:m) allocation. Since the (n:m) ratio determines th percentage of strips used for storing user data, the larger th ratio is, the less the memory is wasted, the fewer strips th OS shall mark, and thus the larger performance degradatio we expect.

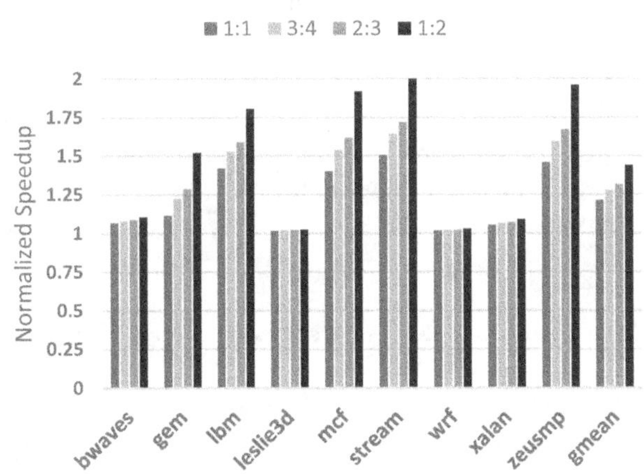

Figure 16. Performance when using different (n:m) allocators.

From the figure, 1:2 ratio achieves no performance degradation as it effectively eliminates VnC by allocating one strip as thermal band between any two strips that store data. From ratio 3:4 to 2:3 until 1:2, performance increases monotonically. This helps to achieve predictable performance at runtime, and adjust the allocation to the need of high priority applications.

6.7 Lifetime Comparison

Figure 17 and 18 present the normalized lifetime degradation on data and ECP chip, respectively. The lifetime degradation of data chip is mainly due to correction accesses. While WD brings up reliability concern, the absolute error number is still low when comparing to the number of cell changes in a normal line write. The figure shows that data chips expects 0.04% lifetime degradation.

Since each WD error translates to writing 10 bits (=9-bit address and 1-bit value) in ECP chip, the lifetime degradation of ECP chip is more significant. We observed an average of 8% degradation. However, ECP was used for protecting hard errors. The cell change rate in ECP chip is low. Without considering WD, ECP chip exhibits 10x longer lifetime than data chip — it is the data chip that determines the DIMM lifetime. Therefore, the lifetime is about the same in SD-PCM.

An alternative ECP design allows intra-row wear leveling across data and ECP chips. This improves DIMM lifetime about 12.5% [28]. Due to low-density ECP design, SD-PCM does not support this design alternative, which leads to a potential of 12.5% lifetime degradation. Note SD-PCM supports intra-row wear leveling among multiple data chips.

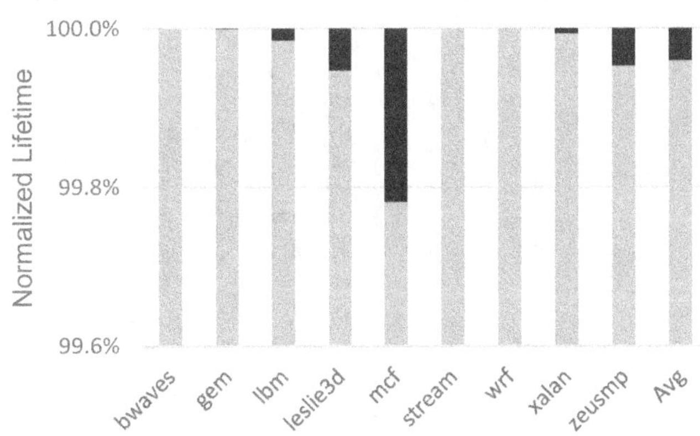

Figure 17. Normalized lifetime degradation on data chips.

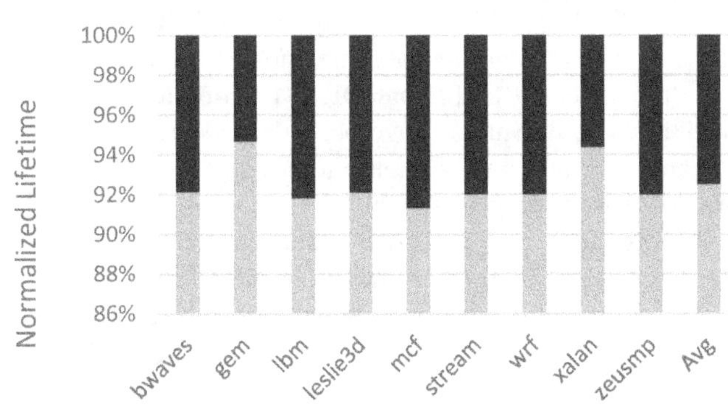

Figure 18. Normalized lifetime degradation on ECP chip.

6.8 Integration with Write Cancellation

VnC effectively prolongs write latency as it performs extra verification and correction operations for many writes. We next studied the effectiveness of combining SD-PCM with write cancellation, a scheme for reducing the impact of long PCM write latency on system performance [22].

Figure 19 summarizes the normalized performance under different schemes. Write cancellation `WC` improves VnC but not significantly. This is because WD errors appear more frequently, which significantly prolong write operations — a write operation becomes 2 pre-write reads, 1 write, 2 post-write read and verify, plus 2 correction write operations(RESET), and additional verifications for correction writes not further affecting their adjacent lines. Canceling writes in super dense PCM is not desirable as repeated write operations tend to introduce more WD errors on adjacent lines, which increases the possibility of cascading verification.

By combining `WC` with `LazyC`, we improve the performance from 21% to 31%, indicating that `WC` and `LazyC` explores different benefits. `WC` improves performance by prioritize read operations while `LazyC` focuses on minimizing correction overhead. We did not integrate `PreRead` due to different scheduling choices in handling write operations.

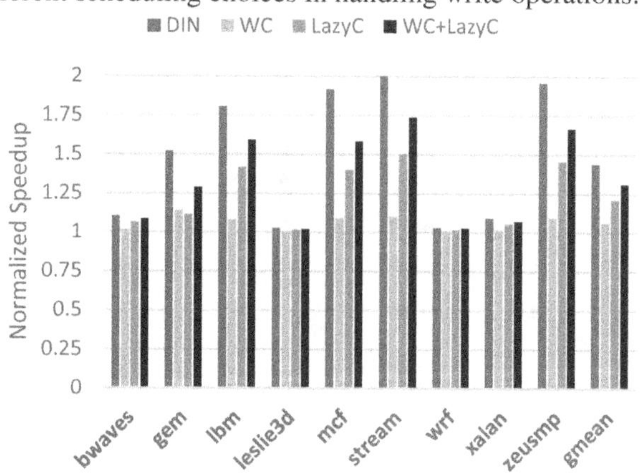

Figure 19. Integrating `LazyC` with Write Cancellation.

7. Related Work

Phase change memory has become one of the most promising alternatives to traditional DRAM to implement main memory system. Studies have been done on reliability issues in PCM, but mainly focusing on hard errors and resistant drift based soft errors.

PCM suffers from short cell endurance, which becomes even worse due to process variations. PCM chip lifetime can be greatly prolonged by schemes that reduces the number of cell change per write, such as differential-write [35] and flip-n-write [7]. By creating randomized mapping between physical and device addresses, Start-gap [20] and security-refresh [29] spreads writes evenly to all PCM lines. ECP [28], Safer [30], Free-p [33], and PAYG [19] address cell endurances under process variations.

Resistance drift [11] introduces drift-based "soft" errors in MLC PCM. The drift-based error can be mitigated through encoding [34] or periodical scrubbing over the physical memory space [5]. A recent work [31] utilized three out of four states of 2-bit MLC to tolerate the resistance drifting of the most drifting vulnerable intermediate resistance state.

For write disturbance in PCM, a recent work [10] shrinks the thermal band along word-lines and presents thermal isolation data encoding scheme to ensure write reliability.

8. Conclusions

WD in PCM is becoming a major obstacle for scaling PCM [4, 13]. Existing approaches such as VnC and allocating large inter-cell space either introduce large performance overhead or greatly reduce memory density.

In this paper, we propose SD-PCM that consists of three schemes — LazyCorrection, PreRead, and (n:m)-Alloc. The first two target at reducing correction and verification overheads in VnC, respectively. (n:m)-alloc targets at achieving good tradeoff between VnC overhead minimization and memory capacity loss. These schemes can be adopted all together or independently. For example, given a 5% performance degradation constraint, we may meet it by either adopting the first two schemes or adopting (n:m)-alloc with proper n and m. The latter disables a subset of rows while the former does not. Combining all three techniques together helps to achieve the best trade off between capacity loss and performance degradation, in addition, it helps to minimize capacity loss with given performance loss constraint, and vice versa. Our experimental results showed that SD-PCM achieves about 80% capacity improvement in memory cell arrays, while incurs 0-10% performance degradation over the state-of-the-art design, depending on the (n:m) allocator to choose at runtime.

Acknowledgments

This work is supported in part by NSF grants 1422331 and 1012070. The authors thank all the anonymous reviewers for their advice and comments.

References

[1] Pin tool. `https://software.intel.com/en-us/articles/pintool`.

[2] Spec2006 benchmarks. `http://www.spec.org/cpu2006/`.

[3] Stream benchmark. `http://www.cs.virginia.edu/stream/`.

[4] S. J. Ahn, Y. Song, H. Jeong, B. Kim, Y.-S. Kang, D.-H. Ahn, Y. Kwon, S.-W. Nam, G. Jeong, H. Kang, and C. Chung. Reliability perspectives for high density pram manufacturing. In *IEDM*, 2011.

[5] M. Awasthi, M. Shevgoor, K. Sudan, B. R. R. Balasubramonian, and V. Srinivasan. Efficient scrub mechanisms for error-prone emerging memories. In *HPCA*, 2012.

[6] G. W. Burr, M. J. Breitwisch, M. Franceschini, D. Garetto, K. Gopalakrishnan, B. Jackson, B. Kurdi, C. Lam, L. A. Lastras, A. Padilla, et al. Phase change memory technology. *Jour-*

nal of Vacuum Science & Technology B: Microelectronics and Nanometer Structures, 28(2), 2010.

[7] S. Cho and H. Lee. Flip-n-write: A simple deterministic technique to improve pram writeperformance, energy and endurance. In *MICRO*, 2009.

[8] Y. Choi, I. Song, and M.-H. Park. A 20nm 1.8v 8gb pram with 40mb/s program bandwidth. In *ISSCC*, 2012.

[9] B. Gleixner, F. Pellizzer, and R. Bez. Reliability characterization of phase change memory. In *EPCOS*, 2009.

[10] L. Jiang, Y. Zhang, and J. Yang. Mitigating write disturbance in super dense phase change memory. In *DSN*, 2014.

[11] D. Kang, J. Lee, J. Kong, D. Ha, and et. al. Two-bit cell operation in diode-switch phase change memory cells with 90nm technology. In *VLSI Technology*, 2008.

[12] M. Kang, T. J. Park, Y. W. Kwon, D. Ahn, Y. Kang, H. Jeong, S. Ahn, Y. Song, B. Kim, S. Nam, H.-K. Kang, G. Jeong, and C. Chung. Pram cell technology and characterization in 20nm node size. In *IEDM*, 2011.

[13] B. Kim, Y. Song, D. Ahn, Y. Kang, H. Jeong, D. Ahn, S. Nam, G. Jeong, and C. Chung. Current status and future prospect of phase change memory. In *ASICON*, 2011.

[14] B. C. Lee, E. Ipek, O. Mutlu, and D. Burger. Architecting phase change memory as a scalable dram alternative. In *ISCA*, 2009.

[15] S. Lee, M. Kim, G. S. Do, S. Kim, H. Lee, J. S. Sim, N. G. Park, S. B. Hong, Y. H. Jeon, K. Choi, H. Park, T. Kim, J. Lee, H. Kim, M. R. Choi, S. Lee, Y. Kim, H. J. Kang, J. Kim, H. Kim, Y. S. Son, B. Lee, J.-H. Choi, S. Kim, J. Lee, S. J. Hong, and S.-W. Park. Programming disturbance and cell scaling in pcm: for up to 16nm based $4f^2$ cell. In *VLSIT*, 2010.

[16] J. Liu, B. Jaiyen, R. Veras, and O. Mutlu. Raidr: Retention-aware intelligent dram refresh. In *ISCA*, 2012.

[17] H. Park, J. Choi, D. Lee, and S. H. Noh. Regularities considered harmful: Forcing randomness to memory accesses to reduce buffer conflicts for multi-bank, multi-core systems. In *ASPLOS*, 2013.

[18] F. Pellizzer, A. Pirovano, F. Ottogalli, M. Magistretti, M. Scaravaggi, P. Zuliani, M. Tosi, A. Benvenuti, P. Besana, S. Cadeo, T. Marangon, R. Morandi, R. Piva, A. Spandre, R. Zonca, A. Modelli, E. Varesi, T. Lowrey, A. Lacaita, G. Casagrande, P. Cappelletti, and R. Bez. Novel utrench phase-change memory cell for embedded and stand-alone non-volatile memory applications. In *VLSIT*, 2004.

[19] M. K. Qureshi. Pay-as-you-go: Low-overhead hard-error correction for phase change memories. In *MICRO*, 2011.

[20] M. K. Qureshi, J. Karidis, M. F. andVijayalakshmi Srinivasan, L. Lastras, and B. Abali. Enhancing lifetime and security of pcm-based main memory with start-gapwear leveling. In *MICRO*, 2009.

[21] M. K. Qureshi, V. Srinivasan, and J. A. Rivers. Scalable high performance main memory system using phase-change memorytechnology. In *ISCA*, 2009.

[22] M. K. Qureshi, M. M. Franceschini, and L. A. Lastras-Montano. Improving read performance of phase change memories via write cancellationand write pausing. In *HPCA*, 2010.

[23] M. K. Qureshi, M. Franceschini, and L. L. andAshish Jagmohan. Preset: Improving read write performance of phase change memoriesby exploiting asymmetry in write times. In *ISCA*, 2012.

[24] S. Raoux, G. W. Burr, M. J. Breitwisch, C. Rettner, Y.-C. Chen, R. M. Shelby, M. S. D. Krebs, S.-H. Chen, H.-L. Lung, and C. Lam. Phase-change random access memory: A scalable technology. *IBM J. RES. & DEV.*, 2008.

[25] U. Russo, D. Ielmini, A. Redaelli, and A. Lacaita. Intrinsic data retention in nanoscaled phase-change memories - part i: Monte carlo model for crystallization and percolation. *TED*, 53(12), 2006.

[26] U. Russo, D. Ielmini, A. Redaelli, and A. Lacaita. Modeling of programming and read performance in phase-change memories - part i: Cell optimization and scaling. *TED*, 55(2), 2008.

[27] U. Russo, D. Ielmini, A. Redaelli, and A. Lacaita. Modeling of programming and read performance in phase-change memories - part ii: Program disturb and mixed-scaling approach. *TED*, 55(2), 2008.

[28] S. Schechter, G. H. Loh, K. Strauss, and D. Burger. Use ecp, not ecc, for hard failures in resistive memories. In *ISCA*, 2010.

[29] N. H. Seong, D. H. Woo, and H.-H. S. Lee. Security refresh: Prevent malicious wear-out and increase durabilityfor phase-change memory with dynamically randomized address mapping. In *ISCA*, 2010.

[30] N. H. Seong, D. H. Woo, V. Srinivasan, J. A. Rivers, and H.-H. S. Lee. Safer:stuck at fault error recovery for memories. In *micro*, 2010.

[31] N. H. Seong, S. Yeo, and H.-H. S. Lee. Tri-level-cell pcm: toward an efficient and reliable memory system. In *ISCA*, 2013.

[32] C. Wilkerson, A. R. Alameldeen, Z. Chishti, W. Wu, D. Somasekhar, and S.-l. Lu. Reducing cache power with low-cost, multi-bit error-correcting codes. In *ISCA*, 2010.

[33] D. H. Yoon, N. Muralimanohar, J. Chang, ParthasarathyRanganathan, N. P. Jouppi, and M. Erez. Free-p: Protecting nonvolatile memory against both hard and softerrors. In *HPCA*, 2011.

[34] W. Zhang and T. Li. Helmet: A resistance drift resilient architecture for multi-levelcell phase change memory system. In *DSN*, 2011.

[35] P. Zhou, B. Zhao, J. Yang, and Y. Zhang. A durable and energy efficient main memory using phase change memorytechnology. In *ISCA*, 2009.

DEUCE: Write-Efficient Encryption for Non-Volatile Memories

Vinson Young   Prashant J. Nair   Moinuddin K. Qureshi

School of Electrical and Computer Engineering
Georgia Institute of Technology
{vyoung,pnair6,moin}@ece.gatech.edu

Abstract

Phase Change Memory (PCM) is an emerging Non Volatile Memory (NVM) technology that has the potential to provide scalable high-density memory systems. While the non-volatility of PCM is a desirable property in order to save leakage power, it also has the undesirable effect of making PCM main memories susceptible to newer modes of security vulnerabilities, for example, accessibility to sensitive data if a PCM DIMM gets stolen. PCM memories can be made secure by encrypting the data. Unfortunately, such encryption comes with a significant overhead in terms of bits written to PCM memory, causing half of the bits in the line to change on every write, even if the actual number of bits being written to memory is small. Our studies show that a typical writeback modifies, on average, only 12% of the bits in the cacheline. Thus, encryption causes almost a 4x increase in the number of bits written to PCM memories. Such extraneous bit writes cause significant increase in write power, reduction in write endurance, and reduction in write bandwidth. To provide the benefit of secure memory in a write efficient manner this paper proposes *Dual Counter Encryption (DEUCE)*. DEUCE is based on the observation that a typical writeback only changes a few words, so DEUCE re-encrypts only the words that have changed. We show that DEUCE reduces the number of modified bits per writeback for a secure memory from 50% to 24%, which improves performance by 27% and increases lifetime by 2x.

Categories and Subject Descriptors B.3.2 [*Hardware*]: Primary Memory

Keywords PCM, Encryption, Tamper-proof Design.

1. Introduction

As DRAM scaling becomes challenging, architects are looking for alternative technologies for designing future memory systems. Emerging Non-Volatile Memory (NVM) technologies, such as Phase Change Memory (PCM), Spin-Torque Transfer RAM (STT-RAM), and Resistive RAM (RRAM), have the potential for building high-density power-efficient memory systems due to enhanced scalability and non-volatility properties [1]. Without loss of generality, this paper analyzes PCM as a representative example of NVM, however the problem, insight, and solutions we develop are applicable to other NVM technologies as well.

One of the key challenges in designing a PCM system tends to be the efficient handling of write operations [2, 3]. Writes not only have a higher latency compared to reads, but they also tend to consume significant power and have limited endurance [4]. Therefore, PCM systems are optimized to reduce the write traffic, in order to improve power efficiency, write bandwidth, and endurance limited lifetime [5, 6]. Fortunately, when a write operation is performed to the main memory system, only a small number of bits get modified, and PCM systems leverage this observation to optimize the number of bits written to memory on each write operation. For example, PCM systems employ a technique called *Data Comparison Write (DCW)* [7] whereby only modified bits in the cache line get written to PCM memory. A further enhancement on this scheme, called *Flip-N-Write (FNW)* [8] reduces the bit writes to PCM even further by inverting the data if more than half of the bits get modified. FNW bounds the number of bit flips on each write to a maximum of half the number of bits in the line. With these optimizations, the number of bits written on each write operation to memory gets reduced to only 10% to 15%, on average. Thus, such optimizations are highly effective at reducing the number of bits written to PCM, and, given the reduced write performance and limited endurance of PCM memories, are vital to achieving high-performance and durability for PCM.

PCM systems are non-volatile and can store data for long after the system is powered down. While the non-volatility of PCM is a desirable property for reducing leakage power, this property can make PCM systems vulnerable to new security issues. For example, in traditional systems if a DRAM DIMM gets lost or stolen, the data is lost within a few seconds due to the low retention of DRAM. However, if a PCM DIMM gets stolen, then it is possible to access sensitive data even after several days or months. An adversary (such as a malicious repairman) with access to the DIMM can stream out the data stored in the PCM array and obtain sensitive information [9, 10]. Therefore, securing the memory against

ASPLOS '15, March 14–18, 2015, Istanbul, Turkey.
Copyright © 2015 ACM 978-1-4503-2835-7/15/03...$15.00.
http://dx.doi.org/10.1145/2694344.2694387

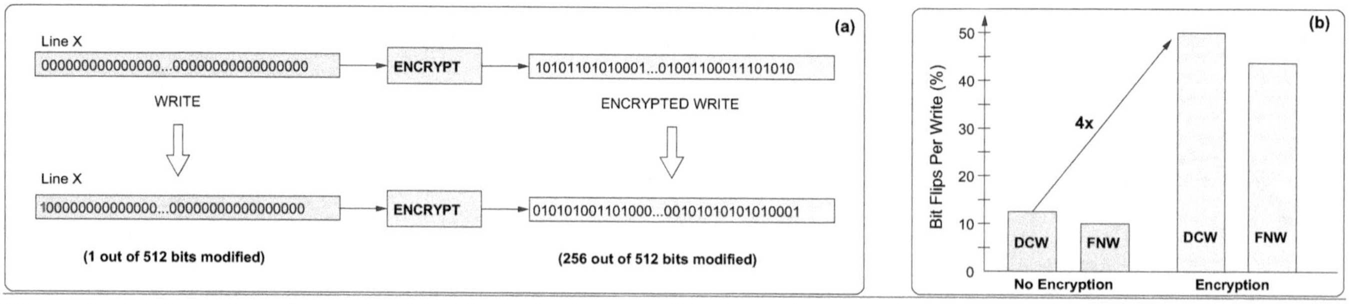

Figure 1. (a) Encryption changes half the bits in the line, even if only one bit in the line changes (b) Our evaluations show that encryption increases the number of bit flips in PCM by 4x for both Data Comparison Write (DCW) and Flip-N-Write (FNW).

such unintended access has become an even bigger concern for PCM systems compared to DRAM. Furthermore, PCM DIMMs are likely to be implemented using conventional bus-based interface standards such as LPDDR-NVM, making them susceptible to traditional attacks such as those that rely on bus snooping [11]. To prevent loss of sensitive data, it is important to make PCM memories secure against both bus snooping attacks as well as stolen DIMM attacks.

The security of PCM memories can be enhanced by encrypting the data. Unfortunately, all good encryption algorithms follow the Avalanche Effect [12], whereby a change of even a single bit in the input data causes half of the bits in the encrypted data to be changed. While this Avalanche property is essential to providing security, it causes the number of bits written on each memory write to be 50% regardless of the number of bits modified in the line. For example, consider Figure 1(a) where a write operation modifies only the MSB of a line that has been initialized to all zeros. This will cause only 1 bit to flip in the memory system without encryption. However, when encryption is employed, the difference between the two encrypted values will be half the number of bits. Thus, encryption causes the number of bits written to encrypted memory to be large, rendering optimizations such as DCW and FNW ineffective.

We analyze PCM memory system with benchmarks from the SPEC suite. Figure 1(b) shows the average number of bits modified per write for the unencrypted memory and encrypted memory when DCW and FNW are employed. We implement FNW at a granularity of two bytes, where 1 flip bit is provisioned per 16 bits. A write to memory modifies only 12.2% of the bits (as optimized by DCW) on average, and FNW reduces this to 10.5%. Unfortunately, encryption causes DCW and FNW to flip 50% and 43% of the bits per write, respectively. Thus, encryption increases the number of bits written to PCM memory by almost a factor of 4. This increase in bit writes can correspondingly increase the power consumption of writes by 4x, reduce endurance-related lifetime by 4x, and cause significant reduction in PCM write bandwidth due to power limitations. Ideally, we want to secure memory, without having to pay the power overheads, lifetime overheads, and performance overheads that happen due to extra writes from encryption. The goal of this paper is devise such a write efficient architecture for secure memory.

We implement memory encryption in the baseline using counter mode encryption [13, 14] scheme which uses One Time Pad (OTP) to implement low latency encryption. Each line has a counter associated with it which gets incremented on each write to the line. The line address and the counter is provided to the AES engine to generate the OTP, and this OTP is ex-ored with the data for encryption, or for decrypting the encrypted data. We leverage the observation that a typical writeback only modifies a few words, so it is not necessary to re-encrypt all the words with the new OTP. If we can keep track of the words that have been modified then we can continue to use the older OTP for the unmodified words. With this insight, we propose *Dual Counter Encryption (DEUCE)*. DEUCE maintains bits to track which words in the line have been modified. Words that have been modified use the current value of the line counter for encryption and decryption, whereas the unmodified words use an older value (obtained from masking few LSB of the current counter) of line counter for decryption. Periodically, the entire line is re-encrypted which resets the modified bits.

Our evaluations show that DEUCE reduces the number of bit flips for a write to encrypted memory by more than 2x, lowering it from 50% to 24%. The write reduction of DEUCE improves the performance of encrypted memory by 27% and EDP by 43%, while incurring a storage overhead of only 32 bits per line for a system with encrypted memory.

Reducing the bit writes by 2x with DEUCE does not result in a equivalent increase of 2x in lifetime, because certain bit locations continue to receive more writes than other locations. We propose *Horizontal Wear Leveling (HWL)* based on algebraic functions that provides near perfect intra line wear leveling, while avoiding the per line storage for tracking the rotation amount. We show that DEUCE with HWL improves the lifetime of encrypted memory by 2x.

While we evaluate DEUCE for a system that performs encryption at the line level, DEUCE is applicable to Block Level Encryption (BLE) schemes that perform re-encryption at the granularity of the AES block (16 bytes). For example, DEUCE lowers the average number of bit flips for a memory encrypted with BLE from 33% to 19.9%.

2. Background and Motivation

2.1 Attack Models

In this paper we specifically seek to protect PCM memories from two types of attacks. First, the traditional attack of bus snooping, where an adversary has access to the bus between the processor and memory and can obtain memory data by simply doing hardware probes of this memory bus [9]. Second, the stolen DIMM attack, whereby an adversary (or a malicious machine repairman) can get access to the PCM DIMM. The attacker can then simply stream the data out of the PCM memory to obtain all the data contained in the PCM DIMM. As PCM DIMM is non-volatile, the attack of the second type becomes much more severe in PCM compared to DRAM DIMM. We seek an efficient solution that will protect PCM DIMM from both types of attacks.

2.2 Security via Data Encryption with Line Counters

PCM memories can be protected against security threats by encrypting the memory contents. The straightforward way to encrypt data at runtime is to employ a one-way function such as AES, and use a global key, as shown in Figure 2(a). However, if the same key is used for all lines, one can simply compare encrypted lines to figure out which lines store the same content, and employ a dictionary-based attack.

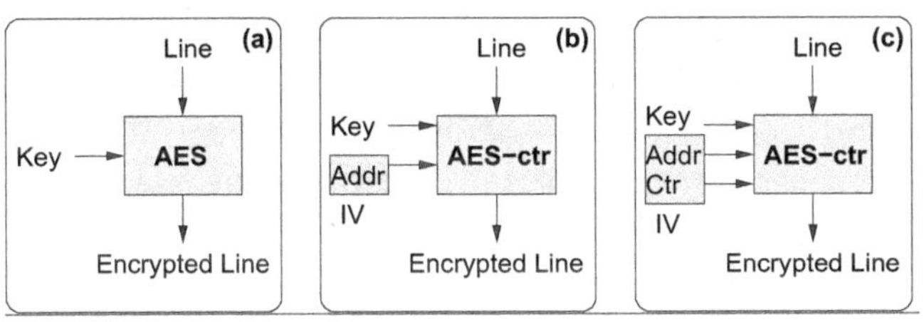

Figure 2. Enhancing security of (a) encrypted memory by adding (b) line address and (c) line counter to encryption.

A more secure approach is to use the line address along with the key to perform encryption, as shown in Figure 2(b). This ensures that each line gets encrypted with its own key, thwarting stolen DIMM attacks. However, this scheme is still vulnerable to bus snooping attacks that can monitor consecutive writes to the same line. An even stronger approach to data security is to employ a per-line counter in conjunction with the line address and key to perform encryption, as shown in Figure 2(c). The per-line counter is incremented on each write, ensuring that each write of each line gets encrypted with a unique key, and thus protects the system from both bus snooping attack and stolen DIMM attack.

2.3 Low Latency Encryption via One Time Pad (OTP)

Memory encryption not only incurs the storage overhead of a per-line counter, but it also incurs the latency overheads of encryption and decryption. Since memory read operations are in the critical path, the decryption latency is of particular importance as it gets added to the overall memory latency, as shown in Figure 3. While this latency may be acceptable when the latency of accessing data is quite high (for example, access from hard drive, which takes a few milli seconds), this latency becomes impractically expensive when the latency for both the data access and decryption are similar, such as for main memory (both take a few tens of nanoseconds).

Prior work [13, 14] on counter mode encryption avoids the serialization of memory access and decryption by employing the One Time Pad (OTP) technique. The key idea is to generate the OTP in parallel with the memory access, and simply XOR the OTP with the memory contents, as shown in Figure 3. As XOR incurs low latency, this scheme removes the decryption latency from the critical path of memory access, while maintaining provable security guarantees because of the uniqueness of the OTP.

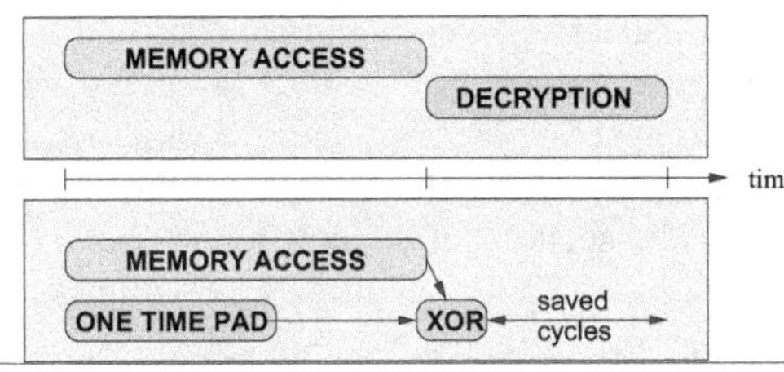

Figure 3. Counter mode encryption uses One Time Pad (OTP) to reduce the impact of decryption latency.

2.4 Operation of Counter Mode Encryption

Counter mode encryption uses a block cipher (such as AES), not to encrypt the data directly but to generate the OTP. To maintain security, the OTP for each line must be generated only once during the lifetime. To ensure this, counter mode encryption uses the line address and the per-line counter as the input data for the AES circuit to generate a unique output, which is used as a PAD. On a write to memory, the cache line is encrypted by XORing the content of the cache line with the OTP, as shown in Figure 4(a). To read the memory contents, the per-line counter and line address is used to regenerate the PAD, and this PAD is XORed with the encrypted contents, as shown in Figure 4(b).

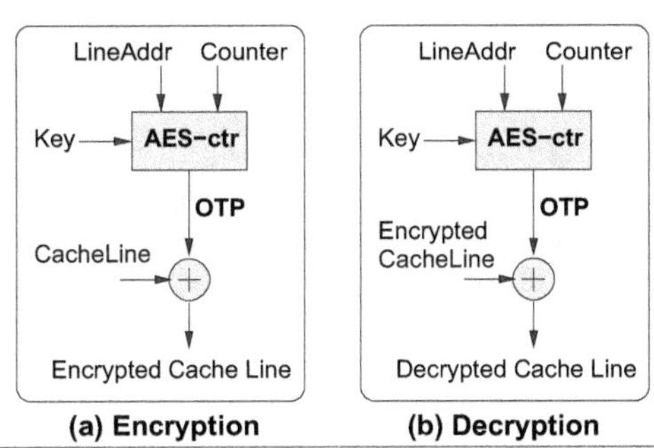

Figure 4. Counter mode generates OTP using line address and counter for both (a) Encryption and (b) Decryption.

The counter used for counter mode encryption need not itself be protected with encryption, as having the knowledge of the value of the counter does not enable the attacker to

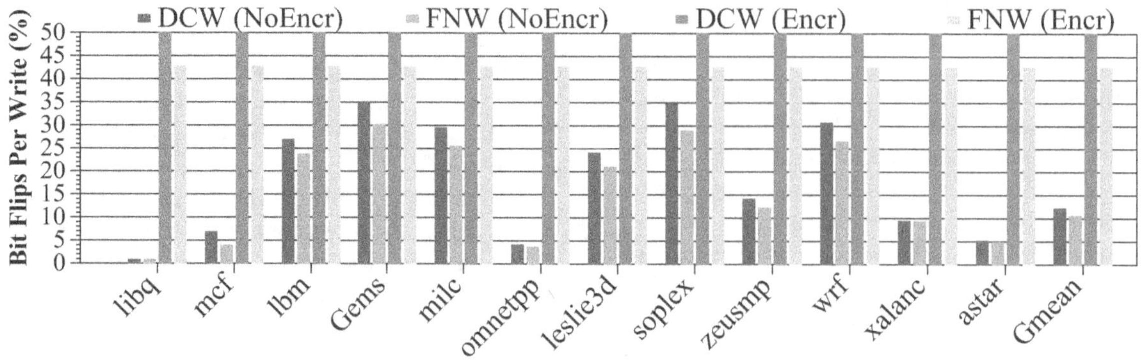

Figure 5. Average number of modified bits per write for unencrypted memory (NoEncr) and encrypted memory (Encr) under Data Comparison Write (DCW) and Flip-N-Write (FNW). Encryption increase the number of bit writes to PCM by almost 4x.

generated the pad [15]. Even if the attacker had access to the counter value, the attacker would still need the key and line address to generate the pad, and it is assumed that the key is well protected. Therefore, we store the line counter in plain text. The security of counter mode encryption has been approved by NIST. In our studies we will assume that memory is encrypted with counter based encryption.[1]

2.5 The Problem: Write Overhead of Encryption

The per-line counter in Counter Mode Encryption is incremented on every write, which allows every cacheline to have a unique PAD for each write. As the PAD is guaranteed to not be reused such systems provide strong security. In PCM systems, this security, however, comes at a cost to write endurance and bandwidth as 50% of the bits will be expected to flip on every writeback, due to the random bits of the PAD, regardless of the input data of the cacheline. Figure 5 shows the average number of bits modified per write for under both no encryption and encryption, when DCW and FNW are applied. For the unencrypted system, the average bits written per write are quite small, 12.4% for DCW and 10.5% for FNW. However, encryption increases this by almost 4x, making it 50% under DCW and 43% under FNW.

2.6 Goal: Write-Efficient Memory Encryption

Encryption causes the number of bit writes to increase by almost 4x, thereby significantly increasing write power, reducing performance, and lowering the lifetime of PCM memory system. Ideally, we would like to have memory security without the significant write overheads of memory encryption. A prior proposal, i-NVMM [17], proposes to employ partial encryption of memory whereby only cold pages are encrypted, and hot pages are encrypted only on power down. This scheme does not protect against bus snooping attacks (as the writeback from processor to memory is kept unencrypted for hot pages). We can also reduce the write overhead by using Block-Level Encryption (BLE) [18], which performs re-encryption at the granularity of AES block (16 bytes) using per block counters. Unfortunately, BLE still incurs high write overhead because even if a byte changes in the 16-byte block, the entire block must get re-encrypted. Our goal is to significantly reduce the write overhead of encryption, while retaining the security of memory contents. To this end, we propose *Dual Counter Encryption (DEUCE)*. We explain our methodology before explaining our design.

[1] Note that if the attacker has the ability to tamper with the memory values or the bus directly, then a new form of attack can be formed, whereby the attacker always resets the counter value to zero. This would make the system reuse the pad, and then the attacker can employ "pad reuse" based attacks to potentially gain access to the encrypted data. While, such *Bus Tampering Attacks* are much harder than *Bus Snooping Attacks*, and are beyond the scope of the attack models we consider, one can use Merkle Trees [14, 16] based authentication techniques to ensure the integrity of memory contents and protect against such attacks.

3. Methodology

3.1 Configuration

The parameters for the baseline system are shown in Table 1. The L4 cache is 64MB, and the L4 cache capacity is partitioned equally between all the cores. The linesize of all cache units is fixed at 64 bytes. Write requests arrive at the PCM memory only on eviction from the L4 cache. Both read and write requests are at the granularity of cache line, and are serviced by one of the PCM banks, based on the address of the line. We assume that relevant pages have already been brought into memory and been initially encrypted as they are placed into the memory via the memory-controller. For counter mode encryption, we assume each line is provisioned with a 28 bit line counter. We implement FNW at a two-byte boundary, so FNW incurs an overhead of 32 bits.

Processors	
Number of cores	8 cores, each 4-wide 4GHz
L1/L2/L3 (private)	32KB/256KB/1MB (8-way each)
L4 cache	64MB (8MB per core), 50 cycles latency
Phase Change Memory	
Capacity	4 ranks, each 8GB = 32 GB total
Read Latency	75 ns
Write Latency	150ns for each slot of 128 bits [19]

Table 1. Baseline Configuration

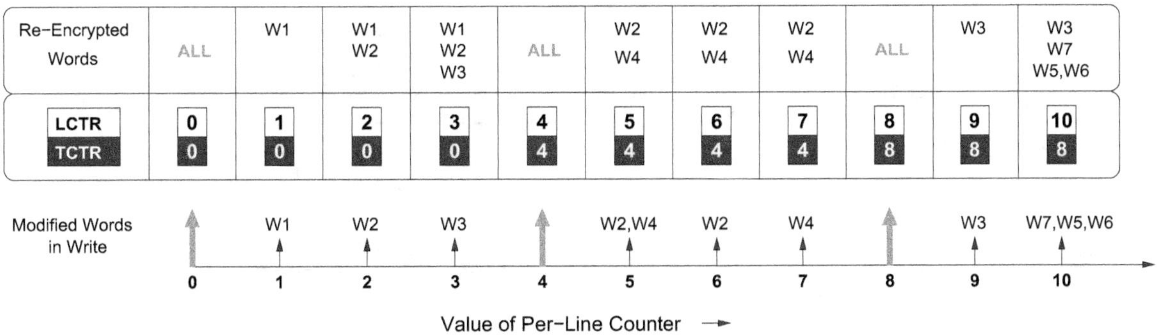

Figure 6. Operation of DEUCE for a system with Epoch Interval of 4 and 8 words per line (W0-W7). At start of each Epoch (red arrow), all words are re-encrypted and TCTR=LCTR. In between Epochs, all words that have been modified at least once since the start of the Epoch get re-encrypted. Such words use LCTR, whereas the unmodified words continue to use TCTR.

3.2 Workloads

We use a representative slice of 4 billion instructions for each benchmark from the SPEC2006 suite. We perform evaluations by executing the benchmark in rate mode, where all the eight cores execute the same benchmark. We perform our studies using all the 12 benchmarks that have at least 1 Writeback per One Thousand Instructions (WBPKI). Table 2 shows the read/write characteristics of our workloads.

Workload (8-copies)	L4 Read Miss (MPKI)	L4 WriteBack (WBPKI)
libq	22.9	9.78
mcf	16.2	8.78
lbm	14.6	7.25
Gems	14.4	7.14
milc	19.6	6.80
omnetpp	10.8	4.71
leslie3d	12.8	4.38
soplex	25.5	3.97
zeusmp	4.65	1.97
wrf	3.85	1.67
xalanc	1.85	1.61
astar	1.84	1.29

Table 2. Benchmark Characteristics.

3.3 Figure of Merit

We measure the average number of bits modified on each writeback as the figure of merit for different systems. While reporting the modified bits per cacheline, we also include the bit flips that happen in metadata (e.g. the Flip bit in FNW).

4. Dual Counter Encryption (DEUCE)

DEUCE leverages the observation that most words in any cacheline are written back unmodified. Fortunately, these unmodified words need not be re-encrypted and only the modified words can be re-encrypted. For example, if only one word in the line is modified, instead of rewriting the whole line, the design could re-encrypt only the modified word with an updated counter and write only that word back. On decryption, the design could decrypt the modified word with the updated counter, decrypt the rest of the cacheline with the previous counter, and combine them to form the newest cacheline. A straightforward way to implement this would be to have a separate counter per word (to avoid PAD reuse). However, this would not only incur high storage overhead but would also require an encryption algorithm that operates at a granularity of a word, making AES an unsuitable choice given that the minimum block length for AES is 16 bytes. To implement re-encryption at word granularity efficiently, we propose DEUCE, a simplified design that relies on generating two PADs to reduce the number of bit writes.

4.1 DEUCE: Overview

DEUCE tracks which words have been modified, and uses the most recent counter value for the modified words, and an older value of the counter for the unmodified words. We provide the overview of DEUCE with an example. Consider that the line has two counters, a *Leading Counter (LCTR)* and a *Trailing Counter (TCTR)*. The LCTR is identical to the line counter. The TCTR is obtained by masking off a few Least Significant Bits (LSBs) of the LCTR. For our example, let us consider that we mask the 2 LSB of LCTR. Thus, LCTR will be equal to TCTR once every 4 writes, a duration which we call *Epoch Interval.* In between the Epoch, the value of TCTR remains unchanged, whereas the LCTR keeps getting incremented. Each word is appended with a bit to indicate if it has been modified since the start of the Epoch. When LCTR equals TCTR, the modified bits associated with all words in the line are reset. On each subsequent write, the modified words are encrypted using LCTR, whereas the unmodified words keep using TCTR. Note that both LCTR and TCTR are virtual counters, whose values get determined by the line counter. Thus, except for the existing line counter, DEUCE does not require separate counters for implementation.

Figure 6 shows the operation of DEUCE for a design when the Epoch Interval is four writes and each line contains 8 words (W0 to W7). The counter is incremented on each write, and, when the two least significant bit of the line counter is 00 (at 0, 4, 8, etc.), all the words in the line are re-encrypted, and TCTR is advanced up to LCTR. Otherwise,

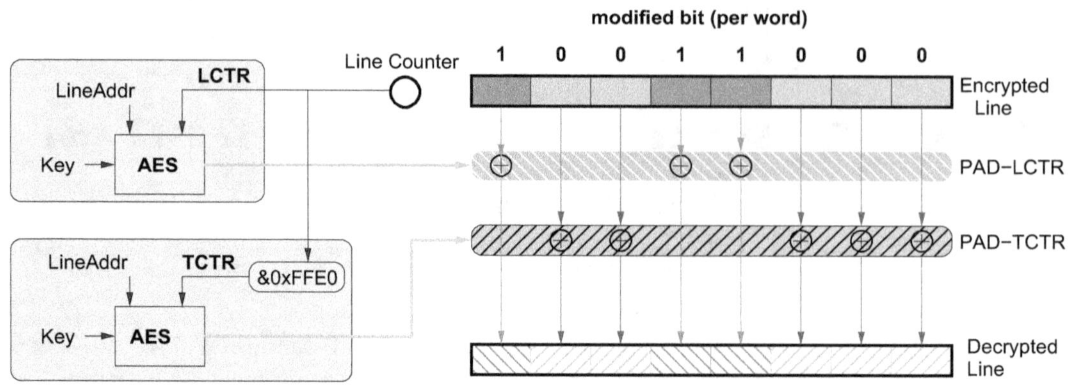

Figure 7. Operation of DEUCE. Two decryptions are performed, one with the PAD generated from the leading counter (PAD-LCTR), and the second with the PAD generated with the trailing counter (PAD-TCTR). The modified bit of the word decides which decrypted value to use. Note: both LCTR and TCTR are virtual counters, their values get determined by the line counter.

on every write LCTR is incremented, while TCTR is not. On every write, all the words that have changed since the last Epoch get re-encrypted. For example, at line counter value 1, W1 gets written, so only W1 is re-encrypted. On next write only W2 gets modified, but now both W1 and W2 get re-encrypted. Similarly, on the next write after that W3 gets written, so W1,W2, and W3 get re-encrypted. The next write triggers the start of the new Epoch so all words get re-encrypted, and TCTR is incremented from 0 to 4. And, so on. Thus, for each write during the Epoch, only a subset of words (that have been modified at least once since the last Epoch) are re-encrypted. This way, the modified words use LCTR, and other unmodified words continue to use TCTR.

4.2 DEUCE Parameters: Epoch and Word Size

The two design parameters for DEUCE are *Epoch Interval* and *Word Size*. The Epoch Interval impacts the effectiveness of DEUCE in terms of reducing bit flips, as there is a full line re-encryption on every Epoch Interval. A larger interval will reduce the full re-encryption overhead. However, a longer Epoch Interval may also cause DEUCE to continuously re-encrypt many words that are modified shortly after the Epoch but have stopped being modified since.

The word size determines the storage overhead and fineness of tracking modified parts of the cacheline. As we need one modified bit per word, we would need 64 bits per line if tracking is done at a byte granularity, and only 8 bits per line if tracking is done at 8 bytes. A finer granularity improves the effectiveness of DEUCE, but incurs higher overhead. So, the word size of DEUCE must be carefully selected.

4.3 Design of DEUCE

4.3.1 Structure

To implement DEUCE on top of a secure memory system, we simply need 1 bit per word in the line to indicate if the word has changed since last Epoch. For example, if tracking is done at a 2 byte granularity then we would need 32 modified bits for each line in memory.

4.3.2 Write Operation

At the start of each Epoch, all words in the line are re-encrypted and all the modified bits are reset. On subsequent writes, a read is performed to identify the words that are modified by the given write. The modified bits corresponding to these words are set. Only the words which have been modified at least once since the start of the Epoch are re-encrypted with the LCTR. The unmodified words (identified by the modified bit equal to zero) are encrypted with the TCTR, and thus continue to remain unchanged in memory.

4.3.3 Read Operation

On a read, decryption is performed as shown in Figure 7. Two PADs are obtained, one with the leading counter (PAD-LCTR), and second with the trailing counter (PAD-TCTR). Decryption is performed based on both PADs; however, the modified bit indicates which of the two values should be used for the given word. If the modified bit for a given word is set then the value decrypted using PAD-LCTR is used, otherwise the value decrypted using PAD-TCTR is used.

4.3.4 Overheads

The storage overhead of DEUCE is simply 1 bit per tracking granularity, so for our default configuration that tracks at a granularity of two bytes, we need 32 bits per line. The latency overhead of DEUCE is negligible, as we generate both PADs in parallel and use a multiplexer to choose between the two decrypted values. Thus, we would need two AES circuits, or we can simply time divison multiplex the AES circuits to generate the two PADs one after the other. As long as both PADs are obtained before the data from the memory arrives, we would avoid the latency overheads.

4.3.5 Security

The security of the counter based scheme relies on the premise that a given OTP is not reused, therefore it is critical to ensure that DEUCE does not use the same PAD multiple times for re-encryption of data. DEUCE always uses a different PAD for re-encrypting the word if the word gets modified. DEUCE simply avoids re-encryption for words that remain unmodified. Given the uniqueness of the PAD for re-encryption of the modified words, the security level of DEUCE is similar to the baseline OTP scheme. The attacker can only retrieve information that a particular word has been modified since the last Epoch, which is similar to knowing which line is modified in a page, based on the line address.

4.4 RESULTS: Sensitivity to DEUCE Word Size

Figure 8 shows the number of modified bits per write, on average, as the tracking granularity of DEUCE is varied from 1 byte (64 bit overhead per line) to 8 bytes (8 bit overhead per line) for an Epoch interval of 32. A smaller granularity is more efficient at reducing write overhead. As the tracking granularity is increased from 1 byte to 2 byte to 4 byte to 8 bytes, the average number of modified bits increases from 21.4% to 23.7% to 26.8% to 32.2%. Our default configuration uses a granularity of 2 bytes, which has a storage overhead of 32 bits per line.

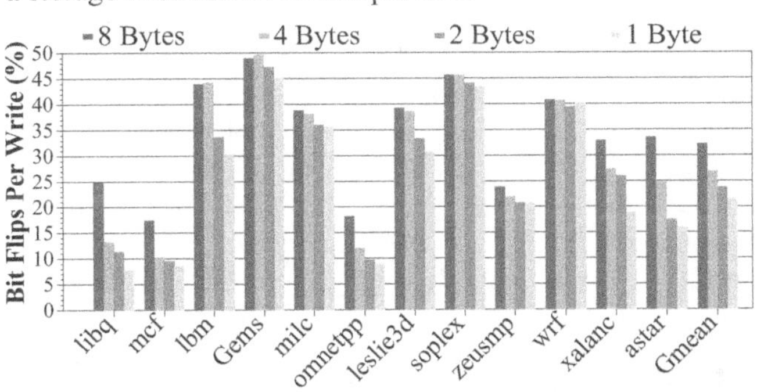

Figure 8. Number of modified bits per write with DEUCE as the tracking granularity is varied. DEUCE with word size of 2 bytes reduces modified bits from 50% to 23.7%.

4.5 RESULTS: Sensitivity to Epoch Interval

Figure 9 shows the number of modified bits per write, on average, with DEUCE as the Epoch interval is varied from 8 to 32. As the Epoch interval increases, the full encryption of the line happens less frequently, reducing the number of modified bits. However, at a much larger Epoch Interval, some words that were modified earlier in the Epoch but are no longer being modified continue to get re-encrypted, resulting in higher bit flips. For example, for wrf and milc there is an increase in bit flips when the Epoch Interval is increased from 8 to 16, and 16 to 32, respectively. The average number of bits modified for Epoch Interval of 8 is 24.8%, for Epoch Interval of 16 is 24.0%, and for Epoch Interval of 32 is 23.7%. Overall, increasing the Epoch Interval has a relatively small effect (less than 1%) on bit writes, as most writebacks tend to be to similar locations. We use a default Epoch Interval of 32 in our studies.

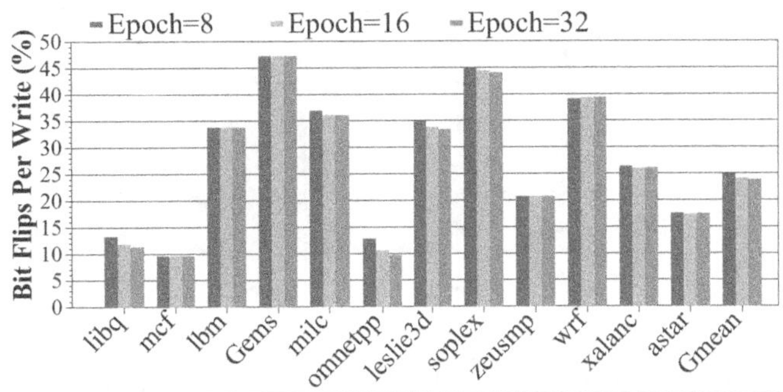

Figure 9. Number of modified bits per write with DEUCE as the Epoch Interval is varied. DEUCE with Epoch Interval of 32 reduces modified bits from 50% to 23.7%.

4.6 DynDEUCE: Morphing from DEUCE to FNW

DEUCE is effective at reducing the average number of bit flips for an encrypted memory by more than 2x (from 50% to 24%). DEUCE performs well when programs write to cachelines in sparse and regular patterns, which tends to be the common case for most general general purpose applications. However, if the applications modifies all the words of the line on every write, then DEUCE will not be able to reduce the number of bit writes to memory, as it will deem all the words as modified and will re-encrypt all the words of the line on each write, thus causing 50% of the bits to flip on each write. In such a scenario, it would have been better to use Flip-N-Write (FNW) and get the 14% fewer bit flips (from 50% to 43%) that FNW can provide. For example, consider the number of modified bits per write shown in Figure 9. Both Gems and soplex have an average of more than 43% bit flips with DEUCE, and would have benefited from FNW instead of DEUCE. Both FNW and DEUCE incur similar storage overheads (32 bits per line). As both FNW and DEUCE are orthogonal, one can potentially implement encrypted memory with both (a configuration we call FNW+DEUCE). However, this configuration will incur double the storage overhead, of 64 bits per line. Ideally, we want benefit of FNW, if FNW is better than DEUCE, without paying for the extra storage overhead. We propose such a configuration that can dynamically switch from DEUCE to FNW, in between the Epoch if FNW provides more benefit than DEUCE. We call this configuration as *DynDEUCE*.

To maintain a constant storage overhead, DynDEUCE reuses the bits allocated for tracking the modified words in DEUCE as the FlipBits in FNW when it is deemed that is FNW is beneficial. Thus, the storage overhead of DynDEUCE is a single bit (ModeBit) per line. If the ModeBit is zero, DynDEUCE operates as DEUCE. When the ModeBit is 1, then DEUCE gets disabled, all words are re-encrypted, and the modified bits allocated for DEUCE are repurposed as FlipBits of FNW. Determining which of the two policies, DEUCE or FNW, is better is done dynamically by measur-

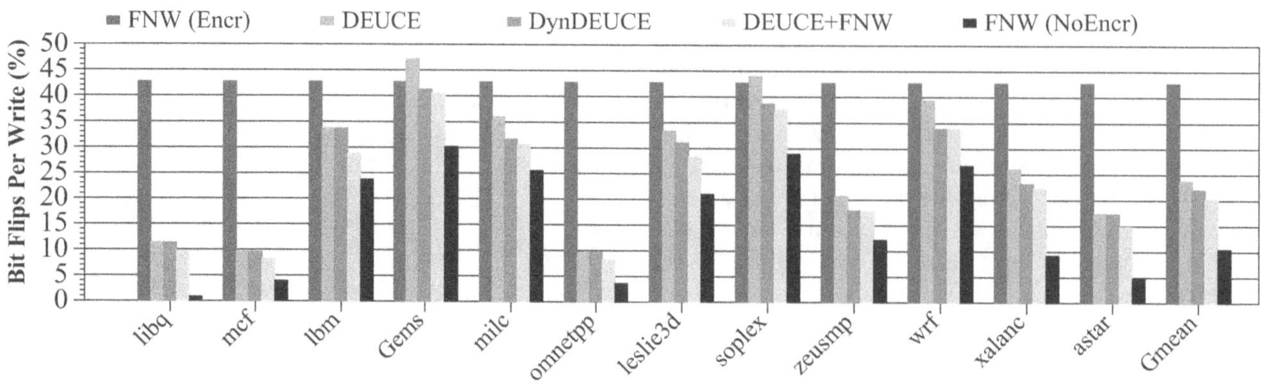

Figure 10. Number of bit flips per write with various schemes. DEUCE and DynDEUCE reduce the bit flips to 24% and 22% respectively. These schemes bridge two thirds of the gap between FNW (with encryption) and FNW (without encryption).

ing the number of bit flips expected with the two policies. If FNW has fewer bit flips then the ModeBit is set to use FNW.

Morphing the mode from DEUCE to FNW is straightforward; however, going from FNW to DEUCE is impractical, as the state at the start of the Epoch is lost when the mode is changed from DEUCE to FNW. DynDEUCE solves this problem by ensuring that the mode returns to DEUCE at the start of every Epoch. Then, at each write during the Epoch, if the number of bit flips with FNW is smaller then the mode is shifted from DEUCE to FNW. Figure 11 shows an example of DynDEUCE. At the start of the Epoch the ModeBit is set to use DEUCE. At the next write (and all subsequent writes till the next Epoch) the number of bit flips with DEUCE and FNW are estimated. For the example, encrypting the line with DEUCE gives 67 bit flips and encrypting the line with FNW gives 55 bit flips. So, DynDEUCE decides to change the mode to FNW, and for all the writes till the next Epoch, the mode continues to be FNW. Thus, DynDEUCE can be implemented with a storage overhead of only 33 bits per line (1 bit for mode selection and 32 bits, which are used either as modified bits for DEUCE or as Flip bits for FNW).

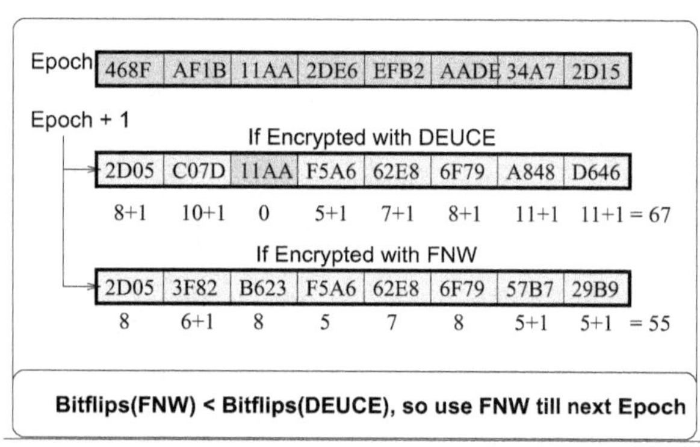

Figure 11. Operation of DynDEUCE. For each write after the Epoch, DynDEUCE calculates the expected number of bit flips with FNW and DEUCE. If FNW has fewer bit flips than DEUCE, the mode is set to FNW till the next Epoch.

4.7 RESULTS: Comparison of Bit Flip Reduction

Figure 10 shows the number of modified bits per write, for various bit flip reductions schemes, such as FNW, DEUCE, DynDEUCE, and DEUCE+FNW (has dedicated bits for both DEUCE and FNW). We compare these schemes to a FNW system with no encryption. The average number of bit flips with FNW with encrypted memory remains constant at 43% regardless of the workload. DEUCE is highly effective at reducing the number of bit flips, especially for workloads such as libq, mcf, and omnetpp. These workloads modify only a small number of words per write, and the footprint of which word gets modified does not change significantly. On average, DEUCE reduces the number of bit flips to 23.7%.

For Gems and Soplex, DEUCE has higher bit flips than FNW. For both these workloads DynDEUCE is more effective than either FNW or DEUCE standalone. On average, DynDEUCE has 22.0% bit flips. DynDEUCE bridges half the gap between DEUCE and FNW+DEUCE, a policy that dedicates dedicated storage to both FNW as well as DEUCE (total of 64 bits per line). Overall, DEUCE and DynDEUCE remove two-thirds of the extra bit flips due to encryption.

4.8 Comparison of Storage Overhead

Table 3 shows the storage overhead of different schemes for an encrypted memory system (already equipped with per line counter). Both FNW and DEUCE are implemented with identical storage overhead; DynDEUCE needs 1 extra mode bit, and DEUCE+FNW needs twice the storage.

Scheme	Overhead	Avg. Bit Flips Per Write
FNW	32 bits/line	42.7%
DEUCE	32 bits/line	23.7%
DynDEUCE	33 bits/line	22.0%
DEUCE+FNW	64 bits/line	20.3%

Table 3. Storage Overhead and Effectiveness

5. Horizontal Wear Leveling for Durability

PCM is an endurance limited memory technology, and reduction in write traffic can enhance the system lifetime significantly. DEUCE reduces the bit writes to PCM by a factor of 2x, so ideally we would expect the lifetime to also increase by 2x. However, we found that the average lifetime with DEUCE increases by only 11%. This happens because some portions of the line continue to get written much more frequently than others causing them to wear out sooner. This section analyzes the problem of non-uniform bit writes within a line, and develops a low cost and highly effective wear leveling algorithm to make bit writes uniform.

5.1 Problem of Non-Uniformity in Bit Writes

Figure 12 show the number of writes to each bit position of a cache line, normalized to the average writes to a bit, for *mcf* and *libquantum*. The bit writes are highly non-uniform, and the most frequently written bit receives as much as 6x (for mcf) to 27x (for libquantum) the writes compared to the average. Such non-uniformity in bit writes not only reduce the lifetime of unencrypted memory but also that of DEUCE, as the same set of words get re-encrypted frequently.

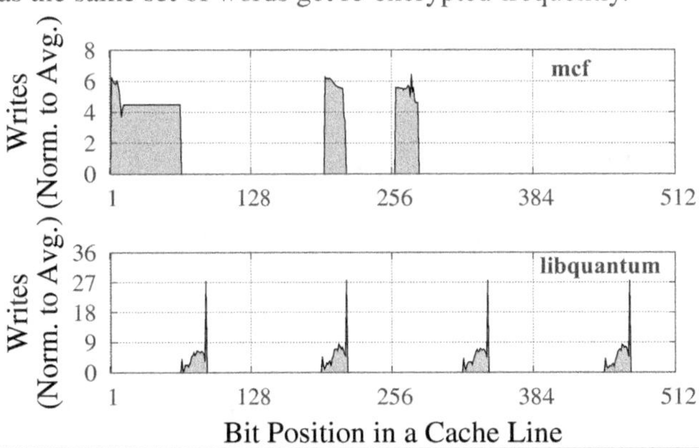

Figure 12. Variation in writes per bit position of a line. The most frequently written bit receives as much as 6x (for mcf) to 27x (for libquantum) more writes than average.

5.2 Background on Vertical Wear Leveling

The problem of non-uniformity in writes can be addressed by wear leveling. We call wear leveling algorithms that operate at a line granularity, such as Start-Gap [20] and Security Refresh [21], as *Vertical Wear Leveling (VWL)* algorithms. Unfortunately, Vertical Wear Leveling is not effective at reducing the bit write variation within a line. Bit writes in a line can be made uniform by rotating the line periodically and keeping track of the rotation amount per line [7]. Ideally, we want uniform bit writes without relying on dedicated storage on a per line or per page basis. We extend vertical wear leveling algorithms, such as Start-Gap and Security Refresh, to provide a storage overhead free intra-line wear leveling, which we call *Horizontal Wear Leveling (HWL)*.

We explain Start-Gap as a low-cost Vertical Wear Leveling algorithm. Figure 13(a) shows the structures for Start-Gap for a memory with 8 lines (A-H). It consists of two pointers, Start and Gap, and one dummy line called the GapLine to aid movement. Every so often (say 100 writes), the Gap line moves by one, by copying the content of the previous line to the next line, as shown in Figure 13(b), After the Gap has gone through all the lines, the Start register is incremented by 1. Thus, Start keeps track of the total number of global rotations, and Gap keeps track of the lines moved in current rotation. Using Start and Gap, the remapped location can be obtained easily.

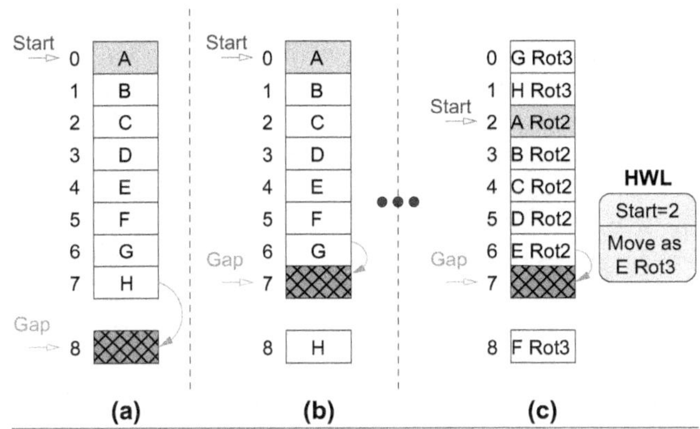

Figure 13. Extending Start-Gap to perform HWL (a) Start-Gap (b) Operation of Start Gap (c) Implementing HWL by rotating a line by (Start+1) on Gap moves.

5.3 Horizontal Wear Leveling via Algebraic Functions

Our insight to develop low cost Horizontal Wear Leveling (HWL) algorithms is to make the rotation amount an algebraic function of the global structures used by Vertical Wear Leveling. For example, we can get the rotation amount as *Rotation Amount = [Start' % BitsInLine]*, where Start' equals (Start+1) if the Gap has already crossed the line, otherwise Start' is equal to Start. This way, rotation amount can increase as Start increases and wrap around when the line has been rotated through all the bits (including any metadata bits associated with the line). Note that, if the Gap has already crossed through the line, then the rotation amount is determined as *Rotation Amount = [(Start+1) % BitsInLine]*. This ensures that when Start increments, all the lines for which the Gap has already passed through have already been rotated by the amount equal to the new value of the Start. Figure 13(c) shows the extension of Start-Gap that supports HWL. For typical applications, the Start register gets incremented by several hundred thousand, so all the bits within each line get rotated several hundred times, ensuring close to uniform bit writes. We found that the lifetime with HWL is within 0.5% of the lifetime of perfect wear leveling.[2]

[2] Given the deterministic nature of HWL, an adversary (or a badly written) program can purposely shift the write pattern at the granularity of the change of Start. The system can be protected against such access patterns easily by calculating a unique rotation amount for each line, as a function of the line address and Start. For example, calculate rotation amount using *Rotation Amount = [Hash(Start',LineAddress) % BitsInLine]*.

To support HWL, the memory is equipped with shifters, for rotating the line on a write and reverse rotating the line on read. Note that our proposed HWL does not incur any storage overhead. It avoids extra writes for line rotation by leveraging the line movement that is incurred by vertical wear leveling.

5.4 RESULTS: Impact on Lifetime

Figure 14 shows the lifetime of FNW, DEUCE, and DEUCE with HWL (DEUCE-HWL), normalized to the lifetime of the encrypted memory. Note that for encrypted memory, all the bits in the line get written with 50% probability, so it achieves an almost uniform bit writes within the line and HWL is not required. FNW reduces bit flips by 14% (50% to 43%) and the writes are spread uniformly across all bits, so it provides a 14% improvement in lifetime. Even though DEUCE reduces bit writes by 2x, the average lifetime improvement is only 11%. This is because DEUCE continues to write to the frequently written parts of the line. However, DEUCE when combined with HWL provides an average lifetime of 2x, which is in proportion to the reduction in bit writes. Thus, HWL achieves lifetime close to uniform bit writes, while incurring no storage overhead, other that what is required for vertical wear leveling.

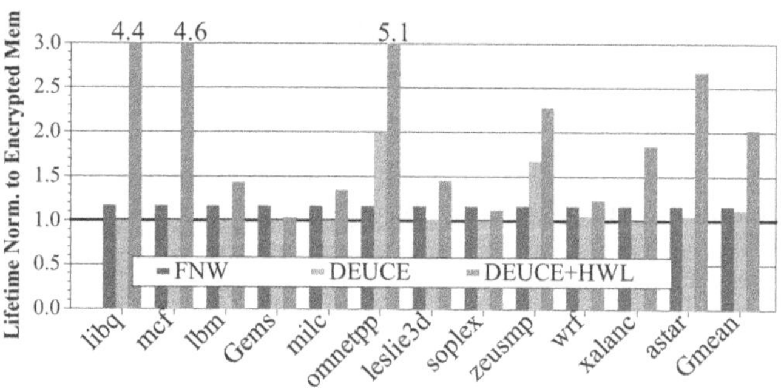

Figure 14. Lifetime normalized to encrypted memory. HWL increases the lifetime of DEUCE from 1.1x to 2x.

6. Impact on Performance and Power

6.1 Impact on Write Throughput

Due to power limitations, PCM memory systems tend to have limited write throughput. Typically, there is not enough current to write all the bits of a 64 byte cache line within one shot. For example, the recent 8Gb PCM prototype [19] shows a write width of 128 bits, and the write of a cache line can take up-to 4 write slots. For our system, we assume a 128 bit width for write (provisioned for handling a maximum of 64 bit flips using internal Flip-N-Write [22]). We also assume that multiple writes can be scheduled concurrently, provided the total number of bit flips does not exceed the current capacity [22].

Bit flip reduction can potentially cause a write to consume fewer write slots, as multiple portions of a cacheline

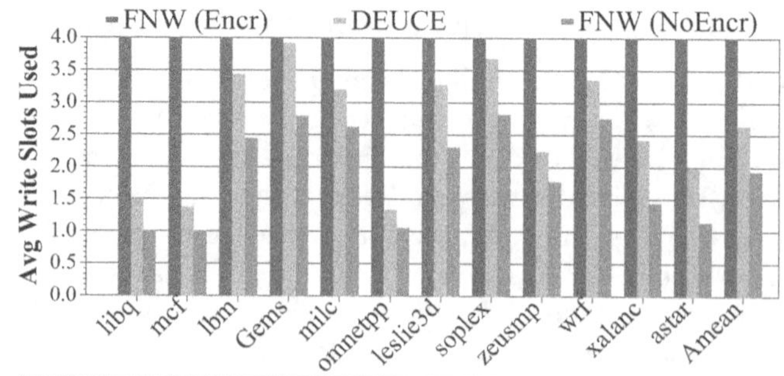

Figure 15. Average number of write slots used per write request. On average, DEUCE consumes 2.64 slots whereas unencrypted memory takes 1.92 slots out of the 4 write slots.

can be serviced concurrently. However, the reduction in bit flips does not always directly translate into fewer write slots because of fragmentation. For example, if the given write causes 70 flips, and one slot can only handle 64 flips, then this write will take two slots. Figure 15 shows the average number of write slots consumed per write. FNW on an encrypted PCM reduces bit flips by 14% (50 to 43), but this reduction is not enough to allow the PCM system to service the request in three slots. DEUCE, on the other hand, reduces the number of write slots from 4.0 to 2.64, which reduces the effective write latency by 34%, thus improving the write throughput by 52%. The unencrypted memory consumes 1.92 write slots on average. Thus, DEUCE bridges two-thirds of the gap for consumption of write slots between encrypted memory and unencrypted memory.

6.2 Impact on System Performance

Servicing the writes quickly can reduce the memory contention for reads and thus improve system performance. Figure 16 shows the system speedup of FNW (with and without encryption) and DEUCE compared to the encrypted memory system. Applying FNW on encrypted memory has negligible impact on performance because of the fragmentation of write slots, which means even with FNW the system tends to have write latency similar to that of the encrypted memory without FNW. DEUCE, however, is able to increase system performance by 27% on average, due to its increased write throughput. Disabling encryption and using FNW would improve the system performance by 40%, on average. Thus, DEUCE bridges two-thirds of the performance gap between encrypted memory and unencrypted memory.

6.3 Impact on Power and Energy

As writes in PCM consume significant power, the reduction in bit writes also has a significant impact on the energy and power of the system. We measure energy and power for the PCM memory system, taking into account the power consumed for each bit written. Figure 17 compares the speedup, energy consumption, power, and Energy Delay Product (EDP), normalized to an encrypted memory system.

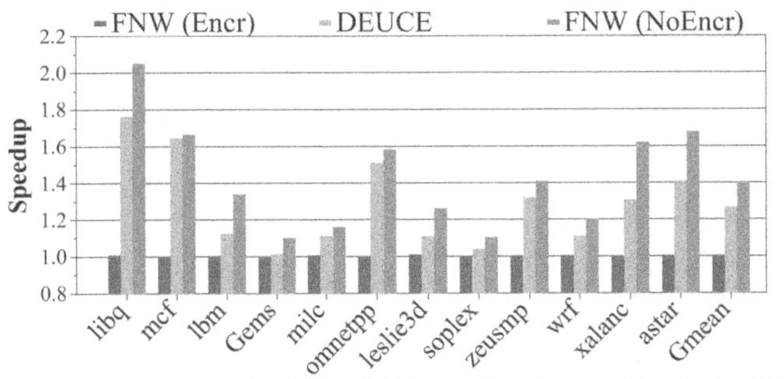

Figure 16. Speedup compared to encrypted memory system. DEUCE bridges two-thirds of the performance gap between encrypted memory and unencrypted memory.

FNW has only a small impact on the energy and power consumption of PCM memory, reducing it by approximately 11%. DEUCE reduces memory energy consumption by 43% and power by 28%. The reduction in power is less than the reduction in energy because of the shorter execution time.

Energy Delay Product (EDP) is often used as a metric combining power and performance. Compared to the baseline encrypted memory, FNW provides a reduction of 4% and DEUCE of 43%. Disabling the encryption and employing FNW would provide an EDP improvement of 56%. Thus, DEUCE bridges three-fourths of the EDP gap between encrypted and unencrypted memory.

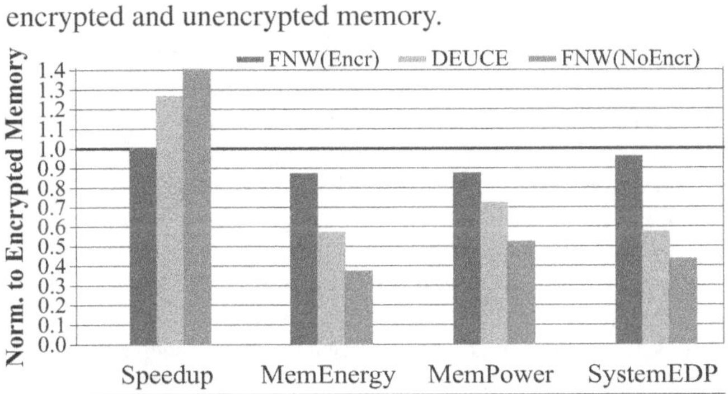

Figure 17. Speedup, memory energy consumption, memory power consumption, and system Energy Delay Product.

7. Related Work

Our study addresses the problem of reducing write traffic for encrypted memory systems. We discuss some of the closely related works that have looked at secure PCM memories.

7.1 Block Level Encryption at AES Granularity

In our studies, we assume counter mode encryption that operates at a line granularity [13, 14]. Each line has one counter, which is incremented on each write, thus causing the entire line to be modified. Block-Level Encryption (BLE) [18] reduces write overhead by performing re-encryption at the granularity of an AES block (16 bytes). As the cacheline is 64 bytes, BLE provisions the line with four separate counters, one per each block. On a write, BLE re-encrypts only the modified blocks in the cacheline and increments the counter of the modified blocks. Unfortunately, BLE still incurs high write overhead as it rewrites 16 bytes, even if one bit in the block gets modified. DEUCE, on the other hand, operates at a much smaller granularity of 2 bytes, and performs fine grained re-encryption. Thus, DEUCE decouples the granularity of re-encryption from the granularity of AES. Nonetheless, DEUCE is orthogonal to BLE and can be combined for greater benefit.

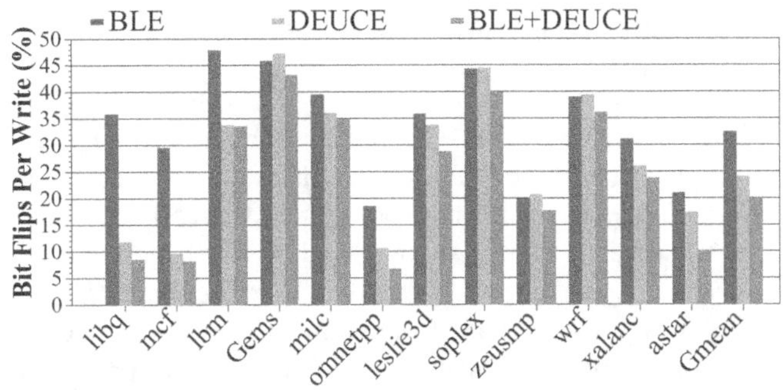

Figure 18. Bit flips with DEUCE and Block Level Encryption at granularity of AES. DEUCE (24%) is orthogonal to BLE (33%) and can be combined for greater benefits (20%).

Figure 18 shows the average number of modified bits per line with BLE, DEUCE, and the combination of BLE+DEUCE. BLE reduces the bit flips to 33%, whereas DEUCE reduces it to 24%. The combination of BLE+DEUCE cause 19.9% bit flips, outperforming either scheme standalone.

7.2 Partial Working-Set Encryption with i-NVMM

i-NVMM [17] tries to reduce the latency overheads of encryption by keeping the hot data in unencrypted form, and encrypting it only on power down. While i-NVMM may protect the system against the stolen DIMM attack, it still leaves the system vulnerable to bus snooping attacks, as writes to hot pages are sent unencrypted on the bus. We seek to protect the memory against both stolen DIMM attack as well as the bus snooping attacks. If one wishes to protect the system only against stolen DIMM attack, then it can be done with low latency (and low bit flips) by eliminating the counter from counter mode encryption, and simply using the line address to generate a unique PAD per line. When the DIMM gets stolen, the adversary will not be able to regenerate the PADs per line without the secret key. This would also ensure that the entire memory content always remains encrypted, which is not the case for i-NVMM.

7.3 Protecting PCM from Endurance Related Attacks

Given that PCM has limited endurance, PCM systems are vulnerable to endurance related attacks that write to a small portion of memory repeatedly [20, 21, 23]. PCM systems can be protected from such lifetime reducing attacks by means of an attack detector [23]. DEUCE is an encryption scheme that focuses on information security as opposed to lifetime security. Techniques that mitigate endurance related attacks could also be applied for systems that use DEUCE.

8. Conclusions

Secure PCM systems rely on data encryption, which increase the bit flips per write by almost 4x. The extra bit flips degrade write throughput, performance, lifetime, and power efficiency. Ideally, we want the security of encryption without significantly increasing the bit writes to PCM. We observe that each writeback writes to only a few words, and we can reduce bit flips by re-encrypting only modified words. With this insight, this paper makes the following contributions:

1. We propose *Dual Counter Encryption (DEUCE)*, a design that selectively re-encrypts cachelines at a fine granularities (two bytes). DEUCE reduces the number of bit flips for an encrypted memory system from 50% to 24%, while incurring a storage overhead of 32 bits per line.
2. We propose a simple *Horizontal Wear Leveling (HWL)* algorithm based on an algebraic function of Start-Gap, to make the bit writes within a line uniform. Our proposed HWL is storage overhead free, and increases the lifetime improvement provided by DEUCE from 1.1x to 2x.
3. We show that DEUCE is orthogonal to, and can be combined with, existing schemes such as Flip-N-Write (FNW) and Block Level Encryption (BLE). For example, DEUCE combined with BLE reduces the bit flips of BLE from 33% to 19.9%. We also develop *DynDEUCE*, which dynamically selects between FNW and DEUCE, depending on which scheme has fewer bit writes.

The reduction in bit flips with DEUCE improves write throughput by 52%, performance by 27%, lifetime by 2x, and EDP by 43% with respect to an encrypted memory system. DEUCE bridges two-thirds of the gap in performance, power, and lifetime between an encrypted memory system and an unencrypted memory system.

With an increase in hardware attacks, secure memory systems are becoming essential. We show how architecture support can mitigate the overheads of encryption, and make security practical. While we analyze PCM as an example of NVM, the scheme, insights, and evaluations should also be useful for other NVM technologies, such as STT-RAM and RRAM, in which write operations are expensive and therefore it is desirable to have write-efficient memory encryption to obtain both security and high performance and durability.

Acknowledgements

We thank the anonymous reviewers, Andrew Chien, Swamit Tannu, and Daniel Wong for their comments and feedback on earlier draft of this paper. We also thank Simha Sethumadhavan and Milos Prvulovic for discussions and providing useful insights on working of counter mode encryption and security analysis of encrypted memoryx. This work was supported by the Center for Future Architectures Research (C-FAR), one of the six SRC STARnet Centers, sponsored by MARCO and DARPA.

References

[1] M. K. Qureshi, S. Gurumurthi, and B. Rajendran, "Phase change memory: From devices to systems," *Synthesis Lectures on Computer Architecture*, vol. 6, no. 4, 2011.

[2] J. Yue and Y. Zhu, "Accelerating write by exploiting pcm asymmetries," in *HPCA-2013*.

[3] L. Jiang *et al.*, "A low power and reliable charge pump design for phase change memories," in *ISCA-2014*.

[4] S. Schechter *et al.*, "Use ecp, not ecc, for hard failures in resistive memories," in *ISCA-2010*.

[5] B. C. Lee, E. Ipek *et al.*, "Architecting phase change memory as a scalable dram alternative," in *ISCA-2009*.

[6] M. Qureshi, M. Franceschini, and L. Lastras-Montano, "Improving read performance of phase change memories via write cancellation and write pausing," in *HPCA-16*, 2010.

[7] P. Zhou, B. Zhao, J. Yang, and Y. Zhang, "A durable and energy efficient main memory using phase change memory technology," in *ISCA*, 2009.

[8] S. Cho and H. Lee, "Flip-n-write: A simple deterministic technique to improve pram write performance, energy and endurance," in *MICRO-2009*.

[9] A. Huang, "The trusted pc: skin-deep security," *Computer*, vol. 35, no. 10, 2002.

[10] A. B. Huang, *Hacking the Xbox: An Introduction to Reverse Engineering*. No Starch Press, 2003.

[11] J. Demme, R. Martin, A. Waksman, and S. Sethumadhavan, "Side-channel vulnerability factor: A metric for measuring information leakage," in *ISCA-2012*.

[12] A. Webster and S. Tavares, "On the design of s-boxes," in *Advances in Cryptology CRYPTO 85 Proceedings*, ser. Lecture Notes in Computer Science, 1986, vol. 218.

[13] Suh *et al.*, "Efficient memory integrity verification and encryption for secure processors," in *MICRO-2003*.

[14] C. Yan, B. Rogers, D. Englender, D. Solihin, and M. Prvulovic, "Improving cost, performance, and security of memory encryption and authentication," in *ISCA-2006*.

[15] H. Lipmaa, P. Rogaway *et al.*, "Ctr-mode encryption," 2000.

[16] B. Rogers, S. Chhabra *et al.*, "Using address independent seed encryption and bonsai merkle trees to make secure processors os-and performance-friendly," in *MICRO-2007*.

[17] S. Chhabra and Y. Solihin, "i-nvmm: A secure non-volatile main memory system with incremental encryption," in *ISCA-2011*.

[18] J. Kong and H. Zhou, "Improving privacy and lifetime of pcm-based main memory," in *DSN-2010*.

[19] Y. Choi *et al.*, "A 20nm 1.8v 8gb pram with 40mb/s program bandwidth," in *ISSCC*, 2012.

[20] M. K. Qureshi, J. Karidis, M. Franceschini *et al.*, "Enhancing lifetime and security of pcm-based main memory with start-gap wear leveling," in *MICRO-42*, 2009.

[21] N. H. Seong, D. H. Woo, and H.-H. S. Lee, "Security refresh: Prevent malicious wear-out and increase durability for phase-change memory with dynamically randomized address mapping," in *ISCA-2010*.

[22] A. Hay, K. Strauss, T. Sherwood *et al.*, "Preventing pcm banks from seizing too much power," in *MICRO-2011*.

[23] M. K. Qureshi, A. Seznec, L. A. Lastras, and M. M. Franceschini, "Practical and secure pcm systems by online detection of malicious write streams," in *HPCA-2011*.

Temporally Bounding TSO for Fence-Free Asymmetric Synchronization

Adam Morrison
Computer Science Department
Technion—Israel Institute of Technology

Yehuda Afek
Blavatnik School of Computer Science
Tel Aviv University

Abstract

This paper introduces a *temporally bounded total store ordering* (TBTSO) memory model, and shows that it enables *nonblocking fence-free* solutions to *asymmetric synchronization* problems, such as those arising in memory reclamation and biased locking.

TBTSO strengthens the TSO memory model by *bounding* the time it takes a store to drain from the store buffer into memory. This bound enables devising fence-free algorithms for asymmetric problems, which require a performance-critical *fast path* to synchronize with an infrequently executed *slow path*. We demonstrate this by constructing (1) a fence-free version of the *hazard pointers* memory reclamation scheme, and (2) a fence-free *biased lock* algorithm which is compatible with unmanaged environments as it does not rely on safe points or similar mechanisms.

We further argue that TBTSO can be implemented in hardware with modest modifications to existing TSO architectures. However, our design makes assumptions about proprietary implementation details of commercial hardware; it thus best serves as a starting point for a discussion on the feasibility of hardware TBTSO implementation. We also show how minimal OS support enables the adaptation of TBTSO algorithms to x86 systems.

Categories and Subject Descriptors C.1.4 [*Computer Systems Organization*]: Processor Architectures—Parallel Architectures; D.1.3 [*Programming Techniques*]: Concurrent Programming

Keywords TSO; bounded TSO; hazard pointers; biased locks; memory fences

ASPLOS '15, March 14–18, 2015, Istanbul, Turkey..

ACM 978-1-4503-2835-7/15/03...$15.00.
http://dx.doi.org/10.1145/2694344.2694374

1. Introduction

Modern multicore architectures implement *relaxed* memory consistency models, which—unlike sequential consistency [21]—allow memory operations to execute out of (program) order. Preventing such reordering, which is crucial for maintaining correctness of synchronization code, requires issuing costly *memory fence* instructions [18].

We focus on the *total store ordering* (TSO) memory model followed by the x86 and SPARC architectures [1, 34], which only allows store/load reordering—i.e., reordering of a store with a later load from a different address. Unfortunately, such a store/load sequence forms the core of the *flag principle* [18], a common synchronization idiom used in algorithms for mutual exclusion [12, 31], memory reclamation [19, 28], and biased locking [33, 40] to name a few. These performance-critical codes must thus issue expensive memory fences that hurt their performance. However, several of these codes are *asymmetric*—they involve synchronization between performance-critical *fast path* code and infrequently executed *slow path* code [11, 28, 33], and only the memory fences on the fast path affect overall performance.

In this paper, we introduce *temporally bounded* TSO (TBTSO)—a strengthening of the TSO memory model that enables asymmetric synchronization with a *fence-free* fast path and a *nonblocking* slow path which can make progress even when the fast path code gets scheduled out. TBTSO facilitates this by guaranteeing a bound Δ on the amount of time it takes a store instruction to become globally visible in memory—i.e., to propagate to memory from the abstract *store buffer* [1, 34] that models store/load reordering in TSO. (TSO store/load reordering occurs when a store remains buffered in the store buffer while a later load from a different address is satisfied from memory.)

1.1 Fence-free asymmetric synchronization

We demonstrate how TBTSO facilitates nonblocking fence-free asymmetric synchronization by developing a fence-free version of the flag principle for TBTSO (§ 3) and applying it to two important problems.

Safe memory reclamation (§ 4) The *safe memory reclamation* (SMR) problem [28] arises in concurrent data structures (particularly *nonblocking* [17] ones) implemented with C/C++, in which multiple operations (e.g., hash table `lookup` and `delete` [27, 38]) access the data structure concurrently. The SMR problem occurs because a thread removing an object O from a data structure cannot immediately reclaim O's memory, since other threads might be reading from the data structure and internally holding a reference to O. Therefore, memory reclamation of an object (slow path) must synchronize with the threads concurrently reading from the data structure (fast path).

We build on *hazard pointers* [28], a nonblocking SMR technique in which each thread maintains a set of *hazard pointers* pointing to objects it may access. After pointing a hazard pointer at an object O, a thread verifies that O has not been removed from the data structure before accessing O for the first time. In standard hazard pointers, this requires issuing a memory fence to order the write of the hazard pointer before the read from the data structure.

TBTSO enables removing this fence. Instead, it is safe to reclaim O's memory if no hazard pointer visibly points to it once Δ time units pass since O is removed from the data structure—even when hazard pointers are written without the subsequent fence. The reason is that any thread holding a reference to O either wrote its hazard pointer at least Δ time units ago, and so its write is globally visible, or it has not yet performed the write and so its (future) validation check will fail since the removal is now globally visible. The hazard pointers method reclaims memory periodically [28], and so Δ time units naturally pass between these periods and no additional waiting is introduced.

Evaluating fence-free hazard pointers (FFHP) on Intel x86 processors shows that they eliminate all overhead associated with hazard pointers, obtaining read-only performance matching that of RCU [26], a reclamation method which imposes no fast path overhead but, unlike FFHP, does not guarantee bounded memory consumption by removed objects.

Biased locking (§ 5) Prior work has shown that many locks in multi-threaded programs are uncontended, and moreover are acquired mostly (or only) by the same thread [20, 30, 33]. This observation lead to the development of *biased lock* algorithms, in which lock acquisition by a designated *owner* thread is cheap—does not use atomic operations—but acquisition by other threads is even more expensive than in standard locks. Existing biased locks either issue fences in the owner acquisition code [30] or block non-owners until the owner reaches a *safe point* outside the critical section [33].

We construct (owner) fence-free biased locks using our TBTSO flag principle. We further adapt the *echo method* [29] to make non-owner lock acquisition speed comparable to standard locks, assuming the owner acquires the lock frequently. Because our lock does not rely on blocking safe points, it (1) can be used in C/C++ programs, which do not naturally define safe points, and (2) enables non-owner acquisition even if the owner is scheduled out or delayed.

Our evaluation shows that the fence-free biased lock (FFBL) outperforms `pthread` locks and performs comparably to safe point based biased locks [33] except for when the owner is delayed outside of the critical section, in which case our FFBL greatly outperform the biased locks.

1.2 Implementing TBTSO

The implementability of TBTSO is an intriguing question. Existing TSO processors do not guarantee bounded time until store visibility, because they do not *fairly arbitrate* [36] the hardware resources (memory units, buses, etc.) involved in propagating stores to memory. In practice, however, stores become visible after only a short delay. Therefore, we propose a hardware design (§ 6) in which the processor *bails out* a store that remains buffered for a long time by *quiescing* the system (this can be done with existing mechanisms [39]).

Unfortunately, we cannot *prove* the feasibility of this design or calculate a worst-case Δ bound, as that entails reasoning about all possible internal interactions that can delay the propagation of a store—many of which are proprietary and undocumented. We thus outline the design and justify—at a high-level—why we believe it is feasible. We also estimate, by extrapolating from measurements on x86 hardware, that this TBTSO design can achieve sub-millisecond Δ bounds. We hope this paper starts a discussion on the implementability of TBTSO and the achievable bounds.

We additionally show that TBTSO algorithms can be adapted to existing x86 systems, provided minimal changes are made in the OS (§ 6). While such adapted TBTSO algorithms experience coarser Δ bounds (1–10 ms) and incur extra work in the slow path, our evaluation shows they perform well.

2. Temporally bounded TSO (TBTSO[Δ])

Here we define TBTSO[Δ], a strengthening of TSO in which a store can remain buffered in a store buffer at most Δ time units. We define TBTSO[Δ] operationally, via an abstract machine whose executions explain observable TBTSO[Δ] behaviors. That is, an execution on a real TBTSO[Δ] machine produces the same read values and final memory state as *some* execution of the abstract TBTSO[Δ] machine.

Technically, the TBTSO[Δ] machine extends Sewell et al.'s x86-TSO abstract machine [34] with a notion of global time. We impose the store buffering bound using this global time by admitting only executions in which the bound holds. Below we describe the TBTSO[Δ] machine informally; the reader can refer to Sewell et al.'s work [34] for the full x86-TSO definitions from which the formal TBTSO[Δ] machine can be derived.

Abstract machine The machine consists of a set of threads, each corresponding to an in-order stream of instructions, that interact through a memory subsystem. The memory subsystem contains one FIFO store buffer for each thread and is protected by a global fair lock. The memory subsystem lock is used to model atomic read-modify-write operations as being performed by a thread holding the lock. (For simplicity, we use atomic operations directly throughout this paper.) The machine also has a global clock (initially 0) readable by the threads.

The execution of the machine proceeds in *time units*. In each time unit the global clock increases by one. Then, at most one of the following actions can be executed for each thread T if it is valid to do so under the rules below. (This does not mean that a valid action must be executed for T—a scheduler decides the actions in each time unit. Thus, despite the presence of a global clock, the execution is asynchronous.)

The following actions are possible only when the memory subsystem lock is unlocked or held by thread T:

1. The memory subsystem can dequeue T's oldest entry from T's store buffer and write it to memory.
2. T may read: If T reads from an address for which a matching write exists in its store buffer, the read returns the newest corresponding value stored in the buffer. Otherwise, the read returns the value from memory.
3. T may acquire the memory lock if it does not hold it.
4. T may release the memory lock if it holds the lock and its store buffer is empty (if T wishes to release the lock when its store buffer is not empty, the memory subsystem must first empty T's store buffer with #1 actions).

The following are allowed at any time:

5. T can execute a `fence` if its store buffer is empty (similarly to #4, the memory subsystem must act to empty T's store buffer first).
6. T may write, enqueuing an entry to its store buffer.
7. T may read the global clock.

Bounding store buffering time In the TBTSO[Δ] model (where $\Delta \geq 1$), we consider only the abstract machine executions in which the following property holds:

> A write enqueued to a thread's store buffer (action #6) at global time t_0 is written to memory (action #1) at global time $t_1 \leq t_0 + \Delta$.

3. TBTSO flag principle

Fence use in TSO often occurs when applying the *flag principle* [18]. The flag principle says that when two threads, T_0 and T_1, each "raise a flag"—writing to a variable in memory—and then "look" at the other's flag by reading it from memory, then at least one will see the other's flag raised [18]. Of course, correctly ordering "raising the flag" to be globally visible before "looking at the other flag" requires a memory fence on TSO (and TBTSO):

	T_0	T_1
	`flag0 := 1`	`flag1 := 1`
Flag	`fence`	`fence`
principle	`if (flag1)`	`if (flag0)`
	`print "saw` T_1`"`	`print "saw` T_0`"`

This section shows a TBTSO variant of the flag principle that is asymmetric: it removes the fence from T_0's code and shifts the responsibility of maintaining correct ordering of T_0's reads and writes to T_1, which does so using the TBTSO Δ bound. We subsequently apply this asymmetric TBTSO flag principle to remove the fence from the fast path of hazard pointers (§ 4) and biased locks (§ 5).

To devise the TBTSO flag principle, we first use TBTSO's global time to rephrase the original flag principle: If, when T_j reads $\texttt{flag}_\texttt{i}$ at time t_j, T_i's write to $\texttt{flag}_\texttt{i}$ does not appear in memory (i.e., is not yet globally visible), then T_i will necessarily see $\texttt{flag}_\texttt{j}$ raised when it reads $\texttt{flag}_\texttt{j}$ at time $t_i > t_j$. This holds because if this happens, then T_i did not yet execute its fence at time t_j, whereas T_j's write is already globally visible at time t_j because of its fence. TBTSO allows us to break this symmetry by removing the fence from T_0 and placing the responsibility of guaranteeing the above property on T_1, which will *wait Δ time units* before reading T_0's flag:

	T_0	T_1
	`flag0 := 1`	`flag1 := 1`
TBTSO		`fence`
flag		`wait` Δ `time units`
principle	`if (flag1)`	`if (flag0)`
	`print "saw` T_1`"`	`print "saw` T_0`"`

Now, if T_0 reads $\texttt{flag}_1$ at time t_0 but T_1's flag write is not yet globally visible, T_0 is still guaranteed that T_1 will see $\texttt{flag}_0$ raised—because in this case T_1 has not yet issued its fence at time t_0 and thus will read $\texttt{flag}_0$ at least Δ time units later, by which time T_0's write is globally visible. In the opposite case, if T_1 reads $\texttt{flag}_0$ at time t_1 but T_0's write is not yet globally visible, then T_0 has not written to its flag before $t_1 - \Delta$. However, T_1's write is globally visible at $t_1 - \Delta$ since T_1 issues a fence, and so T_0 must observe $\texttt{flag}_1$ flag raised.

4. Fence-free hazard pointers (FFHP)

This section describes *fence-free hazard pointers* (FFHP), a nonblocking fence-free SMR algorithm for TBTSO. (Although we build on hazard pointers [28], the ideas described here apply equally well to Herlihy et al.'s *guards* [19]—an SMR method that differs from hazard pointers only in how removed objects are stored before being reclaimed.)

4.1 Standard hazard pointers

In the hazard pointers method, each thread maintains several *hazard pointers*, $\texttt{hp}_0, \texttt{hp}_1, \ldots, \texttt{hp}_\texttt{k}$, which it uses to announce objects it is about to access. Applying hazard pointers in

```
1  Data types:
2  struct MarkPtr {
3    next : pointer to Node
4    mark : boolean ( stored in LSB of next)
5  }
6  struct Node {
7    key : keyType
8    nextPtr : struct MarkPtr
9  }
10 Shared variables:
11   head : MarkPtr ( list head)
12 Per-thread local variables:
13   prev : pointer to MarkPtr
14   cur, next : pointer to Node
15   hp0, hp1, hp2 : hazard pointers (to Node)
16
17 lookup(key : keyType) {
18   return find(&head, key)
19 }
20
21 delete (key : keyType) {
22   while (true) {
23     if (! find(key)) return false
24     // above find() call initialized cur, next & prev
25     if (!CAS(&cur.nextPtr, <next,0>, <next,1>)) continue
26     if (CAS(prev, <cur,0>, <next,0>))
27       retire (cur)
28     return true
29 } }
30 find(head : pointer to MarkPtr, key : keyType) {
31   prev := head
32 retry :
33   ┌ <cur,mark> := *prev
     │ hp1 := cur
     │ fence
     └ if (*prev ≠ <cur,0>) goto retry
34   while (true) {
35     if (cur = null) return false
36     ┌ <next,mark> := cur.nextPtr
       │ hp0 := next
       │ fence
       └ if (cur.nextPtr ≠ <next,mark>) goto retry
37     ckey := ckey.key
38     if (*prev ≠ <cur,0>) goto retry
39     if (!mark) {
40       if (ckey ≥ key) return (ckey = key)
41       prev := &cur.nextPtr
42       hp2 := cur // copy hp1, no need for fence
43                  // Section 4.1 explains why
44     } else {
45       if (CAS(prev, <cur,0>, <next,0>))
46         retire (cur)
47       else
48         goto retry
49     }
50     cur := next
51     hp1 := next // copy hp0, no need for fence
52 } }
```

Figure 1: Hazard pointers usage example in Michael's nonblocking sorted linked list [27] (the `insert` operation is omitted). Boxed code segments show setting of a hazard pointer and verifying that the object has not been removed in the meantime.

a concurrent data structure requires manually changing the algorithm in two ways: First, removed objects may be freed only via the `retire()` method of the hazard pointers. The `retire()` method guarantees that an object is not reclaimed as long as some thread's hazard pointer points to it.

Second, every access to an object must be *protected* by a hazard pointer, that is, one of the thread's hazard pointers must point to the object continuously from a time at which the object was definitely in the data structure (i.e., not `retire()`ed). This entails the following sequence of operations in order to access an object: (1) writing to the hazard pointer, (2) issuing a fence to ensure that the write is globally visible, (3) verifying (in a data structure specific way) that the object is still part of the data structure and has not been retired. Success of this validation implies that the object was part of the data structure throughout steps (1)–(3), so it is successfully protected. If the validation fails, the algorithm typically retries the entire operation, since the state of the data structure has changed under its feet.

Hazard pointers example Figure 1 shows Michael's nonblocking linked list algorithm [27], which uses hazard pointers to safely traverse the list in the presence of concurrent deletions. (Code is presented in C-like pseudo code. Throughout the paper, we ignore the issue of compiler code reordering and assume that memory operations are executed according to the order shown in the pseudo code.) Deletions are done in two steps: first the node is *logically deleted* by setting the least significant bit of its `next` pointer, and only then it is physically removed from the list and passed to `retire()` (Lines 25–27). The `find()` method traverses the list using three pointers, `prev`, `cur` and `next`, and always protects a node with a hazard pointer before reading from it (the boxes at Lines 33 and 36). The hazard pointer validation step consists of verifying that the node being protected is still pointed to by its predecessor. Notice that the shared variable `head` which points to the first element of the list is an immutable sentinel, and therefore `find()` does not need to protect `head` with a hazard pointer.

Copying hazard pointers Figure 1 demonstrates an additional way of setting hazard pointers. In Lines 42 and 51 the value of a hazard pointer is *copied* from one pointer $\mathtt{hp}_i$ to another $\mathtt{hp}_j$. As we explain below, this does not compromise the protection of the hazard pointer, provided that $j > i$.

```
1  Shared variables:
2    hplist : list of all hazard pointers in the system
3  Per-thread local variables:
4    rlist : list of object pointers (removed objects)
5    plist : list of object pointers (copies of hazard pointers)
6    rcount : int
7
8  retire (objp : pointer to object) {
9    rlist .add(objp)
10   rcount += 1
11   if (rcount ≥ R)
12     reclaim ()
13 }
14 reclaim () {
15   // find all non−null hazard pointers in the system
16   plist := ∅
17   foreach (hp ∈ hplist, in ascending index order) {
18     if (hp ≠ null)
19       plist .add(object pointed by hp)
20   }
21   // find all objects which can be removed safely
22   foreach (objp ∈ rlist) {
23     if (objp ∉ plist) {
24       rcount −= 1
25       rlist .remove(objp)
26       free (objp)
27 } } }
28
```

(a) Standard hazard pointers [28]

```
29 Shared variables:
30   hplist : list of all hazard pointers in the system
31 Per-thread local variables:
32 □ rlist : list of <object pointer,time> pairs (removed objects)
33   plist : list of object pointers (copies of hazard pointers)
34   rcount : int
35
36 retire (objp : pointer to object) {
37 □ rlist .add(<objp, global_clock ()>)
38   rcount += 1
39 □ while (rcount ≥ R) // executes at most Δ times
40     reclaim ()
41 }
42 reclaim () {
43   // find all non−null hazard pointers in the system
44   plist := ∅
45 □ now := global_clock ()
46   foreach (hp ∈ hplist, in ascending index order) {
47     if (hp ≠ null)
48       plist .add(object pointed by hp)
49   }
50   // find all objects which can be removed safely
51 □ foreach (<objp,time> ∈ rlist with time < now − Δ) {
52     if (objp ∉ plist) {
53       rcount −= 1
54 □     rlist .remove(<objp,time>)
55       free (objp)
56 } } }
```

(b) Fence-free hazard pointers (FFHP)

Figure 2: Reclamation in hazard pointers and fence-free hazard pointers. Implementation differences are marked by □.

Handling reclamation (Figure 2a) Each thread maintains a list, `rlist`, of all objects it has retired. When the size of `rlist` exceeds a prespecified bound R, the thread calls the `reclaim()` routine to free memory (Lines 9–12). This routine copies the hazard pointers of every thread into a private list, `plist` (Lines 15–20). Next, `reclaim()` frees any previously retired node which is not in `plist`, i.e., not protected by a hazard pointer (Lines 21–27). (Notice that each thread's hazard pointers are scanned in ascending index order, to guarantee that `reclaim()` does not miss a hazard pointer being copied: If thread T copies value v from $\texttt{hp}_\texttt{i}$ to $\texttt{hp}_\texttt{j}$ ($j > i$), overwrites $\texttt{hp}_\texttt{i}$, and the reclaiming thread observes $\texttt{hp}_\texttt{i}$'s new value, then it will necessarily observe v in $\texttt{hp}_\texttt{j}$ because stores are ordered under TSO.)

Progress guarantee The `reclaim()` subroutine is *wait-free* [17], as it completes within a bounded number of steps. As a result, hazard pointers can be used by nonblocking algorithms without comprising their progress guarantee.

Complexity analysis Let N be the number of threads in the system, and $H \geq N$ the total number of hazard pointers. Recall that R is the maximum number of nodes a thread may retire and that have not yet been reclaimed, which is the amount of "waste" memory the thread may hold. If the set `plist` is implemented as a hash table and the set `rlist` as a simple linked list, then a `reclaim()` does $O(H+R)$ work to reclaim at least $R-H$ nodes. Therefore, if $R = H+\Omega(H)$, `reclaim()` does an expected amortized $O(1)$ steps per retired node. In practice, however, it is simpler to implement `plist` as an array, sort it and perform lookups using binary search [28]. Doing this provides a worst-case amortized bound of $O(\log H)$.

4.2 Fence-free hazard pointers implementation

This section presents the new fence-free reclamation method, which we obtain by observing that hazard pointers apply the flag principle: Here, a thread T_0 about to reference an object O interacts with T_1, the thread reclaiming O's memory after removing it from the data structure. T_0 pointing a hazard pointer at O constitutes "raising its flag," and the subsequent validation check "looks" at T_1's flag. Conversely, the removal of O from the data structure forms T_1's "flag raising," and it "looks" at T_0's flag when scanning T_0's hazard pointers. (Note that this implies that the remove of O must be globally visible when O is retired. This holds if the removal performs an atomic operation, which flushes the store buffer. Otherwise, `retire()` must issue a fence.)

In fence-free hazard pointers, we thus apply the TBTSO flag principle as follows: (1) We omit the fence from the hazard pointer validation code (e.g., from the boxes at Lines 33 and 36 of Figure 1). (2) We defer trying to reclaim O's memory for Δ clock ticks since its removal (Figure 2b). Importantly, this additional waiting time does not lie on the critical path of the threads and so does not negatively impact their performance. The Δ clock ticks naturally overlap the time period between consecutive memory reclamation attempts, since a thread accumulates multiple retired objects before trying to reclaim memory.

Retirement For each retired node, the thread records the time (the value of the global clock, which we assume never wraps around) at which the node was retired (Line 37). Reclaiming memory is now done in a loop until some node is freed, because (as explained below) a single invocation of `reclaim()` is not guaranteed to free a node (Line 39). However, as explained below (in Progress guarantee), this loop is still guaranteed to be wait-free.

Reclamation For every retired object O, the reclaiming thread checks whether some hazard pointer protects O only if, at the time that the `reclaim()` has started, more than Δ clock ticks have passed since O was retired (Lines 45 and 51). We implement `rlist` as a linked list to which `retire()` appends, so scanning `rlist` from oldest to newest retired objects is trivial and costs $O(1)$ per object. Notice that if no object O is old enough, `reclaim()` exits without freeing any memory.

Progress guarantee The `while` loop which calls `reclaim()` *is wait-free* [17], provided that $R > H$. Once Δ time units pass since the latest retirement, all R objects in the thread's `rlist` are checked, and thus at least one object is reclaimed. Because Δ is a fixed constant, the loop executes a bounded number of times, overall—there is no indefinite waiting.

4.2.1 Space/time tradeoff

The complexity of the reclamation depends on how large is R relative to Δ. There are two cases. The first is when $R \geq c\Delta \geq H + \Omega(H)$ for some $c > 1$. In this case, a `reclaim()` can find at least $(1 - 1/c)R - H$ objects to reclaim, because in our model every retired node receives a unique time stamp, and so all but the last Δ retired nodes are safe to check against the hazard pointers. Therefore, `reclaim()` has the same amortized complexity as in hazard pointers. In the remaining case, $\Delta > R > H$. This constrained case can be detected in advance (as Δ, R, and H are known) and requires changing the `reclaim()` routine slightly, so that it does not do any work until Δ ticks have passed since the retirement time of the oldest $H+1$ objects in the `rlist`. With this modification, the worst-case running time of reclaim becomes $O(\Delta)$.

To give a practical sense to these parameters, we note that in experiments exercising Michael's nonblocking linked list algorithm [27] on an x86 machine with 80 hardware threads we observe a maximal retirement rate of 1300 nodes per millisecond per thread (see § 7). In § 6 we argue that such a machine can implement TBTSO with Δ on the order of 0.5 to 10 milliseconds. Therefore, setting R to $1300 \times 10 \times 2 = 26000$ nodes—which may take up 2 megabytes—guarantees that a `reclaim()` can always free at least $R/2$ nodes.

5. Fence-free biased locking (FFBL)

This section describes our *fence-free biased lock* (FFBL). A *biased lock* is a lock in which a designated *owner* thread can acquire the lock quickly if there is no contention, possibly at the expense of the other *non-owner* threads whose lock acquisition is slower [20, 30, 33].

5.1 FFBL algorithm

We present a mutual exclusion algorithm based on the flag principle, which we then convert into our FFBL using the TBTSO flag principle. The flag principle can be used to implement two-thread mutual exclusion by having each thread (1) raise its flag and check the other's flag, (2) enter the critical section if the other's flag is not up, otherwise lower its flag and try again, and (3) lower its flag when it exits the critical section. However, such a scheme can *livelock* if the two threads always see each other's flag up and thus never enter the critical section. Thus, mutual exclusion algorithms based on the flag principle, such as Peterson's [31] and Dekker's [12], introduce a mechanism to break such livelocks. These mechanisms are quite intricate, since the classic algorithms use only read and write operations. In contrast, we can use atomic operations, so long as they do not degrade the owner's *fast path*—accessing an uncontended lock. Next, we describe this mechanism.

Baseline biased lock (top row of Figure 3) Because the flag principle works for two threads, we introduce a standard lock, L, to prevent multiple non-owners from participating in the flag protocol. Therefore, from here on we shall speak only of T_0—the owner—and T_1, which is some non-owner that has acquired L. We also use the new lock L to break the flag protocol's symmetry and prevent livelock. If T_0 sees that $\texttt{flag}_1$ is up, it lowers $\texttt{flag}_0$ and tries to acquire L. For its part, if T_1 sees $\texttt{flag}_0$ raised after raising its own $\texttt{flag}_1$, then it waits for T_0 to lower $\texttt{flag}_0$. This maintains the property that a thread that does not see the other's flag raised enters the critical section immediately, but if both see each other's flag T_1 will enter first. Nevertheless, because biased locks are targeted at scenarios in which T_1 participates rarely, *in the common case T_0 immediately enters the critical section.*

Fence-free biased lock (bottom row of Figure 3) Converting the baseline into an FFBL merely requires using the TBTSO flag principle in place of the standard one. However, if the owner T_0 acquires the lock very frequently—as expected from biased locks, otherwise biasing does not make a difference—then it will get delayed for Δ time units

```
1  //
2  // Basic algorithm
3  //
4
5  Shared variables:
6    flag0 , flag1 : bits
7    L : standard lock
8
9
10
```

(a) Variables

```
11 lock() {
12   flag0 := 1
13   fence
14
15   if (flag1) {
16     flag0 := 0
17     L.lock()
18   }
19 }
20
```

(b) Owner lock

```
21 unlock() {
22   if (flag0) {
23     flag0 := 0
24   } else {
25     L.unlock()
26   }
27 }
28
29
30
```

(c) Owner unlock

```
31 lock() {
32   L.lock()
33   flag1 := 1
34   fence
35   await (flag0 = 0)
36 }
37 unlock() {
38   flag1 := 0
39   L.unlock()
40 }
```

(d) Non-Owner

```
41 //
42 // Fence-free
43 // algorithm
44 //
45
46 Shared variables:
47   flag0 , flag1 :
48     struct {v:63bits ,f:1 bit}
49   L : standard lock
50
51
52
53
```

(e) Variables

```
54 lock() {
55   flag0 := <0,1>
56   // no fence
57
58   while (flag1.f) {
59     do
60       flag0 := <flag1.v,0>
61     while (L.is_locked())
62     if (L.try_lock())
63       break
64   }
65 }
66
```

(f) Owner lock

```
67 unlock() {
68   if (flag0.f) {
69     flag0 := <0,0>
70   } else {
71     flag0 := <0,0>
72     L.unlock()
73   }
74 }
75
76
77
78
79
```

(g) Owner unlock

```
80 lock() {
81   L.lock()
82   flag1 := <flag1.v+1,1>
83   fence
84   now = global_clock()
85   await ((global_clock()>now+Δ)
86         or (flag0.v=flag1.v))
87   await (flag0.f = 0)
88 }
89 unlock() {
90   flag1 := <flag1.v+1,0>
91   L.unlock()
92 }
```

(h) Non-Owner

Figure 3: Fence-free biased locking (FFBL) construction. Top: Basic (not fence-free) algorithm. Bottom: FFBL algorithm.

whenever T_1 attempts to acquire the lock, which is suboptimal. This happens because once the owner, T_0, sees T_1's flag raised, it lowers its flag and tries to acquire `L`. But `L` is held by T_1 which is waiting for Δ time units.

We turn this problem around, exploiting the fact that T_0 frequently acquires the lock to speed up T_1's lock acquisition, which in turn speeds up T_0 as well. We do this by having T_0 notify T_1 whenever it sees $\texttt{flag}_1$ raised (which causes T_0 to try to acquire the `L` lock). This signals to T_1 that T_0 is waiting to acquire `L`, so T_1 can stop the Δ delay and enter the critical section. To implement this notification we use *echoing* [29]: We expand the flags to 64-bits, 63 of which are used as *version numbers* that uniquely identify each write—whenever T_1 writes to $\texttt{flag}_1$, it increases $\texttt{flag}_1$'s version. T_0 uses this version to notify T_1 that it is spinning while trying to acquire `L`, by writing—or *echoing*—what it reads from $\texttt{flag}_1$ into $\texttt{flag}_0$ (Lines 59– 63). (For simplicity, the code implements a simple `trylock` loop to do this, but one can incorporate echoing into the spin loop of any lock, e.g., to guarantee that T_0 acquires `L` by using a fair lock implementation.) Similarly, T_1 looks for T_0's echoes as it spins waiting for Δ time units to pass, and stops waiting once it observes an echo (Figure 3h). In practice the echoes reach memory much faster than Δ time units (§ 6.1.2), and so the gains from this optimization can be substantial (§ 7.2).

6. Implementing TBTSO

This section discusses guaranteeing bounded-time store buffering. (Modern x86 systems already support an *invariant timestamp counter* that can be read cheaply and used as a global clock [2, 32], thus satisfying the other requirement for implementing TBTSO.)

We present a simple hardware design for implementing TBTSO[Δ] on x86 systems (§ 6.1). We estimate the design can achieve a Δ bound as low as $\approx 6P\,\mu$s on a system with P hardware threads; as we discuss shortly, we unfortunately cannot prove feasibility of the design and the Δ bound, as that requires proprietary implementation knowledge. We further show how minimal OS support enables adaptation of TBTSO algorithms to existing x86 systems (§ 6.2).

6.1 Enforcing TBTSO with hardware quiescence

x86 processors may delay propagating a store to the memory subsystem indefinitely if a resource required to do so—e.g., a cache port—gets constantly used by another unit. In practice, however, most stores propagate quickly. Our idea is thus to detect a starving store that remains buffered for a long time, and *bail it out* by invoking the system's existing *quiescence* mechanism [39]. This pauses all competing units, which enables the starving store to propagate to the memory subsystem.

We cannot, unfortunately, provide a complete design and calculate an exact worst-case Δ bound. Doing that requires accounting for any possible interaction between hardware mechanisms that can delay the propagation of a store—many of which are proprietary, undocumented, and/or obscure. Instead, we (1) present a high-level design while pointing out—and justifying—its assumptions on internal mechanisms (§ 6.1.1), and (2) estimate its Δ bound by extrapolating from measurements performed on x86 hardware (§ 6.1.2).

6.1.1 TBTSO design

x86 processors retire a store instruction from the reorder buffer without waiting for its value to propagate to the memory subsystem (caches and memory). The processor instead holds a retired store's data in a *store buffer* and propagates it to memory asynchronously [2, 3].

Propagating a store to the memory subsystem—i.e., to the L1 cache—uses hardware resources with limited capacity: for example, (1) the number of *ports* through which an instruction can access the L1 cache [3], (2) the number of *line fill buffers* that are required to hold a missed cache line's data as it comes in [3], (3) the capacity of the communication links and queues through which cache coherence messages go through [16], and so on.

The system *arbitrates* access to these resources to decide, in each cycle, which unit is granted access to each resource. If arbitration is *unfair*, some unit may be prevented from accessing a resource in the face of competition [36, Section 9.3.3]. For example, consider a policy favoring line fill buffer allocation for loads over (buffered) stores (e.g., because a load cannot complete without handling the miss). Then a store followed by a sequence of loads, all of which miss in the L1, will be prevented from being written to the L1 cache. (We have found evidence of unfair policies in performance counter documentation [3, Section B.6.9.3].)

However, the hardware can force a store out of the store buffer by forcing *quiescence*—pausing all competition in order to allow the store to drain out of the buffer. (Without such a mechanism, the system would be vulnerable to absurd situations, e.g., failing to retire a fence instruction because a store cannot be drained.) Because a store may be starved by system-wide competition—on interconnect links or memory controllers—we must obtain *system-wide quiescence*, which is already supported on modern x86 hardware [39].

Hardware design We propose to force quiescence whenever a store remains buffered past a certain amount of time after its retirement (discussed later). Then, once the system is quiescent, propagate every buffered store to the memory subsystem. For this approach to achieve *bounded* store buffering time requires that both forcing quiescence and then propagating a store to the memory subsystem complete in bounded time. Below, we justify these assumptions:

Bounded quiescence time (Assumption 1) We believe quiescence is obtained within bounded time based on the high-level description of the x86 quiescence implementation [39] (however, this property is not explicitly guaranteed). Essentially, a quiescence request is signalled on a sideband channel, instructing cores and memory controllers to block new memory operations (i.e., instructions or DMAs) [39]. Once this happens, we are left with a finite number of pending memory operations—and thus finite levels of competition for resources—so the pending operations drain out within bounded time, achieving quiescence.

Bounded quiescent propagation time (Assumption 2) Propagating a store to the memory subsystem should complete in bounded time on a quiescent system, because the required cache coherence transactions and memory writebacks face no competition on the communication links and queues. Additional delays may occur due to the memory (RAM) itself, but to our knowledge such delays are also bounded—e.g., DRAM refresh events, or recoverable ECC errors that generate exceptions which are handled asynchronously [2, Section 15.5].

The only exception we are aware of is a store to the IO or configuration space of a PCI device. Such a store waits for a completion response from the device, which can delay arbitrarily before responding. (In contrast, writes to general device memory are *posted* and do not wait for an acknowledgment [7, Chapter 2], and thus the former reasoning applies.) Device IO/config stores do not compromise our design, as we explain next.

Putting it together In our design the processor forces system-wide quiescence if a store remains buffered for more than τ cycles since its retirement, where τ is such that most stores propagate to the memory subsystem in $< \tau$ cycles (in § 6.1.2, we estimate τ can be $10\,\mu s$). Stores propagate from the store buffer in retirement order (due to TSO), and so the timeout always expires first for the oldest store in the store buffer, leading to quiescence and subsequent propagation of all buffered stores. Crucially, x86 guarantees that a store to device IO/config space drains the store buffer (including itself) when it retires [2, Section 11.3]. There can thus never be buffered (retired) stores *behind* such an IO/config write, and so the (arbitrary) delays of IO/config writes do not prevent achieving a bound on standard store visibility.

6.1.2 Estimating achievable Δ bound

To get a sense of what a feasible Δ bound might be, we measure the time to force quiescence on real x86 hardware and extrapolate from that. We also measure store visibility times on this system, to estimate what the timeout that triggers quiescence can be—for good performance, we need a timeout that expires rarely but that does not make the Δ bound exceedingly large.

Our measurements use a system with four Xeon E7-4870 (Westmere EX) processors, each of which has 10 2.40 GHz cores that multiplex 2 hardware threads, for a total of 80 hardware threads overall. Based on the measurements below,

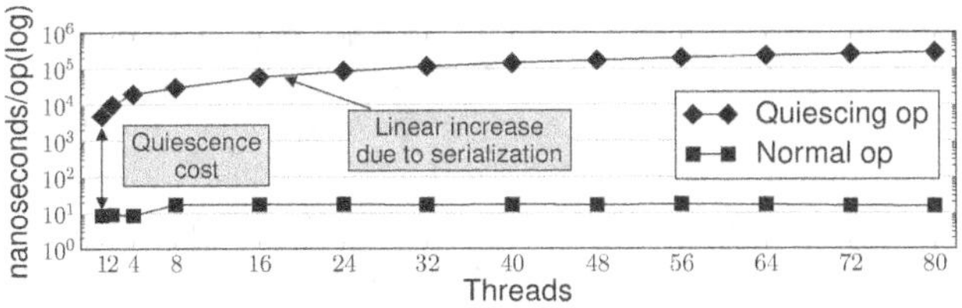

Figure 4: Time to reach system-wide quiescence (log scale) as the number of quiescing threads increases.

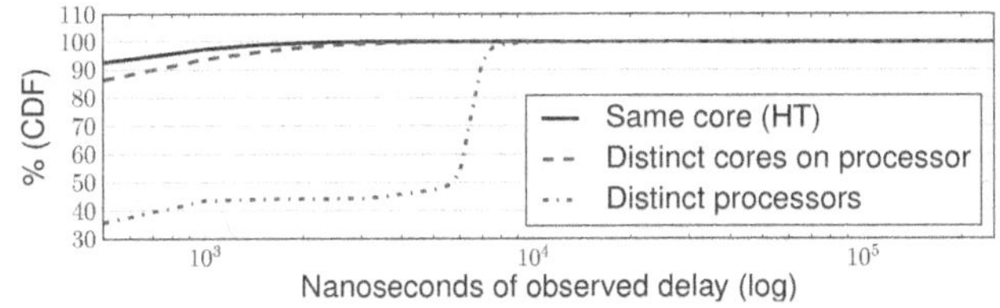

Figure 5: Cumulative distribution of observed store buffering times (log scale) for various writer/reader thread placements.

we estimate that similar TBTSO hardware could be implemented with $\Delta = 500\,\mu$s (or $\approx 6\,\mu$s per hardware thread).

Quiescence time We run a microbenchmark in which all threads repeatedly perform an atomic operation that crosses cache line boundary to a thread-private location, which forces system-wide quiescence on our system [39]. We measure the average latency of an operation. For comparison, we rerun the benchmark with each thread performing a standard atomic operation to a thread-private location.

Figure 4 shows the results: Quiescing the system takes $\approx 5\,\mu$s, about 600× the cost of the normal operation. Because the system must serialize quiescence operations, the time it takes a thread to enforce quiescence grows almost linearly with the number of threads. The results do not change if cores not participating heavily load the system (we omit plots due to space constraints), and thus we believe this measurement represents worst-case time to achieve quiescence.

Store buffering time in practice We use a microbenchmark with two threads: (1) a *writer* that writes the value of the global timestamp counter to a shared variable v (initially 0), and then issues an endless sequence of non-store instructions, and (2) a *reader* which reads v until it sees a non-zero value. The reader then reports the difference between the current time and the time read from v. We vary writers' non-store sequence, to see if different instructions have different effect. For example, to see if the processor delays a store in the store buffer so that it could be read more quickly, we use a benchmark in which the writer repeatedly reads v. To maximally exercise different scenarios, we (1) run the benchmark with different placement of threads—hardware threads of the same core, cores of the same processor, and on different processors, (2) run the benchmarks alone, concurrently, and with the memory-intensive STREAM benchmark [24] in the background. In all, we run $2 \cdot 10^{10}$ executions.

Figure 5 shows the cumulative distribution of the observed delays—99.9% of stores become visible after at most $10\,\mu$s. Notice that this benchmark overestimates the store buffer delay—e.g., it also measures the time it takes the reader to acquire v's cache line.

Estimating Δ: Because quiescence forcing is serialized, we estimate its worst-case time for this system at $80 \times 5\mu\text{s} = 400\,\mu$s (the maximal time measured was $300\,\mu$s). We assume that quiescence time dwarves the time to subsequently drain the store buffer. Still, as a safety margin, we extrapolate that a TBTSO hardware implementation can obtain a Δ of $500\,\mu$s on a system similar to our test machine.

6.2 Adapting TBTSO algorithms to x86 with OS help

On the x86 architecture, a user/kernel transition—i.e., an interrupt or context switch—drains the contents of the store buffer to memory [2, Section 11.10]. By programming the hardware to generate a timer interrupt on every core every Δ time units, the OS can thus force periodic store buffer flushes. (In fact, operating systems already use periodic per-core timer interrupts to trigger expiration of process time quanta and other housekeeping code [9].) Unfortunately, this does not suffice to enforce TBTSO[Δ]: First, timer interrupt precision is not guaranteed—a timer interrupt might fire late. Second, the interrupt only triggers a store buffer flush—current hardware does not bound the time to complete the flush (and hence the delivery of the interrupt).

In practice, however, timer interrupts rarely get delayed arbitrarily, which means that a system with periodic interrupts behaves similarly to a TBTSO system. We now show how simple OS support allows adapting TBTSO algorithms to benefit from this similarity.

OS support The OS maintains an array A in which each core writes the current time when it receives a timer interrupt or enters the kernel. This array is mapped read-only into the address space of every process. (Similarly to how OSes expose their time-keeping variables to implement `gettimeofday()` without trapping into the kernel [8].)

Adapting TBTSO algorithms To establish that every store retired by time t_0 is globally visible, we can adapt the TBTSO policy of "wait Δ ticks" to wait instead for every entry in A to indicate a time $> t_0$. As in TBTSO, this only adds work when we need to wait, and not at time t_0. Thus, in hazard pointers for example, we only add work to the reclamation path and not to every object retirement. (In contrast, the bounded TSO[S] model [29], which does not have a global clock, would require reading A when retiring an object.)

Adapted TBTSO algorithms have two disadvantages. First, the Δ granularity must be *coarse* to minimize the overhead of timer interrupt processing—e.g., current systems use a timer interrupt period of 1 to 10 milliseconds [9].) Second, adapted algorithms incur extra work in the slow path. However, our evaluation shows this overhead is small.

7. Evaluation

This section evaluates our FFHP and FFBL algorithms. We emulate a TBTSO system by using an x86 machine on which we configure the algorithms to use $\Delta = 0.5$ ms. (This corresponds to the estimated obtainable Δ bound for such a machine from § 6.1.2.) We also evaluate the algorithms adapted to run safely on x86 hardware, as described in § 6.2. We emulate the required OS support in user space using POSIX timers to interrupt each thread every $\Delta = 4$ ms (a typical OS timer interrupt period). When describing FFHP and FFBL results, we use the Δ values to distinguish between the TBTSO and the adapted variants that rely on period timers.

Platforms We use two test systems: (1) a server with four Intel Xeon E7-4870 processors, each with 10 2.40 GHz cores that multiplex 2 hardware threads, for a total of 80 hardware threads, and (2) a Core i7-4770 (Haswell) processor, which has 4 3.4 GHz cores, each with 2 hardware threads.

7.1 Safe memory reclamation

We compare FFHP to several SMR algorithms in terms of overhead imposed and memory consumption. We test the following SMR methods: (1) hazard pointers (HP) [28], (2) RCU [26], a widely used scheme [25] that imposes zero overhead on the fast path, (3) drop the anchor (DTA) [6], a quiescence-based method that guarantees bounded memory consumption but requires the fast path to periodically issue an atomic operation, and (4) StackTrack [4], an SMR method that uses hardware transactional memory in the fast path.

Benchmark We use the same methodology as in prior work on SMR [4, 6, 19, 25, 28]— a microbenchmark focusing on a widely used data structure with a read-dominated operation mix, in which memory fences are a significant penalty. Our benchmark, based on McKenney's benchmark [25], is written in C. It consists of n threads performing `lookup()`s, `insert()`s and `remove()`s on a 1024-bucket concurrent hash table with chaining. (Threads are *pinned* to the processors in a round-robin manner, so that every run has threads on all processors.) We vary the size of the universe U from which the key range is picked, allowing us to control the average length L of each chain. We test chains of average length $L = 4$ (short, as in real hash tables), $L = 20$ and $L = 80$ (medium), and $L = 256$ (long). Due to space constraints, we focus on short and long chains, as the results for medium chains are qualitatively similar to the long chains. We test both read-only workloads, and workloads in which readers and updaters work concurrently, as detailed below. Each execution starts with $U/2$ random keys in the hash tables. The chains are implemented with Michael's nonblocking linked lists [27], which support concurrent reading and updating. We report median results from 10 runs, each lasting 10 seconds. Results' variance is negligible (we use a dedicated test machine). The tests use the `jemalloc` memory allocator to prevent the memory allocator from being a bottleneck.

Implementations To obtain the best possible performance, we use the OS in tickless mode. We use McKenney's implementation of hazard pointers [25]. All hazard pointers implementations use $R = 32000$ (which translates to about 2 megabytes). We use the original authors' implementation of RCU [10] and DTA [6], and implement StackTrack following [4]. To avoid irrelevant cache-related effects, the hash table nodes are equally sized in all implementations.

7.1.1 Performance and overheads

Read-only workload (left column of Figure 6) This test evaluates the overhead each SMR method imposes on read-only code, modeling scenarios in which updates are rare. All threads perform random `lookup()`s over the hash table. Since no reclamation is done, the value of Δ has no impact on FFHP performance. FFHP and RCU perform similarly ($\approx 5\%$ difference) in all tests, outperforming HP by 30% on the Westmere-EX machine, and by 60% (short operations) to 15% (long operations) on the Haswell. (We do not include Haswell plots due to space constraints.) FFHP's advantage is solely due to the omission of memory fences compared to HP, as otherwise their lookup code is identical.

DTA and StackTrack do not perform as well as FFHP and RCU. In DTA, every `lookup()` operation updates a per-thread *timestamp* of when it begins and ends (including issuing a fence), and sets a per-thread *anchor* variable using an atomic `compare-and-swap` at least once. This constitutes significant overhead in short operations, causing DTA's throughput to be 30% worse than that of FFHP. Similarly, StackTrack imposes overhead on the fast path by using transactions, leading to 10% less throughput than FFHP for short operations. In long operations, StackTrack starts to experience transaction *capacity aborts* [2], forcing it to *split* each operation into multiple transactions [4]. As a result, StackTrack's throughput is $0.3\times$ that of FFHP.

Read/write workloads (last two columns of Figure 6) In this test, we split the n threads into $\frac{3}{4}n$ *reader* threads and $\frac{1}{4}n$ *updater* threads. A reader performs only `lookup()`s over the entire universe, while an updater alternates between `insert()`ing and `remove()`ing each item in an equally-sized subset of the universe owned by it.

The middle column of Figure 6 shows the throughout obtained by the readers. For all the SMR methods but DTA, the throughput is about $60\% - 70\%$ of the throughput obtained in the read-only case, but with essentially the same throughput ratios between these methods. This is caused by increased reader cache miss rates due to the updaters modifying the hash table. DTA suffers from additional cache misses: updating a reader's timestamp, which is read by updaters, now frequently causes a cache miss. Consequently, DTA's read throughput does not scale past 64 threads. The periodic timer interrupts in the (adapted) FFHP[4 ms] executions have no performance impact, due to their low frequency.

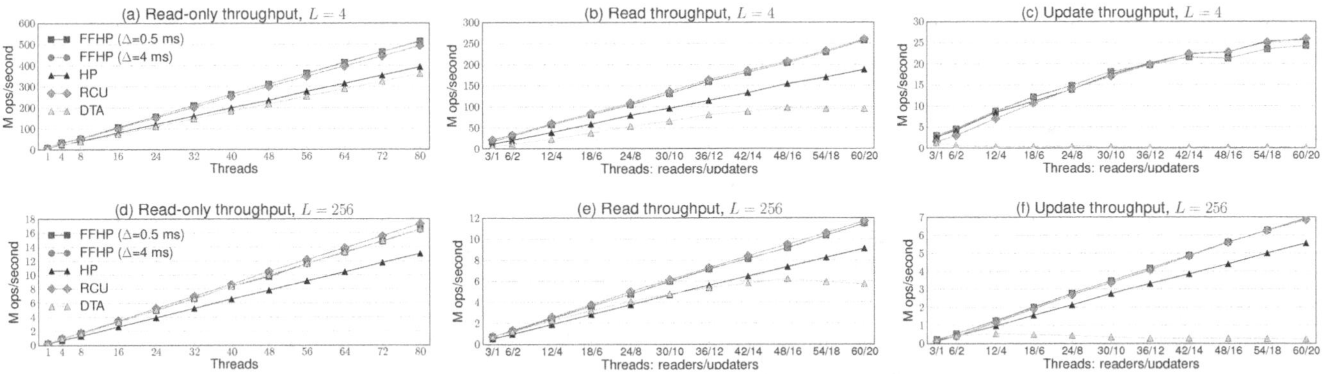

Figure 6: Quad Westmere-EX hash table throughput, for various average bucket list sizes (L).

The right column of Figure 6 shows the updaters' throughout. There is little impact by the Δ parameter, because R provides enough headroom so that a `reclaim()` finds enough nodes to free without waiting. We also see that the extra work in FFHP[4 ms] (scanning the per-core time array, see § 6.2) adds no noticeable overhead compared to the original (TBTSO[0.5 ms]) version. On the Westmere-EX system, FFHP and RCU perform the same ($< 1\%$ difference) on high thread counts, obtaining the same throughput as HP in short operations and improving on HP by 25% in long operations. The reason is that as the chains grow longer, the relative cost of the atomic operations an updater does diminishes, making the traversal cost more significant. On the Haswell system, FFHP outperforms HP by 30% (short operations) to $\approx 50\%$ (long operations). FFHP also outperforms RCU by $\approx 60\%$ and StackTrack by 10% in short operations. Due to aborts and transaction splitting FFHP outperforms StackTrack by 80% in long operations. DTA updates perform $> 100\times$ worse than other methods because an updater reads each thread's timestamp after removing a node [6], an act that can cost more than the original hash chain traversal.

7.1.2 Retired nodes memory consumption

Here we quantify the impact that thread stalls—e.g., due to context switches—have on the SMR schemes. We modify the read/write test done above so that one reader stalls for s milliseconds in one of its `lookup()`s, as would occur on a context switch. We measure the peak memory consumption of the benchmark (as reported by the OS) for various stall times. Figure 7 depicts the results from the Westmere-EX server, in which three trends are apparent.

First, FFHP keeps more removed nodes unreclaimed than HP, because FFHP's `reclaim` frees only the subset that was removed Δ milliseconds ago. In this test, this amounts to at most 7% greater memory consumption than in HP. Second, memory consumption with RCU is 40% greater than when FFHP or HP are used even when there is zero stalling. The reason is that the RCU library handles reclamation more slowly than hazard pointers, since it uses background threads which periodically wake up and free memory. Finally, memory consumption with RCU keeps growing as the stall time increases, because RCU cannot free memory as long as a thread is stalled inside an operation. At maximum stall time, the benchmark using RCU consumes $6\times$ (short operations) to $2\times$ (long operations) more memory than the FFHP.

7.2 Biased locks

We evaluate the FFBL on a benchmark C program that synthesizes various access patterns to the lock. The benchmark consists of two threads, the owner and non-owner, repeatedly acquiring the lock for a period of 10 seconds, with a random *interarrival* delay (simulating application work) between lock acquisitions. We test FFBL versions with and without the echoing optimization, comparing them to the default Linux `pthreads` lock and to our implementation of biased locking using safe points [33], in which we assume that the owner reaches a safe point immediately when it exits the critical section.

Figure 8 shows the throughput—lock acquisitions per seconds—of both owner and non-owner, normalized to the throughput obtained with `pthreads`. The first access pattern, in which the owner arrives frequently and the non-owner rarely (once a millisecond on average) simulates a workload favorable to biased locking. Here the owner path of the FFBL and safe point locks outperforms `pthreads` by 5%–10%, and the non-owner is comparable, except for FFBL[4 ms] without echoing. Here, due to the long delay time, both owner and non-owner perform worse than with `pthreads`.

The next two patterns challenge the locks by increasing the frequency of non-owner arrivals until it equals the owner's frequency. This crystallizes the benefit of echoing, as without it the throughput of the FFBL versions collapses.

The last pattern captures the case in which the owner stalls for a long time—due to a context switch or long computation. While all biased locks collapse compared to pthreads in this case, we see the benefit of bounded delay: the FFBL outperform the safe point lock by $50\times$ (with echoes) and by $7\times$ (without echoes).

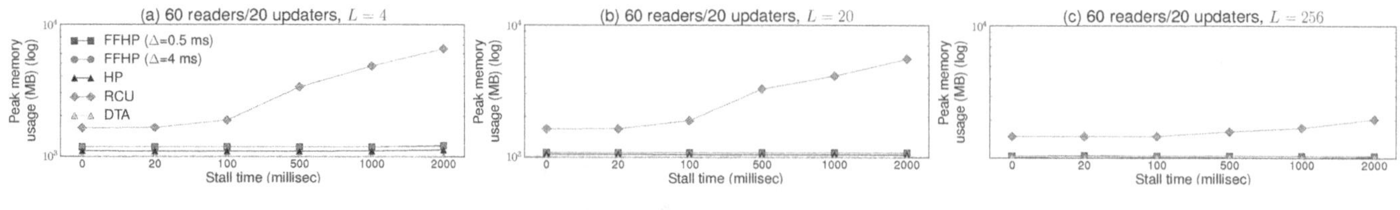

Figure 7: Read/write test memory consumption (log scale) when one reader stalls in its operation.

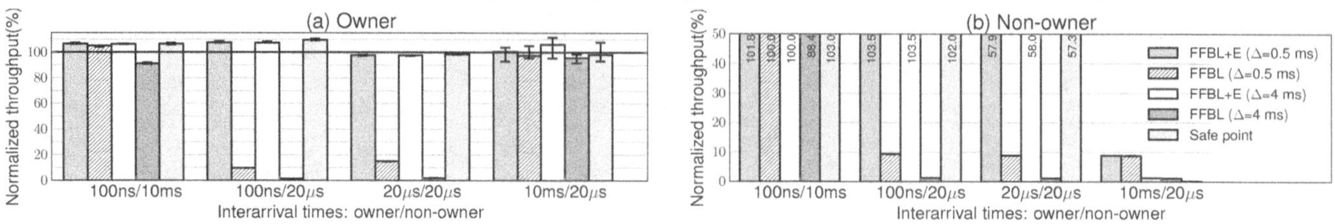

Figure 8: Biased locks throughput, normalized to standard `pthreads` lock.

8. Related work

Bounded reordering TSO[S] [29] is a *spatially* bounded strengthening of TSO in which the store buffer has bounded capacity, S. In TSO[S], a thread's store can remain buffered for an unbounded amount of time if the thread does not issue further stores. This creates uncertainty about the thread's state, making TSO[S] unsuitable for nonblocking fence-free algorithms—indeed, fence-free work stealing algorithms based on TSO[S] require either relaxed semantics or blocking [29]. In contrast, TBTSO's *temporal* reordering bound facilitates nonblocking synchronization without relaxing semantics, making it more broadly applicable.

Liu et al. [23] empirically observe that x86 processors usually propagate stores to memory quickly, and exploit this in designing a fence-free read/write lock. They do not explore how to guarantee bounded store buffering, and instead use inter-processor interrupts to handle cases in which store propagation is delayed. Dice et al. [11] consider methods for an asymmetric fence-free flag principle and mutual exclusion. One of their methods assumes a maximum store buffer delay. However, they do not discuss how to obtain or enforce this delay. They do not use echoing and thus may perform poorly in some workloads (§ 7). Finally, they do not consider safe memory reclamation.

In the context of distributed systems, the *timed consistency* model of Torres-Rojas et al. [37] requires that a write issued by a node become visible to all nodes after at most Δ time units. Torres-Rojas et al. do not apply timed consistency to shared memory systems as we do.

Safe memory reclamation Most quiescence-based memory reclamation methods, such as epoch-based reclamation [15] and RCU [26], cannot be both nonblocking and guarantee bounded memory consumption, in contrast to our FFHP method. Braginsky et al.'s *drop the anchor* (DTA) quiescence-based method [6] achieves both properties, but introduces other limitations not present in FFHP: (1) DTA requires intrusive changes to the data structure to support DTA's *freezing* operation, and (2) it performs poorly on short operations such as in hash tables (see § 7). SMR methods using hardware transactional memory (HTM) [4, 13] are also nonblocking with bounded memory consumption, but using transactions in the fast path imposes overhead (§ 7).

Biased locking FFBLs have a fence-free owner path and allow a non-owner to enter the critical section in bounded time (when the lock is not held). Prior work either blocks the non-owner [33, 40] or uses fences in the owner path [30].

Eliminating fence penalty Several architectural proposals aim at eliminating the penalty of memory fences [5, 14, 22, 35, 41]. However, TBTSO algorithms can be adapted to work on *existing* machines with simple OS changes. In addition, the modifications required to implement TBTSO in hardware are modest compared to these designs, since they rely on triggering existing quiescence mechanisms.

9. Conclusion

We have proposed TBTSO, a temporally bounded TSO memory model that bounds the amount of time it takes for a store to become globally visible, and shown that TBTSO enables nonblocking fence-free asymmetric synchronization.

The TBTSO concept raises several research questions: Are there additional applications for the TBTSO model, perhaps in real-time systems? On the hardware side, we have argued that to our understanding, a TBTSO implementation is feasible. But are there obscure or undocumented internal mechanisms that invalidate our understanding? Can we calculate and verify a TBTSO bound for a real processor?

Acknowledgments

We thank the ASPLOS reviewers for their invaluable comments, which helped us reshape and improve the paper.

This work was supported by the Israel Science Foundation (grants 1227/10, 1749/14 and 1386/11) and by Yad-HaNadiv foundation. Adam Morrison is supported in part at the Technion by an Aly Kaufman Fellowship.

References

[1] *The SPARC Architecture Manual Version 8*. Prentice Hall, 1992.

[2] Intel 64 and IA-32 Architectures Software Developers Manual, Volume 3: System Programming Guide. `http://download.intel.com/products/processor/manual/325384.pdf`, June 2013.

[3] Intel 64 and IA-32 Architectures Optimization Reference Manual. `https://www-ssl.intel.com/content/www/us/en/architecture-and-technology/64-ia-32-architectures-optimization-manual.html`, July 2013.

[4] D. Alistarh, P. Eugster, M. Herlihy, A. Matveev, and N. Shavit. StackTrack: An Automated Transactional Approach to Concurrent Memory Reclamation. In *Proceedings of the 9th European Conference on Computer Systems*, EuroSys '14, pages 25:1–25:14, New York, NY, USA, 2014. ACM. ISBN 978-1-4503-2704-6. .

[5] C. Blundell, M. M. Martin, and T. F. Wenisch. Invisifence: Performance-transparent memory ordering in conventional multiprocessors. In *Proceedings of the 36th Annual International Symposium on Computer Architecture*, ISCA '09, pages 233–244, New York, NY, USA, 2009. ACM. ISBN 978-1-60558-526-0. .

[6] A. Braginsky, A. Kogan, and E. Petrank. Drop the anchor: lightweight memory management for non-blocking data structures. In *Proceedings of the 25th ACM Symposium on Parallelism in Algorithms and Architectures*, SPAA '13, pages 33–42, New York, NY, USA, 2013. ACM.

[7] R. Budruk, D. Anderson, and E. Solari. *PCI Express System Architecture*. Pearson Education, 2003. ISBN 0321156307.

[8] J. Corbet. On vsyscalls and the vdso. `http://lwn.net/Articles/446528/`, 2011. Linux World News.

[9] J. Corbet. (Nearly) full tickless operation in 3.10. `http://lwn.net/Articles/549580/`, 2013. Linux World News.

[10] M. Desnoyers, P. E. McKenney, A. S. Stern, M. R. Dagenais, and J. Walpole. User-Level Implementations of Read-Copy Update. *IEEE Transactions on Parallel and Distributed Systems*, 23(2):375–382, 2012.

[11] D. Dice, H. Huang, and M. Yang. Asymmetric Dekker Synchronization. `http://home.comcast.net/~pjbishop/Dave/Asymmetric-Dekker-Synchronization.txt`, 2001.

[12] E. W. Dijkstra. Cooperating sequential processes. `http://www.cs.utexas.edu/users/EWD/ewd01xx/EWD123.PDF`, 1968.

[13] A. Dragojević, M. Herlihy, Y. Lev, and M. Moir. On the Power of Hardware Transactional Memory to Simplify Memory Management. In *Proceedings of the 30th Annual ACM SIGACT-SIGOPS Symposium on Principles of Distributed Computing*, PODC '11, pages 99–108, New York, NY, USA, 2011. ACM. ISBN 978-1-4503-0719-2. .

[14] Y. Duan, A. Muzahid, and J. Torrellas. WeeFence: toward making fences free in TSO. In *Proceedings of the 40th Annual International Symposium on Computer Architecture*, ISCA '13, pages 213–224, New York, NY, USA, 2013. ACM. .

[15] K. Fraser. *Practical lock-freedom*. PhD thesis, University of Cambridge, Computer Laboratory, University of Cambridge, Computer Laboratory, February 2004.

[16] J. L. Hennessy and D. A. Patterson. *Computer Architecture, Fourth Edition: A Quantitative Approach*. Morgan Kaufmann Publishers Inc., San Francisco, CA, USA, 2006. ISBN 0123704901.

[17] M. Herlihy. Wait-free synchronization. *ACM Transactions on Programming Languages and Systems (TOPLAS)*, 13:124–149, January 1991. .

[18] M. Herlihy and N. Shavit. *The Art of Multiprocessor Programming*. Morgan Kaufmann Publishers Inc., San Francisco, CA, USA, 2008. ISBN 0123705916, 9780123705914.

[19] M. Herlihy, V. Luchangco, P. Martin, and M. Moir. Nonblocking memory management support for dynamic-sized data structures. *ACM Transactions on Computer Systems (TOCS)*, 23(2):146–196, May 2005.

[20] K. Kawachiya, A. Koseki, and T. Onodera. Lock Reservation: Java Locks Can Mostly Do Without Atomic Operations. In *Proceedings of the 17th ACM SIGPLAN Conference on Object-oriented Programming, Systems, Languages, and Applications*, OOPSLA '02, pages 130–141, New York, NY, USA, 2002. ACM. ISBN 1-58113-471-1. .

[21] L. Lamport. How to Make a Multiprocessor Computer That Correctly Executes Multiprocess Programs. *IEEE Transactions on Computers*, 28(9):690–691, Sept. 1979. ISSN 0018-9340. .

[22] C. Lin, V. Nagarajan, and R. Gupta. Address-aware fences. In *Proceedings of the 27th International Conference on Supercomputing*, ICS '13, pages 313–324, New York, NY, USA, 2013. ACM. .

[23] R. Liu, H. Zhang, and H. Chen. Scalable Read-mostly Synchronization Using Passive Reader-Writer Locks. In *Proceedings of the 2014 USENIX Annual Technical Conference*, USENIX ATC '14, pages 219–230, Philadelphia, PA, June 2014. USENIX Association. ISBN 978-1-931971-10-2.

[24] J. D. McCalpin. Memory bandwidth and machine balance in current high performance computers. *IEEE Computer Society Technical Committee on Computer Architecture (TCCA) Newsletter*, pages 19–25, Dec. 1995.

[25] P. E. McKenney. Structured deferral: synchronization via procrastination. *Communications of the ACM*, 56(7):40–49, July 2013. .

[26] P. E. McKenney and J. D. Slingwine. Read-copy update: Using execution history to solve concurrency problems. In *Proceedings of the 10th International Conference on Parallel and Distributed Computing and Systems*, IASTED '98, pages 508–518. ACTA Press, 1998.

[27] M. M. Michael. High performance dynamic lock-free hash tables and list-based sets. In *Proceedings of the 14th Annual ACM Symposium on Parallel Algorithms and Architectures*, SPAA '02, pages 73–82, New York, NY, USA, 2002. ACM.

[28] M. M. Michael. Hazard Pointers: Safe Memory Reclamation for Lock-Free Objects. *IEEE Transactions on Parallel and*

Distributed System, 15(6):491–504, June 2004.

[29] A. Morrison and Y. Afek. Fence-free Work Stealing on Bounded TSO Processors. In *Proceedings of the 19th International Conference on Architectural Support for Programming Languages and Operating Systems*, ASPLOS '14, pages 413–426, New York, NY, USA, 2014. ACM. ISBN 978-1-4503-2305-5. .

[30] T. Onodera, K. Kawachiya, and A. Koseki. Lock Reservation for Java Reconsidered. In M. Odersky, editor, *ECOOP 2004 – Object-Oriented Programming*, volume 3086 of *Lecture Notes in Computer Science*, pages 559–583. Springer Berlin Heidelberg, 2004. ISBN 978-3-540-22159-3.

[31] G. L. Peterson. Myths about the mutual exclusion problem. *Information Processing Letters*, 12(3):115–116, 1981. ISSN 0020-0190.

[32] W. Ruan, Y. Liu, and M. Spear. Boosting Timestamp-based Transactional Memory by Exploiting Hardware Cycle Counters. *ACM Transactions on Architecture and Code Optimization (TACO)*, 10(4):40:1–40:21, Dec. 2013. ISSN 1544-3566. .

[33] K. Russell and D. Detlefs. Eliminating Synchronization-related Atomic Operations with Biased Locking and Bulk Rebiasing. In *Proceedings of the 21st Annual ACM SIGPLAN Conference on Object-oriented Programming Systems, Languages, and Applications*, OOPSLA '06, pages 263–272, New York, NY, USA, 2006. ACM. ISBN 1-59593-348-4. .

[34] P. Sewell, S. Sarkar, S. Owens, F. Z. Nardelli, and M. O. Myreen. x86-TSO: a rigorous and usable programmer's model for x86 multiprocessors. *Communications of the ACM*, 53(7):89–97, July 2010.

[35] A. Singh, S. Narayanasamy, D. Marino, T. Millstein, and M. Musuvathi. End-to-end sequential consistency. In *Proceedings of the 39th Annual International Symposium on Computer Architecture*, ISCA '12, pages 524–535, Washington, DC, USA, 2012. IEEE Computer Society.

[36] D. J. Sorin, M. D. Hill, and D. A. Wood. *A Primer on Memory Consistency and Cache Coherence*. Morgan & Claypool Publishers, 1st edition, 2011. ISBN 1608455645, 9781608455645.

[37] F. J. Torres-Rojas, M. Ahamad, and M. Raynal. Timed Consistency for Shared Distributed Objects. In *Proceedings of the 18th Annual ACM Symposium on Principles of Distributed Computing*, PODC '99, pages 163–172, New York, NY, USA, 1999. ACM. ISBN 1-58113-099-6. .

[38] J. Triplett, P. E. McKenney, and J. Walpole. Resizable, scalable, concurrent hash tables via relativistic programming. In *Proceedings of the 2011 USENIX Annual Technical Conference*, USENIX ATC'11, pages 145–158, Berkeley, CA, USA, 2011. USENIX Association.

[39] J. R. Vash, B. Jung, and R. Tan. System-wide quiescence and per-thread transaction fence in a distributed caching agent. `http://www.google.com/patents/US8443148`, 2013. US Patent 8443148 B2.

[40] N. Vasudevan, K. S. Namjoshi, and S. A. Edwards. Simple and Fast Biased Locks. In *Proceedings of the 19th International Conference on Parallel Architectures and Compilation Techniques*, PACT '10, pages 65–74, New York, NY, USA, 2010. ACM. ISBN 978-1-4503-0178-7. .

[41] T. F. Wenisch, A. Ailamaki, B. Falsafi, and A. Moshovos. Mechanisms for store-wait-free multiprocessors. In *Proceedings of the 34th Annual International Symposium on Computer Architecture*, ISCA '07, pages 266–277, New York, NY, USA, 2007. ACM. .

Reduced Hardware NOrec: A Safe and Scalable Hybrid Transactional Memory

Alexander Matveev
MIT
amatveev@csail.mit.edu

Nir Shavit
MIT
shanir@csail.mit.edu

Abstract

Because of hardware TM limitations, software fallbacks are the only way to make TM algorithms guarantee progress. Nevertheless, all known software fallbacks to date, from simple locks to sophisticated versions of the NOrec Hybrid TM algorithm, have either limited scalability or weakened semantics.

We propose a novel reduced-hardware (RH) version of the NOrec HyTM algorithm. Instead of an all-software slow path, in our RH NOrec the slow-path is a "mix" of hardware and software: one short hardware transaction executes a maximal amount of initial reads in the hardware, and the second executes all of the writes. This novel combination of the RH approach and the NOrec algorithm delivers the first Hybrid TM that scales while fully preserving the hardware's original semantics of opacity and privatization.

Our GCC implementation of RH NOrec is promising in that it shows improved performance relative to all prior methods, at the concurrency levels we could test today.

Categories and Subject Descriptors C.1.4 [*Computer System Organization*]: Parallel Architectures; D.1.3 [*Software*]: Concurrent Programming

General Terms Algorithms, Design

Keywords Transactional Memory

1. Introduction

Transactional memory (TM) is an alternative to using locks for shared-memory synchronization. In TM, the programmer marks code regions as transactions, and the TMs internal implementation ensures a consistent execution of those regions. Transactions provide *external consistency*, that is, a transaction can successfully commit only when it can be totally ordered relative to other (possibly concurrent) transactions without violating their real time order. This is the safety property called serializability. Transactions also provide *internal consistency*: a transaction cannot see inconsistent views of the system state, that is, ones that result from intermediate modifications of another transaction, since this may cause the current transaction to fail unexpectedly or enter an infinite loop. Internal consistency is captured by the safety properties *opacity* [13] and *privatization* [17]. Opacity, which we will refer to many times in this paper, is the property that every transaction sees a snapshot of all the variables it accesses at any time. Given internal and external consistency, the programmer can think of a transaction as one "atomic" (i.e. indivisible) sequence of operations.

Hardware transactional memory (HTM) is currently supported by the mainstream Intel Haswell [14, 21] and the IBM Power8 [3] processors. Intel and IBM provide *best-effort* HTM implementations that are much faster than software transactions, providing serializability, opacity, and privatization, but not providing any progress guarantee. CPU cache capacity limitations, interrupts, page faults, system calls or unsupported instructions, may all cause a hardware transaction to repeatedly fail. To overcome this problem, a software fallback (a *slow-path*) is provided for the cases when the hardware transaction (the *fast-path*) fails. The ability to fall back to the slow-path allows one to provide some form of progress guarantee. The simplest of these software fallbacks is a lock, which provides progress and provides all of the hardware's internal and external consistency properties. However, the lock serializes all of the software and hardware attempts to complete the transaction, and therefore does not scale.

Thus, developers have been looking for alternative software slow-paths that will scale while providing all the consistency properties of the hardware. The approach of choice is hybrid transactional memory (HyTM), in which the slow path is a software transaction that can run concurrently with the hardware ones. Preserving internal consistency, in particular opacity and privatization, in the software slow-path, requires complex coordination protocols that impose non-

ASPLOS '15, March 14–18, 2015, Istanbul, Turkey..

http://dx.doi.org/10.1145/10.1145/2694344.2694393

trivial penalties on the more common hardware fast-path. This is the limitation recent HyTM research is trying to overcome, and for which our new algorithm provides what we believe is the most complete and scalable solution to date.

1.1 HyTM Background

The first HyTM [8, 15] algorithms supported concurrent execution of hardware and software transactions by instrumenting the hardware transactions' shared reads and writes to check for changes in the software path's metadata. This approach, which is the basis of all the generally applicable HyTM proposals, imposes severe overheads on the hardware transaction.

One way to overcome these overheads is through a PhasedTM [16] approach: transactions are executed in phases, each of which is either all hardware or all software. This approach performs well when all hardware transactions are successful, but has poor performance if even a single transaction needs to be executed in software because it must switch all transactions to a slower all-software mode of execution. This is a good approach for some workloads, but in others it is not clear how to overcome frequent switches between phases.

The leading HyTM algorithm to-date is the Hybrid NOrec HyTM of Dalessandro et al. [7], a hybrid version of the Norec STM of Dalessandro, Spear, and Scott [6]. In this algorithm, the commits of write transactions are executed sequentially, and a shared global clock is used to notify concurrent transactions about the updates to memory. The write commits trigger the necessary re-validations and aborts of the concurrently executing transactions. The great benefit the NOrec HyTM scheme over prior HyTM proposals is that no metadata per memory location is required and instrumentation costs are reduced significantly. However, it suffers from limited scalability because it uses a shared clock to ensure serializability and opacity. All hardware transactions must read the clock when they start, which adds this clock location to the HTMs tracking set and causes them to frequently abort; essentially every time the clock gets updated by a software slow-path transaction that writes.

Riegel et al. [19] were aware of this drawback of the Hybrid NOrec algorithm and suggested a way to reduce these overheads by using non-speculative operations inside the hardware transactions. These operations are supported by AMD's proposed ASF transactional hardware [5] but are not supported in the best-effort HTMs that Intel and IBM are bringing to the marketplace [1].

The original authors of the NOrec HyTM, and the recent work by Calciu et al. [4], both state that it is a challenging task to improve the scalability of the NOrec HyTM on existing architectures unless one gives up opacity. They thus propose to sacrifice opacity by implementing efficient but unsafe HyTM protocols that allow non-opaque hardware transactions, ones that may read inconsistent system states. The idea is to use the built-in HTM sandboxing mechanisms to protect non-opaque hardware transactions from runtime errors. If the inconsistent hardware transaction performs a "bad" action that causes it to abort, the hardware together with the runtime can detect and recover from the error. The problem with HTM sandboxing is that it does not protect from *all* possible errors. The authors identify a set of possible scenarios in which transactions might still incorrectly commit in an inconsistent state, and suggest how they can be handled by extending compiler and runtime support.

However, recent work by Dice et al. [10] identifies many additional scenarios of bad executions that escape the HTM sandboxing mechanism. These additional cases rise concerns about the HTM sandboxing approach since on existing hardware they would require a much more complex compiler and runtime support to be handled, overshadowing the advantages of using HTM sandboxing in the first place. Figuring out what hardware modifications and new algorithms would make sandboxing a viable approach is an interesting topic for future research.

We henceforth focus on the performance of HyTM algorithms that can provide the same consistency properties as pure hardware transactions on todays new commodity multicore architectures.

1.2 The RH Approach

In a recent paper, we proposed the reduced hardware approach to HyTM design [18] as a way of minimizing the overhead of the hardware fast-path without restricting concurrency between hardware and software transactions. The idea was that instead of the all-software slow-path used in HyTMs, part of the slow-path will be executed using a reduced size hardware transaction, making the slow path a software-hardware *mixed slow-path*. To show the benefit of this approach [18], we proposed a reduced hardware version of the classic TL2 STM of Dice, Shalev and Shavit [9]. The RH-TL2 algorithm eliminated the instrumentation overheads of the shared reads from the hardware fast-path, and therefore provided a more efficient HyTM fast-path which improved on all prior TL2-style HyTM algorithms. However, there still remain several fundamental problems with the RH-TL2 algorithm which this paper sets out to solve:

- **The RH-TL2 fast-path required instrumentation:** There was no need to instrument the hardware fast-path reads, but there was a need to instrument its writes and update the software metadata for every write location of the fast-path before it performs the HTM commit. Though reads are more frequent than writes, this was still far from the performance of having a fully pure uninstrumented hardware transaction.

[1] IBM Power8 supports a suspend-resume feature that allows to execute non-speculative operations in hardware transactions. The problem is that suspend-resume is intended for debugging and is expensive to use. It cannot be used frequently, for every shared read and write.

- **The RH-TL2 mixed slow-path had high chances of failure:** The mixed slow-path small hardware transaction required a verification phase of the read locations before their write-back. As a result, the chances of the small hardware transaction failing were still high since it included both the read and write locations in HTM.
- **The RH-TL2 algorithm did not provide privatization:** Privatization [17] is a feature provided by hardware transactions, guaranteeing that the modifications of ongoing transactions are not visible to correctly synchronized non-transactional operations. This would be a serious limitation if the algorithm were to be deployed in a commercial setting.

1.3 Our New Reduced Hardware NOrec Algorithm

In this paper, we show how to apply the RH approach of [18] to the NOrec HyTM algorithm, resulting in a new HyTM algorithm that overcomes all the drawbacks of RH TL2 mentioned above, and more importantly, all the scalability limitations of the NOrec HyTM. It provides the first scalable HyTM that has complete internal and external consistency; the same as a pure hardware TM.

Our RH NOrec algorithm, which we describe in detail in the next section, uses two short hardware transactions in the mixed slow-path, to eliminate NOrec HyTM scalability bottlenecks. Both of these bottlenecks are caused by reading of the shared clock too early. In one case too early in the hardware fast-path, and in the other too early in the software slow-path. We execute two hardware transactions, in the mixed slow path, to overcome these problems. One hardware transaction encapsulates all the slow path writes at commit point and executes them all together. This change to the mixed software slow-path enables the fast-path hardware transaction to read the shared NOrec clock at the end of the transaction, just before committing, instead of reading it when it starts, avoiding the frequent false-aborts of the original Hybrid NOrec. The other hardware transaction, in the mixed slow path, executes the largest possible prefix of slow-path reads in a hardware transaction. In other words, it starts the mixed slow-path with a hardware transaction, and as long as it does not encounter a write it keeps on executing in hardware. This hardware prefix allows us to defer the reading of the global clock *in the mixed slow-path itself* to the end of the sequence of reads, which as we will explain, significantly reduces the chances it will have to restart. We believe it is algorithmically surprising that with the hardware support in the mixed path, moving the clock-reads back preserves opacity, enables a pure uninstrumented fast-path, and allows full privatization as in the original Hybrid NOrec algorithm. Finally, we note that if the mixed slow-path fails to commit, the algorithm reverts to the original Hybrid NOrec.

We integrated our new RH NOrec HyTM into the GCC compiler, and performed empirical testing on 16-way Intel Haswell processor. Though one must be cautious given the limited concurrency we could test, our results are rather encouraging: we show that RH NOrec is able to reduce the number of HTM conflicts from 8-20 fold compared to NOrec HyTM for the RBTree microbenchmark, and 2-5 fold for the STAMP applications. Though the reduction in HTM conflicts does not always lead to better throughput results (sometimes the dominant factor is the level of HTM capacity aborts, and sometimes the HTM conflicts are already very low, so reducing them more does not make too much of a difference), in benchmarks that suffer from high HTM conflict rates, RH-NOrec shows a significant improvement over the best previous schemes.

2. Reduced Hardware NOrec

We begin by explaining the Hybrid NOrec algorithm on which RH NOrec is based.

2.1 Hybrid NOrec Overview

The original NOrec STM, that is, the all software one, coordinates transactions based on a global clock that is updated every time a write transaction commits, and also serves as a global lock. It keeps a read set and a write set, that is, logs of all the locations read and written, and their values. A transaction reads the global clock value when it starts, and stores it in a local clock variable. To perform a read, the transaction (1) reads the location, (2) logs its value to a read-set log, and (3) performs a consistency check that ensures opacity: it checks that the local clock value is the same as the global clock value. If the clocks differ, then it means that some writer has committed and maybe even overwrote the current transaction. Thus, the current transaction must perform a full read-set revalidation in order to rule out a possible overwrite. To execute a write, the NOrec algorithm can work in two possible ways: (1) write to a local write-set, deferring the writes to the commit, or (2) write directly to the memory. In both cases, to ensure opacity, the NOrec algorithm locks the global clock before making the actual memory writes (when they are encountered or eventually when commiting), and releases it after the actual writes are done. While the global clock is locked, other transactions are delayed, spinning until it is released.

The original Hybrid NOrec has each transaction start to execute in hardware, and if it repeatedly fails to commit, it falls back to executing the NOrec STM in software. Of course, one must coordinate among the hardware and software to guarantee serializability and opacity. Figure 1 presents a problematic scenario in a hybrid TM execution that one must solve in order to provide opacity. The scenario is a concurrent execution of one hardware fast-path transaction and one software slow-path transaction. We omit many of the hybrid protocol's details and focus only on direct memory reads and writes. In the scenario, the slow-path updates shared variables X and Y and the fast-path reads X and Y. Now, if the slow-path updates X, and before it updates

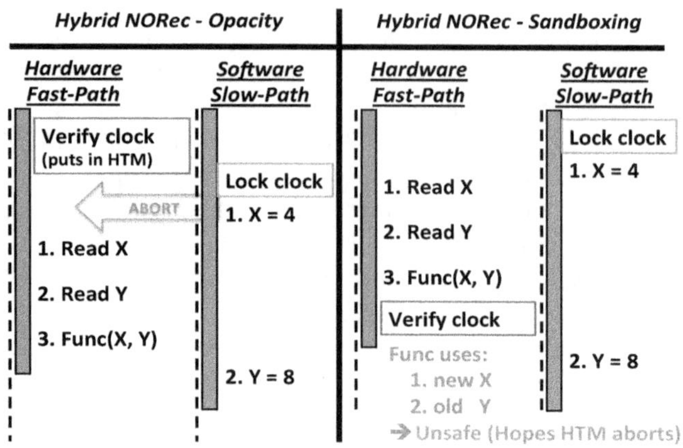

Figure 1. The problematic scenario that a hybrid protocol must handle to provide opacity.

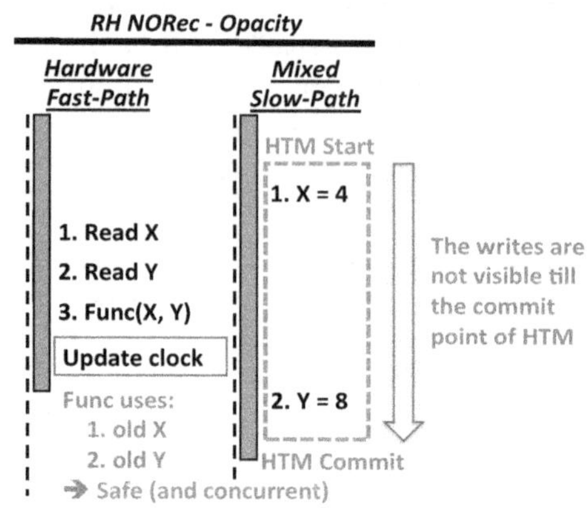

Figure 2. The RH NOrec provides opacity and concurrency between the fast-path and the slow-path by encapsulating the writes in the HTM.

Y, the fast-path reads X and Y, then the fast-path has now a view of a new X and an old Y relative to the slow-path transaction, which is an inconsistent memory view. To avoid this problem, in Hybrid NOrec, when a hardware fast-path transaction starts, it reads the global clock in hardware and verifies it is not locked. Thus, the hardware tracks the clock location from the very start of its execution and will abort whenever any software slow-path that writes to memory locks the global clock to perform its actual memory writes. This creates many false-aborts: aborts by software threads writing to completely unrelated locations.

The way to overcome this problem is to move the verification of the global clock from the start of the hardware fast-path to its end, eliminating the excessive false-aborts. However, as mentioned earlier, doing so in the Hybrid NOrec algorithm requires perfect HTM sandboxing to protect against the inconsistent executions that may corrupt memory and crash the program. Such sandboxing unfortunately does not exist.

2.2 RH NOrec Overview

We now explain our new RH NOrec algorithm. In this algorithm we will move the access and verification of the global clock back in both the hardware and software transactions, while maintaining consistency. We will do so by adding two small hardware transactions to the software slow-path of the Hybrid NOrec. The new slow-path executes using both hardware and software, so we call it the *mixed slow-path.*

The first hardware transaction is *HTM postfix*. It encapsulates all the mixed slow path writes and executes them in one hardware transaction. Executing the writes as an atomic hardware transaction guarantees the fast-path hardware transaction cannot see partial writes of the mixed slow-path, and this enables the fast-path to read the shared NOrec clock at the end of the transaction, just before committing, instead of reading it when it starts. Figure 2 depicts this change and shows how it solves the problematic scenario of the previous Figure 1. Recall, the issue is that the the slow-path may update X, and before it updates Y, the fast-path may read X and Y, where X is new and Y is old relative to the slow-path execution. In the new algorithm, the mixed slow-path writes X and Y together in the HTM postfix transaction, so any concurrent hardware fast-path transaction will see a consistent view.

The second hardware transaction is *HTM prefix*. It tries to execute the largest possible prefix of mixed slow-path reads in a single hardware transaction. In other words, it starts the mixed slow-path with a hardware transaction, and as long as it does not encounter a write it keeps on executing in hardware. The HTM prefix uses the HTM conflict-detection mechanism to detect overwrites of the slow-path reads. This replaces the reading of the shared NOrec clock on the mixed slow-path and validating that it is still the same for each read. In this way, the RH NOrec algorithm defers the read of the shared NOrec clock to the commit point of the HTM prefix, significantly reducing the execution window during which it is possible to abort the mixed slow-path. To make this approach efficient and reduce the false-abort window as much as possible, the length of the HTM prefix adjusts dynamically during the runtime, based on the HTM abort rate feedback, so that the largest amount of mixed slow-path reads can execute in the hardware.

Figure 3 shows an execution example of the RH NOrec mixed slow-path with the two small hardware transactions. The figure presents two fast-path hardware transactions and a one mixed slow-path transaction that are able to execute concurrently (assume no real conflicts) and preserve opacity. The mixed slow-path starts by executing its first reads in the HTM prefix hardware transaction. The first fast-path transaction has this advantage: it executes concurrently with the mixed slow-path HTM prefix, and performs a commit and update of the global clock without forcing the mixed

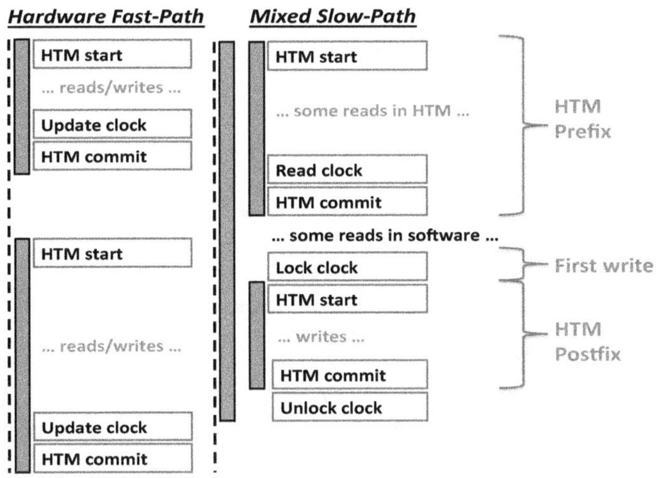

Figure 3. Execution example of RH NOrec that reveals the concurrency advantages of using small hardware transactions in the mixed slow-path: the HTM prefix, for the first reads, and the HTM postfix, for all of the writes. The figure presents two fast-path hardware transactions and a one mixed slow-path transaction, that are able to execute concurrently and preserve opacity.

Algorithm 1 RH NOrec hardware fast-path transaction

```
function FAST_PATH_START(ctx)
    label: retry
    HTM_Start()
    if HTM failed then
        ▷ Handle HTM abort
        ... retry policy ...
        if no retry then
            fallback to mixed slow-path
        end if
        goto retry
    end if
    ▷ HTM started; subscribe to HTM lock
    if global_htm_lock ≠ 0 then
        HTM_Abort()
    end if
end function

function FAST_PATH_READ(ctx, addr)
    ▷ no instrumentation - simple load
    return load(addr)
end function

function FAST_PATH_WRITE(ctx, addr, value)
    ▷ no instrumentation - simple store
    store(addr, value)
end function

function FAST_PATH_COMMIT(ctx)
    if HTM is read only then
        ▷ Detected by compiler static analysis
        HTM_Commit()
        return
    end if
    if num_of_fallbacks > 0 then
        ▷ Notify mixed slow-paths about the update
        if is_locked(global_clock) then
            HTM_Abort()
        end if
        global_clock ← global_clock + 1
    end if
    HTM_Commit()
end function
```

slow-path to restart. When the HTM prefix commits, it reads the global clock to a local clock variable and proceeds to execute the rest of the reads in the software. Upon the first mixed slow-path write, it starts the HTM postfix hardware transaction, and this executes concurrently with the second fast-path transaction. When the HTM postfix commits, it updates the global clock without aborting the second fast-path, and later the fast-path commits successfully.

Finally, when some mixed slow-path small hardware transaction repeatedly fails to commit, the RH NOrec mixed slow-path reverts back to the Hybrid NOrec full software slow-path counterpart. For the HTM prefix, it reads the shared NOrec clock on the slow-path start and validates it is still the same for each read. For the HTM postfix, it aborts all current hardware transactions and executes the writes in the software.

2.3 RH NOrec Algorithm

For clarity, in this section we present a mixed slow-path that uses only the HTM postfix transaction, that encapsulates the writes. In the next section, we add the necessary modifications to support the second, HTM prefix short hardware transaction.

Algorithm 1 and Algorithm 2 show the pseudo-code for the hardware fast-path and the mixed slow-path.

The hybrid protocol coordinates fast-paths and slow-paths by using three global variables:

1. *global_clock:* Implements the conflict-detection mechanism. Every hardware fast-path increments the clock before it commits to notify mixed slow-paths about the memory update, and every mixed slow-path does the same to notify other mixed slow-paths.
2. *global_htm_lock:* Allows to abort all hardware fast-paths when the hardware component of the mixed slow-path fails. Every fast-path subscribes to the htm lock by reading it and verifying it is free on its start. This allows a failed mixed slow-path to abort all of them by setting the htm lock, and execute the mixed slow-path writes as is (in full software) while still ensuring opacity.
3. *num_of_fallbacks:* Represents the current number of mixed slow-paths. Hardware fast-paths use this counter

Algorithm 2 RH NOrec mixed slow-path transaction that supports only HTM postfix.

```
1: function MIXED_SLOW_PATH_START(ctx)
2:     atomic_fetch_and_add(num_of_fallbacks, 1)
3:     ctx.is_write_detected ← 0
4:     ctx.tx_version ← global_clock
5:     if is_locked(ctx.tx_version) then
6:         restart(ctx)
7:     end if
8: end function
9:
10: function MIXED_SLOW_PATH_READ(ctx, addr)
11:     cur_value ← load(addr)
12:     if ctx.tx_version ≠ global_clock then
13:         restart(ctx)
14:     end if
15:     return cur_value
16: end function
17:
18: function MIXED_SLOW_PATH_WRITE(ctx, addr, value)
19:     if ¬ctx.is_write_detected then
20:         handle_first_write(ctx)
21:     end if
22:     store(addr, value)
23: end function
24:
25: function HANDLE_FIRST_WRITE(ctx)
        ▷ Lock the clock and start HTM. If the HTM fails, then set
          the HTM lock to abort all hardware fast-paths.
26:     ctx.is_write_detected ← 1
27:     acquire_clock_lock(ctx)
28:     if ¬ start_rh_htm_postfix(ctx) then
29:         global_htm_lock ← 1
30:     end if
31: end function
32:
33: function START_RH_HTM_POSTFIX(ctx)
34:     label: retry
35:     HTM_Start()
36:     if HTM failed then
37:         ... retry policy ...
38:         if no retry then
39:             return false
40:         end if
41:         goto retry
42:     end if
43:     ctx.is_rh_active ← true
44:     return true
45: end function
46:
47: function ACQUIRE_CLOCK_LOCK(ctx)
48:     new ← set_lock_bit(ctx.tx_version)
49:     expected ← ctx.tx_version
50:     is_locked ← atomic_CAS(global_clock, expected, new)
51:     if ¬is_locked then
52:         restart(ctx)
53:     end if
54:     ctx.tx_version ← new
55:     return true
56: end function
57:
58: function MIXED_SLOW_PATH_COMMIT(ctx)
        ▷ If read-only, then do nothing
59:     if ¬ctx.is_write_detected then
60:         atomic_fetch_and_sub(num_of_fallbacks, 1)
61:         return
62:     end if
        ▷ If RH is on, then commit it
63:     if ctx.is_rh_active then
64:         HTM_Commit()
65:         ctx.is_rh_active ← false
66:     end if
        ▷ If HTM lock is taken, then release it
67:     if global_htm_lock ≠ 0 then
68:         global_htm_lock ← 0
69:     end if
        ▷ Update the clock: clear the lock bit and increment
70:     global_clock ← clear_lock_bit(global_clock) + 1
71:     atomic_fetch_and_sub(num_of_fallbacks, 1)
72: end function
```

to avoid updating the global clock when there is no slow-path executing.

Algorithm 1 shows the hardware fast-path implementation. On start, it initiates a hardware transaction (line 3) and subscribes to the global htm lock (line 11). If the HTM fails, the abort handling code (lines 4 - 9) executes and decides when to perform the fallback. During the HTM execution, reads and writes execute without any instrumentation (line 17 and 21), making them as efficient as pure HTM. Upon commit, a read-only HTM commits immediately. Otherwise, the HTM checks if there are mixed slow-path fallbacks, and if there are, then it increments the global clock to notify the fallbacks about the writer. It then commits the hardware transaction (lines 29-35). The detection of read-only fast-paths is currently based on the GCC compiler static analysis that provides this information to the GCC TM library.

Algorithm 2 shows the mixed slow-path implementation that uses only the HTM postfix short hardware transaction. Upon start, it increments the fallback counter, sets the writer detection flag to 0, and reads the global clock to a local variable called *tx_version* (lines 2 - 7). During the mixed slow-path execution, the reads and writes are performed directly to/from the memory. To execute a read, it loads the memory location, and then verifies that global clock version is still the same as the local version. If there is a change, then this means that some write transaction committed, possibly overwriting the current transaction, and therefore the current transaction restarts (lines 11 - 15). To execute a write, it first

Algorithm 3 RH NOrec mixed slow-path transaction that supports both HTM prefix and HTM postfix.

```
1: function MIXED_SLOW_PATH_START(ctx)
2:     if start_rh_htm_prefix(ctx) then
3:         return
4:     else
5:         ... original code (of Algorithm 2) ...
6:     end if
7: end function
8:
9: function START_RH_HTM_PREFIX(ctx)
10:     label: retry
11:     HTM_Start()
12:     if HTM failed then
13:         ... retry policy and prefix length adjustment ...
14:         if no retry then
15:             return false
16:         end if
17:         goto retry
18:     end if
19:     ctx.is_rh_prefix_active ← true
        ▷ HTM prefix started; subscribe to HTM lock
20:     if global_htm_lock ≠ 0 then
21:         HTM_Abort()
22:     end if
        ▷ Set the prefix expected length
23:     ctx.max_reads ← ctx.expected_length
24:     ctx.prefix_reads ← 0
25:     return true
26: end function
27:
28: function MIXED_SLOW_PATH_READ(ctx, addr)
29:     if ctx.is_rh_prefix_active then
30:         ctx.prefix_reads ← ctx.prefix_reads + 1
31:         if ctx.prefix_reads < ctx.max_reads then
32:             return load(addr)
33:         else
34:             commit_rh_htm_prefix(ctx)
35:         end if
36:     end if
37:     ... original code (of Algorithm 2) ...
38: end function
39:
40: function MIXED_SLOW_PATH_WRITE(ctx, addr, value)
41:     if ctx.is_rh_prefix_active then
42:         commit_rh_htm_prefix(ctx)
43:     end if
44:     ... original code (of Algorithm 2) ...
45: end function
46:
47: function COMMIT_RH_HTM_PREFIX(ctx)
48:     num_of_fallbacks ← num_of_fallbacks + 1
49:     ctx.is_write_detected ← 0
50:     ctx.tx_version ← global_clock
51:     if is_locked(ctx.tx_version) then
52:         HTM_Abort()
53:     end if
54:     HTM_Commit()
55:     ctx.is_rh_prefix_active ← false
56: end function
57:
58: function MIXED_SLOW_PATH_COMMIT(ctx)
59:     if ctx.is_rh_prefix_active then
60:         HTM_Commit()
61:         return
62:     end if
63:     ... original code (of Algorithm 2) ...
64: end function
```

checks if this is the first write (line 19). If so, it sets the writer detected flag to 1, and then locks the global clock by *atomically* (1) setting its lock-bit to 1 and (2) verifying that the global clock is still the same as the local clock (line 26 and lines 48 - 55). Then, it initiates a hardware transaction that is going to perform the rest of the transaction, which includes all of its writes. If this hardware transaction fails to commit, then it sets the *global htm lock*, aborting all current hardware fast-paths, and executes the rest of the transaction as is, with the software NORec algorithm providing full opacity (lines 28 - 30). Upon commit, it checks if the transaction is read-only. If so, then it decrements the fallback counter and it is done (lines 59 - 62). Otherwise, it commits the writes' hardware transaction if it is active, and then releases all locks being held and decrements the fallback counter (lines 63 - 71).

2.4 Reducing Mixed Slow-Path Restarts

In the mixed slow-path using an eager approach (that writes in place as opposed to maintaining a write set that is written upon commit) is lightweight and efficient: It has no read-set or write-set logging and performs direct memory reads and writes. However, eliminating the write-set logs forces a mixed slow-path restart every time the global clock is updated by a concurrent write transaction. In this section, we significantly reduce the amount of these restarts by extending the mixed slow-path to use the second, HTM prefix, short hardware transaction.

A mixed slow-path may perform a restart in any point between the start of the transaction and its first shared memory write. This is because the mixed slow-path reads the global clock upon starting, and only locks it on the first write. So the initial reads, the ones before the first write, execute with a consistency check that may result in a restart. The idea of the HTM prefix short hardware transaction is to execute maximal amount of these reads in the HTM, which effectively eliminates the need to read the global clock on the start and allows to defer it to the commit point of the HTM prefix. To make this effective, the length of the HTM prefix adjusts dynamically based on the HTM abort feedback: at first, the algorithm tries to execute a long prefix, and if this fails to commit in the hardware, then it reduces the length until it finds the right length that will commit with high probability (the adjustment algorithm is similar to that used in [2]).

Algorithm 3 shows modified mixed slow-path that supports the HTM prefix hardware transaction. Upon start, it initiates the prefix hardware transaction (lines 2 - 3). If it fails, then it executes the original start code (of Algorithm 2), and otherwise it skips the original code and proceeds in the HTM. The prefix initiation procedure is implemented in the *start_rh_htm_prefix* function. It starts a hardware transaction, sets the *is_rh_prefix_active* flag to 1, subscribes to the global htm lock to ensure opacity (in a similar way to the fast-paths), and initializes the prefix length parameters (lines 10 - 25). The algorithm adjusts the prefix maximum length (line 13), according to the HTM aborts feedback, and enforces it by counting the number of reads executed (lines 29 - 36). When the maximum number of reads is reached, or a first write is encountered (lines 41 - 43), the HTM prefix executes the commit procedure (lines 48 - 55). This essentially performs the original start code including the initialization of the local version variable. Finally, if none of the threshold conditions are met, and the HTM prefix reaches the mixed slow-path commit, then it simply commits the transaction and returns (lines 59 - 62).

3. Performance Evaluation

We integrated the new RH NOrec algorithm and the original Hybrid NOrec algorithm into the GCC 4.8 compiler. GCC 4.8 provides language-level support for transactional memory (GCC TM) based on the draft specification for C++ of Adl-Tabatabai et. al [1].

The GCC TM compiler generates two execution paths for each GCC transaction: (1) a pure uninstrumented fast-path and (2) a fully instrumented slow-path. In the second path, every shared read and write is replaced with a dynamic function call to the *libitm* runtime library that provides an implementation for the various TM algorithms. In addition, the compiler instrumentation provides the libitm library with runtime hints about the code read-write, write-write and write-read dependencies, and allows the libitm library to identify static read-only transactions. In our implementations, we use all these hints to improve the performance of the Hybrid TMs in the same way as the original libitm library uses the hints to improve the performance of the STMs.

3.1 TM Algorithms

We tested the performance of the following GCC TM algorithms:

Lock Elision: Transactions execute in pure hardware, using the RTM Haswell mechanism [14], and if a transaction fails to commit in hardware, then it acquires the global lock, which aborts all hardware transactions and serializes the execution to ensure progress.

NOrec: All transactions execute as software NOrec [6] transactions with eager encounter-time writes. Upon a first write, a transaction locks the global clock and performs the subsequent writes directly to the memory. In order to perform a read, a transaction reads from the memory and verifies consistency. In this version of NOrec, there are no read-set or write-set logging procedures, so a transaction must restart when a write transaction commits. We also implemented the lazy design of NOrec that does require read-set and write-set logging, but we found that for the low concurrency in our benchmarks, the eager NOrec design delivers better performance.

TL2: All transactions execute in software following the TL2 [9] algorithm with eager encounter-time writes. To write, a transaction locks the metadata of the write location, and performs a direct memory write. To read, it logs the location in the read-set, reads it from the memory, and verifies the associated metadata. Upon commit, it revalidates the read-set, and if successful, releases the locks while advancing the global clock. The TL2 STM imposes high constant overheads, but provides better scalability than the NOrec STM because it uses per location metadata for conflict-detection.

HY-NOrec: The NOrec HyTM algorithm of Dalessandro et. al [7]. The coordination between the hardware fast-path and the software slow-path tries to avoid as many false-aborts as possible. To achieve this, the coordination protocol uses 3 global variables: (1) global htm lock, (2) global NOrec clock, and (3) fallback count. A hardware fast-path reads the global htm lock upon start and verifies it is free. In the fast-path commit, it increments the global clock only if the fallback count is not 0. The software slow-path executes the eager encounter-time NOrec STM, which aborts all of the fast-paths only when the first write is encountered, by setting the global htm lock. As explained above in the case of NOrec, we found this eager HyTM design outperforms the lazy HyTM design for the low concurrency levels available in our benchmarks.

RH-NOrec: This is our new hybrid TM as described in Section 2.

3.2 Execution Environment

In our benchmarks, we use the 16-way Intel Core i7-5960X Haswell processor: It has 8-cores and provides support for HyperThreading of two hardware threads per core. The new Haswell chip RTM system provides support for hardware transactions that can fit into the capacity of the L1 cache. As an optimization, the hardware internally uses bloom filters for the read-sets and write-sets, so it can also provide larger *read-only* hardware transactions that can fit into the capacity of the L2 cache. It is important to notice that the HyperThreading reduces the L1 cache capacity for HTM by a factor of 2, since it executes two hardware threads on the same core (same L1 cache). As a result, in many benchmarks there are significant penalties above the limit of 8 threads, where the HyperThreading executes and generates an increased amount of HTM capacity aborts.

The operating system we use is a Debian OS 3.14 x86_64 with GCC 4.8. All of the benchmarks are compiled with an O3 optimization level and inlining enabled. We found that the malloc/free library provided with the system does not scale and imposes high overheads and many false aborts on the HTM mechanism. We thus switched to the scalable *tc-malloc* [12] memory allocator that maintains per thread memory pools and provides good performance inside the HTM transactions. The GCC libitm library was modified to include the new Hybrid TMs and compiled with the default parameters.

3.3 Retry Policy

Both Hybrid NOrec and RH Norec use the same static retry policy, that we found to perform well for most of the benchmarks. In the next paragraphs, we describe the retry algorithm for the fast-path and the slow-path. Note that for Lock Elision only the fast-path applies.

Fast-path: When a hardware fast-path transaction aborts, the protocol checks the HTM abort flags to see the reason for the abort. If the HTM flags indicate that retrying in the hardware may help (the flag NO_RETRY is false), then the transaction restarts in the hardware. Otherwise it falls back to the software slow-path. The maximum number of hardware restarts we allow is 10, after which the transaction falls back to the software. The effect of this policy is that capacity aborts immediately go to the software, while conflict aborts retry many times in the hardware, giving the hardware a chance to complete as many transactions as possible.

Slow-path: The slow-path of the Hybrid TMs may starve when there are many frequent fast-path write transaction commits: each such commit updates the clock, and this forces a slow-path restart. Note that this starvation scenario is less likely for the RH NOrec, but still may happen when the HTM prefix fails. Therefore, to avoid this and ensure progress, we use a special *serial lock* to serialize the execution of the problematic slow-paths: each slow-path that restarts too often acquires this special lock when it starts, and releases it when it is done. In turn, the HTM fast-paths, that need to increment the global clock (writers), check this lock and abort when it is taken. We set the slow-path restart limit to be 10, since we found this limit to provide the best overall results for most of the benchmarks.

A recent paper [11] presents a dynamic-adaptive retry policy for lock elision schemes. Implementing a dynamic retry policy for Hybrid TMs is an interesting and important topic for future work.

3.4 Mixed Slow-Path HTM Details

The RH NOrec mixed slow-path uses two small hardware transactions: one is the *HTM prefix* that executes the first part of the mixed slow-path and reduces the software restarts, and another is the *HTM postfix* that performs the memory writes and allows the hardware fast-paths to execute concurrently. We found out that the best retry policy for these small HTMs is to try each one only once before using the full software counterpart. This is because many retries increase the execution time of the mixed slow-path, and generate more cache pressure on the HTM fast-paths.

3.5 Red-Black Tree Microbenchmark

The red-black tree we use is derived from the *java.util.TreeMap* implementation found in the Java 6.0 JDK. The red-black tree benchmark exposes a key-value pair interface of *put*, *delete*, and *get* operations, and allows to control the (1) tree size and the (2) mutation ratio (the fraction of write transactions). Each run executes for 10 seconds, and reports the total number of operations completed.

The left to right columns in Figure 4 present results for a 10,000 node red-black tree with 4%, 10% and 40% mutation ratios. The first row (from the top) shows the throughput of the various algorithms, while the next rows present an in-depth execution analysis of the Hybrid NOrec and the RH NOrec. The second row shows (1) the average number of HTM conflict and capacity aborts per completed operation. The third row shows the (2) average number of restarts per slow-path transaction. The fourth row shows the (3) slow-path ratio: the relative number of transactions that failed in the fast-path and made it fall back to the slow-path. The fifth row shows (4) the success ratios of the two small hardware transactions that are used by the RH NOrec mixed slow-path: the HTM prefix that reduces the slow-path restarts, and the HTM postfix that includes the memory writes to allow concurrent fast-path executions.

In Figure 4, we can see that the high instrumentation costs of STMs make them much slower than the HTM-based schemes. However, the performance of Lock Elision and Hybrid NOrec drop when the slow-path fallback ratio increases above 8 threads due to the HyperThreading effect. This performance drop becomes significant with more write transactions and the TL2 STM becomes faster than the Hybrid NOrec for the 40% mutation ratio. In contrast, the new RH NOrec software-hardware mixed fallback path is able to maintain the HTM advantages: it is 1.2, 2.4 and 5.0 times faster than Hybrid NOrec for the respective 4%, 10% and 40% mutation ratios. The execution analysis reveals a significant reduction in the HTM conflict aborts and slow-path restarts for the RH NOrec compared to Hybrid NOrec. This reduction generates a lower slow-path ratio, and is a result of the high success ratio of the HTM prefix and HTM postfix small hardware transactions that the RH NOrec uses in its mixed slow-path. Note that in the 40% mutation case, the

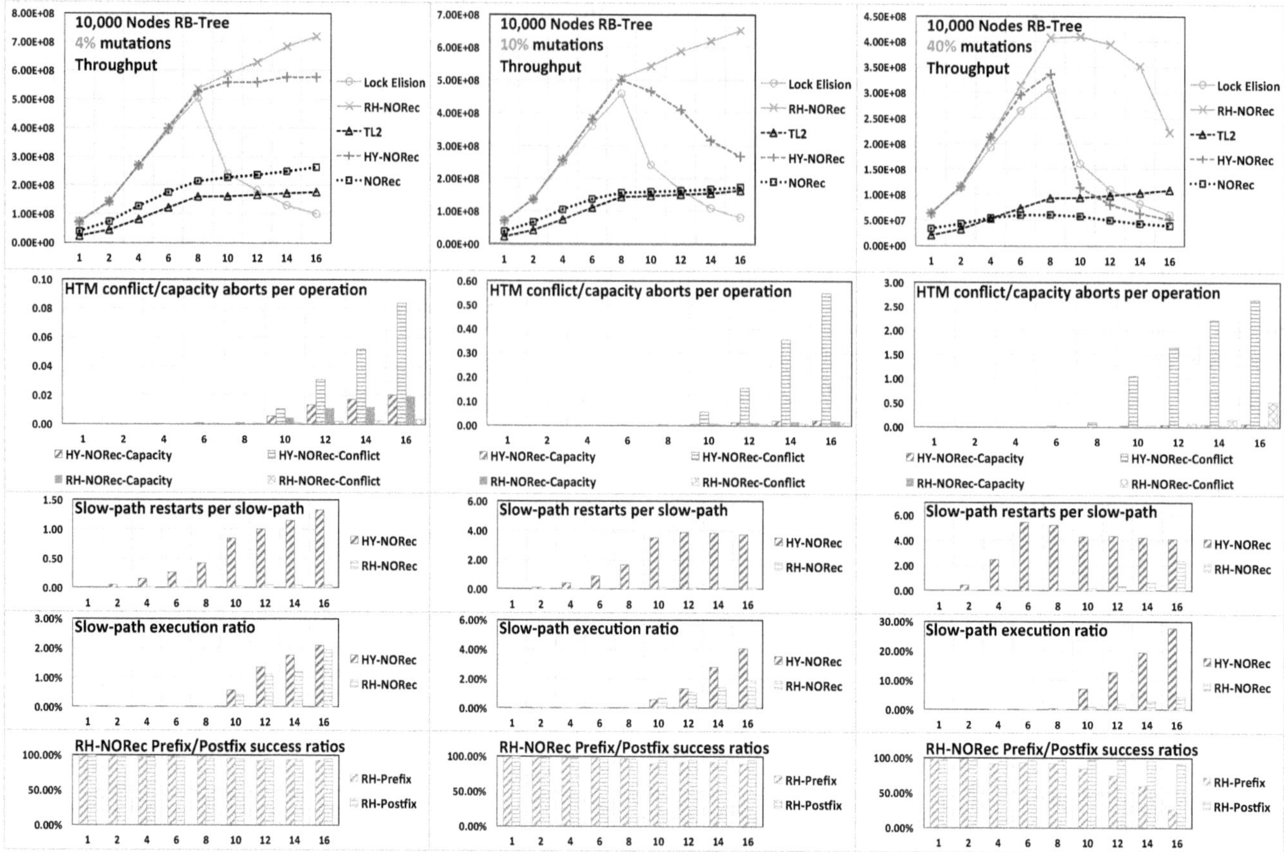

Figure 4. Red-Black tree benchmark. The first (top) row shows the throughput for 4%, 10% and 40% mutation ratios, and the next rows show the execution analysis for the Hybrid TMs.

HTM prefix has a lower success ratio and this aversly affects the RH NOrec scalability.

An interesting side-effect that can be seen in the RBTree analysis is a reduction in HTM capacity aborts for the RH NOrec. The reason for this side-effect is the "sensitivity" of this specific benchmark to the software fallbacks: it executes many "cache-friendly" read-only operations, and therefore the relative L1 cache pressure of the fallbacks is higher compared to benchmarks that execute many write operations. This is typical of the STAMP benchmarks for which this side-effect is small to neligable.

3.6 STAMP Applications

The STAMP suite we use is the most recent version [20] of Ruan et. al, and it includes various real-world applications with different access patterns and behaviors.

The left to right columns in Figure 5 present results for Vacation-Low, Intruder and Genome STAMP applications. The format of the presentation is exactly the same as in Figure 4.

Vacation-Low simulates online transaction processing, and it has a good potential to scale since it generates moderately long transactions with low contention. For this application, the RH NOrec is twice as fast as the Hybrid NOrec for 8 threads, and the analysis shows that this is because the reduction in HTM conflicts. In this case, there is a significant reduction in the HTM conflicts and slow-path restarts just as for the RBTree, but there is no significant difference in the number of slow-path fallbacks. Still RH NOrec is 1.6 times faster than Hybrid NOrec for 8 threads since the overall number of fast-path and slow-path restarts is much lower. Above 8 threads, RH NOrec still reduces the HTM conflicts, slow-path restarts, and even the slow-path fallback ratio, but the HTM capacity aborts increase (due to HyperThreading) and dominate the performance: they increase the slow-path fallback ratio to the point where the RH NOrec reductions are not significant.

Intruder uses transactions to replace coarse-grained synchronization in a simulated network packet analyzer. This workload generates a large amount of short to moderate transactions with high contention, and the poor scalability of the TL2 STM is an indication of this internal behavior. Despite this, the Hybrid TMs significantly improve over the STMs, and RH NOrec is 1.2 and 1.5 times faster than the Hybrid NOrec for 8 and 10 threads. The RH NOrec behavior for 8-16 threads is the opposite of Vacation-Low: there is

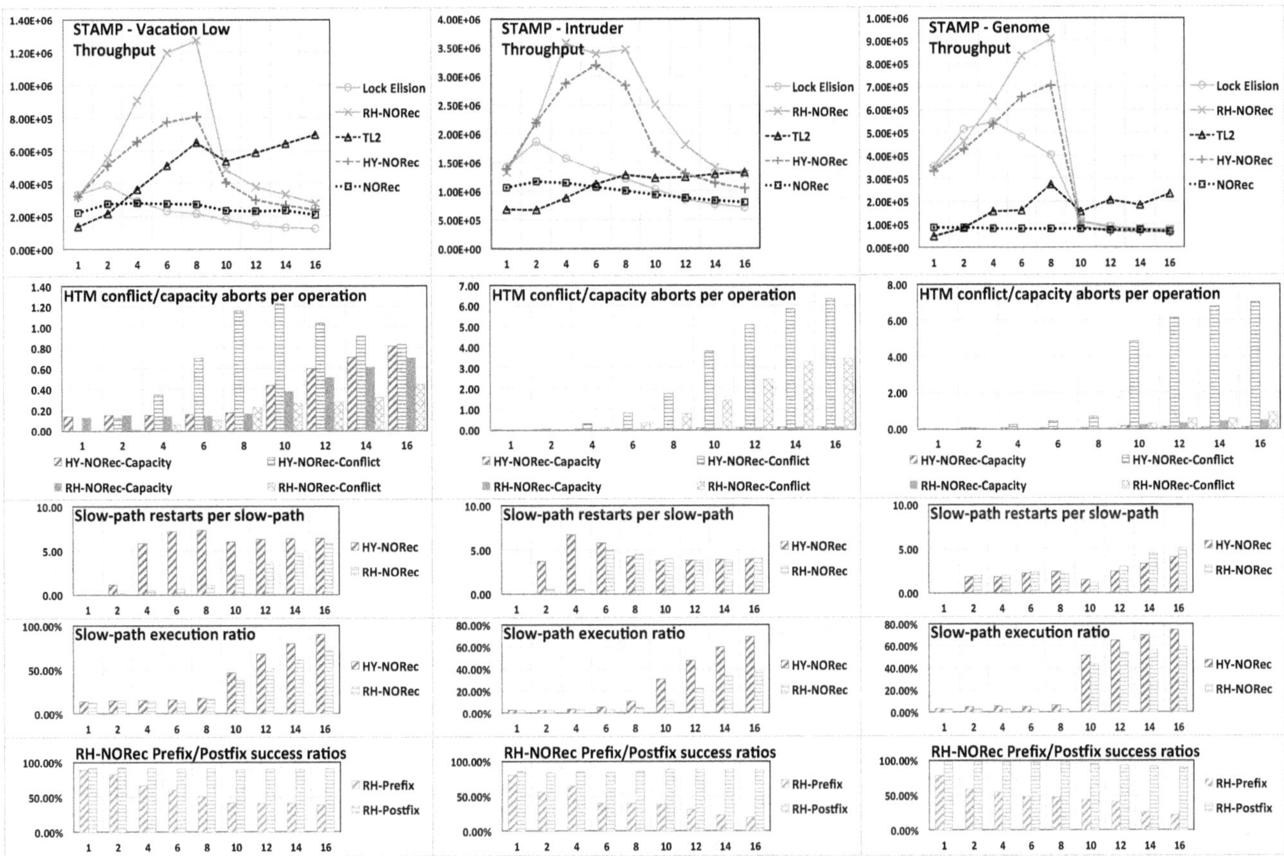

Figure 5. Results for Vacation-Low, Intruder and Genome STAMP applications. The first (top) row shows the throughput, and the next rows show the execution analysis for the Hybrid TMs.

no difference in the number of slow-path restarts, but there is much lower slow-path fallback ratio. So in this case the advantage comes from the HTM postfix small hardware transaction that is able to reduce the HTM conflicts by a factor of 2, and not from the HTM prefix that mostly fails due to high contention. Note that there is a "penalty spike" for RH NOrec at 6 threads. The analysis shows that for more than 4 threads, RH NOrec is not able to reduce slow-path restarts as before, and this adds the additional overhead that results in a spike for 6 threads.

The Genome benchmark employs string matching to reconstruct a genome sequence from a set of DNA segments. This execution generates mostly moderate transactions with a low to moderate contention level, but the instrumentation costs in this benchmark are very high. As a result, the HTM-based schemes that eliminate most of the instrumentation improve significantly over the STMs for 1-8 threads. RH NOrec is 1.3 times faster than Hybrid NOrec for 8 threads, and above 8, the HyperThreading effect significantly increases the HTM capacity aborts, to the point that they dominate the slow-path ratio and eliminate the advantages of the Hybrid TMs. The analysis shows that RH NOrec has no significant effect on the slow-path restarts due to the low success ratio of the HTM prefix small hardware transactions. However, RH NOrec reduces the HTM conflicts by an order of magnitude, and this provides a lower slow-path fallback ratio compared to Hybrid NOrec.

Figure 6 presents the additional STAMP applications: Vacation-High, SSCA2 and Yada. We omit Kmeans and Labyrinth results, since they are similar to SSCA2, and omit Bayes due to its inconsistent behavior (as was also noted by [21]).

Now we explain the results for Figure 6 (from left to right).

Vacation-High is the more contended version of Vacation-Low. It generates additional heavier and slower transactions with moderate contention levels. As a result, all of the HTM-based schemes suffer penalties. However, RH NOrec behaves in the same way as for Vacation-Low: it reduces the HTM conflicts and slow-path restarts, and this allows the RH Norec to be 1.3 times faster than the Hybrid NOrec for 8 threads. In this case, RH NOrec provides less advantage than for Vacation-Low, and the reason for this is the higher number of HTM capacity aborts.

The SSCA2 kernel performs mostly uncontended small read-modify-write operations in order to build a directed,

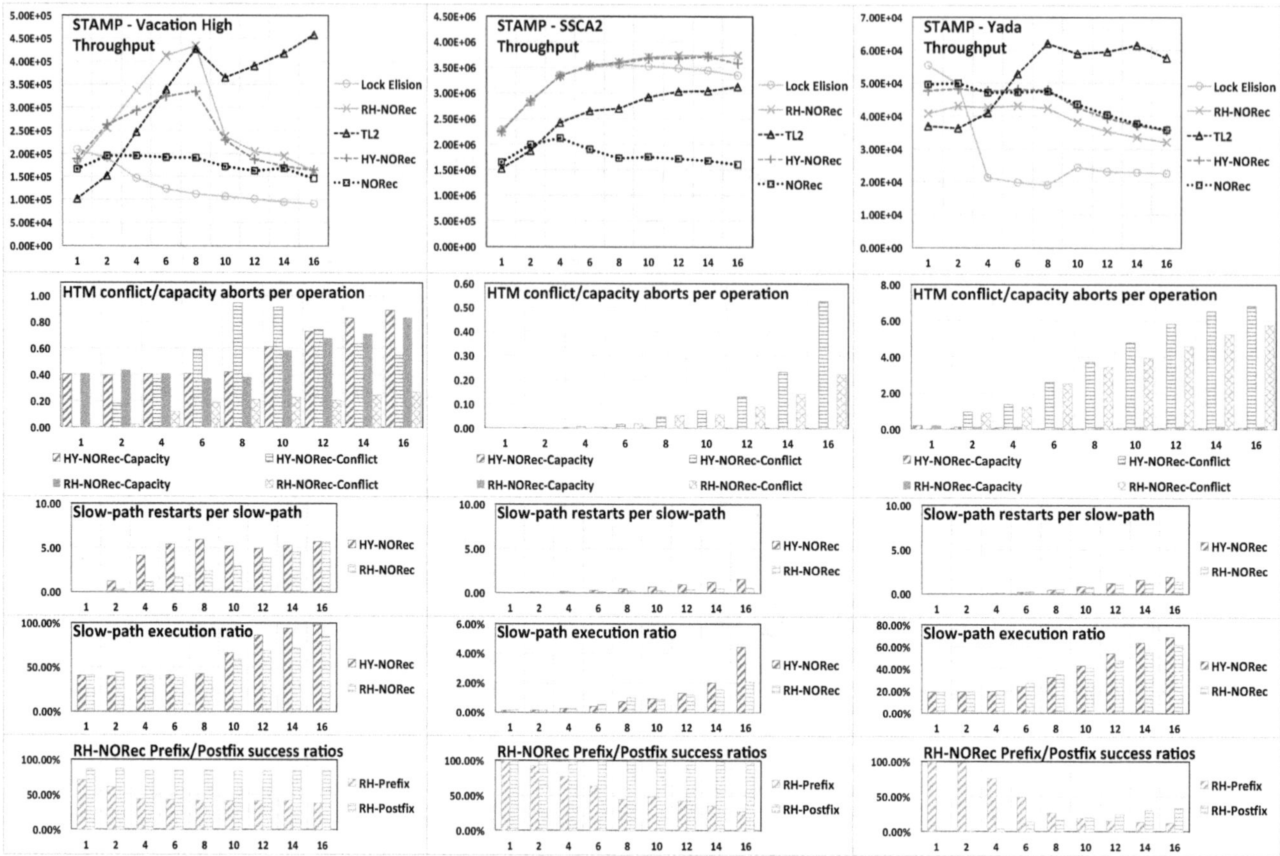

Figure 6. Results for Vacation-High, SSCA2 and Yada STAMP applications. The first (top) row shows the throughput, and the next rows show the execution analysis for the Hybrid TMs.

weighted multi-graph. In this case, the slow-path fallback ratio is very low, so all of the HTM-based schemes provide good results and scalability, and RH NOrec's reduction in HTM conflicts and slow-path restarts is not significant for the overall performance. However, note that the reduction in HTM conflicts and slow-path restarts significantly increases when more threads are added, so for higher concurrency levels RH NOrec should outperform the Hybrid NOrec.

In Yada, threads cooperate to perform a Delaunay refinement, using Ruppert's algorithm. An initial mesh is provided as input, and threads iterate through the triangles of the mesh to identify those whose minimum angle is below some threshold (i.e., they find triangles that are "too skinny"). When such a triangle is found, the thread adds a new point to the mesh, and then re-triangulates a region around that point to produce a more visually appealing mesh. In this benchmark, most of the transactions are heavy, long and contending, so the HTM-based schemes suffer from huge overheads, and the RH-NOrec small hardware transactions only introduce additional overheads, manifested in the low success ratio of the HTM prefix and postfix small hardware transactions.

4. Conclusion

We presented the RH NOrec hybrid TM, a new version of Hybrid NOrec that provides safety and improved scalability at the same time. The RH NOrec HTM fast-paths are fully safe (or opaque), and do not require special code to detect and handle runtime errors.

The core idea of RH NOrec is the mixed NORec slow-path that uses two short hardware transactions, the HTM postfix and HTM prefix, to reduce the HTM conflicts and the slow-path restarts. Of course, because of the limited concurrency available on the Haswell chips and the HyperThreading penalties, one must take our positive results here only as an indicator of the potential of RH NOrec to scale. Our hope is that as higher concurrency processors with HTM support are introduced, this potential will indeed pan out.

Acknowledgments

Support is gratefully acknowledged from the National Science Foundation under grants CCF-1217921, CCF-1301926, and IIS-1447786, the Department of Energy under grant ER26116/DE-SC0008923, and the Oracle and Intel corporations.

References

[1] A. Adl-Tabatabai, T. Shpeisman, and J. Gottschlich. Draft specification of transactional language constructs for c++, 2012. URL `https://sites.google.com/site/tmforcplusplus`.

[2] D. Alistarh, P. Eugster, M. Herlihy, A. Matveev, and N. Shavit. Stacktrack: an automated transactional approach to concurrent memory reclamation. In D. C. A. Bulterman, H. Bos, A. I. T. Rowstron, and P. Druschel, editors, *EuroSys*, page 25. ACM, 2014. ISBN 978-1-4503-2704-6.

[3] H. W. Cain, M. M. Michael, B. Frey, C. May, D. Williams, and H. Le. Robust architectural support for transactional memory in the power architecture. In *ISCA*, pages 225–236, 2013.

[4] I. Calciu, J. Gottschlich, T. Shpeisman, G. Pokam, and M. Herlihy. Invyswell: a hybrid transactional memory for haswell's restricted transactional memory. In J. N. Amaral and J. Torrellas, editors, *International Conference on Parallel Architectures and Compilation, PACT '14, Edmonton, AB, Canada, August 24-27, 2014*, pages 187–200. ACM, 2014. ISBN 978-1-4503-2809-8. . URL `http://doi.acm.org/10.1145/2628071.2628086`.

[5] D. Christie, J.-W. Chung, S. Diestelhorst, M. Hohmuth, M. Pohlack, C. Fetzer, M. Nowack, T. Riegel, P. Felber, P. Marlier, and E. Rivière. Evaluation of amd's advanced synchronization facility within a complete transactional memory stack. In *Proceedings of the 5th European conference on Computer systems*, pages 27–40, New York, NY, USA, 2010. ACM.

[6] L. Dalessandro, M. F. Spear, and M. L. Scott. Norec: streamlining stm by abolishing ownership records. In *Proceedings of the 15th ACM SIGPLAN Symposium on Principles and Practice of Parallel Programming*, PPoPP '10, pages 67–78, New York, NY, USA, 2010. ACM. ISBN 978-1-60558-877-3. . URL `http://doi.acm.org/10.1145/1693453.1693464`.

[7] L. Dalessandro, F. Carouge, S. White, Y. Lev, M. Moir, M. L. Scott, and M. F. Spear. Hybrid norec: a case study in the effectiveness of best effort hardware transactional memory. *SIGPLAN Not.*, 46(3):39–52, Mar. 2011. ISSN 0362-1340. . URL `http://doi.acm.org/10.1145/1961296.1950373`.

[8] P. Damron, A. Fedorova, Y. Lev, V. Luchangco, M. Moir, and D. Nussbaum. Hybrid transactional memory. *SIGPLAN Not.*, 41(11):336–346, Oct. 2006. ISSN 0362-1340. . URL `http://doi.acm.org/10.1145/1168918.1168900`.

[9] D. Dice, O. Shalev, and N. Shavit. Transactional locking II. In *Proc. of the 20th International Symposium on Distributed Computing (DISC 2006)*, pages 194–208, 2006.

[10] D. Dice, T. L. Harris, A. Kogan, Y. Lev, and M. Moir. Hardware extensions to make lazy subscription safe. *CoRR*, abs/1407.6968, 2014.

[11] N. Diegues and P. Romano. Self-tuning intel transactional synchronization extensions. In *11th International Conference on Autonomic Computing (ICAC 14)*, pages 209–219, Philadelphia, PA, June 2014. USENIX Association. ISBN 978-1-931971-11-9.

[12] google-perftools. Tcmalloc : Thread-caching malloc, 2014. URL `http://goog-perftools.sourceforge.net/doc/tcmalloc.html`.

[13] R. Guerraoui and M. Kapalka. On the correctness of transactional memory. In *PPoPP '08: Proceedings of the 13th ACM SIGPLAN Symposium on Principles and practice of parallel programming*, pages 175–184, New York, NY, USA, 2008. ACM. ISBN 978-1-59593-795-7. .

[14] Intel. Transactional synchronization in haswell, 2012. URL `https://software.intel.com/en-us/blogs/2012/02/07/transactional-synchronization-in-haswell`.

[15] S. Kumar, M. Chu, C. J. Hughes, P. Kundu, and A. Nguyen. Hybrid transactional memory. In *Proceedings of the eleventh ACM SIGPLAN symposium on Principles and practice of parallel programming*, PPoPP '06, pages 209–220, New York, NY, USA, 2006. ACM. ISBN 1-59593-189-9. . URL `http://doi.acm.org/10.1145/1122971.1123003`.

[16] Y. Lev, M. Moir, and D. Nussbaum. Phtm: Phased transactional memory. In *In Workshop on Transactional Computing (Transact), 2007. research.sun.com/scalable/pubs/ TRANSACT2007PhTM.pdf*, 2007.

[17] V. Marathe, M. Spear, and M. Scott. Scalable techniques for transparent privatization in software transactional memory. *Parallel Processing, International Conference on*, 0:67–74, 2008. ISSN 0190-3918. .

[18] A. Matveev and N.Shavit. Reduced hardware transactions: a new approach to hybrid transactional memory. In *SPAA*, pages 11–22, 2013.

[19] T. Riegel, P. Marlier, M. Nowack, P. Felber, and C. Fetzer. Optimizing hybrid transactional memory: the importance of nonspeculative operations. In *Proceedings of the 23rd ACM symposium on Parallelism in algorithms and architectures*, SPAA '11, pages 53–64, New York, NY, USA, 2011. ACM. ISBN 978-1-4503-0743-7. . URL `http://doi.acm.org/10.1145/1989493.1989501`.

[20] W. Ruan, Y. Liu, and M. Spear. Stamp need not be considered harmful. In *TRANSACT 2014 Workshop, Salt Lake City, Utah, USA*, 2014.

[21] R. M. Yoo, C. J. Hughes, K. Lai, and R. Rajwar. Performance evaluation of intel transactional synchronization extensions for high-performance computing. In *Proceedings of the International Conference on High Performance Computing, Networking, Storage and Analysis*, SC '13, pages 19:1–19:11, New York, NY, USA, 2013. ACM. ISBN 978-1-4503-2378-9. . URL `http://doi.acm.org/10.1145/2503210.2503232`.

Synchronization Using Remote-Scope Promotion

Marc S. Orr[†§], Shuai Che[§], Ayse Yilmazer[§], Bradford M. Beckmann[§], Mark D. Hill[†§], David A. Wood[†§]

[†]University of Wisconsin–Madison
Computer Sciences

{morr, markhill, david}@cs.wisc.edu

[§]AMD Research

{Shuai.Che, Ayse.Yilmazer, Brad.Beckmann}@amd.com

Abstract

Heterogeneous system architecture (HSA) and OpenCL™ define *scoped synchronization* to facilitate low overhead communication across a subset of threads. Scoped synchronization works well for static sharing patterns, where consumer threads are known *a priori*. It works poorly for dynamic sharing patterns (e.g., work stealing) where programmers cannot use a faster small scope due to the rare possibility that the work is stolen by a thread in a distant slower scope. This puts programmers in a conundrum: optimize the common case by synchronizing at a faster small scope or use work stealing at a slower large scope.

In this paper, we propose to extend scoped synchronization with *remote-scope promotion*. This allows the most frequent sharers to synchronize through a small scope. Infrequent sharers synchronize by promoting that remote small scope to a larger shared scope. Synchronization using remote-scope promotion provides performance robustness for dynamic workloads, where the benefits provided by scoped synchronization and work stealing are hard to anticipate. Compared to a naïve baseline, static scoped synchronization alone achieves a 1.07x speedup on average and dynamic work stealing alone achieves a 1.18x speedup on average. In contrast, synchronization using remote-scope promotion achieves a robust 1.25x speedup on average, across a diverse set of graph benchmarks and inputs.

Categories and Subject Descriptors C.1.4 [**Processor Architectures**]: Parallel Architectures; D.1.3 [**Programming Techniques**]: Concurrent Programming

Keywords graphics processing unit (GPU); memory model; scope promotion; scoped synchronization; work stealing

ASPLOS '15, March 14 - 18, 2015, Istanbul, Turkey

http://dx.doi.org/10.1145/2694344.2694350

1. Introduction

As processors evolve to support more threads, synchronizing among those threads becomes increasingly expensive. This is particularly true for massively-threaded, throughput-oriented architectures, such as graphics processing units (GPUs), which do not support CPU-style "read-for-ownership" coherence protocols. Instead, these systems maintain coherence by "pushing" data to a common level of the memory hierarchy, accessible by all threads, which acts as the global coherence point. After synchronizing, threads must then ensure that they "pull" data from this common memory level (e.g., by invalidating their caches). For discrete and integrated GPU architectures, the global coherence point occurs at the last level cache (LLC) and memory controller, respectively, incurring very high latency. Many applications cannot amortize these high synchronization delays, which limits their performance on GPUs.

One approach to reducing synchronization latency is *scoped synchronization*, which partitions threads into subgroups called scopes. Threads in the same scope can synchronize with each other through a common, but non-global (i.e., scoped) coherence point. General-purpose GPU (GPGPU) languages like OpenCL 1.2 and CUDA have historically provided limited forms of scoped synchronization like work-group barriers [1][2]. Recently, heterogeneous system architecture (HSA) and OpenCL 2.0 (which closely follows HSA) introduced more general scoped synchronization primitives based on acquire/release semantics [3]. For example, in HSA, synchronization operations are tagged with one of the following scope modifiers: work-item (`wi`, a GPU thread), wavefront (`wv`), work-group (`wg`), component (`cmp`), or system (`sys`).

Scoped synchronization works well for static communication patterns, where producers and consumers have well-defined, stable relationships. Figure 1 (a) depicts an example of a *static local* sharing pattern, where two OpenCL work-groups, `wg0` and `wg1`, operate on separate data (`data0` and `data1`, respectively). Work-items within `wg0` use wg-scoped synchronization to coordinate operations on `data0`;

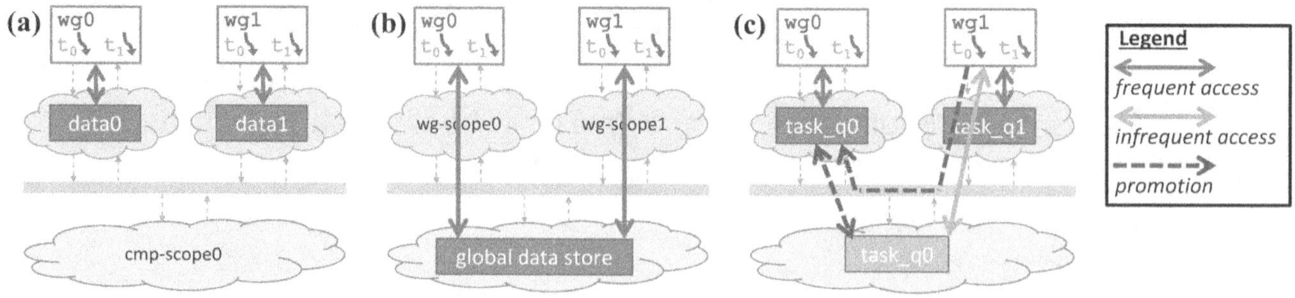

Figure 1. (a) Static local sharing. (b) Dynamic global sharing. (c) Dynamic local sharing.

wg-scoped operations are appropriate because only work-items from wg0 operate on data0. Similarly, work-items in wg1 use wg-scoped synchronization to operate on data1. Static local sharing is supported in OpenCL 2.0.

A larger scope (i.e., cmp scope) is required when data are shared by work-items in different work-groups. An example of this communication pattern, which we call *dynamic global* sharing, is shown in Figure 1 (b). In this scenario, work-items in wg0 and wg1 read and write a global data store. Component scoped synchronization guarantees that reads and writes to the global data store occur at a scope that is visible to all of the work-items. Dynamic global sharing can be expressed in both OpenCL and CUDA [4].

A third important sharing pattern is *dynamic local*, which occurs when a subset of work-items frequently access data within a smaller scope, but non-local work-items occasionally desire ad-hoc access. A common example of dynamic local sharing is work stealing, a scheduling policy that provides dynamic load balancing and is employed by several prominent CPU task runtimes including: Cilk, OpenMP, Intel's Threading Building Blocks (TBB), and Microsoft's Task Parallel Library (TPL) [5][6][7][8]. Figure 1 (c) illustrates work-groups wg0 and wg1 mostly accessing their local task queues: task_q0 and task_q1, respectively. When a work-item finds its local task queue empty, it steals work from another task queue. Stealing mitigates load imbalance.

Ideally, accesses to the local task queue could be optimized with local synchronization. Unfortunately, scoped synchronization, as currently defined in HSA 1.0 and OpenCL 2.0, cannot efficiently support dynamic local sharing. To understand why, consider the work-stealing scenario depicted in Figure 1 (c). There are two scenarios to consider. First, when a work-item accesses its local task queue, it would like to use a smaller scope (e.g., wg scope) to reduce synchronization overheads. However, in the second scenario where a work-item steals work from another task queue, it must use a larger common scope (e.g., cmp scope). Scoped synchronization requires producers to synchronize at a scope that encompasses all of their consumers. Thus, because a stealer can be any work-item in the GPU, a work-stealing runtime requires all task queue synchronization to occur at the larger scope (i.e., cmp scope in this example). This means that smaller scopes cannot be used to optimize dynamic local sharing patterns like work stealing.

In this paper, we extend scoped synchronization to support dynamic local sharing using *remote-scope promotion*. Referring back to Figure 1 (c), work-items in wg1 read from task_q0 by promoting the scope (e.g., wg scope) of the most recent synchronization event on task_q0 to a larger common scope (e.g., cmp scope) that encompasses work-items in wg0 and wg1. Similarly, work-items in wg1 modify task_q0 by promoting the scope of the next future synchronization operation on task_q0 to a common scope.

Remote-scope promotion naturally builds on hardware mechanisms prevalent in GPUs today and only requires a few minor modifications. Detailed simulation results show that remote-scope promotion leads to robust performance improvements across a diverse set of graph benchmarks and inputs.

To summarize, our contributions are:

- We identify that scoped synchronization, as defined in HSA 1.0 and OpenCL 2.0, limits dynamic local sharing.
- We propose a new synchronization semantic—remote-scope promotion— that allows a work-item to communicate outside of its scope hierarchy.
- We propose a hardware implementation for synchronization using remote-scope promotion that requires few changes to a state-of-the-art GPU.
- We evaluate our work for several emerging graph workloads and show that remote synchronization is 17% faster than scoped synchronization alone and 6% faster than work stealing alone.

2. GPU Architecture & Programming

This section reviews the GPU's hierarchical design and relates it to the GPU's relaxed memory model. Specifically, Section 2.1 describes how the HSA hierarchy maps to GPU hardware. Next, Section 2.2 explains how HSA extends acquire/release synchronization with scopes, corresponding to the HSA hierarchy, to minimize the cost of synchronization on GPUs. Finally, Section 2.3 illustrates how GPU synchronization is implemented through an example.

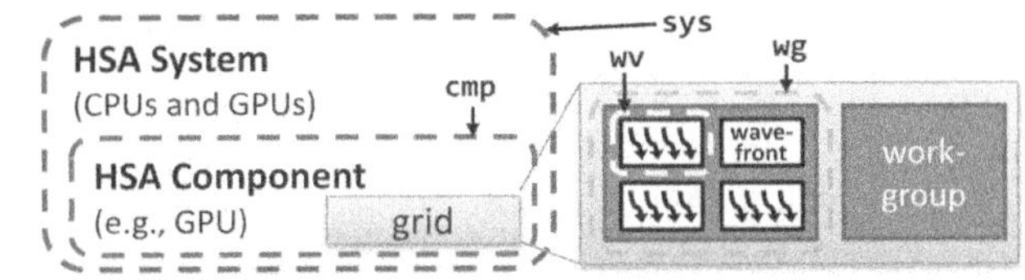

Figure 2. HSA's hierarchy of work-items.

2.1 The GPU Hierarchical Memory Model

GPUs attain high throughput by targeting massively parallel code that can be executed by thousands of threads. The GPU programming model incorporates hierarchy to help programmers organize threads, called work-items in HSA and OpenCL, in a GPU-efficient way. Figure 2 shows the HSA hierarchy of work-items [3]. An *HSA system* is composed of one or more *HSA components*, defined as a GPU for this paper. GPUs execute *grids*, which are sets of work-items that execute the same function at the same time. This organization, called single instruction multiple thread (SIMT), helps GPUs operate efficiently. The work-items within a grid are sub-divided into *work-groups*. Work-items within a work-group are scheduled together and can communicate with each other much faster than with work-items in other work-groups. Finally, an HSA component dynamically partitions work-groups into even smaller sets, called *wavefronts*, to match the GPU's execution width.

The example HSA-compatible GPU architecture illustrated in Figure 3 corresponds to the software hierarchy of work-items. A wavefront executes on single instruction multiple data (SIMD) units, which are sets of functional units that execute in lockstep. A work-group executes on a single compute unit (CU), which is composed of multiple SIMD units (four shown). Typically each CU also includes a private L1 data cache. CUs within a GPU share a common L2 cache that is used to communicate across a grid.

2.2 Scoped Synchronization Overview

HSA adopts acquire/release semantics from the C++ standard [9]. First, we describe how acquire/release synchronization works in C++. Next, we describe how HSA extends these semantics with scopes [10][11]. It is common to couple a synchronization operation with a memory instruction (e.g., *load acquire*, *store release*, etc.). Hardware implementations for acquire and release must do two things. First, they must correctly order memory operations around synchronization (i.e., acquire and release). This means that memory operations that occur after an acquire in program order cannot execute before that acquire (i.e., an acquire acts as a downward memory fence). Similarly, memory operations that occur before a release in program order cannot execute after that release (i.e., a release acts as an upward memory fence). In this work, GPU work-items execute in-order and block on loads; these two properties

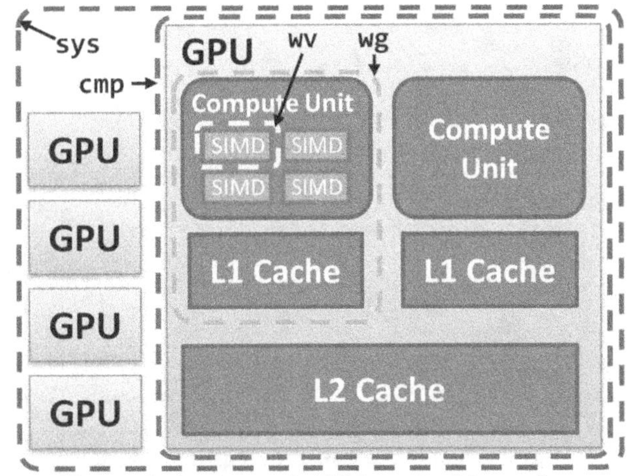

Figure 3. An example HSA cache hierarchy.

guarantee that a load will never be reordered around a synchronization operation. Stores are ordered by tracking their addresses in a hardware first-in/first-out (FIFO) buffer; this mechanism is described in detail in Section 2.3.

The second responsibility of hardware is to ensure that consumers see updates to memory made earlier by producers. Consumer work-items that execute an acquire "pull" the current global view of memory. The GPU implements a pull by invalidating the consumer's private caches, which prevents reading stale data. Producer work-items execute a release to globally "push" their updates to consumers. The GPU implements a push by flushing the producer's dirty cached data, to propagate it to consumers.

To limit synchronization penalties, HSA extends acquire/release semantics with scopes. Specifically, HSA defines the following scopes: work-item (`wi`), wavefront (`wv`), work-group (`wg`), component (`cmp`), and system (`sys`). Each scope corresponds to a different granularity of execution shown in Figure 2. Scopes can be applied to synchronization operations to limit the depth of the hierarchy that they synchronize to. For example, `wg`-scoped synchronization only needs to access the respective work-group's L1 cache since the entire work-group is scheduled on the same CU. Figure 3 shows how scopes are mapped to hardware.

Sequentially consistent for heterogeneous race free (SC for HRF) memory models were proposed to help programmers reason about scoped synchronization [10]. They extend sequentially consistent for data race free (SC for DRF) memory models with scoping rules. Two models were proposed. HRF-direct requires work-items to communicate through the same scope. HRF-indirect extends HRF-direct to allow transitive chains of communication through different scopes. HRF-Relaxed adds scope inclusion to both models [11]. We build on HRF-indirect-relaxed.

2.3 Scoped Synchronization Implementation

GPUs use simple write-through mechanisms to implement a relaxed memory consistency model. For example, many

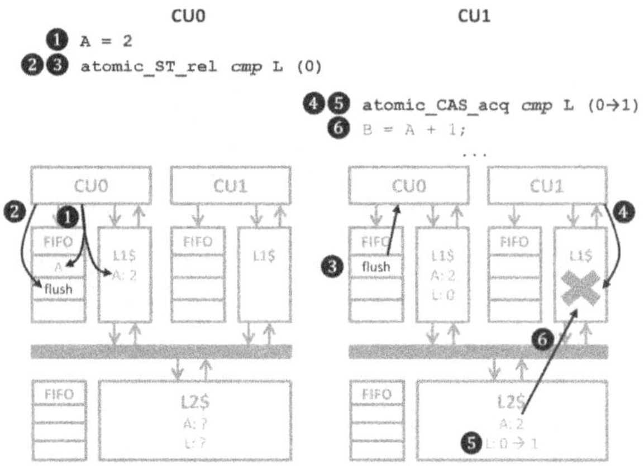

Figure 4. GPU release and acquire operation.

GPU architectures allows stores to complete without waiting for coherence operations, avoiding throughput bottlenecks caused by invalidation traffic [12]. In contrast, CPUs maintain the single-writer/multiple-reader invariant by stalling writes until all of their invalidations are acknowledged [13][14]. The GPU approach avoids invalidation traffic, but synchronization operations are expensive. In particular, release operations must wait until all prior writes reach the correct scope. Naïvely this can be achieved by tracking each outstanding write and waiting until all outstanding writes complete.

A better approach, proposed by Hechtman *et al.* [15], uses a FIFO at each cache level to track dirty addresses. This technique is demonstrated in Figure 4. Every write inserts its address at the FIFO's tail (time ❶), and when an address reaches the FIFO's head, its associated cache block is written to the next level of the hierarchy (if necessary). Release operations are handled by simply inserting flush markers into the FIFO (time ❷); the release completes when all prior addresses in the FIFO are written through to the appropriate scope (time ❸) and the flush marker reaches the FIFO's head. This FIFO approach for releases is assumed for this paper.

Hechtman *et al.* also proposed to use cache-block invalidations, but that adds considerable hardware complexity. Instead, we assume acquire operations simply invalidate all caches encompassed by the acquire's scope. Cache invalidates effectively "pull" the latest version of data from the distant levels of the memory hierarchy by removing closer cached data that have become stale. The invalidations themselves are cheap (i.e., a single-cycle flash-invalidate), but they decrease the effectiveness of caching and cause unnecessary inter-wavefront interference. Referring back to Figure 4, CU1 performs an acquire by invalidating its L1 cache (time ❹). The atomic compare-and-swap (`CAS`) operation is performed at the operation's respective scope. Specifically, the L2 cache controller performs the atomic read-modify-write (RMW) operation at time ❺ on address `L`. Finally, the value of `A` is returned at time ❻.

3. Extending Scoped Synchronization

Scoped synchronization is an exciting development in GPU programming models. Unfortunately, it currently suffers some severe programming limitations. Section 3.1 describes these limitations and Section 3.2 proposes our solution: synchronization using remote-scope promotion.

3.1 Limitations of Scoped Synchronization in HSA 1.0

When using scoped synchronization, programmers must manage both the level of visibility and the order of memory operations [10]. This is different than non-scoped synchronization, which only requires programmers to reason about order. To accommodate scopes, memory models apply scope modifiers to memory operations. In HSA, memory operations are tagged with one of the following scope modifiers: work-item (`wi`), wavefront (`wv`), work-group (`wg`), component (`cmp`), and system (`sys`).

A scope instance is a particular instantiation of a scope. For example, in Figure 5 `wg0`'s work-group scope instance is `wg-scope0` and `wg1`'s work-group scope instance is `wg-scope1`. HSA scope modifiers do not allow different scope instances to be distinguished. A work-item is associated with exactly one scope instance at each level of the scope hierarchy. This means that for a particular memory address to be visible to a work-item, that address must have been "pushed" (i.e., released) to a scope instance that is associated with (i.e., visible to) that work-item. This is because a work-item cannot "pull" (i.e., acquire) from a scope instance with which it is not associated. In other words, HSA defines push-pull semantics that require producers to push data to a scope that they share with their consumers.

These semantics make it difficult to optimize dynamic local sharing because consumers asynchronously read from producers. For example, in a work-stealing runtime, producers do not know when a subset of their consumers (i.e., the stealers) will read their data. Thus, work-items must conservatively push data to a scope that is visible to all consumers. Otherwise, a stealer may read stale data.

This conundrum is demonstrated in Figure 5 (a). Initially, at time ❶, a queue (`task_q0`) is instantiated for work-group 0 (`wg0`) in the component scope. In the common case, `wg0` is the only work-group that reads and writes `task_q0`. Thus the programmer would like to use work-group scoped synchronization to coordinate operations on `task_q0` (time ❷). Unfortunately, doing so would preclude work-items in a different work-group from stealing data from `task_q0`. For example, if a work-item in work-group 1 (`wg1`) were to read from `task_q0` (time ❸), it might find stale data in the component scope. Note that `wg1` cannot correctly use work-group scoped synchronization to operate on `wg0`'s scope instance.

It is important to note that the sequence of events in Figure 5 (a) would be correct in the absence of scopes. For

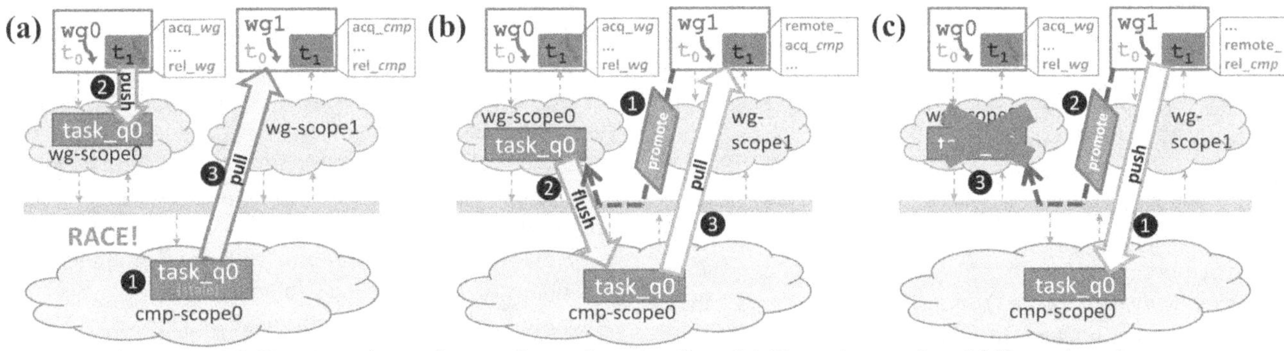

Figure 5. (a) Shortcomings of scoped synchronization. (b) Remote acquire. (c) Remote release.

example, in a traditional CPU, a release operation would make data visible to all threads in the system (i.e., all synchronization would occur at an implicit global scope).

3.2 Motivating Scope Promotion

Today, HSA requires work-items to synchronize through a scope that encompasses all sharers. This is because work-items are only able to synchronize with other work-items that are in the same scope hierarchy. To improve performance for dynamic-local sharing, it would be better if work-items could synchronize through a scope that encompasses the most frequent sharers instead of all possible sharers. Scoped synchronization, as defined in HSA and OpenCL, implicitly targets scope instances within the caller's scope hierarchy. A key insight is that extending this semantic to allow synchronization beyond the caller's scope hierarchy enables better use of scopes.

Towards this end, we propose synchronization using remote-scope promotion: a new semantic that allows a work-item to order memory accesses with a scope instance outside of its scope hierarchy. To access data in a remote scope, a work-item first promotes the remote scope to a larger common scope. After the promotion completes, the work-item synchronizes through the larger common scope. This sequence is shown in Figure 5 (b). At time ❶, wg1 sends a message to promote wg-scope0 to the shared component scope. Promotion is carried out by flushing dirty data in wg-scope0 to cmp-scope0 (time ❷). wg1 can then pull the data with a cmp-scoped acquire (time ❸).

A similar procedure is used to modify data in a remote scope (e.g., task_q0's head pointer). First, the data is written to a larger shared scope. Then the remote scope is promoted to that larger common scope. Figure 5 (c) illustrates how this works. At time ❶, wg1 writes data through to the shared component scope; this is achieved by performing a cmp-scoped release. Next, wg1 sends a message to promote wg-scope0 to the component scope (time ❷). In this case, promotion is carried out by invalidating dirty data in wg-scope0 (time ❸). This sequence guarantees that wg0 will read updates written to the component scope by wg1.

Using scope promotion is surprisingly easy. Consider the tricky lock-free code in Figure 6 for stealing from a queue. This function is a part of an intricate work-stealing algorithm originally proposed by Arora *et al.* [16] and presented in the context of GPUs by Cederman and Tsigas [17]. We have augmented the code with remote synchronization highlighted in ***bold italics***. The primary difference is that the synchronization memory operations are trivially labeled with a remote memory ordering. Also, these operations must synchronize through the correct scope. The next section defines remote-scope promotion more precisely and proposes an implementation.

4. Remote-Scope Promotion

Synchronization using remote-scope promotion allows a work-item to pull and push data from a scope outside of its scope hierarchy without requiring a specific scope instance to be explicitly identified. Instead, programmers identify the common scope that a work-item shares with the target scope instance that the data resides in (e.g., the component scope encompasses wg0 and wg1 in the prior example).

In this section, we extend a current GPU instruction set to support remote synchronization and then we describe how these instructions can be implemented with only modest changes to current GPUs.

```
Task steal(Queue *q, Queue_Elem *val) {
 int tail = remoteRead(q->tail,
                        acq, wg cmp);
 int oldHead = q->head;
 if (tail <= oldHead)
    return NULL;
 Task task = q->contents[oldHead];
 int newHead = oldHead + 1;

 if (remoteCAS(&q->head, oldHead, newHead,
             ar, wg cmp))
    return task;

 return abort;
}
```

Figure 6. Steal with remote synchronization.

4.1 Defining Remote-Scope Promotion

We introduce three remote synchronization operations to carry out the promotion semantic described in Section 3.2:

Remote Acquire (`rm_acq`) ordering allows consumer work-items to acquire data produced at any scope instance. A remote acquire operation on address `L` comprises two steps: (1) promote the scope of the last release on address `L` to match the target scope of this remote acquire, (2) perform an acquire on address `L` at the target scope.

Remote Release (`rm_rel`) ordering allows work-items to propagate their updates to external scope instances. A remote release operation on address `L` comprises two steps: (1) perform a release on address `L` at the target scope, (2) promote the scope of the next acquire on address `L` to match to the target scope of this remote release.

Remote Acquire+Release (`rm_ar`) ordering combines the two remote operations above. To keep the presentation both minimal and complete, we label remote RMW operations with acquire+release ordering.

4.2 Implementing Remote-Scope Promotion

Implementing each remote order in a GPU can be thought of in terms of sub-operations. This sequence of sub-operations ensures that proper synchronization is maintained without directly involving the work-items in the remote scope instance.

Remote Acquire ordering ensures that writes performed at a remote scope instance will be seen by the requestor. Three sub-operations are required. (`rm_acq`.1) The first step is to promote the scope of the last release to match the target scope of this acquire. This is achieved by flushing all remote scope instances that are inclusive with the target scope. For example, if the target scope is `cmp`, then all `wg`, `wv`, and `wi` scope instances encompassed by the requestor's `cmp`-scope instance will flush their dirty data out to the requestor's `cmp`-scope instance. These flushes propagate local updates to the target scope. (`rm_acq`.2) Once these flushes complete, an acquire is carried out by invalidating the requestor's scope instances up to the target scope; this guarantees that the requestor will see the latest data. (`rm_acq`.3) Finally, the requestor performs the actual memory operation, such as a load, at the target scope.

Remote Release ordering ensures that the writes performed by the requestor are guaranteed to be seen by the remote scope instances. Three sub-operations are required. (`rm_rel`.1) First, the requestor performs a release by flushing to the target scope. (`rm_rel`.2) After the flush completes, the associated memory operation, such as a store, proceeds at the target scope[1]. (`rm_rel`.3) Finally, once the memory operation completes, such as the store becomes visible at the target scope, all remote scope instances encompassed by the target scope instance are promoted to the target scope. This is achieved by invalidating them up to the target scope. For example, if the target scope is `cmp`, then all `wg`, `wv`, and `wi` scope instances encompassed by the requestor's `cmp`-scope instance are invalidated, which guarantees that remote work-items will see the latest data.

Remote Acquire+Release ordering combines the sequencing of the other two remote orderings to ensure sequentially consistent execution. Logically, this operation promotes the remote data to the target scope, performs the atomic RMW, and then performs remote invalidations to promote the scope of next acquire to the target scope. Four sub-operations are required. (`rm_ar`.1) The first step is to flush all of the remote scope instances encompassed by the target scope. The requestor also flushes its local data to the target scope to ensure correct operation when the remote scope instance is the same as the requestor's scope instance. (`rm_ar`.2) The requestor also invalidates its local data so that it will execute the RMW at the target scope (this can occur in parallel with the first sub-operation). (`rm_ar`.3) Next, the actual RMW operation is performed at the target scope. (`rm_ar`.4) Finally the instruction completes by invalidating all of the remote scope instances that are encompassed by the target scope, which guarantees that remote work-items will see the update performed by the RMW operation. This implementation ensures that all RMWs to a particular location are globally ordered. Section 4.4.1 discusses this requirement in further detail.

Formalizing Scope Promotion helps to disambiguate corner cases and is discussed in the Appendix. Because we leverage hierarchical memory that provides transitivity, a simple extension of HRF-indirect suffices [10]. Specifically, we build on an extended version of HRF-indirect called HRF-indirect-relaxed [11]. HRF-indirect-relaxed requires each synchronizing release-acquire pair in a transitive sequence to occur at a compatible scope. Our work leverages scope promotion, which allows a work-item to promote the scope of another work-item's acquire/release operations. Thus, the formal model extends HRF-indirect-relaxed to require each synchronizing pair in a transitive sequence to either: (1) have both operations occur at a compatible scope (as in HRF-indirect-relaxed), or (2) one operation must be remote-scoped to promote the pair to a common scope.

4.3 An Example of Remote-Scope Promotion

Figure 7 provides an example of synchronization using remote-scope promotion in a GPU composed of two compute units (CUs). We assume the GPU memory system presented in Section 2, which includes FIFOs at each level of the cache hierarchy to track dirty addresses. The example illustrates how a critical section protected by a lock,

[1] Potential races between the executing the memory operation (step 2) and remote invalidations (step 3) are avoided by stalling accesses to the cache line at the target scope until the remote operation completes.

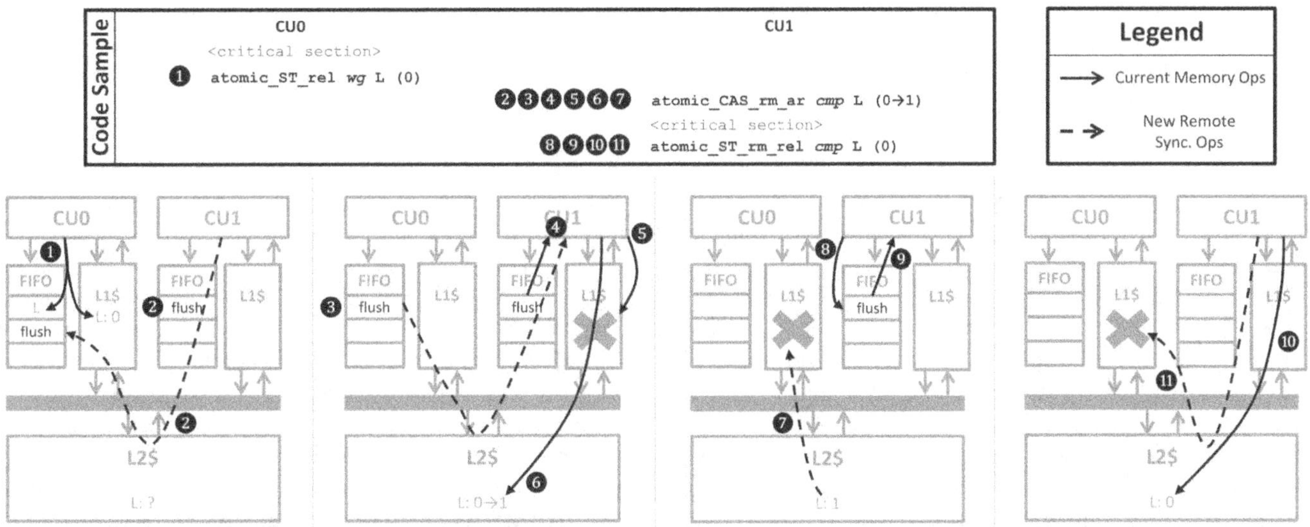

Figure 7. An example of synchronization using remote-scope promotion in a GPU.

which is frequently accessed by a single work-group, can be occasionally accessed in an ad-hoc manner by work-items outside of that work-group. The example assumes that the single work-group frequently accessing the critical section is executing on CU0 and the programmer has specified work-group scope for those synchronizing instructions. The work-items outside of that work-group execute on CU1 and use remote synchronization operations to properly synchronize with the work-group accesses. The example highlights that the work-items performing the remote synchronization operations encounter the primary performance overhead. Meanwhile, the work-group executing on CU0 encounters minimal overhead using work-group scoped instructions in the common case. The text that follows is labeled to clarify the corresponding event.

atomic_ST_rel (store-release on CU0 at wg-scope): The example in Figure 7 begins with a work-item executing on CU0 reaching the end of a critical section. The work-item issues a wg-scoped store release to notify other work-items that the critical section is open. Since the store release is at the work-group scope, no flush marker is inserted into the local FIFO. Instead, the store operation is immediately performed at the local L1 cache and the store's address L is inserted into the local FIFO (time ❶).

atomic_CAS_rm_ar (remote-acquire+release on CU1 at cmp-scope): Next, the work-group on CU1 wants to enter the critical section. It attempts to do so by using a remote synchronization operation to pull the valid data from the work-group executing on CU0. Specifically, at time ❷, a work-item on CU1 executes a CAS at cmp-scope with remote acquire+release ordering. The sub-operations are carried out as follows. (rm_ar.1) First, CU0's wg-scope instance must be promoted (i.e., flushed) to the component scope. This is achieved by broadcasting (via the on-chip network) a cmp-scope flush marker into all FIFOs in the component (including the FIFO of the requestor[2]). At time ❸, the remote flush marker reaches the head of its FIFO indicating that all prior updates by CU0 have propagated to the component scope and CU1 is notified at time ❹. (rm_ar.2) At time ❺, CU1 invalidates its local cache[3]; this is required for the RMW to execute at component scope. The promotion is complete.

An important correctness issue is that all RMW operations must be properly ordered. The remote acquire+release operation has temporarily promoted the wg-scope ordering point to the component scope. Thus, to maintain a single ordering point, all L1 cache controllers connected to the encompassing scope (i.e., component in this example) stall acquires, releases, and RMWs when they begin processing the flush marker sent from CU1.

(rm_ar.3) At time ❻, CU1 proceeds with the RMW (i.e., CAS reads 0 → writes 1) at the L2 cache and the work-item on CU1 gains access to the critical section. Synchronization is re-enabled at CU1's L1 cache. (rm_ar.4) Finally, the operation completes by promoting the scope of the next acquire to component scope. An invalidation message is sent to all remote L1 caches. CU0 receives the message and invalidates its L1 caches at time ❼. This ensures that CU0 will see the latest data at the component scope. The invalidation message also re-enables synchronization at the respective wg-scope. It is important to note that this final remote invalidation does not stall the remote acquire+release instruction. Rather, it just needs to be performed before the next acquire operation executed by each remote CU.

[2] In this example, both work-items reside on different CUs. Flushing the dirty data in the requestor's L1 cache is required when they reside on the same CU because the RMW operates directly at the L2 cache.

[3] The invalidation can execute in parallel with the flushes.

atomic_ST_rm_rel (remote-release on CU1 at cmp-scope): After exiting the critical section, CU1 issues a store with remote release ordering to release the lock. The sub-operations are carried out as follows. (`rm_rel`.1) At time ❽, a flush marker is inserted into CU1's FIFO to release updates, local to CU1, to the component scope. At time ❾, the flush marker reaches the head of the queue, indicating that all prior writes by CU1 are visible at the component scope. (`rm_rel`.2) Now assured that all prior writes are visible, at time ❿, CU1 performs the store operation, writing value '0' to address `L`. (`rm_rel`.3) Finally, at time ⓫, CU1 completes the remote release by invalidating all remote L1 caches encompassed by the component scope, which promotes the next acquire to the component scope.

This example illustrates that synchronization using remote-scope promotion defers overheads to the infrequent case (e.g., stealing) rather than the frequent case (e.g., accessing the local task queue). In addition, the example highlights that remote synchronization seamlessly builds on top of current state-of-the-art GPU memory systems (Section 2) with only a few additional mechanisms.

4.4 Hardware Support for Remote Synchronization

Assuming that GPUs already use per-CU FIFOs to track the partial order of writes and releases, remote-scope promotion requires three additional mechanisms.

The first allows work-items to send commands (e.g., flush and invalidate) and acknowledgments (acks) to other (non-local) CUs. These messages are distinguished in Figure 7 by dashed lines. For example, at time ❷, CU1 inserts a flush marker into CU0's FIFO, and at time ❹, CU1 receives an ack that the remote flush is complete. Similarly, at time ⓫, CU1 invalidates CU0's L1 cache.

The second hardware mechanism is the ability to lock cache lines at the targeted scope for remote-release, as described in Section 4.2. Finally, the third hardware mechanism is enabling remote-acquire+release to block issuing new synchronization operations within the target scope. In particular, Section 4.4.1 describes how remote RMW operations establish a valid *coherence order* using this third mechanism. Alternative solutions may be more efficient, but will require more hardware complexity to handle the longer duration of remote RMWs and merging multiple versions of the cache line within the target scope.

4.4.1 Digging Deep: Ordering Remote RMWs

Correctly ordering remote RMWs is particularly dubious and requires careful consideration. For instance, Hower *et al.* [10] previously identified that race-free code using scoped synchronization must observe a total order of RMWs (referred to as atomics in that work). More recently, Gaster *et al.* [11] and the HSA memory model [3] formally defined this requirement by stating that a GPU implementation must provide a "coherent order" for all accesses to a single memory location. In addition, they state that "the read and write components of an atomic RMW must be adjacent in coherent order." Thus it is necessary for our proposed hardware to ensure that all race-free RMW (both relaxed and non-relaxed) operations are totally ordered.

Our implementation adheres to the principles of the HRF memory models, including the total order of all RMWs. The challenge in ordering RMWs is ensuring that they can immediately observe their place in a location's coherent order (for example, atomic increment instructions that read the previous value). Therefore, remote RMWs must immediately be ordered across all scope instances.

Our solution is to utilize the previously described remote acquire+release ordering rules for all remote RMWs regardless of what ordering the instruction specifies. When a remote RMW is being performed, we stall all RMW operations at L1 caches within the target scope to avoid possible conflicts (i.e., remote scope instance modification vs. modifications at the promoted scope). While heavyweight, this approach ensures correctness and should not impact performance as long as remote RMWs are used sparingly.

5. Methodology

We used gem5 [18] coupled with a proprietary GPU model to evaluate synchronization using remote-scope promotion. The evaluated GPU is based on the design previously shown in Figure 3. It has eight CUs and each CU has four SIMD units. 40 hardware wavefront contexts are time-multiplexed across the four SIMD units using an oldest-job-first scheduling policy. Each CU has a private L1 data cache. There are two instruction caches and each instruction cache is shared by four CUs. All L1 data caches and instruction caches are connected to a unified L2 cache that is then connected to system memory. Details about the baseline GPU configuration can be found in Table 1.

The L1 data caches and L2 cache are write-through and write-no-allocate. Acquire and release operations are implemented as described in Section 2. Specifically, an ac-

Table 1. Simulation configuration

8 Compute Units, each configured as described below:	
Clock	1GHz, 4 SIMD units
Wavefronts (#/scheduler)	40 (each 64 lanes)/oldest-job first
Data cache	16kB, 64B line, 16-way, 4 cycles, delivers one line every cycle
Memory Hierarchy	
L2 cache	512kB, 64B line, 16-way, 24 cycles
1 Instr. cache/4 CUs	32kB, 64B line, 8-way, 4 cycles
DRAM	DDR3, 8 Channels, 500 MHz
Protocol	Write-through, write-no-allocate, acquires trigger scoped flash invalidate, releases trigger scoped FIFO flush
Task Runtime	
8 task queues	1 work-group/queue, 4 wavefronts/work-group

quire operation invalidates the caches between the acquire's wavefront up to the scope of the acquire. Every cache is paired with a FIFO and a release operation flushes the FIFOs from the release's wavefront up to the scope of the release.

We extended the GPU model to support remote-scope promotion. This required adding the new remote synchronization orders proposed in Section 4.1 to the model and modifying the L1-data and L2-cache controllers to carry out remote synchronization, as described in Section 4.2, whenever they encounter a remote operation.

5.1 Workloads

We selected three applications from the Pannotia benchmark suite [19] and evaluated them across a diversity of inputs. Pannotia is a collection of graph workloads implemented in OpenCL. These applications suffer load imbalance when individual work-items process vertices with different numbers of neighbors. It is a challenge to predict the load distributions before running the applications because the resulting load imbalance is dependent on the graph input. The graph applications we evaluated are:

Single-source shortest path (SSSP): Given a source vertex, finds the shortest distances of all other vertices to the source by gradually expanding vertex frontiers.

Graph coloring (color): Iteratively labels a graph with different colors. Individual vertices determine if they should be assigned a new color by evaluating their neighboring vertices each iteration.

PageRank (PR): Estimates the importance of web pages by repeatedly transmitting values among vertices through edges that represent pages and links, respectively.

The graph inputs are chosen from the 9th and 10th DIMACS implementation challenges [20] and a graph for interacting proteins [21]. The inputs that we evaluated for each workload are listed in Table 2. We modified the OpenCL code to use work stealing. Our implementation follows the lock-free algorithm described by Tsigas and Cederman [17]. We allocated and associated a task queue to a work-group composed of four wavefronts. We instantiate eight task queues across the eight CUs. A queue element represents the work consumed by all of the work-items in a work-group. Important operations include: (1) pop, which dequeues an element from the *tail* of the local queue, and (2) steal, which dequeues an element from the *head* of a remote queue. Popping and stealing from different ends of the queues ensures that these operations conflict at most once per queue. Pushing to the tail of the local queue is not necessary for this particular set of workloads.

Table 2. Workloads and inputs

Benchmarks	Graph Inputs
Single Source Shortest Path (SSSP)	dip20090126_MAX (1), USA-road-d.BAY(2), USA-road-d.COL(3)
Graph Coloring (color)	dip20090126_MAX(1), USA-road-d.NY(2), ecology1(3), G3_circuit(4)
PageRank (PR)	cond-mat-2003(1), small-world(2), coAuthorsDBLP(3)

Initially, each task queue is statically assigned work elements (i.e., the graphs' vertices are evenly distributed across the queues). On behalf of the entire work-group, one work-item pops a queue element from its local queue, and application-specific information (e.g., parameters and pointers to the actual work) is provided to all of the work-items in the work-group. When the local queue is empty a work-group attempts to steal an element from a remote queue. The kernel terminates when all of the queues are empty. During the execution, contention may happen, for example, when a pop and steal collide and try to dequeue the same element. The algorithm [17] uses a lock-free solution to ensure these cases are handled efficiently.

5.2 Evaluation Scenarios

Four scenarios are used to evaluate remote synchronization:

Baseline: In the first scenario, called *baseline*, stealing is disabled and global synchronization is used to dequeue elements. Technically, synchronization can be avoided in the baseline scenario because our applications don't enqueue work, but we are interested in how our technique applies beyond this particular set of graph applications.

Scope-only: The second algorithm, called *scope-only*, improves on baseline by replacing global synchronization with scoped synchronization. The scope-only scenario uses optimizations available in OpenCL 2.0 today.

Steal-only: The third algorithm, called *steal-only*, improves on baseline by replacing its static scheduling algorithm with work stealing. Again, this can be achieved using component scoped synchronization in OpenCL 2.0 today.

Rem-sync: Finally, the *rem-sync* scenario applies both scopes and work-stealing to the baseline. This is possible because of the remote-scope promotion technique proposed in this paper.

6. Results

We find that synchronization using remote-scope promotion is able to achieve the benefits of both work stealing and scoped synchronization without compromise. Figure 8 compares remote synchronization (rem-sync) to the other three evaluation scenarios described in Section 5.2. Figure 8 shows that remote synchronization achieves speedups of on average 1.25x over baseline. In contrast, the average scope-only speedup is only 1.07x and the average steal-only speedup is 1.18x. Remote synchronization achieves higher speedup than both the scope-only and steal-only scenarios because is able to optimize for both scopes and dynamic load balancing. As a result, remote synchronization always achieves the maximum or better than the scope-only and steal-only algorithms.

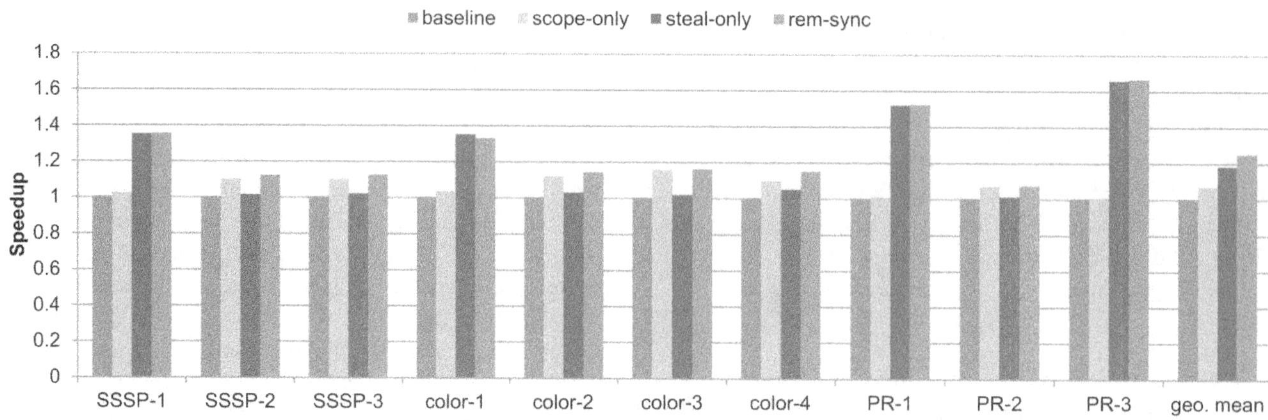

Figure 8. Synchronization using remote-scope promotion quantified.

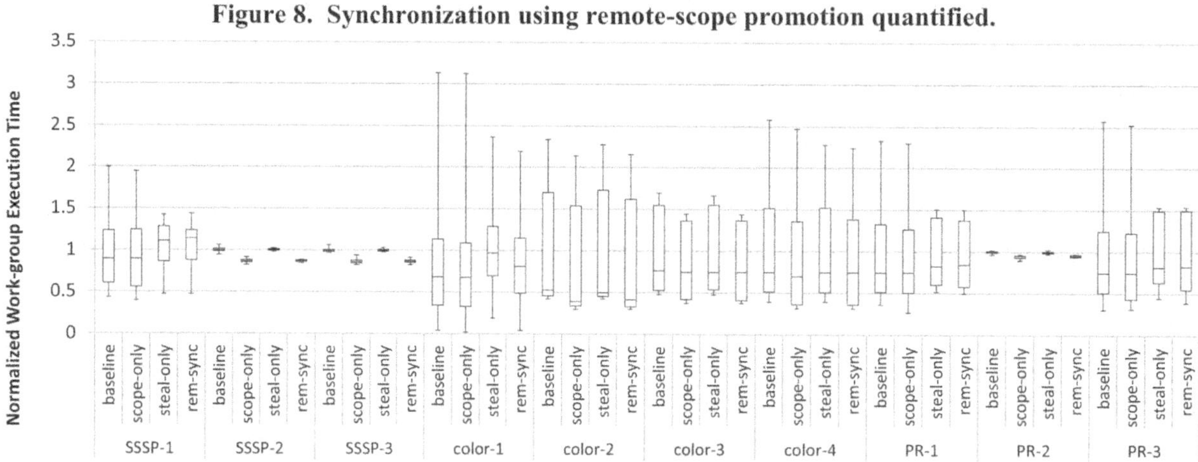

Figure 9. Load imbalance.

The workload/input combinations in Figure 8 clearly demonstrate a variety of behaviors. Some cases benefit from scopes, but are not affected by work stealing. For example, color-3 realizes a 1.16x speedup from scoped synchronization but is hardly impacted by work stealing. At the other extreme is PR-3 which runs more than 1.65x faster with dynamic load balancing, but is not helped by scoped synchronization. Workloads, like color-4, that benefit from both work stealing and scoped synchronization are able to use remote synchronization to optimize both cases at the same time. The key takeaway of Figure 8 is that the dynamic behavior of real workloads cannot be predicted and optimized statically. This fact puts programmers in a dilemma: whether to optimize for scopes or load balance. Remote synchronization eliminates this dilemma.

An important question is: why do some workloads do better with scoped synchronization while others do better with work stealing? In the following sections, we correlate the underlying data movement patterns across the different workload/input combinations to their application behavior.

6.1 Load Balance

Dynamic load balancing is crucial for workloads that have lop-sided data partitions to process. How evenly work is distributed across work-groups largely depends on a workload's input set. We would expect work stealing to accelerate inputs that lead to an uneven distribution of work. Figure 9 shows a box plot that quantifies the load imbalance for each workload/input combination. The box plot shows work-group execution times normalized to the baseline. The boxes in the box plot represent the 25th to 75th percentiles of work-group execution times. The horizontal line inside the box marks the median. Each box also has two tails. The bottom tail marks the minimum work-group execution time and the top tail marks the maximum.

Pannotia workloads execute in iterations. Different iterations may exhibit different load distributions. We find that many workloads with long top tails correspond to inputs that suffer load imbalance within an iteration. For example, SSSP-1, color-1, PR-1, and PR-3 all exhibit long top tails that are effectively reduced by work stealing. This reduction in the maximum work-group execution time ultimately reduces execution time. Interestingly, many of the color benchmarks exhibit long top tails because one iteration takes significantly longer than the others, but the intra-iteration variance is rather small except for color-1, which does benefit from work stealing. In general, the workloads with short boxes and tails correspond to inputs that are

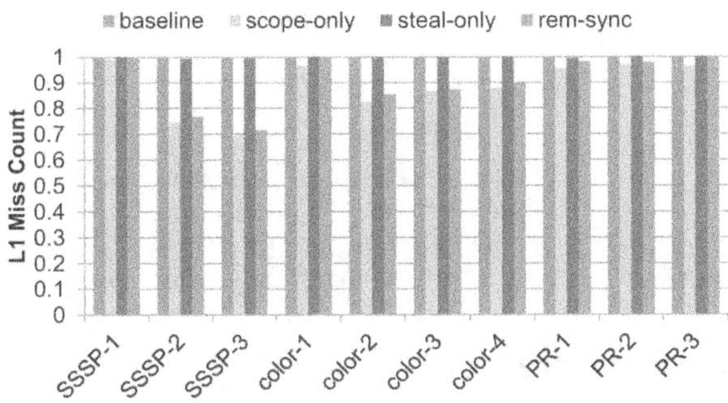

Figure 10. L1 miss rate.

unable to benefit from work stealing because of little variation in work-group execution time within an iteration.

6.2 Cache Behavior

Scoped synchronization is important for workloads that are able to take advantage of the combining provided by the GPU's L1 caches and FIFOs. When global synchronization is used frequently, addresses are unable to reside in the L1 caches long enough to achieve effective combining. In turn, more requests are issued to the L2 cache, which becomes a bandwidth bottleneck. Figure 10 shows the number of L1 cache misses for each algorithm, normalized to the baseline. The baseline, which uses `cmp`-scoped synchronization, suffers many more L1 cache misses than the scope-only algorithm, which uses `wg`-scoped synchronization. The difference in L1 cache misses indicates which workloads will benefit from scoped synchronization. Workload/input combinations that have less than 10% difference in L1 cache misses between the baseline and scope-only scenarios, which includes SSSP-1, color-1, PR-1, PR-2, and PR-3 benefit from scoped synchronization less than workloads with more than 10% difference.

6.3 Limiting Remote Synchronization Overheads

In the dynamic local sharing patterns that remote synchronization is intended for, remote operations should be rare. For example, in a work stealing runtime, the common case is to dequeue work from the local queue. Steals only occur when a local queue becomes empty. The first two columns in Table 3 show the percentage of queue elements that are stolen over each workload's duration. For most workloads, stealing is negligible, which helps explain why many cases don't benefit from work stealing. In contrast, the workloads with the highest amount of load imbalance—SSSP-1, color-1, PR-1, and PR-3—execute the largest number of steals. The surprisingly high number of steals for these workloads is due to our work-stealing algorithm, which steals one task queue element at a time. This policy works best when stolen tasks generate new local tasks, but this is not the case for our workloads. Thus, single-element steals occur frequently when there is significant load imbalance. Table 3 also shows the percentages of failed steal operations. Too many failed steal operations could degrade performance, but fortunately we do not observe significant failures.

Table 3. Steal behavior

	% of queue elements stolen		*% of steals that fail*	
	steal-only	*rem-sync*	*steal-only*	*rem-sync*
SSSP-1	9.0	9.7	1.6	0.7
SSSP-2	0.5	0.6	0.8	3.6
SSSP-3	0.6	0.7	0.6	2.2
color-1	9.6	10.3	0	2.7
color-2	1.2	1.0	0.9	1.1
color-3	0.7	0.4	0	1.2
color-4	1.5	1.4	0.1	0.4
PR-1	5.5	5.5	0	0
PR-2	0.8	0.6	0	0
PR-3	5.1	5.1	0	0

Recall that there are two costs to remote synchronization. The first cost is that caches become less effective (e.g., a remote release will invalidate all non-local caches). The second cost is the up-front latency to carry out a remote operation. For example, a remote acquire has to invalidate the local scope, flush caches in the remote scope, etc. These operations can take hundreds of cycles. Surprisingly, we found that remote synchronization is ~10 times faster than `cmp`-scoped synchronization on average. This is because remote synchronization allows all pop operations to be performed at work-group scope. Replacing `cmp`-scoped synchronization with `wg`-scoped synchronization reduces traffic at the cache controllers because there are less evictions, flushes, and synchronization events. So, in reality, while remote synchronization operations might take more time to service, they take less time overall because they spend less time queued at the cache controllers.

7. Related Work

Prior work studied scoped synchronization in the context of software distributed shared memory for CPUs [22][23]. More recently, Hower *et al.* developed the sequentially consistent for heterogeneous-race-free (SC for HRF) memory model [10] by incorporating scopes into the sequentially consistent for data-race-free (SC for DRF) memory model. Correctly placing synchronization operations in SC for DRF leads to well-defined behavior. In SC for HRF, this is not enough. All synchronization operations must also be labeled with the correct scope. Our work allows a work-item to label a synchronization operation so that it applies to a scope instance other than its own.

In one embodiment of SC for HRF, called HRF-indirect, work-items can transitively push values on behalf of other work-items in their scope instance. HRF-indirect alone is not sufficient to enable dynamic local sharing because the transitive push only applies to a work-item's scope instance hierarchy. In contrast, remote synchronization allows work-items to perform synchronization operations in a scope instance outside of their scope instance hierarchy.

work-item A	work-item B	work-item C
❶ `atomic_CAS_acq_wg &L, 0, 1`		
❷ `enqueue(task_A);`		
❸ `atomic_ST_rel_wg &L, 0`		
	❹ `atomic_CAS_acq_wg &L, 0, 1`	
	❺ `enqueue(task_B);`	
	❻ `atomic_ST_rel_cmp &L, 0`	
		❼ `atomic_CAS_acq_cmp &L, 0, 1`
		❽ `enqueue(task_C);`
		❾ `atomic_ST_rel_cmp &L, 0`

Figure 11. Transitive synchronization. A and B are in the same work-group. A, B, and C are in the same component.

Quickly reacquirable locks (QRL) optimize for dynamic local sharing patterns on CPUs [24]. QRLs can either be in a *biased* state, which reduces the overhead of acquire and release operations, or in a *default* state, which treats the lock normally. To move the QRL from the biased state to the default state (analogous to a *remote acquire* in this paper), a non-biased thread simply updates the state of the lock using the CPU's invalidation-based coherence protocol. This approach cannot be applied to GPUs because their caches do not use an invalidation-based protocol.

Other work on GPU synchronization has not considered scopes. For example, transactional memory (TM) was extended to GPUs to improve the performance of and simplify the use of synchronization [25][26]. One could envision scoped transactions. Singh *et al.* proposed temporal coherence, which is a time-based self-invalidation coherence protocol for GPUs [27]. Scopes could potentially be applied to temporal coherence to reduce self-invalidations.

Previous work surveyed dynamic load-balancing policies for GPUs. Hower *et al.* evaluated work sharing with scoped synchronization [10], but did not consider work stealing due to limitations in SC for HRF. They found that it performs well, but our results are even more impressive. Tseng *et al.* compared work donation and work stealing on a GPU without scoped synchronization [28]. Both scheduling policies showed similar performance, but they preferred work donation because it enables fixed-size queues. However, neither work donation nor work stealing can use scopes without support for remote synchronization.

8. Conclusion

This paper proposed a new synchronization semantic: synchronization using remote-scope promotion. The basic idea is that the work-items that most frequently access shared data do so at the smallest scope possible. Work-items that access that shared data less frequently do so by promoting the small remote scope to a larger compatible scope.

Remote synchronization optimizes scoped synchronization for dynamic local sharing, which occurs when a data structure is shared by many threads, but a subset of those threads desire infrequent, ad-choc access. An important example of this is work stealing. Remote synchronization robustly supports both scoped synchronization and work stealing across a diverse set of graph workloads and inputs.

Acknowledgments

We thank the anonymous reviewers for their helpful feedback. We also thank Derek Hower for answering our questions about HRF-Relaxed. Finally, we thank Tony Tye, Jason Power, and Michael Scott for thoughtful discussions. AMD, the AMD Arrow logo, and combinations thereof are trademarks of Advanced Micro Devices, Inc. OpenCL is a trademark of Apple Inc. used by permission by Khronos.

Appendix: Formalization

We add the notion of scope promotion to HRF-indirect-relaxed. Before presenting these additions, we give some background on the existing HRF models and discuss why we build on HRF-indirect-relaxed in particular.

Prior work proposed two memory models for scoped synchronization: HRF-direct and HRF-indirect [10]. The scoping rules are a defining part of these models. Both models say that a synchronization pair (i.e., a release on an address, executed by one work-item, followed by an acquire on the same address, executed by another work-item) must occur at the same scope. HRF-Relaxed extends the original HRF models by adding scope inclusion, which occurs when: (1) both scopes in the pair are specified such that one is a subset of the other, and (2) both scopes include each work-item in the pair [11]. The HRF-Relaxed paper uses the following notation for scope inclusion: $Rel_{S,A}[\ell] \approx_{\text{incl}} Acq_{S',A'}[\ell]$. This expression says that the scope S of the release Rel on location ℓ executed by work-item, or agent, A is inclusive with the scope S' of the acquire Acq on location ℓ executed by work-item, or agent, A'.

What distinguishes HRF-indirect is that it allows different synchronization pairs to the same location to occur at different scopes; this property is called transitive synchronization. For example, consider the sequence shown in Figure 11. Work-items A and B first synchronize on location `L` at work-group scope. Then, work-items B and C synchronize on location `L` at component scope. This sequence, invalid in HRF-direct, is allowed by HRF-indirect.

Transitivity is useful for scope promotion because it defines the case where synchronization first occurs at the remote scope and then occurs at the promoted scope. Note that without some sort of scope promotion, there is no way for an arbitrary work-item (e.g., a stealer) to guarantee that

Scoped Synchronization Order ($\overrightarrow{so_a}$): Given a release memory action, $Rel_{S,A}[\ell]$, and an acquire memory action, $Acq_{S',A'}[\ell]$, $Rel_{S,A}[\ell]\ \overrightarrow{so_a}\ Acq_{S',A'}[\ell]$ iff $a \in S$, $a \in S'$, $Rel_{S,A}[\ell] \approx_{\text{incl}} Acq_{S',A'}[\ell]$, and $Rel_{S,A}[\ell]\ \overrightarrow{coh_\ell}\ Acq_{S',A'}[\ell]$. Scoped synchronization order captures the synchronization operations visible to a single agent a.

Figure 12. Definition of Scoped Synchronization Order.

the last release occurred at a compatible scope. Thus, we add scope promotion to HRF-indirect-relaxed.

Adding Scope-Promotion to HRF-indirect-relaxed

An important definition in HRF-indirect-relaxed is scoped synchronization order, shown in Figure 12, which describes the order of acquires and releases. We identify where synchronization using remote-scope promotion can violate scoped synchronization order and then propose an addendum to HRF-indirect-relaxed (Figure 13) to fix the issue.

The definition gives three conditions to establish that a release on location ℓ, $Rel_{S,A}[\ell]$, occurs before an acquire on ℓ, $Acq_{S'A'}[\ell]$ (i.e., $Rel_{S,A}[\ell]\ \overrightarrow{so_a}\ Acq_{S',A'}[\ell]$). First, the two scopes S and S' must include agent a. Note, there is a synchronization order for each agent (i.e., work-item) in the execution (e.g., the producer work-item that executes the release and the consumer work-item that executes the acquire). This is depicted in Figure 14. Referring to the figure, the two scopes are `wg0` (i.e., the release executed by agent 0) and `cmp0` (the remote acquire executed by agent 1).

Case 1 shows when agent 0 and agent 1 both execute in the same work-group, the two scopes include both agents. For this case, remote synchronization adheres to HRF-indirect-relaxed.

Case 2 shows agent 0 and agent 1 executing in different work-groups. Both scopes include agent 0, but `wg0` does not include agent 1. To fix this issue, agent 1 *promotes* the scope of agent 0's release. The promotion is signified by back arrow in the figure, which transforms the scoped synchronization order graph. Specifically, the node corresponding to the most recent release on the same location as the remote acquire is updated with a promotion semantic.

The second condition to establish scoped synchronization order is that both scopes are inclusive. Using properly synchronized scope promotion, this is the case. Remote operations (e.g., $RmAcq_{S',A'}[\ell]$) are scoped to encompass the releasing scope, S.

Finally, the third condition says that the release, $Rel_{S,A}[\ell]$, must execute before the acquire, $Acq_{S'A'}[\ell]$, in the total order of all operations on location ℓ (called the coherence order, or $\overrightarrow{coh_\ell}$). This means that a work-item must release a location before another work-item can acquire it. The same is true for scope promotion—a work-item must release a location before another work-item can remotely acquire it.

Thus, we add promotion to HRF-indirect-relaxed (Figure 13) to formalize remote synchronization.

I. New Operators for Scope Promotion

Most Recent Release on ℓ: Given an acquire memory action, $Acq_{S,A}[\ell]$, return the most recent release memory action, $Rel_{S'A'}[\ell]$, in $\overrightarrow{coh_\ell}$:

$$lastRelease(Acq_{S,A}[\ell]) = Rel_{S'A'}[\ell]: (Rel_{S'A'}[\ell]\ \overrightarrow{coh_\ell}\ Acq_{S,A}[\ell]) \wedge (\nexists Rel'_{S''A''}[\ell]: Rel_{S'A'}[\ell]\ \overrightarrow{coh_\ell}\ Rel'_{S''A''}[\ell]\ \overrightarrow{coh_\ell}\ Acq_{S,A}[\ell])$$

Next Acquire on ℓ: Given a release memory action, $Rel_{S,A}[\ell]$, return the next future acquire memory action, $Acq_{S'A'}[\ell]$, in $\overrightarrow{coh_\ell}$:

$$nextAcquire(Rel_{S,A}[\ell]) = Acq_{S'A'}[\ell]: (Rel_{S,A}[\ell]\ \overrightarrow{coh_\ell}\ Acq_{S'A'}[\ell]) \wedge (\nexists Acq'_{S''A''}[\ell]: Rel_{S,A}[\ell]\ \overrightarrow{coh_\ell}\ Acq'_{S''A''}[\ell]\ \overrightarrow{coh_\ell}\ Acq_{S'A'}[\ell])$$

Promote a Scope: Given scopes S' and S:

$$\begin{cases} promote(S',S) = S, & if\ S' \subseteq S \\ promote(S',S) = S', & if\ S \subseteq S' or\ S \cap S' = \emptyset \end{cases}$$

II. New Definitions for Scope Promotion

Remote Acquire: Given a remote acquire memory action, $RmAcq_{S,A}[\ell]$, and the most recent release memory action on ℓ, $Rel_{S'A'}[\ell] = lastRelease(RmAcq_{S,A}[\ell])$, replace $Rel_{S'A'}[\ell]$ with $Rel_{promote(S',S),A'}[\ell]$.

Remote Release: Given a remote release memory action, $RmRel_{S,A}[\ell]$, and the next future acquire memory action on ℓ, $Acq_{S'A'}[\ell] = nextAcquire(RmRel_{S,A}[\ell])$, replace $Acq_{S'A'}[\ell]$ with $Acq_{promote(S',S),A'}[\ell]$.

Figure 13. Scope promotion for HRF-indirect-relaxed.

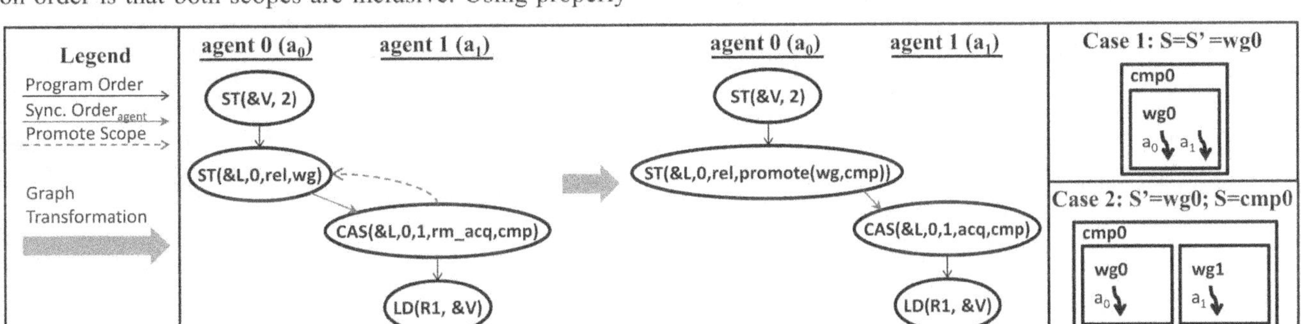

Figure 14. Example synchronization orders.

References

[1] "OpenCL 2.0 Reference Pages." [Online]. Available: http://www.khronos.org/registry/cl/sdk/2.0/docs/man/xhtml/.

[2] "CUDA C Programming Guide." [Online]. Available: http://docs.nvidia.com/cuda/cuda-c-programming-guide/.

[3] "HSA Programmer's Reference Manual: HSAIL Virtual ISA and Programming Model, Compiler Writer's Guide, and Object Format (BRIG) Version 1.0 Provisional," *HSA Foundation*, Spring 2013.

[4] T. Aila and S. Laine, "Understanding the Efficiency of Ray Traversal on GPUs," In *Proceedings of the Conference on High Performance Graphics*, New York, N.Y., USA, 2009, pp. 145–149.

[5] M. Frigo, C. E. Leiserson, and K. H. Randall, "The Implementation of the Cilk-5 Multithreaded Language," In *Proceedings of the ACM SIGPLAN 1998 Conference on Programming Language Design and Implementation*, New York, N.Y., USA, 1998, pp. 212–223.

[6] OpenMP Architecture Review Board, "OpenMP Application Program Interface Version 4.0," [Online]. http://www.openmp.org/mp-documents/OpenMP4.0.0.pdf.

[7] "Intel Threading Building Blocks." [Online]. Available: http://www.threadingbuildingblocks.org/.

[8] D. Leijen, W. Schulte, and S. Burckhardt, "The design of a task parallel library," In *Proceedings of the 24th ACM SIGPLAN conference on Object oriented programming systems languages and applications*, pp. 227-242, 2009.

[9] International Organization for Standardization, "Working Draft, Standard for Programming Language C++," [Online]. Available: http://www.open-std.org/jtc1/sc22/wg21/docs/papers/2012/n3337.pdf

[10] D.R. Hower, B.A. Hechtman, B.M. Beckmann, B.R. Gaster, M.D. Hill, S.K. Reinhardt, and D.A. Wood, "Heterogeneous-race-free Memory Models," In *The 19th International Conference on Architectural Support for Programming Languages and Operating Systems (ASPLOS-19)*, 2014.

[11] B.R. Gaster, D. Hower, and L. Howes, "HRF-Relaxed: Adapting HRF to the complexities of industrial heterogeneous memory models," In *Transactions on Architecture and Code Optimization (TACO)*, 2015.

[12] AMD, "Southern Islands Series Instruction Set Architecture," 2012.

[13] S. Owens, S. Sarkar, and P. Sewell, "A Better x86 Memory Model: x86-TSO," In *Proceedings of the Conference on Theorem Proving in Higher Order Logics*, 2009.

[14] D. J. Sorin, M. D. Hill, and D. A. Wood, "A Primer on Memory Consistency and Cache Coherence," *Morgan and Claypool*, 2011.

[15] B. A. Hechtman, S. Che, D. R. Hower, Y. Tian, B. M. Beckmann, M. D. Hill, S. K. Reinhardt, and D. A. Wood, "QuickRelease: A Throughput-oriented Approach to Release Consistency on GPUs," *presented at the 20th IEEE International Symposium On High Performance Computer Architecture (HPCA-2014)*.

[16] N.S. Arora, R.D. Blumofe, and C. Greg Plaxton, "Thread scheduling for multiprogrammed multiprocessors," In *Proceedings of the ACM Symposium on Parallel Algorithms and Architectures*, ACM, Puerto Vallarta, Mexico, 1998, pp. 119–129.

[17] D. Cederman and P. Tsigas, "Dynamic Load-Balancing Using Work-Stealing," In *GPU Computing Gems Jade Edition*, Wen-Mei Hwu (Editor-in-Chief), Morgan Kaufmann.

[18] N. Binkert, B. Beckmann, G. Black, S. K. Reinhardt, A. Saidi, A. Basu, J. Hestness, D. R. Hower, T. Krishna, S. Sardashti, R. Sen, K. Sewell, M. Shoaib, N. Vaish, M. D. Hill, and D. A. Wood, "The gem5 Simulator," In *SIGARCH Computer Arch. News*, vol. 39, no. 2, pp. 1-7, Aug. 2011.

[19] S. Che, B. M. Beckmann, S. K. Reinhardt, and K. Skadron, "Pannotia: Understanding Irregular GPGPU Graph Applications," In *Proceedings of the International Symposium on Workload Characterizations*, Sept. 2013.

[20] DIMACS Implementation Challenges. http://dimacs.rutgers.edu/Challenges/

[21] Web resource: http://www.sommer.jp/graphs/

[22] B. N. Bershad, M. J. Zekauskas, and W. A. Sawdon, "The Midway distributed shared memory system," In *Proc. 38th IEEE Computer Society Int. Conf.*, pp. 528-537, 1993.

[23] L. Iftode, J. P. Singh, and K. Li, "Scope consistency: a bridge between release consistency and entry consistency," In *Proceedings of the eighth annual ACM symposium on Parallel algorithms and architectures*, p.277-287, June 24-26, 1996, Padua, Italy.

[24] D. Dice, M.S. Moir, and W.N. Scherer III, "Quickly reacquirable locks," *US Patent 7,814,488*, 2010.

[25] W.W.L. Fung and T.M. Aamodt, "Energy Efficient GPU Transactional Memory via Space-Time Optimizations," In *Proceedings of the 46th IEEE/ACM International Symposium on Microarchitecture (MICRO-46)*, pp. 408-420, Davis, CA, Dec. 7-11, 2013.

[26] D. Cederman, P. Tsigas, and M.T. Chaudhry, "Towards a Software Transactional Memory for Graphics Processors," In *Proceedings of the 10th Eurographics Symposium on Parallel Graphics and Visualization (EGPGV 2010)*.

[27] I. Singh, A. Shriraman, W.W.L. Fung, M. O'Connor, and T.M. Aamodt, "Cache Coherence for GPU Architectures," In *Proceedings of the 19th IEEE International Symposium on High-Performance Computer Architecture (HPCA-19)*, pp. 578-590, Shenzhen, China, Feb. 23-27, 2013.

[28] S. Tzeng, A. Patney, and J.D. Owens, "Task Management for Irregular-Parallel Workloads on the GPU," In *Proceedings of High Performance Graphics 2010*, pp. 29–37. June 2010.

GhostRider: A Hardware-Software System for Memory Trace Oblivious Computation

Chang Liu,[†] Austin Harris,[‡] Martin Maas,[*] Michael Hicks,[†] Mohit Tiwari,[‡] and Elaine Shi[†]

[†] University of Maryland, College Park [‡] University of Texas at Austin [*] University of California, Berkeley

Abstract

This paper presents a new, co-designed compiler and architecture called GhostRider for supporting privacy preserving computation in the cloud. GhostRider ensures all programs satisfy a property called *memory-trace obliviousness* (MTO): Even an adversary that observes memory, bus traffic, and access times while the program executes can learn nothing about the program's sensitive inputs and outputs. One way to achieve MTO is to employ Oblivious RAM (ORAM), allocating all code and data in a single ORAM bank, and to also disable caches or fix the rate of memory traffic. This baseline approach can be inefficient, and so GhostRider's compiler uses a program analysis to do better, allocating data to non-oblivious, encrypted RAM (ERAM) and employing a scratchpad when doing so will not compromise MTO. The compiler can also allocate to multiple ORAM banks, which sometimes significantly reduces access times. We have formalized our approach and proved it enjoys MTO. Our FPGA-based hardware prototype and simulation results show that GhostRider significantly outperforms the baseline strategy.

1. Introduction

Cloud computing allows users to outsource both data and computation to third-party cloud providers, and promises numerous benefits such as economies of scale, easy maintenance, and ubiquitous availability. These benefits, however, come at the cost of giving up physical control of one's computing infrastructure and private data. Privacy concerns have held back government agencies and businesses alike from outsourcing their computing infrastructure to the public cloud [9, 52].

ASPLOS '15, March 14–18, 2015, Istanbul, Turkey..

ACM 978-1-4503-2835-7/15/03…$15.00.
http://dx.doi.org/10.1145/2694344.2694385

To protect the confidentiality of sensitive data in the cloud, thwarting software attacks alone is necessary but not sufficient. An attacker with physical access to the computing platform (e.g., an malicious insider or intruder) can launch various *physical attacks*, such as tapping memory buses, plugging in malicious peripherals, or using cold-(re)boots [26, 45]. Such physical attacks can uncover secrets even when the software stack is provably secure.

While memory encryption [19, 31, 47–49] can be used to hide the contents of memory from direct inspection, an adversary can still observe memory addresses transmitted over the memory bus. Perhaps surprisingly, the memory address trace is a side channel that can leak sensitive information, e.g., cryptographic keys [56]. To cryptographically obfuscate the memory access patterns, one can employ Oblivious RAM (ORAM) [20, 21], a cryptographic construction that makes memory address traces computationally indistinguishable from a random address trace. Encouragingly, recent theoretical breakthroughs [44, 46] have allowed ORAM memory controllers to be built [16, 35] – these turn DRAM into oblivious, block-addressable memory banks.

The simplest way to deploy ORAM is to implement a single, large ORAM bank that contains all the code and data (assuming that the client can use standard PKI to safely transmit the code and data to a remote secure processor). A major drawback of this baseline approach is efficiency: every single memory-block access incurs the ORAM penalty which is roughly (poly-)logarithmic in the size of the ORAM [21, 44]. In practice, this translates to almost 100$\times$ additional bandwidth that, even with optimizations, incurs a $\sim$10$\times$ latency cost per block [16, 35]. Another issue is that, absent any padding, the baseline approach reveals the total number of memory accesses made by a program, which can leak information about the secret inputs.

Memory Trace Oblivious (MTO) Program Execution Ultimately, the goal is to ensure that programs satisfy a property called *memory-trace oblivious* (MTO) execution, meaning that an adversary who observes memory contents, address traffic, and access times while the program executes can learn nothing about the program's sensitive inputs and outputs. While allocating code and data in ORAM is one approach toward achieving MTO,[1] our prior work [33] suggested that greater efficiency can be achieved by having the compiler take advantage of the fact that not all parts of a program's memory trace leak sensitive information. As an example, a program that sequentially scans through a sensitive array and computes the sum has a fixed, predictable memory access pattern that is independent of the sensitive array contents. In this case, it suffices to merely encrypt the array, instead of placing the array in ORAM. A further efficiency gain stems from placing data into different ORAM banks, which can now be smaller and in turn faster to access.

While our prior work lays out an initial vision of memory-trace oblivious program execution, this work is conceptual, rather than practical. In particular, we did not target a modern processor architecture, instead assuming unbounded resources and no caching.

1.1 Our Results and Contributions

In this paper, we make the first endeavor to bring the theory of MTO to practice. We design and build GhostRider, a hardware/software platform for provably secure, memory-trace oblivious program execution. Compiling to a realistic architecture while formally ensuring MTO raises interesting challenges in the compiler and type system design, and ultimately requires a co-operative re-design of the underlying processor architecture. Our contributions are:

New compiler and type system We build the first memory-trace oblivious compiler that emits target code for a realistic ORAM-capable processor architecture. The compiler must explicitly handle low-level resource allocation based on underlying hardware constraints, and while doing so is standard in non-oblivious compilers, achieving them while respecting the MTO property is non-trivial. Standard resource allocation mechanisms would fail to address the MTO property. For example, register allocation spills registers to the stack, thereby introducing memory events. Furthermore, caching serves memory requests from an on-chip cache, which suppresses memory events. If these actions are correlated with secret data, they can leak information. We introduce new techniques for resolving such challenges. In lieu of implicit caches we employ an explicit, on-chip *scratchpad*. Our compiler implements caching in software when its use does not compromise MTO.

To formally ensure the MTO property, we define a new type system for a RISC-style low-level assembly language. We show that any well-typed program in this assembly language will respect memory-trace obliviousness during execution. When starting from source programs that satisfy a standard information flow type system [13], our compiler generates type-correct, and therefore safe, target code. Specifically, we implement a type checker that can verify the type-correctness of the target code.

[1] In fact, ORAM allocation is not entirely sufficient: the *length* of an address trace can also reveal information, so additional steps are necessary.

```
void histogram(secret int a[],    // ERAM
               secret int c[]) { // ORAM (output)
  public int i;
  secret int t, v;
  for(i=0;i<100000;i++) // 100000 <= len(c)
    c[i]=0;
  i=0;
  for(i=0;i<100000;i++) { // 100000 <= len(a)
    v=a[i];
    if(v>0) t=v%1000;
      else t=(0-v)%1000;
    c[t]=c[t]+1; } }
```

Figure 1. Motivating source program.

Processor architecture for MTO program execution To enable an automated approach for efficient memory-trace oblivious program execution, we need new hardware features that are not readily available in existing ORAM-capable processor architectures [15, 17, 35]. GhostRider builds on the Phantom processor architecture [35] but exposes new features and knobs to the software. In addition to supporting a scratchpad, as mentioned above, the GhostRider architecture complements Phantom's ORAM support with *encrypted RAM* (ERAM), which is not oblivious and therefore more efficiently supports variables whose access patterns are not sensitive. Section 6 describes additional hardware-level contributions. We prototyped the GhostRider processor on a Convey HC2 platform [10] with programmable FPGA support. The GhostRider processor supports the RISC-V instruction set [51].

Implementation and Empirical Results Our empirical results are obtained through a combination of software emulation and experiments on an FPGA prototype. Our FPGA prototype supports one ERAM bank, one code ORAM bank, and one data ORAM bank. The real processor experiments demonstrate the feasibility of our architecture, while the software simulator allows us to test a range of configurations not limited by the constraints of the current hardware. In particular, the software simulator models multiple ORAM banks at a higher clock rate.

Our experimental results show that compared to the baseline approach of placing everything in a single ORAM bank, our compile-time static analysis achieves up to nearly an order-of-magnitude speedup for many common programs.

2. Architecture and Approach

This section motivates our approach and presents an overview of GhostRider's hardware/software co-design.

2.1 Motivating example

We wish to support a scenario in which a client asks an untrusted cloud provider to run a computation on the client's private data. For example, suppose the client wants the provider to run the program shown in Figure 1, which is

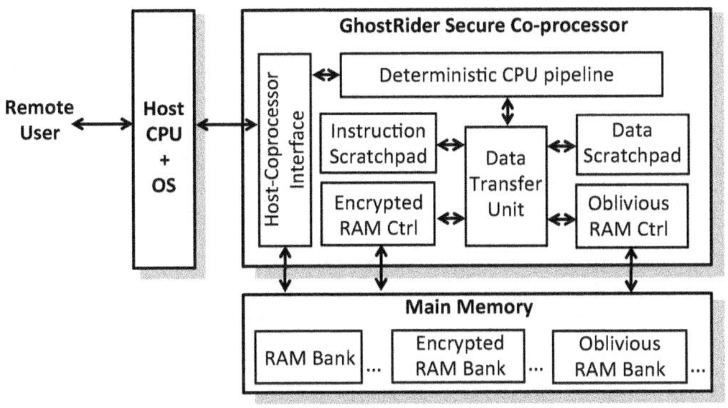

Figure 2. GhostRider architecture.

a simple histogram program written in a C-like source language. As input, the program takes an integer array a, and as output it modifies integer array parameter c. We assume both arrays have size 100,000. The function's code is straightforward, computing the histogram of the absolute values of integers modulo 1000 appearing in the input array. The client's security goal is *data confidentiality*: the cloud provider runs the program on input array a, producing output array c, but nevertheless learns nothing about the contents of either a or c. We express this goal by labeling both arrays with the qualifier `secret` (data labeled `public` is non-sensitive).

2.2 Threat model

The adversary has physical access to the machine(s) being used to run client computations. As in prior work that advocates the minimization of the hardware trusted computing base (TCB) [47–49], we assume that trust ends at the boundary of the secure processor. Off-chip components are considered *insecure*, including memory, system buses, and peripherals. For example, we assume the adversary can observe the contents of memory, and can observe communications on the bus between the processor and the memory. By contrast, we assume that on-chip components are secure. Specifically, the adversary cannot observe the contents of the cache, the register file, or any on-chip communications. Finally, we assume the adversary can make fine-grained timing measurements, and therefore can learn, for example, the gap between observed events. Analogous side channels such as power consumption are outside the scope of this paper, and have received orthogonal treatment in related work [29].

2.3 Architectural Overview

As mentioned in the introduction, one way to defend against such an adversary is to place all data in a single (large) ORAM; e.g., for the program in Figure 1 we place the arrays a and c in ORAM. Unfortunately this *baseline* approach is not only expensive, but also leaks information through the total number of ORAM accesses (if the access trace is not padded to a value that is independent of secret data). We now provide an architectural overview of GhostRider (Figure 2) and contrast it with this baseline.

Joint ORAM-ERAM memory system In the GhostRider architecture, main memory is split into three types—normal (unencrypted) memory (RAM), encrypted memory (ERAM), and oblivious RAM (ORAM)—with one or more (logical) banks of each type comprising the system's physical memory. The differentiation of memory into banks allows a compiler to place only arrays with sensitive access patterns inside the more expensive ORAM banks, while keeping the remaining data in the significantly faster RAM or ERAM banks. For example, notice that in the program in Figure 1 the array a is always accessed sequentially while access patterns to the array c can depend on secret array contents. Therefore, our GhostRider compiler can place the array a inside an ERAM bank, and place the array c inside an ORAM bank. The program accesses different memory banks at the level of blocks using instructions that specify the bank and a block-offset within the bank (after moving data to on-chip memory as described below). Our hardware prototype fixes block sizes to be 4KB for both ERAM and ORAM banks (which is not an inherent limitation of the hardware design).

Software-directed scratchpad As mentioned earlier, cache hit and miss behavior can lead to differences in the observable memory traces. To prevent such cache-channel information leakage, the GhostRider architecture turns off implicit caching, and instead offers software-directed scratchpads for both instructions and data. These scratchpads are mapped into the program's address space so that the compiler can generate code to access them explicitly, and thereby avoid information leaks. For example, the indices of array a in Figure 1 are deterministic; they do not depend on any secret input. As such, it is safe to use the scratchpad to cache array a's accesses. The compiler generates code to check whether the relevant block is in the scratchpad, and if not loads the block from memory. On the other hand, all accesses to array c depend on the secret input a, so a memory request will always be issued independent of whether the requested block is in the scratchpad or not.

Deterministic Processor Pipeline To avoid timing-channel leakage, our pipelined processor ensures that instruction timings are deterministic. We do not use dynamic branch prediction and fix variable-duration instructions, such as division, to take the worst-case execution time, and disable concurrent execution of other instructions.

Initialization We design the oblivious processor and memory banks as a *co-processor* that runs the application natively (i.e., without an OS) and is connected to a networked host computer that can be accessed remotely by a user. We assume that the secure co-processor has non-volatile memory for storing a long-term public key (certified using PKI), such that the client can securely ship its encrypted code and data to the remote host, and initialize execution on the secure co-processor. Implementing the secure attestation is standard [25], and we leave it to future work.

$m, n \in$	$\mathbb{Z}$	$o_1, ..., o_n \in$ **ORAMbanks**	
k	$\in$ **Block IDs**	$r \in$ **Registers**	
l	$\in$ **Labels** $= \{D, E\} \cup$ **ORAMbanks**		
ι	$::=$ **ldb** $k \leftarrow l[r]$	load block to scratchpad	
	$\mid$ **stb** k	store block to memory	
	$\mid$ $r \leftarrow$ **idb** k	retrieve the block ID	
	$\mid$ **ldw** $r_1 \leftarrow k[r_2]$	load a scratchpad val. to reg.	
	$\mid$ **stw** $r_1 \rightarrow k[r_2]$	store a reg. val. to scratchpad	
	$\mid$ $r_1 \leftarrow r_2 \ aop \ r_3$	compute an operation	
	$\mid$ $r_1 \leftarrow n$	assign a constant to a register	
	$\mid$ **jmp** n	(relative) jump	
	$\mid$ **br** $r_1 \ rop \ r_2 \hookrightarrow n$	compare and branch	
	$\mid$ **nop**	empty operation	
I	$::= \iota \mid I; \iota$	instruction sequence	

Figure 3. Syntax for $\mathcal{L}_T$ language, comprising (1) **ldb** and **stb** *i*nstructions that move data blocks between scratchpad and a specific ERAM or ORAM bank, and (2) scratchpad-to-register moves and standard RISC instructions.

`; v=a[i]`
1 $t_1 \leftarrow r_i$ **div** $size_{blk}$
2 $t_2 \leftarrow r_i$ **mod** $size_{blk}$
3 **ldb** $k_1 \leftarrow E[t_1]$
4 **ldw** $r_v \leftarrow k_1[t_2]$
`; if(v>0) t= ...`
5 **br** $r_v \leq 0 \hookrightarrow 3$
6 $r_t \leftarrow r_v \ \% \ 1000$
7 **jmp** 3
`; else t= ...`
8 $t_1 \leftarrow 0 - r_v$
9 $r_t \leftarrow t_1 \ \% \ 1000$

`; c[t]=c[t]+1`
10 $t_1 \leftarrow r_t \gg 9$
11 $t_2 \leftarrow r_t \ \& \ 511$
12 **ldb** $k_2 \leftarrow O[t_1]$
13 **ldw** $t_3 \leftarrow k_2[t_2]$
14 $t_4 \leftarrow t_3 + 1$
15 **stw** $t_4 \rightarrow k_2[t_2]$
16 **stb** k_2

Figure 4. $\mathcal{L}_T$ code implementing (part of) Figure 1

3. Target language

This section presents a small formalization of GhostRider's instruction set, which we call $\mathcal{L}_T$. The next section presents a type system for this language that guarantees security, and the following section describes our compiler from a C-like source language to well-typed $\mathcal{L}_T$ programs.

3.1 Instruction set

The core instructions of $\mathcal{L}_T$ are in the style of RISC-V [51], our prototype's instruction set, and are formalized in Figure 3. We define *labels* l that distinguish the three kinds of main memory: D for normal (D)RAM, E for ERAM, and o_i for ORAM. For the last, the i identifies a particular ORAM bank. We can view each label as defining a distinct address space.

The instruction **ldb** $k \leftarrow l[r]$ loads a block from memory into the scratchpad.[2] Here, l is the address space, r is a register containing the address of the block to load from within that address space, and k is the scratchpad block identifier. Our formalism refers to scratchpad blocks by their identifier, treating them similarly to registers. Our architecture remembers the address space and block address within that address space that the scratchpad block was loaded from so that writebacks, via the **stb** k instruction, will go to the original location. We enforce this one-to-one mapping to avoid information leaks via write-back from the scratchpad (e.g., that where a scratchpad block is written to, in memory, could reveal information about a secret, or that the effect of a write could do so, if blocks are aliased).

To access values from the scratchpad, we have scratchpad-load and scratchpad-store instructions. The scratchpad-load instruction loads a word from a scratchpad block, having the form **ldw** $r_1 \leftarrow k[r_2]$. Assuming register r_2 contains n, this instruction loads the n-th word in block k into register r_1 (notice that we use word-oriented addressing, not byte-oriented). The scratchpad-store instruction is similar, but goes in the reverse direction. The instruction $r \leftarrow$ **idb** k retrieves the block offset of a scratchpad block k.

We have two kinds of assignment instructions, one in the form of $r_1 \leftarrow r_2 \ aop \ r_3$, and the other in the form of $r \leftarrow n$. In $\mathcal{L}_T$ we only model integer arithmetic operations, such as addition, subtraction, multiplication, division, and modulus.

Jumps and branches use relative addressing. The jump instruction **jmp** n bumps the program counter by n instructions (where n can be negative). Branches, having the form **br** $r_1 \ rop \ r_2 \hookrightarrow n$, will compare the contents of r_1 and r_2 using *rop*, and will bump the pc by n if the comparison result is true. An instruction sequence I is defined to be a sequence of instructions concatenated using a logical operation ;. We overload ; to operate over two instruction sequences such that $I; (I'; \iota) \triangleq (I; I'); \iota$ and $I_1; I_2; I_3 \triangleq (I_1; I_2); I_3$.

Note that our formalism does not model the instruction scratchpad; essentially it assumes that all code is loaded on-chip prior to the start of its execution. Section 5 discusses how the instruction scratchpad is used in practice.

3.2 Example

Figure 4 shows $\mathcal{L}_T$ code that corresponds to the body of the second `for` loop in the source program from Figure 1. We write r_X for a register corresponding to variable X in the source program (for simplicity) and write t_i for $i \in \{1, 2, ...\}$ for temporary registers. In the explanation we refer to the names of variables in the source program when describing what the target program is computing.

The first four lines load the `i`th element of array `a` into `v`. Line 1 computes the address of the block in memory that contains the `i`th element of array `a` and line 2 computes the offset of the element within that block. Here $size_{blk}$ is the size of each block, which is an architecture constant.

[2] In our hardware prototype the scratchpad is mapped into addressable memory, so this instruction and its counterpart, **stb**, are implemented as data transfers. In addition, the compiler implements **idb**. We model them in $\mathcal{L}_T$ explicitly for simplicity; see Section 6 for implementation details.

Line 3 then loads the block from ERAM, and line 4 loads the appropriate value from the loaded block into v.

The next five lines implement the conditional. Line 5 jumps three instructions forward if v is *not* greater than 0, else it falls through to line 6, which computes t. Line 7 then jumps past the else branch, which begins on line 8, which negates v to make it positive before computing t.

The final seven lines increment c[t]. Lines 10–13 are analogous to lines 1–4; they compute the address of tth element of array c and load it into temporary t_3. Notice that this time the block is loaded from ORAM, not ERAM. Line 14 increments the temporary; line 15 stores it back to the block in the scratchpad; and line 16 stores the entire block back to ORAM.

4. Security by typing

This section presents a type system[3] for $\mathcal{L}_T$ that guarantees programs obey the strong *memory trace obliviousness* (MTO) security property.

4.1 Memory Trace Obliviousness

Memory trace obliviousness is a noninterference property that also considers the address trace, rather than just the initial and final contents of memory [43]. MTO's definition relies on the notion of *low equivalence* which relates memories whose RAM contents are identical. We formally define this notion below, using the following formal notation:

$$\begin{array}{rcl} M & \in & \textbf{Addresses} \to \textbf{Blocks} \\ a & \in & \textbf{Addresses} = \textbf{Labels} \times \textbf{Nat} \\ b & \in & \textbf{Blocks} = \textbf{Nat} \to \mathbb{Z} \end{array}$$

We model a *memory* M as a map from addresses to blocks, where an address is a pair consisting of a label l (corresponding to an ORAM, ERAM, or RAM bank, as per Figure 3) and an address n in that bank. A block is modeled as a map from an address n to a (integer) value. Here is the definition of memory low-equivalence:

DEFINITION 1 (Memory low equivalence). *Two memories* M_1, M_2 *are* low equivalent, *written* $M_1 \sim_L M_2$, *if and only if for all* n *such that* $0 \leq n < size(D)$ *we have* $M_1(D,n) = M_2(D,n)$.

The definition states that memories M_1 and M_2 are low equivalent when only the RAM bank's values of the memories are the same, but all of the other values could differ.

Intuitively, memory trace obliviousness says two things given two low-equivalent memories. First, if the program will terminate under one memory, then it will terminate under the other. Second, if the program will terminate and lead to a trace t under one memory, then it will do so under the other memory as well while also finishing with low-equivalent memories.

To state this intuition precisely, we need a formal definition of a $\mathcal{L}_T$ execution, which we give as an operational semantics. The semantics is largely standard, and can be found in the technical report [32]. The key judgment has the form $I \vdash (R, S, M, pc) \longrightarrow_t (R', S', M', pc')$, which states that program I, with a register file R, a (data) scratchpad S, a memory M, and a program counter pc, executes some number of steps, producing memory trace t and resulting in a possibly modified register file R', scratchpad S', memory M', and program counter pc'.

DEFINITION 2 (Memory trace obliviousness). *A program* I *is* memory trace oblivious *if and only if for all memories* $M_1 \sim_L M_2$ *we have* $I \vdash (R_0, S_0, M_1, 0) \longrightarrow_{t_1} (R'_1, S'_1, M'_1, pc_1)$, *and* $I \vdash (R_0, S_0, M_2, 0) \longrightarrow_{t_2} (R'_2, S'_2, M'_2, pc_2)$, *and* $|t_1| = |t_2|$ *implies* $t_1 \equiv t_2$ *and* $M'_1 \sim_L M'_2$.

Here R_0 is a mapping that maps every register to 0, and S_0 maps every address to a all-0 block. Traces t consist of reads/writes to RAM (both address and value) and ERAM (just the address), accesses to ORAM (just the bank), and instruction fetches. For the last we only model that a fetch happened, not what instruction it is, as we assume code will be stored in a scratchpad on chip. We write $t_1 \equiv t_2$ to say that traces t_1 and t_2 are *indistinguishable* to the attacker; i.e., they consist of the same events in the same order. Our formalism models every instruction as taking *unit* time to execute – thus the trace event also models the time taken to execute the instruction. On the real GhostRider architecture, each instruction takes *deterministic but non-uniform* time; as this difference is conceptually easy to handle (by accounting for instruction execution times in the compiler), we do not model it formally, for simplicity (see Section 5).

4.2 Typing: Preliminaries

Now we give a type system for $\mathcal{L}_T$ programs and prove that type correct programs are MTO.

Symbolic values To ensure that the execution of a program cannot leak information via its address trace, we statically approximate what events a program can produce. An important determination made by the type system is when a secret variable can be stored in ERAM—because the address trace will leak no information about it—and when it must be accessed in ORAM. As an example, suppose we had the source program

```
if(s) then x[i]=1 else x[i]=2;
```

If x is secret but stored in RAM, then the value in x[i] after running this program will leak the contents of secret variable s. We could store x in ORAM to avoid this problem, but this is unnecessary: both branches will modify the same element of x, so encrypting the content of x is enough to prevent the address trace from leaking information about s. The type

[3] For space reasons, the type system is simplified from the full version, given in the extended technical report [32]. The full system models a stack to support function calls, which we discuss briefly at the end of Section 5.

Sym. vals.	sv	$\in$ **SymVals** $= n \mid ? \mid sv_1\ aop\ sv_2 \mid \mathtt{M}_l[k, sv]$
Sym. Store	Sym	$\in$ **Registers** $\cup$ **Block IDs** $\rightarrow$ **SymVals**
Sec. Labels	ℓ	$\in$ **SecLabels** $= \mathtt{L} \mid \mathtt{H}$
Label Map	Υ	$\in$ (**Registers** $\rightarrow$ **SecLabels**) $\cup$ (**Block IDs** $\rightarrow$ **Labels**)

$\boxed{sv_1 \equiv sv_2}$

$$\frac{\vdash_{safe} sv_1 \quad \vdash_{safe} sv_2 \quad sv_1 = sv_2}{sv_1 \equiv sv_2}$$

$\boxed{\vdash_{safe} sv}$

$$\frac{l = D \quad \vdash_{safe} sv}{\vdash_{safe} \mathtt{M}_l[k, sv]} \qquad \vdash_{safe} n$$

$$\frac{\vdash_{safe} sv_1 \quad \vdash_{safe} sv_2}{\vdash_{safe} sv_1\ aop\ sv_2}$$

$\boxed{\vdash_{const} sv}$

$$\vdash_{const} n \qquad \vdash_{const} ?$$

$$\frac{\vdash_{const} sv_1 \quad \vdash_{const} sv_2}{\vdash_{const} sv_1\ aop\ sv_2}$$

$\boxed{\vdash_{const} Sym}$

$$\frac{\forall r.\ \vdash_{const} Sym(r) \quad \forall k.\ \vdash_{const} Sym(k)}{\vdash_{const} Sym}$$

Auxiliary Functions

$$select(l, a, b, c) = \begin{cases} a & \text{if } l = D \\ b & \text{if } l = E \\ c & \text{if otherwise.} \end{cases}$$

$$slab(l) = select(l, \mathtt{L}, \mathtt{H}, \mathtt{H})$$

$$ite(x, a, b) = \begin{cases} a & \text{if } x \text{ is true.} \\ b & \text{otherwise.} \end{cases}$$

Figure 5. Symbolic values, labels, auxiliary judgments and functions

system can identify this situation by *symbolically* tracking the contents of the registers, blocks, etc.

To do this, the type rules maintain a *symbolic store Sym*, which is a map from register and block IDs to symbolic values. Figure 5 defines symbolic values sv, which consist of constants n, (symbolic) arithmetic expressions, values loaded from memory $\mathtt{M}_l[k, sv]$, and unknowns ?. Most interesting is memory values, which represent the address of a loaded value: l indicates the memory bank it was loaded from, sv corresponds to the offset (i.e., the block number) within that bank, and k is the scratchpad block into which the memory block is loaded.[4]

The type rules also make use of a *label map* Υ mapping registers to security labels and block IDs to (memory) labels; the latter tracks the memory bank from which a scratchpad block was loaded.

The figure defines several judgments; the form of each judgment is boxed. The first defines when two symbolic values can be deemed equivalent, written $sv_1 \equiv sv_2$: they must be syntactically identical and safe static approximations. The latter is defined by the judgment $\vdash_{safe} sv$, which accepts constants, memory accesses to RAM involving safe indexes, and arithmetic expressions involving safe values. Judgement $\vdash_{const} sv$ says that symbolic value sv is not a memory value. That is, sv is either a constant, a ?, or a binary expression not involving memory values. Further, for a symbolic store Sym, if all the symbolic values that it maps to can be accepted by $\vdash_{const} sv$, then we have $\vdash_{const} Sym$. The latter judgment is needed when checking conditionals.

Finally, we give three auxiliary functions used in the type system. Based on whether l is D, E, or an ORAM bank, function $select(l, a, b, c)$ returns a, b, or c respectively. Function $slab(\cdot)$ maps a normal label l to a security label ℓ, which is either L or H. The label H classifies encrypted memory—any ORAM bank and ERAM—while label L classifies RAM. These two labels form the two-point lattice with $\mathtt{L} \sqsubset \mathtt{H}$. Note that L is equivalent to the `public` label used in Figure 1, and H is equivalent to `secret`. Finally, function $ite(x, a, b)$ returns a if x is true, and returns b if x is false.

Trace Pats. $T ::= \mathbf{read}(l, k, sv) \mid \mathbf{write}(l, k, sv) \mid \mathbf{F} \mid o \mid T_1 @ T_2 \mid T_1 + T_2 \mid \mathbf{loop}(T_1, T_2)$

$$\frac{sv_1 \equiv sv_2}{\mathbf{read}(l, k, sv_1) \equiv \mathbf{read}(l, k, sv_2)} \qquad o \equiv o \qquad \frac{T_1 \equiv T_2}{T_2 \equiv T_1}$$

$$\frac{sv_1 \equiv sv_2}{\mathbf{write}(l, k, sv_1) \equiv \mathbf{write}(l, k, sv_2)} \qquad \mathbf{F} \equiv \mathbf{F}$$

$$T_1 @ (T_2 @ T_3) \equiv (T_1 @ T_2) @ T_3 \qquad \frac{T_1 \equiv T_1' \quad T_2 \equiv T_2'}{T_1 @ T_2 \equiv T_1' @ T_2'}$$

Figure 6. Trace patterns and their equivalence

Trace patterns Figure 6 defines *trace patterns* T, which statically approximate traces t. The first line in the definition of T defines single events. The first two indicate reads and writes to RAM or ERAM; they reference the memory bank, block identifier in the scratchpad, and a symbolic value corresponding to the block *address* (not the actual value) read or written. Pattern **F** corresponds to a non memory-accessing instruction. The next pattern indicates a read or write from ORAM bank o: this bank is the trace event itself because the adversary cannot determine whether an access is a read or a write, or which block within the ORAM is accessed. Trace pattern $T_1 @ T_2$ is the pattern resulting from the concatenation of patterns T_1 and T_2. Pattern $T_1 + T_2$ represents *either* T_1 or T_2, and is used to type conditionals. Finally, pattern $\mathbf{loop}(T_1, T_2)$ represents zero or more loop iterations where the guard's trace is T_1 and the body's trace is T_2.

Trace pattern equivalence $T_1 \equiv T_2$ is defined in Figure 6. In this definition, reads are equivalent to other reads accessing exactly the same location; the same goes for writes. Two ORAM accesses to the same ORAM bank are obviously treated as equivalent. Sum patterns specify possibly different trace patterns, and loop patterns do not specify the number

[4] In actual traces t, the block number k is not visible; we track it symbolically to model the scratchpad's contents, in particular to ensure that the same memory block is not loaded into two different scratchpad blocks.

of iterations; as such we cannot determine their equivalence statically. The concatenation operator @ is associative with respect to equivalence.

4.3 Type rules

Figure 7 defines the security type system for $\mathcal{L}_T$. The figure is divided into three parts.

Instructions Judgment $\ell \vdash \iota : \langle \Upsilon, Sym\rangle \to \langle \Upsilon', Sym'\rangle; T$ is used to type instructions ι. Here, ℓ is the *security context*, used in the standard way to prevent implicit flows. The rules are *flow sensitive*: The judgement says that instruction ι has a type $\langle \Upsilon, Sym\rangle \to \langle \Upsilon', Sym'\rangle$, and generates trace pattern T. Informally, we can say by executing ι, a state corresponding to security type $\langle \Upsilon, Sym\rangle$ will be changed to have type $\langle \Upsilon', Sym'\rangle$.

Rule T-LOAD types load instructions. The first premise ensures that the contents of register r, the indexing register, are not leaked by the operation. In particular, the loaded memory bank l must either be ORAM, or else the register r may only contain public data (from RAM). In the latter case, there is no issue with leaking r, and in the former case r will not be leaked indirectly by the address of the loaded memory since it is stored in ORAM. The final two premises determine the final trace pattern. When the memory bank l is D or E, then the trace pattern indicates a read event from the appropriate block and address. When reading from an ORAM bank the event is just that bank itself. The other premises in the rule update Υ to map the loaded block k to the label of the memory bank, and update Sym to track the address of the block.

We defer discussion of rule T-STORE for the moment, and look at the next three rules, T-LOADW, T-STOREW, T-IDB, which are used to load and store values related blocks in the scratchpad. The first two rules resemble standard information flow rules. The second premise of T-LOADW is similar to the first premise of T-LOAD in preventing an indirect leak of index register r_2, which would occur if the label of r_2 was $\texttt{H}$ but the label of k was $\texttt{L}$. Likewise, the premise of T-STOREW prevents leaking the contents of r_1 and r_2 into the stored block, and also prevents an implicit flow from ℓ (the security context). As such, these two rules ensure that a block k with label ℓ never contains information from memory labeled ℓ' such that $\ell' \sqsupset \ell$. The remaining premises of Rule T-LOADW flow-sensitively track the label and symbolic value of the loaded register. In particular, they set the label of r_1 to be that of the block loaded, and the symbolic value of r_1 to be the address of the loaded value in memory. T-STOREW changes neither Υ nor Sym: even though the content of the scratchpad has changed, its memory label and its address in memory has not. Both rules emit trace pattern $\mathbf{F}$ as the operations are purely on-chip. We emit this event to account for the time taken to execute an instruction; assuming uniform times for instructions and memory accesses, MTO executions will also be free of timing channels.

Returning to rule T-STORE, we can see that the store takes place unconditionally—no constraints on the labels of the memory or block must be satisfied. This is because the other type rules ensure that all blocks k never contain information higher than their security label ℓ, and thus the block can be written straight to memory having the same security label. That said, information could be leaked through the memory trace, so the emitted trace pattern will differ depending on the label of the block: If the label is D or E then the trace pattern will be a write event, and otherwise it will be the appropriate ORAM event. Leaks via the memory trace are then prevented by T-IF and T-LOOP, discussed shortly.

Rule T-IDB is similar to rule T-LOADW. For the third premise, if l is either D or E, the block k has a public address, and thus the value assigned to register r is public; otherwise, when l is an ORAM bank, the register r is secret.

Rule T-BOP types binary operations, updating the security label of the target register to be the join of labels of the source registers. Rule T-ASSIGN gives the target register label $\texttt{L}$ as constants are not secret. Rules T-NOP is always safe and has no effect on the symbolic store or label environment. All of these operations occur on-chip, and so have pattern $\mathbf{F}$. Finally, rule T-SEQ types instruction sequences by composing the symbolic maps, label environments, and traces in the obvious way.

Branching Rules T-IF and T-LOOP consider structured control flow. Rule T-IF deals with instruction sequences of the form of $I = \iota_1; I_t; \iota_2; I_f$, where ι_1 is a branching instruction deciding, ι_2 is a jump instruction jumping over the false branch, and I_t and I_f are the true and false branches respectively; the relative offsets n_1 and n_2 are based on the length of these code sequences. We require both branches to have the same type, i.e. $\langle \Upsilon, Sym\rangle \to \langle \Upsilon', Sym'\rangle$, as for the sequence I itself.

When the security context is high, i.e. $\ell = \texttt{H}$, or when the if-condition is private, i.e. $\Upsilon(r_1) \sqcup \Upsilon(r_2) = \texttt{H}$, then ℓ' will be $\texttt{H}$ and we impose three restrictions. First, both of the blocks I_t and I_f must have equivalent trace patterns. (The trace of the true branch is $T_1 @ \mathbf{F}$ where T_1 covers I_t and $\mathbf{F}$ covers the jump instruction ι_2.) Second, if the security context is public, i.e. $\ell = \texttt{L}$, then we restrict $\vdash_{const} Sym$ to enforce $Sym(r)$ does not map to memory values. The reason is that in a public context, two equivalent symbolic memory values may refer to two different concrete values, since the memory region D can be modified. Third, for any register r, its value after taking either branch must be the same, or the register r must have a high security label (i.e. $\Upsilon'(r) = \texttt{H}$). So if $\Upsilon'(r) = \texttt{L}$, the type system enforces that its symbolic values on the two paths are equivalent, i.e. $Sym'(r) \equiv Sym'(r)$, which only requires $\vdash_{safe} Sym'(r)$.

The final premise for rule T-IF states that the sequence's trace pattern T is either $\mathbf{F} @ T_1 @ \mathbf{F}$ when both branches' patterns must be equal, or else is an or-pattern involving the trace T_2 from the else branch.

Instructions

$$\text{T-LOAD}\ \frac{\begin{array}{c} l \notin \textbf{ORAMbanks} \Rightarrow \Upsilon(r) = \mathtt{L} \\ \Upsilon' = \Upsilon[k \mapsto l] \qquad Sym' = Sym[k \mapsto Sym(r)] \\ T_0 = \textbf{read}(l, k, Sym(r)) \qquad T = select(l, T_0, T_0, l) \end{array}}{\ell \vdash \textbf{ldb}\ k \leftarrow l[r] : \langle \Upsilon, Sym \rangle \rightarrow \langle \Upsilon', Sym' \rangle; T}$$

$$\text{T-STORE}\ \frac{\begin{array}{c} Sym(k) = sv \qquad \Upsilon(k) = l \\ T_0 = \textbf{write}(l, k, sv) \qquad T = select(l, T_0, T_0, l) \end{array}}{\ell \vdash \textbf{stb}\ k : \langle \Upsilon, Sym \rangle \rightarrow \langle \Upsilon, Sym \rangle; T}$$

$$\text{T-LOADW}\ \frac{\begin{array}{c} l = \Upsilon(k) \qquad \Upsilon(r_2) \sqsubseteq slab(l) \\ \Upsilon' = \Upsilon[r_1 \mapsto slab(l)] \qquad sv = \mathtt{M}_l[k, Sym(r_2)] \\ Sym' = Sym[r_1 \mapsto sv] \end{array}}{\ell \vdash \textbf{ldw}\ r_1 \leftarrow k[r_2] : \langle \Upsilon, Sym \rangle \rightarrow \langle \Upsilon', Sym' \rangle; \mathbf{F}}$$

$$\text{T-STOREW}\ \frac{\ell \sqcup \Upsilon(r_1) \sqcup \Upsilon(r_2) \sqsubseteq slab(\Upsilon(k))}{\ell \vdash \textbf{stw}\ r_1 \rightarrow k[r_2] : \langle \Upsilon, Sym \rangle \rightarrow \langle \Upsilon, Sym \rangle; \mathbf{F}}$$

$$\text{T-IDB}\ \frac{\begin{array}{c} Sym(k) = sv \qquad \Upsilon(k) = l \\ \Upsilon' = \Upsilon[r \mapsto select(l, \mathtt{L}, \mathtt{L}, \mathtt{H})] \qquad Sym' = Sym[r \mapsto sv] \end{array}}{\ell \vdash r \leftarrow \textbf{idb}\ k : \langle \Upsilon, Sym \rangle \rightarrow \langle \Upsilon', Sym' \rangle; \mathbf{F}}$$

$$\text{T-BOP}\ \frac{\begin{array}{c} \ell' = \Upsilon(r_2) \sqcup \Upsilon(r_3) \qquad \Upsilon' = \Upsilon[r_1 \mapsto \ell'] \\ sv = Sym(r_2)\ aop\ Sym(r_3) \qquad Sym' = Sym[r_1 \mapsto sv] \end{array}}{\ell \vdash r_1 \leftarrow r_2\ aop\ r_3 : \langle \Upsilon, Sym \rangle \rightarrow \langle \Upsilon', Sym' \rangle; \mathbf{F}}$$

$$\text{T-ASSIGN}\ \frac{\Upsilon' = \Upsilon[r \mapsto \mathtt{L}] \qquad Sym' = Sym[r \mapsto n]}{\ell \vdash r \leftarrow n : \langle \Upsilon, Sym \rangle \rightarrow \langle \Upsilon', Sym' \rangle; \mathbf{F}}$$

$$\text{T-NOP}\ \ \ell \vdash \textbf{nop} : \langle \Upsilon, Sym \rangle \rightarrow \langle \Upsilon, Sym \rangle; \mathbf{F}$$

$$\text{T-SEQ}\ \frac{\begin{array}{c} \ell \vdash I : \langle \Upsilon, Sym \rangle \rightarrow \langle \Upsilon', Sym' \rangle; T_1 \\ \ell \vdash \iota : \langle \Upsilon', Sym' \rangle \rightarrow \langle \Upsilon'', Sym'' \rangle; T_2 \end{array}}{\ell \vdash I; \iota : \langle \Upsilon, Sym \rangle \rightarrow \langle \Upsilon'', Sym'' \rangle; T_1 @ T_2}$$

Branching

$$\text{T-IF}\ \frac{\begin{array}{c} I = \iota_1; I_t; \iota_2; I_f \qquad |I_t| = n_1 - 2 \qquad |I_f| + 1 = n_2 \\ \iota_1 = \textbf{br}\ r_1\ rop\ r_2 \hookrightarrow n_1 \qquad \iota_2 = \textbf{jmp}\ n_2 \\ \ell' = \ell \sqcup \Upsilon(r_1) \sqcup \Upsilon(r_2) \\ \ell' \vdash I_t : \langle \Upsilon, Sym \rangle \rightarrow \langle \Upsilon', Sym' \rangle; T_1 \\ \ell' \vdash I_f : \langle \Upsilon, Sym \rangle \rightarrow \langle \Upsilon', Sym' \rangle; T_2 \\ \ell' = \mathtt{H} \Rightarrow \left\{ \begin{array}{l} T_1 @ \mathbf{F} \equiv T_2\ \wedge \\ \ell = \mathtt{L} \Rightarrow \vdash_{const} Sym\ \wedge \\ \forall r.\ \Upsilon'(r) = \mathtt{L} \Rightarrow \vdash_{safe} Sym'(r) \end{array} \right\} \\ T = ite(\ell' = \mathtt{H},\ \mathbf{F} @ T_1 @ \mathbf{F},\ \mathbf{F} @ ((T_1 @ \mathbf{F}) + T_2)) \end{array}}{\ell \vdash I : \langle \Upsilon, Sym \rangle \rightarrow \langle \Upsilon', Sym' \rangle; T}$$

$$\text{T-LOOP}\ \frac{\begin{array}{c} I = I_c; \iota_1; I_b; \iota_2 \\ |I_b| = n_1 - 2 \qquad |I_c| + n_1 = 1 - n_2 \\ \iota_1 = \textbf{br}\ r_1\ rop\ r_2 \hookrightarrow n_1 \qquad \iota_2 = \textbf{jmp}\ n_2 \\ \ell \sqcup \Upsilon(r_1) \sqcup \Upsilon(r_2) \sqsubseteq \mathtt{L} \\ \ell \vdash I_c : \langle \Upsilon, Sym \rangle \rightarrow \langle \Upsilon', Sym' \rangle; T_1 \\ \ell \vdash I_b : \langle \Upsilon', Sym' \rangle \rightarrow \langle \Upsilon, Sym \rangle; T_2 \end{array}}{\ell \vdash I : \langle \Upsilon, Sym \rangle \rightarrow \langle \Upsilon', Sym' \rangle; \textbf{loop}(T_1, T_2)}$$

Subtyping

$$\text{T-SUB}\ \frac{\begin{array}{c} \ell \vdash \iota : \langle \Upsilon, Sym \rangle \rightarrow \langle \Upsilon', Sym' \rangle; T \\ \Upsilon' \preceq \Upsilon'' \qquad Sym' \preceq Sym'' \end{array}}{\ell \vdash \iota : \langle \Upsilon, Sym \rangle \rightarrow \langle \Upsilon'', Sym'' \rangle; T}$$

$$\text{S-LABEL}\ \frac{\begin{array}{c} \forall r. \Upsilon(r) \sqsubseteq \Upsilon'(r) \\ \forall k. \Upsilon(k) = \Upsilon'(k) \end{array}}{\Upsilon \preceq \Upsilon'}$$

$$\text{S-SYM}\ \frac{\begin{array}{c} \forall r. Sym'(r) = ? \vee Sym(r) = Sym'(r) \\ \forall k. Sym'(k) = ? \vee Sym(k) = Sym'(k) \end{array}}{Sym \preceq Sym'}$$

Figure 7. Security Type System for $\mathcal{L}_T$

Rule T-LOOP imposes structural requirements on I similar to T-IF. The premise $\ell \sqcup \Upsilon(r_1) \sqcup \Upsilon(r_2) \sqsubseteq \mathtt{L}$ implies two restrictions. On the one hand, $\ell \sqsubseteq \mathtt{L}$, prevents any loop from appearing in a secret if-statement, because otherwise the number of loop iterations may leak information about which branch is taken. On the other hand, $\Upsilon(r_1) \sqcup \Upsilon(r_2) \sqsubseteq \mathtt{L}$ implies that the loop condition must be public, or otherwise, similarly, the number of iterations would leak secret information about r_1 and/or r_2.

Subtyping Finally, rule T-SUB supports subtyping on the symbolic store and the label map. For the first, a symbolic store Sym can approximated by a store Sym' that either agrees on the symbolic values mapped to be Sym or maps them to ?. For the second, a register's security label can be approximated by one higher in the lattice; block labels may not change. Subtyping is important for typing join points after branches or loops. For example, if a conditional assigned a register r the value 1 in the true branch but assigned r to 2 in the false branch, we would use subtyping to map r to ? to ensure that the symbolic store at the end of both branches agrees, as required by T-IF.

4.4 Security theorem

All well-typed programs are memory-trace oblivious:

THEOREM 1. *Given I, Υ, and Sym, if there exists some Υ', Sym' and T such that $\mathtt{L} \vdash I : \langle \Upsilon, Sym \rangle \rightarrow \langle \Upsilon', Sym' \rangle; T$, where $\forall r. Sym(r) = ?$ and $\Upsilon(r) = L$ and $\forall k. Sym(k) = ?$ and $\Upsilon(k) = D$ then program I is memory-trace oblivious.*

The proof can be found in our technical report [32].

5. Compilation

We have developed a compiler from an imperative, C-like source language, which we call $\mathcal{L}_S$, to $\mathcal{L}_T$. Our compiler is implemented in about 7600 lines of Java, with roughly 400 LoC dedicated to the parser, 700 LoC to the type checker, 3500 LoC to the compiler/optimizer, 950 LoC to the code generator, and the remainder to utility functions. This section informally describes our compilation approach.

5.1 Source Language

Syntax An $\mathcal{L}_S$ program is a collection of (possibly mutually recursive) functions and a collection of (possibly mutually recursive) type definitions. A type definition is simply a mapping of a type name to a type where types are either natural numbers, arrays, or pointers to records (i.e., C-style `structs`). Each type is annotated with a security label which is either `secret` or `public` indicating whether the data should be visible/inferrable by the adversary or not.

A function consists of a sequence of statements s which are either no-ops, variable assignments, array assignments, conditionals, while loops, or returns. As usual, conditional branches and loop bodies may consist of one or more statements. Expressions e appearing in statements (e.g., in assignments) consist of variables x, arithmetic ops e_1 aop e_2, array reads $e[e]$, and numeric constants n. Variables may hold any data other than functions (i.e., there are no function pointers). Guards in conditionals and while loops consist of predicates involving relational operators.

Typing $\mathcal{L}_S$ programs are type checked before they are compiled. We do this using an information flow-style type system (cf. the survey of Sabelfeld and Myers [43]). As is standard, the type system prevents explicit flows and implicit flows. In particular, it disallows assignments like `p = s` where `p` is a public variable and `s` is a secret variable, and disallows conditionals like `if (s == 0) then p = 0 else p = 1`, which leaks information about `s` since after the conditional the adversary knows `p == 0` implies `s == 0`. It also disallows array writes like `p[s] = 5` since the adversary can learn the value of `s` by seeing which element of the public array has changed. Note that accessing `s[p]` is safe because, despite knowing the index, an adversary cannot learn the value being accessed.

To prevent the length of a memory trace from revealing information, we require that loop guard expressions only involve public values (which is a standard restriction [43]). One can work around this problem by "padding out" loop iterations, e.g., by converting a loop like `while (slen > 0) { sarr[slen--]++; }` to be `plen = N; while (plen > 0) { if (plen <= slen) sarr[--plen]++; }` where `N` is a large, fixed constant. For similar reasons we also require that whether a function is called or returned from, and which function it is, may not depend on secret information (e.g., the call or return may not occur in a conditional whose guard involves secret information).

Compilation overview After source-language type checking, compilation proceeds in four stages—memory layout, translation, padding, and register allocation—after which the result is type checked using the $\mathcal{L}_T$ type system, to confirm that it is memory-trace oblivious.[5]

5.2 Memory bank allocation

The first stage of compilation allocates global variables to memory banks. Public variables are always stored in RAM, while secret variables will be allocated either to ERAM or ORAM. Two blocks in the scratchpad are reserved for secret and public variables, respectively, that will fit entirely within the block; these are essentially those that contain numbers, (pointers to) records, and small arrays. Such variables will be loaded into the scratchpad at the start of executing a program, and written back to memory at the end. The remaining scratchpad blocks are used for handling (large) arrays; the compiler will always use the same block for the same array. Public arrays are allocated in RAM, and secret arrays always indexed by public values are allocated in ERAM, and ORAM otherwise. The compiler initially assigns a distinct logical ORAM bank for each secret array, and allocates logical banks up to the hardware limit.

5.3 Basic compilation

The next stage is basic compilation (translation). Expressions are compiled by loading relevant variables/data into registers, performing the computation, and then storing back the result. Statements are compiled idiomatically to match the structure expected by the type rules in Figure 7 (with some work deferred to the padding stage).

Perhaps the most interesting part is handling variable accesses. Variables permanently resident in the scratchpad are loaded at the start of the program, and stored back at the end. Each read/write results in a **ldw**, to load a variable into a temporary register, and a **stw** to store back the result. Accesses to data (i.e., arrays) not permanently stored in the scratchpad will also require a **ldb** to load the relevant block into the scratchpad first and likewise a **stb** to store it back. A standard software cache, rather than a scratchpad, could eliminate repeated loads and stores of blocks from memory but could violate MTO. This is because a non-present block will induce memory traffic while a present block will not, and the presence/absence of traffic could be correlated with secret information. To avoid this, we have the compiler emit instructions that perform caching explicitly, using the scratchpad, with caching only enabled when in a public context, i.e., in a portion of code whose control flow does not depend on secret data. To support software-based caching, the compiler statically maps memory-resident data to particular scratchpad blocks, always loading the same data to the same block. Prior to doing so, and when safe, the compiler uses the **idb** instruction to check whether the relevant scratchpad block contains the memory block we want and loads directly from it, if so.

[5] This is essentially a kind of *translation validation* [38], which removes the compiler from the trusted computing base. We believe that well typed $\mathcal{L}_S$ programs yield well typed $\mathcal{L}_T$ programs, but leave a proof as future work.

Supporting functions requires handling calling contexts and local variables. We do this with two stacks, one in RAM and one in ERAM. Function calls are only permitted in a public context, which means that normal stack allocation and deallocation reveal no information, so no ORAM stack is needed. When a function is called, the current scratchpad variable blocks are pushed on the relevant stacks. At the start of a function, we load the blocks that hold the local variables. Local variables implementing ORAM arrays are stored by reference, with the variable pointing to the actual array stored in ORAM. This array is deallocated when its variable is popped from the stack, when the function returns (which like calls are allowed only in a public context).

The compiler is also responsible for emitting instructions that load code into the instruction scratchpad, as implicit instruction fetches could reveal information [33]. (To bootstrap, the first code block is loaded automatically.) At the moment, our compiler emits code that loads the entire program into the scratchpad at the start; we leave to future work support for on-the-fly instruction scratchpad use.

5.4 Padding and register allocation

Both branches of a secret conditional must produce the same trace. We ensure they do so by inserting extra instructions in one or both branches according to the solution to the *shortest common supersequence* problem [18]. When matching the two branches, we must account for the memory trace and instruction execution times. Only **ldb** and **stb** emit memory events; we discuss these shortly. While our formalism assumes each instruction takes unit time, the reality is different (cf. Table 2): times are deterministic, but non-uniform. For single-cycle operations (e.g., 64b ALU ops), we pad with **nop**s. For two-cycle **ldw** and **stw** instructions, we pad with two **nops**. For multiply and divide instructions, which take 70 cycles each, we could pad with 70 **nops** but this results in a large space overhead. As such, we pad both with the instruction $r0 \leftarrow r0 * r0$, where $r0$ is always 0. For conditionals, we pad the not-taken branch with two **nops**, to account for the hardware-induced delay on the taken branch.

Padding for **stb** and **ldb** requires instructions that generate matching trace events. An access to ORAM is the simplest to pad, since the adversary cannot distinguish a read from a write. We can load any block (e.g., the first block of the ORAM) into a dedicated "dummy" scratchpad block, i.e. this block is used for loading and saving dummy memory blocks only.

For RAM and ERAM, the address being accessed is visible, so we need to make sure that the equivalent padding accesses the same address. To do this, the compiler should insert further instructions to compute the address. These instructions can be computed using the symbolic value: (1) if the symbolic value is a constant, then insert an assign instruction; (2) if the symbolic value is a binary operation of two symbolic values, then insert instructions to compute the two symbolic values respectively, and then another instruction to compute the binary operation; and (3) if the symbolic value is a memory value, then insert instructions to compute the offset first, and then insert a **ldw** instruction.

With instructions inserted to compute the address, we must emit either a load or a store depending on the instruction we are trying to match. For RAM, this instruction will always be a load because we perform padding in the H context, and the type system prevents writing to RAM. To mimic the **read**(l, k, sv) trace pattern, we first compute sv and then insert a **ldb** $k \leftarrow l[r]$ instruction where r stores the value for sv. To handle ERAM writes is challenging because we want the write to be a no-op but not appear to be so. To do this, we require the compiler to *always* follow an ERAM **ldb** with a **stb** back to the same address. In doing so, the compiler also prevents the padded instruction from overwriting a dirty scratchpad block.

At the conclusion of the padding stage we perform standard register allocation to fill in actual registers for the temporaries we have used to this point.

6. Hardware Implementation

We implement our deterministic processor by modifying Rocket, a single-issue, in-order, 6-stage pipelined CPU developed at UC Berkeley [41]. Rocket implements the RISC-V instruction set [51] and is comparable to an ARM Cortex A5 CPU. We modified the baseline processor to remove branch prediction logic (so that conditional branches are always not-taken) and to make each instruction execute in a fixed number of cycles. We describe the remaining changes below.

Instruction-set Extension We customize RISC-V to add a single data transfer instruction that implements **ldb** and **stb** from the formalism. We do this using a Data Transfer accelerator (Figure 2) that attaches to the processor's accelerator interface [50]. We also interface the Data Transfer accelerator with the x86-Linux host through Rocket's control register file so that it can load an `elf`-formatted binary into GhostRider's memory and reset its processor. Once this is done, the host performs processor control register writes to initiate transfers from the co-processor memory to the code ORAM for the code and data sections of the binary. The first code block of a program is loaded into the instruction scratchpad to begin execution; if subsequent instruction blocks are needed they must be loaded explicitly.

Scratchpads GhostRider has two scratchpads, one for code and one for data, each of which can hold eight 4KB blocks. The instruction scratchpad is implemented similar to an 8-way set-associative cache, where each way contains one block. The accelerator transfers one block at a time to a specified way in the instruction scratchpad. Once a block has been written, the valid and tag bits for that block are updated. The architecture does not implement the **idb** instruction from the formalism; instead, the compiler uses the first 8 bytes of every block to remember its address.

ORAM controller We implement ORAM by building on the Phantom ORAM controller [35] and implement an ORAM tree 13 levels deep (i.e., 2^{12} leaf buckets), with 4 blocks per bucket and an effective capacity of 64MB. ORAM controllers include an on-chip *stash* to temporarily buffer ORAM blocks before they are written out to memory. We set this stash to be 128 blocks. The Phantom design (and likewise, Ascend's [15–17]) treats the stash as a cache for ORAM lookups, which is safe when handling timing channels by controlling the memory access rate. GhostRider mitigates timing channels by having the compiler enforce MTO while assuming that events take the same time. As such, we modify Phantom's design to generate an access to a random leaf in case the requested block is found in the stash, to ensure uniform access times.

FPGA Implementation GhostRider is implemented on one of Convey HC-2ex's [10] four Xilinx Virtex-6 LX760 FPGAs. We measure hardware design size in terms of FPGA *slices* for logic and *Block RAMs* for on-chip memory. A slice comprises four 6-input, 2-output lookup tables (implementing configurable logic) and eight flip-flops (as storage elements) in addition to multiplexers, while each BRAM on Virtex-6 is either an 18Kb or 36Kb SRAM with up to two configurable read-write ports. The GhostRider prototype uses 47,357 such slices (39% of total) to implement both the CPU and the ORAM controller, and requires 685 of 1440 18Kb BRAMs (47.5%). Table 1 shows how these resources are broken up between the Rocket CPU and the ORAM controller, with the remaining resources being used by Convey HC-2ex's boilerplate logic to interface with the x86 core and DRAM. Note that this breakdown is a synthesis estimate before place and route.

Our prototype currently supports one data ORAM bank, one code ORAM bank, and one ERAM bank. We do not implement encryption (it is a small, fixed cost and uninteresting in terms of performance trends), and do not have separate DRAM; all public data is stored in ERAM when running on the hardware.

The Convey machine requires the hardware design to be run at 150 MHz while our ORAM controller prototype currently synthesizes to a maximum operating frequecy of 140MHz. Pending further optimization to meet 150 MHz timing, we run *both* the CPU and the ORAM controller in a 75 MHz clock domain, and use asynchronous FIFOs to connect the ORAM controller to the DDR DRAM controllers.

GhostRider simulator timing model In addition to demonstrating feasibility with our hardware prototype, we study the effect of GhostRider's compiler on alternate, more efficient ORAM configurations, e.g., Phantom at 150MHz [35] with two ORAM banks and a distinct (non-encrypting) DRAM bank. Hence we generate a timing model for both the modified processor and ORAM banks based on Phantom's hardware implementation [35], and incorporate the timing model into an ISA-level emulator for the RISC-V architecture; the model is shown in Table 2.

	Slices	BRAMs
Rocket	9287 (8.8%)	36 (10.5%)
ORAM	12845 (12.2%)	211 (61.5%)

Table 1. FPGA synthesis results on Convey HC-2ex.

Feature	**Latency** (# cycles)
64b ALU	1
Jump taken/not taken	3/1
64b Multiply/Divide	70/70
Load/Store from Scratchpad	2
DRAM (4kB access)	634
Encrypted RAM (4kB access)	662
ORAM 13 levels (4kB block)	4262

Table 2. Timing model for GhostRider simulator.

Name	Brief Description	Input Size (KB)
sum	Summing up all positive elements in an array	10^3
findmax	Find the max element in an array	10^3
heappush	insert an element into a min-heap	10^3
perm	computing a permutation executing $a[b[i]] = i$ for all i	10^3
histogram	compute the number of occurances of each last digit	10^3
dijkstra	Single-source shortest path	10^3
search	binary search algorithm	1.7×10^4
heappop	pop the minimal element from a min-heap	1.7×10^4

Table 3. Evaluated programs organized into programs with predictable, partially predictable, and data dependent memory access patterns (in order from top).

7. Empirical Evaluation

Programs Table 3 lists all the programs we use in our evaluation. These programs range from standard algorithms to data structures and include predictable, partially predictable, and predominantly irregular (data-driven) memory access patterns.

Execution time results We present measurements both for the simulator and for the actual FPGA hardware, starting with the former because the simulator allows us to evaluate the benefits from splitting memory into ERAM and ORAM banks v. additionally using a scratchpad. We also discuss the execution time results by categorizing them based on the regularity in the programs' access patterns.

`Non-secure`	Non-secure program: all variables in ERAM, no padding, and uses scratchpad.
`Baseline`	Secure baseline: all secret variables in a single ORAM, no scratchpad.
`Split ORAM`	Variables can be split across multiple ORAM banks, or placed in ERAM. Performs padding. No scratchpad.
`Final`	Scratchpad on top of `Split ORAM`.

(a) Legends.

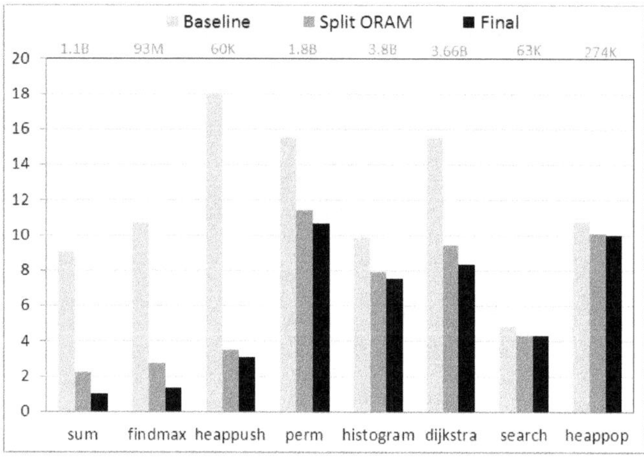

(b) Slowdown in comparison with non-secure version.

Figure 8. Simulator-based execution time results.

Simulator-based results Figure 8 depicts the slowdown of various configurations relative to a non-secure configuration that simply stores data in ERAM and employs the scratchpad. Our non-secure baseline uses a scratchpad instead of a hardware cache in order to isolate the cost of MTO/ORAM. The secure `Baseline` configuration places all secret variables in a single ORAM, while `Split ORAM` employs the GhostRider optimization of using ERAM and multiple ORAM banks, and `Final` further adds the (secure) use of a scratchpad.

Three out of eight programs—`sum`, `findmax`, and `heappush`—have a predictable access pattern and the secure program generated by GhostRider relies mainly on ERAM. Hence, each MTO program (`Final`) has almost no slowdown to 3.08× slowdown in comparison its non-secure counterpart (`Non-secure`), and correspondingly faster than `Baseline` by 5.85× to 9.03×.

For `perm`, `histogram`, and `dijkstra`, which have partially predictable and partially sensitive memory access patterns, our compiler attempts to place sensitive arrays inside both ERAM and ORAM and also favors splitting into several smaller ORAM banks without breaking MTO. As shown in Figure 8, for such programs, `Final` can achieve a 1.30× to 1.85× speedup over `Baseline` (with 7.56× to 10.68× slowdown compared to `Non-secure`, respectively).

For `search` and `heappop`, which have predominantly sensitive memory access patterns, the speedup of `Final` over `Baseline` is not as significant, i.e. 1.07× and 1.12× respectively, and is due mostly to the usage of two ORAMs to store arrays instead of a single ORAM.

Examining the impact of the use of the scratchpad in the results, we can see that for the first six programs, `Final` reduces execution time compared to `Split ORAM` by a factor from 1.05× up to 2.23×.For `search` and `heappop`, the scratchpad provides no benefit because for these programs all data is allocated in ORAM, as array indices are secret (so the access pattern is sensitive), and our type system disallows caching of ORAM blocks. The reason is that the presence of the data in the cache could reveal something about the secret indices. A more sophisticated type system, or a relaxation of MTO, could do better; we plan to explore such improvements in future work.

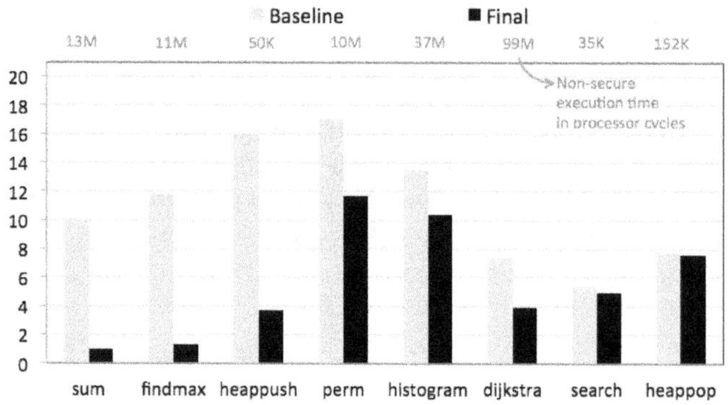

Figure 9. FPGA based execution time results: Slowdown of `Baseline` and `Final` versions compared to non-secure version of the program. Note that unlike Figure 8, `Final` uses only a single ORAM bank and conflates ERAM and DRAM (cf. Section 6).

FPGA-based results For the FPGA we run the same set of programs as in Table 3, but restrict the input size to be around 100 KB, due to limitations of our prototype. Speedups of `Final` over the secure `Baseline` follow a trend similar to the simulator, as shown in Figure 9. Regular programs have speedups in the range of 4.33× (for `heappush`) to 8.94× (for `findmax`). Partially regular programs like `perm` and `histogram` get a speedup of 1.46× and 1.3× respectively. Finally, irregular programs such as `search` and `heappop` see very little improvements (1.08× and 1.02× respectively).

Differences between the simulator and hardware numbers can be attributed to mulitple factors. First, the simulator imperfectly models the Convey memory system's latency, always assuming the worst case, and thus slowdowns compared to the non-secure baseline are often worse on the simulator (cf. `heappop` and `heappush`).

Second, the timing of certain hardware operations is different on the prototype and the simulator (where we consider the latter to be aspirational, per the end of Section 6). In particular, per Table 2, the simulator models access latency for ORAM as 4262 cycles and ERAM as 662 cycles, accounting for both reading data blocks from DRAM and moving the chosen 4KB block into the scratchpad BRAMs on the FPGA. On the hardware, ORAM and ERAM latencies are 5991 and 1312 cycles, respectively, measured using performance counters in the hardware design. The higher ERAM and ORAM access times reduce the slowdown on the simulator by amplifying the benefit of the scratchpad, which is used by the non-secure baseline, but not by the secure baseline (cf. `findmax` and `sum`).

Third, the benefit of using the scratchpad can differ depending on the input size. This effect is particularly pronounced for Dijkstra, where the ratio of secure to non-secure baseline execution is smaller for the hardware than for the simulator. The reason is that the hardware experiment uses a smaller input that fills only about 1/5 of a scratchpad block. Hence, in the non-secure baseline, the block is reloaded after relatively fewer accesses, resulting in a relatively greater number of block loads and thus bringing the performance of the non-secure program closer to that of the secure baseline.

Finally, note that the simulator's use of multiple ORAM banks, and DRAM with different timings, is a source of differences, but this effect is dwarfed by the other effects.

8. Related Work

Oblivious RAM was first proposed by Goldreich and Ostrovsky [21]. Since then, the community has made significant advances [20, 22, 23, 30, 53, 54] such that it evolved from a theoretical concept to real-life hardware prototypes [35, 40].

As an alternative to ORAM, *active RAM* capable of handling programmable logic may also be employed, such that memory addresses must be encrypted when transmitted over the memory bus. One candidate technology is the Hybrid Memory Cube [11]. Our compiler techniques are readily applicable to active RAM as well.

One line of past research has focused on designing customized data oblivious algorithms [7, 14, 24] such that they outperform generic ORAM simulation (i.e., placing all data in a single ORAM). This approach, however, provides point solutions to point problems, whereas our approach is general purpose and requires less human effort.

Secure type systems We build on ideas we previously proposed [33] for type-based enforcement of memory trace obliviousness. Our prior approach worked for a C-like language with only ORAM and RAM, whereas we consider a lower-level assembly language that additionally supports a scratchpad and ERAM; both extensions required nontrivial changes. Our full type system (see the full version [32]) also supports function calls and data structures. We also built a more full-featured compiler targeting a real architecture, rather than evaluating using a simpler simulation.

More generally, our work is the area of work on type-based enforcement of information-flow security [43], a topic sometimes applied to low level languages [3, 4, 6, 8, 28, 36, 39, 55]. Compared to these, our $\mathcal{L}_T$ type system is distinguished by its handling of a novel memory hierarchy. Our type system is essentially a kind of typed assembly language [37], but aims for information flow security rather than memory safety (and related properties). Finally, our compiler and type system are reminiscent of work that transforms programs to eliminate timing channels [2, 5, 12, 27] where inserted padding aims to equalize execution times. Ultimately, however, a program that is without timing leaks may still leak information via the memory trace.

Secure architectures HIDE [56] involves a compiler-assisted technique to obfuscate a processor's memory accesses but stops short of implementing provably secure oblivious RAMs. Shroud [34] is a storage system implementing ORAM using trusted co-processors (TPMs [1]) in datacenters; it uses complementary techniques to exploit parallelism in ORAM algorithms. Ascend [15–17] and Phantom [35] are two recent projects that have introduced adding oblivious computation to processors secure in the XOM model [42, 47, 48]—ORAM controllers presented in these works can be re-used in GhostRider. The key conceptual difference is that our MTO system uses the program's logic to optimize ORAM usage, and to account for the *length* of the memory trace, while Ascend and Phantom address timing and termination channels independent of the program's logic and ignore the length of the trace (hence may not terminate without leaking information).

9. Conclusion

We have presented the first complete memory trace oblivious system—GhostRider—comprising of a novel compiler, type system, and hardware architecture. The compiled programs not only provably satisfy memory trace obliviousness, but also exhibit up to nearly order-of-magnitude performance gains in comparison with placing all variables in a single ORAM bank. By enabling compiler analyses to target a joint ERAM-ORAM memory system, and by employing a compiler-controlled scratchpad, this work opens up several performance optimization opportunities in tuning bank configurations (size and access granularity) and, on a broader level, into co-designing data structures and algorithms for a heterogeneous yet oblivious memory hierarchy.

Acknowledgements We thank the anonymous reviewers, and our shepherd John Criswell, for their helpful feedback. This research was sponsored by NSF grants CNS-1111599 and CNS-1314857, the AFOSR under MURI award FA9550-09-1-0539, and the US Army Research laboratory and the UK Ministry of Defence under Agreement Number W911NF-06-3-0001. The views and conclusions contained in this document are those of the authors and should not be interpreted as representing the official policies, either expressed or implied, of the US Army Research Laboratory, the U.S. Government, the UK Ministry of Defense, or the UK Government. The US and UK Governments are authorized to reproduce and distribute reprints for Government purposes notwithstanding any copyright notation hereon.

References

[1] Trusted Platform Module (TPM) Summary. `http://www.trustedcomputinggroup.org/resources/trusted_platform_module_tpm_summary`.

[2] J. Agat. Transforming out Timing Leaks. In *POPL*, pages 40–53, 2000.

[3] G. Barthe and T. Rezk. Non-interference for a JVM-like language. In *TLDI '05*, pages 103–112, 2005.

[4] G. Barthe, T. Rezk, A. Russo, and A. Sabelfeld. Security of multithreaded programs by compilation. *ACM Trans. Inf. Syst. Secur.*, 13(3):21:1–21:32, 2010.

[5] G. Barthe, T. Rezk, and M. Warnier. Preventing Timing Leaks Through Transactional Branching Instructions. *Electron. Notes Theor. Comput. Sci.*, 153(2):33–55, 2006.

[6] F. Bavera and E. Bonelli. Type-based information flow analysis for bytecode languages with variable object field policies. In *SAC*, pages 347–351, 2008.

[7] M. Blanton, A. Steele, and M. Aliasgar. Data-Oblivious Graph Algorithms for Secure Computation and Outsourcing. In *ASIACCS*, 2013.

[8] E. Bonelli, A. Compagnoni, and R. Medel. Information flow analysis for a typed assembly language with polymorphic stacks. In *CASSIS*, pages 37–56, 2006.

[9] R. Chow, P. Golle, M. Jakobsson, E. Shi, J. Staddon, R. Masuoka, and J. Molina. Controlling data in the cloud: outsourcing computation without outsourcing control. In *ACM Cloud Computing Security Workshop (CCSW)*, pages 85–90, 2009.

[10] C. Computer. The convey HC2 architectural overview. `http://www.conveycomputer.com/files/4113/5394/7097/Convey_HC-2_Architectual_Overview.pdf`.

[11] H. Consortium. Hybrid memory cube. http://hybridmemorycube.org/.

[12] B. Coppens, I. Verbauwhede, K. D. Bosschere, and B. D. Sutter. Practical Mitigations for Timing-Based Side-Channel Attacks on Modern x86 Processors. In *IEEE S & P*, pages 45–60, 2009.

[13] Z. Deng and G. Smith. Lenient array operations for practical secure information flow. In *CSF*, pages 115–124, 2004.

[14] D. Eppstein, M. T. Goodrich, and R. Tamassia. Privacy-preserving data-oblivious geometric algorithms for geographic data. In *GIS*, pages 13–22, 2010.

[15] C. W. Fletcher, M. v. Dijk, and S. Devadas. A secure processor architecture for encrypted computation on untrusted programs. In *STC*, 2012.

[16] C. W. Fletcher, L. Ren, A. Kwon, M. van Dijk, E. Stefanov, and S. Devadas. RAW Path ORAM: A low-latency, low-area hardware ORAM controller with integrity verification. *IACR Cryptology ePrint Archive*, page 431, 2014.

[17] C. W. Fletcher, L. Ren, X. Yu, M. van Dijk, O. Khan, and S. Devadas. Suppressing the Oblivious RAM timing channel while making information leakage and program efficiency trade-offs. In *HPCA*, pages 213–224, 2014.

[18] M. Garey and D. Johnson. *Computers and Intractability: A Guide to the Theory of NP-Completeness*. W.H. Freeman, 1979.

[19] T. Gilmont, J. didier Legat, and J. jacques Quisquater. Enhancing security in the memory management unit. In *EUROMICRO*, 1999.

[20] O. Goldreich. Towards a theory of software protection and simulation by oblivious RAMs. In *STOC*, 1987.

[21] O. Goldreich and R. Ostrovsky. Software protection and simulation on oblivious RAMs. *J. ACM*, 1996.

[22] M. T. Goodrich and M. Mitzenmacher. Privacy-Preserving Access of Outsourced Data via Oblivious RAM Simulation. In *ICALP*, pages 576–587, 2011.

[23] M. T. Goodrich, M. Mitzenmacher, O. Ohrimenko, and R. Tamassia. Privacy-preserving group data access via stateless oblivious RAM simulation. In *SODA*, 2012.

[24] M. T. Goodrich, O. Ohrimenko, and R. Tamassia. Data-oblivious graph drawing model and algorithms. *CoRR*, abs/1209.0756, 2012.

[25] T. C. Group. Trusted computing group. `http://www.trustedcomputinggroup.org/`.

[26] J. A. Halderman, S. D. Schoen, N. Heninger, W. Clarkson, W. Paul, J. A. Calandrino, A. J. Feldman, J. Appelbaum, and E. W. Felten. Lest we remember: cold-boot attacks on encryption keys. *Commun. ACM*, 52(5):91–98, 2009.

[27] D. Hedin and D. Sands. Timing aware information flow security for a javacard-like bytecode. *Electron. Notes Theor. Comput. Sci.*, 141(1):163–182, Dec. 2005.

[28] N. Kobayashi and K. Shirane. Type-based information flow analysis for low-level languages. In *APLAS*, 2002.

[29] P. C. Kocher, J. Jaffe, B. Jun, and P. Rohatgi. Introduction to differential power analysis. *J. Cryptographic Engineering*, 1(1):5–27, 2011.

[30] E. Kushilevitz, S. Lu, and R. Ostrovsky. On the (In)security of Hash-based Oblivious RAM and a New Balancing Scheme. In *SODA*, 2012.

[31] D. Lie, J. Mitchell, C. A. Thekkath, and M. Horowitz. Specifying and Verifying Hardware for Tamper-Resistant Software. In *IEEE S & P*, 2003.

[32] C. Liu, A. Harris, M. Maas, M. Hicks, M. Tiwari, and E. Shi. GhostRider: A hardware-software system for memory trace oblivious computation. Technical Report CS-TR-5041, University of Maryland, Department of Computer Science, Jan. 2015.

[33] C. Liu, M. Hicks, and E. Shi. Memory Trace Oblivious Program Execution. In *CSF*, 2013.

[34] J. R. Lorch, B. Parno, J. W. Mickens, M. Raykova, and J. Schiffman. Shroud: ensuring private access to large-scale data in the data center. In *FAST*, 2013.

[35] M. Maas, E. Love, E. Stefanov, M. Tiwari, E. Shi, K. Asanovic, J. Kubiatowicz, and D. Song. Phantom: Practical Oblivious Computation in a Secure Processor. In *CCS*, 2013.

[36] R. Medel, A. Compagnoni, and E. Bonelli. A typed assembly language for non-interference. In *ICTCS*, pages 360–374, 2005.

[37] G. Morrisett, D. Walker, K. Crary, and N. Glew. From system F to typed assembly language. *ACM Trans. Program. Lang. Syst.*, 21(3):527–568, 1999.

[38] A. Pnueli, M. Siegel, and E. Singerman. Translation Validation. In *TACAS*, 1998.

[39] F. Pottier and V. Simonet. Information flow inference for ML. *ACM Trans. Program. Lang. Syst.*, 25(1):117–158, 2003.

[40] L. Ren, X. Yu, C. W. Fletcher, M. Van Dijk, and S. Devadas. Design space exploration and optimization of path oblivious ram in secure processors. In *ISCA*, 2013.

[41] riscv.org. Launching the Open-Source Rocket Chip Generator, Oct. 2014. `https://blog.riscv.org/2014/10/launching-the-open-source-rocket-chip-generator/`.

[42] B. Rogers, S. Chhabra, Y. Solihin, and M. Prvulovic. Using Address Independent Seed Encryption and Bonsai Merkle Trees to Make Secure Processors OS- and Performance-Friendly. In *MICRO*, pages 183 –196, 2007.

[43] A. Sabelfeld and A. C. Myers. Language-based information-flow security. *IEEE Journal on Selected Areas in Communications*, 21(1):5–19, Jan. 2003.

[44] E. Shi, T.-H. H. Chan, E. Stefanov, and M. Li. Oblivious RAM with $O((\log N)^3)$ worst-case cost. In *ASIACRYPT*, pages 197–214, 2011.

[45] S. Skorobogatov. Low temperature data remanence in static RAM. Technical Report UCAM-CL-TR-536, University of Cambridge, Computer Laboratory, June 2002.

[46] E. Stefanov, M. van Dijk, E. Shi, T.-H. H. Chan, C. Fletcher, L. Ren, X. Yu, and S. Devadas. Path ORAM: an Extremely Simple Oblivious RAM Protocol. IACR Cryptology ePrint Archive, 2013. `http://eprint.iacr.org/2013/280`.

[47] G. E. Suh, D. Clarke, B. Gassend, M. van Dijk, and S. Devadas. AEGIS: architecture for tamper-evident and tamper-resistant processing. In *ICS*, pages 160–171, 2003.

[48] D. L. C. Thekkath, M. Mitchell, P. Lincoln, D. Boneh, J. Mitchell, and M. Horowitz. Architectural support for copy and tamper resistant software. *SIGOPS Oper. Syst. Rev.*, 34(5):168–177, Nov. 2000.

[49] A. Vasudevan, J. McCune, J. Newsome, A. Perrig, and L. van Doorn. CARMA: A Hardware Tamper-Resistant Isolated Execution Environment on Commodity x86 Platforms. In *ASIACCS*, May 2012.

[50] H. Vo, Y. Lee, A. Waterman, and K. Asanović. A Case for OS-Friendly Hardware Accelerators. In *WIVOSCA*, 2013.

[51] A. Waterman, Y. Lee, D. A. Patterson, and K. Asanović. The RISC-V Instruction Set Manual, Volume I: Base User-Level ISA. Technical Report UCB/EECS-2011-62, EECS Department, University of California, Berkeley, May 2011.

[52] L. Whitney. Microsoft Urges Laws to Boost Trust in the Cloud. `http://news.cnet.com/8301-1009_3-10437844-83.html`.

[53] P. Williams and R. Sion. Single round access privacy on outsourced storage. In *CCS*, 2012.

[54] P. Williams, R. Sion, and B. Carbunar. Building castles out of mud: practical access pattern privacy and correctness on untrusted storage. In *CCS*, pages 139–148, 2008.

[55] S. A. Zdancewic. Programming Languages for Information Security. *PhD thesis*, 2002.

[56] X. Zhuang, T. Zhang, and S. Pande. Hide: an infrastructure for efficiently protecting information leakage on the address bus. *SIGARCH Comput. Archit. News*, 32(5):72–84, Oct. 2004.

Freecursive ORAM: [Nearly] Free Recursion and Integrity Verification for Position-based Oblivious RAM

Christopher W. Fletcher†, Ling Ren†, Albert Kwon†, Marten van Dijk‡, Srinivas Devadas†

† Massachusetts Institute of Technology – {cwfletch, renling, kwonal, devadas}@mit.edu
‡ University of Connecticut – vandijk@engr.uconn.edu

Abstract

Oblivious RAM (ORAM) is a cryptographic primitive that hides memory access patterns as seen by untrusted storage. Recently, ORAM has been architected into secure processors. A big challenge for hardware ORAM schemes is how to efficiently manage the Position Map (PosMap), a central component in modern ORAM algorithms. Implemented naïvely, the PosMap causes ORAM to be fundamentally unscalable in terms of on-chip area. On the other hand, a technique called Recursive ORAM fixes the area problem yet significantly increases ORAM's performance overhead.

To address this challenge, we propose three new mechanisms. We propose a new ORAM structure called the PosMap Lookaside Buffer (PLB) and PosMap compression techniques to reduce the performance overhead from Recursive ORAM empirically (the latter also improves the construction asymptotically). Through simulation, we show that these techniques reduce the memory bandwidth overhead needed to support recursion by 95%, reduce overall ORAM bandwidth by 37% and improve overall SPEC benchmark performance by 1.27×. We then show how our PosMap compression techniques further facilitate an extremely efficient integrity verification scheme for ORAM which we call PosMap MAC (PMMAC). For a practical parameterization, PMMAC reduces the amount of hashing needed for integrity checking by $\geq 68\times$ relative to prior schemes and introduces only 7% performance overhead.

We prototype our mechanisms in hardware and report area and clock frequency for a complete ORAM design post-synthesis and post-layout using an ASIC flow in a 32 nm commercial process. With 2 DRAM channels, the design post-layout runs at 1 GHz and has a total area of .47 mm^2. Depending on PLB-specific parameters, the PLB accounts for 10% to 26% area. PMMAC costs 12% of total design area. Our work is the first to prototype Recursive ORAM or ORAM with any integrity scheme in hardware.

ASPLOS '15, March 14–18, 2015, Istanbul, Turkey..

http://dx.doi.org/10.1145/2694344.2694353

1. Introduction

With cloud computing becoming increasingly popular, privacy of users' sensitive data has become a large concern in computation outsourcing. In an ideal setting, users would like to "throw their encrypted data over the wall" to a cloud service that should perform computation on that data without the service learning any information from within that data. It is well known, however, that encryption is not enough to get privacy. A program's memory access pattern has been shown to reveal a large percentage of its behavior [39] or the encrypted data it is computing upon [16, 21].

Oblivious RAM (ORAM) is a cryptographic primitive that *completely* eliminates the information leakage in a program's memory access trace (made up of reads/writes to memory). Conceptually, ORAM works by maintaining all of memory in encrypted and shuffled form. On each access, memory is read and then reshuffled. Under ORAM, any memory access pattern is computationally indistinguishable from any other access pattern of the same length. ORAM was first proposed by Goldreich and Ostrovsky [9, 11], and there has been significant follow-up work that has resulted in more efficient and cryptographically-secure ORAM schemes [4, 5, 14, 18, 23, 24, 30, 34, 36].

An important use case for ORAM is in *trusted hardware* [7, 21, 26, 31, 34]. In this setting, an on-chip ORAM controller intercepts last-level cache (LLC) misses/evictions and turns them into obfuscated main memory requests (i.e., the address pattern is randomized, data read/written is encrypted). Since program performance is very sensitive to cache miss latency, the ORAM controller logic is implemented directly in hardware.

1.1 Problem: Position Map Management

A big challenge for hardware ORAM controllers is that they need to store and manage a large data structure called the *Position Map* (PosMap for short). Conceptually, the PosMap is a page table that maps data blocks to random locations in external memory. Hence, the PosMap's size is proportional to the number of data blocks (e.g., cache lines) in main memory and can be hundreds of MegaBytes in size.

PosMap size has been an issue for all prior hardware ORAM proposals. First, Maas et al. [21] recently built Phantom, the first hardware ORAM prototype on an FPGA. The Phantom design stores the whole PosMap on-chip. As a result, to scale beyond 1 GB ORAM capacities, Phantom requires the use of multiple FPGAs *just to store the PosMap*. Second, Ren et al. [26] evaluate a technique called *Recursive ORAM* [30] in the secure hardware setting. The idea is to store the PosMap in additional ORAMs to reduce the on-chip storage requirement. The cost of Recursive ORAM is performance. One must access all the ORAMs in the recursion on each ORAM access. Even after architectural optimizations [26], a Recursive ORAM spends 39% to 56% of its time looking up PosMap ORAMs, and this percentage only increases with ORAM capacity (§ 3.2.1).

We believe that to be practical and scalable to large ORAM capacities, Recursive ORAM is necessary in secure hardware. To that end, one focus in this paper is to explore novel ways to dramatically reduce the performance overhead of Recursive ORAM.

We then take a new direction and explore what other functions the PosMap can perform on behalf of the processor. We show how our optimized PosMap construction can also, for very little additional cost, be used to perform extremely efficient *integrity verification* for ORAM. Obviously, integrity verification is an important consideration for any secure storage system where data can be tampered with. Yet, prior ORAM integrity schemes based on Merkle trees [25] require large hash unit bandwidth to rate match memory. We show how clever use of our optimized PosMap simplifies this problem dramatically.

1.2 Our Contribution

To accomplish the above goals, we contribute the following mechanisms:

1. We propose the **PosMap Lookaside Buffer** (§ 4), or *PLB* for short, a mechanism that significantly reduces the memory bandwidth overhead of Recursive ORAMs depending on underlying *program address locality*.
2. We propose a way to **compress the PosMap** (§ 5), which reduces the cost of recursion in practice and asymptotically, and improves the PLB's effectiveness.
3. We then show how to further use PosMap compression to create an ORAM integrity scheme, called **PosMap MAC** (§ 6) or *PMMAC* for short, which is extremely efficient in practice and is asymptotically optimal.

With the PLB and PosMap compression, we reduce PosMap-related memory bandwidth overhead by 95%, reduce overall ORAM bandwidth overhead by 37% and improve SPEC performance by 1.27×. As a standalone scheme, PMMAC reduces the amount of hashing needed for integrity checking by $\geq 68\times$ relative to prior schemes. Using PosMap compression and PMMAC as a combined scheme, we demonstrate an integrity checking mechanism for ORAM that increases performance overhead by only 7%.

In addition to evaluating our proposals using software simulation, we prototype a complete ORAM design with the PLB and PMMAC in a 32 nm commercial process and evaluate the entire design post-synthesis and post-layout for area and clock frequency. Our design is open source and available at http://kwonalbert.github.io/oram.

Post-synthesis, PMMAC and the PLB cost $< 13\%$ and 10% (respectively) of total design area. Post-layout, the entire ORAM controller parameterized for 2 DRAM channels is .47 mm^2 and runs at 1 GHz. Our prototype is the first hardware implementation of Recursive ORAM and integrity verification with ORAM.

2. Threat Model

In our setting, trusted hardware (e.g., a secure processor) operates in an untrusted environment (e.g., a data center) on behalf of a remote user. The processor runs a private or public program on private data submitted by the user, and interacts with a trusted on-chip ORAM controller, on last-level cache misses, to access data in untrusted external memory. We assume untrusted memory is implemented in DRAM for the rest of the paper.

The data center is treated as both a passive and active adversary. First, the data center will passively observe how the processor interacts with DRAM to learn information about the user's encrypted data. Second, it may additionally try to tamper with the contents of DRAM to influence the outcome of the program and/or learn information about the encrypted data.

Security definition (privacy)

We adopt the following security definition for ORAM that is implicit in all prior hardware proposals [6, 21, 26]:

For data request sequence $\overleftarrow{a}$, *let* $\mathsf{ORAM}(\overleftarrow{a})$ *be the resulting randomized data request sequence of an ORAM algorithm. Each element in a data request sequence follows the standard RAM interface, i.e., is a (address, op, write data) tuple. We guarantee that for any polynomial-length* $\overleftarrow{a}$ *and* $\overleftarrow{a'}$, *the resulting polynomial-length sequences* $\mathsf{ORAM}(\overleftarrow{a})$ *and* $\mathsf{ORAM}(\overleftarrow{a'})$ *are computationally indistinguishable if* $|\mathsf{ORAM}(\overleftarrow{a})| = |\mathsf{ORAM}(\overleftarrow{a'})|$.

Here, $|\mathsf{ORAM}(\overleftarrow{a})|$ denotes the length of $\mathsf{ORAM}(\overleftarrow{a})$. In other words, the memory request sequence visible to the adversary leaks only its length. Importantly, this definition allows the processor to use conventional on-chip cache. In our terminology, $\overleftarrow{a}$ is the sequence of load/store instructions in the program. $|\mathsf{ORAM}(\overleftarrow{a})|$ is determined by, and thus reveals, the number of LLC misses in $\overleftarrow{a}$, but not $|\overleftarrow{a}|$. The definition captures the essence of ORAM's privacy guarantee: ORAM hides individual elements in the data request sequence, while leaking a small amount of information by exposing the length of the sequence. From an information-theoretic point of view, the former grows linearly with the request sequence length, while the latter only grows logarithmically.

Security definition (integrity)

We guarantee that ORAM behaves like a valid memory with overwhelming probability from the processor's perspective.

Memory has valid behaviors if the value the processor reads from a particular address is the most recent value that it has written to that address (i.e., is *authentic* and *fresh*).

Security definition (integrity+privacy)

In the presence of active adversaries, we guarantee that ORAM behaves like a valid memory and that the resulting ORAM request sequence is computationally indistinguishable up to the point when tampering is detected by the ORAM controller (i.e., that the ORAM request sequence achieves the privacy guarantees described above).

When tampering is detected, the processor receives an exception at which point it can kill the program, or take some measures to prevent leakage from integrity violation detection time.

Threats outside of scope: timing channel leakage

Following Phantom [21], we assume that each DRAM request made *during* an ORAM access occurs at data-independent times and thus does not leak information. Also following Phantom (and work in [26]), we do not obfuscate *when* an ORAM access is made or the time it takes the program to terminate. These two timing channels are orthogonal to our work and have been addressed for ORAM by Fletcher et al. [6]. The schemes in that work can be adopted on top of our work if timing protection is needed.

3. Background

We will evaluate our techniques on top of *Path ORAM* [34], which was the scheme used in [21, 26]. Path ORAM is not only efficient but is also relatively simple algorithmically, making it implementable in hardware. We remark, however, that our optimizations apply to other Position-based (i.e., use a PosMap) ORAM schemes including [8, 30, 32].

3.1 Basic Path ORAM

Hardware Path ORAM is made up of two components: a (trusted) on-chip ORAM controller and (untrusted) external memory.

The untrusted external storage is logically structured as a binary tree, as shown in Figure 1, called the **ORAM tree**. The ORAM tree's levels range from 0 (the root) to L (the leaves). Each node in the tree is called a *bucket* and has a fixed number of slots (denoted Z) which can store blocks, which are the unit of data requested by the processor (e.g., a cache line). Bucket slots may be empty at any point, and are filled with *dummy blocks*. All blocks in the tree including dummy blocks are encrypted with a probabilistic encryption scheme such as AES counter mode [19] with a randomized session key. Thus, any two blocks (dummy or real) are indistinguishable after encryption. We refer to a path from the root to some leaf l as path l.

The **ORAM controller** is made up of the *position map*, the *stash* and control logic. The position map, PosMap for short, is a lookup table that associates each data block with a random leaf in the ORAM tree. Managing and optimizing the PosMap is the focus of this paper. If N is the maximum number of real data blocks in the ORAM, the PosMap capacity is $N * L$ bits: one mapping per block. The stash is a memory that temporarily stores up to a small number of data blocks (we assume 200 following [26]).

3.1.1 Path ORAM Invariant and Operation

At any time, each data block in Path ORAM is mapped to a random leaf via the PosMap. Path ORAM maintains the following invariant: *If a block is mapped to leaf l, then it must be either in some bucket on path l or in the stash.* Blocks are stored in the stash or ORAM tree along with their current leaf and block address.

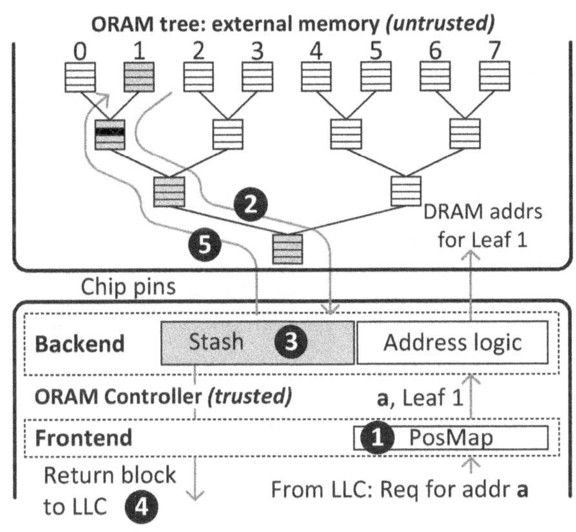

Figure 1. A Path ORAM of $L = 3$ levels and $Z = 4$ slots per bucket. Suppose block a, shaded black, is mapped to path $l = 1$. At any time, block a can be located in any of the shaded structures (i.e., on path 1 or in the stash).

To make a request for a block with address a (block a for short), the LLC calls the ORAM controller via accessORAM(a, op, d'), where op is either read or write and d' is the new data is op =write (the steps are also shown in Figure 1):

1. Look up PosMap with a, yielding the corresponding leaf label l. Randomly generate a new leaf l' and update the PosMap for a with l'.
2. Read and decrypt all the blocks along path l. Add all the real blocks to the stash (dummies are discarded). Due to the Path ORAM invariant, block a must be in the stash at this point.
3. Update block a in the stash to have leaf l'.
4. If op = read, return block a to the LLC. If op = write, replace the contents of block a with data d'.
5. Evict and encrypt as many blocks as possible from the stash to path l in the ORAM tree (to keep the stash occupancy low) while keeping the invariant. Fill any remaining space on the path with encrypted dummy blocks.

To simplify the presentation, we refer to Step 1 (the PosMap lookup) as the Frontend(a), or Frontend, and Steps 2-5 as the Backend(a, l, l', op, d'), or Backend. This work optimizes the Frontend and the techniques can be applied to any Position-based ORAM Backend.

3.1.2 Path ORAM Security

The intuition for Path ORAM's security is that every PosMap lookup (Step 1) will yield a fresh random leaf to

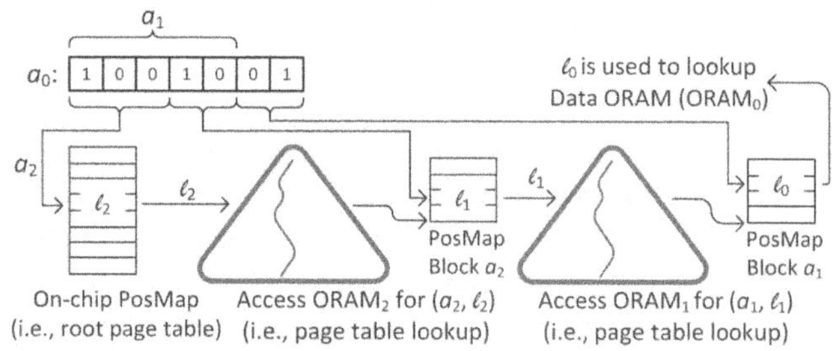

Figure 2. Recursive ORAM with PosMap block sizes $X = 4$, making an access to the data block with program address $a_0 = 1001001_2$. Recursion shrinks the PosMap capacity from $N = 128$ to 8 entries.

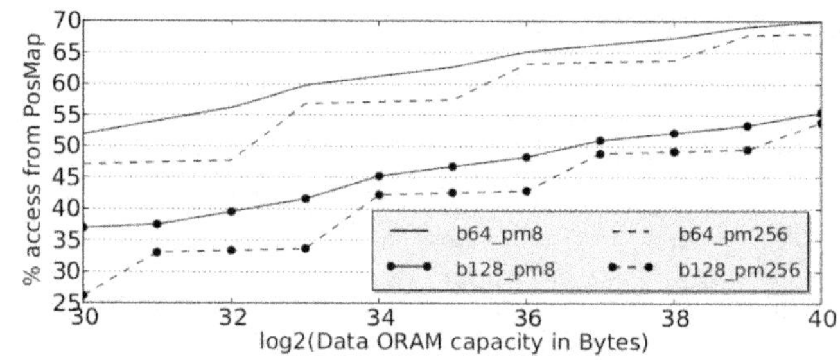

Figure 3. The percentage of Bytes read from PosMap ORAMs in a full Recursive ORAM access for $X = 8$ (following [20]) and $Z = 4$. All bucket sizes are padded to 512 bits to estimate the effect in DDR3 DRAM. The notation b64_pm8 means the ORAM block size is 64 Bytes and the on-chip PosMap is at most 8 KB.

access the ORAM tree for that access. This makes the sequence of ORAM tree paths accessed independent of the actual program address trace. Probabilistic encryption hides *which* block is accessed on the path. Further, stash overflow probability is negligible if $Z \geq 4$ (proven for $Z \geq 5$ [34] and shown experimentally for $Z = 4$ [20]).

3.2 Recursive ORAM

As mentioned in § 3.1, the number of entries in the PosMap scales linearly with the number of data blocks in the ORAM. This results in a significant amount of on-chip storage (hundreds of KiloBytes to hundreds of MegaBytes). To address this issue, Shi et al. [30] proposed scheme called *Recursive ORAM*, which has been studied in simulation for trusted hardware proposals [26]. The basic idea is to store the PosMap in a separate ORAM, and store the new ORAM's (smaller) PosMap on-chip. *We make an important observation that the mechanics of Recursive ORAM are remarkably similar to multi-level page tables in traditional virtual memory systems.* We use this observation to help explain ideas and derive optimizations.

We explain Recursive ORAM through the example in Figure 2, which uses two levels of recursion. The system now contains 3 separate ORAM trees: the *Data ORAM*, denoted as ORam_0, and two *PosMap ORAMs*, denoted ORam_1 and ORam_2. Blocks in the PosMap ORAMs are akin to page tables. We say that PosMap blocks in ORam_i store X leaf labels which refer to X blocks in ORam_{i-1}. This is akin to having X pointers to the next level page table and X is a parameter.[1]

Suppose the LLC requests block a_0, stored in ORam_0. The leaf label l_0 for block a_0 is stored in PosMap block $a_1 = a_0/X$ of ORam_1 (all division is floored). Like a page table, block a_1 stores leaves for neighboring data blocks (i.e., $\{a_0, a_0 + 1, \ldots, a_0 + X - 1\}$ in the case where a_0 is a multiple of X). The leaf l_1 for block a_1 is stored in the block $a_2 = a_0/X^2$ stored in ORam_2. Finally, leaf l_2 for PosMap block a_2 is stored in the on-chip PosMap. The on-chip PosMap is now akin to the root page table, e.g., register CR3 on X86 systems.

[1] Generally, each PosMap level can have a different X. We assume the same X for all PosMaps for simplicity.

To make a Data ORAM access, we must first lookup the on-chip PosMap, ORam_2 and ORam_1 in that order. Thus, a Recursive ORAM access is akin to a full page table walk. Additional PosMap ORAMs ($\text{ORam}_3, \text{ORam}_4, \ldots, \text{ORam}_{H-1}$) may be added as needed to shrink the on-chip PosMap further. H denotes the total number of ORAMs including the Data ORAM in the recursion and $H = \log(N/p)/\log X + 1$ if p is the number of entries in the on-chip PosMap. All logarithms will be base 2 for the rest of the paper.

3.2.1 Overhead of Recursion

It should now be clear that Recursive ORAM increases total ORAM access latency. Unintuitively, with small block sizes, PosMap ORAMs can contribute to more than half of the total ORAM latency as shown in Figure 3. For a 4 GB Data ORAM capacity, 39% and 56% of bandwidth is spent on looking up PosMap ORAMs (depending on block size), and increasing the on-chip PosMap only slightly dampens the effect. Abrupt kinks in the graph indicate when another PosMap ORAM is added (i.e., when H increases).

We now explain this overhead from an asymptotic perspective. We know a single Path ORAM (without recursion) with a block size B of bits transfers $O(B \log N)$ bits per access. In Recursive ORAM, the best strategy to minimize bandwidth is to set X to be constant, resulting in a PosMap ORAM block size of $B_p = \Theta(\log N)$. Then, the number of PosMap ORAMs needed is $\Theta(\log N)$, and the resulting bandwidth overhead becomes

$$O\left(\log N + \frac{H B_p \log N}{B}\right) = O\left(\log N + \frac{\log^3 N}{B}\right)$$

The first term is for Data ORAM and the second term accounts for all PosMap ORAMs combined. In realistic processor settings, $\log N \approx 25$ and data block size $B \approx \log^2 N$ (512 or 1024 in Figure 3). Thus, it is natural that PosMap ORAMs account for roughly half of the bandwidth overhead.

In the next section, we show how insights from traditional virtual memory systems, coupled with security mechanisms, can dramatically reduce this PosMap ORAM overhead (§ 4).

4. PosMap Lookaside Buffer

Given our understanding of Recursive ORAM as a multi-level page table for ORAM (§ 3.2), a natural optimization is to cache PosMap blocks (i.e., page tables) so that LLC accesses exhibiting program address locality require less PosMap ORAM accesses on average. This idea is the essence of the *PosMap Lookaside Buffer*, or PLB, whose name obviously originates from the Translation Lookaside Buffer (TLB) in conventional systems. Unfortunately, unless care is taken, this idea totally breaks the security of ORAM. This section develops the scheme and fixes the security holes.

4.1 High-level Idea and Ingredients

4.1.1 PLB Caches

The key point from § 3.2 is that blocks in PosMap ORAMs contain a set of leaf labels for *consecutive blocks* in the next ORAM. Given this fact, we can eliminate some PosMap ORAM lookups by adding a hardware cache to the ORAM Frontend called the PLB. Suppose the LLC requests block a_0 at some point. Recall from § 3.2 that the PosMap block needed from $\mathsf{ORam_i}$ for a_0 has address $a_i = a_0/X^i$. If this PosMap block is in the PLB when block a_0 is requested, the ORAM controller has the leaf needed to lookup $\mathsf{ORam_{i-1}}$, and can skip $\mathsf{ORam_i}$ *and all the smaller PosMap ORAMs.* Otherwise, block a_i is retrieved from $\mathsf{ORam_i}$ and added to the PLB. When block a_i is added to the PLB, another block may have to be evicted in which case it is appended to the stash of the corresponding ORAM.

A minor but important detail is that a_i may be a valid address for blocks in multiple PosMap ORAMs; to disambiguate blocks in the PLB, block a_i is stored with the tag $i||a_i$ where $||$ denotes bit concatenation.

4.1.2 PLB (In)security

Unfortunately, since each PosMap ORAM is stored in a different physical ORAM tree and PLB hits/misses correlate directly to a program's access pattern, the PosMap ORAM access *sequence* leaks the program's access pattern. To show how this breaks security, consider two example programs in a system with one PosMap ORAM $\mathsf{ORam_1}$ (whose blocks store $X = 4$ leaves) and a Data ORAM $\mathsf{ORam_0}$. Program A unit strides through memory (e.g., touches $a, a+1, a+2, \dots$). Program B scans memory with a stride of X (e.g., touches $a, a+X, a+2X, \dots$). For simplicity, both programs make the same number of memory accesses. Without the PLB, both programs generate the same access sequence, namely: $1, 0, 1, 0, 1, 0, 1, 0, 1, 0, 1, 0, \dots$ where 0 denotes an access to $\mathsf{ORam_0}$, and 1 denotes an access to $\mathsf{ORam_1}$. However, with the PLB, the adversary sees the following access sequences (**0** denotes an access to $\mathsf{ORam_0}$ on a PLB hit):

$$\text{Program A}: 1, 0, \mathbf{0}, \mathbf{0}, \mathbf{0}, 1, 0, \mathbf{0}, \mathbf{0}, \mathbf{0}, 1, 0, \dots$$

$$\text{Program B}: 1, 0, 1, 0, 1, 0, 1, 0, 1, 0, 1, 0, \dots$$

Program B constantly misses in the PLB and needs to access $\mathsf{ORam_1}$ on every access. Clearly, the adversary can tell program A apart from program B in the PLB-enabled system.

4.1.3 Security Fix: Unified ORAM Tree

To hide PosMap access sequence, we will change Recursive ORAM such that *all PosMap ORAMs and the Data ORAM store blocks in the same physical tree* which we denote $\mathsf{ORam_U}$. This is remotely similar to storing all data in one ORAM "bank" as described in [20], which we compare to further in § 8. Organizationally, the PLB and on-chip PosMap become the new Path ORAM Frontend, which interacts with a single ORAM Backend (§ 3.1). Security-wise, both programs from the previous section access *only* $\mathsf{ORam_U}$ with the PLB and the adversary cannot tell them apart (see § 4.3 for more discussion on security).

4.1.4 TLB vs. PLB

We remark that while a traditional TLB caches *single address translations*, the PLB caches entire PosMap blocks (akin to whole page tables). The address locality exploited by both structures, however, is the same.

4.2 Detailed Construction

4.2.1 Blocks Stored in $\mathsf{ORam_U}$

Data blocks and the PosMap blocks originally from the PosMap ORAMs (i.e., $\mathsf{ORam_1}, \dots, \mathsf{ORam}_{H-1}$) are now stored in a single ORAM tree ($\mathsf{ORam_U}$) and all accesses are made to this one ORAM tree. Both data and PosMap blocks now have the same size. Since the number of blocks that used to be stored in some $\mathsf{ORam_i}$ ($i > 0$) is X times smaller than the number of blocks stored in $\mathsf{ORam_{i-1}}$, storing PosMap blocks alongside data blocks adds at most one level to $\mathsf{ORam_U}$.

Each set of PosMap blocks must occupy a disjoint address space so that they can be disambiguated. For this purpose we re-apply the addressing scheme introduced in § 4.1.1: Given data block a_0, the address for the PosMap block originally stored in $\mathsf{ORam_i}$ for block a_0 is given by $i||a_i$, where $a_i = a_0/X^i$. This address $i||a_i$ is used to fetch the PosMap block from the $\mathsf{ORam_U}$ and to lookup the PosMap block in the PLB. To simplify the notation, we don't show the concatenated address $i||a_i$ in future sections and just call this block a_i.

4.2.2 ORAM readrmv and append Operations

We use two new flavors of ORAM access to support PLB refills/evictions (i.e., *op* in § 3.1): read-remove and append. The idea of these two type of accesses appeared in [26] but we describe them in more detail below. Read-remove (readrmv) is the same as read except that it physically deletes the block in the stash after it is forwarded to the ORAM Frontend. Append (append) adds a block to the stash without performing an ORAM tree access. $\mathsf{ORam_U}$ must not contain duplicate blocks: only blocks that are currently not in the ORAM (possibly read-removed previously) can be appended. Further, when a block is appended, the current leaf it is mapped to in $\mathsf{ORam_U}$ must be known so that the block can be written back to the ORAM tree during later ORAM accesses.

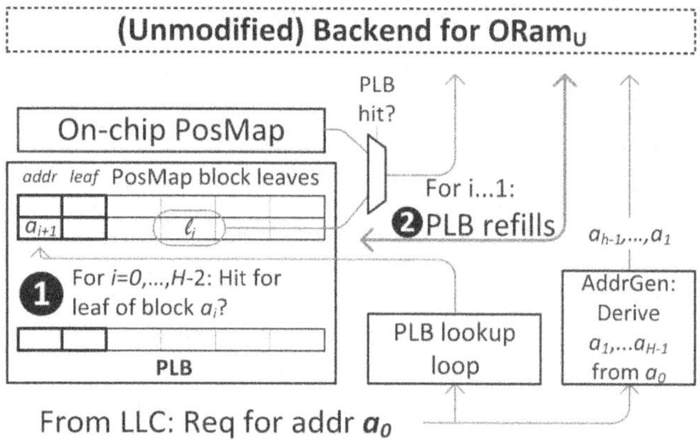

Figure 4. PLB-enabled ORAM Frontend with $X = 4$. Accessing the actual data block a_0 (Step 3 in § 4.2.4) is not shown.

4.2.3 PLB Architecture

The PLB is a conventional hardware cache that stores PosMap blocks. Each PosMap block is tagged with its block address a_i. On a hit, one of the X leaves in the block is read out and remapped. PosMap blocks are read-removed and appended from/to ORam$_U$. Thus, each block is stored in the PLB alongside its *current leaf*. The PLB itself has normal cache parameters (size, associativity), and we explore how this space impacts performance in § 7.1.3.

4.2.4 ORAM Access Algorithm

The steps to read/write a data block with address a_0 are given below (shown pictorially in Figure 4):

1. **(PLB lookup)** For $i = 0, \ldots, H-2$, look up the PLB for the leaf of block a_i (contained in block a_{i+1}). If one access hits, save i and go to Step 2; else, continue. If no access hits for $i = 0, \ldots, H-2$, look up the on-chip PosMap for the leaf of block a_{H-1} and save $i = H-1$.
2. **(PosMap block accesses)** While $i \geq 1$, perform a readrmv operation (§ 4.2.2) to ORam$_U$ for block a_i and add that block to the PLB. If this evicts another PosMap block from the PLB, append that block to the stash. Decrement i. (This loop will not be entered if $i = 0$.)
3. **(Data block access)** Perform an ordinary read or write access to ORam$_U$ for block a_0.

Importantly, aside from adding support for readrmv and append, the above algorithm requires no change to the ORAM Backend.

4.3 Security

We now give a proof sketch that our PLB+Unified ORAM tree construction achieves the security definition in § 2. To do this, we use the fact that the PLB interacts with a normal Path ORAM Backend. We make the following observations, which we will use to argue security:

Observation 1. *If all leaf labels l_i used in* {read, write, readrmv} *calls to* Backend *are random and independent of other l_j for $i \neq j$, the* Backend *achieves the security of the original Path ORAM (§ 3.1.2).*

Observation 2. *If an* append *is always preceded by a* readrmv, *stash overflow probability does not increase (since the net stash occupancy is unchanged after both operations).*

Theorem 1. *The PLB+Unified ORAM tree scheme reduces to the security of the ORAM* Backend.

Proof. The PLB+Unified ORAM Frontend calls Backend in two cases: First, if there is a PLB hit the Backend request is for a PosMap or Data block. In this case, the leaf l sent to Backend was in a PosMap block stored in the PLB. Second, if all PLB lookups miss, the leaf l comes from the on-chip PosMap. In both cases, leaf l was remapped the instant the block was last accessed. We conclude that all {read, write, readrmv} commands to Backend are to random/independent leaves and Observation 1 applies. Further, an append command can only be caused by a PLB refill which is the result of a readrmv operation. Thus, Observation 2 applies. □

Of course, the PLB may influence the ORAM trace *length* $|\mathsf{ORAM}(\overleftarrow{a})|$ by filtering out some calls to Backend for PosMap blocks. Now $|\mathsf{ORAM}(\overleftarrow{a})|$ is determined by, and thus reveals, the sum of LLC misses and PLB misses. We remark that processor cache and the PLB are both on-chip and outside the ORAM Backend, so adding a PLB is the same (security-wise) to adding more processor cache: in both cases, only the total number of ORAM accesses leaks. By comparison, using a PLB in without a Unified ORAM tree leaks the *set* of PosMap ORAMs needed on every Recursive ORAM access (§ 4.1.2), which makes leakage grow linearly with $|\mathsf{ORAM}(\overleftarrow{a})|$.

5. Compressed PosMap

We now show how to compress the PosMap using pseudorandom functions (PRFs, introduced below). The high level goal is to store *more leaves per PosMap block*, thereby reducing the number of Recursive PosMaps.

5.1 Background: PRFs

A pseudorandom Function, or PRF, family $y = \mathsf{PRF}_K(x)$ is a collection of efficiently-computable functions, where K is a random secret key. A PRF guarantees that anyone who does not know K (even given x) cannot distinguish y from a truly random bit-string in polynomial time with non-negligible probability [10]. For the rest of the paper, we implement $\mathsf{PRF}_K()$ using AES-128.

5.2 Construction

5.2.1 Main Idea

Following previous notation, suppose each PosMap block contains X leaf labels for the next ORAM. For example, some PosMap block contains leaf labels for the blocks with addresses $\{a, a+1, \cdots, a+X-1\}$. With the compressed PosMap scheme, the PosMap block's contents are replaced with an α-bit group counter (GC) and X β-bit individual counters (IC):

$$GC \,||\, IC_0 \,||\, IC_1 \,||\, IC_2 \,||\, \cdots \,||\, IC_{X-1}$$

With this format, we can then compute the current leaf label for block $a + j$ through $\mathsf{PRF}_K(a + j||GC||IC_j) \bmod 2^L$. Note that with this technique, the on-chip PosMap is unchanged and still stores an uncompressed leaf per entry.

5.2.2 Block Remap

For $\mathsf{PRF}_K()$ to generate a uniform random sequence of leaves, we must ensure that each $GC||IC_j$ *strictly increases* (i.e., the $\mathsf{PRF}_K()$ must never see the same input twice). This is achieved by the following modified remapping operation:

When remapping block $a + j$, the ORAM controller first increments its individual counter IC_j. If the individual counter rolls over (becomes zero again), the ORAM controller will increment the group counter GC. This changes the leaf label for all the blocks in the group, so we have to read each block through the Backend, reset its individual counter and remap it to the updated path given by $\mathsf{PRF}_K(a + j||GC + 1||0) \bmod 2^L$. In the worst case where the program always requests the same block in a group, we need to reset X individual counters in the group every 2^β accesses.

We remark that this reset operation is very expensive for baseline Recursive ORAM (§ 3.2). In that case, the ORAM controller must make X full Recursive ORAM accesses to reset the individual counters in *a certain* PosMap ORAM block. Otherwise, it reveals that individual counters have overflown in that certain ORAM, which is related to the access pattern. On the other hand, using a single Unified ORAM tree as we do to support the PLB (§ 4.1.3) reduces this to X accesses to ORam_U.

5.2.3 System Impact and the PLB

The compressed PosMap format can be used with or without a PLB and, like the PLB, does not require changes to the Backend. That is, PosMap blocks are stored in their compressed format inside the PLB and ORAM tree/Backend. Uncompressed leaves are generated using the PRF on-demand by the Frontend. Each block stored in the Backend or ORAM tree is still stored alongside its uncompressed leaf label (a one time cost per block), to facilitate ORAM evictions.

5.3 Benefit of Compressed Format (In Practice)

Our scheme *compresses* the PosMap block by setting α, β and X such that $\alpha/X + \beta < L$, implying that the (amortized) bits needed to store each leaf has decreased. A larger X means a fewer number of PosMap ORAMs are needed as discussed in § 3.2. Further, this scheme improves the PLB's hit rate (§ 4.2.4) since more blocks are associated with a given PosMap block.

For concreteness, suppose the ORAM block size in bits is $B = 512$. The compressed PosMap scheme enables $X' = 32$ by setting $\alpha = 64$ and $\beta = 14$, regardless of ORAM tree depth L.[2] In this configuration, the worst case block remap overhead is $X'/2^\beta = .2\%$ (§ 5.2.2). By comparison, the original PosMap representation (up to § 4) only achieves $X = 16$ for ORAM tree depths of $L = 17$ to $L = 32$.

[2] We restrict X' to be a power of two to simplify the PosMap block address translation from § 3.2.

5.4 Benefit of Compressed Format (Theoretical)

We now show that for small data block sizes $B = o(\log^2 N)$, the compressed PosMap with a Unified ORAM asymptotically improves Recursive Path ORAM. In the following analysis, we assume there is no PLB or that the PLB never hits, since there is no good way to model program-dependent locality. We note that by setting $\beta = \log\log N$, and $X' = \log N/\log\log N$, the overhead to reset individual counters is $X'/2^\beta = o(1)$ and we will assume this setting for the rest of the section. Further, as discussed in § 3.2.1 and [33], we always set $B_p = \Theta(\log N)$, because a larger block size for PosMap ORAMs is sub-optimal.

When $B \neq B_p$, we will break each data block into sub-blocks of size B_p, and store them in the Unified ORAM tree as independent blocks. We let these sub-blocks share a single individual counter; the uncompressed leaf for each sub-block is obtained by including the sub-block index k in the PRF input, such that leaves are generated by $\mathsf{PRF}_K(GC \mid\mid IC_j \mid\mid a + j \mid\mid k) \bmod 2^L$. Now a full ORAM access involves H Backend accesses to load the above PosMap block, and another $\lceil B/B_p \rceil$ Backend accesses to load all the data block sub-blocks. The asymptotic bandwidth overhead is

$$(1 + X'/2^\beta) \cdot \frac{2}{B}(B_p \cdot \log N) \cdot \left(\left\lceil \frac{B}{B_p} \right\rceil + H \right) = O\left(\log N + \frac{\log^3 N}{B \log\log N} \right).$$

When $B = o(\log^2 N)$, this result asymptotically outperforms Recursive Path ORAM; When $B = \omega(\log N)$, it beats Kushilevitz et al. [18], the best existing ORAM scheme under small client storage and a small block size. This makes it the best asymptotic ORAM so far for any block size in between.

6. Integrity Verification: PosMap MAC

We now describe a novel and simple integrity verification scheme for ORAM called *PosMap MAC*, or *PMMAC*, that is facilitated by our PosMap compression technique from the previous section. PMMAC achieves asymptotic improvements in hash bandwidth over prior schemes and is easy to implement in hardware.

6.1 Background: MACs

Suppose two parties Alice and Bob share a secret K and Alice wishes to send messages to Bob over an insecure channel where data packets d_i $(i = 0, \dots)$ can be tampered by some adversary Eve. To guarantee message *authenticity*, Alice can send Bob tuples (h_i, d_i) where $h_i = \mathsf{MAC}_K(d_i)$ and $\mathsf{MAC}_K()$ is a Message Authentication Code (e.g., a keyed hash function [5]). For the rest of the paper, we implement $\mathsf{MAC}_K()$ using SHA3-224.

The MAC scheme guarantees that Eve can only produce a message forgery $(h\star, d\star)$ with negligible probability, where

$h\star = \mathsf{MAC}_K(d\star)$ and $d\star$ was not transmitted previously by Alice. In other words, without knowing K, Eve cannot come up with a forgery for a message whose MAC it has never seen.

Importantly Eve can still perform a replay attack, violating *freshness*, by replacing some (h_i, d_i) with a previous legitimate message (h_j, d_j). A common fix for this problem is to embed a *non-repeating counter* in each MAC [29]. Suppose Alice and Bob have shared access to an oracle that, when queried, returns the number of messages sent by Alice but not yet checked by Bob. Then, for message i, Alice transmits (h'_i, d_i) where $h'_i = \mathsf{MAC}_K(i||d_i)$. Eve can no longer replay an old packet (h'_j, d_j) because $\mathsf{MAC}_K(i||d_j) \neq \mathsf{MAC}_K(j||d_j)$ with overwhelming probability. The challenge in implementing these schemes is that Alice and Bob must have access to a shared, *tamper-proof* counter.

6.2 Construction

6.2.1 Main Idea and Non-Recursive PMMAC

Clearly, any memory system including ORAM that requires integrity verification can implement the replay-resistant MAC scheme from the previous section by storing per-block counters in a tamper-proof memory. Unfortunately, the size of this memory is even larger than the original ORAM PosMap making the scheme untenable. *We make a key observation that if PosMap entries are represented as non-repeating counters, as is the case with the compressed PosMap (§ 5.2.1), we can implement the replay-resistant MAC scheme without additional counter storage.*

We first describe PMMAC without recursion and with simple/flat counters per-block to illustrate ideas. Suppose block a which has data d has access count c. Then, the on-chip PosMap entry for block a is c and we generate the leaf l for block a through $l = \mathsf{PRF}_K(a||c) \bmod 2^L$ (i.e., same idea as § 5.2.1). Block a is written to the Backend as the tuple (h, d) where

$$h = \mathsf{MAC}_K(c \mid\mid a \mid\mid d)$$

When block a is read, the Backend returns $(h\star, d\star)$ and PMMAC performs the following check to verify authenticity/freshness:

$$\text{assert } h\star == \mathsf{MAC}_K(c \mid\mid a \mid\mid d\star)$$

where $\star$ denotes values that may have been tampered with. After the assertion is checked, c is incremented for the returned block.

Security follows if it is infeasible to tamper with block counters and no counter value for a given block is ever repeated. The first condition is clearly satisfied because the counters are stored on-chip. We can satisfy the second condition by making each counter is wide enough to not overflow (e.g., 64 bits wide).

As with our previous mechanisms, PMMAC requires no change to the ORAM Backend because the MAC is treated as extra bits appended to the original data block.[3] As with PosMap compression, the leaf currently associated with each block in the stash/ORAM tree is stored in its original (uncompressed) format.

6.2.2 Adding Recursion and PosMap Compression

To support recursion, PosMap blocks (including on-chip PosMap entries) may contain either a flat (64 bits) or compressed counter (§ 5.2.1) per next-level PosMap or Data ORAM block. As in the non-Recursive ORAM case, all leaves are generated via a PRF. The intuition for security is that the tamper-proof counters in the on-chip PosMap form the root of trust and then recursively, the PosMap blocks become the root of trust for the next level PosMap or Data ORAM blocks. Note that in the compressed scheme (§ 5.3), the α and β components of each counter are already sized so that each block's count never repeats/overflows. We give a formal analysis for security with Recursive ORAM in § 6.5.

For realistic parameters, the scheme that uses flat counters in PosMap blocks incurs additional levels of recursion. For example, using $B = 512$ and 64 bit counters we have $X = B/64 = 8$. *Importantly, with the compressed PosMap scheme we can derive each block counter from GC and* IC_j *(§ 5.2.1) without adding levels of recursion or extra counter storage.*

6.3 Key Advantage: Hash Bandwidth and Parallelism

Combined with PosMap compression, the overheads for PMMAC are the bits added to each block to store MACs and the cost to perform cryptographic hashes on blocks. The extra bits per block are relatively low-overhead — the ORAM block size is usually 64-128 Bytes (§ 7.1.5) and each MAC may be 80-128 bits depending on the security parameter.

To perform a non-Recursive ORAM access (i.e., read/write a single path), Path ORAM reads/writes $O(\log N)$ blocks from external memory. Merkle tree constructions [[illegible], 25] need to integrity verify all the blocks on the path to check/update the root hash. Crucially, our PMMAC construction only needs to integrity verify (check and update) 1 block — namely the block of interest — per access, achieving an asympotic reduction in hash bandwidth.

To give some concrete numbers, assume $Z = 4$ block slots per ORAM tree bucket following [24, 34]. Then there are $Z * (L + 1)$ blocks per path in ORAM tree, and our construction reduces hash bandwidth by $68\times$ for $L = 16$ and by $132\times$ for $L = 32$. We did not include the cost of reading sibling hashes for the Merkle tree for simplicity.

Integrity verifying only a single block also prevents a serialization bottleneck present in Merkle tree schemes. Consider the scheme from [25], a scheme optimized for Path ORAM. Each hash in the Merkle tree node must be recomputed based on the contents of the corresponding ORAM tree bucket and *its child hashes*, and is therefore fundamentally sequential. If this process cannot keep up with memory bandwidth, it will be the system's performance bottleneck.

[3] That is, the MAC is encrypted along with the block when it is written to the ORAM tree.

6.4 Adding Encryption: Subtle Attacks and Defenses

Up to this point we have discussed PMMAC in the context of providing integrity only. ORAM must also apply a probabilistic encryption scheme (we assume AES counter mode as done in [26]) to all data stored in the ORAM tree. In this section we first show how the encryption scheme of [26] breaks under active adversaries because the adversary is able to *replay the one-time pads used for encryption.* We show how PMMAC doesn't prevent this attack by default and then provide a fix that applies to PMMAC.

We first show the scheme used by [26] for reference: Each bucket in the ORAM tree contains, in addition to Z encrypted blocks, a seed used for encryption (the $BucketSeed$) that is stored in plaintext. ($BucketSeed$ is synonymous to the "counter" in AES counter mode.) If the Backend reads some bucket (Step 2 in § 3.1) whose seed is $BucketSeed$, the bucket will be re-encrypted and written back to the ORAM tree using the one-time pad (OTP) $\mathsf{AES}_K(BucketID||BucketSeed+1||i)$, where i is the current chunk of the bucket being encrypted.

The above encryption scheme breaks privacy under PMMAC because PMMAC doesn't integrity verify $BucketSeed$. For a bucket currently encrypted with the pad $P = \mathsf{AES}_K(BucketID||BucketSeed||i)$, suppose the adversary replaces the plaintext bucket seed to $BucketSeed - 1$. This modification will cause the contents of that bucket to decrypt to garbage, *but won't trigger an integrity violation under PMMAC unless bucket $BucketID$ contains the block of interest for the current access.* If an integrity violation is not triggered, due to the replay of $BucketSeed$, that bucket will next be encrypted using the *same one-time pad P* again.

Replaying one-time pads obviously causes security problems. If a bucket re-encrypted with the same pad P contains plaintext data D at some point and D' at another point, the adversary learns $D \oplus D'$. If D is known to the adversary, the adversary immediately learns D' (i.e., the plaintext contents of the bucket).

The fix for this problem is relatively simple: To encrypt chunk i of a bucket about to be written to DRAM, we will use the pad $\mathsf{AES}_K(GlobalSeed||i)$, where $GlobalSeed$ is now a single monotonically increasing counter stored in the ORAM controller in a dedicated register (this is similar to the global counter scheme in [27]). When a bucket is encrypted, the current $GlobalSeed$ is written out alongside the bucket as before and $GlobalSeed$ (in the ORAM controller) is incremented. Now it's easy to see that each bucket will always be encrypted with a fresh OTP which defeats the above attack.

6.5 Security

We now give an analysis for our complete scheme's integrity and privacy guarantees.

6.5.1 Integrity

We show that breaking our integrity verification scheme is as hard as breaking the underlying MAC, and thus attains the integrity definition from § 2. First, we have the following observation:

Observation 3. *If the first $k-1$ address and counter pairs (a_i, c_i)'s the* Frontend *receives have not been tampered with, then the* Frontend *seeds a MAC using a unique (a_k, c_k), i.e., $(a_i, c_i) \neq (a_k, c_k)$ for $1 \leq i < k$. This further implies $(a_i, c_i) \neq (a_j, c_j)$ for all $1 \leq i < j \leq k$.*

This property can be seen directly from the algorithm description, with or without the PLB and/or PosMap compression. For every a, we have a dedicated counter, sourced from the on-chip PosMap or the PLB, that increments on each access. If we use PosMap compression, each block counter will either increment (on a normal access) or jump to the next multiple of the group counter in the event of a group remap operation (§ 5.2.2). Thus, each address and counter pair will be different from previous ones. We now use Observation 3 to prove the security of our integrity scheme.

Theorem 2. *Breaking the PMMAC scheme is as hard as breaking the underlying MAC scheme.*

Proof. We proceed via induction on the number of accesses. In the first ORAM access, the Frontend uses (a_1, c_1), to call Backend for (h_1, d_1) where $h_1 = \mathsf{MAC}_K(c_1||a_1||d_1)$. (a_1, c_1) is unique since there are no previous $(a_i, c_i)'s$. Note that a_1 and c_1 cannot be tampered with since they come from the Frontend. Thus producing a forgery (h'_1, d'_1) where $d'_1 \neq d_1$ and $h'_1 = \mathsf{MAC}_K(c_1||a_1||d'_1)$ is as hard as breaking the underlying MAC. Suppose no integrity violation has happened and Theorem 2 holds up to access $n-1$. Then the Frontend sees fresh and authentic (a_i, c_i)'s for $1 \leq i \leq n-1$. By Observation 3, (a_n, c_n) will be unique and $(a_i, c_i) \neq (a_j, c_j)$ for all $1 \leq i < j \leq n$. This means the adversary cannot perform a replay attack (§ 6.1) because all (a_i, c_i)'s are distinct from each other and are tamper-proof. It is also hard to generate a valid MAC with unauthentic data without the secret key. Being able to produce a forgery (h'_i, d'_i) where $d'_i \neq d_i$ and $h'_i = \mathsf{MAC}_K(c_i||a_i||d'_i)$ means the adversary can break the underlying MAC. □

6.5.2 Privacy

The system's privacy guarantees require certain assumptions under PMMAC because PMMAC is an *authenticate-then-encrypt* scheme [17]. Since the integrity verifier only checks the block of interest returned to the Frontend, other (tampered) data on the ORAM tree path will be written to the stash and later be written back to the ORAM tree. For example, if the adversary tampers with the block-of-interest's address bits, the Backend won't recognize the block and won't be able to send any data to the integrity verifier (clearly an error). The adversary may also coerce a stash overflow by replacing dummy blocks with real blocks or duplicate blocks along a path.

To address these cases, we have to make certain assumptions about how the Backend will possibly behave in the presence of tampered data. We require a correct implementation of the ORAM Backend to have the following property:

Property 1. *If the* Backend *makes an ORAM access, it only reveals to the adversary (a) the leaf sent by the* Frontend *for that access and (b) a fixed amount of encrypted data to be written back to the ORAM tree.*

If Property 1 is satisfied, it is straightforward to see that any memory request address trace generated by the Backend is indistinguishable from other traces of the same length. That is, the Frontend receives tamper-proof responses (by Theorem 2) and therefore produces independent and random leaves. Further, the global seed scheme in § 6.4 trivially guarantees that the data written back to memory gets a fresh pad.

If Property 1 is satisfied, the system can still leak the ORAM request trace *length*; i.e., *when* an integrity violation is detected, or when the Backend enters an illegal state. Conceptually, an integrity violation generates an exception that can be handled by the processor. When that exception is generated and how it is handled can leak some privacy. For example, depending on how the adversary tampered with memory, the violation may be detected immediately or after some period of time depending on whether the tampered bits were of interest to the Frontend. Quantifying this leakage is outside our scope, but we remark that this level of security matches our combined privacy+integrity definition from § 2.

7. Evaluation

We now evaluate our proposals in simulation and with a complete hardware prototype.

7.1 Software Simulation

7.1.1 Methodology and Parameters

We first evaluate our proposals using the Graphite simulator [22] with the processor parameters listed in Table 1. The core and cache model remain the same in all experiments; unless otherwise stated, we assume the ORAM parameters from the table. We use a subset of SPEC06-int benchmarks [15] with reference inputs. All workloads are warmed up over 1 billion instructions and then run for 3 billion instructions.

We derive AES/SHA3 latency, Frontend and Backend latency directly from our hardware prototype in § 7.2. Frontend latency is the time to evict and refill a block from the PLB (§ 4.2.4) and occurs at most once per Backend call. Backend latency (approximately) accounts for the cycles lost due to hardware effects such as serializers/buffer latency/etc and is added on top the time it takes to read/write an ORAM tree path in DRAM, which is given in § 7.1.2.

We model DRAM and ORAM accesses on top of commodity DRAM using DRAMSim2 [28] and its default DDR3_micron configuration with 8 banks, 16384 rows and 1024 columns per row. Each DRAM channels runs at 667 MHz DDR with a 64-bit bus width and provides $\sim$ 10.67 GB/s peak bandwidth. All ORAM configurations assume 50% DRAM utilization (meaning a 4 GB ORAM requires 8 GB of DRAM) and use the subtree layout scheme from [26] to achieve nearly peak DRAM bandwidth.

Table 1. Processor Configuration.

Core, on-chip cache and DRAM	
core model	in order, single issue, 1.3 GHz
add/sub/mul/div	1/1/3/18 cycles
fadd/fsub/fmul/fdiv	3/3/5/6 cycles
L1 I/D cache	32 KB, 4-way, LRU
L1 data + tag access time	1 + 1 cycles
L2 Cache	1 MB, 16-way, LRU
L2 data + tag access time	8 + 3 cycles
cache line size	64 B
Path ORAM/ORAM controller	
ORAM controller clock frequency	1.26 GHz
data block size	64 B
data ORAM capacity	4 GB ($N = 2^{26}$)
block slots per bucket (Z)	4
AES-128 latency	21 cycles (§ 7.2)
SHA3-224 latency (PMMAC)	18 cycles (§ 7.2)
Frontend latency	20 cycles (§ 7.2)
Backend latency	30 cycles (§ 7.2)
Memory controller and DRAM	
DRAM channels	2 ($\sim$ 21.3 GB peak bandwidth)
DRAM latency	given by DRAMSim2 [28]

7.1.2 ORAM Latency and DRAM Channel Scalability

ORAM latency is sensitive to DRAM bandwidth and for this reason we explore how changing the channel count impacts ORAM access time in Table 2. ORAM Tree latency refers to the time needed for the Backend to read/write a path in the Unified ORAM tree, given the ORAM parameters in Table 1. All latencies are in terms of *processor* clock cycles, and represent an average over multiple accesses. For reference, a DRAM access for an insecure system without ORAM takes on average 58 processor cycles.

Table 2. ORAM access latency by DRAM channel count.

DRAM channel count	1	2	4	8
ORAM Tree latency (cycles)	2147	1208	697	463

Generally, ORAM latency decreases with channel count as expected but the effect becomes increasingly sub-linear for larger channel counts due to DRAM channel conflicts. Since 2 channels represent realistic mid-range systems and do not suffer significantly from this problem, we will use that setting for the rest of the evaluation unless otherwise specified.

7.1.3 PLB Design Space

Figure 5 shows how direct-mapped PLB capacity impacts performance. For a majority of benchmarks, larger PLBs add small benefits ($\leq$ 10% improvements). The exceptions are bzip2 and mcf, where increasing the PLB capacity from 8 KB to 128 KB provides 67% and 49% improvement, respectively. We tried increasing PLB associativity (not shown for space) and found that, with a fixed PLB capacity, a fully associative PLB improves performance by $\leq$ 10% when compared to direct-mapped. To keep the architecture simple, we therefore assume direct-mapped PLBs from now on. Going from a 64 KB to 128 KB direct-mapped PLB, average performance only increases by only 2.7%, so we assume a 64 KB direct-mapped PLB for the rest of the evaluation.

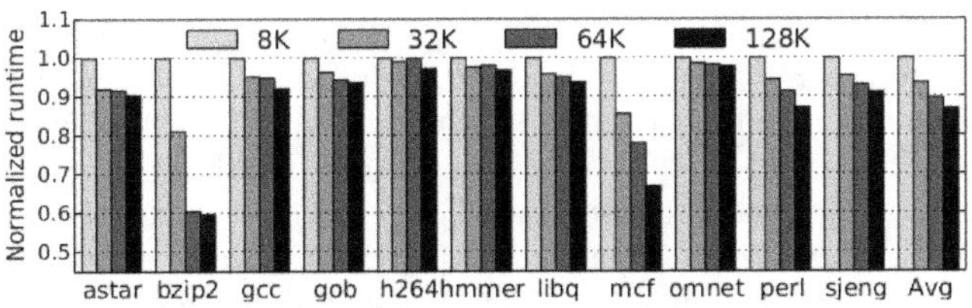

Figure 5. PLB design space, sweeping direct-mapped PLB capacity. Runtime is normalized to the 8 KB PLB point.

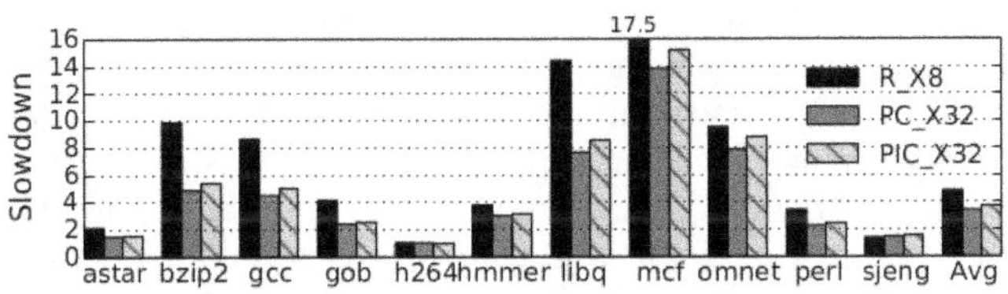

Figure 6. Performance of PLB, Compressed PosMap and PMMAC. Slowdown is relative to an insecure system without ORAM.

7.1.4 Scheme Composability

We now present our main result (Figure 6), the impact on performance when we compose PLB (§ 4), PosMap compression (§ 5) and PMMAC (§ 6). To name our schemes in the discussion, we use the letters P, I and C to indicate the **P**LB, **I**ntegrity verification (PMMAC) and **C**ompressed PosMap, respectively. For example, PC_X32 denotes PLB+Compressed PosMap with $X = 32$. PI_X8 is the flat-counter PMMAC scheme from § 6.2.2. For PC_X32 and PIC_X32, we apply recursion until the on-chip PosMap is $\leq$ 128 KB in size, yielding 4 KB on-chip PosMaps for both points. R_X8 is a Recursive ORAM baseline with $X = 8$ (32-Byte PosMap ORAM blocks following [26]) and $H = 4$, giving it a 272 KB on-chip PosMap.

Despite consuming less on-chip area, PC_X32 achieves a 1.43× speedup (30% reduction in execution time) over R_X8 (geomean). To provide integrity, PIC_X32 only adds 7% overhead on top of PC_X32, which is due to the extra bandwidth needed to transfer per-block MACs (§ 6.3).

To give more insight, Figure 7 shows the average data movement per ORAM access (i.e., per LLC miss+eviction). We give the Recursive ORAM R_X8 up to a 256 KB on-chip PosMap. As ORAM capacity increases, the overhead from accessing PosMap ORAMs grows quickly for R_X8. All schemes using a PLB have much better scalability. For the 4 GB ORAM, on average, PC_X32 reduces PosMap bandwidth overhead by 82% and overall ORAM bandwidth overhead by 38% compared with R_X8. At the 64 GB capacity, the reduction becomes 90% and 57%. Notably the PMMAC scheme without compression (PI_X8) causes nearly half the bandwidth to be PosMap related, due to the large counter width and small X (§ 6.2.2). Compressed PosMap (PIC_X32) solves this problem.

7.1.5 Comparison to Prior-art Recursive ORAM ([26])

While we have applied the ideas from [26] to our baseline in Figure 6, we do change some processor/DRAM parameters

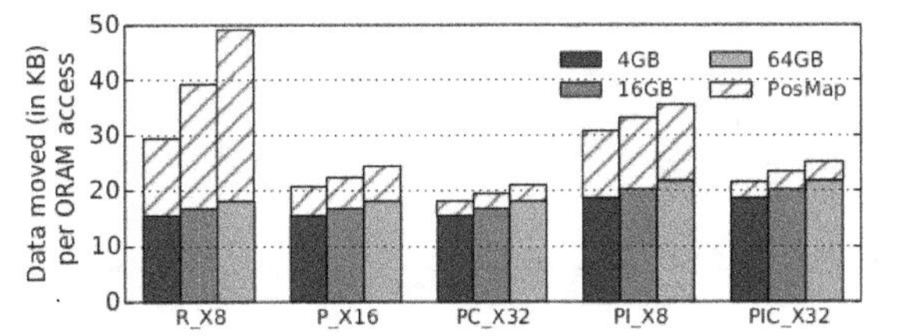

Figure 7. Scalability to large ORAM capacities. White shaded regions indicate data movement from PosMap ORAM lookups. Slowdown is relative to an insecure system without ORAM.

from that work to more realistic values or to be compatible with existing processors, including DRAM bandwidth, processor frequency and cache line size.

For a more apples-to-apples comparison with [26], we now adopt all the parameters from that work: 4 DRAM channels, a 2.6 GHz processor, a 128-Byte cache line and ORAM block size, $Z = 3$, etc. PC_X64 is a PLB-enabled ORAM with a 128-Byte block (cache line) size (thus X doubles). PC_X64 reduces PosMap traffic by 95% and overall ORAM traffic by 37% over the Recursive ORAM configuration from [26].

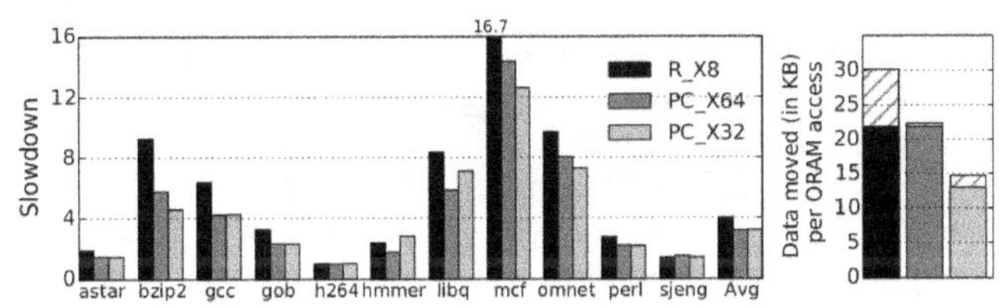

Figure 8. (Left) Performance of Recursive ORAM baseline and our scheme using all parameters from [26]. Slowdown is relative to an insecure system without ORAM. (Right) Average data movement per access. White shaded regions indicate data movement from PosMap ORAM lookups.

PC_X32 is a PLB-enabled ORAM with a 64-Byte block (cache line) size. This configuration has a smaller ORAM latency but also fetches less data per ORAM access. As shown in Figure 8, both PC_X64 and PC_X32 achieve about 1.27× speedup over Recursive ORAM baseline. This shows our scheme is effective for both ORAM block sizes. The larger ORAM block size of PC_X64 benefits benchmarks with good locality (hmmer, libq) but hurts those with poor locality (bzip, mcf, omnetpp).

7.1.6 Comparison to Non-Recursive ORAM with Large Blocks ([21])

In Figure 9, we compare our proposal to the parameterization used by Phantom [21]. Phantom was evaluated with a large ORAM block size (4 KB) so that the on-chip PosMap could be contained on several FPGAs without recursion.

To match § 7.1.4, we model the Phantom parameters on 2 DRAM channels (which matches the DRAM bandwidth reported in [21]) and with a 4 GB ORAM ($N = 2^{20}$, $L = 19$) $Z = 4$, 4 KB blocks and no recursion. For these parameters, the on-chip PosMap is $\sim$ 2.5 MB (which we evaluate for on-chip area in § 7.2.3). To accurately reproduce Phan-

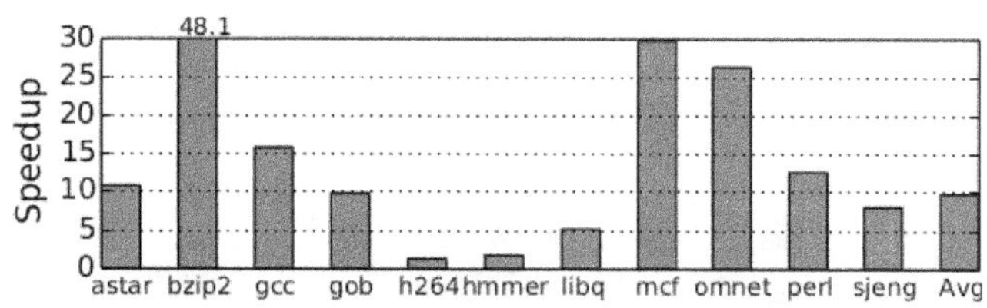

Figure 9. PC_X32 speedup relative to Phantom [21] w/ 4 KB blocks.

Table 3. ORAM area breakdown post-synthesis.

		DRAM channels (nchannel)		
		1	2	4
Area (% of total)	Frontend	31.2	30.0	22.5
	PosMap	7.3	7.0	5.3
	PLB	10.2	9.7	7.3
	PMMAC	12.4	11.9	8.8
	Misc	1.3	1.4	1.1
	Backend	68.8	70.0	77.5
	Stash	28.3	28.9	21.9
	AES	40.5	41.1	55.6
Total cell area (mm^2)		.316	.326	.438

tom's system performance, we implemented the Phantom block buffer (Section 5.7 of that work) as a 32 KB memory with the CLOCK eviction strategy and assume the Phantom processor's cache line size is 128 Bytes (as done in [21]).

On average, PC_X32 from § 7.1.4 achieves 10× speedup over the Phantom configuration with 4 KB blocks. The intuition for this result is that Byte movement per ORAM access for our scheme is roughly $(26*64)/(19*4096) = 2.1\%$ that of Phantom. While PC_X32 needs to access PosMap blocks due to recursion, this effect is outweighed by the reduction in Data ORAM Byte movement.

7.2 Hardware Prototype

We now evaluate a complete hardware ORAM prototype pushed through Synopsis' ASIC synthesis tool Design Compiler and Place and Route tool IC Compiler. Our design (Verilog, tests, etc) is open source and can be found at http://kwonalbert.github.io/oram.

Our first objective is to show that the PLB (§ 4) and PMMAC (§ 6) mechanisms impose a small area overhead. We have not built the compressed PosMap (§ 5) in hardware, but do not think the additional control logic will have a significant effect on area or clock frequency. (Thus, our prototype is equivalent to PI_X8 from § 7.1.4.) More generally, our work is the first to prototype any ORAM through an ASIC hardware flow, and the first to build Recursive ORAM or ORAM with integrity verification in any form of hardware.

7.2.1 Methodology

Our design is written in plain Verilog and was synthesized using a 32 nm commercial standard cell library and memory (SRAM and register file) generator. Our Frontend (the focus of this paper) contains the PLB and PMMAC and has a 64-bit/cycle data interface with the last-level cache for all experiments. ORAM parameters follow Table 1 except that we use an 8 KB PosMap and 8 KB direct-mapped PLB by default (we discuss a 64 KB PLB design in § 7.2.3). Our Backend is similar to the Phantom Backend [21] and has a 64 ∗ nchannel bit/cycle datapath to/from DRAM.[4]

To implement cryptographic operations, we used two AES cores from OpenCores [1]: a 21-cycle pipelined core to implement the Backend's read/write path decryptions/encryptions (§ 3.1) and a non-pipelined 12 cycle core to implement $\mathsf{PRF}_K()$ (§ 5.1). We used a SHA3-224 core from OpenCores to implement $\mathsf{MAC}_K()$ for PMMAC (§ 6.1).

For both synthesis and place and route, we built the design hierarchically as three main components: the Frontend, the stash (Backend) and the AES units used to decrypt/re-encrypt paths (Backend). For synthesis results, we report total cell area; i.e., the minimum area required to implement the design. For layout results, we set a bounding box for each major block that maximized utilization of available space while meeting timing requirements. The entire design required 5 SRAM/RF memories (which we manually placed during layout): the PLB data array, PLB tag array, on-chip PosMap, stash data array and stash tag array. Numerous other (small) buffers were needed and implemented in standard cells.

7.2.2 Results

Post-Synthesis. Table 3 shows ORAM area across several DRAM channel (nchannel) counts. All three configurations met timing using up to a 1.3 GHz clock with a 100 ps uncertainty. The main observation is that the Frontend constitutes a minority of the total area and that this percentage decreases with nchannel. Area decreases with nchannel because the Frontend performs a very small DRAM bandwidth-independent amount of work (∼ 50 clock cycles including integrity verification) per Backend access. The Backend's bits/cycle throughput (AES, stash read/write, etc), on the other hand, must rate match DRAM. Thus, the area cost of the Frontend (and our PMMAC and PLB schemes) is effectively amortized with nchannel (Table 3).[5]

Post-Layout. We now report post-layout area for the nchannel = 2 configuration to give as close an estimate for tape-out as possible. Between synthesis and layout, area increased per-block for nchannel = 2 as follows: Frontend grew by 38%, the stash by 24% and AES by 63%. This configuration met timing at 1 GHz and had a final area of .47 mm^2. In all cases, some space was sacrificed but the overall picture remains the same.

7.2.3 Alternative Designs

To give additional insight, we estimate the area overhead of *not* supporting recursion or having a larger PLB with

[4] Our design, however, does not have a DRAM buffer (see [21]). We remark that if such a structure is needed it should be much smaller than that in Phantom (<10 KB as opposed to hundreds of KiloBytes) due to our 64 Byte block size.

[5] We note the following design artifact: since we use AES-128, area increases only slightly from nchannel = 1 to 2, because both 64-bit and 128-bit datapaths require the same number of AES units.

recursion. For a 4 GB ORAM, the PosMap must contain 2^{26} to 2^{20} entries (for block sizes 64 Bytes to 4 KB). With a 2^{20}-entry on-chip PosMap, without Recursion, the $\mathsf{nchannel} = 2$ design requires ~ 5 mm^2 area — an increase of over 10×. Doubling the ORAM capacity (roughly) doubles this cost. Further, for performance reasons, we prefer smaller block sizes which exacerbates the area problem (§ 7.1.6). On the other hand, we calculate that using Recursion with a 64 KB PLB (to match experiments in § 7.1) increases the area for the $\mathsf{nchannel} = 1$ configuration by 29% (and is 26% of total area).

8. Related Work

Numerous prior works [8, 9, 11–14, 18, 32, 34, 36] have significantly improved the theoretical performance of ORAM over the past three decades. Notably among them, Path ORAM [34] is conceptually simple and the most efficient under small client (on-chip) storage. For these reasons, it was embraced by trusted hardware proposals including our work.

Phantom [21] is the first hardware implementation of non-Recursive Path ORAM. In our terminology, Phantom primarily optimizes the ORAM Backend and is therefore complementary to our work. Our Frontend optimizations (the PLB, PMMAC, and compressed PosMap) can be integrated with the Phantom Backend and this is similar to the design we evaluate in § 7.2. Ren et al. [26] explored the Recursive Path ORAM design space through simulation and proposed several optimizations to Recursive Path ORAM. We use their optimized proposal as a baseline in our work. Ascend [7, 38] is a holistic secure processor proposal that uses ORAM for memory obfuscation and adds timing protection on top of ORAM [6]. We believe our techniques can apply to that work as well.

Liu et al. [20] define memory trace obliviousness which can apply to secure processor settings like this paper. That work allocates different program variables into different ORAM trees to increase performance, when the ORAM tree access sequence can be proven to not leak secrets. Similarly, we store PosMap blocks in the same tree because PosMap accesses *do* leak secrets (§ 4.1). Our complete scheme, the PLB plus Unified ORAM tree, however, is completely counter-intuitive given Liu et al.: we show how using a *single* ORAM tree can unlock great performance *improvement*.

Wang et al. [35] develop mechanisms to reduce the overhead of Recursive ORAM, as does our PLB construction. That work only applies in situations when the data stored in ORAM is a part of a common data structure (such as a tree of bounded degree or list). The PLB can be used given any program access pattern.

Splitting PosMap block entries into two counters (which we do for PosMap compression, § 5.2.1) is similar to the split counter scheme due to Yan et al [37], although the motivation in that work is to save space for encryption initialization vectors. Additionally, that work does not hide *when* individual counters overflow, which we require for privacy and describe in § 5.2.2.

9. Conclusion

In this paper we presented three techniques to manage and optimize the Oblivious RAM Position Map (PosMap). We introduced the PosMap Lookaside Buffer (PLB) to decrease the performance overhead of recursion. We then presented a technique to compress the PosMap, which improves the PLB and improves the Recursive Path ORAM construction asymptotically and in practice. Finally, facilitated by PosMap compression, we propose PosMap MAC (PMMAC) to get integrity verification for ≥ 68× less hashing than prior schemes.

Our simulation results show our techniques decrease PosMap (overall) ORAM performance overhead by 95% (37%), which translates to a 1.27× speedup for SPEC workloads. Using PosMap compression, PMMAC degrades performance by only 7%. Our hardware prototype shows how integrity verification costs ≤ 13% of total design area across various DRAM bandwidths.

Acknowledgments: We thank Charles Herder for helpful suggestions and for reviewing early versions of this paper. We also thank the anonymous reviewers for many constructive comments. This research was partially supported by QCRI under the QCRI-CSAIL partnership and by the National Science Foundation. Christopher Fletcher was supported by a DoD National Defense Science and Engineering Graduate Fellowship.

References

[1] Open cores. http://opencores.org/.

[2] D. Apon, J. Katz, E. Shi, and A. Thiruvengadam. Verifiable oblivious storage. In *PKC*. 2014.

[3] M. Bellare, R. Canetti, and H. Krawczyk. Keying hash functions for message authentication. In *CRYPTO*, 1996.

[4] D. Boneh, D. Mazieres, and R. A. Popa. Remote oblivious storage: Making oblivious RAM practical. Manuscript, http://dspace.mit.edu/bitstream/handle/1721.1/62006/MIT-CSAIL-TR-2011-018.pdf, 2011.

[5] I. Damgård, S. Meldgaard, and J. B. Nielsen. Perfectly secure oblivious RAM without random oracles. In *TCC*, 2011.

[6] C. Fletcher, L. Ren, X. Yu, M. Van Dijk, O. Khan, and S. Devadas. Suppressing the oblivious ram timing channel while making information leakage and program efficiency tradeoffs. In *HPCA*, 2014.

[7] C. Fletcher, M. van Dijk, and S. Devadas. Secure Processor Architecture for Encrypted Computation on Untrusted Programs. In *STC*, 2012.

[8] C. Gentry, K. A. Goldman, S. Halevi, C. S. Jutla, M. Raykova, and D. Wichs. Optimizing oram and using it efficiently for secure computation. In *PET*, 2013.

[9] O. Goldreich. Towards a theory of software protection and simulation on oblivious rams. In *STOC*, 1987.

[10] O. Goldreich, S. Goldwasser, and S. Micali. How to construct random functions. *Journal of the ACM*, 1986.

[11] O. Goldreich and R. Ostrovsky. Software protection and simulation on oblivious rams. In *Journal of the ACM*, 1996.

[12] M. T. Goodrich, M. Mitzenmacher, O. Ohrimenko, and R. Tamassia. Oblivious ram simulation with efficient worst-case access overhead. In *CCSW*, New York, NY, 2011.

[13] M. T. Goodrich, M. Mitzenmacher, O. Ohrimenko, and R. Tamassia. Practical oblivious storage. In *CODASPY*, New York, NY, 2012.

[14] M. T. Goodrich, M. Mitzenmacher, O. Ohrimenko, and R. Tamassia. Privacy-preserving group data access via stateless oblivious RAM simulation. In *SODA*, 2012.

[15] J. L. Henning. Spec cpu2006 benchmark descriptions. *Computer Architecture News*, 2006.

[16] M. Islam, M. Kuzu, and M. Kantarcioglu. Access pattern disclosure on searchable encryption: Ramification, attack and mitigation. In *NDSS*, 2012.

[17] H. Krawczyk. The order of encryption and authentication for protecting communications (or: How secure is ssl?). In *CRYPTO*, 2001.

[18] E. Kushilevitz, S. Lu, and R. Ostrovsky. On the (in) security of hash-based oblivious ram and a new balancing scheme. In *SODA*, 2012.

[19] H. Lipmaa, P. Rogaway, and D. Wagner. Comments to NIST concerning AES-modes of operations: CTR-mode encryption. In *Symmetric Key Block Cipher Modes of Operation Workshop*, 2000.

[20] C. Liu, M. Hicks, and E. Shi. Memory trace oblivious program execution. In *CSF*, 2013.

[21] M. Maas, E. Love, E. Stefanov, M. Tiwari, E. Shi, K. Asanovic, J. Kubiatowicz, and D. Song. Phantom: Practical oblivious computation in a secure processor. In *CCS*, 2013.

[22] J. E. Miller, H. Kasture, G. Kurian, C. G. III, N. Beckmann, C. Celio, J. Eastep, and A. Agarwal. Graphite: A Distributed Parallel Simulator for Multicores. In *HPCA*, 2010.

[23] R. Ostrovsky. Efficient computation on oblivious rams. In *STOC*, 1990.

[24] R. Ostrovsky and V. Shoup. Private information storage (extended abstract). In *STOC*, 1997.

[25] L. Ren, C. Fletcher, X. Yu, M. van Dijk, and S. Devadas. Integrity verification for path oblivious-ram. In *HPCA*, 2013.

[26] L. Ren, X. Yu, C. Fletcher, M. van Dijk, and S. Devadas. Design space exploration and optimization of path oblivious ram in secure processors. In *ISCA*, 2013.

[27] B. Rogers, S. Chhabra, M. Prvulovic, and Y. Solihin. Using address independent seed encryption and bonsai merkle trees to make secure processors os- and performance-friendly. In *MICRO*, 2007.

[28] P. Rosenfeld, E. Cooper-Balis, and B. Jacob. Dramsim2: A cycle accurate memory system simulator. *Computer Architecture Letters*, 2011.

[29] L. F. G. Sarmenta, M. van Dijk, C. W. O'Donnell, J. Rhodes, and S. Devadas. Virtual Monotonic Counters and Count-Limited Objects using a TPM without a Trusted OS. In *STC*, 2006.

[30] E. Shi, T.-H. H. Chan, E. Stefanov, and M. Li. Oblivious ram with $o((\log n)^3)$ worst-case cost. In *Asiacrypt*, 2011.

[31] E. Stefanov and E. Shi. Oblivistore: High performance oblivious cloud storage. In *S&P*, 2013.

[32] E. Stefanov, E. Shi, and D. Song. Towards practical oblivious RAM. In *NDSS*, 2012.

[33] E. Stefanov, M. van Dijk, E. Shi, C. Fletcher, L. Ren, X. Yu, and S. Devadas. Path oram: An extremely simple oblivious ram protocol. volume abs/1202.5150, 2012.

[34] E. Stefanov, M. van Dijk, E. Shi, C. Fletcher, L. Ren, X. Yu, and S. Devadas. Path oram: An extremely simple oblivious ram protocol. In *CCS*, 2013.

[35] X. Wang, K. Nayak, C. Liu, E. Shi, E. Stefanov, and Y. Huang. Oblivious data structures. *IACR*, 2014.

[36] P. Williams and R. Sion. Single round access privacy on outsourced storage. In *CCS*, 2012.

[37] C. Yan, D. Englender, M. Prvulovic, B. Rogers, and Y. Solihin. Improving cost, performance, and security of memory encryption and authentication. *Computer Architecture News*, 2006.

[38] X. Yu, C. W. Fletcher, L. Ren, M. van Dijk, and S. Devadas. Generalized external interaction with tamper-resistant hardware with bounded information leakage. In *CCSW*, 2013.

[39] X. Zhuang, T. Zhang, and S. Pande. HIDE: an infrastructure for efficiently protecting information leakage on the address bus. In *ASPLOS*, 2004.

Beyond the PDP-11: Architectural support for a memory-safe C abstract machine

David Chisnall Colin Rothwell
Robert N. M. Watson
Jonathan Woodruff Munraj Vadera
Simon W. Moore Michael Roe
University of Cambridge
firstname.lastname@cl.cam.ac.uk

Brooks Davis Peter G. Neumann
SRI International
{brooks,neumann}@csl.sri.com

Abstract

We propose a new memory-safe interpretation of the C abstract machine that provides stronger protection to benefit security and debugging. Despite ambiguities in the specification intended to provide implementation flexibility, contemporary implementations of C have converged on a memory model similar to the PDP-11, the original target for C. This model lacks support for *memory safety* despite well-documented impacts on security and reliability.

Attempts to change this model are often hampered by assumptions embedded in a large body of existing C code, dating back to the memory model exposed by the original C compiler for the PDP-11. Our experience with attempting to implement a memory-safe variant of C on the CHERI experimental microprocessor led us to identify a number of problematic idioms. We describe these as well as their interaction with existing memory safety schemes and the assumptions that they make beyond the requirements of the C specification. Finally, we refine the CHERI ISA and abstract model for C, by combining elements of the CHERI capability model and fat pointers, and present a softcore CPU that implements a C abstract machine that can run legacy C code with strong memory protection guarantees.

1. Introduction

A programming language defines both a concrete syntax and an abstract machine. The abstract machine describes the environment that a programmer should expect, such as the range of sizes, behaviors, and representations of primitive types. A fully specified abstract machine for a language encapsulates all assumptions that are safe for a programmer to make about *every* possible implementation of the language.

Concrete implementations may perform native compilation to machine code, provide a virtual machine with a complete environment, or choose an intermediate step with complex parts of the system implemented as operating-system or library routines. The last approach is the most common for the C language, with memory allocation and certain complex floating-point operations implemented in shared libraries, but most language constructs compiled directly to short sequences of machine instructions. A key aspect of mapping the abstract model onto a target platform is the *memory model*, which defines (among other things) how abstract ideas of pointers and objects (ranges of memory with an associated type) are represented on the target—for example, as words and ranges of bytes in a flat address space.

The C abstract machine was originally designed to be sufficiently close to the PDP-11 that a simple compiler could achieve good performance translating C statements into short sequences of PDP-11 instructions. The abstract machine was subsequently extended to allow very different implementations. Early targets included the Honeywell 6000, IBM System/370, and Interdata 8/32 [25]. In spite of this generalization, most contemporary computers designed to support C programs utilize instruction sets that are reminiscent of the PDP-11, particularly in terms of memory model. The PDP-11 model is appealing due to its simplicity and its portability; however, lack of memory-safety properties leaves code compiled to that model subject to memory corruption in the face of bugs. More concerningly, these bugs frequently prove exploitable by attackers with broad scope for malicious data and control-flow modification [29]; for example, CWE/SANS lists "Classic Buffer Overflow", possible due to lack of memory safety, as the third most dangerous software error [21].

ASPLOS '15, March 14–18, 2015, Istanbul, Turkey.

ACM 978-1-4503-2835-7/15/03... $15.00.
http://dx.doi.org/10.1145/2694344.2694367

Bugs with respect to the abstract language model may be vulnerabilities, but the degree to which they are exploitable by attackers depends on concrete implementation choices such as stack layout [2]. Refinements to language implementations (such as *memory protection*) therefore offer opportunities to mitigate vulnerabilities as well as make debugging easier [26]. The potential benefits of bounds checking and other integrity techniques have been well documented by work such as Cyclone [17], CCured [23], SoftBound [22], HardBound [12], and CHERI [35]. Deployment of these techniques is hampered not just by performance concerns but also by whether current software relies on specific implementation choices. Evaluation cases have frequently been limited to benchmarks and application software that might be termed "extremely well-behaved C" rather than the low-level software that would most benefit from their support (e.g., buffer-centered packet parsing).

Understanding and addressing the practical effects of stronger memory models is critical in deploying them to mitigate vulnerabilities. We therefore propose a new interpretation of the C abstract machine that affords stronger memory-protection properties. We evaluate this approach against existing C-language corpora and a practical implementation via our open-source Capability Hardware Enhanced RISC Instructions (CHERI) softcore processor.

We first investigate how commonly held assumptions about pointer behavior go beyond the rules mandated by the C abstract machine, at times incorporating implicit assumptions regarding the PDP-11 memory model. We do this by surveying a variety of pointer-centered C idioms using an LLVM-based static analyzer over a large open-source application corpus. This allows us to identify a tradeoff space between protection and compatibility. Next, we link these ideas to portions of the C abstract machine—as described in the C11 specification [16]—that are implementation defined, investigating the possible implementation space.

We discuss the problems with supporting these idioms on existing models, including our CHERI ISA (a RISC instruction-set architecture that implements fine-grained memory protection). We propose a refinement to the CHERI ISA, *CHERIv3* [34], informed by state-of-the-art hardware-assisted fat-pointer schemes, to improve software compatibility. We evaluate performance and compatibility with respect to both hardware and software by implementing two capability-based memory models and exploring the impact (including lines-of-code changes) on a set of C-language applications, relative to the PDP-11 memory model.

We demonstrate that it is possible for a memory-safe implementation of C to support not just the C abstract machine as specified, but a broader interpretation that is still compatible with existing code. By enforcing the model in hardware, our implementation provides memory safety that can be used to provide high-level security properties for C TCBs, just as memory safety is a building block for higher-level security abstractions in Java.

2. Common idioms

The CHERI ISA [33] introduces memory safety to a RISC ISA by supplementing general-purpose registers with *capability registers* and *tagged memory*, drawn from the capability-system model, providing strong integrity protection and bounds checking for pointers. In attempting to implement a C compiler for early versions of the CHERI ISA, we found that it was very easy to support well-behaved C code. On attempting to compile nontrivial C programs, we discovered a number of programs failed to either compile or run correctly, due to different interpretations of the C abstract machine. We collected examples of these failures and produced the following taxonomy of common C idioms that are difficult for memory-safe implementations to support.

To explore the extent to which existing programs depend on a traditional view of memory, we modified the Clang compiler to identify potentially problematic pointer operations, as well as code that removes the `const` qualifier. LLVM intermediate representation (IR) is typed, with pointers and integers being distinct. Type-safe pointer arithmetic is performed by the `GetElementPtr` instruction. The PDP-11 model allows arbitrary arithmetic to construct valid addresses in a flat address space, but is incompatible with memory safety that requires a substrate to be aware of objects and enforce bounds checking. We can detect assumptions of the PDP-11 model (and violations of the type system), as LLVM must generate `ptrtoint` and `inttoptr` instruction pairs that turn a pointer into an integer, perform arithmetic, and then convert it back.

Our modified LLVM identified all instances of pointer arithmetic that survive optimization and performed some simple categorization. We ignore those that do not survive optimization because they will have no effect on run-time enforcement. We compiled a sample corpus of around 2M lines of popular C code with this modified compiler, categorized violations by inspecting the code, and extracted test cases demonstrating the common patterns.

Table 1 shows a summary of the total number of occurrences of each of the idioms that we have identified. Some of these are entirely valid within the C memory model, some depend on implementation-defined behavior, and some depend on undefined behavior that happens to be implemented in a specific way on common compilers.

Note that these values are a result of machine-assisted human categorization, and are intended to be indicative of the frequency of these idioms rather than accurate measures. Breaking these idioms will break existing code, and our analysis gives a rough idea of the scope of such breakage.

Unlike prior work, such as STACK [32], we are not looking purely for cases where programs rely on *undefined behavior* and therefore work only coincidentally. We are also

PROGRAM	DECONST	CONTAINER	SUB	II	INT	IA	MASK	WIDE	LOC
ffmpeg	150	0	800	4	0	0	4	0	693,010
libX11	117	0	19	9	1	0	0	5	120,386
FreeBSD libc	288	0	216	2	13	50	184	17	136,717
bash	43	0	207	11	0	0	15	4	109,250
libpng	20	0	175	1	0	0	0	0	50,071
tcpdump	579	0	9	1299	0	0	0	0	66,555
perf	575	151	46	0	53	151	31	4	52,033
pmc	2	0	0	0	18	0	0	0	8,886
pcre	98	0	52	0	0	0	0	0	70,447
python	494	0	358	1	109	0	131	8	383,813
wget	55	0	61	0	3	0	1	10	91,710
zlib	4	0	24	0	0	0	0	0	21,090
zsh	29	0	267	0	0	0	5	5	98,664
TOTAL	2491	151	2236	1557	197	201	371	53	1,902,632

Table 1. Summary of difficult idioms in popular C packages.

looking for cases where programs rely on *implementation-defined behavior* related to a specific understanding of the machine's memory model, and thus would be fragile in the presence of different interpretations. When a compiler encounters undefined behavior, it is free to do whatever it wishes. For example, if the value of `a` is the result of undefined behavior, then it is acceptable for the compiler to optimize `a == b` and `a != b` to the same value. In contrast, implementation-defined behavior must be self-consistent. For example, the value of `sizeof(int)` is implementation defined and may be 4, 8, or some other value, but must be consistent within a program.

We assume that all of the code that we inspected works correctly, that all of the idioms that we find are intentional, and that the code depends on them working as expected. We identified the following idioms:

Deconst refers to programs that remove the `const` qualifier from a pointer. This will break with any implementation that enforces the `const` at run time. §6.7.3.4 [16] states:

If an attempt is made to modify an object defined with a const-qualified type through use of an lvalue with non-const-qualified type, the behavior is undefined.

This means that such removal is permitted unless the object identified by the pointer is declared `const`, but this guarantee is very hard to make statically and the removal can violate programmer intent.

We would like to be able to make a `const` pointer a guarantee that nothing that receives the pointer may write to the resulting memory. This allows `const` pointers to be passed across security-domain boundaries.

Container describes behavior in a macro common in the Linux, BSD, and Windows kernels that, given a pointer to a structure member, returns a pointer to the enclosing structure [20]. This may or may not be permitted behavior according to the standard, due to the ambiguous definition of 'object'. Use of this idiom would break with any implementation that associates strict bounds checking with a pointer based on its static type, but not one that employs the bounds of the original object.

This is a special case of pointer subtraction, but its use breaks assumptions that we would like to make for pointer bounds: A compiler can statically insert bounds information on a pointer to a structure field, which can be enforced by the underlying substrate—preventing some categories of pointer error with a fine granularity.

Sub refers to any arbitrary pointer subtraction. High-level languages commonly lack pointer subtraction, preferring a model where pointers are always references to objects (a base and a bounds), and accesses to object fields or array elements require that the programmer have a pointer to the object. With pointer subtraction, bounds checking requires an offset as well as the base and bounds and so bounds-checked pointers are larger.

II refers to computation of *invalid intermediate* results. The C specification allows pointers to point one element after the end of an array, but not be dereferenced when pointing outside of a valid object. This case refers to pointer arithmetic where the end result is within the bounds of an object, but intermediate results are not. This is undefined behavior according to the C specification and makes even conservative garbage collection impossible unless a valid pointer to the object is guaranteed to also exist.

Without this being expected to work, we could trap as soon as a pointer went out of range, rather than waiting until it is dereferenced. This would be useful mostly as a debugging aid, as there are no extra security or reliability guarantees from preventing these operations.

Int refers to storing a pointer in an integer variable in memory—implementation-defined behavior in C. We ignore variables where the store-load sequence is optimized away in calculating these. Disallowing this behavior makes accurate garbage collection possible, as the compiler can statically track every pointer use. It also eliminates a category of error where a value is manipulated as an integer and later interpreted as a pointer.

IA refers to performing integer arithmetic on pointers—such as storing a pointer in an integer value and then performing arbitrary arithmetic on it. This is a more general case of the Int idiom and relies on the same implementation-defined behavior. It also makes conservative garbage collection impossible, as the garbage collector can assume that every integer may be a pointer and still do a reasonable job, but cannot do any collection if pointers can be easily hidden.

Mask refers to simple masking of pointers. For example, to store some other data in the low bits. This relies on pointers having a known representation. Breaking this allows more efficient pointer representations, for example the "low-fat pointers" [18] representation for fat pointers.

Wide refers to storing a pointer in an integer variable of a smaller size. This is undefined according to the C specification, but may work if you are able to guarantee that pointers are within a certain range, for example by allocating memory with `malloc` and the `MAP_32BIT` flag.

Code using this idiom is broken by existing implementations, and most likely reflects bugs in the code. We were surprised to see examples of this in programs that we inspected, but fortunately it is sufficiently rare that fixing all of the cases would be easy in these codebases. This idiom is the result of assuming that `sizeof(int) == sizeof(void*)` or `sizeof(int32_t)== sizeof (void*)`. This assumption was true for desktop computers for a long time, and mobile devices until recently. Had we run the same experiment 15 years ago, we expect we would have seen many more instances of this assumption. We conclude that C codebases adapt (over time) to changes in pointer behavior, and that additional small changes are not impossible to support.

Last Word refers to accessing an object as aligned words without regard for the fact that the object's extent may not include all of the last word. This is used as an optimization for `strlen()` in FreeBSD libc. While this is undefined behavior in C, it works in systems with page-based memory protection mechanisms, but not in CHERI where objects have byte granularity. We have found this idiom only in FreeBSD's libc, as reported by valgrind.

The relatively large number of instances of pointer subtraction in C code that we observed (Table 1) supports our anecdotal observation that the lack of this support in the original C implementation for CHERI (described in detail in the next section) would be problematic. We have not been able to find the Last Word pattern by static analysis and thus have not included it. Note that most of the cases of invalid intermediates also involve subtraction; we have predominantly classified instances as subtraction if the pointers are dereferenced immediately after the subtraction, indicating either that the code is buggy or the pointer is valid.

Arbitrary arithmetic on integers that are then cast to pointers is rare. The majority of the occurrences that we have seen are in the `malloc()` implementation in FreeBSD libc (jemalloc [13]). This is difficult to avoid, as `malloc()` is outside of the C abstract machine. The C specification indicates that each block of memory returned by `malloc()` is an object and that it is undefined behavior to use it after calling `free()`. This means that, with a strict interpretation of the specification, it is impossible for the code inside `free()` to recycle the memory. Similarly, the memory that has not yet been returned by `malloc()` is not yet part of the C abstract machine. In real implementations, the compiler makes sufficient allowances to permit these functions to be implemented in C atop some more primitive functionality (`mmap()` or `brk ()`, which deals with pages of memory.

We investigate tcpdump more closely in §5.2, where we discuss porting it to two CHERI variants. It is worth noting that numerous cases of invalid intermediates involve bounds-checking code: These are not required at all if the underlying implementation supports bounds checking. We therefore observe that, for at least some code, modifications to allow compatibility with a restricted memory-safe implementation of C would simplify the code.

3. The C abstract machine

Having identified a set of idioms that an implementation must support, we now look at the requirements imposed by the language. It is possible to implement the C abstract machine for any Turing-complete target, but that does not mean it is easy or efficient to do so. When considering a low-level language like C, there are three important requirements on a compilation target:

Expressiveness: It must be sufficiently expressive to capture the semantics of the abstract machine.

Efficiency: The primitive operations in the abstract machine must map simply to primitive operations in the underlying system, allowing low-overhead implementation.

Exposure: The features of the underlying system must be exposed to the programmer. For example, the language should expose the register types of the underlying architecture as primitive types.

A language can be described as *low level* with regard to a particular platform only if it meets these requirements. It must be possible to compile the language to run on the target system, but also to do so without introducing significant abstraction layers that hinder performance or hide the details of the underlying architecture.

This section discusses the flexibility that the C abstract machine allows implementers, both with respect to the primitive types used for memory access (integers and pointers), and the layout and semantics of memory itself. We take particular note of changes that can be made to enforce memory safety without compromising the low-level nature of C. The C abstract machine does not include an idea of address translation—intentionally, as not all targets have MMUs—so, from the perspective of userspace C programs running on an operating system, we always mean virtual memory when we refer to memory as described by the abstract machine.

3.1 Primitive types

The C specification is intentionally vague on the representation of most primitive types, allowing significant variety.

3.1.1 Ranges and representations

Before we can consider modifying how pointers are implemented in C, we should examine the requirements that the specification places on the implementations of primitive types. §5.2.4.2.1 [16] is devoted to the ranges of integer types. It defines a minimum range that each can represent. Implementations may support larger ranges, with the exception of the `char` type. C11 requires it to be at least 8 bits, but POSIX requires that it is exactly 8 bits, providing a concrete practical limit for implementations wishing to run code designed for any UNIX-like system.

Within this size, the only constraint is that a signed `char` must be able to represent integers between -127 and 127. Most modern machines opt to use two's complement arithmetic, as it simplifies many operations. Two's complement representation allows values from -128 to 127 to be represented. This leaves one value that can be represented, but which is outside of the range required by the specification.

Most arithmetic operations can overflow. The §6.2.5 [16] defines that overflow of unsigned values should wrap. Signed overflow is undefined and may produce a *trap representation*: A value that may trap if used and whose use makes any subsequent behavior undefined.

These two facts lead to a potential implementation that allows cheap trapping on overflow in hardware. All signed arithmetic that overflowed would be set to this trap value, and all signed arithmetic operations that took this value and an input would raise an exception. This would necessitate different instructions for signed and unsigned addition, but there is some precedent for this. MIPS, for example, includes operations that differ only by whether they trap on overflow.

Trapping on signed overflow is not a new idea. Both clang and gcc provide a `-ftrapv` flag that causes every signed arithmetic operation to be followed by a branch-on-carry with a trap instruction (`ud2` on x86) at the destination. The clang variant also permits a handler function to recover from the overflow. This was used to implement a prototype of the As-if Infinitely Ranged (AIR) proposal by CERT [11]. Similar work was done later by MIT's KINT [31] system, defining an integer equivalent of the not-a-number (NaN) values found in floating point systems. These efforts have all been purely focused on the compiler, and not on extending the underlying architecture.

3.1.2 Pointers

In BCPL [24], an ancestor of C, pointers and integers were both words: pointers were words that could be dereferenced. In contrast, C was intended to support minicomputer and mainframe architectures, including segmented memory models and microcontrollers with separate integer and address registers. The PDP-11 model of C follows closely from BCPL: pointers are integers, any pointer can be cast to any sufficiently large integer type, and results of casting can be used as pointers. Pointer arithmetic is just integer arithmetic.

This behavior is not mandated by the C standard. The abstract machine divides memory into objects: regions of memory with an associated type. Pointer arithmetic that ends outside of the original object is undefined, with the exception that pointers may point one element past the end of arrays, but such a pointer is valid only for comparison, not for dereferencing. §7.20.1.4 [16] defines an optional `intptr_t` as an integer type that can store a pointer and have the pointer value preserved. There is no guarantee that any arithmetic on `intptr_t` will result in a valid pointer and dereferencing any such pointer is implementation defined. Pointer comparisons between pointers to different objects are undefined, allowing the implementation to move objects as long as it does so atomically with respect to the running code.

3.1.3 The null pointer

As per §6.3.2.3 [16], the integer value 0 has a special meaning when cast to a pointer: It must be distinct from any valid object in the system. This value is relevant (according to the specification) only when it is an *integer constant expression* that evaluates to 0. This distinction is important. For example, the specification does not require that the following be a null pointer:

```
int i = 0; void *p = (void*)i;
```

This distinction is difficult to support in modern compilers, as discussed in a recent LLVM mailing list thread [1].

3.2 State of the unions

Footnote 95 in §6.5.2.3 [16] contains the exception to the normal aliasing rules:

If the member used to read the contents of a union object is not the same as the member last used to store a value in the object, the appropriate part of the object representation of the value is reinterpreted as an object representation in the new type...This might be a trap representation.

This requirement is one of the things that makes C useful in low-level contexts: It is possible to subvert the type system and interpret memory as different forms. Supporting unions can be difficult in environments with guarantees about type safety but is important for our *exposure requirement.*

3.3 Code and data memory

C is intended to be usable on microcontrollers with separate address spaces for code and data. A numerical pointer value may be different when interpreted as referring to data and code. In particular, a `void*` may refer to any kind of data, but is not guaranteed to be able to represent function pointers. POSIX breaks this separation by introducing the `void *dlsym(...)` function, used to look up a symbol in a shared library. This is beyond the scope of the C language specification, which has no notion of shared libraries, but is very important, e.g., for finding plugin interfaces. Unfortunately, looking up function pointers is a common use for `dlsym`, and is not defined behavior in C.

3.4 Const enforcement

The `const` qualifier indicates that a pointer should not be used to write memory. In typical C implementations, the immutability of `const`-qualified objects varies. Literal strings are mapped read-only into the running process. Attempting to modify one will cause a segmentation fault. It is therefore safe to remove a `const` qualifier only if you know exactly where it was inserted. Unfortunately, the C specification contains functions such as `memchr`, which takes a `const` -qualified pointer as the first argument, and returns a (non-`const`) pointer derived from it, stripping the `const` qualifier.

This function signature exists because the C type system cannot express the real requirement: that the function has a contract not to modify the buffer, and that the mutability associated with the returned pointer should be equal to the rights that the caller has to the first argument.

3.5 Pointer provenance

The C specification makes the ability to store pointers in integer variables and then recreate the original pointer implementation defined, but many software packages in practice depend on this functionality. In common implementations, as long as the integer is derived from the initial pointer, and the result of arithmetic is within the bounds of the object, then arbitrary arithmetic is permitted. The notion of an integer derived from a pointer is somewhat vague.

The xor linked list is a simple example where this is problematic. Each node has a pointer that is the address of the previous node xor'd with the address of the next node, allowing traversal in both directions. The pointer is derived from the addresses of both objects. This is particularly challenging when attempting to produce a formal semantics of C. This idiom is now very uncommon, due to its poor interaction with pipelined processors.

Relying on the alignment to identify unused bits in a pointer is more common. On a 64-bit platform, most values are 8-byte aligned, and so the low 3 bits in a pointer are zero. It is therefore safe for a program to store information in these bits. The ARMv8 architecture [3] extends this with a mode guaranteeing that the MMU will not use the top 8 bits in a virtual address when performing address translation, allowing them to be used for storing program-specific data.

3.6 Garbage hoarding

To add full memory safety to C would require *temporal* as well as *spatial* safety. We can add spatial safety within the confines of the abstract machine by changing the representation of pointers to include bounds. Efficiently adding temporal safety is more difficult.

Existing conservative garbage collectors for C, such as the Boehm-Demers-Weiser collector [5], fail in cases outlined in §3.5 because they make assumptions about pointer representations. The ability to recover pointers from integers arithmetic makes accurate garbage collection impossible because any integer value may potentially be combined with others to form a valid address.

It is not possible to implement a copying or relocating garbage collector if it is possible for object addresses to escape from the collector. The conservative garbage collectors that are possible allow garbage objects to be accidentally hoarded by integers that contain valid addresses.

We believe that efficient implementations of full temporal safety will require C implementations that are valid within the requirements of the C abstract machine, but have unexpected behavior for much existing code. It is undefined behavior in C to compare two pointers to different addresses but in spite of this it is common to use addresses for comparison in trees or as input to hashes for hash tables. This works in current implementations but would break if a collector is allowed to modify addresses.

4. Refining the CHERI model

Our CHERI processor provides a fine-grained memory protection model via *memory capabilities*, which are hardware-enforced *unforgeable* references to regions of memory. In the CHERI world, all memory is accessed via a memory capability. The ISA is a superset of MIPS IV, an existing 64-bit ISA, and can run unmodified MIPS code.

Version 2 of the CHERI ISA [35] was created based on initial experiences attempting to build a capability system that was a usable compiler target for C. For example, this change propagated tag bits into capability tag bits, rather than preventing memory without tag bits from being loaded into capability registers. This was motivated by the need for `memcpy()` (which is called explicitly by the user and implicitly by the compiler) to be able to copy data without being aware of whether it contained pointers. A similar requirement applies to unions.

CHERIv2 memory capabilities are represented as the triplet *(base, bound, permissions)*, which is loosely packed into a 256-bit value. Here *base* provides an offset into a virtual address region, and *bound* limits the size of the region accessed; for CHERIv2 they are each 64-bits in length. For a discussion of *permissions*, see [33]. Capabilities reside either in a dedicated register file or can be spilled to memory, where their integrity is preserved by hardware-managed *tagged memory*. Capabilities must be naturally aligned and there is a single tag bit per 256 bits of memory. Conventional stores to an in-memory capability cause the tag bit to be cleared, invalidating the capability. Special capability load and store instructions allow capabilities to be spilled to the stack or stored in data structures, just like pointers. CHERIv2 supports use of capabilities as C pointers, with the caveat that pointer subtraction is not allowed.

Memory accesses are indirected via capabilities in three ways. Instruction fetches are relative to the *program counter capability* (PCC). Legacy MIPS loads and stores are relative to the *default data capability*. Finally, the CHERI ISA provides a set of load and store instructions that take an explicit capability register operand. The only instructions that modify a capability strictly reduce its permissions, either by increasing the base (and decreasing the length by the same amount), decreasing the length, or reducing the permissions.

When a process starts, it has a default data capability that covers the entire user address space. This can be partitioned and restricted, for example by limiting its use to the memory allocator, and referring to other memory purely via capabilities returned from the allocator, the linker, or from the stack capability. It is the responsibility of the allocator (or the compiler, for stack allocations) to correctly set the length on capabilities. Once set, it is impossible to use the resulting capability to gain access to memory outside the object.

Code compiled for our extension to the CHERI ISAv2 runs atop the FreeBSD operating system on a modified CHERI processor synthesized to run in FPGA at 100MHz. Our goal is to demonstrate that it is possible to meet all of our requirements for a low-level language compilation target from an instruction set that provides spatial memory safety. In particular, all of the mechanisms provided by the hardware can be exposed to a C programmer directly, and all of the aspects of memory behavior defined by the abstract machine are translated into simple machine instructions without any complex abstraction layers or support libraries.

4.1 Converging capabilities and fat pointers

CHERI ISAv2 capabilities provide C-like pointer semantics subject to non-increasing rights imposed by the capability model. The CHERI ISAv2 compiler allows code authors to qualify suitable pointers for compilation using capabilities, implicitly confirming that any manipulation of the pointer is compatible with those restricted rights; e.g., that subtraction of the *base* field is not required. Ideally, however, the compiler would be able to automatically employ capabilities for all pointers, subject to binary-compatibility concerns with capability-unaware code, which requires more broad support for arbitrary pointer arithmetic. We found, for example, that real-world code such as tcpdump (see §5.2) undertakes pointer arithmetic which, during intermediate steps, goes beyond the bounds of the structure the pointer is supposed to be referencing, but which (usually) ends up within the bounds during a memory access. To make CHERI-style capabilities better fit the C-based pointer idiom, and allow automated use with unqualified pointers, we have therefore extended the memory capabilities found in CHERIv2 with the attributes of *fat pointers*, to produce the CHERIv3 ISA. Our fat-capabilities add an *offset* to the CHERIv2 capability model to form: *(base, bound, offset, permissions)*.

The general idea of a fat pointer is well explored and their benefits in providing spatial memory safety are well documented: pointers are supplemented by base and bounds values that, on dereference, throw a trap if an inappropriate access is requested. CHERIv3 fat-capabilities have two advantages over conventional fat pointers: (1) fat-capability integrity and non-decreasing rights are guaranteed by the hardware capability model while still supporting arbitrary pointer arithmetic; and (2) the permissions field permits additional hardware-checked constraints to be imposed, potentially for garbage collection or information-flow labeling. Integrity is especially important in the presence of concurrency: a thread-safe fat pointer implementation must guarantee that the entire fat pointer is updated atomically.

These distinctions allow memory capabilities to be used as building blocks for higher-level security features. The total memory that is reachable from a piece of code is the transitive closure of the memory capabilities reachable from its capability registers, making it possible for some threads (for example) to have limited rights to memory within a program. The addition of permissions allows capabilities to be tokens granting certain rights to the referenced memory. For example, a memory capability may have permissions to read data and capabilities, but not to write them (or just to write data but not capabilities). Attempting any of the operations that is not permitted will cause a trap.

This allows memory capabilities to enforce the `const` qualifier on pointers, by removing the store permission. We did implement support for this in the original C compiler for CHERIv2, but found that it broke a large amount of code. We subsequently added `__input` and `__output` qualifiers that make it possible to declaratively discard write and read permissions, respectively.

It is possible in the CHERIv2 model to implement fat pointers as a pair of a capability and an (integer) offset. This has several disadvantages. The first is the size. CHERIv2 capabilities are already 256 bits and must be aligned. The alignment requirement would mean that an array of fat point-

INSTRUCTION	USE
CIncOffset	Adds an integer to the offset
CSetOffset	Sets the offset
CGetOffset	Returns the current offset
CPtrCmp	Compares two capabilities
CFromPtr	Converts a MIPS pointer to a capability
CToPtr	Converts capability to a MIPS pointer

Table 2. New CHERI instructions to better support C

ers represented this way would use 64 *bytes* per pointer, although 24 of those would be padding. This approach would also make atomic updates to pointers difficult. Updating a pointer in memory requires writing the capability and the integer value atomically, which is not something that is easy to add with current DRAM memory widths.

To access this new *offset*, we added the instructions described in Table 2. In addition to these extra instructions, we modified `CIncBase` to update the pointer such that the offset remained constant and modified all of the load and store operations to use the pointer value. Our total changes amount to 496 lines of changes to the Bluespec source for the processor and 218 lines of changes to the test suite. These changes did not alter the critical path of the pipeline—the virtual address calculation for loads and stores—which is now done by adding the offset to the pointer, rather than to the base. It did add a small amount of complexity to the bounds checking logic. This now checks the resulting address against the base and top, rather than just against the length, so this pipeline stage (which happens in parallel with the cache fetch) is extended in length by one OR operation.

To avoid accidentally leaking virtual addresses into integer registers, we added a `CPtrCmp` instruction that compares the base plus offset of two capabilities as if they were pointers. This instruction orders all tagged capabilities after all untagged capabilities. Integer values stored in a capability are constructed by setting the offset of the canonical null capability and will never compare equal to any valid capability.

4.2 Interoperability

We added two instructions, `CToPtr` and `CFromPtr`, to convert between a capability and a traditional pointer. These take three operands, the capability and integer registers as the input and output, and a base capability that indicates the capability to which linear pointers are relative.

The `CFromPtr` instruction allows a pointer to be derived from the default data capability. It has special case behavior of giving a canonical null capability (all zeros with the tag bit cleared) if the offset within the default capability is 0, to adhere to C's null pointer semantics. `CToPtr` provides the address of the capability as an offset from a base capability (so that it can be used as a pointer relative to the default data capability) or 0 if this value would be out of range.

As bounds information is not carried by traditional pointers, these instructions must be used carefully and are relevant only in a hybrid environment, where the memory-safe capability view and the traditional view of pointers are mixed. As our canonical null capability is untagged, it can never become a valid capability. Arithmetic may alter the offset of the NULL capability allowing constructions such as returning -1 from `mmap()` to indicate failure.

As long as the appropriate modifications are made for each instance of its use, with CHERIv3, a `__capability` -qualified pointer can be used anywhere (library interfaces permitting) that a traditional pointer can. When a capability-qualified pointer is used in a union and then modified as a non-capability type, the result is an invalid capability that will trap when used for memory access. This is provided by CHERI's tagged memory, which clears the is-a-capability tag bit associated with the memory when a non-capability operation is used to store to a given address.

CHERIv3 C supports storing data in unused bits of a pointer as the pointer can point anywhere in the virtual address space (but must be within the bounds before it can be used). These programmer optimizations rely on the knowledge of implementation-defined behavior (such as the alignment of types and representation of pointers) to be efficient. As such, we consider it sufficient that they work, without requiring that they be efficient.

With CHERIv3, it is possible to use a code capability for every function. Each function invocation becomes a capability jump-and-link-register (`CJALR`) instruction, which replaces the PCC with a new capability register, the PC with a new register, and saves the old ones. This means that when a function is executing, it is impossible to jump out of it without an explicit call. Unfortunately, implementing this in practice is somewhat difficult as compilers and linkers make assumptions about their ability to place constants close to functions and depend on the program counter address to locate globals. Resolving this would require a completely new ABI, which is the subject of ongoing work.

We have implemented a relocating generational garbage collector for CHERIv3 that uses the tagged memory to differentiate between capabilities and other data. Determining how much software will be broken by this is ongoing work.

5. Evaluation

To evaluate our approach, we consider two questions:

- To what extent does compilation of the current C-language corpus depend on C idioms specific to PDP-11-like concrete implementations?
- How do alternative memory models function with respect to correctness and performance of C applications?

We explored the first question earlier, discovering a set of common idioms, and extracting simple test cases for each of them. Having identified these cases, we explored which of them will function with different interpretations of the standard. In addition to the x86 and MIPS baselines, the original CHERIv2 implementation, and our CHERIv3 variant, we implemented a translator for C code into a simple abstract machine interpreter. This runs very slowly but allows us to quickly modify the abstract machine and run the test cases extracted from the idioms to see which fail.

For the second question, we evaluated the two CHERI C implementations against the same code compiled using the MIPS ABI. For this part of the evaluation, we added `__capability` qualifiers to pointers in the application, but retained the non-memory-safe versions for external pointers – for example, for use with system library routines.

5.1 Comparing implementation models

These results are shown in Table 3. They contrast traditional PDP-11-like x86 and MIPS implementations with the following other possibilities:

HardBound refers to the model as described in [12].

Intel MPX refers to the bounds-checking extensions to x86 proposed by Intel.

Relaxed interpreter allows pointers to be constructed from integer values as long as the object is still valid. The top 32 bits of the pointer are used to look up a valid object in a map and the low 32 bits describe an offset.

Strict interpreter allows pointers to be reconstructed from integers if (and only if) they are not modified in their integer representation.

CHERIv2 describes the original C compiler for CHERI, without offset support, where pointer addition decreases the range of the underlying capability.

CHERIv3 describes a new version of the CHERI ISA that allows capabilities to act as fat pointers.

The MIPS and x86 abstract machines do not differ in ways relevant to our analysis.

Several of the results in this table require additional explanation. Both CHERI implementations allow storing capabilities in integers of type `intcap_t`, but not in normal C integers. The CHERIv3 implementation performs arithmetic on these using the offset, and so does permit arbitrary arithmetic. The original CHERI implementation permitted only storing and loading of these values. The Strict implementation has the same restriction: pointers can be stored in integers, but any arithmetic will invalidate the pointers.

These provide five points on a continuum trading safety for compatibility. CHERIv3 supports all of the idioms that we identified as being important to avoid breaking for compatibility with existing code. We address the `const` enforcement issue by making `const` advisory and providing a new qualifier (`__input`) that is hardware enforced. There is also the caveat that storing pointers in integers and performing arbitrary arithmetic is allowed only in places where doing so would not damage the memory-safety model.

The Strict model is close to our ideal interpretation of the C standard, disallowing a large set of operations that are potentially dangerous. Unfortunately, Strict also breaks many assumptions in existing code. Given the amount of time taken to ensure that the majority of C code is 64-bit clean, it is important to provide incremental steps to improve C code. The CHERIv3 target is attainable in the short term with small amounts of work, from which it will be easier to refine code to operate in an environment where pointers are strictly distinct from integers.

Intel's MPX and HardBound both rely on explicit instructions to tag pointer bounds. This approach relies on the compiler being able to determine that it is operating on a pointer. Casting a pointer to an integer and then performing arbitrary arithmetic prevents the compiler from asserting the bounds. These two models (neither is yet available as an implementation, although Intel provides an MPX simulator) provide subtly different tradeoffs. The Intel version leans more in the direction of compatibility. If a pointer is modified in such a way that the MPX extensions are not updated, then the value will fail its check against the copy of the pointer in the look-aside table that the CPU uses to maintain the pointer state. If this occurs, then the bounds checks succeed unconditionally. This preserves compatibility, but at the expense of safety. In contrast, HardBound does not store the pointer in the look-aside table and so will assume the old bounds, even if the pointer now refers to a different object and so will fail closed, preferring a detectable error to compatibility. Both have integer arithmetic on pointers and masking marked as not working, although this does depend on whether the compiler is able to correctly propagate the bounds.

In our simple test cases, MPX failed the Container check because the compiler associated bounds with the inner pointer and so hit a bounds check. Our test cases passed for MPX with arbitrary arithmetic and masking, but this depends on the compiler updating the bounds correctly. This is more difficult in programs where the compiler cannot see that a particular integer contains a pointer value.

MPX also suffers significant problems with atomicity. Its metadata is stored in look-aside tables, in separate pages to the relevant data. This leads to race conditions in multithreaded environments, as both locations must be changed in response to pointer modifications. As MPX relies on explicitly updating pointer metadata, it is also difficult to implement `memcpy` and similar functions, which must copy memory without being aware of the types of its contents.

The "best effort" translation of integers to pointers in the Relaxed model allows accidental construction of valid, but incorrect, pointers. This cannot happen with the CHERI version, as unsafe arithmetic would invalidate the capability, and provides an interesting alternative similar to some attempts at adding bounds checking to C code; it gives little

PROGRAM	DECONST	CONTAINER	SUB	II	INT	IA	MASK	WIDE
x86/MIPS/PDP-11	yes	yes	yes	yes	yes	yes	yes	no
HardBound	yes	yes	yes	yes	(yes)	no	no	no
Intel MPX	yes	no	yes	yes	(yes)	(yes)	(yes)	no
Relaxed	yes	yes	yes	yes	yes	yes	yes	no
Strict	yes	yes	yes	yes	(yes)	no	no	no
CHERIv2	no	no	no	no	(yes)	no	no	no
CHERIv3	yes	yes	yes	yes	(yes)	yes	yes	no

Table 3. Summary of idioms supported by different interpretations of the C abstract machine.

benefit in terms of source compatibility, compared to the capability version, in exchange for a weaker memory model.

All of our original set of requirements for an implementation of a low-level language, meet the expressiveness requirement, according to the specification—except for the original CHERI implementation. The lack of pointer subtraction means that the implementation did not meet the requirements of the abstract machine. More interesting is whether it captures the semantics expected by programmers. From Table 1, we observe that most C code can function with the restrictions imposed by CHERI. The relaxed restrictions in our modified CHERI will still break code that expects to be able to remove a `const` qualifier, but the only other modification required is changing the `intptr_t` typedef to refer to the `intcap_t` type and ensuring that this type is used whenever pointers are stored in integer values.

CHERIv2 and CHERIv3 score very highly on efficiency. Each C operation is a short sequence of machine instructions. Loads and stores are single instructions, and address calculations are either register or immediate offsets, or the result of a `CSetOffset` or `CIncOffset` instruction.

The exposure requirement is a bit more difficult to judge objectively. For the CHERI implementation, all of the functionality of the underlying substrate is exposed, and the properties of a capability (length, permissions, and so on) can be queried via intrinsics.

5.2 Whole program testing

Having demonstrated that our modified CHERI ought to be able to implement almost all of the requirements of C code, we next attempt to validate that assumption by porting a small selection of programs to run on it. We used the Olden benchmark suite (which is heavy in pointer use and so demonstrates a worst case for CHERI), Dhrystone (a less pointer-intensive benchmark), tcpdump (as an illustrative application), and zlib (as an illustrative library).

Table 4 shows the number of lines of code and percentage of the total changed to adapt each to run on CHERIv2 and CHERIv3. All of these results are for CHERI synthesized to run at 100MHz on a Stratix IV FPGA. The L1 data cache is 16KB and the L2 cache is 64KB. This is smaller than most contemporary processors, but the DDR DRAM is faster

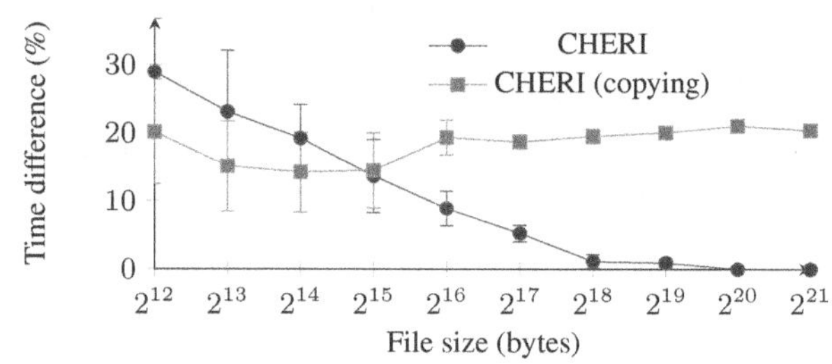

Figure 4. Overhead of CHERI-zlib normalized against zlib compiled for a conventional MIPS ISA.

relative to the CPU speed, so cache misses are more common but less costly than on most modern processors.

The first column shows the lines whose only changes are to mark pointers as capabilities. We made these changes manually to understand their placement, but the compiler can now use capabilities to represent all pointers. The important numbers are the semantic changes required because of the different memory models.

Having ported the code, we benchmarked it with unmodified MIPS code and CHERIv3. The Olden benchmarks were run with the parameters in the CHERI ISCA paper [35]. The Olden results are shown in Figure 1. The Dhrystone benchmark was run for 500,000 iterations on each run and the results are shown in Figure 2. Finally, the performance of tcpdump was measured by processing the first 100,000 packets from the `A.pcap061106170025.pcap` file from a network trace from OSDI 2006[6] is shown in in Figure 3.

The slowdown for tcpdump (unmodified MIPS vs. CHERIv3) was $4\%\pm3\%$. For comparison, small changes to optimizations in our LLVM gave a 15% speedup for tcpdump, so 4% is well within the margin for errors. Changes in cache and TLB pressure resulting from small changes to code layout can be larger. The Dhrystone results show the CHERI version to be around 2% faster than the MIPS code, but this is well within the margin of error simply for changes to instruction cache usage. These results lead us to believe that strong memory protection need not incur a statistically significant slowdown. The T-test places the difference in performance at 95% confidence below the experimental variation from small changes to compiler performance.

Program	Baseline LoC	CHERIv2 Annotation	CHERIv2 Semantic	CHERIv2 Total	CHERIv3 Annotation	CHERIv3 Semantic	CHERIv3 Total
Olden	1519	53 (3.5%)	0 (0%)	53 (3.5%)	53 (3.5%)	0 (0%)	53 (3.5%)
Dhrystone	448	11 (2.4%)	0 (0%)	11 (2.4%)	11 (2.4%)	0 (0%)	11 (2.4%)
tcpdump	66555	3006 (4.5%)	**1,577 (2.4%)**	4583 (6.9%)	3006 (4.5%)	**2 (0.0%)**	3008 (4.5%)

Table 4. Lines of code changed to port from MIPS to CHERIv2 and CHERIv3

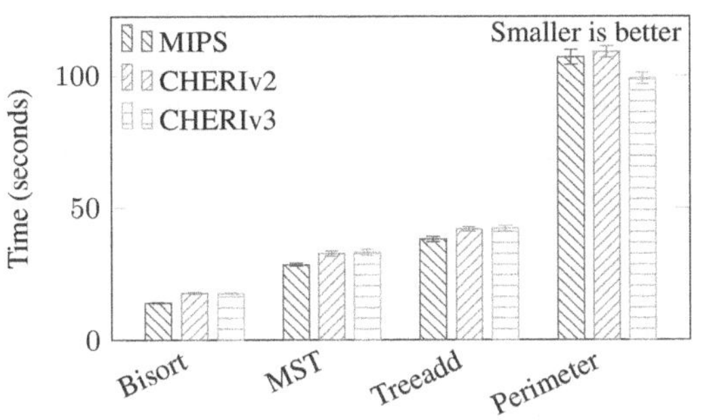

Figure 1. Olden results

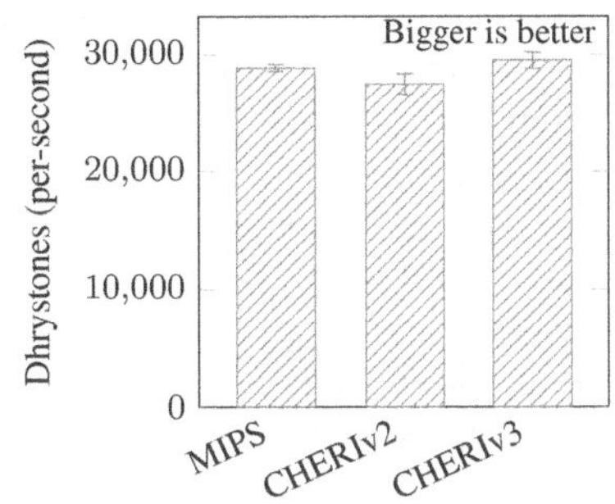

Figure 2. Dhrystone results

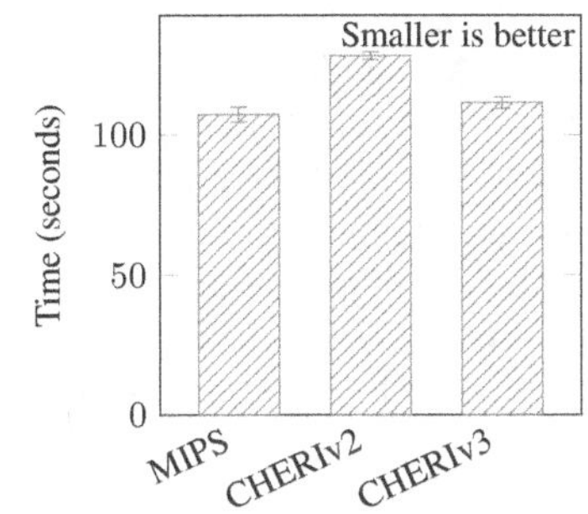

Figure 3. Tcpdump results

The effort required to port C code to a memory-safe environment depends significantly on the coding style employed. We have observed that the code that could most benefit from a memory-safe substrate (judging from published vulnerabilities related to memory errors) is also the code that is harder to port. This observation is one of the motivations for allowing unmodified MIPS code in our CHERI implementation: it allows us to apply coarse-grained sandboxing to such code. This means that even if we have to use non memory-safe code, the damage it can cause can be restricted.

The two benchmark suites that we modified are both conservative in their pointer use. They required changes only to annotate some values with `__capability`, and performed little or no unusual pointer arithmetic. In a pure capability environment, no annotation would be required. This is fairly common in benchmark code. The performance difference between them is primarily due to the larger pointers causing more cache misses. In spite of the relatively small cache on CHERI (16KB L1, 64KB L2), this overhead is significant only in the Olden benchmarks, which create and walk pointer-based data structures. Neither a CPU-focused benchmark nor a real application showed significant slowdown.

The tcpdump codebase is very different from the benchmarks in terms of porting effort. Packet dissection involves substantial pointer arithmetic—ironically, frequently in service of hand-crafted software bounds checking. Unfortunately, tcpdump typically runs as root (to access raw packet data from a network interface), and is often used for inspecting suspicious network traffic. This means that its packet parsers—written using extensive pointer arithmetic—are exposed to malicious data. Crafting malicious packets that crash tcpdump (if not execute arbitrary code) to blind opponents is a common strategy in *capture the flag* uompetitions. The code would benefit substantially from strong memory safety, yet written in a style that makes this very difficult.

Porting tcpdump to CHERIv2 required changes to around 1.6K lines to avoid pointer subtraction: around 2.5% of the total codebase. CHERIv3 is fully able to support the parts of the C standard expected by these codebases. Only, two lines of code had to be changed in just one file, to ensure that tcpdump has read-only access to the packet being parsed rather than the whole packet buffer. This change was not strictly required, but provided stronger and finer-grained protection than would otherwise be possible.

We then modified the compiler to support a new ABI in which all pointers are implemented as capabiliting, including references to on-stack objects, which are derived from a stack capability. We then compiled two versions of zlib using this mode. The first is entirely unmodified internally, but requires some annotations in a header to allow it to be work with code using the MIPS ABI. This was limited to a single pragma at the start and end of the library header, and was required because zlib passes pointers across the library interface. This approach breaks binary compatibility for the library (though it retains source compatibility), so we also implemented a second version that preserves binary compatibility by copying structures whose layouts have changed whenever they are passed across the library boundary.

Figure 4 shows the results for compressing files of varying sizes with the two modified and one unmodified version of zlib, linked to the gzip program. Simply using capabilities incurs no measurable overhead for large files and a small overhead for small files (there is a small constant overhead for setting up the capability environment). Copying data at the library boundaries to maintain binary compatibility incurs around a 21% overhead, independent of file size.

6. Related work

Substantial prior work targets improving C memory safety. Early examples include Cyclone [17], which explicitly broke compatibility with C to define a safer C dialect. Cyclone's abstraction is close to our model, but adds many static annotations. Although Cyclone was not widely adopted, it influenced pointer annotation in current C compilers.

The copious buffer overflow vulnerabilities in C codebases have spurred development of a number of other bounds-checking systems. Research tools HardBound [12] and SoftBound [22] add fine-grained bounds checking to C, followed by commercial work, such as Intel's Memory Protection Extensions [15]. None of these approaches handles some of the complex cases (for example, xor linked lists) outlined here, the key difference being that the HardBound and SoftBound approaches will fail closed (preventing potentially dangerous memory accesses if the can't track pointer provenance), whereas the Intel solution will fail open (allowing unsafe access if the bounds can't be determined).

Memory-related exploit techniques have spawned substantial work in vulnerability scanning and dynamic mitigation [27]. Static analysis tools such as lint [14] and general bug pattern-matching tools [4] are effective for local analyses, but are limited by weak type safety, global program complexity, and difficult-to-analyze dynamic behaviors. Dynamic protections such as stack canaries and address-space layout randomization offer probabilistic protection for specific exploits [7], but suffer a constant escalation [29].

To run untrusted C code within a process that contains other data rights, SFI [30] and Google's Native Client (NaCl) [36] provide coarse-grained isolation for native code. Similar techniques like Robusta [28] (and earlier work on process isolation [10]) isolate almost a million lines of C code libraries from JVM's. Without isolation or a memory-safe substrate, a single pointer error in the native code can damage the entire VM, including the typesafe Java code.

SAFECode and SVA [8, 9] provide control flow integrity and memory safety in TCB code, specifically in kernels, via compiler transforms. We believe that the run-time overhead of these techniques would be lower with hardware assistance described in this paper, and would provide powerful tools for quickly moving existing code to such a substrate.

Emscripten [37] is an interesting example of an unusual deployment target for C, running C code in a JavaScript VM. The runtime violates our exposure requirement by creating the C heap in a single JavaScript object and not exposing the JavaScript memory model. Microsoft's various approaches to running C++ code in the .NET CLR [19] also provide some inspiration. These introduce different types of pointer to differentiate between fully GC'd memory and "pinned" pointers, which have stable integer values. With better hardware support for protection, we argue that it becomes much easier to implement systems like these, with low-level code running in the same environment to managed code.

7. Conclusion

Lack of memory safety in C leads to real and significant vulnerabilities, particularly as near-ubiquitous networking for conventional computers and mobile devices has exposed users to unprecedented malicious activity. This has reinvigorated interest in fine-grained memory protection to mitigate exploit techniques. However, widespread assumptions about pointer behavior, unwarranted by the C abstract machine but consistent with the PDP-11 memory model, produce substantial compatibility problems in real-world programs that might most benefit from additional protection.

To address these problems, we survey C-pointer idioms across a large open-source corpus to understand the effective consensus on pointer use that constrains memory-protection schemes. We are then able to describe a range of points in the protection and compatibility tradeoff space.

Observing potentially significant source-code compatibility, we propose a new model, fully described and implemented as the CHERIv3 ISA, that combines CHERI's capability-system model with results from recent fat-pointer research. Whole-program testing against conventional RISC, CHERIv2, and CHERIv3 illustrates significantly improved source-code compatibility relative to a pure capability-system model, as well as modest performance improvement.

These results confirm that it is possible to retain the strong semantics of a capability-system memory model (which provides non-bypassable memory protection) without sacrificing the advantages of a low-level language.

Acknowledgments

We thank our colleagues – especially Ross Anderson, Gregory Chadwick, Nirav Dave, Khilan Gudka, Steve Hand, Stephen Kell, Ben Laurie, Ilias Marinos, A Theodore Markettos, Ed Maste, Andrew W. Moore, Prashanth Mundkur, Steven J. Murdoch, Robert Norton, Hassen Saidi, Peter Sewell, Stacey Son, and Bjoern Zeeb; we also thank our anonymous reviewers for their feedback.

This work is part of the CTSRD and MRC2 projects that are sponsored by the Defense Advanced Research Projects Agency (DARPA) and the Air Force Research Laboratory (AFRL), under contracts FA8750-10-C-0237 and FA8750-11-C-0249. The views, opinions, and/or findings contained in this paper are those of the authors and should not be interpreted as representing the official views or policies, either expressed or implied, of the Department of Defense or the U.S. Government. We gratefully acknowledge Google, Inc. for its sponsorship.

References

[1] Is address space 1 reserved? URL http://lists.cs.uiuc.edu/pipermail/llvmdev/2015-January/080288.html.

[2] Alelph One. Smashing the stack for fun and profit. *Phrack Magazine*, 7:14–16, 1996.

[3] *ARM Architecture Reference Manual. ARMv8, for ARMv8-A architecture profile*. ARM Limited, 110 Fulbourn Road, Cambridge, England CB1 9NJ, 2013.

[4] A. Bessey, K. Block, B. Chelf, A. Chou, B. Fulton, S. Hallem, C. Henri-Gros, A. Kamsky, S. McPeak, and D. Engler. A few billion lines of code later: Using static analysis to find bugs in the real world. *Commun. ACM*, 53(2):66–75, Feb. 2010. ISSN 0001-0782. URL http://doi.acm.org/10.1145/1646353.1646374.

[5] H.-J. Boehm and M. Weiser. Garbage collection in an uncooperative environment. *Softw. Pract. Exper.*, 18(9):807–820, Sept. 1988. ISSN 0038-0644. . URL http://dx.doi.org/10.1002/spe.4380180902.

[6] R. Chandra, V. Padmanabhan, and M. Zhang. CRAWDAD data set microsoft/osdi2006 (v. 2007-05-23). Downloaded from http://crawdad.org/microsoft/osdi2006/, May 2007.

[7] C. Cowan, P. Wagle, C. Pu, S. Beattie, and J. Walpole. Buffer overflows: attacks and defenses for the vulnerability of the decade. In *DARPA Information Survivability Conference and Exposition, 2000. DISCEX '00. Proceedings*, volume 2, pages 119–129 vol.2, 2000. .

[8] J. Criswell, A. Lenharth, D. Dhurjati, and V. Adve. Secure virtual architecture: A safe execution environment for commodity operating systems. In *SOSP '07: Proceedings of the Twenty First ACM Symposium on Operating Systems Principles*, October 2007.

[9] J. Criswell, N. Geoffray, and V. Adve. Memory safety for low-level software/hardware interactions. In *Proceedings of the Eighteenth Usenix Security Symposium*, August 2009.

[10] G. Czajkowski, L. Daynes, and M. Wolczko. Automated and portable native code isolation. In *Software Reliability Engineering, 2001. ISSRE 2001. Proceedings. 12th International Symposium on*, pages 298–307, Nov 2001. .

[11] R. Dannenberg, W. Dormann, D. Keaton, R. Seacord, D. Svoboda, A. Volkovitsky, T. Wilson, and T. Plum. As-if infinitely ranged integer model. In *Software Reliability Engineering (ISSRE), 2010 IEEE 21st International Symposium on*, pages 91–100, Nov 2010. .

[12] J. Devietti, C. Blundell, M. M. K. Martin, and S. Zdancewic. Hardbound: Architectural support for spatial safety of the C programming language. *SIGPLAN Not.*, 43(3):103–114, Mar. 2008. ISSN 0362-1340. . URL http://doi.acm.org/10.1145/1353536.1346295.

[13] J. Evans. A scalable concurrent malloc(3) implementation for FreeBSD. In *BSDCan*, 2006.

[14] Gimpel Software. FlexeLint for C/C++, August 2014. URL http://www.gimpel.com/html/flex.htm.

[15] Intel Plc. Introduction to Intel® memory protection extensions. http://software.intel.com/en-us/articles/introduction-to-intel-memory-protection-extensions, July 2013.

[16] ISO. *ISO/IEC 9899:2011 Information technology — Programming languages — C*. International Organization for Standardization, Geneva, Switzerland, Dec. 2011. URL http://www.iso.org/iso/iso_catalogue/catalogue_tc/catalogue_detail.htm?csnumber=57853.

[17] T. Jim, J. G. Morrisett, D. Grossman, M. W. Hicks, J. Cheney, and Y. Wang. Cyclone: A safe dialect of C. In *Proceedings of the General Track of the Annual Conference on USENIX Annual Technical Conference*, ATEC '02, pages 275–288, Berkeley, CA, USA, 2002. USENIX Association. ISBN 1-880446-00-6. URL http://dl.acm.org/citation.cfm?id=647057.713871.

[18] A. Kwon, U. Dhawan, J. M. Smith, T. F. Knight, Jr., and A. DeHon. Low-fat pointers: Compact encoding and efficient gate-level implementation of fat pointers for spatial safety and capability-based security. In *Proceedings of the 2013 ACM SIGSAC Conference on Computer and Communications Security*, CCS '13, pages 721–732, New York, NY, USA, 2013. ACM. ISBN 978-1-4503-2477-9. . URL http://doi.acm.org/10.1145/2508859.2516713.

[19] Managed C++. Managed extensions for C++ specification. http://msdn.microsoft.com/en-us/library/Aa712867 (accessed 2014/07/14).

[20] Microsoft Corporation. CONTAINING_RECORD macro. URL http://msdn.microsoft.com/en-us/library/windows/hardware/ff542043%28v=vs.85%29.aspx.

[21] Mitre. CWE/SANS top 25 most dangerous software errors, 2011. URL http://cwe.mitre.org/top25.

[22] S. Nagarakatte, J. Zhao, M. M. Martin, and S. Zdancewic. Softbound: Highly compatible and complete spatial memory safety for C. In *Proceedings of the 2009 ACM SIGPLAN Conference on Programming Language Design and Implementation*, PLDI '09, pages 245–258, New York, NY, USA, 2009. ACM. ISBN 978-1-60558-392-1. . URL http://doi.acm.org/10.1145/1542476.1542504.

[23] G. C. Necula, S. McPeak, and W. Weimer. Ccured: Type-safe retrofitting of legacy code. In *Proceedings of the 29th ACM SIGPLAN-SIGACT Symposium on Principles of Programming Languages*, POPL '02, pages 128–139, New York, NY, USA, 2002. ACM. ISBN 1-58113-450-9. . URL http://doi.acm.org/10.1145/503272.503286.

[24] M. Richards. BCPL: A Tool for Compiler Writing and System Programming. In *Proceedings of the May 14-16, 1969, Spring Joint Computer Conference*, AFIPS '69 (Spring), pages 557–566, New York, NY, USA, 1969. ACM. . URL http://doi.acm.org/10.1145/1476793.1476880.

[25] D. Ritchie, S. Johnson, M. Lesk, and B. Kernighan. UNIX time-sharing system: The C programming language. *Bell System Technical Journal*, 57(6):1991–2019, July-Aug 1978.

[26] J. Saltzer and M. Schroeder. The protection of information in computer systems. *Proceedings of the IEEE*, 63(9):1278–1308, September 1975. URL http://www.multicians.org.

[27] H. Shahriar and M. Zulkernine. Mitigating program security vulnerabilities: Approaches and challenges. *ACM Comput. Surv.*, 44(3):11:1–11:46, June 2012. ISSN 0360-0300. URL `http://doi.acm.org/10.1145/2187671.2187673`.

[28] M. Sun, G. Tan, J. Siefers, B. Zeng, and G. Morrisett. Bringing Java's wild native world under control. *ACM Trans. Inf. Syst. Secur.*, 16(3):9:1–9:28, Dec. 2013. ISSN 1094-9224. . URL `http://doi.acm.org/10.1145/2535505`.

[29] L. Szekeres, M. Payer, T. Wei, and D. Song. Eternal war in memory. In *IEEE Symposium on Security and Privacy*, 2013.

[30] R. Wahbe, S. Lucco, T. E. Anderson, and S. L. Graham. Efficient software-based fault isolation. In *SOSP '93: Proceedings of the fourteenth ACM Symposium on Operating Systems Principles*, pages 203–216, New York, NY, USA, 1993. ACM. ISBN 0-89791-632-8.

[31] X. Wang, H. Chen, Z. Jia, N. Zeldovich, and M. F. Kaashoek. Improving integer security for systems with KINT. In *Proceedings of the 10th USENIX Conference on Operating Systems Design and Implementation*, OSDI'12, pages 163–177, Berkeley, CA, USA, 2012. USENIX Association. ISBN 978-1-931971-96-6. URL `http://dl.acm.org/citation.cfm?id=2387880.2387897`.

[32] X. Wang, N. Zeldovich, M. F. Kaashoek, and A. Solar-Lezama. Towards optimization-safe systems: Analyzing the impact of undefined behavior. In *Proceedings of the Twenty-Fourth ACM Symposium on Operating Systems Principles*, SOSP '13, pages 260–275, New York, NY, USA, 2013. ACM. ISBN 978-1-4503-2388-8. . URL `http://doi.acm.org/10.1145/2517349.2522728`.

[33] R. N. Watson, P. G. Neumann, J. Woodruff, J. Anderson, D. Chisnall, B. Davis, B. Laurie, S. W. Moore, S. J. Murdoch, and M. Roe. Capability Hardware Enhanced RISC Instructions: CHERI Instruction-set architecture. Technical Report UCAM-CL-TR-850, University of Cambridge, Computer Laboratory, Apr. 2014. URL `http://www.cl.cam.ac.uk/techreports/UCAM-CL-TR-850.pdf`.

[34] R. N. M. Watson, P. G. Neumann, J. Woodruff, J. Anderson, D. Chisnall, B. Davis, B. Laurie, S. W. Moore, S. J. Murdoch, and M. Roe. Capability Hardware Enhanced RISC Instructions: CHERI Instruction-set architecture. Technical Report UCAM-CL-TR-864, University of Cambridge, Computer Laboratory, 15 JJ Thomson Avenue, Cambridge CB3 0FD, United Kingdom, phone +44 1223 763500, Dec. 2014. URL `http://www.cl.cam.ac.uk/techreports/UCAM-CL-TR-864.pdf`.

[35] J. Woodruff, R. N. M. Watson, D. Chisnall, S. W. Moore, J. Anderson, B. Davis, B. Laurie, P. G. Neumann, R. Norton, and M. Roe. The CHERI capability model: Revisiting RISC in an age of risk. In *Proceedings of the 41st International Symposium on Computer Architecture (ISCA 2014)*, June 2014.

[36] B. Yee, D. Sehr, G. Dardyk, J. B. Chen, R. Muth, T. Ormandy, S. Okasaka, N. Narula, and N. Fullagar. Native client: A sandbox for portable, untrusted x86 native code. *Commun. ACM*, 53(1):91–99, Jan. 2010. ISSN 0001-0782. . URL `http://doi.acm.org/10.1145/1629175.1629203`.

[37] A. Zakai. Emscripten: An LLVM-to-JavaScript Compiler. In *Proceedings of the ACM International Conference Companion on Object Oriented Programming Systems Languages and Applications Companion*, SPLASH '11, pages 301–312, New York, NY, USA, 2011. ACM. ISBN 978-1-4503-0942-4. . URL `http://doi.acm.org/10.1145/2048147.2048224`.

Supporting Differentiated Services in Computers via Programmable Architecture for Resourcing-on-Demand (PARD)

Jiuyue Ma[1,2] Xiufeng Sui[1] Ninghui Sun[1] Yupeng Li[1] Zihao Yu[1,2] Bowen Huang[1] Tianni Xu[1,2]
Zhicheng Yao[1] Yun Chen[3] Haibin Wang[3] Lixin Zhang[1] Yungang Bao[1]

[1]State Key Laboratory of Computer Architecture, ICT, CAS
[2]University of Chinese Academy of Sciences
[3]Huawei Technologies

Abstract

This paper presents PARD, a programmable architecture for resourcing-on-demand that provides a new programming interface to convey an application's high-level information like quality-of-service requirements to the hardware. PARD enables new functionalities like fully hardware-supported virtualization and differentiated services in computers.

PARD is inspired by the observation that a computer is inherently a network in which hardware components communicate via packets (e.g., over the NoC or PCIe). We apply principles of software-defined networking to this intra-computer network and address three major challenges. First, to deal with the semantic gap between high-level applications and underlying hardware packets, PARD attaches a high-level semantic tag (e.g., a virtual machine or thread ID) to each memory-access, I/O, or interrupt packet. Second, to make hardware components more manageable, PARD implements programmable control planes that can be integrated into various shared resources (e.g., cache, DRAM, and I/O devices) and can differentially process packets according to tag-based rules. Third, to facilitate programming, PARD abstracts all control planes as a device file tree to provide a uniform programming interface via which users create and apply tag-based rules.

Full-system simulation results show that by co-locating latency-critical memcached applications with other workloads PARD can improve a four-core computer's CPU utilization by up to a factor of four without significantly increasing tail latency. FPGA emulation based on a preliminary RTL implementation demonstrates that the cache control plane introduces no extra latency and that the memory control plane can reduce queueing delay for high-priority memory-access requests by up to a factor of 5.6.

Categories and Subject Descriptors C.5.5 [*Computer System Organization*]: Computer System Implementation–Server

Keywords Hardware/Software Interface, QoS, Data Center

ASPLOS '15, March 14 - 18 2015, Istanbul, Turkey.
Copyright © 2015 ACM 978-1-4503-2835-7/15/03. . . $15.00.
http://dx.doi.org/10.1145/2694344.2694382

1. Introduction

Conventional computer organization provides an instruction set architecture (ISA) for software developers and compilers to interact with the hardware. However, as pointed out in the community white paper **21st Century Computer Architecture** [13]:

"Current ISAs fail to provide an efficient means of capturing software-intent or conveying critical high-level information to the hardware. For example, they have no way of specifying when a program requires energy efficiency, robust security, or a desired Quality of Service (QoS) level."

The white paper further suggests that *"new, higher-level interfaces are needed to encapsulate and convey programmer and compiler knowledge to the hardware, resulting in major efficiency gains and valuable new functionality."*

Take data centers as a particular case study, such new architectural interfaces that convey an application's QoS requirements to the hardware can bring significant efficiency benefits for contemporary data centers, because they must manage difficult trade-offs between resource utilization and applications' QoS.

On one hand, to achieve high utilization, one straightforward approach is to co-locate workloads or virtual machines (VM) on each physical server. In this manner, Google's batch-workload data centers achieve 75% CPU utilization, on average [15]. However, co-location induces contention for various shared hardware resources (such as CPU cores, caches, memory bandwidth, and network switches [19]), as well as shared software resources (e.g., page caches, socket buffers, and multiple layers of queueing buffers [19, 35]). Such contention causes unpredictable performance variability [45, 47, 50] that is amplified at data center scales [19] where online services involve tens to hundreds of servers in processing even a single user request [51]. Moreover, such performance variability occurs frequently due to the unpredictability of frequent, short-running workloads. A month of profiling data from a 12,000-server Google data center shows that more than a million jobs ran for only a few minutes [59].

On the other hand, to guarantee QoS of latency-critical online services, data center operators or developers tend to avoid sharing by either dedicating resources or exaggerating reservations for online services in shared environments. Another Google example shows that typical online-service datacenters exhibit only about 30% CPU utilization, on average, much lower than batch-workload data centers [15]. In fact, without co-location industry-wide utilization is even lower — only between 6% [34] to 12% [1]. For shared environments, Reiss et al. [59] verify that developers indeed exaggerate resource requirements: in their 12,000-server data center,

Layer	Contention Points
Application	Background daemon [19], backup job [19, 77]
Network Stacks	Nagle's algorithm, limited buffers, delayed ACK caused RTO [77], TCP congestion control [14, 23], packet scheduling [29, 71, 73, 78], kernel sockets [39]
OS Kernel	Lock contention [35], context switch, kernel scheduling, SMT load imbalance and IRQ imbalance [39]
Hypervisor	Virtual machine scheduling [72, 74, 75], network bandwidth [33, 67, 72, 74]
Hardware	SMT [79], Shared caches [20, 36, 39, 56, 63, 64, 69], memory [20, 49, 69, 76], NIC [57], I/O [20, 48]
Datacenter	Global file system [19]

Table 1. Contention Identified in Prior Work

actual CPU and memory utilizations are only 20% and 40% respectively, while the average reservations are 75% and 60%.

Recognizing the inherent trade-offs, researchers have delved into the contention problem over the recent years. Table 1 highlights efforts to eliminate resource contention points at various levels of the software stack, from the interrupt handler, OS scheduler [39], and hypervisor scheduler [74, 75], to the network stack, queuing buffers, and application locks [35]. Despite these efforts, utilization of practical online-service data centers remains low. First, software-only approaches are limited to coarse-grained management, which results in relatively poor control accuracy. Second, sophisticated software stacks and varying application demands cause contention points to change across different scenarios (as shown in Table 1). Third, finding contention points usually requires tremendous time and effort [74].

Hardware isolation techniques such as cache partitioning [36, 56, 64] and memory channel partitioning [49] suffer from two primary limitations: focusing on only one type rather than multiple types of resources, and lacking uniform interfaces for software to manage various types of resources. Building resource-efficient datacenters thus requires coordinated, cross-layer mechanisms [38].

In this paper, we propose Programmable Architecture for Resourcing-on-Demand (PARD) that provides a new programming interface to convey an application's QoS requirements to the hardware. PARD supports new functionalities such as fully hardware-supported virtualization without software hypervisors and differentiated service (DiffServ) [60] in data center servers. For instance, PARD can accurately isolate performance in shared data centers to improve server utilization without degrading QoS for latency-critical applications.

The key idea of PARD is inspired by software-defined networking (SDN) [2], in which decoupling the control plane from the data plane allows the control plane to be made programmable. We find that a computer can be viewed as a network and then apply SDN principles to computer architecture to form PARD. Specifically, PARD consists of four mechanisms. First, a tagging mechanism labels each intra-computer network (ICN) packet with a high-level entity (e.g. VM, container, process, or thread) ID. Second, a programmable control plane that can be easily integrated into a variety of hardware components uses tag-based rules to differentially process ICN packets. Third, a per-computer IPMI-like [6] platform resource manager (PRM) running Linux-based firmware connects all control planes. Fourth, the firmware abstracts all control planes as a device file tree to provide a uniform programming interface for users to define tag-based rules (e.g., basic priority rules and advanced "trigger⇒action" rules) in the control planes.

We implemented PARD in a full-system simulator based on GEM5 [17]. Simulations of unmodified Linux 2.6.28.4 running Memcached [8] and SPECCPU 2006 [26] workloads show that PARD successfully balances CPU utilization and QoS requirements: On a simulated four-core physical server, without PARD co-running applications achieves 100% CPU utilization but increases Memcached's tail latency by two orders of magnitude, unless the server degrades CPU utilization to 25%. In contrast, when enabling PARD, the server can achieve 100% CPU utilization without substantially increasing Memcached's tail latency.

We evaluate hardware overhead on an FPGA development board [11] with a preliminary RTL implementation based on the OpenSPARC T1 microprocessor [54]. Synthesis results show that when supporting 256 different tags and 64 advanced "trigger⇒action" rules, the last level cache (LLC) and memory control planes introduce about 3.1% and 10.1% FPGA resource overhead, respectively. Since software is still being ported, we run the RTL emulation with microbenchmarks, finding that:

1. the LLC control plane does not introduce extra cycles because its control logic is effectively hidden within the pipeline of the LLC controller (OpenSPARC T1's LLC has eight pipeline stages), and
2. the memory control plane can reduce queueing delays for high-priority memory-access requests by up to 5.6× (from 15.2 cycles to only 2.7 cycles) while reasonably increasing the delay of low-priority memory-access requests by 33.6%.

In summary, our major contributions are:

- a new computer architecture supporting virtualization fully in hardware and providing a new programming interface to convey high-level information to the hardware,
- a programmable control plane structure that applies to various hardware resources and can perform differentiated services,
- a firmware that abstracts all control planes as a device file tree and provides an advanced "trigger⇒action" programming methodology to deploy resourcing-on-demand management policies, and
- a full-system simulation model and a proof-of-concept FPGA implementation.

The rest of the paper is organized as follows: Section §2 introduces background. Section §3 presents an overview of PARD. Section §4 outlines the architecture-level design and Section §5 describes software design. Some implementation details are in Section §6. Section §7 demonstrates case studies based PARD and overhead evaluations. Section §8 further discusses several issues such as overhead, optimization and functionality extension. Section §9 covers related work and Section §10 concludes.

2. Background

We describe the background of DiffServ as well as SDN and then present several challenges in applying SDN's principles to computer architecture.

2.1 DiffServ and SDN: The Origin and Inspiration

Historically, the current trade-offs data centers confront with are similar to the Internet in the 1990s when a lot of network applications emerged, such as streaming video, e-commerce, email and file transfers, which exhibited varying QoS requirements. To deliver end-to-end QoS on an IP-network, the Internet Engineering Task Force (IETF) proposed Differentiated Services (DiffServ) [61] in 1998. Today DiffServ has been one of the most widely adopted traffic engineering mechanism. The key idea of DiffServ is defining an 8-bit Differentiated Services field (DS field) in the IP header to designate an application's requirements so that routers can lever-

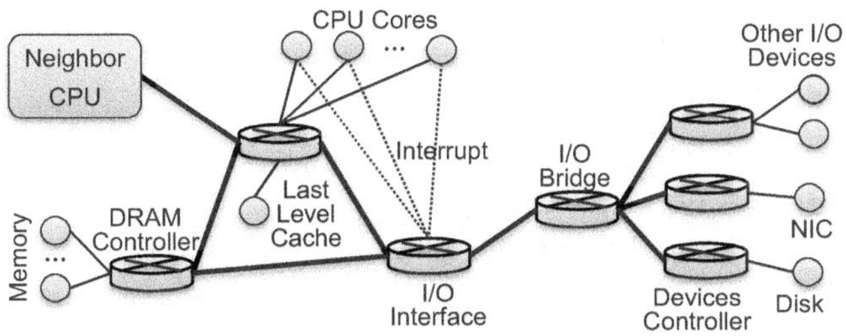

Figure 1. Intra-Computer Network (ICN). A traditional computer can be viewed as a network.

age the DS field to manage each packet for applications' different requirements.

The advent of software-defined networking (SDN) [2] further facilitates network management and traffic engineering. There is one prevalent interpretation of SDN's key principles:

- Each network packet is attached with a tag containing application information like *flowid* in OpenFlow [10].
- For network devices, the control plane is decoupled from the data plane and is responsible for packet management while the data plane is in charge of packet forwarding operations.
- All control planes are logically centralized and are directly programmable via a uniform programming interface.

The prevalence of DiffServ and SDN motivate us to investigate whether it is feasible to apply SDN's principles to computer architecture to address the trade-offs aforementioned. We find a key observation that **a computer is inherently a network**. As shown in Figure 1: a computer can be viewed as an intra-computer network (ICN)[1]; hardware components communicate with each other via different types of packets, such as network-on-chip (NoC), QuickPath Interconnect (QPI) [30] and PCIe packet; apart from processing packets, the controllers of hardware components actually play the role of network routers, i.e., forwarding packets to a next hop. Therefore, it should be possible to apply SDN to computer architecture.

2.2 Challenges of Applying SDN to Computer Architecture

Nevertheless, compared with deploying SDN in a network, there are at least three challenges in applying SDN to computer architecture.

First, in a network, usually the network stack is the only source for generating packets so it is easy to add tagging mechanism into the network stack. In a computer, in contrast, a number of different hardware components can generate different types of packets. Thus, we need to address how to tagging packets generated by various hardware components. (§4.1)

Second, unlike network routers that perform almost the same store-and-forward behavior, hardware components in a computer behave differently. It is challenging to figure out a uniform control plane structure for different hardware components such as LLC, memory and I/O devices. (§4.2)

Finally, there is already a firmware running in a network router for users to access and configure the router's control plane. However, conventional computers lack similar firmware. The current IPMI[2] [6] firmware in servers only performs limited monitoring and management functionality such as temperature, fan speed and power. Thus, it is essential to devise a firmware that provides a uniform interface for server operators to access control planes of hardware components. Moreover, a flexible programming methodology is desirable as well (§5).

3. PARD Overview

To tackle the challenges above, we propose PARD architecture to demonstrate how to apply SDN to computer architecture. (As mentioned in the Introduction section, this paper focuses on data center scenarios.) Figure 2 shows an overview of the architecture, which consists of four mechanisms:

① **Tagging Mechanism**. In shared data center environments, in order to allow shared hardware resources to distinguish different entities such as multiple logic domains (LDoms[3]), a DiffServ ID (DS-id) tag is assigned to each entity by a centralized platform resource manager. We add a DS-id tag register into all sources that generate requests (i.e., ICN packets) such as each CPU core and every I/O device. These registers are used for tagging cache-access, memory-access, DMA and interrupt requests. When a DS-id tag is attached to a request at source-end, the tag will travel along with the request during its whole lifetime until the request is completed.

② **Programmable Control Plane**. Since each request contains a DS-id tag, we introduce a programmable control plane into every shared resource to make use of the DS-id tag. Once receiving a request, a control plane first serves the request according to its DS-id and then generates a new request attached with the same DS-id to a next component.

There are various hardware components that behave differently and use DS-id tags in different ways as well, e.g., LLC using DS-id for capacity allocation while memory controller using DS-id for bandwidth allocation. We devise a basic control plane structure for a variety of components. Specifically, this structure consists of three DS-id indexed tables, i.e., a *parameter table* storing resource allocation policies, a *statistics table* storing resource usage information and a *trigger table* storing performance triggers. Besides, the structure includes a programming interface and an interrupt line. All control planes are connected to a centralized platform resource manager. This control plane structure can be easily instantiated and integrated into LLC, memory and I/O controllers. More details will be described in §4.2.

③ **Per-Computer Centralized Platform Resource Manager (PRM)**. Like IPMI [6] in conventional servers, PARD includes a per-computer centralized platform resource manager (PRM) that connects all control planes and tag registers (see the dash lines in Figure 2). PRM is essentially an embedded system-on-chip (SoC) that consists of an embedded processor, RAM, flash, a local bus, an Ethernet adaptor and several control plane adaptors (CPAs).

A Linux-based firmware running on PRM abstracts all control planes as a device file tree that is logically centralized. The firmware provides a uniform file based programming interface to access different control planes and a more advanced "*trigger⇒action*" programming methodology (see below) for operators to create and deploy resource management policies.

④ ***"Trigger⇒Action"* Programming Methodology**. To facilitate operators to define resource management policies and program control planes, PARD provides not only basic priority-based rules but also an advanced "*trigger⇒action*" programming methodology.

[1] The BarrelFish OS work [16] makes a similar observation that a computer is already a distributed system.

[2] IPMI (Intelligent Platform Management Interface) is used to monitor and manage hardware when a server is powered off or unresponsive.

[3] The term of logic domain (LDom) is originally introduced by SPARC processor [53]. In this paper, a LDom represents a submachine that contains several CPU cores, memory capacity and storage capacity and can run an unmodified OS. A server can be partitioned into multiple LDoms.

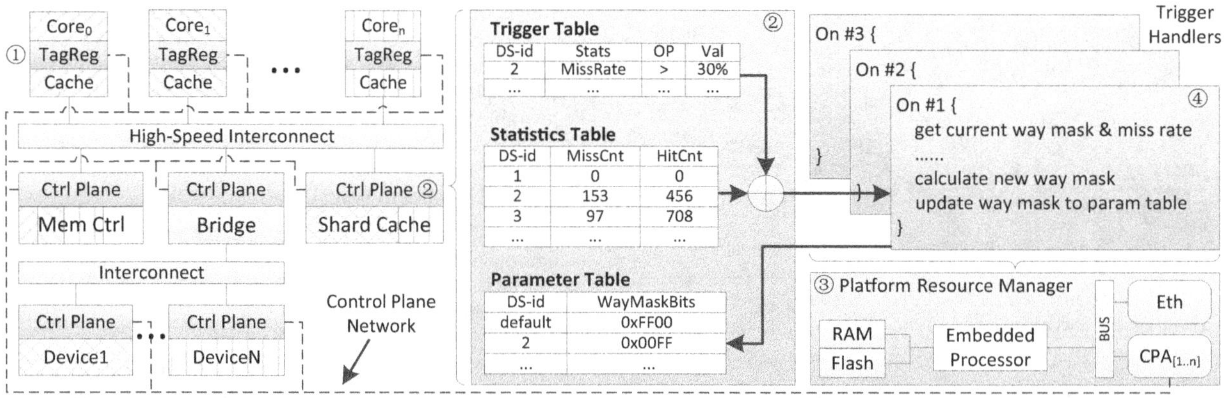

Figure 2. PARD Architecture Overview. The grey boxes represent PARD components.

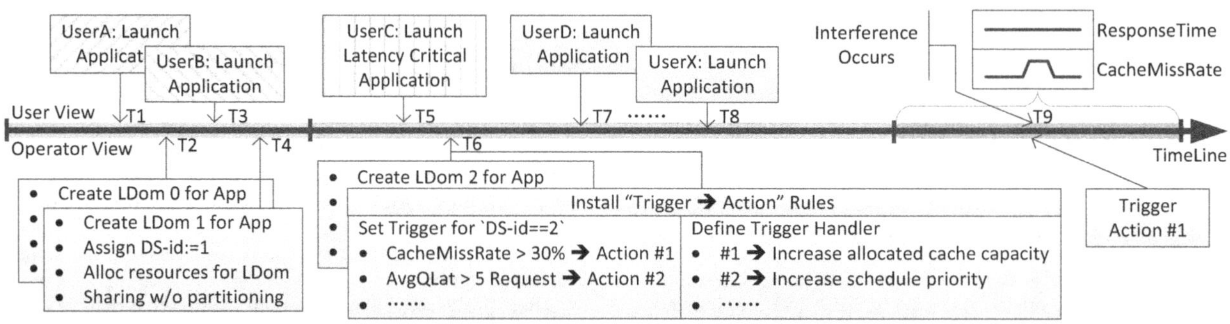

Figure 3. An Illustrative Example of PARD Usages. Above the timeline is users' view and below is data center operators' view.

As shown in Figure 3, operators can define several DS-id tag based "*trigger⇒action*" rules each of which targets a set of hardware resources. Particularly, *triggers* are based on performance metrics such as LLC miss rate and are stored in trigger tables; an *action* (a.k.a., trigger handler) can be written in any languages as long as they support file primitives. Operator-defined rules are installed in the device file tree of the firmware. It is worth noting that thank to the centralized PRM, *trigger* and *action* can be designated to different resources. For instance, if a trigger is created to monitor memory bandwidth, its action can be defined to adjust LLC capacity because LLC miss rate is strongly correlated with both memory bandwidth and LLC capacity.

Data center operators define *actions* and "*trigger⇒action*" rules to represent different resource management policies that are correlated to service-level agreements (SLA) so that users can choose suitable SLA according to their QoS requirements.

3.1 Illustrative Example

The example in Figure 3 demonstrates several usage scenarios on a PARD server in a shared data center.

1. At the time of T1 and T3, user A and user B intend to launch their applications respectively. They submit resource requests to a data center operator, who decides to allocate resources from a same PARD server to user A and B. (A data center operator could be a resource and job management system, such as Mesos [28].)
2. The operator in turn (at T2 and T4) processes users' requests and then sends resource requests to the PRM firmware of the server. Take user B as an example, once receiving his/her request, the firmware first creates a LDom, assigns the LDom's DS-id as "1" (i.e., forming LDom1) and allocates resources for LDom1. Since LDom1 is created for a normal priority application, the firmware adopts default "trigger⇒action" rules for it, which means that LDom1 can share LLC with other LDoms rather than possess dedicated resources. Finally, the firmware executes commands to program control planes (i.e., modify tables in Figure 2) and then launches LDom1 and its OS.
3. At T5, user C wants to run a high-priority latency-critical application and sends a resource request to the firmware. At T6, the firmware creates a LDom2 with DS-id "2" and adopts a set of "trigger⇒action" rules for LDom2. These rules are programmed into related control planes.
4. During T7 and T8, more users submit resource requests to the firmware and the utilization of the server keeps increasing.
5. Unfortunately, at T9, severe interference occurs so that the cache miss rate of user C's application sharply increases (>30%). On a conventional server, high cache miss rate can worsen the tail response time of the application. In contrast, on the PARD server, this change activates LDom2's trigger stored in the LLC control plane, which immediately sends an interrupt signal to the PRM. The firmware running on the PRM captures the interrupt signal and invokes a corresponding trigger handler (see the rightmost Figure 2) to modify the parameter table of the LLC control plane, which thereby allocates more LLC capacity to user C's application. As a result, the response time remains low.

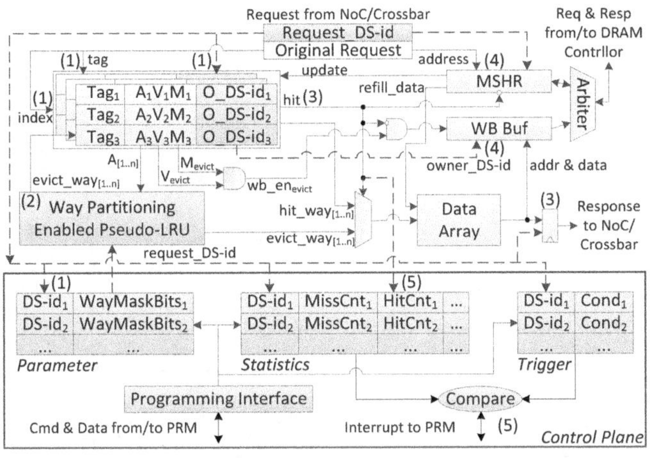

Figure 4. Control Plane for Last Level Cache (LLC).

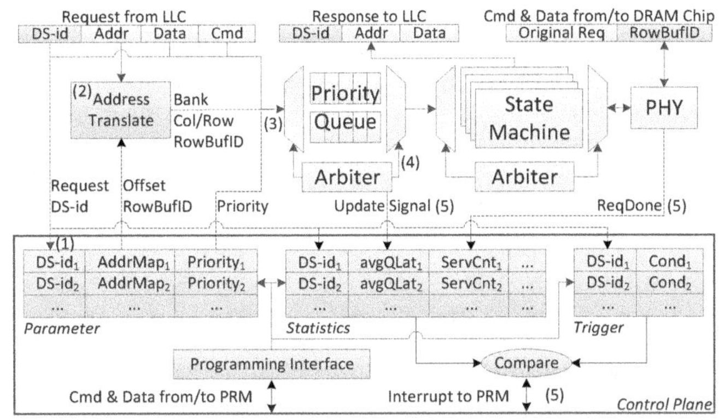

Figure 5. Control Plane for Memory Controller.

4. Architecture Design

This section presents the architecture design of PARD. The emphasis is on the challenges encountered in tagging mechanism and control plane design.

4.1 Tagging Mechanism

Although it is easy to understand the rational of tagging mechanism that every on-the-fly request in a server is associated with a tag, there are two major design issues.

Tagging multi-phase writeback requests. Usually a write operation is divided into multiple phases due to caching. For example, at the LLC level, the first phase of a write request to DRAM only stores data in LLC and marks the data block as dirty. For the second phase, the dirty data block is selected to be evicted when a cache miss occurs, and then written back to DRAM. During these latter phases, we need to determine which tag should be assigned to a writeback request.

To resolve this issue, We find that it is necessary to store DS-id tag if there are multi-phase writeback requests, otherwise resulting in inaccuracy. For example, assume that the current request is attached with DS-id1, the cache block to be written back belongs to another LDom with DS-id2 that does not store in LLC. So the writeback request issued to DRAM has to use the DS-id1 tag. Consequently, the memory control plane applies DS-id1's "trigger⇒action" rules rather than DS-id2's rules and updates cache usage statistics for DS-id1, resulting in wrong behaviors.

Therefore, for current LLC design, once a piece of requested data is filled into LLC, its DS-id tag is stored into the tag array of LLC and is marked as *owner DS-id*. When the data is to be written back to DRAM, the *owner DS-id* will be assigned to the writeback request.

Tagging I/O request and interrupt requests. There are two I/O access modes, i.e, programmed I/O (PIO) and directed memory access (DMA). While it is easy to tagging a PIO request because it is issued by CPU, tagging a DMA request is challenging.

Let us first revisit how DMA works in three steps. Firstly, one device driver first informs a DMA engine of a DMA descriptor's start address, which stores DMA buffers' information such as start address, size and status. Then, after being initialized, the DMA engine loads the descriptor's content to get necessary information for each DMA operation and starts data transfer. Finally, the DMA engine may raise an interrupt after all data transfers are done.

To tag DMA requests, each DMA engine includes a tag register that is used as follows: (1) Initialize the tag register. When a device driver writes a descriptor's information into a DMA engine, the DS-id tag associated with the write request is stored into the tag register of the DMA engine. (2) Tag data transfer requests. The DMA engine attaches the DS-id from the tag register to all DMA data transfer requests, which are issued to a memory controller. (3) Tag interrupt signals. To deal with interrupt, we augment current APIC (advanced programmable interrupt controller) [5] by duplicating multiple interrupt route tables, each of which is associated with a DS-id. When a DMA engine is going to raise an interrupt, it attaches a DS-id to the interrupt request and sends the request to an APIC component. Then the APIC component uses the DS-id to get a corresponding route table and forwards the interrupt to specified CPU cores.

There are two DMA directions, i.e., from-device and to-device. For a disk, our approach works well for both directions. However, for a network interface card (NIC), this is still insufficient for the from-device direction because the sources of incoming packets are unknown. Our current solution is to augment the Intel multi-queue [9] NIC with a control plane that contains a set of tag registers. An augmented NIC can be virtualized as multiple v-NIC with different MAC addresses. Each v-NIC is dedicated to a LDom and stores the LDom's DS-id in v-NIC's tag register. When an incoming packet arrives, the physical NIC checks its destination MAC address and forwards the packet to a corresponding v-NIC, which consequently issues DMA requests with DS-id. It is worth noting that an alternative is to integrate PARD with SDN network (e.g., OpenFlow [2]) to allow a DS-id to travel crosse servers, by correlating a DS-id with network packet's flowid.

4.2 Control Plane Design

This subsection presents how to design component-specific control planes based on the basic control plane structure described in §3. We focus on the LLC control plane and the memory control plane, whose microachitecture are shown in Figure 4 and Figure 5. If comparing the two figures, we can see that their bottom half exhibit almost the same structure with only slightly different table columns. Thus, this basic structure can be easily integrated into a variety of hardware components,

For I/O devices, we add control planes into I/O bridge and IDE. Since the design of these I/O control planes is similar to that of the memory control plane, here we omit their detail design.

LLC control plane. Figure 4 shows the microarchitecture of the LLC control plane, which supports a programmable way-based partitioning mechanism to adjust cache capacity for applications.

The LLC control plane consists of three basic tables, i.e., a *parameter* table, a *statistics* table and a *trigger* table, all of which can be accessed by the PRM firmware through the programming interface. There is also an interrupt line connected to the PRM. Besides, the tag array and pseudo-LRU logic are modified (modification is indicated as shadow part and dash lines in Figure 4).

A key concern on the LLC control plane is whether it introduces extra delay. Fortunately, there is no extra delay because a pipelined cache controller allows the control plane's operations to be hidden into the original pipeline, as shown in Figure 4: (1) When a cache-access request arrives at the controller, its DS-id is used to query the parameter table to get way-partitioning mask bits. For instance, the mask bits "0x00FF" indicate using the rightmost 8 ways of the whole 16 ways. Meanwhile, the request's address is used to find a corresponding entry in the tag array that stores not only normal cache tags and states but also DS-id tags. (2) The pseudo-LRU logic receives the mask bits from the parameter table and the access history information from the tag array, and then calculates which way to be evicted. (3) If the request hits in the LLC, data is retrieved from the data array, attached with the request's DS-id and then sent back to a CPU core via NoC or crossbar. Note that an LLC hit occurs if and only if the request's address matches the original cache tag and the request's DS-id matches the cache block's owner DS-id tag[4]. (4) If a cache miss occurs, the LLC controller allocates a MSHR entry for the request and the DS-id. Assume that the evicted block is dirty, its data will be put into the writeback buffer (WB Buf) with "*owner DS-id*". When the requested data returns, LLC updates the tag array with the original request's DS-id. (5) During the above steps, the LLC control plane performs several operations without being on critical pathes, such as updating the statistics table, sending LLC usage statistic data to the PRM, activating a trigger if necessary, raising an interrupt signal and so forth.

The programming interface allows the PRM firmware to access the three tables of the LLC control plane. Specifically, it receives commands from the PRM, extracts information from the command to select a corresponding table and reads data from the table (or write data to the table). More details are in §5.1.

Memory control plane. Figure 5 shows the microarchitecture of memory control plane. To enable fully virtualized LDoms that are able to run unmodified OSes and applications, the parameter table of the memory control plane stores address mapping information to translate an LDom physical address to a DRAM address. Besides, the table stores priority information for each DS-id.

Regarding performance isolation, unlike the LLC, the memory control plane needs to takes into account two factors, i.e., queuing delay and row buffer locality. To manage queuing delay, we add a priority queuing mechanism into the memory controller. The number of queues depends on the priority levels supported by the memory control plane. Our current design only supports two priories, but it is easy to extend. To avoid memory low-priority requests degrading the row buffer hit rate of high-priority requests, we add one extra row buffer into each DRAM chip for high-priority memory requests. If we want to augment DRAM chip with more buffers, we can leverage some commercial designs such as NEC's virtual-channel memory (VCM).

With these mechanisms above, when a memory access request attached with a DS-id tag arrives at the memory controller, a sequence of operations occur: (1) The control plane uses the DS-id to query the parameter table to get corresponding address mapping mask, priority and row-buffer id. (2) The requested LDom physical address is translated into a DRAM physical address. (3) The original request with DS-id enters a queue specified by the priority information. (4) The DRAM scheduler (arbiter) chooses a request to serve according to two rules: high-priority first and FR-FCFS [62]. (5) The memory control plane updates the statistics table and checks if it needs to activate a trigger. When a trigger takes effect, an interrupt signal will be sent to the PRM.

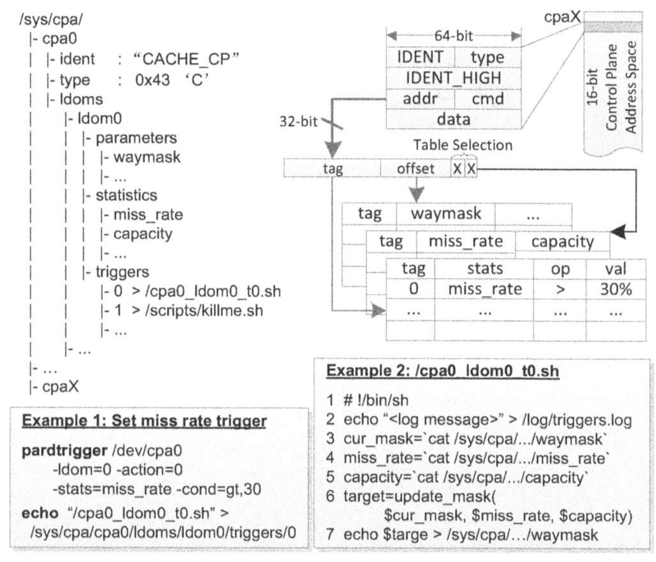

Figure 6. Control Plane Programming Methodology.

5. Software Support

To take the advantage of PARD architecture, we devise a Linux-based firmware that runs on the PRM. This section presents how the firmware interacts with the control planes.

5.1 Control Plane Abstraction and Interface

To provide a uniform interface for firmware users (data center operators) to access various control planes, we leverage Linux's device file mechanism. Figure 6 shows the abstraction of the control planes from a firmware user's perspective. Specifically, each control plane is connected to a PRM's control plane adaptor (CPA) that is abstracted as a file and is mounted to the sysfs [55] of the firmware as "/sys/cpa/cpa[0-9][0-9]*". Thus firmware users can use either bash commands (e.g., *cat* or *echo*) or system calls to access these files.

Each control plane file is organized as a subtree, which contains some general information such as *ident* (e.g., cpa0's "CACHE_CP" in Figure 6) and *type* indicating which type of a control plane is, cache ("C"), memory ("M") or I/O bridge ("B"). Besides, a control plane file further includes several subtrees, each of which represents a LDom with a specific DS-id. When a new LDom is created, the firmware creates a new subtree with root "*ldom[0-9][0-9]**" under the node *ldoms*, where the number represent a DS-id. Take the *ldom0* subtree as an example, there are three tiny trees with roots as *parameters*, *statistics* and *triggers* respectively, which are mapped to several rows of the three tables of the LLC control plane.

For the underlying implementation of the control plane tree, the PRM reserves a 64KB (16 bits) I/O address space for mapping the control plane adaptors (CPA). In particular, each CPA occupies 32

[4] Given two requests contain a same physical address, their DS-id tags are used to distinguish different LDoms. When a PARD server is partitioned into multiple LDoms, each of which has same physical address space starting from 0. Thus, different LDom with different DS-id can issue cache requests for identical physical address. This address mapping mechanism is critical to enable LDom to run unmodified OS and applications (i.e., fully virtualized LDom).

CPU	4 4-issue Out-of-Order X86 cores, 2GHz
L1-I/core	64KB 2-way, hit = 2 cycles
L1-D/core	64KB 2-way, hit = 2 cycles
Shared LLC	4MB 16-way, hit = 20 cycles
DRAM	8GB DDR3-1600 11-11-11 4Gbit chip (Micron MT41J512M8) 1 channel, 2 ranks/channel, 8 banks/Rank Burst Length = 8, Row buffer = 1KB tCK=1.25ns, tRCD = 13.75ns, tCL = 13.75ns tRP = 13.75ns, tRAS = 35ns, tRRD = 6ns
Disks	4-channel IDE controller, 8 disks
Platform Resource Manager (PRM)	1 X86 core, 100MHz 16MB DRAM, 32MB Flash Storage 4 control plane adaptors (CPA) 1 Ethernet adaptor Firmware: tailored Linux kernel 2.6.28.4 with Busybox [3]
Server OS	Gentoo Linux with kernel 2.6.28.4
Workloads	Memcached [8], SPECCPU 2006 [26] Microbenchmark: CacheFlush & DiskCopy

Table 2. Simulation Parameters

Parameter Table	Cache: way mask-bits Memory: row-buffer mask-bits, scheduling priority, address mapping Disk: bandwidth
Statistics Table	Cache: miss rate, capacity Memory: bandwidth, latency Disk: bandwidth
Trigger Table	LLC miss rate ⇒ way mask-bits Memory latency ⇒ row-buffer mask-bits Memory latency ⇒ scheduling priority

Table 3. Control Plane Tables

bytes whose definition is shown in the topright of Figure 6: two fields *IDENT* and *IDENT_HIGH* (12 bytes in total) represents the *ident* node of the tree; the 32-bit *type* field indicates the type of a control plane; the 32-bit *addr* field contains 16-bit DS-id, 14-bit offset designating the column of a table and, 2 bits for table selection; the 32-bit *cmd* field specifies either READ operation or WRITE operation to a selected table; finally, the 64-bit *data* field depends on the *cmd* field. The content of *data* field is filled by users if the *cmd* is WRITE operation. In contrast, it is filled by a control plane and is read by users.

To program a control plane, a driver first writes data into the *addr* field to select a table cell by a DS-id (row) and an offset (column). If a user intends to modify the table, the driver fills the *data* filed and then writes the WRITE command into the *cmd* field. For reading data from the control plane, after the *addr* field is initialized, the driver writes the READ command into the *cmd* field and then reads the *data* field.

5.2 Programming Methodology

As mentioned in §3, we adopt a "*trigger⇒action*" programming methodology. Data center operators predefine a set of *trigger⇒action* rules for different priorities. Usually a trigger is based on performance metrics, e.g., "MissRate>30%".

Example 1 in Figure 6 demonstrates how to install a *trigger⇒action* rule. A data center operator uses the *pardtrigger* command to program the trigger condition "MissRate>30%" for "ldom=0" (i.e., DS-id=0) into the trigger table of the cache control plane (cpa0). The parameter "action=0" guides the command to create a leaf node "0" under ".../cpa0/ldoms/ldom0/triggers". Then the operator calls "echo ..." to install the action script "*/cpa0_ldom0_t0.sh*" shown in Example 2.

There are two programming approaches based on the device file tree. One is invoking system calls (open/read/write etc.) to open and manipulate a CPA file. For example, the *pardtrigger* command is written in C and invokes syscalls to install a trigger into the cache control plane. The advantage of this approach is very fast. A more convenient approach is leveraging bash commands to directly access these CPA files, as shown in Example 2.

6. Implementation

We implemented PARD architecture and the PRM firmware on PARD-gem5[5], a GEM5 [17] based full-system simulator. Moreover, we have been implementing PARD on a Xilinx VC709 FPGA development board.

Full-system simulation. As shown in Table 2, PARD-gem5 is a cycle-accurate simulator that is able to simulate OoO X86 systems. In particular, we added tag registers in CPU cores, implemented LLC, memory controller, I/O bridge and IDE control planes. Table 3 illustrates major content of the three tables of the LLC, memory and IDE control planes. We also implemented the PRM that is also based on an X86 processor running at 100MHz, 16MB DRAM, 32MB Flash, one Ethernet adaptor and four control plane adaptors (CPAs). The firmware running on the PRM is based on a tailored Linux kernel 2.6.28.4 with Busybox [3] toolkit.

With these efforts, PARD-gem5 is able to simulate a PARD server that can be partitioned into multiple LDoms. Each LDom can run unmodified Gentoo Linux with kernel 2.6.28.4 and memcached 1.4.17 [8] of CloudSuite [24] etc.

Preliminary RTL implementation. Our RTL implementation is based on OpenSPARC T1 processor [54]. The original OpenSPARC T1 includes eight 4-thread cores (32 threads in total), a 3MB LLC, a crossbar and four memory controllers etc.. All of these modules make this processor too large to fit into the FPGA development board. Therefore, we first tailored the OpenSPARC T1 processor to a small processor with only two cores, a crossbar, 768KB LLC and a memory controller, which are able to boot an unmodified Linux. Then we added a tag register into each core and propagated its value to LLC, crossbar and memory controller. Finally, we implemented the LLC and memory control plane respectively, which are synthesizable.

Now the LLC control plane is able to distinguish DS-id tags and perform way-based LLC partition according to different DS-id tags. The memory control plane can deliver tagged memory requests into different priority queues in accordance with requests' DS-id. However, we are still working on the PRM, the programming mechanism, the integration of multiple components and software porting. The FPGA prototype aims at fully hardware-supported virtualization, performance isolation, differentiated QoS, and flexible programmability. This goal is still in progress.

Fortunately, current preliminary RTL implementation is sufficient for analyzing latency and logic resources of the control planes, because several major mechanisms and components have been implemented and verified, such as tag mechanisms, LLC and memory control planes.

[5] PARD-gem5 is open-sourced and available at https://github.com/fsg-ict/PARD-gem5.

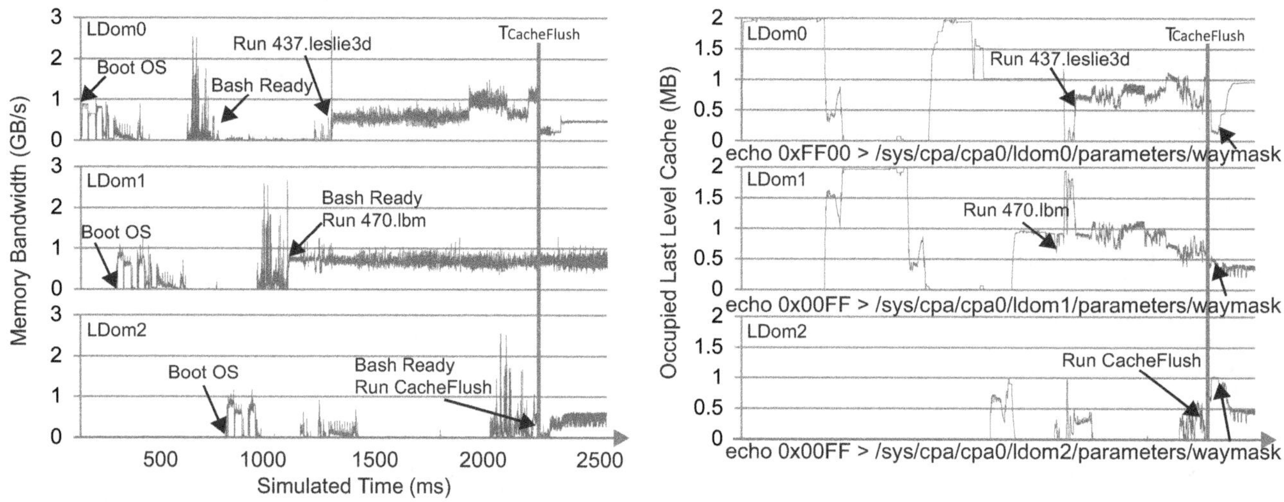

Figure 7. Dynamically Partition a PARD server into Four LDoms and Launch Three LDoms in turn.

7. Evaluation

This section describes the experiments we conducted on both of the simulation and FPGA platforms. The goal is to verify new functionalities enabled by PARD architecture and the overhead of current PARD control plane design.

For experimental methodology, we leveraged GEM5's SimpleTiming mode to boot Linux, launch and warmup workloads, made checkpoints, and then switched to cycle-accurate Out-of-Order (OoO) simulations. Simulation parameters are illustrated in Table 2. Because the full system cycle-accurate OoO simulation is very slow, we ran about 30 hours to simulate three seconds for memcached, during which the first second is for warmuping microarchitecture and the latter two seconds are used for evaluation.

7.1 Functionality

7.1.1 Fully Hardware-Supported Virtualization

This experiment demonstrates the effectiveness of fully hardware-supported virtualization enabled by PARD. We partitioned the four-core PARD server into four LDoms (LDom0 ˜LDom3) that equally share hardware resources. We launched only three LDoms and each LDom ran Linux and a user application. Particularly, LDom0 and LDom1 ran two SPEC CPU2006 workloads (437.leslied3d and 470.lbm) and LDom2 ran CacheFlush microbenchmark.

Figure 7 displays the change of memory bandwidth and occupied LLC capacity of the three LDoms over about two seconds. These usage data are collected by the LLC and memory control planes. For example, the occupied LLC capacity is stored in the statistics table of the LLC cache plane[6]. To obtain these statistics data, we implemented a tool running on the firmware to periodically read data from the two control planes.

Assume that LDom0 is with high priority. According to Figure 7, at the time of $T_{CacheFlush}$ when LDom2 runs CacheFlush, the occupied LLC capacity of LDom0 substantially decreases (see the top right Figure 7). Actually, this situation mimics a software-based virtualization environment where multiple VMs run together on a physical machine. Although a hypervisor can guarantee resource isolation for these VMs, it is difficult to ensure performance isolation. Thus, these VMs may contend for hardware resources such as LLC capacity, as shown in the figure.

In this experiment, in order to guarantee reasonable LLC capacity for LDom0, we manually ran three *echo* commands (shown in the figure) to adjust LLC capacity. Since the LLC of the simulated server is 16-way, the way mask bits "0xFF00" indicates that the LLC control plane allocates eight ways for LDom0 and the mask bits "0x00FF" means that LDom1 and LDom2 share the other eight ways. Consequently, the percentage of LDom0's LLC capacity increases to 50% while the percentage of LDom2 drops sharply.

7.1.2 "Trigger⇒Action" Mechanism Verification

We partitioned the server into four LDoms and ran latency-critical memcached in LDom0. Because the simulation speed is too slow to simulate network environments, we ran both memcached client and server in one LDom where they share a CPU core. Although the client and server may contend for resources within a LDom, this contention in a blackbox is acceptable while we focus on the interference between LDoms. The other three LDoms all ran STREAM microbenchmark.

Figure 8 illustrates the change of memcached's tail response time over different request loads. When memcached runs in the solo-mode (only LDom0 is active), it can serve 22.5K request per second (RPS) with reasonable 95-percentile response time (0.6ms). However, only one CPU core is fully busy, thus the total server CPU utilization is 25% . If the other three LDoms are launched to share resources with LDom0, All four CPU cores are fully busy so that the server exhibits 100% CPU utilization. Unfortunately, the throughput of memcached drops to 15K RPS while the 95-percentile response time already exceeds 1ms. When the throughput increases to 20K RPS, the 95-percetile response time dramatically increases by two orders of magnitude (62.6ms).

To verify the the effectiveness of the "*trigger⇒action*" mechanism, As shown in Figure 6, we predefined a trigger for LDom0, i.e., "LLC.MissRate $>$ 30% $\Rightarrow$ increasing LLC capacity up to 50%".

Next we installed the LLC trigger into the LLC control plane before launching LDom0 and then launched all four LDoms. Figure 9 shows how LDom0's LLC miss rate varies while the trigger takes effect. After half of LLC capacity is dedicated to LDom0, memcached's LLC miss rate quickly decreases to only about 10%, just slightly larger than the solo-mode's miss rate (7%). As a result, the throughput increases to 22.5K RPS with reasonable 95-

[6] Given an LDom, its occupied LLC capacity is calculated by counting the number of a DS-id in the LLC tag array. Specifically, the number increases by 1 when a block with a DS-id is filled into LLC and decreases by 1 when a block with the DS-id is evicted.

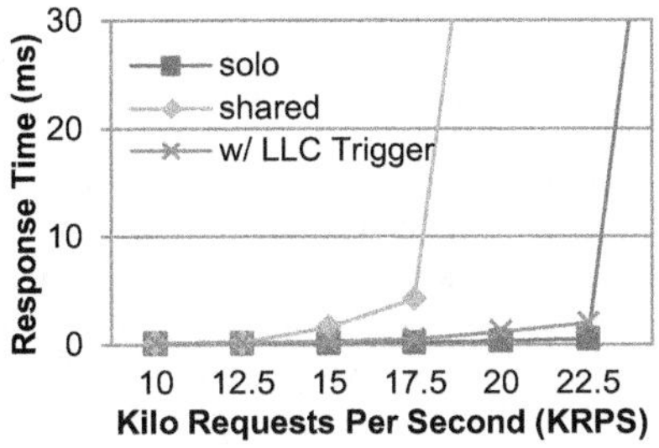

Figure 8. Change of Memcached's Tail Response Time (95-percentile).

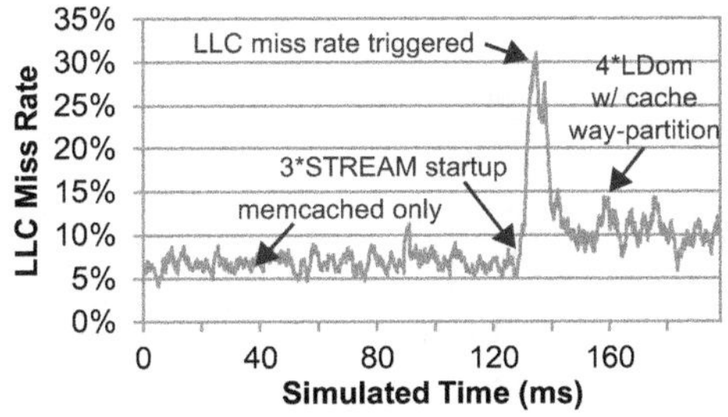

Figure 9. Change of Memcached's LLC Miss Rate (20KRPS).

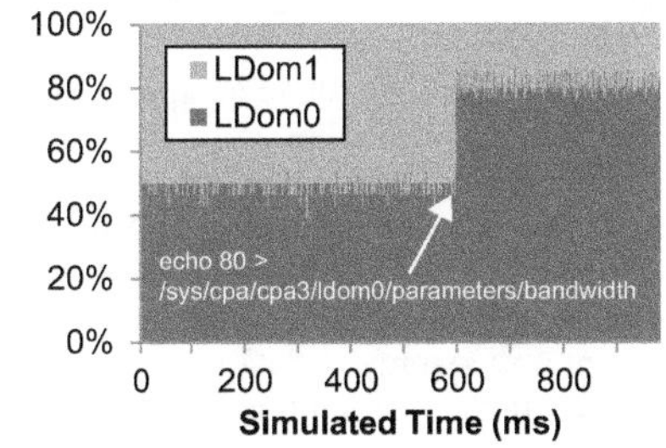

Figure 10. Disk I/O Performance Isolation

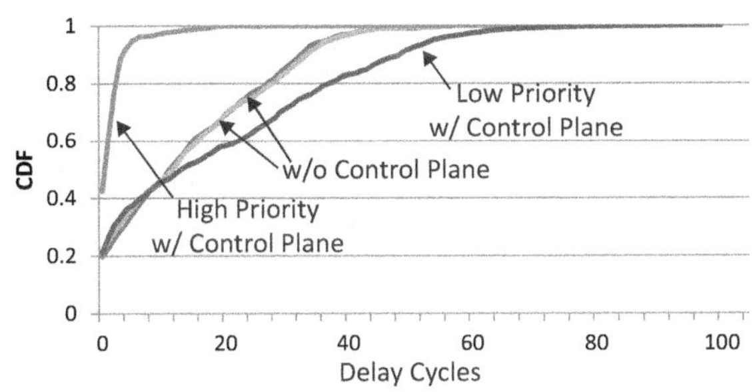

Figure 11. CDF of Queueing Delay of Memory Requests.

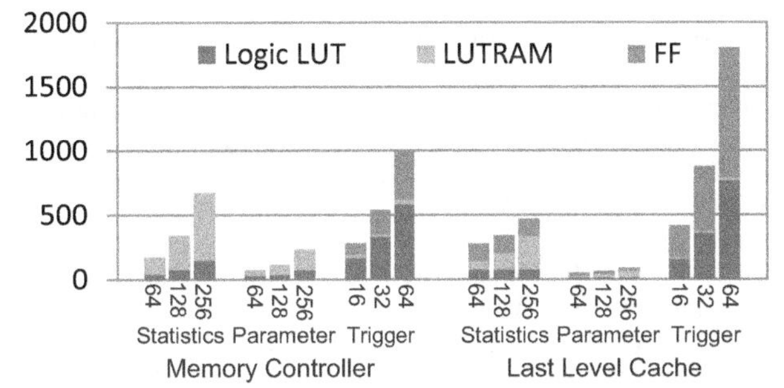

Figure 12. FPGA resource usage of the LLC and memory control control planes. For reference, the original memory controller and 768KB 12-way LLC (w/ tag array only) consume 15178 and 75032 LUT/FF respectively.

percentile response time (1.2ms). Compared with the solo-mode, since LDom0 uses only half of LLC capacity, this tail response time is slightly longer. Overall, these experimental results show that even the total server CPU utilization is 100% (all four cores are fully busy), memcached's behaviors can still approach the solo mode.

This experiment demonstrates that the "*trigger⇒action*" mechanism is able to take the advantage of PARD and is beneficial for balancing the trade-offs between resource utilization and applications' QoS.

7.1.3 Disk I/O Performance Isolation

PARD is able to manage not only capacity resources (e.g., LLC) but also bandwidth resources such as memory and I/O bandwidth. In this experiment, two LDoms are active and each LDom executes disk write operation through this command: "*dd if=/dev/zero of=/dev/sdb bs=32M count=16*".

Initially, two LDoms share the IDE controller so that they exhibit the same disk I/O bandwidth. Assume that the user of LDom1 pays more money in order to get better I/O performance, we manually ran "*echo 80 > /sys/cpa/cpa3/ldom0/parameters/bandwidth*" to program the IDE control plane to increase the disk I/O bandwidth quota of LDom0 to 80%. Figure 10 illustrates the effect of disk I/O bandwidth reallocation.

Although there are other approaches to manage I/O bandwidth such as cgroup [4], PARD provides a more efficient fine-grained I/O management scheme that requires no modifications to OS kernel and applications, reducing the complexity of software stack.

7.2 Overhead

There are two major concerns about adding control planes into the controllers of hardware components: (1) How much extra latency is introduced? (2) How many hardware resources are required? To address these two concerns, we performed evaluation based on the preliminary RTL implementation on an FPGA development board, as described in §6.

Latency. We find that the LLC control plane does not introduce extra latency. According to Figure 4, the processing logic of the LLC control plane can be hidden into the pipeline of the LLC controller. In fact, pipelining is a typical design for modern CPUs' LLC. For example, the L2 cache of OpenSPARC T1 has eight pipeline stages. Furthermore, synthesis data verify that the logic of the LLC control plane is not in critical pathes.

For the memory control plane, we used the RTL implementation to evaluate memory-access requests' queueing latency, which depends on request inject rate (i.e., bandwidth utilization). We present a representative case to show the distribution of queueing delay for the inject rate of 0.44, as shown in Figure 11. There are half high-priority requests and half low-priority requests. According to the figure, the average queueing delay of the original memory controller is 15.2 memory cycles. When we enabled the memory control plane, the average queueing delay of high-priority requests significantly decreases to 2.7 cycles (reduced by 5.6X) while the queing delay of low-priority requests increases to 20.3 cycles (by 33.6%).

FPGA Resources. The required FPGA resources of a control plane mainly depend on the number of table entries of the three tables.

Figure 12 shows the synthesis data reported by Xilinx Vivado Design Suite [12]. Specifically, the 256-entry parameter and statistics tables of the memory control plane require 220 LUT for logic and 688 LUTRAM for storage. The 64-entry trigger table consumes more logic resources (582 LUT + 387 FF) than storages (40 LUTRAM) because it requires many comparators to implement triggers. Two priority queues with 16-depth require only 324 LUT + 30 FF. The total required FPGA resources (1526 LUT/FF) accounts for 10.1% of the original Xilinx MIGv7 memory controller (15178 LUT/FF).

The LLC control plane exhibits similar resources consumption. The 256-entry parameter and statistics tables and the 64-entry trigger table require 2359 LUT/FF, introducing only 3.1% extra FPGA resources compared with the original LLC controller (not counting data array). Additionally, storing *Owner_DS-id* in tag array adds 50% more of blockRAMs (from 12 to 18). This is because the original tag array stores 28 bits for each cache block and the DS-id in our RTL implementation is 8 bits. In fact, the tag array consumes very little FPGA resources compared with the whole cache, thus these extra six blockRAMs are negligible.

8. Discussion

In this section, we will discuss the following issues:

Physical Implementation Cost. PARD's physical implementation is similar with design-for-test (DFT) logic and can even be based on the existing DFT logic or extra logic, so the hardware cost varies from being incremental to being modest. As a particular example, it is a common practice to use fixed-width physical registers from the libraries for logic registers with various widths. For instance, in OpenSPARC T1's RTL, the packets of L2 cache are 128/144-bit wide, but the queues used to store them are composed of customized 160-bit physical register files. Those unused 32/16 bits can be reused for the tagging mechanism of PARD.

For the centralized platform resource manager (PRM), the implementation can be based on prevalent IPMI components. Actually, some IPMI already includes embedded processors and operating systems. For instance, the IPMI component in one of our experimental servers consists of an ARM926EJ-S processor and 128MB memory, running an embedded Linux with kernel 2.6.27.

Functionality Extension. Apart from supporting differentiated QoS, it is also possible to extend PARD to support other differentiated services such as encryption, compression and security check. Take compression as an example, IBM's Memory eXpansion Technology (MXT) [70] integrates a compression engine into a memory controller. if a PARD server includes an MXT engine, the engine can be programmed to compress memory-access packets for only designated DS-id sets. However, there are still many open problems on how to leverage PARD to explore new functionalities.

Control Plane Design Optimization. Current control planes are based on a table structure, which is simple to design and implement but is relatively inflexible. An alternative is to embed a customized microprocessor into control planes. This is not impossible. A recent research demonstrates that a microprocessor with specific instruction set architecture (ISA) can be integrated into high-speed DDRx memory controllers [18]. Although the current ISA can only handle simple scheduling, it may be augmented to support more management policies.

9. Related Work

Table 1 illustrates prior work on eliminating contention at various layers. Companies like Google and Twitter now adopt advanced data center management frameworks (e.g., Borg, Omega [65] and Mesos [28]) to balance the trade-offs between resource utilization and applications' QoS. There are also a number of distributed techniques and OS kernel optimizations, such as multi-level priorities [25], scheduling [21, 22, 39, 46, 52], backup-request [19],cgroup [4], and resource containers [7].

Instead of presenting related work of all layers, in this section we focus on related work within a server.

Software based Partitioning Researchers propose to leverage page-coloring technique to partition cache and DRAM. The key idea of page coloring is leveraging address mapping information to manage hardware resources. Lin *et al.* [42] and Tam *et al.* [68] propose page-coloring based cache partitioning to address the cache contention problem. Liu *et al.* [43] present a practical pagecorloring based DRAM bank partitioning approach to eliminate the memory bank-level interference and further propose an approach to cooperatively partition both cache and DRAM together [44].

Although these software techniques are able to effectively partition shared cache and DRAM banks, there are two major concerns: first, they require reorganizing free-page lists and migrating pages when workload mixtures change. But the overhead is not negligible. Although some work designs different kernel buddy systems for different workload mixtures, this approach requires significant kernel hacking efforts and has limited usage scenarios in production data centers. Second, contemporary processors adopts hashing algorithms to map physical address to cache index (e.g. Intel's Sandy Bridge). These hash algorithms are usually unknown, so it is difficult to apply page-coloring approach to such systems.

In contrast to page coloring, PARD's control planes can expose more underlying information (such as per DS-id cache miss rate and memory bandwidth) to firmware, operators thus can deploy better resource management policy with the information.

Hardware based techniques. Kasture and Sanchez propose Ubik [36], a cache partitioning policy that characterizes and leverages the transient behavior of latency-critical applications to maintain their target tail latency. Vantage [64] implements fine-grained cache partitioning using the statistical properties of Zcaches [63]. Utility-based cache partitioning (UCP) [56] strictly partitions the shared cache depending on the benefit of allocating different number of ways to each application. Muralidhara *et al.* propose an application-aware memory channel partitioning (MCP) [49] to reduce memory system interference. However, these work usually focuses on only one type of resource while PARD is able to simultaneously manage all shared hardware resources winthin a server.

Similar to PARD, NoHype [37] removes the virtualization layer and makes use of hardware virtualization extensions to partition a server into multiple submachines. However, this partitioning is statical. In contrast, PARD allows operators to dynamically partition a physical server into multiple LDoms. Furthermore, PARD supports "*trigger⇒action*" mechanism to deploy resourcing-on-demand resource management policies.

Architectural support for QoS. Rafique *et al.* [58] propose a OS-driven hardware cache partitioning mechanism that tags cache requests and allows OS to adjust cache quota according to the tag. Sharifi *et al.* [66] further propose a feedback-based control architecture for end-to-end on-chip resource management. Iyer *et al.* make substantial contributions in architectural support for QoS [27, 31, 32, 40, 41]. The closest work to PARD is class-of-service based QoS architecture (CoQoS) [40, 41], which assigns a priority tag to each on-chip request and allows cache/DRAM/NoC to schedule the request according to the priority tag.

PARD differs from these prior proposals in the following aspects: (1) Prior work primarily focuses on on-chip resources such as cache, NoC and memory bandwidth (managed by on-chip memory controller) while PARD is able to manage not only on-chip resources but also I/O resources. (2) We design programmable control planes for PARD and a uniform programming interface while prior work does not support programmability. (3) PARD includes a centralized platform resource manager and a Linux-based firmware to facilitate operators's management. (4) PARD supports not only QoS but also NoHype-like virtualization that can partition one server into multiple LDoms. (5) PARD allows users to install "*trigger⇒action*" rules while prior work lacks this useful mechanism.

10. Conclusion and Open Problems

This paper presented a study of building DiffServ in computer servers via architectural support. We proposed programmable architecture for resourcing-on-demand(PARD) and developed a Linux-based firmware to facilitate programming PARD. We implemented PARD on both a full-system simulator and an FPGA development board. Our experiments demonstrated that PARD is able to address the trade-offs between high utilization and high QoS in datacenter environments.

We believe that architectural support for DiffServ in computers is a promising trend as the number of cores keeps increasing. PARD makes a case for this direction and provides new interfaces for users to interact with the hardware. However, there are still a lot of open issues such as

- how to translate applications' QoS requirements into efficient "*trigger⇒action*" rules?
- how to leverage compilers to automatically generate trigger rules?
- how to make OS directly run on PARD server to support process-level DiffServ?
- how to support fine-grain Diffserv for not only process-level but also thread-level or even C++/Java object-level?
- how to support nested DiffServ, i.e., guarantee QoS of a process within a LDom?
- how to deal with simultaneous multithreading (SMT)?
- how to deal with multiple processors issues such as cache coherency?
- how to extend DiffServ to accelerators, e.g., enabling an encryption engine to encrypt/decrypt LDoms with specific DS-id?
- how to integrate PARD and SDN so that DS-id can be propagated in a data center wide?
- how to design and deploy security policy on PARD servers?
- how to develop firmware applications to take advantage of PARD?

To facilitate further optimization and exploration, we release the PARD-gem5 simulator that is available at https://github.com/fsg-ict/PARD-gem5.

Acknowledgments

The authors would like to thank to Kai Li, Babak Falsafi for their insights into the idea and the system. We give special thanks to Sally McKee for her detailed feedback on the paper. We thank our group members, Rui Hou, Xin Jin, Wenjie Li, Pin Li, Yupeng Qu, Rui Ren, Cong Wang, Cheng Yang, Xusheng Zhan, and Jianbo Zhu for their help on the work. We also thank David Brooks, Mingyu Chen, Fred Chong, Mark Hill, Xiaozhou Li, Feng Liu, Jason Mars, Calton Pu, Lingjia Tang, Yida Wang, Jin Xin (Princeton University), Zhiwei Xu, Jianfeng Zhan, Wei Zhang, Xiaodong Zhang, the anonymous reviewers, and our shepherd David Meisner for their valuable comments. This work was supported by the Huawei-ICT Joint Research Lab, National Natural Science Foundation of China (NSFC) under grants No. 61420106013, 61221062, 61202062, and the 973 Program under grant No. 2011CB302500. Yungang Bao is support by CCF-Intel Young Faculty Researcher Program and Xiufeng Sui is supported by 2014 IBM SUR Cycle 2 grant.

References

[1] Gartner says efficient data center design can lead to 300 percent capacity growth in 60 percent less space. `http://www.gartner.com/newsroom/id/1472714`.

[2] Software-Defined Networking. `https://www.opennetworking.org/sdn-resources/sdn-definition/`.

[3] BusyBox. `http://www.busybox.net/`.

[4] Cgroups. `http://en.wikipedia.org/wiki/Cgroups`.

[5] *Intel 64 and IA-32 Architectures Software Developer Manuals*, volume 3: System Programming Guide.

[6] Intelligent Platform Management Interface (IPMI). `http://en.wikipedia.org/wiki/Intelligent_Platform_Management_Interface`.

[7] Linux Container(LXC). `http://lxc.sourceforge.net/`.

[8] Memcached. `http://memcached.org/`.

[9] Intel 82599 10 gigabit ethernet controller: Datasheet. `http://www.intel.com/content/www/us/en/ethernet-controllers/82599-10-gbe-controller-datasheet.html`.

[10] Openflow switch specification. `https://www.opennetworking.org/sdn-resources/openflow/`.

[11] Xilinx Virtex-7 FPGA VC709 Connectivity Kit. `http://www.xilinx.com/products/boards-and-kits/EK-V7-VC709-CES-G.htm`.

[12] Vivado Design Suite. `http://www.xilinx.com/products/design-tools/vivado/`.

[13] Computing Community Consortium (CCC). 21st century computer architecture. *A community white paper*, 2012. URL `http://cra.org/ccc/docs/init/21stcenturyarchitecturewhitepaper.pdf`.

[14] M. Alizadeh, A. Greenberg, D. A. Maltz, J. Padhye, P. Patel, B. Prabhakar, S. Sengupta, and M. Sridharan. Data center TCP (DCTCP). In *Proceedings of the ACM SIGCOMM 2010 Conference*, SIGCOMM '10, New York, NY, USA, 2010.

[15] L. A. Barroso, J. Clidaras, and U. Holzle. The datacenter as a computer: An introduction to the design of warehouse-scale machines. *Synthesis Lectures on Computer Architecture*, 8(3):1–154, 2013.

[16] A. Baumann, P. Barham, P.-E. Dagand, T. Harris, R. Isaacs, S. Peter, T. Roscoe, A. Schüpbach, and A. Singhania. The multikernel: A new os architecture for scalable multicore systems. In *Proceedings of the ACM SIGOPS 22nd Symposium on Operating Systems Principles*, SOSP '09, pages 29–44, New York, NY, USA, 2009.

[17] N. Binkert, B. Beckmann, G. Black, S. K. Reinhardt, A. Saidi, A. Basu, J. Hestness, D. R. Hower, T. Krishna, S. Sardashti, R. Sen, K. Sewell, M. Shoaib, N. Vaish, M. D. Hill, and D. A. Wood. The gem5 simulator. *SIGARCH Comput. Archit. News*, 39(2):1–7, Aug. 2011.

[18] M. N. Bojnordi and E. Ipek. PARDIS: a programmable memory controller for the DDRx interfacing standards. In *Proceedings of the 39th Annual International Symposium on Computer Architecture*, ISCA '12, pages 13–24, Washington, DC, USA, 2012.

[19] J. Dean and L. A. Barroso. The tail at scale. *Commun. ACM*, 56(2):74–80, Feb. 2013.

[20] C. Delimitrou and C. Kozyrakis. ibench: Quantifying interference for datacenter applications. In *Proceedings of the IEEE International Symposium on Workload Characterization*, pages 23–33, 2013.

[21] C. Delimitrou and C. Kozyrakis. Paragon: QoS-aware scheduling for heterogeneous datacenters. In *Proceedings of the eighteenth international conference on Architectural support for programming languages and operating systems*, page 77–88, 2013.

[22] C. Delimitrou and C. Kozyrakis. Quasar: Resource-efficient and QoS-aware cluster management. In *Proceedings of the 19th International Conference on Architectural Support for Programming Languages and Operating Systems*, ASPLOS '14, page 127–144, New York, NY, USA, 2014.

[23] X. L. Dong, B. Saha, and D. Srivastava. Less is more: selecting sources wisely for integration. In *Proceedings of the 39th international conference on Very Large Data Bases*, PVLDB'13, Trento, Italy, 2013.

[24] M. Ferdman, A. Adileh, O. Kocberber, S. Volos, M. Alisafaee, D. Jevdjic, C. Kaynak, A. D. Popescu, A. Ailamaki, and B. Falsafi.

Clearing the clouds: a study of emerging scale-out workloads on modern hardware. In *Proceedings of the seventeenth international conference on Architectural Support for Programming Languages and Operating Systems*, ASPLOS '12, pages 37–48, New York, NY, USA, 2012.

[25] Google. Google Cluster workload traces. `http://code.google.com/p/googleclusterdata`.

[26] J. L. Henning. SPEC CPU2006 benchmark descriptions. *SIGARCH Comput. Archit. News*, 34(4):1–17, Sept. 2006.

[27] A. Herdrich, R. Illikkal, R. Iyer, D. Newell, V. Chadha, and J. Moses. Rate-based QoS techniques for cache/memory in CMP platforms. In *Proceedings of the 23rd international conference on Supercomputing*, page 479–488, 2009.

[28] B. Hindman, A. Konwinski, M. Zaharia, A. Ghodsi, A. D. Joseph, R. Katz, S. Shenker, and I. Stoica. Mesos: A platform for fine-grained resource sharing in the data center. In *Proceedings of the 8th USENIX Conference on Networked Systems Design and Implementation*, NSDI'11, pages 22–22, Berkeley, CA, USA, 2011.

[29] C.-Y. Hong, M. Caesar, and P. B. Godfrey. Finishing flows quickly with preemptive scheduling. *SIGCOMM Comput. Commun. Rev.*, 42 (4), Aug. 2012.

[30] Intel. *An Introduction to the Intel QuickPath Interconnect*. Jan. 2009.

[31] R. Iyer. CQoS: a framework for enabling QoS in shared caches of CMP platforms. In *Proceedings of the 18th annual international conference on Supercomputing*, page 257–266, 2004.

[32] R. Iyer, L. Zhao, F. Guo, R. Illikkal, S. Makineni, D. Newell, Y. Solihin, L. Hsu, and S. Reinhardt. QoS policies and architecture for Cache/Memory in CMP platforms. In *Proceedings of the 2007 ACM SIGMETRICS International Conference on Measurement and Modeling of Computer Systems*, SIGMETRICS '07, page 25–36, New York, NY, USA, 2007.

[33] V. Jeyakumar, M. Alizadeh, D. Mazires, B. Prabhakar, C. Kim, and A. Greenberg. EyeQ: Practical network performance isolation at the edge. In *Proceedings of the 10th USENIX Conference on Networked Systems Design and Implementation*, NSDI'13, Berkeley, CA, USA, 2013.

[34] J. M. Kaplan, W. Forrest, and N. Kindler. Revolutionizing data center energy efficiency. *Technical report, McKinsey & Company*, 2008.

[35] R. Kapoor, G. Porter, M. Tewari, G. M. Voelker, and A. Vahdat. Chronos: Predictable low latency for data center applications. In *Proceedings of the Third ACM Symposium on Cloud Computing*, SoCC '12, pages 9:1–9:14, New York, NY, USA, 2012.

[36] H. Kasture and D. Sanchez. Ubik: Efficient cache sharing with strict qos for latency-critical workloads. In *Proceedings of the 19th International Conference on Architectural Support for Programming Languages and Operating Systems*, ASPLOS '14, page 729–742, New York, NY, USA, 2014.

[37] E. Keller, J. Szefer, J. Rexford, and R. B. Lee. NoHype: virtualized cloud infrastructure without the virtualization. In *Proceedings of the 37th Annual International Symposium on Computer Architecture*, ISCA '10, page 350–361, New York, NY, USA, 2010.

[38] C. Kozyrakis. Resource efficient computing for warehouse-scale datacenters. In *Design, Automation Test in Europe Conference Exhibition (DATE)*, pages 1351–1356, Mar. 2013.

[39] J. Leverich and C. Kozyrakis. Reconciling high server utilization and sub-millisecond quality-of-service. In *Proceedings of the 2014 EuroSys Conference, Amsterdam, Nethelands*, 2014.

[40] B. Li, L. Zhao, R. Iyer, L. S. Peh, M. Leddige, M. Espig, S. E. Lee, and D. Newell. CoQoS: coordinating QoS-aware shared resources in NoC-based SoCs. *Journal of Parallel and Distributed Computing*, 71 (5):700–713, 2011.

[41] B. Li, L. S. Peh, L. Zhao, and R. Iyer. Dynamic QoS management for chip multiprocessors. *ACM Trans. Archit. Code Optim.*, 9(3): 17:1–17:29, Oct. 2012.

[42] J. Lin, Q. Lu, X. Ding, Z. Zhang, X. Zhang, and P. Sadayappan. Gaining insights into multicore cache partitioning: Bridging the gap between simulation and real systems. In *IEEE 14th International Symposium on High Performance Computer Architecture, 2008. HPCA 2008*, pages 367–378, Feb. 2008.

[43] L. Liu, Z. Cui, M. Xing, Y. Bao, M. Chen, and C. Wu. A software memory partition approach for eliminating bank-level interference in multicore systems. In *Proceedings of the 21st international conference on Parallel architectures and compilation techniques*, page 367–376, 2012.

[44] L. Liu, Y. Li, Z. Cui, Y. Bao, M. Chen, and C. Wu. Going vertical in memory management: Handling multiplicity by multi-policy. In *Computer Architecture (ISCA), 2014 ACM/IEEE 41st International Symposium on*, pages 169–180, June 2014. .

[45] J. Mars, N. Vachharajani, R. Hundt, and M. L. Soffa. Contention aware execution: Online contention detection and response. In *Proceedings of the 8th Annual IEEE/ACM International Symposium on Code Generation and Optimization*, CGO '10, pages 257–265, New York, NY, USA, 2010.

[46] J. Mars, L. Tang, and R. Hundt. Heterogeneity in "homogeneous" warehouse-scale computers: A performance opportunity. *Computer Architecture Letters*, 10(2):29–32, 2011.

[47] J. Mars, L. Tang, and M. L. Soffa. Directly characterizing cross core interference through contention synthesis. In *Proceedings of the 6th International Conference on High Performance and Embedded Architectures and Compilers*, HiPEAC '11, pages 167–176, New York, NY, USA, 2011.

[48] M. Mesnier, F. Chen, T. Luo, and J. B. Akers. Differentiated storage services. In *Proceedings of the Twenty-Third ACM Symposium on Operating Systems Principles*, SOSP '11, page 57–70, New York, NY, USA, 2011.

[49] S. P. Muralidhara, L. Subramanian, O. Mutlu, M. Kandemir, and T. Moscibroda. Reducing memory interference in multicore systems via application-aware memory channel partitioning. In *Proceedings of the 44th Annual IEEE/ACM International Symposium on Microarchitecture*, page 374–385, 2011.

[50] O. Mutlu and T. Moscibroda. Stall-time fair memory access scheduling for chip multiprocessors. In *Proceedings of the 40th Annual IEEE/ACM International Symposium on Microarchitecture*, pages 146–160, 2007.

[51] R. Nishtala, H. Fugal, S. Grimm, M. Kwiatkowski, H. Lee, H. C. Li, R. McElroy, M. Paleczny, D. Peek, P. Saab, D. Stafford, T. Tung, and V. Venkataramani. Scaling memcache at facebook. In *Proceedings of the 10th USENIX Symposium on Networked Systems Design and Implementation (NSDI 13)*, pages 385–398, Lombard, IL, 2013.

[52] D. Novaković, N. Vasić, S. Novaković, D. Kostić, and R. Bianchini. Deepdive: Transparently identifying and managing performance interference in virtualized environments. In *the 2013 USENIX Annual Technical Conference (USENIX ATC 13)*, pages 219–230, San Jose, CA, 2013.

[53] Oracle. Oracle VM Server for SPARC (Logical Domains). `http://www.oracle.com/technetwork/systems/logical-domains/index.html`, .

[54] Oracle. OpenSPARC T1 microprocessor. `http://www.oracle.com/technetwork/systems/opensparc/index.html`, .

[55] Patrick Mochel. The sysfs filesystem. In *Linux Symposium*, 2005.

[56] M. K. Qureshi and Y. N. Patt. Utility-based cache partitioning: A low-overhead, high-performance, runtime mechanism to partition shared caches. In *Proceedings of the 39th Annual IEEE/ACM International Symposium on Microarchitecture*, page 423–432, 2006.

[57] S. Radhakrishnan, Y. Geng, V. Jeyakumar, A. Kabbani, G. Porter, and A. Vahdat. Senic: Scalable nic for end-host rate limiting. In *Proceedings of the 11th USENIX Conference on Networked Systems Design and Implementation*, NSDI'14, pages 475–488, Berkeley, CA, USA, 2014.

[58] N. Rafique, W.-T. Lim, and M. Thottethodi. Architectural support for operating system-driven cmp cache management. In *Proceedings of the 15th International Conference on Parallel Architectures and Compilation Techniques*, PACT '06, pages 2–12, New York, NY, USA, 2006.

[59] C. Reiss, A. Tumanov, G. R. Ganger, R. H. Katz, and M. A. Kozuch. Heterogeneity and dynamicity of clouds at scale: Google trace analysis. In *Proceedings of the Third ACM Symposium on Cloud Computing*, SoCC '12, pages 7:1–7:13, New York, NY, USA, 2012.

[60] RFC2474. Definition of the Differentiated Services Field (DS Field) in the IPv4 and IPv6 Headers. `http://tools.ietf.org/html/rfc2474`.

[61] RFC2475. An Architecture for Differentiated Services. `http://tools.ietf.org/html/rfc2475`.

[62] S. Rixner, W. J. Dally, U. J. Kapasi, P. Mattson, and J. D. Owens. Memory access scheduling. In *Proceedings of the 27th Annual International Symposium on Computer Architecture*, ISCA '00, pages 128–138, New York, NY, USA, 2000.

[63] D. Sanchez and C. Kozyrakis. The ZCache: decoupling ways and associativity. In *Proceedings of the 2010 43rd Annual IEEE/ACM International Symposium on Microarchitecture*, MICRO '43, page 187–198, Washington, DC, USA, 2010.

[64] D. Sanchez and C. Kozyrakis. Vantage: scalable and efficient fine-grain cache partitioning. In *ACM SIGARCH Computer Architecture News*, volume 39, page 57–68, 2011.

[65] M. Schwarzkopf, A. Konwinski, M. Abd-El-Malek, and J. Wilkes. Omega: Flexible, scalable schedulers for large compute clusters. In *Proceedings of the 8th ACM European Conference on Computer Systems*, EuroSys '13, pages 351–364, New York, NY, USA, 2013.

[66] A. Sharifi, S. Srikantaiah, A. K. Mishra, M. Kandemir, and C. R. Das. METE: meeting end-to-end QoS in multicores through system-wide resource management. In *Proceedings of the ACM SIGMETRICS joint international conference on Measurement and modeling of computer systems*, page 13–24, 2011.

[67] A. Shieh, S. Kandula, A. Greenberg, C. Kim, and B. Saha. Sharing the data center network. In *Proceedings of the 8th USENIX Conference on Networked Systems Design and Implementation*, NSDI'11, Berkeley, CA, USA, 2011.

[68] D. Tam, R. Azimi, L. Soares, and M. Stumm. Managing shared l2 caches on multicore systems in software. In *In Proc. of the Workshop on the Interaction between Operating Systems and Computer Architecture (WIOSCA)*, 2007.

[69] L. Tang, J. Mars, N. Vachharajani, R. Hundt, and M. L. Soffa. The impact of memory subsystem resource sharing on datacenter applications. In *Proceedings of the 38th Annual International Symposium on Computer Architecture*, ISCA '11, pages 283–294, New York, NY, USA, 2011.

[70] R. B. Tremaine, P. Franaszek, J. Robinson, C. Schulz, T. Smith, M. Wazlowski, and P. M. Bland. IBM memory expansion technology (MXT). *IBM Journal of Research and Development*, 45(2):271–285, Mar. 2001.

[71] B. Vamanan, J. Hasan, and T. Vijaykumar. Deadline-aware datacenter TCP (d2tcp). In *Proceedings of the ACM SIGCOMM 2012 Conference*, SIGCOMM '12, New York, NY, USA, 2012.

[72] G. Wang and T. S. E. Ng. The impact of virtualization on network performance of amazon EC2 data center. In *Proceedings of the 29th Conference on Information Communications*, INFOCOM'10, Piscataway, NJ, USA, 2010.

[73] C. Wilson, H. Ballani, T. Karagiannis, and A. Rowtron. Better never than late: Meeting deadlines in datacenter networks. In *Proceedings of the ACM SIGCOMM 2011 Conference*, SIGCOMM '11, New York, NY, USA, 2011.

[74] Y. Xu, M. Bailey, B. Noble, and F. Jahanian. Small is better: Avoiding latency traps in virtualized data centers. In *Proceedings of the 4th Annual Symposium on Cloud Computing*, SOCC '13, pages 7:1–7:16, New York, NY, USA, 2013.

[75] Y. Xu, Z. Musgrave, B. Noble, and M. Bailey. Bobtail: Avoiding long tails in the cloud. In *Proceedings of the 10th USENIX Conference on Networked Systems Design and Implementation*, NSDI'13, pages 329–342, Berkeley, CA, USA, 2013.

[76] H. Yang, A. Breslow, J. Mars, and L. Tang. Bubble-flux: Precise online QoS management for increased utilization in warehouse scale computers. In *Proceedings of the 40th Annual International Symposium on Computer Architecture*, page 607–618, 2013.

[77] M. Yu, A. Greenberg, D. Maltz, J. Rexford, L. Yuan, S. Kandula, and C. Kim. Profiling network performance for multi-tier data center applications. In *Proceedings of the 8th USENIX Conference on Networked Systems Design and Implementation*, NSDI'11, Berkeley, CA, USA, 2011.

[78] D. Zats, T. Das, P. Mohan, D. Borthakur, and R. Katz. DeTail: Reducing the flow completion time tail in datacenter networks. *SIGCOMM Comput. Commun. Rev.*, 42(4), Aug. 2012.

[79] Y. Zhang, M. Laurenzano, J. Mars, and L. Tang. Smite: Precise qos prediction on real system smt processors to improve utilization in warehouse scale computers. In *Proceedings of the 47th Annual IEEE/ACM International Symposium on Microarchitecture (MICRO)*, Dec. 2014.

Improving Agility and Elasticity in Bare-metal Clouds

Yushi Omote
University of Tsukuba
omote@osss.cs.tsukuba.ac.jp

Takahiro Shinagawa
The University of Tokyo
shina@ecc.u-tokyo.ac.jp

Kazuhiko Kato
University of Tsukuba
kato@cs.tsukuba.ac.jp

Abstract

Bare-metal clouds are an emerging infrastructure-as-a-service (IaaS) that leases physical machines (bare-metal instances) rather than virtual machines, allowing resource-intensive applications to have exclusive access to physical hardware. Unfortunately, bare-metal instances require time-consuming or OS-specific tasks for deployment due to the lack of virtualization layers, thereby sacrificing several beneficial features of traditional IaaS clouds such as agility, elasticity, and OS transparency. We present BMcast, an OS deployment system with a special-purpose *de-virtualizable* virtual machine monitor (VMM) that supports quick and OS-transparent startup of bare-metal instances. BMcast performs streaming OS deployment while allowing direct access to physical hardware from the guest OS, and then disappears after completing the deployment. Quick startup of instances improves agility and elasticity significantly, and OS transparency greatly simplifies management tasks for cloud customers. Experimental results have confirmed that BMcast initiated a bare-metal instance 8.6 times faster than image copying, and database performance on BMcast during streaming OS deployment was comparable to that on a state-of-the-art VMM without performing deployment. BMcast incurred zero overhead after de-virtualization.

Categories and Subject Descriptors C.0 [*Computer Systems Organization*]: General—System architectures; D.4.7 [*Operating Systems*]: Organization and Design

Keywords Operating Systems; Virtualization; Bare-metal Clouds; Device Mediators

1. Introduction

Most infrastructure-as-a-service (IaaS) providers today lease virtual machines (VMs) to their customers. Virtualization helps build their cloud infrastructures and provide certain essential characteristics of cloud computing, such as on-demand self-service, resource pooling, and rapid elasticity. Many research efforts have been devoted to improving the performance of VMs [17, 27, 39, 49], resulting in reasonable performance as a platform for most applications. However, virtualization could still become a significant obstacle to certain types of cutting-edge cloud applications that have significant performance, functionality, and security demands.

For example, big data applications, HPC applications, database servers, and media servers must avoid performance degradation and unpredictability caused by virtualization to maintain consistent high performance for uninterrupted real-time data processing [28, 29]. Google and Facebook do not use virtualization with their primary applications for this reason [2, 3]. In addition, certain applications require special hardware configurations, such as dedicated GPUs [8], InfiniBand network cards [10], specific SSD products [12], and RAID configurations [5]. Companies with strict security requirements hesitate to use virtualized multi-tenant environments [41, 50]. Therefore, a considerable number of today's customers demand physical machines (*bare-metal instances*) rather than VMs as their computing platform [28, 36]. To address this, several cloud providers, including IBM, have begun supporting bare-metal instances [4, 9, 10].

Unfortunately, bare-metal instances require either time-consuming or OS-specific tasks for the initial OS deployment. A straightforward approach to deploying an OS to an instance is to copy the entire OS image from a server to the local disk prior to starting-up the instance. Thus, the customer must wait for up to tens of minutes (depending on the network bandwidth and image size) for the copy procedure to finish. Rebooting the machine after the copy further increases the total wait time by several minutes, especially when the machine has a server-oriented motherboard with slow firmware initialization. This long deployment time significantly impairs the beneficial features of traditional IaaS clouds, such as agility and elasticity, and becomes an obstacle in, for instance, temporal testing, quick scale-up on demand, and hour-based pay-as-you-go services. The importance of startup time in VM instances has been recognized by both users and research communities [35, 40], and the same consideration applies to bare-metal instances.

ASPLOS '15, March 14–18, 2015, Istanbul, Turkey.

http://dx.doi.org/10.1145/2694344.2694349

OS streaming deployment [24] is a promising approach to reducing wait time. This approach first performs a network boot and then copies the OS image to the local disk in the background. This enables quick startup of instances and eventual bare-metal performance after OS deployment is completed. Unfortunately, OS streaming deployment depends heavily on OS functions and configurations, thereby sacrificing another important feature of the IaaS clouds, i.e., OS transparency. Abandoning OS transparency results in crucial limitations for not only cloud providers but also cloud customers because unskilled customers must test and verify the compatibility of special drivers with OS kernels whenever they update, patch, or customize their OSs. Providing pre-configured OS images may allow the customers to avoid such complications but significantly limits the choices of OSs the cloud customers can select. Using conventional virtual machine monitors (VMMs) provides OS transparency and mitigates the compatibility problems while allowing quick OS deployment [22]. However, even state-of-the-art VMMs incur continuous virtualization overhead and have difficulty achieving *pure* bare-metal performance [27, 32, 38, 45, 48].

Our study aims to incorporate several beneficial features of traditional IaaS clouds into bare-metal clouds: to improve agility and elasticity while preserving OS transparency without sacrificing performance. To this end, we introduce BMcast, an OS deployment system with a special-purpose *de-virtualizable* VMM that supports OS-transparent quick startup of bare-metal instances. BMcast performs streaming OS deployment transparently to produce a ready-to-use bare-metal instance quickly, while allowing direct hardware access from the deploying OS to minimize overhead as much as possible. After OS deployment is completed, BMcast turns off virtualization and disappears from underneath the deployed OS.

The key challenge of this approach is achieving two conflicting goals, i.e., sharing devices between the guest OS and VMM for low-overhead streaming OS deployment and seamlessly de-virtualizing devices for eventual bare-metal performance. Using virtual devices makes device sharing easy but makes de-virtualization complicated because device interfaces visible to the guest OS change during de-virtualization. Directly exposing physical devices to the guest OS makes de-virtualization easy but makes device sharing difficult. Although the basic concept of de-virtualization has been proposed previously [30, 34], runtime de-virtualization of I/O devices that are shared between the guest OS and VMM remains an open problem. To address this, we introduce *device mediators* that perform polling-based device-interface-level I/O mediation by carefully monitoring, intercepting, manipulating, and inserting I/O requests in a manner that conforms to device specifications. Device mediators allow physical devices to be first shared and then seamlessly de-virtualized.

The concept of device mediators is novel yet simple and generic. Developing device mediators requires the knowledge of device specifications to some extent; however, the task of device mediators is relatively straightforward, and therefore device mediators are much simpler and smaller than traditional device drivers. In fact, the device mediators we developed for IDE and AHCI devices are only 1,472 lines of code (LOC) and 2,285 LOC, respectively. We also found that MegaRAID SAS and Revo Drive PCIe SSD devices have similar straightforward interfaces. We believe that software interfaces of most storage host controllers have similarities because the types of underlying physical interfaces between the host controllers and disk drives are limited (SATA and SAS). Once implemented at the cloud provider side, device mediators simplify management tasks for customers significantly by providing OS transparency. More issues on the cost of device mediators are discussed in Section 6.

We implemented a prototype VMM of BMcast based on BitVisor [46]. We changed the core of BitVisor 1.4 by only 3,576 LOC. The prototype supports x86 environments with IDE and AHCI disk controllers, and Intel PRO/1000, X540, Realtek RTL816x, and Broadcom NetXtreme network interface controllers (NICs). We also designed and implemented a network storage protocol that extends the ATA-over-Ethernet (AoE) protocol [43] to improve network storage performance. Although sharing a NIC with the guest OS is technically possible, our current implementation uses a dedicated NIC for streaming OS deployment to avoid performance interference. We believe using a dedicated NIC for management is a reasonable configuration because modern server machines typically have multiple NICs. The possibility of sharing a NIC is discussed in Section 6.

Our current implementation does not yet fully support VMXOFF (i.e., completely turning off the CPU's hardware virtualization function). Although its performance benefit is negligible, supporting VMXOFF, in addition to supporting nested virtualization [20], would allow the guest OS to utilize the CPU's hardware virtualization function. Since supporting VMXOFF involves some complications, we currently only have an implementation with the support of a guest kernel module (not used in the performance evaluation). However, fully OS-transparent implementation in the VMM would be possible and is our future work.

The experimental results confirmed that BMcast can deploy Windows (Vista, 7, 8.1, Server 2008) and Linux (Ubuntu 10.04 and later, and CentOS 6.3 and later) without any modifications. BMcast started up a bare-metal instance 8.6 times faster than image copying, and the average database throughput on BMcast was comparable to that on a state-of-the-art VMM, i.e., kernel-based virtual machine (KVM) with exit-less interrupts (ELI) [1, 27] even though BMcast was performing streaming OS deployment while KVM with ELI was not performing that. After de-virtualization, BMcast incurred zero overhead.

The rest of this paper is organized as follows. Section 2 shows related work. Section 3 presents the design and Section 4 describes the implementation. Section 5 shows the results of a performance evaluation and Section 6 describes discussions. Section 7 draws the conclusion of this paper.

2. Related Work

We first present OS deployment approaches and then discuss VMM overhead from an OS deployment perspective.

OS deployment: Image copying, such as in OpenStack Nova [7], is an OS-transparent but time-intensive approach to OS deployment. For example, copying a 30-GB image (default Windows Server 2008 on Amazon EC2) at 130 MB/sec (e.g., transfer from a 1.5 K rpm SAS disk over 10-Gb Ethernet) takes approximately 5 minutes. Using SSDs may reduce the copy time; however, the server or network may saturate when multiple instances are deployed simultaneously. Rebooting machines after the copy further add several minutes due to long firmware initialization time. Network installation, such as Kickstart in Linux, is a similar approach that copies and installs system files from the server to the local disk over the network. However, it is OS-specific and takes tens of minutes to complete the copy operation.

Network booting boots up an OS quickly; however, it does not deploy the OS image to a local disk, which causes continuous overhead as a result of redirecting every disk I/O over the network. Caching data on the local disk [22] reduces I/O overhead but must check cache expiration for every disk access on the critical I/O path, which increases disk access latency. OS streaming deployment [24] is a hybrid approach of network booting and image copying that allows fast OS startup and deployment to the local disk. Although it can reduce startup time and overhead, it still compromises OS transparency. Our approach enhances OS streaming deployment by exploiting a de-virtualizable VMM to provide OS transparency while retaining the low overhead during the OS deployment and eventual bare-metal performance.

VMM overhead: Leveraging conventional VMMs, such as Xen [17] and KVM [31], is an easy approach to starting up an OS quickly while preserving OS transparency. However, despite efforts to reduce virtualization overhead, such as para-virtualization [17] and I/O pass-through [39, 49], such VMMs do not achieve bare-metal performance in compute-intensive and I/O-intensive workloads [18, 29, 37] due to the lock-holder preemption problem [47], cache pollution, nested paging, and interrupt handling overhead [21, 27].

Another possible approach is to uninstall VMMs after OS deployment. Several recent VMMs support raw disks and virtual-to-physical conversion. Therefore, using VMMs during streaming OS deployment and then converting virtual instances to physical instances is possible. However, uninstalling VMMs requires OS reboots, which incurs downtime. A recent study has shown that a more seamless conversion is possible by exploiting OS hibernation [32]. Unfortunately, in addition to slight modifications to the OS, this requires 90 seconds for physical-to-virtual conversion.

Creating virtual devices with the same device interfaces as those of physical devices will ease de-virtualization while preserving OS transparency. However, emulating an entire machine with the identical hardware interface as the underlying physical machine, including all devices (e.g., chipset and ACPI functions), is costly. In addition, synchronizing the internal states of virtual devices with physical devices is an open problem. Therefore, seamless and transparent conversion from virtual instances to physical instances is difficult.

NoHype [30] allows the removal of the virtualization layer to eliminate attack surfaces after booting guest OSs. Microvisor [34] demonstrates run-time de-virtualization for online maintenance of servers. Pass-through-based VMMs that allow direct control of I/O devices from the guest OS [44, 46] can also achieve de-virtualization. However, current de-virtualizable VMMs do not support device sharing between the guest OS and VMM. Therefore, the VMMs do not have access to the local disk to copy the OS image.

BMcast achieves seamless de-virtualization and eventual bare-metal performance, which differs from conventional VMMs. BMcast also achieves low-overhead device sharing with the guest OS, which differs from existing de-virtualizable or pass-through VMMs.

3. Design

In this section, we first explain the deployment process. We then describe the three BMcast functions, such as I/O mediation, background copy, and de-virtualization.

3.1 Deployment Process

BMcast deploys an OS by following four phases: initialization, deployment, de-virtualization, and bare-metal.

In the *initialization phase*, the VMM boots on a target machine. Although booting from the local disk is possible, we employ network booting to simplify VMM management (e.g., patching and updating). To allow fast startup, we minimize the VMM size as much as possible and optimize boot speed by parallelizing the initialization process. The VMM only initializes the dedicated NIC and leaves other hardware devices uninitialized because the guest OS will initialize the devices. The actual boot time is within a few seconds. In this phase, the local disk is uninitialized; all disk blocks are empty and contain no OS image (Figure 1a).

In the *deployment phase*, the VMM performs two tasks for streaming OS deployment: (1) copy-on-read to retrieve data from the server for empty blocks and (2) background copy to actively fill empty blocks. The copy-on-read allows quick startup of OS instances, and the background copy allows eventual bare-metal performance. In copy-on-read, the VMM retrieves data from the server if the blocks requested by the guest OS are empty. The VMM then returns the data

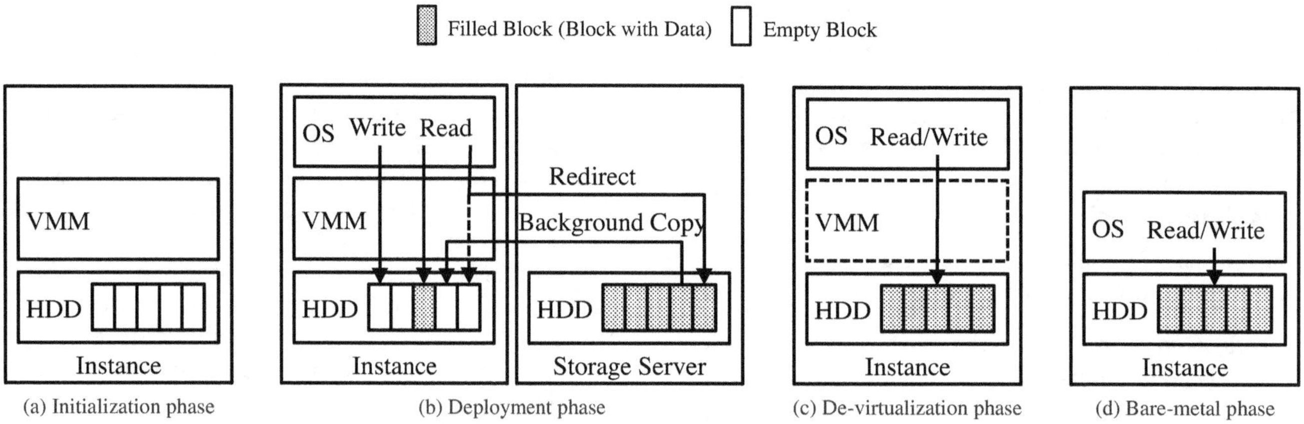

Figure 1. Four phases of deployment process

to the guest OS as if they are read from the local disk (see Redirect in Figure 1b). The VMM also writes the data to the local disk for future use. In other cases, I/O requests from the guest OS pass through the VMM and are served by the local disk (solid arrows from Read and Write in Figure 1b).

Parallel to copy-on-read, the VMM actively fills empty blocks with a background copy operation (see Background Copy in Figure 1b). The local disk is filled with the disk image gradually, and the guest OS eventually gains bare-metal disk performance. To reduce performance interference with the guest OS, the VMM moderates the speed of the background copy. The details of this process are described in Sections 3.2 and 3.3. To facilitate seamless de-virtualization, we use the identical block address space for both the local disk and the disk image on the server; the sector number of the disk image corresponds to that of the local disk.

In the *de-virtualization phase*, the VMM turns off virtualization to allow all hardware accesses to pass through the VMM (Figure 1c). To achieve seamless de-virtualization that is unnoticed by the guest OS, the VMM exposes identical hardware interfaces to the guest OS during de-virtualization, and the VMM waits for a consistent hardware state which is an appropriate time to stop virtualization. The details of this process are discussed in Section 3.4.

In the *bare-metal phase*, the VMM does not exist. The OS runs on the bare-metal instance directly (Figure 1d). At this point, the disk image is the same as that on the server, with the exception of already-written disk regions.

3.2 I/O Mediation by Device Mediators

Device mediators are the key component required to achieve device sharing with the guest OS while exposing the physical hardware interface to the guest OS directly. Device mediators perform I/O mediation; they mediate access to devices from the guest OS and VMM. I/O mediation involves three tasks: *I/O interpretation*, *I/O redirection*, and *I/O multiplexing*. I/O interpretation involves monitoring I/O sequences from the guest OS and determining their context. I/O redirection involves intercepting I/O requests from the guest OS and redirecting them to the server, and I/O multiplexing involves inserting I/O requests from the VMM to devices. Note that I/O interpretation is the basis of I/O redirection and I/O multiplexing. I/O redirection is used in the copy-on-read, and I/O multiplexing is used in the background copy.

I/O interpretation: I/O interpretation determines the context of I/O sequences to properly control I/O access from the guest OS. For example, in disk controllers, device mediators interpret three types of contextual information: *command*, *status*, and *data*. The command information contains the operation type (e.g. read or write), logical block address (LBA), and sector count. The status information determines whether the device is idle or busy, which is required to determine when operations terminate. The data information is about the actual data transfer, such as the DMA buffer address of the guest OS.

Device mediators can easily capture this information by monitoring programmed I/Os (PIOs) and memory-mapped I/Os (MMIOs), in association with in-memory data structures including queues, based on device specifications. Although actual I/O sequences are device-specific, the basic concept can be applied to many different types of disk controllers. In addition, device mediators only need to determine these basic I/O sequences and can ignore other irrelevant sequences, such as device initialization and vendor-specific configurations. Therefore, device mediators are simpler and smaller than conventional full-spec device drivers.

I/O redirection: I/O redirection is used in the deployment phase to redirect read access of empty blocks to the storage server. Device mediators must (1) capture the block information, (2) retrieve the corresponding data from the server, and then (3) pass the data to the guest OS.

Figure 2 illustrates the basic operations of I/O redirection. Device mediators use I/O interpretation to capture the command information ("1. Interpret" in Figure 2). By interpreting I/O requests, device mediators can determine whether an

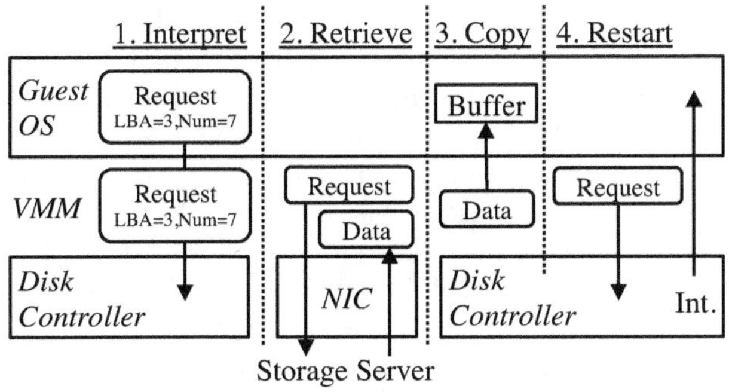

Figure 2. I/O redirection

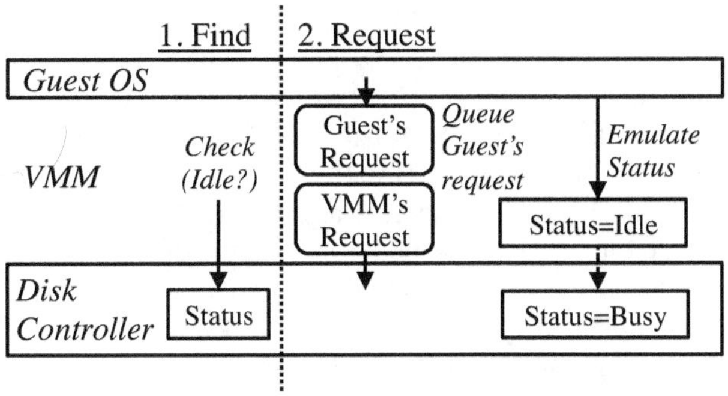

Figure 3. I/O multiplexing

access is read or not, and if read, its location (LBA and sector count). Based on this information, the VMM determines whether the blocks are empty or filled.

When blocks are empty, device mediators must retrieve the corresponding data from the server ("2. Retrieve" in Figure 2). First, device mediators temporarily block I/O access to the device so that the device does not start the data transfer. Device mediators then send the command information over the network and retrieve the data from the server. While retrieving data, device mediators emulate the status information so that the guest OS can determine that the device is busy. After retrieving the data, device mediators pass the data to the guest OS by functioning as a virtual DMA controller; i.e., copying the data to the guest DMA buffer ("3. Copy" in Figure 2). Device mediators obtain the address of the guest DMA buffer using I/O interpretation.

At this point, device mediators must generate an interrupt to indicate that the operation has been completed. The problem here is how to generate this interrupt. One possible approach is to virtualize interrupt controllers; however this complicates de-virtualization. Another possible approach is to share interrupt controllers with the guest OS transparently using techniques that are similar to I/O multiplexing, which is described below. However, sharing interrupt controllers is very complicated, especially when an advanced programmable interrupt controller (APIC) is used. Keeping track of interrupt numbers assigned by the guest OS to the devices is also difficult because it depends on the platform hardware such as low pin counter controllers and PCI bridges in the chipset. Therefore, this approach decreases portability drastically.

Rather than sending virtual interrupts, device mediators simply restart the blocked I/O access to the device so that the device itself generates an interrupt ("4. Restart" in Figure 2). To prevent the device from overwriting the guest DMA buffers, device mediators configure the device to transfer the data to dummy buffers. Device mediators also manipulate the command information (LBA and sector count) so that the device reads a single dummy sector that hits the disk cache. This technique allows easy and transparent generation of interrupts.

I/O multiplexing: I/O multiplexing is used for background copy. I/O multiplexing allows the VMM to issue its own I/O requests to devices while the guest OS controls those devices. Device mediators must (1) find proper timings to insert I/O requests, (2) emulate device status and handle the requests, and (3) manage request queues.

Figure 3 illustrates the basic I/O multiplexing operations. First, device mediators find proper timing to safely share a device in a time-sharing manner ("1. Find" in Figure 3). If the device is processing an I/O request from the guest OS, the device mediators wait for completion of the request. Device mediators detect this using I/O interpretation.

When the request is completed, the device mediators send the I/O request from the VMM to the device ("2. Request" in Figure 3). To preserve consistency, device mediators emulate the status of the device as if the device is not busy even though the device is actually processing the request from the VMM. Therefore, at this time, the guest OS may attempt to send its own I/O request. To prevent conflicts with the guest OS, the device mediators intercept the request and keep it in a queue. After the request from the VMM is completed, the device mediators stop emulating device status and send queued requests to the device.

Sharing devices causes another problem on interrupts. Since obtaining interrupt numbers assigned by the guest OS is difficult, the device mediators cannot detect the exact interrupts generated for the requests from the VMM. In addition, the interrupts for the VMM are also delivered to the guest OS because interrupt controllers are not virtualized. Although device drivers may safely ignore unknown interrupts to support interrupt sharing, extra interrupt delivery should be avoided to preserve portability. Therefore, device mediators temporary disable interrupts and detect completion of requests by polling threads with fine-grained scheduling. The details of this process are described in Section 4.1.

3.3 Background Copy

To fill the entire local disk with the OS image, the VMM actively retrieves the data for empty blocks in the background. Since the retrieval and disk-write rates will differ, the VMM uses a pair of threads, *retriever thread* and *writer thread*, that are connected by a FIFO queue. The retriever thread retrieves data for empty blocks from the server and pushes them to the queue. The writer thread then pops and writes the data to the local disk. The VMM fills blocks in order from low to high LBA. However, to minimize seek, the VMM changes the address adjacent to that of the last-accessed block if the guest OS accessed the disk.

In devices that have multiple request queues, a consistency problem may occur if a local disk is shared by the VMM and guest OS. To illustrate this problem, let us consider the following example. The VMM attempts to fill an empty block and send a request to the server. Before the response arrives, the guest OS issues a write request to the same block. In this case, the data from the guest OS is the most recent and should remain in the local disk. However, the response comes after the write from the guest OS; therefore, simply putting write requests into a queue in a FIFO manner breaks the consistency. To mitigate this problem, the VMM holds a bitmap to manage the status of each disk block and atomically checks the status to prevent the VMM from writing to a filled block. In case of shutdown and reboot, the VMM saves the bitmap on the local disk. The VMM uses an unused region on the local disk (such as unallocated space between two partitions) to save the bitmap. To protect the bitmap from the guest OS, the VMM prevents access to the region by converting it to read access to a dummy sector.

To avoid performance interference, the background copy speed should be moderated. If the write frequency is too high, guest storage performance degrades significantly. If it is too low, the deployment phase takes a long time. To solve this problem, the VMM adjusts the write frequency based on the guest OS load and three configurable parameters: *guest I/O frequency threshold*, *VMM-write interval*, and *VMM-write suspend interval*. If the disk I/O frequency becomes higher than the value of the guest I/O frequency threshold, the VMM waits for the time specified by the VMM-write suspend interval. Otherwise, the VMM writes blocks at the interval specified by the VMM-write interval.

Due to this moderation, the VMM will not perform excessive background copy operations during OS startup. As an optimization technique, we could configure the moderation function to prefetch the disk regions required for OS startup via a background copy operation, which would potentially boost OS startup time. However, we do not assume that this prefetch information is generally available.

3.4 De-virtualization

To make de-virtualization easy, we directly expose physical hardware to the guest OS. For example, all physical CPU cores and I/O devices, including PCI devices and interrupt controllers, and other hardware functionalities such as ACPI are exposed to the guest OS.

Memory address space is identity-mapped; a guest physical address is identical to the machine physical address. However, the VMM must allocate its own memory region and prevent the guest OS from accessing it. Therefore, the VMM reserves the memory region by manipulating the BIOS function such that the guest OS does not allocate the region. The VMM also uses nested paging to prevent the guest OS from accidentally corrupting the memory region.

In the de-virtualization phase, the VMM turns nested paging off to eliminate the paging overhead. At this time, the VMM needs to invalidate TLBs on all CPUs. Unfortunately, the VMM cannot use inter-processor interrupts (IPIs) for TLB shootdown because it does not manage interrupt controllers. Fortunately, page mapping is constant (always identity-mapped) over the life time of the VMM and does not cause a consistency problem among CPUs. Therefore, the VMM no longer needs to synchronize the timing of TLB invalidation for all CPUs. Each CPU can invalidate TLBs and turn nested paging off at different timings. After all CPUs disable nested paging, the VMM terminates virtualization.

4. Prototype Implementation

In this section, we describe our prototype implementation. First, we describe the CPU virtualization and network storage protocol. Then, we discuss the implementation status.

4.1 CPU Virtualization

We assume that the CPU is equipped with a hardware-assisted virtualization feature (Intel VT-x or AMD-V). To minimize overhead, we make the CPU run the guest OS as much as possible and switch to the VMM only when the minimum required events occur. The switch from the guest OS to the VMM is called *VM exits*.

We identified several events that require VM exits. To implement I/O mediation, PIO and MMIO instructions for the storage devices need to trigger VM exits. To detect boot, Startup IPIs and INIT signals need to trigger VM exits. To detect changes in paging and the processor mode of the guest OS, CR0 (PE, ET, WP, AM, NW, CD, PG) and CR4 (PSE, PAE, PGE, VMXE, SMXE, PCIDE, SMAP, SMEP) bit changes should also trigger VM exits. To trigger VM exits on MMIO, the VMM uses nested paging (EPT on Intel VT-x or NPT on AMD-V) and keeps the target memory regions unmapped. To cause other VM exits, the VMM configures the data structure to control the virtual machine (VMCS on Intel VT-x or VMCB on AMD-V). Note that the CPUID instruction unconditionally causes VM exits; however, this instruction occurs infrequently.

To poll devices in I/O mediation, the VMM needs to be scheduled periodically. With Intel VT-x, we exploit *preemption timer* to schedule threads. The preemption timer is supported by latest Intel CPUs that unconditionally causes VM exits at a specified interval. It allows fine-grained control of the timing of VM exits with the granularity of CPU clock cycles. Polling intervals are estimated from recent average network round trip times and I/O latency times. This achieves reasonable performance. If the preemption timer is not available, the VMM enables VM exits on hardware interrupts and uses a technique similar to soft timers [16].

4.2 Network Storage Protocol

The VMM requires a network storage protocol to redirect I/O requests to the server. To reduce overhead and improve transparency, we should select a protocol that allows the conversion of I/O requests to network packets with minimal effort. File-level protocols, such as NFS and CIFS, are therefore not suitable, and a block-level protocol is preferable.

We extended the AoE protocol [43], which has the greater affinity with ATA devices, although other protocols could be used. This protocol has a header that contains a field of device registers, and the VMM can easily convert the values of device registers to an AoE header. Data to be read is transferred as a payload of a packet with the header. If the transferred data is too long for a single Ethernet packet, the VMM splits the data into multiple AoE fragments. In this case, the VMM sets the tag field in an AoE header to determine the offset of a received fragment.

To improve performance, we modified the AoE protocol to support jumbo frames. We also add a retransmission capability to tolerate packet loss. We use *vblade* [15] as the basis of our AoE server implementation. However, the original vblade cannot fully utilize the network bandwidth because it is single-threaded and becomes a performance bottleneck when the VMM sends a significant volume of read requests. Therefore, we implemented a thread pool to vblade.

4.3 Implementation Status

We implemented a prototype VMM based on BitVisor [46]. It supports x86 environments with Intel VT-x or AMD-V CPUs. We implemented device mediators for IDE and AHCI disk controllers and the extended version of the AoE protocol in the VMM and server. We confirmed that the VMM can deploy both Windows (Vista, 7, 8.1, Server 2008) and Linux (Ubuntu 10.04 and later, and CentOS 6.3 and later) without any modifications to the OSs.

The sizes of device mediators are 1,472 LOC for IDE and 2,285 LOC for AHCI. We assume that we can use a dedicated NIC for streaming OS deployment to avoid performance interference. Therefore, we implemented small network drivers for Intel PRO/1000, X540, Realtek 816x, and Broadcom NetXtreme network adapters. The implementation cost is limited because we need minimal functions to send and receive packets with polling: the PRO/1000 driver has 718 LOC, X540 driver has 614 LOC, RTL816x has 757 LOC, and NetXtreme has 620 LOC. Our implementation is based on BitVisor 1.4 and modified the core of BitVisor by only 3,576 LOC. The total size of the VMM is approximately 27 KLOC. When adding device mediators for new devices, the VMM core does not need to be modified.

Our current implementation has some limitations. First, the memory region used for the VMM, currently 128 MB, is not released back to the guest OS after de-virtualization. We can mitigate this by implementing memory hot-plug features. Second, we hide hardware-assisted virtualization features from the guest OS because we have not implemented nested virtualization. However, nested virtualization is known to be implementable [20]. Third, we do not yet fully support VMXOFF (disabling the VMM mode).

To support VMXOFF, we need to perform the following operations on a VM exit: issue a VMXOFF instruction, restore the guest CPU state in memory (VMCS or VMCB) to the real CPU without using a VM enter operation, and jump to the instruction that caused the VM exit. These operations must be performed in the guest context since the VMM context was already lost on the VMXOFF. Therefore, we need memory pages mapped in the guest context to perform these operations. We confirmed that it is possible to implement this with the support of a guest kernel module (not used in the performance evaluation). However, it is theoretically possible to implement without a support of the guest OS by using, e.g., an extra page of device's PCI BAR (Base Address Register) [27]. Therefore, these limitations are not essential and we plan to implement them in the future version.

The NIC dedicated to the VMM is not explicitly released back to the guest OS. However, if the guest OS tries to detect it after de-virtualization, it can be found. If the dedicated NIC was connected to a management network and should not be exposed to the guest OS for the security reason, the VMM should continue to exist without performing VMXOFF and hide the PCI configuration space for that NIC. Its overhead will be negligible since a normal (non-malicious) guest OS will not try to access such a hidden NIC.

5. Performance Evaluation

In this section, we show the experimental results of evaluating the performance of BMcast. First, we show the result of measuring the OS startup time to demonstrate that BMcast achieved quick startup of bare-metal instances. Second, we explain the result of database benchmarks to demonstrate that BMcast achieved low-overhead streaming deployment and eventual bare-metal performance. Third, we show the result of an MPI benchmark to show the performance of BMcast in a cluster environment. Forth, we show the result of a kernel compile benchmark to illustrate the overall performance of BMcast. Fifth, we show the result of micro benchmarks to reveal the effects on threads, memory, storage and network performance. Finally, we show the behavior of the moderation in background copy.

We used a cluster of machines (originally used for HPC applications in practice), each of which was a FUJITSU PRIMERGY RX200 S6 with two Intel Xeon X5680 processors (3.33 GHz, 2 $\times$ 6 cores, hyper-threading disabled), 96-GB memory, a Mellanox MT26428 InfiniBand card (4X QDR), and a Seagate Constellation.2 ST9500620NS (500GB/7200 rpm) SATA hard drive. It also had two Intel 82575EM gigabit NICs, one of which was dedicated to the

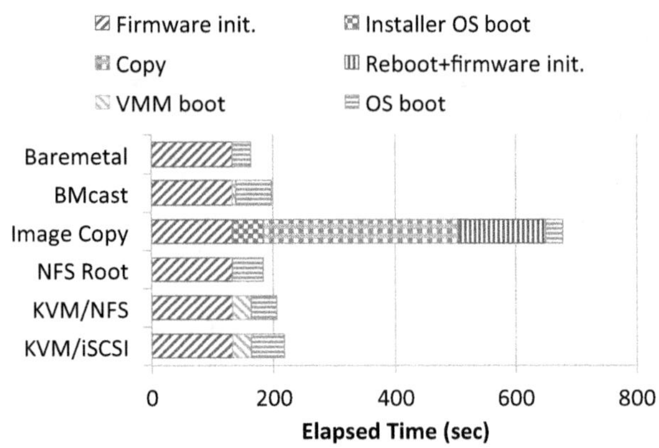

Figure 4. OS startup time

VMM. These machines were connected via a FUJITSU SR-S348TC1 gigabit Ethernet switch with 9000 bytes maximum transmission unit (MTU), and a Mellanox Grid Director 4036E InfiniBand switch. In all experiments, we deployed Ubuntu 14.04 with Linux kernel 3.13.0. For comparison, we used KVM (Linux kernel 3.9.0) with the ELI patch [1].

5.1 OS Startup Time

We first evaluate the OS startup time. We measured the startup time of an instance on both a bare-metal machine (Baremetal) and BMcast (BMcast). For comparison, we also measured the time of image copying over iSCSI (Image Copy). In addition, we measured the startup time of network boot using NFS (NFS Root), and that of a guest OS on KVM using a disk image over either NFS or iSCSI (KVM/NFS and KVM/iSCSI). In all experiments, we used gigabit Ethernet and a 32-GB OS image.

Figure 4 shows the results. The firmware initialization on our machine took 133 seconds, and the OS boot on the bare-metal machine took 29 seconds. On BMcast, the startup time of a bare-metal instance was 63 seconds (including 5 seconds to boot the VMM). On the other hand, image copying took 544 seconds (50 seconds to boot the installer OS over the network, 320 seconds to transfer the disk image, 145 seconds to restart, and 29 seconds for the OS boot from the local disk). Therefore, BMcast started up a bare-metal instance 8.6 times faster (excluding the first firmware initialization) or 3.5 times faster (including the first firmware initialization) than image copying.

The network transfer rate in the image copying was approximately 100 MB/sec, being limited by the bandwidth of gigabit Ethernet. Therefore, using SSDs will not speed up the image copying in this case. Using a faster network such as InfiniBand or 10Gbit Ethernet may reduce the transfer time. However, when multiple instances are started-up at the same time, the performance of the storage server will be saturated and the transfer time will not be reduced so much. On the other hand, BMcast transferred only 72MB of the disk image while booting the OS in 58 seconds, so the average rate was 1.2 MB/sec. This means that there is more room to scale-up the number of instances booted simultaneously. Therefore, BMcast will keep the advantage of fast startup time even if SSDs or faster networks are available.

In Figure 4, the OS startup time of network boot was 49 seconds, which was slightly faster than that on BMcast. However, it did not deploy the OS image to the local disk and took continuous overhead in a database workload. KVM took 30 seconds to boot itself. The BMcast VMM is designed to boot fast, as described in 3.1, and its boot time (5 seconds) was 6 times faster than that of KVM. The startup time of the guest OS on KVM was 42 seconds in the NFS case and 55 seconds in the iSCSI case. The startup time of the OS on BMcast, 58 seconds, was comparable to that in the iSCSI case. Moreover, when we compared the startup time including that of VMMs, BMcast was 1.14 times and 1.35 times faster than KVM with NFS and iSCSI.

From these results, we confirmed that BMcast achieved quick startup of bare-metal instances.

5.2 Database Benchmark

To evaluate the performance throughout the deployment and de-virtualization phase, we simulated a situation in which a user launches a new instance with a NoSQL database that serves data to clients, and traced the performance shift.

We tested two databases widely used in clouds: *memcached* and *Cassandra* [33]. Memcached is an in-memory database often deployed to improve data-serving latency for read-intensive workloads. Cassandra is a database that allows high throughput write access for update-intensive workloads. Both databases are designed to be scalable, spanning multiple instances depending on the amount of data to be handled. We used Yahoo! Cloud Serving Benchmark (YCSB) [23] for the performance evaluation that sends continuous requests from another instance to the database instance. For memcached, we recreated a read-intensive workload with 95% reads and 5% writes ratio and, for Cassandra, a write-intensive workload with 30% reads and 70% writes. We created a 32-GB OS image with the database configured.

Figure 5 shows the throughput and latency results of memcached and Cassandra benchmarks. The horizontal axis in each figure indicates the elapsed time from the beginning of the YCSB test. The vertical axis indicates the ratio to the average performance on the bare-metal machine. We performed the benchmarks on BMcast while streaming OS deployment was in progress and after de-virtualization (BMcast), and on a KVM instance with pass-through access to InfiniBand cards and para-virtual storage devices (KVM). Note that KVM did not perform streaming OS deployment and the overhead of sharing devices were not incurred.

In the memcached benchmark, even while BMcast was in the deployment phase and performing background copy, it showed slightly better performance than KVM. The average throughput was 34.6 kilo-transactions per second (KT/sec)

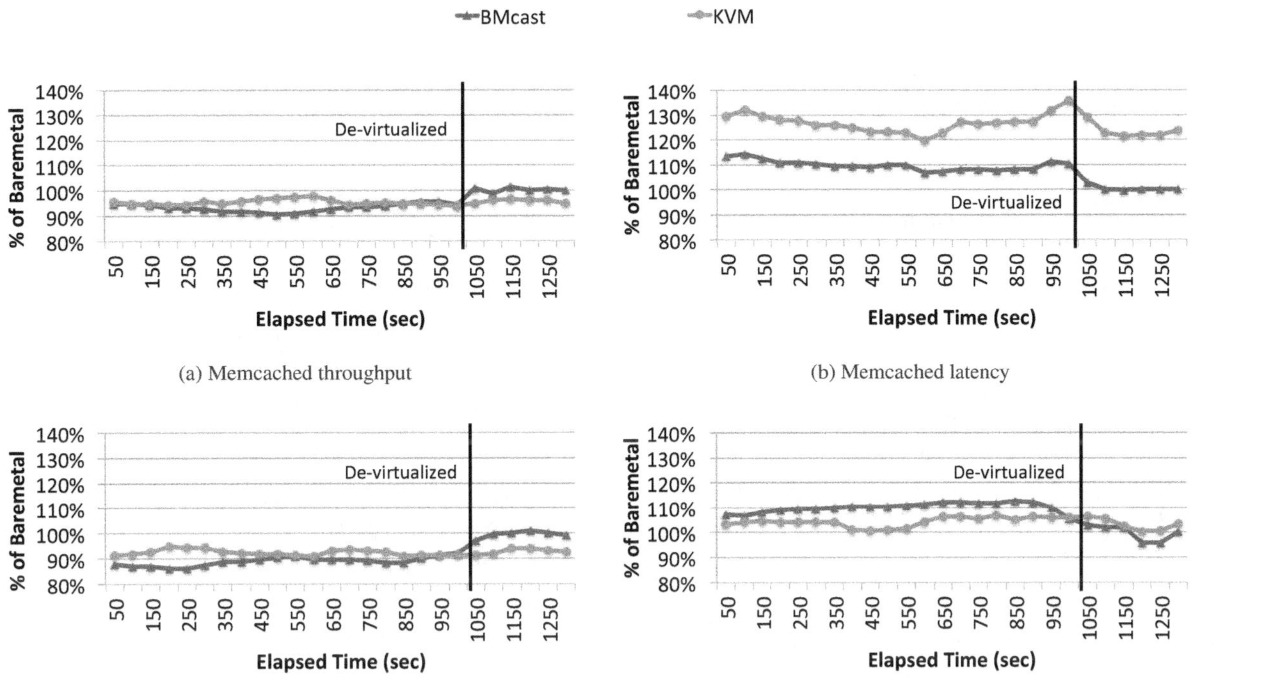

(a) Memcached throughput

(b) Memcached latency

(c) Cassandra throughput

(d) Cassandra latency

Figure 5. Throughput and latency of database benchmark

on BMcast, which was 94.8% of the bare-metal performance and 102% of the KVM performance (see Figure 5a). The average latency was 291 μsec on BMcast, which was 7% slower than the bare-metal performance and 14.8% faster than the KVM performance (see Figure 5b).

The primary reason for the performance degradation by BMcast is TLB pollution; the number of TLB misses increased up to 5 times and the latency on TLB misses doubled due to the two-dimensional page walks of nested paging. BMcast also consumed 6% of the total CPU time: 5% was for handling threads in OS streaming deployment and 1% was for the VMM core itself.

In the memcached benchmark, the deployment phase took 16 minutes. Therefore, in Figures 5a and 5b, the throughput increased and latency decreased after 990 seconds have elapsed; the throughput reached 36.4 KT/sec and the latency reduced to 281 μsec, which were identical to those of the bare-metal performance. There was no suspension or performance degradation during the phase shift. Therefore, we confirmed that BMcast achieved seamless de-virtualization and eventual bare-metal performance.

In the deployment phase, the performance of the Cassandra benchmark on BMcast was slightly lower than that on the memcached benchmark. The average throughput was 51.4 KT/sec, which was 91.4% of the bare-metal performance and 98.7% of the KVM performance (see Figure 5c). The average latency was 2,609 μsec on BMcast, which was 7% slower than the bare-metal performance and 3% slower than the KVM performance (see Figure 5d). The deployment phase took 17 minutes (1020 seconds), which was longer than that in the memcached benchmark because the Cassandra benchmark was more write-intensive. However, after de-virtualization, the throughput on BMcast increased to 60.0 KT/sec and latency decreased to 2,443 μsec, which were almost the same with that of the bare-metal performance.

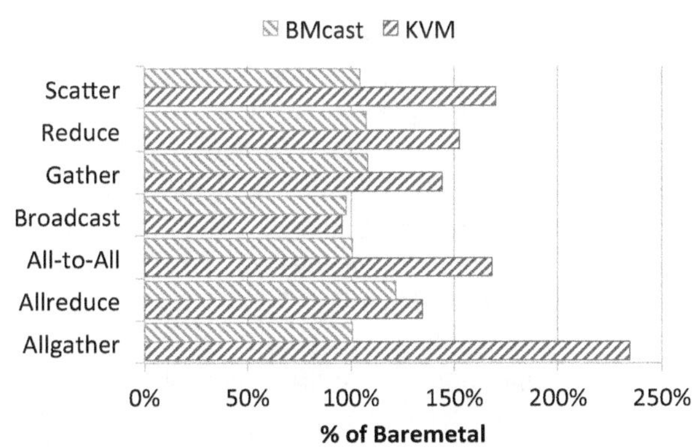

Figure 6. MPI benchmark

5.3 MPI Benchmark

To evaluate the performance effects of BMcast on cluster computing, we ran micro benchmarks of basic MPI operations. The cluster we used consists of 10 machines connected via an InfiniBand switch and OSs are configured to use

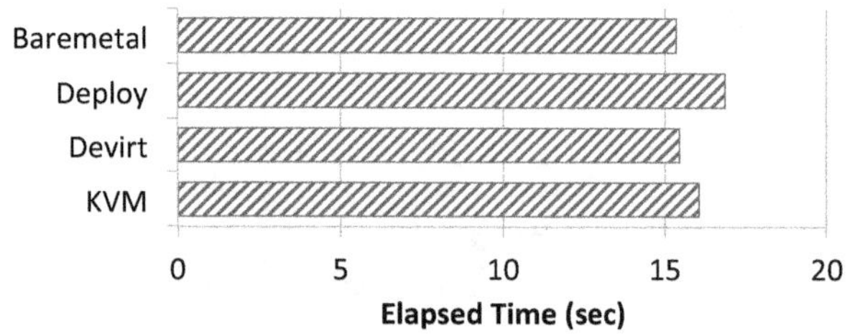

Figure 7. Kernel compile benchmark

MPICH2. We used OSU Micro-Benchmarks [6] and measured the latency of MPI collective communications among all machines. We ran the tests on the cluster with all OSs running on BMcast (BMcast). We also ran the same tests with all OSs running on KVM (KVM). We compared the result with that on the cluster of bare-metal machines.

Figure 6 shows the results. While most results on BMcast were almost the same with that on bare-metal machines, KVM incurred large overhead on many tests. On Allgather, the latency on KVM was 235% of that on bare-metal machines, while that on BMcast was almost identical to that on bare-metal machines. On Allreduce, BMcast incurred 22% overhead but KVM incurred 35% overhead. We guess the latency overhead of InfiniBand (see Section 5.5.3) largely contributes to this severe overhead on the MPI benchmarks.

5.4 Kernel-compile Benchmark

To illustrate the overall performance of BMcast, we used *kernbench*, which compiled a Linux kernel version 2.6.32 with the minimal configuration (`allnoconfig`) and 12 parallel jobs (`make -j 12`), and measured the total elapsed time on the bare-metal machine (Baremetal), on BMcast in the deployment phase (Deploy), on BMcast after de-virtualization (Devirt), and on KVM (KVM).

The benchmark results are shown in Figure 7. The kernel compile took approximately 16 seconds on the bare-metal machine. While OS deployment was in progress, BMcast increased the compile time by 8%. The main reason of this overhead was the cost of sharing the storage device between the guest OS and VMM by I/O multiplexing. However, its performance impact was limited because the moderation of background copy described in Section 3.3 was effective.

KVM (KVM) increased the compile time by 3%. This result does not include the cost of streaming OS deployment because KVM did not perform it. Therefore, this was pure virtualization overhead of KVM. After de-virtualization on BMcast, the compile time became identical to that on the bare-metal machine. These results show that the moderation of background copy is effective, and de-virtualization has the benefit of reducing the overhead of virtualization.

5.5 Micro Benchmarks

We performed three micro benchmarks to measure threads, memory, storage and network performance.

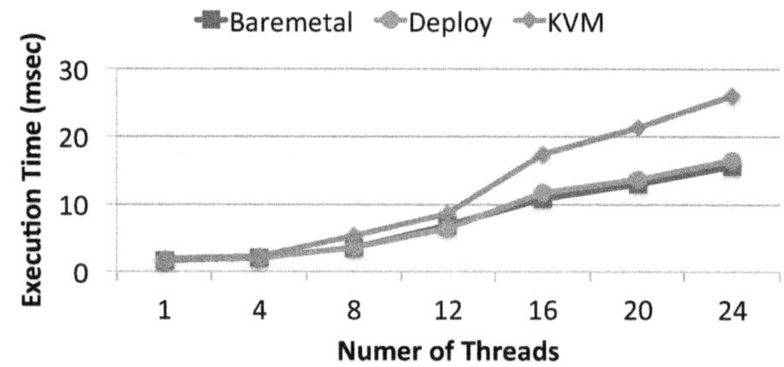

Figure 8. Threads performance

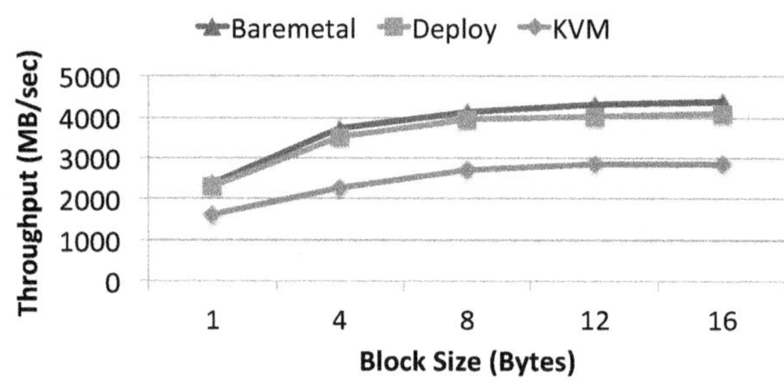

Figure 9. Memory performance

5.5.1 Thread and Memory Benchmark

To evaluate the effect on threads and memory performance, we used SysBench [11]. The thread benchmark repeatedly performed a sequence of acquire-yield-release operations 1,000 times on 8 mutex locks from multiple threads and measures the average execution time. We changed the number of threads from 1 to 24. The memory benchmark repeatedly allocated a memory block and wrote data to the block until the total amount of data written reached 1 MB. We changed the size of memory block from 1 KB to 16 KB. We performed the benchmarks on the bare-metal machine (Baremetal), on BMcast in the deployment phase (Deploy), and on KVM (KVM). We configured KVM to use processor pinning to avoid overhead of scheduling virtual processors, and 2-GB huge paging to reduce overhead of nested paging.

Figure 8 shows the results of the thread benchmark. As the number of threads increased, the overhead of KVM significantly increased (68% on 24 threads). We guess this overhead was incurred by the lock-holder preemption problem [47]; a thread holding a lock was scheduled off from a virtual CPU and other threads must wait until the thread was scheduled back. This virtualization overhead could become a significant problem for highly-concurrent applications. On the other hand, BMcast incurred only moderate overhead (6% on 24 threads) even while streaming OS deployment was in progress. The reason of this was that BMcast traps only minimum events required for streaming OS deployment, and the frequency of VM exits were much lower than conventional VMMs.

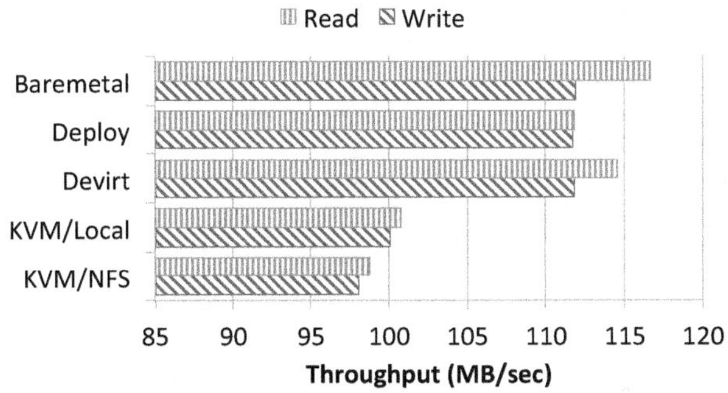

Figure 10. Storage throughput

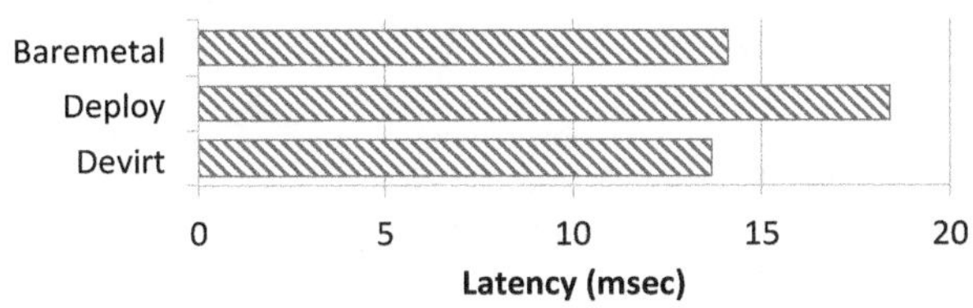

Figure 11. Storage latency

Figure 9 shows the results of the memory benchmark. While the throughput on BMcast incurred only 6% of overhead, KVM incurred 35% of overhead on 16-KB block size. We guess this overhead was caused by the cost of nested paging and cache pollution by the VMM including the host OS. These results confirmed that BMcast incurred low overhead on threads and memory performance during deployment. Note that after de-virtualization, the performance on BMcast became identical to the bare-metal case in both benchmarks.

5.5.2 Storage Benchmark

To evaluate the effects on storage performance, we measured the throughput and latency of disk access on the guest OS. To measure storage throughput, we used Flexible IO Tester (fio) [13] and read 200-MB of data with 1-MB block size using direct I/O and Linux native asynchronous I/O engine (libaio). To measure storage latency, we used ioping [14] and read 1 MB of data 100 times with 4K byte block size. We measured the performance on the bare-metal machine (Baremetal), on BMcast in the deployment phase (Deploy), and on BMcast after the de-virtualization (Devirt). For comparison, we also measured the performance on a network-booted OS (Netboot), on the guest OS on KVM with local disk (KVM/Local), and on that with NFS (KVM/NFS).

Figure 10 shows read & write throughput. On the bare-metal machine, the read and write throughput was 116.6 MB/sec and 111.9 MB/sec, respectively. The read throughput decreased by 4.1% in the Deploy case and 1.7% in the Devirt case. The write throughput was almost the same as the bare-metal case. This result suggests that the moderation of the speed in background copy worked effectively and de-virtualization achieved almost bare-metal performance. On the other hand, KVM decreased the read throughput by 10.5% in KVM/Local and 12.3% in KVM/NFS, and decreased write throughput by 13.6% in KVM/Local and 15.3% in KVM/NFS, respectively. These overhead would be mainly caused by virtual I/O devices.

Figure 11 shows storage latency. BMcast in the Deploy case increased the average latency by 4.3ms. This increase was for the blocking time in accessing storage devices. As described in Section 3.2, if I/O requests from the VMM are being handled, the requests from the guest OS are queued and blocked. This blocking time was measured as the latency overhead. However, in the Devirt case, there was no latency overhead (actually slightly faster due to a mysterious behavior). In this case, no instructions, except for CPUID, triggered VM exits. The intervals of the CPUID exits ranged from a couple of seconds to minutes, and their overhead was negligible. These results confirmed that BMcast achieved eventual bare-metal storage performance.

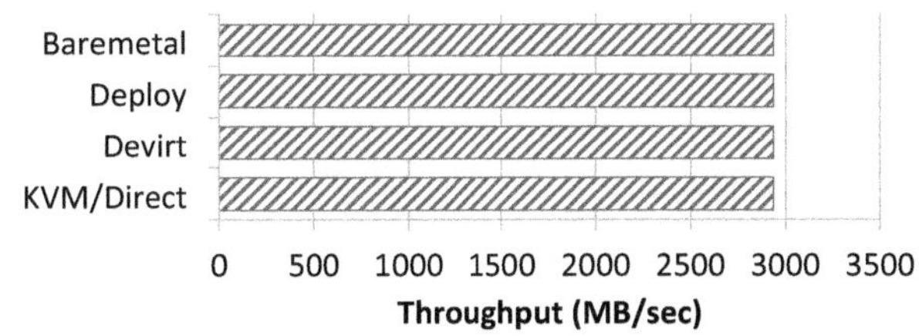

Figure 12. InfiniBand throughput

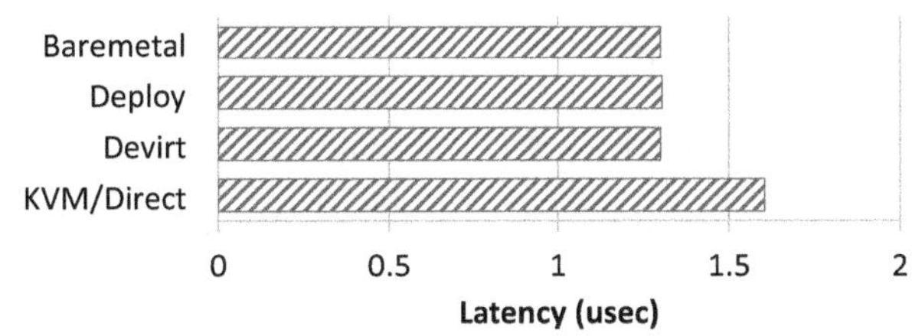

Figure 13. InfiniBand latency

5.5.3 Network Benchmark

To evaluate the effects on network performance, we measured the raw InfiniBand throughput and latency. We used the *ib_rdma_bw* and *ib_rdma_lat* commands in the *perftest* package of the Open Fabrics Enterprise Distribution. These commands sent 64-KB packet 1,000 times and measured the throughput and latency of remote direct memory access (RDMA) over InfiniBand. We measured the performance on the bare-metal machine (Baremetal), on BMcast in the deployment phase (Deploy), on BMcast after de-virtualization (Devirt), and on KVM with direct device assignment (KVM/Direct).

Figure 12 shows the throughput and Figure 13 shows the latency. In our environment, there was no difference

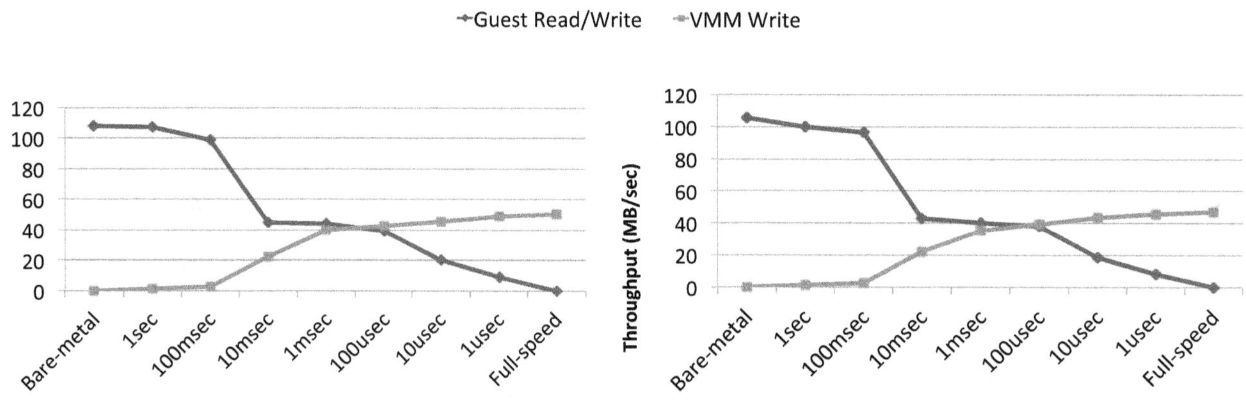

(a) Guest-read and VMM-write I/O throughput

(b) Guest-write and VMM-write I/O throughput

Figure 14. Guest and VMM I/O throughput with changing the intervals of the VMM writes

in throughput. At this time, CPU utilization was very low. This means that network was saturated, and the virtualization overhead was hidden by the command queuing of the RDMA hardware. However, KVM increased the latency by 23.6%. The cause of this would be the overhead of Intel's input/output memory management unit (IOMMU), cache pollution, and nested paging. This overhead become a significant problem in latency-sensitive applications. On the other hand, BMcast incurred negligible overhead (less than 1%). Therefore, these results confirmed that BMcast achieved bare-metal performance in the InfiniBand environment.

5.6 Moderation of Background Copy

In the deployment phase, BMcast moderates the speed of background copy by adjusting the interval between each block write. To clarify the relationship between the interval and the storage performance of the guest OS, we measured read / write throughput of the guest OS and write throughput of the VMM with changing the intervals of the VMM writes. The block size written by the VMM was 1024 KB.

Figure 14a shows the relationship between read throughput of the guest OS and write throughput of the VMM. Figure 14b shows the relationship between write throughput of the guest OS and that of the VMM. On the both graphs, the left-most bar shows the bare-metal throughput (Bare-metal). We reduced the intervals of VMM writes from 1 sec to 1 μsec exponentially, and finally the VMM issued write requests without intervals (Full-speed).

As the intervals of VMM writes were reduced, the guest throughput gradually decreased, and the VMM write throughput gradually increased. The sum of both throughput did not reach the bare-metal throughput in either case because the VMM used a polling-based storage access, and the guest OS and VMM wrote different regions of the disk that increased seek overhead. Overall, however, the total performance was fairly reasonable, showing that adjusting the write intervals in the VMM was an effective approach to moderating the speed of background copy.

6. Discussion

Dedicated v.s. shared NIC: We made a decision to use a dedicated NIC for the VMM to transfer OS images via network. However, sharing a NIC with the guest OS by using a device mediator is technically possible.

To share a NIC, we create a shadow version of ring buffers. The shadow ring buffers are maintained by the VMM and the pointer to the buffers are set to the physical NIC. The guest ring buffers are maintained by the device driver of the guest OS and their contents are copied to and from the shadow ring buffers by the VMM. To perform the copy on the update of buffers, the VMM virtualizes the registers of head and tail pointers to the ring buffers in the NIC. The VMM interleaves its own network requests with the requests from the guest OS into the shadow ring buffers to share the NIC. Most of housekeeping operations on the NIC are performed by the guest device driver and the VMM needs to perform minimal virtualization operations.

This approach is effective while the guest device driver is working. At the OS boot stage when the network device driver is not initialized yet and the shutdown stage when the driver is already terminated, the VMM must handle the NIC with its own device driver. There is some complication on the transition between the VMM device driver and device mediator. The VMM must temporary virtualize the NIC while the guest device driver is performing the initialization and termination because such operations will stop the NIC and the VMM cannot use the network unless virtualized. However, it is possible to handle this situation by partially virtualizing some of hardware registers. We have implemented device mediators for Intel PRO/1000 and Realtek RTL8169. Another possible approach to sharing a NIC is to exploit virtual functions of SR-IOV.

Nevertheless, we did not choose to use a shared NIC mainly because of the performance reason. For example, using a device mediator in the VMM may increase latency and jitter of the guest network performance. These types of network degradation are undesirable for bare-metal cloud applications because the network tends to be a critical path for the performance of such applications. Moreover, guest network throughput could significantly decrease if applications heavily access the local storage because the guest OS and VMM scrambled for the network bandwidth of the shared NIC. In addition, using the combination of device mediators and device drivers in the VMM a little bit complicates the implementation, as described above. Since it is commonplace for modern server machines to have multiple NICs, we believe using a dedicated NIC is a reasonable design choice.

OS transparency v.s. implementation cost: There may be negative opinions against providing OS transparency in exchange for paying implementation cost of device mediators.

Our emphasis here is that providing OS transparency is very important. If the number of OS types used in bare-metal clouds is small, it is reasonable for cloud providers to prepare pre-configured OS images and customers just use them. However, we believe bare-metal cloud providers should support a wide range OSs to maximize the potential benefits for customers. For example, customers may want to use research kernels, such as multikernels (e.g. Barrelfish [19]), microkernels (e.g. L4 [25]), or library OSs (e.g. Exokernel [26]), for the performance reason. Even if they use Linux or Windows, they may want to use various types, versions, and distributions of such OSs and heavily customize their configuration to take advantage of bare-metal clouds. Installing and maintaining customized drivers for various instances are daunting tasks for both providers and customers. Device mediators are, once implemented in the provider side, beneficial for all (many) customers by removing such tasks.

We also emphasize that the cost of implementing device mediators is not so high. Like device drivers for commodity OSs, device mediators also require device-specific knowledge and implementation cost. However, implementation of device mediators is simpler than that of device drivers because device mediators do not need to handle all I/Os but need to handle only key I/Os which are relevant to I/O redirection and multiplexing. For example, they can basically omit handling operations such as device initialization, power management, revision-specific trivial configuration and workarounds for errata.

In addition to the cost of implementing a single device mediator, the cost of supporting various devices may become a subject of discussion because a device mediator must be implemented for each type of devices. However, we believe this issue is not so critical because the variety of server hardware is limited compared to that of client and can be accommodated by software vendors. For example, VMWare ESXi maintains their own set of device drivers for various server hardware. This means that it is recognized as practical for a VMM vendor to support various server hardware.

Given formal device specifications, automatic synthesis of device mediators is theoretically possible and is a future work for covering various devices with minimal development cost. From a high-level viewpoint, device mediators have similar logic with device drivers in the sense that they perform device-specific operations responding to requests from guest OSs. Therefore, existing techniques for automatic device driver synthesis [42] can be applicable to the development of device mediators. Furthermore, device mediators are independent of OS-specific interfaces and are expected to be synthesized with more simplified method.

Overall, therefore, we believe the merit of providing OS transparency outperforms the cost of implementing device mediators.

7. Conclusion

Bare-metal clouds are an emerging and vital service, but the long startup time of instances has been a crucial limitation in providing agility and elasticity. We proposed BMcast, an OS deployment system with a special-purpose de-virtualizable VMM that supports OS-transparent quick startup of bare-metal instances. BMcast performs low-overhead streaming OS deployment transparently via copy-on-read and background copy to local storage from the server, and then disappears after completing the deployment. To achieve seamless de-virtualization of I/O devices, we introduced device mediators that perform polling-based device-interface-level I/O mediation (I/O interpretation, I/O redirection, and I/O multiplexing), allowing physical devices to be directly exposed to and shared with the guest OS.

We implemented a prototype VMM based on BitVisor that supports device mediators for IDE and AHCI devices, small network device drivers for NICs dedicated for the VMM, and a network-storage protocol that extends the AoE protocol. BMcast can deploy Windows and Linux without any modifications and startup a database instance 8.6 times faster than image copying. The database throughput on BMcast during streaming deployment was comparable to that on KVM with ELI. After de-virtualization, BMcast incurred zero overhead. Therefore, we confirmed that BMcast achieved quick startup of bare-metal instances, seamless de-virtualization, and eventual bare-metal performance.

Acknowledgments

We would like to thank the anonymous reviewers for their helpful and constructive comments. We would also like to thank Hideki Eiraku, Tomohiro Kitamura, Katsuya Matsubara, and all others who were involved in the development of BitVisor. This work was partially supported by Adaptable & Seamless Technology Transfer Program through Target-driven R&D (A-STEP) from Japan Science and Technology Agency (JST), JSPS KAKENHI Grant Number 24500031, and Initiative on Promotion of Supercomputing for Young or Women Researchers, Supercomputing Division, Information Technology Center, The University of Tokyo.

References

[1] ELVIS/ELI I/O acceleration code. http://lists.gnu.org/archive/html/qemu-devel/2013-09/msg04610.html.

[2] Facebook: Virtualisation does not scale. http://www.zdnet.com/facebook-virtualisation-does-not-scale-4010021998/.

[3] Containers at scale. https://speakerdeck.com/jbeda/containers-at-scale.

[4] Internap Network Services Corporation. http://www.internap.com/.

[5] Liquid Web Inc. http://www.liquidweb.com/.

[6] OSU Micro-Benchmarks. http://mvapich.cse.ohio-state.edu/benchmarks/.

[7] Openstack. http://www.openstack.org/.

[8] Peer 1 Hosting. http://www.peer1.com/.

[9] Rackspace, Inc. http://www.rackspace.com/.

[10] SoftLayer Technologies, Inc. http://www.softlayer.com/.

[11] Sysbench. https://launchpad.net/sysbench.

[12] Webair Internet Development, Inc. http://www.webair.com/.

[13] fio – Flexible IO Tester. http://git.kernel.dk/?p=fio.git.

[14] ioping. https://code.google.com/p/ioping.

[15] ATA over Ethernet Tools. http://aoetools.sourceforge.net/.

[16] M. Aron and P. Druschel. Soft Timers: Efficient Microsecond Software Timer Support for Network Processing. *ACM Transactions on Computer Systems (TOCS)*, 18(3):197–228, Aug. 2000.

[17] P. Barham, B. Dragovic, K. Fraser, S. Hand, T. Harris, A. Ho, R. Neugebauer, I. Pratt, and A. Warfield. Xen and the Art of Virtualization. In *Proceedings of the 19th ACM Symposium on Operating Systems Principles*, SOSP '03, pages 164–177, Oct. 2003.

[18] S. K. Barker and P. Shenoy. Empirical Evaluation of Latency-sensitive Application Performance in the Cloud. In *Proceedings of the 1st annual ACM SIGMM Conference on Multimedia Systems*, MMSys '10, pages 35–46, Feb. 2010.

[19] A. Baumann, P. Barham, P.-E. Dagand, T. Harris, R. Isaacs, S. Peter, T. Roscoe, A. Schüpbach, and A. Singhania. The Multikernel: A New OS Architecture for Scalable Multicore Systems. In *Proceedings of the ACM SIGOPS 22nd Symposium on Operating Systems Principles*, SOSP '09, pages 29–44, Oct. 2009.

[20] M. Ben-Yehuda, M. D. Day, Z. Dubitzky, M. Factor, N. Har'El, A. Gordon, A. Liguori, O. Wasserman, and B.-A. Yassour. The Turtles Project: Design and Implementation of Nested Virtualization. In *Proceedings of the 9th USENIX Conference on Operating Systems Design and Implementation*, OSDI'10, pages 423–436, Oct. 2010.

[21] R. Bhargava, B. Serebrin, F. Spadini, and S. Manne. Accelerating Two-Dimensional Page Walks for Virtualized Systems. In *Proceedings of the 13th International Conference on Architectural Support for Programming Languages and Operating Systems*, ASPLOS XIII, pages 26–35, Mar. 2008.

[22] R. Chandra, N. Zeldovich, C. Sapuntzakis, and M. S. Lam. The Collective: A Cache-Based System Management Architecture. In *Proceedings of the 2nd Symposium on Networked Systems Design and Implementation (NSDI)*, pages 259–272, May 2005.

[23] B. F. Cooper, A. Silberstein, E. Tam, R. Ramakrishnan, and R. Sears. Benchmarking Cloud Serving Systems with YCSB. In *Proceedings of the 1st ACM symposium on Cloud Computing*, SoCC '10, pages 143–154, June 2010.

[24] C. David, G.-E. Luis, and R. Sean. OS Streaming Deployment. In *Proceedings of the 29th IEEE International Performance Computing and Communications Conference (IPCCC)*, pages 169 –179, Dec. 2010.

[25] K. Elphinstone and G. Heiser. From L3 to seL4 What Have We Learnt in 20 Years of L4 Microkernels? In *Proceedings of the 24th ACM Symposium on Operating Systems Principles*, SOSP '13, pages 133–150, Nov. 2013.

[26] D. R. Engler, M. F. Kaashoek, and J. O'Toole, Jr. Exokernel: An Operating System Architecture for Application-level Resource Management. In *Proceedings of the 15th ACM Symposium on Operating Systems Principles*, SOSP '95, pages 251–266, Dec. 1995.

[27] A. Gordon, N. Amit, N. Har'El, M. Ben-Yehuda, A. Landau, A. Schuster, and D. Tsafrir. ELI: Bare-metal Performance for I/O Virtualization. In *Proceedings of the 17th International Conference on Architectural Support for Programming Languages and Operating Systems*, ASPLOS XVII, pages 411–422, Mar. 2012.

[28] Internap, Inc. Cloud Landscape Report: Price & Performance Obstacles Surface for Fast, Big Data Applications, Jan 2014.

[29] A. Iosup, S. Ostermann, N. Yigitbasi, R. Prodan, T. Fahringer, and D. Epema. Performance Analysis of Cloud Computing Services for Many-Tasks Scientific Computing. *IEEE Transactions on Parallel and Distributed Systems*, 22(6):931–945, June 2011.

[30] E. Keller, J. Szefer, J. Rexford, and R. B. Lee. NoHype: Virtualized Cloud Infrastructure without the Virtualization. In *Proceedings of the 37th Annual International Symposium on Computer Architecture*, ISCA '10, pages 350–361, June 2010.

[31] A. Kivity. kvm: the Linux Virtual Machine Monitor. In *Proceedings of the 2007 Ottawa Linux Symposium*, pages 225–230, July 2007.

[32] T. Kooburat and M. Swift. The Best of Both Worlds with On-Demand Virtualization. In *Proceedings of the 13th Workshop on Hot Topics in Operating Systems*, HotOS XIII, May 2011.

[33] A. Lakshman and P. Malik. Cassandra: A Decentralized Structured Storage System. *ACM SIGOPS Operating Systems Review*, 44(2):35–40, Apr. 2010.

[34] D. E. Lowell, Y. Saito, and E. J. Samberg. Devirtualizable Virtual Machines Enabling General, Single-node, Online Maintenance. In *Proceedings of the 11th International Conference on Architectural Support for Programming Languages and Operating Systems*, ASPLOS XI, pages 211–223, Oct. 2004.

[35] M. Mao and M. Humphrey. A Performance Study on the VM Startup Time in the Cloud. In *Proceedings of the IEEE 5th International Conference on Cloud Computing*, pages 423–430, June 2012.

[36] J. C. Mogul, J. Mudigonda, J. R. Santos, and Y. Turner. The NIC Is the Hypervisor: Bare-Metal Guests in IaaS Clouds. In *Proceedings of the 14th USENIX Conference on Hot Topics in Operating Systems*, HotOS XIV, May 2013.

[37] V. Nae, R. Prodan, T. Fahringer, and A. Iosup. The Impact of Virtualization on the Performance of Massively Multiplayer Online Games. In *Proceedings of the 8th Annual Workshop on Network and Systems Support for Games*, NetGames '09, page 9, Nov. 2009.

[38] S. Ostermann, A. Iosup, N. Yigitbasi, R. Prodan, T. Fahringer, and D. Epema. A Performance Analysis of EC2 Cloud Computing Services for Scientific Computing. In *Cloud Computing*, volume 34 of *Lecture Notes of the Institute for Computer Sciences, Social-Informatics and Telecommunications Engineering*, pages 115–131. Springer Berlin Heidelberg, 2010.

[39] H. Raj and K. Schwan. High Performance and Scalable I/O Virtualization via Self-Virtualized Devices. In *Proceedings of the 16th International Symposium on High Performance Distributed Computing*, HPDC '07, pages 179–188, June 2007.

[40] K. Razavi and T. Kielmann. Scalable Virtual Machine Deployment Using VM Image Caches. In *Proceedings of the International Conference on High Performance Computing, Networking, Storage and Analysis*, SC '13, page 65, Nov. 2013.

[41] T. Ristenpart, E. Tromer, H. Shacham, and S. Savage. Hey, You, Get off of My Cloud: Exploring Information Leakage in Third-party Compute Clouds. In *Proceedings of the 16th ACM Conference on Computer and Communications Security*, CCS '09, pages 199–212, 2009.

[42] L. Ryzhyk, P. Chubb, I. Kuz, E. Le Sueur, and G. Heiser. Automatic Device Driver Synthesis with Termite. In *Proceedings of the ACM SIGOPS 22nd Symposium on Operating Systems Principles*, SOSP '09, pages 73–86, Oct. 2009.

[43] B. C. S. Hopkins. AoE (ATA over Ethernet). February 2009.

[44] A. Seshadri, M. Luk, N. Qu, and A. Perrig. SecVisor: A Tiny Hypervisor to Provide Lifetime Kernel Code Integrity for Commodity OSes. In *Proceedings of the 21st ACM Symposium on Operating Systems Principles*, SOSP '07, pages 335–350, Oct. 2007.

[45] J. Shafer. I/O Virtualization Bottlenecks in Cloud Computing Today. In *Proceedings of the Second Workshop on I/O Virtualization*, WIOV'10, Mar. 2010.

[46] T. Shinagawa, H. Eiraku, K. Tanimoto, K. Omote, S. Hasegawa, T. Horie, M. Hirano, K. Kourai, Y. Oyama, E. Kawai, K. Kono, S. Chiba, Y. Shinjo, and K. Kato. BitVisor: A Thin Hypervisor for Enforcing I/O Device Security. In *Proceedings of the 2009 ACM SIGPLAN/SIGOPS International Conference on Virtual Execution Environments*, VEE '09, pages 121–130, Mar. 2009.

[47] V. Uhlig, J. LeVasseur, E. Skoglund, and U. Dannowski. Towards Scalable Multiprocessor Virtual Machines. In *Proceedings of the 3rd Virtual Machine Research And Technology Symposium*, pages 43 – 56, May 2004.

[48] G. Wang and T. S. E. Ng. The Impact of Virtualization on Network Performance of Amazon EC2 Data Center. In *Proceedings of the 29th IEEE International Conference on Computer Communications*, INFOCOM 2010, pages 1163–1171, Mar. 2010.

[49] P. Willmann, J. Shafer, D. Carr, A. Menon, S. Rixner, A. L. Cox, and W. Zwaenepoel. Concurrent Direct Network Access for Virtual Machine Monitors. In *Proceedings of the IEEE 13th International Symposium on High Performance Computer Architecture*, HPCA '07, pages 306–317, Feb. 2007.

[50] F. Zhang, J. Chen, H. Chen, and B. Zang. CloudVisor: Retrofitting Protection of Virtual Machines in Multi-tenant Cloud with Nested Virtualization. In *Proceedings of the 23rd ACM Symposium on Operating Systems Principles*, SOSP '11, pages 203–216, Oct. 2011.

Few-to-Many: Incremental Parallelism for Reducing Tail Latency in Interactive Services *

Md E. Haque† Yong hun Eom‡ Yuxiong He*
Sameh Elnikety* Ricardo Bianchini†* Kathryn S. McKinley*

†Rutgers University ‡University of California, Irvine *Microsoft Research
mdhaque@cs.rutgers.edu yeom@uci.edu {yuxhe,samehe,ricardob,mckinley}@microsoft.com

Abstract

Interactive services, such as Web search, recommendations, games, and finance, must respond quickly to satisfy customers. Achieving this goal requires optimizing *tail* (e.g., 99th+ percentile) latency. Although every server is multicore, parallelizing individual requests to reduce tail latency is challenging because (1) service demand is unknown when requests arrive; (2) blindly parallelizing all requests quickly oversubscribes hardware resources; and (3) parallelizing the numerous short requests will not improve tail latency.

This paper introduces Few-to-Many (FM) *incremental parallelization*, which dynamically increases parallelism to reduce tail latency. FM uses request service demand profiles and hardware parallelism in an offline phase to compute a policy, represented as an interval table, which specifies when and how much software parallelism to add. At runtime, FM adds parallelism as specified by the interval table indexed by dynamic system load and request execution time progress. The longer a request executes, the more parallelism FM adds. We evaluate FM in Lucene, an open-source enterprise search engine, and in Bing, a commercial Web search engine. FM improves the 99th percentile response time up to 32% in Lucene and up to 26% in Bing, compared to prior state-of-the-art parallelization. Compared to running requests sequentially in Bing, FM improves tail latency by a factor of two. These results illustrate that incremental parallelism is a powerful tool for reducing tail latency.

Categories and Subject Descriptors D.4.1 [*Operating Systems*]: Process Management–Threads

* Haque and Eom contributed equally to this work as interns at Microsoft Research.

ASPLOS '15, March 14–18, 2015, Istanbul, Turkey..
Copyright © 2015 ACM 978-1-4503-2835-7/15/03... $15.00.
http://dx.doi.org/10.1145/2694344.2694384

Keywords Dynamic Parallelism; Interactive Services; Multithreading; Tail Latency; Thread Scheduling; Web Search

1. Introduction

Interactive online services, such as Web search, financial trading, games, and online social networks require consistently low response times to attract and retain users [14, 33]. Interactive service providers therefore define strict targets for *tail latencies* — 99th percentile or higher response times [9, 10, 17, 39] to deliver consistently fast responses to user requests. The lower the tail latency, the more competitive the service. Moreover, reducing each server's tail latency is critical when a request spans several servers and responses are aggregated from these servers. In this case, the slower servers typically dominate the response time [22].

Reducing tail latency is challenging, in part because requests exhibit highly variable demand. For example in finance servers and Web search, most user search requests are short, but a significant percentage are long [9, 17, 32]. Prior work on search engines shows that in a distributed system, the longest requests (99th-percentile execution times) are up to a factor of 10× larger than the average execution times, and even 100× larger than the median [9, 19]. While other sources of variability, such as interference from other workloads, hardware variability, and network congestion, contribute to tail latency, this prior work establishes long requests in computationally intensive workloads are a primary factor in tail latency. A critical component of reducing tail latency is reducing the execution time of long requests.

This paper shows how to reduce tail latency with the judicious use of parallelism at the level of an individual request. We exploit the opportunity afforded by multicore hardware and parallelism in these applications. However, simply parallelizing all requests oversubscribes multicore resources, degrading average and tail latency on search workloads. We therefore seek to parallelize only the long requests, which contribute the most to tail latency. However, when a request arrives, we do not know its service demand (and it is difficult to predict if the request is short or long [26]). Thus, we determine demand as the request executes. We introduce *incremental* parallelism to reduce tail latency, which dynamically adds parallelism to an individual request based on the requests' progress and the system load.

Few-to-Many (FM) incremental parallelization targets interactive services. It progressively increases parallelism by increasing the number of worker threads for a request, from 1 to a given maximum, over the duration of its execution. Short requests execute sequentially, saving resources, and long requests execute in parallel, reducing tail latency. The key challenge for dynamic parallelization is determining *when* to increase the parallelism and by *how much*, as a function of hardware resources, parallelism efficiency, dynamic load, and individual request progress.

FM has an offline and an online phase. The offline phase takes as input a demand profile of requests with (1) their individual sequential and parallel execution times, and (2) hardware parallelism (core resources). We perform a scalability analysis to determine a maximum degree of software parallelism to introduce. Although the individual requests submitted to a service change frequently, the demand profile of these requests changes slowly [26, 32], making periodic offline or online processing practical. The offline phase computes a set of schedules that specify a time and degree of parallelism to introduce based on dynamic load and request progress. The algorithm that produces these schedules seeks to fully utilize available hardware parallelism at all loads. At low load, FM aggressively parallelizes requests. At moderate to high load, FM runs short requests sequentially and incrementally adds parallelism to long requests to reduce their tail latency. Online, each request self-schedules, adding parallelism to itself based on its current progress and the instantaneous system load. Decentralized self-scheduling limits its synchronization costs and therefore improves scalability.

We implement FM in Lucene, an open-source Enterprise search engine, and Microsoft Bing, a commercial Web search engine. On production request traces and service demand profiles, FM reduces tail latency significantly. We compare FM to fixed parallelism polices on a single server and explore sensitivity to load and workload. FM improves the 99th percentile latency by 32% in Lucene and 26% in Bing, compared to state-of-the-art search parallelization techniques [18, 19] because it dynamically adapts to instantaneous load. Compared to sequential processing, incremental parallelization reduces tail latency on a single server by a factor of two. Bing engineers have already deployed incremental parallelization on thousands of production servers.

Our results have implications for the total cost of ownership (TCO) of large services. Given a target tail latency, FM allows higher utilization of servers while meeting the latency target. This higher utilization allows service providers to reduce their infrastructure costs. For example, our Bing results show that the provider can leverage FM to service the same user load with 42% fewer servers. This result is significant because the infrastructure TCO of commercial services is typically dominated by the cost of purchasing servers [9, 15].

This paper makes the following contributions.

- We introduce Few-to-Many (FM) incremental parallelization for interactive services.
- We develop an FM scheduler that determines when and how much parallelism to introduce based on maximum software parallelism, hardware parallelism, dynamic load, and individual request progress to optimize tail latency.
- We evaluate our approach in open-source and commercial search engines, using production workloads and service demand profiles.
- We show substantial improvements in tail latency over prior parallelization approaches that improve users' experiences and reduce service providers' infrastructure cost.

Although we evaluate FM on search, the results apply to other interactive services, such as online ads, financial recommendations, and games, that are computationally intensive, have stable workload distributions, and are easy to parallelize incrementally [13, 21].

2. Background

This section overviews the characteristics and parallelism opportunities of interactive services. It also discusses the production service demand distributions and scalability characteristics of our workloads. Section 3 shows how we exploit these characteristics to reduce tail latency.

Characteristics Many interactive services, such as search, financial trading, games, and social networking are *computationally intensive* [1, 13, 18, 28, 32]. To meet stringent latency constraints, they are carefully engineered such that (1) their working set fits in memory, since any disk access may compromise responsiveness, and (2) although they may frequently access memory, they are not memory-bandwidth constrained.

As an example, consider Web search, which divides the work among many worker servers that compute over a subset of the data, and then a few servers aggregate the responses [3, 6]. In Bing Web search, each worker server has 10s of GBs of DRAM used for caching a partition of the inverted index that maps search keywords to Web documents. This cache is designed to limit disk I/O [18]: the average amount of disk I/O is less than 0.3 KB/s. To attain responsiveness and avoid queuing delay, Bing provisions additional servers to ensure that workers operate at low to modest loads [18]. The average queuing delay at a worker is 0.35 ms even with high 70% CPU utilization. Network I/O is also a small fraction of the overall request latency at 2.13 ms on average. CPU computation is the largest fraction of response time at well over 70% and is even higher for long queries. Consequently, reducing tail latency requires reducing compute time.

Opportunity for parallelism Interactive services today commonly exploit large-scale parallelism in two ways. (1) They distribute the processing over hundreds or thousands of servers at data center scale because they must process requests over vast amounts of data that do not fit on a single server. (2) At each server, they process multiple requests concurrently. In this paper, we exploit parallelism in a third complementary way. We explore intra-request parallelism on a multicore server. In particular, we execute individual requests using concurrent threads on multiple cores to reduce their execution time. Prior work demonstrates that individual requests in interactive systems, such as search, finance trading, and games are easily parallelized [13, 18]. In addition, these workloads are often amenable to dynamic parallelism, in which the scheduler can vary the number of worker threads per request during the request execution. Dynamic parallelism is supported by many parallel libraries and runtimes, such as Cilk Plus [5], TBB [7], TPL [25], and Java [12]. We introduce *incremental parallelism*, a new form of dynamic parallelism that incrementally increases the parallelism degree for individual requests. Section 6.1 and 7.1 demonstrate how to implement incremental parallelism on enterprise search and Web search services.

Demand distributions and scalability To motivate our approach, we study the demand distributions and scalability of Lucene and Bing, our two evaluation systems. However, our approach is more generally applicable than these workloads, because other interactive services have similar demand and parallelism characteristics [13, 21]. We gather production user requests for both Bing and Lucene and measure the sequential and parallel execution times for each request executing alone on a single server. (Sections 6 and 7 describe the methodologies and systems in more detail.)

Figure 1(a) shows the service demand distribution of 30K requests for the Bing Index Server Nodes (ISN). The x-axis is the execution time in 5 ms bins and y-axis is the frequency of requests in each bin. Most requests are short, with more than 85% taking below 15 ms. A few requests are very long, up to 200 ms. The gap between the median and the 99th percentile is a factor of 27×. The slight rise in frequency at 200 ms is because the server terminates any request at 200 ms and returns its partial results. We observe that these workload characteristics are fairly consistent across hundreds of ISN servers with different partitions of the index.

Figure 1(b) presents Bing parallelism efficiency, i.e., the speedup of requests with different parallelization degrees for all requests, the longest 5%, and the shortest 5%. Long requests have over 2 times speedup with 3 threads. In contrast, short requests have limited speedup, a factor of 1.2 with 3 threads. These results show that at degrees higher than 4, additional parallelism does not lead to speed up.

Similarly, Figure 2(a) shows the service demand histogram of 10K Wikipedia search requests for Lucene in 20 ms bins and Figure 2(b) shows the parallelism efficiency.

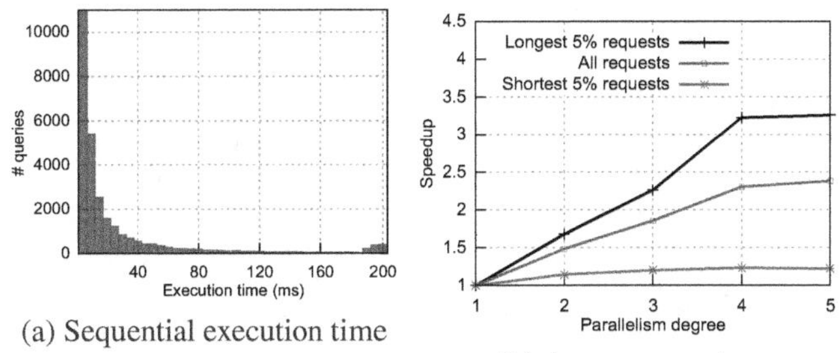

(a) Sequential execution time histogram of 30K requests

(b) Average speedup

Figure 1: Bing demand distribution and average speedup.

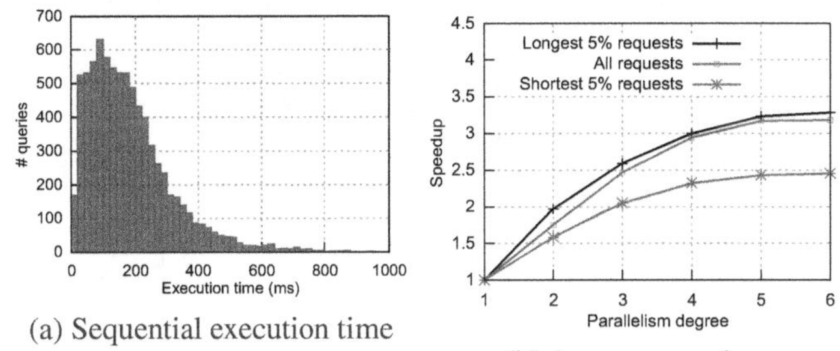

(a) Sequential execution time histogram of 10K requests

(b) Average speedup

Figure 2: Lucene demand distribution and average speedup.

Again, we observe many short requests and few long requests. The maximum number of requests are in the bin around 90 ms and the median service demand is 186 ms. Since the ratio of short to long requests is high, parallelizing the long requests has the potential to reduce tail latency. Figure 2(b) shows that on average, requests exhibit almost linear speedup for parallelism degree 2. Parallelism is slightly less effective for 2 to 4 degrees and is not effective for 5 or more degrees.

Both workloads show diminishing effectiveness of parallelism and motivates limiting the maximum degree of parallelism. Both also show that parallelism is most effective on long requests, which suggests devoting parallel hardware resources to long requests instead of short ones. Moreover, long requests impact tail latency the most.

3. Rationale Behind FM Parallelism

This section discusses the intuition and theory behind FM incremental parallelism and requirements for implementing it effectively.

3.1 Intuition Behind FM Incremental Parallelism

A simple approach to using intra-request parallelism is to use a fixed number of worker threads for each request. Depending on the number of threads per request, *fixed* parallelism would either oversubscribe resources at high systems loads or underutilize them under light loads. To see an example of oversubscription and its impact on response times, consider Figure 3. The figure shows the mean and 99th percentile response times of Lucene as a function of load when all requests run with 1 worker thread (SEQ) and 4 worker threads (FIX-4). (See Section 6 for our methodology.) Clearly, using

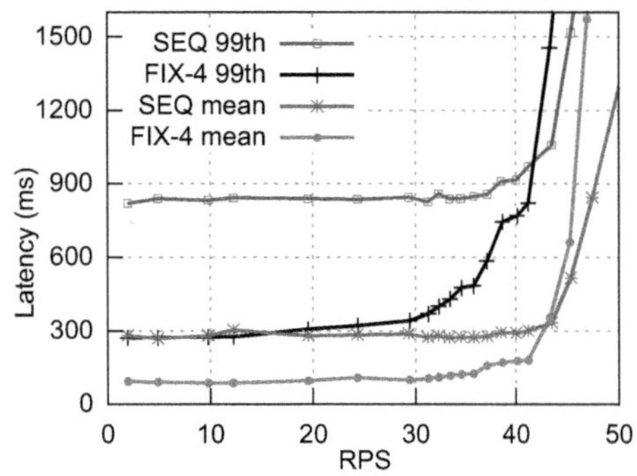

Figure 3: Effect of fixed parallelism on latency in Lucene.

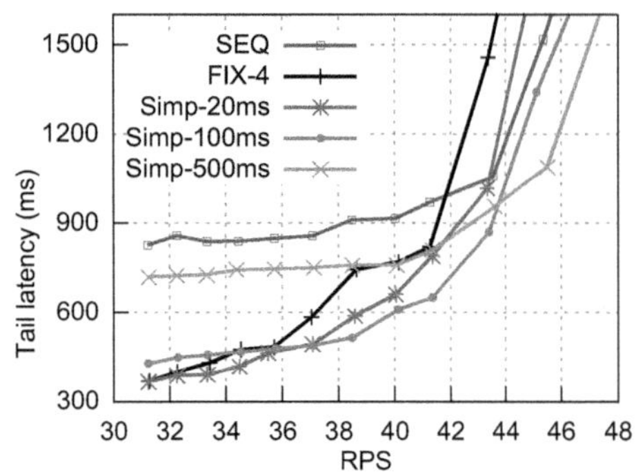

Figure 4: 99th percentile tail latency of sequential, degree 4, and simple fixed addition of dynamic parallelism in Lucene.

4 threads for all requests reduces tail latency well with low load, but gets progressively worse with higher load. In fact, using 4 threads becomes worse than 1 thread around 42 requests per second (RPS). Henceforth, we focus on the range 30 to 48 RPS, since the latency is typically flat below 30 RPS and too high beyond 48 RPS.

Another problem with fixed parallelism is that it targets all requests equally. However, long requests have a greater impact on tail latency than short ones. We prefer to parallelize long requests, but it is difficult to predict if a request will be long or short [26]. Fortunately, requests in many interactive services are amenable to *incremental* parallelization. By dynamically increasing the degree of parallelism as a request executes, long requests will exploit more parallelism than short requests. This insight is the key rationale behind FM incremental parallelization.

3.2 Theoretical Foundation of FM Parallelization

Intuitively, FM parallelization increases the probability that short requests will finish with less parallelism, which saves resources, while it assigns long requests more parallelism, which reduces tail latency. This section presents the theoretical foundation behind this intuition. Theorem 1 shows that, given a tail latency constraint, the optimal policy that minimizes average resource usage assigns parallelism to requests in non-decreasing order. In other words, to minimize resource usage under a latency constraint, if a request ever changes its parallelism, it will only increase, transitioning from *few to many* degrees of parallelism. The theorem makes two assumptions. (1) We do not know if a request is long or short a priori, but we know the service demand distribution, i.e., the distribution of *sequential* request execution times (see Figure 2(a) for an example). (2) Each request exhibits sublinear speedup, i.e., parallelism efficiency decreases with increase in parallelism degree, as we showed in the previous section and is true for many workloads.

THEOREM 1. *Given a request service demand distribution and a sublinear parallelism speedup function, to meet a tail latency constraint, an optimal policy that minimizes average resource usage assigns parallelism to requests in non-decreasing order.*

Proof. Please see Appendix. ■

Intuitively, Theorem 1 means that given an optimal schedule that first adds and then removes parallelism, there exists an equivalent schedule which only adds parallelism. We exploit this theorem to limit our offline search to finding an optimal few-to-many schedule. The dual problem of Theorem 1 also holds: given a fixed amount of resources, few-to-many minimizes latency. For a server system where each request gets a limited amount of resources, FM minimizes tail latency.

3.3 Practical and Effective FM Parallelization

The simplest approach to incremental parallelism is to simply add parallelism periodically, e.g., add one thread to each request after a fixed time interval. Unfortunately, this approach does a poor job of controlling the total parallelism (resource usage and contention), regardless of the interval length. Figure 4 illustrates this problem by comparing the 99th percentile tail latency of Lucene when simply adding parallelism at fixed 20, 100, and 500 ms intervals with executing each request with 1 thread and 4 threads, as a function of load. The figure shows that increasing parallelism dynamically does reduce tail latency more than fixed parallelism at medium and high loads. Short requests use fewer than 4 threads, and thus limit oversubscription of resources. However, no fixed interval is ideal across the entire load spectrum. The shorter the interval, the higher the tail latency at high load. Conversely, the longer the interval, the higher the tail latency at low load. These results suggest that FM parallelization can be effective, but to select intervals correctly FM must carefully consider the system load. Fundamentally, the main requirements for effective incremental parallelization are the following.

FM scheduling must efficiently utilize resources. When the load is low (no resource contention), FM should be aggressive and choose shorter intervals to better utilize the hardware resources. At high load (high contention), it must be conservative and choose longer intervals to apply parallelism more selectively to just the longest requests. We observe that maintaining a fixed overall number of software threads is a good way to control hardware resource utilization as the load varies.

FM scheduling must consider workload characteristics. FM must consider the distribution of the service demand. For example, if the vast majority of requests take less than 100 ms, an interval of 100 ms will not exploit much parallelism. Moreover, FM must consider any overhead due to parallelism. With lower overhead, we choose smaller intervals, parallelizing requests more aggressively. With higher overhead, we choose larger intervals, parallelizing requests more conservatively to avoid wasting resources.

FM scheduling must consider scalability of the workload. When speedups tail off at high degrees, adding more parallelism is a less effective use of hardware resources. FM thus limits parallelism to an effective maximum.

4. Few-to-Many Incremental Parallelization

This section describes Few-to-Many (FM) incremental parallelization for a single server. Our goal is to reduce tail latency. The FM scheduler achieves this goal by exploiting all hardware parallelism and judiciously adding software parallelism. FM has two phases. (1) An offline analysis phase produces an *interval table.* (2) An online dynamic phase schedules requests by indexing the interval table. FM computes the interval table offline using as inputs the maximum software parallelism per request, hardware parallelism, and service demand profiles of sequential and parallel execution times. The interval table specifies when during the execution of a request to add parallelism and how much, as a function of load and request progress. At runtime, the service demand of each request is unknown. FM thus monitors the progress of each request and the total load, and then at the specified intervals, it adds software parallelism to the request. FM is decentralized and each request self-schedules. FM aggressively introduces parallelism under light load, but under high load, it makes efficient use of resources by judiciously executing short requests sequentially and long requests in parallel. The following key insights lead to an efficient solution.

Favoring long requests FM gives more parallelism to long requests. At moderate to high loads, FM assigns only one thread to each new request. Short requests thus execute sequentially, only ever consuming one thread. As long requests continue to execute, FM assigns them more parallelism (software threads). FM performs admission control. At moderate to high load, it may delay adding a new request in favor of adding parallelism to existing requests. Since new requests are more likely short, FM optimizes for tail latency.

Judicious use of hardware parallelism FM explicitly controls total load, neither undersubscribing nor oversubscribing hardware resources. Undersubscribing causes resources to needlessly sit idle when they could be reducing tail latency. Oversubscribing increases contention and thus tail latency, since independent requests and parallel tasks within the same request may interfere, competing for the same resources. Thus, FM slightly oversubscribes the hardware, because threads may occasionally block for synchronization or more rarely I/O. When software parallelism (threads) on occasion exceeds the hardware parallelism (cores), we boost the oldest threads priorities, so they complete without interference from younger requests. FM thus matches software parallelism to hardware parallelism.

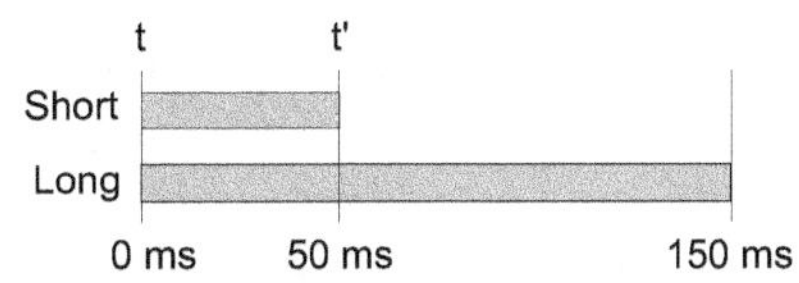

q_r	t	t'
≤ 2	$0, d_3$	
3	$0, d_1$	$50, d_3$
4–6	$50, d_1$	$100, d_3$
≥ 7	e_1, d_1	$100, d_3$

Figure 5: Simple workload and interval table for 50 ms intervals ($t = 0, t' = 50$), number of requests (q_r), parallelism degree (d_j), for 6 cores with speedups $s(2) = 1.5$, $s(3) = 2$.

Judicious use of software parallelism Since parallelism introduces overhead and has diminishing returns, the degree to which software parallelism can reduce tail latency is a function of the service, hardware, and workload. Based on workload speedup efficiency, the service provider specifies a maximum amount of software parallelism per request that will deliver a target tail latency.

4.1 Offline Analysis

Our offline analysis takes as input a request demand profile, maximum software parallelism, and target hardware parallelism. It outputs an *interval table* indexed by load and each request's current processing time.

Example Consider the simple example in Figure 5 that uses the notation defined in Table 1. Short and long requests occur with equal probability. The sequential execution time of short requests is 50 ms and long requests is 150 ms. With parallelism degree 3, both short and long requests obtain a speedup of 2. Assume 6 cores for hardware parallelism and 50 ms intervals for simplicity. The resulting interval table consists of 4 rows indexed by the number of instantaneous requests q_r. For 1 or 2 requests, the pair $t = 0, d_3$ specifies that at time $t = 0$ every request starts immediately with parallelism d_3 degree 3, resulting in tail latency of 75 ms for long requests. Average total parallelism is 3 times active requests q_r. If $q_r = 3$, then $t = 0, d_1$, so short requests run sequentially. With $t' = 50, d_3$, long requests run sequentially until 50 ms, when parallelism degree increases to 3. Long requests finish 50 ms later with a speedup of 2 and a tail latency of 100 ms. The average parallelism per request is $(1 \times 50 + 1 \times 50 + 3 \times 50)/(50 + 100) = 1.67$ since the numbers of short and long requests are equal. With 7 or more requests ($q_r \geq 7$), $t = e_1, d_1$ indicates that new requests must wait until another request exits and then start executing sequentially.

Interval table Formally, we compute a function $f : \mathcal{R} \to \mathcal{I}$, where $\mathcal{R}$ is the set of all potential instantaneous requests in the system and $\mathcal{I}$ is a table indexed by $q_r \in \mathcal{R}$ with each q_r corresponding to one interval selection (or schedule) Φ. A schedule Φ consists of pairs (t_i, d_j), which specify that at load q_r when a request reaches time t_i, execute it with parallelism degree d_j. If $t_0 = 0$, the request immediately starts executing. If $t_0 > 0$, the interval table is specifying admission control and the request must wait to begin its execution until the specified time. If $t_0 = e_1$, the request must wait until another request exits to begin its execution. For example, $f(3) = \{(t_0 = 0, d_1), (t_1 = 50, d_3)\}$ in Figure 5 specifies that all requests start executing immediately with one thread and after a request executes for 50 ms $(t_1 = 50, d_3)$, all requests execute with 3 degrees of software parallelism. Load changes dynamically at runtime. A particular request will consult different entries in the interval table during its execution.

Interval selection algorithm We formulate interval selection as an offline search problem, which takes as inputs the request demand profile, maximum software parallelism, target hardware parallelism *target*$_p$, and parallelism speedup. The profiled sequential and parallel request demand and parallelism speedup are collected offline. The maximum software parallelism per request is selected based on the parallelism efficiency of requests, to limit the parallelism degree to the amount effective at speeding up long requests. We select the target hardware parallelism *target*$_p$ to moderately oversubscribe the hardware threads through profiling. The search algorithm enumerates potential policies that satisfy *target*$_p$, i.e., schedules that use all available hardware resources, and then chooses ones that minimize tail latency.

To ease the presentation, we introduce an intermediate representation of a schedule as $\mathcal{S} = \{v_0, v_1, ..., v_{n-1}\}$: a request starts its first thread at time v_0, and adds parallelism from d_i to d_{i+1} after interval v_{i+1}. It is easy to see that any schedule Φ has an alternative but equivalent representation as $\mathcal{S}$. For example, for $\Phi = \{(t_0 = 0, d_1), (t_1 = 50, d_3)\}$, the equivalent $\mathcal{S} = \{0, 50, 0\}$ when the maximum software parallelism $n = 3$.

The interval selection algorithm has two parts. First, Figure 6 shows the mathematical formulation for computing parallelism and latency of requests for a given interval selection (schedule) $\mathcal{S}$ and load q_r. Equation (1) computes the total time a request takes given the time it spends in its sequential portion (if any) and time it takes in each parallel interval (if any). Equation (2) computes the request average parallelism under the schedule. Equation (3) computes the total parallelism of the system when there are q_r requests. Equation (4) and Equation (5) calculate the average and tail latency of the requests under the schedule.

Second, we enumerate all loads and all potential schedules, evaluate if they satisfy the parallelism target $target_p$, and compute tail and mean latency. If multiple schedules have the same minimum tail latency, we choose the one that minimizes the mean. Figure 7 shows the pseudocode for this search process. For each potential system load q_r, ranging from one request to the maximum system capacity, we generate all candidate schedules $\mathcal{S}$. Each component interval of a candidate schedule $v_i \in \mathcal{S}$ will take a value from 0 to y, where y is the maximum request length in the workload. We choose the schedules whose total average parallelism of all concurrent requests does not exceed the target hardware parallelism *target*$_p$, so we avoid oversubscribing the system. It is also important algorithmically: the formulation in Figure 6 calculates the request latency assuming all software parallelism nicely maps to hardware resources, which no longer holds when the total software parallelism exceeds $target_p$. Note that we do not need a lower bound on total parallelism. While optimizing tail latency, we will find schedules with total parallelism close to *target*$_p$, maximizing the utilization of all resources to reduce tail latency. Moreover, if we include a lower bound of *target*$_p$, we may not find a feasible schedule to meet it under light load, e.g., there is only one request with maximum software parallelism 4, but *target*$_p$ = 20.

Symbol	Definition
$r \in R$	Request profiles
seq_r	Sequential runtime of request r
d_n	Max degree n of software parallelism
$s_r(d_j)$	Speedup of r with d_j, $j \leq n$, $\forall r,\ s_r(1) = 1$
q_r	Instantaneous number of requests
$target_p$	Target hardware parallelism
$\Phi = \{(t_0, d_j), (t_1, d_{j+1}) ..., (t_k, d_n)\}$,	$t_i < t_{i+1}, d_j < d_{j+1}$ schedule, at t_i increase parallelism to degree d_i
$\mathcal{S} = \{v_0, v_1, ..., v_{n-1}\}$,	intermediate representation of schedule Φ start request at time v_0, and add parallelism d_i to d_{i+1} after interval v_i
$time_r(\mathcal{S})$	Execution time of r with schedule $\mathcal{S}$
$ap_r(\mathcal{S})$	Average parallelism of r with $\mathcal{S}$
$ap_R(\mathcal{S}, q_r)$	Total average parallelism of q_r of R $requests$ with $\mathcal{S}$
$time_R(\mathcal{S}, mean)$	Average latency of requests from R with $\mathcal{S}$
$time_R(\mathcal{S}, \beta - tail)$	β-tail latency of R with $\mathcal{S}$ at 99th-percentile latency with $\beta = 0.99$

Table 1: Symbols and definitions for interval selection.

From Figure 7, we can easily derive the complexity of interval table construction as

$$(y/step)^n \times req_{max} \times |R| \ .$$

This search problem is rather compute intensive. We take several steps to make it faster. First, we search in steps. If a target tail latency is in the range of 100 ms, then we limit the intervals to steps of 10 ms. Second, we only search for intervals in the range of the lifetime of the longest request. For example, when searching for intervals to increase par-

$$\mathit{time}_r(\mathcal{S}) = \tag{1}$$

$$\begin{cases} v_0 + \mathit{seq}_r & \mathit{if}\ \mathit{seq}_r \le v_1 \\ v_0 + v_1 + \frac{\mathit{seq}_r - v_1}{s_r(2)} & \mathit{if}\ v_1 < \mathit{seq}_r \le v_1 + s_r(2) \times v_2 \\ \ldots & \\ \sum_{i=0}^{n-1} v_i + \frac{\mathit{seq}_r - \sum_{i=1}^{n-1} s_r(i) \times v_i}{s_r(n)} & \mathit{if}\ \mathit{seq}_r > \sum_{i=1}^{n-1} s_r(i) \times v_i \end{cases}$$

$$\mathit{ap}_r(\mathcal{S}) = \tag{2}$$

$$\begin{cases} \frac{0 \times v_0 + 1 \times \mathit{seq}_r}{\mathit{time}_r(\mathcal{S})} & \mathit{if}\ \mathit{seq}_r \le v_1 \\ \frac{0 \times v_0 + 1 \times v_1 + 2 \times \frac{\mathit{seq}_r - v_1}{s_r(2)}}{\mathit{time}_r(\mathcal{S})} & \mathit{if}\ v_1 < \mathit{seq}_r \le v_1 + s_r(2) \times v_2 \\ \ldots & \\ \frac{\sum_{i=0}^{n-1} i \times v_i + n \times \frac{\mathit{seq}_r - \sum_{i=1}^{n-1} s_r(i) \times v_i}{s_r(n)}}{\mathit{time}_r(\mathcal{S})} & \mathit{if}\ \mathit{seq}_r > \sum_{i=1}^{n-1} s_r(i) \times v_i \end{cases}$$

$$\mathit{ap}_R(\mathcal{S}, q_r) = \frac{\sum_{r \in R} \mathit{time}_r(\mathcal{S}) \times \mathit{ap}_r(\mathcal{S})}{\sum_{r \in R} \mathit{time}_r(\mathcal{S})} \times q_r \tag{3}$$

$$\mathit{time}_R(\mathcal{S}, \text{mean}) = \frac{\sum_{r \in R} \mathit{time}_r(\mathcal{S})}{|R|} \tag{4}$$

$$\mathit{time}_R(\mathcal{S}, \beta\text{-tail}) = L[\lceil \beta \cdot |R| \rceil], \tag{5}$$

L is execution times $time_r(\mathcal{S})$ of all requests $r \in R$ in non-decreasing order.

Figure 6: Mathematical formulation of average parallelism, mean and tail latency for interval $\mathcal{S}$.

allelism from 1 to 4, we only search where the sum of all 3 intervals is less than the lifetime of a request. Third, if some interval does not satisfy $target_p$ for lower number of requests, it will not satisfy the $target_p$, for any higher number of requests. For accuracy, we use individual request profiles for Bing and Lucene. This process takes about four to six hours, as we process 10K - 100K requests one by one for each schedule. We may further reduce the search time by grouping requests into demand distribution bins with their frequencies, which reduces our computation time to a few minutes. The offline analysis can run daily, weekly, or at any other coarse granularity, as dictated by the characteristics of the workload.

Admission control Optimizing for $target_p$ does not directly control the number of active requests in the system. In particular, at high load, we want to determine whether to admit a request or to increase parallelism of the existing requests. Our search algorithm explicitly explores this case by enumerating non-zero values for the first interval (v_0). Furthermore at very high load, if the search returns the maximum value of $v_0 = y$, then the schedule specifies a new request must wait for one to exit and then starts executing with parallelism degree 1. We denote this schedule as (e_1, d_1) in an interval table.

```
Input: reqmax, Maximum number of simultaneous requests
Input: y, step Maximum time interval and interval step values
for qr := 1 to reqmax step 1 do
    mintl = minml = inf  Minimum tail and mean latency
    result = φ
    for v0 = 0 to y step step do
        for v1 = 0 to y step step do
            ...
            for vn-1 = 0 to y step step do
                S = (v0, v1, ..., vn-1)
                if apR(S, qr) ≤ targetp
                    tail = timeR(S, β-tail)
                    mean = timeR(S, mean)
                    if (tail < mintl) or
                       (tail = mintl & mean < minml)
                        mintl = tail, minml = mean, result = S
    Add result to interval table entry qr
```

Figure 7: Pseudocode for interval table construction.

4.2 Online Scheduling

The online FM scheduler is invoked when new requests enter the system and requests terminate. Each request self-schedules itself periodically based on a scheduling quanta, e.g., every 5 or 10 ms. If FM detects oversubscription of hardware parallelism, it boosts the priority of all the threads executing a long request to insure its quick completion.

FM tracks the load by computing the number of requests in the system in a synchronized variable and uses this number to index the interval table. This simple method has several advantages. First, the number of requests is fast and easy to compute compared to other indicators, such as CPU utilization. Second, in contrast with coarse-grained load indicators, such as RPS, it measures the instantaneous load. FM exploits instantaneous spare resources to avoid transient overloading. Third, FM self-corrects quickly. If the number of requests increases due to transient load, FM will index a higher row in the table, which has larger interval values and will introduce parallelism more conservatively. Similarly, when the number of requests decreases, FM will promptly introduce more parallelism for longer requests, as specified by a lower row in the table, which has shorter intervals.

Each time a request enters, FM computes the load, consults the interval table, and either starts or queues the request. When a request leaves, FM computes the load and starts a queued request (if one exists). After a request starts, it self-schedules, regularly examining the current load and its progress at the periods defined by the scheduling quanta. Each self-scheduling request indexes the interval table by the instantaneous load and if it has reached the next interval, adds parallelism accordingly. We choose relatively short scheduling quanta, less than the interval size in the table, because if requests leave the system, then FM can react quickly to add more parallelism. FM self-scheduling increases scalability of the scheduler by limiting synchronization.

FM will on occasion oversubscribe the hardware resources at high load because we choose a target hardware parallelism that exceeds the number of cores. This choice ensures that FM fully utilizes hardware resources when threads are occasionally blocked on synchronization, I/O, or terminating, but under high load will degrade tail latency if long requests must share resources with short requests. For example, operating systems generally implement a round robin scheduling to give equal resources to all the threads. To mitigate this issue, we implement *selective thread boosting*. Boosting increases the priority of all threads executing a single long request. We ensure that the number of boosted threads is always less than the number of cores by using a synchronized shared variable to count the total number of boosted threads. We only boost a request when increasing its parallelism to the maximum degree and when the resulting total number of boosted threads will be less than the number of cores. This mechanism instructs the OS to schedule these threads whenever they are ready. The longer requests will thus finish faster, which improves tail latency.

5. Evaluation

The next two sections evaluate the FM algorithm in two settings. We implement the offline table construction algorithm using around 100 lines of Python that we use for both systems. We compare both systems to the prior state-of-the-art parallelization approaches and find that FM substantially improves tail latencies over these approaches. We compare FM to the following schedulers.

Sequential (SEQ) Each request executes sequentially.

Fixed parallelism (FIX-N) Each request executes with a predefined fixed parallelism degree of N.

Adaptive (Adaptive) This scheduler [18] selects the parallelism degree for a request based on load when the request first enters the system. The parallelism degree remains constant.

Request Clairvoyant (RC) This scheduler is oracular, because it is given all requests' sequential execution times. It is an upper bound on predictive scheduling [19], which estimates request length. It selects a parallelism degree for long requests when they enter the system based on a threshold and executes other requests sequentially. The parallelism degree is constant.

SEQ and *FIX-N* are reference points, and *Adaptive* is the prior state-of-the-art for exploiting parallelism in interactive services. *RC* assumes perfect prediction of request length, but does not adapt to load. An algorithm for an optimal scheduler is unknown and at least NP hard. It is harder than bin packing, since it may divide jobs. It also requires knowledge of future request arrivals. We configure FM to use instantaneous load and each requests' progress to add parallelism and, when necessary, to use selective thread priority boosting. Because FM dynamically adapts to total load, it is significantly better than RC, which only considers the demand of individual requests when they enter the system.

6. Lucene Enterprise Search

This section presents our experimental evaluation of FM in Lucene. Apache Lucene [1] is an open-source Enterprise search engine. We configure it to execute on a single server with a corpus of 33+ million Wikipedia English Web pages [27, 38]. We use 10K search requests from the Lucene nightly regression tests as input to our offline phase and 2K search requests for running the experiments. While the nightly tests use a range of request types, we use the term requests. The client issues requests in random order following a Poisson distribution in an open loop. We vary the system load by changing the average arrival rate expressed as RPS. The index size is 10 GB and it fits in the memory of our server. Figure 2 shows the service demand distribution and the speedup profile of the workload.

6.1 Methodology

Implementation We execute 10K requests in isolation with different degrees of parallelism and gather their execution times. Each time is an average of at least 10 executions. For a specific parallelism degree, we compute the speedup of all requests and the average speedup across all requests. The sequential execution times and speedups of all requests constitute the input to the offline phase. Since the online module of FM implements admission control and assigns work to threads, we implement it within the Lucene request scheduler. Lucene is implemented in Java and we implement the scheduler in Lucene in roughly 1000 lines of Java code.

We make minor changes to the existing Lucene code base. Lucene arranges its index into segments. To add parallelism, we simply divide up the work for an individual request by these segments. We do *not* change how Lucene's default mechanisms create its index and maintain the segments. We note that this type of data organization is common to many services and makes implementing incremental parallelism simple. We extend Lucene to execute each request in parallel by adding a Java *ExecutorService* instance. We use the *ThreadPoolExecutor* class that implements *ExecutorService* and that configures the number of threads in the thread pool. Each main thread retrieves a request from a shared queue and processes the request. The main thread self-schedules periodically (every 5 ms) and checks the system load. As specified by the interval table, it increases parallelism of a request by adding threads. FM adds a thread by simply changing a field of *ThreadPoolExecutor*. Lucene starts a new thread that works on a new segment and synchronizes it with other worker threads.

Hardware We use a server with two 8-core Intel 64-bit Xeon processors (2.30 GHz) and turn off hyperthreading. (Reasoning about job interference with hyperthreading together with parallelism is beyond the scope of this pa-

n_r	t_0	t_1	t_2	t_3
≤6	0, d_4			
7	0, d_3	75, d_4		
8	0, d_2	25, d_3	150, d_4	
9	0, d_2	50, d_3	150, d_4	
10	0, d_1	25, d_2	100, d_3	175, d_4
11	0, d_1	25, d_2	125, d_3	175, d_4
12	0, d_1	75, d_2	150, d_3	200, d_4
13	0, d_1	100, d_2	175, d_3	225, d_4
14	10, d_1	110, d_2	210, d_3	235, d_4
15	30, d_1	130, d_2	205, d_3	255, d_4
16	40, d_1	140, d_2	240, d_3	265, d_4
17	60, d_1	160, d_2	245, d_3	285, d_4
18	60, d_1	185, d_2	260, d_3	310, d_4
19	70, d_1	195, d_2	270, d_3	320, d_4
20	70, d_1	220, d_2	295, d_3	370, d_4
21	80, d_1	255, d_2	305, d_3	375, d_4
22	80, d_1	280, d_2	330, d_3	380, d_4
23	90, d_1	290, d_2	365, d_3	415, d_4
24	90, d_1	315, d_2	390, d_3	440, d_4
≥25	e_1, d_1	315, d_2	390, d_3	440, d_4

Table 2: Lucene interval table in milliseconds for 99th percentile latency with *target*$_p$ = 24 threads and maximum parallelism $n = 4$. When $t_0 = e1$, FM waits for a request to complete and then admits one waiting request. Each entry specifies execution thus far and parallelism d_k to add.

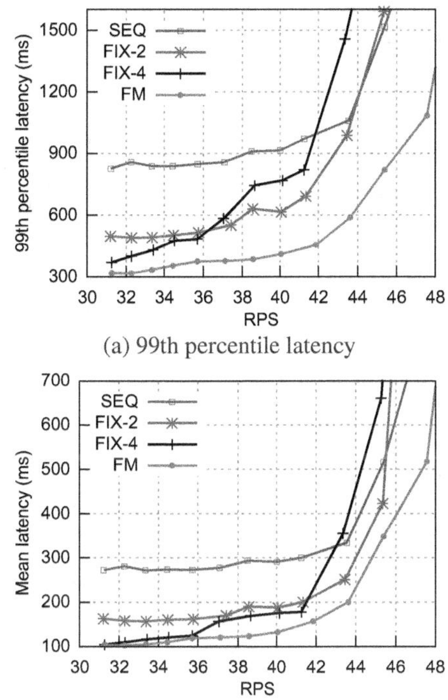

(a) 99th percentile latency

(b) Mean latency

Figure 8: Lucene latency compared to fixed parallelism.

per [32].) The server has 64 GB of memory and runs Windows 8. Out of the available 16 cores, we use 15 cores to run our experiments and 1 core to run the client that generates requests. We empirically set the target hardware parallelism, *target*$_p$ = 24. We explored several values for *target*$_p$ and observed only small differences for *target*$_p \in [20, 28]$.

We report the 99th percentile latency, average latency, and CPU utilization of different policies. Latency includes both queuing delay and execution time. We use Java *NanoTime* for fine-grain time measurements. Our reported tail latency is the 99th percentile of the response times of all requests and the mean is the average response time measured over the 2K requests under various loads.

Interval selection for FM Table 2 shows the intervals generated by the offline phase for a target parallelism of 24. The table is indexed by the number or requests in the system, our metric for system load. Each column shows the time in ms at which FM adds parallelism. We use a step size of 5 ms to generate the interval table. As discussed in Section 4.1, the second column is for admission control. New requests must wait for this time before they start processing. When the load is very low (less than 6 requests), FM starts each request with parallelism degree 4. At other low loads (7 to 13 requests), FM starts a new request whenever it arrives and adds parallelism following the corresponding row. Finally, as load increases (more than 14 requests), FM delays new requests and uses longer intervals to add parallelism.

6.2 Results

Comparison to fixed parallelism policies We compare FM to sequential execution (SEQ) and a fixed degree of parallelism for each request (FIX-2 and FIX-4). Figures 8(a) and 8(b) show the 99th percentile and mean latency. FM has consistently lower tail and average latency than the other policies. At low load, many cores are available; FM is close to but better than FIX-4. Here FM aggressively parallelizes almost all requests with 4 threads (as shown in Table 2, row $n_r <= 6$). Occasional request bursts and short requests reduce intra-request parallelism on occasion even at low load. At high load, FM uses thread boosting and instantaneous load to carefully manage the degree of parallelism per request. At a medium load (40 RPS), FIX-4 is already worse than FIX-2. In contrast, FM reduces the 99th percentile latency by 33% and mean latency by 29% compared to FIX-2. At high load (43 RPS), FM reduces the 99th percentile and mean latency by 40% and 20%, respectively.

FM characteristics We now examine the parallelism degree and number of threads in FM. Figure 9(a) shows the average parallelism degree for all requests, the longest 5%, and the shortest 5%. At low load, FM assigns a high parallelism degree (almost 4) to all requests. As load increases, FM becomes less aggressive and assigns requests less parallelism. On average however, long requests have a higher degree of parallelism than short requests. At high load (47

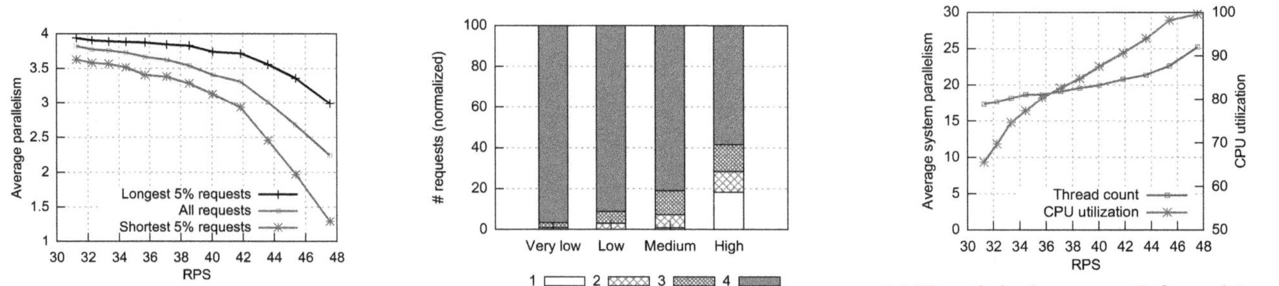

(a) Average request parallelism

(b) Parallelism by degree by load

(c) Threads in the system (left y-axis) and CPU utilization (right y-axis)

Figure 9: Lucene breakdown of parallelism degree by requests and total number of threads in the system.

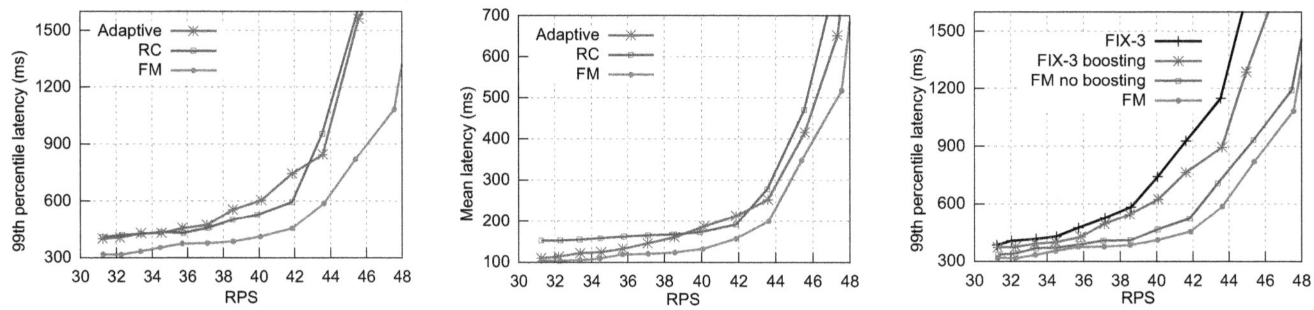

(a) 99th percentile latency

(b) Mean latency

(c) Thread priority boosting

Figure 10: Lucene latency comparison with Adaptive and Predictive policies (a,b). Effect of thread priority boosting (c).

RPS), short requests mostly run sequentially with an average parallelism degree of 1.29 and long requests run with an average degree of 3. These results show that FM adapts parallelism to the system load and favors running longer requests with higher parallelism than shorter requests.

We select four RPS values, (31, 36, 40, 45) to represent ("Very low", "Low", "Medium" and "High") loads. Figure 9(b) shows the parallelism degree distributions over all requests. At very low load, most requests run with degree 4. At high load, 19% of the requests finish sequentially and 41% finish with degree 3 or less. At high load, a request that runs with parallelism degree 4 would have run with a lower parallelism degree for part of its execution. Short requests are thus likely to complete sequentially, which is the most efficient way to execute them, saving processing resources for parallelizing longer requests.

We report the average number of threads in the system and CPU utilization in Figure 9(c). The average number of threads is between 17 and 25, which is close to our target of 24. CPU utilization increases with load. At very high load (48 RPS), CPU utilization is almost 100% and the average number of threads is 25.

Comparison to the state-of-the-art policies We compare FM to state-of-the-art "Adaptive" and perfect prediction "RC" polices described in Section 5. For RC, we execute short requests sequentially and long requests with parallelism degree 4. We experimentally search for the best threshold to divide requests between short and long requests. This threshold is 225 ms.

Figure 10(a) and 10(b) show the 99th percentile latency and mean latency. FM performs consistently better than Adaptive and RC. At low load, FM executes most requests with high degrees of parallelism. Adaptive aggressively runs all requests with high degrees, but does not differentiate between long and short requests. RC misses the opportunity to parallelize requests shorter than its threshold. At medium load (40 RPS), FM reduces the 99th percentile latency by 32% and 22% compared to Adaptive and RC, respectively. Adaptive has higher latency than RC because it executes short requests in parallel, while RC runs short requests sequentially. At high load (43 RPS), RC is worse than Adaptive because it does not adapt to high load by reducing parallelism. At this load, FM reduces the tail latency by 30% and 38% compared to Adaptive and RC, respectively.

FM reduces the tail latency more than Adaptive and RC for three reasons. First, both Adaptive and RC select the parallelism degree at the start and do not dynamically adapt. FM has an extra degree of freedom. It may dynamically increase the parallelism of each individual request. Second, FM favors longer requests with additional parallelism, and shorter requests are more likely to execute sequentially especially under high load. In contrast, Adaptive does not differentiate between short and long requests, and RC, despite being clairvoyant of the request service demand, uses a static threshold,

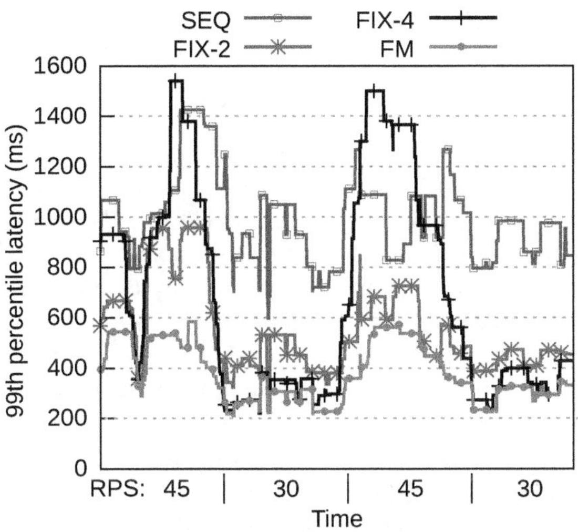

Figure 11: 99th percentile latency for the last 100 requests in a 500-request quanta, while varying the load in Lucene.

fixed parallelism degree, and ignores system load. Third, FM exploits thread boosting to further reduce the tail latency.

Selective thread priority boosting To study benefits of boosting, we disable thread boosting in FM and add it to a fixed parallelism configuration. Since the average parallelism of FM ranges from 2.2 to 3.8 (Figure 9(a)), we select fixed degree 3 (FIX-3) and compare FM with FIX-3 with boosting. Figure 10(c) shows the 99th percentile latencies. Selective thread priority boosting improves the tail latency for both FM and FIX-3. In particular, thread priority boosting reduces the tail latency of FM by 12% at 40 RPS, and by 16% at 43 RPS. Selective thread priority boosting ensures that short requests do not interfere with long requests, reducing tail latency.

Load variation To study the effect of load variation and burstiness on tail latency, we configure the client to vary the request submission rate in quick succession. The client varies load in four quanta: high (45 RPS) to low (30 RPS) to high (45 RPS) to low (30 RPS). The client submits 500 requests in each quanta. Figure 11 compares 99th percentile latencies of the last 100 requests in each quanta for FM, SEQ, FIX-2, and FIX-4. The performance of SEQ is usually the worst, but is slightly better than FIX-4 at the beginning of a load burst. FM adapts well to changes in load and consistently achieves the best tail latency. FIX-4 is the most aggressive and performs almost as well as FM at low load, but performs substantially worse during the load burst. Comparing FIX-2 and FIX-4, we see that FIX-2 performs better than FIX-4 during the high load quanta, but worse at low load. This experiment shows that FM is stable, responding quickly and smoothly to highly variable load. FM tunes its scheduling policy to the load to reduce tail latency.

7. Bing Web Search

This section presents our evaluation of FM in the index servers of Microsoft Bing Web search with a production index and query log. The Bing index serving system consists of aggregators and index serving nodes (ISNs). An entire index, containing information about billions of Web documents, is document-sharded [3] and distributed among hundreds of ISNs. When a user sends a request and the result is not cached, the aggregator propagates the request to all ISNs hosting the index. Each ISN searches its fragment of the index and returns the top-k most relevant results to the aggregator. Because Bing is compute-bound at the ISN servers (see Section 2), a long latency at any ISN manifests as a slow response [9]. To reduce the total tail latency, each ISN must reduce its tail latency. For example, assuming the aggregator has 10 ISNs, if we want to process 90% of user requests within 100 ms, then each ISN needs to reply within 100 ms with probability around 0.99. In other words, for a total latency of 100 ms at the 90th-percentile response time, the response time of each ISN must be at most 100 ms at the 99th-percentile. These results motivate our evaluation of Bing on an individual server.

7.1 Methodology

Implementation We implement FM in the Bing request dispatch code. To eliminate thread creation time, we use a thread pool. Bing organizes its indexes in groups and thus adding incremental parallelism is not onerous. We configure two servers. One server is the index server, which executes requests. A second server is the aggregator, which sends requests to the index server by replaying a trace containing 30K Bing production user requests from 2013. We vary system load by changing the average request arrival rate in RPS. This version of FM does not perform thread boosting. FM uses a target number of threads, $target_p = 16$, a slightly higher number than the 12 available cores (see below). As Section 2 showed, the efficiency of parallelism drops significantly at degree 4, thus we configure FM to increase the parallelism degree of a request up to 3.

Hardware and OS For the index service, we use a server with two 2.27 GHz 6-core Intel 64-bit Xeon processors and 32 GB of main memory with Windows Server 2012. The ISN manages a 160 GB index partition on an SSD, and uses 17 GB of its memory to cache index pages from the SSD.

7.2 Results

We compare FM to fixed parallelism with degree 3 (FIX-3), Adaptive, and SEQ. The production version of FIX-3 applies load protection: it parallelizes each request using degree 3 when the total number of requests in the system is less than 30. Otherwise, it runs requests sequentially.

Figure 12 presents the 99th-percentile latency over different loads. These experimental results show that FM consistently has the lowest tail latency. In particular, it effectively

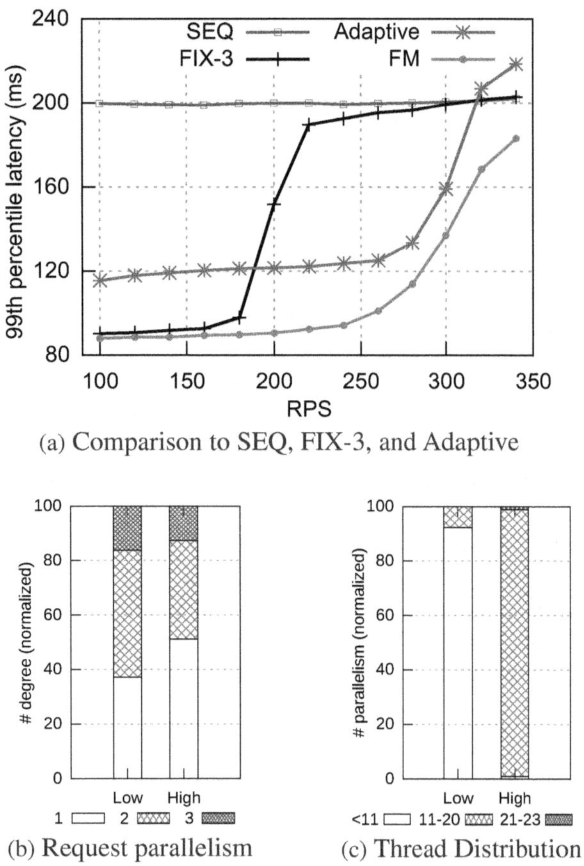

(a) Comparison to SEQ, FIX-3, and Adaptive

(b) Request parallelism

(c) Thread Distribution

Figure 12: Bing comparisons and parallelism.

reduces the tail latency at moderate to high load. For example, up to 260 RPS, FM exhibits a 99th percentile latency of 100 ms. In contrast after 150 RPS, FIX-3 has latencies of over 200 ms because it oversubscribes the resources, parallelizing all requests regardless of system load and the request length. FM also performs better than Adaptive at all load levels. For example, at 180 RPS, the tail latency reduction over Adaptive is 26% and at 260 RPS, the improvement is 24%. FM reduces the tail latency more than Adaptive because it runs long requests with higher parallelism degrees than short requests. These results show that FM enables the provider to service the same load with 42% fewer servers compared to Adaptive for a target tail latency of 120 ms.

To study FM parallelism, we select two representative load values: 200 RPS for "Low" and 280 RPS for "High" load. Figure 12(b) shows the distribution of parallelism per request. Figure 12(c) shows total threads, which are underutilized at low load and match the target load of 16 at high load, as expected. Comparing low to high load, FM uses less intra-request parallelism as load (system parallelism) increases. About 35% of requests execute sequentially at low load, whereas over 50% are sequential at high load.

8. Related Work

This section compares incremental parallelism to related work on parallelism for minimizing latency.

Parallelizing a single job to reduce latency. Many systems adapt parallelism to run-time variability and hardware characteristics [4, 8, 20, 23, 24, 30, 34, 36]. They focus on the execution of a single job to reduce execution time and improve energy efficiency. However, they do not consider a server system running concurrent jobs. Simply applying parallelism to minimize the execution time of every single job will not minimize the response time for concurrent jobs. Our work focuses on a server environment with many requests where parallelizing one request may affect others. We choose the degree of parallelism for a request based on both its impact on the request itself and on other requests.

Parallelization in a multiprogrammed environment for reducing mean response time. Adaptively sharing resources among parallel jobs has been studied empirically [11, 29] and theoretically [2, 16]. However, these studies focus on a multiprogrammed environment, in which jobs have different characteristics unknown *a priori* to the scheduler. The scheduler learns the job characteristics and adjusts the degree of parallelism as the job executes. In contrast, interactive requests in server systems share characteristics that we describe in Section 2 and then exploit. For example, the request service demand distribution and parallelism efficiency are stable over time, and therefore we profile them and use the results to improve scheduling decisions. Moreover, as many requests complete quickly, the scheduler must act quickly. We perform offline processing so that FM makes efficient online decisions. Finally, this prior work focuses only on reducing mean response time, whereas FM reduces tail latency, which requires different techniques.

Parallelization in interactive server systems for reducing mean and tail response time. Adaptive resource allocation for server systems [35, 37] focuses on allocating resources dynamically to different components of the server, while still executing each request sequentially. Raman *et al.* proposed an API and runtime system for dynamic parallelism [31], in which developers express parallelism options and goals, such as minimizing mean response time. The runtime dynamically chooses the degree of parallelism to meet the goals, and does not change it during the execution of the requests. Jeon *et al.* [18] proposed a dynamic parallelization algorithm to reduce the average response time of Web search queries. The algorithm decides the degree of parallelism for each request before the request starts, based on the system load and the average speedup of the requests. Neither approach [18, 31] targets tail latencies. Moreover, since the service demand of each request is typically unknown before the request starts, these approaches cannot differentiate long requests from short ones. Thus, they oversubscribe resources under moderate or high load, and are ineffective at reducing the tail latency. We implement the "Adaptive" algorithm [18] in Section 6, and show FM provides lower tail latency.

To specifically reduce tail latency, Jeon *et al.* [19] predict service demand of Web search requests using machine learning and parallelize the requests predicted to be long, regardless of the system load and workload characteristics. FM considers all of these factors, as well as instantaneous load to deliver better results. Even with a *perfect* predictor, the "Request Clairvoyant" (RC) approach does not outperform FM as shown in Section 6. RC provides an upper-bound on the performance of the predictive technique [19], but it is hard to predict the request service demand in many applications. FM performs better than RC, across all loads, because it continually adapts to total load without requiring prediction.

9. Conclusion

This paper introduces a new parallelization strategy called Few-to-Many (FM) incremental parallelism for reducing high-percentile latency in interactive services. FM uses the demand distribution and a target hardware parallelism to determine dynamically when and how many software threads to add to each request. At runtime, it uses system load and request progress to add parallelism, adapting each request individually. We implement FM in two search engines, Lucene and Bing, and evaluate it using production request traces and service demand profiles. Our results show that FM can significantly reduce tail latencies, and help service providers to reduce their infrastructure costs.

These results and our experience suggest that FM should be extremely useful in practice. In fact, Bing engineers have already deployed a basic version of FM in the production Bing system on thousands of servers.

A. Appendix: Proof of Theorem 1

Suppose a request needs to meet a β-th percentile latency of d. We show any optimal policy that minimizes the average resource usage assigns parallelism in non-decreasing order up to *the latency constraint at time d*. (Requests that take longer than d are in higher percentiles and, thus, may be completed with any degree of parallelism.)

We denote the service demand CDF of request sequential execution times as F and speedup with parallelism i as s_i. As requests have sublinear speedup, the parallelism efficiency decreases with increasing parallelism degree, i.e., $s_i/i > s_j/j$, if $i < j$. Using F, we find the β-th percentile service demand of requests, denoted as w, i.e., $w = F^{-1}(\beta)$. For a schedule to meet β-th percentile latency of d, we want to ensure the β-th percentile longest request can be completed by d, i.e., a work amount w is completed by d.

Let's denote $\mathcal{S}$ as a schedule that specifies how we parallelize a request. For a given piece of work at the x-th cycle where $x \in (0, w]$, and a schedule $\mathcal{S}$, if $\mathcal{S}(x) = i$, this work is parallelized using degree i. The speed to process the work is therefore $s_{\mathcal{S}(x)} = s_i$. We write the resource usage minimization problem as,

$$\min_{\mathcal{S}} \int_0^w [1 - F(x)] \times \frac{\mathcal{S}(x)}{s_{\mathcal{S}(x)}} dx \quad (6)$$

$$s.t. \quad \int_0^w \frac{1}{s_{\mathcal{S}(x)}} dx \leq d\,. \quad (7)$$

Here, the integral in the objective function 6 computes the expected amount of resources a request consumes up to work w and latency d. Constraint 7 guarantees that the processing time of the β-th percentile request is bounded by d.

We now prove the theorem by contradiction. Suppose that there is an optimal schedule $\mathcal{S}'$ that gives higher parallelism to a request earlier and later decreases its parallelism. Thus, there exist x_1 and x_2 such that $0 \leq x_1 < x_1 + dx \leq x_2 < x_2 + dx \leq w$ and $\mathcal{S}'(x_1') > \mathcal{S}'(x_2')$, where $x_1' \in [x_1, x_1 + dx]$, $x_2' \in [x_2, x_2 + dx]$ and dx is a sufficiently small positive number.

Since we assume sublinear speedup, i.e., $s_i/i > s_j/j$ if $i < j$, the following inequality holds:

$$\begin{aligned} &[1 - F(x_1')] \times \left[\frac{\mathcal{S}'(x_1')}{s_{\mathcal{S}'}(x_1')} - \frac{\mathcal{S}'(x_2')}{s_{\mathcal{S}'}(x_2')}\right] \\ &+[1 - F(x_2')] \times \left[\frac{\mathcal{S}'(x_2')}{s_{\mathcal{S}'}(x_2')} - \frac{\mathcal{S}'(x_1')}{s_{\mathcal{S}'}(x_1')}\right] \\ = &\left[\frac{\mathcal{S}'(x_1')}{s_{\mathcal{S}'}(x_1')} - \frac{\mathcal{S}'(x_2')}{s_{\mathcal{S}'}(x_2')}\right] \times [F(x_2') - F(x_1')] > 0 \end{aligned}$$

Thus, $[1 - F(x_1')] \times \frac{\mathcal{S}'(x_1')}{s_{\mathcal{S}'}(x_1')} + [1 - F(x_2')] \times \frac{\mathcal{S}'(x_2')}{s_{\mathcal{S}'}(x_2')}] > [1-F(x_1')] \times \frac{\mathcal{S}'(x_2')}{s_{\mathcal{S}'}(x_2')} + [1-F(x_2')] \times \frac{\mathcal{S}'(x_1')}{s_{\mathcal{S}'}(x_1')}]$. Following the optimization objective in Eqn. 6, the expected resource usage is reduced by exchanging the order of parallelism degree between the x_1'-th cycle and the x_2'-th cycle, while keeping the rest of the schedule $\mathcal{S}'$ unchanged. This contradicts the assumption that $\mathcal{S}'$ minimizes Eqn. 6 and therefore proves Theorem 1. ■

Acknowledgements We thank Xi Yang for helping us with the implementation and configuration of Lucene. We thank our shepherd, Jason Flinn, anonymous reviewers, and Jing Li for their helpful comments and suggestions. We thank Gregg McKnight for his feedback and support of this work.

References

[1] Apache Lucene. `http://lucene.apache.org/`. Retreived July 2014.

[2] N. Bansal, K. Dhamdhere, and A. Sinha. Non-clairvoyant scheduling for minimizing mean slowdown. *Algorithmica*, 40 (4):305–318, 2004.

[3] L. A. Barroso, J. Dean, and U. Hölzle. Web search for a planet: The google cluster architecture. *IEEE Micro*, 23(2):22–28, 2003.

[4] F. Blagojevic, D. S. Nikolopoulos, A. Stamatakis, C. D. Antonopoulos, and M. Curtis-Maury. Runtime scheduling of dynamic parallelism on accelerator-based multi-core systems. *Parallel Computing*, 33(10-11):700–719, 2007.

[5] R. D. Blumofe, C. F. Joerg, B. C. Kuszmaul, C. E. Leiserson, K. H. Randall, and Y. Zhou. Cilk: An efficient multithreaded runtime system. *Journal of Parallel and Distributed Computing*, 37(1):55 - 69, 1996.

[6] B. Cahoon, K. S. McKinley, and Z. Lu. Evaluating the performance of distributed architectures for information retrieval using a variety of workloads. *ACM Transactions on Information Systems (TOIS)*, 18(1):1–43, 2000.

[7] G. Contreras and M. Martonosi. Characterizing and improving the performance of intel threading building blocks. In *IEEE International Symposium on Workload Characterization (IISWC)*, pages 57–66, 2008.

[8] M. Curtis-Maury, J. Dzierwa, C. D. Antonopoulos, and D. S. Nikolopoulos. Online power-performance adaptation of multithreaded programs using hardware event-based prediction. In *ACM International Conference on Supercomputing (ICS)*, pages 157–166, 2006.

[9] J. Dean and L. A. Barroso. The tail at scale. *Communications of the ACM*, 56(2):74–80, 2013.

[10] G. DeCandia, D. Hastorun, M. Jampani, G. Kakulapati, A. Lakshman, A. Pilchin, S. Sivasubramanian, P. Vosshall, and W. Vogels. Dynamo: Amazon's highly available key-value store. In *ACM Symposium on Operating Systems Principles (SOSP)*, pages 205–220, 2007.

[11] D. Feitelson. *A Survey of Scheduling in Multiprogrammed Parallel Systems*. Research report. IBM T.J. Watson Research Center, 1994.

[12] B. Goetz, T. Peierls, J. Bloch, J. Bowbeer, D. Holmes, and D. Lea. *Java Concurrency in Practice*. Addison Wesley Professional, 2006.

[13] R. Guida. Parallelizing a computationally intensive financial R application with zircon technology. In *The R User Conference*, 2010.

[14] J. Hamilton. The cost of latency, 2009. `http://perspectives.mvdirona.com/2009/10/31/-TheCostOfLatency.aspx`.

[15] J. Hamilton. Overall data center costs, 2010. `http://perspectives.mvdirona.com/2010/09/18-/OverallDataCenterCosts.aspx`.

[16] Y. He, W.-J. Hsu, and C. E. Leiserson. Provably efficient online non-clairvoyant adaptive scheduling. *IEEE Transactions on Parallel and Distributed Systems*, 19(9):1263–1279, 2008.

[17] Y. He, S. Elnikety, J. Larus, and C. Yan. Zeta: Scheduling interactive services with partial execution. In *ACM Symposium on Cloud Computing (SOCC)*, page 12, 2012.

[18] M. Jeon, Y. He, S. Elnikety, A. L. Cox, and S. Rixner. Adaptive parallelism for web search. In *ACM European Conference on Computer Systems (EuroSys)*, pages 155–168, 2013.

[19] M. Jeon, S. Kim, S.-W. Hwang, Y. He, S. Elnikety, A. L. Cox, and S. Rixner. Predictive parallelization: taming tail latencies in web search. In *ACM Conference on Research and Development in Information Retrieval (SIGIR)*, pages 253–262, 2014.

[20] C. Jung, D. Lim, J. Lee, and S. Han. Adaptive execution techniques for SMT multiprocessor architectures. In *ACM Symposium on Principles and Practice of Parallel Programming (PPoPP)*, pages 236–246, 2005.

[21] A. Jurgelionis, P. Fechteler, P. Eisert, F. Bellotti, H. David, J. P. Laulajainen, R. Carmichael, V. Poulopoulos, A. Laikari, P. Perälä, A. De Gloria, and C. Bouras. Platform for distributed 3D gaming. *International Journal of Computer Games Technology*, 2009:1:1–1:15, 2009.

[22] S. Kim, Y. He, S.-W. Hwang, S. Elnikety, and S. Choi. Delayed-Dynamic-Selective (DDS) prediction for reducing extreme tail latency in web search. In *ACM International Conference on Web Search and Data Mining (WSDM)*, 2015.

[23] W. Ko, M. N. Yankelevsky, D. S. Nikolopoulos, and C. D. Polychronopoulos. Effective cross-platform, multilevel parallelism via dynamic adaptive execution. In *IEEE International Parallel and Distributed Processing Symposium (IPDPS)*, page 130, 2002.

[24] J. Lee, H. Wu, M. Ravichandran, and N. Clark. Thread tailor: dynamically weaving threads together for efficient, adaptive parallel applications. In *International Symposium on Computer Architecture (ISCA)*, pages 270–279, 2010.

[25] D. Leijen, W. Schulte, and S. Burckhardt. The design of a task parallel library. In *ACM Conference on Object Oriented Programming Systems Languages and Applications (OOPSLA)*, pages 227–242, 2009.

[26] J. R. Lorch and A. J. Smith. Improving dynamic voltage scaling algorithms with PACE. In *ACM International Conference on Measurement and Modeling of Computer Systems (SIGMETRICS)*, pages 50–61, 2001.

[27] Lucene Nightly Benchmarks. http://people.apache.org/~mikemccand/lucenebench. Retreived June 2014.

[28] J. Mars, L. Tang, R. Hundt, K. Skadron, and M. L. Soffa. Bubble-up: increasing utilization in modern warehouse scale computers via sensible co-locations. In *IEEE/ACM International Symposium on Microarchitecture (MICRO)*, pages 248–259, 2011.

[29] C. McCann, R. Vaswani, and J. Zahorjan. A dynamic processor allocation policy for multiprogrammed shared-memory multiprocessors. *ACM Transactions on Computer Systems*, 11 (2):146–178, 1993.

[30] K. K. Pusukuri, R. Gupta, and L. N. Bhuyan. Thread reinforcer: Dynamically determining number of threads via OS level monitoring. In *IEEE International Symposium on Workload Characterization (IISWC)*, pages 116–125, 2011.

[31] A. Raman, H. Kim, T. Oh, J. W. Lee, and D. I. August. Parallelism orchestration using DoPE: the degree of parallelism executive. In *ACM Conference on Programming Language Design and Implementation (PLDI)*, pages 26–37, 2011.

[32] S. Ren, Y. He, S. Elnikety, and K. McKinley. Exploiting processor heterogeneity in interactive services. In *USENIX International Conference on Autonomic Computing (ICAC)*, pages 45–58, 2013.

[33] E. Schurman and J. Brutlag. The user and business impact of server delays, additional bytes, and http chunking in web search. In *Velocity Conference*, 2009.

[34] M. A. Suleman, M. K. Qureshi, and Y. N. Patt. Feedback-driven threading: power-efficient and high-performance exe-

cution of multi-threaded workloads on CMPs. In *ACM International Conference on Architectural Support for Programming Languages and Operating Systems (ASPLOS)*, pages 277–286, 2008.

[35] G. Upadhyaya, V. S. Pai, and S. P. Midkiff. Expressing and exploiting concurrency in networked applications with aspen. In *ACM Symposium on Principles and Practice of Parallel Programming (PPoPP)*, pages 13–23, 2007.

[36] Z. Wang and M. F. O'Boyle. Mapping parallelism to multi-cores: a machine learning based approach. In *ACM Symposium on Principles and Practice of Parallel Programming (PPoPP)*, pages 75–84, 2009.

[37] M. Welsh, D. Culler, and E. Brewer. SEDA: an architecture for well-conditioned, scalable internet services. In *ACM Symposium on Operating Systems Principles (SOSP)*, pages 230–243, 2001.

[38] Wikipedia: Database download. http://en.wikipedia.org/-wiki/wikipedia:database_download#english-language_wikipedia/. Retreived May 2014.

[39] J. Yi, F. Maghoul, and J. Pedersen. Deciphering mobile search patterns: A study of Yahoo! mobile search queries. In *ACM International Conference on World Wide Web (WWW)*, pages 257–266, 2008.

Protecting Data on Smartphones and Tablets from Memory Attacks

Patrick Colp†, Jiawen Zhang‡, James Gleeson‡, Sahil Suneja‡,
Eyal de Lara‡, Himanshu Raj*, Stefan Saroiu*, and Alec Wolman*

†University of British Columbia, ‡University of Toronto, and *Microsoft Research

Abstract

Smartphones and tablets are easily lost or stolen. This makes them susceptible to an inexpensive class of memory attacks, such as cold-boot attacks, using a bus monitor to observe the memory bus, and DMA attacks. This paper describes Sentry, a system that allows applications and OS components to store their code and data on the System-on-Chip (SoC) rather than in DRAM. We use ARM-specific mechanisms originally designed for embedded systems, but still present in today's mobile devices, to protect applications and OS subsystems from memory attacks.

Categories and Subject Descriptors C.0 [*Computer Systems Organization*]: Hardware/software interfaces; D.4.1 [*Operating Systems*]: Process Management; D.4.6 [*Operating Systems*]: Security and Protection

Keywords encrypted memory, encrypted RAM, AES, cold boot, bus monitoring, DMA attack, ARM, cache, iRAM, Android, Nexus, Tegra

1. Introduction

Smartphones and tablets are more easily lost or stolen than desktops or even laptops. This ease of loss makes enterprises and device owners concerned about the security of the data stored on their devices. Many enterprises today mandate that employee laptops use disk encryption, such as TrueCrypt [51] or BitLocker [30], to protect "data at rest". With such systems, the data on disk is always encrypted with a key protected by a password or PIN that the user must enter at boot time. If a device is lost, an attacker cannot retrieve the data without knowing the encryption password. Because laptops are often shutdown or hibernating, such systems provide adequate safety when dealing with lost devices.

In contrast, smartphones and tablets are rarely powered off. Instead, when the screen is off, these devices are in a sleep state where RAM is continually refreshed. While sleeping, these devices periodically check for incoming phone calls or application notifications. When a device is lost, an attacker only needs to press a button to force the device to immediately resume execution. Encrypting data at rest is therefore less useful for smartphones and tablets, as their data can always be decrypted and loaded to RAM with the press of a button.

Instead, smartphones and tablets offer *PIN-unlock*: a user must enter a PIN to unlock her device when the device is idle for more than a short period of time (e.g., 15 minutes). To prevent brute-force attacks on the PIN, many smartphones enter a deep-lock state if an incorrect PIN is entered a few times in a row. A key limitation of PIN-unlock is that even when the device is locked, unencrypted data resides in RAM on the stolen device. This allows attackers to subject lost smartphones and tablets to physical attacks. There are different avenues to read secrets from RAM, such as cold boot attacks [25, 31], attaching a bus monitor to monitor data transfers between the CPU and system RAM [18, 21, 24], or mounting DMA attacks [7, 9, 36]. For example, Müller and Spreitzenbarth describe how to mount a cold boot attack on Android smart phones using only a household freezer, a USB cable and a laptop [31]. Using their tool named Frost, they were able to recover recent emails, photos, and visited web sites from physical RAM.

This paper demonstrates that the ARM *System-on-Chip (SoC)* architecture used by today's smartphones and tablets is amenable to a new security approach – storing users' sensitive data on the ARM SoC rather than in DRAM. By storing the secrets on the SoC, we make physical attacks more difficult to mount because they must target the SoC to retrieve secrets, which is much more expensive. The ARM SoC is already equipped with low-capacity storage that can be used as an adequate alternative to traditional off-the-SoC DRAM. Its primary usage is to store small amounts of data closer to the CPU than DRAM. This storage's presence is (arguably) due to the role ARM plays in embedded systems, which often require both fast and predictable performance. Bringing data closer to the CPU helps these systems meet their real-time performance needs.

This paper presents Sentry, a system that protects against DRAM attacks by leveraging on-SoC storage mechanisms originally intended for realtime predictable performance. Sentry can bootstrap additional secure storage by safely encrypting regions of memory much larger than the capacity of the ARM SoC. Sentry starts with the observation that *protecting sensitive data on an unlocked device offers little value because an attacker can access the data simply by using the device's UI.* Instead, Sentry encrypts the memory of sensitive applications and OS subsystems when a mobile device transitions to a screen-locked state. When the user unlocks the device, Sentry decrypts memory on demand to reduce user-perceived resume latency and to save power.

Sentry supports two alternatives to storing secrets in DRAM. First, Sentry supports iRAM, a small amount of internal SRAM on the SoC, whose primary usage is storing the runtime state of the firmware of the platform's peripherals. Second, Sentry supports

ASPLOS '15, March 14–18, 2015, Istanbul, Turkey..
Copyright © 2015 ACM 978-1-4503-2835-7/15/03... $15.00.
http://dx.doi.org/10.1145/2694344.2694380

cache locking, an old feature of ARM platforms, to "pin" data in the cache and prevent it from being written back to DRAM. Current ARM platforms used by smartphones and tablets are equipped with shared L2 caches with much larger sizes than iRAM.

To enable sensitive applications to run in the background while the device remains locked, Sentry leverages AES_On_SoC. Unlike traditional AES, AES_On_SoC safely encrypts and decrypts without leaking any sensitive code and data to DRAM. This new implementation carefully manages the sensitive encryption/decryption state to eliminate the possibility of accidental leaks to DRAM due to procedure calls (e.g., by passing parameters on the stack) or to context switches. Sentry uses AES_On_SoC and fine-grained software control over the L2 cache to secure the state of sensitive applications running in the background. When an application starts running in the background, Sentry transparently reads its encrypted memory pages from DRAM, stores them on the ARM SoC, and decrypts them. Similarly, pages are encrypted when written back to DRAM. Sentry operates with little or no overhead when the device is unlocked, and can securely run background applications while the device is locked, albeit at lower performance.

We implement Sentry on a Nexus 4 smartphone and on an NVidia Tegra 3 development board. On the Nexus 4, Sentry only uses iRAM to store secrets on the SoC, while on the NVidia board, Sentry can use both iRAM and the L2 cache. We have firmware access to the NVidia Tegra 3 board that allows us to enable L2 cache locking (this feature is often disabled by firmware). We use Sentry to secure a number of Android applications (Twitter, Google Maps, Contacts, MP3), and *dm-crypt*, a generic Linux block-level encryption module. Our evaluation shows that Sentry's performance and energy overheads are modest, and its mechanisms do not affect the rest of the system's performance in a significant manner. On a daily basis, Sentry consumes about 2% of a device's battery life to protect an application assuming the user unlocks the device 150 times a day.

2. Sentry

Sentry secures mobile devices against DRAM attacks by leveraging the limited amount of secure storage available on the ARM SoC to safely encrypt much larger regions of DRAM.

Main Observation. Sentry builds on the observation that securing data in memory while a device is unlocked provides limited protection because any user can access sensitive data by simply interacting with the device's UI. Instead, Sentry secures memory state only while a device's screen is locked.

Sentry encrypts the memory pages of all sensitive applications when the device starts transitioning to a screen-locked state. When the device resumes and is successfully unlocked, Sentry decrypts memory pages on demand as sensitive applications start to run. The encryption/decryption keys are only stored on the ARM SoC when the device is locked, and not in DRAM.

While this encrypt-on-lock and decrypt-on-unlock cycle improves security, it has one major drawback – it does not support background computation. Modern smartphones need to perform limited background computations (e.g., receiving notifications, providing calendar alerts) while the screen is locked. To enable this, Sentry runs sensitive background applications in a mode that guarantees their decrypted state is always confined to the SoC.

This approach makes it possible for Sentry to operate with little or no overhead when the device is unlocked, while simultaneously enabling it to run background applications while the device is locked, albeit at lower performance.

Implementing Sentry requires solving the following three technical challenges:

In Scope Attacks	Out of Scope Attacks
cold boot	software attacks (malware)
bus monitoring	physical side-channel attacks
DMA attacks	code-injection
	JTAG attacks
	sophisticated physical attacks (e.g., using electron microscope)

Table 1. Summary of our threat model.

1. On-SoC Storage: Identifying a location on the SoC where sensitive state (e.g., encryption keys, cleartext pages of sensitive background applications) can be stored and accessed while running background applications. All this state must be preserved between lock and unlock cycles.

2. Encrypted DRAM: To enable background operation while locked, Sentry requires a way to transparently run background applications whose memory pages are always encrypted in DRAM. To run these processes, Sentry uses the virtual memory system to load referenced memory pages onto the SoC, and then decrypt them in place. Similarly, Sentry encrypts them before paging them out of the SoC and back to DRAM.

3. On-SoC Encryption: To bootstap its security guarantees, Sentry requires the encryption/decryption routines to never leak any sensitive information outside the SoC. For example, a generic cryptographic library is insufficient because its function calls may place their arguments on the stack in DRAM, and as a result they would violate Sentry's guarantees.

After we describe our threat model, we then address each of the above challenges in turn.

3. Threat Model

This section describes three classes of memory attacks within our threat model, and additional threats that fall outside the scope of our paper. Table 1 summarizes these threats.

3.1 In-Scope Threats

We are concerned with memory attacks that aim to steal secrets by reading the memory of a stolen/lost smartphone or tablet.

Cold Boot Attacks. Cold boot attacks exploit the data remanence effect of RAM to read secrets stored in memory [25]. There are two ways to mount cold boot attacks. One way is for an attacker to physically remove the RAM modules from a victim device and insert them into a compromised device which outputs the RAM's content. The bolting of DRAM into the motherboard and the growing popularity of package-on-package (PoP), where memory is vertically stacked on top of processor, makes this approach ineffective on today's mobile phones.

A more practical possibility is to reboot a stolen device and boot into an attacker-controlled OS that outputs the memory contents [11]. A typical way to mount this attack is by *reflashing* a device. This requires a short power-disconnect (i.e., tapping a RESET button). Müller and Spreitzenbarth used this technique to mount successful cold boot attacks on Android smart phones [31]. On phones with a locked bootloader, they were able to recover recent emails, photos, and visited web sites from physical RAM dumps. Moreover, on devices with an unlocked bootloader, they recovered encryption keys from RAM and decrypted the user partition[1].

[1] Decrypting the user partition on locked devices is not possible because the unlocking process requires device reflashing which wipes all user data.

Bus Monitoring Attacks. An attacker could attach a bus monitoring tool [18, 21] to the memory bus and wait for the CPU to request sensitive data over the memory bus. For example, a simple reboot ensures that any secrets (e.g., disk encryption keys) are loaded into the CPU as they are needed to start decrypting the disk volume upon startup.

Bus monitoring attacks present a different danger than cold boot. Bus monitoring enables a class of side-channel attacks based on memory access patterns. Consider a sensitive application for which an attacker can monitor its access patterns to its internal state. For example, AES implementations use tables of precomputed values (e.g., the exponentiation of 2 in a particular field, such as $GF(2^8)$) to speed up their computation. While the tables themselves are not secret, the order in which the table entries are accessed can reveal secret information. Previous work has shown fast ways to break AES if its state access patterns are known [50]. Bus monitoring attacks can reveal these access patterns, whereas cold boot attacks cannot.

To the best of our knowledge, all previous work on protecting secrets against memory attacks (on x86 platforms) is susceptible to this attack [32, 33, 41]. Addressing this attack is nontrivial because the above schemes can only protect small quantities of data, such as one set of encryption keys. Protecting the entire state of the encryption/decryption code and data makes the secret state's size grow several fold. Such sizes are beyond the protection capabilities of previous solutions. Our related work section (Section 9) provides a more in-depth discussion of these issues.

DMA Attacks. An attacker could program a DMA-capable peripheral to manipulate the DMA controller and read arbitrary memory regions. This class of attacks is often referred to as *Firewire attacks*, although they can exploit many other DMA interfaces, including PCMCIA, PCI Express, or even the more recent Thunderbolt interface. A DMA interface allows a peripheral to read memory contents without any cooperation from the processor or the OS. DMA attacks are successful even when the mobile device is PIN-locked. As long as the device is not powered-off, one of its DMA controllers can be programmed over a DMA interface.

One form of defense is using an IOMMU, a memory management unit often found on PCs and laptops today. The OS can program the IOMMU to restrict what memory regions different DMA devices can access. Unfortunately, there are two problems with IOMMUs: (1) some mobile devices lack IOMMUs today, and (2) IOMMUs cannot authenticate DMA devices and are thus susceptible to spoofing attacks in which a malicious DMA device can impersonate another device. Therefore, IOMMUs must be programmed to deny access to a restricted memory range from *all* DMA devices.

Although some ARM platforms lack IOMMUs, most of today's ARM platforms are equipped with ARM TrustZone [2], which is ARM's hardware support for trusted computing. ARM TrustZone provides two virtual processors backed by hardware access control. The software stack can switch between the two states, referred to as the *secure world* and the *normal world*. The OS and all applications run in the normal world, whereas a small trusted kernel runs in the secure world. Untrusted code running in the normal world cannot access protected resources, such as memory pages and peripheral registers of the secure world. ARM TrustZone can protect against DMA attacks by giving the secure world control over the memory storing secrets, and denying normal world's DMA requests.

3.2 Out-of-Scope Threats

Data residing on a smartphone face many threats other than those described above.

Software Attacks. This class of attacks compromise the software on a mobile device and can thus access and steal any secrets, such as the owner's PIN number. Such attacks exploit a software vulnerability to install compromised code. Although an important class of attacks to consider, this paper focuses on attacks that do not rely on running compromised software, yet are possible when the device is in an attacker's hands.

Physical Side-channel Attacks. Side-channel attacks aim to obtain sensitive information by exploiting physical properties of the cryptographic implementation, such as timing information or power consumption. For example, different keys could affect the amount of processing time or power required to do the encryption differently, revealing something about the keys' structure. Although our system does address one class of side-channel attacks based on observing memory access patterns using bus monitoring, we do not address physical externally measurable side-channel attacks. Such attacks fall outside our threat model because they require a relatively high level of sophistication particularly when the attacker cannot run arbitrary code on the device.

Code-injection Attacks. This class of attacks inject or modify code running on the platform. One way to mount this attack is to use a compromised DMA-capable device. However, as described above, an ARM TrustZone (or an IOMMU) can protect a memory region against all DMA accesses including writes. Another possibility is to attach a logic analyzer to the memory or I/O bus and issue write commands that bypass any ARM TrustZone or IOMMU protections. We consulted a DRAM hardware expert about these attacks and learned that, albeit possible, these attacks are very challenging to mount because they are electrically unsound [8]. An attacker needs to use a higher drive strength than the bus to effectively "override" the bus protocol. Using a higher strength has the potential to damage the memory controller beyond repair. Also, bus protocols use dynamic time synchronization; the attacker must discover and synchronize the analyzer's timings to match those of the bus. In the expert's opinion, mounting such an attack costs several 100's of thousands of dollars, at a minimum.

JTAG Attacks. JTAG attacks are preventable because JTAG can be disabled. Some mobile vendors disable JTAG by depopulating the JTAG connector. Unfortunately, the JTAG interface can be re-enabled by soldering a JTAG cable back to the JTAG pad [38]. Other mobile vendors use a more secure form of JTAG-blocking based on hardware fuses [46]; such fuses can be disabled at device provisioning time. JTAG is permanently disabled once this fuse is burned. Additionally, manufacturers are also starting to build "authenticated JTAG", an interface that requires a reader to authenticate to enable JTAG [20].

Sophisticated Physical Attacks. It is hard to anticipate all types of physical attacks. One example of an advanced attack is using an electron microscope to examine the internals of the ARM SoC chip and carry attacks on the stored data [49]. Although possible, such an attack requires specialized equipment and can often take several months even when carried out by a skilled attacker.

4. On-SoC Storage

This section presents two alternatives for storing secrets on the SoC when the device is screen-locked.

4.1 Alternative #1: Internal RAM (iRAM)

Many smartphones and tablets are equipped with a small amount of internal SRAM on the SoC, called iRAM. By placing iRAM on the chip, different SoC subsystems (e.g., the DSP and various micro-controllers) have fast access to a little bit of memory to run their

Memory Preserved	iRAM	DRAM
OS Reboot (no power loss)	100%	96.4%
Device Reflash (power loss)	0%	97.5%
2 Second Reset (power loss)	0%	0.1%

Table 2. The iRAM (SRAM) and DRAM's data remanence rates on a commodity tablet.

firmware. For example, our Tegra 3 development board provides 256KB of iRAM.

However, like DRAM, SRAM storage also suffers from *data remanence* – the memory retains its contents for a period of time upon a power disconnect. Data remanence makes memory vulnerable to cold boot attacks [25]. In fact, SRAM decays over time more slowly than DRAM [10], making it even less suitable for storing secrets. We performed the following experiment to characterize iRAM's data remanence.

Methodology. We connected the Tegra 3 tablet to a debugging board and used its reset button to power off the tablet for short periods of time. For each experiment, we varied how long the power was cut from the board and measured the amount of data preserved in DRAM and iRAM, respectively. To do so, we created a process that allocates 1GB of memory (the tablet has 1GB of DRAM and 256KB of iRAM) and fills it with an 8-byte pattern written repeatedly.

We then performed three types of board resets that correspond to mounting different variants of cold boot attacks. First, we just performed a simple OS reboot. Such an attack is possible for *unlocked* mobile devices – an attacker can boot a malicious OS that dumps the memory. Second, we tapped the reset button (i.e., a short power disconnect), which corresponds to the reflashing the device. The final test is a longer power interrupt – we held the reset button pressed for two seconds. This corresponds to an attack in which the memory is yanked out of the device and quickly inserted into a malicious device which dumps all memory contents.

For each test, we used a kernel-level driver to enumerate all DRAM and iRAM before starting the test and after the test ended. We then grepped for the pattern, counted the number of occurrences, and used these results to compute data remanence as a ratio. Each test was per formed at room temperature, and was repeated five times. Table 2 shows the average results. Previous work has characterized DRAM and SRAM's memory remanence as a function of temperature [10, 25, 43].

Results. iRAM lost all its contents every time the device lost power no matter for how long. In contrast, at room temperature, DRAM still preserved a portion of its contents (0.1%) even when losing power for two seconds.

After private conversations with the ARM board's hardware manufacturer, we learned that the board's firmware zeroes out its iRAM upon boot up. This behavior is consistent with our results, and makes iRAM attractive for our security needs.

4.2 Alternative #2: Locked L2 Cache

Cortex-A9 ARM platforms are equipped with a PL310 cache controller [3] whose role is to manage a shared L2 cache. The PL310 offers the ability to lock a portion of the cache to prevent it from being evicted from the cache. ARM platforms have supported cache locking for a long time to improve computation performance as well as the predictability of computation latency. Being able to *pin* data into the cache can make small amount of computation faster and its duration predictable. This piece of functionality is especially attractive for embedded systems that need real-time guarantees. The PL310 controller mandates the ability to lock a cache *by way*, and optionally by *cache-line*. This is done via a Verilog option provided to the SoC vendors. Flushing the cache is done with a single instruction, regardless of the number of ways being flushed. We were able to enable cache locking by way on our NVidia Tegra 3 board. Unfortunately, we could not enable cache locking on the Nexus 4 because we do not have access to the boot firmware.

	iRAM	Locked L2 Cache
Cold Boot	Safe	Safe
Bus Monitoring	Safe	Safe
DMA Attacks	Safe (ARM TrustZone)	Safe

Table 3. Security analysis of different storage alternatives to DRAM.

The locked L2 cache is useful for storing secrets on the SoC only if it *guarantees* that locked ways are not invalidated and remain present in the L2 cache until unlocked. While such a guarantee is not important for performance (the original goal of cache locking), it is crucial to our security needs. Unfortunately, the ARM spec is silent on whether the L2 cache locking implementation offers this guarantee. To validate our hardware behavior, we performed the following two experiments.

Validating PL310's write-back behavior. First, we inspected the codebase of an ARM simulator built by ARM itself (ARM Fast Model [1]) and found that the PL310 does not write back locked entries. Our second experiment was done on our Tegra 3 board. We started by choosing an 8-byte random pattern that never appears in DRAM. We wrote the random pattern at the physical address that maps into a locked cache way, and used DMA reads to read the DRAM directly bypassing the cache.

Finding a way to "hijack" a DMA controller for our testing needs proved to be challenging for several reasons. First, few Linux drivers appeared to use DMA for their data transfers. Second, DMA controllers transfer data from memory to a device only. Reading the DMA-ed data from the device is sometimes impossible. For example, the NIC only allowed DMA-ing data out to a transmit buffer that cannot be DMA-ed back in. Incoming DMA transfers from the NIC were filled from a separate receive buffer. Third, certain devices expect the DMA-ed data to have a certain format; for example, the NIC expects transmitted data to have packet headers.

In the end, we used a driver that offers a high-speed serial channel. We discovered that the UART controller offers a *debugging* port that acts like a loopback interface – it returns all data written to it. We then modified the driver to DMA data to this debugging port and then read the serial port to output its contents. This experiment revealed that the hardware does not evict data from a locked cache way. However, we discovered that flushing the entire cache does unlock all locked ways. To ensure data safety, our system disables flushing of locked cache ways. We validated that the locked way's entries never appear in DRAM once this OS change is made.

4.3 Security Analysis of Storage Options

Table 3 summarizes our analysis of secure storage choices for protecting secrets against memory attacks.

Because the low-level firmware zeroes-out iRAM upon boot, storing secrets in iRAM protects them against cold boot attacks. Unfortunately, we do not know of any published data on how prevalent this behavior is across different types of mobile devices, and as a result we cannot generalize our finding beyond our Tegra 3 device. iRAM is also safe against bus monitoring attacks because secret data never leaves the SoC and thus does not traverse any externally exposed busses. Finally, iRAM is safe against DMA attacks as long as access to iRAM is protected inside the ARM TrustZone only, as described in Section 3.

Similar to iRAM, upon boot the low-level device firmware resets the PL310 L2 cache controller and zeros the L2 cache contents. As a result, sensitive data in the L2 cache is protected from cold boot attacks. Bus monitoring attacks are also ineffective because data does not travel on any exposed busses. On ARM platforms, DMA attacks are ineffective because DMA transfers data directly from DRAM, bypassing the L2 cache.

Because the low-level device firmware implements the zeroing logic for both iRAM and the L2 cache, one attack vector would be to replace this firmware. However, this attack is difficult to mount because the device verifies that the low-level firmware is signed with the manufacturer's key.

4.4 Trade-Offs

Looking at Table 3 one might ask: *What are the security trade-offs between iRAM and L2 cache locking because both appear to be safe to these attacks?* On one hand, any on-SoC storage is "safe" because placing sensitive on the SoC protects it from memory attacks. On the other hand, the hardware, the operating system, or even an application could accidentally copy data off the SoC to DRAM (even if not malicious). It is thus important to examine the security guarantees each on-SoC storage alternative offer.

The key distinction between cache locking and iRAM arises in how they protect against DMA attacks. On today's ARM SoCs, cache coherence for DMA transfers is handled in software. The operating system must explicitly flush the cache before DMA reads, and invalidate the cache before DMA writes. Because software manages the cache for DMA operations, hardware initiated DMA attacks cannot see the contents of the L2 cache, and therefore L2 cache-locking protects against DMA attacks. In contrast, iRAM is just like any other system memory (DRAM) with respect to DMA attacks. iRAM can only be protected from DMA attacks when software in the TrustZone takes explicit steps to protect it.

4.5 Implementation

iRAM. We implemented a simple memory allocator that manages the 192KB of iRAM (out of a total of 256KB) on our Tegra 3 tablet. In our experiments, we discovered that the first 64KB of iRAM appear to be used by our tablet's firmware; overwriting this region of iRAM crashes the tablet.

L2 cache locking. Locking a cache way is done by programming the PL310 controller with a special *enable way* command. This command has two effects. First, it ensures that all new data loaded in the cache will be loaded in the *enabled* way. Second, all data already loaded in the remaining *disabled* ways remains in fact available to reads and writes but no new allocations or evictions will take place. We can leverage this *disable way* command to first load sensitive data into one way, and then lock the way. In pseudocode, cache locking is done with the following four steps:

```
1. flush entire cache
2. enable 1-way
/* cache size is now 128KB */
3. write 0xFF in all sensitive data
/* warm the one-way with data */
4. enable last 7-ways
/* first way is now ''disabled'' */
/* cache size is now 7x128KB */
```

Once a way is locked, we return pointers to free pages mapped to this cache way. Once the entire way has been allocated, we lock an additional way if new requests for locked L2 cache memory are made. Section 8 will show the increasing performance overhead as additional ways are locked. To unlock a cache way, we erase the sensitive data and re-enable all unlocked ways:

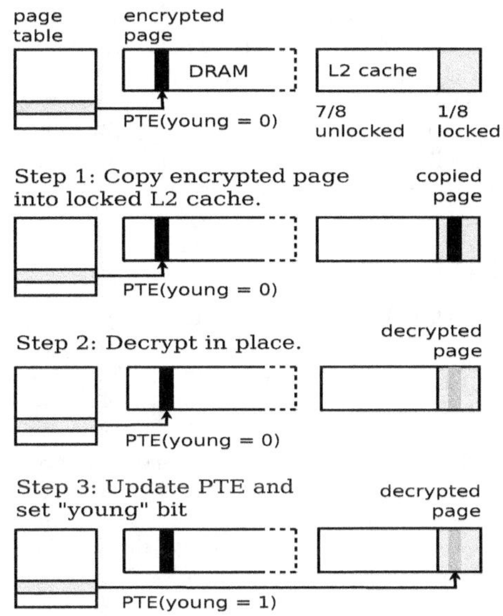

Figure 1. Decrypt on page-in.

```
1. write 0xFF in all sensitive data
/* all sensitive data erased */

2. enable (8-k)-ways
/* restore unlocked cache ways */
```

OS-level changes for handling L2 cache flushes. Flushing the L2 cache unlocks all locked ways. To ensure that data remains locked, we used a feature of the PL310 cache controller – supporting a mask that specifies which ways should be flushed. Each time a way is locked, our system sets this mask appropriately, and resets it when the way is unlocked. We changed all calls to the L2 cache flush routines in Linux to use this mask. As a result of these changes, the code handling L2 cache flushes in Linux grew from 428 to 676 lines of code.

5. Encrypted DRAM

This section describes how Sentry uses paged virtual memory to secure background applications. Sentry uses paging to manage data transfers between on-SoC memory and main memory (DRAM). Sentry ensures that pages stored in DRAM are always encrypted, and Sentry performs decryption on page-in to on-SoC memory, and encryption on page-out of on-SoC memory.

We clear a bit (called the *young* bit in the ARM architecture) of a Page Table Entry (PTE) to ensure we trap (page fault) whenever this page is accessed. Upon a page-in, the trap is fired, and we copy this page into a locked L2 cache way, and decrypt it in place. Once decryption is done, we modify the PTE to point to the decrypted page copy stored in the locked way and reset the "young" bit. Figure 1 illustrates the steps performed by Sentry during decryption on page-in.

If the locked L2 cache is full, Sentry needs to evict a page. For this, the same sequence is repeated in reverse. We encrypt in place, and then copy the page back, modify the PTE to point back to this location, and clear its young bit to ensure future traps.

While this approach supports running unmodified applications securely in the background, it has a couple of limitations. First, system performance is reduced as page faults need to be handled in software to enable careful control of the L2 cache contents. In addition, the limited capacity of the locked cache ways leads to an increase in the frequency of paging content in and out of the cache. Second, direct accesses to physical memory that do not trigger page faults, such as DMA by I/O devices, is not supported. We expect these limitations to be negligible because typical background jobs running on mobile devices (e.g., polling for email, periodically reading sensor data) have modest processing requirements.

6. On-SoC Encryption

To ensure protection from memory attacks, Sentry's implementation of encrypted DRAM cannot use generic encryption and decryption routines. Instead, the encryption and decryption routines used by Sentry must ensure that they do not leak any sensitive state to DRAM. This section presents AES_On_SoC, a secure implementation of the Advanced Encryption Standard (AES) [34] that prevents sensitive encryption state from leaking out to DRAM. We start with an in-depth analysis of AES to classify its state and determine what portion must be protected. We then describe the implementation steps taken to build AES_On_SoC.

6.1 An In-depth Analysis of AES's State

Brief AES Primer. The Advanced Encryption Standard (AES) [34] is a block cipher that operates on 128-bit blocks of plaintext and can use keys of 128, 192, or 256 bits. AES performs up to four different operations repeatedly, where each repetition is called a *round*. In each round, AES uses a specific, per-round encryption key, derived from the original encryption key. For performance reasons all round keys are precomputed and "cached" because they depend on the original encryption key only, and not on any intermediate state. While this optimization speeds up performance, it also increases the amount of AES sensitive state. This raises an interesting trade-off – a faster AES implementation requires more secure storage.

To precompute the round keys, AES uses two lookup tables, called the *S-box* and the *R-con*. While these lookup tables contain no secret state, the specific order in which AES looks up into these tables can leak sensitive information about AES.

To handle input data longer than 128 bits, AES breaks the input data into 128-bit input blocks and applies the single-block operation repeatedly. The ciphertexts corresponding to each block are then combined or chained using different modes of operation. AES supports many different modes (e.g., ECB, CTR, CBC). Sentry uses the CBC mode; CBC is also the default AES mode of operation on Android and Linux.

State Classification. Different types of state can be safe against some types of memory attacks but not against others. AES's state can be classified as follows:

1. Secret state. Secret state is state that, if leaked, will lead to a compromise. In AES, the input text, the encryption key, and most of the state derived from the encryption key is secret. Note that not all state derived from the encryption key is secret; for example, the ciphertext is not secret.

2. Public state. Public state is state that will not lead to a compromise if leaked. For AES, the public state is the ciphertext and any additional state that keeps track of the progress of the encryption. For example, the variable keeping track of the encryption round in AES is public.

3. Access-protected state. Although not secret, this state's access patterns are sensitive. For example, AES (and other symmetric encryption algorithms) use pre-computed lookup tables to speed up computation (e.g., the R-con and S-box tables). The lookup tables' contents are not secret, but monitoring what entries in these tables are accessed during encryption can reveal sensitive information about encryption keys.

	AES-128	AES-192	AES-256	Sensitivity
Input block	16	16	16	Secret
Key	16	24	32	Secret
Round Index	1	1	1	Public
Round Keys	320	368	416	Secret
2 Round Tables	2048	2048	2048	Access-protected
2 S-box	512	512	512	Access-protected
Rcon	40	40	40	Access-protected
Block Index	1	1	1	Public
CBC block/ivec	16	16	16	Public

Table 4. The breakdown of AES state in bytes.

How much state does AES use? Table 4 presents the state AES uses for encrypting with different key sizes. The input block holds the plaintext at the beginning of encryption and the ciphertext at the end as each round is performed on the same input block. We list its size as one block of 16 bytes (128 bits); however, the input can be arbitrarily long. Summing up the sizes of each piece of state leads to 2970 bytes of state for implementing encryption and decryption in AES-128.

What Portion of AES State is Sensitive? The last column of Table 4 classifies AES's state according to its sensitivity. The bulk of the state is access-protected and is due to the round tables. In fact, the round tables alone account for an order of magnitude more state than the rest of the state variables combined. In summary, the OpenSSL AES-128 implementation has 352 bytes of secret state, 2600 bytes of access-protected state, and 18 bytes of public state.

6.2 AES_On_SoC Implementation

Sentry implements the following two AES_On_SoC versions:

1. iRAM AES_On_SoC. This version stores all secret and access-protected stated in iRAM. This required few changes to the generic OpenSSL AES version that loads its state from DRAM.

2. Locked L2 AES_On_SoC. This version ensures that all the secret and access-protected state is allocated in a locked L2 cache way. On our platform, the size of one way is 128KB, which is plentiful to store all AES's sensitive state.

Handling context switches. Irrespective of where it is stored, sensitive state is loaded in the regular CPU registers at runtime to perform computation. If left unhandled, a context switch could evict all the sensitive data from the CPU registers and place it on the stack in DRAM. To avoid this situation, computation handling sensitive state is performed with interrupts raised. For this, we created two different macros called *onsoc_disable_irq()* and *onsoc_enable_irq()*. Our AES_On_SoC implementations encapsulate the computation handling secure state within these two macros. The first macro disables interrupts whereas the second macro zeroes all regular registers and re-enables interrupts. Our implementation raises interrupts for 160 microseconds on average on our Tegra 3 board.

Handling procedure calls. Sensitive state can also be put on the stack when passed as arguments to procedure calls. According to the ARM procedure call standard [4], the first four arguments to a procedure call are passed in registers, and the rest on the stack. The sensitive state is safe as long as is passed in the first four arguments to a procedure call. We inspected the AES_On_SoC implementation and checked that no procedure called used more than four arguments. This guarantees that all state is passed in registers and never put on the stack.

7. Prototypes

We developed two Sentry prototypes: one on an NVidia Tegra 3 ARM development board, and one on a Google Nexus 4 smartphone. Tegra 3 allows us the low-level access needed to enable cache-locking. This prototype fully implements Sentry including support for secure on-SoC encryption and background applications. In contrast, Nexus 4 does not support cache locking, and therefore cannot run background applications while locked. However, Nexus 4 enabled us to run experiments with widely used mobile apps, and to collect meaningful power measurements. Instead, our Tegra board is not as optimized for low energy consumption as a retail device, such as the Nexus 4.

Secure On Suspend. Our Nexus 4 prototype takes advantage of the fact that smartphones seek to suspend their state to DRAM frequently (this corresponds to the ACPI S3 state) to save energy. These suspend events occur after brief periods of user inactivity, or when the user turns off the phone by pressing the power button. Wake-up occurs (1) upon detecting user interaction, such as the user pressing the home or camera buttons, or (2) when some hardware event fires, such as an incoming phone call, or when some period timer fires.

Selective Encryption. On a device lock, a strawman design would encrypt all user-level state and most of the kernel state, except for kernel state needed for resuming the device, some low-level device drivers (e.g., cell telephony driver), and the code that handles decryption and device unlock. Despite its security appeal, such an approach incurs significant latency and energy cost.

Our experiments showed that encrypting 2GB of DRAM contents on a modern smartphone (Nexus 4) takes over a minute even when using all its four CPU cores and its crypto accelerator simultaneously. This also had a steep energy price: a single full-memory (2GB) encryption consumed over 70 Joules, completely depleting the battery after 410 suspend/resume cycles only. Hardware trends also do not look promising – while future smartphones will be equipped with faster CPU cores, their DRAM sizes will also be increasing, and energy consumption will continue to be a bottleneck. Given that a typical user consults her phone on average 150 times per day [5], to be practical Sentry must add little overhead in terms of time and energy.

Instead, Sentry only secures selected applications and OS subsystems identified as sensitive. On Android, users mark applications for encryption using an extension to the systems setting menu to chose the ones from a list of installed apps.

Upon device locking, Sentry walks the page tables of all processes marked sensitive and encrypts them. The Tegra prototype relies on AES_On_SoC for encryption. The Android prototype uses the default Linux Crypto API for encryption, and stores the encryption key in iRAM. In addition, the Android prototype marks encrypted processes as *un-schedulable* and places them in a special queue to prevent them from running in the background while the phone remains locked.

We also ported AES_On_SoC to the Linux Crypto API to ensure that the encryption does not release sensitive data outside the SoC. Any legacy software already designed to use this API automatically works with our system. We register our AES implementation with the API, providing it with a higher priority than the default AES implementation. Thus, if both the generic AES and our AES are loaded, the crypto system will favor ours.

On-demand Decryption. Sentry decrypts on demand using a lazy approach to minimize the impact of decryption to resume latency and energy consumption. We modified the page fault handler to enable on-demand page decryption. Encrypted pages have modified page table entries (PTE) to generate a trap next time the page is accessed. When the page fault is generated, Sentry decrypts the page in the context of the page fault handler. By using a lazy approach, Sentry saves energy and time in the case when users unlock their phones, engage in a just a few interactions, and re-lock their phones.

While most memory is decrypted on demand, Sentry handles DMA regions used by the GPU and I/O devices differently. These regions do not trigger page faults when accessed directly by their I/O devices using physical addresses. To handle these cases, Sentry eagerly decrypts DMA regions once the device is unlocked. These regions can vary in size, from 1MB for the Contacts application, to 3MB for Twitter, and 15MB for Google Maps.

A final case is handling memory pages shared between applications. If a memory page is shared with an application deemed non-sensitive, Sentry assumes that the contents of this memory page are not secret and skips encrypting it. However, if the page is shared only between sensitive applications, Sentry encrypts the page.

Securing Persistent State. Another concern is handling the persistent state of sensitive applications. Using file-system encryption only is not sufficient because the cryptography library could leave sensitive data in DRAM during execution. Instead, we incorporate AES_On_SoC in *dm-crypt*, a transparent block-level encryption module in Linux. At a high-level, *dm-crypt* makes three calls to an AES library, one to set the encryption and decryption keys, and two calls to encrypt and decrypt data. As described earlier, we incorporated AES_On_SoC into the kernel's Crypto API and modified dm-crypt to use AES_On_SoC instead of the default kernel AES library.

Securing Freed Pages. Another concern is handling memory pages that have been de-allocated (i.e. "freed") by a sensitive application because such pages could contain sensitive data. Although Linux has a kernel thread whose job is to zero-out these freed pages, there is no guarantee when this is done. This is not a risk for background applications because Sentry always encrypts these pages when paged out from the L2 cache even when freed. However, this is a potential risk for applications encrypted at screen-lock. This risk is eliminated by waiting for the kernel thread to zero-out all freed pages before locking the screen. We measured this overhead on our Nexus 4 device and found it negligible – the kernel thread can zero-out pages at a rate of 4.014 GB/s and an energy cost of 2.8 micro-Joules per MB.

Bootstrapping. Sentry uses two root keys for AES encryption, a volatile root key and a persistent one. The volatile key is used to encrypt all sensitive applications' memory pages. The volatile key is stored on the SoC and is generated upon each platform reboot with different values. The persistent key is used to encrypt all on-disk, persistent state (using dm-crypt). This key is derived from a combination of user input (a password entered at boot time) and a secret value stored in a secure hardware fuse on the device. Present mobile devices are already equipped with such a secure fuse storing a random, hard-to-guess number only readable by code running inside ARM TrustZone. We implemented code that reads the secure fuse and generates an AES persistent root key, although this code is not integrated into Sentry yet.

Minimum On-SoC Memory Requirements. The minimum amount of on-SoC memory required to implement Sentry is only two pages. Sentry requires at least one page for AES_On_SoC, and another for the code and data of the sensitive application being decrypted/encrypted. We verified that our Tegra 3 Sentry prototype works in this configuration, although the system becomes very slow because of very frequent page faults.

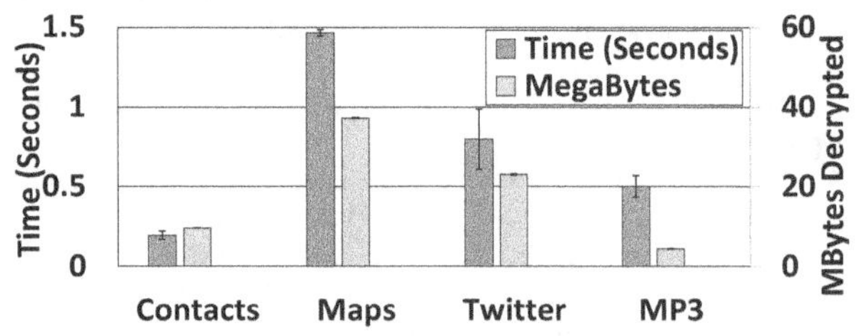

Figure 2. Performance overhead upon device unlock.

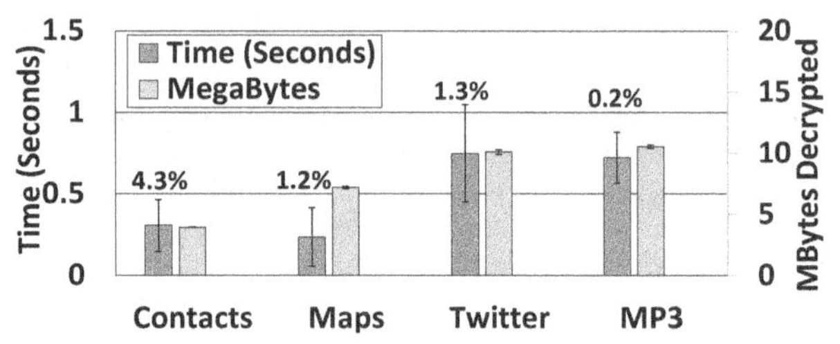

Figure 3. Performance overhead at runtime.

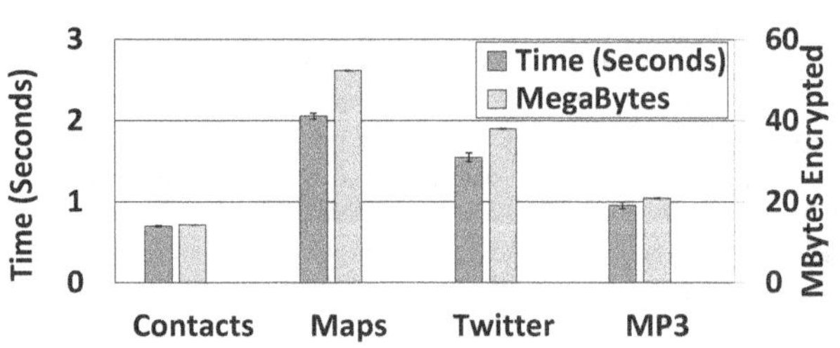

Figure 4. Performance overhead upon device lock.

8. Evaluation

This section evaluates the energy and performance overheads of Sentry in its various modes of protection.

8.1 Methodology

To evaluate Sentry, we use our two different hardware platforms: (1) an NVidia Tegra 3 ARM development board running Ubuntu Linux that allows us the low-level access needed to enable cache-locking, and (2) a Google Nexus 4 smartphone running a full-featured version of the Android OS. On the Tegra, we run a custom version of the Linux kernel v3.1.10, and on the Nexus the Linux kernel version is v3.4.0. The Tegra 3 contains a quad-core Cortex A9 CPU running at 1.2 GHz with 1GB of RAM, and the Nexus 4 contains a quad-core SnapdragonS4 CPU running at 1.5 GHz with 2 GB of RAM. All experiments are repeated at least ten times. All our graphs plot the average and the standard deviation, although sometimes the standard deviation is so low that it can barely be seen in the graph.

All mobile devices we are familiar with disable L2 cache locking in firmware. Because we only have access to the Tegra board's firmware, this is the sole platform where we can run our cache locking experiments. We only perform energy measurements on the Nexus 4 platform because our Tegra development board is not optimized for low energy consumption required by retail devices.

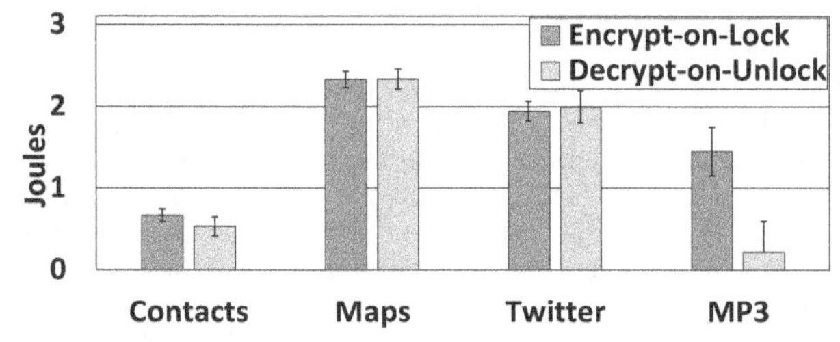

Figure 5. Energy overhead of encrypt-on-lock and decrypt-on-unlock.

8.2 Performance and Energy Overheads

We use a series of application-level benchmarks to characterize the performance and energy overheads of Sentry. We then follow with microbenchmarks that show the raw AES energy and performance characteristics on our platforms.

Macrobenchmarks

We consider five different aspects of Sentry's overhead.

1. What is the performance overhead of Sentry on device lock and unlock? We run four Android applications, Contacts, Maps, Twitter, and ServeStream (an MP3 streaming app) both with and without Sentry on the Nexus 4. We measure their performance throughout their lifetime, from device unlock (where the memory pages of these applications start being decrypted), to running the applications, to device lock (where the memory pages of these applications must be all encrypted).

Device Unlock: Our first experiment measures the overhead added by Sentry of unlocking the Nexus 4 and performing a simple resume step of a single, sensitive application. This step decrypts only that portion of the application's memory pages needed to resume the application. Figure 2 shows Sentry's overhead in terms of both time and megabytes of data decrypted. We find that resuming sensitive applications has modest overhead, taking anywhere from 200 ms (Contacts) to a second and a half (Maps). This overhead is roughly proportional to the amount of data to be decrypted.

Sensitive Application Performance: We scripted each of these applications to perform a series of typical tasks. We run the script right after unlocking the screen and measure its duration; the scripts for the four applications take about 17 seconds for Twitter, 20 seconds for Maps, 23 seconds for Contacts, and 5 minutes for the MP3 app. With Sentry, the script takes longer to run because the applications are decrypting their memory pages on demand. Figure 3 presents Sentry's overhead in terms of time and megabytes of data decrypted. While these applications run, Sentry's overhead is small ranging between 0.2% and 4.3%.

Device Lock: Finally, all memory pages of the applications must be encrypted before the device is locked. Figure 4 shows this performance overhead. Again, the overhead is modest adding between 700 ms to 2 seconds per application. As before, the overhead is proportional to the amount of data needed to be encrypted.

Energy Profile: Figure 5 shows the energy overhead of device lock and unlock operations for protecting one sensitive application. These results do not include the energy consumed by an application at runtime; our benchmarking results later will show the energy costs of encryption/decryption at runtime. As Figure 5 shows,

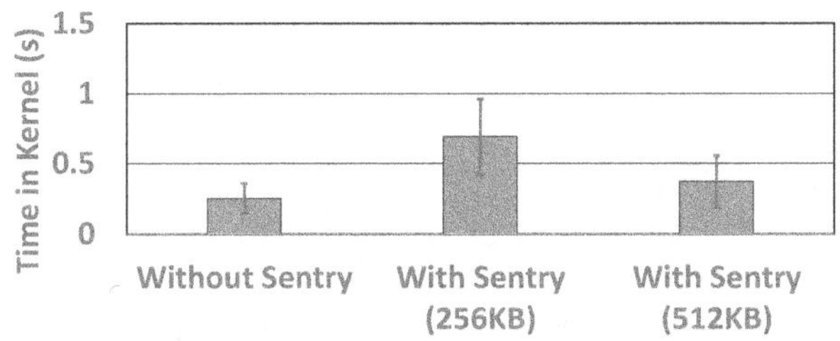

Figure 6. Performance of background computation for alpine.

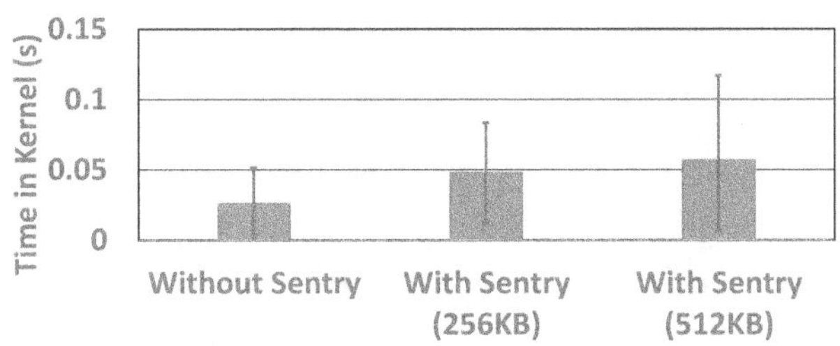

Figure 7. Performance of background computation for vlock.

the overhead is minimal for all apps. Even for Google Maps, a relatively large application that needs to decrypt 38 MB of memory pages during device lock, and encrypt 48 MB, the energy overhead of device lock/unlock is modest consuming up to 2.3 Joules. We measure the unlock overhead conservatively because applications' memory pages are decrypted on demand rather than all at once as is the case with our experiment. Even so, Sentry will consume daily about 2% of a device's battery life to protect an application assuming the user locks and unlocks a phone 150 times a day.

2. What is the performance of Sentry's encryption and decryption for background computation?

On our Tegra 3 board, we ported three applications to Sentry: *alpine* (an e-mail reader based on *pine*), *vlock* (a text-based lock screen application), and *xmms2* (an MP3 player). These applications represent the types of actions users do when their smartphones are locked – they listen to music (xmms2), receive e-mail (alpine), and lock and unlock their devices' screens (vlock).

We run each application in the background for several seconds and measure the elapsed time spent inside of the kernel with and without Sentry. Figures 6, 7, and 8 show the results of our experiments. Sentry's overhead varies from a factor of 2.74 in the case of alpine when running with 256KB of locked L2 cache, to 48% in the case of xmms2 when running with 512KB of locked L2 cache. Although these overheads are high, we find Sentry's performance adequate because applications are generally not performance-critical while running in the background. Furthermore, these overheads are all relative to kernel time only, and not user time. Sentry's performance overhead is lower when considering an application's total time both in kernel and user-space. In all our experiments, we found that applications remain responsive when run in the background with Sentry.

3. What is Sentry's performance overhead for protecting file-system access with dm-crypt?

One of the most common ways to encrypt a file-system is using the *dm-crypt* Linux kernel module. Using Sentry to protect dm-

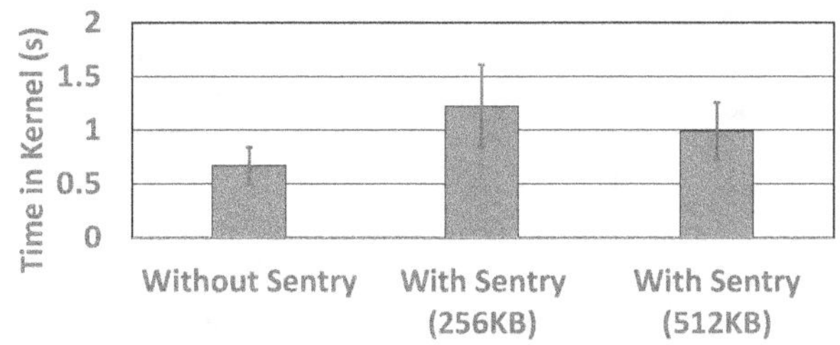

Figure 8. Performance of background computation for xmms2.

crypt provides appealing security properties because it ensures that all persistent data in the system is secured against memory attacks.

We start by devising an experiment that isolates the performance overhead of Sentry when used on *dm-crypt*. *dm-crypt* performance is usually disk-bound, so we setup an in-memory disk partition of 450 MB and protect it with dm-crypt. We use three filebench [19] workloads: sequential reads, random reads, and random read/writes. All the dm-crypt benchmarks are run on the Tegra platform with cache-locking enabled.

For each run, the benchmark first creates a variety of files and then runs a sequence of I/O operations on these files, according to each workload. The initial file creation warms up the file system's buffer cache, and most of the I/O operations end up being serviced from the cache, without exercising the block-level AES encryption. To eliminate this effect, we also run the workloads using *direct I/O* to bypass the buffer cache.

Figure 9 shows the throughput in megabytes per second of two workloads – running random reads (on the left) and random read/writes (on the right). Each graph has groups of three bars; the first bar corresponds to running with *dm-crypt* disabled, the second bar corresponds to running *dm-crypt* without Sentry, and the last bar corresponds to running *dm-crypt* with Sentry. The presence of the file system buffer cache "masks" some of the performance overhead of Sentry. Encryption adds no performance overhead for the randread benchmark. However, encryption cuts throughput by a factor of two for the randrw benchmark (the y-axis of Figure 9 is shown with a log-scale). When we eliminate the system buffer cache by using direct I/O, the impact of encryption on throughput is clearly visible.

4. What is the performance impact on the rest of the system when the L2 cache size is effectively reduced by cache locking?

Locking L2 cache ways can affect the performance of the rest of the system. We quantify this effect by running a CPU intensive task while locking different numbers of cache ways. Figure 10 shows, on the Tegra platform, the average duration of a Linux kernel compilation as a function of the number of locked cache ways. We use *"make -j 5"* as our build command, which runs up to five commands simulatenously during the build. As expected, the full compilation process takes longer as more ways are locked. However, the effect of locking a single way, which reduces the effective cache size by 128 KB (out of a total cache size of 1 MB) is not large. It takes 14.53 minutes to compile the Linux kernel with one locked way versus 14.41 minutes with no locked ways, an increase of 7.2 seconds (less than 1%).

Microbenchmarks

These microbenchmarks are useful in understanding sources of overhead in the application macrobenchmarks. On Tegra, we use three AES implementations: unsafe AES (unmodified OpenSSL AES), cache-locked AES, and iRAM AES. On the Nexus 4, we use three versions of AES: unsafe AES (unmodified OpenSSL AES)

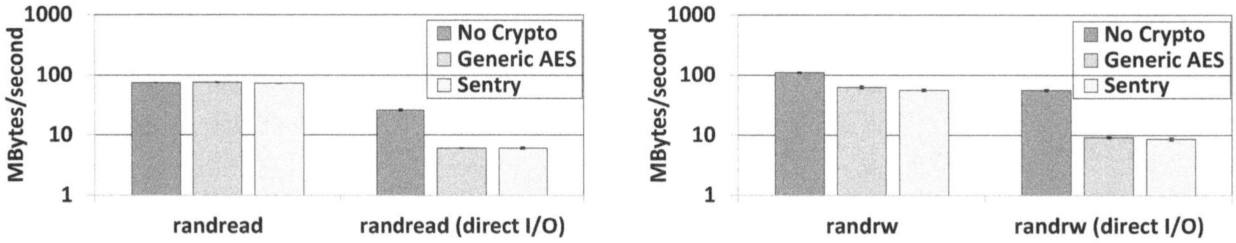

Figure 9. Performance of dm-crypt for random reads (left) and random read/writes (right).

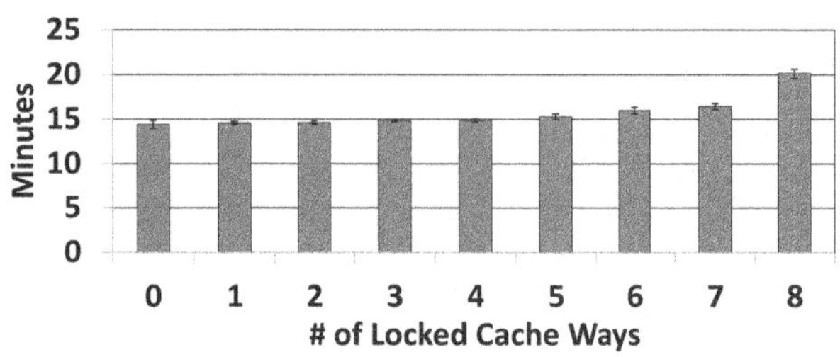

Figure 10. Performance of Linux kernel compile. Compiling Linux gets gradually slower as more cache ways are locked.

both at running in user-level and in the kernel, and the hardware accelerator AES.

Figure 11 shows the performance of AES for all the different AES variants on both platforms, with the Nexus 4 on the left and Tegra 3 on the right. At first, we were surprised to discover that AES is slower when running on the crypto hardware accelerator than on the CPU. However, upon investigation, this discrepancy is due to two factors. First, we are using 4KB blocks of data (the page size) to encrypt/decrypt. Crypto accelerators exhibit higher performance when encrypting large amounts of data. Second, our experiment is done upon phone lock and we suspect that the crypto accelerator is down-scaling its frequency. We repeated this experiment with the phone fully awake and the crypto accelerator is 4× faster. However, we were unable to prevent the crypto hardware from being down-scaled in our experiments. Without downscaling, the performance of our crypto accelerator is similar to previously published results [28].

Figure 11 also shows that Nexus 4 is much faster than our Tegra development board. Finally, and more importantly, on Tegra using AES_On_SoC adds negligible overhead (less than 1%).

Figure 12 shows the full-system energy overhead of CPU-based encryption versus hardware-accelerated encryption on Nexus 4. These results are driven by how long encryption takes using each method. Hardware-accelerated encryption is much less energy-efficient than the CPU due to the lower throughput of the AES hardware accelerator when encrypting 4 KB memory pages.

9. Related Work

9.1 On Chip AES Schemes

A few previous projects have investigated the idea of storing AES keys in CPU registers. In addition of being AES-for-x86-specific, most of these previous solutions fail to guard access-protected state and thus are subject to bus monitoring attacks. Furthermore, to us, it is unclear how to extend these solutions to safeguard the voluminous access-protected state.

In AESSE [32], Müller et al. implement AES for x86 processors by leveraging the SSE functionality of Pentium III and later processors to both store encryption and decryption keys and to perform the AES computation. Their initial implementation, based on the FIPS documentation [34], performed all the calculations sequentially on the input data, producing a very slow implementation. Their final implementation makes use of the table lookup optimization, improving performance from a 100× slowdown to a 6× slowdown over regular AES. In this implementation, all of the AES lookup tables (i.e., access-protected state) are stored in DRAM.

Their later work, TRESOR [33] expands on the AESSE functionality to support 64-bit CPUs with support for Intel's encryption instructions (AES-NI). This version is resilient to memory attacks because all AES's state is stored in AES-NI in the CPU. However, such an approach is not extensible beyond protecting AES implementations only.

Simmons [41] disables model-specific registers used for debugging and instead re-purposes them to store a single 128-bit AES key. This key is used to decrypt other keys stored encrypted in DRAM. This improves the performance to only a 2× slowdown over regular AES. The implementation's description specifies that no temporary data is stored in DRAM, although the paper offers no clear explanation on how large round tables are being stored in model-specific registers.

9.2 Other Forms of Defense

Encrypted RAM. Encrypted RAM schemes aim at storing data encrypted in DRAM. There are two main differences between our approach and encrypted RAM: (1) encrypted RAM's performance overhead is typically high and (2) it is unclear whether encrypted DRAM can protect against DMA attacks. In particular DMA transfers should be automatically decrypted otherwise there is little benefit of using DMA for fast memory access.

Cryptkeeper [35] expands the traditional memory hierarchy by proposing to encrypt a large portion of DRAM. Their implementation stores DRAM's encryption keys in the clear portion of RAM.

Another project [12] proposed the idea of encrypting the memory for processes when evicted from the cache. Like Sentry, they use a form of cache locking to ensure that sensitive data leaving the SoC is encrypted. However, this previous work differs from Sentry in four aspects. First, it only describes a preliminary design with no implementation. Second, the evaluation is all done in simulation on top of a Pentium-based architecture (whereas their design is aimed at ARM SoC) while artificially injecting hypothetical costs, such as the number of cycles encryption might take. Third, it is aimed at embedded systems and does not meet the needs of smartphones today. For example, there is no notion of "pin lock", no background processes, no discussion of DMA capabilities. Instead, a different set of assumptions are made, such as whether MMU is present or what types of crypto engines could be found on embedded systems. Finally, the cache-locking mechanism discussed is hypothet-

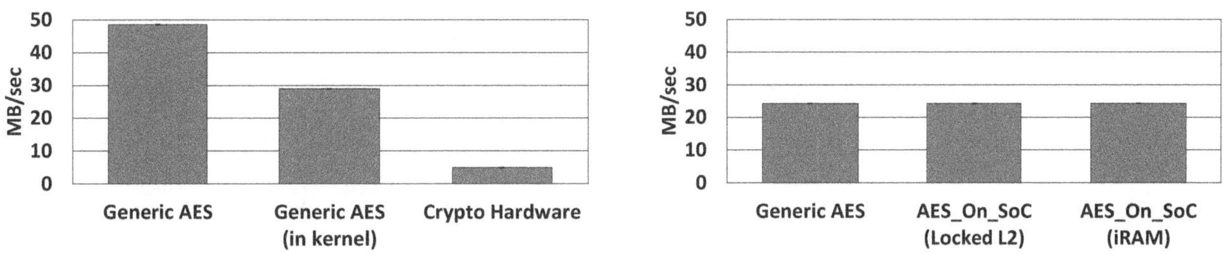

Figure 11. AES performance. Comparison of OpenSSL AES, the kernel CryptoAPI AES, and hardware-accelerated AES on Nexus (left), and OpenSSL AES, cache-locked Sentry, and iRAM Sentry on Tegra.

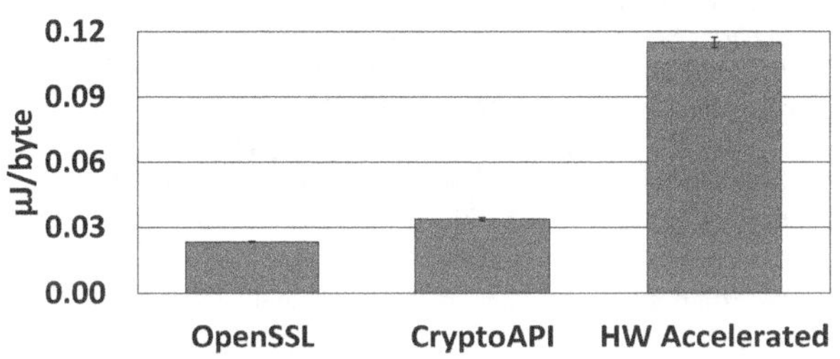

Figure 12. Energy overhead. Comparison of OpenSSL AES, the kernel Crypto API AES, the hardware-accelerated AES on Nexus.

ical, and thus it is unclear how the cache locks its contents (e.g., by way or by line).

Other methods have been proposed that store encryption keys in a secret place. ZIA [14] and Transient Authentication [15] use user-carried, small hardware tokens, and CleanOS [48] uses cloud servers for storing encryption keys. Unlike Sentry, such schemes rely on additional external infrastructure in the form of an Internet connection [48] or short-range wireless interfaces [14, 15]. Transient Authentication also does not support running background application securely while the phone is locked. Another difference lies in the type of abstractions used. CleanOS provides APIs that let applications define their sensitive data that needs protection. Instead, Sentry reduces the programmer's burden by encrypting all sensitive applications' state.

Auditing file-systems. Keypad [23] keeps logs of file-system accesses. While such an approach does not explicitly defend against memory attacks, it enables the victim to determine what portion of their data has been compromised when the mobile is lost.

9.3 Complementary Threat Models

A large body of work aims at protecting the integrity and confidentiality of trusted applications' code and data [13, 16, 17, 22, 26, 29, 37, 39, 40, 42, 44, 45, 47, 52]. These related works defend against a compromised OS (e.g., malware) or a compromised privileged VM, whereas Sentry relies on the OS to defend against DRAM attacks.

10. Discussion

ARM TrustZone: Today's ARM platforms offer TrustZone [2], a set of hardware extensions for code and data isolation. TrustZone can be used to isolate a set of secure services from the general purpose operating system. With TrustZone, the processor can execute instructions in one of two processor modes, referred to as the *normal world*, where untrusted code executes, and the *secure world*, where secure services run. One CPU instruction allows the software stack to switch back and forth between these two worlds. All memory allocated to the secure world remains inaccessible to the normal world. This offers a form of protection where malware in the normal world cannot infect the secure world. ARM TrustZone does not encrypt secure world memory.

Sentry uses TrustZone to enable cache-locking. This requires configuring certain co-processor registers which are only accessible from the secure world of TrustZone. We have access to TrustZone only on our Tegra 3 device, but not on the Nexus 4 (due to locked firmware). This is why we cannot test cache locking behavior on the Nexus 4.

Unfortunately, ARM TrustZone cannot help prevent cold boot or bus monitoring attacks. Removing RAM modules (one form of cold boot attack) and bus monitoring make the entire contents of RAM vulnerable, including any RAM allocated to the TrustZone. Reflashing the device firmware (another form of cold boot attack) also can bypass TrustZone's protection of secure world memory.

Running 3rd-party applications inside TrustZone makes them immune to DMA attacks. However, this approach brings significant challenges: running an OS/browser/DalvikVM in the TrustZone [39] and porting each app to it. The TrustZone's software stack could become very large, increasing the TCB of any other security services that rely on TrustZone.

Intel Software Guard Extensions (SGX): Intel has recently announced SGX [6, 27], a new set of CPU instructions for code and data isolation. Unlike TrustZone, the memory allocated to an "enclave" is encrypted in hardware, which renders cold boot and bus monitoring attacks ineffective. However, SGX brings in a set of additional challenges. First, OS code cannot run inside of SGX (SGX runs ring 3 code only). Second, based on the current documentation, SGX offers no form of protection against rollback attacks (i.e., no secure counters). Third, SGX technology appears to be aimed at the server market targetting cloud computing datacenters.

Architecture suggestions: This work demonstrates the feasibility and security benefits of locking data on the SoC. We believe that modern CPUs could offer a small amount of memory on the SoC together with a pin-on-SoC abstraction. Operating systems can make use of this abstraction to store cryptographic keys used to bootstrap additional system security, such as encrypted main memory. Such keys will be much better protected from memory attacks. In Sentry, we went to great lengths to use ARM-based mechanisms designed for computation performance and predictability (e.g., cache locking and internal RAM), and applied them to our security needs. However, Sentry's design would be greatly simplified in the presence of a simple abstraction that would guarantee a small amount of memory pinned on the SoC. This memory should be inaccessible to DMA controllers to further prevent DMA-based attacks.

To increase the security of on-SoC storage, we also recommend that low-level firmware should always erase it (i.e., zero it) upon device boot up. Additionally, this low-level firmware should not be modifiable to guarantee an attacker cannot simply disable it. Although this step would increase the time required for the device to boot up, the increase should be modest because zero-ing out a small amount of memory should be relatively fast. We believe this overhead is justified given the additional security gains.

11. Conclusions

This paper shows that today's smartphones and tablets have several performance features that can be retrofitted to defend against memory attacks. We implement Sentry, a system that leverages these features to guarantee that the sensitive state of a program is never stored in DRAM, but always stored on the ARM SoC. Our main observation is that sensitive state only needs to be encrypted when the device is screen-locked. However, to run computation in the background when the screen is locked, Sentry decrypts and encrypts the memory pages of sensitive applications as they are paged in and out. Sentry uses a carefully engineered AES crypto library (called AES_On_SoC) that never stores any sensitive state in DRAM. This combination of mechanisms ensures Sentry never leaks any sensitive state to DRAM when the device is screen-locked.

Acknowledgments

We would like to thank our shepherd, Gernot Heiser, and the anonymous reviewers for their thorough feedback. We would also like to thank Andrew Baumann and Jay Lorch for their feedback on earlier drafts of this paper.

References

[1] ARM. Fast models. http://www.arm.com/products/tools/models/fast-models/index.php. Accessed: 2014-12-10.

[2] ARM. ARM security technology – building a secure system using trustzone technology. http://infocenter.arm.com/help/topic/com.arm.doc.prd29-genc-009492c/PRD29-GENC-009492C_trustzone_security_whitepaper.pdf, 2005–2009.

[3] ARM. PL310 cache controller reference manual, 2007. http://infocenter.arm.com/help/topic/com.arm.doc.ddi0246a/DDI0246A_l2cc_pl310_r0p0_trm.pdf.

[4] ARM. Procedure Call Standard for the ARM Architecture. http://infocenter.arm.com/help/topic/com.arm.doc.ihi0042e/IHI0042E_aapcs.pdf, 2012.

[5] T. T. Athonen and A. Moore. Commununities dominate brands. http://communities-dominate.blogs.com/brands/2013/03/. Accessed: 2014-12-10.

[6] A. Baumann, M. Peinado, and G. Hunt. Shielding applications from an untrusted cloud with haven. In *Proc. of the 11th Symposium on Operating System Design and Implementation (OSDI)*, Broomfield, CO, 2014.

[7] M. Becher, M. Dornseif, and C. N. Klein. Firewire - all your memory are belong to us. In *Proc. of CanSecWest Applied Security Conference*, 2005.

[8] R. Bittner. Personal Communication, April 2014.

[9] A. Boileau. Hit by a bus: Physical access attacks with firewire. In *Proc. of 4th Annual Ruxcon Conference*, 2006.

[10] C. Cakir, M. Bhargava, and K. Mai. 6T SRAM and 3T DRAM data retention and remanence characterization in 65nm bulk CMOS. In *Custom Integrated Circuits Conference (CICC)*, 2012.

[11] E. M. Chan, J. C. Carlyle, F. M. David, R. Farivar, and R. H. Campbell. Bootjacker: compromising computers using forced restarts. In *Proceedings of the 15th ACM conference on Computer and communications security (CCS)*.

[12] X. Chen, R. P. Dick, and A. Choudhary. Operating system controlled processor-memory bus encryption. In *Proceedings of the conference on Design, automation and test in Europe*, 2008.

[13] X. Chen, T. Garfinkel, E. C. Lewis, P. Subrahmanyam, C. A. Waldspurger, D. Boneh, J. Dwoskin, and D. R. K. Ports. Overshadow: A Virtualization-Based Approach to Retrofitting Protection in Commodity Operating Systems. In *Proc. of 13th International Conference on Architectural Support for Programming Languages and Operating Systems (ASPLOS)*, Seattle, WA, 2008.

[14] M. D. Corner and B. D. Noble. Zero-interaction authentication. In *Proc. of the 8th Annual International conference on Mobile computing and networking (Mobicom)*, 2002.

[15] M. D. Corner and B. D. Noble. Protecting applications with transient authentication. In *Proc. of the 1st International Conference on Mobile systems, applications and services (MobiSys)*, 2003.

[16] J. Criswell, N. Dautenhahn, and V. Adve. Virtual ghost: Protecting applications from hostile operating systems. In *Proc. of 19th International Conference on Architectural Support for Programming Languages and Operating Systems (ASPLOS)*, 2014.

[17] O. H. A. Dunn, S. Kim, M. Lee, and E. Witchel. Inktag: Secure applications on an untrusted operating system. In *Proc. of 18th International Conference on Architectural Support for Programming Languages and Operating Systems (ASPLOS)*, 2013.

[18] EPN Solutions. Analysis tools for DDR1, DDR2, DDR3, embedded DDR and fully buffered DIMM modules. http://www.epnsolutions.net/ddr.html. Accessed: 2014-12-10.

[19] Filebench. Filebench: File system benchmark. http://sourceforge.net/projects/filebench/. Accessed: 2014-12-10.

[20] Freescale Semiconductor. Configuring secure JTAG for the i.MX 6 series family of applications processors. http://cache.freescale.com/files/32bit/doc/eng_bulletin/AN4686.pdf, 2013.

[21] FuturePlus System. DDR2 800 bus analysis probe. http://www.futureplus.com/download/datasheet/fs2334_ds.pdf, 2006.

[22] T. Garfinkel, B. Pfaff, J. Chow, M. Rosenblum, and D. Boneh. Terra: A Virtual Machine-Based Platform for Trusted Computing. In *Proc. of 19th ACM Symposium on Operating Systems Principles (SOSP)*, Lake George, NY, 2003.

[23] R. Geambaşu, J. P. John, S. D. Gribble, T. Kohno, and H. M. Levy. Keypad: An Auditing File System for Theft-prone Devices. In *Proc. of the European Conference on Computer Systems (EuroSys)*, 2011.

[24] G. Gogniat, T. Wolf, W. Burleson, J.-P. Diguet, L. Bossuet, and R. Vaslin. Reconfigurable hardware for high-security/high-performance embedded systems: The SAFES perspective. *IEEE Transactions on Very Large Scale Integration (VLSI) Systems*, 16(2): 144–155, 2008.

[25] J. A. Halderman, S. D. Schoen, N. Heninger, W. Clarkson, W. Paul, J. A. Calandrino, A. J. Feldman, J. Appelbaum, and E. W. Felten. Lest we remember: Cold boot attacks on encryption keys. In *Proc. of the 17th USENIX Security Symposium*, 2008.

[26] H. Härtig, M. Hohmuth, N. Feske, C. Helmuth, A. L. orzynski, F. Mehnert, and M. Peter. The Nizza secure-system architecture. In *Proc. of 1st International Conference on Collaborative Computing: Networking, Applications and Worksharing (CollaborateCom)*, 2005.

[27] Intel. Software Guard Extensions Programming Reference. https://software.intel.com/sites/default/files/329298-001.pdf, 2013.

[28] V. Keränen. Cryptographic algorithm benchmarking in mobile devices. Technical Report Master's Thesis, University of Oulu, 2013.

[29] J. M. McCune, Y. Li, N. Qu, Z. Zhou, A. Datta, V. Gligor, and A. Perrig. TrustVisor: Efficient TCB Reduction and Attestation. In *Proc. of IEEE Symposium on Security and Privacy*, Oakland, CA, May 2010.

[30] Microsoft. BitLocker Drive Encryption. http://windows.microsoft.com/en-us/windows7/products/features/bitlocker.

[31] T. Müller and M. Spreitzenbarth. FROST - forensic recovery of scrambled telephones. In *Proc. of the International Conference on Applied Cryptography and Network Security (ACNS)*, 2013.

[32] T. Müller, A. Dewald, and F. C. Freiling. AESSE: a cold-boot resistant implementation of AES. In *Proc. of the 3rd European Workshop on System Security (EUROSEC)*, 2010.

[33] T. Müller, A. Dewald, and F. Freiling. TRESOR runs encryption securely outside RAM. In *Proc. of the 20th USENIX Security Symposium*, 2011.

[34] NIST. Pub. 197 – advanced encryption standard (AES). `http://csrc.nist.gov/publications/fips/fips197/fips-197.pdf`, 2001.

[35] P. A. Peterson. Cryptkeeper: Improving security with encrypted RAM. In *Proc. of IEEE International Conference on Technologies for Homeland Security*, 2010.

[36] D. R. Piegdon. Hacking in physically addressable memory - a proof of concept. Presentation to the Seminar of Advanced Exploitation Techniques, 2006.

[37] H. Raj, D. Robinson, T. Tariq, P. England, S. Saroiu, and A. Wolman. Credo: Trusted computing for guest VMs with a commodity hypervisor. Technical Report MSR-TR-2011-130, 2011.

[38] Riff Box. `http://www.riffbox.org/`, 2014. Accessed: 2014-12-10.

[39] N. Santos, H. Raj, S. Saroiu, and A. Wolman. Using ARM TrustZone to build a trusted language runtime for mobile applications. In *Proc. of 19th International Conference on Architectural Support for Programming Languages and Operating Systems (ASPLOS)*, 2014.

[40] F. B. Schneider, K. Walsh, and E. G. Sirer. Nexus Authorization Logic (NAL): Design Rationale and Applications. *ACM Transactions on Information and System Security*, 14(1), 2011.

[41] P. Simmons. Security through amnesia: A software-based solution to the cold boot attack on disk encryption. In *Proc. of the 27th Annual Computer Security Applications Conference (ACSAC)*, 2011.

[42] E. G. Sirer, W. de Bruijn, P. Reynolds, A. Shieh, K. Walsh, D. Williams, and F. B. Schneider. Logical attestation: An authorization architecture for trustworthy computing. In *Proc. of 23rd ACM Symposium on Operating Systems Principles (SOSP)*, 2011.

[43] S. Skorobogatov. Low temperature data remanence in static RAM. Technical Report UCAM-CL-TR-536, University of Cambridge, Computer Laboratory, 2002.

[44] J. Sorber, M. Shin, R. Peterson, and D. Kotz. Plug-n-Trust: Practical trusted sensing for mHealth. In *Proc. of the International Conference on Mobile Systems, Applications, and Services (MobiSys)*, 2012.

[45] U. Steinberg and B. Kauer. NOVA: A microhypervisor-based secure virtualization architecture. In *Proc. of European Conference on Computer Systems (Eurosys)*, 2010.

[46] STMicroelectronics. STM32F205/215, STM32F207/217 Flash programming manual. `http://www.st.com/st-web-ui/static/active/en/resource/technical/document/programming_manual/CD00233952.pdf`, 2013.

[47] R. Ta-Min, L. Litty, and D. Lie. Splitting interfaces: Making trust between applications and operati ng systems configurable. In *Proc. of the 7th Symposium on Operating System Design and Implementation (OSDI)*, 2006.

[48] Y. Tang, P. Ames, S. Bhamidipati, A. Bijlani, R. Geambaşu, and N. Sarda. CleanOS: Limiting mobile data exposure with idle eviction. In *Proc. of the 10th USENIX Symposium on Operating Systems Design and Implementation (OSDI)*, 2012.

[49] C. Tarnovsky. Attacking hardware: Unsecuring [once] secure devices. Black Hat USA Training Session, 2009.

[50] E. Tromer, D. A. Osvik, and A. Shamir. Efficient cache attaks on AES, and countermeasures. *Journal of Cryptology*, 23(1):37–31, 2010.

[51] TrueCrypt. Truecrypt – free open source disc encryption software. `http://www.truecrypt.org/`. Accessed: 2014-04-01; Product and website retired on: 2014-05-28.

[52] F. Zhang, J. Chen, H. Chen, and B. Zang. CloudVisor: Retrofitting protection of virtual machines in multi-tenant cloud with nested virtualization. In *Proc. of 23rd ACM Symposium on Operating Systems Principles (SOSP)*, 2011.

Nested Kernel: An Operating System Architecture for Intra-Kernel Privilege Separation

Nathan Dautenhahn[1], Theodoros Kasampalis[1], Will Dietz[1], John Criswell[2], and Vikram Adve[1]

[1]University of Illinois at Urbana-Champaign, [2]University of Rochester

{dautenh1, kasampa2, wdietz2, vadve}@illinois.edu, criswell@cs.rochester.edu

Abstract

Monolithic operating system designs undermine the security of computing systems by allowing single exploits anywhere in the kernel to enjoy full supervisor privilege. The *nested kernel operating system architecture* addresses this problem by "nesting" a small isolated kernel within a traditional monolithic kernel. The "nested kernel" interposes on all updates to virtual memory translations to assert protections on physical memory, thus significantly reducing the trusted computing base for memory access control enforcement. We incorporated the nested kernel architecture into FreeBSD on x86-64 hardware while allowing the entire operating system, including untrusted components, to operate at the highest hardware privilege level by write-protecting MMU translations and *de-privileging* the untrusted part of the kernel. Our implementation inherently enforces *kernel code integrity* while still allowing dynamically loaded kernel modules, thus defending against code injection attacks. We also demonstrate that the nested kernel architecture allows kernel developers to isolate memory in ways not possible in monolithic kernels by introducing write-mediation and write-logging services to protect critical system data structures. Performance of the nested kernel prototype shows modest overheads: $< 1\%$ average for Apache and 2.7% for kernel compile. Overall, our results and experience show that the nested kernel design can be retrofitted to existing monolithic kernels, providing important security benefits.

Categories and Subject Descriptors D.4.6 [*Operating Systems*]: Organization and Design

Keywords intra-kernel isolation; operating system architecture; malicious operating systems; virtual memory

ASPLOS '15, March 14–18, 2015, Istanbul, Turkey.

ACM 978-1-4503-2835-7/15/03... $15.00.

http://dx.doi.org/10.1145/2694344.2694386

1. Introduction

Critical information protection design principles, e.g., fail-safe defaults, complete mediation, least privilege, and least common mechanism [34, 40, 41], have been well known for several decades. Unfortunately, monolithic commodity operating systems (OSes), like Windows, Mac OS X, Linux, and FreeBSD, lack sufficient protection mechanisms with which to adhere to these design principles. As a result, these OS kernels define and store access control policies in main memory which any code executing within the kernel can modify. The impact of this default, *shared-everything* environment is that the entirety of the kernel, including potentially buggy device drivers [12], forms a single large trusted computing base (TCB) for all applications on the system. An exploit of any part of the kernel allows complete access to all memory and resources on the system. Consequently, commodity OSes have been susceptible to a range of kernel malware [27] and memory corruption attacks [5]. Even systems employing features such as non-executable pages, supervisor-mode access prevention, and supervisor-mode execution protection are susceptible to both user level attacks [25] and kernel level threats that directly disable these protections.

Traditional methods of applying these principles in OS kernels either completely abandon monolithic design (e.g., microkernels [3, 9, 28]) or rely upon transparent enforcement of isolation via an external virtual machine monitor (VMM) [15, 35, 44, 55, 56]. Microkernels require extensive redesign and implementation of the operating system. VMMs suffer from both performance issues and a lack of semantic knowledge at the OS level to transparently support protection easily; also, generating semantic knowledge has been shown to be circumventable [6]. More recent techniques to split existing commodity operating systems into multiple protection domains using page protections [46] or software fault isolation (SFI) [18] incur high overhead and continue to trust "core" kernel code (which may not be all that trustworthy [15, 16]).

To address this problem, we present a new OS organization, the **nested kernel architecture**, which restricts MMU control to a small subset of kernel code, effectively "nesting" a memory protection domain within the larger kernel. The key design feature in the nested kernel architecture is that a very small portion of the kernel code and data operate within an isolated environment called the *nested kernel*; the rest of the kernel, called the *outer kernel*, is untrusted. The nested kernel architecture can be incorporated into an existing monolithic commodity kernel through a minimal *reorganization* of the kernel design, as we demonstrate using FreeBSD 9.0. The nested kernel isolates and mediates modifications to itself and other protected memory by 1) configuring the MMU such that all mappings to protected pages (minimally the page-table pages (PTPs)) are read-only, and 2) ensuring that those policies are enforced at runtime while the untrusted code is operating. Although similar to a microkernel, the nested kernel only requires MMU isolation and maintains a single monolithic address space abstraction between trusted and untrusted components.

We present a concrete prototype of the nested kernel architecture, called PerspicuOS, that implements the nested kernel design on the x86-64 [2] architecture. PerspicuOS introduces a novel isolation technique where both the outer kernel and nested kernel operate at the same hardware privilege level—contrary to isolation in a microkernel where untrusted code operates in user-mode. PerspicuOS enforces read-only permissions on outer kernel code by employing existing, simple hardware mechanisms, namely the MMU, IOMMU, and the Write-Protect Enable (WP) bit in *CR0*, which enforces read-only policies even on supervisor-mode writes. By using the *WP-bit*, PerspicuOS efficiently toggles write-protections on transitions between the outer kernel and nested kernel without swapping address spaces or crossing traditional hardware privilege boundaries.

PerspicuOS ensures that the outer kernel never disables write-protections (e.g., via the *WP-bit*) by 1) *de-privileging* the outer kernel code and 2) maintaining that *de-privileged* code state by enforcing lifetime kernel code integrity—a key security property explored by several previous works, most notably SecVisor [43] and NICKLE [38]. PerspicuOS *de-privileges* outer kernel code by replacing instances of writes to *CR0* with invocations of nested kernel services and enforces lifetime kernel code integrity by restricting outer kernel code execution to validated, write-protected code. In this way PerspicuOS *creates two virtual privileges within the same hardware privilege level*, thus virtualizing ring 0.

By isolating the MMU, the nested kernel architecture can enforce *intra-kernel* memory isolation policies that trust only the nested kernel. Therefore, the nested kernel architecture exposes two *intra-kernel* write-protection services to kernel developers: write-mediation and write-logging. Write-mediation enables kernel developers to deploy security policies that isolate and control access to critical kernel data, including kernel code. In some cases, data may require valid updates from a large portion of the kernel, making it hard to protect kernel objects in place, or otherwise not have an applicable write-mediation policy; consequently, we present the write-logging interface that ensures all modifications to protected kernel objects are recorded (a design principle suggested by Saltzer et al. [41]).

To demonstrate the benefit of the write-mediation and write-logging facilities—for enhancing commodity OS security—we present three intra-kernel write-protection policies and applications. First, we introduce the write-once mediation policy that only allows a single update to protected data structures, and apply it to protect the system call vector table, defending against kernel call hooking [27]. In general, the write-once policy presents a novel defense against non-control data attacks [11]. Second, we introduce the append-only mediation policy that only allows append operations to list type data structures, and apply it to protect data generated by a system call logging facility. Additionally, the system call logging facility guarantees invocation of monitored events, a feature made possible by PerspicuOS's code integrity property, and therefore supports a pivotal feature required by a large class of security monitors [35, 44]. Third, we deploy a write-logging policy to track modifications to FreeBSD's process list data structures, allowing our system to detect direct kernel object manipulation (DKOM) attacks used by rootkits to hide malicious processes [27].

We have retrofitted the nested kernel architecture into an existing commodity OS: the FreeBSD 9.0 kernel. Our experimental evaluation shows that this reorganization requires approximately 2000 lines of FreeBSD code modifications while significantly reducing the TCB of memory isolation code to less than 5000 lines of nested kernel code. Our prototype also demonstrates that it is feasible to completely remove MMU modifying instructions from the untrusted portion of the kernel while allowing it to operate in ring 0. Furthermore, our experiments show that the nested kernel architecture incurs very low overheads for relatively OS-intensive system benchmarks: $< 1\%$ for Apache and 2.7% for a full kernel compile. In summary, the key contributions of this paper include

- A new OS organization strategy, the nested kernel architecture, which nests, within a monolithic kernel, a higher privilege protection domain that enables kernel developers to explicitly apply *intra-kernel* security policies through the use of write-mediation and write-logging services.
- A novel x86-64 implementation of the nested kernel architecture, PerspicuOS, that virtualizes supervisor privilege, thereby keeping the outer kernel and the nested kernel at the highest protection level; PerspicuOS uses only the MMU and control registers to protect memory, in lieu of VMM extensions, expensive page table manipulation, or costly compiler techniques.
- An evaluation of three *intra-kernel* memory access control policies: a write-once policy to protect access to

the system call table, a write-logging policy that detects rootkits attempting to hide processes, and an append-only system call logging facility with incorruptible logs and guaranteed invocation.

- An OS design that provides lifetime kernel code integrity, defending against a large class of kernel malware.

2. Nested Kernel Approach

The primary insight and contribution of the nested kernel architecture is to demonstrate how to virtualize a minimal subset of hardware functionality, specifically the MMU, to guarantee mediation and therefore isolation of *intra-kernel* protection domains. By virtualizing the MMU, the nested kernel architecture enables a new set of protection policies based upon physical page resources and their mappings within the kernel. This section presents the nested kernel architecture overview, our foundational design principles, and the challenges of virtualizing the MMU; it concludes with a description of the nested kernel write protection service made available to kernel developers.

2.1 System Overview

The nested kernel architecture partitions and reorganizes a monolithic kernel into two privilege domains: the *nested kernel* and the *outer kernel*. The nested kernel is a subset of the kernel's code and data that has full system privilege, and most importantly, the nested kernel has sole privilege to modify the underlying physical MMU (pMMU) state. The nested kernel mediates outer kernel modifications to the MMU via a virtual interface, which we refer to as the virtual MMU (vMMU). The outer kernel is then modified to use the vMMU.

Similar to previous work [15, 43], the nested kernel architecture isolates pMMU updates at the final stage of creating a virtual to physical translation: the point at which a virtual-to-physical translation is made *active* on the processor (i.e., when the processor can use the translation). For example, on the x86-64, address mappings are added to the system by storing a value to a virtual memory location, called a page-table entry (PTE), that resides on a page-table page (PTP) [2]. By selecting this abstraction, the outer kernel still manages all aspects of the virtual memory subsystem; however, the nested kernel interposes on all pMMU updates, thereby allowing the nested kernel to isolate the pMMU and enforce any other access control policy in the system, such as the one used to protect nested kernel code and data.

2.2 Design Principles

The nested kernel architecture comprises the mechanism and interface to establish virtual address mappings. As such, we seek to accomplish the following:

Separate resource control (e.g., policy) from protection mechanism (e.g., MMU). We seek the lowest level of abstraction possible to virtualize the MMU, providing only a mechanism that performs updates to virtual-to-physical address mappings. This principle has several benefits: it minimizes the TCB of the privileged domain, maximizes the portability of the nested kernel, and gives maximum flexibility to the types of policies implemented in the outer kernel while maintaining isolation of the nested kernel.

Operating system co-design and explicit interface. OS designers are experts in how their systems work: they represent the best opportunity to enhance the security of the system. Therefore, the nested kernel architecture presents a unified design to realize protections explicitly within the OS rather than transparently enforcing protections via external tools, such as in the case with prior work [35, 43, 44].

Privilege separation based upon MMU state, not instructions. Traditionally, systems use the notion of rings of protection, where each ring prescribes what instructions may be executed by code in that ring. In contrast, we enforce privilege separation in terms of access to the pMMU, including both memory (e.g,. PTPs) and CPU state (e.g., *WP-bit* in *CR0*).

Minimal architecture dependence. We want to make the nested kernel architecture design as hardware agnostic as possible, assuming only a hardware paging mechanism with page-granularity protections and the ability to enforce write-protections on outer kernel code.

Fine grained resource control. The protections enabled by virtualizing the MMU can be expressed in many ways; we seek to enable fine grained resource control, i.e., protections at byte-level granularity, so that *intra-kernel* isolation policies can be applied to arbitrary OS data structures.

Negligible performance impact. The nested kernel architecture provides isolation and privilege separation without requiring separate address spaces so that it can be applied to operating system architectures with minimal overhead. In our x86-64 prototype, we also run both the outer kernel and nested kernel in the same protection ring (ring 0) rather than via hardware virtualization extensions to avoid costly hypercalls, as evidenced by measurements in Section 5.3.

2.3 Virtualizing the MMU via API Emulation

We summarize the runtime isolation of the pMMU as the following property, which Invariants I1 and I2 enforce:

Nested Kernel Property. *The nested kernel interposes on all modifications of the pMMU via the vMMU.*

Invariant 1. Active *virtual-to-physical mappings for protected data are configured read-only while the outer kernel executes.*

Invariant 2. *Write-protection permissions in* active *virtual-to-physical mappings are enforced while the outer kernel executes.*

Active virtual-to-physical mappings are those mappings that may be used by the processor to determine page protections; inactive mappings do not affect memory access privileges. Invariant I2 applies to those processors (such as the x86 [2]) which can disable page protections while still performing virtual-to-physical address translation. While these definitions are independent of whether the MMU uses hardware- or software-managed TLBs, we will assume a hardware-managed TLB to simplify discussion.

On a hardware-TLB system, the nested kernel architecture enforces Invariant I1 by 1) requiring explicit initialization of PTPs, 2) creating an explicit interface to update the page-table entries (PTEs), and 3) configuring all PTEs that map PTPs as read-only. Therefore, any PTP that has not been explicitly initialized at boot time by the nested kernel or declared by the outer kernel via the vMMU is rejected from use, enforcing Invariant I1.

Invariant I2 can be enforced by a variety of mechanisms, including internal page protection mechanisms such as used in our prototype or external mechanisms such as a virtual machine monitor running at a higher hardware privilege level. Section 3.2 details how we ensure Invariant I2 is enforced in PerspicuOS on the x86-64 architecture.

2.4 Intra-Kernel Memory Write Protection Services

By isolating the pMMU from the outer kernel, the nested kernel can fully enforce memory access control policies on any physical page in the system. For example, the nested kernel can write-protect all statically defined constant data or a subset of system call function pointers that never change at runtime. Therefore, the nested kernel architecture provides a simple, robust API for specifying and enforcing such policies on kernel memory. The write-protection services API, listed in Table 1, comprises memory allocation and a data write function with an accompanying byte-granularity mediation policy.

Clients use the *intra-kernel* protection services to allocate regions of memory that are protected by and only written from nested kernel code. When an allocation is requested, either statically via `nk_declare` or dynamically via `nk_alloc`, the nested kernel initializes a write descriptor and allocates an associated memory region. The nested kernel also establishes the memory bounds for the region and sets the mediation callback function (as defined below) that implements the write-protection policy. The nested kernel returns to the client both the write descriptor and virtual address of the newly allocated write protected region, and finally, write-protects all existing mappings to the physical pages containing the memory region.

Clients specify write-protection policies in the form of *mediation functions*. Mediation functions enforce the update policies for write-protected kernel objects, and are invoked by the nested kernel prior to any writes. One example of a simple mediation function is a no-write policy for constant data, with function body, `return false;`, which rejects all writes to the memory region. A more complex example is a write-once policy, such as described in Section 4.1.1, where the nested kernel initializes a bitmap for each byte in the allocated memory region, then upon an `nk_write`, validates that the write is only made to memory not previously written. A significant value of the write-protection interface is that even in the absence of a mediation function (e.g., all writes to the object are permitted), the updates must use `nk_write`, thus thwarting overwrites from memory corruption bugs.

Once a write descriptor, `nk_wd`, is created, the outer kernel executes mediated writes via the `nk_write` function. `nk_write` operates similarly to a simple byte-level memory copy operation. `nk_write` performs two checks prior to executing the write: 1) it verifies that the write is within the boundary of the region specified by `nk_wd`, and 2) it invokes the mediation function, if any. By allowing clients to write only a subset of the memory region, the nested kernel allows protection of aggregate data types without requiring any knowledge about its fields. The interface also makes bounds checking fast by including the write descriptor for constant-time lookup of the descriptor information for the given region.

To fully support dynamically allocated memory, the nested kernel provides `nk_free`, which deallocates memory previously allocated by `nk_alloc`. Because an OS exploit could prematurely force `nk_free` to be called on a memory region and then attempt to store to it, any freed memory must be retained in protected memory, and so we design a simple interface that assumes the allocator is part of the nested kernel.

2.5 Preventing DMA Memory Writes

The nested kernel must also prevent DMA writes to protected memory. We require that the system have an IOMMU [1] that the nested kernel can use to ensure that DMA operations do not modify any pages protected by the nested kernel.

3. PerspicuOS: A Nested Kernel Prototype

We present a concrete implementation of the nested kernel architecture, named PerspicuOS, for x86-64 processors. PerspicuOS introduces a novel method for ensuring privilege separation between the outer kernel and the nested kernel while running both at the highest hardware privilege level, effectively creating two virtual privilege levels in *ring 0*. PerspicuOS achieves this goal by taking advantage of x86-64 hardware support for efficiently enabling and disabling MMU write protection enforcement and by controlling which privileged instructions can be used by outer kernel code. More specifically, PerspicuOS applies the design presented in Section 2.3, by configuring all mappings to PTPs as read-only and *de-privileging* the outer kernel so that it cannot disable write-protection enforcement at ring 0. PerspicuOS *de-privileges* the outer kernel by scanning

Function	Selected Arguments	Purpose
nk_declare	mem_start, size, mediation_func	Marks all pages RO; initializes an NK write descriptor nk_wd; returns the nk_wd and the pointer to the region.
nk_alloc	size, mediation_func, nk_wd_p	Allocates memory region; invokes nk_declare on it; stores write descriptor in nk_wd; returns nk_wd and pointer to the region.
nk_free	nk_wd	Deallocates memory identified by nk_wd. Memory must have been allocated by nk_alloc. Freed pages can be reused only by a future nk_alloc.
nk_write	dest, src, size, nk_wd	Verifies write bounds; invokes mediation_func, if any; then copies size bytes from src to dest.

Table 1. Nested Kernel Write Protection API. nk_declare is for static allocation and nk_alloc is for dynamic allocation.

all outer kernel code to ensure that it does not contain instructions that disable the *WP-bit* or the MMU. Additional hardware features (described in Section 3.5) prevent user-space code or kernel data from being used to disable protections.

In this section, we describe our threat model, specify a set of invariants to maintain the *Nested Kernel Property*, and then discuss how PerspicuOS maintains the invariants through a combination of virtual privilege switch management, MMU configuration validation, and lifetime kernel code integrity.

3.1 Threat Model and Assumptions

In this work, we assume that the outer kernel may be under complete control of the attacker who can attempt to arbitrarily modify CPU state. Furthermore, we assume that an attacker can modify outer kernel source code, i.e., that outer kernel code may be malicious. Moreover, we do not assume or require outer kernel control flow integrity, which means that an attacker can arbitrarily target any memory location on the system for execution. For example, since nested kernel and outer kernel code may reside in a unified address space, an attacker could attempt to redirect execution to arbitrary locations within nested kernel code, including instructions that toggle write-protections (i.e., the nested kernel must take explicit steps to prevent such control transfers or render them harmless).

We assume that the nested kernel source code and binaries are trusted and that the nested kernel is loaded with a secure boot mechanism such as in AEGIS [45] or UEFI [48]. We also trust mediation functions, a necessary requirement to ensure security checks execute in PerspicuOS. We assume that the nested kernel and mediation functions are free of vulnerabilities, and given the small source code size (less than 5,000 lines-of-code), the nested kernel could be formally or manually verified. Furthermore, we assume that the hardware is free of vulnerabilities and do not protect against hardware attacks.

3.2 Protection Properties and Invariants

The nested kernel design specifies two invariants that must hold to enforce the *Nested Kernel Property*. Invariant I1 requires that all active mappings to PTPs be configured as read-only; Invariant I2 requires that these configurations be

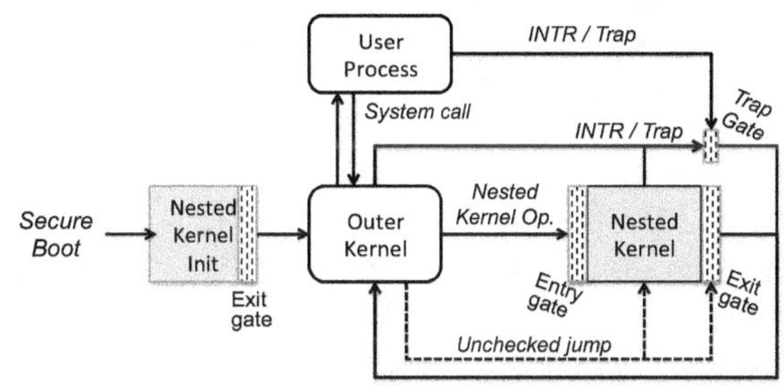

Figure 1. PerspicuOS State Transition Diagram. Only shaded blocks can execute PerspicuOS privileged operations (Table 2). All transitions out of the nested kernel must go through the Exit Gate.

enforced while the outer kernel is in operation. We systematically assessed the x86-64 architecture specification [2] to identify both the necessary hardware configurations to realize invariants I1 and I2 and the hardware configurations that may violate those invariants. For example, write-protections are enforced on supervisor-mode accesses when both the *WP-bit* is set and the mapping is configured as read-only; however, alternative execution modes, such as System Management Mode (SMM), can bypass write-protections when invoked. From this assessment, we derive the following invariants that ensure that invariants I1 and I2 hold.

3.2.1 Supporting Invariant I1

The set of active mappings in x86-64 is controlled by the *CR3* register and a set of in-memory PTPs [2]. *CR3* specifies the base address of a "top-level" page serving as the root for a hierarchical translation data structure that is traversed by the MMU [2]. To ensure that all translations to protected physical pages are marked as read-only (thereby asserting I1), PerspicuOS enforces the following invariants:

Invariant 3. *Ensure that there are no unvalidated mappings prior to outer kernel execution.*

Invariant 4. *Only declared PTPs are used in mappings.*

Invariant 5. *All mappings to PTPs are marked read-only.*

Invariant 6. *CR3 is only loaded with a pre-declared top-level PTP.*

3.2.2 Supporting Invariant I2

PerspicuOS must ensure that, while the outer kernel is operating, MMU write-protections are continually enforced. Read-only permissions are enforced by x86-64 when the processor is operating in long mode with write-protections enabled, i.e., Protected Mode Enable (*PE-bit*), Paging Enabled (*PG-bit*), and Write-Protect Enable (*WP-bit*) bits are set in *CR0*; Physical Address Extensions (*PAE-bit*) bit is set in *CR4*; and Long Mode Enable (*LME-bit*) bit is set in the *EFER* model specific register (MSR) [2]. Therefore, PerspicuOS considers scenarios where the outer kernel attempts to 1) disable the *WP-bit* while in operation, 2) disable paging by modifying the *PG-bit*, or 3) subvert control flow of the nested kernel so that the outer kernel gains control of execution while the *WP-bit* has been legitimately disabled for nested kernel operations. PerspicuOS ensures that the *WP-bit* is always set while the outer kernel is in operation and that any instantaneous mode changes that could disable paging, such as an SMM interrupt, are directed to nested kernel control.

Invariants I7 and I8 capture the requirements of the *WP-bit*.

Invariant 7. *The WP and PG flags in CR0 are set prior to any outer kernel execution.*

Invariant 8. *The WP-bit in CR0 is never disabled by outer kernel code.*

When the *PG-bit* is disabled, the processor immediately interprets virtual addresses as physical addresses [2]. As Section 3.7 describes, preventing the outer kernel from clearing the *PG-bit* is impossible. Instead, PerspicuOS enforces the following invariant:

Invariant 9. *Disabling the PG-bit directs control flow to the nested kernel.*

Additionally, SMM may be invoked by the outer kernel and therefore, PerspicuOS must also assert control on the SMI interrupt.

Invariant 10. *The nested kernel controls the SMM interrupt handler and operation.*

Given that the previous set of invariants hold, the outer kernel might attempt to manipulate CPU state or outer kernel memory in such a way as to cause control-flow to move from nested kernel code to outer kernel code without re-enabling the *WP-bit*. Therefore, to ensure write-protections are always enforced, PerspicuOS must protect against control-flow attacks on nested kernel execution in two specific cases: interrupt control flow paths and nested kernel stack state manipulation.

PerspicuOS ensures that all exit paths from the nested kernel to the outer kernel enable the *WP-bit* (shown in Figure 3), which is captured in the following invariant:

Invariant 11. *Enable the WP-bit on interrupts and traps prior to calling outer kernel interrupt/trap handlers.*

Because the trap handlers are a part of the nested kernel, the Interrupt Descriptor Table (IDT) [2] must be placed in protected memory and modifications of the Interrupt Descriptor Table Register (IDTR) must be solely a nested kernel operation.

Invariant 12. *The IDT must be write-protected, and the IDTR is only updated by the nested kernel.*

On a multiprocessor system, code running in outer kernel context on one core could modify the return address stored on the stack by code running in nested kernel on another core if the stack is in outer kernel memory. This would cause nested kernel code to return to outer kernel context without enabling the *WP-bit*. Therefore, PerspicuOS must ensure that code running in the nested kernel uses its own stack located in nested kernel memory.

Invariant 13. *The nested kernel stack is write-protected from outer kernel modifications.*

3.3 System Initialization

PerspicuOS must ensure that all mappings to protected pages (e.g. PTPs, code, nested kernel data, etc.) are configured as read-only and that paging is enabled prior to outer kernel execution, as suggested by invariants I3 and I7. Therefore, PerspicuOS, as depicted in Figure 1, initializes the paging system so that invariants I3—where validation implies invariants I4, I5, and I6 by registering all protected pages in nested kernel data structures—and I7 are enforced prior to outer kernel execution by using secure boot and "nested kernel init" functionality, thereby initializing all PTEs in the system.

3.4 Virtual MMU Interface

PerspicuOS provides a set of functions, called the nested kernel operations, that allow the outer kernel to configure the pMMU. The nested kernel operations interpose on underlying x86-64 instructions, called *protected instructions*, to isolate the pMMU. There are two classes of nested kernel operations: those that control the configuration of the hardware PTPs via memory writes and those that control updates to processor control registers.

The nested kernel enforces pMMU update policies by assigning types to physical pages based upon the kind of data stored in each physical page. The page types include PTPs, nested kernel code and data, outer kernel code and data, user code and data, and data protected by the intra-kernel write-protection service. This type information, along with the number of active mappings and a list of all virtual address mappings to the page, is kept in a *physical page descriptor*.

The outer kernel uses the `nk_declare_PTP` operation to specify the physical pages to be used as PTPs. The

Operation	x86 Instruction	Description	Constraints
nk_declare_PTP	None	Initialize physical page descriptor as usable in page tables	Asserting invariant I4
nk_write_PTE	mov VAL, PTEADDR	Update *p*MMU mapping	Asserting invariants I4 and I5
nk_remove_PTP	mov VAL, PTEADDR	Remove physical page from being used as PTP	Supporting invariants I4, I5, and I6.
nk_load_*CR0*	mov %REG, %*CR0*	Controls enforcement of read-only mappings	*WP-bit* must be set: invariant I8
nk_load_*CR3*	mov %REG, %*CR3*	Controls MMU mapping base PML4 page	Value must be a declared PML4-PTP
nk_load_*CR4*	mov %REG, %*CR4*	Controls user mode execution with *SMEP* flag	*CR4 SMEP* flag must be 1
nk_load_MSR	wrmsr Value, MSR	Control enforcement of no-execute permissions	*EFER* NX-Bit must be set to 1

Table 2. Nested Kernel Operations, *Protected Instructions*, Description, and Constraints

`nk_declare_PTP` operation takes, as arguments, the level within the page table hierarchy at which the physical page will be used and the address of the physical page being declared, then zeros each page to eliminate any stale data, write-protects all existing virtual mappings to the physical page, and registers the physical page as a PTP by updating the page's physical page descriptor.

Once declared, a physical page cannot be modified directly by outer kernel code. Instead, the outer kernel uses the `nk_write_PTE` operation, which inspects and validates all mappings prior to insertion. The nested kernel uses the previously described physical page type information along with a list of existing mappings to each page to ensure that 1) if the PTE does not point to a data page then it targets a declared PTP and 2) all mappings to PTPs are write-protected, thereby ensuring invariants I4 and I5 respectively. The nested kernel also protects nested kernel code, data, and stack pages to avoid code modifications that would eliminate mediation or functionality of the *p*MMU update process. We also ensure that the update does not write to any kernel data protected by the nested kernel; this is done via a simple check that ensures that the physical page being updated was previously declared as a page table page.

The second group of operations configure the paging hardware itself. We expose an interface for updating *CR3* to ensure that it only points to a declared top-level PTP, called PML4-PTP, thereby ensuring invariant I6. The interface for modifying other registers ensures that paging and lifetime kernel code integrity protections are not disabled by outer kernel code. The description of these mechanisms are in Sections 3.5 and 3.7.

3.5 Lifetime Kernel Code Integrity

To prevent *protected instructions* from being executed while in outer kernel context, PerspicuOS first validates all code before making it executable in supervisor-mode, and second, protects the runtime integrity of validated code by enforcing lifetime kernel code integrity, thereby maintaining invariants I6 and I8. PerspicuOS enforces *load time outer kernel code validity* by scanning binary code to ensure that it does not contain any *protected instructions*, including at unaligned instruction boundaries. Then PerspicuOS enforces dynamic lifetime outer kernel code integrity by configuring the processor and *p*MMU so that 1) by default all kernel pages are mapped as non-executable (enforced by the no-

```
entry:
  pushfq                         Save current flags
  cli                            Disable interrupts
  mov %rax, -8(%rsp)             Spill regs for temps
  mov %rcx, -16(%rsp)
  mov %rsp, %rcx                 Save stack ptr in rcx
  mov %cr0, %rax                 Get current CR0 value
  and ~CR0_WP,%rax               Clear WP bit in copy
  mov %rax, %cr0                 Write back to CR0
  cli                            Disable interrupts
  mov PerCPUSecureStack,%rsp     Switch to secure stack
  push %rcx                      Save orig stack ptr
  mov -0x8(%rcx), %rax           Restore spilled regs
  mov -0x10(%rcx), %rcx
```

Figure 2. Nested Kernel Entry.

```
exit:
  mov 0(%rsp), %rsp              Restore orig stack ptr
  push %rax                      Spill scratch reg
  mov %cr0, %rax                 Get current CR0 value
1:
  or CR0_WP, %rax                Set WP in CR0 copy
  mov %rax, %cr0                 Write back to CR0
  test CR0_WP, %eax              Ensure WP set
  je 1b                          If not, loop back
  pop %rax                       Restore clobbered reg
  popfq                          Restore flags
                                 (incl interrupt status)
```

Figure 3. Nested Kernel Exit

execute bit (*NX-bit*) in the *EFER* MSR), 2) validated kernel code pages are mapped with read-only permissions, and 3) user-space code and data are mapped as non-executable in supervisor-mode by employing supervisor-mode execution prevention (*SMEP* in *CR4*) [2], thereby preventing the outer kernel from executing any *protected instructions* contained within user-mode pages. Note that because protecting the nested kernel depends upon kernel code integrity both *EFER* and *CR4* must also be removed from outer kernel's ability to execute and are thus *protected instructions* as depicted in Table 2.

3.6 Virtual Privilege Switches

In PerspicuOS, the nested kernel and outer kernel share a single address space. Therefore, nested kernel operations are essentially function calls to nested kernel functions that are wrapped by entry and exit gates that (among other things) disable and enable the *WP-bit*. Virtual privilege switches occur when write-protection is disabled (which only occurs on nested kernel operations). In this section, we detail PerspicuOS entry and exit gates and describe the ways in which PerspicuOS ensures that the outer kernel does not gain control while write protections are disabled (enforcing I11, I13) and how the gates ensure that mediation functions execute (ensuring I4 and I5).

3.6.1 Nested Kernel Entry and Exit Gates

The nested kernel entry and exit gates ensure that there is a clear and protected privilege boundary between the nested kernel and the outer kernel. The routines depicted in Figures 2 and 3 perform the virtual privilege switch. The entry gate (Figure 2) disables interrupts, turns off system-wide write protections, disables interrupts, and then switches to a secure nested kernel stack; the exit gate (Figure 3) executes the reverse sequence. PerspicuOS by default disables interrupts while in operation; however, we include the second interrupt disable instruction to avoid instances where the outer kernel invokes interrupts that may corrupt internal nested kernel state.

3.6.2 Interrupts

PerspicuOS disables interrupts when executing in the nested kernel. Because the nested kernel is limited to a very small set of functionality, disabling interrupts is not expected to impact performance. Disabling interrupts simplifies the design of nested kernel operations because they can execute atomically: they do not need to contend with the possibility of being interrupted. However, long-running mediation functions may need to run with interrupts enabled—we leave supporting this feature as future work.

PerspicuOS must also ensure that the *WP-bit* is set whenever either a trap occurs or if the outer kernel directly invokes the *WP-bit* disable instruction and subsequently manages to execute an interrupt prior to the second interrupt disable instruction. This is necessary because an attacker could feed inputs to a mediated function that causes it to generate a trap; if the handler runs in the outer kernel, it would be running with write-protection disabled. PerspicuOS protects against these attacks by isolating the x86-64 interrupt handler table [2], enforcing invariant I12, and configuring it to send all interrupts and traps through the nested kernel trap gate first—depicted in Figure 1; the nested kernel trap gate sets the *WP-bit* before transferring control to an outer kernel trap handler, following a similar loop as the exit gate starting at assembly label "1" in Figure 3, thus enforcing invariant I11.

3.6.3 Nested Kernel Stack

To enforce invariant I13, PerspicuOS includes separate stacks for the nested kernel. Upon entry to the nested kernel, PerspicuOS saves the existing outer kernel stack pointer and switches to a preallocated nested kernel stack, as shown in Figure 2. When exiting the nested kernel, PerspicuOS restores the original outer kernel stack pointer (Figure 3).

3.6.4 Ensuring Write Mediation

By mapping the nested kernel code into the same address space as the outer kernel, PerspicuOS gains in efficiency on privilege switches; however, the outer kernel can directly jump to instructions that modify the protected state. For example, the outer kernel can target the instruction that writes to PTP entries, thus, bypassing the vMMU mediation. However, such a write will fail with a protection trap because the jump would have bypassed the entry gate, which is the only way to turn off the system-wide write protections enforced by the *WP-bit* (Figure 2). In this way, PerspicuOS ensures that either mediation will occur or the system will detect a write violation.

3.7 Privileged Register Integrity

While the protections in Section 3.5 prevent the outer kernel from directly modifying privileged registers (e.g., *CR0*, *CR3*, *IDTR*), it is possible for the outer kernel to jump to instructions within the nested kernel that configure these registers. To protect against this, the nested kernel unmaps pages containing these instructions from the virtual address space when the outer kernel is executing and maps them only when needed. Invariants I6, protecting *CR3*, and I12, protecting *IDTR*, are enforced using this method because direct modification of these registers can allow the outer kernel to instantly gain control.

While this works for most privileged registers, it does not work for *CR0* (to enforce I8) because the entry and exit gates must toggle write protections, and therefore the instruction to disable *CR0* must be mapped into the same address space as the outer kernel. Therefore, the outer kernel could load a value into the RAX register and jump to the instruction in the entry and exit gates that move RAX into *CR0*. Ideally, the entry and exit gates would use bit-wise OR and AND instructions with immediate operands to set and clear the *WP-bit* in *CR0*. Unfortunately, the x86-64 lacks such instructions; it can only copy a value in a general purpose register into a control register [2]. Note that the *protected instruction* "mov %REG, %*CR0*" is only mapped at three code locations, the entry, exit, and trap gates.

Entry gates do not require verification of the value loaded to *CR0* because the purpose of the entry gate is to disable the *WP-bit*; in contrast, exit and trap gates return control-flow to the outer kernel after modifying *CR0*. The exit and trap gates must therefore ensure that the *WP-bit* is enabled. To do so, PerspicuOS inserts a simple check and loop in the exit gate to ensure that the value of *RAX* has the *WP-bit* enabled, thus ensuring invariant I8. Since these are the only instances of writes to *CR0* in the code, PerspicuOS ensures that outer kernel attacks cannot bypass write-protections by using these instructions.

In the x86-64 architecture, paging is enabled when the processor is in either protected mode with paging enabled (both *PG-bit* and *PE-bit* set) or long mode (PG, PE, PAE, and the LME bits set). To handle the situation where the outer kernel disables the *PG-bit* (regardless of whether the CPU is in long or protected mode), PerspicuOS configures the MMU so that the virtual address of the entry gate matches a physical address containing code that traps into the nested kernel. Therefore, enforcing invariant I9 whenever the *PG-bit* is disabled.

If either the *PAE-bit* or *LME-bit* are disabled while the CPU is in long mode a general protection fault occurs. Because the bits are not updated but instead a trap occurs, the write-protections continue to be enabled and do not require any other solution. According to the Intel Architecture Reference Manual, the *PE-bit* cannot be disabled unless the *PG-bit* is also disabled [2], which is handled by the previously described solution.

3.8 Allocating Protected Data Structures

PerspicuOS presents the intra-kernel write-protection interface as described in Section 2.4 for allocating and updating write protected data structures. PerspicuOS establishes a predefined ELF memory region to protect global statically-defined data structures. Kernel developers declare write-protected data structures with a C macro that uses a special compiler directive to notify the linker to allocate the object into the specified region. The macro then registers the object into the write descriptor table along with the precomputed bounds and generates both the `nk_wd` and pointer to the region. PerspicuOS provides for dynamic allocation via the interface as described in Section 2.4. The shadow process list example uses this interface, which is described in Section 4.1.3.

One of the primary challenges of implementing the nested kernel write protection services is to devise a method for conquering the protection granularity gap [51], specifically the issue of protecting data co-located on pages with non-protected data. The nested kernel interface can fully support in-place protections but would result in poor performance: each unprotected object would require a trap and emulate cycle. Therefore, we modify the linker script to put this protected ELF region onto its own set of separate pages so that only write-protected data is placed in the region. At boot time, pages belonging to this protected ELF section are write-protected via MMU configuration to ensure the *Nested Kernel Property* for each of these data structures.

3.9 Mediation Functions

In an ideal nested kernel implementation, mediation functions would not be in the TCB. This would keep the TCB small regardless of the number of policies and would allow policies to be mutally distrusting. However, to simplify implementation, and to ensure that the mediation functions are executed prior to writes, mediation functions are incorporated into PerspicuOS's TCB. In our evaluation of the write protection interface, we present a set of predefined trusted mediation functions (which, like the mediation functions in an ideal design, do not write to nested kernel memory).

3.10 Implementation

We implemented PerspicuOS in FreeBSD 9.0. We replaced all instances of writes to PTPs to use the appropriate nested kernel API function and inserted validation checks as Section 3.4 describes. We modified the trap handlers to check for and enable the *WP-bit*; however, we did not implement the IDT and IDTR protections. We believe that these will not impact performance as modern OS kernels rarely modify the IDT and IDTR. We ported and implemented nested kernel calls for each function in Table 2. These calls perform the requested operation and verify that the value in the register is correct. We ported all instances of writes to MSRs to ensure the NX bit is always set in *EFER*; however, we did not fully implement no-execute page permissions in the PTPs. We do not believe these will negatively impact performance as the nested kernel already interposes on all MMU updates and sets other protection bits accordingly. We also implemented an offline scanner for the kernel binary; we have applied this to the entire core kernel but not to dynamically loaded kernel modules (this is a minor matter of engineering).

Our current implementation uses coarse-gained synchronization even though our evaluation is on a uni-processor. It uses a single nested kernel stack with a lock to protect it from concurrent access. We did not implement protections for DMA writes or enforce nested kernel control on SMI events; however, we do not believe they will negatively impact performance because these are rare events under normal operation. Last, we did not fully implement all features to enforce Invariant I6; however, we did implement code that updates a PTE and flushes the TLB to simulate mapping and unmapping the code that modifies *CR3*. We believe this faithfully represents the performance costs of the full solution.

4. Enforcing Intra-Kernel Security Policies

The nested kernel architecture permits kernel developers to employ fundamental design principles such as least privilege and complete mediation [41]. In this section, we explore several intra-kernel security policies enabled by the nested kernel. Our examples demonstrate the nested kernel's ability to combat key mechanisms used by well-known classes of kernel malware such as rootkits [27].

We emphasize that our use cases do not completely solve specific high-level security goals (such as preventing rootkits from evading detection). However, they demonstrate specific key elements for complete solutions. Developing complete solutions is part of our ongoing work.

4.1 Nested Kernel Write Mediation Policies

The nested kernel provides kernel developers with the ability to prevent or monitor memory writes at run-time. We illustrate three write-protection policies that this interface can enforce; each can be used for multiple security goals.

4.1.1 Write-Once Data

Several kernel data structures are written to only once, when they are initialized. Other structures are initialized to default values and are only changed once during operation (e.g., the system call table). Our interface can protect these data with very low overhead.

As such, PerspicuOS implements a simple, byte-granularity, *write-once* policy within the nested kernel. It is enforced by maintaining a bit-vector with one bit per byte, initialized to zeroes. When `nk_write` is called, it uses a mediation function that checks whether each bit is set for the memory to be modified; if all the bits are clear, it writes the data and marks those corresponding bits as being written.

We apply the write-once policy to protect the FreeBSD system call table by allocating the table within nested kernel-protected pages and selecting the *write-once* policy, guaranteeing that it can never be overwritten by malware after initialization. This application defends against kernel malware that "hook" system call dispatch by overwriting entries in the system call table to invoke exploit code [27], and could be extended to protect other key kernel code pointers.

4.1.2 Append-Only Data

Operating systems also have append-only data structures such as circular buffers and event logs. These data structures reside in ordinary kernel memory and are vulnerable to kernel exploits, making them unreliable for forensics use.

To protect such data structures, PerspicuOS implements an *append-only* write policy within the nested kernel. It is enforced by maintaining a "tail" pointer to a list structure within the nested kernel. Each call to `nk_write` increments the tail pointer to ensure that writes never overwrite existing data within the region. A stricter policy could ensure that no gaps exist between successive writes. A full solution must also be able to securely write the log to disk when full, which our prototype does not yet do.

We used this policy to implement a system call event logger that records system call entry and exit events in a statically allocated, append-only buffer. System call recording has been a popular target in both research systems [22, 23, 32, 36] and security monitoring applications [19, 21, 26, 33, 35, 44, 52]. However, these systems are susceptible to attack [49]. By protecting the log buffer, we ensure that rootkits cannot hide traces of malicious system call events and strengthen security staffs' ability to conduct forensics investigations after breakins. Further effort is required to write the logs out to another media for long term storage, and to defend against an attacker that spoofs security events.

4.1.3 Write Logging

A rootkit's primary goal is to hide itself and malicious processes and files. Therefore, they often modify kernel data such as network counters, process lists, and system event logs [27]. Some of these data are challenging to protect due to being co-located within large kernel data structures; others cannot be protected by simple write-once and append-only policies. However, the ability to reliably *monitor* writes to such data enables detection of all malicious modifications.

Therefore, we implement a general *write-logging* mechanism that records (and can later reconstruct) all writes to selected data structures. All calls to `nk_write` for a memory region declared with this policy record the range of addresses modified and the values written into the memory. Again, this buffer must be periodically written to disk.

As an example use case of the interface, we use *write-logging* to detect rootkits that attempt to hide processes by corrupting FreeBSD's process list data structure: `allproc`. Instead of logging writes to `allproc` directly, we created a shadow *allproc* data structure that exactly mirrors the original list. Each shadow list entry contains a pointer back to the corresponding `allproc` entry, and any updates to the `allproc` list structure (e.g., unlinking a node) are also performed on the shadow list. More importantly, to fully hide the presence of a particular process from the kernel, the rootkit must use `nk_write` to remove the shadow entry from the shadow list (which is logged).

The logging of shadow list writes enables effective forensics. Security monitors can easily reconstruct the list updates and identify the prior existence of hidden processes. Moreover, we modified the `ps` program to query the shadow list instead of the `allproc` list so that the `ps` program can detect the presence of hidden processes.

4.2 System Protection Policies

The nested kernel architecture can also realize several system security properties because it controls all virtual memory mappings in the system. One example is *lifetime kernel code integrity* (as Section 3.5 explains). This single use case effectively thwarts an entire class of kernel malware (namely code injection attacks). In addition to code integrity, PerspicuOS also marks memory pages as non-executable by default and enables superuser mode execution prevention of user-mode code and data. Even if commodity kernels use these hardware features, they cannot prevent malware from disabling them. PerspicuOS, in contrast, enables these protections *and* prevents malicious code from disabling them. PerspicuOS can also be used for any type of security monitor that inserts explicit calls into source code to ensure that the monitor both executes and is isolated from the untrusted code.

5. Evaluation

We evaluate PerspicuOS by investigating the impact on the TCB, FreeBSD porting effort, *de-privileging* scanner, and performance overheads.

We evaluated the overheads of PerspicuOS on a Dell Precision T1650 workstation with an Intel® Core™ i7-3770 processor at 3.4 GHz with 8 MB of cache, 16 GB of RAM, and an integrated PCIE Gigabit Ethernet card. Experiments requiring a network used a dedicated Gigabit ethernet network; the client machine on the network was an Acer Aspire Revo R3700 with an Intel® Atom™ D525 processor at 1.8 GHz with 2 GB of RAM. We evaluate five systems for each of our tests: the *original* (unmodified) FreeBSD system, the base PerspicuOS, and each of our three use cases: append-only, which is used for system call entry and exit recording; write-once, used for the system call table protection; and write-log, used for the shadow process list. The baseline for the syscall use case was the original FreeBSD modified so that it is logging system call entry and exit events.

5.1 Trusted Computing Base and Kernel Porting

The nested kernel requires porting existing functionality in a commodity kernel to use the nested kernel operations. Our port of FreeBSD to the nested kernel architecture modified 52 files totalling $\sim$1900^{+} LOC changed, including comments. The vast majority of deleted lines were to configuration or build system files—ignoring these, only $\sim$100^{-} LOC were eliminated in the port. Code modifications were measured using Git change logs. We measure the number of lines in the nested kernel with the SLOCCount tool [53]: the implementation consists of $\sim$4000 C SLOC and $\sim$800 assembly SLOC; the scanner was implemented in 248 python SLOC.

5.2 Code Scanning Results

To evaluate the feasibility of eliminating all instances of *protected instructions* from the outer kernel, we scanned our compiled kernels and subsequently used manual methods to eliminate all unaligned *protected instructions*. We found a total of 40 implicit instructions for writing to *CR0* (2) and *wrmsr* (38). Most of these instances are due to constants embedded in the code used for relative addressing; therefore, we eliminated them by adjusting alignments, rearranging functions, and inserting *nops*. A few were due to particular sequences of arithmetic expressions; these were addressed by replacing them with equivalent computation. Finally, a small number of constants in the outer kernel code contained implicit instructions. These were addressed by replacing the each constant with two others that were dynamically combined to create the equivalent value.

5.3 Privilege Boundary Microbenchmark

To investigate the impact of different privilege crossings against the nested kernel architecture approach, we developed a simple microbenchmark that evaluates the round trip cost into a null function for each privilege boundary: syscall, nested kernel call, and VMM call (hypercall).

Privilege Boundary	Time (μsecs)	Time / NK Call
NK Call	0.1390	1.00x
Syscall	0.08757	0.62x
VMCALL	0.5130	3.69x

Table 3. Privilege Boundary Crossing Costs.

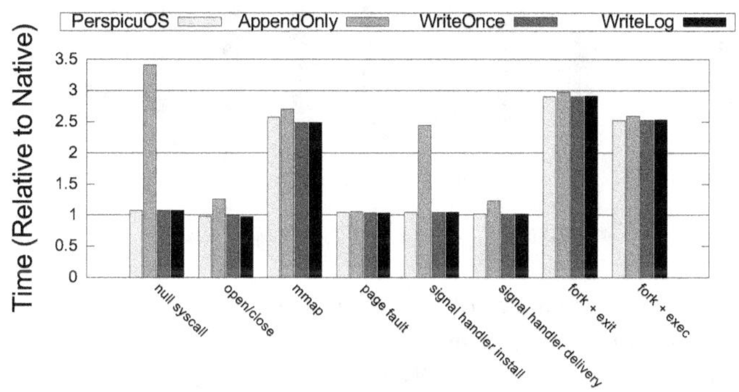

Figure 4. LMBench results.

For the syscall boundary experiment we used the *syscall* instruction to invoke a special system call added to the kernel that immediately returns. The VMM boundary cost experiment is performed using a guest kernel consisting solely of *VMCALL* instructions in a loop executing within a VMM modified to resume the guest immediately after this instruction traps to the VMM. The nested kernel cost experiment uses an empty function wrapped with the entry and exit gates as described in Section 3.6.1.

The microbenchmark performs each call one million times and reports total elapsed time. Each microbenchmark configuration was executed 5 times with negligible variance, and the computed average time per call is reported.

Our results, shown in Table 3, indicate that a nested kernel call is approximately 3.69 times *less* expensive than a hypercall, thus motivating the performance benefits of implementing the nested kernel architecture at a single supervisor privilege level. User-mode to supervisor-mode calls are faster than nested kernel calls, which take approximately 1.59 times as long.

5.4 Micro-benchmarks

To evaluate the effect that PerspicuOS has on system call performance, we ran experiments from the LMBench benchmark suite [30]. Figure 4 shows the results for our four systems relative to the original FreeBSD. In most cases, our systems are, at most, 1.25 times slower relative to the baseline (unmodified) FreeBSD kernel. `mmap`, `fork+exit`, and `fork+exec`, however, exhibit higher execution time overheads of approximately 2.5 to 3 times. This is because these benchmarks stress the vMMU with several consecutive calls to set up new address spaces. Upon investigation, we

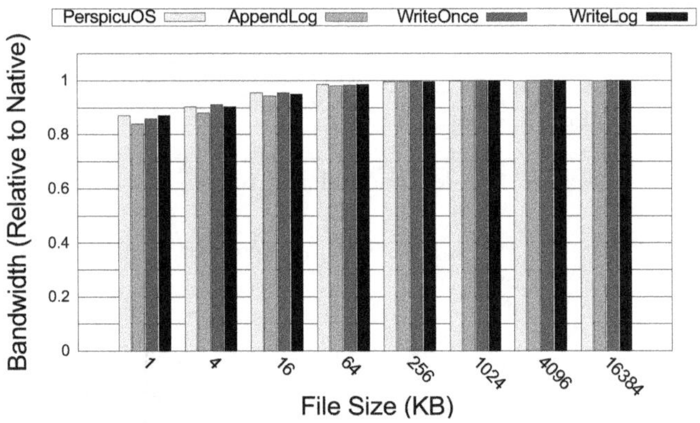

Figure 5. SSHD Average Bandwidth.

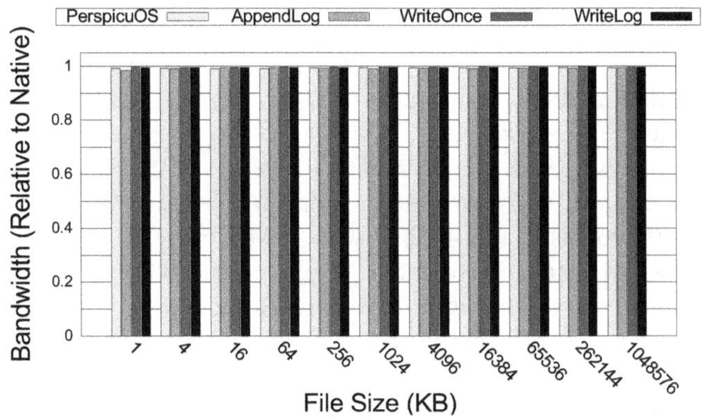

Figure 6. Apache average bandwidth.

identified a small set of functions that were responsible for most of this behavior, and preliminary experiments showed a reduction by more than 60% when converting these to batch operations. In the future, we plan to extend the nested kernel interface to allow for batch updates to the vMMU in order to reduce overheads for these operations.

We also observe that the write-once and write-log policies incur the same overheads as the base PerspicuOS system, whereas the append-only policy used for system call entry and exit recording incurs higher overheads. In fact, the worst *relative* overhead for this system is the `null syscall` benchmark; it occurs because each null system call makes two nested kernel operations calls.

5.5 Application Benchmarks

To evaluate the overheads on real applications, we measured the performance of the FreeBSD OpenSSH server, the Apache httpd server running on the PerspicuOS kernel, and a kernel compile. We opted to use network servers as they exercise kernel functionality more heavily than many compute bound applications and are therefore more likely to be impacted by kernel overhead.

OpenSSH Server: For the OpenSSH experiments, we transferred files ranging from 1 KB to 16 MB in size from the server to the client. We transferred each file 20 times, measuring the bandwidth achieved each time. Figure 5 shows the average bandwidth overhead, relative to native, for each file size transferred. The maximum bandwidth reduction is 20% for 1 KB files. Transferring files above 64 KB in size has less than 2% reduction in bandwidth.

Apache: For the Apache experiments, we used Apache's benchmark tool `ab` to perform 10000 requests using 32 concurrent connections over a 1Gbps network for file sizes ranging from 1 KB to 1 GB. We performed this experiment 20 times for each file size, and present the results in Figure 6. The experiment results reveal negligible, if any, overheads that are within the standard deviation error.

Kernel Build: The kernel build experiment cleaned and built a FreeBSD kernel from scratch for a total of 3 runs (the variance was virtually negligible). The worst run times are shown in Table 4. The results show an overhead of about 2.6% for the base PerspicuOS, system call table, and process list configurations; and an overhead of 3% for the system call entry/exit case.

PerspicuOS	AppendOnly	WriteOnce	WriteLog
2.6%	3.0%	2.6%	2.7%

Table 4. Kernel Build Overhead over Native.

6. Future Work

There are several directions for future work. First, we plan to investigate methods for removing mediation functions from the TCB. Mediation functions do not need to write to protected memory and could be excluded from the TCB by running them with write-protections enabled. Second, although the nested kernel provides a sufficient interface to protect data structures, techniques are needed to ensure that policy-enforcing code stores all critical data within the nested kernel. Third, we plan to formally verify PerspicuOS's design to improve assurance of its correctness.

Additionally, we will explore applications of PerspicuOS. For example, moving the kernel memory allocator into the nested kernel could protect the kernel from memory safety attacks that overwrite allocator meta-data [5]. Additionally, we could move the access control functionality into the nested kernel, thereby ensuring that attacks on the operating system kernel cannot subvert its access controls.

7. Related Work

The core contributions of this work include a new OS organization, the nested kernel architecture, for providing privilege separation and isolation within a single monolithic kernel, and a unique method for implementing it on commodity hardware with PerspicuOS.

Operating System Organizations. Several alternative operating system designs provide privilege separation and memory isolation, including microkernels [3, 9, 28], ExoKernels [8, 17], and separation kernels [39]. OSes written in type safe languages also provide inherent security improvements [4, 9, 42]. While these approaches isolate kernel components and mediate access to critical data structures, they completely abandon commodity OS design.

MMU Protections. The nested kernel architecture isolates the MMU by modifying the outer kernel so that MMU updates can be mediated, and exports an interface similar to those of related efforts including Xen [7], SVA-OS [13–15, 20] and `paravirtops` [54]. Although the interface is similar, the nested kernel architecture employs different *p*MMU policies to protect and virtualize the MMU, as well as introduces *de-privileging* to isolate the nested kernel. SecVisor employs similar MMU policies to enforce kernel code integrity [43] as PerspicuOS; however, SecVisor uses special nested paging hardware support that uses implicit traps on certain hardware events, which is both external to the kernel and has higher costs per invocation than PerspicuOS.

Intra-Kernel Memory Isolation. SILVER [55] and UCON [56] specify policy frameworks (similar to mandatory access control) to enforce access control policies on internal kernel objects using VMM hardware. SILVER exports an access control service that is used by the operating system to specify principals and object ownership access policies through the memory allocator, which are then enforced by the VMM. In contrast, PerspicuOS uses the x86-64 *WP-bit* to provide a memory isolation mechanism on which SILVER access control polices could be overlaid.

Nooks [46] provides lightweight protection domains for kernel drivers and modules. Nooks uses the hardware MMU to create protection domains and changes hardware page tables when transferring control between the core kernel and the kernel driver. Although Nooks provides reliability guarantees, it does not consider isolation from malicious entities, and therefore is susceptible to attack.

Compiler Based Intra-Kernel Memory Isolation. Several previous efforts [10, 18] employ software fault isolation (SFI) and control-flow integrity (CFI) to isolate kernel components. These systems utilize heavy weight compiler instrumentation in addition to address translation policies to isolate kernel components. LXFI [29] uses programmer annotations to specify interface policy rules between kernel extensions and the core kernel and inserts run-time checks to enforce these rules. In contrast, PerspicuOS does not require compiler-based enforcement mechanisms, alleviates the need for kernel control-flow integrity, and removes the core kernel from the TCB.

Hypervisor Based Isolation. Both SVA [15] and HyperSafe [50] employ the MMU and the *WP-bit* to prevent privileged system software from making errant changes to page tables. However, these approaches require control flow integrity, and furthermore the HyperSafe work claimed that using the WP approach on a monolithic kernel would be too challenging due to shared code and data pages.

Several approaches deploy security monitors to protect and record certain kernel events: each has drawbacks. Several such approaches place the monitor in the same TCB as the untrusted code, leaving them vulnerable to attack [31, 37, 47]. Other systems, namely Lares [35] and the In-VM monitor SIM [44], place the monitor in a VMM (using nested paging support) to provide integrity guarantees about the isolation and invocation of the security monitor. These systems suffer from high performance costs [35] or assume integrity of the code region [44]. VMM-based monitors must also address VMM introspection problems: the monitor does not understand the semantics of kernel data structures [19, 24]. In PerspicuOS, security monitors are isolated from the monitored system, can be invoked much more efficiently via direct nested kernel operations instead of expensive VMM hypercalls, and completely avoid the VMM introspection problem.

KCoFI [13], SecVisor [43], and NICKLE [38] provide kernel code integrity. SecVisor and NICKLE also ensure that only authorized code runs in the processor's privileged mode. PerspicuOS enforces the same policies, but also includes a novel memory isolation mechanism.

8. Conclusion

This paper presents the nested kernel architecture, a new OS organization that provides important security benefits to commodity operating systems that was retrofitted to an existing monolithic kernel. We show that the two nested kernel architecture components, the nested kernel and the outer kernel, can co-exist in the highest hardware protection level in a common address space without compromising the isolation guarantees of the system. The nested kernel architecture can efficiently support useful write-mediation policies, such as write-once and append-only, which OS developers can use to incorporate new security policies with very low performance overheads. More broadly, we expect that the nested kernel architecture can improve OS security by enabling OS developers to incorporate richer security principles like complete mediation, least privilege, and least common mechanism, for selected OS functionality.

Acknowledgments

The authors would like to thank Audrey Dautenhahn for her editorial services, and Maria Kotsifakou, Prakalp Srivastava, and Matthew Hicks for refining our ideas via technical and writing discussions. Our shepherd Peter Druschel and the anonymous reviewers provided valuable feedback that greatly enhanced the quality of this paper. This work was sponsored by ONR via grant number N00014-12-1-0552 and supported in part by ONR via grant number N00014-4-1-0525, MURI via contract number AF Subcontract UCB 00006769, and NSF via grant number CNS 07-09122.

References

[1] AMD64 architecture programmers manual volume 2: System programming. Manual, Advancd Micro Devices, 2006.

[2] Intel 64 and IA-32 architectures software developers manual. Manual 325384-051US, Intel, June 2014.

[3] M. Accetta, R. Baron, W. Bolosky, D. Golub, R. Rashid, A. Tevanian, and M. Young. Mach: A new kernel foundation for UNIX development. In *Proceedings of the USENIX Annual Technical Conference*, USENIX ATC'10, pages 93–112, Altanta, GA, USA, 1986. USENIX Association.

[4] M. Aiken, M. Fhndrich, C. Hawblitzel, G. Hunt, and J. Larus. Deconstructing process isolation. In *Proceedings of the 2006 Workshop on Memory System Performance and Correctness*, MSPC '06, pages 1–10, New York, NY, USA, 2006. ACM.

[5] argp and Karl. Exploiting UMA, FreeBSD's kernel memory allocator. *.:: Phrack Magazine ::.*, 0x0d(0x42), Nov. 2009.

[6] S. Bahram, X. Jiang, Z. Wang, M. Grace, J. Li, D. Srinivasan, J. Rhee, and D. Xu. DKSM: Subverting virtual machine introspection for fun and profit. In *Proceedings of the 2010 29th IEEE Symposium on Reliable Distributed Systems*, SRDS '10, pages 82–91, Washington, DC, USA, 2010. IEEE Computer Society.

[7] P. Barham, B. Dragovic, K. Fraser, S. Hand, T. Harris, A. Ho, R. Neugebauer, I. Pratt, and A. Warfield. Xen and the art of virtualization. In *Proceedings of the Nineteenth ACM Symposium on Operating Systems Principles*, SOSP '03, pages 164–177, New York, NY, USA, 2003. ACM.

[8] A. Belay, A. Bittau, A. Mashtizadeh, D. Terei, D. Mazires, and C. Kozyrakis. Dune: Safe user-level access to privileged CPU features. In *Proceedings of the 10th USENIX Conference on Operating Systems Design and Implementation*, OSDI'12, pages 335-348, Berkeley, CA, USA, 2012. USENIX Association.

[9] B. N. Bershad, S. Savage, P. Pardyak, E. G. Sirer, M. E. Fiuczynski, D. Becker, C. Chambers, and S. Eggers. Extensibility safety and performance in the SPIN operating system. In *Proceedings of the Fifteenth ACM Symposium on Operating Systems Principles*, SOSP '95, pages 267–283, New York, NY, USA, 1995. ACM.

[10] M. Castro, M. Costa, J.-P. Martin, M. Peinado, P. Akritidis, A. Donnelly, P. Barham, and R. Black. Fast byte-granularity software fault isolation. In *Proceedings of the ACM SIGOPS 22nd symposium on Operating Systems Principles*, SOSP '09, pages 45–58, New York, NY, USA, 2009. ACM.

[11] S. Chen, J. Xu, E. C. Sezer, P. Gauriar, and R. K. Iyer. Non-control-data attacks are realistic threats. In *Proceedings of the 14th Conference on USENIX Security Symposium - Volume 14*, SSYM'05, pages 12–12, Berkeley, CA, USA, 2005. USENIX Association.

[12] A. Chou, J. Yang, B. Chelf, S. Hallem, and D. Engler. An empirical study of operating systems errors. In *Proceedings of the Eighteenth ACM Symposium on Operating Systems Principles*, SOSP '01, pages 73–88, New York, NY, USA, 2001. ACM.

[13] J. Criswell, N. Dautenhahn, and V. Adve. KCoFI: Complete control-flow integrity for commodity operating system kernels. In *Proceedings of the 2014 IEEE Symposium on Security and Privacy*, SP '14, pages 292–307, Washington, DC, USA, 2014. IEEE Computer Society.

[14] J. Criswell, N. Dautenhahn, and V. Adve. Virtual ghost: Protecting applications from hostile operating systems. In *Proceedings of the 19th International Conference on Architectural Support for Programming Languages and Operating Systems*, ASPLOS '14, pages 81–96, New York, NY, USA, 2014. ACM.

[15] J. Criswell, N. Geoffray, and V. Adve. Memory safety for low-level software/hardware interactions. In *Proceedings of the 18th Conference on USENIX Security Symposium*, SSYM'09, pages 83–100, Berkeley, CA, USA, 2009. USENIX Association.

[16] J. Criswell, A. Lenharth, D. Dhurjati, and V. Adve. Secure virtual architecture: A safe execution environment for commodity operating systems. In *Proceedings of Twenty-first ACM SIGOPS Symposium on Operating Systems Principles*, SOSP '07, pages 351–366, New York, NY, USA, 2007. ACM.

[17] D. R. Engler, M. F. Kaashoek, and J. O'Toole, Jr. Exokernel: An operating system architecture for application-level resource management. In *Proceedings of the Fifteenth ACM Symposium on Operating Systems Principles*, SOSP '95, pages 251–266, New York, NY, USA, 1995. ACM.

[18] Ú. Erlingsson, M. Abadi, M. Vrable, M. Budiu, and G. C. Necula. XFI: Software guards for system address spaces. In *Proceedings of the 7th Symposium on Operating Systems Design and Implementation*, OSDI '06, pages 75–88, Berkeley, CA, USA, 2006. USENIX Association.

[19] T. Garfinkel and M. Rosenblum. A virtual machine introspection based architecture for intrusion detection. In *Proceedings of the Network and Distributed System Security Symposium, NDSS 2003, San Diego, California, USA*. The Internet Society, 2003.

[20] O. S. Hofmann, S. Kim, A. M. Dunn, M. Z. Lee, and E. Witchel. InkTag: Secure applications on an untrusted operating system. In *Proceedings of the Eighteenth International Conference on Architectural Support for Programming Languages and Operating Systems*, ASPLOS '13, pages 265–278, New York, NY, USA, 2013. ACM.

[21] S. A. Hofmeyr, S. Forrest, and A. Somayaji. Intrusion detection using sequences of system calls. *J. Comput. Secur.*, 6(3):151–180, Aug. 1998.

[22] N. Honarmand, N. Dautenhahn, J. Torrellas, S. T. King, G. Pokam, and C. Pereira. Cyrus: Unintrusive application-level record-replay for replay parallelism. In *Proceedings of the Eighteenth International Conference on Architectural Support for Programming Languages and Operating Systems*, ASPLOS '13, pages 193–206, New York, NY, USA, 2013. ACM.

[23] N. Honarmand and J. Torrellas. Replay debugging: Leveraging record and replay for program debugging. In *Proceeding of the 41st Annual International Symposium on Computer Architecuture*, ISCA '14, pages 445–456, Piscataway, NJ, USA, 2014. IEEE Press.

[24] B. Jain, M. B. Baig, D. Zhang, D. E. Porter, and R. Sion. SoK: Introspections on trust and the semantic gap. In *Proceedings of the 2014 IEEE Symposium on Security and Privacy*, SP '14, pages 605–620, Washington, DC, USA, 2014. IEEE Computer Society.

[25] V. P. Kemerlis, M. Polychronakis, and A. D. Keromytis. ret2dir: Rethinking kernel isolation. In *Proceedings of the 23rd USENIX Conference on Security Symposium*, SEC'14, pages 957–972, Berkeley, CA, USA, 2014. USENIX Association.

[26] S. T. King and P. M. Chen. Backtracking intrusions. In *Proceedings of the Nineteenth ACM Symposium on Operating Systems Principles*, SOSP '03, pages 223–236, New York, NY, USA, 2003. ACM.

[27] J. Kong. *Designing BSD Rootkits*. No Starch Press, San Francisco, CA, USA, 2007.

[28] J. Liedtke. On micro-kernel construction. In *Proceedings of the Fifteenth ACM Symposium on Operating Systems Principles*, SOSP '95, pages 237–250, New York, NY, USA, 1995. ACM.

[29] Y. Mao, H. Chen, D. Zhou, X. Wang, N. Zeldovich, and M. F. Kaashoek. Software fault isolation with API integrity and multi-principal modules. In *Proceedings of the Twenty-Third ACM Symposium on Operating Systems Principles*, SOSP '11, pages 115–128, New York, NY, USA, 2011. ACM.

[30] L. McVoy and C. Staelin. lmbench: Portable tools for performance analysis. In *Proceedings of the 1996 Annual Conference on USENIX Annual Technical Conference*, ATEC '96, pages 23–23, Berkeley, CA, USA, 1996. USENIX Association.

[31] Microsoft. Kernel patch protection: frequently asked questions (windows drivers), 2007.

[32] P. Montesinos, M. Hicks, S. T. King, and J. Torrellas. Capo: A software-hardware interface for practical deterministic multiprocessor replay. In *Proceedings of the 14th International Conference on Architectural Support for Programming Languages and Operating Systems*, ASPLOS XIV, pages 73–84, New York, NY, USA, 2009. ACM.

[33] D. Mutz, F. Valeur, G. Vigna, and C. Kruegel. Anomalous system call detection. *ACM Trans. Inf. Syst. Secur.*, 9(1):61–93, Feb. 2006.

[34] E. I. Organick. *The Multics System: An Examination of Its Structure*. MIT Press, Cambridge, MA, USA, 1972.

[35] B. D. Payne, M. Carbone, M. Sharif, and W. Lee. Lares: An architecture for secure active monitoring using virtualization. In *Proceedings of the 2008 IEEE Symposium on Security and Privacy*, SP '08, pages 233–247, Washington, DC, USA, 2008. IEEE Computer Society.

[36] G. Pokam, K. Danne, C. Pereira, R. Kassa, T. Kranich, S. Hu, J. Gottschlich, N. Honarmand, N. Dautenhahn, S. T. King, and J. Torrellas. QuickRec: Prototyping an intel architecture extension for record and replay of multithreaded programs. In *Proceedings of the 40th Annual International Symposium on Computer Architecture*, ISCA '13, pages 643–654, New York, NY, USA, 2013. ACM.

[37] C. Ries. Defeating windows personal firewalls: Filtering methodologies, attacks, and defenses. Technical report, 2005.

[38] R. Riley, X. Jiang, and D. Xu. Guest-transparent prevention of kernel rootkits with VMM-based memory shadowing. In *Proceedings of the 11th International Symposium on Recent Advances in Intrusion Detection*, RAID '08, pages 1–20, Berlin, Heidelberg, 2008. Springer-Verlag.

[39] J. M. Rushby. Design and verification of secure systems. In *Proceedings of the Eighth ACM Symposium on Operating Systems Principles*, SOSP '81, pages 12–21, New York, NY, USA, 1981. ACM.

[40] J. H. Saltzer. Protection and the control of information sharing in multics. *Commun. ACM*, 17(7):388–402, July 1974.

[41] J. H. Saltzer and M. D. Schroeder. The protection of information in computer systems. *Proceedings of the IEEE*, 63(9):1278–1308, 1975.

[42] T. Saulpaugh and C. A. Mirho. *Inside the JavaOS operating system*. Addison-Wesley Reading, 1999.

[43] A. Seshadri, M. Luk, N. Qu, and A. Perrig. SecVisor: A tiny hypervisor to provide lifetime kernel code integrity for commodity OSes. In *Proceedings of Twenty-first ACM SIGOPS Symposium on Operating Systems Principles*, SOSP '07, pages 335–350, New York, NY, USA, 2007. ACM.

[44] M. I. Sharif, W. Lee, W. Cui, and A. Lanzi. Secure in-VM monitoring using hardware virtualization. In *Proceedings of the 16th ACM Conference on Computer and Communications Security*, CCS '09, pages 477–487, New York, NY, USA, 2009. ACM.

[45] G. E. Suh, D. Clarke, B. Gassend, M. van Dijk, and S. Devadas. AEGIS: Architecture for tamper-evident and tamper-resistant processing. In *Proceedings of the 17th Annual International Conference on Supercomputing*, ICS '03, pages 160–171, New York, NY, USA, 2003. ACM.

[46] M. M. Swift, B. N. Bershad, and H. M. Levy. Improving the reliability of commodity operating systems. *ACM Trans. Comput. Syst.*, 23(1):77–110, Feb. 2005.

[47] A. Tereshkin. Rootkits: Attacking personal firewalls. In *Proceedings of the Black Hat USA 2006 Conference*, 2006.

[48] I. Unified EFI. Unified extensible firmware interface specification: Version 2.2d, November 2010.

[49] D. Wagner and P. Soto. Mimicry attacks on host-based intrusion detection systems. In *Proceedings of the 9th ACM Conference on Computer and Communications Security*, CCS '02, pages 255–264, New York, NY, USA, 2002. ACM.

[50] Z. Wang and X. Jiang. HyperSafe: A lightweight approach to provide lifetime hypervisor control-flow integrity. In *Proceedings of the 2010 IEEE Symposium on Security and Privacy*, SP '10, pages 380–395, Washington, DC, USA, 2010. IEEE Computer Society.

[51] Z. Wang, X. Jiang, W. Cui, and P. Ning. Countering kernel rootkits with lightweight hook protection. In *Proceedings of the 16th ACM Conference on Computer and Communications Security*, CCS '09, pages 545–554, New York, NY, USA, 2009. ACM.

[52] C. Warrender, S. Forrest, and B. A. Pearlmutter. Detecting intrusions using system calls: Alternative data models. In *1999 IEEE Symposium on Security and Privacy*, SP '99, pages 133–145, Oakland, California, USA, May 1999. IEEE Computer Society.

[53] D. Wheeler. SLOCCount, 2015. http://www.dwheeler.com/sloccount/.

[54] C. Wright. Para-virtualization interfaces, 2006. http://lwn.net/Articles/194340.

[55] X. Xiong and P. Liu. SILVER: Fine-grained and transparent protection domain primitives in commodity OS kernel. In S. J. Stolfo, A. Stavrou, and C. V. Wright, editors, *Research in Attacks, Intrusions, and Defenses*, number 8145 in Lecture Notes in Computer Science, pages 103–122. Springer Berlin Heidelberg, Jan. 2013.

[56] M. Xu, X. Jiang, R. Sandhu, and X. Zhang. Towards a VMM-based usage control framework for OS kernel integrity protection. In *Proceedings of the 12th ACM Symposium on Access Control Models and Technologies*, SACMAT '07, pages 71–80, New York, NY, USA, 2007. ACM.

DIABLO: A Warehouse-Scale Computer Network Simulator using FPGAs

Zhangxi Tan Zhenghao Qian Xi Chen Krste Asanović David Patterson

University of California, Berkeley

{xtan,peterfly,c.xi,krste,pattrsn}@eecs.berkeley.edu

Abstract

Motivated by rapid software and hardware innovation in warehouse-scale computing (WSC), we visit the problem of warehouse-scale network design evaluation. A WSC is composed of about 30 arrays or clusters, each of which contains about 3000 servers, leading to a total of about 100,000 servers per WSC. We found many prior experiments have been conducted on relatively small physical testbeds, and they often assume the workload is static and that computations are only loosely coupled with the adaptive networking stack. We present a novel and cost-efficient FPGA-based evaluation methodology, called Datacenter-In-A-Box at LOw cost (DIABLO), which treats arrays as whole computers with tightly integrated hardware and software. We have built a 3,000-node prototype running the full WSC software stack. Using our prototype, we have successfully reproduced a few WSC phenomena, such as TCP Incast and memcached request latency long tail, and found that results do indeed change with both scale and with version of the full software stack.

Categories and Subject Descriptors C.5.3 [*Computer System Implementation*]: Microprocessors; I.6.8 [*Simulation and Modeling*]: Discrete Event

Keywords Warehouse-scale computing; FPGA; Performance Evaluation

1. Introduction

Modern datacenters are no longer just a collection of servers running traditional commercial workloads. The tremendous success of Internet services has led to the rise of Warehouse-Scale Computers (WSCs) [25] with 50,000 to 100,000 servers [41] treated as a massive computer system. The continuing push for greater cost efficiency and scalability has driven leading Internet companies, such as Facebook and Google, to innovate in new software infrastructure and even custom hardware [15, 18].

As noted in many recent papers [35, 58], the network is perhaps the most critical component in a WSC. The growing scale of WSCs leads to increasing and more variable network delays, while demand for more ports increases cost in an already expensive switching fabric. Consequently, many researchers have proposed novel datacenter network architectures, mostly focusing on new switch designs [36, 37, 40, 50, 57, 58], and several new networking products emphasize simple switch designs with low latency [9, 10].

When comparing these network proposals, we observe a wide variety of design choices made for almost every aspect of the design space, including switch design, network topology, protocol, and applications. We believe these basic disagreements about fundamental design decisions are due to the different assumptions taken by various existing WSC infrastructures and applications, and the lack of a sound methodology to evaluate new options. Most proposed designs have only been tested with a small testbed running unrealistic microbenchmarks, as it is very difficult to evaluate network infrastructure innovations at scale without first building a WSC. We surveyed WSC-related papers in the SIGCOMM conference from 2008 to 2013 and found that the median size of physical testbeds contained only 16 servers and 6 switches (see Figure 2).

In this paper, we present the design of DIABLO (Datacenter-In-A-Box at LOw cost), an FPGA-based WSC simulator that enables the at-scale and in-depth modeling of WSC arrays as complete computer systems with tightly integrated hardware and software. DIABLO can run unmodified WSC applications and operating systems at the scale of O(1,000) to O(10,000) nodes while providing detailed models of every instruction executed on every node, the operation of the network interfaces on each node, and the movement of every byte in every packet through multiple levels of datacenter switches.

ASPLOS '15, Month 14–18, 2015, Istanbul, Turkey.

http://dx.doi.org/10.1145/2694344.2694362

The specific target of DIABLO is the building block of the WSC, called an *array* [38] or *cluster* [25]. A WSC is composed of about 20–40 such arrays, each of which contains about 2000–3000 servers, summing to a total of about 50,000–100,000 servers per WSC. The array is often the target of an application, with multiple arrays used for both dependability and to distribute workload. DIABLO is fast enough to model O(10) seconds of runtime of a whole WSC array in a few hours instead of the weeks that would be required for an equivalent software simulator. To increase FPGA efficiency and flexibility, DIABLO is not based on FPGA prototyping, where hardware designs are directly mapped to FPGAs, but instead uses FPGAs to accelerate parameterized abstract performance models of the system [55].

The number of compute nodes in the DIABLO prototype is two orders-of-magnitude greater than recent testbeds used by academic researchers, but the FPGA-based simulation approach makes it plausible for many research groups to acquire their own private platform. The projected full-system hardware cost of an O(10,000)-node DIABLO system using modern state-of-the-art FPGAs is around $150K. An equivalent real WSC array would cost around $36M in CAPEX and $800K in OPEX/month. Furthermore, unlike real hardware, DIABLO is fully parameterizable and fully instrumented, and supports repeatable deterministic experiments.

In our evaluation, we show how results obtained from large-scale DIABLO runs can be dramatically different from those obtained from smaller testbeds. In particular, DIABLO allows us to record the same behavior administrators observe when deploying equivalently scaled WSC software, such as TCP Incast throughput collapse [60] and the long tails of memcached request latency.

2. Background and Related Work

In this section, we first review the structure of WSCs, then discuss existing evaluation approaches and previous studies, and conclude with a summary of WSC simulation needs.

2.1 WSC Network Architecture

WSCs use a hierarchy of local-area networks (LAN) and off-the-shelf switches. Figure 1 shows a typical WSC network arranged in a Clos topology with three networking layers. At the bottom layer, each rack typically holds 20–40 servers, each singly connected to a commodity *Top-of-Rack (ToR)* switch with a 1 Gbps link. These ToR switches usually offer two to eight uplinks, which leave the rack to connect up to several *array switches* to provide redundancy and bandwidth. At the top of the hierarchy, *datacenter switches* carry traffic between array switches usually using 10 Gbps links. All links use Ethernet physical-layer protocol, with either copper or fiber cabling depending on connection distance.

One of the most challenging design problems is that the bandwidth "over-subscription" ratio (i.e. bandwidth entering from below versus bandwidth available to level above) worsens rapidly as we move up the hierarchy. This imbalance is due to the cost of switch bandwidth, which grows quadratically in the number of switch ports. The resulting limited WSC bisection bandwidth significantly affects the design of software and the placement of services and data, hence the current active interest in improving network switch designs.

Recent novel network architectures employ a simple, low-latency, supercomputer-like interconnect. For example, the Sun Infiniband datacenter switch [10] has a 300 ns port-port latency as opposed to the 7–8 μs of common Gigabit Ethernet switches. Even at the WSC level, where huge traditional Cisco and Juniper switches or routers have dominated to handle inter-WSC traffic, simple switches with minimal software are now preferred. For example, the Google G-scale OpenFlow switch [47] runs almost no software except the OpenFlow agent using just BGP and ISIS protocols.

2.2 Evaluation Approaches

We next compare the different methodologies that have been used to evaluate designs for WSC networks.

Production prototyping: In industry, perhaps the ideal way to test new hardware is to build the real system at a smaller scale and run it alongside a production system [34]. In this way, new hardware evaluation will benefit from running production software and a more realistic workload. However, this approach suffers from scalability issues. First, it is expensive to build a large number of prototypes. Second, it is risky to deploy experimental hardware at a large-scale in a production environment. Third, the majority of the testing workload will be generated by older and slower computers.

Testing clusters: Another popular approach is to deploy the test equipment in medium-scale shared testing clusters. For instance, the Yahoo M45 [7] cluster has 4,000 processors and 1.5 petabytes of data storage, and is designed to run data-intensive distributed computing platforms such as Hadoop [13]. Larger Internet companies can afford much larger testing clusters, e.g. 20,000 nodes at Google [8]. Although these test clusters have enough computing nodes to help diagnose interesting scalability problems, their construction and maintenance costs are enormous. Bringing up an equivalent production software stack is also another practical issue [8]. Because of cost, researchers in academia use much smaller in-house clusters at the scale of 40–80 nodes (1–2 racks) [36, 51, 61] of off-the-shelf hardware. Commer-

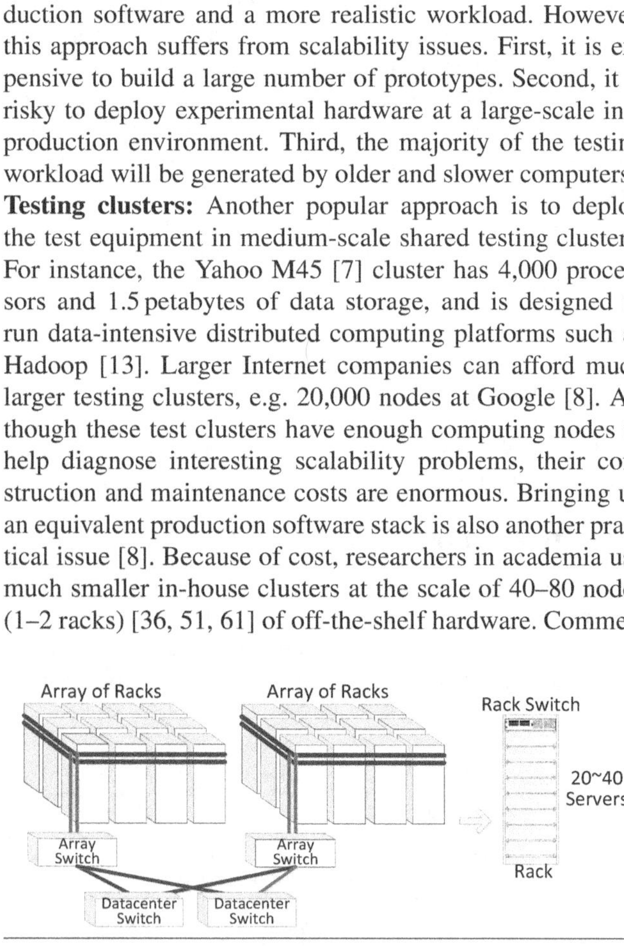

Figure 1. A typical WSC network architecture.

cial hardware usually has few controllable parameters, so experiments can only explore a limited design space, and has limited observability to help understand behavior, which complicates analysis given that experimental runs with real hardware are not generally reproducible.

Cloud computing: Cloud computing platforms such as Amazon EC2 offer a pay-per-use service based on virtual machine (VM) technology to enable users to share their WSC infrastructure at an O(1,000) scale. Researchers can pay $0.10/hour/node to rapidly deploy a functional-only testbed for network management and control plane studies [30, 63]. The cloud is a straightforward approach for software developers to acquire a large-scale infrastructure. Such services, however, provide almost no visibility or control over the network and have no mechanism for accurately experimenting with new networking architectures.

Full-system software simulations: To avoid the high capital cost of hardware prototyping, researchers have long used software simulators to explore new architectural ideas at all levels, from microarchitectures and instruction sets [46] to full systems [27]. Alas, the recent abrupt transitions to massively distributed architectures and high-radix switches have both increased the complexity and scale of simulation. The complex interaction of networking software with networking hardware renders popular techniques, such as sampling and simple analytical models, unreliable at reproducing actual steady-state behavior even in the simplest TCP/IP networking environments [39].

Analytical simulation models: Researchers have used stochastic queuing models in simulations [43, 48] to gain insight into existing systems. Instead of simulating the detailed microarchitecture, such analytical models raise the level of abstraction, provided measurements of distributions of arrival and service times for various tasks in the system are available. Although analytical models are much faster than full-scale simulation, it is challenging to build faithful models for new HW/SW that captures interesting interactions at the 100,000-server scale when there is no system to measure.

2.3 Recent WSC Network Evaluation Studies

We next survey previous WSC-network evaluation studies. Figure 2 plots the scale of the physical testbeds used by datacenter networking papers published in SIGCOMM from 2008 to 2013. To be generous in our survey, we count VMs as physical nodes, although VMs time-share hardware resources and might not reflect accurate timing in the real physical network. In addition, when EC2 is used, there is no visibility into network performance. We optimistically estimate the maximum number of switches assuming each physical machine only hosts one VM.

Clearly, the biggest issue is evaluation scale. Although a mid-size WSC contains tens of thousands of servers and thousands of switches, recent evaluations have been limited to relatively small testbeds with less than 100 servers and 10–20 switches. Small-scale systems are understandable, but results obtained may not be predictive of systems deployed at large scale. As we show later in this paper, sometimes design decisions drawn from O(100) testbeds are completely reversed when scaling to O(1,000) nodes.

For workloads, most evaluations run synthetic programs, microbenchmarks, or even pattern generators, but real WSC workloads include web search, email, and Map-Reduce jobs. In large companies, like Google and Microsoft, researchers typically use trace-driven simulation, due to the abundance of production traces. Nevertheless, production traces are collected on existing systems with drastically different network architectures. They cannot capture the effects of timing-dependent execution on a new proposed architecture. In the past, when looking at networking designs, researchers tend to focus on networking hardware and ignore server computation and client OS interaction for large-scale experiments. We find that not only does OS software affect the system results at scale, but it can be the dominant factor.

Types	*Microbenchmark*	*Trace*	*Application*
Number of Papers	16	3	2

Table 1. *Workload in recent SIGCOMM papers*

Finally, many evaluations make use of existing commercial off-the-shelf switches, with proprietary architectures that have poor documentation of their existing structure and little opportunity to change parameters such as link speed and switch buffer configurations, which may have significant impact on fundamental design decisions.

2.4 WSC Network Evaluation Needs

As pointed out in [25], the technical challenges of designing WSCs are no less worthy of the expertise of computer systems and networking architects than any other class of machines. Their size alone makes them difficult to experiment with or simulate efficiently, therefore, system designers must develop new techniques to guide design decisions. We believe to evaluate new WSC network architectures using high-performance supercomputing-style interconnects with a rapidly evolving set of application workloads and OS software requires simulations with the following four properties:

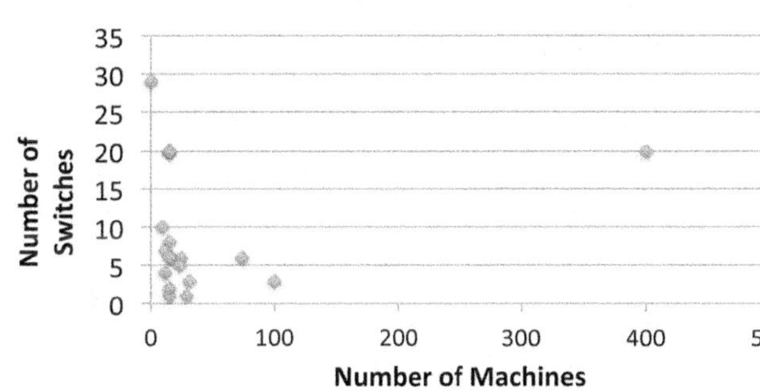

Figure 2. Size of physical testbeds used in recent SIGCOMM papers.

1. *Scale*: WSCs contain O(100,000) servers or more. Although few single apps use all servers in a WSC, O(10,000) nodes are desired to study networking phenomena at aggregate and array-level switches.
2. *Performance*: Current large datacenter switches have 48/96 ports, and are massively parallel. Each port has 1–4 K flow tables and several input/output packet buffers. In the worst case, there are ~200 concurrent events every clock cycle. In addition, high-bandwidth switch processors often employ multicore architectures [1].
3. *Accuracy*: A WSC network operates at nanosecond time scales. For example, transmitting a 64-byte packet on a 10 Gbps link takes only ~50 ns, which is comparable to DRAM access latency. This precision implies many fine-grained synchronizations during simulation if timing models are to be accurate.
4. *Flexibility*: The simulator should support experimentation with radical new switch designs and network software stacks. It is unlikely slight tweaks to existing designs will lead to large improvements.

3. DIABLO Implementation

Although software simulation is a flexible and low-cost technique for systems evaluation, it cannot scale to the size and performance levels required for WSC-scale network experiments while maintaining accuracy. In this section, we describe the design of DIABLO, which exploits FPGAs to provide programmable hardware acceleration of simulation models, achieving two orders of magnitude performance improvement over software simulators. In addition, DIABLO can be scaled using multiple tightly coupled FPGAs to provide scalable high-performance simulations that retain accuracy and flexibility. Overall, we designed DIABLO to answer questions about how new systems behave after changes to the hardware, the software, and/or the scale. We use *target* to refer to the proposed system under evaluation, and *host* to refer to the system running the simulation.

3.1 FAME-Based WSC Array Simulation

The most obvious approach to experimenting with WSC arrays on FPGAs is to build a WSC array *emulator* by mapping processor and switch RTL designs directly to the FPGAs. But this naive mapping is inefficient and inflexible, and makes it impractical to model key WSC array architecture features at scale. DIABLO instead uses FPGAs to accelerate *simulation models* of the various components, an approach known as FPGA Architecture Model Execution (FAME) [55]. Groups in both academia and industry have built various types of FAME simulators, which can be classified in five levels that are analogous to different RAID levels [55]. Higher FAME levels lower simulator cost and improve performance over lower levels, while moving further away from the concrete RTL design of the target. DIABLO is a FAME-7 simulator using the following three key techniques to improve efficiency [55].

1. *Abstracted Models:* To reduce host hardware resource requirements, we employ high-level abstract models of each simulated component, capturing important features but simplifying or removing features that are rarely used. We also separate functional models from timing models to simplify parameterization of target timing. For example, the functional model for a router interprets headers to send packets to the correct output port, while the router's timing model calculates how many target clock cycles this takes. Thus, we can change the timing without altering the router's functional model.
2. *Decoupled Design:* We use a variable number of FPGA host clock cycles and FPGA-resource-friendly structures to simulate a single target clock cycle. For example, a simple ring network on the host FPGA can model an expensive multiport crossbar in the target datacenter switch.
3. *Host Multithreading:* We run multiple target model threads simulating different target instances in a single host hardware model pipeline. Multithreading improves FPGA resource utilization and hides host platform latencies, such as those from host DRAM access and timing-model synchronization across different FPGAs.

3.2 DIABLO Modular Architecture

DIABLO employs a modular design with only two distinct FPGA configurations. Figure 3 shows the high-level simulator architecture for the typical target WSC array configuration presented in Figure 1. We map all server models along with the ToR switch models into *Rack FPGAs*, and array and datacenter switch models to separate *Switch FPGAs*. To further simplify switch model design, we keep any switch model within a single FPGA. Mirroring the physical topology of the target system, we connect Rack FPGAs to Switch FPGAs through several time-shared 2.5 Gbps serial transceivers. Each FPGA has its own simulation scheduler that synchronizes with adjacent FPGAs over the serial links at a fine granularity to satisfy the nanosecond-scale simulation accuracy requirements mentioned in Section 2.

To make the design simpler and more modular, we only use multi-gigabit serial transceivers for inter-FPGA connections. The serial transceivers provide enough bandwidth between FPGAs considering our overall simulation slowdown of between 250–1000× of real time. For example, the bandwidth of a 2.5 Gbps host transceiver translates to 625–2500 Gbps in the target, which far exceeds the bandwidth between a few racks and several array switches today. Moreover, recent FPGAs have significantly enhanced serial transceiver performance, supporting up to 28 Gbps bandwidth [14] in the 28 nm generation.

We reduce host communication latency by using our own protocol over the serial links. Including all packet payload

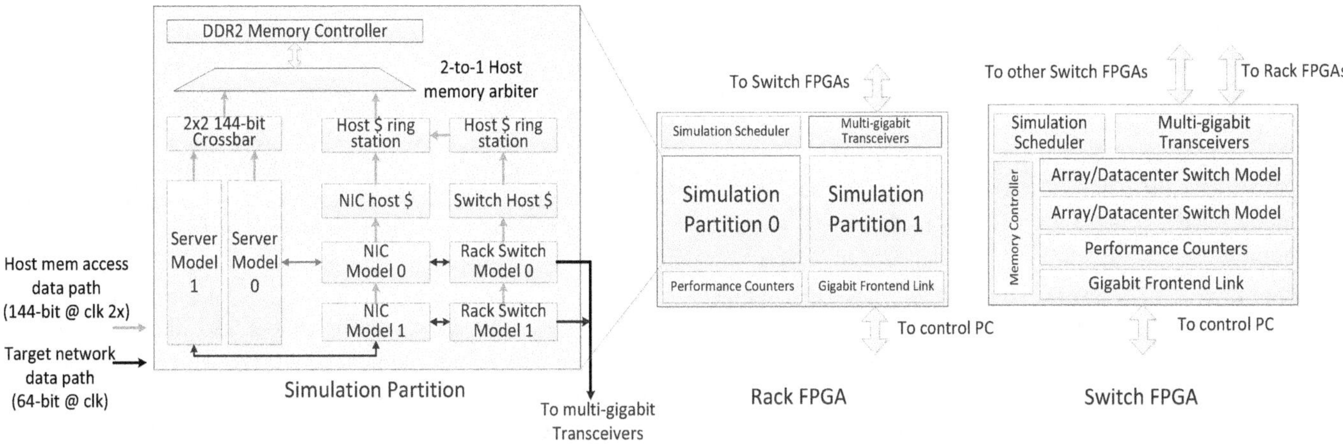

Figure 3. DIABLO FPGA simulator architecture. Only two FPGA configurations are used: Rack FPGA and Switch FPGA.

and overhead, the overall round-trip latency between FAME models on different FPGAs is only around 1.6 μs. In addition, the host-multithreaded FAME-7 design further helps to hide host communication latency, removing model synchronization latency as a simulator performance bottleneck.

3.3 DIABLO FPGA Models

DIABLO contains three FPGA models corresponding to three basic components in WSC array network infrastructure: compute servers, network interface cards, and network switches. To enable design-space exploration without time-consuming FPGA re-synthesis, all the models have runtime-configurable parameters. All the modules were custom-built in SystemVerilog with minimal use of 3rd-party IP blocks.

Server Model

The server model is built on top of RAMP Gold [54], which is an open-source cycle-level full-system FAME-7 architecture simulator supporting the full 32-bit SPARC v8 ISA. RAMP Gold also models MMUs, timers, and interrupt controllers, and boots Linux 2.6.39.3 and 3.5.7 kernels as well as a many-core research OS [45]. The server model is binary compatible with existing SPARC32 machines, and runs unmodified binaries from Debian Linux distributions.

We map one target server running an independent Linux instance to one hardware thread in the host server model pipeline, with each host pipeline in DIABLO simulating a WSC rack holding up to 32 servers. Each simulated server uses a simplified runtime-configurable fixed-CPI timing model, where all instructions take a fixed number of cycles. The goal of the simple server model is not to model WSC server microarchitecture with 100% accuracy but run a full software stack with an approximate performance estimate or bound. More detailed timing models could be implemented, but would require additional host hardware resources and would thus reduce simulation scale.

Even though the RAMP Gold pipeline improves server model performance by two orders-of-magnitude over state-of-the-art software simulators, the server models are still the simulation bottleneck for the whole DIABLO system.

Switch Model

To demonstrate the flexibility of our approach, we build FAME-7 models for two broad categories of WSC array switch: those using *connectionless packet switching*, also known as *datagram switching*, and those using *connection-oriented virtual-circuit switching*.

Although packet switches dominate current WSC networks, some researchers are proposing new circuit-switching designs for WSCs to provide more predictable latencies and to take advantage of new high-speed switching technologies. The proposed designs are only available as early research prototypes but details are open, and some have been directly implemented on FPGAs [59], simplifying construction of highly accurate models. An earlier publication [56] showed that the fully detailed model for a 128-port 10-Gbps high-radix array/datacenter circuit-switching switch can fit on a single FPGA.

In contrast, the packet switches used in existing production WSCs pose a considerable modeling challenge due to their design complexity and their hidden proprietary microarchitecture. To make modeling tractable, we simplify our abstract models by removing features that are seldom used in a WSC. Here are the simplifications we employed and the rationale behind our choice:

Ignore Ethernet QoS-related features: Although QoS features (e.g. support of IEEE 802.1p class of service (CoS)) are available on almost every switch today, many WSCs only utilize switches for basic connectivity without turning on QoS features.

Use simplified source routing: Many switches [11, 12] already support TCAM-based flow tables that have at least 32 K entries. Given the total number of machines in a WSC, the slow-path flow-table update is rarely executed, making the flow-table lookup time constant in practice. Besides, WSC topologies do not change frequently, and routes can be pre-configured statically. We use source routing to simplify modeling of packet routing, and we note that source routing is actually a component of many WSC-switch research proposals. To emulate more complicated flow-table operations, we could implement d-left hash tables [49] using host DRAM. This technique has already been applied by recent datacenter switches implementing large flow tables [11].

Abstract packet processors: Commercial datacenter switches include many pipelined packet processors that handle different tasks such as MAC address learning, VLAN membership, and so on. The processing time of each stage is relatively constant regardless of packet size, and the time can be as short as a few hundred nanoseconds [31] to a few microseconds [11].

Although commercial switch implementation details are generally not publicly available, the fundamentals of these switch architectures are well known. Examples include the architecture of a virtual-output-queue switch and common scheduling algorithms. We build our abstracted model focusing on these central well-known architectural features, and allow other parts that are unclear or of special interest to researchers (for example, packet buffer layout) to be configurable during simulation. Specifically, in our switch models, we focus on the data path features, such as switch buffer management and configuration, which have become an active area for packet-switch researchers [26]. We base our packet buffer models after that of the Cisco Nexus 5000 switch, with configurable parameters selected according to a Broadcom switch design [42]. We also model high link bandwidth and cut-through switching fabrics with low port-to-port latencies. These are all essential features for exploring future high-performance WSC switches, which are not very easy to deploy at scale for testing in the real world because of high cost.

There has been an increasing research interest in the area of Software Defined Networks (SDNs) using Openflow-capable switches in the WSC. The datapaths of these SDN switches are actually identical to those of conventional switches, and our simplified source-routed switch models can be easily extended to support the flow-table architecture used by an SDN switch.

In DIABLO, we use a unified abstract virtual output-queue switch model with a simple round-robin scheduler for all levels of switch. Switch models in different layers of the network hierarchy differ only in their link latency, bandwidth, and buffer configuration parameters. An earlier publication provides more details of our switch model [56]. Our FAME-7-based switch model is four times faster than a software single-threaded network simulator used at Google [8] that does not simulate packet payloads or support full software-stack scaling to 10,000 nodes as does DIABLO.

NIC Models

The DIABLO NIC models an abstracted Ethernet device, whose internal architecture resembles that of the Intel 8254x Gigabit Ethernet controller on the popular Intel PRO/1000 MT server adapter. It is also popular among many VM implementations such as Virtual Box [20], VMWare Virtual Server [21], QEMU [19], and Microsoft Hyper-V [16]. Figure 4 shows the target architecture of our abstracted NIC model. The core feature of the NIC is a scatter/gather DMA with ring-based packet buffers stored in the main system DRAM. The scatter/gather DMA is used to support the zero-copy feature in Linux, and is essential for any high-performance networking interface. In our current prototype, we support only one hardware ring buffer for each of the receive (RX) and transmit (TX) queues. For model simplicity, we did not model any hardware checksum offloading. Instead, we turn off the packet checksum feature in the Linux kernel to emulate having a hardware checksum offloading engine in the NIC without taking additional CPU time. Our

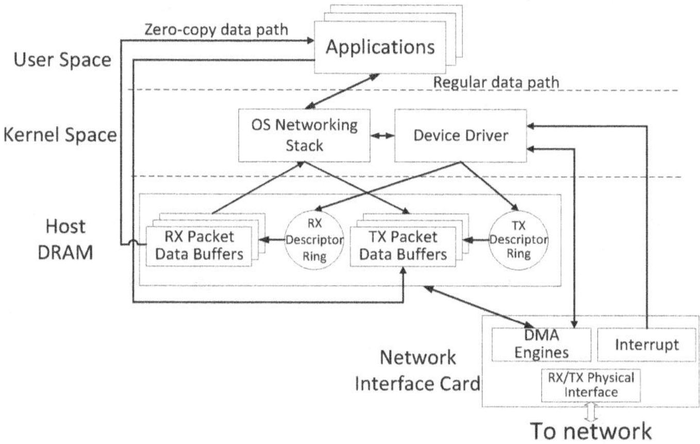

Figure 4. Software and hardware architecture of generic network interface cards

NIC device driver supports all features of a generic Linux Ethernet device driver. We can run unmodified TCP/IP user applications using the standard socket programming interface. To model high performance NICs, our driver supports advanced features such as Zero-copy, RX/TX interrupt mitigation and the NAPI polling interface [52].

The NIC model is a straightforward FAME-7 implementation of the target hardware. The basic functionality of a NIC is to manipulate packet data stored in the DRAM, but DRAM performance is much less an issue for FAME models so the NIC model is not on the simulator critical path.

3.4 DIABLO Cluster Prototype

The DIABLO prototype was built using a rack of BEE3 boards [32]. Each board has four Xilinx Virtex-5 LX155T FPGAs, each with 16 GB of DDR2 memory across two independent DRAM channels, resulting in 64 GB total per board. Each FPGA provides eight 2.5 Gbps SERDES lanes in two CX4 ports to connect to other FPGAs.

On each Rack FPGA of the current BEE3 boards, we evenly distribute four 32-thread server models to two host DRAM channels and partition the host DRAM for server computations, simulating four racks with 124 servers. Each server model has one ToR switch model attached to the same DRAM controller.

Component Name	*LUT*	*Register*	*BRAM*	*LUTRAM*
Server Models	28,445	37,463	96	6,584
NIC Models	9,467	4,785	10	752
Rack Switch Models	4,511	3,482	52	345
Miscellaneous	3,395	16,052	31	5,058
Total	45,818	62,811	189	12,739

Table 2. *Rack FPGA resource utilization on Xilinx Virtex-5 LX155T after place and route using Xilinx ISE 14.3.*

Table 2 shows the overall resource utilization of the Rack FPGA on the BEE3 board. Including the resources dedicated for FPGA routing, the device is almost fully utilized with 95% of logic slices occupied at a 90 MHz host clock rate. The chip resources are dominated by structures to simulate server computation. On each FPGA, we equally divide the 16 GB physical DRAM into 128×128 MB partitions. Each simulated server uses one partition for target memory storage. For each server pipeline, we use 31 threads out of the 32 available threads and save the DRAM storage of the remaining thread for simulating packet buffers on the ToR switch. Each DIABLO model has a dedicated on-chip host cache to optimize simulator DRAM accesses.

All DIABLO models on the same FPGA share a single Gigabit Ethernet connection as the frontend connection for bootstrapping, console output and functional I/O, such as keyboard and disk access.

The Switch FPGA is just a cut-down version of the Rack FPGA containing only switch models and fewer server model pipelines. A single server functional model pipeline, without a timing model, is used to run functional configuration for our switch models. The server functional model can also act as a control-plane processor for a simulated switch.

We emphasized reliability over performance in physical design. We protect all physical links, such as Gigabit Ethernet and serial links, with hardware checksums and retries to handle occasional soft errors, which we've observed occur a few times per day in our prototype. We also use ECC to protect all memory data paths that interact with the ECC memory DIMMs on our FPGA board.

A 3,000-node DIABLO system

We used 9 BEE3 boards totalling 36 FPGAs to build a sizable prototype, as Figure 5 shows. We use off-the-shelf CX4 breakout cables to connect arbitrary transceiver pairs on different FPGAs from the front panel following the target network topology. We populate six boards with the Rack-FPGA design simulating 2,976 servers with 96 rack switches. We load the remaining three boards with the Switch-FPGA design to simulate 6 array switches and one datacenter switch. Using an additional 13 boards, we could scale the existing system to build an emulated large WSC array with 11,904 servers and 385 rack switches.

(a) Without inter-board connections (b) Fully-connected with high-speed cables

Figure 5. DIABLO cluster prototype

The whole FPGA cluster has a total memory capacity of 576 GB in 72 independent DRAM channels with an aggregated bandwidth of 268 GB/s. All FPGA boards fit into a standard server rack, and the prototype consumes about 1.5 kW when active. Each FPGA has a Gigabit frontend control link connected to a shared 48-port gigabit switch. We use two 12-core Intel Xeon X5680 servers to drive all nine FPGA boards using our custom protocol over Ethernet. Each server has four 1 Gbps interface card connected to the 48-port switch to balance the control traffic to different boards. We store boot disk images and console I/O logs of all 2,976 servers on a striped RAID-0 partition on each front-end server. This setup is used to optimize the simulated Linux booting process, where all simulated servers access disk images over 8×1 Gbps links simultaneously.

The BEE3 boards used have 2007-era FPGAs and older DRAM DIMMs, and the BEE3 board was not designed with low-cost simulations in mind. Each BEE3 cost $15K, and the total cost of a 9-board system was about $140K. Although the BEE3 hardware is now somewhat dated, the system was sufficient to develop and evaluate the approach and gather experience for the next system. Because DIABLO uses a modular design and uses only the serial links between FPGAs, we can readily port DIABLO to lower-cost single-FPGA boards. Using the latest 20nm FPGAs in 2015 and with a redesigned board, we estimate we could now potentially build a 32,000-node DIABLO system using just 32 FPGAs and an overall cost of $150K including DRAM.

4. Case Studies

In this section, we demonstrate the capabilities of the DIABLO prototype and validate its performance models using case studies drawn from classic networking problems run at scale. We show the effects of changing both hardware and software parameters of the system, including switch bandwidth, latency, buffer configuration, target server CPU performance, operating systems, and application logic.

4.1 Reproducing TCP Incast

Incast is a classic many-to-one communication pattern commonly found in many WSCs implementing scale-out distributed storage and computing frameworks, such as Hadoop and Map-Reduce. In particular, the TCP Incast problem [53, 60] refers to the application-level throughput collapse that occurs as the number of servers returning data to a client increases past the ability of an Ethernet switch to buffer packets. Previous work [28, 60] has focused on studying the interplay between the TCP retransmission timeout (RTO) value and the limited capacity of buffers in low-cost ToR switches. However, as pointed out in [53], TCP Incast is only obvious under specific hardware and software setups, for instance with switches that have very small shared packet buffers.

Our first experiment uses DIABLO to reproduce the application throughput collapse observed with shallow-buffer Gigabit switches, as used in many previous studies. We configured the DIABLO packet-switching model for 1 Gbps links, switch port-to-port delay of 1 μs, and 4 KB packet buffers per port, as found in a Nortel 5500 switch [29]. Compared to existing *ns2* [4] and analytical switch models, DIABLO models a more advanced packet buffer architecture that supports virtual queues to prevent head-of-line blocking, as usually used in high-end Cisco [11] and Fulcrum switches [31]. The test program [3] we ran has been used to test 10 Gbps production datacenter switches from Arista and Cisco [9]. We selected a typical request block size of 256 KB for the client application. We configured our server models to simulate a single-core 4 GHz CPU and ran Linux 2.6.39.3 on our simulated servers. We used up to 24 ports of the simulated switch and ran the network transaction for 40 iterations.

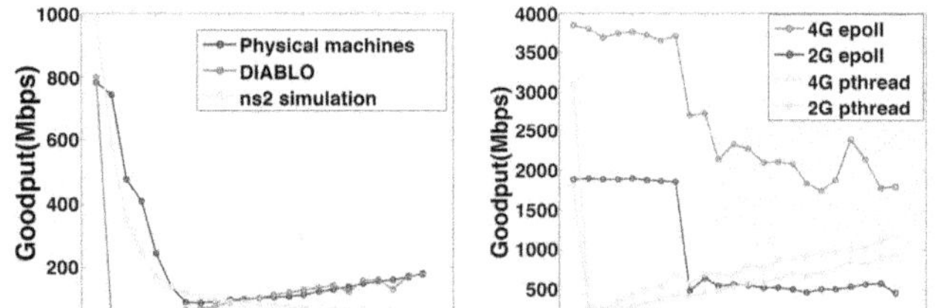

(a) 1 Gbps shallow-buffer switch (b) 10 Gbps simulated switch

Figure 6. Reproducing the *goodput* of TCP Incast under different configurations

We compare DIABLO results against an *ns2* simulation configured to match these parameters, and validate our results against a real hardware cluster containing 16 Intel Xeon D7950 servers and a 16-port Asante IntraCore 35516-T switch, where the commercial switches have a shared packet buffer architecture. Figure 6(a) compares the average *goodput* of the three systems. With its abstract virtual-output-queue switch model, DIABLO has a faster application throughput collapse than measured on the hardware with a shared-buffer switch. However, DIABLO captures the throughput recovery trend after the collapse better than *ns2*. The simulated throughput before collapse also matches that on the real system at around 800 Mbps. Note that many details are different between the DIABLO system and the real hardware, including instruction set, processor performance, and NIC and switch architecture, yet DIABLO captures the overall shape of the performance curve at the larger scale.

Traditional network simulators like *ns2* focus on network protocols but not the implementation of the OS network stack and application interface, which become more important for high-speed networks. To investigate the impact of target OS and application interface, we modified the TCP Incast benchmark to use the *epoll* syscall instead of the original *pthread* with blocking socket syscalls. The *epoll* syscall has been used by many WSC applications, such as *memcached*, to efficiently handle many client network connections. Applications using *epoll* proactively poll the kernel for available data. This behavior is different from that of using blocking syscalls to wait for OS notifications from multiple user threads. We also configured the DIABLO server timing model to simulate target computations of a 2 GHz CPU versus a 4 GHz CPU.

Figure 6(b) plots *goodput* curves of experiments under different server hardware and software configurations using a 10 Gbps network. With the same switch and TCP configuration, the results show that CPU speed and choice of OS syscalls significantly affects the application throughput. As pointed out in early work on 10 Gbps TCP performance at the Fermi High Energy Physics Lab [62], there are many other factors in the Linux kernel that could contribute to packet losses, such as different queues for slow and fast path handling of received packets. With 10 Gbps links, it is challenging for applications to sustain wire speed without significant tuning. Even when using scatter/gather zero-copy features in the NIC, the simulated single-core 2 GHz CPU using *pthread* could only achieve 1.8 Gbps throughput when there is no throughput collapse. Using *epoll* significantly delays the onset of throughput collapse. In addition, we only observed a moderate throughput collapse to 2.7 Gbps starting from 9 servers and 1.8 Gbps with 23 servers using 4 GHz CPUs. Using 2 GHz CPUs, the collapse is much more significant at 400–500 Mbps, which is less than a third of the throughput with 4 GHz CPUs. The collapsed throughput with the *epoll* client is only half of that of the original *pthread* client. However, using the *pthread* version, the throughput collapses quickly even with a faster CPU. The throughput recovers to only 10% of the link capacity, which again matches the observations from measurements and simulations in [60]. Moreover, the absolute throughput numbers do not seem to be correlated with the target processor performance when collapse happens.

In conclusion, switch buffers are not always the one and only limiting factor for TCP Incast. The long TCP retransmission timeout is just a consequence of an imbalanced system. Simple analytical or network simulation models might allow parameters to be set to match results for a small number of faster machines connected by a slower network, but then the models will not correctly predict behavior of a scaled system.

4.2 Studying memcached Latency Long Tail at Scale

One of the greatest challenges in building responsive large-scale computer systems is the nature of request service variations. For example, Google researchers found long-tail distributions for web query latencies, where some request latencies are multiple orders of magnitude longer than the median [24, 33]. Moreover, more requests fall into the tail as the system scale increases. There are multiple complex underlying causes of the long tail, including queuing in both software and hardware, kernel schedulers, shared hardware resources and many others [33]. Hence, reproducing the long tail and understand the contributing factors requires analyzing hardware along with the full software stack at large scale. In this section, we use DIABLO to illustrate the impact on tail latency of many factors including: implementation of the application, versions of the OS kernel, network transport protocols, as well as switch design.

Experiment setup

To demonstrate running production WSC software, we ran the popular *memcached* [2, 5, 17] distributed key-value store application on DIABLO. We used unmodified *memcached* source code versions 1.4.15 and 1.4.17.

In a real production environment, the client workloads of *memcached* servers are generated by the front-end web tier. Although the API is simple, it is difficult to accurately represent a *memcached* workload. In particular, previous studies show that the object size distribution has a large impact on the system behavior [44]. Simple microbenchmark tools like *memslap* do not attempt to reproduce the statistical characteristics of real traffic. To provide a more realistic workload, we built our own client based on recently published Facebook live traffic statistics [23]. At Facebook, *memcached* servers are partitioned based on the concept of *pools*. We focused on one of the pools that is the most representative, and validated our workload generator against the Facebook data [23].

Figure 7 shows the simulated target topology. Each rack contains 31 servers with one Top-of-Rack switch. We used the 32nd port on the rack switch to connect to an array switch, creating a bandwidth over-subscription ratio of 31 to 1. Each array switch supports up to 16 inward-facing links and one uplink to the datacenter switch, thus having a bandwidth over-subscription ratio of 16-to-1. With the runtime configurable switch timing models, we are able to simulate a 1 Gbps interconnect with 1 μs port-to-port switch latency as well as a 10 Gbps interconnect with 100 ns port-to-port switch latency. We used the same simulated switch buffer configuration as in section 4.1, and used the simple 4 GHz fixed-CPI timing model for server CPUs. This simulation required six BEE3 boards: four boards to simulate 64 server racks of 1,984 servers, one board to simulate all array switches, and the remaining board for the datacenter switch simulation.

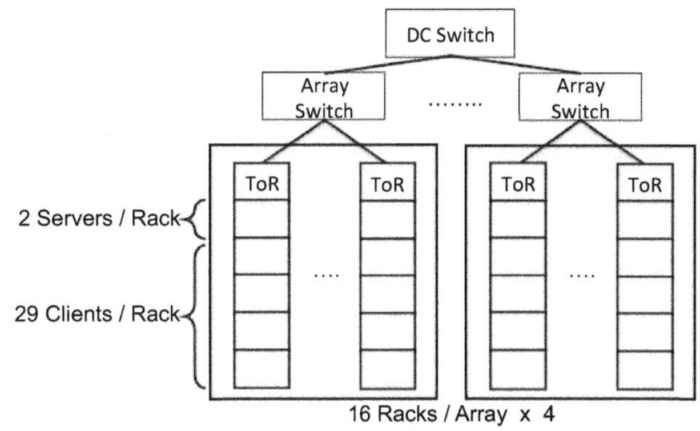

Figure 7. Memcached experimental setup.

We distributed 128 *memcached* servers evenly across all 64 racks to minimize potential hot spots in the network, and used the remaining machines as clients. This creates a configuration of two *memcached* servers and 29 clients in a single rack. Each client sends 30K requests to a randomly selected server from all 128 servers, each configured with a 64 MB memory pool.

We performed experiments at several scales: 496-node, 992-node, and 1984-node. For convenience when presenting results, we round up the exact number of nodes to 500, 1000 and 2000 respectively in the rest of this paper. We scale down the number of servers when running a smaller configuration, maintaining a constant server-to-client ratio. The 500-node setup uses only one 16-port array switch without a datacenter switch, while both 1000-node and 2000-node experiments exercise all three levels of switches. We also performed our load tests using both TCP and UDP protocols. CPU utilization in all servers is moderate, at under 50%. There is also no packet retransmission due to switch buffer overruns.

Validating *memcached* on real clusters and Reproducing the latency long tail on DIABLO

First, to validate our DIABLO models at an understandable scale, we deployed a set of *memcached* experiments at the single-rack scale using a real cluster. Our single-rack 16-node testbed includes 3 GHz Intel Xeon D7950 servers running Linux 2.6.34 connected with a 16-port Asante IntraCore 35516-T Gigabit switch. We used two machines as *memcached* servers with the rest as clients. We let each client thread send 30,000 requests till completion. We also tried 100,000 requests with up to 256 MB server memory pool, and the steady-state performance numbers were similar. We configured each server with several parameter combinations, for example 4 or 8 worker threads using TCP or UDP connections.

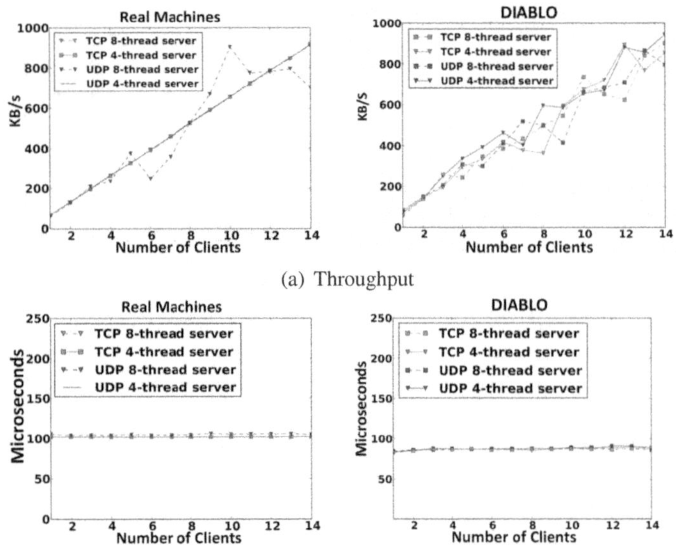

(a) Throughput

(b) Latency

Figure 8. Real machines vs. simulated memcached servers.

We compared results from the perspective of both server and client. Figure 8(a) shows the throughput of a measured server versus a simulated server under different number of clients. We only show results from one server, as throughput curves of other servers are similar. Figure 8(b) illustrates the average request latencies measured at every client. For all configurations we tested at this small scale, DIABLO successfully reproduced the shapes of performance curves. The client latency stays low and scales linearly with a small number of clients, while more clients saturate the server. We expect absolute performance differences between real and simulated clusters, as DIABLO uses a different simulated hardware specification. However, the goal is to reproduce the trend at scale.

As with prior studies using real physical testbeds, our validation efforts are limited by available networking and computing hardware. To perform scale-out validations, we ran the same experiments on an 8-rack 120-node Intel Xeon E5-2620 v2 cluster with 10 Gbps rack switches and a 40 Gbps aggregate switch [6]. As we could not obtain dedicated access to this large shared cluster, we had to run the same experiments many times and choose 10 runs without a significant background workload in the cluster. Figure 9 compares the client request latency tail measured from the large physical cluster with the simulation results from DIABLO. To show the robustness of our data from the shared physical cluster, we plotted the error bars in Figure 9. At the scale of 120 machines, we do see $< 0.1\%$ of total requests finish orders of magnitude slower than regular requests. The newer memcached 1.14.17 has a slightly better tail performance than the older 1.14.15 on both simulated and real cluster. The simulated 120-node setup is a more ideal environment with less software services running in the background. Therefore, there are fewer requests falling into the tail compared to a real system. Similarly, the difference between the two versions of memcached becomes less obvious.

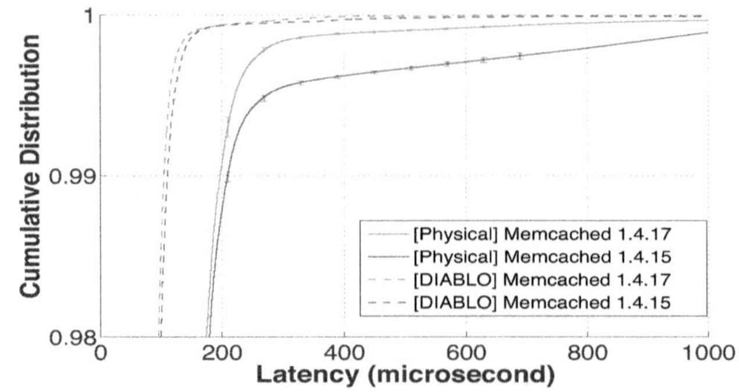

Figure 9. Client latency CDF on a 120-node real cluster vs. DIABLO

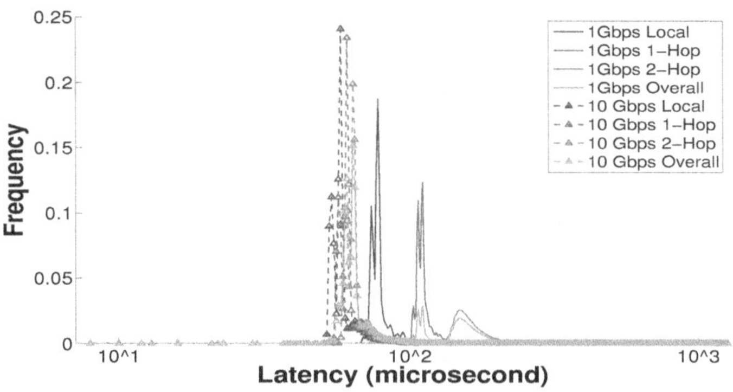

Figure 10. PMF of client request latency at 2000-node on DIABLO using UDP.

Figure 10 plots the Probability Mass Function (PMF) of all client queries for the 2k-node DIABLO simulation running UDP over different interconnects. The shape of PMF is similar at the scale of 500-node and 1k-node. We also observed similar latency long tails using TCP. We found the majority of requests finished in less than $100\mu s$, but there are a small number of requests that finished more than two orders of magnitude slower than the average, reproducing the long tail distribution. To understand the long tail better, we classified all queries into three different categories based on the number of physical switches they traverse, with *local* indicating requests hit the same rack. From Figure 10, we know that all three types of requests exhibit a long tail distribution. The more switches the query traverses, the greater the latency variation. Moreover, 2-hop requests dominate the overall latency distribution at large scale, as the majority of requests travel to a remote rack.

From Figure 11, we can also tell the impact of system scale on the latency tail. For example, the 99-percentile latency of a 2K-node system is more than an order-of-magnitude worse than that of a 500-node system. These observations from DIABLO match those reported in a recent Google publication [33].

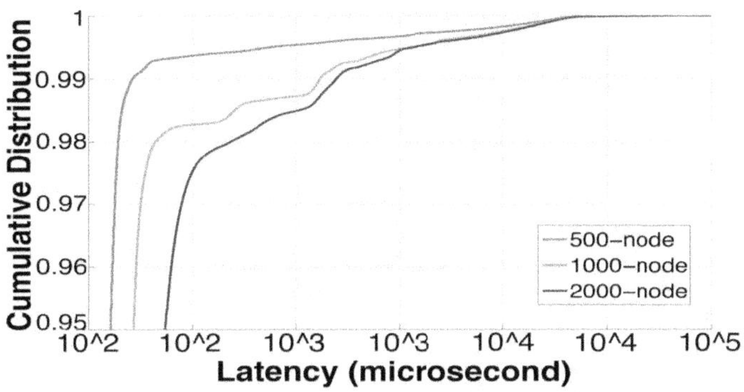

Figure 11. $95^{th} - 100^{th}$ percentile CDF of client latency at different scales on a 1 Gbps interconnect running UDP.

Impact of network hardware

One straightforward solution to reduce request latency is to upgrade the network hardware, and we next explore the potential performance gain via DIABLO simulations. We simulate a low-latency 10 Gbps switch with 10× bandwidth and 10× shorter latency compared to the simulated 1 Gbps network. From our results, the improved cut-through switch does help to reduce request latencies, but the improvement is no more than 2×. This indicates that the full OS networking stack dominates the request latency. Google showed similar results from their large-scale testbed using O(100 ns) low-latency switches [24].

Further, to evaluate the robustness of our simulation results, we simulated the client latency tail with an additional 50 ns and 100 ns port-to-port latency at all switch levels, with results in Figure 12. The error bars on the figure are very small showing that the cycle-level DIABLO simulator is quite stable when tweaking simulated hardware configurations. We found that the extra switch latency does not affect the shape of the tail curves, although the 99-percentile latency increases to 364 μs from 253 μs. In addition, the extra switch latency does not impose a significant tax on regular non-tail request latencies.

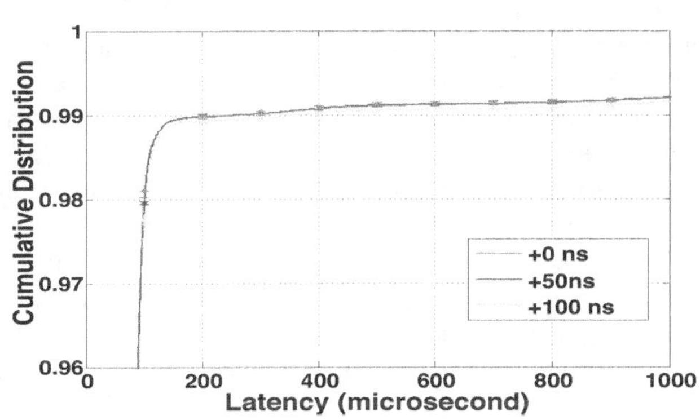

Figure 12. Client latency tail with different switch latencies.

Impact of the network transport protocol at scale

As mentioned earlier, current evaluation technologies only allow most networking researchers to conduct full-system experiments at scales of O(10) to O(100). Often the most intuitive solution to a networking issue is to change the network transport protocol. However, one big question is whether we can generalize O(10)–O(100) node results to a larger scale at O(1000)–O(10,000). In this section, we conduct a simple experiment using DIABLO to quantitatively analyze which network protocol (TCP or UDP) is better at reducing the long-tail at scale, by sweeping through several system parameters including interconnect performance and system scale.

Figure 13 shows the cumulative tail distribution of using different protocols. For the 1 Gbps interconnect, at the 500-node scale the UDP protocol is a clear winner compared to TCP. However, UDP's advantage disappears when moving to 1000 nodes, as TCP slightly outperforms UDP. When we move to the 2000-node scale, TCP is better. The conclusion at 2000-node scale is completely reversed to that at 500 nodes. On the other hand, upgrading the interconnect to 10 Gbps shows a very different result. Now, there is much less difference between UDP and TCP.

The 500-node setup represents a small cluster in a full-scale datacenter, with 13–14 fully populated standard server racks connected to a single aggregate array switch. For the given topology we simulated, both 1000-node and 2000-node setups require an extra aggregate switch. The extra aggregate switch contributes to the tail latency more than using more ports (2000 vs. 1000) on the same extra switch.

Impact of target operating system

DIABLO is different from prior simulators in that it can run 1,000s of full OS instances while modeling time accurately. This enables experiments that are difficult even in a real WSC, e.g., deploying an experimental kernel on thousands of machines.

We ported a more recent Linux 3.5.7 kernel and compared its performance running our large-scale *memcached* experiments against those from the one-year-older 2.6.39.3 kernel used earlier in this section. We compare them at 2K nodes with the same 10 Gbps interconnect and server hardware. Figure 14 plots the cumulative distribution of 95-percentile client request latencies. We can see that there are significant improvements in terms of request responsiveness in the new 3.5.7 kernel. The average request latency is almost halved, and the better kernel scheduler and more efficient networking stack also helps to alleviate the latency long-tail issue.

This result shows that OS optimizations play a critical role in the performance of distributed applications, and OS behaviour should be modeled when evaluating any new proposed new network designs.

Impact of application implementation

In addition to OS network stack design, another factor that affects client request latency is the application's implementation and choice of system calls. We ran two versions of memcached, 1.4.17 and 1.4.15 on both the physical testbed

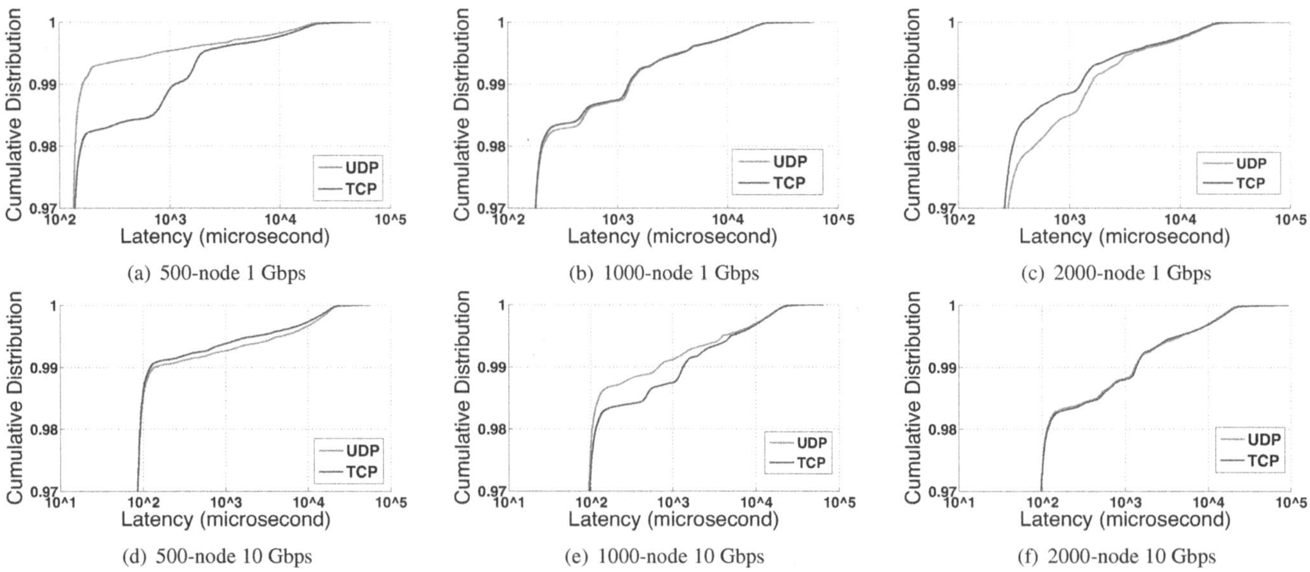

(a) 500-node 1 Gbps (b) 1000-node 1 Gbps (c) 2000-node 1 Gbps

(d) 500-node 10 Gbps (e) 1000-node 10 Gbps (f) 2000-node 10 Gbps

Figure 13. Comparing TCP vs UDP on CDFs of client request latency at different scale with different interconnect.

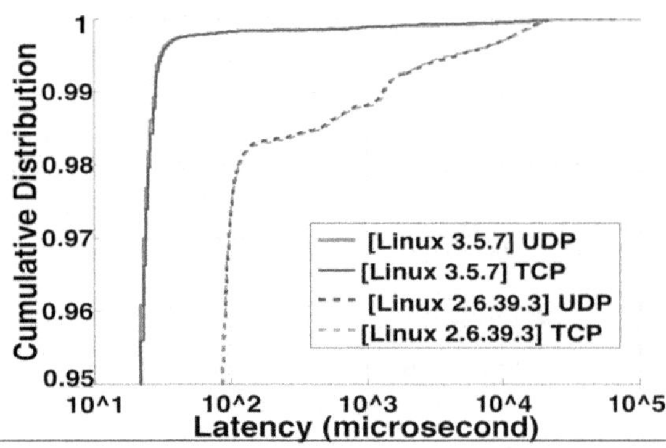

Figure 14. Impact of OS kernel versions on the 2,000-node system.

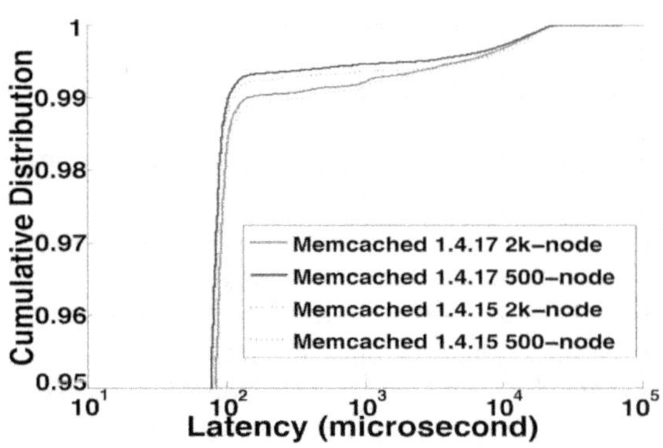

Figure 15. Impact of memcachd versions on the latency CDF. 1.4.17 has a slightly better tail performance similar to our validation results in Figure 9.

and DIABLO. One of the major differences for the slight newer 1.4.17 is the support of the *accept4* syscall, which eliminates one extra syscall for each new TCP connection [22].

For both versions, there is no significant difference between the client request latencies on the real cluster at the scale of 120 nodes. The 1.4.17 memcached has a marginal better 99 percentile latency of 197 μs, while the older 1.4.15 is at 210 μs.

To investigate the effectiveness of the *accept4* syscall at a larger scale, we simulate a configuration with 500 nodes and another configuration with 2,000 nodes on DIABLO. Figure 15 shows the CDF of client latency of both configurations. At the 500-node scale, both versions of memcached on the simulated cluster behave similarly to the 120-node real cluster. The 99-percentile client request latency of 1.4.17 memcached is only 8 μs faster on the simulated hardware. Note that the absolute latency difference between the simulated hardware and real cluster is due to the fact that we configure our abstract model with a slightly faster switch.

On the other hand, when scaling to the 2,000-node scale with one more aggregate switch in the network hierarchy, the benefit of fewer syscalls in the newer version of memcached becomes more apparent. The 99-percentile client request latency of version 1.4.17 is 145 μs versus 345 μs of version 1.4.15. This again shows how the scale of the system amplifies the latency tail effect.

To summarize, in our case studies, the impact of software implementation of OS and application interface are far more important than all the hardware and network transport protocol changes we have studied. The detailed execution-driven DIABLO models show that there are many more aspects in both HW and SW stacks that could significantly affect the application tail latency at scale.

5. Discussion and Future Work

When simulating 4 GHz servers with a 10 Gbps interconnect, around 50 minutes of simulation wall-clock time are required for one second of target time; software simulation would take almost two weeks. Moreover, DIABLO's simulation performance scales perfectly. We observed no performance drop from simulating 500 nodes with two boards, to 2,000 nodes using six boards. The simulation performance is dominated by simulating the server computation using RAMP Gold, which can be improved by reducing the number of model threads per host hardware pipeline at the cost of reduced system scale or increased hardware cost [54].

The FAME-7 modeling technique gives us the capability of emulating larger target systems with fewer virtualized FPGA resources. However, the target memory capacity is very hard to virtualize with limited physical DRAM storage. We should note that this is an open topic for any work that is trying to emulate a WSC with limited hardware resources. Another limitation is that we have only simulated fixed-CPI single-CPU servers with one hardware thread per server model. A more complex timing model supporting multi-core CPUs is planned for DIABLO-2.

Neither limitation is intrinsic to the methodology, but instead reflects our use of a 5-year-old FPGA board. We are developing a new FPGA board using upcoming 20 nm FPGAs that should support a quad-core 64-bit server model with 4 GB/node memory capacity. Additional simulated DRAM storage will be provided through PCIe-attached NAND FLASH storage.

Our current prototype used FAME-7 style NIC/switch models, which run far faster than necessary for the simulation while consuming considerable FPGA resources. We will replace these hardware models with a software-programmable microcoded model, to provide additional flexibility as well as reduced resource usage.

6. Conclusion

We believe the research community needs a boost in evaluation technology to look at systems with scale of O(1,000) to O(10,000), as behavior is drastically different compared to O(10) to O(100) systems. The working DIABLO prototype enables networking researchers to conduct controllable, reproducible, full-stack WSC simulations at much larger scales than previously possible. We show that considering end-to-end server computation, including full OS and application code, is essential to understanding network system performance, and has much greater impact than networking hardware and protocols.

Acknowledgments

This research is supported in part by gifts from Oracle, Google, Microsoft, Amazon Web Services, Cisco Systems, Cloudera, eBay, Facebook, Fujitsu, Hewlett-Packard, Intel, Network Appliance, SAP, VMWare and Yahoo! and by matching funds from the State of California's MICRO program (grants 06-152, 07-010, 06-148, 07-012, 06-146, 07-009, 06-147, 07-013, 06-149, 06-150, and 07-008), the National Science Foundation (grant #CNS-0509559), AFOSR under MURI award FA9550-09-1-0539 (Air Force Office of Sponsored Research in MURI program), and the University of California Industry/University Cooperative Research Program (UC Discovery) grant COM07-10240. The testbed for validation work was supported in part by the by the National Basic Research Program of China Grant 2011CBA00300, 2011CBA00301, the National Natural Science Foundation of China Grant 61033001, 61361136003. We thank the anonymous reviewers for their many insightful comments and suggestions.

References

[1] XGS Core Switch Series - BCM88030 Series. http://www.broadcom.com/products/Switching/Carrier-and-Service-Provider/BCM88030-Series.

[2] Facebook Memcached. https://github.com/amanuel/facebook-memcached.

[3] R2D2: RAPID AND RELIABLE DATA DELIVERY IN DATA CENTERS. http://www.stanford.edu/~atikoglu/r2d2/.

[4] Network simulator, ns-2 : http://www.isi.edu/nsnam/ns/.

[5] Twemcache. https://twitter.com/twemcache.

[6] Tsinghua IIIS test cluster. http://wiki.iiis.systems/w/index.php/Cluster.

[7] Yahoo! Reaches for the Stars with M45 Supercomputing Project. http://research.yahoo.com/node/1884, 2007.

[8] Glen Anderson, private communications, 2009.

[9] Switching Architectures for Cloud Network Designs. http://www.aristanetworks.com/en/SwitchingArchitecture_wp.pdf, 2009.

[10] Sun Datacenter InfiniBand Switch 648. http://www.sun.com/products/networking/infiniband.jsp, 2009.

[11] Cisco Nexus 5000 Series Architecture: The Building Blocks of the Unified Fabric. http://www.cisco.com/en/US/prod/collateral/switches/ps9441/ps9670/white_paper_c11-462176.html, 2010.

[12] Force10 S60 High-Performance 1/10 GbE Access Switch. http://www.force10networks.com/products/s60.asp, 2010.

[13] Hadoop. http://hadoop.apache.org/, 2010.

[14] Xilinx Virtex 7 Series FPGAs. http://www.xilinx.com/technology/roadmap/7-series-fpgas.htm, 2010.

[15] Google G-Scale Network. http://www.eetimes.com/electronics-news/4371179/Google-describes-its-OpenFlow-network, 2012.

[16] Microsoft Hyper-V virtualization platform. http://www.microsoft.com/en-us/server-cloud/windows-server/server-virtualization.aspx, 2012.

[17] memcached: a distributed memory objec caching system. http://memcached.org, 2012.

[18] Open Compute Project. http://opencompute.org, 2012.

[19] QEMU open source processor emulator. http://wiki.qemu.org, 2012.

[20] Oracle Virtualbox VM. http://www.virtualbox.org/, 2012.

[21] VMware Virtual Server. http://www.vmware.com, 2012.

[22] Memcache 1.14.17 release notes. https://code.google.com/p/memcached/wiki/ReleaseNotes1417, 2013.

[23] B. Atikoglu, Y. Xu, E. Frachtenberg, S. Jiang, and M. Paleczny. Workload analysis of a large-scale key-value store. In *Proceedings of the 12th ACM SIGMETRICS/PERFORMANCE joint international conference on Measurement and Modeling of Computer Systems*, SIGMETRICS '12, pages 53–64, New York, NY, USA, 2012. ACM. ISBN 978-1-4503-1097-0. . URL http://doi.acm.org/10.1145/2254756.2254766.

[24] L. A. Barroso. Warehouse-scale computing: Entering the teenage decade. In *Proceedings of the 38th annual international symposium on Computer architecture*, ISCA '11, pages –, New York, NY, USA, 2011. ACM. ISBN 978-1-4503-0472-6.

[25] L. A. Barroso and U. Hölzle. *The Datacenter as a Computer: An Introduction to the Design of Warehouse-Scale Machines*. Synthesis Lectures on Computer Architecture. Morgan & Claypool Publishers, 2009.

[26] A. Bechtolsheim. Moore's Law and Networking. In *The Linley Group Processor Conference*, San Jose, CA, USA, 2012.

[27] N. L. Binkert, R. G. Dreslinski, L. R. Hsu, K. T. Lim, A. G. Saidi, and S. K. Reinhardt. The M5 simulator: Modeling networked systems. *IEEE Micro*, 26(4):52–60, 2006. ISSN 0272-1732.

[28] Y. Chen, R. Griffith, J. Liu, R. H. Katz, and A. D. Joseph. Understanding TCP incast throughput collapse in datacenter networks. In *WREN '09: Proceedings of the 1st ACM workshop on Research on enterprise networking*, pages 73–82, New York, NY, USA, 2009. ACM. ISBN 978-1-60558-443-0.

[29] Y. Chen, R. Griffit, D. Zats, and R. H. Katz. Understanding tcp incast and its implications for big data workloads. Technical Report UCB/EECS-2012-40, EECS Department, University of California, Berkeley, Apr 2012. URL http://www.eecs.berkeley.edu/Pubs/TechRpts/2012/EECS-2012-40.html.

[30] M. Chowdhury, M. Zaharia, J. Ma, M. I. Jordan, and I. Stoica. Managing data transfers in computer clusters with orchestra. In *SIGCOMM*, pages 98–109, 2011.

[31] U. Cummings, D. Daly, R. Collins, V. Agarwal, F. Petrini, M. Perrone, and D. Pasetto. Fulcrum's FocalPoint FM4000: A Scalable, Low-Latency 10GigE Switch for High-Performance Data Centers. In *Proceedings of the 2009 17th IEEE Symposium on High Performance Interconnects*, pages 42–51, Washington, DC, USA, 2009. IEEE Computer Society. ISBN 978-0-7695-3847-1. . URL http://portal.acm.org/citation.cfm?id=1633800.1634467.

[32] J. Davis, C. Thacker, and C. Chang. BEE3: Revitalizing Computer Architecture Research. Technical Report MSR-TR-2009-45, Microsoft Research, Apr 2009. URL http://research.microsoft.com/apps/pubs/default.aspx?id=80369.

[33] J. Dean and L. A. Barroso. The tail at scale. *Communications of the ACM*, 56(2):74–80, 2013.

[34] A. Ganesan, D. Lee, A. Leinwand, A. Shaikh, and M. Shaw. What is the impact of cloud computing on the data center interconnect? In *Hot Interconnects*, 2011.

[35] A. Greenberg, J. Hamilton, D. A. Maltz, and P. Patel. The cost of a cloud: research problems in data center networks. *SIGCOMM Comput. Commun. Rev.*, 39(1):68–73, 2009. ISSN 0146-4833.

[36] A. Greenberg, J. R. Hamilton, N. Jain, S. Kandula, C. Kim, P. Lahiri, D. A. Maltz, P. Patel, and S. Sengupta. VL2: a scalable and flexible data center network. In *SIGCOMM '09*, pages 51–62, New York, NY, USA, 2009. ACM. ISBN 978-1-60558-594-9.

[37] C. Guo, G. Lu, D. Li, H. Wu, X. Zhang, Y. Shi, C. Tian, Y. Zhang, and S. Lu. BCube: a high performance, server-centric network architecture for modular data centers. In *SIGCOMM '09*, pages 63–74, New York, NY, USA, 2009. ACM. ISBN 978-1-60558-594-9.

[38] J. L. Hennessy and D. A. Patterson. *Computer architecture: a quantitative approach*. Elsevier, 2012.

[39] L. R. Hsu, A. G. Saidi, N. L. Binkert, and S. K. Reinhardt. Sampling and stability in tcp/ip workloads. In *Proceedings of the First Annual Workshop on Modeling, Benchmarking, and Simulation*, MoBS '05, pages 68–77, 2005.

[40] D. A. Joseph, A. Tavakoli, and I. Stoica. A policy-aware switching layer for data centers. In *SIGCOMM '08*, pages 51–62, New York, NY, USA, 2008. ACM. ISBN 978-1-60558-175-0.

[41] R. Katz. Tech titans building boom: The architecture of internet datacenters. *IEEE Spectrum*, February 2009.

[42] B. Kwan, P. Agarwal, and L. Ashvin. Flexible buffer allocation entities for traffic aggregate containment. US Patent 20090207848, August 2009.

[43] J. Li, N. K. Sharma, D. R. K. Ports, and S. D. Gribble. Tales of the tail: Hardware, OS, and application-level sources of tail latency. In *Proceedings of the ACM Symposium on Cloud Computing (SoCC)*, Seattle, WA, USA, 11 2014. ACM. URL papers/latency-socc14.pdf.

[44] K. Lim, D. Meisner, A. Saidi, P. Ranganathan, and T. F. Wenisch. Thin Servers with Smart Pipes: Designing SoC Accelerators for Memcached. In *Proceedings of the 40th annual international symposium on Computer architecture*, ISCA '13, 2013.

[45] R. Liu et al. Tessellation: Space-Time partitioning in a manycore client OS. In *HotPar09*, Berkeley, CA, 03/2009 2009. URL http://www.usenix.org/event/hotpar09/tech/.

[46] P. S. Magnusson et al. Simics: A Full System Simulation Platform. *IEEE Computer*, 35, 2002.

[47] N. McKeown, T. Anderson, H. Balakrishnan, G. Parulkar, L. Peterson, J. Rexford, S. Shenker, and J. Turner. Openflow: enabling innovation in campus networks. *SIGCOMM Comput. Commun. Rev.*, 38(2):69–74, Mar. 2008. ISSN 0146-4833. . URL `http://doi.acm.org/10.1145/1355734.1355746`.

[48] D. Meisner, J. Wu, and T. F. Wenisch. BigHouse: A Simulation Infrastructure for Data Center Systems. *ISPASS '12: International Symposium on Performance Analysis of Systems and Software*, April 2012.

[49] M. Mitzenmacher and A. Broder. Using multiple hash functions to improve ip lookups. In *In Proceedings of IEEE INFOCOM*, pages 1454–1463, 2000.

[50] R. Niranjan Mysore, A. Pamboris, N. Farrington, N. Huang, P. Miri, S. Radhakrishnan, V. Subramanya, and A. Vahdat. PortLand: a scalable fault-tolerant layer 2 data center network fabric. In *SIGCOMM '09*, pages 39–50, New York, NY, USA, 2009. ACM. ISBN 978-1-60558-594-9.

[51] D. Ongaro, S. M. Rumble, R. Stutsman, J. K. Ousterhout, and M. Rosenblum. Fast crash recovery in ramcloud. In *SOSP*, pages 29–41, 2011.

[52] J. H. Salim, R. Olsson, and A. Kuznetsov. Beyond softnet. In *Proceedings of the 5th annual Linux Showcase & Conference - Volume 5*, ALS '01, pages 18–18, Berkeley, CA, USA, 2001. USENIX Association. URL `http://dl.acm.org/citation.cfm?id=1268488.1268506`.

[53] H. Shah. *Solving TCP Incast in Cluster Storage Systems*. Technical report (Information Networking Institute). Carnegie Mellon University. Information Networking Institute, 2009. URL `http://books.google.com/books?id=Rl2jYgEACAAJ`.

[54] Z. Tan, A. Waterman, R. Avizienis, Y. Lee, H. Cook, D. Patterson, and K. Asanović and. RAMP gold: An FPGA-based architecture simulator for multiprocessors. In *Design Automation Conference (DAC), 2010 47th ACM/IEEE*, pages 463 – 468, June 2010.

[55] Z. Tan, A. Waterman, H. Cook, S. Bird, K. Asanović, and D. Patterson. A case for FAME: FPGA architecture model execution. In *Proceedings of the 37th annual international symposium on Computer architecture*, ISCA '10, pages 290–301, New York, NY, USA, 2010. ACM. ISBN 978-1-4503-0053-7.

[56] Z. Tan, K. Asanovic, and D. Patterson. Datacenter-scale network research on fpgas. In *Proc. Workshop on Exascale Evaluation and Research Techniques*, 2011.

[57] A. Tavakoli, M. Casado, T. Koponen, and S. Shenker. Applying NOX to the datacenter. In *HotNets*, 2009.

[58] C. Thacker. Rethinking data centers. October 2007.

[59] C. Thacker. A data center network using FPGAs, May 2010.

[60] V. Vasudevan, A. Phanishayee, H. Shah, E. Krevat, D. G. Andersen, G. R. Ganger, G. A. Gibson, and B. Mueller. Safe and effective fine-grained TCP retransmissions for datacenter communication. In *SIGCOMM '09*, pages 303–314, New York, NY, USA, 2009. ACM. ISBN 978-1-60558-594-9.

[61] G. Wang, D. G. Andersen, M. Kaminsky, K. Papagiannaki, T. S. E. Ng, M. Kozuch, and M. P. Ryan. c-through: part-time optics in data centers. In *SIGCOMM*, pages 327–338, 2010.

[62] W. Wu and M. Crawford. Potential performance bottleneck in linux tcp. *Int. J. Commun. Syst.*, 20(11):1263–1283, Nov. 2007. ISSN 1074-5351. . URL `http://dx.doi.org/10.1002/dac.v20:11`.

[63] M. Zaharia, D. Borthakur, J. S. Sarma, K. Elmeleegy, S. Shenker, and I. Stoica. Delay scheduling: a simple technique for achieving locality and fairness in cluster scheduling. In *EuroSys*, pages 265–278, 2010.

Sirius: An Open End-to-End Voice and Vision Personal Assistant and Its Implications for Future Warehouse Scale Computers

Johann Hauswald, Michael A. Laurenzano, Yunqi Zhang, Cheng Li, Austin Rovinski, Arjun Khurana, Ronald G. Dreslinski, Trevor Mudge, Vinicius Petrucci[1], Lingjia Tang, Jason Mars

Clarity Lab
University of Michigan - Ann Arbor, MI, USA
{jahausw, mlaurenz, yunqi, elfchris, rovinski, khuranaa, rdreslin, tnm, lingjia, profmars}@umich.edu

Abstract

As user demand scales for *intelligent personal assistants* (IPAs) such as Apple's Siri, Google's Google Now, and Microsoft's Cortana, we are approaching the computational limits of current datacenter architectures. It is an open question how future server architectures should evolve to enable this emerging class of applications, and the lack of an open-source IPA workload is an obstacle in addressing this question.

In this paper, we present the design of **Sirius**, an open end-to-end IPA web-service application that accepts queries in the form of voice and images, and responds with natural language. We then use this workload to investigate the implications of four points in the design space of future accelerator-based server architectures spanning traditional CPUs, GPUs, manycore throughput co-processors, and FPGAs. To investigate future server designs for Sirius, we decompose Sirius into a suite of 7 benchmarks (**Sirius Suite**) comprising the computationally intensive bottlenecks of Sirius. We port Sirius Suite to a spectrum of accelerator platforms and use the performance and power trade-offs across these platforms to perform a total cost of ownership (TCO) analysis of various server design points. In our study, we find that accelerators are critical for the future scalability of IPA services. Our results show that GPU- and FPGA-accelerated servers improve the query latency on average by 10× and 16×. For a given throughput, GPU- and FPGA-accelerated servers can reduce the TCO of datacenters by 2.6× and 1.4×, respectively.

ASPLOS '15, March 14–18, 2015, Istanbul, Turkey.

http://dx.doi.org/10.1145/2694344.2694347

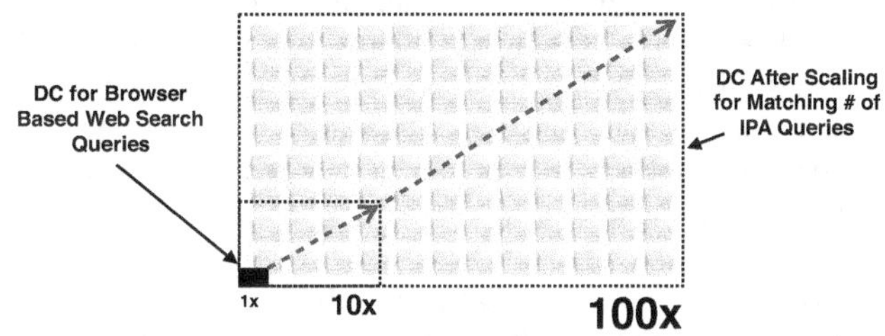

Figure 1: Impact of Higher Computational Requirements for IPA Queries on Datacenters (DCs)

Categories and Subject Descriptors C.0 [*Computer Systems Organization*]: General—System architectures; C.5.5 [*Computer System Implementation*]: Servers

Keywords datacenters; warehouse scale computers; emerging workloads; intelligent personal assistants

1. Introduction

Apple's Siri [1], Google's Google Now [2] and Microsoft's Cortana [3] represent a class of emerging web-service applications known as *Intelligent Personal Assistants* (IPAs). An IPA is an application that uses inputs such as the user's voice, vision (images), and contextual information to provide assistance by answering questions in natural language, making recommendations, and performing actions. These IPAs are emerging as one of the fastest growing Internet services as they have recently been deployed on well known platforms such as iOS, Android, and Windows Phone, making them ubiquitous on mobile devices worldwide [4]. In addition, the usage scenarios for IPAs are rapidly increasing with recent offerings in wearable technologies such as smart watches [5] and smart glasses [6]. Recent projections predict the wearables market to be at 485 million annual device shipments by 2018 [7]. This growth in market share, coupled with the fact that the design of wearables is heavily reliant on voice

[1] Work conducted as a postdoctoral fellow in Clarity Lab at the University of Michigan. He is now a professor at Federal University of Bahia.

and image input, further indicates that rapid growth in user demand for IPA services is on the horizon.

IPAs differ from many of the web-service workloads currently present in modern warehouse-scale computers (WSCs). In contrast to the queries of traditional browser-centric services, IPA queries stream through software components that leverage recent advances in speech recognition, natural language processing and computer vision to provide users a speech-driven and/or image-driven contextually-based question-and-answer system [8]. Due to the computational intensity of these components and the large data-driven models they use, service providers house the required computation in massive datacenter platforms in lieu of performing the computation on the mobile devices themselves. This offloading approach is used by both Apple's Siri and Google's Google Now as they send compressed recordings of voice command/queries to datacenters for speech recognition and semantic extraction [9]. However, datacenters have been designed and tuned for traditional web services such as Web Search and questions arise as to whether the current design employed by modern datacenters, composed of general-purpose servers, is suitable for emerging IPA workloads.

IPA queries require a significant amount of compute resources compared to traditional text-based web services such as Web Search. As we show later in this work, the computational resources required for a single leaf query is in excess of 100× more than that of traditional Web Search. Figure 1 illustrates the scaling of compute resources in a modern datacenter required to sustain an equivalent throughput of IPA queries compared to Web Search. Due to the looming *Scalability Gap* shown in the figure, there has been significant interest in both academia and industry to leverage hardware acceleration in datacenters using various platforms such as GPU, manycore co-processors and FPGAs to achieve high performance and energy efficiency. To gain further insight on whether there are sufficient acceleration opportunities for IPA workloads and what the best acceleration platform is, several challenges need to be addressed, including:

1. Identifying critical compute and performance bottlenecks throughout the end-to-end lifetime of an IPA query;
2. Understanding the performance, energy and cost trade-offs among popular accelerator options given the characteristics of IPA workloads;
3. Designing future server and datacenter solutions that can meet the amount of future user demand while being cost and energy efficient.

However, the lack of a representative, publicly available, end-to-end IPA system proves prohibitive for investigating the design space of future accelerator-based server designs for this emerging workload. To address this challenge, we first construct an end-to-end standalone IPA service, **Sirius**, that implements the core functionalities of an IPA such as speech recognition, image matching, natural language processing and a question-and-answer system. Sirius takes as input user dictated speech and/or image(s) captured by a camera. There are three pathways of varying complexity through the Sirius back-end based on the nature of the input query. A voice command primarily exercises speech recognition on the server-side to execute a command on the mobile device. A voice query additionally leverages a sophisticated natural language processing (NLP) question-and-answer system to produce a natural language response to the user. A voice and image question such as *"When does this restaurant close?"* coupled with an image of the restaurant, also leverages image matching with an image database and combines the matching output with the voice query to select the best answer for the user. We have constructed Sirius by integrating three services built using well-established open source projects that include techniques and algorithms representative of those found in commercial systems. These open projects include CMU's Sphinx [10], representing the widely-used Gaussian Mixture Model based speech recognition, Kaldi [11] and RWTH's RASR [12], representing industry's recent trend toward Deep Neutral Network based speech recognition, OpenEphyra [13] representing the-state-of-the-art question-and-answer system based on IBM's Watson [14], and SURF [15] implemented using OpenCV [16] representing state-of-the-art image matching algorithms widely used in various production applications.

With this end-to-end workload in hand, we perform an in-depth investigation of the viability of various acceleration strategies, and provide insights on future datacenter and server designs for this emerging workload. Specifically, this paper makes the following contributions:

- **Sirius** - We construct Sirius, an open end-to-end intelligent personal assistant system with both speech and image front-ends. In addition to Sirius itself, we compile a query taxonomy spanning three classes of queries: Voice Command, Voice Query, and Voice/Image Query. (Section 2)
- **Scalability Gap** - We characterize Sirius on commodity hardware and demonstrate the *Scalability Gap* for this type of workload. We observe that the compute resources needed to sustain this workload is orders of magnitude higher than traditional datacenter workloads. We also perform an analysis of the cycle breakdown of IPA queries and analyze the computational bottlenecks of Sirius. We show that there is a limited speedup potential for this workload on general-purpose processors and acceleration is indeed needed to address the scalability gap. (Section 3)
- **Accelerating Sirius** - Based on our cycle breakdown analysis, we extract 7 computational bottlenecks comprising 92% of the cycles consumed by Sirius to compose a C/C++ benchmark suite (**Sirius Suite**) for acceleration. We port these workloads and conduct a thorough performance evaluation on a spectrum of accelerator platforms. The end-to-end Sirius, query taxonomy, input set, Sirius Suite benchmarks, and the full source code ported across accelerators are available online [17]. (Section 4)

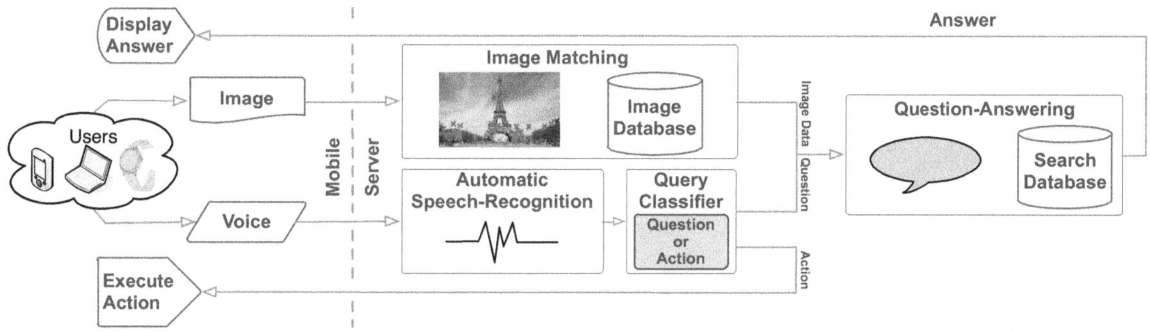

Figure 2: End-to-end Diagram of the Sirius Pipeline

- **Future Server and Datacenter Design** - Based on our acceleration results, we investigate the implications for future server designs. After evaluating the trade-offs between performance, power efficiency and the total cost of ownership of a datacenter, we propose server and datacenter designs that significantly reduce the computation gap between user demand and the current datacenter's computation capability. (Section 5)

In summary, we find that among the popular acceleration options including GPU, Intel Phi and FPGA, the FPGA-accelerated server is the best server option for a homogeneous datacenter design when the design objective is minimizing latency or maximizing energy efficiency with a latency constraint. FPGA achieves an average 16× reduction on the query latency across various query types over the baseline multicore system. On the other hand, GPUs provide the highest TCO reduction on average. GPU-accelerated servers can achieve an average 10× query latency reduction, translating to a 2.6× TCO reduction. When excluding FPGAs as an acceleration option, GPUs provide the best latency and cost reduction among the rest of the accelerator choices. On average, replacing FPGAs using GPUs leads to a 66% longer latency, but in return achieves a 47% TCO reduction and simpler software engineering costs.

2. Sirius: An End-to-End IPA

In this section we present **Sirius**: an end-to-end intelligent personal assistant (IPA). We first describe the design objectives for Sirius, then present an overview of Sirius and a taxonomy of query types it supports. Finally, we detail the underlying algorithms and techniques used by Sirius.

2.1 Sirius Design Objectives

There are three key objectives in the design for Sirius:

1. **[Completeness]** - Sirius should provide a complete IPA service that takes the input of human voice and images and provide a response to the user's question with natural language.
2. **[Representativeness]** - The computational techniques used by Sirius to provide this response should be representative of state-of-the-art approaches used in commercial domains.
3. **[Deployability]** - Sirius should be deployable and fully functional on real systems.

2.2 Sirius Overview: Life of an IPA Query

Figure 2 presents a high-level diagram of the end-to-end Sirius query pipeline. The life of a query begins with a user's voice and/or image input through a mobile device. Compressed versions of the voice recording and image(s) are sent to a server housing Sirius. The user's voice is then processed by an Automatic Speech Recognition (ASR) front-end that translates the user's speech question into its text equivalent using statistical models. The translated speech then goes through a Query Classifier (QC) that decides if the speech is an action or a question. If it is an action, the command is sent back to the mobile device for execution. Otherwise, the Sirius back-end receives the question in plain text. Using natural language processing (NLP) techniques, the Question- Answering (QA) service extracts information from the input, searches its database, and chooses the best answer to return to the user. If an image accompanies the speech input, Sirius uses computer vision techniques to attempt to match the input image to its image database and return relevant information about the matched image using the Image Matching (IMM) service. For example, a user can ask *"What time does this restaurant close?"* while image(s) of the restaurant are captured via smart glasses [6]. Sirius can then return an answer to the query based not only on the speech, but also information from the image.

As shown in Figure 2, there are a number of pathways a single query can take based on the type of directive, whether it be question or action, and the type of input, speech only or accompanied by images. In order to design the input set used with Sirius we have identified a query taxonomy of three classes that covers these pathways. Table 1 summarizes these query classes providing an example for each, the Sirius services they exercise, the resulting behavior of Sirius, and the number of queries of that type in our input set. Figure 3 illustrates a tiered view of Sirius spanning the query taxonomy it supports, the services that comprise Sirius, and the algorithmic sub-components that compose each service. We describe these services and algorithms in the following section.

Table 1: Query Taxonomy

Query Type	Example	Service	Result	# of Queries
Voice Command (VC)	"Set my alarm for 8am."	ASR	Action on user's device	16
Voice Query (VQ)	"Who was elected 44th president?"	ASR & QA	Best answer from QA	16
Voice-Image Query (VIQ)	"When does this restaurant close?"	ASR, QA & IMM	Best results from IMM and QA	10

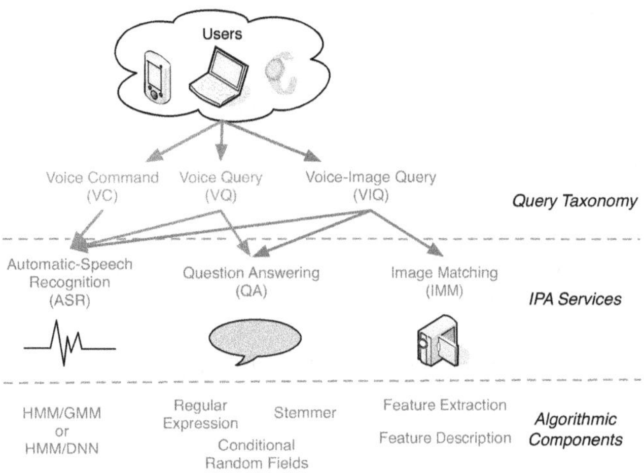

Figure 3: Tier-level View of Sirius

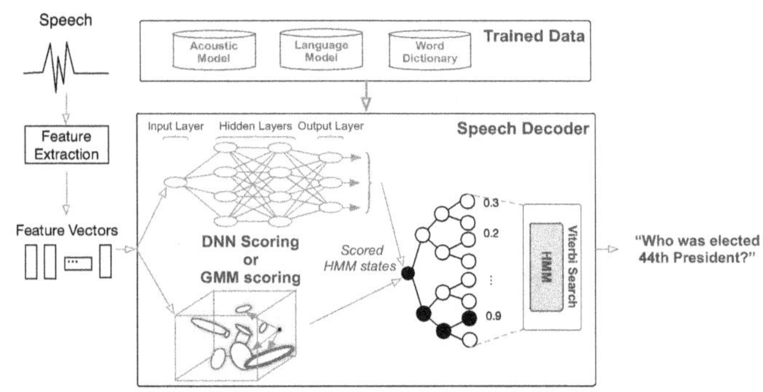

Figure 4: Automatic Speech Recognition Pipeline

Figure 5: Image Matching Pipeline

2.3 The Design of Sirius: IPA Services and Algorithmic Components

As shown in Figure 3, Sirius is composed of three IPA services: speech recognition (ASR), question-answering (QA), and image matching (IMM). These services can be further decoupled into their individual algorithmic components. In order to design Sirius to be representative of production grade systems, we leverage well-known open infrastructures that use the same algorithms as commercial applications. Speech recognition in Google Voice, for example, has used speaker-independent Gaussian Mixture Model (GMM) and Hidden Markov Model (HMM) and is adopting Deep Neural Networks (DNNs) [18, 19]. The OpenEphyra framework used for question-answering is an open-source release from CMU's prior research collaboration with IBM on the Watson system [14]. OpenEphyra's NLP techniques, including conditional random field (CRF), have been recognized as state-of-the-art and are used at Google and in other industry question-answering systems [20]. We design our image matching pipeline based on the SURF algorithm, which is widely used in industry [15, 21, 22]. We implement SURF using the open source computer vision (OpenCV) library [16], which is employed in commercial products from companies like Google, IBM, and Microsoft. The design of these services are described in the remainder of this section.

2.3.1 Automatic-Speech Recognition (ASR)

The inputs to the ASR are feature vectors representing the speech segment, generated by fast pre-processing and feature extraction of the speech. The ASR component relies on a combination of a Hidden Markov Model (HMM) and either a Gaussian Mixture Model (GMM) or a Deep Neural Network (DNN). Sirius' GMM-based ASR uses CMU's Sphinx [10], while the DNN-based ASR includes Kaldi [11] and RWTH's RASR [12].

As shown in Figure 4, the HMM builds a tree of states for the current speech frame using input feature vectors. The GMM or DNN scores the probability of the state transitions in the tree, and the Viterbi algorithm [23] then searches for the most likely path based on these scores. The path with the highest probability represents the final translated text output. The GMM scores HMM state transitions by mapping an input feature vector into a multi-dimensional coordinate system and iteratively scores the features against the trained acoustic model.

DNN, however, scores using probabilities from a neural network. The depth of a DNN is defined by the number of hidden layers where scoring amounts to one forward pass through the network. In recent years, industry and academia have moved towards DNN over GMM due to its higher accuracy [24, 25].

2.3.2 Image Matching (IMM)

The image matching pipeline receives an input image, attempts to match it against images in a pre-processed image database, and returns information about the matched

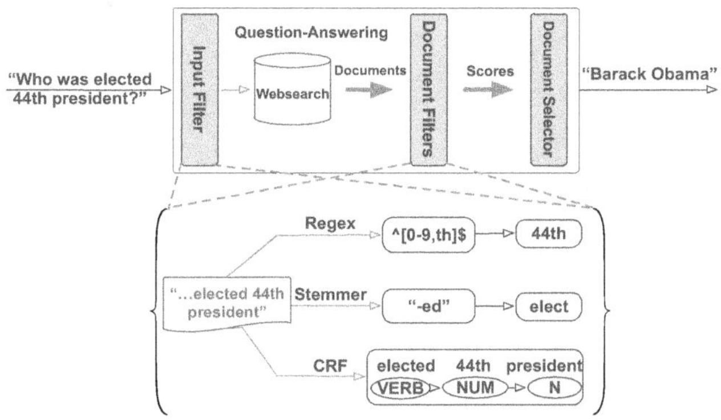

Figure 6: OpenEphyra Question-Answering Pipeline

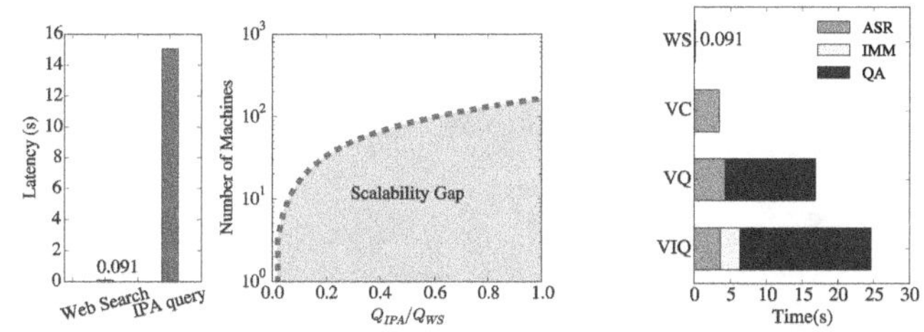

(a) Scalability Gap

(b) Latency Across Query Types

Figure 7: Scalability Gap and Latency

images. The database that is used in Sirius is the Mobile Visual Search [26] database. Image keypoints are first extracted from the input image using the SURF algorithm [15]. In Feature Extraction (FE), the image is downsampled and convolved multiple times to find interesting points at different scales. After thresholding the convolution responses, the local maxima responses are stored as image keypoints. Figure 5 details the steps in this process. The keypoints are then passed to the Feature Descriptor (FD) component where they are assigned an orientation vector, and similarly oriented keypoints are grouped into feature descriptors. This process reduces variability across input images, increasing chances of finding the correct match. The descriptors from the input image are matched to pre-clustered descriptors representing the database images by using an approximate nearest neighbor (ANN) search; the database image with the highest number of matches is returned.

2.3.3 Question-Answering (QA)

The text output from the ASR is passed to OpenEphyra (OE) [13], which uses three core processes to extract textual information: word stemming, regular expression matching, and part-of-speech tagging. Figure 6 shows a diagram of the OE engine incorporating these components, generating Web Search queries and filtering the returned results. The Porter Stemming [27] algorithm (stemmer) exposes the root of a word by matching and truncating common word endings. OE also uses a suite of regular-expression patterns to match common query words (what, where, etc) and filter any special characters in the input. The Conditional Random Field (CRF) classifier [28] takes a sentence, the position of each word in the sentence, and the label of the current and previous word as input to makes predictions on the part-of-speech for each word of an input query. Each input query is parsed using the aforementioned components to generate queries to the web search engine. Next, filters using the same techniques are used to extract information from the returned documents; the document with the highest overall score after score aggregation is returned as the best answer.

3. Real System Analysis for Sirius

In this section, we present a real-system analysis of Sirius. The experiments throughout this section are performed using an Intel Haswell server (details in Table 3).

Scalability Gap - To gain insights on the required resource scaling for IPA queries in modern datacenters, we juxtapose the computational demand of an average Sirius query with that of an average Web Search query. To perform this experiment, we compare the average query latency (execution time) for both applications on a single core at a very low load. Both Sirius and Web Search are configured to be memory resident and go no further than main memory to process a query (i.e., minimum I/O activities).

Figure 7a (left) presents the average latency of both Web Search using open source Apache Nutch [29, 30] and Sirius queries. As shown in the figure, the average Nutch-based Web Search query latency is 91ms on the Haswell based server. In contrast, Sirius query latency is significantly longer, averaging around 15s across 42 queries spanning our three query classes (VC, VQ and VIQ from Table 1). Based on this significant difference in the computational demand, we perform a back-of-the-envelope calculation of how the compute resources (machines) in current datacenters must scale to match the throughput in queries for IPAs and Web Search.

Figure 7a (right) presents the number of machines needed to support IPA queries as the number of these queries increases. The x-axis shows the ratio between IPA queries and traditional Web Search queries. The y-axis shows the ratio of compute resources needed to support IPA queries relative to Web Search queries. As shown in the figure, current datacenter infrastructures will need to scale its compute resources to 165× its current size when the number of IPA queries scale to match the number of Web Search queries. We refer to this throughput difference as the *scalability gap.*

Sirius Query Deep Dive - To better understand the IPA query characteristics, we further investigate the average latency and latency distributions of various query types for Sirius. Figure 7b presents the average latency across query types including traditional Web Search (WS), Voice Command (VC), Voice Query (VQ) and Voice Image Query (VIQ). As shown in the figure, the latency of all three Sirius query types are significantly higher than that of Web

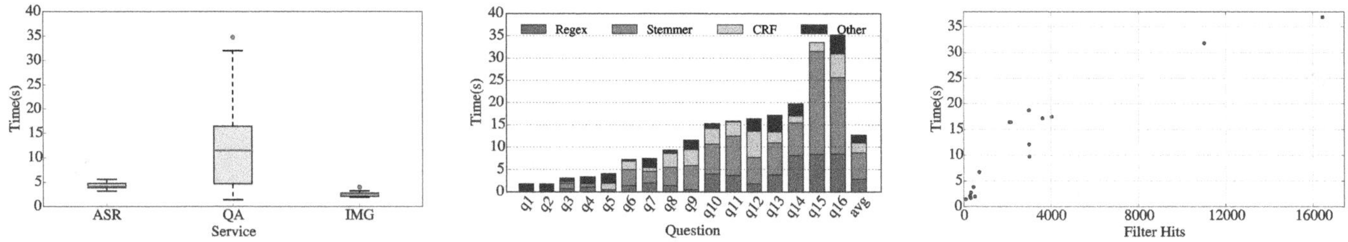

(a) Latency Variability Across Services (b) OpenEphyra Breakdown (c) Latency and Filter Hits in OpenEphyra

Figure 8: Sirius Variability Across Query Types and Causes

Search queries. The shortest query type is VC, which only uses the ASR service. Yet it still requires orders of magnitude more computation than Web Search. The longest query type is VIQ, which uses all three services including ASR, IMM, and QA. Among all three services, QA consistently consumes the most compute cycles.

Table 2: Voice Query Input Set

Q#	Query
q1	"Where is Las Vegas?"
q2	"What is the capital of Italy?"
q3	"Who is the author of Harry Potter?"
...	...
q15	"What is the capital of Cuba?"
q16	"Who is the current president of the United States?"

Figure 8a presents the latency distribution for each Sirius service. As shown in the figure, QA has the highest variability in latency, ranging from 1.7s to 35s depending on the input query. Figure 8b further presents the breakdown of execution time among QA's hot components (described later in this section) across the complete VQ query input set (shown in Table 2). The reason for this high latency variability is not immediately clear from inspecting the query input set, especially when considering the small difference between Q2 and Q15 in Table 2. However, after further investigation, we identified that the high variance is primarily due to the runtime variability of various document filters in the NLP component used to select the most fitting answer for a given query. Figure 8c demonstrates the correlation between latency and the number of hits in the document filters. The other services, ASR and IMM, have very low query to query variability. Next, we investigate the cycle breakdown of the algorithmic components that comprise each service.

Cycle Breakdown of Sirius Services - To identify the computational bottlenecks of each service, we perform top-down profiling of hot algorithmic components for each service, shown in Figure 3, using Intel VTune [31]. Figure 9 presents the average cycle breakdown results. Across services, a few hot components emerge as good candidates for acceleration. For example, a high percentage of the execution for ASR is spent on scoring using either GMM or DNN. For QA, on average 85% of the cycles are spent in three components including stemming, regular expression pattern matching and CRF, and for IMM, the majority of cycles are spent either performing feature extraction or description using the SURF algorithm.

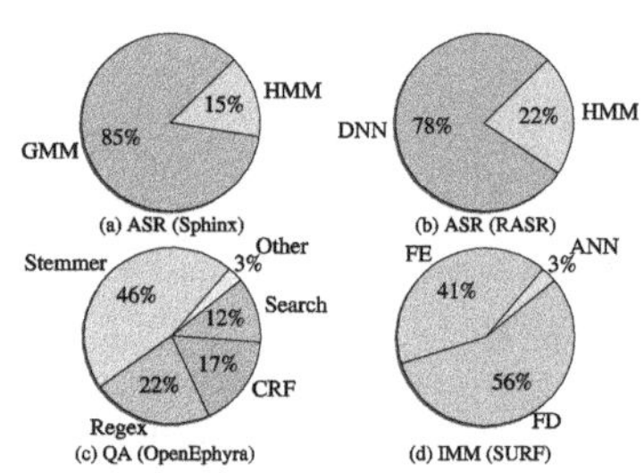

Figure 9: Cycle Breakdown per Service

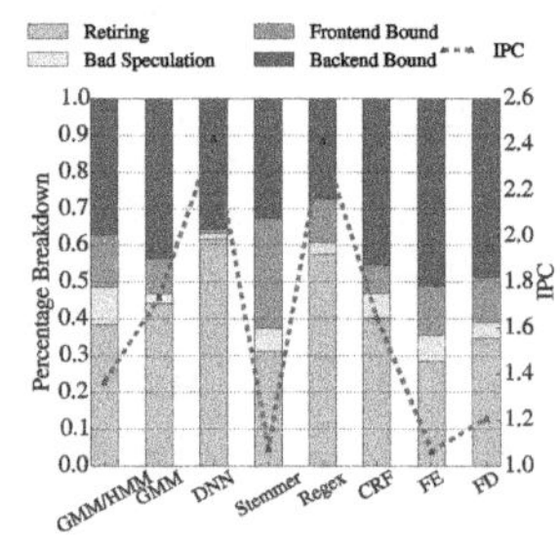

Figure 10: IPC and Bottleneck Breakdown

We then identify the architectural bottlenecks for these hot components to investigate the performance improvement potential for a general-purpose processor. Figure 10 presents the instructions per cycle (IPC) and potential architectural bottlenecks (including front-end, speculation and back-end) for each component, identified using Intel VTune [31]. A few of the service components including DNN and Regex execute relatively efficiently on Xeon cores. This graph indicates that even with all stall cycles removed (i.e., perfect branch prediction, infinite cache, etc) the maximum speedup is bound by around 3×. Considering the orders of magnitude difference indicated by the scalability gap, further acceleration is needed to bridge the gap.

4. Accelerating Sirius

In this section, we describe the platforms and methodology used to accelerate the key components of Sirius. We also present and discuss the results of accelerating each of these components across 4 different accelerator platforms.

4.1 Accelerator Platforms

We use a total of four platforms, summarized in Table 3, to accelerate Sirius. Our baseline platform is an Intel Xeon Haswell CPU running single-threaded kernels.

We summarize the advantages and disadvantages of each accelerator platform below.

Table 3: Platform Specifications

Model	Multicore Intel Xeon E3-1240 V3	GPU NVIDIA GTX 770	Phi Intel Xeon Phi 5110P	FPGA Xilinx Virtex-6 ML605
Frequency	3.40 GHz	1.05 GHz	1.05 GHz	400 MHz
# Cores	4	8*	60	N/A
# HW Threads	8	12288	240	N/A
Memory	12 GB	2 GB	8 GB	512 MB
Memory BW	25.6 GB/s	224 GB/s	320 GB/s	6.40 GB/s
Peak TFLOPS	0.5	3.2	2.1	0.5

** Core = SM (Streaming Multiprocessor), 2048 threads/SM*

Table 4: Sirius Suite and Granularity of Parallelism

Service	Benchmark	Baseline	Input Set	Data Granularity
ASR	*Gaussian Mixture Model (GMM)*	CMU Sphinx [10]	HMM states	For each HMM state
	Deep Neural Network (DNN)	RWTH RASR [12]	HMM states	For each matrix multiplication
QA	*Porter Stemming (Stemmer)*	Porter [27]	4M word list	For each individual word
	Regular-Expression (Regex)	SLRE [32]	100 expressions/400 sentences	For each regex-sentence pair
	Conditional Random Fields (CRF)	CRFsuite [33]	CoNLL-2000 Shared Task [34]	For each sentence
IMM	*Feature Extraction (FE)*	SURF [15]	JPEG Image	For each image tile
	Feature Description (FD)	SURF [15]	Vector of Keypoints	For each keypoint

- **Multicore CPU** - *Advantages:* High clock frequency, not limited by branch divergence. *Disadvantages:* Least amount of threads available.
- **GPU** - *Advantages:* Massively parallel. *Disadvantages:* Power hungry, custom ISA, hard to program, large data transfer overheads, limited branch divergence handling.
- **Intel Phi** - *Advantages:* Many core, standard programming model (same ISA), manual porting optional / compiler help, handles branch divergence, high bandwidth. *Disadvantages:* Data transfer overheads, relies on compiler. *Note:* 1 core is used for the operating system running on the device itself.
- **FPGA** - *Advantages:* Can be tailored to implement very efficient computation and data layout for the workload. *Disadvantages:* Runs at a much lower clock frequency, expensive, hard to develop for and maintain with software updates.

4.2 Sirius Suite: A Collection of IPA Compute Bottlenecks

To investigate the viability and trade-offs of accelerating IPAs, we extract the key computational bottlenecks of Sirius (described in Section 3) to construct a suite of benchmarks we call **Sirius Suite**. Sirius Suite as well as its implementations across the described accelerator platforms are available alongside the end-to-end Sirius application [17]. As a basis for Sirius Suite, we port existing open-source C/C++ implementations available for each algorithmic component to our target platforms. We additionally implemented standalone C/C++ benchmarks based on the source code of Sirius where none were currently available. The baseline implementations are summarized in column 2 of Table 4. For each Sirius Suite benchmark, we built an input set representative of IPA queries. Table 4 shows the granularity at which each thread performs the computation on the accelerators. For example, both GMM and DNN kernels receive input feature vectors from the HMM search, which are all scored in parallel but at different levels of abstraction, respectively, based on each implementation.

4.3 Porting Methodology

The common porting methodology used across all platforms is to exploit the large amount of data-level parallelism available throughout the processing of a single IPA query. We describe the platform-specific highlights of our porting efforts in the following subsections.

4.3.1 Multicore CPU

We use the Pthread library to accelerate the kernels on the multicore platform by dividing the size of the data. Each thread is responsible for a range of data over a fixed number of iterations. This approach allows each thread to run concurrently and independently, synchronizing only at the end of the execution.

For the image matching kernels, we pre-process the input images for feature extraction by tiling the images. Each thread of the CPU is assigned one or more tiles of the input image (depending on the size of each tile). This allows us to spawn threads once at the beginning of execution and synchronize threads at the end, instead of parallelizing at a smaller granularity within the SURF algorithm, which would require multiple synchronizations between loops. However, as the tile size decreases, the number of "good" keypoints decreases, so we fix the tile size to a minimum of 50×50 per thread.

4.3.2 GPU

We use NVIDIA's CUDA library to port the Sirius components to the NVIDIA GPU. To implement each CUDA kernel, we varied and configured the GPU block and grid sizes to achieve high resource utilization, matching the input data to the best thread layout. We ported additional string manipulation functions currently not supported in CUDA for the stemmer kernel.

4.3.3 Intel Phi

We port our Pthread versions to the Intel Phi platform, leveraging the ability of the target compiler to parallelize the loops on the target platform. For this, we use Intel's ICC cross-compiler. The Phi kernel is built and run directly on the target device allowing for rapid prototyping and debugging. On the Phi platform, we sweep the total amount of threads spawned in increments of 60, increasing the number of hardware threads per core. For some kernels, the maximum number of threads (with enough input data) did not always yield the highest performance. To investigate the potential of this platform to facilitate ease of programming, we use the standard programming model and custom compiler to extract performance from the platform. As such, the results represent what can be accomplished with minimal programmer effort.

4.3.4 FPGA

We use previously published details of FPGA implementations for a number of our Sirius Benchmarks in this work. However, due to limited published details for two of our workloads and to gain further insights, we design our own FPGA implementations for both GMM and Stemmer and evaluate them on a Xilinx FPGA.

GMM The major computation of the algorithm lies in three nested loops that iteratively score the feature vector against the training data. This training data comes from an acoustic model, a language model, and a dictionary in the forms of a means vector, a pre-calculated (precs) vector, a weight vector, and a factor vector. All of this data is used to generate a score for the probability of an HMM state transition. Our focus when implementing the algorithm on the FPGA was to maximize parallelization and pipeline utilization, which led to the design presented in Figure 11. This figure depicts both a core that computes the score of a single iteration of the outermost loop and a callout of a log differential unit. The log differential unit is used to fully parallelize the innermost loop, while the entire core can be instantiated multiple times to parallelize the outermost loop. Because of this, the design is highly scalable as multiple cores can be used to fill the FPGA fabric. The middle loop of the algorithm was not parallelizable, however, and is represented by the Log Summation unit. With this design, we were able to create a high throughput device with a linear pipeline.

Stemmer The Stemmer algorithm computes the root of a word by checking for multiple conditions, such as the word's suffixes or roots. Figure 12 summarizes a single step for our stemmer implementation. By taking advantage of the mutual exclusivity of test conditions, we were able to parallelize these comparisons, which allowed the FPGA to achieve a much lower latency than the original Porter algorithm. Our implementation performs multiple vector operations simultaneously to count vowels, vowel-consonant pairs, and compare suffixes. Together, these operations select the correct word shift for the specific step. We formed a single pipelined core based upon six steps dealing with the different possibilities of suffixes. We instantiate multiple cores to fill the FPGA fabric to deliver maximum performance.

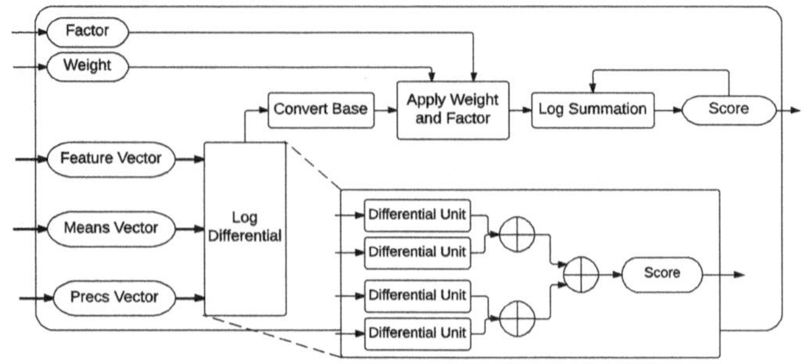

Figure 11: FPGA GMM Diagram

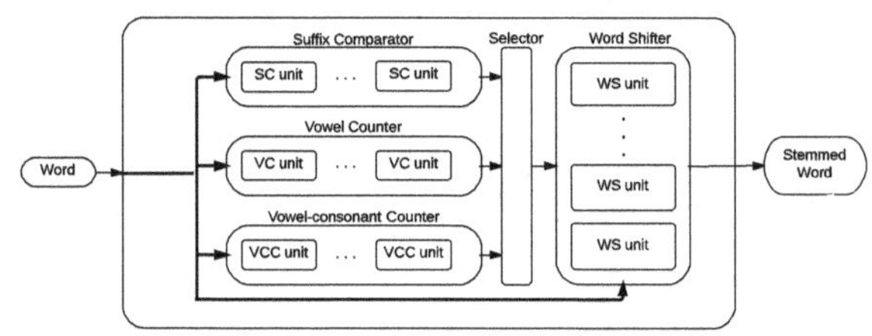

Figure 12: FPGA Stemmer Diagram

4.4 Accelerator Results

Table 5 and Figure 13 present the performance speedup achieved by the Sirius kernels running on each accelerator platform, organized by service type. For the numbers from the prior literature, we scale the FPGA speedup number to match our FPGA platform based on fabric usage and area reported in prior work. We also use numbers from the literature for kernels (Regex and CRF) that were already ported to the GPU architecture and yielded better speedups than our implementations.

4.4.1 ASR

The GMM implementation, extracted from CMU Sphinx's acoustic scoring, had the best performance on the GPU (70×) after optimizations. These custom optimizations on the GPU achieved an order of magnitude improvement by optimizing the data structure layout to ensure coalesced global memory accesses. This leveraged concurrent reads to sequential memory positions for a warp of 32 threads. In addition, it was possible to store the entire data required for the GMM in the GPU memory (2GB) during the deployment time reducing communication between the host and device. The Phi platform did not perform as well as the GPU, indicating that the custom compiler may not have achieved the optimal data layout. The FPGA implementation using a single GMM core achieved a speedup of 56×; when fully utilizing the FPGA fabric we achieved a 169× speedup using 3 GMM cores. RWTH's DNN includes both multithreaded and GPU versions out-of-the-box. The RWTH's DNN parallelizes the entire framework (both HMM search and DNN scoring) and achieves good speedup in both cases. In the cases where we use a custom kernel or cite literature, we assume a 3.7× speedup for the HMM [35] as a reasonable lower bound.

4.4.2 QA

The NLP algorithms as a whole have very similar performance across platforms because of the nature of the workload: high input variability with many test statements causes high branch divergence. Fine tuning the stemming algorithm on the Phi to spawn 120 threads instead of the maximum and switching from allocating a range of data per thread to interlaced array accesses yields a better performance given the lower number of threads used. The FPGA stemmer implementation achieved a 6× speedup over the baseline with a single core using only 17% of the FPGA. Scaling the number of cores to fully utilize the resources of the FPGA yielded a 30× speedup over the baseline. The stemmer algorithm contains many test statements and is not well suited for SIMD operations. We attempted to improve our initial stemmer implementation for GPU by replacing most of the conditional branches with efficient XOR operations [36]. However, our fine-grained XOR-based implementation performed worse than our initial version due to additional synchronization between threads.

4.4.3 IMM

The image processing kernels achieved the best speedup on the GPU which uses heavily optimized OpenCV [16] SURF implementations yielding speedups of 10.5× and 120.5× for FE and FD, respectively. Prior work shows that FPGA yields better FE speedups but does not show similar increases for FD. The tiled multicore version yields good speedup but the performance does not scale as well on the Phi because the number of tiles is fixed, which means there is little advantage to having more threads available. The GPU version has better performance because it uses a data layout explicitly optimized for a larger number of threads.

5. Implications for Future Server Design

In this section, we investigate the performance, power and cost-efficiency trade-offs when configuring servers with different accelerator platforms for Sirius.

Table 5: Speedup of Sirius Suite Across Platforms

Service	Benchmark	CMP	GPU	Phi	FPGA
ASR	*GMM*	3.5	70.0	1.1	169.0
	DNN	6.0*	54.7*	11.2	110.5 [37]
QA	*Stemmer*	4.0	6.2	5.6	30.0
	Regex	3.9	48.0 [38]	1.1	168.2 [39]
	CRF	3.7	3.8 [40]	4.7	7.5 [41]
IMM	*FE*	5.2	10.5	2.5	34.6 [42]
	FD	5.9	120.5	12.7	75.5 [42]

* This includes DNN and HMM combined.

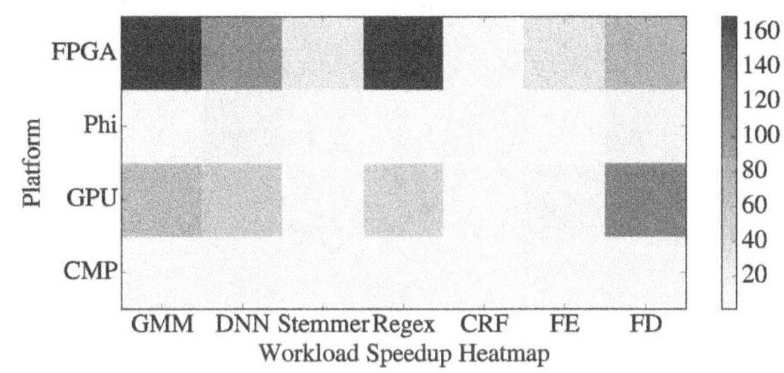

Figure 13: Heat Map of Acceleration Results

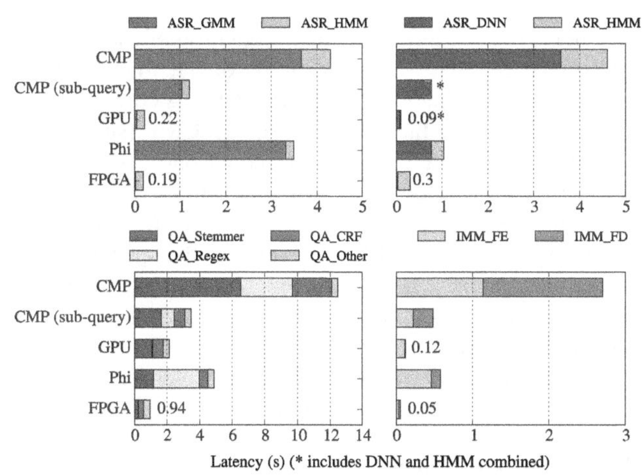

Figure 14: Latency Across Platforms for Each Service

5.1 Server Level Design

We first investigate the end-to-end latency reduction and the power efficiency achieved across server configurations for Sirius' services including ASR, QA and IMM.

5.1.1 Latency Improvement

Figure 14 presents the end-to-end query latency across Sirius' services on a single leaf node configured with each accelerator. We present both results for ASRs that use GMM/HMM and DNN/HMM as key algorithms. The latency breakdown for all hot components within a service is also presented in the figure. For QA, we focus on the NLP components comprising 88% of the cycles of QA as search has already been well studied [30].

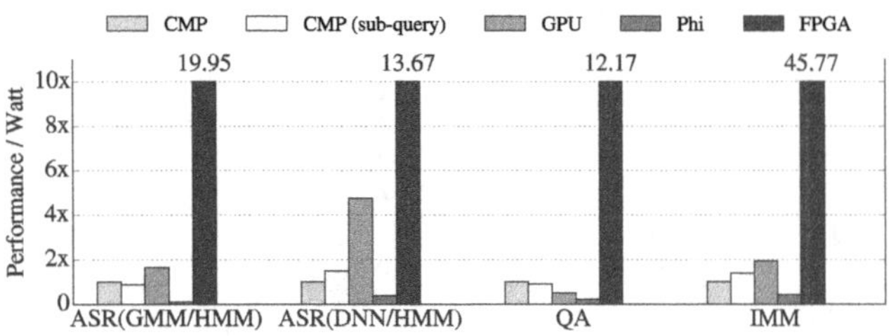

Figure 15: Performance per Watt

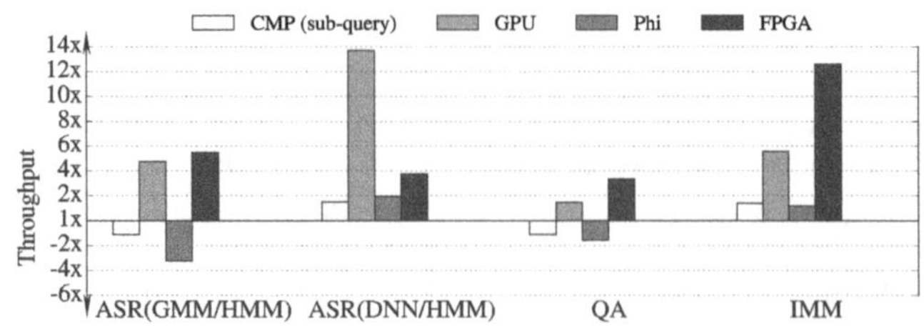

Figure 16: Throughput Across Services

Table 6: Platform Power and Cost

Platform	Power TDP (W)	Cost ($)
Intel Xeon CPU E3-1240	80	250
NVIDIA GPU GTX 770	230	399
Intel Xeon Phi 5110P	225	2,437
Xilinx Virtex-6 FPGA	22	1,795

Our baseline in this figure, CMP, is the latency of the original algorithm implementations of Sirius running on a single core of an Intel Haswell server, described in Table 3. CMP (sub-query) is our Pthreaded implementation of each service exploiting parallelism within a single query, thus reducing the single query latency. This is executed on 4 cores (8 hardware threads) of the Intel Haswell server. CMP (sub-query) in general achieves a 25% latency reduction over the baseline. Across all services, the GPU and FPGA significantly reduce the query latency. For example, the FPGA implementation of ASR (GMM/HMM) reduces the speech recognition query latency from 4.2s to only 0.19s. The FPGA outperforms the GPU for most of the services except ASR (DNN/HMM). Although Intel Phi can reduce the latency over the single core baseline (CMP), Phi is generally slower than the Pthreaded multicore baseline.

5.1.2 Energy Efficiency

Figure 15 presents the energy efficiency (performance/watt) for each accelerator platform across four services of the Sirius pipeline, normalized by the performance/watt achieved by using all cores on a multicore CPU by query-level parallelism. Here performance is defined as $1/latency$. Table 6 presents the power (TDP) for each accelerator platform. The FPGA has the best performance/watt, exceeding every other platform by a significant margin, with more than 12× energy efficiency over the baseline multicore. The GPU's performance/watt is also higher than the baseline for 3 of 4 services. Its performance/watt is worse than the baseline for QA, mainly due to its moderate performance improvement for this service.

5.2 Datacenter Design

Based on the latency and energy efficiency trade-offs for server platforms discussed in the previous section, we evaluate multiple design choices for datacenters composed of accelerated servers to improve performance (throughput) and reduce the total cost of ownership (TCO).

5.2.1 Throughput Improvement

The latency reduction shown in Figure 14 can translate to significant throughput improvement. Figure 16 presents the throughput improvement achieved using various acceleration platforms without degrading latency beyond the baseline. Similar to Figures 14 and 15, the CMP baseline executes the original Sirius workload on the Intel Haswell platform, where all four cores are utilized to serve queries, thus achieving similar throughput as CMP (sub-query level). Note that CMP's query latency is however significantly longer because CMP (sub-query level) exploits parallelism within a single query. Figure 16 demonstrates that significant latency reductions achieved by the GPU and FPGA translate to significant throughput improvement. For example, the GPU provides 13.7× throughput improvement over the baseline CMP for ASR (DNN/HMM), while the FPGA achieves 12.6× throughput for IMM. For QA, the throughput improvement across the platforms is generally more limited than other services.

Figure 17 presents the throughput improvement achieved using each acceleration platform at various load levels (the server is modeled as M/M/1 queue). Compared to Figure 16, which presents the throughput improvement at 100% load, when considering queuing effect, the lower the server load, the bigger impact latency reduction would have on throughput improvement. In other words, Figure 16 demonstrates a lower bound of throughput improvement for a queuing system. Since datacenter servers often operate at medium-to-low load, as shown in Figure 17, significant higher throughput improvement can be expected.

5.2.2 TCO Analysis

Improving throughput allows us to reduce the amount of computing resources (servers) needed to serve a given load. However, reducing the number of servers may or may not lead to reduction in the total cost of ownership of a datacenter (DC). Although reducing the machines leads to reduction on DC construction cost and power/cooling infrastructure cost, we may increase the per server capital or operational expenditure cost either by additional accelerator purchase cost or the energy cost. Here we present a cost analysis to

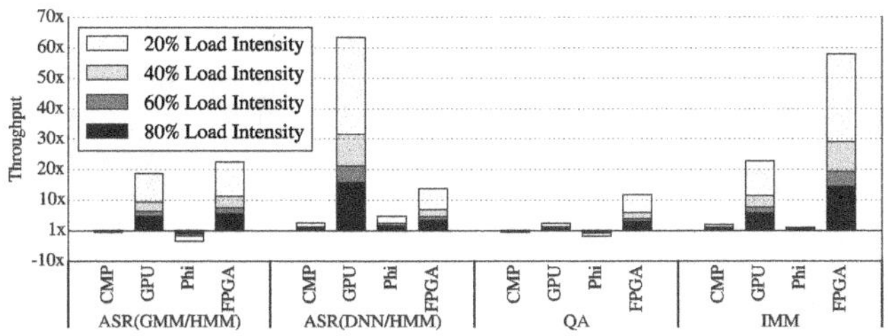

Figure 17: Throughput Improvement at Various Load Levels Modeled as M/M/1 Queue (darker is a higher load intensity for each platform)

Table 7: TCO Model Parameters [43]

Parameter	Value
DC Depreciation Time	12 years
Server Depreciation Time	3 years
Average Server Utilization	45%
Electricity Cost	$0.067/kWh
Datacenter Price	$10/W
Datacenter Opex	$0.04/W
Server Opex	5% of Capex / year
Server Price (baseline)	$2,102 [44]
Server Power (baseline)	163.6 W [44]
PUE	1.1

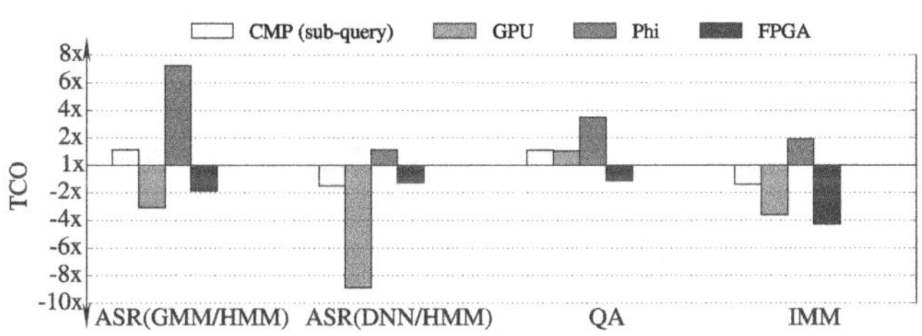

Figure 18: TCO Across Platforms for Each Service

evaluate the implication on the datacenter cost when using each accelerated server platform.

We perform our TCO analysis using the TCO model recently proposed by Google [43]. The parameters used in our TCO model are described in Table 7. The server price and power usage are based on the following server configuration based on the OpenCompute Project: 1 CPU Intel Xeon E3-1240 V3 3.4 GHz, 32 GB of RAM, and two 4TB disks [44].

Figure 18 presents the datacenter TCOs with various acceleration options, normalized by the TCO achieved by a datacenter that uses only CMPs. Overall, FPGA and GPU provide high TCO reduction. For example, GPU achieves over 8× TCO reduction for ASR(DNN) and FPGA achieves over 4× TCO reduction for IMM. We will further discuss the TCO results and use them to derive our DC designs in the next section.

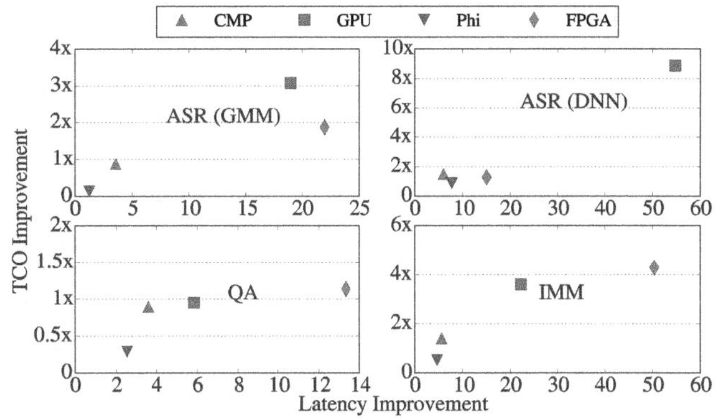

Figure 19: Trade-off Between TCO and Latency

5.2.3 Homogeneous Datacenter Design

Based on latency results from Figure 14 and TCO results from Figure 18, we first investigate the trade-offs when designing a homogeneous datacenter, that is, all servers in the datacenter have the same configuration. Homogeneous datacenters are often desirable as they minimize the management and maintenance overhead [45].

When designing a datacenter, it would be ideal to maximize performance (e.g, minimize query latency or improve throughput for a given latency constraint) and minimize the total cost of ownership. However, trade-offs may need to be made as which objective should be prioritized if both cannot be optimized by the same design. Figure 19 presents the trade-offs between the query latency improvement and the TCO improvement for each server option across four Sirius services. The x-axis presents latency improvement and the y-axis shows the TCO improvement.

As shown in the figure, FPGA achieves the lowest latency (highest latency improvement) among all accelerating platforms for 3 out of 4 services that we studied. However, the FPGA's relatively high purchase cost allows GPUs to achieve similar or higher TCO savings as FPGAs with smaller latency reduction. When the FPGA is not considered an option, the GPU achieves the optimal latency and TCO for all services. Even with the FPGA as an accelerator candidate, a GPU-accelerated datacenter provides the best latency and TCO for ASR using DNN.

Table 8 summarizes the homogeneous datacenter design for each of the main Sirius services under different conditions and optimization objectives. We present three first-order design objectives: minimizing latency, minimizing TCO with a latency constraint, and maximizing energy efficiency with a latency constraint, shown as three rows of the table. The latency constraint here is CMP (sub-query) latency shown in Figure 14. The first row (with FPGA, without FPGA, without FPGA or GPU) also shows the design constraints for the accelerator candidates.

Key Observation - *In conclusion, FPGAs and GPUs are the top 2 candidates for homogeneous accelerated datacenter designs across all three design objectives. An FPGA-accelerated datacenter allows DCs to minimize latency and*

Table 8: Homogeneous DC

	With FPGA				Without FPGA				Without {FPGA, GPU}			
	ASR (GMM)	ASR (DNN)	QA	IMM	ASR (GMM)	ASR (DNN)	QA	IMM	ASR (GMM)	ASR (DNN)	QA	IMM
Hmg-latency	FPGA				GPU				CMP			
Hmg-TCO (w/ L constraint)	GPU											
Hmg-power eff. (w/L constraint)	FPGA											

Table 9: Heterogeneous DC

	With FPGA				Without FPGA				Without {FPGA, GPU}			
	ASR (GMM)	ASR (DNN)	QA	IMM	ASR (GMM)	ASR (DNN)	QA	IMM	ASR (GMM)	ASR (DNN)	QA	IMM
Hetero-latency	FPGA	GPU (3.6x)	FPGA		GPU				CMP			
Hetero-TCO (w/ L constraint)	GPU		FPGA (20%)	FPGA (19%)								
Hetero-power eff. (w/L constraint)	FPGA											

maximize energy efficiency for most of the services and is the best homogeneous design option for those objectives. Its power efficiency is desirable for datacenters with power constraints, especially for augmenting existing filled datacenters that are equipped with capped power infrastructure support. It also improves TCO for all four services. On the other hand, FPGA-accelerated datacenters incur higher engineering cost than the rest of the platforms. For DCs where engineering cost needs to be under a certain constraint, GPU-accelerated homogeneous datacenters achieve relatively low latency and high throughput. They also achieve similar or higher TCO reduction than FPGA due to its low purchase cost. GPUs could be a desirable option over FPGAs when the high engineering overhead of FGPA implementation is a concern, especially given the quick workload churn (e.g., binaries are updated on the monthly basis) in modern datacenters.

5.2.4 Heterogeneous (Partitioned) Datacenter Design

Next, we explore the design options for partitioned heterogeneous datacenters. Because each service can run on its most suitable platform in a partitioned heterogeneous datacenter, this strategy may provide additional opportunities for further latency reduction or TCO reduction. Table 9 shows various DC design choices for different design objectives (rows), accelerator candidate sets (with FPGA, without FPGA, and without FPGA and GPU) and services (columns). The numbers in parenthesis show the improvement on the metric of the specific design objective of that row when the DC design switches from a homogeneous baseline to a heterogeneous partitioned design.

As shown in the first row of the table, when designing a partitioned heterogeneous DC for ASR, QA and IMM services, if all accelerators are considered viable candidates, GPUs can be used to optimize the latency for ASR (DNN) and achieves 3.6× latency reduction for that service compared to the homogeneous DC using FPGA across all services. Similarly, using FPGAs for QA and IMM achieves 20% and 19% TCO improvement, respectively.

Key Observation - *In conclusion, the partitioned heterogeneity in our study does not provide much benefit over the homogeneous design. The amount of benefit is certainly dependant on the workload partition across services. However, overall, most of the algorithms and services in Sirius workload exhibit a similar trend in terms of preferences for accelerators for FPGA and GPU, etc. There is also additional cost associated with managing a heterogeneous/partitioned datacenter that needs to be justifiable by the performance gain.*

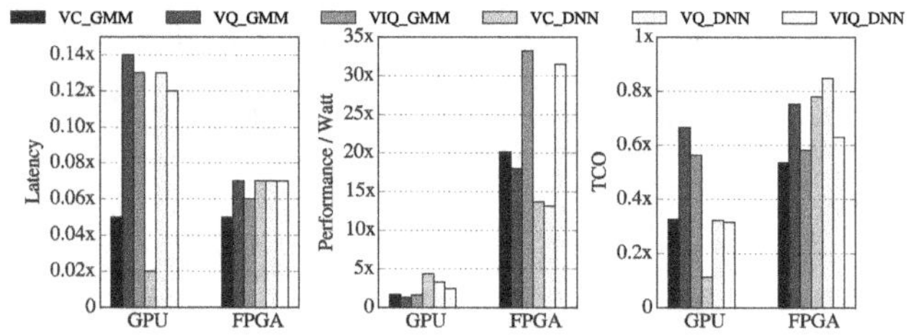

Figure 20: Latency, Energy Efficiency and TCO of GPU and FPGA Datacenters

5.2.5 Query-level Results for DC designs

In previous sections, we focused on latency, energy-efficiency and TCO trade-offs for various acceleration options across three services in Sirius. In this section, we focus on these trade-offs across three query types supported by Sirius, namely, VC, VQ and VIQ. Figure 20 presents the query latency of three query types achieved by the best two homogeneous datacenters, composed of GPU- and FPGA-accelerated servers, respectively. In addition to query latency, energy efficiency of the servers and the TCO of the datacenters to support these query types are also presented. GPU-accelerated homogeneous datacenters achieve on average 10× latency reduction, and FPGA-accelerated datacenters achieve a 16× reduction. The accelerated datacenters also reduce the TCO on average by 2.6× and 1.4×, respectively.

Figure 21 further presents the latency reduction of these two accelerated datacenters and how homogeneous accelerated datacenters can significantly reduce the scalability gap for datacenters, from the current 165× resource scaling, shown in Figure 7, down to 16× and 10× for GPU- and FPGA-accelerated datacenters, respectively.

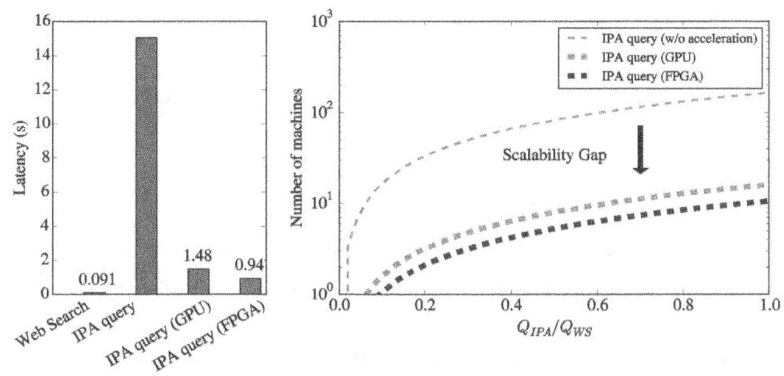

Figure 21: Bridging the Scalability Gap

6. Related Work

In addition to prior work focusing on datacenter efficiency [45–54], a heterogeneous server design [55] was proposed for speech and image recognition, where the GMM scoring and image matching algorithms were ported to hardware accelerators. However their work does not address the acceleration of NLP algorithms or DNN-based speech recognition. Custom accelerators for specific cloud applications have also been proposed, for example for memcached [56] and database systems [57] showing the growing need for specialized hardware in server applications. The Catapult project [58] at Microsoft Research has ported key components of Bing's page ranking to FPGAs. In this work, we focus on accelerating the components that make up an intelligent personal assistant focusing on their impact in the end-to-end system.

Prior work has also investigated acceleration of individual components of Sirius on various platforms. For speech recognition systems using GMM/HMM, prior work characterizes and accelerates the workload in hardware [59, 60]. In the past, GPUs have been successful in accelerating speech recognition's GMM [61] and more recently ASR was ported using a hybrid CPU-GPU approach [62]. The Carnegie Mellon *In Silicon Vox* [63] project has implemented an FPGA based GMM/HMM speech recognizer with a relatively small vocabulary. Image processing algorithms have been shown to map well to accelerators [64–66]. Key natural language processing techniques also show promising results when ported to hardware [67, 68]. Additionally, low-power accelerators for deep neural networks [69, 70] have garnered the interest of researchers as DNNs can be parallelized easily but have better accuracy compared to conventional machine learning techniques [71].

7. Conclusion

This work introduces **Sirius**, an open end-to-end intelligent personal assistant application, modeled after popular IPA services such as Apple's Siri. Sirius leverages well-established open infrastructures for speech recognition, computer vision, and question-answering systems. We use Sirius to investigate the performance, power, and cost implications of hardware accelerator-based server architectures for future data center designs. We show that GPU- and FPGA-accelerated servers can improve the query latency on average by 10× and 16×. Leveraging the latency reduction, GPU- and FPGA-accelerated servers can reduce the TCO by 2.6× and 1.4×, respectively.

8. Acknowledgment

We thank our anonymous reviewers for their feedback and suggestions. This work was partially sponsored by Google, ARM, the Defense Advanced Research Projects Agency (DARPA) under agreement HR0011-13-2-000, and by the National Science Foundation (NSF) under grants CCF-SHF-1302682 and CNS-CSR-1321047.

References

[1] Apple's Siri. https://www.apple.com/ios/siri/.

[2] Google's Google Now. http://www.google.com/landing/now/.

[3] Microsoft's Cortana. http://www.windowsphone.com/en-us/features-8-1.

[4] Smartphone OS Market Share, Q1 2014. http://www.idc.com/prodserv/smartphone-os-market-share.jsp.

[5] Google's Android Wear. www.android.com/wear/.

[6] Google's Google Glass. www.google.com/glass.

[7] ABI Research. Wearable Computing Devices, Like Apple iWatch, Will Exceed 485 Million Annual Shipments by 2018. 2013. https://www.abiresearch.com/press/wearable-computing-devices-like-apples-iwatch-will.

[8] Marti A. Hearst. 'Natural' Search User Interfaces. *Commun. ACM*, 54(11):60–67, November 2011.

[9] M. G. Siegler. Apple's Massive New Data Center Set To Host Nuance Tech. http://techcrunch.com/2011/05/09/apple-nuance-data-center-deal/.

[10] David Huggins-Daines, Mohit Kumar, Arthur Chan, Alan W Black, Mosur Ravishankar, and Alex I Rudnicky. Pocketsphinx: A free, real-time continuous speech recognition system for hand-held devices. In *Acoustics, Speech and Signal Processing, 2006. ICASSP 2006 Proceedings. 2006 IEEE International Conference on*, volume 1, pages I–I. IEEE, 2006.

[11] Daniel Povey, Arnab Ghoshal, Gilles Boulianne, Lukas Burget, Ondrej Glembek, Nagendra Goel, Mirko Hannemann, Petr Motlicek, Yanmin Qian, Petr Schwarz, Jan Silovsky, Georg Stemmer, and Karel Vesely. The kaldi speech recognition toolkit. In *IEEE 2011 Workshop on Automatic Speech Recognition and Understanding*. IEEE Signal Processing Society, December 2011.

[12] David Rybach, Stefan Hahn, Patrick Lehnen, David Nolden, Martin Sundermeyer, Zoltan Tüske, Siemon Wiesler, Ralf Schlüter, and Hermann Ney. RASR - the RWTH Aachen University Open Source Speech Recognition Toolkit, 2011.

[13] Frank Seide, Gang Li, and Dong Yu. Conversational speech transcription using context-dependent deep neural networks. In *Interspeech*, pages 437–440, 2011.

[14] David Ferrucci, Eric Brown, Jennifer Chu-Carroll, James Fan, David Gondek, Aditya A. Kalyanpur, Adam Lally, J. William Murdock, Eric Nyberg, John Prager, Nico Schlaefer, and Chris Welty. Building Watson: An Overview of the DeepQA Project

— Ferrucci — AI Magazine. *AI MAGAZINE*, 31(3):59–79, September 2010.

[15] Herbert Bay, Tinne Tuytelaars, and Luc Van Gool. Surf: Speeded up robust features. In *Computer Vision–ECCV 2006*, pages 404–417. Springer, 2006.

[16] G. Bradski. *Dr. Dobb's Journal of Software Tools*, 2000.

[17] Sirius: An Open End-to-End Voice and Vision Personal Assistant. http://sirius.clarity-lab.org.

[18] Geoffrey Hinton, Li Deng, Dong Yu, George Dahl, Abdel rahman Mohamed, Navdeep Jaitly, Andrew Senior, Vincent Vanhoucke, Patrick Nguyen, Tara Sainath, and Brian Kingsbury. Deep neural networks for acoustic modeling in speech recognition. *Signal Processing Magazine*, 2012.

[19] Jeffrey Dean, Greg S. Corrado, Rajat Monga, Kai Chen, Matthieu Devin, Quoc V. Le, Mark Z. Mao, Marc Aurelio Ranzato, Andrew Senior, Paul Tucker, Ke Yang, and Andrew Y. Ng. Large scale distributed deep networks. In *NIPS*, 2012.

[20] Oscar Tckstrm, Dipanjan Das, Slav Petrov, Ryan McDonald, and Joakim Nivre. Token and type constraints for cross-lingual part-of-speech tagging. *Transactions of the Association for Computational Linguistics*, 1:1–12, 2013.

[21] Kooaba, inc. http://www.vision.ee.ethz.ch/~surf/download.html.

[22] Qualcomm Acquires Kooaba Visual Recognition Company. http://mobilemarketingmagazine.com/qualcomm-acquires-kooaba-visual-recognition-company/.

[23] G David Forney Jr. The viterbi algorithm. *Proceedings of the IEEE*, 61(3):268–278, 1973.

[24] George E Dahl, Dong Yu, Li Deng, and Alex Acero. Context-dependent pre-trained deep neural networks for large-vocabulary speech recognition. *Audio, Speech, and Language Processing, IEEE Transactions on*, 20(1):30–42, 2012.

[25] Xuedong Huang, James Baker, and Raj Reddy. A historical perspective of speech recognition. *Commun. ACM*, 57(1):94–103, January 2014.

[26] Vijay R. Chandrasekhar, David M. Chen, Sam S. Tsai, Ngai-Man Cheung, Huizhong Chen, Gabriel Takacs, Yuriy Reznik, Ramakrishna Vedantham, Radek Grzeszczuk, Jeff Bach, and Bernd Girod. The stanford mobile visual search data set. In *Proceedings of the Second Annual ACM Conference on Multimedia Systems*, MMSys '11, pages 117–122, New York, NY, USA, 2011. ACM.

[27] Martin F Porter. An algorithm for suffix stripping. *Program: electronic library and information systems*, 14(3):130–137, 1980.

[28] John Lafferty, Andrew McCallum, and Fernando CN Pereira. Conditional random fields: Probabilistic models for segmenting and labeling sequence data. 2001.

[29] Apache nutch. http://nutch.apache.org.

[30] Michael Ferdman, Almutaz Adileh, Onur Kocberber, Stavros Volos, Mohammad Alisafaee, Djordje Jevdjic, Cansu Kaynak, Adrian Daniel Popescu, Anastasia Ailamaki, and Babak Falsafi. Clearing the clouds: A study of emerging scale-out workloads on modern hardware. In *Proceedings of the Seventeenth International Conference on Architectural Support for Programming Languages and Operating Systems*, ASPLOS XVII, pages 37–48, New York, NY, USA, 2012. ACM.

[31] Intel vtune. https://software.intel.com/en-us/intel-vtune-amplifier-xe.

[32] SLRE: Super Light Regular Expression Library. http://cesanta.com/.

[33] Naoaki Okazaki. CRFsuite: a fast implementation of Conditional Random Fields (CRFs), 2007. http://www.chokkan.org/software/crfsuite/.

[34] Erik F. Tjong Kim Sang and Sabine Buchholz. Introduction to the conll-2000 shared task: Chunking. In *Proceedings of the 2Nd Workshop on Learning Language in Logic and the 4th Conference on Computational Natural Language Learning - Volume 7*, ConLL '00, pages 127–132, Stroudsburg, PA, USA, 2000. Association for Computational Linguistics.

[35] Jike Chong, Ekaterina Gonina, and Kurt Keutzer. Efficient automatic speech recognition on the gpu. *Chapter in GPU Computing Gems Emerald Edition, Morgan Kaufmann*, 1, 2011.

[36] A Singh, N. Kumar, S. Gera, and A Mittal. Achieving magnitude order improvement in porter stemmer algorithm over multi-core architecture. In *Informatics and Systems (INFOS), 2010 The 7th International Conference on*, pages 1–8, March 2010.

[37] Clément Farabet, Yann LeCun, Koray Kavukcuoglu, Eugenio Culurciello, Berin Martini, Polina Akselrod, and Selcuk Talay. Large-scale FPGA-based convolutional networks. *Machine Learning on Very Large Data Sets*, 2011.

[38] Giorgos Vasiliadis, Michalis Polychronakis, Spiros Antonatos, Evangelos P. Markatos, and Sotiris Ioannidis. Regular expression matching on graphics hardware for intrusion detection. In *Proceedings of the 12th International Symposium on Recent Advances in Intrusion Detection*, RAID '09, pages 265–283, Berlin, Heidelberg, 2009. Springer-Verlag.

[39] Yi-Hua E. Yang, Weirong Jiang, and Viktor K. Prasanna. Compact Architecture for High-throughput Regular Expression Matching on FPGA. In *Proceedings of the 4th ACM/IEEE Symposium on Architectures for Networking and Communications Systems*, ANCS '08, pages 30–39, New York, NY, USA, 2008. ACM.

[40] Nico Piatkowski. Linear-Chain CRF@GPU, 2011. http://sfb876.tu-dortmund.de/crfgpu/linear_crf_cuda.html.

[41] Sriram Swaminathan, Russell Tessier, Dennis Goeckel, and Wayne Burleson. A dynamically reconfigurable adaptive viterbi decoder. In *Proceedings of the 2002 ACM/SIGDA Tenth International Symposium on Field-programmable Gate Arrays*, FPGA '02, pages 227–236, New York, NY, USA, 2002. ACM.

[42] Dimitris Bouris, Antonis Nikitakis, and Ioannis Papaefstathiou. Fast and Efficient FPGA-Based Feature Detection Employing the SURF Algorithm. In *Proceedings of the 2010 18th IEEE Annual International Symposium on Field-Programmable Custom Computing Machines*, FCCM '10, pages 3–10, Washington, DC, USA, 2010. IEEE Computer Society.

[43] Luiz Andre Barroso, Jimmy Clidaras, and Urs Holzle. *The Datacenter as a Computer: An Introduction to the Design of Warehouse-Scale Machines, Second Edition.* Synthesis Lectures on Computer Architecture. 2013.

[44] Thinkmate high performance computing, 2014. http://www.thinkmate.com/system/rax-xf2-1130v3-sh.

[45] Jason Mars and Lingjia Tang. Whare-map: Heterogeneity in homogeneous warehouse-scale computers. In *ISCA '13: Proceedings of the 40th annual International Symposium on Computer Architecture*. IEEE/ACM, 2013.

[46] Jason Mars, Lingjia Tang, Robert Hundt, Kevin Skadron, and Mary Lou Soffa. Bubble-up: Increasing utilization in modern warehouse scale computers via sensible co-locations. In *Proceedings of the 44th Annual IEEE/ACM International Symposium on Microarchitecture (MICRO)*, MICRO-44, pages 248–259, New York, NY, USA, 2011. ACM.

[47] Jason Mars, Lingjia Tang, Kevin Skadron, Mary Lou Soffa, and Robert Hundt. Increasing utilization in modern warehouse-scale computers using bubble-up. *IEEE Micro*, 32(3):88–99, May 2012.

[48] Lingjia Tang, Jason Mars, Xiao Zhang, Robert Hagmann, Robert Hundt, and Eric Tune. Optimizing google's warehouse scale computers: The numa experience. In *Proceedings of the 2013 IEEE 19th International Symposium on High Performance Computer Architecture (HPCA)*, HPCA '13, pages 188–197, Washington, DC, USA, 2013. IEEE Computer Society.

[49] Lingjia Tang, Jason Mars, Wei Wang, Tanima Dey, and Mary Lou Soffa. Reqos: Reactive static/dynamic compilation for qos in warehouse scale computers. In *Proceedings of the Eighteenth International Conference on Architectural Support for Programming Languages and Operating Systems (ASPLOS)*, ASPLOS '13, pages 89–100, New York, NY, USA, 2013. ACM.

[50] Hailong Yang, Alex Breslow, Jason Mars, and Lingjia Tang. Bubble-flux: Precise online qos management for increased utilization in warehouse scale computers. In *Proceedings of the 40th Annual International Symposium on Computer Architecture (ISCA)*, ISCA '13, pages 607–618, New York, NY, USA, 2013. ACM.

[51] Yunqi Zhang, Michael Laurenzano, Jason Mars, and Lingjia Tang. Smite: Precise qos prediction on real system smt processors to improve utilization in warehouse scale computers. In *Proceedings of the 47th Annual IEEE/ACM International Symposium on Microarchitecture (MICRO)*, MICRO-47, New York, NY, USA, 2014. ACM.

[52] Michael Laurenzano, Yunqi Zhang, Lingjia Tang, and Jason Mars. Protean code: Achieving near-free online code transformations for warehouse scale computers. In *Proceedings of the 47th Annual IEEE/ACM International Symposium on Microarchitecture (MICRO)*, MICRO-47, New York, NY, USA, 2014. ACM.

[53] Vinicius Petrucci, Michael A. Laurenzano, Yunqi Zhang, John Doherty, Daniel Mosse, Jason Mars, and Lingjia Tang. Octopus-man: Qos-driven task management for heterogeneous multicore in warehouse scale computers. In *Proceedings of the 2015 IEEE 21st International Symposium on High Performance Computer Architecture (HPCA)*, HPCA '15, Washington, DC, USA, 2015. IEEE Computer Society.

[54] Chang-Hong Hsu, Yunqi Zhang, Michael A. Laurenzano, David Meisner, Thomas Wenisch, Lingjia Tang, Jason Mars, and Ron Dreslinski. Adrenaline: Pinpointing and reigning in tail queries with quick voltage boosting. In *Proceedings of the 2015 IEEE 21st International Symposium on High Performance Computer Architecture (HPCA)*, HPCA '15, Washington, DC, USA, 2015. IEEE Computer Society.

[55] Ravi Iyer, Sadagopan Srinivasan, Omesh Tickoo, Zhen Fang, Ramesh Illikkal, Steven Zhang, Vineet Chadha, Paul M. Stillwell Jr., and Seung Eun Lee. Cogniserve: Heterogeneous server architecture for large-scale recognition. *IEEE Micro*, 31(3):20–31, 2011.

[56] Kevin Lim, David Meisner, Ali G. Saidi, Parthasarathy Ranganathan, and Thomas F. Wenisch. Thin servers with smart pipes: Designing soc accelerators for memcached. In *Proceedings of the 40th Annual International Symposium on Computer Architecture*, ISCA '13, pages 36–47, New York, NY, USA, 2013. ACM.

[57] Onur Kocberber, Boris Grot, Javier Picorel, Babak Falsafi, Kevin Lim, and Parthasarathy Ranganathan. Meet the walkers: Accelerating index traversals for in-memory databases. In *Proceedings of the 46th Annual IEEE/ACM International Symposium on Microarchitecture*, MICRO-46, pages 468–479, New York, NY, USA, 2013. ACM.

[58] Andrew Putnam, Adrian Caulfield, Eric Chung, Derek Chiou, Kypros Constantinides, John Demme, Hadi Esmaeilzadeh, Jeremy Fowers, Gopi Prashanth Gopal, Jan Gray, Michael Haselman, Scott Hauck, Stephen Heil, Amir Hormati, Joo-Young Kim, Sitaram Lanka, Jim Larus, Eric Peterson, Simon Pope, Aaron Smith, Jason Thong, Phillip Yi Xiao, and Doug Burger. A reconfigurable fabric for accelerating large-scale datacenter services. In *41st Annual International Symposium on Computer Architecture (ISCA)*, June 2014.

[59] Rajeev Krishna, Scott Mahlke, and Todd Austin. Architectural optimizations for low-power, real-time speech recognition. In *Proceedings of the 2003 International Conference on Compilers, Architecture and Synthesis for Embedded Systems*, CASES '03, pages 220–231, New York, NY, USA, 2003. ACM.

[60] Binu Mathew, Al Davis, and Zhen Fang. A low-power accelerator for the sphinx 3 speech recognition system. In *Proceedings of the 2003 International Conference on Compilers, Architecture and Synthesis for Embedded Systems*, CASES '03, pages 210–219, New York, NY, USA, 2003. ACM.

[61] Paul R. Dixon, Tasuku Oonishi, and Sadaoki Furui. Harnessing graphics processors for the fast computation of acoustic likelihoods in speech recognition. *Comput. Speech Lang.*, 23(4):510–526, October 2009.

[62] Jungsuk Kim, Jike Chong, and Ian R. Lane. Efficient On-The-Fly Hypothesis Rescoring in a Hybrid GPU/CPU-based Large Vocabulary Continuous Speech Recognition Engine. In *INTERSPEECH*. ISCA, 2012.

[63] Edward C. Lin, Kai Yu, Rob A. Rutenbar, and Tsuhan Chen. A 1000-word Vocabulary, Speaker-independent, Continuous Live-mode Speech Recognizer Implemented in a Single FPGA. In *Proceedings of the 2007 ACM/SIGDA 15th International Symposium on Field Programmable Gate Arrays*, FPGA '07, pages 60–68, New York, NY, USA, 2007. ACM.

[64] J Hauswald, T Manville, Q Zheng, R Dreslinski, C Chakrabarti, and T Mudge. A hybrid approach to offloading mobile image classification. In *Acoustics, Speech and Signal Processing (ICASSP), 2014 IEEE International Conference on*, pages 8375–8379. IEEE, 2014.

[65] Ethan Rublee, Vincent Rabaud, Kurt Konolige, and Gary Bradski. Orb: an efficient alternative to sift or surf. In *Computer Vision (ICCV), 2011 IEEE International Conference on*, pages 2564–2571. IEEE, 2011.

[66] Tung H Dinh, Dao Q Vu, Vu-Duc Ngo, Nam Pham Ngoc, and Vu T Truong. High throughput fpga architecture for corner detection in traffic images. In *Communications and Electronics (ICCE), 2014 IEEE Fifth International Conference on*, pages 297–302. IEEE, 2014.

[67] Yuliang Sun, Zilong Wang, Sitao Huang, Lanjun Wang, Yu Wang, Rong Luo, and Huazhong Yang. Accelerating frequent item counting with fpga. In *Proceedings of the 2014 ACM/SIGDA International Symposium on Field-programmable Gate Arrays*, FPGA '14, pages 109–112, New York, NY, USA, 2014. ACM.

[68] Jan Van Lunteren, Christoph Hagleitner, Timothy Heil, Giora Biran, Uzi Shvadron, and Kubilay Atasu. Designing a programmable wire-speed regular-expression matching accelerator. In *Proceedings of the 2012 45th Annual IEEE/ACM International Symposium on Microarchitecture*, MICRO-45, pages 461–472, Washington, DC, USA, 2012. IEEE Computer Society.

[69] Tianshi Chen, Zidong Du, Ninghui Sun, Jia Wang, Chengyong Wu, Yunji Chen, and Olivier Temam. DianNao: A Small-footprint High-throughput Accelerator for Ubiquitous Machine-learning. In *Proceedings of the 19th International Conference on Architectural Support for Programming Languages and Operating Systems*, ASPLOS '14, pages 269–284, New York, NY, USA, 2014. ACM.

[70] Hadi Esmaeilzadeh, Adrian Sampson, Luis Ceze, and Doug Burger. Neural acceleration for general-purpose approximate programs. In *Proceedings of the 2012 45th Annual IEEE/ACM International Symposium on Microarchitecture*, MICRO-45, pages 449–460, Washington, DC, USA, 2012. IEEE Computer Society.

[71] Alex Graves, Abdel-rahman Mohamed, and Geoffrey Hinton. Speech recognition with deep recurrent neural networks. In *Acoustics, Speech and Signal Processing (ICASSP), 2013 IEEE International Conference on*, pages 6645–6649. IEEE, 2013.

Automated OS-level Device Runtime Power Management

Chao Xu
Rice University

Felix Xiaozhu Lin
Purdue University

Yuyang Wang
Tsinghua University

Lin Zhong
Rice University

Abstract

Non-CPU devices on a modern system-on-a-chip (SoC), ranging from accelerators to I/O controllers, account for a significant portion of the chip area. It is therefore vital for system energy efficiency that idle devices can enter a low-power state while still meeting the performance expectation. This is called device runtime Power Management (PM) for which individual device drivers in commodity OSes are held responsible today. Based on the observations of existing drivers and their evolution, we consider it harmful to rely on drivers for device runtime PM.

This paper identifies three pieces of information as essential to device runtime PM, and shows that they can be obtained without involving drivers, either by using a software-only approach, or more efficiently, by adding one register bit to each device. We thus suggest a structural change to the current Linux runtime PM framework, replacing the PM code in all applicable drivers with a single kernel module called the central PM agent. Experimental evaluations show that the central PM agent is just as effective as hand-tuned driver PM code. The paper also presents a tool called PowerAdvisor that simplifies driver PM efforts under the current Linux runtime PM framework. PowerAdvisor analyzes execution traces and suggests where to insert PM calls in driver source code. Despite being a best-effort tool, PowerAdvisor not only reproduces hand-tuned PM code from stock drivers, but also correctly suggests PM code never known before. Overall, our experience shows that it is promising to ultimately free driver developers from manual PM.

Categories and Subject Descriptors D.4.7 [*OPERATING SYSTEMS*]: Organization and Design

Keywords Power management; Mobile system; System-on-a-chip; Operating system

ASPLOS '15, March 14–18, 2015, Istanbul, Turkey..
Copyright © 2015 ACM 978-1-4503-2835-7/15/03. . . $15.00.
http://dx.doi.org/10.1145/2694344.2694360

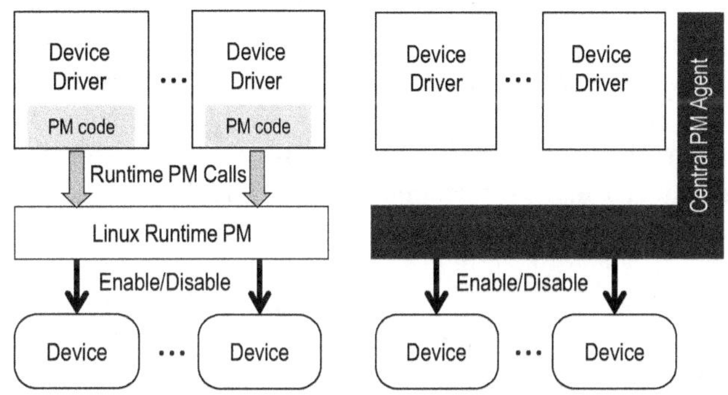

(a) Current Linux PM (b) Central PM in This Work

Figure 1: An overview of this work. (a) In the current Linux, each driver is responsible for implementing its PM under the runtime PM framework, which incurs high development burden and is error-prone. (b) The central PM agent relieves drivers from PM.

1. Introduction

A System-on-a-chip (SoC) [1–4] is often the heart of a wide spectrum of embedded systems from tablets to wearables. It is complex, incorporating not only multiple general purpose cores (CPU) but also dozens of IP (intellectual property) modules, most notably I/O controllers and accelerators such as multimedia codec, DSP, and GPU. These IP modules not only bring specialized functions to an SoC efficiently, but also account for the majority of the SoC chip area [5]. Because commodity operating systems (OSes) treat these non-CPU modules as I/O devices and manage them with device drivers, we refer to them as *devices* in this work.

In a system that employs an SoC, power management (PM) is an important design issue that requires software and hardware collaboration. Its goal is to ensure that performance requirements of workloads are met with the lowest possible energy consumption. PM is critical to the energy efficiency and therefore usability of the overall system.

This paper focuses on *device runtime PM* that enables/disables individual devices properly and timely when the system is in use. Its actions are bubbled up to the hardware clock and power hierarchy, finally leading to clock (un)gating, power supply switching, or voltage change. Note that device runtime PM is not concerned with the CPU, which is an orthogonal research problem [6] addressed by other OS subsystems, e.g., `cpufreq` and `cpuidle` in Linux.

Although device runtime PM has been recognized as vital [7] due to emerging always-on workloads, it is poorly implemented in commodity OSes such as Linux. In this paper, we highlight the shortcomings of Linux device runtime PM: as SoCs appear in the market, their device runtime PM support is often long overdue, and is likely to be minimal when finally implemented.

The root cause of these problems is that today's commodity OSes hold drivers responsible for PM. To understand this problem, we identify three pieces of information as essential to runtime PM: (*i*) the Quality of Service (QoS) requirements, such as device wakeup latency, (*ii*) characteristics of hardware low-power states, such as power consumption and (*iii*) whether there are pending tasks for the device, that is, tasks buffered either in the driver or in the device. While (*i*) and (*ii*) are conveniently available to the OS, Linux obtains (*iii*) by relying on drivers' correct behaviors in invoking runtime PM API, as shown in Figure 1(a). This reliance effectively makes the runtime PM driver-directed.

As SoC design life cycles tighten and the software/hardware stack bloats, we consider driver-directed PM to be harmful. We argue for an architectural overhaul as shown in Figure 1(b): introducing a central OS component, or central PM agent, to relieve device drivers from their runtime PM responsibilities. To build a central PM agent, our key insight is that the above information (*iii*) can be made available without the help of device drivers. We present two alternative ways to infer this information: using software to monitor device register access or adding one register bit to the device for exposing device busy/idle status.

Built atop the two alternative inference approaches, the central PM agent is effective. Under interactive workloads that frequently exercise the devices, it can automatically put the devices into the disabled mode over 77% of the time. Compared to manual, fine-tuned PM that already exists in a couple of Linux drivers, this disabled time is only 3.3 percentage points less. The central PM agent incurs very low overhead: in our FPGA-based implementation, the added hardware register introduces at most 34 gates as estimated by the synthesis tool; the device performance loss is unnoticeable.

To ease driver development under the *current* PM framework, we further develop a best-effort tool called PowerAdvisor. It observes the target driver's behaviors in test runs, and advises developers on where to add calls to runtime PM API in source code. We show that PowerAdvisor is effective: it discovers previously unknown locations for adding PM in a complicated display controller driver with 22 thousand lines of code.

In summary, this paper makes three major contributions:

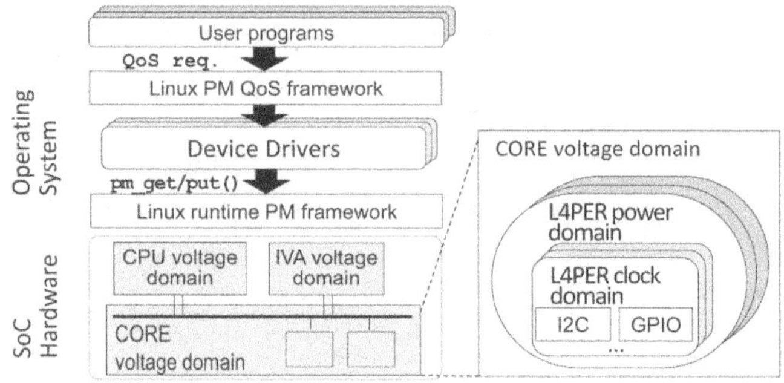

Figure 2: Hardware PM infrastructure in SoC (as exemplified by OMAP4) and the Linux PM frameworks

- We experimentally show that device runtime PM can be effectively done outside of drivers, either using a software approach based on existing hardware, or using software with small hardware support.
- A complete design and implementation of the central PM agent, whose performance is comparable with manual runtime PM code in Linux device drivers.
- PowerAdvisor, a tool that effectively simplifies the development of runtime PM in drivers under the current Linux framework.

All source code and trace data used in this paper can be downloaded from `http://www.recg.org`.

2. Background

Other than a powerful, multicore CPU, a modern SoC integrates tens of hardware devices from computational devices like GPU and face detection integrated circuit, to controllers for I/O like I2C and display. These devices are connected together via on-chip interconnects, and expose functions to the CPU via their registers. As shown in Figure 2, device runtime PM on SoC is a collaboration between hardware and software.

2.1 Hardware PM Infrastructure

We next sketch the hardware support for PM available on SoCs. Although our descriptions are based on our understanding of the TI OMAP4, a popular mobile SoC with abundant public information [2], we observe similar hardware support on other SoCs [1, 3, 4, 8–12].

A Hierarchy of Domains Device is the basic unit of power management from the perspective of software. A device can be configured by software to be in either ENABLED or DISABLED mode: it is functional only when it is ENABLED, and when DISABLED, it stops receiving clocks to conserve energy. Note that software, e.g., device drivers, only decides when to disable a device, leaving the rest of the power management decisions to hardware. To save chip area, devices on an SoC may share clocks and power supplies. This effectively organizes all devices into a hierarchy of domains.

Table 1: Device drivers of SoC families and the delay (in months) between the driver initial release and the implementation of runtime PM. Asterisks indicate the absence of fine-grained runtime PM at the time of writing (Jan. 2015).

Driver	Delay	Driver	Delay
OMAP UART	12 [13]	Exynos Keypad	18 [14]
OMAP WDT	22 [15]	Exynos USB	14 [16]
OMAP USB	45 [17]	OMAP GPIO	32 [18]
i.MX SD Ctrl	37 [19]	i.MX I2C	9 [20]
Tegra SD Ctrl	48 *	i.MX SPI	31 [21]

- A *clock domain* is a group of devices sharing the same clock source. A domain-level clock gating shuts down the clock source, putting the clock domain as INACTIVE and resulting in further energy saving.
- A *power domain* encompasses one or more clock domains. Its devices are powered by the same power rails controlled by the same switch. The domain could either be ON, RETENTION (a subset of transistors are on to preserve hardware state) or OFF (all transistors are off and hardware state is lost).
- A *voltage domain* encompasses one or more power domains. Its devices share the same voltage source controlled by the same regulator. It can be either ON, SLEEP (supplying regular voltage, but limited current), RETENTION (supplying minimum voltage for preserving hardware state) or OFF (voltage drops to zero).

For these domains, software only chooses the target low-power states (e.g., RETENTION, OFF); hardware decides when to perform the actual state transitions, as discussed below. Notably domains introduce inter-device dependence in runtime PM, because for a domain to enter a low-power state, all its devices must be disabled.

Global Power Manager Global power manager is a special on-chip hardware device that coordinates devices and domains in performing power state transitions. It sets a domain to a low-power state if all encompassed devices of the domain have been configured by software as DISABLED; it brings the domain back to a high-power state if any encompassed device is configured by software as ENABLED. The manager is always on. Even when the entire SoC has been suspended, it listens for external events and wakes up the SoC accordingly.

2.2 Linux Support for Device Runtime PM

Linux, like other OSes, plays two key roles in device runtime PM. Note that the Linux community often abbreviates device runtime PM as *runtime PM*. We will respect the convention when describing the related Linux API.

First, the *Linux runtime PM framework* provides generic set of API for device drivers to track the number of concurrent users of a device in the form of a per-device reference counter. When the reference counter drops to zero, the framework calls a driver callback to set the device to DISABLED. Built under this framework, a device driver should never directly change device modes. Instead, it is responsible for making runtime PM calls, `pm_get()` and `pm_put()`, which increase and decrease the reference counter respectively. In a well-designed driver, the reference counter will reach zero whenever there is no pending task for the device, neither buffered inside the driver nor in the device.

Second, the *PM QoS frameworks* allow users to express QoS requirements (e.g., wakeup latency) to be met by the OS. The device driver is responsible for mapping such QoS requirements to driver parameters, such as timeout value before disabling the device, or hardware configurations, such as the target low-power state of the encompassing domain.

This work aims at replacing the Linux runtime PM framework but retains compatibility with the PM QoS frameworks.

3. Driver-directed PM Considered Harmful

As discussed above, the current Linux runtime PM is essentially driver-directed: its correctness and efficiency fully depend on a driver properly maintaining its reference counter. For modern SoCs, we consider this approach harmful. In this section, we provide three reasons and elaborate upon each with a real-world case.

Runtime PM often supported after long delay. Driver developers almost always consider functionality as their first priority, leaving PM as an afterthought. While many drivers keep receiving new functionality over time, they get stuck for a long time with preliminary, coarse-grained PM. Proper PM support, if any, appears much later than the driver's initial release.

Real-world Case: Samsung Exynos SPI controller

The SPI controller driver for the Exynos family had preliminary PM code for 25 months after its first commit [22]. The preliminary PM, as shown in Listing 1, is very coarse-grained and saves no energy at run time. It simply enables the SPI controller in `probe()`, which is invoked during system boot, and disables it in `remove()`, which is invoked during system shutdown, keeping the SPI controller on as long as the CPU is on. The much delayed patch shown in Listing 2 fixed the problem with a finer-grained PM, which only keeps the controller enabled for configuration and transmission tasks. More cases are listed in Table 1.

Complex drivers make it hard to do runtime PM. Many devices on modern SoCs are complex. So are the drivers that harness the hardware. The complexity makes it hard for developers to reason about how a driver works and write correct PM code accordingly.

Real-world Case: OMAP4 display controller driver

The display controller in modern SoC is notoriously complex. The OMAP4 technical reference manual [2] dedi-

```
int s3c64xx_spi_probe(platform_device
    *pdev)
{
  /* allocate controller resources...*/
  pm_runtime_get_sync(dev);
  /*initialize the controller...*/
}

int s3c64xx_spi_remove(platform_device
    *pdev)
{
  /* deinitialize controller...*/
  pm_runtime_put(dev);
  /* free controller resources...*/
}
```

Listing 1: Preliminary PM that has existed in the Exynos SPI driver for more than two years.

```
void s3c64xx_spi_work(work_struct *work)
{
  pm_runtime_get_sync(dev);
  while (!list_empty(queue)) {
    /* transmitting message... */
  }
  pm_runtime_put(dev);
}

int s3c64xx_spi_setup(spi_device *spi)
{
  pm_runtime_get_sync(dev);
  /* set up SPI, like tx rate... */
  pm_runtime_put(dev);
}
```

Listing 2: Hand-tuned PM in the Exynos SPI driver after patching [22].

cates 565 pages to the display controller. The corresponding Linux driver consists of 22K SLoC, featuring extensive asynchronous execution (e.g., bottom-halves for completing frame composition) and tens of callbacks. Not surprisingly, the Linux driver only has preliminary power management, leaving the controller ENABLED as long as the screen is on. In our own attempts to patch the driver with finer-grained PM, we found it very difficult, if not impossible, to manually identify where in the driver source code to add runtime PM calls while still keeping the reference counter balanced in various interleavings of execution paths.

Inter-device dependence amplifies the impact of bad drivers Because the state of a domain depends on the state of all its encompassed devices (§2.1), one device that is mistakenly left on will prevent the entire domain from entering a low-power state, ruining the PM efforts of other drivers.

Real-world Case: OMAP4 UART controller

During one entire year after its first release, the OMAP4 UART controller driver did no power management, keeping the whole L4_PER power domain on as long as the CPU was on [13]. Although the ENABLED UART controller consumes a relatively small amount of power, the L4_PER domain drains 17 mW more power for not being able to enter the default low-power state RETENTION, leading to significant runtime inefficiency.

4. Fundamental PM Information

To fix the problems caused by driver-directed PM, we identify information that is essential to device runtime PM. Note that much research focuses on optimizing PM policy by exploiting complex workloads information [23–25]. Unlike these research works, the policy of Linux PM is simple, as has been discussed in §2.2. It requires the following three pieces of information:

(*i*) The QoS requirements supplied by users, such as wakeup latency.

(*ii*) Specifications of power states, including their power consumption, and the latency and energy consumption for transition between states.

(*iii*) Whether a device has pending tasks: only after a device has finished *all* pending tasks that are buffered in the driver and in the device, can the device be DISABLED. When there is a new pending task for a disabled device, the device needs to be enabled. Note that the functionality of a device is not broken if it is disabled after finishing *one* task and enabled before handling the next one, as long as the driver preserves and then restores the device context, respectively. However, this incurs unnecessary overhead due to power-state transition. Therefore, a good PM policy keeps the device enabled until it finishes *all* pending tasks.

We observe that (*i*) is provided by the user of the device, e.g., user-space software or other dependent device drivers. (*ii*) is static information and is available offline, either from the vendor or by profiling.

The Linux PM infers (*iii*) from the value of the reference counter (whether it is zero), and relies on the driver to properly invoke runtime PM API to maintain the reference counter. This approach incurs high development burden [26] and is error-prone as has been discussed in §3.

Our key insight is that information (*iii*) can be made available without device drivers' efforts. We next demonstrate that it can be inferred by monitoring memory access, or with small modification to device hardware.

5. Pending Task Inference

As discussed above, knowing if a device has pending tasks is key to its runtime power management. In this section, we present two alternative ways to acquire this knowledge outside device drivers, i.e., without device drivers' support: (*i*) a software-only approach that infers the knowledge by monitor memory access, and (*ii*) a small modification, a register bit, to device hardware that exposes whether the device is busy or idle.

5.1 Software-based Inference

The software approach infers if there are pending tasks by monitoring device register access initiated by the CPU. More specifically, it is based on the following two insights:

1. If CPU has not accessed a device's registers for a period of time longer than a threshold $T_{threshold}$, it is safe to assert that the device has no pending task.

   Taking I2C transmission as an example: the device registers are frequently accessed until the task is completed. In preparing sending a message, the CPU writes to the controller's registers for configuring speed mode, message length, etc. When the message is being transmitted, the controller frequently interrupts the CPU to provide updates, e.g., FIFO status, and the CPU accesses the controller's registers to examine and clear the interrupts.

2. On ARM-based SoCs, the memory protection mechanism can be used to effectively detect device register access. This is because ARM maps all device registers in the global physical address space. Therefore, CPU's accesses to device registers will go through MMU, and can be captured as memory exceptions when required.

The choice of $T_{threshold}$ We face a trade off in choosing $T_{threshold}$: with a smaller value of $T_{threshold}$, the software approach can infer in a more timely manner if a device has pending tasks and can capture shorter periods in which a device has no pending task. Thus, a smaller $T_{threshold}$ leads to more aggressive PM; however, to avoid false report of no pending task, $T_{threshold}$ needs to be greater than the largest possible interval between register accesses when a device has pending tasks. According to our observation of mobile SoCs, the largest interval appears when a DMA transaction is in progress. Given that the typical mobile SoC memory bandwidth is a few hundred MB/s to a few GB/s, we choose $T_{threshold}$=100 ms which is much larger than the time for a 4 MB transfer, a typical maximum size of contiguous memory allocation in Linux. We will evaluate our choice in §7.1.

Applicability of Insight 1 Insight 1 applies to most, but not all types of devices. The deciding factor is whether, for a given device, the length of a processing period without register access is bounded such that Insight 1 holds. For I/O devices the length of such periods is bounded by the longest DMA transaction as discussed above. For accelerators with periodic tasks, the length of such periods is bounded as well: for example, the OMAP4 face detection device interrupts the CPU upon finishing each frame, which happens every 33ms. However, this is not the case for complex computational units, such as GPU or DSP, whose processing duration can be unbounded in theory.

Limitations Although effective and immediately deployable, we recognize that the software approach has the following limitations: (*i*) it is less aggressive than the PM code in device drivers, as the device always lingers in ENABLED after there has been no pending task for $T_{threshold}$, which is lower bounded by the largest register access interval; (*ii*) it incurs memory exceptions, which comes with overhead, though small, as evaluated in §7.1.

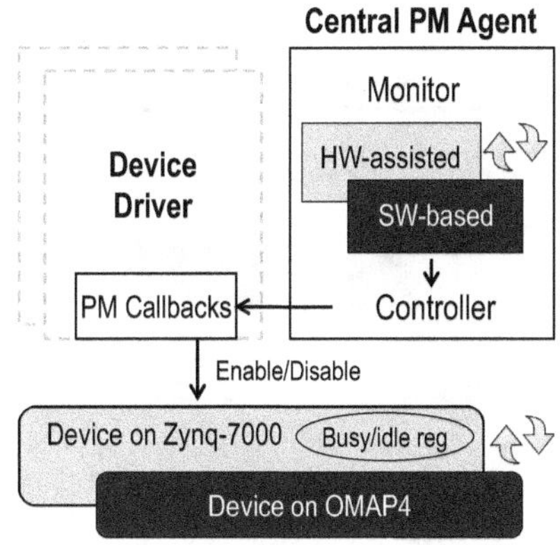

Figure 3: The structure of the Central PM agent, a concrete design following the conceptual model shown in Figure 1(b). The monitor employs one of the two ways for pending task inference, which are prototyped on two respective SoCs.

5.2 Hardware-assisted Inference

In order to avoid the limitations of the software approach, we find that small hardware modifications will suffice: a busy/idle register bit per device.

By polling this register bit periodically, the OS can estimate how long a device has been idle and then infer whether a device has pending tasks. Note that even if a device has been idle for only a few milliseconds, the OS can be certain that the device has no pending task because a device always starts processing pending tasks immediately after finishing the current one. Hence, by applying a small polling period, the OS can infer if a device has pending tasks in a timely manner, which enables more aggressive PM than the software approach in §5.1 does. Moreover, the polling does not incur memory exceptions and is thus more lightweight.

The modifications can be easily implemented on modern SoC hardware. A device already possesses the knowledge on whether it is busy processing a task or not: in its implementation, a device hardware is typically designed as a state machine using a hardware description language. Among all possible states, a subset represent the device being idle. Therefore, the busy/idle register is essentially a mapping from these states to a single bit.

6. Central PM Agent

With the pending task information inferred, we can realize device runtime PM of all applicable devices in a single kernel module, called *central PM agent*. The central PM agent relieves driver developers from reasoning where to insert runtime PM calls in driver source code (§2.2). In this section, we first describe the overall structure of the central

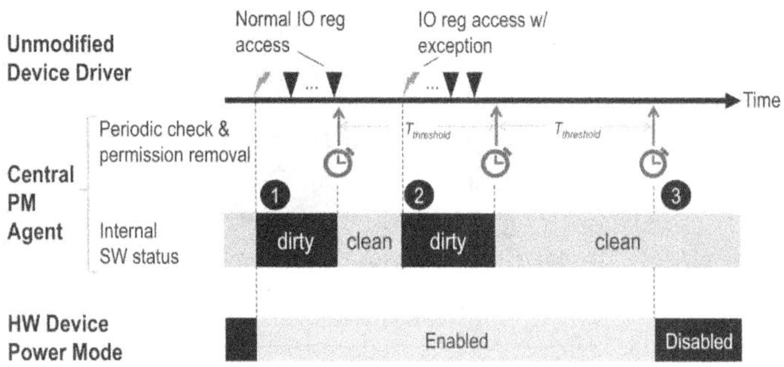

Figure 4: An example timeline of central PM agent execution, which infers the existence of pending tasks using the software-based approach.

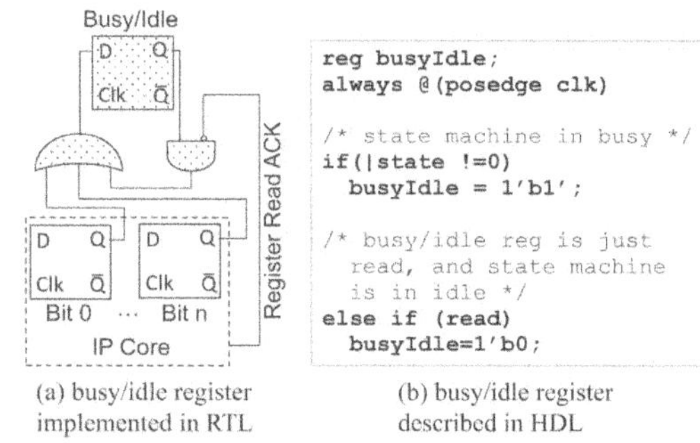

(a) busy/idle register implemented in RTL

(b) busy/idle register described in HDL

Figure 5: Example implementation of the one-bit busy/idle register, (a) in several tens of gates and (b) in several lines of code in Verilog.

PM agent and then how the software and hardware-assisted solutions for pending task inference fit in the design.

6.1 Overall Structure

As shown in Figure 3, the central PM agent consists of two major components: the monitor and the controller. The monitor infers whether a device has pending tasks, which can be implemented in software on top of the existing hardware or with the assistance of the busy/idle register bit. Based on the monitor output, the controller calls the PM callbacks provided by the driver to set the device to ENABLED/DISABLED mode.

6.2 Software Pending Task Monitor

The software pending task monitor is based on the insights presented in §5.1: a device has no pending task if CPU has not accessed its registers for $T_{threshold}$. Every $T_{threshold}$ period, the monitor checks if a device's registers have been accessed since the last check, i.e., in the past $T_{threshold}$. In order to do so, the monitor maintains a per-device software status: `dirty` means that CPU has accessed the device's registers since the last check; `clean` otherwise.

Figure 4 illustrates how the central PM agent works for a device through an example timeline. During initialization, the monitor sets the software status to `clean` and sets up a check timer that will fire every $T_{threshold}$ interval.

Every time the timer fires, the monitor does two things. First, it checks the software status: `clean` (❸) indicates that none of the device's registers have been accessed in the past $T_{threshold}$. Based on Insight 1 in §5.1, the monitor concludes that the device has no pending task, and notifies the controller to disable the device. If the status is `dirty`, the monitor simply sets it to `clean`.

Second, the monitor invalidates the page table entries that correspond to the device's registers, so the next access to any of these registers will trigger memory exception, which will be handled by the central PM agent. This is based on Insight 2 in §5.1.

A memory exception occurs upon the first access to any of the device's registers since last check. The monitor handles the exception and sets the software status to `dirty`, indicating that an access has occurred. Then it checks the device mode: if DISABLED (❶), the monitor notifies the controller to enable the device; otherwise, if the device is already ENABLED (❷), the monitor takes no action. Finally, it validates the page table entries to allow further register access to pass through without incurring any exception.

Implementation on OMAP4 SoC We implement the central PM agent based on the above monitor design as a kernel module on the OMAP4 SoC. We choose OMAP4 because it has abundant public information.

6.3 Hardware-assisted Pending Task Monitor

We add the busy/idle register bit to existing devices, so that (*i*) the runtime PM can be more aggressive and (*ii*) the design of the monitor is simplified and incurs less overhead. We next describe how we design the busy/idle register and revise the design of the monitor accordingly.

Mapping device state machine to busy/idle register As discussed in §5.2, device hardware is described as state machines, with a subset of the states representing the device being idle. We design the semantics of the busy/idle register as follows:

The busy/idle register is set to busy when the state machine leaves the idle states; it resets to idle immediately after a read if the state machine is in an idle state when the read happens. Thus, if the register shows busy, it does not necessarily mean the device is busy at the moment. Instead, it indicates the device has been busy at least once since the last read of the busy/idle register. On the other hand, if the register shows idle, the device must have been idle since the last read of the busy/idle register.

Because the logic of a busy/idle register re-uses the state machine in the hardware, it requires very little hardware resources and development effort to implement. As the conceptual design in Figure 5(a) shows, aside from a busy/idle

Table 2: The cost of adding the busy/idle register. Development time is in man-hours. *unknown because Xilinx specific FPGA primitives cannot be synthesized to ASIC.

Module	Development Effort		FPGA Resources		ASIC Resources
	LoC	Time	LUTs	Registers	Gates
Xilinx I2C	93 (+1.2%)	12	16 (+3.8%)	8 (+2.4%)	N/A*
Opencores SPI	15 (+6%)	5	1 (+1.3%)	1 (+1.5%)	15 (+1.1%)
Opencores I2C	20 (+2%)	10	4 (1.8%)	1 (+0.6%)	34 (+1.6%)

register bit, the design merely requires several gates to extract the needed information from the state machine. Figure 5(b) shows that several lines of Verilog code suffice to describe the logic of the busy/idle register.

Using the busy/idle register Instead of triggering memory exceptions, the monitor polls the busy/idle register periodically to estimate how much time has elapsed since the completion of the most recent task. Based on this information, the monitor infers whether the device has pending tasks. As discussed in §5.2, a smaller polling period enables more aggressive PM. However, frequently polling the busy/idle register wastes CPU cycles and energy. In practice, we expect that a polling interval of tens of milliseconds is aggressive enough.

Implementation on Zynq-7000 SoC We choose Zynq [27] for using its on-chip FPGA to prototype the busy/idle register. Moreover, the FPGA has dedicated clocks that can be gated in software without affecting the rest of the system. We add a busy/idle register to an Xilinx I2C controller [28], and instantiate the modified I2C controller in the FPGA. We run the central PM agent on Zynq's CPU. As shown in Table 2, the development effort in modifying the I2C controller is small. The extra FPGA resources and the estimated number of extra gates required for ASIC implementation are also small. Note that our modification is largely unoptimized and the resource usage should be read as upper bounds.

In order to further experiment with the busy/idle register, we implement it by modifying an Opencores I2C controller [29] and an Opencores SPI controller [30] written in Verilog. As shown in Table 2, the involved development effort and extra resources are similarly small.

7. Evaluation

In the evaluation, we experimentally answer the following questions:

1. Can the central PM agent effectively save power, as compared to manual PM?
2. What is the associated runtime overhead introduced by the central PM agent?
3. Can the central PM agent correctly use the added busy/idle register?

7.1 Software Central PM

We evaluate the software central PM agent on Pandaboard Rev B2, which employs OMAP4460 SoC. It runs Linaro Android release 13.10. The kernel version is 3.2, the latest kernel that supports Android on OMAP SoC. Its driver code base receives contributions regularly from TI and Google.

7.1.1 Methodology

We use the central PM agent to automatically control four widely used and representative devices: the multimedia card (MMC) controller, the secure digital input/output (SDIO) controller, the I2C controller, and the display controller (DISPC). We use a trace collected from interacting with the Pandaboard to test the central PM agent. The trace is of 600 seconds and contains 48 user input events, including reading emails with the Android email application and browsing the web with the default Android browser. These activities exercise the drivers of the four devices extensively.

In running the benchmark for each device, we measure the total length of DISABLED periods. We run the benchmark with the central PM agent, and with the existing PM code if there is any.

7.1.2 Effectiveness of Central PM Agent

We show that the central PM agent is able to manage devices as effectively as the hand-tuned PM code in the MMC controller and I2C controller drivers: the difference in the disabled time is within 3.3 percentage points (with $T_{threshold}$=100 ms). Moreover, the central PM agent provides PM to the SDIO controller and DISPC drivers that lack PM code. We next describe the results for the four devices in detail.

MMC controller. On many embedded systems, the CPU accesses the root filesystem through a MMC controller. The Linux MMC controller driver comes with hand-tuned PM code. To examine how well the central PM agent works for it, we disable the PM code and run the benchmark, which generates extensive file operations (e.g., saving email attachment, application launch) to exercise the MMC controller driver. As shown in Figure 6(a), when $T_{threshold}$ is 100 ms, the central PM agent keeps the MMC controller in DISABLED for 77.2% of the time, which is only 3.3 percentage points less than the hand-tuned PM. If we aggressively reduce $T_{threshold}$ to 50 ms, the disabled time under the control of the central PM agent is actually 1.9 percentage points more, as the hand-tuned PM chooses to disable the controller after a 100 ms idle timeout.

I2C and SDIO controllers. The I2C and SDIO controllers on Pandaboard together bridge the CPU with the Wi-Fi interface. The I2C controller driver comes with hand-tuned PM; the SDIO driver does not, leaving the SDIO controller always on as long as the Wi-Fi interface is enabled, even when no data is being transmitted. The benchmark exercises

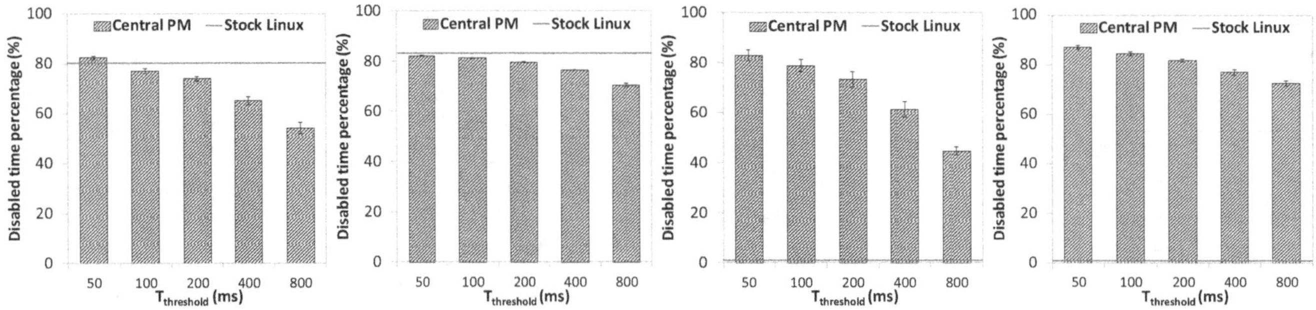

(a) MMC Controller (b) I2C Controller (c) SDIO Controller (d) Display Controller

Figure 6: Device DISABLED time with different $T_{threshold}$, with the default being 100 ms in this paper. The Linux stock drivers in (a) and (b) come with hand-tuned PM code while that of (c) and (d) does not. In (c) and (d), we have slightly shifted up the lines for Linux stock drivers to make them visible since they are 0. With $T_{threshold}$=100 ms, the central PM agent saves at most 17 mW by disabling (c) the SDIO controller, and 10 mW by disabling (d) the display controller.

the two drivers with rich network activities generated from web browsing and email fetch. The results are shown in Figure 6(b) and Figure 6(c). When $T_{threshold}$ is 100 ms, the central PM agent keeps I2C controller DISABLED for 81.2% of the time , which is only 2.1 percentage points less than the hand-tuned PM; the central PM agent keeps SDIO controller DISABLED for 78.8% of the time.

DISPC. The display controller, or DISPC, overlays multiple rendered frames into a final buffer that is co-located with the video output interface, HDMI in our setup. Its driver comes with no runtime PM, keeping DISPC ENABLED as long as the display is on, missing the power-saving opportunity when the displayed image is still and DISPC has no task. The results are shown in Figure 6(d). When $T_{threshold}$ is 100 ms, the central PM agent keeps the DISPC DISABLED for 84.5% of the time.

Impact of $T_{threshold}$. When $T_{threshold}$ is larger than 100 ms, the time in which the central PM agent keeps the four devices in DISABLED state decreases noticeably. With a larger $T_{threshold}$, a device not only lingers in a high-power state for longer time after the last task is finished, but also misses power-saving opportunities for periods without pending tasks but shorter than $T_{threshold}$. We have also tried a reduced $T_{threshold}$ of 50 ms, which at most leads to a trivial 5.2% increase of device DISABLED time. We believe this is because most periods without pending tasks are longer than 50 ms. Hence, we choose $T_{threshold}$=100 ms as the default value, which is safe as stated in §5.1.

7.1.3 Estimated Overall Energy Saving

We have shown that the central PM agent provides effective runtime PM to drivers that lack PM code, i.e., the SDIO controller and DISPC. We next show that the resulting energy savings are significant.

We measure the power consumed by the two devices by physically sampling current on power rails [31]. By disabling the DISPC, the central PM agent saves 10 mW. Although the SDIO controller itself consumes very little power, disabling it saves 17 mW because an enabled SDIO controller blocks the encompassing power domain from entering RETENTION.

The resulting energy savings are significant, estimated from smartphone daily usage reported in LiveLab [32]. For the SDIO controller, the stock driver keeps it always ENABLED as long as the user has not manually switched off the Wi-Fi; compared to the stock driver, the central PM agent saves up to 71.4 mWh daily which extends the standby time by 2.4 hours. For the DISPC, the stock driver keeps it always ENABLED as long as the screen is on; compared to the stock driver, the central PM agent saves around 18.5 mWh daily, which extends the standby time by 0.6 hours. Given that a smartphone usually lasts for 0.7 to 2 days with average use [33], extending the standby time by a total of 3 hours is a significant gain. We note the LiveLab data was collected about four years ago; the gain would be more if the user uses the smartphone more because runtime PM saves power when the system is in use. We further estimate that the relative gain may be considerably higher on systems like Google Glass that use a similar SoC but have lower overall power consumption due to smaller displays.

7.1.4 Overhead of Central PM Agent

The central PM agent incurs very small overhead at run time, which mainly comes from the memory exceptions introduced by software inference. By using CPU performance counters, we measure that each memory exception takes around 2500 cycles, which is 8 µs if the CPU is at the lowest frequency 300 MHz. Note this overhead occurs only once for each device every $T_{threshold}$, which is typically 100 ms.

To understand the impact of this overhead, we stress the SD card (backed by the MMC controller) and the Wi-Fi interface (backed by the SDIO and I2C controllers) and measure the performance loss due to the central PM agent.

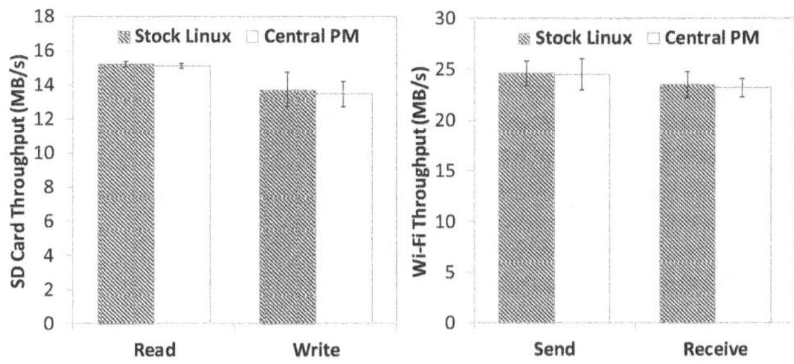

(a) SD Card Throughput (b) Wi-Fi Throughput

Figure 7: Performance of devices managed by central PM agent under stress tests, as compared to the stock Linux.

All results are averaged over 10 iterations. To stress the SD card, we invoke `dd` to read/write a 100MB file. We force dropping pagecache before each read test and use the `fdatasync` option in the write test. To stress the Wi-Fi interface, we use *iperf* [34] to measure the maximum TCP throughput. We run each iteration for 10 seconds, and manually interleave two types of runs (with and without the central PM agent) to exclude the impact of possible wireless signal fluctuation. As shown in Figure 7, the throughput loss due to the central PM agent is smaller than the standard deviations and thus negligible, for both the SD card and the Wi-Fi interface.

7.2 Hardware-assisted Central PM

We prototype the hardware-assisted central PM agent on the Zynq SoC. As described in §6.3, we instantiate the modified I2C controller on Zynq's FPGA. We then develop test software running on Zynq's CPU to validate that the busy/idle register has the expected behavior. We further connect Zynq with an external accelerometer [35] over the I2C bus. Managed by the central PM agent, Zynq can communicate with the accelerometer correctly, showing that the central PM agent supported by our busy/idle register is working without breaking any device functionality. In addition, our effort in bringing up the central PM agent on Zynq is small.

8. PowerAdvisor for PM Code Suggestion

So far we have argued for an overhaul to the Linux PM. Can we simplify driver development under the *current* runtime PM framework without such an overhaul? To answer this question, we build PowerAdvisor, a software tool that suggests where to add runtime PM calls in existing driver source code. Consisting of an instrumenter and an offline analyzer, the tool analyzes historical execution trace and makes suggestions accordingly.

Figure 8 shows the workflow of PowerAdvisor. A developer first instruments the driver with the tool. In test runs, the developer exercises the instrumented driver with various user workloads. The instrumented driver will generate a trace; the analyzer then examines the trace and outputs a list of source locations where `pm_get()` or `pm_put()` shall be inserted.

8.1 Division of Responsibility between PowerAdvisor and Developers

PowerAdvisor is best-effort. It greatly simplifies, but does not completely relieve driver developers from, PM efforts. It provides the following guarantees to the developer. If the driver were patched with the suggested runtime PM calls, in the test run from which the trace has been generated:

G1 During any no-pending-task period (that is, any period longer than $T_{threshold}$ during which no device register access occurs, as described in Insight 2 in §5.1), the PM reference counter would remain as zero, implying that the hardware device remains DISABLED.

G2 At the moment of any device register access, the reference counter would be above zero, implying that the hardware device is ENABLED at that moment.

Given the guarantees, the developers need to further reason about the following two questions:

Will the added PM code break device functionality? PowerAdvisor cannot guarantee that the suggested PM calls will not break device functionality. This is due to the incompleteness of the tool's knowledge about device internals: although the tool can safely assume that no task is being processed in a device during no-pending-task periods, at an arbitrary moment *outside* of such periods, it has no visibility into the device to decide if a task is being processed there. Note that the tool cannot assume that the device has to be always ENABLED outside of no-pending-task periods, a constraint so strong that it suppresses useful suggestions.

Will the added runtime PM calls be effective in future executions? PowerAdvisor makes suggestions purely based on historical observations. The above two guarantees only apply to the trace it has observed; developers need to reason if the PM code is effective under different execution paths.

We believe it is feasible to reason about the two questions above in practice. For the first question, as the number of suggested PM calls is usually moderate, reasoning about whether these calls break device functionality is often tractable. For the second question, moderately extending the length of test runs and increasing workload variation is effective. For instance, a test run longer than a few minutes is often sufficient for the tool to reproduce hand-tuned PM. Furthermore, symbolic execution tools, such as KLEE [36], are able to produce high-coverage test runs. Because of these, we believe PowerAdvisor as a best-effort tool is useful in practice. We will show experimental evidences in §8.3.

8.2 PowerAdvisor Internals

For suggesting runtime PM calls, PowerAdvisor considers the following candidate locations:

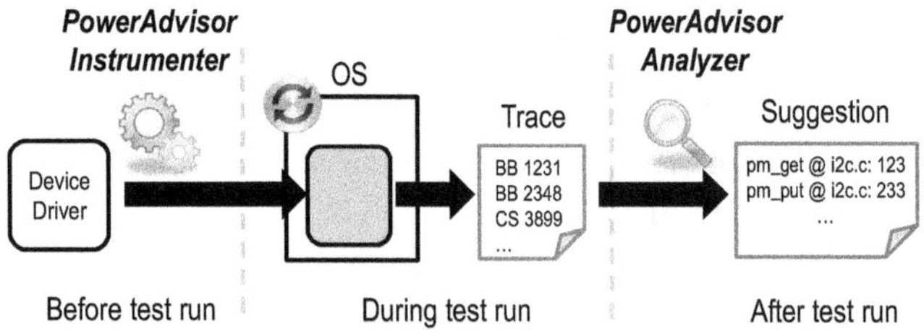

Figure 8: The workflow of PowerAdvisor

- `pm_get()`: the *start* of any basic block that contains device register access; the location *before* call sites that may lead to device register access.
- `pm_put()`: the *end* of any basic block that contains device register access; the location *after* call sites that may lead to device register access.

The choice of these candidate locations is based on the following rationale. Intuitively, the tool should consider the start and the end of basic blocks that contain device register access to fulfill G1 and G2 in §8.1. Furthermore, as one of such basic blocks may be included in various execution paths, we want the tool to be able to insert runtime PM calls that only affect a subset of these paths. On the other hand, we need to limit the number of candidate locations and make the resulting problem tractable. As a trade-off, we choose to instrument all call sites that may lead to such basic blocks.

8.2.1 Inserting Tracepoints

At compile time, the driver is firstly compiled as Intermediate Representation (IR). The instrumenter's job is to insert trace points into the driver IR to collect runtime information about candidate locations for PM calls.

To do so, the instrumenter first marks basic blocks that contain device register access, and call sites that may lead to the functions that contain device register access. This is a fairly easy job, as Linux kernel uses dedicated macros to encapsulate device register access.

With the markings, the instrumenter inserts trace points at four types of code locations: the start and the end of each marked basic block, and the locations before and after each marked call site. The instrumenter statically assigns each tracepoint a unique identifier that can be retrieved at run time.

8.2.2 Collecting Trace

As shown in Figure 8, in a test run, whenever a tracepoint is reached by the control flow, it appends its identifier into an global trace buffer. In addition, an entry for a no-pending-task period is inserted in the same buffer when the interval between two consecutive tracepoints is larger than $T_{threshold}$. This is done by a small piece of code added to the kernel.

After the test run, the resulting trace is a sequence of tracepoint identifiers delimited by no-pending-task periods.

8.2.3 Analyzing Trace

Overall, the PowerAdvisor analyzer looks for legal PM calls that, when applied to the collected trace, satisfy the guarantees in §8.1. The analyzer translates the problem into a Satisfiability Modulo Theories (SMT) problem, with the linear integer arithmetic as the background theory. It establishes SMT constraints based on the trace, and invokes the Z3 SMT solver [37] to identify the PM calls that should be inserted.

We next briefly describe the SMT problem in an informal way. All variables in the SMT problem correspond to the candidate PM call locations that have appeared in the trace, which are the union of four subsets: the start (S_{BB_GET}) and the end (S_{BB_PUT}) of the marked basic blocks, before (S_{CS_GET}) and after (S_{CS_PUT}) the marked call sites:

$$V = S_{BB\_GET} \cup S_{BB\_PUT} \cup S_{CS\_GET} \cup S_{CS\_PUT} \quad (1)$$

We define the possible values of the SMT variables as the delta applied to the reference counter by the corresponding PM calls.

$$\begin{aligned} &\forall v \in S_{BB\_GET} \cup S_{CS\_GET}, v \in \{0, 1\} \\ &\forall v \in S_{BB\_PUT} \cup S_{CS\_PUT}, v \in \{0, -1\} \end{aligned} \quad (2)$$

The analyzer further translates the collected trace into a set of SMT constraints. In order to do so, the analyzer first splits the trace into multiple subsequences delimited by no-pending-task periods, and generates constraints from each subsequence.

We next zoom in on one subsequence $Q = \{q_i\}_{i=1..N}$. According to our discussion of trace collection, each element of the subsequence is an appearance of one SMT variable in V. A SMT variable from V might appear one or multiple times in Q.

Based on Q, the analyzer asserts the following two sets of constraints that are directly mapped to the two guarantees G1 and G2 in §8.1. First, G1 requires the reference counter to be zero in the no-pending-task period following the subsequence. That is, all `pm_get()` and `pm_put()` in the subsequence are balanced.

$$\sum_{q_i \in Q} q_i = 0 \quad (3)$$

Second, G2 requires the device to be enabled when the control flow enters any basic block containing device register access, i.e., the PM reference counter to be larger than zero.

$$\forall j \in \{1...N\}, \text{if } q_j \in S_{BB\_GET}, \text{then } \sum_{i=1}^{j} q_i > 0 \quad (4)$$

Note that the analyzer generates the constraints (3) and (4) for all subsequences in the trace.

At last, the analyzer minimizes the number of introduced PM calls $C = \sum_{v_i \in V} |v_i|$.

In order to do so, the analyzer assigns different constants to C, from the smallest possible value $C = 2$ upward, and invokes the SMT solver on each resulting SMT problem. It stops when a solution is found.

Table 3: Driver traces used in evaluating PowerAdvisor. *#NPT stands for the number of no-pending-task periods.

Device	Trace			SMT Problem	
	Time (s)	#Entries	#NPT*	#Vars	#Constraints
MMC ctrl.	50.2	20,000	19	58	4,930
I2C ctrl.	33.9	5,000	13	32	1,480
SDIO ctrl.	24.4	5,000	78	14	1,708
DISPC	183.2	679,915	275	294	126,274

With the found solution, the analyzer maps the SMT variables with non-zero values to the corresponding source lines, and suggests that the developer insert PM calls there.

We note that the above SMT problem can be expressed as a Integer Linear Programming problem and solved more efficiently by an linear programming solver like CPLEX [38]. In our prototype of PowerAdvisor, we use the Z3 SMT solver because we are more familiar with it.

8.3 Evaluation of PowerAdvisor

We experimentally show that the PowerAdvisor can offer useful and correct suggestions. To do so, we study the drivers of the four devices used in §7.1. We generate driver traces by using the Android system to browse the web and navigate among multiple applications; for validating the suggested PM code, we replay the user trace described in §7.1 on the Android system.

Statistics of collected driver traces and resulting SMT problems are shown in Table 3. Note that the driver trace for the DISPC is much longer as its driver is significantly more complex than others.

As mentioned in §7.1, the drivers of the MMC and I2C controllers come with hand-tuned PM code, which has been removed by us before the test runs. Based on the driver traces, PowerAdvisor suggests PM calls identical to the hand-tuned code.

The drivers of the SDIO controller and DISPC come with no PM code. For the SDIO controller driver, PowerAdvisor suggests two pairs of `pm_get()` and `pm_put()`, which disable the SDIO controller for more than 85% of the time in the validation run. For the DISPC driver, whose complexity defeated our attempts of manually adding PM code, PowerAdvisor discovers a pair of `pm_get()/pm_put()` to be invoked when any interrupt handler is registered and unregistered, respectively. With the suggested PM code applied, the driver is able to disable the display controller for 90.5% of the time during the validation run. We further stress-test the driver with continuous animation on the screen. The driver runs for more than 48 hours without breaking the device functionality, and correctly disables the device in no-pending-task periods.

9. Related Work

Power management (PM) is critical not only to system efficiency but also to performance as we enter the dark silicon era [39]. We roughly categorize prior PM works into system suspension management and runtime PM. We also discuss model checking and code synthesis tools that are related to PowerAdvisor.

System suspension management. In system suspension, most SoC components (including CPU) are off, leaving on only the necessary circuitry for wakeup. Although effective and popular, system suspension challenges software to properly and timely drive hardware in and out of the suspension state. Android opportunistically suspends the entire SoC if no user interaction has occurred recently. In addition, it allows applications to override this policy by holding wakelocks. This relies on application developers for correct PM, leading to many power bugs, e.g., no-sleep [40] and sleep conflict [41], and has stirred up long debates in the Linux community [42]. Many have suggested ways to detect power bugs due to wakelock misuse, e.g., by detecting abnormal energy-hungry phases in applications [43], monitoring I/O bus traffic [41], and static analysis of source code [40]. Notably, the static analysis techniques used by Pathak et al. [40] only work well for programs having single entry/exit point. Unfortunately, device drivers usually have multiple entry/exit points, e.g., callbacks registered with various Linux frameworks and interrupt handlers. Moreover, the static analysis techniques only handle wakelocks that are not reference counted, while the Linux runtime PM framework indeed relies on reference counters. In contrast, our PowerAdvisor is based on execution trace generated from test runs and thus is not subject to the limitations discussed above.

Runtime power management. The goal of runtime PM is to reduce power consumption when the system is still in use.

Runtime PM for Computational Unit: A rich set of works focus on matching the performance of computational units, e.g., CPU or GPU, with the expectation of given workloads. Vertigo[6] uses a hierarchy of performance-setting algorithms to choose the CPU operating point for interactive applications. The Process Cruise Control framework [44] and the Koala framework [45] adjust the CPU performance for given workloads according to the workloads characteristics captured with performance counters. Pathania *et al.* adjust the performance point of CPU and GPU together according to 3D game workloads history to save energy [46]. Gupta *et al.* point out that the power consumed by uncore components, e.g., memory controller, should be considered in making runtime PM decisions for the CPU [47].

Runtime PM for Device: Device runtime PM aims at disabling individual devices that are not in use when the system is in use. Compared to system suspension, device runtime PM is finer-grained and can leverage more power-saving opportunities. If done properly, device runtime PM can bring the power consumption by an SoC to as low as system suspension does [42] while allowing the system to remain responsive to external events. It is recognized by the Linux kernel community that device runtime PM is becoming increasingly important as more always-on applications emerge on personal computing devices [7].

The central challenge to device runtime PM is to turn off unused devices in a timely manner. This is difficult as the OS and the SoC hardware are complicated. Intel engineers report great engineering efforts in implementing runtime PM for their Medfield SoC. They also advocate hardware-supplied information for detecting pending tasks [26]. ICEM [48] integrates PM code into locks for device drivers. However, the approach only focuses on a specific class of device drivers ("shared drivers") which is uncommon in Linux for modern SoCs, according to our observation. Anand *et al.*[49] propose a new I/O API for applications to disclose hints for better device PM. Although sharing the similar goal of device runtime PM with such prior work, we seek to maintain the existing Linux API and are not restricted to a subset of devices. In a previous paper [50], we present a preliminary implementation and the results of the software central PM agent.

Formal methods and synthesis tools. PowerAdvisor (§8) is related to software tools that use formal methods for bug finding or code synthesis. However, these tools, when applied to PM, cannot make the developer's task much easier. Model checking tools like CBMC [51] and symbolic execution tools like KLEE [36] can be used to verify if a device is disabled when the control flow reaches given source code locations. However, it is up to the developers to manually identify those locations where the device must have no pending task. In theory, automatic device driver synthesis tools like Termite [52] can synthesize PM code given formal device specifications, either derived from the documentation or RTL (register transfer level) description of a device. However, it is unclear whether deriving such formal specifications is any easier, if not harder, than writing driver PM code.

10. Concluding Remarks

How far can hardware PM support go? We have shown that a small hardware modification (§5.2) can go a long way. However, shifting the runtime PM responsibility entirely to hardware is unwise as it may result in much higher hardware complexity: (*i*) each device must fully preserve its hardware context before hitting off, possibly by implementing a RETENTION state, instead of relying on the software to preserve the hardware context; (*ii*) each device must be capable of interpreting various PM QoS requests expressed by users.

How general is the central PM agent? As mentioned in §5.1, the central PM agent is applicable to an SoC device as long as it is (*i*) memory-mapped, (*ii*) with bounded register-access interval. Additionally, if an SoC device serves as a slave in a communication protocol, e.g., an I2C slave, then it has to be (*iii*) interruptible when in a low-power state. These conditions are true for most devices on ARM-based SoCs. In particular, to satisfy (*iii*), most devices rely on platform-specific hardware mechanisms, e.g., asynchronous wakeup or re-routing interrupt signal through GPIO. However, a device such as an Ethernet controller on a TV SoC lacks such hardware support as of now, making its runtime PM difficult in general.

Conclusion Device runtime PM requires the OS to disable devices that have no pending task in a timely manner. Currently, Linux places this burden on driver developers, who unfortunately implement runtime PM poorly in most cases. To address this issue, we relieve drivers from PM by building a central PM agent that automatically performs runtime PM, according to its observation and inference on whether there are pending tasks for the device. We propose two alternatives for performing the inference, one with existing hardware and the other with added hardware support. In addition, we demonstrate it is possible and useful to have a best-effort software tool that suggests where to add PM calls in driver source code, an approach reducing (but not eliminating) developers' efforts in reasoning about PM without structural changes to the OS.

Acknowledgments

The work was supported in part by NSF Awards #1054693, #1065506, and #1218041. The authors thank Aaron Carroll for injectevents [53], Jie Liao for helping process the LiveLab data, and Kevin Boos for helping revise the paper. The authors also thank anonymous reviewers for their useful feedbacks.

References

[1] NVIDIA, "NVIDIA Tegra K1 mobile processor technical reference manual," 2014.

[2] Texas Instruments, "OMAP4460 multimedia device technical reference manual," 2011.

[3] Samsung, "Samsung Exynos 5 Quad (Exynos 5250) RISC microprocessor user's manual," 2012.

[4] Texas Instruments, "Multicore DSP+ARM KeyStone II System-on-Chip (SoC) technical reference manual," 2013.

[5] M. Mehendale, S. Das, M. Sharma, M. Mody, R. Reddy, J. Meehan, H. Tamama, B. Carlson, and M. Polley, "A true multistandard, programmable, low-power, full HD video-codec engine for smartphone SoC," in *Digest of Technical Papers of IEEE Int. Solid-State Circuits Conf. (ISSCC)*, pp. 226–228, 2012.

[6] K. Flautner and T. Mudge, "Vertigo: automatic performance-setting for Linux," in *Proc. USENIX Symp. Operating Systems Design and Implementation (OSDI)*, pp. 105–116, 2002.

[7] R. J. Wysocki, "Power management in the Linux kernel: current status and future." http://events.linuxfoundation.org/sites/events/files/slides/kernel_PM_plain.pdf, 2013.

[8] NVDIA, "NVIDIA Tegra 4 4-plus-1 quad-core processors technical reference manual," 2013.

[9] Freescale, "i.MX 6Dual/6Quad applications processor reference manual," 2013.

[10] Intel, "Intel Atom processor Z36xxx and Z37xxx series datasheet," 2013.

[11] P. Choudhary and D. Marculescu, "Power management of voltage/frequency island-based systems using hardware-based methods," *IEEE Transactions on Very Large Scale Integration (VLSI) Systems*, pp. 427–438, 2009.

[12] T. Hattori, T. lrita, M. Ito, E. Yamamoto, H. Kato, G. Sado, Y. Yamada, K. Nishiyama, H. Yagi, T. Koike, Y. Tsuchihashi, M. Higashida, H. Asano, I. Hayashibara, K. Tatezawa, Y. Shimazaki, N. Morino, K. Hirose, S. Tamaki, S. Yoshioka, R. Tsuchihashi, N. Arai, T. Akiyama, and K. Ohno, "A power management scheme controlling 20 power domains for a single-chip mobile processor," in *Digest of Technical Papers of IEEE Int. Solid-State Circuits Conf. (ISSCC)*, pp. 2210–2219, 2006.

[13] G. Raja, "OMAP2+: UART: add runtime pm support for OMAP-serial driver." http://www.spinics.net/lists/linux-omap/msg58443.html, 2011.

[14] M. Brown, "Input: samsung-keypad: implement runtime power management support." http://www.spinics.net/lists/linux-input/msg18796.html, 2011.

[15] P. Walmsley, "Watchdog: OMAP_wdt: add fine grain runtime PM." http://permalink.gmane.org/gmane.linux.ports.arm.omap/54608, 2011.

[16] V. Gautam, "DWC3/xHCI: enable runtime power management." https://lkml.org/lkml/2013/1/28/229, 2013.

[17] R. Quadros, "USB: implement runtime idling and remote wakeup for OMAP EHCI controller." https://lkml.org/lkml/2013/7/10/355, 2013.

[18] F. Balbi, "GPIO: OMAP: be more aggressive with pm_runtime." http://www.spinics.net/lists/linux-omap/msg64196.html, 2012.

[19] A. Dong, "MMC: sdhci-esdhc-imx: add runtime PM support." http://lists.infradead.org/pipermail/linux-arm-kernel/2013-October/208191.html, 2013.

[20] R. Zhao, "I2C: IMX: disable clock when it's possible to save power." http://lists.infradead.org/pipermail/linux-arm-kernel/2009-October/002455.html, 2009.

[21] S. Huang, "SPI: spi-imx: only enable the clocks when we start to transfer a message." http://lists.infradead.org/pipermail/linux-arm-kernel/2013-October/206797.html, 2013.

[22] M. Brown, "SPI/s3c64xx: implement runtime PM support." http://www.spinics.net/lists/linux-samsung-soc/msg08912.html, 2012.

[23] S. Irani, S. Shukla, and R. Gupta, "Online strategies for dynamic power management in systems with multiple power-saving states," *ACM Transaction on Embedded Computing Systems (TECS)*, vol. 2, no. 3, pp. 325–346, 2003.

[24] T. Simunic, L. Beniani, and G. De Micheli, "Event-driven power management of portable systems," in *Proc. Int. Symp. System Synthesis*, pp. 18–23, 1999.

[25] Q. Qiu and M. Pedram, "Dynamic power management based on continuous-time Markov decision processes," in *Proc. ACM/IEEE Design Automation Conf. (DAC)*, 1999.

[26] R. Muralidhar, H. Seshadri, V. Bhimarao, V. Rudramuni, I. Mansoor, S. Thomas, B. Veera, Y. Singh, and S. Ramachandra, "Experiences with power management enabling on the Intel Medfield phone," in *Proc. Linux Symposium*, 2012.

[27] Xilinx, "Zynq-7000 all programmable soc technical reference manual," 2014.

[28] Xilinx, "LogiCORE IP AXI IIC Bus Interface v2.0." http://japan.xilinx.com/support/documentation/ip_documentation/axi_iic/v2_0/pg090-axi-iic.pdf, 2014.

[29] R. Herveille, "Opencores project: I2C." http://opencores.org/project,i2c.

[30] R. Herveille, "Opencores project: simple SPI." http://opencores.org/project,simple_spi.

[31] eLinux.org, "PandaBoard Power Measurements." http://elinux.org/PandaBoard_Power_Measurements.

[32] C. Shepard, A. Rahmati, C. Tossell, L. Zhong, and P. Kortum, "Livelab: Measuring wireless networks and smartphone users in the field," *SIGMETRICS Performance Evaluation Review*, vol. 38, pp. 15–20, Jan. 2011.

[33] Verizon Wireless, "A smartphone is only as good as its battery life." http://www.verizonwireless.com/mobile-living/tech-smarts/smartphones-with-long-lasting-battery-life/, 2013.

[34] M. Gates, A. Tirumala, J. Ferguson, J. Dugan, F. Qin, K. Gibbs, and J. Estabrook, "Iperf: The TCP/UDP bandwidth measurement tool, version 2.0.5." https://iperf.fr/.

[35] Freescale, "Xtrinsic MMA8452Q 3-axis, 12-bit/8-bit digital accelerometer." http://www.freescale.com/files/sensors/doc/data_sheet/MMA8452Q.pdf, 2014.

[36] C. Cadar, D. Dunbar, and D. Engler, "KLEE: unassisted and automatic generation of high-coverage tests for complex systems programs," in *Proc. USENIX Symp. Operating Systems Design and Implementation (OSDI)*, pp. 209–224, 2008.

[37] L. De Moura and N. Bjørner, "Z3: an efficient SMT solver," in *Tools and Algorithms for the Construction and Analysis of Systems*, pp. 337–340, 2008.

[38] IBM, "CPLEX Optimizer." `http://www-01.ibm.com/software/commerce/optimization/cplex-optimizer/`.

[39] H. Esmaeilzadeh, E. Blem, R. St. Amant, K. Sankaralingam, and D. Burger, "Dark silicon and the end of multicore scaling," in *Proc. ACM/IEEE Int. Symp. Computer Architecture (ISCA)*, pp. 365–376, 2011.

[40] A. Pathak, A. Jindal, Y. C. Hu, and S. P. Midkiff, "What is keeping my phone awake? Characterizing and detecting no-sleep energy bugs in smartphone apps," in *Proc. Int. Conf. Mobile Systems, Applications, and Services (MobiSys)*, pp. 267–280, 2012.

[41] A. Jindal, A. Pathak, Y. C. Hu, and S. Midkiff, "Hypnos: understanding and treating sleep conflicts in smartphones," in *Proc. ACM European Conf. Computer System (EuroSys)*, pp. 253–266, 2013.

[42] R. J. Wysocki, "Technical background of the Android suspend blockers controversy." `lwn.net/images/pdf/suspend_blockers.pdf`, 2010.

[43] X. Ma, P. Huang, X. Jin, P. Wang, S. Park, D. Shen, Y. Zhou, L. K. Saul, and G. M. Voelker, "eDoctor: automatically diagnosing abnormal battery drain issues on smartphones," in *Proc. USENIX Symp. Networked Systems Design and Implementation (NSDI)*, pp. 57–70, 2013.

[44] A. Weissel and F. Bellosa, "Process cruise control: Event-driven clock scaling for dynamic power management," in *Proc. Int. Conf. Compilers, Architecture, and Synthesis for Embedded Systems (CASES)*, pp. 238–246, 2002.

[45] D. C. Snowdon, E. Le Sueur, S. M. Petters, and G. Heiser, "Koala: a platform for OS-level power management," in *Proc. ACM European Conf. Computer Systems (EuroSys)*, pp. 289–302, 2009.

[46] A. Pathania, Q. Jiao, A. Prakash, and T. Mitra, "Integrated CPU-GPU power management for 3D mobile games," in *Proc. ACM/IEEE Design Automation Conf. (DAC)*, pp. 40:1–40:6, 2014.

[47] V. Gupta, P. Brett, D. A. Koufaty, D. Reddy, S. Hahn, K. Schwan, and G. Srinivasa, "The forgotten 'uncore': on the energy-efficiency of heterogeneous cores," in *USENIX Annual Technical Conf. (ATC)*, pp. 367–372, 2012.

[48] K. Klues, V. Handziski, C. Lu, A. Wolisz, D. Culler, D. Gay, and P. Levis, "Integrating concurrency control and energy management in device drivers," in *Proc. ACM Symp. Operating Systems Principles (SOSP)*, pp. 251–264, 2007.

[49] M. Anand, E. B. Nightingale, and J. Flinn, "Ghosts in the machine: interfaces for better power management," in *Proc. ACM Int. Conf. Mobile Systems, Applications, and Services (MobiSys)*, pp. 23–35, 2004.

[50] C. Xu, X. Lin, and L. Zhong, "Device drivers should not do power management," in *Proc. ACM SIGOPS Asia-Pacific Wrkshp. Systems (APSYS)*, June 2014.

[51] E. Clarke, D. Kroening, and F. Lerda, "A tool for checking ANSI-C programs," in *Tools and Algorithms for the Construction and Analysis of Systems*, pp. 168–176, 2004.

[52] L. Ryzhyk, P. Chubb, I. Kuz, E. Le Sueur, and G. Heiser, "Automatic device driver synthesis with Termite," in *Proc. ACM Symp. Operating Systems Principles (SOSP)*, pp. 73–86, 2009.

[53] N. FitzRoy-Dale and A. Carroll, *injectevents*. `https://github.com/xaaronc/injectevents`.

CoolAir: Temperature- and Variation-Aware Management for Free-Cooled Datacenters

Íñigo Goiri[†]*, Thu D. Nguyen[‡], and Ricardo Bianchini[†‡]

[‡]Rutgers University {tdnguyen,ricardob}@cs.rutgers.edu

[†]Microsoft Research {inigog,ricardob}@microsoft.com

Abstract

Despite its benefits, free cooling may expose servers to high absolute temperatures, wide temperature variations, and high humidity when datacenters are sited at certain locations. Prior research (in non-free-cooled datacenters) has shown that high temperatures and/or wide temporal temperature variations can harm hardware reliability.

In this paper, we identify the runtime management strategies required to limit absolute temperatures, temperature variations, humidity, and cooling energy in free-cooled datacenters. As the basis for our study, we propose CoolAir, a system that embodies these strategies. Using CoolAir and a real free-cooled datacenter prototype, we show that effective management requires cooling infrastructures that can act smoothly. In addition, we show that CoolAir can tightly manage temperature and significantly reduce temperature variation, often at a lower cooling cost than existing free-cooled datacenters. Perhaps most importantly, based on our results, we derive several principles and lessons that should guide the design of management systems for free-cooled datacenters of any size.

Categories and Subject Descriptors C.m [*Computer Systems Organizations*]: Miscellaneous; D.4.m [*Operating systems*]: Miscellaneous

Keywords Thermal management, energy management, free cooling, datacenters.

* This work was done while Íñigo was at Rutgers University.

ASPLOS '15, March 14–18, 2015, Istanbul, Turkey..

ACM 978-1-4503-2835-7/15/03...$15.00.
http://dx.doi.org/10.1145/2694344.2694378

1. Introduction

Recently, datacenter operators have started building their datacenters in cold and dry climates, where outside air can be used to cool the servers [14, 18]. In this approach, known as "air-side economizer" or simply "free" cooling, fans blow the cool outside air into the datacenter so that it reaches the server inlets, while the warm air heated up by the servers is guided back outside [33]. Free cooling significantly reduces energy consumption, and may obviate the need for water chillers, cooling towers, and air conditioners (ACs) in many geographical locations. Free cooling can be useful *across the spectrum of datacenter sizes,* from small enterprise datacenters to warehouse-scale datacenters run by large Internet companies.

Motivation. In recent years, free cooling has received attention in the popular media [28, 29] and in the scientific literature [2, 12, 15, 22, 23, 27, 41]. There is a consensus that free cooling reduces cooling costs and should be used whenever and wherever possible. However, the potential impact of free cooling on hardware reliability is not yet fully understood. For example, researchers have recently studied the impact of temperature on hardware (especially, hard disk drive) reliability in *non*-free-cooled datacenters [10, 34, 36] with conflicting results. Pinheiro *et al.* [34] studied Google datacenters and observed the impact of absolute disk temperature on reliability to be small up to roughly 50°C. El-Sayed *et al.* [10] studied a variety of datacenters (including some from Google) and reached a similar conclusion, but found wide temporal temperature variations to increase sector errors more significantly and consistently. Sankar *et al.* [36] studied Microsoft datacenters and observed that absolute disk temperature has a significant impact on reliability, whereas wide temperature variation does not.

Regardless of how these conflicting results will be reconciled, it is clear that free-cooled datacenters may expose servers to high absolute temperatures and/or wide temporal temperature variations at locations where outside temperatures are high and/or highly variable. At these locations, free-cooled datacenters would exhibit higher temperatures and wider temperature variations than those shown in the disk reliability papers we cite above. However, for latency reasons or other restrictions on siting (*e.g.*, an enterprise's desire to build its datacenter next to its offices), it may be desirable to build free-cooled datacenters at such locations.

To the best of our knowledge, there has been no *publicly available* study of the temperatures and variations to which servers are exposed in free-cooled datacenters. Similarly, there has been no study of techniques that can manage absolute temperature and temperature variations in those datacenters. Importantly, such techniques should keep the cooling energy consumption low, as many locations exhibit a tradeoff between the cooling energy savings due to free cooling and hardware maintenance and replacement costs.

This paper fills these large gaps in the literature. Specifically, we propose CoolAir, a workload and cooling management system for free-cooled datacenters. As a case study, we apply CoolAir to our real free-cooled datacenter prototype, called Parasol [17]. Parasol combines free cooling with a direct-expansion (DX) AC, and embodies a commercial feedback-driven cooling controller that periodically selects the cooling regime (*e.g.*, free cooling at 50% fan speed, or free cooling off with AC on). Despite this controller, Parasol exhibits high inlet air temperatures and wide daily inlet air temperature variations. We refer to Parasol running this controller as the "baseline" system.

CoolAir. CoolAir manages absolute temperature, temperature variation, relative humidity, and cooling energy in free-cooled datacenters. It uses machine learning, simulation, and weather forecasts to model and predict temperatures, humidity, and cooling energy. To achieve its goals, CoolAir manages the workload placement and schedule, the servers' power state, as well as the cooling regime. In contrast, the baseline system only controls the cooling regime and does so in a more limited fashion (*e.g.*, without concern for future outside temperatures or internal temperature variations).

Although we study CoolAir for Parasol and Hadoop workloads, it can be easily adapted to other cooling infrastructures and software systems. Interestingly, our multiple day-long real experiments with CoolAir on Parasol show that it is impossible to control temperature variation with Parasol's cooling infrastructure; the cooling units react too abruptly during certain regime transitions.

Evaluation. To evaluate CoolAir for an entire year, we build a simulator of Parasol and *validate* it against multiple (day-long) real experiments on Parasol. To study a more controllable setup, we simulate a free cooling unit with fine-grained fan speed ramp up, and a variable-speed AC. These types of cooling units are available commercially [7, 11, 37]. Using the simulator, we study CoolAir in detail for five locations: Iceland (cold year-round), Chad (hot year-round), Santiago de Chile (mild year-round), Singapore (hot and humid year-round), and Newark (hot in the summer, cold in the winter). Like Newark, Parasol is located in New Jersey, USA. We also explore 1500+ locations world-wide.

Our results for the manageable version of Parasol demonstrate that CoolAir can limit temperatures and significantly reduce daily variations, while keeping Power Usage Efficiencies (PUEs) low, compared to the baseline system. Interestingly, managing temperature variation incurs a substantial cooling energy penalty. Nevertheless, CoolAir's management of cooling energy produces cooling costs that are often even lower than those of the baseline system. In fact, CoolAir is broadly useful: at locations where it reduces variations significantly, it does so at little or no cost in PUE; at locations where it tends to reduce variations less substantially, it lowers PUEs. Importantly, our results quantify the energy cost of lowering absolute temperature and temperature variation, as a function of location. Overall, our results demonstrate that *CoolAir can effectively manage temperatures (and consequently disk reliability) and cooling energy all over the world.*

Principles and lessons. From our case study, we derive *general* lessons that should apply to free-cooled datacenters of any size. For example, we find that effective management requires fine-grain management knobs, and temperature setpoints based on outside temperature. Moreover, we find that *existing energy-driven spatial and temporal workload scheduling techniques* (e.g., *[2, 22, 27, 30, 32]) have a negative impact on variation,* suggesting that these techniques should be avoided in free-cooled datacenters.

Contributions. In summary, our main contributions are:

1. We show that free cooling may expose servers to high absolute temperatures and wide daily temperature variations.

2. We propose CoolAir, a general workload and cooling manager for free-cooled datacenters. No prior work has considered temperature variation or future outside temperatures in managing internal temperatures. Moreover, some existing thermal management techniques actually *increase* variation.

3. As a case study, we evaluate CoolAir using day-long experiments on a real free-cooled datacenter prototype, and on a simulated system with a more sophisticated cooling infrastructure for a year at more than 1500 locations.

4. We derive principles and lessons for the management systems of free-cooled datacenters of any size.

2. Background

Datacenters have traditionally used different cooling infrastructures depending on their sizes. Large datacenters have often used water chillers and cooling towers outside the datacenter, and air handlers inside of it. Medium datacenters often forgo the cooling tower, but retain the chiller and air handling units. Small datacenters often replace the chiller and air handler with in-datacenter DX ACs. These ACs utilize compressors to remove heat. All datacenters now create "cold aisles" in front of the servers, and isolate them from the "hot aisles" behind the servers.

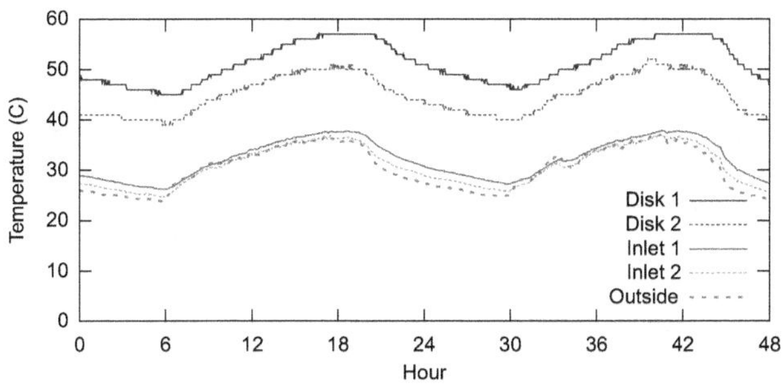

Figure 1. Disk, inlet, and outside temps under free cooling.

Recently, datacenters of all sizes have started to leverage free cooling by using fans to blow cool (filtered) outside air into the datacenter. Again using fans, the warm return air is guided back out of the datacenter. When outside temperature and humidity are appropriate, free cooling obviates the need to run power-hungry water chillers or compressors. In fact, in cool climates, free cooling enables the forgoing of chillers and compressors altogether. In warmer climates, some free-cooled datacenters also apply adiabatic cooling (via water evaporation, within the humidity constraint) to lower the temperature of the outside air before letting it reach the servers. Another approach (the one we study in this paper) is to combine free cooling with more power-hungry, "backup" cooling (*e.g.*, ACs), for use when outside air temperature or humidity is too high.

Free cooling operation. Typically, the cooling system uses a (feedback-based) controller that modulates the fan speed to keep the inside temperature below a setpoint. The controller is also responsible for (turning free cooling off and) activating the backup cooling system when necessary.

3. CoolAir

The main goal of CoolAir is to manage absolute temperatures and daily temperature variations in free-cooled datacenters, while keeping energy consumption low. In addition, CoolAir manages relative humidity and the rate of air temperature change per hour. CoolAir achieves its goals by intelligently (1) selecting the best setpoint for the inlet air temperatures on a daily basis (leverages predictions of outside temperatures); (2) placing the offered workload around the datacenter (spatial placement); (3) possibly scheduling the workload for later execution (temporal scheduling, when the workload is deferrable); and (4) periodically selecting the best cooling regime according to all air temperature and humidity sensors. It also decides how many servers to keep active. We refer to datacenter "utilization" as the fraction of active servers; *e.g.*, 50% utilization means that half of the servers are active and the other half is asleep (in ACPI's S3 state).

CoolAir assumes: at least one air temperature sensor and at least one humidity sensor outside the datacenter; the datacenter is organized into "pods" of servers (*i.e.*, sets of servers that are spatially close) [30]; at least one air temperature sensor representing the inlet temperature of each pod; and a humidity sensor in one of the cold aisles.

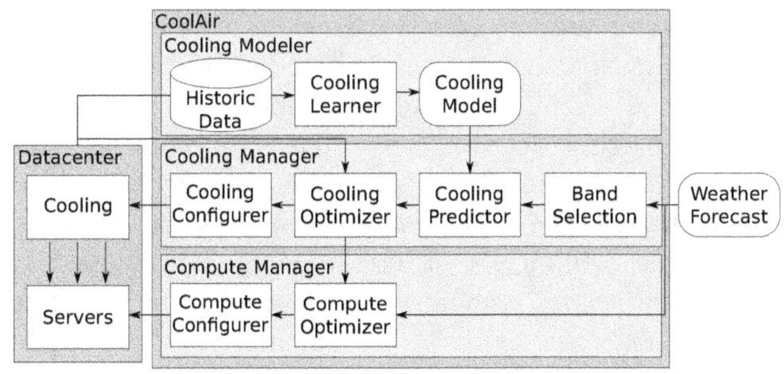

Figure 2. Architecture. Rectangles with square corners represent modules, whereas round corners represent derived or input data.

Importantly, CoolAir manages air temperatures and humidity to prevent disk reliability from suffering under free cooling. Disks are the most sensitive components to temperature and temperature variation. Figure 1 illustrates the relationship between outside air temperature, inside inlet air temperature, and disk temperature during Parasol's free cooling operation. The figure plots the lowest and highest disk temperatures on July 6th and 7th 2013, when we ran a workload that constantly left the disk 50% utilized. Clearly, there is a strong correlation between air and disk temperatures. *Any datacenter exposed to outside temperatures would exhibit this same correlation.*

Figure 2 overviews the CoolAir architecture. It comprises three main components: the *Cooling Modeler*, the *Cooling Manager*, and the *Compute Manager*. The following subsections describe each component in detail.

3.1 Cooling Modeler

The Cooling Modeler is responsible for modeling temperatures and the cooling system. It collects air temperature and humidity for each available sensor, the utilization of each server, the current status of the cooling infrastructure, and the cooling power currently being consumed. The *Cooling Learner* then executes a linear regression algorithm to learn a model (the *Cooling Model*) for the thermal behavior in multiple locations of the cold aisles and the humidity in one location of the cold aisles, as a function of many parameters. The Cooling Modeler runs offline and only once, after enough data has been collected under the default cooling controller.

Temperature. We model the thermal behavior of each area of interest inside a datacenter, *i.e.* the location of a temperature sensor, using a set of equations of the form $T = F(I)$, where the predicted temperature T is a linear function of the inputs I. The inputs are the current and last inside air temperature (at the sensor's location), the current and last outside air temperature, the current and last fan speed of the free cooling system, the current datacenter utilization, the product of the current fan speed and the current inside air temperature, and the product of the current fan speed and the current outside air temperature. Note that we use composed inputs (*e.g.*, current fan speed × current temperature) to allow linear regression.

Using machine learning and extensive monitoring data, CoolAir generates *a distinct function F for each possible cooling regime and transition between regimes*, including neither free cooling nor air conditioning, free cooling at different speeds, AC compressor-on, and transition from free cooling to AC compressor-on. For simplicity, we assume that a given datacenter utilization always causes the same servers to be active.

Humidity. We similarly model absolute humidity inside the datacenter using a set of equations $H = G(I')$, where the humidity H is a linear function of the inputs I'. The inputs are the current inside air humidity, the current outside air humidity, the current fan speed of the free cooling system, the product of the fan speed and the inside humidity, and the product of the fan speed and the outside humidity. Again, *CoolAir produces a function G for each cooling regime and transition between regimes.* It uses the predicted inside air temperature (at a chosen location) to convert the predicted absolute inside air humidity to a relative inside air humidity.

Cooling power. We model it as a constant amount drawn in each regime: (1) per each fan speed during free cooling operation; and (2) when free cooling is off and backup cooling is on (possibly in different operating modes).

3.2 Cooling Manager

The Cooling Manager selects the best operating region, selects and installs good cooling configurations, and produces cooling predictions for the Compute Manager. Since CoolAir seeks to limit variation, it uses a target *range (or band) of temperatures* within which it tries to keep inlet temperatures.

Temperature band selection. The Cooling Manager first selects the band that would be easiest to maintain throughout the day while limiting temporal variation. For example, on a cool day, it can maintain a relatively low temperature range by alternating between free cooling and simply closing the datacenter (*i.e.*, using neither free cooling nor backup cooling). On a warm day, it can maintain a relatively higher temperature by using free cooling, and backup cooling only if necessary.

CoolAir selects the band by querying a Web-based weather forecast service to find the hourly outside temperature predictions at the datacenter's location for the rest of the day. With these predictions, it selects a band of temperatures *Width* degrees wide around the average predicted outside temperature for the day plus an *Offset*. Intuitively, the width of the band should be selected based on the expected temperature variations over any one day, and how much energy one wants to spend limiting temperature variations. Since the outside air naturally heats up before arriving at the server inlets, the *Offset* corresponds to the typical difference between outside and inside air temperatures (*e.g.*, see Figure 1, where *Offset* is 2.5°C). Figure 3 illustrates the band selection. However, no part of the band can be higher than the *Max* temperature or lower than the *Min* temperature; the band slides back just below *Max* or just above *Min* in those cases.

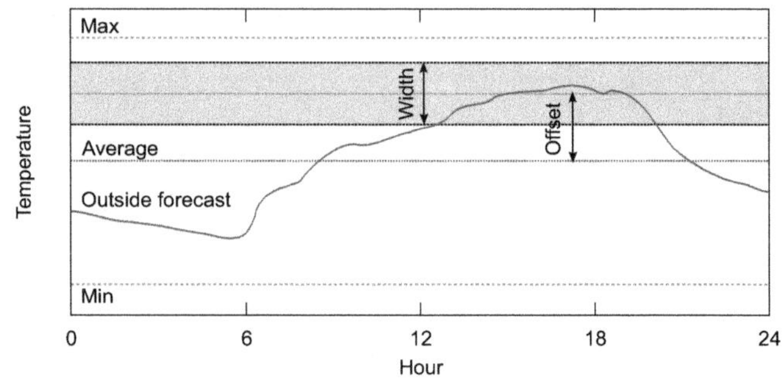

Figure 3. Temperature band selection in CoolAir.

Selecting a temperature band for each day independently of other days could contribute to increases in long-term temperature variation. However, this is not a problem since: (1) variation is most harmful to reliability when it happens quickly (*e.g.*, ASHRAE recommends a temperature change rate of at most 20°C/hour [3]); and (2) we set *Width* wide enough that transitions between days are smooth, *i.e.* bands for consecutive days almost always overlap.

Cooling Optimizer. This module periodically (every 10 minutes) selects the best cooling regime to use for the next period. It uses the *Cooling Predictor* (described below) and information about the current datacenter utilization, air temperatures, and humidity to predict the thermal behavior that would result from using each of the regimes for the next period (10 minutes). To select one of these choices, the Cooling Optimizer uses a simple *utility function*.

The utility function considers the predictions for: (1) absolute temperature; (2) temperature variation; (3) relative humidity; and (4) cooling energy. To guide the system towards the CoolAir goals, we assign a penalty to any violation of these goals. Specifically, the following violations all carry the same penalty: each 0.5°C higher than the maximum temperature threshold, each 1°C of temperature variation higher than 20°C/hour, each 0.5°C outside of the temperature band, each 5% of relative humidity outside of the humidity band, and turning on the AC at full speed. The overall function value for each cooling regime is the sum of the penalties for the sensors of all active pods. In Section 5, we also consider simplified versions of CoolAir that disregard certain components of the utility function.

Cooling Predictor. The Cooling Optimizer calls the Cooling Predictor when it needs temperature and relative humidity predictions for a cooling regime it is considering. The Predictor then uses the Cooling Model to produce the predictions. However, as the Cooling Model predicts temperatures for a short term, the Cooling Predictor has to use it repeatedly (each time passing the results of the previous use as input).

Cooling Configurer. This is the only module that interacts directly with the cooling infrastructure, according to the behavior the Cooling Optimizer wants to achieve.

3.3 Compute Manager

The Compute Manager is responsible for the execution of the workload, and for activating and deactivating servers.

Compute Optimizer. This module optimizes the set of active servers and the *spatial placement* of the workload. To do so, it uses a ranking of pods in terms of their potential for heat recirculation.[1] This ranking comes from the Cooling Modeler, which creates it by observing changes in inlet temperature when load is scheduled on each pod.

CoolAir selects the set of servers that are most prone to heat recirculation as targets for the current workload. Although this may seem counter-intuitive, this approach makes it easier to manage temperature variation. The reason is that lower recirculation pods tend to be more exposed to the effect of the cooling infrastructure and, thus, may experience wider variations. In Section 5, we consider simplified versions of CoolAir that make different activation/placement decisions.

For deferrable workloads, CoolAir also performs *temporal scheduling*, *i.e.* it schedules the jobs that have already arrived 24 hours into the future. This scheduling may determine that certain jobs should be delayed. However, CoolAir will not delay any job beyond its user-provided *start deadline*. Within these deadlines, CoolAir tries to place as much load as possible during periods when the hourly predictions of outside air temperature for the day are within its temperature band. It does not temporally schedule jobs for a day, if (1) the band needs to slide back below *Max* or above *Min*, or (2) the band does not overlap with predicted outside temperatures (outside temperatures will constantly be higher than *Max* or lower than *Min*). Temporal scheduling provides no benefits for such days.

Compute Configurer. This module configures the number of active servers and is the only one that interacts with the system running on the datacenter (Hadoop in this paper).

4. CoolAir for Parasol

CoolAir can be adapted to any free-cooled datacenter. In this section, we describe its implementation for Parasol.

4.1 Parasol and Its Cooling Infrastructure

We built Parasol for research on several topics, including free cooling and wimpy servers. Parasol combines free cooling with DX air conditioning, allowing it to be used in a wide range of climates, as we study in this paper.

Internal view. Parasol comprises a small custom container (7'×12') that houses the servers. Figure 4 shows the internal

[1] Heat recirculation is a feature (not a bug) in free-cooled datacenters, and is used to increase temperature (when the outside air is too cold) and decrease humidity (when the outside air is too humid).

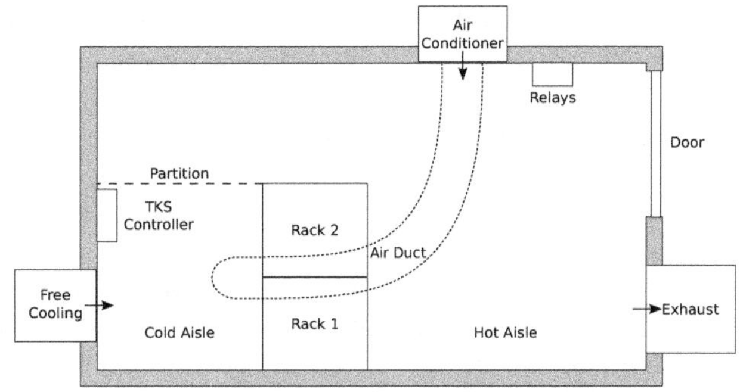

Figure 4. Internal layout of Parasol.

layout of the container in scale. The free cooling unit (Dantherm Flexibox 450) and its controller (TKS 3000) appear on the left, the servers in the two racks in the middle, the exhaust damper on the right, and the AC (Dantherm iA/C 19000) at the top-right part of the figure. Using simple partitions (the dashed line), we create a small, sealed cold aisle in front of the servers, and a "wind-tunnel" effect between the free cooling unit, the servers, and the damper. To seal the cold aisle, we also place a partition at the top of the racks (not shown). The location of the AC is not ideal, requiring an air duct (the snake-like shape across the figure) into the cold aisle. The AC's hot air intake is above the end of the duct in the hot aisle. The sealed cold aisle minimizes hot air recirculation during free cooling or AC operation. When the container is closed and both cooling units are off, recirculation occurs around the partitions and through any sleeping servers.

System operation. The TKS controller manages Parasol's cooling. It selects the cooling mode based on how the outside temperature relates to a configurable setpoint SP (25°C by default). Below the setpoint, it operates in the Low Outside Temperature (LOT) mode, and uses free cooling as much as possible. Above the setpoint, the TKS starts operating in the High Outside Temperature (HOT) mode. It then closes the damper, turns the free cooling unit off, and turns the AC on. The TKS uses hysteresis (1°C) around the setpoint. The AC operates in cycles: it stops the compressor when the inside temperature is lower than $SP - 2$°C, and starts it when the inside temperature is higher than SP. The AC consumes either 135W (fan only) or 2.2kW (compressor and fan on).

In LOT mode, the TKS operates based on the temperature of a control sensor located in a typically warmer area in the cold aisle. When the temperature at this sensor is low, the TKS turns free cooling off and closes the container, which increases temperatures via recirculation. When the internal temperature is between SP and $SP - P$ (P is set to 5°C by default), the TKS uses free cooling, and selects the fan speed based on the difference between the outside and the inside temperatures. The closer the two temperatures are, the faster the fan blows. The minimum speed is 15% of the maximum speed. If the outside temperature is much lower than the inside temperature, the fan blows slowly but the inside temperature still drops fast due to the cold outside air. The free cooling unit draws between 8W and 425W, depending on fan speed.

The above description identifies the main cooling regimes in Parasol: (1) free cooling with a fan speed above 15%; (2) air conditioning with the compressor on or off; or (3) neither (the datacenter is closed).

Though a successful commercial product, the TKS lacks key CoolAir features: daily temperature setpoint selection based on future outside temperature; all-sensor temperature, variation, and humidity control; spatial and temporal workload management; and energy management. In the absence of these features, Parasol's disk reliability could suffer severely. Our evaluation compares CoolAir to a baseline that extends the TKS control scheme, as we describe in Section 5.1.

4.2 CoolAir Implementation

Monitoring Parasol. Parasol has one air temperature sensor for each server pod, which includes the servers that behave similarly (*e.g.*, same temperature changes, same potential for recirculation) in response to the cooling regimes. Parasol also monitors humidity with one sensor in each aisle. It uses the periodic temperature and humidity measurements in modeling the thermal behavior (Section 3).

Cooling Configurer for Parasol. CoolAir translates its desired actions into changes to the TKS temperature setpoint SP. To translate the temperature band, it sets the top of the band to be SP and *Width* to be the P value. By changing the TKS setpoint, we can also turn off the free cooling (which stops the flow of air into and out of Parasol), change the free cooling fan speed, and activate the AC (turning free cooling off). When the AC is on, we can also control its internal setpoint, and whether the compressor should be off.

Compute Configurer for Hadoop. In our implementation, CoolAir manages a slightly modified version of Hadoop [17]. The modification enables energy management by implementing three server power states: active, decommissioned, and sleep. Active and sleep (the S3 state) are self-explanatory. The decommissioned state is an intermediate state that prevents new jobs from starting on the server. We configure our Hadoop setup to the Covering Subset scheme [24], *i.e.* we store a full copy of the dataset on the smallest possible number of servers; any server out of the Covering Subset can be sent to sleep without affecting data availability.

The Compute Configurer transitions servers between the server power states in three ways: (1) it transitions any active server that need not be active but still stores (temporary) data required by running jobs to the decommissioned state. In a following iteration, if the data stored at the decommissioned server is no longer needed, the Configurer transitions it to the sleep state; (2) it transitions any active server that need not be active and does not store relevant data to the sleep state; and (3) it transitions sleeping servers to the active state if they are required for computation during an iteration. The Configurer keeps the Covering Subset active at all times.

In the absolute worst case, by transitioning power states, the Compute Configurer could cause a set of disks to power-cycle every 20 minutes, *i.e.* 3 times per hour. Fortunately, modern disks use load/unload technology [21], which enables them to power-cycle at least 300,000 times without failure. This means that disks can be power-cycled 8.5 times per hour on average, during their 4-year typical lifetime. For our workloads, no disk gets power-cycled more than 2.2 times per hour on average.

Data collection and model learning. To create our models, *we collected temperature, humidity, power consumption data from Parasol for 1.5 months.* To get a richer dataset within this period of time, we intentionally generated extreme situations by changing the cooling setup (*e.g.*, temperature setpoint), and monitored the resulting behaviors. We then use regression on this dataset to generate the specific set of functions F and G that together comprise the models (one model per cooling regime or transition between regimes) for predicting air temperature and humidity (Section 3.1). We use a similar approach to build the power model. We use Weka [19] to generate these regressions. For behaviors that are non-linear (*e.g.*, power consumption as a function of free cooling speed), we generate piece-wise linear models using M5P. For linear behaviors, we try linear and least median square approaches and pick the one with the lowest error. Prior works [25, 31] have shown regressions to work well for this problem.

Validation of the temperature and humidity models. *We compare the predicted temperatures to measured values in Parasol, during two entire (and non-consecutive) days* that were not in the learning dataset. Figure 5 plots the CDFs for the prediction error (in °C) for four cases: (1) *2-minutes:* the absolute value of the difference between the predicted temperature 2 minutes into the future and the measured temperature; (2) *2-minutes no-transition:* same as (1) except that we consider only 2-minute intervals that did not involve a transition in cooling regime; (3) *10-minutes:* the absolute value of the difference between the predicted temperature 10 minutes into the future and the measured temperature; and (4) *10-minutes no-transition:* same as (3) except that we consider only 10-minute intervals that did not involve a regime transition.

These results show that the temperature models are quite accurate, especially for periods without transitions between cooling regimes. Specifically, without transitions, 95% of the 2-minutes and 90% of the 10-minutes predictions are within 1°C of measured values. Even when including transitions, over 90% of the 2-minutes and over 80% of the 10-minutes predictions are within 1°C of measured values.

We used the same approach to validate our relative humidity models. Again, the results show that the models are quite accurate: 97% of our predictions are within 5% (in absolute terms) of the measured humidities.

CoolAir version	Workload type	Utility function	Spatial placement	Temporal scheduling
Temperature	Non-deferrable	Lower max temp + energy + humidity	Low recirculation	No
Variation	Non-deferrable	Adaptive band (max 30°C) + humidity	High recirculation	No
Energy	Non-deferrable	Max temp (30°C) + energy + humidity	Low recirculation	No
All-ND	Non-deferrable	Adaptive band (max 30°C) + energy + humidity	High recirculation	No
All-DEF	Deferrable	Adaptive band (max 30°C) + energy + humidity	Low recirculation	Yes

Table 1. CoolAir versions. All-ND: CoolAir for non-deferrable workloads. All-DEF: CoolAir for deferrable workloads.

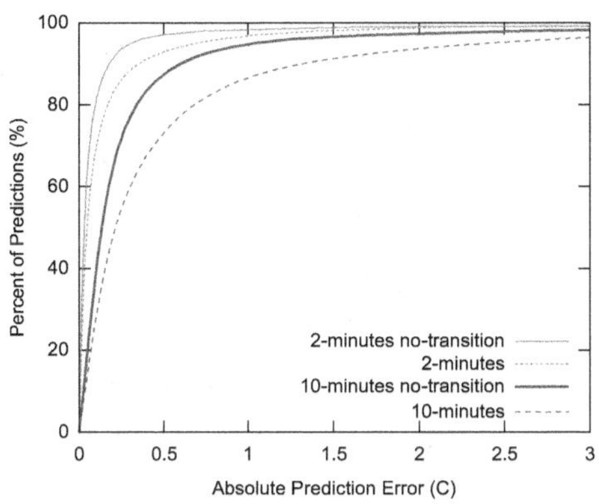

Figure 5. Modeling errors for 5/1/13 and 6/20/13.

4.3 Example Behavior

As an example of the behavior of CoolAir for Parasol, consider Figures 7(a) and 7(b). Figure 7(b) illustrates how CoolAir tried to keep the inlet temperatures between 24 and 29°C, given the workload described in Figure 7(a), on 06/15/2013. For example, around 7:30am, the inlet temperatures were starting to exceed 29°C and the outside temperature was low enough, so CoolAir opened up Parasol for free cooling (lightly shaded area labeled FC). CoolAir did not react to lower the temperatures sooner because this would have caused a higher utility function penalty. It then modulated the fan speed to regulate temperature until around 5:45pm, when the workload increased and inlet temperatures again started to exceed 29°C. At that point, it activated the AC (darkly shaded area labeled AC), since the workload was too heavy for it to lower temperatures enough with free cooling. As we show in Section 5, CoolAir can do an even better job of managing temperatures when the cooling infrastructure can react more smoothly to changes in cooling regime (Figure 7(d)).

5. Evaluation

5.1 Methodology

CoolAir and baseline system configurations. We configure CoolAir with *Offset* = 8°C, which is the offset that we normally observe in Parasol. We set *Width* = 5°C, as narrower bands tend to make it harder to control temperature variations (higher cooling energy and more regime changes) and wider bands needlessly allow temperatures to vary. We set *Min* and *Max* to 10°C and 30°C, respectively. We configure CoolAir to keep the relative humidity below 80% and air temperature changes below 20°C/hour. These settings roughly correspond to the "allowable" values suggested by ASHRAE [3].

We study multiple versions of CoolAir, called *Temperature*, *Variation*, *Energy*, *All-ND*, and *All-DEF*. The Temperature version only focuses on limiting absolute air temperatures below a low setpoint. This version represents what energy-aware thermal management systems do in non-free-cooled datacenters today. We set the setpoint to the lowest value that achieves the same PUE as the baseline system (described below). The Variation version focuses solely on limiting the amount of air temperature variation. The Energy version manages absolute temperatures, while attempting to conserve cooling energy. However, it does not manage temperature variation. This version is the same as Temperature, but it targets a higher maximum temperature to lower the cooling energy further. The All-ND version is the complete CoolAir implementation, which manages absolute temperatures, temperature variation, and cooling energy. All versions above are for non-deferrable workloads. We also study All-DEF, which manages absolute temperatures, temperature variation, and cooling energy for deferrable workloads. Table 1 lists the characteristics of each version.

We compare these versions to a baseline system that extends Parasol's default control scheme (Section 4.1) in two ways: (1) we set the setpoint to 30°C, instead of the default 25°C; and (2) we add humidity control to it, with a maximum limit of 80% relative humidity. These extensions make the baseline more efficient and comparable to CoolAir.

Parasol setup. Parasol currently hosts 64 half-U servers, each of which has a 2-core Atom D525MW CPU, 4GB of DRAM, a 250GB hard disk, and a 64GB solid-state drive. CoolAir's Compute Manager runs on one of these servers. Each server draws from 22W to 30W. Parasol also hosts a 4-core Xeon server, which runs Cooling Modeler and Cooling Manager. Parasol's sensors are accurate to within 0.5°C.

Workloads. We run our modified version of Hadoop on the 64 servers. We use a remote client to submit the Hadoop jobs. Each real experiment runs for a full day.

We study two widely different Hadoop traces, called "Facebook" and "Nutch". Facebook comes from a larger trace of 600 machines at Facebook [8]. We use Statistical Workload Injector for MapReduce (SWIM) [9] to generate a day-long, scaled-down version of the trace for 64 machines. In the resulting trace, each job comprises 2–1190 map tasks and 1–63 reduce tasks. There are roughly 5500 jobs and 68000 tasks.

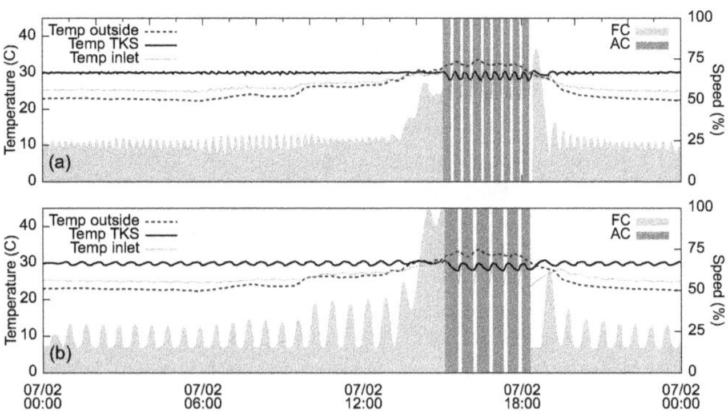

Figure 6. Real (a) and Real-Sim (b) baseline runs on 7/2/13.

The map phase of each job takes 25–13000 seconds, whereas the reduce phase takes 15–2600 seconds. Jobs have inputs of 64MB–74GB and outputs of up to 4GB. These characteristics lead to an average datacenter utilization of 27%.

Nutch is the indexing part of the Web search system in CloudSuite [13]. The day-long trace consists of 2000 jobs that index groups of pages previously fetched from our Web domain. Each job runs 42 map tasks and 1 reduce task. Each map phase takes 15–40 seconds, whereas the reduce phase takes 150 seconds. On average, each job touches 85MB of data. Jobs arrive according to a Poisson distribution with mean inter-arrival time of 40 seconds. These characteristics lead to an average utilization of 32%.

We study both non-deferrable and deferrable (all jobs have 6-hour start deadlines) versions of these workloads.

Simulation and validation. Though we built CoolAir for real datacenters, we need to use simulations for multiple reasons, including (1) we cannot compare two real executions, because the same weather conditions never repeat exactly; (2) we want to run CoolAir multiple times, each time for an entire year, which is not feasible in real time; and (3) we want to study many geographical locations.

Thus, we built two simulators: Real-Sim and Smooth-Sim. *Real-Sim* simulates Hadoop on Parasol with or without CoolAir. Figure 6 compares a real execution of the baseline system (a) and the Real-Sim execution (b) on 07/02/2013 for the Facebook workload. Similarly, Figure 7 compares a real execution of CoolAir (b) and the Real-Sim execution (c) on 06/15/2013 for this workload (a). On this day, CoolAir tried to keep temperatures between 24 and 29°C. It is clear from the figures that Real-Sim is accurate. For the baseline system, maximum temperatures, temperature variations, and cooling energy are all within 8% of the real execution. For CoolAir, these values are within 15% of the real execution. In absolute terms, 89% of all real baseline measurements are within 2°C of its simulation, while 70% of the CoolAir measurements are within 2°C of its simulation. Overall, *we validate Real-Sim for 8 full random days,* with average simulation errors of 3.3% (baseline) and 6.6% (CoolAir).

Figure 7(b) illustrates a problem with Parasol's cooling infrastructure: it reacts too abruptly to changes in regime,

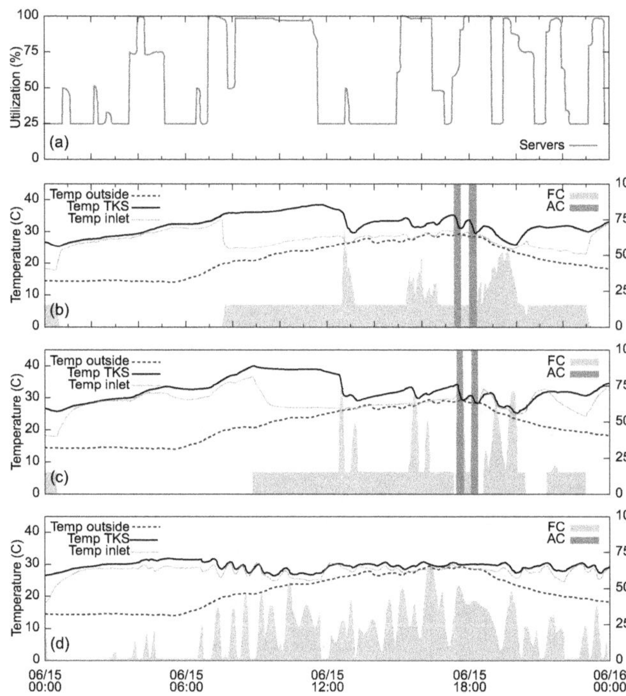

Figure 7. Workload (a), real (b), Real-Sim (c), and Smooth-Sim (d) CoolAir runs on 6/15/13.

making it difficult to manage variations accurately. For example, opening up Parasol to allow outside air to come in (causing free cooling to start running at 15% of the maximum speed) around 7:30am caused the inlet air temperature to decrease 9°C in only 12 minutes. Similarly, shutting down free cooling and turning on the AC (causing the compressor to run full-blast) caused a decrease of 7°C in 10 minutes.

Due to this limitation of Parasol, *Smooth-Sim* simulates CoolAir and Hadoop for a version of Parasol with a smoother, more controllable cooling infrastructure. Specifically, we simulate (1) a free cooling unit with fine-grained fan speed ramp up starting from 1% fan speed (ramp down still goes from 15% directly to off); and (2) an AC with fixed fan speed (ramp up is also fine-grained from 1% and settling at 100%), and variable and fine-grained compressor speed. Both the AC fan and compressor go straight from 15% to 0% when shutting down. These types of cooling units are available commercially [7, 11, 37]. Figure 7(d) shows the CoolAir behavior with this smoother infrastructure. Clearly, CoolAir keeps temperatures more stable with the new infrastructure.

Smooth-Sim cannot be validated in full, since we do not have access to a real fine-grained cooling infrastructure. However, we expect its behavior to also be close to reality, since the two simulators are almost exactly the same. To compute temperatures and humidity over time, they repeatedly call the same code implementing CoolAir's Cooling Predictor. We model the temperature, humidity, and power consumption of the smooth free cooling unit by extrapolating the earlier models to lower speeds. We model the temperature and humidity of the smooth AC by interpolating the models for the

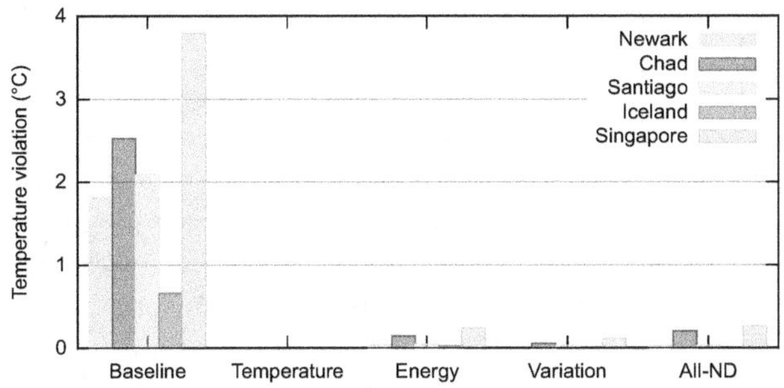

Figure 8. Average temperature violations.

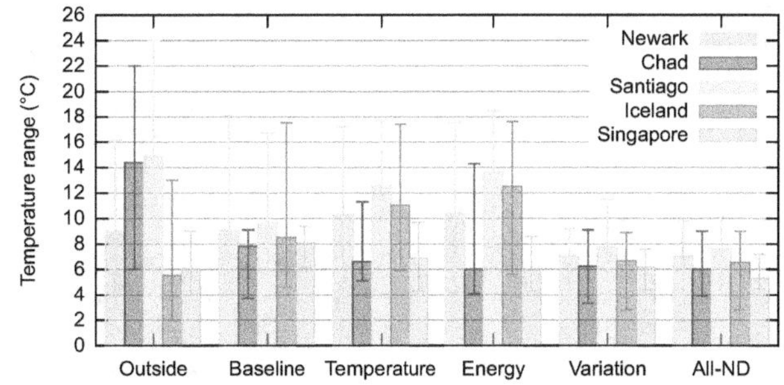

Figure 9. Temperature ranges.

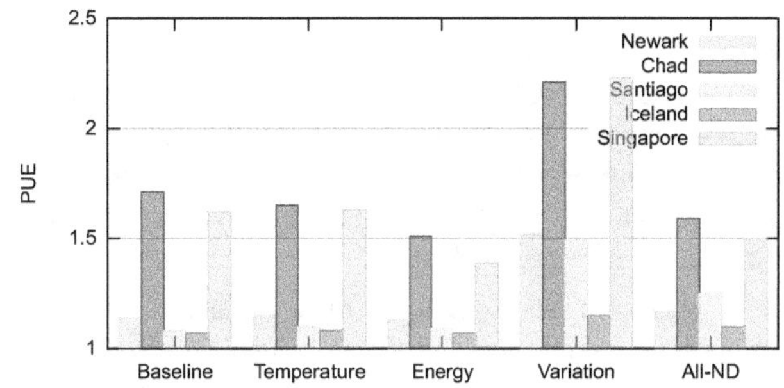

Figure 10. PUEs (including 0.08 for power delivery).

AC with the compressor on and off. For the power model, we assume the air conditioning fan consumes 1/4 of the power of the entire unit, and that the compressor consumes power linearly with speed. We base our assumptions, extrapolations, and interpolations in Smooth-Sim on [26].

To limit the length of our year-long Smooth-Sim simulations, we only simulate the first day of each week of the year. We repeat the workload for each of those days. We collect the typical meteorological year (TMY) temperature and humidity data for those days from [38]. We have compared our results for TMY and for actual temperatures for 2012 at two locations and found similar behaviors. Newark is the closest location to Parasol for which we found TMY data.

5.2 Results

Absolute internal temperatures. Figure 8 shows the average temperature "violations", *i.e.* the number of °C by which the systems exceed the desired maximum absolute air temperature of 30°C, during a year of running the non-deferrable Facebook workload at the five locations we consider. We compute this average by considering all sensor readings at or below 30°C to be a violation of 0°C. Each reading above 30°C contributes $reading - 30$ degrees to the overall sum.

These results show that the baseline system cannot limit all absolute temperatures well at warmer locations, especially in Singapore. As the other systems manage every sensor, they are more successful, with average violations lower than 0.5°C in all cases. Note that the bars for the Temperature version are *not* missing; this version is always able to keep average temperatures below 30°C (we set 29°C as the setpoint for Temperature at these locations) for the same PUE as the baseline system. All-ND is not as good as Temperature, but still leads to very low average violations. In fact, the CoolAir results are so good that we do not consider violations further.

Internal temperature variations. We measure the daily variation for each sensor as the difference between its maximum and minimum readings. From these variations, we select the worst sensor variation for each day. In Figure 9, the bars depict the average of these worst daily ranges over the year, while the vertical lines connect the minimum worst daily range to the maximum worst daily range. We also show the outside temperature variations (measured the same way).

These results show that the baseline system exhibits wide daily temperature ranges. Its average daily ranges hover around 9°C, and its maximum daily ranges are even wider. The maximum ranges are important because they represent an upper-bound on how variable a system is. For example, the maximum daily range for locations with cold or cool seasons (Newark, Santiago, and Iceland) is at least 16.5°C. The Temperature and Energy versions make maximum ranges even worse in some cases. As one would expect, Variation and All-ND lower the average daily ranges consistently, with respect to the baseline system. Most importantly, they lower the maximum daily range by a significant amount, except for Chad where it remains the same. For example, All-ND cuts the maximum daily range in *half* for Iceland, and *almost half* for Newark and Santiago. The most challenging days for All-ND are those when the outside temperature exhibits little overlap with CoolAir's temperature band.

Interestingly, the average outside temperature ranges can be lower than those inside under the baseline system (Iceland and Singapore). The same is the case for maximum ranges (Newark and Iceland). We mention the potential reasons for such behaviors in the Introduction.

PUEs. Figure 10 shows the yearly PUEs, assuming the power delivery losses of Parasol (0.08 in terms of PUE).

As one would expect, the baseline system exhibits high PUEs in Chad and Singapore. The Energy version reduces PUEs significantly at those locations. Interestingly, the Variation results show that trying to limit temperature ranges has a significant cooling energy penalty. All-ND brings PUEs back down to nearly the same values as the Energy version, except

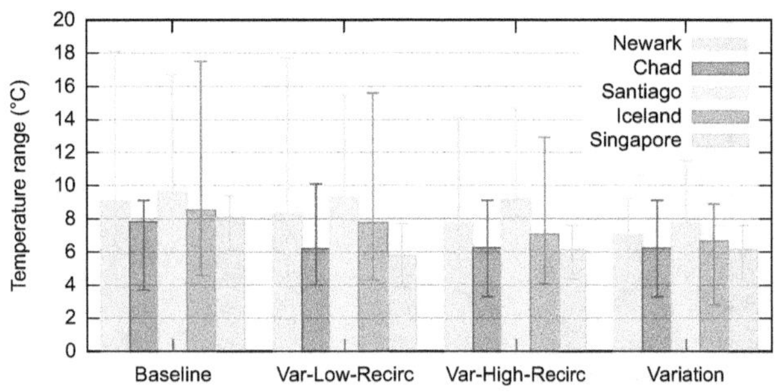

Figure 11. Temperature ranges, as a function of spatial placement and approach for limiting variation.

for Santiago. In this location, the baseline system does not need to consume much energy to keep temperatures below 30°C, whereas CoolAir does so to limit variation. However, two factors contribute to this: the relatively high power draw of air conditioning in our setup, and the low average IT power (servers are sent to sleep when not needed).

Cost of managing temperature and variation. We now quantify the yearly (energy) cost of controlling these measures. Lowering 1°C of absolute temperature costs more than reducing 1°C of maximum daily range in Newark (232 vs 53kWh), Chad (1275 vs 131kWh), and Singapore (2145 vs 716kWh). In Santiago (110 vs 171kWh) and Iceland (7 vs 29kWh), the opposite is true. Clearly, managing absolute temperature costs more than managing variation in places with warmer seasons, and less in places with colder ones.

Spatial placement. To understand why CoolAir achieves such large reductions in variation, we plot Figure 11. The figure depicts the temperature ranges for the baseline system, the Variation version of CoolAir, and two other systems: *Var-Low-Recirc* and *Var-High-Recirc*. Var-Low-Recirc attempts to keep temperatures between 25 and 30°C and uses a spatial placement that selects the pods with the lowest recirculation first. This placement has been used in prior works on energy-aware cooling in non-free-cooled datacenters [30, 32]. Var-High-Recirc tries to keep the temperature in the same range, but uses the same spatial placement as Variation. Var-High-Recirc uses no temperature band or weather prediction.

Comparing Var-Low-Recirc and Var-High-Recirc isolates the impact of the spatial placement. As the figure shows, placing loads on pods with higher recirculation reduces maximum temperature ranges somewhat; this tends to keep those areas consistently warm, with low variation. This is interesting because this spatial placement is the *opposite* as prior research has identified as ideal for energy savings [30, 32]. Nevertheless, high-recirculation placement increases PUE only slightly (not shown) in free-cooled datacenters.

However, the largest reductions in maximum range come from our temperature band (and the weather prediction it requires). Comparing Var-High-Recirc and Variation isolates its impact. As we can see, the maximum range goes down substantially for locations with cold or cool seasons when the band is used. The average ranges for these locations also go down but by smaller amounts.

Temporal scheduling. Now we consider whether the ability to defer workloads would enable reductions in temperature variation in All-DEF. Our results indicate that All-DEF provides only minor reductions in both average range and maximum range, compared to All-ND. The reason is that the days when All-ND does poorly in terms of variation are exactly those days when All-DEF decides to forgo temporal scheduling; All-DEF would perform worse if it tried to schedule for those days. For this reason, we argue that All-ND is the best implementation of CoolAir.

Temporal scheduling has been proposed recently for conserving cooling energy in free-cooled datacenters [2, 22, 27]. Though these techniques do conserve energy, *they also widen temperature variations*, compared to All-ND. We observe this by studying *Energy-DEF*, a system that combines the Energy version with temporal scheduling based solely on cooling energy. Like previous techniques, Energy-DEF schedules loads for periods when the outside temperature is low, but still within the jobs' start deadlines. As a sampling of the results, we find that the maximum range for Newark grows from 10 (All-ND) to 19°C (Energy-DEF), in exchange for a reduction in PUE from 1.17 to 1.13. For Santiago, the maximum range grows from 10 to 18°C, while PUE decreases from 1.25 to 1.10. For all five locations, the Energy-DEF maximum ranges are even worse than those of the baseline system.

Impact of the desired maximum temperature. Now we investigate the impact of trying to keep absolute temperatures below different maximum values. For the baseline system, this means setting the temperature setpoint to those values. For CoolAir, this means not allowing the top of the adaptive temperature band to exceed those values, which can be done by setting *Max* to each of them.

We find that the CoolAir benefits tend to be greater when datacenter operators are willing to accept higher maximum temperatures (to allow for lower cooling costs). For example, the reductions in maximum range achieved by CoolAir tend to be greater for a desired maximum temperature of 30°C than 25°C. For locations where PUE is high for a desired maximum temperature of 30°C, CoolAir tends to lower PUEs. However, CoolAir tends to increase PUEs for those same locations when the desired maximum temperature is 25°C.

Impact of weather forecast accuracy. As we only have the TMY data, our simulated predictions of average outside temperature are perfectly accurate. Fortunately, weather services predict daily average temperatures accurately. For example, at our location, predictions are within 2.5°C of the actual daily averages 83% of the time, *i.e.* plenty accurate given CoolAir's 5°C-wide temperature band.

Nevertheless, we next quantify the impact of inaccurate outside temperature predictions on CoolAir. Specifically, we consider scenarios in which average outside temperature predictions are consistently too high by 5°C, and consistently

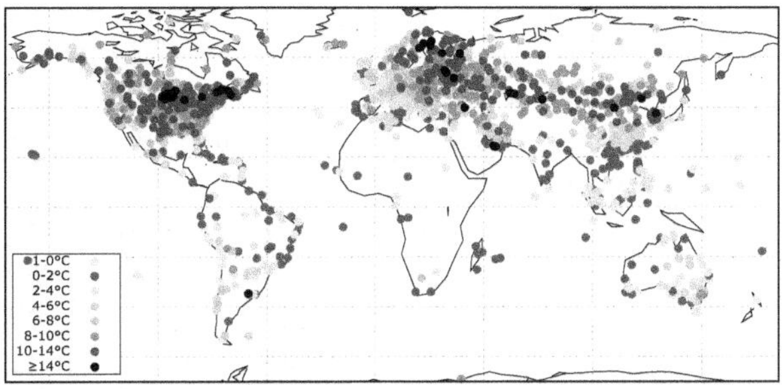

Figure 12. World-wide reduction in max range.

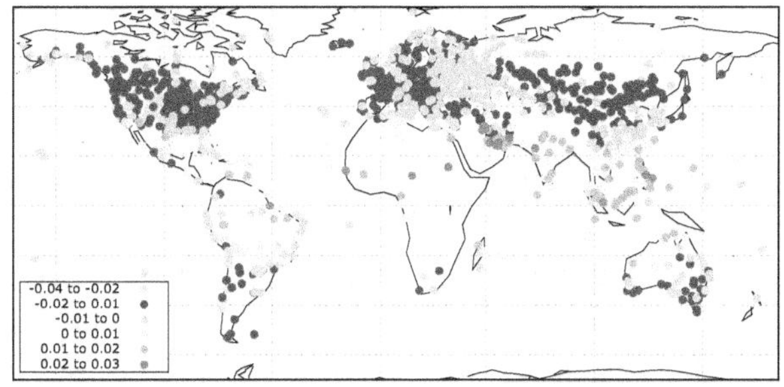

Figure 13. World-wide reduction in yearly PUE.

too low by 5°C. For the former case, our results show increases of the maximum ranges but always by less than 1°C, and reductions in PUE. For the latter case, our results show reductions in the maximum ranges, and increases in PUE but always by less than 0.01. Clearly, the impact of inaccuracies is small, mostly because of CoolAir's temperature band.

Impact of workload. The results above have been for the Facebook workload. We now study the widely different Nutch trace. The results with Nutch exhibit the exact same trends we observe with the Facebook workload (Figures 9 and 10). For example, All-ND cuts the maximum daily temperature range in roughly half for Newark, Santiago, and Iceland, while also lowering the average daily range for all locations. These benefits come with significant PUE reductions for Chad and Singapore, and a small PUE increase for Santiago.

More geographical locations. Finally, we now extend our study to 1520 locations world-wide, assuming the Facebook workload. We do not argue that datacenters could be built at all locations, since there are other issues to consider [16]; rather, we quantify the potential impact of using CoolAir at the locations were datacenters to be built there.

Compared to the baseline system, CoolAir reduces the maximum range from 18.6 to 12.1°C on average, for a slight increase in yearly PUE from 1.08 to 1.09 on average. In more detail, Figures 12 and 13 depict the reductions in maximum range and PUE, respectively, compared to the baseline system. The figures show that CoolAir can reduce maximum ranges significantly in colder locations. Specifically, it can reduce these ranges by between 2 and 14°C in a large number of locations in North America, Europe, and Asia. Similarly, it can reduce the maximum ranges by between 2 and 8°C in many locations in the south of South America and Australia. These reductions come with only a slight penalty in PUE. In fewer than 2% of locations, CoolAir increases the maximum range, but always by less than 1°C.

CoolAir is also useful for locations closer to the Equator, which exhibit higher PUEs. For those locations, CoolAir lowers PUEs without increasing internal temperature variations. Thus, CoolAir should be useful all over the world.

6. Principles and lessons

In summary, our results prompt many observations:

1. If not managed explicitly in free-cooled datacenters, absolute temperatures and variations can be high in many locations (Figures 8 and 9), especially when temperature setpoints are higher. In fact, internal variations can be higher than those outside (Figure 9). These effects have been shown to degrade disk reliability [10, 34, 36].

2. Effectively managing temperature variation requires fine-grain cooling (Figures 7(b) and (d)) and workload control (Figures 9 and 11).

3. Managing absolute temperature costs more than managing variation in regions with warmer seasons, and less in regions with colder ones (Cost of managing temperature and variation, Section 5.2).

4. Adaptive temperature bands and smart spatial workload placement are useful in managing temperature variation (Figure 11), whereas temporal workload scheduling is not (Temporal scheduling, Section 5.2). Moreover, existing energy-driven techniques for spatial and temporal thermal management increase temperature variation (Figure 11 and Temporal scheduling, Section 5.2).

5. Managing absolute temperature and temperature variation is easier when internal temperatures can be higher (Impact of the desired maximum temperature, Section 5.2).

6. The accuracy of weather forecast services is not a problem when managing variations with temperature bands (Impact of weather forecast accuracy, Section 5.2).

7. Managing temperature variation is most critical and successful in cold climates (Figures 12 and 13).

8. Using CoolAir, it is possible to manage absolute temperature and variation at little or no energy cost even in very hot climates (Figures 12 and 13). *This significantly broadens the set of locations where free cooling can be used.*

Generalizing from the case study. Clearly, the results of Section 5.2 are influenced by the characteristics of Parasol. However, we expect that *the observations above should apply to any datacenter,* as our modeling of air temperature and cooling power is similar to that of very different datacenters in the literature. Specifically, the model we learned for air temperature is similar to that in [20]. The power model for free cooling models power as a cubic function of fan speed, as in [27]. Our AC power model was derived experimentally in [26]. For datacenters that combine free cooling with chillers (instead of DX AC), we can use [23] to strike the proper ratio of power consumptions. For a large datacenter with multiple independent "cooling zones" (*e.g.*, containers), each of them would have its own CoolAir-like manager.

Thus, applying our ideas to another datacenter would lead to different temperatures, variations, and PUEs, but the trends (*e.g.*, impact of climate on variation) should be the same.

Practical considerations. CoolAir can be used in a variety of real scenarios, from small-scale datacenters found in universities to large-scale datacenters operated by Internet companies. Free-cooled datacenters, especially large-scale ones, embody temperature, humidity, and power sensors. These sensors facilitate the creation of the corresponding CoolAir models over time (*e.g.*, 6 months or 1 year), *during the normal operation of the datacenter.* (We explicitly generated scenarios for Parasol simply to speedup our learning of the temperature and humidity models.)

Selecting the CoolAir *Offset* and *Width* parameters can be easily done via observation and experimentation, respectively, for a desired tradeoff between ambient control and energy consumption. In fact, our simulation infrastructure would allow the datacenter operator to evaluate multiple settings even before real deployment.

Finally, many real systems and workloads enable flexibility in spatial and temporal scheduling. Spatial flexibility needs to exist for fault tolerance and performance optimization, whereas temporal flexibility exists in real deferrable workloads (*e.g.*, typical batch and data-processing loads).

7. Related Work

To our knowledge, this paper is the *first publicly available study* of the internal absolute temperatures and temperature variations in a real free-cooled datacenter. Though companies like Google and Facebook use free cooling [14, 18], they have not published data on temperature or humidity effects in these datacenters or their disk reliability. Our paper is also the *first study* of techniques for managing temperature and variation in free-cooled datacenters. Finally, our paper is the *first to argue* for (1) fine-grained control of the cooling infrastructure for managing variation; and (2) selecting temperature setpoints based on predictions of outside temperature. Nevertheless, CoolAir does relate to works on the following three topics.

Disk reliability in datacenters. Our motivation to manage absolute temperature and temporal temperature variation in free-cooled datacenters came from papers on disk reliability in non-free-cooled datacenters [10, 34, 36].

Energy-aware thermal management of non-free-cooled datacenters. Similarly to CoolAir, previous efforts have used: machine learning for modeling thermals (*e.g.*, [25, 31]); programmatic control of the cooling infrastructure (*e.g.*, [6, 40]); simulations to predict thermal behavior into the future (*e.g.*, [35]); energy-aware spatial placement of workloads (*e.g.*, [1, 4, 5, 30, 32]); and energy-aware temporal scheduling of workloads (*e.g.*, [4, 32]). The CoolAir contributions here are simulator-based predictions, *spatial placement, and temporal scheduling that seek to manage temperature variation primarily,* not cooling energy. In fact, our results show that the best spatial placement for variation is the *opposite* of the best placement for energy.

Energy-efficiency in free-cooled datacenters. Researchers have studied free cooling and its impact on energy efficiency (*e.g.*, [15, 39]); programmatic control of it (*e.g.*, [12, 41]); techniques for temporal scheduling based on outside temperatures (*e.g.*, [2, 22, 27]); and geographical load balancing based on outside temperatures (*e.g.*, [23]). However, as mentioned above, *none of these studies* considered internal temperature variations, selecting setpoints based on predicted outside temperatures, or techniques for managing variations. In fact, our results demonstrate that temporal scheduling for energy [2, 22, 27] *increases* temperature variations significantly compared to CoolAir.

8. Conclusions

We designed, implemented, and evaluated CoolAir, a system for managing temperature, variation, humidity, and energy in free-cooled datacenters. Though our case-study results are based on Parasol, a real free-cooled datacenter prototype, we derived lessons that apply to other datacenters as well. Importantly, these lessons are useful regardless of how researchers eventually resolve the issue of whether absolute temperature or temperature variation has the strongest impact on hardware reliability. As CoolAir shows, it is possible to manage *both* effects while keeping cooling energy consumption low.

Acknowledgments

We would like to thank our shepherd, Hillery Hunter, as well as Georgios Varsamopoulos, Cristian Perfumo, and Sriram Sankar for comments that helped improve our paper. We are also indebted to NSF grant CSR-1117368 and the Rutgers Green Computing Initiative for their funding of our work.

References

[1] F. Ahmad and T. Vijaykumar. Joint Optimization of Idle and Cooling Power in Data Centers while Maintaining Response Time. In *ASPLOS*, 2010.

[2] M. Arlitt, C. Bash, S. Blagodurov, Y. Chen, T. Christian, D. Gmach, C. Hyser, N. Kumari, Z. Liu, M. Marwah, A. McReynolds, C. Patel, A. Shah, Z. Wang, and R. Zhou. Towards the Design and Operation of Net-zero Energy Data Centers. In *ITherm*, 2012.

[3] ASHRAE Technical Committee. 2011 thermal guidelines for data processing environments – expanded data center classes and usage guidance. *Whitepaper*, 2011.

[4] A. Banerjee, T. Mukherjee, G. Varsamopoulos, and S. Gupta. Cooling-Aware and Thermal-Aware Workload Placement for Green HPC Data Centers. In *IGCC*, 2010.

[5] C. Bash and G. Forman. Cool Job Allocation: Measuring the Power Savings of Placing Jobs at Cooling-Efficient Locations in the Data Center. In *USENIX ATC*, 2007.

[6] C. Bash, C. Patel, and R. Sharma. Dynamic Thermal Management of Air Cooled Data Centers. In *ITherm*, 2006.

[7] Carbon Trust. Variable Speed Drives, 2013. `http://www.carbontrust.com`.

[8] Y. Chen, A. Ganapathi, R. Griffith, and R. Katz. The Case for Evaluating MapReduce Performance Using Workload Suites. In *MASCOTS*, 2011.

[9] Y. Chen, S. Alspaugh, A. Ganapathi, R. Griffith, and R. Katz. Statistical Workload Injector for MapReduce, 2012. `https://github.com/SWIMProjectUCB/SWIM`.

[10] N. El-Sayed, I. Stefanovici, G. Amvrosiadis, A. Hwang, and B. Schroeder. Temperature Management in Data Centers: Why Some (Might) Like it Hot. In *SIGMETRICS*, 2012.

[11] Emerson Network Power. Liebert DSE – DX Cooling and Refrigerant Economizer System, 2013. `http://www.emersonnetworkpower.com`.

[12] H. Endo, H. Kodama, H. Fukuda, T. Sugimoto, T. Horie, and M. Kondo. Effect of Climatic Conditions on Energy Consumption in Direct Fresh-Air Container Data Centers. In *IGCC*, 2013.

[13] EPFL. CloudSuite, 2012. `http://parsa.epfl.ch/cloudsuite/`.

[14] Facebook. Prineville - Facebook Power, 2013. `https://fbpuewue.com/prineville`.

[15] B. Gebrehiwot, K. Aurangabadkar, N. Kannan, D. Agonafer, D. Sivanandan, and M. Hendrix. CFD Analysis of Free Cooling of Modular Data Centers. In *SEMI-THERM*, 2012.

[16] I. Goiri, K. Le, J. Guitart, J. Torres, and R. Bianchini. Intelligent Placement of Datacenters for Internet Services. In *ICDCS*, 2011.

[17] I. Goiri, W. Katsak, K. Le, T. D. Nguyen, and R. Bianchini. Parasol and GreenSwitch: Managing Datacenters Powered by Renewable Energy. In *ASPLOS*, 2013.

[18] Google. Efficiency: How We Do It - Data Centers - Google, 2013. `http://www.google.com/about/datacenters/efficiency/internal/`.

[19] M. Hall, E. Frank, G. Holmes, B. Pfahringer, P. Reutemann, and I. Witten. The WEKA Data Mining Software: An Update. *ACM SIGKDD Explorations Newsletter*, 11(1), 2009.

[20] T. Heath, A. P. Centeno, P. George, L. Ramos, Y. Jaluria, and R. Bianchini. Mercury and Freon: Temperature Emulation and Management for Server Systems. In *ASPLOS*, 2006.

[21] Hitachi. Ramp Load/Unload Technology in Hard Disk Drives, 2007. `http://www.hgst.com`.

[22] N. Kumari, A. Shah, C. Bash, Y. Chen, Z. Liu, Z. Wang, T. Cader, M. Slaby, D. Cepulis, C. Felix, A. Aviles, and M. Figueroa. Optimizing Data Center Energy Efficiency via Ambient-Aware IT Workload Scheduling. In *ITherm*, 2012.

[23] K. Le, J. Zhang, J. Meng, R. Bianchini, Y. Jaluria, and T. D. Nguyen. Reducing Electricity Cost Through Virtual Machine Placement in High Performance Computing Clouds. In *SC*, 2011.

[24] J. Leverich and C. Kozyrakis. On the Energy (In)efficiency of Hadoop Clusters. In *HotPower*, 2009.

[25] L. Li, C. Liang, J. Liu, S. Nath, A. Terzis, and C. Faloutsos. Thermocast: A Cyber-Physical Forecasting Model for Data Centers. In *KDD*, 2011.

[26] Z. Li and S. Deng. An Experimental Study on the Inherent Operational Characteristics of a Direct Expansion (DX) Air Conditioning (A/C) Unit. *Building and Environment*, 42, 2007.

[27] Z. Liu, Y. Chen, C. Bash, A. Wierman, D. Gmach, Z. Wang, M. Marwah, and C. Hyser. Renewable and Cooling Aware Workload Management for Sustainable Data Centers. In *SIGMETRICS*, 2012.

[28] R. Miller. Free Cooling, Illustrated, 2009. `http://www.datacenterknowledge.com/archives/2009/02/03/free-cooling-illustrated/`.

[29] R. Miller. The Evolution of Facebook's Data Center Cooling, 2012. `http://www.datacenterknowledge.com/archives/2012/12/04/evolution-of-facebooks-cooling/`.

[30] J. Moore, J. Chase, P. Ranganathan, and R. Sharma. Making Scheduling "Cool": Temperature-Aware Workload Placement in Data Centers. In *USENIX ATC*, 2005.

[31] J. Moore, J. Chase, and P. Ranganathan. Weatherman: Automated, Online and Predictive Thermal Mapping and Management for Data Centers. In *ICAC*, 2006.

[32] T. Mukherjee, A. Banerjee, G. Varsamopoulos, S. Gupta, and S. Rungta. Spatio-Temporal Thermal-aware Job Scheduling to Minimize Energy Consumption in Virtualized Heterogeneous Data Centers. *Computer Networks*, 53(17), 2009.

[33] J. Park. Open Compute Project–Data Center. Technical report, Facebook, 2011.

[34] E. Pinheiro, W.-D. Weber, and L. A. Barroso. Failure Trends in a Large Disk Drive Population. In *FAST*, 2007.

[35] L. Ramos and R. Bianchini. C-Oracle: Predictive Thermal Management for Data Centers. In *HPCA*, 2008.

[36] S. Sankar, M. Shaw, K. Vaid, and S. Gurumurthi. Datacenter Scale Evaluation of the Impact of Temperature on Hard Disk Drive Failures. *ACM Transactions on Storage*, 9(2), 2013.

[37] Stulz. Stulz Solutions and Services, 2013. `http://www.stulz-ats.com`.

[38] US DOE. Weather Data. `http://apps1.eere.energy.gov/buildings/energyplus/weatherdata_about.cfm`.

[39] B. Weerts, D. Gallaher, R. Weaver, and O. V. Geet. Green Data Center Cooling: Achieving 90% Reduction: Airside Economization and Unique Indirect Evaporative Cooling. In *GreenTech*, 2012.

[40] R. Zhou, Z. Wang, C. B. E, A. McReynolds, C. Hoover, R. Shih, N. Kumari, and R. Sharma. A Holistic and Optimal Approach for Data Center Cooling Management. In *ACC*, 2011.

[41] R. Zhou, Z. Wang, A. McReynolds, C. Bash, T. Christian, and R. Shih. Optimization and Control of Cooling Microgrids for Data Centers. In *ITherm*, 2012.

A Probabilistic Graphical Model-based Approach for Minimizing Energy Under Performance Constraints

Nikita Mishra Huazhe Zhang John D. Lafferty Henry Hoffmann

University of Chicago

{nmishra,huazhe,hankhoffmann}@cs.uchicago.edu, lafferty@galton.uchicago.edu

Abstract

In many deployments, computer systems are underutilized – meaning that applications have performance requirements that demand less than full system capacity. Ideally, we would take advantage of this under-utilization by allocating system resources so that the performance requirements are met and energy is minimized. This optimization problem is complicated by the fact that the performance and power consumption of various system configurations are often application – or even input – dependent. Thus, practically, minimizing energy for a performance constraint requires fast, accurate estimations of application-dependent performance and power tradeoffs.

This paper investigates machine learning techniques that enable energy savings by learning Pareto-optimal power and performance tradeoffs. Specifically, we propose LEO, a probabilistic graphical model-based learning system that provides accurate online estimates of an application's power and performance as a function of system configuration. We compare LEO to (1) offline learning, (2) online learning, (3) a heuristic approach, and (4) the true optimal solution. We find that LEO produces the most accurate estimates and near optimal energy savings.

This work was funded by the U.S. Government under the DARPA PERFECT program, the Dept. of Energy under DOE DE-AC02-06CH11357, NSF grant IIS-1116730 and ONR grant N000141210762. The views and conclusions contained herein are those of the authors and should not be interpreted as representing the official policies, either expressed or implied, of the U.S. Government.

ASPLOS '15, March 14-18, 2015, Istanbul, Turkey..

http://dx.doi.org/10.1145/2694344.2694373

Categories and Subject Descriptors

C.4 [*Modeling Techniques*]: Design Techniques; I.6.5 [*Computing Methodologies*]: Model Development—Modeling methodologies

General Terms

Design, Experimentation, Measurement, Performance

Keywords

Adaptation; Dynamic systems; Statistics; Probabilistic Graphical models; Energy minimization.

1. Introduction

This paper addresses two trends in modern computing systems. First, energy is increasingly important; reducing energy consumption reduces operating costs in datacenters and increases battery life in mobile devices. Second, computer systems are often underutilized, meaning there are significant portions of time where application performance demands do not require the full system capacity [3, 41].

These two trends raise the problem of allocating available resources to meet the current performance demand while minimizing energy consumption. This problem is a *constrained optimization* problem. The current utilization level represents a performance constraint (*i.e.,*an amount of work that must be completed in a given time); system energy consumption represents the objective function to be minimized.

This problem is challenging because it requires a great deal of knowledge to solve. More than knowledge of the single fastest, or most energy efficient system configuration solving this problem requires knowledge of the power and performance available in all configurations and the extraction of those configurations that represent Pareto-optimal tradeoffs. Acquiring this knowledge is additionally complicated by the fact that these power/performance tradeoffs are often application – or even input – dependent. Thus, there is a need for techniques that accurately estimate these application-dependent parameters during run-time.

Machine learning techniques represent a promising approach to addressing this estimation problem. *Offline learning* approaches collect profiling data for known applications and use that to predict optimal behavior for unseen applications (examples include [10, 33, 35, 50, 59]). *Online learning* approaches use information collected while an application is running to quickly estimate the optimal configuration (examples include [1, 34, 37, 40, 44, 45, 52]). Offline methods require minimal runtime overhead, but suffer because they estimate only trends and cannot adapt to particulars of the current application. Online methods customize to the current application, but cannot leverage experience from other applications. In a sense, offline approaches are dependent on a rich training set that represents all possible behavior, while the online approaches generate a statistically weak – *i.e.,*inaccurate – estimator due to small sample size.

In this paper, we present LEO (Learning for Energy Optimization), a learning framework that combines the best of both worlds, *i.e.,*the statistical properties both offline and online estimation. We assume that there is some set of applications for which the power and performance tradeoffs are gathered offline. LEO uses a graphical model to integrate a small number of observations of the current application with knowledge of the previously observed applications to produce accurate estimations of power and performance tradeoffs for the current application in all configurations. LEO's strength is that it quickly matches the behavior of the current application to a subset of the previously observed applications. For example, if LEO has previously seen an application that only scales to 8 cores, it can use that information to quickly determine if the current application will be limited in its scaling.

LEO is a fairly general approach in that it supports many types of applications with different resource needs. It is not, however, appropriate for all computer systems, especially ones, which run many small, unique jobs. Instead, it focuses on supporting systems that 1) execute longer running jobs (in the 10s of seconds) or many repeated instances of short jobs, 2) run at a wide range of utilizations, and 3) might have phases where optimal tradeoffs may change online. For systems that meet these criteria, LEO provides a powerful ability to reduce the energy consumption. For systems that service short ($<$ 1 second), largely unique jobs, LEO will work, but other approaches are probably better matched to those specific needs.

We have implemented LEO on a Linux x86 server and tested its ability to minimize energy for 25 different applications from a variety of different benchmark suites. We first compare LEO's performance and power prediction accuracy to (1) the true value, (2) an offline approach, and (3) an online approach (See Section 6.2). On average, LEO is within 97% of the true value while the offline and online approaches only achieve 79% and 86% accuracy, respectively. We then use LEO to minimize energy for various performance requirements (or system utilizations) (See Section 6.4). Overall we find that our approach is within 6% of the true optimal energy, while the offline approach exceeds optimal energy consumption by 29% and online approach by 24%. Finally, we show that LEO provides near optimal energy savings when adapting to phases within an application.

This paper makes the following contributions:

- To the best of our knowledge, this is the first application of probabilistic graphical models for solving crucial system optimization problems such as energy minimization.
- It presents a graphical model capable of accurately estimating the application-specific performance and power of computer system configurations without prior knowledge of the application. (See Section 5).
- It makes the source code for this learning system available in both Matlab and C++[1].
- It evaluates LEO on a real system. (See Section 6).
- It compares the accuracy of LEO's estimations to both the truth and to offline and online learning approaches (See Section 6.3).
- It integrates LEO into a runtime for energy optimization and finds this learning framework achieves near-optimal energy savings. Furthermore, LEO significantly reduces energy compared to both offline and online approaches as well as the popular race-to-idle heuristic. (See Section 6.4).

The rest of the paper is organized as follows. Section 2 provides a motivational example to build intuition. Section 3 presents notation. Section 4 formalizes the energy minimization problem as a linear program and discusses the application-specific parameters of this problem. Section 5 elaborates our probabilistic graphical model and describes LEO in full detail. Section 6 presents empirical studies on LEO. Related work is discussed in Section 7 and the paper concludes in Section 8.

2. Motivational Example

This section presents an example to motivate LEO and build intuition for the formal models presented subsequently. We consider energy optimization of the `Kmeans` benchmark from Minebench [43]. Kmeans is a clustering algorithm used to analyze large data sets. For this example, we run on a 16-core Linux x86 server with hyperthreading (allowing up to 32 cores to be allocated)[2]. We assume that `Kmeans` may be run with different performance demands and we would like to minimize energy for any given performance demand. To do so for `Kmeans` on our 32-core system we must estimate its performance and power as a function of the number of cores allocated to the application. Given this information, we can easily select the most energy efficient number of cores to use for any performance demand.

To illustrate the benefits of LEO, we will compare it with three other approaches: a heuristic, offline learning, and online learning. The heuristic uses the well know *race-to-idle*

[1] leo.cs.uchicago.edu

[2] Our full system evaluation tests more parameters than simply core allocation. See Section 6 for details.

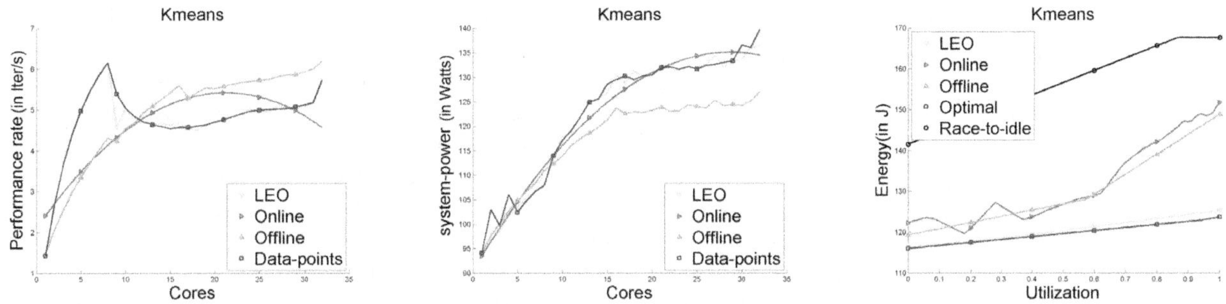

(a) (b) (c)

Figure 1. Power estimation for Kmeans clustering application using LEO, *Online* and *Offline* algorithms. The estimations are made using only 6 observed values (Cores) out of 32.

strategy – simply allocating all resources (cores, clockspeed, etc.) to Kmeans and then idling the system once the application completes. The offline learning approach builds a statistical model of performance and power for each configuration based on prior measurements of other applications. The online approach uses polynomial regression to learn the tradeoffs for each configuration while Kmeans is running. (More details on the specifics of these approaches can be found in Section 6.2).

Each of these three approaches has their limitations. The heuristic approach simply assumes that the most energy efficient configuration is the one where all the system resources are in use, but that has been shown to be a poor assumption for this type of application [21, 41]. The offline approach predicts average behavior for a range of applications, but it may be a poor predictor of specific applications (Kmeans, in this case). The online approach will produce a good prediction if it takes a sufficient number of samples, but the required number of samples may be prohibitive.

LEO combines the best features of both the offline and online approaches. At runtime, it changes core allocation (using process affinity masks), observes the power and performance, and combines this data with that from previously seen applications to obtain the most probable estimates for other unobserved cores. The key advantage of LEO's graphical model approach is that it quickly finds similarities between Kmeans and previously observed applications. It builds its estimation not from every previous application, but only those that exhibit similar performance and power responses to core usage. This exploitation of similarity is the key to quickly producing a more accurate estimate than either strictly online or offline approaches.

Figure 1 shows the results for this example. Figure 1a shows each approach's performance estimates as a function of cores, while Figure 1b shows the estimate of power consumption. These runtime estimates are then used to determine the minimal energy configuration for various system utilizations. Figure 1c shows the energy consumption data where higher utilizations mean more demanding performance requirements. As can be seen in the figures, LEO is the only estimation method that captures the true behavior of the application and this results in significant energy savings across the full range of utilizations.

Learning the performance for Kmeans is hard because the application scales well to 8 cores, but its performance degrades sharply with more. It is quite challenging to find the peak without exploring every possible number of cores. We observe the power and performance at 6 uniformly distributed values ($5, 10, \cdots, 30$ cores). The offline learning method predicts the highest performance at 32 cores because that is the general trend over all applications. The online method predicts peak performance at 24 cores, so it learns that performance degrades, but requires many more samples to correctly place the peak. LEO – in contrast – leverages its prior knowledge of an application whose performance peaks with 8 cores. Because LEO has previously seen an application with similar behavior, it is able to quickly realize that Kmeans follows this pattern and LEO produces accurate estimates with just a small number of observations.

The next three sections formalize this example. Section 3 describes the notation we will use. Section 4 presents a general formalization of this energy minimization problem for any configurable system (not just cores). Section 5 presents the technical description of how LEO incorporates online and offline approaches to find similar applications and produce accurate runtime estimates of power and performance.

3. Notations

The set of real numbers is denoted by $\mathbb{R}$. $\mathbb{R}^d$ denotes the set of d-dimensional vectors of real numbers; $\mathbb{R}^{d\times n}$ denotes the set of real $d \times n$ dimensional matrices. We denote the vectors by lower-case and matrices with upper-case boldfaced letters. The transpose of a vector $\mathbf{x}$ (or matrix $\mathbf{X}$) is denoted by $\mathbf{x}^T$ or just $\mathbf{x}'$. $\|\mathbf{x}\|_2$ is the $\mathcal{L}_2$ norm of vector $\mathbf{x}$, i.e. $\mathbf{x} = \sqrt{\sum_{i=1}^{d} x^2[i]}$. $\|\mathbf{X}\|_F$ is the Frobenius norm of matrix $\mathbf{X}$; *i.e.*, $\|\mathbf{X}\|_F = \sqrt{\sum_{i=1}^{d}\sum_{i=1}^{n} X^2[i][j]}$. Let $\mathbf{A} \in \mathbb{R}^{d\times d}$ denote a d-dimensional square matrix. $\mathrm{tr}(\mathbf{A})$ is the trace of the matrix $\mathbf{A}$ and is given as, $\text{tr}(\mathbf{A}) = \sum_{i=1}^{d} \mathbf{A}[i][i]$. And, $\text{diag}(\mathbf{x})$ is a d-dimensional diagonal matrix $\mathbf{B}$ with the diagonal elements given as, $\mathbf{B}[i][i] = x[i]$ and off-diagonal elements being 0.

We now review the standard statistical notation used below. Let $\mathbf{x}, \mathbf{y}$ denote any random variables in $\mathbb{R}^d$. The notation $\mathbf{x} \sim \mathcal{D}$ represents that $\mathbf{x}$ is drawn from the distribution $\mathcal{D}$. Similarly, the notation $\mathbf{x}, \mathbf{y} \sim \mathcal{D}$ represents that $\mathbf{x}$ and $\mathbf{y}$ are jointly drawn from the distribution $\mathcal{D}$, and finally $\mathbf{x}|\mathbf{y} \sim \mathcal{D}$ represents that $\mathbf{x}$ is drawn from the distribution after observing (or conditioned on) the random variable $\mathbf{y}$. The following are the operators on $\mathbf{x}$: $\mathbb{E}[\mathbf{x}]$: expected value of $\mathbf{x}$, $\text{var}[\mathbf{x}]$: variance of $\mathbf{x}$, $\text{Cov}[\mathbf{x}, \mathbf{y}]$: covariance of $\mathbf{x}$ and $\mathbf{y}$. $\hat{\mathbf{x}}$ denotes the estimated value for the random variable $\mathbf{x}$.

4. Energy Minimization

This section formalizes the problem of minimizing an application's energy consumption for some *performance constraint*; *i.e.,*work that should be accomplished by a particular deadline. We assume a configurable system where each configuration has different application-specific performance and power characteristics. Our aim is to select the configuration that finishes the work by the deadline while minimizing the energy consumption.

Formally, the application must accomplish W work units in time T. The system has a set of configurations (*e.g.,*combinations of cores and clockspeeds) denoted by $\mathcal{C}$. Assuming that each configuration $c \in \mathcal{C}$ has an application-specific performance (or work rate) r_c and power consumption p_c, then we formulate the energy minimization problem as a linear program in Equation (1):

$$\begin{aligned} \min_{\mathbf{t} \geq \mathbf{0}} \quad & \sum_{c \in \mathcal{C}} p_c t_c, \\ \text{subject to} \quad & \sum_{c \in \mathcal{C}} r_c t_c = W, \\ & \sum_{c \in \mathcal{C}} t_c \leq T. \end{aligned} \tag{1}$$

where p_c: Power consumed when running on c^{th} configuration; r_c: Performance rate when running on c^{th} configuration; W: Work that needs to be done by the application; t_c: Time spent by the application in c^{th} configuration; T: Total run time of the application. The linear program above finds the times t_c during which the application runs in the cth configuration so as to minimize the total energy consumption and ensure all work is completed by the deadline. The values p_c and r_c are the key to solving this problem. If they are known, the structure of this linear program allows the minimal energy schedule to be found using convex optimization techniques [6].

This formulation is abstract so that it can be applied to many applications and systems. To help build intuition, we relate it to our `Kmeans` example. For `Kmeans` the workload is the number of samples to cluster. The deadline T is the time by which the clustering must be completed. Configurations represent assigning `Kmeans` different resources. In Section 2, we restricted configurations to be assignment of cores. In Section 6, we will expand configurations to include assignment of cores, clockspeed, memory controllers, and hyperthreads. For `Kmeans`, each assignment of resources results in a different rate of computation (points clustered per time) and power consumption.

Unfortunately, power and performance are entirely application dependent. For many applications, these values also vary with varying inputs. Hence, for any new application in use we do not know the values of these coefficients. One way to solve the problem would be run this new application on each configuration in a brute force manner. But, as we pointed out earlier, we might have very large number of configurations and the brute force approach may not be tractable. Alternatively, we can just run the application in small subset of configurations and use these measurements to estimate the behavior of unmeasured configurations. We might also consider using the data from other applications from the same system to estimate these parameters (we can collect this data offline). The question now is how do we utilize this data to find our estimates. One simple yet clever thing would be to simply take a mean of p_c (similarly for r_c) across all the applications. Now, this offline method will work well for any application that follows the general trend exhibited by all prior applications. Another quick solution could be to just use the small subset of collected sample and run a multivariate polynomial regression on the configuration parameters vs p_c (or r_c) to predict power (performance) in all other configurations. This online method might not work for all the applications s because they might have local minima or maxima that are not captured by a small sample. In the next section, Section 5 we give details of LEO, our solution to this problem which uses both the data from the current application and previously seen applications for fast, accurate estimates.

5. Modeling Power and Performance

5.1 Introduction to Probabilistic Graphical Models

We present an introduction to graphical models in general before we delve into the details of LEO specifically. Directed graphical models (or Bayesian networks) are a type of graphical model capturing dependence between random variables. Each node in these models denotes a random variable and the edges denote a conditional dependence among the connecting nodes. The nodes which have no edges connecting them are conditionally independent. By convention shaded nodes denote an observed variable (*i.e.,*one whose value is known), whereas the unshaded ones denote an unobserved variable. In Figure 2a, variables A and B are dependent on C. If C is observed, A and B would be independent in Figure 2b.

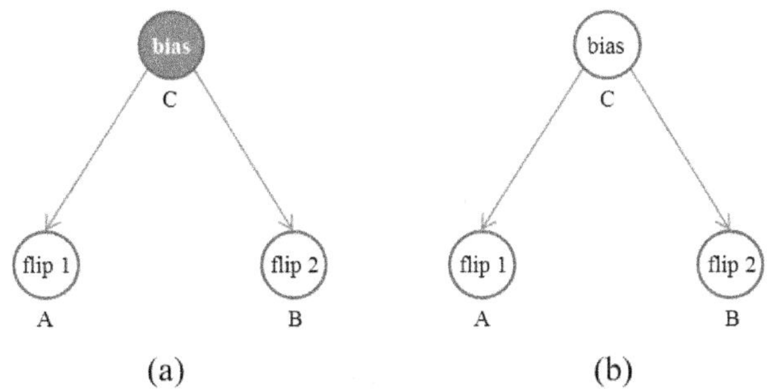

Figure 2. Conditional dependence in Bayesian Model.

The dependence structure in Bayesian networks can be understood using a coin flipping example with a biased coin. Suppose A represents the outcome of the first coin flip, B represents that of second coin flip and C represents the coin's bias. Suppose we know this bias is $P(Heads) = 0.7$, then both the flips are independent — irrespective of the first flip the second flip gives *heads* with probability 0.7. If the bias is unknown, however, then the value of B is conditionally dependent on A. Thus, knowing that $A = Heads$ increases belief that the bias is towards *Heads* – that $C > 0.5$. Therefore, the probability that the second coin flip gives *Heads* (*i.e.*,$B = Heads$) increases.

LEO exploits this conditional dependence in the presence of hidden, or unobserved, random variables. LEO models the performance and power consumption of every system configuration as a random variable drawn from a Gaussian probability distribution with unknown mean and standard deviation. *Therefore, previously observed applications will condition LEO's estimations of the performance and power for new, unobserved applications.*

5.2 Hierarchical Bayesian Model

Hierarchical Bayesian Models are slightly more complex Bayesian networks, usually with more than one layer of hidden nodes representing unobserved variables. LEO utilizes these hidden nodes to improve its estimates for a new application using prior observations from other applications. The intuition is that *knowing about one application should help in producing better predictors for other applications.* In our examples, learning about one biased coin flip should tell us something about another. Similarly, learning about another application that scales up to 8 cores should tell us something about Kmeans. LEO utilizes this conditional dependence in the problem of performance and power prediction for an application using other applications. LEO's model is explained in the figure Figure 3,

Suppose we have $n = |\mathcal{C}|$ configurations in our system. We have a *target application* whose energy we wish to minimize, while meeting a performance requirement (as in (1)). Additionally, we have a set of $M-1$ applications whose performance and power are known (as they have been measured offline).

We will illustrate how LEO estimates power as a function of system configuration. The identical process is used to estimate performance. Let the vector $\mathbf{y}_i \in \mathbb{R}^n$ represent the power estimate of application i in all n configurations of the system; *i.e.*,the cth component of $\mathbf{y}_i$ is the power for application i in configuration c (or $\mathbf{y}_i[c] = p_c$). Also, let $\{\mathbf{y}_i\}_{i=1}^{M}$ be the shorthand for the power estimates for all applications. Without loss of generality, we assume that the first $M-1$ columns, *i.e.*,$\{\mathbf{y}_i\}_{i=1}^{M-1}$ represent the data for those applications whose power consumption is known (this data is collected offline). The Mth column, $\mathbf{y}_M$ represents the power consumption for the new, unknown application. We have some small number of observations for this application. Specifically, for the Mth application we have observed configurations belonging to the set Ω_M where $|\Omega_M| \ll n$; *i.e.*,we have a very small number of observations for this application. Our objective is to estimate the power for application M for all configurations that we have not observed. The model is described in terms of statistical equations below,

$$\begin{aligned} \mathbf{y}_i|\mathbf{z}_i &\sim N(\mathbf{z}_i, \sigma^2\mathbb{I}), \\ \mathbf{z}_i|\mu, \Sigma &\sim N(\mu, \Sigma), \\ \mu, \Sigma &\sim N(\mu_0, \Sigma/\pi) IW(\Sigma|\nu, \Psi), \end{aligned} \tag{2}$$

where $\mathbf{y}_i \in \mathbb{R}^n$, $\mathbf{z}_i \in \mathbb{R}^n$, $\mu \in \mathbb{R}^n$, $\Sigma \in \mathbb{R}^{n \times n}$. It describes that the power (denoted by $\mathbf{y}_i$) for each of the ith application, is drawn from multivariate-Gaussian distribution with mean $\mathbf{z}_i$ and a diagonal covariance matrix $\sigma^2\mathbb{I}$. Similarly, $\mathbf{z}_i$ is from multivariate-Gaussian distribution with mean μ and covariance Σ. And, μ and Σ are jointly drawn from normal-inverse-Wishart distribution with parameters μ_0, π, Ψ, ν. The parameters for our model are μ, Σ, whereas, μ_0, π, Ψ, ν are the hyper-parameters, which we set as $\mu_0 = 0, \pi = 1, \Psi = \mathbb{I}, \nu = 1$.

The first layer in this model as described in Figure 3, is the filtration layer and accounts for the measurement error for each application. Interestingly, even if we have just a single measurement of each configuration for each application, this layer plays a crucial role as it creates a shrinkage effect. The shrinkage effect penalizes large variations in the application and essentially help in reducing the risk of the model (See [15] for shrinkage effect and [42] for shrinkage in hierarchical models). The second layer on the other hand binds the variable $\mathbf{z}_i$ for each application and enforces that they are drawn from the same distribution with unknown mean and covariance. We work with a normal-inverse-Wishart distribution as described in [19] as our hyper prior on μ, Σ, since this distribution is the conjugate prior for a multivariate Gaussian distribution. Thus, we essentially have a normal means model at the first level of our hierarchy for each of the different apps and we have a Gaussian prior on the parameter of this model. Now, if the mean μ, covariance Σ and noise σ were known, $\mathbf{y}_i$ are conditionally independent given these

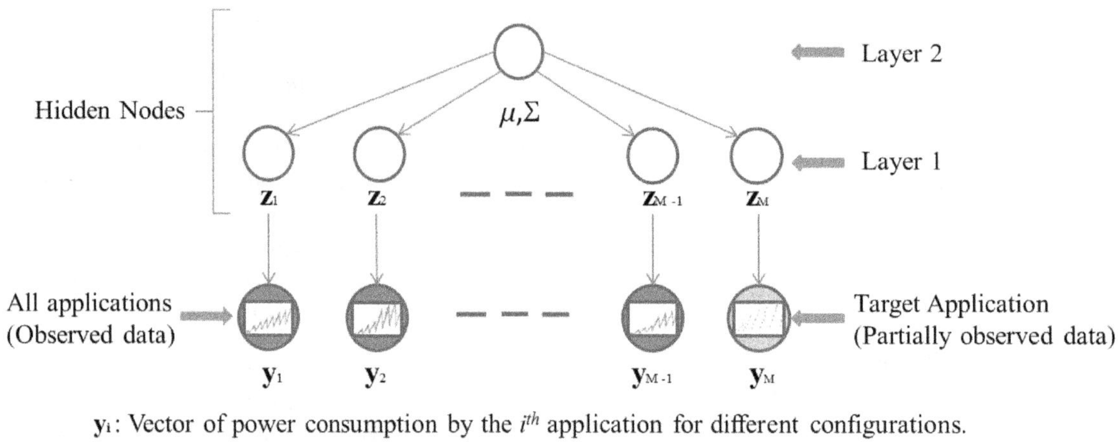

Figure 3. Hierarchical Bayesian Model.

parameters. Since they are unknown we have introduced a dependence amongst all the $\mathbf{y}_i$s. This is a similar situation to our coin flipping example in Figure 2, where the value of one coin influences our prediction about the other coin. Σ captures the correlation between different configurations as depicted in Figure 4.

We use $\theta = \{\mu, \Sigma, \sigma\}$ to denote the unknown parameters in the model. It can be shown that $\mathbf{y}_M$ is Gaussian given θ (See [60]). Thus, the problem boils down to estimating θ. Maximum-likelihood estimators are the set of values of the model parameters that maximizes the likelihood function (or the probability function of the observed outcomes given the parameter values). Essentially, the maximum-likelihood estimates of parameters are those values which most agree with the model. Suppose $\phi(\mathbf{y})$ is the set of the observed entries in vector $\mathbf{y}$. Ideally, we would like to find the maximum likelihood estimate of the parameter θ by maximizing the probability of $\mathbf{y}_M$ conditioned on $\phi(\mathbf{y}_i)_{i=1}^{M}$ and then use the expectation of $\mathbf{y}_M$ given $\phi(\mathbf{y}_i)_{i=1}^{M}$ and $\hat{\theta}$ and as our estimator for $\mathbf{y}_M$. Due to the presence of latent variables (layer 1 and layer 2 in Figure 3) , we do not have a closed form for $\Pr(\mathbf{y}_M|\{\phi(\mathbf{y}_i)\}_{i=1}^{M}, \theta)$ and we have to resort to the iterative algorithms like Expectation Maximization algorithm to solve this problem.

5.3 Expectation Maximization Algorithm

The EM (Expectation Maximization) algorithm is a popular approach in statistics for optimizing over analytically intractable problems. The EM algorithm switches between two steps: *expectation* (E) and *maximization* (M) until convergence. During the E step, a function for the expectation of the log of the likelihood is found using the current estimate for the parameters. In the M step, we compute parameters maximizing the expected log-likelihood found on the E step. These parameter estimates are then used to determine the distribution of the latent variables in the next E step. We have left out some details of the algebra here, but a more detailed proof on similar lines can be found here [60].

As described earlier, Ω_i is the set of observed indices for i^{th} application. Let L denote the indicator matrix with $L(i,j) = 1$ if $j \in \Omega_i$ and 0 otherwise. That is, $L(i,j) = 1$ if we have observed application i in system configuration j. We are using L_i for $L(:,i)$ for i^{th} application for shorter notation. We can write the expectation and covariance for $\mathbf{z}_i$ given θ as following,

$$\begin{aligned} \mathrm{Cov}(\mathbf{z}_i) &= \left(\frac{\mathrm{diag}(L_i)}{\sigma^2} + \Sigma^{-1}\right)^{-1} \quad \text{and} \\ \mathbb{E}(\mathbf{z}_i) &= \hat{\mathbf{C}}_i\left(\frac{\mathrm{diag}(L_i)\mathbf{y}_i}{\sigma^2} + \Sigma^{-1}\mu\right). \end{aligned} \tag{3}$$

We use $\hat{\mathbf{C}}_i$ as shorthand for $\mathrm{Cov}(\mathbf{z}_i)$ and $\hat{\mathbf{z}}_i$ denotes $\mathbb{E}(\mathbf{z}_i)$. Later, we maximize log-likelihood w.r.t. θ and taking derivative w.r.t. Σ, σ and μ and setting them to 0 gives,

$$\begin{aligned} \mu &= \frac{1}{M+\pi}\sum_{i=1}^{M}\hat{\mathbf{z}}_i, \\ \Sigma &= \frac{1}{M+1}\left(\sum_{i=1}^{M}\hat{\mathbf{C}}_i + (\hat{\mathbf{z}}_i - \mu)(\hat{\mathbf{z}}_i - \mu)'\right) + \pi\mu\mu' + \mathbb{I}, \\ \sigma^2 &= \frac{1}{\|L\|_F^2}\sum_{i=1}^{M}\mathrm{tr}\left(\mathrm{diag}(L_i)(\hat{\mathbf{C}}_i' + (\hat{\mathbf{z}}_i - \mathbf{y}_i)(\hat{\mathbf{z}}_i - \mathbf{y}_i)')\right), \end{aligned} \tag{4}$$

LEO iterates over the E step (equation (3)) and M step (equation (4)) until convergence to obtain the estimated parameters θ. Then, conditioned on those values of the parameters, LEO sets $\mathbf{y}_M$ as $\mathbb{E}(\mathbf{z}_M|\theta)$ given by (3). LEO uses the same algorithm to estimate performance as well.

Given performance and power estimates, the energy minimization problem can be solved using existing convex optimization techniques [24, 27, 36, 61]. LEO simply first take the estimates, then finds the set of configurations that represent Pareto-optimal performance and power tradeoffs, and

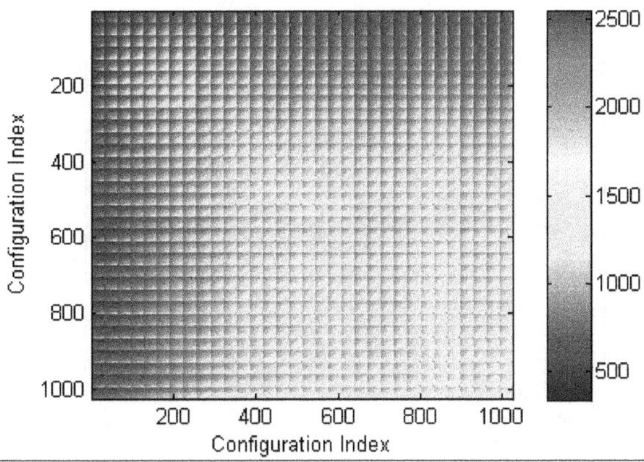

Figure 4. A illustrative example of covariance Σ between different configurations, in equation (2)

finally walks along the convex hull of this optimal tradeoff space until the performance goal is reached. The configuration representing this this point in the Pareto-optimal space is the desired tradeoff.

5.4 Example

We illustrate how LEO can be applied to our running example of `Kmeans` from Section 2. We have 32 configurations (hence $n = 32$) corresponding to cores. We also have 24 other applications (hence $M = 25$) with all the data for different configurations collected offline and denoted by $\{\mathbf{y}_i\}_{i=1}^{M-1}$; $\mathbf{y}_M$ denotes the power data for `Kmeans`. Referring to Figure 3, `Kmeans` is the final node, labeled "Target Application," whereas the rest of the applications would be the remaining nodes in any order. LEO estimates $\mathbf{z}_M$, the node above $\mathbf{y}_M$ in Figure 3, which is an unbiased estimator for $\mathbf{y}_M$. LEO collects data $\mathbf{y}_M$ for 6 different configurations (5, 10, $\cdots$, 30 cores). Hence, $\Omega_M = \{5, 10, \cdots, 30\}$ and $\mathbf{y}_M[j]$ is known iff $j \in \Omega_M$. Also, L_i or $L(:, i)$ is an all one vector of length n if $i \neq M$ and $L(j, i) = 1$ if $j \in \Omega_M$ and $L(j, i) = 0$ otherwise.

Now, we describe the main steps of LEO. The algorithm starts by setting some initialization for the parameter $\theta = \{\mu, \Sigma, \sigma\}$ and then evaluates equation (3) for each ith and later uses these values of $\hat{\mathbf{z}}_i$ and $\hat{C}_i$ to evaluate equation (4), which is fed back to expectation (3) and so on. This alternating step between equation (3) and (4) runs until the algorithm converges. The algorithm uses $\hat{\mathbf{z}}_M$ as the estimate of `Kmeans` power (*i.e.*,$p_c = \hat{\mathbf{z}}_M[c], \forall c \in \mathcal{C}$ in equation (1)). Similarly, LEO estimates the performance r_c. After the estimation step the linear program in equation (1) is solved to obtain the best configuration.

5.5 Discussion

The key to LEO is that it does not assume any parametric function to describe how the power varies along the underlying configuration knobs such as cores, memory controllers or speed settings. The upside of this representation is that LEO captures a much wider variety of applications, whereas the downside is a higher computational load. LEO finds covariance in the configurations and exploits these relationships to estimate the data for each of the configurations (See Figure 4). We want to again point out how our modeling of the problem is markedly different from some of the previous approaches (such as [12]), which assume that power and performance are convex functions of the configuration knobs and employ algorithms similar to gradient descent to find the optimal configuration. While such methods work well for most applications, it may not be suitable for more complicated applications. *In contrast, LEO assumes that there will be many local minima and maxima in the functions mapping system configuration to power and performance – LEO is designed to be robust to the presence of local extrema, but this property is achieved at a cost of higher computational complexity.*

We describe some of the properties of LEO. The EM algorithm's convergence is dependent on the initial model [56]. We can initialize the algorithm randomly. Empirically, however, we observe that the initialization of μ with the estimates from the online or offline approaches (given in Section 6.2) improves LEO's accuracy. Experimentally we have observed that the algorithm converges quickly for our benchmark sets, generally requiring 3-4 iterations to reach the desired accuracy. We discuss the overhead of LEO further in Section 6.7.

6. Experimental Results

This section evaluates LEO's performance and power estimates, and its ability to use those estimates to minimize energy across a range of performance requirements. We begin by describing our experimental setup and the approaches to which we compare LEO. We discuss LEO's accuracy for performance and power estimates. We then show that LEO provides near optimal energy savings using these estimates. We conclude the evaluation with a sensitivity analysis showing how LEO performs with respect to different sample sizes and a measurement of LEO's overhead.

6.1 Experimental Setup

Our test platform is a dual-socket Linux 3.2.0 system with a SuperMICRO X9DRL-iF motherboard and two Intel Xeon E5-2690 processors. We use the `cpufrequtils` package to set the processor's clock speed. These processors have eight cores, fifteen DVFS settings (from 1.2 – 2.9 GHz), hyper-threading, and TurboBoost. In addition, each chip has its own memory controller, and we use the `numactl` library to control access to memory controllers. In total, the system supports 1024 user-accessible configurations, each with its own power/performance tradeoffs[3]. According to Intel's documentation, the thermal design power for these proces-

[3] 16 cores, 2 hyperthreads, 2 memory controllers, and 16 speed settings (15 DVFS settings plus TurboBoost)

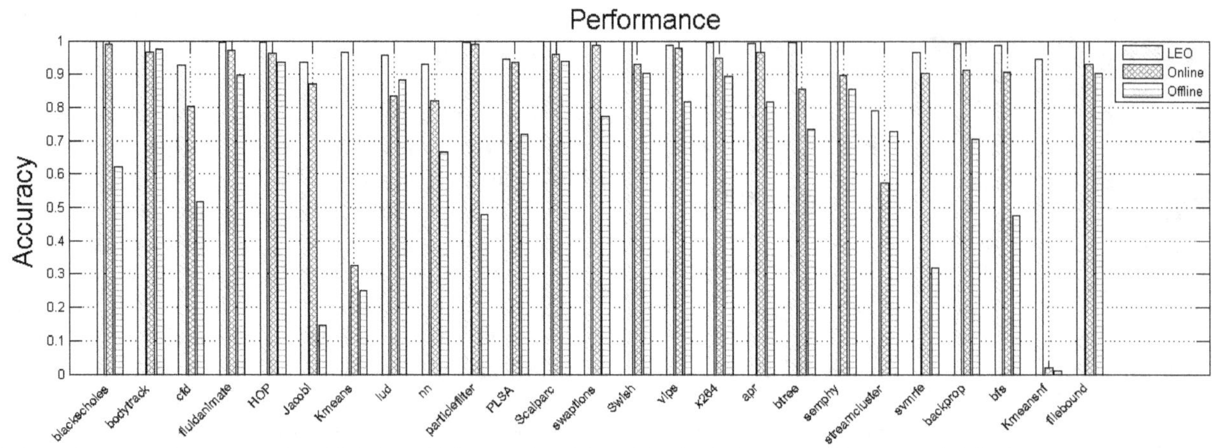

Figure 5. Comparison of performance (measured as speedup) estimation by different techniques for various benchmarks. On an average (over all benchmarks), *LEO*'s accuracy is 0.97 compared to 0.87 and 0.68 for *Online* and *Offline* respectively. The results are normalized with respect to the *Exhaustive search* method.

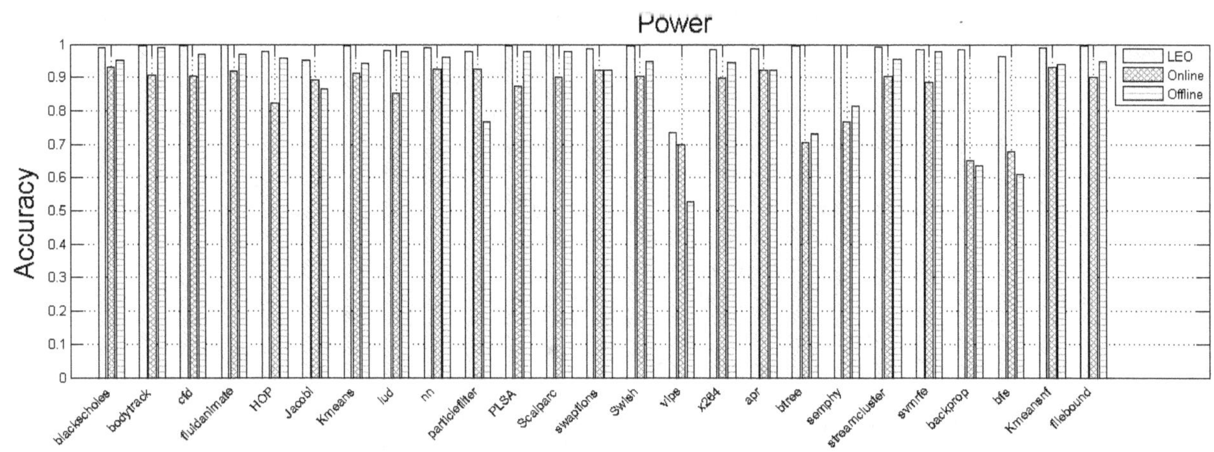

Figure 6. Comparison of power (measured in Watts) estimation by different techniques for various benchmarks. On an average (over all benchmarks), *LEO*'s accuracy is 0.98 compared to 0.85 and 0.89 for *Online* approach and *Offline* approach respectively. Again, the results are normalized with respect to the *Exhaustive search* method.

sors is 135 Watts. The system is connected to a WattsUp meter which provides total system power measurements at 1s intervals. In addition, we use Intel's RAPL power monitor to measure chip power for both sockets at finer-grain intervals. We use 25 benchmarks from three different suites including PARSEC (`blackscholes`, `bodytrack`, `fluidanimate`, `swaptions`, `x264`) [4], Minebench (`ScalParC`, `apr`, `semphy`, `svmrfe`, `Kmeans`, `HOP`, `PLSA`, `non fuzzy kmeans` (`Kmeansnf`)) [43], and Rodinia (`cfd`, `nn`, `lud`, `particlefilter`, `vips`, `btree`, `streamcluster`, `backprop`, `bfs`) [8]. We also use a partial differential equation solver (`jacobi`), a file intensive benchmark (`filebound` and the `swish++` search web-server [25]. These benchmarks test a range of important multi-core applications with both compute-intensive and i/o-intensive workloads. All the applications run with up to 32 threads (the maximum supported in hardware on our test machine). In addition, all workloads are long running, taking at least 10 seconds to complete. This duration gives sufficient time to measure system behavior. All applications are instrumented with the Application Heartbeats library which provides application specific performance feedback to LEO [22, 27]. Thus LEO is ensured of optimizing the performance that matters to the application. All performance results are then estimated and measured in terms of heartbeats/s. In the `Kmeans` example, this metric would represent the samples clustered per second.

To evaluate LEO quantitatively, we measure the *accuracy* of the predicted performance and power values $\hat{\mathbf{y}}$ with respect to the true data $\mathbf{y}$ is measured as,

$$\text{accuracy}(\hat{\mathbf{y}}, \mathbf{y}) = \max\left(1 - \frac{\|\hat{\mathbf{y}} - \mathbf{y}\|_2^2}{\|\mathbf{y} - \bar{\mathbf{y}}\|_2^2}, 0\right). \tag{5}$$

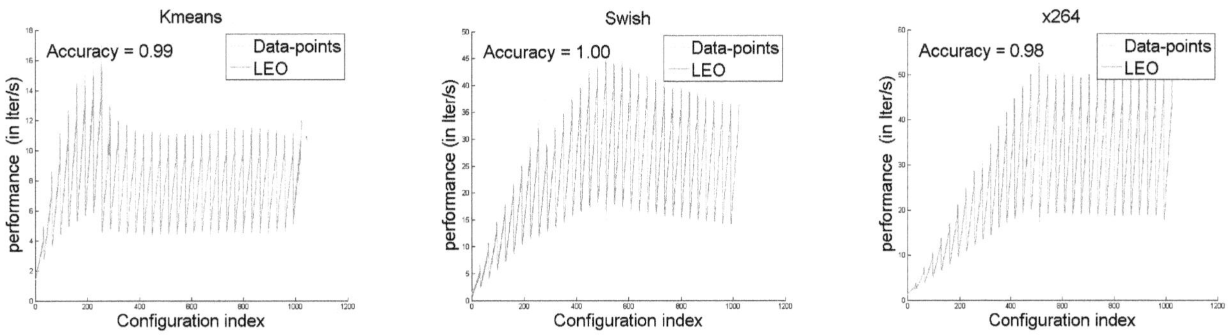

(a) (b) (c)

Figure 7. Examples of performance estimation using LEO. Performance is measured as application iterations (or heartbeats) per second. (See Section 6.1).

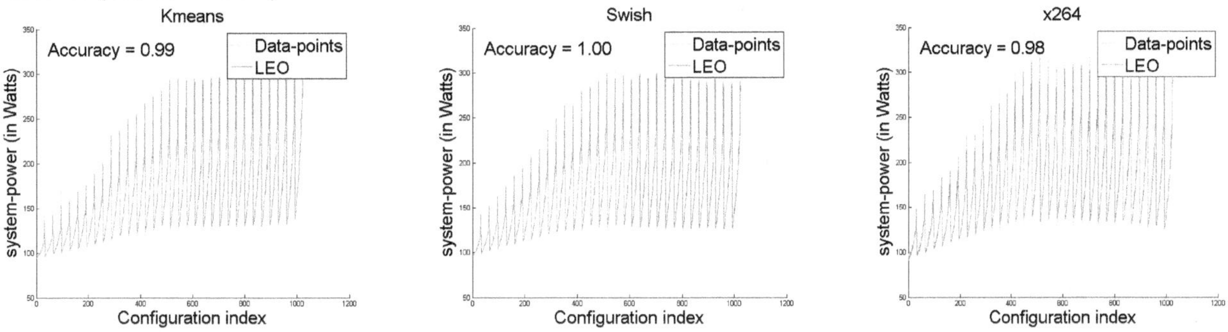

(a) (b) (c)

Figure 8. Examples of power estimation using LEO. Power is measured as total system power.

6.2 Points of Comparison

We evaluate LEO in comparison to four baselines:

1. *Race-to-idle* – This approach allocates all resources to the application and once it is finished the system goes to idle. This strategy incurs almost no runtime overhead, but may be suboptimal in terms of energy, since maximum resource allocation is not always the best solution to the energy minimization equation (1) [7, 21, 32].
2. *Online* – This strategy carries out polynomial multivariate regression on the observed dataset using configuration values (the number of cores, memory control and speed-settings) as predictors, and estimates the rest of the data-points based the same model. Then it solves the linear program given by (1). This method uses only the observations and not the prior data.
3. *Offline* – This method takes the mean over the rest of the applications to estimate the power and performance of the given application and uses these predictions to solve for minimal energy. This strategy only uses prior information and we does not update based on runtime observations.
4. *Exhaustive search* – This brute-force approach searches every possible configuration to determine the true performance, power, and optimal energy for all applications.

6.3 Power and Performance using LEO

We compare LEO's estimates to the *online*, *offline*, and exhaustive search methods described in Section 6.2. We deploy each of our 25 applications on our test system and estimate performance and power. We allow LEO and the online method to sample randomly select 20 configurations each. Unlike online method, which only uses these 20 samples, LEO utilizes these 20 samples along with all the data from the other applications for the estimation purpose. For both LEO and the online approach, we take the average estimates produced over 10 separate trials to account for random variations. The offline approach does no sampling. The exhaustive approach samples all 1024 configurations.

The performance and power estimation accuracies are shown in Figure 5 and Figure 6, respectively. Each chart shows the benchmarks on the x-axis and estimation accuracy (computed using Equation 5) on the y-axis. Unity represents perfect accuracy. As seen in these charts, LEO produces significantly higher accuracy for both performance and power. On average – across all benchmarks and all configurations – LEO's estimations achieve 0.97 accuracy for performance and 0.98 for power. In contrast, the online approach achieves accuracies of 0.87 and 0.85, while the offline approach's accuracies are 0.68 and 0.89. Even for difficult benchmarks

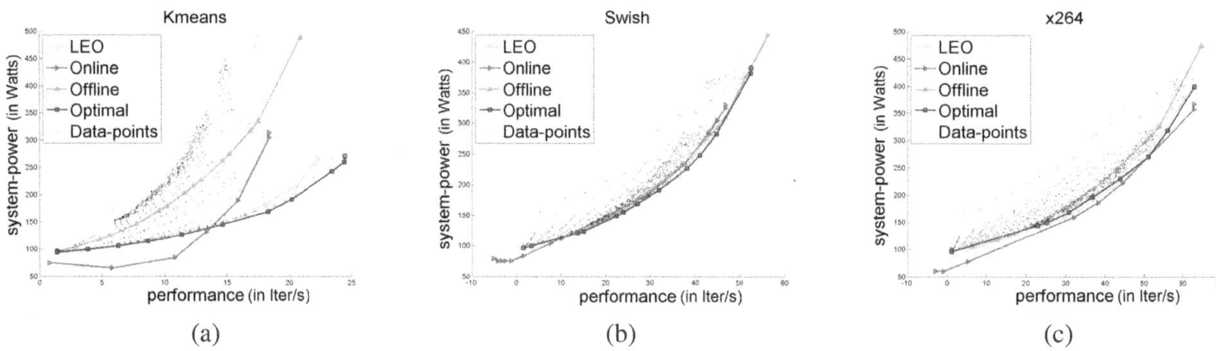

Figure 9. Pareto frontier for power and performance estimation using different estimation algorithms. We compare estimated Pareto-optimal frontiers to the true frontier found with exhaustive search, providing insight into how LEO solves equation (1). When the estimated curves are below optimal plots, it represents worse performance i.e. missed deadlines, whereas the estimations above the optimal waste energy.

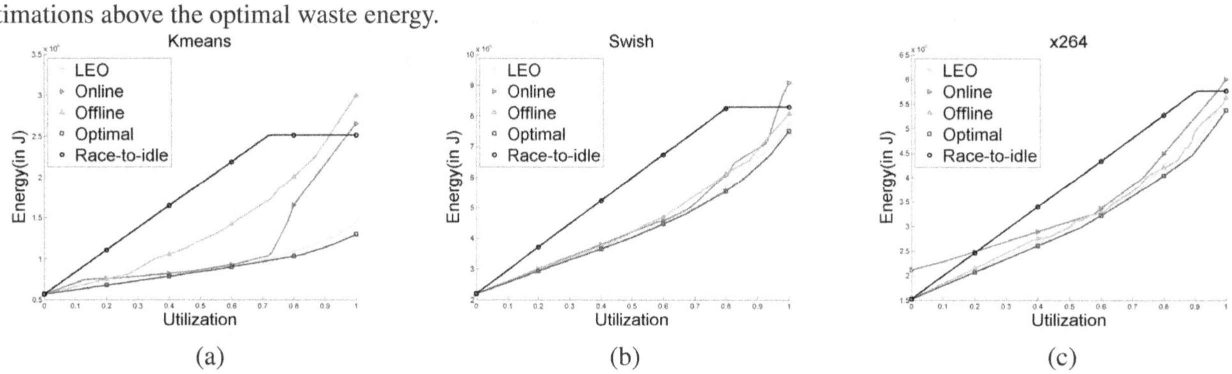

Figure 10. Energy consumption vs utilization for different estimation algorithms.

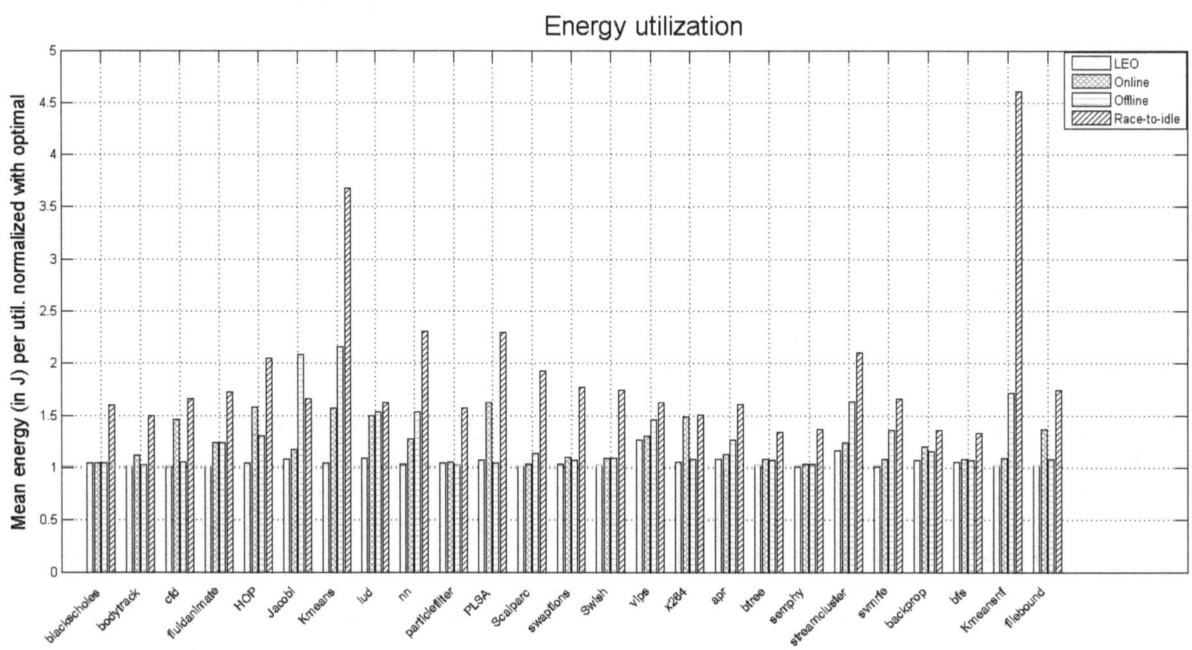

Figure 11. Comparison of average energy (normalized to optimal) by different estimation techniques for various benchmarks. On an average (taken over all the benchmarks); *LEO* consumes 6% over optimal, as compared to the *Online*, *Offline*, and *Race-to-idle* approaches, which respectively consume 24%, 29% and 90% more energy than optimal.

(like Kmeans), LEO produces accurate estimations despite sampling less than 2% of the possible configuration space.

To further illustrate LEO, we include some individual estimations for three representative applications: Kmeans, Swish, and x264. Kmeans is the same application used in our example (Section 2), now extended to consider all 1024 configurations of the test system. Swish is an open source search web server. x264 is a video encoder. All three are representative of our target applications: they are long running and they may be launched with different performance demands. Furthermore, all three represent some unusual trends: performance for Kmeans peaks at 8 cores, for Swish it peaks at 16 cores, and for x264 it is (essentially) constant after 16 cores.

Despite this behavior, LEO produces highly accurate estimates of performance (Figure 7) and power (Figure 8). Each figure shows the configuration index on the x-axis and the predicted performance (or power) on the y-axis. Each chart shows both the estimated values and the measured data points, but LEO is so accurate that it is hard to distinguish the two. The figures (Figure 7 and Figure 8) are saw-tooth in appearance since the speed settings vary from low to high along the *Configuration index* multiple times. The saw-tooth nature of the curves arises from two sources: (1) the extrema that naturally arise (*e.g.,*response to cores) and (2) we have flattened a multi-dimensional configuration space into the configuration index. The number of memory controllers is the fastest changing component of configuration, followed by clockspeed, followed by number of cores. LEO captures the peak performance configuration for all three applications and it captures local minima and maxima. These accurate estimates of unusual behavior make LEO well-suited for use in energy minimization problems.

6.4 Minimizing Energy

Our original goal, of course, is not just to estimate performance and power, but to minimize energy for a performance (or utilization) target. As described in Section 5.3, LEO uses its estimates to form the Pareto-optimal frontier of performance and power tradeoffs. Figure 9 shows the true convex hull and those estimated by the LEO, Offline and Online approaches. Due to space limitations, we show only the hulls for our three representative applications: Kmeans, Swish, and x264. In these figures performance (measured as speedup) is shown on the x-axis and system wide power consumption (in Watts) on the y-axis. These figures clearly show that LEO's more accurate estimates of power and performance produce more accurate estimates of Pareto-optimal tradeoffs.

To evaluate energy savings, we deploy each application with varying performance demands. Technically, we fix the deadline and vary the workload W from Equation 1 so that $W \in [minPerformance, maxPerformance]$ for each application. We test 100 different values for W – each representing a different utilization demand from 1 to 100% – for each application. We then use each approach to estimate power and performance and form the estimated convex hull and select the minimal energy configuration.

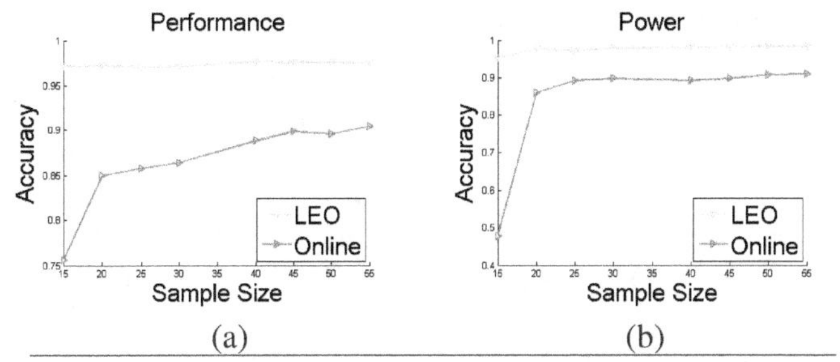

Figure 12. Sensitivity analysis of LEO and Online estimation. Our baseline method (online regression) cannot perform below 15 samples because the design matrix of regression model would be rank deficient – effectively 0 accuracy. On the other hand, with 0 samples, LEO behaves as the offline method and its accuracy increases with the sample size until it quickly reaches near optimal accuracy.

Figure 10 shows the results for our three representative benchmarks. Each chart shows the utilization demand on the x-axis and the measured energy (in Joules) on the y-axis. Each chart shows the results for the LEO, Online, and Offline estimators as well as the race-to-idle approach and the true optimal energy. As shown in these figures, LEO produces the lowest energy results across the full range of different utilization targets. LEO is always close to optimal and outperforms the other estimators. Note that all approaches do significantly better than race-to-idle. We repeat the above experiment for all applications, then average the energy consumption for each application across all utilization levels. These results are shown in Figure 11, which displays the benchmark on the x-axis and the average energy (normalized to optimal) on the y-axis. On an average across all the applications, LEO does only 6% worse than optimal. In contrast, Online, Offline and race-to-idle methods are 24% , 29% and 90% worse respectively. These results demonstrate that LEO not only produces more accurate estimates of performance and power, but that these estimates produce significant – near optimal – energy savings.

6.5 Sensitivity to Measured Samples

One of the key parameters of LEO is the number of samples it must measure to produce an accurate estimate. All of the above measurements were taken with the system configured to sample 20 configurations. In this section, we investigate the effect of the number of configurations on the accuracy of performance and power estimation. In Figure 12, we show the accuracy (averaged over all benchmarks) for performance (a) and power (b) estimation as a function of sample size. We observe that LEO performs well with an even smaller sample size, whereas the Online approach does poorly for very small sample sizes.

6.6 Reacting to Dynamic Changes

This section shows that LEO can quickly react to changes in application workload. In this section we run `fluidanimate`, which renders frames, with an input that has two distinct phases. Both phases must be completed in the same time, but the second phase requires significantly less work. In particular, the second phase requires 2/3 the resources of the first phase. Our goal is to demonstrate that LEO can quickly react to phase changes and maintain near optimal energy consumption.

Table 1. Relative energy consumption by various algorithms with respect to optimal.

Algorithm	Phase#1	Phase#2	Overall
LEO	1.045	1.005	1.028
Offline	1.169	1.275	1.216
Online	1.325	1.248	1.291

The results of this experiment are shown in Figure 13. Each chart shows time (measured in frames) on the x-axis. Figure 13a shows performance normalized to real-time on the x-axis, while Figure 13b shows power in Watts (subtracting out idle power) on the y-axis. The dashed vertical line shows where the phase change occurs. Each chart shows the behavior for LEO, Offline, Online, and optimal approaches.

All approaches are able to meet the performance goal in both phases. This fact is not surprising as all use gradient ascent to increase performance until the demand is met. The real difference comes when looking at power consumption, however. Here we see that LEO again produces near optimal power consumption despite the presence of phases. Furthermore, this power consumption results in near optimal energy consumption as well, as shown in Table 1. These results indicate that LEO produces accurate results even in dynamically changing environments.

6.7 Overhead

The runtime takes several measurements, incurring minuscule sampling overhead. After collecting these samples, it incurs a one-time cost of executing LEO. After executing this algorithm, the models are sufficient for making predictions and LEO does not need to be executed again for the life of the application under control. This is the reason we believe LEO is best suited for long running applications which may operate at a range of different utilizations. The one-time estimation process is sufficient to provide accurate estimates for the full range of utilizations (see Section 6.4).

Therefore, we measure overhead in two ways. First, we measure the average time required to execute LEO on our system. The average execution time is 0.8 seconds across each benchmarks for each power and performance. Second, we measure the average total system energy consumption while executing the runtime, obtaining an energy overhead of 178.5 Joules. These overheads are not trivial, and they indicate (as stated in the introduction) that LEO is not appropriate for all deployments. For applications that run in the 10s of seconds to minutes or more, however, LEO's overheads are easily amortized by the large energy savings it enables. For comparison, the exhaustive search approach takes more than 5 days to produce the estimates for `semphy`. For the fastest application in our suite, `HOP`, exhaustive search takes at least 3 hours.

7. Related Work

We discuss related work on energy and power optimization. Offline optimization techniques have been proposed (*e.g.*,[2, 10, 33, 35, 59], but they are limited by reliance on a robust training phase. If behavior occurs online that was not represented in the training data, then these approaches may produce suboptimal results.

Several approaches augment offline model building with online measurement. For example, many systems employ control theoretic designs which couple offline model building with online feedback control [9, 24, 27, 36, 39, 46, 47, 51, 57, 61]. Over a narrow range of applications the combination of offline learning and control works well, as the offline models capture the general behavior of the entire class of application and require negligible online overhead. This focused approach is extremely effective for multimedia applications [17, 18, 30, 39, 54] and web-servers [26, 38, 53]. The goal of LEO, however, is to build a more general framework applicable to a broad range of applications. LEO's approach is complementary to control based approaches. For example, incorporating LEO into control-based approaches might extend them to other domains even when the application characteristics are not known ahead of time.

Some approaches have combined offline predictive models with online adaptation [11, 14, 48, 50, 55, 58, 62]. For example, Dubach et al. propose such a combo for optimizing the microarchitecture of a single core [14]. Such predictive models have also been employed at the OS level to manage system energy consumption [48, 50]. [58].

Other approaches adopt an almost completely online model, optimizing based only on dynamic runtime feedback [1, 34, 37, 44, 45, 52]. For example, Flicker is a configurable architecture and optimization framework that uses only online models to maximize performance under a power limitation [44]. Another example, ParallelismDial, uses online adaptation to tailor parallelism to application workload.

Perhaps the most similar approaches to LEO are others that combine offline modeling with online model updates [5, 16, 28]. For example, Bitirgen et al use an artificial neural network to allocate resources to multiple applications in a multicore [5]. The neural network is trained offline and then adapted online using measured feedback. This approach optimizes performance but does not consider power or energy minimization.

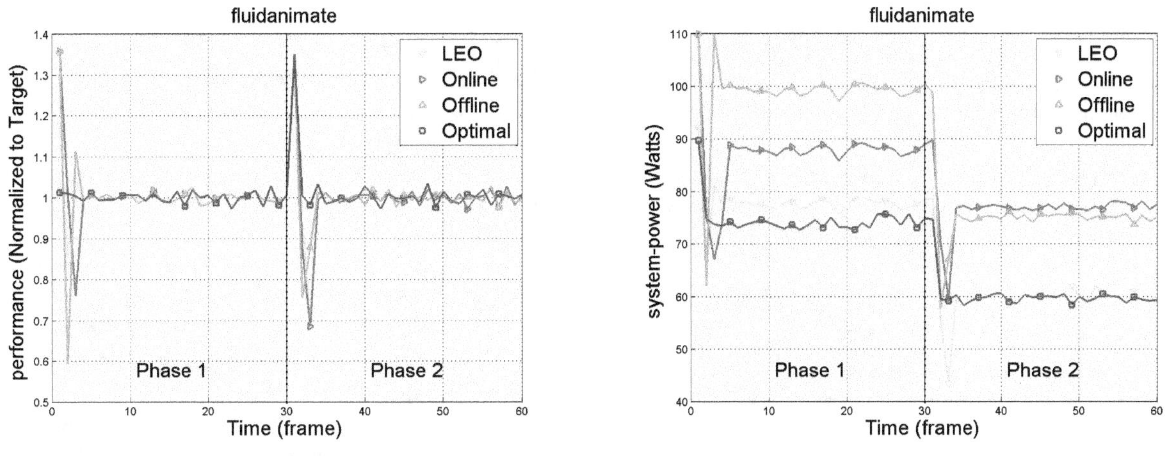

(a) (b)

Figure 13. Power and performance for `fluidanimate` transitioning through phases with different computational demands.

Like these approaches, LEO combines offline model building and with online model updates. *Unlike prior approaches, LEO learns not a single best state, but rather all Pareto-optimal tradeoffs in the power/performance space (like those illustrated in Figure 9).* These tradeoffs can be used to maximize performance or to minimize energy across an application's entire range of possible utilization. There is a cost for this added benefit: LEO's online phase is likely higher overhead than these prior approaches that focus only on maximizing performance. In that sense, however, these approaches complement each other. If fastest performance is the goal, then prior approaches are likely the best option. If the goal is to minimize energy for a range of possible performance, then LEO produces near optimal energy.

8. Conclusion

This paper has presented LEO, a system capable of learning Pareto-optimal power and performance tradeoffs for an application running on a configurable system. LEO combines some of the best features of both online and offline learning approaches. Offline, LEO acquires knowledge about a range of application behaviors. Online, LEO quickly matches the observed behavior of a new application to previously seen behavior from other applications to produce highly accurate estimates of performance and power. We have implemented LEO, made the source code available, and tested it on a real system with 25 different applications exhibiting a range of behaviors. Across all applications, LEO achieves greater than 97% accuracy in its performance and power estimations despite only sampling less than 2% of the possible configuration space for an application it has never seen before. These estimations are then used to allocate resources and save energy. LEO produces energy savings within 6% of optimal while purely Offline or Online approaches are both over 24% of optimal. LEO's learning framework represents a promising approach to help generalize resource allocation in energy limited computing environments and could be used in conjunction with other control techniques to help develop a *self-aware* computing system [13, 20, 23, 29, 31, 49].

References

[1] Jason Ansel, Maciej Pacula, Yee Lok Wong, Cy Chan, Marek Olszewski, Una-May O'Reilly, and Saman Amarasinghe. Siblingrivalry: online autotuning through local competitions. In *CASES*, 2012.

[2] Jason Ansel, Yee Lok Wong, Cy Chan, Marek Olszewski, Alan Edelman, and Saman Amarasinghe. Language and compiler support for auto-tuning variable-accuracy algorithms. In *CGO*, 2011.

[3] L.A Barroso and U. Holzle. The case for energy-proportional computing. *Computer*, 40(12):33–37, Dec 2007.

[4] C. Bienia, S. Kumar, J. P. Singh, and K. Li. The PARSEC benchmark suite: Characterization and architectural implications. In *PACT*, 2008.

[5] Ramazan Bitirgen, Engin Ipek, and Jose F. Martinez. Coordinated management of multiple interacting resources in chip multiprocessors: A machine learning approach. In *MICRO*, 2008.

[6] S.P. Bradley, A.C. Hax, and T.L. Magnanti. *Applied mathematical programming*. Addison-Wesley Pub. Co., 1977.

[7] Aaron Carroll and Gernot Heiser. Mobile multicores: Use them or waste them. In *Proceedings of the Workshop on Power-Aware Computing and Systems*, HotPower '13, pages 12:1–12:5, New York, NY, USA, 2013. ACM.

[8] Shuai Che, Michael Boyer, Jiayuan Meng, David Tarjan, Jeremy W. Sheaffer, Sang-Ha Lee, and Kevin Skadron. Rodinia: A benchmark suite for heterogeneous computing. In *IISWC*, 2009.

[9] Jian Chen and Lizy Kurian John. Predictive coordination of multiple on-chip resources for chip multiprocessors. In *ICS*, 2011.

[10] Jian Chen, Lizy Kurian John, and Dimitris Kaseridis. Modeling program resource demand using inherent program characteristics. *SIGMETRICS Perform. Eval. Rev.*, 39(1):1–12, June 2011.

[11] Ryan Cochran, Can Hankendi, Ayse K. Coskun, and Sherief Reda. Pack & cap: adaptive dvfs and thread packing under power caps. In *MICRO*, 2011.

[12] Qingyuan Deng, David Meisner, Abhishek Bhattacharjee, Thomas F Wenisch, and Ricardo Bianchini. Coscale: Coordinating cpu and memory system dvfs in server systems. In *Microarchitecture (MICRO), 2012 45th Annual IEEE/ACM International Symposium on*, pages 143–154. IEEE, 2012.

[13] Petre Dini, Wolfgang Gentzsch, Mark Potts, Alexander Clemm, Mazin Yousif, and Andreas Polze. Internet, GRID, self-adaptability and beyond: Are we ready? Aug 2004.

[14] Christophe Dubach, Timothy M. Jones, Edwin V. Bonilla, and Michael F. P. O'Boyle. A predictive model for dynamic microarchitectural adaptivity control. In *MICRO*, 2010.

[15] Bradley Efron and Carl Morris. Data analysis using stein's estimator and its generalizations. *Journal of the American Statistical Association*, 70(350):311–319, 1975.

[16] Antonio Filieri, Henry Hoffmann, and Martina Maggio. Automated design of self-adaptive software with control-theoretical formal guarantees. In *ICSE*, 2014.

[17] J. Flinn and M. Satyanarayanan. Energy-aware adaptation for mobile applications. In *SOSP*, 1999.

[18] Jason Flinn and M. Satyanarayanan. Managing battery lifetime with energy-aware adaptation. *ACM Trans. Comp. Syst.*, 22(2), May 2004.

[19] Andrew Gelman, John B Carlin, Hal S Stern, David B Dunson, Aki Vehtari, and Donald B Rubin. *Bayesian data analysis*. CRC press, 2013.

[20] W. Gentzsch, K. Iwano, D. Johnston-Watt, M.A. Minhas, and M. Yousif. Self-adaptable autonomic computing systems: An industry view. In *Proceedings of the 16th International Workshop on Database and Expert Systems Applications*, pages 201–205, Aug 2005.

[21] Henry Hoffmann. Racing vs. pacing to idle: A comparison of heuristics for energy-aware resource allocation. In *HotPower*, 2013.

[22] Henry Hoffmann, Jonathan Eastep, Marco D. Santambrogio, Jason E. Miller, and Anant Agarwal. Application heartbeats: a generic interface for specifying program performance and goals in autonomous computing environments. In *ICAC*, 2010.

[23] Henry Hoffmann, Jim Holt, George Kurian, Eric Lau, Martina Maggio, Jason E. Miller, Sabrina M. Neuman, Mahmut Sinangil, Yildiz Sinangil, Anant Agarwal, Anantha P. Chandrakasan, and Srinivas Devadas. Self-aware computing in the angstrom processor. In *DAC*, 2012.

[24] Henry Hoffmann, Martina Maggio, Marco D. Santambrogio, Alberto Leva, and Anant Agarwal. A generalized software framework for accurate and efficient managment of performance goals. In *EMSOFT*, 2013.

[25] Henry Hoffmann, Stelios Sidiroglou, Michael Carbin, Sasa Misailovic, Anant Agarwal, and Martin Rinard. Dynamic knobs for responsive power-aware computing. In *ASPLOS*, 2011.

[26] T. Horvath, T. Abdelzaher, K. Skadron, and Xue Liu. Dynamic voltage scaling in multitier web servers with end-to-end delay control. *Computers, IEEE Transactions on*, 56(4), 2007.

[27] Connor Imes, David H. K. Kim, Martina Maggio, and Henry Hoffmann. Poet: A portable approach to minimizing energy under soft real-time constraints. In *RTAS*, 2015.

[28] Engin Ipek, Onur Mutlu, José F. Martínez, and Rich Caruana. Self-optimizing memory controllers: A reinforcement learning approach. In *ISCA*, 2008.

[29] J.O. Kephart. Research challenges of autonomic computing. In *ICSE*, 2005.

[30] Minyoung Kim, Mark-Oliver Stehr, Carolyn Talcott, Nikil Dutt, and Nalini Venkatasubramanian. xtune: A formal methodology for cross-layer tuning of mobile embedded systems. *ACM Trans. Embed. Comput. Syst.*, 11(4), January 2013.

[31] Robert Laddaga. Guest editor's introduction: Creating robust software through self-adaptation. *IEEE Intelligent Systems*, 14, 1999.

[32] Etienne Le Sueur and Gernot Heiser. Slow down or sleep, that is the question. In *Proceedings of the 2011 USENIX Annual Technical Conference*, Portland, OR, USA, June 2011.

[33] B.C. Lee, J. Collins, Hong Wang, and D. Brooks. Cpr: Composable performance regression for scalable multiprocessor models. In *MICRO*, 2008.

[34] Benjamin C. Lee and David Brooks. Efficiency trends and limits from comprehensive microarchitectural adaptivity. In *ASPLOS*, 2008.

[35] Benjamin C. Lee and David M. Brooks. Accurate and efficient regression modeling for microarchitectural performance and power prediction. In *ASPLOS*, 2006.

[36] Baochun Li and K. Nahrstedt. A control-based middleware framework for quality-of-service adaptations. *IEEE Journal on Selected Areas in Communications*, 17(9), 1999.

[37] J. Li and J.F. Martinez. Dynamic power-performance adaptation of parallel computation on chip multiprocessors. In *HPCA*, 2006.

[38] C. Lu, Y. Lu, T.F. Abdelzaher, J.A. Stankovic, and S.H. Son. Feedback control architecture and design methodology for service delay guarantees in web servers. *IEEE TPDS*, 17(9):1014–1027, September 2006.

[39] Martina Maggio, Henry Hoffmann, Marco D. Santambrogio an d Anant Agarwal, and Alberto Leva. Power optimization in embedded systems via feedback control of resource allocation. *IEEE Transactions on Control Systems Technology (to appear)*.

[40] Martina Maggio, Henry Hoffmann, Alessandro V. Papadopoulos, Jacopo Panerati, Marco D. Santambrogio, Anant Agarwal, and Alberto Leva. Comparison of decision-making strategies for self-optimization in autonomic computing systems. *ACM Trans. Auton. Adapt. Syst.*, 7(4):36:1–36:32, December 2012.

[41] David Meisner, Christopher M. Sadler, Luiz André Barroso, Wolf-Dietrich Weber, and Thomas F. Wenisch. Power management of online data-intensive services. *ISCA*, 2011.

[42] Carl N Morris. Parametric empirical bayes inference: theory and applications. *Journal of the American Statistical Association*, 78(381):47–55, 1983.

[43] R. Narayanan, B. Ozisikyilmaz, J. Zambreno, G. Memik, and A. Choudhary. Minebench: A benchmark suite for data mining workloads. In *IISWC*, 2006.

[44] Paula Petrica, Adam M. Izraelevitz, David H. Albonesi, and Christine A. Shoemaker. Flicker: A dynamically adaptive architecture for power limited multicore systems. In *ISCA*, 2013.

[45] Dmitry Ponomarev, Gurhan Kucuk, and Kanad Ghose. Reducing power requirements of instruction scheduling through dynamic allocation of multiple datapath resources. In *MICRO*, 2001.

[46] R. Raghavendra, P. Ranganathan, V Talwar, Z. Wang, and X. Zhu. No "power" struggles: coordinated multi-level power management for the data center. In *ASPLOS*, 2008.

[47] R. Rajkumar, C. Lee, J. Lehoczky, and Dan Siewiorek. A resource allocation model for qos management. In *RTSS*, 1997.

[48] Arjun Roy, Stephen M. Rumble, Ryan Stutsman, Philip Levis, David Mazières, and Nickolai Zeldovich. Energy management in mobile devices with the cinder operating system. In *EuroSys*, 2011.

[49] Mazeiar Salehie and Ladan Tahvildari. Self-adaptive software: Landscape and research challenges. *ACM Trans. Auton. Adapt. Syst.*, 4(2):1–42, 2009.

[50] David C. Snowdon, Etienne Le Sueur, Stefan M. Petters, and Gernot Heiser. Koala: A platform for os-level power management. In *EuroSys*, 2009.

[51] Michal Sojka, Pavel Písa, Dario Faggioli, Tommaso Cucinotta, Fabio Checconi, Zdenek Hanzálek, and Giuseppe Lipari. Modular software architecture for flexible reservation mechanisms on heterogeneous resources. *Journal of Systems Architecture*, 57(4), 2011.

[52] Srinath Sridharan, Gagan Gupta, and Gurindar S. Sohi. Holistic run-time parallelism management for time and energy efficiency. In *ICS*, 2013.

[53] Q. Sun, G. Dai, and W. Pan. LPV model and its application in web server performance control. In *ICCSSE*, 2008.

[54] Vibhore Vardhan, Wanghong Yuan, Albert F. Harris III, Sarita V. Adve, Robin Kravets, Klara Nahrstedt, Daniel Grobe Sachs, and Douglas L. Jones. Grace-2: integrating fine-grained application adaptation with global adaptation for saving energy. *IJES*, 4(2), 2009.

[55] Jonathan A. Winter, David H. Albonesi, and Christine A. Shoemaker. Scalable thread scheduling and global power management for heterogeneous many-core architectures. In *PACT*, 2010.

[56] CF Jeff Wu. On the convergence properties of the em algorithm. *The Annals of statistics*, pages 95–103, 1983.

[57] Qiang Wu, Philo Juang, Margaret Martonosi, and Douglas W. Clark. Formal online methods for voltage/frequency control in multiple clock domain microprocessors. In *ASPLOS*, 2004.

[58] Weidan Wu and Benjamin C Lee. Inferred models for dynamic and sparse hardware-software spaces. In *Microarchitecture (MICRO), 2012 45th Annual IEEE/ACM International Symposium on*, pages 413–424. IEEE, 2012.

[59] Joshua J. Yi, David J. Lilja, and Douglas M. Hawkins. A statistically rigorous approach for improving simulation methodology. In *HPCA*, 2003.

[60] Kai Yu, Volker Tresp, and Anton Schwaighofer. Learning gaussian processes from multiple tasks. In *Proceedings of the 22nd international conference on Machine learning*, pages 1012–1019. ACM, 2005.

[61] R. Zhang, C. Lu, T.F. Abdelzaher, and J.A. Stankovic. Controlware: A middleware architecture for feedback control of software performance. In *ICDCS*, 2002.

[62] Xiao Zhang, Rongrong Zhong, Sandhya Dwarkadas, and Kai Shen. A flexible framework for throttling-enabled multicore management (temm). In *ICPP*, 2012.

More is Less, Less is More: Molecular-Scale Photonic NoC Power Topologies

Jun Pang
Department of Computer Science
Duke University
pangjun92@gmail.com

Chris Dwyer
Department of Electrical and Computer Engineering
Duke University
dwyer@ece.duke.edu

Alvin R. Lebeck
Department of Computer Science
Duke University
alvy@cs.duke.edu

Abstract

Molecular-scale Network-on-Chip (mNoC) crossbars use quantum dot LEDs as an on-chip light source, and chromophores to provide optical signal filtering for receivers. An mNoC reduces power consumption or enables scaling to larger crossbars for a reduced energy budget compared to current nanophotonic NoC crossbars. Since communication latency is reduced by using a high-radix crossbar, minimizing power consumption becomes a primary design target. Conventional Single Writer Multiple Reader (SWMR) photonic crossbar designs broadcast all packets, and incur the commensurate required power, even if only two nodes are communicating.

This paper introduces power topologies, enabled by unique capabilities of mNoC technology, to reduce overall interconnect power consumption. A power topology corresponds to the logical connectivity provided by a given power mode. Broadcast is one power mode and it consumes the maximum power. Additional power modes consume less power but allow a source to communicate with only a statically defined, potentially non-contiguous, subset of nodes. Overall interconnect power is reduced if the more frequently communicating nodes use modes that consume less power, while less frequently communicating nodes use modes that consume more power. We also investigate thread mapping techniques to fully exploit power topologies. We explore various mNoC power topologies with one, two and four power modes for a radix-256 SWMR mNoC crossbar. Our results show that the combination of power topologies and intelligent thread mapping can reduce total mNoC power by up to 51% on average for a set of 12 SPLASH benchmarks. Furthermore performance is 10% better than conventional resonator-based photonic NoCs and energy is reduced by 72%.

Categories and Subject Descriptors C.1.2 [*Multiple Data Stream Architectures (Multiprocessors)*]: Interconnection architectures

Keywords Nanophotonics; Interconnection Network; Energy Efficiency

1. Introduction

Nanophotonic Network-on-Chips (NoC) exhibit superior power delay product and bandwidth compared to electrical NoCs [19, 27, 28, 36] and are likely to play an important role in next generation NoCs. The ideal NoC is one large crossbar that enables communication between all pairs of nodes in the absence of output conflicts. Unfortunately, current ring resonator based crossbars are difficult to scale larger than 64×64 due to ring thermal tuning, ring nonlinearity, and external light source inefficiency.

Recently proposed Molecular-scale Network-on-Chip (mNoC) designs use emerging molecular-scale devices to construct nanophotonic networks [29, 30]. Quantum dot LEDs (QD_LED) provide on-chip electrical to optical signal generation/modulation and chromophores provide optical signal filtering for receivers. These molecular devices replace the ring resonators and external laser source used in current nanophotonic NoCs. For a simple Single Writer Multiple Reader (SWMR) crossbar, mNoC reduces energy consumption or enables scaling to larger crossbars (more than radix-256) for a smaller energy budget and with better performance compared to ring resonator NoCs.

Communication latency and power consumption are two important factors in NoC design. Communication latency is reduced in high radix (e.g., 256 × 256) SWMR mNoC crossbars since there are no intermediate routers and optical signals transmit at the speed of light. Therefore, power consumption becomes a top concern in mNoC design. In con-

ASPLOS '15, March 14–18, 2015, Istanbul, Turkey.

http://dx.doi.org/10.1145/2694344.2694377

ventional SWMR crossbars, a source node broadcasts every packet and consumes power necessary to reach every destination even with only one or a few destination nodes. Furthermore, broadcast ignores frequency of communication between a source and specific destination nodes. The challenge is to design a single physical interconnect that provides the latency benefits of high-radix crossbars, but without the worst case broadcast power consumption for frequent communication to subsets of destinations.

To meet the above challenge, this paper introduces mNoC power topologies, a unique capability where connectivity is dynamically controlled as a function of source power (**Contribution 1**). For a given source on a single waveguide, broadcast requires the highest power since it reaches all destinations, whereas lower power modes provide connectivity to progressively smaller subsets of destination nodes. The ability to control the on-chip QD_LED light source power and the appropriate design of optical waveguides enables different power modes. In particular, we use asymmetric waveguide splitters to allow potentially non-contiguous destinations in each power mode.

This paper explores static power topologies with a fixed set of source power modes. The specific power mode is selected dynamically based on destination. Our designs are guided by examining program communication patterns. The general design problem is NP-hard, therefore we use heuristic methods to design several power topologies with one, two, and four power modes (**Contribution 2**). We also explore the impact of thread mapping, since overall power is reduced if frequently communicating nodes use the lowest power modes, while less frequently communicating nodes use higher power modes (**Contribution 3**).

We use Graphite [25] to evaluate performance and to gather execution traces of several SPLASH-2 benchmarks [37] executing on a 256 core system. The traces are used to examine communication patterns and to compute NoC power consumption. Our results show that total mNoC power consumption is reduced by around 13% for naive power topologies, whereas a communication-aware power topology that utilizes intelligent thread mapping reduces power by 51%. The best overall design achieves performance 10% better than conventional resonator-based photonic NoCs while reducing energy by 72% (**Contribution 4**).

The remainder of this paper is organized as follows. Section 2 introduces background information for mNoC and the motivation of our work. We present power topologies and their implementation in Section 3 and Section 4 discusses architecting power topologies. In Section 5 we evaluate several power topologies and the impact of thread mapping. Related work is discussed in Section 6 and we conclude in Section 7.

2. Background and Motivation

Nanophotonic NoCs are promising since they provide high bandwidth and lower power than conventional electrical NoCs. Previously proposed ring resonator-based NoCs (rNoC) have the following main components: 1) an external laser source to provide highly coherent light, 2) a waveguide to provide connectivity, and 3) ring resonators for both modulation and detection. Despite the advantages over electrical NoCs, there still exist significant limitations to resonator-based NoCs, including: 1) high static power consumption due to the power inefficiency from the activity independent off-chip laser source and the non-negligible ring thermal tuning power (20-100μW/ring over 20K temperature range) [19, 26, 27], and 2) poor scalability due to ring resonators' nonlinearity [5]. Recently proposed molecular-scale nanophotonic network on-chip (mNoC) seeks to overcome these limitations [29, 30].

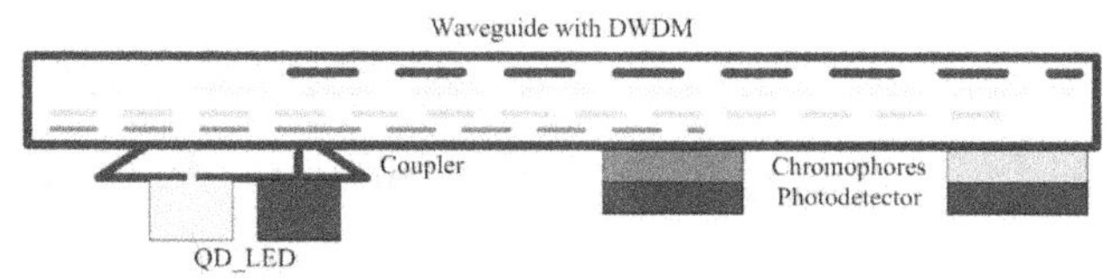

Figure 1. mNoC Main Components

2.1 Enabling Molecular-Scale Nanophotonic Technology

Our work on power topologies builds on the base mNoC designs, but is applicable to any similar technology (e.g., VCSELs as light sources). We provide a brief summary of mNoC technology and a comparison to rNoC, further details are available elsewhere [29, 30]. Figure 1 shows the main mNoC components, which includes QD_LEDs, chromophores and waveguides. Transmitters are composed of silicon compatible QD_LEDs [13] which inject light directly into the waveguide and provide both the light source and modulation in a single on-chip device. QD_LEDs operate as a current controlled light source, more current leads to more photons, and have small size, narrow emission bandwidth, good stability and fast excitation rate [14, 24, 33, 38]. Receivers are composed from chromophores [23, 35] that filter the desired optical signals and couple the energy from the waveguide to a photodetector for O/E conversion. Subwavelength-diameter silica (SiO_2) waveguides [34] transmit visible light from the transmitters to receivers. These components have been individually experimentally demonstrated [1, 13, 14, 20, 30, 34, 38] and are silicon compatible, however a fully integrated mNoC has not yet been demonstrated.

Table 1 summarizes the key differences between mNoC and rNoC for a 256-node system. In this table mNoC uses a single writer multiple reader (SWMR) 256×256 crossbar with a serpentine layout whereas rNoC uses a clustered topology with a 64×64 optical crossbar and 4 nodes per crossbar port (a clustered mNoC is also possible). Communication within a 4-node cluster uses the electrical domain.

Metric of Interest	rNoC	mNoC
Technology Characteristics		
Wavelength (nm)	1550	390-750
Requires Thermal Tuning	Yes	No
Activity/traffic independent light source	Yes	No
Nonlinearity (transmitters & receivers)	Yes	No
System Evaluation Metrics		
Scalability (Max crossbar size)	64×64	> 256×256
Normalized energy (256-node)	1	< 0.51
Normalized performance (256-node)	1	1.1

Table 1. Comparison between rNoC and mNoC

- ***Scalability***: rNoC scalability is limited by either nonlinear device behavior or ring thermal tuning power. Since mNoCs do not utilize rings and neither QD_LEDs [31] or chromophores exhibit nonlinear behavior, waveguide nonlinearity is the primary limitation to mNoC scalability. An mNoC crossbar can easily scale to more than radix-256 even with a $2dB/cm$ loss waveguide. With multilayer silicon integration [5] even higher scalability may be achievable.
- ***Energy and Performance***: Overall energy consumption is reduced because mNoC eliminates the large ring thermal tuning power. Moreover, the off-chip activity-independent laser source is replaced with on-chip QD_LEDs, where the waveguide link utilization and per packet 1-to-0 ratio play an important role in further reducing energy consumption. Previous work [29, 30] shows that for a 256-node clustered design with a radix-64 optical crossbar, the clustered mNoC (c_mNoC) reduces energy by 77% for the same performance compared to rNoC. When scaled to a single 256×256 crossbar (not possible for rNoC), mNoC achieves a 49% energy reduction with a 10% increase in performance vs. the clustered rNoC topology.

2.2 Motivation

The above results demonstrate the potential benefit of mNoC technology over rNoC technology by providing more scalability (and thus performance) with lower energy consumption. We also observe that, for a 256-node system, c_mNoC achieves the largest energy reduction while the full 256×256 mNoC crossbar achieves the highest performance. Although it is possible to construct multiple networks to provide either low power or high performance when needed (e.g., catnap [11]), *ideally we want a single physical network that provides the performance of the high radix crossbar (mNoC) with the energy savings of the lower-radix clustered topology (c_mNoC).*

Our work toward achieving this goal is motivated by three primary observations: 1) source power consumption dominates overall mNoC power consumption, 2) waveguide loss determines mNoC source power requirements, and 3) workloads exhibit non-uniform communication patterns.

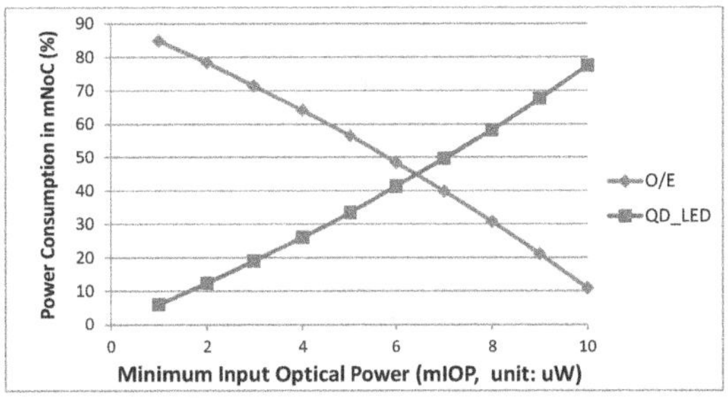

Figure 2. Percent of mNoC Power for QD_LED and O/E

Observation 1: Source power dominates overall mNoC power consumption. The total power consumption of an mNoC is composed of three parts: QD_LED source power, O/E conversion power due to photoreceiver power dissipation, and electrical circuit power (buffers, etc.). The O/E power is a function of the photoreceiver's minimum input optical power (mIOP) [8, 20]; a low mIOP requires a high gain photoreceiver and thus increases O/E power while high mIOP can reduce O/E power but requires higher source power [5, 6]. This relationship enables mNoC designs to tradeoff O/E power for source power while keeping total power relatively constant. The impact of this tradeoff for rNoC is minimal since thermal tuning dominates total power.

Figure 2 shows how the QD_LED and O/E power changes as a percentage of the total power as mIOP increases from $1\mu W$ to $10\mu W$, assuming O/E conversion power decreases linearly with mIOP[1]. From this figure, we see that as mIOP increases, the dominant power is shifted from O/E to QD_LED source power. Using a $10\mu W$ mIOP photoreceiver, QD_LED source power is 80% of the total power and becomes the new optimization target.

Observation 2: Waveguide loss determines source power required to reach a particular destination for a given photodetector mIOP. The waveguide loss dominates other losses due to chromophore receivers which are dependent on the specific mIOP for a photodetector. The two main sources of waveguide loss for mNoC are transmission loss given the distance to a destination and various insertion loss along the optical path (e.g., splitter and photodetector insertion loss). Consider the distance dependence loss; Figure 3 shows that mNoC source power increases exponentially vs. maximum broadcast distance to a destination on the waveguide.

Observation 3: Applications exhibit non-uniform communication patterns. Analysis of the SPLASH benchmarks shows that not every packet needs to traverse the full broadcast range. The average communication distance between

[1] Linearity is achieved by changing the number of gain stages and/or tuning the photoreceiver's bias voltage (*Vbias*).

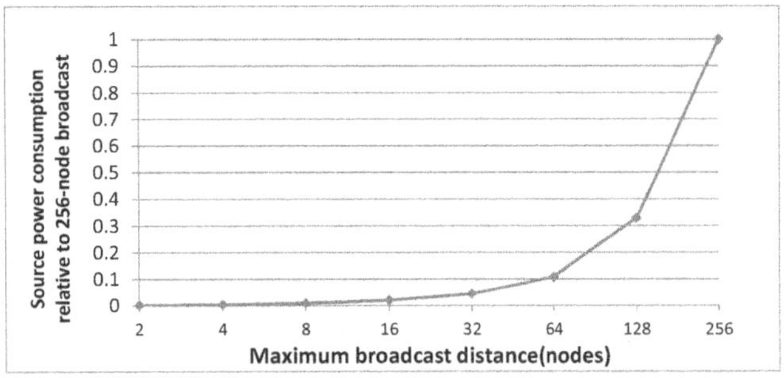

Figure 3. Source Power Consumption vs. Broadcast Distance

threads, based on thread ID numbered from 0 to 255, is 102 across 12 SPLASH benchmarks. Therefore, broadcasting to all the nodes is not always power efficient and it should be used only when needed. Furthermore, the amount of communication between nodes is not evenly distributed, some nodes communicate more frequently than others, similar observations for both SPLASH and Parsec are presented by Barrow-Williams, et al. [3].

These observations motivate us to explore alternative mNoC designs. Ideally, we want to match NoC power consumption to application communication patterns. Specifically, *destinations with more frequent communication should use a mode that consumes less power, while destinations with less frequent communication should use modes that consume more power.* Importantly, all the modes incur the same latency. The remainder of this paper describes our initial steps toward achieving this objective.

3. mNoC Power Topologies

This section describes the foundational concepts that enable mNoC designs that achieve the performance of a full crossbar with energy savings approaching low-radix clustered designs. The key insight is to create a crossbar structure where connectivity (reachable destination nodes from a given source) is a function of source power—called a *power topology*. **The destinations reachable in a given power mode do not need to be contiguous on the physical waveguide.** To our knowledge, this is the first work to define a communication system for on-chip optical networks where on a given waveguide (and thus fixed physical topology) a source node can communicate with a given set of destinations as a function of the source input power. Our goal in this section is to first define the concept of a power topology and then to introduce the design parameters and methods available for architects to create various power topologies. The next section discusses architecting specific power topologies.

3.1 Power Topology Definition

The intuition behind a power topology is to augment a crossbar structure with a set of power modes where different sets of destination nodes are reachable in each power mode. Broadcast is the highest power mode and can reach all possible destinations, additional lower power modes can only reach decreasing subsets of destinations. Importantly, destinations in a low power mode are also reachable in all higher power modes, and power modes do not need to be uniform across all sources.

More formally, the global power topology PT of an $N \times N$ crossbar is the union of each source's local power topology $PT = \bigcup_{n=0}^{N-1} PT_n$. A local power topology PT_n is an ordered set of M_n power modes with $Pmode_{n,i}$ Watts, such that $Pmode_{n,i}; Pmode_{n,i} < Pmode_{n,j}, \forall i < j$, where $i, j \in \{0..M_n - 1\}$, and the set of destination nodes reachable in each power mode ($Mdest_{n,i} \subseteq \{0..N-1\}$). The destination nodes reachable in a given power mode are also reachable in all higher power modes ($Mdest_{n,i} \subset Mdest_{n,j}, \forall i < j$). The highest power mode contains all destinations ($Mdest_{n,M_n} = \{0..N-1\}$) and requires the maximum source power. Specifying the number of modes and which nodes are in each mode of the power topology is the architect's job, as described in Section 4. The remainder of this section describes how to implement a given power topology, and obtain the values of $Pmode_{n,i}$ to minimize the total power for a given topology.

3.2 Implementing Power Topologies

In this paper we focus on the SWMR crossbar structure, where each source node has its own dedicated waveguide(s); however, the approach is general and could be applied to other photonic crossbar structures. Without loss of generality, we consider a single waveguide with a single source and N-1 destinations and describe how to create different power modes. For clarity we omit the subscript n.

Different power modes are enabled by two key aspects of mNoC technology: 1) waveguide design and 2) current controlled QD_LED emission (any current controlled light source could be used). Our power topologies are static since they are defined at design time. As part of our ongoing research we are exploring the feasibility of dynamic power topologies. Below we elaborate on the two design aspects for designing static power topologies.

3.2.1 Waveguide Design

Our goal is to implement a power topology to achieve the lowest overall power consumption by minimizing the total source power. Recall, a source QD_LED injects power into the waveguide, which is dissipated due to waveguide loss, insertion loss incurred by various optical devices (usually fixed), and splitters that divert a fraction of the power to each destination's receiver. The last factor is the key parameter for creating power topologies and is dependent on waveguide splitter design. Below we outline how to compute appropriate splitter parameters for a given power topology.

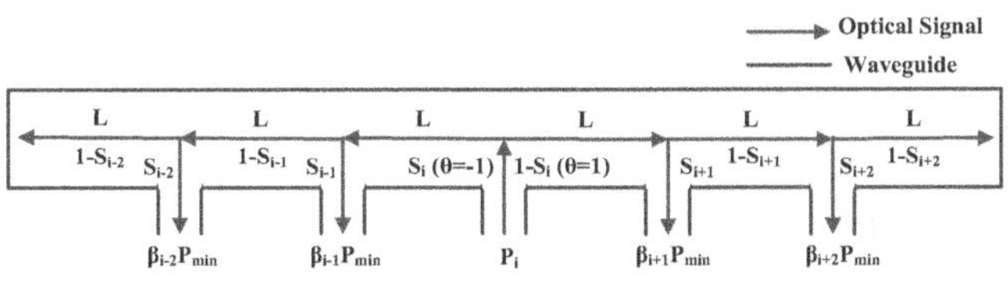

Figure 4. Source Power Model

Assume we are provided a local power topology (i.e., the number of power modes and the set of destination nodes in each power mode) and an expected fraction of overall communication in each mode w_m. The total source power is the sum of the power for each mode weighted by the fraction of communication in each mode (see Equation 1).

$$Psrc = \sum_{m=0}^{M-1} w_m Pmode_m \tag{1}$$

Equation 2 represents the relationship between source power and waveguide losses (including splitters) for an arbitrary source injected power P_i at source i (See one illustration in Fig. 4).

$$P_i = \sum_{j=0, j\neq i}^{N-1} \frac{\beta_j P_{min}}{L^{|j-i|} S_j (0.5(1+\theta) - S_i\theta) \prod_{\substack{k=min(i,j),\\ k\neq i,j}}^{max(i,j)} (1 - S_k)} \tag{2}$$

The sum is over all destinations on the waveguide. The numerator in Equation 2 represents the amount of power incident on j's receiver in terms of the minimum required power P_{min} (which considers the insertion loss of various optical devices and photoreceiver mIOP) where in general $\beta_j \geq 0$. In the denominator, $L^{|j-i|}$ is the power loss along the waveguide between the source i and the destination j. S_j is the fraction of power diverted by the destination's splitter. The third term in the denominator represents how the source power splits (S_i) into two directions ($\theta \in \{1, -1\}$ identifies the direction relative to the source node i). The product term accounts for the power diverted by all splitters between i and j.

For a single mode power topology (broadcast) total power is minimized if $\beta_j = 1, \forall j$. However, β_j is not a directly available design knob, it simply reflects the relative amount of P_{min} received by the destination, which depends on the distance from the source and the splitter design. If node layout is fixed along the waveguide, then splitter design (S_j) is the only remaining design option available to ensure $\beta_j = 1$ and to minimize total power.

When we consider multiple power modes, the goal is to minimize total power, $Psrc$ in Equation 1, not minimize power for a single mode. To achieve this we seek to design splitters, S_j, that minimize $Psrc$. The intuition behind our design process is that for a given power mode m all nodes reachable using power $Pmode_m$ must receive at least $Pmin$ (i.e., $\beta_j \geq 1$) and that the nodes unique to that mode receive exactly $Pmin$ (i.e., $\beta_j = 1$). This basic observation allows us to set up a system of equations (one for each mode) that can be used to solve computationally for S_j's that minimize $Psrc$. Appendix A provides further details on the splitter design process.

The primary constraint in our designs is that destinations in low power modes are also reachable in higher power modes. It is important to note that nodes in a given power mode can be non-contiguous; that is nodes reachable only in a higher power mode may be physically closer to the source than nodes reachable in lower power modes. The intuition is that the high power node's splitter diverts a very small fraction of the power to its receiver, therefore a much higher power is required to reach $Pmin$ at the receiver. In contrast, the low power node's splitters divert a larger fraction of power. This unique capability enables the creation of arbitrary power topologies.

3.2.2 Implementing Source Power Modes

Similar to micro-ring resonators, the QD_LED can be driven by an integrated high-speed current driver. The QD_LED output intensity can be adjusted either through pulse-width modulation or dynamic gain adjustment of the driver. Since the required output power (per source-destination pair) is static, software can store a table of constants for each power mode and augment packet transmission with control bits which set the QD_LED output power. This same table can also store the mapping of logical thread IDs to physical cores, or vice versa. On the receiving side, when the input power is below mIOP, especially in low power modes, the input should be treated as noise. Therefore, to reduce the bit error rate (BER), a simple threshold circuit [4] can be used.

4. Architecting Power Topologies

The architecture of an mNoC crossbar specifies the global crossbar power topology: the number of power modes and the set of destination nodes in each power mode, for each source node. Power toplogies are created on top of an underlying physical topology; in our case an mNoC SWMR crossbar with a serpetine layout. Designing an optimal power topology requires a global optimization which is NP-hard. Therefore, we decompose the problem into a series of steps that enables us to explore progressively more sophisticated designs. For simplicity, we limit our investigations to power topologies where each source has the same number of power modes ($M_n = M, \forall n$). We begin by mapping conventional topologies onto a power topology. This is followed by power topologies that group destination nodes based on distance from the source. We then introduce communication-aware topologies that account for locality of communication between nodes.

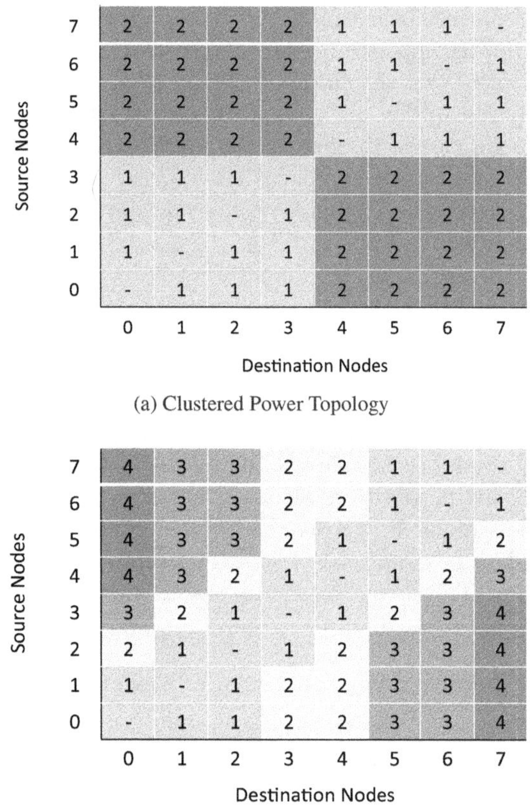

(b) Distance-Based Power Topology

Figure 5. Example Power Topologies: Each row represents the waveguide(s) for the source in a SWMR crossbar mNoC. Numbers indicate the power mode required to reach a destination in a given column (lower numbers = lower power mode).

4.1 Conventional Topologies

A simple approach is to map known topologies into a power topology. One way to accomplish this is to set the number of power modes based on the diameter of the conventional network. For each source, destination nodes are assigned to power modes based on the number of hops in the shortest path from the source.

To visualize a power topology we use an adjacency matrix where each entry indicates the power mode for a source (row) to reach a specific destination (column). Each row represents the waveguide(s) for the source in a SWMR crossbar mNoC. We note that different sources may have very different values for their respective power modes. For example, power mode 2 for some sources may be much higher power than power mode 2 for other sources due to the maximum propagation distance along the waveguide.

Figure 5a shows an 8-node clustered power topology with four nodes per cluster. This corresponds loosely to the clustered topology used in rNoC and c_mNoC as described in Section 2. In this power topology there are two power modes: a low power mode (1) for nodes within the source's cluster and a high power mode (2) with nodes outside the source's cluster. Each source has three destinations in its lowest power mode, corresponding to the local communication in the conventional physical topology. The remaining destinations are reachable only in the high power mode. For the 256-node rNoC or c_NoC systems, there are 252 nodes in the high power mode.

This approach can be used to map any known topology (e.g., trees, binary n-cubes, etc.) into a power topology. However, these architectures may not produce the lowest overall power due to a mismatch between the power characteristics of the waveguides and the defined power topology. For example, nodes three and four in Figure 5a are physically close on the waveguide, yet any communication between them requires the high power mode.

4.2 Distance-Based Topologies

An alternative to naively mapping conventional physical topologies into power topologies is to design new power topologies. One simple approach is to specify a power topology based on the n nearest destinations. Figure 5b shows a 4-mode power topology based on the two nearest destinations. In this design all sources' local power topologies have the same value of $n = 2$. This is not a requirement in architecting power topologies, and we could explore using different distance parameters per source to create a global power topology with unique local power topologies.

Distance-based topologies are well-matched to the underlying power characteristics of the waveguide and capture localized communication between consecutive neighboring nodes on a line. Unfortunately, they may be a mismatch for communication patterns with higher dimensional locality (non-consecutive nodes on a line).

4.3 Communication-Aware Topologies

To achieve the full benefit of power topologies, we'd like to assign destinations with the highest traffic to the low power modes. Achieving this requires more than an architect's intuition about traffic patterns, but instead must be data driven through profiling. By utilizing communication patterns and frequency we can potentially identify the optimal number of modes and the assignment of destinations to each mode. Nonetheless, it may be difficult to create a single static power topology that is the best for all benchmarks.

Our goal is to find the power topology that provides the lowest power, which could be achieved by searching over the entire power topology space. In the extreme case, a power topology could have a dedicated mode for each destination. However, finding an optimal power topology has complexity $O(M^{N-1})$, which is intractable for large systems with more than a few modes (i.e., $N = 256$). In this case, heuristic methods must be utilized, and may result in suboptimal power topologies. Developing appropriate algorithmic techniques to fully explore the power topology space is beyond the scope of this paper.

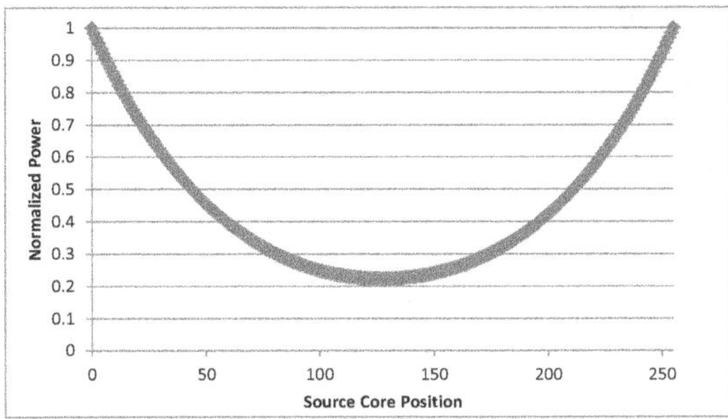

Figure 6. mNoC Single-Mode Power Profile

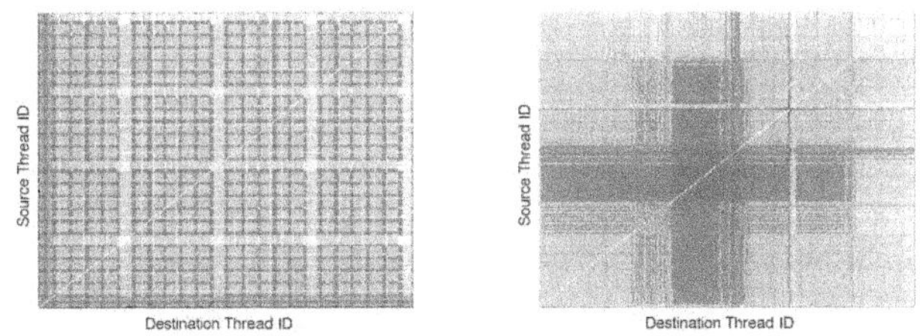

(a) Naive Mapping (b) QAP Mapping

Color indicates communication intensity (dark = high, light = low)

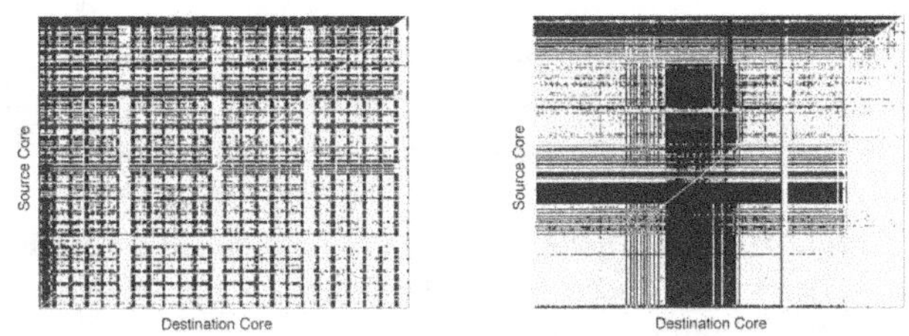

(c) Naive 2-mode Power Topology (d) QAP 2-mode Power Topology

Color indicates power mode (dark = low, light = high). Each row represents the waveguide(s) for a source node in a SWMR crossbar. Note the non-contiguous destinations in each power mode.

Figure 7. Thread Mapping and Power Topologies (water_spatial). Rows are sources and columns are destinations.

We explore communication-aware power topologies with two and four modes. In general, we apply the "*more is less, less is more*" philosophy and sort the destinations by communication frequency with the source. For the two-mode case, we iterate over all possible binary partitions of the sorted destinations into the two power modes to create $N-2$ two mode power topologies. Starting with only the highest frequency destination in the low power mode, we then progressively move destinations to the low power mode until only the lowest frequency destination is in the high power mode. We then choose the power topology with the lowest overall power.

For the four-mode case we apply various *ad hoc* heuristics to assign destinations from the sorted list to the four power modes. We consider several partitions of the sorted destinations into the four modes, such as {64,64,64,63}, {1,1,2,251}, {4,120,53,78}, but found the latter to be best, based on manual greedy assignment. We leave a methodical exploration of this space to future work.

Application specific power topologies can be created by applying the above methods to a single application. This could be important for embedded or high-performance ASIC designs where there are limited and well-known usage scenarios. We also note that even the distance-based power topologies could potentially benefit from more accurate information on communication frequency since it might impact splitter design, as discussed previously.

4.4 Thread Mapping

The base mNoC power topology operates by having each source broadcast a packet on its dedicated waveguide(s) and each node locally determine if it is the destination. This single mode topology provides the maximum connectivity: each source can reach all destinations. However, even in this single-mode topology, different source nodes can require different power. Consider the serpentine waveguide layout where all waveguides terminate in the same regions of the chip. For this layout, source nodes occupy locations on their respective waveguide that range from either end of the waveguide to the middle of the waveguide. The nodes in the middle do not require as much source power as the end nodes since their signals propagate only half the distance as the end node signals.

The variation in required source power creates a power profile for the overall crossbar. Although each source has a single fixed power, the power for each source depends on its location (see Figure 6). Given this power profile and the observation of workload communication locality, it is beneficial to map frequently communicating threads to the cores located near the center of the waveguide.

Even for different layouts where waveguides terminate in different regions of the chip, a power profile still exists. Cores are arranged in a 2D plane, even a more complex layout of waveguides cannot create a uniform distance from each source to each destination.

Thread mapping can be achieved either offline or online if the workload runs long enough to warrant migration. Our mapping problem is an instance of the quadratic assignment problem (QAP), which is NP-hard, therefore we use heuristic methods. We explore both Taboo [32] and simulated annealing [10], and find that Taboo generally performs best.

4.5 Discussion

Figure 7 shows the communication pattern for the water_spatial benchmark before (Figure 7a) and after running Taboo (Figure 7b). Each row is a source node (thread) and each column is a destination node, darker colors represent a larger amount of communication. In contrast to the naive

Router pipeline stages	4 cycles
Electrical link latency	1 cycles
Optical link latency	1-9 cycles for mNoC; 1-5 for rNoC
Clock	5GHz
Flit size	256-bit
Core model	in-order model, private 32KB L1D, 32KB L1I, 512KB L2 Cache

Table 2. Simulation configuration

QD_LED energy efficiency	10%
QD_LED 1-to-0 ratio	1
Waveguide loss	$1dB/cm$
Coupler loss	$1dB$
Photodetector mIOP	$10\mu W$
Power loss of chromophores	$5\mu W$ for $10\mu W$ mIOP
Optical splitter	$0.2dB$

Table 3. Optical energy parameters

mapping, the new mapping has very high density communication clustered around the middle nodes, which require lower overall power than the nodes near the ends of the waveguide.

Figure 7 also shows the mode assignment for a 2-mode power topology specific to water_spatial before (Figure 7c) and after running Taboo (Figure 7d). Each row represents a source node's waveguide(s) and each column is a destination node, a dark color indicates a specific destination node (x axis) is in the low power mode of a source node (y axis). We observe that this power topology matches the communication patterns from Figure 7a and 7b, with more frequently communicating nodes in the low power mode. These figures also show the non-uniform nature of communication-aware power topologies: *source nodes have different local power topologies, and the general framework does not require consecutive destinations within a given power mode.*

In this paper we perform thread mapping based on the single mode power topology and thus the assignment accounts for only the waveguide loss between a source and destination. A more general approach would perform a joint optimization of power topology design and thread mapping. We leave exploring additional heuristic techniques to perform this even more complex assignment as future research.

5. Evaluation

In this section, we evaluate the power consumption of mNoC for various power topologies, using naive and QAP thread mapping. Our results show that power topologies combined with QAP thread mapping achieves the goal of performance equal to a full crossbar, but with power consumption close to the smaller clustered topology. Thread mapping is critical for achieving this goal, where two power modes capture a significant fraction of the opportunity (46% reduction), but a 4-mode power topology can provide an additional 5% reduction. We first present our evaluation methodology and then discuss the impact on power consumption of several different design options. The options include naive distance-based power topology, thread mapping, communication-aware power topologies, and application-specific power topologies.

5.1 Methodology

We create our mNoC topology in the Graphite [25] simulator and run all the simulations in full simulator mode. We explore 256-core systems and the simulation configuration is summarized in Table 2. We use the MOSI directory-based cache coherence protocol provided in Graphite along with its built-in models for contention in the system. The total O/E and E/O latency is about 200 ps and is modeled as 1 cycle in the nanophotonic link traversal time. We assume a die size of $400mm^2$, therefore the waveguide's total length is approximately $18cm$. We conservatively assume the speed of light in the waveguide is about $10cm/ns$, which means $1.8ns$ to travel the longest distance, corresponding to a worst case of 9 cycles for a $5GHz$ clock. All electrical links are modeled as 1 cycle [8] for the rNoC and clustered mNoC (c_mNoC).

We run 12 benchmarks from the SPLASH benchmark suite [37] to evaluate performance. As mentioned in Section 2, a SWMR single-mode mNoC crossbar improves the performance by 10% compared with rNoC, while c_mNoC has similar performance to rNoC. To evaluate power consumption, we obtain traces of communication packets from all 12 benchmarks executing on mNoC and build a power model to explore the impact of power topologies and thread mapping on power consumption. The key parameters used in the power model are shown in Table 3. The baseline for comparison is total network power for a 256×256 single mode mNoC with naive thread mapping, shown in Table 4. For rNoC we calculate power using similar methodology to Pang et al. [30]; however we bias in favor of rNoC by using $0.1\mu W$ for photodetector mIOP vs. the $10\mu W$ mIOP for mNoC as descrbied in 2.2. We further bias results toward rNoC by assuming 10% QD_LED efficiency instead of the 18% assumed in [30]. The electrical buffer power is deteremined using models decribed by others [19, 27, 28] which may slightly bias in favor of mNoC due to our increased number of buffers.

Our baseline results reveal that the clustered rNoC (radix-64 optical crossbar) consumes 36W, with 23W in ring trimming and a 5W laser source, lower than previous results [27, 36] for SWMR optical crossbars (see Figure 10 in Section 5.7 for a complete breakdown). The average power for the base mNoC is 20.94W, lower than the clustered rNoC. Furthermore, mNoC is energy proportional, applications with higher network utilization (e.g., radix) require

Benchmark	Power (W)	Benchmark	Power (W)
barnes	7.05	water_s	5.28
radix	120.34	water_ns	6.08
ocean_c	12.31	cholesky	5.14
ocean_nc	24.23	lu_cb	7.79
raytrace	3.99	lu_ncb	43.70
fft	11.41	volrend	3.99
average	20.94		

Table 4. Base mNoC Power Consumption

Symbol	Definition
M	Mode
T	Thread mapping with QAP
N	Naive distance-based mode assignment
G	General mode assignment based on sampled weights
C	Custom power topology design
U	Uniform traffic pattern for splitter design
W	Weighted traffic pattern for splitter design
S	Sampled traffic weights for splitter design

Table 5. Design Symbols

high power (> 100W); however we show that power aware thread mapping and power topologies reduce this below rNoC, to $\sim$ 20W, while maintaining the performance benefits of high-radix crossbars. We use the symbols shown in Table 5 to create a notation for the various power topologies in our figures; for example, 2M_T_N_S4 means 2 modes, QAP thread mapping, naive distance-based, and splitter design based on weights from sampling 4 applications.

5.2 Naive Distance-Based Power Topologies

We evaluate two distance-based power topologies: 1) a 2-mode topology with the 128 closest destinations assigned to the low power mode of a source, and the remaining destinations assigned to the higher power mode, and 2) a 4-mode power topology based on groups of 64 nearest nodes. To calculate overall source power (Equation 1), and the corresponding splitter design, we explored several communication weightings (e.g., 66% / 33%, uniform, etc.) and found qualitatively similar results across all weightings (see Section 5.6). For clarity we only present results for uniform weights. Figure 8 shows the power consumption of the two distance-based power topologies with naive and QAP thread mapping normalized to the single-mode mNoC with naive thread mapping (1M). Here we consider only the naive thread mapping, we discuss QAP thread mapping below. The 4-mode distance-based power topology reduces the total mNoC power by 12% while the 2-mode distance-based power topology reduces power by 10% on average (harmonic mean). Ocean_nc and radix show the largest benefits of power topologies with reductions 15%-20%. We also implement 256-node clustered 2-mode power topology similar to Fig. 5a with naive thread mapping; however it only reduces mNoC power by 1% on average, demonstrating that distance-based power topologies are superior to clustered power topologies.

5.3 Impact of Thread Mapping

Clustering communication so that frequently communicating threads are allocated to cores near the center of the waveguide provides greater opportunity to exploit the different power modes in a given power topology. Figure 8 supports this hypothesis; QAP thread mapping helps all three power topologies. The average power reductions over the base mNoC are 27%, 38%, and 39% for the 1-mode, 2-mode, and 4-mode power topologies, respectively. Ocean_nc and radix show the most improvement from QAP thread mapping with power topologies providing as low as 26%-32% of total network power vs. the base single-mode mNoC power topology. Although QAP thread mapping has larger impact on total mNoC power than power topologies alone, the best overall design uses a 4-mode power topology along with QAP thread mapping.

5.4 Communication-Aware Mode Assignment

Communication-aware power mode assignment follows the *"more is less, less is more"* philosophy by utilizing communication information from benchmarks. We first sort all the destination nodes according the communication frequency with a given source node and then assign more frequent destinations to lower power mode and less frequent destinations to higher power modes. In this section we explore two methods for obtaining communication frequency: sampling from four benchmarks (lu_cb, radix, raytrace, water_s) and averaging across all 12 benchmarks. A more statistically significant exploration of sampling, while interesting, is beyond the scope of this paper.

To isolate the impact of communication-aware mode assignment, we compare to a distance-based power topology that uses the sampled traffic for splitter design. Therefore, the difference in total mNoC power is mainly due to different mode assignment. As shown in Fig. 9, communication-aware mode assignment generally works better than naive distance-based mode assignment. Using weights from the average of all 12 benchmarks reduces power by 7% compared with the distance-based mode assignment for the 2-mode design. The reduction is increased to 10% for the 4-mode design. Moreover, communication-aware mode assignment based on the average of 12 benchmarks works better than the one based on 4 sampled benchmarks. As expected, when more communication information is available, the better the design.

A 4-mode power topology produces qualitatively similar results, but quantitatively is the best overall design when sampling across all 12 benchmarks with 49% of the base mNoC's power on average vs. 53% for the 2-mode power topology. Compared to the best distance-based power topol-

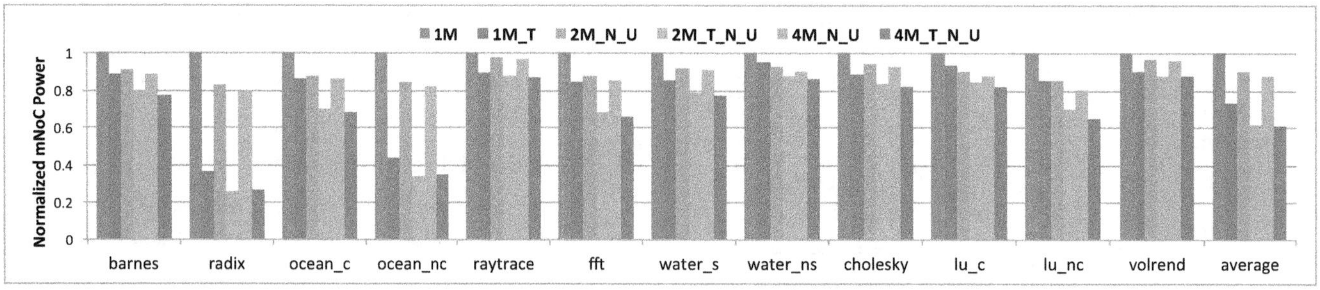

Figure 8. Distance-Based Power Topology With and Without Thread Mapping

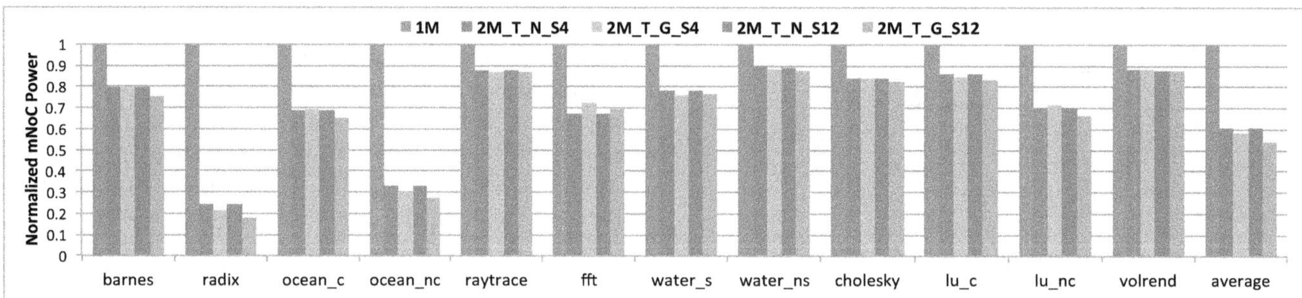

(a) Two-Mode Power Topologies

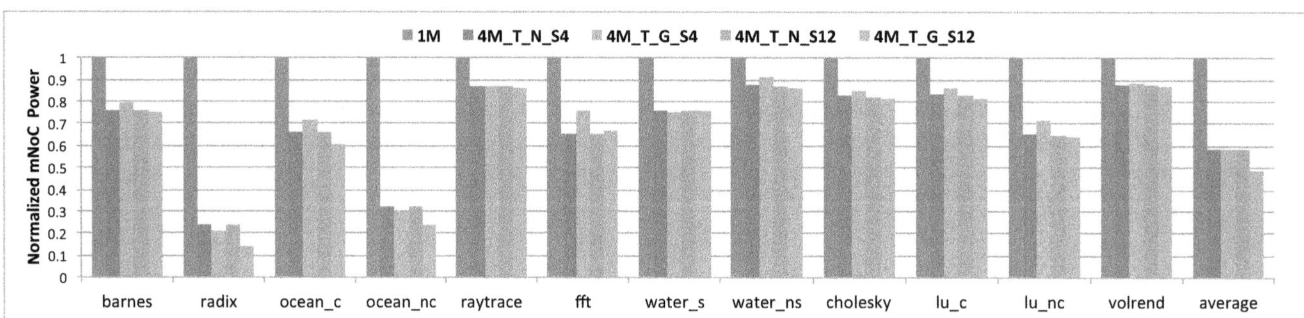

(b) Four-Mode Power Topologies

Figure 9. Communication-Aware Mode Designs vs Distance-Based Mode Designs

ogy that uses the uniform traffic for splitter design in Fig. 8, the best 4-mode power topology with communication-aware mode assignment reduces the total mNoC power by 12%. This demonstrates the benefit of communication aware power topologies.

5.5 Application Specific Designs

To understand how well the various general power topologies work, we create application specific power topologies tailored to each benchmark. We examine the source power consumption for the application specific designs with QAP thread mapping and naive mapping. They both have similar characteristics, but do not have a significant improvement over naive distance-based power topologies (about 8%). The *"keep it simple"* design philosophy may apply. However, for embedded systems or situations with known specific communication patterns, a custom power topology may be beneficial.

5.6 Splitter Design Sensitivity Analysis

As explained in Section 3.2 and Section 4.3, the communication patterns of benchmarks could potentially affect the splitter design. We evaluated the sensitivity of splitter design to communication traffic weights using the application specific 2-mode power topology with QAP thread mapping as the basic design. The different communication weights we consider are: uniform, 66%/33%, 33%/66%, samples from 4 benchmarks (S4), and the average across all 12 benchmarks (S12).

Our results reveal minimal variation in power reduction across the different weights (within 2%), but all produce over a 40% reduction in total mNoC power on average. One potential explanation for this limited impact of weights on

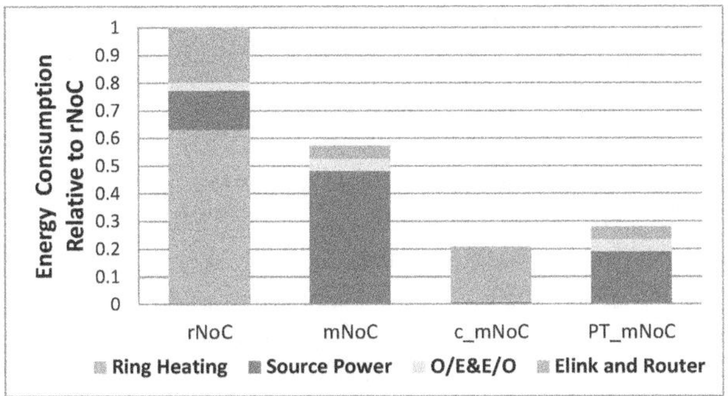

Figure 10. Total NoC Energy Consumption

splitter designs is that the total source power for given a source core is a function of both weights and splitter ratios. Changes in the weights can be compensated by changes in the splitter ratios resulting in similar overall power. Therefore, the traffic pattern, as it relates to splitter design, has minimal impact on overall power consumption.

5.7 Overall mNoC Energy Consumption

As mentioned in Section 2.2, our goal is to design a single physical network with the same performance as the high-radix mNoC, but with the power savings of the lower-radix clustered topology (c_mNoC). Figure 10 shows the total energy normalized to rNoC for baseline (mNoC), c_mNoC, and the best power topology mNoC (PT_mNoC=4M_T_G_S12) with static splitters. The power model for rNoC is similar to the one proposed by Joshi et al. [19]. We use $20\mu W$/ring over 20K temperature range as thermal tuning power to favor rNoC. More accurate ring models [26, 39] indicate much higher ring tuning power. Since the dominant power for rNoC is ring tuning instead of O/E, it shows little or no benefit to increase mIOP for rNoC (see Section 2.2). Therefore, we keep rNoC's photodetector mIOP as $1\mu W$ instead of $10\mu W$ used by all mNoC related topologies. From these results we see that the best power topology with thread mapping requires only 28% of rNoC's energy, close to the 21% required by c_mNoC and much lower than the base mNoC (1M power topology) of 57%. Note that c_mNoC has smaller source and OE/EO power than mNoC, because the lower radix requires shorter waveguide length and fewer optical devices.

Our power topology has at least the same performance as the base radix-256 mNoC (1M). Performance could be improved by considering QAP thread mapping, because it reduces the distance between source and destination, and potentially reduces latency. Thread mapping will have minimal impact on rNoC's power consumption since it is dominated by thermal ring tuning. Similarly, c_mNoC's power is dominated by electrical components. There may be some impact on performance of the clustered topologies (rNoC and c_NoC) by thread mapping, however only three nodes are near neighbors and communication with all others requires traversal of two local routers and the larger crossbar. Therefore, we don't expect to observe too much benefit from thread mapping, nonetheless, we are currently exploring this design point.

6. Related Work

We discuss related work based on three broad categories: current nanophotonic NoC designs, power optimization in both on-chip networks and wireless networks, and thread mapping methods to optimize the network in terms of energy, performance or congestion in NoCs. Although different power optimization methods have been proposed for on-chip networks, the concepts proposed in this paper such as logical power mode and power topology in nanophotonic NoCs are new.

Bus-based crossbars are very popular in the current nanophotonic NoCs. A typical nanophotonic crossbar is usually designed using one of the following structures: Multi-Write-Single-Read (MWSR) as proposed for Corona [36], Single-Write-Multi-Read (SWMR) shared-bus crossbar proposed by Kirman et al. [21] and Pan et al. [28], or Multi-Write-Multi-Read (MWMR) which combines the above two and proposes a reduced number of channels design as proposed for Flexishare [27]. However, due to the power inefficiency from the off-chip laser source and thermal ring tuning power, and the ring resonator's nonlinearity, these designs are difficult to scale to more than radix-64. Nitta et al. [26] presents a thermal model to calculate the ring tuning power, which is much bigger than the heating power calculated with the popular per ring fixed cost method. Even with further optimization techniques [39], the ring power consumption is still a dominant factor. Other topologies based on ring resonator switches are also explored, such as a 2D grid NoC from Phastlane [9] and a torus-based hierarchical hybrid NoC called THOE [41]. Xue et al. [40] proposes a freespace optical interconnect that uses VCSELs as light sources.

As power becomes a larger concern in current computing systems, various power optimization methods are proposed for on-chip networks. Recent work from Koka et al. [22] presents a power constrained method for designing and evaluating the nanophotonic interconnects. Their results show that under reasonable device assumptions for a given input optical power, point-to-point networks have better power and performance characteristics than switched-based networks. Catnap [11] proposes a power proportional NoC design which divides a single NoC into multiple subnetworks to exploit the benefits of power gating. We could apply this same method on mNoC by deactivating waveguides per source to decrease bandwidth and reduce power. Other work explores different physical topologies to reduce NoC energy and/or latency [12, 17, 18]. Finally, any transmission line or wireless communication system can utilize the same principles of power modes based on distance to destinations, e.g., [2, 7].

Thread mapping is previously used to design energy and/or latency-aware on-chip networks. Hu et al. [16] proposes an efficient branch-and-bound algorithm to map cores to a regular tile-based network to save total energy. Hoefler et al. [15] discusses efficient application communication pattern mapping to sparse network topologies. They demonstrate a heuristic method based on graph similarity to reduce network congestion and also improve application communication performance. Their methods could potentially be used for joint optimization of thread mapping and power topology design.

7. Conclusion

Energy efficiency and power dissipation are increasingly important design goals for computer systems. Manycore processors exacerbate this problem since on-chip interconnect (NoC) can become a significant portion of overall power consumption. This paper utilizes a new molecular-scale photonic NoC technology (mNoC) and shows how to architect power efficient designs through the use of power topologies. A power topology is a set of power modes and an assignment of destination nodes reachable in these power modes, for each source node in the system. Power topology implementations are enabled by careful waveguide design and the unique mNoC capability of current-controlled on-chip QD_LEDs for light sources.

The benefits of mNoC power topologies include scaling to high-radix crossbars, to achieve high performance, while providing power savings close to smaller-radix crossbars. We present several different power topologies for a 256-core system with two and four power modes, including distance-based and communication-aware topologies that reduce network power by $\geq 10\%$ compared to a baseline mNoC with a single power mode that can reach all destinations. Further improvements, additional 40% reduction, are possible with intelligent thread mapping that maps frequently communicating threads to cores with lower power communication requirements. We find that distance-based power topologies capture a significant fraction of the overall benefit in mNoC power reduction 40%, but that utilizing application information for mode assignment can achieve over a 50% reduction. Overall, mNoC with power topologies achieves performance 10% higher than a clustered ring-resonator photonic NoC, while reducing energy by 72%.

The work in this paper represents our initial efforts at exploiting emerging molecular-scale photonics to architect novel power efficient on-chip interconnects. The design space is very large, and we've explored only a small portion. Areas of future work include, but are not limited to: dynamic power modes, joint optimization of thread mapping and power topology design, applying power topologies to embedded systems with well-defined IP blocks and communication patterns, and exploring mNoC's ability to multicast/broadcast when used in coherence protocol design.

Acknowledgements

This material is based upon work supported by, or in part by, the National Science Foundation (CCF-0702434), the Defense Advanced Research Projects Agency and the U. S. Army Research Office under grant number W911NF-13-1-0096 (Distribution Statement A: Approved for Public Release, Distribution Unlimited). The views, opinions, and/or findings contained in this article are those of the author(s) and should not be interpreted as representing the official views or policies of the Department of Defense or the U.S. Government. We thank the anonymous reviewers and the Duke self-assembled systems group for their comments that improved the quality of the paper.

Appendix A

For a $N \times N$ crossbar, to solve for S_j at the destination j given a source node i, where $i, j \in \{0..N-1\}$, we build on the observation that destination nodes unique to a given power mode $m \in \{0..M\}$ have the same β_j values which we call γ_m: $\beta_i = \beta_j = \gamma_m, \forall i, j \in Mdest_m - Mdest_{m-1}$, and for each source mode power $Pmode_k, k \in \{0..M\}$ we define unique $\gamma_{k,m}$. We then further simplify by defining all $\gamma_{k,m}$ in terms of $\gamma_{0,m}$ in power mode 0 to obtain $\alpha_m = \gamma_{0,m}, m \in \{0..M\}$, where $\alpha_m \in (0..1], \alpha_0 = 1$.

Equations 3-6 show abbreviated versions of Equation 2 for a four mode($M = 4$) power topology, which connect Equation 2 to Equation 1. The equations are based on an observation that given a fabricated waveguide, a given source power is proportional to *any* destination's received power, and that a change in the source power results in a proportional change in *all* destination's received power.

$$Pmode_0 = f(P_{min}, \alpha_1 P_{min}, \alpha_2 P_{min}, \alpha_3 P_{min}) \quad (3)$$

$$Pmode_1 = f(\frac{1}{\alpha_1} P_{min}, P_{min}, \frac{\alpha_2}{\alpha_1} P_{min}, \frac{\alpha_3}{\alpha_1} P_{min}) \quad (4)$$

$$Pmode_2 = f(\frac{1}{\alpha_2} P_{min}, \frac{\alpha_1}{\alpha_2} P_{min}, P_{min}, \frac{\alpha_3}{\alpha_2} P_{min}) \quad (5)$$

$$Pmode_3 = f(\frac{1}{\alpha_3} P_{min}, \frac{\alpha_1}{\alpha_3} P_{min}, \frac{\alpha_2}{\alpha_3} P_{min}, P_{min}) \quad (6)$$

We can then rearrange the summand of Equation 2 to express S_j in terms of $\alpha_m, Pmin, \& L$. We then iterate over all α_m from 0 to 1 in increments of 0.1 to obtain values for each power mode.

Note that by determining the values that minimize $Pmode_0$, all higher power modes can be computed by $Pmode_i = \frac{Pmode_0}{\alpha_i}$. Once we have the alpha values we can substitute into the splitter equation to obtain the appropriate splitter values for use in fabrication. Since we have one equation with many unknowns, we solve for alpha values computationally by iterating over all alpha values (better results may be achieved by using steps smaller than 0.1).

References

[1] R. Arians, A. Gust, T. Kummell, C. Kruse, S. Zaitsev, G. Bacher, and D. Hommel. Electrically driven single quantum dot emitter operating at room temperature. *Applied Physics Letters*, 93(17):173506–173506, 2008.

[2] Wonseok Baek, David SL Wei, and C-CJ Kuo. Power-aware topology control for wireless ad-hoc networks. In *Wireless Communications and Networking Conference, 2006. WCNC 2006. IEEE*, volume 1, pages 406–412. IEEE, 2006.

[3] N. Barrow-Williams, C. Fensch, and S. Moore. A communication characterisation of splash-2 and parsec. In *Workload Characterization, 2009. IISWC 2009. IEEE International Symposium on*, pages 86–97. IEEE, 2009.

[4] Valeriu Beiu, José M Quintana, and María J Avedillo. Vlsi implementations of threshold logic-a comprehensive survey. *Neural Networks, IEEE Transactions on*, 14(5):1217–1243, 2003.

[5] A. Biberman, K. Preston, G. Hendry, N. Sherwood-Droz, J. Chan, J.S. Levy, M. Lipson, and K. Bergman. Photonic network-on-chip architectures using multilayer deposited silicon materials for high-performance chip multiprocessors. *ACM Journal on Emerging Technologies in Computing Systems (JETC)*, 7(2):7, 2011.

[6] J. Chan, G. Hendry, K. Bergman, and L.P. Carloni. Physical-layer modeling and system-level design of chip-scale photonic interconnection networks. *Computer-Aided Design of Integrated Circuits and Systems, IEEE Transactions on*, 30(10):1507–1520, 2011.

[7] Benjie Chen, Kyle Jamieson, Hari Balakrishnan, and Robert Morris. Span: An energy-efficient coordination algorithm for topology maintenance in ad hoc wireless networks. In *Proceedings of the 7th annual international conference on Mobile computing and networking*, pages 85–96. ACM, 2001.

[8] G. Chen, H. Chen, M. Haurylau, N.A. Nelson, D.H. Albonesi, P.M. Fauchet, and E.G. Friedman. Predictions of cmos compatible on-chip optical interconnect. *Integration, the VLSI journal*, 40(4):434–446, 2007.

[9] M.J. Cianchetti, J.C. Kerekes, and D.H. Albonesi. Phastlane: a rapid transit optical routing network. In *36th annual international symposium on Computer architecture*, pages 441–450, 2009.

[10] David T Connolly. An improved annealing scheme for the qap. *European Journal of Operational Research*, 46(1):93–100, 1990.

[11] Reetuparna Das, Satish Narayanasamy, Sudhir K Satpathy, and Ronald G Dreslinski. Catnap: Energy proportional multiple network-on-chip. In *to appear in Proceeding of the 40th annual international symposium on Computer architecture*, 2013.

[12] Haytham Elmiligi, Ahmed A Morgan, M Watheq El-Kharashi, and Fayez Gebali. Power-aware topology optimization for networks-on-chips. In *Circuits and Systems, 2008. ISCAS 2008. IEEE International Symposium on*, pages 360–363. IEEE, 2008.

[13] Ashwini Gopal, Kazunori Hoshino, Sunmin Kim, and Xiaojing Zhang. Multi-color colloidal quantum dot based light emitting diodes micropatterned on silicon hole transporting layers. *Nanotechnology*, 20(23):235201, 2009.

[14] F Hargart, CA Kessler, T Schwarzback, E Koroknay, S Weidenfeld, M Jetter, and P Michler. Electrically driven quantum dot single-photon source at 2 ghz excitation repetition rate with ultra-low emission time jitter. *Applied Physics Letters*, 102(1):011126–011126, 2013.

[15] Torsten Hoefler and Marc Snir. Generic topology mapping strategies for large-scale parallel architectures. In *Proceedings of the international conference on Supercomputing*, pages 75–84. ACM, 2011.

[16] Jingcao Hu and Radu Marculescu. Energy-aware mapping for tile-based noc architectures under performance constraints. In *Design Automation Conference, 2003. Proceedings of the ASP-DAC 2003. Asia and South Pacific*, pages 233–239. IEEE, 2003.

[17] Yuanfang Hu, Hongyu Chen, Yi Zhu, Andrew A Chien, and Chung-Kuan Cheng. Physical synthesis of energy-efficient networks-on-chip through topology exploration and wire style optimization. In *Computer Design: VLSI in Computers and Processors, 2005. ICCD 2005. Proceedings. 2005 IEEE International Conference on*, pages 111–118. IEEE, 2005.

[18] Yuanfang Hu, Yi Zhu, Hongyu Chen, Ronald Graham, and Chung-Kuan Cheng. Communication latency aware low power noc synthesis. In *Proceedings of the 43rd annual Design Automation Conference*, pages 574–579. ACM, 2006.

[19] A. Joshi, C. Batten, Y.J. Kwon, S. Beamer, I. Shamim, K. Asanovic, and V. Stojanovic. Silicon-photonic clos networks for global on-chip communication. In *Proceedings of the 2009 3rd ACM/IEEE International Symposium on Networks-on-Chip*, pages 124–133. IEEE Computer Society, 2009.

[20] Pawan Kapur. Scaling induced performance challenges/limitations of on-chip metal interconnects and comparisons with optical interconnects. Ph.D. Dissertation, Stanford University, Stanford, California, 2002.

[21] N. Kirman, M. Kirman, R.K. Dokania, J.F. Martinez, A.B. Apsel, M.A. Watkins, and D.H. Albonesi. Leveraging optical technology in future bus-based chip multiprocessors. In *Proceedings of the 39th Annual IEEE/ACM International Symposium on Microarchitecture*, pages 492–503. IEEE Computer Society, 2006.

[22] Pranay Koka, Michael O McCracken, Herb Schwetman, Chia-Hsin Owen Chen, Xuezhe Zheng, Ron Ho, Kannan Raj, and Ashok V Krishnamoorthy. A micro-architectural analysis of switched photonic multi-chip interconnects. In *Proceedings of the 39th International Symposium on Computer Architecture*, pages 153–164. IEEE Press, 2012.

[23] J.R. Lakowicz. *Principles of fluorescence spectroscopy*, volume 1. Springer, 2006.

[24] Benjamin S Mashford, Matthew Stevenson, Zoran Popovic, Charles Hamilton, Zhaoqun Zhou, Craig Breen, Jonathan Steckel, Vladimir Bulovic, Moungi Bawendi, Seth Coe-Sullivan, et al. High-efficiency quantum-dot light-emitting devices with enhanced charge injection. *Nature Photonics*, 7(5):407–412, 2013.

[25] J.E. Miller, H. Kasture, G. Kurian, C. Gruenwald, N. Beckmann, C. Celio, J. Eastep, and A. Agarwal. Graphite: A distributed parallel simulator for multicores. In *High Performance Computer Architecture (HPCA), 2010 IEEE 16th International Symposium on*, pages 1–12. IEEE, 2010.

[26] Christopher Nitta, Matthew Farrens, and Venkatesh Akella. Addressing system-level trimming issues in on-chip nanophotonic networks. In *High Performance Computer Architecture (HPCA), 2011 IEEE 17th International Symposium on*, pages 122–131. IEEE, 2011.

[27] Y. Pan, J. Kim, and G. Memik. Flexishare: Channel sharing for an energy-efficient nanophotonic crossbar. In *High Performance Computer Architecture (HPCA), 2010 IEEE 16th International Symposium on*, pages 1–12. IEEE, 2010.

[28] Yan Pan, Prabhat Kumar, John Kim, Gokhan Memik, Yu Zhang, and Alok Choudhary. Firefly: Illuminating future network-on-chip with nanophotonics. In *In Proc. of the International Symposium on Computer Architecture*, 2009.

[29] Jun Pang, Christopher Dwyer, and Alvin R Lebeck. Exploiting emerging technologies for nanoscale photonic networks-on-chip. In *Proceedings of the Sixth International Workshop on Network on Chip Architectures*, pages 53–58. ACM, 2013.

[30] Jun Pang, Christopher Dwyer, and Alvin R. Lebeck. mNoC: Large nanophotonic network-on-chip crossbars with molecular scale devices. *ACM Journal on Emerging Technologies in Computing Systems (JETC)*, to appear.

[31] I.K. Park, M.K. Kwon, J.O. Kim, S.B. Seo, J.Y. Kim, J.H. Lim, S.J. Park, and Y.S. Kim. Green light-emitting diodes with self-assembled in-rich ingan quantum dots. *Applied Physics Letters*, 91:133105, 2007.

[32] E Taillard. Robust taboo search for the quadratic assignment problem. *Parallel computing*, 17(4):443–455, 1991.

[33] Dmitri V Talapin and Jonathan Steckel. Quantum dot light-emitting devices. *Mrs Bulletin*, 38(09):685–691, 2013.

[34] Limin Tong, Rafael R Gattass, Jonathan B Ashcom, Sailing He, Jingyi Lou, Mengyan Shen, Iva Maxwell, and Eric Mazur. Subwavelength-diameter silica wires for low-loss optical wave guiding. *Nature*, 426(6968):816–819, 2003.

[35] Bernard Valeur et al. *Molecular fluorescence: principles and applications*. John Wiley & Sons, 2013.

[36] Dana Vantrease, Robert Schreiber, Matteo Monchiero, Moray McLaren, Norman P. Jouppi, Marco Fiorentino, Al Davis, Nathan Binkert, Raymond G. Beausoleil, and Jung Ho Ahn. Corona: System implications of emerging nanophotonic technology. In *Proceedings of the 35th Annual International Symposium on Computer Architecture*, pages 153–164, Washington, DC, USA, 2008. IEEE Computer Society.

[37] Steven Cameron Woo, Moriyoshi Ohara, Evan Torrie, Jaswinder Pal Singh, and Anoop Gupta. The splash-2 programs: characterization and methodological considerations. In *Proceedings of the 22nd annual international symposium on Computer architecture*, pages 24–36. ACM, 1995.

[38] V. Wood and V. Bulović. Colloidal quantum dot light-emitting devices. *Nano Reviews*, 1(0), 2010.

[39] Yi Xu, Jun Yang, and Rami Melhem. Tolerating process variations in nanophotonic on-chip networks. In *Proceedings of the 39th International Symposium on Computer Architecture*, pages 142–152. IEEE Press, 2012.

[40] Jing Xue, Alok Garg, Berkehan Ciftcioglu, Jianyun Hu, Shang Wang, Ioannis Savidis, Manish Jain, Rebecca Berman, Peng Liu, Michael Huang, Hui Wu, Eby Friedman, Gary Wicks, and Duncan Moore. An intra-chip free-space optical interconnect. In *Proceedings of the 37th Annual International Symposium on Computer Architecture*, ISCA '10, pages 94–105, New York, NY, USA, 2010. ACM.

[41] Y. Ye, J. Xu, X. Wu, W. Zhang, W. Liu, and M. Nikdast. A torus-based hierarchical optical-electronic network-on-chip for multiprocessor system-on-chip. *ACM Journal on Emerging Technologies in Computing Systems (JETC)*, 8(1):5, 2012.

Memory Errors in Modern Systems

The Good, The Bad, and The Ugly

Vilas Sridharan[1], Nathan DeBardeleben[2], Sean Blanchard[2], Kurt B. Ferreira[3], Jon Stearley[3], John Shalf[4], Sudhanva Gurumurthi[5]

[1]RAS Architecture, [5]AMD Research, Advanced Micro Devices, Inc., Boxborough, MA
[2]Ultrascale Systems Research Center, Los Alamos National Laboratory, Los Alamos, New Mexico *
[3]Scalable System Software, Sandia National Laboratories, Albuquerque, New Mexico †
[4]National Energy Research Scientific Computing Center, Lawrence Berkeley National Laboratory, Berkeley, CA ‡
{vilas.sridharan, sudhanva.gurumurthi}@amd.com, {ndebard, seanb}@lanl.gov
{kbferre, jrstear}@sandia.gov, jshalf@lbl.gov

Abstract

Several recent publications have shown that hardware faults in the memory subsystem are commonplace. These faults are predicted to become more frequent in future systems that contain orders of magnitude more DRAM and SRAM than found in current memory subsystems. These memory subsystems will need to provide resilience techniques to tolerate these faults when deployed in high-performance computing systems and data centers containing tens of thousands of nodes. Therefore, it is critical to understand the efficacy of current hardware resilience techniques to determine whether they will be suitable for future systems.

In this paper, we present a study of DRAM and SRAM faults and errors from the field. We use data from two leadership-class high-performance computer systems to analyze the reliability impact of hardware resilience schemes that are deployed in current systems. Our study has several key findings about the efficacy of many currently-deployed reliability techniques such as DRAM ECC, DDR address/command parity, and SRAM ECC and parity. We also perform a methodological study, and find that counting errors instead of faults, a common practice among researchers and data center operators, can lead to incorrect conclusions about system reliability. Finally, we use our data to project the needs of future large-scale systems. We find that SRAM faults are unlikely to pose a significantly larger reliability threat in the future, while DRAM faults will be a major concern and stronger DRAM resilience schemes will be needed to maintain acceptable failure rates similar to those found on today's systems.

Categories and Subject Descriptors B.8.1 [*Performance and Reliability*]: Reliability, Testing, and Fault-Tolerance

Keywords Field studies; Large-scale systems; Reliability

1. Introduction

Current predictions are that exascale systems in the early 2020s will have between 32 and 100 petabytes of main memory (DRAM), a 100x to 350x increase compared to 2012 levels [8]. Similar increases are likely in the amount of cache memory (SRAM) in such systems. Future data centers will also contain many more nodes than existing data centers. These systems and data centers will require significant increases in the reliability of both DRAM and SRAM memories in order to maintain hardware failure rates comparable to current systems.

The focus of this work is to provide insight and guidance to system designers and operators on characteristics of a reliable system. In particular, our focus is on analyzing the efficacy of existing hardware resilience techniques, their impact on reliable system design, and whether they will be adequate for future systems.

For our analysis, we use data collected over the past several years from two leadership-class production sys-

* A portion of this work was performed at the Ultrascale Systems Research Center (USRC) at Los Alamos National Laboratory, supported by the U.S. Department of Energy contract DE-FC02-06ER25750. The publication has been assigned the LANL identifier LA-UR-14-26219.

† Sandia is a multiprogram laboratory operated by Sandia Corporation, a Lockheed Martin Company, for the United States Department of Energy under Contract DE-AC04-94AL85000. The publication has been assigned the Sandia identifier SAND2014-16515J

‡ A portion of this work used resources of the National Energy Research Scientific Computing Center supported by the Office of Science of the U.S. Department of Energy under Contract No. DE-AC02-05CH11231.

ASPLOS '15, March 14–18, 2015, Istanbul, Turkey.

http://dx.doi.org/10.1145/2694344.2694348

tems: Hopper, a 6,000-node supercomputer located at the NERSC center at Lawrence Berkeley Labs in Oakland, California; and Cielo, an 8,500-node supercomputer located at Los Alamos National Laboratory (LANL) in Los Alamos, New Mexico. Both supercomputers are based on AMD Opteron™CPUs and contain DDR3 DRAM. In aggregate, the data that we analyze (which is a subset of the full data available) comprises over 314 million CPU socket-hours and 45 billion DRAM device-hours. This scale gives us the ability to gather statistically representative data on faults observed during production lifetimes of CPU and DRAM devices. While our data is collected primarily from supercomputing centers, the results of our analysis are applicable to any large data center or compute cluster where hardware reliability is important.

This paper adds several novel insights about system reliability to the existing literature and also highlights certain aspects of analyzing field data that are critical to perform correctly in order to derive correct insights. Broad contributions include:

- A detailed analysis of DRAM and SRAM faults on Hopper. This data complements existing studies on faults in other production systems, including Jaguar, Cielo, and Blue Waters, thus furthering our understanding of DRAM and SRAM faults [12][33][34].
- The effect of altitude on DRAM fault rates. To our knowledge, this is the first study to present an analysis of altitude effects on DRAM in production systems.
- The impact of counting errors instead of faults to evaluate system reliability. Counting errors is common among researchers and data center operators (e.g., [12][30]), but no one has quantified the effect of this methodology on the accuracy of the reliability conclusions obtained.
- The effect of several hardware-based resilience techniques on system reliability, including SEC-DED ECC, chipkill ECC, and command/address parity in DRAM subsystems. We also examine SRAM resilience schemes, and analyze in-depth the impact of design choices on SRAM reliability.
- A projection of the impacts of SRAM and DRAM faults on future exascale-class systems.

Our study has several key findings that are of interest to system designers and operators. These findings are wide ranging and cover a variety of hardware resilience techniques in common use in the industry. We group these findings into three categories: the good, the bad, and the ugly.

The Good. Our study highlights several advances made in the understanding of fault behavior and system reliability. These include:

- DDR command and address parity, an addition to JEDEC's DDR-3 and DDR-4 specifications, has a substantial positive effect on system reliability, detecting errors at a rate comparable to the uncorrected error rate of chipkill ECC.
- The majority of observed SRAM faults in the field are transient faults from particle strikes. This further confirms that SRAM faults are a well-understood phenomenon in current and near-future process technologies.
- The majority of uncorrected SRAM errors are due to single-bit faults; therefore, reducing SRAM uncorrected error rates is a matter of engineering time and effort (e.g., replacing parity codes with ECCs) rather than new research and novel techniques. Furthermore, appropriate multi-bit fault protection reduces or eliminates the expected increase in uncorrected error rate from SRAM faults due to high altitude.

The Bad. Unfortunately, some of our findings point to areas where more work needs to be done, or more understanding is required. These include:

- Altitude increases the fault rate of some DRAM devices, though this effect varies by vendor. This is evidence that some (but not all) DRAM devices are susceptible to transient faults from high-energy particle strikes.
- Unlike on-chip SRAM, external memory (e.g., DRAM) of future systems will require stronger resilience techniques than exist in supercomputing systems today.

The Ugly. Finally, some of our results show potential problems in commonly-used practices or techniques:

- Performing field studies is difficult. For instance, we demonstrate that counting errors instead of faults can lead to incorrect conclusions about system reliability. We examine results from recent studies that have used error counts, and use our data to show that using this methodology can result in misleading or inaccurate conclusions.
- SEC-DED ECC, a commonly used ECC technique, is poorly suited to modern DRAM subsystems and may result in *undetected* errors (which may cause silent data corruption) at a rate of up to 20 FIT per DRAM device, an unacceptably high rate for many enterprise data centers and high-performance computing systems.

The rest of this paper is organized as follows. Section 2 defines the terminology we use in this paper. Section 3 discusses related studies and describes the differences in our study and methodology. Section 4 explains the system and DRAM configurations of Cielo and Hopper. Section 5 describes our experimental setup. Section 6 presents baseline data on faults. Section 7 examines the impact of counting errors instead of faults. Section 8 presents our analysis of existing hardware resilience techniques. Section 9 extracts lessons from our data for system designers. Section 10 presents our projections for future system reliability, and Section 11 concludes.

2. Terminology

In this paper, we distinguish between a fault and an error as follows [6]:

- A fault is the underlying cause of an error, such as a stuck-at bit or high-energy particle strike. Faults can be *active* (causing errors), or *dormant* (not causing errors).
- An error is an incorrect portion of state resulting from an active fault, such as an incorrect value in memory. Errors may be *detected* and possibly *corrected* by higher level mechanisms such as parity or error correcting codes (ECC). They may also go *uncorrected*, or in the worst case, completely *undetected* (i.e., silent).

Hardware faults can further be classified as *transient*, *intermittent*, or *hard* [7] [10] [11]. Distinguishing a hard fault from an intermittent fault in a running system requires knowing the exact memory access pattern to determine whether a memory location returns the wrong data on every access. In practice, this is impossible in a large-scale field study such as ours. Therefore, we group intermittent and hard faults together in a category of *permanent* faults.

In this paper, we examine a variety of error detection and correction mechanisms. Some of these mechanisms include: *parity*, which can detect but not correct any single-bit error; single-error-correction double-error-detection *error correcting codes* (SEC-DED ECCs), which can correct any single-bit error and detect any double-bit error; and *chipkill* ECCs. We discuss two levels of chipkill ECC: *chipkill-detect* ECC, which can detect but not correct any error in a single DRAM chip; and *chipkill-correct*, which can correct any error in a single DRAM chip. To protect against multi-bit faults, structures with ECC or parity sometimes employ *bit interleaving*, which ensures that physically adjacent bitcells are protected by different ECC or parity words.

3. Related Work

During the past several years, multiple studies have been published examining failures in production systems. In 2006, Schroeder and Gibson studied failures in supercomputer systems at LANL [29]. In 2007, Li *et al.* published a study of memory errors on three different data sets, including a server farm of an Internet service provider [21]. In 2009, Schroeder *et al.* published a large-scale field study using Google's server fleet [30]. In 2010, Li *et al.* published an expanded study of memory errors at an Internet server farm and other sources [20]. In 2012, Hwang *et al.* published an expanded study on Google's server fleet, as well as two IBM Blue Gene clusters [16], Sridharan and Liberty presented a study of DRAM failures in a high-performance computing system [33], and El-Sayed *et al.* published a study on temperature effects of DRAM in data center environments [14].

In 2013, Siddiqua *et al.* presented a study of DRAM failures from client and server systems [31], and Sridharan *et al.* presented a study of DRAM and SRAM faults, with a focus on positional and vendor effects [34]. Finally, in 2014, Di Martino *et al.* presented a study of failures in Blue Waters, a high-performance computing system at the University of Illinois, Urbana-Champaign [12].

Parameter	Cielo	Hopper
Nodes	8568	6000
Sockets / Node	2	2
Cores / Socket	8	12
DIMMs / Socket	4	4
Location	Los Alamos, NM	Oakland, CA
Altitude	7,320 ft.	43 ft.

Table 1. System Configuration Information.

Our study contains larger scale and longer time intervals than many of the prior studies, allowing us to present more representative data on faults and errors. Among those studies with similar or larger scale to ours, many count errors instead of faults [12][14][16][30], which we show in Section 7 to be inaccurate. In addition, few of these prior studies examine the efficacy of hardware resilience techniques such as SEC-DED, chipkill, and DDR command/address parity.

There has been laboratory testing on DRAM and SRAM dating back several decades (e.g., [9][13][23][24][27]), as well as a recent study by Kim *et al.* on DRAM disturbance faults [19]. Lab studies such as these allow an understanding of fault modes and root causes, and complement field studies that identify fault modes which occur in practice.

4. Systems Configuration

Our study comprises data from two production systems in the United States: Hopper, a supercomputer located in Oakland, California, at 43 feet in elevation; and Cielo, a supercomputer in Los Alamos, New Mexico, at around 7,300 feet in elevation. A summary of relevant statistics on both systems are given in Table 1.

Hopper contains approximately 6,000 compute nodes. Each *node* contains two 12-core AMD Opteron™processors, each with twelve 32KB L1 data caches, twelve 512KB L2 caches, and one 12MB L3 cache. Each node has eight 4GB DDR-3 registered DIMMs for a total of 32GB of DRAM.

Cielo contains approximately 8,500 compute nodes. Each node contains two 8-core AMD Opteron™processors, each with eight 32KB L1 data caches, eight 512KB L2 caches, and one 12MB L3 cache. Each node has eight 4GB DDR-3 registered DIMMs for a total of 32GB of DRAM.

The nodes in both machines are organized as follows. Four nodes are connected to a *slot* which is a management module. Eight slots are contained in a *chassis*. Three chassis are mounted bottom-to-top (numerically) in a *rack*. Cielo has 96 racks, arranged into 6 *rows* each containing 16 racks.

4.1 DRAM and DIMM Configuration

In both Hopper and Cielo, each DDR-3 DIMM contains two *ranks* of 18 DRAM devices, each with four data (DQ) signals (known as an x4 DRAM device). In each rank, 16 of the

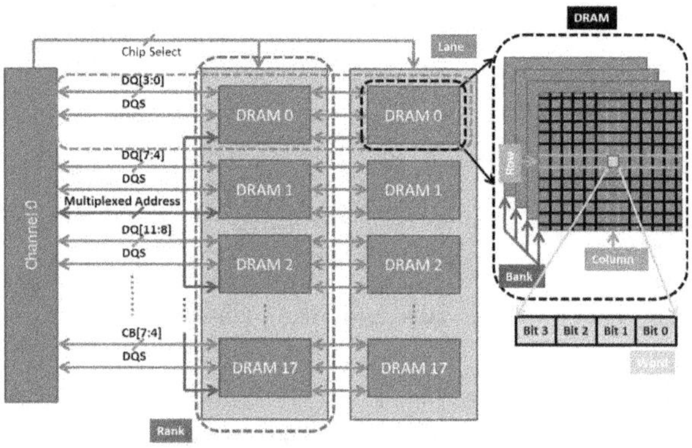

Figure 1. A simplified logical view of a single channel of the DRAM memory subsystem on each Cielo and Hopper node.

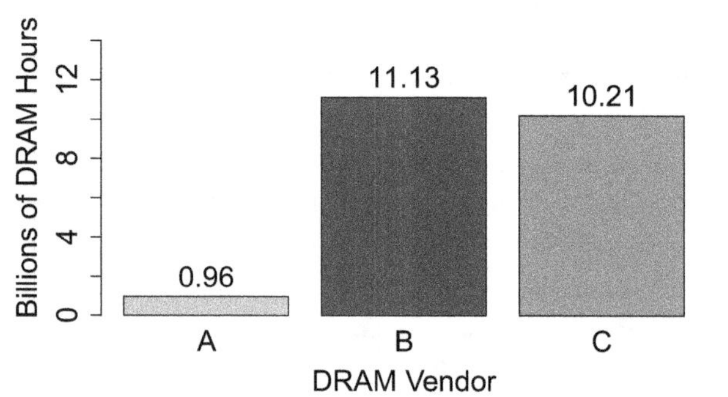

Figure 2. DRAM device-hours per vendor on Hopper. Even for the least-populous vendor (A), we have almost 1B device-hours of data.

DRAM devices are used to store data bits and two are used to store check bits. A *lane* is a group of DRAM devices on different ranks that shares data (DQ) signals. DRAMs in the same lane also share a strobe (DQS) signal, which is used as a source-synchronous clock signal for the data signals. A memory *channel* has 18 lanes, each with two ranks (i.e., one DIMM per channel). Each DRAM device contains eight internal *banks* that can be accessed in parallel. Logically, each bank is organized into *rows* and *columns*. Each row/column address pair identifies a 4-bit *word* in the DRAM device. Figure 1 shows a diagram of a single memory channel.

Physically, all DIMMs on Cielo and Hopper (from all vendors) are identical. Each DIMM is double-sided. DRAM devices are laid out in two rows of nine devices per side. There are no heatsinks on DIMMs in Cielo or Hopper.

The primary difference between the two memory subsystems is that Cielo uses chipkill-correct ECC on its memory subsystem, while Hopper uses chipkill-detect ECC.

5. Experimental Setup

For our analysis we use three different data sets - corrected error messages from console logs, uncorrected error messages from event logs, and hardware inventory logs. These three logs provided the ability to map each error message to specific hardware present in the system at that point in time.

Corrected error logs contain events from nodes at specific time stamps. Each node in the system has a hardware memory controller that logs corrected error events in registers provided by the x86 machine-check architecture (MCA) [5]. Each node's operating system is configured to poll the MCA registers once every few seconds and record any events it finds to the node's console log.

Uncorrected error event logs are similar and contain data on uncorrected errors logged in the system. These are typically not logged via polling, but instead logged after the node reboots as a result of the uncorrected error.

Both console and event logs contain a variety of other information, including the physical address and ECC syndrome associated with each error. These events are decoded further using configuration information to determine the physical DRAM location associated with each error. For this analysis, we decoded the location to show the DIMM, as well as the DRAM bank, column, row, and chip.

We make the assumption that each DRAM device experiences a single fault during our observation interval. The occurrence time of each DRAM fault corresponds to the time of the first observed error message per DRAM device. We then assign a specific type and mode to each fault based on the associated errors in the console log. Our observed fault rates indicate that fewer than two DRAM devices will suffer multiple faults within our observation window, and thus the error in this method is low. Prior studies have also used and validated a similar methodology (e.g., [34]).

Hardware inventory logs are separate logs and provide snapshots of the hardware present in each machine at different points in its lifetime. These files provide unique insight into the hardware configuration that is often lacking on other systems. In total we analyzed over 400 individual hardware inventory logs that covered a span of approximately three years on Hopper and two years on Cielo. Each of these files consist of between 800 thousand and 1.5 million lines of explicit description of each host's hardware, including configuration information and information about each DIMM such as the manufacturer and part number.

We limit our analysis to the subset of dates for which we have both hardware inventory logs as well as error logs. For Hopper, this includes 18 months of data from April 2011 to January 2013. For Cielo, this includes 12 months of data from July 2011 to November 2012. For both systems, we exclude the first several months of data to avoid attributing hard faults that occurred prior to the start of our dataset to the first months of our observation. Also, in the case of both systems, time periods where the system was not in a consistent state or was in a transition state were excluded.

For confidentiality purposes, we anonymize all DIMM vendor information. Because this is not possible for the CPU vendor, we present all CPU data in arbitrary units (i.e., all data is normalized to one of the data points in the graph). While this obscures absolute rates, it still allows the ability to observe trends and compare relative rates. Since every data center and computing system is different, this is often the most relevant information to extract from a study such as this.

5.1 Methodology

Both Cielo and Hopper include hardware scrubbers in DRAM, L1, L2, and L3 caches. Therefore, we can identify permanent faults as those faults that survive a scrub operation. Thus, we classify a fault as permanent when a device generates errors in multiple scrub intervals (i.e., when the errors are separated by a time period that contains at least one scrub operation), and transient when it generates errors in only a single scrub interval. For example, Cielo's DRAM scrub interval is 24 hours. A fault that generates errors separated by more than 24 hours is classified as permanent, while a fault that generates errors only within a 24-hour period is classified as transient.

Our observed fault rates indicate that fewer than two DRAM devices will suffer multiple faults within our observation window. Therefore, similar to previous field studies, we make the simplifying assumption that each DRAM device experiences a single fault during our observation interval [33]. The occurrence time of each DRAM fault corresponds to the time of the first observed error message from that DRAM device. We then assign a specific type and mode to each fault based on the subsequent errors from that device in the console logs. We use a similar methodology (based on fault rates) for SRAM faults.

6. Baseline Data on Hopper Faults

In this section, we present our baseline data on DRAM and SRAM fault modes and rates in Hopper. We have published similar information on Cielo in prior work [34].

6.1 DRAM Faults

Figure 2 shows the number of DRAM-hours per vendor during our measurement interval on Hopper. Our data consists of approximately 1 billion DRAM-hours of operation or more for each vendor, enough to draw statistically meaningful conclusions.

Figure 3 shows the DRAM fault rate over time in Hopper. Similar to other systems, Hopper experienced a declining rate of permanent DRAM faults and a constant rate of transient faults during our measurement interval [33] [34].

Table 2 shows a breakdown of DRAM fault modes experienced in Hopper. Similar to prior studies, we identify several unique DRAM fault modes: single-bit, in which all errors map to a single bit; single-word, in which all errors map to a single word; single-column, in which all errors map to a single column; single-row, in which all errors map to a single row; single-bank, in which all errors map to a single bank; multiple-bank, in which errors map to multiple banks; and multiple-rank, in which errors map to multiple DRAMs in the same lane.

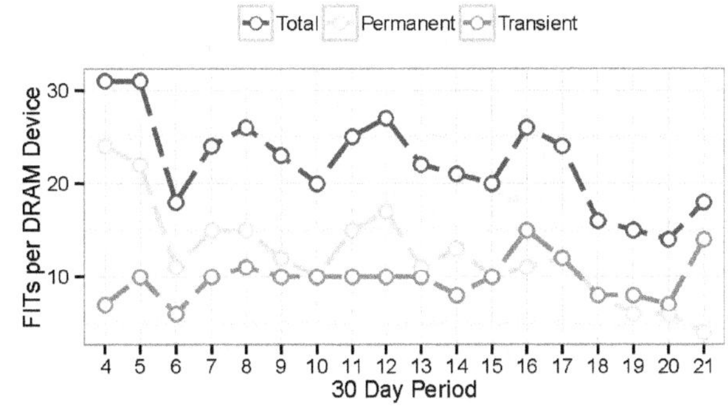

Figure 3. Hopper DRAM device fault rates per month (30-day period); 22.3 billion DRAM device hours total. The rate of permanent faults decreases over time, while the rate of transient faults remains approximately constant.

Fault Mode	Total Faults	Transient	Permanent
Single-bit	78.9%	42.1%	36.8%
Single-word	0.0%	0.0%	0.0%
Single-column	5.9%	0.0%	5.9%
Single-row	9.2%	1.8%	7.4%
Single-bank	4.3%	0.4%	3.9%
Multiple-bank	0.6%	0.0%	0.6%
Multiple-rank	1.0%	0.2%	0.8%

Table 2. DRAM fault modes in Hopper.

Similar to other DDR-2 and DDR-3 systems, a majority of DRAM faults are single-bit faults, but a non-trivial minority of faults are large multi-bit faults, including row, column, bank, and chip faults.

Figure 4 shows the transient and permanent fault rate in Hopper in FIT per DRAM device, broken down by DRAM vendor. Vendors A, B, and C in Hopper are the same as vendors A, B, and C in Cielo [34]. The figure shows substantial variation in per-vendor FIT rates, consistent with data from Cielo [34]. This implies that the choice of DRAM vendor is an important consideration for system reliability.

6.1.1 Effect of Altitude It is well-known that altitude will have an effect on modern SRAM devices due to high-energy neutrons from cosmic radiation [7], and particle strikes in DRAM were a problem in the past [23]. It is uncertain, however, whether high-energy neutrons are a significant source of faults in modern DRAM devices. We have previously published data on DRAM faults in Cielo [34]. We use this data in conjunction with Hopper data to examine the effect of altitude on DRAM faults by comparing fault rates of similar DRAM devices in Cielo and Hopper.

The Hopper and Cielo memory subsystems are extremely similar: the systems use memory from the same three

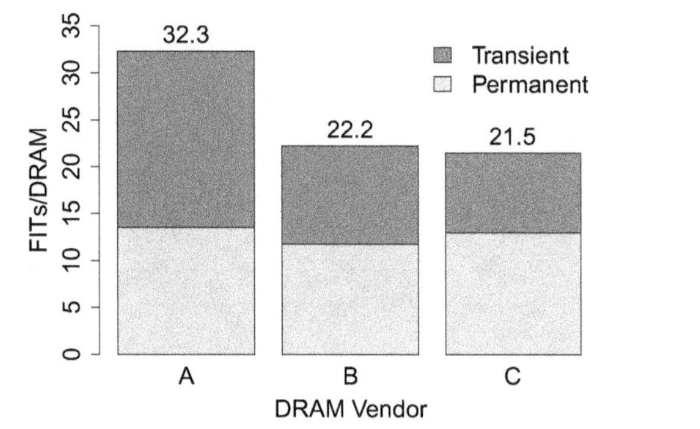

Figure 4. Fault rate per DRAM vendor. Hopper sees substantial variation in fault rates by DRAM vendor.

DRAM vendors, share the same DDR-3 memory technology, and use the same memory controllers. A major difference between the two systems is their altitude: the neutron flux, relative to New York City, experienced by Cielo is 5.53 and the relative neutron flux experienced by Hopper is 0.91[1]. Therefore, by comparing fault rates in Cielo and Hopper, we can determine what effect, if any, altitude has on DRAM fault rates.

Figure 5 plots the rate of transient faults on Cielo relative to the rate of transient faults on Hopper, using Cielo data from [34]. The figure shows that vendor A experiences a substantially higher transient fault rate on Cielo, while vendor B experiences a modestly higher transient fault rate and vendor C experiences virtually the same transient fault rate.

Table 3 breaks down this data and shows the single-bit, single-column, and single-row transient fault rates for each system by DRAM vendor. The table shows that the single-bit transient fault rates for vendors A and B are substantially higher in Cielo than in Hopper, as are the single-column and single-bank transient fault rates for vendor A. The rates of all other transient fault modes were within 1 FIT of each other on both systems. Due to the similarities between the two systems, the most likely cause of the higher single-bit, single-column, and single-bank transient fault rates in Cielo is particle strikes from high-energy neutrons.

Our main observation from this data is that particle-induced transient faults remain a noticeable effect in DRAM devices, although the susceptibility varies by vendor and there are clearly other causes of faults (both transient and permanent) in modern DRAMs. Also, our results show that while altitude does have an impact on system reliability, judicious choice of the memory vendor can reduce this impact.

6.1.2 Multi-bit DRAM Faults Figure 6 shows an example of a single-bank fault from Hopper of multiple adjacent DRAM rows with bit flips. The figure shows that errors from this fault were limited to several columns in three logically adjacent rows. Multiple faults within our dataset matched this general pattern, although the occurrence rate was relatively low. All errors from this fault were corrected by ECC.

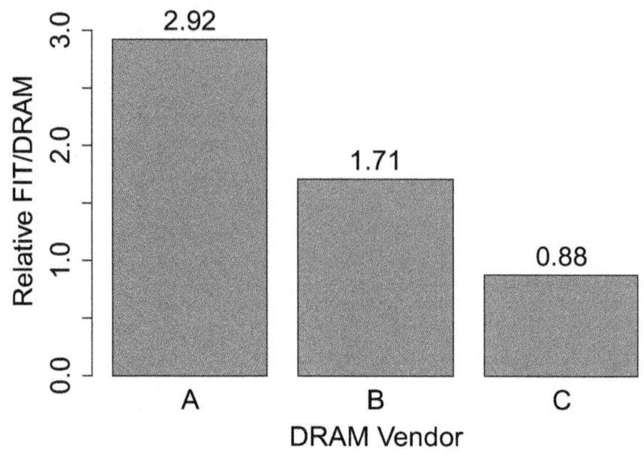

Figure 5. Cielo DRAM transient fault rates relative to Hopper (Hopper == 1.0). Vendor A shows a significantly higher transient fault rate in Cielo, likely attributable to altitude.

Fault Mode	Vendor	Cielo	Hopper
Single-bit	A	31.85	18.75
	B	15.61	9.70
	C	6.10	7.93
Single-column	A	6.05	0.0
	B	0.55	0.0
	C	0.18	0.0
Single-bank	A	14.65	0.0
	B	0.07	0.09
	C	0.18	0.10

Table 3. Rate of single-bit, single-column and single-bank transient DRAM faults in Cielo and Hopper (in FIT). The higher rate of transient faults in Cielo may indicate that these faults are caused by high-energy particles.

The pattern of errors from this fault appears to be similar to a fault mode called DRAM disturbance faults or "row-hammer" faults [19] [26]. This fault mode results in corruption of a "victim row" when an "aggressor row" is opened repeatedly in a relatively short time window. We did not do root-cause analysis on this part; therefore, we cannot say for certain that the fault in question is a disturbance fault. However, it is clear that fault modes with similar characteristics do occur in practice and must be accounted for.

Our primary observation from data in this section is that new and unexpected fault modes may occur after a system is architected, designed, and even deployed: row-hammer faults were only identified by industry after Hopper was designed, and potentially after it began service [26]. Prior work has looked at tailoring detection to specific fault modes (e.g., [35]), but the data show that we need to be able to handle a larger variety of fault modes and that robust detection is crucial.

6.2 SRAM Faults

In this section, we examine fault rates of SRAM in the AMD Opteron^{TM}processors in Hopper.

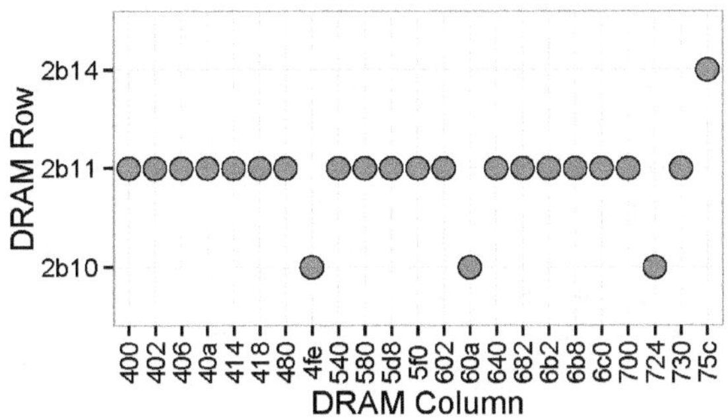

Figure 6. A single-bank fault from one Hopper node.

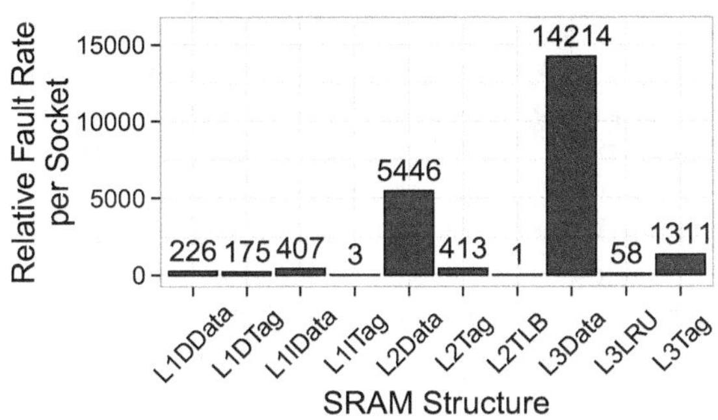

Figure 7. Rate of SRAM faults per socket in Hopper, relative to the fault rate in the L2TLB. The fault rate is affected by structure size and organization, as well as workload effects.

6.2.1 SRAM Fault Rate Figure 7 shows the rate of SRAM faults per socket in Hopper, broken down by hardware structure. The figure makes clear that SRAM fault rates are dominated by faults in the L2 and L3 data caches, the two largest structures in the processor. However, it is clear that faults occur in many structures, including smaller structures such as tag and TLB arrays.

A key finding from this figure is that, at scale, faults occur even in small on-chip structures, and detection and correction in these structures is important to ensure correctness for high-performance computing workloads running on large-scale systems. This result is significant for system designers considering different devices on which to base their systems. Devices should either offer robust coverage on all SRAM and significant portions of sequential logic, or provide alternate means of protection such as redundant execution [36].

6.2.2 Comparison to Accelerated Testing Accelerated particle testing is used routinely to determine the sensitivity of SRAM devices to single-event upsets from energetic particles. To be comprehensive, the accelerated testing must include all particles to which the SRAM cells will be exposed to in the field (e.g., neutrons, alpha particles) with energy spectra that approximate real-world conditions. Therefore, it is important to correlate accelerated testing data with field data to ensure that the conditions are in fact similar.

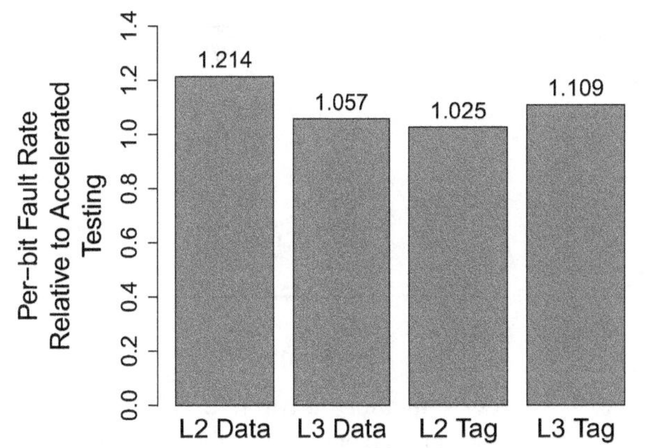

Figure 8. Rate of SRAM faults in Hopper compared to accelerated testing.

Accelerated testing on the SRAM used in Hopper was performed using a variety of particle sources, including the high-energy neutron beam at the LANSCE ICE House[22] at LANL and an alpha particle source. The testing was "static" testing, rather than operational testing. Static testing initializes SRAM cells with known values, exposes them to the beam, and then compares the results to the initial state to look for errors.

The L2 and L3 caches employ hardware scrubbers, so we expect the field error logs to capture the majority of bit flips that occur in these structures. Figure 8 compares the per-bit rate of SRAM faults in Hopper's L2 and L3 data and tag arrays to results obtained from the accelerated testing campaign on the SRAM cells. The figure shows that accelerated testing predicts a lower fault rate than seen in the field in all structures except the L2 tag array. The fault rate in the L2 tag is approximately equal to the rate from accelerated testing.

Overall, the figure shows good correlation between rates measured in the field and rates measured from static SRAM testing. Our conclusion from this correlation is that the majority of SRAM faults in the field are caused by known particles. While an expected result, confirming expectations with field data is important to ensure that parts are functioning as specified, to identify potential new or unexpected fault modes that may not have been tested in pre-production silicon, and to ensure accelerated testing reflects reality.

7. Fallacies in Measuring System Health

All data and analyses presented in the previous section refer to fault rates, not error rates. Some previous studies have reported system error rates instead of fault rates [12][14][16][30]. Error rates are heavily dependent on a system's software configuration and its workloads' access patterns in addition to the health of the system, which makes error rates an imperfect measure of hardware reliability. In this section, we show that measuring error rates can lead to erroneous conclusions about hardware reliability.

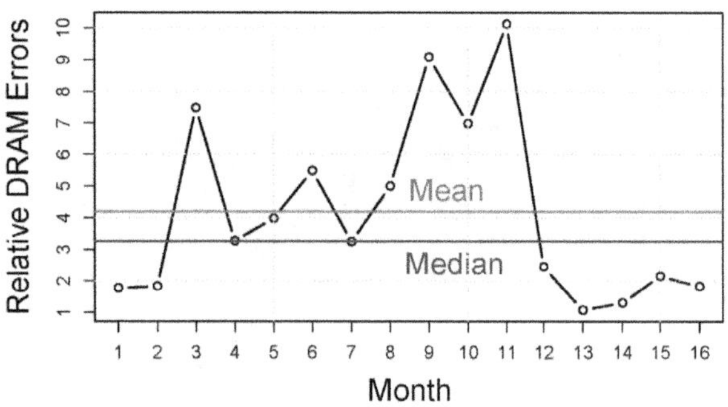

Figure 9. Hopper's memory error rate relative to Cielo. Hopper has a memory error rate 4x that of Cielo, but a memory fault rate 0.625x that of Cielo. Because error counts are confounded by other factors such as workload behavior, they are not an accurate measure of system health.

7.1 Error Logging Architecture

In most x86 CPUs, DRAM errors are logged in a register bank in the northbridge block [4] [31]. Each register bank can log one error at a time; x86 architecture dictates that the hardware discard subsequent corrected errors until the bank is read and cleared by the operating system [5]. The operating system typically reads the register bank via a polling routine executed once every few seconds [2]. Therefore, on a processor which issues multiple memory accesses per nanosecond, millions of errors may be discarded between consecutive reads of the register bank.

The error logging architecture described above means that the console logs represent only a sample of all corrected errors that have occurred on a system. Moreover, the number of logged corrected errors is highly dependent on the polling frequency set by the operating system. For instance, if the operating system is using a 5-second polling frequency, only one error per node can be reported per 5-second interval.

Uncorrected errors in x86 processors, on the other hand, are collected through a separate machine check exception mechanism [5]. These exceptions are individually delivered to the operating system, and thus uncorrected error counts do not suffer this sampling problem.

7.2 Counting Errors vs. Counting Faults

Using our data, we provide two concrete examples of how counting errors can lead to incorrect conclusions about system reliability. Our first example is a study by Di Martino *et al.* on the Blue Waters system [12]. The second example is a study by Schroeder *et al.* on memory errors in Google data centers [30].

Example 1. First, we examine the Di Martino *et al.* claim that the chipkill ECCs used on Blue Waters' DRAM corrected 99.997% of all logged errors. Because corrected errors are sampled while uncorrected errors are not, the chipkill codes on Blue Waters almost certainly corrected a much larger fraction of the total errors experienced by the system. More importantly, however, this type of analysis can lead to incorrect conclusions about the efficacy of ECC. For instance, using the authors' methodology, we find that Hopper's chipkill-detect ECC corrected 99.991% of all logged errors, while Cielo's chipkill-correct ECC corrected 99.806% of all logged errors. This implies that Hopper's ECC performs better than Cielo's ECC. However, Cielo's ECC actually had a 3x lower uncorrected error rate than that on Hopper, leading to the opposite conclusion: the chipkill-correct code on Cielo performs substantially better than the chipkill-detect code on Hopper.

Example 2. Our second example comes from a paper by Schroeder *et al.*, where the authors quote a memory error rate of 25,000-75,000 FIT/Mbit, and claim that DRAM is orders of magnitude less reliable than previously thought [30]. The rate measured by the authors is the rate of logged errors, not the rate of faults [28]. Using this methodology, we find Hopper's memory error rate was slightly more than 4x that of Cielo, again giving the impression that Hopper's DRAM is less reliable than Cielo's (see Figure 9). As stated in Section 6, however, Hopper has a fault rate of 25 FIT/device, compared to Cielo's 40 FIT/device [34], demonstrating that Hopper's DRAM is actually more reliable than Cielo's.

7.3 Importance of Counting Faults

The key observation in this section is, in order to obtain an accurate picture of system reliability, it is imperative to analyze the error logs to identify individual faults, rather than treating each error event as separate. Error event counts: (a) are more indicative of the OS's polling frequency than of hardware health; and (b) overemphasize the effects of permanent faults, which can lead to thousands or millions of errors, while underreporting the effects of transient faults, which typically only result in a few errors but can be equally deleterious to system reliability.

8. Analysis of Hardware Resilience Schemes

In this section, we use our data to examine various hardware resilience schemes in both DRAM and SRAM. Our goal is to understand the effectiveness of current hardware schemes. This data is useful for silicon and system designers who must consider a range of resilience techniques.

8.1 Comparing DRAM ECC Schemes

Many DRAM ECC schemes are used in the industry. The most common schemes are SEC-DED ECCs, chipkill-detect ECCs, and chipkill-correct ECCs [18]. SEC-DED ECC corrects single-bit errors and detects double-bit errors. Chipkill-detect ECC detects any error from a single DRAM device, while chipkill-correct ECC corrects any error from a single device. Prior studies show that chipkill-correct reduces the uncorrected error rate by 42x relative to SEC-DED ECC [33]. However, no prior study has quantified the difference in undetected errors between SEC-DED and chipkill.

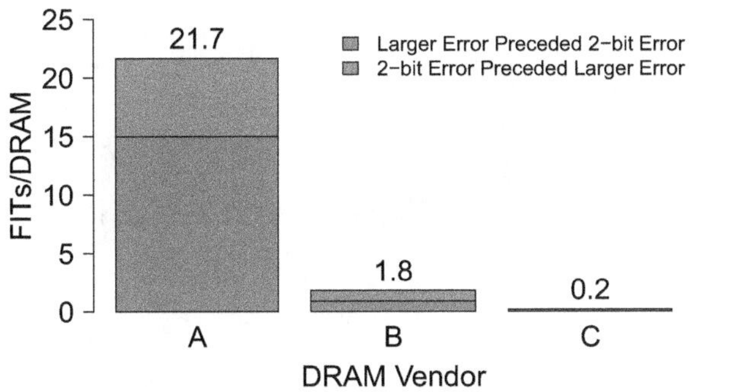

Figure 10. Rate of faults that generate errors which are potentially undetectable by SEC-DED ECC.

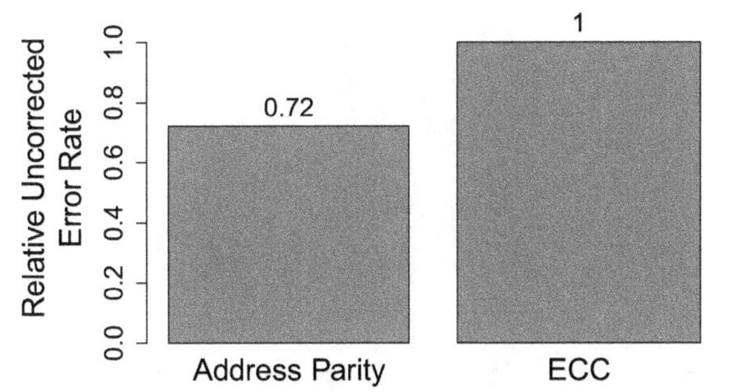

Figure 11. Rate of DRAM address parity errors relative to uncorrected data ECC errors.

Both Cielo and Hopper log the bits in error for each corrected error. By analyzing each error, we can determine whether a given error would be undetectable by SEC-DED ECC. For the purposes of this study, we assume that errors larger than 2 bits in a single ECC word are undetectable by SEC-DED (an actual SEC-DED ECC typically can detect some fraction of these errors). We call a fault that generates an error larger than 2 bits in an ECC word an *undetectable-by-SECDED* fault. A fault is undetectable-by-SECDED if it affects more than two bits in any ECC word, and the data written to that location does not match the value produced by the fault. For instance, writing a 1 to a location with a stuck-at-1 fault will not cause an error.

Not all multi-bit faults are undetectable-by-SECDED faults. For instance, many single-column faults only affect a single bit per DRAM row [33], and manifest as a series of ECC words with a single-bit error that is correctable by SEC-DED ECC.

Figure 10 shows the rate of undetectable-by-SECDED faults on Cielo, broken down by vendor. The rate of these faults exhibits a strong dependence on vendor. Vendor A has an undetectable-by-SECDED fault rate of 21.7 FIT per DRAM device. Vendors B and C, on the other hand, have much lower rates of 1.8 and 0.2 FIT/device, respectively. A Cielo node has 288 DRAM devices, so this translates to 6048, 518, and 57.6 FIT per node for vendors A, B, and C, respectively. This translates to one undetected error every 0.8 days, every 9.5 days, and every 85 days on a machine the size of Cielo.

Figure 10 also shows that 30% of the undetectable-by-SECDED faults on Cielo generated 2-bit errors (which are detectable by SEC-DED) before generating a larger (e.g., 3-bit) error, while the remaining 70% did not. We emphasize, however, that this detection is not a guarantee - different workloads would write different data to memory, and thus potentially exhibit a different pattern of multi-bit errors.

Our main conclusion from this data is that SEC-DED ECC is poorly suited to modern DRAM subsystems. The rate of undetected errors is too high to justify its use in very large scale systems comprised of thousands of nodes where fidelity of results is critical. Even the most reliable vendor (vendor C) has a high rate of undetectable-by-SECDED faults when considering multiple nodes operating in parallel.

Hopper and Cielo use chipkill-detect ECC and chipkill-correct ECC, respectively, and therefore exhibit much lower undetected error rates than if they used SEC-DED ECC.

8.2 DDR Command and Address Parity

A key feature of DDR3 (and now DDR4) memory is the ability to add parity-check logic to the command and address bus. The wires on this bus are shared from the memory controller to each DIMM's register. Therefore, errors on these wires will be seen by all DRAM devices on a DIMM. Though command and address parity is optional on DDR2 memory systems, we are aware of no prior study that examines the potential value of this parity mechanism.

The on-DIMM register calculates parity on the received address and command pins and compares it to the received parity signal. On a mismatch, the register signals the memory controller of a parity error. The standard does not provide for retry on a detected parity error, but requires the on-DIMM register to disallow any faulty transaction from writing data to the memory, thereby preventing data corruption.

The DDR3 sub-system in Cielo includes command and address parity checking. Figure 11 shows the rate of detected command/address parity errors relative to the rate of detected, uncorrected data ECC errors. The figure shows that the rate of command/address parity errors was 72% that of the rate of uncorrected ECC errors.

The conclusion from this data is that command/address parity is a valuable addition to the DDR standard. Furthermore, increasing DDR memory channel speeds will likely cause an increase in signaling-related errors. Therefore, we expect the ratio of address parity to ECC errors to increase with increased DDR frequencies.

8.3 SRAM Error Protection

In this section, we examine uncorrected errors from SRAM in Hopper and Cielo.

Figure 12 shows the rate of SRAM uncorrected errors on Cielo in arbitrary units. The figure separately plots uncorrected errors from parity-protected structures and uncor-

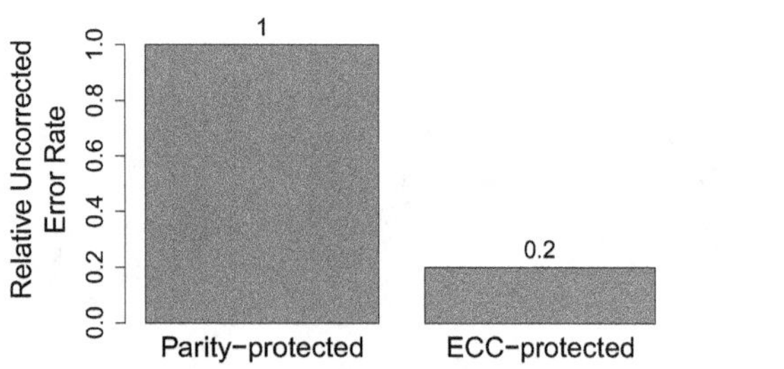

Figure 12. Rate of SRAM uncorrected errors in Cielo from parity- and ECC-protected structures.

rected errors from ECC-protected structures, and includes structures in the core, all caches, and a variety of non-core arrays and FIFOs. ECC-protected structures include the L1, L2, and L3 caches, which comprise the majority of the die area in the processor.

The figure shows that the majority of uncorrected errors in Cielo come from parity-protected structures, even though these structures are far smaller than the ECC-protected structures. Parity can detect, but cannot correct, single-bit faults, while ECC will correct single-bit faults. Therefore, the majority of SRAM uncorrected errors in Cielo are the result of single-bit, rather than multi-bit, faults.

Our primary conclusion in this section is that the best way to reduce SRAM uncorrected error rates simply is to extend single-bit correction (e.g., SEC-DED ECC) through additional structures in the processor. While this is a non-trivial effort due to performance, power, and area concerns, this solution does not require extensive new research or novel technologies.

Once single-bit faults are addressed, the remaining multi-bit faults may be more of a challenge to address, especially in highly scaled process technologies in which the rate and spread of multi-bit faults may increase substantially [17]. In addition, novel technologies such as ultra-low-voltage operation will likely change silicon failure characteristics [37]. Current and near-future process technologies, however, will see significant benefit from increased use of on-chip ECC.

8.4 Analysis of SRAM Errors

In this section, we delve further into the details of observed SRAM uncorrected errors, to determine the root cause and potential avenues for mitigation.

Figure 13 shows the rate of uncorrected errors (in arbitrary units) from several representative SRAM structures in Hopper. In the processors used in Hopper, the L1 data cache tag (L1DTag) is protected by parity, and all errors are uncorrectable. The L2 cache tag (L2Tag), on the other hand, is largely protected by ECC. However, a single bit in each L2 tag entry is protected by parity. Because the L2 cache is substantially larger than the L1, there are approximately half as many parity-protected bits in the L2 tag as there are bits in the entire L1 tag. This is reflected in the observed un-

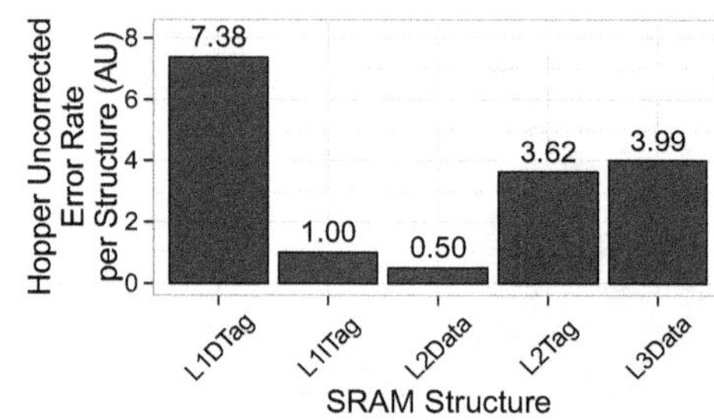

Figure 13. Rate of SRAM uncorrected errors per structure in Hopper from cache data and tag arrays. Each Hopper socket contains 12 L1 instruction and data caches, 12 L2 caches, and 2 L3 caches.

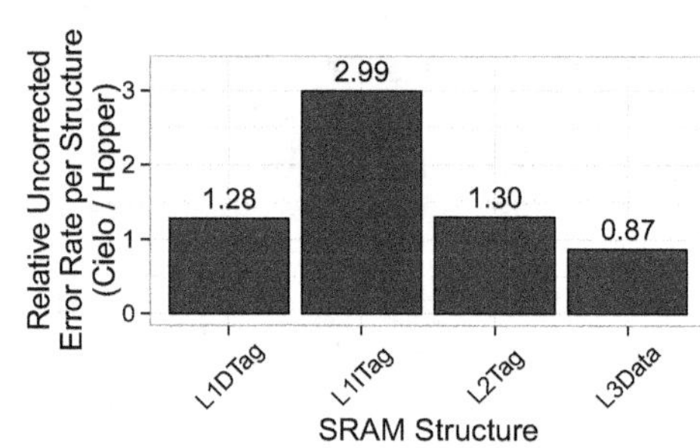

Figure 14. Rate of SRAM uncorrected errors in Cielo relative to Hopper. ECC and aggressive interleaving seem to mitigate the expected increase in uncorrected error rate due to altitude.

corrected error rate from the L2 tag, which is approximately half the rate of uncorrected errors from the L1 tag[1].

Our observation from this data is that seemingly small microarchitectural decisions (e.g., the decision to exclude a single bit from ECC protection) can have a large impact on overall system failure rates. Therefore, detailed modeling and analysis of the microarchitecture (e.g., AVF analysis [25]) is critical to ensuring a resilient system design.

Prior field studies have shown that SRAM fault rates have a strong altitude dependence due to the effect of atmospheric neutrons [34]. True to this trend, Cielo experiences substantially more corrected SRAM faults than Hopper. While first principles would predict a similar increase in SRAM uncorrected errors at altitude, prior studies have not quantified whether this is true in practice.

Figure 14 shows the per-bit SRAM uncorrected error rate in Cielo relative to Hopper in the L1 instruction tag, L2 tag, and L3 data arrays. The figure shows that Cielo's error rate in the L2 and L3 structures is not substantially higher than Hopper's error rate, despite being at a significantly higher altitude. We attribute this to the error protection in these structures. These structures have both ECC and aggressive bit interleaving; therefore, a strike of much larger than two bits is required to cause an uncorrected error. Therefore, the

[1] This L2 Tag behavior has been addressed on more recent AMD processors.

data points to the conclusion that the multi-bit error rate from high-energy neutrons in these structures is smaller than the error rate from other sources, such as Alpha particles, and a variety of hard fault mechanisms.

Therefore, the data in this section suggest that appropriate error protection mechanisms can successfully offset the increase in raw fault due to altitude. We conclude that an appropriately-designed system need not be less reliable when located at higher elevations.

9. Lessons for Reliable System Design

There are several lessons about reliable system design to be gleaned from our study. We believe this study both confirms and rebuts many widely-held assumptions and also provides new insights valuable to system designers and researchers.

- **Faults are unpredictable.** Some faults may occur much more often than expected (e.g., DDR address parity) and some fault modes may not be known at design time (e.g., DRAM disturbance faults). Therefore, providing a robust set of error detectors is key.
- **Details matter.** For instance, simply describing a cache as "ECC-protected" does not convey adequate information, since excluding even a single bit from this protection can have a large negative effect on system reliability. Careful analysis and modeling (e.g., AVF analysis) are required to predict the expected failure rate of any device.
- **The ability to diagnose is critical.** This includes both ensuring that hardware logs have adequate diagnosis information as well as having access to appropriate software tools. For example, knowing exactly which bits are in error is critical to understanding fault modes and determining what went wrong. Adding this level of diagnosability to the hardware can require a much larger investment of time and effort than adding ECC to a structure in the first place.
- **Analysis is tricky.** Qualitatively, our experience is that this type of field study is difficult to perform correctly. These studies require understanding the details of hardware and software behavior (some of which may be undocumented), mining extremely large data sets to separate the signal from the noise, and carefully interpreting the results. Quantitatively, our data shows that not following these steps can lead to incorrect conclusions about system reliability.
- **Scale changes everything.** In large systems, even very small structures require protection due to the sheer number of components in a modern-day supercomputer or data center. Components that neglect this type of protection run the risk of corrupting data at non-trivial rates.

10. Projections to Future Systems

In this section, we examine the impact of DRAM and SRAM faults on a potential exascale supercomputer. Our goal is to understand whether existing reliability mechanisms can cope with the challenges presented by likely increases in system capacity and fault rates for future large-scale systems and data centers. To accomplish this, we scale our observed DRAM and SRAM error rates to likely exascale configurations and system sizes. We also model the impact of different process technologies such as FinFET transistors [15].

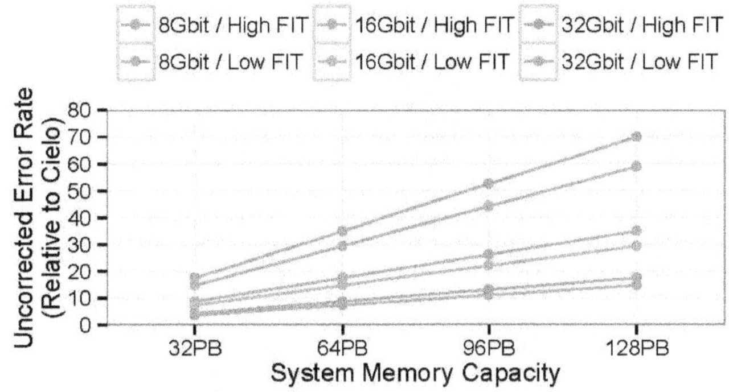

Figure 15. Rate of DRAM uncorrected errors in an exascale supercomputer relative to Cielo.

All analysis in this section refers to detected errors. Our projections are for currently-existing technologies and do not consider the impact of new technologies such as die-stacked DRAM, ultra-low-voltage CMOS, or NVRAM.

10.1 DRAM

Exascale supercomputers are predicted to have between 32PB and 128PB of main memory. Due to capacity limitations in die-stacked devices [32], much of this memory is likely to be provided in off-chip memory. The interface to these off-chip devices is will likely resemble current DDR memory interfaces. Therefore, it is critical to understand the reliability requirements for these off-chip sub-systems.

Prior work has shown that DRAM vendors maintain an approximately constant fault rate per device across technology generations, despite reduced feature sizes and increased densities [9]. Therefore, we expect the per-device fault rates in an exascale computer will be similar to those observed in todays DRAM devices. Our goal is to determine whether current error-correcting codes (ECCs) will suffice for an exascale supercomputer. Therefore, we assume that each memory channel in an exascale system will use the same single-chipkill code in use on Cielo. As a result, we project that the per-device uncorrected error rate in an exascale supercomputer will be the same as the per-device error rate in Cielo.

Because we do not know the exact DRAM device capacity that will be in mass production in the exascale timescale, we sweep the device capacity over a range from 8Gbit to 32Gbit devices. A larger DRAM device can deliver a specified system memory capacity with fewer total devices.

Figure 15 shows the results of this analysis. The figure plots the system-wide DRAM uncorrected error rate for an exascale system relative to the DRAM uncorrected error

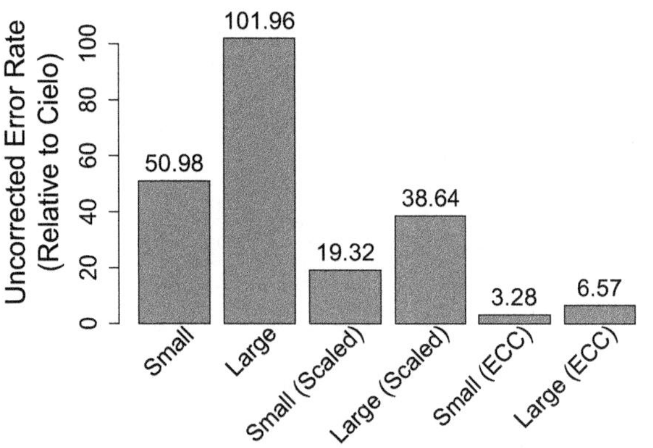

Figure 16. Rate of SRAM uncorrected errors relative to Cielo in two different potential exascale computers composed of CPU and GPU/APU nodes.

rate on Cielo. The figure plots two per-device error rates at each point, each taken from field data on different systems. The figure shows that uncorrected error rate for an exascale system ranges from 3.6 times Cielos uncorrected error rate at the low end to 69.9 times Cielos uncorrected error rate at the high end.

At a system level, the increase in DRAM uncorrected error rates at the high end of memory capacity is comparable to the 40x reduction in DRAM uncorrected errors achieved when upgrading from SEC-DED ECC to chipkill ECC [33]. If we assume that SEC-DED ECC provides insufficient reliability for todays memory subsystems, our conclusion from these results is that higher-capacity exascale systems may require stronger ECC than chipkill.

10.2 SRAM

We now turn our attention to SRAM failures on future systems. A socket in Cielo contains 18MB of SRAM in the L2 and L3 cache data arrays. Exascale-class processors are projected to see a substantial increase in processing power per socket, and thus will contain significantly more SRAM per node. Taking into account technology trends and reported structure sizes for CPU and GPU processors [3], we project that an exascale socket will contain over 150MB of SRAM, or an 8-10x increase in SRAM per socket over current supercomputers. The increase in SRAM relative to todays systems is less than the increase in DRAM because of the switch to general-purpose graphical processing units (GPGPUs) and/or GPGPUs integrated with CPU cores in an accelerated processing unit (APU), both of which rely less on large SRAM caches than traditional CPU cores.

Assuming that SRAM fault rates remain constant in future years, the per-socket fault rates will increase linearly with SRAM capacity. Therefore, an exascale processor will see 8-10x the number of SRAM faults experienced by a current processor, and potentially 8-10x the rate of uncorrected SRAM errors. This translates to a system-level uncorrected error rate from SRAM errors of 50-100 times the SRAM uncorrected error rate on Cielo, depending on the system size. This is shown in the first group of bars of Figure 16, labeled Small for a low node-count system (50k nodes) and Large for a high node-count system (100k nodes).

Per-bit SRAM transient fault rates have trended downwards in recent years [17]. If this trend continues, the SRAM uncorrected error rate per socket will be lower than our projections. For instance, according to Ibe et al. the per-bit SER decreased by 62% between 45nm and 22nm technology. If we see a corresponding decrease between current CMOS technologies and exascale technologies, the exascale system SRAM uncorrected error rate decreases to 19-39 times the uncorrected error rate on Cielo, shown in the second group of bars of Figure 16.

Finally, as noted previously, the majority of uncorrected SRAM errors are due to single-bit faults. If these errors are eliminated in an exascale processor (e.g. by replacing parity with ECC), the exascale system SRAM uncorrected error rate would be only 3-6.5 times Cielos uncorrected error rates, shown in the third group of bars in Figure 16.

Our conclusion from this analysis is that, vendors should focus aggressively on reducing the rate of uncorrected errors from SRAM faults. However, large potential reductions are available through reductions in SER due to technology scaling, and much of the remainder may be possible through expanding correction of single-bit faults. Once practical limits are reached, however, more advanced techniques to reduce the rate of multi-bit faults may be needed.

11. Summary

Reliability will continue to be a significant challenge in the years ahead. Understanding the nature of faults experienced in practice can benefit all stakeholders, including processor and system architects, data center operators, and even application writers, in the quest to design more resilient large-scale data centers and systems.

In this paper, we presented data on DRAM and SRAM faults, quantified the impact of several hardware resilience techniques, and extracted lessons about reliable system design. Our findings demonstrate that, while systems have made significant strides over the years (e.g., moving from SEC-DED ECC to chipkill on the DRAM subsystem), there is clearly more work to be done in order to provide a robust platform for future large-scale computing systems.

Acknowledgments

We thank R. Balance and J. Noe from Sandia, and K. Lamb and J. Johnson from Los Alamos for information on Cielo, and T. Butler and the Cray staff at NERSC for data and information from Hopper.

References

[1] Flux calculator. http://seutest.com/cgi-bin/FluxCalculator.cgi.

[2] mcelog: memory error handling in user space. `http://halobates.de/lk10-mcelog.pdf`.

[3] AMD. AMD graphics cores next (GCN) architecture. `http://www.amd.com/us/Documents/GCN\_Architecture\_whitepaper.pdf`.

[4] AMD. Bios and kernel developer guide (BKDG) for AMD family 10h models 00h-0fh processors. `http://developer.amd.com/wordpress/media/2012/10/31116.pdf`.

[5] AMD. AMD64 architecture programmer's manual volume 2: System programming, revision 3.23. `http://amd-dev.wpengine.netdna-cdn.com/wordpress/media/2012/10/24593_APM_v21.pdf`, 2013.

[6] A. Avizienis, J.-C. Laprie, B. Randell, and C. Landwehr. Basic concepts and taxonomy of dependable and secure computing. *IEEE Transactions on Dependable and Secure Computing*, 1(1):11–33, Jan.-Mar. 2004.

[7] R. Baumann. Radiation-induced soft errors in advanced semiconductor technologies. *IEEE Transactions on Device and Materials Reliability*, 5(3):305–316, Sept. 2005.

[8] K. Bergman, S. Borkar, D. Campbell, W. Carlson, W. Dally, M. Denneau, P. Franzon, W. Harrod, J. Hiller, S. Karp, S. Keckler, D. Klein, R. Lucas, M. Richards, A. Scarpelli, S. Scott, A. Snavely, T. Sterling, R. S. Williams, and K. Yelick. Exascale computing study: Technology challenges in achieving exascale systems, Peter Kogge, editor & study lead, Sep. 2008.

[9] L. Borucki, G. Schindlbeck, and C. Slayman. Comparison of accelerated DRAM soft error rates measured at component and system level. In *IEEE International Reliability Physics Symposium (IRPS)*, pages 482–487, 2008.

[10] C. Constantinescu. Impact of deep submicron technology on dependability of VLSI circuits. In *International Conference on Dependable Systems and Networks (DSN)*, pages 205–209, 2002.

[11] C. Constantinescu. Trends and challenges in VLSI circuit reliability. *IEEE Micro*, 23(4):14–19, Jul.-Aug. 2003.

[12] C. Di Martino, Z. Kalbarczyk, R. K. Iyer, F. Baccanico, J. Fullop, and W. Kramer. Lessons learned from the analysis of system failures at petascale: The case of blue waters. In *International Conference on Dependable Systems and Networks (DSN)*, pages 610–621, 2014.

[13] A. Dixit, R. Heald, and A. Wood. Trends from ten years of soft error experimentation. In *IEEE Workshop on Silicon Errors in Logic - System Effects (SELSE)*, 2009.

[14] N. El-Sayed, I. A. Stefanovici, G. Amvrosiadis, A. A. Hwang, and B. Schroeder. Temperature management in data centers: why some (might) like it hot. In *International Conference on Measurement and Modeling of Computer Systems (SIGMETRICS)*, pages 163–174, 2012.

[15] X. Huang, W.-C. Lee, C. Kuo, D. Hisamoto, L. Chang, J. Kedzierski, E. Anderson, H. Takeuchi, Y.-K. Choi, K. Asano, V. Subramanian, T.-J. King, J. Bokor, and C. Hu. Sub 50-nm FinFET: PMOS. In *International Electron Devices Meeting (IEDM)*, pages 67–70, 1999.

[16] A. A. Hwang, I. A. Stefanovici, and B. Schroeder. Cosmic rays don't strike twice: understanding the nature of DRAM errors and the implications for system design. In *International Conference on Architectural Support for Programming Languages and Operating Systems (ASPLOS)*, pages 111–122, 2012.

[17] E. Ibe, H. Taniguchi, Y. Yahagi, K. i. Shimbo, , and T. Toba. Impact of scaling on neutron-induced soft error in SRAMs from a 250 nm to a 22 nm design rule. In *IEEE Transactions on Electron Devices*, pages 1527–1538, Jul. 2010.

[18] X. Jian, H. Duwe, J. Sartori, V. Sridharan, and R. Kumar. Low-power, low-storage-overhead chipkill correct via multi-line error correction. In *International Conference on High Performance Computing, Networking, Storage and Analysis (SC)*, pages 24:1–24:12, 2013.

[19] Y. Kim, R. Daly, J. Kim, C. Fallin, J. H. Lee, D. Lee, C. Wilkerson, K. Lai, and O. Mutlu. Flipping bits in memory without accessing them: An experimental study of DRAM disturbance errors. In *International Symposium on Computer Architecture (ISCA)*, pages 361 – 372, 2014.

[20] X. Li, M. C. Huang, K. Shen, and L. Chu. A realistic evaluation of memory hardware errors and software system susceptibility. In *USENIX Annual Technical Conference (USENIX-ATC)*, pages 6–20, 2010.

[21] X. Li, K. Shen, M. C. Huang, and L. Chu. A memory soft error measurement on production systems. In *USENIX Annual Technical Conference (USENIXATC)*, pages 21:1–21:6, 2007.

[22] P. W. Lisowski and K. F. Schoenberg. The Los Alamos neutron science center. In *Nuclear Instruments and Methods*, volume 562:2, pages 910–914, June 2006.

[23] T. May and M. H. Woods. Alpha-particle-induced soft errors in dynamic memories. *IEEE Transactions on Electron Devices*, 26(1):2–9, Jan. 1979.

[24] A. Messer, P. Bernadat, G. Fu, D. Chen, Z. Dimitrijevic, D. Lie, D. Mannaru, A. Riska, and D. Milojicic. Susceptibility of commodity systems and software to memory soft errors. *IEEE Transactions on Computers*, 53(12):1557–1568, Dec. 2004.

[25] S. S. Mukherjee, C. Weaver, J. Emer, S. K. Reinhardt, and T. Austin. A systematic methodology to compute the architectural vulnerability factors for a high-performance microprocessor. In *International Symposium on Microarchitecture (MICRO)*, pages 29–40, 2003.

[26] J. T. Pawlowski. Memory errors and mitigation: Keynote talk for SELSE 2014. In *IEEE Workshop on Silicon Errors in Logic - System Effects (SELSE)*, 2014.

[27] H. Quinn, P. Graham, and T. Fairbanks. SEEs induced by high-energy protons and neutrons in SDRAM. In *IEEE Radiation Effects Data Workshop (REDW)*, pages 1–5, 2011.

[28] B. Schroeder. Personal Communication.

[29] B. Schroeder and G. Gibson. A large-scale study of failures in high-performance computing systems. In *International Conference on Dependable Systems and Networks (DSN)*, pages 249–258, 2006.

[30] B. Schroeder, E. Pinheiro, and W.-D. Weber. DRAM errors in the wild: a large-scale field study. *Commun. ACM*, 54(2):100–107, Feb. 2011.

[31] T. Siddiqua, A. Papathanasiou, A. Biswas, and S. Gurumurthi. Analysis of memory errors from large-scale field data collection. In *IEEE Workshop on Silicon Errors in Logic - System Effects (SELSE)*, 2013.

[32] J. Sim, G. H. Loh, V. Sridharan, and M. O'Connor. Resilient die-stacked DRAM caches. In *International Symposium on Computer Architecture (ISCA)*, pages 416–427, 2013.

[33] V. Sridharan and D. Liberty. A study of DRAM failures in the field. In *International Conference on High Performance Computing, Networking, Storage and Analysis (SC)*, pages 76:1–76:11, 2012.

[34] V. Sridharan, J. Stearley, N. DeBardeleben, S. Blanchard, and S. Gurumurthi. Feng shui of supercomputer memory: Positional effects in DRAM and SRAM faults. In *International Conference for High Performance Computing, Networking, Storage and Analysis (SC)*, pages 22:1–22:11, 2013.

[35] A. N. Udipi, N. Muralimanohar, R. Balsubramonian, A. Davis, and N. P. Jouppi. LOT-ECC: Localized and tiered reliability mechanisms for commodity memory systems. In *International Symposium on Computer Architecture (ISCA)*, pages 285–296, 2012.

[36] J. Wadden, A. Lyashevsky, S. Gurumurthi, V. Sridharan, and K. Skadron. Real-world design and evaluation of compiler-managed GPU redundant multithreading. In *International Symposium on Computer Architecture (ISCA)*, pages 73–84, 2014.

[37] C. Wilkerson, A. R. Alameldeen, Z. Chishti, W. Wu, D. Somasekhar, and S.-l. Lu. Reducing cache power with low-cost, multi-bit error-correcting codes. In *International Symposium on Computer Architecture (ISCA)*, pages 83–93, 2010.

CommGuard: Mitigating Communication Errors in Error-Prone Parallel Execution

Yavuz Yetim
Princeton University
yyetim@gmail.com

Sharad Malik
Princeton University
sharad@princeton.edu

Margaret Martonosi
Princeton University
mrm@princeton.edu

Abstract

As semiconductor technology scales towards ever-smaller transistor sizes, hardware fault rates are increasing. Since important application classes (e.g., multimedia, streaming workloads) are data-error-tolerant, recent research has proposed techniques that seek to save energy or improve yield by exploiting error tolerance at the architecture/microarchitecture level. Even seemingly error-tolerant applications, however, will crash or hang due to control-flow/memory addressing errors. In parallel computation, errors involving inter-thread communication can have equally catastrophic effects.

Our work explores techniques that mitigate the impact of potentially catastrophic errors in parallel computation, while still garnering power, cost, or yield benefits from data error tolerance. Our proposed CommGuard solution uses FSM-based checkers to pad and discard data in order to maintain semantic alignment between program control flow and the data communicated between processors. CommGuard techniques are low overhead and they exploit application information already provided by some parallel programming languages (e.g. StreamIt). By converting potentially catastrophic communication errors into potentially tolerable data errors, CommGuard allows important streaming applications like JPEG and MP3 decoding to execute without crashing and to sustain good output quality, even for errors as frequent as every $500\mu s$.

Categories and Subject Descriptors Computer Systems Organization [*Performance of Systems*]: Fault tolerance

Keywords Application-level error tolerance, high-level programming languages, parallel computing

ASPLOS '15, March 14–18, 2015, Istanbul, Turkey..
Copyright is held by the owner/author(s). Publication rights licensed to ACM.
ACM 978-1-4503-2835-7/15/03...$15.00.
http://dx.doi.org/10.1145/2694344.2694354

1. Introduction

Achieving reliable, cost-effective computation with acceptable semiconductor yields becomes more challenging with each new technology generation. Resilience challenges arise due to extreme operating temperatures and currents, and due to increased susceptibility to soft errors [6, 12, 14, 17, 26]. Originally handled primarily at the circuit level or below, the challenges of semiconductor reliability have become pressing enough that architecture-level solutions must also be explored. Our goal is to find low-overhead methods to exploit application-level error tolerance in order to improve the cost or yield.

Not all errors are equally worrisome. In particular, while many applications may be tolerant of modest *data* error rates, other errors—in control flow, memory addressing, or parallel communication—are often catastrophic. Thus, in most prior work, programs are separated at design-time, compile-time, or run-time into the operations (calculations, loop control, etc.) that must be run on fully-reliable hardware versus those that can be run on potentially error-prone hardware. In some cases, the fully-reliable hardware represents the bulk of the machine (all instruction decode, sequencing, and control) while the error-prone hardware is limited to calculation units, a small fraction of processor die area [25]. In other prior work, a single fully-reliable processor manages loop-level control sequencing and timeouts for a set of potentially unreliable processors [18]. This allows more error-prone area (and thus increases potential benefits), but limits the types of applicable programs, e.g., do-all parallelism with idempotent loop bodies [18].

Our work proposes and evaluates techniques that support the data-error-tolerant execution of a fairly broad set of workloads, and that greatly decrease the amount of fully-reliable hardware required. In particular, we focus on parallel systems in which each component core is itself only partially reliable, and we explore methods to mitigate the catastrophic effects of error-prone interprocessor communication between such cores. *Our work enables low-cost error-tolerant execution by converting potentially catastrophic control flow or communication errors into potentially tolerable data errors.*

Our approach centers on CommGuard, a simple FSM-based technique for dynamically monitoring that the program abides by expectations about how many data communications will occur between different parallel entities. For example, in a producer-consumer interaction, resiliency hinges on the consumer receiving the correct number of data items; incorrect data counts lead to deadlock, livelock, permanent misalignments, or other fatal issues. CommGuard pads or discards communicated items when too many or too few have arrived. Discarded items are chosen arbitrarily and padding items fills data frames with arbitrary values to use. Such techniques succeed because data errors are generally more tolerable than the control-oriented errors that stem from incorrect item counts.

This paper shows how a CommGuard checker can be very effective, can be built at very low-overhead, and can exploit program-level information already frequently provided by languages like StreamIt [29] or Concurrent Collections [3]. CommGuard allows important streaming applications (e.g., jpeg, mp3 decode) to execute without crashing and to sustain good output quality, even for errors as frequent as every $500\mu s$. Furthermore, it requires low overhead, almost all of which is off the critical path of instruction execution.

2. Motivation

2.1 Tolerating Hardware Errors

Device scaling increases hardware fault rates for several reasons and ITRS has identified reliability as a major design challenge for newer technology nodes [16]. Hardware faults (e.g., transistor aging, process variation, energized particle strikes, and others) come in three types: permanent, intermittent or transient [12, 17, 26]. Intermittent and transient faults are particularly expected to increase for newer technologies [7]; this work focuses on them. Faults may or may not result in application-level errors depending on where and when they occur [23]. For this paper, in accordance with prior literature [24], we use the term *error* to refer to an architecture-level value change caused by a hardware-level *fault* .

With increasing fault rates, conventional redundancy techniques to detect and correct errors result in high overheads. In SRAM and other storage units, protection is achieved through error correction codes (ECC) but increasing fault rates require stronger codes with higher latencies and storage overheads [1]. Further, protecting data storage is only part of the issue; one must also address errors in control-flow, data-flow, computation and communication. Various forms of redundant execution [22] protect against these errors. Redundant execution can be temporal (e.g., executing instructions twice on the same core) or spatial (e.g., executing instructions in parallel on another core). Different choices trade-off hardware area, performance, and energy in different ways, but none effectively avoid the high overhead of redundancy.

Certain application classes, e.g. multimedia, have some degree of error tolerance. They are *data* error tolerant in that their output can be acceptable even without 100% error correction. They are still susceptible, however, to control flow and memory addressing errors, which can be catastrophic. Fully-reliable processors can avoid these errors completely [18, 19, 25] but will incur high performance and energy overheads and may be cost-prohibitive for future technologies.

Some control-flow and memory addressing errors may be acceptable as long as their effects on the execution are managed. For example, architectures proposed in [18, 32] handle control-flow and memory-addressing errors when they may cause crashes or hangs. The reliability analysis proposed in [4] allows cores that may have bounded control-flow and memory addressing errors in its execution model. Here, we refer to such processors as *partially protected uniprocessors (PPU)* and show that existing PPU microarchitectural techniques are either insufficient or incur high overheads for parallel computation. This paper addresses this with a low-overhead microarchitectural solution to manage communication errors in parallel systems built on PPU cores.

2.1.1 Requirements

Our design will not eliminate errors entirely, but rather seeks to limit their impact. In particular, our operational requirements are as follows. First, an error-tolerant execution needs to **progress** (i.e., not crash, hang, or corrupt I/O devices). Second, achieving long-term execution with acceptable output quality requires that the effects of errors must be **ephemeral**. That is, if errors occur, their effect on execution should diminish with time. The third design requirement is that the technique be **low-overhead**.

2.2 Coarse-Grain Error Management and High-Level Application Constructs

CommGuard exploits application-level constructs to identify coarse-grained linkages between control flow and communication operations. With appropriate knowledge of control-flow and communication relationships, small reliable hardware modules can detect and mitigate the error effects seen as violations of the operational requirements.

As a concrete example, this paper uses streaming applications. A streaming application consists of coarse-grain compute operations each of which inputs and outputs data streams. CommGuard uses static information, such as explicit producer/consumer connections, and monitors the communication and control-flow construct invocations at run-time. This allows CommGuard to identify groups of items in the data streams and establish a run-time link between control-flow and inter-core data-flow.

Our implementation examples are based on StreamIt [29], a programming language and a compiler for streaming applications. StreamIt offers constructs to support do-all, data, and pipeline (producer-consumer) parallelism, as well as streaming communication between threads. Figure

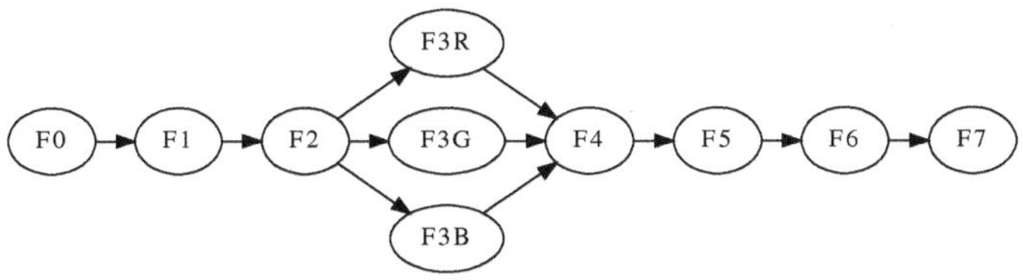

Figure 1: jpeg streaming computation graph with explicit communication between processing nodes.

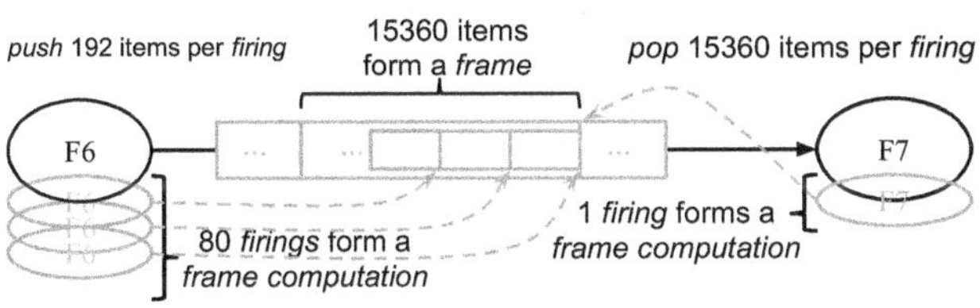

Figure 2: Example jpeg subgraph showing relations of items, firings, and frames

1 shows an example streaming graph for the jpeg application. The graph is composed of 10 parallel nodes connected with producer-consumer edges. The graph represents the producer-consumer pipelined execution flow of each image pixel, with the R, G, and B elements of a pixel being handled with data parallelism at one stage. For the rest of the paper, *node* refers to a chunk of computation and *edge* refers to communication streaming between two nodes. To execute this application, a node runs as a separate *thread* pinned to a processor and a *queue* implements the communication along an edge. StreamIt uses a concurrent queue data structure to implement a queue manager with head/tail pointers pointing to queue buffers.

As Figure 2 shows, StreamIt expresses communication through *push* and *pop* constructs. On each node *firing*, the node consumes items from its incoming edges and produces items to its outgoing edges. The amount of algorithm-specific communication determines the per-firing item counts. For example, the figure shows that F6 produces 192 items, and this refer to an 8-pixel by 8-pixel image region, where each pixel consists of 3 items, the red, green and blue values.

From StreamIt constructs, one can link the control-flow and data-flow of communicating threads by matching node production and consumption rates. In Figure 2, a group of 192 items forms exactly one firing worth of output for F6 but forms only a part of the input for F7. However, 15360 items correspond to exact multiples of firings in both filters. For this edge, 1 firing of F7 depends on the output of the 80 most recent firings of F6. This analysis relates groups of producer firings to groups of items and transitively to groups of consumer firings, and thus links producer and consumer control-flows to the communication. In the following sections, we will use the terms *frames* to refer to the groups of items and *frame computations* to refer to the groups of firings that are linked through this analysis.

(a) Error-free processor cores

(b) Error-prone PPU cores

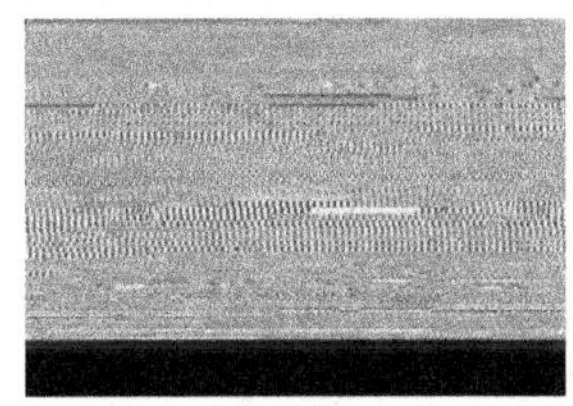

(c) Error-prone PPU cores with reliable data transmission

(d) CommGuard: Error-prone PPU cores with framed computation.

Figure 3: Output of jpeg running on 10 threads with varying protection mechanisms. Systems in Figures 3b-d had a mean time between errors of 1M instructions.

2.3 Example Scenario

As a motivational example, Figure 3 shows the result of running a 10-core execution of jpeg [31] with different error rates and error protection mechanisms. Figure 3a shows the output when the cores do not experience any errors. Next, Figure 3b shows the output when random bit errors in architectural registers occur on average every 1M instructions. Even with PPU cores, the effects of errors corrupt the queue data structure that manages the item transmissions between the nodes. As a result, execution proceeds less than 25 million instructions before the queue starts to transmit most of items incorrectly. With frequent communication being the norm (a communication event occurs as often as every 7 compute instructions on average in our benchmarks) it is clear that errors can quickly corrupt inter-thread communication.

A first recourse might be to error-protect the communication subsystem itself, but Figure 3c—obtained with fully-reliable queues interconnecting the PPU cores—shows that this too is insufficient. The reliable communication substrate is not enough to overcome alignment problems if the producer cores produce more or fewer data items than what downstream consumer cores expect. Much like Figure 3b, this scenario also quickly experiences significant error degradation; the running program loses or garbles many output pixels. *In addition to protecting the data being communicated, one must also be able to check and realign the number and type of data communications being sent and received.*

CommGuard provides low-overhead, coarse-grained communication checkers that detect when errors must be mitigated in order to avoid permanent corruptions for parallel streaming applications. Figure 3d shows the result of the same 10-core `jpeg` execution at the same error rate with the same PPU cores, but now with this paper's new CommGuard state machines to check and realign communications between cores. While errors still have mild data effects, CommGuard allows the parallel execution to complete with acceptable image quality.

3. How Errors Affect Communication

Data Transmission Errors (DTE): Bitflips can cause data to have the incorrect value when it is being stored or transmitted (e.g., in non-ECC memory or unreliable interconnect). If these errors only cause value changes in the items being transmitted but still ensure the transmission of the correct number of items then their effects are usually ephemeral as we focus on applications with data error tolerance running on PPU cores.

Queue Management Errors (QME): In some error scenarios, errors may corrupt the inter-thread communication management state, such as the head and tail pointers of a StreamIt queue. These corruptions degrade output quality significantly or cause catastrophic failure. In some cases, such errors cause deadlock, e.g, when cores have inconsistent views about the full/empty status of the queue. In other cases, corrupted head/tail pointers point to incorrect addresses and the values returned from the queue become incorrect for the rest of the computation. Therefore, either (i) these pointers and their operations must be reliable, or (ii) pointer corruptions need to be periodically repaired.

To avoid permanent errors due to data transmission, a reliable hardware queue may communicate items between producer-consumer pairs through error correction mechanisms. However, as shown in Figure 3c, an error-free queue is not enough. This is due to alignment errors discussed below.

Alignment Errors ($AE_{(I|F)(E|I)}$): Alignment errors occur when the number of communicated data items produced or consumed depends on program control flow that might itself be error-prone. For example, PPU cores allow small control-flow perturbations that change iteration counts, and that may partially construct a collection of items, possibly missing some. Operations on such a collection will execute incorrectly if they are written to expect properly-constructed collections with a particular item count.

We denote alignment errors with respect to the consumer using the notation $A_{(I|F)(E|L)}$ where the subscripts denote (i) misalignment granularity, i.e. if (I)tems (i.e., the smallest transmission units) in a frame or (F)rames are misaligned, and (ii) misalignment amount, i.e. if misalignment caused (E)xtra data or (L)ost data. Note that, we define errors in their effect, not by their causes. Misalignments can happen due to control-flow errors in the producer or consumer thread or due to queue management errors. A *realignment* (of a misalignment due to producer, consumer or the queue between them) operation ensures that every new frame, which is constructed by the frame computation of the producer, aligns with the start of a frame computation of the consumer.

For example misalignments, consider Figures 1 and 2. In Figure 2, an internal control-flow error in `F6` may cause it to push one extra pixel. `F7` would not be aware of the extra item and would *pop* the extra item as if it is the next item to be processed (A_{IE}). Then, `F7` compute operations would apply to incorrect items (e.g., a scalar vector multiplication of the incoming vectors, i.e. frames, with a constant vector). Frame-level misalignments may be benign for `F6` and `F7` but would still be catastrophic for split-joins. If `F3R` drops a full frame but `F3G` does not, then the following `F4` node will start merging different frames (A_{FI}). Both of these misalignment scenarios would shift items for the rest of the computation; without repair, they will never realign.

To summarize: a control-flow error in a producer thread can translate to a permanent control-flow corruption in a consumer thread. It is cost-prohibitive to prevent control-flow errors entirely and PPU cores prevent control flow errors from resulting in permanent hangs or crashes. As a result, multiprocessors built using such processors must be prepared for the control-flow error effects on interprocessor communication. To protect against such alignment errors, CommGuard draws inspiration from reliability solutions in data networking and uses headers and frame IDs to identify frames. Using these constructs, CommGuard handles alignment errors by discarding or padding items. This has the attribute of converting potentially catastrophic errors into potentially tolerable data errors, with much lower overhead than checkpointing or recomputation.

4. CommGuard: Communication Guards for Error-Tolerant Multiprocessor Execution

Figure 4 gives an overview of CommGuard's organization. To manage inter-processor communication effects, CommGuard includes three new modules per processor core; a *header inserter (HI)*, an *alignment manager (AM)*, and a *queue manager (QM)*. Figure 5 gives a more detailed logical view of how producer and consumer nodes interact with CommGuard modules. CommGuard interfaces with the normal program execution through *push* and *pop* operations. The *push* operation supplies the modules with a queue identifier (QID) and the data item, and the *pop* operation supplies only a queue identifier and receives data. (These can be implemented either in hardware as special instructions or in software as additions to the push/pop implementations.) The modules access the Queue Information Table (QIT) entries using QIDs.

The AM monitors the items being popped from the communication queue by the consumer thread. It uses the frame

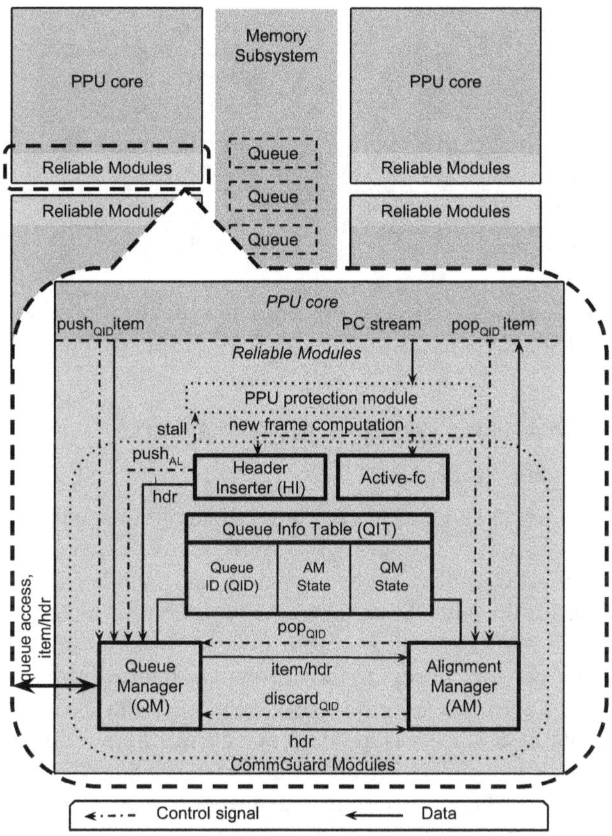

Figure 4: CommGuard modules attach to processor cores and the PPU protection module.

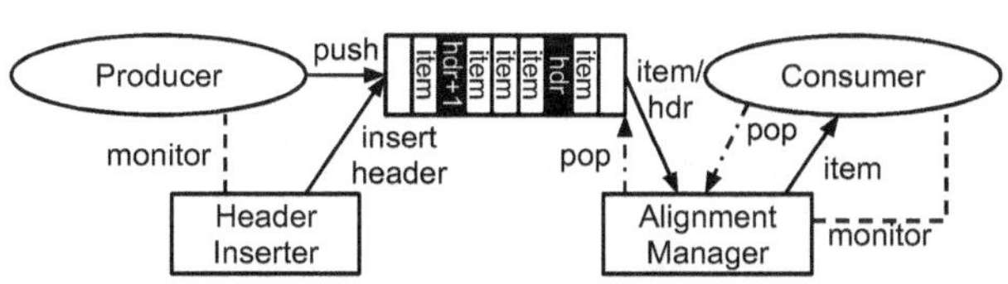

Figure 5: Logical placement of CommGuard modules between a producer and a consumer.

headers inserted by the HI to check and maintain alignment. The QM handles the data transmission to other threads. The PPU core increments the *active-fc* counter (i.e., active frame computation) for every new frame computation and this counter represents the frame progress of the thread. These modules must be built from error-free circuits. (As in prior work [13, 18, 19, 25], reliable hardware is considered feasible by increasing transistor sizes or voltage margins for that portion of the design.)

4.1 Header Inserter

On the producer side of a producer-consumer queue, at the start of every frame computation, the HI inserts a frame header with an ID into all outgoing queues to identify the frames as a sequence. This frame header is an alignment marker in the outgoing stream of data. Even if the count of data items or their specific bit values are incorrect in the stream that follows, the frame header gives downstream AMs specific points at which alignment can be restored. The HI inserts the value of active-fc as the frame ID. When active-fc reaches its limit, indicating the end of this thread's computation, a special frame ID indicating the end of computation is inserted to every outgoing queue. A thread is oblivious to the HI actions. Header reliability is ensured using ECC.

Table 1: Alignment manager FSM states and transitions. FSM receives events when local thread starts a new frame computation or issues a pop instruction. The FSM transitions to new states depending on the incoming header ID and the *active-fc*.

State	State Activity	Event	Next State
RcvCmp	Receiving and computing on items for active frame computation	New frame computation started	ExpHdr
		Received future header	Pdg
		Received past header	Disc
ExpHdr	New frame computation started and expecting header from queue	Received correct header	RcvCmp
		Received item or past header	DiscFr
		Received future header	Pdg
DiscFr	Discarding frames from queue (AE_{FE})	Received correct header	RcvCmp
		Received future header	Pdg
Disc	Discarding items and frames from queue (AE_{IE}, AE_{FE})	Received future header	Pdg
Pdg	Padding thread for lost data (AE_{IL}, AE_{FL})	New frame computation matched header	RcvCmp

4.2 Alignment Manager

The AM within a consumer core aligns incoming data with the execution of a consumer thread using the frame ID's in the communicated headers and the active-fc counter. The AM controls the data that is being transferred to the currently executing thread by discarding or padding items when necessary.

Table 1 summarizes the checking and control operations in AM in the form of a state transition table. The AM checks and responds to each *pop* instruction and to the start of a new frame computation. In response to a *pop* instruction, the QM is invoked to return the next item, which may be a regular item or a header. If a misalignment is detected, it may *pad* items to respond to the *pop* requests from the thread or *discard* items in the queue until the misalignment is resolved.

The normal consuming state of the thread is *RcvCmp*. The state *ExpHdr* denotes that the thread's control-flow has just rolled over to a new frame computation. That is, the*RcvCmp* state expects an item and *ExpHdr* expects a frame header from the queue. Failure to get what is expected indicates a misalignment, and puts the AM into one of the erroneous states— *Disc*, *DiscFr* or *Pdg*—to handle the specific alignment error. (These are shown in parentheses in Table 1.) The AM resolves erroneous states by advancing the local computation or communication to the correct frame boundaries. More specifically, either items are discarded to bring an incoming queue to the correct frame boundary (communication realignment) or items are padded to bring the local computation to the correct frame boundary (computation realignment).

4.3 Queue Manager

As shown in Figure 4, the QM interacts directly with cores and the CommGuard modules. Its responsibility is to transfer items/headers to the AM or to other threads when requested. The QM responds to *pop* and *discard* requests of the AM, and the *push* requests of the core and the HI. Hence, the QM performs these actions; (i) sending/receiving of items through the memory subsystem (ii) separating items and headers, and (iii) ECC checking of headers. Reliable queue management eliminates the errors belonging to the QME group from Section 3.

Here, we consider a hardware implementation for the data queue with ISA-visible push and pop operations. The queues (i.e., the items and their head and tail pointers) reside in a static location in memory and the QM implements the operations for a queue data structure. Section 5.1 elaborates on details of this design choice.

4.4 Guided Execution Management and Its Integration With CommGuard

We now describe CommGuard's integration with the PPU cores in [32]. The application is divided into coarse-grained (potentially nested) control-flow regions termed *scopes*. These are demarcated in the StreamIt benchmarks and are at the granularity of function calls or loop nests. The PPU cores ensure: (i) the thread running on a core sequences correctly from one scope to the next, and (ii) it does not loop indefinitely within some scope. This ensures acceptable coarse-grained forward progress for the application.

The PPU protection module monitors computation inside a thread and increments the active-fc, which the HI and AM use as explained in Sections 4.1 and 4.2. For the StreamIt programs as written, a scope encompasses each frame computation. Choosing coarser scopes or down-sampling the active-fc increment frequency through a saturating counter allows the CommGuard modules to monitor alignment at larger granularities. Lastly, to determine when the computation in a thread ends, the PPU protection module signals CommGuard when a thread's outermost global scope exits.

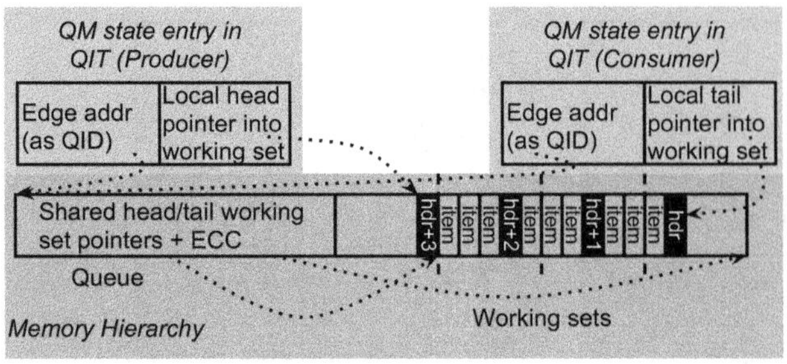

Figure 6: QM uses local pointers to access the local working set and shared pointers to share working sets across threads.

5. Hardware Design Considerations

5.1 Queue Manager

For this work we assume a hardware queue implementation as shown in Figure 6. The QM protects head/tail pointers through ECC and shares them with QM's in other cores. The QM follows the StreamIt implementation for a parallel queue; a 320KB memory region divided to 8 sub-regions to avoid per-item access to the head/tail pointers. Further, a blocked queue that spins on a condition does not repeatedly compute ECC since it is looking for a change in its value.

QM employs blocking operations when the queue is full or empty. PPU cores determine the queue state, e.g., number of items in the queue can overflow due to erroneous control-flow. Therefore, the QM needs timeout mechanisms to avoid indefinite blocking. A timeout may cause incorrect data to be transmitted but frame checking would still ensure alignment at the frame boundaries.[1]

5.2 Hardware Operations

Table 2 shows the hardware suboperations CommGuard executes in response to the CommGuard interface events. The *push* event adds the item to the local working set and gets a new working set if the working set becomes full. In response to a *pop* event, the FSM in Pdg state responds to the request with a 0. Otherwise, the next data unit is popped from the queue. Depending on if the data unit is a regular item or a header and the state of the FSM CommGuard may issue more pops and discard items (see Table 1 for different cases). *New frame computation* event triggers header insertions for all outgoing queues. Table 3 shows the overheads of the suboperations from Table 2.

5.3 Timing, Pipeline and Speculation

CommGuard's ECC and header bit pattern operations (Table 3), are off the critical path of execution in steady-state operation. Header bit patterns and ECC can be computed prior to insertion. At the receiver, the header-bit-pattern and ECC operations can be performed for the head of the queue before the item is needed.

[1] We did not observe any timeouts in any of our experiments.

Table 2: CommGuard Suboperations

Architectural Operation	CommGuard Suboperations
push	QM-push-local item if QM-local-full QM-get-new-workset
pop	if FSM-check not Pdg do QM-pop-local if QM-local-empty QM-get-new-workset if is-header then check-ECC for header FSM-check/update while FSM not DONE
new frame computation	prepare-header compute-ECC for header for out-queues: FSM-update QM-push-local header if QM-local-full QM-get-new-workset

Table 3: CommGuard Suboperations and Their Overheads

CommGuard Suboperation	Operational Overhead
prepare-header	Read then increment active-fc, set header-bit
is-header	Check header-bit
check/compute-ECC	Single-word ECC set/check
FSM-check/update	Checking/updating a 5-state FSM (see Table 1)
QM-push/pop-local, QM-local-full/empty	Additional memory events for header transmissions (No CommGuard overhead for regular item transmissions)
QM-get-new-workset	10 check/compute-ECC operations for shared pointer access through QM

Frame computation invocations are serializing operations for push/pop instructions, because CommGuard compares headers coming from the incoming streams with active-fc as set by frame computation invocations. While this dependency may incur stalls, the resulting performance hit is small since frame computations usually contain more instructions than typical pipeline depths. The number of instructions per frame computation in the median threads of our applications ranges from 72 and 33 for `audiobeamformer` and `complex-fir`, to thousands for the other applications. We evaluate the run-time overhead of the stalls in Section 7.2.2.

We propose three options regarding speculation for CommGuard's architecturally visible push and pop operations: (i) A processor may execute instructions speculatively until it encounters a push/pop. (ii) CommGuard QM stores speculative state for buffer pointers and committed push/pop instructions alter the visible queue state. This adds one copy in the QIT (Figure 4) for each speculative local pointer (Figure 6). (iii) QM operations use processor load/store operations to utilize the existing speculative hardware. Here, we consider option (ii) as the speculative storage overhead is small (Section 5.5).

5.4 Varying Frame Sizes Throughout an Application

Frame sizes are design knobs for adjusting CommGuard alignment granularity. The CommGuard implementation explained here targets a uniform frame definition across an application. That is, for all threads every frame received from the incoming queues matches a frame computation and every frame computation triggers a header insertion to the outgoing queues indicating a new frame. CommGuard can increase the application-wide frame definitions by downscaling the frame computation frequencies through one saturating counter for frame computation invocations. In addition, CommGuard can also support varying frame definitions across an application. This requires a redundant active-fc counter per frame domain. We do not detail this design here since our experiments showed that the default application-wide frame definitions provide sufficient output quality for our benchmarks.

5.5 Hardware Area

We do not provide circuit-level implementations for the logic of AM, HI and QM but we expect this to be small based on the storage needed. CommGuard modules need reliable storage for maintaining static and dynamic state and here we show that this storage is small enough to reside on core.

In our implementation, CommGuard modules store 2 counters and their limits; active-fc and a saturating counter to optionally down-scale frame computation frequency for larger frame sizes. Further, the modules need to store the following for each incoming queue; 3-bits and 1 word for header, queue ID, the local buffer pointer and its speculative copy in the QIT (Table 1, and Figure 6). The number of queues per thread varies and for our benchmarks this number was at most 4. Therefore, with 4 queues per core the total reliable storage would account to $4 \times 4B + 4 \times (3bits + 4B + 4B + 4B + 4B) \approx 82B$. Hence we assume this is completely cached on core.

6. Experimental Methodology

Simulation: To validate CommGuard, we implement the proposed hardware modules in a detailed Virtutech Simics functional architecture simulator [20] extended with error injection capabilities. Our baseline system is a 32-bit Intel x86 architecture simulating 10 processor cores. Our simulator models hardware errors through architectural error injection and implements the PPU cores described in [32].

Every core in our simulator implements an error injection module that randomly flips bits in the register file. Each error injector picks a random target cycle in the future following the mean error rate, and flips a random bit in the register file when the simulation reaches the target cycle. Register-based error injection has been used in prior work [18, 30].

We vary mean-time-between-errors (MTBE) to capture the trends in output quality changes, run-time and error handling statistics. Each core's error injection is independent and has its own random number generator. Therefore, the MTBE mentioned in our experiments represents the MTBE of each core, i.e. not the MTBE of the whole multi-core processor. (So errors in the full multi-core are more frequent.) For every MTBE, we ran the application 5 times using different random number generator seeds and observed the deviation across different runs.

To model realistic error rates, we use functional ISA simulation, which allows us to run applications fully at error rates of interest and compare output qualities. Our simulator does not use detailed microarchitectural models [2], which would provide accurate performance models but at the cost of simulation speed. CommGuard events are triggered by instructions modeled as ISA extensions. We implemented the new hardware modules, QM, HI, and AM as explained in Section 4. The hardware events of the CommGuard modules are implemented using the Simics API for hardware modules.

We implemented StreamIt's *push* and *pop* operations as ISA extensions that use x86 registers for hand-off for data and edge identifiers. Therefore, data transmissions are also error-prone due to our register-based error injector. This models uncore error sources. Headers are not error-prone because we assume they are end-to-end ECC protected and account for their overhead. Headers with their ECC are also word-sized items since header values in the order of thousands are enough to identify frames across a streaming graph.

Power Estimation: As a proxy for power estimates, we record processor event counts (i.e., all instructions committed, memory accesses), and CommGuard overhead event counts (Tables 2 and 3) during all simulation runs. CommGuard's remaining hardware operations are simple comparisons and arithmetic operations. CommGuard sub-operations are on par with or simpler than instruction processing pipestages. Aside from *push* and pop instructions, they are not implemented as software visible instructions, but to give some intuition regarding their relative frequency, we show hardware operation counts as a percentage of processor instruction counts.

Real-System Measurements: To estimate pipeline performance effects (Section 5.3) we use real hardware measurements of slightly-modified StreamIt applications running on an 8-core Xeon E3-1230 (3.30GHz) *without* Simics. We modify applications by inserting an *lfence* instruction at all frame boundaries. The lfence instruction in Intel x86 architecture is a serializing instruction, i.e. all instructions complete before lfence executes [15]. This serialization reflects the fact that our CommGuard implementation requires that pushes&pops that follow a new frame computation stall until the instruction for the new frame computation commits. lfence instructions at frame computation boundaries serialize all instructions and (conservatively) observe CommGuard dependencies.

Benchmarks: Our experiments use 6 benchmarks from the StreamIt benchmark suite: `audiobeamformer`, `channelvocoder`, `complex-fir`, `fft`, and widely-used multimedia applications `jpeg` and `mp3`. We used the cluster backend of StreamIt to automatically parallelize these applications for 10 cores using the shared-memory model. We modified the StreamIt compiler backend to use the new instructions for hardware-push and hardware-pop instead of library calls to the existing StreamIt software implementation of communication.

`mp3` and `jpeg` are lossy compression/decompression algorithms. Lossiness is commonly measured using signal-to-noise-ratio (SNR) for audio, and using peak-signal-to-noise-ratio (PSNR) for image [27]. The image quality obtained by standard lossy compression levels [28, 31] is a baseline in our experiments. To provide this quality reference we first encode the raw input file. We decode the raw data through an error-free decoder to establish the baseline SNR under lossy compression. We then decode the encoded file through the decoder running on error-prone hardware, and compare the result quality (both algorithmic and error-prone lossiness) with the baseline (only algorithmic). For the remaining four applications, we calculate SNR to compare the outputs of error-prone runs directly with the outputs of error-free runs.

7. Experimental Results

Our experiments show that (i) CommGuard avoids permanent corruptions due to communication and control-flow errors and has good output quality even at high error rates (Section 7.1) and (ii) it does this with low overhead (Section 7.2).

7.1 Quality of Results

Figure 7 shows an example run of the `jpeg` application on error-prone processors (MTBE of 512K instructions) with CommGuard modules. `jpeg` decoding the full image required 16 padding and discard operations. The frames at the `jpeg` output are rows 8-pixels high and pad/discard events are denoted on the right hand side of these rows.[2] Without CommGuard, Figure 3c showed that the output of `jpeg` is completely corrupted at this error rate even with a reliable queue and PPU cores. On the other hand, Fig-

[2] A misalignment may have happened in any thread. Because all threads share the frame definitions, we can annotate them visually at the application output.

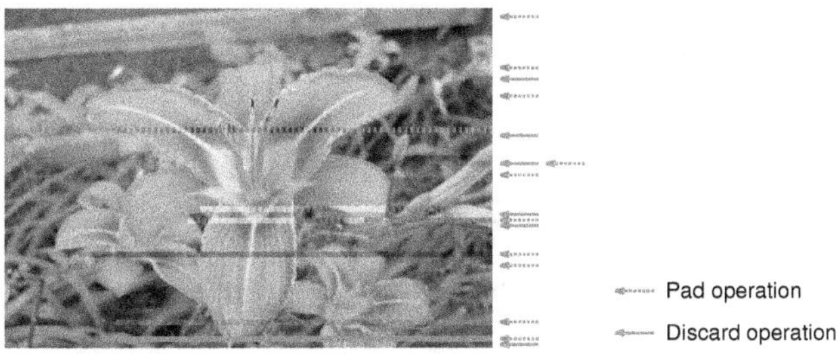

Figure 7: Example jpeg output running with CommGuard (MTBE of 512k instructions) with PSNR of 20.2dB. Arrows for pad/discard actions are shown adjacent to the frames for which CommGuard detected misalignment.

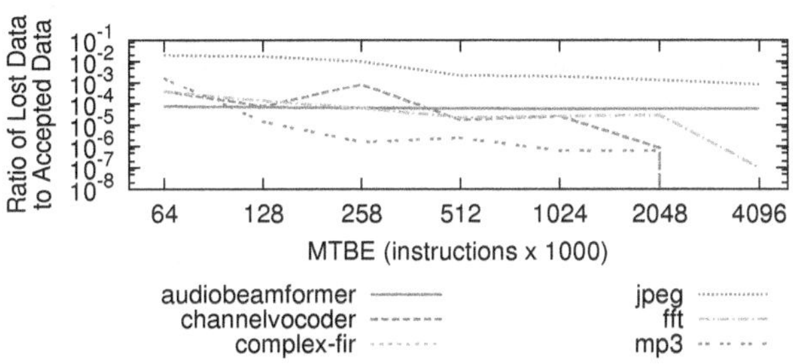

Figure 8: Realignment may result in data loss of correct items. We calculate data loss as the sum of padded and discarded bytes.

ure 7 shows only some 8-pixel-high erroneous lines. As CommGuard aligns computation and communication at every frame boundary, the frames following the corrupted frames start without the effects of misalignment. This is critical for the effects of control-flow errors to be ephemeral and not cumulative.

Figure 8 shows the amount of data loss (i.e. padded or discarded items) due to realignment across different error rates. Even at extreme error rates (MTBE of 64K instructions) the loss is less than 0.2% for five benchmarks. Jpeg loses more data than other benchmarks because it has the lowest frame/item ratio for default frame size (1 frame for every $7K$ items on average). However, the loss is still less than 0.2% at an MTBE of 512K instructions. This shows that data loss due to padding and discarding actions are small. The visible error clusters are largely due to intra-thread control-flow and memory addressing errors.

Figure 9 shows different outputs and PSNR values for the jpeg application at varying MTBE values. PSNRs of 20dB or more are quite acceptable, and for PSNRs larger than 30dB, the errors are hardly visible. When errors are quite frequent (MTBE=128k), the image is more corrupted, but the flower is still recognizable. Thus this technique is useful even at extreme error rates.

Figure 10 shows output quality averages and standard deviations for varying MTBEs for jpeg and mp3, respectively. For MTBEs as frequent as 512K instructions, output quality

(a) MTBE=128k (PSNR: 14.7dB)

(b) MTBE=512k (PSNR: 18.6dB)

(c) MTBE=2048k (PSNR: 28.6dB)

(d) MTBE=8192k (PSNR: 35.6dB)

Figure 9: Visual results with PSNR values at varying MTBE values. Output quality reaches error-free PSNR, 35.6dB, at an MTBE of 8192k instructions.

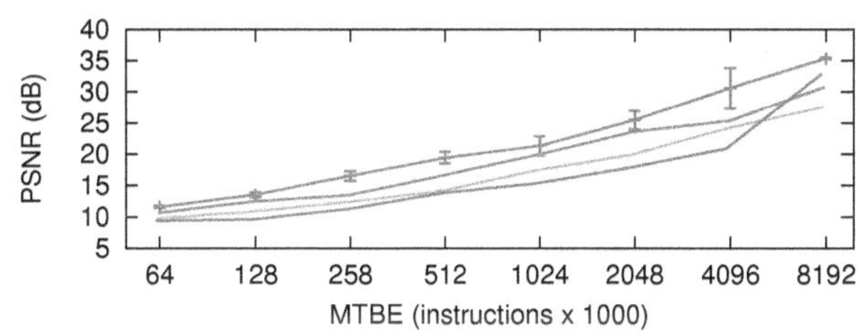

(a) jpeg (error-free PSNR: 35.6dB)

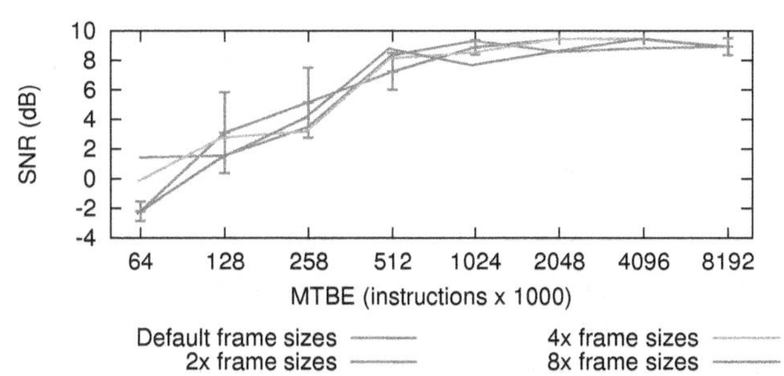

(b) mp3 (error-free SNR: 9.4dB)

Figure 10: Comparison of quality loss due to "error-free lossy compression" and "error-prone lossy compression with CommGuard" at varying MTBEs and varying frame sizes. (Deviations are shown only for default frame sizes.)

is maintained at very good levels: 20dB (error free PSNR of 35.6dB) and 7.6dB (error free SNR of 9.4dB), respectively. Example audio outputs for different error rates for the mp3 application may be heard at: http://youtu.be/k72hTg5zbik. With larger frame sizes, realignment operations less frequent. Therefore, run-time overheads decrease (as discussed

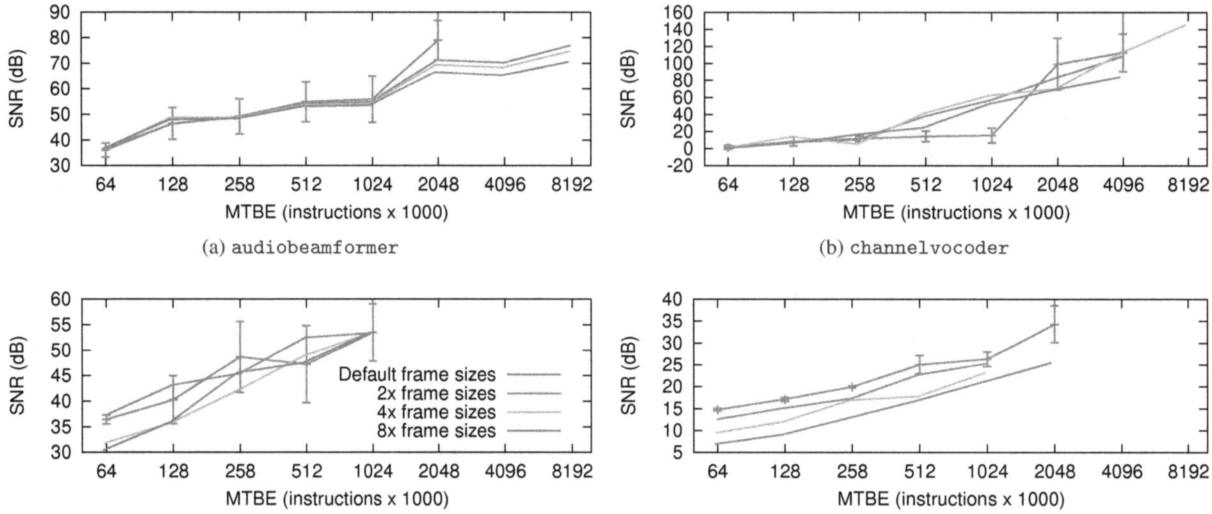

(a) `audiobeamformer` (b) `channelvocoder`

(c) `complex-fir` (d) `fft`

Figure 11: Output quality loss of error-prone runs with CommGuard with respect to the error-free execution (error-free SNR is infinity).

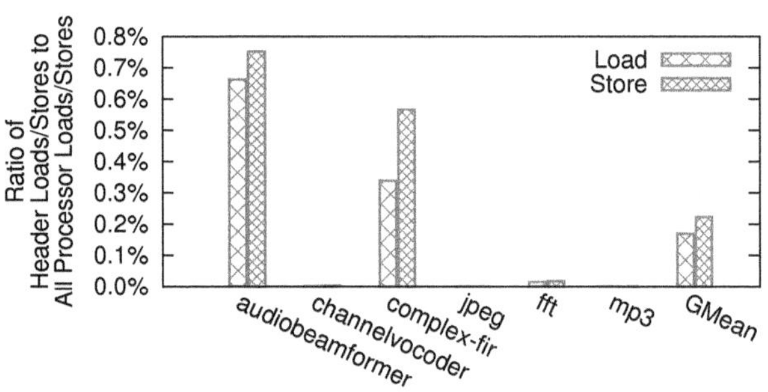

Figure 12: CommGuard overhead on memory events.

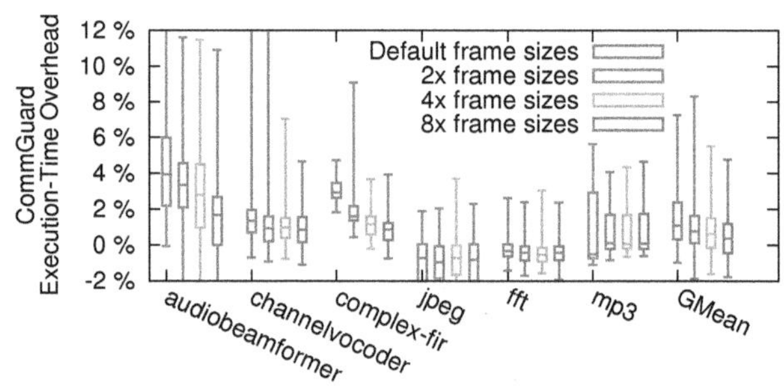

Figure 13: Runtime overhead of additional header pushes and pops, and pipeline serialization at frame boundaries. Measured on real hardware (100 runs) for varying frame sizes. Headers are additional item pushes&pops and pipeline stalls at frame boundaries are implemented by lfence instructions. Reference is execution without CommGuard.

in Section 7.2) but a misalignment is likely to corrupt more data.

Figure 11 shows SNR values for the remaining benchmarks. Among these benchmarks, `complex-fir` maintains error-free output quality for MTBEs as frequent as 1024K, while `channelvocoder` shows the same improvement at higher MTBEs (4096K). Similarly, `channelvocoder`, `fft`, and `mp3` approach 0dB quickly, whereas the remaining benchmarks are more resilient even at extreme error rates.

7.2 Hardware Overheads

CommGuard dynamically monitors execution and communication, induces additional memory events due to header pushes and pops and may affect the pipeline. Our evaluations show that coarse-grained protection keeps overheads low.

7.2.1 Extra Memory Events due to Headers:

CommGuard induces extra queue pushes and pops for the headers it inserts. The CommGuard QM implements the header pushes by storing the inserted headers in the software queue (just like data items in the queue). Since the queue is implemented as a software data structure in normal program memory, there is no extra storage overhead per se, but headers may lead to energy and performance overheads. As a proxy for power/energy influence in the memory hierarchy, Figure 12 shows the additional memory events due to header pushes and pops. (Performance effects are below.) Across benchmarks, our experiments show that the geometric mean increase in memory events is less than 0.2%. The maximum effect is for `audiobeamformer`, and even that is very small: Frame headers increase the number of data loads by only 0.66% and data stores by only 0.75%.

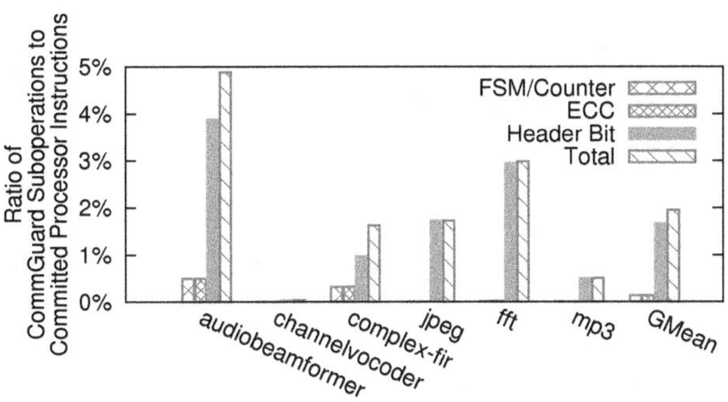

Figure 14: CommGuard operations normalized to processor instruction commits.

7.2.2 Execution Time Overheads:

Here, we measure CommGuard runtime overhead using the techniques described in Section 6, which account for extra pushes, pops, and pipeline serialization at frame boundaries. Figure 13 shows that extra CommGuard operations do not affect the performance for `jpeg`, `fft`, or `mp3`. `audiobeamformer` and `complex-fir` show the worst behaviors but their execution time increase is still less than 4%. The mean runtime overhead across all benchmarks is only 1%. Increasing frame sizes slightly reduces the already low execution time overheads, but since some applications, such as `jpeg`, have output quality sensitive to frame size (Figure 11) it is preferred to use the StreamIt-default frame size rather than anything larger.

7.2.3 Run-time Activity of CommGuard Modules

Tables 2 and 3 show the hardware operations that CommGuard may execute during run-time. CommGuard operations occur very infrequently relative to other processor activity. While some of our benchmarks (`audiobeamformer`, `channelvocoder`) contain threads that have a frame size of 1 item (i.e., one header overhead for every data item), the operations in the processor core still dominate all CommGuard hardware activities.

Figure 14 shows that the CommGuard operations are only as frequent as 2% of processor instruction commits (geometric mean). Even in the worst-case (`audiobeamformer`) all operations occur as frequently as 4.9% of processor instruction commits. The *header bit-pattern* operations (to indicate if a data unit is a regular item or a header) are the most frequent operations and are simple less-than-a-word size sets/checks. ECC computation for the headers (a relatively more complicated operation even though only for word-sized data) occurs only for 0.5% of instructions for `audiobeamformer`.

8. Applicability to Other Programming Models

In this work, CommGuard utilizes high-level information from StreamIt's programming model. However, CommGuard's principles of modular error-tolerance through coarse-grain control-flow/data identification apply more broadly to other programming models. The key attribute used by CommGuard is a frame structure linking shared data or communication to coarse-grained program control flow. Other StreamIt attributes, such as strict producer/consumer relationships and static definition of the size of data transfers are not needed by CommGuard.

Programming models that can express high-level control-flow constructs and how these control-flow constructs in different threads relate may easily implement CommGuard. For example, Concurrent Collections [3] expresses control-flow by *tagging* produced items of a thread and *steps* threads with a matching tag. Similarly, *keys* in MapReduce [8] programs identify a group of items and express the sequencing of parallel operations. CommGuard's headers are identifiers for data frames, and alignment manager modules use these identifiers for realignment. Other research such as DeNovo also proposes hardware-software constructs for coherence and communication that can similarly be employed [5].

9. Discussion and Related Work

Modularity and Self-Stabilization: CommGuard allows each local thread to make control-flow, memory addressing, and data errors without considering their effects on other threads. In addition to the design advantages of core-local management, this modular structure makes CommGuard easy to reason about and verify.

The concept of *Self-stabilization* [9] from distributed systems formalizes the *ephemeral* effects of errors. Self-stabilizing systems guarantee that a perturbation resulting in an erroneous state will eventually be corrected to bring the system to a valid state. Our design principles align with this goal. Errors may cause degradation of the output quality but the reliable protection modules repair the system to continue producing useful output. Existing techniques can rely on CommGuard's modularity to verify global self-stabilization properties using self-stabilizing local execution. Related work [10] shows verification of self-stabilizing Java programs. Work in [4] further shows how error-tolerant hardware models can be specified to verify such program-level properties.

Reliable Hardware: To address hardware errors, SRAM and other storage units use error correction codes [1], and other hardware units (i.e., logic) can use larger transistors or higher voltage [17, 24]. Razor [11] is a lower-level example of low-overhead error recovery. It detects timing errors using shadow latches and recovers from them by pipeline flush and re-execution. Razor provides low overhead error protection by targeting timing errors in critical paths. Redundant program execution [22] at different pipelines/hardware threads/processors helps recover from errors but incurs very high energy/performance overheads due to double redundancy for error detection and triple redundancy or re-execution for error recovery. These techniques are all directed towards maintaining an error-free hardware abstraction. In this work, we target applications that are tolerant to data errors and propose using these hardware reliability techniques only for small reliable modules. The rest of the micro-architecture permits errors that are potentially acceptable at the application level. Argus [21] detects errors separately for control-flow, data-flow, computation and memory. Like Argus, our work also distinguishes these concerns, and further includes inter-core communication errors. However, Argus targets error detection, while we go further with limited error correction to provide useful computation results.

Application-Level Error Tolerance: Some work has, like ours, leveraged application-level information while handling errors in computation. ANT (Algorithmic Noise Tolerance) [13] uses an estimator block to mitigate the effects of errors for circuits implementing signal processing algorithms. This is a hardware solution that does not need to deal with control-flow issues addressed in our work. Placing checkers using heuristics [30] strives to improve detection of control-flow and memory addressing errors. In contrast, CommGuard uses coarse-grain application information to detect the catastrophic errors and manage their effects.

Program-Level Specification and Analyses: EnerJ [25] partitions computation into error-tolerant and error-intolerant instructions to be implemented using "error-prone but low power" and "error-free but high power" components. EnerJ does not allow any errors on control-flow or memory addressing and requires a fully-reliable processor for error-intolerant instructions; this requires over half of the processor to be designed with reliable hardware. While EnerJ targets reducing energy consumption through using error-prone functional units on an otherwise-error-free processor, CommGuard more aggressively targets error-tolerant computation on unreliable processors that can only afford small reliable components.

Rely [4] lets programmers express application-level properties for error-tolerance and uses probabilistic hardware models to prove these properties. Further, Rely allows some control-flow and memory addressing errors. Here, we have shown that relaxed control-flow and memory addressing quickly cause catastrophic errors due to inter-core communication. Therefore, without CommGuard, Rely's reliability analysis would capture the misalignments and conclude that the application has virtually zero reliability. However, with CommGuard, the reliability analysis can capture that error effects do not propagate across frame boundaries. As a result, Rely's reliability analysis may compute the overall application reliability for streaming data. We experimentally verified CommGuard and have laid out this verification possibility using Rely-style analysis as future work.

Error-Tolerant Architectures ERSA [18] uses one reliable processor core to control algorithmic flow and many unreliable processors cores to execute error-tolerant worker tasks. ERSA requires application rewrite to fit this partitioned do-all execution model and the overhead of the reliable processor core can only be amortized when the application has many parallel threads. In contrast, CommGuard has fewer demands on the programming model, is fully automated in the StreamIt compiler and can also handle do-all parallelism which can be easily written in StreamIt. CommGuard could potentially enhance ERSA by enabling inter-core cooperation among the unreliable cores and thus help expand its programming model.

10. Conclusions

This work investigates the challenges of parallel program execution on error-prone hardware, and proposes CommGuard as a low-overhead communication protection mechanism. CommGuard uses small reliable hardware modules designed as simple FSMs to manage the coarse-grained computation progress of a core within which they reside, and the communication to/from that core. CommGuard uses application-level constructs that express how coarse-grain control-flow operations are related to data-flow operations. We use already existing constructs in StreamIt as a concrete example, however these constructs exist in other high-level programming languages as well.

Our results show that CommGuard can sustain correct operation and provide good output quality: 20dB for `jpeg` and 7.6dB for `mp3`, running on 10 error-prone cores, for errors occurring as frequently as every 500μs at each core. CommGuard avoids catastrophic degradation of output quality and only introduces mean overheads of 0.3% on the memory subsystem events, 2% as additional hardware operations relative to the committed instructions, and 1% on execution time.

11. Acknowledgements

The authors acknowledge the support of C-FAR and SONIC (under the grants HR0011-13-3-0002 and 2013-MA-2385), two of six SRC STARnet centers by MARCO and DARPA. In addition, this work was supported in part by the National Science Foundation (under the grant CCF-0916971).

References

[1] A. R. Alameldeen, I. Wagner, Z. Chishti, W. Wu, C. Wilkerson, and S.-L. Lu, "Energy-efficient cache design using variable-strength error-correcting codes," in *Proceedings of the Annual International Symposium on Computer Architecture*, 2011.

[2] N. Binkert, B. Beckmann, G. Black, S. K. Reinhardt, A. Saidi, A. Basu, J. Hestness, D. R. Hower, T. Krishna, S. Sardashti, R. Sen, K. Sewell, M. Shoaib, N. Vaish, M. D. Hill, and D. A. Wood, "The gem5 simulator," *SIGARCH Computer Architecture News*, vol. 39, no. 2, pp. 1–7, 2011.

[3] Z. Budimlic, M. Burke, V. Cave, K. Knobe, G. Lowney, R. Newton, J. Palsberg, D. Peixotto, V. Sarkar, F. Schlimbach, and S. Tasirlar, "Concurrent collections," *Scientific Programming*, vol. 18, no. 3-4, pp. 203–217, 2010.

[4] M. Carbin, S. Misailovic, and M. C. Rinard, "Verifying quantitative reliability for programs that execute on unreliable hardware," in *Proceedings of the International Conference on Object Oriented Programming Systems Languages and Applications*, 2013.

[5] B. Choi, R. Komuravelli, H. Sung, R. Smolinski, N. Honarmand, S. V. Adve, V. S. Adve, N. P. Carter, and C.-T. Chou, "Denovo: Rethinking the memory hierarchy for disciplined parallelism," in *Proceedings of the International Conference on Parallel Architectures and Compilation Techniques*, 2011.

[6] M. Clemens, B. Sierawski, K. Warren, M. Mendenhall, N. Dodds, R. Weller, R. Reed, P. Dodd, M. Shaneyfelt, J. Schwank, S. Wender, and R. Baumann, "The effects of neutron energy and high-z materials on single event upsets and multiple cell upsets," *IEEE Transactions on Nuclear Science*, 2011.

[7] C. Constantinescu, "Trends and challenges in vlsi circuit reliability," *IEEE Micro*, vol. 23, no. 4, pp. 14–19, 2003.

[8] J. Dean and S. Ghemawat, "MapReduce: Simplified data processing on large clusters," *Commun. ACM*, vol. 51, no. 1, pp. 107–113, 2008.

[9] E. W. Dijkstra, "Self-stabilizing systems in spite of distributed control," *Commun. ACM*, vol. 17, no. 11, pp. 643–644, 1974.

[10] Y. h. Eom and B. Demsky, "Self-stabilizing java," in *Proceedings of the Conference on Programming Language Design and Implementation*, 2012.

[11] D. Ernst, N. S. Kim, S. Das, S. Pant, R. Rao, T. Pham, C. Ziesler, D. Blaauw, T. Austin, K. Flautner, and T. Mudge, "Razor: A low-power pipeline based on circuit-level timing speculation," in *Proceedings of the Annual International Symposium on Microarchitecture*, 2003.

[12] G. Gielen, P. De Wit, E. Maricau, J. Loeckx, J. Martín-Martínez, B. Kaczer, G. Groeseneken, R. Rodríguez, and M. Nafría, "Emerging yield and reliability challenges in nanometer cmos technologies," in *Proceedings of the Conference on Design, Automation and Test in Europe*, 2008.

[13] R. Hegde and N. R. Shanbhag, "Energy-efficient signal processing via algorithmic noise-tolerance," in *Proceedings of the International Symposium on Low Power Electronics and Design*, 1999.

[14] W. Huang, M. Stan, S. Gurumurthi, R. Ribando, and K. Skadron, "Interaction of scaling trends in processor architecture and cooling," in *Semiconductor Thermal Measurement and Management Sym.*, 2010.

[15] Intel Corporation, vol. 3A, pp. 8–16, 2014. [Online]. Available: http://www.intel.com/content/dam/www/public/us/en/documents/manuals/64-ia-32-architectures-software-developer-manual-325462.pdf

[16] ITRS, "ITRS process integration, devices, and structures," http://public.itrs.net/Links/2011ITRS/2011Chapters/2011PIDS.pdf, ITRS, 2011.

[17] K. Kuhn, M. Giles, D. Becher, P. Kolar, A. Kornfeld, R. Kotlyar, S. Ma, A. Maheshwari, and S. Mudanai, "Process technology variation," *IEEE Transactions on Electron Devices*, 2011.

[18] L. Leem, H. Cho, J. Bau, Q. A. Jacobson, and S. Mitra, "ERSA: Error resilient system architecture for probabilistic applications," in *Proceedings of the Conference on Design, Automation and Test in Europe*, 2010.

[19] S. Liu, K. Pattabiraman, T. Moscibroda, and B. G. Zorn, "Flikker: Saving dram refresh-power through critical data partitioning," in *Proceedings of the International Conference on Architectural Support for Programming Languages and Operating Systems*, 2011.

[20] P. S. Magnusson, M. Christensson, J. Eskilson, D. Forsgren, G. Hållberg, J. Högberg, F. Larsson, A. Moestedt, and B. Werner, "Simics: A full system simulation platform," *Computer*, vol. 35, no. 2, pp. 50–58, 2002.

[21] A. Meixner, M. E. Bauer, and D. Sorin, "Argus: Low-cost, comprehensive error detection in simple cores," in *Proceedings of the Annual International Symposium on Microarchitecture*, 2007.

[22] S. S. Mukherjee, M. Kontz, and S. K. Reinhardt, "Detailed design and evaluation of redundant multithreading alternatives," in *Proceedings of the Annual International Symposium on Computer Architecture*, 2002.

[23] S. S. Mukherjee, C. Weaver, J. Emer, S. K. Reinhardt, and T. Austin, "A systematic methodology to compute the architectural vulnerability factors for a high-performance microprocessor," in *Proceedings of the Annual International Symposium on Microarchitecture*, 2003.

[24] S. Mukherjee, *Architecture Design for Soft Errors*. Morgan Kaufmann Publishers Inc., 2008.

[25] A. Sampson, W. Dietl, E. Fortuna, D. Gnanapragasam, L. Ceze, and D. Grossman, "EnerJ: Approximate data types for safe and general low-power computation," in *Proceedings of the Conference on Programming Language Design and Implementation*, 2011.

[26] B. Sierawski, R. Reed, M. Mendenhall, R. Weller, R. Schrimpf, S.-J. Wen, R. Wong, N. Tam, and R. Baumann, "Effects of scaling on muon-induced soft errors," in *International Reliability Physics Symposium*, 2011.

[27] T. Stathaki, *Image Fusion: Algorithms and Applications*. Academic Press, 2008.

[28] G. Stoll and K. Brandenburg, "The iso/mpeg-audio codec: A generic standard for coding of high quality digital audio," in *Audio Engineering Society Convention*, 1992.

[29] W. Thies, M. Karczmarek, and S. P. Amarasinghe, "StreamIt: A language for streaming applications," in *Proceedings of the International Conference on Compiler Construction*, 2002.

[30] A. Thomas and K. Pattabiraman, "Error detector placement for soft computation," in *Proceedings of the Conference on Dependable Systems and Networks*, 2013.

[31] G. K. Wallace, "The JPEG still picture compression standard," *Commun. ACM*, vol. 34, no. 4, 1991.

[32] Y. Yetim, M. Martonosi, and S. Malik, "Extracting useful computation from error-prone processors for streaming applications," in *Proceedings of the Conference on Design, Automation and Test in Europe*, 2013.

Dual Execution for On the Fly Fine Grained Execution Comparison

Dohyeong Kim[1] Yonghwi Kwon[1] William N. Sumner[2] Xiangyu Zhang[1] Dongyan Xu[1]

[1]Department of Computer Science, Purdue University, USA

[2]School of Computing Science, Simon Fraser University, Canada

[1]{kim1051,kwon58,xyzhang,dxu}@purdue.edu [2]wsumner@sfu.ca

Abstract

Execution comparison has many applications in debugging, malware analysis, software feature identification, and intrusion detection. Existing comparison techniques have various limitations. Some can only compare at the system event level and require executions to take the same input. Some require storing instruction traces that are very space-consuming and have difficulty dealing with non-determinism. In this paper, we propose a novel dual execution technique that allows on-the-fly comparison at the instruction level. Only differences between the executions are recorded. It allows executions to proceed in a coupled mode such that they share the same input sequence with the same timing, reducing nondeterminism. It also allows them to proceed in a decoupled mode such that the user can interact with each one differently. Decoupled executions can be recoupled to share the same future inputs and facilitate further comparison. We have implemented a prototype and applied it to identifying functional components for reuse, comparative debugging with new GDB primitives, and understanding real world regression failures. Our results show that dual execution is a critical enabling technique for execution comparison.

Categories and Subject Descriptors D.2 [*Software Engineering*]

General Terms Algorithms

Keywords Execution Comparison, Dynamic Analysis

1. Introduction

Execution comparison techniques compare multiple executions from the same program or highly similar programs to identify state differences including control flow differences and variable value differences. Execution comparison has been used to debug sequential, concurrent, and regression failures, by reasoning about the causality between execution differences and input differences [50], thread scheduling differences [47], and syntactic differences among program versions [8, 36, 41], respectively. It has also been used to identify and extract functional features for legacy software reuse [25]. For example, to identify the "send email" functionality from an email client, two executions are compared. In one execution, an email is composed and sent, whereas in the other, the same email is composed but not sent. Execution comparison is also used in malware behavior analysis [24]. Advanced malware often has logic to decide whether or not to activate its payload depending on the environment such as the platform, the running applications on the victim machine, the current date and time, and the presence of debuggers or virtual machines. To understand the activation logic and the payload, malware is executed in different environments and the resulting executions are compared. Software diversification creates executables with different structures, e.g. different stack layouts [38]. At runtime, multiple such versions are executed simultaneously. The executions are compared to detect intrusion because an exploit to one version often crashes others.

Execution comparison can be classified into *online* and *offline* techniques. In online comparison, the executions are compared on-the-fly. The intrusion detection technique from Salamat in 2009 is one such online approach [38]. However, such comparison is at the system event level. In particular, the executions of the multiple diversified versions are driven by the same input event sequence and the output event sequences are then compared. This technique assumes all executions consume the same input, which does not hold for debugging, where executions may have different paths and hence consume different sequence of input events. Most execution comparison techniques are offline [24, 25, 36, 47]. They first collect traces and compare them offline. A prominent challenge is hence the space required to store such traces, which can grow to a few GB within a few milliseconds of execution.

ASPLOS '15, March 14–18, 2015, Istanbul, Turkey..

http://dx.doi.org/10.1145/2694344.2694394

Since executions are performed independently, many execution differences are caused by nondeterminism such as input events being received at different times. These differences are not helpful in understanding functional differences. Note that many existing logging and replay techniques [15, 20] cannot both preclude nondeterminism and allow for functional differences. Viennot et al. [45] can handle functional differences but it requires explorations and it cannot be used in online analysis. For UI applications, comparing their executions also requires repeated manual effort.

In this paper, we propose a novel *dual execution* engine to overcome the aforementioned limitations. It performs on-the-fly instruction level comparison of two executions and only stores traces for parts of executions that are different. There are several challenges in on-the-fly execution comparison. The executions may diverge because of (1) different inputs, (2) different outcomes from interactions with the environment, and (3) nondeterminism in the program. Our technique allows the executions to differ and consume different inputs. It suppresses the differences caused by interactions with the environment and nondeterminism. In particular, it has three execution modes. Initially, the two executions run in a *coupled* mode, in which they are synchronized and one of them, the *slave*, receives most of its system events from the other, the *master*, instead of from the environment. When the user indicates that different inputs should be provided, the two executions get into the *decoupled* mode, in which they execute independently. After introducing the differences, the user indicates the two executions should be coupled again such that they can share the same future inputs to avoid unnecessary nondeterminism. Since the two executions may be at different points when the coupling signal is received, in the *resynchronization* mode, the engine blocks the faster execution until the other one catches up. After that, the two execute in the *coupled* mode again. Since the two executions then have different states, even though they execute in the *coupled* mode, their paths and system event sequences may differ, so our engine detects and handles all these differences.

Our contributions are summarized as follows.

- We have proposed the novel dual execution technique that allows on-the-fly fine-grained execution comparison. It allows executions to take different inputs.
- We have addressed a set of underlying technical challenges such as how to synchronize two executions at the instruction level; how to share system events such that nondeterminism can be suppressed; how to prevent sharing in some cases such that the slave can still have its independent visible interface; how to resynchronize the two executions after they are decoupled; how to handle signals and threading.
- We have implemented a prototype and applied it to three applications: functional component extraction, on-the-fly comparative debugging with new GDB primitives, and understanding regression failures. The results show that the engine is a critical enabling technique. It also substantially reduces the space and time overhead compared to offline comparison.

```
1 busy_cue() {
2   if (status_message_remaining()) ...
3 }
4 status_message_remaining() {
5   return display_time - time() + min_time > 0;
6 }
```

Figure 1. Nondeterminism in pine.

2. Motivation

In this section, we use a real world example to explain why dual execution is preferable in execution comparison and illustrate some of the technical challenges in dual execution.

Suppose we want to identify the functional components that change an email subject and log a sent email in `pine`, an email client. In `pine`, a user can get to the email composition interface through a sequence of menu operations, where he/she can provide the email body, subject, and recipient. He/she can also choose whether a copy of the email will be saved in the `sent_mail` file after it is sent, through the `ctrl-r` hot-key. During the whole process, `pine` periodically pulls incoming emails from the server through a timer control. While an email is being sent, `pine` shows busy messages on the screen.

To identify the desired components, the user provides two executions. In the first, he/she composes an email and sends it, and a copy of the email is saved by default. The second execution is almost identical, except that the user changes the subject and reconfigures `pine` so that a copy is not saved.

We first use an offline technique similar to that of Kim et al. [25], in which the two executions run independently, and we collect instruction level traces for offline comparison. We observe the following problems. *First*, we must repeat the almost identical sequence of user interactions. We must be very careful to not introduce any human error. For example, in the second execution, when we try to type the same email, suppose we mistype a character and use `backspace` to fix it. Although the two emails are identical after the mistake is fixed, the instruction level trace faithfully records the interaction error, which will be identified as a difference during comparison.

Second, even if we manage to avoid introducing human error, there is substantial low level nondeterminism, e.g. from timers, that leads to unnecessary execution differences. Fig. 1 shows a code snippet from `pine` that has nondeterministic behavior. busy_cue() is a function that shows a busy message on the screen. Before showing a message it checks whether there already is a message by calling status_message_remaining() at line 2, which checks whether the current message is shown on screen for at least a minimum amount of time (line 5). The program behavior is thus dependent on execution timing that

```
1  pico() {
2    while(...) {
3      c = GetKey();
4      if (c == empty || time_to_check())
5        check_new_mail();
6      execute (c);
7    }
8  }
9  GetKey() {
10   if (ReadyForKey(STDIN, timeout))
11     return read(STDIN);
12   else
13     return empty;
14 }
```

Figure 2. Input handling loop in `pine`.

is nondeterministic. There are additional such timing related behaviors in `pine`. We show in Section 5 that execution differences caused by nondeterminism can be as large as half of the overall differences.

Third, we observe that the trace for even one of these executions is over 30GB even though the execution is already very small. It is not surprising given the large number of instructions executed within a second by a modern CPU. Storing and processing such huge trace files is a heavy burden even for modern systems. Note that the two traces are mostly identical.

Next, we use our dual execution engine. Initially, the engine spawns two executions of `pine` at the same time. Then, we only interact with one of the executions, called the *master*. All the interactions between the master and the environment, including user interactions, are relayed to the *slave*. This allows us to avoid repeating the same error-prone user interactions. In addition, the two executions run exactly the same way, without any differences caused by nondeterminism. Since only differences are recorded, we also avoid tracing in this phase.

After composing the email, we press a predefined hot-key. Now we can control the master and the slave separately. We provide different subjects to the two executions and set the save_to_sent_mail option differently. After that, we couple the two executions again by pressing another hot-key. Once again we only interact with the master to confirm sending the email and terminate the program. In this phase, since the engine aligns the two executions at the instruction level and executes them in locksteps, instruction level differences are detected on the fly and recorded. The resulting trace file is only less than 90MB.

We note several technical challenges. *First*, our system relays system events in the master to the slave, but we cannot relay every event. For example, if the slave did not execute the write() system call but rather simulated it using a relayed result during coupled execution, it could not show any interface and thus we could not provide different inputs when decoupled. The engine must identify the events that can be relayed.

Second, when we indicate our intent to recouple the executions after providing different inputs, the engine cannot

```
1  pico();
2  ...
3  call_mailer();
4  ...
5  if (fcc)
6    write_fcc(sentmail);
```

Figure 3. Send-mail function from `pine`.

simply resume relaying events because the two executions may be in different stages due to the different inputs. Fig. 2 shows a code segment in which `pine` receives user inputs. Lines 2-7 use a loop to handle user inputs. At line 3, it reads a key from the user. At lines 4-5, if a certain amount of time has passed, the program checks whether there is a new email. At line 6, the program processes the keystroke. Therefore, depending on the time we spent providing the different inputs, the two executions will be in the different instances of the loop upon recoupling. They may even be in different child functions of the pico() function. The engine needs to resynchronize the two executions at the instruction level.

Third, even though the engine manages to recouple the two executions, they may execute differently due to the input differences. Fig. 3 shows another code snippet from `pine`. At line 1, the program executes pico() to allow the user to compose the email. It also contains the confirmation menu. Recoupling happens inside pico(). At line 3, the program calls call_mailer(), which constructs the email packet and sends it to the SMTP server. After that at line 5, the program checks fcc, which corresponds to the save_to_sent_mail option. If it is set, `pine` makes a copy of the sent mail (line 6). Since we set fcc differently in the two executions, one execution will execute write_fcc(), but the other will not. Note that write_fcc() relies on several events such as file open and file write. Therefore in this case, the engine needs to detect such differences and provide the events appropriately.

3. Design

Our discussion follows the order of the three execution modes: the *coupled* mode in which the master and the slave share system events; the *decoupled* mode in which they execute independently; and the *resynchronization* mode in which the faster execution is blocked until the slower one catches up, when the user wants to recouple the two executions.

3.1 Coupled Execution Mode

The master and slave are in coupled mode when they start and also after different inputs are provided and the executions are resynchronized. Note that after differences are introduced, the two executions may take different paths and have different syscalls, even though they are resynchronized. Thus we focus on detecting and handling such differences that may prevent the executions from sharing events.

We first present the semantics of the master and slave executions and then discuss the monitor that coordinates their behavior.

Table 1. Semantic Rules for Master Execution.

Instruction	Action	Rule
regular instruction $y=^l$ instr(op, x_1,...x_n)	execute the instruction; send_trace_entry($\langle INSTR, l, \sigma[y]^1\rangle$);	M-INSTR

$y=^l$ syscall (sid, x_1,...x_n);	send_trace_entry($\langle SYSCALL, l, sid, \sigma[x_1], ..., \sigma[x_n]\rangle$);
	execute the system call;
	send_syscall_outcome($\sigma[y]$);
		M-SYSCALL

1. σ stands for the store that maps a variable to a value.

$TraceEntry$	$t ::=$	$\langle INSTR, l, v\rangle$
		$\mid \langle SYSCALL, l, sid, P\rangle$
$Label$	$l ::=$	$\{l_1, l_2, l_3, ...\}$
$Value$	$v ::=$	$\{true, false, 0, 1, 2, ...\}$
$SysCallId$	$sid ::=$	$\{1, 2, ...\}$
$SysCallParameters$	$P ::=$	$\overline{v}$

Figure 4. Trace Syntax

3.1.1 Master Execution in the Coupled Mode.

In coupled mode, the master tracks each instruction execution and sends a trace entry to the monitor. It performs all syscalls faithfully and sends syscall parameters and outcomes to the monitor, who decides if the syscall outcomes need to be relayed to the slave. The semantics is shown in Table 1. We model instructions into two kinds: system calls and others (or *regular instructions*). A regular instruction, with opcode op, takes n operands and produces the result in y. According to rule M-INSTR, the instruction is first executed, then a trace entry is sent to the monitor.

Trace Entry Syntax. As shown in Fig. 4, there are two kinds of trace entries, identified by the types $INSTR$ (denoting regular instructions) and $SYSCALL$, respectively. A regular instruction entry consists of the label (or the program counter) of the instruction and the left hand side value of the instruction. A syscall entry consists of the label, the syscall id, and the parameters. □

Upon a syscall invocation (rule M-SYSCALL), the master first sends the corresponding trace entry containing the syscall id and the parameters to the monitor. It then executes the syscall and sends the outcome to the monitor.

3.1.2 Slave Execution in the Coupled Mode.

As shown in Fig. 2, the slave handles a regular instruction in the same way as the master. For a syscall, the slave sends the trace entry containing the parameters to the monitor, which allows the monitor to decide if the slave should *copy* the syscall outcome from the master or *execute* the syscall. After that, the slave receives the decision from the monitor and acts accordingly. recv_syscall_outcome() is a blocking call, preventing the situation in which the slave execution is faster than the master and manages to perform a syscall before the master reaches the corresponding syscall.

3.1.3 Monitor in the Coupled Mode.

The monitor is the most complex component. It is responsible for synchronizing the two executions, comparing their trace

Algorithm 1 Monitor Algorithm for the Coupled Mode

Input: a pair of executions e_m, e_s

Definition: $\mathcal{I}_{m/s}$ denotes the execution index of the current trace entry from master/slave;

```
MONITOR (e_m, e_s)
1:  while e_m and e_s are not finished do
2:     t_m = recv_trace_entry(e_m)
3:     I^p_m = I_m
4:     I_m = update_index(t_m.l, I_m)
5:     t_s = recv_trace_entry(e_s)
6:     I^p_s = I_s
7:     I_s = update_index(t_s.l, I_s)
8:     if t_m.type==SYSCALL then
9:        y_m = recv_syscall_outcome(e_m)
10:       if policy(t_m.sid)==COPY && t_m.P==t_s.P
          then
11:          send_2_slave(y_m)
12:       else
13:          send_2_slave(EXEC)
14:    if t_m.l != t_s.l then
15:       /* Lines 16-21 run parallel with lines 22-27*/
16:       while I_m != dyn_ipdom(I^p_m) do
17:          record(t_m, nil)
18:          t_m = recv_trace_entry(e_m)
19:          I_m = update_index(t_m.l, I_m)
20:          if t_m.type==SYSCALL then
21:             y_m = recv_syscall_outcome(e_m)
22:       while I_s != dyn_ipdom(I^p_s) do
23:          record(nil, t_s)
24:          t_s = recv_trace_entry(e_s)
25:          I_s = update_index(t_m.l, I_s)
26:          if t_m.type==SYSCALL then
27:             send_2_slave(EXEC)
28:    if t_m.v != t_s.v then
29:       record(t_m, t_s)
```

entries on the fly, and instructing the slave how to handle its syscalls.

Background: Execution Indexing. Our execution synchronization is built on *execution indexing* (EI) [48]. For completeness of the paper, we briefly introduce the EI technique. It computes a unique identifier for an execution point called an *execution index*, or index. Execution points across multiple runs align when they have the same index. The index of an

Table 2. Semantic Rules for Slave Execution.

Instruction	Action	Rule
regular instruction $y =^l$ instr(op, x_1,...x_n)	execute the instruction; send_trace_entry($\langle INSTR, l, \sigma[y]\rangle$)	S-INSTR

$y=^l$ syscall (sid, x_1,...x_n)	send_trace_entry($\langle SYSCALL, l, sid, \sigma[x_1], ..., \sigma[x_n]\rangle$);
	t=recv_syscall_outcome();
	if (t == EXEC) execute the system call;
	else $\sigma[y] = t$;
		S-SYSCALL

$$ExecIndex \quad \mathcal{I} ::= \bar{l}$$

$$\text{update\_index} : Label \times ExecIndex \rightarrow ExecIndex$$

$$\text{update\_index}(l, nil) = l \qquad \text{update\_index}(l, \mathcal{I}_{head} \cdot l_{tail}) = \begin{cases} \mathcal{I}_{head} \cdot l_{tail} \cdot l & \text{if } l \text{ control dep. on } l_{tail} \\ \text{update\_index}(l, \mathcal{I}_{head}) & \text{otherwise} \end{cases}$$

$$\text{dyn\_ipdom} : ExecIndex \rightarrow ExecIndex$$

$$\text{dyn\_ipdom}(\mathcal{I}_{head} \cdot l_{tail}) = \mathcal{I}_{head} \cdot l, \text{ with } l \text{ the immediate postdom. of } l_{tail}$$

Figure 5. Execution indexing primitives. The syntax is presented in boxes.

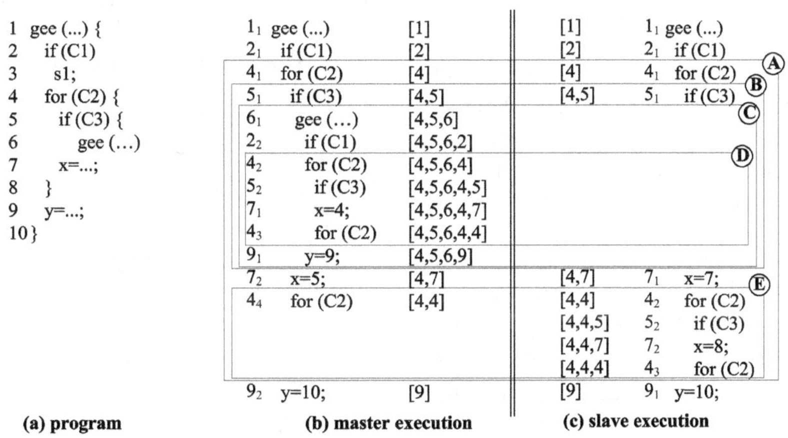

Figure 6. Example for execution indexing and synchronization.

execution point is analogous to the calling context of the point, but instead of describing the nesting of function calls, the index describes the nesting of the control dependence regions of the execution point. Note that multiple instances of an instruction may share the same calling context (and hence calling contexts cannot be used to distinguish the instances), but they must have different control dependence region nestings.

The syntax of execution indexing and the primitives to compute indices are described in Fig. 5. Syntactically, an index is a sequence of labels (or PCs). It is constructed by the update_index() primitive, which takes the label of the current execution point and the index of the previous point, produces the new index. According to the rules, if the previous index is nil, the resulting index is the label. If the previous index is not nil, and if the current label l is control dependent on the tail label l_{tail} of the previous index, indicating l is nesting in the region of l_{tail}, l is appended to the previous index. Otherwise, labels at the tail of the previous index are popped one by one until l finds its control dependence region.

Consider Fig. 6. A code snippet is presented in (a) and two executions are presented in (b) and (c). The two executions differ due to some state differences introduced earlier. The indices of the execution points are presented in the center for easy comparison. Lets look at the master execution (b). Initially, the index of the first instance of statement 1 $\mathcal{I}(1_1) = [1]$ as its previous index is nil; then update_index(2, $\mathcal{I}(1_1)$)= update_index(2, $[1]$)= update_index(2, nil)=$[2]$, because 2 is not control dependent on 1; update_index(5, $\mathcal{I}(4_1)$)= update_index(5, $[4]$)=$[4, 5]$ because 5 is control dependent on 4. Intuitively, it means 5 is nesting in the region of 4, denoted by the box Ⓐ. Similarly, $\mathcal{I}(5_2) = [4, 5, 6, 4, 5]$, denoting 5_2 is nesting inside regions Ⓓ, Ⓒ, Ⓑ, and then Ⓐ. Note that our system only maintains the index for the current execution point, similar to maintaining the call stack.

The indices for the slave (c) are similarly computed. By comparing the indices, only $1_1, 2_1, 4_1, 5_1, 7_2, 4_4, 9_2$ in the master have correspondence in the slave. We can see the essence of EI is to align the control dependence regions. For example, the alignment of 5_1 in both executions indicates the Ⓑ regions align. But inside the region, different branch outcomes are taken such that there are no further alignments. □

Synchronizing Master and Slave Executions. The monitor component continuously updates the current indices of the master and the slave based on the trace entries received. The indices allow the monitor to achieve lockstep synchronization of the two executions. Initially, the two executions follow the same path such that they are perfectly synchronized, indicated by identical indices. When a predicate is encountered but its branch outcomes are different in the two runs, the paths start to diverge. As such, the monitor decouples the two executions, allowing them to proceed independently to the immediate postdominator of the predicate. Note that since the predicates in the two runs share the same immediate postdominator, they are perfectly synchronized again.

Details are in Algorithm 1, in which a **while** loop continuously processes trace entries until the two executions finish. In the loop, it first receives an entry from the master and updates the current index for the master (lines 2-4). We use $t_m.l$ to represents the label field of the trace entry. Lines 5-7 do the same thing for the slave. In normal cases, the two entries from the two respective runs have the identical labels. But if the previous label is a predicate with different branch outcomes, the pair of entries will have different labels (line 14). In this case, the monitor processes trace entries from the two executions in parallel (lines 16-21 and 22-27), until the *dynamic* immediate postdominator (IPDOM) of the previous predicate is encountered (line 16 and line 22). Note that the trace entries are recorded (line 17 and line 23) because they denote *control flow differences*. In contrast, in lines 28-29, if the values are different, the two entries (with the same label) are also recorded. Note that the monitor must leverage indices to identify the *dynamic* IPDOM (lines 16 and 22). It cannot simply looks for the next occurrence of the *static* IPDOM, because in the presence of recursive functions, the next occurrence of the static IPDOM may not mean the end of the control dependence region. In Fig. 5, dyn_ipdom($\mathcal{I}$) computes the dynamic IPDOM of $\mathcal{I}$ by replacing the tail label, a predicate label, with its static IPDOM label, demanding the prefixing control dependence regions remain the same.

Example. Consider the example in Fig. 6. The first four pairs of trace entries have identical labels. Only the entries for 5_1 are recorded as the branch outcomes are different. The monitor detects that the fifth pair have different labels, i.e. 6_1 from the master and 7_1 from the slave. As such, it computes dyn_ipdom($\mathcal{I}[5_1]$)=dyn_ipdom($[4, 5]$)=$[4, 7]$. Thus, both executions proceed to index $[4, 7]$, that is, 7_2 in (b) and 7_1 in (c). Note that if the static IPDOM 7 were used, due to the recursive call of gee(), we would mistakenly consider 7_1 to be the end of region Ⓑ. □

Handling Syscalls. The monitor also needs to handle syscalls because we want the two executions to share the sequence of external inputs as much as possible to reduce nondeterminism and hence the meaningless differences caused by such nondeterminism. It also reduces error-prone manual efforts. From the earlier discussion, we know both the master and the slave send their syscall parameters to the monitor. In addition, the master also sends its syscall outcome. For a syscall that occurs in both executions, the monitor compares their parameters, e.g. the size of a file read. If they are identical, the monitor relays the syscall outcome from the master to the slave. In the case that they are different due to differences introduced earlier, the monitor instructs the slave to execute the syscall instead of copying from the master.

In Algorithm 1, when the monitor receives a pair of syscall trace entries (line 8), it first retrieves the syscall outcome from the master (line 9). Then it consults a *policy table* that defines the actions for different kinds of syscalls. While the details of the policy table are discussed in Section 4, all we need to know now is that there are two possible actions for each syscall ID. COPY indicates the slave should copy the result from the master, and EXEC indicates the slave should execute the syscall. At line 10, the algorithm checks whether the action is COPY and if the parameters are identical. If so, it relays the outcome from the master (line 11). Otherwise, it instructs the slave to execute (line 13). When the two executions take different branches, the monitor retrieves and discards the syscall outcome from the master (lines 20-21), and instructs the slave to always execute its syscall (lines 26-27).

```
1   /* different file names are provided*/
2   filename = read();
3   ...
4   while (1) {
5     menu = selectMenu();
6     if (menu == MENU_QUIT)
7       quit();
8     else if (menu == MENU_WRITE_MESSAGE) {
9       message = read();
10      if (exists(filename))
11        rename(filename, filename + ".bak");
12      fd = open(filename);
13      write (fd, message);
14    }
15  }
```

Figure 7. Example for syscall handling.

Example. Consider an example in Fig. 7. When the user selects the menu item `write message`, the program reads a message and writes it to a file with a name provided earlier. If the file already exists, the program first makes a backup. Suppose the user wants to compare two executions with two different file names `A` and `B`, and there is already a file with name `B`. Fig. 8 shows the master and the slave executions. Note that since the file name is different at 2_1, the following syscalls at 10_1, 11_1, 12_1, and 13_1 in the slave are executed instead of copied, which correctly exercises the intended different semantics. In contrast, the syscalls at 5_1 and 9_1 are copied. □

Master		Slave		
2_1	`filename = read();`	2_1	`filename = read();`	E
4_1	`while (1)`	4_1	`while (1)`	
5_1	`menu = selectMenu()`	5_1	`menu = selectMenu()`	C
6_1	`if (menu == ...)`	6_1	`if (menu == ...)`	
8_1	`else if (menu == ...)`	8_1	`else if (menu == ...)`	
9_1	`message = read();`	9_1	`message = read();`	C
10_1	`if ( exists (filename ))`	10_1	`if ( exists (filename ))`	E
-		11_1	`rename(filename, ...) ;`	E
12_1	`fd = open(filename) ;`	12_1	`fd = open(filename) ;`	E
13_1	`write (fd, message) ;`	13_1	`write (fd, message) ;`	E

Figure 8. Executions of the example in Fig. 7. The last column shows if the slave executes (E) the syscall or copies (C) result. The boxed entries are affected by the differences from 2_1.

3.2 Decoupled Execution Mode

When the user wants to decouple the two executions and provide different inputs, he/she presses `ctrl-c` in the master execution, which sends an interrupt to the master. Note that the user does not interact with the slave execution (in most cases). The master checks for the interrupt before executing a system call. If it was received, the master informs the monitor. When the slave is about to execute the corresponding system call, the monitor notifies the slave to start executing its syscalls. In other words, the two start to interact with the environment directly. Both continue to send their trace entries to the monitor to update their indices.

3.3 Resynchronizing Master and Slave Executions

After providing the different inputs, the user presses another hot-key in both the master and the slave to indicate that he/she wants to resynchronize the two executions such that they can share the same input events again to reduce nondeterminism and manual interactions. However, when the interrupts are received, the two executions may be at different locations. The monitor needs to determine which execution is faster and block it until the slower one catches up. After the two resynchronize, they resume in the coupled mode.

We leverage execution indices to determine which execution is ahead of the other. Intuitively, an index represents the nesting of control dependence regions. Two indices sharing some common prefix means that the current execution points in the two runs are nesting in a common set of control dependence regions, called *aligned regions*. By comparing the relative positions of the two points inside the aligned regions, we can decide which execution is ahead. Consider Fig. 6. Point 7_1 in (c) is ahead of 5_1 in (b) because $\mathcal{I}_m(5_1) = [4,5]$ and $\mathcal{I}_s(7_1) = [4,7]$; they share a prefix $[4]$ and 7 is ahead of 5 inside the region of 4. Similarly, 7_2 in (c) is ahead of 5_2 in (b). In particular, their indices share the prefix $[4]$; 7_2 in (c) is in the region denoted by index $[4,4]$, i.e. Ⓔ representing the second iteration of the loop, whereas 5_2 in (b) is in the region denoted by $[4,5]$, i.e. Ⓑ representing the **if** statement at line 5 in the first iteration of the loop). Ⓔ is ahead of Ⓑ.

```
1  while (1) {
2     if (select(STDIN, ...) == SUCCESS)
3       /* process the user input */
4       s1;
5       ...
6  }
```

Figure 10. Event handling loop example.

The ahead_of() primitive in Fig. 9 defines how to decide index order. If the two indices share the same head label, it recursively checks the order of their tails. If the head labels l_1 and l_2 are different, and there is a path from l_2 to l_1, the first index is ahead. In Fig. 6,

$$\text{ahead\_of}(\mathcal{I}_s(7_2), \mathcal{I}_m(5_2)) = \text{ahead\_of}([4,4,7],[4,5,6,4,5]) = \text{ahead\_of}([4,7],[5,6,4,5]) = true.$$

There are cases where neither execution is ahead of the other if they are in the different branches of a predicate. In this case, the monitor will resynchronize the two executions at the dynamic IPDOM of the predicate.

Dealing With Event Handling Loops. When the user sends a resynchronization signal, the two executions are likely inside some event handling loop, which receives and handles external events. During the independent executions in decoupled mode, the two runs may have received different events, e.g. different numbers of key strokes, causing them to execute a different number of iterations. Index based resynchronization recognizes that the execution that iterated more is ahead[1]. As such, it tries to execute the other that iterated less, but in fact the other execution cannot make progress as it has received all the needed external inputs and expects no more. When the user signals resynchronization, he/she knows that the two executions have received the different inputs, and they should start to receive the same inputs again from then on. Hence, the iteration number differences of the event loop are not important. We introduce a normalization step to remove the excessive entries (in the indices) corresponding to unnecessary iteration differences. The primitive is defined in Fig. 9. It takes three indices, with the first two requiring normalization and the third an auxiliary parameter whose initial value is *nil*, and it produces two normalized indices. The auxiliary parameter represents the current common prefix during computation. According to the rules, it initially compares the two head labels. If different, the differences are not caused by the event loop, so it returns the two input indices as normalized (rule N-INIT-NEQ). Rules N-INIT-EQ and N-EQ-HEADER detect equivalent heads and move it to the tail of the common prefix. In rule N-RM-FIRST, if the two heads are different but the head of the first index is identical to the tail of the prefix, indicating repetitive entries, i.e. loop iterations, the head is removed. Rule N-RM-SECOND is symmetric. Rule N-END states the termination condition, in which the difference is not caused by repetition. The final normalized indices are the common prefix concatenated with the two current indices.

Example. Fig. 10 shows a very simple event loop. Assume it iterates two times and stops at line 5 in the master when

[1] In indexing, an iteration nests within the region of the previous iteration such that the one iterating more has a longer index.

ahead_of : $ExecIndex \times ExecIndex \rightarrow Boolean$

$$\text{ahead\_of}(l_1 \cdot \mathcal{I}_1, l_2 \cdot \mathcal{I}_2) = \begin{cases} false & \texttt{if } l_1 \neq l_2 \wedge \text{ there is not a path from } l_2 \text{ to } l_1; \\ true & \texttt{if } l_1 \neq l_2 \wedge \text{ there is a path from } l_2 \text{ to } l_1; \\ \text{ahead\_of}(\mathcal{I}_1, \mathcal{I}_2) & \texttt{otherwise} \text{ i.e., } l_1 \equiv l_2 \end{cases}$$

normalize : $ExecIndex \times ExecIndex \times ExecIndex \rightarrow ExecIndex \times ExecIndex$

$$\text{normalize}(l_1 \cdot \mathcal{I}_1,\ l_2 \cdot \mathcal{I}_2,\ nil) = \begin{cases} \langle l_1 \cdot \mathcal{I}_1,\ l_2 \cdot \mathcal{I}_2 \rangle & \texttt{if } l_1 \neq l_2 & \text{[N-INIT-NEQ]} \\ \text{normalize}(\mathcal{I}_1,\ \mathcal{I}_2,\ l_1) & \texttt{if } l_1 \equiv l_2 & \text{[N-INIT-EQ]} \end{cases}$$

$$\text{normalize}(l_1 \cdot \mathcal{I}_1,\ l_2 \cdot \mathcal{I}_2,\ \mathcal{I}_p \cdot l_p) = \begin{cases} \langle \mathcal{I}_p \cdot l_p \cdot l_1 \cdot \mathcal{I}_1,\ \mathcal{I}_p \cdot l_p \cdot l_2 \cdot \mathcal{I}_2 \rangle & \texttt{if } l_1 \neq l_2 \wedge l_2 \neq l_p \wedge l_1 \neq l_p & \text{[N-END]} \\ \text{normalize}(l_1 \cdot \mathcal{I}_1,\ \mathcal{I}_2,\ \mathcal{I}_p \cdot l_p) & \texttt{if } l_1 \neq l_2 \wedge l_2 \equiv l_p & \text{[N-RM-SECOND]} \\ \text{normalize}(\mathcal{I}_1,\ l_2 \cdot \mathcal{I}_2,\ \mathcal{I}_p \cdot l_p) & \texttt{if } l_1 \neq l_2 \wedge l_1 \equiv l_p & \text{[N-RM-FIRST]} \\ \text{normalize}(\mathcal{I}_1,\ \mathcal{I}_2,\ \mathcal{I}_p \cdot l_p \cdot l_1) & \texttt{if } l_1 \equiv l_2 & \text{[N-EQ-HEADER]} \end{cases}$$

Figure 9. Resynchronization Primitives.

the user signals resynchronization, and it iterates four times and stops at 3 in the slave, yielding the indices $\mathcal{I}_m = [1, 1, 2, 5]$ and $\mathcal{I}_s = [1, 1, 1, 2, 4]$, respectively. Recall that loop iterations produce consecutive entries in the indices as an iteration directly nests in the region of the previous iteration. We have the following:

$$\begin{aligned} &\text{normalize}(\mathcal{I}_m, \mathcal{I}_s, nil) \\ &= \text{normalize}([1,2,5],\ [1,1,2,4],\ [1]) && \text{[N-INIT-EQ]} \\ &= \text{normalize}([2,5],\ [1,2,4],\ [1,1]) && \text{[N-EQ-HEADER]} \\ &= \text{normalize}([2,5],\ [2,4],\ [1,1]) && \text{[N-RM-SECOND]} \\ &= \text{normalize}([5],\ [4],\ [1,1,2]) && \text{[N-EQ-HEADER]} \\ &= [1,1,2,5],\ [1.1,2,4]) && \text{[N-NED]} \end{aligned}$$

The rules applied are presented on the right. Note that at the second step, the heads of the indices are different, but the second head is the same as the tail of the prefix, indicating repetition. The head is thus removed. Observe that after normalization, the two executions are within the same control dependence region, and the master is ahead.

Overall Resynchronization Procedure. The procedure is informally described as follows. Assume $\mathcal{I}_m$ and $\mathcal{I}_s$ are the indices when a resynchronization signal is received. The monitor first normalizes $\mathcal{I}_m$ and $\mathcal{I}_s$. If one execution is ahead of the other, it is blocked until the other one catches up. If neither is ahead, meaning they are in the two branches of some predicate, the monitor allows both to execute independently until the dynamic IPDOM of the predicate.

4. Handling Practical Challenges

Syscall Policy for Slave Execution in Coupled Mode. In previous discussion, whether the slave should execute a syscall mainly depended on whether the syscall corresponded to one in the master and whether they had different parameters. However, the decision also depends on the type of the syscall. This is reflected by the policy table look up on line 10 of Algorithm 1. For example, we would like to execute user interface (UI) related syscalls such that the slave has its own UI.

We categorize syscalls into 7 groups. Table 3 presents the groups and their policies. There are two possible policies: *execute* and *copy*. The former means that the slave executes the syscall whereas the latter means that the slave copies the result from the master and does not execute the syscall.

Table 3. Category of syscalls and the default policy. 'E' and 'C' stand for execute and copy, respectively.

Category	Description	Policy
Memory	Allocate/free memories (mmap(), munmap(), ...)	E
Process	Create/kill/block processes (fork(), clone(), ...)	E[1]
Open	Open a file descriptor (open(), create(), ...)	E
Input	Read data from a file/environment (read(), stat(), ...)	C
Output	Write data to a file (write(), ...)	C,E[2]
GUI	Special case of network syscalls with X-Windows server	E,C[1,3]
Utility	Nondeterministic library functions (time(), ...)	C

1. there is ID translation during execution.
2. outputs to stdout and UI are executed, others copied.
3. requests and replies are executed and events are copied.

Process management syscalls follow the execute policy. In addition, the slave and the master both manage a mapping between process IDs. Syscalls creating new processes such as fork() and clone() return different process IDs in the two executions. To prevent propagating these different values to other parts of the executions, we would like the corresponding processes in the two runs to have the same IDs. In particular, when clone() is called to create a thread, both runs assign the same logical thread ID to the newly created thread and map the real thread ID returned by the syscall to the logical ID. Our wrapper around clone() then returns the logical ID. Later, when the logical ID is used in other syscalls such as exit(), our wrapper maps it to the original real ID.

Open syscalls also use an execute policy because the descriptors they return may be used by other syscalls such as mmap or when the user introduces differences between the executions. It is possible that the master succeeds in opening a file but the slave fails to open the same file, for instance, when the master creates a file with the O_EXCL option first. In this case, the slave opens a new temporary file. Since I/O syscalls in the slave mostly copy their outcomes from the master, opening a different file will not affect the slave execution.

Most *input/output syscalls* follow the copy policy. One exception is that we *execute* output syscalls emitting to standard output or user interfaces to allow the slave to have its interface. In addition, both the master and the slave record

Table 4. Applications in feature identification.

Program	Feature Description
alpine-1	Send an e-mail
alpine-2	Create a directory in remote imap server
xv	Convert two different bitmap images to jpeg images
smbc	Create a directory in remote samba server
ncmpc	Add a song to playlist

the buffer content of an output syscall and meta information such as the definition point of the buffer, for further analysis, e.g. slicing.

GUI applications in Linux communicate with the X server through sockets. There are three types of messages: *requests*, *replies*, and *events*. Requests are sent from a client to the server to request a service such as creating a window and querying properties. Upon a request, the server sends the requested information with a reply. Events are sent by the server without the corresponding requests, denoting user interactions. Requests/replies are handled in a way similar to process management syscalls, which use the execute policy and ID translation, to provide the proper user interface. The master and the slave must map their window IDs to the same logical ID when the windows correspond to each other. Events have the copy policy, meaning the slave copies events from the master and ignores its own events.

The slave also copies signals from the master in coupled mode, ignoring its own signals except segfaults. We support threads by implementing a deterministic scheduler [31] that allows one thread to execute at a time. This suppresses nondeterminism caused by different thread schedules.

5. Evaluation

We implement a prototype on Pin [26]. It can work on stripped binaries as it can generate dynamic control flow graphs (for indexing). In our experiments, we first quantitatively evaluate the space and time savings by our technique in comparison with offline techniques. We then apply the prototype to three comparative analysis tasks.

5.1 Examined Comparative Tasks

Feature identification. As seen in Sec. 2, feature identification involves locating the portion of a program responsible for a feature [2, 11, 17–19, 34, 35, 46], and this can be done by comparing executions of a program over different inputs [25]. Table 4 presents the full set of examined feature identification tasks, which have appeared in published work [25].

Comparative Debugging. To help developers, we integrate our technique into gdb and provide a few new gdb primitives that allow developers to modify variables and compare the execution with changes to an execution without them. Details on the changes to gdb are presented in a later case study.

Understanding regression. We also apply our technique to executions of an old, working version of a program and a new, failing version to understand regressions.

All the examined bugs are real world bugs from [7, 41]. Table 5 describes them with GNU Savannah bug IDs if any.

Table 5. Subjects in comparative debugging and regression understanding. The regression bugs are tagged with *.

Program	Bug #	Description
grep-1	12128	Numeric parameters are incorrectly interpreted
grep-2	16567	-i option does not work with a regular expression
grep-3	27919	
grep-4	27919	
grep-5	21199	-w option causes incorrect search results
make-1	25493	Incorrectly handle dependencies in rules
make-2	18622	User-defined rules conflict with default rules
tar-1	508199	Cannot restore files from backup
tar-2	598636	Cannot handle broken symbolic links
tar-3	637085	Cannot handle longer filenames
grep-6*		Search incorrect if -i, -n options are used together
grep-7*	36567	-i does not work with multi-byte characters
grep-8*		
find-1*	34976	Fail to save working directory
find-2*	29949	-execdir does not change working directory
make-3*	31155	Incorrect order in parsing patterns
make-4*	39310	Commandline options are applied multiple times
rm*		-I, –interactive=once does not work same
seq*		[seq 1 3 1] treated as [seq 1 3]
cp*		–no-preserve=mode exits 1
cut*		Incorrect error message
expr*		Incorrect computation with negative value

5.2 Disk Usage and Performance

In this experiment, we examine the impact of dual execution on the running time and disk usage, when compared with offline techniques. We first collect traces of the two executions for all the subjects (in the three tasks). We then perform offline comparison. The results are used as the base line. We then use our prototype to generate difference traces on the fly and compare the results. We used an Intel Core i7 machine running Arch Linux 3.15.5 with 16GB RAM.

Table 6 presents the trace size comparison. The Traces column shows the size of full traces. The Diffs (W/O Dual Exec.) column shows the size after offline trace comparison. The Diffs (W/ Dual Exec.) column shows the size of difference traces generated online. The % Full column shows the size of the difference traces as a percentage of the full traces. Note that we do not use any trace compression technique. However, our technique is orthogonal to those techniques and users can combine the techniques to achieve smaller traces. Also many trace compression techniques targets specific trace abstractions but our technique can be used on a fine-grained trace including data and control dependencies.

Observe that using dual execution always produces much smaller (difference) traces than the *full traces* (5.41% on average). This is because the full traces include every instruction of both executions, while dual execution only records differences. For tasks comparing executions, there is often substantial similarity between the executions. There is also a lot of similarity across executions from initialization and configuration behavior that is irrelevant to the analysis tasks.

Dual execution also consistently produces smaller differences than the differences by offline comparison. This occurs because many applications have nondeterministic behaviors

Table 6. Trace size comparison.

Program	W/O Dual Exec.		W/ Dual Exec.	
	Traces	Diffs	Diffs	% Full
seq	62MB	15MB	15MB	24.19
make-3	1.8GB	409MB	358MB	19.42
make-4	4.6GB	887MB	886MB	18.81
grep-7	4.0GB	978MB	653MB	15.94
find-1	4.2GB	562MB	541MB	12.58
find-2	4.0GB	462MB	447MB	10.91
grep-8	4.0GB	432MB	424MB	10.35
grep-5	12.5GB	2.7GB	1.0GB	8.00
cut	79MB	6.0MB	6.0MB	7.59
grep-4	13GB	438MB	428MB	3.22
rm	3.8GB	117MB	117MB	3.00
xv	14GB	559MB	380MB	2.65
cp	68MB	1.4MB	1.3MB	1.91
tar-1	377MB	17MB	6.8MB	1.80
ncmpc	6GB	120MB	93MB	1.51
tar-2	457MB	6MB	4.0MB	0.88
smbc	55GB	627MB	432MB	0.77
make-1	15.7GB	1.5GB	105.2MB	0.65
expr	58MB	306KB	305KB	0.51
make-2	7.3GB	104.9MB	32.2MB	0.43
alpine-2	57GB	320MB	205MB	0.35
grep-3	14GB	41.2MB	40.7MB	0.28
grep-6	4.0GB	9.1MB	7.7MB	0.19
tar-3	11.4GB	35MB	6.4MB	0.055
grep-1	10.6GB	8.6MB	832KB	0.0074
alpine-1	60GB	344MB	170MB	0.0003
grep-2	14.8GB	3.4KB	1KB	0.000006
			Geometric Mean	5.41

Table 7. Execution time comparison.

Program	Native	W/O Dual Execution			W/ Dual Execution		
		Tracing	Comp	Total_1	Total_2	$\text{Tot}_2/\text{Tot}_1$	Tot_2/Nat
expr	.002s	3s	0.5s	4s	6s	1.50	3000
seq	.002s	4s	0.5s	5s	7s	1.40	3500
cut	.002s	4s	0.7s	5s	7s	1.40	3500
grep-6	.01s	10s	29s	39s	49s	1.26	4900
cp	.01s	4s	0.5s	5s	6s	1.20	600
make-3	.01s	19s	21s	40s	36s	0.90	3600
grep-7	.01s	11s	42s	53s	42s	0.79	4200
find-2	.03s	11s	39s	50s	38s	0.76	1267
find-1	.02s	12s	46s	58s	44s	0.76	2200
ncmpc	14s	1m 12s	1m 3s	2m 15s	1m 42s	0.76	*
tar-1	.03s	18s	1s	19s	12s	0.63	400
tar-2	.01s	20s	2s	22s	12s	0.55	1200
grep-5	.05s	1m 16s	1m 45s	3m 1s	1m 32s	0.51	1840
make-4	.01s	42s	38s	80s	40s	0.50	4000
grep-8	.01s	12s	45s	57s	28s	0.49	2800
rm	2s	11s	32s	43s	19s	0.44	*
tar-3	.02s	1m 0s	1m 58s	2m 58s	1m 15s	0.42	3750
xv	16s	2m 20s	3m 42s	6m 2s	2m 31s	0.42	*
grep-3	.03s	1m 10s	1m 9s	2m 19s	45s	0.32	1500
grep-2	.02s	1m 16s	1m 11s	2m 27s	47s	0.32	2350
grep-4	.02s	1m 6s	59s	2m 5s	38s	0.30	1900
make-2	.03s	52s	39s	1m 31s	27s	0.30	900
smbc	40s	5m 32s	7m 2s	12m 34s	3m 10s	0.25	*
grep-1	.02s	1m 0s	1m 15s	2m 15s	26s	0.19	1300
alpine-2	16s	5m 20s	6m 31s	9m 51s	1m 47s	0.18	*
alpine-1	12s	6m 42s	8m 59s	15m 41s	2m 14s	0.14	*
make-1	.01s	1m 28s	1m 59s	3m 27s	20s	0.10	2000
					Geometric Mean	0.49	2022

that the user cannot control, which introduce additional differences. For example, `alpine` reads and uses the system time quite often, causing a lot of non-deterministic differences. Dual execution eliminates such differences by sharing system events as much as possible.

Table 7 presents the time comparison. The Native column shows the original native execution time, i.e. sum of the master and the slave. Tracing and Comp present the time taken for whole execution tracing and offline comparison. Total_1 is their sum. Total_2 presents the time for dual execution. The last two columns shows the comparison. Running times of interactive programs are not comparable against Native, denoted by '*'. Entries in the table are sorted by $\text{Tot}_2/\text{Tot}_1$. A lower number means that dual execution improved the running time.

Observe that the time spent on dual execution is almost always lower than the time for full execution tracing and offline comparison, 0.49% on average. The benefits are more obvious for larger programs and longer runs. These improvements are mostly due to the smaller traces that are actually recorded when using dual execution. The slowdown of our system is 2022× relative to native on average. It is more suitable for inhouse testing and debugging.

5.3 Case Studies

5.3.1 Feature Identification

In this case study, we use our prototype to identify 5 functional features from 4 real world applications. We use our prototype to trace and compare executions and use an offline technique similar to [25] to identify functions from the trace. For each case, we compare two executions that exercise the feature with different inputs by using our prototype, and we identify the relevant differences, which are supposed to correspond to the features. For example, in alpine-1 case, we compare two executions sending two different mails. The differences between the executions should be the feature responsible for sending different emails if there is no nondeterminism that is not relevant to the input differences. Our prototype suppresses those nondeterminism. Once we get the changes, we consider the highest function(s) on the call graph that can cover all the differences to be the functional component for the feature. The differences generated by our tool allow us to precisely locate the correct functions. For example, all the differences in `xv` can be covered by two functions with the names of `LoadBMP()` and `SaveJPEG()`, which clearly indicate they are the intended functions. For `alpine`, we have located `call_mailer()` for email sending and `add_new_folder()` for directory creation. For `smbc`, `RcreateDir()`. For `ncmpc`, `mpd_async_send_command_v()`.

All these applications contain event handling loops that behave differently between two executions because different user input timings or packet arrival timings perturb the loop behavior, causing undesirable execution differences.

For the `xv` case, from the results in Table 6, 559MB-380MB=179MB trace differences are due to such nondeterminism, which largely originates from an event han-

```
1   _XReply() {
2       while (1) {
3           reply = poll_for_reply();
4           if (reply->sequence == expected) break;
5           ...
6   }
7   poll_for_reply() {
8       while (poll() == -1) ...;
9   }
```

Figure 11. Simplified event handling loop in libX11

dling loop for reply messages from the X server, as shown in Fig. 11. In the de-coupled mode, the different sequences of X messages make the loop at line 2 iterate different times. As a result, full traces cannot be properly aligned, leading to lots of undesirable differences during offline comparison. In contrast, the normalization step in the re-synchronization mode in our technique suppresses such differences.

5.3.2 Comparative Debugging Using GDB.

Table 8. New gdb commands supported by dual execution.

Command	Interface
`dslice`	`dslice [instruction address] [instance]`
`dset`	`dset [variable] [value1] [value2]`
`dprint`	`dprint [variable]`

We integrated our prototype with gdb and provided new debugging commands as shown in Table 8. `dslice` generates a dual slice [47] of the given instruction and instance. The slice contains execution differences causally related to the difference at the given slicing criterion. `dset` sets a variable in two executions to different values; `dprint` shows two values of a variable side by side. Basic commands such as setting a breakpoint and continuing the execution are applied to both executions by default. We then used the enhanced gdb to debug the 10 non-regression failures. Each required fewer than 15 manual steps to capture the causality of the failure. We also tried to use the vanilla gdb to achieve the same results for three cases, `grep-5`, `tar-2`, and `tar-3`, but failed due to the prohibitively tedious manual interactions involved.

Next, we present our experience with the `grep-5` bug. The "-w" option in `grep` selects lines containing whole word matches. The buggy program prints out only a substring of a matched line. We launched the buggy program in our enhanced gdb. Two processes were automatically created and run in coupled mode. We set a breakpoint at prtext(), which printed the incorrect output. Few places in the immediate source code were affected by the "-w" option; the match_word variable was one of them. It had value 1 in the buggy run. We wanted to perturb its value and observe the effect, and more important, the causality. We used `dset` to set it to 0 and 1 in the two respective runs. At the breakpoint, we observed output differences: the execution with match_word set to 0 produced the whole line. We then used `dslice` to slice from this output difference. Fig. 12 presents the resulting dual slice. The results from the correct run are on the left side and

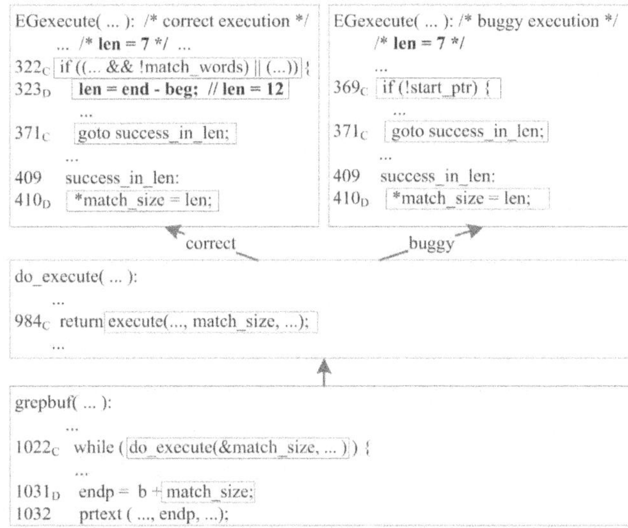

Figure 12. Slicing results for `grep`

those from the buggy run are on the right. do_execution() and grepbuf() are common to both executions, though they have different dependencies in EGexecution(). The subscript C and D on line numbers represent control and data dependencies respectively. The bug manifests when prtext() prints different results at line 1032 in grepbuf() because of the differences in the variable endp. The slice result shows that the two executions have different match_size values, 12 versus 7. It also shows that the control dependencies include do_execute(), execute(), and EGexecution(). Observe that in the correct run, len is defined at line 324, which eventually allows printing the whole line, whereas there is no such definition in the buggy run. Therefore, the root cause is that such a definition is missing when the option is set, which is confirmed by the bug report.

Next, we show our experience in doing the same comparative debugging with the vanilla gdb. We started two executions of the buggy program and attached them to two separate gdb instances. Then we set the match_word variable to 0 and 1 again. But the challenges lie in monitoring the propagation of the value differences. We first tried to single-step the two executions. But the definition point of match_word and the output point are separated by a substantial amount of computation in EGexecute(). Even worse, there were control flow differences due to our perturbations such that we had to somehow manually align the two executions. The process quickly became unmanageable. Another attempted option was to identify related variables and set break-points and watch-points. However, we could not solely use watch-points as many related variables were stack variables. However, using break points was also problematic. In particular, when we set a break point at the access to match_size in do_execute(), we found that the access occurs more than 200 times and only the 150th instance shows a difference across the two runs. The process is prohibitively tedious and error-prone. In con-

Table 9. Dual slicing regressions.

Program	# of Instr. in differences	# of Instr. in slice	Time
grep-6	44K	35K	0.1s
grep-7	15K	7.7K	16s
grep-8	213K	76K	6s
find-1	42K	2.0K	6s
find-2	172K	120K	5s
make-3	888K	127K	4s
make-4	753K	108K	3s
rm	3.4K	214	1.5s
seq	902	516	0.2s
cp	2179	332	0.05s
cut	952	541	0.05s
expr	787	62	0.03s

trast, our new commands and the underlying dual execution engine make interactive comparative-debugging feasible.

We also point out that the enhanced gdb is more flexible than a stand-alone slicing tool as it allows interactively perturbing program state at any point.

5.3.3 Understanding Regressions

In this case study, we applied an existing dual slicing [47] tool on the difference traces generated by the dual execution engine to understand regressions. As mentioned earlier, dual slicing computes the execution differences related to the difference at the slicing criterion. In the experiment, we use a text differencing tool to generate syntactic mappings between statements in the two program versions and propagate such mappings down to the instruction level to facilitate our engine. The slicing criteria are output differences. In the case of crashing bugs, they are the pointer dereferences. The results are shown in Table 9. The second column shows the total instructions in the difference traces, which are already a very small portion of the full traces (Table 6). The third column shows the slice size. Observe that the slices are much smaller than the differences for most cases. We also confirm that all of them include the root causes. We suspect the slice sizes can be further reduced if we use a better syntactic mapping algorithm. But that is beyond our scope.

6. Related Work

Execution comparison. Execution comparison is used in debugging [1, 3, 37, 50], concurrency failure understanding [47], vulnerability detection [24], and binary reuse [25]. Comparative causality [41] produces bug explanations by replacing program states on the fly. Sieve [36] compares traces from program versions to identify the root causes of regressions. Hoffman et al. proposed a semantic-aware trace analysis [22] for understanding executions, particularly identifying the cause of regressions. In comparison to these works, the dual execution engine avoids generating full traces. Instead, it performs online comparison and only records differences.

Execution Replication and Replay. Execution replication has been widely studied [4–6, 10, 13, 42]. The premise is similar to n-version programming [12], which runs different implementations of the same service specification in parallel. Then, voting is used to produce a common result tolerating occasional faults. Vandiver et al. [43] proposed a technique that handles Byzantine faults in database transaction processing using replicated systems. Chun et al. [14] run diversified replicas on multi-core processors to handle Byzantine faults. There are also many security applications [9, 16, 27, 38] of n-variant execution. McDermott et al. [28] proposed a defense technique based on logical replication. They re-execute commands on each replicated system and detect differences among the replicas. TightLip [49] runs a replicated process in parallel to an original process and analyzes the replica to prevent information leakage. There is also a large body of works in execution replay [23, 30, 32, 33, 39, 44] that aim to faithfully reproduce an execution. Compared to these works, our technique allows differences in executions and handles the complex consequences of these differences.

Viennot et al. [45] proposed a technique that replays events from one version of a program with another version of the program. It hence also allows sharing syscalls across different executions. However, it requires exploration steps to find the best replay. In contrast, our technique exploits fine-grained traces and can align executions on-the-fly.

Execution Alignment. Alignment techniques identify corresponding points [21, 21, 29, 48] and memory locations [40] across different executions. Xin et al. proposed Execution Indexing (EI) [48] to precisely locate corresponding points across executions. Our technique is built on EI. We have overcome many new challenges such as lockstep synchronization, resynchronization, and syscall dispatching for our purpose.

7. Conclusion

We develop a dual execution engine that allows two executions to proceed simultaneously in coupled mode, in which they share system inputs, or in decoupled mode, in which different inputs can be provided. On the fly comparison identifies instruction level differences between executions for later analysis. Our experiments on three comparative analyses demonstrate the engine is highly effective.

Acknowledgments

This research has been supported in part by DARPA under contract 12011593 and under cooperative agreement HR0011-12-2-0006, and by NSF under awards 0845870, 0917007, 1320326 and 1409668. Any opinions, findings, and conclusions in this paper are those of the authors only and do not necessarily reflect the views of DARPA and NSF.

References

[1] David Abramson, Ian Foster, John Michalakes, and Rok Sosič. Relative debugging: A new methodology for debugging scientific applications. *Commun. ACM*, 39(11):69–77, November 1996.

[2] G. Antoniol and Y.-G. Gueheneuc. Feature identification: a novel approach and a case study. In *Proceedings of the IEEE*

International Conference on Software Maintenance (ICSM), 2005.

[3] Ansuman Banerjee, Abhik Roychoudhury, Johannes A. Harlie, and Zhenkai Liang. Golden implementation driven software debugging. In *Proceedings of the Eighteenth ACM SIGSOFT International Symposium on Foundations of Software Engineering*, FSE '10, pages 177–186, New York, NY, USA, 2010. ACM.

[4] Emery D. Berger and Benjamin G. Zorn. Diehard: Probabilistic memory safety for unsafe languages. In *Proceedings of the 2006 ACM SIGPLAN Conference on Programming Language Design and Implementation*, PLDI '06, pages 158–168, New York, NY, USA, 2006. ACM.

[5] Kenneth P. Birman. Replication and fault-tolerance in the isis system. *SIGOPS Oper. Syst. Rev.*, 19(5):79–86, December 1985.

[6] Dave Black, C. Low, and Santosh K. Shrivastava. The voltan application programming environment for fail-silent processes. *Distributed Systems Engineering*, 5(2):66–77, 1998.

[7] Marcel Böhme and Abhik Roychoudhury. Corebench: studying complexity of regression errors. In *ISSTA*, pages 105–115, 2014.

[8] David Brumley, Juan Caballero, Zhenkai Liang, James Newsome, and Dawn Song. Towards automatic discovery of deviations in binary implementations with applications to error detection and fingerprint generation. In *Proceedings of 16th USENIX Security Symposium on USENIX Security Symposium*, SS'07, pages 15:1–15:16, Berkeley, CA, USA, 2007. USENIX Association.

[9] Danilo Bruschi, Lorenzo Cavallaro, and Andrea Lanzi. Diversified process replicæ for defeating memory error exploits. *Performance, Computing, and Communications Conference, 2002. 21st IEEE International*, 0:434–441, 2007.

[10] Miguel Castro, Rodrigo Rodrigues, and Barbara Liskov. Base: Using abstraction to improve fault tolerance. *ACM Trans. Comput. Syst.*, 21(3):236–269, August 2003.

[11] Kunrong Chen and Vaclav Rajlich. Ripples: Tool for change in legacy software. In *Proceedings of the IEEE International Conference on Software Maintenance (ICSM)*, 2001.

[12] Liming Chen and A Avizienis. N-version programminc: A fault-tolerance approach to rellablllty of software operatlon. In *Fault-Tolerant Computing, 1995, Highlights from Twenty-Five Years., Twenty-Fifth International Symposium on*, pages 113–, Jun 1995.

[13] M. Chereque, D. Powell, P. Reynier, J.-L. Richier, and J. Voiron. Active replication in delta-4. In *Fault-Tolerant Computing, 1992. FTCS-22. Digest of Papers., Twenty-Second International Symposium on*, pages 28–37, July 1992.

[14] Byung-Gon Chun, Petros Maniatis, and Scott Shenker. Diverse replication for single-machine byzantine-fault tolerance. In *USENIX 2008 Annual Technical Conference on Annual Technical Conference*, ATC'08, pages 287–292, Berkeley, CA, USA, 2008. USENIX Association.

[15] Asaf Cidon, Kanthi Nagaraj, Sachin Katti, and Pramod Viswanath. Flashback: Decoupled lightweight wireless control. In *Proceedings of the ACM SIGCOMM 2012 Conference on Applications, Technologies, Architectures, and Protocols for Computer Communication*, SIGCOMM '12, pages 223–234, New York, NY, USA, 2012. ACM.

[16] Benjamin Cox, David Evans, Adrian Filipi, Jonathan Rowanhill, Wei Hu, Jack Davidson, John Knight, Anh Nguyen-Tuong, and Jason Hiser. N-variant systems: A secretless framework for security through diversity. In *Proceedings of the 15th Conference on USENIX Security Symposium - Volume 15*, USENIX-SS'06, Berkeley, CA, USA, 2006. USENIX Association.

[17] Dennis Edwards, Sharon Simmons, and Norman Wilde. An approach to feature location in distributed systems. *Journal of Systems and Software*, 2006.

[18] Thomas Eisenbarth, Rainer Koschke, and Daniel Simon. Locating features in source code. *IEEE Transactions on Software Engineering*, 2003.

[19] A.D. Eisenberg and K. De Volder. Dynamic feature traces: finding features in unfamiliar code. In *Proceedings of the IEEE International Conference on Software Maintenance (ICSM)*, 2005.

[20] Andrew D. Ferguson, Peter Bodik, Srikanth Kandula, Eric Boutin, and Rodrigo Fonseca. Jockey: Guaranteed job latency in data parallel clusters. In *Proceedings of the 7th ACM European Conference on Computer Systems*, EuroSys '12, pages 99–112, New York, NY, USA, 2012. ACM.

[21] Liang Guo, Abhik Roychoudhury, and Tao Wang. Accurately choosing execution runs for software fault localization. In *Proceedings of the 15th International Conference on Compiler Construction*, CC'06, pages 80–95, Berlin, Heidelberg, 2006. Springer-Verlag.

[22] Kevin J. Hoffman, Patrick Eugster, and Suresh Jagannathan. Semantics-aware trace analysis. In *Proceedings of the 2009 ACM SIGPLAN Conference on Programming Language Design and Implementation*, PLDI '09, pages 453–464, New York, NY, USA, 2009. ACM.

[23] Derek R. Hower and Mark D. Hill. Rerun: Exploiting episodes for lightweight memory race recording. In *Proceedings of the 35th Annual International Symposium on Computer Architecture*, ISCA '08, pages 265–276, Washington, DC, USA, 2008. IEEE Computer Society.

[24] Noah M. Johnson, Juan Caballero, Kevin Zhijie Chen, Stephen McCamant, Pongsin Poosankam, Daniel Reynaud, and Dawn Song. Differential slicing: Identifying causal execution differences for security applications. In *Proceedings of the 2011 IEEE Symposium on Security and Privacy*, SP '11, pages 347–362, Washington, DC, USA, 2011. IEEE Computer Society.

[25] Dohyeong Kim, William N. Sumner, Xiangyu Zhang, Dongyan Xu, and Hira Agrawal. Reuse-oriented reverse engineering of functional components from x86 binaries. In *Proceedings of the 36th International Conference on Software Engineering*, ICSE 2014, pages 1128–1139, New York, NY, USA, 2014. ACM.

[26] Chi-Keung Luk, Robert Cohn, Robert Muth, Harish Patil, Artur Klauser, Geoff Lowney, Steven Wallace, Vijay Janapa Reddi, and Kim Hazelwood. Pin: Building customized program analysis tools with dynamic instrumentation. In *Proceedings of the 2005 ACM SIGPLAN Conference on Programming*

Language Design and Implementation, PLDI '05, pages 190–200, New York, NY, USA, 2005. ACM.

[27] Vitaliy B. Lvin, Gene Novark, Emery D. Berger, and Benjamin G. Zorn. Archipelago: Trading address space for reliability and security. In *Proceedings of the 13th International Conference on Architectural Support for Programming Languages and Operating Systems*, ASPLOS XIII, pages 115–124, New York, NY, USA, 2008. ACM.

[28] J. McDermott, R. Gelinas, and S. Ornstein. Doc, wyatt, and virgil: prototyping storage jamming defenses. In *Computer Security Applications Conference, 1997. Proceedings., 13th Annual*, pages 265–273, Dec 1997.

[29] Subrata Mitra, Ignacio Laguna, Dong H. Ahn, Saurabh Bagchi, Martin Schulz, and Todd Gamblin. Accurate application progress analysis for large-scale parallel debugging. In *PLDI*, page 23, 2014.

[30] Pablo Montesinos, Matthew Hicks, Samuel T. King, and Josep Torrellas. Capo: A software-hardware interface for practical deterministic multiprocessor replay. In *Proceedings of the 14th International Conference on Architectural Support for Programming Languages and Operating Systems*, ASPLOS XIV, pages 73–84, New York, NY, USA, 2009. ACM.

[31] Madanlal Musuvathi, Shaz Qadeer, and Thomas Ball. Chess: A systematic testing tool for concurrent software. Technical Report MSR-TR-2007-149, Microsoft Research, November 2007.

[32] Satish Narayanasamy, Cristiano Pereira, and Brad Calder. Recording shared memory dependencies using strata. *SIGPLAN Not.*, 41(11):229–240, October 2006.

[33] Soyeon Park, Yuanyuan Zhou, Weiwei Xiong, Zuoning Yin, Rini Kaushik, Kyu H. Lee, and Shan Lu. Pres: Probabilistic replay with execution sketching on multiprocessors. In *Proceedings of the ACM SIGOPS 22Nd Symposium on Operating Systems Principles*, SOSP '09, pages 177–192, New York, NY, USA, 2009. ACM.

[34] Maksym Petrenko and VáClav Rajlich. Concept location using program dependencies and information retrieval (depir). *Information and Software Technology*, 2013.

[35] D. Poshyvanyk, Y.-G. Gueheneuc, A. Marcus, G. Antoniol, and V. Rajlich. Feature location using probabilistic ranking of methods based on execution scenarios and information retrieval. *IEEE Transactions on Software Engineering*, 2007.

[36] Murali Krishna Ramanathan, Ananth Grama, and Suresh Jagannathan. Sieve: A tool for automatically detecting variations across program versions. *2011 26th IEEE/ACM International Conference on Automated Software Engineering (ASE 2011)*, 0:241–252, 2006.

[37] Manos Renieris and Steven P. Reiss. Fault localization with nearest neighbor queries. In *ASE*, pages 30–39, 2003.

[38] Babak Salamat. *Multi-variant Execution: Run-time Defense Against Malicious Code Injection Attacks.* PhD thesis, Irvine, CA, USA, 2009. AAI3359500.

[39] Francesco Sorrentino, Azadeh Farzan, and P. Madhusudan. Penelope: Weaving threads to expose atomicity violations. In *Proceedings of the Eighteenth ACM SIGSOFT International Symposium on Foundations of Software Engineering*, FSE '10, pages 37–46, New York, NY, USA, 2010. ACM.

[40] William N. Sumner and Xiangyu Zhang. Memory indexing: Canonicalizing addresses across executions. In *Proceedings of the Eighteenth ACM SIGSOFT International Symposium on Foundations of Software Engineering*, FSE '10, pages 217–226, New York, NY, USA, 2010. ACM.

[41] William N. Sumner and Xiangyu Zhang. Comparative causality: Explaining the differences between executions. In *Proceedings of the 2013 International Conference on Software Engineering*, ICSE '13, pages 272–281, Piscataway, NJ, USA, 2013. IEEE Press.

[42] A Tulley and S.K. Shrivastava. Preventing state divergence in replicated distributed programs. In *Reliable Distributed Systems, 1990. Proceedings., Ninth Symposium on*, pages 104–113, Oct 1990.

[43] Ben Vandiver, Hari Balakrishnan, Barbara Liskov, and Samuel Madden. Tolerating Byzantine Faults in Transaction Processing Systems Using Commit Barrier Scheduling. In *ACM SOSP*, Stevenson, WA, October 2007.

[44] Kaushik Veeraraghavan, Dongyoon Lee, Benjamin Wester, Jessica Ouyang, Peter M. Chen, Jason Flinn, and Satish Narayanasamy. Doubleplay: Parallelizing sequential logging and replay. *ACM Trans. Comput. Syst.*, 30(1):3:1–3:24, February 2012.

[45] Nicolas Viennot, Siddharth Nair, and Jason Nieh. Transparent mutable replay for multicore debugging and patch validation. In *Proceedings of the Eighteenth International Conference on Architectural Support for Programming Languages and Operating Systems*, ASPLOS '13, pages 127–138, New York, NY, USA, 2013. ACM.

[46] Jinshui Wang, Xin Peng, Zhenchang Xing, and Wenyun Zhao. Improving feature location practice with multi-faceted interactive exploration. In *Proceedings of the 2013 International Conference on Software Engineering (ICSE)*, 2013.

[47] Dasarath Weeratunge, Xiangyu Zhang, William N. Sumner, and Suresh Jagannathan. Analyzing concurrency bugs using dual slicing. In *Proceedings of the 19th International Symposium on Software Testing and Analysis*, ISSTA '10, pages 253–264, New York, NY, USA, 2010. ACM.

[48] Bin Xin, William N. Sumner, and Xiangyu Zhang. Efficient program execution indexing. In *Proceedings of the 2008 ACM SIGPLAN Conference on Programming Language Design and Implementation*, PLDI '08, pages 238–248, New York, NY, USA, 2008. ACM.

[49] Aydan R. Yumerefendi, Benjamin Mickle, and Landon P. Cox. Tightlip: Keeping applications from spilling the beans. In *Proceedings of the 4th USENIX Conference on Networked Systems Design & Implementation*, NSDI'07, pages 12–12, Berkeley, CA, USA, 2007. USENIX Association.

[50] Andreas Zeller. Yesterday, my program worked. today, it does not. why? In *Proceedings of the 7th European Software Engineering Conference Held Jointly with the 7th ACM SIGSOFT International Symposium on Foundations of Software Engineering*, ESEC/FSE-7, pages 253–267, London, UK, UK, 1999. Springer-Verlag.

VARAN the Unbelievable

An Efficient N-version Execution Framework

Petr Hosek   Cristian Cadar

Department of Computing
Imperial College London
{p.hosek, c.cadar}@imperial.ac.uk

Abstract

With the widespread availability of multi-core processors, running multiple diversified variants or several different versions of an application in parallel is becoming a viable approach for increasing the reliability and security of software systems. The key component of such N-version execution (NVX) systems is a runtime monitor that enables the execution of multiple versions in parallel.

Unfortunately, existing monitors impose either a large performance overhead or rely on intrusive kernel-level changes. Moreover, none of the existing solutions scales well with the number of versions, since the runtime monitor acts as a performance bottleneck.

In this paper, we introduce VARAN, an NVX framework that combines selective binary rewriting with a novel event-streaming architecture to significantly reduce performance overhead and scale well with the number of versions, without relying on intrusive kernel modifications.

Our evaluation shows that VARAN can run NVX systems based on popular C10k network servers with only a modest performance overhead, and can be effectively used to increase software reliability using techniques such as transparent failover, live sanitization and multi-revision execution.

Categories and Subject Descriptors D.4.5 [*Operating Systems*]: Reliability—Fault-tolerance

General Terms Reliability, Performance

Keywords N-version execution; selective binary rewriting; event streaming; transparent failover; multi-revision execution; live sanitization; record-replay

ASPLOS '15, March 14–18, 2015, Istanbul, Turkey.

ACM 978-1-4503-2835-7/15/03...$15.00.
http://dx.doi.org/10.1145/2694344.2694390

1. Introduction

Recent years have seen a growing interest in using diversity as a way to increase the reliability and security of software systems. One form of software diversity that has attracted significant interest from the research community is the idea of running multiple diversified versions of a program in parallel in order to survive bugs and detect security attacks [5, 10, 13, 14, 40, 44, 48]. In essence, diversity can offer probabilistic guarantees that at least one variant survives a bug, or that a security attack will be flagged by divergent behaviour across variants.[1]

On the security side, these diversified variants are constructed in such a way as to reduce the probability of an attack succeeding in all of them. For example, one may generate versions with stacks growing in opposite directions [40] to prevent attacks whose success depends on the stack layout.

On the reliability side, which forms the main focus of this paper, these diversified versions are either automatically-generated variants, multiple revisions of the same application, or different programs implementing the same interface. For example, one may run in parallel multiple variants that employ complementary thread schedules to survive concurrency errors [44], multiple versions of the same software to survive update bugs [21], or multiple web browsers to benefit from the fact that many errors do not affect all browser implementations [47]. In this paper, we show that running multiple versions in parallel can be used in other reliability scenarios, such as running expensive error detectors ("sanitizers") during deployment.

To enable these scenarios, a monitor process coordinates the parallel execution of these variants and synchronises their execution, making them appear as a single application to any outside entities. While synchronisation can be performed at different levels, the most common approach is to do it at the level of system calls, for two main reasons: first, many existing diversification transformations, such as the ones discussed above, do not change the sequence of system calls (the program's *external behaviour*), and the ordering is often preserved even across different software revisions [21]. Sec-

[1] The terms *version* and *variant* are used interchangeably.

ond, system calls are the main way in which the application communicates with the outside environment, and therefore must be virtualised in order to enable the multiple versions to act as one to the outside world.

The main challenge in implementing an NVX monitor at the system call level is the trade-off between performance, security, flexibility and ease of debugging. Many implementations [7, 21, 40] use the `ptrace` mechanism offered by most UNIX-based operating systems. While easy-to-use and not requiring kernel modifications, `ptrace` is slow, and these systems see performance degradations of up to two orders of magnitude. An alternative approach is to implement the monitor in kernel space [13], which is much faster, but requires kernel patches and/or new kernel modules, and the monitor must be run in privileged mode. Furthermore, none of these approaches scales well with the number of variants (as the monitor is both a communication and synchronisation bottleneck), none are debug-friendly (`ptrace` disallows the use of *GDB*, while kernel debugging has its well-known set of limitations) and none of them have been designed to be flexible with respect to small variations in system call sequences (which can occur for certain diversification transformations and across software revisions).

In this paper, we propose VARAN,[2] a novel architecture for implementing NVX monitors. VARAN monitors operate at the system call level, run in user space (and therefore in unprivileged mode), introduce a small performance overhead for popular C10k network servers[3] and scale well with the number of versions, and provide a flexible mechanism for handling small divergences in the system call sequences issued across versions.

The rest of this paper is structured as follows. Section 2 gives a high-level overview of our approach and Section 3 presents our prototype implementation in detail. Then, Section 4 evaluates our prototype on a set of micro- and macrobenchmarks, Section 5 shows the applicability to different application scenarios, and Section 6 discusses the main implications of our design. Finally, Section 7 presents related work and Section 8 concludes.

2. Overview

Two key aspects influence the performance and flexibility of an NVX system: system call interception and version coordination. We discuss each in turn below.

2.1 System call interception

The biggest downside of existing system call monitors based on the `ptrace` interface is the high performance overhead [21, 33, 40]. For each system call performed by each version, execution must switch to the monitor process, which has to perform several additional system calls in order to copy buffers to and from the version being monitored, nullify the system call, *etc.*

For CPU-intensive applications which perform few system calls, this overhead will be amortised, translating into a modest overall slowdown. However, for heavily I/O-bound applications, the slowdown can be up to two orders of magnitude, which is unacceptable for many real-world deployments. Consequently, in order to implement a system call monitor with acceptable overhead even for heavily I/O-bound applications, we need to eliminate context switching to the monitor and back during interception and eliminate the need for additional system calls. This is accomplished through a combination of selective binary rewriting and an interprocess communication mechanism based on a fast shared memory ring buffer.

Whenever code is loaded into memory, VARAN scans each code page to selectively rewrite all system calls with jump instructions to dedicated handlers. Section 3.2 discusses in detail the main steps and challenges associated with this binary rewriting approach.

To eliminate the need for additional system calls during interception, VARAN uses a shared ring buffer to communicate between versions. This ring buffer is heavily optimised for performance: it is stored in memory, allows largely lock-free communication, and does not require the dispatch of events to different queues. These aspects are discussed in detail in Section 3.3.

2.2 Event-streaming architecture

In prior NVX systems, versions are typically run in lockstep, with a centralised monitor coordinating and virtualising their execution. Essentially, at each system call, the versions pass control to the monitor, which waits until all versions reach the same system call. Once this happens, the monitor executes the system call and communicates the result to each individual version. If two or more versions try to break the lockstep by executing different system calls, the monitor needs to either terminate the entire application or continue executing a subset of the versions in lockstep.

This approach has two key disadvantages. First, the centralised monitor is a bottleneck, which can have a significant impact on performance. Note that in addition to the synchronisation overhead, this centralised monitor makes the NVX application execute at the speed of the slowest individual version.

Second, this approach is totally inflexible to any divergence in the sequence of system calls executed across versions. This is an issue both when running automatically-diversified variants, where certain transformations may affect the external behaviour, and when running existing software revisions, where changes in the sequences of system calls can occur between revisions.

[2] VARAN's name comes from the scientific name *Varanus*, commonly known as the *monitor* lizard. Varan is also a name of the Kaiju monster that first appeared in the 1958 movie *Varan the Unbelievable*.

[3] Numeronym used for servers capable of concurrently handling ten thousand connections.

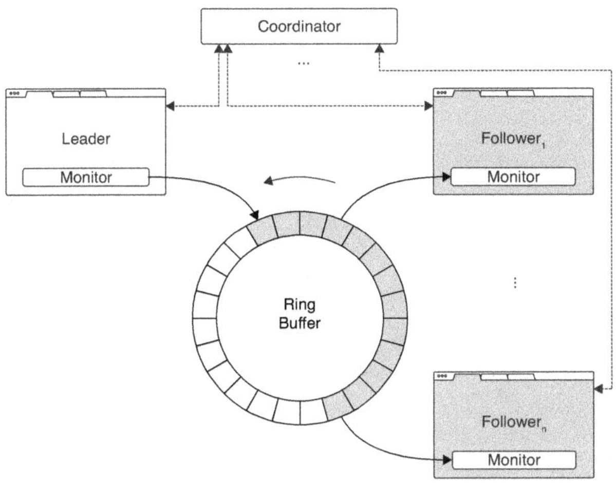

Figure 1. The event-streaming architecture of VARAN.

To address these limitations, VARAN uses a new approach which we call *event streaming*. In this decentralised architecture, depicted in Figure 1, one of the versions is designated as the *leader*, while the others are *followers*. During execution, the leader records all events into a shared ring buffer, which are later read by followers to mimic the leader's external behaviour (§3.3). Events consist primarily of regular system call invocations, but also of signals, process forks (*i.e.* `clone` and `fork` system calls) and exits (*i.e.* `exit` and `exit_group` system calls).

In general, any version can be the leader, although in some situations some may be a better choice than others–*e.g.*, when running multiple software revisions in parallel, one might prefer to designate the newest one as leader. However, the leader can be easily replaced if necessary, *e.g.*, if it crashes (§3.3.2).

The only centralised component in this architecture is the *coordinator*, whose main job is to prepare the versions for execution and establish the necessary communication channels. At a high level, the coordinator first loads the variants into memory, injects several special handlers and memory objects into their address spaces, rewrites any system calls in their code with jumps to the special handlers and then starts executing the variants (§3.1) in a decentralised manner.

2.3 Rewrite rules for system call sequences

In addition to eliminating the central monitor bottleneck, our event-streaming architecture also supports (small) divergences between the system call sequences of different variants. For example, different software revisions can be run inside a classical NVX system only as long as they all issue the same sequence of system calls [21]. However, software patches sometimes change the external behavior of an application. In particular, many divergences in system call traces fall into the following two categories: (i) *addition/removal*, characterising situations when one of the versions performs (or conversely does not perform) an additional system call, typically as a consequence of an additional check, and (ii) *coalescing*, covering the situations when a (repeated) sequence of system calls is executed a different number of times in each version (*e.g.*, one version might execute two `write` system calls, while another version executes only one `write` system call to write the same bytes because extra buffering is used).

VARAN is the first NVX system that is able to deal with such changes. When followers process the event sequence streamed by the leader, they can rewrite it to account for any such differences: *e.g.*, they can skip and merge system calls, or perform some calls themselves. We provide a flexible implementation of such rewrite rules using Berkeley Packet Filters (§3.4).

3. Prototype

We have implemented our approach in a prototype (to which we will also refer as VARAN), targeted at multi-core processors running x86-64 Linux. VARAN works on off-the-shelf binaries (both stripped and unstripped) and supports single- as well as multi-threaded applications.

When it starts, VARAN first sets up the address spaces of all program versions and establishes the needed communication channels (§3.1). It then performs selective binary rewriting to replace all system calls with jump instructions (§3.2). After these initial stages, the event streamer component of VARAN ensures the coordination of the leader and its followers (§3.3).

3.1 Setup of address spaces and communication channels

The main steps involved in the setup of version address spaces and the needed communication channels are shown in Figure 2. To run multiple versions in parallel, the user launches VARAN's *coordinator* providing the paths to all versions, together with any command line arguments required to start them (Step Ⓐ in Figure 2).

The *coordinator* first creates the shared memory segment used for communication among versions, and then spawns the *zygote* process (Ⓑ), which is responsible for starting the individual versions. The coordinator communicates with the zygote via a UNIX domain socket. For each version i that needs to be spawned, the coordinator sends a fork request to the zygote over this socket pair, which includes the path to that version executable, the command line arguments, and the end-point of a socket pair which will be used for the subsequent communication between the coordinator and that version ((C_i)). After receiving this request, the zygote spawns a new process, which first finalises the communication with the coordinator ((D_i)). The coordinator then sends the shared memory segment descriptor to this process, which maps it inside its address space.

In the final step, the new process starts executing inside the monitor code, which loads the specified ELF executable and sets up the initial address space as described in the ELF

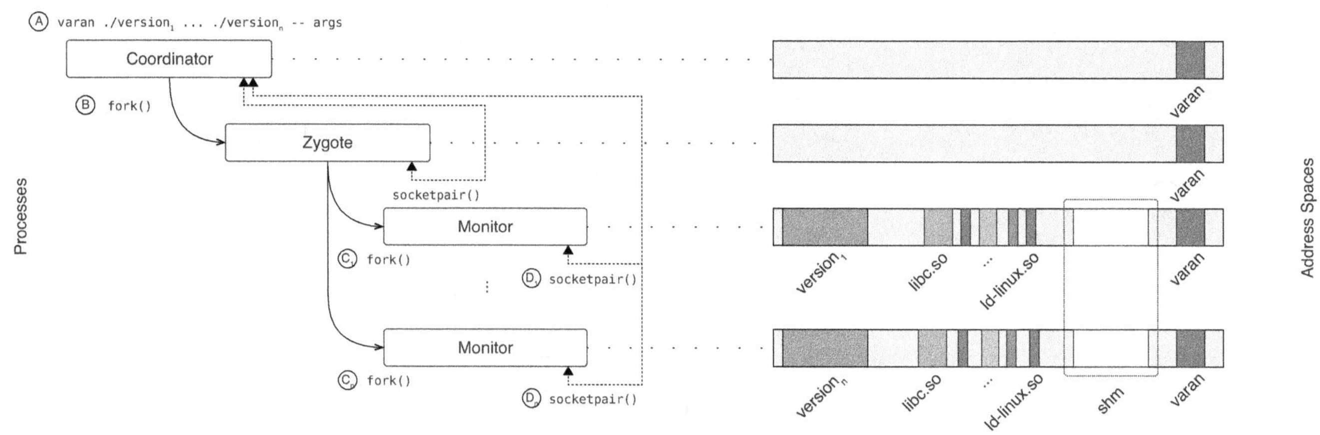

Figure 2. Setup of address spaces and communication channels.

headers. If the program requires a dynamic linker, VARAN loads the linker image specified in the header as well. The text segments of both the application and the dynamic linker are then processed by the binary rewriter (§3.2). Finally, VARAN jumps to the application entry point as specified in the ELF header, starting the execution of the application version.

The right-hand side of Figure 2 shows the address spaces of the coordinator, zygote, and program versions. When run with VARAN, program versions have two new segments mapped into their address spaces: the shared memory segment used for communication among versions ("shm") and the VARAN statically-linked library ("varan"). Note that VARAN does not prevent address-space layout randomisation schemes to be used by the operating system.

Coordinator. To set up the address spaces of the versions, the coordinator acts as a specialized preloader, inspired by *rtldi*.[4] However, the coordinator does not attempt to replace the existing dynamic linker, which would be unnecessarily complex and may affect compatibility with existing applications. Instead, it simply intercepts the system calls performed by the linker to enable the binary rewriter (§3.2) to rewrite the code of dynamically-linked shared libraries. One important advantage of our interception mechanism is that we do not make use of `ptrace` to intercept calls to the dynamic linker—instead, the binary rewriter is used to rewrite all the system calls done by the linker with jumps into the coordinator code. As a result, VARAN can be used in combination with existing `ptrace`-based tools such as *GDB* or *strace*, which greatly simplifies debugging.

Zygote. The role of the zygote is to spawn new processes on request from the coordinator. Zygote processes are already used in systems such as *Android* and *Chrome* [12]—in this paper, we use the term to refer to the architectural pattern rather than a particular implementation, as VARAN provides its own clean-slate implementation. While it would be technically possible for the coordinator to create the processes in which versions run, this would bring some complications regarding the communication channels: for example, the second version spawned would inherit the communication channel between the first version and the coordinator, which would be undesirable.

Monitor. The monitor code is built as a statically-linked, position-independent library, to make sure it does not stand in the way of any segments which have to be loaded by the application at fixed addresses. To ensure that the code can be compiled like this, we must avoid using any global variables (*i.e.* those in the `.data` section). One consequence is that VARAN cannot use any of the existing C libraries such as *GNU C Library*, as these are not typically built to support this requirement. Instead, VARAN provides its own implementation of the necessary C library functions based on the *Bionic C library*.[5] To support the use of Linux system calls, VARAN uses a modified version of the `linux_syscall_support.h` header.[6]

3.2 Binary Rewriting

To intercept system calls, VARAN uses selective binary rewriting [35]. Unlike traditional dynamic binary rewriting implemented by tools like DynamoRIO [26] or Pin [32], where the entire process image is being rewritten, often introducing a significant performance overhead, VARAN only replaces the instructions for performing system calls (*i.e.* **`int`** `$0x80` on x86 and **`syscall`** on x86-64).

The rewriting itself is done when a segment is mapped into memory with executable permissions, or an existing memory segment is marked as executable. During rewriting, VARAN scans the segment searching for system call instructions using a simple x86 disassembler. Every system call found is

[4] `http://www.bitwagon.com/rtldi/rtldi.html`

[5] `https://android.googlesource.com/platform/bionic`

[6] `https://code.google.com/p/linux-syscall-support/`

rewritten with a jump to an internal system call entry point. This process is complicated by the fact that while a system call instruction is only one byte long, a jump instruction requires five bytes. Therefore, in order to rewrite the system call with a jump, we also need to relocate some of the instructions surrounding the system call—*i.e.* perform binary detouring via trampolines [22]. On the rare occasions when this is not possible (*e.g.*, because the surrounding instructions are potential branch targets), we replace the system call with an interrupt (`INT 0x0`). This interrupt is handled by VARAN through a signal handler installed during initialisation, which redirects the control flow to the system call entry point as for other system calls.

The system call entry point first saves all registers, and then consults an internal system call table to check whether there is a handler installed for that particular system call; if so, it calls that handler, otherwise it invokes the default handler. After processing the system call, the entry point handler restores all registers and returns to the original caller (using `sigreturn` in the case of system calls intercepted via an interrupt). The system call entry point also implements support for restarting system calls (*i.e.* signaled by the `-ERESTARTSYS` error code). This is used in certain scenarios supported by VARAN such as transparent failover (§5.1).

The internal system call table can be easily changed to accommodate various application scenarios. In particular, the only difference between the leader and the followers is the system call table. For example, the `write` system call would be redirected in the leader to a function that performs the call and records its result in the shared ring buffer, while in the followers it would be redirected to a function that reads the results from the shared buffer without making the call. VARAN also provides a Python script which can produce new tables and their implementations using templates.

Finally, note that in order to prevent potential attackers to easily inject system calls into the program, the binary rewriter follows a W⊕X discipline throughout execution, making sure that segments are not marked as both writable and executable at the same time.

3.2.1 Virtual System Calls

Certain Linux system calls are accelerated through the *vsyscall* page and the *vDSO* segment. These are mapped into the address space of each Linux process, and contain system call implementations. These *virtual system calls* do not incur the context switch overhead between kernel and user space associated with standard system calls.

The *vsyscall* page was introduced first, but is being deprecated in favor of the *vDSO* segment. The main reason for this development is that the *vsyscall* page is mapped to a fixed address, making it susceptible to return-oriented programming attacks [37]. To address this issue, the vDSO segment is mapped to a random address. Since the segment is dynamically allocated, it can also support an arbitrary number of virtual system calls (currently `clock_gettime`, `getcpu`, `gettimeofday` and `time`).

Virtual system calls represents one of the major limitations of `ptrace`-based monitors. Since these system calls are entirely implemented in user space, they cannot be intercepted via `ptrace` . This is an important limitation: as these system calls provide access to timing information, they are often used as a source of non-determinism (*e.g.*, for random number generators) and their handling is critical for any NVX system.

To our knowledge, VARAN is the first NVX system which handles virtual system calls, using binary rewriting. Handling calls made via the *vsyscall* page is easier because the function symbols are always mapped to the same address. To handle *vDSO* calls, we first need to determine the base address of the *vDSO* segment; this address is passed by the kernel in the ELF auxiliary vector via the `AT_SYSINFO_EHDR` flag.[7] Second, we need to examine the ELF headers of the *vDSO* segment to find all symbols. Identifying calls to these symbols is more complicated than in the *vsyscall* case because these symbols are allocated at arbitrary addresses. Instead, we replace the entry point of each function with a jump to dynamically generated code which sets up the stack and then issues a call to the VARAN system call entry point as in the case of regular system calls. Furthermore, we provide a trampoline, which allows the invocation of the original function, by moving the first few instructions of each function to a new place, followed by a jump to the original code. This allows VARAN to take advantage of the virtual system call mechanism to further improve performance.

3.3 Event Streaming

As we discussed briefly in Section 2 and illustrated graphically in Figure 1, the leader records all external events into a shared ring buffer, while the followers replay them to mimic the leader's behavior. The leader is the only version interacting with the environment, *i.e.* executing the system calls, with the exception of system calls which are local to the process (*e.g.*, `mmap`).

As in any NVX system operating at the level of system calls, VARAN has to be aware of the system call semantics, in order to transfer the arguments and results of each system call. VARAN currently implements 86 system calls, which were all the system calls encountered across our benchmarks.[8]

3.3.1 Shared ring buffer

For fast communication, the leader and its followers share a common ring buffer of fixed size, which is held entirely in memory. Our initial solution used a separate shared queue for each process [18, 29], with the coordinator acting as an event pump—reading events from the leader's queue and dispatching them into followers' queues. This approach

[7] `https://www.gnu.org/software/libc/manual/html_node/Auxiliary-Vector.html`

[8] We configured VARAN to emit an error message when an unhandled system call is encountered, and have implemented system call handlers on demand.

worked well for a low system call rate, but at higher rates the event pump quickly became a bottleneck.

As a result, we have instead opted for a design based on the Disruptor pattern [42], which uses a shared ring buffer allowing concurrent access by multiple producers and consumers, eliminating the need to dispatch events among queues, and thus improving both performance and memory consumption. Our implementation uses C11 atomics, in combination with cache aligning to achieve maximum performance with minimal use of locking (locks are used only during memory allocation and deallocation).

The size of the ring VARAN uses is configurable and has a default value of 256 events. Each event has a fixed size of 64 bytes; the size has been deliberately chosen to fit into a single cache line on modern x86 CPUs. This is sufficient for sending signals and system calls for which all arguments are passed by value (on x86-64, a system call can have up to six arguments of eight bytes, to fit into general purpose registers). However, for system call arguments passed by reference, the payload might have variable size and can be potentially larger than the event itself. In this case, we use events only to transfer shared pointers, which identify memory shared across versions.

The use of a shared memory buffer may result in a waste of system resources when the leader process performs a system call which blocks for a long period of time, as the followers use busy waiting to check for new events. To address this problem, we have introduced the concept of a *waitlock*. Whenever a follower makes a blocking system call, it acquires the waitlock. If there is no event available, the thread will block until the leader wakes up and notifies it. The waitlocks are efficiently implemented using a combination of C11 atomics and futexes [15].

3.3.2 Transferring file descriptors and leader replacement

Apart from the ring buffer, each version has a *data channel*, implemented using UNIX domain sockets. The data channel is used to send information which cannot be transferred via shared memory, in particular open file descriptors. Whenever the leader obtains a new file descriptor (*e.g.*, by opening a file), it sends this descriptor to all followers, effectively duplicating the descriptor into their processes. This is a crucial mechanism which enables the leader to be replaced transparently when it crashes. When the leader crashes, the follower that is elected as the new leader can simply continue executing using existing descriptors (*e.g.*, responding to requests coming over the network) without any disruption of service.

3.3.3 Multi-process and multi-threaded applications

Handling processes and threads is crucial in supporting many modern applications. In our design, we have opted to have separate ring buffers for each tuple of processes or threads in the system: for instance, when a process forks, the parent processes in the leader and all followers form one tuple, and

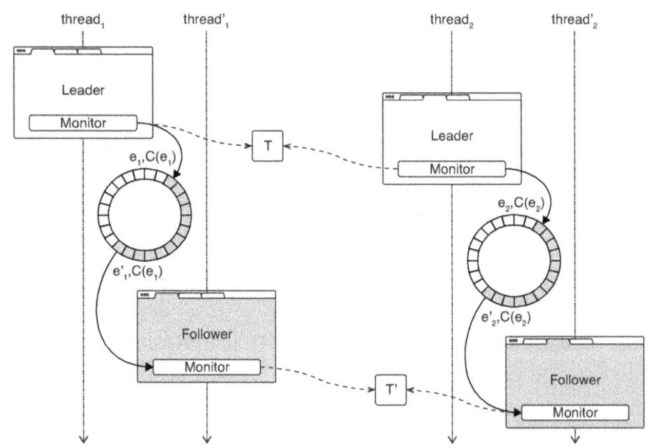

Figure 3. Event delivery in a multi-threaded NVX program, with the ordering of events enforced using logical clocks.

the child processes another, with a process in each tuple acting as the leader. More exactly, when a new process is forked, a new socket pair is established between the process and the coordinator and a new ring buffer is allocated. The leader then continues execution, but the coordinator waits until all followers fork a new process, establishing appropriate socket pairs for communication, and setting the child processes to read events from the newly-allocated ring buffer.

To alleviate non-determinism issues due to scheduling, VARAN enforces system call ordering across all tuples using Lamport's *happens-before* relation [28]. Currently, this is only implemented for multi-threaded applications, which make intensive use of synchronisation primitives, but the same solution could be employed for multi-process applications too.

Each variant has an internal Lamport clock, shared by all threads, and each event e_i sent through the ring buffer is annotated with a timestamp $C(e_i)$. Then, when replaying events from the buffer, each thread checks the timestamp of every new event and only receives the event if it does not violate the happens-before relation. This scenario is depicted in Figure 3. If $e_1 \to e_2$ (e_1 happens before e_2), then $C(e_1) < C(e_2)$ and VARAN enforces $e'_1 \to e'_2$. Without the ordering, there could be a situation where $e_1 \to e_2$, but $e'_1 \not\to e'_2$, which could lead to a divergence. A similar approach has been proposed in the past for record-replay in shared-memory systems [30].

To implement the internal clocks shared by the threads of a variant (T and T' in Figure 3), we use an atomic counter allocated in the shared memory space and updated using C11 atomics for efficiency. When the leader thread writes a new event into the ring buffer, it increments its variant's clock value and attaches it to the event. When a follower thread reads an event from the ring buffer, it compares its variant's clock value with the event's timestamp. If they are equal, the thread increments its variant's clock value and processes the event, otherwise it continues waiting. Our current implementation uses busy waiting, as the wait times are expected to be small. However, shall this become a problem in the future, it is possible to use blocking wait instead (*e.g.*, a futex).

Our solution resembles existing deterministic multi-threading (DMT) mechanisms [4, 31]. The guarantees provided by VARAN are weaker than those typically provided by these systems as we do not enforce ordering across atomics-based synchronisation primitives. We have not detected any system call divergences caused by related data races in our benchmarks, which include multi-threaded applications (*e.g.*, *Redis*), similar to the experience reported for prior NVX systems. However, shall this become a problem, we could address it by employing a stronger form of determinism similar to existing DMT systems.

3.3.4 Memory allocation scheme

Efficient shared memory allocation plays an important role in a system like VARAN. We use a custom shared memory pool allocator implementation. The allocator has the notion of buckets for different allocation sizes, where each bucket holds a list of segments, and each segment is divided into chunks of the same size; each bucket holds a free list of chunks. When there are no more unused chunks in a bucket, the allocator requests a new segment from the memory pool, and divides it into chunks which are then added to the free list. Each bucket also has a lock associated with it which has to be held prior to an allocation from that bucket.

3.4 Rewrite rules for system call sequences

VARAN uses Berkeley Packet Filters (BPF) [34] to implement the system call rewrite rules introduced in Section 2.3. BPF is a machine language for writing rules and an interpreter shipped with many UNIX implementations, including Linux and BSD. BPF filters have been traditionally used to filter network packets, but recently also for system call filtering as a part of seccomp "mode 2" (also known as seccomp-bpf).

We have integrated a BPF interpreter in VARAN to allow for system call rewrite rules. Our implementation is based on the Linux kernel code which was ported to user space and extended for NVX execution. VARAN provides BPF extensions on top of the instruction set used by seccomp-bpf.[9] The `event` extension allows access to the event stream, which can be used to compare the system calls executed across versions, as we will show in Section 5.2.

The use of BPF has a number of advantages. First, it does not require the user to modify and recompile the monitor on every rule change. This is particularly important as rewrite rules can be application specific. Second, the BPF machine language was designed to be simple enough to prevent certain classes of errors—in particular, all filters are statically verified when loaded to ensure termination.

[9] `https://www.kernel.org/doc/Documentation/networking/filter.txt`

4. Performance evaluation

One of the main contributions of VARAN is a significantly lower performance overhead compared to existing state-of-the-art NVX systems. Therefore, we have conducted an extensive performance evaluation, using microbenchmarks (§4.1), high-performance C10k servers (§4.2) and applications used to evaluate prior NVX systems (§4.3).

The microbenchmarks were run on a four-core/eight-thread machine with a 3.50 GHz Intel Xeon E3-1280 CPU and 16 GB RAM running 64-bit Ubuntu 14.04 LTS, while the servers were run on a pair of such machines, one running the server under VARAN and the other the client. The machines are located in the same rack, connected by a 1 Gb Ethernet link.

4.1 Microbenchmarks

To measure the overhead introduced by VARAN while processing individual system calls, we designed a series of experiments that compare a system call intercepted and executed by VARAN against the same system call executed natively. We used five different system calls:

1. `close(-1)` is representative of an inexpensive system call, which returns immediately.
2. `write(DEV_NULL, ..., 512)` is representative of system calls which involve expensive I/O, but whose result can be sent entirely as a single event in the ring buffer.
3. `read(DEV_NULL, ..., 512)` is representative of system calls which involve expensive I/O, and whose result cannot be fully included in the associated event in the ring buffer. Instead, it has to be copied via additional shared memory (§3.3.1).
4. `open("/dev/null", O_RDONLY)` is representative of system calls that require transferring file descriptors (§3.3.2).
5. `time(NULL)` is a virtual system call implemented via the *vDSO* segment (§3.2.1). It internally calls `__vdso_time` (since glibc 2.15). We could not measure the overhead of using the *vsyscall* page, because it is deprecated on our system (and all recent versions of Linux), with all *vsyscalls* now redirected to their *syscall* versions.

We executed each system call one million times and computed the average of all execution times. Time measurements were done using the time stamp counter (*i.e.* the RDTSC instruction). Each set of measurements was preceded by a warm-up stage in which we executed the system call 10,000 times.

Figure 4 shows the results. The first set of bars labeled *native* shows the execution time without VARAN. The second set of bars labeled *intercept* shows the execution time with interception, measuring the cost of binary rewriting: for

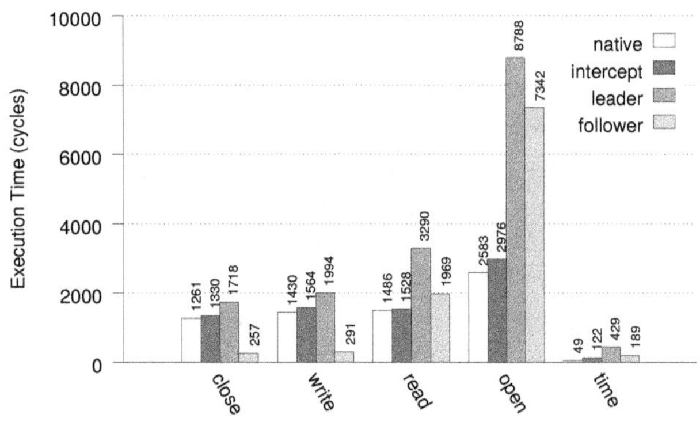

Figure 4. System call microbenchmarks.

these experiments, the intercepted system call is immediately executed, without any additional processing. As it can be seen, the interception cost is small, at under 15% in all cases except for `time`. The overhead of intercepting virtual system calls is high in relative terms, but low in absolute ones: 122 cycles vs 49 cycles for native execution for `time`.

The set of bars labeled *leader* shows the execution time for each system call to be intercepted, executed and recorded by the leader. That is, it is the sum of the *intercept* cost and the cost of recording the system call. For `close` and `write`, the overhead is only 36% and 39% respectively on top of native execution, because the arguments and results of these system calls can be recorded in a single event. For `read`, it is more expensive, at 139%, because transferring the result also involves accessing additional shared memory. Finally, the cost for `open` is the highest, since it also involves the slower transfer of the returned file descriptor via a UNIX domain socket.

Finally, the set of bars labelled *follower* shows the execution time of the follower, which has to intercept each system call and read its results from the ring buffer and (if necessary) shared memory. As expected, the costs for `close` and `write` are low (and significantly lower than executing the system call), because the entire result fits into a single event on the ring buffer. The costs for `read` and `open` are higher, because they involve additional shared memory and transferring a file descriptor, respectively, but they are still lower than the costs incurred by the leader.

4.2 C10k servers

Existing NVX systems, including those based on `ptrace`, can already run many (two-version) CPU-bound applications efficiently with an overhead typically less than 20%. As a result, we focus our evaluation on high-performance, heavily I/O-bound C10k servers which (1) represent the worst-case scenario for a system call monitor; and (2) form the backbone of modern, highly-scalable web applications, for which reliability is critical.

The five server applications used in our evaluations are summarized in Table 1 (the size is measured in lines of

Application	Size	Threading
Beanstalkd	6365	single-threaded
Lighttpd	38,590	single-threaded
Memcached	9779	multi-threaded
Nginx	101,852	multi-process
Redis	34,625	multi-threaded

Table 1. Server applications used in the evaluation.

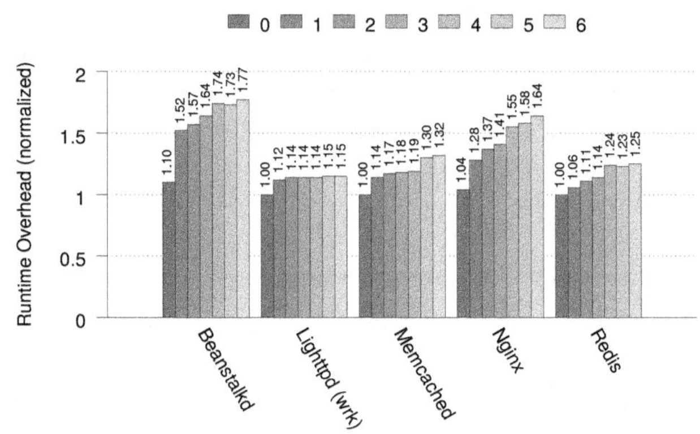

Figure 5. Performance overhead for the *Beanstalkd*, *Lighttpd*, *Memcached*, *Nginx* and *Redis* servers for different number of followers. The client and server are located on the same rack, simulating a worst-case scenario.

code, as reported by the *cloc* tool). For our performance experiments, we ran multiple instances of the same version of each application. Each experiment was performed six times, with the first measurement used to warm up the caches and discarded. The overhead was calculated as the median of the remaining five measurements.

We give a short overview of each benchmark and the way in which we measure performance (namely throughput) in our experiments:

Beanstalkd is a simple and fast work queue, used by a number of websites to distribute jobs among workers. We used revision `157d88b` from the official *Git* repository, the latest revision at the time of writing. To measure performance, we used `beanstalkd-benchmark` with 10 concurrent workers each performing 10,000 push operations using 256 B of data per operation.

Lighttpd is a lightweight web server optimized for high performance environments. The version used for the measurements was 1.4.36, the latest version in the 1.4.x series at the time of writing. We measured the performance of serving a 4 kB page using `wrk`, which was run for 10 s with 10 clients.

Memcached is a high-performance, distributed memory object caching system, used by many high-profile websites to alleviate database load. We used revision 1.4.17, the latest at the time of writing. To measure the performance overhead, we used the *memslap* benchmark, part of the *libMemcached* library. We used the default workload, *i.e.* an initial load of 10,000 key pairs and 10,000 test executions.

Nginx is a highly popular reverse proxy server often used as an HTTP web server, load balancer or cache. We used version 1.5.12, the latest at the time of writing. We measured performance using the same workload as for *Lighttpd*.

Redis is a high-performance in-memory, key-value data store, used by many well-known services. We used version 2.9.11 in our experiments. To measure performance, we used *redis-benchmark*, distributed as part of Redis. The benchmark issues different types of commands supported by Redis and measures both the throughput and the latency for each type. We used the default workload, *i.e.* 50 clients issuing 10,000 requests and calculated the average overhead across all commands.

Figure 5 shows the results for all servers. All performance numbers are obtained using the client-side tools mentioned above. Since the client machine is located on the same rack as the server, these numbers represent a worst-case scenario, as the network latency would hide some of the overhead for a more distant client machine.

For each benchmark, we show one bar, normalised relative to native execution, showing the performance of VARAN using a given number of followers. We stop at six followers, because our machine has eight threads, and we also need one thread for the leader and one for the coordinator.

The set of bars for 0 followers measure the interception overhead of VARAN using binary rewriting. This overhead is negligible for *Lighttpd*, *Memcached* and most *Redis* operations, 4% for *Nginx*, and 10% for *Beanstalkd*.

For all benchmarks, we see that the performance overhead increases slightly with the number of followers. For instance, the overhead for *Beanstalkd* increases from 1.52× for one follower to 1.77× for six followers, while the overhead for *Lighttpd* increases from 1.12× to 1.15×.

The figure also shows that there is a significant difference across benchmarks: the worst performer is *Beanstalkd*, which sees performance degradations in the range of 52% to 77%, while the best performers are *Lighttpd*, with only 12% to 15% overhead and some operations in *Redis* (not shown separately in Figure 5) with under 3% overhead.

4.3 Comparison with prior NVX systems

While Sections 4.1 and 4.2 illustrate the worst-case synthetic and real-world scenarios for a system call monitor, in order to compare VARAN directly with prior NVX systems, we have also run it on the same set of benchmarks used to evaluate prior systems. In particular, we chose to compare against three state-of-the-art NVX systems: *Mx* [21], *Orchestra* [40], and *Tachyon* [33]. These systems and their benchmarks are briefly described in the first three columns of Table 2. To our knowledge, we are the first to perform an extensive performance comparison of existing NVX systems.

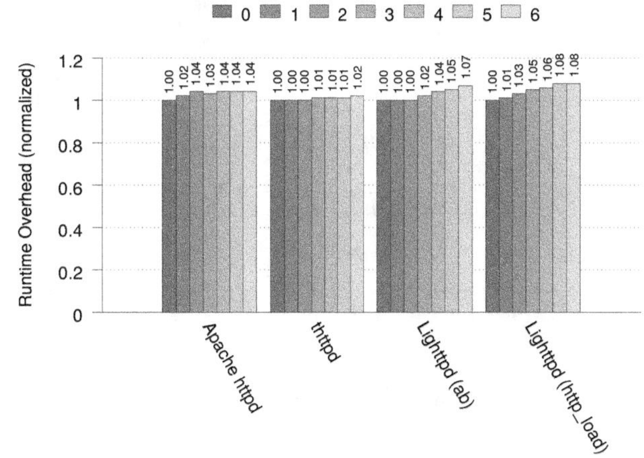

Figure 6. Performance overhead for the *Apache httpd*, *thttpd*, and *Lighttpd* servers for different numbers of followers to allow for comparison with existing systems.

The last two columns of Table 2 show the cumulative results. Since prior systems only handle two versions, the comparison is done against VARAN configured in the same way. However, we remind the reader that one of the strengths of VARAN's decentralised architecture is that it can often handle multiple versions with minimum additional overhead, and below we also show how VARAN performs on these benchmarks when more than two versions are used.

Apache httpd was used by *Orchestra*. We used version 1.3.29, the same as in the original work [40]. The overhead reported for *Orchestra* is 50% using the *ApacheBench* benchmark. VARAN introduces 2.4% overhead using the same benchmark, which is a significant improvement. Figure 6 shows the overhead introduced by VARAN for *Apache httpd* (and the other servers used to evaluate prior work) with different numbers of followers. As it can be seen, VARAN scales very well with increasing numbers of followers for these benchmarks.

Lighttpd has been used to evaluate both *Mx* and *Tachyon*. We used version 1.4.36. *Mx* used the *http_load* benchmark and reported 3.49× overhead while *Tachyon* used the *ApacheBench* benchmark and reported a 3.72× overhead. When benchmarked using *http_load*, VARAN introduced only 1.01× overhead, while with *ApacheBench* it introduced no noticeable overhead. In both cases, this marks a significant improvement over previous work.

thttpd was shown to introduce 1.17× overhead when run on top of *Tachyon* using the *ApacheBench* benchmark. When run on top of VARAN using the same settings as in [33], we have not measured any noticeable overhead.

Redis 1.3.8 was used in the evaluation of *Mx*. The performance overhead reported by *Mx* was 16.72× using the `redis-benchmark` utility. When run with VARAN using the same benchmark and the same workload, the overhead we

System	Mechanism	Benchmarks	Overhead	VARAN
Mx [21]	ptrace	*Lighttpd* (http_load)	3.49×	1.01×
		Redis (redis-benchmark)	16.72×	1.06×
		SPEC CPU2006	17.9%	14.2%
Orchestra [40]	ptrace	*Apache httpd* (ApacheBench)	50%	2.4%
		SPEC CPU2000	17%	11.3%
Tachyon [33]	ptrace	*Lighttpd* (ApacheBench)	3.72×	1.00×
		thttpd (ApacheBench)	1.17×	1.00×

Table 2. Comparison with *Mx*, *Orchestra* and *Tachyon* on the benchmarks used to evaluate these systems.

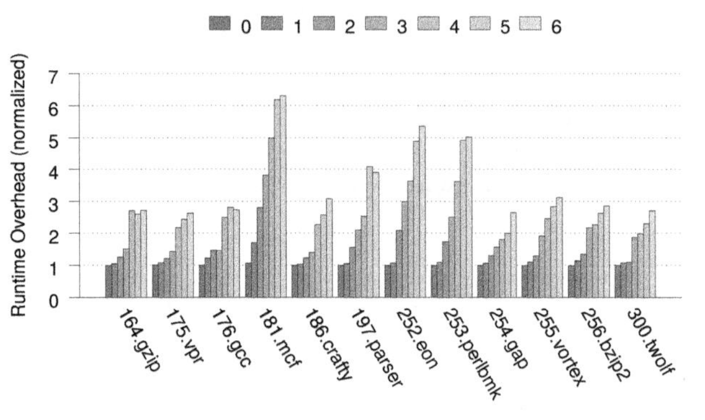

Figure 7. *SPEC CPU2000* performance overhead for different numbers of followers.

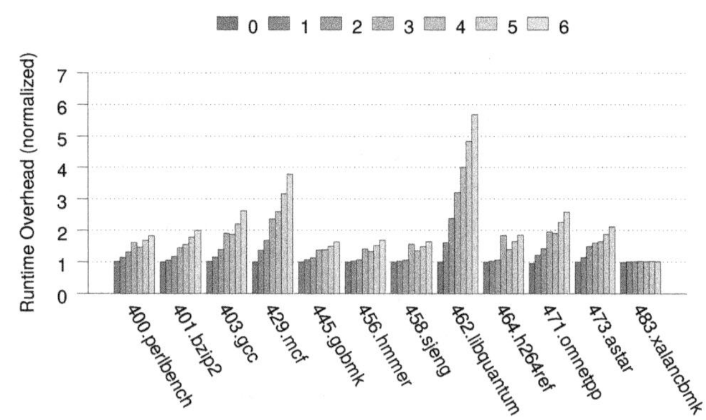

Figure 8. *SPEC CPU2006* performance overhead for different numbers of followers.

measured was 1.06×, which is again a significant improvement over previous work.

SPEC CPU2000 was used to evaluate *Orchestra*. We used the latest available version 1.3.1. *Orchestra* reported a 17% overhead, while VARAN introduced only a 11.3% overhead. The results for the individual applications contained in the *SPEC CPU2000* suite and for different numbers of followers can be seen in Figure 7. The reason these applications scale poorly with the number of followers is likely due to memory pressure and caching effects [24], and to the fact that our machine has only four physical cores (with two logical cores each). We plan to investigate these results in more detail in future work.

SPEC CPU2006 was previously used to evaluate *Mx*. We used the latest version 1.2. The overhead reported by *Mx* was 17.9%, while VARAN introduced only a 14.2% overhead. Individual results can be seen in Figure 8.

5. Application scenarios

VARAN is designed as a flexible framework that can support a variety of application scenarios involving NVX systems. In this section, we discuss four such scenarios: transparent failover (§5.1), multi-revision execution (§5.2), live sanitization (§5.3) and record-replay (§5.4).

5.1 Transparent Failover

NVX systems introduce a variety of opportunities for increasing software reliability and availability via transparent failover. For instance, one can run in parallel multiple variants of an application with different memory layouts, different software revisions or different implementations of a given interface to survive bugs that occur only in some of them.

VARAN makes it easy to implement transparent failover. When one of the versions crashes, the `SIGSEGV` signal handler installed in each version notifies the coordinator, which decides what restart strategy to use. When one of the followers crashes, the coordinator unsubscribes it from the list of currently-running followers, and discards it without affecting other followers. When the leader crashes, it designates one of the followers as the new leader (currently the one with the smallest internal ID), and notifies it to switch its system call table (§3.2) to that of the leader, and to restart the last system call while discarding the old (crashed) leader.

To demonstrate support for transparent failover, we reproduced a *Redis* bug[10] which was also used in the evaluation of *Mx* [21]. We ran in parallel eight consecutive revisions of *Redis* from the range `9a22de8` to `7fb16ba`, where the last revision introduced a bug which crashes the server by causing a segmentation fault. We then set up a client to send an `HMGET`

[10] `https://code.google.com/p/redis/issues/detail?id=344`

command that triggers the bug, and measured the increase in latency for that command. When the buggy version is a follower, we do not observe any increase in latency, as expected. When the buggy version is the leader, the latency increases from 42.36 µs to 122.62 µs. In both cases, we observed no extra degradation in throughput for the commands that follow.

As an additional experiment, we ran revisions `2437` and `2438` of *Lighttpd* (also used in the evaluation of *Mx*), the latter of which introduced a crash bug. We then set up a client that triggers the bug and measured the latency for that request. Both when the buggy version was the leader or a follower, there was no significant increase in latency, which remained at around 5 ms.

5.2 Multi-revision execution

Different software versions (revisions) can be run inside an NVX system as long as they all issue the same sequence of system calls [21]. This limitation is due to the fact that prior NVX systems run versions in lockstep (§2.3).

Because VARAN does not run the versions in lockstep and can use system call rewrite rules, it can often overcome this limitation. To illustrate, we used several *Lighttpd* revisions from the *Mx* [21] feasibility study which introduced new system calls and as such cannot be run in parallel by prior NVX systems that rely on lockstep execution.

As a first experiment, we ran revision `2435` as leader together with revision `2436` as follower. Revision `2436` introduces two additional checks using the `getuid` and `getgid` system calls. More precisely, revisions until and including `2435` used `geteuid()` and `getegid()` C library functions to check the user account under which the server is being run, before issuing an `open` system call. This resulted in a sequence of `geteuid`, `getegid` and `open` system calls. Revision `2436` replaced the use of the aforementioned functions with `issetugid()` which changed the system call sequence to `geteuid`, `getuid`, `getegid`, `getgid`, followed by `open` as before.

To allow for this divergence, we used the custom BPF filter shown in Listing 1. The filter is executed by the follower whenever a divergence is detected. In our experiment, this happens when the follower executes the newly introduced `getuid` system call. The filter first loads the system call number executed by the leader into the implicit BPF accumulator (line 1) and checks whether the call is either `getegid` (line 2) or `open` (line 3). The former will be true in this case, so control will transfer to line 6, which loads the system call number executed by the follower into the accumulator, checks whether it is `getuid` (line 7) and finally transfers control to line 12 returning the value `SECCOMP_RET_ALLOW`, which instructs VARAN to execute the additional system call (*i.e.* `getuid`) in the follower. Any other combination of system calls would have killed the follower (line 11). After executing the `getuid` system call and replaying the execution of `getegid` (which the leader also executed), VARAN would detect a second divergence when the follower tries to execute

```
1  ld event[0]
2  jeq #108, getegid /* __NR_getegid */
3  jeq #2, open /* __NR_open */
4  jmp bad
5  getegid:
6  ld [0] /* offsetof(struct seccomp_data, nr) */
7  jeq #102, good /* __NR_getuid */
8  open:
9  ld [0] /* offsetof(struct seccomp_data, nr) */
10 jeq #104, good /* __NR_getgid */
11 bad: ret #0 /* SECCOMP_RET_KILL */
12 good: ret #0x7fff0000 /* SECCOMP_RET_ALLOW */
```

Listing 1. Example of a BPF rewriting rule.

`getgid` instead of `open`. This divergence would be resolved using the same filter, taking the path on lines 3, 9, 10 and 12.

Note this is only one possible filter for allowing this divergence; in particular, one could write a filter that takes into account more information about the context in which it should be applied, *e.g.*, by inspecting some system call arguments.

We used a similar filter to run revisions `2523` and `2524`, the latter of which introduces an additional `read` system call to access the `/dev/urandom` file to obtain an additional source of entropy. We were also able to run revisions `2577` and `2578` where the difference consists of an additional `fcntl` system call to set a `FD_CLOEXEC` flag on one of the file descriptors.

Currently, VARAN's implementation can use BPF filters only to allow adding or removing system calls in followers. However, this is not a fundamental limitation, and in the future we plan to support other types of transformations, such as replacing one sequence of system calls with another.

5.3 Live Sanitization

Sanitization is one of the most effective testing techniques for revealing low-level bugs such as uninitialised pointer dereferences and use-after-free errors. Both Clang and GNU C Compiler now include a set of sanitizers—AddressSanitizer (ASan), MemorySanitizer (MSan), ThreadSanitizer (TSan)—which can be used to statically instrument the code with various checks. Unfortunately, these checks introduce extra overhead (*e.g.*, 2× for ASan, 3× for MSan and 5-15× for TSan). which is why these sanitizers are typically only used in offline testing. However, during testing developers only use a limited set of inputs which might not reveal all bugs.

One possible solution is to record execution traces during deployment and then replay them in a testing environment with sanitization enabled. However, this approach is unlikely to work in practice for several reasons. First, since we do not know in advance which traces are potentially interesting (*e.g.*, trigger sanitization checks) and which are not, we have to potentially collect and replay a huge number of execution traces. Even with some form of deduplication, this is usually impractical. Second, for long-running applications such as servers, the log will quickly grow to a large size. Third, many customers will refuse to share the logs from their production deployment.

With VARAN, we can perform live sanitization by running the native unsanitized version as the leader, with sanitized versions as followers. While sanitization itself introduces a performance overhead, since followers do not need to execute any I/O operations and merely replay them, they can often keep up with the leader, allowing users to run sanitized versions in production without introducing any significant overhead. Note that VARAN's architecture also provides the ability to run several sanitizers concurrently, which is important because many sanitizers are mutually incompatible.

To demonstrate this, we build revision `7f77235` of *Redis* twice: once with Clang without any sanitization, once with ASan enabled. We then ran both versions in parallel using VARAN and used the same benchmark with the same settings as for our performance evaluation (§4.2). As expected, we have not measured any additional slowdown in the leader compared to the scenario with two non-sanitized versions being run in parallel. To get a better insight into the effect of running the sanitized version with VARAN, we have also measured the median size of the log, *i.e.* the distance between the leader and the follower. This value is only six events, which does not impose any problems.

5.4 Record-Replay

Although VARAN shares similarities with record-replay systems, there are significant differences; in particular, the log is of fixed size and only kept in-memory. However, it is possible to easily extend VARAN to provide full record-replay capabilities by implementing two artificial clients: (i) during the record phase, one acting as a follower whose only goal is to write the content of the ring buffer to persistent storage, and (ii) during the replay phase, one acting as the leader, reading the content of the log from the persistent storage and publishing events into the ring buffer for consumption by replay clients.

Compared to some of the previous record-replay systems, VARAN has a number of advantages. First, decoupling the logic responsible for reading/writing the log from the actual application into a separate process allows the application to run at nearly full speed and utilise the multiple cores available in modern CPUs. Second, since VARAN was designed to run multiple instances at the same time, we can replay multiple versions at once, *e.g.*, to determine which versions of the application from a given range are susceptible to a crash reported by the user.

We have implemented a simple prototype of the two aforementioned clients on top of VARAN and compared its performance against *Scribe* [27], a state-of-the-art record-replay system implemented in the kernel. Unfortunately, because *Scribe* is implemented in the kernel and is only maintained for an old 32-bit Linux kernel (2.6.35), we had to run our experiments inside a virtual machine (kindly provided to us by *Scribe*'s authors, as the source tree was broken at the time of our experiments). To allow for a more faithful comparison, we ran VARAN inside the same virtual machine.

We used *Redis* as a benchmark, running the same workload as before, and configured both systems to record the execution to persistent storage. We recorded an overhead of 53% for *Scribe*,[11] compared to 14% for VARAN.

6. Discussion

This section discusses some of the implications of VARAN's design, including its main limitations, many of which are inherent to all existing NVX systems.

CPU utilisation and memory consumption. The performance evaluation reported in Section 4 considers the overhead in terms of throughput or clock time. However, an NVX framework introduces a CPU utilisation overhead linear in the number of versions. While this might be a serious concern in some scenarios, leaving cores idle has a cost as well [3] and in many cases idle cores can be profitably used to increase software reliability and security [5, 8, 9, 13, 40].

Similarly, the memory overhead imposed by VARAN is linear in the number of versions, as in prior NVX systems. This can lead to degradations in performance due to memory pressure and caching effects, as we have observed in Section 4.3.

Memory-based communication. As prior NVX systems, VARAN does not support memory-based communication. More exactly, VARAN only allows files to be mapped into memory as read-only—if the file would be mapped as read-write, any writes by the leader would likely lead to divergences in followers, as they would read the value written by the leader rather than the original value. This limitation comes from the fact that memory-based communication cannot be intercepted by interposing upon the system call interface, and as such is invisible to NVX systems operating at the system call level.

Synchronisation. While VARAN supports multi-threaded and multi-process applications (§3.3.3), there is a potential issue with synchronisation primitives implemented entirely in user space, as these primitives will be invisible to VARAN. While it is possible to use entirely user-space synchronisation primitives, in our experience, they are not that frequent and standard synchronisation primitives combine atomics with system calls (*i.e.* futex). We have not observed any related problems in our concurrent benchmarks (§4.2, §4.3).

Security. Although our focus with VARAN has been on improving software reliability, VARAN could be also used to implement existing NVX security defences [13, 40]. However, there are two additional problems that VARAN introduces, as discussed below.

[11] The overhead we measured for *Scribe* is higher than that reported in [27]; however, note that the original work used less I/O intensive benchmarks such as *Apache httpd* and that the use of a virtual machine also affected the result.

First, the use of buffering, while essential for improving performance, leads to delayed detection of divergences, providing attackers with a window of opportunity in which to perform malicious system calls. However, VARAN's buffer size is configurable, and could be set to one to disable buffering. Even without buffering, VARAN's binary rewriting mechanism is more efficient than `ptrace`-based solutions.

Second, since VARAN resides in the same address space as the application, a return-oriented programming (ROP) attack can bypass VARAN's tracing mechanism and thus escape detection. Furthermore, VARAN's code could be a primary target of such an attack. However, this is partially mitigated by the fact that VARAN's code is loaded at a random memory address.

7. Related Work

N-version programming was introduced in the seventies by Chen and Avizienis [11]. The core idea was to have multiple teams of programmers develop the same software independently and then run the produced implementations in parallel in order to improve the fault tolerance of the overall system. Both version generation and the synchronisation mechanism required manual effort.

Recent work on NVX systems has moved in the direction of opportunistically using existing versions—*e.g.*, different browser implementations [47] or different software revisions [21]—or automatically synthesising them—*e.g.*, by varying the memory layout [5] or the direction of stack growth [40]. Significant effort has also been expended on running multiple versions in parallel in the context of online and offline testing [33, 41, 43, 45]. VARAN targets NVX systems that use system call level synchronisation and is oblivious to the way in which the versions are generated.

Recent NVX systems that synchronise versions at the level of system calls use either the `ptrace` interface [21, 33, 40] or kernel modifications [13] to implement monitors. As discussed, `ptrace`-based systems incur an unacceptable overhead on I/O-bound applications—for instance, *Tachyon* [33] reports an overhead of 3.72× on *Lighttpd* and *Mx* [21] an overhead of 16.72× in one of the Redis experiments. By contrast, kernel-based systems [13] achieve overheads competitive to VARAN—but the main disadvantages are the additional privileges required for deployment and the difficulty of maintaining and debugging the kernel patches. Finally, all existing NVX systems operating at the level of system calls, both user- and kernel-level, require lockstep execution, which introduces significant limitations both in terms of performance and flexibility, as discussed in detail in Sections 2.2 and 3.4.

Event streaming in VARAN can be seen as a variant of record-replay. However, unlike traditional record-replay systems that require a persistent log [17, 20, 38, 39], VARAN keeps the shared ring buffer in memory, and deallocates events as soon as they are not needed, which minimises performance overhead and space requirements in the NVX context. As we showed in Section 5.4, VARAN can also be efficiently extended into a traditional record-replay framework.

RR [6] replicates an application into multiple instances for fault tolerance. It also uses a variant of record-replay to synchronise the multiple instances, but in contrast to VARAN RR is focused on fail-stop scenarios involving identical replicas. RR was implemented as a Linux kernel extension, which as discussed above presents several disadvantages compared to a user-level solution like VARAN, and was evaluated on a single benchmark.

More generally, system call interposition has been an active area of research [1, 2, 19, 23, 25, 36, 46]. VARAN draws inspiration from the Ostia delegating architecture [16], and from the selective binary rewriting approach implemented by *BIRD* [35] and *seccompsandbox*[12] (our binary rewriting implementation being based on the latter).

8. Conclusion

Recent years have seen a growing interest in using NVX systems as a way to increase the reliability and security of software systems. While NVX systems hold promise, frameworks for implementing them efficiently have lagged behind.

In this paper, we have introduced VARAN, a novel architecture for implementing NVX monitors. VARAN combines selective binary rewriting with high-performance event streaming to deliver a flexible and efficient user-space solution that incurs a low performance overhead, can scale to large numbers of versions, is easier to debug than prior systems, and can handle small divergences in the sequences of system calls issued across versions.

Our experimental evaluation has demonstrated that VARAN can run C10k network servers with low performance overhead and can be used in various scenarios such as transparent failover, multi-revision execution, live sanitization and record-replay.

For up-to-date information about the project, please visit `http://srg.doc.ic.ac.uk/projects/varan`.

Acknowledgments

We would like to thank Oscar Dustmann, Paul Marinescu, Luis Pina, Bennet Yee and the anonymous reviewers for their valuable comments on the paper. Special thanks to our ASPLOS shepherd, Andrew Baumann, for his time and constructive feedback. Petr is a recipient of a Google Europe Fellowship in Software Engineering, and Cristian of an Early-Career EPSRC Fellowship, and this research has been generously supported by these fellowships.

[12] `https://code.google.com/p/seccompsandbox/`

References

[1] A. Acharya and M. Raje. MAPbox: Using parameterized behavior classes to confine applications. In *Proc. of the 9th USENIX Security Symposium (USENIX Security'00)*, Aug. 2000.

[2] A. Alexandrov, P. Kmiec, and K. Schauser. Consh: Confined execution environment for Internet computations. `http://itslab.inf.kyushu-u.ac.jp/ssr/Links/alexandrov98consh.pdf`, Dec. 1998.

[3] L. A. Barroso and U. Hölzle. The case for energy-proportional computing. *Computer*, 40:33–37, 2007.

[4] T. Bergan, O. Anderson, J. Devietti, L. Ceze, and D. Grossman. CoreDet: A compiler and runtime system for deterministic multithreaded execution. In *Proc. of the 15th International Conference on Architectural Support for Programming Languages and Operating Systems (ASPLOS'10)*, Mar. 2010.

[5] E. D. Berger and B. G. Zorn. Diehard: probabilistic memory safety for unsafe languages. In *Proc. of the Conference on Programing Language Design and Implementation (PLDI'06)*, June 2006.

[6] P. Bergheaud, D. Subhraveti, and M. Vertes. Fault tolerance in multiprocessor systems via application cloning. In *Proc. of the 27th IEEE International Conference on Distributed Computing Systems (ICDCS'07)*, June 2007.

[7] D. Bruschi, L. Cavallaro, and A. Lanzi. Diversified process replicae for defeating memory error exploits. In *Proc. of the International Performance, Computing, and Communications Conference (IPCCC'07)*, Apr. 2007.

[8] C. Cadar and P. Hosek. Multi-version software updates. In *Proc. of the 4th Workshop on Hot Topics in Software Upgrades (HotSWUp'12)*, June 2012.

[9] C. Cadar, P. Pietzuch, and A. L. Wolf. Multiplicity computing: A vision of software engineering for next-generation computing platform applications. In *Proc. of the FSE/SDP workshop on the Future of Software Engineering Research (FoSER'10)*, Nov. 2010.

[10] R. Capizzi, A. Long, V. Venkatakrishnan, and A. P. Sistla. Preventing information leaks through shadow executions. In *Proc. of the 24th Annual Computer Security Applications Conference (ACSAC'08)*, Dec. 2008.

[11] L. Chen and A. Avizienis. N-version programming: A fault-tolerance approach to reliability of software operation. In *Proc. of the 8th IEEE International Symposium on Fault Tolerant Computing (FTCS'78)*, June 1978.

[12] Chromium.org. Linux Zygote: The use of zygotes on Linux. `https://code.google.com/p/chromium/wiki/LinuxZygote`.

[13] B. Cox, D. Evans, A. Filipi, J. Rowanhill, W. Hu, J. Davidson, J. Knight, A. Nguyen-Tuong, and J. Hiser. N-variant systems: a secretless framework for security through diversity. In *Proc. of the 15th USENIX Security Symposium (USENIX Security'06)*, July-Aug. 2006.

[14] D. Devries and F. Piessens. Noninterference through secure multi-execution. In *Proc. of the IEEE Symposium on Security and Privacy (IEEE S&P'10)*, May 2010.

[15] H. Franke, R. Russell, and M. Kirkwood. Fuss, futexes and furwocks: Fast userlevel locking in Linux. In *Proc. of the 2002 Ottawa Linux Symposium (OLS'02)*, June 2002.

[16] T. Garfinkel, B. Pfaff, and M. Rosenblum. Ostia: A delegating architecture for secure system call interposition. In *Proc. of the 11th Network and Distributed System Security Symposium (NDSS'04)*, Feb. 2004.

[17] D. Geels, G. Altekar, S. Shenker, and I. Stoica. Replay debugging for distributed applications. In *Proc. of the 2006 USENIX Annual Technical Conference (USENIX ATC'06)*, May-June 2006.

[18] J. Giacomoni, T. Moseley, and M. Vachharajani. FastForward for efficient pipeline parallelism: a cache-optimized concurrent lock-free queue. In *Proc. of the 13th ACM Symposium on Principles and Practice of Parallel Programming (PPoPP'08)*, Feb. 2008.

[19] I. Goldberg, D. Wagner, R. Thomas, and E. A. Brewer. A secure environment for untrusted helper applications confining the wily hacker. In *Proc. of the 6th USENIX Security Symposium (USENIX Security'96)*, July 1996.

[20] Z. Guo, X. Wang, J. Tang, X. Liu, Z. Xu, M. Wu, M. F. Kaashoek, and Z. Zhang. R2: An application-level kernel for record and replay. In *Proc. of the 8th USENIX Symposium on Operating Systems Design and Implementation (OSDI'08)*, Dec. 2008.

[21] P. Hosek and C. Cadar. Safe software updates via multi-version execution. In *Proc. of the 35th International Conference on Software Engineering (ICSE'13)*, May 2013.

[22] G. Hunt and D. Brubacher. Detours: Binary interception of Win32 functions. In *Proc. of the 3rd USENIX Windows NT Symposium (USENIX NT'99)*, July 1999.

[23] K. Jain and R. Sekar. User-level infrastructure for system call interposition: A platform for intrusion detection and confinement. In *Proc. of the 6th Network and Distributed System Security Symposium (NDSS'99)*, Feb. 1999.

[24] A. Jaleel. Memory characterization of workloads using instrumentation-driven simulation. Technical report, Intel Corporation, 2007.

[25] T. Kim and N. Zeldovich. Practical and effective sandboxing for non-root users. In *Proc. of the 2013 USENIX Annual Technical Conference (USENIX ATC'13)*, June 2013.

[26] V. Kiriansky, D. Bruening, and S. P. Amarasinghe. Secure execution via program shepherding. In *Proc. of the 11th USENIX Security Symposium (USENIX Security'02)*, Aug. 2002.

[27] O. Laadan, N. Viennot, and J. Nieh. Transparent, lightweight application execution replay on commodity multiprocessor operating systems. In *Proc. of the ACM SIGMETRICS 2010 (SIGMETRICS'10)*, June 2010.

[28] L. Lamport. Time, clocks, and the ordering of events in a distributed system. *Communications of the Association for Computing Machinery (CACM)*, 21(7):558–565, July 1978. ISSN 0001-0782.

[29] P. P.-C. Lee, T. Bu, and G. Chandranmenon. A lock-free, cache-efficient multi-core synchronization mechanism for line-rate network traffic monitoring. In *Proc. of the 24th IEEE International Parallel & Distributed Processing Symposium (IPDPS'10)*, Apr. 2010.

[30] L. Levrouw, K. Audenaert, and J. Van Campenhout. A new trace and replay system for shared memory programs based on Lamport clocks. In *Proc. of the 6th IEEE International Parallel & Distributed Processing Symposium (IPDPS'94)*, Oct. 1994.

[31] T. Liu, C. Curtsinger, and E. D. Berger. DTHREADS: Efficient deterministic multithreading. In *Proc. of the 23rd ACM Symposium on Operating Systems Principles (SOSP'11)*, Oct. 2011.

[32] C.-K. Luk, R. Cohn, R. Muth, H. Patil, A. Klauser, G. Lowney, S. Wallace, V. J. Reddi, and K. Hazelwood. Pin: building customized program analysis tools with dynamic instrumentation. In *Proc. of the Conference on Programing Language Design and Implementation (PLDI'05)*, June 2005.

[33] M. Maurer and D. Brumley. TACHYON: Tandem execution for efficient live patch testing. In *Proc. of the 21st USENIX Security Symposium (USENIX Security'12)*, Aug. 2012.

[34] S. McCanne and V. Jacobson. The BSD packet filter: A new architecture for user-level packet capture. In *Proc. of the 1993 Winter USENIX Conference*, Jan. 1993.

[35] S. Nanda, W. Li, L.-C. Lam, and T. cker Chiueh. BIRD: Binary interpretation using runtime disassembly. In *Proc. of the 4th International Symposium on Code Generation and Optimization (CGO'06)*, Mar. 2006.

[36] N. Provos. Improving host security with system call policies. In *Proc. of the 11th USENIX Security Symposium (USENIX Security'02)*, Aug. 2002.

[37] R. Roemer, E. Buchanan, H. Shacham, and S. Savage. Return-oriented programming: Systems, languages, and applications. *ACM Transactions on Information and System Security (TISSEC)*, 15(1):2:1–2:34, Mar. 2012.

[38] M. Ronsse and K. De Bosschere. RecPlay: A fully integrated practical record/replay system. *ACM Transactions on Computer Systems (TOCS)*, 17(2):133–152, May 1999. ISSN 0734-2071.

[39] Y. Saito. Jockey: a user-space library for record-replay debugging. In *Proc. of the 6th International Workshop on Automated Debugging (AADEBUG'05)*, Sept. 2005.

[40] B. Salamat, T. Jackson, A. Gal, and M. Franz. Orchestra: intrusion detection using parallel execution and monitoring of program variants in user-space. In *Proc. of the 4th European Conference on Computer Systems (EuroSys'09)*, Mar.-Apr. 2009.

[41] S. Sidiroglou, S. Ioannidis, and A. D. Keromytis. Band-aid patching. In *Proc. of the 3rd Workshop on Hot Topics in System Dependability (HotDep'07)*, June 2007.

[42] M. Thompson, D. Farley, M. Barker, P. Gee, and A. Stewart. Disruptor: High performance alternative to bounded queues for exchanging data between concurrent threads. Technical report, LMAX, 2011. URL `http://lmax-exchange.github.io/disruptor/files/Disruptor-1.0.pdf`.

[43] J. Tucek, W. Xiong, and Y. Zhou. Efficient online validation with delta execution. In *Proc. of the 14th International Conference on Architectural Support for Programming Languages and Operating Systems (ASPLOS'09)*, Mar. 2009.

[44] K. Veeraraghavan, P. M. Chen, J. Flinn, and S. Narayanasamy. Detecting and surviving data races using complementary schedules. In *Proc. of the 23rd ACM Symposium on Operating Systems Principles (SOSP'11)*, Oct. 2011.

[45] M. A. Vouk. Back-to-back testing. *Information and Software Technology (IST)*, 32:34–45, Jan.-Feb. 1990.

[46] D. A. Wagner. Janus: an approach for confinement of untrusted applications. Technical Report UCB/CSD-99-1056, University of California at Berkley, 1999. URL `http://www.eecs.berkeley.edu/Pubs/TechRpts/1999/5271.html`.

[47] H. Xue, N. Dautenhahn, and S. T. King. Using replicated execution for a more secure and reliable web browser. In *Proc. of the 19th Network and Distributed System Security Symposium (NDSS'12)*, Feb. 2012.

[48] A. R. Yumerefendi, B. Mickle, and L. P. Cox. Tightlip: Keeping applications from spilling the beans. In *Proc. of the 4th USENIX Symposium on Networked Systems Design and Implementation (NSDI'07)*, Apr. 2007.

rIOMMU: Efficient IOMMU for I/O Devices that Employ Ring Buffers

Moshe Malka Nadav Amit Muli Ben-Yehuda Dan Tsafrir

Technion – Israel Institute of Technology

{moshemal,namit,muli,dan}@cs.technion.ac.il

Abstract

The IOMMU allows the OS to encapsulate I/O devices in their own virtual memory spaces, thus restricting their DMAs to specific memory pages. The OS uses the IOMMU to protect itself against buggy drivers and malicious/errant devices. But the added protection comes at a cost, degrading the throughput of I/O-intensive workloads by up to an order of magnitude. This cost has motivated system designers to trade off some safety for performance, e.g., by leaving stale information in the IOTLB for a while so as to amortize costly invalidations.

We observe that high-bandwidth devices—like network and PCIe SSD controllers—interact with the OS via circular ring buffers that induce a sequential, predictable workload. We design a ring IOMMU (rIOMMU) that leverages this characteristic by replacing the virtual memory page table hierarchy with a circular, flat table. A flat table is adequately supported by exactly one IOTLB entry, making every new translation an implicit invalidation of the former and thus requiring explicit invalidations only at the end of I/O bursts. Using standard networking benchmarks, we show that rIOMMU provides up to 7.56x higher throughput relative to the baseline IOMMU, and that it is within 0.77–1.00x the throughput of a system without IOMMU protection.

Categories and Subject Descriptors B.3.2 [*memory structures*]: design styles—virtual memory; B.4.2 [*I/O and data communications*]: I/O devices—channels and controllers; D.4.2 [*operating systems*]: storage management—virtual memory, allocation/deallocation strategies

General Terms design, experimentation, performance

Keywords I/O memory management unit

ASPLOS '15, March 14–18, 2015, Istanbul, Turkey.
Copyright © 2015 ACM 978-1-4503-2835-7/15/03...$15.00.
http://dx.doi.org/10.1145/2694344.2694355

1. Introduction

I/O device drivers initiate direct memory accesses (DMAs) to asynchronously move data from their devices into memory and vice versa. In the past, DMAs used physical memory addresses. But such unmediated access made systems vulnerable to (1) rogue devices that might perform errant or malicious DMAs [9, 12, 28, 32, 52], and to (2) buggy drivers that account for most operating system (OS) failures and might wrongfully trigger DMAs to arbitrary memory locations [8, 13, 23, 36, 47, 50]. Subsequently, all major chip vendors introduced I/O memory management units (IOMMUs) [3, 7, 25, 28], which allow DMAs to execute with I/O virtual addresses (IOVAs). The IOMMU translates the IOVAs into physical addresses according to I/O page tables that are setup by the OS. The OS thus protects itself by adding a translation just before the corresponding DMA, and by removing the translation right after [11, 16, 51]. We explain in detail how the IOMMU is implemented and used in §2.

DMA protection comes at a cost that can be substantial in terms of performance [4, 10, 51], for newer, high-throughput I/O devices like 10/40 Gbps network controllers (NICs), which can deliver millions of packets per second. Our measurements indicate that using DMA protection with such devices can reduce the throughput by up to 10x. This penalty has motivated OS developers to trade off some protection for performance. For example, when employing the "deferred" IOMMU mode, the Linux kernel defers IOTLB invalidations for a short while instead of performing them immediately, because invalidations are slow. Later, the kernel processes the accumulated invalidations en masse by flushing the entire IOTLB, thus amortizing the overhead at the risk of allowing devices to erroneously utilize stale IOTLB entries. While this tradeoff can double the performance relative to the stricter IOMMU mode, the throughput is still 5x lower than when the IOMMU is disabled. We analyze and model the overheads associated with using the IOMMU in §3.

We argue that the degraded performance is largely due to the IOMMU needlessly replicating the design of the regular MMU, which is based on hierarchical page tables. Our claim pertains high-bandwidth I/O devices, such as NICs and PCIe

SSD drives, which utilize circular "ring" buffers to interact with the OS. A ring is an array of descriptors that the OS driver sets when initiating DMAs. Descriptors encapsulate the DMA details, including the associated IOVAs. Importantly, ring semantics dictate that (1) the driver work through the ring in order, one descriptor after the other, and that (2) the I/O device process these descriptors in the same order. Thus, IOVAs are short-lived and the sequence in which they are used is linearly predictable: each IOVA is allocated, placed in the ring, used in turn, and deallocated.

We propose a ring IOMMU (rIOMMU) that supports this pervasive sequential model using flat (1D) page tables that directly correspond to the nature of rings. RIOMMU has three advantages over the baseline IOMMU that significantly reduce the overhead of DMA protection. First, building/destroying an IOVA translation in a flat table is quicker than in a hierarchical structure. Second, (de)allocation of IOVAs—the actual integers serving as virtual addresses—is faster, as IOVAs are indices of flat tables in our design. Finally, the frequency of IOTLB invalidations is substantially reduced, because the rIOMMU designates only one IOTLB entry per ring. One is enough because IOVAs are used sequentially, one after the other. Consequently, every translation inserted to the IOTLB removes the previous translation, eliminating the need to explicitly invalidate the latter. And since the OS handles high-throughput I/O in bursts, explicit invalidations become rare. We describe rIOMMU in §4.

We evaluate the performance of rIOMMU using networking benchmarks and find that it improves throughput by 1.00—7.56x, shortens latency by 0.80–0.99x, and reduces CPU consumption by 0.36–1.00x relative to the existing IOMMU. Our fastest rIOMMU variant is within 0.77–1.00x the throughput, 1.00–1.04x the latency, and 1.00–1.22x the CPU consumption of a system that disables the IOMMU entirely. We describe our experimental evaluation in §5.

2. Background

2.1 Operating System DMA Protection

The role the IOMMU plays for I/O devices is similar to the role the regular MMU plays for processes, as illustrated in Figure 1. Processes typically access the memory using virtual addresses, which are translated to physical addresses by the MMU. Analogously, I/O devices commonly access the memory via DMAs associated with IOVAs. The IOVAs are translated to physical addresses by the IOMMU.

The IOMMU provides *inter-* and *intra-OS protection* [4, 49, 51, 53]. Inter-OS protection is applicable in virtual setups. It allows for "direct I/O", where the host assigns a device directly to a guest virtual machine (VM) for its exclusive use, largely removing itself from the guest's I/O path and thus improving its performance [22, 36]. In this mode of operation, the VM directly programs device DMAs using its notion of (guest) "physical" addresses. The host uses the IOMMU to redirect these accesses to where the VM memory truly resides, thus protecting its own memory and the memory of the other VMs. With inter-OS protection, IOVAs are mapped to physical memory locations infrequently, typically only upon such events as VM creation and migration. Such mappings are therefore denoted *static* or *persistent* [51]; they are not the focus of this paper.

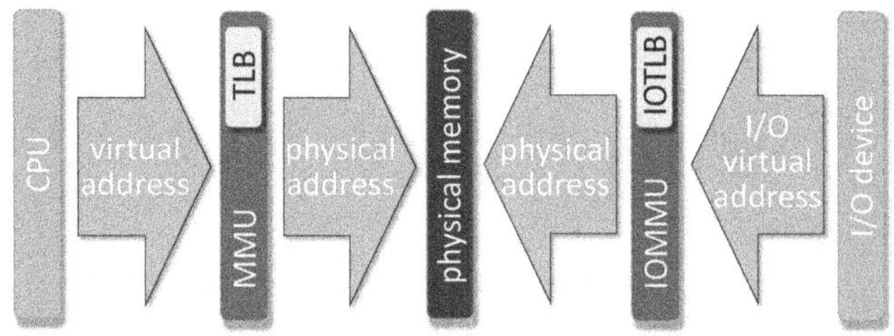

Figure 1. The IOMMU is for devices what the MMU is for processes.

Intra-OS protection allows the OS to defend against the DMAs of errant/malicious devices [9, 12, 17, 28, 32, 52] and of buggy drivers, which account for most OS failures [8, 13, 23, 36, 47, 50]. Drivers and their I/O devices can perform DMAs to arbitrary memory addresses, and IOMMUs allow OSes to protect themselves (and their processes) against such accesses, by restricting them to specific physical locations. In this mode of work, *map* operations (of IOVAs to physical addresses) and *unmap* operations (invalidations of previous maps) are frequent and occur within the I/O critical path, such that each DMA is preceded and followed by the mapping and unmapping of the corresponding IOVA [32, 40]. Due to their short lifespan, these mappings are denoted *dynamic* [11], *streaming* [16] or *single-use* [51]. This strategy of IOMMU-based intra-OS protection is the focus of this paper. It is recommended by hardware vendors [24, 28, 32] and employed by operating systems [6, 11, 16, 26, 38, 51].[1] It is applicable in non-virtual setups where the OS has direct control over the IOMMU. It is likewise applicable in virtual setups where IOMMU functionality is exposed to VMs via paravirtualization [10, 36, 45, 51], full emulation [4], and, more recently, hardware support for nested IOMMU translation [3, 28].

2.2 IOMMU Design and Implementation

Given a *target memory buffer* of a DMA, the OS associates the physical address (PA) of the buffer with an IOVA. The OS maps the IOVA to the PA by inserting the IOVA⇒PA

[1] For example, the DMA API of Linux notes that "DMA addresses should be mapped only for the time they are actually used and unmapped after the DMA transfer" [40]. In particular, "once a buffer has been mapped, it belongs to the device, not the processor. Until the buffer has been unmapped, the [OS] driver should not touch its contents in any way. Only after [the unmap of the buffer] has been called is it safe for the driver to access the contents of the buffer" [16].

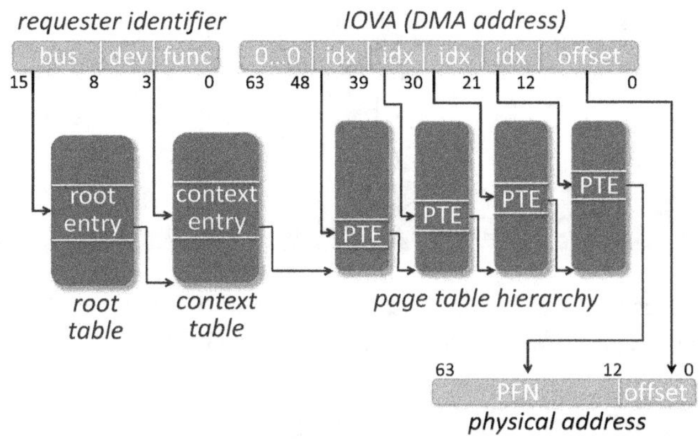

Figure 2. IOVA translation with the Intel IOMMU.

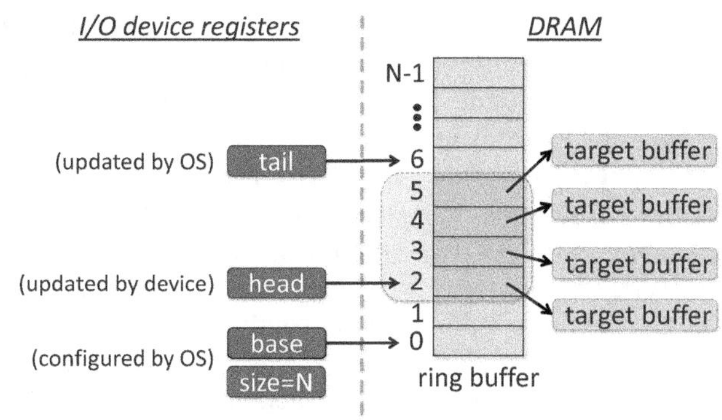

Figure 3. The driver drives its device via a ring. With an IOMMU, register/target pointers are IOVAs.

translation to the IOMMU data structures. Figure 2 depicts these structures as implemented by Intel x86-64 [28]. The PCI protocol dictates that each DMA operation is associated with a 16-bit *request identifier* comprised of a *bus-device-function* triplet that uniquely identifies the corresponding I/O device. The IOMMU uses the 8-bit bus number to index the *root table* in order to retrieve the physical address of the *context table*. It then indexes the context table using the 8-bit concatenation of the device and function numbers. The result is the physical location of the root of the page table hierarchy that houses all of the IOVA⇒PA translations of that I/O device.

The purpose of the IOMMU page table hierarchy is similar to that of the MMU hierarchy: recording the mapping from virtual to physical addresses by utilizing a 4-level radix tree. Each 48-bit (I/O) virtual address is divided into two: the 36 high-order bits, which constitute the *virtual page number*, and the 12 low-order bits, which are the *offset* within the page. The translation procedure applies to the virtual page number only, converting it into a *physical frame number* (PFN) that corresponds to the physical memory location being addressed. The offset is the same for both physical and virtual pages.

Let T_j denote a page table in the j-th radix tree level for $j = 1,2,3,4$, such that T_1 is the root of the tree. Each T_j is a 4KB page containing up to $2^9 = 512$ pointers to physical locations of next-level T_{j+1} tables. Last-level—T_4—tables contain PFNs of target buffer locations. Correspondingly, the 36-bit virtual page number is split into a sequence of four 9-bit indices i_1, i_2, i_3 and i_4, such that i_j is used to index T_j in order to find the physical address of the next T_{j+1} along the radix tree path. Logically, in C pointer notation, $T_1[i_1][i_2][i_3][i_4]$ is the PFN of the target memory location.

Similarly to the MMU translation lookaside buffer (TLB), the IOMMU caches translations using an IOTLB, which it fills on-the-fly as follows. Upon an IOTLB miss, the IOMMU hardware hierarchically *walks* the page table as described above, and it inserts the IOVA⇒PA translation to the IOTLB. IOTLB entries are invalidated explicitly by the OS as part of the corresponding unmap operation.

An IOMMU table walk fails if a matching translation was not previously established by the OS, a situation which is logically similar to encountering a null pointer value during the walk. A walk additionally fails if the DMA being processed conflicts with the read/write permission bits found within the page table entries along the traversed radix tree path. We note in passing that, at present, in contrast to MMU memory accesses, DMAs are typically not restartable. Namely, existing systems usually do not support "I/O page faults", and hence the OS cannot populate the IOMMU page table hierarchy on demand. Instead, IOVA translations of valid DMAs are expected to be successful, and the corresponding pages must be pinned to memory. (Albeit I/O page fault standardization does exist [42].)

2.3 I/O Devices Employing Ring Buffers

Many I/O devices—notably NICs and disk drives—deliver their I/O through one or more producer/consumer *ring* buffers. A ring is an array shared between the OS device driver and the associated device, as illustrated in Figure 3. The ring is circular in that the device and driver wrap around to the beginning of the array when they reach its end. The entries in the ring are called DMA *descriptors*. Their exact format and content vary between devices, but they specify at least the address and size of the corresponding target buffers. Additionally, the descriptors commonly contain status bits that help the driver and the device to synchronize.

Devices must also know the *direction* of each requested DMA, namely, whether the data should be transmitted from memory (into the device) or received (from the device) into memory. The direction can be specified in the descriptor, as is typical for disk controllers. Or the device can employ different rings for receive and transmit activity, in which case the direction is implied by the ring. The receive and transmit rings are denoted *Rx* and *Tx*, respectively. NICs employ at least one Rx and one Tx per port. They may employ multiple Rx/Tx rings per port to promote scalability, as different rings can be handled concurrently by different cores.

Upon initialization, the OS device driver allocates the rings and configures the I/O device with the ring sizes and base locations. For each ring, the device and driver utilize a *head* and a *tail* pointers to delimit the ring content that can be used by the device: $[head, tail)$. The device iteratively consumes (removes) descriptors from the head, and it increments the head to point to the next descriptor to be used next. Similarly, the driver adds descriptors to the tail, incrementing the tail to point to the entry it will use subsequently.

A device asynchronously informs its OS driver that data was transmitted or received by triggering an interrupt. The device coalesces interrupts when their rate is high. Upon receiving an interrupt, the driver of a high-throughput device handles the entire I/O burst. Namely, it sequentially iterates through and processes all the descriptors whose corresponding DMAs have completed,

3. Cost of Safety

This section enumerates the overhead components involved in using the IOMMU in the Linux/Intel kernel (§3.1). It experimentally quantifies the overhead of each component (§3.2). And it provides and validates a simple performance model that allows us to understand how the overhead affects performance and to assess the benefits of reducing it (§3.3).

3.1 Overhead Components

Suppose that a device driver that employs a ring wants to transmit or receive data from/to a target buffer. Figure 4 lists the actions it carries out. First, it allocates the target buffer, whose physical address is denoted p (1). (For simplicity, let us assume that p is page aligned.) It pins p to memory and then asks the IOMMU driver to map the buffer to some IOVA, such that the I/O device would be able to access p (2). The IOMMU driver invokes its IOVA allocator, which returns a new IOVA v—an integer that is not associated with any other page currently accessible to the I/O device (3). The IOMMU driver then inserts the $v \Rightarrow p$ translation to the page table hierarchy of the I/O device (4), and it returns v to the device driver (5). Finally, when updating the corresponding ring descriptor, the device driver uses v as the address for the target buffer of the associated DMA operation (6).

Assume that the latter is a receive DMA. Figure 5 details the activity taking place when the I/O device gets the data. The device reads the DMA descriptor through its head register. The address held by the head is an IOVA, so it is intercepted by the IOMMU (1). The IOMMU consults its IOTLB to find a translation for the head IOVA. If the translation is missing, the IOMMU walks the page table hierarchy of the device to resolve the miss (2). Equipped with the head's physical address, the IOMMU translates the head descriptor for of the device (3). The head descriptor specifies that v (IOVA defined above) is the address of the target buffer (4), so the device writes the received data to v (5). The IOMMU intercepts v, walks the page table if the $v \Rightarrow p$ translation is missing (6), and redirects the received data to p (7).

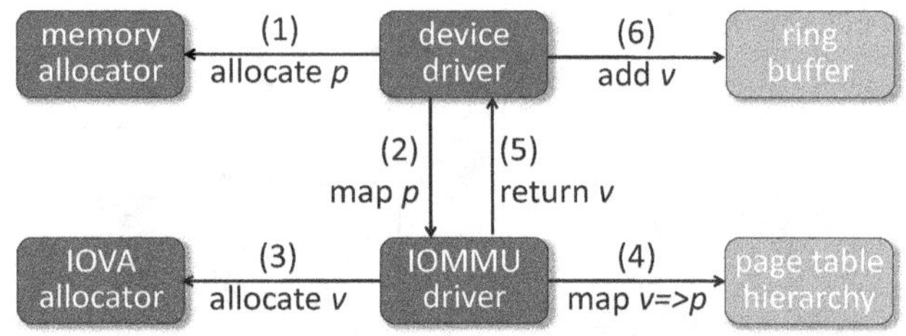

Figure 4. The I/O device driver maps an IOVA v to a physical target buffer p. It then assigns v to the DMA descriptor.

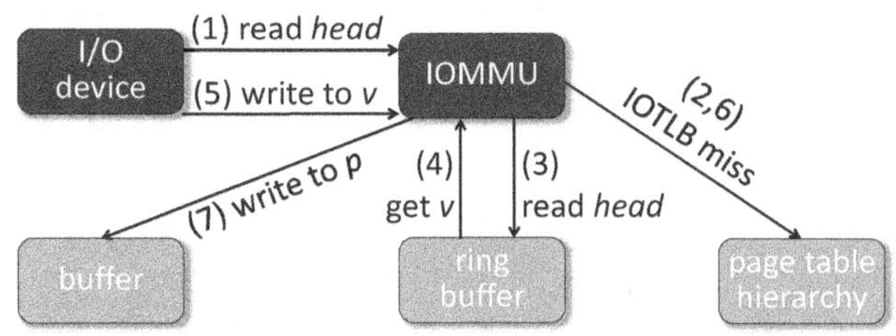

Figure 5. The I/O device writes the packet it receives to the target buffer through v, which the IOMMU translates to p.

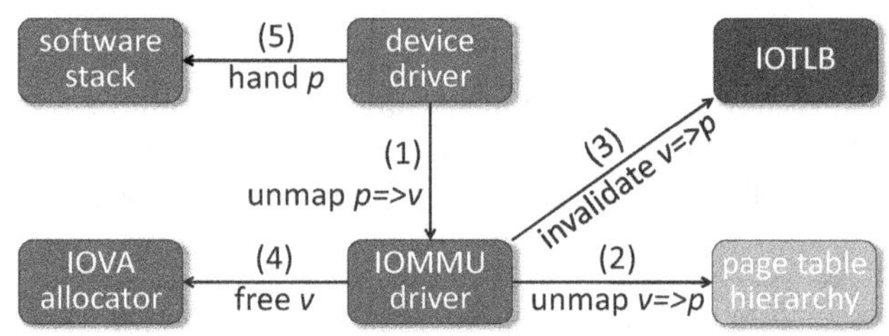

Figure 6. After the DMA completes, the I/O device driver unmaps v and passes p to a higher-level software layer.

Figure 6 shows the actions the device driver carries out after the DMA operation is completed. The device driver asks the IOMMU driver to unmap the IOVA v (1). In response, the IOMMU driver removes the $v \Rightarrow p$ mapping from the page table hierarchy (2), purges the mapping from the IOTLB (3), and deallocates v (4). (The order of these actions is important.) Once the I/O device can no longer access p, it is safe for the device driver to hand the buffer to higher levels in the software stack for further processing (5).

3.2 Protection Modes and Measured Overhead

We experimentally quantify the overhead components of the map and unmap functions—outlined in Figures 4 and 6—of the IOMMU driver. To this end, we execute the standard Netperf TCP stream benchmark, which attempts to maximize network throughput between two machines over a TCP connection. (The experimental setup is detailed in §5.)

function	*component*	*strict*	*strict+*	*defer*	*defer+*
map	iova alloc	3986	92	1674	108
	page table	588	590	533	577
	other	44	45	44	42
	sum	4618	727	2251	727
unmap	iova find	249	418	263	454
	iova free	159	62	189	57
	page table	438	427	471	504
	iotlb inv	2127	2135	9	9
	other	26	25	205	216
	sum	2999	3067	1137	1240

Table 1. Average cycles breakdown of the (un)map functions of the IOMMU driver for different protection modes.

Strict Protection We begin by profiling the Linux kernel in its safer IOMMU mode, denoted *strict*, which strictly follows the map/unmap procedures described in §3.1. Table 1 shows the average duration of the components of these procedures in cycles. The strict/map breakdown indicates that its most costly component is, surprisingly, IOVA allocation (Step 3 in Figure 4). Upon further investigation, we found that the reason for this high cost is a nontrivial pathology in the Linux IOVA allocator that regularly causes some allocations to be linear in the number of currently allocated IOVAs. We were able to come up with a more efficient IOVA allocator, which consistently allocates/frees in constant time [37]. We denote this optimized IOMMU mode—which is quicker than strict but equivalent to it in terms of safety—as *strict+*. Table 1 shows that strict+ indeed reduces the allocation time from nearly 4,000 cycles to less than 100.

The remaining dominant strict(+)/map overhead is the insertion of the IOVA to the IOMMU page table (Step 4 in Figure 4). The 500+ cycles of the insertion are due to explicit memory barriers and cacheline flushes that the driver performs when updating the hierarchy. Flushes are required, as the I/O page walk is incoherent with the CPU caches on our system. (This is common nowadays; Intel started shipping servers with coherent I/O page walks only recently.)

Focusing on the unmap components of strict/strict+, we see that finding the unmapped IOVA in the allocator's data structure is costlier in strict+ mode. The reason: like the baseline strict, strict+ utilizes a red-black tree to hold the IOVAs. But the strict+ tree is fuller, so the logarithmic search is longer. Conversely strict+/free (Step 4 in Figure 6) is done in constant time, rather than logarithmic, so it is quicker. The other unmap components are: removing the IOVA from the page tables (Step 2 in Figure 6) and the IOTLB (Step 3). The removal takes 400+ cycles, which is comparable to the duration of insertion. IOTLB invalidation is by far the slowest unmap component at around 2,000 cycles; this result is consistent with previous work [4, 53].

Deferred Protection In order to reduce the high cost of invalidating IOTLB entries, the Linux *deferred* protection mode relaxes strictness somewhat, trading off some safety for performance. Instead of invalidating entries right away, the IOMMU driver queues the invalidations until 250 freed IOVAs accumulate. It then processes all of them in bulk by invalidating the entire IOTLB. This approach affects the cost of (un)mapping in two ways, as shown in Table 1 in the defer and defer+ columns. (Defer+ is to defer what strict+ is to strict.) First, as intended, it eliminates the cost of invalidating individual IOTLB entries. And second, it reduces the cost of IOVA allocation in the baseline deferred mode as compared to strict (1,674 vs. 3,986), because deallocating IOVAs in bulk reduces somewhat the aforementioned linear pathology.

The drawback of deferred protection is that the I/O device might erroneously access target buffers through stale IOTLB entries after the buffers have already been handed back to higher software stack levels (Step 5 in Figure 6). Notably, at this point, the buffers could be (re)used for other purposes.

3.3 Performance Model

Let C denote the average number of CPU cycles required to process one packet. Figure 7 shows C for each of the aforementioned IOMMU modes in our experimental setup. The bottommost horizontal grid line shows C_{none}, which is C when the IOMMU is turned off. We can see, for example, that C_{strict} is nearly 10x higher than C_{none}.

Our experimental setup employs a NIC that uses two target buffers per packet: one for the header and one for the data. Each packet thus requires two map and two unmap invocations. So the processing of the packet includes: two IOVA (de)allocations; two page table insertions and deletions; and two invalidations of IOTLB entries. The corresponding aggregated cycles are respectively depicted as the three top stacked sub-bars in the figure. The bottom, "other" sub-bar embodies all the rest of the packet processing activity, notably TCP/IP and interrupt processing. As noted, the deferred modes eliminate the IOTLB invalidation overhead, and the "+" modes reduce the overhead of IOVA (de)allocation. But even C_{defer+} (the most performant mode, which introduces a vulnerability window) is still over 3.3x higher than C_{none}.

We find that the way the value of C affects the overall throughput of Netperf is simple and intuitive. Specifically, if S denotes the cycles-per-second clock speed of the core, then S/C is the number of packets the core can handle per second. And since every Ethernet packet carries 1,500 bytes, the throughput of the system in Gbps should be $Gbps(C) = 1500 \text{ byte} \times 8 \text{ bit} \times \frac{S}{C}$, assuming S is given in GHz. Figure 8 shows that this simple model (thick line) is accurate. It coincides with the throughput obtained when systematically lengthening C_{none} using a carefully controlled busy-wait loop (thin line). It also coincides with the throughput measured under the different IOMMU modes (cross points).

Consequences As our model is accurate, we conclude that the translation activity carried out by the IOMMU (as depicted in Figure 5) does not affect the performance of the system, even when servicing demanding benchmarks like

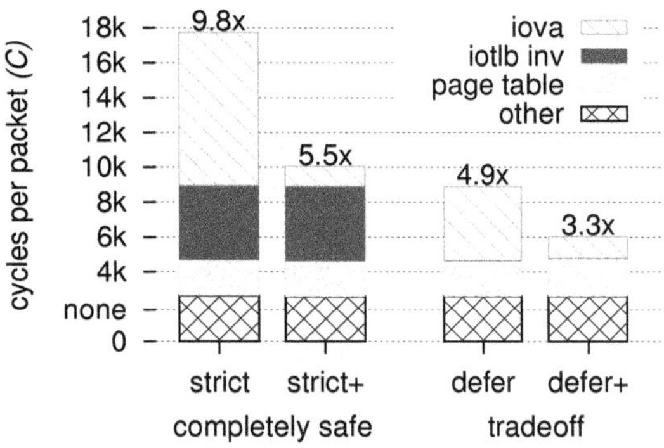

Figure 7. CPU cycles for processing one packet. The top bar labels are relative to C_{none}=1,816 (bottommost grid line).

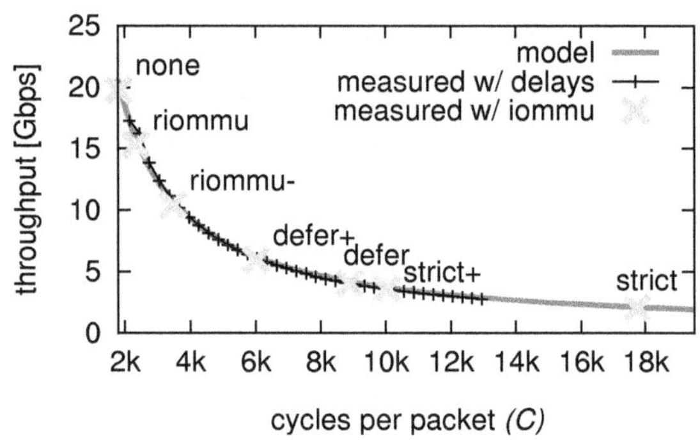

Figure 8. Throughput of Netperf as a function of the average number of cycles spent on processing one packet.

Netperf. Instead, the cost of IOMMU protection is entirely determined by the number of cycles the *core* spends creating and destroying IOVA mappings. Consequently, we can later simulate and accurately assess the expected performance of our proposed IOMMU by likewise spending cycles; there is no need to simulate the actual IOMMU hardware circuitry external to the core. A second conclusion rests on the understanding that throughput is proportional to $1/C$. If C is high (right-hand side of Figure 8), incrementally improving it would make little difference. The required change must be significant enough to bring C to the proximity of C_{none}.

4. Design

Our goal is to design rIOMMU—an efficient IOMMU for devices that employ rings. We aim to substantially reduce all IOVA-related overheads: (de)allocation, insertion/deletion to/from the page table hierarchy, and IOTLB invalidation (see Figure 7). We base our design on the observation that ring semantics (§2.3) dictate a well-defined memory mapping order, caused by the fact that the OS maps ring entries and shortly after unmaps them in the exact same order.

We contend that the x86 hierarchical structure of page tables is poorly suited for the ring model. For each DMA, the OS has to walk the hierarchical page table in order to map the associated IOVA. Then, the device faults on the IOVA and so the IOMMU must walk the table too. Shortly after, the OS has to walk the table yet again in order to unmap the IOVA. Contributing to this overhead are the aforementioned memory barriers and cacheline flushes required for propagating page table changes.

In a nutshell, we propose to replace the table hierarchy with a per-ring *flat* page table (1D array). IOVAs would constitute indices of the array, thus eliminating IOVA (de)allocation overheads. Not having to walk a hierarchical structure would additionally reduce the table walk cost. In accordance with Figure 9e, we propose an IOTLB that holds at most one entry per ring, such that each table walk removes the previous IOVA translation. Consequently, given a burst of unmaps, only the last IOVA in the sequence requires explicit invalidation. We further discuss this point later on.

We next describe the rIOMMU design in detail. There are several ways to realize the rIOMMU concept, and our description should be viewed as an example. Contrary to the baseline IOMMU, which provides protection in page granularity, our rIOMMU facilitates finer-grained protection of any specified size. This property is appealing because different target buffers can, and often do, reside on the same page. Therefore, the existing IOMMU allows the I/O device to access an already unmapped buffer if the page in which it resides additionally houses a still-mapped buffer. In contrast, rIOMMU eliminates this type of vulnerability.

Data Structures Figure 9 defines the rIOMMU data structures. The rDEVICE (Figure 9a) is to the rIOMMU what the root page table is to the baseline IOMMU. It is uniquely associated with a bus-device-function (bdf) triplet and is pointed to by the context table (Figure 2). As noted, each DMA carries with it a bdf, allowing the rIOMMU to find the corresponding rDEVICE when needed. The rDEVICE consists of a physical pointer to an array of rRING structures (Figure 9b) and a matching size. Each rRING entry represents a flat page table. It likewise contains the table's physical address and size. The OS associates with each rRING: (1) a tail pointing to the next entry to be allocated in the flat table, and (2) the current number of valid mappings in the table. The latter two are not architected and are unknown to the rIOMMU hardware. We include them in rRING to simplify the description.

Each ring buffer of the I/O device is associated with *two* rRINGs in the rDEVICE array. The first corresponds to IOVAs pointing to the device ring buffer (Step 1 of Figure 5 for translating the head register). The second corresponds to IOVAs that the device finds within its ring descriptors (Step 5 in Figure 5 for translating target buffers). The IOVAs that reside in the first flat table are mapped as part of the I/O device initialization. They will be unmapped only when the device is brought down, as the device rings are always accessible to the device. IOVAs residing in the second flat table are asso-

```
a) struct rDEVICE {
   u16   size;
   rRING rings[size];
};

b) struct rRING {
   u18 size;
   rPTE ring[size];
   u18 tail;     // SW only
   u18 nmapped; // SW only
};

c) struct rPTE {
   u64 phys_addr;
   u30 size;
   u02 dir;
   u01 valid;
   u31 unused;
}; // = 128bit

d) struct rIOVA {
   u30 offset;
   u18 rentry;
   u16 rid;
}; // = 64bit

e) struct rIOTLB_entry {
   u16  bdf;
   u16  rid;
   u18  rentry;
   rPTE rpte;
   rPTE next;
};
```

Figure 9. The rIOMMU data structures. rDEVICE is used only by hardware. Last two fields of rRING are used only by software.

ciated with DMA target buffers; they are mapped/unmapped repeatedly and are valid only while their DMA is in flight.

The flat table pointed to by rRING.ring is an array of rPTE structures (Figure 9c). An rPTE consists of the physical address and size associated with the corresponding IOVA; two bits that specify the DMA *direction*, which can be from the device, to it, or both; and a bit that indicates whether the rPTE (and thus the corresponding IOVA) are valid. The physical address need not be page aligned and the associated size can have any value, allowing for fine-grained protection.

The rIOVA structure (Figure 9d) defines the format of IOVAs. As noted, every DMA has a bdf that uniquely identifies its rDEVICE. The rIOVA.rid (ring ID) serves as an index to the corresponding rDEVICE.rings array, and thus it uniquely identifies the rRING of the rIOVA. Likewise, rIOVA.rentry serves as an index to the rRING.ring array, and thus it uniquely identifies the rPTE of the rIOVA. The target address of the rIOVA is computed by adding rIOVA.offset to rPTE.phys_addr.

The data structures discussed so far are used by both software and hardware. They are setup by the OS and utilized by the rIOMMU to translate rIOVAs. The last one (Figure 9e) is a hardware-only structure, representing one rIOTLB entry. The combination of its first two fields (bdf+rid) uniquely identifies a rRING flat page table, which we denote as T. The rIOTLB utilizes at most one rIOTLB_entry per T. The combination of the first three fields (bdf+rid+rentry) uniquely identifies T's "current" rPTE—the PTE associated with the most recently translated rIOVA that belongs to T. The current rPTE is cached by rIOTLB_entry.rpte (holds a copy). The rIOTLB_entry.next field may or may not contain a prefetched copy of T's subsequent rPTE. (Our design does not depend on the latter field and works just as well without it.)

Hardware The rtranslate routine (Figure 10 top/left) outlines how rIOMMU translates a rIOVA to a physical address. First, it searches for e, the rIOTLB_entry of the rRING that is associated with the rIOVA. (Recall that there is only one such entry per rRING.) If e is missing from the rIOTLB, rIOMMU walks the table using the data structures defined above, finds the rPTE, and inserts to the rIOTLB a matching entry. Doing the table walk ensures that e.rpte is the rPTE of the given rIOVA. However, if e was initially found in the rIOTLB, then e and the rIOVA might mismatch. RIOMMU therefore compares the rentry numbers of e and the IOVA, and it updates e if they are different. Now that e is up-to-date, rIOMMU checks that the direction of the DMA is permitted according to the rPTE. It also checks that the offset of the IOVA is in range, namely, smaller than the associated rPTE.size. Violating these conditions constitutes an error, causing rIOMMU to trigger an I/O page fault (IOPF). IOPFs are not expected to occur (drivers pin target buffers to memory), and OSes typically reinitialize the I/O device if they do. If no violation is detected, rIOMMU finally performs the translation by adding the offset of the IOVA to rPTE.phys_addr.

The rtable_walk routine (Figure 10 top/right) ensures that the rIOVA complies with the rIOMMU data structure limits as well as points to a valid rPTE. Noncompliance might be the result of, e.g., an errant DMA or a buggy driver. After validation, rtable_walk initializes the rIOTLB_entry in a straightforward manner based on the rIOVA and its rPTE. It additionally attempts to prefetch the subsequent rPTE by invoking rprefetch (Figure 10 bottom/right), which succeeds if the next rPTE is valid. Prefetching can be asynchronous.

The riotlb_entry_sync routine (Figure 10 bottom/left) is used by rtranslate to synchronize e (the rIOTLB_entry) with the current IOVA. The two become unsynchronized, e.g., whenever the device handles a new DMA descriptor. The required rPTE can be found in e.next if prefetching was previously successful, in which case the routine assigns e.next to e.rpte. Otherwise, it uses rtable_walk to fetch the needed rPTE. Finally, it attempts to prefetch the subsequent rPTE.

Software The (un)map functions comprising the rIOMMU OS driver are shown in Figure 11. Their prototypes are logically similar to the associated Linux functions from the baseline IOMMU OS driver (Figures 4 and 6), with minor adjustments. The map flow corresponds to Figure 4. It gets a device, a ring ID, a physical address to be mapped, and the associated size and direction of the DMA. The first part of the code allocates a ring entry rPTE at the ring's tail and then updates the tail/nmapped fields accordingly. This allocation—which consists of incrementing two integers—is analogous to the costly IOVA allocation of baseline Linux.

The second part of map initializes the newly allocated rPTE. When the rPTE is ready, the map function invokes sync_mem, which ensures that the rPTE memory updates are visible to the rIOMMU. This part of the code is analogous to walking and updating the page table hierarchy of the baseline IOMMU, but it is simpler since the page table is flat. The return statement of the map function packs the rentry index and its ring ID into an IOVA as dictated by the rIOVA data structure (Figure 9d). The offset is always set to be 0 by the rIOMMU driver. Callers of map can later manipulate the offset as they please,

```
u64 rtranslate(u16 bus_dev_func, rIOVA iova, u2 dir) {
    rIOTLB_entry e = riotlb_find( bus_dev_func, iova.rid );
    if( ! e  ) {
        e = rtable_walk( bus_dev_func, iova );
        riotlb_insert( e );
    }
    if( e.rentry != iova.rentry )
        riotlb_entry_sync( bus_dev_func, iova, e );
    if( iova.offset >= e.rpte.size || ! (e.rpte.dir & dir) )
        io_page_fault();
    return e.rpte.phys_addr + iova.offset;
}
void riotlb_entry_sync(u16 bus_dev_func, rIOVA iova,
                       rIOTLB_entry e)
{
    rDEVICE d = get_domain( bus_dev_func );
    u18 next = (e.rentry + 1) % d.rings[e.rid].size;

    if( e.next.valid && (iova.rentry===next) ) {
        e.rpte = e.next;  e.rentry = next;
        e.next.valid = 0;
    } else
        e = rtable_walk( bus_dev_func, iova );
    rprefetch( d, e );
}
```

```
rIOTLB_entry
rtable_walk(u16 bus_dev_func, rIOVA iova)
{
    rDEVICE d = get_domain( bus_dev_func );
    if( iova.rid     >= d.size ||
        iova.rentry >= d.rings[iova.rid].size ||
        ! d.rings[iova.rid].ring[iova.rentry].valid )
        io_page_fault();

    rIOTLB_entry e;
    rRING r  = d.rings[iova.rid];
    e.bdf    = bus_dev_func;
    e.rid    = iova.rid;
    e.rentry = iova.rentry;
    e.rpte   = r.ring[e.rentry]; // copy
    rprefetch( d, e );
    return e;
}
void rprefetch(rDEVICE d, rIOTLB_entry e) // async
{
    rRING r  = d.rings[e.rid];
    u18 next = (e.rentry + 1) % r.size;
    if( r.size > 1 && r.ring[next].valid )
        e.next = r.ring[next];  // copy
}
```

Figure 10. Outline of the rIOMMU hardware logic. All DMAs are carried out with IOVAs that are translated by rtranslate.

```
rIOVA map(rDEVICE d, u16 rid, u64 pa, u30 size, u2 direction)
{
    rRING r = d.rings[rid];
    locked { if( r.nmapped == r.size ) return OVERFLOW;
             u18 t  = r.tail;
             r.tail = (r.tail + 1) % r.size;
             r.nmapped++;  }

    r.ring[t].phys_addr = pa;
    r.ring[t].size      = size;
    r.ring[t].dir       = direction;
    r.ring[t].valid     = 1;
    sync_mem( & r.ring[t] );
    return pack_iova( 0/*offset*/, t/*rentry*/, rid );
}
```

```
void unmap(rDEVICE d, rIOVA iova, bool end_of_burst) {
    rRING r = d.rings[iova.rid];
    r.ring[iova.rentry].valid = 0;
    locked { r.nmapped--; }
    sync_mem( & r.ring[iova.rentry] );
    if( end_of_burst )
        riotlb_invalidate( bus_dev_func(d), iova.rid );
}
void sync_mem(void * line) {
    if( ! riommu_pt_is_coherent() ) {
        memory_barrier();
        cache_line_flush( line );
    }
    memory_barrier();
}
```

Figure 11. Outline of the rIOMMU OS driver map and unmap routines, which respectively correspond to Figures 4 and 6.

provided they conform to the size constraint encoded into the corresponding rPTE.

The flow of unmap (Figure 11/right) corresponds to Figure 6. Unmap gets an rIOVA, marks the associated rPTE as invalid (analogous to walking the table hierarchy), decrements the ring's nmapped counter (analogous to IOVA deallocation), and synchronizes the memory to make the rPTE update visible to the rIOMMU. Recall that when the device driver is notified that its device has finished some DMAs, it loops through the relevant descriptors and sequentially unmaps their IOVAs (§2.3). The driver sets the end_of_burst parameter of unmap to true at the end of this loop upon the last IOVA, signifying that an rIOTLB_entry invalidation is required. One such invalidation is sufficient for the entire burst because, by design, each rRING has at most one rIOTLB_entry allocated in the rIOTLB.

Our experimental measurements indicate that the average loop length of a throughput-sensitive workload such as Netperf is ~200 iterations. This is long enough to make the amortized cost of IOTLB invalidations negligible, as in the deferred mode, but without sacrificing safety. Amortization, however, does not apply to latency-sensitive workloads. Nonetheless, the invalidation cost is small in comparison to the overall latency as will shortly be demonstrated.

Finally, we consider the problem of synchronizing the memory between the IOMMU and its driver. In sync_mem (Figure 11 bottom/right), we see support for two hardware modes, corresponding to whether the IOMMU table walk is coherent with the CPU caches. The baseline Linux kernel queries the relevant IOMMU capability bit. If it finds that the two are not in the same coherency domain, it introduces an additional memory barrier followed by a cacheline flush. In the following section, we experimentally evaluate two simulated rIOMMU versions corresponding to these two modes.

Applicability and Limitations We note in passing that rIOMMU relies on the predictability of the order of IOVA (un)mappings—not the order by which the IOVAs are used by the device. That is, so long as IOVAs are valid (mapped), they can be used out of order. They are merely indices to a

1D-array. The only implication of an out of order access is that the rIOTLB prefetched 'next' entry would not satisfy that access, so the translation would have to be fetched from DRAM. (Namely, the riotlb_entry_sync hardware routine will be re-invoked; see left of Figure 10.)

Let R be a ring. Let D be the number of DMA descriptors comprising R. Let L be the maximal number of R's live IOVAs whose DMAs are currently in flight. And let N be the size of the associated rRING. N is set by the device driver upon startup. Optimally, $N \geq L$, or else the driver would experience overflow (2nd line of map in Figure 11). While suboptimal, overflow is legal as with other devices employing rings; it just means that the driver should slow down. D is typically hundreds or a few thousands. In some I/O devices, each descriptor can hold a constant number of IOVAs (K), so setting $N = D \times K$ would prevent overflow. Some devices support scatter-gather lists, whose K might be large or unbounded. Developers of device drivers must therefore make a judicious decision regarding N based on their domain-specific knowledge about L. (In our experiments, L was at most 8K for all rings.) Alternatively, developers can opt for using the baseline IOMMU as discussed below.

The IOMMU induces noticeable overhead only for high bandwidth I/O devices, notably NICs and PCIe SSDs. We have thus far focused on the former, but rIOMMU is also applicable to the latter. Specifically, PCIe SSDs adhere to the NVM Express (NVMe) specification for fast non-volatile memory devices [41], which dictates that OS-device interactions are conducted via circular rings that impose a strict (un)mapping order. (There can be up to 64K such rings, which are denoted "queues"; each queue may contain up to 64K descriptors, which are denoted "commands".)

Conversely, rIOMMU is inapplicable to slower SATA drives, which adhere to the Advanced Host Controller Interface Specification (AHCI) [29]. A SATA drive has a single queue with 32 slots (DMA descriptors) that can be processed by the drive in arbitrary order. It would be easy to extend rIOMMU to support this work mode as well. But such support seems unneeded, because SATA drives are too slow to benefit. Our measurements indicate indistinguishable performance results when running the Bonnie++ benchmark [15, 39] executing sequential I/O with (1) strict IOMMU protection and with (2) a disabled IOMMU. Regardless of whether we use a SATA HDD or a SATA SSD.

rIOMMU is likewise inapplicable in setups that exploit remote direct memory access (RDMA), where fine-grained protection is impractical. The reason: all the memory that could be accessed by the passive, receiving NIC must be persistently mapped by the IOMMU, as it is unknown which location would be accessed. We therefore do not propose to entirely replace the baseline IOMMU, only to supplement it. (PCIe allows for multiple IOMMUs and existing systems routinely support such configurations.)

5. Evaluation

5.1 Methodology

Simulating rIOMMU We experimentally evaluate the seven IOMMU modes defined in §3–4: (1) strict, which is the completely safe Linux baseline; (2) strict+, which enhances strict with our faster IOVA allocator; (3) defer, which is the Linux variant that trades off some protection for performance by batching IOTLB invalidations; (4) defer+, which is defer with our IOVA allocator; (5) riommu- (in lowercase), which is the newly proposed rIOMMU when assuming no I/O page table coherency; (6) riommu, which does assume coherent I/O page tables; and (7) none, which turns off the IOMMU.

The five non-rIOMMU modes are executed as is. They constitute full implementations of working systems and do not require a simulation component. To simulate the two rIOMMU modes, we start with the none mode as the baseline. We then supplement the baseline with calls to the (un)map functions, similarly to the way they are called in the non-simulated IOMMU-enabled modes. But instead of invoking the native functions of the Linux IOMMU driver (Figures 4 and 6), we invoke the (un)map functions that we implement in the simulated rIOMMU driver (Figure 11). All the code of the rIOMMU driver can be—and is—executed, with one exception. Since there is no real rIOTLB, we must simulate the invalidation of rIOTLB entries. We do so by busy waiting for 2,150 cycles upon each entry invalidation, in accordance to the measurements specified in Table 1.

Notice that our methodology does not account for differences between the existing and proposed IOMMU translation mechanism. We only account for actions shown in Figures 4 and 6 but not those in Figure 5. Notably, we ignore the fact that the IOMMU works harder than the rIOMMU due to IOTLB misses that rIOMMU avoids via prefetching. We likewise ignore the fact that rIOMMU works harder than the no-IOMMU mode, since it translates addresses whereas the no-IOMMU mode does not. We ignore these differences, as the model validated in §3.3 shows that throughput is entirely determined by the number of cycles it takes the core—not the device or the IOMMU—to process a DMA request, even for the most demanding I/O-intensive workloads. The system behaves this way probably because the device and IOMMU operate in parallel to the CPU and are apparently fast enough so as not to constitute a bottleneck.

We revalidate our methodology and show that it is also applicable for latency-sensitive workloads by using the standard Netperf UDP request-response (RR) benchmark, which repeatedly sends one byte to its peer and waits for an identical response. We run RR under two IOMMU modes: hardware pass-through (HWpt) and software pass-through (SWpt). With HWpt, the IOMMU is enabled, but it translates each IOVA to an identical physical address without consulting the IOTLB or any page table. SWpt provides an equivalent functionality by using a page table that maps the entire physical memory and associates each physical page address with an identical IOVA. Under SWpt, Netperf RR experiences an IOTLB miss on every packet it sends and receives. Nonetheless, we find that the performance of HWpt and SWpt is identical, because the network stack and interrupt processing introduce far greater latencies that hide the IOTLB miss penalty. Moreover, we find that the RR performance of HWpt/SWpt is identical to that of no-IOMMU.

Throughput performance of Netperf stream with HWpt and SWpt is smaller by ~10% relative to no-IOMMU. But here too the difference is entirely caused by the core: about 200 CPU cycles spent on unrelated kernel abstraction code that executes under HWpt/SWpt but not under no-IOMMU.

Experimental Setup In an effort to get more general results, we conduct the evaluation using two setups involving two different NICs, as follows.

The Mellanox setup (mlx for short) is comprised of two identical Dell PowerEdge R210 II Rack Server machines that communicate through Mellanox ConnectX3 40Gbps NICs connected back to back and configured to use Ethernet. We use one machine as the server and the other as a workload generator client. Each machine has a 8GB 1333MHz memory and a single-socket 4-core Intel Xeon E3-1220 CPU running at 3.10GHz. The chipset is Intel C202, which supports VT-d, Intel's Virtualization Technology that provides IOMMU functionality. We configure the server to utilize one core only and turn off all power optimizations—sleep states (C-states) and dynamic voltage and frequency scaling (DVFS)—to avoid reporting artifacts caused by nondeterministic events. The machines run Ubuntu 12.04 with the Linux 3.4.64 kernel. All experimental findings described thus far were obtained with the mlx setup.

The Broadcom setup (brcm for short) is similar, likewise utilizing two R210 machines. The differences are that the two machines communicate through Broadcom NetXtreme II BCM57810 10GbE NICs (connected by a CAT7 10GBASE-T cable for fast Ethernet); that they have 16GB memory; and that they run the Linux 3.11.0 kernel.

The mlx and brcm device drivers differ substantially. Notably, mlx utilizes more ring buffers and allocates more IOVAs (we observed a total of ~12K addresses for mlx and ~3K for brcm). The mlx driver uses two target buffers per packet (header and body) and thus two IOVAs, whereas the brcm driver allocates only one buffer/IOVA per packet.

Benchmarks To drive our experiments we utilize the following benchmarks. Netperf TCP stream [30] is a standard tool to measure networking throughput. It maximizes the amount of data sent over one TCP connection, simulating an I/O-intensive workload. Its default message size is 16KB. This is the application we used in §3.

Netperf UDP RR (request-response) models a latency sensitive workload by exchanging one byte messages in a ping-pong manner. The per message latency can be calculated as the inverse of the number of messages per second.

Apache [18, 19] is a HTTP web server. We drive it with ApacheBench [5] (distributed with Apache) that measures the number of requests per second that the server is capable of handling, issuing (32) concurrent requests of a static page of a given size. We run two instances of the benchmark, requesting a smaller (1KB) and a bigger (1MB) file.

Memcached [20] is an in-memory key-value storage server. We drive it with the Memslap benchmark [2] (part of the libmemcached client library), which measures the completion rate of the requests that it generates. By default, Memslap generates a workload comprised of 90% get and 10% set operations, with 64B and 1KB key and value sizes, respectively. It too is set to use 32 concurrent requests.

5.2 Results

We run each benchmark 100 times. Each individual run is configured to take ~10 seconds. We treat the first 10 runs as warmup and report the average of the remaining 90 runs. Figure 12 shows the resulting throughput and CPU consumption for the mlx (top) and brcm (bottom) setups. The corresponding normalized performance is shown in Table 2, specifying the relative improvement of the two rIOMMU variants over the other modes. The top/left plot in Figure 12 corresponds to the analysis and data shown in Figures 7–8.

Let us discuss the results in Figure 12, left to right. The greatest observed improvement by rIOMMU is attained with mlx / Netperf stream (Figure 12/top/left). This result is to be expected considering the model from §3.3 showing that every cycle shaved off the IOVA (un)mappings translates into increased throughput. CPU cycles constitute the bottleneck resource, as is evident from the mlx/stream/CPU curve, which is at 100% for all IOMMU modes. The notable difference between riommu- and riommu is due to ~1.1K cycles that the former adds to the latter, which is the cost of four additional memory barriers and four additional cacheline flushes, per packet. (Specifically, a barrier and a cacheline flush in both map and unmap for two IOVAs corresponding to the packet's header and data.) Riommu- and riommu provide 2.90–7.56x higher throughput relative to the completely safe IOMMU modes strict and strict+, and 1.74–3.79x higher throughput relative to the deferred modes. The latter, however, does not constitute an apple-to-apples comparison, since the deferred modes are vulnerable whereas the rIOMMU modes are safe. Riommu- and riommu deliver 0.52x and 0.77x lower throughout relative to the unprotected, no-IOMMU optimum.

The brcm/stream results (Figure 12/bottom/left) are quantitatively and qualitatively different. In particular, all IOMMU modes except strict have enough cycles to saturate the Broadcom NIC and achieve its line-rate, which is 10 Gbps. The brcm setup requires fewer cycles per packet because its device driver is more efficient, e.g., due to utilizing only one IOVA per packet instead of two. In setups of this type—where

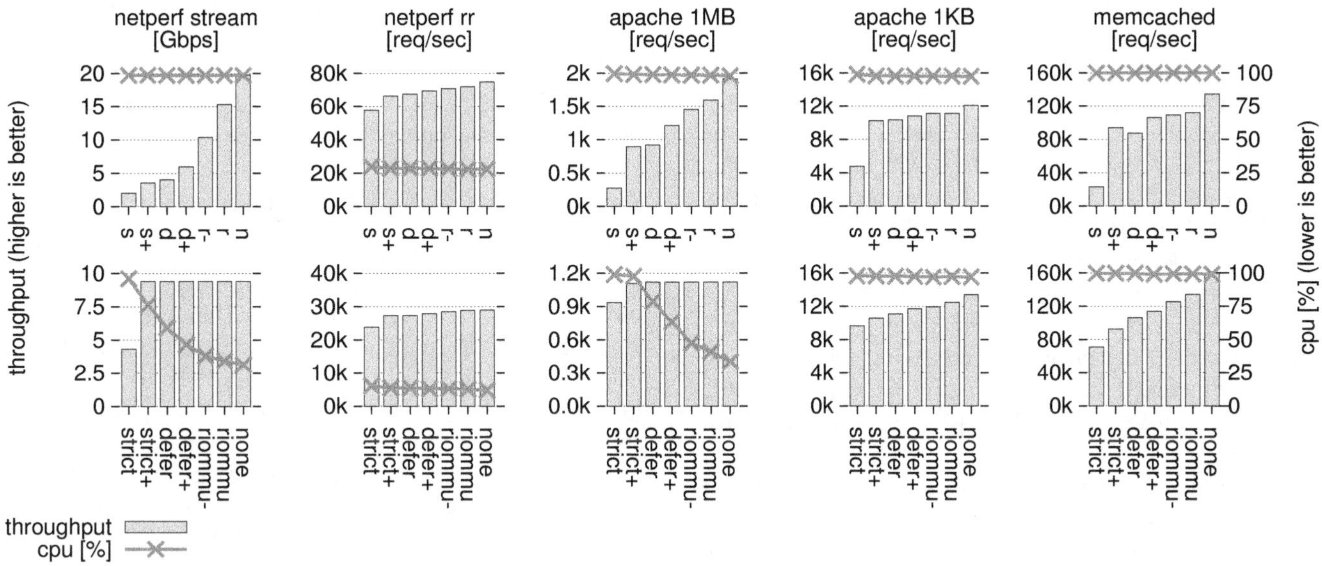

Figure 12. Performance of the IOMMU modes when using the Mellanox (top) and Broadcom (bottom) NICs.

NIC	*benchmark*	*throughput*										*cpu*									
		riommu- divided by					*riommu divided by*					*riommu- divided by*					*riommu divided by*				
		strict	*strict+*	*defer*	*defer+*	*none*	*strict*	*strict+*	*defer*	*defer+*	*none*	*strict*	*strict+*	*defer*	*defer+*	*none*	*strict*	*strict+*	*defer*	*defer+*	*none*
mlx	stream	5.12	2.90	2.57	1.74	0.52	7.56	4.28	3.79	2.57	0.77	1.00	1.00	1.00	1.00	1.00	1.00	1.00	1.00	1.00	1.00
	rr	1.23	1.07	1.05	1.02	0.95	1.25	1.09	1.07	1.03	0.96	0.94	0.99	0.98	0.99	1.01	0.93	0.98	0.96	0.98	1.00
	apache 1M	5.30	1.62	1.58	1.20	0.76	5.80	1.77	1.73	1.31	0.83	0.99	0.99	1.00	1.00	1.00	0.99	0.99	0.99	1.00	1.00
	apache 1K	2.32	1.08	1.07	1.03	0.92	2.32	1.08	1.07	1.03	0.92	0.99	1.00	1.00	1.00	1.00	0.99	1.00	1.00	1.00	1.00
	memcached	4.77	1.17	1.25	1.03	0.82	4.88	1.19	1.28	1.05	0.83	1.00	1.00	1.00	1.00	1.00	1.00	1.00	1.00	1.00	1.00
brcm	stream	2.17	1.00	1.00	1.00	1.00	2.17	1.00	1.00	1.00	1.00	0.40	0.50	0.64	0.81	1.21	0.36	0.45	0.58	0.73	1.09
	rr	1.19	1.05	1.04	1.02	0.99	1.21	1.06	1.05	1.03	1.00	0.86	0.96	0.96	1.00	1.11	0.84	0.93	0.93	0.98	1.08
	apache 1M	1.20	1.01	1.00	1.00	1.00	1.20	1.01	1.00	1.00	1.00	0.48	0.49	0.60	0.75	1.41	0.41	0.42	0.52	0.65	1.22
	apache 1K	1.24	1.13	1.08	1.02	0.89	1.29	1.18	1.13	1.07	0.93	0.99	0.99	0.99	1.00	1.00	0.99	1.00	1.00	1.00	1.00
	memcached	1.76	1.35	1.18	1.10	0.78	1.88	1.45	1.27	1.18	0.84	1.00	1.00	1.00	1.00	1.00	1.00	1.00	1.00	1.00	1.00

Table 2. Relative (normalized) performance numbers.

the network is saturated—the performance metric of interest becomes the CPU consumption. By Table 2, we can see that riommu and riommu- consume 0.36–0.50x fewer CPU cycles than the two strict modes; 0.58–0.81x fewer cycles than the deferred modes; and 1.09x and 1.21x more cycles than the no-IOMMU optimum, respectively.

The improvement by rIOMMU is less pronounced when running RR, in both mlx and brcm, with 1.02–1.25x higher throughput and 0.84–1.00x lower CPU consumption relative to the strict and deferred variants. It is less pronounced due to RR's ping-pong nature, which implies that CPU cycles are in low demand, as indicated by the CPU curves at 28–30% for mlx and at 12–15% for brcm. For this reason, in comparison to mlx/RR/none, rIOMMU has 4–5% lower throughput and nearly identical CPU consumption. In comparison to brcm/RR/none, rIOMMU has 8–11% higher CPU consumption and nearly identical throughput. Although the per-packet processing time at the core is smaller in brcm, overall, the mlx hardware transmits packets faster, as indicated by its higher RR throughput. The corresponding round-trip time of the different modes (which, as noted, is the inverse of the throughput in RR's case) is shown in Table 3.

NIC	*strict*	*strict+*	*defer*	*defer+*	*riommu-*	*riommu*	*none*
mlx	17.3	15.1	14.9	14.4	14.1	13.9	13.4
brcm	41.9	36.7	36.6	35.8	35.1	34.7	34.6

Table 3. Netperf RR round-trip time in microseconds.

The results of Apache 1MB are qualitatively identical to those of Netperf stream, because the benchmark transmits a lot of data per request and is thus throughput sensitive. Conversely, Apache 1KB is not throughput sensitive. Its smaller 1KB requests make the performance of mlx and brcm look remarkably similar despite their networking infrastructure difference. In both cases, the bottleneck is the CPU, while the volume of the transmitted data is only a small fraction of the NICs capacity. (Both deliver ~12K requests per second of 1KB files, yielding a transfer rate of ~0.1 Gbps.) The reason: Apache requires heavy processing for each http request. This overhead is amortized over hundreds of packets in the case of Apache 1MB but over only one packet in the case of 1KB. Thus, the computational processing dominates the throughput of Apache 1KB and the role of the networking infrastructure is marginalized. Even so, rIOMMU demonstrates a ~1.24x and ~2.32x throughput improvement over brcm/strict and mlx/strict, respectively. It is up to 1.18x higher relative to the other IOMMU-enabled modes. And ~0.9x lower relative to the unprotected optimum.[2]

The network activity of Apache 1KB is somewhat similar to that of the Memcached benchmark, because both are configured with 32 concurrent requests, both receive queries comprised of a few dozens of bytes (file name or key item), and both transmit 1KB responses (file content or data item). The difference is that the Memcached internal logic is simpler, as its purpose is merely to serve as an in-memory LRU cache. For this reason, it achieves an order of magnitude higher throughput relative to Apache 1KB.[3] The shorter per-request processing time makes the differences between the IOMMU configurations more pronounced, with rIOMMU throughput that is 1.17–4.88x higher than the completely safe modes, 1.03–1.28x higher than the deferred modes, and 0.78–0.84x lower than the optimum.

5.3 When IOTLB Miss Penalty Matters

Our experiments thus far indicated that using the IOMMU affects performance because it mandates the OS to spend CPU cycles on creating and destroying IOVA mappings. We were unable to measure the overhead caused by the actual IOMMU translation activity of walking the page tables upon an IOTLB miss (Figures 2 and 5). In §5.1, we attributed this inability to the substantially longer latencies induced by interrupt processing and the TCP/IP stack. In Table 3, we specified the round-trip latencies, whose magnitude (13–42 μs) seems to suggest that the occasional cost of 4 memory references per table walk is negligible in comparison.

There are, however, high performance environments that enjoy lower latencies in the order of a μs [14, 21, 43, 48], which is required, e.g., "where a fraction of a microsecond can make a difference in the value of a transaction" [1]. User-level I/O, for example, might permit applications to (1) utilize raw Ethernet packets to eliminate TCP/IP overheads, and to (2) poll the I/O device to eliminate interrupt delays.

With the help of the ibverbs library [27, 35], we established such a configuration on top of the mlx setup. We ran two experiments. The first iteratively and randomly selects a buffer from a large pool of previously mapped buffers and transmits it, thus ensuring that the probability for the corresponding IOVA to reside in the IOTLB is low. The second experiment does the same but with only one buffer, thus ensuring that the IOTLB always hits. The latency difference—which is the cost of an IOTLB miss—was ~0.5 μs (1532 cycles on average); we believe it is reasonable to assume that it approximates the benefit of using rIOMMU over the existing IOMMU in high performance environments of this type.

5.4 Comparing to TLB Prefetchers

RIOMMU is not a prefetcher. Rather, it is a new IOMMU design that allows for efficient IOVA (un)mappings while minimizing costly IOTLB invalidations. (Unrelated to prefetching.) But rIOMMU does have a prefetching component, since it loads to the rIOTLB the next IOVA to be used ahead of time. While this component turned out to be useful only in specialized setups (§5.3), it is still interesting to compare this aspect of our work to previously proposed TLB prefetchers.

For lack of space, we only briefly describe the bottom line. We modified the IOMMU layer of KVM/QEMU to log the DMAs that its emulated I/O devices perform. We ran our benchmarks in a VM and generated DMA traces. We fed the traces to three simulated TLB prefetchers: Markov [31], Recency [44], and Distance [34], as surveyed by Kandiraju and Sivasubramaniam [33]. We found their baseline versions to be ineffective, as IOVAs are invalidated immediately after being used. We modified them and allowed them to store invalidated addresses, but mandated them to walk the page table and check that their predictions are mapped before making them. Distance was still ineffective. Recency and Markov, however, were able to predict most accesses, but only if the number of entries comprising their history data structure grew larger than the ring. In contrast, rIOTLB requires only two entries per ring and its "predictions" are always correct.

6. Conclusions

The IOMMU design is similar to that of the regular MMU, despite the inherent differences in their workloads. This design worked reasonably well when I/O devices were relatively slow as compared to the CPU. But it hampers the performance of contemporary devices like 10/40 Gbps NICs. We foresee that this problem will get worse due to the ever increasing speed of such devices. We thus contend that it makes sense to rearchitect the IOMMU such that it directly supports the unique characteristics of its workload. We propose rIOMMU as an example for such a redesign and show that the benefits of using it are substantial.

Acknowledgments We thank the anonymous reviewers for their feedback. We thank Ilya Lesokhin and Igor Smolyar for providing much appreciated technical help. This research was funded in part by the Intel Collaborative Research Institute for Computational Intelligence (ICRI-CI) and by the Israeli Ministry of Science and Technology grant #3-9779. Mellanox graciously donated NICs.

[2] We note in passing that our Apache 1KB throughput results coincide with that of Soares et al. [46], who reported a latency of 22ms for 256 concurrent requests, which translate to $1000/22 \times 256 \approx 12$K requests/second.

[3] Our Memcached results are comparable to that of Gordon et al. [22].

References

[1] Dennis Abts and Bob Felderman. A guided tour through data-center networking. *ACM Queue*, 10(5):10:10–10:23, May 2012.

[2] Brian Aker. Memslap - load testing and benchmarking a server. `http://docs.libmemcached.org/bin/memslap.html`. libmemcached 1.1.0 documentation. Accessed: Jan 2015.

[3] AMD Inc. AMD IOMMU architectural specification, rev 2.00. `http://support.amd.com/TechDocs/48882.pdf`, Mar 2011. Accessed: Jan 2015.

[4] Nadav Amit, Muli Ben-Yehuda, Dan Tsafrir, and Assaf Schuster. vIOMMU: efficient IOMMU emulation. In *USENIX Annual Technical Conference (ATC)*, pages 73–86, 2011.

[5] Apachebench. `http://en.wikipedia.org/wiki/ApacheBench`. Accessed: Jan 2015.

[6] Apple Inc. Thunderbolt device driver programming guide: Debugging VT-d I/O MMU virtualization. `https://developer.apple.com/library/mac/documentation/HardwareDrivers/Conceptual/ThunderboltDevGuide/DebuggingThunderboltDrivers/DebuggingThunderboltDrivers.html`, 2013. Accessed: May 2014.

[7] ARM Holdings. ARM system memory management unit architecture specification — SMMU architecture version 2.0. `http://infocenter.arm.com/help/topic/com.arm.doc.ihi0062c/IHI0062C_system_mmu_architecture_specification.pdf`, 2013. Accessed: Jan 2015.

[8] Thomas Ball, Ella Bounimova, Byron Cook, Vladimir Levin, Jakob Lichtenberg, Con McGarvey, Bohus Ondrusek, Sriram K. Rajamani, and Abdullah Ustuner. Thorough static analysis of device drivers. In *ACM Eurosys*, pages 73–85, 2006.

[9] Michael Becher, Maximillian Dornseif, and Christian N. Klein. FireWire: all your memory are belong to us. In *CanSecWest applied security conference*, 2005.

[10] Muli Ben-Yehuda, Jimi Xenidis, Michal Ostrowski, Karl Rister, Alexis Bruemmer, and Leendert van Doorn. The price of safety: Evaluating IOMMU performance. In *Ottawa Linux Symposium (OLS)*, pages 9–20, 2007.

[11] James E.J. Bottomley. Dynamic DMA mapping using the generic device. `https://git.kernel.org/cgit/linux/kernel/git/stable/linux-stable.git/tree/Documentation/DMA-API.txt?id=refs/tags/v3.18.3`. Linux kernel documentation. Accessed: Jan 2015.

[12] Brian D. Carrier and Joe Grand. A hardware-based memory acquisition procedure for digital investigations. *Digital Investigation*, 1(1):50–60, Feb 2014.

[13] Andy Chou, Junfeng Yang, Benjamin Chelf, Seth Hallem, and Dawson Engler. An empirical study of operating systems errors. In *ACM Symposium on Operating Systems Principles (SOSP)*, pages 73–88, 2001.

[14] Cisco. Understanding switch latency. `http://www.cisco.com/c/en/us/products/collateral/switches/nexus-3000-series-switches/white_paper_c11-661939.html`, Jun 2012. White paper. Accessed: Aug 2014.

[15] Russell Coker. The Bonnie++ benchmark. `http://www.coker.com.au/bonnie++/`. Accessed: Jan 2015.

[16] Jonathan Corbet. *Linux Device Drivers*, chapter 15: Memory Mapping and DMA. O'Reilly, 3rd edition, 2005.

[17] John Criswell, Nicolas Geoffray, and Vikram Adve. Memory safety for low-level software/hardware interactions. In *USENIX Security Symposium*, pages 83–100, 2009.

[18] The Apache HTTP server project. `http://httpd.apache.org`. Accessed: Jan 2015.

[19] Roy T. Fielding and Gail Kaiser. The Apache HTTP server project. *IEEE Internet Computing*, 1(4):88–90, Jul 1997.

[20] Brad Fitzpatrick. Distributed caching with memcached. *Linux Journal*, 2004(124), Aug 2004.

[21] Brice Goglin. Design and implementation of Open-MX: High-performance message passing over generic Ethernet hardware. In *IEEE International Parallel and Distributed Processing Symposium (IPDPS)*, 2008.

[22] Abel Gordon, Nadav Amit, Nadav Har'El, Muli Ben-Yehuda, Alex Landau, Assaf Schuster, and Dan Tsafrir. ELI: Bare-metal performance for I/O virtualization. In *ACM International Conference on Architectural Support for Programming Languages and Operating Systems (ASPLOS)*, pages 411–422, 2012.

[23] Jorrit N. Herder, Herbert Bos, Ben Gras, Philip Homburg, and Andrew S. Tanenbaum. Failure resilience for device drivers. In *IEEE/IFIP Annual International Conference on Dependable Systems and Networks (DSN)*, pages 41–50, 2007.

[24] Brian Hill. Integrating an EDK custom peripheral with a LocalLink interface into Linux. Technical Report XAPP1129 (v1.0), XILINX, May 2009. `http://www.xilinx.com/support/documentation/application_notes/xapp1129.pdf`. Accessed: Jan 2015.

[25] IBM Corporation. PowerLinux servers — 64-bit DMA concepts. `http://pic.dhe.ibm.com/infocenter/lnxinfo/v3r0m0/topic/liabm/liabmconcepts.htm`. Accessed: May 2014.

[26] IBM Corporation. AIX kernel extensions and device support programming concepts. `https://publib.boulder.ibm.com/infocenter/aix/v7r1/topic/com.ibm.aix.kernelext/doc/kernextc/kernextc_pdf.pdf`, 2013. Accssed: May 2014.

[27] ibverbs evaluation. `http://www.scalalife.eu/book/export/html/434`. Accessed: Aug 2014.

[28] Intel Corporation. Intel virtualization technology for directed I/O - architecture specification - specification - Rev. 2.2.

http://www.intel.com/content/dam/www/public/us/en/documents/product-specifications/vt-directed-io-spec.pdf, Sep 2013. Accessed: Jan 2015.

[29] Intel Corporation. Serial ATA advanced host controller interface (AHCI) 1.3.1. http://www.intel.com/content/www/us/en/io/serial-ata/serial-ata-ahci-spec-rev1-3-1.html, Mar 2014. Accessed: Jan 2015.

[30] Rick A. Jones. A network performance benchmark (Revision 2.0). Technical report, Hewlett Packard, 1995. http://www.netperf.org/netperf/training/Netperf.html. Accessed: Jan 2015.

[31] Doug Joseph and Dirk Grunwald. Prefetching using Markov predictors. In *ACM International Symposium on Computer Architecture (ISCA)*, pages 252–263, 1997.

[32] Asim Kadav, Matthew J. Renzelmann, and Michael M. Swift. Tolerating hardware device failures in software. In *ACM Symposium on Operating Systems Principles (SOSP)*, pages 59–72, 2009.

[33] Gokul B. Kandiraju and Anand Sivasubramaniam. Characterizing the d-TLB behavior of SPEC CPU2000 benchmarks. In *ACM SIGMETRICS International Conference on Measurement and Modeling of Computer Systems*, pages 129–139, Jun 2002.

[34] Gokul B. Kandiraju and Anand Sivasubramaniam. Going the distance for TLB prefetching: An application-driven study. In *ACM International Symposium on Computer Architecture (ISCA)*, pages 195–206, 2002.

[35] Gregory Kerr. Dissecting a small InfiniBand application using the Verbs API. *Computing Research Repository (arxiv)*, abs/1105.1827, 2011. http://arxiv.org/abs/1105.1827.

[36] Joshua LeVasseur, Volkmar Uhlig, Jan Stoess, and Stefan Götz. Unmodified device driver reuse and improved system dependability via virtual machines. In *USENIX Symposium on Operating System Design and Implementation (OSDI)*, pages 17–30, 2004.

[37] Moshe Malka, Nadav Amit, and Dan Tsafrir. Efficient intra-operating system protection against harmful DMAs. In *USENIX Conference on File and Storage Technologies (FAST)*, Feb 2015.

[38] Vinod Mamtani. DMA directions and Windows. http://download.microsoft.com/download/a/f/d/afdfd50d-6eb9-425e-84e1-b4085a80e34e/sys-t304_wh07.pptx, 2007. Accessed: May 2014.

[39] Ben Martin. Using Bonnie++ for filesystem performance benchmarking. Linux.com article. http://archive09.linux.com/feature/139742, 2008. Accessed: Jan 2015.

[40] David S. Miller, Richard Henderson, and Jakub Jelinek. Dynamic DMA mapping guide. https://git.kernel.org/cgit/linux/kernel/git/stable/linux-stable.git/tree/Documentation/DMA-API-HOWTO.txt?id=refs/tags/v3.18.3. Linux kernel documentation. Accessed: Jan 2015.

[41] NVM Express Workgroup. NVM Express (NVMe) specification – Revision 1.2. http://www.nvmexpress.org/wp-content/uploads/NVM-Express-1_2-Gold-20141209.pdf, Nov 2014. Accessed: Jan 2015.

[42] PCI-SIG. Address translation services Revision 1.1. https://www.pcisig.com/specifications/iov/ats, Jan 2009. Accessed: Jan 2015.

[43] Simon Peter, Jialin Li, Irene Zhang, Dan R. K. Ports, Doug Woos, Arvind Krishnamurthy, Thomas Anderson, and Timothy Roscoe. Arrakis: The operating system is the control plane. In *USENIX Symposium on Operating System Design and Implementation (OSDI)*, pages 1–16, 2014.

[44] Ashley Saulsbury, Fredrik Dahlgren, and Per Stenström. Recency-based TLB preloading. In *ACM International Symposium on Computer Architecture (ISCA)*, pages 117–127, 2000.

[45] Arvind Seshadri, Mark Luk, Ning Qu, and Adrian Perrig. SecVisor: A tiny hypervisor to provide lifetime kernel code integrity for commodity OSes. In *ACM Symposium on Operating Systems Principles (SOSP)*, pages 335–350, 2007.

[46] Livio Soares and Michael Stumm. FlexSC: Flexible system call scheduling with exception-less system calls. In *USENIX Symposium on Operating System Design and Implementation (OSDI)*, pages 33–46, 2010.

[47] Michael Swift, Brian Bershad, and Henry Levy. Improving the reliability of commodity operating systems. *ACM Transactions on Computer Systems (TOCS)*, 23(1):77–110, Feb 2005.

[48] Transpacket Fusion Networks. Ultra low latency of 1.2 microseconds for 1G to 10G Ethernet aggregation. http://tinyurl.com/transpacket-low-latency, Dec 2012. Accessed: Jan 2015.

[49] Carl Waldspurger and Mendel Rosenblum. I/O virtualization. *Communications of the ACM (CACM)*, 55(1):66–73, Jan 2012.

[50] Dan Williams, Patrick Reynolds, Kevin Walsh, Emin Gün Sirer, and Fred B. Schneider. Device driver safety through a reference validation mechanism. In *USENIX Symposium on Operating System Design and Implementation (OSDI)*, pages 241–254, 2008.

[51] Paul Willmann, Scott Rixner, and Alan L. Cox. Protection strategies for direct access to virtualized I/O devices. In *USENIX Annual Technical Conference (ATC)*, pages 15–28, 2008.

[52] Rafal Wojtczuk. Subverting the Xen hypervisor. In *Black Hat*, 2008. http://www.blackhat.com/presentations/bh-usa-08/Wojtczuk/BH_US_08_Wojtczuk_Subverting_the_Xen_Hypervisor.pdf. Accessed: May 2014.

[53] Ben-Ami Yassour, Muli Ben-Yehuda, and Orit Wasserman. On the DMA mapping problem in direct device assignment. In *ACM International Systems and Storage Conference (SYSTOR)*, pages 18:1–18:12, 2010.

PuDianNao: A Polyvalent Machine Learning Accelerator

Daofu Liu
SKLCA, ICT, China

Tianshi Chen *
SKLCA, ICT, China

Shaoli Liu
SKLCA, ICT, China

Jinhong Zhou
USTC, China

Shengyuan Zhou
SKLCA, ICT, China

Olivier Teman
Inria, France

Xiaobing Feng
SKLCA, ICT, China

Xuehai Zhou
USTC, China

Yunji Chen
SKLCA, CAS Center for Excellence in Brain Science, ICT, China

Abstract

Machine Learning (ML) techniques are pervasive tools in various emerging commercial applications, but have to be accommodated by powerful computer systems to process very large data. Although general-purpose CPUs and GPUs have provided straightforward solutions, their energy-efficiencies are limited due to their excessive supports for flexibility. Hardware accelerators may achieve better energy-efficiencies, but each accelerator often accommodates only a single ML technique (family). According to the famous No-Free-Lunch theorem in the ML domain, however, an ML technique performs well on a dataset may perform poorly on another dataset, which implies that such accelerator may sometimes lead to poor learning accuracy. Even if regardless of the learning accuracy, such accelerator can still become inapplicable simply because the concrete ML task is altered, or the user chooses another ML technique.

In this study, we present an ML accelerator called PuDianNao, which accommodates seven representative ML techniques, including k-means, k-nearest neighbors, naive bayes, support vector machine, linear regression, classification tree, and deep neural network. Benefited from our thorough analysis on computational primitives and locality properties of different ML techniques, PuDianNao can perform up to 1056 GOP/s (e.g., additions and multiplications) in an area of 3.51 mm^2, and consumes 596 mW only. Compared with the NVIDIA K20M GPU (28nm process), PuDianNao (65nm process) is 1.20x faster, and can reduce the energy by 128.41x.

* Tianshi Chen is the corresponding author. Address: State Key Laboratory of Computer Architecture, Institute of Computing Technology, Chinese Academy of Sciences, Beijing, China. Email: chentianshi@ict.ac.cn

ASPLOS '15, March 14–18, 2015, Istanbul, Turkey..

http://dx.doi.org/10.1145/2694344.2694358

1. Introduction

In the era of data explosion, Machine Learning (ML) techniques have become pervasive tools in emerging large-scale commercial applications such as social network, recommendation system, computational advertising, and image recognition. Facebook generates over 10 Petabyte (PB) log data per month [6]. Taobao.com, the largest online retailer in China, generates tens of Terabyte (TB) data every day [6]. The increasing amount of data poses great challenges to ML techniques, as well as computer systems accommodating those techniques.

The most straightforward way to accelerate large-scale ML is to design more powerful general-purpose CPUs and GPUs. However, such processors must consume a large fraction of transistors to flexibly support diverse application domains, thus can often be inefficient for specific workloads. In this context, there is a clear trend towards hardware accelerators that can execute specific workloads with very high energy-efficiency or/and performance. For ML techniques that have broad yet important applications in both cloud servers and mobile ends, of course, there have been some successful FPGA/ASIC accelerators, but each of which often targets at only a single ML technique or technique family. DianNao [7, 8] is one such example, which effectively accelerates representative neural network algorithms to benefit different ML scenarios (e.g., regression and classification).

While valid to support different ML scenarios at different scales, DianNao still has disadvantages. To be specific, when using DianNao to solve an ML problem, one has no choice but to use a neural network. Although recent studies have reported the large success of neural network (e.g., deep neural network), they were often achieved at great computational efforts, and involve too many parameters to tune. Even if regardless of the high computational complexity, neural network can still be worse than other ML techniques under certain scenarios. For example, in the classification of linearly-separable data, complex neural networks can easily become over-fitting, and perform worse than even a linear classifier. In application domains such as financial quantitative trading, linear regression is more widely-used than neural network due to the simplicity and interpretability of linear model [5]. The famous no-free-lunch theorem from the ML domain is a good summary of the above situation: any learning technique cannot perform universally better than another learning technique [39]. The insight here is that an ML accelerator should be able to support diverse ML techniques, in order to address needs under different scenarios.

However, unlike neural networks which share similar computational patterns, there is significant diversity among existing ML techniques, making it hard to design a pervasive ML accelerator. The diversity is two-fold. First, different ML techniques may differ a lot in their *computational primitives*. Here we take two classification algorithms, naive bayes and k-nearest neighbors (k-NN), as examples. The most time-consuming part of naive bayes is estimating the conditional probabilities, but that of k-NN is calculating distances between instances (each represented as a feature vector). Second, different ML techniques may differ a lot in their *locality properties*. For example, a large number of instances in k-NN may be frequently reused to classify unseen instances, while each feature (vector component) of an instance is not frequently reused in naive bayes. In this case, one must identify and factor in computational primitives and locality properties of representative ML techniques before deciding the overall accelerator architecture.

In this paper, we present an accelerator accommodating seven representative ML techniques, i.e., k-means, k-NN, naive bayes, support vector machine, linear regression, classification tree, and deep neural network. We conduct a thorough analysis of the ML techniques to extract critical computational primitives and locality optimizations that need to be supported by the accelerator. We present PuDianNao, an architecture design at TSMC 65nm process. On 13 critical phases of 7 representative ML techniques, the accelerator, clocked at 1GHz, is 1.20x faster and 128.41x more energy-efficient than the NVIDIA K20M GPU on average.

Our contributions are the following. First, we thoroughly analyze several representative ML techniques to extract their key computational tasks and locality properties, which establishes a solid foundation for the design of ML accelerator. Second, we design novel functional units to cover common computational primitives of different ML techniques, as well as on-chip storage that comprehensively factors in locality properties of different ML techniques. Third, we present PuDianNao, an accelerator accommodating seven representative ML techniques and multiple ML scenarios (e.g., classification, regression and clustering).

The rest of this paper proceeds as the following. Section 2 conducts a thorough analysis on computational primitives and locality properties of seven ML techniques. Section 3 presents the accelerator architecture of PuDianNao. Section 4 introduces the control module and code format of PuDianNao. Section 5 and 6 provide the experimental methodology and experimental results, respectively. Section 7 presents the related work.

2. Analysis of Representative ML Techniques: A Computer Architecture Perspective

In the machine learning community, an ML technique is conventionally characterized by its mathematical model (e.g., linear or non-linear), its learning style (e.g., supervised or unsupervised), its training algorithm (e.g., maximum-a-posteriori or gradient descent) and so on. From a computer architecture perspective, however, an ML technique is mainly characterized by its computational primitives and locality property. In this section, we do not repeat too much the context of ML textbooks, but provide an architect's-eye analysis of seven ML techniques.

For each ML technique, our analysis consists of two parts. In the first part, we identify the most time-consuming step of the technique. In the second part, we analyze the locality property of the identified time-consuming step of the ML technique, and leave the analysis/optimization on the rest of the technique to later sections. This divide-and-conquer idea well reflects the spirit of our accelerator (see Section 3.1): it accommodates the most time-consuming operations of ML techniques with dedicated hardware computational structures as well as optimized on-chip buffers, but supports the rest operations by integrating lightweight general-purpose Arithmetic Logic Units (ALUs).

Based on our locality analysis, we also investigate how to reduce off-chip memory bandwidth requirements of different ML techniques, and empirically check potential off-chip memory bandwidth reductions with an in-house cache simulator, which has 32KB cache (clocked at 1GHz) which has enough banks to support a 256-bit SIMD engine. To focus on memory behaviors, we assume that the SIMD engine can calculate any function with three 256-bit inputs (e.g., $f(a, b, c)$) at one cycle. We provide a sufficiently large num-

```
//Na is the number of testing instances
//Nb is the number of reference instances
for (i = 0; i < Na; i++){
  for(j = 0; j < Nb; j ++){
    Dis[i,j] = dis(t(i),r(j));
} }
```

Figure 1: Original code of distance calculations.

ber of training/testing/reference instances (each is a 32x32-bit floating-point vector) for each ML technique when evaluating the off-chip memory bandwidth requirement.

2.1 k-Nearest Neighbors

k-Nearest Neighbors (k-NN) [2] is a simple yet widely-used learning algorithm that directly uses the k nearest neighbors of a testing instance to determine the label (classification or regression result) of the instance. For each testing instance, the k-NN has two major steps. First, it computes distances between the testing instance and reference instances. Second, it finds the k nearest reference instances to the testing instance, and assigns the testing instance the most frequent label among labels of the k nearest reference instances (classification), or the average label in the k nearest reference instances (regression). The most time-consuming operations in k-NN are calculating distances between instances. On UCI Gas datasets, distance calculations averagely account for.84.44% the computation time on an Intel Xeon E5-4620 CPU.

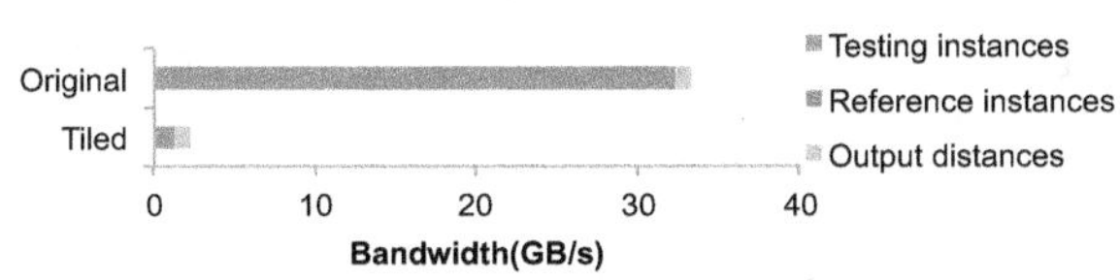

Figure 2: Memory bandwidth requirements for distance calculations of k-NN.

Figure 1 presents the original code of distance calculations. We observe that a reference instance can be reused after $N_b - 1$ distance calculations (N_b is the number of testing instances), while a testing instance can always be reused in its own loop. When N_b is very large, the reuse distance of a reference instance is also very large, and the chip cannot simultaneously store all reference instances, leading to frequent off-chip memory accesses that re-fetch the same reference instances for different testing instances. To exploit the locality of reference instances, we tile loops of both testing and reference instances, and define each *tiling block* to be distance calculations between T_i testing instances and T_j reference instances (see Figure 3). Tiling significantly reduces the reuse distance of reference instances, and can significantly reduce off-chip memory transfers. In our experiment comparing the off-chip memory bandwidth requirements before and after tiling, we set $T_i = T_j = 32$, i.e., $T_i + T_j = 64$ instances (each is a 32x32-bit floating-point vector) in a tiling block (64x32x4 Byte = 8KB) can be simultaneously stored in the cache (32KB). We observe that tiling reduces the off-chip memory bandwidth requirement of distance calculations by 93.9% (see Figure 2).

```
//Ti is the tiled testing block size
//Tj is the tiled reference block size
for (i = 0; i < Na/Ti; i++){
  for(j = 0; j < Nb/Tj; j ++){
    //tiled block
    for (ii = i*Ti; ii < (i+1)*Ti; ii++){
      for(jj = j*Tj; jj < (j+1)*Tj; jj++){
        Dis[ii,jj] = dis(t(ii),r(jj));
} } } }
```

Figure 3: Tiled code of distance calculations.

2.2 k-Means

k-Means [16] is an unsupervised ML technique which partitions N instances into k clusters. k-Means starts with k random cluster centroids, and iteratively performs two steps. First, it assigns each instance to the cluster whose current centroid (mean) is the nearest. Second, it computes the new mean of each cluster with the current members of the cluster, which then becomes the new centroid of the cluster. The most time-consuming operations in k-Means are distance calculations. On UCI Gas datasets, distance calculations account for 89.83% the computation time of k-Means on an Intel Xeon E5-4620 CPU.

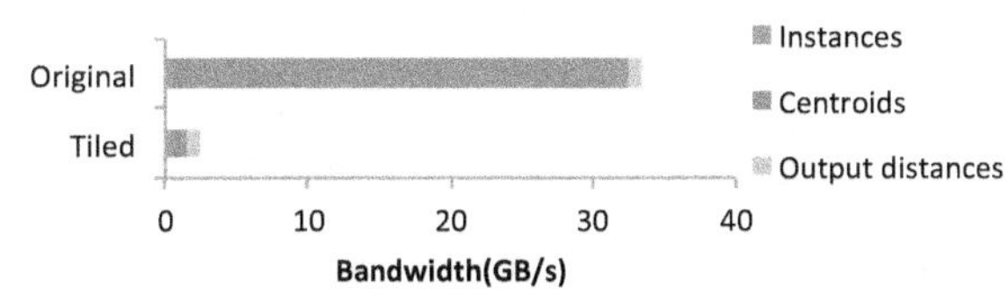

Figure 4: Memory bandwidth requirements for distance calculations of k-Means ($k = 64$).

In locality optimization, distance calculations in k-Means can be treated in a way (i.e., tiling) similar to what is done to k-NN. The minor difference here is that reference instances and testing instances in the locality analysis of k-NN are respectively replaced with cluster centroids (means), and instances to be clustered. We follow the same experimental setting of tiling in k-NN (e.g., instance length and tiling block size), and observe that tiling both cluster centroids and instances can reduce the off-chip memory bandwidth requirement of distance calculations by 92.5% (see Figure 4).

2.3 Deep Neural Network

Multi-Layer Perceptron (MLP) [12] is a classical artificial neural network that can model the non-linear relationship between inputs and outputs. Over the past decade, an emerging type of MLP called Deep Neural Network (DNN) has attracted broad interests of both the machine learning community and industry [10, 13, 20].

DNN is known to have a deep structure consisting of many hidden layers, and neurons in adjacent layers are often fully connected. A DNN has three computation modes, feedforward computation which computes the network output for each given input under the current network setting, pre-training which locally tune the synapses (connection weights) between each pair of adjacent layers, and global training which globally tune synapses with the Back Propagation (BP) algorithm [35].

We first analyze the feedforward computation, which computes neuron values of the $(g+1)$-th layer with neuron values of the g-th layer ($g \geq 1$). Without losing any generality, assume that we already know the neuron values of the g-th layer, a layer having N_a neurons $(x_1, \dots, x_{N_a})$. We are going to compute the neuron values of the $(g+1)$-th layer, a layer having N_b neurons $(y_1, \dots, y_{N_b})$. The value of the i-th neuron in the $(g+1)$-th layer, y_i, is computed by $y_j = f\left(\sum_{i=1}^{N_a} w_{ij}x_i + s_j\right)$, where f represents the activation function (e.g., sigmoid and tanh), w_{ij} is the synapse between neurons x_i and y_j, and s_j is the bias. The feedforward computation, which computes all N_b neurons in the same layer, can be written in a matrix form $Y = X \otimes W$, where

$$W = \begin{bmatrix} s_1 & s_2 & \cdots & s_{N_b} \\ w_{11} & w_{12} & \cdots & w_{1N_b} \\ w_{21} & w_{22} & \cdots & w_{2N_b} \\ \vdots & \vdots & \ddots & \vdots \\ w_{N_a1} & w_{N_a2} & \cdots & w_{N_aN_b} \end{bmatrix} \quad (1)$$

$X = (1, x_1, \dots, x_{N_a})$, $Y = (y_1, \dots, y_{N_b})$, and the operator $\otimes$ is similar to the conventional matrix/vector multiplication except that the dot product performed between each row vector of the left multiplier and each column vector of the right multiplier, say, $p \cdot q$ is now replaced with $f(p \cdot q)$. Here f is the activation function of neurons.

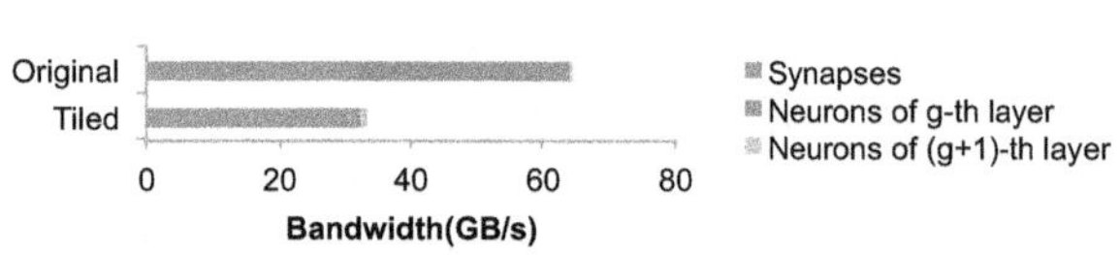

Figure 5: Memory bandwidth requirements for DNN feedforward computation ($N_a = 16384$).

It can be observed that neurons of the g-th layer ($x[i]$ in Figure 5) will be used for N_b times to calculate neurons in the next layer ($y[j]$ in Figure 5), while each synapse ($w[i,j]$ in Figure 6) is only be used once. In the original code, however, $x[i]$ can be reused after a total of $2N_a$ floating-point operations (multiplications and additions). When the number of neurons in the vector X (i.e., N_a) is very large, the reuse distance is also very large. In the meantime, the cache of a chip may not be sufficiently large to simultaneously store values of all N_a neurons, and have to re-fetch them when reusing. In order to reduce memory transfers, we tile the loop with respect to neurons in the vector X (see Figure 7). We also empirically evaluate the impact of tiling on feedforward computations, where we set $N_a = 16384$ (16384 neurons need a total of $16384 \times$ 4Byte=64KB). We observe that tiling reduces the memory bandwidth requirement of feedforward computation by 46.7%.

```
//x is the input neurons, y is output
   neurous
//w is the weights, w[0,i] = s[i]
y(all) = 0; //initialize all neurons
for(i = 0; i < Nb; i++){
  for(j = 0; j < (Na+1); j ++){
    y[i] += w[j,i]*x[j];
    if(j == Na)
        y[i] = f(y[i]);
} }
```

Figure 6: Original code of DNN feedforward computation.

```
//T is the tiled block size
y(all) = 0; //initialize all output
   neurons
for (j = 0; j < (Na+1)/T; j ++){
    //tiled block
    for(i = 0; i < Nb; i++){
        for(jj = j*T; jj < T; jj ++){
          y[i] += w[jj,i]*x[jj];
          if(jj == Na)
              y[i] = f(y[i]);
} } }
```

Figure 7: Tiled code of DNN feedforward computation.

Pre-training locally tunes synapses (weights) between each pair of adjacent layers, such synapses then serves as the initial synapses of global training. Pre-training can be done by training Restricted Boltzmann Machines (RBMs) [21], in which the most time-consuming steps are iterative feedforward computation and backforward computation (which includes similar operations to feedforward computation)[1]

[1] Given two adjacent layers A, B and synapses between them, a feedforward pass computes neuron values of layer B with neuron values of layer A and the synapses, while a backforward pass computes neuron values of layer A with neuron values of layer B and the same synapses. From a computer architecture perspective, they are the same.

invoked by Gibbs sampling. Global training uses the Back Propagation (BP) algorithm [35] to globally tune synapses, and the most-time consuming step is still analogous to feedforward/backforward computation. Therefore, the locality optimization done for feedforward computation also provides hints to pre-training and global training. We do not repeat details for the sake of brevity.

2.4 Linear Regression

Linear Regression (LR) [14] is a supervised learning technique which models the relationship between a scalar response variable y and a d-dimensional vector variable $x = (x_1, x_2 x_d)^T$ with a linear function $y = \sum_{i=0}^{d} \theta_i x_i$ (where x_0 always equals to 1). LR consists of two phases, the training phase which establishes the linear function from data, and the prediction phase which uses the existing linear model to predict the response (label) of each testing instance.

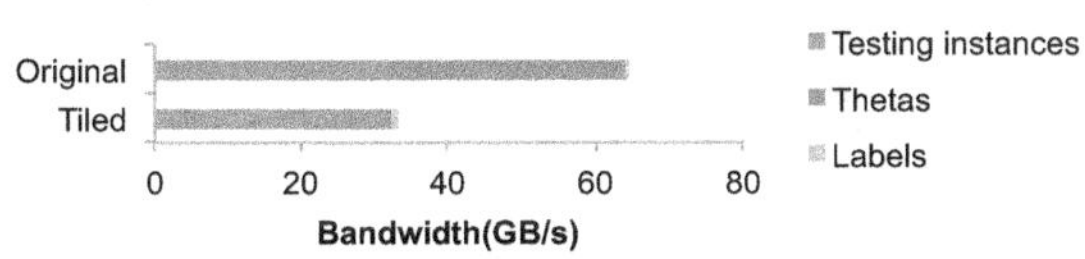

Figure 8: Memory bandwidth requirements for prediction phase of LR ($N_a = 16384$).

We starts with the prediction phase as it is simpler and more fundamental. At this phase, predicted responses of n different testing instances can be computed as

$$Y = \theta X, \tag{2}$$

where

$$X = \begin{bmatrix} 1 & 1 & 1 & \cdots & 1 \\ x_1^{(1)} & x_1^{(2)} & x_1^{(3)} & \cdots & x_1^{(n)} \\ x_2^{(1)} & x_2^{(2)} & x_2^{(3)} & \cdots & x_2^{(n)} \\ \vdots & \vdots & \vdots & \ddots & \vdots \\ x_d^{(1)} & x_d^{(2)} & x_d^{(3)} & \cdots & x_d^{(n)} \end{bmatrix}, \tag{3}$$

$\theta = (\theta_0, \theta_1, \dots, \theta_d)$, and $Y = (y^{(1)}, \dots, y^{(n)})$ are predicted responses of testing instances $x^{(1)}, \dots, x^{(n)}$, respectively. This can be viewed as a multiplication between a vector and a matrix. The locality analysis is similar to that for feedforward computations in DNN (see Section 2.3). Briefly, the coefficients θ need to be reused, and there is no reuse of data in X. When the number of coefficients in a linear model is very large, we need to tile θ to reduce the reuse distance of those coefficients. Our empirical study on a setting of $d = 16384$ reveals that tiling reduces the memory bandwidth requirement of LR prediction phase by 46.7%.

At the training phase, the aim is to find appropriate coefficients $\theta = (\theta_0, \dots, \theta_d)$ minimizing the Mean Square Error (MSE) over m training instances $\{x^{(1)}, y^{(1)}\}, \dots, \{x^{(m)}, y^{(m)}\}$, where $y^{(i)}$ is observed response (label) of training instance $x^{(i)}$. Gradient descent is a common solution to this training task [41]. Briefly, gradient descent starts with an initial values of $\theta = (\theta_0, \dots, \theta_d)$, and iteratively updates θ along the negative gradient direction. In gradient descent, the most-time consuming operations are calculating $\theta x^{(i)}$ ($i = 1, \dots, m$) with the latest θ. Such operations can also be written as Eq. (2). Therefore, the locality optimization for the prediction phase is also applicable here.

2.5 Support Vector Machine

Support Vector Machine (SVM) is a supervised learning technique for classification and regression [11]. The central idea of SVM is finding a hyperplane in a high-dimensional space, such that the distance between the hyperplane and the nearest training instance (i.e., geometric margin) is the largest. Like other supervised learning techniques, SVM has two phases, the training phase which constructed a model from the training data, and the prediction phase which use the trained model to predict the label of each testing instance. The SVM model, which predicts the label (y) of input instance x, has the form $y = \sum_{i=1}^{N} \alpha_i y^{(i)} k(x, x^{(i)}) + b$, where N is the number of training instances, $x^{(i)}$ and $y^{(i)}$ are the i-th training instance and its label respectively, α_i is a constant coefficient, $k(\cdot,\cdot)$ is a kernel function (e.g., radial basis function, tanh function) serves as the surrogate of computing the dot product between two instances at a high-dimensional space, and b is a constant. When $x^{(i)}$ is not a support vector[2], the corresponding coefficient α_i equals to 0.

At the SVM training phase, the goal is finding appropriate coefficients α_i that maximize the geometric margin, and a common training algorithm is Sequential Minimal Optimization (SMO) [32]. The most time-consuming step in SMO is to compute the $N \times N$ kernel matrix K (N is the total number of training instances), a symmetric matrix recording kernel function values of all possible pairs of training instances. Let k_{ij} ($i, j = 1, \dots, N$) be the entry at the i-th row and j-th column of matrix K, which is the kernel function value of training instances $x^{(i)}$ and $x^{(j)}$, i.e., $k_{ij} = k(x_i, x_j)$. Kernel matrix computation shares a similar locality property to distance calculations in k-NN, except that for each pair of instances, kernel matrix computation computes the value of kernel function instead of computing the distance. Therefore, we reuse the tiling mechanism designed for distance calculations. Tiled kernel matrix computation reduces the memory bandwidth requirement by 93.9%.

Assume that we have already constructed an SVM model involving N_a support vectors (see Footnote [2]). At the prediction phase, we use the constructed SVM model to predict labels of N_b testing instances. The most time-consuming computations at this phase are calculating kernel function values between each pair of support vector and testing in-

[2] A support vector is one of the training instances that are nearest to the decision hyperplane of SVM.

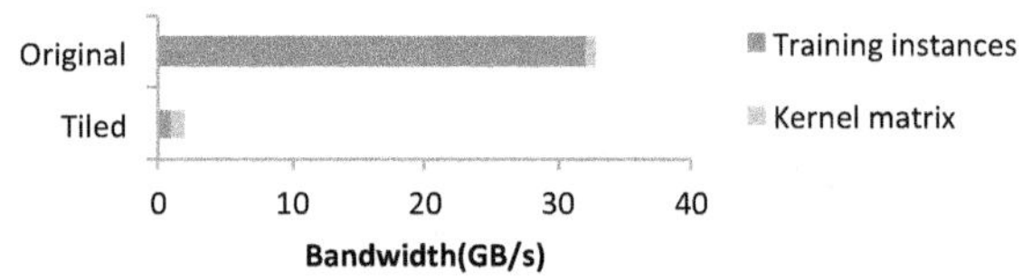

Figure 9: Memory bandwidth requirements for kernel matrix computation of SVM (d=32).

stance. The locality analysis is similar to that of distance calculations in k-NN, and the minor differences are that reference instances in k-NN are replaced with support vectors in the context of SVM, and for each pair of support vector and testing instance we calculate the kernel function value instead of their distance. Similarly, we can tile both support vectors and testing instances to reduce memory bandwidth requirement.

2.6 Naive Bayes

Naive Bayes (NB) is a probabilistic classifier based on Bayes' theorem and the Maximum-a Posteriori (MAP) paradigm [23]. It also relies on a strong assumption that instance features are independent with each other. NB has two phases: the training phase which estimates individual conditional probabilities from training instances, the prediction phase which classifies testing instances.

The goal of the training phase is to construct probability tables for estimating the posterior probability $p(C|F_1, \ldots, F_d)$, where C represents the label (class index), F_i $(i = 1, \ldots, d)$ represents the i-th feature. Here C and F_i are random variables, not specific values. By applying the Bayes' theorem and the independence assumption, $p(C|F_1, \ldots, F_d)$ can be written as $(1/Z)p(C)\prod_{i=1}^{d} p(F_i|C)$, where Z is a scaling factor that does not influence the results of NB. The central task of the training phase is to estimate conditional probabilities $p(F_i|C)$ $(i = 1, \ldots, d)$. Here we consider the discrete version of NB, thus those conditional probabilities can be obtained by performing frequency estimate on the training data. Assume that F_i $(i = 1, \ldots, d)$ can only take the value from $\{f_{ij}\}_{j=1}^{a}$, C can only take the value from $\{c_k\}_{k=1}^{b}$, then each conditional probability can be written as $p(F_i = f_{ij}|C = c_k)$, and there are a total of $d \times a \times b$ such items. NB maintains a *temporary counter* for each item to assist the frequency estimate. By streaming in features and label of training instances, NB completes all frequency estimates, and normalize the frequencies to get all conditional probabilities. In training an NB classifier, each dimension (feature value) of an instance is fetched to cache for a single time, but could be reused for multiple times when it is involved in, for example, multiple bitwise AND operations for comparing it with several candidate values that the feature can take (comparisons are due to conditional assignment/branching statements for choosing the right counter). Because each reuse of a feature value happens almost immediately after the last use, there is no need to tile instances as well as their feature values. During counting, however, temporary counters have to be frequently updated. When there are too many conditional probabilities to estimate, it is possible that the cache cannot store all temporary counters. To reduce memory transfers of temporary counters, one can pre-process training instances so that they are grouped according to their labels. Moreover, it is better to fetch from off-chip memory the corresponding features of different instances, rather than fetching each instance as a whole.

The prediction phase is relatively simpler. For each testing instance $x = (\hat{f}_1, \ldots, \hat{f}_d)$, NB calculates posterior probabilities $p(C = c_k|F_1 = \hat{f}_1, \ldots, F_d = \hat{f}_d)$ $(k = 1, \ldots, b)$, and assigns the class index that maximize the posterior probability as the label of instance X. The most time-consuming operations are multiplications of d numbers. Moreover, there is no significant locality here, as no one can predict the feature values of an unseen instance (which determine the data required by the follow-up multiplications).

2.7 Classification Tree

Classification Tree (CT) is a type of supervised learning techniques which construct tree-like classifiers from training instances. CT consists of two phases, the training phase which constructs a tree-like classifiers from training instances, and the prediction phase which predicts labels of testing instances.

At the training phase, CT starts with the root node representing the whole set of training instances, and recursively split non-leaf nodes into smaller nodes under the guide of a learning metric. Different CTs may use different learning metrics. For example, CART uses Gini impurity [3], ID3 uses information gain [33], and C4.5 uses information gain ratio [34]. However, the most time-consuming operations of all CTs are counting, which are indispensable steps for computing values of different learning metrics. There are often three types of counting tasks: counting the number of instances whose specific feature takes a specific value (for discrete feature space), counting the number of instances whose specific feature exceeds a threshold (for continuous feature space), and counting the number of instances having a specific label value. In each round of counting, the same feature value (vector component) of the same training instance (vector) will be frequently reused, because it is involved in, for example, multiple bitwise AND operations for comparing it with several candidate values that the feature can take (comparisons are due to conditional assignment/branching statements for choosing the right counter). Because each reuse of a feature value happens almost immediately after the last use, there is no need to tile instances as well as their feature values. In different rounds of counting, the same training instance could also be reused, but the reuse distance depends on data characteristics (instead of algorithm characteristics), thus is not deterministic. Therefore, we cannot expect a predefined tiling strategy that can reduce the corresponding memory accesses.

At the prediction phase, the constructed CT classifier predicts the label of each testing instance. In this process, each testing instance needs to travel along the path from the root node to a leaf node, and the leaf node assigns the testing instance its label. When the size of the CT is very large, it is possible that the cache cannot store the whole tree, and there is an unacceptable cost if we reload the whole tree for each testing instance. To address this issue, we can follow the divide-and-conquer strategy and decompose the tree into sub-trees, each of which can be stored by cache. When a sub-tree is stored in the cache, it processes all testing instances that have not yet been labeled. This strategy can also be interpreted as tiling the tree, which avoids to frequently reload the whole tree.

2.8 Summary

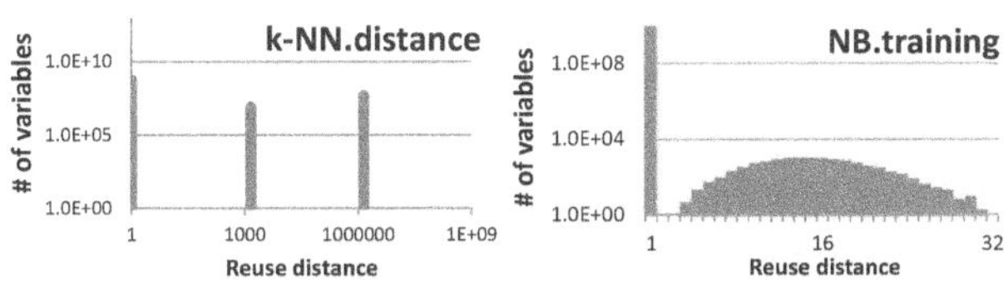

(a) (b)

Figure 10: Average reuse distances of variables.

We provide a brief summary to this section. First, we identify some critical computational primitives of ML techniques, such as distance calculation, dot product, counting, as well as some non-linear functions, providing hints to implementing functional units of the accelerator. Second, and more importantly, we discover from our locality analysis that tiling can effectively exploit the data locality of k-NN, k-Means, DNN, LR, and SVM, but is not very helpful to NB and CT since they do not exhibit remarkable or predictable data locality. Figure 10 illustrates the average reuse distance (i.e., the average number of instructions between two consecutive accesses) of each variable (excluding loop variables) in k-NN (tiled distance calculations) and NB (training) on an x86 machine. As illustrated in Figure 10a, variables of distance calculations in k-NN naturally cluster into three classes in terms of their average reuse distances (similar behaviors can be observed from k-Means, DNN, LR, and SVM). This observation motivates us to use three separate on-chip buffers in the accelerator, each buffer stores variables having similar reuse distances (see Section 3.2 for details). Moreover, we observe from Figure 10b that variables in NB also cluster into two classes (similar behaviors can be observed from CT). The left class corresponds to feature and label values of training instances, whose reuse distances are always 1 (see Section 2.6 for more details). The right class corresponds to temporary counters, whose average reuse distances spread over a large interval. This is because the reuse of a temporary counter happens only when a specific feature of the current instance takes a specific value, which is a stochastic event decided by data characteristics instead of algorithm characteristics. For ML techniques like NB and CT, we need at least two on-chip buffers to fit two levels of reuse distances. When designing the accelerator, we carefully factor in observations made in this section. In follow-up sections, we will present the concrete accelerator architecture and show how the architecture accommodates different ML techniques.

3. Accelerator Architecture

In this section, we present the detailed architecture of PuDianNao, a hardware accelerator supporting seven representative ML techniques. As illustrated in Figure 11, the PuDianNao consists of several Functional Units (FUs), three data buffers (HotBuf, ColdBuf, and OutputBuf), an instruction buffer (InstBuf), a control module, and a DMA. In the rest of this section, we will elaborate the microarchitecture of each component.

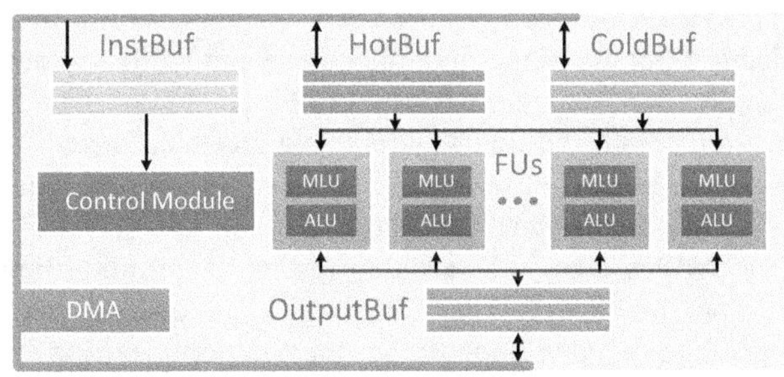

Figure 11: Accelerator architecture of PuDianNao.

3.1 Functional Units

Functional Units (FUs) are the basic execution units of the PuDianNao ML accelerator. Specifically, each FU consists of two parts, a Machine Learning functional Unit (MLU) and an Arithmetic Logic Unit (ALU).

3.1.1 Machine Learning Unit (MLU)

The MLU is designed to support several basic yet important computational primitives which are common in representative ML techniques, including dot product (LR, SVM, and DNN), distance calculations (k-NN and k-Means), counting (ID3 and NB), sorting (k-NN and k-Means), non-linear functions (e.g., sigmoid and tanh) and so on. As illustrated in Figure 12, the MLU is divided into 6 pipeline stages (Counter, Adder, Multiplier, Adder tree, Acc, and Misc).

In the **Counter** stage, each pair of inputs will be fed to a bitwise-AND unit or be compared by a comparer unit, and the value will then be added to an accumulator. After that, results of accumulators will be directly forwarded to

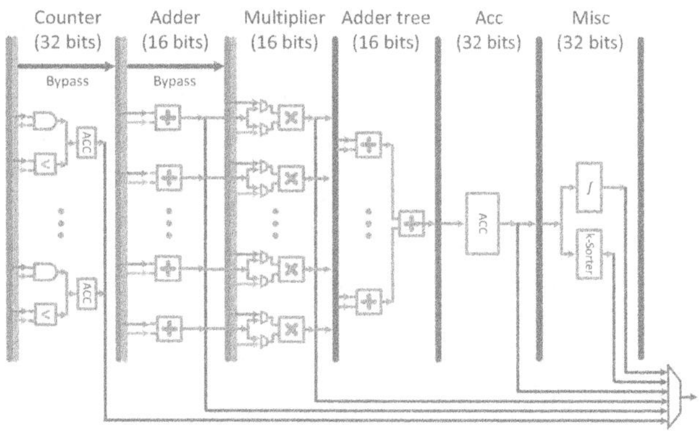

Figure 12: Implementation of MLU.

the output buffer rather than the next stage. This stage is used to accelerate counting operations in naive bayes and classification tree. When there is no need to execute counting operations, the counter stage will be bypassed.

The **Adder** stage is leveraged to operate vector addition, which is a very common operation in ML techniques. The adder stage may also be bypassed (e.g., in DNN), and results can be forwarded to either the next stage or the output port.

The **Multiplier** stage is leveraged to operate vector multiplication. Inputs of the multiplier stage can be the outputs of the previous stage (gray arrows in Figure 12) or data directly read from the input buffers (red and blue arrows in Figure 12). Results of the multiplier stage can be forwarded to either the next stage or the output port.

The **Adder tree** stage adds up results of all multipliers in the previous stage. The Adder tree stage and the Multiplier stage together support the dot product operation, an operation widely used in ML techniques (e.g. LR, SVM, and DNN). When the dimension of instance is larger than the size of adder tree, results of this stage are partial sums, which will be accumulated in the **Acc** stage. After obtaining the final result of dot product, the Acc stage will forward it to either the next stage or the output port.

The **Misc** stage integrates two modules, linear interpolation module and k-sorter module. The linear interpolation module is used to approximatively calculate non-linear functions involved in ML techniques (e.g. sigmoid and tanh in neural network). Different non-linear functions correspond to different interpolation tables. The k-sorter module is used to find the smallest k values from the outputs of Acc stage, which is a common operation in k-Means and k-NN. Results of linear interpolation module and k-sorter module will be forwarded to the output port respectively. Finally, the output port will select one out of the six collected results as the final output of the MLU module, as illustrated in Figure 12.

Furthermore, to reduce the area/power consumption of the PuDianNao accelerator, we implement 16-bit floating-point arithmetic units for stages Adder, Multiplier, and Adder tree. In the meantime, we still implement 32-bit floating-point units for the rest three stages (Counter, Acc,

ML techniques	accuracy	
	all 16bits	32bits&16bits
SVM	37.7%	98.2%
k-NN	99.9%	100%
k-Means	93.9%	100.1%
LR	78.2%	99.0%
DNN	99.4%	100.1%

Table 1: Training accuracy of ML techniques under different sizes of arithmetic units (normalized to *all 32bits*).

and Misc) to avoid potential overflow. We empirically evaluate the impact of the above hardware optimizations on the accuracies of k-NN, k-Means, SVM, LR, and MLP. We observe that it incurs negligible accuracy loss to these ML techniques (see Table 1), but significantly reduces the area of MLU. For example, we implemented the verilog of both 16-bit and 32-bit floating-point multipliers, placed/routed them, and found that the area of the 16-bit multiplier is only 20.07% the area of the 32-bit multiplier. Besides, here we do not evaluate naive bayes and classification tree, because they are not involved in stages Adder, Multiplier, and Adder tree, and will not be influenced by the 16-bit arithmetic units at all.

3.1.2 Arithmetic Logic Unit (ALU)

In addition to computational primitives discussed above, in some ML techniques there are some other miscellaneous operations that are not supported by the MLU (e.g., division and conditional assignment). Although such operations are not very frequent in ML techniques, executing them on a host general-purpose core will still cause long-distance data movements as well as synchronization overheads. Therefore, we add a small Arithmetic Logic Unit (ALU) in each FU, which contains an adder, a multiplier, and a divider, as well as the converter of 32-bit float to 16-bit float and 16-bit float to 32-bit float. In addition, to support the log function required in training classification trees, we use ALU to compute approximations with the Taylor expansion of $\log(1-x)$. Our experiments of the ID3 classification tree on UCI datasets [1] suggest that computing $\log(\cdot)$ with the first 10 items of the Taylor series have been sufficient to remove the accuracy loss brought by approximations.

3.2 On-Chip Data Buffers

We reveal in Section 2 that tiling can effectively exploit the locality of many ML techniques, and we also observe that average reuse distances of variables in tiled ML techniques cluster into two or three classes (see Section 2.8). Motivated by this observation, we put three separate on-chip data buffers in the PuDianNao accelerator: HotBuf (8KB), ColdBuf (16KB) and OutputBuf (8KB). HotBuf stores the input data which have short reuse distance, and ColdBuf stores the input data with relative longer reuse distance. OutputBuf stores output data or temporary results.

In addition to the locality property, read width is another factor that motivates us to use multiple buffers. Here we take tiled distance calculations in k-Means as an example. Suppose that each time an MLU can only process f features (dimensions) of a testing instance and f features of a centroid. As the accelerator has a total of u MLUs, it can calculate partial square distances between one centroid and u testing instances at each cycle. Correspondingly, the MLUs need to read $f \times 16$ bits of centroids and $u \times f \times 16$ bits of testing instances at each cycle. In other words, the read width of centroids and testing instances are different. Therefore, we set two separate buffers (HotBuf and ColdBuf) to reduce the overhead brought by different read widths. HotBuf stores centroids, thus the read width is $f \times 16$ bits. HotBuff stores testing instances, thus the read width is $u \times f \times 16$ bits.

All three buffers are connected to the same DMA. Moreover, we use single-port SRAMs to construct HotBuf and ColdBuf, which can reduce the area and power consumption. As FUs may read (e.g. partial sum) or write the OutputBuf, we use dual-port SRAM to construct the OutputBuf.

CM	HotBuf				ColdBuf				OutputBuf								FU						
Inst Name	READ OP	READ ADDR	READ STRIDE	READ ITER	READ OP	READ ADDR	READ STRIDE	READ ITER	READ OP	WRITE OP	READ ADDR	WRITE ADDR	READ STRIDE	WRITE STRIDE	READ ITER	WRITE ITER	MLU-1 OP	MLU-2 OP	MLU-3 OP	MLU-4 OP	MLU-5 OP	MLU-6 OP	ALU OP

Table 2: Instruction format of PuDianNao.

CM	HotBuf				ColdBuf				OutputBuf								FU						
k-means	LOAD	0	16	128	LOAD	16384	256	16	NULL	STORE	NULL	1064960	NULL	16	NULL	16	NULL	SUB	MULT	ADD	NULL	SORT	NULL
k-means	READ	0	16	128	LOAD	20480	256	16	NULL	STORE	NULL	1065216	NULL	16	NULL	16	NULL	SUB	MULT	ADD	NULL	SORT	NULL
k-means	READ	0	16	128	LOAD	24576	256	16	NULL	STORE	NULL	1065472	NULL	16	NULL	16	NULL	SUB	MULT	ADD	NULL	SORT	NULL
......																							
k-means	LOAD	2048	16	128	LOAD	16384	256	16	LOAD	STORE	1064960	1064960	16	16	16	16	NULL	SUB	MULT	ADD	NULL	SORT	NULL
......																							

Table 3: An example of k-Means code ($f = 16$, $k = 1024$, $N = 65536$).

4. Control and Code Generator

The simplest way of controlling the accelerator is to hardwire all seven ML techniques. However, if the user wants to use another ML technique that is only slightly different from a hardwired ML technique, we might have to provide the user a new accelerator. To improve the flexibility of the accelerator, we use control instructions to support potential minor changes made on ML techniques. The accelerator only needs a single control module because all FUs will synchronously execute the same operations. The control module fetches instructions from the InstBuf, decodes the instructions, and sends operation signals to all FUs.

For each ML technique, the execution can be decomposed into several instructions. Table 2 presents the instruction format. More specifically, each instruction contains five slots: CM, HotBuf, ColdBuf, OutputBuf, and FU. This instruction format is customized for the PuDianNao architecture, thus a programmer needs to know implementation details of the accelerator. In order to facilitate programmers, we implement a code generator to generate instructions for different ML techniques.

We provide an example of generated k-Means code in Table 3. In this example, the number of features in each instance is $f = 16$, the number of centroids is $k = 1024$, and the number of testing instances is $N = 65536$. Centroids will be stored in the HotBuf (8KB), and testing instances will be stored in the ColdBuf (16KB). In order to hide the DMA memory access behind the computation, we leverage the HotBuf and ColdBuf in the ping-pong manner. Specifically, in the first instruction, the accelerator LOADs 128 centroids (4KB) and 256 testing instances (8KB) from the memory via the DMA, which occupy half of the HofBuf and ColdBuf, respectively. Then the accelerator calculates distances between the loaded centroids and testing instances. At the same time, another 256 testing instances are loaded to the other half of the ColdBuf, which will be leveraged by the second instruction. In the second instruction, the 128 centroids loaded in the first instruction will be reused, which are READ from the HotBuf. When distance calculations between the 128 centroids and all 65536 testing instances have been processed (after the 256-th instruction), a new block of 128 centroids will be loaded (in the 257th instruction). The process is repeated until distance calculations between all centroids and testing instances have been done.

5. Experimental Methodology

Evaluation. We use both Verilog and C simulator implementations of PuDianNao to measure the performance and power.

Verilog design. The design is synthesized by Synopsys Design Compiler with TSMC 65nm GP process in standard VT. The synthesized design is also placed and routed with the Synopsys ICC compiler. We then simulate and verify the design with the Synopsys VCS, and estimate the power consumption with Synopsys Prime-Tame PX based on the simulated Value Change Dump (VCD) file.

C simulator. Due to the slow simulation speed of the VCS, it is extremely time-consuming to run large-scale datasets on the verilog design of PuDianNao. To alleviate this problem, we implemented an in-house cycle-by-cycle C simulator of PuDianNao, and carefully calibrated it to the verilog design and TSMC library on small-scale datasets with <0.3% performance errors and $<7\%$ energy errors across all scenarios. The simulator allows a memory band-

ML technique	Dataset	Problem Size
k-NN	MNIST	60000 reference instances, 10000 testing instance 784 features, k=20
k-Means	MNIST	60000 instances, 784 features, k=10
DNN	MNIST	data size same with k-NN, L1=784,L2=L3=L4=L5=4096,L6=10
LR	MNIST	data size same with k-NN
SVM	MNIST	data size same with k-NN
NB	UCI Nursery	12960 instances, 8 features, 5 classes
Classification Tree(ID3)	UCI Covertype	522000 training instances, 59012 testing instances

Table 4: Benchmarks and dataset used in this paper.

width of up to 250GB/s, and is used to estimate the performance of PuDianNao on large-scale datasets.

Benchmarks. We evaluate PuDianNao and baseline processor on 7 ML techniques, including k-NN, k-Means, deep neural network, linear regression, support vector machine, naive bayes, and classification tree (ID3 [33]). We use MNIST [25] and UCI data [1] as benchmarks of ML techniques, see Table 4.

Baseline. GPUs have been widely used to support ML in industry due to their speed advantage over SIMD CPU. Hence, we take a modern GPU card (NVIDIA K20M, 3.52 TFlops peak, 5GB GDDR5, 208GB/s memory bandwidth, 28nm technology, CUDA SDK5.5) as the baseline. To validate the performance of the GPU baseline on ML applications, we compare it against a CPU with 256-bit SIMD (Intel Xeon E5-4620 Sandy Bridge-EP, 2.2GHz, 1TB memory, gcc compilation flag "-O3 -ftree-vectorize -march=native") over all benchmarks introduced above. As shown in Figure 13, our GPU baseline achieves an average speedup of 17.74x with respect to the SIMD CPU implementation. This result complies with two recent investigations which reported GPU to have 15x-49x [38] and 10x-60x [9] speedups over SIMD CPU for ML applications.

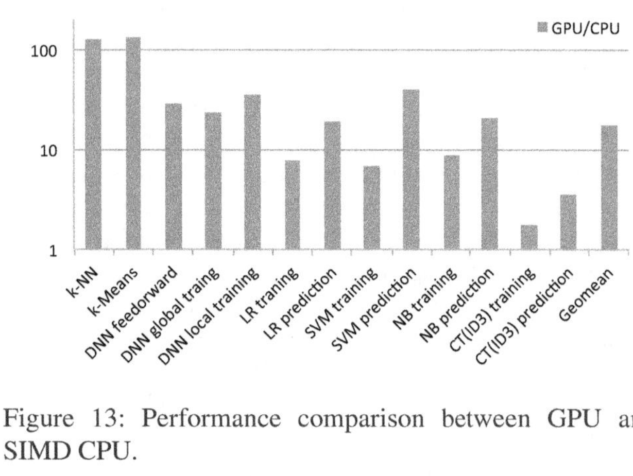

Figure 13: Performance comparison between GPU and SIMD CPU.

6. Experimental Results

In this section, we present characteristics of PuDianNao after layout, and quantitatively compare PuDianNao against the GPU baseline.

6.1 Characteristics after Layout

The current version of PuDianNao has 16 MLUs, each MLU can process 16 instance features (dimensions) at each cycle. Each MLU contains 16+16+15+1+1=49 adders, coming from the Counter stage, the Adder stage, the Adder tree stage, the Acc stage, and the Misc stage respectively. Each MLU contains 16+1=17 multipliers, coming from the Multiplier stage and the Misc stage, respectively. With 16 MLUs[3], PuDianNao can achieve a peak performance of $16 \times (49 + 17) \times 1 = 1056$ Gop/sec at 1GHz frequency, almost approaching the performance of a modern GPU.

However, the area and power consumption of PuDianNao are remarkably smaller than those of a modern GPU, by two orders of magnitude. According to the DC and ICC reports, the total area of PuDianNao is 3.51 mm^2, and the total power consumption is 596 mW. The critical path delay of PuDianNao is 0.99ns, suggesting that the accelerator can work at 1GHz frequency. The concrete area/power breakdowns are listed in Table 5. The on-chip buffers consume 62.64% and 31.37% of the total area and power. The combinational logic only consumes 21.97% area and 29.02% power. Among functional blocks, the most area-consuming part is ColdBuf (33.22%). All 16 FUs uses 19.38% area and 35.57% power. The concrete layout of PuDianNao is presented in Figure 14.

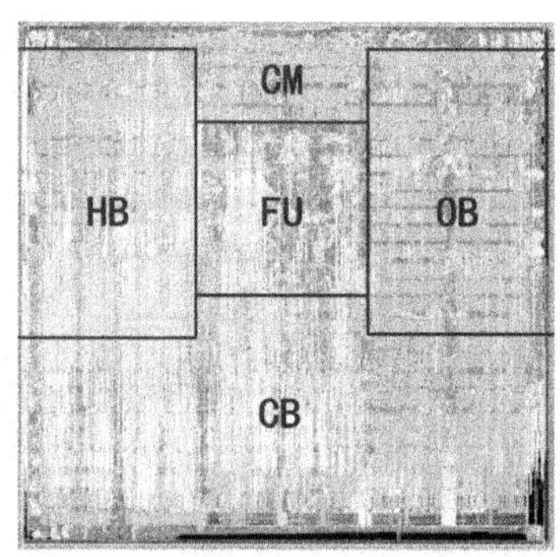

Figure 14: Layout of PuDianNao. CM, FU, HB, CB, and OB stand for Control Module, Functional Unit, HotBuf, ColdBuf, and OutputBuf, respectively.

6.2 Performance and Energy Consumption

We compare the performance of PuDianNao with GPU baseline across 13 phases of 7 ML techniques.[4] As shown in

[3] When calculating the peak performance, we voluntarily ignore contributions of ALUs, because ALU cannot work with MLU simultaneously.

[4] Many ML techniques have two phases each (training and prediction phases), but k-NN and k-Means only have one phase, and DNN has two different training phases, pre-training and global training.

Table 5: Characteristics of PuDianNao layout.

Component or Block	Area in μm^2	(%)	Power in mW	(%)	Critical path in ns
ACCELERATOR	3,513,437		596		0.99
Combinational	771,943	(21.97%)	173	(29.02%)	
On-chip buffers	2,201,138	(62.64%)	187	(31.37%)	
Registers	200,196	(14.23%)	86	(16.10%)	
Clock network	40,154	(1.14%)	143	(23.99%)	
Function Units	681,012	(19.38%)	117	(35.57%)	
ColdBuf	1,167,232	(33.22%)	78	(16.44%)	
HotBuf	578,829	(16.47%)	47	(9.56%)	
OutputBuf	586,361	(16.68%)	51	(10.23%)	
Control Module	481,737	(13.71%)	127	(21.30%)	
Other	18,266	(0.52%)	41	(0.06%)	

Figure 15, PuDianNao outperforms GPU on 6 phases out of the total 13 phases, and the average speedup of PuDianNao over the GPU is 1.20x. The maximal speedup of PuDianNao is achieved on *SVM prediction* (2.92x) , and an important reason is that PuDianNao provides dedicated linear interpolation functionality to efficiently compute kernel functions. The worst speedup of PuDianNao is achieved on *NB prediction* (0.37x). This phase needs frequent multiplications of different numbers (conditional probabilities) to obtain the overall posterior probabilities. PuDianNao does not have a large register file as the GPU, thus has to frequently move data between FUs and on-chip buffers, resulting in the observed performance loss. In contrast, the other phase of NB (*NB training*) does not have such operations, thus PuDianNao achieves a 2.22x speedup over the GPU on *NB training*.

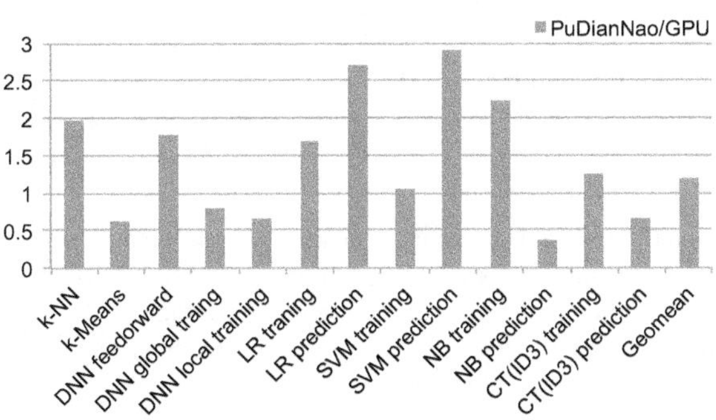

Figure 15: Performance speedup of PuDianNao over GPU.

We also compare energy consumptions of PuDianNao and the GPU baseline. As shown in Figure 16, PuDianNao averagely reduces the energy consumption of the GPU by 128.41x. This observation is not surprising, because PuDianNao is equipped with dedicated functional units and on-chip buffers optimized for the ML techniques. The largest energy reduction of PuDianNao is achieved on k-NN (262.20x), which is mainly because PuDianNao has efficiently supported sorting, a frequent and time-consuming operation (each finds top 20 instances out of 60000 reference instances in our experiment) in k-NN. In contrast, the GPU consumes remarkable energy on sorting with its general-purpose functional units. The smallest energy reduction of PuDianNao is achieved on *CT(ID3) prediction* (50.32x). That is because PuDianNao frequently reconfigures its DMA to support irregular memory accesses (e.g., linked list) for loading components of the ID3 classification tree. The above observations and discussions provide hints for further optimizations of the PuDianNao accelerator.

We do not factor in the energy/area of memory controller and off-chip memory of PuDianNao, but our energy/area comparison is still rather conservative: PuDianNao uses a 65nm process, while the GPU baseline uses a 28nm process. Although the energy/area reported for the GPU baseline does include the memory controller, this is far from compensating for the area ratio between 28nm and 65nm processes.

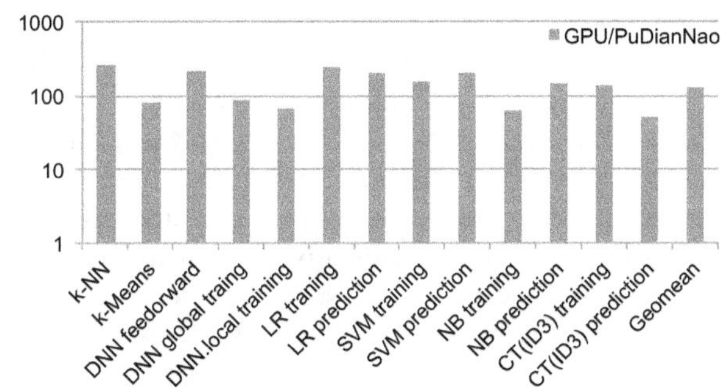

Figure 16: Energy reduction of PuDianNao over GPU.

7. Related Work

Machine learning has a broad application scope, but has to be accommodated by powerful computer systems to achieve high efficiency. Although it is straightforward to run ML techniques on general-purpose CPUs and GPUs (e.g., [18]), the efficiency is limited, because they spend too many efforts on flexibly supporting diverse application domains. For example, their functional units and memory hierarchies are not specifically designed to support ML applications.

There have been some successful ML accelerators that manage to implement dedicated hardware to accelerate machine learning. Yeh et al. designed a k-NN accelerator on FPGA [40]. Manolakos and Stamoulias designed two high-performance parallel array architectures for k-NN [29, 36]. There are also many dedicated accelerators for k-Means [17, 22, 30] or SVM [4, 31], due to their broad applications in industry. Recent debates on deep learning [24] even triggers the rebirth of *hardware neural network* [37], a hot topic in 1990s [19]. In this trend, a number of successful neural network accelerators have been proposed [7, 15, 26].

While remarkably increasing the energy-efficiency and performance compared with general-purpose processors, each of the above accelerators only accommodates a single technique or technique family (e.g.,neural network). When the ML task shifts from, for example, classification to clustering, or the user favors another ML technique having better accuracy/efficiency, such an accelerator might easily become useless. Recently, Majumdar et al. proposed an accelerator called MAPLE which can accelerate matrix/vector operation and ranking used in five ML technique families (including neural network, SVM, k-means) [27, 28]. However, there are still many widely-used ML techniques (e.g., decision tree and naive bayes) whose major computational primitives are neither matrix nor vector operations (e.g., counting, linear interpolation), and such techniques cannot be supported by MAPLE. Furthermore, MAPLE does not excavate the locality properties of tiled ML algorithms, thus its memory bandwidth requirement might become the main bottleneck that prevents MAPLE from achieving high energy-efficiency/performance in large-scale ML applications common in industry.

Unlike previous investigations on ML accelerators which do not simultaneously address (a)*computational primitives* and (b)*locality properties* of (c)*diverse representative ML techniques*, we factor in all three dimensions during the design of PuDianNao accelerator. Although PuDianNao has not yet supported all representative ML techniques, the design methodology may shed some light on developing *general-purpose machine learning accelerator* in the future.

8. Conclusion

In this paper we present a machine learning accelerator called PuDianNao, which supports multiple ML scenarios (e.g., classification, regression and clustering) as well as multiple ML techniques (k-NN, k-Means, linear regression, SVM, DNN, naive bayes, classification tree). When executing the seven ML techniques, PuDianNao is 1.20x faster and 128.41x more energy-efficient than the NVIDIA K20M GPU on average. Compared with previous ML accelerators designed for narrow ranges of ML techniques, PuDianNao is more robust when the data characteristics change, or the application scenario is altered, because it provides users a basket of candidate techniques. This is somewhat similar to a common strategy adopted by Wallstreet traders: they usually invest to a basket of currencies to reduce the overall risk. Our future work on this topic includes extending PuDianNao to support some other mature ML techniques, as well as a tape-out of PuDianNao.

Acknowledgements

This work is partially supported by the NSF of China (under Grants 61100163, 61133004, 61222204, 61221062, 61303158, 61473275, 61432016, 61472396), the 973 Program of China (under Grants 2015CB358800, 2011CB302500), the Strategic Priority Research Program of the CAS (under Grant XDA06010403), the International Collaboration Key Program of the CAS (under Grant 171111KYSB20130002), a Google Faculty Research Award, the Intel Collaborative Research Institute for Computational Intelligence (ICRI-CI), the 10,000 talent program, and the 1,000 talent program.

References

[1] UC Irvine Machine Learning Repository. `http://archive.ics.uci.edu/ml/`. [Online; accessed 31-July-2014].

[2] Naomi S Altman. An introduction to kernel and nearest-neighbor nonparametric regression. *The American Statistician*, 46(3):175–185, 1992.

[3] Leo Breiman, Jerome Friedman, Richard Olshen, Charles Stone, D Steinberg, and P Colla. Cart: Classification and regression trees. *Wadsworth: Belmont, CA*, 156, 1983.

[4] Srihari Cadambi, Igor Durdanovic, Venkata Jakkula, Murugan Sankaradass, Eric Cosatto, Srimat Chakradhar, and Hans Peter Graf. A massively parallel fpga-based coprocessor for support vector machines. In *Field Programmable Custom Computing Machines, 2009. FCCM'09. 17th IEEE Symposium on*, pages 115–122. IEEE, 2009.

[5] Ernie Chan. *Algorithmic trading: winning strategies and their rationale*, volume 625. John Wiley & Sons, 2013.

[6] Min Chen, Shiwen Mao, Yin Zhang, and Victor CM Leung. *Big Data-Related Technologies, Challenges and Future Prospects*. Springer, 2014.

[7] Tianshi Chen, Zidong Du, Ninghui Sun, Jia Wang, Chengyong Wu, Yunji Chen, and Olivier Temam. Diannao: a small-footprint high-throughput accelerator for ubiquitous machine-learning. In *Proceedings of the 19th International Conference on Architectural support for programming languages and operating systems*, pages 269–284. ACM, 2014.

[8] Yunji Chen, Tao Luo, Shaoli Liu, Shijin Zhang, Liqiang He, Jia Wang, Ling Li, Tianshi Chen, Zhiwei Xu, Ninghui Sun, and Olivier Temam. Dadiannao: A machine-learning supercomputer. In *Proceedings of the 47th IEEE/ACM International Symposium on Microarchitecture (MICRO'14)*, pages 1–14. IEEE, 2014.

[9] Dan C Ciresan, Ueli Meier, Jonathan Masci, Luca Maria Gambardella, and Jürgen Schmidhuber. Flexible, high performance convolutional neural networks for image classification. In *IJCAI Proceedings-International Joint Conference on Artificial Intelligence*, volume 22, page 1237, 2011.

[10] Ronan Collobert and Jason Weston. A unified architecture for natural language processing: Deep neural networks with multitask learning. In *Proceedings of the 25th international conference on Machine learning*, pages 160–167. ACM, 2008.

[11] Corinna Cortes and Vladimir Vapnik. Support-vector networks. *Machine learning*, 20(3):273–297, 1995.

[12] George Cybenko. Approximation by superpositions of a sigmoidal function. *Mathematics of control, signals and systems*, 2(4):303–314, 1989.

[13] George E Dahl, Dong Yu, Li Deng, and Alex Acero. Context-dependent pre-trained deep neural networks for large-vocabulary speech recognition. *IEEE Transactions on Audio, Speech, and Language Processing*, 20(1):30–42, 2012.

[14] Allen L Edwards. An introduction to linear regression and correlation. 1976.

[15] Clément Farabet, Berin Martini, Benoit Corda, Polina Akselrod, Eugenio Culurciello, and Yann LeCun. Neuflow: A runtime reconfigurable dataflow processor for vision. In *Computer Vision and Pattern Recognition Workshops (CVPRW), 2011 IEEE Computer Society Conference on*, pages 109–116. IEEE, 2011.

[16] Edward W Forgy. Cluster analysis of multivariate data: efficiency versus interpretability of classifications. *Biometrics*, 21:768–769, 1965.

[17] AC Frery, CC de Araujo, Haglay Alice, Jorge Cerqueira, Juliana A Loureiro, Manoel Eusebio de Lima, Mdas Oliveira, MM Horta, et al. Hyperspectral images clustering on reconfigurable hardware using the k-means algorithm. In *Integrated Circuits and Systems Design, 2003. SBCCI 2003. Proceedings. 16th Symposium on*, pages 99–104. IEEE, 2003.

[18] Vincent Garcia, Eric Debreuve, and Michel Barlaud. Fast k nearest neighbor search using gpu. In *Computer Vision and Pattern Recognition Workshops, 2008. CVPRW'08. IEEE Computer Society Conference on*, pages 1–6. IEEE, 2008.

[19] Jan NH Heemskerk. Overview of neural hardware. *Neurocomputers for Brain-Style Processing. Design, Implementation and Application*, 1995.

[20] Geoffrey Hinton, Li Deng, Dong Yu, George E Dahl, Abdelrahman Mohamed, Navdeep Jaitly, Andrew Senior, Vincent Vanhoucke, Patrick Nguyen, Tara N Sainath, et al. Deep neural networks for acoustic modeling in speech recognition: The shared views of four research groups. *Signal Processing Magazine, IEEE*, 29(6):82–97, 2012.

[21] Geoffrey E Hinton. Training products of experts by minimizing contrastive divergence. *Neural computation*, 14(8):1771–1800, 2002.

[22] Hanaa M Hussain, Khaled Benkrid, Huseyin Seker, and Ahmet T Erdogan. Fpga implementation of k-means algorithm for bioinformatics application: An accelerated approach to clustering microarray data. In *Adaptive Hardware and Systems (AHS), 2011 NASA/ESA Conference on*, pages 248–255. IEEE, 2011.

[23] Pat Langley, Wayne Iba, and Kevin Thompson. An analysis of bayesian classifiers. In *AAAI*, volume 90, pages 223–228. Citeseer, 1992.

[24] Quoc V Le. Building high-level features using large scale unsupervised learning. In *Acoustics, Speech and Signal Processing (ICASSP), 2013 IEEE International Conference on*, pages 8595–8598. IEEE, 2013.

[25] Yann LeCun, Léon Bottou, Yoshua Bengio, and Patrick Haffner. Gradient-based learning applied to document recognition. *Proceedings of the IEEE*, 86(11):2278–2324, 1998.

[26] Ahmed Al Maashri, Michael Debole, Matthew Cotter, Nandhini Chandramoorthy, Yang Xiao, Vijaykrishnan Narayanan, and Chaitali Chakrabarti. Accelerating neuromorphic vision algorithms for recognition. In *Proceedings of the 49th Annual Design Automation Conference*, pages 579–584. ACM, 2012.

[27] Abhinandan Majumdar, Srihari Cadambi, Michela Becchi, Srimat T Chakradhar, and Hans Peter Graf. A massively parallel, energy efficient programmable accelerator for learning and classification. *ACM Transactions on Architecture and Code Optimization (TACO)*, 9(1):6, 2012.

[28] Abhinandan Majumdar, Srihari Cadambi, and Srimat T Chakradhar. An energy-efficient heterogeneous system for embedded learning and classification. *Embedded Systems Letters, IEEE*, 3(1):42–45, 2011.

[29] Elias S Manolakos and Ioannis Stamoulias. Ip-cores design for the knn classifier. In *Circuits and Systems (ISCAS), Proceedings of 2010 IEEE International Symposium on*, pages 4133–4136. IEEE, 2010.

[30] Tsutomu Maruyama. Real-time k-means clustering for color images on reconfigurable hardware. In *Pattern Recognition, 2006. ICPR 2006. 18th International Conference on*, volume 2, pages 816–819. IEEE, 2006.

[31] Markos Papadonikolakis and C Bouganis. A heterogeneous fpga architecture for support vector machine training. In *Field-Programmable Custom Computing Machines (FCCM), 2010 18th IEEE Annual International Symposium on*, pages 211–214. IEEE, 2010.

[32] John C Platt, Nello Cristianini, and John Shawe-Taylor. Large margin dags for multiclass classification. In *nips*, volume 12, pages 547–553, 1999.

[33] J. Ross Quinlan. Induction of decision trees. *Machine learning*, 1(1):81–106, 1986.

[34] J Ross Quinlan. Bagging, boosting, and c4. 5. In *AAAI/IAAI, Vol. 1*, pages 725–730, 1996.

[35] DE Rummelhart. Learning representations by back-propagating errors. *Nature*, 323(9):533–536, 1986.

[36] Ioannis Stamoulias and Elias S Manolakos. Parallel architectures for the knn classifier–design of soft ip cores and fpga implementations. *ACM Transactions on Embedded Computing Systems (TECS)*, 13(2):22, 2013.

[37] Olivier Temam. The rebirth of neural networks. In *International Symposium on Computer Architecture*, 2010.

[38] George Teodoro, Rafael Sachetto, Olcay Sertel, Metin N Gurcan, W Meira, Umit Catalyurek, and Renato Ferreira. Coordinating the use of gpu and cpu for improving performance of compute intensive applications. In *Cluster Computing and Workshops, 2009. CLUSTER'09. IEEE International Conference on*, pages 1–10. IEEE, 2009.

[39] David H Wolpert. The lack of a priori distinctions between learning algorithms. *Neural computation*, 8(7):1341–1390, 1996.

[40] Yao-Jung Yeh, Hui-Ya Li, Wen-Jyi Hwang, and Chiung-Yao Fang. Fpga implementation of knn classifier based on wavelet transform and partial distance search. In *Image Analysis*, pages 512–521. Springer, 2007.

[41] Tong Zhang. Solving large scale linear prediction problems using stochastic gradient descent algorithms. In *Proceedings of the twenty-first international conference on Machine learning*, page 116. ACM, 2004.

ApproxHadoop: Bringing Approximations to MapReduce Frameworks

Íñigo Goiri[†*] Ricardo Bianchini[†‡] Santosh Nagarakatte[‡] Thu D. Nguyen[‡]

[‡]Rutgers University
{ricardob, santosh.nagarakatte, tdnguyen}@cs.rutgers.edu

[†]Microsoft Research
{inigog, ricardob}@microsoft.com

Abstract

We propose and evaluate a framework for creating and running approximation-enabled MapReduce programs. Specifically, we propose approximation mechanisms that fit naturally into the MapReduce paradigm, including input data sampling, task dropping, and accepting and running a precise and a user-defined approximate version of the MapReduce code. We then show how to leverage statistical theories to compute error bounds for popular classes of MapReduce programs when approximating with input data sampling and/or task dropping. We implement the proposed mechanisms and error bound estimations in a prototype system called ApproxHadoop. Our evaluation uses MapReduce applications from different domains, including data analytics, scientific computing, video encoding, and machine learning. Our results show that ApproxHadoop can significantly reduce application execution time and/or energy consumption when the user is willing to tolerate small errors. For example, ApproxHadoop can reduce runtimes by up to 32× when the user can tolerate an error of 1% with 95% confidence. We conclude that our framework and system can make approximation easily accessible to many application domains using the MapReduce model.

Categories and Subject Descriptors C.4 [*Computer Systems Organizations*]: Performance of Systems; D.m [*Software*]: Miscellaneous

Keywords MapReduce, approximation, multi-stage sampling, extreme value theory

* This work was done while Íñigo Goiri was at Rutgers University.

ASPLOS '15, March 14–18, 2015, Istanbul, Turkey..

ACM 978-1-4503-2835-7/15/03...$15.00.
http://dx.doi.org/10.1145/2694344.2694351

1. Introduction

Motivation. Despite the enormous computing capacity that has become available, large-scale applications such as data analytics and scientific computing continue to exceed available resources. Furthermore, they consume significant amounts of time and energy. Thus, approximate computing has and continues to garner significant attention for reducing the resource requirements, computation time, and/or energy consumption of large-scale computing (*e.g.*, [5, 6, 10, 17, 38]). Many classes of applications are amenable to approximation, including data analytics, machine learning, Monte Carlo computations, and image/audio/video processing [4, 14, 25, 30, 41]. As a concrete example, Web site operators often want to know the popularity of individual Web pages, which can be computed from the access logs of their Web servers. However, relative popularity is often more important than the exact access counts. Thus, estimated access counts are sufficient if the approximation can significantly reduce processing time.

In this paper, we propose and evaluate a framework for creating and running approximation-enabled MapReduce programs. Since its introduction [13], MapReduce has become a popular paradigm for many large-scale applications, including data analytics (*e.g.*, [2, 3]) and compute-intensive applications (*e.g.*, [15, 16]), on server clusters. Thus, embedding a general approximation approach in MapReduce frameworks can make approximation easily accessible to many applications.

MapReduce and approximation mechanisms. A MapReduce job consists of user-provided code executed as a set of map tasks, which run in parallel to process input data and produce intermediate results, and a set of reduce tasks, which process the intermediate results to produce the final results. We propose three mechanisms to introduce a general approximation approach to MapReduce: (1) *input data sampling*: only a subset of the input data is processed, (2) *task dropping*: only a subset of the tasks are executed, and (3) *user-defined approximation*: the user provides a precise and an approximate version of a task's code. These mechanisms can be easily applied to a wide range of MapReduce applications (Section 5).

Computing error bounds for approximations. Critically, in Section 3, we show how multi-stage sampling theory [27] and extreme value theory [11] can be used to compute error bounds (*i.e.*, confidence intervals) for approximate MapReduce computations. Specifically, we apply the former theory to develop a unified approach for computing error bounds when using input data sampling and/or task dropping in applications that use a set of aggregation (*e.g.*, sum) reduce operations. We apply the latter theory to compute error bounds when using task dropping in applications that use extreme value (*e.g.*, min/max) reduce operations. Such error bounds allow users to intelligently trade accuracy to improve other metrics (*e.g.*, performance and/or energy consumption).

ApproxHadoop. We have implemented our proposed mechanisms and error bound estimations in a prototype system called ApproxHadoop, which we describe in Section 4. (In this paper, we limit our discussions to the first two mechanisms, input data sampling and task dropping, because of space constraints. The description and evaluation of user-defined approximation can be found in our longer technical report [19].) For MapReduce programs that use ApproxHadoop's error estimation, the user can specify the desired error bounds at a particular confidence level when submitting a job. As the job is executed, ApproxHadoop gathers statistics and determines a mix of task dropping and/or input data sampling to achieve the desired error bounds. Alternatively, the user can explicitly specify the fraction of tasks that can be dropped (*e.g.*, 25% of map tasks) and/or the data sampling ratio (*e.g.*, 10% of data items). In this case, ApproxHadoop computes the error bounds for the specified levels of approximation. This second approach can also be used for running arbitrary ApproxHadoop programs that can tolerate approximations, but for which ApproxHadoop's error-bounding techniques do not apply; of course, ApproxHadoop cannot compute error bounds for such jobs.

Evaluation. We use ApproxHadoop to implement and study approximation-enabled applications in several domains, including data analytics, scientific computing, video encoding, and machine learning. In Section 5, we present representative experimental results for some of these applications. These results show that ApproxHadoop allows users to trade small amounts of accuracy for significant reductions in execution time and energy consumption. For example, the execution time of an application that counts the popularity of projects (subsets of articles) in Wikipedia from Web server logs for one week (217GB) decreases by 60% when the user can tolerate a maximum error of 1% with 95% confidence. This runtime decrease can be even greater for larger input data (and the same maximum error and confidence); *e.g.*, 32× faster when processing a year of log entries (12.5TB).

Our results also show that, for a wide range of error targets, ApproxHadoop successfully chooses combinations of data sampling and task dropping ratios that achieve close to the best possible savings while *always achieving the target error bounds*. For the same project popularity application, ApproxHadoop reduces the execution time by 79% when given a target maximum error of 5% with 95% confidence.

Contributions. In summary, we make the following contributions: (1) we propose a general set of mechanisms for approximation in MapReduce, (2) we show how statistical theories can be used to compute error bounds in MapReduce for rigorous tradeoffs between approximation accuracy and other metrics, (3) we implement our approach in the ApproxHadoop prototype, and (4) via extensive experimentation with real systems, we show that ApproxHadoop is widely applicable to many MapReduce applications, and that it can significantly reduce execution time and/or energy consumption when users can tolerate small amounts of inaccuracy.

2. Background

MapReduce. MapReduce is a computing model designed for processing large data sets on server clusters [13]. Each MapReduce computation processes a set of input key/value pairs and produces a set of output key/value pairs. Each MapReduce program defines two functions: `map()` and `reduce()`. The `map()` function takes one input key/value pair and processes it to produce a set of intermediate key/-value pairs. The `reduce()` function performs a reduction computation on all the values associated with a given intermediate key to produce a set of final key/value pairs.

A MapReduce computation is executed in two phases by a MapReduce framework, a Map phase and a Reduce phase. To execute the Map phase, the framework divides the input data into a set of blocks, and runs a *map task* for each block that invokes `map()` for each key/value pair in the block. To execute the Reduce phase, the framework first collects all the values produced for each intermediate key. Then, it partitions the intermediate keys and their associated values among a set of *reduce tasks*. Each reduce task invokes `reduce()` for each of its assigned intermediate key and associated values, and writes the output into an output file.

In practice, it has been observed that MapReduce executions often take the form of *waves* of map and reduce tasks, where most map/reduce tasks require similar amounts of processing time as each other [48]. We leverage this observation later in our implementation of ApproxHadoop.

Hadoop. Hadoop is the best-known, publicly available implementation of MapReduce [1]. Hadoop comprises two main parts: the Hadoop Distributed File System (HDFS) and the Hadoop MapReduce framework. Input and output data to/from MapReduce programs are stored in HDFS. HDFS splits files across the local disks of the servers in the cluster. A cluster-wide *NameNode* process maintains information about where to find each data block. A *DataNode* process at each server services accesses to data blocks.

The framework is responsible for executing MapReduce jobs. Users submit jobs to the framework using a client interface; the user provides configuration parameters via this interface to guide the splitting of the input data and set the number of map and reduce tasks. Jobs must identify all input data at submission time. The interface submits each job to the *JobTracker*, a cluster-wide process that manages job execution. Each server runs a configurable number of map and reduce tasks concurrently in compute *slots*. The *JobTracker* communicates with the *NameNode* to determine the location of each job's data. It then selects servers to execute the jobs, preferably ones that store the needed data locally if they have slots available. Each server runs a *TaskTracker* process, which initiates and monitors the tasks assigned to it. The *JobTracker* starts a duplicate of any straggler task, *i.e.* a task that is taking substantially longer than its sibling tasks.

3. Approximation with error bounds

We propose three mechanisms for approximation in MapReduce: (1) input data sampling, (2) task dropping, and (3) user-defined approximation [19]. In this section, we use theories from statistics to rigorously estimate error bounds when approximating using input data sampling and/or task dropping.

3.1 Aggregation

Multi-stage sampling theory. We leverage multi-stage sampling [27] to compute error bounds for approximate MapReduce applications that compute aggregations (*e.g.*, counting accesses to Web pages from a log file). The set of supported aggregation functions includes *sum*, *count*, *average*, and *ratio*. For simplicity, we next discuss two-stage sampling. Depending on the computation, it may be necessary to use additional sampling stages as discussed at the end of the section.

Two-stage sampling works as follows. Suppose we have a population of T units, and the population is partitioned into N clusters. Each cluster i contains M_i units so that $T = \sum_{i=1}^{N} M_i$. Suppose further that each unit j in cluster i has an associated value v_{ij}, and we want to compute the sum of these values across the population, *i.e.* $\sum_{i=1}^{N}\sum_{j=1}^{M_i} v_{ij}$. (We describe the approximation of sum in the remainder of the subsection; approximations for the other operations are similar [27].)

To compute an approximate sum, we can create a sample by randomly choosing n clusters, and then randomly choosing m_i units from each chosen cluster i. Two-stage sampling then allows us to estimate the sum from this sample as:

$$\hat{\tau} = \frac{N}{n}\sum_{i=1}^{n}\left(\frac{M_i}{m_i}\sum_{j=1}^{m_i} v_{ij}\right) \pm \epsilon \quad (1)$$

where the error bound ϵ is defined as:

$$\epsilon = t_{n-1,1-\alpha/2}\sqrt{\widehat{Var}(\hat{\tau})} \quad (2)$$

$$\widehat{Var}(\hat{\tau}) = N(N-n)\frac{s_u^2}{n} + \frac{N}{n}\sum_{i=1}^{n} M_i(M_i - m_i)\frac{s_i^2}{m_i} \quad (3)$$

where (s_u^2) is the inter-cluster variance (computed using the sum and average of the values associated with units from each cluster in the sample), (s_i^2) is the intra-cluster variance for cluster i, and $t_{n-1,1-\alpha/2}$ is the value of the Student t-distribution with $n-1$ degrees of freedom at the desired confidence $1-\alpha$. Thus, to compute the error bound with 95% confidence, we use the value $t_{n-1,0.975}$ [27].

Applying two-stage sampling to MapReduce. To apply two-stage sampling to MapReduce, we associate population, clusters, and the value associated with each unit in the population to the respective components in MapReduce. As an example, consider a program that counts the occurrence of a word W in a set of Web pages, where the Map phase counts the occurrence of W in each page, and the Reduce phase sums the counts. Suppose that the program is then run on an input data set with T pages (input data items), and the framework partitions the input into N data blocks. In this case, the population corresponds to the T pages, with each page being a unit. Each data block i is a cluster, where M_i is the number of units (pages) in the block. The Map phase would produce $<W, v_{ij}>$ for each unit (page) j in cluster (data block) i, where v_{ij} is the value associated with that unit.

With the above associations, an approximate computation can be performed by executing only a subset of randomly chosen map tasks, using task dropping to avoid the execution of the remaining map tasks. Further, each map task only processes a subset of randomly chosen pages (input data items) from its data block using input data sampling. Together, these actions are equivalent to choosing a sample using two-stage sampling. Thus, in the Reduce phase, Equations 1 and 2 can be used to compute the approximate sum and error bounds.

For jobs that produce multiple intermediate keys, we view the summation of the values associated with each key as a distinct computation. As an example, consider a program that counts the occurrence of every word that appears in a set of Web pages. The Map phase now produces a set of counts for each word appearing in the input pages. Assuming there are z words, Equations 1 and 2 are used in the Reduce phase to produce z approximate sums, each with its own error bound.

Figure 1 illustrates an approximate computation that produces several final keys and their associated sums. In this computation, the sample comprises the 2nd and 4th input data items from block 1, all data items from block 2, the 1st, 3rd, and 5th data items from block 4, and the 2nd data item from block 6. The Map phase produces three intermediate keys k_1, k_2, k_3. Thus, Equations 1 and 2 are used three times to compute $\hat{\tau}_1 \pm \epsilon_1$, $\hat{\tau}_2 \pm \epsilon_2$, and $\hat{\tau}_3 \pm \epsilon_3$.

In some computations, the Map phase may *not* produce a value for every intermediate key from each processed input data item (*e.g.*, in the example in Figure 1, a value was produced for k_1 from the 2nd data item in block 1 but not for the 4th data item.). This means that some units (input data items) do not have associated values for that intermediate key. When this happens, there are two cases: (1) the missing values are 0, or (2) there are no defined values (*i.e.*, part of the Map computation is to filter out these input data items). Our approximation approach works correctly for the first case but not the second. Going back to the second word counting example above, if a page p does not contain a word w (but other pages do), then the Map phase will not produce a count for w from data item p. However, we can correctly view the Map phase as also (implicitly) producing $<w, 0>$ for p. Thus, our approximation with error bounds works for this application.

We cannot handle the second case because the number of data items in a block is no longer the correct unit count for some intermediate keys; the data items that do not have associated values for an intermediate key have to be dropped from the population for the key. It is then impossible to compute accurate unit counts for the block for all intermediate keys without processing all data items in the block. Thus, our use of two-stage sampling depends on the assumption that a value of 0 can be correctly associated with an input data item, if the Map phase did not produce a value for the item for some intermediate key. This is the only assumption that we make in our application of multi-stage sampling.

Finally, we can either adjust the task dropping and input data sampling ratios to achieve a target error bound (*e.g.*, a maximum error of $\pm 1\%$ across all output keys), or compute the error bound for specific dropping/sampling ratios.

Three-stage sampling. In some MapReduce computations, it may be desirable to associate the population units with the intermediate <key, value> pairs produced by the Map phase for each intermediate key, rather than the input data items. For example, we might want to compute the average number of occurrences of a word W in a paragraph, and each input data item is a Web page. In this case, the Map phase would produce $<W, count>$ for each paragraph, so that the average should be computed over the number of pairs produced rather than the number of input pages. We use three-stage sampling to handle such computations. The programmer must understand her application and explicitly add the third sampling level.

Limitation: Missed intermediate keys. With our approach to sampling, it is possible to completely miss the generation of an intermediate key. In the second word counting example above, suppose that a word w only appears in one input Web page. If the sampling skips this page, the computation will not output an estimated count for w. If the set of all words are known *a priori*, we can correctly estimate the count for all words not in the output as 0 plus a bound, with a certain level of confidence. Otherwise, it is impossible to know whether words with non-zero counts were lost in the approximate computation. Thus, our online sampling approach is not appropriate if it is important to discover *all* intermediate keys, including the rarely occurring ones. Nevertheless, we could estimate the overall number of keys (with a certain confidence interval) by extrapolating from a sample, as described in [20]. Further, creating a stratified sample via pre-processing of the input data can help address this limitation.

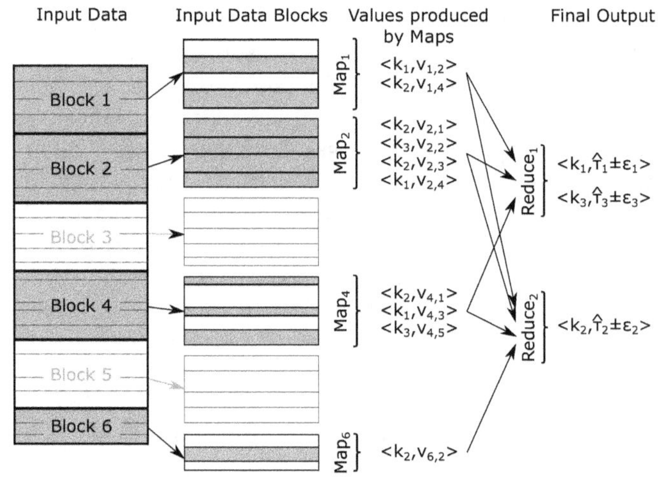

Figure 1. Example usage of two-stage sampling in a MapReduce job. Only 4 map tasks (1, 2, 4, and 6) are executed, processing 10 input data items. $v_{x,y}$ is the value produced for an intermediate key by Map_x from data item y in block x.

3.2 Extreme values

Extreme value theory. We leverage extreme value theory [11, 26] to estimate results and compute error bounds for approximate MapReduce applications that compute extreme values (*e.g.*, optimizing for minimum cost). The supported operations include *minimum* and *maximum*.

In extreme value theory, the Fisher-Tippett-Gnedenko theorem states that the cumulative distribution function (CDF) of the minimum/maximum of n independent, identically distributed (*IID*) random variables will converge to the Generalized Extreme Value (GEV) distribution as $n \to \infty$, if it converges. The GEV distribution is parameterized by three parameters μ, σ, and ξ, which define location, scale, and shape, respectively. This theorem can be used to estimate the min/max in a practical setting, where a finite set of observations is available. Specifically, given a sample of n values, it is possible to estimate a fitting GEV distribution using the Block Minima/Maxima and Maximum Likelihood Estimation (MLE) methods [11, 26].

The fitting process for estimating a minimum when given a sample of n values $v_1, v_2, ..., v_n$ is as follows. (Estimating a maximum is similar.) First, divide the sample into m equal size blocks, and compute the minimum value $v_{i,min}$ for each block i; this Block Minima method transforms the original sample to a sample of minima. Next, compute a fitting GEV distribution G for $v_{1,min}, v_{2,min}, ..., v_{m,min}$ using MLE. This fitting will give values for μ, σ, and ξ for G, as well as the confidence intervals around them (*e.g.*, 95% confidence intervals). These confidence intervals are used to compute G_l and G_h, the fitted GEV distributions that bound the errors around G.

G is then used to estimate the minimum by computing the value min where $G(min) = p$ for some low percentile p (*e.g.*, 1st percentile). The confidence interval around min is defined by $[min_l, min_h]$, where $G_l(min_l) = p$ and $G_h(min_h) = p$.

Applying extreme value theory to MapReduce. We apply the above to approximate MapReduce min/max computations as follows. First, assume that the Map phase produces values (for a specific intermediate key) corresponding to a sample of random variables. (This is our only assumption about the Map computation.) To approximate, we can then simply drop some of the map tasks, leading to a smaller sample being produced. In the Reduce phase, we would use the above GEV fitting approach to estimate the min/-max and the confidence interval. Of course, smaller samples lead to larger confidence intervals (error bounds) for the GEV fitting. Thus, similar to multi-stage sampling, the amount of approximation (*i.e.*, the percentage of dropped map tasks) must be adjusted properly to achieve the desired error bounds.

In some computations, each map task may compute multiple values and output only the min/max of these values. Thus, the values already comprise a sample of min/max, allowing them to be used directly without applying the Block Minima/Maxima method. In turn, this increases the sample size for GEV fitting and so may allow many more map tasks to be dropped when targeting a specific error bound.

Figure 2 shows an example approximate computation that uses GEV. Each map task computes a part of an optimization procedure and outputs the minimum value that it finds. (There is only one intermediate key.) The reduce uses the GEV fitting and estimation approach to determine that the desired error bound has been achieved after map tasks 1 and 2 complete. Thus, map task 3 is discarded.

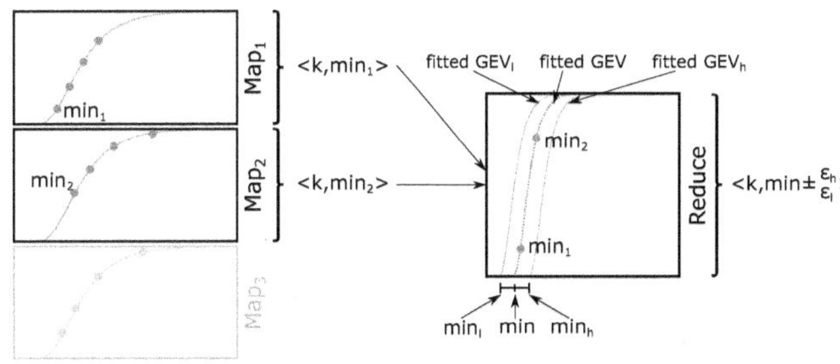

Figure 2. Example usage of GEV theory in a MapReduce job. Each map task computes the values shown (red points) and reports the minimum. Only maps 1 and 2 are executed.

4. ApproxHadoop

We have implemented the three approximation mechanisms [19], along with the error estimation techniques described in Section 3, in a prototype system called ApproxHadoop that extends the Hadoop MapReduce framework. This section describes ApproxHadoop's interfaces for application development and job submission, and the changes required to implement the approximation mechanisms and error estimation. As previously mentioned, we limit our discussion to input data sampling and task dropping.

4.1 Developing ApproxHadoop programs

Hadoop offers a set of pre-defined reduce functions (via Java classes) that can be used by programmers (*e.g.*, a reduce function that sums the values for a given intermediate key). ApproxHadoop similarly offers a set of pre-defined approximation-aware map templates and reduce functions—*e.g.*, classes `MultiStageSamplingMapper` and `MultiStageSamplingReducer` for aggregation and `ApproxMinReducer` for extreme values; see [19] for a complete list. These classes implement the desired approximation (by leveraging the ApproxHadoop mechanisms), collect the needed information for error estimation (*e.g.*, the total number of data items in a sampled input data block), perform the reduce operation, estimate the final values and the corresponding confidence intervals, and output the approximated results. To perform approximations with dropping/sampling, the user inherits ApproxHadoop's pre-defined classes instead of the regular Hadoop classes. The rest of the program remains the same as in regular Hadoop, including the code for `map()` and `reduce()`.

Using ApproxHadoop, the word count example from [13] would be adapted as in Figure 3. Only lines #2, #8, and #17 are different than the corresponding Hadoop code.

4.2 Job submission

When the user wants to run an approximate program that uses input data sampling and/or map dropping, she can direct the approximation by specifying either:

1. The percentage of map tasks that can be dropped (*dropping ratio*) and/or the percentage of input data that needs to be sampled (*input data sampling ratio*); or,
2. The desired *target error bound* (either as a percentage or an absolute value) at a confidence level.

Users who understand their applications well (*e.g.*, from repeated execution) can use the first approach. In this case, ApproxHadoop will randomly drop the specified percentage

```
class ApproxWordCount:
  class Mapper extends
        MultiStageSamplingMapper:
    //key: document name
    //val: document contents
    void map(String key, String val):
      for each word w in val:
        context.write(w, 1);
  class Reducer extends
        MultiStageSamplingReducer:
    //key: a word
    //vals: a list of counts
    void reduce(String key, Iterator vals):
      int result=0;
      for each v in vals:
        result+=v;
      context.write(key, result);
  void main():
    setInputFormat(ApproxTextInputFormat);
    run();
```

Figure 3. An example approximate word count MapReduce program using ApproxHadoop.

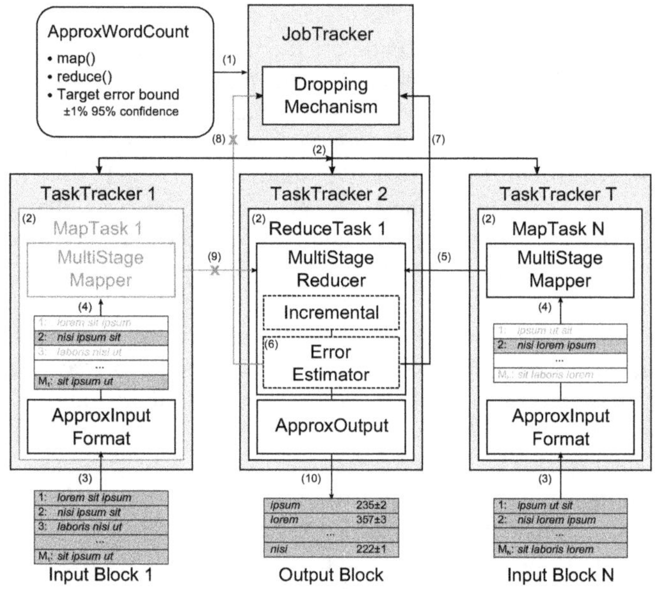

Figure 4. Example execution of the ApproxWordCount program with multi-stage sampling in ApproxHadoop.

of map tasks and/or sample each data block with the specified sampling ratio. For supported reduce operations, ApproxHadoop will also compute and output error bounds.

In the second case, for the supported reduce operations, ApproxHadoop will determine the appropriate sampling and dropping ratios. For other computations, the user would need to provide code for estimating errors. When the Map phase produces multiple intermediate keys, ApproxHadoop assumes that the specified error bound is the maximum error desired for any intermediate key.

4.3 The ApproxHadoop framework

Input data sampling. We implement input data sampling in new classes for input parsing. These classes parse an input data block and return a random sample of the input data items according to a given sampling ratio. For example, we implement `ApproxTextInputFormat`, which is similar to Hadoop's `TextInputFormat`. Like `TextInputFormat`, `ApproxTextInputFormat` parses text files, producing an input data item per line in the file. Instead of returning all lines in the file, however, `ApproxTextInputFormat` returns a sample that is a random subset of appropriate size.

Task dropping. We modified the *JobTracker* to: (1) execute map tasks in a random order to properly observe the requirements of multi-stage sampling, and (2) be able to kill running maps and discard pending ones when they are to be dropped; dropped maps are marked with a new state so that job completion can be detected despite these maps not finishing. We also modified the Reducer classes to detect dropped map tasks and continue without waiting for their results.

Error estimation. As already mentioned, our pre-defined approximate Mapper and Reducer classes implement error estimation. Specifically, the Mapper collects the necessary information, such as the number of data items in the input data block, and forwards it to the Reducer. The Reducer computes the error bounds using the techniques described in Section 3. We have also modified the *JobTracker* to collect error estimates from all reduce tasks, so that it can track error bounds across the entire job. This is necessary for choosing appropriate ratios of map dropping and input data sampling.

Incremental reduce tasks. To estimate errors and guide the selection of sampling/dropping ratios at runtime, reduce tasks must be able to process the intermediate outputs before all the map tasks have finished. We accomplish this by adding a barrier-less extension to Hadoop [44] that allows reduce tasks to process data as it becomes available.

Example execution. Figure 4 depicts a possible approximate execution of the ApproxWordCount program. The user first submits the job (arrow 1), specifying a target error bound and confidence level. The *JobTracker* then starts N map tasks (only two are shown) and 1 reduce task (2). Each map task executes by sampling its input data block (3 & 4). Map task N finishes first and reports its statistics to the reduce task (5). The reduce task estimates the error bounds (6), decides that the target has been achieved, and so asks the *JobTracker* to terminate the remaining map tasks (7). The *JobTracker* then kills map task 1, which may still be executing (8). The reduce task is informed that map task 1 will not complete (9), allowing it to complete its execution and output the results (10).

4.4 Estimating and bounding errors for aggregation

To compute the error bounds when multi-stage sampling is used, we need to know which cluster (*i.e.*, input data block) each key/value pair came from. Thus, each map task tags each key/value pair that it produces with its unique task ID. Each map task processing an input data block i also tracks the number of units (*i.e.*, data items) M_i in the block, as well as the number of sampled units m_i. This information is passed to all of the reduce tasks. We implement this functionality in our pre-defined Mapper and Reducer classes.

User-specified dropping/sampling ratios. The computation is straightforward when the user specifies the ratios. The framework randomly chooses the appropriate number of map tasks and executes them. Each task is directed to sample the input data block at the user-specified sampling ratio. The reduce tasks then compute the error bounds as discussed in Section 3.1.

User-specified target error bound. Selecting dropping/sampling ratios is more challenging when the user specifies a target error bound, because the ratios required to achieve the bound depend on the variance of the intermediate values. Also, different combinations of n (number of clusters) and m_i/M_i (sampling ratio within each cluster) will achieve similar error bounds.

Our approach for choosing n and m_i is as follows. Suppose that a subset n_1 of map tasks are executed first and the target error is X%. The framework collects information from these tasks to guide the sampling of the remaining map tasks. Specifically, we want to find the minimum amount of time required to complete the job while meeting the constraint:

$$t_{n-1,1-\alpha/2}\sqrt{\widehat{Var}(\hat{\tau})} \leq X\% \times \hat{\tau} \quad (4)$$

Thus, we set up an optimization problem and solve it. The optimization problem is to minimize the remaining execution time $RET = n_2 t_{map}(\bar{M}, \bar{m})$, where n_2 is the number of remaining map tasks, and $t_{map}(\bar{M}, \bar{m})$ is the time required to execute a map task with $\bar{M}$ input data items, processing only $\bar{m}$ items. Note that this assumes that the input data is equally divided among the map tasks, and that processing time for each data item does not vary greatly. We model the running time of a map task as:

$$t_{map}(M, m) = t_0 + Mt_r + mt_p \quad (5)$$

where t_0 is the base time to start a map and t_r and t_p are the average times required to read and process one data item, respectively. We do not model or optimize the running time of reduce tasks, because the Map phase is typically the most time-consuming, and optimizing for the map tasks usually decreases the reduces' runtime.

We also rewrite Equation 3 as:

$$\widehat{Var}(\hat{\tau}) = N(N-n)\frac{s_u^2}{n} + \frac{N}{n}CVar \quad (6)$$

where

$$CVar = n_2\bar{M}(\bar{M}-\bar{m})\frac{\bar{s}^2}{\bar{m}} + \sum_{i=1}^{n_1} M_i(M_i - m_i)\frac{s_i^2}{m_i} \quad (7)$$

Finally, we estimate t_o, t_r, t_p, $\bar{M}$, and $\bar{s}$ using statistics gathered from the execution of the n_1 completed map tasks. We then solve for n_2 and $\bar{m}$ using binary search, under the constraint given by Equation 4, $n = n_1 + n_2$, and $n_2 \leq N - n_1$. The time required to solve the problem is negligible (compared to the time to compute the approximate result and its error bounds), even for large numbers and sizes of clusters.

By default, for a job using multi-stage sampling with a user-specified target error bound, ApproxHadoop executes the first wave of map tasks without sampling. It then uses statistics from this first wave to solve the optimization problem and set the dropping/sampling ratios for the next wave. After the second wave, it selects ratios based on the previous two waves, and so on.

The above approach implies that a job with just one wave of map tasks cannot be approximated. However, the user can set parameters to direct ApproxHadoop to run a small number of maps at a specific sampling ratio in a first pilot wave. Statistics from this pilot wave are then used to select dropping/sampling ratios for the next (full) wave of maps. This reduces the amount of precise execution and allows ApproxHadoop to select dropping/sampling ratios even for jobs whose maps would normally complete in just one wave. Running such a pilot wave may lengthen job execution time (*e.g.*, by running two waves of maps instead of one), but can increase system throughput and decrease energy consumption because fewer maps are executed without sampling.

4.5 Estimating and bounding errors for extreme values

To compute the error bounds when GEV is used, the Reducer needs to know whether the values it receives for each key are already in Block Minima/Maxima format. If not, the Reducer transforms the data to this format.

User-specified dropping ratio. The framework only runs a randomly chosen subset of maps as specified by the user. The reduce then estimates the min/max and corresponding error bounds, as discussed in Section 3.2.

User-specified target error bound. The reduce estimates the min/max and the error bounds as each map completes. The overhead of this estimation is negligible. When the target error bound has been achieved, the reduce asks the *JobTracker* to kill and/or drop all remaining maps. The reduce will then observe that all maps have completed (or been dropped) and will complete the overall computation.

5. Evaluation

We evaluate ApproxHadoop using applications with varying characteristics (see Table 1) and using various approximations for each application. We first explore the approximation mechanisms and errors for some of the applications when users specify the dropping/sampling ratios. Next, we evaluate ApproxHadoop's ability to dynamically adjust its approximations to achieve user-specified target error bounds

Application	Input data	Size	Approx. S	Approx. D	Approx. U	Err.
Page Length	Wikipedia dump	9.8GB	✓	✓		MS
Page Rank		(40GB)	✓	✓		MS
Request Rate	Wikipedia log	46GB	✓	✓		MS
Project Popul			✓	✓		MS
Page Popul		(217GB)	✓	✓		MS
Request Rate	Webserver log	330MB	✓	✓		MS
Page Popul		(11GB)	✓	✓		MS
Page Traffic			✓	✓		MS
Total Size			✓	✓		MS
Request Size			✓	✓		MS
Clients			✓	✓		MS
Client Browser			✓	✓		MS
Attack Freq			✓	✓		MS
DC Placement	US and Europe	480KB		✓	✓	GEV
Video Encoding	Movie	816MB			✓	U
K-Means	Apache mail list	7.3GB			✓	U

Table 1. List of evaluated applications. Approximations: sample input data (S), drop computation (D), and user-defined approximation (U). Error estimation: multi-stage sampling (MS), generalized extreme values (GEV), and user-defined (U).

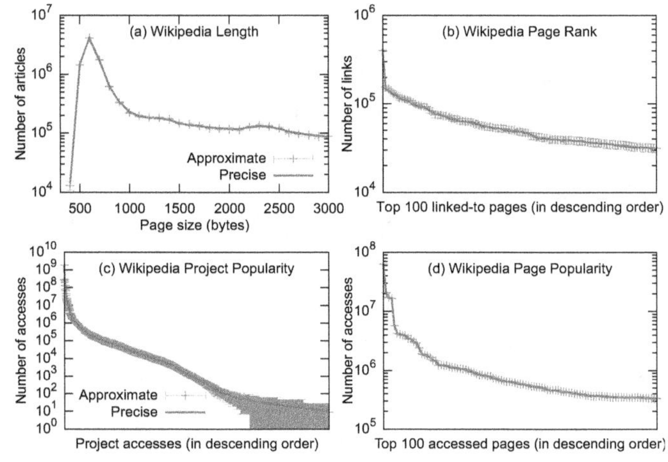

Figure 5. Results of data analysis for (a) WikiLength and (b) WikiPageRank; and log analysis for (c) Project Popularity and (d) Page Popularity. The error bars show the intervals of one approximated run at 1% input data sampling ratio.

while minimizing execution time. Finally, we explore ApproxHadoop's sensitivity to the distribution of key values, job sizes (and the impact on energy consumption), and input data sizes.

5.1 Methodology

Hardware. We run our experiments on a cluster of 10 servers (larger experiments on a 60 server cluster). Each server is a 4-core (with 2 hardware threads each) Xeon machine with 8GB of memory and one 164GB 7200rpm SATA disk. The cluster is interconnected with 1Gb Ethernet. Each server consumes 60 Watts when idle and 150 Watts at peak. Reported energy consumption numbers are based on a power model we built from measuring one server. We use a separate client machine to submit jobs, measuring job execution times on this client.

Software. ApproxHadoop extends Hadoop 1.1.2. Each server hosts a *TaskTracker* and *DataNode*, while one server also hosts the *JobTracker* and *NameNode*. We configure each server to have 8 map slots and 1 reduce slot. Experiments with multiple reduce tasks always run with the number of reduce tasks equal to the cluster size.

Metrics and measurements. Evaluation metrics include job execution time, energy consumption, and accuracy. For accuracy, we report the actual errors between approximate and precise executions, as well as the estimated 95% confidence intervals for the approximate executions. When a job outputs multiple key-value pairs, we report the actual error and confidence interval for the key with the maximum predicted absolute error. We repeat each experiment 20 times and often report the average, minimum, and maximum for each metric.

5.2 Results for user-specified dropping/sampling ratios

Data Analysis. We study two publicly available large-scale data analysis applications, WikiLength and WikiPageRank, that analyze all English Wikipedia articles. These applications are representative of large-scale processing on collections of Web pages (*e.g.*, for Web search). WikiLength produces a histogram of lengths of the articles [45], with the Map phase producing a key-value pair $<s, 1>$ for each article whose size is in bin s and the Reduce phase summing the count for each key s. WikiPageRank counts the number of articles that point to each article [24], emulating one of the main processing components of PageRank [32]. The Map phase of this application produces a pair $<a, 1>$ for each link that it finds to article a and the Reduce phase sums the count for each key a.

We use the Mapper and Reducer classes that implement multi-stage sampling to create approximation-enabled versions of WikiLength and WikiPageRank. We then use the applications to analyze the May 2014 snapshot of Wikipedia [45, 46]. This snapshot contains more than 14 million articles and is compressed into 9.8GB using bzip2 to allow random access by the map tasks. (Uncompressed, the snapshot requires 40GB of storage.) The 9.8GB partitions into 161 blocks and thus our jobs have 161 maps, running in a little more than two waves in the Xeon cluster.

Figures 5(a) and 5(b) plot parts of the results for a precise execution and an approximate execution with an input data sampling ratio of 1% (each map task processes 1 out of every 100 input data items) for each application. The error bars show the 95% confidence intervals of the approximated values. Taking one size for WikiLength as an example, consider the values for 1000B articles; the precise value is 230,793,

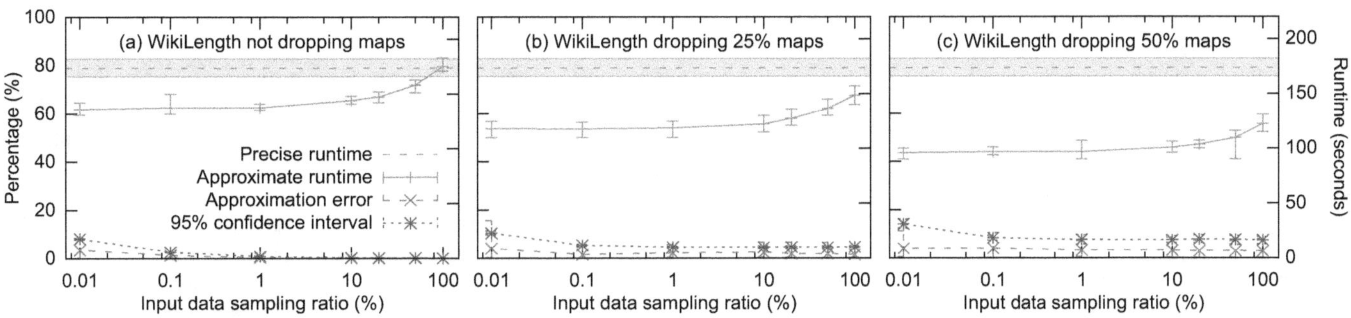

Figure 6. Performance and accuracy of WikiLength for different dropping/sampling ratios.

while the approximated value is 221,802±9,165. The actual error is 8,991 (*i.e.*, 3.89% = (230,793 - 221,802)/230,793).

Figure 6 shows the impact of approximations on the runtime (Y-axis on right) and estimation errors (Y-axis on left) for WikiLength. Each data point along a curve in the graphs plots the average value (over 20 executions) for the corresponding metric, and a range bar limited by the minimum and maximum values (over the 20 executions) of the metric. The gray horizontal band across each graph depicts the range of runtimes from multiple runs of the precise program.

Figure 6(a) shows the impact of different input data sampling ratios when no map tasks were dropped. Observe that runtime can be reduced by 21% (173.6 $\rightarrow$ 137.5 secs) by processing 1% of the articles, resulting in a 95% confidence interval of 0.81% and an actual error of 0.34%. Figures 6(b)-(c) show the impact of combining task dropping with input data sampling. Observe that dropping tasks reduces execution times more than input data sampling, but with wider confidence intervals. For example, by dropping 50% of the maps, we can reduce the runtime to below 105 secs. However, even without input data sampling (*i.e.*, 100% sampling ratio), the confidence interval at this dropping ratio is 7.38% while the actual error is 2.83%.

Task dropping has a stronger impact on execution times because it eliminates all processing (data block I/O accesses and computation on data items) for each dropped block, whereas input data sampling still requires all data items in a block to be read even though some of them will not be processed as part of the chosen sample. On the other hand, task dropping leads to wider confidence intervals for two reasons: (1) data within blocks usually has "locality" (*e.g.*, the data was produced close in time), and (2) sampling within blocks (input data sampling) adds more randomization than sampling blocks (task dropping), because in our setup, block sizes are substantially larger than the number of blocks ($M \gg N$).

Though not shown in the figures, the approximate version of WikiLength does miss sizes for which counts are small (rare occurrences). For example, in the case of 1% input data sampling, counts were reported for 1028 sizes compared to 5018 in the precise computation. For these missing sizes, the error bound was ±197, which is substantially smaller than the maximum error bound, ±33,480, for the sizes that we did find. This is consistent with our discussion of the limitations of multi-stage sampling in Section 3.1.

To quantify the *overhead* of our implementation, we compare the runtime of the precise version against the approximation with no sampling and no dropping. In this case, the average runtime increases from 173.6 to 175.0 secs, which is less than 1%.

While not shown here, results for WikiPageRank show the exact same trends (although the overhead is somewhat larger at close to 8%) [19]. Thus, in summary, we observe that input data sampling and map dropping can lead to significantly different impacts on job runtime and error bounds. Properly combining the two via multi-stage sampling can lead to the lowest runtime for specific error bound targets (and vice versa).

Log Processing. Log processing is a second important type of data analysis commonly done using MapReduce [8]. Thus, we use ApproxHadoop to process the access log for Wikipedia [46]. This log contains log entries for the first week of 2013 and is compressed into 46.0GB (216.9GB uncompressed).

In this case, each unit is an access log entry containing information like access date, access page, and request size. We compute the Project Popularity (the English project, rooted at `http://en.wikipedia.org`, is the most popular project across more than 2,064 projects with more than 1.9 billion accesses) and Page Popularity (`http://en.wikipedia.org/wiki/Main_Page` is the most accessed page).

Figures 5(c) and 5(d) plot the results for a precise execution and an approximate execution with an input data sampling ratio of 1% for the two programs. Though the confidence intervals for unpopular projects may seem large in Figure 5(c), this effect is caused by reporting small numbers in log scale. These intervals are actually narrower than those for more popular projects. Figure 7 plots the runtime and errors for Project Popularity, as a function of the dropping/sampling ratios. The figure shows very similar trends to

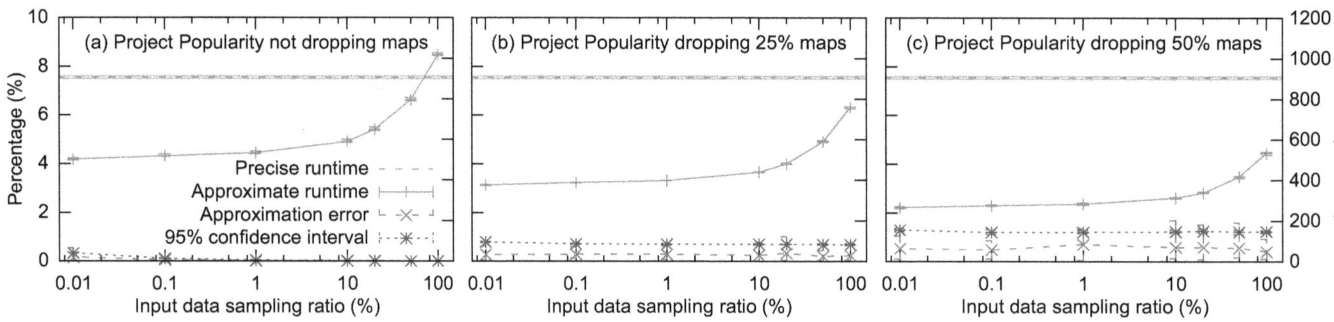

Figure 7. Performance and accuracy of Wikipedia log processing for Project Popularity.

those for WikiLength. The overhead when executing the approximate version without sampling/dropping is 12%. (Note that, when dropping maps, some of the actual errors are larger than the confidence intervals; only 95% of the estimations are expected to fall in the 95% confidence intervals).

Datacenter (DC) Placement. We now explore the impact of approximation on an optimization application. Specifically, the application uses simulated annealing to find the lowest costing placement of a set of datacenters in a geographic area (*e.g.*, the US), constrained by a maximum latency to clients (*e.g.*, 50ms) [18]. The area is divided into a two dimensional grid, with each cell in the grid as a potential location for a datacenter. In the MapReduce program, each map executes an independent search through the solution space, outputting the minimum cost placement that it finds. The single reduce task outputs the overall minimum cost placement.

Note that this application itself is already an approximation: the optimization is not guaranteed to produce an optimal result, but will produce better results as the search becomes more comprehensive and/or a finer grid is used. We enhance the capabilities for approximations in this application by allowing the dropping of map tasks. We use the Mapper and Reducer classes implementing extreme value to estimate an approximate minimum value and the confidence interval along with the actual minimum cost solution found.

Figure 8 shows the impact of map dropping on the optimization with a 50ms maximum latency constraint and the default grid size. We run the experiments with 80 map tasks, with each server configured with only 4 map slots, which is the most efficient setting for this CPU-bound application. Note that the runtime decreases slowly with map dropping (right-to-left) until about 50% of the maps are dropped. This sharp drop in runtime results from the dropping of an entire wave of maps. Error bounds also grow relatively slowly until we drop more than 50% of the maps. Targeting error bounds of at most 10%, we drop 70% of the maps to reduce the runtime by 51%.

5.3 Results for user-specified target error bounds

We now demonstrate ApproxHadoop's ability to achieve a given target error bound by dynamically adjusting the drop-

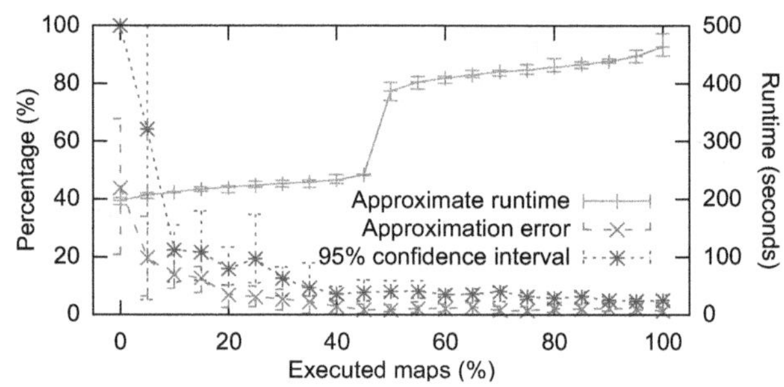

Figure 8. Performance and accuracy of DC Placement for different dropping ratios. The optimization targets a network of datacenters with a 50ms max latency.

ping/sampling ratios. We consider two applications, log processing and optimization, which use multi-stage sampling and extreme value theory for approximation, respectively.

Log Processing. Figure 9(a) plots the runtime and errors as a function of the target error bound for Project Popularity. For small target errors (<0.05%), ApproxHadoop decides that no approximation is possible. Thus, in these cases, there are no errors and the runtimes are the same as for the precise version (the overheads are negligible). From 0.05% to 0.5%, ApproxHadoop is able to use different input data sampling ratios to reduce the runtimes by more than 37%. Above 0.5%, ApproxHadoop can start dropping maps to further reduce the runtimes. For example, for a 1% target error, ApproxHadoop reduces the runtime from 908 to 360 secs (60%). Finally, for target errors above 2%, the required error bound is achieved after the 1st wave of map tasks complete, allowing all remaining maps to be dropped. Thus, ApproxHadoop cannot reduce runtime further, giving a maximum runtime reduction of 79%. Importantly, ApproxHadoop achieved the target error bounds in all experiments, as shown by the 95% confidence interval curve.

Page Popularity presents a more interesting case. The precise version cannot be executed without memory-swapping in our cluster. In fact, our memory capacity is not even large enough to run the first wave of maps precisely without swapping. However, it is possible to compute Page Popularity ef-

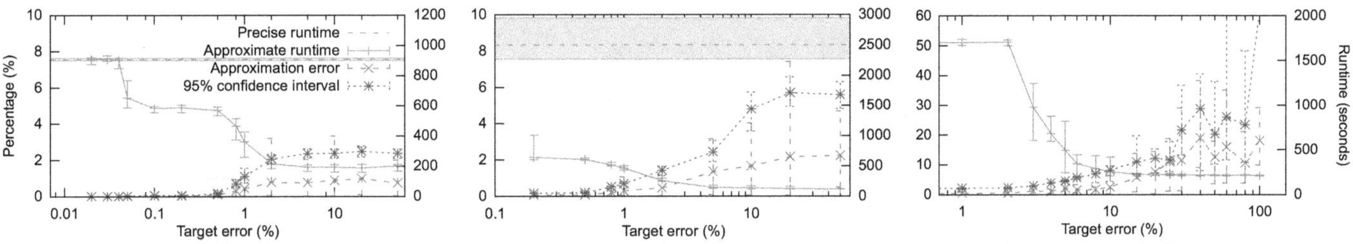

(a) Project Popularity (b) Page Popularity using a pilot sample (c) DC Placement with 50ms max latency

Figure 9. Performance and accuracy for Project Popularity when targeting different maximum errors.

ficiently for this log by directing ApproxHadoop to use a small pilot wave (see end of Section 4.4).

Figure 9(b) plots the behavior of Page Popularity, when ApproxHadoop relies on a pilot sample ran with a 1% input data sampling ratio. (The pilot takes an average of 93 ± 11 secs to complete for this application.) The results show that we cannot target errors lower than 0.2%. Note that the execution time is somewhat variable at the 0.2% target error, as the reduce tasks memory-swap in some experiments. For larger target bounds, ApproxHadoop can approximate enough that swapping does not occur. Overall, the use of the pilot sample improves performance significantly. For example, assuming a target bound of 1%, the pilot sample reduces the execution time by 78% compared to the precise execution, and 80% compared to ApproxHadoop without the pilot sample. (We include the time to perform the pilot in these calculations.) Finally, note again that all confidence intervals are smaller than the target error bounds.

DC Placement. Figure 9(c) plots the runtime and errors, as a function of the target error bounds, for an execution with 320 map tasks. Since this application uses only task dropping and the errors introduced by dropping maps are relatively large, ApproxHadoop cannot improve execution time until the target bound is larger than 2%. (Note that we are showing errors for these cases, even though ApproxHadoop is not performing any approximation, because the application itself is an approximation.) At 6%, ApproxHadoop reduces the runtime by more than 80% by dropping 285 maps. For targets higher than 6%, ApproxHadoop achieves the target error after processing the first wave of maps, and so it drops all remaining maps. Thus, ApproxHadoop can reduce runtime by up to 87%, while consistently achieving the target bound.

5.4 Sensitivity analysis

Impact of the distribution of key values. An important factor when estimating errors is the distribution of the program outputs (key values). We now evaluate the impact of this distribution by considering Log Processing on a log with different characteristics, our department's Web server access log. The log spans 80 weeks from November 2012 to June 2014 and contains more than 40 million requests. The compressed size of the log is 330MB, while the original size is 11GB. The data is divided into 80 files (one per week), each of which fits in a single data block (*i.e.*, <64MB). Each unit in the files is an access (a line), which contains information like timestamp, accessed page, and page size.

We study two applications that analyze: (1) *Request Rate:* computes the average number of requests per time unit (*e.g.*, each hour within a week), and (2) *Attack Frequencies:* computes the number of attacks (for a set of well-known attack patterns) on the Web server per client.

Figure 10(a) plots a precise and an approximate execution of Request Rate with an input data sampling ratio of 1%. The figure shows the pattern of request rates that one would expect for a Web site, as well as small errors and narrow confidence intervals. For the same execution, Figure 10(b) plots the request rates in descending order. This figure shows that request rates are fairly stable (they vary by roughly 33%), *i.e.* quite a different distribution than what we see in Figure 5. Despite this significantly different distribution, Figure 11(a) shows that the impact of varying the input data sampling ratio is very similar to Figures 6 and 7.

More interestingly, consider the precise and approximate results for Attack Frequencies in Figure 10(c), again with 1% input data sampling ratio. Since this application computes rare values, we see larger errors and wider confidence intervals. Figure 11(b) shows that ApproxHadoop can reduce execution time significantly at the cost of higher errors and wider intervals. This application emphasizes the fact that approximation is most effective for estimating values computed from a large number of input data items, rather than those from only a few.

Impact of job size on energy consumption. One of the goals of approximate computing is to conserve energy. By reducing the execution time, as in the experiments so far, and not increasing the power consumption, we save energy. The energy savings is roughly proportional to the reduction in execution time. However, in certain scenarios, ApproxHadoop can also save energy independently of reductions in execution time.

To see this, consider the experiments processing our department's Web server log. They show that input data sampling reduces the runtime (Figure 11), but dropping maps has

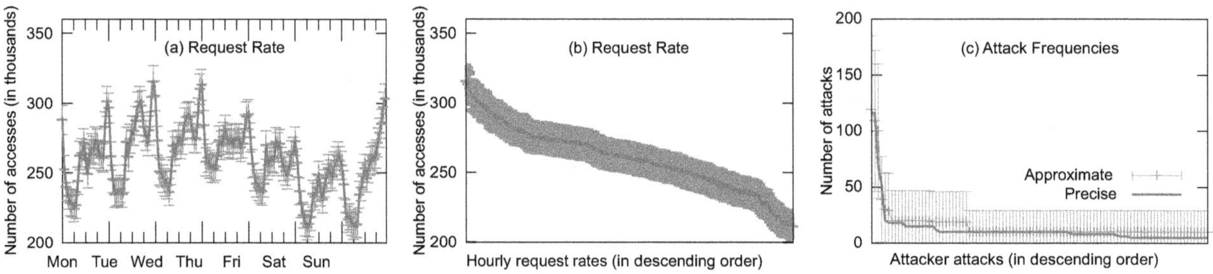

Figure 10. Results of processing our Web server log.

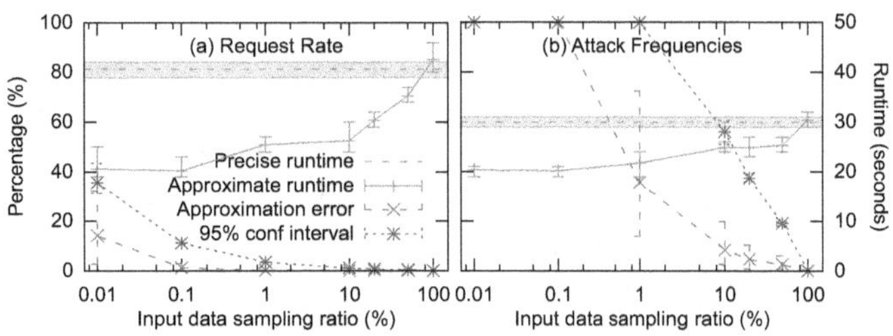

Figure 11. Performance and accuracy of Web server log processing: (a) Request Rate and (b) Attack Frequencies.

no significant effect when jobs have a single wave of maps. (Recall that when the user specifies the dropping/sampling rates, they can be applied in the first wave of maps.) The same may occur for applications that have a few more waves as well. For applications where dropping maps does not reduce the runtime, we can transition the servers that have no maps to execute (corresponding to the maps that were dropped) to a low-power state (*i.e.*, ACPI S3) when they become idle. Figure 12 shows the energy consumptions resulting from both dropping maps and input data sampling for Request Rate and Attack Frequencies. As we would expect, decreasing the amount of input data ApproxHadoop samples reduces energy consumption, as this reduces execution time. However, dropping more maps also saves energy, even though this does not reduce execution time.

Impact of data size. Finally, we evaluate the impact of the dataset size on ApproxHadoop by running Log Processing on a larger Wikipedia access log. The log has one file per day of the year for a total of 365 files and 12.5TB, which become 2.3TB when compressed. We experiment with different subsets of the log, as we list in Table 2. Our Log Processing experiments on Wikipedia so far have only used the first week's data.

Because our Xeon cluster does not have enough disk space, for these experiments, we use another cluster with 60 nodes and a total disk capacity of 14TB. Each server in this cluster is a 2-core (with 2 hardware threads each) Atom machine with 4GB of memory, one 250GB 7200rpm SATA disk (200GB for data), interconnected with 1Gb Ethernet.

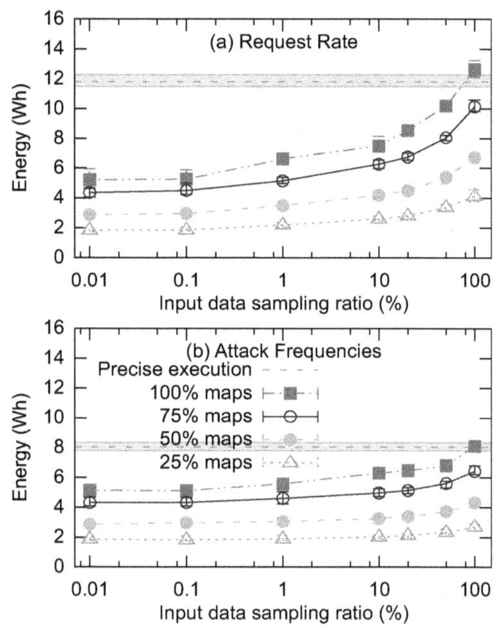

Figure 12. Energy in processing our Web server log using (a) Request Rate and (d) Attack Frequencies for multiple dropping/sampling ratios.

We configure each Atom server with 4 map slots and 1 reduce slot.

Figure 13 compares the runtime of the precise and approximate (targeting a 1% maximum error with 95% confidence) executions of Project and Page Popularity. As one would expect for these applications, the figure shows that the runtime of the precise program scales linearly with the input size. More importantly, approximating the results shortens runtimes significantly, *especially for the larger input sizes.* For example, the approximate executions of Project and Page Popularity for the year are more than 32× and 20× faster, respectively, while always achieving error bounds lower than 1%.

6. Related work

Researchers have explored numerous approximation techniques at the language [6, 38] and hardware [39] levels, for query processing [4, 10, 42], and for distributed sys-

Period	Accesses	Compress	Uncompress	#Maps
1 day	499M	5.7 GB	27.0 GB	92
2 days	1.1G	12.4 GB	58.7 GB	201
5 days	2.8G	32.1 GB	151.7 GB	518
1 week	4.0G	46.0 GB	216.9 GB	740
10 days	5.9G	67.5 GB	317.9 GB	1086
15 days	9.0G	103.2 GB	484.9 GB	1661
1 month	19.4G	221.8 GB	1.0 TB	3567
3 months	55.8G	633.1 GB	2.9 TB	10172
6 months	109.2G	1.2 TB	5.7 TB	19947
1 year	234.2G	2.3 TB	12.5 TB	38246

Table 2. Sizes of the Wikipedia access log [46] for different periods starting on January 1st 2013.

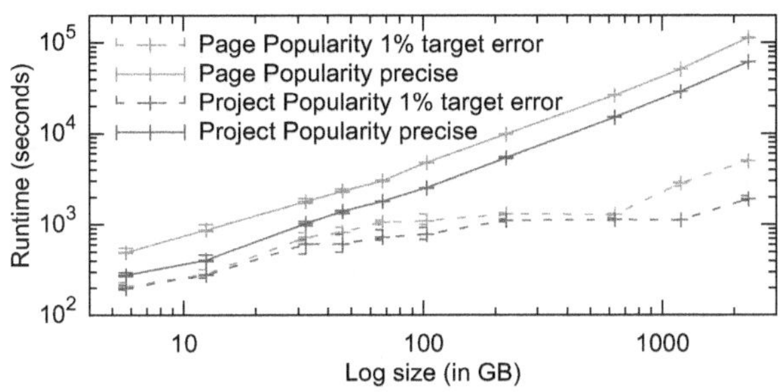

Figure 13. Performance of Page and Project Popularity for different log sizes. Both axes are in log scale.

tems [12, 21, 33]. They have also explored techniques for probabilistic reasoning about approximate programs [7, 9, 23, 28, 34, 40, 47]. We discuss the most closely related works on approximation in this section.

Approximation mechanisms. Slauson and Wan [43] have studied map task dropping in Hadoop. Riondato *et al.* [36] have used input data sampling with error estimation in a specific MapReduce application. However, these works have not considered the two mechanisms together, nor did they consider a general framework for error estimation in the presence of both mechanisms. Rinard [35] has also studied task dropping, albeit in an entirely different approach that requires previous executions with known output and significant pre-computation for estimating errors.

Our proposed sampling/dropping mechanisms are also related to loop/code perforation techniques in SpeedPress for sequential code [22, 29–31, 41]. Green [6] similarly provides a framework to adapt the approximation level based on the defined quality of service for sequential code. Bornholt *et al.* [9] propose uncertain data types to abstract approximations at the language level (*e.g.*, C#) and estimate errors from approximate data sources (*e.g.*, GPS). Unlike these systems for sequential code, ApproxHadoop proposes mechanisms for distributed MapReduce programs.

Paraprox [37] creates approximate data-parallel kernels using function memoization and runtime tuning. The execution is checked a posteriori using an easily checkable quality metric. In contrast, ApproxHadoop provides statistical error bounds around the computed approximate results within a distributed MapReduce framework.

Approximations in query processing. In the domain of database query processing, Garofalakis *et al.* [17] use wavelet-coefficient synopses and Chaudhuri *et al.* [10] use stratified sampling to build samples to provide bounded errors. SciBorq [42] also builds samples based on past query results. BlinkDB [4] uses stratified sampling to produce data samples with the desired characteristics before the execution of the queries. In contrast, we focus on the MapReduce paradigm, and use multi-stage sampling (stratified sampling is a subset) to compute approximations online without precomputation. Online sampling is a powerful tool for MapReduce environments, where large data sets (*e.g.*, logs) are often processed only a few times (or even just once).

MapReduce and Hadoop. MapReduce Online [12] modifies Hadoop to avoid the barrier between the Map and Reduce phases, and outputs intermediate (called "approximate") results during the execution of the reduce tasks. However, unlike ApproxHadoop, it does not attempt to compute error bounds. GRASS [5] uses speculation to reduce the impact of straggler tasks in jobs that need not complete all their tasks. In contrast, ApproxHadoop drops remaining map tasks when a target error bound has been achieved or a target percentage of map tasks has been completed.

7. Conclusions

In this paper, we proposed a general set of mechanisms for approximation in MapReduce, and demonstrated how to use existing statistical theories to compute error bounds (95% confidence intervals) for popular classes of approximate MapReduce programs. We also implemented and evaluated ApproxHadoop, an extension of the Hadoop data-processing framework that supports our rigorous approximations. Using extensive experimentation with real systems and applications, we show that ApproxHadoop is widely applicable, and that it can significantly reduce execution time and/or energy consumption when users can tolerate small amounts of inaccuracy. Based on our experience and results, we conclude that our framework and system can make efficient and controlled approximation easily accessible to MapReduce programmers.

Acknowledgments

We thank A. Verma and his co-authors for the barrier-less extension to Hadoop [44]. We also thank David Carrera and the reviewers for comments that helped us improve this paper. This work was partially supported by NSF grant CSR-1117368 and the Rutgers Green Computing Initiative.

References

[1] Apache Hadoop. http://hadoop.apache.org.

[2] Apache Mahout. `http://mahout.apache.org`.

[3] Apache Nutch. `http://nutch.apache.org`.

[4] S. Agarwal, B. Mozafari, A. Panda, H. Milner, S. Madden, and I. Stoica. BlinkDB: Queries with Bounded Errors and Bounded Response Times on Very Large Data. In *Proceedings of the European Conference on Computer Systems (EuroSys)*, 2013.

[5] G. Ananthanarayanan, M. Hung, X. Ren, I. Stoica, A. Wierman, and M. Yu. GRASS: Trimming Stragglers in Approximation Analytics. In *Proceedings of the USENIX Symposium on Networked Systems Design and Implementation (NSDI)*, 2014.

[6] W. Baek and T. M. Chilimbi. Green: A Framework for Supporting Energy-Conscious Programming using Controlled Approximation. In *Proceedings of the ACM SIGPLAN Conference on Programming Language Design and Implementation (PLDI)*, 2010.

[7] S. Bhat, J. Borgström, A. D. Gordon, and C. Russo. Deriving Probability Density Functions from Probabilistic Functional Programs. In *Proceedings of the International Conference on Tools and Algorithms for the Construction and Analysis of Systems (TACAS)*, 2013.

[8] S. Blanas, J. M. Patel, V. Ercegovac, J. Rao, E. J. Shekita, and Y. Tian. A Comparison of Join Algorithms for Log Processing in MapReduce. In *Proceedings of the ACM SIGMOD International Conference on Management of Data (SIGMOD)*, 2010.

[9] J. Bornholt, T. Mytkowicz, and K. S. McKinley. Uncertain<T>: A First-Order Type for Uncertain Data. In *Proceedings of the International Conference on Architectural Support for Programming Languages and Operating Systems (ASPLOS)*, 2014.

[10] S. Chaudhuri, G. Das, and V. Narasayya. Optimized Stratified Sampling for Approximate Query Processing. *ACM Transactions on Database Systems (TODS)*, 32(2), 2007.

[11] S. Coles. *An Introduction to Statistical Modeling of Extreme Values*. Springer, 2001.

[12] T. Condie, N. Conway, P. Alvaro, J. M. Hellerstein, K. Elmeleegy, and R. Sears. MapReduce Online. In *Proceedings of the USENIX Symposium on Networked Systems Design and Implementation (NSDI)*, 2010.

[13] J. Dean and S. Ghemawat. MapReduce: Simplified Data Processing on Large Clusters. In *Proceedings of the Symposium on Operating Systems Design and Implementation (OSDI)*, 2004.

[14] A. Doucet, S. Godsill, and C. Andrieu. On Sequential Monte Carlo Sampling Methods for Bayesian Filtering. *Statistics and Computing*, 10(3), 2000.

[15] J. Ekanayake, S. Pallickara, and G. Fox. MapReduce for Data Intensive Scientific Analyses. In *Proceedings of the IEEE International Conference on e-Science (e-Science)*, 2008.

[16] Z. Fadika, E. Dede, M. Govindaraju, and L. Ramakrishnan. Adapting MapReduce for HPC environments. In *Proceedings of the International ACM Symposium on High-Performance Parallel and Distributed Computing (HPDC)*, 2011.

[17] M. N. Garofalakis and P. B. Gibbons. Approximate Query Processing: Taming the TeraBytes. In *Proceedings of the International Conference on Very Large Databases (VLDB)*, 2001.

[18] I. Goiri, K. Le, J. Guitart, J. Torres, and R. Bianchini. Intelligent Placement of Datacenters for Internet Services. In *Proceedings of the International Conference on Distributed Computing Systems (ICDCS)*, 2011.

[19] I. Goiri, R. Bianchini, S. Nagarakatte, and T. D. Nguyen. ApproxHadoop: Bringing Approximations to MapReduce Frameworks. Technical Report DCS-TR-709, Department of Computer Science, Rutgers University, 2014.

[20] P. J. Haas, J. F. Naughton, S. Seshadri, and L. Stokes. Sampling-Based Estimation of the Number of Distinct Values of an Attribute. In *Proceedings of the International Conference on Very Large Databases (VLDB)*, 1995.

[21] J. M. Hellerstein, P. J. Haas, and H. J. Wang. Online Aggregation. In *Proceedings of the ACM SIGMOD International Conference on Management of Data (SIGMOD)*, 1997.

[22] H. Hoffmann, S. Sidiroglou, M. Carbin, S. Misailovic, A. Agarwal, and M. Rinard. Dynamic Knobs for Responsive Power-Aware Computing. In *Proceedings of the International Conference on Architectural Support for Programming Languages and Operating Systems (ASPLOS)*, 2011.

[23] O. Kiselyov and C.-C. Shan. Embedded Probabilistic Programming. In *Proceedings of the IFIP TC 2 Working Conference on Domain-Specific Languages (DSL)*, 2009.

[24] J. Lin. Cloud9: A Hadoop Toolkit for Working with Big Data. `http://lintool.github.io/Cloud9`.

[25] J. W. Liu, W.-K. Shih, K.-J. Lin, R. Bettati, and J.-Y. Chung. Imprecise Computations. *Proceedings of the IEEE*, 82(1), 1994.

[26] S. Liu and W. Q. Meeker. Statistical Methods for Estimating the Minimum Thickness Along a Pipeline. *Technometrics*, 2014.

[27] S. Lohr. *Sampling: Design and Analysis*. Cengage Learning, 2009.

[28] T. Minka, J. Winn, J. Guiver, S. Webster, Y. Zaykov, B. Yangel, A. Spengler, and J. Bronskill. Infer.NET 2.6. Microsoft Research Cambridge, 2014. `http://research.microsoft.com/infernet`.

[29] S. Misailovic, S. Sidiroglou, H. Hoffmann, and M. Rinard. Quality of Service Profiling. In *Proceedings of the ACM/IEEE International Conference on Software Engineering (ICSE)*, 2010.

[30] S. Misailovic, D. M. Roy, and M. C. Rinard. Probabilistically Accurate Program Transformations. In *Proceedings of the International Static Analysis Symposium (SAS)*, 2011.

[31] S. Misailovic, S. Sidiroglou, H. Hoffmann, M. Carbin, A. Agarwal, and M. Rinard. Code Perforation: Automatically and Dynamically Trading Accuracy for Performance and Power, 2014. `http://groups.csail.mit.edu/cag/codeperf/`.

[32] L. Page, S. Brin, R. Motwani, and T. Winograd. The PageRank Citation Ranking: Bringing Order to the Web. Technical

report, Stanford InfoLab, 1999.

[33] N. Pansare, V. R. Borkar, C. Jermaine, and T. Condie. Online Aggregation for Large MapReduce Jobs. *Proceedings of the VLDB Endowment (PVLDB)*, 4(11), 2011.

[34] A. Pfeffer. A General Importance Sampling Algorithm for Probabilistic Programs. Technical Report TR-12-07, Harvard University, 2007.

[35] M. Rinard. Probabilistic Accuracy Bounds for Fault-tolerant Computations That Discard Tasks. In *Proceedings of the Annual International Conference on Supercomputing (ICS)*, 2006.

[36] M. Riondato, J. A. DeBrabant, R. Fonseca, and E. Upfal. PARMA: A Parallel Randomized Algorithm for Approximate Association Rules Mining in MapReduce. In *Proceedings of the International Conference on Information and Knowledge Management (CIKM)*, 2012.

[37] M. Samadi, J. Lee, A. Jamshidi, A. Hormati, and S. Mahlke. SAGE: Self-Tuning Approximation for Graphics Engines. In *Proceedings of the IEEE/ACM International Symposium on Microarchitecture (MICRO)*, 2013.

[38] A. Sampson, W. Dietl, E. Fortuna, D. Gnanapragasam, L. Ceze, and D. Grossman. EnerJ: Approximate Data Types for Safe and General Low-Power Computation. In *Proceedings of the ACM SIGPLAN Conference on Programming Language Design and Implementation (PLDI)*, 2011.

[39] A. Sampson, J. Nelson, K. Strauss, and L. Ceze. Approximate Storage in Solid-State Memories. In *Proceedings of the IEEE/ACM International Symposium on Microarchitecture (MICRO)*, 2013.

[40] A. Sampson, P. Panchekha, T. Mytkowicz, K. S. McKinley, D. Grossman, and L. Ceze. Expressing and Verifying Probabilistic Assertions. In *Proceedings of the ACM SIGPLAN Conference on Programming Language Design and Implementation (PLDI)*, 2014.

[41] S. Sidiroglou-Douskos, S. Misailovic, H. Hoffmann, and M. Rinard. Managing Performance vs. Accuracy Trade-offs with Loop Perforation. In *Proceedings of the Joint Meeting of the European Software Engineering Conference and the ACM SIGSOFT Symposium on the Foundations of Software Engineering (ESEC/FSE)*, 2011.

[42] L. Sidirourgos, M. L. Kersten, and P. A. Boncz. SciBORQ: Scientific data management with Bounds On Runtime and Quality. In *Proceedings of the Conference on Innovative Data Systems Research (CIDR)*, 2011.

[43] J. Slauson and Q. Wan. Approximate Hadoop, 2012. `http://www.joshslauson.com/pdf/cs736_project.pdf`.

[44] A. Verma, N. Zea, B. Cho, I. Gupta, and R. H. Campbell. Breaking the MapReduce Stage Barrier. In *Proceedings of the IEEE International Conference on Cluster Computing (Cluster)*, 2010.

[45] Wikipedia. Wikipedia Database, 2014. `http://en.wikipedia.org/wiki/Wikipedia_database`.

[46] Wikipedia. Wikimedia Downloads, 2014. `http://dumps.wikimedia.org`.

[47] D. Wingate, A. Stuhlmueller, and N. D. Goodman. Lightweight Implementations of Probabilistic Programming Languages Via Transformational Compilation. In *Proceedings of the International Conference on Artificial Intelligence and Statistics (AISTATS)*, 2011.

[48] M. Zaharia, A. Konwinski, A. D. Joseph, R. H. Katz, and I. Stoica. Improving MapReduce Performance in Heterogeneous Environments. In *Proceedings of the USENIX Symposium on Operating Systems Design and Implementation (OSDI)*, 2008.

Monitoring and Debugging the Quality of Results in Approximate Programs

Michael Ringenburg
Adrian Sampson
University of Washington
{miker,asampson}@cs.washington.edu

Isaac Ackerman
Cornell University *
ica23@cornell.edu

Luis Ceze Dan Grossman
University of Washington
{luisceze,djg}@cs.washington.edu

Abstract

Energy efficiency is a key concern in the design of modern computer systems. One promising approach to energy-efficient computation, *approximate computing*, trades off output accuracy for significant gains in energy efficiency. However, debugging the actual cause of output quality problems in approximate programs is challenging. This paper presents dynamic techniques to debug and monitor the quality of approximate computations. We propose both offline debugging tools that instrument code to determine the key sources of output degradation and online approaches that monitor the quality of deployed applications.

We present two offline debugging techniques and three online monitoring mechanisms. The first offline tool identifies correlations between output quality and the execution of individual approximate operations. The second tracks approximate operations that flow into a particular value. Our online monitoring mechanisms are complementary approaches designed for detecting quality problems in deployed applications, while still maintaining the energy savings from approximation.

We present implementations of our techniques and describe their usage with seven applications. Our online monitors control output quality while still maintaining significant energy efficiency gains, and our offline tools provide new insights into the effects of approximation on output quality.

Categories and Subject Descriptors D.2.5 [*Testing and Debugging*]: Debugging aids; D.2.5 [*Testing and Debugging*]: Monitors

Keywords Approximate computing; debugging; monitoring

* Research performed while at the University of Washington.

ASPLOS '15, March 14–18, 2015, Istanbul, Turkey..

ACM 978-1-4503-2835-7/15/03... $15.00.
http://dx.doi.org/10.1145/2694344.2694365

1. Introduction

Energy efficiency has become a critical component of computer system design. Battery life is a major concern in mobile and embedded devices; power bills make up a large part of the cost of running data centers; and the dark silicon problem limits the amount of usable silicon resources [9].

Approximate computing is a promising approach that allows systems to trade accuracy for energy efficiency or performance [2, 3, 8, 10, 15, 22, 27, 28]. These techniques exploit applications' tolerance to occasional errors and provide imprecise but efficient computation for certain parts of the program. For example, a lossy image compression algorithm can tolerate some small errors: users are unlikely to notice minor image imperfections and lossy codecs already compromise on image fidelity. To exploit this tolerance, the algorithm can selectively use unreliable hardware components or unsound code transformations. For example, reducing the DRAM refresh rate saves energy at the cost of occasional memory errors [20] and loop perforation skips some loop iterations [28].

Imprecise computation must be used carefully to avoid compromising too much on software quality. Previous work has given programmers control over the use of approximation [2, 3, 8, 22, 27]. In Relax [8], programmers mark regions of code where hardware errors can safely go uncorrected. In EnerJ [27], a type system distinguishes data that can tolerate errors from data that requires full precision and typing rules prevent approximate-to-precise information flow. Carbin et al. [3] propose a proof system for reasoning about acceptability properties in the face of imprecision. The Rely system [4] statically determines the probability that values produced by an approximate computation are correct.

These static approaches are valuable and help bound the negative effects of approximation. However, even with static safety guarantees that prevent outright crashes and bound error margins (such as Relax's spatial error bounding or EnerJ's noninterference), some approximations can be more pernicious than others in terms of their effect on the program's *quality of result* (QoR). Hence, dynamic tools are important too. The situation is analogous to conventional software development, where static tools like Coverity [7] or Lint [16] and dynamic tools like Valgrind [24] play important and complementary roles in software quality.

This paper presents tools that use dynamic analysis to help debug and control the QoR of approximate programs. We first propose *offline* debugging tools that instrument programs to determine the critical data locations and code points that most affect QoR—to the best of our knowledge, these are the first tools to address debugging approximate code. We then propose *online* mechanisms to monitor quality and let programs adjust approximation levels or re-execute code.

We argue that both styles are important pieces of an approximate programming ecosystem. Offline tools, while too heavyweight for usage in deployment, are well-suited for pre-deployment debugging and QoR investigation. They help programmers better understand why QoR suffers and where approximation is valuable. Conversely, online monitoring can be lightweight enough to run in deployed code and adaptively adjust approximation levels or correct erroneous results when faced with QoR issues that arise post-deployment (due, for example, to unanticipated program inputs or variations in approximate hardware).

Our contributions include:

- a debugging tool for dynamically tracking approximate dataflow,
- a debugging tool for identifying correlations between approximate operations and output quality,
- three approaches to online quality monitoring, and
- an extensible online monitoring framework.

Section 2 describes a strawman approach to quality control, and explains why it is too heavyweight for the online setting and too weak for offline debugging. Section 3 discusses two novel styles of offline approximate code instrumentation and tracing that can be used to identify problematic code points and data locations for debugging. We also describe where these fit into the design space of offline approximation debugging tools. Section 4 introduces three approaches to low-overhead online monitoring. Two of our approaches (precise sampling and verification functions) are similar to previous proposals, but, to the best of our knowledge, the third (fuzzy memoization) is novel in the context of online quality monitoring. Section 5 describes the design space of online quality monitors, and where our approaches fit into this space. Section 6 describes salient implementation details of our systems. Section 7 describes our experience with using the prototypes to investigate and control QoR, including three use cases where we combined offline debugging with online monitoring. Using our tools in concert typically lets us prevent 50–100% of the errors due to approximation while retaining 44–78% of the original energy savings. The final two sections discuss related work and conclude.

2. The Quality-Control Strawman

When writing code that trades off accuracy for resource usage, it is essential to understand how this trade-off affects computation quality. While resource usage—time or power, for example—can be measured directly, quality must be assessed using a program-specific metric. We refer to this application-defined notion of output quality as the *quality of result*, or QoR. For example, in an object recognition application, the QoR metric may be the rate of correct classifications.

One way to measure QoR is to run the approximate portion(s) of a program twice for each input—once approximately, once precisely—and compare results. In an offline setting, this could be done repeatedly in a controlled environment with a variety of inputs. We refer to this as *approximation profiling*. In an online setting, we could do this in real time with each input seen "in the wild." We refer to this as *complete online monitoring*. This section argues that approximation profiling is insufficient and complete online monitoring is inappropriate.

For example, consider evaluating approximate pixel computations in a ray tracer:

```
evaluate { tracePx(x, y); }
```

The strawman would effectively execute this as:

```
approx = tracePx(x, y);
precise = runPrecise { tracePx(x, y); }
if (abs(approx - precise) > Threshold)
  throw new FailedQoR();
```

In an online tool, this approach provides real-time quality updates as each approximate computation completes. This enables programs to respond immediately, e.g., by adjusting energy parameters, or by re-executing erroneous computations. Unfortunately, such an approach also has fundamental problems. First, the code assumes idempotence of the monitored code block, but approximate computations can and often do have side effects. To run a non-idempotent code block twice, we need to buffer or roll back side effects. Second, comparing numeric return values is insufficient for measuring the QoR of many applications. QoR is inherently domain-specific, so we must support application-specific metrics. For example, a video application may prefer neighboring frames that are distorted in the same way (thus preventing jitter) over neighboring frames with less distortion but which are distorted in different ways. Another example is an algorithm that searches for local optima. An approximate version that selects a different optimum from the precise version can have equal—or possibly even superior—result quality. Lastly, and most importantly, an online monitoring scheme *must not cost more than the savings provided by the original approximation*. Executing twice clearly violates this requirement.

Section 4 addresses the online cost problem by proposing three significantly cheaper monitoring schemes, each of which work for different application scenarios. Any approach to QoR monitoring will also need to address side effects and provide flexible QoR metrics. We address these needs with a flexible monitoring API that provides hooks for programmer-specified quality metrics (see [25] for details on our API) and with a framework that provides transparent side effect isolation (see Sections 5.3 and 6.2).

In the offline case, on the other hand, cost is not an issue. During pre-deployment quality testing and debugging, spending extra time and energy to improve performance in the field is wise. In fact, we can do much more than just approximation profiling. The strawman tells us only *what* the final QoR was, with no reason *why*. It gives no indication of which operations or data are critical to QoR. Developers need more program introspection when working with approximation. We propose approaches that let us track approximation and errors at a much finer grain (individual operations or variables) and correlate them with output quality. These tools thus help identify the source of a quality issue rather than merely determining that an issue exists.

3. Offline QoR Debugging

This section describes two offline tools for investigating the QoR of approximate applications. *Dataflow instrumentation* (Section 3.1) tracks the number of approximate operations that flow into each approximate variable. *Correlation instrumentation* (Section 3.2) tracks the number of times each approximate operation executes and the number of times it produces an incorrect result. By running the instrumented program multiple times, we can identify the operations and errors that are most correlated with poor QoR and thus may represent quality bugs.

3.1 Dataflow Instrumentation

There can be wide variance in how many approximate operations flow into the computation of various values. This variance may not be proportional to the savings provided by approximation. In such cases, the approximate computation of values can degrade QoR much more than the energy savings would justify. For example, an image transform may compute a scaling factor for its output by traversing the input to compute the difference between the maximum and minimum pixels. If the input image is approximate data, this computation requires many approximate operations. If any such operation experiences a bit flip, the scaling factor and hence *every* output pixel will be incorrect. Thus, even though this computation likely comprises only a small portion of the program's energy usage, it can have disastrous impact on QoR.

Such scenarios motivate our dataflow instrumentation tool. Given an approximate operation O_1 and an operation O_2 with inputs $i_1, ..., i_n$ and result R, we say O_1 *flows* into R if $O_1 = O_2$ *or* if O_1 flows into one of $i_1, ..., i_n$. Our tool tracks the number of approximate operations that flow into each result and memory location.

We built our tool on top of a version of LLVM enhanced with approximate versions of the IR operations for arithmetic and memory access. We use a compiler pass to add code after every IR operation to compute the number of approximate operations that flow into the result of the operation. For each IR data location (e.g., user variable, memory address, SSA name), we create a shadow counter that tracks the approximate flow into the result held in that location. For most operations, we simply sum the shadow counters associated with the operands, add 1 if the operation is approximate, and assign the result into the shadow counter for the result of the operation. For store operations, we add code to store the counter associated with the store's value operand into a shadow memory (after adding one if the store itself is approximate). For load operations, we retrieve the associated counter from the shadow memory and add one if the load operation is approximate. Finally, for calls, we utilize a shadow parameter-return stack to keep track of counts for parameters and results.

We also provide API-level access to these counters. See [25] for details.

3.2 Correlation Instrumentation

In many approximate applications, particular *approximate code points* (operations that are executed approximately) are more likely to cause poor QoR than others. For example, a code point that always executes may have much more impact than one in a rarely used control flow branch. Our second offline approach, *correlation instrumentation*, helps developers identify these critical points by tracking the execution and error frequencies of every approximate code point during multiple program executions with varied QoRs. The result is a series of correlation vectors, where each vector consists of a QoR and execution and error counts for every approximate code point. Off-the-shelf tools can then determine which vector coordinates are most highly correlated with QoR.

Our instrumentation maintains two counters for each approximate code point (approximate LLVM bytecodes in our implementation). One counter records the number of times the code point executes. The other counts the number of errors, determined as follows: For operations other than memory references, we re-execute the operation precisely and compare the result. For stores, we precisely store an identical value into a shadow memory (e.g., a hash table keyed on memory addresses—see Section 6.1), along with the code point performing the store. At loads, we look up the loaded address in the shadow memory and compare the result to the approximately loaded value. If there is a mismatch, we can charge the error counters of the store (obtained from the shadow memory), the load, or both. This decision can be programmer-driven or chosen by the tool. Here we have assumed a model where approximate data is only accessed via approximate loads *and* approximate stores. We can generalize this by simply using the shadow memory for *every* store.

This approach is not context-sensitive—we are tracking correlations to individual program counters. Nothing conceptually prevents adding context sensitivity, but we have not found it necessary for the applications we studied. It would greatly increase the number of counters and could obscure some correlations.

3.3 Offline Debugging Design Space

Our offline debugging approaches can be viewed as flow analysis (dataflow instrumentation) and statistical correlation (correlation instrumentation). To our knowledge, these are *the* two general ways of assigning blame to a program point. Variants on these approaches are possible, including:

- **Context sensitivity**: As mentioned above, our correlation instrumentation approach is not context-sensitive: We analyze code points inside library functions as single points even for common functions like `memset` where uses from some callers may correlate more with QoR than uses from other callers.
- **Interactivity**: Our prototypes do not offer user interactivity. For example, one could imagine supporting *breakpoints* (like in a debugger) and providing access to our counters while execution is paused.
- **Granularity of instrumentation**: Our prototypes instrument at a fine-grained level (IR operations for correlation, and individual expression results for dataflow). Aggregating information at coarser granularity may provide complementary insights.

4. Online QoR Monitoring

Next, we turn our attention to online quality monitoring in order to detect and compensate for QoR problems in the field. As code that is deployed with the application, these tools must have very low overheads. If the monitoring cost outweighs the approximation savings, it is trivially better to run precise code rather than monitor approximate code.

4.1 Precise Sampling

The first approach we consider is *precise sampling*. Like our strawman, precise sampling compares the results of the precise and approximate versions of the monitored code. Unlike the strawman, this strategy checks only a random subset of the executions. In the sampled executions, a developer-provided function compares the output of the two executions. The developer can tune the sampling frequency to manage the trade-off between overhead and monitoring precision.

In a ray tracer, a sampling monitor might execute as follows:

```
res = tracePx(x, y);
if (random() < sampleFreq) {
  prec = runPrecise {tracePx(x, y);}
  if (!compare(result, prec, approxOut,
               preciseOut))
    throw new FailedQoR();
}
image[x][y] = res;
```

Here `compare` is a developer-supplied function that compares precise and approximate results to decide whether the QoR is acceptable. The `approxOut` and `preciseOut` arguments capture any memory side effects of the two executions. This is left intentionally vague here; side effects are an orthogonal issue discussed in Section 5.3.

Precise sampling is appropriate for applications where quality properties can be checked by looking at a random subset of the output. We can monitor—with probabilistic guarantees—the fraction of correct executions of a code block or its average error. We cannot use precise sampling for applications that require a bound on the worst-case error. Precise sampling also assumes good quality inputs to the monitored computation, otherwise the precise run may not generate a high quality output to compare with.

Our monitoring framework and API (described in [25]) includes support for precise sampling with customized QoR metrics and sampling parameters. We discuss example use cases in Section 7.3.

4.2 Verification Functions

Verification functions are routines supplied by the developer to check the QoR of a computation. Verification functions are useful whenever we can *check* a result at significantly lower cost than *computing* the result.

Our framework supports three distinct forms of verification functions. Each form requires different inputs and is useful in different situations. The first, *traditional verification*, verifies the outputs of the current execution based on its inputs. For example, a 3-SAT verifier could check that the variable assignments satisfy the formula clauses. The second, *streaming verification*, verifies the output of the current execution based on the output of past executions. For example, a video decoder could check that the current frame bears a sufficient resemblance to past frames. The final form, *consistent output verification*, looks only at the output of the current computation and verifies that it holds some desired property: for example, that a computed probability distribution sums to 1.0 or that a number lies within an expected range. Like precise sampling, traditional verification functions rely on good quality inputs to the computation, since the inputs are used to check the output. The other two forms rely only on outputs, so they are less sensitive to problems with the input.

Our monitoring APIs (described in [25]) support all three forms of verification function.

4.3 Fuzzy Memoization

Our third approach to quality monitoring is *fuzzy memoization*. Fuzzy memoization records previous inputs and outputs of the checked code and predicts the output of the current execution from past executions with *similar* inputs. We estimate the QoR by checking how different the current output is from the predicted output. Similar ideas have been used by Chaudhuri et al. [6] and Alvarez et al. [1] to *provide* approximate execution rather than to check execution quality.

We identify several variations distinguished by their prediction mechanisms. The simplest, which we call *simple fuzzy memoization*, predicts the previously recorded output with the most similar input. Another variation (*interpolated fuzzy memoization*) performs interpolation between a set of similar previous inputs. Finally, *learned fuzzy memoization* applies machine learning techniques to learn the relation between inputs and outputs. Like verification functions, fuzzy memoization solves the overhead issue with frequent cheap checks rather than rare expensive checks. It is applicable when the function computed by the checked code is relatively continuous (or easily learnable). Our framework implements the interpolated style.

QoR monitors based on fuzzy memoization become more accurate as they observe more executions of the monitored code. In the early stages, the prediction model contains few inputs. As execution proceeds, the monitor adds more results to the model and predictions improve. However, if a poorly approximated result is added to the model, it can hurt future estimates. Also, depending on the memoization implementation, adding results may increase memory overheads and eventually outweigh the energy savings from approximation. In addition, even after many results have been added to the model, new results in poorly sampled (or discontinuous) regions of the input space may have poor predictions.

To address these issues, we propose a three-pronged approach. First, the monitor should use some precise runs to ensure that the model is seeded with known-good values. Precise runs should be used early in the program execution to seed the model with some initial values, and with random sampling throughout execution to enhance the model with data from additional regions of the input space. Second, the monitor should limit the number of approximate results added to the model and add only those whose QoR estimates meet a developer-specified threshold. This prevents the model from growing too large and may keep some bad data from corrupting the model. However, as mentioned above, it is also possible that a negative prediction is due to a poor model rather than poor QoR. This may be caused, for example, by a sparsely sampled input region. Thus, our third proposal is that some failed checks lead to precise re-execution to improve the model.

For example, a fuzzy memoization monitor running our ray tracer might execute as follows:

```
if (preciseSeedingRun()) {
  result = runPrecise { tracePx(x, y); }
  addMemo(x, y, result, sideEffects);
} else {
  result = tracePx(x, y);
  if (!compNearestMemos(x, y, result,
                          sideEffects))
    if (updateModel())
      // Rerun precisely, update memos
    else throw new FailedQoR();
}
image[x][y] = result;
```

Here, the addMemo call adds a new result to the model and compNearestMemos finds nearby memoized results to compare with our current result.

Efficient fuzzy memoization requires storing previous results as input–output pairs that can be efficiently retrieved when we encounter nearby inputs. A self-balanced binary search tree ($O(\log n)$ lookup) worked well in our prototype.

Our monitoring APIs (described in [25]) provide support for interpolated fuzzy memoization.

5. The Online Monitoring Design Space

We now consider the broader design space of online quality monitoring. We begin with a discussion of the dimensions of the design space (Section 5.1). We then mention a possible additional dimension—code-centric versus data-centric annotation—and argue why code-centric is the better choice (Section 5.2). Finally, we discuss how to handle side effects and re-execution (Section 5.3).

5.1 Design Space Dimensions

We can describe the design space of online QoR monitoring algorithms in terms of four (mostly) orthogonal dimensions:

- **What is Checked**: Do we check every execution, or a sample? If we sample, what is the distribution?
- **Checkable Quality Properties**: What can we verify? Do we want every execution to be within some error bound? Or do we want the average error over all executions to be within the bound? Do we want at least some percentage of the executions to match the precise result? Also, how configurable is the QoR metric—must it be reducible to a number that we verify is close to an expected value, or can developers create arbitrary code to check correctness?
- **Checking Parameters**: What inputs are supplied to the checking algorithm? Do we look only at the outputs of the current execution? Or do we look at the inputs as well? Can we also look at inputs and outputs of past executions? Or at the results of a precise execution?
- **Side Effects**: How do we deal with the side effects of approximate computations? This is a significant issue, so we devote Section 5.3 to discussing it.

Approach	What Is Checked	Checking Parameters	Applicability and Checkable Quality Properties
Precise Sampling	Sampled executions	Approximate and precise outputs	Applicable to code that can be re-executed. Desired properties must not require examining every execution.
Verification Functions	Every execution		Applicable when checking a result is cheaper than computing it.
Traditional		Approximate inputs and outputs	
Streaming		Current and old approximate outputs	
Consistency		Approximate outputs	
Fuzzy Memoization	Every execution	Current and old inputs and outputs	Applicable to computations with easily learnable outputs. The desired property must be representable as a distance metric.

Table 1. How each of our monitoring approaches fits into the full design space. Handling side effects (not shown) is orthogonal.

Certain regions of this space are undesirable or impossible. For example, requiring the results of a precise computation combined with checking every execution leads to the prohibitive overhead of our strawman. Similarly, it is impossible to use sampling to provide error bounds on every execution.

Table 1 fits the approaches from Section 4 into this space.

5.2 The Code-Centric Nature of Quality Measurement

QoR monitoring can be expressed in either a code-centric or a data-centric style. In this section, we describe and contrast both styles and argue for the benefits of a code-centric style.

Code-centric annotations specify requirements on regions of code. For example, the following annotation might specify that the value of a pixel should be similar to the previously computed pixel:

```
pixel = checkComp(computePixel, args,
                  compareToPrevious);
```

Here `checkComp` will call `computePixel(args)` and pass its result to `compareToPrevious`, which will compare that result to the last result it saw.

Data-centric annotations, in contrast, apply to pieces of approximate data. Such requirements are typically relative to the corresponding value at the same time during a precise execution of the program. For example, the following annotation could specify that the value of `pixelA` should vary at most 5% compared to its value during a precise execution:

```
@Approx<0.05> double pixelA;
```

The two opposing annotation styles have two important similarities. First, the choice of code-centric versus data-centric *monitoring* is orthogonal to the choice of code-centric versus data-centric *approximation*. For instance, the `computePixel` function in the code-centric example above may base its approximation on data-centric annotations on values used to compute the pixel. Second, code-centric annotations are not limited to checking return values: they can check any data that is live at the end of the computation. The two approaches differ less in which data is checked and more in the frequency and granularity of checks.

Code-centric monitoring has three important advantages:

Developer expectations. Code-centric annotations apply to the result of a computation, which is generally what programmers care about. Appropriate QoR constraints are less obvious on intermediate values. Data-centric annotations on intermediate values may also generate false positives. For example, a ray tracer computes a pixel by adding the contributions of many rays. If the initial rays have small contributions compared to later rays, even large relative errors in those rays may have little impact on the final computed value.

Checking flexibility. Limiting checking to specific times lets code-centric monitors perform more expensive checks. If we must constantly monitor all intermediate values of a variable, the checks must be extremely cheap. Conversely, with a code-centric specification, QoR requirements can be represented by arbitrary functions, as long as they are cheap *relative to the cost of the computation being checked.* If this computation is, for example, the tracing and summing of all of the rays that contribute to a pixel value, the checking function can be fairly complex. If we attempt to loosen the semantics of data-centric annotations to check the value at only certain points, they essentially become code-centric annotations.

Implementation of monitoring and recovery. Limiting checking to explicit points in the computation simplifies the implementation of the monitoring framework. Monitoring need only be invoked via explicit library calls; we do not need to instrument variable accesses. In addition, code-centric annotations make it easy to take recovery actions, such as re-execution, in response to quality monitoring.

5.3 Dealing With Side Effects

Monitored computations naturally have inputs (arguments) and outputs (return values) that can be checked by a QoR monitor. But what if approximate computations mutate other data or have other side effects? These side effects impact quality and may differ in an approximate execution. For example, control flow changes in the approximate execution may cause a write to execute that does not occur in the precise version.

Unanticipated side effects can harm quality in ways that the developer-specified metrics do not account for, violating the expectation that quality monitoring catches all unacceptable precision losses. Any monitoring solution needs to account for this difficulty. We identify three general approaches:

- **Ignore side effects**: This is the simplest approach, but it shifts the burden entirely to the developer. The monitor assumes that the inputs to the QoR function or verifier are the only things that matter. Developers must ensure that any other possible side effects are incidental and will not affect the overall quality of the computation. This can be difficult, however, due to the possibility of unanticipated side effects. It may be more appropriate in a mostly functional language where side effects are less common.
- **Ensure precise and approximate side effects are identical**: In this approach, the compiler and runtime system ensure that if an approximate execution modifies any data that is not checked by the monitor, then an equivalent precise execution would have produced the same modification. In the general case this requires significant, high-overhead, dynamic cooperation from the runtime system.
- **Restrict side effects**: Our final approach simply detects and forbids side effects in monitored code except for data that is local to the computation *or* explicitly marked as an output of the computation. The monitor can check this explicitly marked output data and verify its quality. If the runtime detects disallowed side effects, it raises an exception. This approach again requires runtime cooperation, but can be done relatively cheaply (as shown in Section 6.2).

We contend that ignoring side effects pushes too much of the burden onto the developer and that ensuring identical side effects creates too much overhead. Thus our monitoring framework pursues the third option, as discussed in Section 6.2.

6. Implementation Issues

This section describes some of the most interesting details of our QoR tool implementations. Section 6.1 describes implementing shadow memories for our offline approaches. Section 6.2 discusses handling side effects in monitored code, including controlling their impact on quality and buffering/rollback for approaches that may require multiple executions. More details can be found in [25].

6.1 Shadow Memories

Both our offline tools require a shadow memory. Dataflow instrumentation uses the shadow memory to track dataflow counts across loads and stores. Correlation instrumentation, on the other hand, uses the shadow memory to track the actual values stored in approximate memory. When we load from an address in approximate memory, we check the corresponding shadow memory address to see if the loaded value is correct (if it is not correct, we increment the appropriate error counter).

Both forms of shadow memory are implemented as hash tables keyed on the real memory address. The values are either the dataflow counter for dataflow instrumentation or the stored value and the address of the store's error counter for correlation instrumentation.[1] Stores correspond to hash table inserts and loads to table lookups. Key reinsertions (i.e., stores to a previously-used address) replace the old value.

6.2 Side Effects in Monitored Code

Our monitoring system restricts side effects by allowing monitored code to write only to objects that are either part of the output list or local to the monitored code. Other memory writes result in an exception. Possible implementation strategies include reusing existing memory protection mechanisms or keeping per-object data indicating which checked computations may write to the object. Our prototype uses the latter since it is built on top of the EnerJ simulator [27], which already tracks per-object state for other purposes.

In particular, our prototype tracks whether objects are writable by augmenting heap-allocated objects with per-object state containing a region number. This state is updated and tracked by the same runtime routines that manage our framework's dynamic monitors. Specifically, users of our framework monitor computations by wrapping the computation in an implementation of a function object interface that we provide. They then pass the computation to our primary monitoring API [25], `checkApprox`. They may also optionally provide a list of *output data*: objects that the computation is allowed to modify.[2] When we call

[1] We track the store's error counter so that we can assign "blame" to the store in the event of an error due to the approximate memory.

[2] If an output list is specified, our framework also automatically passes it to the QoR metric, verification function, or fuzzy memoization predictor, so that modifications to these objects may also be monitored.

`checkApprox`, our framework creates a new region by incrementing a global region counter. To support nested calls, each call to `checkApprox` also records the region number of the parent call and restores the counter when it returns. Thus, as we return from the `checkApprox` invocations on the call stack, we also unwind the region number stack. If any output objects were specified, we set their region number to the number of region we are entering. Similarly, if any objects are allocated inside a checked region, we set their region number to the number of the current region. When entering a nested region, we first check that any output objects were writable by the parent region. (It is unsafe to make an object writable by the child when it is not writable by the parent.) Before returning from a region, we reset the output objects' region numbers to the parent region number. Thus, to enforce side effect restrictions, all stores to heap objects inside monitored code must simply check that the destination object's region number matches the current region number. If there is a mismatch, we throw an exception.

Our implementation requires a static list of output/side-effectable objects, which we found adequate for all of the use cases we examined. If necessary, the implementation could made more flexible by allowing users to register objects-that-can-change midway through an approximate computation. Also note that this approach requires non-reversible side-effects to be buffered as writes to side-effectabe objects.

In addition to restricting side effects, our implementation needs to buffer and roll back side effects for monitoring approaches that incorporate re-execution (e.g., precise sampling). We provide buffering using a copy-on-write policy for non-local objects. To implement copy-on-write, we add a boolean to each object indicating whether it should be copied when written and a pointer to the copy (initially null). If buffering is needed (e.g., during the first execution of a sampled execution), we iterate through the list of objects marked as outputs (i.e., the objects for which side effects are allowed) and set the copy-on-write flag. If a store occurs to an object whose flag is set, we check the copy pointer and create a copy if it is null. We then perform the store to the copy instead of the original object. When we load from an object with the copy-on-write boolean set, we again check the copy pointer and read the copy if it is present. After the first execution completes, we remove all the copies and unset the copy-on-write flag. This allows the subsequent run to start as if from scratch.

7. Use Cases

To evaluate our dynamic QoR tools, we experimented with seven approximate applications. For three, we used offline debugging in concert with online monitoring,[3] for one we used just offline debugging, and for three we added just monitoring. For two programs, we created two monitored versions using different monitoring approaches, resulting in a total of eight monitoring configurations.

Section 7.1 describes our approximate applications. Section 7.2 discusses insights gained via our offline debugging tools. Section 7.3 details our online monitoring results.

7.1 Applications

We considered the following applications, which cover a variety of approximation use cases, including scientific computing, image processing, simulations, and games:

- We used precise sampling online monitoring with an approximate **simple ray tracer** (from [27]).
- We used two types of verification function monitoring (streaming and consistency) with an approximated version of the classic **Asteroids** game [17].
- We used traditional verification to monitor the approximated **JME triangle intersection kernel** from [27].
- We used both dataflow and correlation instrumentation to debug the QoR of a **Sobel filter**, and used fuzzy memoization to monitor and correct the remaining errors.
- We used dataflow instrumentation to better understand the approximation patterns of an **FFT kernel** (from [27]) and used this to inform our design of two online monitors: a consistency verification monitor and a fuzzy memoization monitor.
- We used correlation instrumentation to better understand the approximation present in an approximate version of the PARSEC `canneal` **simulated annealing** benchmark. This convinced us that the error patterns were such that a monitor was not necessary.
- We used correlation instrumentation to debug the quality of an approximate version of the PARSEC **Black Scholes** benchmark (and a Java port of it). We then built a consistency verification monitor to detect any remaining errors.

7.2 Offline Debugging Tool Results

Results summary. Our offline debugging tools enabled us to narrow in on the key quality issues in our applications, and to better understand their key characteristics. In one case, we were able to solve an intermittent segmentation fault. In others, we were able to identify and correct the issues that most commonly led to poor output QoR, and in another, we were able to gain insights that led us to design a better monitor. Figure 1 shows how correlations are distributed in the applications where we used correlation instrumentation. Overall, our tools helped us improve quality, understand behavior, and design better monitors.

Sobel filter. Our instrumentation of the approximate Sobel filter enabled us to debug two problems: an intermittent seg-

[3] Our offline tools were built on top of the LLVM-based EnerC infrastructure for approximate computing in C/C++, and our monitoring prototype was built on top of the EnerJ infrastructure for approximate computing in Java, so we were able to use both tools only in applications where we could find similarly coded C and Java versions.

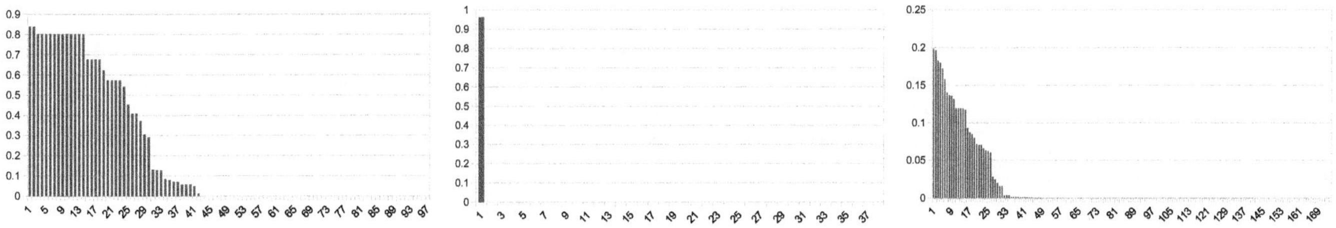

(a) (b) (c)

Figure 1. Graphs showing correlations between code points and QoR in (a) `canneal`, (b) Sobel filtering, and (c) Black Scholes. The x-axes represent source lines, and the y-axes represent QoR correlations. The x-axes are sorted by correlation value to show how the correlations are distributed: a relatively small number of code points have high correlation to QoR.

mentation fault and frequent poor quality filter results (e.g., no edges). To track down the crash, we created correlation vectors where the QoR component was determined entirely by whether or not we crashed. These vectors quickly pointed us to a code point where the application was reading from an array. Dataflow instrumentation confirmed that the array index could be influenced by approximate operations.

To investigate the poor quality results, we created correlation vectors whose QoR was based on the number of correct elements of the result and determined that the highest correlation was with code that computed a scaling factor which was later applied to every pixel. This scaling factor was being computed approximately by scanning the initial image. Dataflow instrumentation confirmed that there were a large number of approximate operations in this scan. Since this value impacts every output pixel, it was causing our frequent garbage results.

FFT. Our primary insights with FFT came from dataflow instrumentation. We checked the approximate dataflow into each element of the result and determined that, even with the relatively small FFT we used in testing (32K elements), each element of the output vector was dependent on many approximate operations (almost 180K). Due to the structure of the FFT, if an error corrupts an intermediate array value early in the computation, errors can propagate through the rest of the FFT result. This insight led us to design a monitor for the FFT application that catches any errors early so that we could either attempt to correct them or simply restart the computation.

Simulated annealing. For `canneal`, we created correlation vectors where the QoR component was determined by the difference in route length from the precisely computed version. When we plugged our vectors into a spreadsheet to compute correlations, we determined that the results with lower quality were strongly correlated with errors in approximate operations inside the random number generation routines and nothing else. The random number generation is used to compute random steps in the simulation, and these errors appeared to effectively be altering the randomization. This was causing our annealer to simply find different local minima. In fact, a number of these different minima were *better* than the one found by the precise version. This investigation gave us increased confidence in the results of our approximation, and convinced us that monitoring was unnecessary for this application.

Black Scholes. In Black Scholes, our correlation instrumentation identified two locations with particularly high correlation to QoR. In both cases, we were loading a value from a location in approximate storage that had not been accessed in a long time. In our EnerJ-based approximation model, the decay of an approximate memory value is based on the amount of time since it was last accessed. This suggests that future approximate languages may want a language feature that forces a refresh of approximate storage.

7.3 Monitoring Results

Results summary. The overheads of our monitored applications appear in Table 3. All applications were run five times. The final column displays the percentage of the original energy savings that are retained with monitoring, which ranges from 44% to 78%. The second to last column displays the energy usage of the monitored approximate computation relative to the original precise (and unmonitored) computation. Table 2 contains a detailed breakdown of overheads. Memory overhead is related to the amount of data that must be remembered in order to verify results, and can be reduced through clever monitor design by application developers. Table 4 shows our monitoring accuracy.

A Note on our Energy Model. To evaluate the energy overhead of online monitoring, we reuse the energy simulation model from the evaluation of EnerJ [27]. The model quantifies the normalized energy consumed by the CPU and memory systems during an entire program execution. This technique assumes a hardware substrate capable of enabling approximation for each instruction and each cache line as in Truffle [10]. However, our techniques would also work with approximation applied to regions of code instead of individual instructions.

For each program, we consider four configurations: fully precise (the baseline), approximate without monitoring, fully precise with monitoring, and approximate with monitoring. The difference between the approximate executions with and without monitoring reflects the energy "given

Application	Instruction Compute	Instruction Check	Instruction Overhead	Memory Compute	Memory Check	Memory Overhead
Triangle intersect, traditional verifier	95.8%	4.2%	**4.4%**	99.0%	1.0%	**1.0%**
Asteroids, streaming verifier	64.7%	35.3%	**54.6%**	89.1%	10.9%	**12.3%**
Asteroids, consistency verifier	74.1%	25.9%	**35.0%**	94.8%	5.2%	**5.5%**
Simple ray tracer, precise sampling	85.7%	14.7%	**17.2%**	69.9%	30.1%	**43.1%**
Sobel filter, fuzzy memoization	93.2%	6.8%	**7.3%**	75.4%	24.7%	**32.7%**
FFT, consistency verifier	93.5%	6.5%	**7.0%**	90.9%	9.1%	**10.0%**
FFT, fuzzy memoization	92.3%	7.7%	**8.3%**	99.7%	0.3%	**0.3%**
Black Scholes, consistency verifier	96.7%	3.3%	**3.4%**	74.2%	24.8%	**34.8%**

Table 2. The percentage of instructions and memory dedicated to the original computation (compute) and the monitoring (check) for each application and online monitor. We measure these dynamically, as total instructions executed and total memory footprint of the monitored versus unmonitored applications.

Application	Type of Monitor	Precise	Approx	Precise Monitored	Approx Monitored	Savings Retained
Simple Ray Tracer	Precise Sampling	100%	67.3%	117.2%	85.5%	**44.3%**
Asteroids, 10k frames	Streaming Verifier	100%	91.2%	103.7% (130.0%)	95.0% (121.5%)	**56.8%**
Asteroids, 10k frames	Consistency Verifier	100%	91.2%	104.8% (119.2%)	95.2% (107.4%)	**54.5%**
Triangle Intersection	Traditional Verifier	100%	83.2%	104.3%	86.8%	**77.7%**
Sobel Filter	Fuzzy Memoization	100%	85.6%	107.0%	92.9%	**49.0%**
FFT	Consistency Verifier	100%	72.8%	106.9%	82.5%	**64.3%**
FFT	Fuzzy Memoization	100%	73.4%	108.4%	81.6%	**69.2%**
Black Scholes	Consistency Verifier	100%	73.1%	117.0%	88.1%	**44.4%**

Table 3. The modeled energy consumption of each monitored application. Energy is measured relative to the precise, unmonitored execution energy (the **Precise** column). The **Approx** column shows the energy use of an unmonitored approximate execution. The **Precise Monitored** column shows the energy use of a precise, monitored execution (this would not be useful in practice, but is included to show the overall energy overhead of monitoring). **Approx Monitored** shows the energy use of an approximate monitored execution and **Savings Retained** is the percentage of the unmonitored energy savings that are retained after we add monitoring. Because the Asteroids results include a mix of monitored and unmonitored (post-training) frames, we have included the relative costs of the monitored portion in parentheses in the appropriate columns.

back" to enable online monitoring. Although a monitored precise execution is not useful in practice, it shows the overall energy overhead of monitoring. To compare monitored and unmonitored executions, we scale the processor energy by the increase in the number of instructions executed and scale the memory energy by the increase in the time that the memory must remain active. In most cases, the latter is also represented by the increase in instruction count. However, in one case (the Asteroids application), the execution time does *not* increase because the application uses `sleep` calls to maintain the proper frame rate. Thus we did not scale its memory energy. We apply the above energy scaling factors to the precise unmonitored execution to determine the energy usage of the precise monitored execution. We then apply the approximation scaling factors from the EnerJ model to the precise monitored energy to determine the approximate monitored energy level.

Ray tracer. For the ray tracer, we applied precise sampling with a sampling rate of 1% around the computation of each pixel. Our overheads were relatively high due to the simplicity of the pixel computation kernel (it only traces a scene with a single known plane and texture). Despite the overheads, we still managed to retain nearly 50% of the original energy savings. Our sampling also achieved an accurate estimate of the QoR. The mean average error of the monitor's estimate of the number of bad pixels was just 9.6%.

To demonstrate the utility of monitoring in practice, we also built an end-to-end system on top of our monitored ray tracer. This system takes advantage of the fact that certain areas of the image are more susceptible to errors than other areas (e.g., areas with smaller features). Our end-to-end monitored application decreases approximation whenever the error rate of sampled pixels gets above a configurable maximum threshold over a window of samples. Similarly, we lower the energy if the error rate drops below a configurable minimum threshold. This system reduced the error rate to 4.6%, compared with a rate of 8.6% for the monitored ray tracer without automatic adjustments. In addition, it used slightly less energy than the regular monitored system (84.8% versus 85.5%).

Asteroids. We tried two varieties of verification functions to monitor our approximate Asteroids game: a streaming verifier and a consistent output verifier. The streaming verifier compares the positions of the asteroids and the ship with their last known positions and verifies that they have not moved by more than the maximum velocity. To reduce overhead, we record and check only every fifth time step. Our consistent output verifier simply checks that the velocities are in the allowable range and that the positions are within the screen bounds.

We also explored an end-to-end use case of monitoring in the context of the Asteroids game. To do this, we added hooks to the EnerJ runtime that allow developers to adjust the simulated energy levels of the processor and memory. We then set up our constraint function to check whether the detected error rate was higher than 0.002% of positions. Subjectively, we found that this error rate was sufficient to make the game very playable. When our constraint function detected a higher error rate, we raised the energy. Once our monitor detected that the error rate had stayed below the desired rate for 1000 (for streaming verification) or 2000 (for consistent output verification) frames, we declared the training phase over. The higher count was necessary for consistent output verification because it detects fewer errors (see Table 4). After declaring training complete, we turned the monitor off. For our results, we let the game run for 10,000 frames to capture an adequate mix of pre- and post-training energy savings. Streaming verification did slightly better than consistent output verification because it was able to settle on the correct energy level more quickly and thus turn off monitoring sooner. If we look at just the overhead during the training phase, consistent output verification's overhead was better.

Triangle intersection. Our traditional verifier for triangle intersection was based on the insight that triangles that are close together are more likely to intersect than triangles that are far apart. Thus, a traditional verifier could pick a point on each of the two triangles and compute the Euclidean distance between them. If the distance between them was high and the computation returned `true` (intersection), the monitor could declare a possible error. Similarly, if the distance was small and the computation returned `false`, we could also declare an error. We quickly noticed, however, that cases where we declared an intersection between two triangles that were far apart were almost always real errors, but cases where nearby triangles don't intersect were a mixed bag—many were false positives. So, we changed our verifier to look only for the far-apart/intersecting case. We then corrected errors we caught by declaring that they did not intersect (since we only flagged erroneous intersections). This optimization allowed us to retain 78% of the energy savings, with a false positive rate of just 0.2%. We detected 47.7% of errors, and our correction reduced the error rate from 5.2%to 2.7%.

Sobel filter. For the Sobel filter, we used fuzzy memoization to monitor the computation of each pixel gradient. For our memoization input, we summed the absolute values of the differences between the north and south neighbors and the east and west neighbors. For the output, we chose the magnitude of the gradient vector (this is what edge detectors look at). Our constraint accepted the computed value if it was within 60 of the predicted value (we found empirically that this threshold gave good results). Whenever the monitor indicated a potential quality violation, we re-executed the computation precisely. Our monitor successfully identified and corrected 86.7% of the erroroneus computations, reducing the error rate from 0.66% to 0.09%. This reduction was achieved with an overhead of just 7% and allowed us to retain nearly 50% of the original energy savings. Our false positive rate was just 2.5%.

FFT. Based on the insights from our offline tools, we designed a consistent output verification monitor for the FFT kernel. Rather than applying the verification only at the end of the computation, we checked the intermediate results after every 10 iterations. Our verifier checks that every element of the array is within the maximum possible range based on the size of the input array. This allows us to catch errors early, rather than continuing with a computation that is bound to have poor QoR. In addition, we also implemented a fuzzy memoization monitor that predicts the magnitude of the output array based on the magnitude of the input array. Both monitors caught over 90% of the errors, had less than 2% false positives, and retained over 60% of the energy savings.

Black Scholes. Finally, we implemented consistency verification monitoring for Black Scholes. We simply check if the option value is within the maximum possible range, and if not, declare an error. Our monitor reduced the error rate from 3.68% to 1.26%, and retained 44.4% of the energy savings.

8. Related Work

Many systems are designed to relax output quality to improve performance or energy consumption via software [2, 15, 28, 30] or hardware [5, 8, 10, 11, 19, 20, 23] techniques. Dynamic QoR monitoring and debugging tools help make these approximate computing techniques more feasible by helping programmers understand and control quality degradations.

Online quality monitoring. Our monitoring work is the first (to our knowledge) to explore the design space of dynamic quality monitoring for approximate computations and to implement a framework supporting multiple approaches to monitoring. Here we review related efforts.

Green [2] is a framework for controlling approximation that can, optionally, invoke user code on a sampling of executions to assess quality. The programmer must provide an appropriate monitoring scheme. One example application

Application	Type of Monitor	Errors caught vs. perfect monitor	False Positives
Simple Ray Tracer	Precise Sampling	Sampling rate (with a 9.6% MAE)	0.0%
Asteroids, 10k frames	Streaming Verifier	54.8%	0.0%
Asteroids, 10k frames	Consistency Verifier	8.0%	0.0%
Triangle Intersection	Traditional Verifier	47.7%	0.2%
Sobel Filter	Fuzzy Memoization	86.7%	2.5%
FFT	Consistency Verifier	100.0%	0.0%
FFT	Fuzzy Memoization	90.1%	1.3%
Black Scholes	Consistency Verifier	65.8%	0.0%

Table 4. The percentage of errors caught by our online monitors. For precise sampling, the percentage of errors caught will be approximately the sampling rate, with some level of error. We account for this in the table above by indicating that the percentage caught will be the sampling rate, plus or minus the mean average error of the rate of sampled versus real errors. We also show the percentage of executions that result in a false positive (i.e., the monitor reports a QoR error that does not occur).

uses a manual implementation of precise sampling (with no support for controlling side effects). Our work is complementary: it explores the design space of monitoring schemes and provides reusable implementations for a variety of practical approaches.

Grigorian et al. [13, 14] propose Light Weight Checks that are similar to the verification functions we describe. Their success reinforces our assertion that this is an important coordinate in the monitoring design space.

PowerDial [15] also dynamically controls an application's degree of approximation. It monitors run-time conditions (e.g., real-time deadlines) and adjusts quality accordingly. Similarly, Eon [29] adjusts system energy at runtime based on the availability and cost of energy and computational resources. Whereas those systems monitor resource consumption, our work focuses on monitoring quality.

Quality-of-service profiling [22] uses offline profiling runs during development to examine the QoR impact of unsound code transformations. The offline calibration steps in Green and PowerDial work similarly. Online quality monitoring, as in our work, requires efficient mechanisms that do not overwhelm the benefits of approximation.

Previous work [1, 6] uses approximate (or fuzzy) memoization to *provide* approximation rather than to check the quality of approximation. In that setting, fuzzy memoization can be more expensive—since it replaces a baseline computation instead of augmenting it—but must also be more accurate.

Offline quality debugging. Our dynamic, instrumentation-based debugging tools pinpoint program points that lead to poor output quality. These techniques complement prior static and dynamic approaches.

Static approaches conservatively bound the quality impacts of approximate computing. Carbin et al. [3] propose a proof system for verifying programmer-specified correctness properties and other work [21, 30] uses probabilistic reasoning to prove accuracy bounds on program transformations. EnerJ [27] provides noninterference guarantees. Rely [4] bounds the probability that values produced by an approximate computation are correct by examining the static data flow of nondeterministic operations. In this sense, it represents a static complement to our dataflow instrumentation technique. Static techniques provide important safety properties but are necessarily conservative; our dynamic techniques are critical to addressing run-time events that static analyses cannot rule out.

There is also relevant work in the field of dynamic instrumentation. Lam et. al. [18] use instrumentation to determine where they can safely reduce floating point precision (a specific form of approximation). Roth et al. [26] and Ganai et al. [12] apply dynamic dataflow analyses to debugging in other environments, namely MPI and multi-threading.

The aforementioned work on quality-of-service profiling [22] describes an exhaustive search process for identifying program loops that do not need full precision. In contrast, our instrumentation approaches apply to finer-grained sources of error without resorting to brute-force search.

9. Conclusion

Dynamic tools are invaluable for debugging and monitoring quality-of-result for approximate computations. We have shown that offline quality debugging is useful for understanding quality tradeoffs during pre-deployment development and testing, and online quality monitoring can detect and correct quality degradations in approximate applications. Just as static and dynamic tools complement each other in other aspects of software development, we view our dynamic tools as a key addition to the tools available for using approximate computing.

Acknowledgments

This work was supported in part by C-FAR, one of six centers of STARnet, a Semiconductor Research Corporation program sponsored by MARCO and DARPA. It was also supported by NSF award number 1216611 and gifts from Microsoft Research.

References

[1] Carlos Alvarez, Jesus Corbal, and Mateo Valero. Fuzzy memoization for floating-point multimedia applications. *IEEE Transactions on Computers*, 54(7):922 – 927, July 2005.

[2] Woongki Baek and Trishul M. Chilimbi. Green: a framework for supporting energy-conscious programming using controlled approximation. In *PLDI*, 2010.

[3] Michael Carbin, Deokhwan Kim, Sasa Misailovic, and Martin C. Rinard. Reasoning about relaxed programs. In *PLDI*, June 2012.

[4] Michael Carbin, Sasa Misailovic, and Martin C. Rinard. Verifying quantitative reliability for programs that execute on unreliable hardware. In *OOPSLA*, 2013.

[5] Lakshmi N. Chakrapani, Bilge E. S. Akgul, Suresh Cheemalavagu, Pinar Korkmaz, Krishna V. Palem, and Balasubramanian Seshasayee. Ultra-efficient (embedded) SOC architectures based on probabilistic CMOS (PCMOS) technology. In *DATE*, 2006.

[6] Swarat Chaudhuri, Sumit Gulwani, Roberto Lublinerman, and Sara Navidpour. Proving programs robust. In *FSE*, 2011.

[7] `www.coverity.com`.

[8] Marc de Kruijf, Shuou Nomura, and Karthikeyan Sankaralingam. Relax: an architectural framework for software recovery of hardware faults. In *ISCA*, 2010.

[9] Hadi Esmaeilzadeh, Emily Blem, Renee St. Amant, Karthikeyan Sankaralingam, and Doug Burger. Dark silicon and the end of multicore scaling. In *ISCA*, 2011.

[10] Hadi Esmaeilzadeh, Adrian Sampson, Luis Ceze, and Doug Burger. Architecture support for disciplined approximate programming. In *ASPLOS*, 2012.

[11] Hadi Esmaeilzadeh, Adrian Sampson, Luis Ceze, and Doug Burger. Neural acceleration for general-purpose approximate programs. In *MICRO*, 2012.

[12] Malay Ganai, Dongyoon Lee, and Aarti Gupta. Dtam: dynamic taint analysis of multi-threaded programs for relevancy. In *ACM SIGSOFT 20th International Symposium on the Foundations of Software Engineering (FSE)*, 2012.

[13] Beayna Grigorian and Glenn Reinman. Dynamically adaptive and reliable approximate computing using light-weight error analysis. In *NASA/ESA Conference on Adaptive Hardware and Systems (AHS)*, 2014.

[14] Beayna Grigorian and Glenn Reinman. Improving coverage and reliability in approximate computing using application-specific, light-weight checks. In *First Workshop on Approximate Computing Across the System Stack (WACAS)*, 2014.

[15] Henry Hoffmann, Stelios Sidiroglou, Michael Carbin, Sasa Misailovic, Anant Agarwal, and Martin Rinard. Dynamic knobs for responsive power-aware computing. In *ASPLOS*, 2011.

[16] Steve C. Johnson. Lint, a C Program Checker. *Unix Programmer's Supplementary Documents*, vol. 1, 1986.

[17] Matthias Kalisch. Asteroid field. `http://jcolorexpansion.sourceforge.net/asteroid_field.html`.

[18] Michael O. Lam, Jeffrey K. Hollingsworth, Bronis R. de Supinski, and Matthew P. Legendre. Automatically adapting programs for mixed-precision floating-point computation. In *27th ACM International Conference on Supercomputing*, 2013.

[19] Larkhoon Leem, Hyungmin Cho, Jason Bau, Quinn A. Jacobson, and Subhasish Mitra. ERSA: Error resilient system architecture for probabilistic applications. In *DATE*, 2010.

[20] Song Liu, Karthik Pattabiraman, Thomas Moscibroda, and Benjamin G. Zorn. Flikker: Saving refresh-power in mobile devices through critical data partitioning. In *ASPLOS*, 2011.

[21] Sasa Misailovic, Daniel M. Roy, and Martin C. Rinard. Probabilistically accurate program transformations. In *SAS*, 2011.

[22] Sasa Misailovic, Stelios Sidiroglou, Hank Hoffman, and Martin Rinard. Quality of service profiling. In *ICSE*, 2010.

[23] Sriram Narayanan, John Sartori, Rakesh Kumar, and Douglas L. Jones. Scalable stochastic processors. In *DATE*, 2010.

[24] Nicholas Nethercote and Julian Seward. Valgrind: a framework for heavyweight dynamic binary instrumentation. In *PLDI*, 2007.

[25] Michael F. Ringenburg. *Dynamic Analyses of Result Quality in Energy-Aware Approximate Programs*. PhD thesis, Department of Computer Science and Engineering, University of Washington, Feb 2014.

[26] Philip Roth and Jeremy Meredith. Value influence analysis for message passing applications. In *28th ACM International Conference on Supercomputing*, 2014.

[27] Adrian Sampson, Werner Dietl, Emily Fortuna, Danushen Gnanapragasam, Luis Ceze, and Dan Grossman. EnerJ: Approximate data types for safe and general low-power computation. In *PLDI*, 2011.

[28] Stelios Sidiroglou, Sasa Misailovic, Henry Hoffman, and Martin Rinard. Managing performance vs. accuracy trade-offs with loop perforation. In *FSE*, 2011.

[29] Jacob Sorber, Alexander Kostadinov, Matthew Garber, Matthew Brennan, Mark D. Corner, and Emery D. Berger. Eon: a language and runtime system for perpetual systems. In *Proceedings of the 5th international conference on Embedded networked sensor systems*, 2007.

[30] Zeyuan Allen Zhu, Sasa Misailovic, Jonathan A. Kelner, and Martin Rinard. Randomized accuracy-aware program transformations for efficient approximate computations. In *POPL*, 2012.

Watson and the Era of Cognitive Computing

Guruduth S Banavar
Vice President, Cognitive Computing
Thomas J Watson Research Center, Yorktown Heights, New York
banavar@us.ibm.com

Abstract

In the last decade, the availability of massive amounts of new data, and the development of new machine learning technologies, have augmented reasoning systems to give rise to a new class of computing systems. These "Cognitive Systems" learn from data, reason from models, and interact naturally with us, to perform complex tasks better than either humans or machines can do by themselves. In essence, cognitive systems help us perform like the best by penetrating the complexity of big data and leverage the power of models. One of the first cognitive systems, called Watson, demonstrated through a Jeopardy! exhibition match, that it was capable of answering complex factoid questions as effectively as the world's champions. Follow-on cognitive systems perform other tasks, such as discovery, reasoning, and multi-modal understanding in a variety of domains, such as healthcare, insurance, and education. We believe such cognitive systems will transform every industry and our everyday life for the better. In this talk, I will give an overview of the applications, the underlying capabilities, and some of the key challenges, of cognitive systems.

Author Keywords: Cognitive Computing, Cognitive Systems, Big Data, Watson.

Biography

Guruduth Banavar is vice president of cognitive computing at IBM Research, responsible for creating the next generation of cognitive systems in the Watson family. He has worked across IBM's businesses to co-innovate with clients, for example, to build a city operations center in Rio de Janeiro.

Guru has served on Governor Cuomo's commission for improving New York state's resilience to natural disasters after Hurricane Sandy. His work has been featured in The New York Times, The Economist, and other international media.

Earlier, Guru was the Director of IBM Research in India, which he helped establish as a pre-eminent center for Services Research and Mobile Computing. There, he and his team received a National Innovation Award by the President of India in 2009 for the Spoken Web project. His early work was on distributed systems and programming models at IBM's TJ Watson Research Center in New York, which he joined in 1995 after his PhD in Computer Science.

ASPLOS'15, March 14–18, 2015, Istanbul, Turkey.
ACM 978-1-4503-2835-7/15/03.
http://dx.doi.org/10.1145/2694344.2694376

Ziria: A DSL for wireless systems programming

Gordon Stewart
Princeton University
jsseven@cs.princeton.edu

Mahanth Gowda
UIUC
gowda2@illinois.edu

Geoffrey Mainland
Drexel University
mainland@cs.drexel.edu

Božidar Radunović
MSR Cambridge
bozidar@microsoft.com

Dimitrios Vytiniotis
MSR Cambridge
dimitris@microsoft.com

Cristina Luengo Agulló
Universitat Politècnica de Catalunya
cristinaluengoagullo@gmail.com

Abstract

Software-defined radio (SDR) brings the flexibility of software to wireless protocol design, promising an ideal platform for innovation and rapid protocol deployment. However, implementing modern wireless protocols on existing SDR platforms often requires careful hand-tuning of low-level code, which can undermine the advantages of software.

Ziria is a new domain-specific language (DSL) that offers programming abstractions suitable for wireless physical (PHY) layer tasks while emphasizing the pipeline reconfiguration aspects of PHY programming. The Ziria compiler implements a rich set of specialized optimizations, such as lookup table generation and pipeline fusion. We also offer a novel – due to pipeline reconfiguration – algorithm to optimize the data widths of computations in Ziria pipelines. We demonstrate the programming flexibility of Ziria and the performance of the generated code through a detailed evaluation of a line-rate Ziria WiFi 802.11a/g implementation that is on par and in many cases outperforms a hand-tuned state-of-the-art C++ implementation on commodity CPUs.

1. Introduction

The past few years have seen increased innovation in the design and implementation of wireless protocols, both in industry and academia (cf. [8, 28, 44]). Much of this work – especially at the physical (PHY) layer of the protocol stack, managing the translation between radio hardware signals and protocol packets – has been driven by the increased availability of *software-defined radio (SDR)* platforms. SDR platforms, unlike ASIC designs, enable wireless devices to be programmed by researchers and other end users. In industry, low-cost SDR platforms have paved the way for new business models to disrupt the traditionally conservative telecom sector [23, 34, 51].

In order to meet the processing requirements of wireless protocols, SDR platforms have traditionally been FPGA-based, and were therefore difficult to program and extend. Despite some recent efforts [35], these FPGA-based SDR platforms still haven't achieved wide-spread adoption. Recently, however, projects such as Sora [45] and USRP [50] have demonstrated that CPU-based platforms can also meet the processing demands of contemporary wireless standards. Sora, for example, was the first to achieve interoperability with commercial WiFi hardware while executing all signal processing on the CPU.

Writing realtime PHY code for a CPU, though easier than programming FPGAs, is still difficult. Wireless PHY algorithms have to process tens of millions of I/Q samples per second – equivalent to a rate of around one gigabit per second. To achieve such speed a programmer has to have a good understanding of the underlying hardware and the effects of design choices on performance. As evidence of the difficulty of the problem, the initial Sora WiFi implementation – the first to solve the problem in software – merited a best-paper award [45]; the first WiFi receiver for GNU Radio appeared only a year ago [11].

A PHY design typically consists of a pipeline of signal processing stages. So far, much of the effort has been devoted to generating efficient implementations (using advanced CPU features) of the digital signal processing (DSP) algorithms that sit within these pipelines – such as FFT, correlation, encoding, and decoding. Such implementations are developed by human experts [45] or are auto-generated from high-level algebraic specifications [40, 52].

However, wireless PHY programming is not only about generating fast DSP code and efficient matrix computations.

ASPLOS '15, March 14–18, 2015, Istanbul, Turkey.

ACM 978-1-4503-2835-7/15/03...$15.00.
http://dx.doi.org/10.1145/2694344.2694368

It is also about expressing and correctly and efficiently compiling *pipeline reconfigurations* when system state (e.g. channel information, index of element in the LTE resource grid, coding and modulation rates) changes. Pipeline reconfigurations do appear in a PHY implementation and a programmer needs to maintain state that persists across the processing of multiple entities (header, resource blocks, packets, etc.), specify when a state changes, and how that change will affect the functionality of other blocks.

This pipeline reconfiguration aspect of PHY design is largely overlooked in previous work on SDR programming, yet it is of paramount importance. For example, the 4G/LTE standard – the state-of-the-art wireless cellular technology – contains over 400 pages of specifications defining the PHY layer alone [1–3]. The signal processing blocks used in LTE are mainly standard (e.g. FFT, turbo coding); most of the specification actually describes the control flow and state changes. The IEEE WiFi standard and typical textbooks give simplified block diagrams [25, Figure 118] that look like straightline dataflow composition. Unfortunately, these diagrams completely ignore pipeline reconfigurations. The full specification of state changes is instead given in 90 pages of text [25] and is nontrivial to implement correctly and efficiently due to the delicate synchronization required between pipeline reconfiguration and data processing.

Our key contribution is a new programming language, Ziria, specifically designed to expose high-level pipeline reconfiguration and control flow in PHY protocols without sacrificing the performance required for line-rate SDR. Ziria has a layered design. The main novelty is the higher-layer *computation* language for specifying and composing stream processing pipelines. Ziria also offers a lower-layer *expression* language for implementing DSP algorithms and data manipulation within pipeline components. This language is similar to those used by domain experts (C or Matlab), with a subset of features and low-level optimizations carefully selected to maintain expressiveness yet guarantee efficient compilation. The main benefits of a new domain-specific language over a library-based approach implemented in a general-purpose language are (a) domain-specific programming abstractions and a rich type system that allow programmers to express and confidently reason about state changes in their pipelines, and (b) support for aggressive optimizations on Ziria ASTs, which is crucial for compiling high-level programs to meet the tight performance constraints of modern PHYs on commodity CPUs. In this work we focus on CPUs because they are adopted by wide-spread SDR platforms [45, 50].

An important optimization in SDRs involves increasing the data widths of the components in a processing pipeline. For instance, although an encoder may naturally be defined to operate on single bit inputs, it will be much more efficient if implemented to operate on bytes. Wide data paths bring clear benefits: the ability to use SIMD instructions and wider lookup tables, efficient data manipulation, and more data locality. However, having to optimize data widths *manually* compromises ease of programming and flexibility. The acceptable data widths of a component may depend in complex ways on the rest of the pipeline (Section 3). As a consequence, a programmer needs to jointly optimize all the data widths in a pipeline, which is error-prone and tedious. Additionally, optimizing each component for the data widths of the specific pipeline in which it is used can lead to code that cannot easily be reused in other pipelines.

The Ziria compiler instead offers a *vectorization* transformation that automates this process. Thanks to this transformation, a component can be written once and reused – without any changes – in different pipelines or in different positions in the same PHY implementation with possibly different vectorizations. A well-typed pipeline modification does not require manual modifications in the constituent components. The main novelty of our vectorization transformation (compared to more traditional coarsening transformations of data paths [4, 48]) is that – for correctness – it must take into account pipeline reconfigurations (Section 3). In addition, our algorithm must jointly optimize the data path widths for *all* the components in a pipeline, which (we have empirically confirmed) can easily cause compilation times to blow up. To address this problem, we employ an idea from a distributed convex optimization framework [26] that, for a large class of utility functions, allows our vectorizer to make a local decision for each sub-computation in the pipeline without compromising global optimality. Local pruning dramatically reduces the number of vectorization candidates. As a consequence, full-featured WiFi transmit (TX) and receive (RX) PHY pipelines can compile (from Ziria to C) in 2-4 seconds.

In addition to vectorization, the Ziria compiler implements numerous other optimizations, including: automatic lookup table (LUT) creation, inlining, partial evaluation, memory management optimizations, fusion, a variant of static scheduling and others that are fundamental in achieving the desired processing speeds.

In summary, our contributions are:

- We present a new programming language, Ziria, with domain-specific abstractions well-suited for programming wireless SDRs with reconfigurable pipelines and a compilation scheme that supports limited coarse-grained pipeline parallelism and produces efficient executables for commodity CPUs (Section 2).
- We design and implement a novel *vectorization* algorithm to optimize the data widths of components in processing pipelines (Section 3). We measure the effects of this optimization and show that it also dramatically amplifies the effects of other optimizations (a combined $10\times - 100\times$ speedup over baseline).
- To demonstrate the viability of Ziria for developing SDR applications, we implement a IEEE 802.11a/g PHY. Our implementation meets the protocol *throughput* and *latency* constraints, its performance matches and often outper-

forms hand-tuned C++ code, and it is tested with live transmissions on Sora boards, delivering $< 2\%$ packet error rate on a nonrealtime OS (Section 5).

To the best of our knowledge, we are the first to present a *high-level* programming language that – in addition to being performant – can concisely capture and optimize for reconfigurations in PHY pipelines. Our compiler, testsuite, and WiFi implementation are publicly available [22].

2. Programming in Ziria

In this section we present the basic programming abstractions of Ziria and show how these abstractions help programmers compose complex pipelines such as those required for 802.11a/g. We then show how programmers familiar with imperative C-like languages can implement the basic processing blocks of those pipelines as imperative code in Ziria's expression language. A small number of signal processing concepts are introduced along the way.

2.1 Ziria stream programming abstractions

Ziria programs process *streams* of values. At a high level, a WiFi receiver is just one such computation that reads a stream of complex numbers (I/Q samples) from the A/D converter of a radio and outputs a stream of bytes corresponding to MAC-layer packets. Ziria programmers can create and compose together computations of two *types*.

Stream transformers are computations that resemble traditional stream processing "blocks" or "bricks" commonly found in existing SDR platforms like GnuRadio and Sora. They execute indefinitely by taking values from input streams and emitting values onto output streams, perhaps also maintaining some internal state. A *scrambler* block is a simple example: scramblers are used, e.g., in a WiFi transmitter, to XOR input data with a pseudorandom sequence in order to shape the transmitted signal.

Stream computers, on the other hand, are a novel concept in SDR programming. Like stream transformers, they take values from input streams and emit onto output streams. In contrast to stream transformers, they execute for a while, consuming input and producing output, but eventually *halt* and return an additional value, which we refer to as a *control value*. The WiFi packet header decoder is an example of a stream computer: it decodes the header of a packet in a streaming fashion but eventually halts, returning a *control value* containing coding and modulation parameters from the header, which can subsequently be used to decode the packet payload. The fact that computers continuously process and output data while computing the final return value allows downstream components to continuously use these outputs, reducing overall program latency.

The Ziria type system distinguishes between these two abstractions. It assigns type ($\mathsf{Zr}\ \mathsf{T}\ a\ b$) to Ziria transformers that take inputs of type a and emit outputs of type b and type ($\mathsf{Zr}\ (\mathsf{C}\ c)\ a\ b$) to Ziria computers that take inputs of type a and emit outputs of type b while eventually returning a control value of type c. Value types a, b, c are more conventional and include bit, integer and complex types of various widths, structures, arrays of statically known length, etc.

2.2 Composition on the control path

Control values returned by stream computers are *the only* Ziria mechanism for reconfiguring the processing pipeline. In our decoding example, the runtime – upon termination of the header decoder – will use the returned control value to initialize and configure the payload decoder and serve it the rest of the input stream. This is in sharp contrast to other SDR platforms [35, 46, 48], in which reconfiguration and initialization of different parts of the processing pipeline is achieved via shared global variables, asynchronous message passing, or has to be manually programmed in a low-level fashion with extra messages in data paths. These alternatives can hamper code maintainability and reusability.

In Ziria, this pattern of control flow is expressed using the `seq`-uence combinator (excerpt from our WiFi receiver):

```
seq { (h : HeaderInfo) ← DecodePLCP()
    ; Decode(h) }
```

This code runs the stream computer `DecodePLCP()` until it produces a control value `h`, of type `HeaderInfo`, and then switches to the stream computer `Decode(h)`. Because this sequencing expresses control flow in a program, we refer to the sequence operator as composition "on the control path." The Ziria type system ensures that in a sequence `seq { x ← c1; c2 }`, the component `c1` is indeed a stream computer, and not a transformer (`c2` may be either a stream computer or transformer). The (simplified) typing rule is:

$$\frac{\vdash \texttt{c1} : \mathsf{Zr}\ (\mathsf{C}\ c)\ a\ b \quad (\texttt{x}{:}c) \vdash \texttt{c2} : \mathsf{Zr}\ t\ a\ b}{\vdash \texttt{seq \{ x} \leftarrow \texttt{c1; c2 \}} : \mathsf{Zr}\ t\ a\ b}$$

where t is either T or $\mathsf{C}\ d$. Notice that both `c1` and `c2` take values of the same type (a) and emit values of the same type (b), albeit at different points in time.

Dynamic reconfiguration using `seq` directly reflects the control flow of many PHY-layer protocols. Another typical example is WiFi packet reception, in which the receiver first uses a sample preamble to estimate the characteristic of the communication channel and uses this estimation to invert the effects of the channel and decode the packet.

2.3 Composition on the data path

Whereas control path composition combines two components that take from the same input stream and emit to the same output stream (although at different points in time), Ziria also supports the more convential form of composition "on the data path": this is composition in which the stream output of one block becomes the stream input of another. For instance, in a WiFi transmitter the output stream of the CRC block is piped to a scrambler, followed by an encoder. We express this composition with the >>> combinator. In Ziria code (again, an excerpt from our WiFi transmitter):

```
crc24(len) >>> scrambler() >>> encode12()
```

The general form of this combinator c1>>> c2 allows at most one of c1 and c2 to be a stream computer, in which case the whole c1>>> c2 becomes a computer, halting and returning back the return value of the computer component. If both components are transformers, then so is their composition. The (simplified) typing rule is:

$$\frac{t = t_1 \oplus t_2 \quad \vdash \texttt{c1} : \mathsf{Zr}\, t_1\, a\, b \quad \vdash \texttt{c2} : \mathsf{Zr}\, t_2\, b\, c}{\vdash \texttt{c1} >\!\!>\!\!> \texttt{c2} : \mathsf{Zr}\, t\, a\, c}$$

where $\top \oplus t = t \oplus \top = t$.[1] In addition, only one of c1 and c2 can have read-write access to shared variables, to guarantee race-freedom in a pipeline parallel execution of >>> composition.

2.4 Example: WiFi receiver pipeline

We now show how these abstractions fit together to form complex pipelines. Our example in this section is an implementation of a WiFi 802.11a/g receiver in Ziria, based on the Sora implementation [45].

```
1  let comp Decode(h : struct HeaderInfo) =
2    DemapLimit(0) >>>
3      if h.modulation == M_BPSK then
4        DemapBPSK() >>> DeinterleaveBPSK()
5      else if h.modulation == M_QPSK then
6        DemapQPSK() >>> DeinterleaveQPSK()
7      else ... -- QAM16, QAM64 cases
8    >>> Viterbi(h.coding, h.len*8 + 8)
9    >>> scrambler()
10 let comp detectSTS() = removeDC() >>> cca()
11 let comp receiveBits() =
12   seq { h <- DecodePLCP()
13       ; Decode(h) >>> check_crc(h.len)
14       }
15 let comp receiver() =
16   seq { det <- detectSTS()
17       ; params <- LTS(det.shift)
18       ; DataSymbol(det.shift) >>>
19         FFT() >>>
20         ChannelEqualization(params) >>>
21         PilotTrack() >>>
22         GetData()    >>>
23         receiveBits() }
```

Listing 1: Ziria WiFi 802.11a/g receiver pipeline

The main phases of the WiFi pipeline are: channel detection (line 16), channel estimation (line 17), and packet demodulation and decoding (lines 22 to 23). Lines 18 to 22 convert from the time into the frequency domain and remove channel impairments.

Channel detection determines if there is a WiFi transmission by searching for a known preamble in the input stream. The first block, detectSTS, consists of a block that removes the signal DC component (removeDC), followed by the actual detection algorithm (clear channel assessment, cca). Detection returns fine-grained timing information, bound to det.

[1] Readers may recognize the combination of a monad [32] and arrow [24] structure in Ziria computation types, an idea that appears in several variations in the functional progrmaming literature [14, 38, 39].

Syntax	Description
c ::= seq$\{x \leftarrow c;\ c\}$	Sequence
$\mid c >\!\!>\!\!> c$	Data path composition
$\mid$ if e then c_1 else c_2	Conditionals
$\mid$ var $\overline{x{:}\tau := v}$ in c	Mutable variables
$\mid$ let $f(\overline{x{:}\tau}) = m$ in c	Function definition
$\mid$ let comp $f(\overline{x{:}\tau}) = c_1$ in c_2	Computation definition
$\mid c(\overline{e})$	Call computation function
$\mid$ take	Take from input
$\mid$ emit e	Emit on output
$\mid$ do m $\mid$ return e	Lift expression
$\mid$ repeat c	Repeat c indefinitely
$\mid$ while e c	Repeat c while e
$\mid$ times e c	Repeat c e-times
$\mid$ map f	Map function over input
$\mid \ldots$	
e, m ::= $x \mid v \mid x := e \mid m_1; m_2 \mid f(\overline{e}) \mid \ldots$	Expressions
v ::= unit $\mid i \mid \ldots$	Values

Figure 1: Simplified syntax of Ziria

Channel estimation estimates physical effects (multipath fading) on the transmitted signal (block LTS). The channel estimate is returned as control value params.

OFDM demodulation converts the received data from the time to the frequency domain (lines 18 to 22), and the receiver removes the effects of the channel, as estimated in the previous phase, using ChannelEqualization followed by PilotTrack. Finally, the processed symbols are passed to receiveBits for demodulation and decoding.

Discussion. The WiFi example highlights key high-level features of the Ziria computation language. First, component composition is intuitive and code is well-structured, short, and guaranteed type-correct by the compiler. Second, configuration parameters are explicitly passed to and from components, and all reconfigurations – contrary to Sora – become explicit in the seq-structure of the programs.

2.5 Implementing processing blocks

Ziria is a two-layer language consisting of (i) a computation language and (ii) an imperative and by-and-large conventional language for computing with bits, integers, complex values, structures, arrays, etc. The most important syntactic forms of the language are given in Figure 1. We use c to denote computations and e, m to denote expressions from the imperative fragment. The details of the imperative fragment, which we omit, are unsurprising. As a notational convention, we use m for statements (e.g. y := y+1) and e for expressions (e.g. y+42). Formally, statements are just expressions that return unit.

Computations c include the seq and >>> combinators, conditionals, bindings for mutable variables, functions, computations, and calls.

In addition, Ziria provides a set of primitives:

- emit e. A stream *computer* that evaluates its argument and emits the value on the output stream. It is a computer, since it halts after emitting its value, returning a `unit` control value.

- take. A stream *computer* that takes one element from the input stream and returns it as a control value. For instance:

```
seq { (x : int) ← take
    ; emit (x+1) }
```

will take one value x from the input stream and emit $x+1$.

- do m and return e. These primitives *lift* an m or e from the low-level imperative fragment to the computation language. They are both stream *computers* that execute their argument and return the final result as a control value. For instance, given a mutable variable y, the following code will take an input value, update y, and emit $y+1$:

```
seq { (x : int) ← take
    ; do { y := y+x+1; }
    ; emit (y+1) }
```

The do and return primitives have identical semantics, but as a programmer convenience we use do for imperative code that returns `unit` (such as `y := x+y+1`) and return for expressions that will return a value, e.g. return$(y+1)$.

- repeat c. A stream *transformer* that executes the stream *computer* c. When c halts, repeat re-initializes it and restarts, effectively implementing: seq$\{c; c; \ldots\}$. Here is a component that filters out all 0-value elements of its input stream.

```
repeat { (x : int) ← take
       ; if x == 0 then return ()
         else emit x }
```

Ziria also provides a few more combinators for: repeating computers n times, mapping (expression) functions over input streams, and more. The typing rules for the most important primitives are summarized below:

$$
\begin{array}{rll}
\vdash \mathsf{take}: & \forall ab.\, \mathsf{Zr}\ (\mathsf{C}\ a)\ a\ b & \\
\vdash \mathsf{emit}\ e: & \forall a.\, \mathsf{Zr}\ (\mathsf{C}\ \mathsf{unit})\ a\ \tau, & \text{if } \vdash e:\tau \\
\vdash \mathsf{return}\ e: & \forall ab.\, \mathsf{Zr}\ (\mathsf{C}\ \tau)\ a\ b, & \text{if } \vdash e:\tau \\
\vdash \mathsf{map}\ f: & \mathsf{Zr}\ \mathsf{T}\ \tau\ \sigma, & \text{if } \vdash f:\tau\rightarrow\sigma \\
\vdash \mathsf{repeat}\ c: & \mathsf{Zr}\ \mathsf{T}\ \tau\ \sigma, & \text{if } \vdash c:\mathsf{Zr}\ (\mathsf{C}\ \mathsf{unit})\ \tau\ \sigma
\end{array}
$$

2.6 Executing Ziria pipelines

Ziria programs target commodity CPUs and large parts of program pipelines run on dedicated cores. The design of the Ziria *intrathread* execution model is motivated by performance, namely (a) processing with low latency, and (b) avoiding compiler-introduced buffering – even for programs that use >>> .

The fundamental insight is that there exist computations that can spontaneously produce output and push it downstream (the simplest being `emit e`), and computations that must first pull input in order to execute (the simplest being `take`). Many complex Ziria processing blocks will need to both push *and* pull data during their execution. Consequently, every Ziria computation compiles to a pair of code blocks, called `tick` and `proc`. The `tick` code block determines if the computation has a result readily available, and if so, immediately pushes it to the `proc` code block of the *downstream* component for processing. On the other hand, if input needs to be pulled, `tick` jumps to the `tick` code block of the *upstream* component. A `proc` code block consumes a pushed input and can push output to the downstream `proc` code block.

Two subtle points deserve attention:

- The `tick` or `proc` block can determine that the computation – if it is a stream computer – should halt. This will happen when `c1` halts in a `seq { x ←c1; c2}` computation. For this reason, `seq` compiles with a switchtable that selects which of the two `tick`/`proc` blocks is active at any point in time. Termination of `c1` activates the `tick`/`proc` blocks associated with `c2`.
- The `tick` and `proc` blocks for `c1` >>> `c2` *are* `c2`'s `tick` and `c1`'s `proc`, respectively. This means pipelines are drained from the right, and thus there is no need for variable-sized queues between >>> . It also implies that values are pushed *as soon* as they become available, which is beneficial for latency.

On top of this basic compilation scheme, the Ziria compiler also makes static scheduling decisions, such as eliminating `tick` code blocks for components that can never spontaneously produce output but always require input (e.g. `map f` or `take`). This optimization reduces the administrative overhead of `tick`-ing through the data path.[2]

Pipeline parallelization. A `c1` >>> ... >>> `cn` in isolation can naturally be mapped onto multiple cores by introducing interthread queues and compiling each constitutent component according to the previous intrathread model. We generalize this observation to programs where the last computation in a `seq`-uence is a data-path composition:

```
seq { x ← c0
    ; c1 >>> ... >>> cn }
```

We allow programmers to replace any of the >>> operators above with a variant |>>>| to explicitly indicate partitioning onto multiple cores. Pipeline-parallelizing arbitrary uses of >>> is more delicate and left as future work. The reason is, upon termination and reconfiguration of a data path, we need to synchronously notify all participating threads, making sure that no upstream thread in that path has erroneously consumed data not intended for this particular data path. The currently supported form of pipeline parallelization is sufficient for our workloads, however. Section 5 gives performance evaluation for WiFi TX/RX parallel pipelines.

3. Vectorization

A central optimization in the Ziria compiler is the *vectorization transformation*. It rewrites pipeline components that take values of type a and emit values of type b to take instead values of type (array$[d_{\text{in}}]$ a) and emit values of type (array$[d_{\text{out}}]$ b) for appropriate d_{in} and d_{out}, thus systematically

[2] In Section 5 we evaluate execution model overhead with program size.

transforming pipelines data paths to operate on vectors rather than scalars.

The benefits of compiler-based vectorization were outlined in the introduction. The alternative – manually adjusting the implementations of processing blocks for a specific placement in a pipeline – not only departs from intuitive protocol specifications and hampers reusability, but as the next paragraph shows, is also challenging to get right.

The challenge of vectorization. Let us examine a simple transformer `t` in isolation:

```
let comp t = repeat { (x:int) ← take
                    ; emit f(x); }
```

We could vectorize `t` to take arrays instead of singleton values of type `int`:[3]

```
let comp t_vect =
  repeat { (xa:arr[8] int) ← take
         ; for i in 0..7 { emit f(xa[i]); }}
```

Consider now placing `t` inside a pipeline that can be *reconfigured* with a `seq` block:

```
seq { x ← (t >>> c1); c2 }
```

Suppose that `c1` returns after consuming 4 values (one by one). The original `t` transformer can produce those 4 values by consuming 4 values from the input stream. On the other hand, `t_vect` can produce 4 values only after consuming a full array of 8 values. Hence, the moment the pipeline reconfigures to `c2`, `t_vect` has erroneously consumed 4 extra values, originally destined for `c2`. We conclude that the `t_vect` vectorization is incorrect for this pipeline.

The example illustrates the subtlety of vectorization and the challenge we address. The set of *feasible* vectorizations of a component depends on the placement of the component inside the pipeline, as well as on the data widths of adjacent blocks (as we have to – at the very least – produce well-typed pipelines to avoid buffer overruns and segmentation faults).

Overview of our algorithm. Guided by this intuition, we design a decentralized vectorization algorithm that:

1. In a top-down fashion, identifies sets of feasible vectorizations for transformers and computers based on the number of values they take and emit (Section 3.1) and their pipeline placement (Section 3.2), then
2. In a bottom-up fashion, composes feasible vectorization candidates together to re-assemble vectorization candidates for the original pipeline (Section 3.3).

To avoid search space explosion, the second step uses ideas from distributed optimization to locally prune the set of candidates and finally return a single candidate that maximizes a (parameter) utility function.

We implement vectorization as an AST transformation (versus a code-generation-time optimization) to allow for further waves of optimizations on the vectorized ASTs, as we illustrate in Section 4.

[3] Though valid, this may not be the most efficient vectorization since the output is not vectorized.

3.1 Cardinality analysis

As the examples above demonstrate, central to vectorization is a static analysis that we refer to as "cardinality analysis." Cardinality analysis infers for each computer `c` the number α_{in} of values the computer will take from its input and the number α_{out} of values the component will emit on its output before returning. All transformers in our WiFi workload use `repeat`-ed computers of statically deducible cardinalities, but a few computers take or emit a dynamic number of values. For these few cases Ziria provides several forms of annotations to force vectorizations, e.g., when we know that some multiple of a fixed number of values will be emitted, such as in the CRC implementation in our repository.

3.2 Feasible vectorization sets

In a top-down fashion, our algorithm determines feasible vectorizations, distinguishing the following three cases.

Computer vectorizations. For correctness, vectorization of a computer `c` needs to ensure that the vectorized computer takes (one or more) arrays of size d_{in} and emits (one or more) arrays of size d_{out} for some *divisors* d_{in} and d_{out} of cardinalities α_{in} and α_{out} respectively. We call this a *down-vectorization* of the computer because the final array sizes are less or equal to the cardinality parameters.

Transformer-before-computer vectorization. Consider now the example from the beginning of this Section,

```
seq { x ← (t >>> c1); c2 }
```

and assume `t` is of the form `repeat c` for some computer `c` with input cardinality α_{in} and output cardinality α_{out}.

Suppose `t` vectorizes so that in each iteration it takes one array of size $2\alpha_{\text{in}}$ and emits two arrays of size α_{out} each. The downstream computer `c1` may also be vectorized to take an array of α_{out} input values, so the types match. This vectorization candidate is nevertheless incorrect because `c1` could stop after reading the first α_{in} inputs from `t`'s output, leaving `t` with extra α_{in} values which should have been processed by `c2`.

The solution is to never increase the output rate per input in a "transformer-before-computer" vectorization. A transformer in a data path with a computer to the right can only safely *up-vectorize* to take arrays of size $d \cdot \alpha_{\text{in}}$ and emit arrays of size $d \cdot k \cdot \alpha_{\text{out}}$ for some d and k. We refer to this mode as up-vectorization because it takes and emits arrays with larger width than the cardinality parameters.

Finally, we can also *down-vectorize* to take arrays d_{in} and emit arrays d_{out} where d_{in} and d_{out} are divisors of α_{in} and α_{out} taken and emitted per iteration.

Transformer-after-computer vectorization. The symmetric situation is also interesting. Consider a transformer `t` that consumes the output of computer `c1`:

```
seq { x ← (c1 >>> t); c2 }
```

Although transformers do not themselves return control values, in this case `t` will process a *finite* amount of data because the component upstream is a computer.

Again, consider an example of a transformer `t` in the form `repeat c` for some computer `c` that has input cardinality α_{in} and output cardinality α_{out}. Suppose `t` vectorizes so that in each iteration it takes one array of α_{in} values and in every second iteration emits an array of $2\alpha_{\text{out}}$ values, leading to an input–output rate of 2-to-1. If the computer `c1` emits an array of size α_{in} (so the types match) and then immediately returns, the expected α_{out} output values will never be emitted since the output granularity is $2\alpha_{\text{out}}$.

Unsurprisingly, the solution is to never decrease the output rate per input in a "transformer-after-computer" vectorization. A transformer in a data path with a computer to the left can only safely *up-vectorize* to take arrays of size $d \cdot k \cdot \alpha_{\text{in}}$ and emit arrays of size $d \cdot \alpha_{\text{out}}$ for some d and k. Finally, as before, down-vectorizations are also acceptable.

3.3 Assembling vectorization candidates

Having collected constraints describing all feasible vectorizations for simple components, our algorithm proceeds to compose these sets to form well-typed vectorized pipelines. Let $\mathcal{D}(\texttt{c})$ denote the feasible set for computation `c` as a set of triples $(\texttt{cv}, d_{\text{in}}, d_{\text{out}})$, where `cv` takes and emits arrays $(\mathsf{array}[d_{\text{in}}]\ a)$ and $(\mathsf{array}[d_{\text{out}}]\ b)$ respectively. The following rules describe how feasible sets compose over >>> and `seq`:

$$\begin{array}{l} \mathcal{D}(\texttt{c1} \ggg \texttt{c2}) = \\ \quad \{\ (\texttt{cv1} \ggg \texttt{cv2}, d_{\text{in}}, d_{\text{out}}) \text{ where} \\ \quad\quad \exists d.\ (\texttt{cv1}, d_{\text{in}}, d) \in \mathcal{D}(\texttt{c1}) \text{ and } (\texttt{cv2}, d, d_{\text{out}}) \in \mathcal{D}(\texttt{c2})\ \} \\ \mathcal{D}(\texttt{seq x}{\leftarrow}\texttt{c1;c2}) = \\ \quad \{\ (\texttt{seq x}{\leftarrow}\texttt{cv1;cv2}, d_{\text{in}}, d_{\text{out}}) \text{ where} \\ \quad\quad (\texttt{cv1}, d_{\text{in}}, d_{\text{out}}) \in \mathcal{D}(\texttt{c1}) \text{ and } (\texttt{cv2}, d_{\text{in}}, d_{\text{out}}) \in \mathcal{D}(\texttt{c2})\ \} \end{array}$$

The sets of vectorizations that the aforementioned strategy introduces can grow large very quickly (tens or hundreds of thousands, for WiFi-scale pipelines), even if we impose limits on the maximum size of arrays.

To avoid search space explosion, we perform local pruning of candidates. Consider the example of `c1` >>> `c2`. There will be multiple feasible input (d_{in}) and output (d_{out}) data widths that this component can vectorize into. Moreover, for each feasible pair of d_{in} and d_{out}, there may be several possible internal vectorizations arising from the set of intermediate widths d in the first rule above.

Locally pruning the candidates for `c1` >>> `c2` for a given d_{in} and d_{out} amounts to deciding, for a choice of two intermediate widths d and d' (and consequently two vectorization candidates), which of the two we should prefer. A natural choice, guided by the need for "fat" pipelines, is to choose the one with the highest intermediate width.

However, at top-level we must choose a *single vectorization* among a set of vectorizations, irrespectively of input and output widths. A simple generalization of the aforementioned local choice is to choose the vectorization with the highest sum of all input, intermediate, and output widths in the pipeline. However, that choice is not always desirable. Consider two pipelines vectorized to input, intermediate, and output widths of 256-4-256 and 128-64-128, respectively,[4] where the unvectorized constituent components emit one value for each value they take. Choosing the pipeline with the highest sum of all widths means the first candidate ($256 + 4 + 256 > 128 + 64 + 128$) is selected, but the intermediate narrow width, 4, in the first pipeline is a clear bottleneck.

An alternative is to pick the candidate with the highest minimal width – this strategy would happily select the second candidate above. But highest-minimal-width is not always good either, since it will prefer 8-8-8-8 over 256-256-256-4 even though the second candidate is better in this case: candidate 256-256-256-4 sends 256 elements directly through the first two blocks and only pays the cost of breaking the result into arrays of size 4 at the end, causing 1+1+64 = 66 `tick`/`proc` executions. By contrast the 8-8-8-8 candidate induces $4 \cdot 32 = 128$ `proc`s.

From the above discussion, it is evident that the two extreme metrics, maximizing the sum of all block widths and maximizing the smallest of all widths, are conflicting. A similar issue is often encountered in computer network design. The seminal work of Kelly et al. [26] presents a utility framework parameterized over a set of concave (utility) functions that is amenable to decentralized optimization. The trade-off between the two extremes can be balanced through the choice of the utility function. Let f be such a utility function. Choosing $f(d) = d$ results in maximizing the sum of widths, whereas choosing $f(d) = 1/d^a$ for large a is known to be equivalent to maximizing the minimum width.

Here we adapt this framework. Specifically, we choose $f(d) = \log(d)$, a function that is known to strike a good balance between the two extremes [26]. We extend the earlier composition rules with local pruning and decentralized utility calculation, as given in Figure 2. We evaluate the effects of the resulting vectorizations in Section 5.

$$\begin{array}{l} \mathcal{D}(\texttt{c1} \ggg \texttt{c2}) = \\ \quad \{\ (\texttt{cv1} \ggg \texttt{cv2}, d_{\text{in}}, d_{\text{out}}, u) \text{ where} \\ \quad\quad (\texttt{cv1}, d_{\text{in}}, d, u_1) {\in} \mathcal{D}(\texttt{c1}) \text{ and } (\texttt{cv2}, d, d_{\text{out}}, u_2) {\in} \mathcal{D}(\texttt{c2}) \\ \quad\quad \text{and } u = u_1 + f(d) + u_2 \text{ is maximal }\ \} \\ \\ \mathcal{D}(\texttt{seq x}{\leftarrow}\texttt{c1;c2}) = \\ \quad \{\ (\texttt{seq x}{\leftarrow}\texttt{cv1;cv2}, d_{\text{in}}, d_{\text{out}}, u_1 + u_2) \text{ where} \\ \quad\quad (\texttt{cv1}, d_{\text{in}}, d_{\text{out}}, u_1) \in \mathcal{D}(\texttt{c1}) \text{ and} \\ \quad\quad (\texttt{cv2}, d_{\text{in}}, d_{\text{out}}, u_2) \in \mathcal{D}(\texttt{c2})\ \} \end{array}$$

Figure 2: Vectorization composition and utility calculation

[4] In light of the previous discussion on rates, this may occur if the pipeline is composed just of transformers.

4. Other Optimizations

The Ziria compiler implements a series of type- and semantics-preserving optimizations that eliminate computations over expressions, reduce memory copying, and fuse multiple computations for more efficient execution. These optimizations are mainly based on standard techniques but are instrumental in producing performant code. We review the most important in this section and illustrate their synergy.

Static scheduling optimizations. One set of optimizations focuses on converting sequences of computations that include `seq` and >>> into imperative code wherever possible. One particular form of this optimization is called *auto-mapping* and is essential for producing performant code, as the overhead measurements in Section 5.2 (Figure 4) show. Figure 3 illustrates auto-mapping: the vectorized scrambler kernel is pulled out in a separate local function, and the `repeat` block is replaced with a call to `map`. A whole set of optimizations, such as inlining, pushing around `let`-bound definitions and conditionals, and replacing computation-level loops with expression-level loops, are specifically designed to enable auto-mapping. Auto-mapping is a form of static scheduling, since the code generator is aware that `map` cannot proceed without consuming input (cf. Section 2.6) – for instance a long sequence of >>> compositions of `map` will only push values downstream without using `tick` blocks.

Lookup table generation. Many PHY operations are defined to operate at a bit-level granularity, but direct implementation of such code is inefficient on CPUs with wide data buses. A common optimization is to identify such operations and speed them up by memoizing the results as lookup tables (LUTs) (manually created LUTs are used pervasively in Sora and GNU Radio for performance, for example). However, writing functions that use LUTs is tedious and results in code that is hard to read and modify.

The Ziria compiler solves this problem by automatically detecting portions of a program that are amenable to a LUT implementation (e.g., expressions complex enough to be worth converting to a LUT but whose LUT sizes are not too large) and automatically converting these expressions to LUTs. For instance, the auto-mapped version of the scrambler in Figure 3 is compiled to use a LUT with an index consisting of the current input (8 bits) and the scrambler state (7 bits), a total of 2^{15} entries. Packing input values to LUT indices and unpacking results required delicate performance tuning in the Ziria compiler; Section 5 evaluates the results of this optimization in our WiFi pipeline.

5. Evaluation

In this section we seek to answer the following questions about the performance of Ziria: (1) What is the overhead of Ziria's execution engine? (2) What is the speedup of various compiler optimizations? (3) Can we implement WiFi PHY in Ziria to meet the protocol specifications and how does this implementation compare with a state-of-the-art, manually optimized implementation on the same platform?

5.1 Methodology

We evaluate the performance of our framework on various DSP algorithms that are part of a standard WiFi transceiver. We choose Sora's WiFi implementation [45] as our reference implementation (since it is the most stable available) and port it to Ziria. Our port consists of $\approx$ 3k lines of Ziria code in total and it is verified against Sora's implementation. As part of Ziria, we provide a basic signal processing library with a high-level interface for SIMD instructions and efficient implementations (borrowed from Sora) of FFT, IFFT and Viterbi decoding.[5] The rest is written entirely in Ziria and available online [22].

We evaluate data throughput of a number of the processing blocks and compare the performance of our Ziria implementation with the manually optimized Sora implementation [45] and the WiFi requirements. We compile both on the Sora-supported C compiler [31], and we adapt our runtime to use Sora's runtime libraries. In particular, we use Sora's user-mode threading library, which allows us to run threads at the highest priority and pinned to a specific core, effectively preventing the OS from preempting their execution. Our evaluation machine is a 2-year-old Dell T3600 PC with an Intel Xeon E5-1620 CPU[6] at 3.6 GHz running Windows 8.1 and the WinDDK compiler [31], together with the SoraMIMO SDR platform. When we measure the maximum rates of our software components (which are faster than the line speed of WiFi), we feed the input samples directly from memory and discard the output. We also evaluate the performance of the full SDR system using live wireless transmissions.

5.2 Overheads of nonoptimized execution model

Control-flow composition (`seq`). We measure the overhead of `seq` by measuring the runtime of a program containing n computation components in sequence, with each component consisting of a single call to `sin()`. As a performance baseline, we use the runtime of the equivalent program in which all n `sin` operations are executed in the same block. The results are depicted in Figure 4, top. The dashed line gives runtime of the baseline program for n `sin` computations. The solid line gives runtimes for n `sin` components bound in sequence. Both are average over 200 million inputs and we report average execution time per data item (confidence intervals are very small). We verify that the runtime data fit a linear model as a function of n, indicating that the cost of `seq` grows linearly with the number of components. The cost of a single `seq` operation on our system, given by the difference of the slopes of the two lines, is around 3ns.

[5] These blocks are standard and are reused across all modern physical layers (WiFi, WiMax, LTE). Efficient implementations are already available across a large range of SDR platforms.

[6] We observe very similar results on a laptop with an Intel i7.

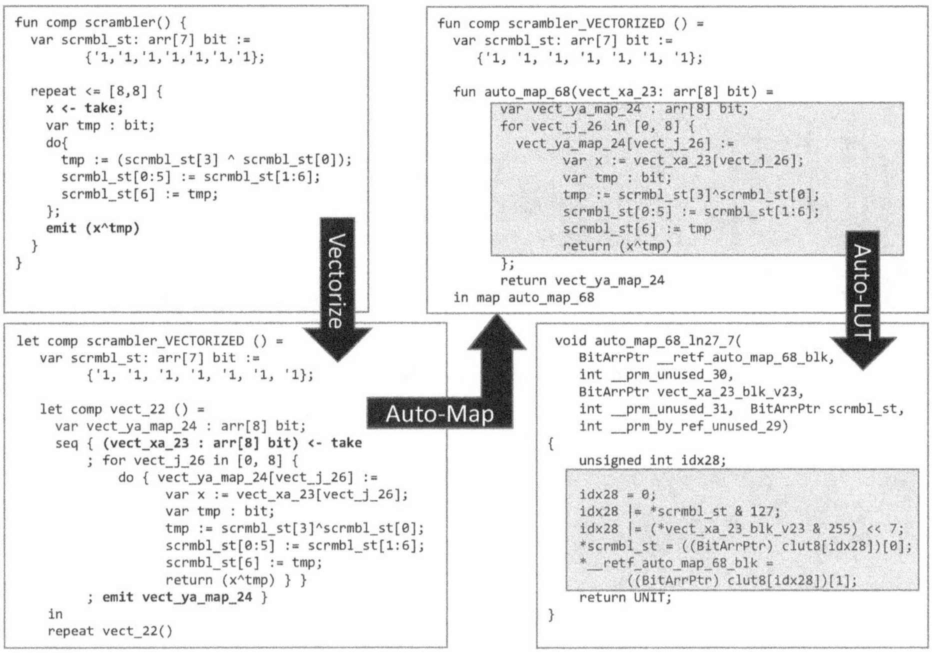

Figure 3: Optimization synergy: original scrambler, auto-vectorized, auto-mapped, and generated C code with a LUT.

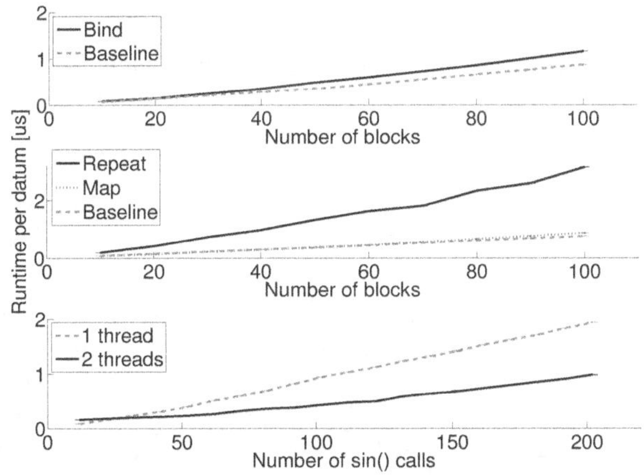

Figure 4: Overheads of various Ziria components: `seq` (top), >>> (middle), |>>>| (bottom)

***Dataflow composition* >>> .** To evaluate the overhead of >>>, we measured the runtime of a program containing n >>>-composed code blocks, with each block executing the computation `repeat {x←take; emit(sin(x))}`. We also measured the runtime of a version of this program optimized to use `map`. The baseline is the runtime of a program in which all n `sin` calls are merged into a single block. We average over 200 million inputs and report average execution time per data item (confidence intervals are very small). The results are depicted in Figure 4, middle. The cost of a single >>> with repeat on our system, given by the difference of the slopes of Repeat and Baseline, is ≈ 24ns, while the cost of a single >>> with map is ≈ 1ns. The difference stems from the fact that the `repeat` block executes several `ticks` and `procs` in each round, whereas `map` execution is completely streamlined. As shown in Section 5.3, the overhead of >>> is usually significantly reduced by auto-mapping (Section 4), which converts certain `repeat` blocks into `maps`. The cost is further amortized by vectorization (Section 3), except in a few cases in which automapping and vectorization cannot be applied because not all sizes are statically known. Examples where this occurs include CRC, for which the input size depends on packet length and is therefore not known at compile time, and Viterbi, whose output frequency and size may depend on the amount of noise present at the received signal.

***Pipelined dataflow composition* |>>>|.** To gauge the overhead of pipelining Ziria programs onto multiple cores using |>>>|, we measured the runtime of n `sin` calls both on a single core and divided evenly onto two cores. Figure 4, bottom, shows the results of this experiment. We average over 200 million inputs and report average execution time per data item (confidence intervals are very small). The red dashed line and solid black line give the execution time when running on a single core and on two cores, respectively. The point at which these two lines intersect, approximately 30 computations per datum, is the point at which we break even, i.e., when pipelining gives speedup rather than slowdown. The speedup is approximately 1.7x at 60 calls and 2x at 90 calls.

(a) Vect. **WiFi RX** blocks (green) vs. all (yellow), relative to no opts.

(b) Vect. **WiFi TX** blocks (green) vs. all (yellow), relative to no opts.

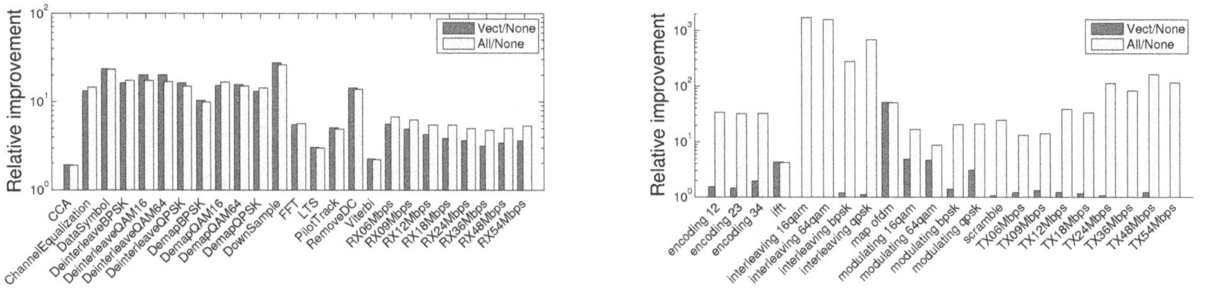

Figure 5: Benefits of optimizations

(a) WiFi receiver throughputs at various data rates

(b) WiFi transmitter throughputs at various data rates

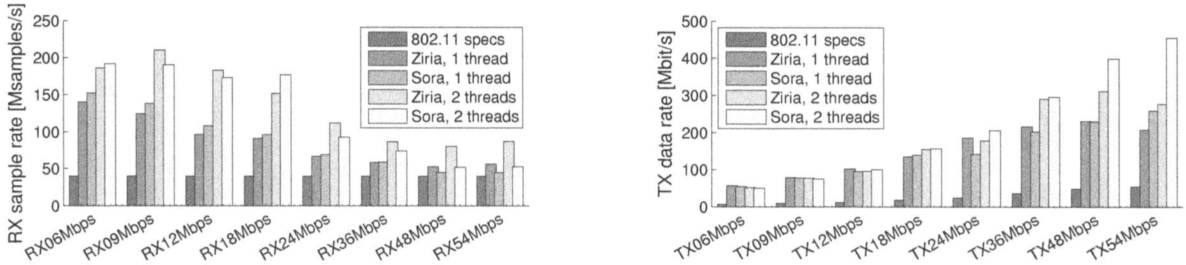

Figure 6: WiFi throughput

5.3 Ziria optimizations

Vectorization is instrumental in achieving good performance, both on its own and in combination with LUTs. In plot 5a and 5b, we give the relative improvement of vectorization (green) and vectorization+LUT (yellow) over no optimization for receiver (RX) and transmitter (TX) blocks. Vectorization brings large benefits to the receiver, with order-of-magnitude speedups. Vectorization alone is not as effective on the transmitter side, since most TX blocks perform bit-level operations that dominate performance. However, vectorization enables LUT generation, and the combined speedup of both optimizations is up to 1000× (in the full TX pipeline at 54 Mbps the compiler automatically identifies 40 LUT opportunities). Note that wherever we measure the performance of vectorization, we also include other control flow optimizations mentioned in Section 4.

5.4 WiFi performance

Finally, we compare our WiFi implementation in Ziria with the IEEE WiFi standard requirements and the Sora implementation in terms of compile time, throughput, and latency. We also evaluate its real world performance.

Compile time. We begin by measuring the compile times in Sora (C++ with templates to executable code) and Ziria (Ziria high-level code to executable code) using the same WinDDK C compiler [31]. Both Sora and Ziria take 8s to compile the transmitter at 54 Mbps to an executable file. Ziria is faster when compiling the receiver at 54 Mbps: it takes 15s compared to the 26s taken by Sora.

Throughput. We next inspect the receiver's performance, plot 6a. The specification mandates a sampling (input) rate of 40 million samples/second (dark green bars). We measure the maximum throughputs of the Sora implementations of receivers at various data rates and compare with the equivalent implementations in Ziria, with 1 and 2 threads. We see that all Ziria implementations meet the WiFi specifications at all data rates. We are also at most 15% slower than the corresponding manually optimized Sora implementations and even faster than Sora in several of the most demanding cases.

In particular, our 2-threaded implementation of the receiver at 54 Mbps is more than 60% faster than Sora's. This is because our vectorizer finds the optimal width of the Viterbi decoder for this particular pipeline (288 samples), whereas Sora uses the default width (48 samples). Since Viterbi is placed on a different core from the rest of the pipeline, we reduce the number of synchronization messages 6-fold.

In plot 6b we give the results for the same experiment applied instead to the WiFi transmitter. The inputs to the TX pipeline are data bits, so the required input rates correspond to the WiFi data rates (dark green bars). Ziria again meets the WiFi requirements and in most cases is faster than Sora. The main exceptions are the transmitters at 48 and 54 Mbps.

These data rates use 64QAM modulation and require packing chunks of 6 bits of data per symbol; our current bit operations are not very efficient for nonaligned data.

Latency. We also evaluate the latency of our single thread WiFi implementation. We measure two types of latencies: the read latency at input and the write latency at output. To measure read latency, we randomly sample 10000 latencies between two consecutive read operations, and we do the same for write latency. Since read and write operations are vectorized, we plot an average latency per sample for each measured vectorized read/write. We normalize all latencies with respect to the maximum average latency per datum for each data rate ($1/\text{data rate}$ for TX reads and $1/\text{sampling rate} = 1/40\text{MHz}$ for TX writes and RX reads).

We plot the CDFs of normalized latencies in Figure 7. Plot 7a shows that latencies at transmitter reads are highly nonuniform. This is because the time it takes to process one input datum may vary widely depending on the order in which we execute various blocks. For example, it will be small while we are reading data to fill an FFT buffer. But the FFT will get executed once the buffer is filled, which will introduce high latency before the subsequent read. However, since the FFT is the transmitter block with the largest vectorization and also the last component in the TX pipeline, the latencies at write are much more uniform (Plot 7b). The read latencies for the receiver are shown in Plot 7c.

For the performance of WiFi, it is important that the write latency of the transmitter is below the maximum latency dictated by the line rate of WiFi ($1/40\text{MHz}$). This is because a sudden excessive write delay can cause an interruption in transmission. Similarly, if the read latency of the receiver is above the maximum latency dictated by the line rate, a buffer overflow can occur causing dropped RX samples. WiFi is not designed to cope with dropped samples or interruptions, and such events will yield immediate packet losses.

However, occasional large delays are not catastrophic; all SDR hardware uses buffers to amortize such delays. The sizes of these buffers are dimensioned according to the protocol specs. For example, WiFi requires hardware to finish processing packet reception and start transmitting in $10\mu s$ (SIFS, "short interframe space" time), so any buffering and processing delays smaller than SIFS are acceptable.

We see that only 0.2% of all observed write latencies at the TX and read latencies at the RX are above the maximum allowed by the device line speed, and the highest of all observed latencies is $5\times$ the maximum, which is still more than $100\times$ smaller than the SIFS time.

Testbed evaluation. In order to further verify that our implementation meets the system requirements in practice and that no excessive delay between consecutive samples, caused by our nonrealtime OS scheduler, will cause packet transmission or reception errors, we set up a realtime wireless transmission using Ziria WiFi code and Sora SDR hardware. High data rates (24-54 Mbps) involve amplitude modulation (16QAM and 64QAM) and require a more accurate implementation of an automatic gain control algorithm, which is currently provided neither in Sora nor in Ziria. We therefore experiment with the four lowest data rates (6-18 Mbps). For each of these rates we send a sequence of packets encoded at the selected rate at a constant pace. Each packet has a unique ID so we can detect losses accurately. We count how many packets are correctly received and calculate the packet error rate. In our experiment, we lose around 2% of 10,000 packets transmitted [18]. This is on par with loss observed with commercial WiFi cards (cf. [41]). As discussed before, WiFi cannot cope with sample losses, and the low loss rate we observe here implies that we meet WiFi timing requirements.

6. Related work

Software-defined radio. SDR platforms have traditionally been FPGA- [29, 33, 35] and DSP-based [43, 49]. More recently, CPU-based platforms [6, 23, 34, 45, 50] have gained popularity, in particular due to widespread use of USRP radios and GNU Radio [12, 50]. Similarly, there are numerous programming platforms and approaches for SDRs [7, 12, 13, 19, 30, 35, 36, 42, 48, 52].

As we motivated in the introduction, however, the existing SDR platforms typically fail to provide convenient abstractions for programming pipeline reconfiguration, an important aspect of PHY design. For example, the Sora [13] transmitter consists of a single data pipeline with global shared state for (re)configuration. GNU Radio [37] encodes control flow in the data stream (e.g., using a stream of 0's and 1's to convey the presence or absence of a preamble). StreamIt [48] uses asynchronous teleport messages for pipeline reconfiguration, which can obscure control flow. Spiral [52] does not offer an easy way to mix control and data flow.

Further, many of the software platforms require tedious manual optimization, which can limit code reuse and lead to subtle errors. Examples include Sora and GNU Radio components that are programmed with predefined, manually adjusted widths and therefore may not be compatible with arbitrary pipelines. In Sora, the programmer must also manually identify and implement lookup tables, which can lead to verbose code (for example, the scrambler implementation is 90 lines of C++ code in Sora but only 20 lines in Ziria).

Dataflow languages. In addition to work on SDR, Ziria builds on a significant body of programming languages research. Synchronous dataflow (SDF) languages [9, 15, 16] have been used in embedded and reactive systems for modeling and verification but – to our knowledge – never to implement line-rate software PHY designs. Parameterized SDF [10], like Ziria, supports dynamic reconfiguration of the dataflow graph but does not develop language abstractions for reconfiguration like our `seq` combinator. StreamIt [48], also based on synchronous dataflow, was one of the early works to target DSP applications, including software WiFi and 3GPP PHY, though it is not clear whether these implementations can

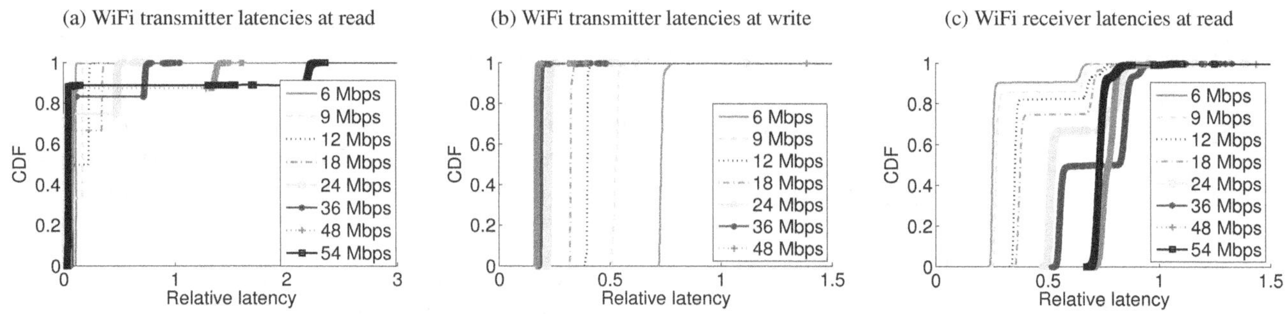

Figure 7: WiFi latency at various data rates for single-threaded WiFi transmitter and receiver

operate at line rate. More recently, Liquid Metal [4] showed how to compile a high-level Java-like language with streaming primitives to a combination of Java bytecode, C code, and FPGA bitfiles, with runtime support for dynamically selecting from among the implementations. Both StreamIt and Liquid Metal support forms of cardinality-aware vectorization, although simpler in the absence of pipeline reconfigurations.

Functional programming and FRP. The design of Ziria and its key combinators draws from monads [32] and arrows [24]. A flavor of our `seq` combinator (called "switch") is used in Yampa [17], a popular functional reactive programming (FRP) framework that lacks an efficient execution model. The Haskell Pipes [39] library includes monad transformers that provide high-level functionality similar to Ziria's stream combinators, but it does not guarantee implementation in constant space. Ziria's tick and process semantics resemble the push–pull model of streaming popular in FRP [20, 21, 47]. Feldspar [5], a language for DSP embedded in Haskell, uses a novel vector representation that supports vector fusion, which could be profitably incorporated into the Ziria compiler. Spiral [40] generates efficient implementations of a wide variety of linear transforms (e.g., DFT) from high-level algebraic specifications and compares favorably to Sora in benchmarks of a Spiral-generated WiFi PHY [53]. In principle, Spiral could be used to generate architecture-tuned versions of some of the basic stream-processing blocks we currently use in Ziria. Bitvector program synthesis using, e.g., sketching [27] may be another way to generate optimized low-level processing blocks.

7. Conclusion

We presented Ziria, the first high-level SDR platform with a performant execution model. To validate our design, we built a compiler that performs optimizations done manually in existing CPU-based SDR platforms: vectorization, lookup table generation, and annotation-guided pipelining. To demonstrate Ziria's viability, we used Ziria to build a rate-compliant PHY layer for WiFi 802.11a/g.

References

[1] 3GPP 36.211. Evolved universal terrestrial radio access (e-utra) - physical channels and modulation. URL `http://www.3gpp.org/DynaReport/36211.htm`.

[2] 3GPP 36.212. Evolved universal terrestrial radio access (e-utra) - multiplexing and channel coding. URL `http://www.3gpp.org/DynaReport/36212.htm`.

[3] 3GPP 36.213. Evolved universal terrestrial radio access (e-utra) - physical layer procedures. URL `http://www.3gpp.org/DynaReport/36213.htm`.

[4] Joshua Auerbach, David F. Bacon, Perry Cheng, and Rodric Rabbah. Lime: A java-compatible and synthesizable language for heterogeneous architectures. In *Proceedings of the ACM International Conference on Object Oriented Programming Systems Languages and Applications*, OOPSLA '10, pages 89–108, 2010. ISBN 978-1-4503-0203-6.

[5] Emil Axelsson, Koen Claessen, Gergely Dévai, Zoltán Horváth, Karin Keijzer, Anders Persson, Mary Sheeran, Josef Svenningsson, András Vajda, et al. Feldspar: A domain specific language for digital signal processing algorithms. In *FMMC*, 2010.

[6] H. V. Balan, M. Segura, S. Deora, A. Michaloliakos, R. Rogalin, K. Psounis, and G. Caire. USC SDR, an easy-to-program, high data rate, real time software radio platform. In *Software Radio Implementation Forum*, 2013.

[7] Manu Bansal, Jeffrey Mehlman, Sachin Katti, and Philip Levis. OpenRadio: a programmable wireless dataplane. In *HotSDN*, 2012.

[8] T. Bansal, B. Chen, P. Sinha, and K. Srinivasan. Symphony: Cooperative packet recovery over the wired backbone in enterprise WLANs. In *MOBICOM*, 2013.

[9] Gérard Berry and Georges Gonthier. The ESTEREL synchronous programming language: Design, semantics, implementation. *SCP*, 19(2), 1992.

[10] Bishnupriya Bhattacharya and Shuvra S Bhattacharyya. Parameterized dataflow modeling for dsp systems. *Signal Processing, IEEE Transactions on*, 49(10):2408–2421, 2001.

[11] B. Bloessl, M. Segata, C. Sommer, and F. Dressler. An IEEE 802.11a/g/p OFDM receiver for GNU radio. In *SRIF*, 2013.

[12] Eric Blossom. GNURadio: tools for exploring the radio frequency spectrum. *Linux Journal*, 2004(122):4, 2004.

[13] Bricks. Microsoft Research, Brick specification, 2011. URL http://research.microsoft.com/apps/pubs/default.aspx?id=160800.

[14] Magnus Carlsson and Thomas Hallgren. *Fudgets - Purely Functional Processes with applications to Graphical User Interfaces*. Doktorsavhandlingar vid Chalmers tekniska högskola. Ny serie, no: 1366. Institutionen för datavetenskap, Chalmers tekniska högskola, 1998. ISBN 91-7197-611-6.

[15] Paul Caspi. Lucid Synchrone. In *Actes du colloque INRIA OPOPAC, Lacanau*. HERMES, November 1993.

[16] Paul Caspi and Marc Pouzet. Lucid Synchrone, a functional extension of Lustre. Technical report, Univ. Pierre et Marie Curie, Lab. LIP6, 2000.

[17] Antony Courtney and Conal Elliott. Genuinely functional user interfaces. In *Haskell Workshop*, 2001.

[18] Demo. Ziria WiFi demo. URL http://research.microsoft.com/apps/video/default.aspx?id=228361.

[19] A. Dutta, D. Saha, D. Grunwald, and D. Sicker. CODIPHY: Composing on-demand intelligent physical layers. In *SRIF*, 2013.

[20] Conal Elliott. Push-pull functional reactive programming. In *Haskell Symposium*, 2009.

[21] Conal Elliott and Paul Hudak. Functional reactive animation. In *ACM SIGPLAN Notices*, volume 32, pages 263–273. ACM, 1997.

[22] GitHub. Ziria github repository. URL https://github.com/dimitriv/Ziria.

[23] GSM. Fairwaves GSM base-station. URL https://fairwaves.co/wp/.

[24] John Hughes. Generalising monads to arrows. *SCP*, 37(1-3), 2000.

[25] IEEE. Part 11: Wireless LAN MAC and PHY specifications high-speed physical layer in the 5 GHz band, 1999. URL http://standards.ieee.org/getieee802/download/802.11a-1999.pdf.

[26] F. P. Kelly. Charging and rate control for elastic traffic. *European Transactions on Telecommunications*, 8:33–37, 1997.

[27] A Solar Lezama. *Program synthesis by sketching*. PhD thesis, Citeseer, 2008.

[28] T. Li, M. K. Han, A. Bhartia, L. Qiu, E. Rozner, Y. Zhang, and B. Zarikoff. CRMA: Collision-resistant multiple access. In *MOBICOM*, 2011.

[29] Lyrtech. Lyrtech. URL http://intrinsic.lyrtech.com/.

[30] Mathworks. Simulink. URL http://www.mathworks.co.uk/products/simulink/.

[31] Microsoft. Windows driver kit version 7. URL http://www.microsoft.com/en-us/download/details.aspx?id=11800.

[32] Eugenio Moggi. Notions of computation and monads. *Inf. Comput.*, 93(1), 1991.

[33] Patrick Murphy, Ashu Sabharwal, and Behnaam Aazhang. Design of WARP: a wireless open-access research platform. In *ESPC*, 2006.

[34] Myriad. MyriadRF open source wireless hardware. URL http://myriadrf.org/.

[35] Man Cheuk Ng, Kermin Elliott Fleming, Mythili Vutukuru, Samuel Gross, Arvind, and Hari Balakrishnan. Airblue: a system for cross-layer wireless protocol development. In *Proceedings of the 6th ACM/IEEE Symposium on Architectures for Networking and Communications Systems*, ANCS '10, page 4:1–4:11, New York, NY, USA, 2010. ACM. ISBN 978-1-4503-0379-8.

[36] NI. National instruments, LabVIEW. URL http://www.ni.com/labview/.

[37] OFDM. GNU Radio OFDM implementation. URL http://gnuradio.org/redmine/projects/gnuradio/repository/changes/gr-digital/python/digital/ofdm_receiver.py?rev=master.

[38] John Peterson, Paul Hudak, and Conal Elliott. Lambda in motion: Controlling robots with haskell. In *Proceedings of the First International Workshop on Practical Aspects of Declarative Languages*, PADL '99, pages 91–105, London, UK, UK, 1998. Springer-Verlag. ISBN 3-540-65527-1. URL http://dl.acm.org/citation.cfm?id=645769.667757.

[39] Pipes. Haskell Pipes Tutorial. URL http://hackage.haskell.org/package/pipes-4.0.0/docs/Pipes-Tutorial.html.

[40] Markus Püschel, José M. F. Moura, Jeremy Johnson, David Padua, Manuela Veloso, Bryan Singer, Jianxin Xiong, Franz Franchetti, Aca Gacic, Yevgen Voronenko, Kang Chen, Robert W. Johnson, and Nicholas Rizzolo. SPIRAL: Code generation for DSP transforms. *Proceedings of the IEEE, special issue on "Program Generation, Optimization, and Adaptation"*, 93(2):232– 275, 2005.

[41] S. Rayanchu, A. Mishra, D. Agrawal, S. Saha, and Suman Banerjee. Diagnosing wireless packet losses in 802.11: Separating collision from weak signal. In *INFOCOM 2008. The 27th Conference on Computer Communications. IEEE*, April 2008.

[42] T. Rondeau, N. McCarthy, and T. O'Shea. SIMD programming in GNURadio: Maintainable and user-friendly algorithm optimization with VOLK. In *SDR WinnComm*, 2013.

[43] Saankhya. Saankhya labs, multi-standard modems. URL http://www.saankhyalabs.com.

[44] S. Sen, R. R. Choudhury, and S. Nelakuditi. No time to countdown: Migrating backoff to the frequency domain. In *MOBICOM*, 2011.

[45] K. Tan, J. Zhang, J. Fang, H. Liu, Y. Ye, S. Wang, Y. Zhang, H. Wu, W. Wang, and G. Voelker. Sora: High performance software radio using general purpose multi-core processors, 2009.

[46] Kun Tan, Jiansong Zhang, Ji Fang, He Liu, Yusheng Ye, Shen Wang, Yongguang Zhang, Haitao Wu, Wei Wang, and Geoffrey M. Voelker. Sora: high performance software radio using general purpose multi-core processors. In *Proceedings of the 6th USENIX symposium on {N}etworked {S}ystems {D}esign and {I}mplementation*, NSDI'09, pages 75—90, Berkeley, CA, USA, 2009. USENIX Association. URL http://dl.acm.org/citation.cfm?id=1558977.1558983.

[47] Colin J Taylor. *Formalising and reasoning about Fudgets*. PhD thesis, University of Nottingham, 1998.

[48] William Thies, Michal Karczmarek, and Saman Amarasinghe. StreamIt: A language for streaming applications. In *CC*, 2002.

[49] TMS320. Texas Instruments TMS320TCI6616 Communications Infrastructure KeyStone SoC. URL `http://www.ti.com/lit/ds/sprs624d/sprs624d.pdf`.

[50] USRP. Ettus Research, USRP: Universal Software Radio Peripheral. URL `http://www.ettus.com/`.

[51] Volo. Volo Wireless, low-cost last mile broadband. URL `http://www.volowireless.com/`.

[52] Y. Voronenko, V. Arbatov, C. Berger, R. Peng, M. Puschel, and F. Franchetti. Computer generation of platform-adapted physical layer software. In *Proc. Software Defined Radio (SDR)*, 2010.

[53] Y Voronenko, V Arbatov, CR Berger, R Peng, M Pueschel, and F Franchetti. Computer generation of platform-adapted physical layer software. *Proceedings Software Defined Radio (SDR)*, 2010.

PolyMage: Automatic Optimization for Image Processing Pipelines

Ravi Teja Mullapudi
Department of Computer Science and Automation,
Indian Institute of Science
Bangalore 560012, INDIA
ravi.mullapudi@csa.iisc.ernet.in

Vinay Vasista
Department of Computer Science and Automation,
Indian Institute of Science
Bangalore 560012, INDIA
vinay.vasista@csa.iisc.ernet.in

Uday Bondhugula
Department of Computer Science and Automation,
Indian Institute of Science
Bangalore 560012, INDIA
uday@csa.iisc.ernet.in

Abstract

This paper presents the design and implementation of PolyMage, a domain-specific language and compiler for image processing pipelines. An image processing pipeline can be viewed as a graph of interconnected stages which process images successively. Each stage typically performs one of point-wise, stencil, reduction or data-dependent operations on image pixels. Individual stages in a pipeline typically exhibit abundant data parallelism that can be exploited with relative ease. However, the stages also require high memory bandwidth preventing effective utilization of parallelism available on modern architectures. For applications that demand high performance, the traditional options are to use optimized libraries like OpenCV or to optimize manually. While using libraries precludes optimization across library routines, manual optimization accounting for both parallelism and locality is very tedious.

The focus of our system, PolyMage, is on automatically generating high-performance implementations of image processing pipelines expressed in a high-level declarative language. Our optimization approach primarily relies on the transformation and code generation capabilities of the polyhedral compiler framework. To the best of our knowledge, this is the first model-driven compiler for image processing pipelines that performs complex fusion, tiling, and storage optimization automatically. Experimental results on a modern multicore system show that the performance achieved by our automatic approach is up to 1.81× better than that achieved through manual tuning in Halide, a state-of-the-art language and compiler for image processing pipelines. For a camera raw image processing pipeline, our performance is comparable to that of a hand-tuned implementation.

Categories and Subject Descriptors D.3.4 [*Programming Languages*]: Processors – compilers, optimization, code generation

Keywords Domain-specific language; image processing; polyhedral optimization; locality; parallelism; tiling; multicores; vectorization

1. Introduction

Image processing is pervasive, spanning several areas including computational photography, computer vision, medical imaging, and astronomy. Applications in these areas range from enhancing the capabilities of digital cameras and emerging devices like Google Glass [18], autonomous driving cars, to Magnetic Resonance Imaging (MRI) and analyzing astronomical data. Processing and analyzing the data generated from imaging systems often demands high performance. This need is due to: (a) the sheer volume of data compounded by high resolution and frame rates, (b) increasing complexity of algorithms used to process the data, and (c) potential real-time requirements of interactive and mission-critical applications. The emergence and evolution of multicore architectures, GPUs, FPGAs, single instruction multiple data (SIMD) instruction sets through MMX, SSE, and AVX, are examples of advances on the hardware front that have benefited the image processing domain. Coping up with the increased demand in performance requires software to effectively utilize multiple cores, SIMD parallelism and caches.

A wide range of algorithms for processing image data can be viewed as *pipelines* consisting of several interconnected processing stages. Each pipeline can be represented as a directed acyclic graph, with the stages as nodes and producer-consumer relationships between the stages as edges. Pipeline structure can vary from a few stages, with only point-wise

ASPLOS '15, March 14–18, 2015, Istanbul, Turkey.

ACM 978-1-4503-2835-7/15/03. . . $15.00.
http://dx.doi.org/10.1145/2694344.2694364

operations, to tens of stages having a combination of point-wise, stencil, sampling and data dependent access patterns. Individual stages in a pipeline typically exhibit abundant data parallelism that can be exploited with relative ease. However, the stages also require high memory bandwidth necessitating locality optimization for achieving high performance. Manually exploiting parallelism and locality on modern architectures for complex pipelines is a daunting task. Libraries such as OpenCV [32], CImg [12] and MATLAB image processing toolboxes only provide tuned implementations for a limited set of algorithms on specific architectures. Even when optimized implementations of the individual routines required for a task are available, the inability to optimize across them prevents achieving high performance.

A promising way to address the tension between ease of programming and high performance is to provide a high-level domain-specific language (DSL) to express algorithms, and use an optimizing compiler to map them to a target architecture. Such an approach has been used successfully in the context of several DSLs [15, 28, 39]. For image processing, languages like CoreImage [35] and functional image synthesis [16] have focused on creating easy-to-use abstractions with minimal compiler optimization. Halide [36, 37] a recent domain-specific language and compiler for image processing pipelines focuses on both productivity and performance. However, the Halide compiler requires a schedule specification to generate an implementation. Determining an effective schedule requires manual effort and expertise, or relying on extensive and prolonged autotuning over a vast space of schedules.

In this paper, we describe our framework, PolyMage, comprising a DSL, an optimizer, and an autotuner, for generating high performance implementations of image processing pipelines. We first briefly describe the input language in Section 2; it also serves the purpose of describing the class of image processing computations we currently handle. We then describe our automatic optimization framework, our main contribution, in Section 3. The key optimization techniques that we present are:

- a method for overlapped tiling tailored for heterogeneous image processing stages,
- a heuristic, modeling the trade-off between locality and redundant computation, for partitioning a pipeline into groups of stages that are later fused together with overlapping tiles,
- storage optimization and code generation for general-purpose multicores accounting for SIMD parallelism,
- and an autotuning mechanism for exploring a small parameter space resulting from our model-driven approach.

Section 4 details our experimental evaluation on a 16-core Intel Xeon (Sandybridge) server. We use a set of seven applications of varying structure and complexity to demonstrate the effectiveness of our approach when compared to highly-tuned schedules manually specified using Halide and implementations using the OpenCV library. In cases where feasible, we show that the schedule determined by our system when specified using Halide provides improved performance. In Section 5 we discuss related work, and conclusions are presented in Section 6.

2. Language Specification

In this section, we give a brief overview of our DSL and also provide a description of the computation patterns that can be expressed with it.

The design of our language is inspired by Halide [36], and allows a user to intuitively express common computation patterns that emerge in image processing. These patterns include point-wise operations, stencils, upsampling and downsampling, histograms, and time-iterated methods. Table 1 shows the data access patterns corresponding to some of these operations. The language abstracts an image as a function on a multi-dimensional integer grid, i.e., it maps a multi-dimensional integer coordinate to an intensity value. Using this abstraction, new images can be constructed as expressions involving other images, thus enabling implicit expression of producer-consumer relationships that are a characteristic of image processing pipelines. Rather than building a standalone language, we chose to embed our language in Python.

Operation	Example
Point-wise	$f(x, y) = g(x, y)$
Stencil	$f(x, y) = \sum_{\sigma_x=-1}^{+1} \sum_{\sigma_y=-1}^{+1} g(x + \sigma_x, y + \sigma_y)$
Upsample	$f(x, y) = \sum_{\sigma_x=-1}^{+1} \sum_{\sigma_y=-1}^{+1} g((x + \sigma_x)/2, (y + \sigma_y)/2)$
Downsample	$f(x, y) = \sum_{\sigma_x=-1}^{+1} \sum_{\sigma_y=-1}^{+1} g(2x + \sigma_x, 2y + \sigma_y)$
Histogram	$f(g(x)) += 1$
Time-iterated	$f(t, x, y) = g(f(t - 1, x, y))$

Table 1. Typical computation patterns in image processing

The specification of Harris corner detection [25] algorithm in our PolyMage DSL is shown in Figure 1. Parameters like width, height, and other constants, which are inputs to the pipeline, can be declared using the `Parameter` construct as shown in Line 1. The input data to the pipeline is declared using the `Image` construct, as in Line 2, by specifying both its data type and its extent along each dimension. Extents are restricted to expressions involving parameters and constants. `Function` is a central construct in the language, and is used to declare a function mapping a multi-dimensional integer domain to a scalar value. The domain of a function is a list of variables followed by their ranges. `Variable` is used to declare integer variables which serve as labels for function dimensions. The range of a variable is declared using the `Interval` construct. An interval is defined by a lower bound, an upper bound, and a step value.

```
1 R, C = Parameter(Int), Parameter(Int)
2 I = Image(Float, [R+2, C+2])
3
4 x, y = Variable(), Variable()
5 row, col = Interval(0,R+1,1), Interval(0,C+1,1)
6
7 c = Condition(x,'>=',1) & Condition(x,'<=',R) &
8     Condition(y,'>=',1) & Condition(y,'<=',C)
9
10 cb = Condition(x,'>=',2) & Condition(x,'<=',R-1) &
11      Condition(y,'>=',2) & Condition(y,'<=',C-1)
12
13 Iy = Function(varDom = ([x,y],[row,col]),Float)
14 Iy.defn = [ Case(c, Stencil(I(x,y), 1.0/12,
15                         [[-1, -2, -1],
16                          [ 0,  0,  0],
17                          [ 1,  2,  1]]) ]
18
19 Ix = Function(varDom = ([x,y],[row,col]),Float)
20 Ix.defn = [ Case(c, Stencil(I(x,y), 1.0/12,
21                         [[-1, 0, 1],
22                          [-2, 0, 2],
23                          [-1, 0, 1]]) ]
24
25 Ixx = Function(varDom = ([x,y],[row,col]),Float)
26 Ixx.defn = [ Case(c, Ix(x,y) * Ix(x,y)) ]
27
28 Iyy = Function(varDom = ([x,y],[row,col]),Float)
29 Iyy.defn = [ Case(c, Iy(x,y) * Iy(x,y)) ]
30
31 Ixy = Function(varDom = ([x,y],[row,col]),Float)
32 Ixy.defn = [ Case(c, Ix(x,y) * Iy(x,y)) ]
33
34 Sxx = Function(varDom = ([x,y],[row,col]),Float)
35 Syy = Function(varDom = ([x,y],[row,col]),Float)
36 Sxy = Function(varDom = ([x,y],[row,col]),Float)
37 for pair in [(Sxx, Ixx), (Syy, Iyy), (Sxy, Ixy)]:
38     pair[0].defn = [ Case(cb, Stencil(pair[1], 1,
39                                    [[1, 1, 1],
40                                     [1, 1, 1],
41                                     [1, 1, 1]]) ]
42
43 det = Function(varDom = ([x,y],[row,col]),Float)
44 d =  Sxx(x,y) * Syy(x,y) - Sxy(x,y) * Sxy(x,y)
45 det.defn = [ Case(cb, d) ]
46
47 trace = Function(varDom = ([x,y],[row,col]),Float)
48 trace.defn = [ Case(cb, Sxx(x,y) + Syy(x,y)) ]
49
50 harris = Function(varDom = ([x,y],[row,col]),Float)
51 coarsity = det(x,y) - .04 * trace(x,y) * trace(x,y)
52 harris.defn = [ Case(cb, coarsity) ]
```

Figure 1. PolyMage specification for Harris corner detection

Lower and upper bounds are restricted to affine expressions involving constants and parameters. Lines 4 and 5 show how variables and intervals are created.

For a function, the expressions which define it over the domain need to be specified. A function can be defined in a piece-wise manner using a list of cases. Each `Case` construct takes a condition and an expression as arguments. Piece-wise definitions allow for expressing custom boundary conditions, interleaving, and other complex patterns. `Condition` can be used to specify constraints involving variables, function values, and parameters as shown in lines 7 and 10. Two conditions can be combined to form a disjunction or a conjunction using the operators | and & respectively. All the cases defining a function are expected to be mutually exclusive; otherwise, the function definition is considered ambiguous. The `Case` construct is optional for functions that

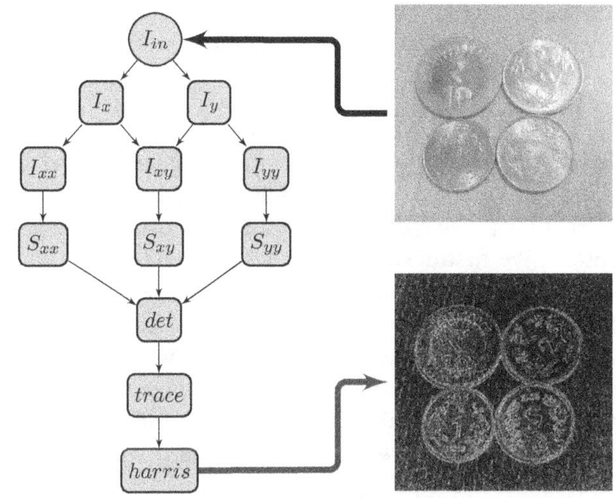

Figure 2. Harris corner detection pipeline as a graph of stages

are defined by a single expression over the entire domain. Expressions defining a function can involve its domain variables, parameters, and other function values. The `Stencil` construct is a compact way to specify a spatial filtering operation; it can also be expressed using simple arithmetic operations. Lines 37 and 38 show how the host language Python is used for meta-programming, enabling compact specification of complex pipelines. Function definitions allow referencing image values under the function being defined – this allows expression of important patterns like time-iterated computations and summed area tables [14].

Functions in our language do not have any state associated with them. Expressing histograms and other reduction operations however requires a mechanism which retains state. `Accumulator` is a function-like construct that serves this purpose. An accumulator has two domains, a reduction domain and a variable domain. Evaluation of the accumulator is done on the reduction domain while the accumulator is defined on the variable domain. Figure 3 shows an accumulator used to compute a histogram by counting the number of pixels of each intensity value, ranging from 0-255, in the image I.

```
R, C = Parameter(Int), Parameter(Int)
I = Image(UChar, [R, C])
x, y = Variable(), Variable()

row, col = Interval(0, R, 1), Interval(0, C, 1)
bins =  Interval(0, 255, 1)
hist = Accumulator(redDom = ([x,y],[row,col]),
                   varDom = ([x],bins), Int)
hist.defn = Accumulate(hist(I(x,y)), 1, Sum)
```

Figure 3. Grayscale histogram

Overall, our language allows intuitive and compact expression of image processing pipelines at the algorithm level. The number of lines of code required to specify such pipelines in our DSL is significantly less than that in an equivalent naive C/C++ implementation.

3. Pipeline Compiler

This section describes how our compiler translates pipelines specified in the PolyMage DSL into high-performance implementations. The sequence of compiler phases is shown in Figure 4. We first describe the front-end, which constructs a polyhedral representation of pipelines, performs static bounds checking and inlining. We then discuss the rationale behind our choice of tiling technique, which forms the core of our optimization, and describe a new approach for constructing overlapped tiles for a group of heterogeneous pipeline stages. Next, we detail the model-driven heuristic to decompose the pipeline into groups. Finally, we discuss the code generation and autotuning approach.

The PolyMage compiler takes the pipeline specification and the names of live-out functions as input. Pipelines are represented as a directed acyclic graph (DAG), where each stage (a function or an accumulator) in the user specification is mapped to a node, and the producer-consumer relations among the stages are captured by the edges between nodes. In the rest of the discussion, we use the terms function and stage interchangeably to refer to a stage in the pipeline. The *pipeline graph* is automatically extracted from the input specification; Figure 2 shows the pipeline graph for Harris corner detection discussed earlier. Cycles in the pipeline graph result in an invalid specification. After extracting the pipeline graph, the compiler statically checks if the values of a function used in defining other functions are within its domain. Function accesses which are affine combinations of variables and parameters are the only accesses analyzed. References to values outside the domain of a function are considered invalid and reported to the user.

Inlining substitutes producer function definitions into consumer functions. In the Harris corner detection example, the function `Ix` can be substituted into both the consumers `Ixx` and `Ixy`, resulting in `Ix` being evaluated twice. Inlining functions trades-off redundant computation for improved locality. For point-wise functions, `Ixx`, `Ixy`, `Iyy`, `det`, and `trace` in Figure 1, inlining is an obvious choice since it introduces minimal or no redundant computation. However, for stencil or sampling operations as consumer functions, the redundant computation introduced by inlining can be quite significant. Therefore, we restrict our inlining to cases where the consumer functions are point-wise functions, and rely on our schedule transformations to enhance locality for the other operations.

3.1 Polyhedral Representation of Pipelines

The polyhedral model is a mathematical framework well-suited to represent and transform loop nests. Image processing computations have regular dependence patterns which are amenable to polyhedral analysis. The strengths of the polyhedral model are in enabling complex transformations, precise dependence analysis, and code generation to realize the complex transformations. The PolyMage language allows a user to express pipelines naturally while capturing the essential details required to extract a polyhedral representation. A function *domain* in the language directly maps to a parametric integer set. The domain of `harris` function in Figure 1 is represented by the following integer set:

$$\texttt{harris}_{dom} = \{\ (x,y)\ \mid\ x \geq 2\ \wedge\ x \leq R-1\ \wedge\ y \geq 2\ \wedge\ y \leq C-1\ \}.$$

A geometric view of pipeline functions is shown in Figure 5. The functions f_1, f_2, and f_{out} are represented on the vertical axis, and the individual points in each function's domain are shown along the horizontal axis. We omit the bounds on the domain of a function when they are evident from the context, or not relevant to the discussion.

Schedules in the polyhedral framework can be represented as parametric relations from one integer set to another. The domain of the relation corresponds to a function domain, and the range to a multi-dimensional time stamp, whose lexicographic ordering gives a schedule for evaluating the function. The following shows a scheduling relation and the corresponding evaluation order for the `harris` function in the corner detection example:

$$\texttt{harris}_{sched} = \{(x,y) \rightarrow (y,x)\ \mid\ x \geq 2\ \wedge\ x \leq R-1\ \wedge\ y \geq 2\ \wedge\ y \leq C-1\ \}$$

```
for y in [2 ... C-1]:
    for x in [2 ... R-1]:
        harris(x, y)
```

A schedule can alternatively be described using hyperplanes, which provide better geometric intuition when dealing with tiling transformations. A hyperplane is an $n-1$ dimensional affine subspace of an n-dimensional space. It maps an n-dimensional vector, which corresponds to a point in a pipeline function's domain, to a scalar value. When viewed as a scheduling hyperplane, the scalar value is the time stamp at which the function value will be evaluated. A k-dimensional schedule is defined by k scalars, each given by the hyperplane corresponding to the dimension. Equation 1 describes a scheduling hyperplane for a function f. If $\vec{i_f} = (x,y)$ is a point in the function's domain, $\vec{h}$ is the normal to the hyperplane, and h_0 is the translation or the constant shift component, then

$$\phi(\vec{i_f}) = \vec{h} \cdot \vec{i_f} + h_0. \tag{1}$$

The scheduling hyperplanes corresponding to the relation $\texttt{harris}_{sched}$, representing a 2-dimensional schedule, are $\vec{h_1}$ = [0 1] and $\vec{h_2}$ = [1 0] with no translation ($h_0 = 0$).

After extracting the domain for a function, the compiler builds an initial schedule by using both the pipeline graph and the domain order in the function definition. The leading dimension of the initial schedule for a function is given by

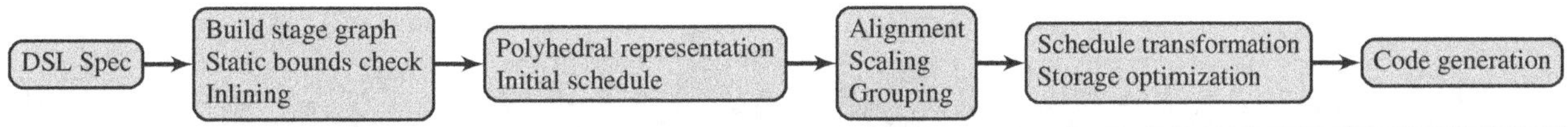

Figure 4. Phases of the PolyMage compiler

its *level* in a topological sort of the pipeline graph, and the remaining ones are given by its domain variables. The initial schedules for the functions Ix, Ixx, and Sxx in Figure 1 are as follows:

$$\begin{aligned}\texttt{Ix}_{sched} &= \{(x,y) \rightarrow (0,x,y) \mid x \geq 1 \ \wedge \ x \leq R \ \wedge \\ &\qquad y \geq 1 \ \wedge \ y \leq C \ \} \\ \texttt{Ixx}_{sched} &= \{(x,y) \rightarrow (1,x,y) \mid x \geq 1 \ \wedge \ x \leq R \ \wedge \\ &\qquad y \geq 1 \ \wedge \ y \leq C \ \} \\ \texttt{Sxx}_{sched} &= \{(x,y) \rightarrow (2,x,y) \mid x \geq 2 \ \wedge \ x \leq R-1 \ \wedge \\ &\qquad y \geq 2 \ \wedge \ y \leq C-1 \ \}.\end{aligned}$$

The compiler uses the initial schedule, which is implicit from the pipeline specification, and derives dependence information from it.

Dependences between consumer and producer functions, which are determined by analyzing the function definitions, are captured using *dependence vectors*. Initial function schedules give the time stamps at which function values are produced and consumed. The dependence vectors are computed by subtracting the time stamp at which a value is produced from the time stamp at which it is consumed. For example, the function Sxx at $(2, x, y)$ consumes the values of Ixx produced at $(1, x-1, y-1)$, $(1, x+1, y-1)$, $(1, x-1, y+1)$ and $(1, x+1, y+1)$: this is captured by the dependence vectors $(1, 1, 1)$, $(1, -1, 1)$, $(1, 1, -1)$ and $(1, -1, -1)$. Figures 5 and 6 show functions, schedules, and corresponding dependence vectors.

3.2 Transformation Criteria

While optimizing schedules for functions in a pipeline, one needs to account for the key factors of parallelism and locality. These factors have been studied well in the context of time-iterated stencils, which are closely related to stencil functions in image processing pipelines. Several tiling techniques have been developed for time-iterated stencils to allow for a high degree of concurrent execution while preserving locality. Among these techniques, parallelogram [8, 44], split [26], overlapped [27, 29], diamond [5], and hexagonal [21] tiling use the polyhedral model. Figure 5 shows overlapped, split, and parallelogram tiling for a group of pipeline functions. Each of the tiling strategies provide different trade-offs with respect to parallelism, locality, redundant computation and ease of storage optimization.

Parallelogram tiling improves locality but only allows for wavefront parallelism, which effectively reduces to sequential execution of the tiles due to the small number of functions relative to the spatial tile size. This can be seen in Figure 5 where the second parallelogram tile is dependent on the first. Split tiling evaluates functions in two phases. The tiles with a larger base (upward pointing) are scheduled in the first phase, and the remaining ones (downward pointing) are scheduled next. All tiles in a single phase can be processed in parallel. Tiles in the second phase consume values produced at the boundaries of tiles in the first phase (encircled in the figure); hence, these values have to be kept live for consumption in the second phase. Overlapped tiling recomputes function values which are in the intersecting region of two neighboring tiles. Since the required values are recomputed within each tile, all the tiles can be executed in parallel without any communication across tile boundaries. This key difference allows for aggressive storage optimization making overlapped tiling a more suitable choice for image processing pipelines.

Tiling shown in Figure 5 is across several functions rather than multiple time iterations of the same function. Functions that describe complex pipelines are heterogeneous in nature as they potentially involve stencil, sampling and data dependent references to function values. Current techniques for overlapped tiling [27, 29] are designed only for time-iterated stencil dependence patterns and cannot be directly applied in our context. We now discuss the schedule transformations required to enable overlapped tiling for a group of heterogeneous functions.

3.3 Alignment and Scaling of Functions

Constructing overlapped tiles for a group of functions is only possible when the dependences can be captured by constant vectors, as shown in Figures 5 and 6. In general, a group of heterogeneous functions can have different dimensions and complex access patterns, requiring alignment and scaling transformations to make the dependence vectors constant. Consider the following example which shows a color to gray scale conversion.

```
gray(x,y) = 0.299×I(2,x,y) + 0.587×I(1,x,y) +
            0.114×I(0,x,y)
```

I represents a color image where the first dimension corresponds to the color channel c, and the others to the spatial coordinates x and y. The initial schedules for gray and I are $(x, y) \rightarrow (1, x, y, 0)$ and $(c, x, y) \rightarrow (0, c, x, y)$ respectively. According to the initial schedule, the value I(0,x,y) required to compute gray(x,y) at $(1, x, y, 0)$ is produced at $(0, 0, x, y)$, resulting in the non-constant dependence vector $(1, x, y-x, -y)$. However, if the schedule for gray is transformed to $(x, y) \rightarrow (1, 0, x, y)$, the dependence vector becomes $(1, 0, 0, 0)$.

For the functions in Figure 6, value dependences are not near-neighbor like in stencils; evaluating $f_{out}(x)$ and $g(x)$ requires the values $f_{\uparrow}(x/2)$ and $f(2x-1)$ respectively. Under the initial schedule of these functions, both dependences

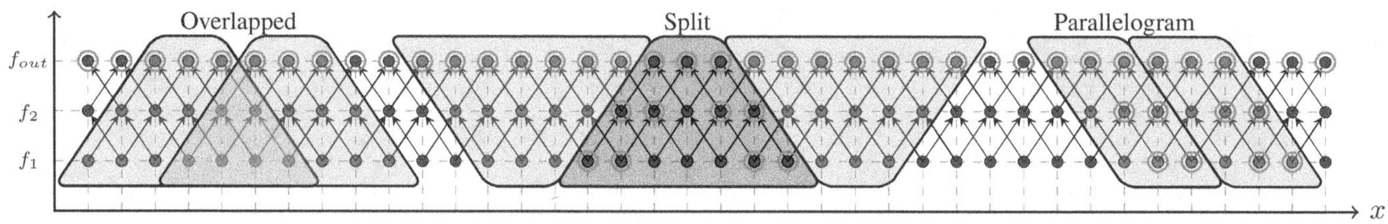

Function	Schedule	Dependence Vectors
$f_{out}(x) = f_2(x-1) \cdot f_2(x+1)$	$(x) \rightarrow (2, x)$	$(1,1), (1,-1)$
$f_2(x) = f_1(x-1) + f_1(x+1)$	$(x) \rightarrow (1, x)$	$(1,1), (1,-1)$
$f_1(x) = f_{in}(x)$	$(x) \rightarrow (0, x)$	

	Overlapped	Split	Parallelogram
Parallelism	✓	✓	×
Locality	✓	✓	✓
Redundancy	✓	×	×

Figure 5. Functions fused using overlapped, split and parallelogram tiling (left to right). Live-outs at tile boundaries are circled. Function definitions are on the bottom left. Characteristics of the tiling techniques are on the bottom right.

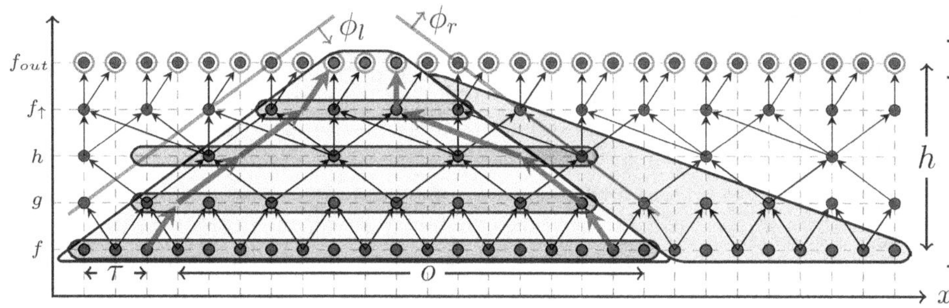

Function	Schedule
$f_{out}(x) = f_\uparrow(x/2)$	$(x) \rightarrow (4, x)$
$f_\uparrow(x) = h(x/2) \cdot h(x/2+1)$	$(x) \rightarrow (3, 2x)$
$h(x) = g(2x-1) \cdot g(2x+1)$	$(x) \rightarrow (2, 4x)$
$g(x) = f(2x-1) \cdot f(2x+1)$	$(x) \rightarrow (1, 2x)$
$f(x) = f_{in}(x)$	$(x) \rightarrow (0, x)$

Figure 6. Anatomy of an overlapped tile for a group of heterogeneous functions. The functions and their scaled schedules are shown on the right. A tight tile shape is computed by analyzing dependence vectors between the stages. Extended region shows overlap with over-approximation. Horizontal boxes within the tile show scratchpad allocations.

cannot be captured by constant dependence vectors. Dependences of this form are characteristic of up-sampling and down-sampling operations. These dependences can be made near-neighbor by scaling the function schedules appropriately, as shown in Figure 6. The compiler determines the schedule alignment and scaling factors for each function in the group. This is done by analyzing the accesses to other function values in the function definitions. It may not always be possible to align and scale schedules to make the value dependence vectors constant, for instance, for the functions $f(x, y) = g(x, y) + g(y, x)$ and $f(x) = g(x/2) + g(x/4)$. Our grouping heuristic, which is presented in Section 3.5, takes the scaling and alignment factors into account while partitioning the pipeline into groups. Only functions whose schedules can be scaled and aligned to make the dependences near-neighbor are grouped together. We now present the method to construct overlapped tiles for a group of functions.

3.4 Generating Schedules for Overlapped Tiling

Tiling is only relevant for a group of functions whose dependence vectors are constant in at least one dimension after scaling and alignment transformations. The compiler constructs schedules for overlapped tiling of functions, one dimension after another. For each dimension, the shape of an overlapped tile is determined by analyzing the dependence vectors. The tile shape is given by the left and right bounding hyperplanes denoted by ϕ_l and ϕ_r respectively. For the tile shape to be valid, the cone formed by ϕ_l and ϕ_r from any of the live-out values should contain all the values required to compute it. Figure 6 shows hyperplanes which define a valid tile shape. A naive approach to determine the tile shape is to assume that every dependence vector exists uniformly at every point in the space. This over-approximates the dependence cone increasing the redundant computation by a significant amount, as shown in Figure 6. It is desirable to minimize the redundant computation by determining the tightest *slope* possible for ϕ_l and ϕ_r.

Our compiler accounts for the heterogeneity of the functions, and determines the tile shape by examining the dependence vectors between two *levels* in isolation from the other dependence vectors. *Level* refers to the level in a topological sort of the pipeline DAG formed by the functions in the group, it is also the first dimension in every function's initial schedule. To determine ϕ_l for a particular dimension, only the dependence vectors with non-negative components in that dimension are considered. Similarly, only the vectors with non-positive components are considered for ϕ_r. In Figure 6, the thick arrows shown at the left tile boundary are the maximum non-negative dependence vectors at each level. Similarly, the minimum non-positive vectors at each level are shown at the right tile boundary. Using the dependences at the boundaries both ϕ_l and ϕ_r are determined. Then the overlapped tile schedule for each function f_k in the group is constructed as follows.

Let the scaled and aligned schedule for a function f_k in the group be $(\vec{i_k}) \rightarrow (\vec{s_k})$. For a tile, let h be the tile height which is one less than number of levels in the group, l and r be the slopes corresponding to ϕ_l and ϕ_r respectively. The amount of overlap for a dimension, denoted by o, is given by:

$$o = h \cdot (|l| + |r|).$$

With traditional tiling where both the lower and the upper bounding faces are parallel to each other and given by a single hyperplane, ϕ, the tiling constraints [2, 45] are given by:

$$\tau \cdot T \leq \phi(\vec{s_k}) \leq \tau \cdot (T+1) - 1,$$

where T is a newly added dimension corresponding to the iterator on the tile space, and τ is the tile size. For an overlapped tile with ϕ_l and ϕ_r as its lower and upper bounding faces respectively, the constraints are now given by the conjunction:

$$\begin{aligned} \tau \cdot T \leq \phi_l(\vec{s_k}) \leq \tau \cdot (T+1) + o - 1 \ \wedge \\ \tau \cdot T \leq \phi_r(\vec{s_k}) \leq \tau \cdot (T+1) + o - 1. \end{aligned} \quad (2)$$

Note that o, h and τ are known at code generation time. The schedule for f_k is updated to $(\vec{i_k}) \rightarrow (T, \vec{s_k})$, and the constraints in Equation (2) are added to the schedule relation. Since the overlapped tile is for the entire group of stages, the schedules for all the functions in the group are modified similarly.

3.5 Grouping

Our algorithm to group stages is shown as Algorithm 1. The algorithm takes the directed acyclic graph, (S, E), where S is the set of stages or functions and E, the set of edges, as input. Initially, each function in the pipeline is in a separate group. The tile sizes, an overlap threshold and the approximate estimates of all pipeline parameters, are also part of the input. Typically, the user has an idea of the range of image dimensions on which the processing algorithm will be applied. The generated pipeline is optimized for the parameter values around the estimates. However, the implementation is valid for all parameter sizes. Generating an optimized implementation for all possible parameter values is often not feasible. The grouping algorithm uses the estimates to avoid considering functions of very small size for merging. At any point, the groups in G are disjoint and their union is the set of all stages, S.

The grouping algorithm iteratively merges groups until no further merging is possible. For every iteration, it finds all groups that have only a single child or successor group, with respect to the pipeline graph (line 6). These candidate groups are sorted (line 7) in the decreasing order of their sizes determined from the parameter estimates. Next, the algorithm iterates over the sorted groups to check for merging opportunities. An iteration finishes when either a child is merged or there is no opportunity to merge, in which case the algorithm terminates.

Algorithm 1: Iterative grouping of stages

```
Input : DAG of stages, (S, E); parameter estimates, P; tile
        sizes, T; overlap threshold, o_thresh
/* Initially, each stage is in a separate group              */
1  G ← ∅
2  for s ∈ S do
3  |  G ← G ∪ {s}
4  repeat
5  |  converge ← true
6  |  cand_set ← getGroupsWithSingleChild(G, E)
7  |  ord_list ← sortGroupsBySize(cand_set, P)
8  |  for each g in ord_list do
9  |  |  child = getChildGroup(g, E)
10 |  |  if hasConstantDependenceVectors(g, child) then
11 |  |  |  o_r ← estimateRelativeOverlap(g, child, T)
12 |  |  |  if o_r < o_thresh then
13 |  |  |  |  merge ← g ∪ child
14 |  |  |  |  G ← G − g − child
15 |  |  |  |  G ← G ∪ merge
16 |  |  |  |  converge ← false
17 |  |  |  |  break
18 until converge = true
19 return G
```

Lines 10, 11, and 12 show the criteria used for a profitable merge. The first criterion is that it should be possible to make the dependence vector components constant by aligning and scaling the functions in child and parent groups. Otherwise, overlapped tiling cannot be performed on the group and merging the groups is not desirable. The second criterion is the amount of redundant computation that would be introduced. The algorithm merges groups only when the size of overlapping region, as a fraction of the tile size, is less than the overlap threshold. The size of the overlapping region along a dimension is independent of the tile size along that dimension, and is determined only by the slopes of the bounding hyperplanes and the group size. Recall that the slope itself was determined by dependences among functions in the group, as shown in Figure 6. The tile size in effect restricts group sizes. This is exploited by our auto-tuner to explore a range of implementations with a very small parameter space, as described later in Section 3.8.

Algorithm 1 is greedy, but fast and effective. A characteristic of the algorithm is that it groups maximally in a greedy fashion subject to the constraints on redundant computation, scaling and alignment. The pipeline graphs we consider have a single sink node (stage), which is the final output of the pipeline. Therefore, there exists at least one node with a single child group, i.e., the parent(s) of the sink node. When the sink node and its parents are grouped together, they form the new sink node. Now, the new sink node will be the only child of it's parents. By repeatedly merging the sink node with its parents, the entire DAG can be grouped together if the overlap and alignment criteria permit. Hence, the algorithm, (1) *tends* to maximize reuse as it only groups stages connected by producer-consumer relationships and (2) prevents merging of groups *only* when the overlap threshold and alignment criteria do not permit such a merge. Once the groups are formed, overlapped tiling for each group is performed as described in Section 3.4. The algorithm is not provably optimal in minimizing the number of groups or maximizing any pre-defined notion of reuse. However, our experiments demonstrate that it is effective in practice when combined with auto-tuning in a restricted space. As an example, the grouping obtained for the Pyramid Blending pipeline is shown in Figure 8.

Validity A grouping is valid if there is no cycle between the groups with reference to the pipeline DAG. Since algorithm 1 merges a group with its single child into itself, it does not create cycles.

Termination Every iteration of the repeat-until loop that does not lead to termination, reduces the cardinality of G by one. The algorithm thus terminates in $|S| - 1$ iterations in the worst case.

3.6 Storage Mapping

Functions that are outputs of the pipeline need to be stored in memory after they are computed, and we allocate arrays to store values of both output and intermediate functions. Array layout for the output functions is dictated by the domain order in their definitions and cannot be altered. However, the data layout for intermediate functions closely follows the schedule transformations applied to them, thus considering them in an integrated manner. For example, a function $f(x, y)$ whose schedule is given by $(x, y) \rightarrow (y, x)$ will be stored in a 2-dimensional array with y and x as the outer and inner dimensions respectively.

For a group of functions that are tiled, the values of the intermediate functions are used only within the tile. This can be seen in Figure 6, in the case of intermediate functions f, g, h and $f_\uparrow$. These intermediate values can be discarded after computing the live-out values at the top of a tile. Therefore, the intermediate functions need not be allocated as full buffers, instead they can be stored in small scratchpads which are private to each tile. Horizontal boxes in Figure 6 indicate such scratchpad allocations. All tiles which are executed sequentially by a single thread can reuse the same set of scratchpads. The only full allocations required are for the live-out functions in a group. For tile sizes which are small relative to the size of the functions, the reduction in storage is quite significant, leading to better locality.

```
void pipe_harris(int C, int R, float* I,
                 float*& harris)
{
   /* Live out allocation */
   harris = (float*) (malloc(sizeof(float)*
                             (2+R)*(2+C)));
#pragma omp parallel for
   for (int Ti = -1; Ti <= R/32; Ti+=1){
      /* Scratchpads */
      float  Ix[36][260];
      float  Iy[36][260];
      float  Syy[36][260];
      float  Sxy[36][260];
      float  Sxx[36][260];
      for (int Tj = -1; Tj <= C/256; Tj+=1) {
         int lbi = max(1, 32*Ti);
         int ubi = min(R, 32*Ti + 35);
         for (int i = lbi; i <= ubi; i+=1) {
            int lbj = max(1, 256*Tj);
            int ubj = min(C, 256*Tj + 259);
#pragma ivdep
            for (int j=lbj; j<=ubj; j+=1) {
               Iy[-32*Ti+i][-256*Tj+j] = ...;
               Ix[-32*Ti+i][-256*Tj+j] = ...;
            }
         }
         lbi = max(2, 32*Ti + 1);
         ubi = min(R - 1, 32*Ti + 34);
         for (int i = lbi; i <= ubi; i+=1) {
            int lbj = max(2, 256*Tj + 1);
            int ubj = min(C-1, 256*Tj + 258);
#pragma ivdep
            for (int j=lbj; j<=ubj; j+=1) {
               Syy[-32*Ti+i][-256*Tj+j] = ...;
               Sxy[-32*Ti+i][-256*Tj+j] = ...;
               Sxx[-32*Ti+i][-256*Tj+j] = ...;
            }
         }
         if (Tj >= 0 && Ti >= 0) {
            lbi = 32 * Ti + 2;
            ubi = min(R - 1, 32*Ti + 33);
            for (int i = lbi; i <= ubi; i+=1) {
               int lbj = 256*Tj + 2;
               int ubj = min(C-1, 256*Tj+257);
#pragma ivdep
               for (int j=lbj; j<=ubj; j+=1)
                  harris[i*(R+2)+j] = ...;
            }
         }
      }
   }
}
```

Figure 7. Generated code for Harris corner detection

In order to perform scratchpad allocation for intermediate functions, their accesses have to be remapped to the scratchpads. The compiler generates index expressions into scratchpads relative to the origin of each tile: in Figure 6, the origin is the left bottom corner of the tile shown. Relative indexing generates simple indexing expressions for scratchpads allowing for easier code generation and vectorization. The generated code shown in Figure 7 shows the indexing ex-

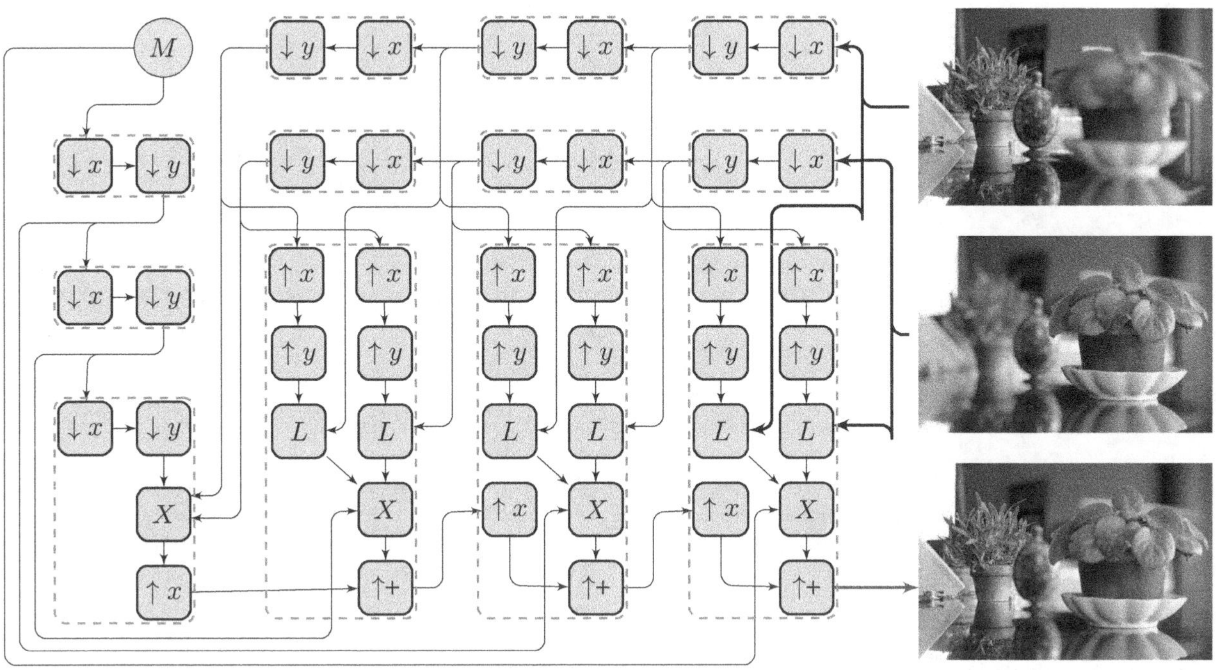

Figure 8. Pyramid Blending pipeline with four pyramid levels. The grouping generated by our compiler is shown by the dashed boxes, all the stages in one group are enclosed by a dashed box. Inputs to the pipeline are the two images on the top right, each with one of the halves out of focus, and a mask image *M*. The image on the bottom right is the blended output where both halves of the image are in focus. (Image courtesy Kyros Kutulakos)

pressions for scratchpad allocations. Without storage reduction, the tiling transformations are not very effective due to the streaming nature of image processing pipelines. The reduction of memory footprint coupled with a schedule optimized for parallelism and locality results in a dramatic improvement in performance.

3.7 Code Generation

After partitioning the pipeline into groups, building overlapped tiled schedules and optimizing storage, the compiler generates a C++ function implementing the pipeline. Figure 7 shows the code generated for Harris corner detection specification (Figure 1). The integer set library (isl) [42] is used to generate loops to scan each group of functions as per the ordering implied by our schedules. The outermost parallel dimension for each group is marked parallel using OpenMP pragmas. Scratchpad allocations are placed at the start of the parallel loop's body. For the code in Figure 7, scratchpads are allocated in the T_i loop. Our alignment and scaling method always ensures that the innermost loop iterator has a unit stride. The compiler also avoids branching in the innermost loops by splitting function domains and unrolling loops. Unit stride loops are annotated using `ivdep` pragmas which inform the downstream C++ compiler of the absence of any vector dependences. From our experiments, we found the Intel C++ compiler's cost model for vectorization to be very effective, and we relied on it to decide which loops to vectorize and in what way.

3.8 Autotuning

Our grouping heuristic (Section 3.5) and overlapped tiling (Section 3.4) use fixed tile sizes and overlap threshold to generate an implementation of the pipeline. It is tedious for a user to infer the right choice of parameters that lead to the best performance. Given that the solution space is narrowed down only to tile size choices, we use an autotuning mechanism to infer the right ones. The grouping heuristic we proposed takes a tile size configuration, and determines a grouping structure considering the overlap. This model-driven approach reduces the search space to one of a very tractable size. The parameter space we explore comprises seven tile sizes – 8, 16, 32, 64, 128, 256, 512, for each dimension, and three threshold values, 0.2, 0.4, 0.5, for o_{thresh}. Even for a pipeline that has four tilable dimensions, the size of the parameter space is $7^4 \times 3$ configurations. We however note that even the complex pipelines in our benchmarks have only 2 dimensions that can be tiled, and the parameter space we consider for them is thus $7^2 \times 3 = 147$. Figure 9 shows the single and 16-thread performance for various configurations explored by the auto-tuner for three of our benchmarks. For all the benchmarks we considered, the autotuner took under 30 minutes to explore the parameter space.

4. Experimental Evaluation

Setup: All experiments were conducted on an Intel Xeon E5-2680 based on the Sandybridge microarchitecture. The ma-

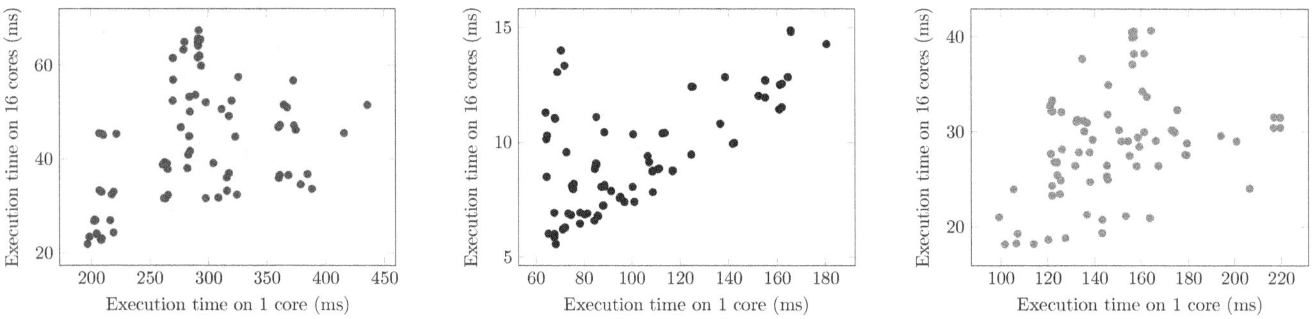

(a) Pyramid Blending (b) Camera Pipeline (c) Multiscale Interpolation

Figure 9. Autotuning results (note: origin of the plots is not (0,0); it has been shifted for better illustration)

chine is a dual-socket NUMA with an 8-core Xeon E5 2680 processor in each socket and 64 GB of non-ECC RAM, running Linux 3.8.0-38 (64-bit). Each Xeon E5 2680 runs at 2.7 GHz and with a 32 KB L1 cache/core, 512 KB L2 cache/-core, and a shared 20 MB L3 cache. The Sandybridge includes the 256-bit Advanced Vector Extensions (AVX). The experiments were conducted with hyperthreading disabled. All codes generated by PolyMage were compiled with Intel C/C++ compiler 14.0.1 with flags "-O3 -xhost". The Halide version [23] used for benchmarking uses LLVM 3.4 as its backend, and the OpenCV version used was 2.4.9. The PolyMage performance numbers were taken with 6 runs; the first warm up run was discarded, and the average of the other five is reported.

We use seven image processing application benchmarks which vary widely in structure and complexity. The number of stages and the lines of PolyMage code for each of these applications is shown in Table 2. We evaluate our results relative to other implementations of the same benchmarks in the following ways.

- We compare with the highly tuned schedules available in the Halide repository for the applications evaluated by Ragan-Kelley et al. [37]. We tuned those schedules further for our target machine by varying tile sizes, vector lengths and unroll factors, and we call these *H-tuned*.
- We evaluate schedules generated by our compiler in conjunction with Halide. This is done by specifying a schedule, referred to as *H-matched*, that closely matches our best schedule for the benchmark. Coming up with a matching Halide schedule is not practically feasible for all the applications considered. It is too tedious in cases where the pipelines have a large number of stages – since schedules generated by our compiler are complex.
- We used the OpenTuner [3] framework and the associated Halide autotuner to generate schedules for all the benchmarks, by running the autotuner for 12 hours on each application.
- We also compare with OpenCV implementations for applications which could be written solely using optimized OpenCV library routines available.

An expert hand-tuned version is publicly available for *camera pipeline*, but other expert versions evaluated by Ragan-Kelley et al. [37] are either proprietary or not publicly available. In such cases, our comparison relative to *H-tuned* can be used to place PolyMage in relation to hand-tuned versions.

Table 2 shows absolute execution times for the implementations generated by PolyMage that are fully optimized for 16 cores, their speedup over *H-tuned* and schedules generated by OpenTuner. Speedups on applications not from Halide's repository are marked with $*$. The table also provides the number of stages in each benchmark, lines of code in PolyMage, and execution times for OpenCV versions with optimized library routines. Figure 10 shows performance comparing various configurations of PolyMage and Halide to provide insight into the benefits of grouping, tiling, and vectorization separately. The baseline is the sequential version generated by PolyMage without schedule transformations and vectorization: this is the same as *PolyMage (base)* for 1 thread.

Multiscale Interpolation interpolates pixel values at multiple scales. The *H-tuned* schedule does loop reordering, vectorization, tiling, and parallelization but no fusion. Our best schedule performs non-trivial grouping of the pipeline stages and outperforms *H-tuned* by $2\times$. Specifying our best schedule using Halide (*H-matched*) completely bridged the $2\times$ gap in performance between *H-tuned* and *PolyMage (opt+vec)*. Also, the *H-matched* schedule provided better vectorization gains than the *H-tuned* one.

Harris Corner Detection [25] is a widely used method to detect interest points in an image. The feature or interest points are used in various computer vision tasks. A full description of the algorithm in our DSL is shown in Figure 1. The best schedule generated by PolyMage inlines all pointwise operations, and groups all stencil functions together. The speedup of the tiled and vectorized implementation is $46.78\times$ over the baseline. An interesting point to note is that, without the tiling transformation, vectorization improves the single thread performance only by $1.12\times$. This shows the importance of locality transformations to effectively utilize

Benchmark	Stages	Lines	Image size	Execution times (ms) PolyMage (opt + vec) 1 core	4 cores	16 cores	OpenCV (1 core)	PolyMage speedup (16 cores) over OpenTuner	H-tuned
Unsharp Mask	4	16	2048×2048×3	42.21	11.43	3.95	84.44	1.39×	*1.63×
Bilateral Grid [11]	7	43	2560 × 1536	89.76	27.30	8.47	-	1.09×	0.89×
Harris Corner [25]	11	43	6400 × 6400	233.79	68.03	18.69	810.24	2.61×	*2.59×
Camera Pipeline	32	86	2528 × 1920	67.87	19.95	5.86	-	10.05×	1.04×
Pyramid Blending [10]	44	71	2048×2048×3	196.99	57.84	21.91	197.28	27.61×	*4.61×
Multiscale Interpolate	49	41	2560×1536×3	101.70	34.73	18.18	-	12.72×	1.81×
Local Laplacian [4]	99	107	2560×1536×3	274.50	76.60	32.35	-	9.41×	1.54×

Table 2. Columns from left to right: Application, number of pipeline stages, lines of code in PolyMage, input size, execution times in milliseconds of PolyMage (opt+vec) and OpenCV (those for Halide can be derived from Figure 10 and this table), speedup of PolyMage (opt+vec) over auto-tuned (OpenTuner) and hand-tuned Halide schedules (16 thread execution in all three cases).

vector parallelism. *H-tuned* schedule uses a different grouping and performs reasonably well. *H-matched* schedule uses the same grouping and inlining as our schedule, and performs much better than *H-tuned*. The performance gap between *H-matched (tuned+vec)* and *PolyMage (opt+vec)* is due to *icc* generating better vectorized code than Halide. This can be observed from the single thread vectorization speedups.

Pyramid Blending [10] blends two images into one using a mask and constructing a Laplacian pyramid. The complex grouping performed by PolyMage is shown in Figure 8. Writing a similar schedule in Halide (*H-matched*) for such a complex grouping is a non-trivial task. The *H-tuned* schedule is provided by us along the lines of the tuned schedule available for the Local Laplacian Filter benchmark. The *H-matched* schedule provides a clear performance improvement over *H-tuned*.

Bilateral Grid [11, 34] is a structure used for computing a fast approximation of the bilateral filter. The benchmark constructs a bilateral grid, and then uses it to perform edge-aware smoothing on the input image. The pipeline is a histogram operation followed by stencil and sampling operations. Our compiler fuses all the stencil and sampling stages into one group, and the histogram into another. *H-tuned* schedule is quite different as it fuses the histogram computation with one of the stencil operations. Our current implementation does not attempt to fuse reduction operations. However, the schedule we generate is quite competitive to *H-tuned*.

Camera Pipeline processes raw images captured by the camera into a color image. The pipeline stages have stencil-like, interleaved, and data-dependent access patterns. Our best schedule fuses all stages except small lookup table computations into a single group. Performance of the PolyMage optimized code is slightly better than *H-tuned*, and matches that of an expert tuned version labeled 'FCam' [1] in Figure 10e.

Local Laplacian Filter [4, 33] enhances the local contrast in an image. It is the most complex of our benchmarks, involving both sampling and data-dependent operations. The best schedule PolyMage generates is very complex and is tedious to manually express in Halide. We only compare with the *H-tuned* schedule which does not group any of the stages but exploits parallelism and vectorization.

Unsharp Mask is a simple pipeline used to sharpen image edges, and comprises a series of stencil operations. The *H-tuned* schedule we use is very similar to our best schedule.

Summary For applications from the Halide repository, PolyMage obtains a mean (geometric) speedup of 1.27× over *H-tuned* while running on 16 cores. The corresponding speedup over manually tuned Halide schedules for all the seven applications is 1.75×. When compared with Halide schedules automatically tuned with OpenTuner, PolyMage is 5.39× faster on average. We believe that automatically obtaining this level of parallel performance while requiring the programmer to only provide a high-level specification of the computation is a significant result. Determining and applying a similar sequence of transformations manually is often either very tedious or infeasible (cf. Figure 8). For *camera pipeline*, our 86 line input code was transformed to 732 lines of C++ code, and performs only 10% slower than an expert-tuned version (FCam).

5. Related Work

In this section, we discuss related work from image processing pipeline compilation, stencil computation optimization and past polyhedral optimization efforts.

Halide is a recent domain-specific language for image processing pipelines [36] that decouples the algorithm and schedule specification. The Halide DSL allows the user to experiment with a wide variety of schedules without changing the algorithm specification, facilitating rapid experimen-

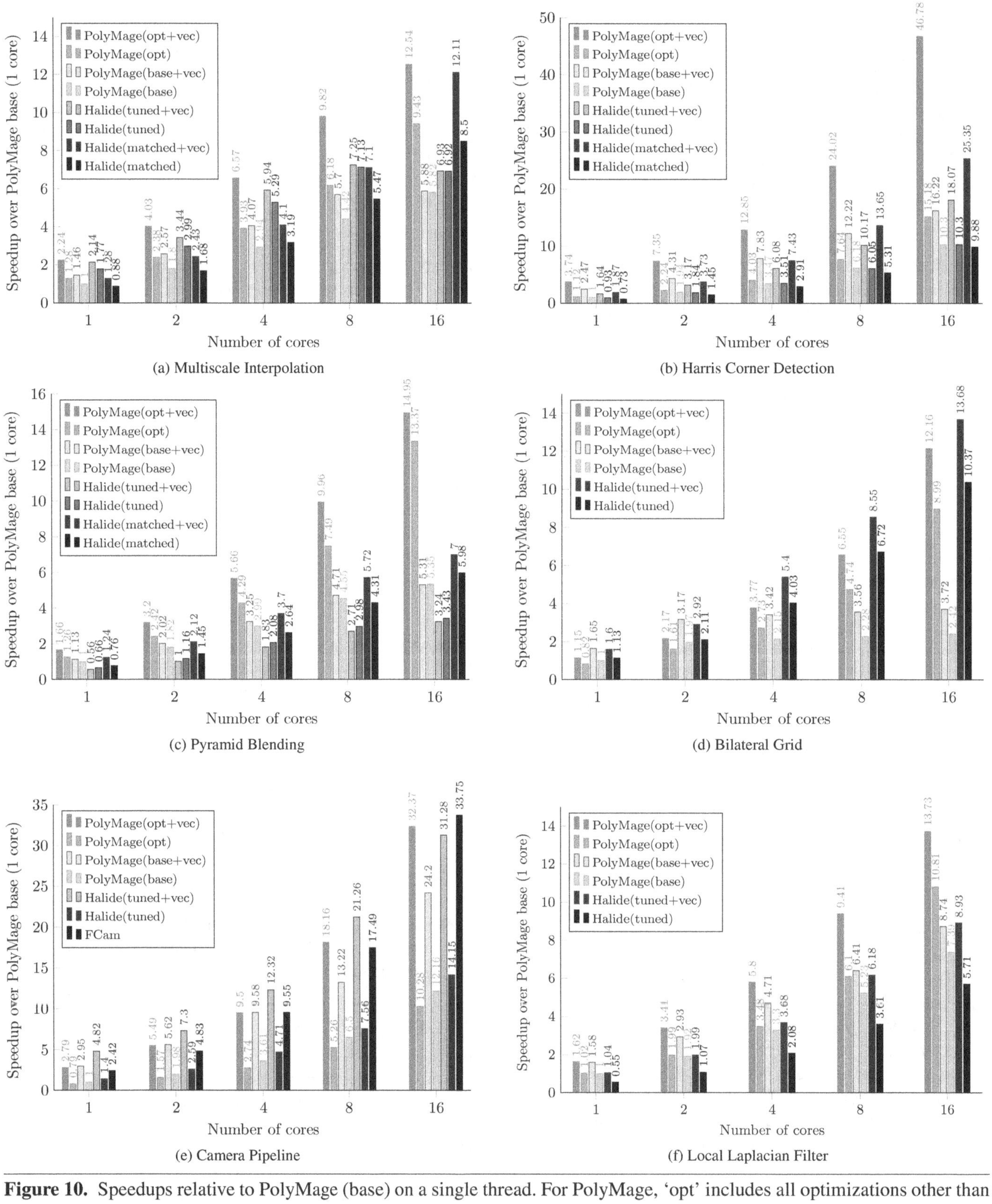

(a) Multiscale Interpolation (b) Harris Corner Detection

(c) Pyramid Blending (d) Bilateral Grid

(e) Camera Pipeline (f) Local Laplacian Filter

Figure 10. Speedups relative to PolyMage (base) on a single thread. For PolyMage, 'opt' includes all optimizations other than enabling *icc* auto-vectorization. 'base' implies all scalar optimizations including stage inlining, but not grouping, tiling, and storage optimizations. Absolute execution times can be determined in conjunction with Table 2.

tation. However, providing a good schedule often requires a lot of effort, prior knowledge, and expertise in manual optimization. Autotuning based on genetic search [37] was used in conjunction with Halide to explore the vast space of schedules. However, this method converges on good schedules very slowly, taking hours to days, and requires seed schedules for fast convergence. This approach is no longer maintained or available with Halide ([3], section 4.2).

A more recent approach for autotuning Halide programs is based on the OpenTuner [3] framework. Although more robust, the underlying approach still relies on combining several search techniques to stochastically explore the schedule space. This is only effective for small pipelines due to the exponential increase in the schedule space with pipeline size. Though the schedule space is vast, only a small subset of the space matters in practice. Our model-driven approach allows us to target such a subset and find schedules that outperform highly tuned schedules specified using Halide. Additionally, we employ a flexible transformation and code generation machinery that allows us to model a richer variety of transformations. For example, expressing parallelogram or split tiling [22] is currently not feasible with the Halide scheduling language.

Stencil optimization efforts have extensively focused on improving locality and parallelism for time-iterated stencil computations, resulting in parallelogram [8, 43, 44], diamond [5], split [22], and hybrid hexagonal [21] tiling techniques. The latter three techniques allow for concurrent start of tiles along a boundary, and are particularly effective in maximizing parallelism. These techniques exploit temporal locality across time steps without introducing any redundant computation. However, storage reduction and reuse using private scratchpads, a crucial optimization for image processing pipelines, is very difficult with these approaches due to the complex scratchpad indexing and management (and thus code generation) required. Overlapped tiling [27, 29, 46] is attractive in this context due to the dismissal of dependence between neighboring tiles – this greatly simplifies scratchpad allocation, indexing, and management. In addition, dependences between stages of an image processing pipeline are of a heterogeneous nature, and more complex than those in time-iterated stencils. Our technique to construct overlapped tiles takes this heterogeneity into account, and minimizes overlap further in comparison to prior polyhedral approaches [27, 29].

Polyhedral compilation frameworks, since the works of Bastoul [6], Cohen et al [13, 17], and Hall et al. [24, 41] have taken a decoupled view of computation (as a set of iteration domains) and schedules (as multi-dimensional affine functions). Schedules could be transformed and complex ones composed without worrying about domains. However, most subsequent works remained general-purpose, both in the techniques to determine schedules, and in the extraction of initial representation from input. Among existing fusion heuristics in the polyhedral framework [7, 30, 31], there is none suitable for image processing pipelines. The heuristics do not consider overlapped tiling of the fused groups as a possibility. In our context, we observe that the interactions between fusion, tile sizes and the overlap threshold are very important to capture for optimization. Using a domain-specific approach here is thus clearly the pragmatic one.

Other prior work on image processing languages [16, 35, 38] has focused more on the language, programmability and expressiveness aspects while proposing simple and limited optimization. There is a large body of work on compilation of stream languages [9, 19, 20, 40]. However, these works do not consider the space of optimizations that we do, in particular, the tradeoff between redundant computation and locality. Most work on stream programs dealt with one-dimensional streams while image processing pipelines involve two or higher dimensional data entities. The polyhedral framework makes it convenient to deal with such higher dimensional spaces.

6. Conclusions

We presented the design and implementation of a domain-specific language along with its optimizing code generator, for a class of image processing pipelines. Our system, PolyMage, takes a high-level specification as input, and automatically transforms it into a high-performance parallel implementation. Such an automation was possible due to the effectiveness of our model-driven approach to fuse image processing stages, and our tiling strategy and memory optimizations for the fused stages. Experimental results on a modern multicore system with complex image processing pipelines show that the performance achieved by our automatic approach is up to 1.81× better than that achieved through tuned schedules with Halide, another state-of-the-art DSL and compiler for image processing pipelines. For a camera raw image processing pipeline, the performance of code generated by PolyMage is comparable to that of an expert-tuned version. We believe that our work is a significant advance in improving programmability while delivering high performance automatically for an important class of image processing computations.

Acknowledgments

We gratefully acknowledge the authors of Halide for developing and actively maintaining Halide as an open-source project. We are very thankful to the anonymous reviewers of ASPLOS for their constructive comments. We thank Intel Labs, Bangalore for donation of software and equipment with which the experiments presented in this paper were conducted. We also thank Google India for supporting Ravi Teja Mullapudi's travel to ASPLOS'15.

References

[1] Andrew Adams, Eino-Ville Talvala, Sung Hee Park, David E. Jacobs, Boris Ajdin, Natasha Gelfand, Jennifer Dolson, Daniel Vaquero, Jongmin Baek, Marius Tico, Hendrik P. A. Lensch, Wojciech Matusik, Kari Pulli, Mark Horowitz, and Marc Levoy. The Frankencamera: An Experimental Platform for Computational Photography. In *ACM Transactions on Graphics*, pages 29:1–29:12, 2010.

[2] Corinne Ancourt and Francois Irigoin. Scanning polyhedra with do loops. In *ACM SIGPLAN symposium on Principles and Practice of Parallel Programming*, pages 39–50, 1991.

[3] Jason Ansel, Shoaib Kamil, Kalyan Veeramachaneni, Jonathan Ragan-Kelley, Jeffrey Bosboom, Una-May O'Reilly, and Saman Amarasinghe. Opentuner: An extensible framework for program autotuning. In *International conference on Parallel Architectures and Compilation Techniques*, pages 303–316, 2014.

[4] M. Aubry, S. Paris, S. Hasinoff, J. Kautz, and F. Durand. Fast local laplacian filters: Theory and applications. *ACM Transactions on Graphics*, 2014.

[5] Vinayaka Bandishti, Irshad Pananilath, and Uday Bondhugula. Tiling stencil computations to maximize parallelism. In *International conference for High Performance Computing, Networking, Storage, and Analysis*, pages 40:1–40:11, 2012.

[6] Cédric Bastoul. Code generation in the polyhedral model is easier than you think. In *International conference on Parallel Architectures and Compilation Techniques*, pages 7–16, 2004.

[7] Uday Bondhugula, Oktay Gunluk, Sanjeeb Dash, and Lakshminarayanan Renganarayanan. A model for fusion and code motion in an automatic parallelizing compiler. In *International conference on Parallel Architectures and Compilation Techniques*, pages 343–352, 2010.

[8] Uday Bondhugula, Albert Hartono, J. Ramanujam, and P. Sadayappan. A practical automatic polyhedral parallelizer and locality optimizer. In *ACM SIGPLAN conference on Programming Languages Design and Implementation*, pages 101–113, 2008.

[9] Ian Buck, Tim Foley, Daniel Reiter Horn, Jeremy Sugerman, Kayvon Fatahalian, Mike Houston, and Pat Hanrahan. Brook for GPUs: stream computing on graphics hardware. In *ACM Transactions on Graphics*, 2004.

[10] Peter J. Burt and Edward H. Adelson. A multiresolution spline with application to image mosaics. *ACM Transactions on Graphics*, 2(4):217–236, 1983.

[11] Jiawen Chen, Sylvain Paris, and Frédo Durand. Real-time edge-aware image processing with the bilateral grid. In *ACM Transactions on Graphics*, 2007.

[12] The CImg Library: C++ Template Image Processing Toolkit. http://cimg.sourceforge.net/.

[13] Albert Cohen, Sylvain Girbal, David Parello, M. Sigler, Olivier Temam, and Nicolas Vasilache. Facilitating the search for compositions of program transformations. In *International conference on Supercomputing*, pages 151–160, 2005.

[14] Franklin C. Crow. Summed-area tables for texture mapping. In *Annual conference on Computer Graphics and Interactive Techniques*, pages 207–212, 1984.

[15] Zachary DeVito, Niels Joubert, Francisco Palacios, Stephen Oakley, Montserrat Medina, Mike Barrientos, Erich Elsen, Frank Ham, Alex Aiken, Karthik Duraisamy, Eric Darve, Juan Alonso, and Pat Hanrahan. Liszt: A domain specific language for building portable mesh-based pde solvers. In *International conference for High Performance Computing, Networking, Storage, and Analysis*, pages 9:1–9:12, 2011.

[16] Conal Elliott. Functional image synthesis. In *Proceedings of Bridges*, 2001.

[17] Sylvain Girbal, Nicolas Vasilache, Cédric Bastoul, Albert Cohen, David Parello, Marc Sigler, and Olivier Temam. Semi-automatic composition of loop transformations. *International Journal of Parallel Programming*, 34(3):261–317, 2006.

[18] Google Glass. http://www.google.com/glass.

[19] Michael I. Gordon, William Thies, and Saman P. Amarasinghe. Exploiting coarse-grained task, data, and pipeline parallelism in stream programs. In *International conference on Architectural Support for Programming Languages and Operating Systems*, pages 151–162, 2006.

[20] Michael I. Gordon, William Thies, Michal Karczmarek, Jasper Lin, Ali S. Meli, Andrew A. Lamb, Chris Leger, Jeremy Wong, Henry Hoffmann, David Maze, and Saman P. Amarasinghe. A stream compiler for communication-exposed architectures. In *International conference on Architectural Support for Programming Languages and Operating Systems*, pages 291–303, 2002.

[21] Tobias Grosser, Albert Cohen, Justin Holewinski, P Sadayappan, and Sven Verdoolaege. Hybrid hexagonal/classical tiling for GPUs. In *International symposium on Code Generation and Optimization*, page 66, 2014.

[22] Tobias Grosser, Albert Cohen, Paul HJ Kelly, J Ramanujam, P Sadayappan, and Sven Verdoolaege. Split tiling for GPUs: automatic parallelization using trapezoidal tiles. In *Proceedings of the 6th Workshop on General Purpose Processor Using Graphics Processing Units*, pages 24–31, 2013.

[23] Halide git version. `https://github.com/halide/Halide` Commit: 8a9a0f7153a6701b6d76a706dc08bbd12ba41396.

[24] Mary W. Hall, Jacqueline Chame, Chun Chen, Jaewook Shin, Gabe Rudy, and Malik Murtaza Khan. Loop transformation recipes for code generation and auto-tuning. In *International workshop on Languages and Compilers for Parallel Computing*, pages 50–64, 2009.

[25] Chris Harris and Mike Stephens. A combined corner and edge detector. In *Fourth Alvey Vision Conference*, pages 147–151, 1988.

[26] Tom Henretty, Richard Veras, Franz Franchetti, Louis-Noël Pouchet, J. Ramanujam, and P. Sadayappan. A stencil compiler for short-vector simd architectures. In *International conference on Supercomputing*, pages 13–24, 2013.

[27] Justin Holewinski, Louis-Noël Pouchet, and P Sadayappan. High-performance code generation for stencil computations on GPU architectures. In *International conference on Supercomputing*, pages 311–320, 2012.

[28] Sungpack Hong, Hassan Chafi, Edic Sedlar, and Kunle Olukotun. Green-marl: A dsl for easy and efficient graph analysis. In *International conference on Architectural Support for*

Programming Languages and Operating Systems, pages 349–362, 2012.

[29] Sriram Krishnamoorthy, Muthu Baskaran, Uday Bondhugula, J. Ramanujam, A. Rountev, and P. Sadayappan. Effective Automatic Parallelization of Stencil Computations. In *ACM SIGPLAN conference on Programming Languages Design and Implementation*, 2007.

[30] A. Leung, N.T. Vasilache, B. Meister, and R.A. Lethin. Methods and apparatus for joint parallelism and locality optimization in source code compilation, June 3 2010. WO Patent App. PCT/US2009/057,194.

[31] Sanyam Mehta, Pei-Hung Lin, and Pen-Chung Yew. Revisiting loop fusion in the polyhedral framework. In *ACM SIGPLAN symposium on Principles and Practice of Parallel Programming*, pages 233–246, 2014.

[32] OpenCV: Open Source Computer Vision. http://opencv.org.

[33] Sylvain Paris, Samuel W. Hasinoff, and Jan Kautz. Local laplacian filters: Edge-aware image processing with a laplacian pyramid. In *ACM Transactions on Graphics*, pages 68:1–68:12, 2011.

[34] Sylvain Paris, Pierre Kornprobst, JackTumblin Tumblin, and Frédo Durand. Bilateral filtering: Theory and applications. *Foundations and Trends® in Computer Graphics and Vision*, 4(1):1–75, 2009.

[35] CoreImage. Apple Core Image programming guide.

[36] Jonathan Ragan-Kelley, Andrew Adams, Sylvain Paris, Marc Levoy, Saman Amarasinghe, and Frédo Durand. Decoupling algorithms from schedules for easy optimization of image processing pipelines. *ACM Transactions on Graphics*, 31(4):32:1–32:12, 2012.

[37] Jonathan Ragan-Kelley, Connelly Barnes, Andrew Adams, Sylvain Paris, Frédo Durand, and Saman Amarasinghe. Halide: a language and compiler for optimizing parallelism, locality, and recomputation in image processing pipelines. In *ACM SIGPLAN conference on Programming Languages Design and Implementation*, pages 519–530, 2013.

[38] Michael A. Shantzis. A model for efficient and flexible image computing. In *ACM Transactions on Graphics*, pages 147–154, 1994.

[39] Arvind K. Sujeeth, Kevin J. Brown, Hyoukjoong Lee, Tiark Rompf, Hassan Chafi, Martin Odersky, and Kunle Olukotun. Delite: A compiler architecture for performance-oriented embedded domain-specific languages. *ACM Transactions on Embedded Computing*, 13(4s):134:1–134:25, 2014.

[40] William Thies, Michal Karczmarek, and Saman P. Amarasinghe. Streamit: A language for streaming applications. In *International conference on Compiler Construction*, pages 179–196, 2002.

[41] Ananta Tiwari, Chun Chen, Jacqueline Chame, Mary Hall, and Jeffrey K. Hollingsworth. A scalable auto-tuning framework for compiler optimization. In *International Parallel and Distributed Processing Symposium*, pages 1–12, 2009.

[42] Sven Verdoolaege. isl: An integer set library for the polyhedral model. In *International Congress Conference on Mathematical Software*, volume 6327, pages 299–302. 2010.

[43] M. Wolf. More iteration space tiling. In *International conference for High Performance Computing, Networking, Storage, and Analysis*, pages 655–664, 1989.

[44] D. Wonnacott. Using time skewing to eliminate idle time due to memory bandwidth and network limitations. In *International Parallel and Distributed Processing Symposium*, pages 171 –180, 2000.

[45] Jingling Xue. *Loop tiling for parallelism.* Kluwer Academic Publishers, Norwell, MA, USA, 2000.

[46] Xing Zhou, Jean-Pierre Giacalone, María Jesús Garzarán, Robert H. Kuhn, Yang Ni, and David Padua. Hierarchical overlapped tiling. In *International symposium on Code Generation and Optimization*, pages 207–218, 2012.

Compiler Management of Communication and Parallelism for Quantum Computation

Jeff Heckey
UC Santa Barbara
jheckey@ece.ucsb.edu

Shruti Patil
Princeton University
spatil@princeton.edu

Ali JavadiAbhari
Princeton University
ajavadia@princeton.edu

Adam Holmes
Cornell University
ah744@cornell.edu

Daniel Kudrow
UC Santa Barbara
dkudrow@cs.ucsb.edu

Kenneth R. Brown
Georgia Inst. of Technology
ken.brown@chemistry.gatech.edu

Diana Franklin
UC Santa Barbara
franklin@cs.ucsb.edu

Frederic T. Chong
UC Santa Barbara
chong@cs.ucsb.edu

Margaret Martonosi
Princeton University
mrm@princeton.edu

Abstract

Quantum computing (QC) offers huge promise to accelerate a range of computationally intensive benchmarks. Quantum computing is limited, however, by the challenges of decoherence: i.e., a quantum state can only be maintained for short windows of time before it decoheres. While quantum error correction codes can protect against decoherence, fast execution time is the best defense against decoherence, so efficient architectures and effective scheduling algorithms are necessary. This paper proposes the Multi-SIMD QC architecture and then proposes and evaluates effective schedulers to map benchmark descriptions onto Multi-SIMD architectures. The *Multi-SIMD* model consists of a small number of SIMD regions, each of which may support operations on up to thousands of qubits per cycle.

Efficient Multi-SIMD operation requires efficient scheduling. This work develops schedulers to reduce communication requirements of qubits between operating regions, while also improving parallelism.We find that communication to global memory is a dominant cost in QC. We also note that many quantum benchmarks have long serial operation paths (although each operation may be data parallel). To exploit this characteristic, we introduce Longest-Path-First Scheduling (LPFS) which pins operations to SIMD regions to keep data in-place and reduce communication to memory. The use of small, local scratchpad memories also further reduces communication. Our results show a 3% to 308% improvement for LPFS over conventional scheduling algorithms, and an additional 3% to 64% improvement using scratchpad memories. Our work is the most comprehensive software-to-quantum toolflow published to date, with efficient and practical scheduling techniques that reduce communication and increase parallelism for full-scale quantum code executing up to a trillion quantum gate operations.

Categories and Subject Descriptors B.3.2 [*Memory Structures*]: Design Styles – cached memories, shared memory; D.2.8 [*Software Engineering*]: Metrics – performance metrics; D.3.2 [*Programming Languages*]: Language Classifications – design languages; D.3.4 [*Programming Languages*]: Processors – compilers, optimization, memory management

Keywords Quantum, LLVM, Compilers, Scheduling

1. Introduction

Quantum computing (QC) is a powerful paradigm with a potential for massive computational speedup. QC-based algorithms, in contrast to classical algorithms, traverse large solution spaces exponentially fast by manipulating *qubits*, which are superpositions of 0 and 1 states, instead of individual bits. Taking advantage of this, QC algorithms have been devised for important scientific problems that have high computational complexity. For example, recent work required 8400 MIPS-years to factor RSA-155 on a classical machine [4], while Shor's QC factoring algorithm offers the potential for a significant speedup on large problems due to a reduction in asymptotic complexity.

Although the QC algorithms we use as benchmarks offer dramatic reductions in computational complexity, it is also important to optimize their actual runtimes. Quantum bits (qubits) are highly error-prone, susceptible to decoherence over time, and require expensive Quantum Error Correcting Code (QECC) operations for reliable computation. Accelerating quantum computation is important because it allows the computation to "stay ahead of the errors".

In this paper, we propose the Multi-SIMD(k,d) architecture for quantum computation. Multi-SIMD approaches combine operation-level parallelism (with k different gates or operating regions) along with data-level parallelism (up to d qubits can be operated on within a single gate). We show that QC machines of this type are well-suited to the parallelism and computational needs of large-scale

ASPLOS '15, March 14–18, 2015, Istanbul, Turkey.

http://dx.doi.org/10.1145/2694344.2694357

QC benchmarks. In addition, we explore parallelism and locality scheduling techniques as a means to optimize the performance of quantum computations onto Multi-SIMD hardware.

A natural source of state degradation in this architecture is communication delay, due to the fact that qubits need to be moved between regions in order to undergo an operation or to interact with other qubits (to support data and instruction parallelism). QECC requires many *physical* qubits to represent a single *logical* qubit. This makes compute regions and memories large in area, which results in large communication distances. When we add support for operation- and data-level parallelism, distances become even larger.

These high communication costs push us towards a communication-centric scheduling model. Exploiting the "mostly-serial" nature (at the operation level) of many of our applications, we adopt a Longest-Path-First scheduling (LPFS) strategy that keeps operands in-place for computations. Small scratchpad memories can further avoid global communication by capturing some temporal locality. In fact, the scratchpad memories are critical to leveraging the locality generated by LPFS, since it is often the case that one operand stays in a region for the next operation, but other operands must temporarily be moved aside. To maintain scheduling quality while reducing analysis times, we have developed a hierarchical approach that performs fine-grained scheduling in leaf modules with higher-level coarse-grained scheduling to stitch them together. Our results show an increase in speedup when incorporating communication from 3% to 308% and when incorporating local memories from 3% to 64%. With both modifications, total speedups can reach 9.83X.

This paper makes the following contributions:

- To exploit parallelism while mitigating control complexity, we propose a novel Multi-SIMD(k,d) quantum architectural model. Ion trap technology with microwave control provides a practical basis for our model.
- We propose a hierarchical scheme to apply the scheduling algorithms to large-scale QC benchmarks. Through remodularization and application of the algorithms at coarse-grained and fine-grained levels, we show that our algorithms can effectively analyze large-scale QC benchmarks and generate schedules that are comparable to their estimated critical path lengths.
- We propose and evaluate communication-aware scheduling algorithms that reduce communication overheads while maximizing parallelism. We compare a traditional scheduling algorithm to the designed algorithm that considers the structure of quantum programs, and evaluate the speedup of both algorithms over sequential execution and naive communication models.
- We analyze the benefits of scheduling for local, scratchpad memories next to each compute region in reducing long communication delays to the global memory and overall execution speedup.

The rest of the paper is organized as follows: Section 2 discusses the technology and architectural model proposed. Section 3 discusses the design of the ScaffCC compiler and the program execution model. Section 4 discusses the scheduling algorithms in depth. Section 5 discusses the schedules found. Sections 6 and 7 discuss related work, future work, and conclusions of the paper.

2. Architectural Model

We propose Multi-SIMD(k,d), a family of quantum architectures motivated by practical constraints in *ion trap* technology. Multi-SIMD architectures support parallelism at both the operation and data levels. In this section, we describe the concept, feasibility and challenges of trapped ion quantum computation. Our proposed architectural model and the choice of its parameters are based on

Figure 1: Microwave control for Ion Traps. Note the large off-chip coaxial connectors for the microwave signals. Figure is reproduced from [40] with permission.

ion trap QC, but are applicable to other technologies as discussed later.

2.1 Background on Quantum Computation

This section briefly describes background on aspects of QC most relevant to the work described here. In particular, one key constraint in quantum computation is the *no cloning theorem* [33], which states that a superposition state cannot be perfectly copied from one qubit to another qubit, without destroying the first one. Thus, in order to use the state of a qubit in another part of the architecture, that qubit must be physically moved. This can be costly on computation time, therefore in Section 2.3 we describe the use of a technique called *quantum teleportation*, which allows these movements to be hidden by pipelining them into the computation.

Another consequence of the no-cloning theorem, and also the fact that quantum operations have to be norm-preserving unitaries, is that these operations cannot have fan-in or fan-out, and all quantum computations must be reversible. This general property of quantum circuits means that normal, irreversible classical circuits cannot be directly written as quantum circuits, and we have to equip the compiler with a feature to convert classical operations to quantum ones. This is described in Section 3.1.

2.2 Ion Trap Technology

A trapped-ion system is currently the most promising candidate for realizing large-scale quantum computers. These include well characterized qubits, long decoherence, and the ability to initialize, measure and perform a universal set of gates [9, 27, 31, 38]. Experimental results with ion traps have demonstrated all the requirements of a viable quantum technology for realistic quantum computation [3, 6, 13, 37, 50], as laid down in the *DiVincenzo criteria* [12].

In trapped-ion systems, operations are typically performed by focusing lasers on each ion, which represents a physical qubit. Because these lasers must have precisely tuned relative phase, they can be extremely large in size, currently the size of a small room, limiting current visions for QCs to roughly 6-12 lasers.

However, recent experiments with microwaves demonstrated multi-qubit control that could scale from 10 to 100 ions for a single microwave emitter [40], like the example hardware shown in Fig. 1. Another level of fanout could create a small number of SIMD regions each capable of performing a different operation ("gate") on roughly 100 to 10000 qubits. Microwaves are a natural choice for driving single qubit gates and coupled with gradients they can also drive two-qubit gates [22, 36]. The signals for different regions can be tuned to cancel microwaves for some regions, effectively shielding some ions from neighboring signals [11].

Microwave control does not currently allow for qubit measurement, although schemes are under development. For this work, we assume laser-controlled measurement, which has better fanout

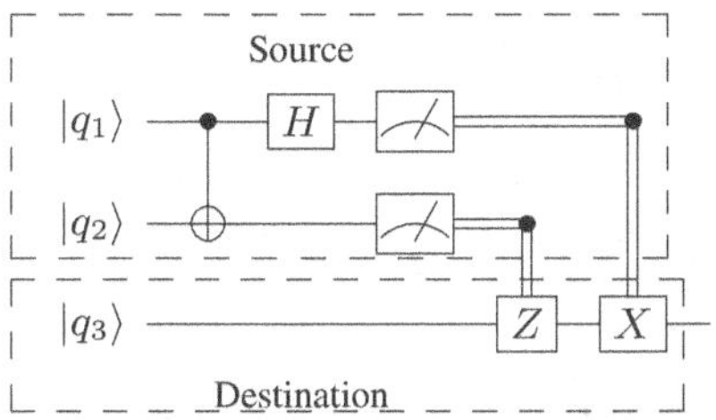

Figure 2: Communicating the state of q_1 using quantum teleportation: The EPR pair of q_2/q_3 is distributed prior to teleportaion, keeping q_2 near the communication source q_1, and using q_3 as the communication destination. By measuring the states of q_1 and q_2, and classically transmitting those measurement results (classical 0 and 1 bits), the state of q_3 takes on that of q_1 using none, one, or both of the X and Z operations at the target side. This completes the transmission of q_1 to q_3, while the state of q_1 is destroyed in the process.

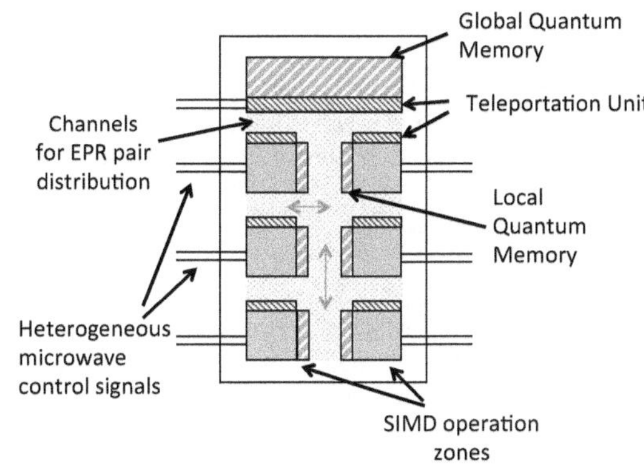

Figure 3: Block diagram of Multi-SIMD quantum architecture based on ion traps controlled by microwave technology. k operating regions each support quantum operations on d qubits simultaneously. Each operating region has a local memory for storing qubits. EPR qubit pairs are prepared near the global memory and distributed among regions via quantum teleportation.

characteristics than operation gates. This is because measurement requires only a single laser and the phase between multiple ions is not important.

All our analyses are performed at the logical level and ignore the lowest-level physical operations. The logical gate operations are actually sequences of microwave signals that operate on a group of physical qubits to produce a single logical qubit state. The encoding we assume is some form of concatenated code for QECC [17, 42, 43]. As the need for better reliability increases some of these codes can have an exponential overhead costs and resulting runtime increases. By keeping the runtimes below these boundaries, we can avoid these expenses.

2.3 Handling Data Movement and Teleportation

At a physical level, communication in the Multi-SIMD architecture is assumed to be achieved through *quantum teleportation* (QT), a phenomenon that makes transmission of exact qubit states possible. QT requires a pre-distribution of entangled Einstein-Podolsky-Rosen (EPR) pairs of qubits between the regions where communication will occur. EPR pairs are generated at the global memory, and distributed to the required regions. Fig. 2 illustrates the computations required. The communication cost is four times as high as a single quantum gate per move; in a naive movement model, this quintuples the actual compute cost because of repeatedly moving qubits between SIMD regions and the global memory. In many cases our compiler can schedule QT operations in parallel with the computation steps. It should be noted that in the context of our logical compiler, we treat all logical gates as having the same latency, which effectively means we assume the system will be clocked at the rate of the longest gate. More precise latencies can be found in [18]. For example, 2-qubit gates may physically take up to 10 times the latency of 1-qubits gates. Moreover, by choosing QT as the method of communication, we mask the latency of moving qubits around. This masking is possible by *pre-distribution* of these pairs before they are needed for the teleportation.

For a teleportation operation to occur, EPR pairs must be distributed to each SIMD region and global memory so that the sender and receiver each have one half of the pair. The distribution of such EPR pairs has been studied in detail in [49]. Since repeated movement of qubits on the physical fabric is error-prone, QT reduces quantum decoherence by communicating information through a classical channel. Our compiler schedules the pre-distribution of EPR pairs statically, as with other parts of the overall schedule. While QT has constant latency with communication distance, longer distances do imply higher EPR bandwidth requirements (larger communication channels to move enough EPR pairs throughout the architecture). To minimize EPR bandwidth requirements, future work will investigate distributed global memory and compiler algorithms for mapping to such a non-uniform memory architecture. Additionally, the issue of correctly dealing with the problem of decoherence at the physical level when moving EPR pairs, which may arise in long communication channels, is studied in [10].

2.4 The Multi-SIMD Architectural Model

Based on the ion trap technology with microwave signaling mechanism, we propose to build a scalable system with multiple independent operation regions, each offering gate-level parallelism. Fig. 3 shows the block diagram for our proposed architecture. Within each SIMD region, a large amount of data-level parallelism is available—100 - 10,000 qubits. In this manner, the architecture can support k independent regions each allowing d bits of SIMD computation, where k is limited by the number of microwave signals and the complexity of generating interference to shield neighboring regions. The value of d is limited by the ability to fan out the microwaves signal to all d qubits without disrupting the rest of the system.

These k SIMD regions serve two purposes. First, they allow active computation on qubits. Second, when idle, they can be used as passive short-term storage for qubits between compute operations. We also optionally provision each SIMD region with a small amount of scratchpad memory (or local memory) for temporary storage of qubits during intermediate computations on other qubits in the same region, similar to a traditional hierarchical memory system. During a scheduled run of the benchmark, active qubits must be moved between SIMD regions and idle qubits must be moved to the global memory. Storing some qubits in the local memories can potentially reduce overall communication cost to and from the global memory.

Note that the centralized global memory is a simplification that results from QT which makes the latency of long-distance communication constant. This constant global communication cost favors parallelism, since the serial version of our computations pay just as much to access global memory as our parallel versions do. In fact, parallelism breaks the computation into finer-grain chunks on separate regions. This reduces global memory accesses by leveraging local storage in regions and optional local memories, which is analogous to spatial computing approaches in classical computing [14, 45, 46].

Overall, efficient use of Multi-SIMD requires orchestration of qubits to maximize parallelism and to reduce qubit motion. Devising and evaluating effective scheduling techniques for Multi-SIMD is the focus of this paper.

2.5 Optimizing Communication using Local Memory

The communication overhead of four cycles per qubit movement in QT can be reduced even further by adding a local memory storage to each SIMD region. A local memory region bordering an operating region acts as a temporary store for a qubit that must be moved out of the SIMD region for one or more cycles, and moved back into the same region for the next computation on it. Due to the proximity of the local memory region, qubits can be moved back and forth physically using ballistic control. This eliminates the need for computational cycles required for teleportation to global memory reducing the communication overhead considerably. While the latency of ballistic transport of a qubit depends on the size of the operating region (or the distance to be traversed), note that even teleportation operation involves a similar ballistic latency for accomplishing the interaction of data qubits with an EPR qubit. In our experiments, we assume a one-cycle latency overhead for local communication.

2.6 Adaptability for Other Technologies

We use trapped-ion technology as a motivating example since its scaling properties and parameters are well understood. Our toolflow and the Multi-SIMD model, however, are not tied to any particular physical implementation and can be applied so long as the scaling properties hold. For example, superconducting qubits could be electronically tuned in and out of resonance in parallel, allowing SIMD operation in regions. Recent work with quantum dots using rotating frames and microwaves also could support Multi-SIMD in a manner very similar to trapped ions. A global operation can also be applied to a lattice of neutral atoms. Further, work by [5] utilized another SIMD approach based on electron spins on helium technology.

3. Computation and Compilation Framework

Our evaluation framework consists of a set of large-scale quantum benchmarks and a LLVM-based compiler toolchain designed to perform deep analysis at scale. Since large-scale quantum benchmarks can not be simulated on any classical computer, our compiler is also designed to estimate the performance and resource requirements of the code we generate.

3.1 ScaffCC Compiler Framework

Our scheduler implementation is built within ScaffCC, a compiler framework for synthesis of logical quantum circuits from a high-level language description [21]. As input, ScaffCC takes programs written in Scaffold, a C-like programming language for quantum computing [20]. Scaffold includes data types to distinguished quantum and classical bits and offers built-in functions for quantum gates. It also offers additional constructs for parallelism and control, such as parallel *for* loops and conditional statements based on the (probabilistic) state of qubits.

ScaffCC operates largely at the logical level, translating high-level quantum algorithms (benchmarks) described in Scaffold into the LLVM [26] intermediate representation and ultimately back-end-targeting QASM which is a technology-independent quantum assembly language [33, 44]. The basic data types in QASM are qubits and cbits, and the instruction set includes a universal set of gates (X, Y, and Z), and operations for measurement, as well as preparation in the states of $|0\rangle$ and $|1\rangle$. Quantum gates of Controlled NOT (CNOT), Hadamard (H) and Phase (S), referred to as the *Clifford* group of gates, along with the $\pi/8$ phase (T) gate form a minimum set for universal quantum computing. These logical gates are assumed to incorporate QECC sub-operations; no attempt in this paper is made to optimally schedule these sub-operations.

Many classical operations, such as $a + b = c$, cannot be expressed traditionally in reversible logic. To allow programmers to work in more familiar ways, we incorpoarate a tool called *Classical-To-Quantum-Gates* (CTQG) [21] into the compiler flow. This tool decomposes certain common programming syntax, such as arithmetic operations and if-then-else control structures, into QASM operations suitable for linking into the more quantum code.

The set of gates allowed in QASM is a subset of the full vocabulary allowed in Scaffold. To target just this subset (akin to an instruction set architecture in classical processors) the compiler uses a decomposition stage to translate arbitrary-angle *Rotation* gates and *Toffoli* gates into either approximate or precise equivalents. For Rotations, this is an approximate process implemented through the SQCT [25] toolbox. We perform our compiler analysis and scheduling on the quantum program after gate decomposition has been applied.

To incorporate parallelism/communication analysis and scheduling, we extend the ScaffCC compiler framework (based on the LLVM intermediate format) with new analysis passes. The current state-of-the-art in quantum programming is that nearly all of the program control flow, iteration counts, and gate operations can be determined classically, before program run time. As a result of this deeply-analyzable program control flow, most work on synthesis and optimization of quantum circuits has assumed a completely flat and unrolled circuit format [8, 29]. While *full* linearization was viable for early small QC benchmarks, quantum benchmarks have now progressed to the point where the benchmarks we study (Section 3.3) require $10^7$to 10^{12} operations or more, and thus this full unrolling is no longer tractable. We therefore incorporate a hierarchical scheduling technique, dividing the benchmark up along module boundaries into *leaf* and *non-leaf* modules. Leaf modules make no calls to other modules and are composed solely of QC primitive gates; non-leaves may use a mix of gates and submodule calls. Fine grained scheduling of the leaves are discussed in Sections 4.1 and 4.2. Coarse-grained parallel scheduling of the non-leaves is discussed in Section 4.3.

3.1.1 Leaf Module Flattening

Our hierarchical process allows scheduling of very large codes, but this comes at the cost of reduced parallelism being detected by the scheduler. Larger leaf modules provide more opportunities for good fine-grained scheduling, but when leaf modules are too large the scheduling time becomes unacceptably long. Here we look at how to flatten non-leaves into larger leaf modules optimally.

Fig. 4 illustrates a simple example of possible parallelism loss at module boundaries. Here, a program to be scheduled on a Multi-SIMD$(4, \infty)$ system, a Toffoli operation is followed by a dependent Toffoli operation i. *Toffoli(x,y,z)* is a three-qubit operation that flips the state of qubit z depending on states of x and y. Since qubits are subject to the no-cloning theorem any common operand in two operations presents a data dependency in quantum programs. In this case, the two gates share the input *a* and therefore the second is dependent on the first.

In the example, the Toffoli operation is decomposed into a circuit containing QASM-compatible gates. If these two modules were conjoined and scheduled together using fine-grained scheduling, they could be scheduled in 21 cycles, with $k = 2$. Maintaining modularity, on the other hand, serializes the resulting blackboxes due to the data dependency. At this granularity, we must execute

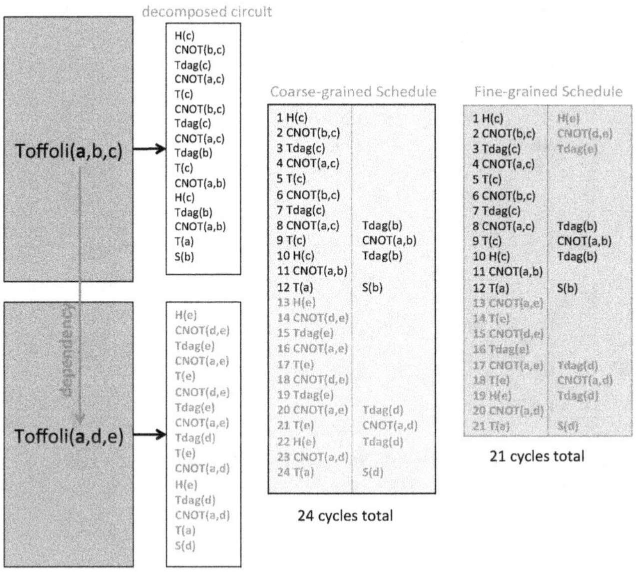

Figure 4: Scheduling of two dependent Toffoli operations with flattened and modular code. The Toffoli(x,y,z) operation is decomposed into gates supported by QASM. In the modular case, the scheduler treats the Toffoli operations as blackboxes and does not detect the inter-blackbox parallelism that exists between the decomposed circuits.

all of the scheduled sub-operations for *Toffoli(a,b,c)* before any of those for *Toffoli(a,d,e)*. In this case, the resulting $k = 2$ schedule for the two Toffoli operations is 24 cycles.

This example motivates our desire to choose the appropriate degree of modularity and flattening. To this end, we define and explore here a *Flattening Threshold (FTh)*. Namely, by performing resource estimation analysis on each module, we determine the number of gates within the module. If this is less than the flattening threshold, then the module is flattened, i.e. all the function calls contained within it are inlined. This results in leaf modules that consist of at most *FTh* operations.

The flattening threshold is determined by characterizing the initial modularity within a program. Fig. 5 shows the percentage of modules with gate counts falling within specified ranges. This reveals the proportion of modules that could be flattened for a certain *FTh*. Based on these and other experiments, the remainder of our studies use *FTh* set to 2 million operations. This flattened 80% or more of the modules contained within all benchmarks except *SHA-1*. For *SHA-1*, we used a flattening threshold for 3 million which flattened the entire benchmark.

3.2 Execution Model

The Multi-SIMD(k,d) model allows 1 to k discrete, simultaneous gates to be executed in a single *logical* timestep, each of which can be applied on 1 to d qubits apiece. For example, if 10 different qubits all require a CNOT operation applied to them, these can be positioned within a single operation region and the CNOT will be applied in a single timestep.

In this compiler, we assume that modules are blackboxes, so all active qubits are flushed to global memory during calls. This is mitigated by the fact that module calls are relatively infrequent and only cause a fixed overhead of a single teleportation cycle. It is also assumed that all ancilla qubits are generated by global and teleported to the SIMD region where they are needed.

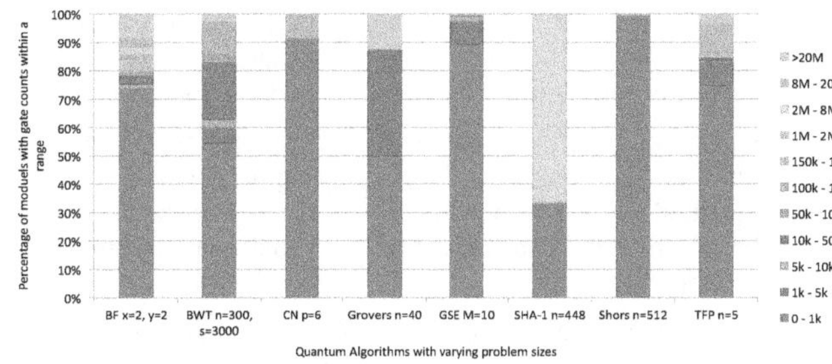

Figure 5: Histogram of gate counts represented as percentage of total modules in benchmarks. Using a flattening threshold of 2M operations, 80% or more modules were flattened for fine-grained scheduling for all benchmarks except SHA-1. For SHA-1, a flattening threshold of 3M was used to flatten the entire benchmark.

Teleporting data between SIMD regions also must be orchestrated by the scheduler so the quantum teleportation (QT) sub-operations shown in Fig. 2 can be scheduled. If a qubit physically residing in one region is scheduled in a different region in the next timestep, it is moved to that region. If no operation is scheduled on that qubit and that region is active in the next timestep, it is moved to a memory region. In later variations, a local memory is used to store qubits without teleporting them to global memory if they will be reused in the same region next.

Our execution models and evaluations assume that each gate operation takes 1 timestep. We also account for communication latencies. Some models of QC communication have a latency that varies proportionally to distance traveled, but QT approaches are distance insensitive. Rather, in QT, the bulk of the latency of each communication operation is the sequence of four qubit manipulation steps shown in Fig. 2. Their schedule can be integrated into the computation schedule for the program. In order to simplify timestep sequencing and accounting, each timestep is constrained to the longest operational time, for example $10\mu s$ for a CNOT [33].

3.3 Benchmarks

Finally, we also describe the quantum benchmarks our work studies. Promising quantum algorithms now exist for a range of problems such as factorization, searching, order and period finding, eigenvalue estimation, phase estimation and discrete logarithms [32]. We study eight quantum benchmarks of significant scale. Fully implemented in Scaffold, these are the largest and most sophisticated quantum computing programs produced to date. They are described below:

- Grover's Search (GS): Uses a quantum concept called *amplitude amplification* to search a database of 2^n elements [15]. The benchmark is parameterized by n.
- Binary Welded Tree (BWT): Uses quantum random walk algorithm to find a path between an entry and exit node of a binary welded tree [7]. The benchmark is parameterized by height of the tree (n) and a time parameter (s) within which to find the solution.
- Ground State Estimation (GSE): Uses quantum phase estimation algorithm to estimate the ground state energy of a molecule [48]. The benchmark is parameterized by the size of the molecule in terms of its molecular weight (M).
- Triangle Finding Problem (TFP): Finds a triangle within a dense, undirected graph [28]. The benchmark is parameterized by the number of nodes n in the graph.

- Boolean Formula (BF): Uses the quantum algorithm described in [2], to compute a winning strategy for the game of Hex. The benchmark is parameterized by size of the Hex board (x, y).
- Class Number (CN). A problem from computational algebraic number theory, to compute the class group of a real quadratic number field [16]. The benchmark is parameterized by p, the number of digits after the radix point for floating point numbers used in computation.
- Secure Hash Algorithm 1 (SHA-1): An implementation of the reverse cryptographic hash function [34]. The message is decrypted by using the SHA-1 function as the oracle in a Grovers search algorithm. The benchmark is parameterized by the size of the message in bits (n).
- Shor's Factoring Algorithm (Shors): Performs factorization using the Quantum Fourier Transform [41]. The benchmark is parameterized by n, the size in bits of the number to factor.

The benchmarks modularly describe the quantum circuit acting on logical qubits. The parameters dictate the problem size of the benchmarks. Our studied benchmarks ranged from 10^7 to 10^{12} gates with their various problem sizes.

4. Scheduling

Efficient scheduling of large-scale benchmarks requires a scalable approach and a delicate balance between maximizing parallelism and minimizing communication. We implement and study two different scheduling algorithms with different approaches to scheduling for parallelism with communication awareness. We also use a hierarchical, coarse-grained scheduler to limit final program size.

As discussed in Section 2.3, the primary means of communication within the MultiSIMD architecture is QT, which potentially requires an additional overhead of 4 timesteps per operation. If each operation timestep requires QT to receive its operands, then the full runtime could be 5X longer than the computation critical path. By adapting our schedulers to account for data movement costs and to reduce unnecessary movements, our runtimes remain much closer to the computation-only ideal.

Schedules are stored as a list of sequential timesteps. Each timestep consists of an array of $k + 1$ SIMD regions. The 0th region contains a list of the qubits that will be moved and their sources and destinations timestep. The remaining SIMD regions contain an unsorted list of operations to be performed in that region. Operations consist of an operation type (X, Z, CNOT, etc.), a list of qubit operands and a list of pointers to each operand's next operation.

4.1 Communication-Aware Scheduling with RCP

The Ready Critical Path (RCP) algorithm is a traditional parallel computing algorithm described in [51, 52]. The primary distinguishing feature is that it maintains a ready list instead of a free list for all tasks, only queuing the tasks that have all of their dependencies met. This prevents tasks from waiting for data during execution and reduces the overall run time. The ready list is a simple, unsorted list of operations.

Here RCP is extended to support the Multi-SIMD execution model by providing a priority scheduling mechanism that evaluates the operation type, movement cost, and *slack*. The operation type is used for grouping qubits to expose data parallelism. The movement cost indicates whether a bit needs to move (0) or is already in the present SIMD region (1); minimized movement is preferred. *Slack* is the graph distance between uses of a particular qubit, so if many operations need to occur before the next use that qubit does not need to be scheduled as soon; this is negatively correlated with the priority. The metrics can be multiplied by weights, w_op, w_dist,

```
Function rcp(Module my_module) is
    int simd, ts = 0;
    OPTYPE optype;
    RCP schedule;
    OP rcpq[] = my_module.top();
    while not rcpq.empty() do
        int simds[] = 1..k; while not (simds.empty() or
        rcpq.empty()) do
            {simd, optype} =
            getMaxWeightSimdOpType(rcpq, simds);
            schedule[ts][simd] = extract_optype(rcpq,
            optype);
            simds.delete(simds.find(simd));
        end
        updateRcpq(ts, rcpq); ts++;
    end
end
Function getMaxWeightSimdOpType(OP rcpq, list of int
simds) : {int, OPTYPE} is
    for each op in rcpq do
        optype_cnt[op.optype()]++
        for each qubit in op.args() do
            locs[op] —= 1 ¡¡ qubit.simd();
        end
        // foreach location
    end
    // foreach op for each simd in simds do
        for each op in rcpq do
            weight = w_op * op.optype() + w_dist *
            (locs[op] & (1 ¡¡ simd)) - w_slack * op.slack();
            if weight ¿ max then
                max = weight;
                max_simd = simd;
                max_optype = op.optype();
            end
        end
    end
    return {max_simd, max_optype};
end
Function updateRcpq(int ts, OP rcpq[], RCP schedule) is
    for each op in schedule[ts] do
        for each child in op.children() do
            if child.ready() then
                rcpq.push_unique(child);
            end
        end
        op.slack–;
    end
end
```

Algorithm 1: The RCP algorithm. At each timestep, it computes the relative weight for scheduling an operation type to each SIMD region based on the prevelence of that operation, the distance of each qubit from that SIMD region, and the graph distance to the next use of that qubit. The highest weighted operation type is then scheduled to its preferred SIMD region and the calculation is repeated until no more operations can be scheduled.

and w_slack respectively, though in this paper all weights are set to 1.

As shown in Algorithm 1, at each timestep the priority for each operation type in each SIMD region is calculated. A maximum priority is maintained along with the SIMD region and operation type. As the priority for each configuration is calculated, this maximum and its corresponding values are updated. When all configurations'

```
Function lpfs(DAG G, list of int simds, int l) : Schedule S is
    for i in 0 to l-1 do
        // Get longest paths for allocated SIMD regions
        simd[i] = getNextLongestPath(G.top);
    end
    ready = G.top();
    while (! ready.empty() && ! simd.forall().empty() ) do
        // Schedule each time
        for i in 0 to l-1 do
            // Schedule allocated SIMD regions
            if (refill && simd[i].empty()) then
                // Reuse SIMD region if it is out of
                operations
                simd[i] = getNextLongestPath(ready);
            end
            op = simd[i].pop();
            S[time][i].push(op);
            if (opportunistic_simd) then
                // Schedule ready operations of the same
                type
                S[time][i].push(ready.getAllOps(op.op_type));
            end
        end
        for i in l to k-1 do
            // Schedule unallocated SIMD regions
            optype = ready.top().op_type;
            S[time][i].push(ready.getAllOps(op.op_type));
        end
        for op in S[time].forall().getAllOps() do
            // Update ready list
            ready.push(op.getReadyChildren());
        end
        ready.uniq();
        time++;
    end
    return S;
end
```

Algorithm 2: The Longest Path First Scheduling algorithm. First, the longest paths for l allocated SIMD regions. At each timestep first schedule the allocated regions, then any unallocated regions are assigned from the free list. If the SIMD option is set, add data parallel operations to all regions. If refill is set, anytime a region completes its path find a new one from the current free list.

priority have been computed, the SIMD region and operation type with the highest priority is scheduled, the ready list is updated, and the SIMD region is removed from the list of available regions. This priority computation is repeated until all operations in the ready list are scheduled or all SIMD regions are occupied. The scheduler then updates the ready list with the operations that will be ready after the current timestep completes. The scheduler completes once the ready queue is empty.

4.2 Communication-Aware Scheduling with LPFS

Many of our benchmarks are highly serial, with an average critical path speedup of around 1.5x (Fig. 6). This serialization prevents the data dependencies from being accelerated significantly through parallelization, but it does provide ample opportunity for reducing expensive communication by optimizing the location of qubits throughout the execution. To this end, the Longest Path First Scheduling (LPFS) algorithm was developed (see Algorithm 2).

LPFS assigns l SIMD regions, where $l < k$, to be dedicated to computing l longest paths. These longest paths are statically assigned to those regions and so any qubits in their operational paths will have relatively few movements. This is especially useful when arbitrary rotations are decomposed, where a single qubit may have up to several thousand operations performed sequentially with no movement of the target qubit.

The longest path algorithm initially finds the critical path in the program DAG generated by LLVM. It starts at the top of the DAG and sets a tag at each node with the furthest distance from the top. After finding the largest depth at the bottom, the path is traced back and recorded. Multiple longest paths can be found sequentially, and at arbitrary positions in the execution based on the current free list. By being able to find multiple longest paths, further movement can potentially be reduced. All longest paths are returned as an ordered list of the operations to be performed in that path. These longest paths are stored in an array of size l for each statically scheduled region.

All operations that are not on any of the active longest paths are added to a free list. These are scheduled in any of the SIMD regions in the range [l+1, k] based on their order in the free list. This order is not prioritized, but is instead populated based on the order of operations as they are scheduled, and their descendants.

Two additional options can be used to control LPFS, *SIMD* and *Refill*. *SIMD* scheduling allows any SIMD region dedicated to a longest path execution to execute other free list operations of the same type; this setting also allows any timesteps where that SIMD region would have to stall for dependencies to execute arbitrary operations from the free list as well, thus providing SIMD parallelism. The *Refill* option is for the case when multiple longest paths are used and they are of unequal lengths. Once the shorter path completes, the next longest un-executed path will be found and scheduled in the region that completed. Our experiments were run with l = 1, and both SIMD and Refill enabled.

4.3 Hierarchical Scheduling

To allow benchmarks to scale beyond tractable sizes, we employ a coarse-grained schedule which stitches together optimized schedules for leaf modules scheduled by RCP and LPFS in our call tree. The scheduler uses a simple, list-based approach to schedule leaf modules and operations in non-leaf modules with the goals of improving parallelism and/or reducing communication overheads. Algorithm 3 illustrates the overall approach.

Given a set of pre-scheduled leaf nodes, the coarse-grained scheduler completes the program scheduling by using a list scheduler to compose together a full schedule. Operations are assigned priorities based on criticality and scheduled in priority order. The quantum gate operations in non-leaf modules are scheduled along with invocations to other modules. The invoked modules have been previously scheduled by one of the fine-grained schedulers discussed next and are now treated as blackbox functions. Once the schedule for a module is determined, it is characterized as a blackbox with a length dimension equal to schedule length, and a width dimension equal to highest degree of parallelism found in the schedule.

To allow the coarse-grained scheduler to effectively parallelize the invoked blackboxes within the width (k) constraint, we consider flexible rectangular dimensions for each blackbox. During fine-grained scheduling of each module, multiple schedules are determined to find schedule lengths with widths between 1 to k. The coarse-grained scheduler is presented these blackboxes with multiple dimensions. When parallelizable modules are encountered, the combination of blackboxes that yields the minimal length subject to the width constraint is chosen. Algorithm 3 shows the pseudo-code for coarse-grained scheduling with flexible blackbox dimensions.

In a k-resource constrained schedule, the width for any invoked module is at most k. Any operations (other than invoked modules)

```
for each non-flat module do
    //Track schedule in terms of blackbox dimensions
    totalL = 0; totalW = 0; // total length and width
    currL = 0; currW = 0; //current length and width
    for each operation F_i in a priority-ordered set of operations
    {F: Priority(F_i) ≥ Priority(F_j) if (i < j)} do
        Check predecessors to find the earliest timestep t_e in which
        F_i can be scheduled
        Get width W and length L for F_i
        if (t_e ≤ totalL + currL) then
            // dependencies show that F_i can be parallelized with
            previous schedule
            if (currW + W ≤ K) then
                //parallelize the operation F_i
                timestep(F_i) = max(totalL+1, t_e)
                currW = currW+W
                currL = max(currL, timestep(F_i)+L)
                F_p = {F_p,F_i} //Add to set of parallel functions
                in current schedule
            else
                //k-constraint would be violated if parallelized
                for set of functions {F_p,F_i} do
                    Try all combinations of possible widths, and
                    compute length.
                end
                if one or more combinations found with
                combined width ≤ K then
                    Choose combination with smallest length.
                    currW = Width of combination
                    currL = Length of combination
                    F_p = {F_p,F_i} //Add to set of parallel
                    functions in current schedule
                else
                    //serialize F_i due to k-constraint
                    totalW = max(totalW, currW)
                    totalL = totalL + currL
                    timestep(F_i) = totalL+1
                    currW = W; currL = L
                    F_p = {F_i} //set of parallel functions in
                    current schedule
                end
            end
        else
            // serialize F_i due to data dependency
            totalW = max(totalW, currW)
            totalL = totalL + currL
            timestep(F_i) = totalL+1
            currW = W; currL = L
            F_p = {F_i} //set of parallel functions in current
            schedule
        end
    end
    //merge current box with total box dimensions
    totalW = max(totalW, currW)
    totalL = totalL + currL
    Store totalW and totalL in data structure
end
```

Algorithm 3: Hierarchical scheduling algorithm for k SIMD regions. Operations are scheduled in priority order similar to list scheduling. Flexible blackbox dimensions are considered for parallelizable modules to find the best combination for them.

encountered by the coarse-grained scheduler have an operation execution cost of 1 and a movement cost of 4.

4.4 Scheduling Communication using Local Memory

To reduce communication overheads, we study further optimizations using local memories attached to the SIMD regions. Once computations are mapped to SIMD regions and the necessary communication schedules are determined, some qubits can be moved to local memories using a lower overhead ballistic movement instead of teleportation to the global memory. Distinguishing a move as a local move or teleportation primarily depends on where its next computation is scheduled, but local memory regions may also be constrained by capacity. With prior information about the next computation and available space in the local memory, a move can be directed to a local or global memory by the scheduler.

When a qubit in a SIMD region (source) must be stored for a few cycles before being used in a *different* SIMD region (destination), there are multiple options for storage: the global memory, the source local memory, the destination local memory, or if idle, either of the two SIMD regions. With limited local memory capacity, holding qubits for other regions or holding additional qubits before they are required can both reduce the space available for qubits being currently operated upon. For simplicity, unless the source SIMD region is idle, we move such qubits to the global memory for storage.

After a computation or communication cycle, qubits which are not scheduled for the next operation are moved to global or scratchpad memory, while those which undergo further operations in the same region will stay in place. Physically, any qubits left behind from the teleportation of state can be reinitialized and reused as ancilla or EPR pairs.

The local moves are derived from the RCP or LPFS schedules on leaf modules. The schedules are updated to reflect the single cycle local move if its next operation location is in the same region and there is space in the local memory, otherwise the original teleportation movement is kept. If any SIMD regions in a timestep have a global move, the full four cycle move time is retained to avoid disrupting the schedule.

5. Results

We present three sets of results. First, we evaluate the amount of parallelism our schedulers can expose when communication is assumed to be zero-cost. Second, we demonstrate the benefits of communication-aware schedulers when accounting for communication costs to global memory. Finally, we evaluate the benefits of local scratchpad memories associated with each SIMD region.

In each set of results we look at all eight benchmarks under the LPFS and RCP scheduling algorithms. Both algorithms are run with $k = 2$ and 4 (the number of regions). For simplicity, we assume infinite d (number of qubits in a region). LPFS also uses Refill and SIMD options. Refill lets a region with a longest path schedule a new path if the current one completes, and SIMD allows non-path operations to be SIMD scheduled in a longest path region. All experiments were run at the logical level, omitting physical qubit sub-operations and error-correction, as these are constant multipliers to the overall runtimes within the range of runtimes involved.

5.1 Characterizing Logical Parallelism

In our first set of results, looking solely at the parallelism in the benchmarks, we are able to compare the speedups provided by a Multi-SIMD architecture against the theoretical maximum based on the estimated critical path. As seen in Fig. 6, all of the benchmarks except Shor's were able to achieve near-theoretical speedup on the Multi-SIMD architecture, at either $k = 2$ or 4. This is assisted by using $d = \infty$, which allows for clustering as many qubits as possible into SIMD regions. In Section 5.4 we explain the difference in trend for Shor's.

RCP speedups are lower than or equal to LPFS in every benchmark except TFP, in some cases tying at $k = 4$ with LPFS at $k = 2$. This is due to RCP being better suited to coarse-grained scheduling in classical functions, looking predominantly at data dependencies, then operation- and data-level parallelism, and finally slack

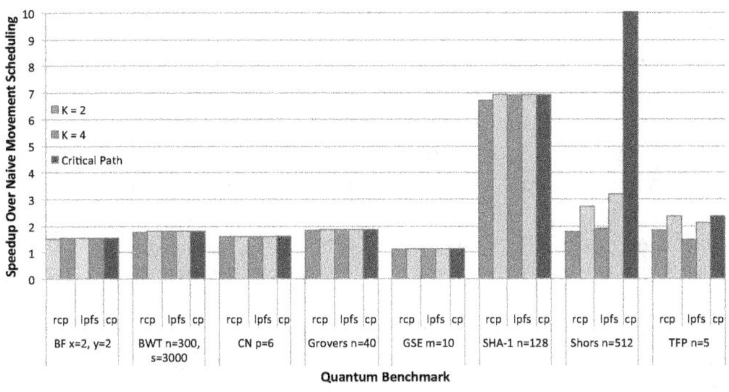

Figure 6: The speedup over sequential execution of each benchmark with each scheduling algorithm, compared to the estimated critical path. Almost all benchmarks, except Shor's, achieve near-complete speedup by $k = 4$.

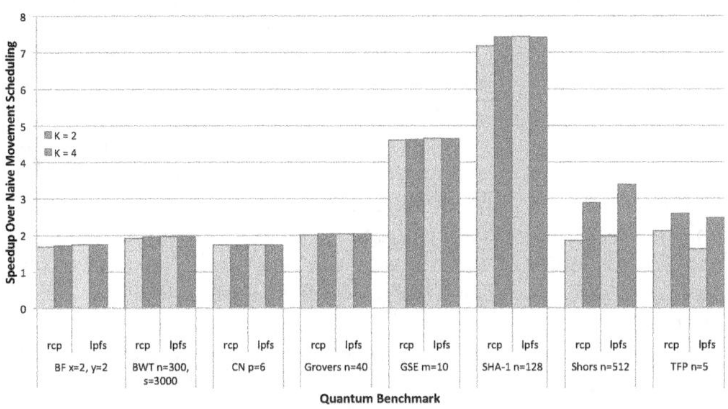

Figure 7: Speedups using a communication-aware scheduler over a sequential, naive movement model. All benchmarks show improvement over Fig. 6, with GSE showing the largest gains. Notice the renormalization of the y-axis in comparison to Fig. 6, as a result of introducing the communication costs.

based on graph distance. LPFS on the other hand focuses much more heavily on critical path prioritization.

TFP under RCP behaved interestingly, where all of the leaves scheduled by RCP had longer runtimes than those scheduled with LPFS. However, under the coarse-grained hierarchical scheduler the longer schedules were narrower, allowing for the blackboxes to be scheduled in parallel instead of in serial. This higher level parallelism allows for a shorter overall schedule.

5.2 Runtime Speedup with Data Movement Analysis

Fig. 7 shows all scheduling algorithm speedups over a naive movement model where data is moved between SIMD regions and global memory every timestep, effectively increasing the overall runtime by 5X. All benchmarks show some speedup over communication-unaware runtime models due to reduced movement. An average increase in speedup of 46% is seen across all benchmarks. The largest gain is seen in GSE (308%). The critical path was not used for a theoretical bound in these or the next results because we did not have a viable critical path model for incorporating movement.

Some benchmarks, such as BF, CN, Grovers, SHA-1 and Shor's, have a large number of highly dependent, serial operations. BF, CN and SHA-1 are composed of several CTQG modules, which produces unoptimized code that is highly locally serialized. This results in benchmarks that have a low degree of parallelism and cannot be well optimized. The interactions between data dependencies

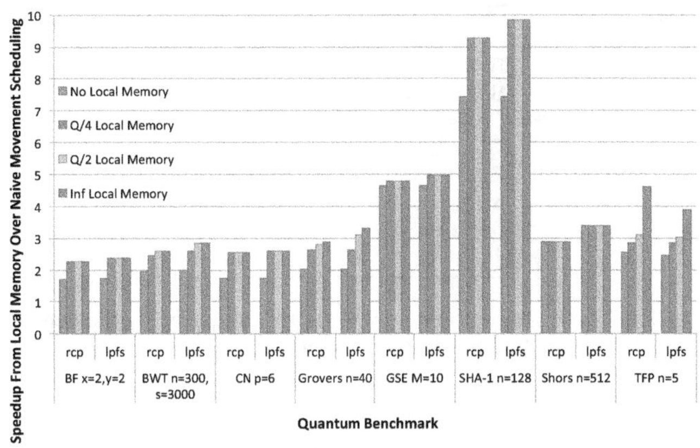

Figure 8: Speedups due to the addition of local memory to operating regions, computed over a sequential, naive movement model. Results are shown for a Multi-SIMD($4,\infty$) architecture.

also result in many small (1-2 qubit) moves between global memory and various SIMD regions that cannot be removed to improve performance.

GSE shows the largest gains due to its distinctive structure. The two key qubit registers containing the primary active qubits are rarely moved out of an SIMD region once they are in place and typically have long sequences of operations on the same qubits. This results in very few moves either between SIMD regions or memory.

5.3 Runtime Speedup with Local Memories

Fig. 8 illustrates the performance benefits of adding local memory to SIMD regions. To study the effectiveness of a small amount of local memory in each SIMD region, we experiment with varying memory sizes. For each benchmark, we limit the capacity of local memory to one-half and one-quarter of the minimum qubits Q required by the benchmark. Q is computed by scheduling the benchmark run sequentially, with maximal possible reuse of ancilla qubits across functions. Table 1 shows the value of Q determined for each benchmark. A parallel schedule of the benchmark may require more than Q qubits, thus the global memory may be much larger than the size of Q. The maximum benefit of local memory is demonstrated with an infinite capacity memory region.

Algorithms that are effective at reducing communication overheads do so by scheduling maximally interacting qubits in a single region. Adding local memory to SIMD regions raises the effectiveness of these algorithms since it allows the frequently interacting qubits to stay close. Thus, LPFS naturally sees higher benefits than RCP with local memory for most benchmarks.

These data movement based speedups show that, at least in some cases, it is possible to minimize the communications within the system to achieve a reasonable speedup (up to 9.82X in the case of SHA-1) in a practical system with physical limits on EPR distribution for teleportation and limited parallelism.

5.4 Sensitivity to d and k parameters:

The preceding results show that in most quantum benchmarks, data-level parallelism (d) achieved through microwave signaling is able to capture most of the parallelism, even with modest numbers of distinct SIMD regions. In fact, even though we practically assumed infinite amount of data-parallelism available in our SIMD regions, our other experiments have shown that decreasing this to below 32 qubits only causes marginal changes. This is important, since we have solely focused on the logical level, but we can see

Benchmark	Q
BF x=2, y=2	1895
BWT n=300, s=3000	2719
CN p=6	60126
Grovers n=40	120
GSE M=10	13
SHA-1 n=448	472746
Shors n=512	5634
TFP n=5	176

Table 1: The minimum number of qubits Q required by the benchmarks, computed with sequential execution and maximum reuse of ancilla qubits.

Rotation Operation	Primitive Operations Approximating Rotations
$R_z(q_1, \theta_1)$	$T(q_1) - S^{\dagger}(q_1) - H(q_1) - Z(q_1) - ...$
$R_z(q_2, \theta_2)$	$H(q_2) - Y(q_2) - X(q_2) - H(q_2) - ...$
...	...
$R_z(q_n, \theta_n)$	$S(q_n) - X(q_n) - T(q_n) - T^{\dagger}(q_n) - ...$

Table 2: Parallel rotations cannot be executed simultaneously on a hardware with primitive operations, unless there are enough SIMD regions to accommodate them.

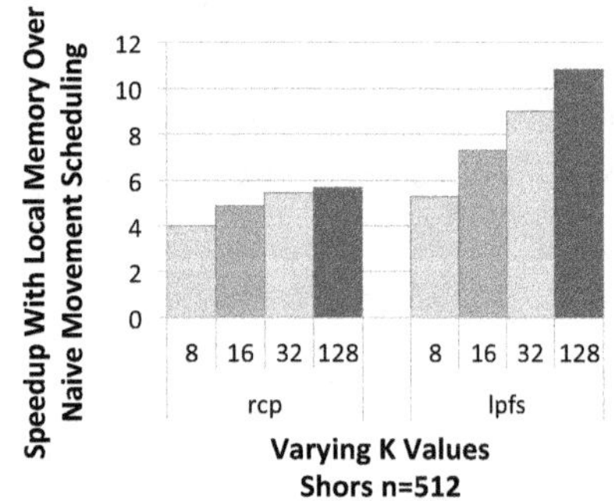

Figure 9: Shor's speedups as scheduled with a communication-aware scheduler on a Multi-SIMD architecture with local memories. High numbers of rotations cause long serial threads of operations to each execute on a separate SIMD region, thus getting better gains with higher k.

that even with added qubits for error correction, the architecture is able to cope and perform well.

Shor's showed a greater sensitivity to the number of SIMD regions available (k). The reason for this can be traced to the large number of rotation operations that exists in this code. These rotation operations can theoretically execute at the same time because they are on distinct qubits, except for the fact that practically they need to be decomposed into primitive, standard operations (as described in 3.1). This can prohibit the parallelization of operations unless more SIMD regions are created to accommodate them, as illustrated in Table. 2. Since many of these rotations were not inlined into the code, to keep the size manageable, they remain as black-boxes in the course-grained schedule. That causes the scheduler to allocate a separate region to each, effectively increasing the need for these regions. In Fig. 9, we show how the speedups vary with k for this benchmark.

6. Related and Future Work

This paper builds on several important previous studies relating to SIMD parallelism [5, 24, 39], ancilla preparation [19, 23], and quantum architecture [5, 30, 47]. Our work is the first to use a complete compiler infrastructure to discover this parallelism, allowing us to evaluate a non-trivial set of benchmarks (previous work focused almost exclusively on Shor's and Grover's, or other small quantum circuits). It is also the first to incorporate data movement analysis and optimizations within the compiler framework established.

Some prior work has explored optimization of execution latencies with SIMD architectures, but in a more limited context. Chi *et.al.* [5] proposed a SIMD architecture based on the technology of *electron spins on liquid helium*. For a quantum carry-lookahead adder circuit, they evaluated pipelining of ancilla preparation for CNOT and Toffoli gates to reduce latency, and optimization of width of SIMD regions to reduce area requirements. Our work builds on this model, with the implementation of a complete compiler and the study of a much larger and more diverse benchmark suite.

Schuchman *et.al.* [39] identify a high-level parallelism pertaining to specific quantum tasks of *uncomputation* (analogous to garbage collection for qubits) and propose a multi-core architecture to minimize latency and expensive inter-core communication during their execution. This kind of parallelism fits well into our Multi-SIMD model; it can be easily extended to support the proposed multiple cores. Some degree of uncomputation already exists in the compiled code of our benchmarks and is naturally parallelized by our model, and more can be added in the future to reclaim unused qubits.

The SIMD regions in our architecture are well-suited for a commonly used class of error-correction codes known as concatenated codes [1, 42]. A new class of ensemble codes, known as surface codes [17], have the potential of lowering ECC overhead for very large problems. Future research will explore whether surface code operations are amenable to SIMD parallelism.

7. Conclusion

We have proposed a Multi-SIMD architectural target for this compiler that incorporates practical physical constraints in quantum computing technology. To fully exploit its computational power, our work has also developed a scalable compiler that uses deep analysis to create logical schedules that enable parallelism and minimize communication. Largely as a result of SIMD parallelism, efficient communication and fine-grained data locality, we achieve speedups over our sequential baseline of 2.3X to 9.8X. Since quantum error correction can have overhead exponential in program execution time [1, 35, 42], these speedups can be even more significant than they appear, because they offer important leverage in allowing complex QC programs to complete with manageable levels of QECC. The source for ScaffCC and benchmarks is available on GitHub at https://github.com/ajavadia/ScaffCC.git.

Acknowledgments

This work was funded in part by NSF PHY-1415537. Many researchers have contributed to our benchmarks, including John Black, Lukas Svec, Aram Harrow, Amlan Chakrabarti, Chen-Fu Chiang, Oana Catu and Mohammad Javad Dousti.

References

[1] P. Aliferis and A. Cross. Subsystem fault tolerance with the Bacon-Shor code. *arXiv preprint quant-ph/0610063*, 2006.

[2] A. Ambainis, A. M. Childs, B. W. Reichardt, R. Spalek, and S. Zhang. Any AND-OR formula of size N can be evaluated in time $N^{1/2+o(1)}$ on a quantum computer. In *Proceedings of the 48th Annual IEEE Symposium on Foundations of Computer Science*, FOCS '07. IEEE Computer Society, 2007. ISBN 0-7695-3010-9.

[3] B. Blinov, D. Moehring, L.-M. Duan, and C. Monroe. Observation of entanglement between a single trapped atom and a single photon. *Nature*, 428(6979):153–157, 2004.

[4] S. Cavallar, B. Dodson, A. Lenstra, W. Lioen, P. Montgomery, B. Murphy, H. te Riele, K. Aardal, J. Gilchrist, G. Guillerm, P. Leyland, J. Marchand, F. Morain, A. Muffett, C. Putnam, and P. Zimmermann. Factorization of a 512–bit RSA modulus. In B. Preneel, editor, *Advances in Cryptology – EUROCRYPT 2000*, volume 1807 of *Lecture Notes in Computer Science*, pages 1–18. Springer Berlin Heidelberg, 2000. ISBN 978-3-540-67517-4.

[5] E. Chi, S. A. Lyon, and M. Martonosi. Tailoring quantum architectures to implementation style: a quantum computer for mobile and persistent qubits. In *Proceedings of the 34th Annual International Symposium on Computer Architecture*, ISCA '07. ACM, 2007. ISBN 978-1-59593-706-3.

[6] J. Chiaverini, D. Leibfried, T. Schaetz, M. Barrett, R. Blakestad, J. Britton, W. Itano, J. Jost, E. Knill, C. Langer, R. Ozeri, and D. J. Wineland. Realization of quantum error correction. *Nature*, 432 (7017):602–605, 2004.

[7] A. M. Childs, R. Cleve, E. Deotto, E. Farhi, S. Gutmann, and D. A. Spielman. Exponential algorithmic speedup by a quantum walk. In *Proceedings of the Thirty-Fifth Annual ACM Symposium on Theory of Computing*, STOC '03. ACM, 2003. ISBN 1-58113-674-9.

[8] I. Chuang. Quantum architectures: qasm2circ. URL `http://www.media.mit.edu/quanta/qasm2circ/`.

[9] J. I. Cirac and P. Zoller. Quantum computations with cold trapped ions. *Phys. Rev. Lett.*, 74:4091–4094, May 1995.

[10] D. Copsey, M. Oskin, F. Impens, T. Metodiev, A. Cross, F. T. Chong, I. L. Chuang, and J. Kubiatowicz. Toward a scalable, silicon-based quantum computing architecture. *Selected Topics in Quantum Electronics, IEEE Journal of*, 9(6):1552–1569, 2003.

[11] D. P. L. A. Craik, N. M. Linke, T. P. Harty, C. J. Ballance, D. M. Lucas, A. M. Steane, and D. T. C. Allcock. Microwave control electrodes for scalable, parallel, single-qubit operations in a surface-electrode ion trap, August 2013. URL `http://arxiv.org/pdf/1308.2078.pdf`.

[12] D. P. DiVincenzo. The physical implementation of quantum computation. *Fortschritte der Physik*, 48(9-11):771–783, 2000. ISSN 1521-3978.

[13] J. Garcıa-Ripoll, P. Zoller, and J. Cirac. Speed optimized two-qubit gates with laser coherent control techniques for ion trap quantum computing. *Phys. Rev. Lett*, 91(15):157901, 2003.

[14] M. Gebhart, B. A. Maher, K. E. Coons, J. Diamond, P. Gratz, M. Marino, N. Ranganathan, B. Robatmili, A. Smith, J. Burrill, S. W. Keckler, D. Burger, and K. S. McKinley. An evaluation of the TRIPS computer system. In *Proceedings of the Fourteenth International Conference on Architectural Support for Programming Languages and Operating Systems*. ACM, Mar. 2009.

[15] L. K. Grover. A fast quantum mechanical algorithm for database search. In *Proceedings of the Twenty-Eighth Annual ACM Symposium on Theory of Computing*, STOC '96, 1996. ISBN 0-89791-785-5.

[16] S. Hallgren. Fast quantum algorithms for computing the unit group and class group of a number field. In H. N. Gabow and R. Fagin, editors, *STOC*. ACM, 2005. ISBN 1-58113-960-8.

[17] C. Horsman, A. G. Fowler, S. Devitt, and R. V. Meter. Surface code quantum computing by lattice surgery. *New Journal of Physics*, 14 (12):123011, 2012.

[18] N. Isailovic. *An investigation into the realities of a quantum datapath*. PhD thesis, University of California, Berkeley, 2010.

[19] N. Isailovic, M. Whitney, Y. Patel, and J. Kubiatowicz. Running a quantum circuit at the speed of data. In *ACM SIGARCH Computer Architecture News*, volume 36, pages 177–188. IEEE Computer Society, 2008.

[20] A. JavadiAbhari, A. Faruque, M. J. Dousti, L. Svec, O. Catu, A. Chakrabati, C.-F. Chiang, S. Vanderwilt, J. Black, F. Chong, M. Martonosi, M. Suchara, K. Brown, M. Pedram, and T. Brun. Scaffold: Quantum programming language. Technical report, Princeton University, 2012.

[21] A. JavadiAbhari, S. Patil, D. Kudrow, J. Heckey, A. Lvov, F. Chong, and M. Martonosi. ScaffCC: A framework for compilation and analysis of quantum computing programs. *ACM International Conference on Computing Frontiers (CF 2014)*, May 2014.

[22] M. Johanning, A. Braun, N. Timoney, V. Elman, W. Neuhauser, and C. Wunderlich. Individual addressing of trapped ions and coupling of motional and spin states using RF radiation. *Phys. Rev. Lett.*, 102: 073004, Feb 2009.

[23] N. C. Jones, R. Van Meter, A. G. Fowler, P. L. McMahon, J. Kim, T. D. Ladd, and Y. Yamamoto. Layered architecture for quantum computing. *Physical Review X*, 2(3):031007, 2012.

[24] J. Kim, S. Pau, Z. Ma, H. McLellan, J. Gates, A. Kornblit, R. E. Slusher, R. M. Jopson, I. Kang, and M. Dinu. System design for large-scale ion trap quantum information processor. *Quantum Information & Computation*, 5(7):515–537, 2005.

[25] V. Kliuchnikov, D. Maslov, and M. Mosca. SQCT: Single qubit circuit toolkit. URL `https://code.google.com/p/sqct/`.

[26] C. Lattner and V. Adve. LLVM: a compilation framework for lifelong program analysis and transformation. In *Code Generation and Optimization, 2004. CGO 2004. International Symposium on*, pages 75–86, 2004.

[27] D. Leibfried, B. DeMarco, V. Meyer, D. Lucas, M. Barrett, J. Britton, B. J. WM Itano, C. Langer, and D. T Rosenband. Experimental demonstration of a robust, high-fidelity geometric two ion-qubit phase gate. *Nature*, 422(6930):412–415, 2003.

[28] F. Magniez, M. Santha, and M. Szegedy. Quantum algorithms for the triangle problem. In *Proceedings of the Sixteenth annual ACM-SIAM Symposium on Discrete Algorithms*, SODA '05, pages 1109–1117, 2005. ISBN 0-89871-585-7.

[29] T. Metodi, D. Thaker, A. Cross, F. T. Chong, and I. L. Chuang. Scheduling physical operations in a quantum information processor. *Proceedings for the SPIE Defense & Security symposium, Orlando, FL, April*, 2006.

[30] T. S. Metodi, D. D. Thaker, and A. W. Cross. A quantum logic array microarchitecture: Scalable quantum data movement and computation. In *MICRO*, pages 305–318. IEEE Computer Society, 2005. ISBN 0-7695-2440-0.

[31] C. Monroe, D. Meekhof, B. King, W. Itano, and D. Wineland. Demonstration of a fundamental quantum logic gate. *Physical Review Letters*, 75(25):4714, 1995.

[32] M. Mosca. Quantum algorithms. In R. A. Meyers, editor, *Encyclopedia of Complexity and Systems Science*, pages 7088–7118. Springer New York, 2009. ISBN 978-0-387-75888-6.

[33] M. A. Nielsen and I. L. Chuang. *Quantum computation and quantum information*. Cambridge university press, 2010.

[34] N. I. of Standards and Technology. *FIPS PUB 180-4: Secure Hash Standard (SHS)*. U.S. Department of Commerce, 2012.

[35] M. Oskin, F. Chong, and I. Chuang. A practical architecture for reliable quantum computers. *Computer*, 35(1):79–87, 2002. ISSN 0018-9162.

[36] C. Ospelkaus, U. Warring, Y. Colombe, K. R. Brown, J. M. Amini, D. Leibfried, and D. J. Wineland. Microwave quantum logic gates for trapped ions. *Nature*, 476:181–184, 2011.

[37] M. Riebe, H. Häffner, C. Roos, W. Hänsel, J. Benhelm, G. Lancaster, T. Körber, C. Becher, F. Schmidt-Kaler, and D. James. Deterministic quantum teleportation with atoms. *Nature*, 429(6993):734–737, 2004.

[38] F. Schmidt-Kaler, H. Häffner, M. Riebe, S. Gulde, G. P. Lancaster, T. Deuschle, C. Becher, C. F. Roos, J. Eschner, and R. Blatt. Realiza-

tion of the Cirac–Zoller controlled-NOT quantum gate. *Nature*, 422 (6930):408–411, 2003.

[39] E. Schuchman and T. N. Vijaykumar. A program transformation and architecture support for quantum uncomputation. *SIGARCH Comput. Archit. News*, 34(5):252–263, Oct. 2006. ISSN 0163-5964.

[40] C. M. Shappert, J. T. Merrill, K. R. Brown, J. M. Amini, C. Volin, S. C. Doret, H. Hayden, C.-S. Pai, and A. W. Harter. Spatially uniform single-qubit gate operations with near-field microwaves and composite pulse compensation. *New Journal of Physics*, 15(083053), 2013.

[41] P. W. Shor. Algorithms for quantum computation: discrete logarithms and factoring. In *Foundations of Computer Science, 1994 Proceedings., 35th Annual Symposium on*, pages 124–134. IEEE, 1994.

[42] A. Steane. Error correcting codes in quantum theory. *Physical Review Letters*, 77(5):793–797, 1996.

[43] A. M. Steane. Active stabilization, quantum computation, and quantum state synthesis. *Phys. Rev. Lett.*, 78:2252–2255, Mar 1997.

[44] K. Svore, A. Aho, A. Cross, I. Chuang, and I. Markov. A layered software architecture for quantum computing design tools. *Computer*, 39(1):74–83, 2006. ISSN 0018-9162.

[45] S. Swanson, A. Schwerin, M. Mercaldi, A. Petersen, A. Putnam, K. Michelson, M. Oskin, and S. J. Eggers. The WaveScalar architecture. *ACM Trans. Comput. Syst.*, 25(2):4:1–4:54, May 2007. ISSN 0734-2071.

[46] M. B. Taylor, W. Lee, J. Miller, D. Wentzlaff, I. Bratt, B. Greenwald, H. Hoffmann, P. Johnson, J. Kim, J. Psota, A. Saraf, N. Shnidman, V. Strumpen, M. Frank, S. Amarasinghe, and A. Agarwal. Evaluation of the Raw Microprocessor: An Exposed-Wire-Delay Architecture for ILP and Streams. In *Proceedings of the 31st Annual International Symposium on Computer Architecture*, ISCA '04, pages 2–. IEEE Computer Society, 2004. ISBN 0-7695-2143-6.

[47] D. D. Thaker, T. S. Metodi, A. W. Cross, I. L. Chuang, and F. T. Chong. Quantum memory hierarchies: Efficient designs to match available parallelism in quantum computing. In *ISCA*, pages 378–390. IEEE Computer Society, 2006. ISBN 0-7695-2608-X.

[48] J. D. Whitfield, J. Biamonte, and A. Aspuru-Guzik. Simulation of electronic structure Hamiltonians using quantum computers. *Molecular Physics*, 109(5):735, 2010.

[49] M. G. Whitney, N. Isailovic, Y. Patel, and J. Kubiatowicz. A fault tolerant, area efficient architecture for shor's factoring algorithm. In *Proceedings of the 36th annual international symposium on Computer architecture*, ISCA '09, pages 383–394, New York, NY, USA, 2009. ACM. ISBN 978-1-60558-526-0.

[50] D. Wineland, C. Monroe, W. Itano, B. King, D. Leibfried, D. Meekhof, C. Myatt, and C. Wood. Experimental primer on the trapped ion quantum computer. *Spectroscopy*, 7:8, 1998.

[51] T. Yang and A. Gerasoulis. PYRROS: static task scheduling and code generation for message passing multiprocessors. In *Proceedings of the 6th ACM International Conference on Supercomputing*, pages 428–437, 1992.

[52] T. Yang and A. Gerasoulis. List scheduling with and without communication delays. *Parallel Comput.*, 19(12):1321–1344, Dec. 1993. ISSN 0167-8191.

Kinetic Dependence Graphs *

M. Amber Hassaan
Dept. of Electrical and Computer Engineering
The University of Texas at Austin
m.a.hassaan@utexas.edu

Donald Nguyen Keshav Pingali
Dept. of Computer Science
The University of Texas at Austin
ddn@cs.utexas.edu, pingali@cs.utexas.edu

Abstract

Task graphs or dependence graphs are used in runtime systems to schedule tasks for parallel execution. In problem domains such as dense linear algebra and signal processing, dependence graphs can be generated from a program by static analysis. However, in emerging problem domains such as graph analytics, the set of tasks and dependences between tasks in a program are complex functions of runtime values and cannot be determined statically. In this paper, we introduce a novel approach for exploiting parallelism in such programs. This approach is based on a data structure called the *kinetic dependence graph* (KDG), which consists of a dependence graph together with update rules that incrementally update the graph to reflect changes in the dependence structure whenever a task is completed.

We have implemented a simple programming model that allows programmers to write these applications at a high level of abstraction, and a runtime within the Galois system [15] that builds the KDG automatically and executes the program in parallel. On a suite of programs that are difficult to parallelize otherwise, we have obtained speedups of up to 33 on 40 cores, out-performing third-party implementations in many cases.

Categories and Subject Descriptors: D.3.3 [Programming Languages]: Concurrent programming structures.

Keywords: ordered algorithms; kinetic dependence graph; stable-source and unstable-source algorithms;

1. Introduction

A task graph is a directed acyclic graph (DAG) in which nodes represent computational tasks that must be performed atomically and edges represent dependences between tasks. A node without any predecessors in the task graph is called a *source*, and the corresponding task can be scheduled for execution on any free processor. When a task has completed, the corresponding node and its incident edges are removed from the graph, potentially creating new sources. Program execution terminates when the task graph becomes empty.

In some application areas such as dense numerical linear algebra, task graphs can be constructed statically because tasks and dependences are independent of runtime data values. Restructuring compilers can sometimes build the task graph automatically by analyzing the text of the program [23]. Static analyses can be fragile, so systems like DAGuE [38, 39], Intel CnC [8] and TBB [20] allow the programmer to explicitly specify tasks and dependences. Other systems like SMPSs, OpenMP 4.0, and XKaapi [16, 32, 33] require the programmer to specify the read and write sets (*i.e.* accesses to elements of shared data) of each task, and the system builds the task graph using this information. Finally, fork-join style programming models like Cilk [7, 10] implicitly specify a task graph through the parent-child relationship between a task and its children.

Conventional task graphs are not adequate for many applications, particularly in problem domains like graph analytics, time-based simulations and unstructured mesh computations. Applications considered in this paper include (i) asynchronous variational integrators (AVI), which are used in computational mechanics and in graphics for solving complicated contact mechanics problems [27] like simulating the tying of ribbons and the crushing of rabbits in a trash compactor [1, 18], (ii) discrete-event simulation (DES) [9], (iii) the simulation of collisions between a set of moving bodies like billiard balls [2, 18], and (iv) graph analytics algorithms such as Breadth-First Search (BFS), Minimum-weight Spanning Tree (MST), and tree traversals. The inadequacy of conventional task graphs for these applications arises from the fact that the dependence graph computed from a particular program state may not remain valid after a task has executed because new tasks may have been created and dependences between existing tasks may have changed. In particular, the following issues may arise upon executing a task.

* The work presented in this paper has been supported by the National Science Foundation grants CNS 1111766, CCF 1218568, XPS 1337281, and CNS 1406355.

ASPLOS '15, March 14–18, 2015, Istanbul, Turkey..
Copyright © 2015 ACM 978-1-4503-2835-7/15/03... $15.00.
http://dx.doi.org/10.1145/2694344.2694363

1. A new task may be created that must be executed before some or all of the pending tasks. The execution order of tasks in these applications is problem-specific and input dependent. One example is Discrete-Event Simulation (DES), in which events have time-stamps based upon simulation time, and must appear to have been processed in time-stamp order to preserve causality. Executing tasks in task creation order or parent-child order, as is done in existing systems, may be incorrect.
2. Dependences between pending tasks may have changed. This happens when read and write sets of a task depend on values modified by execution of another task. Examples discussed in this paper include Kruskal's minimum-weight spanning tree algorithm and sparse matrix factorization. Most existing systems do not support this feature.
3. An incoming edge may be created to a source in the dependence graph. This may result from either of the behaviors mentioned above. This implies that it is not always safe to schedule multiple source from the dependence graph in parallel. We call algorithms with this property *unstable-source*. Examples include DES and asynchronous algorithms for simulating collisions.

These issues are not a concern in sequential implementations of these algorithms because they typically use a priority queue to organize tasks and execute tasks one at a time in priority order. For example, sequential DES implementations process events in increasing time order by maintaining a priority queue of events sorted by their time-stamp; it can be shown that it is correct to process the earliest event, which is a safe source in the DAG. These kinds of algorithms are called *ordered* algorithms in the TAO classification of algorithms [34] because the execution of the program must respect the priority order between tasks (in contrast, tasks in *unordered* algorithms can be executed in any order without violating program semantics)[1].

Some of these applications have been parallelized previously by other researchers using problem-specific techniques: for example, AVI has been parallelized by Huang *et al.* [19] using "edge-flipping" DAGs, described in Sections 2.1 and 4.1, but this technique cannot be used for any of the other problems considered in this paper. In the Galois project, we have shown that optimistic or speculative parallelization [11, 36] can be used effectively for unordered algorithms like Delaunay mesh refinement [31]; for ordered algorithms, the overheads of optimistic parallelization appear to outweigh benefits, as we show in this paper.

In this paper, we present a generalization of the task graph called the *kinetic dependence graph* (KDG), and show that it can be used to systematically parallelize ordered algorithms in a problem independent way. Problem-specific techniques used in the literature to parallelize these applications emerge as optimizations of the general KDG-based approach that

[1] Ordered and unordered algorithms are similar to hyperbolic and elliptic partial differential equations respectively in the theory of PDEs [22].

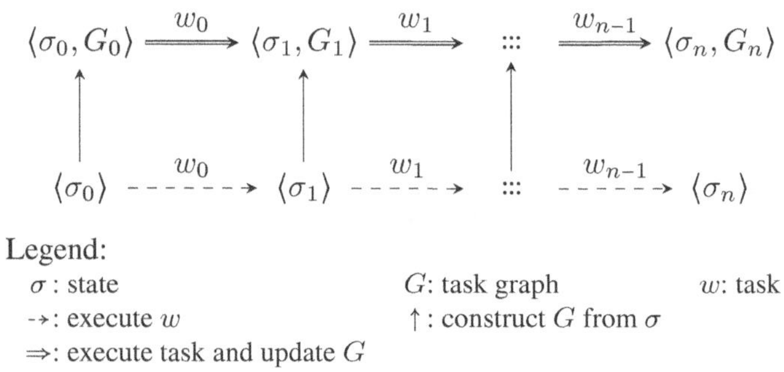

Figure 1: Kinetic dependence graph approach

exploit problem structure to reduce KDG overheads, and can easily be incorporated into our general approach. For example, in AVI, all sources in the task graph are guaranteed to be safe, which simplifies the implementation. We call such algorithms *stable-source*.

Figure 1 is a pictorial representation of how the KDG is used for parallelization. A KDG has three components: (i) a task graph, (ii) a predicate called the *safe source test* for finding tasks that can be safely executed in parallel, and (iii) an *update rule* that specifies how the task graph should be updated incrementally when a task is completed. Given a program and an initial program state σ_0, we build the initial task graph G_0 at runtime, use the safe source test to select a task w_0, and execute that task to produce the new program state σ_1. Applying the (incremental) update rule to G_0 produces the new task graph G_1, which is the task graph that would have been produced from state σ_1, had we rebuilt the task graph from scratch[2]. Program execution terminates when the task graph becomes empty. The safe source test can be used to find multiple tasks that can be performed safely in parallel; the underlying system ensures that the resulting execution is serializable, i.e., the final state is equivalent to the state that would have been produced by executing these tasks serially. Conventional parallelization using task graphs is a special case of the KDG approach in which all sources of the task graph are safe sources, and the update rule just deletes the completed task and its associated edges from the task graph.

We have implemented KDGs for shared-memory machines within the Galois system [15]. Application programmers write sequential descriptions of ordered algorithms, while the Galois system builds and updates the KDG at runtime, yielding a correct and efficient parallelization. The programming model for these sequential descriptions is explained in Section 3. Our experimental results show speedups of up to 33 on a 40 core platform, demonstrating that the KDG approach can deliver substantial speedups from programs written at a high level of abstraction.

The rest of this paper is organized as follows. In Section 2, we introduce the KDG informally using AVI as the

[2] Strictly speaking, G_1 can be conservative in the sense that it may have more dependence edges.

```
Mesh M

struct Update {
  Element* elem; double t; // time stamp;
};
WorkList<Update> Q;
for(Element* e: M.elements())
  Q.push(Update(e, e->timestamp))

foreach (Update up ∈ Q) orderedby up.t:
  Vec initial;
  for (Vertex v: M.vertices(up.elem)):
    initial.push(v.data);
  Vec updated = AVI_update(up.elem, initial);
  int i = 0;
  for (Vertex v: M.vertices(up.elem)):
    v.data = updated[i++];

  up.elem->timestamp += up.elem->step;

  if(up.elem->timestamp < endtime)
    Q.push(Update(up.elem, up.elem->timestamp));
```

Figure 2: Asynchronous Variational Integrator (simplified)

running example. In Section 3, we describe the programming model and the KDG formally. We also give general procedures that can be used to construct the KDG for any application in this programming model, and show how to use the KDG for parallelization. In Section 3.6, we describe optimized KDG versions that can be used for applications with special structure. In Section 4, we describe the rest of the ordered applications considered in this paper. Experimental results are presented in Section 5. In these results, we compare the performance of the KDG approach with the performance of third-party implementations for our benchmark problems, if they are available. Related work is discussed in Section 6.

2. Informal introduction to KDGs

In this section, we use asynchronous variational integrators (AVI) to motivate and introduce the KDG.

2.1 AVI: Example Application

AVI is a finite-element method for solving PDEs. The domain of interest is discretized into a mesh of elements (triangles), such as the mesh shown in the Figure 3(a). When an element is updated, values stored at its vertices, e.g., position, force, velocity, etc., are updated. In a traditional explicit-time finite-element simulation, simulation time advances at a uniform rate for all mesh elements. In AVI, in contrast, elements advance in time with different time-steps.

In a sequential implementation, elements are updated in strict time order by maintaining a priority queue of elements and processing elements in time order. Figure 2 shows an outline of AVI; $t(w)$ is the time at which element w should execute. One way to parallelize AVI is to advance time in lock-step over the entire mesh; when the global clock is at time τ, all elements whose scheduled time or time-stamp are τ are processed in parallel before time is advanced (if some of these elements share vertices, independent subsets are processed in rounds). In this paper, we call this synchronous or *level-by-level* execution. This is a common parallelization technique for problems like breadth-first search in power-

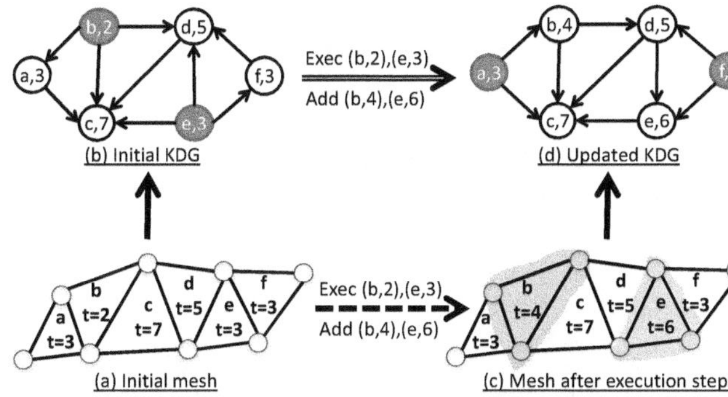

Figure 3: Using the KDG to parallelize AVI

```
AVI-BuildTaskGraph(Tasks W, TaskGraph G):
  for (Task w ∈ W):
    G.addNode(w)
  for (Node w ∈ G):
    for (Node w' ∈ G):
      if (M.vertices(w) ∩ M.vertices(w') ≠ ∅):
        if ((t(w) < t(w')) ∨ (t(w) = t(w') ∧ w ≺ w')):
          G.addEdge(w → w')
        else:
          G.addEdge(w' → w)

AVI-ExecAndUpdate(Task wP, TaskGraph G):
  //update state of corresponding element and
  //discover new tasks
  Task wC = Execute(wP)
  if (t(wC) < endtime):
    G.addNode(wC)
    //assert M.vertices(wP) = M.vertices(wC)
    for (Node n ∈ G.neighbors(wP)):
      if (t(wC) < t(n) ∨ (t(wC) = t(n) ∧ wC ≺ n):
        G.addEdge(wC → n)
      else:
        G.addEdge(n → wC)
  //as in conventional task graphs,
  //remove node and incident edges
  G.removeNode(wP)

AVI-SafeSourceTest: //any source is safe source
```

Figure 4: KDG Procedures for AVI

law graphs [26], but it is not useful for AVI, as we show in Figure 5, because few elements have the same time-stamp.

2.2 Asynchronous parallel execution of AVI

To exploit more parallelism, elements with different time-stamps must be processed concurrently, an approach that we call *asynchronous* parallel execution. One possible approach is to build a task graph and execute sources in parallel. Unfortunately, when tasks can create other tasks, it is not always safe to execute sources of the task graph in parallel.

As an example, consider Figure 3(b), which shows the task graph for AVI for the mesh in Figure 3(a). It has a node for the pending update to each element, and it has a dependence edge $(w_1 \rightarrow w_2)$ if the elements represented by tasks w_1 and w_2 have a vertex in common and the time-stamp of w_1 is less than the time-stamp of w_2. If they have the same time-stamp, as tasks $(e, 3)$ and $(f, 3)$ do, the tie is broken using some total order $\prec$ on tasks, such as the lexicographical order on element names. Procedure

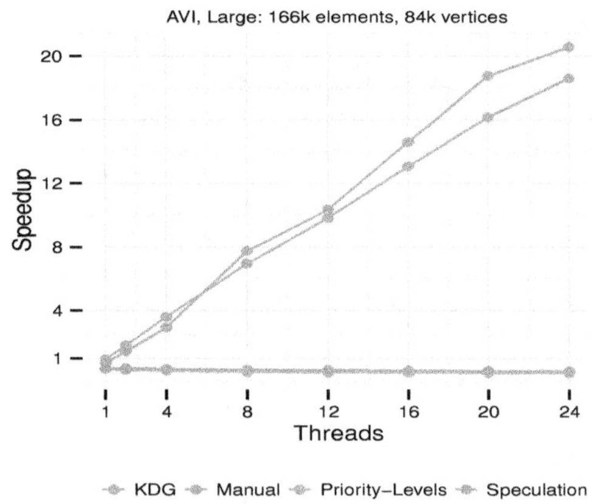

Figure 5: Speedup of different parallel implementations for AVI relative to an optimized serial implementation

`AVI-BuildTaskGraph` in Figure 4 shows pseudocode for building this graph.

There are two sources in the task graph, task $(b, 2)$ and task $(e, 3)$. It is safe to execute task $(b, 2)$ since it has the lowest time-stamp among all tasks in the system, but executing task $(e, 3)$ in parallel with $(b, 2)$ can result in an incorrect execution because, in principle, $(b, 2)$ could create a new task $(c, 2.5)$ that reads and writes the same vertex as task $(e, 3)$, and this new task should be executed before task $(e, 3)$ even though $(e, 3)$ is a source in Figure 3(b).

Although task graphs are not sufficient for this application, examination of the AVI code reveals that if a task w_P (parent task) is executed, it creates at most one new task w_C (child task), which must have a later time-stamp; also both w_P and w_C read and write the same portion of the mesh. The net effect in the task graph of executing w_P is to replace w_P with w_C and to flip the directions of some incident edges due to the new time-stamp. The effect of executing task w_P can be reflected in a simple, local update to the task graph as shown in procedure `AVI-ExecAndUpdate` in Figure 4. We also note that procedure `AVI-ExecAndUpdate` in Figure 4 never adds an edge to source in the original task graph. We call this the *stable-source property*, and it is useful because it means that a source in the task graph can always be safely executed, just like in conventional task graphs. In Figure 3(b) therefore, it is safe to execute tasks b and e in parallel; the task graph is incrementally updated whenever a task is completed, producing the task graph shown in Figure 3(d) after both tasks are completed.

To summarize, the pseudocode of Figure 4, together with the application code, is an implementation of the abstract diagram in Figure 1 for the particular case of AVI. The vertical arrows in Figure 1 are implemented by procedure `AVI-BuildTaskGraph`, the safe source test is implemented by `AVI-SafeSourceTest`, the horizontal arrows at the bottom of the diagram are implemented by the application code, and the horizontal arrows at the top of the diagram are implemented by procedure `AVI-ExecAndUpdate`, which invokes the application code.

2.3 Experimental results

Figure 5 shows experimental results that demonstrate the performance potential of using the KDG for parallelization. All experiments were performed on an Intel Xeon E7540 with 24 cores running at 2 GHz. To provide a sequential baseline, we implemented an AVI code using a priority queue to schedule tasks. To provide a reference parallel implementation, we implemented the AVI-specific edge-flipping DAG approach of Huang *et al.* [19]. In Figure 5, we call this implementation Manual. The line labeled KDG shows the performance our KDG-based runtime, described in more detail in Section 3; we see that this general and automatic parallelization approach achieves performance comparable to the application-specific approach of Huang *et al.*

In order to study existing parallelization schemes for ordered tasks, we implemented (i) a speculation-based executor, based on the work by Kulkarni et al. [25], which generalized the idea of out-of-order execution and in-order commit from TLS [36, 37], and (ii) a level-by-level executor. Figure 5 shows that thread-level speculation does not perform well for AVI. In most of our applications, including AVI, tasks take a very short amount of time, and most of the execution time is spent waiting on the commit queue, which limits scalability. More sophisticated commit mechanisms combined with hardware support may make speculation a viable parallelization strategy for our applications, but this remains to be seen. Figure 5 also shows the performance of the level-by-level executor (Priority-Levels) is poor due to little parallelism per level and large number of levels. For the input mesh used here, we observed that the level-by-level executor created 1.47×10^7 different levels, and the average number of elements per level was just 1.38.

3. Programming model and the KDG

Section 3.1 introduces the programming model. Section 3.3 describes the KDG formally. We describe two different approaches for parallelizing programs using the KDG. The first approach (§3.4) builds the KDG explicitly and updates it incrementally during execution. The second approach (§3.5) maintains the KDG implicitly by keeping sufficient metadata to find only sources in the KDG. These two approaches make different tradeoffs, as explained later. In our current system, these approaches are implemented by pieces of code called *executors*, which are concurrent schedulers based on different implementations of the KDG, and incorporate a few optimizations described in Section 3.6. Application programmers use flags in their code to choose an executor and the desired optimizations. We show the code for AVI in Section 3.7 to describe the programming interface.

3.1 Programming model

Unlike other task-based parallelization systems, such as OpenMP 4.0, XKaapi, and SMPSs, where the user invokes tasks, we provide *ordered foreach* loop to express parallelism in an ordered algorithm. Ordered foreach is an ordered set-iterator [34], which iterates over a set of work items ordered by some priority metric. In the AVI pseudocode, shown in Figure 2, the *foreach-orderedby* statement shows an example of the ordered set iterator. The ordered foreach iterates over Q, to which new elemental updates are added inside the loop body. The *orderedby* clause of the ordered foreach specifies the priority ordering of tasks, which in the case of AVI is the timestamp of an elemental update. A *task* under this programming model is an iteration of ordered foreach loop. The loop body can contain code that reads or modifies shared data. The programmer must use concurrent data structures from Galois library [15, 34], which are thread-safe and contain hooks into our runtime so that the runtime can monitor accesses of a task (iteration) to shared data. The shared data structure in the case of AVI is the mesh M, and the values on its vertices are updated inside the loop body. Notice that this programming model is implicitly parallel: there are no threads, locks or barriers in the code. Also, serial code would look very similar, where instead of a an ordered foreach iterating over a worklist, the programmer would use a while loop iterating over a priority queue.

The execution model is similar to Galois [15, 34], where a main thread starts executing the serial portion of the code. Upon encountering the ordered foreach loop, the runtime will build a KDG internally, using the elements in the worklist and execute the safe sources from the KDG in parallel on a thread pool. An implicit barrier follows after the loop finishes and serial execution resumes from there.

Tasks under our programming model are iterations of the ordered foreach loop, which perform computation and read and write data locations such as the mesh in the AVI application. The set of global data locations read or written by a task is called the *rw-set* for that task (for AVI, the rw-set for a task (e, t) is the time-stamp of element e and its vertices). We require tasks to be *cautious*: a task must read all elements in its rw-set before it writes to any of them [34]. In our experience, this is not a significant restriction since many applications are naturally written like this while others can be transformed so that all the shared data is read before the first modification. Cautiousness is a useful property because the rw-set of a task can be determined by executing it up to the first global data structure write; since no updates are made to global data structures in this process, rw-sets can be computed without having to buffer or undo changes to global state.

The only requirement on the relative order in which tasks execute is that the final result should be identical to that obtained by executing the tasks atomically in the application-specific priority order, specified using the *orderedby* constraint on the iterator, such as the time-stamp order in the AVI code. This order is a total order, like time, in most applications, but it is useful to generalize it to a partial order to handle applications like tree traversals. We will assume that the order is specified by a function $t : W \to P$, where W is the domain of tasks for the application, and P is a partially ordered set $(T, \leq)$. One legal execution order is a sequential execution that always picks a task minimal in P from the worklist. Following standard notation, we will write $t(w_1) = t(w_2)$ if $t(w_1) \leq t(w_2) \wedge t(w_2) \leq t(w_1)$; this means that the priorities of the two tasks are the same. Relational operators such as $>$ and $\not>$ are defined similarly. If $t(w_1) < t(w_2)$, we will say that the priority of task w_1 is *earlier than* that of task w_2, and that the priority of task w_2 is *later than* that of task w_1.

We have implemented this programming model as a C++ template library. In Section 3.7, we describe its implementation in C++.

3.2 Program Properties

Program properties can be used to optimize the KDG implementation. In the following, we have identified some general properties found in many ordered programs. In §3.6, we describe how these properties can be used to optimize the KDG runtime. In §4, we discuss how sometimes problem-specific properties can be used to further customize the KDG implementation manually, in the user code.

An important class of algorithms are those for which every source in the KDG is a safe source.

DEFINITION 1. *An application is* **stable-source** *if every source in its KDG is a safe source.*

This property not only forms the basis of classical DAG-based scheduling but is also present in more complex applications, such as AVI, Kruskal's Minimum-weight Spanning Tree algorithm and Tree Traversals. Algorithms where not all sources are safe are called *unstable-source*. Examples are Discrete-Event Simulation (DES), and Asynchronous Collisions Simulation (Billiards).

Another important property is *monotonicity*. For example, in AVI, the time-stamp of a new task is always greater than the time-stamp of the parent task that created it. This property is defined below in a generalized form in which the new task may have the same priority as the parent task. Note that it applies even when priorities form a partial order.

DEFINITION 2. *An application is* **monotonic** *if whenever the execution of a task w_P creates task w_C, $t(w_P) \leq t(w_C)$.*

In conventional task graphs, the execution of a task does not change dependences between other existing tasks; i.e., the set of data locations that form the rw-set of a task is not a function of values updated by other tasks. We call this property *non-increasing rw-sets*.

DEFINITION 3. *An application has* **non-increasing rw-sets** *if the execution of a task does not introduce new locations in the rw-sets of other tasks.*

This property implies that dependences among existing tasks need not be recomputed during execution. Besides conventional task graphs, this property is observed the more complex applications considered in this paper such as AVI, DES and tree traversals. A counter-example of this property is Kruskal's MST algorithm, where rw-set of a task increases when components are merged. Notice that the property ignores the possibility of execution of a task causing locations to be removed from rw-set of other tasks. A stronger form of non-increasing rw-sets property called *structure-based rw-sets* is also seen in AVI, DES and traversals etc:

DEFINITION 4. *An application has* **structure-based rw-sets** *if the locations that comprise the rw-set of a task w_c are either (i) not a function of values updated by other tasks, or (ii) w_c is created by a parent task w_p and rw-set of w_c is a subset of w_p.*

This property allows the computation of the rw-set of a task correctly even while other tasks are being executed.

3.3 KDG

Given an application, let V be the domain of values, and let L be the set of abstract locations (for AVI, V might contain floating-point numbers and L might contain vertices, edges and elements for example). States are functions $\Sigma : L \to (V + L)^*$ (for example, in a minimal spanning tree (MST) computation, the abstract location for a weighted edge might contain the two end points of the edge and a value that is the edge weight). Tasks are functions from states to states $W : \Sigma \to \Sigma$. A task graph is an acyclic graph whose nodes correspond to some subset of W.

DEFINITION 5. *Given a domain of tasks W, a* task graph *is an acyclic directed graph $G = (V, E)$ where $V \subseteq W$, and $E \subseteq V \times V$.*

We let G_W denote the domain of task graphs for W.

DEFINITION 6. *Given a domain of tasks W, a* kinetic dependence graph *(KDG) is a three tuple $\langle G, P, U\rangle$ where*

- *$G : G_W$ is a task graph,*
- *$P : G_W \times \Sigma \times W \to \{true, false\}$ is a* safe source test, *and*
- *$U : G_W \times \Sigma \times W \to G_W \times \Sigma$ is an* update rule.

The safe source test P takes as input a task graph, the state of the computation, and a task, and returns true if the task is a safe source and can be executed in the current state of the computation. The update rule U takes as input a task graph, the state of the computation, and a task (which must be a safe source), and executes that task to update the task graph and the state. This update rule invokes the application code to execute task.

Not all triples $\langle G, P, U\rangle$ are semantically meaningful. KDGs of interest must satisfy two conditions called *safety* and *liveness*. Safety says that the safe source test and the update rule must be mutually consistent: applying the update rule repeatedly to the task graph never creates an incoming edge to a safe source. Liveness ensures forward progress: it says that if the task graph is non-empty, the safe source test must be true for at least one task of earliest priority. In the rest of the paper, we consider only KDGs that satisfy the safety and liveness properties.

- *Safety:* If w is a safe source in a KDG $\langle G, P, U\rangle$, the transitive closure of U applied to G never creates an incoming edge to w.
- *Liveness:* For any non-empty task graph G and state σ, the test $P(G, \sigma, w)$ must be true for at least one task w in G for which $t(w)$ is minimal among the tasks in G.

3.4 Explicit KDG Implementation

This section describes a general approach to parallelizing applications by maintaining a KDG explicitly. In the pseudocode, we use **for** to indicate standard sequential loops, **doall** to indicate parallel loops with independent iterations, and **foreach** to indicate parallel loops whose iterations may have overlapping reads and writes. Any implementation of a foreach loop must guarantee that iterations are serializable. In the loops in this paper, we use fine-grain locking to implement concurrent data structure operations by hand. A more general technique would be to use the Galois system [34].

Building the KDG: Given the initial set of tasks, we can compute the rw-set of each task by executing it up to the point in that task where the first write to a global data location occurs, keeping track of all reads to data locations. Given the rw-sets and priorities of all tasks, one can build the task graph. As in the case of AVI, some total order on tasks, such as the lexicographical order on task names, is used to break ties between tasks of the same priority.

Incrementally updating the KDG requires keeping track of the rw-sets of all tasks. It is convenient to think of the association between tasks and their rw-sets as a bipartite graph B in which the two sets of nodes are tasks and data locations; if location l is in the rw-set of a task w, there is an undirected edge (w, l) in graph B. Thus, the rw-set of task w is simply the set of its neighbors in B.

Procedure `General-BuildTaskGraph`, shown in Figure 6, builds the task graph G and the rw-set graph B for a set of tasks. This is a generalization of procedure AVI-BuildTaskGraph. In line 8 of the procedure AddTask, the rw-set is computed by executing task w to its fail-safe point, which is in respect to the state seen by w before the fail-safe point denoted by σ_w in the figure. In line 10, the neighbors of l in B are the tasks whose rw-sets contain location l.

Executing a task and updating the KDG: In Figure 6, procedure `General-Execute` executes a task w_P by invoking the application code, which reads and updates some subset of state denoted by σ_{w_P}. If new tasks are created, they are returned by the Execute method. Procedures `General-Execute` and `General-Update` then update the KDG. There are three kinds of updates that must be performed:

```
1  TaskGraph G
2  RWSets B
3  State σ
4
5  AddTask(Task w):
6    G.addNode(w)
7    B.addNode(w)
8    Locations RW = ComputeRWSet(w, σ_w)
9    for (Location l ∈ RW):
10     for (Task w_i ∈ B.neighbors(l)):
11       if ((t(w_i) < t(w))
12       ∨(t(w_i) ≯ t(w) ∧ w_i ≺ w):
13         G.addEdge(w_i → w)
14       else:
15         G.addEdge(w → w_i)
16      B.addEdge(w ↔ l)
17
18 RemoveTask(Task w):
19   G.removeNode(w)
20   B.removeNode(w)

22 General-BuildTaskGraph(Tasks T):
23   foreach (Task w ∈ T)
24     AddTask(w)
25
26 General-Execute(Task w_P):
27   w_P.newTasks = Execute(w_P, σ_{w_P})
28   w_P.neighbors = G.neighbors(w_P)
29   //subrule R
30   RemoveTask(w_P)
31
32 General-Update(Task w_P):
33   //subrule N
34   for (Task w ∈ w_P.neighbors):
35     RemoveTask(w)
36     AddTask(w) //recomputes rw-sets
37   //subrule A
38   for (Task w_C ∈ w_P.newTasks):
39     AddTask(w_C)

40 KDG-RNA-Executor(Tasks initial):
41   General-BuildTaskGraph(initial)
42   while (G.notEmpty()):
43     Tasks E = {}
44
45     //parallel phase 1
46     doall (Task w ∈ G.sources()):
47       //apply safe source test
48       if (P(G,σ,w)):
49         E = E ∪ {w}
50
51     //parallel phase 2
52     foreach (Task w ∈ E):
53       General-Execute(w)
54
55     //parallel phase 3
56     foreach (Task w ∈ E):
57       General-Update(w)
```

Figure 6: General procedures for Explicit KDG (KDG-RNA): initial construction, update and execution

- *Subrule Remove:* Nodes corresponding to w in the task graph G and the rw-set graph B must be removed, together with incident edges.
- *Subrule Neighbors:* Updates to the global state by w may change the rw-sets of some pending tasks. These tasks share state with w, and must be immediate neighbors of w in the task graph G. The rw-sets of these tasks must be recomputed, and edges in G and B must be updated to reflect these new sets.
- *Subrule Add:* New nodes and edges must be added to G and B for each new task created by the execution of w.

We will refer to this basline explicit KDG implementation as *KDG-RNA*, based on the above three subrules.

Parallel execution: We combine the basic KDG procedures into a parallel executor. The executor proceeds in rounds; each round contains three phases, which are executed in parallel and are separated by global barriers.

In the first phase (Figure 6 lines 46–49), the executor finds safe sources by applying the safe source test in parallel. The safe source test reads the global state σ but does not write to it, so this phase is completely data-parallel.

Phases 2 and 3 apply the procedures `General-Execute` and `General-Update` over all the safe sources.

In general, executing a task (line 27 in Figure 6), must not be done concurrently with computing the rw-set of other tasks (line 8), which is reachable via lines 36 and 39. This is because executing a task may update state that is read while computing the rw-set of another task (i.e., σ_{w_P} in line 27 and σ_w in line 8 are not disjoint). Performing all tasks executions first and then updating the KDG second avoids this problem. Section 3.6 shows how to exploit certain program properties that allow these two phases to be done concurrently.

In phase 2, executing safe sources (Figure 6 line 27) is data-parallel because sources have disjoint rw-sets, but removing tasks (Figure 6 line 30) requires some synchronization because multiple sources may share neighbors in both graphs.

Phase 3, which implements subrules N and A, can also be done in parallel as long as adding and removing nodes and edges of the task graph and rw-sets are properly synchronized. As stated earlier, we use simple atomic operations and fine-grained locking to implement these graph manipulations.

3.5 Implicit KDG Implementation

The cost of explicit KDG, described in Section 3.4, is that it maintains the association between tasks and their rw-sets (through graphs G and B). In this section, we describe an *implicit KDG* (IKDG) executor that finds KDG sources without building the graph G, or the rw-sets data structure B explicitly, but at the cost of having to compute rw-sets of tasks repeatedly.

Parallel execution proceeds in rounds, where each round consists of three parallel phases separated by global barriers.

Phase I: The runtime executes each task up to its first global write, and tries to mark all the locations in its rw-set with the ID of the task. Marks are updated atomically using primitives like compare-and-set (CAS instruction). A task with earlier priority overwrites the marks made by another task, so that at the end of the phase, each location stores the ID of the earliest priority task that accessed it.

Phase II: Each task w checks if its marks have been changed since the first phase. If so, there is another task that has an overlapping rw-set and has precedence. Otherwise, task w has precedence over all tasks whose rw-sets overlap with its own; therefore, the task is a source. The safe-source test is applied to such tasks, and the task is added to a work-list if it passes this test.

Phase III: Tasks in the work-list of safe-sources are executed in parallel, and all marks are reset to an unused value.

3.6 KDG optimizations

The baseline KDG implementations described above can be expensive for applications with fine-grained tasks that perform relatively simple operations. Therefore, it is crucial to identify opportunities to optimize the KDG implementation. Starting from the algorithmic properties specified by the user (introduced in §3.2), we can optimize the representation of the KDG and code required to maintain it. We can broadly group the optimizations in to following categories.

3.6.1 Windowing

Rather than compute the KDG for *all* tasks as is done in Figure 6, we can build the KDG for a subset of tasks, provided this subset forms a *prefix* of the set of tasks under priority ordering, i.e., if a task (w, t) with priority t is included in the subset, then all tasks with priority lesser than (or equal to) t are included in the subset. Pending tasks can be added to the window incrementally, as tasks in the window complete. We choose the size of the window adaptively: if threads lack work in the current window, the size of the next window is increased. Newly created tasks must be processed in a way that satisfies the prefix condition; for example, if $t_{\max}$ is the latest priority in the current window and a task of priority $t < t_{\max}$ is created, it must be processed within the current window.

This optimization can be applied to both the explicit and implicit KDG. It controls the cost of graphs G and B for explicit KDG, and the cost of repeatedly marking rw-sets for implicit KDG.

The level-by-level executor described in Section 2.1 can be viewed as a particular windowing strategy for the implicit KDG in which windows correspond to priority levels. Implementations of level-by-level execution usually assume that all sources with earliest priority are safe sources, an assumption that is satisfied by monotonic algorithms (Definition 2) such as BFS and AVI. Level-by-level execution is useful when the number of priority levels is small, as is the case for BFS on social network graphs.

3.6.2 Update Rule Optimizations

No-Adds: The execution of a task does not create new tasks, so subrule A can be eliminated.

Non-increasing RW-sets: The execution of a task does not add new elements to the rw-sets of other tasks, so subrule N can be eliminated.

No-Adds + Non-increasing RW-sets: When an application has non-increasing rw-sets and no new tasks are created during execution, the KDG executor can be simplified to a conventional task graph scheduler (update rule is subrule-R).

3.6.3 Removal of parallel phases and barriers

Stable-source: If the application is stable-source, all sources are safe sources and no safe source test is needed. In these applications, phase 1 of the explicit KDG executor can be eliminated, and the loop beginning on line 52 of Figure 6 and the one beginning on line 56 can be rewritten to iterate over sources in G. Similarly, phases II and III of IKDG implementation can be combined into one phase, after eliminating the safe-source test.

Local Safe-source test: In general, a safe source test $P(G, \sigma, w)$ is a function of the entirety of σ. For some applications like discrete event simulation, P is, at most, only a function of σ_w (the state accessed by task w). In this case, phase 1 and phase 2 of the KDG-RNA executor can be combined.

Structure-based RW-set: When an application has structure-driven rw-sets, the barrier between phase 2 and phase 3 of the KDG-RNA executor can also be eliminated. This is because the portion of σ needed for computing the rw-sets (line 8 in Figure 6) is not affected by the execution of other tasks (line 27), and the intervening global barrier can be eliminated. When the application is stable-source, the optimized executor is asynchronous, i.e., does not need multiple rounds.

Comments: In our current system, programmers must request these optimized KDG versions through flags indicating algorithmic properties. Compiler analysis of the application code can determine some of these algorithmic properties. If no algorithmic properties are specified, our runtime falls back to IKDG executor with windowing optimization as the default.

3.7 Example: Galois program for AVI

```
Mesh M; // Galois data structure

// 1. work item
struct Update {
  Element* elem; double t; // time stamp;
};
// 2. priority comparator
auto comparator = [&](const Update& u1, const Update& u2){
  return u1.t < u2.t;
};
// 3. visit RW sets (prefix of loop body)
auto visitRWsets = [&] (Update& up) {
  for (Vertex v: M.vertices(up.elem)
    Runtime::write(v); // intent to write
};
// 4. loop body
auto applyUpdate = [&] (Update& up, W& wlHandle) {
  Vcc initial;
  for (Vertex v: M.vertices(w.elem)):
    initial.push(v.data);
  Vec updated = AVI_update(up.elem, initial);
  int i = 0;
  for (Vertex v: M.vertices(w.elem)):
    v.data = updated[i++];

  up.elem->timestamp += up.elem->step;

  if(up.elem->timestamp < endtime)
    wlHandle.push(Update(up.elem, up.elem->timestamp));
};
// 5. initial set of work items
vector<Update> init;
for(Elcmcnt c: M.clcmcnts())
  init.push_back(Update(e, e->timestamp));

// 6. Ordered loop
Runtime::for_each_ordered(init.begin(), init.end(),
  comparator, visitRWsets, applyUpdate,
  Runtime::has_structure_based_rw_sets, // 7. flags
  Runtime::is_stable_source,
  Runtime::chunk_size<4>()); // and hints
```

Figure 7: AVI using KDG-based programming model

To make the programming model concrete, we present a portion of the Galois program for AVI in Figure 7. This C++ program corresponds to the pseudo-code for AVI shown in Figure 2. Because the Galois system is library-based, there are differences between the pseudocode of Figure 2 and the C++ code, but the overall structure is similar; the main difference is the loop body in the pseudo-code must be split into two parts, a prefix that visits the rw-set (the lambda called `visitRWsets` in Figure 7) and a suffix that implements the rest of the loop body (the lambda called `applyUpdate` in Figure 7. The lambda for loop body takes two parameters, the item to work on and a handle to the worklist, which is maintained internally by the runtime. The mesh M is implemented using a graph implementation from the Galois library. The ordered foreach is a library call, similar to `std::foreach`, but takes extra parameters: (i) a priority-based comparison function, which implements the *orderedby* clause, (ii) a set of initial tasks, (iii) flags to choose the executor and to enable optimizations, and (iv) for unstable-source algorithms, a safe source test.

4. Applications

In this section, we describe the applications in our benchmark suite. For each one, we describe (i) the program properties that we specified to our runtime in order to choose the best automatic KDG executor (user code written in our programming model §3.1), (ii) problem-specific optimizations to the KDG, done manually by implementing the KDG in the user code, and (iii) non-KDG parallel implementations.

4.1 AVI

AVI is described in Section 2.1.

Automatic executor: AVI is stable-source, and although it creates new tasks, new task's rw-set is the same as the parent tasks, therefore it has structure-based rw-sets. We choose the KDG-RNA executor, which gets optimized to an asynchronous executor that implements only subrule-R, and subrule-A.

Manual executor: This is a variation of the edge-flipping approach of Huang *et al.* [19]. We create an explicit dependence graph initially. Since (i) the rw-set of a child task is the same as its parent task (task that generated it), and (ii) the child task has a later time-stamp than the parent, we can update the node for the parent task in-place by changing the time-stamp and flipping its edges as needed.

Alternate parallelization: We obtained an MPI implementation from Adrian Lew [27] but it was orders of magnitude slower than our KDG implementation, so we did not use it.

4.2 Kruskal's MST algorithm

Kruskal's algorithm computes a minimal weight spanning tree (MST) of a weighted undirected graph [12]. It proceeds by applying edge contraction to the edges of a graph in increasing weight order. Each contraction is a task, and each edge successfully contracted is part of the MST. Figure 8 shows an example of edge contraction and its corresponding effect on the KDG. Tasks (nodes in KDG) are edges in the input graph. Edges that share a node in the input graph are neighbors in the task graph. Given two nodes a and b and the edge (a, b) between them, an *edge contraction* removes the edge (a, b) and replaces nodes a and b with a new node c that has the union of the edges incident on a and b. Edge contractions can create multiple edges between the same endpoints, in which case only the lightest weight edge should be retained. For efficiency, instead of explicitly removing an edge and performing the union of edges, edge contraction is implemented using a union-find data structure [12]. Another common optimization is to partition the edges into light and heavy edges. Light edges are processed first, and the result is used to filter edges connecting the same component amongst the heavy edges [6].

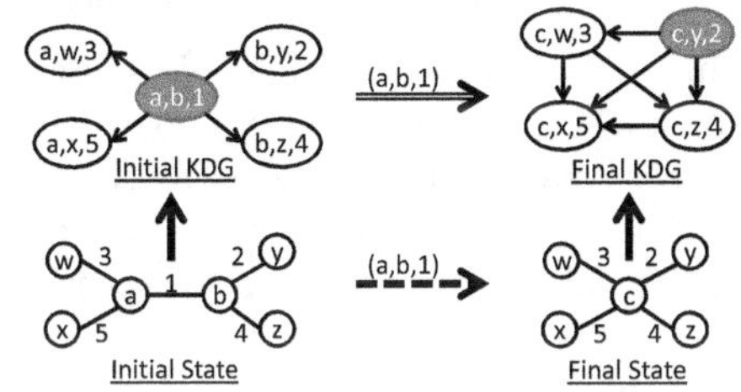

Figure 8: Using the KDG to parallelize Kruskal's algorithm

Edge-contraction may cause the rw-sets of existing tasks (edges in input graph) to increase, because the two nodes of edge being contracted are replaced by a new node with potentially larger adjacency set. For example, in Figure 8, edges incident on a and b are neighbors of each other in task graph, after c replaces (a, b). However, this algorithm is stable-source, since edge contraction only affects the neighbors of a source node in the task graph, which are not sources by definition.

Automatic executor: This application is stable-source but processing an edge may require recomputing the rw-sets of non-source tasks. We choose the IKDG executor with windowing.

Alternate parallelization: Blelloch et al. have parallelized this application by hand [6]. For capturing dependences correctly, they use *reservation stations* and priority-writes much in the same way as the IKDG exeuctor, but specialized to Kruskal, which does not generate new tasks and is stable-source.

Manual executor: Here we in-line the IKDG code into Kruskal application and specialize it by removing support for new tasks. The resulting implementation is similar to Blelloch et al., but with a different policy to control the window size.

4.3 Billiard Balls Simulation

Colliding billiard balls are a useful abstraction of complex phenomena such as molecular dynamics [2] and deformable contact [18]. The problem is stated as follows: given the positions and initial velocities of some balls on a billiards table, simulate the motion of these balls for some amount of time. Collisions are assumed to be elastic and to conserve both energy and momentum. Tasks are potential collision events. The rw-set of a collision consists of the two balls involved in the collision. A collision is a source in the KDG if it is the earliest collision of both the balls involved. Simulating the collision between two balls a and b causes the rescheduling of events involving a and b with other balls. In the KDG, this requires adding new nodes for new collisions and marking some existing collisions as invalid.

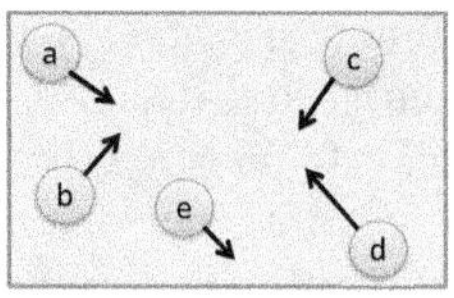

Figure 9: Billiards: Balls with initial velocities on a table

To see that this algorithm is not stable-source, consider the scenario shown in Figure 9 and suppose that collisions (a, b), and, (c, d) are sources in the KDG. Upon colliding with b, ball a may speed up and collide with c before c can collide with d, invalidating task (c, d). However, if we put a bound on how fast the balls can move, we can determine if the collision between balls c and d is sufficiently far away that even if a were to move with maximum velocity, it could not affect the collision between balls c and d. We use this *maximum velocity test* on all pairs of sources in the KDG as the safe-source test.

Automatic executor: We choose the IKDG executor over KDG-RNA because most of the non-source collisions become invalid.

Manual executor: Finding sources can be improved by keeping track of the earliest collision for each ball. The number of safe source test invocations can be reduced by maintaining per-thread priority queues to help determine earlier collisions.

4.4 Sparse LU factorization

We took the LU factorization code from Barcelona OpenMP Task Suite (BOTS) [14], which performs LU factorization (without pivoting) of a sparse matrix using *right-looking* algorithm [13]. It iterates left-to-right over the diagonal entries, of an $N \times N$ matrix M, and updates the bottom-right sub-matrix $M[i : N, i : N]$. The update consists of three parts: type I updates the diagonal entry at $M[i, i]$, type II updates the non-zero entries in the sub-row $M[i, j + 1 : N]$, and the sub-column $M[i + 1 : N, j]$, type III updates the sub-matrix $M[i + 1 : N, j + 1 : N]$ by computing $M[k, j] = M[k, j] - M[k, i] \times M[i, j]$, if $M[k, i]$ and $M[i, j]$ are non-zero; $M[k, j]$ may be zero before the update and may need to be allocated (i.e., *fill*) . Conceptually, we create a task of type I for each diagonal entry, a task of type II for each non-zero entry in the corresponding sub-row and sub-column, and a task for each entry of the sub-matrix that will be updated by type III update. Updates corresponding to diagonal entry i have priority over j if $i < j$, and, for a particular diagonal entry$i$: type I update must precede all type II updates, and all type II updates must precede any type III updates. In practice, to amortize the cost of task-creation and to improve locality, updates are performed on a block of the matrix at a time.

Alternate Implementation: The BOTS code implements a level-by-level parallelization approach, where tasks corresponding to one diagonal block are performed in two parallel phases. Type I update is performed serially, after which the first parallel phase performs updates of type II in parallel, while the second parallel phase performs updates of type III in parallel.

Manual Executor: We use the level-by-level parallelization similar to BOTS.

Automatic Executor: We modified the BOTS code to use the IKDG with windowing for parallelization. We perform a pre-processing pass similar to *symbolic factorization* that simply allocates blocks for the *fill* introduced by type III updates. The initial tasks are of type I, whose rw-set is all the non-zero entries in the sub-matrix $M[i : N, i : N]$ that are in the union of rw-sets of updates of type I, II and III corresponding to diagonal entry i. The rw-set of a type II task consists of the non-zero entry $M[i, k]$ in the row i that it updates, and the entries in the sub-column $M[i+1 : N, k]$ that depend on $M[i, k]$ and will be updated by type III updates. This strategy enforces the precedence constraints among type I, II, III tasks for a particular diagonal entry i, and those among different diagonal entries. Additionally, the algorithm becomes stable-source and has structure-based rw-sets. We can also choose asynchronous KDG-RNA with subrules R and A, as in the case of AVI.

4.5 Discrete-Event Simulation

In discrete-event simulation (DES), there is a network of processing stations each of which has internal state. Stations communicate by sending events along FIFO links. When a station consumes an event, it may update its internal state and send events to some of its outgoing neighbors. In the simulation, events are assigned time-stamps and are processed in global time-stamp order to maintain time causality.

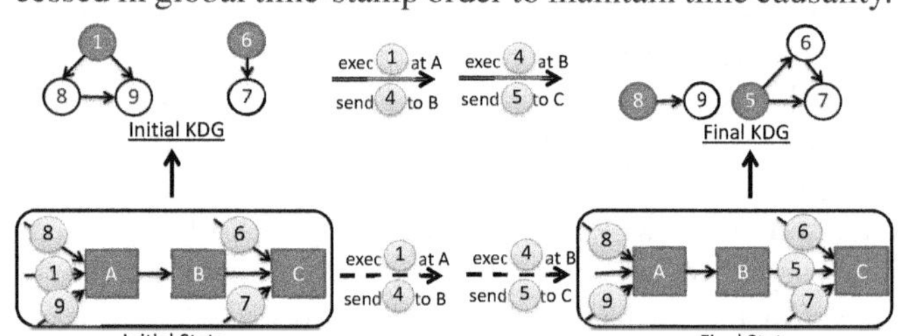

Figure 10: DES: Network of Stations A, B & C

A task corresponds to the processing of an event. The rw-set of an event is its target station. Hence the KDG has a node for every event, and edges among pending events on a particular station. DES is unstable-source, because a station can receive an event, on a particular input edge, that has a time-stamp earlier than events previously received on other inputs. For example, in Figure 10, events 1 and 6 are sources initially (we will refer to events by their time-stamps for simplicity). Let us assume that station A processes event 1 and sends an event 4 to B. B processes event 4 and sends an event 5 to C. Now 5 is a source in the KDG, while 6 is no longer a source.

Chandy and Misra [9] observed that with FIFO-links, a station must receive events on a particular input edge in increasing time-order. Therefore, a station that has received at least one event on all inputs can safely process the earliest of them, regardless of the global time-stamp order. We devised a safe-source test for DES using this insight. The test is local and relatively cheap, but may fail to identify certain safe sources in a cyclic network.

Automatic executor: DES has structure-based rw-sets, and although it is not stable-source, our safe source test depends on local state only. The resulting KDG-RNA executor is asynchronous, just like AVI.

Alternate implementation: The Chandy-Misra approach sends null messages carrying timing information, and these messages are used by stations to determine when they can fire safely. We compare against Chandy-Misra implemented in Lonestar suite [15].

Manual executor: In DES the size of the rw-set of an event is exactly one (i.e., the receiving station). Therefore, the KDG can be represented by using a priority queue for each station, whose earliest event is a source in the KDG.

4.6 Breadth-first Search

A BFS task is a tuple (n, L), which represents updating the distance label (i.e., number of hops from some starting node) of node n to value L. These updates must be processed in increasing distance order. BFS is not stable-source. A common parallelization strategy for BFS is to process updates in a level-by-level fashion. We use this insight to devise a safe source test for BFS. A source task is safe if it has a distance label equal to the current global minimum level.

Automatic executor: For most inputs, the number of priority levels is small. We use the IKDG executor with level-by-level windowing strategy.

Manual executor: In BFS, only two levels need to be maintained at a time.

Alternate Implementation: We use parallel BFS code released by Leiserson et al. [26].

4.7 Bottom-up tree traversal algorithms

Bottom-up tree traversal requires visiting children of a node in tree before the node itself. In our experiments, we use a particular instance of bottom-up tree traversal: the center-of-mass computation in Barnes-Hut [3].

Automatic executor: This application is stable-source, has non-increasing rw-sets and does not create new tasks. We use the KDG-RNA executor with only subrule-R. Additionally, since the dependences are only between parent and child tasks, we disable the computation of rw-sets.

Manual executor: We embed the information for task graph in the tree being traversed because they are isomorphic. This is done when building the tree.

Alternate implementation: We used Cilk to parallelize the recursive implementation.

5. Evaluation

We performed all our experiments on an Intel Xeon E7-4860 server with 40 cores running at 2.2 GHz, organized in 4 packages with 10 cores each, and 24 MB L3 per package. The machine has 128GB of RAM, and runs Scientific Linux 6.3. All programs were compiled with GCC 4.8 at the -O3 optimization level; the only exceptions were Cilk-Plus implementations used for comparisons, which were compiled with the Intel Compiler 14.0. Figure 11a lists the small and large inputs used for each of our applications.

5.1 KDG Performance Comparison

To evaluate the relative performance of KDG-based implementations, we used two kinds of alternative implementations: (i) sequential implementations, to provide a baseline for speedup estimates, and (ii) third-party parallel implementations, when they were available (described in §4, and referred to as *Other* in Figure 11b). Sequential implementations do not use any parallel constructs. For LU, BFS, and MST, we use highly optimized serial implementations released by BOTS [14], Schardl [26], and Blelloch et al. [6], respectively. AVI, Billiards and DES use priority-queues; Tree Traversal is a recursive implementation.

We show results for two kinds of KDG-based implementations, as discussed in §4: (i) KDG-Auto: code written in our programming model that chooses an executor from our KDG-based runtime by specifying flags indicating program properties, (ii) KDG-Manual: KDG implemented in user code, customized to the application.

Figure 11b plots the speedup of KDG-Auto, KDG-Manual and Other against sequential baseline. The best running times of both sequential and parallel implementations are listed in Figure 11a. Both KDG-Auto and KDG-Manual achieve good parallel speedup for many applications, e.g., for AVI, KDG-Auto achieves a speedup of 27 on 40 cores, while for LU, the speedup is 33. Overall, KDG-Auto performs either better than, or within 10-20% of third-party parallel implementations, which often incorporate application specific optimizations. KDG-Manual performs equal to, or, better than third-party parallel implementations, which shows the true potential of the KDG abstraction. The performance difference between KDG-Auto and KDG-Manual are due to overheads related to KDG-Auto being general. Finally, for applications like AVI and Billiards, which are hard to parallelize by hand and no existing system supports their easy parallelization, KDG provides good parallel performance (best case speedups of 27 and 25 respectively).

5.2 Overhead of KDG executors

We analyzed the over-heads and scalability problems of automatic KDG runtime (KDG-Auto), using Vtune Amplifier to collect a profile of total cycles. Figure 12 shows a breakdown of total cycles aggregated over all the threads,

	Inputs		Serial		KDG-Auto		KDG-Manual		Other	
	Small	Large	Small	Large	Small	Large	Small	Large	Small	Large
AVI	42 K elements	166 K elements	55.5	98.1	2.0	3.7	1.7	3.7	-	-
MST	2D Grid $\|V\| = 16$ M, $\|E\| = 33$ M	Random $\|V\| = 67$ M, $\|E\| = 268$ M	10.0	82.1	1.4	6.9	0.9	6.1	1.1	7.4
Bill.	7 K balls, $7K \times 7K$ table	15 K balls, $15K \times 15K$ table	36.7	156.9	1.8	6.1	1.8	6.2	-	-
LU	$12K \times 12K$, 140 K non-zeros	$23K \times 23K$, 1.1M non-zeros	195.7	355.1	5.9	10.8	5.3	9.6	5.5	10.0
DES	12-bit Tree Multiplier	64-bit Kogge-Stone Adder	26.9	32.6	6.0	7.2	3.1	3.7	3.3	4.8
BFS	USA road $\|V\| = 23$ M, $\|E\| = 59$ M	Random $\|V\| = 67$ M, $\|E\| = 268$ M	1.3	18.2	0.78	1.8	0.28	1.0	0.98	1.5
Tree	40 M bodies, Plummer dist. [35]	100 M bodies, Plummer dist. [35]	10.1	28.2	0.70	1.77	0.73	1.85	0.92	2.4

(a) Inputs and best running times (in seconds)

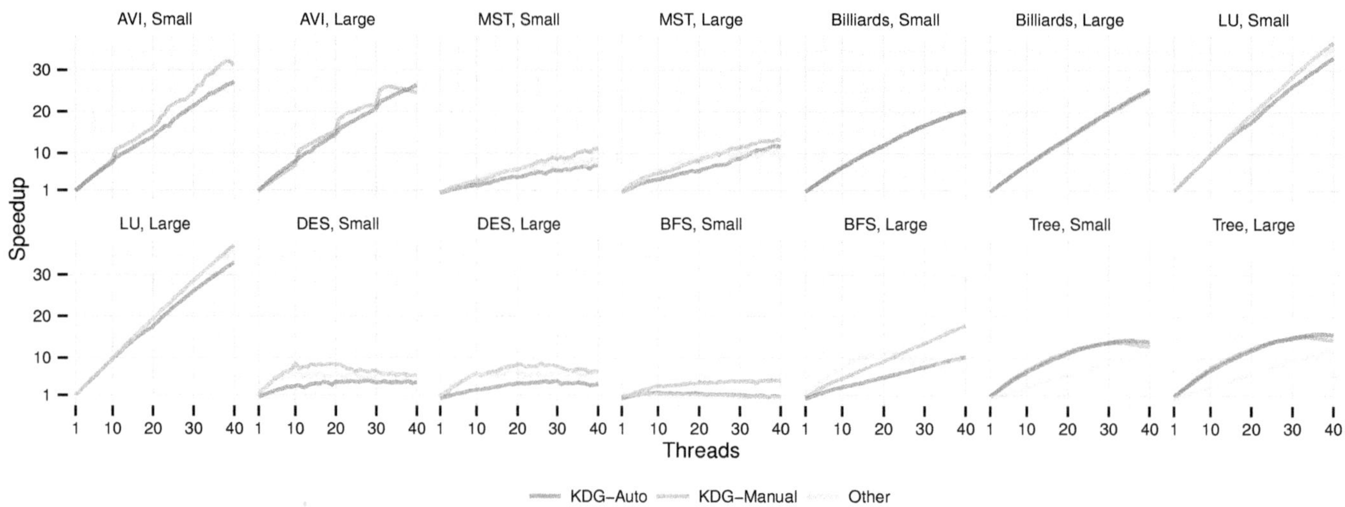

(b) Speedup relative to best serial time, showing small input only (due to space limitations)

Figure 11: KDG performance

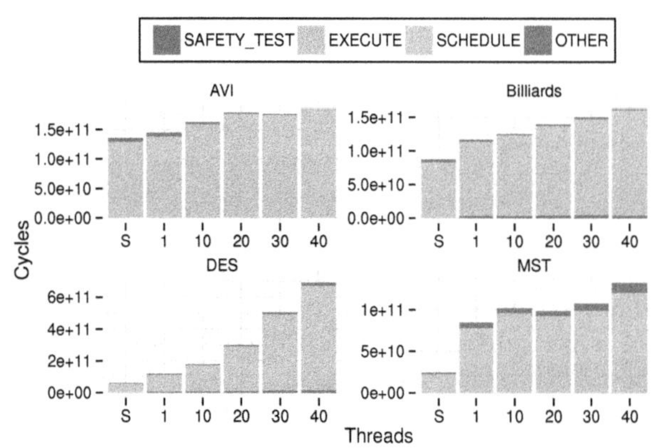

Figure 12: Breakdown of total cycles (summed over all threads). Small Input was used.

for a particular run. We chose four benchmarks for this study, using small inputs. Out of these, AVI and DES were configured to choose explicit KDG implementation from the runtime, while Billiards and MST were configured to choose implicit KDG implementation. The first bar, labeled *S*, shows the breakdown of serial baseline. We group the cycles from the profile into (1) SAFETY_TEST: safe source test (DES and Billiards only) (2) SCHEDULE: KDG maintenance (3) EXECUTE: task execution (4) Other: cost that could not be categorized, e.g., cycles spent in functions called by both user code and runtime. SCHEDULE for serial implementation accounts for the cost of maintaining priority queues or sorting etc.

In general, the cost of KDG (SCHEDULE) scales with the number of threads, with the exception of DES. Further investigation showed that DES suffers from low parallelism (small number of sources), which causes contention on the internal worklist for sources. DES has tasks that perform very little work, which magnifies the overheads of automatic KDG runtime. Notice that the bandwidth consumed by such contention causes EXECUTE to consume more cycles on higher number of threads in some cases. Additionally, task execution when using KDG executors takes longer than when using serial priority-queue because of the cache space and memory bandwidth consumed by KDG runtime.

5.3 Speculation and Level-by-Level Parallelization

In the following, we show experimental results highlighting the problems with using speculation and level-by-level parallelization for these applications (introduced in §??).

Figure 13 shows a breakdown of time spent by threads, when using the speculation-based executor, for three applications. We observed that the commit queue and sequential commits inhibit the scalability of the speculative executor. Tasks in our applications are fine-grain so threads spend most of their time waiting to commit. Additionally, the overhead of copying state and storing undo actions is significant.

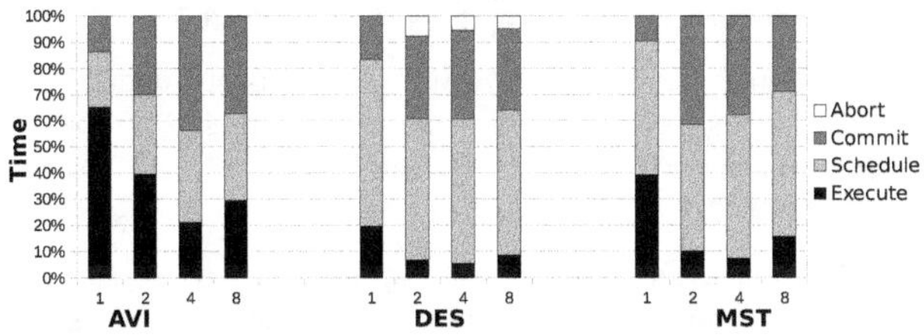

Figure 13: Speculative overheads:Breakdown of time spent by each thread

Application	#levels	avg. #tasks/level
AVI	1.47×10^7	1.38
BFS (on Random graph)	22	6.35×10^6
BFS (on Road Net.)	6262	4607
Billiards	6.03×10^5	1.12
DES	5.2×10^4	1717.21
MST	10^4	2.7×10^4
Tree Traversal	23	2.51×10^6

Figure 14: Amount of parallelism exposed by Level-by-Level executor. Number of levels indicates critical path; Average number of tasks per level indicates parallelism.

The performance of level-by-level execution depends on (1) the number of tasks within each level, which is a measure of parallelism, and (2) the total number of priority levels, which is a measure of the critical path. Figure 14 shows these statistics for our applications, using the level-by-level executor. The level-by-level executor performs well only for BFS (Large input) and Tree Traversal, where there are only a few levels and each level has lots of tasks. On the other hand, level-by-level execution does not discover any useful parallelism in Billiards and AVI. Timestamps are real numbers in these applications and two tasks rarely have the same timestamp. For DES, events have integer timestamps, while in MST, edge weights are integers. Therefore, level-by-level finds some parallelism, but it does not scale beyond a few threads. This is due to the overheads introduced by stopping threads at a barrier after completing each level.

6. Related work

The term Kinetic Dependence Graph was inspired by Guibas's Kinetic Data Structures [4], which are data structures used in computational geometry and graphics. These data structures capture time-varying information and allow incremental and efficient updates at runtime.

General parallelization approaches: Thread-level speculation (TLS) [24, 29, 36] is a general technique for exploiting parallelism in DO loops with statically unpredictable dependences. In our experience, speculation is useful for parallelization of atomic tasks that can commit in any order such as Galois-style unordered set iterators [34], on the other hand, the overheads of in-order commit make it less attractive for parallelizing tasks that must commit in a particular order.

Task graphs have been used for parallelization in dense linear algebra [38, 39], sparse linear algebra [17], and linear transforms [40]. The KDG is a generalization of classic task graphs because it can handle the creation of new tasks and changes in dependences during execution.

Fork-join style programming models such as Cilk [7], NESL [5] and X10 [10] require dependences to be between child and parent tasks only. Task graphs in these systems can be seen as a special case of the KDG. The restriction makes it difficult to express applications such as billiard balls, DES and AVI.

Application-specific parallelization: In the literature, there are many application-specific parallelizations of the benchmarks considered in this paper. However, most of them can be viewed as using application-specific specializations of the KDG.

For example, parallelization of AVI by Huang et al. [19] uses a dependence DAG with a specific update rule (*i.e.*, edge flipping) to incorporate newly created tasks. This is a special case of the KDG. The parallel implementation of Kruskal's MST algorithm in the PBBS benchmark suite [6] uses a special case of IKDG, optimized for the fact that the application has the stable-source property and does not generate new tasks. Our general IKDG executor was inspired by this work. Lubachevsky describes a billiard balls algorithm that is based on dividing up the physical region between processors, and processing events in different partitions in parallel. It exploits an upper bound on the velocity of balls to process in parallel balls that are sufficiently far away [28].

Discrete-event simulation has been parallelized using both optimistic techniques like Time Warp [21] and conservative techniques like the Chandy-Misra-Bryant algorithm [30]. Our safe-source test is based on Chandy-Misra's null messages, which allows stations to find safe events locally. Time Warp uses speculative execution, so it is quite different from the KDG-based approach described in this paper.

7. Conclusion

In this paper, we have described a new approach to parallelizing many algorithms with priority ordered tasks, dynamic task creation, and changing dependences. Our approach is based on the Kinetic Dependence Graph, which can be viewed as a generalization of the static dependence graph. The KDG is used to schedule tasks for parallel execution, and it can be computed and updated efficiently at runtime. We presented experimental results for several important ordered algorithms showing that our approach outperforms hand-tuned third-party parallel implementations in several cases and gives good parallel performance for other algorithms that are otherwise difficult to parallelize.

References

[1] S. Ainsley, E. Vouga, E. Grinspun, and R. Tamstorf. Speculative Parallel Asynchronous Contact Mechanics. *ACM Transactions on Graphics (SIGGRAPH Asia)*, 31(6):8, Nov 2012.

[2] B. J. Alder and T. E. Wainwright. Studies in molecular dynamics. i. general method. *J. Chem. Phys. 31 (2)*, page 459, 1959.

[3] J. Barnes and P. Hut. A hierarchical o(n log n) force-calculation algorithm. *Nature*, 324(4), December 1986.

[4] J. Basch, L. J. Guibas, and J. Hershberger. Data structures for mobile data. In *JOURNAL OF ALGORITHMS*, pages 747–756, 1997.

[5] G. Blelloch. Programming parallel algorithms. *Communications of the ACM*, 39(3), March 1996.

[6] G. E. Blelloch, J. T. Fineman, P. B. Gibbons, and J. Shun. Internally deterministic parallel algorithms can be fast. In *Proceedings of the 17th ACM SIGPLAN symposium on Principles and Practice of Parallel Programming*, PPoPP '12, pages 181–192, New York, NY, USA, 2012. ACM.

[7] R. D. Blumofe, C. F. Joerg, B. C. Kuszmaul, C. E. Leiserson, K. H. Randall, and Y. Zhou. Cilk: an efficient multithreaded runtime system. *SIGPLAN Not.*, 30(8):207–216, 1995.

[8] M. G. Burk, K. Knobe, R. Newton, and V. Sarkar. The concurrent collections programming model. Technical Report Department of Computer Science Technical Report TR 10-12, Rice University, December, 2010.

[9] K. M. Chandy and J. Misra. Distributed simulation: A case study in design and verification of distributed programs. *IEEE Trans. Software Eng.*, 5(5):440–452, 1979.

[10] P. Charles, C. Grothoff, V. Saraswat, C. Donawa, A. Kielstra, K. Ebcioglu, C. von Praun, and V. Sarkar. X10: An object-oriented approach to non-uniform cluster computing. In *Proceedings of the 20th Annual ACM SIGPLAN Conference on Object-oriented Programming, Systems, Languages, and Applications*, OOPSLA '05, pages 519–538, New York, NY, USA, 2005. ACM.

[11] M. Cintra, J. F. Martínez, and J. Torrellas. Architectural support for scalable speculative parallelization in shared-memory multiprocessors. In *International Symposium on Computer Architecture (ISCA)*, pages 13–24, Vancouver, Canada, June 2000.

[12] T. Cormen, C. Leiserson, R. Rivest, and C. Stein, editors. *Introduction to Algorithms*. MIT Press, 2001.

[13] T. A. Davis. *Direct Methods for Sparse Linear Systems (Fundamentals of Algorithms 2)*. Society for Industrial and Applied Mathematics, Philadelphia, PA, USA, 2006.

[14] A. Duran, X. Teruel, R. Ferrer, X. Martorell, and E. Ayguade. Barcelona openmp tasks suite: A set of benchmarks targeting the exploitation of task parallelism in openmp. In *Proceedings of the 2009 International Conference on Parallel Processing*, ICPP '09, pages 124–131, Washington, DC, USA, 2009. IEEE Computer Society.

[15] `http://iss.ices.utexas.edu/?p=projects/galois`.

[16] T. Gautier, J. V. Lima, N. Maillard, and B. Raffin. Xkaapi: A runtime system for data-flow task programming on heterogeneous architectures. *Parallel and Distributed Processing Symposium, International*, 0:1299–1308, 2013.

[17] A. Gupta, S. Koric, and T. George. Sparse matrix factorization on massively parallel computers. In *SC '09*, 2009.

[18] D. Harmon, E. Vouga, B. Smith, R. Tamstorf, and E. Grinspun. Asynchronous contact mechanics. In *ACM SIGGRAPH 2009 papers*, SIGGRAPH '09, pages 87:1–87:12, New York, NY, USA, 2009. ACM.

[19] J.-C. Huang, X. Jiao, R. M. Fujimoto, and H. Zha. Dag-guided parallel asynchronous variational integrators with super-elements. In *Proceedings of the 2007 summer computer simulation conference*, SCSC, pages 691–697, San Diego, CA, USA, 2007. Society for Computer Simulation International.

[20] Intel Corporation. Intel thread building blocks 2.0. `http://osstbb.intel.com`.

[21] D. R. Jefferson. Virtual time. *ACM TOPLAS*, 7(3), 1985.

[22] F. John. *Partial Diffeential Equations*. Springer Publishers, 1984.

[23] K. Kennedy and J. Allen, editors. *Optimizing compilers for modren architectures:a dependence-based approach*. Morgan Kaufmann, 2001.

[24] V. Krishnan and J. Torrellas. A chip-multiprocessor architecture with speculative multithreading. *IEEE Trans. Comput.*, 48(9):866–880, Sept. 1999.

[25] M. Kulkarni, K. Pingali, B. Walter, G. Ramanarayanan, K. Bala, and L. P. Chew. Optimistic parallelism requires abstractions. *SIGPLAN Not. (Proceedings of PLDI)*, 42(6):211–222, 2007.

[26] C. E. Leiserson and T. B. Schardl. A work-efficient parallel breadth-first search algorithm (or how to cope with the nondeterminism of reducers). In *Proceedings of the 22nd ACM symposium on Parallelism in algorithms and architectures*, SPAA '10, 2010.

[27] A. Lew, J. E. Marsden, M. Ortiz, and M. West. Asynchronous variational integrators. *ARCHIVE FOR RATIONAL MECHANICS AND ANALYSIS*, 2003.

[28] B. Lubachevsky. Simulating colliding rigid disks in parallel using bounded lag without time warp. In *SCS Multiconference*, 1990.

[29] P. Marcuello, A. González, and J. Tubella. Speculative multithreaded processors. In *Proceedings of the 12th international conference on Supercomputing*, ICS '98, pages 77–84, New York, NY, USA, 1998. ACM.

[30] J. Misra. Distributed discrete-event simulation. *ACM Comput. Surv.*, 18(1):39–65, 1986.

[31] D. Nguyen, A. Lenharth, and K. Pingali. A lightweight infrastructure for graph analytics. In *Proceedings of the Twenty-Fourth ACM Symposium on Operating Systems Principles*, SOSP '13, pages 456–471, New York, NY, USA, 2013. ACM.

[32] OpenMP Architecture Review Board. OpenMP Application Program Interface, Version 4.0, July, 2013.

[33] J. Perez, R. Badia, and J. Labarta. A dependency-aware task-based programming environment for multi-core architectures. In *Cluster Computing, 2008 IEEE International Conference on*, pages 142–151, Sept 2008.

[34] K. Pingali, D. Nguyen, M. Kulkarni, M. Burtscher, M. A. Hassaan, R. Kaleem, T.-H. Lee, A. Lenharth, R. Manevich, M. Méndez-Lojo, D. Prountzos, and X. Sui. The Tao of Parallelism in Algorithms. In *PLDI 2011*, pages 12–25, New York, NY, USA, 2011. ACM.

[35] H. Plummer. On the problem of distribution in globular star clusters. *Mon. Not. R. Astron. Soc.*, 71(460), 1911.

[36] L. Rauchwerger and D. A. Padua. The LRPD test: Speculative run-time parallelization of loops with privatization and reduction parallelization. *IEEE Trans. Parallel Distrib. Syst.*, 10(2):160–180, 1999.

[37] J. G. Steffan, C. B. Colohan, A. Zhai, and T. C. Mowry. A scalable approach to thread-level speculation. In *ISCA '00*, 2000.

[38] `http://icl.cs.utk.edu/dague/`.

[39] `http://www.cs.utexas.edu/~flame/web/`.

[40] `http://www.spiral.net/`.

Targeted Automatic Integer Overflow Discovery Using Goal-Directed Conditional Branch Enforcement

Stelios Sidiroglou-Douskos Eric Lahtinen Nathan Rittenhouse Paolo Piselli Fan Long
Deokhwan Kim Martin Rinard
MIT CSAIL
{stelios,elahtinen,nathan_,ppiselli,fanl,dkim,rinard}@csail.mit.edu

Abstract

We present a new technique and system, DIODE, for automatically generating inputs that trigger overflows at memory allocation sites. DIODE is designed to identify relevant sanity checks that inputs must satisfy to trigger overflows at target memory allocation sites, then generate inputs that satisfy these sanity checks to successfully trigger the overflow.

DIODE works with off-the-shelf, production x86 binaries. Our results show that, for our benchmark set of applications, and for every target memory allocation site exercised by our seed inputs (which the applications process correctly with no overflows), either 1) DIODE is able to generate an input that triggers an overflow at that site or 2) there is no input that would trigger an overflow for the observed target expression at that site.

1. Introduction

Integer overflow errors are an insidious source of software failures and security vulnerabilities [1, 14, 41]. Because programs with latent overflow errors often process typical inputs correctly, such errors can easily escape detection during testing only to appear later in production. Overflow errors that occur at memory allocation sites can be especially problematic as they comprise a prime target for code injection attacks. A typical scenario is that a malicious input exploits the overflow to cause the program to allocate a memory block that is too small to hold the data that the program will write into the allocated block. The resulting out-of-bounds writes can easily enable code injection attacks [14].

ASPLOS '15', March 14–18, 2015, Istanbul, Turkey..
Copyright © 2015 ACM 978-1-4503-2835-7/15/03. . . $15.00.
http://dx.doi.org/10.1145/10.1145/2694344.2694389

1.1 DIODE

We present a new technique and system, DIODE (Directed Integer Overflow Discovery Engine), for automatically generating inputs that trigger integer overflow errors at critical sites. DIODE starts with a *target site* (such as a memory allocation site) and a *target value* (such as the size of the allocated memory block). It then uses symbolic execution to obtain an *target expression* that characterizes how the program computes the target value as a function of the input. It then transforms the target expression to obtain a *target constraint*. If the input 1) satisfies the target constraint while 2) causing the program to execute the target site, then it will trigger the error.

Sanity Checks: A key observation behind the design of DIODE is that programs often perform sanity checks on the input before they use the input to compute target values. If the input does not pass the sanity checks, the program typically emits an error or warning message and does not further process the input. To trigger an overflow, an input must therefore take the *same path* through the sanity checks as typical inputs that the program processes successfully.

One obvious way to obtain an input that satisfies the sanity checks is start with a *seed input* that causes one or more target sites to execute, then use a solver to obtain a new input that 1) satisfies the target constraint as well as 2) additional constraints that force the solver to generate an input that takes the *same path* to the target site as the seed input. This approach ensures that the input passes the sanity checks.

Blocking Checks: Unfortunately, our results indicate that this approach often fails because, in most cases, the path that the seed input takes through the computation contains additional *blocking checks* that prevent any input that satisfies these checks from triggering the error. To trigger an overflow, an input must take a *different path* through these blocking checks. The challenge is therefore to find inputs that 1) satisfy the target constraint, 2) satisfy the sanity checks, and 3) find a path through the blocking checks to execute the target site. DIODE meets this challenge as follows:

- **Target Site Identification:** Using a fine-grained dynamic taint analysis on the program running on the seed input,

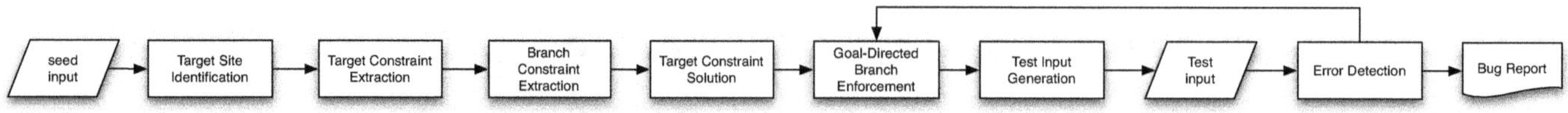

Figure 1: System Overview

DIODE identifies all memory allocation sites that are influenced by values from the seed input. These sites are the *target sites*.

- **Target Constraint Extraction:** Based on instrumented executions of the program, DIODE extracts a symbolic target expression that characterizes how the program computes the target value (the size of the allocated memory block) at each target memory allocation site. The inputs that appear in this expression are the *relevant inputs*. Using the target expression, DIODE generates a *target constraint* that characterizes all inputs that would cause the computation of the target value to overflow (as long as the input also causes the program to compute the target value).
- **Branch Constraint Extraction:** Again based on instrumented executions of the program, DIODE extracts the sequence of conditional branch instructions that the program executes to generate the path to the target memory allocation site. To ensure that DIODE considers only relevant conditional branches, DIODE discards all branches whose condition is not influenced by relevant inputs.

  For each remaining conditional branch, DIODE generates a *branch constraint* that characterizes all input values that cause the execution to take the same path at that branch as the seed input. DIODE will use these branch constraints to generate candidate test inputs that force the program to follow the same path as the seed input at selected conditional branches.
- **Target Constraint Solution:** DIODE invokes the Z3 SMT solver [13] to obtain input values that satisfy the target constraint. If the program follows a path that evaluates the target expression at the target memory allocation site, DIODE has successfully generated an input that triggers the overflow. If the program performs no sanity checks on the generated values, this step typically delivers an input that triggers the overflow.
- **Goal-Directed Conditional Branch Enforcement:** If the previous step failed to deliver an input that triggers an overflow, DIODE compares the path that the seed input followed with the path that the generated input followed. These two paths must differ (otherwise the generated input would have triggered an overflow).

  DIODE then finds the first (in the program execution order) relevant conditional branch where the two paths diverge (i.e., where the generated input takes a different path than the seed input). We call this conditional branch the *first flipped branch*.

  DIODE adds the branch constraint from the first flipped branch to the constraint that it passes to the solver, forcing the solver to generate a new input that takes the same path as the seed input at the that first flipped branch. DIODE then runs the program on this new generated input to see if it triggers the overflow.

  DIODE continues this goal-directed branch enforcement algorithm, incrementally adding the branch constraints from first flipped branches, until either 1) it generates an input that triggers the overflow or 2) it generates an unsatisfiable constraint.

If the program does not contain relevant sanity checks, DIODE will typically find an input that triggers the overflow immediately when it solves the target constraint. If the program does contain relevant sanity checks, DIODE enforces flipped sanity checks in the order in which they are executed by the program. Each iteration of the goal-directed conditional branch enforcement algorithm forces the solver to produce an input that satisfies the next relevant unsatisfied sanity check.

As soon as DIODE enforces enough relevant sanity checks, it typically obtains an input that triggers the overflow (if such an input exists). Because the test inputs enforce only relevant branch conditions associated with previously failed relevant sanity checks, this approach gives the input the freedom it needs to navigate the blocking checks that would, if enforced, cause the program to fail to execute the target site (and therefore fail to generate an overflow).

1.2 Experimental Results

We evaluate DIODE on five applications: Dillo 2.1, VLC 08.6h, SwfPlay 0.5.5, CWebP 0.3.1, and ImageMagick 6.5.2. We start by using DIODE to locate the target memory allocation sites (there are 40 of these sites) and extract, for each site, the target constraint. The target constraint for 17 of the 40 target sites is unsatisfiable. For 9 of the remaining 23 target sites, DIODE was unable to generate an overflow-triggering input. Our manual inspection of the source code verified that the applications contain sanity checks that prevent any input from triggering an overflow at these target sites.

DIODE was able to generate inputs that trigger overflows at all of the remaining 14 sites. We were aware of 3 of these overflows prior to starting the study; the remaining 11 were new. We verified that at least 4 of the new overflow errors are still present in the latest versions of these applications as of the submission date of this paper. For 2 of the 14 sites, DIODE was able to generate an overflow-triggering input with a constraint that forced the input to take the same path as the seed input. For the remaining 12 sites, the presence of relevant blocking checks requires any overflow-triggering input to take a different path to the target site.

For 9 of the 14 sites DIODE was able to generate an overflow-triggering input without enforcing any conditional branches. The remaining 5 sites require the enforcement of a minimum of 2, average of 4, and maximum of 5 conditional branches. Our manual inspection of the source code indicates that all of the enforced conditional branches involve sanity checks on relevant inputs (all but one of which were apparently not specifically designed to check for overflows). Our results also indicate that, if the application does perform relevant sanity checks and the input generation strategy does not take these checks into account, the input generation strategy is unlikely to find inputs that trigger an overflow even when such inputs exist (Section 5).

1.3 Engineering Challenges and Solutions

DIODE works directly on off-the-shelf, production stripped x86 binaries with no need for symbol information or source code. Given a binary and one or more seed inputs, DIODE executes instrumented versions of the binary to extract the symbolic target expressions and branch conditions for each target memory allocation site. For scalability reasons, DIODE stages the symbolic expression extraction as follows.

The first stage runs the application using fine-grained taint tracing to find memory allocation sites in which the input influences the size of the allocated memory block. This size is the target value of the site. This stage also obtains, for each target value, the *relevant input bytes*, i.e., the input bytes that influence the target value. The second stage runs the application again, recording a (compressed for efficiency) symbolic representation of each computation that the relevant input bytes influence. The third stage reads the symbolic representation of the computation to automatically derive the symbolic target expressions at the target memory allocation sites (these expressions capture the computation that the application performs on the relevant input bytes to obtain the target value) and the symbolic branch condition expressions at the relevant conditional branches. This staging is essential in enabling DIODE to scale to real-world applications — attempting to record a symbolic representation of all computations that the application performs is clearly infeasible for real-world applications.

Given a seed input and candidate values from the Z3 SMT solver for relevant input fields within the seed input, DIODE uses Hachoir [3] and Peach [4] to generate a new input file with the candidate values. Together, Hachoir and Peach reconstruct the input file to accommodate the values, applying techniques such as checksum recalculation.

1.4 DIODE and Multi-Application Code Transfer

Once DIODE has identified the error, the next step is to eliminate the error. The standard approach is to report the error to the developers of the application, then wait for them to develop and distribute a patch [12]. Drawbacks of this approach include the patch development and distribution time and the difficulty of obtaining any patch at all if the application is no longer under development or maintained.

In response to this problem, we have developed CodePhage, an automatic code transfer system [37]. CodePhage starts with an input that exposes an error, a related input that the application processes correctly, and a donor application that processes both inputs correctly (such applications are typically readily available for standard input file formats). CodePhage automatically discovers code in the donor that eliminates the error, then transfers this code into the original application to eliminate the error. CodePhage operates directly on stripped x86 binary donors to generate source-level patches. The code transfer includes automatic data structure translation and the automatic location of appropriate code insertion points in the recipient. Combining CodePhage with DIODE produces a system that automatically discovers and eliminates integer overflow errors — DIODE generates inputs that expose errors; CodePhage uses these inputs to locate and transfer code from donor applications to eliminate the errors. To the best of our knowledge, CodePhage is the first system to automatically transfer code between applications.

1.5 Continuous Automatic Improvement

Given a the ability to automatically expose errors via tools such as DIODE and the ability to automatically repair these errors via tools such as CodePhage [37] (as well as the ability to automatically generate repairs using techniques such as ClearView [27], Error Virtualization [35, 36], Failure-Oblivious Computing [29], and RCV [23]), the next step is to build *continuous automatic improvement* systems that automatically search for errors and generate patches that repair the encountered errors. ClearView's automatic patch generation capability provides continuous improvement driven by responses to attacks and errors that users encounter in production use [27]. Augmenting the ClearView continuous improvement approach with continuously executing automatic error detection tools would make it possible to detect and repair errors before users encounter them and before attackers can exploit them. The result would be significantly more secure and robust software systems.

1.6 Contributions

This paper makes the following contributions:

- **Targeted Input Generation:** It introduces the approach of automatically generating error-triggering inputs that target potentially vulnerable program sites.
- **Sanity and Blocking Checks:** It identifies sanity and blocking checks as an important challenge for techniques that aspire to discover error-triggering inputs. Critically, our results indicate that if the program contains relevant sanity checks, one way to identify relevant sanity checks and generate inputs that satisfy these checks is to incrementally find and enforce first flipped conditional branches.

- **DIODE:** It presents DIODE, an implemented system that works with programs that contain relevant sanity checks to automatically generate inputs that trigger overflow errors. Starting with seed inputs that execute a set of target memory allocation sites, DIODE uses (optimized) symbolic execution to obtain symbolic expressions that characterize how input values determine the path through the computation to the target site and control the target value (the number of bytes that the target site allocates).

  Using a targeted approach, DIODE generates a sequence of inputs, each of which enforces the next relevant conditional branch to find and satisfy the sanity checks that would otherwise prevent the input from triggering the overflow at the target site. The goal is to find inputs that satisfy the relevant sanity checks while preserving the ability of the input to successfully traverse relevant blocking checks and reach the target site.

- **Experimental Results:** It presents experimental results that characterize the effectiveness of DIODE in discovering overflow errors. For our benchmark applications, DIODE discovers 14 overflows, 11 of which are new. For 9 of these overflows, DIODE generates overflows without enforcing any conditional branches. We attribute this success to a lack of relevant sanity checks in the program.

  For the remaining 5 overflows, DIODE discovers the overflow after enforcing a modest (2 to 5) number of conditional branches. We attribute this success to the ability of DIODE to 1) successfully identify and satisfy relevant sanity checks that appear in these programs while 2) preserving the ability of the input to traverse relevant blocking checks that would otherwise prevent the execution of the target site.

Fuzzing [4, 6] and concolic execution [9, 10, 18, 25] have been shown to be effective in discovering errors in the initial input parsing stages of computations, but have had little to no success in exposing errors that lie deep within the program. DIODE shows that discovering and targeting specific potentially vulnerable program sites can effectively expose such deep errors. One of the keys to success is new techniques that work appropriately with sanity and blocking checks to obtain inputs that can successfully traverse these obstacles to reach the target site. The success of DIODE in exposing integer overflow vulnerabilities opens up the field to the further development of other targeted techniques that work effectively with sanity and blocking checks to expose deep errors.

The remainder of the paper is structured as follows. Section 2 presents an example that illustrates the operation of DIODE. Section 3 presents the DIODE goal-directed conditional branch enforcement algorithm. Section 4 discusses the engineering challenges that we had to overcome to enable DIODE to operate on stripped x86 binaries. We present experimental results in Section 5, related work in Section 6, and conclude in Section 7.

```
// libpng main data process function.
void png_process_data(png_structp png_ptr,
 png_infop info_ptr, ...) {
  ...
  while (png_ptr->buffer_size) {
   // This is a wrapper for png_push_read_chunk
   png_process_some_data(png_ptr, info_ptr);
  }
}
void png_push_read_chunk(png_structp png_ptr,
 png_infop info_ptr) {
  if (!png_memcmp(png_ptr->chunk_name,png_IHDR,4)){
   ...
   png_handle_IHDR(png_ptr, info_ptr, ...);
  }
  else if (!png_memcmp(png_ptr->chunk_name,png_IDAT, 4)) {
   // Datainfo callback is called
   png_push_have_info(png_ptr, info_ptr);
  }
}
png_check_IHDR(png_structp png_ptr,
  png_uint_32 width, png_uint_32 height, int bit_depth...) {
   ...
   //Check 3: Height < 1000000L
   if (height > PNG_USER_HEIGHT_MAX) {
     png_warning(png_ptr,
           "Image width exceeds user limit in IHDR");
     error = 1;
   }
   //Check 4: Width < 1000000L
   if (width > PNG_USER_WIDTH_MAX) {
     png_warning(png_ptr,
           "Image width exceeds user limit in IHDR");
     error = 1;
   }
}
png_get_uint_31(png_structp png_ptr, png_const_bytep buf) {
   png_uint_32 uval = png_get_uint_32(buf);
   // Checks 1 & 2: Checks that width/height < 0x7fffffffL
   if (uval > PNG_UINT_31_MAX)
     png_error(png_ptr,
            "PNG unsigned integer out of range");
   return (uval);
}
#define PNG_ROWBYTES(pixel_bits,width) ((pixel_bits)>=8? \
  ((width)*(((png_uint_32)(pixel_bits))>>3)):\
  ((((width)*((png_uint_32)(pixel_bits)))+7)>>3))
void png_handle_IHDR(png_structp png_ptr,
 png_infop info_ptr, ...) {
  ...
  // read individual png fields from input buffer
  width     = png_get_uint_31(png_ptr, buf);
  height    = png_get_uint_31(png_ptr, buf + 4);
  bit_depth = buf[8];
  ...
  png_ptr->width      = width;
  png_ptr->height     = height;
  png_ptr->bit_depth  = (png_byte)bit_depth;
  ...
  png_ptr->pixel_depth = (png_byte)(
      png_ptr->bit_depth * png_ptr->channels);
  png_ptr->rowbytes = PNG_ROWBYTES(
      png_ptr->pixel_depth, png_ptr->width);
}
png_memset_check (png_structp png_ptr, png_voidp s1, int value,
        png_uint_32 length)
{
  png_size_t size;
  size = (png_size_t)length;
  if ((png_uint_32)size != length)
    png_error(png_ptr, "Overflow in png_memset_check.");
  return (png_memset (s1, value, size));
}
// Dillo datainfo initialization callback
static void
Png_datainfo_callback(png_structp png_ptr, png_infop info_ptr)
{
  DilloPng *png;
  ...
  // Check 5:  Incorrect check of max image size
  if (abs(png->width*png->height) > IMAGE_MAX_W * IMAGE_MAX_H) {
    MSG("suspicious image size request %ldx%ld\n",
       png->width, png->height);
    return;
  }
  // Where the overflow happens
  png->image_data = (uchar_t *)dMalloc(png->rowbytes * png->height);
}
```

Figure 2: Simplified source code from Dillo 2.1 and libpng

2. Example

We next present an example that illustrates how DIODE automatically generates an input that triggers an integer overflow in Dillo 2.1, a lightweight open source web browser [2]. Figure 2 presents the simplified source code for this example. This code is from the libpng library, which Dillo uses to read PNG images.

Target Site Discovery: DIODE runs Dillo on the seed input, using a fine-grained dynamic taint analysis to track the propagation of input bytes through the program. The libpng runtime calls `png_process_data()` (line 2) to process each PNG image. This function then calls `png_push_read_chunk()` (line 10) to process each chunk in the PNG image. When the libpng runtime reads the first data chunk (the IDAT chunk), it calls the Dillo callback `png_datainfo_callback()` (lines 76-88) in the Dillo PNG processing module. At line 87, Dillo invokes `dMalloc()` to allocate the image buffer. Because the size of the allocated memory block is influenced by the input, DIODE identifies the site as a *target memory allocation site*.

Dillo computes the size of the allocated image buffer as `png->rowbytes * png->height`. This is the *target value*. DIODE's goal is to generate an input that 1) executes the target site at line 87 and 2) causes the computation of the target value `png->rowbytes * png->height` to overflow. The taint information indicates that the target value is influenced by the PNG width, height, and bitdepth fields in the seed input file. These fields are the *relevant input bytes*.

Target Expression Extraction: Next, DIODE runs the application again, this time with additional instrumentation that records all calculations that involve the relevant input bytes. DIODE uses the recorded information to extract the symbolic *target expression*, which characterizes how the application computes the target value (recall that this target value is the size of the allocated image buffer) as a function of the input bytes. Conceptually, this expression is `((width*(4*bitdepth))>>3)*height`, where `width`, `bitdepth`, and `height` are the PNG width, bitdepth, and height fields in the input file. Large values of these fields will cause this expression to overflow. Because of endianness conversions that take place when Dillo reads in the input field values, the actual target expression is:

```
MallocArg(Mul(32,Mul(32,Add(32,ToSize(32,UShr(32,BvAnd(32,
HachField(32, '/header/width'),Constant(0xFF000000)),
Constant(24))),Add(32,Add(32,Shl(32,ToSize(32,
BvAnd(32,HachField(32, '/header/width'), Constant(0xFF))),
Constant(24)),Shl(32,ToSize(32,UShr(32,BvAnd(32,HachField(32,
'/header/width'),Constant(0xFF00)),Constant(8))),
Constant(16))),Shl(32,ToSize(32,UShr(32,BvAnd(32,
HachField(32, '/header/width'),Constant(0xFF0000)),
Constant(16))),Constant(8)))),ToSize(32,Shrink(8,
UShr(32,ToSize(32,Shrink(8,Mul(32,ToSize(32,
HachField(8, '/header/bit_depth')),Constant(4)))),
Constant(3))))),Add(32,ToSize(32,UShr(32,BvAnd(32,
HachField(32, '/header/height'),Constant(0xFF000000)),
Constant(24))),Add(32,Add(32,Shl(32,ToSize(32,
BvAnd(32,HachField(32, '/header/height'),
Constant(0xFF))),Constant(24)),Shl(32,ToSize(32,
UShr(32,BvAnd(32,HachField(32, '/header/height'),
Constant(0xFF00)),Constant(8))),Constant(16))),Shl(32,
ToSize(32,UShr(32,BvAnd(32,HachField(32,
'/header/height'),Constant(0xFF0000)),Constant(16))),
Constant(8))))),Constant(0xFFFFFFFF))
```

Here `TargetSite` indicates that, to overflow, the expression must be greater than the constant `0xFFFFFFFF` (at the end of the last line of the expression). The expression itself references the PNG width, bitdepth, and height fields from the input file as `/header/width`, `/header/bit_depth`, and `/header/height`. The remainder of the expression captures the computation of the target value as described above. It also incorporates constructs (such as `Shl` and `BvAnd`) that capture the conversion of the input values from big-endian to little-endian form. From this target expression, DIODE extracts a target constraint that is satisfied if and only if the computation of the target expression overflows. The variables in this target constraint represent the `/header/width`, `/header/bit_depth`, and `/header/height` PNG input file fields. The target constraint faithfully represents integer arithmetic as implemented in the hardware.

Target Constraint: DIODE next uses the Z3 solver [13] to obtain *candidate values* for the relevant input byte values that would cause the target value to overflow. In this example, the solution sets `/header/width` to 3880563055L, `/header/bit_depth` to 4, and `/header/height` to 689749785L. It then uses Hachoir [3] and Peach [4] to generate a new input file with the candidate values (we call this input file the *initial input file*) and executes Dillo on this new input file. Dillo and libpng contain sanity checks that together prevent the input from triggering the overflow.

Sanity Checks: Dillo and libpng collectively contain five sanity checks. The first two checks occur in `png_get_uint_31` (line 37), which checks that the PNG height and width values are less than `0x7fffffffL`. The third and fourth sanity checks occur in `png_check_IHDR` (lines 21–36), which check that the PNG height and width values are less than one million. The fifth and final sanity check occurs at line 72, immediately before the target memory allocation site at line 87. This final sanity check attempts to ensure that the size of the allocated image does not exceed a specified value (`IMAGE_MAX_W * IMAGE_MAX_H`) (which is 6000 * 6000). This final check contains an overflow error that prevents it from recognizing and correctly rejecting some inputs that cause overflows at the target memory allocation site at line 87.

Symbolic Branch Condition Extraction: DIODE uses the recorded instrumentation information to extract symbolic expressions (the branch conditions) that characterize how the application computes the values of the branch conditions at conditional branch instructions that are directly influenced by the relevant input bytes. For Dillo, the extracted branch conditions characterize how Dillo computes the branch conditions for the sanity checks described above.

Blocking Checks: DIODE is capable of generating a constraint over the relevant input bytes that 1) cause the target value to overflow and 2) cause the application to follow the same path through the conditional branches to the target site as the seed input. If this constraint were satisfiable, DIODE could then use the solution to generate an input file that would trigger the overflow. This constraint is not satisfiable. Dillo and libpng contain *blocking checks* that prevent any input that would trigger an overflow from following the same path through the relevant branches to the target site.

The blocking checks occur in the png_memset procedure, which initializes a block of memory whose size is a function of the PNG width and bitdepth input fields. The png_memset procedure is hand coded in assembly language using the SSE2 extensions. This procedure contains a loop that iterates over the block of memory initializing the values in the block. The number of iterations of this loop is a function of the size of the block of memory. The conditional branch that controls the number of iterations is therefore a relevant branch — its condition depends on the PNG width and bitdepth fields. Any input that follows the same path as the seed input through the relevant conditions must therefore have PNG width and bitdepth fields that produce the same number of iterations of the loop as the seed inputs. This additional *blocking constraint* makes it impossible to obtain an input that both 1) triggers the overflow and 2) follows the same path through the relevant branches as the seed input.

In our example, the PNG width field is 280. The number of iterations is 8 and the constraint is width $\times$ bitdepth$/8 \leq 1154$. The target expression is (width $\times$ bitdepth$/8$) $\times$ height (which is rowbytes $\times$ height). This value cannot overflow because the maximum value of rowbytes is 1154 and the maximum value of height is 1,000,000 (line 24). These values produce 1154 $\times$ 1,000,000 = 1,154,000,000, which is less than 2^{32}.

Goal-Directed Conditional Branch Enforcement: DIODE next starts goal-directed conditional branch enforcement. It initializes the *current constraint* to the target constraint and the *current input* to the initial input (recall that the initial input was generated to satisfy only the target constraint). It then executes Dillo on the seed input and the current input to find the first (in the program execution order) relevant branch where the seed and current input take different paths. In our example this relevant branch corresponds to the sanity check at function png_get_uint_31, line 48 — the seed input satisfies this sanity check, while the current input fails the sanity check (because the generated height is too large).

DIODE therefore adds the branch constraint from the corresponding conditional to the current constraint. Given this new current constraint, Z3 produces a solution that sets /header/width to 1632109428L, /header/bit_depth to 4, and /header/height to 872360950L. The resulting current input fails to generate an overflow because it fails the sanity check at png_check_IHDR, line 25.

DIODE adds the branch constraint from the conditional branch that implements the sanity check to the current constraint and obtains a new /header/width of 1081489513L and /header/height of 732927L. The resulting input file fails to trigger an overflow because it fails the sanity check at png_check_IHDR, line 31. After adding the corresponding branch constraint, the solver comes back with /header/width 966175L and /header/height 484094L. The sanity check at Png_datainfo_callback, line 81, which checks for an overly large image size, rejects the resulting current input.

$$
\begin{array}{rcrcl}
x,y & \in & \text{Var} & = & \text{PgmVar} \cup \text{InpVar} \\
A,A_1,A_2 & \in & \text{Aexp} & ::= & n \mid x \mid \texttt{-}A \mid A_1\, aop\, A_2 \\
B,B_1,B_2 & \in & \text{Bexp} & ::= & \texttt{true} \mid \texttt{false} \mid A_1\, cmp\, A_2 \mid \\
 & & & & \texttt{!}B \mid B_1 \,\texttt{\&\&}\, B_2 \mid B_1 \,\texttt{||}\, B_2 \\
C,C_1,\cdots,C_n & \in & \text{Stmt} & ::= & \texttt{skip} \mid x \texttt{=} A \mid \\
 & & & & x \texttt{=} \texttt{alloc(}y\texttt{)} \mid x \texttt{=} y\texttt{[}A\texttt{]} \mid x\texttt{[}A\texttt{]} \texttt{=} y \mid \\
 & & & & \texttt{if}\, B\, S_1\, S_2 \mid \texttt{while}\, B\, S
\end{array}
$$

$$S,S_1,S_2 \in \text{Seq} ::= C_1\,;\,\cdots\,;\,C_n$$

Figure 3: Syntax

Successful Generation of Overflow-Triggering Input: This sanity check, designed to detect overflows, is itself vulnerable to an overflow — carefully chosen values can overflow the checked value and cause the sanity check to incorrectly accept an input that overflows the target value at line 87. After adding the branch condition from line 81 to the current constraint, the solver comes back with /header/width 689853L and /header/height 915210L. With these values, the generated input successfully navigates the sanity checks and the blocking checks to trigger the overflow. The resulting out of bounds writes cause Dillo to crash with a SIGSEGV exception.

3. Goal-Directed Conditional Branch Enforcement Algorithm

We next present the basic DIODE goal-directed conditional branch enforcement algorithm. We first define a core imperative language and a small-step operational semantics for this language. This semantics defines both concrete and symbolic executions for programs written in the core language. We then use this semantics to present the algorithm.

3.1 Core Language

Figure 3 presents the syntax of a core imperative language with variables, arithmetic expressions, boolean expressions, assignments, dynamic memory allocation, memory read/write, conditional statements, while loops, and sequential composition.

Variables: We divide variables into two classes, PgmVar and InpVar. A *program variable* $\in$ PgmVar is a conventional variable and can store integer values or memory addresses as usual. On the other hand, an *input variable* $\in$ InpVar represents an external input value to a program. DIODE uses input variables to symbolically express how the program computes a target value (such as the size of the allocated memory block) from the input values.

Labels: All program statements have a unique label $\ell \in$ Label. before(C) and after(C) denote the labels before and after the statement C, respectively. In a sequence $S = C_1\,;\,\cdots\,;C_n$, after$(C_i) =$ before(C_{i+1}). We define before$(C_1\,;\,\cdots\,;C_n)$ and after$(C_1\,;\,\cdots\,;C_n)$ as follows:

$$
\begin{array}{rcl}
\text{before}(C_1\,;\,\cdots\,;C_n) & = & \text{before}(C_1) \\
\text{after}(C_1\,;\,\cdots\,;C_n) & = & \text{after}(C_n)
\end{array}
$$

$$\rho \vdash n \Rightarrow \langle n,n\rangle \qquad \frac{x \in \text{PgmVar}}{\rho \vdash x \Rightarrow \rho(x)} \qquad \textsc{InpVar}\ \frac{x \in \text{InpVar}}{\rho \vdash x \Rightarrow \langle \pi_1(\rho(x)), x\rangle} \qquad \frac{\rho \vdash A \Rightarrow \langle n,n\rangle}{\rho \vdash \text{-}A \Rightarrow \langle -n,-n\rangle} \qquad \frac{\rho \vdash A \Rightarrow \langle n,A'\rangle}{\rho \vdash \text{-}A \Rightarrow \langle -n,\text{-}A'\rangle}$$

$$\frac{\rho \vdash A_1 \Rightarrow \langle n_1,n_1\rangle \qquad \rho \vdash A_2 \Rightarrow \langle n_2,n_2\rangle}{\rho \vdash A_1 + A_2 \Rightarrow \langle n_1+n_2, n_1+n_2\rangle}$$

$$\frac{\rho \vdash A_1 \Rightarrow \langle n_1,A_1'\rangle \qquad \rho \vdash A_2 \Rightarrow \langle n_2,n_2\rangle}{\rho \vdash A_1 + A_2 \Rightarrow \langle n_1+n_2, A_1' + n_2\rangle} \qquad \frac{\rho \vdash A_1 \Rightarrow \langle n_1,n_1\rangle \qquad \rho \vdash A_2 \Rightarrow \langle n_2,A_2'\rangle}{\rho \vdash A_1 + A_2 \Rightarrow \langle n_1+n_2, n_1 + A_2'\rangle} \qquad \frac{\rho \vdash A_1 \Rightarrow \langle n_1,A_1'\rangle \qquad \rho \vdash A_2 \Rightarrow \langle n_2,A_2'\rangle}{\rho \vdash A_1 + A_2 \Rightarrow \langle n_1+n_2, A_1' + A_2'\rangle}$$

Figure 4: Semantics of Arithmetic Expressions

ℓ and ℓ' denote before(C) and after(C) of statement C in question

$$\langle \ell,\rho,m,\phi\rangle =\!\!\llbracket \mathtt{skip} \rrbracket\!\!\Rightarrow_{\text{Stmt}} \langle \ell',\rho,m,\phi\rangle \qquad \frac{x \in \text{PgmVar} \qquad \rho \vdash A \Rightarrow \langle v,w\rangle}{\langle \ell,\rho,m,\phi\rangle =\!\!\llbracket x \mathtt{=} A \rrbracket\!\!\Rightarrow_{\text{Stmt}} \langle \ell',\rho[x \mapsto \langle v,w\rangle],m,\phi\rangle}$$

$$\frac{x \in \text{PgmVar} \qquad \rho \vdash y \Rightarrow \langle n,\_\rangle \qquad n > 0 \qquad a \notin \text{dom}(m)}{\langle \ell,\rho,m,\phi\rangle =\!\!\llbracket x \mathtt{=alloc(}y\mathtt{)} \rrbracket\!\!\Rightarrow_{\text{Stmt}} \langle \ell',\rho[x \mapsto \langle a,a\rangle],m[(a,0)\mapsto\langle 0,0\rangle,\cdots,(a,n-1)\mapsto\langle 0,0\rangle],\phi\rangle} \qquad \frac{x \in \text{PgmVar} \qquad \rho \vdash y \Rightarrow \langle a,\_\rangle \qquad \rho \vdash A \Rightarrow \langle n,\_\rangle}{\langle \ell,\rho,m,\phi\rangle =\!\!\llbracket x \mathtt{=} y\mathtt{[}A\mathtt{]} \rrbracket\!\!\Rightarrow_{\text{Stmt}} \langle \ell',\rho[x \mapsto m(a,n)],m,\phi\rangle}$$

$$\frac{\rho \vdash y \Rightarrow \langle v,w\rangle \qquad \rho \vdash x \Rightarrow \langle a,\_\rangle \qquad \rho \vdash A \Rightarrow \langle n,\_\rangle}{\langle \ell,\rho,m,\phi\rangle =\!\!\llbracket x\mathtt{[}A\mathtt{]} \mathtt{=} y \rrbracket\!\!\Rightarrow_{\text{Stmt}} \langle \ell',\rho,m[(a,n)\mapsto\langle v,w\rangle],\phi\rangle} \qquad \frac{\rho \vdash B \Rightarrow \langle \text{true},\text{true}\rangle}{\langle \ell,\rho,m,\phi\rangle =\!\!\llbracket \mathtt{if}\ B\ S_1\ S_2 \rrbracket\!\!\Rightarrow_{\text{Stmt}} \langle \text{before}(S_1),\rho,m,\phi\rangle}$$

$$\frac{\rho \vdash B \Rightarrow \langle \text{true},B'\rangle}{\langle \ell,\rho,m,\phi\rangle =\!\!\llbracket \mathtt{if}\ B\ S_1\ S_2 \rrbracket\!\!\Rightarrow_{\text{Stmt}} \langle \text{before}(S_1),\rho,m,\phi \to \langle \ell,B'\rangle\rangle} \qquad \frac{\langle \ell_1,\rho,m,\phi\rangle =\!\!\llbracket S_1 \rrbracket\!\!\Rightarrow_{\text{Seq}} \langle \ell_1',\rho',m',\phi'\rangle}{\langle \ell_1,\rho,m,\phi\rangle =\!\!\llbracket \mathtt{if}\ B\ S_1\ S_2 \rrbracket\!\!\Rightarrow_{\text{Stmt}} \langle \ell_1',\rho',m',\phi'\rangle} \qquad \langle \text{after}(S_1),\rho,m,\phi\rangle =\!\!\llbracket \mathtt{if}\ B\ S_1\ S_2 \rrbracket\!\!\Rightarrow_{\text{Stmt}} \langle \ell',\rho,m,\phi\rangle$$

$$\frac{\rho \vdash B \Rightarrow \langle \text{false},\text{false}\rangle}{\langle \ell,\rho,m,\phi\rangle =\!\!\llbracket \mathtt{if}\ B\ S_1\ S_2 \rrbracket\!\!\Rightarrow_{\text{Stmt}} \langle \text{before}(S_2),\rho,m,\phi\rangle} \qquad \frac{\rho \vdash B \Rightarrow \langle \text{false},B'\rangle}{\langle \ell,\rho,m,\phi\rangle =\!\!\llbracket \mathtt{if}\ B\ S_1\ S_2 \rrbracket\!\!\Rightarrow_{\text{Stmt}} \langle \text{before}(S_2),\rho,m,\phi \to \langle \ell,\mathtt{!}B'\rangle\rangle}$$

$$\frac{\langle \ell_2,\rho,m,\phi\rangle =\!\!\llbracket S_2 \rrbracket\!\!\Rightarrow_{\text{Seq}} \langle \ell_2',\rho',m',\phi'\rangle}{\langle \ell_2,\rho,m,\phi\rangle =\!\!\llbracket \mathtt{if}\ B\ S_1\ S_2 \rrbracket\!\!\Rightarrow_{\text{Stmt}} \langle \ell_2',\rho',m',\phi'\rangle} \qquad \langle \text{after}(S_2),\rho,m,\phi\rangle =\!\!\llbracket \mathtt{if}\ B\ S_1\ S_2 \rrbracket\!\!\Rightarrow_{\text{Stmt}} \langle \ell',\rho,m,\phi\rangle \qquad \frac{\rho \vdash B \Rightarrow \langle \text{true},\_\rangle}{\langle \ell,\rho,m,\phi\rangle =\!\!\llbracket \mathtt{while}\ B\ S \rrbracket\!\!\Rightarrow_{\text{Stmt}} \langle \text{before}(S),\rho,m,\phi\rangle}$$

$$\frac{\langle \ell_1,\rho,m,\phi\rangle =\!\!\llbracket S \rrbracket\!\!\Rightarrow_{\text{Seq}} \langle \ell_1',\rho',m',\phi'\rangle}{\langle \ell_1,\rho,m,\phi\rangle =\!\!\llbracket \mathtt{while}\ B\ S \rrbracket\!\!\Rightarrow_{\text{Stmt}} \langle \ell_1',\rho',m',\phi'\rangle} \qquad \langle \text{after}(S),\rho,m,\phi\rangle =\!\!\llbracket \mathtt{while}\ B\ S \rrbracket\!\!\Rightarrow_{\text{Stmt}} \langle \ell,\rho,m,\phi\rangle \qquad \frac{\rho \vdash B \Rightarrow \langle \text{false},\_\rangle}{\langle \ell,\rho,m,\phi\rangle =\!\!\llbracket \mathtt{while}\ B\ S \rrbracket\!\!\Rightarrow_{\text{Stmt}} \langle \ell',\rho,m,\phi\rangle}$$

Figure 5: Small-Step Operational Semantics of Statements

3.2 Operational Semantics

The language has three different kinds of values

$$\begin{array}{rcl} n & \in & \text{Int} \\ b,b_1,b_2 & \in & \text{Bool} = \{\text{true},\text{false}\} \\ a & \in & \text{Addr} \end{array}$$

where Int is a set of machine integers of finite bit-width, Bool is the standard set of boolean values, and Addr is an address space with an unbounded number of memory addresses.

An *environment* $\rho \in \text{Env}$ is a partial mapping from variables to pairs of values and symbolic values. A *value* $v \in \text{Val}$ is either an integer or an memory address. A *symbolic value* $w \in \text{SymVal}$ can be a symbolic arithmetic expression, integer, or memory address. We use symbolic values to characterize how values were computed as a function of input variables.

$$\begin{array}{rcccl} \rho & \in & \text{Env} & = & \text{Var} \to \text{Val} \times \text{SymVal} \\ v,v_1,v_2 & \in & \text{Val} & = & \text{Int} \cup \text{Addr} \\ w,w_1,w_2 & \in & \text{SymVal} & = & \text{Int} \cup \text{Addr} \cup \text{Aexp} \end{array}$$

Similar to an environment, a *memory* $m \in \text{Mem}$ receives a base address and an offset to the base address as its arguments and returns a pair of a value and a symbolic value.

$$m,m_1,m_2 \in \text{Mem} = \text{Addr} \to \text{Offset} \to \text{Val} \times \text{SymVal}$$

$$\frac{\ell \text{ is a label in } C_i \qquad \langle \ell,\rho,m,\phi\rangle =\!\!\llbracket C_i \rrbracket\!\!\Rightarrow_{\text{Stmt}} \langle \ell',\rho',m',\phi'\rangle}{\langle \ell,\rho,m,\phi\rangle =\!\!\llbracket C_1\mathtt{;}\cdots\mathtt{;}\ C_n \rrbracket\!\!\Rightarrow_{\text{Seq}} \langle \ell',\rho',m',\phi'\rangle}$$

Figure 6: Small-Step Operational Semantics of Sequences

A *branch condition* $\phi \in \text{BranchCond}$ is a sequence. Each element $\langle \ell, B\rangle$ in this sequence records the symbolic branch condition that determines the path taken at the conditional branch at label ℓ. The elements appear in ϕ in the program execution order.

$$\phi \in \text{BranchCond} := \varepsilon \mid \langle \ell, B\rangle \to \phi$$

A *program state* $\sigma = \langle \ell,\rho,m,\phi\rangle$ is composed of the current program point (represented by a label ℓ), an environment ρ, a memory m, and a branch condition ϕ. At a state $\langle \ell,\rho,m,\phi\rangle$, the program is about to execute a statement C labelled ℓ (i.e. before$(C) = \ell$) in the environment ρ and memory m at the program point ℓ reached by taking the path recorded by the conditional branches in the sequence ϕ.

$$\sigma \in \text{State} = \text{Label} \times \text{Env} \times \text{Mem} \times \text{BranchCond}$$

Expressions: Figure 4 presents the semantics of arithmetic expressions. Each expression evaluates to a pair $\langle v, w\rangle$, where

$v \in$ Val is a concrete value and $w \in$ SymVal is a symbolic expression. The INPVAR rule, for example, defines that the evaluation of an input variable $x \in$ InpVar produces a pair $\langle \pi_1(\rho(x)), x \rangle$, where $\pi_1(\rho(x))$ is the actual input value and x is the variable that symbolically represents that value. The semantics of boolean expressions is defined in a similar way.

Statement: Figures 5 and 6 present the small-step operational semantics of DIODE's core language. Note that the meaning of ℓ and ℓ' is slightly different in Figures 5 and 6. In Figure 5, ℓ is the label for the program point before the relevant statement C; ℓ' is the label for the program point after C. In Figure 6, ℓ and ℓ' are the labels of some program points within (including before for ℓ and after for ℓ') some statement C_i in $C_1; \cdots; C_n$.

3.3 Algorithm

Figure 7 presents the DIODE goal-directed conditional branch enforcement algorithm. Given a program S, an initial program state σ, and a target site ℓ, the algorithm first extracts the symbolic target expression B and the observed path ϕ (from the seed input) for that site (line 1). target$(\langle S, \sigma \rangle, \ell)$ is defined as follows:

$$\text{target}(\langle S, \sigma \rangle, \ell) = \{\langle \pi_2(\rho(y)), \phi \rangle \mid \langle \sigma, \langle \ell, \rho, m, \phi \rangle \rangle \in \tau^*(S)\}$$
$$\text{where } \ell = \text{before}(x = \texttt{alloc}(y))$$

The function target$(\langle S, \sigma \rangle, \ell)$ is defined in terms of the reflexive transitive closure $\tau^*(S)$ of the transition relation of the program S, which contains all possible transitions from a starting state to all reachable states.

The algorithm next uses the overflow(B) function to extract the target constraint β (line 2). The overflow(B) function returns a target constraint β such that any input that satisfies the target constraint β will trigger an overflow during the computation of the target expression B.

The algorithm next compresses the path ϕ to coalesce multiple occurrences of conditional branch constraints of a conditional statement into a single constraint (line 7 and Figure 8). This single constraint is the conjuction of all of the observed branch constraints. The algorithm then extracts the relevant branch constraints (line 8) and performs the goal-directed conditional branch enforcement algorithm (lines 10-16).

The relevant(ϕ, β) function takes a branch condition ϕ and a target constraint β as its arguments, and removes conditions that are not relevant to the target constraint β from the branch condition ϕ. A condition $\langle \ell, B \rangle$ in a branch condition is relevant to a target constraint β if the condition B and the target constraint β share the same input variable.

```
Input  : a program S, an initial state σ, a target label ℓ
Output : an input I that triggers an integer overflow at label ℓ

1  for ⟨B, φ⟩ in target(⟨S, σ⟩, ℓ) do
2      β ⟵ overflow(B)
3      if the solver generates an input I that satisfies β then
4          if the input I triggers an overflow at label ℓ then
5              return the input I
6      else continue
7      φ ⟵ compress(φ)
8      φ ⟵ relevant(φ, β)
9      φ' ⟵ true
10     while true do
11         if the previous input I satisfies φ then break
12         φ' ⟵
           φ' ∧ (the first condition in φ that the previous input I
           does not satisfy)
13         if the solver generates an input I that satisfies φ' ∧ β
           then
14             if the input I triggers an overflow at label ℓ then
15                 return the input I
16         else break
17 return not found
```

Figure 7: Goal-Directed Conditional Branch Enforcement

```
Parameters : φ ∈ BranchCond
Returns    : φ's compressed form ∈ BranchCond

Function compress(φ) =
begin
    if φ is ε then
        return ε
    else if φ is ⟨ℓ, B⟩ → φ then
        B ⟵ B ∧ (⋀_{⟨ℓ,B'⟩ in φ} B')
        φ ⟵ filter out all ⟨ℓ, B'⟩ from φ
        return ⟨ℓ, B⟩ → compress(φ)
```

Figure 8: Branch Condition Compression

4. System Design and Implementation

We next discuss how DIODE deals with the many complications that it must overcome to effectively operate on stripped x86 binaries. DIODE consists of approximately 9,000 lines of C (most of this code implements the taint and symbolic expression tracking) and 6,000 lines of Python (the target and branch constraint generation algorithms, code that interfaces with Z3, code that manages the database of relevant experimental results, and a distributed work queue system). We first describe our techniques for target site identification. Second, we introduce the dynamic instrumentation used for target and branch constraint extraction. Third, we discuss how DIODE generates and solves target constraints. Fourth, we discuss how DIODE generates new inputs. Fifth, we discuss the implementation of our goal-directed conditional branch enforcement algorithm. Finally, we discuss how DIODE detects any errors caused by the overflow.

4.1 Target Site Identification

To extract the set of symbolic target expressions that characterizes how the application computes the target value at critical program sites, DIODE uses a fine-grained dynamic taint analysis built on top of the Valgrind [26] binary analysis framework. Our analysis takes as input a specified taint source, such as a filename or a network connection, and marks all data read from the taint source as tainted. Each input byte is assigned a unique label and is tracked by the execution monitor as it propagates through the program until it reaches a potential target site (e.g., malloc). To track the data-flow dependencies from source to sink, our analysis instruments arithmetic instructions (e.g., ADD, SUB), data movement instructions (e.g., MOV, PUSH) and logic instructions (e.g., AND, XOR). Using the dynamic taint analysis on the application and a seed input, DIODE generates the set of target sites and relevant input bytes.

4.2 Target and Branch Constraint Extraction

Next, DIODE reruns the program with additional instrumentation that enables DIODE to reconstruct the full symbolic target expression. Conceptually, DIODE generates a symbolic record of all calculations that the application performs (Section 3). Obviously, attempting to record all calculations would produce an unmanageable volume of information. DIODE reduces the volume of recorded information with the following optimizations:

- **Relevant Input Bytes:** DIODE only records calculations that involve the relevant input bytes. Specifically, DIODE maintains an expression tree of relevant calculations that only tracks calculations that operate on tainted data (i.e., relevant input bytes). This optimization drastically reduces the amount of recorded information.
- **Simplify Expressions:** DIODE further reduces the amount of recorded information by simplifying recorded expressions at runtime. Specifically, DIODE identifies and simplifies resize, move and arithmetic operations. For example, DIODE can convert the following sequence of VEX IR instructions:

```
t15 = Add32(t10, 0x1:I32)
t16 = Add32(t15,0x1:I32)
t17 = Add32(t16,0x1:I32)
```

  that would result in: `Add32(Add32(Add32(t10, 0x1), 0x1),0x1)`

  into: `Add32(t10, 0x3)`

To convert relevant input bytes to symbolic representations of the input format, DIODE uses the Hachoir [3] tool to convert byte ranges into input fields (e.g., in the PNG format, bytes 0-3 represent /header/height).

DIODE also uses the recorded information to extract symbolic expressions that characterize how the application computes the values of conditional branch instructions that relevant input bytes directly influence.

4.3 Target Constraint Solution

DIODE uses the Z3 SMT solver [13] to obtain new input values that satisfy the target constraint. Note that the generated target constraint is designed to capture any overflow in the evaluation of the expression, including in the evaluation of subexpressions. For example, if $bbp_8 \in \{8, 16, 32\}$, there are no values that cause the following expression to overflow:

$$((width_{16} \times height_{16}) \times 4)/bbp_8) > 2^{32}$$

But there are values that cause the following subexpression to overflow:

$$((width_{16} \times height_{16}) \times 4)) > 2^{32}$$

4.4 Test Input Generation

DIODE uses a combination of Hachoir [3] and Peach [4] to generate input files with the values obtained from the SMT solver for the target expression. Together, these tools reconstruct the input file such that it satisfies any checksum calculations or any required field orderings. If DIODE needs to operate on an unknown input format, it also supports a raw-byte option, where modifications are made directly on the input bytes. To deal with any required checksum calculations in raw-byte mode, DIODE can use standard checksum reconstruction techniques [40].

4.5 Goal-Directed Branch Enforcement

If a test input that is generated from a target constraint solution fails to trigger an integer overflow error, DIODE turns on instrumentation that records the path taken at all conditional branches that the seed input executes. DIODE uses this instrumentation to find the first conditional branch at which the generated input takes a different path from the seed input. DIODE uses this information to drive the goal-directed branch enforcement algorithm described above (Section 3).

4.6 Error Detection

We use Valgrind's *memcheck* to detect errors (invalid reads and writes; uninitialized reads and writes) that occur as a result of the overflow. Our automated system therefore does not directly detect the overflow; it only detects the overflow indirectly through its effect on the computation (for our benchmark applications, we manually verify that the generated input actually produces an overflow and generates the reported errors as a result of the overflow). Our automated system first filters any errors that occur during t he execution on the seed input.

5. Evaluation

We evaluate DIODE on five applications: Dillo 2.1, VLC 08.6h, SwfPlay 0.5.5, CWebP 0.3.1, and ImageMagick 6.5.2. For each application we obtain a seed input, then use DIODE to automatically generate input files that trigger overflows in the applications. We perform all tests on a quad Intel i7 2.2 GHz machine with 8 GB RAM.

5.1 Benchmark Selection

The benchmark applications were selected as follows. First, we select applications that process input formats supported by Hachoir [3] and Peach [4]. Second, we filter applications that cannot be successfully processed by DIODE's dynamic instrumentation engine. Third, we select applications that contain at least one known integer overflow vulnerability,

Application	Total Target Sites	DIODE Exposes Overflow	Target Constraint Unsatisfiable	Sanity Checks Prevent Overflow
Dillo 2.1	12	3	1	8
VLC 08.6h	4	4	0	0
SwfPlay 0.5.5	8	3	5	0
CWEBP 0.3.1	7	1	6	0
ImageMagick 6.5.2	9	3	5	1

Table 1: Target Site Classification

5.2 Target Site Classification

Table 1 classifies the target sites in our benchmark applications. There is one row for each application. The first column (Application) identifies the application. The second column (Total Target Sites) presents total number of exercised memory allocation sites from the executions on the seed inputs. These sites are the target sites. The third column (DIODE Exposes Overflow) presents the number of sites for which DIODE was able to generate an input that triggered an overflow at the site. The fourth column (Target Constraint Unsatisfiable) presents the number of sites for which the target constraint, by itself, is unsatisfiable. We verified, via a manual inspection, that there is *no* input that will cause an overflow at any of these sites. The fifth column (Sanity Checks Prevent Overflow) presents the number of remaining sites. For all of these remaining sites, we manually verified that the application contains sanity checks that ensure that there is *no* input that triggers an overflow at that site.

Note that, for each target site, either 1) DIODE finds an input that triggers an overflow at that site, or 2) no such input exists. Our analysis indicates that, except for VLC 0.8.6h, whenever DIODE is able to generate an input that triggers an overflow at a given site, the application is missing overflow sanity checks for that site (of course, the applications contain other relevant sanity checks that DIODE must successfully navigate to trigger the overflow). VLC 0.8.6h contains ineffective overflow sanity checks that are designed to protect the application against overflow, but do not, in fact, do so. DIODE is able to generate inputs that successfully evade these checks to trigger overflows at the target sites.

5.3 Overflow Characteristics

Table 2 summarizes the results for each overflow. The table contains one line for each overflow that DIODE discovers. The first column (Application) identifies the application that contains the overflow. The second column (Target) presents the source code file and line that contains the memory allocation statement for which the overflow occurs. The third column (CVE Number) presents either the CVE number of the overflow (if the overflow was known) or "New" if the overflow was new. We note that all but three of the 14 overflows were new. Four of the 11 new overflows persist in the latest versions of the benchmark applications as of the submission date of this paper. Specifically, the latest versions of CWebP and Display, CWebP 0.4.1 and Display 6.8.9-8, are still vulnerable to error triggering inputs discovered by DIODE. We have notified the developers and are awaiting confirmation.

The fourth column (Error Type) characterizes the effect of the overflow on the application for the first input (that DIODE discovers) that triggers the overflow. In most cases the overflow causes the program to generate a SIGSEGV exception and crash, either from an invalid read or from an invalid write as presented in the table. The remaining two overflows cause the application to perform invalid reads and/or writes that do not crash the application. We detect these invalid reads and writes using the Valgrind memcheck tool [26], which monitors the reads and writes and detects invalid reads and writes. All of the invalid reads or writes occur because the overflow makes the memory block allocated at the target allocation site too small to contain the data.

The fifth column (Analysis and Discovery Time) presents the initial analysis time required for each application (performed once) and the subsequent time to generate an error input for each bug. Each entry in this column is of the form (A) B, where A is the analysis time and B is the time required to generate the error input.

The sixth column (Enforced Branches) presents the number of relevant conditional branches that DIODE enforced before generating an input that triggered the overflow. Each entry in this column is of the form X/Y, where X is the number of enforced conditional branches and Y is the total number of relevant conditional branches on the path that the seed input takes to the target memory allocation site. We note that the number of enforced conditional branches is small, especially relative to the total number of relevant conditional branches — to discover the overflow, DIODE enforces only between two to five out of the 35 to 5779 total relevant conditional branches. Our manual inspection of the code indicates that all of the enforced branches are sanity checks, but that (apparently) only one of these checks is designed (obviously incorrectly) to detect an overflow (Section 2).

5.4 Blocking Checks

Recall that DIODE can generate a constraint that requires 1) the computation of the target value to overflow and 2) the input to follow the same path through the relevant conditional branches as the seed input. If this constraint is satisfiable, the solution typically immediately provides an input that will trigger an overflow at the site. Because of blocking checks, this constraint is unsatisfiable for all but two of the sites, specifically SwfPlay 0.5.5 at jpeg.c@192 and CWebP 0.3.1 at jpegdec.c@248.

Application	Target	CVE Number	Error Type	Analysis and Discovery Time	Enforced Branches	Target Success Rate	Target + Enforced Success Rate
Dillo 2.1	png.c@203	CVE-2009-2294	SIGSEGV/InvalidRead	(42m) 8m	4/35	0/200	190/200
Dillo 2.1	fltkimagebuf.cc@39	New	SIGSEGV/InvalidRead	(42m) 7m	5/69	0/200	189/200
Dillo 2.1	Image.cxx@741	New	SIGSEGV/InvalidRead	(42m) 7m	4/5779	0/200	190/200
VLC 0.8.6h	messages.c@355	New	SIGSEGV/InvalidRead	(6m) 1m	2/117	32/200	108/200
VLC 0.8.6h	wav.c@147	CVE-2008-2430	InvalidRead/Write	(6m) 1m	0/62	2/2	N/A
VLC 0.8.6h	dec.c@277	New	SIGSEGV/InvalidRead	(6m) 8m	5/291	57/200	97/200
VLC 0.8.6h	block.c@54	New	InvalidRead	(6m) 4m	0/151	200/200	N/A
SwfPlay 0.5.5	jpeg_rgb_decoder.c@253	New	SIGSEGV/InvalidWrite	(7m) 13m	0/1736	200/200	N/A
SwfPlay 0.5.5	jpeg_rgb_decoder.c@257	New	SIGSEGV/InvalidWrite	(7m) 13m	0/1736	200/200	N/A
SwfPlay 0.5.5	jpeg.c@192	New	SIGABRT/InvalidWrite	(7m) 1m	0/1012	200/200	N/A
CWebP 0.3.1	jpegdec.c@248	New	SIGSEGV/InvalidWrite	(11m) 2s	0/651	155/200	N/A
ImageMagick 6.5.2	xwindow.c@5619	CVE-2009-1882	SIGSEGV/InvalidWrite	(6m) 1m	0/2521	200/200	N/A
ImageMagick 6.5.2	cache.c@803	New	SIGSEGV/InvalidWrite	(6m) 1m	0/306	199/200	N/A
ImageMagick 6.5.2	display.c@4393	New	SIGSEGV/InvalidWrite	(6m) 2m	0/154	200/200	N/A

Table 2: Evaluation Summary

5.5 Inputs That Satisfy Target Constraint Alone

The seventh column (Target Success Rate) presents the results from the experiment in which DIODE generated 200 inputs that satisfied the target constraint by itself (with none of the conditional branch constraints added to the target constraint passed to the solver). Note that all of these inputs will trigger an overflow at the target memory allocation site if they follow a path that evaluates the target expression at that site. Note also that every discovered input that triggers the overflow is in the set of inputs that satisfy the target constraint alone and therefore could potentially be generated as one of the sampled 200 inputs.

Each entry in the column is of the form X/200, where X is the number of generated inputs that actually trigger the overflow. We note that there is a bimodal distribution — in general, either all or the vast majority of the 200 generated inputs trigger the overflow or none or few of the 200 generated inputs trigger the overflow. This bimodal distribution is correlated with the presence or absence of sanity checks on relevant input values — without sanity checks, all or the vast majority of the generated inputs trigger the overflow. If the application contains sanity checks, the generated inputs are unlikely to pass the sanity checks to trigger the overflow. These data indicate that, if the application contains sanity checks and the input generation strategy does not take these checks into account, the input generation strategy is unlikely to find inputs that trigger an overflow (even when such inputs exist).

For CVE-2008-2430, the target expression is of the form $x+2$, where x is an input field. The target constraint for this expression has only two solutions (because there are only two values of x that cause the target expression to overflow).

5.6 Target and Enforced Branch Success Rate

The eighth column (Target + Enforced Success Rate) presents experimental results for those overflows that DIODE discovered only after enforcing some of the conditional branches. DIODE generated 200 inputs that satisfied the corresponding constraint (i.e., the target constraint plus the constraints that enforced the discovered first flipped branches in Algorithm 7). Each entry in the column is of the form X/200, where X is the number of generated inputs that trigger the overflow (note that we do not run this experiment if the majority of the inputs that satisfy the target constraint alone also trigger the overflow).

We note that, for three of the five overflows, the vast majority of the generated inputs trigger the overflow. For the remaining two overflows, approximately half of the generated inputs trigger the overflow. We attribute this success to DIODE's ability to produce inputs that satisfy the sanity checks while preserving their flexibility to satisfy the blocking checks and traverse alternate paths through the computation to reach the target memory allocation site and trigger the overflow.

The success of DIODE in generating these overflows also illustrates the difficulty of writing sanity checks that detect inputs that cause overflows — even though Dillo 2.1 and VLC 0.8.6h contain sanity checks, these checks do not detect all inputs that trigger overflows.

6. Related Work

Random and Directed Fuzzing: Random fuzzing has been shown to be surprisingly effective in uncovering errors [24, 38] and is heavily used by security researchers [4, 6, 30]. But because most randomly generated inputs fail input sanity checks, random fuzzing has been relatively ineffective at generating inputs that trigger errors (such as integer overflows) deep inside applications. Their ability to generate such inputs can be especially limited for programs that process deeply structured formats such as videos.

Motivated by the need to expose errors deep inside applications, researchers have proposed directed fuzzing techniques [15, 16, 40]. BuzzFuzz [16] and TaintScope [40] use taint tracking to identify input bytes that influence values at critical program sites such as memory allocation sites and system calls. In contrast with random fuzzing techniques that modify the entire input, these techniques then fuzz the input bytes that influence critical program points. While successful at reducing the size of the mutation space, our results indicates that these directed techniques are ineffective at finding the carefully crafted inputs required to navigate the sanity checks and expose integer overflow errors. Because these directed fuzzing systems operate directly on the raw binary input bytes, the modifications can also produce syntactically incorrect inputs that immediately fail the sanity checks.

Symbolic Test Generation: Symbolic test generation (i.e., concolic testing) has been proposed as an alternative to random and directed fuzzing [9, 10, 17–19, 25, 33, 39]. These systems execute programs both concretely and symbolically on a seed input until an interesting program expression is reached (e.g., an assert, a conditional or a specific expression). Although successful in many cases [9, 10, 18, 25], symbolic test generation faces several challenges [8, 34]. Specifically, once past the initial parsing stages, the resulting deeper program paths may produce very large constraints with complex conditions that are currently beyond the capabilities of current state of the art constraint solvers. Our results also show that the path taken by a seed input may contain additional blocking checks that can prevent a constraint solver from generating inputs that satisfy the checks and trigger an overflow.

SmartFuzz [25] is a symbolic test generation tool to discover integer overflows, non-value-preserving width conversions, and potentially dangerous signed/unsigned conversions. SmartFuzz, like other concolic systems, is limited by deep program paths and blocking checks.

Dowser [19] is a fuzzer that combines taint tracking, program analysis, and symbolic execution to find buffer overflows. The key idea is to use program analysis to guide symbolic execution (e.g.,KLEE [9]) along a path that is more likely to discover buffer overflows than running symbolic execution over the entire program. Like most concolic systems, Dowser optimizes for path coverage and is thus unlikely to discover integer overflow errors.

DIODE differs from all of these techniques in that it is *targeted* — instead of exploring paths to find critical sites, it starts with a critical site that is executed by a seed input, then uses a variety of techniques that are designed to produce inputs that successfully navigate sanity and blocking checks to trigger an overflow at the critical site.

Runtime and Library Support: To alleviate the problem of false positives, several research projects have focused on runtime detection tools that dynamically insert runtime checks before integer operations [7, 14, 42]. Another technique is to use safe integer libraries such as SafeInt [5] and CERT's IntegerLib [32] to perform sanity checks at runtime. Using these libraries requires developers to rewrite existing code to use safe versions of integer operations. DIODE, in contrast, pro-actively finds integer errors during testing (i.e., does not rely on observing a malicious input in the wild) and imposes no runtime overhead.

Input Rectification is another technique that can protect applications from integer overflow errors [20, 21, 28] by empirically learning input constraints from benign training inputs and then monitoring inputs for violations of the learned constraints. Instead of discarding inputs that violate the learned constraints, input rectification modifies the input so that it satisfies the constraints. The goal is to nullify potential errors while still enabling the program to successfully process as much input data as possible. Because it learns the constraints from examples, the technique is susceptible to false positives. In contrast, DIODE has no false positives and can proactively discover integer overflow errors.

Static Analysis For Finding Integer Errors: Several static analysis tools have been proposed to find integer overflow and/or sign errors [11, 31, 41]. KINT [41], for example, analyzes individual procedures, with the developer optionally providing procedure specifications that characterize the value ranges of the parameters. Despite substantial effort, KINT reports a large number of false positives [41]. In contrast, DIODE generates inputs that prove the existence of integer errors without any false positives.

SIFT [22] is a system for generating input filters that nullify integer overflow errors associated with critical program sites such as memory allocation and block copy sites. SIFT uses a sound static program analysis to generate filters that discard inputs that may trigger overflow errors. SIFT requires access to source code and is not designed to identify errors. DIODE, in contrast, operates directly on stripped x86 binaries with no need for source code to generate overflow-triggering inputs.

7. Conclusion

We present a system, DIODE, for discovering integer overflow errors in real-world applications. DIODE is designed to work with programs that first perform sanity checks on relevant input fields, then use the input fields to compute target values such as the sizes of allocated memory blocks. Leveraging this pattern, DIODE generates inputs that are designed to satisfy the relevant sanity checks, generate an overflow in the target expression, and impose no other constraints on the specific path that the input takes to trigger the overflow. Our experimental results show that DIODE is effective at generating inputs that trigger integer overflow errors, including previously unknown errors in widely used applications.

Acknowledgements

We thank Jeff Perkins, Michael Gordon and the anonymous reviewers for their insightful comments. This research was supported by DARPA (Grant FA8650-11-C-7192).

References

[1] Common vulnerabilities and exposures. `http://cve.mitre.org/`.

[2] Dillo. `http://www.dillo.org/`.

[3] Hachoir. `http://bitbucket.org/haypo/hachoir/wiki/Home`.

[4] Peach fuzzing platform. `http://peachfuzzer.com/`.

[5] SafeInt. `http://safeint.codeplex.com/`.

[6] SPIKE fuzzing platform. `http://www.immunitysec.com/resources-freesoftware.shtml`.

[7] D. Brumley, T. Chiueh, R. Johnson, H. Lin, and D. Song. RICH: Automatically protecting against integer-based vulnerabilities. *Department of Electrical and Computing Engineering*, page 28, 2007.

[8] D. Brumley, P. Poosankam, D. Song, and J. Zheng. Automatic patch-based exploit generation is possible: Techniques and implications. In *Security and Privacy, 2008. SP 2008. IEEE Symposium on*, pages 143–157. IEEE, 2008.

[9] C. Cadar, D. Dunbar, and D. Engler. KLEE: Unassisted and automatic generation of high-coverage tests for complex systems programs. In *Proceedings of the 8th USENIX conference on Operating systems design and implementation*, OSDI'08, pages 209–224, Berkeley, CA, USA, 2008. USENIX Association.

[10] C. Cadar, V. Ganesh, P. M. Pawlowski, D. L. Dill, and D. R. Engler. EXE: Automatically generating inputs of death. *ACM Transactions on Information and System Security (TISSEC)*, 12(2):10, 2008.

[11] E. Ceesay, J. Zhou, M. Gertz, K. Levitt, and M. Bishop. Using type qualifiers to analyze untrusted integers and detecting security flaws in C programs. *Detection of Intrusions and Malware & Vulnerability Assessment*, pages 1–16, 2006.

[12] C. Cowan, H. Hinton, C. Pu, and J. Walpole. The cracker patch choice: An analysis of post hoc security techniques. 2000.

[13] L. De Moura and N. Bjørner. Z3: an efficient smt solver. In *Proceedings of the Theory and practice of software, 14th international conference on Tools and algorithms for the construction and analysis of systems*, TACAS'08/ETAPS'08, pages 337–340, Berlin, Heidelberg, 2008. Springer-Verlag.

[14] W. Dietz, P. Li, J. Regehr, and V. Adve. Understanding integer overflow in C/C++. In *Proceedings of the 2012 International Conference on Software Engineering*, pages 760–770. IEEE Press, 2012.

[15] W. Drewry and T. Ormandy. Flayer: Exposing application internals. In *Proceedings of the first USENIX workshop on Offensive Technologies*, pages 1–9. USENIX Association, 2007.

[16] V. Ganesh, T. Leek, and M. Rinard. Taint-based directed whitebox fuzzing. In *ICSE '09: Proceedings of the 31st International Conference on Software Engineering*. IEEE Computer Society, 2009.

[17] P. Godefroid, N. Klarlund, and K. Sen. DART: Directed automated random testing. In *Proceedings of the 2005 ACM SIGPLAN conference on Programming language design and implementation*, PLDI '05, pages 213–223, New York, NY, USA, 2005. ACM.

[18] P. Godefroid, M. Y. Levin, and D. Molnar. SAGE: Whitebox fuzzing for security testing. *Queue*, 10(1):20, 2012.

[19] I. Haller, A. Slowinska, M. Neugschwandtner, and H. Bos. Dowsing for overflows: a guided fuzzer to find buffer boundary violations. In *Proceedings of the 22nd USENIX conference on Security*, pages 49–64. USENIX Association, 2013.

[20] F. Long, V. Ganesh, M. Carbin, S. Sidiroglou, and M. Rinard. Automatic input rectification. In *Proceedings of the 2012 International Conference on Software Engineering*, ICSE 2012, pages 80–90, Piscataway, NJ, USA, 2012. IEEE Press.

[21] F. Long, V. Ganesh, M. Carbin, S. Sidiroglou, and M. Rinard. Automatic input rectification. MIT-CSAIL-TR-2011-044.

[22] F. Long, S. Sidiroglou-Douskos, D. Kim, and M. Rinard. Sound input filter generation for integer overflow errors. 2014.

[23] F. Long, S. Sidiroglou-Douskos, and M. Rinard. Automatic runtime error repair and containment via recovery shepherding. In *Proceedings of the 35th ACM SIGPLAN Conference on Programming Language Design and Implementation*, page 26. ACM, 2014.

[24] B. P. Miller, L. Fredriksen, and B. So. An empirical study of the reliability of UNIX utilities. *Communications of the ACM*, 33(12):32–44, 1990.

[25] D. Molnar, X. C. Li, and D. A. Wagner. Dynamic test generation to find integer bugs in x86 binary Linux programs. In *Proceedings of the 18th conference on USENIX security symposium*, pages 67–82. USENIX Association, 2009.

[26] N. Nethercote and J. Seward. Valgrind: a framework for heavyweight dynamic binary instrumentation. In *Proceedings of the 2007 ACM SIGPLAN conference on Programming language design and implementation*, PLDI '07. ACM, 2007.

[27] J. H. Perkins, S. Kim, S. Larsen, S. Amarasinghe, J. Bachrach, M. Carbin, C. Pacheco, F. Sherwood, S. Sidiroglou, G. Sullivan, W.-F. Wong, Y. Zibin, M. D. Ernst, and M. Rinard. Automatically patching errors in deployed software. In *Proceedings of the ACM SIGOPS 22nd symposium on Operating systems principles*, SOSP '09, pages 87–102, New York, NY, USA, 2009. ACM.

[28] M. Rinard. Acceptability-oriented computing. In *Proceedings of the 2003 ACM SIGPLAN Conference on Object-Oriented Programming Systems, Languages, and Applications (OOPSLA '03) Companion, Onwards! Session*, Anaheim, California, Oct. 2003.

[29] M. C. Rinard, C. Cadar, D. Dumitran, D. M. Roy, T. Leu, and W. S. Beebee. Enhancing server availability and security through failure-oblivious computing. In *OSDI*, volume 4, pages 21–21, 2004.

[30] J. Röning, M. Lasko, A. Takanen, and R. Kaksonen. PROTOS — systematic approach to eliminate software vulnerabilities. *Invited presentation at Microsoft Research*, 2002.

[31] D. Sarkar, M. Jagannathan, J. Thiagarajan, and R. Venkatapathy. Flow-insensitive static analysis for detecting integer anomalies in programs. In *Proceedings of the 25th conference on IASTED International Multi-Conference: Software Engineering*, pages 334–340. ACTA Press, 2007.

[32] R. Seacord. *The CERT C Secure Coding Standard*. Addison-Wesley Professional, 2008.

[33] K. Sen, D. Marinov, and G. Agha. *CUTE: A Concolic Unit Testing Engine for C*, volume 30. ACM, 2005.

[34] M. I. Sharif, A. Lanzi, J. T. Giffin, and W. Lee. Impeding malware analysis using conditional code obfuscation. In *NDSS*, 2008.

[35] S. Sidiroglou, O. Laadan, C. Perez, N. Viennot, J. Nieh, and A. D. Keromytis. Assure: automatic software self-healing using rescue points. *ACM SIGARCH Computer Architecture News*, 37(1):37–48, 2009.

[36] S. Sidiroglou, M. E. Locasto, S. W. Boyd, and A. D. Keromytis. Building a reactive immune system for software services. *Proceedings of the general track, 2005 USENIX annual technical conference: April 10-15, 2005, Anaheim, CA, USA*, pages 149–161, 2005.

[37] S. Sidiroglou-Douskos, E. Lahtinen, F. Long, P. Piselli, and M. Rinard. Automatic error elimination by multi-application code transfer. Technical Report MIT-CSAIL-TR-2014-024, MIT CSAIL, August 2014.

[38] M. Sutton, A. Greene, and P. Amini. *Fuzzing: Brute Force Vulnerability Discovery*. Pearson Education, 2007.

[39] W. Tielei, W. Tao, L. Zhiqiang, and Z. Wei. IntScope: Automatically detecting integer overflow vulnerability in X86 binary using symbolic execution. In *16th Annual Network & Distributed System Security Symposium*, 2009.

[40] T. Wang, T. Wei, G. Gu, and W. Zou. TaintScope: A checksum-aware directed fuzzing tool for automatic software vulnerability detection. In *Proceedings of the 31st IEEE Symposium on Security & Privacy (Oakland'10)*, 2010.

[41] X. Wang, H. Chen, Z. Jia, N. Zeldovich, and M. Kaashoek. Improving integer security for systems with KINT. In *Proceedings of the 10th USENIX conference on Operating Systems Design and Implementation*, pages 163–177. USENIX Association, 2012.

[42] C. Zhang, T. Wang, T. Wei, Y. Chen, and W. Zou. IntPatch: Automatically fix integer-overflow-to-buffer-overflow vulnerability at compile-time. *Computer Security–ESORICS 2010*, pages 71–86, 2010.

Architectural Support for Software-Defined Metadata Processing

Udit Dhawan[1] Cătălin Hriţcu[2] Raphael Rubin[1] Nikos Vasilakis[1] Silviu Chiricescu[3]
Jonathan M. Smith[1] Thomas F. Knight Jr.[4] Benjamin C. Pierce[1] André DeHon[1]

[1]University of Pennsylvania [2]INRIA, Paris [3]BAE Systems [4]Ginkgo Bioworks

Contact author: udit@seas.upenn.edu

Abstract

Optimized hardware for propagating and checking software-programmable metadata tags can achieve low runtime overhead. We generalize prior work on hardware tagging by considering a generic architecture that supports software-defined policies over metadata of arbitrary size and complexity; we introduce several novel microarchitectural optimizations that keep the overhead of this rich processing low. Our model thus achieves the efficiency of previous hardware-based approaches with the flexibility of the software-based ones. We demonstrate this by using it to enforce four diverse safety and security policies—spatial and temporal memory safety, taint tracking, control-flow integrity, and code and data separation—plus a composite policy that enforces all of them simultaneously. Experiments on SPEC CPU2006 benchmarks with a PUMP-enhanced RISC processor show modest impact on runtime (typically under 10%) and power ceiling (less than 10%), in return for some increase in energy usage (typically under 60%) and area for on-chip memory structures (110%).

Categories and Subject Descriptors C.1 [*Processor Architecture*]: Miscellaneous—security

Keywords security, metadata, tagged architecture, CFI, Taint Tracking, Memory Safety

1. Introduction

Today's computer systems are notoriously hard to secure, and conventional processor architectures are partly to blame, admitting behaviors (pointer forging, buffer overflows, ...) that blatantly violate higher-level abstractions. The burden of closing the gap between programming language and hardware is left to software, where the cost of enforcing airtight abstractions is often deemed too high.

Several recent efforts [2, 37, 53, 57] have demonstrated the value of propagating metadata during execution to enforce policies that catch safety violations and malicious attacks as they occur. These policies can be enforced in software [3, 8, 28, 48, 69], but typically with high overheads that discourage their deployment or motivate coarse approximations providing less protection [23, 31]. Hardware support for fixed policies can often reduce the overhead to acceptable levels and prevent a large fraction of today's attacks [19, 25, 40, 63]. Following this trend, Intel recently announced hardware for bounds checking [36] and isolation [42]. While these mitigate many of today's attacks, fully securing systems will require more than memory safety and isolation. Some needs we can already identify (like control-flow integrity and information flow control) but the complete set remains unknown. Attacks rapidly evolve to exploit any remaining forms of vulnerability. What is needed is a flexible security architecture that can be quickly adapted to this ever-changing landscape. Some recent designs have made the hardware metadata computation configurable [24, 66] but have limited bits to represent metadata and only support a limited class of policies. A natural question, then, is: *Is it possible to provide hardware to support extensible, software-defined metadata processing with low overhead?* In particular, in the spirit of the 0-1-∞ rule, can we efficiently support fine-grained, software-defined metadata propagation without placing a visible, hard bound on the number of bits allocated to metadata or a bound on the number of policies simultaneously enforced?

To achieve this goal, we introduce a rich architectural model, the Programmable Unit for Metadata Processing (PUMP), that indivisibly associates a metadata tag with every word in the system's main memory, caches, and registers. To support unbounded metadata, the tag is large enough to indirect to a data structure in memory. On every instruction, the tags of the inputs are used to determine if the operation is allowed, and if so to determine the tags for the results. The tag checking and propagation rules are defined in software; however, to minimize performance impact, these rules are cached in a hardware structure, the *PUMP rule cache*, that

ASPLOS 2015, March 14–18, 2015, Istanbul, Turkey.

ACM 978-1-4503-2835-7/15/03...$15.00.
http://dx.doi.org/10.1145/694344.2694383

operates in parallel with the ALU. A software *miss handler* services cache misses based on the policy rule set currently in effect.

We measure the performance impact of the PUMP using a composition of four different policies (Tab. 1) that stress the PUMP in different ways and illustrate a range of security properties: (1) a *Non-Executable Data and Non-Writable Code (NXD+NWC)* policy that uses tags to distinguish code from data in memory and provides protection against simple code injection attacks; (2) a *Memory Safety* policy that detects all spatial and temporal violations in heap-allocated memory, extending [17] with an effectively unlimited (2^{60}) number of colors ("taint marks" in [17]); (3) a *Control-Flow Integrity* (CFI) [3] policy that restricts indirect control transfers to only the allowed edges in a program's control flow graph, preventing return-oriented-programming-style attacks [59] (we enforce fine-grained CFI [3, 50], not coarse-grained approximations [20, 72] that are potentially vulnerable to attack [23, 31]); and (4) a fine-grained *Taint Tracking* policy (generalizing [49]) where each word can potentially be tainted by multiple sources (libraries and IO streams) simultaneously. Since these are well-known policies whose protection capabilities have been established in the literature, we focus only on measuring and reducing the performance impact of enforcing them using the PUMP. Except for NXD+NWC, each of these policies needs to distinguish an essentially unlimited number of unique items; by contrast, solutions with a limited number of metadata bits can, at best, support only grossly simplified approximations.

As might be expected, a simple, direct implementation of the PUMP is rather expensive. Adding pointer-sized (64b) tags to 64b words at least doubles the size and energy usage of all the memories in the system; rule caches add area and energy on top of this. For this simple implementation, we measured area overhead of 190% and geomean energy overhead around 220%; moreover, runtime overhead is disappointing (over 300%) on some applications (see §3). Such high overheads would discourage adoption, if they were the best we could do.

However, we find that most policies exhibit spatial and temporal locality for both tags and the rules defined over them. The number of unique rules can be significantly reduced by defining them over a group of identical instructions, reducing compulsory misses and increasing the effective capacity of the rule caches. Off-chip memory traffic can be reduced by exploiting spatial locality in tags. On-chip area and energy overhead can be minimized by using a small number of bits to represent the subset of the pointer-sized tags in use at a time. Runtime costs of composite policy miss handlers can be decreased by providing hardware support for caching component policies. These optimizations allow the PUMP to achieve low overheads without compromising its rich policy model.

The main contributions of this work are (a) a metadata processing architecture supporting unbounded metadata and fully software-defined policies (§2); (b) an empirical evaluation (§3) of the runtime, energy, power ceiling, and area impacts of a simple implementation of the PUMP integrated with an in-order Alpha microarchitecture (§2) on the SPEC CPU2006 benchmark set under four diverse policies and their combination; (c) a set of microarchitectural optimizations (§4); and (d) an assessment of their impact (§5), showing typical runtime overhead under 10%, a power ceiling impact of 10%, and typically energy overhead under 60% by using 110% additional area for on-chip memory structures. Tab. 2 summarizes related work, which is discussed in §6; §7 concludes and highlights future work.

2. The PUMP

We illustrate the PUMP as an extension to a conventional RISC processor (we use an Alpha [1], but the mechanisms are not ISA-specific) and an in-order implementation with a 5-stage pipeline suitable for energy-conscious applications [10]. In this section, we describe the ISA-level extensions that constitute the PUMP's hardware interface layer, the basic microarchitectural changes, and the accompanying low-level software.

Metadata Tags Every word in a PUMP system is associated with a pointer-sized tag. These tags are uninterpreted in the hardware. At the software level, a tag may represent metadata of unbounded size and complexity, as defined by the policy. Simple policies that need only a few bits of metadata may store it directly in the tag; if more bits are needed, indirection is used to store the metadata as a data structure in memory, with the address of this structure used as the tag. The basic addressable word is indivisibly extended with a tag, making all value slots, including memory, caches, and registers, suitably wider. The program counter is also tagged. This notion of software-defined metadata and its representation as a pointer-sized tag extends previous tagging approaches, where only a few bits are used for tags and/or they are hardwired to fixed interpretations (see Tab. 2).

All tag manipulation is defined and implemented with PUMP rules. Metadata tags are not addressable by user programs, only by software policy handlers invoked on rule cache misses as detailed below.

Tag-propagation rules We define metadata computations in terms of *rules* of the form $opcode\ :\ (PC, CI, OP1, OP2, MR)\ \Rightarrow\ (PC_{new}, R)$, which should be read: "If the current opcode is *opcode*, the current tag on the program counter is PC, the tag on the current instruction is CI, the tags on its input operands (if any) are $OP1$ and $OP2$, and the tag on the memory location (in case of load/store) is MR, then the tag on the program counter in the next machine state should be PC_{new} and the tag on the instruction's result (a destination register or a memory location, if any) should be R". Instead of (PC_{new}, R), the function can also fail, indicating that the operation is not allowed. The PUMP can enforce any pol-

Policy	Threat	Metadata	Max Unique Tags	Tag Check (allow?)	Tag Propagation Rules	Ref.
NXD+NWC	code injection	DATA or CODE on memory locations	2	CI=CODE; MR≠CODE on write	no	
Memory Safety	spatial/temporal memory safety violation on heap	color on pointers; region color + payload color on memory locations	$(\#mallocs)^2$	pointer color == referenced region color	$R \leftarrow OPi$ on mov/add/sub; $R \leftarrow payload(MR)$ on load	[17]
CFI	control-flow hijacking (JOP/ROP/code reuse)	unique id on each indirect control-flow source and target	#sources+#targets	$(PC, CI) \in$ program's control-flow graph	$PC \leftarrow CI$ on indirect jumps (including call, return)	[3]
Taint Tracking	untrusted code, low-integrity data from IO	source-taint-id on instructions and IO; set of input taint-ids on words	$2^{(\#code+\#IO\ ids)}$	user-defined check	$R \leftarrow CI \cup OP1 \cup OP2 \cup MR$	[49]
Composite	all of the above	structure with 4 elements	product of above	all of the above (Alg. 2 with $N = 4$)		

Table 1: Summary of Investigated Policies (simplified for brevity; details not critical to understand architecture and optimizations)

Tag Bits	Propagate?	Outputs: allow?	Outputs: R (result)	Outputs: PC	Inputs: PC	Inputs: CI	Inputs: $OP1$	Inputs: $OP2$	Inputs: MR	Usage (Example)
2	✗	soft	✗	✗	✗	✗	✗	✗	✓	memory protection (Mondrian [67])
word	✗	limited prog.	✗	✗	✗	✗	✗	✗	✓	memory hygiene, stack, isolation (SECTAG [5])
32	✗	limited prog.	✗	✗	✗	✗	✗	✗	✓	unforgeable data, isolation (Loki [71])
2	✗	fixed	fixed	✗	✗	✗	✗	✗	✓	fine-grained synchronization (HEP [61])
1	✓	fixed	✗	✗	✗	✗	✓	✗	✗	capabilities (IBM System/38 [34], Cheri [68])
2–8	✓	fixed	fixed	✗	✗	✗	✓	✓	✗	types (Burroughs B5000, B6500/7500 [51], LISP Machine [44], SPUR [64])
128	✓	fixed	copy	✗	✗	✗	✓	✗	✓	memory safety (HardBound [25], Watchdog [46, 47])
0	✓	software defined		✗	propagate only one					invariant checking (LBA [14])
1	✓	fixed	fixed	✗	✗	✗	✓	✓	✓	taint (DIFT [63], [15], Minos [19])
4	✓	limited programmability		✗	✗	✗	✓	✓	✗	taint, interposition, fault isolation (Raksha [22])
10	✓	limited prog.	fixed	✗	✗	✗	✓	✓	✓	taint, isolation (DataSafe [16])
unspec.	✓	software defined		✗	✗	✗	✓	✓	✓	flexible taint (FlexiTaint [66])
32	✓	software defined		✗	✗	✗	✓	✓	✓	programmable, taint, memory checking, reference counting (Harmoni [24])
0–64	✓	software defined			✓	✓	✓	✓	✓	information flow, types (Aries [11])
Unbounded	✓	software defined			✓	✓	✓	✓	✓	fully programmable, pointer-sized tags (PUMP)

Table 2: Taxonomy of Tagging Schemes (Propagate = tag propagates with data (✓) or is a property of memory address (✗); allow? = logic for allowing / disallowing operations; R = policy impacts tag of result; PC = programmable tag on program counter; CI = is current instruction tag checked or propagated; $OP1$, $OP2$, MR = is tag on these inputs checked or propagated)

icy that can be expressed as a function of this form. The mapping should be "purely functional"; i.e., it should neither depend on nor modify any mutable state. The policy function is defined and resolved entirely in software (see App. A [27] for an example). This rule format, allowing two output tags to be computed from up to five input tags, is markedly more flexible than those considered in prior work (see Tab. 2), which typically compute one output from up to two inputs. It should also generalize easily across most RISC architectures. Beyond previous solutions that only track data tags ($OP1$, $OP2$, MR, R), we add a current instruction tag (CI) that can be used to track and enforce provenance, integrity, and usage of code blocks; as well as a PC tag that can be used to record execution history [4], ambient authority [43], and "control state" including implicit information flows [39]. The CFI policy (Tab. 1) exploits the PC tag for recording the sources of indirect jumps and the CI tag for identifying jump targets, NXD+NWC leverages the CI to enforce that data is not executable, and Taint Tracking uses the CI to taint data based on the code that produced it.

Rule Cache The other main feature of the PUMP is hardware support for single-cycle common-case computation on metadata. To resolve the rules in a single cycle in the common case, we provide a *hardware cache* of the most recently used rules; as long as we hit in this cache, we do not add any extra cycles. Fig. 1 shows the microarchitecture of our current rule cache implementation. Specifically, the rule cache does nothing more than perform an associative mapping between the instruction opcode and the 5 input tags and the two output tags. Since rules are purely functional, the rule cache can directly map between pointer tag inputs and pointer tag outputs without dereferencing the pointers or examining the metadata structures they point to. Failure cases are never inserted into the PUMP rule cache since they must transfer control to software cleanup.

While the PUMP can, in principle, implement any policy function, the rule cache can only effectively accelerate policy functions that generate small working sets and hence can be cached well, including: (i) policies that use only a limited number of distinct tags, and hence rules, and (ii) policies where the potential universe of tags is large but the set of tags actually encountered is still modest (e.g., library and file taint-tracking with up to 34 unique taints could see 2^{34} distinct sets in principle, but only about 5–10,000 are seen in practice). Good performance depends upon temporal locality, just as good performance in the instruction and data caches also depend on temporal locality. As with data caches and virtual memory, the PUMP allows the policy programmer to express the policy without being concerned with arbitrary hard limits on the number of tags or rules. If the policies do have (or mostly do have) small tag and rule sets, the policy will perform well. If the policies occasionally need to use more tags or rules, performance degrades only in proportion to the cases where many rules are required. If the policy

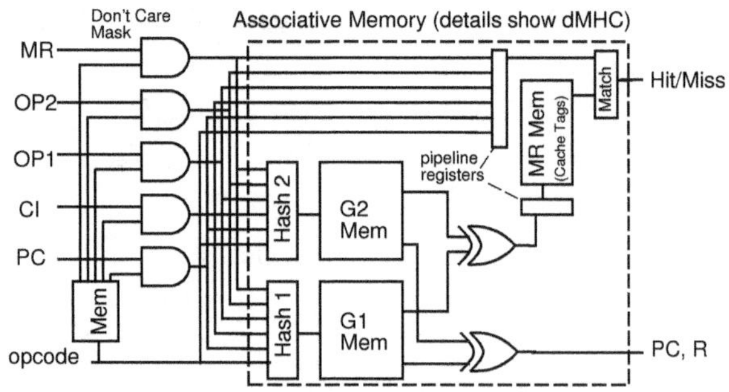

Figure 1: PUMP Rule Cache Dataflow and Microarchitecture

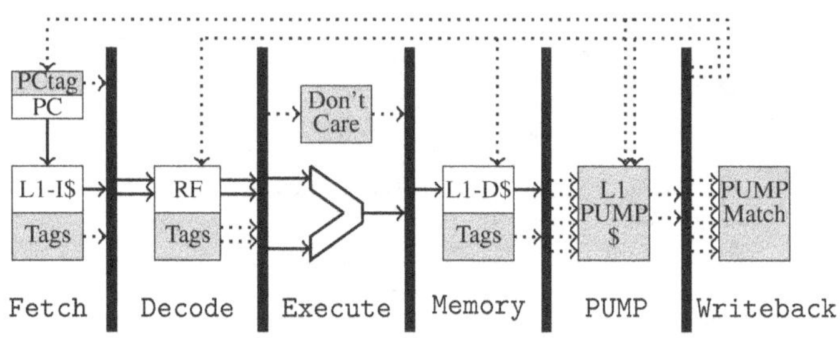

Figure 2: L1 PUMP Rule Cache in a Processor Pipeline

writer develops a policy with poor locality, the rule cache will thrash, just as a program with poor locality will thrash virtual memory and instruction and data caches. The experimental data in this paper shows that the PUMP rule caches can be engineered to efficiently support four quite different example policies, and their composition.

Depending on the instruction and policy, one or more of the input slots in a rule may be unused. For example, a register-to-register `add` will never depend on the value of the unused MR tag. To avoid polluting the cache with rules for all possible values of the unused slots, the rule-cache lookup logic refers to a bit vector containing a *don't-care bit* for each input slot–opcode pair (shown in the `Execute` stage in Fig. 2), which determines whether the corresponding tag is actually used in the rule cache lookup. To handle these "don't care" inputs efficiently, we mask them out before presenting the inputs to the PUMP rule cache (`AND` gates in Fig. 1). The don't-care bit vectors are set by a privileged instruction as part of the miss handler installation. The implementation details of the rule cache are presented in §3.

Pipeline Integration Fig. 2 shows how we revise the 5-stage processor pipeline to incorporate the PUMP hardware. We add the rule cache lookup as an additional stage and bypass tag and data independently so that the `PUMP` stage does not create additional stalls in the processor pipeline.

Placing the PUMP as a separate stage is motivated by the need to provide the tag on the word read from memory (`load`), or to be overwritten in memory (`store`), as an input to the PUMP. Since we allow rules that depend on the existing tag of the memory location that is being written, write operations become `read-modify-write` operations. The existing tag is read during the `Memory` stage like

Algorithm 1 Taint Tracking Miss Handler (Fragment)

switch (op)
case `add`, `sub`, `or`:
  $PC_{new} \leftarrow PC$
  $R \leftarrow$ canonicalize($CI \cup OP1 \cup OP2$)
(... cases for other instructions omitted ...)
default: trap to error handler

a read, the rule is checked in the `PUMP` stage, and the write is performed during the `Commit` stage. As with any caching scheme, we can use multiple levels of caches for the PUMP; in this paper, we use two.

Miss Handler When a last-level miss occurs in the rule cache, it is handled as follows: (i) the current opcode and tags are saved in a (new) set of processor registers used only for this purpose and (ii) control is transferred to the policy miss handler (described in more detail below), which (iii) invokes the policy function to decide if the operation is allowed and, if so, generates an appropriate rule. When the miss handler returns, the hardware (iv) installs this rule into the rule caches, and (v) re-issues the faulting instruction. To provide isolation between the privileged miss handler and the rest of the system software and user code, we add a *miss-handler operational mode* to the processor, controlled by a bit in the processor state that is set on a last-level rule cache miss and reset when the miss handler returns. To avoid the need to save and restore registers on every miss handler invocation, we expand the integer register file with 16 additional registers that are available only to the miss handler. Additionally, the rule inputs and outputs appear as registers while in miss handler mode (*cf.* register windows [52]), allowing the miss handler (but nothing else) to manipulate the tags as ordinary values.

We add a new `miss-handler-return` instruction to finish installing the rule into the PUMP rule caches and return to user code; this instruction can only be issued when in miss-handler mode. While in miss-handler mode, the rule cache is ignored and the PUMP instead applies a single, hardwired rule: all instructions and data touched by the miss handler must be tagged with a predefined MISSHANDLER tag, and all instruction results are given the same tag. In this way, the PUMP architecture prevents user code from undermining the protection provided by the policy. User code cannot: (1) divide, address or replace tags; (2) touch metadata data structures and miss handler code; and (3) directly insert rules into the rule cache.

Alg. 1 illustrates the operation of the miss handler for our Taint-Tracking policy. To minimize the number of distinct tags (and hence rules), the miss handler takes care to use a single tag for logically equivalent metadata by "canonicalizing" any new data structures that it builds. While it would be functionally correct to create a new data structure, with a new metadata pointer, for the set resulting from the unions

Algorithm 2 N-Policy Miss Handler

1: **for** i=1 to N **do**
2: $M_i \leftarrow \{op, PC[i], CI[i], OP1[i], OP2[i], MR[i]\}$
3: $\{pc_i, res_i\} \leftarrow$ policy$_i$ (M_i)
4: $PC_{new} \leftarrow$ canonicalize($[pc_1, pc_2, ..., pc_N]$)
5: $R \leftarrow$ canonicalize($[res_1, res_2, ..., res_N]$)

in Line 4, it is important for performance to make sure that equivalent sets are assigned the same tag—i.e., the same canonical name—to increase reuse and sharing of rules in the rule cache, thereby increasing its effectiveness.

Rather than forcing users to choose a single policy, we want to enforce multiple policies simultaneously and add new ones later. An advantage of our "unbounded" tags is that we can in principle enforce any number of policies at the same time. This can be achieved by letting tags be *pointers to tuples* of tags from several component policies. For example, to combine the NXD+NWC policy with the taint-tracking policy, we can let each tag be a pointer to a tuple (s, t), where s is a NXD+NWC tag (either DATA or CODE) and t is a taint tag (a pointer to a set of taints). The rule cache lookup is exactly the same, but when a miss occurs, both component policies are evaluated separately: the operation is allowed only if both policies allow it, and the resulting tags are pairs of results from the two component policies. Alg. 2 shows the general behavior of the composite miss handler for any N policies. Depending on how correlated the tags in the tuple are, this could result in a large increase in the number of tags and hence rules. In order to demonstrate the ability to support multiple policies simultaneously and measure its effect on working set sizes, we implement the composite policy ("Composite") comprising all four policies described in §1. The Composite policy represents the kind of policy workloads we would like to support; hence we use it for most of the experiments described later.

Most policies will dispatch on the opcode to select the appropriate logic. Some, like NXD+NWC, will just check whether the operation is allowed. Others may consult a data structure (e.g., the CFI policy consults the graph of allowed indirect call and return ids). Memory safety checks equality between address and memory region colors. Taint tracking computes fresh result tags by combining the input tags (Alg. 1). Policies that must access large data structures (CFI) or canonicalize across large aggregates (Taint Tracking, Composite) may make many memory accesses that could miss in the on-chip caches and go to DRAM. On average across all of our benchmarks, servicing misses for NXD+NWC required 30 cycles, Memory Safety 60, CFI 85, Taint Tracking 500, and Composite 800.

If the policy miss handler determines that the operation is *not* allowed, it invokes a suitable security fault handler. What this fault handler does is up to the runtime system and the policy; typically, it would shut down the offending process, but in some cases it might return a suitable "safe value" instead [35, 54]. For incremental deployment with UNIX-style [55] operating systems, we assume policies are applied per process, allowing each process to get a different set of policies. It also allows us to place the tags, rules, and miss handling support into the address space of the process; together with the *miss-handler operational-mode*, this allows fast transitions to and from the miss-handler software without the software bookkeeping, data copying, or management of address translation tables that would be necessary for an OS-level context switch. Longer term, perhaps PUMP policies can be used to protect the OS as well.

3. Evaluation of a Simple Implementation

We next describe our evaluation methodology for measuring runtime, energy, area, and power overheads and apply it on a simple implementation of the PUMP hardware and software, using 128b words (64b payload and 64b "integrated" tag [38]) and the modified pipeline sketched in Fig. 2. Although the optimized implementation of §4 is the one whose overheads (relative to the baseline processor) we really care about, it is useful to describe and measure the simple PUMP implementation first, both because it gives us a chance to show basic versions of the key mechanisms before getting to more sophisticated versions and because it allows us to confirm the natural intuition that the simple implementation does not perform very well.

Resource Estimates To estimate the physical resource impact of the PUMP, we focus on memory costs, since the memories are the dominant area and energy consumers in a simple RISC processor [21] and in the PUMP hardware extensions. We consider a 32 nm Low Operating Power (LOP) process for the L1 memories and Low Standby Power (LSTP) for the L2 memories and use CACTI 6.5 [45] for modeling the area, access time, energy per access, and static (leakage) power of the main memory and the processor on-chip memories.

Baseline Processor: Our (no-PUMP) baseline processor has separate 64KB L1 caches for data and instructions and a unified 512KB L2 cache. We use delay-optimized L1 caches and an energy-optimized L2 cache. All caches use a write-back discipline. The baseline L1 cache has a latency around 880 ps; we assume that it can return a result in one cycle and set its clock to 1 ns, giving us a 1 GHz-cycle target—comparable to modern embedded and cell phone processors. Tab. 3 shows the parameters for this processor.

PUMP Implementation: The PUMP hardware implementation has two parts: extending all memories with integrated tags, and adding PUMP rule caches to the processor. Extending each 64b word in the on-chip memories with a 64b tag increases their area and energy per access and worsens their access latency. This is potentially tolerable for the L2 cache, which already has a multi-cycle access latency and is not used every cycle. But adding an extra cycle of latency to ac-

Unit	Design	Organization	Area (mm^2)	Access Energy Read/Write (pJ)	Static Power (pJ/cyc)	Latency (ps)	Cyc
Register File (Int. and FP)	Baseline	64b, 2R1W, {32 Integer, 32 Floating}	0.002	0.3/0.5	0.080	264	1
	64b tag extended	128b, 2R1W, {48 Integer, 32 Floating}	0.007	1.0/1.4	0.23	295	1
L1-$ (I and D)	Baseline	64KB, 4-way, 64B/line	0.236	17/11	14.4	880	1
	64b tag extended	64KB, 4-way, 128B/line (eff. 32KB, 64B/line)	0.244	19/14	14.5	880	1
L2-$ (unified)	Baseline	512KB, 8-way, 64B/line	1.207	393/481	0.111	4000	5
	64b tag extended	1MB, 8-way, 128B/line (eff. 512KB, 64B/line)	2.350	758/1223	0.214	4930	5
TLB (I and D)	Either	1KB, 2-way set-assoc.	0.040	3.6/4.5	2.0	800	1
DRAM	Baseline	1GB, access 64B line per transfer	-	15,000	-	-	100
	64b tag extended	1GB, access 128B line (eff. 64B line per transfer)	-	31,000	-	-	130
L1 PUMP-$	64b tag	fully associative 1024 entry, 328b match, 128b out (not used; shown only for reference)	1.500	750/900		3000	4
		1024 entry, 328b match, 128b out `Fast-Value dMHC(4,2)`	0.683	51/62	32.0	500	1
L2 PUMP-$	64b tag	4096 entry, 328b match, 128b out `2-level dMHC(4,2)`	0.994	173/444	0.085	3300	4
		Total Baseline Area	**1.485mm^2**				
		Total 64b-tagged Area	**4.318mm^2 (+190% over baseline)**				

Table 3: Memory Resource Estimates for the Baseline and Simple PUMP-extended Processors at 32nm node

cess the L1 caches can lead to stalls in the pipeline. To avoid this, in this simple implementation we reduce the effective capacity of our L1 caches to half of those in the baseline design and then add tags; this gives the same single-cycle access to the L1 caches, but can degrade performance due to increased misses.

The PUMP rule caches require a long match key (5 pointer-sized tags plus an instruction opcode, or 328b) compared to a traditional cache address key (less than the address width), and they return a 128b result. Using a fully associative L1 rule cache would lead to high energy and delay (Tab. 3). Instead, we use a four-hash-function instance of a dynamic Multi-Hash Cache (dMHC) [26], a near-associative multi-hash cache scheme. The L1 rule cache, illustrated concretely with a two-hash function instance in Fig. 1, is designed to produce a result in a single cycle, checking for a false hit (MR Mem lookup and comparison) in the second cycle, while the L2 rule cache is designed for low energy, giving a multi-cycle access latency. Entries are added to the dMHC in such a way that the XOR of the values stored in the hashed memory locations (G1 and G2 in Fig. 1) produce the desired output. As long as one of the hashed table entries is empty, a new rule mapping can be added without evicting or displacing existing rule mappings. Tab. 3 shows the parameters for 1024-entry L1 and 4096-entry L2 rule caches used in the simple implementation. When these caches reach capacity, we use a simple FIFO replacement policy, which appears to work well in practice for our current workloads (FIFO is within 6% of LRU here).

Evaluation Methodology To estimate the performance impact of the PUMP, we use a combination of ISA, PUMP, and address-trace simulators (Fig. 3). We use the gem5 simulator [9] to generate instruction traces for the SPEC CPU2006 [33] programs on a 64-bit Alpha baseline ISA (omitting xalancbmk and tonto, on which gem5 fails). We simulate each program for each of the four policies listed in §1 and the Composite policy for a warm-up period of 1B instructions and then evaluate the next 500M instructions. In gem5, each benchmark is run on the baseline processor with no tags or policies. The resulting instruction trace is then run through a PUMP simulator that performs metadata computation for each instruction. This "phased" simulation strategy is accurate for fail-stop policies (the only ones we consider), where the PUMP's results cannot cause a program's control flow to diverge from its baseline execution. While address-trace simulations can be inaccurate for highly pipelined and out-of-order processors, they are quite accurate for our simple, in-order, 5- and 6-stage pipeline. On the baseline configuration, the gem5 instruction simulation and address trace generation followed by our custom address-trace simulations and accounting were within 1.2% of gem5's cycle-accurate simulations.

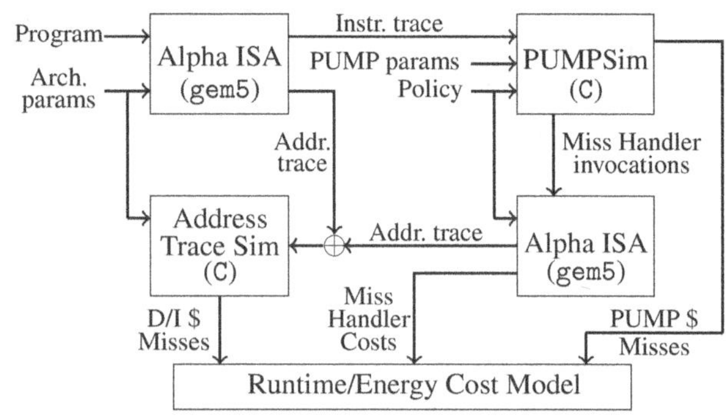

Figure 3: PUMP Evaluation Framework

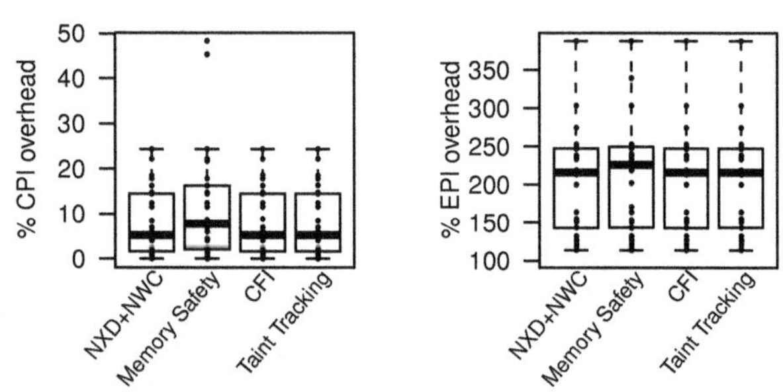

Figure 4: Single Policies with Simple Implementation

We provide the PUMP simulator with miss-handler code (written in C) to implement each policy, and we assign meta-

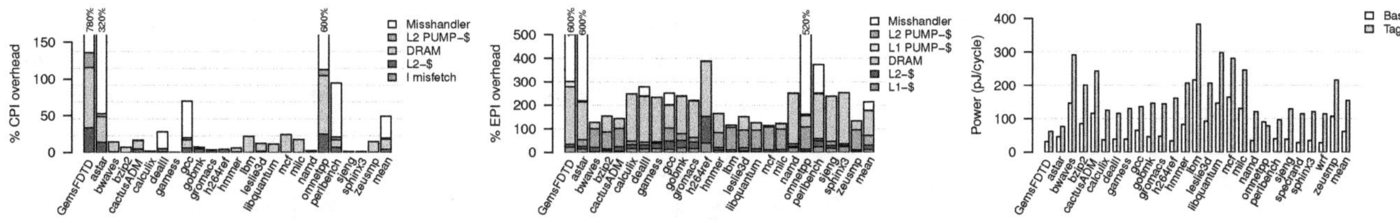

(a) Composite Policy Runtime (b) Composite Policy Energy (c) Absolute Power

Figure 5: Overhead of Simple Implementation with 64b Tags Compared to Baseline

data tags on the initial memory depending on the policy. Our PUMP simulator allows us to capture the access patterns in the PUMP rule caches and estimate the associated runtime and energy costs, accounting for the longer wait cycles required to access the L2 rule cache. Since the PUMP miss handler code also runs on the processor, we separately simulate our miss handler on `gem5` to capture its dynamic behavior. Since the miss-handler code potentially impacts the data and instruction caches, we create a merged address trace that includes properly interleaved memory accesses from both user and miss-handler code, which we use for the final address-trace simulation to estimate the performance impact of the memory system.

Tag and Rule Usage One of the contributions of the PUMP model is support for unbounded metadata. The Composite policy applied to the benchmark set exercises this support. The Composite policy uses from 400 (`specrand`) to 2M (`GemsFDTD`) tags, requiring 1700 (`specrand`) to 14M (`GemsFDTD`) rules. (The large number of tags and rules in `GemsFDTD` are driven largerly by the memory safety policy, which itself uses 640K memory component tags.) The composite tags are pointers that point to metadata structures for the component policies. The Taint Tracking policy tag component is itself a set represented as an ordered list. The largest single metadata structure is 176B. The total metadata structure memory ranges from 1KB (`specrand`) to 56MB (`GemsFDTD`). As a fraction of the maximum heap allocated memory, this represents only 1–10%.

Simple Implementation We evaluate the simple PUMP implementation, comparing it to the no-PUMP baseline.

Area Overhead: The overall area overhead of the PUMP on top of the baseline processor is 190% (Tab. 3). The dominant portion of this area overhead (110%) comes from the PUMP rule caches. The unified L2 cache contributes most of the remaining area overhead. The L1 D/I caches stay roughly the same, since we halved their effective capacity. This high memory area overhead roughly triples the static power, contributing to 24% of the energy overhead.

Runtime Overhead: For all single policies on most benchmarks, the average runtime overhead of even this simple implementation is only 10% (see Fig. 4; to read boxplots [12]: bar is the median, box covers one quartile above and below (middle 50% of cases), dots represent each individual data point, whiskers denote full range except for outliers (more than 1.5× respective quartile)), with the dominant overhead coming from the additional DRAM traffic required to transfer tag bits to and from the processor. For the Memory Safety policy, we see a few benchmarks that exhibit high miss handler overhead, pushing their total overhead up to 40-50% due to compulsory misses on newly allocated memory blocks. For the Composite policy, five of the benchmarks suffer from very high overheads in the miss handler (Fig. 5a), with the worst case close to 780% and the geomean reaching 50%. Two factors contribute to this overhead: (1) the large number of cycles required to resolve a last-level rule cache miss (since every component miss handler must be consulted), and (2) an explosion in the number of rules, which expands the working set size and increases the rule cache miss rate. In the worst case, the number of unique composite tags could be the product of the unique tags in each component policy. However, we do not see this worst case—rather, total rules increase by a factor of 3–5 over the largest single policy, Memory Safety.

Energy Overhead: Moving more bits, due to wider words, and executing more instructions, due to miss handler code, both contribute to energy overheads, impacting both the single and composite policies (Figs. 4 and 5b). The CFI and Memory Safety policies—and hence also the Composite policy—access large data structures that often require energy-expensive DRAM accesses. The worst-case energy overhead is close to 400% for single policies, and about 1600% for the Composite policy, with geomean overhead around 220%.

Power Ceiling: For many platform designs the worst-case power, or equivalently, energy per cycle, is the limiter. This power ceiling may be driven by the maximum current they can draw from a battery or the maximum sustained operating temperature either in a mobile or in a wired device with ambient cooling. Fig. 5c shows that the simple implementation raises the maximum power ceiling by 76% with `lbm` driving the maximum power in both the baseline and simple PUMP implementations. Note that this power ceiling increase is lower than the worst-case energy overhead in part because some benchmarks slow down more than the extra energy they consume and in part because the benchmarks with high energy overhead are the ones consuming the least absolute energy per cycle in the baseline design. Typically the data working set of these energy-efficient programs fits

Unit	Parameter	Range	Final
L1 PUMP-$	Capacity	512–4096	1024
	Tag Bits	8–12	10
L2 PUMP-$	Capacity	1024–8192	4096
	Tag Bits	13–16	14
UCP-$	Capacity	512–4096	2048
CTAG-$	Capacity	128–1024	512

Table 4: PUMP Parameter Range Table

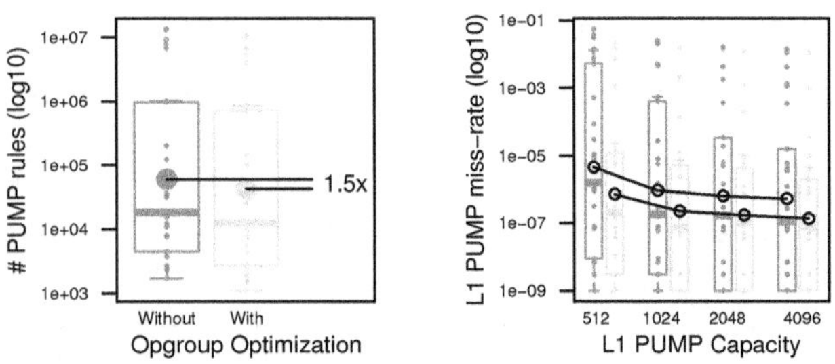

(a) Number of PUMP Rules (b) L1 PUMP-$ Miss-Rate

Figure 6: Impact of Opgroup Optimization

into the on-chip caches, so they seldom pay the higher cost of DRAM accesses.

4. Optimizing the PUMP

Though the simple implementation described above achieves reasonable performance on most benchmarks, the runtime overhead for the Composite policy on some of them and the energy and power overheads on all policies and benchmarks seem unacceptably high. To address these overheads, we introduce a series of targeted microarchitecture optimizations and examine the impact of the architectural parameters associated with the PUMP components (Tab. 4) on the overall costs. We use groupings of opcodes with identical rules to increase the effective capacity of the rule caches, tag compression to reduce the delay and energy of DRAM transfers, short tags to reduce the area and energy in on-chip memories, and Unified Component Policy and Composition Tag caches to decrease the overheads in the miss handlers.

Opgroups In practical policies, it is common to define similar rules for several opcodes. For example, in the Taint Tracking policy, the rules for the `add` and `sub` instructions are identical (Alg. 1). However, in the simple implementation, these rules occupy separate entries in the rule caches. Consequently, we group instruction opcodes with the same rules into "opgroups", reducing the number of rules needed. Which opcodes can be grouped together depends on the policy; we therefore expand the don't-care SRAM in the `Execute` stage (Fig. 2, also shown as "Mem" in Fig. 1) to also translate opcodes to opgroups before the rule cache lookup. For the Composite policy, we can reduce 300+ Alpha opcodes to 14 opgroups and the total number of rules by a factor of 1.1×–6×, with an average of 1.5× (Fig. 6a measures this effect across all the benchmarks). This effectively increases the rule cache capacity for a given investment in silicon area. Opgroups also reduce the number of compulsory misses, since a miss on a single instruction in the group installs the rule that applies to every instruction opcode in the group. Fig. 6b summarizes the miss-rate across all the benchmarks for different L1 rule cache sizes for the Composite policy with and without opgrouping. This figure shows that both the range and the mean of the miss-rates are reduced by opgrouping. With opgroup optimization, a 1024-entry rule cache has a lower miss rate than a 4096-entry rule cache without it. A lower miss-rate naturally reduces the time and energy spent in miss handlers (Fig. 14), and smaller rule caches directly reduce area and energy.

Main Memory Tag Compression Using 64b tags on 64b words doubles the off-chip memory traffic and hence roughly doubles the associated energy. Typically, though, tags exhibit spatial locality—many adjacent words have the same tag. For example, Fig. 7a plots the distribution of unique tags for each DRAM transfer for the `gcc` benchmark with the Composite policy, showing that most words have the same tag: on average we see only 1.14 unique tags per DRAM transfer of an 8-word cache line. We exploit this spatial locality to compress the tag bits that must be transferred to and from the off-chip memory. Since we are already transferring data in cache lines, we use cache lines as the basis for this compression. We allocate 128B per cache line in the main memory, to keep addressing simple. However, rather than storing 128b tagged words directly, we store eight 64b words (payloads) followed by eight 4b indexes and then up to eight 60b tags (see Fig. 7b). The index identifies which of the 60b tags goes with the associated word. We trim the tag to 60b to accommodate the indexes, but this does not compromise the use of tags as pointers: assuming byte addressing and 16B (two 64b words) aligned metadata structures, the low 4b of the 64b pointer can be filled in as zeros. As a result, after transferring the 4B of indexes, we only need to transfer the unique 7.5B tags in the cache line. For instance, if the same tag is used by all the words in the cache line, we transfer 64B+4B=68B in a first read, then 8B in a second read for a total of 76B instead of 128B. The second read is to the same DRAM page, needing only CAS cycles and not the full random-access cycle time. The 4b index can be either a direct index or a special value. We define a special index value to represent a default tag, so that there is no need to transfer any tag in this case. By compressing tags in this manner we are able to reduce the average energy overhead per DRAM transfer from 110% to 15%.

We chose this compression scheme for its combination of simplicity and effectiveness at reducing off-chip memory energy. Many clever schemes for fine-grained memory tagging exist—including multi-level tag page tables [60], variable-grained TLB-like structures [67, 71], and range caches [65]—and these could also be used to reduce the DRAM footprint.

Tag Translation The simple PUMP rule caches are large (adding 110% area) since each cached rule is 456b wide.

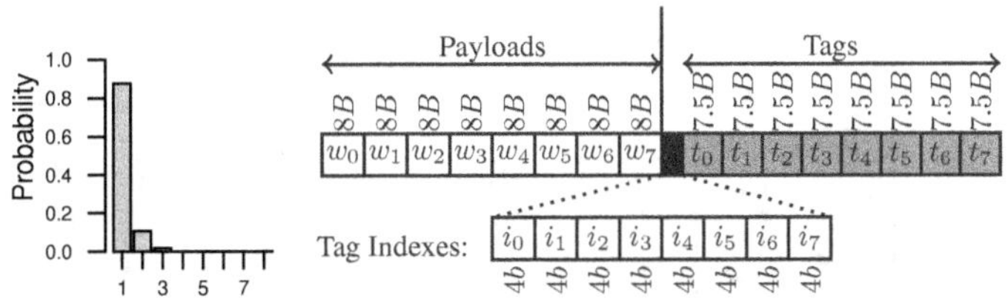

(a) Unique tags per DRAM transfer for gcc

(b) Cache line compression in DRAM

Figure 7: Main Memory Tag Compression

Supporting the PUMP also required extending the baseline on-chip memories (RFs and L1/L2 caches) with 64b tags. Using a full 64b (or 60b) tag for each 64b word here incurs heavy area and energy overheads, as we saw in §3. However, a 64KB L1 D-\$ holds only 8192 words and hence at most 8192 unique tags. Along with a 64KB L1 I-\$, we can have at most 16384 unique tags in the L1 memory subsystem; these can be represented with just 14b tags, reducing the delay, area, energy, and power in the system. Caches exist to exploit temporal locality, and this observation suggests we can leverage that locality to reduce area and energy. If we reduce the tag bits to 14b, the PUMP rule cache match key is reduced from 328b to 78b.

To get these savings without losing the flexibility of full, pointer-sized tags, we use different-width tags for different on-chip memory subsystems and translate between these as needed. For example, one might use 12b tags in the L1 memories and 16b tags in the L2 memories. Fig. 8 shows how we manage tag translation between L1 and L2 memory subsystems. Moving a word from L2 cache to L1 cache requires translating its 16b tag to the corresponding 12b tag, creating a new association if needed. We use a simple SRAM for the L2-tag-to-L1-tag translation, with an extra bit indicating whether or not there is an L1 mapping for the L2 tag. Translating an L1 tag to L2 tag (on a write-back or an L2 lookup) is again performed with an SRAM lookup using the L1 tag as the address. A similar translation occurs between the 60b main memory tags and 16b L2 tags.

When a long tag is not in the long-to-short translation table, we must allocate a new short tag, potentially reclaiming a previously allocated short tag that is no longer in use. There is a rich design space to explore for determining when a short tag can be reclaimed, including garbage collection and tag-usage counting. For simplicity, we allocate short tags sequentially and flush all caches above a given level (instruction, data, PUMP) when the short tag space is exhausted, avoiding the need to track when a specific short tag is available for reclamation. We assume all caches are designed with a lightweight gang clear [41], making flushes inexpensive.

Compared to Tab. 3, where each L1 rule cache access costs 51pJ, we get down to 10pJ with 8b L1 tags or 18pJ with 16b L1 tags, with the energy scaling linearly with tag length between these points. The energy impact on the L1 instruction and data caches is small. Similarly, with 16b L2 tags, L2 rule cache access costs 120pJ, down from 173pJ with 64b tags.

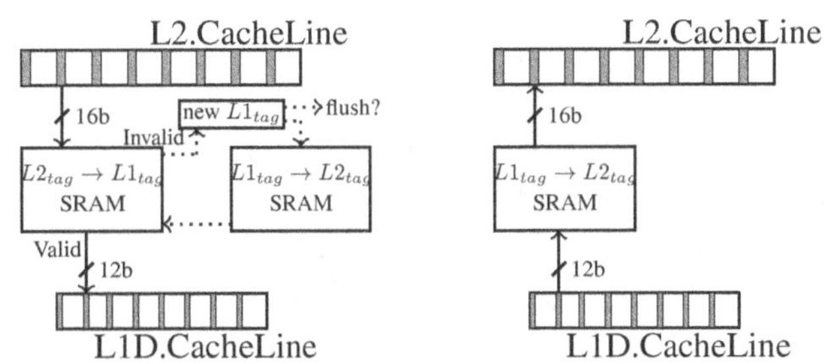

(a) L1 miss, L2 hit

(b) L1 to L2 writeback

Figure 8: Translation Between 12b L1 Tags and 16b L2 Tags

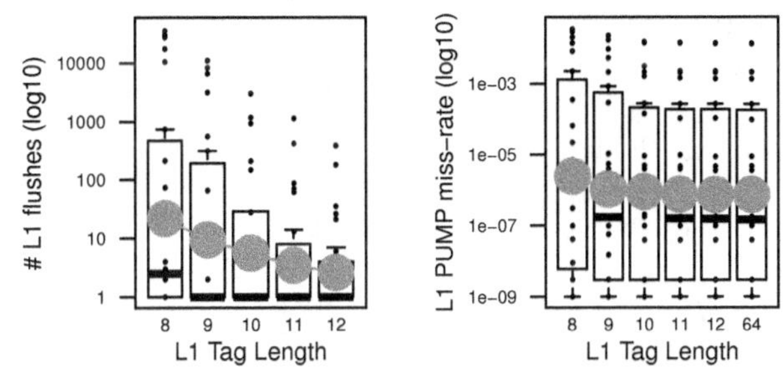

Figure 9: Impact of L1 Tag Length on L1 PUMP Miss-Rates

Slimming L1 tags also allows us to restore the capacity of the L1 D/I caches. With 12b tags, the full-capacity (76KB, effective 64KB) L1 cache will meet single-cycle timing requirements, reducing the performance penalty the simple implementation incurred from the reduced cache capacity. As a result, we limit L1 tag length exploration to 12 bits or less. While even shorter tags reduce energy, they also increase the frequency of flushes. Fig. 9 shows how flushes decrease with increasing L1 tag length, as well as the impact on the L1 rule cache miss-rate.

Miss-Handler Acceleration Enforcing large policies obtained by the orthogonal combination of smaller policies is, not surprisingly, expensive. We illustrated this by combining *four* policies into a single Composite policy. As shown in Alg. 2, each invocation of a N-policy miss handler must take apart a tuple of tags, compute result tags for each component policy, reassemble them into tuples, and canonicalize these tuples to prevent duplication. Moreover, the greater number of tags and rules needed for the Composite policy increases the rule cache miss rates—in Fig. 10a, even though the Taint Tracking and CFI policies individually have a low miss-rate, a higher miss-rate from the Memory Safety policy drives the miss-rate for the Composite policy high as well. The lower miss rates of the individual policies suggest that their results may be cacheable even when the composite rules are not.

Microarchitecture: We introduce two hardware structures to optimize composite policy miss handlers. First we add a Unified Component Policy (UCP) cache where we simply cache the most recent component policy results. The general miss-handler for composite policies is modified to perform lookups in this cache while resolving component policies

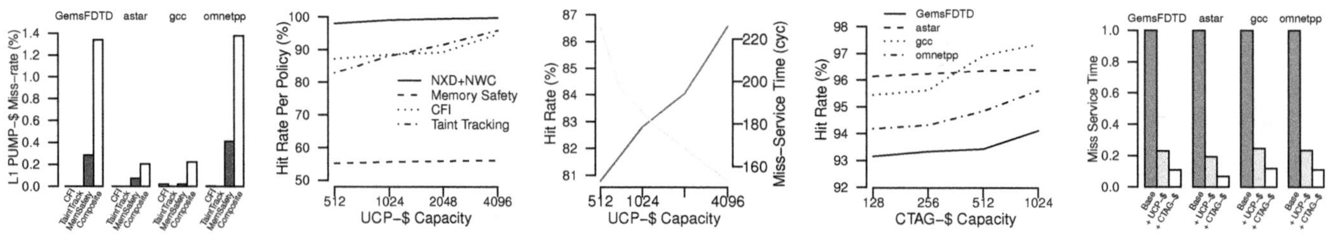

(a) Per policy miss-rates (b) UCP Cache Hit-rate (c) Miss Service Performance (d) Miss-Handler CTAG-$ (e) Miss Handler Cost

Figure 10: Optimizing Composite Policy Miss Handler

Algorithm 3 N-Policy Miss Handler with HW support

1: **for** i=1 to N **do**
2: $M_i \leftarrow \{op, PC[i], CI[i], OP1[i], OP2[i], MR[i]\}$
3: $\{hit, pc_i, res_i\} \leftarrow$ UCP-$ (i, M_i)
4: **if** $!hit$ **then**
5: $\{pc_i, res_i\} \leftarrow$ policy$_i$ (M_i)
6: insert $\{i, pc_i, res_i\}$ into UCP-$
7: $pc[1..N] \leftarrow \{pc_1, pc_2, ..., pc_N\}$
8: $\{hit, PC_{new}\} \leftarrow$ CTAG-$ $(pc[1..N])$
9: **if** $!hit$ **then**
10: $PC_{new} \leftarrow$ canonicalize$(pc[1..N])$
11: insert $\{pc[1..N], PC_{new}\}$ into CTAG-$
12: $res[1..N] \leftarrow \{res_1, res_2, ..., res_N\}$
13: $\{hit, R\} \leftarrow$ CTAG-$ $(res[1..N])$
14: **if** $!hit$ **then**
15: $R \leftarrow$ canonicalize$(res[1..N])$
16: insert $\{res[1..N], R\}$ into CTAG-$

(Alg. 3, line 3). When this cache misses for a component policy we perform its policy computation in software (and insert the result in this cache). We implement the UCP cache with the same hardware organization as the regular PUMP rule cache, with an additional policy identifier field. For simplicity we use a FIFO replacement policy for this cache, but it may be possible to achieve better results by prioritizing space using a metric such as the re-computation cost for the component policies. With modest capacity, this cache filters out most policy recomputations (Fig. 10b; the low hit rate for memory safety is driven by compulsory misses associated with new memory allocations). As a result, we are able to reduce the average number of miss handler cycles by a factor of 5 for our most challenging benchmarks (Fig. 10e). It is possible for every policy to hit in the UCP cache when there is a miss in the L2 PUMP since the composite rules needed could be a product of a small number of component policy rules. For `GemsFDTD`, we hit in 3 or more component policies about 96% of the time.

Second, we add a cache that translates a tuple of result tags into its canonical composite result tag (Alg. 2, Line 4). This identifies the single pointer tag that points to the component result tag tuple, when such a pointer already exists; it is canonicalized so there is a single, unique tag for any distinct combination of components in order to maximize the effectiveness of the rule caches. This Composition Tag (CTAG) cache is implemented by hashing together all the tuple components to get an index into a small CTAG memory. Multiple hashes and memories are used to minimize conflicts as in the PUMP rule cache (Fig. 1). Once the CTAG cache returns a candidate composite tag, the hardware dereferences the pointer result to check that the hashed result is a valid hit. This CTAG cache is effective (Fig. 10d) because it is common for several component policy rules to return the same tuple of result tags. For example, in many cases the PC_{tag} will be the same, even though the result tag is different. Furthermore, many different rule inputs can lead to the same output. For example, in Taint Tracking we perform set unions, and many different unions will have the same result; e.g., $(Blue, \{A, B, C\})$ is the composite answer for writing the result of both $\{A\} \cup \{B, C\}$ and $\{A, B\} \cup \{B, C\}$ (Taint Tracking) into a *Blue* slot (Memory Safety). We also use a FIFO replacement policy for this cache. The CTAG cache reduces the average miss handler cycles by another factor of 2 (Fig. 10e). Taken together, a 2048-entry UCP cache and a 512-entry CTAG cache reduce the average time spent on each L2 rule cache miss from 800 cycles to 80 cycles.

Rule Prefetch: Another way to reduce the compulsory miss rate is to pre-compute rules that might be needed in the near future. A full treatment of prefetching is beyond the scope of this paper. However, one easy case has high value for the Memory Safety rules. When we allocate a new memory tag, we will likely need the 7 rules (initialize (1), add offset to pointer and move (3), scalar load (1), scalar store (2)) for that tag in the near future. Consequently, we add all of these rules to the UCP cache at once. For the single-policy Memory Safety case, we add the rules directly into the rule caches. This reduces the number of Memory Safety miss-handler invocations by 2×.

Fig. 11 shows how the optimizations discussed in this section extend the PUMP-microarchitecture.

5. Overall Evaluation

Design-Point Selection For the most part, the architecture parameters (Tab. 4) monotonically impact a particular cost, providing tradeoffs among energy, delay, and area, but not defining a minimum within a single cost criteria. There is

Unit	Design	Organization	Area (mm^2)	Access Energy Read/Write (pJ)	Static Power (pJ/cyc)	Latency (ps)	Cyc
Register File	Extended 10b	74b, 2R1W, {48 Integer, 32 Floating}	0.005	0.4/0.5	0.13	360	1
L1 Cache	10b-tag	74KB, 4-way, 74B/line (eff. 64KB, 64B/line)	0.272	19/13	16.4	975	1
L2 Cache	14b-tag	592KB, 8-way, 78B/line (eff. 512KB, 64B/line)	1.247	343/640	0.133	4600	5
TLB	–	1KB, 2-way set-assoc.	0.040	3.6/4.5	2.0	800	1
DRAM	64b-tag	1GB, access 128B line (move 76B)		17,500			112
L1 PUMP Cache	10b L1 tag	1024-entry, 58b match, 20b out `Fast-Value dMHC(4,2)`	0.095	15/43.2	2.22	520	1
L2 PUMP Cache	14b L2 tag	4096-entry, 78b match, 28b out `2-level dMHC(4,2)`	0.287	99.4/267	0.032	2800	3
full→L2-tag	64b→14b	8196-entry, 64b match, 14b out `dMHC(4,2)`	0.432	166/436	0.052	3400	4
L2-tag→full	14b→64b	16K×64 SRAM	0.216	55.5/31.5	0.027	1700	2
L2-tag→L1-tag	14b→10b	16K×11 SRAM	0.038	8.8/4.7	0.0040	1420	2
L1-tag→L2-tag	10b→14b	1K×14 SRAM	0.004	0.8/1	0.0004	780	1
UCP Cache	64b tags	2048-entry, 328b match, 128b out `2-level dMHC(4,2)`	0.377	196/479	0.035	2730	3
CTAG Cache	64b tags	512-entry `2-level dMHC(4,2)`	0.107	56/139	0.009	1700	2
		Total area	**3.120mm^2 (+110% over baseline)**				

Table 5: Memory Resource Estimates for the PUMP-optimized Processor at 32nm node

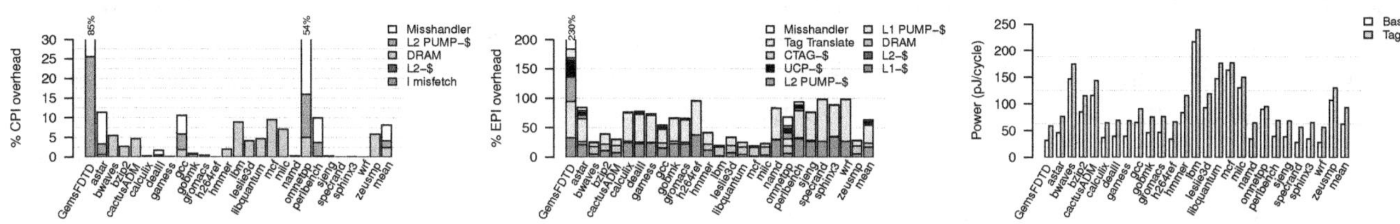

(a) Runtime Overhead (b) Energy Overhead (c) Absolute Power

Figure 12: Overhead of Optimized Implementation as Shown in Tab. 5 (Composite Policy)

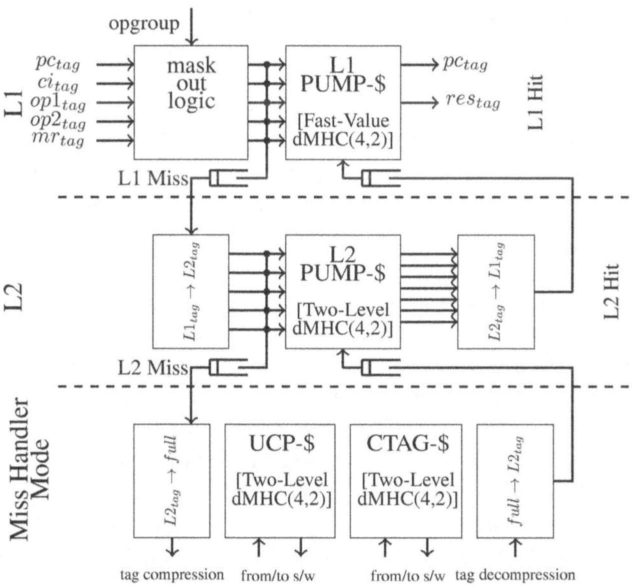

Figure 11: PUMP Microarchitecture

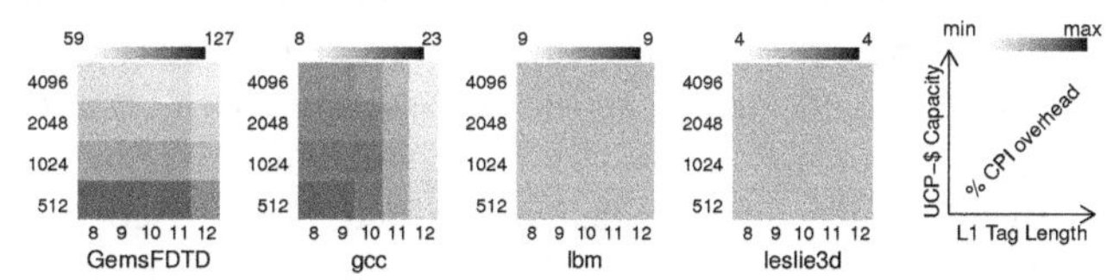

(a) Runtime Overhead

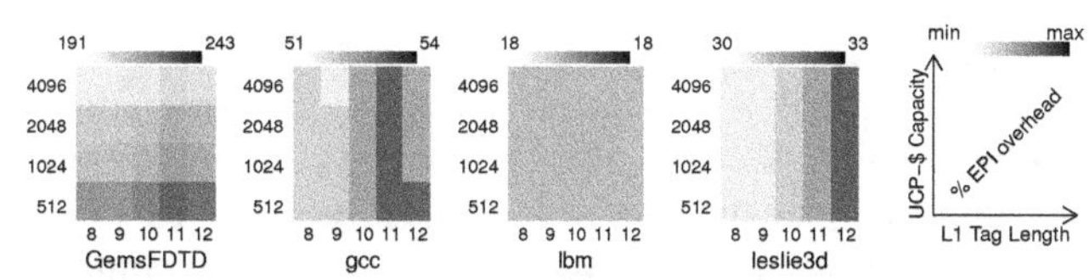

(b) Energy Overhead

Figure 13: Impact of Tag Bits and UCP-$ Capacity

the threshold effect that, once the tag bits are small enough, the L1 D/I caches can be restored to the capacity of the baseline, so we adopt that as our upper bound to explore for L1 tag length, but beyond that point, decreasing tag length reduces energy with small impact on performance. Fig. 13b shows that reducing tag length is the dominant energy effect for most benchmark programs (e.g., `leslie3d`, `mcf`), with a few programs showing equal or larger benefits from increasing UCP cache capacity (e.g., `GemsFDTD`, `gcc`). Ignoring other cost concerns, to reduce energy, we would select large miss handler caches and few tag bits. Runtime overhead (Fig. 13a) is also minimized with larger miss handler caches, but benefits from more rather than fewer tag bits (e.g., `GemsFDTD`, `gcc`). The magnitude of the benefits vary across benchmarks and policies. Across all benchmarks, the benefit beyond 10b L1 tags is small for the SPEC CPU2006 benchmarks, so we use 10b as the compromise between energy and delay and use a 2048-entry UCP cache and a 512-entry CTAG cache to reduce area overhead while coming close to the minimum energy level within the space of the architecture parameters explored.

Runtime and Energy Impact of Optimizations Fig. 14 shows the overall impact on runtime and energy overheads of applying the optimizations from §4 in sequence. Every optimization is dominant for some benchmark (e.g., op-

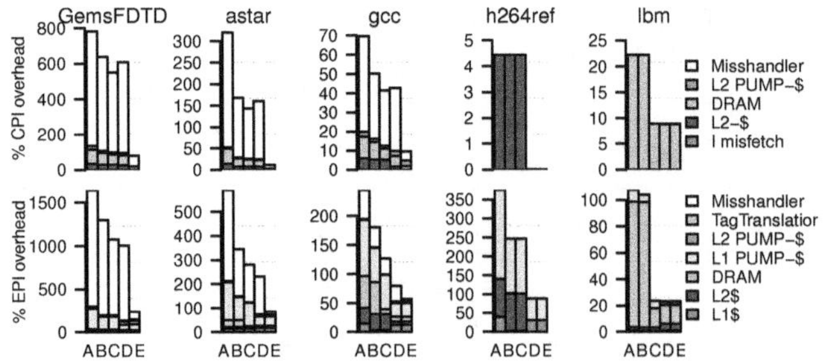

Figure 14: Runtime and Energy Impact of Optimizations on Representative Benchmarks (Composite Policy) (A: Simple; B: A+Opgrouping; C: B+DRAM Compression; D: C+(10b L1,14b L2) short tags; E: D+(2048-UCP, 512-CTAG))

groups for `astar`, DRAM tag compression for `lbm`, short tags for `h264ref`, miss handler acceleration for `GemsFDTD`), and some benchmarks see benefits from all optimizations (e.g., `gcc`), with each optimization successively removing one bottleneck and exposing the next. The different behavior from the benchmarks follows their baseline characteristics as detailed below.

Applications with low locality have baseline energy and performance driven by DRAM due to high main memory traffic. The overhead in such benchmarks (e.g., `lbm`) trends to the DRAM overhead, so reductions in DRAM overhead directly impact runtime and energy overhead. Applications with more locality are faster in the baseline configuration, consume less energy, and suffer less from DRAM overheads; as a result, these are more heavily impacted by the reduced L1 capacity and the tag energy in the L1 D/I and rule caches. DRAM optimization has less effect on these applications, but using short tags has a large effect on energy and removes the L1 D/I cache capacity penalty (e.g., `h264ref`).

The benchmarks with heavy dynamic memory allocation have higher L2 rule cache miss rates due to compulsory misses as newly created tags must be installed in the cache. This drove the high overheads for several benchmarks (`GemsFDTD, omnetpp`) in the simple implementation. The miss handler optimizations reduce the common-case cost of such misses, and the opgroup optimization reduces the capacity miss rate. For the simple implementation, `GemsFDTD` took an L2 rule cache miss every 200 instructions and took 800 cycles to service each miss driving a large part of its 780% runtime overhead. With the optimizations, it services an L2 rule cache miss every 400 instructions and takes only 140 cycles on average per miss, reducing its runtime overhead to 80%.

Overall, these optimizations bring runtime overhead below 10% for all benchmarks except `GemsFDTD` and `omnetpp` (Fig. 12a), which are high on memory allocation. The mean energy overhead is close to 60%, with only 4 benchmarks exceeding 80% (Fig. 12b).

Power Ceiling The optimizations reduce the impact on power ceiling to 10% (Fig. 12c), suggesting the optimized PUMP will have little impact on the operating envelope of the platform. The programs that still have the worst energy overhead (`GemsFDTD, h264ref`) are well below the baseline absolute power ceiling set by `lbm`. DRAM compression reduces the energy overhead for `lbm` to 20%; since it also slows down by 9%, its power requirement increases by 10%.

Area The area overhead of the optimized design is around 110% (Tab. 5), compared to the 190% of the simple design (Tab. 3). On the one hand, short tags significantly reduce the area of the L1 and L2 caches (now adding only 5% over the baseline) and of the rule caches (adding only 26%). On the other hand, the optimized design spends some area to reduce runtime and energy overhead. The UCP and CTAG caches add 33% area overhead, while the translation memories for short tags (both L1 and L2) add another 46%. While these additional hardware structures add area, they provide a net reduction in energy, since they are accessed infrequently and the UCP and CTAG caches also substantially reduce the miss-handler cycles.

Policy Scaling A key goal of our model (and optimizations) is to make it relatively painless to add additional policies that are simultaneously enforced. The Composite policy on the simple PUMP design incurred more than incremental costs for several benchmarks due to the large increase in miss handler runtime, but we reduced these with the miss handler optimizations. For most benchmarks, one policy (typically Memory Safety) dominates the performance of the composition. Adding more policies to this dominant one incurs little further performance degradation—the runtime overhead is increased by less than 1% per policy. This is shown in Fig. 15 where we first show the overhead of each single policy, then show composites that incrementally add one policy at a time to Memory Safety, our most complex single policy. Between the Memory-Safety-only case and the full composite, the average runtime overhead grows from 5% to 8% and the average energy overhead grows from 50% to 60%. The progression makes it clearer what overhead comes simply from adding any policy as opposed to adding a higher-overhead policy. These results show that the caches are effective for these benchmarks: the working set does not grow substantially, and the time spent in miss-handlers resolving all the policies is effectively contained such that it does not degrade performance.

To provide a sense of scaling beyond the four policies measured here, we have decomposed the CFI policy into returns (CFI1) and indirect jumps (CFI2) and the Taint Tracking policy into code tainting and I/O tainting. This does not increase the main PUMP cache working set, as it requires the same number of distinct composite rules, but it does increase the miss-handler complexity and pressure in the UCP and CTAG caches. The fact that we do not see overhead jumps between code and I/O tainting and between CFI1 and CFI2 suggests the working set remains small enough that the additional miss-handler complexity has only incremental impact on overall overhead.

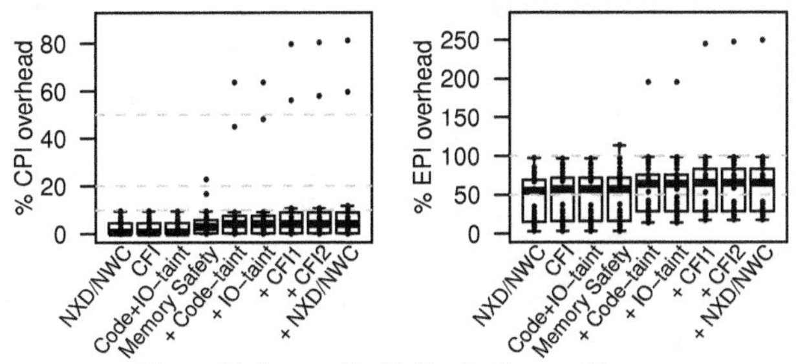

Figure 15: Impact Per Policy in Composition

Two outliers (`GemsFDTD` and `omnetpp`) have a larger increase in runtime overhead (20–40%), with only one (`GemsFDTD`) showing a larger increase in energy. The increases occur only when we add the first taint and first CFI policy, due mostly to higher memory safety compulsory miss rates for these benchmarks coupled with the increased miss-handler resolution complexity.

6. Related Work

The idea of using metadata for safety and security has been around since the 1960s [29]. During the past decade [63], it has been greatly refined and expanded (see Tab. 2). Our proposal extends previous work by offering a unified architecture for metadata tags and making it fully programmable.

The earliest uses of tags were for types, capabilities, and synchronization [34, 51, 61]. More recent uses include taint tracking [15, 19, 63] and bounds checking [17, 46]. Raksha [22] and DataSafe [16] generalize from the 1-bit taints and hardwired policies of earlier systems to larger taint fields (4b and 10b, respectively) and taint-specific configurable propagation rules. Our proposal further generalizes these systems by offering pointer-sized tags and fully programmable, software-defined rules for metadata validation and propagation.

Metadata has long been used for page-size units; later work has associated metadata at finer granularities, down to individual words or bytes [5, 67]. These systems can also trap to software for handling, though the tags do not propagate with the data and no tag results are computed.

DISE [18], Log-Based Architecture (LBA) [13, 14], and FADE [30] provide software-defined checking by inserting instructions in the processor's instruction stream (DISE) or running software on a processor core dedicated to checking (LBA, FADE). Aside from performance gains from code compactness, the performance and energy of DISE are comparable to software-only solutions. LBA adds hardware accelerators for checking and simple propagation (but not computation) of metadata, and FADE adds the the ability to perform programmable `AND` or `OR` computations. Some of the innovations in these accelerators (e.g., the restriction of taint propagation to unary inheritance tracking, excluding taint combining in LBA or the programmable `AND` or `OR` in the FADE Event Table) give up generality that our solution retains. LBA and FADE were demonstrated on simpler policies than our single policies, but have $\sim$50% (LBA) and 20–80% (FADE) runtime overhead compared to our 6% single-policy overhead (Fig. 15). The PUMP can cache any rule for single-cycle PUMP resolution, even rules involving composite tags, while FADE can only capture a subset of operations in a single cycle ("single-shot"), with others requiring multi-cycle resolution. Using a second processor for log processing incurs roughly 100% energy overhead—higher than our worst-case single-policy energy overhead of 60%. Conversely, FADE is designed to work with superscalar, out-of-order cores, while the PUMP design presented here is only for in-order cores.

Other work aims to support software-defined metadata processing with hardware acceleration, similar to our approach. Aries sketches a vision for cached metadata propagation rules [11], and more recently Harmoni shows where a rule cache would fit in a programmable tag processing architecture [24], though neither shows how to map policies into rule tables or evaluates the runtime characteristics of rule-cache-supported policies. FlexiTaint [66] is closest to our design; it demonstrates support for two taint propagation policies and their combination. The policies we show here are richer than the ones supported by FlexiTaint, due both to the extra tag inputs and outputs and to the richer tag metadata. FlexiTaint could in principle be scaled to wide metadata; it would then suffer performance and energy problems similar to our simple design (§3) and would likely benefit from our optimizations.

7. Conclusions and Future Work

With evidence mounting for the value of metadata-based policy enforcement, the time is ripe to define an architecture for software-defined metadata processing and identify accelerators to remove most of the runtime overhead. The PUMP architecture neither bounds the number of metadata bits nor the number of policies simultaneously supported; its microarchitectural optimizations (opgroups, tag compression, tag translation, and miss handler acceleration—see §4) achieve performance comparable to dedicated, hardware metadata propagation solutions (§5). We believe the software-defined metadata policy model and its acceleration will be applicable to a large range of policies beyond those illustrated here, including sound information-flow control [7, 8, 32, 56, 62], fine-grained access control [67, 71], integrity, synchronization [6, 61], race detection [58, 73], debugging, application-specific policies [70], and controlled generation and execution of dynamic code.

Acknowledgments

This material is based upon work supported by the DARPA CRASH program through the United States Air Force Research Laboratory (AFRL) under Contract No. FA8650-10-C-7090. The views expressed are those of the authors and do not reflect the official policy or position of the Department of Defense or the U.S. Government.

References

[1] *Alpha Architecture Handbook*. Digital Equipment Corporation, 1992.

[2] M. Abadi, M. Budiu, Ú. Erlingsson, and J. Ligatti. Control-flow integrity. In *12th ACM Conference on Computer and Communications Security*, pages 340–353. ACM, 2005.

[3] M. Abadi, M. Budiu, Ú. Erlingsson, and J. Ligatti. Control-flow integrity principles, implementations, and applications. *ACM Transactions on Information System Security*, 13(1), 2009.

[4] M. Abadi and C. Fournet. Access control based on execution history. In *Proceedings of the 10th Annual Network and Distributed System Security Symposium*, pages 107–121. The Internet Society, 2003.

[5] D. Arora, S. Ravi, A. Raghunathan, and N. K. Jha. Architectural support for run-time validation of program data properties. *IEEE Transactions on Very Large Scale Integration (VLSI) Systems*, 15(5):546–559, May 2007.

[6] Arvind, R. S. Nikhil, and K. K. Pingali. I-structures: Data structures for parallel computing. In *Proceedings of the Workshop on Graph Reduction (Springer-Verlag Lecture Notes in Computer Science 279)*, Sept. 1986.

[7] T. H. Austin and C. Flanagan. Efficient purely-dynamic information flow analysis. In *Workshop on Programming Languages and Analysis for Security (PLAS)*, PLAS, pages 113–124. ACM, 2009.

[8] A. Bichhawat, V. Rajani, D. Garg, and C. Hammer. Information flow control in WebKit's JavaScript bytecode. In *3rd International Conference on Principles of Security and Trust*, volume 8414 of *Lecture Notes in Computer Science*, pages 159–178. Springer, 2014.

[9] N. Binkert, B. Beckmann, G. Black, S. K. Reinhardt, A. Saidi, A. Basu, J. Hestness, D. R. Hower, T. Krishna, S. Sardashti, R. Sen, K. Sewell, M. Shoaib, N. Vaish, M. D. Hill, and D. A. Wood. The gem5 simulator. *SIGARCH Comput. Archit. News*, 39(2):1–7, Aug. 2011.

[10] E. Blem, J. Menon, and K. Sankaralingam. Power Struggles: Revisiting the RISC vs. CISC Debate on Contemporary ARM and x86 Architectures. In *Proc. HPCA*, pages 1–12, 2013.

[11] J. Brown and T. F. Knight, Jr. A minimally trusted computing base for dynamically ensuring secure information flow. Technical Report 5, MIT CSAIL, November 2001. Aries Memo No. 15.

[12] J. M. Chambers, W. S. Cleveland, B. Kleiner, and P. A. Tukey. *Graphical Methods for Data Analysis*. Wadsworth Statistics/Probability Series. Duxbury Press, 1983.

[13] S. Chen, B. Falsafi, P. B. Gibbons, M. Kozuch, T. C. Mowry, R. Teodorescu, A. Ailamaki, L. Fix, G. R. Ganger, B. Lin, and S. W. Schlosser. Log-based architectures for general-purpose monitoring of deployed code. In *1st Workshop on Architectural and System Support for Improving Software Dependability (ASID)*, pages 63–65. ACM, 2006.

[14] S. Chen, M. Kozuch, T. Strigkos, B. Falsafi, P. B. Gibbons, T. C. Mowry, V. Ramachandran, O. Ruwase, M. P. Ryan, and E. Vlachos. Flexible hardware acceleration for instruction-grain program monitoring. In *35th International Symposium on Computer Architecture (ISCA)*, pages 377–388. IEEE, 2008.

[15] S. Chen, J. Xu, N. Nakka, Z. Kalbarczyk, and R. Iyer. Defeating memory corruption attacks via pointer taintedness detection. In *International Conference on Dependable Systems and Networks (DSN)*, pages 378–387, 2005.

[16] Y.-Y. Chen, P. A. Jamkhedkar, and R. B. Lee. A software-hardware architecture for self-protecting data. In *ACM Conference on Computer and Communications Security*, pages 14–27. ACM, 2012.

[17] J. A. Clause, I. Doudalis, A. Orso, and M. Prvulovic. Effective memory protection using dynamic tainting. In *22nd IEEE/ACM International Conference on Automated Software Engineering (ASE)*, pages 284–292. ACM, 2007.

[18] M. L. Corliss, E. C. Lewis, and A. Roth. DISE: a programmable macro engine for customizing applications. *SIGARCH Comput. Archit. News*, 31(2):362–373, May 2003.

[19] J. R. Crandall, F. T. Chong, and S. F. Wu. Minos: Architectural support for protecting control data. *ACM Transactions on Architecture and Code Optimization*, 5:359–389, December 2006.

[20] J. Criswell, N. Dautenhahn, and V. Adve. KCoFI: Complete control-flow integrity for commodity operating system kernels. In *IEEE Security and Privacy Symposium*, 2014.

[21] W. J. Dally, J. Balfour, D. Black-Shaffer, J. Chen, R. C. Harting, V. Parikh, J. Park, and D. Sheffield. Efficient embedded computing. *IEEE Computer*, 41(7):27–32, July 2008.

[22] M. Dalton, H. Kannan, and C. Kozyrakis. Raksha: a flexible information flow architecture for software security. In *International Symposium on Computer Architecture (ISCA)*, pages 482–493, 2007.

[23] L. Davi, A. Sadeghi, D. Lehmann, and F. Monrose. Stitching the gadgets: On the ineffectiveness of coarse-grained control-flow integrity protection. In *23rd USENIX Security Symposium*, pages 401–416, 2014.

[24] D. Y. Deng and G. E. Suh. High-performance parallel accelerator for flexible and efficient run-time monitoring. In *IEEE/IFIP International Conference on Dependable Systems and Networks (DSN)*, pages 1–12. IEEE Computer Society, 2012.

[25] J. Devietti, C. Blundell, M. M. K. Martin, and S. Zdancewic. HardBound: Architectural support for spatial safety of the C programming language. In *13th International Conference on Architectural Support for Programming Languages and Operating Systems*, pages 103–114, 2008.

[26] U. Dhawan and A. DeHon. Area-efficient near-associative memories on FPGAs. In *Proceedings of the International Symposium on Field-Programmable Gate Arrays*, pages 191–200, 2013.

[27] U. Dhawan, C. Hriţcu, R. Rubin, N. Vasilakis, S. Chiricescu, J. M. Smith, T. F. Knight, Jr., B. C. Pierce, and A. DeHon. Online appendix to Architectural support for software-defined metadata processing. Available from `http://ic.ese.upenn.edu/abstracts/sdmp_asplos2015.html`, January 2015.

[28] Ú. Erlingsson, M. Abadi, M. Vrable, M. Budiu, and G. C. Necula. XFI: Software guards for system address spaces. In *7th Symposium on Operating Systems Design and Implementation*, pages 75–88. USENIX Association, 2006.

[29] E. A. Feustel. On the advantages of tagged architectures. *IEEE Transactions on Computers*, 22:644–652, July 1973.

[30] S. Fytraki, E. Vlachos, Y. O. Koçberber, B. Falsafi, and B. Grot. FADE: A programmable filtering accelerator for instruction-grain monitoring. In *20th IEEE International Symposium on High Performance Computer Architecture*, pages 108–119, 2014.

[31] E. Göktaş, E. Athanasopoulos, H. Bos, and G. Portokalidis. Out of control: Overcoming control-flow integrity. In *IEEE Symposium on Security and Privacy*, 2014.

[32] D. Hedin and A. Sabelfeld. Information-flow security for a core of JavaScript. In *25th IEEE Computer Security Foundations Symposium (CSF)*, CSF, pages 3–18. IEEE, 2012.

[33] J. L. Henning. SPEC CPU2006 benchmark descriptions. *SIGARCH Comput. Archit. News*, 34(4):1–17, Sept. 2006.

[34] M. E. Houdek, F. G. Soltis, and R. L. Hoffman. IBM System/38 Support for Capability-based Addressing. In *Proceedings of the Eighth Annual Symposium on Computer Architecture*, pages 341–348, 1981.

[35] C. Hriţcu, M. Greenberg, B. Karel, B. C. Pierce, and G. Morrisett. All your IFCException are belong to us. In *34th IEEE Symposium on Security and Privacy*, pages 3–17. IEEE Computer Society Press, May 2013.

[36] Introduction to Intel Memory Protection extensions. `http://software.intel.com/en-us/articles/introduction-to-intel-memory-protection-extensions`. Accessed: 2014-05-24.

[37] M. G. Kang, S. McCamant, P. Poosankam, and D. Song. DTA++: Dynamic taint analysis with targeted control-flow propagation. In *Network and Distributed System Security Symposium (NDSS)*. The Internet Society, 2011.

[38] H. Kannan. Ordering decoupled metadata accesses in multiprocessors. In *Proceedings of IEEE/ACM International Symposium on Microarchitecture*, MICRO 42, pages 381–390, 2009.

[39] D. King, B. Hicks, M. Hicks, and T. Jaeger. Implicit flows: Can't live with 'em, can't live without 'em. In *4th International Conference on Information Systems Security*, ICISS, pages 56–70, 2008.

[40] A. Kwon, U. Dhawan, J. M. Smith, T. F. Knight, Jr., and A. DeHon. Low-fat pointers: compact encoding and efficient gate-level implementation of fat pointers for spatial safety and capability-based security. In *ACM SIGSAC Conference on Computer and Communications Security (CCS)*, pages 721–732. ACM, 2013.

[41] K. Mai, R. Ho, E. Alon, D. Liu, Y. Kim, D. Patil, and M. Horowitz. Architecture and Circuit Techniques for a 1.1GHz 16-kb Reconfigurable Memory in 0.18um-CMOS. *IEEE J. Solid-State Circuits*, 40(1):261–275, January 2005.

[42] F. McKeen, I. Alexandrovich, A. Berenzon, C. V. Rozas, H. Shafi, V. Shanbhogue, and U. R. Savagaonkar. Innovative instructions and software model for isolated execution. In *Workshop on Hardware and Architectural Support for Security and Privacy*, pages 10:1–10:1, 2013.

[43] M. S. Miller, K.-P. Yee, and J. Shapiro. Capability myths demolished. Version submitted to Usenix Security 2003., 2003.

[44] D. A. Moon. Architecture of the Symbolics 3600. In *Proceedings of the 12th Annual International Symposium on Computer Architecture*, ISCA, pages 76–83, Los Alamitos, CA, USA, 1985. IEEE Computer Society.

[45] N. Muralimanohar, R. Balasubramonian, and N. P. Jouppi. CACTI 6.0: A tool to model large caches. HPL 2009-85, HP Labs, Palo Alto, CA, April 2009. Latest code release for CACTI 6 is 6.5.

[46] S. Nagarakatte, M. M. K. Martin, and S. Zdancewic. Hardware-Enforced Comprehensive Memory Safety. *IEEE Micro*, 33(3):38–47, May-June 2013.

[47] S. Nagarakatte, M. M. K. Martin, and S. Zdancewic. WatchdogLite: Hardware-accelerated compiler-based pointer checking. In *12th Annual IEEE/ACM International Symposium on Code Generation and Optimization*, page 175. ACM, 2014.

[48] S. Nagarakatte, J. Zhao, M. M. K. Martin, and S. Zdancewic. CETS: compiler enforced temporal safety for C. In *9th International Symposium on Memory Management*, pages 31–40. ACM, 2010.

[49] J. Newsome and D. X. Song. Dynamic taint analysis for automatic detection, analysis, and signature generation of exploits on commodity software. In *the Network and Distributed System Security Symposium (NDSS)*. The Internet Society, 2005.

[50] B. Niu and G. Tan. Modular control-flow integrity. In *ACM SIGPLAN Conference on Programming Language Design and Implementation*, page 58. ACM, 2014.

[51] E. I. Organick. *Computer System Organization: The B5700/B6700 Series*. Academic Press, 1973.

[52] D. A. Patterson and C. H. Sequin. RISC I: A Reduced Instruction Set VLSI Computer. In *Proceedings of the 8th Annual Symposium on Computer Architecture*, ISCA '81, pages 443–457, 1981.

[53] F. Qin, C. Wang, Z. Li, H. Kim, Y. Zhou, and Y. Wu. LIFT: A low-overhead practical information flow tracking system for detecting security attacks. In *39th IEEE/ACM International Symposium on Microarchitecture (MICRO-39)*, pages 135–148, 2006.

[54] M. Rinard, C. Cadar, D. Dumitran, D. M. Roy, T. Leu, and W. S. Beebee, Jr. Enhancing Server Availability and Security Through Failure-Oblivious Computing. In *Proceedings of the Symposium on Operating Systems Design and Implementation (OSDI)*, December 2004.

[55] D. Ritchie and K. Thompson. The UNIX Time-Sharing System. *Bell System Technical Journal*, 57(6):1905–1930, 1978.

[56] A. Russo and A. Sabelfeld. Dynamic vs. static flow-sensitive security analysis. In *23rd Computer Security Foundations Symposium (CSF)*, CSF, pages 186–199. IEEE Computer Society, 2010.

[57] O. Ruwase and M. S. Lam. A Practical Dynamic Buffer Overflow Detector. In *Proc. NDSS*, pages 159–169, 2004.

[58] S. Savage, M. Burrows, G. Nelson, P. Sobalvarro, and T. Anderson. Eraser: A dynamic race detector for multi-threaded programs. *ACM Transactions on Computer Systems*, 15(4), 1997.

[59] H. Shacham. The Geometry of Innocent Flesh on the Bone: Return-into-libc without Function Calls (on the x86). In *Proc. ACM CCS*, pages 552–561, Oct. 2007.

[60] R. Shioya, D. Kim, K. Horio, M. Goshima, and S. Sakai. Low-overhead architecture for security tag. In *Proceedings of the 2009 15th IEEE Pacific Rim International Symposium on Dependable Computing*, PRDC '09, pages 135–142, Washington, DC, USA, 2009. IEEE Computer Society.

[61] B. J. Smith. A pipelined, shared-resource MIMD computer. In *Proc. ICPP*, pages 6–8, 1978.

[62] D. Stefan, A. Russo, J. C. Mitchell, and D. Mazières. Flexible dynamic information flow control in Haskell. In *4th Symposium on Haskell*, pages 95–106. ACM, 2011.

[63] G. E. Suh, J. W. Lee, D. Zhang, and S. Devadas. Secure program execution via dynamic information flow tracking. In *International Conference on Architectural Support for Programming Languages and Operating Systems*, pages 85–96, 2004.

[64] G. S. Taylor, P. N. Hilfinger, J. R. Larus, D. A. Patterson, and B. G. Zorn. Evaluation of the SPUR lisp architecture. In *Proceedings of the 13th annual International Symposium on Computer architecture*, ISCA, pages 444–452, 1986.

[65] M. Tiwari, B. Agrawal, S. Mysore, J. Valamehr, and T. Sherwood. A Small Cache of Large Ranges: Hardware Methods for Efficiently Searching, Storing, and Updating Big Dataflow Tags. In *Proc. MICRO*, pages 94–105, 2008.

[66] G. Venkataramani, I. Doudalis, Y. Solihin, and M. Prvulovic. FlexiTaint: A programmable accelerator for dynamic taint propagation. In *14th International Symposium on High Performance Computer Architecture (HPCA)*, pages 173–184, Feb. 2008.

[67] E. Witchel, J. Cates, and K. Asanović. Mondrian memory protection. In *10th International Conference on Architectural Support for Programming Languages and Operating Systems*, ASPLOS X, pages 304–316, New York, NY, USA, 2002. ACM.

[68] J. Woodruff, R. N. Watson, D. Chisnall, S. W. Moore, J. Anderson, B. Davis, B. Laurie, P. G. Neumann, R. Norton, and M. Roe. The CHERI capability model: Revisiting RISC in an age of risk. In *Proc. of the International Symposium on Computer Architecture (ISCA)*, pages 457–468, June 2014.

[69] B. Yee, D. Sehr, G. Dardyk, J. B. Chen, R. Muth, T. Ormandy, S. Okasaka, N. Narula, and N. Fullagar. Native Client: a sandbox for portable, untrusted x86 native code. *Communications of the ACM*, 53(1):91–99, 2010.

[70] A. Yip, X. Wang, N. Zeldovich, and M. F. Kaashoek. Improving application security with data flow assertions. In *Proceedings of the Symposium on Operating Systems Principles*, Big Sky, MT, USA, October 2009.

[71] N. Zeldovich, H. Kannan, M. Dalton, and C. Kozyrakis. Hardware enforcement of application security policies using tagged memory. In *Proceedings of the 8th USENIX Conference on Operating Systems Design and Implementation*, OSDI, pages 225–240. USENIX Association, 2008.

[72] C. Zhang, T. Wei, Z. Chen, L. Duan, L. Szekeres, S. McCamant, D. Song, and W. Zou. Practical Control Flow Integrity & Randomization for Binary Executables. In *IEEE Symposium on Security and Privacy*, 2013.

[73] P. Zhou, R. Teodorescu, and Y. Zhou. HARD: Hardware-assisted lockset-based race recording. In *Proc. HPCA*, 2007.

A Hardware Design Language for Timing-Sensitive Information-Flow Security

Danfeng Zhang Yao Wang G. Edward Suh Andrew C. Myers

Cornell University
Ithaca, NY 14853

zhangdf@cs.cornell.edu yao@csl.cornell.edu suh@csl.cornell.edu andru@cs.cornell.edu

Abstract

Information security can be compromised by leakage via low-level hardware features. One recently prominent example is cache probing attacks, which rely on timing channels created by caches. We introduce a hardware design language, SecVerilog, which makes it possible to statically analyze information flow at the hardware level. With SecVerilog, systems can be built with verifiable control of timing channels and other information channels. SecVerilog is Verilog, extended with expressive type annotations that enable precise reasoning about information flow. It also comes with rigorous formal assurance: we prove that SecVerilog enforces timing-sensitive noninterference and thus ensures secure information flow. By building a secure MIPS processor and its caches, we demonstrate that SecVerilog makes it possible to build complex hardware designs with verified security, yet with low overhead in time, space, and HW designer effort.

Categories and Subject Descriptors B.6.3 [*Hardware/Design Aids*]: Hardware Description Languages

Keywords Timing channels, hardware description language, information flow control, dependent types

1. Introduction

Information flow control offers a powerful way to prevent improper release and modification of information in complex systems. It has been applied successfully at multiple levels of abstraction: the language level, the operating system level, and the hardware level. Because hardware behavior can create additional information flows that violate a security policy, it is not enough to control information flow only at the software level.

ASPLOS '15, March 14–18, 2015, Istanbul, Turkey.

http://dx.doi.org/10.1145/2694344.2694372

Recent work has demonstrated the danger of hardware-level information flows by showing that timing channels can be used to communicate sensitive information between processes and even across virtual machines. For example, cache probing attacks (e.g., [15, 30]) exploit the timing channel that arises because accesses to memory locations by one process affect the cache, and thereby observably affect the timing behavior of later accesses by other processes. The cache is not the only problem. Attacks have also been shown that exploit timing channels arising from other components: instruction and data caches [2], branch predictors and branch target buffers [3], and shared functional units [44].

Motivated by such vulnerabilities, we have developed a method for designing hardware that correctly, precisely, and efficiently enforces secure information flow. This method is based on a new hardware description language (HDL) called SecVerilog, which adds a security type system to Verilog so that hardware-level information flows can be checked statically. In combination with software-level information flow control, our hardware design method enables building computing systems in which all forms of information flow are tracked, including implicit flows and timing channels.

Our approach has several advantages over the state of the art in secure hardware design. SecVerilog checks information flows statically while providing formal security assurance and guidance to hardware designers; security assurance is obtained directly from the design process. The language is also expressive enough to prove security of a design even when hardware resources are shared among multiple security levels that are changed at per-cycle granularity. The novel dependent type system of the language integrates with external program analyses, avoiding both the duplication of hardware resources and run-time tracking of information flow. Consequently, run-time overhead is lower than in prior work. Our prototype secure pipelined MIPS processor with a cache adds area and clock cycle overheads of about 1%.

In summary, our work makes multiple contributions:

- SecVerilog, a new hardware description language that extends Verilog with fine-grained tracking of information flows within hardware,

- expressive static annotations incorporating dependent security types, enabling flexible, fine-grained reuse and sharing of hardware across security levels,
- a formal proof that the HDL type system soundly controls information flow, and
- the design of a secure microprocessor using SecVerilog, demonstrating the practicality and the power of this methodology. We show that overheads in delay, area, power, performance and designer effort are all low.

The paper is structured as follows. Section 2 gives an overview of our approach for controlling hardware-level information flow, including timing channels. Sections 3 and 4 describe SecVerilog and its security type system. The formal proof that SecVerilog enforces security is sketched in Section 5. An evaluation of using SecVerilog in building a pipelined MIPS processor is in Section 6. Section 7 covers related work, and Section 8 concludes.

2. Background and Approach

2.1 Information flow control

Information flow control aims to ensure that all information flows in a system respect a security policy. For this purpose, information in the system is associated with a *security level* drawn from a lattice $\mathcal{L}$ whose partial ordering $\sqsubseteq$ specifies which information flows are allowed. For example, a lattice with two security levels L (low, public) and H (high, secret) can be used to forbid information labeled as H from flowing into L ($H \not\sqsubseteq L$) while allowing the other direction ($L \sqsubseteq H$).

The goal of SecVerilog is to enforce fine-grained information flow control for hardware designs in a statically verifiable fashion. With SecVerilog, hardware designers specify hardware-level information flow policies by annotating wires and registers with security labels and specifying a security lattice. Then, the SecVerilog type system statically checks and verifies timing-sensitive information flow properties within hardware at design time. While we use a simple lattice with two security levels (L and H) in our examples, the approach applies to an arbitrary security lattice.

2.2 Threat model

We target synchronous circuits driven by a fixed-frequency clock. We assume a *software-level* adversary, who can observe *all* information at or below a certain security level that we will call low (L). The adversary can also measure timing of hardware operations at the granularity of a clock cycle. Hence, both storage and timing channels [21] are considered. However, we assume the adversary has no physical access to the hardware, and we do not consider physical attacks such as directly tapping internal circuits or side channels that require physical proximity, such as power consumption analysis.

2.3 Controlling timing channels

The ability to verifiably control fine-grained information flow in hardware can enhance security in many applications. One notable example, and a focus of this paper, is designing efficient hardware that controls timing channels. These channels are perhaps the most challenging aspect of information flow security, because confidential information can affect timing in various ways: at the software level, a branch or loop conditioned on secret values creates timing channels [20]; at the hardware level, sharing hardware resources such as the data cache also creates timing channels [8, 15, 30, 32].

```
1 if (h1)[L]
2   h2:=11;[H]
3 else
4   h2:=12;[H]
5 l3:=l1;[L]
```

Restrictions on secure hardware designs:

1) The high partition cannot affect the timing of instructions with label L,
2) the low partition cannot be modified when the timing label is H, and
3) the contents of the high partition cannot affect those of the low partition.

Figure 1. An example of full-system timing channel control. The well-typed program on the left is secure if the hardware enforces the constraints on the right.

Our goal is an efficient hardware design that enforces the complex security policy required by the full-system timing channel control mechanism proposed by Zhang et al. [49]. In this approach, the security of the whole system rests on a concise contract between the software and hardware, provably controlling timing channels if both meet their requirements.

The contract treats the hardware implementation as an abstract *machine environment* whose state is partitioned by security level. For example, with two levels L and H, hardware resources such as caches are conceptually partitioned into a low part and a high part. At the software level, the contract is manifested as one *timing label* for each statement in a source program[1]. With this abstraction, a type system generates *timing labels* at the software layer that should be communicated to hardware. For example, the code fragment in Figure 1 illustrates a well-typed program, in which timing labels are shown in brackets; `h1` and `h2` are confidential, and other variables are public. Since the existence of `h1` in data cache, rather than the value of `h1`, can affect the execution time of line 1, line 1 has a timing label of L. The benefit of these timing labels is that only the timing of instructions with H timing labels needs to be controlled and mitigated at software level, as long as the security policy in Figure 1 is enforced on hardware.

2.4 Example: secure cache design

Designing hardware to meet the complex security policy in Figure 1 is challenging. As an illustration, we consider designing a secure cache, statically partitioned between security levels L (low) and H (high) as proposed in prior work [31,

[1] The general contract in [49] uses two timing labels, called the *read* and *write* labels. SecVerilog is expressive enough to verify the general case, which is implemented in our verified MIPS processor (Section 6). For simplicity, we assume these two labels are equal in most of examples.

```
reg[18:0] {L} tag0[256],tag1[256];
reg[18:0] {H} tag2[256],tag3[256];
wire[7:0] {L} index;
//Par(0)=Par(1)=L  Par(2)=Par(3)=H
wire[1:0] {Par(way)} way;
wire[18:0] {Par(way)} tag_in;
wire {Par(way)} write_enable;

always @(posedge clock) begin
  if (write_enable) begin
    case (way)
    0: begin tag0[index]=tag_in; end
    1: begin tag1[index]=tag_in; end
    2: begin tag2[index]=tag_in; end
    3: begin tag3[index]=tag_in; end
    endcase
  end
end
```

(a) SecVerilog code for cache tags

```
1  wire {L} isLoad,isStore;
2  wire {L} hit0,hit1; // hitX: 1 iff way X gets a cache hit
3  wire {H} hit2,hit3;
4  //LH(0)=L  LH(1)=H
5  wire {LH(timingLabel)} stall, hit, timingLabel;
6  reg[2:0] {LH(timingLabel)} dFsmState;
7
8  assign stall = ((isLoad | isStore) &
9    (~hit | (dFsmState != DFSM_IDLE)));
10 assign hit = (timingLabel == 0) ?
11   ((hit0|hit1)?1:0) : ((hit0|hit1|hit2|hit3)?1:0);
12 ...
13 case (dFsmState)
14   DFSM_IDLE: begin
15     // load hit
16     if (isLoad && hit) begin
17       dFsmState <= DFSM_IDLE; // nonblocking assignment
18   ...
19 endcase
```

(b) SecVerilog code for a cache controller

Figure 2. SecVerilog extends Verilog with security label annotations (shaded in gray).

45]. The L and H partition correspond to the L and H machine environment respectively.

Figure 2(a) presents a simplified fragment of SecVerilog code to update cache tags. For now, ignore the shaded annotations. This design logically partitions a 4-way set-associative cache so that ways 0 and 1 (`tag0` and `tag1`) are used as the L partition, and the other ways (`tag2` and `tag3`) are used as the H partition. The code writes a new cache tag to a way specified by `way` when `write_enable` is asserted.

This simple example shows the intricacy of correctly enforcing the aforementioned security policy in hardware. First, `tag_in` must not contain high information when `way` is 0 or 1, to prevent the H partition from affecting the state of the L partition (`tag0` and `tag1`). Second, `write_enable`, which controls whether a write occurs, cannot be influenced by high information when `way` is 0 or 1 (an instance of implicit flows [35]). Verifying these restrictions is tricky since the cache partition that `tag_in` and `write_enable` belong to can change at run time.

More challenging is to enforce secure timing: the H partition cannot affect the timing of instructions with timing label L. A simplified fragment of the SecVerilog code for the cache controller is shown in Figure 2(b), where `timingLabel` represents the timing label of a cache access, propagated from the software level, `hit`i ($0 \leq i \leq 3$) indicates if way i gets a cache hit, and the `stall` signal indicates when a cache access completes.

Since the `stall` signal affects the execution time of an instruction, a secure design must ensure that only the L partition can affect it when `timingLabel` is 0 (encoding L). Verifying this property is difficult, since the cache controller may access H data even when `timingLabel` is 0 (e.g., to execute line 1 of the example in Figure 1). Perhaps counterintuitively, this access is secure: timing may be affected by the *existence* of H data in the cache but not by the value of the data. Moreover, the `hit` and `dFsmState` signals, which affect `stall` (line 8), are shared across both cache partitions. A secure design must ensure that no information leaks through these shared variables, which is difficult since their uses are spread across multiple statements (lines 13–19 only show a snippet).

2.5 The SecVerilog approach

SecVerilog extends Verilog with the ability to give each variable a *label* that specifies the security level of the variable. In Figure 2, these labels are the shaded annotations, which indicate, e.g., that variables `tag0` and `tag1` are labeled L whereas `tag2` and `tag3` are labeled H. Using these annotations, the SecVerilog type system automatically verifies information flow properties of Verilog code at compile time.

Programming languages that provide the ability to label variables have been developed before [6, 25, 36], but their labels are not expressive enough to handle practical hardware designs where resources need to be shared across security levels. In effect, the security levels change at run time. We use dependent types to address this challenge.

Consider the example in Figure 2(a). The labels of `way`, `write_enable`, and `tag_in` depend on which cache way is being accessed. In fact, we observe that a precise dependent label can be assigned to these variables without any change to the Verilog code. The proper label is `Par(way)`, where the name `Par` denotes a type-level function that maps 0 and 1 to level L, and 2 and 3 to level H (concisely, `Par` $= \{0 \mapsto \mathrm{L}, 1 \mapsto \mathrm{L}, 2 \mapsto \mathrm{H}, 3 \mapsto \mathrm{H}\}$). Intuitively, these dependent labels express a lightweight invariant on variables (e.g., when `way` is 0, `write_enable` must have level L).

For the example in Figure 2(b), `stall`, `hit` and `dFsmState` can be labeled with `LH(timingLabel)` where `LH` $= \{0 \mapsto \mathrm{L}, 1 \mapsto \mathrm{H}\}$ to ensure that they can be affected only by the low partition when `timingLabel` is 0.

Program	Prog	$::= B_1 \dots B_n$
Thread	B	$::=$ `always` $@(\gamma)\ c$
Trigger	γ	$::=$ `posedge clock` | `negedge clock` | $\vec{v}$
Cmds	c	$::=$ $\mathtt{skip}_\eta$ | `begin` $c_1; \dots; c_n;$ `end`
		| $v =_\eta e$ | $v \Leftarrow_\eta e$ | $\mathtt{if}_\eta\ (e)\ c_1$ `else` c_2
Expr	e	$::= v \mid n \mid$ uop $e \mid e$ bop e
Vars	x, y, v	$\in$ **Vars**

Figure 3. Syntax of SecVerilog.

Such invariants can be maintained by the type system described in Section 4. For instance, to ensure that the explicit flow from `tag_in` to `tag0` at line 12 in Figure 2(a) is secure, the type system generates a proof obligation (`way` $= 0 \Rightarrow$ `Par(way)` $\sqsubseteq L$), meaning that when `way` is 0, information flow from `tag_in` (with label `Par(way)`) to `tag0` (with label L) is permissible. This proof obligation can easily be discharged by an external solver.

The soundness of our type system (Section 5) guarantees that all security violations are detected at compile time. For example, consider the case when `timingLabel` is 0 in line 11 in Figure 2(b). If the H partition, such as variable `hit2`, were accessed in that case, an error would be reported because the type system would generate an invalid proof obligation: (`timingLabel` $= 0) \Rightarrow H \sqsubseteq$ `LH(timingLabel)`.

2.6 Benefits over previous approaches

Our approach enjoys several benefits compared with prior efforts with verifiable information-flow security for hardware [22, 23, 42]. First, verification is done at compile time, avoiding run-time overhead and detecting errors at an early design stage. This is not possible with GLIFT [42] and Sapper [22]. Second, variables and logic can be shared across multiple security levels (e.g., `way` and `hit` are shared with various timing labels), which is not possible with Caisson [23]. Moreover, SecVerilog adds little programming effort: Verilog code can be verified almost as-is, with annotations (security labels) required only for variable declarations.

3. SecVerilog: Syntax and semantics

Except for added annotations, SecVerilog has essentially the same syntax and semantics as Verilog [13]. It builds on the synthesizable subset of the Verilog language. We restrict to synthesizable code because unsynthesizable Verilog code is used only for testing purposes: it has no effect on the final hardware. The target language of our compiler is synthesizable Verilog from which hardware can be generated using existing tools.

A core subset of SecVerilog is shown in Figure 3. We choose this subset because it includes all interesting features, and the omitted features (e.g., `case`, `assign` and the ternary conditional) can be translated into the core language.

Level	$\ell \in \mathcal{L}$
Family	$f \in \mathbb{Z}_n \to \mathcal{L}$
Label	$\tau ::= \ell \mid f(v) \mid \tau_1 \sqcup \tau_2 \mid \tau_1 \sqcap \tau_2$

Figure 4. Syntax of security labels.

A SecVerilog program (`Prog`) consists of a set of variable declarations and a set of thread definitions that use these variables. Variable v can represent either a register or a wire. The difference is that wires are stateless, and must be driven by other signals. We do not distinguish them in the syntax.

"Always blocks" (B) in (Sec)Verilog are similar to *threads* from the software perspective. Each `always` block translates into a hardware module that operates in parallel to other modules.

Threads are activated by triggers. A trigger γ can either be a change to the clock signal (`posedge`/`negedge` means the rising/falling edge of the clock signal), or a change to a variable in a variable list $\vec{v}$. For example, commands in the `always` block at line 9 in Figure 2(a) are activated at every rising edge of the clock signal.

Commands c are similar to those in software languages. Symbols η are unique identifiers for program points and can be ignored for now. A feature of Verilog not found in most programming languages is the distinction between blocking assignment $v =_\eta e$ and nonblocking assignment $v \Leftarrow_\eta e$. The effects of blocking assignments are visible immediately, but those of nonblocking assignments are delayed until the end of the current time unit. For example, consider the two code fragments $x = 1; y \Leftarrow x$ and $x \Leftarrow 1; y \Leftarrow x$. If the value of x is initially 0, then y becomes 1 in the first piece of code, but 0 in the second.

We provide a formal operational semantics for SecVerilog in the supplementary material [50].

4. SecVerilog: Type system

The SecVerilog type system statically controls information flow in a rigorous and verifiable way. The most novel features of the type system include: 1) mutable, dependent security labels, 2) a permissive yet sound way of controlling label channels, and 3) a modular design that decouples the program analyses required for precision from the type system. These novel features are essential for statically verifying highly efficient, practical hardware designs.

4.1 Type syntax

Types in SecVerilog are simply Verilog types extended with security label expressions, whose syntax is shown in Figure 4. The simplest form of label τ is a concrete security level ℓ drawn from the security lattice $\mathcal{L}$.

Unlike in most previous work on language-based security, SecVerilog supports *dynamic labels*: labels that can change

$$\frac{}{\Gamma, pc, \mathcal{M} \vdash \texttt{skip}_\eta}\ \textsc{T-Skip} \qquad \frac{\Gamma, pc, \mathcal{M} \vdash c_1 \quad \Gamma, pc, \mathcal{M} \vdash c_2}{\Gamma, pc, \mathcal{M} \vdash c_1; c_2}\ \textsc{T-Seq} \qquad \frac{\Gamma \vdash e : \tau \quad v \notin \texttt{FV}(\Gamma(v)) \quad \models P(\bullet\eta) \Rightarrow \tau \sqcup pc \sqsubseteq \Gamma(v)}{\Gamma, pc, \mathcal{M} \vdash v =_\eta e \quad \Gamma, pc, \mathcal{M} \vdash v \Leftarrow_\eta e}\ \textsc{T-Assign}$$

$$\frac{\Gamma \vdash e : \tau \quad \begin{array}{c} v \in \texttt{FV}(\Gamma(v)) \\ v' \notin \Gamma \end{array} \quad \begin{array}{c} \models P(\bullet\eta) \Rightarrow pc \sqsubseteq \Gamma(v)\ ^{\text{if } v \notin \mathcal{M}} \\ \models P(\bullet\eta), v' = \lfloor e \rfloor_a \Rightarrow \tau \sqcup pc \sqsubseteq \Gamma(v)\,\{v'/v\} \end{array}}{\Gamma, pc, \mathcal{M} \vdash v =_\eta e \qquad \Gamma, pc, \mathcal{M} \vdash v \Leftarrow_\eta e}\ \textsc{T-Assign-Rec} \qquad \frac{\Gamma \vdash e : \tau \quad \begin{array}{c} \Gamma, pc \sqcup \tau, \mathcal{M} \cap \texttt{DA}(\eta) \vdash c_1 \\ \Gamma, pc \sqcup \tau, \mathcal{M} \cap \texttt{DA}(\eta) \vdash c_2 \end{array}}{\Gamma, pc, \mathcal{M} \vdash \texttt{if}_\eta\ (e)\ c_1\ \texttt{else}\ c_2}\ \textsc{T-If}$$

Figure 5. Typing rules: commands.

at run time. A dynamic label $f(v)$ is constructed using a type-valued function f applied to a variable v. Type-valued functions are needed in order to decode the simple values that the hardware can convey into labels from the lattice $\mathcal{L}$.

Dynamic labels are needed to accurately describe information flows in complex hardware designs, where hardware resources can be used by multiple security levels. One example is the label `Par(way)` used in Figure 2(a). Note that all security labels in SecVerilog, including dynamic labels and label-decoding functions, only exist for compile-time type checking; they have no run-time manifestation.

Because security labels can mention terms (in particular, variables such as `way`), the type system has dependent types. Dependent security types have been explored in some prior work on security type systems that track information flow (e.g., [25, 43, 51]), where they provide valuable expressive power. However, in order to support analysis of hardware security, the type system for SecVerilog includes some unique features: first, the use of type-valued functions for label decoding, and second, even more unusual, the presence of mutable variables in types—that is, types may depend on variables whose value can change at run time.

The design philosophy of SecVerilog is to offer an expressive language with a low annotation burden, along with fast, automatic type checking. Following this philosophy, the only kind of term to which a label decoding function can be applied is a variable. This restriction ameliorates two problems: first, the undecidability of type equality involving general program expressions, and second, side effects changing the meaning of types.

Despite this restriction, dependent types in SecVerilog nevertheless turn out to be expressive enough for the intended use in hardware design. Restricting dependent types allows type checking to be fast (e.g., two seconds to verify a complete MIPS CPU in Section 6.1) and fully automatic. The syntax also alleviates the resulting limitations on expressiveness by allowing joins ($\sqcup$) and meets ($\sqcap$) of labels.

4.2 Typing rules

Typing rules for expressions have the form $\Gamma \vdash e : \tau$ where Γ is a typing environment that maps variables to security labels, e is the expression, and τ is its label. Since these rules are mostly standard [35], we leave the details in the supplementary material [50].

The typing rules for commands are shown in Figure 5. The typing judgment has the form $\Gamma, pc, \mathcal{M} \vdash c$. Similar to the usual program-counter label [35] for software languages, pc is used to control implicit flows. More interesting is $\mathcal{M}$, which tracks a set of variables that *must* be modified in all alternative executions. The type system uses $\mathcal{M}$ to improve its precision, as we see shortly.

In the next three sections, we explore the challenges of designing the SecVerilog type system and along the way explain the rules of Figure 5 in more depth.

4.3 Mutable dependent security labels

Dependent types need to mention mutable variables in practical hardware designs. For example, variable `way` in Figure 2(a) can be modified whenever a new read request comes to the data cache, updating which cache way to use. Mutability creates some challenges for the soundness of the type system. We begin by illustrating these challenges.

Implicit declassification. Whenever a variable changes, the meaning of any security label that depends on it also changes. To be secure, SecVerilog needs to prevent such changes from implicitly declassifying information. Consider the example in Figure 6. This code is clearly insecure since it copies `secret` into `public` when `x` changes from 1 to 0 (not shown for brevity).

At the assignment to `y` in the first branch, its level is H, but at the assignment to `public`, the level of `y` has become L. The insecurity arises from the change to the label of `y` during the execution, while its content remains the same. In other words, if `x` changes from 1 to 0, the label of `y` cannot protect its content.

We rely on a dynamic mechanism to erase register contents when the old label is not bounded by the new one. Code to dynamically zero out registers is automatically inserted as part of the translation to Verilog. Note that wires in hardware are stateless, so dynamic erasure only applies to registers.

```
reg[7:0] {H} secret, {L} public, {L} x;
reg[7:0] {LH(x)} y; // LH(0)=L LH(1)=H
always@(posedge clock) begin
  if (x==1) begin y ⇐ secret; end
  else      begin public ⇐ y; end
  end
end
```

Figure 6. An example of implicit declassification.

```
1  reg{H} high;
2  reg{L} low, low';
3  reg{LH(x)} x;//LH(0)=L LH(1)=H
4  ...
5  if (high) begin
6    x <= 1;
7  end
8  if (x==0 && low==1) begin
9    low' <= 0;
10 end
11 low <= 1;
12 ...
```

(a) Insecure program with a label channel.

```
1  reg{H} hit2, hit3;
2  reg[1:0]{Par(way)} way;
3  // Par(0)=Par(1)=L
4  // Par(2)=Par(3)=H
5  ...
6  if (hit2 || hit3) begin
7    way <= (hit2 ? 2'b10 : 2'b11);
8  end
9  else begin
10   way <= 2'b10;
11 end
12 ...
```

(b) No-sensitive-upgrade rejects secure code.

```
1  reg{H} high;
2  reg{L} low, low';
3  reg{Par(x)} x;
4  // Par(0)=Par(1)=L
5  // Par(2)=Par(3)=H
6  ...
7  if (x==0) begin
8    low <= 1;
9  end
10 else begin
11   high <= 1;
12 end
13 low' <= low;
14 ...
```

(c) Flow-sensitive systems reject secure code.

Figure 7. Examples illustrating the challenges of controlling label channels.

While this dynamic mechanism may affect the functionality of the original hardware design, we believe that it is not a major issue in practice for the following reasons:

1. Dynamic erasure happens very rarely in our design experience. Most variables with dynamic labels are wires in our prototype processor design (e.g., `way`, `tag_in` and `write_enable` in Figure 2(a)). So the dynamic mechanism has no effect on these variables.
2. For registers with dynamic labels, this clearing is indeed necessary for security; hardware designers need to explicitly implement it anyway. Consider `dFsmState` in Figure 2(b), the state of the cache controller. It is reset anyway in a secure design, when the pipeline is flushed in the case that the timing label changes from H to L.
3. Further, the compiler can notify a designer when automatic clearing is generated, and ask the designer to explicitly approve such changes.

Label channels. Mutable dependent types create *label channels* in which the value of a label becomes an information channel. For instance, consider the code snippet in Figure 7(a). This example appears secure as the assignment to `low'` only occurs when the label of `x` is L (when `x` is 0). When `high` is 1, the label of `x` becomes H, which correctly protects the secrecy of `high`. However, this code is insecure because the *change of label* `x` also leaks information. Suppose that the variables represent flip-flops that are initialized to $(\texttt{x} = 0, \texttt{low} = 0, \texttt{low}' = 1)$ on a reset. The value of `x` in the second clock cycle after a reset is determined by the value of `high` in the first cycle; 1 if `high` is 1, 0 if `high` is 0. Then, `low'` in the third clock cycle reflects the value of `x` in the second cycle, leaking information from `high` to `low'`.

Similar vulnerabilities have also been observed in the literature on flow-sensitive security types, in which security labels of a variable may change dynamically (e.g., [5, 18, 34]). However, prior solutions are all too conservative (i.e., they reject secure programs) for practical hardware designs.

The first approach is *no-sensitive-upgrade* [5], which forbids raising a low label to high in a high context. However, this restriction rules out useful secure code, such as the secure code in Figure 7(b), adapted from our partitioned cache design. This code selects a cache way to write to. Variables `hit2` and `hit3`, representing the existence of a hit in high cache, have label H. No-sensitive-upgrade rejects this program, since `way` might be L before the assignment.

The second approach [18, 34] raises the label of variables modified in any branch to the context label (the label of the branch condition). Returning to the example in Figure 7(a), the label of `x` would become H because of the if-statement at lines 5–7. This over-approximation can be too conservative as well. For example, consider the secure code in Figure 7(c). Here, the label of `x` specifies an invariant: whenever `x` is 0 or 1 (i.e., `Par(x)`=L), nothing is leaked by the value of `x` nor by the time at which its value changes. Hence, `low`'s transition to 1 at line 8 is secure. However, the approach in [18] raises the label of `low` to `Par(x)` after the if-else statement. This conservative label of `low` makes checking at line 13 fail, since there is a flow from H to L when `x` is 2 or 3. Even a more permissive approach rejects this secure code. When `x` is 2 or 3, the dynamic monitor described in [34] tracks a set of variables that may be modified in another branch (`low` in this case), and raises their label to the context label (H). Hence, line 13 is still rejected.

We propose a more permissive mechanism that accepts secure programs in Figure 7(b) and 7(c). Our insight is that no-sensitive-upgrade is needed for security, but only when the modified variable *might not* be assigned in an alternative path. For example, in Figure 7(b), the variable `way` is modified in both branch paths. Here, the label of `way` is checked for both branch paths on the assignments to `way` (line 7 and 10), ensuring that the label of `way` must be higher than the context label (H) at the merge point. In other words, the fact that the label of `way` becomes H leaks no information. Hence, the no-sensitive-upgrade check is unnecessary in this case. This insight is formally justified in our soundness proof in the supplementary material [50].

This insight motivates using a *definite-assignment analysis*, which identifies variables that must be assigned to in any possible execution. Definite assignment analysis is a common static program analysis useful for detecting uninitialized variables. Since SecVerilog, like Verilog, has no aliasing, definite-assignment analysis is simple; we omit the details.

We assume an analysis that returns $\mathtt{DA}(\eta)$, variables that must be assigned to in any possible execution of the command at location η. The type system propagates this information to branches, so that for an assignment to v, the no-sensitive-upgrade check is avoided if v must be assigned to in other paths. For example, the program in Figure 7(b) is well-typed because `way` is modified in both branches, avoiding the limitations of [5]. Moreover, the type system still enables the remaining (necessary) no-sensitive-upgrade checks. So there is no need to raise the label of a variable assigned to in an alternative path. For example, there is no need to check the assignment to `low` at line 8 of Figure 7(c) in a high context (the else branch), avoiding the limitations of [18, 34]. Soundness is preserved despite the extra permissiveness (see Section 5).

4.4 Constraints and hypotheses

The design goal of SecVerilog is to achieve both soundness and precision, with a low annotation burden. The key to precision is to make enough information about the run-time values of variables available to the type system. For instance, consider the assignment to `hit` at line 10 in our cache controller (Figure 2(b)). To rule out an insecure flow from `hit2` and `hit3` (with label H) to `hit` (with label `LH(timingLabel)`), the type system must ensure $\mathrm{H} \sqsubseteq \mathtt{LH(timingLabel)}$. In other words, in any possible evaluation of the assignment, the label H must be bounded by `LH(timingLabel)`. In fact, this must be true because the condition `timingLabel=1` holds whenever the assignment happens (note that `timingLabel` is a single bit). However, a naive type system without knowledge of run-time values of `timingLabel` has to conservatively reject the program.

We use a modular design to separate the concerns of soundness and precision of our type system. In this design, the type system, along with a race-condition analysis in Section 5.3, ensures soundness (i.e., *observational determinism* in Section 5.2). The precision of the type system is improved further, without harming soundness, by integrating two program analyses: a *predicate transformer* analysis and the definite-assignment analysis already discussed.

Specifically, the type system generates proof obligations: partial orderings that must hold on pairs of security labels, regardless of the run-time values of those labels. To statically check a partial ordering on labels, we might require the partial ordering to hold for *any* possible values of free variables:

$$\tau_1 \sqsubseteq \tau_2 \Leftrightarrow \forall \vec{n}\,.\,\tau_1\{\vec{n}/\vec{v}\} \sqsubseteq \tau_2\{\vec{n}/\vec{v}\}$$

where $\vec{v} = \mathtt{FV}(\tau_1) \cup \mathtt{FV}(\tau_2)$, and $\mathtt{FV}(\tau)$ is the free variables in τ. However, this static approximation is too conservative.

To escape this conservatism, the type system uses a more precise approximation of the possible hardware states that can arrive at each program point. We denote the facts that program analysis has derived about the hardware states as predicates indexed by command identifiers η. The predicates $P(\bullet\eta)$ and $P(\eta\bullet)$ respectively denote overapproximations of the hardware states that can exist before and after the execution of the command at location η. Using even simple program analyses to generate these predicates considerably improves the precision of information flow analysis without harming soundness. Returning to our example, supposing that the program analysis can derive $P(\bullet\eta) = (\mathtt{timingLabel} = 1)$. The type system then only needs to know that the flow from H to `LH(timingLabel)` is secure when `timingLabel` is 1. This requirement can be expressed as an (easily verified) constraint:

$$\mathtt{timingLabel} = 1 \Rightarrow \mathrm{H} \sqsubseteq \mathtt{LH(timingLabel)}$$

$$\lfloor n \rfloor_a = n \qquad \lfloor v \rfloor_a = v \qquad \lfloor e \rfloor_a = \top \text{ (otherwise)}$$

$$\lfloor e_1 \ \mathsf{bop}\ e_2 \rfloor_b = \begin{cases} \lfloor e_1 \rfloor_b \ \mathsf{bop}\ \lfloor e_2 \rfloor_b \text{ if } \mathsf{bop} \in \{\wedge, \vee\} \\ \lfloor e_1 \rfloor_a \ \mathsf{bop}\ \lfloor e_2 \rfloor_a \text{ if } \mathsf{bop} \in \{=, \neq\} \\ \top \text{ otherwise} \end{cases}$$

$$\lfloor \mathsf{uop}\ e \rfloor_b = \begin{cases} \neg \lfloor e \rfloor_b \text{ if } \mathsf{uop} \in \{\neg\},\ \lfloor e \rfloor_b \neq \top \\ \top \text{ otherwise} \end{cases}$$

$$\frac{}{\{P\}\,\mathtt{skip}_\eta\,\{P\}} \qquad \frac{\{P\}\,c_1\,\{Q\} \quad \{Q\}\,c_2\,\{R\}}{\{P\}\,c_1; c_2\,\{R\}}$$

$$\frac{Q = \mathtt{remove}(v, P)}{\{P\}\ v =_\eta e\ \{Q \wedge (v = \lfloor e \rfloor_a)\}} \qquad \frac{}{\{P\}\ v \Leftarrow_\eta e\ \{P\}}$$

$$\frac{\{P \wedge (\lfloor e \rfloor_b)\}\,c_1\,\{Q\} \quad \{P \wedge (\neg \lfloor e \rfloor_b)\}\,c_2\,\{R\}}{\{P\}\,\mathtt{if}_\eta\,(e)\,c_1\ \mathtt{else}\ c_2\,\{Q \cap R\}}$$

Figure 8. Predicate generation in Hoare logic.

4.5 Generating state predicates

Many techniques can be used to generate predicates describing the run-time state, with a tradeoff between precision and complexity. For example, weakest preconditions [10] could be used. However, shallow knowledge of run-time state is enough for our type system to be effective. We use a simple abstract interpretation to propagate predicates forward through each thread definition, starting from the predicate `true` and overapproximating the postcondition at each program point. The rules defining this analysis are given in Figure 8. The algorithm generates predicates in linear time.

Expression results are coarsely approximated by tracking only constant values and variables, and replacing more complex expressions with the "unknown" value $\top$. Operators $\lfloor e \rfloor_a$ and $\lfloor e \rfloor_b$ estimate the arithmetic and boolean values of e, respectively. The result of binary operators is $\top$ if any operand is $\top$. The translation rules on commands are written as admissible weakenings of the rules of Hoare Logic [17]. They should be read as specifying how to compute a postcondition from a precondition. To make reasoning practical, the rules do not derive the strongest possible postcondition—but of course it is sound to weaken postconditions. Consequently, postconditions and preconditions are represented as conjunctions. The rule for assignment weakens the strongest-postcondition rule [11] by discarding all conjuncts that mention the assigned variable, in $\texttt{remove}(v, P)$. For efficiency, the rule for `if` weakens the obvious postcondition, $Q \vee R$, by syntactically intersecting the sets of conjuncts in Q and R.

4.6 Discussion of typing rules

The most interesting rules in Figure 5 are (T-ASSIGN), (T-ASSIGN-REC) and (T-IF). Proof obligations are generated for assignments $v =_\eta e$ and $v \Leftarrow_\eta e$. These proof obligations are discharged by an external solver; our implementation uses Z3 [9]. The informal invariants the type system maintains are 1) the new label of v is more restrictive than both the context label pc and label of e, 2) the no-sensitive-upgrade check is enabled if there might not be an assignment to v in an alternative branch. Rule (T-ASSIGN-REC) checks these invariants explicitly. To check the invariant after update, the rule generates a fresh variable v' to represent the new value of v. Though pc and the security level of e may also change after the assignment, the rule checks against the old value since semantically, information flows from the old state to variable v. The no-sensitive-upgrade check is enforced with the condition $v \notin \mathcal{M}$ adding precision in the case where the variable is assigned in every branch. The single check in Rule (T-ASSIGN) is sufficient for these invariants since $\Gamma(v)$ remains the same when there is no self-dependency, and the check entails no-upgrade-check (because $pc \sqsubseteq \tau \sqcup pc$). To improve precision of the type system, predicates on states are used only as hypotheses in these proof obligations. Blocking and nonblocking assignments use the same typing rule, differing only on when the assignment takes effect.

Rule (T-IF) propagates the set of variables that must be modified in both branches ($\texttt{DA}(\eta)$) to c_1 and c_2. Taking the intersection of $\mathcal{M}$ and $\texttt{DA}(\eta)$ is needed for nested if-statements.

4.7 Scalability of type checking

Queries sent to Z3 are generated by typing rules (T-ASSIGN) and (T-ASSIGN-REC) in Figure 5. Note that these queries are essentially predicates on a (finite) lattice of security labels. In another word, only simple theories (e.g., no quantifiers, no real numbers) of the full-fledged Z3 solver are utilized by the type system. These queries can be efficiently solved by Z3.

Moreover, the static analyses used by SecVerilog to enable precise type checking (definite assignment analysis and predicate generation) are both modular. Race condition analysis may vary depending on the hardware design tool, but is scalable for most tools.

For the complete MIPS CPU in Section 6.1, it takes a total of only two seconds to generate all 1257 constraints by the type system, and solve them with Z3, suggesting that type checking is likely to scale to larger hardware designs.

4.8 Well-formed typing environments

The use of dynamic labels also puts constraints on the typing environment Γ: Γ is *well-formed*, denoted $\vdash \Gamma$, when 1) no variable depends on a more restrictive variable, preventing secrets from flowing into a label, and 2) no dependencies are chained, preventing cyclic dependencies. If $\texttt{FV}(\tau)$ is the free variables in τ, this can be expressed formally as follows:

DEFINITION 1 (Well-formedness). *Γ is well-formed iff*

$$\begin{aligned}\forall v \in \mathbf{Vars}\,.\,&(\forall v' \in \texttt{FV}(\Gamma(v))\,.\,\Gamma(v') \sqsubseteq \Gamma(v))\\ &\wedge(\forall v' \in \texttt{FV}(\Gamma(v))\,.\,v' \neq v \Rightarrow \texttt{FV}(\Gamma(v')) = \emptyset)\end{aligned}$$

5. Soundness

Central to our approach is rigorous enforcement of a strong information security property. We formalize this property and sketch a soundness proof of our type system; the full proof is available in the supplementary material [50].

5.1 Proving hardware properties from HDL code

Our goal is to prove that the actual hardware implementation controls information flow. However, information flow is analyzed at the level of the HDL. The argument that language-level reasoning is accurate has two steps. First, the operational semantics of SecVerilog correspond directly to hardware simulation at the RTL (Register Transfer Level) of abstraction. Second, for a synchronously clocked design, these RTL simulations accurately reflect behavior of synthesized hardware; in fact, functional verification of modern hardware relies mainly on RTL simulation. Thus, HDL-level reasoning suffices to prove hardware-level security properties.

5.2 Observational determinism

Our formal definition of information flow security is based on *observational determinism* [33, 48], a generalization of noninterference [12] that provides a strong end-to-end security guarantee even for nondeterministic systems. Observational determinism requires that in any two executions that receive the same low (adversary-visible) input, the system's low behavior must also be indistinguishable regardless of both high inputs and (possibly adversarial) nondeterministic choices.

Formalizing this property in the presence of dynamic labels presents some challenges, since the security level of a variable may differ in two hardware states. We start by defining a *low-equivalence* relation $\approx_\ell$ on hardware states σ, indexed by a level $\ell \in \mathcal{L}$. Two states are low-equivalent at level ℓ if they cannot be distinguished by an adversary able to observe information only at that level or below.

We assume a typing environment Γ that maps variables to security labels. Given state σ, the security level of a variable x is: $\mathcal{T}(x, \sigma) = \ell'$, where ℓ' is the value of label $\Gamma(x)$ in σ. We formalize the low-equivalence relation as follows:

DEFINITION 2 (Low equivalence at level ℓ). *Two states are low-equivalent at level ℓ iff any variable whose label is below ℓ in one state must have the same label and value in the other:*

$$\forall \sigma_1, \sigma_2 \,.\, \sigma_1 \approx_\ell \sigma_2 \iff \forall x \in \textbf{Vars}\,.$$
$$(\mathcal{T}(x,\sigma_1) \sqsubseteq \ell \Leftrightarrow \mathcal{T}(x,\sigma_2) \sqsubseteq \ell)$$
$$\wedge\, (\mathcal{T}(x,\sigma_1) \sqsubseteq \ell \Rightarrow \sigma_1(x) = \sigma_2(x))$$

It is straightforward to check that $\approx_\ell$ is an equivalence relation. Note that we require the level of x to be bounded by ℓ in σ_2 whenever $\mathcal{T}(x,\sigma_1) \sqsubseteq \ell$. This definition corresponds to our adversary model: all variables below ℓ are observable to the adversary. For example, consider the case $\Gamma(x) = \mathtt{LH}(x), \sigma_1(x) = 0$ and $\sigma_2(x) = 1$. Since x has different labels in the two states, $\sigma_1 \not\approx_L \sigma_2$. This is necessary because the ability to make the observation itself leaks information.

An *event* is a pair (t, σ), meaning that state σ occurred at clock cycle t. Assuming synchronous logic, events are produced only when a clock tick occurs. A *trace* T is a countably infinite sequence of events. We write $\langle \sigma, \mathtt{Prog}\rangle \hookrightarrow T$ if executing Prog with initial states σ produces a trace T. Since the semantics is nondeterministic, there can be multiple traces T such that $\langle \sigma, \mathtt{Prog}\rangle \hookrightarrow T$. Two traces are low-equivalent when the states in traces are clockwise low-equivalent.

We formalize observational determinism as follows:

DEFINITION 3 (Observational Determinism). *Program* Prog *obeys observational determinism if for any low-equivalent states σ_1 and σ_2, execution from those states always produces low-equivalent traces:*

$$\sigma_1 \approx_L \sigma_2 \;\wedge\; \langle \sigma_1, \mathtt{Prog}\rangle \hookrightarrow T_1 \wedge \langle \sigma_2, \mathtt{Prog}\rangle \hookrightarrow T_2 \implies T_1 \approx_L T_2$$

Note that traces include the clock-cycle counter, so this definition is timing-sensitive, controlling timing channels.

5.3 Soundness of SecVerilog

The type system in Section 4 along with a race-condition analysis ensures that well-typed SecVerilog programs satisfy observational determinism.

Race freedom. Today's synchronous hardware design methods disallow race conditions in order to produce deterministic systems. Existing synthesis tools prevent races by ensuring that only one thread updates each variable once per clock cycle. Intuitively, a program is race-free if the sequence of thread executions does not affect the synchronized state.

Soundness proof. We use the notation $\langle c, \sigma\rangle \Downarrow \sigma'$ to denote a big step: fully evaluating command c in state σ results in state σ'. To simplify notation, $\mathcal{V}(\tau,\sigma)$ represents the security level resulting from evaluating type τ in σ.

The first lemma states that any variable assigned to in a high context has a high label in the final state.

LEMMA 1 (Confinement). *Let $\langle \sigma, c\rangle \Downarrow \sigma'$. If c can be typed under a given program counter label pc and well-formed typing environment Γ, then for every variable v assigned in command c, we have*

$$\mathcal{V}(pc,\sigma) \sqsubseteq \mathcal{T}(v,\sigma')$$

Proof. By induction on the structure of c. The correctness of the predicate transformer analysis is used for assignments. □

The next theorem states that running a command atomically to finish enforces noninterference.

THEOREM 1 (Single-command noninterference). *If the states σ_1, σ_2 are low-equivalent at the beginning of a clock cycle, running any well-typed command c in σ_1 and σ_2 produces low-equivalent states at the beginning of next cycle as well:*

$$(\vdash \Gamma) \wedge (\Gamma \vdash c) \wedge (\sigma_1 \approx_L \sigma_2) \wedge \langle \sigma_1, c\rangle \Downarrow \sigma_1' \wedge \langle \sigma_2, c\rangle \Downarrow \sigma_2' \implies \sigma_1' \approx_L \sigma_2'$$

Proof. By induction on the structure of c. The interesting case is an if-statement that takes different branches in σ_1 and σ_2. When both branches assign to v, the label of v must be higher than L in both σ_1' and σ_2' by Lemma 1. When v is assigned in only one branch, the correctness of definite-assignment analysis implies $v \notin \mathcal{M}$. Lemma 1 and the no-sensitive-upgrade check (T-ASSIGN-REC) together ensure the label of v is higher than L in σ_1' and σ_2'. □

Finally, any well-typed SecVerilog program obeys observational determinism and is therefore secure:

THEOREM 2 (Soundness of the type system). *If a SecVerilog program is well-typed under any well-formed typing environment, the program obeys observational determinism:*

$$(\vdash \Gamma) \wedge (\Gamma \vdash \mathtt{Prog}) \wedge (\sigma_1 \approx_L \sigma_2) \wedge \langle \sigma_1, \mathtt{Prog}\rangle \hookrightarrow T_1 \wedge \langle \sigma_2, \mathtt{Prog}\rangle \hookrightarrow T_2 \implies T_1 \approx_L T_2$$

Proof. By induction on the length of T_1. For the inductive step, consider two atomic runs in σ_1 and σ_2 where all threads run to finish without being preempted, producing σ_1' and σ_2'. By Theorem 1, states σ_1' and σ_2' are low-equivalent. By the correctness of the race-freedom analysis, all possible runs from σ_1 and σ_2 produce the same states σ_1' and σ_2'. Hence, the final states must be low-equivalent in all runs. □

6. Evaluation

We used SecVerilog to design and verify a secure MIPS processor. We sketch the processor design, and show how SecVerilog helped avoid security vulnerabilities, including some not identified in prior work. We then provide results on the overhead of SecVerilog and timing channel protection. Overall, we found that the capability to statically control information flow at a fine granularity enables efficient secure hardware designs, and that the SecVerilog type system only requires a small number of changes to the Verilog code with no added run-time overhead.

6.1 A secure MIPS processor design

We implemented a SecVerilog compiler based on Icarus Verilog [1]. The constraints generated by the type system are

Module Name	LOC
Fetch	60
Decode + Register File	465
Execute + ALU	218
FPU	N/A
Memory + Cache	537
Write Back	20
Control Logic + Forwarding + Stalling	419
Total w/o FPU	1719

Table 1. Lines of Code (LOC) for each processor component.

Instruction type	Instructions
Additive Arithmetic	add, addi, addiu, addu, sub, subu
Binary Arithmetic	and, or, xor, nor, srl, sra, sll, sllv srlv, srav, slt, sltu, slti, sltiu, andi, ori, xori
Multiply/divide	mult, multu, div, divu
Floating point	add.s, sub.s, mul.s, div.s, neg.s, abs.s mov.s, cvt.s.w, cvt.w.s, c.lt.s, c.le.s
Branch and jump	bne, beq, blez, bgtz, jr, jalr, j, jal
Memory operation	lw, lhu, lh, lbu, lb, sw, sh, sb, swc1, lwc1
Others	mfhi, mflo, lui, mtc1, mfc1 syscall, break
Security-related	setr, setw

Table 2. Complete ISA of our MIPS processor.

solved by Z3 [9]. Using this implementation, we designed a complete MIPS processor that enforces the timing label contract discussed in Section 2.3. Our processor is based on a classic 5-stage in-order pipeline with separate instruction and data caches, both of which are 32kB and 4-way associative. The processor also includes typical pipelining techniques, such as data hazard detection, stalling and data bypassing, as well as a floating point unit (FPU) that we constructed using the Synopsys DesignWare library.

The Verilog code for our processor has more than 1700 LOC excluding the FPU, as shown in Table 1. LOC for the FPU is not reported because the source for the DesignWare library component is not available. Table 2 summarizes the processor's ISA, which is rich enough that we can compile a recent OpenSSL release with an off-the-shelf GCC compiler. The ISA is at least comparable to the ISAs of prior processors with formally verified security (e.g., [22]). New instructions `setr` and `setw` are used to set timing labels.

Our secure processor design supports fine-grained sharing of hardware resources between different security levels. For example, the design allows both high and low cache partitions to be securely used by a single program. This effectively increases the cache size and improves performance for applications with multiple security levels.

To implement such a rich policy, we divide a 4-way cache into a low partition and a high partition. When the timing label is H, both low and high partitions can be used securely. When the timing label is L, both the low and high partitions are still searched. However, to ensure that timing can be affected only by the low cache partition, a cache access is treated as a miss even when there is a hit in the high partition. To avoid data duplication, the cache line moves from the high partition to the low partition when the data arrives from memory, achieving functional correctness without violating the timing constraint. Since cache states have static labels, they are not zeroed out when timing label changes.

The pipeline, on the other hand, is dynamically partitioned using the timing label. When the timing label changes, the pipeline is flushed to avoid leaking information. A pipeline that interleaves high and low instructions without flushing is indeed insecure, since high instructions may stall low ones.

We found that implementing such a complex policy securely would be difficult without using SecVerilog. For example, the SecVerilog type checker caught a security flaw not foreseen by the authors: the dirty bit copied from the high partition to the low partition created a potential timing channel. Our solution is to set the dirty bit for every cache line immediately after it is fetched. This change still allows store hits to write directly to cache line without writing to memory.

Another security issue caught by the SecVerilog type checker is a stall at the instruction fetch stage affecting the memory stage: in our pipeline implementation, a load miss in an instruction could stall instructions in later pipeline stages. Thus, when the timing label changes, an instruction with timing label H can stall another instruction with label L, breaking the timing-label contract. To make the design type-check, the pipeline is flushed at every timing-label switch.

6.2 Overhead of SecVerilog

SecVerilog may require designers to add additional branches to establish invariants needed to convince the type system of the security of the design. For instance, the type system fails to infer in our cache design that variable `way` can only be 2 or 3 at a particular point in the code. In this case, the design needs to include an if-statement establishing this fact. These added branches represents the overhead of using SecVerilog.

To measure this overhead, we compare our secure MIPS processor written in SecVerilog ("Verified") with another secure design written in Verilog ("Unverified"). The Unverified design is essentially the same as Verified, including the same timing channel protections. Because it eliminates the if-statements necessary for type checking, it cannot be verified.

Designer effort and verification time. The Unverified MIPS processor comprises 1692 lines of Verilog code. Converting this design to the Verified processor in SecVerilog required adding only 27 lines of extra code to the cache module, in order to establish necessary invariants to convince the type checker, suggesting that very little overhead is imposed by imprecision of the type system.

The current implementation of SecVerilog requires a programmer to explicitly write down one security label for each variable declaration, unless the variable has the default label L. However, most security labels can be automatically inferred via adding type inference (e.g., as in [7, 26, 46]) to the SecVerilog compiler, which we leave as future work.

The verification process is also fast. For our processor design, it takes a total of two seconds to both generate all obligations and then discharge them with Z3.

Delay, area and power. We synthesized the processor designs using the Synopsys synthesis flow, using the 90nm `saed90nm_max` digital standard cell library. For all designs, we increased the frequency of the processors to the maximum achievable to see what overhead the Verified design adds to the critical path. The synthesis results are shown in Table 3. Here "Insecure" represents the baseline, unmodified MIPS processor without timing channel protection. We discuss the baseline result in the next subsection.

The Verified design only adds 27 lines of code to Unverified, so we found that the delay, area, and power consumption of the two designs are almost identical. For example, area overhead is only 0.16% even without including cache SRAM, which is identical for all designs. This overhead is much lower than that of other secure design techniques, as reported in [22]: GLIFT, 660%; Caisson, 100%; and Sapper, 4%. Power consumption of the two designs is identical. Critical path delay is slightly lower for Verified, likely due to randomness in synthesis. The results show the benefit of sharing hardware across security levels and of controlling information flow at design time, without run-time checks.

Performance. The Verified design does not add any performance overhead over the Unverified design because the added logic does not change cycle-by-cycle behavior.

6.3 Overhead of timing channel protection

The timing channel protection mechanisms in our processor ("Verified") adds overheads compared to the unmodified baseline ("Baseline") without any protection.

Delay, area and power. When an FPU is included, we found that the critical path delay is identical for both Verified and Baseline, as shown in Table 3. This is because the critical path of the processor lies in the FPU, which is largely unmodified for secure designs. To more meaningfully evaluate the impact of secure design, we also measured the maximum achievable frequency without an FPU. Nevertheless, the delay overhead is still only 1.22%. The area overhead of 0.67% is also quite low, and power overhead is almost negligible. Because SecVerilog allows hardware resources to be shared across security levels while properly restricting their allocations, timing channel protection mostly does not require duplicating or adding hardware.

Performance. The timing channel protection in our secure processor design imposes restrictions on cache usage and results in additional pipeline flushes and cache write-backs. We measured the performance overhead of the Verified processor and tested its correctness on two security benchmarks.

	Baseline	Unverified	Verified
Delay w/ FPU (ns)	4.20	4.20	4.20
Delay w/o FPU (ns)	1.64	1.67	1.66
Area (μm^2)	399400	401420	402079
Power (mW)	575.5	575.6	575.6

Table 3. Comparing processor designs.

Our benchmarks include three security programs (blowfish, rijndael, SHA-1) from MiBench, a popular embedded benchmark suite for architectural designs[2] [16], as well as ciphers and hash functions in a recent release (version 1.0.1g) of OpenSSL, a widely used open-source SSL library.

Thanks to the rich ISA of our MIPS processor, compiling and running these benchmarks requires only modest effort. We use an off-the-shelf GCC compiler to cross-compile the benchmarks to the MIPS 1 platform. We use Cadence NCVerilog to simulate our processor design running these binaries. Because we lack an operating system on the processor, system calls (e.g., open, read, close, time) are emulated by Programming Language Interface (PLI) routines. Dynamic memory allocation is implemented by simple code using preallocated static memory.

Most test programs in these benchmarks were used as is. The only exceptions are a few tests in OpenSSL that take a long time to simulate. To make evaluation feasible on these tests, we replace long inputs with shorter ones.

We evaluate two security policies: "nomix", a coarse-grained policy where the entire program is labeled H, corresponding to the security policy targeted by previous secure hardware design methods, and "mixed", a fine-grained policy allowing mixed H and L instructions, enabled by the new features of SecVerilog. In the latter case, we use a simple policy to decide timing labels: for ciphers (e.g., AES, RSA), the encryption and decryption functions are marked as H; for secure hash functions (e.g., MD4, SHA512), we pretend part of the input is secret, and mark the hash functions on these inputs as H. Performance results for a single run of each test are shown in Figure 9. Multiple runs are unnecessary for our evaluation since the simulation is deterministic.

From the MiBench suite, only rijndael shows noticeable performance overhead, at 19.6%. Overhead is reduced to 12.2% when the fine-grained model with mixed labels is used. Overhead on OpenSSL ranges from 0.3% (Blowfish) to 34.9% (SHA-0), with an average of 21.0%. For the fine-grained model, the overhead on OpenSSL ranges from −3.9% (CAST5) to 21.7% (DES), with an average of 8.8%. CAST5 runs faster with the partitioned cache because H instructions cannot evict frequently used data in the L partition.

The results clearly show the benefit of fine-grained information flow control within a single application. Most slowdown comes from the restriction that H instructions cannot write to the low cache partition. Allowing mixed H and L in-

[2] The only benchmark omitted is PGP, which requires a full-featured OS.

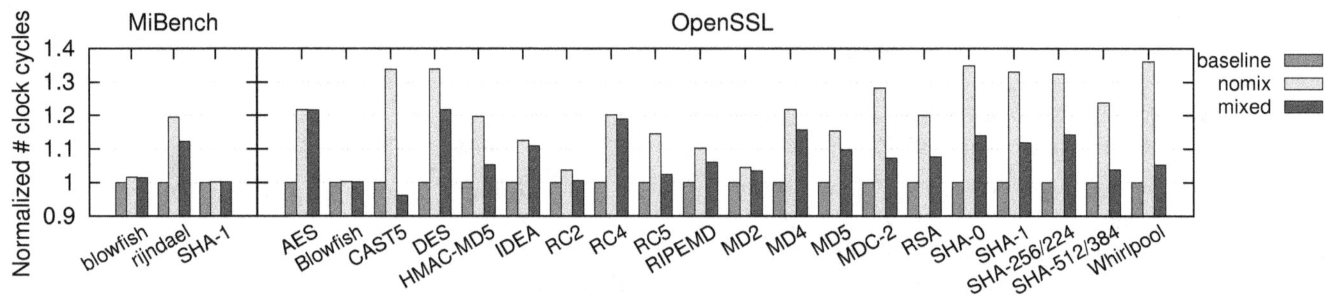

Figure 9. Performance overhead of timing channel protection.

structions in a single program improves performance because the restrictions only apply to a subset of program instructions.

We could not compare our performance overhead with prior work [22, 23, 42] because they do not report the performance overhead over a baseline with unpartitioned cache[3].

7. Related work

Verifiable secure hardware. Dynamic information flow tracking is applied at the logic-gate level in GLIFT [28, 29, 40–42]. Dynamic checks in the initial GLIFT design [42] add high overheads in area, power, and performance. Subsequent work [28, 29, 41] checks designs before fabrication, but enumerates all possible states through gate-level simulation, an approach unlikely to scale to large designs without rigid time-and-space multiplexing. SecVerilog allows more flexible resource sharing and identifies security issues early in the design process.

Sapper [22] also adds logic for tracking information flows, incurring run-time overhead. Sapper cannot capture the dependencies between types and values needed for complex security policies. For example, it would not be possible to use the label `LH(timingLabel)` for variable `stall`, as shown in Figure 2(b), to capture the policy that the label of `stall` must be L when `timingLabel` is 0.

Caisson [23] supports static analysis but with purely static security levels that prevent fine-grained sharing of hardware resources across security levels. E.g., `write_enable`, `tag_in` and `stall` in Figure 2 would require duplication (per security level) since their labels cannot be determined at compile time. Duplicated resources must be controlled by extra encoders and decoders, adding run-time overhead.

Dynamic security labels. Some prior type systems for information flow also support limited forms of dynamic labels [14, 19, 24, 25, 39, 43, 51]. The type-valued functions needed to express the communication of security levels at the hardware level are absent in most of these, and none permit dynamic labels to depend on mutable variables, a feature key to allowing SecVerilog to verify practical hardware designs. The modular design of the SecVerilog type system makes it more amenable to future extension. Fine [37] and F* [38] can verify stateful information flow policies, modeling state changes with affine types. Affine types suffice for functional programming, but HDLs need SecVerilog's new feature of dependence on mutable variables.

Flow-sensitive information flow control. Flow-sensitive information flow control [5, 18, 34], where security labels may change during execution, encounters label channels similar to those observed in our type system. Our type system controls these channels more permissively (Section 4.3) because it captures the dependency between types and values.

Dependent type systems. Dependent types have been widely studied and have been applied to practical programming languages (e.g., [4, 7, 25, 46, 47]). Information flow adds new challenges, such as precise, sound handling of label channels. RHTT [27] supports rich information flow policies with dependent types, but has much more complex specifications and verification is not automatic.

8. Conclusion

We have shown SecVerilog makes it possible to efficiently design complex hardware with strong security assurance. This is enabled by novel features such as type-valued functions for dependent labels, the ability to soundly and precisely use mutable variables within labels, and the modular incorporation of program analyses to improve precision. Using SecVerilog, a reasonably complex processor can be designed in such a way that it satisfies a software–hardware contract for comprehensive control of information flows, including timing channels. The added overhead and effort required to design hardware in this way were both small. Our experience with SecVerilog suggests it will be a useful tool for designing complex hardware with strong security assurance.

Acknowledgments

We thank Tao Chen, Chinawat Isradisaikul, Jed Liu, Dan Lo, Derek Lockhart, Stephen Longfield, Tom Magrino, Matthew Milano and the anonymous reviewers for their helpful suggestions.

This work was partially supported by Office of Naval Research grant N00014-13-1-0089, MURI grant FA9550-12-1-0400, Air Force grant FA8750-11-2-0025, and by National Science Foundation grants CNS-0746913, CCF-0905208, and CCF-0964409.

[3] The previous method [22] calls a secure but unverified design "insecure", and reports the overhead of verified vs. unverified as we do in Section 6.2.

References

[1] Icarus Verilog. http://iverilog.icarus.com/.

[2] O. Acıiçmez. Yet another microarchitectural attack: Exploiting I-cache. In *Proc. ACM Workshop on Computer Security Architecture (CSAW '07)*, pages 11–18, 2007.

[3] O. Acıiçmez, C. Koç, and J. Seifert. On the power of simple branch prediction analysis. In *ASIACCS*, pages 312–320, 2007.

[4] L. Augustsson. Cayenne—a language with dependent types. In *Proc. 3rd ACM SIGPLAN Int'l Conf. on Functional Programming (ICFP)*, pages 239–250, 1998.

[5] T. H. Austin and C. Flanagan. Efficient purely-dynamic information flow analysis. In *Proc. 4th ACM SIGPLAN Workshop on Programming Languages and Analysis for Security (PLAS)*, pages 113–124, 2009.

[6] J. Barnes. *High Integrity Software: The SPARK Approach to Safety and Security*. Addison Wesley, Apr. 2003. ISBN 0321136160.

[7] J. Condit, M. Harren, Z. Anderson, D. Gay, and G. C. Necula. Dependent types for low-level programming. In *Proc. European Symposium on Programming (ESOP)*, pages 520–535, 2007.

[8] B. Coppens, I. Verbauwhede, K. D. Bosschere, and B. D. Sutter. Practical mitigations for timing-based side-channel attacks on modern x86 processors. *IEEE Symposium on Security and Privacy*, pages 45–60, 2009.

[9] L. M. de Moura and N. Bjørner. Z3: An efficient SMT solver. In *Proc. Conf. on Tools and Algorithms for the Construction and Analysis of Systems (TACAS)*, 2008.

[10] E. W. Dijkstra. Guarded commands, nondeterminacy and formal derivation of programs. *CACM*, 18(8):453–457, Aug. 1975.

[11] R. W. Floyd. Assigning meanings to programs. In *Proc. Sympos. Appl. Math.*, volume XIX, pages 19–32, 1967.

[12] J. A. Goguen and J. Meseguer. Security policies and security models. In *Proc. IEEE Symp. on Security and Privacy*, pages 11–20, Apr. 1982.

[13] M. Gordon. The semantic challenge of Verilog HDL. In *LICS*, pages 136–145, 1995.

[14] R. Grabowski and L. Beringer. Noninterference with dynamic security domains and policies. In *Advances in Computer Science - ASIAN 2009. Information Security and Privacy*, pages 54–68, 2009. LNCS 5913.

[15] D. Gullasch, E. Bangerter, and S. Krenn. Cache games—bringing access-based cache attacks on AES to practice. In *IEEE Symposium on Security and Privacy*, pages 490–505, 2011.

[16] M. R. Guthaus, J. S. Ringenberg, D. Ernst, T. M. Austin, T. Mudge, and R. B. Brown. Mibench: A free, commercially representative embedded benchmark suite. In *Workload Characterization, 2001. WWC-4. 2001 IEEE International Workshop on*, pages 3–14, 2001.

[17] C. A. R. Hoare. An axiomatic basis for computer programming. *CACM*, 12(10):576–580, Oct. 1969.

[18] S. Hunt and D. Sands. On flow-sensitive security types. In *POPL 33*, pages 79–90, 2006.

[19] L. Jia, J. A. Vaughan, K. Mazurak, J. Zhao, L. Zarko, J. Schorr, and S. Zdancewic. Aura: A programming language for authorization and audit. In *Proc. 13th ACM SIGPLAN Int'l Conf. on Functional Programming (ICFP)*, pages 27–38, 2008.

[20] P. Kocher. Timing attacks on implementations of Diffie–Hellman, RSA, DSS, and other systems. In *Advances in Cryptology—CRYPTO'96*, Aug. 1996.

[21] B. W. Lampson. A note on the confinement problem. *Comm. of the ACM*, 16(10):613–615, Oct. 1973.

[22] X. Li, V. Kashyap, J. K. Oberg, M. Tiwari, V. R. Rajarathinam, R. Kastner, T. Sherwood, B. Hardekopf, and F. T. Chong. Sapper: A language for hardware-level security policy enforcement. In *Proc. 19th Int'l Conference on Architectural Support for Programming Languages and Operating Systems (ASPLOS)*, pages 97–112, 2014.

[23] X. Li, M. Tiwari, J. Oberg, V. Kashyap, F. Chong, T. Sherwood, and B. Hardekopf. Caisson: a hardware description language for secure information flow. In *ACM SIGPLAN Conf. on Programming Language Design and Implementation (PLDI)*, pages 109–120, 2011.

[24] L. Lourenço and L. Caires. Dependent information flow types. *FCT/UNL Technical Report*, Oct. 2013.

[25] A. C. Myers. JFlow: Practical mostly-static information flow control. In *POPL 26*, pages 228–241, Jan. 1999.

[26] A. C. Myers, L. Zheng, S. Zdancewic, S. Chong, and N. Nystrom. Jif 3.0: Java information flow. Software release, `http://www.cs.cornell.edu/jif`, July 2006.

[27] A. Nanevski, A. Banerjee, and D. Garg. Verification of information flow and access control policies with dependent types. In *Proc. IEEE Symp. on Security and Privacy*, pages 165–179, 2011.

[28] J. Oberg, W. Hu, A. Irturk, M. Tiwari, T. Sherwood, and R. Kastner. Theoretical analysis of gate level information flow tracking. In *Proc. 47th Design Automation Conference*, pages 244–247, 2010.

[29] J. Oberg, W. Hu, A. Irturk, M. Tiwari, T. Sherwood, and R. Kastner. Information flow isolation in I2C and USB. In *Proc. 48th Design Automation Conference*, pages 254–259, 2011.

[30] D. Osvik, A. Shamir, and E. Tromer. Cache attacks and countermeasures: the case of AES. *Topics in Cryptology–CT-RSA 2006*, Jan. 2006.

[31] D. Page. Partitioned cache architecture as a side-channel defense mechanism. In *Cryptology ePrint Archive, Report 2005/280*, 2005.

[32] C. Percival. Cache missing for fun and profit. In *Proc. BSDCan*, 2005.

[33] A. W. Roscoe. CSP and determinism in security modeling. In *Proc. IEEE Symp. on Security and Privacy*, 1995.

[34] A. Russo and A. Sabelfeld. Dynamic vs. static flow-sensitive security analysis. In *Proc. 23rd IEEE Computer Security Foundations Symposium (CSF)*, CSF '10, pages 186–199, 2010.

[35] A. Sabelfeld and A. C. Myers. Language-based information-flow security. *IEEE Journal on Selected Areas in Communications*, 21(1):5–19, Jan. 2003.

[36] V. Simonet. The Flow Caml System: documentation and user's manual. Technical Report 0282, Institut National de Recherche en Informatique et en Automatique (INRIA), July 2003.

[37] N. Swamy, J. Chen, and R. Chugh. Enforcing stateful authorization and information flow policies in Fine. In *Proc. European Symposium on Programming (ESOP)*, pages 529–549, 2010.

[38] N. Swamy, J. Chen, C. Fournet, P.-Y. Strub, K. Bhargavan, and J. Yang. Secure distributed programming with value-dependent types. In *Proc. 16th ACM SIGPLAN Int'l Conf. on Functional Programming (ICFP)*, pages 266–278, 2011.

[39] N. Swamy, B. J. Corcoran, and M. Hicks. Fable: A language for enforcing user-defined security policies. In *Proc. IEEE Symp. on Security and Privacy*, pages 369–383, 2008.

[40] M. Tiwari, X. Li, H. M. G. Wassel, F. T. Chong, and T. Sherwood. Execution leases: A hardware-supported mechanism for enforcing strong non-interference. In *Micro '09*, Dec. 2009.

[41] M. Tiwari, J. Oberg, X. Li, J. K. Valamehr, T. Levin, B. Hardekopf, R. Kastner, F. T. Chong, and T. Sherwood. Crafting a usable microkernel, processor, and I/O system with strict and provable information flow security. In *Proc. International Symposium on Computer Architecture (ISCA)*, June 2011.

[42] M. Tiwari, H. M. Wassel, B. Mazloom, S. Mysore, F. T. Chong, and T. Sherwood. Complete information flow tracking from the gates up. In *ASPLOS XIV*, pages 109–120, 2009.

[43] S. Tse and S. Zdancewic. Run-time principals in information-flow type systems. *ACM Transactions on Programming Languages and Systems (TOPLAS)*, 30(1):6, 2007.

[44] Z. Wang and R. Lee. Covert and side channels due to processor architecture. In *ACSAC '06*, pages 473–482, 2006.

[45] Z. Wang and R. Lee. New cache designs for thwarting software cache-based side channel attacks. In *Proc. International Symposium on Computer Architecture (ISCA)*, pages 494–505, 2007.

[46] H. Xi. Imperative programming with dependent types. In *Proc. IEEE Symposium on Logic in Computer Science*, pages 375–387, 2000.

[47] H. Xi and F. Pfenning. Dependent types in practical programming. In *POPL*, pages 214–227, 1999.

[48] S. Zdancewic and A. C. Myers. Observational determinism for concurrent program security. In *Proc. 16th IEEE Computer Security Foundations Workshop*, pages 29–43, June 2003.

[49] D. Zhang, A. Askarov, and A. C. Myers. Language-based control and mitigation of timing channels. In *Proc. SIGPLAN Conf. on Programming Language Design and Implementation (PLDI)*, pages 99–110, 2012.

[50] D. Zhang, Y. Wang, G. E. Suh, and A. C. Myers. A hardware design language for efficient control of timing channels. Technical report, Cornell University, Apr. 2014. `http://hdl.handle.net/1813/36274`.

[51] L. Zheng and A. C. Myers. Dynamic security labels and static information flow control. *Intl' J. of Information Security*, 6(2–3), Mar. 2007.

SPECS: A Lightweight Runtime Mechanism for Protecting Software from Security-Critical Processor Bugs

Matthew Hicks
University of Michigan
mdhicks@umich.edu

Cynthia Sturton
University of North Carolina at Chapel Hill
csturton@cs.unc.edu

Samuel T. King
Twitter, Inc.
sking@twitter.com

Jonathan M. Smith
University of Pennsylvania
jms@cis.upenn.edu

Abstract

Processor implementation errata remain a problem, and worse, a subset of these bugs are security-critical. We classified 7 years of errata from recent commercial processors to understand the magnitude and severity of this problem, and found that of 301 errata analyzed, 28 are security-critical.

We propose the SECURITY-CRITICAL PROCESSOR ERRATA CATCHING SYSTEM (SPECS) as a low-overhead solution to this problem. SPECS employs a dynamic verification strategy that is made lightweight by limiting protection to only security-critical processor state. As a proof-of-concept, we implement a hardware prototype of SPECS in an open source processor. Using this prototype, we evaluate SPECS against a set of 14 bugs inspired by the types of security-critical errata we discovered in the classification phase. The evaluation shows that SPECS is 86% effective as a defense when deployed using only ISA-level state; incurs less than 5% area and power overhead; and has no software run-time overhead.

Categories and Subject Descriptors C.0 [*General*]: Hardware/software interfaces; C.0 [*General*]: System architectures; K.6.5 [*Security and Protection*]: Invasive software (e.g., viruses, worms, Trojan horses)

Keywords Processor errata; hardware security exploits; security-critical processor errata

1. Introduction

Modern processors are imperfect. Processors are built from millions of lines of code [42], yielding chips with billions of transistors [22]. Verifying the functional correctness of hardware at such scales remains intractable. The resulting gaps in functional verification mean that today's production hardware typically ships with bugs. For example, the errata document for Intel's Core 2 Duo processor family [20] lists 129 *known* bugs.

ASPLOS '15, March 14–18, 2015, Istanbul, Turkey.

ACM 978-1-4503-2835-7/15/03.
http://dx.doi.org/10.1145/2694344.2694366

	Catch All Bugs?	Catch Security-Critical Bugs?	Low Overhead?
SW-only	✗	✗	✓
HW-only	✓	✓	✗
SPECS	✗	✓	✓
SPECS+SW	✓	✓	✓

Table 1: The design space for catching processor bugs: existing software-only approaches are limited, but practical; existing hardware-only approaches are powerful, but impractical; and SPECS, combined with existing software approaches, is both powerful and practical.

Some processor bugs have the potential to weaken the security of software by allowing unprivileged code to modify or control privileged processor state. We deem these bugs *security critical* (we do not claim that this set is unique). While some effects of bugs are detectable by software through periodic checks [8, 27] or special encodings [6, 40], other processor bugs affect software in a manner that software cannot detect practically. Such bugs are security-critical because they affect a critical subset of processor functionality trusted by the software tasked with detecting and recovering from imperfections. One example of a security-critical bug is a design flaw in the MIPS R4000 processor that allows user-mode code to control the location of an exception vector [26]. The effect of this bug is user-mode code that runs at the supervisor level—privilege escalation.

These types of flaws compromise otherwise correct software—especially software that implements security policies. There are many documented examples [4, 5, 29–32] of the impact security-critical bugs have on software. Software-only patching approaches have been explored (e.g., microcode [16, 43], re-compilation [28], and binary translation [35]), but are not able to address all processor bugs [33]. Further, many of the existing patching mechanisms incur large performance penalties [38, 39], mainly due to the coarse granularity and heavyweight nature of their consistency checks.

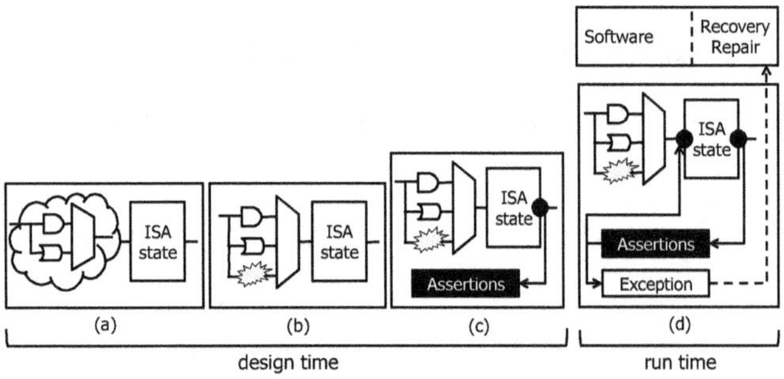

Figure 1: Processor design flow with SPECS: (a) Hardware description language implementation of the instruction set (b) At some point during design, a bug is introduced. (c) Assertions that implement SPECS invariants are added to the processor, with taps directly on the outputs of ISA state storage elements. (d) To squash in-flight state, SPECS adds write gating to the inputs of ISA state storing elements and attaches the result of dynamic verification to the exception logic, which triggers existing recovery/repair software in the event of an invariant violation.

Alternatively, hardware-based bug defenses can address all processor bugs using checks on every cycle, but this comprehensiveness comes at a prohibitive cost in terms of hardware area and power. One example illustrating the tradeoffs of hardware patching mechanisms is Diva [1]. Diva relies on modular redundancy; a second formally-verified but lower-performance processor core checks the calculations of the buggy, high-performance core. Diva can protect against all processor bugs, but is complex (potentially creating new processor bugs) and has a high hardware cost. A second example is Phoenix [37], which detects potentially inconsistent processor state by comparing the hardware-level state of the processor to known buggy state values; Phoenix requires more hardware than Diva and cannot respond to unknown bugs.

Rather than incur the costs of protecting software from all processor bugs, we propose a hybrid approach, shown in Table 1: SPECS adds a small amount of additional hardware to the processor that dynamically verifies a subset of processor functionality. The goal is to protect software from security-critical processor bugs, especially those that it cannot protect itself from efficiently. SPECS works by enforcing instruction-set-specification-derived invariants on security-critical processor state dynamically. The invariants are enforced by a series of simple assertions in hardware (Figure 1(c)). The assertions analyze ISA-level state and events to validate in-flight (i.e., not yet visible at the software level) ISA-level state updates. If in-flight state violates a SPECS invariant, a combination of assertions fire that then triggers an exception that squashes the inconsistent in-flight state (Figure 1(d)). From here, existing software recovery/repair mechanisms take over—while SPECS continues to work in the background. Essentially, SPECS acts as an interposition layer for a range of existing processor repair and recovery approaches that allows software to execute past security-critical bugs safely.

AMD ID#	Synopsis	Class	Sub class
418	Incorrect translation tables used		
561	Incorrect page walks	MA	
731	Using large pages causes incorrect IO address translations		
77	Using unaligned descriptor table allows software to jump past the end of the table without causing an exception	XR	
170	May use instructions from old page tables pointed to by old CR3		
578	Branch prediction causes invalid control flow	EI	
639	CALL instruction treated as a NOP		
776	Branch prediction causes invalid control flow		
144	Shadow RAM not invalidated	IR	
784	Control register data leaked through load operation		
165	Guest can clear data in VMCB		
503	Writes to APIC task priority register use the wrong register	IU	IL
573	Instruction pointer updated incorrectly		
734	Incorrect data stored to and past VMCB		
770	Privilege escalation		
171	Execute breakpoint handler with mixed guest and host state		
248	TLB pages not invalidated		
342	Interrupts disabled for guest		
385	Incorrect error address reported		
401	Hypervisor doesn't get correct IP		
440	CR3 not saved correctly	IU	IX
563	Flags not stored correctly in VMCB		
564	Auto halt flag not set in SMM save state		
659	VMCB flag bit not cleared		
691	Cache not invalidated correctly		
704	Incorrect IP stored		
738	Incorrect SP stored in VMCB		
744	A CC6 transition may not restore trap registers		

Table 2: Security-critical errata mined from AMD processors manufactured between 2006 and 2013. The security-critical errata fit into five classes: MA (arbitrary memory access), XR (exception related), EI (execute incorrect instruction), IR (incorrect results), and IU (invalid register update). Further, there are two types of IU: IL (illegal) and IX (incorrect).

We make three contributions in this paper:

- We identify and classify security-critical errata from recent commercial processors and discover that these bugs involve invalid updates to privileged ISA-level state, which is updated in a few simple ways (Section 2).
- We introduce a lightweight dynamic-verification strategy against security-critical processor bugs, providing an introspection point whenever security-critical state is updated outside the specification (Section 3).
- We implement (Section 4) and evaluate (Section 5) SPECS, showing that it is possible to protect software from a range of realistic security-critical processor bugs. The evaluation shows that SPECS: (1) is able to detect 86% of the implemented processor bugs using only ISA-level state; (2) requires less than 5% additional hardware; and (3) has no software run-time overhead. [1]

[1] We make the errata used for our analysis and our hardware and software source code available publicly [19].

2. Security-Critical Errata

Existing work on processor bugs as security vulnerabilities takes the approach of finding a single processor bug and realizing a usable software-level attack with that bug as a foothold [3, 11, 12, 23]. While this level of analysis highlights the threat of a specific security-critical processor bug, it does not give an idea of how pervasive security-critical bugs are, their range of effects, or what they have in common. We take a wider approach in an attempt to learn about security-critical bugs in general and to guide evaluation of our detection mechanism SPECS.

We took a systematic approach to identifying security vulnerabilities in processors. First, we collected the errata documents from the most popular commercial desktop, mobile, and embedded processors. To place a reasonable limit on this work, we limited ourselves to errata documents covering processors released in the last seven years (i.e., since 2007). For each errata document, we read the vendor's description of each erratum and determine if it represents a bug that *can* be used to allow unprivileged software to gain access to or control the behavior of privileged state of the processor in a way that contradicts the ISA. If the erratum is a possible attack foothold, we mark it as security critical. When errata documents are unclear about how software triggers the erratum, we mark it as security critical if, and only if, we believe it *possible* for a user process or guest OS to trigger it.

Table 2 gives the results from our classification of AMD errata. From a total of 301 AMD errata, we found 28 to be security critical, and split these into 5 classes: IU (invalid register update) (64%), EI (execute incorrect instruction) (14%), MA (arbitrary memory access) (11%), IR (incorrect results) (7%), XR (exception related) (4%). Figure 2 presents a visualization of the distribution of errata into the five classes.

Since it is not immediately clear from the class names what properties of a security-critical bug cause it to be in that class, here is an example bug for each class:

IU - invalid register update: There are two sub-classes of IU bugs: IL and IX. Regardless of sub-class, this class of bug is marked by the contamination of a privileged ISA-level register. The sub-class IL refers to contaminations that low-privilege software can use to bypass security policies implemented by higher-privileged software (e.g., if a user process could execute a sequence of instructions that caused the processor to execute in supervisor mode). The sub-class IX refers to when a processor bug causes security-related commands from privileged software to be essentially ignored. From the perspective of SPECS these two sub-classes are the same because SPECS focuses on the state itself, agnostic of how it became contaminated.

EI - execute incorrect insn: This class of bug is marked by the processor executing a different instruction than a perfect processor would. In this class, the processor correctly executes the instruction, but somewhere earlier in the pipeline, the instruction itself was contaminated. This is usually due to incorrect control flows caused by the processor bug.

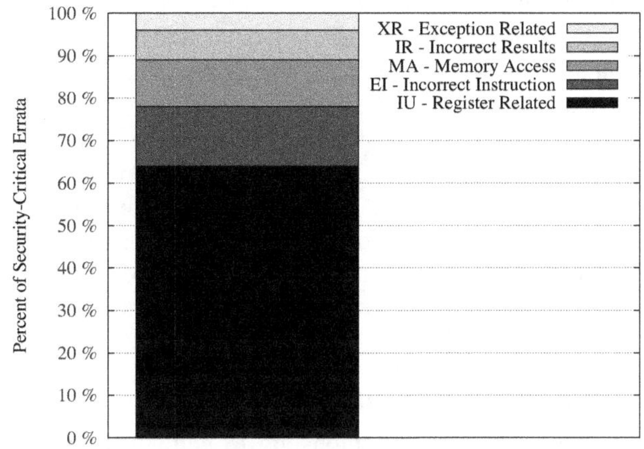

Figure 2: Class-wise composition of the security-critical errata.

MA - memory access: This class of bug is marked by the ability for any software to access memory that it should not have access to given the specification. This includes memory caches, but does not include valid accesses to shared memory buffers that were not cleared correctly (see IR).

IR - incorrect results: This class of bug is marked by an operation returning an incorrect result or not correctly updating the state (micro-architectural or ISA) of the processor correctly given the executed instruction.

XR - exception related: This class of bug is marked by an exception being ignored when it should have been handled, by the handling of an exception that should have been ignored, or by passing control to the wrong exception handler.

3. SPECS Design

SECURITY-CRITICAL PROCESSOR ERRATA CATCHING SYSTEM (SPECS) is a lightweight, hardware-based approach to protecting software from the processor bugs that can compromise system security. SPECS protects against bugs that affect reads and writes of privileged processor state. Included in this set are the bugs that software-only approaches are not be able to protect against. To detect processor bugs, it is necessary to know when and in what way processor state changes. Software-only approaches necessarily rely on privileged state as a key component of their consistency check implementation. When a security-critical processor bug compromises this privileged state, then so to are the consistency checks. Furthermore, SPECS provides a precise introspection point when privileged state changes, without which software must rely on polling or other, more coarse grain, introspection points (e.g., page faults); both decrease common case performance and leave gaps that make the system vulnerable.

SPECS catches security-critical processor bugs precisely by enforcing a select set of invariants dynamically. SPECS invariants are properties over architecturally visible processor state and events (i.e., ISA-state). They are derived from the instruction set specification and govern how and when updates to privileged processor state can occur. An example of the type of bug that SPECS will catch is privilege escalation: a change in processor mode from low to high privilege that is not consistent with the instruction set specification. Privilege escalation bugs have occurred in recent commercial processors (see Section 2).

3.1 An example invariant and assertion

We use the privilege escalation bug to help illustrate the concepts of a SPECS invariant and the implementation of that invariant using a combination of simple assertions. To start, we describe privilege escalation as a violation of the following invariant: $I_0 \doteq$ **A change in processor mode from low privilege to high privilege is caused only by an exception or a reset.**

Invariant I_0 is a statement that the instruction set specification says must be true of the system at all points of execution.

In SPECS, invariants are enforced by composing (with Boolean operations) one or more simple assertions on ISA-level processor state. For example, SPECS enforces I_0 in the following way:

$$\begin{aligned} A_0 \doteq \mathit{assert}(&\mathit{risingEdge}(\texttt{SR[SM]}) \rightarrow (\texttt{NPC}[31:12]=0) \wedge \\ &\mathit{risingEdge}(\texttt{SR[SM]}) \rightarrow (\texttt{NPC}[7:0]=0) \vee \\ &\mathit{risingEdge}(\texttt{SR[SM]}) \rightarrow (\texttt{reset}=1)). \end{aligned}$$

`SR[SM]` represents the supervisor mode bit of the processor's status register and an exception is indicated by the next program counter, `NPC`, pointing to an exception vector start address. In our implementation (see Section 5), the exception vector start address is of the form `0x00000X00` (the "X" indicates a don't-care value).[2]

3.2 Design principles

The high-level design of SPECS follows three principles;

1. *Maintain current ISA abstractions.* SPECS should detect processor imperfections automatically, without changes to existing software.
2. *Keep the common case fast.* SPECS should only interrupt software in the rare case that a processor violates one of SPECS's security invariants—precise introspection.
3. *Be practical.* To maximize practicality, we aim to implement invariants using only ISA-level state. The ISA is more stable across processor families and less complex than micro-architectural state. Additionally, SPECS implements invariants using improved versions of industry-standard assertions.

[2] This might seem as if it leaves the door open for a processor attack that escalates privilege while executing at an address that matches the form `0x00000X00`, but it does not. Pages in that address range have supervisor permissions set which implies that code executing in that address range is already in supervisor mode. If software that exercises a security-critical processor bug attempts to allow user mode execution of supervisor mode pages, SPECS includes an invariant to detect such misbehavior.

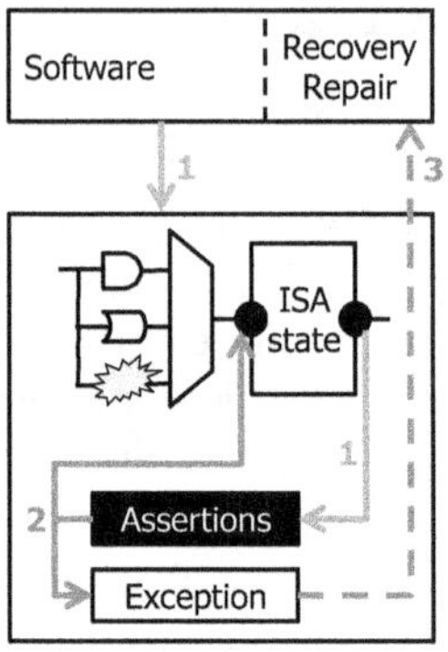

Figure 3: Flow of detection and recovery in SPECS: 1) Software executes normally on the processor while invariants implemented using hardware assertions check the processor's state for specification violations. 2) A violation of a SPECS invariant triggers an exception and prevents state updates. 3) The exception causes any in-flight (i.e., contaminated) state to be flushed and control passes to existing recovery/repair software. 1) SPECS continues to protect the recovery/repair software.

3.3 Assumptions

SPECS relies on three assumptions. The first is that the instruction set specification is correct. Ambiguities in the specification lead to implementation differences, which lead to security vulnerabilities [45]. For SPECS, the specification drives the design and implementation of the invariants; thus, specification ambiguities can lead to false detections or worse, missed detections.

The second assumption is that it is possible to dynamically verify the correctness of an ISA-level state update using only the current ISA-level state and the instruction. This forms the basis of our approach: SPECS invariants are defined over the proposed ISA-level state update, the current instruction, and the current ISA-level state. When this assumption does not hold, we have to implement security invariants using low-level state (see Section 5 for one exception) or risk missing bug activations.

Finally, the focus of our work is the pipeline core of the processor; we assume the memory hierarchy is correct. Note that we do not foresee any fundamental limitations to applying the SPECS approach to other units in a processor. Our experience indicates that the SPECS approach works well where it is possible to precisely define expected behavior and where there is a subset of critical behaviors that need protecting.

3.4 SPECS components and interactions

Figure 3 shows the key components of SPECS and their interactions. Software executes normally on the processor while assertions in hardware check processor ISA-level state and events for specification violations. The assertions verify that a proposed ISA-level state update is valid—i.e., does not violate an invariant—for security-critical state given the instruction and the current (already verified) ISA-level state. If the proposed ISA-level state update is valid, then: (1) no combination of assertions fire to signify an invariant violation; (2) the processor is allowed to commit the proposed state to the ISA level; and (3) execution continues. On the other hand, if a state update violates an invariant, SPECS triggers an exception causing any contaminated in-flight state to be flushed. From this point, existing recovery/repair software can take control as required to push the state of software forward. Note that SPECS continues to protect the recovery/repair software; this added safety requires that any recovery/repair approach be able to handle recursive detections.

3.5 History

Some invariants require more history than the current and proposed ISA-level state provide. For invariants over control flow (Section 4) we need to check previous instructions for valid causes of control flow discontinuities. Valid causes of control flow discontinuities in our implementation are branches and jumps; return from exception; system calls and traps; and exceptions. For exceptions and system calls/traps (which we treat as exceptions) the assertion logic doesn't need any extra history information because the current PC informs us whether we got here due to one of the listed events. For this, we look to see if we are at an address associated with a exception handler. For return from exception instructions, we need to know the instruction before the break in control flow. The remaining control flow disrupting events require the ability to see the instruction associated with the current (most recently verified) ISA-level state to verify that it was a jump or branch. Making the history problem worse is an architectural feature known as a branch delay slot. In many architectures, including the one we implement SPECS in, the processor always executes the instruction directly after the branch/jump instruction; thus the instruction after jumps/branches is also executed. The goal of the branch delay slot is to reduce the number of pipeline bubbles due to breaks in control flow. This means that when SPECS's continuous control flow invariant gets violated, we have to look back two instructions previous for a branch or jump instruction.

There are two ways to solve this problem: we can store the previous two instructions or we can store—and use in our assertions—the previous two assertion results. We choose to implement the latter since it requires two extra flip-flops for each micro assertion that is impacted by a delay slot and one for those that are not (7 total), since the result of all assertions is a single bit. In comparison, keeping the previous two instructions around would require 64 additional flip-flops.

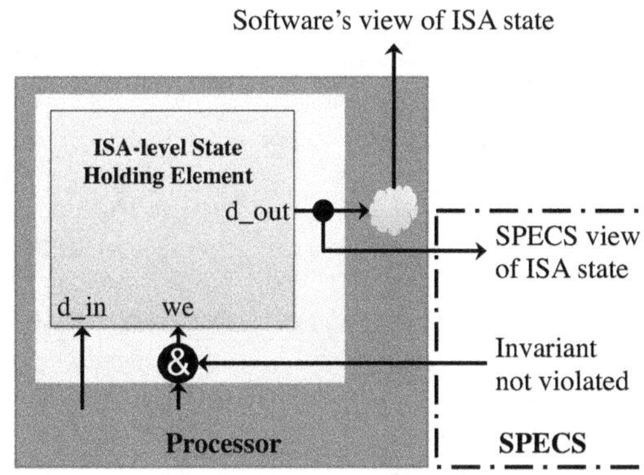

Figure 4: Low-level hardware support required for SPECS: SPECS requires direct access to state holding elements (i.e., before any other circuit manipulates the value) and requires the ability to prevent updates to ISA-level state in the event of invariant violations. Without either of these, SPECS misses bugs in our evaluation platform.

3.6 Instruction stability

A preliminary evaluation showed that SPECS missed security-critical bugs that changed the instruction in the pipeline. For example, a security-critical processor bug could change a privilege de-escalation into a no-op, causing it to be ignored and resulting in a privileged escalation. SPECS misses such bugs because it must trust the instruction as a state input. Additionally, there is only a single instruction at the ISA-level (SPECS reads the decode stage version), but in reality each pipeline stage may see a different instruction.

To ensure that we can trust that SPECS's view of the instruction is what the pipeline sees, we add a micro-architectural-level invariant that enforces instruction integrity as it moves through the pipeline. The invariant states that the instruction loaded from memory is seen at each pipeline stage. Refer to Section 4 for detailed information on this invariant.

3.7 Local state taps

It is critical that the assertions get their view of ISA-level state from as close to the state holding element as possible. Any logic between the state holding element and SPECS's state taps is vulnerable to bugs. In fact, in the first SPECS prototype, we missed catching bugs (bug 5) due to buggy logic between the state taps and the state holding element. Figure 4 shows our general approach to solving this problem. We find the actual memory that holds the state value, and read the state directly from that memory's output. Often times, this reduces to inserting SPECS's state taps between the state holding element and the rest of the processor.

3.8 Invariant state update gating

Similar to where we place SPECS's state taps, we found that we need to add write gates directly to the inputs of state holding elements. It is essential that SPECS squashes in-flight state when invariants are violated. We do this is by guarding writes at each privileged ISA-level state element using the

<table>
<tr><th>ID</th><th>SPECS Invariant</th><th>OVL Implementation</th></tr>
<tr><td>1</td><td>Execution privilege matches page privilege</td><td>always((SR_SM & MMU_SXE) || ($\overline{SR\_SM}$ & MMU_UXE))</td></tr>
<tr><td>2</td><td>SPR = GPR in register move instructions</td><td>posedge(INSN = l.MTSPR, SPR = GPR)</td></tr>
<tr><td>3</td><td>Updates to exception registers make sense</td><td>posedge((PC & 0xFFFFF0FF) = 0, (EEAR = EA) && (EPCR = SR[DSX] ? PPC-4 : PPC) && (ESR = (SR & 0xFFFFDFFF)))</td></tr>
<tr><td>4</td><td>Destination matches the target</td><td>posedge(GPR_WRITTEN, GPR_TARGET = (INSN & TARGET_MASK))</td></tr>
<tr><td>5</td><td>Memory value in = register value out</td><td>posedge((INSN = l.LWZ) || (INSN = l.LHZ) || (INSN = l.LHS) || (INSN = l.LBZ) || (INSN = l.LBS), GPR = MEM_BUS)</td></tr>
<tr><td>6</td><td>Register value in = memory value out</td><td>posedge((INSN = l.SW) || (INSN = l.SH) || (INSN = l.SB), GPR = MEM_BUS)</td></tr>
<tr><td>7</td><td>Memory address = effective address</td><td>posedge((INSN = l.SW) || (INSN = l.SH) || (INSN = l.SB) || (INSN = l.LWZ) || (INSN = l.LHZ) || (INSN = l.LHS) || (INSN = l.LBZ) || (INSN = l.LBS), ADDR_CPU = ADDR_BUS)</td></tr>
<tr><td>8</td><td>Privilege escalates correctly</td><td>posedge(SR['OR1200_SR_SM], (RST = 1) || (PC = 0x00000X00))</td></tr>
<tr><td>9</td><td>Privilege deescalates correctly</td><td>posedge(INSN = l.RFE, SR['OR1200_SR_SM] = ESR['OR1200_SR_SM]) && posedge((INSN = l.MTSPR) && (INSN_target = SR), SR['OR1200_SR_SM] = GPR_SOURCE['OR1200_SR_SM])</td></tr>
<tr><td>10</td><td>Jumps update the PC correctly</td><td>next((INSN = JMP) || (INSN = BR), PC = EA, 2)</td></tr>
<tr><td>11</td><td>Jumps update the LR correctly</td><td>next((INSN = JMPL) || (INSN = JMPLR), LR = PPC+4, 2)</td></tr>
<tr><td>12</td><td>Instruction is in a valid format</td><td>always((INSN & Class_Mask) = Class) && ((INSN & Reserved_Mask) = 0)</td></tr>
<tr><td>13</td><td>Continuous Control Flow</td><td>delta(PC, 4, 4) || assert((INSN = JMP) || (INSN = BR) || (INSN = RFE)) || assert((PC & 0xFFFFF0FF) = 0)</td></tr>
<tr><td>14</td><td>Exception return updates state correctly</td><td>next(INSN = l.RFE, (SR = ESR) && (PC = EPCR), 1)</td></tr>
<tr><td>15</td><td>Reg change implies that it is the instruction target</td><td>(posedge(GPR_Written, (INSN & OPCODE_MASK) = (20-2F, 06, 38)) && posedge(GPR_Written, (INSN & TARGET_MASK) = GPR_Written_Addr)) || posedge(GPR9_Written, ((INSN & OPCODE_MASK) = JAL) || ((INSN & OPCODE_MASK) = JALR))</td></tr>
<tr><td>16</td><td>SR is not written to a GPR in user mode</td><td>posedge(GPR_WRITTEN, GPR_TARGET $\neq$ SR)</td></tr>
<tr><td>17</td><td>Interrupt implies handled</td><td>next((INSN & 0xFFFF0000) = 0x20000000, ((PC & 0x00000F00) = 0xE00) || ((PC & 0x00000F00) = 0xC00), 1)</td></tr>
<tr><td>18</td><td>Instruction not changed in the pipeline</td><td>next($\overline{IF\_flush}$ & ICPU_ack & $\overline{IF\_freeze}$, INSN_F = INSN_MEM) || next($\overline{ID\_freeze}$, INSN = INSN_F) || next($\overline{EX\_freeze}$, INSN_E = INSN)</td></tr>
</table>

Table 3: Invariants developed to protect against security-critical processor bugs: The first 14 invariants were developed by only looking at the specification. The next three invariants were added in response to what we learned in classifying existing commercial processor errata (Section 2). The final invariant was added after one of our errata-based bugs evaded the initial SPECS implementation (Section 5).

result of SPECS's invariants. Figure 4 shows how we add write gating: we add an AND gate to the pre-existing write enable signal that controls updates to the state item. The AND gate takes the original write enable and a signal which takes the value zero whenever any invariant fires. Write gating causes writes to any protected state to be ignored if the current execution violates any SPECS invariant.

4. SPECS Invariants

This section details the SPECS invariants for our OR1200-based prototype.[3] Table 3 contains an identification number, concise description, and assertion-level implementation for each SPECS invariant. These invariants are *not* ad hoc: 1–14 come directly from the specification, 15–17 come from our analysis of AMD errata, and 18 comes from our preliminary evaluation. Additionally, there are fewer errata than there are security-critical errata because many security-critical have the same effect (i.e., they are in the same class) even though the activation mechanism is different and SPECS is concerned only with effect.

[3] Since we do not have access to the source code for any AMD processor covered by our errata analysis, we experiment on the OR1200. The OR1200 is a RISC processor with a Harvard architecture, five-stage pipeline, memory management unit, and caches—comparable to a mid-range mobile part.

4.1 Assertions

Before tackling the invariant descriptions, it is important to understand the behavior of the assertions we construct them out of. In keeping with our design goals, we modify industry standard Open Verification Library (OVL) assertions [14] so that they are synthesizable (originally, some were simulation-only). We are able to construct all 18 of the SPECS invariants using only 4 of the more simple OVL assertions:

- *always*(`expression`): `expression` must always be true
- *edge*(`trigger, expression`): `expression` must be true when the `trigger` goes from 0 to 1
- *next*(`trigger, expression, cycles`): `expression` must be true `cycles` instruction clock ticks after `trigger` goes from 0 to 1
- *delta*(`signal, min, max`): when `signal` changes value, the difference must be between `min` and `max`, inclusive

4.2 Invariant descriptions

Table 4 contains written descriptions of each invariant in Table 3 and provides details of the OR1200 as needed. It is numbered to coincide with the ID listed in Table 3.

ID	SPECS Invariant Description
1	The privilege of the memory page the current instruction comes from matches the privilege of the processor.
2	Instructions that load a special-purpose register (privileged) with a value from a general-purpose register load do not modify the general-purpose register value.
3	The OR1200 has three registers that save the state of software when an exception occurs. The EPCR stores the PC at the time of the exception, the ESR stores the status register (SR), and the EEAR stores the effective address at the time of the exception. This invariant fires when any of these exception registers are not updated correctly.
4	The register update as the result of executing an instruction is the register specified as the target register by the instruction.
5	In memory loads, the value stored in the target register is exactly the value from the memory subsystem.
6	In memory stores, the value sent to the memory subsystem is exactly the value of the register specified in the store instruction.
7	The address sent to the memory subsystem is exactly the effective address given the GPR values and instruction contents (i.e., addressing mode and immediate).
8	If the execution privilege, stored in SR, goes from 0 (user mode) to 1 (supervisor mode), then it must be the result of taking an exception or a processor reset.
9	The execution privilege goes from 1 to 0 when a value with a 0 in the mode bit position is loaded into SR or when a return from exception is executed and the mode bit in the ESR is 0.
10	Branch and jump instructions generate the correct effective address and that effective address is loaded correctly into the program counter (PC).
11	Jump and link instructions store the address of the instruction immediately following the delay slot instruction to the link register (LR).
12	The reserved bits of a given instruction are set to 0 for each instruction encoding class
13	The address of the current instruction is the address of the previous instruction plus four. This invariant is a building block used to trigger other invariants that verify control flow discontinuities.
14	The return from exception instruction causes the PC to be loaded from EPCR and the SR to be loaded from ESR.
15	When a register changes, it must be specified as the target of the instruction.
16	When a target unprivileged register changes, the value written to that register is not equal to the SR.
17	When a software created interrupt occurs the processor passes control to the appropriate exception handler. In the OR1200, the exception handlers are at fixed address in the start of the system's address space.
18	Once the instruction fetch stage latches a new instruction, that instruction stays the same as it transitions between pipeline changes. In the OR1200, the instruction is not needed by the memory or write-back stages, so the invariant only checks up to the execute stage. Additionally, the OR1200 squashes mid-pipeline instructions by changing the instruction to a special no-op instruction, so we have to gate invariant 18 on a check to see if the instruction changed to this special no-op.

Table 4: Detailed descriptions of invariants; IDs correspond to the invariant IDs in Table 3.

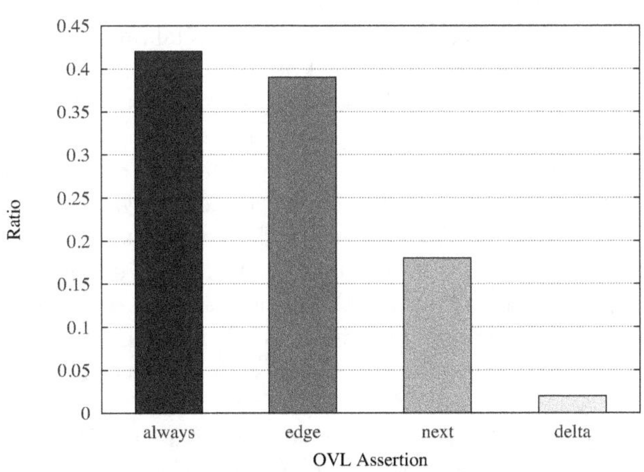

Figure 5: The proportion of each OVL assertion that we use in implementing SPECS invariants. The OVL assertions are ordered left to right in terms of increasing hardware complexity.

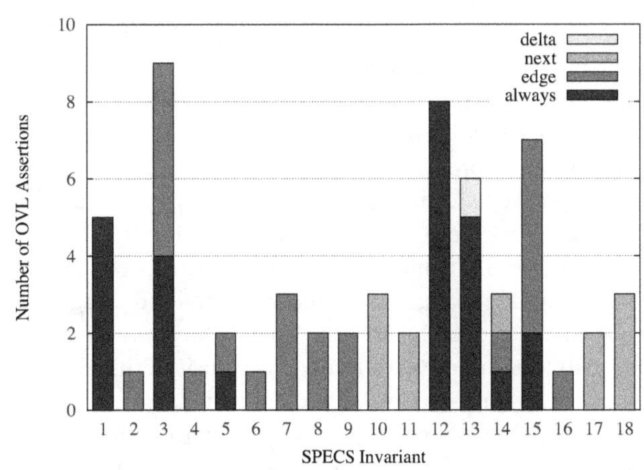

Figure 6: For each SPECS invariant, the number and type of OVL assertions required to implement the invariant and the composition of OVL assertions.

4.3 Invariant analysis

Figure 5 shows that the most common OVL assertion is *always*, followed closely by *edge*. *delta* is used only once. One observation is that the use of an assertion is inversely proportional to its complexity: we use the simplest assertions most often. Another observation is that we can implement all of our invariants using only 4 of the 33 assertions provided by OVL.

Figure 6 shows how many of each OVL assertion it takes to construct each SPECS invariant. 13 of the 18 invariants use only a single type of assertion. For the invariants that require multiple types of assertions, there is no clear pattern

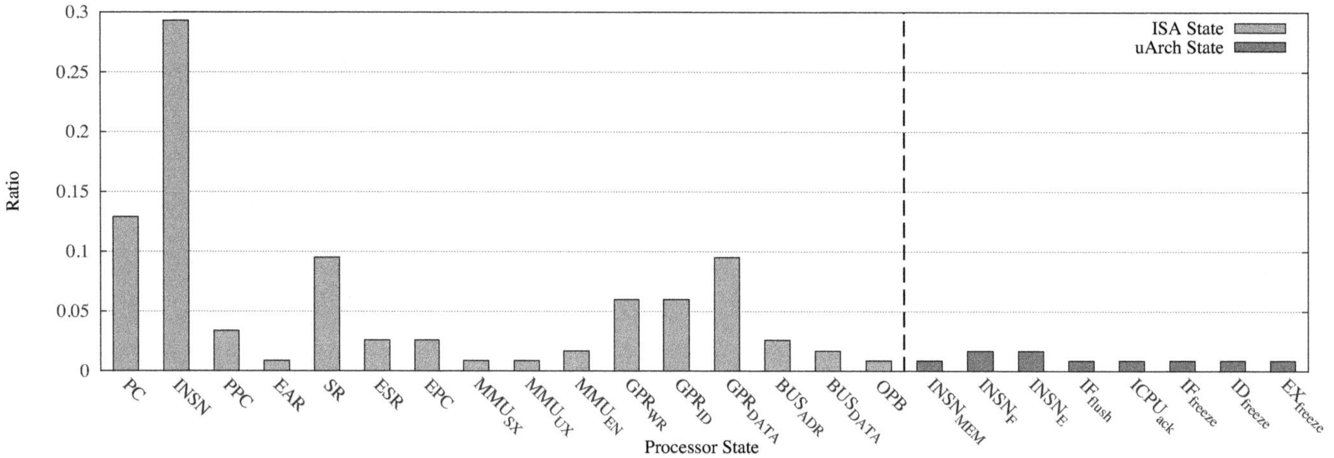

Figure 7: The ISA and micro-architectural state required to implement the 18 SPECS invariants and a tally of how many times each state item is referenced.

on which types of assertions tend to go together. The most complex invariants use more assertions, but are no more diverse with respect to assertion type than simple invariants.

Figure 7 shows the ISA and micro-architectural state that SPECS invariants rely on when dynamically verifying ISA-level state updates. The most important state item is the instruction (INSN) itself—which is why we added invariant 18 to protect the instruction as it moves through the pipeline. The other important state items are the program counter (PC) and information about register file updates, i.e., is this a write (GPR_WR), what register are we updating (GPR_ID), and what value is being written (GPR_DATA). As it resides outside of the register file, the status register (SR)—which contains the mode bit—is also frequently used by SPECS invariants. To get an idea of what SPECS looks like in an AMD-class processor, look at the difference between uses of SR and ESR (the exception-backup of SR). SR is involved in three times more invariants than ESR even though the both are privileged and hold roughly the same data. The difference in popularity comes from the ability to directly manipulate the SR using software-level instructions, while the only way to change the value of ESR is to trigger an exception. We expect this trend to hold for processors of any complexity: the more ways to update security-critical state, the more invariants required to protect that state.

Another point to note is that the one micro-architectural-level invariant tends to use more state than the ISA-level invariants. A wider footprint makes the invariant more complex and less portable.

5. Evaluation

To demonstrate that SPECS can detect and recover from a realistic and diverse set of security-critical processor bugs, we built a prototype implementation in the OR1200 processor [34] and tested it against 14 processor bugs modeled after the classes of errata from Figure 2 and associated bug-activating programs.[4] We choose the OR1200 processor because it is an open source processor implementation of non-trivial complexity that allows us to build and evaluate our SPECS design. Ideally, we would implement SPECS in an AMD processor, but complete, open source implementations are not available for x86/x64 architectures. The OpenRISC OR1200 processor is a mature, open source, 32-bit, RISC processor implementing the OR1K instruction set. It has a five stage pipeline, separate instruction and data caches, and support for virtual memory. These traits make it popular in research prototypes and it has even been used in commercial products [2, 21, 36]. Inside the OR1200, we craft each of the 14 buggy systems to model the security-critical bug classes that we mined from recent commercial processor errata (Section 2); this ensures that our test cases represent realistic design defects. For each buggy system, we create a program that activates the bug, violating some security policy.

For our prototype, we implemented the 18 invariants described in Table 3. The majority of the invariants, 14, come directly from our analysis of the specification, 3 come from the results of our AMD errata analysis, and the last invariant comes from a preliminary evaluation of our SPECS prototype. Of the 18 invariants, 17 keep with our goal of using only ISA-level state.

The goal of this evaluation is to show that SPECS (1) is versatile enough to detect the activations of a wide variety of security-critical processor bugs; (2) has low hardware and software overheads; and (3) supports existing software-only recovery and repair mechanisms.

5.1 Detecting the errata-based bugs

As shown in Table 5, SPECS assertions correctly detect all of the errata-based buggy systems. SPECS detects 12 of the 14 bugs (87%) using only ISA-level state. The two

[4] There is no relationship between the AMD, Bug, and Invariant ID numbers.

Bug ID	Synopsis	Class	Detected	Pre-recovery Cleanup
1	Privilege escalation by direct access	IU	✓	Correction
2	Privilege escalation by exception	IU	✓	Correction
3	Privilege anti-de-escalation	IU	✓	Correction
4	Register target redirection	IU	✓	Correction
5	Register source redirection	IU	✓	None
6	ROP by early kernel exit	IU	✓+	Backtrack
7	Disable interrupts by SR contamination	IU	✓	None
8	EEAR contamination	IU	✓	Correction
9	EPCR contamination on exception entry (from PC)	IU	✓	Correction
10	EPCR contamination on exception exit (to PC)	IU	✓	None
11	Code injection into kernel	EI	✓	Backtrack
12	Selective function skip	EI	✓+	Backtrack
13	Register source redirection	IR	✓	None
14	Disable interrupts via micro arch	XR	✓	Backtrack

Table 5: Errata-based buggy systems: For each errata-based bug, a description of its effect, its class (from Section 2), whether SPECS can detect the bug (Detected: ✓= yes, + = requires micro-architectural state), and the expected minimum recovery required after SPECS squashes in-flight state: in order of complexity, None: no special action required; Correction: need to reset some ISA state to a default/safe value; and Backtrack: need to rollback some ISA state to its previous value.

bugs that bypass the ISA-only invariants do so in the same way: they change the instruction as it moves through the pipeline. This bypasses SPECS because its assertions trust that the instruction is correct. To detect this type of bug we define an invariant using micro-architectural-level state that ensures that the instruction the ISA-level assertions see is the instruction that was loaded from memory. Adding a single invariant (#18) to ensure instruction integrity is enough to detect the remaining two bugs (bugs 6 and 12).

5.2 Protection versus time

We believe that because SPECS focuses on the effect of the problem as opposed to the cause of the problem, processor designers will incorporate SPECS in a model where security-critical bugs from previous generation processors become SPECS invariants in next generation processors. To support this point, we investigate how SPECS protects later processors by looking at the invariants required to protect earlier processors. For this, we add invariants in the order of the AMD bug that motivated them. The first 14 invariants came directly from the specification, before analyzing any errata. With just these 14 invariants, SPECS detects 7 of the 14 bugs we implement and the chronologically first 11 of the 28 security-critical errata from recent AMD processors (39%). After adding an invariant to detect activations of the 12th AMD bug, SPECS detects 12 of the 14 buggy systems and addresses the first 15 of the 28 AMD bugs (54%). Finally, after adding an invariant to handle the 16th AMD bug, SPECS detects all of our 14 bugs and the remaining AMD bugs (100%). We feel that this result supports our classification of AMD bugs into equivalence classes and provides a good model for the life-cycle of SPECS.

5.3 False detections

In our experiments, there are no false detections given the final set of SPECS invariants, but it did not start that way. When it is not possible to precisely define an invariant for a given security-critical state update, there is a tradeoff between missing bug activations and firing when no bug has been activated. SPECS supports erring on either side of the tradeoff space, but for this paper, we prefer the safety of false detections. This section presents each initial false positive and the approach used to eliminate it.

Invariant 3 can produce false detections because of the limits of implementing the invariant at the ISA level. Invariant 3 verifies that the processor updates the exception registers correctly in the event of an exception. False detections occur when an exception interrupts the first instruction in a basic block (a continuous and contiguous dynamic trace of instructions). When this occurs, there is no record of the address that should have been saved to Exception Program Counter Register (EPCR; it holds the PC to return to after the exception returns): the invariants only see the current state and the state about to be committed. Since the instruction was interrupted by the exception, its state was flushed, along with it the PC value that should be saved to EPCR. This means that invariant 3 fires even when the processor updates EPCR correctly—a false detection. We can avoid this by looking for impending exceptions in the invariant.

To determine the rate of this false detection, we run a gamut of software on our FPGA-based prototype, including Linux and MiBench [15] benchmarks. We find that the rate of false detections is approximately 1 detection per 20,000 instructions. These detections all occur in a single burst while booting Linux—which is exception heavy (the upper limit is the rate of exceptions). A deeper analysis reveals that the most common cause of false detections is jumping

	Baseline	Minimum	All
Logic	7911 LUTs	2.16%	4.26%
State	10549 Bits	2.74%	4.95%
Power	4.17 W	.17%	.58%
Delay	13.3 ns	0%	0%

Table 6: SPECS overheads: baseline for the OR1200, Xilinx xupv5-lx110t-based System-on-Chip compared to the overheads of SPECS with only the invariants required to detect all bugs in Table 5 (Minimum) and all 18 invariants listed in Table 3 (All).

to an address not in the translation lookaside buffer (TLB). The OR1200 has software-managed TLBs that handle the ensuing TLB miss which causes the effective address to be lost.

Another source of false detections is invariant 1. Invariant 1 fires in a series of bursts early during Linux boot-up, but then ceases. We find that this is due to Linux not correctly assigning page protections—an incomplete implementation of a security policy. Once Linux's boot-up routines correctly set page permissions, invariant 1 no longer fires.

5.4 Evaluating the cost of SPECS

Experiments show that SPECS effectively addresses all errata-based bugs that make up our evaluation platform. Experiments also show that false detections (and by extension, activations of recovery/repair software) are rare. The goal of this section is to measure the hardware overhead of SPECS. We look at all invariants as a group, the relative overheads of individual invariants, and the relative overheads of each OVL assertion that SPECS employs.

Table 6 shows less than 5% hardware overhead and no run-time overhead (in the common case) due to SPECS. Table 6 explores the hardware overheads at two design points: *Minimum* represents SPECS with only the invariants required to detect all of the errata-based bugs, while *All* represents all invariants being implemented in the OR1200. The invariants from Table 3 that make up *Minimum* are 3, 8, 9, 14, 15, 17, and 18.

There is a sizable jump in overhead when going from the 7 invariants in *Minimum* to all 18 invariants. Figure 8 shows how each invariant contributes to the total overhead of SPECS. Invariants 3, 5, and 13 stand out as the most costly invariants. One might assume that these three invariants are the most complex or require the most OVL assertions, but by comparing Figures 6 and 8, we see that is not always the case. For example, invariants 1 and 12 both use relatively many assertions, but they have relatively low overheads. This is because these invariants read ISA-level state that is much smaller than 32-bits. This allows the tools to optimize the assertions, reducing their gate count.

It is also difficult to determine the hardware cost of a given invariant due to the different hardware cost of the individual assertions. Figure 9 presents the hardware overheads of the OVL assertions that SPECS invariants use. Figure 9 also includes a parameter exploration for the assertions that are configurable. These results show the the hardware overheads vary greatly across assertion types. Fortunately, *delta*, the most expensive assertion, is also the least used, while the most used is the simplest!

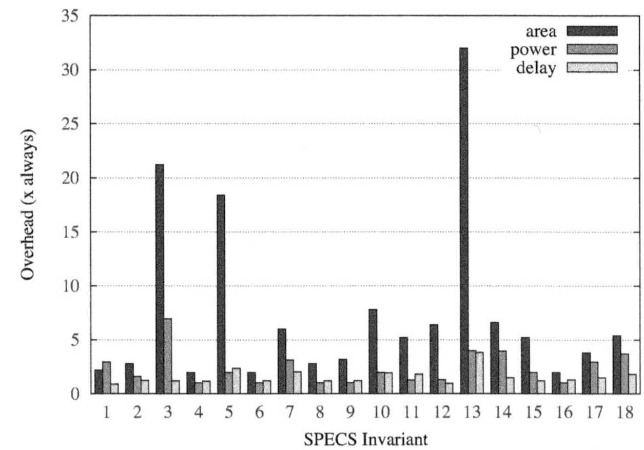

Figure 8: Hardware overheads of each SPECS invariant relative to the OVL always assertion.

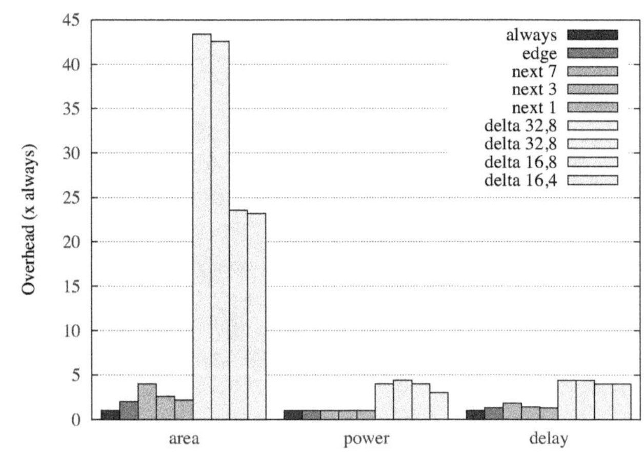

Figure 9: Hardware overheads of each OVL assertion relative to the OVL always assertion. For assertions that have configuration parameters, i.e., next and delta, we explore the effects of selecting different parameters. next x: x is the maximum number of ticks between the triggering event and the expected event. delta x,y: x is the number of bits in the input data and y is the number of bits in the maximum allowed delta (e.g., 8 bits = +/-256).

5.5 Recovering from invariant violations

SPECS supports existing software-level recovery and repair approaches by providing precise introspection points when software activates security-critical processor bugs. To aid fitting existing recovery and repair approaches to SPECS, this section provides details on the consistency of ISA-level state after SPECS squashes in-flight state updates.

Table 5 lists, for each buggy system, the amount of ISA-level state clean-up necessary post detection. Sometimes SPECS write gating is enough to ensure a consistent state, but other times a rollback to the previous state value is required. There are three distinct levels of state clean-up. Aside from no correction being required (*None*), the simplest clean-up is *Correction*, which involves resetting the contaminated ISA-level state to a safe value (e.g., setting the processor mode to user mode in the event of a privilege escalation) and then continuing execution. The most complex clean-up is *Backtrack*. *Backtrack* differs from *Correction* in that there is no safe or obvious previous value. This means that the previous value needs to be restored by the recovery or repair software. One approach to *Backtrack* is to provide a few cycles of checkpointing for security-critical state. Another approach is to recalculate the value by retracing execution.

6. Discussion

Our presentation of SPECS's implementation and evaluation did not address two important points, namely, scaling SPECS to x86 class processors and limitations of SPECS. We address these questions now.

6.1 Implementing SPECS in x86

Section 5 shows that SPECS is effective and efficient at detecting x86-like bugs implemented in a more simple processor architecture. The longer-term goal, however, is to have SPECS adopted by commercial processor manufacturers, thus it is important to address how SPECS scales with processor complexity. Lacking an open source x86 implementation we can augment with SPECS, we address how SPECS scales in a qualitative manner, but we do expect SPECS to scale to x86 processors.

We expect SPECS to scale to x86 processors. Complexity in commercial processors stems largely from logic devoted to increasing performance—as opposed to the functionality that SPECS must protect. These optimizations add state below the level of the software interface, i.e., without changing the architecturally visible state (e.g., out-of-order execution). SPECS monitors only the architecturally visible state (e.g., special-purpose registers). This means that x86-class processors are likely to have proportionally less ISA-level state than the OR1200 we evaluate with, resulting in relatively lower overheads due to SPECS. We also expect SPECS to scale because the types of architecturally visible state and rules guarding state updates are similar in the OR1200 and x86, with the x86 just having much more state and instructions: we do not know of a unique aspect of x86 at the ISA-level fundamentally different from the OR1200.

6.2 Limitations

SPECS is not able to detect all possible processor bugs, nor can it guarantee that all inconsistent state is flushed (Section 5.5). By construction, SPECS cannot detect contaminations to general-purpose state. General-purpose state is updated in a myriad of ways; as opposed to the few and simple ways that security-critical state is updated. To apply SPECS to general-purpose functionality, the number and complexity of invariants must greatly increase. Since the assertions are at the same level of abstraction as the functional description, the increase in number and complexity of invariants is the same order of magnitude as the increase in processor functionality that SPECS must protect. While SPECS is capable, the result amounts to a second implementation of the ISA. As stated earlier, software is better suited for general-purpose protection [6].

Another limitation of SPECS is that it cannot defend against processor bugs that change ISA-level state before SPECS taps the signal. Section 3.6 showed how to use micro-architectural state to prevent the the instruction from being contaminated in this fashion (from bugs 6 and 12). Another possibility is a manufacturing defect, a single-event upset, or a wear-out that contaminates the state holding element itself or the wires that feed SPECS's view of ISA-level state. Two options to address this problem outside of SPECS are to add error correction logic to state holding memories or to manufacture security critical components of the processor at a more resilient process node.

7. Additional related work

This section covers work related to SPECS. Specifically, we cover processor errata as software-level security vulnerabilities, alternative approaches to patching design-time processor bugs, and a overview of recovery approaches and how SPECS supports them.

7.1 Processor imperfections

The idea that processor errata can impact the security of a system is not new. Theo de Raadt was the first to link Intel errata to potential security vulnerabilities in the OpenBSD operating system [11]. Inspired by de Raadt's ideas, others implemented software-level attacks that used Intel errata as a foothold [3, 12, 23]. The difference between previous efforts in exploiting a single erratum as a foothold for a software-level attack and our work is that our analysis extends beyond a single attack; we identify both a set of errata that make it past functional verification and the different classes of vulnerabilities created by these errata that software can not protect itself from.

7.2 Patching processor bugs

Ideally, all design-time processor imperfections should be addressed. The best way to do this is by proving correctness using formal verification. Although formal methods have made great strides in recent years, full formal verification of modern processors remains out of reach—as is evident from the number of errata in commercial processors [20, 24]. One approach to patching processor bugs that escape verification is to add redundant but diverse computations. DIVA [1], as mentioned in Section 1, is a processor bug patching mechanism that leverages redundant implementations of the instruction set combined inside a single processor. In DIVA, a simplified checker core verifies the computation results of the full-featured core before the processor commits the results to the ISA level. Since the checker core must be simple enough to formally verify, its performance is reduced and slows execution; in contrast, SPECS provides introspection points that enable recovery approaches that add overhead *only* when the processor violates security invariants.

Another approach to patching arbitrary processor bugs is signature-based detection of processor bug activations. Constantinides et al. [7] and Phoenix [37] use low-level hardware state (flip-flops) to form bug signatures and monitor the run time state of the processor for matches. Such techniques can detect more imperfections than SPECS, but at a cost: (1) they require two extra flip-flops for every flip-flop in the design and (2) heavy contention on opcode flip-flops limits how many bugs the approaches can monitor concurrently [17]. These overheads can be significant; Phoenix, for example incurs up to 200% additional hardware.

Similar to signature-based detectors, but at the opposite end of the design tradeoff space is the idea of Semantic Guardians [44]. Semantic Guardians are assertions on low-level state that fire whenever the processor enters a state at runtime that was not functionally verified. This does not suffer from the heavy contention on a shared resource seen in signature-based approaches, as each unverified state has its own assertion circuit. The problem with this approach is that many states are not seen during verification and building an assertion for each state is not practical.

7.3 Recovery

The most common recovery strategy is to use a checkpointing and rollback mechanism. While there are a range of low overhead checkpointing options available [10, 13, 41], our analysis of recent errata shows that re-executing is not enough to move software state past the malicious circuit. Even in the case of a homogeneous multiprocessor, re-executing the bug-inducing instruction sequence may activate the bug. This means that a form of processor repair or recoding of software is required to handle arbitrary security invariant violations.

Changing software to recover from incomplete hardware is not a new idea; before the ubiquity of hardware floating point (FP) units, processors lacking FP hardware supported ISA-mandated FP instructions by triggering an exception and using FP emulation firmware to produce a correct result [25]. Narayanasamy et al. [33] extend this idea to processor bug patching by using simple, ad hoc, instruction rewriting routines that run on the macro expander DISE [9] in an attempt to avoid activating the bug, and suggest specific software-based recovery strategies for five errata. BlueChip [18], a further elaboration of this scheme, is a recovery mechanism targeted at malicious circuits implemented as a Linux device driver. SPECS provides a low overhead way of invoking the BlueChip recovery routines when they are needed.

8. Conclusion

SPECS is a new approach to patching processor bugs. SPECS adds a small amount of hardware to a processor that dynamically verifies security invariants. SPECS works in the background, not affecting software in the common case of a bug-free execution. Should software activate a processor bug that causes a violation of a security invariant, SPECS creates an introspection point for existing repair and recovery schemes. Experiments with a SPECS implementation show its practicality and effectiveness at detecting a range of errata-inspired processor bugs.

Our results validate the hybrid approach of SPECS. Previous research shows that software can practically address a wide range of processor bugs—but not all. Previous research also shows hardware can address the processor bugs that software cannot, but a system powerful enough to address all possible processor bugs is impractical. SPECS represents a middle ground: where small amounts of hardware ensure a baseline of processor functionality and software is free to protect itself, as it sees fit, from the bugs in the rest.

Acknowledgments

The paper was improved with constructive comments from anonymous reviewers; we appreciate your work, expertise, and insights. The work also benefited from discussions with Kevin Fu, Milo M. K. Martin, and David Wagner. This research was supported in part by Intel through the ISTC for Secure Computing, by the AFOSR under MURI Award FA9550-09-1-0539, by MARCO and DARPA via C-FAR (one of the six SRC STARnet Centers), and by the National Science Foundation under grants CCF-0810947, CNS-1331652 and CNS-1040672. Any opinions, findings, conclusions, and recommendations expressed in this paper are solely those of the authors.

References

[1] T. M. Austin, "DIVA: a reliable substrate for deep submicron microarchitecture design," in *International Symposium on Microarchitecture*, 1999.

[2] Beyond Semiconductor, "Beyond BA22 Embedded Processor," http://www.beyondsemi.com/25/beyond-ba22-embedded-processor.

[3] E. Biham, Y. Carmeli, and A. Shamir, "Bug attacks," in *Conference on Cryptology: Advances in Cryptology*, 2008.

[4] bjornstar. (2011) nacl_cpuid.c uses vendor string in features check. NativeClient Bug Tracker. Google. [Online]. Available: https://code.google.com/p/nativeclient/issues/detail?id=2508

[5] cbiffle@google.com. (2010) Nacl should accept x86 'int3' instruction or offer a plausible alternative. NativeClient Bug Tracker. Google. [Online]. Available: https://code.google.com/p/nativeclient/issues/detail?id=645

[6] J. Chang, G. A. Reis, and D. I. August, "Automatic Instruction-Level Software-Only Recovery," in *International Conference on Dependable Systems and Networks*, 2006.

[7] K. Constantinides, O. Mutlu, and T. Austin, "Online Design Bug Detection: RTL Analysis, Flexible Mechanisms, and Evaluation," in *International Symposium on Microarchitecture*, 2008.

[8] K. Constantinides, O. Mutlu, T. Austin, and V. Bertacco, "Software-Based Online Detection of Hardware Defects: Mechanisms, Architectural Support, and Evaluation," in *International Symposium on Microarchitecture*, 2007.

[9] M. L. Corliss, E. C. Lewis, and A. Roth, "DISE: a programmable macro engine for customizing applications," in *International Symposium on Computer Architecture*, 2003.

[10] M. de Kruijf, S. Nomura, and K. Sankaralingam, "Relax: An Architectural Framework for Software Recovery of Hardware Faults," in *International Symposium on Computer Architecture*, 2010.

[11] T. de Raadt. (2007) Intel Core 2. openbsd-misc mailing list. openbsd-misc mailing list. [Online]. Available: http://marc.info/?l-openbsd-isc&m=118296441702631;

[12] L. Duflot, "CPU Bugs, CPU Backdoors and Consequences on Security," in *European Symposium on Research in Computer Security*, 2008.

[13] S. Feng, S. Gupta, A. Ansari, S. A. Mahlke, and D. I. August, "Encore: Low-cost, Fine-grained Transient Fault Recovery," in *International Symposium on Microarchitecture*, 2011.

[14] H. Foster, K. Larsen, and M. Turpin, "Introduction to the new accellera open verification library," 2006.

[15] M. R. Guthaus, J. S. Ringenberg, D. Ernst, T. M. Austin, T. Mudge, and R. B. Brown, "MiBench: A free, commercially representative embedded benchmark suite," in *Workshop on Workload Characterization*, 2001.

[16] L. C. Heller and M. S. Farrell, "Millicode in an IBM zSeries processor," *IBM Journal of Research and Development*, vol. 48, pp. 425–434, 2004.

[17] M. Hicks, "Practical systems for overcoming processor imperfections," Ph.D. dissertation, University of Illinois Urbana-Champaign, 2013.

[18] M. Hicks, M. Finnicum, S. T. King, M. M. K. Martin, and J. M. Smith, "Overcoming an Untrusted Computing Base: Detecting and Removing Malicious Hardware Automatically," in *Symposium on Security and Privacy*, 2010.

[19] M. Hicks, C. Sturton, S. T. King, and J. M. Smith. Specs public repository. [Online]. Available: https://github.com/impedimentToProgress/specs

[20] Intel Corporation, "Intel Core 2 Extreme Processor X6800 and Intel Core 2 Duo Desktop Processor E6000 and E4000 Sequence – Specification Update," 2008.

[21] Jennic Limited, "JN5148 Wireless Microcontroller Modules."

[22] Jon Stokes, "Two billion-transistor beasts: POWER7 and Niagara 3," http://arstechnica.com/business/2010/02/two-billion-transistor-beasts-power7-and-niagara-3/.

[23] S. Lemon. (2008) Researcher to Demonstrate Attack Code for Intel Chips. PCWorld. [Online]. Available: http://www.pcworld.com/article/148353/security.html

[24] Advanced Micro Devices, "Revision Guide for AMD Athlon 64 and AMD Opteron Processors," 2005.

[25] ARM, "ARMv4 Instruction Set, Issue C," 1998.

[26] MIPS Technologies, "MIPS R4000PC/SC errata, processor rev. 2.2 and 3.0," 1994.

[27] A. Meixner, M. E. Bauer, and D. Sorin, "Argus: Low-Cost, Comprehensive Error Detection in Simple Cores," in *International Symposium on Microarchitecture*, 2007.

[28] A. Meixner and D. J. Sorin, "Detouring: Translating Software to Circumvent Hard Faults in SimpleCores," in *International Conference on Dependable Systems and Networks*, 2008.

[29] mseaborn@chromium.org. (2009) Check for trailing HLT in x86 is unnecessary. NativeClient Bug Tracker. Google. [Online]. Available: https://code.google.com/p/nativeclient/issues/detail?id=155

[30] mseaborn@chromium.org. (2010) Dynamic loading syscall insists on a trailing HLT on x86-32. NativeClient Bug Tracker. Google. [Online]. Available: https://code.google.com/p/nativeclient/issues/detail?id=585

[31] mseaborn@chromium.org. (2011) Escape from x86-64 inner sandbox using BSF instruction. NativeClient Bug Tracker. Google. [Online]. Available: https://code.google.com/p/nativeclient/issues/detail?id=2010

[32] mseaborn@chromium.org. (2012) x86-64: DATA16 prefix on direct jumps allows sandbox escape on AMD CPUs. NativeClient Bug Tracker. Google. [Online]. Available: https://code.google.com/p/nativeclient/issues/detail?id=2578

[33] S. Narayanasamy, B. Carneal, and B. Calder, "Patching Processor Design Errors," in *International Conference on Computer Design*, 2006.

[34] OpenCores.org, "OpenRISC OR1200 processor," http://opencores.org/or1k/OR1200_OpenRISC_Processor.

[35] G. A. Reis, J. Chang, D. I. August, R. Cohn, and S. S. Mukherjee, "Configurable Transient Fault Detection via Dynamic Binary Translation," in *Workshop on Architectural Reliability*, 2006.

[36] R. Rubenstein, "Open Source MCU core steps in to power third generation chip," 2014, http://www.newelectronics.co.uk/electronics-technology/open-source-mcu-core-steps-in-to-power-third-generation-chip/59110/.

[37] S. R. Sarangi, A. Tiwari, and J. Torrellas, "Phoenix: Detecting and Recovering from Permanent Processor Design Bugs with Programmable Hardware," in *International Symposium on Microarchitecture*, 2006.

[38] S. Shebs, "GDB tracepoints, redux," in *GCC Developer's Summit*, 2009.

[39] A. L. Shimpi. (2008) AMD's B3 Stepping Phenom Previewed, TLB Hardware Fix Tested. AnandTech. AnandTech. [Online]. Available: http://anadtech.com/show/2477/2

[40] S. Shyam, K. Constantinides, S. Phadke, V. Bertacco, and T. Austin, "Ultra Low-Cost Defect Protection for Microprocessor Pipelines," in *International Conference on Architectural Support for Programming Languages and Operating Systems*, 2006.

[41] D. J. Sorin, M. M. K. Martin, M. D. Hill, and D. A. Wood, "SafetyNet: Improving the Availability of Shared Memory Multiprocessors with Global Checkpoint/Recovery," in *International Symposium on Computer Architecture*, 2002.

[42] Sun, "OpenSPARC T2 Source Code," http://www.opensparc.net/opensparc-t2/download.html.

[43] S. G. Tucker, "Microprogram control for System/360," *IBM Syst. J.*, vol. 6, pp. 222–241, 1967.

[44] I. Wagner and V. Bertacco, "Engineering Trust with Semantic Guardians," in *Conference on Design, Automation and Test in Europe*, 2007.

[45] Xen.org security team. [Xen-announce] Xen Security Advisory 7 (CVE-2012-0217) - PV. [Online]. Available: http://lists.xen.org/archives/html/xen-announce/2012-06/msg00001.html

Asymmetric Memory Fences: Optimizing Both Performance and Implementability *

Yuelu Duan, Nima Honarmand, † and Josep Torrellas
University of Illinois at Urbana-Champaign
{duan11,torrella}@illinois.edu nhonarmand@cs.stonybrook.edu
http://iacoma.cs.uiuc.edu

Abstract

There have been several recent efforts to improve the performance of fences. The most aggressive designs allow post-fence accesses to retire and complete before the fence completes. Unfortunately, such designs present implementation difficulties due to their reliance on global state and structures.

This paper's goal is to optimize both the performance and the implementability of fences. We start-off with a design like the most aggressive ones but without the global state. We call it *Weak Fence* or *wF*. Since the concurrent execution of multiple *wF*s can deadlock, we combine *wF*s with a conventional fence (i.e., *Strong Fence* or *sF*) for the less performance-critical thread(s). We call the result an *Asymmetric* fence group. We also propose a taxonomy of Asymmetric fence groups under TSO. Compared to past aggressive fences, Asymmetric fence groups both are substantially easier to implement and have higher average performance. The two main designs presented (*WS*+ and *W*+) speed-up workloads under TSO by an average of 13% and 21%, respectively, over conventional fences.

Categories and Subject Descriptors C.1.2 [**Processor Architectures**]: Multiple Data Stream Architectures (Multiprocessors) - Multiple-instruction-stream, multiple-data-stream processors (MIMD); D.1.3 [**Programming Techniques**]: Concurrent Programming - Parallel programming.

Keywords Fences; Sequential Consistency; Synchronization; Parallel Programming; Shared-Memory Machines.

1. Introduction

Fence instructions prevent the compiler and the hardware from reordering memory accesses [13, 32]. In its basic form, a fence instruction prevents post-fence accesses from being observed by other processors before all pre-fence accesses have completed.

Programmers and compilers use fence instructions to coordinate threads with low overhead — where more popular synchronization primitives would be too heavyweight. For example, programmers insert fences in performance-critical codes with fine-grain communication. Examples include runtime systems such as Cilk [9] and Threading Building Blocks [27], synchronization libraries, operating systems, and Software Transactional Memory (STM) systems [30]. Compilers also insert fences, e.g., when generating code for accesses to variables declared atomic in C++ (or volatile in Java). Often, fences appear in performance-critical codes.

Successive generations of processors have steadily reduced fence overhead. One useful technique is to execute post-fence loads speculatively within the reorder buffer before the fence completes — i.e., before all the pre-fence loads retire and all the pre-fence stores drain from the write buffer. A post-fence load only stalls when it is about to retire. If, before the fence completes, an external coherence message conflicts with a speculative load, the load is retried.

In practice, however, a fence is often costly, especially if the write buffer is full with several pre-fence stores that miss in the cache, and the memory consistency model requires draining stores one at a time, such as in TSO. Recently, we measured the stall of a fence preceded by many writes in an 8-threaded Intel Xeon E5530 desktop to be ≈200 cycles [8].

As a result, there have been several recent proposals of high-performance fence designs (e.g., [8, 15, 19, 20]). The most aggressive of these are WeeFence [8] and Address-Aware Fences (AAF) [19], which allow post-fence accesses to *retire and complete* before the fence completes.

However, these two schemes present implementation difficulties. When a processor encounters a fence, it needs to obtain some global state. In a distributed-directory environment, with multiple processors updating and reading this global state, obtaining a consistent view is very challenging — in fact, we believe that the problem is still unsolved. In addition, supporting the global state requires non-trivially augmenting protocol messages and adding hardware structures. It would be most helpful to have a fence with the access reordering abilities of WeeFence or AAF, but *without* any global state. We call such a design a *Weak Fence (wF)*.

Fences prevent a Sequential Consistency Violation (SCV) when multiple fences execute concurrently, each one invoked by a different thread and, as a group, prevent a cycle of dependences [29]. We call an instance of these dynamic groups a *Fence Group*. Unfortunately, we find that, if all the fences in

---

* This work was supported in part by NSF under grants CCF-1012759 and CNS-1116237, and Intel under the Illinois-Intel Parallelism Center (I2PC).

† Nima Honarmand is now with the Department of Computer Science, Stony Brook University.

ASPLOS '15, March 14–18, 2015, Istanbul, Turkey.
Copyright © 2015 ACM 978-1-4503-2835-7/15/03…$15.00.
http://dx.doi.org/10.1145/2694344.2694388

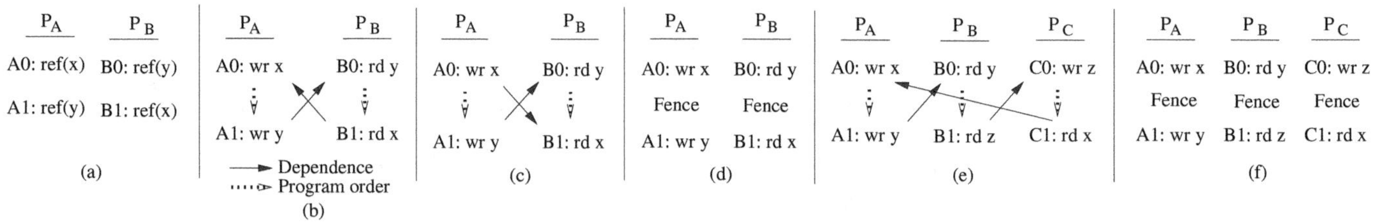

Figure 1. Examples of SC violations and uses of fences.

a group are *wF*s, when they prevent an SCV, they deadlock. Hence, this design is not acceptable. However, a key insight of this paper is that, if at least one of the fences in a group is a conventional one, then there can be no deadlock or SCV. We call a conventional fence a *Strong Fence (sF)*, and a fence group that contains one or more *sF*s and one or more *wF*s an *Asymmetric* fence group. Implementing Asymmetric groups is much simpler than implementing WeeFences or AAFs.

Interestingly, a fence group often contains one or more threads that are more performance-critical than the other(s). This idea was pointed out by Ladan-Mozes et al. [15] for two-fence groups. Hence, we use *wF*s in the critical threads and *sF*s in the other threads. For example, in the Cilk runtime [9], a thread accessing its own task queue is the common case and can use a *wF*, while a second thread stealing a task from the first thread's task queue is rarer, and can use an *sF*. With this strategy, Asymmetric fences perform comparably to or *even better* than WeeFences.

Based on these insights, this paper proposes *Asymmetric Fences*, which provide the best fence performance-cost tradeoff that we are aware of. It also proposes a *taxonomy* of Asymmetric fence groups under TSO, with various designs optimized for different needs. While Asymmetric fences introduce interesting programming issues, in this paper, we do not address such issues, and leave them for future work. However, we expect Asymmetric fences to be used by expert programmers, as they write performance-critical code.

Overall, the main contributions of this paper are:

- The proposal of Asymmetric fences, which combine *sF*s and *wF*s in the same fence group.
- A taxonomy of Asymmetric fence groups under TSO.
- The description of a few uses of Asymmetric fences.
- An evaluation of the performance, characteristics, and scalability of Asymmetric fences. The average performance of the two main designs (*WS+* and *W+*) under TSO is higher than past aggressive fences, and is 13% and 21% higher, respectively, than conventional fences.

In this paper, Section 2 gives a background; Section 3 presents Asymmetric fences; Section 4 discusses several example uses; Section 5 discusses hardware and programming issues; Sections 6-7 evaluate Asymmetric fences; and Section 8 covers related work.

2. Motivation

2.1 Background on Fences

To understand the use of fences, we begin by defining *performed*, *retired*, and *completed* for a memory instruction. A load *performs* when the data loaded returns from the memory system and is deposited into a register. It *retires* when it reaches the head of the Reorder Buffer (ROB) and has performed. After retirement, the load has *completed.*

A store *retires* when it reaches the head of the ROB and its address and data are available. The store goes into the write buffer. Later, when the memory consistency model allows, the store merges with the memory system, potentially triggering a coherence transaction. When the latter terminates (e.g., when all the invalidation acknowledgments have been received), the store has *performed*, and is now *completed.* Then, the store is removed from the write buffer.

The memory consistency model determines the access reorderings allowed. TSO [32] allows reodering between a store and a subsequent load, but not between two loads or between two stores. Release Consistency (RC) [10] allows all these three reorderings. In the write buffer, TSO only allows one write to merge with the memory system at a time, while RC allows multiple writes to merge concurrently.

Fences are instructions that prevent the compiler and the hardware from reordering memory accesses [13, 32]. While there are different flavors of fences, the basic idea is that: (1) a fence *completes* when all pre-fence accesses have *completed*, and (2) a fence has to complete before any post-fence access can be observed by other processors. Of course, post-fence loads can execute speculatively. However, they have to stall when they are about to retire and the prior fence is not completed. If an incoming coherence message conflicts with a speculative load, the load is squashed and retried.

Fences prevent access reorderings that, while allowed by the memory consistency model of the platform, can cause SCVs. Recall that SC requires that the memory accesses of a program appear to execute in some global sequence as if the threads where multiplexed on a uniprocessor [17]. An SCV occurs when the memory accesses reorder in a non-SC conforming interleaving. An SCV is typically a harmful bug.

An SCV is caused by two or more overlapping data races where the dependences end up ordered in a cycle [29]. Figure 1a shows the required program pattern for two threads (where each variable x and y is written at least once). Figure 1b shows the required order of the dependences at runtime to cause an SCV (where we assigned reads and writes to the references arbitrarily). Due to access reordering in one of the threads (or in both), *A1* occurs before *B0*, and *B1* occurs before *A0*. The cycle *A1*→*B0*→*B1*→*A0*→*A1* is now created, and this order does not conform to any SC interleaving.

If at least one of the dependences occurs in the opposite direction (e.g., as in Figure 1c), no SCV occurs. To force one or both dependences to go in the opposite direction, we must place one fence between references *A0* and *A1*, and another between *B0* and *B1* [29] (Figure 1d). It can be seen that, if *A1* is not seen by P_B until *A0* is completed, and *B1* is not seen by P_A until *B0* is completed, no cycle is possible.

This idea extends to any number of threads. For example, Figure 1e shows three threads with accesses that could potentially cause a cycle. To prevent a cycle, we need to prevent the reordering of accesses in each of the threads and, therefore, we need three fences (Figure 1f).

In this paper, we say that two or more fences running on different threads *collide* when their execution overlaps in time. When two or more colliding fences end up preventing a cycle, we say that these fences form a *Fence Group*. Note that a fence group is a dynamic concept.

2.2 Aggressive Techniques to Speed-up Fences

There have been four recent proposals of high-performance fence designs: WeeFence [8], Address-Aware Fences (AAF) [19], Conditional Fences (C-Fences) [20], and Location-Based Memory Fences (l-mfences) [15]. The first two are the most aggressive ones, and directly motivate our work. Hence, we discuss them here. The other two are discussed in detail in the related work section (Section 8).

The ideas in WeeFence [8] and AAF [19] are similar. Post-fence accesses are allowed to *complete* before the fence completes, but only if the resulting reordering is not about to cause an SCV. If it is, these post-fence accesses are stalled until the SCV cannot occur anymore. Since most of the time a fence will not collide with another one to form a fence group, the approach is beneficial. However, to detect if a reordering may cause an SCV, both schemes need *global* state. They need to know if there is any concurrently-executing fence and, if so, the pending pre-fence accesses of such a fence. These are the accesses to watch for to avoid a cycle.

To see the difficulties involved, we describe WeeFence; AAF has similar issues. Figure 2a shows two fences that prevent a cycle. Assume that WeeFence1 is in progress and P1:rd_y tries to complete. P1:rd_y needs to be careful not to cause dependence arrow *B* if there is any chance that an arrow like *A* may already exist. Such pair of arrows would cause a cycle and induce an SCV.

To avoid this case, when a WeeFence starts executing, it collects the addresses of its pending pre-fence accesses (the Pending Set (PS)) and deposits them in a global table called Global Reorder Table (GRT). At the same time, from the GRT, it grabs the PSs of all the currently-executing fences and brings them to a local structure called Remote PS. From then on, every local post-fence access checks its address against the Remote PS. If there is a match, it stalls.

This strategy prevents arrow *B* in Figure 2a. Indeed, if WeeFence2 was executing, it would have left address *y* in the GRT. WeeFence1 would have brought *y* into its Remote PS and P1:rd_y would stall, preventing arrow *B*.

However, this is not all. WeeFence still needs to do more. Figure 2b shows a pattern under TSO where a single fence prevents a cycle. P2 needs no fence because, under TSO,

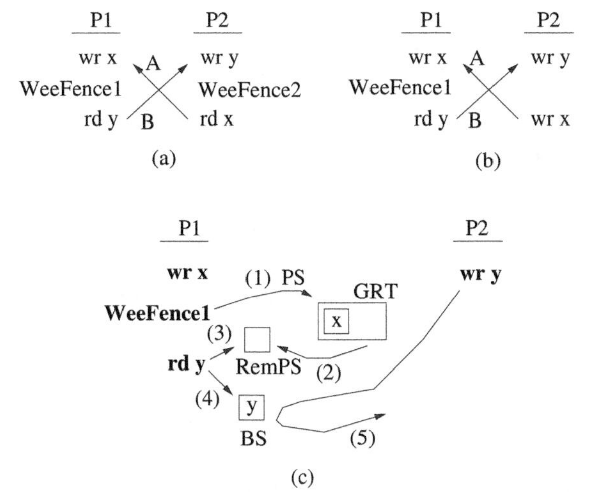

Figure 2. Operation of WeeFence.

there is no write-write reorder. Therefore, WeeFence1 will not find any PS state left in the GRT by any concurrently-executing fence. Therefore, WeeFence1 cannot use the Remote PS to stall P1:rd_y and prevent arrow *B*. However, if we allow arrow *B* to happen, and then arrow *A* happens, we have a cycle. Hence, WeeFence1 has to delay the occurrence of an arrow like *B* with any processor that has not already registered its PS in the GRT when WeeFence1 checks the GRT.

To accomplish this, when a post-WeeFence access does not find a match in its Remote PS, as it executes, it stores its address in a local Bypass Set (BS). The BS is in the cache controller, and all incoming coherence requests will be checked against it. In case of a match, the coherence request is rejected. The BS remains until the local fence completes.

This strategy delays the creation of the arrow *B* in Figure 2b. Assume P1:rd_y completed. As request P2:wr_y reaches P1 and checks the BS, it finds a match and gets bounced. Arrow *B* will not be allowed until WeeFence1 completes, at which point arrow *A* cannot occur.

Figure 2c shows the operation of WeeFence. The execution of WeeFence1 involves collecting its PS (i.e., *x*), storing it in the GRT (1), and bringing the combined PSs of all other active fences into the Remote PS (2). Then, every post-WeeFence1 access compares its address against the Remote PS (3). On a match, the access stalls; else, it executes and puts its address in the BS (4). The access may complete before WeeFence1 completes. Any incoming coherence access is checked against the BS (5). On a match, the incoming transaction bounces.

AAFs [19] work similarly. When an AAF executes, it collects global information on pending accesses in other processors, and brings it into a local Watchlist. Local accesses that hit in the Watchlist stall. The processor has a local Active Buffer like the BS that stalls incoming coherence transactions that hit there. While WeeFence is described for TSO and AAF for RC, both schemes can be adapted to either model.

2.3 Limitations

These two fence designs, while effective, are challenging to implement in a distributed-directory environment. There are

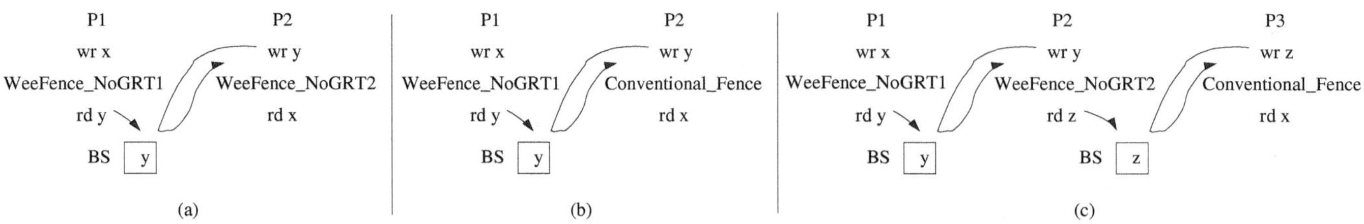

Figure 3. Eliminating global state without suffering from deadlock.

two reasons, which stem from the schemes' reliance on updating and collecting global state. First and foremost, they are subject to having coherence protocol races. In general, a fence needs to collect Remote PS state from different directory modules (since the state is distributed according to physical addresses). Such state needs to be consistent. Unfortunately, multiple processors may be depositing PSes and reading PSes from multiple directory modules with some unknown interleaving. Obtaining a consistent view is hard. We believe that this problem is still unsolved. To avoid this problem, if a WeeFence needs to deposit/access PS to/from more than one directory module, it is turned it into a conventional fence [8] — which lowers performance.

The second reason is that handling the global state adds complexity. It requires: adding new coherence messages to get pending sets (AAF and WeeFence), augmenting protocol messages with address sets (AAF and WeeFence), adding the GRT hardware table in the directory (WeeFence), and collecting addresses into signatures (AAF and WeeFence).

3. Asymmetric Fences

3.1 Main Idea

Our goal is to design a fence architecture that optimizes both performance and hardware implementability. Our contribution is to eliminate the global-state requirements of aggressive fences like WeeFence or AAF, and use the resulting fence in combination with conventional fences. With this, we greatly simplify the implementation and retain the performance. We call this approach *Asymmetric* fences. Next, we describe the ideas in the context of WeeFence.

3.1.1 Minimizing Hardware Cost

The reason why WeeFence needs to save state in the GRT global table is to avoid deadlock when preventing an SCV. If there was no such global state, at the onset of an SCV, the processors would deadlock. This can be seen in Figure 3a, which is WeeFence without GRT or PS. In the figure, P1:rd_y has completed, while P1:wr_x is still pending (and hence address *y* is in P1's BS). Moreover, P2:wr_y is incomplete. As P2:wr_y's transaction is issued into the network, it bounces off P1's BS and keeps retrying. WeeFence_NoGRT2 is then bypassed, and P2:rd_x executes, placing address *x* in P2's BS. The execution of P1:wr_x issues a transaction that bounces off P2's BS and keeps retrying. The system is deadlocked.

In WeeFence, however, P1 deposits its PS (i.e., address *x*) in the GRT while bypassing WeeFence1, and P2 reads the GRT when it finds WeeFence2. Then, P2:rd_x is unable to execute because its address matches what was read from the GRT. Later, P1:wr_x finishes, WeeFence1 completes, P1's BS is cleared, and P2:wr_y can make progress.

Our insight is that, if *at least one of the fences* in the fence group is a conventional fence, there is no need for the GRT or PS state. This is shown in Figure 3b for a 2-fence group, and in Figure 3c for a 3-fence group.

Consider Figure 3b first, where P2 now uses a conventional fence. The execution state is the same as in Figure 3a: P1:rd_y has completed, P1's BS has address *y*, and P2:wr_y is bouncing. However, the conventional fence prevents P2:rd_x from executing *non-speculatively* — i.e., if P2:rd_x executes, it must remain speculative, and a coherence message from P1:wr_x will squash it. As a result, P1:wr_x does not stall. Its completion will complete WeeFence_NoGRT1, clear P1's BS, and enable P2:wr_y to make progress.

Similarly, in Figure 3c, where only P3 uses a conventional fence, there is no deadlock possible. In the worst case, P2:wr_y is stalled by P1's BS and P3:wr_z is stalled by P2's BS. However, P3:rd_x cannot stall P1:wr_x.

In summary, we have transitioned from an N-fence group with all WeeFences, to one where N-1 fences are WeeFences without global state and one is a conventional fence. This simplifies the hardware implementation substantially.

3.1.2 Retaining High Performance

In many cases, a program where individual fence groups have both WeeFence_NoGRTs and conventional fences can deliver as much performance as if all the fence groups only had WeeFences. This is because, in a fence group, there are often one or more threads that execute performance-critical operations, while the other threads do not. Hence, we use WeeFence_NoGRTs in the former threads and conventional fences in the latter. The result is that the overall program performance is the same as if all the threads used WeeFences.

Ladan-Mozes et al. [15] observed that, in a two-fence group, there is sometimes a thread that is more important than the other. In this paper, we consider fence groups with any number of threads.

Two examples where we can combine WeeFence_NoGRT and conventional fences are algorithms in work stealing and software transactional memory (STM). Specifically, in the Cilk runtime system [9], a thread may be dequeuing a task from its task queue *Q* while a second thread is stealing a task from *Q*. Both owner and thief use fences to avoid an SCV. Since, typically, the owner dequeues from *Q* much more frequently than a thief, we use a WeeFence_NoGRT in the owner code and a conventional fence in the thief code.

In STM, there are fences when threads read a variable, write a variable, and commit a transaction. In the STM scheme that we use later, when a thread that reads a variable conflicts with another that writes the same variable, their fences prevent an SCV. Since reads are more frequent and time-critical than writes, we use a WeeFence_NoGRT in the read code and a conventional fence in the write code.

3.2 Strong Fence and Weak Fence

We define an *Asymmetric* fence group as one that is composed of one or more *Strong Fences* (*sF*s) and one or more *Weak Fences* (*wF*s). An *sF* is a conventional fence. It allows post-fence reads to execute speculatively, but not to complete, before the fence completes. On a conflict with an incoming coherence message, a speculative read is squashed.

A *wF* is a WeeFence with no GRT or PS, augmented with a few small additions that we will describe. It allows the same post-fence accesses as WeeFence to execute, retire, and complete before the fence completes. The addresses referenced by post-fence accesses are put in the BS. When one such access cannot be squashed anymore, the BS rejects incoming requests that conflict with its address. In TSO, which is the focus of this paper, the following holds: (i) the accesses in the BS are *post-fence reads*; (ii) these reads cannot be squashed anymore after they retire; and (iii) the rejected incoming requests are *write* transactions that attempt to *invalidate* the line. In other consistency models, other conditions apply.

Recall from WeeFence [8] that the BS is stored in a hardware list in the cache controller, and that it can include a front-end Bloom-filter to reduce the number of comparisons.

BS addresses and coherence transaction addresses are compared at line granularity. This is because the coherence protocol, which detects the dependences, uses line addresses. Figure 4a shows why using finer-grain addresses (e.g., word-level) would be incorrect. The example is like Figure 3b, except that P2 writes to word *y'* before writing to *y*, where words *y'* and *y* share the same line. If the comparison between the BS and the transaction (1) induced by P2:wr_y' was done at word granularity, there would be no match. Hence, the line would be brought to P2 and, later, P2:wr_y would complete execution locally, potentially causing an SCV.

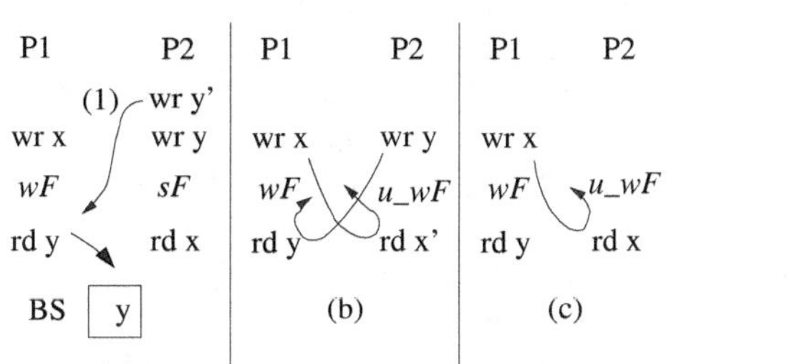

Figure 4. Examples using Asymmetric fences. In the figure, u_wF means *unrelated* Weak fence.

We expect Asymmetric fences to be used in codes that require high performance — possibly in libraries such as those for work-stealing scheduling, STM, or synchronization. These codes are typically programmed by expert programmers. It is reasonable for these programmers, for example, to place a *wF* in the code of the owner thread in a work-stealing runtime, and an *sF* in the code of the thief thread.

However, it is unreasonable for these programmers to know or worry about false sharing. Consequently, when two or more unrelated *wF*s whose pre- and post-fence accesses could form a cycle due to false sharing end up executing concurrently, the hardware has to work seamlessly. With the microarchitecture that we propose in Section 3.3, the programmer is unaware of any false-sharing related effects.

In the following, we present a taxonomy of Asymmetric fence groups, and describe the implementation of the *wF*s for the different design points. We assume the TSO model.

3.3 Taxonomy of Asymmetric Fence Groups in TSO

We design the *wF* slightly differently depending on our assumptions on what Asymmetric fence groups are possible. We propose three *wF* designs: *WS+*, *SW+*, and *W+*. First, *WS+* is the preferred design if we can assume that all Asymmetric fence groups will include at most one *wF* — i.e., the rest of the fences in the fence group will be *sF*s. Next, *SW+* is a design that works for all Asymmetric fence groups. It relies on the presence of at least one *sF* in the fence group to avoid deadlocks. Finally, *W+* is a design that works for all Asymmetric fence groups and even when *all* the fences in the group are *wF* — which, strictly speaking, is not an Asymmetric fence group anymore.

For comparison, we also consider two known environments: WeeFence and the conventional case where all fence groups only contain *sF*s (*S+*). Table 1 lists all the environments. The *S+* design has the lowest hardware complexity and the lowest performance. At the other extreme, the design with all-WeeFence fence groups (*Wee*) has the highest complexity because it uses global state. Next, we present our proposed designs.

3.3.1 At Most One Weak Fence in the Group (*WS+*)

If we can guarantee that any Asymmetric fence group will have at most one *wF*, the design of the *wF* requires relatively minor changes over a WeeFence without GRT or PS. The reason is that, in these groups, the accesses preceding the *wF* *never* need to bounce-off from another processor's BS to prevent SCVs. This is because the other processors participating in the fence group execute *sF*s, which have no BS.

Therefore, if, at runtime, an access preceding a *wF* bounces, it is due to interference with an *unrelated wF* that happens to be executing concurrently. Such interference cannot create an SCV and, hence, can be handled as such.

Specifically, the bouncing of a pre-*wF* write can be due to two cases. The first one is a cycle with another *wF* due to false sharing. This is shown in Figure 4b, where *x* and *x'* are two words from the same line. P1:wr_x bounces off P2's BS because P2:rd_x' has completed. Recall that the comparison between BS addresses and coherence transaction addresses is done at line granularity. In this case, the threads could deadlock and the bouncing continue indefinitely. The second case is a short-lived bouncing due to a true-sharing (or

wF Design Point		Hardware Support Required
Name	Corresponding Fence Group	
S+	Fence groups with only *sF*s	None (conventional fence)
WS+	Asymmetric groups with at most one *wF*	BS, Order bit, and Order operation
SW+	Any Asymmetric group	BS, Order bit, fine-grain info, and Conditional Order operation
W+	Any Asymmetric group and *wF*-only groups	BS, checkpoint, detect bouncing & being bounced, timeout, and recovery
Wee	WeeFence [8]	BS and global state (GRT and PS)

Table 1. *wF* designs with a taxonomy of Asymmetric fence groups under TSO.

false-sharing) dependence that does not cause a cycle. This is shown in Figure 4c. In all of these cases, no SCV is possible.

To handle these cases, we cannot simply transform the bouncing transaction into a plain coherence one — e.g., in Figure 4c, by letting P1:wr_x invalidate the line from P2's cache and bringing it to P1's cache. The reason is that P2's BS still has to see all the future coherence transactions directed to *x*. Invalidating the line from P2's cache would prevent that.

Our goal is to ensure both that (i) P1 makes progress (i.e., P1:wr_x completes, getting ordered after P2:rd_x), and (ii) P2's BS keeps its ability to monitor all the future coherence transactions directed to *x*. We accomplish this with the *Order* operation, which *orders* P1:wr_x after P2:rd_x, but allows P2 to retain its monitoring ability on *x*.

Specifically, we augment request messages with a bit called Order (*O*). Typically, *O* is zero. Assume that a request issued by P1 reaches the BS of P2 and there is a match (at line granularity). The transaction bounces and keeps retrying. If P1 then executes a *wF*, we know that the bouncing is unneeded, and the hardware sets the *O* bit of all of P1's currently-bouncing requests. Each of these write requests becomes an *Order* request in its next retry.

An Order request carries its update in the message. When the request reaches the directory, the latter sends an invalidation to all the sharers. The sharers invalidate the line but, in their response, tell the directory if they still have the line's address in their BS. Those that do are kept as sharers in the directory. This ensures that they will see future coherence accesses to the line. Also, if the line was dirty in a cache, it is written back to memory. The directory returns the line to the requester (or just an ack if the requester was a sharer), and merges the requester's update into memory. On reception of the response from the directory, the requester merges its update into the line and keeps the line in Shared cached state.

Overall, going back to Figure 4c, we have completed P1:wr_x and kept P2 as a sharer of the line, allowing it to see future writes to *x*. For as long as P2 has the address of *x*'s line in its BS, P2 will see any external write transaction to *x*. If the transaction's *O* is clear, it is bounced; if it is set, P2 asks the directory to keep P2 as sharer. In one of these external writes, P2 will not have the address of *x*'s line in its BS anymore, and not tell the directory to keep P2 as sharer.

Note that if P1's bouncing writes are followed by an *sF*, no special action is taken; *O* is kept zero and bouncing continues. Also, recall that the programmer guarantees that the execution will not find any other type of Asymmetric fence group. If this is incorrect, an SCV may silently occur.

Table 1 shows that the *WS+* *wF* is a WeeFence without GRT or PS, plus the Order bit and the Order operation.

3.3.2 Any Asymmetric Fence Group (*SW+*)

To handle any Asymmetric fence group, we require a more advanced *wF* design that we call *SW+* (named after the most challenging case of only one *sF* and many *wF*s in the group). The reason why we cannot reuse the *WS+* design is because some pre-*wF* accesses may now need to bounce for correctness. This is the case for the fence in P2 in Figure 3c. P2's pre-fence access needs to bounce until another processor in the group (P1 in the example) completes its fence, clears its BS, and enables P2's progress. Progress is guaranteed thanks to the presence of an *sF* in the group. If, instead of bouncing, we set the Order bit in P2's pre-fence request, we force an order that can cause a cycle and, hence, an SCV.

At the same time, as described in Section 3.3.1, pre-*wF* accesses may interfere with unrelated, concurrent *wF*s and experience unnecessary bouncing. The bouncing can be indefinite when there is a dependence cycle due to false sharing (Figure 4b), or short-lived when there is a true- or false-sharing dependence that does not cause a cycle (Figure 4c).

We solve this problem by continuing to bounce when there is a true dependence between threads, and by triggering an Order operation when the bouncing is due to false sharing. We call this idea *Conditional Order*. Note that some true-sharing induced bouncing may be unnecessary. However, such bouncing is short-lived and eventually stops.

The required hardware support is two-fold. First, the BS now keeps fine-grain addresses — i.e., those of the words (or bytes) accessed. Second, requests contain the *O* bit and a bitmask with as many bits as words (or bytes) in a line.

By default, the BS is checked against external coherence transactions at line granularity. Assume that a write issued by P1 reaches P2's BS and there is a match at line granularity. The request bounces and continues retrying as usual. However, if P1 then executes a *wF*, P1's hardware changes each pre-*wF* bouncing request as follows: (i) it sets the *O* bit and (ii) it sets the bits in the bitmask for the words (or bytes) in the line that are being requested. Note that it is possible that P1 requests multiple words of the same line; the requests are combined into a single one. These changes transform the bouncing request into a Conditional Order (CO) request.

A CO request starts-off as an Order request: all the sharers are forced to invalidate their cached copies of the line. However, the sharers that have the line's address in their BS tell the directory if the *match is due to true or false sharing*. Both types of processors are kept as sharers in the directory. However, the directory proceeds differently depending on whether there are any true-sharers at all among them.

If there are not, the CO transaction completes as an Order transaction in *WS+*. Otherwise, the CO transaction fails and bounces back to the requester, and the hardware retries it again as a CO request. Moreover, the directory discards the requester's update. Overall, the failed CO request had no effect except invalidating the caches; the processors with matching line-addresses in the BS are still sharers.

Eventually, the BSes with true-sharing addresses will clear: in the case of a normal fence group, thanks to having an *sF* in the group; in the case of a short-lived interference with an unrelated *wF*, when the latter completes. After that, when the sharers receive invalidations, they will inform the directory that all BSes match only due to false sharing. Then, the transaction will complete as an Order transaction.

Again, if P1's bouncing writes are followed by an *sF*, no special action is taken and bouncing continues. We could stop bouncing if it was false sharing, but such an optimization is unnecessary, given that *sF*s are used by non-critical threads.

Table 1 shows that the *wF* in *SW+* is a WeeFence without GRT or PS, plus the Order bit, the fine-grain address information in the BS and in requests, and the CO operation.

3.3.3 All Fences in the Group Can Be Weak (*W+*)

The *W+* design supports all Asymmetric fence groups and all fence groups where all the fences are *wF*s. As discussed in Section 3.1.1, a *wF*-only group, where *wF*s are implemented as WeeFences without GRT or PS, ends up deadlocking as it prevents an SCV. In *W+*, we allow the hardware to deadlock, trigger a time out, rollback the state to before the *wF*s, and retry execution while avoiding the deadlock again.

W+ does not distinguish between genuine fence groups, and cycles due to false sharing. In all cases, when multiple colliding *wF*s end up trying to avoid a cycle, the threads will deadlock. The recovery process is the same.

In TSO, recovery is not too costly. Since the post-*wF* accesses that can complete before the *wF* completes are necessarily loads, we can recover by mostly reusing mechanisms already present in current processors. However, recovery in models such as RC would be costly.

The hardware implementation is as follows. *wF*s are largely WeeFences without GRT or PS. There is no fine-grain address information — i.e., both BS and request transactions use line-level addresses. As usual, pre-*wF* writes bounce if they hit in another processor's BS, and post-*wF* reads can complete before the *wF*. However, a difference is that, when a *wF* reaches the head of the ROB, the hardware takes a register checkpoint, in case a rollback is later needed. Note that there may be many pending pre-*wF* writes.

After the checkpoint creation, as soon as the hardware detects that (1) at least one pre-fence write is being bounced and (2) the BS bounces external requests, it starts a timeout. When the timeout goes off, the hardware assumes there is a deadlock. Hence, it restores the checkpoint and clears the BS. This brings the processor to right at the *wF*. At this point, the processor waits until its write buffer is drained, which completes all the pre-*wF* accesses, and then resumes execution. The same deadlock is not possible anymore.

As shown in Table 1, the *wF* in *W+* needs support for checkpointing, detecting when a processor's requests are being bounced and the processor bounces requests, timing out, and performing a rollback recovery — all in hardware.

4. Examples of Asymmetric Fence Uses

4.1 Runtime Schedulers with Work Stealing

Cilk, TBB, and other runtime schedulers use work stealing. In work stealing, each thread owns a task queue. A thread removes (*take()*) tasks from the tail to execute. It may also append new tasks to the tail. When the queue becomes empty, a thread tries to steal a task from the head of the queue of another thread. Hence, *take()* and *steal()* may conflict with each other. To coordinate them without expensive synchronization, the Cilk THE algorithm [9] adopts a Dekker-like protocol, as shown in Figure 5a.

take()	*steal()*	*read(M,tid)*	*write(M,tid)*
Tail = t	Head = h	Lock(M).readers[tid] = 1	Lock(M).writer = tid
fence	fence	fence	fence
h = Head	t = Tail	w = Lock(M).writer	r = Lock(M).readers
(a)		(b)	

Figure 5. Examples from work stealing (a) and STM (b).

In *take()*, the worker first decrements the tail pointer, then checks the head to see if anyone is trying to steal the same task. If so, it will fall into a lock-based path to compete with the thief; if not, it will take the task. In *steal()*, the thief first increments the head pointer, then checks the tail to see if the owner is trying to take the task. If not, it steals the task. The protocol works if: (1) the thief observes the worker decrementing the tail before it observes the worker performing the check, and (2) the worker observes the thief incrementing the head before it observes the thief performing the check. Otherwise, an SCV can occur and a task can be executed multiple times.

To ensure the two requirements, the protocol needs two fences like in Figure 5a. Such fences are typically unnecessary because very little stealing occurs — in our workloads we see less than 0.5% of the total tasks being stolen. However, the fences must be there for correctness. Unfortunately, they cause an average of $\approx$15% execution time overhead.

These fences can form two-fence groups. We can use Asymmetric fences to optimize them. For example, since the worker executes much more frequently than the thief, we can use a *wF* in the former and an *sF* in the latter.

4.2 Software Transactional Memory

To enable optimistic concurrency between threads that might make conflicting accesses to shared-memory locations, STM programs enclose accesses inside Read and Write Barriers. These are software routines that, in addition to performing the requested read or write, also update the STM metadata to ensure proper serialization of the transactions. Typically, these metadata accesses use ad-hoc synchronization mechanisms that rely on fences.

We use the open-source Rochester Software Transactional Memory (RSTM) library [1], and consider its implementation of the TLRW algorithm [6]. TLRW is an eager-locking, eager-versioning algorithm based on read/write locks. There is one lock per shared-memory location. Each lock object has two parts: (1) an array of per-thread "reader" flags, and (2) a "writer" field. Hence, there can be multiple readers or a single writer for a memory location.

These locks are used to detect conflicts when performing transactional accesses. In Figure 5b, *M* is the memory location being accessed transactionally, *Lock(M)* is its lock metadata, and *tid* is the ID of the thread performing the access. A reading transaction writes its "reader" flag and then checks the "writer" field to see if there is any concurrent writer. A writing transaction writes to the "writer" field and then reads all the "reader" flags to determine if there are any concurrent readers. To be correct, these accesses have to be made visible to other threads in program order. Hence, fences are used.

The fences in a read and a write operation can form two-fence groups. Typically, reads are considerably more frequent than writes (3.5x in our workloads). Thus, we can use a *wF* in *read()* and an *sF* in *write()*.

4.3 Bakery Algorithm

Lamport's Bakery algorithm [16] is a lock-free mutual-exclusion algorithm of an arbitrary number of threads. It simulates a baker's shop where each customer grabs an increasing number and waits for his turn to be serviced. The algorithm uses two shared arrays (*E* and *N*), each with as many entries as threads. *E[i]* denotes whether thread *i* is trying to grab a number, while *N[i]* is the number currently held by *i*. A thread grabs a number, waits for its turn, goes to execute some critical section, and then repeats.

Figure 6a shows a code snippet with a fence. The code is executed by all threads. First, a thread writes its own *E* entry (*E[ownpid]*) and then, in a loop, goes on to read the other threads' entries (*E[pid]*). The execution can induce fence groups with any combination of thread count and pid — e.g., Figures 6b and 6c show a group with threads *T0* and *T2*, and one with threads *T4*, *T1*, and *T3*, respectively.

```
E[ownpid] = ...
fence
for all pid
    ... = E[pid]
```
(a)

```
E[T0] = ...        E[T2] = ...
fence              fence
... = E[T2]        ... = E[T0]
```
(b)

```
E[T4] = ...      E[T1] = ...      E[T3] = ...
fence            fence            fence
... = E[T1]      ... = E[T3]      ... = E[T4]
```
(c)

Figure 6. Asymmetric fences in the Bakery algorithm.

If we want to give priority to one thread, Bakery can use *WS+*. For example, if we want to give priority to *T0*, then, we use a *wF* in its code, while we use an *sF* in the other threads' code. *T0* will execute faster than the others, and we will observe *WS+* fence groups every time that *T0* participates in one of them. On the other hand, if we want all threads to run equally fast, we can use *W+*.

4.4 Other Algorithms and Domains

There are other algorithms and domains where Asymmetric fences can be used. One example is distributed lock-free lists, queues, or other structures. Another is many aspects of STM libraries. Since such libraries come in many flavors (e.g., eager or lazy, or optimized for performance or for readability) and are written by experts, they are a promising area. Other examples are environments that use biased locking such as Java Monitors [5, 14] and garbage collectors in a Java Virtual Machine (JVM). Such locking may be translated into Asymmetric fences. Finally, another example is double-checked locking [28] under relaxed memory models.

5. Discussion

5.1 Hardware Implementation Issues

The *wF* designs that we use in this paper are largely WeeFence for TSO without GRT or PS [8], plus relatively small modifications. Note that, under TSO, a BS entry only rejects incoming matching coherence transactions that attempt to *invalidate* the local line. Incoming read transactions are always serviced, even if they downgrade a local cached line from Dirty to Shared. Such downgrade does not hurt the BS ability to intercept future external writes to the line. We did not explicitly made this point in [8].

However, our *wF* designs differ from WeeFence without GRT or PS in one aspect: the handling of cache evictions of Dirty lines whose address happens to be in the BS. In [8], such evictions required storing the line's address in the GRT. Now, there is no GRT. Hence, we use the support described in Section 3.3.1, where a cache can get invalidated but, if it has the line's address in its BS, it requests the directory to keep the node as sharer. This support was described in the context of Order transactions.

Hence, in all of our designs (*WS+*, *SW+*, and *W+*), when a Dirty line is displaced and its address is in the BS, we do the following. As the line is written back, the cache requests the directory to keep it as sharer, so that it can see future writes to it (and can potentially bounce them). Note that evictions of clean lines are not a problem. Since they are silent, the directory still considers the displacing cache a sharer.

Overall, our three designs significantly simplify the hardware over WeeFence, by eliminating global hardware and state. Each design has slightly different hardware requirements, as shown in Table 1.

5.2 Implementing Asymmetric Fences in RC

Supporting Asymmetric fences in RC requires redesigning the *wF* implementations. This is because, in RC, when the *wF* executes, there may be incomplete pre-fence writes and reads. Moreover, before the *wF* completes, the post-fence accesses in the BS may include reads executed and writes potentially merged with the memory system.

As an example, the *W+* design under RC will need to recover from completed post-*wF* reads and writes. Hence, after the *W+* hardware creates a register checkpoint at the *wF*, it needs to buffer the post-*wF* writes that complete early. One approach is to place such writes into a speculative buffer or cache, while the regular cache issues exclusive prefetches for the lines. If rollback is required, the checkpoint is restored and the state in this speculative buffer or cache is discarded. We leave the design of *wF*s under RC for future work.

5.3 Programming Challenges

While this paper focuses on hardware issues, we note that *wF*s introduce programming challenges. In this section, we discuss two of them. Addressing them is beyond our scope.

One challenge is that all of the *wF*s and *sF*s that participate in a given fence group have to be contained in a code region or library that the programmer can realistically understand. If the programmer is unaware of the full extent of a possible fence group, the code may operate incorrectly. Consequently, fence groups in code that crosses software module and abstraction boundaries are unlikely to be good candidates for Asymmetric fences. Future work involves developing tools that help programmers isolate fence groups and avoid incorrect code. It also involves understanding what classes of algorithms are suitable for Asymmetric fences.

A second issue occurs with code that has an SCV and still functions as intended. For example, Figure 7a shows two threads that first release a lock and then acquire another one. Assume that a release is implemented as a store, an acquire as a test-and-test&set (using an exchange instruction), and that value 0 is free and 1 is taken. We have the code in Figure 7b. The first two accesses of this code are shown in Figure 7c. If there is an SCV, the code still works as intended.

P1	P2
release(L1)	release(L2)
acquire(L2)	acquire(L1)

(a)

P1	P2
wr L1	wr L2
rd L2	rd L1

(c)

```
P1                          P2
L1 = 0                      L2 = 0
while( L2!=0 ||             while( L1!=0 ||
    exch(L2,1)!=0 ) { }         exch(L1,1)!=0 ) { }
fence                       fence
```

(b)

Figure 7. Code with an existing SCV.

Our Asymmetric fence designs assume that the input code does not have SCVs to start with. Consequently, they may not work with the code in Figure 7c. For example, assume that, in between P1:wr_L1 and P1:rd_L2, there is code with a *wF* and, in between P2:wr_L2 and P2:rd_L1 there is code with an unrelated *wF*. If these *wF*s are implemented as *SW+*, the system may deadlock as both *wF*s attempt Conditional Order operations. On the other hand, if they are implemented as either *WS+* or *W+*, the code executes correctly. Future work involves examining the interaction of *wF* implementations with codes that contain SCVs.

Overall, we expect Asymmetric fences to be used mostly by expert programmers, as they develop performance-sensitive codes — e.g., synchronization, TM, or task scheduling libraries.

6. Evaluation Setup

To evaluate Asymmetric fences, we use detailed cycle-level execution-driven simulations. We model a multicore with 8 cores connected in a mesh network with a directory-based MESI coherence protocol under TSO. Each core has a private L1 cache, a bank of a shared L2 cache, a portion of the directory and, for WeeFence, a module of the distributed GRT. For some experiments, we change the number of cores from 4 to 32. Table 2 shows the architecture parameters. For WeeFence, we use the default parameters in [8].

Architecture	Multicore with 4-32 cores (default is 8)
Core	Out of order, 4-issue wide, 2.0 GHz
ROB; write buffer	140 entries; 64 entries
L1 cache	Private 32KB WB, 4-way, 2-cycle RT, 32B lines
L2 cache	Shared with per-core 128KB WB banks A bank: 8-way, 11-cycle RT (local), 32B lines
Bypass Set (BS)	Up to 32 entries per core, 4B per entry
Cache coherence	MESI under TSO, full-mapped NUMA directory
On-chip network	2D-mesh, 5 cycles/hop, 256-bit links
Off-chip memory	Connected to one network port, 200-cycle RT

Table 2. Architecture modeled. RT means round trip.

We tune our simulator so that a conventional fence has approximately the same overhead as indicated in [8] for a desktop with a 4-core Intel Xeon E5530 processor.

For the evaluation, we use three workload groups. They are listed in Table 3. The first one is a set of Cilk applications (*CilkApps*) that use the THE work-stealing algorithm [9]. As indicated in Section 4.1, all fence groups are formed by 2 fences, one in the worker code and one in the code for the thief. For both *SW+* and *WS+*, we use a *wF* in the worker code and an *sF* in the thief code.

Workload Group	Applications
Cilk Apps. (*CilkApps*)	bucket, cholesky, cilksort, fft, fib, heat, knapsack, lu, matmul, plu
STM Micro-benchs. (*uSTM*)	Counter, DList, Forest, Hash, List, MCAS, ReadNWrite1, ReadWriteN, Tree, TreeOverwrite
STAMP Apps.	genome,intruder,kmeans,labyrinth,ssca2,vacation

Table 3. Applications used in the evaluation.

The second workload is a set of STM microbenchmarks (*uSTM*). They are obtained from the Rochester Software Transactional Memory (RSTM) library [1] and use the TLRW algorithm discussed in Section 4.2. Each microbenchmark consists of a concurrent data structure and transactions that look-up, insert, or delete data in the structure. 50% of the transactions are lookups, and the rest are equally divided between insertions and deletions. As per Section 4.2, fence groups are formed by two fences, one in the read operation and one in the write operation. For both *SW+* and *WS+*, we use a *wF* in the read code and an *sF* in the write code.

The third workload has applications from the STAMP suite [23] distributed with RSTM. The fence groups and the assignment of *wF* and *sF* are the same as in *uSTM*.

In both *CilkApps* and *STAMP*, we report performance as execution time. For *uSTM*, since there is no standard input set, we run each microbenchmark for a certain fixed time and measure the number of transactions committed. We report performance as throughput.

We find that the performance of our workloads under *SW+* and *WS+* is practically the same. This is unsurprising, given that our fence groups have two fences. Hence, to simplify the evaluation, we do not show data for *SW+*.

Recall that *sF*s allow *speculative* execution of post-fence reads. Also, when a WeeFence cannot confine its PS and BS into a single directory module, it turns into an *sF* [8].

7. Evaluation

7.1 Performance Comparison

Figure 8 compares the execution time of *CilkApps* for different types of fences. For each application, we show, from left to right, bars for *S+*, *WS+*, *W+* and *Wee* fences, all normalized to *S+*. The time is broken down according to whether the processor is retiring instructions (*Busy*), is stalled for fences (*Fence Stall*) or is stalled for other reasons such as memory or pipeline hazards (*Other Stall*). The rightmost set of four bars shows the average of all applications.

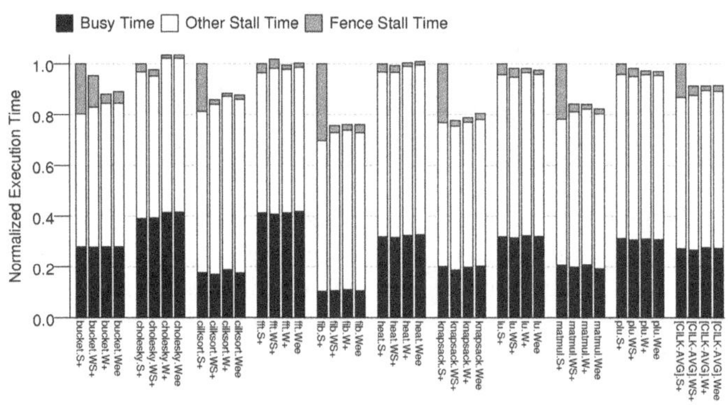

Figure 8. Execution time of *CilkApps*.

Looking at the average bars, we see that, with conventional fences (*S+*), *CilkApps* spend 13% of their time stalled in fences. *WS+*, *W+* and *Wee* eliminate most of such stall. With these designs, the remaining fence stall time amounts to an average of 2-4% of the application time. The result is that, with either of these three designs, the overall execution time of *CilkApps* is reduced by an average of 9%.

The overall average performance impact is necessarily limited by the average fraction of original time spent on fence stall. However, we see that there are applications with 20-30% of the time spent on fence stall and, in those cases, *WS+* and *W+* eliminate most of it. As fence stall decreases, other stall sometimes increases — e.g., memory operations that bypass fences then induce memory contention.

WS+, *W+* and *Wee* perform similarly because, in work-stealing, most of the executed fences are *wF*. Moreover, there are very few recoveries in *W+*. Overall, *WS+* are *W+* are equally attractive and much more cost-effective than *Wee*.

We now consider the *uSTM* workload. As shown in Figure 9, we measure performance as transactional throughput — i.e., the number of transactions committed per second. Therefore, higher is better. For each microbenchmark, we show bars for *S+*, *WS+*, *W+* and *Wee*, all normalized to *S+*. The rightmost set of bars is the average.

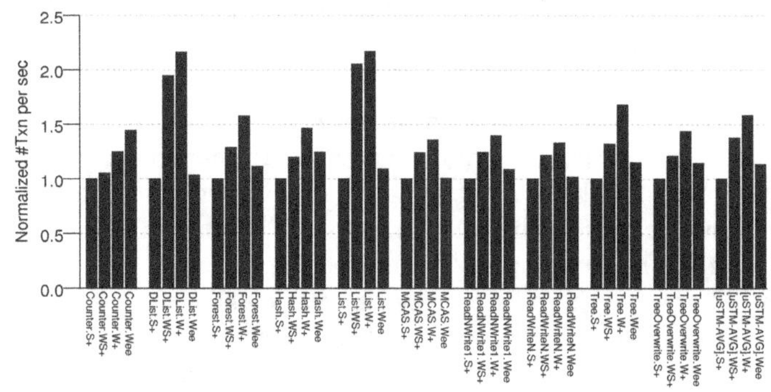

Figure 9. Transactional throughput of *uSTM*.

As shown in the figure, *WS+*, *W+* and *Wee* all outperform *S+*. This is because, by reducing the fence stall time, these designs are able to speed-up the execution. On average, *WS+*, *W+* and *Wee* increase the transactional throughput by 38%, 58%, and 14%, respectively, over *S+*. We see that *W+* and *WS+* are much more cost-effective than *Wee*.

To understand these results better, Figure 10 shows the per-transaction breakdown of processor cycles. This figure breaks down the bars into the usual categories. Compared to *CilkApps* in Figure 8, these microkernels spend a much higher fraction of their time in fence stall. On average, in *S+*, *uSTM* spend 54% of their time stalled in fences.

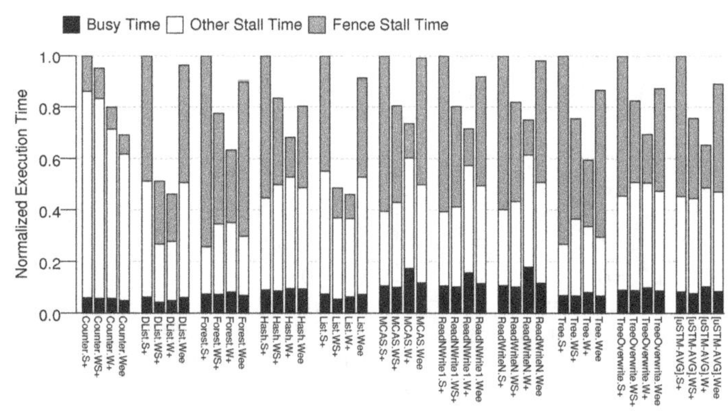

Figure 10. Per-transaction breakdown of processor cycles.

The figure shows that Asymmetric fences are very effective. *WS+* and *W+* eliminate half and two thirds of the average fence stall time, respectively. As a result, the average transaction takes 24% and 35% fewer cycles in *WS+* and *W+*, respectively, than in *S+*. *W+* reduces more fence stall time than *WS+*. However, in part because of its deadlock recoveries, it has a higher busy time than *WS+*. Interestingly, *Wee* reduces the fence stall time little. The reason is that *Wee* ends-up turning many of its fences into *sF*s. *Wee* only manages to reduce the average transaction time by 11%.

Workload	S+	WS+						W+			Wee		
	#sFs /1000i	#sFs /1000i	#wFs /1000i	#lines /BS	#wr bounc /wF	#retries /wr	%traffic incr.	#wFs /1000i	#recov. /wF	%traffic incr.	#sFs /1000i	#wFs /1000i	#lines /BS
CilkApps	1.1	0.3	0.8	4.7	0.1	1.3	3.6	1.1	0.0	1.1	0.0	1.1	4.6
uSTM	5.7	1.8	4.5	2.6	0.3	0.6	2.3	6.5	0.2	1.3	3.1	2.9	2.4
STAMP	1.3	0.6	0.7	2.5	0.0	0.6	0.6	1.7	0.0	0.9	0.6	1.1	2.4

Table 4. Characterization of Asymmetric fences.

Finally, Figure 11 compares the execution time of *STAMP* applications for different fence types. The bars are broken down as usual. In the figure, we see a lot of variation. This is because each application's potential depends on the amount and type of transactional work that it does.

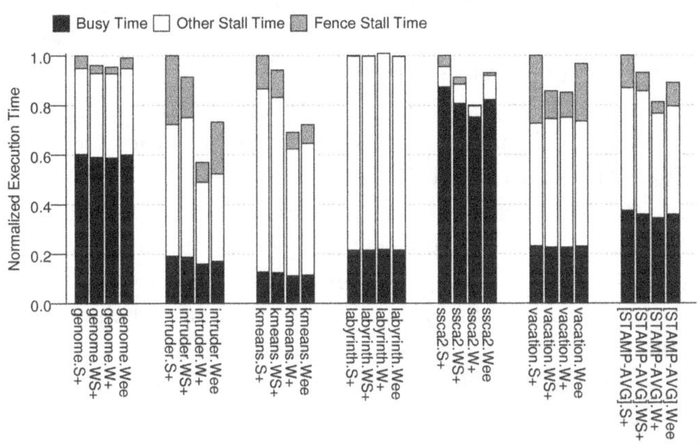

Figure 11. Execution time of STAMP.

For example, *intruder* includes many write operations and, hence, *W+* decreases the fence stall time more than *WS+*. Its changes in fence stall time also affect the other stall time. *Labyrinth* has very few transactions in the first place, and hence cannot get noticeable improvements. *Genome* sees moderate improvements because most of its stall time is due to reasons other than fences. On average, with conventional fences, these applications spend 13% of their time stalled in fences. *WS+*, *W+* and *Wee* reduce the average execution time by 7%, 19%, and 11%, respectively.

Based on the many workloads analyzed, we conclude that, under TSO, *W+* is faster than *WS+*. Across all the workload sets, *W+* and *WS+* reduce the execution time over *S+* by an average of 21% and 13%, respectively. The selection of which scheme is more cost-effective depends on implementation issues. As shown in Table 1, *WS+* requires the Order bit and operation, while *W+* requires detecting a potential cycle, triggering a timeout, and supporting checkpointed recovery. In any case, both schemes are much more cost-effective than *Wee*, which only reduces the execution time by an average of 10% and is more complex.

7.2 Performance Characterization

Table 4 characterizes the *S+*, *WS+*, *W+*, and *Wee* designs for 8 processors. Column 2 shows the average number of *sF*s per 1,000 dynamic instructions in *S+*. For *CilkApps* and *STAMP*, the number is around 1, while for *uSTM* this number is 5.7. Such higher fence frequency is why *WS+* and *W+* get better speedups in *uSTM*.

The next few columns correspond to *WS+*. Columns 3-4 show the average number of *sF*s and *wF*s per 1,000 instructions. The sum of Columns 3 and 4 is not equal to Column 2 for *uSTM* because the *uSTM* experiments measure throughput and execute slightly different code every time. In *STAMP*, *sF*s are about as frequent as *wF*s. Hence, there is a bigger performance gap between *W+* and *WS+* in *STAMP*.

Column 5 shows the average number of line addresses in the BS of a *wF*. We see that this value is 3-5 for the workloads. It can be shown that it corresponds to 12-24 different word addresses. Columns 6-7 consider an average *wF* and show the average number of writes that bounce off it and, for each of these writes, the average number of retries until it can commit. In all cases, the two numbers are low. Hence, the stalls caused by bouncing are largely hidden by the write buffer and do not cause pipeline stall. Column 8 shows the increase in bytes transferred in the network due to write retries. We can see that the increase is negligible.

The next three columns correspond to *W+*. Column 9 shows the average number of *wF*s per 1,000 instructions. Recall that *W+* does not have any *sF*s. Column 10 shows the average number of recoveries per *wF*. This number is only noticeable for *uSTM*, which causes a slightly higher busy time for *W+* in Figure 10. Column 11 shows the increase in network traffic due to *W+*, which is again negligible.

Finally, we show data for *Wee*. Columns 12-13 show the average number of *sF*s and *wF*s per 1,000 instructions. Recall that *Wee* only has the equivalent of *wF*s. However, when a fence's PS and BS cannot be confined into a single directory module, the fence becomes an *sF*. We see that, for *CilkApps*, fences remain *wF*s. However, for *uSTM*, about half of the fences turn into *sF*s. For *STAMP*, about one third do. This effect explains why *Wee* has a higher fence stall time than *WS+* and *W+* in Figures 10 and 11. Column 14 shows the number of line addresses in the BS. These values are similar to those for *WS+* (Column 5). They are higher than in [8] because, in that paper, we used Private Access Filtering. Finally, it can be shown that the number of writes that get bounced per *wF*, and number of retries until a bouncing write can commit are very small, as in *WS+* (Columns 6-7).

7.3 Scalability Analysis

Finally, we assess the scalability of Asymmetric fences' effectiveness to reduce fence stall time. For a given design (say, *WS+*), we compare its fence stall time to that of *S+*, and compute the ratio (stall*WS+*/stall*S+*). This ratio is shown in Figure 12 for different numbers of cores. The figure organizes the data per workload and fence design. For each case, it shows bars for 4, 8, 16, and 32-core runs.

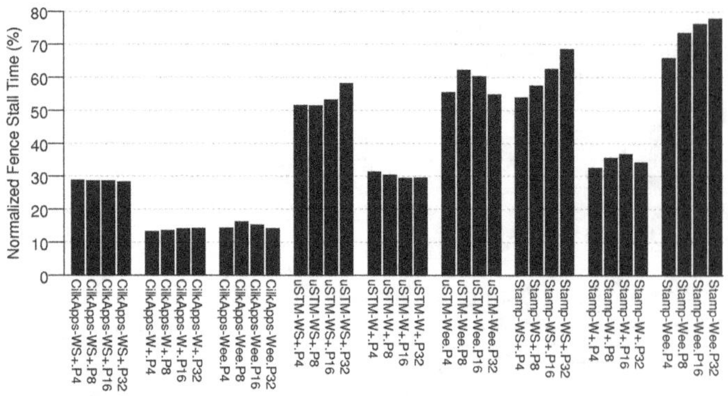

Figure 12. Scalability of Asymmetric fence stall time.

For a given workload and fence design, as we go from 4 to 32 cores, the bars remain flat or increase only modestly. For example, for *CilkApps* with *WS+*, the bars remain at 28%. While the total fence stall time for *CilkApps* with *S+* may change with the core count, *WS+* manages to reduce it always to about 28% of it. This means that *WS+* is scalable. Its effectiveness is not reduced with higher core counts.

Overall, while the various designs have different impacts on different loads, they all keep their effectiveness across different core counts. Hence, Asymmetric fences are scalable.

8. Related Work

Location-based memory fences (l-mfences) [15] is a design that speeds-up the execution of a fence in a thread when no other thread accesses the location protected by the fence often. It is implemented with instructions like Load-Linked (LL) and Store-Conditional (SC). The operation takes as arguments the address of a write that precedes the fence and the value it wants to write. If the memory line accessed by the operation is in the cache in Exclusive state, the operation only involves a cached load and a store. However, if a second thread has accessed the location in the meantime, when the first thread tries to access it again, its SC fails, and it has to perform a conventional fence.

*wF*s and l-mfences have four main differences. First, *wF*s allow *reordering* of accesses across fences: post-fence accesses can *complete* before pre-fence accesses complete. In l-mfences, the SC has to complete before post-fence accesses can complete. Second, *wF*s are more general: an l-mfence takes as argument a write, while a *wF* protects many writes. In addition, the l-mfence only works well if a fence protects the *same* address across invocations. Third, with l-mfences, every time that another thread accesses the location, the line's coherence state changes, and a future l-mfence will fail. A *wF* works well no matter how many times another *sF* executes. Finally, the l-mfence design focuses on two conflicting threads only, while our *wF*s work for any fence group size.

The idea of Conditional Fences (C-Fences) [20] is for the compiler or user to statically classify fences into groups called Associates. These are fences that may appear in a fence group at runtime. At runtime, when a fence executes, the hardware checks a centralized table to see if any other associate fence is executing. If so, the fence stalls until its associate completes. This scheme requires global hardware, and such hardware is centralized. *wF*s eliminate global hardware and any centralization points. It is unclear how the difficulty of grouping fences into associates compares to that of choosing *wF*s and *sF*s. However, *wF*s are compatible with conventional fences in other code modules, but C-Fences are not.

A related approach is post-retirement speculation (e.g., [3, 4, 11, 26]) — a technique that tries to reduce stalls due to access reorders disallowed by the memory model (not just fences). This technique completes writes speculatively and, therefore, needs to buffer speculative state. Depending on the design, the speculative state is stored in large purposely-built post-retirement buffers or in L1 caches modified with speculative read/write bits. In some cases, the speculation is performed in chunks of instructions. None of our schemes completes writes speculatively, not even *W+*.

Our work is also related to schemes that enforce SC or identify SC violations. Examples are Conflict Ordering (CO) [21], End-to-End SC [22, 31], Vulcan [24], and Volition [25]. These schemes are concerned about the reordering of all accesses; in Asymmetric fences, we are concerned only about the reordering of the accesses across fences.

Software researchers have built on a cycle-detection algorithm [29] to insert fences in codes to guarantee SC (e.g., [7, 18, 33]). Their goal is to minimize the number of fences added to guarantee SC. Our work is complementary, as we help them minimize the overhead of SC guarantees.

In C/C++ and Java, it is possible to avoid exposing fences and, instead, provide implicit ordering with respect to a single update. This is supported by the ARMv8 [2] and Itanium [12] load-acquire and store-release instructions. Adapting *wF*s to these environments is interesting future work.

9. Conclusions

Past fence proposals improved performance by allowing post-fence accesses to complete before the fence completes. Unfortunately, such proposals present implementation challenges caused by requiring global state and structures.

The goal of this paper was to improve both the performance and the implementability of fences. We used a fence design like the most aggressive ones but without the global state (*Weak Fence* or *wF*) combined with a conventional fence (*Strong Fence* or *sF*) for the less performance-critical threads. We called the result an Asymmetric fence group. We proposed a taxonomy of Asymmetric fence groups. Compared to past aggressive fences, Asymmetric fences both are substantially easier to implement and have higher average performance. Hence, they offer the best performance-cost tradeoff that we are aware of. The two main designs presented (*WS+* and *W+*) speed-up workloads under TSO by an average of 13% and 21%, respectively, over conventional fences. The designs require different hardware: *WS+* requires the Order bit and operation, while *W+* requires checkpointing, triggering a timeout when a cycle is suspected, and rolling back.

Acknowledgments

We thank Hans Boehm and the anonymous reviewers.

References

[1] Rochester Software Transactional Memory. http://www.cs.rochester.edu/research/synchronization/rstm/.

[2] ARM. ARMv8-A Reference Manual, Issue A.d. http://infocenter.arm.com.

[3] Colin Blundell, Milo M. K. Martin, and Thomas F. Wenisch. InvisiFence: Performance-Transparent Memory Ordering in Conventional Multiprocessors. In *International Symposium on Computer Architecture*, June 2009.

[4] Luis Ceze, James Tuck, Pablo Montesinos, and Josep Torrellas. BulkSC: Bulk Enforcement of Sequential Consistency. In *International Symposium on Computer Architecture*, June 2007.

[5] Dave Dice, Mark Moir, and William Scherer. Quickly Reacquirable Locks. *Technical Report, Sun Microsystems Inc.*, 2003.

[6] Dave Dice and Nir Shavit. TLRW: Return of the Read-write Lock. In *Symposium on Parallelism in Algorithms and Architectures*, June 2010.

[7] Yuelu Duan, Xiaobing Feng, Lei Wang, Chao Zhang, and Pen-Chung Yew. Detecting and Eliminating Potential Violations of Sequential Consistency for Concurrent C/C++ Programs. In *International Symposium on Code Generation and Optimization*, March 2009.

[8] Yuelu Duan, Abdullah Muzahid, and Josep Torrellas. WeeFence: Toward Making Fences Free in TSO. In *International Symposium on Computer Architecture*, June 2013.

[9] Matteo Frigo, Charles E. Leiserson, and Keith H. Randall. The Implementation of the Cilk-5 Multithreaded Language. In *Conference on Programming Language Design and Implementation*, June 1998.

[10] Kourosh Gharachorloo, Daniel Lenoski, James Laudon, Phillip Gibbons, Anoop Gupta, and John Hennessy. Memory Consistency and Event Ordering in Scalable Shared-memory Multiprocessors. In *International Symposium on Computer Architecture*, June 1990.

[11] Chris Gniady, Babak Falsafi, and T. N. Vijaykumar. Is SC + ILP = RC? In *International Symposium on Computer Architecture*, June 1999.

[12] Intel. Intel Itanium Architecture Software Developer's Manual, Revision 2.3. http://www.intel.com/design/itanium/ manuals/iiasdmanual.htm, May 2010.

[13] Intel Corp. *IA-32 Intel Architecture Software Developer Manual, Volume 2: Instruction Set Reference*. 2002.

[14] Kiyokuni Kawachiya, Akira Koseki, and Tamiya Onodera. Lock Reservation: Java Locks Can Mostly Do without Atomic Operations. In *Conference on Object-Oriented Programming, Systems, Language, and Applications*, November 2002.

[15] Edya Ladan-Mozes, I-Ting Angelina Lee, and Dmitry Vyukov. Location-Based Memory Fences. In *Symposium on Parallelism in Algorithms and Architectures*, June 2011.

[16] L. Lamport. A New Solution of Dijkstra's Concurrent Programming Problem. *Communications of the ACM*, August 1974.

[17] L. Lamport. How to Make a Multiprocessor Computer that Correctly Executes Multiprocess Programs. *IEEE Transactions on Computers*, July 1979.

[18] Jaejin Lee and D.A. Padua. Hiding Relaxed Memory Consistency with Compilers. In *International Conference on Parallel Architectures and Compilation Techniques*, October 2000.

[19] C. Lin, V. Nagarajan, and R. Gupta. Address-aware Fences. In *International Conference on Supercomputing*, June 2013.

[20] Changhui Lin, Vijay Nagarajan, and Rajiv Gupta. Efficient Sequential Consistency using Conditional Fences. In *International Conference on Parallel Architectures and Compilation Techniques*, September 2010.

[21] Changhui Lin, Vijay Nagarajan, Rajiv Gupta, and Bharghava Rajaram. Efficient Sequential Consistency via Conflict Ordering. In *International Conference on Architectural Support for Programming Languages and Operating Systems*, March 2012.

[22] Daniel Marino, Abhayendra Singh, Todd Millstein, Madanlal Musuvathi, and Satish Narayanasamy. A Case for an SC-preserving Compiler. In *Conference on Programming Language Design and Implementation*, June 2011.

[23] Chi Cao Minh, Jaewoong Chung, Christos Kozyrakis, and Kunle Olukotun. STAMP: Stanford Transactional Applications for Multi-Processing. In *International Symposium on Workload Characterization*, September 2008.

[24] Abdullah Muzahid, Shanxiang Qi, and Josep Torrellas. Vulcan: Hardware Support for Detecting Sequential Consistency Violations Dynamically. In *International Symposium on Microarchitecture*, December 2012.

[25] Xuehai Qian, Benjamin Sahelices, Josep Torrellas, and Depei Qian. Volition: Scalable and Precise Sequential Consistency Violation Detection. In *International Conference on Architectural Support for Programming Languages and Operating Systems*, March 2013.

[26] Parthasarathy Ranganathan, Vijay S. Pai, and Sarita V. Adve. Using Speculative Retirement and Larger Instruction Windows to Narrow the Performance Gap Between Memory Consistency Models. In *Symposium on Parallelism in Algorithms and Architectures*, June 1997.

[27] James Reinders. *Intel Threading Building Blocks*. O'Reilly & Associates, Inc., 2007.

[28] Douglas C. Schmidt and Tim Harrison. Double-Checked Locking: An Optimization Pattern for Efficiently Initializing and Accessing Thread-Safe Objects. In *Conference on Pattern Languages of Programming*, 1996.

[29] D. Shasha and M. Snir. Efficient and Correct Execution of Parallel Programs that Share Memory. *ACM Transactions on Programming Languages and Systems*, April 1988.

[30] Nir Shavit and Dan Touitou. Software Transactional Memory. In *Symposium on Principles of Distributed Computing*, August 1995.

[31] Abhayendra Singh, Satish Narayanasamy, Daniel Marino, Todd D. Millstein, and Madanlal Musuvathi. End-to-End Sequential Consistency. In *International Symposium on Computer Architecture*, June 2012.

[32] SPARC International, Inc. *The SPARC Architecture Manual (Version 9)*. 1994.

[33] Zehra Sura, Xing Fang, Chi-Leung Wong, Samuel P. Midkiff, Jaejin Lee, and David Padua. Compiler Techniques for High Performance Sequentially Consistent Java Programs. In *Symposium on Principles and Practice of Parallel Programming*, June 2005.

DeNovoSync: Efficient Support for Arbitrary Synchronization without Writer-Initiated Invalidations *

Hyojin Sung and Sarita V. Adve

Department of Computer Science
University of Illinois at Urbana-Champaign
denovo@cs.illinois.edu

Abstract

Current shared-memory hardware is complex and inefficient. Prior work on the DeNovo coherence protocol showed that disciplined shared-memory programming models can enable more complexity-, performance-, and energy-efficient hardware than the state-of-the-art MESI protocol. DeNovo, however, severely restricted the synchronization constructs an application can support. This paper proposes DeNovoSync, a technique to support arbitrary synchronization in DeNovo. The key challenge is that DeNovo exploits race-freedom to use reader-initiated local self-invalidations (instead of conventional writer-initiated remote cache invalidations) to ensure coherence. Synchronization accesses are inherently racy and not directly amenable to self-invalidations. DeNovoSync addresses this challenge using a novel combination of registration of all synchronization reads with a judicious hardware backoff to limit unnecessary registrations. For a wide variety of synchronization constructs and applications, compared to MESI, DeNovoSync shows comparable or up to 22% lower execution time and up to 58% lower network traffic, enabling DeNovo's advantages for a much broader class of software than previously possible.

1. Introduction

Both software and hardware in today's multicore systems face a major challenge in efficiently exploiting parallelism. Shared-memory remains a popular programming model due to its global address space, but it is unfortunately plagued with complexities arising from undisciplined programming practices; e.g., data races, unstructured parallelism with implicit side-effects, and unstructured non-determinism. Such "wild" shared memory behavior undermines the efficiencies that can be achieved through parallelism. It makes it difficult to test and maintain software as well as complicates hardware, preventing energy-efficient scaling.

Recently, there has been active research in exploiting information about memory accesses to improve the complexity and performance of hardware coherence and consistency [10, 11, 32, 35]. Specifically, the DeNovo project [10, 21, 35, 36] showed that hardware coherence can be simpler and more efficient if shared-memory programs are more "disciplined;" i.e., if parallelism is explicitly requested through structured parallel constructs with memory side-effects statically or dynamically identified. DeNovo eliminates directory storage for sharer lists, writer-initiated invalidation traffic, false sharing, and protocol transient states. Compared to the state-of-the-art MESI protocol, DeNovo offers a more complexity-, performance-, and energy-efficient solution.

DeNovo has primarily focused on supporting data accesses, assuming restricted forms of synchronization (global barriers for determinism in the original DeNovo [10] and disciplined locks for safe non-determinism in the later DeNovoND [35]) supported with special hardware support. For DeNovo to be widely adopted, however, it must relax its software requirements and support programs with arbitrary synchronization without expensive hardware support. This paper proposes DeNovoSync, an extension to DeNovo that supports programs with arbitrary synchronization without sacrificing DeNovo's benefits.

The primary insight behind DeNovo's efficiency is that for data-race-free programs with restricted synchronization, it is possible to determine statically (for deterministic programs) or dynamically (for disciplined non-deterministic programs) which memory locations are protected by the allowed forms of synchronization. DeNovo uses software-initiated self-invalidation instructions at the reader's cache to invalidate stale cached data in lieu of writer-initiated invalidations in traditional coherence protocols (e.g., MESI). This enables DeNovo to eliminate the overhead of sharers lists in directories, useless invalidation and ack messages, and protocol complexities due to myriad transient states caused from protocol races.

* This work was supported in part by Intel Corp. through the Illinois/Intel Parallelism Center at Illinois, by the National Science Foundation under grants CCF-1018796 and CCF-1302641, and by the Center for Future Architectures Research (C-FAR), one of six centers of STARnet, a Semiconductor Research Corporation program sponsored by MARCO and DARPA.

ASPLOS '15, March 14–18, 2015, Istanbul, Turkey.

http://dx.doi.org/10.1145/2694344.2694356

The challenge with synchronization accesses is that they are *inherently "racy"* and depend on writer-initiated invalidation for a reader to see a new value. DeNovo's use of reader-initiated self-invalidations worked well for race-free data, where appropriate self-invalidations (to known writeable regions) at synchronization points ensured that a data read would see any newly written value (which would be written before the synchronization). Racy synchronization accesses, however, do not have any a priori knowledge of when a value may be updated. DeNovoND solved this problem for well-structured locks by building special hardware for such locks [35]; however, it is unclear how such a custom approach could be used for arbitrary synchronization. To our knowledge, no previous systems without writer-initiated invalidations allow caching of synchronization variables for arbitrary synchronization constructs We could revert back to writer-initiated self-invalidations with directories for sharers lists only for synchronization variables, but this would eliminate the simplicity advantage of DeNovo.

This paper proposes DeNovoSync, a simple and efficient mechanism to support racy synchronization accesses on DeNovo, without impacting any of DeNovo's advantages. Specifically, we do not require adding any new states to the protocol and retain the properties of no writer-initiated invalidations and no sharers lists.

Our implementation is derived from a careful study of various common synchronization patterns and non-blocking data structures. We use sequential consistency as the correctness semantics for synchronization. From the conditions required for such semantics and the behavior of synchronization, we propose a single-reader constraint for such accesses, requiring synchronization reads to the same location to be serialized by registering for ownership. DeNovo already provides a single writer constraint requiring write serialization. Adding read serialization ensures that synchronization reads always get up-to-date values without writer-initiated invalidations. This already provides reasonable performance, but in some cases, incurs excessive read traffic under high read-sharing contention. Inspired by software backoff based algorithms, we judiciously integrate a hardware-backoff to reduce contention. We call the resulting protocols DeNovoSync0 (no backoff) and DeNovoSync.

Although our focus is on synchronization, we must provide a way to ensure data consistency as well. If there is no further information available from the program, we can simply self-invalidate all cached data (or shared writeable data) at a synchronization acquire, similar to the method used in [32]. With more information, we can perform selective self-invalidations as in DeNovo (using purely software information) or DeNovoND (using hardware signatures). Since our focus is on synchronization, we assume that we have software information similar to DeNovo to determine which data to self-invalidate at a synchronization acquire.

We compare DeNovoSync0 and DeNovoSync with a state-of-the-art MESI implementation for 24 synchronization kernels on 16 and 64 cores and for 13 applications on 64 cores (2 on 16 cores). For the kernels, for all but four out of the 48 cases studied, DeNovoSync shows comparable or lower execution time (22% lower on average) and lower network traffic (58% lower on average), which can be translated into energy savings. For larger applications where data accesses prevail, for all but one application, DeNovoSync provides comparable execution time (4% lower on average) and lower traffic (24% lower on average).

To our knowledge, this is the first work to show an efficient implementation of such a variety of synchronization patterns for a coherence protocol that does not rely on writer-initiated invalidations. The paper takes a large step in broadening the software that can enjoy the advantages of DeNovo and presenting DeNovo hardware as a complete and comprehensive software-aware hardware coherence solution.

2. Background

This section describes how disciplined programming languages drove the design of the previous DeNovo systems [10, 35]. We focus on the original DeNovo system for deterministic programs [10] since it covers most of the relevant concepts. We emphasize that DeNovoSync does not impose the software constraints in this section.

2.1 Software Assumptions for Original DeNovo [10]

Most disciplined programming models use some form of metadata about program structures and memory access patterns to prove certain desirable properties of programs. DeNovo used information in the Deterministic Parallel Java (DPJ) language [7, 8], as an example driver of the approach. (DeNovoSync does not assume DPJ.)

DPJ is an extension to Java that enforces deterministic-by-default semantics via compile-time type checking. DPJ provides (1) structured parallel constructs of *foreach* and *cobegin* supporting nested fork-join parallelism, and (2) a type and effect system for programmers to safely express common access patterns in object-oriented programs. Programmers assign a "region" to memory locations and annotate a method with "effects" summarizing the regions read and written by the method. The compiler uses this information to (1) type-check operations in the region type system and (2) ensure that no two parallel tasks conflict. With the above constraints, DPJ provides strong safety guarantees such as data-race-freedom and determinism.

2.2 Previous DeNovo Systems

DeNovo [10] divided the coherence problem for "data accesses" into two parts:

(1) *No stale data:* A read should never see stale data in its private cache(s).

(2) *Locatable up-to-date data:* When a read misses in its private cache(s), it should know where to get an up-to-date copy.

For (1), DeNovo uses DPJ-provided information on regions that could be potentially written in a parallel phase (each DPJ parallel construct forms a phase, with an implicit barrier at the join). DeNovo issues compiler-inserted self-invalidations for all writeable regions in the previous phase at phase boundaries, so that reads in subsequent phases cannot see stale data. (This requires the cache to store region information as described in [10].)

For (2), DeNovo uses a structure called the *registry* to keep track of one up-to-date copy of each cache line. This is analogous to a conventional directory, but unlike the latter, it does not track all sharers of a cache line (eliminating a source of unscalability). With systems with a shared last-level cache (LLC), the data bank of the cache doubles as the registry, storing either the data or a pointer to it (the core ID that last registered to write the data).

Thus, the DeNovo protocol has three states – *Registered, Valid*, and *Invalid*. These are analogous to the M, S, and I states in an MSI protocol. The key difference is that a real MSI implementation has numerous additional transient states to deal with races while DeNovo implementations have exactly three states (because there are no data races).

The key aspects of the protocol's operation are as follows (assuming a two level cache hierarchy without loss of generality) [10]. A read hits in the L1 if the line is *Valid* or *Registered*. A read miss request goes to the registry (the shared L2) and either finds the data there or a pointer to the L1 that contains the data in *Registered* state. In the latter case, the request is routed to the registered data for service. A write to data in *Registered* state at the L1 updates the data. A write to data in *Valid* or *Invalid* state at the L1 immediately transitions the data to *Registered* and updates it (no transient states) and generates a registration request. If the data is not registered elsewhere, the L2 immediately registers it and sends an acknowledgment. Otherwise, the L2 records the new registration and forwards the request to the previously registered core to relinquish its registration.

DeNovoND [35, 36] extended DeNovo to support disciplined non-deterministic data accesses using (i) dynamic access signatures to determine what data to self-invalidate at a synchronization point and (ii) a queue-based hardware implementation for locks. In this paper, we seek simple implementations for arbitrary synchronization patterns and leverage the original DeNovo style static self-invalidations for data consistency.

DeNovo [10] provides the following advantages: (1) There are no transient states and so it is much easier to verify and extend (incorporating optimizations did not introduce any protocol state changes) than MESI [10, 21]. (2) DeNovo does not rely on writer-initiated invalidations; it therefore eliminates invalidation message traffic and does not require storage overhead for sharer lists in directories, removing a key source of unscalability. (3) DeNovo keeps coherence state at the granularity at which data is shared and so does not suffer from false sharing (the added state overhead is much less than the reduced directory state). Overall, compared to MESI, DeNovo is much simpler, performs comparably or better than MESI, and is more energy-efficient (since it reduces cache misses and network traffic). However, so far its efficacy has only been demonstrated for deterministic codes and codes with disciplined lock-based non-determinism.

3. Software Assumptions for DeNovoSync

As we extend DeNovo to support broader classes of applications, we relax our assumptions about disciplined software. We assume the following software properties, which are already enforced by most modern programming languages: (1) Software obeys the standard data-race-free memory model adopted by C++, Java, and other languages [9, 26] that define sequentially consistent semantics for data-race-free programs. (2) Software distinguishes between synchronization and data accesses (also part of the requirement of data-race-free). Mainstream languages all require this; e.g., programmers are required to use volatile (Java) or atomic (C++) declarations for synchronization variables [9, 26]. We assume this distinction is conveyed to the hardware as well.

DeNovoSync can run any applications that obey the above requirements. However, data consistency performance is improved with more information. Without further information, DeNovoSync will work correctly by invalidating all (shared, writable) data that is not registered in a core's cache at an acquire synchronization. However, with more information at acquires, these invalidations can be selective, possibly yielding better performance. This information may be in the form of compiler-specified shared writeable regions that are synchronized by the acquire (as in DeNovo [10]) or it may be generated dynamically through hardware signatures (as in DeNovoND [35]). In this paper, we assume the program provides static regions that need to be invalidated at an acquire. Although determining this information may be difficult in the general case,[1] for the programs we examined, it was generally easy to identify because most of them were written in a disciplined manner using high-level parallel constructs that made clear which data was being protected by which synchronization. We leave the question of how to (semi-)automatically (statically or dynamically) deduce such information in the general case to future work.

4. Protocols for Synchronization Accesses

Our focus here is on correctly implementing synchronization accesses; i.e., accesses involved in a race [1]. We assume the correctness criteria for synchronization is sequential consistency, the strongest hardware-level guarantee possible. Translating this to high-level safety properties when such synchronization constructs are used in the context of otherwise disciplined code is outside the scope of this work. Without loss of generality, we assume below that there is a two level cache hierarchy with private L1 caches and a shared L2 cache.

[1] To determine which region needs to be invalidated at an acquire more formally, we use the standard happens-before definition [1]. If X is the last conflicting write ordered before a read Y by happens-before, then either (1) X must be program ordered before Y, or (2) there must be an acquire A program ordered before Y such that X happens-before A and there is a self-invalidation for the region of X (which is the same as the region of Y) between A and Y. This ensures that Y never sees a "stale" value. (Note that a self-invalidation only affects non-registered data in the cache; registered data stays in the cache across synchronization boundaries.)

4.1 The DeNovoSync0 Protocol

The following conditions are sufficient for sequential consistency of synchronization accesses [1]:

- *Write propagation:* A write is eventually visible to all cores.
- *Write atomicity:* A write is not made visible to a read until it is visible to all cores.
- *Write serialization:* Writes to the same synchronization location are serialized (i.e., seen by all cores in the same order).
- *Program order:* A synchronization access must not be issued until the previous (by program order) synchronization access completes (i.e., a write is visible to all cores and a read returns its value).

We next describe how we modify the DeNovo protocol [10] to satisfy the above conditions.

Write propagation: Since we do not have writer-initiated invalidations, a synchronization read to a word in valid state will never see a new write. To ensure the write propagation condition, we need to perform periodic self-invalidation for such reads so that they miss and go to the last level cache and see the values of any newly registered writes. DeNovoSync0 always performs such a self-invalidation for synchronization reads to valid state; i.e., unless the word is in registered state, a synchronization read always incurs a miss.

Write atomicity: For write atomicity, DeNovoSync0 simply uses a single-reader protocol for synchronization (at the word granularity, which is the coherence granularity for DeNovo). Thus, a synchronization read is always required to register itself at the LLC and only one read can be registered at a time. Read registration produces read-read "races" in the protocol, which we discuss further below. Since all synchronization reads seek registration, once a synchronization write is visible to a synchronization read, no later read can see an older value. This ensures write atomicity.

Write serialization: DeNovo already provides write serialization by requiring writes to be registered and allowing only a single registered write to a given location. However, with synchronization, we can have write-write races, which the baseline DeNovo protocol did not have to handle. This is discussed below.

Program order: The program order requirement is easily met by not issuing a synchronization access until the previous synchronization access (by program order) is complete (i.e., registered).

Handling races: The baseline DeNovo protocol is built on the assumption of race-freedom; i.e., there are no concurrent conflicting accesses to the same location at any time. Specifically, when a registration request reaches the LLC in registered state, the LLC immediately updates the current registrant in its registry and forwards the new request to the previous registrant – the previous registrant invalidates itself and sends an ack to the new registrant without any need to inform the directory. In contrast, many MESI protocols (including the one we study) implement a blocking transaction

```
void queue.enqueue(value v):
  node *pw := new node(v, null)
  ptr pt, pn
  loop
(1)   pt := tail
(2)   pn := pt->next
(3)   if pt == tail
(4)     if pn == null
(5)       if (CAS(&pt->next, pn, pw))
            break;
(6)     else CAS(&tail, pt, pn)
(7)CAS(&tail, pt, pw)
```

(a) enqueue().

```
value queue.dequeue():
  ptr ph, pt, pn
  loop
  ph := head
  pt := tail
  pn := ph->next
  if ph == head
    if ph.p == pt.p
      if pn.p == null return <failure>
      CAS(&tail, pt, pn)
    else
      rtn := pn->val
      if CAS(&head, ph, pn) break
  free for reuse(ph)
  return rtn
```

(b) dequeue().

Figure 1: Pseudo code for Michael-Scott Queue.

where the directory serves as the intermediary for transferring the ownership from the previous to the new owner – until the full transaction is completed (with all invalidation acks collected), the directory does not service any new requests to that line to avoid even more complex transient states.

We continue to maintain a non-blocking registry; i.e., the registry (LLC) forwards a new registration request to the previous registrant and continues to service other requests to the same word (including forwarding new registrations). This can result in an L1 cache receiving a forwarded registration request before it receives an ack for its own registration request by a remote L1. This is indicated by the word being in invalid state – the forwarded registration is simply stored in the MSHR entry of the pending registration. When the pending registration's ack arrives, the cache services the stored request in its MSHR, forwarding the registration ack (or data for a read) to the requesting core (keeping itself invalid). Thus, instead of serializing registrations at the LLC, we build a queue distributed among the L1 caches with pending registrations (similar to [12, 13, 34]). [2]

Summary and Example: In summary, the DeNovoSync0 protocol effectively treats a synchronization read like a read-modify-write (RMW), requiring registration. It does not add any new states to the protocol and requires only a few small changes to the actions on state transitions to accommodate registration request races.

To illustrate the working of the protocol, we apply it to an example. Figure 1 (adapted from [33]) shows pseudo-code for the enqueue and dequeue functions for the Michael-Scott queue [28]. Figure 2 shows two concurrent threads executing the enqueue function with MESI (part (a)), DeNovoSync0 (part (b)), and DeNovoSync (part (c), to be discussed later) protocols. We focus on the two synchronization variables, `tail` and `tail->next` here. All solid arrows represent legitimate invalidation of stale copy or ownership transfer by R-W and W-W races respectively on MESI and DeNovo, while dashed arrows indicate invalidation caused by read registration on false races (R-R and W-R races) for DeNovo. Rippled lines connect a read hit and a read/write that brought in the value. Rounded and rectangular boxes indi-

[2] We did not implement a non-blocking directory for MESI because of the much higher complexity. Exploring its potential impact on performance is part of future work.

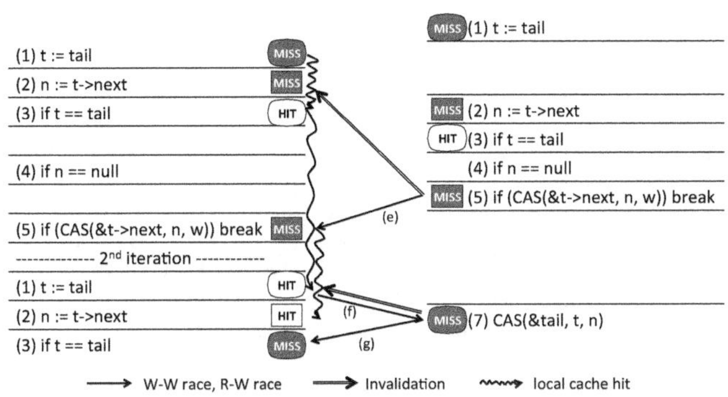

(a) MESI.

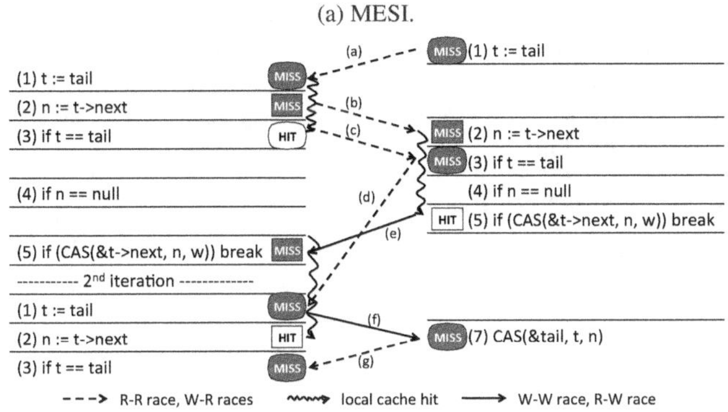

(b) DeNovoSync0.

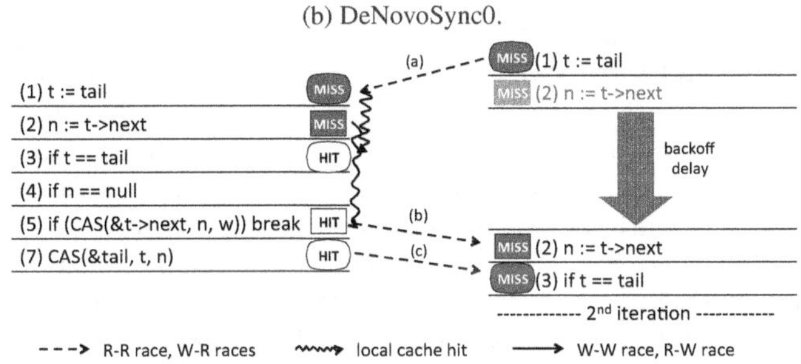

(c) DeNovoSync.

Figure 2: Example interleavings for enqueue() of Michael-Scott queue on MESI, DeNovoSync0, and DeNovoSync.

cate whether memory accesses to `tail` and `tail->next` in each line respectively result in a cache hit or miss.

Figures 2a and 2b show the following key differences between MESI and DeNovoSync0:

- False R-R and W-R races (edges (a), (b), (c), (d), and (g) in Figure 2b) trigger registration transfer and unnecessary invalidation of unchanged values for DeNovoSync0, while MESI does not incur any inter-thread communication for read accesses once valid copies are cached. These conservative invalidations on DeNovoSync0 cause the additional read misses in line 1 of the second iteration on thread 1 and line 3 on thread 2 relative to MESI.
- Rippled lines in Figure 2b show synchronization read/write hits enabled by earlier writes and read registrations by DeNovoSync0. Without an intervening read/write, thread 1 can safely re-read a valid copy of `tail` in line (3) and (2) of the second iteration in Registered state (similar to MESI). In addition, on thread 2, the rippled line from line (2) to (5) enables a write hit for DeNovoSync0 as `tail->next` is brought in Registered state in line (2). MESI, on the other hand, incurs a write miss on line (5).

Overall, compared to MESI, DeNovoSync0's read registrations suffer from two extra read misses but save a future write miss. Section 6 qualitatively analyzes the net impact.

4.2 The DeNovoSync Protocol

DeNovoSync0 is a reasonable solution for certain scenarios; e.g., with a single producer and consumer. However, in many scenarios, requiring all synchronization reads to register results in unnecessary misses. Specifically, with multiple waiting consumers, the synchronization data will ping-pong between the readers unnecessarily even while there is no intervening write.

The DeNovoSync protocol continues to require registration on synchronization reads, but attempts to delay such registration requests (in hardware) based on the perceived contention in the system. It is inspired by the idea of software backoff in conventional synchronization mechanisms [2]. Hardware backoff shares with software backoff the main goal of reducing contention in the system by delaying synchronization attempts. However, hardware backoff implements more fine-grained contention control than software backoff. Efficient, finer-granularity backoff is critical for many scenarios. For example, for non-blocking synchronization (e.g., the Michael-Scott queue described earlier), there are often several synchronization reads in succession and it is not reasonable to insert a software backoff before each of them. We therefore enhance the use and scope of conventional software backoff with a hardware backoff mechanism that adaptively delays synchronization reads to a location in non-registered state as follows.

4.2.1 Backoff Counter

DeNovoSync uses one hardware backoff counter per core to delay the core's synchronization read misses (i.e., reads to non-registered state). The size of the counter determines the maximum backoff cycles and should be determined by the system configuration; e.g., the number of cores, average miss latency, and network characteristics. The backoff counter logic performs the following operations.

Update counter: The backoff cycles value stored in the counter should adapt to the contention in the system. Our design uses *remote synchronization read requests* coming into a core as a symptom of system contention. On receiving a remote synchronization read request, a core downgrades from Registered to Valid state, sends a response to the remote requester, and increments the backoff counter. The increment is determined by a separate counter described in Section 4.2.2. The next time the core issues a synchronization read request to a value in Valid state, it stalls for the number of cycles indicated in the updated counter, delaying the issue of the synchronization read miss request. A synchronization variable in Valid state is not considered a usable valid copy. We simply reuse the state to differentiate from initial reads to Invalid state and trigger backoff delay. A synchronization read request to a value in Registered state will be a read hit and will not trigger backoff. When the counter overflows, it wraps around to zero.

Reset counter: The backoff counter is reset on a synchronization read to registered state (i.e., a read or RMW hit). Such a hit means that no other core intervened between the core's last access and the current access to the accessed location. We translate this as a low-contention status and do not delay subsequent requests.

Wakeup from backoff: When the backoff delay expires, it unstalls the core and issues the delayed synchronization read request. Since backoff delay is triggered only when the accessed location is in non-registered state, the core ignores any cached copy and issues a miss.

4.2.2 Increment Counter

The backoff counter efficiently adapts to changing contention levels in the system by increasing its value on a remote synchronization read registration request. However, a fixed increment value may not be flexible enough to handle both extremely low and extremely high contention. If the increment is fixed too low, the backoff counter may not climb fast enough to reduce unnecessary read registration requests under high contention. On the other hand, the increment of a large value may cause unnecessarily long stalls under low contention. Therefore, we introduce another level of adaptivity for the increment counter.

Update Increment: Again, we use the number of incoming remote synchronization read registration requests to indicate the contention level and update the increment counter accordingly. The size of the increment and the frequency of update should be determined by considering the system configuration. We found that the number of cores is a good indicator. For example, the increment counter is increased by the default increment value on receiving every 16th remote synchronization read registration request for the 16-core system evaluated in the paper (64th request for the 64-core system). The updated increment counter is then used to increase the backoff counter for the next remote read registration request.

Reset Increment: The increment counter is reset to a default value on a release. A release indicates the successful completion of a synchronization construct and the reset prepares the core to adapt for the next synchronization.

4.2.3 Example

Figure 2c shows how the Michael-Scott enqueue() function results in a different number of misses for the DeNovoSync0 and DeNovoSync systems. On the R-R race (a), the Registered copy of `tail` at thread 2 is downgraded to Valid state and the backoff counter is updated. When the thread tries to read `tail->next` in line (2), it recognizes the backoff counter is non-zero and starts the delay (assuming `tail->next` is in Valid state).

While the read of `tail->next` is being delayed on thread 2, thread 1 can proceed with its read and write of `tail` and `tail->next`. As a result, thread 1 can escape the loop in one iteration. Depending on when thread 2 wakes up, it may or may not fail the test in line (3). Compared to DeNovoSync0 in Figure 2b, DeNovoSync can save three misses in thread 1 – line (5) in the first iteration and (1) and (3) in the second iteration, allowing thread 1 to finish early. As will be seen in Section 7, DeNovoSync quickly adapts to different levels of contention in the system. Especially under high contention, contending cores can save on numerous read and write misses that are doomed to fail and repeat.

# of cores	16 cores	64 cores
Core frequency	2 GHz	
L1 data cache (private)	32KB, 64 bytes line	
L2 (shared, NUCA)	4MB, 16 banks	8 MB, 64 banks
	64 bytes line	
Memory	4GB, 4 on-chip controllers	
L1 hit latency	1 cycle	
L2 hit latency	28 to 68 cycles	28 to 140 cycles
Remote L1 hit latency	37 to 97 cycles	37 to 205 cycles
Memory hit latency	197 to 277 cycles	197 to 421 cycles
Network parameters	2D mesh, 16 bit flits	

Table 1: Simulated system parameters.

4.2.4 Protocol States

We still have only three protocol states for DeNovoSync/0 (meaning "both DeNovoSync0 and DeNovoSync" from now on): *Invalid, Valid* and *Registered*. When the word is Invalid or not present in the private cache, both reads and writes request registration and bring the address in Registered state. When the word is Registered, both reads and writes hit in the cache. While DeNovoSync0 makes the same transitions for Invalid and Valid state for all synchronization requests, DeNovoSync uses Valid state to trigger backoff on a synchronization read request. To this end, DeNovoSync distinguishes synchronization read and synchronization write requests and handles them differently in the protocol – synchronization write requests will be immediately issued in Invalid/Valid states while synchronization read requests may be delayed based on the backoff counter value.

5. Evaluation Methodology

5.1 Simulation Environment

For our evaluation, we use the Wind River Simics [25] full-system functional simulator to drive the Wisconsin GEMS detailed memory timing simulator [27] that we modified to implement our protocols. We also use the Princeton Garnet [3] interconnection network simulator to model network communication. To keep simulation times reasonable, as is common practice, we employ a simple, single-issue, in-order core model with blocking loads and 1 CPI for all non-memory instructions. We assume 1 CPI for all instructions executed inside the OS. We model 16 and 64 core systems. Table 1 shows the key parameters of our simulated systems.

5.2 Simulated Systems

We evaluated the following systems:

- **MESI:** We used the GEMS implementation of the MESI protocol [27], modified to support non-blocking writes for a fair comparison with DeNovo (where writes are non-blocking by default).
- **DeNovoSync0:** DeNovoSync0 implements the protocol as described in Section 4.1.

- **DeNovoSync:** DeNovoSync enhances DeNovoSync0 with the hardware backoff mechanism from Section 4.2, using the following parameters: 9-bit backoff counter with 1-cycle default increment for 16 cores and 12-bit backoff counter with 64-cycle default increment for 64 cores.

5.3 Workloads

We study several synchronization kernels as well as applications from standard benchmark suites. The kernels allow analyzing the new protocols in detail and showing that they can efficiently support a large variety of synchronization patterns. The applications are dominated by data accesses, but show that DeNovo can fully support common workloads.

5.3.1 Synchronization Kernels

We evaluated 24 synchronization kernels covering several lock-based concurrent data structures, non-blocking data structures, and barriers.

For lock-based structures, we adapted 5 kernels from [29]: single-lock queue, double-lock queue, stack, heap, and counter. The original kernels in [29] used Test-and-Test-and-Set (TATAS) locks. We also evaluated them using the more efficient array/list based queuing locks [4]. The critical sections of most of the above kernels have a small number of data accesses for one or two shared variables (e.g., pointers to queue head/tail or stack top) which allows us to isolate protocol behaviors for synchronization accesses. To cover a larger space, we also wrote a small kernel, *large CS*, with larger critical sections of fixed length, again both with TATAS and array locks. We did not use software backoff for any of the above kernels because our preliminary experiments with TATAS based kernels showed increased benefit of DeNovo over MESI for software backoff (further discussed in Section 7.1.1).

For non-blocking data structures, we adapted 6 kernels from [29]: Michael-Scott queue, PLJ queue, Treiber stack, Herlihy stack, Herlihy heap, and FAI counter. Each kernel has a software exponential delay in the range of [128, 2048) cycles to backoff after a failed attempt.

For barriers, we evaluated a static binary tree barrier, a static tree barrier with non-binary fan-in of 4 and fan-out of 2, and a centralized sense-reversing barrier derived from pseudo codes in [33]. To examine how the variance in the amount of parallel work between barriers can affect barrier performance, we evaluated a load-balanced and an unbalanced version for each barrier.

As mentioned, we insert region-based static self-invalidation instructions for data consistency. We ran 100 iterations of each kernel (1,000 for *FAI counter* due to its very small size) with dummy computations in between to spread out iterations. In each iteration, a queue, stack, or a heap kernel executes one insertion and one retrieval (or deletion) function call for one entry to/from the shared data structure, a counter kernel performs a single increment, and a barrier kernel executes two barrier instances around dummy computation. The length of the dummy computations is randomly chosen in the range of [1400, 1800) cycles for 16 cores and [6200, 6600) cycles for 64 cores, except that the unbalanced versions of barriers use [400, 2800) cycles for 16 cores and [1600, 11,200) cycles for 64 cores.

SPLASH-2	Input	PARSEC	Input
FFT	m16	fluidanimate	sim_small
LU	n256	blackscholes	sim_medium
barnes	8192	swaptions	sim_small
radix	524288	canneal	sim_small
water	512	ferret	sim_small
ocean	258	x264	sim_medium
		bodytrack	sim_medium

Table 2: Benchmark inputs.

5.3.2 Benchmarks

We evaluated 13 benchmarks from SPLASH-2 [37] and PARSEC 3.1 benchmark suites [6]. Table 2 shows the benchmarks and their input parameters. The benchmarks are chosen to represent programs with different synchronization patterns including locks, barriers, producer-consumer synchronization (pipeline parallelism), and aggressive lock-free synchronization. We show results with 64 cores for all except two benchmarks. Results for *ferret* and *x264* are for 16 cores because the simulation inputs provided do not fully utilize 64 cores concurrently. In all cases, we inserted region-based static self-invalidation instructions, both in the application code and in the POSIX thread library synchronization routines that were used.

6. Qualitative Analysis

This section qualitatively analyzes the performance of the different synchronization mechanisms on MESI and DeNovoSync/0, using the notion of *linearization points* [14]. Commonly used synchronization objects are *linearizable*; i.e., the operations on the object appear to occur in some total order that is consistent with the program order in each thread and also with any ordering observable by threads [33]. With linearizable synchronization objects, we can typically identify a linearization point within each method whose ordering determines the ordering of the method itself. To repeat on a synchronization failure, the linearization point for acquire synchronization is usually enclosed in a loop. This loop often includes synchronization accesses that are not linearization points; i.e., accesses that do not determine if an attempt is successful. For example, the first Test part of Test-and-Test-and-Set (TATAS) or equality checks before the final CAS instruction in non-blocking algorithms do access the shared synchronization object in the same loop, but their purpose is only to filter unsuccessful attempts early before reaching the linearization point.

To systematically understand protocol overheads for each synchronization mechanism, we divide the overheads into two parts: (1) *Linearization cost* is the cost to execute the instruction at the linearization point, including all coherence activities involved. (2) *Pre-linearization cost* is the cost of executing all the other synchronization accesses in the synchronization loop. Note that the coherence overhead for data accesses protected by these synchronizations may vary between the protocols, further affecting synchronization cost;

e.g., by changing contention. Further, DeNovo may inherently see lower traffic because it has word-based coherence state and does not transfer locations in a cache line known to be invalid. Since these overheads are orthogonal to the synchronization focus of this paper, we do not discuss them here, but they do affect our results in Section 7.

6.1 Locks

Atomicity synchronization ensures that a sequence of instructions executes as a single, indivisible unit [33], and its most common form is a lock. Here we explore the commonly used single variable based Test-and-Test-and-Set (TATAS) lock as well as the distributed array (or list) lock.

6.1.1 TATAS Locks

For individual TATAS lock acquire and release, we identify their linearization points at a successful Test-and-Set instruction for acquire, and the release write of a lock for release.
Linearization cost: When there are no or only two competing cores, the linearization cost for MESI and DeNovo is simply a two-hop or three-hop write miss acquiring the Modified (Registered) state from the shared LLC or the other core's cache respectively. As the number of contending cores increases, MESI is expected to have increasingly high linearization cost, since invalidating all cached copies increases the release write latency for the lock. While the release write may be overlapped with subsequent instructions at the releasing core, its latency is on the critical path of the next acquirer; the release write will be made visible to the next acquirer only after invalidations are complete for all cores (to ensure the write atomicity requirement for sequential consistency). In terms of network traffic, MESI incurs increasingly high network traffic for invalidation and acknowledgment messages. On the other hand, DeNovoSync/0 has no invalidation message overheads and only needs point-to-point registration transfer. Thus, DeNovo's linearization cost is expected to be independent of the number of competing cores and generally lower than MESI's.
Pre-linearization cost: Pre-linearization cost occurs only for acquires and consists of reads that perform preliminary checks to determine if it is worth proceeding to the linearization point. For MESI, waiting cores efficiently spin on a cached copy, incurring read misses only after the lock is released. For DeNovo, every synchronization read incurs a miss, unless the lock is Registered. Since registration can be revoked by remote synchronization reads, read misses by such false R-R races can be a source of performance inefficiencies for DeNovo. However, unless critical sections are very long, the percentage of false races relative to the total registration transfers will not be high since writes (CAS acquire and write release) by a winning core will frequently intervene between pre-linearization reads (which will trigger legitimate registration transfer). If critical sections are long and there are multiple waiting cores, DeNovoSync0 will suffer excessive ping-ponging of registrations between these cores, but DeNovoSync is expected to reduce this inefficiency through its hardware backoff.

Overall, for most cases, we expect that the linearization cost will dominate since it is on the critical path of the lock handoff; therefore, DeNovoSync/0 will perform better than MESI for execution time and network traffic. An exception is the case of long critical sections with multiple waiters, where DeNovoSync0's higher pre-linearization costs may or may not be offset by its lower linearization cost.

6.1.2 Array Locks

To reduce synchronization overheads for highly contended locks, array locks distribute synchronization points in space so that cores wait on different locations (array entries) in order. The linearization points are (1) a synchronization read in the acquire loop indicating the lock for the given entry is available, and (2) the release write of the next entry's lock.
Linearization cost: Array locks allocate a unique memory location for each acquiring core. Linearization involves setting of this location by the releaser and reading of the new value by the acquirer. For DeNovoSync/0, this is a simple 2 or 3 hop registration transfer for both the release and the acquire. For MESI, the critical path is similar (there are no excessive invalidations as for TATAS), but there are two subtle effects. First, the transactions are slightly more complex; e.g., the acquire involves a potential writeback to the directory and accompanying unblock messages for a blocking directory. Second, the successful acquire read is immediately followed by a write to reset the same lock so it can be reused in the next invocation. For DeNovoSync/0, this write is a hit since the lock is already registered by the acquire, but MESI needs to separately request ownership. This write latency for MESI can be on the critical path if the critical section is too small and the ensuing data accesses cannot overlap the latency. In that case, the write latency will be visible as an additional linearization cost for MESI. A read for ownership transaction in MESI would eliminate that cost, but our system does not implement such a transaction.
Pre-linearization cost: Pre-linearization includes spinning on the unique lock entry for each waiter. Since there is only one waiter per entry, both DeNovo and MESI spin on a cached copy, with minimal overhead.

Overall, for array locks, we expect comparable performance except for very small critical sections (where MESI may be worse) and higher traffic for MESI due to its more complex transactions and additional ownership request.

6.2 Non-Blocking Algorithms

It is common that non-blocking algorithms (1) linearize at their final CAS instruction, and (2) perform relatively many reads for equality checks to guarantee fast forward progress until the linearization point (e.g., Figure 1).
Linearization cost: Non-blocking algorithms provide atomicity of concurrent operations by linearizing cores that successfully execute the final CAS instruction. Similar to TATAS locks, MESI adds significant invalidation overheads for linearization cost with many competing cores, while DeNovo requires only a single point-to-point communication.
Pre-linearization cost: Non-blocking algorithms tend to have many repeated reads for equality checks on multiple

synchronization variables before the linearization point. In this case where synchronization read-to-write ratio is high, DeNovo with pessimistic reader-initiated self-invalidation is likely to suffer from spurious read misses from R-R and W-R registration transfer. While MESI can perform such reads without any cost unless there is a true race, we expect DeNovo to have high pre-linearization cost proportional to the number of synchronization read accesses.

Overall, under relatively low contention, DeNovoSync/0 may offset its high pre-linearization cost with its lower linearization cost compared to MESI. Under high contention, DeNovoSync0 will likely see the negative impact of pre-linearization cost while DeNovoSync can mitigate the impact with hardware backoff.

6.3 Barriers

For barriers, separate linearization and pre-linearization points can be defined for arrival and departure phases. Signaling arrival (e.g., incrementing the arrived core counter for centralized barriers or reversing and propagating parent's flag for tree barriers) and departure (e.g., reversing the sense(s) and propagating the updated sense to waiting cores) belongs to linearization, while pre-linearization includes unsuccessful checks (synchronization reads) of sense/flags (in a loop).

Linearization cost: For a centralized barrier, for arrival, both MESI and DeNovo incur high linearization cost by serializing cores incrementing the arrived core counter. MESI with blocking directory may suffer from extra queuing and messaging delays than DeNovo when the counter is severely contended. On departure, the release of a centralized barrier allows many readers to proceed. For MESI, this adds invalidation related overheads to linearization cost similar to TATAS locks. For DeNovo, we expect a potentially higher cost because all the waiting readers incur serialized registrations, adding to the critical path.

The linearization cost for both MESI and DeNovo is lowered with tree barriers since these reduce the number of threads synchronizing on a given location. Trees in tree barriers can be configured with different width and depth, depending on the number of child threads synchronized for the same parent thread. Regardless of the tree structure, there is only one reader and one writer for each node in the trees: an owner thread for a given tree node and its parent thread. For arrival, the owner thread updates its node (flag) and its parent thread reads it to see if the thread has arrived and vice versa for departure. Thus, the case of a distributed tree barrier is similar to that of an array lock, and we expect similar latency for both DeNovo and MESI.

Pre-linearization cost: Pre-linearization cost for barriers comes from synchronization reads by cores waiting for their flag to be reversed. Again, MESI efficiently spins from the local cache. DeNovoSync/0 pays similar costs for distributed tree barriers with only one reader per node. For scenarios with a large number of readers (i.e., centralized barrier), DeNovoSync0 sees a negative effect on network traffic through ping-ponging registrations, while DeNovoSync partly mitigates this effect through the hardware backoff.

Overall, MESI and DeNovo perform comparably for distributed tree barriers, behaving similar to array-based locks. DeNovo, however, can potentially suffer from higher pre-linearization and linearization costs with worse performance and traffic for centralized barriers. We note, however, that centralized barriers with many readers and one writer contending for a single variable is not a scalable synchronization pattern regardless of the coherence protocol. For best absolute performance, tree barriers with limited read sharing per synchronization variable are preferred. DeNovoSync is expected to be comparable to MESI in both execution time and traffic for such scalable barriers.

7. Results

We next validate our qualitative analysis by evaluating a variety of synchronization kernels (Section 7.1) and applications (Section 7.2).

7.1 Results for Synchronization Kernels

Figure 3, 4, 5, and 6 show results for synchronization kernels using TATAS locks, array locks, non-blocking algorithms, and barriers respectively. In each figure, parts (a) and (b) respectively show the execution time and network traffic for MESI (denoted M), DeNovoSync0 (denoted DS0), and DeNovoSync (denoted DS) protocols, all normalized to MESI, for a 16 core system. Parts (c) and (d) show the analogous data for a 64 core system. We measure time in cycles and network traffic in terms of flit crossings across all network links (i.e., a flit going over one network link constitutes one unit of network traffic).

Parts (a) and (c) in each figure divide the execution time into multiple components. The gray (non-synch) component is the computation time spent between iterations of the studied synchronization kernels. These non-synchronization cycles are not affected by our techniques, but changing their length may increase/decrease the contention level. The rest of the components all represent the time spent strictly within invocations of the synchronization kernels for computation and memory accesses to data and synchronization variables (as described in Section 5, most kernels are dominated by synchronization accesses). These components consist of compute time (1 cycle per instruction, not including software backoff cycles), memory stall time for both synchronization and data accesses inside the kernel, software backoff time, hardware backoff time (only for DeNovoSync), and barrier stall time. Barrier stall time measures the time spent in the barrier at the end of the kernels for non-barrier kernels, which can indicate possible load imbalance caused by contention in synchronization methods. Note that a large part of compute time is from spinning synchronization read accesses (cache hits), so it can vary across protocols.

Parts (b) and (d) in each figure divide the network traffic based on the message type. For MESI, we show load, store, writeback, and invalidation (including ack) messages. For

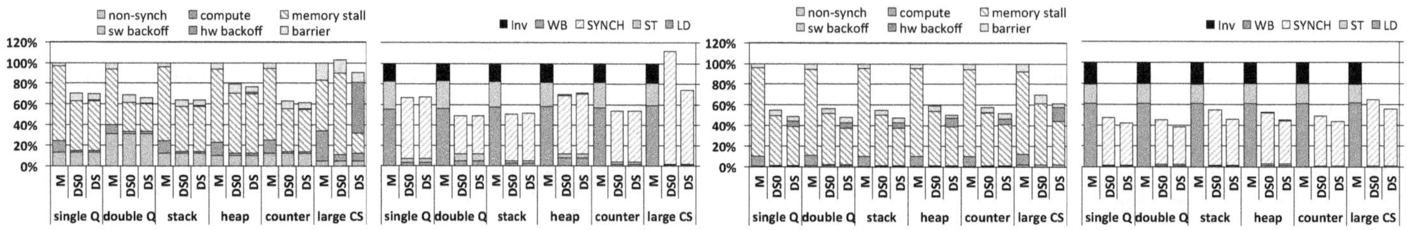

(a) Execution time (16 cores) (b) Network traffic (16 cores) (c) Execution time (64 cores) (d) Network traffic (64 cores)

Figure 3: Test-and-Test-and-Set (TATAS) locks based synchronization.

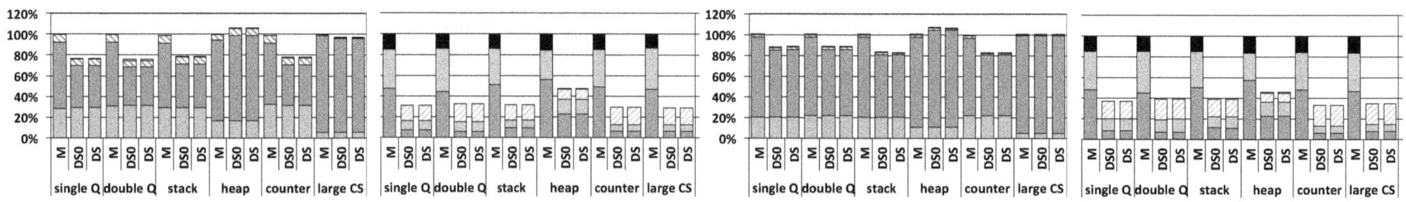

(a) Execution time (16 cores) (b) Network traffic (16 cores) (c) Execution time (64 cores) (d) Network traffic (64 cores)

Figure 4: Array locks based synchronization.

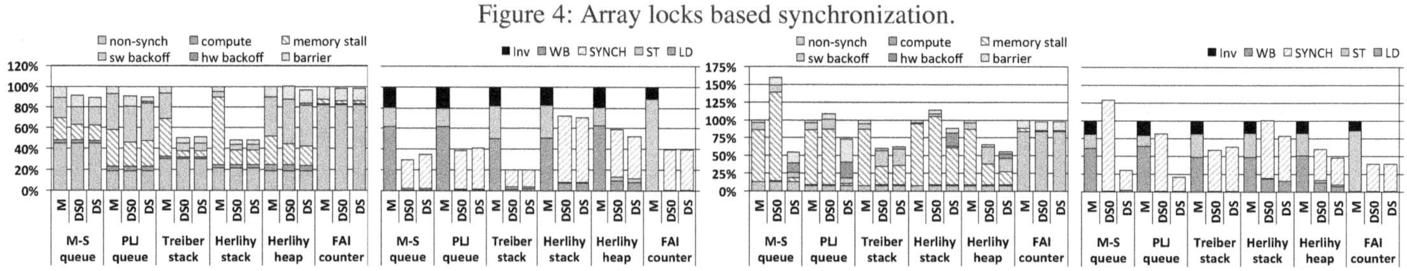

(a) Execution time (16 cores) (b) Network traffic (16 cores) (c) Execution time (64 cores) (d) Network traffic (64 cores)

Figure 5: Non-blocking algorithms.

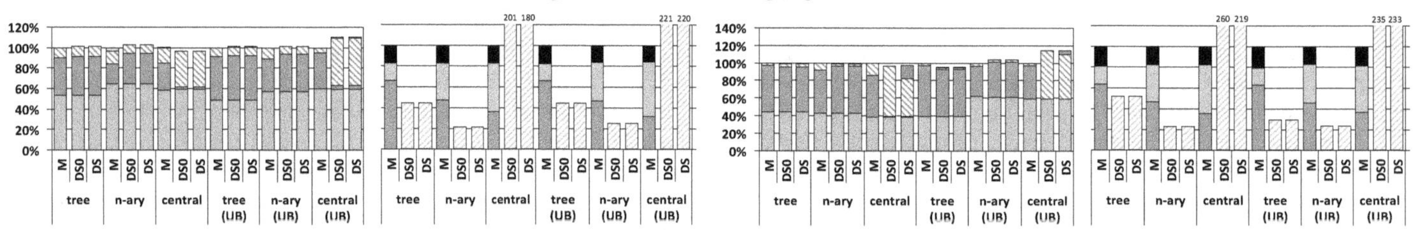

(a) Execution time (16 cores) (b) Network traffic (16 cores) (c) Execution time (64 cores) (d) Network traffic (64 cores)

Figure 6: Barrier synchronization (UB = unbalanced computations).

DeNovo, we show data load, data store, synchronization (load, store, and RMW), and writeback messages.[3]

7.1.1 Test-and-Test-and-Set (TATAS) Locks

Figure 3 shows that across all synchronization kernels using TATAS locks, DeNovoSync outperforms MESI in terms of execution time (31% on average) and network traffic (42% on average) for 16 and 64 cores.

MESI vs. DeNovoSync0: DeNovoSync0 outperforms MESI on both systems except for *large CS* on 16 cores. The benefit in execution time ranges from 20% to 36% (average 25%) on 16 cores and an even higher 40% to 45% (average 41%) on 64 cores. Based on the analysis in Section 6, this benefit occurs because MESI incurs higher linearization cost in the form of invalidation/ack latencies on the critical path from lock release to the next successful acquire. For these kernels, which have small critical sections, the linearization cost dominates pre-linearization cost as explained in Section 6. Further, this cost increases in larger systems when more cores need to be invalidated, explaining the higher benefit for 64 core systems. For the *large CS* kernel, on the other hand, higher pre-linearization cost from false registration transfers makes DeNovoSync0 perform slightly (3%) worse than MESI on 16 cores. On 64 cores, however, this effect is mitigated by MESI's higher linearization cost and DeNovoSync0 shows 29% reduction in execution time.

DeNovoSync0 reduces network traffic by 35% on average over MESI on 16 and 64 cores, except for *large CS* where it suffers from high read miss rates as discussed above. The main reasons for reduced traffic on DeNovo are: (1) lack of invalidation/ack traffic (which contributes about 20% of

[3] For MESI, our system does not explicitly identify loads and stores as synchronization or data. We use fences to enforce ordering at the acquire and release synchronization points. We therefore do not separate LD/ST traffic into data and synchronization for MESI. For DeNovo, on the other hand, such information was readily available and we report it here.

network traffic for MESI), and (2) per-word coherence granularity for DeNovo which allows sending only valid data. The latter significantly reduces response traffic for synchronization requests on DeNovo since most software pads lock variables to avoid false sharing.

DeNovoSync0 vs. DeNovoSync: DeNovoSync is comparable or better than DeNovoSync0 for all TATAS-based kernels on 16 and 64 cores (average 5% and 13% lower execution time and 14% and 16% lower network traffic). The benefit comes from delaying unnecessary synchronization read registrations, improving both network traffic and execution time through reduced contention.

Impact of lock padding: We ran all TATAS kernels without lock padding and found that most showed worse performance for MESI than the original versions due to false sharing. However, performance gaps between MESI and DeNovoSync/0 are also reduced by removing the padding because DeNovo has to issue more read/write requests separately for locks and data in the same cache line.

Impact of software backoff: We conducted a sensitivity study to see the impact of software backoff on TATAS-based kernels. We ran the kernels with exponential software backoff in the range of [128,2048) cycles. We found that the performance gap between DeNovoSync0 and MESI increased significantly (up to 70% on 64 cores), relative to kernels without software backoff. Similar to hardware backoff, software backoff also separates failed synchronization read accesses. As a result, it reduces read misses from false races for DeNovoSync/0. On the other hand, its does not affect invalidation latency for MESI, which is the largest source of memory stall time in these kernels.

7.1.2 Array Locks

Figure 4 shows that for array lock based kernels, DeNovoSync0 and DeNovoSync show similar performance and traffic. As analyzed in Section 6, the single-reader design of array locks does not generate spurious registrations and does not benefit from DeNovoSync's backoff.

Compared to MESI, DeNovoSync/0 provides comparable or (up to 24%) better performance except for *heap* and reduces network traffic by 64% on average. As discussed in Section 6, for the most part, synchronization related pre-linearization and linearization costs for MESI and DeNovo are largely similar except for subtle effects; e.g., DeNovo saves one write miss whose latency may or may not be overlapped in MESI, depending on the critical section length. Based on detailed analysis of our experiments, we find that the overall performance of array lock kernels is therefore sensitive to the nature of the critical section computation.

Four of the six kernels (all except *large CS* and *heap*) have very small critical sections; therefore, the additional write miss for MESI adversely impacts performance, giving DeNovo an advantage. *Large CS* has a large critical section, which removes this advantage, and both MESI and DeNovo see comparable performance. *Heap* also has a high number of data accesses, but their unpredictability makes DeNovo suffer from conservative region-based static self-invalidations as follows. *Heap* re-balances its tree as entries are inserted/deleted, requiring a data-dependent traversal of the tree nodes. Without a priori knowledge of which nodes have been previously updated, DeNovo conservatively self-invalidates all nodes, resulting in unnecessary data misses as well as increasing synchronization wait times for subsequent acquirers. DeNovo therefore performs 6% and 7% worse than MESI on 16 and 64 cores respectively. This can be remedied using dynamic hardware signatures to more precisely determine what data to invalidate as in [35], but is orthogonal to the synchronization focus of this work.

Finally, DeNovo's traffic savings are for the same reasons as for the TATAS locks and saved write misses.

7.1.3 Non-Blocking Algorithms

Figure 5 shows that the non-blocking data structures exhibit varying performance depending on their access patterns and system contention. On 16 cores, both DeNovoSync0 and DeNovoSync perform comparably or better than MESI (average of 14% better execution time and 60% better traffic). On 64 cores, DeNovoSync outperforms MESI (by an average of 28% for execution time and 54% for traffic). DeNovoSync0, however, often does worse than MESI on 64 cores; e.g., up to 60% worse execution time.

MESI vs. DeNovoSync0: As discussed in Section 6, DeNovoSync0 suffers from high pre-linearization cost caused by unnecessary registration transfers for many synchronization reads on multiple variables. On 16 cores, this cost is offset by MESI's higher linearization cost (due to invalidations). Thus, all kernels show comparable or better performance and network traffic for DeNovoSync0. With increased number of cores, threads experience more failed equality checks before reaching the linearization point, and DeNovoSync0 is likely to suffer from increased unnecessary read registrations and misses due to interference from remote synchronization reads. For 3 of the 6 non-blocking kernels, DeNovoSync0 therefore performs worse than MESI by 28% on average on 64 cores.

DeNovoSync0 vs. DeNovoSync: Under low contention and with software backoff delay, DeNovoSync's hardware backoff does not provide visible performance boost over DeNovoSync0 (2% better on average for 16 cores). On the other hand, as contention increases on 64 cores, DeNovoSync performs much better than DeNovoSync0 (by 30% and 41% on average for execution time and network traffic respectively). Figure 5 shows that the improved performance directly comes from replacing memory stall time with smaller hardware backoff cycles.

Software Modifications: We observed that many non-blocking algorithms are designed to perform well on systems with a writer-initiated invalidation protocol. Since a core can spin on a cached copy on such systems, most non-blocking algorithms have repeated equality checks comparing a shared variable's current value and a core's local snapshot. These checks help non-blocking algorithms make faster progress on a failed attempt. The same checks do more harm than good for reader-initiated invalidation protocols like DeNovo. If synchronization reads occur much more frequently than writes in a synchronization loop, read registration requests will end up ping-ponging registration between readers, forcing them to miss even if shared variables are not updated at all. Since many equality checks exist only for performance but not for correctness, removing/adding some checks is safe. In our experiments, we modified *Herlihy stack* and *Herlihy heap* from [29] to reduce the number of such checks (these kernels had the most equality checks among those we tested).

We saw that the modifications significantly shortened execution time for both MESI and DeNovo, but DeNovoSync saw much higher improvement than MESI, with 41% and 79% lower execution time on average on 16 and 64 cores compared to the unmodified version. Network traffic also reduced by up to 78% on 64 cores. Studying how implementation details of synchronization algorithms may affect their behaviors on different coherence protocols is an interesting future research direction.

7.1.4 Barriers

Figure 6 shows that DeNovo performs comparably or better than MESI for the barrier kernels studied on 16 and 64 cores except for centralized barrier with highly unbalanced computations (denoted UB) on 64 cores. For network traffic, the DeNovo protocols are better (67% on average) than MESI for the tree barriers, but much worse for the centralized barrier.

As discussed in Section 6, since the tree barriers exhibit a single producer and single consumer scenario for the linearization synchronization variable, all protocols behave similarly for execution time. DeNovoSync/0 sees much lower traffic for reasons similar to other kernels above.

For centralized barriers, MESI has higher linearization cost during arrival than DeNovo while DeNovo has higher linearization cost during departure, as discussed in Section 6. With load balanced computations, these effects offset each other and the execution times for all protocols are comparable. In case of higher load imbalance, however, DeNovo suffers from even more read registrations (and higher pre-linearization cost) than the load-balanced case, delaying the linearization point. As a result, DeNovoSync/0 performs worse than MESI by 9% and 14% on 16 and 64 cores respectively. The excessive registrations in the pre-linearization and linearization phases for DeNovo result in high traffic in both load-balanced and imbalanced cases.

Nevertheless, comparing absolute performance of centralized and tree barriers, we confirmed that tree barriers are better for both our 16 and 64 core systems. Our results thus show that as long as designed in a distributed and scalable fashion, DeNovo can provide reasonable performance even for barrier synchronization (and more generally, conditional synchronization) where the synchronization accesses are mostly reads.

7.2 Results for Applications

Figure 7 shows execution time and network traffic for 13 benchmarks (*ferret* and *x264* on 16 cores, others on 64 cores) on MESI (denoted M) and DeNovoSync (denoted DS), normalized to MESI. The components for each bar are as for the synchronization kernels except that there is no separation of non-synchronization time. We see that DeNovoSync provides comparable execution time to MESI (4% better on average) – it is noticeably better for *LU, water, ocean,* and *ferret* (up to 36% better), but 7% worse for *fluidanimate*. For network traffic, DeNovoSync is 24% better than MESI on average for all benchmarks. We next discuss the applications in more detail, classified by the synchronization patterns they include.

Barrier-only: FFT, LU, blackscholes, swaptions, and *radix* use only barrier synchronization (with tree barriers). For execution time, as expected, DeNovoSync is comparable to MESI. It provides a slight advantage for *LU* since *LU* exhibits data false sharing with MESI (which DeNovo avoids due to word-level coherence [10]). DeNovoSync significantly reduces network traffic because it does not incur invalidations, load responses do not contain invalid parts of the cache line, and stores involve only registration [10].

Barriers and locks: Bodytrack, barnes, water, ocean, and *fluidanimate* use both barriers and locks. Except for *fluidanimate*, DeNovoSync shows comparable or (up to 30%) better execution time than MESI for these applications. For *fluidanimate*, DeNovoSync is 7% worse because of the use of static self-invalidations for shared data protected by critical sections. Self-invalidating all data in writeable regions at every lock acquire results in unnecessary invalidation of valid data for this application. As discussed in the previous section for array-based lock heap in Section 7.1.2, we can reduce unnecessary read misses with more dynamic solutions. DeNovoSync shows substantial savings in network traffic for these applications as expected.

Non-blocking synchronization: canneal is a unique benchmark that synchronizes shared pointers in an aggressive lock-free loop with CAS instructions. Unlike other applications, synchronization forms a large fraction of the memory accesses in *canneal*. Again, DeNovoSync shows comparable execution time and reduced network traffic relative to MESI.

Pipeline parallelism: ferret and *x264* use pipeline parallelism, a parallel pattern that has not been previously evaluated for DeNovo. Again, relative to MESI, DeNovoSync shows comparable or better (by 5% for *ferret*) execution time, with an average network traffic reduction of 29%.

Overall, DeNovoSync efficiently supports a variety of applications, without restrictions on synchronization patterns.

8. Related Work

There has been a vast body of work on software-driven coherence protocols and various shared-memory optimizations that inspired the DeNovo system [16, 19, 20, 22, 24, 30, 31, 38]. This section focuses mainly on closely related work in efficiently supporting synchronization mechanisms.

Research in software distributed shared-memory (DSM) proposed several software techniques to provide an illusion of a consistent global address space for DSMs [5, 16, 18]. The work focused mainly on consistency for data accesses, and assumed explicit and customized software interfaces for a limited set of synchronization patterns. DeNovoSync

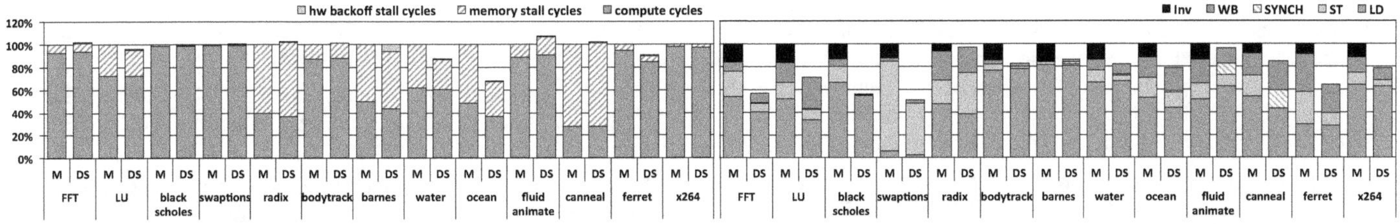

(a) Execution Time.

(b) Network Traffic.

Figure 7: Execution time and network traffic for MESI and DeNovoSync for applications.

aims to provide integrated hardware coherence solutions for synchronization and data accesses on tightly-coupled multicores, and supports arbitrary synchronization.

VIPS-M [32], a recent version of SARC [17], proposed a protocol somewhat similar to DeNovo. It uses private/shared information about data to perform self-invalidations and eliminates the directory by performing write-through at synchronization points. The work also implemented a write-through protocol for synchronization accesses, but claimed that delaying the completion of such a write-through helps reducing spinning by other cores, which is similar to delaying of QOLB attempts in [31]. However, VIPS-M is not clear about how it efficiently deals with synchronization algorithms with multiple synchronization variables and frequent reads to them such as with non-blocking algorithms considered here. If many variables cause delayed write-through, they may interfere with each others' progress causing degraded synchronization latency. DeNovoSync, on the other hand, supports arbitrary synchronization, including non-blocking algorithms, through a novel combination of synchronization read registration and hardware backoff.

Dir_1SW [15] proposes a simplified directory protocol that adds little complexity to message-passing hardware by using software traps, but efficiently supports programs written within the CICO model [23]. Dir_1SW supports synchronization accesses separately from data accesses with non-cacheable pages, since they do not fit with the CICO model, ruining performance. DeNovoSync allows both data and synchronization accesses to be cached locally and maintained by coherence protocols.

More recently, TSO-CC [11] proposed a self-invalidation based coherence protocol for the TSO memory model. It leverages relaxed write-to-read ordering in TSO to introduce lazy self-invalidations for reads and eliminate sharers and invalidation traffic for writes. However, without distinction between data and synchronization accesses, every read miss has to self-invalidate all shared cache lines in private caches to guarantee read-to-read ordering. To avoid cache-wide flushes, TSO-CC introduces many additional hardware mechanisms such as timestamps and epoch tables and complicated logic to maintain them.

Read-for-Ownership has been explored as an optimization for reducing write misses on synchronization accesses. [31] explores how Queue-On-a-Lock-Bit (QOLB), a hardware distributed lock mechanism, can be applied to individual synchronization accesses. While they propose a range of solutions with different trade-off, Read-for-Ownership was dismissed as it is expected to generate spurious read misses. We show that for many synchronization algorithms, a judicious use of RFO can be a simple yet effective solution.

It is worthwhile to note that many of the above and other related work assume that data and non-data (synchronization) accesses are distinguished and provide different solutions for these two classes. To our knowledge, no previous writer-invalidation-free system has supported arbitrary synchronization with cacheable synchronization variables. We expect that the ideas underlying DeNovoSync for synchronization can also be adapted to other writer-invalidation-free systems to improve the efficiency and generality of their supported synchronization mechanisms.

9. Conclusion

The DeNovo system has shown that hardware coherence for data accesses can be made much simpler and more efficient by leveraging software information and properties like data-race-freedom. However, adding support for races on a protocol driven by race-free software could potentially undermine all the benefits of the existing systems. This paper showed that leveraging access patterns of synchronization operations can help design a simple yet flexible mechanism that can support the coherence and consistency requirements of synchronization accesses. While the simple "single-reader" approach proposed for DeNovoSync0 may suffer from conservative invalidations and traffic under high contention, delaying these reads with a contention-dependent backoff as in DeNovoSync can improve performance significantly. We compared our new protocols with the state-of-the-art MESI on several synchronization constructs including those for challenging non-blocking data structures. We found our technique to be quite competitive and in many cases much better. For future work, we would like to integrate more dynamic signature-based coherence support for data accesses with DeNovoSync, reaching towards a comprehensive coherence solution. Studying protocol-aware synchronization design further and exploring the potential for applying DeNovoSync to other writer-invalidation free systems are also promising future work directions.

References

[1] S. V. Adve and K. Gharachorloo. Shared memory consistency models: A tutorial. *IEEE Computer*, 29(12):66–76, 1996.

[2] A. Agarwal and M. Cherian. Adaptive backoff synchronization techniques. In *Proceedings of the 16th Annual International Symposium on Computer Architecture*, ISCA '89, 1989.

[3] N. Agarwal, T. Krishna, L.-S. Peh, and N. Jha. Garnet: A detailed interconnection network model inside a full-system simulation framework. Technical Report CE-P08-001, Princeton University, 2008. URL http://www.princeton.edu/~niketa/garnet.

[4] T. E. Anderson. The performance of spin lock alternatives for shared-memory multiprocessors. *IEEE Trans. Parallel Distrib. Syst.*, 1(1), Jan. 1990.

[5] B. Bershad, M. Zekauskas, and W. Sawdon. The midway distributed shared memory system. In *Compcon Spring '93, Digest of Papers.*, Feb 1993.

[6] C. Bienia. *Benchmarking Modern Multiprocessors.* PhD thesis, Princeton University, Jan. 2011.

[7] R. L. Bocchino, Jr., V. S. Adve, D. Dig, S. V. Adve, S. Heumann, R. Komuravelli, J. Overbey, P. Simmons, H. Sung, and M. Vakilian. A type and effect system for deterministic parallel java. In *Proceedings of the 24th ACM SIGPLAN Conference on Object Oriented Programming Systems Languages and Applications*, OOPSLA '09, 2009.

[8] R. L. Bocchino, Jr., S. Heumann, N. Honarmand, S. V. Adve, V. S. Adve, A. Welc, and T. Shpeisman. Safe nondeterminism in a deterministic-by-default parallel language. In *Proceedings of the 38th Annual ACM SIGPLAN-SIGACT Symposium on Principles of Programming Languages*, POPL '11, 2011.

[9] H.-J. Boehm and S. V. Adve. Foundations of the c++ concurrency memory model. In *Proceedings of the 2008 ACM SIGPLAN Conference on Programming Language Design and Implementation*, PLDI '08, 2008.

[10] B. Choi, R. Komuravelli, H. Sung, R. Smolinski, N. Honarmand, S. V. Adve, V. S. Adve, N. P. Carter, and C.-T. Chou. Denovo: Rethinking the memory hierarchy for disciplined parallelism. In *Proceedings of the 20th International Conference on Parallel Architectures and Compilation Techniques*, PACT '11, 2011.

[11] M. Elver and V. Nagarajan. Tso-cc: Consistency directed cache coherence for tso. In *IEEE 20th International Symposium on High Performance Computer Architecture*, HPCA-20, Feb 2014.

[12] J. R. Goodman and P. J. Woest. The wisconsin multicube: A new large-scale cache-coherent multiprocessor. In *Proceedings of the 15th Annual International Symposium on Computer Architecture*, ISCA '88, 1988.

[13] J. R. Goodman, M. K. Vernon, and P. J. Woest. Efficient synchronization primitives for large-scale cache-coherent multiprocessors. In *Proceedings of the Third International Conference on Architectural Support for Programming Languages and Operating Systems*, ASPLOS III, 1989.

[14] M. Herlihy. A methodology for implementing highly concurrent data structures. In *Proceedings of the Second ACM SIGPLAN Symposium on Principles &Amp; Practice of Parallel Programming*, PPOPP '90, 1990.

[15] M. D. Hill, J. R. Larus, S. K. Reinhardt, and D. A. Wood. Cooperative shared memory: Software and hardware for scalable multiprocessor. In *Proceedings of the Fifth International Conference on Architectural Support for Programming Languages and Operating Systems*, ASPLOS V, 1992.

[16] L. Iftode, J. P. Singh, and K. Li. Scope consistency: A bridge between release consistency and entry consistency. In *Proceedings of the Eighth Annual ACM Symposium on Parallel Algorithms and Architectures*, SPAA '96, 1996.

[17] S. Kaxiras and G. Keramidas. SARC Coherence: Scaling Directory Cache Coherence in Performance and Power. *IEEE Micro*, 30(5), Sept.-Oct. 2010.

[18] P. Keleher, A. L. Cox, and W. Zwaenepoel. Lazy Release Consistency for Software Distributed Shared Memory. In *Proceedings of the 19th Annual International Symposium on Computer Architecture*, ISCA '92, 1992.

[19] J. H. Kelm, D. R. Johnson, M. R. Johnson, N. C. Crago, W. Tuohy, A. Mahesri, S. S. Lumetta, M. I. Frank, and S. J. Patel. Rigel: An Architecture and Scalable Programming Interface for a 1000-core Accelerator. In *Proceedings of the 36th Annual International Symposium on Computer Architecture*, ISCA '09, 2009.

[20] J. H. Kelm, D. R. Johnson, W. Tuohy, S. S. Lumetta, and S. J. Patel. Cohesion: A Hybrid Memory Model for Accelerators. In *Proceedings of the 37th Annual International Symposium on Computer Architecture*, ISCA '10, 2010.

[21] R. Komuravelli, S. V. Adve, and C.-T. Chou. Revisiting the complexity of hardware cache coherence and some implications. *ACM Trans. Archit. Code Optim.*, Dec. 2014.

[22] D. Koufaty, X. Chen, D. Poulsen, and J. Torrellas. Data forwarding in scalable shared-memory multiprocessors. *IEEE Transactions on Parallel and Distributed Systems*, 7(12), dec 1996.

[23] J. R. Larus, S. Chandra, and D. A. Wood. Cico: A practical shared-memory programming performance model. In *Workshop on Portability and Performance for Parallel Processing*, 1993.

[24] A. R. Lebeck and D. A. Wood. Dynamic self-invalidation: Reducing coherence overhead in shared-memory multiprocessors. In *Proceedings of the 22nd Annual International Symposium on Computer Architecture*, ISCA '95, 1995.

[25] P. S. Magnusson, M. Christensson, J. Eskilson, D. Forsgren, G. Hallberg, J. Hogberg, F. Larsson, A. Moestedt, and B. Werner. Simics: A full system simulation platform. *Computer*, 35:50–58, 2002.

[26] J. Manson, W. Pugh, and S. V. Adve. The java memory model. In *Proceedings of the 32Nd ACM SIGPLAN-SIGACT Symposium on Principles of Programming Languages*, POPL '05, 2005.

[27] M. M. K. Martin, D. J. Sorin, B. M. Beckmann, M. R. Marty, M. Xu, A. R. Alameldeen, K. E. Moore, M. D. Hill, and D. A. Wood. Multifacet's General Execution-driven Multiprocessor Simulator (GEMS) Toolset. *SIGARCH Computer Architecture News*, 33(4):92–99, 2005.

[28] M. M. Michael and M. L. Scott. Simple, fast, and practical non-blocking and blocking concurrent queue algorithms. In *Proceedings of the fifteenth annual ACM symposium on Principles of distributed computing*, PODC '96, 1996.

[29] M. M. Michael and M. L. Scott. Nonblocking algorithms and preemption-safe locking on multiprogrammed shared memory multiprocessors. *J. Parallel Distrib. Comput.*, 51(1), May 1998.

[30] S. L. Min and J.-L. Baer. Design and analysis of a scalable cache coherence scheme based on clocks and timestamps. *IEEE Trans. on Parallel and Distributed Systems*, 3(2):25–44, January 1992.

[31] R. Rajwar, A. Kagi, and J. Goodman. Improving the throughput of synchronization by insertion of delays. In *Proceedings of the Sixth International Symposium on High-Performance Computer Architecture*, HPCA-6, 2000.

[32] A. Ros and S. Kaxiras. Complexity-effective multicore coherence. In *Proceedings of the 21st international conference on Parallel architectures and compilation techniques*, PACT '12, 2012.

[33] M. Scott. *Shared Memory Synchronization*. Synthesis Lectures on Computer Architecture. Morgan & Claypool, 2013. ISBN 9781608459568. URL `http://books.google.com/books?id=N4YcnQEACAAJ`.

[34] S. Subramaniam, S. C. Steely, W. Hasenplaugh, A. Jaleel, C. Beckmann, T. Fossum, and J. Emer. Using in-flight chains to build a scalable cache coherence protocol. *ACM Trans. Archit. Code Optim.*, 10(4), Dec. 2013.

[35] H. Sung, R. Komuravelli, and S. V. Adve. DeNovoND: efficient hardware support for disciplined non-determinism. In *Proceedings of the eighteenth international conference on Architectural support for programming languages and operating systems*, ASPLOS '13, 2013.

[36] H. Sung, R. Komuravelli, and S. V. Adve. DeNovoND: efficient hardware for disciplined nondeterminism. *IEEE Micro*, 34(3), 2014.

[37] S. C. Woo, M. Ohara, E. Torrie, J. P. Singh, and A. Gupta. The splash-2 programs: Characterization and methodological considerations. In *Proceedings of the 22nd Annual International Symposium on Computer Architecture*, ISCA '95, 1995.

[38] J. Zebchuk, V. Srinivasan, M. K. Qureshi, and A. Moshovos. A tagless coherence directory. In *Proceedings of the 42Nd Annual IEEE/ACM International Symposium on Microarchitecture*, MICRO 42, 2009.

Hybrid Static–Dynamic Analysis for Statically Bounded Region Serializability *

Aritra Sengupta Swarnendu Biswas Minjia Zhang Michael D. Bond
Ohio State University
{sengupta,biswass,zhanminj,mikebond}@cse.ohio-state.edu

Milind Kulkarni
Purdue University
milind@purdue.edu

Abstract

Data races are common. They are difficult to detect, avoid, or eliminate, and programmers sometimes introduce them intentionally. However, shared-memory programs with data races have unexpected, erroneous behaviors. Intentional and unintentional data races lead to atomicity and sequential consistency (SC) violations, and they make it more difficult to understand, test, and verify software. Existing approaches for providing stronger guarantees for racy executions add high run-time overhead and/or rely on custom hardware.

This paper shows how to provide stronger semantics for racy programs while providing relatively good performance on commodity systems. A novel hybrid static–dynamic analysis called *EnfoRSer* provides end-to-end support for a memory model called *statically bounded region serializability* (SBRS) that is not only stronger than weak memory models but is strictly stronger than SC. EnfoRSer uses static compiler analysis to transform regions, and dynamic analysis to detect and resolve conflicts at run time. By demonstrating commodity support for a reasonably strong memory model with reasonable overheads, we show its potential as an always-on execution model.

Categories and Subject Descriptors D.3.4 [*Programming Languages*]: Processors—Compilers, Run-time environments

Keywords Dynamic analysis; static analysis; region serializability; memory models; atomicity; synchronization

1. Introduction

Shared-memory parallel programs have many possible behaviors due to the ways in which threads' memory accesses can interleave and can be reordered by compilers and hardware. Modern languages and systems provide a strong guarantee for any well-synchronized, or *data-race-free*, execution: its synchronization-free regions (SFRs) appear to execute atomically. However, executions with data races have few or no guarantees [1, 7, 8, 39], leading to unexpected, erroneous behaviors. Furthermore, handling the possibility of data races complicates static and dynamic analyses. Prior work has proposed stronger memory models, but they have lacked a compelling tradeoff between costs and benefits.

This paper's goal is to provide end-to-end support for a memory model that achieves a compelling balance between the benefits of stronger guarantees and the costs of providing those guarantees. Inspired by ideas from prior work on using *region serializability* (RS) to provide SC [4, 23, 37, 40], we focus on a new memory model called *statically bounded region serializability* (SBRS) that enforces serializability (atomicity) of statically bounded regions: regions bounded by synchronization operations, loop back edges, and method calls. SBRS offers an interesting cost–benefit tradeoff: it is strictly stronger than SC, yet we show that the bounded nature of its regions offers opportunities for static–dynamic analysis to enforce *end-to-end* SBRS with reasonable performance on commodity systems.

This paper presents a hybrid static–dynamic analysis for enforcing end-to-end SBRS called *EnfoRSer*. EnfoRSer enforces SBRS through (i) a static, intraprocedural compiler pass that partitions code into statically bounded regions, and transforms and instruments each region so that (ii) a runtime system can guarantee that regions appear to execute atomically. The key to EnfoRSer's operation is the interaction between the static transformations and the runtime system.

At a high level, EnfoRSer guarantees region atomicity using two-phase locking: each thread acquires lightweight, mostly-synchronization-free reader–writer locks before each memory access and does not release locks until the region ends. We present two distinct approaches for implementing this basic technique while overcoming its inherent tendency to deadlock. The first approach *executes regions idempotently* by deferring side effects (stores) until the region has acquired all of its locks. The second approach *executes regions speculatively*, rolling back speculative state when regions potentially conflict. While these approaches are related to *software transactional memory* (e.g., [25]), statically bounded regions enable a significantly different,

* This material is based upon work supported by the National Science Foundation under Grants CSR-1218695, CAREER-1253703, and CCF-1421612.

ASPLOS'15, March 14–18, 2015, Istanbul, Turkey.
Copyright is held by the owner/author(s). Publication rights licensed to ACM.
ACM 978-1-4503-2835-7/15/03... $15.00.
http://dx.doi.org/10.1145/2694344.2694379

higher-performance design based on hybrid static–dynamic analysis (Section 9).

We have implemented EnfoRSer in a high-performance Java virtual machine and applied it to benchmarked version of large multithreaded applications. EnfoRSer adds 43 and 36% overhead on average for the idempotent and speculation approaches, respectively—without relying on custom hardware or whole-program analysis. After we extend EnfoRSer to use the results of whole-program static analysis that identifies definitely data-race-free (DRF) accesses [44], it adds 32 and 27% average overhead for the idempotent and speculation approaches, respectively. Thus, enforcing SBRS can incur reasonable overhead even in commodity systems, meaning that it is a feasible always-on memory model that could improve software reliability today—and perhaps be supported more efficiently by future hardware systems.

2. Background and Motivation

An execution is *data race free* (DRF) if every pair of conflicting accesses (i.e., accesses to the same variable where at least one is a write) is well synchronized [3]—meaning they are ordered by the *happens-before* relation, a partial order that is the union of program and synchronization order [28].

The DRF0 memory model. Modern shared-memory languages such as Java and C++ use variants of the *DRF0* memory model [2, 8, 39]. DRF0 provides a strong guarantee for any DRF execution: *serializability* (i.e., atomicity) of *synchronization-free regions* (SFRs).

However, DRF0 provides weak guarantees for racy executions. Java tries to preserve the memory and type safety of racy executions [39], although the resulting memory model has flaws [58]. C++ provides essentially no guarantees [8].

Eliminating data races effectively and efficiently is a challenging, unsolved problem (e.g., [11, 21, 43]). Moreover, developers often avoid synchronization in pursuit of performance, deliberately introducing data races that lead to unexpected, ill-defined behaviors. Adve and Boehm and Ceze et al. argue that languages and hardware must provide stronger memory models to avoid impossibly complex semantics [1, 7, 14]. According to Adve and Boehm: "The inability to define reasonable semantics for programs with data races is not just a theoretical shortcoming, but a fundamental hole in the foundation of our languages and systems." They "call upon software and hardware communities to develop languages and systems that *enforce* data-race-freedom ..." [1].

Existing stronger memory models. Under the *sequential consistency* (SC) memory model, operations appear to interleave in an order respecting program order [29]. Providing end-to-end SC involves limiting memory access reordering by both the compiler and hardware, which slows programs and/or relies on custom hardware support [1, 32, 33, 41, 47, 51, 53, 55] (Section 9).

A promising approach for providing SC (and/or for detecting data races) is to provide *region serializability* (RS) of dynamically executed regions of code [4, 18, 23, 37, 38, 40, 52]. RS can be an advantageous mechanism since it can avoid unduly limiting compiler and hardware reordering of accesses. However, prior work that uses RS for SC relies on new hardware, adds high overhead, and/or *checks* SC instead of enforcing it, risking unexpected failures (Section 9).

While SC is stronger than DRF0-based memory models, it is not particularly strong. Under SC, it is still difficult and unnatural for programmers to reason about all interleavings, and for program analyses and runtime support to deal with all interleavings. Some operations that many programmers expect to execute atomically do not execute atomically under SC (e.g., 64-bit integer accesses in Java; multi-access operations such as x++ or buffer[index++] = ...). Adve and Boehm argue that "programmers do not reason about correctness of parallel code in terms of interleavings of individual memory accesses, and sequential consistency does not prevent common sources of concurrency bugs ..." [1].

While most work on RS-based memory models has focused on bounded regions, some work supports RS of regions bounded only by synchronization operations, a memory model we call *full-SFR RS* [37, 45]. While full-SFR RS is clearly a strong memory model, it may not be practical to enforce it—even with custom hardware support. Existing approaches rely on complex custom hardware and check (rather than enforce) full-SFR RS [37], or they rely on page-protection-based speculation and slow programs by two times or more (unless extra cores are available) [45].

3. Statically Bounded Region Serializability

This paper seeks to provide a strong memory model that can be supported with reasonable efficiency in commodity systems. Inspired by prior work that provides RS, our approach is based on enforcing RS. While providing full-SFR RS is appealing, it seems inherently difficult to enforce without heavyweight support for conflict detection and speculation, which would be expensive in software and complex in hardware. Thus, we seek a compromise memory model that balances strength and practicality.

Our choice is guided by two insights. First, enforcing RS of *dynamically bounded* regions (i.e., each executed region performs a bounded number of operations) permits simple, conservative region conflict detection, since the cost of misspeculation is bounded. Second, enforcing RS of not only dynamically but also *statically bounded* regions (i.e., an executing region executes each static instruction at most once) enables powerful static compiler transformations for enforcing region atomicity. Based on these insights, we propose to enforce a memory model called *statically bounded region serializability* (SBRS), which provides RS of statically bounded regions—regions demarcated at loop back edges and method calls as well as synchronization operations.

Section 8 evaluates SBRS's efficacy at avoiding real program errors. Here we discuss potential advantages and disadvantages of SBRS relative to other memory models.

Potential advantages and disadvantages. SBRS makes software automatically more reliable than under DRF0-based models. In addition to providing SC and thus avoiding hard-to-reason-about SC violations (e.g., double-checked locking errors), SBRS eliminates all violations of atomicity of statically bounded regions, e.g., common patterns such as improperly synchronized read–modify–write accesses and accesses to multiple variables. The following code snippets—which programmers may already expect to execute atomically—will execute atomically under SBRS:

- `x += 42` (read–modify–write)
- `if (o != null) { ... = o.f; }` (check before use)
- `buffer[pos++] = value` (multi-variable operation)

Furthermore, because SBRS restricts possible behaviors, the job of various static and dynamic analyses or runtime systems can be simplified by assuming SBRS. Current analyses and runtimes either (unsoundly) ignore the effects of possible data races,[1] or they consider the effects but incur increased complexity or overhead. The model checker CHESS must consider many more possible executions because of the effects of data races [12, 42]. Static dataflow analysis must account for racy interleavings to be fully sound [16]. The primary performance challenge of software-based multithreaded record & replay is dealing with the possibility of data races [56]: RecPlay assumes data race freedom unsoundly to reduce costs [49]; Chimera shows that handling data races leads to prohibitively high overhead [30]; other approaches sidestep this problem but incur other disadvantages or limitations such as not supporting both online and offline replay [31, 46] or requiring extra available cores [56].

We note that code expansion optimizations, such as method inlining and loop unrolling, increase the size of statically bounded regions beyond those anticipated at the source-code level, eliminating more atomicity violations and increasing the scope of possible compiler reordering optimizations. Since code expansion makes regions strictly larger than they appear to be at the source-code level, the atomicity of source-code-level regions still holds.

SBRS is clearly not as strong as full-SFR RS, which will avoid more errors and provide fewer interleavings for static and dynamic analyses to consider. Programmers might find it easier to reason about full-SFR RS, which requires considering only synchronization operations, than SBRS, which requires thinking about method and loop boundaries as well. On the other hand, full-SFR RS requires interprocedural reasoning: a region is synchronization free only if (transitively) all of its callee methods are synchronization free.

In any case, we suspect that SBRS and full-SFR RS are mainly useful *not* for helping programmers reason about their code, but rather for enforcing behaviors that many programmers *already assume*.

Extending SBRS. While we expect most programmers can and should be unaware of runtime support for SBRS, experts might want more control. They could mark code regions as atomic, e.g., with `atomic {}` blocks. EnfoRSer could naturally enforce atomicity of marked, statically bounded regions, and use method inlining and loop unrolling on larger regions to allow EnfoRSer to execute them atomically. The largest regions could be handled by using software transactional memory (STM) integrated with EnfoRSer. These extensions are beyond this paper's scope.

Progress. If SC guarantees progress[2] for a program, SBRS guarantees progress for that program. A proof sketch of this claim is available in an extended technical report [50].

A program can be *unable* to make progress under SBRS even though it *might* make progress under SC. For example, the following program *might* terminate—but is *not guaranteed* to terminate—under SC:

Initially x = false, y = false, done = false

```
// T1:                 // T2:
while (!done) {        while (true) {
  x = !x;                if (x != y) break;
  y = !y;              }
}                      done = true;
```

In contrast, under SBRS, each loop body executes atomically, so the program *cannot* terminate.

Interestingly, *full-SFR RS* can impede the progress of a program for which SC guarantees progress, although full-SFR RS guarantees progress for any program for which *DRF0* guarantees progress. For example, the following program always terminates under SC; cannot terminate under full-SFR RS (any terminating execution would violate full-SFR RS); and may or may not terminate under DRF0 (e.g., the compiler can legally hoist each load out of its loop):

Initially x = false, y = false

```
// T1:            // T2:
y = true;         x = true;
while (!x);       while (!y);
```

Under SBRS, this program always terminates because regions are dynamically bounded.

4. Hybrid Static–Dynamic Analysis

This section describes EnfoRSer, a hybrid static–dynamic analysis that enforces end-to-end SBRS.

4.1 Overview

To enforce SBRS, EnfoRSer's compiler pass partitions the program into regions bounded by synchronization operations, method calls, and loop back edges. Dynamic analysis then enforces atomicity of regions. A naïve approach for enforcing atomicity is as follows. First, associate a "lock" with each potentially shared object[3] (e.g., by adding a header word to each object that tracks the object's ownership state). Henceforth, this paper uses the term "lock" to refer to per-objects locks that are added by EnfoRSer and acquired by its

[1] In theory, a static or dynamic analysis for C++ can provide any behavior for racy executions and still be sound, since C++ (unlike Java) provides no semantics for racy executions [8]. In practice, real-world programs have data races, so it is useful for analyses to behave sensibly in their presence.

[2] We assume a fair scheduler that does not allow any thread to starve.

[3] This paper uses the term "object" to refer to any unit of shared memory.

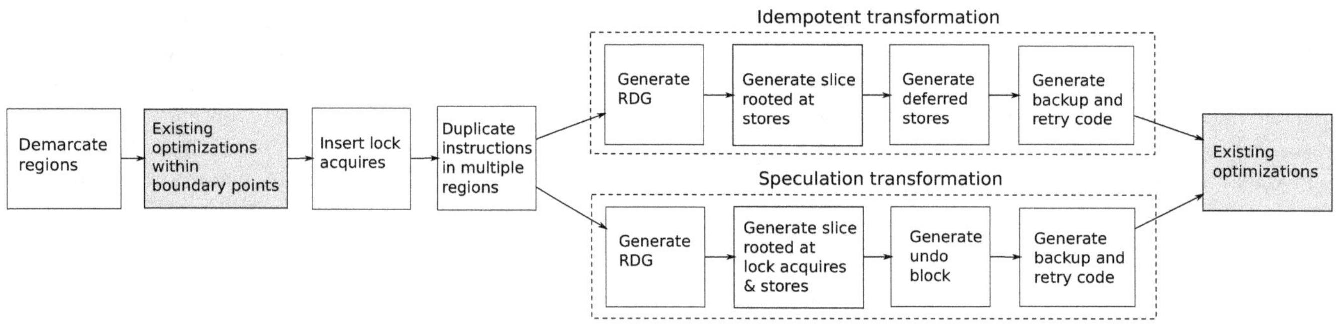

Figure 1. The transformations performed by an EnfoRSer-enabled optimizing compiler. Boxes shaded gray show existing compiler optimizations. Dashed boxes indicate transformations performed once on each region.

instrumentation and are *not* visible to programmers. Second, instrument the region to ensure that (1) a thread holds a lock on an object before the region accesses it and (2) the region releases locks only when it ends. This approach implements two-phase locking, so the execution will be equivalent to a serialized execution of regions.

This naïve approach suffers from two drawbacks. First, because threads can access objects in arbitrary orders, and per-object locks must be held until the end of the region to satisfy two-phase locking, a thread can deadlock while executing a region that attempts to acquire multiple locks. EnfoRSer solves this problem by applying a compile-time *atomicity transformation*: if a thread cannot acquire a lock because another thread holds it—we call this situation a "conflict," as all region conflicts result in a failed lock acquire—the transformed region is restarted, avoiding the deadlock. Second, acquiring a lock on each object access seems to require an atomic operation such as compare-and-swap (CAS), which would add unreasonable overhead. EnfoRSer uses special locks that mostly avoid atomic operations [10] (Section 4.3).

The key challenge is ensuring that a transformed region can be safely restarted without losing atomicity. If a region restarts after modifying shared objects, then either another thread could see those effects, or the region may behave incorrectly after restart. Either way, region atomicity is violated. We design, implement, and evaluate two atomicity transformations that address this challenge. (We investigate two different transformations in order to explore the space.)

The *idempotent* transformation modifies each region to defer stores until all per-object locks have been acquired. If a region encounters a conflict when acquiring a lock, it can safely restart since it executes idempotently up to that point. The challenge is generating correct code for deferring stores in the face of object aliasing and conditional statements.

The *speculation* transformation modifies the region to perform stores speculatively as it executes. The transformed region backs up the original value of stored-to memory locations. On a conflict, the modified region can restart safely by using the backed-up values to restore memory to its original state. The challenges are maintaining the backup values efficiently and restoring them correctly on retry.

Putting it all together, EnfoRSer's compiler pipeline operates as shown in Figure 1. First, it demarcates a program into regions (Section 4.2), and any optimizing passes in the compiler are performed, modified to operate within region boundaries. Next, the compiler inserts lock acquire operations before object accesses (Section 4.3). The compiler then performs a duplication transformation (Section 4.4) and builds an intermediate representation (Section 4.5), before transforming each region using one of the two atomicity transformations (Sections 4.6 and 4.7). Finally, any remaining compiler optimizations are performed.

At run time, if a thread executing a region detects a potential conflict, it restarts the region safely, preserving atomicity. The atomicity of regions guarantees equivalence to some serialized execution of regions.

4.2 Demarcating Regions

The first step in EnfoRSer's compiler pass is to divide the program into regions; later steps ensure that these regions execute atomically. The following program points are region *boundary points*: synchronization operations, method calls, and loop back edges.[4] Since method calls are boundary points, regions are demarcated at method entry and return, i.e., EnfoRSer's analysis is intraprocedural. An EnfoRSer region is a maximal set of instructions such that (1) for each instruction i, all (transitive) successors of i are in the region provided that the successors are reachable without traversing a region boundary point; and (2) there exists a "start" instruction s such that each instruction i in the region is reachable from s by only traversing edges in the region. Note that an instruction can be in multiple regions statically, i.e., reachable from multiple boundary points without an intervening boundary point—a situation that Section 4.4 addresses.

Reordering within and across regions. To ensure region atomicity, the compiler cannot be permitted to reorder instructions across region boundary points. Similar to DRFx's soft fences [40], EnfoRSer prohibits inter-region optimizations, by modifying optimization passes, such as common subexpression elimination, that may reorder memory accesses to ensure they do not reorder across boundary points. We find that prohibiting reordering across region boundaries

[4] A loop *back edge* is any control-flow edge to a loop header from a basic block dominated by the loop header. Loop *headers* are not boundary points.

impacts performance negligibly for our implementation; details are in an extended technical report [50].

4.3 Lightweight Reader–Writer Locks

The next step after demarcating regions is instrumenting program loads and stores with lock acquire operations. Acquiring traditional locks on every object access would be prohibitively expensive. EnfoRSer instead uses lightweight reader–writer locks that differ from traditional locks in two key ways. (1) A lock is always "acquired" in some state such as write-exclusive or read-shared, and acquiring the lock does not require an atomic operation if the thread already holds the lock in a compatible state. (2) A thread never automatically "releases" a lock; instead, another thread may acquire the lock, but it must first *coordinate* with the thread(s) that currently hold the lock. The design and implementation of these reader–writer locks (called "locks" for the remainder of the paper) are based closely on *Octet* locks [10]. We summarize their operation here.

Each object has a lock, denoted by o.lockState but not visible to programmers, that is always acquired in one of the following states:

- $WrEx_T$: Thread T may read or write the object.
- $RdEx_T$: T may read but not write the object.
- RdSh: Any thread may read but not write the object.

At each program store and load to the object referenced by o, the compiler inserts instrumentation denoted by acq_wr(o) and acq_rd(o), respectively, as the following pseudocode shows:

```
acq_wr(o); // instrumentation
o.f = ...; // program store

acq_rd(p); // instrumentation
... = p.g; // program load
```

The following pseudocode shows the definitions of acq_wr() and acq_rd() (T is the executing thread):

```
acq_wr(Object obj) {
  if (obj.lockState != WrEx_T)
    wrSlowPath(obj); /* change obj.lockState */
}

acq_rd(Object obj) {
  if (obj.lockState != WrEx_T &&
      obj.lockState != RdEx_T) {
    if (obj.lockState != RdSh)
      rdSlowPath(obj); /* change obj.lockState */
    load_fence; // see footnote 5
  }
}
```

To acquire a lock to obtain read or write access to its associated object, a thread T checks the state of the lock. If the lock's state is compatible with the access being performed (e.g., T wants to read or write an object in $WrEx_T$ state), the lock is already "acquired" without any synchronization operations. This check is called the *fast path*.

Code path(s)	Transition type	Old state	Program access	New state	Sync. needed
Fast	Same state	$WrEx_T$	R/W by T	Same	None
		$RdEx_T$	R by T	Same	
		RdSh	R by T	Same	
Fast & slow	Upgrading	$RdEx_T$	W by T	$WrEx_T$	Atomic op.
		$RdEx_{T1}$	R by T2	RdSh	
	Conflicting	$WrEx_{T1}$	W by T2	$WrEx_{T2}$	Roundtrip coord.
		$WrEx_{T1}$	R by T2	$RdEx_{T2}$	
		$RdEx_{T1}$	W by T2	$WrEx_{T2}$	
		RdSh	W by T	$WrEx_T$	

Table 1. State transitions for lightweight locks.

Otherwise, a thread encounters a lock in an incompatible state, and it must change the lock's state. Table 1 shows all possible state transitions.[5] The first three rows (*Same state*) correspond to the fast path. The remaining rows show cases that must change a lock's state. Collectively, all operations that change a lock's state are called the *slow path*. An *upgrading* transition (e.g., from $RdEx_T$ to RdSh) expands the set of accesses allowed by the lock; it requires an atomic operation to change the lock's state.

The slow path triggers a *conflicting* transition in cases where the program access conflicts with accesses allowed under the lock's current state. Because other thread(s) might be accessing the object without synchronization, merely changing the lock's state—even with an atomic operation—is insufficient. Instead, the thread executing the conflicting transition, called the *requesting thread*, must *coordinate* with every other thread, called a *responding thread*, that has access to the object, to ensure the responding thread(s) "see" the state change. For $WrEx_T$ and $RdEx_T$ states, T is the responding thread; for RdSh states, every other thread is a responding thread.

A responding thread participates in coordination only at a *safe point*: a point that does not interrupt instrumentation–access atomicity (i.e., atomicity of lock acquire instrumentation together with the program access it guards). Conveniently, managed language virtual machines already place safe points throughout the code, e.g., at every method entry and loop back edge. Furthermore, all blocking operations (e.g., *program* lock acquires and I/O) must act as safe points. If a responding thread is actively executing program code, the requesting and responding threads coordinate *explicitly*: the requesting thread sends a request, and the responding thread responds when it reaches a safe point. Otherwise, the responding thread is at a blocking safe point, so the threads coordinate *implicitly*: the requesting thread atomically modifies a flag that the responding thread will later see. Finally, in either case, the requesting thread finishes changing the lock's state and proceeds with the access.

Thus, while traditional locks add synchronization at every access, the locks used by EnfoRSer add no synchronization

[5] EnfoRSer does not need nor use Octet's RdSh counter [10]. Instead, EnfoRSer ensures that reads to RdSh locks happen after the prior write by issuing a load fence on the RdSh fast path.

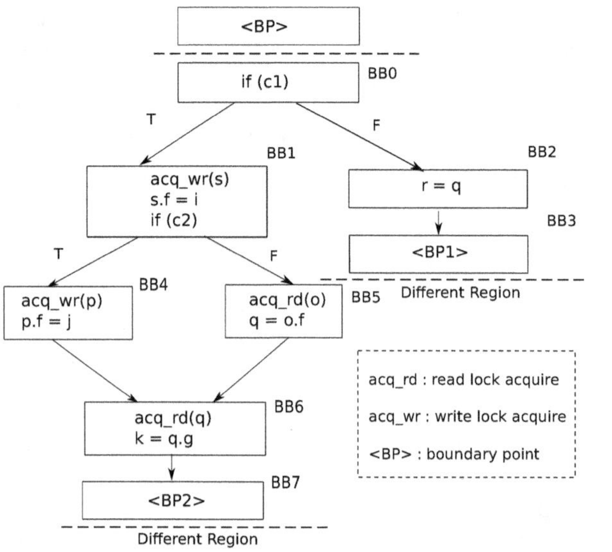

Figure 2. A region instrumented with lock acquire operations.

at non-conflicting accesses (the fast path), but they require coordination with other threads at conflicting accesses (the slow path). This tradeoff works well in practice for many programs, which aim for good thread locality by design.

Avoiding deadlock. As described so far, locks are deadlock prone: two threads each waiting to acquire a lock held by the other thread will wait indefinitely. To prevent deadlock, if a thread T is waiting for other thread(s) to relinquish a lock, T *allows other threads to acquire locks held by T.*

This behavior has interesting implications for EnfoRSer. When a thread tries to acquire an object's lock, it might give up *other objects' locks acquired in the same region.* As a result, rather than suffering from deadlock, as in traditional two-phase locking, regions may lose atomicity when they conflict. Hence, EnfoRSer's transformed regions actually restart *whenever a lock may have been released*—indicated by responding to another thread's coordination request.

Example. Figure 2 shows a region instrumented with lock acquire operations (acq_rd and acq_wr). The rest of this section uses this region as a running example.

4.4 Duplication Transformation

If a lock acquire (acq_rd(o) or acq_wr(o)) detects a potential conflict, it must retry the region by returning control to the region start. For the compiler to generate control flow for retry, the lock acquire must be statically in a single region.

The modified compiler thus performs a *duplication* transformation prior to atomicity transformations (Figure 1). This transformation duplicates instructions and control flow so that every instruction (not including boundary points) is in a single region. First, a simple dataflow analysis determines which boundary point(s) reach each instruction (i.e., which region(s) each instruction resides in). Second, in topological order starting at method entry, the duplication algorithm replicates each instruction that appears in $k > 1$ regions $k-1$ times, and retargets each of the original instruction's predecessors to the appropriate replicated instruction.

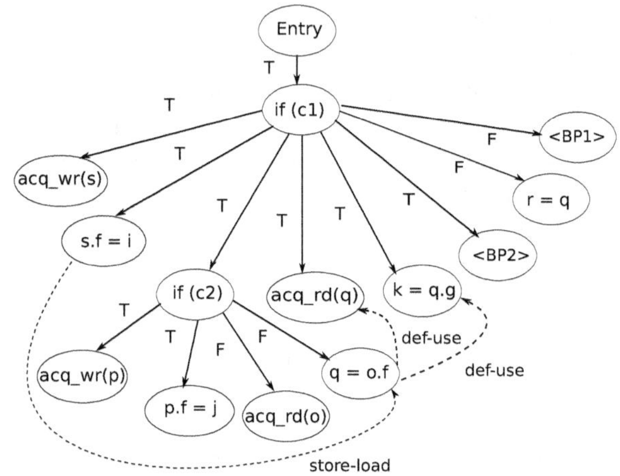

Figure 3. A region dependence graph for the region in Figure 2.

The duplication transformation does not duplicate any region boundary points. Since the number of region boundary points remains fixed, duplication cannot result in an exponential blowup in code size.

4.5 The Region Dependence Graph

In order to transform regions, the atomicity transformations require static *slices* [27]: the set of instructions that are data and control dependent on some instruction. Thus, for each region, an atomicity transformation first builds a *region dependence graph* (RDG), based on Ferrante et al.'s program dependence graph [20], which captures both data and control dependences in a region. The RDG needs to track true (write–read) dependences, but not output (write–write) or anti (read–write) dependences. It can ignore loop-carried dependences since regions are acyclic.

EnfoRSer's RDG construction algorithm uses a reaching-definitions analysis to compute intraprocedural data dependences in a region. The algorithm treats lock acquire operations acq_rd(o) and acq_wr(o) like a use of the object referenced by o. Because RDG construction is performed at the region level, aliasing relationships that arise due to operations outside the region cannot be inferred. Hence, the RDG construction algorithm adopts a conservative, type-based approach, e.g., it assumes that a load from field f of object o can have a dependence with any earlier store to the same field f of object p, since p and o could potentially alias. It also conservatively assumes that loads from arrays may have dependences from stores to type-compatible arrays. The construction algorithm uses the data dependences computed by the reaching-definitions analysis, as well as control dependences computed by a standard post-dominance analysis, to construct the final RDG.

Figure 3 shows the RDG for the region from Figure 2. The dotted lines depict store–load dependences (between accesses to object fields or array locations) and def–use dependences (between definitions and uses of local variables). The construction algorithm's aliasing assumptions lead to a store–load dependence between s.f = i and q = o.f, since s and o may be aliased. The Entry node is the root of the RDG and has control dependence edges marked as T to all nodes (only one in this case) that are not control dependent on any other nodes. Other edges labeled T and F are control dependence edges from conditionals to dependent statements.

Slicing of the RDG. Each atomicity transformation must identify which parts of the region are relevant for the transformation. The transformation performs static program slicing of the RDG (based on static program slicing of the program dependence graph [27]) to identify relevant instructions. A *backward* slice *rooted* at an instruction i includes all instructions on which i is *transitively* dependent. Dependences include both data (store–load and def–use) and control dependences. A slice rooted at a set of instructions is simply the union of the slices of each instruction.

4.6 Enforcing Atomicity with Idempotence

The *idempotent* transformation defers side effects (program stores) until the end of the region. The side-effect-free part of the region, which includes all lock acquires, executes *idempotently*, so it can be restarted safely if a lock acquire detects a potential region conflict.

To defer program stores, the transformation replaces each static store with a definition of a new local variable. Figure 4 shows the region from Figure 2 after the idempotent transformation. The stores s.f = i and p.f = j from Figure 2 are replaced with assignments to fresh locals i' and j' in BB1 and BB3 of Figure 4. The two main challenges are (1) modifying loads that might alias with stores so that they read the correct value and (2) generating code at the end of the region that performs the stores that should actually execute.

Loads aliased with deferred stores. Any load that aliases a deferred store needs to read from the local variable that backs up the stored value, rather than from the deferred store's memory location. The RDG in Figure 3 includes a store–load edge from s.f = i to q = o.f because RDG construction conservatively assumes all type-compatible accesses might alias. As shown in BB1 of Figure 4, the transformation substitutes a definition of a new temporary variable i' = i in place of the store s.f = i. If s and o alias, then q = i' should execute in place of q = o.f; otherwise q = o.f should execute normally.

For each load, the transformation emits a series of alias checks to disambiguate the scenarios: one for each potentially aliased store that may reach the load. BB4–BB6 in Figure 4 show the result of this transformation. The transformation first emits the original load (BB4). Then, for each store on which the load appears to be dependent, the transformation generates an assignment from the corresponding local variable, guarded by an alias check (BB6, guarded by the check in BB5). By performing these checks in program order, the load will ultimately produce the correct value, even if multiple aliasing tests pass. If a possibly-aliased store executes conditionally, the transformed load is guarded by a conditional check in addition to the alias check to ensure that the store executed. A similar situation arises with array accesses, in which case the aliasing checks must not only compare the array references, but also the index expressions.

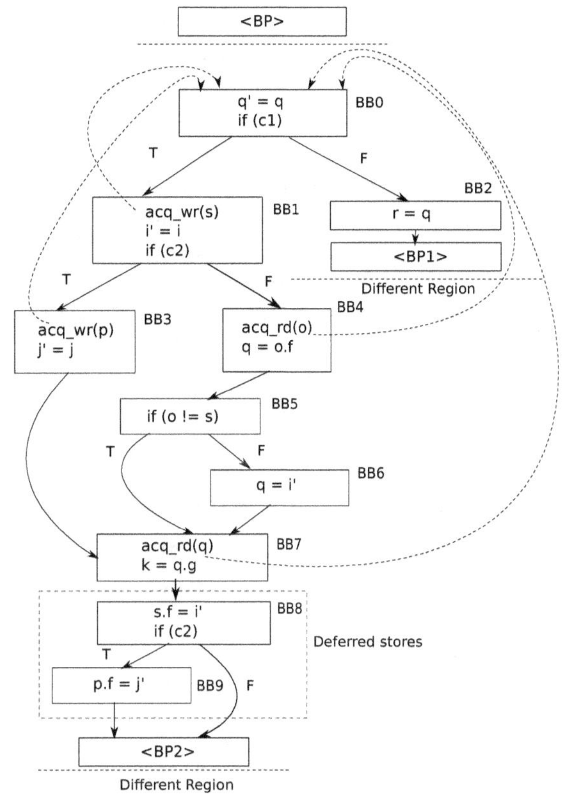

Figure 4. Region from Figure 2 after idempotent transformation.

Although this approach may generate substantial code per load, in practice later compiler passes can simplify it significantly. For example, if the compiler can prove two object references definitely do or do not alias, constant propagation and dead code elimination will remove unnecessary checks.

Deferred stores. It is nontrivial to generate code at the end of a region to perform the region's stores, because the code should perform only the stores that actually would have executed. The transformation generates code at each region exit based on a slice of the region's stores from the RDG. It generates each deferred store using the mapping from static stores to local variables. To ensure a deferred store only executes if it would have in the original region, the slice includes all condition variables on which stores are control dependent. The generated code checks these conditions before performing any deferred store. For example, BB8 in Figure 4 checks condition c2, executing the deferred store in BB9 only if the store would have occurred in the original region (note that the same condition guards j' = j in BB3).

Note that it is possible that the conditional variables guarding stores are overwritten during the execution of the idempotent portion of the region; if so, those conditionals may resolve differently while executing deferred stores. To avoid this problem, the transformation "backs up" the results of any conditional in the idempotent region in fresh local variables, and uses these locals in the conditionals guarding deferred stores. Similarly, any store to an object field or array in the original region is dependent on the base reference of the object or array. If these base references may change during execution, the transformation backs them up at the point of the original store and uses the backups when executing the deferred stores.

Supporting retry. Although the idempotent transformation defers stores, the region can still have side effects if it modifies *local* variables that may be used in the same or a later region. For each region, the idempotent (and speculation) transformations identify such local variables and insert code to (1) back up their values in new local variables at region start and (2) restore their values on region retry. In Figure 4, local variable q is backed up in q' at the beginning of the region (BB0). If a lock acquire detects a potential conflict, the code restores the value of q from q' (not shown) and control returns to the region start (a dashed arrow indicates the edge is taken if the operation detects a potential conflict).

4.7 Enforcing Atomicity with Speculation

EnfoRSer's second atomicity transformation enables *speculative execution*. This transformation leaves the order of operations in the region unchanged, but it transforms the region to perform stores speculatively: before a store executes, instrumentation saves the old value of the field or array element being updated. If a lock acquire detects a possible conflict, the region restarts safely by "rolling back" the region's stores. Figure 5 shows the region from Figure 2 after applying the speculation transformation. The primary challenge is generating code that correctly backs up stored-to variables and (when a conflict is detected) rolls back speculative state.

Supporting speculative stores. Since regions are acyclic and intraprocedural, every static store executes at most once per region execution. Hence, the speculation approach's transformation can associate each store with a unique, new local variable. Before each store to a memory location (i.e., field or array element), the transformation inserts a load from the location into the store's associated local variable.

Generating code to roll back executed stores is complex due to the challenge of determining *which* stores have executed. The solution depends on the subpath executed through the region. To tackle this challenge, the transformation generates an *undo block* for each region. In reverse topological order, it generates an undo operation for each store s in the region that "undoes" the effects of s using the associated backup variable. To ensure that s is only undone if it executed in the original region, this undo operation executes conditionally. The transformation determines the appropriate conditions by traversing the RDG from s up through its control ancestors. As in the idempotent approach, conditional variables and object base references are backed up if necessary, so they can be used during rollback. The undo block in Figure 5 illustrates the result of this process. The store to p.f is topologically after the store to s.f, so it appears first in the undo block. The store to p.f is performed if both c1 and c2 are true, so the old value is restored under the same conditions. Likewise, the store to s.f is only performed, and hence only undone, if c1 is true.

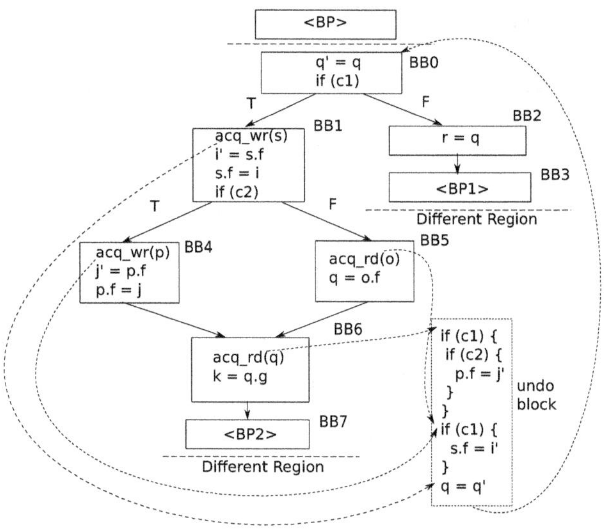

Figure 5. Region from Figure 2 after speculation transformation.

Supporting retry. The transformation generates control flow for each lock acquire to jump to the appropriate location in the undo block if the lock acquire detects a potential conflict. The jump target is the first undo operation associated with a store that is a control-flow predecessor of the lock acquire. Figure 5 shows these conditional jumps with dashed lines. As with the idempotent transformation, local variables must be backed up and restored during retry. In the figure, q is backed up in q' at the beginning of the region, and restored at the end of the undo block.

5. Optimizations

EnfoRSer's compiler analysis identifies accesses that do not need lock acquires, which in turn enables reducing the size of regions that need to be analyzed and transformed.

Statically redundant lock acquires. A lock acquire for an object access is "redundant" if each incoming path definitely performs a sufficiently strong lock acquire on the same object in the same region. An acq_rd() is redundant if definitely preceded by acq_rd() or acq_wr() on the same object; an acq_wr() is redundant if definitely preceded by acq_wr() on the same object. A lock is guaranteed to be in a compatible state at a redundant lock acquire; another thread cannot change the state without triggering restart of the current region. The compiler uses an intraprocedural, flow-sensitive dataflow analysis (based on an analysis used by prior work [10]) to identify redundant lock acquires.

Static data race detection. EnfoRSer's transformations can optionally use the results of sound static analysis that identifies all accesses that might be involved in data races. Remaining accesses are definitely data race free (DRF). An access that is DRF does not need a corresponding lock acquire. Prior work has also leveraged sound static race detection to simplify dynamic analysis [15, 19, 30, 57].

Whole-program static analysis is somewhat impractical in the real world since it relies on all code being available and all call graph edges being known at analysis time, which is difficult in the presence of dynamic class loading and reflection. An implementation could handle unexpected dynamic behavior by dynamically recompiling *all* code to treat all accesses as potentially racy, or by using incremental static analysis to identify and recompile new potentially racy accesses. Our experiments sidestep this challenge by making all code and calls known to the static analysis.

Optimizing region demarcation. We optimize region demarcation to take advantage of optimizations that remove lock acquires. Optimized region demarcation distinguishes between *programmatic regions*—regions delimited at boundary points—and *enforced regions*—the regions whose atomicity is explicitly enforced by EnfoRSer's atomicity transformations. Optimized region demarcation starts and ends an enforced region at the first and last lock acquire of a programmatic region, respectively. Because any memory accesses outside of these boundaries are guaranteed to be DRF or guarded by locks earlier in the region, providing atomicity for these enforced regions automatically guarantees atomicity for programmatic regions.

An access that has no lock acquire but is inside of an enforced region must still be handled by the atomicity transformations: the idempotent transformation handles every possible store–load dependence in an enforced region, and the speculation transformation backs up every store in an enforced region. Although the endpoint of an enforced region may come before the end of a programmatic region, EnfoRSer does not treat the end of an enforced region as a safe point, so a thread will not release locks between the end of the enforced region and the end of the programmatic region.

6. Implementation

We have implemented EnfoRSer in Jikes RVM 3.1.3, a high-performance Java virtual machine [5] that provides performance competitive with commercial JVMs. We have made our implementation publicly available.[6]

Although the implementation targets a managed language VM, it should be possible to implement EnfoRSer's design for a native language such as C or C++. The main challenge would be adapting Octet to a native language [10].

Modifying the compilers. Jikes RVM uses two just-in-time dynamic compilers that perform method-based compilation. The first time a method executes, the *baseline* compiler compiles it directly from Java bytecode to machine code. If a method becomes hot, the *optimizing* compiler recompiles it at successively higher levels of optimization. The optimizing compiler performs standard intraprocedural optimizations. It performs aggressive method inlining but does not otherwise perform interprocedural optimizations.

We modify the optimizing compiler to demarcate regions and restrict reordering across regions throughout compilation; to insert lock acquires (we use the publicly available Octet implementation of lightweight locks [10]); and to perform EnfoRSer's atomicity transformations on the optimizing compiler's intermediate representation (IR).

[6] `http://www.jikesrvm.org/Research+Archive`

The baseline compiler does not use an IR, making it hard to implement atomicity transformations. Instead, in baseline-compiled code only, our implementation *simulates* the cost of enforcing SBRS without actually enforcing SBRS. The baseline compiler inserts (1) lock acquires, (2) instrumentation that logs each store in a memory-based undo log, and (3) instrumentation that resets the undo log pointer at each boundary point. This approach does not soundly enforce SBRS since it does not perform rollback on region conflicts. Since conflicts are infrequent and (by design) a small fraction of time is spent executing baseline-compiled code, this approach should closely approximate the performance of a fully sound implementation.

The compiler performs EnfoRSer's transformations on application and library code. Since Jikes RVM is written in Java, in a few cases VM code gets inlined into application and library code. Our prototype implementation cannot correctly handle inlined VM code that performs certain low-level operations or that does not have safe points in loops. To execute correctly, we identify and exclude 25 methods across all benchmarks and 10 methods in the Java libraries from EnfoRSer's transformations, instead inserting only lock acquires into these methods.

Demarcating regions. EnfoRSer demarcates regions at synchronization operations (lock acquire, release, and wait; thread fork and join), method calls, and loop back edges. These are essentially the same program points that are GC-safe points in Jikes RVM and other VMs. Since Jikes RVM makes each loop header a safe point, the implementation bounds regions at loop headers instead of back edges. To simplify the implementation, we currently bound regions along special control-flow edges for switch statements.

The optimizing compiler is able to identify all synchronization operations when it compiles application and library code, since synchronization in Java is part of the language. The implementation does not bound regions at `volatile` variable accesses, which does not affect progress guarantees.

Object allocations can trigger GC, so they are safe points and thus boundary points in our implementation. A production implementation could either define regions as being bounded at allocation (non-array allocations already perform a constructor call); defer GC past allocations; or speculatively hoist memory allocation above regions.

Retrying regions. A region must retry if another thread may have performed accesses that conflict with the region's accesses so far. This case can occur only if the region, while waiting for coordination, responds to coordination requests (Section 4.3). In the idempotent approach, lock acquires use this criterion to decide whether to retry a region. However, the speculation approach cannot easily use this criterion: a region must not lose access to objects until after it executes its undo block—at which point the region must re-execute—so the decision to retry the region must be made before the region responds to coordination requests and potentially loses needed access to an object. The speculation approach instead triggers retry whenever a lock acquire takes the slow path. As a result, the idempotent approach provides lower retry rates than speculation—but the more precise retry criterion has a negligible performance impact (Section 7.3).

Retrying regions could lead to *livelock*, where conflicting regions repeatedly cause each other to retry. EnfoRSer could avoid livelock with standard techniques such as exponential backoff. Livelock is not an issue in our experiments, presumably because regions are short and conflicts are infrequent.

Runtime exceptions. A runtime exception (e.g., null pointer exception) can cause a region to exit early. This behavior can affect correctness for the idempotent approach since it reorders loads and stores, but we have not observed any problems in our experiments. We find that runtime exceptions are sufficiently rare (experimental details are in an extended technical report [50]) that just-in-time deoptimized recompilation could handle them efficiently.

7. Evaluation

This section evaluates EnfoRSer's run-time characteristics and performance.

7.1 Methodology

Benchmarks. The experiments execute our modified Jikes RVM on the multithreaded DaCapo benchmarks [6] versions 2006-10-MR2 and 9.12-bach (2009) with the large workload size (excluding programs Jikes RVM cannot run), distinguished by suffixes 6 and 9; and fixed-workload versions of SPECjbb2000 and SPECjbb2005.[7]

Platform. We build a high-performance configuration of Jikes RVM that adaptively optimizes the application as it runs (FastAdaptive) and uses the default high-performance garbage collector and adjusts the heap size automatically.

Experiments run on an AMD Opteron 6272 system with eight 8-core processors running Linux 2.6.32. We limit experiments to only four processors (32 cores) due to an anomalous result with 64 cores where EnfoRSer actually outperforms the baseline for some programs. (We find that adding *any* kind of instrumentation can improve performance, due to anomalies we have been able to attribute to Linux thread scheduling decisions [10].)

We have also evaluated EnfoRSer on an Intel Xeon E5-4620 system with four 8-core processors running Linux 2.6.32, in order to test EnfoRSer's sensitivity to the system architecture. On this platform, EnfoRSer adds nearly the same overhead as on the AMD platform (within 1% relative to baseline execution).

Static race detection. EnfoRSer can use any sound static analysis to identify definitely data-race-free (DRF) accesses (Section 5). We use the publicly available implementation of Naik et al.'s 2006 race detection algorithm, *Chord* [44]. By default, Chord is unsound (i.e., it misses races) because it uses a may-alias lockset analysis.[8] We thus *disable* lockset analysis, using only Chord's thread escape and thread fork–join analyses to identify DRF accesses.

	Threads		Insts.	Insts. /	Dyn. regions retried	
	Total	Live	executed	region	Idem.	Spec.
eclipse6	18	12	5.6×10^{10}	27	<0.01%	<0.01%
hsqldb6	402	102	5.7×10^{9}	32	<0.01%	0.50%
lusearch6	65	65	5.7×10^{9}	31	<0.01%	<0.01%
xalan6	9	9	8.5×10^{10}	29	0.05%	1.07%
avrora9	27	27	3.8×10^{10}	36	<0.01%	0.81%
jython9	3	3	8.5×10^{10}	29	<0.01%	<0.01%
luindex9	2	2	4.2×10^{9}	23	<0.01%	<0.01%
lusearch9	c	c	2.4×10^{9}	26	<0.01%	<0.01%
pmd9	5	5	1.2×10^{9}	22	<0.01%	0.11%
sunflow9	$2\times c$	c	3.0×10^{9}	26	<0.01%	0.03%
xalan9	c	c	9.9×10^{9}	23	0.37%	8.16%
pjbb2000	37	9	3.0×10^{9}	21	<0.01%	1.29%
pjbb2005	9	9	9.7×10^{9}	22	1.30%	17.91%

Table 2. Dynamic execution characteristics. A few programs launch threads proportional to the number of cores c, which is 32 in our experiments.

	Without static race detection					With static race detection				
	0	1	2–3	4–7	≥8	0	1	2–3	4–7	≥8
eclipse6	9%	25%	10%	38%	17%	9%	25%	10%	38%	17%
hsqldb6	7%	14%	11%	60%	8%	9%	13%	11%	59%	8%
lusearch6	5%	44%	14%	29%	8%	22%	43%	14%	19%	2%
xalan6	15%	27%	5%	30%	23%	45%	21%	9%	11%	13%
avrora9	6%	32%	5%	19%	38%	8%	31%	5%	18%	38%
jython9	24%	35%	5%	28%	8%	73%	18%	0%	8%	1%
luindex9	2%	28%	9%	35%	26%	23%	32%	8%	26%	11%
lusearch9	3%	42%	10%	32%	12%	24%	44%	10%	17%	5%
pmd9	5%	45%	7%	31%	12%	37%	30%	4%	20%	7%
sunflow9	18%	22%	16%	25%	19%	34%	30%	14%	13%	8%
xalan9	15%	33%	6%	21%	25%	42%	30%	4%	11%	12%
pjbb2000	42%	3%	26%	24%	4%	44%	23%	22%	7%	4%
pjbb2005	14%	17%	24%	37%	8%	18%	23%	14%	38%	7%

Table 3. Percentage of dynamic regions executed with various complexity (static accesses), without and with identifying statically DRF accesses to optimize region demarcation.

The programs we evaluate use reflection and custom class loading, which present a challenge for static analysis. To handle reflection, we use a feature of Chord that executes the program to identify reflective call sites and targets. Chord does not run eclipse6 correctly in our environment, so EnfoRSer runs eclipse6 assuming all accesses are racy. jython9 has custom-loaded classes that present a challenge for Chord, so EnfoRSer assumes all accesses in custom-loaded classes are racy. We cross-checked Chord's results with a dynamic race detector's output; we found one class (in jbb2005) that Chord does not analyze at all (for unknown reasons), so EnfoRSer fully instruments this class.

Static analysis is a one-time cost, incurred only when the program changes. In any case, Chord's cost is low: analyzing any of the programs we evaluate takes at most 90 seconds.

7.2 Run-Time Characteristics

The *Threads* columns of Table 2 report the total number of threads created and the maximum number of live threads.

The table's remaining columns report characteristics of executed regions, averaged across 10 trials. The *Insts.* columns report total dynamic IA-32 instructions and dynamic instructions per executed region, measured without

[7] `http://www.spec.org/jbb200{0,5}`, `http://users.cecs.anu.edu.au/~steveb/research/research-infrastructure/pjbb2005`

[8] We have confirmed that there is no available implementation of their 2007 algorithm, which uses conditional must-not-alias analysis to be sound [43].

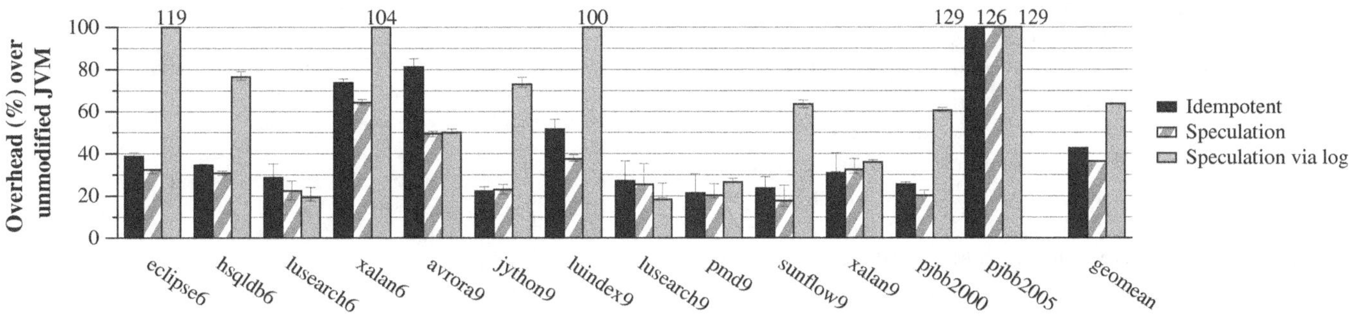

Figure 6. Run-time overhead over an unmodified JVM of providing SBRS with EnfoRSer's two atomicity transformations and speculation that uses a log to simulate a stripped-down version of STM.

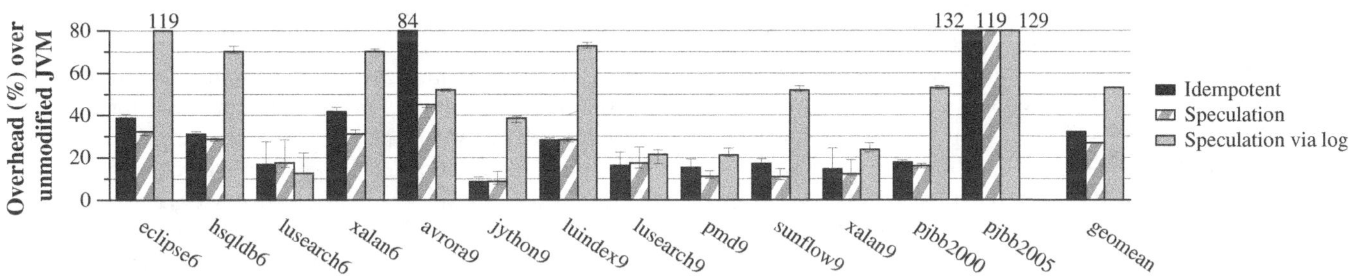

Figure 7. Run-time overhead over an unmodified JVM when transformations use whole-program static analysis to identify definitely data-race-free accesses. Otherwise, configurations are the same as Figure 6.

any EnfoRSer instrumentation. The programs each execute billions of instructions, divided into regions that execute 21–36 IA-32 instructions each on average. Across all programs, each region executes 27 instructions on average. EnfoRSer's regions are comparable in size to DRFx's statically bounded regions (about 10 instructions per region [40]).

The last two columns show that the vast majority of regions do not detect a conflict. The idempotent approach provides a substantially lower retry rate than the speculation approach, since the idempotent transformation uses a more precise retry check (Section 6), but we have found that making the check more precise does not significantly improve the idempotent approach's performance. The program pjbb2005 has the highest retry rate; unsurprisingly it has the highest rate of conflicts [10]. The high cost of coordination to handle these conflicts leads to high overhead for both the idempotent and speculation approaches (Section 7.3).

Table 3 evaluates the complexity of executed regions. We measure a region's complexity using the *static* count of accesses in the region, after performing the shrinking optimization from Section 5. Unsurprisingly, static data race detection helps simplify regions, i.e., executed regions tend to be less complex overall. Even so, all programs still rely on EnfoRSer's transformations for a significant number of complex regions (i.e., regions with $\geq$2 static accesses).

7.3 Performance

Figure 6 shows the overhead EnfoRSer's transformations add over unmodified Jikes RVM, *without* making use of static race detection. Each bar is the median of 15 trials (to minimize effects of machine noise); each bar shows 95% confidence intervals centered at the mean. The compiler duplicates instructions that are in multiple regions statically, adding 7% alone (not shown). The idempotent and speculation approaches add 43 and 36% total overhead, respectively.

The idempotent approach incurs costs to buffer and replay stores correctly and to check for aliasing at loads. Speculation is the better-performing approach since (in the common, non-conflicting case) it incurs only the cost of backing up each store's old value to a local variable. In a more aggressive compiler, the idempotent approach might have an advantage by enabling more intra-region reordering.

EnfoRSer adds the highest overhead for pjbb2005 (126–129%). This overhead primarily comes from the lightweight locks, which alone add 114% to pjbb2005 due to a relatively high conflicting access rate [10], which leads to expensive coordination among threads. EnfoRSer could achieve lower overhead for high-conflict executions by making use of "hybrid" lightweight locks that adaptively avoid coordination for high-conflict objects [13].

Static race detection. Figure 7 shows the same configurations when the transformations make use of statically identified DRF accesses. Identifying DRF accesses eliminates about a quarter of the overhead on average: the idempotent and speculation transformations enforce SBRS at 32 and 27% overhead, respectively. Although using static race detection seems to have a small adverse effect on idempotent performance for pjbb2005, this effect is likely due to high run-to-run variation for this program (we have confirmed that the confidence intervals overlap).

Log-based speculation. The *Speculation via log* configuration in Figures 6 and 7 measures a stripped-down version of STM that uses memory-based undo logs instead of local variables for backing up stores, but still relies on EnfoRSer's lightweight locks and efficient conflict detection. On average it adds 64 and 53% total overhead, without and with sound static race detection, respectively, significantly more than EnfoRSer's speculation approach. The memory-based log incurs these high costs despite adding just one of several costs that STMs typically incur over EnfoRSer (Section 9).

Compilation time. The overheads in Figures 6 and 7 naturally include the costs of just-in-time compilation. EnfoRSer slows the optimizing compiler by performing additional analyses and transformations, and by bloating the internal representation (IR) and slowing downstream passes. Since EnfoRSer's analysis is intraprocedural, its complexity scales well with program size. We find that compile time increases over unmodified Jikes RVM by 2.5X and 2.1X without static race detection, and 1.9X and 1.7X with static race detection, for the idempotent and speculation approaches, respectively. However, the effect of EnfoRSer's compilation overhead on overall execution time is modest: a few percent, relative to baseline execution time.

Scalability. EnfoRSer's overhead scales well when varying the number of application threads. Results are available in an extended technical report [50].

Summary. Overall, these results show that EnfoRSer enforces SBRS at a reasonable cost of 27% average overhead (using the speculation approach with sound static race detection). To our knowledge, this represents the lowest reported overhead of any kind of end-to-end RS enforcement on commodity systems. The best-performing prior work (which, admittedly, provides full-SFR RS) requires additional available cores to avoid adding over 100% overhead [45]—a fundamentally different, replication-based approach that would *not* benefit from identifying statically DRF accesses.

8. Avoiding Erroneous Behavior

This section describes a limited study of one of SBRS's potential benefits: its ability to automatically avoid errors caused by data races. To help expose such errors, we have implemented *adversarial memory* (AM), a dynamic analysis that helps expose behaviors that are allowed under the Java memory model [22, 39]. (Similar behaviors are possible under other language memory models including C++'s [8].) Under AM, each load from memory can choose from a buffer of stored values; the load may choose any value that does not violate established happens-before relationships. AM instruments potentially racy memory locations, identified by a sound dynamic race detector based on the FastTrack algorithm [9, 21].

We first identify potential errors by executing programs with AM. We use the DaCapo and SPECjbb benchmarks, as well as the smaller Java Grande benchmarks [54] evaluated by the AM paper [22]. Since the EnfoRSer implementation enforces SBRS only in Jikes RVM's optimizing compiler, our experiments forcibly compile all methods with the optimizing compiler. Table 4 reports a row for each error exposed by AM. AM exposes two different errors in SPECjbb2000. Each result is repeatable across many trials. The *JMM* column shows erroneous behaviors allowed under the Java memory model, exposed using AM.

	Erroneous behavior		
	JMM (AM alone)	**SC** (perturbation & inspection)	**SBRS** (AM + EnfoRSer)
hsqldb6	Infinite loop	None	None
sunflow9	Null ptr exception	None	None
jbb2000	Corrupt output	Corrupt output	None
jbb2000	Infinite loop	None	None
sor	Infinite loop	None	None
lufact	Infinite loop	None	None
moldyn	Infinite loop	None	None
raytracer	Fails validation	Fails validation	None

Table 4. Errors exposed by adversarial memory (AM) that are possible under the Java memory model, and whether the errors are possible under SC and SBRS.

To evaluate EnfoRSer's ability to avoid these errors, we use AM and EnfoRSer in the same execution. The compiler performs either of EnfoRSer's atomicity transformations, followed by AM's instrumentation of racy loads and stores. We integrate EnfoRSer and AM by making AM aware of the happens-before edges established by EnfoRSer's locks (e.g., coordination between threads). The *SBRS* column shows that EnfoRSer successfully avoids all erroneous behavior, by providing atomicity of statically bounded regions even in the presence of data races.

We have also determined whether these erroneous behaviors are possible under sequential consistency (SC). Despite the fact that these errors do not occur in typical runs (i.e., runs without AM), two of the errors are still possible under SC (the *SC* column):

SPECjbb2000 uses unsynchronized updates to a shared (64-bit) long field to keep track of elapsed time in milliseconds. Java makes no guarantees for the atomicity of accesses to the low and high 32 bits of a long [22, 34]. We confirmed an atomicity violation by inspecting the code. We were not able to reproduce a violation since it would take a very long time to overflow the counter's low bits (AM in fact exposes a *visibility* error by reading a stale value). SBRS avoids the errors since it inherently makes accesses to long fields atomic.

In raytracer, multiple threads perform additions to a shared int field called checksum1:

```
checksum1 = checksum1 + val; // val is thread local
```

Under SC, the program still computes an incorrect checksum if two threads' load–add–store operations interleave. SBRS eliminates the error by making the load–add–store atomic.

SC eliminates the other errors exposed by AM. We find that five out of six of these errors are *visibility* errors: a thread sees a "stale" value not possible under an SC execution. For each of these errors, a loop cannot terminate because it repeatedly sees a shared variable's stale value instead of an up-to-date value. The sixth error is in sunflow9, which throws an exception when it reads and then dereferences a stale value of null. We have been unable to expose this error under SC (or SBRS), suggesting that it is an SC violation.

In general, many real-world atomicity violations are possible under SC (e.g., [35, 36, 61]). If the region that requires atomicity is small enough, SBRS eliminates the error.

9. Related Work

Section 2 covered related work on enforcing RS-based memory models. This section covers other approaches.

Software transactional memory. *Transactional memory* (TM) guarantees atomicity of programmer-annotated code regions [25, 26]. EnfoRSer's approach is analogous to using *software* TM (STM) [25] to provide atomicity of every statically bounded region. In particular, EnfoRSer's idempotent transformation behaves similarly to a lazy-versioning STM, while its speculation transformation behaves similarly to an eager-versioning STM. However, EnfoRSer provides atomicity much more efficiently than STM for three reasons:

1. STMs maintain read/write sets (i.e., the last transaction(s) to read and write each object) to detect precisely whether an access conflicts with another thread's ongoing transaction. In contrast, EnfoRSer avoids maintaining read/write sets, at the cost of false region conflicts. The rollbacks these false conflicts trigger incur only a small penalty since statically bounded regions are short.
2. STMs that use eager or lazy versioning maintain *undo logs* or *redo logs*, respectively. At each store, the STM appends an entry to the memory-based log containing the address of the stored-to location and its old or new value. EnfoRSer can instead map each store to a dedicated local variable for deferring or backing up the store, because regions are statically bounded.
3. The locks used by EnfoRSer are a lighter-weight mechanism for conflict detection than STMs typically use, as long as relatively few accesses conflict. (Recent work introduces an STM that uses similar lightweight locks [60].)

Hardware TM. Hammond et al. introduce a memory model and associated hardware where all code is in transactions [24]. However, manufacturers have been reluctant to incorporate general-purpose *hardware* TM (HTM) support into already-complex cache and memory subsystems.

Intel's recently released Haswell architecture provides *restricted transactional memory* (RTM) support with an upper bound on shared-memory accesses in a transaction [59]. It might seem at first that RTM would be well suited to enforcing SBRS. However, two studies find that the overhead of an RTM transaction is substantial: the startup and tear-down costs of each transaction are about the same as three compare-and-swap operations [48, 59]. In contrast, EnfoRSer's approach avoids atomic operations at most accesses, most likely achieving substantially lower overhead than an approach based on atomic operations or RTM transactions (except perhaps for high-conflict workloads), although an empirical comparison is beyond the scope of this paper. Future limited HTM implementations might provide lower-overhead transactions, enabling efficient support for SBRS. In the meantime, EnfoRSer can provide reasonably efficient support for SBRS in commodity systems.

Checking for region conflicts. Prior work *checks* region conflict freedom (RCF) in order to detect SC violations and/or data races [18, 23, 37, 40, 52]. Regions can be delimited only by synchronization operations [18, 37] or statically bounded to simplify the hardware [40, 52]. These approaches rely on custom hardware [23, 37, 40, 52] or add high overhead [18]. Furthermore, checking RCF can generate errors unexpectedly, even for executions for which RS is not violated. In contrast, EnfoRSer *enforces* RCF and thus RS in commodity systems.

Enforcing atomicity in hardware. Prior work relies on custom hardware support to enforce atomicity of regions. *Atom-Aid* avoids some atomicity violations [38], while *BulkCompiler* focuses on providing SC [4]. Their regions do not correspond to well-defined regions at the source-code level (which could help programmers and analyses), although they could potentially be made to do so.

Sequential consistency. Providing end-to-end SC requires restricting reordering in both the compiler and hardware. Whole-program static analysis called *delay sets* detects possible SC violations and introduces memory fences conservatively (e.g., [51, 55]).

Hardware can reorder loads and stores speculatively (e.g., [32, 33, 47]). Compilers can be modified to enforce SC, with additional hardware support providing end-to-end SC [41, 53]. Providing end-to-end SC—a weaker property than SBRS—seems destined to add nontrivial overhead due to restricting reordering by the compiler and hardware.

Idempotent execution. De Kruijf and Sankaralingam transform regions to execute idempotently [17]. Their approach targets hardware fault recovery and thus does not detect shared-memory conflicts. The approach handles def–use dependences but not store–load dependences—the primary challenge for EnfoRSer's idempotent transformation.

10. Conclusion

EnfoRSer leverages hybrid static–dynamic analysis to ensure that statically bounded, synchronization-free regions execute atomically on commodity systems. By providing reasonable efficiency in commodity systems, EnfoRSer can help make SBRS the default memory model, spurring development of new hardware for even faster SBRS support.

Acknowledgments

We thank our shepherd, Serdar Tasiran, and the anonymous reviewers for detailed and insightful suggestions for improving this work. Thanks to Hans Boehm, Man Cao, Meisam Fathi Salmi, Jipeng Huang, Brandon Lucia, Todd Millstein, Madan Musuvathi, Andrew Myers, Satish Narayanasamy, and Chris Stone for valuable discussions, suggestions, and other feedback; and to Mayur Naik for help with Chord.

References

[1] S. V. Adve and H.-J. Boehm. Memory Models: A Case for Rethinking Parallel Languages and Hardware. *CACM*, 53:90–101, 2010.

[2] S. V. Adve and M. D. Hill. Weak Ordering—A New Definition. In *ISCA*, pages 2–14, 1990.

[3] S. V. Adve, M. D. Hill, B. P. Miller, and R. H. B. Netzer. Detecting Data Races on Weak Memory Systems. In *ISCA*, pages 234–243, 1991.

[4] W. Ahn, S. Qi, M. Nicolaides, J. Torrellas, J.-W. Lee, X. Fang, S. Midkiff, and D. Wong. BulkCompiler: High-performance Sequential Consistency through Cooperative Compiler and Hardware Support. In *MICRO*, pages 133–144, 2009.

[5] B. Alpern, S. Augart, S. M. Blackburn, M. Butrico, A. Cocchi, P. Cheng, J. Dolby, S. Fink, D. Grove, M. Hind, K. S. McKinley, M. Mergen, J. E. B. Moss, T. Ngo, and V. Sarkar. The Jikes Research Virtual Machine Project: Building an Open-Source Research Community. *IBM Systems Journal*, 44:399–417, 2005.

[6] S. M. Blackburn, R. Garner, C. Hoffman, A. M. Khan, K. S. McKinley, R. Bentzur, A. Diwan, D. Feinberg, D. Frampton, S. Z. Guyer, M. Hirzel, A. Hosking, M. Jump, H. Lee, J. E. B. Moss, A. Phansalkar, D. Stefanović, T. VanDrunen, D. von Dincklage, and B. Wiedermann. The DaCapo Benchmarks: Java Benchmarking Development and Analysis. In *OOPSLA*, pages 169–190, 2006.

[7] H.-J. Boehm. Position paper: Nondeterminism is Unavoidable, but Data Races are Pure Evil. In *RACES*, pages 9–14, 2012.

[8] H.-J. Boehm and S. V. Adve. Foundations of the C++ Concurrency Memory Model. In *PLDI*, pages 68–78, 2008.

[9] M. D. Bond, K. E. Coons, and K. S. McKinley. Pacer: Proportional Detection of Data Races. In *PLDI*, pages 255–268, 2010.

[10] M. D. Bond, M. Kulkarni, M. Cao, M. Zhang, M. Fathi Salmi, S. Biswas, A. Sengupta, and J. Huang. Octet: Capturing and Controlling Cross-Thread Dependences Efficiently. In *OOPSLA*, pages 693–712, 2013.

[11] C. Boyapati, R. Lee, and M. Rinard. Ownership Types for Safe Programming: Preventing Data Races and Deadlocks. In *OOPSLA*, pages 211–230, 2002.

[12] S. Burckhardt and M. Musuvathi. Effective Program Verification for Relaxed Memory Models. In *CAV*, pages 107–120, 2008.

[13] M. Cao, M. Zhang, and M. D. Bond. Drinking from Both Glasses: Adaptively Combining Pessimistic and Optimistic Synchronization for Efficient Parallel Runtime Support. In *WoDet*, 2014.

[14] L. Ceze, J. Devietti, B. Lucia, and S. Qadeer. A Case for System Support for Concurrency Exceptions. In *HotPar*, 2009.

[15] J.-D. Choi, K. Lee, A. Loginov, R. O'Callahan, V. Sarkar, and M. Sridharan. Efficient and Precise Datarace Detection for Multithreaded Object-Oriented Programs. In *PLDI*, pages 258–269, 2002.

[16] R. Chugh, J. W. Voung, R. Jhala, and S. Lerner. Dataflow Analysis for Concurrent Programs using Datarace Detection. In *PLDI*, pages 316–326, 2008.

[17] M. de Kruijf and K. Sankaralingam. Idempotent Code Generation: Implementation, Analysis, and Evaluation. In *CGO*, pages 1–12, 2013.

[18] L. Effinger-Dean, B. Lucia, L. Ceze, D. Grossman, and H.-J. Boehm. IFRit: Interference-Free Regions for Dynamic Data-Race Detection. In *OOPSLA*, pages 467–484, 2012.

[19] T. Elmas, S. Qadeer, and S. Tasiran. Goldilocks: A Race and Transaction-Aware Java Runtime. In *PLDI*, pages 245–255, 2007.

[20] J. Ferrante, K. J. Ottenstein, and J. D. Warren. The Program Dependence Graph and Its Use in Optimization. *TOPLAS*, 9(3):319–349, 1987.

[21] C. Flanagan and S. N. Freund. FastTrack: Efficient and Precise Dynamic Race Detection. In *PLDI*, pages 121–133, 2009.

[22] C. Flanagan and S. N. Freund. Adversarial Memory For Detecting Destructive Races. In *PLDI*, pages 244–254, 2010.

[23] K. Gharachorloo and P. B. Gibbons. Detecting Violations of Sequential Consistency. In *SPAA*, pages 316–326, 1991.

[24] L. Hammond, V. Wong, M. Chen, B. D. Carlstrom, J. D. Davis, B. Hertzberg, M. K. Prabhu, H. Wijaya, C. Kozyrakis, and K. Olukotun. Transactional Memory Coherence and Consistency. In *ISCA*, pages 102–113, 2004.

[25] T. Harris and K. Fraser. Language Support for Lightweight Transactions. In *OOPSLA*, pages 388–402, 2003.

[26] M. Herlihy and J. E. B. Moss. Transactional Memory: Architectural Support for Lock-Free Data Structures. In *ISCA*, pages 289–300, 1993.

[27] S. Horwitz, T. Reps, and D. Binkley. Interprocedural Slicing Using Dependence Graphs. In *PLDI*, pages 35–46, 1988.

[28] L. Lamport. Time, Clocks, and the Ordering of Events in a Distributed System. *CACM*, 21(7):558–565, 1978.

[29] L. Lamport. How to Make a Multiprocessor Computer That Correctly Executes Multiprocess Programs. *IEEE Computer*, 28:690–691, 1979.

[30] D. Lee, P. M. Chen, J. Flinn, and S. Narayanasamy. Chimera: Hybrid Program Analysis for Determinism. In *PLDI*, pages 463–474, 2012.

[31] D. Lee, B. Wester, K. Veeraraghavan, S. Narayanasamy, P. M. Chen, and J. Flinn. Respec: Efficient Online Multiprocessor Replay via Speculation and External Determinism. In *ASPLOS*, pages 77–90, 2010.

[32] C. Lin, V. Nagarajan, and R. Gupta. Efficient Sequential Consistency Using Conditional Fences. In *PACT*, pages 295–306, 2010.

[33] C. Lin, V. Nagarajan, R. Gupta, and B. Rajaram. Efficient Sequential Consistency via Conflict Ordering. In *ASPLOS*, pages 273–286, 2012.

[34] T. Lindholm and F. Yellin. *The Java Virtual Machine Specification*. Prentice Hall PTR, 2nd edition, 1999.

[35] S. Lu, S. Park, E. Seo, and Y. Zhou. Learning from Mistakes: A Comprehensive Study on Real World Concurrency Bug Characteristics. In *ASPLOS*, pages 329–339, 2008.

[36] S. Lu, J. Tucek, F. Qin, and Y. Zhou. AVIO: Detecting Atomicity Violations via Access-Interleaving Invariants. In *ASPLOS*, pages 37–48, 2006.

[37] B. Lucia, L. Ceze, K. Strauss, S. Qadeer, and H.-J. Boehm. Conflict Exceptions: Simplifying Concurrent Language Semantics with Precise Hardware Exceptions for Data-Races. In *ISCA*, pages 210–221, 2010.

[38] B. Lucia, J. Devietti, K. Strauss, and L. Ceze. Atom-Aid: Detecting and Surviving Atomicity Violations. In *ISCA*, pages 277–288, 2008.

[39] J. Manson, W. Pugh, and S. V. Adve. The Java Memory Model. In *POPL*, pages 378–391, 2005.

[40] D. Marino, A. Singh, T. Millstein, M. Musuvathi, and S. Narayanasamy. DRFx: A Simple and Efficient Memory Model for Concurrent Programming Languages. In *PLDI*, pages 351–362, 2010.

[41] D. Marino, A. Singh, T. Millstein, M. Musuvathi, and S. Narayanasamy. A Case for an SC-Preserving Compiler. In *PLDI*, pages 199–210, 2011.

[42] M. Musuvathi and S. Qadeer. Iterative Context Bounding for Systematic Testing of Multithreaded Programs. In *PLDI*, pages 446–455, 2007.

[43] M. Naik and A. Aiken. Conditional Must Not Aliasing for Static Race Detection. In *POPL*, pages 327–338, 2007.

[44] M. Naik, A. Aiken, and J. Whaley. Effective Static Race Detection for Java. In *PLDI*, pages 308–319, 2006.

[45] J. Ouyang, P. M. Chen, J. Flinn, and S. Narayanasamy. ...and region serializability for all. In *HotPar*, 2013.

[46] S. Park, Y. Zhou, W. Xiong, Z. Yin, R. Kaushik, K. H. Lee, and S. Lu. PRES: Probabilistic Replay with Execution Sketching on Multiprocessors. In *SOSP*, pages 177–192, 2009.

[47] P. Ranganathan, V. Pai, and S. Adve. Using Speculative Retirement and Larger Instruction Windows to Narrow the Performance Gap between Memory Consistency Models. In *SPAA*, page pages, 1997.

[48] C. G. Ritson and F. R. Barnes. An Evaluation of Intel's Restricted Transactional Memory for CPAs. In *CPA*, pages 271–292, 2013.

[49] M. Ronsse and K. De Bosschere. RecPlay: A Fully Integrated Practical Record/Replay System. *TOCS*, 17:133–152, 1999.

[50] A. Sengupta, S. Biswas, M. Zhang, M. D. Bond, and M. Kulkarni. Hybrid Static–Dynamic Analysis for Statically Bounded Region Serializability. Technical Report OSU-CISRC-11/12-TR18, Computer Science & Engineering, Ohio State University, 2015. `http://www.cse.ohio-state.edu/~mikebond/papers.html#EnfoRSer`.

[51] D. Shasha and M. Snir. Efficient and Correct Execution of Parallel Programs that Share Memory. *TOPLAS*, 10(2):282–312, 1988.

[52] A. Singh, D. Marino, S. Narayanasamy, T. Millstein, and M. Musuvathi. Efficient Processor Support for DRFx, a Memory Model with Exceptions. In *ASPLOS*, pages 53–66, 2011.

[53] A. Singh, S. Narayanasamy, D. Marino, T. Millstein, and M. Musuvathi. End-to-End Sequential Consistency. In *ISCA*, pages 524–535, 2012.

[54] L. A. Smith, J. M. Bull, and J. Obdrzálek. A Parallel Java Grande Benchmark Suite. In *SC*, pages 8–8, 2001.

[55] Z. Sura, X. Fang, C.-L. Wong, S. P. Midkiff, J. Lee, and D. Padua. Compiler Techniques for High Performance Sequentially Consistent Java Programs. In *PPoPP*, pages 2–13, 2005.

[56] K. Veeraraghavan, D. Lee, B. Wester, J. Ouyang, P. M. Chen, J. Flinn, and S. Narayanasamy. DoublePlay: Parallelizing Sequential Logging and Replay. In *ASPLOS*, pages 15–26, 2011.

[57] C. von Praun and T. R. Gross. Static Conflict Analysis for Multi-Threaded Object-Oriented Programs. In *PLDI*, pages 115–128, 2003.

[58] J. Ševčík and D. Aspinall. On Validity of Program Transformations in the Java Memory Model. In *ECOOP*, pages 27–51, 2008.

[59] R. M. Yoo, C. J. Hughes, K. Lai, and R. Rajwar. Performance Evaluation of Intel Transactional Synchronization Extensions for High-Performance Computing. In *SC*, pages 19:1–19:11, 2013.

[60] M. Zhang, J. Huang, M. Cao, and M. D. Bond. LarkTM: Efficient, Strongly Atomic Software Transactional Memory. In *PPoPP*, 2015. To appear.

[61] W. Zhang, M. de Kruijf, A. Li, S. Lu, and K. Sankaralingam. ConAir: Featherweight Concurrency Bug Recovery via Single-threaded Idempotent Execution. In *ASPLOS*, pages 113–126, 2013.

GPU Concurrency: Weak Behaviours and Programming Assumptions

Jade Alglave[1,2] Mark Batty[3] Alastair F. Donaldson[4] Ganesh Gopalakrishnan[5]
Jeroen Ketema[4] Daniel Poetzl[6] Tyler Sorensen[1,5] John Wickerson[4]

[1] University College London [2] Microsoft Research [3] University of Cambridge
[4] Imperial College London [5] University of Utah [6] University of Oxford

Abstract

Concurrency is pervasive and perplexing, particularly on graphics processing units (GPUs). Current specifications of languages and hardware are inconclusive; thus programmers often rely on folklore assumptions when writing software.

To remedy this state of affairs, we conducted a large empirical study of the concurrent behaviour of deployed GPUs. Armed with litmus tests (i.e. short concurrent programs), we questioned the assumptions in programming guides and vendor documentation about the guarantees provided by hardware. We developed a tool to generate thousands of litmus tests and run them under stressful workloads. We observed a litany of previously elusive weak behaviours, and exposed folklore beliefs about GPU programming—often supported by official tutorials—as false.

As a way forward, we propose a model of Nvidia GPU hardware, which correctly models every behaviour witnessed in our experiments. The model is a variant of SPARC Relaxed Memory Order (RMO), structured following the GPU concurrency hierarchy.

Categories and Subject Descriptors B.3.0 [*Memory structures*]: General

Keywords memory consistency, GPU, Nvidia PTX, OpenCL, litmus testing, test generation, formal model

1. Introduction

GPUs have cemented their position in computer systems: no longer restricted to graphics, they appear in critical applications, e.g. [29]. Thus programming them correctly is crucial.

Yet GPU concurrency is poorly specified. The vendors' documentation and programming guides suffer from significant omissions and ambiguities, which force programmers to rely on folklore assumptions when writing software.

To distinguish assumptions from ground truth, we questioned the hardware guarantees and the assumptions made in programming guides. Thus we conducted a large empirical study of deployed Nvidia and AMD GPUs (see Tab. 1).

vendor	architecture	chip	short name	year
Nvidia	Tesla	GTX 280	GTX 280	2008
	Fermi	GTX 540m	GTX5	2011
		Tesla C2075	TesC	2011
	Kepler	GTX 660	GTX6	2012
		GTX Titan	Titan	2013
	Maxwell	GTX 750	GTX7	2014
AMD	TeraScale 2	Radeon HD 6570	HD6570	2011
	Graphics Core Next (GCN) 1.0	Radeon HD 7970	HD7970	2012

Table 1: The GPU chips we tested

Our methodology relies on executing short programs (*litmus tests*), probing specific hardware behaviours [6, 7, 14, 17]. Central to the success of our method is a test harness: we run each test thousands of times under stressful workloads, to provoke the behaviour that the test characterises.

Our litmus tests uncovered *weak GPU behaviours*, similar to those of CPUs (e.g. IBM Power [6, 7]), which "no existing literature has been able to show how to trigger" and have been dismissed as "infinitesimally unlikely" to occur [19].[7] We observed weak behaviours on all the chips listed in Tab. 1 except the GTX 280; we henceforth omit this particular chip from our results tables. Moreover, our tests exposed as false several *programming assumptions* made in academic works [22, 42] and literature endorsed by vendors [26, 36, 38]. We summarise our findings in Tab. 2 and detail them in Sec. 3; we illustrate two key findings below.

[7] In fairness to the authors of [19], we were unable to observe weak behaviours using our method on the Nvidia GTX 280 chip they used.

ASPLOS '15, March 14–18, 2015, Istanbul, Turkey..

http://dx.doi.org/10.1145/2694344.2694391

Weak behaviours The litmus test of Fig. 1 (written in Nvidia's low level language PTX) tests for *read-read coherence* ***coRR*** violations. The left thread stores 1 into the location x, which is in global memory and initialised to 0, and the right thread, which is in the same CTA (see Sec. 2.1), loads twice from x. Read-read coherence violations occur for executions ending with register r1 holding 1 and register r2 holding 0. This behaviour seems to spark debate for CPUs: it is allowed by SPARC Relaxed Memory Order (RMO) [43, Chap. D.4], but is considered a bug on some ARM chips [12]. Yet on several Nvidia GPUs, we observed coRR violations several thousand times; for instance, the results reported at the bottom of Fig. 1 show that the GTX 540m exhibited coRR violations on 11642 out of 100k runs.

init: global x=0 **final:** r1=1 $\wedge$ r2=0 **threads:** intra-CTA

0.1	st.cg [x],1	1.1	ld.cg r1,[x]
		1.2	ld.cg r2,[x]

obs/100k	GTX5	TesC	GTX6	Titan	GTX7	HD6570	HD7970
	11642	8879	9599	9787	0	0	0

Figure 1: PTX test for coherent reads (**coRR**)

Programming assumptions Fig. 2 shows a spin lock from Nvidia's *CUDA by Example* [38, App. 1]. We show experimentally (see Sec. 3.2.2) that without the fences that we added (indicated by (+), i.e. lines 3 and 5), a critical section protected by the lock can read both stale and future values, and that clients using the lock can produce incorrect results.

```
1     __device__ void lock( void ) {
2       while( atomicCAS( mutex, 0, 1 ) != 0 );
3(+)    __threadfence();}
4     __device__ void unlock( void ) {
5(+)    __threadfence();
6       atomicExch( mutex, 0 );}
```

Figure 2: CUDA spin lock of [38, p. 253] with added fences

After we reported this issue, Nvidia published an erratum stating that their code "did not consider [weak behaviours] and requires the addition of __threadfence() instructions [...] to ensure stale values are not read" [33].

On AMD, an OpenCL analogue of Fig. 2 (see [1]) allows stale values to be read on TeraScale 2 and GCN 1.0.

Hardware vs. language We emphasise that this paper focuses on hardware behaviours. Our figures show either PTX litmus tests (i.e. Fig. 1, 3,4, 7, 8, 9, 11), or CUDA programs (i.e. Fig. 2, 6, 10). For the CUDA programs, we extracted a snippet that was susceptible to weak memory behaviours and translated it to PTX by using the mapping in Tab. 5. We then compiled the PTX litmus test to machine code, and checked that the PTX assembler did not reorder or remove memory accesses (see Sec. 4.4). Executing the litmus test on a GPU thus reveals the hardware behaviour.

As a way forward, we propose a model of Nvidia GPU hardware. Our model is based on SPARC RMO, and is stratified according to the thread hierarchy found on GPUs. We validated it against 10930 litmus tests on the Nvidia chips of Tab. 1, each executed 100k times, to confirm that it accounts for every observed behaviour.

affected	litmus tests	comment	sec.
		Nvidia	
Fermi/Kepler architectures	**coRR**	sparks debate for CPUs	3.1.1
Fermi architecture	**mp-L1**, **coRR-L2-L1**	fences do not restore orderings	3.1.2
PTX ISA [36]	**mp-volatile**	volatile documentation disagrees with testing	3.1.2
GPU Computing Gems [26]	**dlb-lb**, **dlb-mp**	fenceless deque allows items to be skipped	3.2.1
CUDA by Example [38]	**cas-sl**	fenceless lock allows stale values to be read	3.2.2
Stuart–Owens lock [42]	**exch-sl**	fenceless lock allows stale values to be read	3.2.2
He–Yu lock [22]	**sl-future**	lock allows future values to be read	3.2.3
CUDA 5.5 [32]	**coRR**	compiler reorders volatile loads	4.4
		AMD	
GCN 1.0	**mp**	compiler removes fences between loads	3.1.2
TeraScale 2	**dlb-lb**	compiler reorders load and CAS	3.2.1

Table 2: Summary of the issues revealed by our study

Contributions In essence, we present:

1. a framework for generating and running litmus tests to question memory consistency on GPU chips (see Sec. 4);
2. a set of *incantations*: heuristics for provoking weak behaviour during testing (see Sec. 4);
3. an extensive empirical evaluation across seven GPUs from Nvidia and AMD (see Tab. 1, Sec. 3 and Sec. 5);
4. details of ten correctness issues in GPU hardware, compilers and public software (see Tab. 2 and Sec. 3); and
5. a formal model of Nvidia GPUs, informed by our evaluation, providing a foundation on which to build more reliable chips, compilers and applications (see Sec. 5).

Online material We give our complete experimental reports online [1], along with extra examples and explanations.

2. Background on GPUs

A GPU (graphics processing unit) features *streaming multiprocessors* (*SMs*; *compute units* on AMD), each with multiple *cores* [36, Chap. 2–3] [34, App. G] [11, Chap. 1].

2.1 Execution hierarchy

Programs map to hardware in a hierarchical way. A *thread* (*work-item* in OpenCL) executes instructions on a core. A *warp* (*wavefront* on AMD) is a group of 32 threads (64 on AMD), which execute following the "single instruction multiple threads" model (SIMT). Thus threads in a warp execute in lock step, i.e. run the same code and share a program counter. A *cooperative thread array* (*CTA*; *block* in CUDA and *work-group* in OpenCL) consists of a configurable number of warps, all executing on the same SM. A *grid* (*NDRange* in OpenCL) can consist of millions of CTAs. A *kernel* refers to a GPU program executed by a grid.

We focus on thread interactions either in the same CTA but different warps, or in the same grid but different CTAs. We do not test inter-grid or inter-GPU interactions as we did not find any example using these features in the literature.

Additionally we do not test intra-warp interactions; this would require threads in the same warp to execute different instructions; several of our incantations (see Sec. 4) require that all threads in a warp execute the same instructions.

2.2 Memory hierarchy

Global memory is shared between all threads in a grid, and may be cached in L1 or L2 caches. The SMs each have their own L1, and share an L2. There is also one region of *shared memory* per SM, shared only by threads in the same CTA.

GPUs also provide read-only regions (e.g. CUDA *constant* and *texture* memory [34, Chap. 3.2.11]). We ignore these as they are uninteresting from a weak memory perspective: reads from a constant location all yield the same result.

2.3 Parallel Thread Execution (PTX) and OpenCL

To test hardware, we run assembly litmus tests. Nvidia's assembly, SASS, is largely undocumented, except for a list of instructions [35, Chap. 4] which does not describe their semantics. Moreover, there is no openly available assembler from SASS to binary. The AMD TeraScale 2 and GCN 1.0 architectures use the Evergreen [9] and Southern Islands [10] instruction set architectures (ISAs), respectively. These ISAs are documented but assemblers are not openly available. Below we explain how we circumvent these challenges.

Nvidia: PTX For Nvidia chips, we write our tests in Nvidia's *Parallel Thread Execution* (PTX) low-level intermediate language [36]. PTX abstracts over the ISAs of Nvidia GPUs. Sec. 4.4 explains how we relate our PTX tests to the hardware behaviours that we observe, using our optcheck tool based on Nvidia's cuobjdump [35, Chap. 2]: we inspect the SASS code and check that it has not introduced reorderings w.r.t. the initial PTX code that would alter the intention of our tests.

Our formal model of PTX (see Sec. 5) includes the following instructions: loads (`ld`), stores (`st`), ALU operations (`add`, `and`), fences (`membar`), unconditional jumps (`bra`), setting a predicate register if two operands are equal (`setp.eq`), and predicated instructions that only execute if a predicate register is set (`@p1 ...`) or unset (`@!p1 ...`). Fences are parameterised by a *scope*: `membar.cta` (resp. `.gl` or `.sys`) provides ordering within a CTA (resp. within the GPU or with the host). Other instructions bear a *cache operator*: for example, load instructions may be annotated with the cache operator `.ca` (resp. `.cg`) which specify that the load targets the L1 (resp. L2) cache. Several instructions bear a type specifier indicating their bit width and signedness [36, Chap. 5.2]. For brevity, we omit the type specifier in our examples and use the signed single word size (i.e. `.s32`) for all instructions.

Some of our examples use compare-and-swap (`atom.cas`), exchange (`atom.exch`), and `volatile` instructions (which inform the compiler that the value in memory "can be changed or used at any time by another thread" [34, p. 170] in CUDA, and "inhibit optimization" [36, p. 131] in PTX), but these instructions are not included in our model.

AMD: OpenCL AMD intermediate language (AMD IL) [8] is analogous to Nvidia PTX; but AMD does not provide compilation tools for it, so we cannot use the same approach as for Nvidia. To test AMD chips we write our tests in OpenCL, relying on the AMD OpenCL compiler to translate them into Evergreen [9] and Southern Islands [10] code. Our testing is thus constrained by the compiler; we can inspect the generated code, but unlike in the case of Nvidia PTX we cannot issue memory accesses to specific caches, apply scopes to fences, or prevent the insertion of fences by the compiler. We discuss the impact of these constraints in Sec. 3, and explain how we guard against compiler optimisations in Sec. 4.4. We give mappings that reflect how the AMD tools translate OpenCL into Evergreen and Southern Islands online [1].

3. A plea for rigour

Our testing uncovered weak behaviours, and exposed several programming assumptions as false. Tab. 2 summarises our findings; we detail them below, and discuss their implications. In essence, this litany of examples is a plea for more rigour in vendor documentation and programming guides. Otherwise, we are bound to find issues in our hardware, compilers and software, such as the ones that we present below.

The behaviours that we expose correspond to classic litmus idioms, gathered in Tab. 3, together with a brief description and the figures where the idiom appears.

name	description	figures
coRR	coherence of read-read pairs	1, 4
mp	message passing (viz. handshake)	3, 5, 7, 9
lb	load buffering	8, 11
sb	store buffering	12

Table 3: Glossary of idioms

Experimental setup For each test, we give the memory region and initial value of each location (see **init** in Fig. 3) and the placement of threads in the execution hierarchy (**threads**), and we report the number of times the final condition (**final**) is observed (**obs**) on our chips during 100k executions of the test using the most effective incantations (Sec. 4.3). The complete histogram of results for each test can be found in the online material [1]. We conducted our Nvidia experiments on four machines running Ubuntu 12.04, and our AMD experiments on a single machine running Windows 7 SP1. In the Nvidia case, Tab. 4 lists the CUDA SDK and driver versions we used, and gives the PTX architecture specification, i.e. the argument of the `-arch` compiler option. In the AMD case, Tab. 4 lists the AMD Accelerated Parallel Processing SDK and Catalyst driver versions. The SDKs include the compilation tools for the respective platforms.

	Nvidia					AMD
	GTX5	TesC	GTX6	Titan	GTX7	
SDK	5.5	5.5	5.0	6.0	6.0	2.9
driver	331.20	334.16	331.67	331.62	331.62	14.4
options	sm_21	sm_20	sm_30	sm_35	sm_50	default

Table 4: Compilers and drivers used

3.1 Weak behaviours

3.1.1 Sequential Consistency (SC) per location

This principle ensures that the values taken by a memory location are the same as if on SC [28]. Nearly all CPU models guarantee this [7], except SPARC RMO [43, Chap. D.4], which allows the weak behaviour of **coRR** (Fig. 1). As discussed in Sec. 1, this behaviour seems to spark debate for CPUs: indeed, it has been deemed a bug on some ARM chips [12]. Fig. 1 shows that we observed **coRR** on Nvidia Fermi and Kepler. We did not observe **coRR** on AMD TeraScale 2 or GCN 1.0 chips.

3.1.2 Cache operators

Message passing mp On Nvidia we test **mp** with the loads bearing the cache operator which targets the L1 cache, i.e. `.ca`, (**mp-L1**, see Fig. 3) and all threads in different CTAs. The stores bear the cache operator `.cg` because our reading of the PTX manual implies that there is no cache operator for stores that target the L1 cache [36, p. 122]. We instantiate the fence at different PTX levels [36, p. 169]: `cta`, `gl`, and `sys`, and also report our observations when the fence is removed.

We observe the weak behaviour on the Tesla C2075, no matter how strong the fences are. Note that `.ca` is the default cache operator for loads in the CUDA compiler. [36, p. 121]. *Thus no fence (i.e. membar or CUDA equivalent in Tab. 5) is sufficient under default CUDA compilation schemes (i.e. loads targeting the L1 with the .ca cache operator) to compile **mp** correctly for Nvidia Tesla C2075 (e.g. the example in the CUDA manual [34, p. 95]).*

We experimentally fix this issue by setting cache operators to `.cg` (using the CUDA compiler flags `-Xptxas -dlcm=cg -Xptxas -dscm=cg`) and using `membar.gl` fences (see test **mp+membar.gls** online [1]).

init: (`global x=0`, `global y=0`) **final:** `r1=1` $\wedge$ `r2=0` **threads:** inter-CTA

0.1	`st.cg [x],1`	1.1	`ld.ca r1,[y]`
0.2	*fence*	1.2	*fence*
0.3	`st.cg [y],1`	1.3	`ld.ca r2,[x]`

obs/100k	*fence*	GTX5	TesC	GTX6	Titan	GTX7
	`no-op`	4979	10581	3635	6011	3
	`membar.cta`	0	308	14	1696	0
	`membar.gl`	0	187	0	0	0
	`membar.sys`	0	162	0	0	0

Figure 3: PTX **mp** w/ L1 cache operators (**mp-L1**)

On AMD we cannot directly test **mp-L1**, because we do not have direct access to the caches when working with OpenCL (as explained in Sec. 2.3). Instead, we revert to the classic **mp** test, with threads in distinct OpenCL work-groups, all variables in global memory, and OpenCL global fences (`mem_fence(CLK_GLOBAL_MEM_FENCE)`) between the loads and between the stores. Without the fences, we observe **mp** on AMD GCN 1.0 (**obs**: 2956) and TeraScale 2 (**obs**: 9327). With the fences we do not observe **mp** on TeraScale 2. On GCN 1.0 we still observe **mp** when fences are inserted; inspection of the Southern Islands ISA generated by the compiler shows that the fence between load instructions is removed. It is not clear from the OpenCL specification whether this is a legitimate compiler transformation. On the one hand the specification states that "loads and stores preceding the `mem_fence` will be committed to memory before any loads and stores following the `mem_fence`" [27, p. 277]; on the other hand it states that "There is no mechanism for synchronization between work-groups" [27, p. 30]. We have reported this issue to AMD.

Coherent reads coRR We tested whether using different cache operators within the **coRR** test can restore SC. The PTX manual states that after an L2 load (i.e. `.cg`) "existing cache lines that match the requested address in L1 will be evicted" [36, p. 121]. This seems to suggest that a read from the L2 cache can affect the L1 cache.

Let us revisit **coRR** (see Fig. 1). We run a variant that we call **coRR-L2-L1** (see Fig. 4), where we first read from the L2 cache via the `.cg` operator and then from the L1 cache via the `.ca` operator. Thus the load 1.3 in Fig. 1 now holds the `.ca` operator, all the others being the same.

Fig. 4 shows that *on the Tesla C2075, no fence guarantees that updated values can be read reliably from the L1 cache even when first reading an updated value from the L2 cache.*

This issue does not apply to AMD chips for which, as discussed in Sec. 3.1.1, we did not observe **coRR**.

Volatile accesses PTX accesses can be marked `.volatile`, which supposedly [36, p. 131 for loads; p. 136 for stores] "may be used [...] to enforce sequential consistency between threads accessing shared memory". We test whether `.volatile` restores SC with shared memory with the test **mp-**

init: `global x=0`		**final:** `r1=1` $\wedge$ `r2=0`	**threads:** intra-CTA
0.1	`st.cg [x],1`	1.1	`ld.cg r1,[x]`
		1.2	*fence*
		1.3	`ld.ca r2,[x]`

obs/100k	*fence*	GTX5	TesC	GTX6	Titan	GTX7
	`no-op`	2556	2982	2	141	0
	`membar.cta`	1934	2180	0	0	0
	`membar.gl`	0	1496	0	0	0
	`membar.sys`	0	1428	0	0	0

Figure 4: PTX **coRR** mixing cache operators (**coRR-L2-L1**)

volatile (Fig. 5), a variant of **mp** where all accesses bear the `.volatile` annotation and locations are in the shared memory region and threads are in the same CTA (but different warps, see Sec. 2.1). We observe violations on Fermi and Kepler; thus, *contrarily to the PTX manual, the* `.volatile` *annotation does not restore SC for shared memory.*

init: (`shared x=0`, `shared y=0`)		**final:** `r1=1` $\wedge$ `r2=0`	**threads:** intra-CTA
0.1	`st.volatile [x],1`	1.1	`ld.volatile r1,[y]`
0.2	`st.volatile [y],1`	1.2	`ld.volatile r2,[x]`

obs/100k	GTX5	TesC	GTX6	Titan	GTX7
	6301	4977	2753	2188	0

Figure 5: PTX **mp** with volatiles (**mp-volatile**)

3.2 Programming assumptions

This section studies the assumptions that several CUDA examples from the literature make about GPUs. Each paragraph header is an assumption that we have encountered.

We give CUDA or PTX code snippets. We show the original code snippets that are susceptible to undesirable behaviours due to weak memory effects, and how they can be modified to prevent those behaviours. To show the differences between the original and the modified versions, we prefix some lines with `(-)` or `(+)`. The original code contains the lines without a prefix or prefixed with `(-)`; the modified version can be obtained by removing the lines prefixed with `(-)` and adding the lines prefixed with `(+)`.

Because our framework for testing Nvidia chips tests PTX code, we must translate CUDA to PTX. We use the mapping summarised in Tab. 5, which we discovered by examining code generated by the CUDA compiler, release 5.5 (with the compiler flags `-Xptxas -dlcm=cg -Xptxas -dscm=cg` to set cache operators to `.cg`, to guard against the behaviour shown in Sec. 3.1.2).

For the examples in Sec. 3.2.1 and 3.2.2 we have also written OpenCL litmus tests for evaluation on AMD GPUs; this was not possible for the examples in Sec. 3.2.3 because, as discussed in Sec. 2.3, we were unable to avoid automatic placement of fences by the AMD OpenCL compiler.

CUDA	PTX
`atomicCAS`	`atom.cas`
`atomicExch`	`atom.exch`
`__threadfence`	`membar.gl`
`__threadfence_block`	`membar.cta`
`atomicAdd(...,1)`	`atom.inc`
store to global int	`st.cg`
load from global int	`ld.cg`
store to volatile int	`st.volatile`
load from volatile int	`ld.volatile`
control flow (`while`, `if`)	jumps & predicated instructions

Table 5: CUDA to PTX mapping (for CUDA 5.5)

3.2.1 "GPUs exhibit no weak memory behaviours"

Several sources (e.g. [15, 26, 45]) simply omit memory model considerations. For example, Cederman and Tsigas [26, Chap. 35] describe a concurrent work-stealing double-ended queue (deque), adapting the queue of Arora et al. [13] to GPUs. The implementation seems to assume the absence of weak behaviour: it does not use fences. *Our testing shows that two bugs result from the absence of fences.*

```
    volatile int head, tail;
    void push(task){
      tasks[tail] = task;
(+)   __threadfence();
      tail++; }
    Task steal(){
      int oldHead = head;
      if (tail <= oldHead.index) return EMPTY;
(+)   __threadfence();
      task = tasks[oldHead.index];
(+)   __threadfence();
      newHead = oldHead; newHead.index++;
      if (CAS(&head,oldHead,newHead)) return task;
      return FAILED; }
    Task pop(){
      ...
      tail--;
      ...
      if( oldTail == oldHead.index )
        if( CAS(&head, oldHead, newHead) ) {
(+)       __threadfence();
          return task; }
(+)   atomicExch(head, newHead);
(-)   head = newHead;
      return FAILED; }
```

Figure 6: CUDA code for queue of [26, p. 490-491]

In the implementation of [26, Chap. 35], each CTA owns a deque that it can `push` to and `pop` from. If a CTA's deque is empty then it attempts to `steal` a task from another CTA. Each deque is implemented as an array with two indices: `tail` is incremented by `push` and decremented by `pop`, and `head` is incremented by `steal`; `tail` and `head` are declared as volatile. Fig. 6 gives part of the implementation.

Message passing The first bug arises when executing two threads T_0 and T_1 in different CTAs. T_0 pushes to its deque, writes the `tasks` array (Fig. 6, line 3) and then increments `tail` (line 5). Assume that T_1 steals from T_0, sees the increment made by T_0 (line 8), and reads the `tasks` array at index `head` (line 10). Without fences, T_1 can see a stale value of the `tasks` array, rather than the write of T_0.

init: (`global t=0`, `global d=0`) **final:** `r0=1` $\wedge$ `r1=0` **threads:** inter-CTA

		*			*
0.1	`st.cg [d],1`	3	1.1	`ld.volatile r0,[t]`	8
0.2(+)	`membar.gl`	4	1.2	`setp.eq p4,r0,0`	8
0.3	`ld.volatile r2,[t]`	5	1.3(+)	`@!p4 membar.gl`	9
0.4	`add r2,r2,1`	5	1.4	`@!p4 ld.cg r1,[d]`	10
0.5	`st.volatile [t],r2`	5			

**original line in Fig. 6*

obs/100k	GTX5	TesC	GTX6	Titan	GTX7	HD6570	HD7970
	0	4	36	65	0	0	0

Figure 7: PTX **mp** from load-balancing (**dlb-mp**)

We distilled this execution into the dynamic-load-balancing test **dlb-mp** (Fig. 7) by applying the mapping of Tab. 5 to Cederman and Tsigas' implementation [16]. Each instruction in Fig. 7 is cross-referenced to the corresponding line in Fig. 6. Without fences, the load 1.1 can read 1 and the load 1.4 can read 0, as observed on Fermi (Tesla C2075) and Kepler (GTX 660, GTX Titan). *This means reading a stale value from the task array, and results in the deque losing a task.* Adding the lines prefixed with (+) forbids this behaviour. We did not observe the weak behaviour on Maxwell or AMD.

Load buffering The second bug arises again when executing T_0 and T_1 in different CTAs. T_0 pushes to its deque, T_1 steals, reads the `tasks` array (Fig. 6, line 10) and increments `head` (line 13). T_0 pops, reads the incremented `head` with a compare-and-swap (CAS) instruction, resets `tail` and returns empty. Then T_0 pushes a new task `t`, writing to `tasks` at the original index (line 3). The implementation allows T_1's steal to read `t`, the second value pushed to the deque.

init: (`global t=0`, `global h=0`) **final:** `r0=1` $\wedge$ `r1=1` **threads:** inter-CTA

		*			*
0.1	`atom.cas r0,[h],0,1`	20	1.1	`ld.cg r1,[t]`	10
0.2(+)	`membar.gl`	21	1.2(+)	`membar.gl`	11
0.3	`mov r2,1`	3	1.3	`atom.cas r3,[h],0,1`	13
0.4	`st.cg [t],r2`	3			

**original line in Fig. 6*

obs/100k	GTX5	TesC	GTX6	Titan	GTX7	HD6570	HD7970
	0	750	399	2292	0	n/a	13591

Figure 8: PTX **lb** from load-balancing (**dlb-lb**)

We distilled this execution into the dynamic-load-balancing test (**dlb-lb**, Fig. 8), again following Tab. 5 and Cederman and Tsigas' code [16]. Without fences, the load 1.1 can read from the store 0.4, and the CAS 0.1 can read from the CAS 1.3, as observed on Fermi (Tesla C2075) and Kepler (GTX 660, GTX Titan). *This corresponds to the steal reading from the later pop, and hence the deque losing a task.* Adding the lines prefixed with (+) forbids this behaviour.

On AMD TeraScale 2 we find that the OpenCL compiler reorders T_1's load and CAS. We regard this as a miscompilation: it invalidates code that uses a CAS to synchronise between threads, even if the threads are in the same workgroup. Therefore we do not present the number of weak behaviours for HD6570 in Fig. 8 and write "n/a" instead. We reported this issue to AMD. On AMD GCN 1.0, we observe the weak behaviour of an OpenCL version of **dlb-lb**.

Adding fences (see lines prefixed with (+) in Fig. 6) forbids the behaviours of Fig. 7 and 8 in our experiments, on all Nvidia chips and on AMD GCN 1.0. As we explain in Sec. 3.2.3, pop's store to `head` requires an atomic exchange.

3.2.2 "Atomic operations provide synchronisation"

Several sources assume that read-modify-writes (RMW) provide synchronisation across CTAs (e.g. [30, 38, 42]). For example, Stuart and Owens "use `atomicExch()` instead of a volatile store and `threadfence()` because the atomic queue has predictable behavior, `threadfence()` does not (i.e. it can vary greatly in execution time if other memory operations are pending)" [42, p. 3]. Communication with the authors confirms that the weak behaviour is unintentional.

Nvidia's *CUDA by Example* [38, App. 1] makes similar assumptions. Fig. 2 shows the `lock` and `unlock` from [38, App. 1]. For now we ignore the lines prefixed with a `(+)`, which we added. Stuart and Owens' implementation [42, p. 3] is similar, but uses *atomic exchange* (an unconditional RMW) instead of CAS. The `lock` and `unlock` of Fig. 2 are used in a dot product [38, App. 1.2] (a linear algebra routine), where each CTA adds a local sum to a global sum, using locks to provide mutual exclusion. The absence of synchronisation in the lock permits stale values of the local sums to be read, leading to a wrong dot product calculation.

init: (`global x=0`, `global m=1`) **final:** `r1=0` $\wedge$ `r3=0` **threads:** inter-CTA

		*			*
0.1	`st.cg [x],1`		1.1	`atom.cas r1,[m],0,1`	2
0.2(+)	`membar.gl`	5	1.2	`setp.eq r2,r1,0`	2
0.3	`atom.exch r0,[m],0`	6	1.3(+)	`@r1 membar.gl`	3
			1.4	`@r1 ld.cg r3,[x]`	

**original line in Fig. 2*

obs/100k	GTX5	TesC	GTX6	Titan	GTX7	HD6570	HD7970
	0	47	43	512	0	508	748

Figure 9: PTX compare-and-swap spin lock (**cas-sl**)

In Fig. 9, we show the `lock` and `unlock` functions of Fig. 2, distilled into a variant of the **mp** test called **cas-sl** ("spin lock using compare-and-swap"), using the mapping in Tab. 5. We ignore the additional fences (lines 0.2 and 1.3) for now. Lines 0.1 and 1.4 correspond to a store and a load inside a critical section; the other lines cross-reference Fig. 2.

Location `m` holds the mutex, which is initially locked (i.e. `m` = 1), and `x` is the data accessed in the critical section. The left thread stores to `x` and then releases the mutex with an atomic exchange. The right thread attempts to acquire the lock with a CAS instruction (1.1), and if the lock was acquired successfully (1.2), loads from `x` (1.4). The final constraint checks whether the lock is successfully acquired (i.e. `r1 = 0`), yet a stale value of `x` is read (i.e. `r3 = 0`).

Fig. 9 gives the outcome for threads in different CTAs using global memory. *On Fermi and Kepler we observed stale values, violating the lock specification of [42], and showing the implementation from [38, App. 1] is wrong.*

Our reading of the PTX manual implies that the `.gl` fences (prefixed with a (+) in Fig. 9) forbid the weak behaviour [36, Chap. 8.7.10.2], and with them, we no longer observe it during testing. As pointed out in the introduction, our findings prompted Nvidia to publish an erratum [33] confirming the false programming assumptions of [38, App. 1].

On AMD TeraScale 2 and GCN 1.0, we observe stale values for an OpenCL version of **cas-sl** (see [1]). Thus replacing CUDA atomics with their OpenCL counterparts in the dot product of [38, App. 1] would result in an incorrect implementation. This weak behaviour is not observed experimentally by inserting OpenCL global memory fences.

3.2.3 "Only unlocks need fences"

He and Yu [22] describe how to execute transactions for databases stored in global memory. They aim to guarantee the *isolation* property [21], i.e. the database state resulting from a concurrent execution of transactions should match some serial execution of the transactions. We distill litmus tests to experimentally validate the locks used by the database operations.

Spin lock Fig. 10 shows the CUDA spin lock of [22, p. 322]. For now, we ignore the lines marked (+). The locking is handled by the CAS on line 3, the critical section is on line 7, and the write on line 10 implements the unlock.

```
1      bool leaveLoop = false;
2      while(!leaveLoop) {
3        int lockValue = atomicCAS(lockAddr,0,1);
4        if(lockValue == 0) {
5          leaveLoop = true;
6(+)       __threadfence();
7          // critical section
8(+)       __threadfence();
9(+)       atomicExch(lockAddr, 0);
10(-)      *lockAddr = 0;}
11(-)   __threadfence();}
```

Figure 10: CUDA spin lock implementation of [22, p. 322]

To investigate the correctness of the lock, we distilled the **sl-future** test, given in Fig. 11, from the CUDA code of

init: (`global x=0`, `global m=1`) **final:** `r0=1` ∧ `r2=0` **threads:** inter-CTA

		*			*
0.1	`ld.cg r0,[x]`	7	1.1	`atom.cas r2,[m],0,1`	3
0.2(+)	`membar.gl`	8	1.2	`setp.eq p,r2,0`	4
0.3(+)	`atom.exch r1,[m],0`	9	1.3	`@p mov r3,1`	5
0.4(-)	`st.cg [m],0`	10	1.4(+)	`@p membar.gl`	6
0.5(-)	`membar.gl`	11	1.5	`@p st.cg [x],1`	7

**original line in Fig. 10*

obs/100k	GTX5	TesC	GTX6	Titan	GTX7	HD6570	HD7970
	0	99	41	58	0	n/a	n/a

Figure 11: PTX spin lock future value test (**sl-future**)

Fig. 10. We assume that the threads are in different CTAs. Again, we first ignore the lines marked (+). The test checks whether a thread in the critical section can read a value from the future, i.e. written by the next critical section. The left thread reads a value within a critical section (line 0.1) then releases the lock (line 0.4). The right thread attempts to acquire the lock (line 1.1), and if successful, writes 1 to `x` in another critical section (line 1.5). The final condition checks whether the left thread can read the value written by the right thread when the right thread acquires the lock. Fig. 11 shows that this behaviour can be observed. *This effect can lead to a violation of the isolation property described above.*

The bugs arise because the CAS at the entry of the critical section (Fig. 10, line 3) does not provide any ordering nor does the release of the lock (line 10). As is, the `__threadfence()` does not help, because it appears *after* the release of the lock: this does not prevent the lock release (line 10) from being reordered with the accesses in the critical section (line 7). The fence would need to be placed before the release of the lock.

A possible fix for Fig. 10 is to remove the lines prefixed with (-), and add the lines prefixed with (+). The corrected version has fences both at the entry and exit points of the critical section. The spin lock uses CAS before entering the critical section in an attempt to provide mutual exclusion, but PTX annuls the guarantees afforded to atomic operations if other stores access the same location [36, p. 170], so we replace the normal store that releases the lock (the only other access to `lockAddr`) with an atomic exchange operation. We applied the equivalent transformations to the distilled test in Fig. 11, and did not observe the weak behaviour anymore.

4. Our testing methodology

Our testing tool takes a litmus test (as given in the previous sections) and produces a CUDA or OpenCL executable that runs the test many times while stressing the memory system, and produces a histogram of all observed outcomes.

4.1 Writing and generating litmus tests

Fig. 12 illustrates the GPU litmus format. Parts of it come from CPU litmus tests [5, 6]; others are specific to GPUs. We focus on the PTX case, the AMD case being similar.

		1	2	3	4	5	6	7	8	9	10	11	12	13	14	15	16
memory stress										●	●	●	●	●	●	●	●
general bank conflicts						●	●	●	●					●	●	●	●
thread synchronisation				●	●			●	●			●	●			●	●
thread randomisation			●		●		●		●		●		●		●		●
Nvidia GTX Titan	**coRR** (intra-CTA)	0	0	0	0	0	1235	0	9774	161	118	847	362	632	3384	3993	**9985**
	lb (inter-CTA)	0	0	0	0	0	0	0	0	181	1067	1555	**2247**	4	37	83	486
	mp (inter-CTA)	0	0	0	0	0	621	0	2921	315	1128	2372	**4347**	7	94	442	2888
	sb (inter-CTA)	0	0	0	0	0	0	0	0	462	1403	3308	**6673**	3	50	88	749
AMD Radeon HD 7970	**coRR** (intra-CTA)	0	0	0	0	0	0	0	0	0	0	0	0	0	0	0	0
	lb (inter-CTA)	10959	8979	31895	29092	13510	12729	29779	26737	5094	9360	37624	**38664**	5321	10054	32796	34196
	mp (inter-CTA)	212	31	243	158	277	46	318	247	473	217	1289	563	611	339	**2542**	1628
	sb (inter-CTA)	0	0	0	0	**2**	0	**2**	0	0	0	0	0	0	0	0	0

Table 6: Observations out of 100k executions for combinations of incantations (all tests target global memory)

```
1  GPU_PTX SB
2  {0:.reg .s32 r0;        0:.reg .s32 r2;
3   0:.reg .b64 r1 = x;  0:.reg .b64 r3 = y;
4   1:.reg .s32 r0;        1:.reg .s32 r2;
5   1:.reg .b64 r1 = y;  1:.reg .b64 r3 = x;}
6  T0                     | T1                     ;
7  mov.s32 r0,1           | mov.s32 r0,1           ;
8  st.cg.s32 [r1],r0      | st.cg.s32 [r1],r0      ;
9  ld.cg.s32 r2,[r3]      | ld.cg.s32 r2,[r3]      ;
10 ScopeTree(grid(cta(warp T0) (warp T1)))
11 x: shared, y: global
12 exists (0:r2=0 /\ 1:r2=0)
```

Figure 12: GPU PTX litmus test **sb**

Line 1 states the architecture (here GPU_PTX) and test (here SB for "store buffering", the typical x86-TSO scenario [37]). Lines 2–5 declare and initialise registers; note that PTX registers are typed (see [36, Chap. 5.2]).

Lines 6–9 list the test program with each column describing the sequential program to be executed by a thread. Each sequential program starts with an identifier (e.g. T_0), followed by a sequence of PTX instructions. The list of supported instructions is described in Sec. 2.3.

The test ends with an assertion about the final state of registers or memory. In Fig. 12, line 12 asks if T_0's register r2 and T_1's register r2 can both hold 0 at the end.

Execution hierarchy A test specifies the location of its threads in the concurrency hierarchy (see Sec. 2.1) through a *scope tree* (borrowing the term *scope* from [24, 25]). In Fig. 12, we declare the scope tree on line 10: T_0 and T_1 are in the same CTA but different warps.

Memory hierarchy A test specifies a region for each location (viz. shared or global, see Sec. 2.2) in a *memory map*, immediately after the scope tree: e.g. line 11 in Fig. 12 specifies that x is in shared memory and y is in global memory.

Automatic test generation We extended diy—a tool for systematically generating CPU litmus tests (see [6] and `http://diy.inria.fr`)—to generate GPU tests. The diy tool assumes an axiomatic modelling style (see Sec. 5.1), where non-SC executions are encoded as cyclic graphs. It takes as input a set of edges, enumerates the possible cycles that can be formed with those edges, and generates a litmus test from each cycle. The main challenge in extending diy from CPUs to GPUs was the need for a much larger set of edges, to accommodate for GPU features such as scope trees and memory maps. Additionally, because we write our tests in an intermediate language, registers must be declared before use (see lines 2–5, Fig. 12), and dependencies must be protected against compiler optimisations (see Sec. 4.5).

4.2 Running litmus tests

Our tool generates code that is split into two parts: the CPU code and the GPU kernel code.

Testing locations The tests' memory locations (viz. *testing locations*) are either in the global or shared memory region. Global testing locations are allocated and freed by the CPU while shared testing locations are statically allocated. For incantations (see Sec. 4.3), we allocate an array of global memory, distinct from the testing locations.

Testing threads In GPU programming, threads have access to their CTA id, CTA size and thread id (within the CTA) [34, p. 92]. These values can be combined to give each thread a unique *global id* within the grid. These ids differ from CPU affinity since they are part of the programming model, e.g. the semantics of CUDA's `__syncthreads()` and OpenCL's `barrier()` differs for threads in the same or distinct CTAs.

The kernel function, executed by all threads, switches based on the global id of a thread. A set of *testing threads* runs the test and records register values into a global array that the CPU can copy and record. Unused threads either exit the kernel or participate in incantations (see Sec. 4.3).

Scope tree Our tool computes global ids of the testing threads matching the scope tree specified in the litmus test: if the scope tree requires T_0 and T_1 to be in different CTAs, we compute T_0's and T_1's global id so that their CTA ids differ. Unless the thread randomisation incantation (Sec. 4.3.3) is enabled, global ids are assigned in ascending order.

4.3 Incantations

The setup of Sec. 4.2 only witnessed weak behaviours in combination with *incantations* on Nvidia chips; these incantations also influenced the incidence of weak behaviours on AMD chips. We benchmarked them on a subset of our litmus tests (see complete results online [1]). Tab. 6 gives a selection of results for the GTX Titan and Radeon HD 7970, highlighting for each test the column (i.e. combination of incantations) with the greatest incidence of weak behaviours. We write intra-CTA (resp. inter-CTA) for tests with threads in the same CTA (resp. different CTAs).

We present absolute numbers of observations over 100k runs to demonstrate the extent to which our incantations provoke weak behaviour during testing; we emphasise that for correct GPU programming the *possibility*, not *probability* of weak behaviours is what matters.

4.3.1 Memory Stress

Hypothesis Stressing caching protocols might trigger weak behaviours. For example, a bus may be more likely to transfer data out of order when it is under heavy stress than when it is only servicing a few requests.

Implementation All non-testing threads branch to a code block and repeatedly access non-testing memory locations.

Efficacy Tab. 6 shows that we did not observe **sb** and **lb** on Titan without this incantation. Combined with thread randomisation (column 12), this incantation provokes the most weak behaviours for inter-CTA tests (**lb**, **mp** and **sb**). For AMD HD7970 we did not need memory stress to observe weak behaviour, although we observe **mp** consistently more when this incantation is enabled.

4.3.2 General bank conflicts

Hypothesis GPUs access shared memory through *banks*, which can handle only one access at a time. *Bank conflicts* occur when multiple threads in a warp seek simultaneous access to locations in the same bank. Hardware might handle accesses out of order to hide the latency of bank conflicts.

Implementation Bank conflicts apply only within a warp, so this incantation is performed only by threads in the same warp as a testing thread. The non-testing threads perform the same actions as the testing thread, but on locations that are offset from the testing locations. These offsets can be calculated either to produce bank conflicts or to avoid them, and we randomly oscillate between these on each iteration of the test. For warps that do not contain a testing thread, the threads either exit as in the basic testing setup (see Sec. 4.2), or perform the memory stress incantation (see Sec. 4.3.1).

Efficacy Tab. 6 shows that for intra-CTA tests (**coRR**), this incantation combined with all others (column 15) provokes the most weak behaviours on Titan. However, general bank conflicts alone do not expose any weak behaviours (see column 5), and even consistently reduce the number of inter-CTA weak behaviours when combined with memory stress: comparing columns 12 and 16 (which differ only by general bank conflicts), the number of weak behaviours for **lb** decreased from 2247 to 486. On HD7970 we only observed **sb** when bank conflicts were enabled, but this weak behaviour is still notably infrequent; we observe **mp** consistently more often when the incantation is enabled.

4.3.3 Thread randomisation

Hypothesis Varying the layout, e.g. the thread ids of testing threads and the number of threads per kernel, of a test in the execution hierarchy, in a way that is consistent with the scope tree of the test, might exercise different components and paths through the hardware and hence, increase the likelihood of weak behaviours

Implementation We randomly select the ids of testing threads and the number of non-testing threads, while respecting the scope tree, on each test execution.

Efficacy Tab. 6 shows that for all tests, thread randomisation contributes to the columns yielding the most weak behaviours on Titan. In intra-CTA tests (**coRR**) thread randomisation increases the number of weak behaviours observed dramatically: comparing columns 15 and 16 (which differ only by thread randomisation), the number of weak behaviours for **coRR** increased from 3993 to 9985. On HD7970, thread randomisation consistently decreases the extent to which we observe **mp**, but consistently increases observations of **lb** when combined with memory stress.

4.3.4 Thread synchronisation

Hypothesis Synchronising testing threads immediately before running the test pomotes interactions while values are actively moving through the memory system, which might increase the likelihood of weak behaviours.

Implementation Testing threads synchronise immediately before running the test by atomically incrementing a counter and busy-waiting until the counter reaches the number of threads participating in the test. Compared with a similar incantation used in CPU testing [5] we had to take care to avoid deadlock due to the lack of progress guarantees across CTAs [34, p. 12] and within warps [20].

Efficacy Tab. 6 records the most weak behaviours on Titan when thread synchronisation is enabled. In inter-CTA tests (**lb**, **mp**, and **sb**) thread synchronisation increases the number of weak behaviours dramatically: comparing columns 10 and 12 (which differ only by thread synchronisation), the number of weak behaviours observed for **sb** increased from 1403 to 6673. For HD7970, thread synchronisation consistently increases observations of **lb** and **mp**.

4.4 Checking for optimisations

We now discuss how we guard against unwanted compiler optimisations in the case of Nvidia and AMD.

For Nvidia, recall from Sec. 2.3 that we write our tests in PTX. We compile this to SASS machine-level assembly with the ptxas assembler, which optimises the code for efficiency.

If we invoke the assembler with minimal optimisations (-O0), we find that although each PTX load or store has a corresponding SASS load or store, instructions that were adjacent in the PTX code are separated by several instructions in the SASS code. This is undesirable for testing: it can make the difference between observing weak behaviours or not.

If we invoke the assembler with maximal optimisations (-O3), most intermediate instructions are optimised away. However, we found that on rare occasions some instructions were reordered. For example, testing **coRR** on Maxwell uncovered cases where the CUDA 5.5 compiler reordered volatile loads to the same address; we did not observe this for CUDA 6.0. This is again harmful for testing, as we could attribute weak behaviours to the hardware, when in fact they were introduced by the compiler. In fact, such optimisations can occur at any optimisation level, in principle even at -O0 (which does not fully disable optimisations).

To overcome these challenges, we developed the optcheck tool that detects whether SASS code has been optimised. To do this, we first add instructions to the PTX code of a litmus test that specify certain properties of the test, such as the order of instructions within a thread. The compiled code thus contains both the litmus test code and the specification. Our optcheck tool takes a binary, obtains the corresponding SASS code using cuobjdump [35, Chap. 2], and then checks whether the SASS code and the specification are consistent.

A specification (in PTX) consists of a sequence of `xor` instructions, placed at the end of each thread, for example:

```
register used ─────┐              ┌─ instruction type
      xor.b32 r2, rb, 0x07f3a001
constant ─────────────────┘    └──── position
```

Each `xor` instruction corresponds to exactly one memory access instruction. The integer literal of an `xor` instruction (last operand) specifies several properties of the corresponding access: which register it uses, what type of instruction it is (e. g. 00 for a load with cache operator `.cg`), and its position in the order of memory access instructions. The constant serves to distinguish these specification instructions from any `xor` instructions that appear in the code. In the litmus tests we generate, the accesses within a thread use different registers, so we can always create a one-to-one correspondence between memory accesses and `xor` instructions.

Our optcheck tool was essential in checking the data which informs our model of PTX (Sec. 5); this data comes from running 10930 tests on the Nvidia chips of Tab. 1. Our AMD testing is for now more modest: 12 distinct litmus tests to assess weak behaviours and programming assumptions in Sec. 3 and 14 tests to evaluate the incantations of Sec. 4.3.

For all these tests we checked the generated Evergreen (for TeraScale 2) and Southern Islands (for GCN 1.0) ISA files by hand to guard against unwanted compiler optimisations. We observed that multiple loads from the same location (e.g in Fig. 1) get optimised into a single load. We explain online [1] how to suppress this optimisation. We also explain how to check whether the order of loads and stores is consistent with the original litmus test.

4.5 Manufacturing dependencies

We also want to test whether dependencies between memory accesses have an effect on memory consistency. For CPUs, such litmus tests use *false dependencies* [6]: ones that have no effect on the computed values. For example, in the PTX code snippet in Fig. 13a, there is an *address dependency* between the load in line 1 and the load in line 5, since the result of the first load is used to compute the address of the memory location accessed by the second load. The dependency is a false dependency as the result of the `xor` is always 0, so the subsequent `add` never changes the value of the address register `r4`.

```
1 ld.s32 r1, [r0]
2 xor.b32 r2, r1, r1
3 cvt.u64.u32 r3, r2
4 add.u64 r4, r4, r3
5 ld.s32 r5, [r4]
```

(a) Optimised by ptxas (-O3)

```
1 ld.s32 r1, [r0]
2 and.b32 r2, r1, 0x80000000
3 cvt.u64.u32 r3, r2
4 add.u64 r4, r4, r3
5 ld.s32 r5, [r4]
```

(b) Not optimised by ptxas (-O3)

Figure 13: Load-load address dependencies

Since we compile our litmus tests with the highest optimisation settings (cf. Sec. 4.4), the PTX assembler would recognise that the result of the `xor` is always 0, and hence remove lines 2–4, thereby removing the dependency. Therefore, we use a different scheme for testing dependencies, exemplified in Fig. 13b. It is based on `and`-ing with a constant that has just the high bit set. The result of this operation will always be 0, since in our litmus tests all memory locations are initialised to 0 and the store instructions only write small positive values (with the high bit being 0). However, determining that the result is 0 would require an inter-thread analysis (which the PTX assembler does not perform). Thus, the dependency is left intact.

5. A model of Nvidia GPUs

Sec. 3 illustrates some difficulties faced by GPU programmers. One crucial issue is to reliably predict the possible behaviours of concurrent GPU programs. As a step forward, we present a formal model for a fragment of PTX. We also propose a simulation tool that determines the allowed behaviours of PTX litmus tests w.r.t. our formal model.

5.1 Axiomatic models

Our model is axiomatic (see e.g. [6, 7]), thus discriminates, for a given program, its *candidate executions*. Given a PTX program we build a set of candidate executions which our model partitions into executions that are *allowed* (the program *may* behave in this manner) or *forbidden* (the program *cannot* behave in this manner).

init: (`global x=0`, `global y=0`)		**final:** `r0=1` ∧ `r2=0`	**threads:** intra-CTA
0.1	`st.cg [x],1`	1.1	`ld.cg r0,[y]`
0.2	`membar.cta`	1.2	`membar.gl`
0.3	`st.cg [y],1`	1.3	`ld.cg r2,[x]`

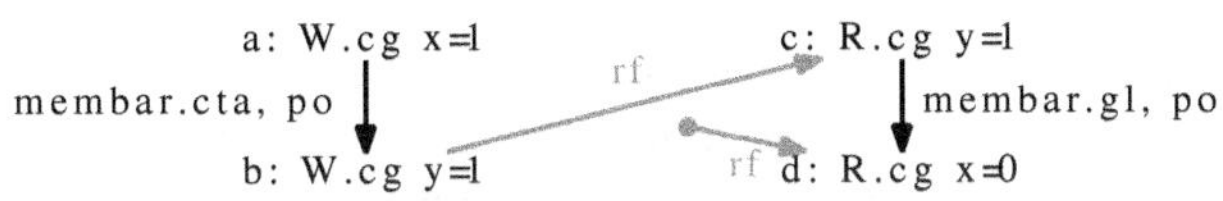

Figure 14: An execution of the **mp** test, similar to Fig. 3

5.1.1 Candidate executions

Informally, a candidate execution is a graph (see e.g. Fig. 14), which consists of a set of *memory events* for each thread, and relations over these events. These relations describe the *program order* within a thread, the *communications* between threads, and specifically for GPUs, the *scopes* of threads along the memory hierarchy.

Memory events give a semantics to instructions (we omit the formal instruction semantics for brevity). Essentially, loads give rise to *reads*, and stores to *writes*.

For example in the test of Fig. 14, the first thread issues two stores, the first one to memory location x and the second one to location y, separated by a fence (`membar.cta`). In the execution graph of Fig. 14, we have two corresponding write events, bearing the same cache operator (cg), and mentioning the same locations and values as the store instructions. The second thread issues two loads from y and x, separated by a fence (`membar.gl`). In the execution graph, we have two corresponding read events, bearing the same cache operator (cg), and mentioning the same locations as the load instructions. The values of the reads are given by the final state of the litmus test.

Scope relations link events from threads in the same CTA (`cta`), same grid (`gl`) and anywhere in the system (`sys`). Note that the `sys` relation is simply the universal relation between all events.

The program order relation (`po`) totally orders events in a thread, and does not relate events from different threads.

The *dependency* relation `dp`, included in `po`, relates events in program order whose instructions are separated by an *address* (`addr`), *data* (`data`) or *control* (`ctrl`) dependency.

Similarly, the `membar` *fence* relations, included in `po`, relate events whose instructions are separated by a fence. There is one relation per strength of fence, `sys`, `gl` and `cta`. In Fig. 14 the fence on the first thread corresponds to the `membar.cta` relation between the writes a and b.

Communication relations The *read-from relation* (`rf`) associates every read r with a unique corresponding write that agrees with r on variable and value components. In Fig. 14, the load of y on the second thread reads from the store of y on the first thread, as indicated by the final state (`r0=1`). Thus we have a read-from between the two corresponding events b and c. The load of x on the second thread reads from the initial state (since `r2=0` in the final state), which is depicted as a `rf` arrow with no source pointing to the read d.

Writes to a single location are totally ordered by *coherence* `co`, i.e. the order in which they hit the memory.

5.1.2 From a PTX litmus to its candidate executions

Recall that a PTX litmus test (see Sec. 4.1 and Fig. 12) specifies the shared variables, with initial values, the sequence of instructions for each thread, and a scope tree describing how the threads are organised into warps and CTAs.

We can enumerate the candidate execution graphs of a litmus test by unwinding the body of each thread: this gives us the program order `po` for each thread, as well as the dependency and fence relations, which are included in `po`. The scope relations come directly from the scope tree. Once these relations are established, any choice for the read-from and coherence relations respecting the above definitions yields a candidate execution graph.

5.2 Defining our model

Given a candidate execution graph, originating from a PTX litmus test, we seek to answer the question of whether the execution is allowed or not. As mentioned earlier, we achieve this through an axiomatic model. Essentially, an axiomatic model lists a set of constraints over execution graphs, built from the primitive relations described above, such that an execution is *allowed* if and only if it satisfies the constraints.

5.2.1 Derived relations over events

The following derived relations are useful in defining the constraints of our model.

The relation `po-loc` is the program order `po` restricted to events having the same memory location.

The relation `rfe` is the `rf` relation restricted to *external* events, i.e. events coming from different threads. For example in Fig. 14 the read-from relation between b and c is in fact an `rfe` relation, as b and c belong to distinct threads.

The from-read relation `fr` relates a read r to all the writes overwriting the value r reads from. Formally, (r, w) relates by `fr` when r reads from a write w' (i.e. (w', r) is in `rf`) such that w' hits the memory before w (i.e. (w', w) is in `co`).

In Fig. 14, the read of x on the second thread reads from the initial state. By convention the initial state for a given location hits the memory before any update to this location; thus the read d of x is in `fr` with the update a of x.

```
1  let com = rf | co | fr
2  let po-loc-llh =
3    WW(po-loc) | WR(po-loc) | RW(po-loc)
4  acyclic (po-loc-llh | com) as sc-per-loc-llh
5  let dp = addr | data | ctrl
6  acyclic (dp | rf) as no-thin-air
7  let rmo(fence) = dp | fence | rfe | co | fr
```

Figure 15: RMO `.cat` file

5.2.2 The `.cat` format illustrated on Sparc RMO

The `.cat` format of [7] uses a small language that allows the user to describe an axiomatic model in a succinct way. A `.cat` file, together with a litmus test, can be given to the herd tool (see [7] and `http://diy.inria.fr/herd`). Given an instruction semantics module (i.e. a way to translate a program into a set of candidate executions) for the language under scrutiny (in our case PTX), the tool takes a `.cat` file (e.g. the one in Fig. 16) to produce a simulator that enumerates all the valid executions of a litmus test.

Syntax of* `.cat` *files In Fig. 15 and 16, we use several syntactic constructs that we list here. One declares new relations with `let`. The union of relations is written `|`, and their intersection is `&`. One can obtain a subrelation of a relation `r` using various filters: for example `WW(r)` returns only the pairs of write events related by `r`; `RW(r)` returns the read-write pairs related by `r`. One can enforce the acyclicity of a relation `r` by declaring the check `acyclic r`. One can give a name to such a check with the keyword `as`; for example `acyclic (po | com) as sc` declares a new check `sc`, that enforces the acyclicity of the union of program order and communication relations.

Our model resembles Sparc's Relaxed Memory Order (RMO) [43], factoring in the GPU concurrency hierarchy. As an introduction to the `.cat` syntax, we present here the `.cat` transcription of Sparc RMO as formalised in [3].

Intuitively, RMO allows any pair of memory accesses to different locations to be reordered, unless separated by a dependency or a fence. For example, RMO allows the non-SC behaviour of **mp** (see Fig. 14). To forbid this behaviour, one can use a fence between instructions 0.1 and 0.3 and a dependency between instructions 1.1 and 1.3. Additionally, RMO allows the test **coRR** of Fig. 1.

Formally, RMO relies on three principles, detailed below.

SC PER LOCATION WITH LOAD-LOAD HAZARD Most CPU hardware guarantees what we call SC PER LOCATION, explained in Sec. 3.1.1. RMO relaxes this constraint, as it allows **coRR** (Fig. 1). As shown in Fig. 1, Nvidia chips exhibit this behaviour; thus our model allows it.

Formally, following [3, 4, 7], this corresponds to the constraint `sc-per-loc-llh` on line 4 of Fig. 15, which builds on the definitions on lines 1 and 3. More precisely, line 1 defines the relation `com` (for communication) as the union of

```
8   let sys-fence = membar.sys
9   let gl-fence = membar.gl | sys-fence
10  let cta-fence = membar.cta | gl-fence
11  let rmo-cta = rmo(cta-fence) & cta
12  let rmo-gl = rmo(gl-fence) & gl
13  let rmo-sys = rmo(sys-fence) & sys
14  acyclic rmo-cta as cta-constraint
15  acyclic rmo-gl as gl-constraint
16  acyclic rmo-sys as sys-constraint
```

Figure 16: RMO per scope

`rf`, `co` and `fr`. Line 3 defines `po-loc-llh`: program order over single locations without read-read pairs. We require on line 4 that communications do not contradict `po-loc-llh`.

The weak behaviour of **coRR** is allowed by our model, because we excluded the read-read pairs from the `sc-per-loc-llh` check at line 3.

NO THIN AIR prevents *causal loops*: where the dependency and reads-from, that intuitively suggest causation, form a cycle. Load buffering tests, e.g. **dlb-lb** (Fig. 8), check for violations of this principle. Formally, following [3, 4, 7], this corresponds to lines 5-6. Line 5 defines the relation `dp` (for dependencies), made of the union of address, data, and control dependencies. Line 6 declares the check `no-thin-air`, which requires that the union of `dp` and `rf` is acyclic.

The* `rmo` *relation declared at line 7 collects the orderings due to dependencies `dp`, inter-thread communication `rfe`, `co` and `fr`, and fences `fence`, where the behaviour of fences is left parametric. Constraints over `rmo` can be used to forbid the weak behaviour of idioms such as message passing **mp** or store buffering **sb**, when using the appropriate ordering, e.g. fences between writes and dependencies between reads. Such constraints are at the heart of our PTX model.

5.3 Our PTX model

Our model is the concatenation of Fig. 15 and 16, and implements RMO *per scope*. In contrast to RMO for CPUs, for which Fig. 15 suffices, our PTX model duplicates the `rmo` relation at each scope (see lines 11, 12 and 13).

More precisely, lines 8–10 declare the relations `sys-fence`, `gl-fence` and `cta-fence`, which provide ordering within the named scopes. Lines 11–13 then instantiate the generic `rmo` relation (see Fig. 15, line 7) for each scope of fence, using the intersection operator (`&`) to restrict to the appropriate scope. Lines 14–16 enforce the acyclicity of the three `rmo` relations; this implements RMO at each scope.

In Fig. 14, the execution of **mp** exhibits a cycle in the union of `membar.cta`, `rfe`, `fr` and `membar.gl`, i.e. a cycle in `rmo-cta`. Our model forbids this execution by the constraint `cta-constraint` at line 14.

5.4 Validating our model

We developed a PTX simulator as part of the herd tool [7]: it enumerates, for a litmus test, its candidate executions (see Sec. 5.1.1), then discriminates them following our PTX model (see Fig. 15 and 16). We automatically generated 10930 tests with our extension of the diy tool (see Sec. 4.1).

We supplied all our tests to herd, and our PTX .cat model: our model is experimentally sound w.r.t. our 10930 tests for the Nvidia chips of Tab. 1. This means that whenever the hardware exhibits a behaviour, our model allows it. We provide all experimental data for all chips online [1].

5.5 Limitations of our model

Our model reflects the hardware behaviour of a PTX program, compiled in the setup given in Tab. 1, in which accesses of shared data have not been reordered or optimised, as checked by our optcheck tool (see Sec. 4.4). The limitations of our model are as follows: we only handle the instructions listed in Sec. 2.3, and we assume that all accesses use the .cg cache operator (which targets the L2 cache).

The reason for choosing .cg is that our observations on Fermi (see 3.1.2) show that it is not possible to restore ordering between accesses marked .ca (targeting the L1).

6. Related work

Testing and modelling Our method follows the work of Alglave et al. [4–7] for CPUs, which follows the steps of Collier [17]. More precisely, in [17] Collier presents the ARCHTEST tool for CPUs, which runs a small number of fixed tests to check for discrepancies with Lamport's Sequential Consistency [28], e.g. **coRR** (see Fig. 1). Using few handwritten tests has limitations, as rich sets of litmus tests were required to inform the formalisation of weak architectures such as IBM Power [6, 7, 39]. Alglave et al. [6] developed a method to automatically generate litmus tests for CPUs based on the axiomatic framework of [4, 6], and implemented their approach in the diy toolsuite (see [5–7] and http://diy.inria/fr). The toolsuite generates and runs systematic families of litmus tests, and collects their outcomes. As detailed in Sec. 4, we implemented several novel extensions to make these tools suitable for GPUs.

Microbenchmarking is loosely related to our approach. While we are concerned with semantics, microbenchmarking gathers performance data. The GPUBench [2] suite gathers statistics such as memory bandwidth and instruction throughput of AMD and Nvidia GPUs. Wong et al. [44] developed a test suite to reveal microarchitectural aspects of Nvidia GeForce GT200 and GTX280 GPUs: they draw conclusions about the latency of memory accesses, or the structure of the caches. Feng and Xiao [19] analyse the overhead of barrier synchronisation.

Checking for optimisations Our checking whether a litmus test has been optimised (see Sec. 4.4) is related to testing of compiler optimisations for concurrent programs.

Eide and Regehr check whether accesses to C volatile variables are compiled correctly [18]. They compile a test case both with and without optimisations (e.g. -O3 and -O0), then run both versions with the same input while logging the accesses to volatile variables. If the traces of the two versions differ, an invalid optimisation has been detected. Morisset et al. extend this work to a subset of C++11 [31].

Our approach differs from these in that we do not make use of an unoptimised version of the code, but instead embed a specification of the expected instruction sequence into the optimised version. Moreover, we statically check whether the compiled code conforms to the specification. Finally, the methods have different aims: our aim is not to find compiler bugs but to detect unwanted reorderings due to compilation.

GPU models Hower et al. proposed several models for GPUs [24, 25]. All of these models are "SC-for-DRF" models, i.e. only concern data race free programs, and ensure that such programs have an SC semantics. Somewhat relatedly, Hechtman and Sorin show that weak memory has negligible performance benefits on their set of benchmarks, thus argue that SC is an attractive model for GPUs [23]. By contrast, and since we are concerned with hardware, we give semantics to race free and racy programs alike.

Sorensen et al. [40, 41] proposed an operational model of Nvidia hardware, based on reading the Nvidia documentation and communication with Nvidia representatives; they provide intuition about their model using GPU litmus tests similiar to the ones we present (e.g. Fig. 1). However, this model is unsound w.r.t. hardware: the inter-CTA **lb+membar.ctas** test, i.e. a variant of **dlb-lb** (Fig. 8) without atomics and with membar.cta fences between all accesses, is *forbidden* by the model, but observed 586 times on GTX Titan and 19 times on GTX 660 out of 100k iterations (see [1]).

7. Perspectives

The present work uncovered weak behaviours, and exposed several programming assumptions as false, summarised in Tab. 2. We use these examples to plead for clarity and rigour in vendor documentations. We believe that formal models, such as the one we propose in Sec. 5, can help remedy this situation, providing a rigorous basis on which to build our systems. Further steps towards that goal include building language level models (e.g. for OpenCL), and sound compilation mappings from language to hardware.

Acknowledgments We thank Luc Maranget for feedback on extending litmus and diy, Mary Hall for lending us her group's machines, Tom Stellard for feedback on setting up our AMD testbed, Matt Arsenault and Brad Beckmann for clarification on the AMD OpenCL compiler behaviour, and Benedict Gaster, Peter Sewell, Tatiana Shpeisman and our reviewers for their feedback.

Support EPSRC grants EP/{H005633, H008373, K008528, K011499, K039431}, EU FP7 project CARP (287767), NSF CCF Awards 1346756 and 1302449, and SRC project 2269.002.

References

[1] Online companion material. http://virginia.cs.ucl.ac.uk/sunflowers/asplos15/.

[2] GPUBench, June 2014. http://graphics.stanford.edu/projects/gpubench.

[3] J. Alglave. *A Shared Memory Poetics*. PhD thesis, Université Paris 7, 2010.

[4] J. Alglave. A formal hierarchy of weak memory models. *Formal Methods in System Design (FMSD)*, 41(2):178–210, 2012.

[5] J. Alglave, L. Maranget, S. Sarkar, and P. Sewell. Litmus: Running tests against hardware. In *Tools and Algorithms for the Construction and Analysis of Systems (TACAS)*, pages 41–44, 2011.

[6] J. Alglave, L. Maranget, S. Sarkar, and P. Sewell. Fences in weak memory models (extended version). *Formal Methods in System Design (FMSD)*, 40(2):170–205, 2012.

[7] J. Alglave, L. Maranget, and M. Tautschnig. Herding cats: Modelling, simulation, testing, and data mining for weak memory. *ACM Transactions on Programming Languages and Systems (TOPLAS)*, 36(2):7, 2014.

[8] AMD. AMD intermediate language (IL), version 2.4, Oct. 2011.

[9] AMD. Evergreen family instruction set architecture: Instructions and microcode, revision 1.1a, Nov. 2011.

[10] AMD. Southern Islands series instruction set architecture, revision 1.1, Dec. 2012.

[11] AMD. AMD accelerated parallel processing OpenCL programming guide, Nov. 2013.

[12] ARM. Cortex-A9 MPCore, programmer advice notice, read-after-read hazards ARM reference 761319, Sept. 2011.

[13] N. S. Arora, R. D. Blumofe, and C. G. Plaxton. Thread scheduling for multiprogrammed multiprocessors. In *Symposium on Parallelism in Algorithms and Architectures (SPAA)*, pages 119–129, 1998.

[14] H. Boehm and S. V. Adve. Foundations of the C++ concurrency memory model. In *Programming Language Design and Implementation (PLDI)*, pages 68–78, 2008.

[15] D. Cederman and P. Tsigas. On dynamic load balancing on graphics processors. In *SIGGRAPH/Eurographics*, pages 57–64, 2008.

[16] D. Cederman and P. Tsigas. Dynamic load balancing on graph ics processors, Feb. 2014. http://www.cse.chalmers.se/research/group/dcs/gpuloadbal.html.

[17] W. Collier. *Reasoning About Parallel Architectures*. Prentice-Hall, 1992.

[18] E. Eide and J. Regehr. Volatiles are miscompiled, and what to do about it. In *Embedded software (EMSOFT)*, pages 255–264, 2008.

[19] W. Feng and S. Xiao. To GPU synchronize or not GPU synchronize? In *International Symposium on Circuits and Systems (ISCAS)*, pages 3801–3804, 2010.

[20] A. Habermaier and A. Knapp. On the correctness of the SIMT execution model of GPUs. In *European Symposium on Programming (ESOP)*, pages 316–335, 2012.

[21] T. Härder and A. Reuter. Principles of transaction-oriented database recovery. *Computing Survey (CSUR)*, 15(4):287–317, 1983.

[22] B. He and J. X. Yu. High-throughput transaction executions on graphics processors. *The Proceedings of the VLDB Endowment (PVLDB)*, 4(5):314–325, 2011.

[23] B. A. Hechtman and D. J. Sorin. Exploring memory consistency for massively-threaded throughput-oriented processors. In *International Symposium on Circuits and Systems (ISCA)*, pages 201–212, 2013.

[24] D. R. Hower, B. M. Beckmann, B. R. Gaster, B. A. Hechtman, M. D. Hill, S. K. Reinhardt, and D. A. Wood. Sequential consistency for heterogeneous-race-free. In *Memory Systems Performance and Correctness (MSPC)*, 2013.

[25] D. R. Hower, B. A. Hechtman, B. M. Beckmann, B. R. Gaster, M. D. Hill, S. K. Reinhardt, and D. A. Wood. Heterogeneous-race-free memory models. In *Architectural Support for Programming Languages and Operating Systems (ASPLOS)*, pages 427–440, 2014.

[26] W.-m. W. Hwu. *GPU Computing Gems Jade Edition*. Morgan Kaufmann Publishers Inc., 2011.

[27] Khronos OpenCL Working Group. The OpenCL specification (version 1.2, revision 19), Nov. 2012.

[28] L. Lamport. How to make a multiprocessor computer that correctly executes multiprocess programs. *IEEE Transactions on Computers*, 28(9):690–691, 1979.

[29] S. Lee, Y. Kim, J. Kim, and J. Kim. Stealing webpages rendered on your browser by exploiting GPU vulnerabilities. In *Symposium on Security and Privacy (SP)*, pages 19–33, 2014.

[30] P. Misra and M. Chaudhuri. Performance evaluation of concurrent lock-free data structures on GPUs. In *International Conference on Parallel and Distributed Systems, (ICPADS)*, pages 53–60, 2012.

[31] R. Morisset, P. Pawan, and F. Z. Nardelli. Compiler testing via a theory of sound optimisations in the C11/C++11 memory model. In *Programming Language Design and Implementation (PLDI)*, pages 187–196, 2013.

[32] Nvidia. CUDA C programming guide, version 5.5, July 2013.

[33] Nvidia. CUDA by example — errata, June 2014. http://developer.nvidia.com/cuda-example-errata-page.

[34] Nvidia. CUDA C programming guide, version 6, July 2014.

[35] Nvidia. CUDA binary utilities, Aug. 2014. http://docs.nvidia.com/cuda/pdf/CUDA_Binary_Utilities.pdf.

[36] Nvidia. Parallel thread execution ISA: Version 4.0, Feb. 2014.

[37] S. Owens, S. Sarkar, and P. Sewell. A better x86 memory model: x86-tso. In *Theorem Proving in Higher Order Logics (TPHOLs)*, pages 391–407, 2009.

[38] J. Sanders and E. Kandrot. *CUDA by Example: An Introduction to General-Purpose GPU Programming*. Addison-Wesley Professional, 2010.

[39] S. Sarkar, P. Sewell, J. Alglave, L. Maranget, and D. Williams. Understanding POWER multiprocessors. In *Programming Language Design and Implementation (PLDI)*, pages 175–186, 2011.

[40] T. Sorensen. Towards shared memory consistency models for GPUs. Bachelor's thesis, University of Utah, 2013.

[41] T. Sorensen, G. Gopalakrishnan, and V. Grover. Towards shared memory consistency models for GPUs. In *International Conference on Supercomputing (ICS)*, pages 489–490, 2013.

[42] J. A. Stuart and J. D. Owens. Efficient synchronization primitives for GPUs. *Computing Research Repository (CoRR)*, abs/1110.4623, 2011. `http://arxiv.org/pdf/1110.4623.pdf`.

[43] D. L. Weaver and T. Germond. *The SPARC Architecture Manual Version 9*. SPARC International Inc., 1994.

[44] H. Wong, M.-M. Papadopoulou, M. Sadooghi-Alvandi, and A. Moshovos. Demystifying GPU microarchitecture through microbenchmarking. In *Performance Analysis of Systems Software (ISPASS)*, pages 235–246, 2010.

[45] S. Xiao and W. Feng. Inter-block GPU communication via fast barrier synchronization. In *International Symposium on Parallel and Distributed Processing (IPDPS)*, pages 1–12, 2010.

Chimera: Collaborative Preemption for Multitasking on a Shared GPU

Jason Jong Kyu Park
University of Michigan
Ann Arbor, MI
jasonjk@umich.edu

Yongjun Park *
Hongik University
Seoul, Korea
yongjun.park@hongik.ac.kr

Scott Mahlke *
University of Michigan
Ann Arbor, MI
mahlke@umich.edu

Abstract

The demand for multitasking on graphics processing units (GPUs) is constantly increasing as they have become one of the default components on modern computer systems along with traditional processors (CPUs). Preemptive multitasking on CPUs has been primarily supported through context switching. However, the same preemption strategy incurs substantial overhead due to the large context in GPUs. The overhead comes in two dimensions: a preempting kernel suffers from a long preemption latency, and the system throughput is wasted during the switch. Without precise control over the large preemption overhead, multitasking on GPUs has little use for applications with strict latency requirements.

In this paper, we propose *Chimera*, a collaborative preemption approach that can precisely control the overhead for multitasking on GPUs. *Chimera* first introduces streaming multiprocessor (SM) flushing, which can instantly preempt an SM by detecting and exploiting idempotent execution. *Chimera* utilizes flushing collaboratively with two previously proposed preemption techniques for GPUs, namely context switching and draining to minimize throughput overhead while achieving a required preemption latency. Evaluations show that *Chimera* violates the deadline for only 0.2% of preemption requests when a 15μs preemption latency constraint is used. For multi-programmed workloads, *Chimera* can improve the average normalized turnaround time by 5.5x, and system throughput by 12.2%.

Categories and Subject Descriptors D.4.1 [*Operating Systems*]: Process Management - Multitasking; I.3.1 [*Computer Graphics*]: Hardware Architecture - Graphics processors

Keywords Graphics Processing Unit; Preemptive Multitasking; Context Switch; Idempotence

* Co-corresponding authors.

ASPLOS '15, March 14–18, 2015, Istanbul, Turkey.

http://dx.doi.org/10.1145/2694344.2694346

1. Introduction

Modern computer systems are increasingly adopting graphics processing units (GPUs) to aid traditional processors (CPUs). In these heterogeneous systems, one typically offloads throughput-oriented workloads (or kernels) from CPUs to GPUs. GPUs can accelerate highly data-parallel applications effectively with the help of new programming models, such as OpenCL [14] or CUDA [20], which put an emphasis on thread level parallelism. Threads are distributed among hundreds of processing units on a GPU to obtain high throughput.

These systems often have multiple CPUs that share a single GPU. When multiple CPUs offload data-parallel kernels simultaneously onto a shared GPU, multitasking must be supported. Recently, Nvidia's Kepler architecture [21] introduced the Hyper-Q feature to maintain multiple independent kernel queues to concurrently execute independent kernels on a shared GPU. However, this feature is limited to the kernels *within* a single process. Multi-Process Service (MPS) [22] achieves multitasking with a software solution, but is limited to MPI applications. With current generation GPUs, kernels have to wait until a previously running kernel finishes, if multiple processes are trying to share a GPU.

Traditionally, preemptive multitasking on CPUs has been achieved through context switching, which has a reasonable preemption latency and throughput overhead on CPUs. However, supporting preemptive multitasking on GPUs through context switching can incur a higher overhead compared to CPUs, where the context of an SM can be as large as 256kB of register file and 48kB of on-chip scratch-pad memory [1, 24, 29]. Not only does a kernel have to endure a long preemption latency, the GPU also wastes execution resources while context switching. Although Tanasic et al. [29] has shown that the average normalized turnaround time can still be improved with high context switching overhead, such overhead wastes the GPU's computing power and may be ineffective for latency-sensitive applications [3, 12, 13].

To overcome these challenges, we propose *Chimera*, a collaborative preemption approach for GPUs that can precisely control the preemption overhead. *Chimera* can achieve a specified preemption latency while minimizing throughput overhead. Since GPUs consist of multiple SMs, a preemption request can have multiple solutions with diverse overheads by preempting different subsets of SMs with different preemption techniques. Given a preemption request, *Chimera* explores the possible solutions to minimize throughput overhead while conforming to the required preemption latency. *Chimera* achieves the goal by intelligently selecting *which* SMs to preempt and *how* each thread block will be preempted.

Chimera first introduces SM flushing, a GPU-specific preemption technique that is enhanced to exploit the semantics of thread blocks in the GPU programming model and the concept of idempotence to achieve low preemption latency. A kernel is *idempotent* if it generates the same result even if it is restarted in the middle of its execution [6, 8, 15, 17]. *Chimera* further relaxes the idempotence condition to enable flushing for more kernels. We say that a thread block is *idempotent at the time of preemption* if it produces the same result up to preemption point even if it is restarted from the beginning. Thus, the context of a thread block can be safely dropped with the relaxed idempotence condition even if the kernel is non-idempotent. Because non-idempotent execution regions tend to be clustered at the end of execution in GPU kernels, relaxed idempotence is effective for increasing the opportunities for flushing.

With flushing, *Chimera* has three preemption techniques in its toolbox: context switching, draining, and flushing. Context switching [17, 29] stores the context of currently running thread blocks, and preempts an SM with a new kernel. Draining [12, 29] stops issuing new thread blocks to the SM and waits until the SM finishes its currently running thread blocks. Flushing drops the execution of running thread blocks and preempts the SM almost instantly.

These three preemption techniques exhibit different tradeoffs between preemption latency and throughput overhead. Context switching has an almost constant mid-range preemption latency and throughput overhead. Draining has the least throughput overhead, but preemption latency can be long if preemption happens near the beginning of thread block execution. Flushing has almost zero preemption latency, but throughput overhead can be large if preemption occurs near the end of thread block execution.

Chimera recognizes the different tradeoffs of these three preemption techniques and chooses which SMs to preempt and how each thread block will be preempted. *Chimera* estimates the costs of the three preemption techniques for the candidate SMs, and intelligently selects SMs and corresponding preemption technique by comparing the costs.

This paper makes the following contributions:

- We introduce SM flushing, a GPU-specific adaptation of a classic preemption technique that can instantly preempt an SM. We combine the concept of idempotence with the semantics of thread blocks in the GPU programming model to enable efficient SM flushing.
- We show that relaxing the idempotence condition is essential for SM flushing to achieve its promised preemption latency. Detecting the relaxed idempotence condition can be done in software.
- We show that the three available preemption techniques for GPUs, namely context switching, draining, and flushing, make different tradeoffs between preemption latency and throughput overhead. Moreover, these tradeoffs change as a thread block makes execution progress on an SM.
- We propose *Chimera*, a collaborative preemption approach for a shared GPU that achieves a specified preemption latency while minimizing throughput overhead. *Chimera* recognizes tradeoffs of available preemption techniques, and makes an intelligent decision as to which SMs to preempt and how to preempt each thread block.

2. Background and Motivation

This section provides an overview of the GPU programming and execution models, and introduces the three preemption techniques used in *Chimera*. This section also motivates the need for collaboration among the preemption techniques. We will use Nvidia's terminology throughout the paper.

2.1 GPU Programming Model and Execution Model

A GPU program consists of host code, which contains the sequential code sections of the program, and a *kernel*, which has the parallel code sections. The host code is run on the CPU, while the kernel code is offloaded from the CPU to the GPU for acceleration.

The GPU programming model is based on a single instruction multiple thread (SIMT) model to explicitly express the parallelism in the kernel code. In the SIMT model, a programmer only writes a code for the basic unit of execution, called a *thread*. A group of threads called a *thread block* is also specified by the programmer. Within a thread block, the programmer can synchronize threads through an explicit barrier operation. Also, threads within a thread block can access a common, fast, on-chip scratch-pad memory called *shared memory*. The entire kernel is executed by launching *grids* of thread blocks to the GPUs.

Figure 1 illustrates a GPU architecture and its execution model. The top left box shows a kernel with the notion of a GPU programming model. The bottom box depicts the GPU architecture with a memory hierarchy. The top right box represents a GPU execution model with the contexts of running thread blocks. In a GPU, each streaming multiprocessor

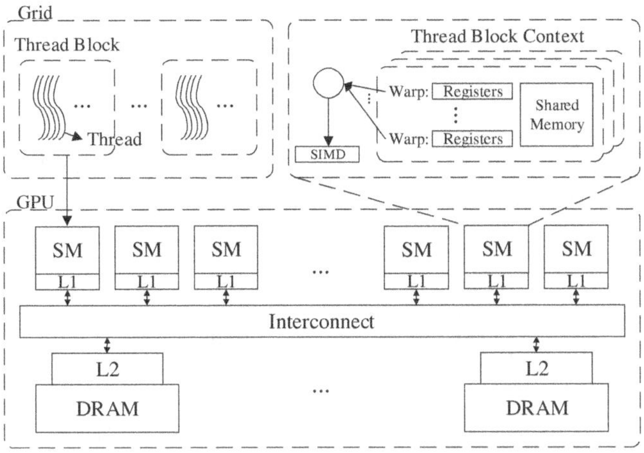

Figure 1. GPU architecture and execution model.

(SM) has a private L1 data cache, a read-only texture cache, and a read-only constant cache. The memory subsystem of the GPU consists of multiple memory partitions. Each memory partition contains a shared L2 cache bank and a memory controller.

The GPU execution model relies on the notion of a thread block. Thread blocks from a kernel can run in arbitrary order because thread block executions are independent from each other. When a kernel is launched, each thread block is scheduled to one of the SMs. Depending on the resource constraints, the number of thread blocks that can run simultaneously on an SM may vary. Also, current generation GPUs only allow thread blocks from the same kernel to be executed on the same SM. When a thread block is dispatched to an SM, the thread block is split into groups of 32 threads called *warps*, where threads within a warp operate on a single common instruction. Each warp has its own register contents, and shares the state of a shared memory if they are in the same thread block.

SMs do not share any states among themselves. Spatial multitasking [1] exploits this property to allow GPUs to run multiple kernels on different subsets of SMs. Preemptive multitasking can also exploit the same property by preempting only a subset of SMs to yield to a new kernel. Starvation can also be avoided by scheduling at least one SM to each available kernel.

2.2 Prior Preemption Techniques

Supporting preemptive multitasking incurs overheads in terms of latency and throughput. For example, context switching for preemption in CPUs involves saving context of the currently running process/thread, running the operating system (OS) scheduler to choose the next process/thread to run, and loading context of the selected process/thread. Preempting a process/thread experiences increased response time due to preemption latency. Also, system throughput is degraded because no progress is made during context switching. The overhead of context switching is proportional to the size of the context.

Modern GPUs can have up to 2048 threads concurrently running on a single SM [21]. Because each thread accesses its own registers, the context size for a SM can grow quickly. Moreover, each SM has its own on-chip scratch-pad memory, which is shared by the threads within a thread block. For modern GPUs, the context of a single SM can be as large as 256kB of register file and 48kB of shared memory [1, 24, 29]. With such a large context, preempting with context switching has high overhead in both preemption latency and wasted throughput.

To avoid throughput overhead of context switching, SM draining [29] has been proposed, which exploits the GPU execution model. Because thread block executions are independent from each other, a thread block does not have to remember its context when it finishes execution. When an SM is preempted with draining, new thread blocks are no longer issued to that SM. When the SM finishes all the running thread blocks, the SM is preempted and can be assigned to another kernel. As the SM is continuously making progress during preemption, throughput overhead of draining is much less than that of context switching.

Draining, however, does not solve the preemption latency problem. Because the preemption latency of draining is dependent on the remaining execution time of thread blocks in the SM, it can be much higher than that of context switching.

2.3 SM Flushing

To enable low preemption latency, we introduce SM flushing, which further exploits the independence of thread block execution in the GPU execution model. Flushing drops an execution of a thread block without context saving and re-executes the dropped thread block from the beginning on another SM. Because thread block executions are independent, other thread blocks do not notice whether a thread block has been rerun from the beginning. Flushing reduces the preemption latency to almost zero. However, certain conditions have to be met to ensure the correctness of the thread block execution that was dropped and rerun from the beginning.

A GPU kernel is *idempotent* if it produces the same result regardless of the number of times it is executed [6, 8, 15, 17]. Because there is no interaction between thread blocks, idempotence conditions for a GPU kernel are much simpler than those in general CPU applications. To be idempotent, a kernel should not have any 1) atomic operations, and 2) overwrites to a global memory location that is read in the kernel. In the benchmarks we studied, 12 out of 27 kernels were found to be idempotent. The idempotence conditions are listed in Table 2. Without enabling flushing in all the kernels, flushing loses its effectiveness because it cannot preempt non-idempotent kernels. We discuss the details of relaxing the idempotence conditions, and implementation of flushing in Section 3.4.

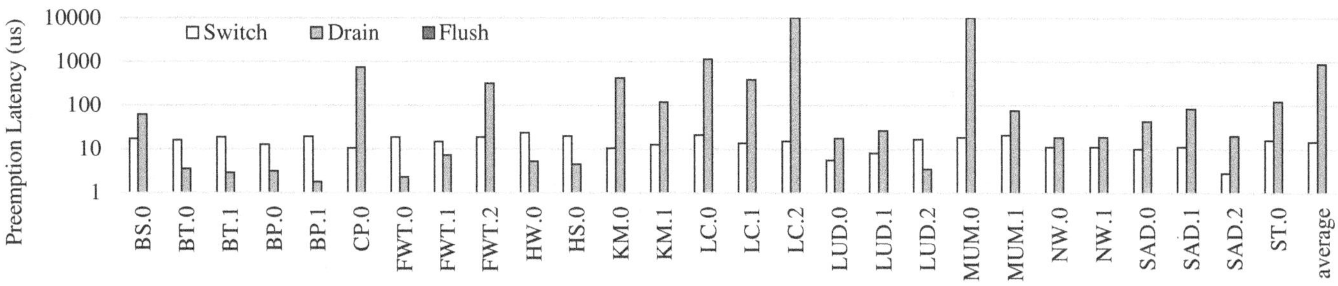

Figure 2. Estimated preemption latency for each preemption technique. For draining, a uniform random distribution on the preemption point across thread block execution is assumed. For flushing, zero preemption latency is assumed.

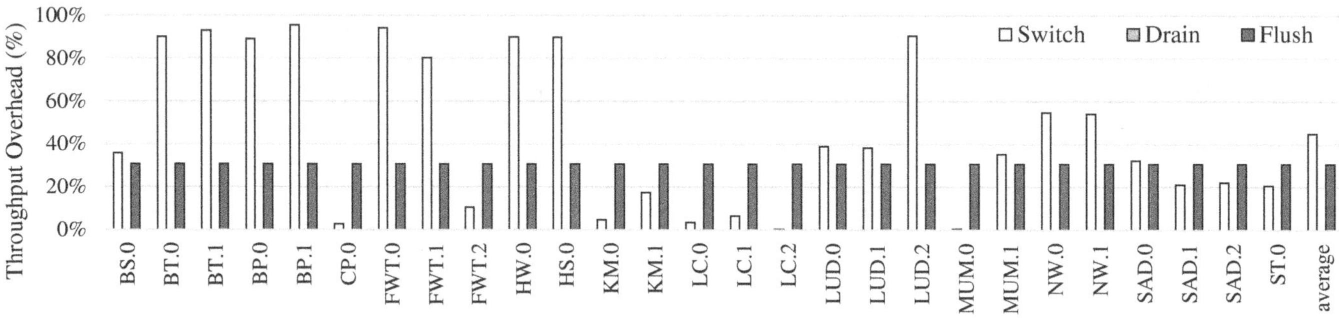

Figure 3. Estimated throughput overhead for each preemption technique when thread blocks running on an SM are assumed to be in sync. For flushing, a uniform random distribution on the preemption point across thread block execution is assumed.

2.4 Tradeoff

Context switching, draining, and flushing make different tradeoffs between preemption latency and throughput overhead. Figure 2 shows the estimated preemption latency for each preemption technique. In the figure, the y-axis shows preemption latency on a logarithmic scale, and the x-axis shows the kernels in the benchmarks. If multiple kernels are launched in a benchmark, they are differentiated with numbers after the benchmark name and a dot. All the labels and numbers for benchmarks and kernels are listed in Table 2. To estimate the preemption latency of context switching, an SM is assumed to have only its share of global memory bandwidth to save its context. Context size can be calculated from the kernel's resource usage even before the kernel launch. The same method was used in [29] to project the estimated preemption latency for context switching. To estimate the preemption latency for draining, the average time to execute a thread block is first measured through simulation. Assuming uniform random distribution on the preemption point across the execution of a thread block, the preemption latency for draining can be calculated. The preemption latency for flushing is assumed to be zero.

In Figure 2, context switching shows a relatively constant response time in the order of 10 μs, while draining exhibits diverse response time ranging from 0.8 μs to 10212.8 μs. On average, context switching, draining, and flushing require 14.5 μs, 830.4 μs, and 0 μs, respectively, to preempt an SM. They are equivalent to an order of 10,000, 500,000, and 0 cycles, respectively, in current generation GPUs.

Figure 3 shows the estimated throughput overhead for each preemption technique. In the figure, the y-axis shows the percentage of throughput overhead for each preemption technique compared to the throughput without preemption. Thread blocks running on an SM are assumed to be in sync. The throughput overhead of context switching is twice the preemption latency divided by the thread block execution time, where the preemption latency is doubled because throughput overhead comes both from context saving and context loading. SM draining is assumed to have zero throughput overhead because it continuously does useful work until the thread block finishes. In reality, thread blocks can be out of sync, which will cause draining to incur some throughput overhead. To estimate the throughput overhead of flushing, a uniform random distribution on the preemption point across the execution of a thread block is again assumed. The throughput overhead of flushing is independent of the kernel, and is constant across all the benchmarks. Overall, context switching, draining, and flushing have throughput overhead of 47.7%, 0%, and 30.7%, respectively.

2.5 Motivation

Different tradeoffs from the three preemption techniques encourage using different preemption techniques for each kernel. In fact, different tradeoffs can be further exploited by

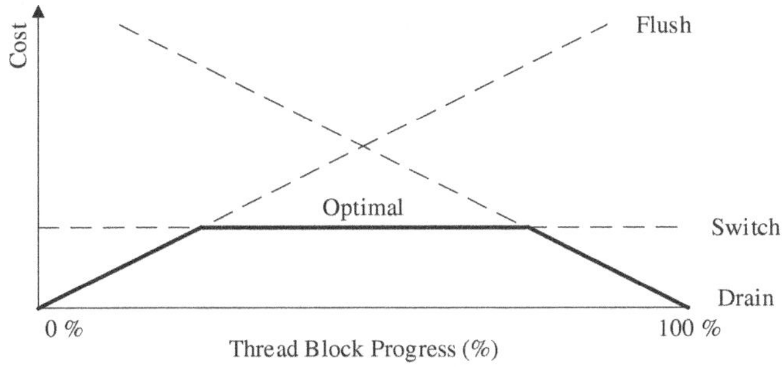

Figure 4. Theoretical cost of each preemption technique when preempting a thread block at a given amount of execution progress. Context switching has constant cost across the execution, draining has lower cost as a thread block is near the end of execution, and flushing has lower cost as a thread block is closer to the beginning of execution.

using different preemption techniques within one preemption request. Because a preemption request would typically want multiple SMs at the same time, each SM can be preempted with a different preemption technique. Moreover, each thread block in the SM can be preempted with a different preemption technique.

Figure 4 depicts the theoretical cost of each preemption technique if a thread block at given progress is preempted. The cost can be thought of as an aggregate measure of preemption latency and throughput overhead. The cost of context switching is dependent on the context size and the available bandwidth for an SM, which is almost constant across thread block execution. The cost of draining, which is primarily preemption latency, is dependent on the remaining execution time of a thread block. It decreases toward the end of the thread block progress. The cost of flushing, on the other hand, is primarily throughput overhead, which is dependent on the work thrown away by flushing. More work is thrown away as the thread block progresses; hence, the cost increases accordingly.

The figure motivates to preempt with flushing if a thread block is in the early stage of execution, with context switching if a thread block is in the middle stage of execution, and with draining if a thread block is near the end of execution. The exact points at which to switch the preemption decision is based on the cost estimation of each preemption technique.

3. Architecture

Chimera is a collaborative preemption with three individual techniques: context switching, draining, and flushing. Context switching is implemented with a software trap routine. Draining is performed by adding logic in a thread block scheduler that stops issuing new thread blocks. Flushing requires reset logic in SMs, which clears all the states and in-flight instructions in the SM. For context switching and flushing, an SM has to send the stopped thread blocks' IDs back to the thread block scheduler so that they can be reissued to the other SMs.

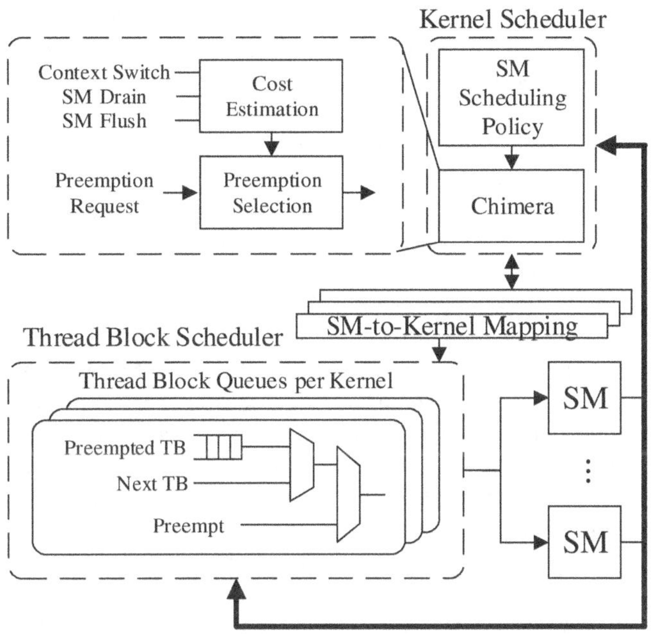

Figure 5. GPU scheduler with preemptive multitasking. The scheduler is two-level: the kernel scheduler assigns SMs to each kernel that may involve preemption decisions, and the thread block scheduler executes the decision by dispatching or preempting thread blocks from each SM. SMs can feedback the schedulers when an event that can change the scheduling decision occurs.

Chimera decides which SMs to preempt and which preemption technique to use for each thread block in the SMs, given the number of SMs to preempt. *Chimera* makes the decision based on the upper bound for preemption latency given by the preempting application or kernel. *Chimera* first estimates preemption latency and throughput overhead for each thread block in an SM when it is preempted with each preemption technique. *Chimera* chooses preemption techniques with the least throughput overhead that satisfy the given preemption latency for an SM, which can give the total cost of preemption for each SM. With the calculated costs, *Chimera* selects SMs which can minimize throughput overhead while meeting the required preemption latency.

3.1 GPU Scheduler with Preemptive Multitasking

Figure 5 illustrates the GPU scheduler with preemptive multitasking when multiple GPU kernels are running concurrently. The scheduler is a two-level scheduler: the kernel scheduler assigns kernel to each SM, which may involve preemption decisions, and the thread block scheduler carries out the decision. The thread block scheduler dispatches a new thread block to an SM, or preempts an SM with the given preemption techniques based on the decisions from the kernel scheduler. The kernel scheduler is a part of an operating system that manages a GPU device, while the thread block scheduler is a hardware module in a GPU, which is an extension of GigaThread engine in Fermi [19] with a preemption support.

An SM partitioning policy in the kernel scheduler tells how many SMs each kernel will run on. The policy is orthogonal to the preemption decisions. It may be dependent on a characteristic of a kernel [1] or a priority of a kernel [29]. *Chimera* in the kernel scheduler achieves an SM partitioning policy by making preemption decisions. The kernel scheduler communicates to the thread block scheduler through SM-to-kernel mapping information which contains per-SM information about which kernel to schedule, whether preemption is necessary or not, and which preemption technique to use. The thread block scheduler always prefers to schedule the preempted thread blocks first so that the size of the preempted thread block queue can be limited.

Chimera consists of two parts: estimating costs of preemption for each technique, and selecting SMs to preempt with corresponding preempting techniques. To estimate the costs, *Chimera* gathers statistics for SMs. The statistics are measured using hardware and reported directly to *Chimera*. Based on these statistics, *Chimera* estimates preemption latency in cycles, and throughput in the number of instructions rather than IPC. *Chimera* can directly compare the estimated cost of each preemption technique because they are calculated in the same units.

3.2 Cost Estimation

To distinguish different tradeoffs between different preemption techniques, *Chimera* has to estimate the cost of each preemption technique precisely for each SM. First, *Chimera* measures the total number of executed instructions for each thread block to determine the progress of each thread block. Note that instructions are counted not in thread granularity, but in warp granularity so that control divergence in a warp has minimal effect on the total executed instructions. Second, *Chimera* also measures the progress of each thread block in cycles. *Chimera* can calculate the average instructions-per-cycle (IPC) or cycles-per-instruction (CPI) of a thread block with these two statistics.

We estimate the preemption latency of context switching using the same method as detailed in Section 2.4. To estimate the throughput overhead of context switching, the average IPC of preempted kernel on a single SM is multiplied by twice the preemption latency of context switching. Note that preemption latency is doubled because throughput overhead not only comes from context saving, but also from context loading. The preemption latency of draining is estimated by multiplying the remaining instructions to execute in a thread block by the average CPI of the preempted kernel. We avoid using the average execution cycles per thread block directly because it has much larger variance compared to the average executed instructions, leading to less accurate estimations. The throughput overhead of draining is estimated by

Algorithm 1 Preemption Selection

```
    Input: LatLimit, Kernel, NumPreempts ▷ From SM Scheduling Policy
    Output: SM_Preemptions[1..NumPreempts]
 1: for each SM in Kernel do
 2:     for each TB in the SM do
 3:         for each Preemption Technique do
 4:             TBCosts.push(EstimateCost(TB, Technique))
 5:         end for
 6:     end for
 7:     TBSorted = SortByThroughputOverhead(TBCosts)
 8:     while !TBSorted.empty() do
 9:         TBCandidate = TBSorted.pop()
10:         if meets_latency(TBCandidate) and TBCandidate.TB not in SingleSMCost then
11:             SingleSMCost.add(TBCandidate)
12:         end if
13:     end while
14:     for each TB not in SingleSMCost do
15:         SingleSMCost.add(EstimateCost(TB, Switch))
16:     end for
17:     SMCosts.push(SingleSMCost)
18: end for
19: SMSorted = SortByThroughputOverhead(SMCosts)
20: for i = 1 to NumPreempts do
21:     while !SMSorted.empty() do
22:         SMCandidate = SMSorted.pop()
23:         if meets_latency(SMCandidate) then
24:             SM_Preemptions[i] = SMCandidate
25:             break
26:         end if
27:     end while
28: end for
29: return SM_Preemptions[1..NumPreempts]
```

summing the difference between the number of executed instructions for each thread block and the maximum number of executed instructions among them. Flushing is always assumed to have zero preemption latency. The total number of executed instructions for thread blocks in the SM is used to estimate the throughput overhead of flushing. When the cost cannot be estimated due to the lack of gathered statistics, we conservatively use the maximum value as the estimated cost to avoid selecting affected techniques.

3.3 Preemption Selection

Chimera is a collaborative preemption that achieves low overhead multitasking through multiple preemption techniques with different overheads. SM scheduling policy, which is independent of these decisions, provides *Chimera* a preemption latency constraint, a kernel to preempt, and the number of SMs to preempt. Given the inputs, *Chimera* generates combinations of which SM to preempt and how to preempt, while satisfying the latency constraint.

Algorithm 1 illustrates how *Chimera* selects a subset of SMs and techniques to preempt. The algorithm starts by estimating the cost of each preemption technique for the thread blocks in an SM (line 2-6). The costs for the thread blocks are sorted by throughput overhead (at line 7), and a preemption technique for a particular thread block is selected if the preemption latency constraint is met and it is not already selected with another preemption technique (line 8-13). If a thread block cannot meet the constraint with any preemption technique, *Chimera* performs context switching for the thread block (line 14-16). Now, *Chimera* knows the preemption costs for each SM that is running the given kernel. It sorts all the costs by throughput overhead (at line 19). From the list of sorted candidates, *Chimera* finalizes the preemption selection (line 20-28). When finalizing the decision, *Chimera* checks whether the candidate satisfies the preemption latency constraint (at line 23). Because only one candidate exists for an SM, *Chimera* does not have to check whether the candidate SM is already selected.

The time complexity of algorithm 1 is $O(NTlogT + NlogN)$, where N is the number of SMs that a kernel to preempt is occupying, and T is the number of available thread blocks in an SM. The first term comes from the first loop (line 1-18), where preemption techniques are selected for particular thread blocks. Two loops (line 2-6 and line 8-13) take the linear time complexity of $O(PT)$, where P is the number of preemption techniques. In *Chimera*, P is a maximum of 3. The third loop (line 14-16) only takes the linear time complexity of $O(T)$. Therefore, sorting (at line 7) defines the time complexity with $O(PTlogPT) = O(TlogT)$. Since the outer loop runs N times, the entire loop (line 1-18) takes $O(NTlogT)$. The second term, which is $O(NlogN)$, comes from sorting for SMs (at line 19). The last loop (line 20-28) only takes the linear time complexity of $O(N)$. In general, N is in the order of 10 for current GPU generations. Furthermore, N will be reduced as more kernels run concurrently on the GPU because each kernel is likely to occupy a lower number of SMs. Also, T is a fixed number (maximum of 16 in Kepler [21]), but is typically less than the maximum (8 is the largest number of thread blocks per SM for simulated benchmarks in Table 2). Thus, the impact of the selection algorithm in *Chimera* is negligible to the preemption latency.

3.4 SM Flushing

SM flushing can be effective if it can preempt all kernels, whether they are idempotent or not. Flushing may still violate the required preemption latency if it cannot preempt an SM due to non-idempotence. Implementation of flushing is fairly straightforward as an SM already has a circuit that resets or clears itself.

We relax the idempotence condition by looking at thread blocks individually with the notion of time. A GPU thread block is *idempotent at a given time* if it neither 1) has executed any atomic operations yet, nor 2) has overwritten a global memory location that is read by the thread block. Because atomic operations or global memory overwrites tend to be performed at the end of a thread block execution, a thread block can remain idempotent for the most of its execution time even if the kernel itself is non-idempotent.

With the relaxed idempotence condition, SMs have to notify the GPU scheduler when thread blocks have progressed beyond the non-idempotent point. The notification is implemented in software by inserting a store instruction in front of atomic operations or global overwrite operations. The store is made to a pre-defined address, which is non-cacheable. SMs will prepend their ID to the store so that the store address is unique for each SM. As SMs are in-order cores, these inserted stores are guaranteed to take place before the atomic or global overwrite operations. The GPU scheduler looks at these pre-defined addresses to check whether each SM can be preempted with flushing.

As atomic operations are separate hardware instructions, they are trivial to find. Global overwrite operations are found by compiler analysis to distinguish between global writes and global overwrites. While pointer alias analysis is undecidable [10] in general, pointers are used in a more restricted fashion in GPU kernels, which allows the compiler to find global overwrites precisely in most cases.

System	Parameters
SM	30 SMs, 1400 MHz, 8 SIMT width 32768 registers per SM 8 maximum thread blocks per SM 48 kB shared memory
Memory Subsystem	6 memory partitions 177.4 GB/s bandwidth

Table 1. System configuration

4. Results

We use the GPGPU-Sim v3.2.2 [2] to evaluate *Chimera*. GPGPU-Sim only models the GPU, while the host code runs natively on CPUs. GPGPU-Sim does not model the overhead of data transfers between the CPU and GPU as well. We model a Fermi [19] architecture with 30 SMs. All the system configuration parameters are summarized in Table 1. We implement context switching by halting an SM for the estimated context switch time instead of using software trap routine. The result for context switching will be rather optimistic in the sense that the memory bandwidth consumed by context switching will affect other SMs to slow down in reality and vice versa, whereas our implementation does not account for the effect.

For all the preemption techniques, we use the same SM scheduling policy, which is similar to the mix of **Smart Even** and **Rounds** in spatial multitasking [1]. SMs are distributed evenly across the kernels except when the kernel requires less SMs than the even split. A kernel can request less SMs than the even split for two reasons: if a kernel is size-bound, where the grid size or the number of thread blocks for the kernel cannot fully occupy its portion of SMs at its launch, or if the remaining number of thread blocks is insufficient to fully occupy the given number of SMs near the end of execution.

We use a wide range of GPGPU applications from Nvidia Computing SDK [18], Rodinia [4], and Parboil [28] bench-

Benchmark (Label) [Input]	Source	Kernel (Label)	Average Drain Time	Context /TB	TBs /SM	Switching Time	Idempotent
BlackScholes (BS) [4M Options]	Nvidia SDK [18]	BlackScholesGPU (0)	60.9 μs	24 kB	4	17.0 μs	Yes
B+ Tree (BT) [1M Nodes]	Rodinia [4]	findRangeK (0)	3.5 μs	46 kB	2	15.9 μs	No
		findK (1)	2.8 μs	36 kB	3	18.7 μs	No
Back Propagation (BP) [128K Nodes]	Rodinia [4]	bpnn_layerforward (0)	3.1 μs	12 kB	6	12.5 μs	No
		bpnn_adjust_weights (1)	1.8 μs	22 kB	5	19.0 μs	No
Coulombic Potential (CP) [2K Atoms on 256x256 Grid]	Parboil [28]	cenergy (0)	746.9 μs	7 kB	8	10.4 μs	No
Fast Walsh Transform (FWT) [8M]	Nvidia SDK [18]	fwtBatch2Kernel (0)	2.3 μs	21 kB	5	18.2 μs	No
		fwtBatch1Kernel (1)	7.2 μs	28 kB	3	14.5 μs	No
		modulateKernel (2)	321.8 μs	18 kB	6	18.7 μs	No
Heart Wall Tracking (HW) [656x744 Pixels/Frame]	Rodinia [4]	kernel (0)	5.2 μs	67 kB	2	23.4 μs	No
HotSpot (HS) [1024x1024 Data Points]	Rodinia [4]	calculate_temp (0)	4.5 μs	38 kB	3	19.7 μs	Yes
Kmeans (KM) [0.5M Data Points, 34 Features]	Rodinia [4]	invert_mapping (0)	424.3 μs	10 kB	6	10.4 μs	Yes
		kmeansPoint (1)	118.8 μs	12 kB	6	12.5 μs	Yes
Leukocyte Tracking (LC) [640x480 Pixels/Frame]	Rodinia [4]	GICOV_kernel (0)	1162.0 μs	17 kB	7	20.9 μs	Yes
		dilate_kernel (1)	391.7 μs	9 kB	8	13.5 μs	Yes
		IMGVF_kernel (2)	10173.2 μs	87 kB	1	15.2 μs	No
LU Decomposition (LUD) [512x512 Data Points]	Rodinia [4]	lud_diagonal (0)	17.4 μs	4 kB	8	5.6 μs	No
		lud_perimeter (1)	26.2 μs	5 kB	8	8.1 μs	No
		lud_internal (2)	3.5 μs	16 kB	6	16.6 μs	No
MUMmer (MUM) [50000 25-character Queries]	Rodinia [4]	mummergpuKernel (0)	10212.8 μs	18 kB	6	18.7 μs	Yes
		printKernel (1)	76.4 μs	24 kB	5	20.8 μs	Yes
Needleman-Wunsch (NW) [4096x4096 Data Points]	Rodinia [4]	needle_cuda_shared_1 (0)	18.2 μs	8 kB	8	11.1 μs	No
		needle_cuda_shared_2 (1)	18.7 μs	8 kB	8	11.1 μs	No
SAD [1920x1072 Pixels]	Parboil [28]	mb_sad_calc (0)	42.3 μs	7 kB	8	10.1 μs	Yes
		larger_sad_calc_8 (1)	82.9 μs	8 kB	8	11.1 μs	Yes
		larger_sad_calc_16 (2)	19.7 μs	2 kB	8	2.8 μs	Yes
Stencil (ST) [512x512x64 Grid]	Parboil [28]	block2D_hybrid_coarsen_x (0)	122.3 μs	11 kB	8	15.9 μs	Yes

Table 2. Benchmark Specification

mark suite. Table 2 lists all the evaluated benchmarks, their inputs, and their kernels with their characteristics. We show the estimated average drain time, the size of the context for one thread block, the maximal number of concurrent thread blocks per SM, the estimated context switch time, and idempotence of the kernel. Note that kernel idempotence can be relaxed in flushing. We selected a subset of benchmarks from each benchmark suite so that they show diverse characteristics in terms of the context switching time, draining time, and the idempotence condition.

4.1 Periodic Task with Deadline

We first analyze each GPGPU benchmark, when it is concurrently run with a synthetic GPU benchmark, which mimics a periodic, real-time task that has a hard deadline. The synthetic GPU benchmark is launched every 1ms, preempting half of the SMs, and executed for 200μs. The deadline for the synthetic benchmark is the execution time plus the required preemption latency. The synthetic benchmark is killed if it misses the deadline. The simulation is run until a GPGPU benchmark executes 1 billion instructions or finishes its execution.

Figure 6 illustrates the percentage of preemptions that violate the deadline of the synthetic benchmark when the preemption latency constraint is set to 15μs. On average, context switching, draining, flushing, and *Chimera* miss the deadline for 56.0%, 61.3%, 7.3%, and 0.2% of preemptions, respectively. Flushing, despite its zero preemption latency, violates the deadline for BT and FWT because these benchmarks have non-idempotent kernels with short thread block execution time. In such cases, flushing is more likely to miss the deadline because thread blocks have higher chances to be in a non-idempotent region even with the relaxed idempotence condition. On the other hand, *Chimera* misses the dealine in 0.2% cases only. These misses are primarily due to the incorrect estimation of draining latency. However, the error is in the range of few hundred cycles ($< 1\mu s$), and can be avoided by providing a headroom to preemption latency constraint against the deadline.

Figure 7 shows the overhead on throughput for each preemption technique in the same scenario. If the deadline of the synthetic benchmark is missed, we ignore the throughput additionally gained by running GPGPU benchmark more during that period so that the measured overhead is fair among the preemption techniques. Also, we neglect the throughput of the synthetic benchmark on purpose, to isolate throughput overhead of each preemption technique. Overall, context switching, draining, flushing, and *Chimera* have

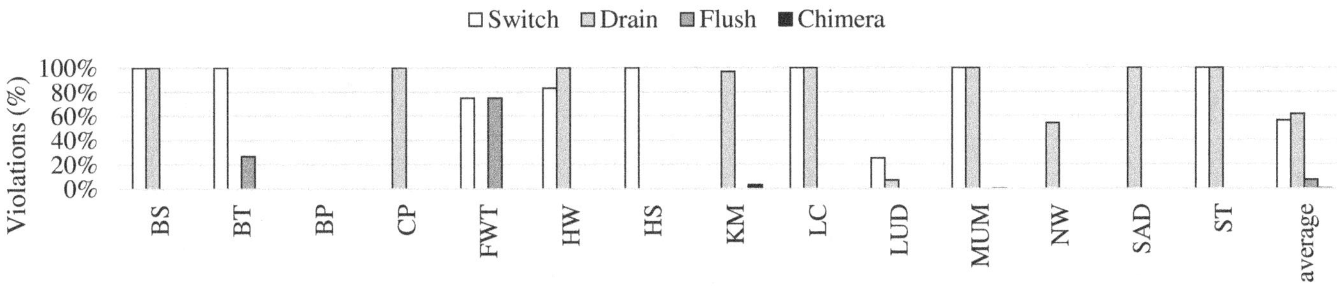

Figure 6. The percentage of preemptions that violate the deadline of a periodic, real-time task when GPGPU benchmarks are run together. The preemption latency constraint is 15 μs.

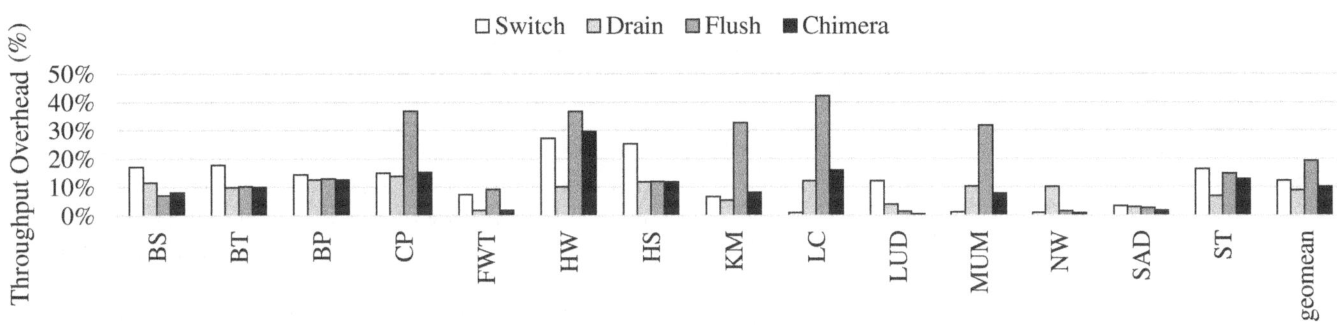

Figure 7. Throughput overhead of each preemption technique when GPGPU benchmarks are run with a periodic, real-time task. The preemption latency constraint is 15 μs. Effective throughput is used to avoid giving unfair advantage to the preemption techniques that frequently miss the deadline.

throughput overhead of 12.2%, 8.9%, 19.3%, and 10.1%, respectively. Draining does not have zero throughput overhead as explained in Section 2.4 because the assumption that thread blocks are running in sync is not true in practice. However, it still achieves the minimum throughput overhead compared to switching, and flushing. *Chimera* shows similar throughput overhead with significantly fewer deadline misses. FWT, LUD, and NW show least throughput overhead for *Chimera* because they include kernels that either have short execution time (SMs will be quickly freed) or occupy less than half of all available SMs from the beginning. In such case, preemption can be performed with low overhead since a new kernel can be launched to the idle SMs.

As shown by the figures, *Chimera* can almost always meet the preemption latency constraint while individual preemption technique cannot. *Chimera* achieves this goal while maintaining the low throughput overhead of draining. In fact, *Chimera* can have lower throughput overhead than individual preemption technique as in LUD by collaboratively utilizing all the techniques.

4.2 Impact of Preemption Latency Constraint

Chimera is a collaborative preemption with controlled overhead. Figure 8 demonstrates the impact of preemption latency constraint when it is varied from 5μs to 20μs. We use the same multi-programmed workloads as in Section 4.1.

Figure 8 (a) shows the percentage of preemptions that *Chimera* violates the deadline when the preemption latency constraint is varied from 5μs to 20μs. When the preemption latency is 5μs, 10μs, 15μs, and 20μs, violations happen for 2.00%, 1.08%, 0.24%, and 0.00% of preemptions, respectively. As explained with Figure 6, flushing may fail to meet the deadline if a kernel is non-idempotent, and has short thread block execution time. Since flushing is what *Chimera* relies on to achieve low preemption latency, *Chimera* also suffers from the same problem when the preemption latency constraint is extremely low as in the case of 5μs.

Figure 8 (b) shows throughput overhead of *Chimera* when the preemption latency constraint is varied from 5μs to 20μs. Again, we use effective throughput to measure throughput overhead to avoid giving unfair advantage to the preemption techniques that miss the deadline. *Chimera* have 16.5%, 12.2%, 10.0%, and 9.0% throughput overhead when the preemption latency constraint is 5μs, 10μs, 15μs, and 20μs, respectively. As shown in the figure, *Chimera* can reduce more throughput overhead when the preemption latency constraint is increased. If only one preemption technique is utilized, the loose deadline cannot be exploited.

Figure 8 (c) shows distribution of each preemption technique used in *Chimera* when the preemption latency constraint is varied from 5μs to 20μs. As the preemption latency constraint is reduced, *Chimera* exploits flushing more because flushing is the only preemption technique that pro-

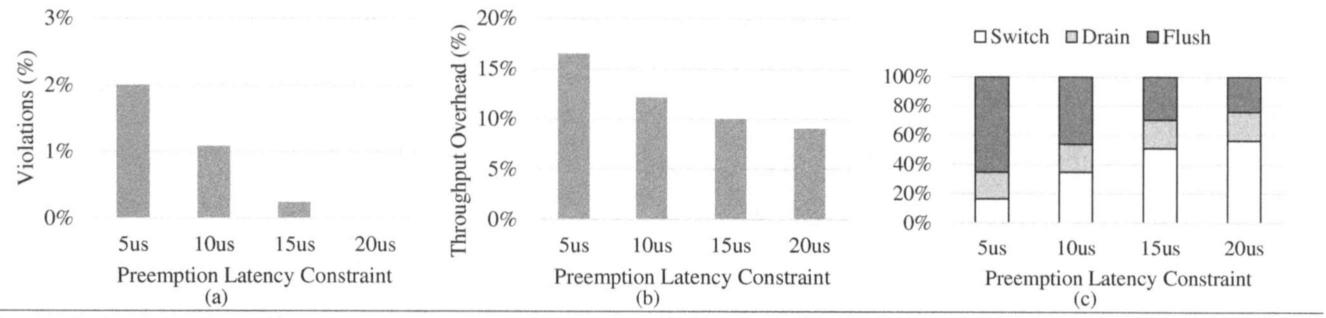

Figure 8. Impact of varying preemption latency constraint on (a) the percentage of deadline violations, (b) throughput overhead, and (c) distribution of each preemption technique used in *Chimera*.

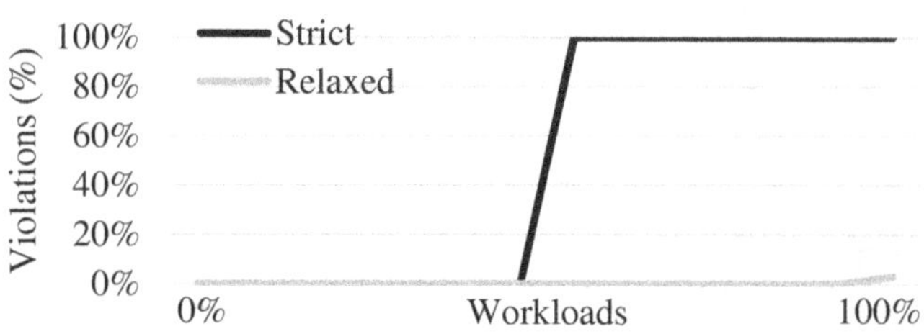

Figure 9. The percentage of preemptions that violate $15\mu s$ preemption latency constraint when SM flushing uses strict or relaxed idempotence condition.

vides low preemption latency at the expense of throughput overhead. About 19% of preemptions constantly utilize draining because thread blocks near the end of their execution always exist even for low preemption latency constraint. Context switching has constant preemption latency regardless of the constraint hence its utilization quickly drops as the preemption latency constraint is reduced.

4.3 Relaxed Idempotence Condition in SM Flushing

Figure 9 illustrates the effectiveness of relaxing the idempotence condition for flushing. We refer to the original idempotence condition as strict, and the relaxed idempotence condition as relaxed. The percentage of preemptions that violate $15\mu s$ preemption latency constraint is shown for all the workloads used in Section 4.1. On average, flushing violates the deadline for 50.0%, and 0.2% of the total preemptions with strict and relaxed idempotence condition, respectively.

When strict idempotence condition is used, the kernel idempotence decides whether an SM can be preempted with flushing or not. With relaxed idempotence condition, thread blocks in such kernel can still be preempted with flushing if they have not reached non-idempotent region. Without the relaxed idempotence condition, flushing cannot achieve its promised low preemption latency because non-idempotent kernels cannot be preempted. The violations for strict idempotence condition will be the same regardless of the preemption latency constraint. The results show that it is mandatory for flushing to have relaxed idempotence condition to provide instant preemption.

4.4 Case Study

In this section, we further investigate *Chimera* when a combination of GPGPU benchmarks without hard deadline is concurrently executed. Each multi-programmed workload is a combination of LUD with one of the benchmarks in Table 2. LUD is chosen because it launches multiple kernels that require different number of SMs, which results in numerous preemption requests. GPGPU benchmarks do not have hard deadline hence we chose preemption latency constraint to be $30\mu s$, which is the maximum possible preemption latency for context switching in our configuration.

Each simulation runs until *all* benchmarks either execute 1 billion instructions or finish its execution. Among the benchmarks, FWT, HW, KM, LC, MUM, SAD, and ST run more than 1 billion instructions. When one benchmark finishes earlier than the others, it is restarted from the beginning to prohibit the last remaining benchmark from running on its own. The reported results are gathered only for the first 1 billion instructions or first execution whichever is reached first. All the benchmarks are started simultaneously at the beginning. This is a typical setting for simulating multi-programmed workloads [1, 25, 29–31]. For the baseline, we use non-preemptive scheduling, where each kernel has to wait until previous kernel has finished its execution. Kernels are launched following first-come, first-serve (FCFS) policy.

To compare the performance of preemption techniques, we use the metrics suggested by Eyerman et al. [7]. Average normalized turnaround time (ANTT) quantifies the user-perceived slowdown due to multitasking using Equation 1, where N denotes the number of kernels, CPI_i^{multi} is the CPI when a kernel is executed in the multi-programmed workload, and CPI_i^{single} is the CPI when the kernel is executed on its own. System throughput (STP) measures the progress of the system under multitasking using Equation 2, where parameters are the same as in ANTT.

$$ANTT = \frac{1}{N}\sum_{i=1}^{N}\frac{CPI_i^{multi}}{CPI_i^{single}} \quad (1)$$

$$STP = \sum_{i=1}^{N}\frac{CPI_i^{single}}{CPI_i^{multi}} \quad (2)$$

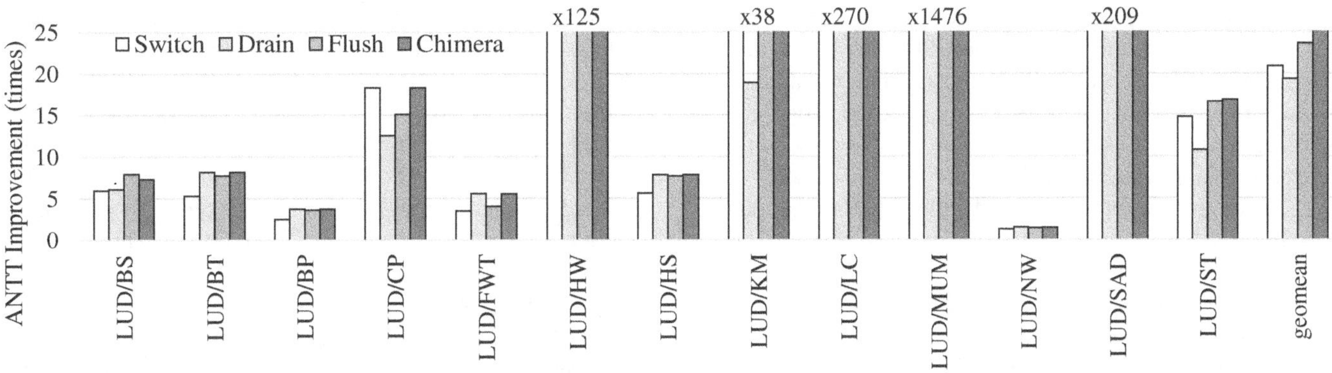

Figure 10. ANTT improvement over the non-preemptive FCFS when LUD is concurrently executed with another benchmark.

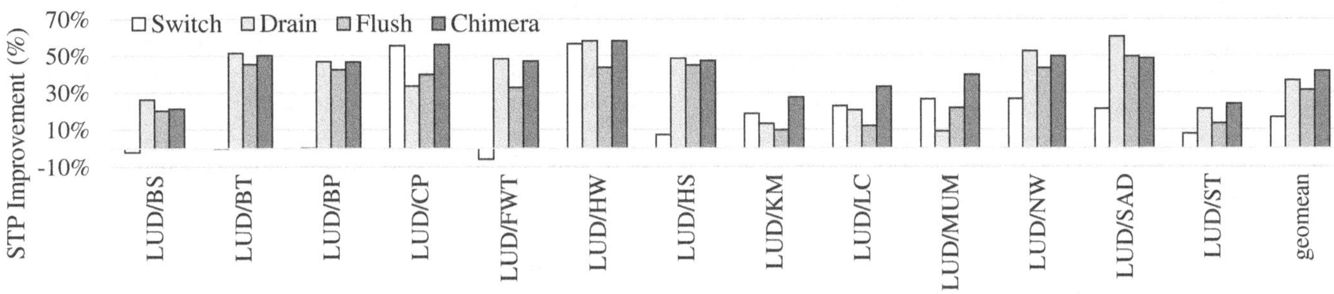

Figure 11. STP improvement over the non-preemptive FCFS when LUD is concurrently executed with another benchmark.

Figure 10 presents the ANTT improvement of each preemption technique over the non-preemptive FCFS. On average, context switch, draining, flushing, and *Chimera* improves the ANTT by 20.9x, 19.3x, 23.6x, and 25.4x, respectively. HW, KM, LC, MUM, and SAD have a kernel, whose execution time is extremely long. Preemptive multitasking improves ANTT drastically over non-preemptive FCFS because non-preemptive FCFS has to wait until these kernels finish their execution. Among single preemption techniques, flushing has the most ANTT improvement as it has the least preemption latency. *Chimera* can improve the ANTT more than flushing because it can preempt non-idempotent thread blocks using other preemption techniques.

Figure 11 shows the STP improvement of each preemption technique over the non-preemptive FCFS. Overall, context switch, draining, flushing, and *Chimera* improves the STP by 16.5%, 36.6%, 31.4%, and 41.7%, respectively. Since LUD does not occupy all the available SMs, STP is significantly improved despite the throughput overhead of preemption techniques. Here, spatial multitasking is effectively improving STP. In LUD/SAD, *Chimera* improves STP much less than the top single preemption technique, which is draining. *Chimera* shows such behavior when the cost estimation is not accurate enough for context switching, and draining. Cost estimation is not precise if thread blocks have large variations in the execution time or in the CPI. Again, *Chimera* achieves the most STP improvement over any single preemption technique because *Chimera* can choose alternative low overhead preemption technique if one preemption technique incurs larger overhead compared to the others while a single preemption technique is forced to endure the overhead. We see larger difference in STP compared to throughput overhead in the Section 4.1 because preemptions occur more frequently than 1ms interval in the simulated multi-programmed workloads.

Chimera can improve ANTT and STP for GPGPU benchmarks without hard deadlines as it utilizes adequate preemption technique when preemption request occurs. When all the combinations of GPGPU benchmarks are used, *Chimera* improves ANTT and STP by 5.5x, and 12.2%, respectively, on average. Other combinations of GPGPU benchmarks have smaller number of preemption requests, which results in smaller improvement compared to LUD combinations.

5. Related Work

Multitasking on GPUs is receiving a lot of attention from the research community as GPUs are becoming common in modern computer systems. First, we list recent works on enabling multitasking on GPUs. Next, we present previous studies on reducing the overhead of context switching on CPUs. Lastly, we discuss prior research that exploit the notion of idempotence.

Multitasking on GPUs: First attempts on GPU multitasking have been made on top of current GPUs by providing an illusion of single process to GPU or using cooperative multitasking. Context funneling [32] merges GPU contexts of multiple processes into a shared GPU context so that they can run concurrently on a single GPU. KernelMerge [9] makes GPUs only see a single scheduler kernel instead of individual independent kernels. Ino et al. [11] used cooperative multitasking to allow the concurrent execution of scientific and graphics applications on GPUs.

Some of the recent works study the scheduling policy when multitasking is enabled. Elastic kernels [24] transform kernels to enable fine grain control over the resource usage of kernels so that they can utilize SMs more efficiently. They study their scheme with multitasking by timeslicing a kernel to launch only a range of thread blocks at a time. Lee et al. [16] studies the interaction between thread block scheduling and warp scheduling. They also propose to run multiple kernels on the same SM, but do not present any detailed implementation.

Several works have paid attention to the independence of thread block execution. RGEM [12] splits memory transfers to GPU into smaller chunks so that they can be preempted at the chunk boundary. PKM [3] partitions a kernel into subkernels, where each subkernel executes a subset of thread blocks. SM draining [29] stops issuing a thread block and waits until all the running thread blocks are finished. Independence of thread block execution is a unique property of GPUs and creates opportunities for efficient preemption specific to GPUs. *Chimera* also utilizes the independence of thread block execution to enable SM flushing.

Spatial multitasking [1] observes that kernels may not fully occupy all the available SMs and shows that kernels can run on different subset of SMs. However, spatial multitasking still requires preemption if one kernel wants to dynamically take SM that is already running another kernel. Tanasic et al. [29] implement context switching to show that it still improves ANTT, however, they do not solve the problems of long preemption latency and large throughput overhead.

Chimera can control the overhead in preemptive multitasking with collaborative preemption. *Chimera* is the only solution so far that can meet a given preemption latency with minimized throughput overhead.

Context switching: Reducing the overhead of context switching has been researched for CPUs as well. One approach is finding fast context switch points, where there are only few live registers so that the amount of context to be stored can be reduced [27, 33]. But they either achieve small amount of gain or require code specific to each switch point for context switching. Another approach is to mark registers with additional bits to annotate whether corresponding register should be stored during the context switch [23]. With tens of thousands of registers in GPUs, the extra storage overhead is not acceptable. ASTI [26] statically sets context switching points during compile time, thus needs to know which applications will be running concurrently in advance.

All of these studies are limited in their applicability, and cannot be directly used in GPUs for low overhead context switching. In *Chimera*, context switching collaborates with preemption techniques that are specialized for GPUs to achieve low overhead preemption.

Idempotence: Idempotence has been primarily exploited to reduce the overhead of checkpointing in hardware. Reference idempotency [15] optimizes speculative execution by not tracking idempotent references, thus reduces speculative storage. Idempotent processor [6] and iGPU [17] implement low overhead exception support for CPUs and GPUs, respectively. They reconstruct a consistent program state for precise exception by re-executing from the beginning of idempotent region to the point of exception. Relax [5] and Encore [8] recover from soft errors with low overhead by selectively rerunning the idempotent regions rather than checkpointing all the states.

Chimera shares the idea of idempotence and is the first solution to try the notion of idempotence to eliminate preemption latency on GPUs with flushing. Moreover, flushing can be implemented with minimal overhead because the flush logic already exists, and relaxed idempotence condition is detected in software.

6. Conclusion

In this paper, we presented *Chimera*, a collaborative preemption approach on a shared GPU, that enables multitasking with controlled overhead. *Chimera* utilizes two GPU-specific preemption techniques called draining and flushing on top of traditional context switching. Draining exploits the independence of thread block execution to allow low throughput overhead preemption. Flushing brings the concept of idempotent execution to preemption, which can be combined with the independence of thread block execution to enable low preemption latency. By intelligently selecting a subset of SMs to be preempted as well as the preemption techniques for thread blocks, *Chimera* can meet a given preemption latency constraint with minimal throughput overhead. Evaluations show that *Chimera* violates a $15\mu s$ preemption latency constraint for only 0.2% of the preemption requests. For multi-programmed workloads, *Chimera* can improve the average normalized turnaround time by 5.5x, which can go up to 25.4x when a large number of preemption requests occur. System throughput can be improved by 12.2%, which can go up to 41.7% when a large number of preemption requests exist. *Chimera* demonstrates that preemptive multitasking on a shared GPU requires a different strategy from a traditional CPU, but is practical to implement.

Acknowledgments

We would like to thank the anonymous reviewers as well as Daya S. Khudia, Shruti Padmanabha, and Ankit Sethia for their valuable comments and feedbacks. This work is supported by the National Science Foundation under grants CNS-0964478 and CCF-1438996.

References

[1] Jacob T. Adriaens, Katherine Compton, Nam Sung Kim, and Michael J. Schulte. The case for GPGPU spatial multitasking. In *Proc. of the 18th International Symposium on High-Performance Computer Architecture*, pages 1–12, 2012.

[2] Ali Bakhoda, George L. Yuan, Wilson W. L. Fung, Henry Wong, and Tor M. Aamodt. Analyzing CUDA workloads using a detailed GPU simulator. In *Proc. of the 2009 IEEE Symposium on Performance Analysis of Systems and Software*, pages 163–174, April 2009.

[3] Can Basaran and Kyoung-Don Kang. Supporting preemptive task executions and memory copies in GPGPUs. In *2012 24th Euromicro Conference on Real-Time Systems*, pages 287–296, 2012.

[4] Shuai Che, Michael Boyer, Jiayuan Meng, David Tarjan, Jeremy W. Sheaffer, Sang-Ha Lee, and Kevin Skadron. Rodinia: A benchmark suite for heterogeneous computing. In *Proc. of the IEEE Symposium on Workload Characterization*, pages 44–54, 2009.

[5] Marc de Kruijf, Shuou Nomura, and Karthikeyan Sankaralingam. Relax: An architectural framework for software recovery of hardware faults. In *Proc. of the 37th Annual International Symposium on Computer Architecture*, pages 497–508, June 2010.

[6] Marc de Kruijf and Karthikeyan Sankaralingam. Idempotent processor architecture. In *Proc. of the 44th Annual International Symposium on Microarchitecture*, pages 140–151, 2011.

[7] Stijn Eyerman and Lieven Eeckhout. System-level performance metrics for multiprogram workloads. *IEEE Micro*, 28(3):42–53, 2008.

[8] Shuguang Feng, Shantanu Gupta, Amin Ansari, Scott Mahlke, and David August. Encore: Low-cost, fine-grained transient fault recovery. In *Proc. of the 44th Annual International Symposium on Microarchitecture*, pages 398–409, 2011.

[9] Chris Gregg, Jonathan Dorn, Kim Hazelwood, and Kevin Skadron. Fine-grained resource sharing for concurrent GPGPU kernels. In *Proceedings of the 4th USENIX Conference on Hot Topics in Parallelism*. USENIX, 2012.

[10] Michael Hind. Pointer analysis: Haven't we solved this problem yet? In *Proc. of the 2001 ACM SIGPLAN-SIGSOFT workshop on Program analysis for software tools and engineering*, pages 54–61, June 2001.

[11] Fumihiko Ino, Akihiro Ogita, Kentaro Oita, and Kenichi Hagihara. Cooperative multitasking for GPU-accelerated grid systems. *Concurrency and Computation: Practice and Experience*, 24(1):96–107, 2012.

[12] Shinpei Kato, Karthik Lakshmanan, Aman Kumar, Mihir Kelkar, Yutaka Ishikawa, and Ragunathan Rajkumar. RGEM: A responsive GPGPU execution model for runtime engines. In *2011 IEEE 32nd Real-Time Systems Symposium*, pages 57–66, 2011.

[13] Shinpei Kato, Karthik Lakshmanan, Ragunathan (Raj) Rajkumar, and Yutaka Ishikawa. TimeGraph: GPU scheduling for real-time multi-tasking environments. In *2011 USENIX Annaul Technical Conference (USENIX ATC'11)*, pages 17–30, 2011.

[14] KHRONOS Group. OpenCL - the open standard for parallel programming of heterogeneous systems, 2010.

[15] Seon Wook Kim, Chong-Liang Ooi, Rudolf Eigenmann, Babak Falsafi, and T.N. Vijaykumar. Reference idempotency analysis: A framework for optimizing speculative execution. In *Proc. of the 6th ACM SIGPLAN Symposium on Principles and Practice of Parallel Programming*, pages 2–11, 2001.

[16] Minseok Lee, Seokwoo Song, Joosik Moon, John Kim, Woong Seo, Yeongon Cho, and Soojung Ryu. Improving GPGPU resource utilization through alternative thread block scheduling. In *Proc. of the 20th International Symposium on High-Performance Computer Architecture*, pages 260–271, 2014.

[17] Jaikrishnan Menon, Marc de Kruijf, and Karthikeyan Sankaralingam. iGPU: Exception support and speculative execution on GPUs. In *Proc. of the 39th Annual International Symposium on Computer Architecture*, pages 72–83, 2012.

[18] NVIDIA. GPU Computing SDK. http://developer.nvidia.com/gpu-computing-sdk.

[19] NVIDIA. Fermi: Nvidias next generation CUDA compute architecture, 2009. http://www.nvidia.com/content/PDF/fermi_white_papers/NVIDIA_Fermi_Compute_Architecture_Whitepaper.pdf.

[20] NVIDIA. *CUDA C Programming Guide*, May 2011.

[21] NVIDIA. NVIDIA's next generation CUDA compute architecture: Kepler GK110, 2012. www.nvidia.com/content/PDF/NVIDIA_Kepler_GK110_Architecture_Whitepaper.pdf.

[22] NVIDIA. Sharing a GPU between MPI processes: Multi-process service (MPS) overview, 2014. http://docs.nvidia.com/deploy/mps/index.html.

[23] Andris Padegs, Brian B. Moore, Ronald M. Smith, and Werner Buchholz. The IBM system/370 vector architecture: Design considerations. *IEEE Transactions on Computers*, 37(5):509–520, 1988.

[24] Sreepathi Pai, Matthew J. Thazhuthaveetil, and Ramaswamy Govindarajan. Improving GPGPU concurrency with elastic kernels. In *18th International Conference on Architectural Support for Programming Languages and Operating Systems*, pages 407–418, March 2013.

[25] Moinuddin K. Qureshi and Yale N. Patt. Utility-based cache partitioning: A low-overhead, high-performance runtime mechanism to partition shared caches. In *Proc. of the 39th Annual International Symposium on Microarchitecture*, pages 423–432, 2006.

[26] Siddhartha Shivshankar, Sunil Vangara, and Alexander G. Dean. Balancing register pressure and context-switching delays in ASTI systems. In *Proc. of the 2005 International Conference on Compilers, Architecture, and Synthesis for Embedded Systems*, pages 286–294, September 2005.

[27] Jeffrey S. Snyder, David B. Whalley, and Theodore P. Baker. Fast context switches: Compiler and architectural support for preemptive scheduling. *Microprocessors and Microsystems*, 19(1):35–42, 1995.

[28] John A. Stratton, Christopher Rodrigues, I-Jui Sung, Nady Obeid, Li-Wen Chang, Nasser Anssari, Geng Daniel Liu, and

Wen mei Hwu. Parboil: A revised benchmark suite for scientific and commercial throughput computing. Technical Report IMPACT-12-01, University of Illinois at Urbana-Champaign, March 2012.

[29] Ivan Tanasic, Isaac Gelado, Javier Cabezas, Alex Ramirez, Nacho Navarro, and Mateo Valero. Enabling preemptive multiprogramming on GPUs. In *Proc. of the 41st Annual International Symposium on Computer Architecture*, pages 193–204, 2014.

[30] Nathan Tuck and Dean M. Tullsen. Initial observations of the simultaneous multithreading pentium 4 processor. In *Proc. of the 12th International Conference on Parallel Architectures and Compilation Techniques*, pages 26–34, 2003.

[31] Javier Vera, Francisco J. Cazorla, Alex Pajuelo, Oliverio J. Santana, Enrique Fernandez, and Mateo Valero. FAME: Fairly measuring multithreaded architectures. In *Proc. of the 16th International Conference on Parallel Architectures and Compilation Techniques*, pages 305–316, 2007.

[32] Lingyuan Wang, Miaoqing Huang, and Tarek El-Ghazawi. Exploiting concurrent kernel execution on graphic processing units. In *2011 International Conference on High Performance Computing and Simulation*, pages 24–32, 2011.

[33] Xiangrong Zhou and Peter Petrov. Rapid and low-cost context-switch through embedded processor customization for real-time and control applications. In *Proc. of the 43rd Design Automation Conference*, pages 352–357, 2006.

Page Placement Strategies for GPUs within Heterogeneous Memory Systems

Neha Agarwal[‡] * David Nellans[†] Mark Stephenson[†] Mike O'Connor[†] Stephen W. Keckler[†]

University of Michigan[‡] NVIDIA[†]

nehaag@umich.edu, {dnellans,mstephenson,moconnor,skeckler}@nvidia.com

Abstract

Systems from smartphones to supercomputers are increasingly heterogeneous, being composed of both CPUs and GPUs. To maximize cost and energy efficiency, these systems will increasingly use globally-addressable heterogeneous memory systems, making choices about memory page placement critical to performance. In this work we show that current page placement policies are not sufficient to maximize GPU performance in these heterogeneous memory systems. We propose two new page placement policies that improve GPU performance: one application agnostic and one using application profile information. Our application agnostic policy, bandwidth-aware (BW-AWARE) placement, maximizes GPU throughput by balancing page placement across the memories based on the aggregate memory bandwidth available in a system. Our simulation-based results show that BW-AWARE placement outperforms the existing Linux INTERLEAVE and LOCAL policies by 35% and 18% on average for GPU compute workloads. We build upon BW-AWARE placement by developing a compiler-based profiling mechanism that provides programmers with information about GPU application data structure access patterns. Combining this information with simple program-annotated hints about memory placement, our hint-based page placement approach performs within 90% of oracular page placement on average, largely mitigating the need for costly dynamic page tracking and migration.

Categories and Subject Descriptors D.4.2 [*Operating Systems*]: Storage management—Main memory

Keywords Bandwidth, Page placement, Linux, Program annotation

1. Introduction

GPUs are now ubiquitous in systems ranging from mobile phones to datacenters like Amazon's elastic compute cloud (EC2) and HPC installations like Oak Ridge National Laboratory's Titan supercomputer. In all of these systems, GPUs are increasingly being used for processing beyond traditional computer graphics, including image processing, computer vision, machine learning, physical dynamics in games, and modeling high energy particle interactions. Regardless of the class of system being considered, GPU/CPU architectures are evolving towards general-purpose cache coherent non-uniform memory access (CC-NUMA) designs with both CPUs and GPUs being able to access a unified globally-addressable memory [18]. While some of these systems may share a single homogeneous pool of memory, an increasing number of systems use heterogeneous memory technologies. Specifically, cost and/or energy concerns are driving memory system architects to provide a pool of high-bandwidth memory as well as a higher-capacity pool of lower-cost and/or lower-power memory.

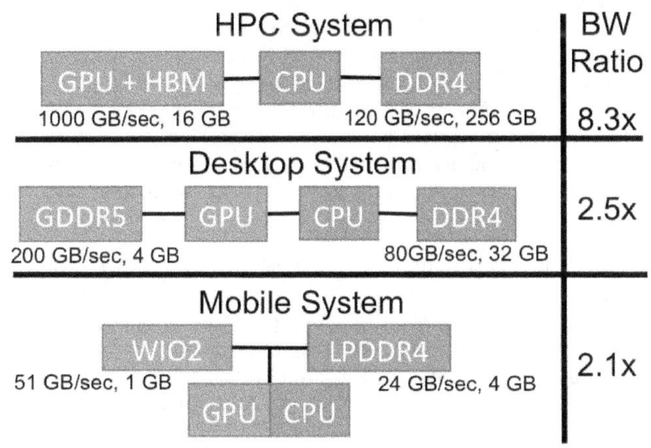

Figure 1: BW-Ratio of high-bandwidth vs high-capacity memories for likely future HPC, desktop, and mobile systems

Figure 1 shows several processor and memory topology options that are likely to be common over the next several years. While traditional systems are likely to continue using commodity DDR3 and soon DDR4, many future GPUs and mobile systems are moving to also include higher bandwidth, but capacity limited, on-package memories such as High Bandwidth Memory (HBM) or Wide-IO2 (WIO2). Regardless the type of machine, both memories will be globally accessible to maximize aggregate capacity and performance, making all systems non-uniform memory access (NUMA) due to variations in latency, bandwidth, and connection topology. Depending on the memories paired the bandwidth ratio between the bandwidth-optimized (BO) and capacity or cost optimized (CO) memory pools may be as low as 2× or as high as 8×.

To date, GPU-attached bandwidth optimized (BO) memory has been allocated and managed primarily as the result of explicit, programmer-directed function calls. As heterogeneous GPU/CPU

* This work was done while Neha Agarwal was an intern at NVIDIA.

ASPLOS '15, March 14–18, 2015, Istanbul, Turkey.

http://dx.doi.org/10.1145/2694344.2694381

systems move to a transparent unified memory system, the OS and runtime systems will become increasingly responsible for memory management functions such as page placement, just as they are in CPU-only NUMA systems today. In CC-NUMA systems, the notion of local versus remote memory latency is exposed to the operating system via the Advanced Configuration and Power Interface (ACPI). The latency differences between local and remote memory account for the additional latency incurred due to accessing remote memory across the system interconnect. In these systems, latency information, alone, is adequate, as CPUs are generally more performance sensitive to memory system latency, rather than other memory characteristics.

In contrast, massively parallel GPUs and their highly-threaded programming models have been designed to gracefully handle long memory latencies, instead demanding high bandwidth. Unfortunately, differences in bandwidth capabilities, read versus write performance, and access energy are not exposed to software; making it difficult for the operating system, runtime, or programmer to make good decisions about memory placement in these GPU-equipped systems. This work explores the effect on GPU performance of exposing memory system bandwidth information to the operating system/runtime and user applications to improve the quality of dynamic page placement decisions. Contributions of this work include:

1. We show that existing CPU-oriented page placement policies are not only sub-optimal for placement in GPU-based systems, but simply do not have the appropriate information available to make informed decisions when optimizing for bandwidth-asymmetric memory. Exposing additional bandwidth information to the OS, as is done for latency today, will be required for optimized decision making.
2. Perhaps counter-intuitively we show that, placing all pages in the bandwidth optimized memory is not the best performing page placement policy for GPU workloads. We propose and simulate a new bandwidth-aware (BW-AWARE) page placement policy that can outperform Linux's current bandwidth-optimized INTERLEAVE placement by 35% and the default latency optimized LOCAL allocation policy by as much as 18%, when the application footprint fits within bandwidth-optimized memory capacity.
3. For *memory capacity constrained* systems (i.e. bandwidth-optimized memory capacity is insufficient for the workload footprint), we demonstrate that using simple application annotations to inform the OS/runtime of hot versus cold data structures can outperform the current Linux INTERLEAVE and LOCAL page placement policies. Our annotation based policy combined with bandwidth information can outperform these page placement policies by 19% and 12% respectively, and get within 90% of oracle page placement performance.

2. Motivation and Background

2.1 Heterogeneous CC-NUMA Systems

Systems using heterogeneous CPU and GPU computing resources have been widely used for several years. Until recently, the GPU has been managed as a separate accelerator, requiring explicit memory management by the programmer to transfer data to and from the GPU's address space and (typically) the GPU's locally-attached memory. To increase programmer productivity and broaden the classes of workloads that the GPU can execute, recent systems have introduced automatic memory management enabling the CPU and GPU to access a unified address space and transparently migrate data at a page-level granularity [36]. The next step in this evolution is making the GPU a cache-coherent peer to the

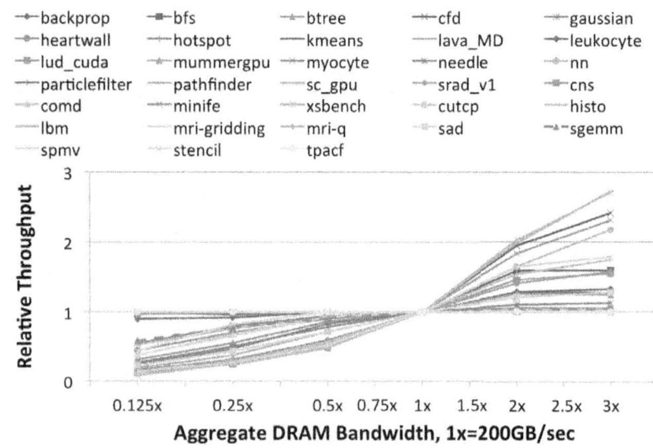

(a) Bandwidth sensitivity

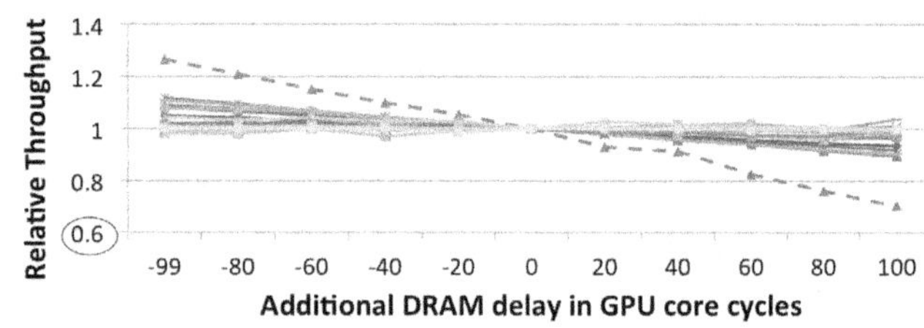

(b) Latency sensitivity

Figure 2: GPU performance sensitivity to bandwidth and latency changes.

CPU in the memory system, which is the stated goal of a number of commercial vendors [18].

While some heterogeneous CPU/GPU systems share a single unified physical memory [12], discrete GPUs are already using specialized DRAM optimized to meet their high bandwidth demands. To highlight the sensitivity of GPU performance to memory characteristics, Figures 2a and 2b show the performance variation as memory bandwidth and latency vary for a variety of GPU compute benchmarks from the Rodinia [10] and Parboil [44] suites, as well as a number of recent HPC [8, 17, 35, 46] workloads. Most of these GPU workloads are sensitive to changes in bandwidth, while showing much more modest sensitivity to varying the latency; only `sgemm` stands out as highly latency sensitive among these 33 workloads. Some application kernels are neither bandwidth nor latency sensitive and do not see significant performance variation as modifications are made to the memory subsystem. While GPU-equipped systems generally require bandwidth-optimized memories to achieve peak performance, these memory technologies have significant cost, capacity, and/or energy disadvantages over alternative DRAM technologies.

The most common bandwidth-optimized (BO) memory technology today is GDDR5 [19]. Providing a per-pin data rate of up to 7Gbps, this memory technology is widely used with discrete GPUs used in HPC, workstation, and desktop systems. Due to the high data rates, GDDR5 systems require significant energy per access and are unable to support high-capacity multi-rank systems. In contrast, the roadmap for the next several years of cost/capacity-optimized (CO) DRAM (DDR4 and LPDDR4) provides a per-pin data rate that reaches only 3.2 Gbps. However, these CO DRAM technologies provide similar latency at a fraction of the cost and lower energy per access compared to the BO GDDR5 memories.

Looking forward, systems requiring more bandwidth and/or reduced energy per access are moving to die-stacked DRAM technologies [24, 26]. These bandwidth-optimized stacked memories are significantly more energy-efficient than off-package memory technologies like GDDR5, DDR4, and LPDDR4. Unfortunately, the number of DRAM die that can be economically stacked in a single package is limited, necessitating systems to also provide a pool of off-package capacity-optimized DRAM.

This disaggregation of memory into on-package and off-package pools is one factor motivating the need to revisit page placement within the context of GPU performance. Future GPU/CPU systems are likely to take this disaggregation further and move capacity-optimized memory not just off the GPU package, but across a high speed interconnect where it is physically attached to the CPU rather than the GPU, or possibly further [30]. In a CC-NUMA system, the physical location of this capacity-optimized memory only changes the latency and bandwidth properties of this memory pool – it is functionally equivalent regardless of being CPU or GPU locally attached. A robust page placement policy for GPUs will abstract the on-package, off-package, and remote memory properties into performance and power characteristics based on which it can make optimized decisions.

2.2 Current OS NUMA Page Placement

In modern symmetric multiprocessor (SMP) systems, each socket typically consists of several cores within a chip multi-processor (CMP) that share last-level caches and on-chip memory controllers [22]. The number of memory channels connected to a processor socket is often limited by the available pin count. To increase the available memory bandwidth and capacity in a system, individual sockets can be connected via a cache coherent interconnect fabric such as Intel's Quick Path [21], AMD's HyperTransport [20], or NVIDIA's NVLink [38]. A single socket, the processors within it, and the physically attached memory comprise what an operating system sees as a local NUMA zone. Each socket is a separate NUMA zone. While a processor within any given zone can access the DRAM within any other zone, there is additional latency to service this memory request compared to a locally serviced memory request because the request must be routed first to its own memory controller, across the socket interconnect, and through the remote memory controller.

Operating systems such as Linux have recognized that, unless necessary, it is typically better for applications to service memory requests from their own NUMA zone to minimize memory latency. To get the best performance out of these NUMA systems, Linux learns system topology information from the Advanced Configuration and Power Interface (ACPI) System Resource Affinity Table (SRAT) and memory latency information from the ACPI System Locality Information Table (SLIT). After discovering this information, Linux provides two basic page placement policies that can be specified by applications to indicate where they prefer their physical memory pages to be placed when using standard `malloc` and `mmap` calls to allocate memory.

LOCAL: The default policy inherited by user processes is *LOCAL* in which physical page allocations will be from memory within the local NUMA zone of the executing process, unless otherwise specified or due to capacity limitations. This typically results in allocations from memory physically attached to the CPU on which the process is running, thus minimizing memory access latency.

INTERLEAVE: The second available allocation policy, which processes must specifically inform the OS they would like to use, is *INTERLEAVE*. This policy allocates pages round-robin across all (or a subset) of the NUMA zones within the SMP system to balance bandwidth across the memory pools. The downside of this policy is that the additional bandwidth comes at the expense of increased memory latency. Today, the OS has no knowledge about the relative bandwidth of memories in these different NUMA zones because SMP systems have traditionally had bandwidth-symmetric memory systems.

In addition to these OS placement policies, Linux provides a library interface called *libNUMA* for applications to request memory allocations from specific NUMA zones. This facility provides low-level control over memory placement but requires careful programming because applications running on different systems will often have different NUMA-zone layouts. Additional difficulties arise because there is no performance feedback mechanism available to programmers when making memory placement decisions, nor are they aware of which processor(s) their application will be running on while writing their application.

With the advent of heterogeneous memory systems, the assumptions that operating system NUMA zones will be symmetric in bandwidth, latency, and power characteristics break down. The addition of heterogeneous GPU and CPU computing resources further stresses the page placement policies since processes may not necessarily be migrated to help mitigate performance imbalance, as certain phases of computation are now pinned to the type of processor executing the program. As a result, data placement policies combined with bandwidth-asymmetric memories can have significant impact on GPU, and possibly CPU, performance.

2.3 Related Work

With the introduction of symmetric multiprocessors, significant work has examined optimal placement of processes and memory in CC-NUMA systems [6, 7, 23, 29, 48, 50]. While much of this early work focused on placing processes and data in close proximity to each other, more recent work has recognized that sharing patterns, interconnect congestion, and even queuing delay within the memory controller are important metrics to consider when designing page and process placement policies [2, 5, 11, 13, 27, 45, 53]. Nearly all of these works focus on improving traditional CPU throughput where reduced memory latency is the primary driver of memory system performance. Recent work from Gerofi et al. [16] examines TLB replacement policies for the Xeon Phi co-processor with a focus on highly parallel applications with large data footprints.

Using non-DRAM technologies or mixed DRAM technologies for main memory systems to improve power consumption on traditional CPUs has also been explored by several groups [4, 9, 28, 34, 40–42]. Much of this work has focused on overcoming the performance peculiarities that future non-volatile memory (NVM) technologies may have compared to existing DRAM designs. In addition to mixed technology off-package memories, upcoming on-package memories provide opportunities for latency reduction by increasing the number of banks available to the application [14] and may one day be configurable to balance bandwidth application needs with power consumption [51]. An alternative to treating heterogeneous memory systems as a flat memory space is to use one technology as a cache for the other [25, 32]. While this approach has the advantage of being transparent to the programmer, OS, and runtime systems, few implementations [43] take advantage of the additive bandwidth available when using heterogeneous memory.

In the GPU space, Zhao et al. [52] have explored the affect of hybrid DRAM-NVM systems on GPU compute workloads, making the observation that modern GPU designs are very good at hiding variable memory system latency. Wang et al. [49] explore a mixed NVM-DRAM system that uses compiler analysis to identify near-optimal data placement across kernel invocations for their heterogeneous memory system. While their system does not significantly improve performance, it offers improved power efficiency through use of NVM memory and shows that software based page placement, rather than hardware caching, can be a viable alternative to managing heterogeneous memory for use with GPUs.

3. BW-AWARE Page Placement

Using all available memory bandwidth is a key driver to maximizing performance for many GPU workloads. To exploit this observation, we propose a new OS page placement algorithm which accounts for the bandwidth differential between different bandwidth-optimized and capacity-optimized memories when making page placement decisions. This section discusses the need, implementation, and results for a bandwidth-aware (BW-AWARE) page placement policy for systems where the application footprint fits within BO memory, the common case for GPU workloads today. Later in Section 5, we discuss an extension to BW-AWARE placement for systems where memory placement decisions are constrained by the capacity of the bandwidth-optimized memory. Both HPC systems trying to maximize in-memory problem footprint and mobile systems which are capacity limited by cost and physical part dimensions may soon encounter these capacity constraints with heterogeneous memories.

3.1 Bandwidth Maximized Page Placement

The goal of bandwidth-aware page placement is to enable a GPU to effectively use the total combined bandwidth of *all* the memory in the system. Because GPUs are able to hide high memory latency without stalling their pipelines, all memories in a system can be used to service GPU requests, even when those memories are off-package or require one or more hops through a system interconnect to access. To exploit bandwidth-heterogeneous memories, our BW-AWARE policy places physical memory pages in the ratio of aggregate bandwidths of the memories in the system without requiring any knowledge of page access frequency. Below we derive that this placement policy is optimal for maximizing bandwidth.

Consider a system with bandwidth-optimized and capacity-optimized memories with bandwidths b_B and b_C respectively, where unrestricted capacity of both memories are available. Let f_B represent fraction of data placed in the BO memory and $1 - f_B$ in the CO memory. Let us assume there are total of N memory accesses uniformly spread among different pages. Then the total amount of time spent by the BO memory to serve $N * f_B$ memory accesses is $N * f_B/b_B$ and that by the CO memory to serve $N(1 - f_B)$ memory accesses is $N(1 - f_B)/b_C$. Since requests to these two memories are serviced in parallel, the total time T to serve the memory requests is:

$$T = max(N * f_B/b_B, N(1 - f_B)/b_C)$$

To maximize performance, T must be minimized. Since, $N*f_B/b_B$ and $N(1 - f_B)/b_C$ are linear in f_b and $N * f_B/b_B$ is increasing function while $N(1 - f_B)/b_C$ is decreasing, the minimum of T occurs when both are equal:

$$T_{opt} = N * f_B/b_B = N(1 - f_B)/b_C$$

Therefore,

$$f_{Bopt} = b_B/(b_B + b_C)$$

Because we have assumed that all pages are accessed uniformly, the optimal page placement ratio is the same as the bandwidth service ratio between the bandwidth-optimized and capacity-optimized memory pools. From this derivation we make two additional observations. First, BW-AWARE placement will generalize to an optimal policy where there are more than two technologies by placing pages in the bandwidth ratio of all memory pools. Second, a practical implementation of a BW-AWARE policy must be aware of the bandwidth provided by the various memory pools available within a system. Hence there is a need for a new System Bandwidth Information Table (SBIT), much like there is already a ACPI System Locality Information Table (SLIT) which exposes memory latency information to the operating system today. We will re-visit the assumption of uniform page access later in Section 4.1.

Simulator	GPGPU-Sim 3.x
GPU Arch	NVIDIA GTX-480 Fermi-like
GPU Cores	15 SMs @ 1.4Ghz
L1 Caches	16kB/SM
L2 Caches	Memory Side 128kB/DRAM Channel
L2 MSHRs	128 Entries/L2 Slice
Memory system	
GPU-Local GDDR5	8-channels, 200GB/sec aggregate
GPU-Remote DDR4	4-channels, 80GB/sec aggregate
DRAM Timings	RCD=RP=12,RC=40,CL=WR=12
GPU-CPU Interconnect Latency	100 GPU core cycles

Table 1: Simulation environment and system configuration for mixed memory GPU/CPU system.

3.2 Experimental Results

While it would be ideal to evaluate our page placement policy on a real CC-NUMA GPU/CPU system with a heterogeneous memory system, such systems are not available today. Mobile systems containing both ARM CPU cores and NVIDIA GPU cores exist today in products such as the NVIDIA Shield Portable, but use a single LPDDR3 memory system. Desktop and HPC systems today have heterogeneous memory attached to CPUs and discrete GPUs but these processors are not connected through a cache coherent interconnect. They require explicit user management of memory if any data is to be copied from the host CPU memory to the GPU memory or vice versa over the PCIe interconnect. Pages can not be directly placed into GPU memory on allocation by the operating system. Without a suitable real system to experiment on, we turned to simulation to evaluate our page placement improvements.

3.2.1 Methodology

To evaluate BW-AWARE page placement, we simulated a heterogeneous memory system attached to a GPU comprised of both bandwidth-optimized GDDR and cost/capacity-optimized DDR where the GDDR memory is attached directly to the GPU. No contemporary GPU system is available which supports cache-coherent access to heterogeneous memories. Commonly available PCIe-attached GPUs are constrained by interconnect bandwidth and lack of cache-coherence; while cache-coherent GPU systems, such as AMD's Kaveri, do not ship with heterogeneous memory.

Our simulation environment is based on GPGPU-Sim [3] which has been validated against NVIDIA's Fermi class GPUs and is reported to match hardware performance with up to 98.3% accuracy [1]. We modified GPGPU-Sim to support a heterogeneous GDDR5-DDR4 memory system with the simulation parameters listed in Table 1. We model a baseline system with 200GB/s of GPU-attached memory bandwidth and 80GB/s of CPU-attached memory bandwidth, providing a bandwidth ratio of 2.5×. We made several changes to the baseline GTX-480 model to bring our configuration in-line with the resources available in more modern GPUs, including a larger number of MSHRs and higher clock frequency. With a focus on memory system performance, we evaluate GPU workloads which are sensitive to memory bandwidth or latency from three benchmark suites: Rodinia [10], Parboil [44] and recent HPC [8, 17, 35, 46] workloads; those which are compute-bound see little change in performance due to changes made to the mem-

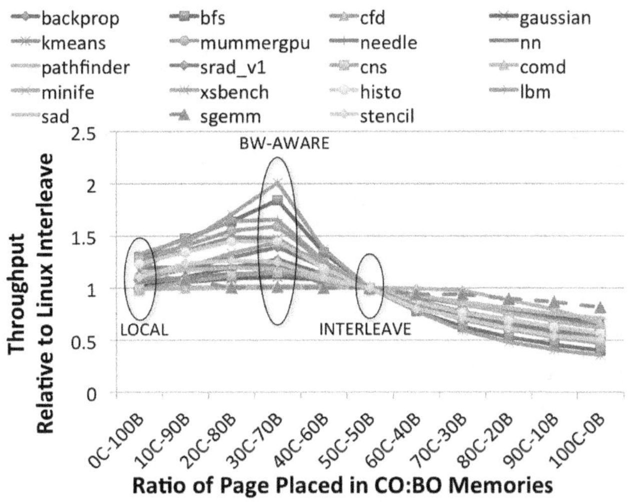

Figure 3: GPU workload performance with different page placement policies. xC-yB policy represents $x : y$ data transfer ratio from CO and BO memory respectively.

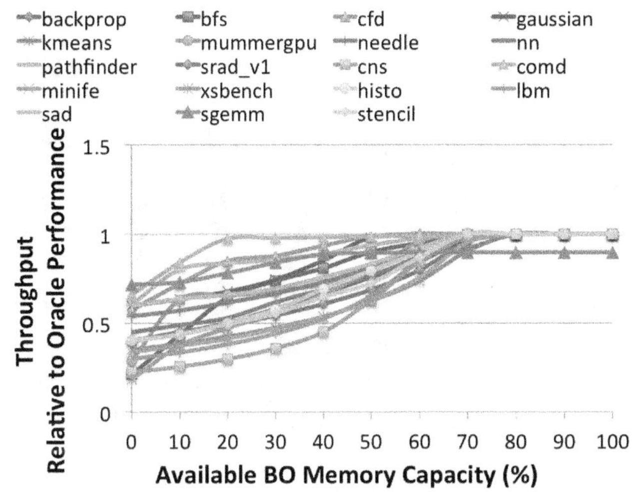

Figure 4: Performance of BW-AWARE placement as application footprint exceeds available high-bandwidth memory capacity.

ory system. For the remainder of the paper we show results for 19 benchmarks, 17 of which are sensitive to memory bandwidth while also providing `comd` and `sgemm` results to represent applications which are memory insensitive and latency sensitive respectively.

As noted in Section 2.1, attaching the capacity-optimized memory directly to the GPU is functionally equivalent to remote CPU attached memory, but with different latency parameters. To simulate an additional interconnect hop to remote CPU-attached memory, we model a fixed, pessimistic, additional 100 cycle latency to access the DDR4 memory from the GPU. This overhead is derived from the single additional interconnect hop latency found in SMP CPU-only designs such as the Intel XEON [22]. Our heterogeneous memory model contains the same number of MSHRs per memory channel as the baseline memory configuration. The number of MSHRs in the baseline configuration is sufficient to effectively hide the additional interconnect latency to the DDR memory in Figure 2b. Should MSHR quantity become an issue when supporting two level memories, previous work has shown that several techniques can efficiently increase MSHRs with only modest cost [33, 47].

Implementing a BW-AWARE placement policy requires adding another mode (`MPOL_BWAWARE`) to the `set_mempolicy()` system call in Linux. When a process uses this mode, the Linux kernel will allocate pages from the two memory zones in the ratio of their bandwidths. These bandwidth ratios may be obtained from future ACPI resources or dynamically determined by the GPU runtime at execution time.

3.2.2 BW-AWARE Performance

We define our BW-AWARE page placement policy xC-yB, where x and y denote the percentage of pages placed in a given memory technology, C stands for capacity-optimized memory and B stands for bandwidth-optimized memory. By definition $x + y = 100$. For our baseline system with 200GB/sec bandwidth-optimized memory and 80GB/sec of capacity-optimized memory the aggregate system bandwidth is 280GB/sec. In this notation, our BW-AWARE policy will then be $x = 80/280 = 28\%$ and $y = 200/280 = 72\%$, represented as $28C$-$72B$. However, for simplicity we will round this to $30C$-$70B$ for use as the placement policy. For processes running on the GPU, the LOCAL policy would be represented as $0C$-$100B$; $50C$-$50B$ corresponds to the bandwidth spreading Linux INTERLEAVE policy.

To achieve the target $30C$-$70B$ bandwidth ratio, we implemented BW-AWARE placement as follows. On any new physical page allocation, a random number in the range $[0, 99]$ is generated. If this number is ≥ 30, the page is allocated from the bandwidth-optimized memory; otherwise it is allocated in the capacity-optimized memory. A LOCAL allocation policy can avoid the comparison if it detects either B or C has the value zero. While this implementation does not exactly follow the BW-AWARE placement ratio due to the use of random numbers, in practice this simple policy converges quickly towards the BW-AWARE ratio. This approach also requires no history of previous placements nor makes any assumptions about the frequency of access to pages, minimizing the overhead for making placement decisions which are on the software fast-path for memory allocation.

Figure 3 shows the application performance as we vary the ratio of pages placed in each type of memory from 100% BO to 100% CO. For all bandwidth-sensitive applications, the maximum performance is achieved when using the correct BW-AWARE $30C$-$70B$ placement ratio. We find that, on average, a BW-AWARE policy performs 18% better than the Linux LOCAL policy and 35% better than the Linux INTERLEAVE policy. However, for latency sensitive applications, such as `sgemm`, the BW-AWARE policy may perform worse than a LOCAL placement policy due to an increased number of accesses to higher latency remote CO memory. The BW-AWARE placement policy suffers a worse case performance degradation of 12% over the LOCAL placement policy in this scenario.

Because the current Linux INTERLEAVE policy is identical to BW-AWARE for a bandwidth-symmetric DRAM $50C$-$50B$ memory technology pairing, we believe a BW-AWARE placement policy could simply replace the current Linux INTERLEAVE policy without having significant negative side affects on existing CPU or GPU workloads. Because maximizing bandwidth is more important than minimizing latency for GPU applications, BW-AWARE placement may be a good candidate to become the default placement policy for GPU-based applications.

3.2.3 Effective Improvement in Problem Sizing

Figure 4 shows the application throughput as we reduce the capacity of our bandwidth-optimized memory pool as a fraction of

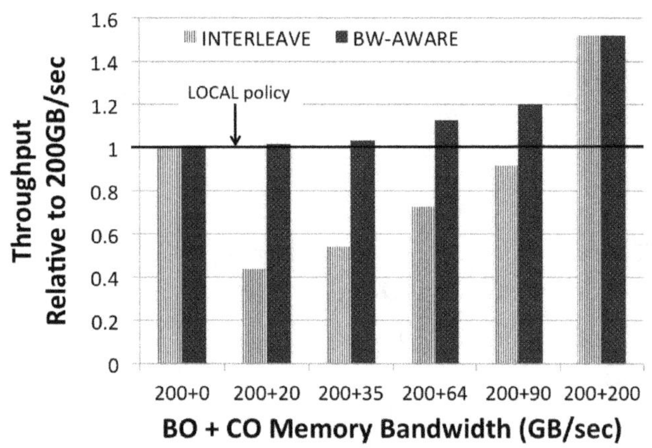

Figure 5: Performance comparison between BW-AWARE, INTERLEAVE, and LOCAL page placement policies while varying the memory bandwidth ratio.

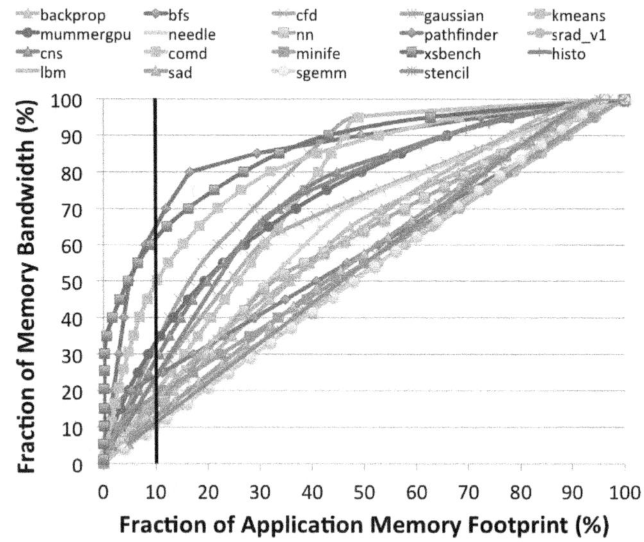

Figure 6: Data bandwidth cumulative distribution function with pages sorted from hot (most memory accesses) to cold (least memory accesses).

the total application footprint. BW-AWARE placement is able to achieve near peak performance even when only 70% of the application footprint fits within the BO memory because BW-AWARE placement places only 70% of pages in BO memory, with the other 30% is placed in the less expensive capacity-optimized memory. Thus, GPU programmers who today tune their application footprint to fit entirely in the GPU-attached BO memory could gain an extra 30% effective memory capacity by exploiting the CPU-attached CO memory with a BW-AWARE placement policy. However, as the bandwidth-optimized memory capacity drops to less than 70% of application footprint, performance begins to fall off. This effect is due to the ratio of bandwidth service from the two memory pools no longer matching the optimal ratio of $30C$-$70B$, with more data being serviced from the capacity optimized ratio than is ideal. Applications which are insensitive to memory bandwidth (shown as having little change in Figure 3), tend to maintain their performance at reduced capacity points (shown as having little change in Figure 4), because the average bandwidth reduction does not strongly affect their performance. Conversely, those applications with strong BW-performance scaling tend to see larger performance reduction as the average bandwidth available is reduced, due to capacity constraints forcing a disproportionate number of memory accesses to the lower bandwidth CO memory. The performance at 70% memory capacity does not exactly match 100% of ideal because the actual ratio of bandwidth in our system is $28C$-$72B$ not $30C$-$70B$.

3.2.4 Sensitivity to NUMA BW-Ratios

Heterogeneous memory systems are likely to come in a variety of configurations. For example, future mobile products may pair energy efficient and bandwidth-optimized Wide-IO2 memory with cost-efficient and higher capacity LPDDR4 memory. Using the mobile bandwidths shown in Figure 1, this configuration provides an additional 31% in memory bandwidth to the GPU versus using the bandwidth-optimized memory alone. Similarly, HPC systems may contain GPUs with as many as 4 on-package bandwidth-optimized HBM stacks and high speed serial interfaces to bulk capacity cost/capacity-optimized DDR memory expanders providing just 8% additional memory bandwidth. While we have explored BW-AWARE placement in a desktop-like use case, BW-AWARE page placement can apply to all of these configurations.

Figure 5 shows the average performance of BW-AWARE, INTERLEAVE, and LOCAL placement policies as we vary the additional bandwidth available from the capacity-optimized memory from 0GB/s–200GB/s. As the bandwidth available from capacity-optimized memory increases, the LOCAL policy fails to take advantage of it by neglecting to allocate any pages in the capacity-optimized memory. The Linux INTERLEAVE policy, due to its fixed round-robin allocation, loses performance in many cases because it oversubscribes the capacity-optimized memory, resulting in less total bandwidth available to the application. On the other hand, BW-AWARE placement is able to exploit the bandwidth from the capacity-optimized memory regardless the amount of additional bandwidth available. Because BW-AWARE placement performs identically to INTERLEAVE for symmetric memory and outperforms it in all heterogeneous cases, we believe that BW-AWARE placement is a more robust default policy than INTERLEAVE when considering bandwidth-sensitive GPU workloads.

4. Understanding Application Memory Use

Section 3 showed that optimal BW-AWARE placement requires the majority of the application footprint to fit in the bandwidth-optimized memory to match the bandwidth service ratios of the memory pools. However, as shown in Figure 1, systems may have bandwidth-optimized memories that comprise less than 10% the total memory capacity, particularly those using on-package memories which are constrained by physical dimensions. If the application footprint grows beyond the bandwidth-optimized capacity needed for BW-AWARE placement, the operating system has no choice but to steer remaining page allocations into the capacity-optimized memory. Unfortunately, additional pages placed in the CO memory will skew the ratio of data transferred from each memory pool away from the optimal BW-AWARE ratio.

For example, in our simulated system if the bandwidth-optimized memory can hold just 10% of the total application memory footprint, then a BW-AWARE placement would end up placing 10% pages in the BO memory; the remaining 90% pages must be spilled exclusively to the capacity-optimized memory. This ratio of $90C$-$10B$ is nearly the inverse of the performance-optimized ratio of $30C$-$70B$. To improve upon this capacity-induced placement problem, we recognize that not all pages have uniform access frequency, and we can selectively place hot pages in the BO memory and cold pages in the CO memory. In this work we define page *hotness* as the number of accesses to that page that are served from DRAM.

4.1 Visualizing Page Access Distribution

Figure 6 shows the cumulative distribution function (CDF) for memory bandwidth as a fraction of the total memory footprint for each of our workloads. The CDF was generated by counting accesses to each 4kB page, after being filtered by on-chip caches, and then sorting the pages from greatest to least number of accesses. Applications that have the same number of accesses to all pages have a linear CDF, whereas applications in which some pages are accessed more than others have a non-linear CDF skewed towards the left of the graph. For example, we see that for applications like `bfs` and `xsbench`, over 60% of the memory bandwidth stems from within only 10% of the application's allocated pages. Skewing the placement of these hot pages towards bandwidth-optimized memory will improve the performance of GPU workloads which are capacity constrained by increasing the traffic to the bandwidth-optimized memory. However, for applications which have linear CDFs, there is little headroom for improved page placement over BW-AWARE placement.

Figure 6 also shows that some workloads have sharp inflection points within the CDF, indicating that distinct ranges of physical addresses appear to be clustered as hot or cold. To determine if these inflection points could be correlated to specific memory allocations within the application, we plotted the virtual addresses that correspond to application pages in the CDF, and then reverse-mapped those address ranges to memory allocations for program-level data structures, with the results shown in Figure 7. The x-axis shows the fraction of pages allocated by the application, where pages are sorted from greatest to least number of accesses. The primary y-axis (shown figure left) represents the CDF of memory bandwidth among the pages allocated by the application (also shown in Figure 6). Each point on the secondary scatter plot (shown figure right) shows the virtual address of the corresponding page on the x-axis. The points (pages) are colored according to different data structures they were allocated from in the program source.

We analyze three example applications, `bfs`, `mummergpu`, and `needle` which show different memory access patterns. For `bfs`, we can see three data structures: `d_graph_visited`, `d_updating_graph_mask`, and `d_cost` consume $\approx$ 80% of the total application bandwidth while accounting for $\approx$ 20% of the memory footprint. However for `mummergpu`, the memory hotness does not seem to be strongly correlated to any specific application data structures. Several sub-structures have similar degrees of hotness and some virtual address ranges (10,000-19,000 and 29,000-37,000) are allocated but never never accessed. In `needle`, which has a fairly linear CDF, the degree of memory hotness actually varies within the same data structure. While we examined all applications with this analysis, we summarize our two key observations.

Individual pages can and often do have different degrees of hotness. Application agnostic page placement policies, including BW-AWARE placement, may leave performance on the table compared to a placement policy that is aware of page frequency distribution. Understanding the relative hotness of pages is critical to further optimizing page placement. If an application does not have a skewed CDF, then additional effort to characterize and exploit hotness differential will only introduce overhead without any possible benefit.

Workloads with skewed cumulative distribution functions often have sharp distinctions in page access frequency that map well to different application data structures. Rather than attempting to detect and segregate individual physical pages which may be hot or cold, application structure and memory allocation policy will likely provide good information about pages which will have similar degrees of hotness.

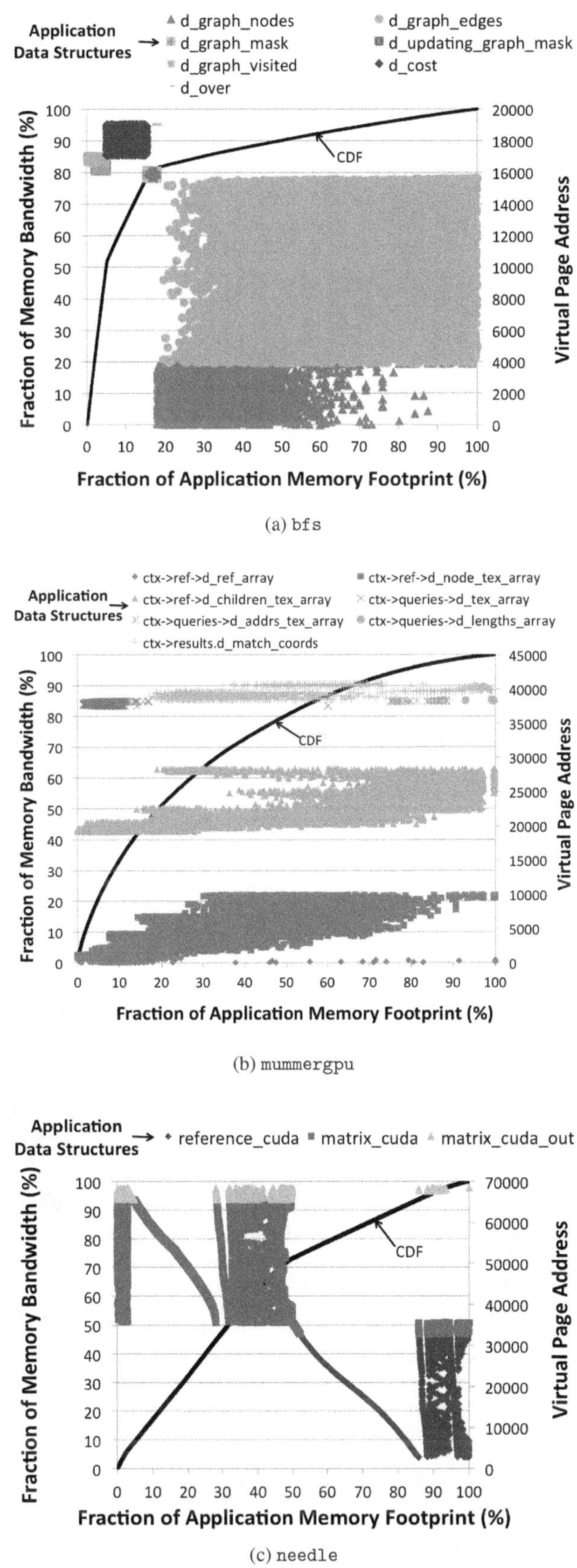

(a) `bfs`

(b) `mummergpu`

(c) `needle`

Figure 7: Application CDF of data footprint versus virtual address data layout.

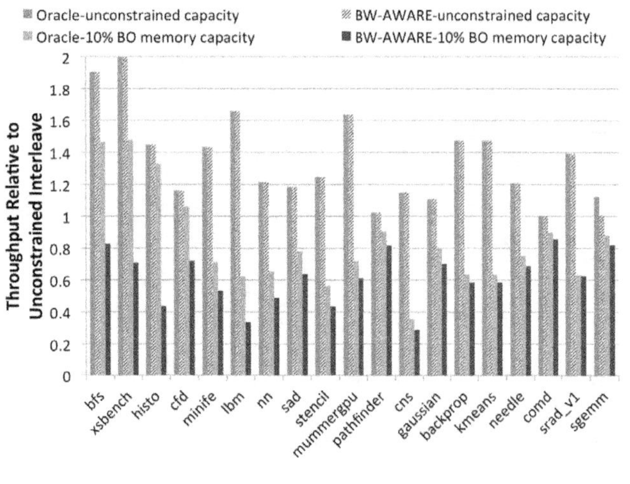

Figure 8: Oracle application performance of a constrained capacity system vs unconstrained capacity system

4.2 Oracle Page Placement

With knowledge that page accesses are highly differentiated for some applications, we implemented an oracle page placement policy to determine how much more application performance could be achieved compared to BW-AWARE placement in capacity constrained situations. Using perfect knowledge of page access frequency, an oracle page placement policy will allocate the hottest pages possible into the bandwidth-optimized memory until the target bandwidth ratio is satisfied, or the capacity of this memory is exhausted. We implemented this policy using two phase simulation. First, we obtained perfect knowledge of page access frequency. Then in a second simulation pass, we used this information to allocate pages to achieve the best possible data transfer ratio under a 10% capacity constraint where only 10% of the application memory footprint fits within the bandwidth-optimized memory.

Figure 8 compares the performance of the oracle and BW-AWARE placement policies in both the unconstrained and 10% capacity constrained configuration. Figure 8 confirms that BW-AWARE placement is near-optimal when applications are not capacity limited. This is because both BW-AWARE and oracle placement are both able to achieve the ideal bandwidth distribution, though the oracle policy is able to do this with a smaller memory footprint by placing fewer, hotter, pages in the BO memory. Under capacity constraints, however, the oracle policy can nearly double the performance of the BW-AWARE policy for applications with highly skewed CDFs and it outperforms BW-AWARE placement in all cases. This because the random page selection of BW-AWARE placement is not able to capture enough hot pages for placement in BO memory, before running out of BO memory capacity, to achieve the ideal bandwidth distribution. On average the oracle policy is able to achieve nearly 60% the application throughput of a system for which there is no capacity constraint. This additional performance, achievable through application awareness of memory access properties, motivates the need for further improvements in memory placement policy.

5. Application Aware Page Placement

Figure 7 visually depicts what may be obvious to performance-conscious programmers: *certain data structures are accessed more frequently than others.* For these programmers, the unbiased nature of BW-AWARE page placement is not desirable because all data structures are treated equally. This section describes compiler tool-flow and runtime modifications that enable programmers to intelligently steer specific allocations towards bandwidth- or capacity-optimized memories and achieve near-oracle page placement performance.

To correctly annotate a program to enable intelligent memory placement decisions across a range of systems, we need two pieces of information about a program: (1) the relative memory access hotness of the data structures, and (2) the size of the data structures allocated in the program. To understand the importance of these two factors, let us consider the following scenario. In a program there are two data structure allocations with hotness H1 and H2. If the bandwidth-optimized memory capacity is large enough for BW-AWARE placement to be used without running into capacity constraints, then BW-AWARE page placement should be used irrespective of the hotness of the data structures. To make this decision we must know the application runtime memory footprint. However, if the application is capacity-constrained, then ideally the memory allocation from the hotter data structure should be preferentially placed in the BO memory. In this case, we need to know both the relative hotness and the size of the data structures to optimally place pages.

5.1 Profiling Data Structure Accesses in GPU Programs

While expert programmers may have deep understanding of their application characteristics, as machines become more complex and programs rely more on GPU accelerated libraries, programmers will have a harder time maintaining this intuition about program behavior. To augment programmer intuition about memory access behavior, we developed a new GPU profiler to provide information about program memory access behavior.

In this work we augmented `nvcc` and `ptxas`, NVIDIA's production compiler tools for applications written in CUDA [39] (NVIDIAs explicitly parallel programming model), to support data structure access profiling. When profiling is enabled, our compiler's code generator emits memory instrumentation code for all loads and stores that enables tracking of the relative access counts to virtually addressed data structures within the program. As with the GNU profiler `gprof` [15], the developer enables a special compiler flag that instruments an application to perform profiling. The developer then runs the instrumented application on a set of "representative" workloads, which aggregates and dumps a profile of the application.

When implementing this GPU memory profiling tool, one of the biggest challenges is that `nvcc` essentially generates two binaries: a host-side program, and a device-side program (that runs on the GPU). The profiler's instrumentation must track the execution of both binaries. On the host side, the profiler inserts code to track all instances and variants of `cudaMalloc`. The instrumentation associates the source code location of the `cudaMalloc` with the runtime virtual address range returned by it. The host side code is also instrumented to copy this mapping of line numbers and address ranges to the GPU before each kernel launch. The GPU-side code is instrumented by inserting code before each memory operation to check if the address falls within any of the ranges specified in the map.

For each address that falls within a valid range, a counter associated with the range is incremented, using atomic operations because the instrumentation code is highly multi-threaded. At kernel completion, this updated map is returned to the host which launched the kernel to aggregate the statistics about virtual memory location usage. Our profiler generates informative data structure mapping plots, like those shown in Figure 7, which application programmers can use to guide their understanding of the relative access frequencies of their data structures, one of the two required pieces of information to perform intelligent near-optimal placement within an application.

5.2 Memory Placement APIs for GPUs

With a tool that provides programmers a profile of data structure hotness, they are armed with the information required to make page placement annotations within their application, but they are lacking a mechanism to make use of this information. To enable memory placement hints (which are not a functional requirement) for where data should be placed in a mixed BO-CO memory system, we also provide an alternate method for allocating memory. We introduce an additional argument to the `cudaMalloc` memory allocation functions that specifies in which domain the memory should be allocated (BO or CO) or to use BW-AWARE placement (BW). For example:

```
cudaMalloc(void **devPtr, size_t size, enum hint)
```

This hint is not machine specific and simply indicates if the CUDA memory allocator should make a best effort attempt to place memory within a BO or CO optimized memory using the underlying OS libNUMA functionality or fall back to the bandwidth-aware allocator. By providing an abstract hint, the CUDA runtime, rather than the programmer, becomes responsible for identifying and classifying the machine topology of memories as bandwidth or capacity optimized. While we have assumed bandwidth information is available in our proposed system bandwidth information table, programmatic discovery of memory zone bandwidth is also possible as a fall back mechanism [31]. In our implementation, memory hints are honored unless the memory pool is filled to capacity, in which case the allocator will fall back to the alternate domain. If no placement hint is provided, the CUDA runtime will fall back to using the application agnostic BW-AWARE placement for unannotated memory allocations. When a hint is supplied, the `cudaMalloc` routine uses the `mbind` system call in Linux to perform placement of the data structure in the corresponding memory.

5.3 Program Annotation For Data Placement

Our toolkit now includes a tool for memory profile generation and a mechanism to specify abstract memory placement hints. While programmers may choose to use this information directly, optimizing for specific machines, making these hints performance portable across a range of machines is harder as proper placement depends on application footprint as well as the memory capacities of the machine. For performance portability, the hotness and allocation size information must be annotated in the program before any heap allocations occur. We enable annotation of this information as two arrays of values that are linearly correlated with the order of the memory allocations in the program. For example Figure 9 shows the process of hoisting the size allocations manually into the `size` array and hotness into the `hotness` array.

We provide a new runtime function `GetAllocation` that then uses these two pieces of information, along with the discovered machine bandwidth topology, to compute and provide a memory placement hint to each allocation. `GetAllocation` determines appropriate memory placement hints by computing the ideal (BO or CO) memory location by first calculating the cumulative footprint of all data structures and then calculating the total number of identified data structures from `[1:N]` that will fit within the bandwidth-optimized memory before it exhausts the BO capacity.

It is not critical that programmers provide annotations for all memory allocations, only large or performance critical ones. For applications that make heavy use of libraries or dynamic decisions about runtime allocations, it may not be possible to provide good hinting decisions because determining the size of data structures allocated within libraries calls is difficult, if not impossible, in many cases.. While this process may seem impractical to a traditional high level language programmer, examining a broad range of GPU compute workloads has shown that in almost all GPU-optimized programs, the memory allocation calls are already hoisted to the beginning of the GPU compute kernel. The CUDA C Best Practices Guide advises the programmer to minimize memory allocation and de-allocation in order to achieve the best performance [37].

```
// n:input parameter
cudaMalloc(devPtr1, n*sizeof(int));
cudaMalloc(devPtr2, n*n);
cudaMalloc(devPtr3, 1000);
```

(a) Original code dependent allocations

```
// n: input parameter
// size[i]: Size of data structures
// hotness[i]: Hotness of data structures
size[0] = n*sizeof(int);
size[1] = n*n;
size[2] = 1000;
hotness[0] = 2;
hotness[1] = 3;
hotness[2] = 1;

// hint[i]: Computed data structure placement hints
hint[] = GetAllocation(size[], hotness[]);
cudaMalloc(devPtr1, size[0], hint[0]);
cudaMalloc(devPtr2, size[1], hint[1]);
cudaMalloc(devPtr3, size[2], hint[2]);
```

(b) Final code

Figure 9: Annotated pseudo-code to do page placement at runtime taking into account relative hotness of data structures and data structure sizes

5.4 Experimental Results

Figure 10 shows the results of using our feedback-based optimization compiler workflow and annotating our workloads using our new page placement interfaces. We found that on our capacity-limited machine, annotation-based placement outperforms the Linux INTERLEAVE policy performance by 19% and naive BW-AWARE 30C-70B placement by 14% on average. Combining program annotated placement hints and our runtime placement engine achieves 90% of oracular page placement on average. In all cases our program-annotated page placement algorithm outperforms BW-AWARE placement, making it a viable candidate for optimization beyond BW-AWARE placement if programmers choose to optimize for heterogeneous memory system properties.

One of the drawbacks to profile-driven optimization is that data dependent runtime characteristics may cause different behaviors than were seen during the profiling phase. While GPU applications in production will be run without code modification, the data set and parameters of the workload typically vary in both size and value from run-to-run. Figure 11 shows the sensitivity of our workload performance to data input set changes, where placement was trained on the first data-set but compared to the oracle placement for each individual dataset. We show results for the four example applications which saw the highest improvement of oracle placement over BW-AWARE. For `bfs`, we varied the number of nodes and average degree of the graph. For `xsbench`, we changed three parameters: number of nuclides, number of lookups, and number of gridpoints in the data set. For `minife`, we varied the dimensions of the finite element problem by changing the input matrix. Finally,

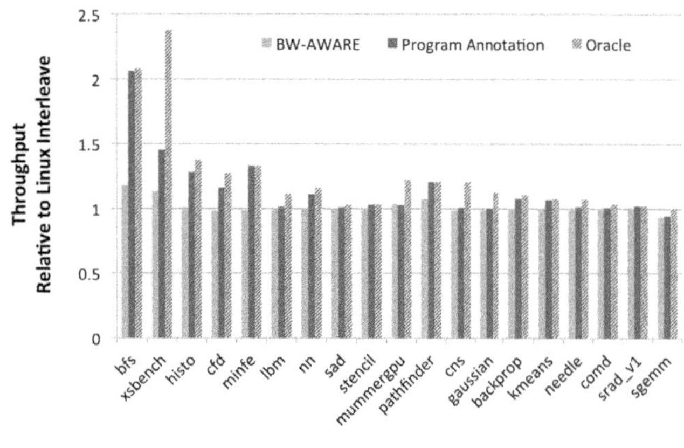

Figure 10: Profile-driven annotated page placement performance relative to INTERLEAVE, BW-AWARE and oracular policies under at 10% capacity constraint.

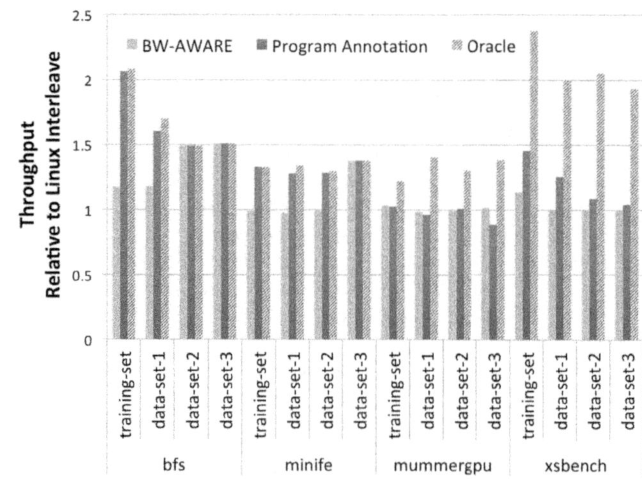

Figure 11: Annotated page placement effectiveness versus data sets variation after training phase under at 10% capacity constraint.

for mummergpu, we changed the number of queries and length of queries across different input data sets.

Using the profiled information from only the training set, we observe that annotated placement performs 29% better than the baseline Linux INTERLEAVE policy, performs 16% better than our own BW-AWARE 30C-70B placement, and achieves 80% of the oracle placement performance. This result indicates that for GPU compute applications, feedback-driven optimization for page placement is not overly sensitive to application dataset or parameter variation, although pessimistic cases can surely be constructed.

5.5 Discussion

The places where annotation-based placement falls short primarily come from three sources. First, our application profiling relies on spatial locality of virtual addresses to determine page hotness. We have shown that this spatial locality holds true for many GPU applications, but this is not guaranteed to always be the case. Allocations within libraries or larger memory ranges the programmer chooses to logically sub-allocate within the program will not exhibit this property. The second shortcoming of our annotation-based approach is for applications which show high variance within a single data structure. For example, when using a hashtable where the application primarily accesses a small, dynamically determined portion of the total key-space, our static hotness profiling will fail to distinguish the hot and cold regions of this structure. Finally, although our runtime system abstracts the programming challenges of writing performance portable code for heterogeneous machines, it is still complex and puts a large onus on the programmer. Future work will be to learn from our current implementation and identify mechanisms to reduce the complexity we expose to the programmer while still making near-ideal page placement decisions.

In this work we have focused on page placement for applications assuming a static placement of pages throughout the application runtime. We recognize that temporal phasing in applications may allow further performance improvement but have chosen to focus on initial page placement rather than page migration for two reasons. First, software-based page migration is a very expensive operation. Our measurements on the Linux 3.16-rc4 kernel indicate that it is not possible to migrate pages between NUMA memory zones at a rate faster than several GB/s and with several microseconds of latency between invalidation and first re-use. While GPUs can cover several hundred nanoseconds of memory latency, microsecond latencies encountered during migration will induce high overhead stalls within the compute pipeline. Second, online page migration occurs only after some initial placement decisions have been made. Focusing on online page migration before finding an optimized initial placement policy is putting the cart before of the horse. With improved default page placement for GPU workloads, the need for dynamic page migration is reduced. Further work is needed to determine if there is significant value to justify the expense of online profiling and page-migration for GPUs beyond improved initial page allocation.

6. Conclusions

Current OS page placement policies are optimized for both homogeneous memory and latency sensitive systems. We propose a new BW-AWARE page placement policy that uses memory system information about heterogeneous memory system characteristics to place data appropriately, achieving 35% performance improvement on average over existing policies without requiring any application awareness. In future CC-NUMA systems, BW-AWARE placement improves the performance optimal capacity by better using all system resources. But some applications may wish to size their problems based on total capacity rather than performance. In such cases, we provide insight into how to optimize data placement by using the CDF of the application in combination with application annotations enabling intelligent runtime controlled page placement decisions. We propose a profile-driven application annotation scheme that enables improved placement without requiring any runtime page migration. While only the beginning of a fully automated optimization system for memory placement, we believe that the performance gap between the current best OS INTERLEAVE policy and the annotated performance (min 1%, avg 20%, max 2x) is enough that further work in this area is warranted as mobile, desktop, and HPC memory systems all move towards mixed CPU-GPU CC-NUMA heterogeneous memory systems.

Acknowledgments

The authors would like to thank the numerous anonymous reviewers and R. Govindrajan for their valuable feedback. This work was supported by US Department of Energy and NSF Grant CCF-0845157.

References

[1] T. M. Aamodt, W. W. L. Fung, I. Singh, A. El-Shafiey, J. Kwa, T. Hetherington, A. Gubran, A. Boktor, T. Rogers, A. Bakhoda, and

H. Jooybar. GPGPU-Sim 3.x Manual. http://gpgpu-sim.org/manual/index.php/GPGPU-Sim_3.x_Manual, 2014. [Online; accessed 4-December-2014].

[2] M. Awasthi, D. Nellans, K. Sudan, R. Balasubramonian, and A. Davis. Handling the Problems and Opportunities Posed by Multiple On-Chip Memory Controllers. In *International Conference on Parallel Architectures and Compilation Techniques (PACT)*, pages 319–330, September 2010.

[3] A. Bakhoda, G. L. Yuan, W. W. L. Fung, H. Wong, and T. M. Aamodt. Analyzing CUDA Workloads Using a Detailed GPU Simulator. In *International Symposium on Performance Analysis of Systems and Software (ISPASS)*, pages 163–174, April 2009.

[4] R. A. Bheda, J. A. Poovey, J. G. Beu, and T. M. Conte. Energy Efficient Phase Change Memory Based Main Memory for Future High Performance Systems. In *International Green Computing Conference (IGCC)*, pages 1–8, July 2011.

[5] S. Blagodurov, S. Zhuravlev, M. Dashti, and A. Fedorova. A Case for NUMA-aware Contention Management on Multicore Systems. In *USENIX Annual Technical Conference (USENIXATC)*, pages 1–15, June 2011.

[6] W. Bolosky, R. Fitzgerald, and M. Scott. Simple but Effective Techniques for NUMA Memory Management. In *Symposium on Operating Systems Principles (SOSP)*, pages 19–31, December 1989.

[7] T. Brecht. On the Importance of Parallel Application Placement in NUMA Multiprocessors. In *Symposium on Experiences with Distributed and Multiprocessor Systems (SEDMS)*, pages 1–18, September 1993.

[8] C. Chan, D. Unat, M. Lijewski, W. Zhang, J. Bell, and J. Shalf. Software Design Space Exploration for Exascale Combustion Co-design. In *International Supercomputing Conference (ISC)*, pages 196–212, June 2013.

[9] N. Chatterjee, M. Shevgoor, R. Balasubramonian, A. Davis, Z. Fang, R. Illikkal, and R. Iyer. Leveraging Heterogeneity in DRAM Main Memories to Accelerate Critical Word Access. In *International Symposium on Microarchitecture (MICRO)*, pages 13–24, December 2012.

[10] S. Che, M. Boyer, J. Meng, D. Tarjan, J. W. Sheaffer, S.-H. Lee, and K. Skadron. Rodinia: A Benchmark Suite for Heterogeneous Computing. In *International Symposium on Workload Characterization (IISWC)*, pages 44–54, October 2009.

[11] J. Corbet. AutoNUMA: the other approach to NUMA scheduling. http://lwn.net/Articles/488709/, 2012. [Online; accessed 29-May-2014].

[12] M. Daga, A. M. Aji, and W.-C. Feng. On the Efficacy of a Fused CPU+GPU Processor (or APU) for Parallel Computing. In *Symposium on Application Accelerators in High-Performance Computing (SAAHPC)*, pages 141–149, July 2011.

[13] M. Dashti, A. Fedorova, J. Funston, F. Gaud, R. Lachaize, B. Lepers, V. Quema, and M. Roth. Traffic Management: A Holistic Approach to Memory Placement on NUMA Systems. In *International Conference on Architectural Support for Programming Languages and Operating Systems (ASPLOS)*, pages 381–394, March 2013.

[14] X. Dong, Y. Xie, N. Muralimanohar, and N. Jouppi. Simple but Effective Heterogeneous Main Memory with On-Chip Memory Controller Support. In *International Conference on High Performance Networking and Computing (Supercomputing)*, pages 1–11, November 2010.

[15] Free Software Foundation. GNU Binutils. http://www.gnu.org/software/binutils/, 2014. [Online; accessed 5-August-2014].

[16] B. Gerofi, A.Shimada, A. Hori, T. Masamichi, and Y. Ishikawa. CMCP: A Novel Page Replacement Policy for System Level Hierarchical Memory Management on Many-cores. In *International Symposium on High-performance Parallel and Distributed Computing (HPDC)*, pages 73–84, June 2014.

[17] M. Heroux, D. Doerfler, J. Crozier, H. Edwards, A. Williams, M. Rajan, E. Keiter, H. Thornquist, and R. Numrich. Improving Performance via Mini-applications. Technical Report SAND2009-5574, Sandia National Laboratories, September 2009.

[18] HSA Foundation. HSA Platform System Architecture Specification - Provisional 1.0. http://www.slideshare.net/hsafoundation/hsa-platform-system-architecture-specification-provisional-verl-10-ratifed, 2014. [Online; accessed 28-May-2014].

[19] Hynix Semiconductor. Hynix GDDR5 SGRAM Part H5GQ1H24AFR Revision 1.0. http://www.hynix.com/datasheet/pdf/graphics/H5GQ1H24AFR(Rev1.0).pdf, 2009. [Online; accessed 30-Jul-2014].

[20] HyperTransport Consortium. HyperTransport 3.1 Specification. http://www.hypertransport.org/docs/twgdocs/HTC20051222-0046-0035.pdf, 2010. [Online; accessed 7-July-2014].

[21] Intel Corporation. An Introduction to the Intel QuickPath Interconnect. http://www.intel.com/content/www/us/en/io/quickpath-technology/quick-path-interconnect-introduction-paper.html, 2009. [Online; accessed 7-July-2014].

[22] Intel Corporation. Intel Xeon Processor E7-4870 . http://ark.intel.com/products/75260/Intel-Xeon-Processor-E7-8893-v2-37_5M-Cache-3_40-GHz, 2014. [Online; accessed 28-May-2014].

[23] R. Iyer, H. Wang, and L. Bhuyan. Design and Analysis of Static Memory Management Policies for CC-NUMA Multiprocessors. *Journal of Systems Architecture*, 48(1):59–80, September 2002.

[24] JEDEC. High Bandwidth Memory(HBM) DRAM - JESD235. http://www.jedec.org/standards-documents/docs/jesd235, 2013. [Online; accessed 28-May-2014].

[25] X. Jiang, N. Madan, L. Zhao, M. Upton, R. Iyer, S. Makineni, D. Newell, Y. Solihin, and R. Balasubramonian. CHOP: Integrating DRAM Caches for CMP Server Platforms. *IEEE Micro*, 31(1):99–108, March 2011.

[26] J. Y. Kim. Wide IO2 (WIO2) Memory Overview. http://www.cs.utah.edu/events/thememoryforum/joon.PDF, 2014. [Online; accessed 30-Jul-2014].

[27] R. Knauerhase, P. Brett, B. Hohlt, T. Li, and S. Hahn. Using OS Observations to Improve Performance in Multicore Systems. *IEEE Micro*, 28(3):54–66, May 2008.

[28] E. Kultursay, M. Kandemir, A. Sivasubramaniam, and O. Mutlu. Evaluating STT-RAM as an Energy-efficient Main Memory Alternative. In *International Symposium on Performance Analysis of Systems and Software (ISPASS)*, pages 256–267, April 2013.

[29] R. LaRowe, Jr., C. Ellis, and M. Holliday. Evaluation of NUMA Memory Management Through Modeling and Measurements. *IEEE Transactions on Parallel Distribibuted Systems*, 3(6):686–701, November 1992.

[30] K. Lim, J. Chang, T. Mudge, P. Ranganathan, S. K. Reinhardt, and T. F. Wenisch. Disaggregated Memory for Expansion and Sharing in Blade Servers. In *International Symposium on Computer Architecture (ISCA)*, pages 267–278, June 2009.

[31] J. D. McCalpin. Memory Bandwidth and Machine Balance in Current High Performance Computers. *IEEE Technical Committee on Computer Architecture (TCCA) Newsletter*, pages 19–25, December 1995.

[32] J. Meza, J. Chang, H. Yoon, O. Mutlu, and P. Ranganathan. Enabling Efficient and Scalable Hybrid Memories Using Fine-Granularity DRAM Cache Management. *IEEE Computer Architecture Letters*, 11 (2):61–64, July 2012.

[33] A. Minkin and O. Rubinstein. Circuit and method for prefetching data for a texture cache. US Patent 6,629,188, issued September 20, 2003.

[34] J. Mogul, E. Argollo, M. Shah, and P. Faraboschi. Operating System Support for NVM+DRAM Hybrid Main Memory. In *Workshop on Hot Topics in Operating Systems (HotOS)*, pages 14–18, May 2009.

[35] J. Mohd-Yusof and N. Sakharnykh. Optimizing CoMD: A Molecular Dynamics Proxy Application Study. In *GPU Technology Conference (GTC)*, March 2014.

[36] NVIDIA Corporation. Unified Memory in CUDA 6. http://devblogs.nvidia.com/parallelforall/unified-memory-in-cuda-6/, 2013. [Online; accessed 28-May-2014].

[37] NVIDIA Corporation. CUDA C Best Practices Guide. https://docs.nvidia.com/cuda/cuda-c-best-practices-guide/index.html#allocation, 2014. [Online; accessed 28-July-2014].

[38] NVIDIA Corporation. NVIDIA Launches World's First High-Speed GPU Interconnect, Helping Pave the Way to Exascale Computing. http://nvidianews.nvidia.com/News/NVIDIA-Launches-World-s-First-High-Speed-GPU-Interconnect-Helping-Pave-the-Way-to-Exascale-Computin-ad6.aspx, 2014. [Online; accessed 28-May-2014].

[39] NVIDIA Corporation. Compute Unified Device Architecture. https://developer.nvidia.com/cuda-zone, 2014. [Online; accessed 28-May-2014].

[40] M. Pavlovic, N. Puzovic, and A. Ramirez. Data Placement in HPC Architectures with Heterogeneous Off-chip Memory. In *International Conference on Computer Design (ICCD)*, pages 193–200, October 2013.

[41] S. Phadke and S. Narayanasamy. MLP-Aware Heterogeneous Memory System. In *Design, Automation & Test in Europe (DATE)*, pages 1–6, March 2011.

[42] L. Ramos, E. Gorbatov, and R. Bianchini. Page Placement in Hybrid Memory Systems. In *International Conference on Supercomputing (ICS)*, pages 85–99, June 2011.

[43] J. Sim, G. Loh, H. Kim, M. O'Connor, and M. Thottethodi. A Mostly-Clean DRAM Cache for Effective Hit Speculation and Self-Balancing Dispatch. In *International Symposium on Microarchitecture (MICRO)*, pages 247–257, December 2012.

[44] J. A. Stratton, C. Rodrigues, I.-J. Sung, N. Obeid, v.-W. Chang, N. Anssari, G. D. Liu, and W.-m. W. Hwu. Parboil: A Revised Benchmark Suite for Scientific and Commercial Throughput Computing. Technical report, IMPACT Technical Report, IMPACT-12-01, University of Illinois, at Urbana-Champaign, March 2012.

[45] D. Tam, R. Azimi, and M. Stumm. Thread Clustering: Sharing-aware Scheduling on SMP-CMP-SMT Multiprocessors. In *European Conference on Computer Systems (EuroSys)*, pages 47–58, March 2007.

[46] J. Tramm, A. Siegel, T. Islam, and M. Schulz. XSBench - The Development and Verification of a Performance Abstraction for Monte Carlo Reactor Analysis. *The Role of Reactor Physics toward a Sustainable Future (PHYSOR)*, September 2014.

[47] J. Tuck, L. Ceze, and J. Torrellas. Scalable Cache Miss Handling for High Memory-Level Parallelism. In *International Symposium on Microarchitecture (MICRO)*, pages 409–422, December 2006.

[48] B. Verghese, S. Devine, A. Gupta, and M. Rosenblum. Operating System Support for Improving Data Locality on CC-NUMA Compute Servers. In *International Conference on Architectural Support for Programming Languages and Operating Systems (ASPLOS)*, pages 279–289, September 1996.

[49] B. Wang, B. Wu, D. Li, X. Shen, W. Yu, Y. Jiao, and J. Vetter. Exploring Hybrid Memory for GPU Energy Efficiency Through Software-hardware Co-design. In *International Conference on Parallel Architectures and Compilation Techniques (PACT)*, pages 93–103, September 2013.

[50] K. Wilson and B. Aglietti. Dynamic Page Placement to Improve Locality in CC-NUMA Multiprocessors for TPC-C. In *International Conference on High Performance Networking and Computing (Supercomputing)*, pages 33–35, November 2001.

[51] J. Zhao, G. Sun, G. Loh, and Y. Xie. Energy-efficient GPU Design with Reconfigurable In-package Graphics Memory. In *International Symposium on Low Power Electronics and Design (ISLPED)*, pages 403–408, July 2012.

[52] J. Zhao, G. Sun, G. Loh, and Y. Xie. Optimizing GPU Energy Efficiency with 3D Die-stacking Graphics Memory and Reconfigurable Memory Interface. *ACM Transactions on Architecture and Code Optimization*, 10(4):24:1–24:25, December 2013.

[53] S. Zhuravlev, S. Blagodurov, and A. Fedorova. Addressing Shared Resource Contention in Multicore Processors via Scheduling. In *International Conference on Architectural Support for Programming Languages and Operating Systems (ASPLOS)*, pages 129–142, March 2010.

On-the-Fly Principled Speculation for FSM Parallelization

Zhijia Zhao
Computer Science Department
College of William and Mary, USA
zzhao@cs.wm.edu

Xipeng Shen
Computer Science Department
North Carolina State University, USA
xshen5@ncsu.edu

Abstract

Finite State Machine (FSM) is the backbone of an important class of applications in many domains. Its parallelization has been extremely difficult due to inherent strong dependences in the computation. Recently, principled speculation shows good promise to solve the problem. However, the reliance on offline training makes the approach inconvenient to adopt and hard to apply to many practical FSM applications, which often deal with a large variety of inputs different from training inputs.

This work presents an assembly of techniques that completely remove the needs for offline training. The techniques include a set of theoretical results on inherent properties of FSMs, and two newly designed dynamic optimizations for efficient FSM characterization. The new techniques, for the first time, make principle speculation applicable on the fly, and enables swift, automatic configuration of speculative parallelizations to best suit a given FSM and its current input. They eliminate the fundamental barrier for practical adoption of principle speculation for FSM parallelization. Experiments show that the new techniques give significantly higher speedups for some difficult FSM applications in the presence of input changes.

Categories and Subject Descriptors D3.4 [*Programming Languages*]: Processors

General Terms Languages, Performance

Keywords Finite State Machine, FSM, DFA, Speculative Parallelization, Multicore, Online Profiling

1. Introduction

Finite State Machine (FSM) is the backbone of many important applications in various domains. It consumes most time in pattern matching [3], XML validation [23], front end of a compiler [2], compression and decompression [16], model checking, network intrusion detection [13], and many other important applications. The performance of these applications is often critical for improving user experienced responsiveness, supporting large-scaled network traffics, or meeting the quality of service provided by commercial servers. Given that processors are gaining more parallelism rather than higher frequency, it is hence essential to parallelize FSM computations to achieve sustained performance improvement.

However, FSM applications are challenging to parallelize —so challenging that they are known as "embarrassingly essential" applications [3]. Dependences exist between every two steps of the computations of an FSM application. Consider the string matching example in Figure 1. On a machine with two computing units, a natural way to parallelize the pattern matching is to evenly divide the input string, S, into two segments as illustrated by the broken vertical line in Figure 1, and let the threads process the segments concurrently, one segment per thread. The difficulty is in determining the correct start state to use by the second thread. It should equal the state at which the FSM ends when the first thread finishes

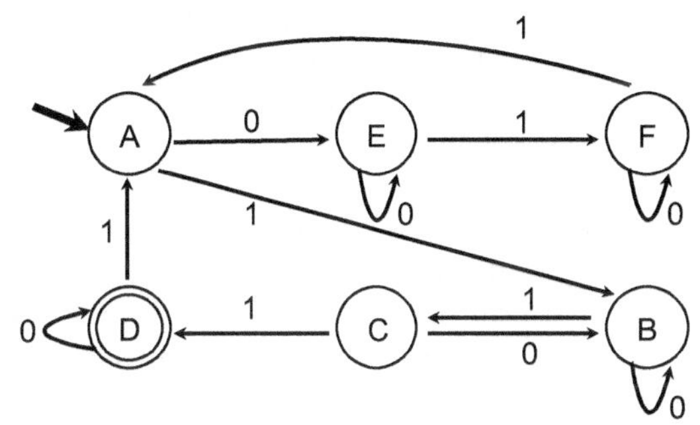

An example input:
... 10011010 ⋮ 11010011 ...

Figure 1. An FSM for string pattern matching and an example input string to it. Each circle on the graph represents an FSM state. State A is the initial state (marked by the extra incoming edge), and state D is an acceptance state. The symbols on the edges indicate conditions for state transitions.

ASPLOS '15, March 14–18, 2015, Istanbul, Turkey.

ACM 978-1-4503-2835-7/15/03... $15.00.
http://dx.doi.org/10.1145/2694344.2694369

processing the first segment. In general, such dependences connect all threads into a dependence chain, preventing concurrent executions of any two threads.

Driven by the importance and challenges of FSM parallelization, recent years have seen an increasing research efforts in enabling high performance parallel FSM executions [22, 31]. A traditional way to parallelize FSM is through prefix-sum parallelization or its variations [18]. A recent study [22] shows that a careful implementation of the method on vector units on modern machines can produce large speedup. However, as that study also acknowledges, the approach is fundamentally subject to scalability issues: The number of threads that conduct useless computations increase linearly with the number of states.

An orthogonal approach is speculative parallelization [14, 23, 31]. The basic idea is to take a guess of the starting state for every thread (other than the first) such that all threads can process their chunks of inputs concurrently. The part of inputs that are processed incorrectly by a thread due to the speculation errors will be reprocessed after the correct ending state of the previous thread (i.e., the correct starting state of this thread) becomes known.

The quality of state speculation is apparently critical for the performance. It depends on a number of design choices, including where to draw hints for speculation, how to use those hints, what state to take as the starting state to execute the FSM speculatively, and so on. A recent work [31] presents a rigorous approach to finding the design that best suits a FSM and its inputs. The approach is called *principled speculation*, which employs a probabilistic make-span model to formulate the profits of a speculation, through which, speculations can be customized to the probabilistic properties of the FSM and hence maximize the overall performance of its parallel executions.

Although the method outperforms previous ad-hoc designs significantly, it is based on offline training. Before using the speculative parallelization, users in most cases have to conduct some tedious, time-consuming training runs of the FSM to collect some probabilistic properties of the states of the FSM and its inputs. The offline training imposes much burden on users. More importantly, it limits the applicability of principled speculation to cases in which the real inputs to the FSM are similar to the training inputs. Otherwise, the offline collected probabilistic properties fail to match with the real inputs, throttling the effectiveness of principled speculation significantly (up to 7x in our experiments shown in Section 6). In practice, many FSM applications need to deal with various kinds of inputs. A compression tool may be used to compress images, videos, texts, and other types of data; a compiler may need to scan or parse programs of various sizes, complexity, and styles; a network intrusion detector may have to go through all kinds of data packages go through the network. Therefore, the lack of cross-input adaptivity forms a fundamental barrier for practical deployment of principled speculation.

This paper addresses the problem by, for the first time, enabling on-the-fly principled speculation for FSM. It proposes a novel static FSM property analysis and two new dynamic optimizations for collecting statistical properties of an FSM. By lowering the cost in collecting expected convergent lengths by orders of magnitude, it makes the principled speculation able to get deployed on the fly, and hence fundamentally removes the input sensitivity issue faced by the state-of-the-art design. With the solution, an FSM application can automatically equip the speculative parallelization with design configurations that best suite the properties of the FSM and its current input. The entire process happens during production runs of an FSM, requiring no offline training or user intervention. Experiments show that the technique reduces the time needed to collect the statistical properties of an FSM by tens to thousands of times, and improve the parallel performance of seven FSMs by up to 7x (1.5x on average).

To our best knowledge, this work is the first that makes on-the-fly principled speculation possible. By removing a fundamental limitation of the basic principled speculation, it eliminates the major barrier for practical adoption of principled speculation, and hence opens new opportunities for maximizing the performance of real-world FSM applications that deal with data in an increasing variety.

2. Background and Problem

In this section, we first present the background of principled parallelization, and then explain the key barrier for its practical deployment.

Principled Speculation At the center of principled speculative parallelization is a make-span formula, which offers the statistical expectation of the make-span of a speculatively parallelized execution of an FSM. Here, *make-span* means end to end execution time, including all speculation overhead and reexecutions upon speculation errors. An important feature of the method is that the make-span formula is based on the statistical properties of the given FSM. So if the statistical properties of an FSM are known, from the formula, the method can analytically figure out how good a design of speculative parallelization is for that FSM. Through the method, the authors of the previous work [31] have shown the feasibility to automatically customize the design of speculative parallelization based on the properties of a given FSM such that its parallel performance can be maximized.

Barrier for Practical Deployment A challenge for practical deployment of the method is in how to obtain the statistical properties of an FSM. These properties include the following:

- *size*: the number of states in the FSM
- *state feasibilities*: the probability of each of its states to get reached in an execution. For instance, if the FSM is at state A in 10% time of an execution, the state feasibility of state A is 10%.
- *character probabilities*: the probability for the next input character to be a particular character while the FSM is at a given state. For instance, if 20% of time, the next character to the FSM is "a" while the current state of the FSM is B, the character probability is $P(a|B) = 0.2$.
- *expected convergent lengths*: Consider two copies of an FSM that start processing the same input string independently from two states, s_i and s_j. If the two FSM copies move into the same state after they finish processing l-character of the input string but not before that, we say that the two states s_i and s_j converge into the same state, and their convergent length is l. For instance, no matter whether the FSM in Figure 1 starts from state C or E, it always moves into the same state A after processing string "11". Therefore, the convergent length between C and E on that input is 2. For a long input string, two states may have different convergent lengths at different sections of the input. The expected convergent length of the two states is the average (or statistical expectation) of all those possible convergent lengths, denoted as $L_M(s_i, s_j)$.

Except *size*, all the other properties are decided by not only the FSM, but also its input. Prior work has shown that *state feasibilities* and *character probabilities* can be easily obtained through lightweight online profiling of the execution of the FSM. But *expected convergent lengths* cannot for most FSMs due to the large cost of collecting convergent lengths.

The large cost comes from three reasons. First, since $L_M(s_i, s_j) = L_M(s_j, s_i)$ and $L_M(s_i, s_i) = 0$, there are $N \cdot (N-1)/2$ pairs of states needed to profile for an FSM with N states. Second, for each pair of states, it usually requires a number of samples to get a reliable average value. Third, to get one sample for a pair of states (s_i, s_j), it takes $(L_M(s_i, s_j) \cdot 2)$ state transitions. Suppose the average number of transitions among all state pairs is L. (If some pairs of states never converge on the given input, a large number is used, denoted as $MAXLEN$.) Let the number of needed samples of convergent lengths per pair of states is $SAMPLE$ ($SAMPLE = 10$ in prior work). The complexity for collecting all expected convergent lengths for an FSM is $O(N^2 \cdot SAMPLE \cdot L)$. Algorithm 1 shows the default algorithm used for profiling the state convergent length.

The actual cost of this default profiling algorithm could range from several seconds to tens of minutes (details in Section 6). As that is comparable or even longer than the parallel execution time of many FSM applications, doing it online is often not affordable. In the prior work, it is affordable on only two out of seven benchmarks [31].

Algorithm 1 Default Convergent Length Profiling

```
for each pair of states (s_i, s_j) do
    result[s_i][s_j].sum = 0
    result[s_i][s_j].cnt = 0
    while result[s_i][s_j].cnt ¡ SAMPLE do
        l = 0
        s_a = s_i, s_b = s_j
        while (s_a ≠ s_b —— l ¡ MAXLEN) do
            c = read()
            s_a = transit(s_a, c), s_b = transit(s_b, c)
        end
        result[s_i][s_j].sum += l
        result[s_i][s_j].cnt++
    end
    print result[s_i][s_j].sum / SAMPLE
end
```

For that reason, convergent length profiling has been mostly done offline on some training runs of an FSM. It is acceptable if the inputs in the production runs of the FSM are similar to the training inputs. But that condition often do not hold for many real-world FSM applications, which often need to process a variety of inputs. As data variety rapidly increases with the trends towards "big data", the issue is a critical barrier for practical usage of the principled speculative parallelization for FSM.

3. Overview of Solutions

The solution developed in this work addresses the issue by completely eliminating the need for offline training. By lowering the cost in collecting expected convergent lengths by orders of magnitude, it makes the principled speculation able to get deployed on the fly, and hence fundamentally removes the input sensitivity issue faced by the state-of-the-art design.

The removal of the high collection cost is through a synergy between a novel static FSM property analysis and two new dynamic optimizations. With this solution, the speculative parallelization runs in this way. At the beginning of a production run, the FSM application calls our static FSM analyzer (through an inserted library function call), which examines the FSM and infers some inherent properties that can hold regardless of what inputs are used. Then, it invokes a lightweight online profiling of the FSM on a small portion of the current input. The profiling, guided by the properties from the static analyzer and facilitated with two new dynamic optimizations, goes orders of magnitude faster than the previous FSM profilings. After obtaining all the statistical properties of the FSM, the FSM application automatically equips the speculative parallelization with the best suitable design configurations accordingly, processes the input in parallel, and returns the output to the user.

The next two sections explain the static analysis and the two dynamic optimizations respectively.

4. Static Analysis on FSMs

The objective of the static analysis is to infer some inherent properties of an FSM, which may guide the online FSM profiling. Specifically, our static FSM analyzer infers two properties of an FSM as follows:

- *FSM convergence:* whether there is any pair of states in the FSM that are ever possible to converge.
- *Minimal convergent lengths:* what is the minimal convergent length of each pair of states in the FSM.

The two properties both relate with convergent length collection of an FSM; the first helps avoid convergent length profiling at a coarse grain, while the second helps the avoidance at a finer grain. If the first property says that no two states in the FSM converge, the convergent length collection can be safely skipped entirely; otherwise, if the second property says that the minimal convergent length of a certain pair of states is infinity, the collection can simply avoid profiling on that pair of states.

The static analysis is based on a series of theoretical results developed in this work. This section presents them. For the theoretical nature, the presentation contains some formalism, which we find indispensable for the rigorous inference. However, we try to ease the understanding efforts through examples and graphs. As Deterministic Finite Automaton (DFA) is the most common form of FSM, it has been the focus of recent studies and also this current study on FSM parallelization. The following of this section uses the term DFA rather than FSM to be specific.

4.1 Preliminaries

Before explaining how the static analysis infers the two properties of FSM, we first introduce some concepts and notations to be used in the follow-up explanation. Some concepts have been mentioned in earlier sections but in an informal way; for rigor and completeness, we give their formal definitions here as well.

A *deterministic finite automaton* is a 5-tuple $(Q, \Sigma, \delta, q_0, F)$, where Q is a finite state set called *states*, Σ is a finite set called the *alphabet*, $\delta : Q \times \Sigma \to Q$ is the *transition function*, $q_0 \in Q$ is the *initial state*, and $F \subseteq Q$ is the *set of accept states*. The members of the alphabet are called *symbols*. A *string* over an alphabet is a finite sequence of symbols from that alphabet. We use α, β, or γ to denote strings. The set of all possible strings over Σ is denoted as Σ^*. If α is a string over Σ, the *length* of α, written $|\alpha|$, is the number of symbols that it contains. The string of length zero is called the *empty string*, denoted as ϵ. If α has length n, we can write $\alpha = a_1 a_2 \cdots a_n$, where $a_i \in \Sigma$. If there exists a transition function from state s and symbol a to state s' in δ, we say s transits to s' on symbol a, denoted as $s \xrightarrow{a} s'$.

For convenience, we introduce the following terms and notations.

Definition 1 (State Combination). *A* <u>*k-state combination*</u> *of $\mathcal{M}$ is a k-element subset of the states of a DFA, denoted as $c^{(k)}$. The set of all k-state combinations of a DFA is called* <u>*k-state combination set,*</u> *denoted as $C_Q^{(k)}$. Clearly, $C_Q^{(1)} = Q$, where Q is the state set of the DFA.*

As $c^{(1)}$ contains only one state, we sometimes use it to also refer to the state it contains.

Definition 2 (State Combination Transition). *Let $c^{(k)}$ be a k-state combination of a DFA $\mathcal{M}$ and $c^{(k')}$ be a k′-state combination of $\mathcal{M}$, we say $c^{(k)}$* <u>*transits*</u> *to $c^{(k')}$ on input symbol a, if and only if $c^{(k')} = \{s' | s \xrightarrow{a} s', \forall s, s \in c^{(k)}\}$, denoted as $c^{(k)} \xrightarrow{a} c^{(k')}$.*

Note that if $c^{(k)} \xrightarrow{a} c^{(k')}$, k' must be no greater than k, guaranteed by the deterministic transitions in the DFA. Actually, k' could be smaller than k in the cases multiple states in $c^{(k)}$ transit to a single state on symbol a.

Definition 3 (Convergence). *Let $c^{(k)}$ be a k-state combination of a DFA, if there is a string α such that $c^{(k)} \xrightarrow{\alpha} c^{(1)}$, then we say $c^{(k)}$* <u>*converges*</u> *on string α, or $c^{(k)}$ is* convergent. *The state in $c^{(1)}$ is called* <u>*convergence state.*</u>

Since $c^{(1)} \xrightarrow{\epsilon} c^{(1)}$, we consider every $c^{(1)}$ is convergent. According to Definition 3, it is obvious that if a k-state combination $c^{(k)}$ converges on α, then it converges on any string with α as the prefix, that is $c^{(k)} \xrightarrow{\alpha\beta} c^{(1)}$, where β is any string in Σ^*.

Definition 4 (Convergent Length). *Let $c^{(k)}$ be a k-state combination of a DFA that converges on a string α, then the* <u>*convergent prefix*</u> *of α is the shortest prefix of α that $c^{(k)}$ can converge on, denoted as α_c. The length of α_c is called the* <u>*convergent length*</u> *of $c^{(k)}$ on α, denoted as $L_\alpha(c^{(k)})$.*

It is obvious that $L_\alpha(c^{(k)}) \geq 1$ for any string $\alpha \in \Sigma^*$, when $k > 1$.

Definition 5 (Minimal Convergent Length). *Let $c^{(k)}$ be a k-state combination of a DFA, the* <u>*minimal convergent length*</u> *of $c^{(k)}$ is the minimum of convergent lengths on all possible strings in Σ^*, denoted as $L_{min}(c^{(k)})$.*

If $c^{(k)}$ converges on no strings in Σ^*, we say that its minimal convergent length is infinite, denoted as $L_{min}(c^{(k)}) = \infty$.

Example We illustrate the concepts with the DFA in Figure 1. Let's consider the 2-state combination $\{A, B\}$. When reading symbol "1", it transits to another 2-state combination $\{B, C\}$; then reading symbol "0" would let it transit to a 1-state combination $\{B\}$, hence the 2-state combination $\{A, B\}$ is convergent, and it converges on string "10".

In the example, since the 2-state combination $\{A, B\}$ converges on string "10", but does not converge on the prefix "1", its convergent length on string "10" is 2.

The minimal convergent length for the 2-state combination $\{A, B\}$ is 2, since it converges on string "10", but converge on neither "1" nor "0".

4.2 Property I: FSM Convergence

We now present a theorem that allows quick determination of the first property, *FSM convergence*—that is, to decide whether there is any pair of states in the FSM that are ever possible to converge.

We first introduce the following lemma:

Lemma 1. *Let $c^{(k)}$ and $c^{(k')}$ be two state combinations of a DFA, $c^{(k)} \supseteq c^{(k')}$, if there is a string α such that $c^{(k)}$ converges on α, then $c^{(k')}$ must also converge on α.*

The correctness of the lemma is obvious. On the other hand, even if every $c^{(k-1)} \subset c^{(k)}$ is convergent, $c^{(k)}$ may be not.

Based on the lemma, we have the following theorem:

Theorem 1. *Given a DFA $\mathcal{M}$, if and only if none of its states has two or more incoming edges that carry the same symbol, no state combinations of $\mathcal{M}$ are convergent except single-state combinations.*

Proof. It is easy to see that the condition is necessary for the conclusion to hold: If the condition is not met, the sources of the two edges must converge on the common symbol. To prove that the condition is sufficient, we assume that under that condition, there is still a k-state combination $c^{(k)}$ that converges on a string α, where $1 < k \leq |Q|$. That means there is a 1-state combination $c^{(1)}$ such that $c^{(k)} \xrightarrow{\alpha} c^{(1)}$. Then according to Lemma 1, there is a 2-state combination $c^{(2)} \subseteq c^{(k)}$ such that $c^{(2)} \xrightarrow{\alpha} c^{(1)}$. Suppose the two states in $c^{(2)}$ are s_1 and s_2, and the convergence prefix of α is $\alpha_c = a_1 a_2 \cdots a_l$, then we must have $s_1 \xrightarrow{a_1 a_2 \cdots a_{l-1}} s_1' \xrightarrow{a_l} c^1$, $s_2 \xrightarrow{a_1 a_2 \cdots a_{l-1}} s_2' \xrightarrow{a_l} c^1$. According to Definition 4, $s_1' \neq s_2'$. Thus, state c^1 is the state with two transitions from s_1' and s_2' leading to it, both on symbol a_l, which is contradicts the assumption. □

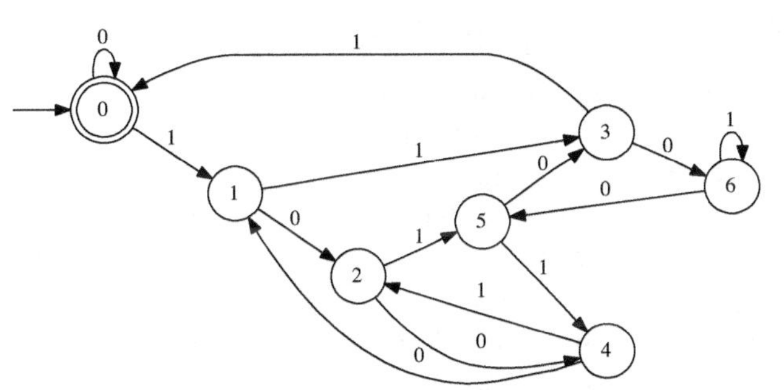

Figure 2. DFA for Testing Divisibility by Seven

Discussion. Theorem 1 tells us that to find out whether states in an FSM are going to ever converge, one only needs to check the incoming edges of every state in the DFA. The time complexity is $O(|Q| \cdot |\Sigma|)$ since the algorithm only needs to examine each edge once. It may significantly cut cost in some existing DFA parallelizations. For example, Figure 2 shows a DFA used for testing whether a binary number is seven-divisible. Previously, for speculative parallelization, people empirically collect the convergent lengths between every pair of its states by running it on many inputs [31]. With Theorem 1, all these collection work can be safely saved as it can immediately tell that no two states of the DFA are convergent.

4.3 Property II: Minimal Convergent Lengths

As aforementioned, directly collecting convergent lengths is time consuming. Even worse, when a combination does not merge, the empirical approach is difficult to tell no matter how long the profiling runs.

In this section, we give an in-depth study on convergent length, especially, on the computations of the minimal convergent lengths of state combinations of a DFA. We prove that it can be computed in polynomial time for a given k by providing a concrete algorithm with $O(k \cdot |Q|^k \cdot |\Sigma|)$ time complexity. The algorithms leverage the relationships of convergent length among different state combinations. They are applicable to all kinds of DFA, including those whose convergent lengths of some or all state combinations are infinity.

The minimal convergent length of a state combination reflects how fast these states could converge. Our algorithm for computing minimal convergent lengths is based on the following lemma.

Lemma 2. *Let $c^{(k)}$ be a k-state combination of a DFA, and $c^{(k')}$ be the state combination that $c^{(k)}$ transits to on symbol a, $a \in \Sigma$, then*

$$L_{min}(c^{(k)}) \leq L_{min}(c^{(k')}) + 1.$$

Now we describe the algorithm for computing the minimal convergent length of every k-state combinations, $L_{min}(c^{(k)})$ for given k, $1 \leq k \leq |Q|$.

Step 1. Check whether the condition of Theorem 1 is met. If so, set all $L_{min}(c^{(k)}) = \infty$ and terminate; otherwise, continue.

Step 2. Construct a graph based on the following rules:

1. For each minimal convergent length of $c^{(i)}$, where $1 \leq i \leq k$, create a node;
2. For each k-state combination $c^{(k)}$, if there is a symbol a, such that $c^{(k)} \xrightarrow{a} c^{(i)}$, where $c^{(i)} \in C_Q^{(i)}$ and $2 \leq i \leq k$, create an edge from $c^{(i)}$ to $c^{(k)}$;
3. Iterate state combination set from $C_Q^{(k-1)}$ to $C_Q^{(2)}$: If an i-state combination $c^{(i)}$, $2 \leq i < k$ has at least

one outgoing edge and there exists symbol a, such that $c^{(i)} \xrightarrow{a} c^{(i')}$, create an edge from $c^{(i')}$ to $c^{(i)}$;

Figure 3 illustrates such a graph. The nodes are aligned by layers, each layer corresponds to a state combination set, with the 1-state combination set on the top. Based on the discussion in Section 4.1, edges may exist among nodes in the same layer or from a higher layer to a lower layer, but not the other way.

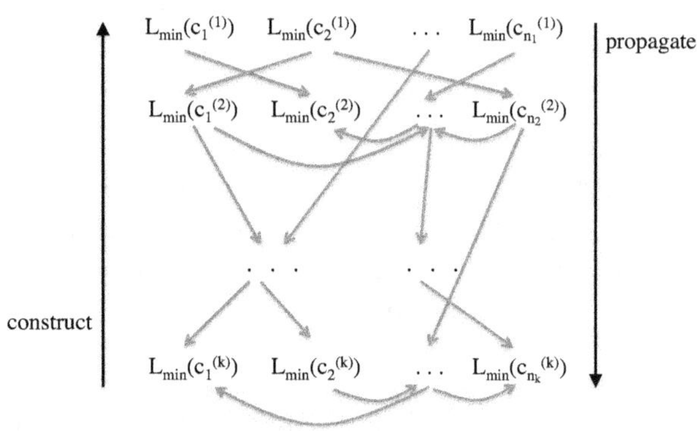

Figure 3. Minimal Convergent Length Propagation Graph

Step 3. Compute the minimal convergent lengths through propagation:

1. Label all nodes in the graph with UNSET;
2. Set nodes $L_{min}(c^{(1)}) = 0$, $c^{(1)} \in C_Q^{(1)}$ and label them with SET;
3. Propagate the minimal convergent lengths from top layer to bottom layer: If there is an edge from $L_{min}(c^{(i)})$ to $L_{min}(c^{i'})$ and $L_{min}(c^{i'})$ is UNSET, then set $L_{min}(c^{i'}) = L_{min}(c^{(i)}) + 1$;
4. Check if any $L_{min}(c^{(k)})$ is UNSET, if so, set $L_{min}(c^{(k)}) = \infty$.

With this solution, we can compute the minimal convergent lengths for all k-state combinations in $C_Q^{(k)}$, for any given k, $1 \leq k \leq |Q|$.

Theorem 2. *Let $c^{(k)}$ be a k-state combination in a DFA, if the minimal convergent length of $c^{(k)}$ is finite, then it is bounded by $\sum_{i=2}^{k} |C_Q^{(i)}|$.*

Proof. On its convergent prefix, $c^{(k)}$ cannot transit to a combination more than once. Otherwise, removing the part of the prefix between the two visits to the state would still make $c^{(k)}$ converge. There are only $\sum_{i=1}^{k} |C_Q^{(i)}|$ unique combinations a transit could reach, and for $c^{(k)}$ to converge, it only needs to transit to one c^1. Therefore, the length of its convergent prefix can be no greater than $\sum_{i=2}^{k} |C_Q^{(i)}|$. □

Corollary 1. *Given a DFA, if the minimal convergent length of all the states, that is, $c^{|Q|}$ is finite, then it is bounded by $2^{|Q|} - |Q| - 1$.*

Theorem 3. *The time complexity of the minimal convergent length algorithm is $O(k \cdot |Q|^k \cdot |\Sigma|)$.*

Proof. The complexity mainly comes from two parts: graph construction in *Step 2* and minimal convergent length propagation in *Step 3*. The number of nodes in the graph is $\sum_{i=2}^{k} |C_Q^{(i)}|$, which is $O(|Q|^k)$. Each node has at most $|\Sigma|$ edges, with each corresponding to one unique input character. The construction of an edge coming out of a node $c^{(i)}$ requires i checks to determine the target combination, with each check figuring out what target state one state in $c^{(i)}$ connects to on the input character in the original DFA. So the graph construction time complexity is bounded by $O(k \cdot |Q|^k \cdot |\Sigma|)$. Given that the propagation time cost is bounded by the number of edges, the whole algorithm time complexity is $O(k \cdot |Q|^k \cdot |\Sigma|)$. □

Algorithm 3 in appendix shows the pseudocode of this algorithm.

Discussion. The minimal convergent length of a state combination provides several insights to help reduce the cost and penalty in the speculation-centered DFA parallelization. For example, if one state has very long minimal convergent length with every other state, then it would be quite risky to select it as the predicted state, since a wrong prediction in this case would cause a very large penalty. For the principled speculation in particular, the static inferences of the minimal convergent lengths can help avoid spending time in collecting the empirical convergent length between two states if the minimal convergent length between them is known to be infinity. Since empirical profiling of such cases would not find out that they can never converge, it usually goes through the maximum length of the training inputs before it gives up. The savings by the minimal convergent length inference hence can be substantial.

Inference of the two properties can avoid the profiling on some if not all combinations of states for an FSM in the collection of expected convergent lengths. Next we introduce two dynamic optimizations that take place during the profiling of the remaining state combinations. They further reduce the profiling cost substantially.

5. Dynamic Profiling Optimizations

We introduce two dynamic optimizations to further accelerate the collection of FSM convergent lengths. They are both built on some simple observations. However, when used together, they cut the overhead by up to thousands of times on our experimented FSMs.

To help analyze the benefits of the optimizations, we first introduce a metric, called *transition reduction ratio.*

Definition 6. Transition Reduction Ratio (TRR) *is the ratio of state transitions between the optimized profiling and the default profiling.*

Apparently, the inverse of TRR reflects the speedup that the optimization can bring: *Speedup = 1/TRR.*

5.1 Optimization I: IR Reuse

The first method is called *Intermediate Results Reuse*, or *IR Reuse* for short. The basic idea is simple: when profiling the convergent length between a pair of states s_i and s_j on training input I_{train} starting at position 0, the intermediate transition states could be also considered as the state pairs on the same training input, but with different starting positions. For instance, suppose that the FSM in Figure 1, when running on an input "01..." from state pair (A, C), converges after l characters. one can infer a convergent length sample for state pair (E, B) as $l-1$ because the FSM reaches those two states after processing the first input character. In the same vein, we get a sample for (F, D) as $l-2$, and so on. In total, the IR reuse helps produce l samples of convergent lengths for the FSM through the one profiling on a single pair of states.

We show the implementation of the idea together with the second optimizations later in this section.

Complexity Analysis *IR Reuse* optimization helps reduce the S factor in the complexity of the default algorithm. Since the reuse of intermediate state transitions can potentially contribute to the sample collection of some other state pairs, some sample runs for those state pairs could be eliminated. The actual reduction of S depends on the FSM, training input and the profiling order of state pairs.

The TRR of IR reuse can be expressed symbolically as the following:

$$TRR(\text{IR Reuse}) = \frac{O(N^2 \cdot S' \cdot L)}{O(N^2 \cdot SAMPLE \cdot L)} = O(\frac{S'}{SAMPLE}) \quad (1)$$

where S' is the average number of samples after IR reuse is applied. Since the lower bound of the IR reuse optimized profiling is $O(N^2 \cdot L)$, we have $O(1/SAMPLE) \leq TRR(\text{IR reuse}) \leq 1$.

5.2 Optimization II: Early Stop

The second optimization method is called *Early Stop*. As the name implies, it terminates state transitions before state converge actually happen. The rational of this method is based on the conditional correlations among state pairs. Still use the example in Figure 1. When it is profiling state pair (A, C) on an input "01...", it notices that the FSM will reach states E and B respectively after processing the first character. So if the expected convergent length of (E, B) is already known, then it would stop after processing the first character, and infer the convergent length as $L_M(E, B) + 1$. We show the implementation of the idea in the next section.

Complexity Analysis *Early stop* helps reduce the L factor in the complexity of the default profiling algorithm. Since early stop terminates the profiling of a sample before it ends, the averaged number of transitions for one sample (i.e., L) could decrease. Similar to IR reuse, the actual reduction depends on the FSM, training input and the state pair profiling order.

The TRR of early stop can be expressed symbolically as the following:

$$TRR(\text{Early Stop}) = \frac{O(N^2 \cdot SAMPLE \cdot L')}{O(N^2 \cdot SAMPLE \cdot L)} = O(\frac{L'}{L}) \quad (2)$$

where L' is the average number of transitions for profiling one sample when early stop is applied. It is straightforward to get the similar conclusion as IR reuse, that is, $O(1/L) \leq TRR(\text{Early Stop}) \leq 1$, assuming $L' \leq L$.

5.3 Compound Effects

It is important to note that when the two optimizations are used together, they manifest a compound effect, which dramatically magnifies the benefits by the optimizations. On one hand, by reducing the transition length (L) for profiling one sample, early stop also reduces the cost of "reusing" the intermediate results. On the other hand, by reusing the intermediate results, much more samples are generated within a short period, hence more state pairs obtain their convergent length quickly. This greatly increases the chance of early stop happening, thus further reduces the transition length L. Such an interplay results in more and more powerful optimizations as profiling continues.

Algorithm 2 shows how the two optimizations are implemented together. Line 14 and Lines 20 to 25 correspond to the IR reuse optimization; line 9 to line 11 and line 16 to line 17 correspond to the early stop optimization. In actual implementation, an assistance table, `ready[N][N]`, is created to indicate whether a state pair already has enough samples. With it, the checks of `result[`s_a`][`s_b`].cnt` $\geq$ `SAMPLE` could be more a more efficient table lookup. Since both IR reuse and early stop need these checks, and they occurs at every iteration, the benefit could be substantial.

Complexity Analysis In terms of complexity, both the factors S and L can be reduced drastically. The TRR becomes:

$$TRR(\text{IR Reuse + Early Stop}) = O(\frac{S' \cdot L'}{SAMPLE \cdot L}). \quad (3)$$

Thanks to the compound effects, our experiments show that on typical FSMs, $S' \ll SAMPLE$ and $L' \ll L$. As to the TRR range, we have $O(1/SAMPLE \cdot L) \leq TRR(\text{IR Reuse + Early Stop}) \leq 1$.

6. Evaluation

We evaluate our techniques using the benchmark suite used in a recent study [31] but with more inputs added. Table 1 lists their basic information, including the number of states and input sizes for training and testing. They come from a variety of communities: XML processing (*lexing, xval*), Decompression (*huff*), Pattern Searching and Validation(*str1,*

Algorithm 2 IR Reuse + Early Stop

```
for each pair of states (s_i, s_j) do
    result[s_i][s_j].sum = 0
    result[s_i][s_j].cnt = 0
    while result[s_i][s_j].cnt ¡ SAMPLE do
        l = 0
        s_a = s_i, s_b = s_j
        flag = false
        while (s_a ≠ s_b —— l ¡ MAXLEN) do
            /* Early stop transitions */
            if result[s_a][s_b].cnt ≥ SAMPLE then
                flag = true, break
            c = read()
            s_a = transit(s_a, c), s_b = transit(s_b, c)
            states_a[l] = s_a, states_b[l] = s_b
        end
        if flag then
            l = result[s_a][s_b].sum/result[s_a][s_b].cnt
        result[s_i][s_j].sum += l
        result[s_i][s_j].cnt++
        /* Reuse intermediate transitions */
        for (i = 0; i ¡ l; i++) do
            s_a = states_a[i], s_b = states_b[i]
            result[s_a][s_b].sum += l - i
            result[s_a][s_b].cnt++
        end
    end
    print result[s_i][s_j].sum / SAMPLE
end
```

str2, pval) and Mathematics (*div*). They also have a spectrum of complexities, ranging from 3 to more than 700 states. This range covers the sizes of commonly used FSMs that we have examined, which echoes the observations from prior studies [22, 31]. The default benchmark suite comes with two inputs per program, a small one and a large one. The small one is the first 2% of the large one and was used for training in the previous work [31]. To test the capability of the FSM parallelizations in dealing with different inputs, we added one new small input to each program. The inputs were collected from some public sources. For example, the input to pval is a segment randomly extracted from a novel; the input to huff is a 1.6MB pre-encoded text file; the input to lexing is a 1.7MB segment of an XML file. We kept these inputs of a size similar to the default small inputs in the benchmark suite for a direct comparison. Also for the comparison, we use the default large input as the testing input in all our experiments. The new small input is used for the offline training of the previous principled speculative parallelization to expose its sensitivity to inputs. Our on-the-fly method needs no training inputs.

Our implementation is built on the *SpecOpt* library created by Zhao and others [31] in C language. We mainly replaced its profiling component with the new one supported by our static analyzer and dynamic optimizations. The interface remains the same. In this way, the existing applications using *SpecOpt* can transparently upgrade to our new library. GCC 4.8 is used for compiling the library. The optimization level is set to O3. The results are collected on a server equipped with Intel Xeon E5-4650L CPU (8 physical cores).

Table 1. Benchmarks

Name	Description	States	Train Input	Test Input
lexing	XML Lexing	3	1.6MB	76MB
huff	Huffman Decoding	46	1.6MB	209MB
pval	Pattern Validation	28	1.7MB	96MB
str1	String Pattern Search 1	496	1.5MB	70MB
str2	String Pattern Search 2	131	1.5MB	70MB
xval	XML Validation	742	1.7MB	170MB
div	Unary Divisibility	7	1.7MB	97MB

Results: Static Analysis Table 2 shows the results of the static analysis. The second column lists the overall number of state pairs in each of those programs, which ranges from 3 to 274,911. The FSM convergence property analysis swiftly recognizes that no state pairs of *div* converge on any inputs. The minimum convergent length analysis further recognizes two other benchmarks *pval* and *xval* respectively contain 24 and one state pairs that have infinite minimal convergent length. The fourth column of the table lists the range of the minimal convergent lengths of the FSM state pairs that the analysis finds out. The rightmost column reports the time taken by the static analyses. Generally the more state pairs there are, the longer the time is. But it is not absolute; the time also depends on the structure of the FSM. For instance, *xval* has twice as many as the state pairs *str1* has, but the analysis takes only about half of the time. Overall, the static analysis takes negligible overhead for those benchmarks.

Table 2. Static Analysis Results

	total state pairs	pairs w/ infinite len	min converg length	exec. time
lexing	3	0	0–1	< 1ms
huff	1035	0	0–6	1ms
pval	378	24	0–∞	1ms
str1	122760	0	0–42	139ms
str2	8515	0	0–44	19ms
xval	274911	1	0–∞	62ms
div	21	21	∞–∞	< 1ms

Results: Dynamic Optimizations Table 3 shows the FSM profiling cost reduction by the proposed dynamic optimizations. The profiling times in the "optimized" column are the ones when all the proposed dynamic optimizations in Section 5 are applied after the static analysis. Comparing to the default profiling, the speedup goes from tens of times to thousands of times. The largest speedup is 6381x, shown on benchmark *str1*. The FSM has 496 states that have much more connections among them than many other FSMs in the suite. The many connections offer more chances for both IR reuses and early stops.

Table 3. Profiling Time

	default (s)	optimized (s)	speedup
lexing	0.50	0.016	31X
huff	1.03	0.033	31X
pval	4.54	0.023	195X
str1	1353.5	0.212	6381X
str2	16.99	0.069	247X
xval	148	2.272	65X
div	1.84	0.019	98X

The dynamic optimizations, especially the early stop, use expected convergent lengths in the inference, which could introduce some differences in the profiling results compared to the results produced by the default offline profiling. Table 4 reports the convergent length profiles of the default and optimized profiling respectively. It shows that the results are quite close in most cases. The most significant differences show up on *lexing* and *xval*. The former has only three states and hence is sensitive to changes; the latter has a complicated FSM with the largest number of states but relatively few connections. Even with the differences, the method still shows good help to FSM parallel performance as shown next.

Table 4. Average Convergent Length

	default	optimized
lexing	2.9	5.9
huff	19.2	21.3
pval	17002.5	18466.6
str1	77997.9	89139.2
str2	66973.0	69068.0
xval	699.3	342.4
div	85714.3	85714.3

Results: On-the-fly Speculation With the enhancement from static analysis and dynamic optimization, the profiling costs are greatly reduced, making on-the-fly speculation possible. To examine its potential, we evaluate three method:

- **offline**: Speculation with the default offline profiling. Profiling cost is not counted in the overall time.
- **online (naive)**: Speculation with online profiling but without the static analysis or dynamic optimizations. Profiling cost is included.
- **online (optimized)**: Speculation with online profiling equipped with both static and dynamic optimizations. Profiling cost is included.

Table 5. Speedups over sequential executions

	offline	online (naive)	online (optimized)
lexing	6.47X	4.46X	6.60X
huff	6.76X	4.05X	6.68X
pval	0.94X	1.53X	6.49X
str1	3.29X	0.01X	3.76X
str2	3.79X	0.39X	3.98X
xval	1.52X	0.12X	3.50X
div	1.26X	1.00X	1.26X
geomean	2.68X	0.49X	4.08X

Table 5 reports the speedups produced by the three parallelization methods over the performance of the sequential execution of the programs. The offline profiling-based approach gives good speedups on *lexing* and *huff*. These two programs have been shown before to be the simplest to parallelize; even simple heuristic-based speculation can already work well on them [23, 31]. They feature very short convergent lengths among all state pairs. Hence, even though the offline profiling-based approach does not lead to accurate speculation results, the FSMs still converge to the correct states quickly and enjoys good speedups. But for the other programs, the input sensitivity causes the approach some substantial degrees of loss in the parallelization benefits. Compared to the offline approach, the optimized online approach gives substantially higher speedups on four out of the five challenging benchmarks. Overall, on average it brings 1.4x extra speedups over the offline method, demonstrating the promise of the on-the-fly speculative parallelization of FSM enabled by the new techniques.

The comparison between the optimized online approach and the naive online approach highlights the importance of the static and dynamic optimizations introduced in this work. Although the naive online profiling method is also able to adapt to input changes, it suffers from the large profiling overhead. With it, most of the parallelized FSMs run even slower than their sequential counterpart.

The program *div* is an extreme case. As none of its state pairs converge, it is not input sensitive in terms of the suitable configurations of the speculation. Our static analysis recognizes this property and avoids any online profiling. It achieves the same 1.26x speedup as the offline approach does. In contrast, without such analysis, the profiling overhead of the naive online approach completely cancels the parallelization benefit.

7. Related Work

There have been many efforts spent on program parallelization. The efforts are from various angles, from language design (e.g. Cilk [11], X10 [7]), to hardware support (e.g., TLS [12, 27]) and programming models (e.g., STM [1, 6]). In section, we focus the discussion on the studies that closely relate with FSM and software speculation.

Parallelization of FSM To parallelize FSM, a traditional way is through prefix-sum parallelization or its variations [18]. A recent study [22] shows that a careful implementation of the method on vector units on modern machines can produce large speedup. The approach is however subject to large FSMs as the number of threads that conduct useless computations increase linearly with the number of states.

There have been some studies on parallelizing some specific FSM applications. An example is the work by Jones and others on parallelizing a browser's front-end [14]. They introduce the concept of lookback (called overlap) for enhancing speculation accuracy. Other examples include the parallelization of JPEG decoder by Klein and Wiseman [16], hot state prediction in a pattern matching FSM to identify intrusions by Luchaup and others [21], speculative parsing [15], and speculative simulated annealing [30]. There have been many efforts in parallel parsing. They can be roughly classified into two categories. The first tries to decompose the grammar among threads [4, 5] by exploiting some special properties of the target language or parsing algorithm (e.g., LR parsing in Fischer's seminal work [10]). The second tries to decompose the input [20], and can often leverage more parallelism than the first approach. All these prior studies employ simple heuristics for speculation. Zhao and others [31] introduce the concept of principled speculation, which is the first rigorous approach to speculative parallelization. There have been some studies in implementing parallel Non-deterministic Finite Automata (NFA) [32]. Unlike other types of FSM, the non-determinism in NFA inherently exposes a large amount of parallelism and is hence easier to parallelize.

Speculative Parallelization Beyond a specific domain, there are also a number of studies in speculative parallelization. Prabhu and others [23] proposed two new language constructs to simplify programmers' job in using speculation schemes. There are some software frameworks developed to speculatively parallelize programs with dynamic, uncertain parallelism, either at the level of processes [8] or threads [9, 25, 28]. They are mainly based on simple heuristics exposed in program runtime behaviors (e.g., speculation success rate). Llanos and others use probabilities of a dependence violation to guide loop scheduling of randomized incremental algorithms in the context of speculative parallelization [19]. Kulkarni and others have showed the usage of abstraction to find parallelism in some irregular applications [17]. The pre-computation used by Quinones and others for speculative threading [24] shares the spirit with lookback in exploiting some part of the program execution for speculation. They construct no rigorous speculation models, but relies on subset of instructions to resolve dependences.

FSM Static Analysis Finite state machine or finite state automaton, as the abstract machine of computing, has been studied for a long time. It is one of the oldest topics in theoretical computer science, and has formed its own theory, automata theory. Our discussion here focuses on work closely related to this study. One of them is from the system testing community. FSMs are used there for testing and discovering the properties of given systems [26, 29]. An important concept is synchronizing string, which is the input string that can lead a set of states transiting to a common state. The length of the shortest synchronizing string is similar to minimal convergent length. However, research on synchronizing strings emphasizes on finding synchronizing strings, while our static analysis emphasizes the connections with convergent length profiling for speculation, and practical algorithms for leveraging the connections.

8. Conclusion

This paper presents a two-fold solution to remove a key barrier that has been preventing practical deployment of principled speculation for FSM parallelization. The solution is a synergy of a series of theoretical results regarding the inherent properties of FSMs and two dynamic optimizations on effectively reusing state profiling results. Through static analysis, it first examines the FSM and infers its inherent properties on state convergence, with which, the profiling space could be safely pruned. Second, by exploring the convergence correlations among state pairs, it further reduces the cost at runtime via IR reuse and early stop. The synergy and the compound effects of the two dynamic optimizations save up to thousands of times of profiling overhead. Together, they yield the first approach to enabling on-the-fly deployment of principled speculation, which demonstrates substantial improvement in speeding up FSM computations.

Acknowledgments

We thank Weizhen Mao for her feedback to this work. This material is based upon work supported by DOE Early Career Award, and the National Science Foundation grant No. 1320796 and CAREER Award. Any opinions, findings, and conclusions or recommendations expressed in this material are those of the authors and do not necessarily reflect the views of the National Science Foundation or DOE.

A. Pseudocode of Minimal Convergent Length Algorithm

Algorithm 3 Minimal Convergence Length Computation

```
L_min ← −1 /*L_min is N-D min convergence len. matrix*/
l ← 0 /*Value of minimal convergence length*/
diagonal(L_min) ← l
l ++
while true do/*Iteratively compute new values*/
    converge ← true /*Any new value in last iteration*/
    for e in uppertrangular(L_min) do /*e is an N-D vector*/
        if L_min(e) = −1 then
            for c in Σ do
                e -c-> e' /*States transit on character c*/
                e'' ← sort(e') /*To ascending order*/
                if L_min(e'') = −1 and L_min(e'') < l then
                    L_min(e) ← l
                    converge ← false
                    break for-loop c
    if converge = true then
        for e in uppertrangular(L_min) do
            if L_min(e) = −1 then /*States don't converge*/
                L_min(e) = ∞
        break while-loop
end while
```

References

[1] M. Abadi, A. Birrell, T. Harris, and M. Isard. Semantics of transactional memory and automatic mutual exclusion. In *Proceedings of ACM Symposium on Principles of Programming Languages*, 2008.

[2] A. V. Aho, M. S. Lam, R. Sethi, and J. D. Ullman. *Compilers: Principles, Techniques, and Tools*. Addison Wesley, 2nd edition, August 2006.

[3] K. Asanovic, R. Bodik, B. Catanzaro, J. Gebis, P. Husbands, K. Keutzer, D. Patterson, W. Plishker, J. Shalf, S. Williams, and K. Yelick. The landscape of parallel computing research: A view from berkeley. Technical Report UCB/EECS-2006-18, University of California at Berkele, 2006.

[4] F. Baccelli and T. Fleury. On parsing arithmetic expressions in a multiprocessing environment. *Acta Inf.*, 17:287–310, 1982.

[5] F. Baccelli and P. Mussi. An asynchronous parallel interpreter for arithmetic expressions and its evaluation. *IEEE Trans. Computers*, 35(3):245–256, 1986.

[6] B. Carlstrom, A. McDonald, H. Chafi, J. Chung, C. Minh, C. Kozyrakis, and K. Olukotun. The atomos transactional programming langauges. In *Proceedings of ACM SIGPLAN Conference on Programming Language Design and Implementation*, 2006.

[7] P. Charles, C. Grothoff, V. Saraswat, C. Donawa, A. Kielstra, K. Ebcioglu, C. von Praun, and V. Sarkar. X10: an object-oriented approach to non-uniform cluster computing. In *OOPSLA*, 2005.

[8] C. Ding, X. Shen, K. Kelsey, C. Tice, R. Huang, and C. Zhang. Software behavior-oriented parallelization. In *PLDI*, 2007.

[9] M. Feng, R. Gupta, and Y. Hu. Spicec: Scalable parallelism via implicit copying and explicit commit. In *Proceedings of the ACM SIGPLAN Symposium on Principles Practice of Parallel Programming*, 2011.

[10] C. N. Fischer. *On Parsing Context Free Languages in Parallel Environments*. PhD thesis, Cornell University, 1975.

[11] M. Frigo, C. E. Leiserson, and K. H. Randall. The implementation of the Cilk-5 multithreaded language. In *Proceedings of ACM SIGPLAN Conference on Programming Language Design and Implementation*, 1998.

[12] M. Herlihy and J. E. Moss. Transactional memory: Architectural support for lock-free data structures. In *Proceedings of the International Symposium on High Performance Computer Architecture (HPCA)*, 1993.

[13] K. Ingham, A. Somayaji, J. Burge, and S. Forrest. Learning dfa representations of http for protecting web applications. *Computer Networks*, 51(5):1239–1255, Apr. 2007.

[14] C. Jones, R. Liu, L. Meyerovich, K. Asanovic, and R. Bodik. Parallelizing the web browser. In *HotPar*, 2009.

[15] B. Kaplan. Speculative parsing path. `http://bugzilla.mozilla.org`.

[16] S. Klein and Y. Wiseman. Parallel huffman decoding with applications to jpeg files. *Jounal of Computing*, 46(5), 2003.

[17] M. Kulkarni, K. Pingali, B. Walter, G. Ramanarayanan, K. Bala, and L. Chew. Optimistic parallelism requires abstractions. In *PLDI*, 2007.

[18] R. E. Ladner and M. J. Fischer. Parallel prefix computation. *J. ACM*, 27(4):831–838, Oct. 1980. ISSN 0004-5411.

[19] D. Llanos, D. Orden, and B. Palop. New scheduling strategies for randomized incremental algorithms in the context of speculative parallelization. *IEEE Transactions on Computers*, 2007.

[20] W. Lu, K. Chiu, and Y. Pan. A parallel approach to xml parsing. In *Proceedings of the 7th IEEE/ACM International Conference on Grid Computing*, GRID '06, pages 223–230, 2006.

[21] D. Luchaup, R. Smith, C. Estan, and S. Jha. Multi-byte regular expression matching with speculation. In *RAID*, 2009.

[22] T. Mytkowicz, M. Musuvathi, and W. Schulte. Data-parallel finite-state machines. In *ASPLOS '14: Proceedings of 19th International Conference on Architecture Support for Programming Languages and Operating Systems*. ACM Press, 2014.

[23] P. Prabhu, G. Ramalingam, and K. Vaswani. Safe programmable speculative parallelism. In *Proceedings of ACM SIGPLAN Conference on Programming Languages Design and Implementation*, 2010.

[24] C. Quinones, C. Madriles, J. Sanchez, P. Marcuello, A. Gonzalez, and D. M. Tullsen. Mitosis compiler: an infrastructure for speculative threading based on pre-computation slices. In *PLDI*, 2005.

[25] A. Raman, H. Kim, T. R. Mason, T. B. Jablin, and D. I. August. Speculative parallelization using software multi-threaded transactions. In *Proceedings of the international conference on Architectural support for programming languages and operating systems*, 2010.

[26] S. Sandberg. Homing and synchronizing sequences. *Model-based testing of reactive systems*, 2005.

[27] J. G. Steffan, C. Colohan, A. Zhai, and T. C. Mowry. The STAMPede approach to thread-level speculation. *ACM Transactions on Computer Systems*, 23(3):253–300, 2005.

[28] C. Tian, M. Feng, V. Nagarajan, and R. Gupta. Copy or discard execution model for speculative parallelization on multicores. In *Proceedings of the International Symposium on Microarchitecture*, 2008.

[29] M. V. Volkov. Synchronizing automata and the ern conjecture. *Lecture Notes in Computer Science*, pages 11–27, 2008.

[30] E. Witte, R. Chamberlain, and M. Franklin. Parallel simulated annealing using speculative computation. *IEEE Transactions on Parallel and Distributed Systems*, 2(4):483–494, 1991.

[31] Z. Zhao, B. Wu, and X. Shen. Challenging the "embarrassingly sequential": Parallelizing finite state machine-based computations through principled speculation. In *ASPLOS '14: Proceedings of 19th International Conference on Architecture Support for Programming Languages and Operating Systems*. ACM Press, 2014.

[32] Y. Zu, M. Yang, Z. Xu, L. Wang, X. Tian, K. Peng, and Q. Dong. Gpu-based nfa implementation for memory efficient high speed regular expression matching. In *PPoPP '12: Proceedings of the ACM SIGPLAN symposium on Principles and practice of parallel programming*, pages 129–140, 2009.

Asynchronized Concurrency: The Secret to Scaling Concurrent Search Data Structures

Tudor David Rachid Guerraoui Vasileios Trigonakis *

School of Computer and Communication Sciences,
École Polytechnique Fédérale de Lausanne (EPFL), Switzerland
{tudor.david, rachid.guerraoui, vasileios.trigonakis}@epfl.ch

Abstract

We introduce *"asynchronized concurrency (ASCY),"* a paradigm consisting of four complementary programming patterns. ASCY calls for the design of concurrent search data structures (CSDSs) to resemble that of their sequential counterparts. We argue that ASCY leads to implementations which are *portably scalable*: they scale across different types of hardware platforms, including single and multi-socket ones, for various classes of workloads, such as read-only and read-write, and according to different performance metrics, including throughput, latency, and energy. We substantiate our thesis through the most exhaustive evaluation of CSDSs to date, involving 6 platforms, 22 state-of-the-art CSDS algorithms, 10 re-engineered state-of-the-art CSDS algorithms following the ASCY patterns, and 2 new CSDS algorithms designed with ASCY in mind. We observe up to 30% improvements in throughput in the re-engineered algorithms, while our new algorithms out-perform the state-of-the-art alternatives.

Categories and Subject Descriptors D.1.3 [*Programming Techniques*]: Concurrent Programming

Keywords Concurrent data structures, scalability, multi-cores, portability

1. Introduction

A *search data structure* consists of a set of elements and an interface for accessing and manipulating these elements. The three main operations of this interface are a *search* operation and two update operations (one to *insert* and one to *delete* an element), as shown in Figure 1. Search data structures are said to be *concurrent* when they are shared by several processes. Concurrent search data structures (CSDSs) are commonplace in today's software systems. For instance, concurrent hash tables are crucial in the Linux kernel [40]

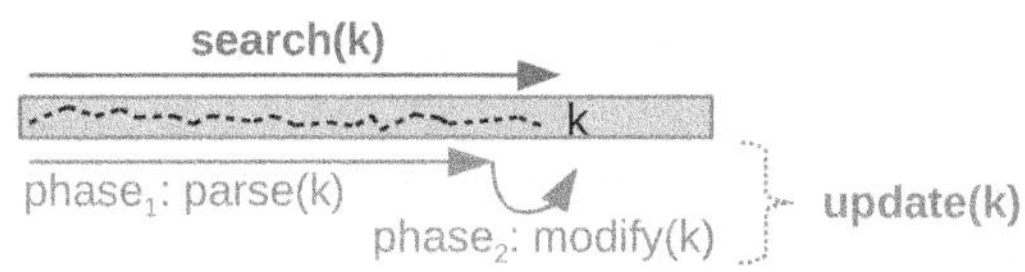

Figure 1: Search data structure interface. Updates have two phases: a parse phase, followed by a modification phase.

and in Memcached [42], while skip lists are the backbone of key-value stores such as RocksDB [18]. As the tendency is to place more and more workloads in the main memory of multi-core machines, the need for CSDSs that effectively accommodate the sharing of data is increasing.

Nevertheless, devising CSDSs that scale and leverage the underlying number of cores is challenging [4, 5, 8, 19, 47]. Even the implementation of a specialized CSDS that would scale on a specific platform, with a specific performance metric in mind, is a daunting task. Optimizations that are considered effective on a given architecture might not be revealed as such on another [4, 12]. For example, NUMA-aware techniques provide no benefits on uniform architectures [12]. Similarly, if a CSDS is optimized for a specific type of workload, slightly different workloads can instantly cause a bottleneck. For instance, read-copy update (RCU) [41] is extensively used for designing CSDSs that are suitable for read-dominated workloads. However, it could be argued that this is achieved at the expense of scalability in the presence of updates.

The motivation of this work is to ask whether we can determine characteristics of CSDS algorithms that favor implementations which achieve what we call *portable scalability*, namely that *scale* across various platforms, workloads, and performance metrics. At first glance, this goal might look fuzzy for it raises a fundamental question: what scalability can we ideally expect from a given data structure, architecture, performance metric, and workload combination?

In fact, we can provide a practical estimation of an upper bound for a data structure's scalability, on a particular hardware and workload combination. We step on the observation that the coherence traffic induced by stores on shared data is the biggest impediment to the scalability of concurrent software. This is valid for practically any contemporary multi-core. Yet, some stores cannot be removed because

* Authors appear in alphabetical order.

ASPLOS '15, March 14–18, 2015, Istanbul, Turkey.

http://dx.doi.org/10.1145/2694344.2694359

they are inherent to the semantics of the data structure; typically those stores are employed by any standard sequential implementation of the same data structure (one that is not supposed to be shared by several processes). Assume however that we deploy, as is, such a sequential implementation on a multi-core and have it shared by multiple threads. Obviously, this deployment would result in incorrect (e.g., non-linearizable [31]) executions. The performance of these *asynchronized executions*, however, constitutes a reasonable indication of what can be ideally expected from a correct, *synchronized* implementation of the same structure.

We thus consider that a CSDS achieves *portable scalability* when its scalability closely matches that of asynchronized executions (a) across different types of hardware, including single and multi-sockets, (b) for various classes of workloads, such as read-dominated and read-write, and (c) according to different performance metrics. In the CSDS context, aspect (c) means that as we increase the number of threads, we want to remain as close as possible to the asynchronized execution in terms of *throughput* and *latency*, without sacrificing *energy* (i.e., without consuming more *power* than implementations that do not scale as well in terms of throughput or latency).

With this pragmatic objective in mind, we perform an exhaustive evaluation of CSDSs on six different processors: a 20-core and a 40-core Intel Xeon, a 48-core AMD Opteron, a 32-core Oracle SPARC T4-4, a 36-core Tilera TILE-Gx36, and a 4-core Intel Haswell. We measure four dimensions of scalability: throughput, latency, latency distribution, and power. We consider the state-of-the-art algorithms for linked lists, hash tables, skip lists, and BSTs. To the best of our knowledge, this is the most extensive CSDS evaluation to date. We find that for each data structure, there are CSDS algorithms whose performance is within 10% of the asynchronized versions. We observe that in general, the algorithms whose memory accesses to shared state best resemble those of a sequential – asynchronized – algorithm tend to achieve portable scalability. We further identify four patterns through which this resemblance to sequential implementations is achieved:

ASCY$_1$: The search operation should not involve any waiting, retries, or stores.

ASCY$_2$: The parse phase of an update operation should not perform any stores other than for cleaning-up purposes and should not involve any waiting, or retries.

ASCY$_3$: An update operation whose parse is unsuccessful (i.e., the element not found in case of a remove, the element already present in case of an insert) should not perform any stores, besides those used for cleaning-up in the parse phase.

ASCY$_4$: The number and region of memory stores in a successful update should be close to those of a standard sequential implementation.

None of these patterns is fundamentally counter-intuitive and each of them has already been identified as important in some form or another. We find that the existing algorithms that scale the best already apply some of these patterns. To our knowledge however, they have never been put in a coherent form and collectively applied and evaluated. We refer to these patterns as *asynchronized concurrency (ASCY)*, for together they indeed call for the design of concurrent algorithms to resemble that of their sequential counterparts in terms of access to shared state.

We apply ASCY to several existing state-of-the-art algorithms and obtain up to 30% improvements in throughput, accompanied by reduced latencies. Interestingly, ASCY not only leads to better throughput, but also results in CSDSs that consume less power (by 1.4% in average), hence further improving energy efficiency. We also present a hash table (CLHT) and a BST (BST-TK), two *new algorithms* designed and implemented from scratch with ASCY in mind. CLHT (cache-line hash table) places each hash-table bucket on a single cache line and performs in-place updates so that operations complete with at most one cache-line transfer. CLHT outperforms state-of-the-art hash tables in virtually every scenario. BST-TK (BST Ticket) is a new concurrent BST that significantly reduces the number of acquired locks per update over existing algorithms. BST-TK is consistently the best lock-based BST, compared to the state of the art.

Our evaluation also highlights a number of other interesting observations. We show, for instance, that the fact that an algorithm is lock-based or lock-free does not have a major effect on the scalability of CSDSs. Similarly, we show that the use of hardware transactional memory also makes little difference. We highlight however a number of hardware-related bottlenecks that should be taken into consideration by system designers.

In summary, the main contributions of this paper are:

- The analysis and comparison of a large number of state-of-the-art CSDS algorithms in a wide range of settings (i.e., platforms, workloads, and metrics), representing the most extensive evaluation to date. This evaluation helps identify characteristics of *portably scalable* algorithms and revisit some beliefs regarding CSDSs.
- *Asynchronized Concurrency*: A design paradigm which yields portably scalable CSDSs. When ASCY is applied, increasing throughput, reducing latency, and reducing power consumption go hand in hand.
- ASCYLIB: a CSDS library, including 34 highly optimized and portable implementations of linked lists, hash tables, skip lists, and BSTs, together with a companion memory allocator with garbage collection. ASCYLIB includes two novel CSDS algorithms designed from scratch, namely CLHT and BST-TK, and re-engineered versions of ten state-of-the-art CSDS algorithms. ASCYLIB is available at `http://lpd.epfl.ch/site/ascylib`.

Our patterns are not very precise guidelines and cannot be used to automatically generate the implementation of a CSDS from its sequential counterpart. They cannot be used to derive any theoretical lower bound either. Yet, as we show in the paper, they provide very useful hints both for optimizing existing CSDSs and for designing new algorithms.

The rest of the paper is organized as follows. We provide in Section 2 some background related to search data structures. We present ASCYLIB in Section 3. In Section 4, we provide our evaluation of CSDS algorithms. In Section 5 we identify and illustrate the benefits of ASCY. We describe in Section 6 the use of ASCY in the design of CLHT and BST-TK. We present related work in Section 7. We discuss the limitations of ASCY, and conclude the paper in Section 8.

2. Search Data Structures

Basic interface. A search data structure consists of a set of elements and three main operations: *search*, *insert*, and *remove*. An element consists of a *key* and a *value*. The key uniquely identifies the element in the set. The value is often a pointer to a structure that contains the actual data.

The three main operations have the following semantics:

- *search(key)* looks for an element with the given key; if it is found, returns the value of the element, otherwise returns `NULL`.
- *insert(key, val)* attempts to insert a new element in the data structure; the insertion is successful iff there is no other element with the same key.
- *remove(key)* attempts to remove the element with the given key; it is successful iff such an element exists.

A common attribute of search data structures is that the updates (insertions and removals) comprise two distinct phases. First, they *parse* the structure until the update point is reached. Then the actual modification is attempted.

Concurrent search data structures. We study the most basic and commonly-used CSDSs: *linked lists, hash tables, skip lists*, and *binary search trees (BSTs)*. We are interested in *linearizable* [31] implementations of the aforementioned data structures.

It is common to classify linearizable implementations based on whether and how they make use of locks [29]. One can distinguish *fully lock-based, hybrid lock-based*, and *lock-free* [20] algorithms. Fully lock-based algorithms use locks to protect all three operations and are *blocking* [29], in the sense that a thread might have to wait for a lock to be released. Hybrid lock-based (henceforth called "lock-based") algorithms use locks to protect the actual updates to the structure. They are otherwise lock-free. For instance, a removal might parse the list (in a lock-free manner) until the target node is found, get the lock, and then do the actual deletion. Hybrid algorithms are also blocking. Finally, lock-free algorithms do not use locks and are *non-blocking* [20, 27]. They typically use the underlying atomic operations, such as compare-and-swap (CAS), provided by the hardware.

3. The ASCYLIB Library

ASCYLIB contains 32 fully/hybrid lock-based and lock-free CSDSs, as well as 5 sequential implementations.[1] These include existing state-of-the art designs, and optimized versions, which we adapt in order to enable one, or more, ASCY patterns. In addition, ASCYLIB contains two novel CSDS algorithms built from scratch based on ASCY. Some implementations in ASCYLIB were initially based on the Synchrobench benchmark suite [22].

Algorithms. Table 1 contains a short description of the existing algorithms we implement.[2] ASCYLIB further contains 10 re-engineered (using ASCY) state-of-the-art CSDS designs. In particular, we apply $ASCY_{1-2}$ on *harris* linked list and *fraser* skip list. We also apply $ASCY_3$ on *pugh*, *lazy*, and *copy* linked lists/hash tables, on *java* hash table, on *pugh* and *herlihy* skip lists, and on *drachsler* BST. Finally, we create a *urcu* hash-table variant that uses SSMEM (see below) instead of RCU for memory management and is closer to $ASCY_4$. In all our experiments, these optimizations result in better performance (see §4 and §5). We then use ASCY as the base to design two new CSDS algorithms, a lock-based and a lock-free variants of a hash table and a BST (see §6).

Memory management. We develop SSMEM, a memory allocator with epoch-based garbage collection (GC) [20]. SSMEM uses ideas similar to the RCU [41] mechanism: freed memory can only be reused once it is certain that no other thread holds a reference to this location. When some memory is freed, it does not become available until a GC pass decides that it is safe to be reused. The amount of garbage SSMEM allows before performing GC is configurable. Furthermore, SSMEM is non-blocking: it is based on per-thread counters that are incremented to indicate activity.

4. Evaluating the State of the Art CSDSs

In this section, we present a cross-platform evaluation of the state-of-the-art CSDS implementations and compare them with their asynchronized counterparts. We observe that regardless of the platform, the asynchronized executions perform the best. We further note that the algorithms with memory accesses to shared state that best resemble the asynchronized implementations are also the closest to these asynchronized upper bounds. Our evaluation also enables us to quantify the impact that various hardware features have on CSDS algorithms.

We start by describing the platforms and experimental settings used throughout this paper. We consider four multi-processors (with multiple sockets) and a chip multiprocessor (with one socket). We also briefly experiment with an Intel Haswell desktop processor with hardware transactional-memory support.

[1] We use these as incorrect asynchronized CSDSs.

[2] The *urcu* and the *tbb* hash tables belong to the corresponding libraries and are not our own implementations.

	Name	Type	Short description
linked list	*async*	seq	A sequential linked list. We use it as an *incorrect asynchronized* concurrent set for performance upper bounds.
	coupling [29]	flb	All operations use hand-over-hand locking (grab next lock and release the previous) while parsing the list.
	pugh [49]	lb	Operations search/parse the list optimistically. Updates lock and then validate the target node. Removals employ pointer reversal so that a search/parse always finds a correct path.
	lazy [25]	lb	Nodes are deleted in two steps: marking and physical deletion. Searching/Parsing the list simply ignores marked nodes. Updates parse the list, grab the locks, validate the locked nodes, and perform the update.
	copy [48]	lb	Similar to Java's *CopyOnWriteArrayList*. Updates create new copies of the list and are protected by a global lock.
	harris [23]	lf	Nodes are deleted in two steps: mark with CAS and delete with a second CAS. Operations remove the logically deleted nodes while searching/parsing the list. If cleaning-up fails, searching/parsing is restarted.
	michael [44]	lf	A refactored implementation of *harris* for easier memory management.
hash table	*async*	seq	A sequential hash table. We use it as an *incorrect asynchronized* concurrent set for performance upper bounds.
	coupling [29]	flb	Uses one *coupling* list per bucket, with a single per-bucket lock.
	pugh [49]	lb	Uses one *pugh* list per bucket, with a single per-bucket lock.
	lazy [25]	lb	Uses one *lazy* list per bucket, with a single per-bucket lock.
	copy [48]	lb	Uses one *copy* list per bucket, with a single per-bucket lock.
	urcu [13]	lb	Part of the URCU (User-space RCU) (version 0.8) library. After each successful removal, it waits for all ongoing operations to complete before freeing the memory. Supports resizing.
	java [37]	lb	Similar to Java's *ConcurrentHashMap*. Protects the hash table with a fixed number of locks (we use 512 locks). Supports resizing.
	tbb [36]	flb	Part of Intel's Thread Building Blocks (version 4.2) library. Uses reader-writer locks. Supports resizing.
	harris [23]	lf	Uses one *harris-opt* list per bucket.
skip list	*async*	seq	A sequential skip list. We use it as an *incorrect asynchronized* concurrent set for performance upper bounds.
	pugh [49]	lb	Maintains several levels of *pugh* lists. Parses towards the target node without locking.
	herlihy [26]	lb	Update operations optimistically find the node to update and then acquire the locks at all levels, validate the nodes, and perform the update. Searches simply traverse the multiple levels of lists.
	fraser [20]	lf	Optimistically searches/parses the list and then does CAS at each level (for updates). A search/parse restarts if a marked element is met when switching levels. The same applies if a CAS fails.
bst	*async-int*	seq	A sequential internal BST. We use it as an *incorrect asynchronized* concurrent set for performance upper bounds.
	async-ext	seq	A sequential external BST. We use it as an *incorrect asynchronized* concurrent set for performance upper bounds.
	bronson [7]	lb	Partially external. A search/parse can block waiting for a concurrent update to complete.
	drachsler [15]	lb	Internal tree. Uses logical ordering to allow sequential read operations. Acquires ≥ 3 locks for removals.
	ellen [17]	lf	External tree. Updates help outstanding operations on the nodes that they intend to modify.
	howley [32]	lf	Internal tree. All three operations perform helping and might need to restart.
	natarajan [46]	lf	External tree. Minimizes the number of atomic operations and optimistically searches/parses the tree.

Table 1: A short description of the existing CSDS algorithms we consider. "seq" stands for sequential, "flb" for fully lock-based, "lb" for (hybrid) lock-based, and "lf" for lock-free.

Opteron. The 48-core AMD Opteron contains four Opteron 6172 [10] multi-chip modules (MCMs). Each MCM has two 6-core dies. It operates at 2.1 GHz and has 64 KB, 512 KB, and 5 MB (per die) L1, L2, and LLC data caches respectively.

Xeon20. The 20-core Intel Xeon consists of two sockets of Xeon E5-2680 v2 Ivy-Bridge 10-core (20 hyper-threads). It runs at 2.8 GHz and includes 32 KB, 256 KB, and 25 MB (per die) L1, L2, and LLC, respectively.

Xeon40. The 40-core Intel Xeon consists of four sockets of Xeon E7-8867L Westmere-EX 10-core (20 hyper-threads). It clocks at 2.13 GHz and offers 32 KB L1, 256 KB L2, and 30 MB (per die) LLC, respectively.

Tilera. The Tilera TILE-Gx36 [51] is a 36-core chip multi-processor. It clocks at 1.2 GHz and has 32 KB, 256 KB, and 9 MB[3] L1, L2, and L3 data caches, respectively.

T4-4. The Oracle SPARC T4-4 is a four-socket multi-processor with 8 cores per socket and a total of 256 hardware threads (chip multi-threading). It operates at 2.85/3 GHz and has 16 KB, 256 KB, and 4 MB (per die) L1, L2, and LLC data caches, respectively.

Experimental settings. Each of our measurements represents the median value of 11 repetitions of 5 seconds each. We manually pin threads on cores in order to take advantage of the locality within sockets. Each operation is either a search, or an update, based on the update percentage we select. In general, we initialize the structure with a number of elements (N). The operations choose a key at random in the $[1 \ldots 2N]$ range. This provides the guarantee that on average, half of the operations are successful and that the structure size remains close to N (the update percentage is split to half insertions and half removals). On all architectures, except Tilera, we set SSMEM to trigger GC when 512 memory locations have been freed. On Tilera, we set this value to 128 in order to optimize for the smaller TLBs of 32 entries. On the asynchronized implementations, we disable GC to avoid data corruption. Finally, we use 64-bit long keys and values. It is straightforward to replace both with larger structures.

Cross-Platform evaluation. We now look at the behavior of a large sample of the state-of-the-art CSDS algorithms, as presented in Table 1. Figure 2 shows cross-platform results on various workloads, spanning low, average, and high degrees of contention. The histograms plot the throughput and the scalability ratio compared to the single-threaded execution (on top of each bar) on 20 threads.

On average and low-contention levels, algorithms exhibit good scalability in terms of throughput: in the experiments with 20 threads, the average scalability of the best

[3] The 36 L2 caches are utilized as a distributed LLC.

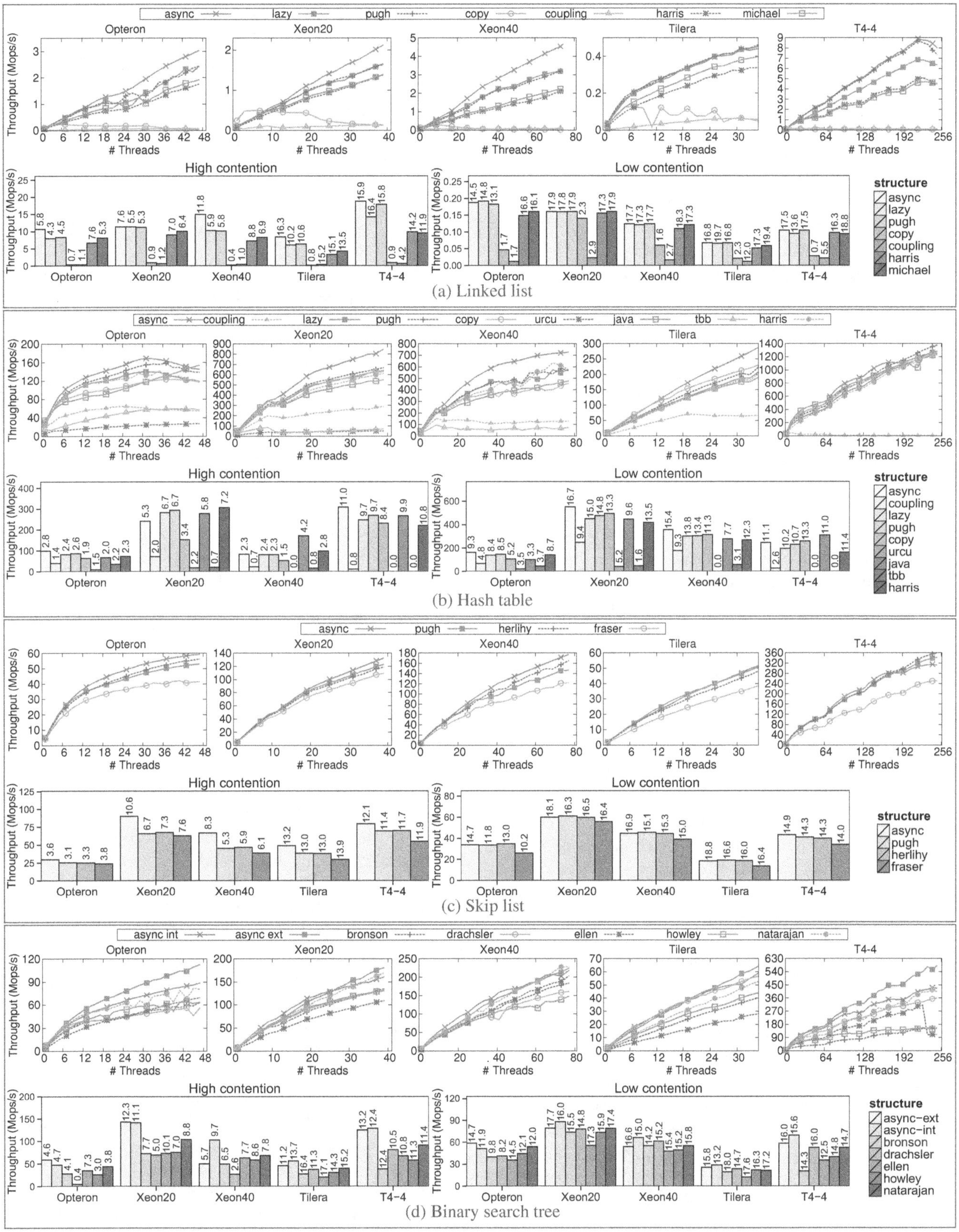

Figure 2: Cross-platform results of the data structures in ASCYLIB on average (top graphs – 4096 elements, 10% updates), high (20 threads, 512 elements, 25% updates), and low contention (20 threads, 16384 elements, 10% updates).

performing CSDS algorithm (per data structure) is 16.2 in the low contention case, whereas for the average and high-contention levels, this value is 14.1 and 9.8, respectively. While trends are generally valid across platforms, we do notice a certain variability: for each workload, the standard deviation of the average scalability values of different platforms is ~2. In some cases, scalability trends differ significantly between platforms. For instance, on the Opteron the hash tables do not scale beyond 32 threads (including *async*), due to bandwidth limitations. In short, the main hash table structure is initialized from a single memory node, thus all requests are directed to that node. This problem does not emerge on *java*, because of the fine-grained resizing (per one of the 512 regions) that spreads the hash table on multiple nodes.

In addition, we observe that there are various algorithms per data structure that are the "best". On linked lists (Figure 2a), *pugh* is consistently competitive across workloads and platforms, but *lazy* is close in throughput. On hash tables (Figure 2b), several algorithms perform close to each other (e.g., *pugh*, *lazy*, *copy*, *harris*). On skip lists (Figure 2c), *herlihy* and *pugh* perform similarly. Finally, on BSTs (Figure 2d), *natarajan* is generally the best. Overall, we see that, per data structure, both lock-based and lock-free algorithms are close in terms of performance. Lock-freedom is more important when we employ more threads than hardware contexts (not shown in the graphs). In these deployments, lock-freedom provides better scalability than lock-based designs.

It is worth noting that the workloads we evaluate are uniform: the frequency and the distribution of updates are constant. We briefly experiment with non-uniform workloads (not shown in the graphs), such as those with update spikes and continuously increasing structure size. We notice that our observations are valid in these scenarios as well.

Dissecting asynchronized executions. In Figure 2, we also depict the behavior of the asynchronized implementations for each data structure. We notice that except for some corner cases, the asynchronized implementations outperform alternatives on all the platforms. The reason for the rare corner cases in which some concurrent implementations can perform better than *async* is that asynchronized structures can become malformed in concurrent scenarios. For instance, an update operation on a skip list could update several pointer fields. We observe that these pointers are sometimes not properly set due to concurrency, leading to longer average path lengths.

For each data structure and regardless of the platform and workload, there is at least one concurrent algorithm that performs and scales close to the asynchronized implementation (*async*) of the data structure. On average, the best concurrent implementations are 10% slower than their asynchronized counterparts and exhibit similar scalability trends. The next section explores methods in which the portable scalability of these algorithms can be improved even further. Our

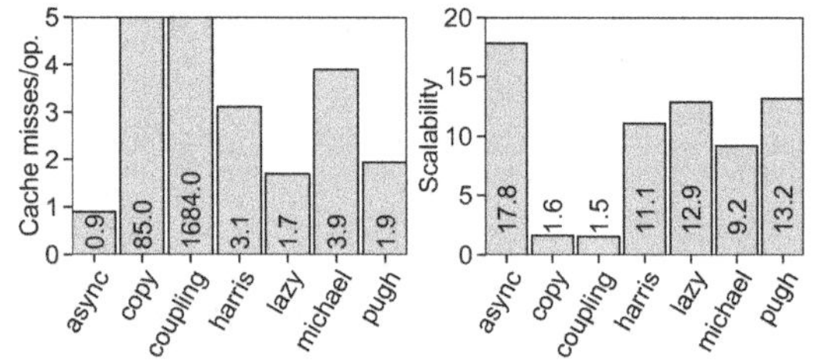

Figure 3: Cache misses per operation and scalability for various linked-list algorithms.

empirical results thus confirm our intuition: asynchronized executions represent good approximations for the ideal behavior of CSDSs.

Intuitively, the asynchronized implementations perform and scale better than the concurrent alternatives because they trigger cache coherence less (i.e., fewer cache-line transfers): they modify only the data that is semantically necessary, as they do not employ synchronization, thus leading to a smaller number of memory stores. Cache coherence is the source of the most significant scalability bottleneck for concurrent algorithms on multi-cores, because the number of cache-line transfers tends to increase with the number of threads. Hence, it is essential for a CSDS algorithm to limit the amount of cache traffic it performs during each operation, which is directly linked to the number of stores on shared data. Stores cause cache-line invalidations, which in turn generate cache misses of future accesses.

We confirm this line of reasoning by showing a practical correspondence between the number of cache misses and the performance of an algorithm. In doing so, we use linked-list algorithms as an example. Figure 3 shows the number of cache misses per operation generated by various linked-list algorithms, as well as their scalability compared to single-thread throughput. We use a workload where the list has 4096 elements on average, 10% of the operations are updates, and 20 threads concurrently access the data structure. Clearly, the asynchronized execution has the fewest number of cache misses. It is also interesting to note that the number of cache misses per operation is directly correlated to the scalability and performance of the algorithms: the fewer cache misses an algorithm generates, the better it scales. This correlation pertains to the other data structures as well.

We also take a closer look at how the "best" concurrent algorithms access memory. We look at the memory access pattern of a CSDS algorithm by studying the number of loads and stores (often performed through read-modify-write instructions), as well as the branches in each operation and phase of the algorithm. We notice that the CSDS algorithms that tend to scale and perform the best also tend to have an average number of loads, stores, and branches closer to the asynchronized implementations than the alternatives. This is generally valid for all the operations and phases. Thus, we make the observation that the more an algorithm's memory access pattern resembles that of the asynchronized execu-

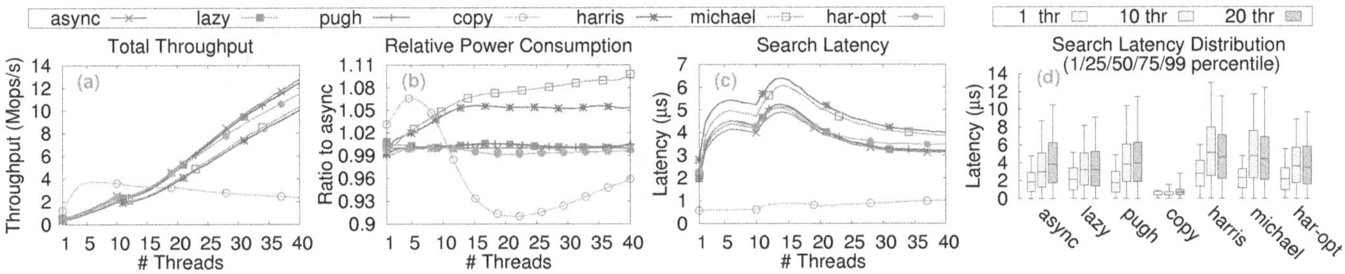

Figure 4: Linked list with 1024 elements and 5% updates (2.5% successful).

tion, the better it scales regardless of the platform and workload. In the next section, we look at ways in which this similarity can be achieved and validate this observation.

Hardware considerations. Our evaluation has revealed a number of other hardware-related observations.

We fine-tune several algorithms in ASCYLIB using Intel's TSX [34] hardware transactional memory (HTM), in order to assess whether HTM can be used to optimize CSDSs. Basically, in 60% of the scenarios, HTM improves throughput with up to 5%. In the remaining 40%, the results are either unaffected, or the throughput decreases (up to 5% as well). We use a 4-core desktop processor (8 hyper-threads) with the first iteration of Intel's TSX. As larger machines become available and the technology matures,[4] HTM might become even more helpful.

We also encounter a number of hardware-related bottlenecks, not specific to CSDSs. For example, the small TLBs on the Tilera (32 entries) require feeding SSMEM with small chunks of memory and keeping the amount of garbage low. Otherwise, if the threads use largely fragmented memory, the TLB misses become a bottleneck. Similarly, on Xeon40, large chunks of memory with a lot of garbage can lead to an excessive number of hardware prefetches that decrease performance up to an order of magnitude. On the Opteron, the interconnect bandwidth becomes a bottleneck when the structure is allocated on a single memory node. If a structure fits on one memory page, there is no straightforward solution to this problem, other than restructuring the data structure. System designers should be aware of the aforementioned issues as they can emerge in all types of software.

5. The ASCY Patterns

Having observed that CSDSs that resemble sequential algorithms scale and perform best, we now look at how this similarity can be achieved. We identify four patterns which are applicable to a broad class of CSDS algorithms and we show that when they are applied, the performance and scalability of CSDSs is systematically improved. These patterns collectively represent *asynchronized concurrency (ASCY).*

For brevity, we select Xeon20 as the platform in our experiments. This is the most modern processor within our platform set. Also for brevity, we break down the results for each pattern using one of the four data structures. Note that we get similar results on any platform and data-structure combination: the patterns are globally beneficial.

ASCY$_1$. We first examine the search operation of CSDSs and use linked lists as a case study. Figure 4 depicts the behavior of the various linked lists of ASCYLIB on a search-dominated workload (only 2.5% successful updates).

Out of the existing algorithms, the *async*, *lazy* and *pugh* lists deliver the highest total throughput. Both *lazy* and *pugh* linked lists have a search that is identical to the sequential algorithm. Essentially, no stores, waiting, or restarting is involved. These algorithms perform within 10% of *async*. In comparison, the lock-free lists (*harris* and *michael*) diverge from the sequential code as they try to physically remove logically-deleted nodes using CAS. If a physical removal fails, the operation is restarted. Additionally, they also need to unmark[5] every pointer while traversing the list.

Overall, the results can be largely explained by the average search latencies (Figure 4(c)): the closer to the sequential an implementation is, the lower the latency is. On more than 20 threads, the search latencies decrease due to the effects of hyper-threading; the two hyper-threads of a core help each other by keeping the list nodes warm in the shared L1 cache.

We thus identify ASCY$_1$ as a generic pattern: *The search operation should not involve any stores, waiting, or retries.*

We apply this pattern to the search operation of existing algorithms: in the case of linked lists, we apply it to the *harris* lock-free list by removing the physical removal of logically deleted elements from the search operation. We refer to the resulting algorithm as *harris-opt.*

If we now look at the three lock-free algorithms, namely *harris*, *michael*, and *harris-opt*, the effects of applying ASCY$_1$ become evident. In both *harris* and *michael*, the search tries to unlink logically deleted nodes and restarts if it fails, hence violating ASCY$_1$. In contrast, *harris-opt* ignores the deleted nodes while searching. The latency improvements due to ASCY$_1$ are approximately 10-30% as we can observe on the latency graphs (Figure 4(c) & (d)). Additionally, *harris-opt* has a tighter latency distribution (Figure 4(d)) than the other two. *harris-opt* provides more stable

[4] A recent announcement by Intel [35] suggests that this might take a while.

[5] Clear the least significant bit that indicates a logically deleted element.

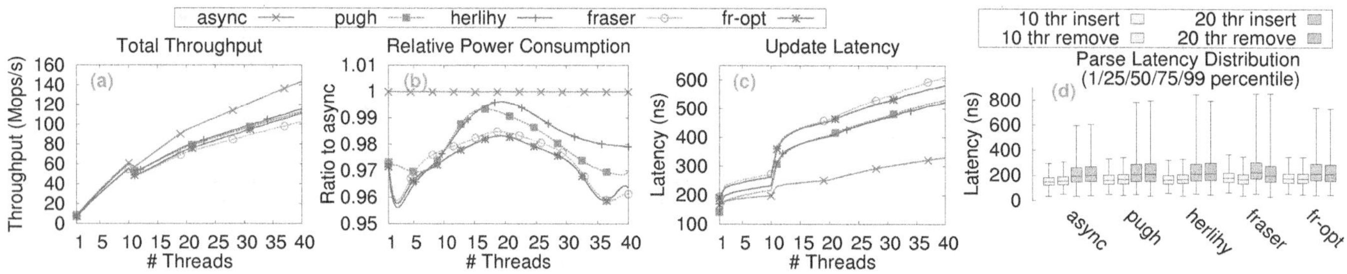

Figure 5: Skip list with 1024 elements and 20% updates (10% successful).

executions because it never restarts or invokes work that is unnecessary to the search. Furthermore, Figure 4(b) plots the power consumption relative to *async*. We observe that *harris* and *michael*, which do not follow ASCY_1, deliver lower performance while consuming more power than the rest.

Additionally, the behavior of the *copy* list is worth analyzing. It is apparent from the latency graphs that structuring the data as an array can bring tremendous benefits on serial data accesses. However, *copy* has two major limitations: (i) high memory overhead, as every update creates a new list copy, and (ii) synchronization of updates with a global lock, which easily becomes a bottleneck. In §6.1, we use the idea of array-based structures in the design of a hash table.

Finally, we apply ASCY_1 to the *fraser* skip list (not shown in the graphs) and observe performance improvements. In most cases, applying ASCY_1 means deferring cleaning-up and helping to the update methods. ASCY_1 also requires that updates always leave the data structure in a state that allows any existing node to be found. In addition, when removing nodes, their memory should not be freed while there is the possibility of an ongoing search accessing it. Memory reclaimation is handled by SSMEM in ASCYLIB.

ASCY_2. We now focus on the parse phase of the update operations. In a sequential algorithm, this phase is basically identical to the search operation. In CSDSs however, parsing might involve helping, cleaning-up the data structure, or restarting the operation (e.g., due to a failed clean-up attempt). We study this phase more closely using skip-list algorithms.

Figure 5 depicts the behavior of the five skip lists in ASCYLIB on a workload with 10% successful updates. The best performing pre-existing algorithms are *pugh* and *herlihy*, which are within 22% of the asynchronized version. Looking closer at their parse phase, we note that the only stores that are performed are for cleaning-up purposes and that the parse is never restarted. In contrast, a parse in *fraser* might have to restart due to a failed clean-up attempt, or accessing a logically deleted node when changing levels.

Taking these results into account, we establish ASCY_2: *The parse phase of an update operation should not perform any stores other than for cleaning-up purposes and should not involve waiting, or retries.*

We apply this pattern in conjunction with ASCY_1 (based on [30]) to the *fraser* skip list and refer to the resulting algorithm as *fraser-opt*. *fraser-opt* delivers up to 8% better throughput than *fraser* and has a 5% lower average update latency (Figure 5(c)). Furthermore, Figure 5(d) plots the latency distribution of the parsing phase only. The behavior of both *fraser* and *fraser-opt* is similar. However, the latter eliminates the overhead of useless parses that have to be restarted. *fraser* performs 0.38%, 1.07%, and 1.82% more parses than updates on 10, 20, and 40 threads, respectively. *fraser-opt* has lower overheads: 0.03%, 0.09%, and 0.17%, respectively.

In terms of power consumption (Figure 5(b)), there are two main observations. First, ASCY not only improves the throughput of *fraser*, but also leads to an algorithm that consumes slightly less power than the initial design. Second, in the case of skip lists, the lock-based algorithms seem to consume more power than their lock-free counterparts.

Finally, we also apply ASCY_2 to the *harris* linked list. In practice, applying ASCY_2 means (i) not helping other threads while parsing the data structure and (ii) avoiding restarting if cleaning-up fails. Similar to ASCY_1, for ASCY_2 to work, concurrent updates should not render portions of the data structure unreachable.

ASCY_3. Another characteristic of sequential algorithms is that if an update operation cannot be completed (i.e., the parse does not find the node in case of a remove, or it finds the node in case of an insert), no additional stores are performed and the update method simply returns "false". This is not always the case in existing CSDS algorithms.

We quantify the impact of this issue by looking at hash-table algorithms. Figure 6 depicts the performance of various hash tables with and without (suffixed with "*-no*") the "read-only fail" of the sequential algorithms. In terms of throughput, algorithms doing no additional stores after unsuccessful parses perform up to 12.5% better than their counterparts doing stores. Additionally, they are within 19-30% of the *async* version. Although this change alters the behavior of only 5% of all operations in this workload, we observe throughput benefits up to 12.5% on *java*. This difference can be attributed to (i) the increased number of cache misses caused by unnecessary synchronization, and (ii) the increase of con-

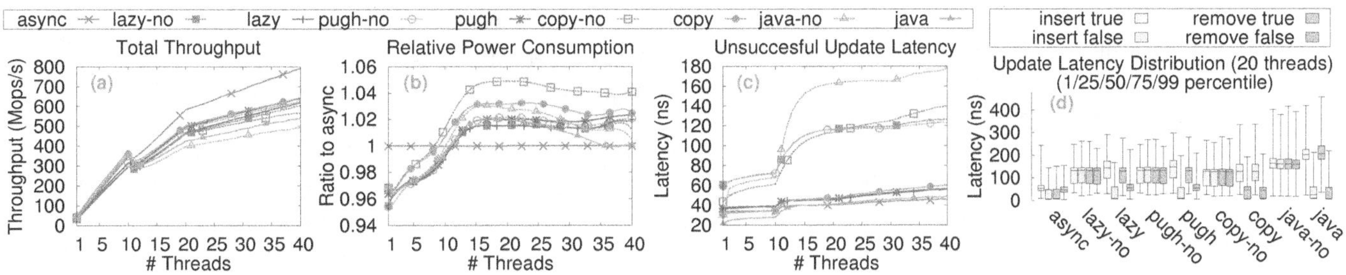

Figure 6: Hash table with 8192 elements, 8192 (initial) buckets, and 10% updates (5% successful).

tention on locks. Basically, (i) manifests as a 2.8% increase in the cache-miss ratio on 40 threads, and (ii) as a 14% increased chance to find a lock occupied.

Given the apparent benefits, we model the behavior of the sequential algorithms through ASCY$_3$: *An update operation whose parse phase is unsuccessful should not perform any stores, besides those used for cleaning-up in the parse phase.*

Figure 6(c) details the benefits of ASCY$_3$ on the average latency of unsuccessful updates. It is clear that turning a failed update into a read-only operation yields a significant (1.5-4x) decrease in latencies. Nevertheless, depending on the algorithm, applying ASCY$_3$ can incur some overhead on successful updates, as we notice on the graph (d). For instance, enabling ASCY$_3$ on *java* requires an additional search to either decide that the update cannot succeed, or proceed to the actual update. In general ASCY$_3$ also reduces the power consumption of the CSDSs. This is achieved by decreasing the number of cache-line transfers.

Finally, we apply this pattern to multiple other existing algorithms: the *pugh*, *lazy*, and *copy* linked lists, the *pugh* and *herlihy* skip lists, and the *drachsler* BST. In many cases, applying ASCY$_3$ simply means checking the outcome of the parse and returning "false" without locking. The algorithms to which we apply ASCY$_3$ trivially maintain correctness, as unsuccessful updates can be seen as search operations.

ASCY$_4$. We now focus on the modification phase of the update operation. We use BSTs as an example for this scenario. Figure 7 includes the corresponding results.

Aside from the asynchronized algorithms, the best performing concurrent implementation is *natarajan*. We argue that the other four concurrent trees synchronize more than the minimum. Indeed, we measure the ratio of atomic operations to the number of successful updates on the same workload as Figure 7. *natarajan* uses two atomic operations per update on average, which is close to the asynchronized versions, whereas the other concurrent trees require more than three. In fact, *natarajan* is also the closest to *async* in terms of the number of stores and the number of affected cache lines. This major difference, together with the differences in the first three ASCY patterns, is reflected in the results, in terms of throughput, latency, and power consumption.

More precisely, *howley* employs helping even while searching or parsing the tree. *ellen* uses helping only on elements that the current operation wants to update. Helping is generally expensive, as it requires additional synchronization in order to be implemented. *bronson* is a complex algorithm that can block waiting for an update to complete. Finally, *drachsler* acquires a large number of locks (3.15 on average) for each successful update.

Figure 7(d) depicts the latency distribution of successful-only operations, isolating the effects of the modification phases. Clearly, the *natarajan* tree has lower latencies and a tighter distribution than the rest. Interestingly, *natarajan* consumes less power than two of the other four concurrent trees, similar power to *drachsler*, and more power than *howley*. *natarajan* simply performs at speeds different than the rest: on 40 threads, it issues 797M memory accesses per second with 13.4% cache-miss ratio, compared to the 578M/23.8% of *drachsler* and the 395M/18.7% of *howley*.

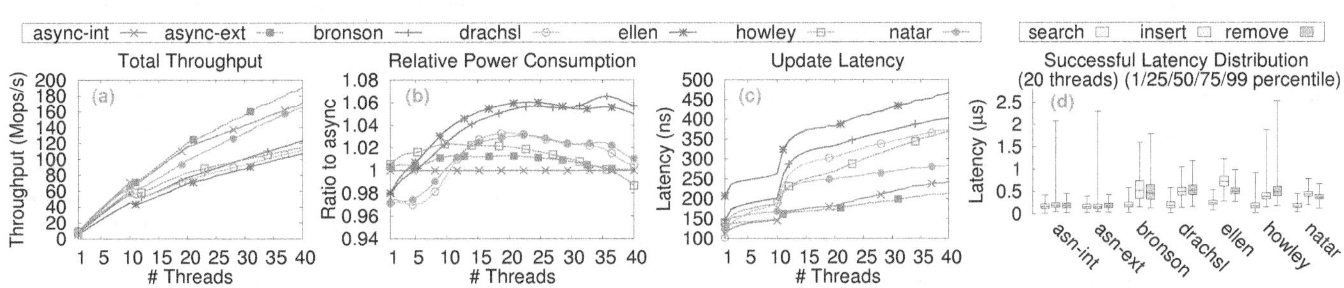

Figure 7: BST with 2048 elements and 20% updates (10% successful).

Still, *drachsler* and *howley* consume 41% and 49% more energy per operation than *natarajan*, respectively.

We can thus identify $ASCY_4$: *The number and region of memory stores in a successful update should be close to those of a standard sequential implementation.*

Essentially, $ASCY_4$ means that updates should not block each other or write to the same memory addresses unless they operate on semantically related elements, such as adjacent nodes in the data structure.

Discussion. It is worth noting that while each pattern can be identified in some of the existing algorithms, we have shown that CSDS algorithms can be improved even further when the ASCY patterns are applied collectively. Moreover, as seen in §4, for each data structure and platform combination, there is an algorithm that is reasonably close in performance to the asynchronized executions, in general a CSDS that resembles the sequential algorithm. In this section, by applying ASCY and bringing these algorithms even closer to their sequential counterparts, we have further improved their performance and scalability. We can therefore conclude that ASCY can help reach implementations that are portably scalable.

6. Designing with ASCY from Scratch

We illustrate the use of ASCY on the design of two new search data structure algorithms: (i) a hash table (CLHT), and (ii) a binary search tree (BST-TK). Due to the limited space, we only present the high-level ideas of the algorithms and refer the reader to [11] for further details.

6.1 Cache-Line Hash Table (CLHT)

CLHT captures the basic idea behind ASCY: avoid cache-line transfers. To this end, CLHT uses cache-line-sized buckets and, of course, follows the four ASCY patterns. As a cache-line block is the granularity of the cache-coherence protocols, CLHT ensures that most operations are completed with *at most* one cache-line transfer.

CLHT uses the 8 words of a cache line as:

concurrency	k_1	k_2	k_3	v_1	v_2	v_3	next

The first word is used for concurrency-control; the next six are the key/value pairs; the last is a pointer that can be used to link buckets. Updates synchronize based on the `concurrency` word and do in-place modifications of the key/value pairs of the bucket. To support in-place updates, the basic idea behind CLHT is that a search/parse does not simply traverse the keys, but obtains an *atomic snapshot* of each key/value pair[6]:

```
val_t val = bucket->val[i];
if (bucket->key[i] == key && bucket->val[i] == val)
    /* atomic snapshot of key/value */
```

[6] For an atomic snapshot to be possible, the memory allocator of the values must guarantee that the same address cannot appear twice during the lifespan of an operation. Additionally, the implementation has to handle possible compiler and CPU re-orderings (not shown in the pseudo-code)

We design and implement two variants of CLHT, lock-based (CLHT-LB) and lock-free (CLHT-LF).

CLHT-LB. The lock-based variant of CLHT uses the `concurrency` word as a lock. Search operations traverse the key/value pairs and return the value if a match is found. Updates first perform a search to check whether the operation is at all feasible (recall $ASCY_3$) and if so, they grab the lock, apply the update, and release the lock. If there is not enough space for an insertion, the operation either links a new bucket by using the `next` pointer, or resizes the hash table.

CLHT-LF. The lock-free variant of CLHT is more elaborate than the lock-based. This is due to the fact that the key/value-pair insertions have to appear atomic. With locks, we implement atomicity by allowing for a single concurrent writer per bucket. However, without locks, several updates can concurrently alter the same key or value. Even worse, if concurrent insertions on the same bucket do not synchronize, there is no way to avoid duplicate keys on different slots.

In order to solve these complications, we devise the `snapshot_t` object. `snapshot_t` handles a word (8 bytes) as an array of bytes (*map*) with a *version* number:

```
struct snapshot_t {
  uint32_t version;    /* a 4-bytes integer */
  uint8_t  map[4];     /* an array of 4 bytes */
};
```

Naturally, `snapshot_t` occupies the `concurrency` word of a bucket. `snapshot_t` provides an interface to atomically get or set the value of an index in the map. The `version` number is used to enable sets/gets to do atomic changes with respect to the other spots in the map. In short, atomicity is implemented by reading the value of the `snapshot_t` object before the atomic section and by using the version number to get/set the target index in the map using a CAS on the whole object. For instance, if a another concurrent insertion has already been completed, the current operation will fail the CAS, because the version number will be different. We then use the fields of the map as flags that indicate whether a given key/value pair is valid, invalid, or is being inserted.

Evaluation. We compare CLHT to *pugh*, one of the best performing hash tables in §4. In contrast to the linked-based hash tables, CLHT performs in-place updates, thus avoiding memory allocation and garbage collection of hash-table nodes. Nevertheless, we use the SSMEM allocator for values.

Figure 8 includes the results. Noticeably, *clht-lb* and *clht-lf* outperform *pugh* by 23% and 13% on average, respectively. CLHT's design significantly reduces the number of cache-line transfers. For example, on the Opteron for 20% updates, *clht-lb* requires 4.06 cycles per instruction, *clht-lf* 4.24, and *pugh* operates with 6.57. Interestingly, *clht-lb* is consistently better than *clht-lf* on 20 threads. On more threads (e.g., 40), however, *clht-lf* often outperforms *clht-lb*.

Discussion. CLHT supports operations with keys up to 64-bits. To support longer keys, the 64-bit keys in CLHT can be used as a first filter. The operation has to compare the full key, that is stored separately, only if there is a match with

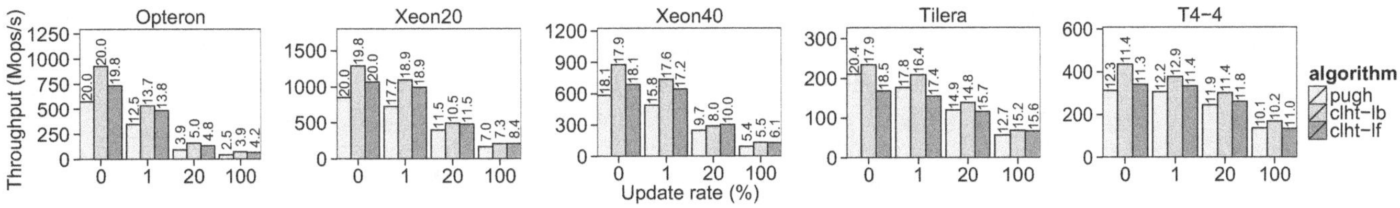

Figure 8: CLHT with 4096 elements on 20 threads for various update rates.

the 64-bit filter. This technique has already been shown to work well in practice [19].

6.2 BST Ticket (BST-TK)

BST-TK reduces the number of cache-line transfers by acquiring less locks than existing BSTs. Intuitively, on any lock-based BST an update operation parses to the node to modify and, if possible, acquires a number of locks and performs the update. This is precisely how BST-TK proceeds.

More specifically, BST-TK is an external tree, where every internal, router node is protected by a lock and contains a version number. The version numbers are used in order to be able to optimistically parse the tree and later detect concurrency. Update operations proceed as described in Figure 10. We are able to simplify the design of BST-TK by making the simple observation that a ticket lock already contains a version field. Accordingly, we consolidate steps 3 and 6, with steps 4 and 7 respectively. We do this by modifying the interface of the ticket lock in order to try to acquire a specific version of the lock (i.e., the one that the parsing phase has observed). If the lock acquisition fails, the version of the lock has been incremented by a concurrent update, hence the operation has to be restarted. We further optimize the tree by assigning two smaller (32-bits) ticket locks to each node, so that the left and the right pointers of the tree can be locked separately. Overall, BST-TK acquires one lock for successful insertions and two locks for successful removals.

Evaluation. We compare BST-TK to *natarajan*, the best performing BST in §4. Figure 9 depicts the results. In general, *bst-tk* behaves very similarly to *natarajan* (within 1% on average). It might have been expected that *bst-tk* would outperform the latter, because it uses less atomic operations per update. Although this is true, *bst-tk* has slightly increased parsing overhead compared to *natarajan* (0.045% vs. 0.032% with 20% updates on the Opteron). For simplicity, we did not implement certain optimizations that could prove beneficial

```
update()
1. parse() /* keeps track of the versions numbers */
2. if (!can_update()) { return false; } /* ASCY3 */
3. lock() /* 1 node for insert, 2 nodes for remove */
4. if (!validate_version()) { goto 1; }
5. apply_update()
6. increase_version()
7. unlock()
```

Figure 10: Update operations in BST-TK.

under high contention. For instance, an insertion does not have to be restarted if the router node is locked by another insertion. Instead, it can be blocked and wait for the ongoing insertion to finish and then proceed almost normally.

7. Related Work

CSDS design. A large body of work has been dedicated to the design of efficient CSDSs [7, 15, 17, 20, 25, 29, 32, 41, 43, 44, 46, 49, 50, 52, 53]. These efforts usually aim at optimizing a specific CSDS (e.g., BST) in terms of throughput, for a specific set of workloads and platforms. In contrast, ASCY is a paradigm that targets the scalability of various CSDSs across different platforms, for various workloads, and according to several performance metrics.

Memory reclamation is of key importance in CSDSs [6, 14, 16, 28, 45]. Various techniques have been proposed, such as *quiescent state* [13, 23, 24], *epochs* [20], *reference counters* [14, 21, 53], *pointers* [6, 28, 45], and, recently, hardware transactional memory [1, 16]. ASCYLIB uses an epoch-based allocator that reduces the performance overheads.

Read-copy update (RCU) [41] is a concurrent programming technique that is heavily used in the Linux Kernel [3]. In short, RCU guarantees that readers always find a consistent view of the data structure. Writers perform atomic updates, after which, in the case of removals, they wait for all concurrent readers to finish in order to perform memory reclamation. Relativistic programming [52] is a technique

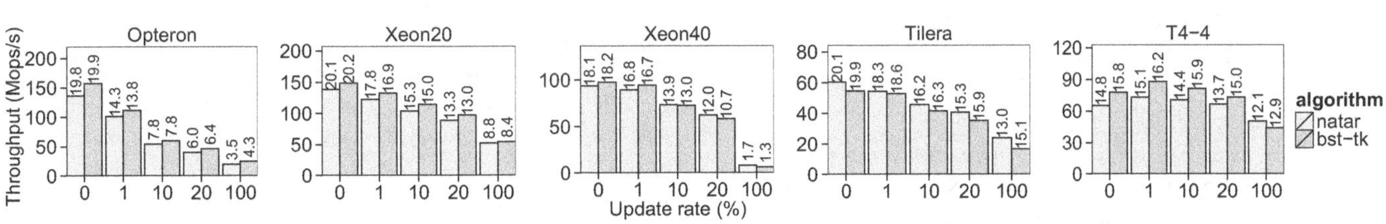

Figure 9: BST-TK with 4096 elements on 20 threads for various update rates.

that is related to RCU and maintains efficient reads even with large updates to the data structure (e.g., a resize). Arbel and Attiya [2] present an RCU-like search tree which allows concurrent updates. While out-performing classic RCU-based structures, the design is still shown to lag behind other state-of-the-art CSDSs that are closer to ASCY, in particular in write-intensive scenarios. In general, RCU-like approaches purposefully optimize the performance of search operations at the possible expense of updates. Our $ASCY_1$ pattern is similar in the sense that it dictates that readers must be unaware of concurrency. However, our three remaining patterns achieve the benefits of sequential reads without sacrificing the performance of updates.

Hunt et al. [33] study the energy efficiency of lock-free and lock-based concurrent data structures (queues and linked lists). They find that lock-free algorithms tend to be more energy efficient than their lock-based counterparts. We observe that in the context of CSDSs, as long as the algorithms apply ASCY, there is no inherent difference between lock-free and lock-based algorithms. Essentially, this is because the ASCY patterns help reduce the number and the granularity of locks.

Scalability. Recent work [12] has argued that scalability of synchronization is mainly a property of the hardware. In particular, synchronization primitives are shown to be inherently non-scalable on NUMA architectures due to expensive cache-line transfers. To bypass these problems, ASCY reduces the amount of synchronization on CSDSs, leading to designs that scale even in the presence of non-uniformity.

Clements et al. [9] link commutative interfaces to the existence of scalable implementations. In essence, they argue that commutative operations can lead to cache conflict-free implementations, that are inherently scalable from the memory-system point of view. Although basic CSDS interfaces commute, as defined by Clements et al., certain structures such as lists and trees do not allow for conflict-free implementations. We show, however, that even in these cases, scalable algorithms can be devised following ASCY.

Data structures in systems. Boyd-Wickizer et al. [5] performed a scalability study of the Linux kernel. They identify several bottlenecks, among which, one in the directory entry lookup operation (even though it is optimized using RCU). In general, numerous key-value stores, such as Memcached [42], SILT [38] or Masstree [39] are based on a CSDS. In some cases, these structures have been shown to be scalability bottlenecks, as for example in Memcached [5, 19, 47]. Fan et al. [19] achieve a 3-fold performance increase over the traditional Memcached, mainly by optimizing its hash table. ASCY can be used to recognize possible optimizations in systems such as Memcached and develop scalable CSDS implementations.

Baumann et al. [4] argue that in principle, non-portable, hardware-specific optimizations in the OS kernel should be removed. They attribute the existence of such optimizations to "the basic structure of a shared-memory kernel with data structures protected by locks" and propose to rethink the OS structure. We show that, by applying ASCY, we reach portably-scalable implementations. We believe that ASCY can help alleviate the difficult problem of CSDSs in OSes.

8. Concluding Remarks

This paper introduced *asynchronized concurrency (ASCY)*: a paradigm consisting of four complementary programming patterns to govern the design of portably scalable concurrent search data structures (CSDSs). We showed that ASCY can be used both to optimize existing algorithms and to assist in the design of new ones. In particular, using ASCY, we have optimized 10 state-of-the-art algorithms and designed 2 new algorithms from scratch, a hash table (CLHT) and a binary search tree (BST-TK). These are part of ASCYLIB, a new CSDS library that contains 34 highly-optimized cross-platform implementations of linked lists, hash tables, skip lists, and BSTs. ASCYLIB is available at `http://lpd.epfl.ch/site/ascylib`.

It is important to note that it is not always straightforward to apply some of the ASCY patterns. For instance, internal BSTs require either helping (e.g., *ellen*) or additional structures (e.g., *drachsler*) to implement $ASCY_{1-2}$. Similarly, in order to apply $ASCY_3$ on some lock-based hash tables, such as *java* and CLHT, we have to add a complete search operation before starting with the code of the update. As conveyed by our results, doing so is beneficial overall, because it reduces the coherence traffic. Enabling ASCY in these cases, however, results in overhead in successful updates.

Clearly, we expect ASCY to be applicable to other *search* data structures, such as prefix-trees, or B-trees. However, given that the ASCY patterns are based on the breakdown of operations to search and to parse-then-modify updates, some of the patterns might be meaningless for other abstractions such as queues and stacks. Still, we argue that the basic principle of ASCY (i.e., bring the concurrent-software design close to the asynchronized one) is generally beneficial.

Finally, it is important to note that we have focused this work on the basic CSDS interface, which is the common denominator for all search data structures. We did not consider data-structure-specific operations, such as *iterations, move*, or *max*. It is not clear whether it is easy, or possible, to implement these on top of ASCY-compliant CSDSs.

Acknowledgments

We wish to thank the anonymous reviewers for their helpful comments. We also like to thank Anne-Marie Kermarrec for her comments in the early stages of this work, as well as, Eric Ruppert for the fruitful discussions while designing the CLHT hash table. Finally, we wish to thank Oracle Labs, the EPFL DIAS lab, and EcoCloud for providing us with some of the platforms employed in this work. Part of this work was funded from the SNSF projects 200021-143915 (Reusable Concurrent Data Types) and 200021-147067 (Scalable and Secure Computing in Social Networks).

References

[1] Dan Alistarh, Patrick Eugster, Maurice Herlihy, Alexander Matveev, and Nir Shavit. StackTrack: An Automated Transactional Approach to Concurrent Memory Reclamation. EuroSys 2014.

[2] Maya Arbel and Hagit Attiya. Concurrent Updates with RCU: Search Tree As an Example. PODC 2014.

[3] Andrea Arcangeli, Mingming Cao, Paul E McKenney, and Dipankar Sarma. Using Read-Copy-Update Techniques for System V IPC in the Linux 2.5 Kernel. USENIX ATC 2003.

[4] Andrew Baumann, Paul Barham, Pierre-Evariste Dagand, Tim Harris, Rebecca Isaacs, Simon Peter, Timothy Roscoe, Adrian Schüpbach, and Akhilesh Singhania. The multikernel: a new OS architecture for scalable multicore systems. SOSP 2009.

[5] Silas Boyd-Wickizer, Austin T Clements, Yandong Mao, Aleksey Pesterev, M Frans Kaashoek, Robert Morris, and Nickolai Zeldovich. An Analysis of Linux Scalability to Many Cores. OSDI 2010.

[6] Anastasia Braginsky, Alex Kogan, and Erez Petrank. Drop the anchor: lightweight memory management for non-blocking data structures. SPAA 2013.

[7] Nathan G Bronson, Jared Casper, Hassan Chafi, and Kunle Olukotun. A Practical Concurrent Binary Search Tree. PPoPP 2010.

[8] Austin T Clements, M Frans Kaashoek, and Nickolai Zeldovich. Scalable address spaces using RCU balanced trees. In *ACM SIGARCH Computer Architecture News*, volume 40, pages 199–210. ACM, 2012.

[9] Austin T Clements, M Frans Kaashoek, Nickolai Zeldovich, Robert T Morris, and Eddie Kohler. The Scalable Commutativity Rule: Designing Scalable Software for Multicore Processors. SOSP 2013.

[10] Pat Conway, Nathan Kalyanasundharam, Gregg Donley, Kevin Lepak, and Bill Hughes. Cache Hierarchy and Memory Subsystem of the AMD Opteron Processor. *IEEE Micro*, 30(2):16–29, March 2010.

[11] Tudor David, Rachid Guerraoui, Tong Che, and Vasileios Trigonakis. Designing ASCY-compliant Concurrent Search Data Structures. Technical report, EPFL, Lausanne, 2014.

[12] Tudor David, Rachid Guerraoui, and Vasileios Trigonakis. Everything You Always Wanted to Know About Synchronization but Were Afraid to Ask. SOSP 2013.

[13] Mathieu Desnoyers, Paul E McKenney, Alan S Stern, Michel R Dagenais, and Jonathan Walpole. User-level implementations of read-copy update. *Parallel and Distributed Systems, IEEE Transactions on*, 23(2):375–382, 2012.

[14] David L Detlefs, Paul A Martin, Mark Moir, and Guy L Steele Jr. Lock-free reference counting. *Distributed Computing*, 15(4):255–271, 2002.

[15] Dana Drachsler, Martin Vechev, and Eran Yahav. Practical Concurrent Binary Search Trees via Logical Ordering. PPoPP 2014.

[16] Aleksandar Dragojević, Maurice Herlihy, Yossi Lev, and Mark Moir. On the power of hardware transactional memory to simplify memory management. PODC 2011.

[17] Faith Ellen, Panagiota Fatourou, Eric Ruppert, and Franck van Breugel. Non-blocking Binary Search Trees. PODC 2010.

[18] Facebook. RocksDB. `http://rocksdb.org`.

[19] Bin Fan, David G Andersen, and Michael Kaminsky. MemC3: Compact and Concurrent MemCache with Dumber Caching and Smarter Hashing. NSDI 2013.

[20] Keir Fraser. *Practical Lock-Freedom*. PhD thesis, University of Cambridge, 2004.

[21] Anders Gidenstam, Marina Papatriantafilou, Håkan Sundell, and Philippas Tsigas. Efficient and reliable lock-free memory reclamation based on reference counting. *Parallel and Distributed Systems, IEEE Transactions on*, 20(8):1173–1187, 2009.

[22] Vincent Gramoli. More than You Ever Wanted to Know about Synchronization. PPoPP 2015.

[23] Timothy L Harris. A Pragmatic Implementation of Non-blocking Linked Lists. DISC 2001.

[24] Thomas E Hart, Paul E McKenney, Angela Demke Brown, and Jonathan Walpole. Performance of memory reclamation for lockless synchronization. *Journal of Parallel and Distributed Computing*, 67(12):1270–1285, 2007.

[25] Steve Heller, Maurice Herlihy, Victor Luchangco, Mark Moir, III Scherer, William N, and Nir Shavit. A Lazy Concurrent List-Based Set Algorithm. In *Principles of Distributed Systems*, volume 3974. 2006.

[26] Maurice Herlihy, Yossi Lev, Victor Luchangco, and Nir Shavit. A simple optimistic skiplist algorithm. SIROCCO 2007.

[27] Maurice Herlihy, Victor Luchangco, and Mark Moir. Obstruction-free synchronization: Double-ended queues as an example. ICDCS 2003.

[28] Maurice Herlihy, Victor Luchangco, and Mark Moir. The repeat offender problem: a mechanism for supporting dynamic-sized lock-free data structures. Technical report, 2002.

[29] Maurice Herlihy and Nir Shavit. *The Art of Multiprocessor Programming, Revised First Edition*. 2012.

[30] Maurice P Herlihy, Yosef Lev, and Nir N Shavit. Concurrent lock-free skiplist with wait-free contains operator, May 3 2011. US Patent 7,937,378.

[31] Maurice P Herlihy and Jeannette M Wing. Linearizability: A correctness condition for concurrent objects. *ACM Transactions on Programming Languages and Systems*, 12(3):463–492, 1990.

[32] Shane V Howley and Jeremy Jones. A non-blocking internal binary search tree. SPAA 2012.

[33] Nicholas Hunt, Paramjit Singh Sandhu, and Luis Ceze. Characterizing the performance and energy efficiency of lock-free data structures. INTERACT 2011.

[34] Intel. Intel Transactional Synchronization Extensions Overview. 2013.

[35] Intel. Intel xeon processor e3-1200 v3 product family - specification update. `http://www.intel.com/content/dam/www/public/us/en/documents/specification-updates/xeon-e3-1200v3-spec-update.pdf`, 2014.

[36] Intel Thread Building Blocks. https://www.threadingbuildingblocks.org.

[37] Doug Lea. Overview of package util.concurrent Release 1.3.4. http://gee.cs.oswego.edu/dl/classes/EDU/oswego/cs/dl/util/concurrent/intro.html, 2003.

[38] Hyeontaek Lim, Bin Fan, David G Andersen, and Michael Kaminsky. SILT: A Memory-efficient, High-performance Key-value Store. SOSP 2011.

[39] Yandong Mao, Eddie Kohler, and Robert Tappan Morris. Cache craftiness for fast multicore key-value storage. EuroSys 2012.

[40] Paul E McKenney, Dipankar Sarma, and Maneesh Soni. Scaling Dcache with RCU. *Linux Journal*, 2004(117), January 2004.

[41] Paul E McKenney and John D Slingwine. Read-copy update: Using execution history to solve concurrency problems. In *Parallel and Distributed Computing and Systems*, pages 509–518, 1998.

[42] Memcached. http://www.memcached.org.

[43] Zviad Metreveli, Nickolai Zeldovich, and M Frans Kaashoek. CPHASH: A Cache-partitioned Hash Table. PPoPP 2012.

[44] Maged M Michael. High performance dynamic lock-free hash tables and list-based sets. SPAA 2002.

[45] Maged M Michael. Hazard pointers: Safe memory reclamation for lock-free objects. *Parallel and Distributed Systems, IEEE Transactions on*, 15(6):491–504, 2004.

[46] Aravind Natarajan and Neeraj Mittal. Fast Concurrent Lock-free Binary Search Trees. PPoPP 2014.

[47] Rajesh Nishtala, Hans Fugal, Steven Grimm, Marc Kwiatkowski, Herman Lee, Harry C Li, Ryan McElroy, Mike Paleczny, Daniel Peek, Paul Saab, David Stafford, Tony Tung, and Venkateshwaran Venkataramani. Scaling Memcache at Facebook. NSDI 2013.

[48] Oracle. CopyOnWriteArrayList in Java docs. http://docs.oracle.com/javase/7/docs/api/java/util/concurrent/CopyOnWriteArrayList.html.

[49] William Pugh. Concurrent Maintenance of Skip Lists. Technical report, 1990.

[50] Håkan Sundell and Philippas Tsigas. Fast and lock-free concurrent priority queues for multi-thread systems. IPDPS 2003.

[51] Tilera. Tilera TILE-Gx. http://www.tilera.com/products/processors/TILE-Gx_Family.

[52] Josh Triplett, Paul E McKenney, and Jonathan Walpole. Resizable, scalable, concurrent hash tables via relativistic programming. USENIX ATC 2011.

[53] John D Valois. Lock-free linked lists using compare-and-swap. PODC 1995.

iThreads: A Threading Library for Parallel Incremental Computation

Pramod Bhatotia
MPI-SWS
bhatotia@mpi-sws.org

Pedro Fonseca
MPI-SWS
pfonseca@mpi-sws.org

Umut A. Acar
Carnegie Mellon University & Inria
umut@cs.cmu.edu

Björn B. Brandenburg
MPI-SWS
bbb@mpi-sws.org

Rodrigo Rodrigues
NOVA University of Lisbon / CITI / NOVA-LINCS
rodrigo.rodrigues@fct.unl.pt

Abstract

Incremental computation strives for efficient successive runs of applications by re-executing only those parts of the computation that are affected by a given input change instead of recomputing everything from scratch. To realize these benefits automatically, we describe `iThreads`, a threading library for parallel incremental computation. `iThreads` supports unmodified shared-memory multithreaded programs: it can be used as a replacement for `pthreads` by a simple exchange of dynamically linked libraries, without even recompiling the application code. To enable such an interface, we designed algorithms and an implementation to operate at the compiled binary code level by leveraging MMU-assisted memory access tracking and process-based thread isolation. Our evaluation on a multicore platform using applications from the PARSEC and Phoenix benchmarks and two case-studies shows significant performance gains.

Categories and Subject Descriptors D.1.3 [*Programming Techniques*]: Concurrent Programming; D.4.1 [*Operating Systems*]: Process Management; F.1.2 [*Computation by Abstract Devices*]: Modes of Computation

General Terms Algorithms; Design; Performance

Keywords Incremental computation; shared-memory multithreading; self-adjusting computation; memoization; Concurrent Dynamic Dependence Graph (CDDG); Release Consistency (RC) memory model

ASPLOS '15, March 14 - 18 2015, Istanbul, Turkey.

http://dx.doi.org/10.1145/2694344.2694371

1. Introduction

Many applications operate incrementally by repeatedly invoking an algorithm or a program over input data that differs slightly from that of the previous invocation [25, 30, 37, 38, 42, 46, 68]. In such a workflow, small, localized changes to the input often require only small updates to the output, creating an opportunity to update the output incrementally instead of recomputing it from scratch. Since the work done is often proportional to the change size [6], rather than the total input size, incremental computation can achieve significant performance gains and efficient use of computing resources.

To obtain the benefits of incremental computation automatically, researchers in the programming-languages community have proposed compiler- and language-based approaches. While this has been an area of active research for several decades (§7), *almost* all prior work targets sequential programs—with the notable exceptions of two recent approaches for *parallel* incremental computation [27, 48].

Importantly, by leveraging a language-based approach, these two prior proposals [27, 48] have demonstrated substantial speedups, thus establishing that the promise of incremental computation can be realized in parallel programs. Specifically, these systems enable efficient and correct incremental updates to the output through the use of new programming languages with special data types (§7), and by requiring a *strict* fork-join programming model, where threads communicate *only* at end points (i.e., when forking/joining).

These choices reflect a difficult design tradeoff: they provide the compiler and runtime system with the information required to maximize reuse, but they also impose a cost on the programmer, who has to provide appropriate type annotations and, in some cases, also application-specific functions to safely implement the new type system. Furthermore, due to the restricted programming model, they also preclude support for many existing shared-memory multithreaded programs

```
$ LD_PRELOAD=iThreads.so                           // preload iThreads
$./<program_executable> <input-file>               // initial run
$ emacs <input-file>                               // input modified
$ echo "<off> <len>" >> changes.txt                // specify changes
$./<program_executable> <input-file>               // incremental run
```

Figure 1. How to run an executable using `iThreads`

```
                      Thread 1 (T1)          Thread 2 (T2)
/* T1.a */            lock();
read={y}              z = ++y;
write={y, z}          unlock();
                                   ↘
                                      lock();            /* T2.a */
                                      x++;               read={x}
                                      unlock();          write={x}
                                         ↓
                                      lock();            /* T2.b */
                                      y = 2*x + z;       read={x, z}
                                      unlock();          write={y}
```

Figure 2. An example of shared-memory multithreading

and synchronization primitives (such as *R/W locks, mutexes, semaphores, barriers*, and *conditional wait/signal*).

In this paper, we instead target increased generality, and to this end propose an OS-based approach to parallel incremental computation. More specifically, we present `iThreads`, a threading library for parallel incremental computation, which achieves the following goals.

- Practicality: `iThreads` supports the shared-memory multi-threaded programming model with the full range of synchronization primitives in the `POSIX` API.
- Transparency: `iThreads` supports unmodified programs (e.g., `C/C++`) without requiring the use of a new language with special data types.
- Efficiency: `iThreads` achieves efficiency, without limiting the available application parallelism, as its underlying algorithms are parallel as well.

The `iThreads` library is easy to use (see Figure 1 for the workflow): the user just needs to preload `iThreads` to replace `pthreads` by using the environment variable `LD_PRELOAD`. The dynamically linkable shared library interface allows existing executables to benefit from `iThreads`.

For the first run of a program (or the *initial run*), `iThreads` computes the output from scratch and records an execution trace. All subsequent runs for the program are *incremental runs*. For an incremental run, the user modifies the input and specifies the changes; e.g., assuming that the program reads the input from a file, the user specifies the `offset` and `len` for the changed parts of the file. Thereafter, `iThreads` incrementally updates the output based on the specified input changes and the recorded trace from the previous run.

Our approach relies on recording the data and control dependencies in a computation during the initial run by constructing a *Concurrent Dynamic Dependence Graph (CDDG)*. The CDDG tracks the input data to a program, all sub-computations (a *sub-computation* is a unit of the computation that is either reused or recomputed), the data flow between them, and the final output. For the incremental run, a (parallel) *change propagation* algorithm updates the output and the CDDG by identifying sub-computations that are affected by the changes and recomputing only those sub-computations.

We make the following main contributions:

- We present parallel algorithms for incremental multithreading (§4).
- We present an implementation of the algorithms encapsulated in a dynamically linkable shared library built using `Dthreads` [63], which we call `iThreads` (§5).
- We empirically demonstrate the effectiveness of `iThreads` by applying it to applications taken from the PARSEC [24] & Phoenix [74] benchmark suites and case studies (§6).

Our experience with `iThreads` shows that significant performance gains (time savings) and efficient resource utilization (work savings) can be achieved in many parallel applications without requiring any effort from the programmer.

2. Design Overview

We base our design on `POSIX` threads, or `pthreads`, a widely used threading library for shared-memory multithreading with a rich set of synchronization primitives.

2.1 The Basic Approach

Our design adapts the principles of self-adjusting computation [6] for shared-memory multithreading, and also makes use of techniques from record-replay systems employed for reliable multithreading (§7). At a high level, the basic approach proceeds in the following three steps:

1. Divide a computation into a set of sub-computations N.
2. During the initial run, record an execution trace to construct a Concurrent Dynamic Dependence Graph (or CDDG). The CDDG captures a partial order $O = (N, \rightarrow)$ among sub-computations with the following property: given a sub-computation n (where $n \in N$) and the subset of sub-computations M that precede it according to $\rightarrow$, i.e., $M = \{M \subset N \mid \forall m \in M, m \rightarrow n\}$, if the inputs to all $m \in M$ are unchanged and the incremental run follows the partial order $\rightarrow$, then n's input is also unchanged and we can reuse n's memoized effect without recomputing n.
3. During the incremental run, propagate the changes through the CDDG. That is, the incremental run follows an order that is consistent with the recorded partial order $\rightarrow$, reusing sub-computations whose input is unchanged and re-computing those whose input has changed.

Case	Input	Thread schedule	Sub-computations	
			Reused	Recomputed
A	x, y^*, z	$T_1.a \rightarrow T_2.a \rightarrow T_2.b$	$T_2.a$	$T_1.a, T_2.b$
B	x, y, z	$(T_2.a \rightarrow T_2.b \rightarrow T_1.a)^*$	$T_2.a$	$T_1.a, T_2.b$
C	x, y, z	$T_1.a \rightarrow T_2.a \rightarrow T_2.b$	$T_1.a, T_1.b, T_2.a$	—

Figure 3. For the incremental run, some cases with changed input or thread schedule (changes are marked with *)

2.2 Example

We next use a simple example, shown in Figure 2, to explain how our basic approach works. The example considers a multi-threaded execution with two threads (T_1 & T_2) modifying three shared variables (x, y, & z) using a lock.

Step #1: Identifying sub-computations. We divide a thread execution into sub-computations at the boundaries of `lock()` / `unlock()`. (We explain this design choice in §3.) We identify these sub-computations as $T_1.a$ for thread T_1, and $T_2.a$ & $T_2.b$ for thread T_2. For the initial run, let us assume that thread T_2 acquired the lock after the execution of sub-computation $T_1.a$. This resulted in the following thread schedule for sub-computations: $T_1.a \rightarrow T_2.a \rightarrow T_2.b$.

Step #2: Construct the CDDG. To understand the dependencies that need to be recorded to build the CDDG, we consider incremental runs with changes either in the input data or the thread schedule (shown in Figure 3).

We first consider the case of change in the input data. An important function of the CDDG is to propagate the changes through the graph by determining whether a sub-computation is transitively affected by the input change. For example consider **case *A*** in Figure 3, when the value of variable y is changed—in this case, we need to recompute $T_1.a$ because it reads the modified value of y. In contrast, we can still reuse $T_2.a$ because it is independent of y and also not affected by the writes made by $T_1.a$. However, we need to recompute $T_2.b$ even though it does not directly depend on y, since it is still transitively affected (via modified z) by the writes made by $T_1.a$. Therefore, the CDDG needs to record *data dependencies* (meaning which sub-computations modify a value that is read by another sub-computation) to determine whether a sub-computation can be reused or if it has to be recomputed.

We next consider the case of a change in the thread schedule. In general, multi-threaded programs are non-deterministic because the OS scheduler is free to interleave sub-computations in different ways. As a result, a problem can arise if the initial and the incremental runs follow different schedules. This might alter the shared state, and therefore cause unnecessary re-computations even without any input changes. For example consider **case *B*** in Figure 3: if thread T_1 acquires the lock after the execution of $T_2.b$ (i.e., a changed thread schedule of $T_2.a \rightarrow T_2.b \rightarrow T_1.a$) then sub-computations $T_1.a$ and $T_2.b$ need to be recomputed because of the changed value of y. Therefore, (and as observed by prior work on reliable multithreading (§7)) the partial order

Algorithm 1: Basic algorithm for the incremental run

```
dirty-set ← {changed input};
executeThread(t)
forall sub-computations in thread t do
    // Check a sub-computation's validity in happens-before order
    if (read-set ∩ dirty-set) then
        – recompute the sub-computation
        – add the write-set to the dirty-set
    else
        – skip execution of the sub-computation
        – write memoized value of the write-set to address space
    end
end
```

captured by the CDDG ($\rightarrow$) is a *happens-before* order among synchronization events, which ensures that, given unchanged input and that all threads acquire locks in the same order as dictated by $\rightarrow$, all sub-computations remain unchanged, as shown in **case *C*** in Figure 3. We explain how to build this partial order in §4.

Step #3: Change propagation. The previous observations allow us to reach a refined explanation of our basic algorithm (see Algorithm 1). The starting point is the CDDG that records the happens-before order ($\rightarrow$) between sub-computations, according to the synchronization events. Furthermore, data dependencies are recorded implicitly in the CDDG by recording the read and write sets: if we know what data is read and written by each sub-computation, we can determine whether a data dependency exists, i.e., if a sub-computation is reading data that was modified by another sub-computation. Therefore, the incremental run visits sub-computations in an order that is compatible with $\rightarrow$, and, for each sub-computation, uses the read and write sets to determine whether part of its input was modified during the incremental run. If the read-set is modified then the sub-computation is re-computed, otherwise we skip the execution of the sub-computation, and directly write the memoized value of the write-set to the address space.

3. System Model

Memory consistency model. As we explained in the previous section, the CDDG implicitly records read-after-write data dependencies between sub-computations using the read and write sets. The efficiency of the mechanism that records these dependencies is related to the memory model we use, and consequently on the granularity of sub-computations. As a design choice, our approach relies on the use of the Release Consistency [44] (RC) memory model. To understand this design choice, consider a possible option of using a strict memory model such as Sequential Consistency [58] (SC). Under the SC model, one would have to define the regions of code bounded by shared-memory accesses as the granularity of sub-computations. This is because any write made by a thread can potentially affect the execution of another thread since it may read the same memory location. Intercepting this inter-thread communication would be prohibitively expensive, essentially requiring tracking of shared-memory accesses at the granularity of individual load/store instructions.

In contrast, the RC model only requires writes made by one thread to become visible to other threads at synchronization points, thus restricting inter-thread communication to such points. This allows us to define the granularity of a sub-computation at the boundaries of synchronization points, which is essential to achieving feasible runtime overheads.

Note that the RC model still guarantees correctness and liveness for applications that are data-race-free [9]. Consequently, `iThreads` assumes that the programs are data-race-free w.r.t. `pthreads` synchronization primitives. In fact, the semantics provided by `iThreads` is no more restrictive than `pthreads` semantics [4], which mandate that all accesses to shared data structures must be properly synchronized using `pthreads` synchronization primitives, and which guarantees only that any updates become visible to other threads when invoking a `pthreads` synchronization primitive.

Synchronization model. We support the full range of synchronization primitives in the `pthreads` API. However, due to the weakly consistent RC memory model, our approach does not support *ad-hoc synchronization mechanisms* [82] such as user-defined spin locks. (We will revisit this limitation in §8.) Our current implementation also does not handle `C/C++` atomic synchronization constructs.

4. Algorithms

In this section we present two parallel algorithms for incremental multithreading. The first algorithm is for the initial run that executes the program from scratch and constructs the CDDG. The second algorithm is for the incremental run that performs change propagation through the CDDG. Both algorithms rely on the CDDG, which we explain first.

4.1 Concurrent Dynamic Dependence Graph (CDDG)

The CDDG is a directed acyclic graph with vertices representing sub-computations (or thunks), and two types of edges to record dependencies between thunks: happens-before edges and data-dependence edges. We next explain how to derive vertices and edges.

Thunks (or sub-computations). We define a *thunk* as the sequence of instructions executed by a thread between two `pthreads` synchronization API calls. We model an execution of thread t as a sequence of thunks (L_t). Thunks in a thread are totally ordered based on their execution order using a monotonically increasing thunk counter (α). We refer to a thunk of thread t using the counter α as an index in the thread execution sequence (L_t), i.e., $L_t[\alpha]$.

Happens-before edges. There are two types of happens-before edges: control edges, which record the intra-thread execution order; and synchronization edges, which record explicit inter-thread synchronization events.

Control edges are simply derived by ordering thunks of the same thread based on their execution order. Synchronization edges are derived by modeling synchronization primitives as *acquire* and *release* operations. In particular, during synchronization, a synchronization object s is *released* by one set of threads and subsequently *acquired* by a corresponding set of threads blocked on the synchronizing object. For example, an `unlock(s)` operation releases s and a corresponding `lock(s)` operation acquires it. Similarly, all other synchronization primitives can also be modeled as acquire and release operations [43, 71].

Under the acquire-release relation, a release operation happens-before the corresponding acquire operation. Given that a thunk's boundaries are defined at synchronization points, the acquire and release operations also establish the happens-before ordering between thunks of different threads. Formally, two thunks $L_{(t_1)}[\alpha]$ & $L_{(t_2)}[\beta]$ are connected by a

- *control edge* iff they belong to the same thread ($t_1 = t_2$) and $L_{(t_1)}[\alpha]$ was executed immediately before $L_{(t_2)}[\beta]$;
- *synchronization edge* iff $L_{(t_1)}[\alpha]$ releases a synchronization object s and $L_{(t_2)}[\beta]$ is a thunk that acquires s next.

Data-dependence edges. Data dependencies are tracked to establish the *update-use relationship* between thunks. Intuitively, such a relationship exists between two thunks if one reads data written by the other. More formally, for a thunk $L_t[\alpha]$, the *read-set* $L_t[\alpha].R$ and the *write-set* $L_t[\alpha].W$ are the set of addresses that were read-from and written-to, respectively, by the thread t while executing the thunk. Two thunks $L_{(t_1)}[\alpha]$ and $L_{(t_2)}[\beta]$ are then connected by a

- *data-dependence edge* iff $L_{(t_2)}[\beta]$ is reachable from $L_{(t_1)}[\alpha]$ via happens-before edges and $L_{(t_1)}[\alpha].W \cap L_{(t_2)}[\beta].R \neq \emptyset$.

4.2 Algorithm for the Initial Run

During the initial run, we record the execution of the program to construct the CDDG. Algorithm 2 presents the high-level overview of the initial run algorithm, and details of the subroutines used in the algorithm are presented in Algorithm 3. The algorithm is executed by threads in parallel. The algorithm employs run-time techniques to derive the information needed for the CDDG. In particular, during a thread execution, the thread traces memory accesses on `load/store` instructions (using routine `onMemoryAccess()`), and adds them to the read and the write set of the executing thunk. (Our implementation, described in §5, derives the read and write sets at the granularity of memory pages using the OS memory protection mechanism.) The thread continues to execute instructions and perform memory tracing until a synchronization call is made to the `pthreads` library. At the synchronization point, we define the end point for the executing thunk and memoize its end state (using routine `endThunk()`). Thereafter, we let the thread perform the synchronization. Next, we start a new thunk and repeat the process until the thread terminates.

Algorithm 2: The initial run algorithm

```
/* Let S be the set of synchronization objects and T be the number
of threads in the system. */
∀s ∈ S, ∀i ∈ {1, ..., T} : C_s[i] ← 0; // All sync clocks set to zero
executeThread(t)
begin
    initThread(t);
    while t has not terminated do
        startThunk(); // Start new thunk
        repeat
            Execute instruction of t;
            if (instruction is load or store) then
                onMemoryAccess();
            end
        until t invokes synchronization primitive;
        endThunk(); // Memoize the end state of thunk
        α ← α + 1; // Increment thunk counter
        // Let s denote invoked synchronization primitive
        onSynchronization(s);
    end
end
```

Algorithm 3: Subroutines for the initial run algorithm

```
initThread(t)
begin
    α ← 0; // Initializes thunk counter (α) to zero
    ∀i ∈ {1, ..., T} : C_t[i] ← 0; // t's clock set to zero
end
startThunk()
begin
    C_t[t] ← α; // Update thread clock
    ∀i ∈ {1, ..., T} : L_t[α].C[i] ← C_t[i]; // Update thunk clock
    L_t[α].R/W ← ∅; // Initialize read/write sets to empty set
end
onMemoryAccess()
begin
    if load then
        L_t[α].R ← L_t[α].R ∪ {memory-address}; // Read
    else
        L_t[α].W ← L_t[α].W ∪ {memory-address}; // Write
    end
end
endThunk()
begin
    memo (L_t[α].W) ← content(L_t[α].W); // Globals & heap
    memo (L_t[α].Stack) ←content(Stack);
    memo (L_t[α].Reg) ←content(CPU_Registers);
end
onSynchronization(s)
begin
    switch Syncronization type do
        case release(s):
            // Update s's clock to hold max of its and t's clocks
            ∀i ∈ {1, ..., T} : C_s[i] ← max(C_s[i], C_t[i]);
            sync(s); // Perform the synchronization

        case acquire(s):
            sync(s); // Perform the synchronization
            // Update t's clock to hold max of its and s's clocks
            ∀i ∈ {1, ..., T} : C_t[i] ← max(C_s[i], C_t[i]);

    end
end
```

To infer the CDDG, control and synchronization edges are derived by ordering thunks based on the happens-before order. To do so, we use vector clocks (C) [65] to record a partial order that defines the happens-before relationship between thunks during the initial run, and in the incremental run we follow this partial order to propagate the changes. Our use of vector clocks is motivated by its efficiency for recording a partial order in a decentralized manner, rather than having to serialize all synchronization events in a total order.

Our algorithm maintains one vector clock for each thread, thunk, and synchronization object. These vector clocks are an array of size T, where T denotes the number of threads in the system, which are numbered from 1 to T.

Each thread t has a vector clock, called its *thread clock* C_t, to track its local logical time, which is updated at the start of each thunk (using routine `startThunk()`) by setting $C_t[t]$ to the thunk index α. Further, each thunk $L_t[\alpha]$ has a *thunk clock* $L_t[\alpha].C$, which stores a snapshot of $C_t[t]$ to record the thunk's position in the CDDG.

Finally, each synchronization object s has a *synchronization clock* C_s that is used to order release and acquire operations (see `onSynchronization()`). More precisely, if a thread t invokes a release operation on s, then t updates C_s to the component-wise maximum of its own thread clock C_t and C_s. Alternatively, if t invokes an acquire operation on s, it updates its own thread clock C_t to the component-wise maximum of C_t and s's synchronization clock C_s. This ensures that a thunk acquiring s is always ordered after the last thunk to release s.

At the end of the initial run algorithm, the CDDG is defined by the read/write sets and the thunk clock values of all thunks.

4.3 Algorithm for the Incremental Run

The incremental run algorithm takes as input the CDDG ($\forall t : L_t$) and the modified input (named the dirty set M), and performs change propagation to update the output as well as the CDDG for the next incremental run. As explained in the basic change propagation algorithm (Algorithm 1), each thread transitions through its list of thunks by following the recorded happens-before order to either reuse or recompute thunks. To make this algorithm work in practice, however, we need to address the following three challenges.

(1) Missing writes. When a thunk is recomputed during the incremental run, it may happen that the executing thread no longer writes to a previously written location because of a data-dependent branch. For such cases, our algorithm should update the dirty set with the new write-set of the thunk as well as the *missing writes*. These consist of the set of memory locations that were part of the thunk's write-set in the previous run, but are missing in the current write-set.

(2) Stack dependencies. As mentioned previously, we transparently derive read and write sets by tracking the global memory region (heap/globals) using the OS memory protection mechanism (detailed in §5). Unfortunately, this mechanism is inefficient for tracking the per-thread stack region

Algorithm 4: The incremental run algorithm

```
Data: Shared dirty set M ← { modified pages } and L_t
∀s ∈ S, ∀i ∈ {1, ..., T} : C_s[i] ← 0; // All sync clocks set to 0
executeThread(t)
begin
    initThread(t); // Same as initial run algorithm
    while (t has not terminated and isValid(L_t[α]) ) do
        // Thread t is valid
        await (isEnabled(L_t[α]) or ! isValid(L_t[α]) );
        if (isEnabled(L_t[α]) then
            resolveValid(L_t[α]);
            C_t[t] ← α; // Update thread clock
            α ← α + 1; // Increment thunk counter
        end
    end
    // The thread has terminated or a thunk has been invalidated
    L'_t ← L_t; // Make a temp copy for missing writes
    while (t has not terminated or α < |L'_t|) do
        // Thread t is invalid
        if (α < |L'_t|) then
            M ← M ∪ L'_t[α].W; // Add missing writes
            C_t[t] ← α; // Update thread clock
        end
        if (t has not terminated) then
            resolveInvalid(L_t[α]);
        end
        α ← α + 1; // Increment thunk counter
    end
    // The thread has terminated
end
```

Algorithm 5: Subroutines for the incremental run algorithm

```
isEnabled(L_t[α])
begin
    if (∀i ∈ {1, ..., T} \ {t} : (C_i[i] > L_t[α].C[i])) then
        // All thunks happened-before are resolved
        return (isValid(L_t[α])); // check if it's valid
    end
    return false;
end
isValid(L_t[α])
begin
    if ((L_t[α].R ∩ M) = ∅) then
        return true; // Read set does not intersects with dirty set
    end
    return false;
end
resolveInvalid(L_t[α])
begin
    startThunk(); // Same as initial run algorithm
    repeat
        Execute instruction of t;
        if (instruction is load or store) then
            onMemoryAccess(); // Same as initial run algorithm
        end
    until t invokes synchronization primitive;
    M ← M ∪ L_t[α].W; // Add the new writes
    endThunk(); // Same as initial run algorithm
    onSynchronization(s); // Same as initial run algorithm
end
resolveValid(L_t[α])
begin
    address space ← memo(L_t[α].W); // Globals and heap
    stack ← memo(L_t[α].Stack);
    CPU registers ← memo(L_t[α].Reg); // Also adjusts PC
    onSynchronization(s); // Same as initial run algorithm
end
```

(which usually resides in a single page storing local variables) because the stack follows a *push/pop* model, where the stack is written (or gets dirty) when a call frame is pushed or popped, even without a local variable being modified. To avoid the overheads of tracking local variables, we do not track the stack. Instead, we follow a conservative strategy to capture the intra-thread data dependencies. In our design, once a thunk is recomputed (or invalidated) in a thread, all remaining thunks of the thread are also invalidated in order to capture a possible change propagation via local variables.

(3) Control flow divergence. During the incremental run, it may happen that the control flow diverges from the recorded execution. As a result of the divergence, new thunks may be created or existing ones may be deleted. As in the previous challenge, the algorithm we propose takes a simple approach of only reusing a prefix of each thread (before the control flow diverges), and subsequently recording the new CDDG for enabling change propagation in subsequent runs.

Details. Algorithm 4 presents the overview of the incremental run algorithm, and details of subroutines used in the algorithm are presented in Algorithm 5. The incremental run algorithm allows all threads to proceed in parallel, and associates a state with each thunk of every thread. The state of each thunk follows a state machine (shown in Figure 4), which enforces that each thread waits until all thunks that happened-before its next thunk to be executed are resolved (i.e., either recomputed or reused), and only when it is certain that reusing memoized results is not possible will it start to re-execute

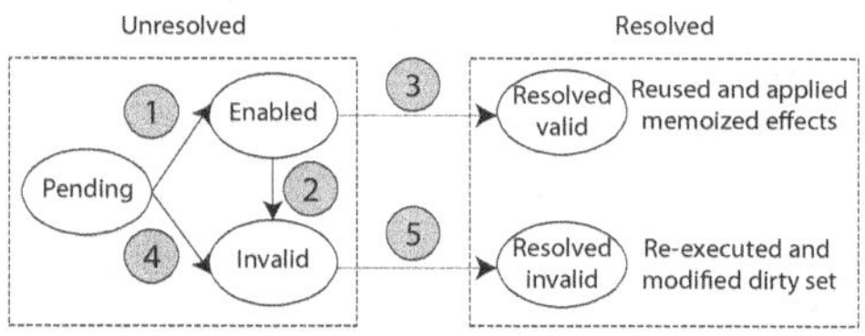

Figure 4. State transition for thunks during incremental run

its next thunk. In particular, the state of a thunk is either resolved or unresolved. The state of a thunk is resolved when the thunk has either been reused (`resolved-valid`) or re-executed (`resolved-invalid`). Otherwise, the thunk is still unresolved. An unresolved thunk is in one of the following states: `pending`, `enabled` or `invalid`.

Initially, the state of all thunks is `pending`, except for the initial thunk, which is `enabled`. A pending thunk is not "ready" to be considered for re-computation or reuse. A `pending` thunk of a thread is `enabled` (state transition ①) when all thunks (of any thread) that happened-before are resolved (either `resolved-valid` or `resolved-invalid`). To check for this condition (using routine `isEnabled()`), we make use of the strong clock consistency condition [65] provided by vector clocks to detect causality ($a \rightarrow b$ iff $C(a) < C(b)$). In particular, we compare the recorded clock value of the thunk against the current clock value of all threads to check that all threads have passed the time recorded in the thunk's clock.

An `enabled` thunk transitions to `invalid` (state transition ②) if the read set of the thunk intersects with the dirty set. Otherwise, the `enabled` thunk transitions to `resolved-valid` (state transition ③), where we skip the execution of the thunk and directly apply the memoized write-set to the address space, including performing the synchronization operation (using the `resolveValid()` routine).

A `pending` thunk transitions to `invalid` (state transition ④) if any earlier thunk of the same thread is `invalid` or `resolved-invalid`. The `invalid` thunk transitions to `resolved-invalid` (state transition ⑤) when the thread re-executes the thunk and adds the write set to the dirty set (including any missing writes). The executing thread continues to resolve all the remaining `invalid` thunks to `resolved-invalid` until the thread terminates. To do so, we re-initialize the read/write sets of the new thunk to the empty set and start the re-execution, similarly to the initial run algorithm (using the `resolveInvalid()` routine). While re-executing, the thread updates the CDDG, and also records the state of the newly formed thunks for the next run.

5. Implementation

We implemented `iThreads` as a 32-bit dynamically linkable shared library for the GNU/Linux OS (Figure 5). `iThreads` reuses two mechanisms of the `Dthreads` implementation [63]: the memory subsystem (§5.1) and a custom memory allocator (§5.4). Additionally, our implementation also includes the `iThreads` memoizer, which is a stand-alone application. We next describe the implementation in detail.

5.1 iThreads Library: Memory Subsystem

The `iThreads` memory subsystem implements the RC memory model and derives per-thunk read/write sets.

Release consistency memory model. To implement the RC memory model, `iThreads` converts threads into separate processes using a previously proposed mechanism [17]. This "thread-as-a-process" approach provides each thread with its own private address space, and thus allows `iThreads` to restrict inter-thread communication. In practice, `iThreads` forks a new process on `pthread_create()` and includes a *shared memory commit* mechanism [28, 56] that enables communication between processes at the synchronization points, as required by the RC memory model.

At a high level, throughout the application execution, `iThreads` maintains a copy of the address space contents in a (shared) reference buffer, and it is through this buffer, with instrumentation provided by `iThreads` at the synchronization points, that the processes transparently communicate (Figure 6). Communication between processes is implemented

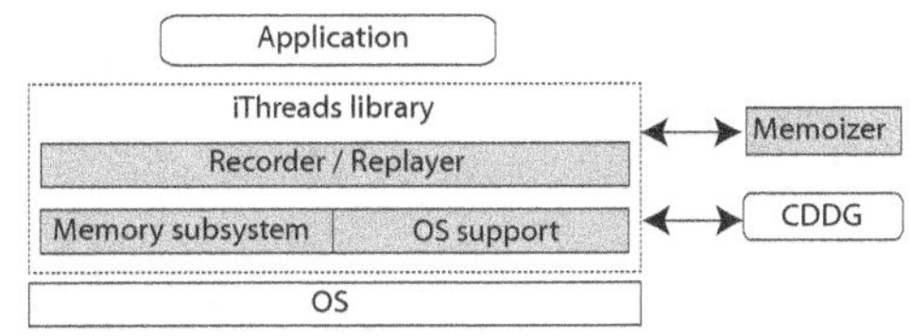

Figure 5. `iThreads` implementation architecture. Shaded boxes represent the main components of the system.

by determining the thunk write-set, as explained next, which is then used to calculate a byte-level delta [63].

To compute the byte-level delta for each dirty page, `iThreads` performs a byte-level comparison between the dirty page and the corresponding page in the reference buffer, and then applies atomically the deltas to the reference buffer. In case there are concurrent writes by different processes to the same memory location, `iThreads` resolves the conflict by using a last-writer wins policy.

Furthermore, for efficiency reasons, the implementation of the communication mechanism relies on private memory-mapped files—this allows different processes to share physical pages until processes actually write to the pages, and still keeps performance overheads low by virtue of the OS copy-on-write mechanism.

Read and write set. Besides serving as the foundation for the RC memory model, the adopted thread-as-a-process mechanism is also essential for easily deriving *per-thread* read and write sets. More specifically, `iThreads` uses the OS memory protection mechanism to efficiently track the read and write sets. In particular, `iThreads` renders the address space inaccessible by invoking `mprotect(PROT_NONE)` at the beginning of each thunk, which ensures that a signal is triggered the first time a page is read or written by the thunk. Hence, within the respective signal handler, `iThreads` is able to record the locations of the accesses made to memory at the granularity of pages. Immediately after recording a memory access, the `iThreads` library proceeds to reset the page protection bits, allowing the thunk to resume the read/write operation as soon as the handler returns. In addition, resetting the permissions also ensures that subsequent accesses proceed without further page faults. In this way, `iThreads` incurs at most two page faults (one for reads & one for writes) for each accessed page during a thunk execution.

5.2 iThreads Library: Recorder and Replayer

The `iThreads` library executes the application in either *recording* or *replaying* mode. We next describe the two subcomponents, recorder and replayer, that realize these modes of execution by implementing the algorithms described in §4.

Recorder. Since `iThreads` reuses the `Dthreads` memory subsystem, which serializes memory commit operations from different threads, the implementation of the recording algorithm is greatly simplified. Due to the resulting implicit serialization of thunk boundaries, the employed thread, thunk,

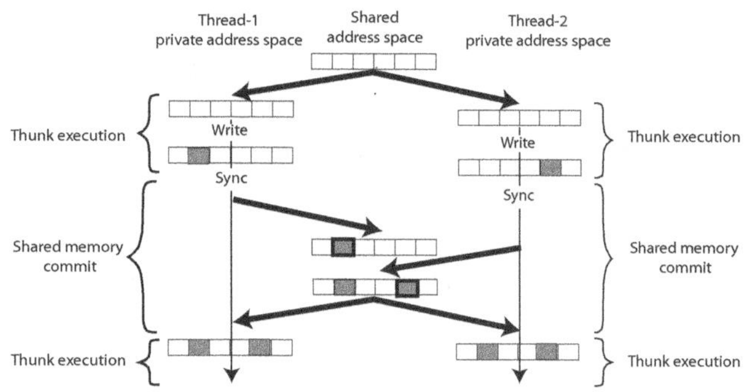

Figure 6. Overview of the RC model implementation

and synchronization vector clocks effectively reduce to scalar sequence numbers, which allows the recorder to simply encode the thread schedule using thunk sequence numbers.

The recorder is further responsible for memoizing the state of the process at the end of each thunk. To this end, using an assembly routine, `iThreads` stores the register values on the stack, takes a snapshot of the dirty pages in the address space, and stores the snapshot in the memoizer (§5.4). In addition, the recorder also stores the CDDG, consisting of thunk identifiers (thread number and thunk sequence number) and their corresponding read/write sets, to an external file.

Replayer. Similarly to the recorder, the replayer relies on thunk sequence numbers to enforce the recorded schedule order. The replayer first reads the file with the input changes and the CDDG to initialize the replay algorithm. During an incremental run, whenever memoized thunks can be reused, the replayer retrieves the appropriate state from the memoizer, patches the address space and restores the state of registers.

5.3 iThreads Library: OS Support

As practical applications depend on OS services, there are two important aspects related to the OS that `iThreads` needs to address. First, system calls are used by the application to communicate with the rest of the system, so the effects of system calls (on the system and application) need to be addressed; in particular, input changes made by the user need to be handled. Second, there are OS mechanisms that can unnecessarily change the memory layout of the application across runs, preventing the reuse of memoized thunks.

System calls and input changes. Since `iThreads` is a user-space library running on top of an unmodified Linux kernel, it has no access to kernel data structures. The effects of system calls thus cannot be memoized or replayed. To support system calls, `iThreads` instead considers system calls to be thunk delimiters (in addition to synchronization calls). Hence, immediately before a system call takes place, `iThreads` memoizes the thunk state, and immediately after the system call returns, `iThreads` determines whether it still can reuse the subsequent thunks according to the replayer algorithm.

To ensure that system calls *take effect* (externally and internally), `iThreads` invokes system calls in all executions, even during replay runs. To guarantee that effects of system calls on the application (i.e., the return values and writes made to the address space) are *accounted for* by the thunk invalidation rules, `iThreads` infers the write-set of the system calls and checks whether the write-set contents match previous runs by leveraging knowledge of system call semantics (e.g., some system call parameters return pointers where data is written).

An important special case is that of reading the potentially large input to the computation (e.g., using `mmap`). In this case, `iThreads` efficiently identifies the content that does not match across runs by allowing the user to specify input changes explicitly. This relies on an external file, either written manually by users or produced by external tools, that lists the modified offset ranges (Figure 1).

In practice, our implementation intercepts system calls through wrappers at the level of `glibc` library calls.

Memory layout stability. To avoid causing unnecessary data dependencies between threads, `iThreads` reuses the custom memory allocator of `Dthreads`, which is based on HeapLayer [16]. The allocator isolates allocation and deallocation requests on a per-thread basis by dividing the application heap into a fixed number of per-thread sub-heaps. This ensures that the sequence of allocations in one thread does not impact the layout of allocations in another thread, which otherwise might trigger unnecessary re-computations.

In addition, `iThreads` disables Address Space Layout Randomization (ASLR) [1], an OS feature that deliberately randomizes the memory layout.

5.4 iThreads Memoizer

The memoizer is responsible for storing the end state of each thunk so that its effects can be replayed in subsequent incremental runs. The memoizer is implemented as a separate program that stores the memoized state in a shared memory segment, which serves as the substrate to implement a key-value store that is accessible by the recorder/replayer.

6. Evaluation

Our evaluation answers the following three main questions:

- What performance gains does `iThreads` provide for the incremental run? (§ 6.1)
- How do these gains scale with increases in the size of the input, the computation, and the input change? (§ 6.2)
- What overheads does `iThreads` impose for memoization and for the initial run? (§ 6.3)

Experimental setup. We evaluated `iThreads` on a six-core Intel(R) Xeon(R) CPU X5650 platform with 12 hardware threads running at 2.67 GHz and 32 GB of main memory.

Applications and datasets. We evaluated `iThreads` with applications from two benchmark suites: PARSEC [24] and Phoenix [74]. Table 1 lists the applications evaluated and their

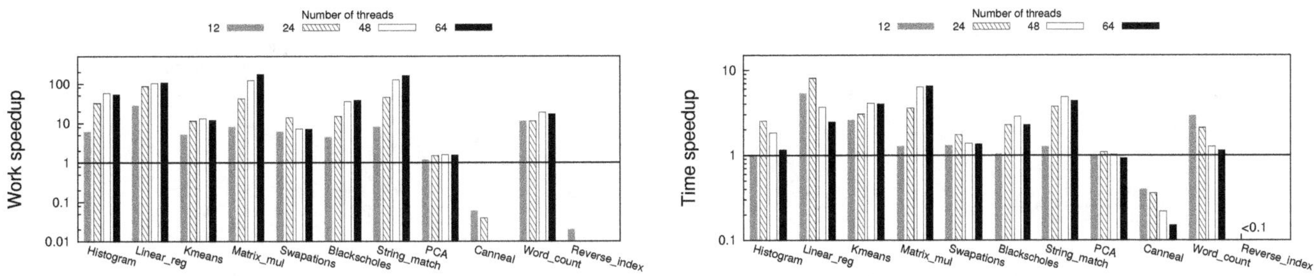

Figure 7. Performance gains of `iThreads` with respect to `pthreads` for the incremental run

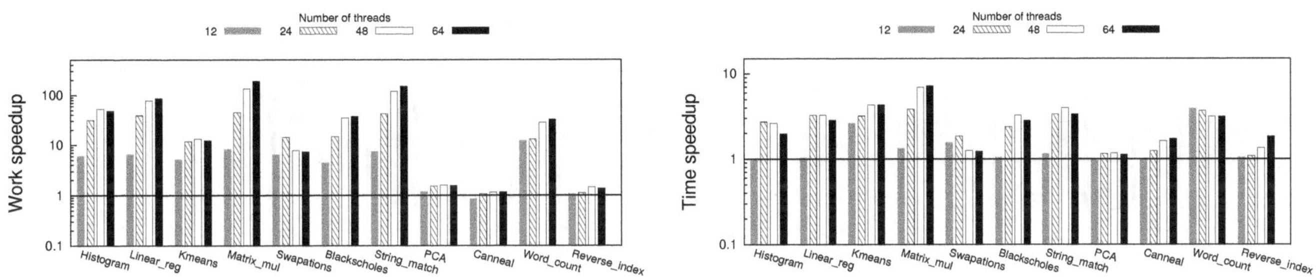

Figure 8. Performance gains of `iThreads` with respect to `Dthreads` for the incremental run

respective input sizes in terms of 4KB pages. In addition, we also report the gains with two case studies (§6.4).

Metrics: work and time. We consider two types of measures, *work* and *time*. Work refers to the total amount of computation performed by all threads and is measured as the sum of the total runtime of all threads. Time refers to the end-to-end runtime to complete the parallel computation. Time savings reflect reduced end user perceived latency, whereas work savings reflect improved resource utilization.

Measurements. For all measurements, each application was executed 12 times. We exclude the lowest and highest measurements, and report the average over the 10 remaining runs.

6.1 Performance Gains

We first present a comparison of `iThreads`'s incremental run with `pthreads` and `Dthreads`, as shown in Figures 7 and 8 respectively. In this experiment, we modified one randomly chosen page of the input file prior to the incremental run. We then measured the work and time required by `iThreads`'s incremental run, as well as by `pthreads` and `Dthreads`, which re-compute everything from scratch. We report the work and time speedups (i.e., `iThreads`'s performance normalized by the performance of `pthreads/Dthreads`) for a varying number of threads ranging from 12 to 64 threads. When comparing the performance, we use the same number of threads in `iThreads` and `pthreads/Dthreads`.

The experiment shows that the benefits of using `iThreads` vary significantly across applications. In over half of the evaluated benchmarks (7 out of 11), `iThreads` was able to achieve at least $2X$ time speedups. In contrast, for applications such as `canneal` and `reverseindex`, `iThreads` can be very inefficient, by a factor of more than $15X$, an effect that we explain in further detail in §6.3. Overall, the results show that `iThreads` is effective across a wide range of applications, but also that the library is not a one-size-fits-all solution.

As expected, we observed that increasing the number of threads tended to yield higher speedups. This is because, for a fixed input size, a larger number of threads translates to less work per thread. As a result, `iThreads` is forced to recompute fewer thunks when a single input page is modified.

Note that work speedups do not directly translate into time speedups. This is because even if just a single thread is affected by changes, the end-to-end runtime is still dominated by the (slowest) invalidated thread's execution time.

6.2 iThreads Scalability

In a second experiment, we investigated the scalability of `iThreads` w.r.t. increases in the size of the input, the amount of computation (work), and the size of the input change.

Input size. We first present the performance of `iThreads` as we increase the input data size for the three application benchmarks (`histogram, linear regression`, and `string match`) that are available in three input sizes: small (S), medium (M), and large (L). (We used the large size in §6.1.) Figure 9 shows a bar plot of the work and time speedups w.r.t. `pthreads` for different input sizes (S, M, L) with a single modified page for 64 threads. For reference, the normalized input size is also shown by the line plot in the same figure. In summary, this result shows that speedups increase with the input size due to increased work savings.

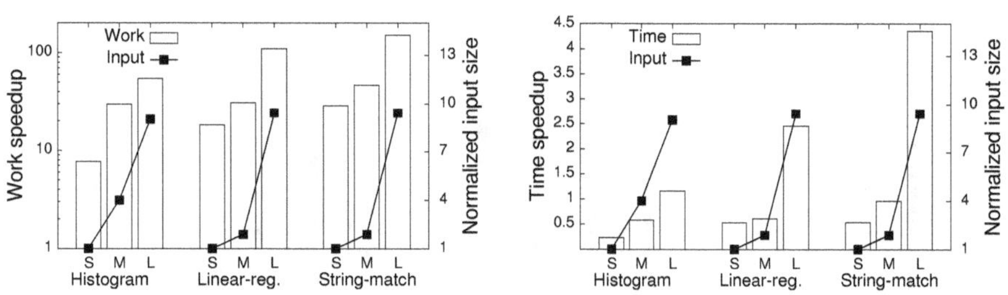

Figure 9. Scalability with data (work and time speedups)

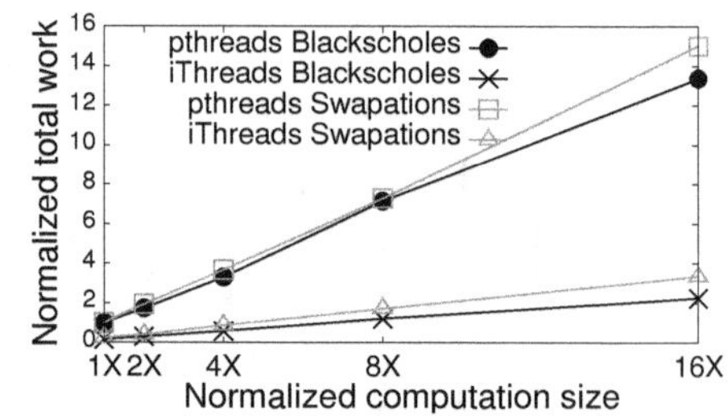

Figure 10. Scalability with work

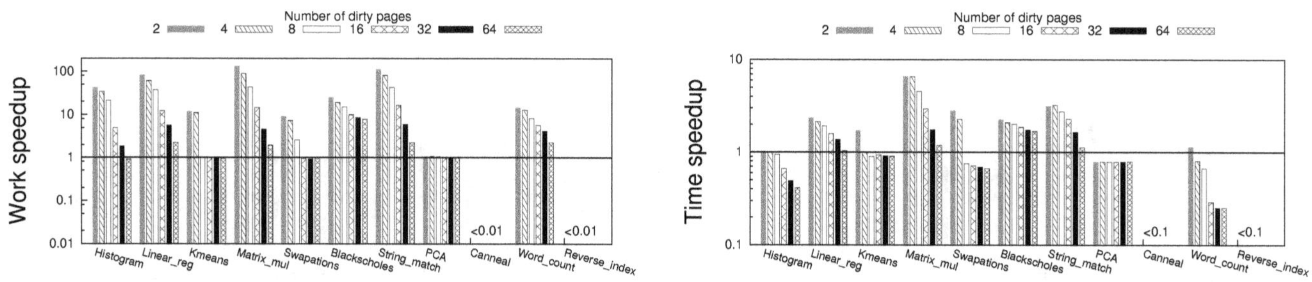

Figure 11. Scalability with input change compared to `pthreads` for 64 threads

Computation (work). We next present `iThreads`'s incremental run performance for two applications (`swapations` and `blackscholes`) that allow the amount of work required to be tuned with a parameter. Figure 10 reports work speedups as the normalized work is increased (from $1X$ to $16X$) for a single modified page and 64 threads. The result shows the gap between `pthreads` and `iThreads` widens as the total work increases, which directly translates to higher speedups.

Input change. Finally, we present `iThreads`'s incremental run performance in the case of multiple modified input pages. To avoid confining changes to a single thread, we modified multiple non-contiguous pages of the input that are read by different threads. Figure 11 shows speedups w.r.t. `pthreads` with different change sizes (ranging 2 to 64 dirty pages) for 64 threads. As expected, the results show that speedups decrease as larger portions of the input are changed because more threads are invalidated.

6.3 Overheads

`iThreads` imposes two types of overheads: (1) space overheads; and (2) performance overheads during the initial run.

Space overheads. Table 1 shows the space overheads for memoizing the end state of the thunks and storing the CDDG. We report the overheads in terms of 4KB pages for 64 threads (space overhead grows with the number of threads). To put the overheads into perspective, we also report overheads as a percentage of the input size.

The space overheads varied significantly across applications. We found that three applications (`canneal`, `swapations` and `reverse-index`) incur very high overheads (exceeding 1000% of the input size), but, interestingly,

Application	Input size	Memoized state		CDDG	
Histogram	230400	347	(0.15%)	57	(0.02%)
Linear-reg.	132436	192	(0.14%)	33	(0.02%)
Kmeans	586	1145	(195.39%)	27	(4.61%)
Matrix-mul.	41609	4162	(10.00%)	64	(0.15%)
Swapations	143	1473	(1030.07%)	1	(0.70%)
Blackscholes	155	201	(129.68%)	1	(0.65%)
String match	132436	128	(0.10%)	33	(0.02%)
PCA	140625	3777	(2.69%)	43	(0.03%)
Canneal	9	15381	(170900.00%)	4	(44.44%)
Word count	12811	10191	(79.55%)	24	(0.19%)
Rev-index	359	260679	(72612.53%)	64	(17.83%)

Table 1. Space overheads in pages and input percentage

nearly half of the applications (5/11) have a very low overhead (ranging from 0.1% to 10% of the input size).

Performance overheads. We measured `iThreads`'s performance overheads during the initial run (in terms of work and time) by comparing it against both `pthreads` and `Dthreads` (Figures 12 and 13). Our results show that most of the applications (7/11) incur modest overheads when compared with either `pthreads` (i.e., lower than 50%) or `Dthreads` (i.e., lower than 25%). In fact, `linear-reg` and `string-match` even performed better during the initial run of `iThreads` than with `pthreads`, which is explained by the fact that private address space mechanism avoid false sharing, as previously noted by Sheriff [62]. At the other end of the spectrum, applications such as `canneal` and `reverse-index` incur high overheads mainly due to the high number of memory pages written by these applications (as shown in Table 1).

When compared to `Dthreads` as the baseline, `iThreads` incurs work overheads of up to $3.58X$ and time overheads of up to $3.13X$. `iThreads` incurs additional overheads on

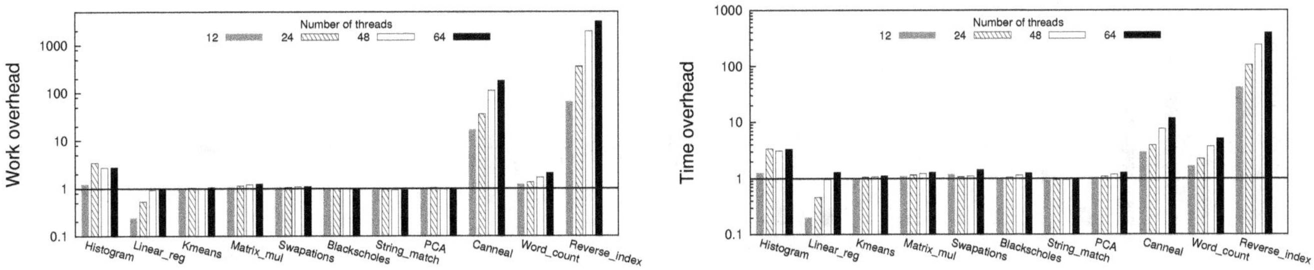

Figure 12. Performance overheads of `iThreads` with respect to `pthreads` for the initial run

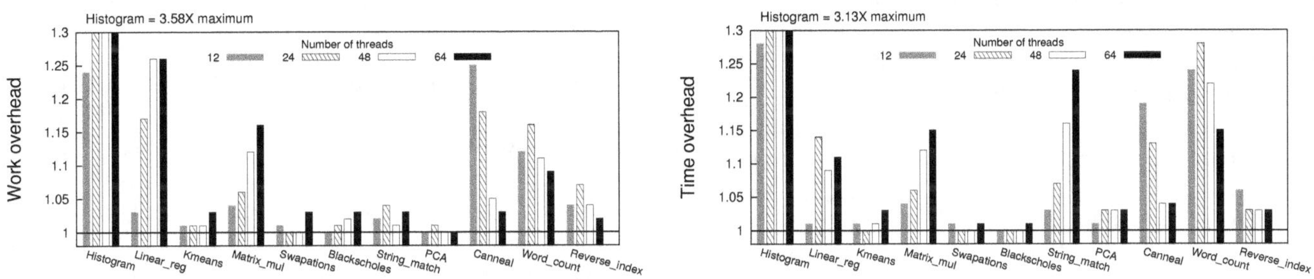

Figure 13. Performance overheads of `iThreads` with respect to `Dthreads` for the initial run

top of `Dthreads` mainly from two sources: memoization of the intermediate address space state and read page faults (`Dthreads` incurs write faults only). We show the work overheads along with a breakdown of these two sources of overheads with respect to `Dthreads` for 64 threads in Figure 14. The overheads are dominated by read page faults (around 98%) for most applications. For instance, `histogram` incurs overheads of roughly 3.5X due the large number of page faults while reading a large input file (as shown in Table 1). In contrast, some application such as `canneal` and `reverse-index` suffer a significant overhead for memoization (around 24%) due to a large number of dirtied pages.

6.4 Case-study Applications

In addition to the benchmark applications, we report the performance gains for two case-study applications: (1) Pigz [3], a parallel gzip compression library compressing a 50MB file, and (2) a monte-carlo simulation [2]. To compute speedups, we modified a random input block and compared the performance of the `iThreads` incremental run with the `pthreads` run. Figure 15 shows the work and time speedups with a varying number of threads (from 12 to 64). The performance gains peak at 24 threads for both applications. In particular, `iThreads` achieves a time speedup of $1.45X$ and a work speedup of $4X$ for Pigz, and a time speedup of $2.28X$ and a work speedup of $22.5X$ for the monte-carlo simulation.

To conclude, while there exist specific workloads for which our OS-based approach is not suitable, our evaluation is overall positive: `iThreads` is able to achieve significant time and work speedups both for many of the benchmark applications and also for the two considered case-studies.

7. Related Work

Researchers in the algorithms community proposed several *dynamic algorithms*, a class of algorithms that take advantage of application-specific properties to incrementally update the output. Dynamic algorithms have been shown to be asymptotically more efficient than their conventional non-dynamic versions (e.g., [25, 30, 37, 38, 42, 46, 68]). However, they can be difficult to design, implement, and maintain even for simple problems [10, 45]. Moreover, most dynamic algorithms are sequential, and cannot be easily parallelized due to their highly specialized nature. In contrast, `iThreads` provides incremental computation in a transparent way.

Incremental computation is a well-studied area in the programming languages community; see [73] for a classic survey. Earlier work on incremental computation was primarily based on dependence graphs [36, 53] and memoization [5, 51, 72]. In the past decade, with the development of self-adjusting computation [6–8, 29, 49, 50, 60, 61], the efficiency of incremental computation has much improved. In contrast to `iThreads`, however, most prior work in this area targets sequential programs only. Nonetheless, `iThreads`'s central data structure, the CDDG, is based on these foundations.

For supporting parallel incremental computation, existing proposals [27, 48] require a strict fork-join programming model without supporting other synchronization primitives. Furthermore, these proposals rely on the use of a new programming language with special data types (e.g., *isolation,*

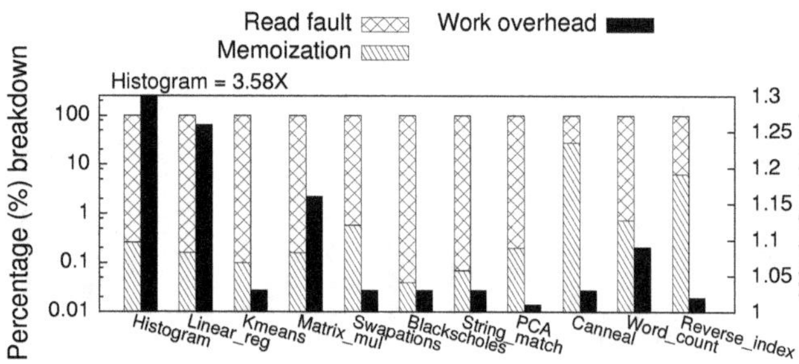

Figure 14. Work overheads breakdown w.r.t Dthreads

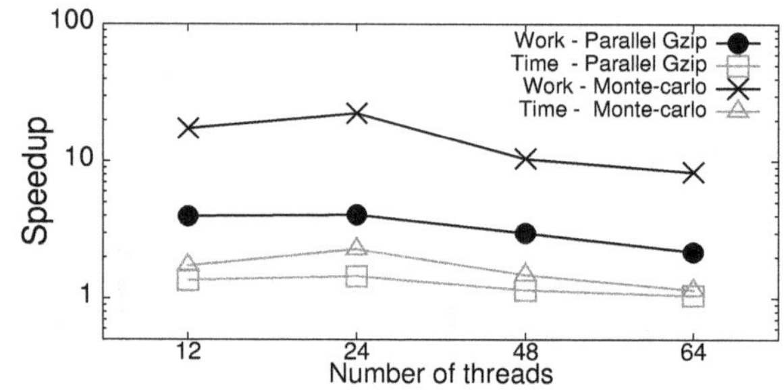

Figure 15. Work & time speedups for case-studies

versioned, cumulative, merge function [27] and *read, write, mod, and letpar* [48]). In contrast, our approach targets unmodified multithreaded programs supporting the full range of synchronization primitives in the POSIX API.

In very recent work, Tseng and Tullsen [78] proposed compiler-based whole-program transformations to eliminate redundant computation, which can be leveraged for faster incremental computation. The transformed programs rely on underlying hardware [76] and software [77] support to dynamically identify redundant code that can be skipped. In contrast, our approach directly operates at the binary level without requiring access to source code. A further design difference is that iThreads realizes incremental computation based on explicit change propagation, and that iThreads memoizes and reuses intermediate results of previous runs.

Incremental processing of "big data" is an active area of research [18–20, 22, 23, 26, 31, 47, 64, 70]. These "big data" systems exploit the underlying data-parallel programming model such as MapReduce [35] or Dryad [55] for supporting incremental computation. In contrast to these structured approaches where the dependence graph is explicitly available based on the programming model, iThreads is designed to support general shared-memory multithreaded programs.

In the context of increased reliability, prior work has yielded a large range of solutions to eliminate *non-determinism* from multithreaded programs. Most relevant to iThreads are the wide range record and replay techniques (e.g., [12, 41, 52, 57, 59, 69, 75, 79–81]) and deterministic multithreading approaches (e.g., [13–15, 17, 32–34, 39, 40, 54, 63, 67]). As described throughout the paper, these proven techniques are leveraged by iThreads, which applies them in a novel context, namely *transparent* parallel incremental computation.

8. Conclusion

We have presented iThreads, a *practical, transparent*, and *efficient* solution for parallel incremental computation. Our approach targets unmodified, multithreaded programs and supports the full range of synchronization primitives in the POSIX API. The iThreads library is easy to use: it simply replaces the pthreads library. Our experience with iThreads shows that significant performance gains (time savings) and efficient resource utilization (work savings) can be achieved for incremental workflows in many applications.

Limitations and future work. While iThreads is a significant step towards general and practical support for parallel incremental computation, plenty of opportunities remain to further increase the range of supported workloads.

For one, iThreads's memory model currently lacks support for ad-hoc synchronization mechanisms [82]. While such mechanisms are error-prone [82], they are nonetheless used for either flexibility or performance reasons in some applications. Replacing the ad-hoc synchronization calls with equivalent pthread calls might solve the problem in some cases, but perhaps a better solution would be to extend iThreads with an interface for annotating ad-hoc synchronization primitives (e.g., at the level of gcc's built-in atomic primitives).

Another interesting research challenge is improving support for small, localized insertions and deletions in the input data. Since iThreads is currently tuned for in-place modifications of the input data, insertions and deletions lead to the displacement of otherwise unchanged data, which causes an excessively large dirty-set. Prior work has solved the displacement problem in the context of data-deduplication by replacing fixed-size input chunking with variable-size, content-based chunking [21, 66]. We plan to explore similar approaches in the context of iThreads.

Lastly, our current implementation assumes the number of threads in the system remains the same. However, our approach can be extended to handle dynamically varying number of threads by considering newly forked threads or deleted threads as invalidated threads, where the writes of deleted threads are handled as "missing writes". The happens-before relationship for dynamically varying number of threads can be detected using interval tree clocks [11].

Acknowledgments

We are thankful to Remzi Arpaci-Dusseau, Rose Hoberman, Tongping Liu, and the reviewers for their valuable feedback. Umut Acar is partially supported by ERC (ERC-2012-StG-308246) and NSF (CCF-1320563 and CCF-1408940). Rodrigo Rodrigues is partially supported by ERC (ERC-2012-StG-307732).

References

[1] PaX Team. PaX Address Space Layout Randomization (ASLR). (http://pax.grsecurity.net/docs/aslr.txt).

[2] Monte-Carlo Method. (http://cdac.in/index.aspx?id =ev_hpc_pthread_benchmarks_kernels).

[3] Pigz: A parallel implementation of gzip for modern multiprocessor, multi-core machines. (http://zlib.net/pigz/).

[4] Pthreads Memory Model. (http://pubs.opengroup.org /onlinepubs/9699919799/basedefs/v1_chap04.html).

[5] M. Abadi, B. W. Lampson, and J.-J. Lévy. Analysis and caching of dependencies. In *proceedings of the First ACM SIGPLAN International Conference on Functional Programming (ICFP)*, 1996.

[6] U. A. Acar. *Self-Adjusting Computation*. PhD thesis, Department of Computer Science, Carnegie Mellon University, May 2005.

[7] U. A. Acar, G. E. Blelloch, M. Blume, R. Harper, and K. Tangwongsan. An experimental analysis of self-adjusting computation. In *proceedings of the 2006 ACM SIGPLAN Conference on Programming Language Design and Implementation (PLDI)*, 2009.

[8] U. A. Acar, A. Cotter, B. Hudson, and D. Türkoğlu. Dynamic well-spaced point sets. In *proceedings of the Twenty-sixth Annual Symposium on Computational Geometry (SoCG)*, 2010.

[9] S. V. Adve and H.-J. Boehm. Memory models: A case for rethinking parallel languages and hardware. *Communication of ACM (CACM)*, 2010.

[10] P. K. Agarwal, L. J. Guibas, H. Edelsbrunner, J. Erickson, M. Isard, S. Har-Peled, J. Hershberger, C. Jensen, L. Kavraki, P. Koehl, M. Lin, D. Manocha, D. Metaxas, B. Mirtich, D. Mount, S. Muthukrishnan, D. Pai, E. Sacks, J. Snoeyink, S. Suri, and O. Wolefson. Algorithmic issues in modeling motion. *ACM Computing Survey*, 2002.

[11] P. S. Almeida, C. Baquero, and V. Fonte. Interval tree clocks. In *proceedings of the 12th International Conference on Principles of Distributed Systems (OPODIS)*, 2008.

[12] G. Altekar and I. Stoica. ODR: Output-deterministic Replay for Multicore Debugging. In *proceedings of the ACM SIGOPS 22nd Symposium on Operating Systems Principles (SOSP)*, 2009.

[13] A. Aviram, S.-C. Weng, S. Hu, and B. Ford. Efficient System-enforced Deterministic Parallelism. In *proceedings of the 9th USENIX Conference on Operating Systems Design and Implementation (OSDI)*, 2010.

[14] T. Bergan, O. Anderson, J. Devietti, L. Ceze, and D. Grossman. CoreDet: A Compiler and Runtime System for Deterministic Multithreaded Execution. In *proceedings of the fifteenth edition of Architectural Support for Programming Languages and Operating Systems (ASPLOS)*, 2010.

[15] T. Bergan, N. Hunt, L. Ceze, and S. D. Gribble. Deterministic Process Groups in dOS. In *proceedings of the 9th USENIX conference on Operating Systems Design and Implementation (OSDI)*, 2010.

[16] E. D. Berger, B. G. Zorn, and K. S. McKinley. Composing High-Performance Memory Allocators. In *proceedings of the ACM SIGPLAN 2001 conference on Programming Language Design and Implementation (PLDI)*, 2001.

[17] E. D. Berger, T. Yang, T. Liu, and G. Novark. Grace: Safe Multithreaded Programming for C/C++. In *proceedings of the 24th ACM SIGPLAN conference on Object Oriented Programming Systems Languages and Applications (OOPSLA)*, 2009.

[18] P. Bhatotia, A. Wieder, I. E. Akkus, R. Rodrigues, and U. A. Acar. Large-scale incremental data processing with change propagation. In *USENIX Workshop on Hot Topics in Cloud Computing (HotCloud)*, 2011.

[19] P. Bhatotia, A. Wieder, R. Rodrigues, U. A. Acar, and R. Pasquini. Incoop: MapReduce for Incremental Computations. In *proceedings of the 2nd ACM Symposium on Cloud Computing (SoCC)*, 2011.

[20] P. Bhatotia, M. Dischinger, R. Rodrigues, and U. A. Acar. Slider: Incremental Sliding-Window Computations for Large-Scale Data Analysis. In *Technical Report: MPI-SWS-2012-004*, 2012.

[21] P. Bhatotia, R. Rodrigues, and A. Verma. Shredder: GPU-Accelerated Incremental Storage and Computation. In *proceedings of the 10th USENIX conference on File and Storage Technologies (FAST)*, 2012.

[22] P. Bhatotia, U. A. Acar, F. Junqueira, and R. Rodrigues. Slider: Incremental Sliding Window Analytics. In *proceedings of the 15th Annual ACM/IFIP/USENIX Middleware conference (Middleware)*, 2014.

[23] P. Bhatotia, A. Wieder, R. Rodrigues, and U. A. Acar. Incremental MapReduce Computations. In *book chapter of advances in data processing techniques in the era of Big Data, CRC Press*, 2014.

[24] C. Bienia, S. Kumar, J. P. Singh, and K. Li. The PARSEC Benchmark Suite: Characterization and Architectural Implications. In *proceedings of the 17th international conference on Parallel Architectures and Compilation Techniques (PACT)*, 2008.

[25] G. S. Brodal and R. Jacob. Dynamic planar convex hull. In *proceedings of the 43rd Annual IEEE Symposium on Foundations of Computer Science*, 2002.

[26] Y. Bu, B. Howe, M. Balazinska, and M. D. Ernst. HaLoop: efficient iterative data processing on large clusters. In *proceedings of VLDB Endowment (VLDB)*, 2010.

[27] S. Burckhardt, D. Leijen, C. Sadowski, J. Yi, and T. Ball. Two for the Price of One: A Model for Parallel and Incremental Computation. In *proceedings of the 2011 ACM international conference on Object Oriented Programming Systems Languages and Applications (OOPSLA)*, 2011.

[28] J. B. Carter, J. K. Bennett, and W. Zwaenepoel. Implementation and Performance of Munin. In *proceedings of the Thirteenth ACM Symposium on Operating Systems Principles (SOSP)*, 1991.

[29] Y. Chen, J. Dunfield, and U. A. Acar. Type-Directed Automatic Incrementalization. In *proceedings of the 33rd ACM SIGPLAN conference on Programming Language Design and Implementation (PLDI)*, Jun 2012.

[30] Y.-J. Chiang and R. Tamassia. Dynamic algorithms in computational geometry. *proceedings of the IEEE*, 1992.

[31] T. Condie, N. Conway, P. Alvaro, J. M. Hellerstein, K. Elmeleegy, and R. Sears. MapReduce online. In *proceedings of the 7th USENIX Conference on Networked Systems Design and Implementation (NSDI)*, 2010.

[32] H. Cui, J. Wu, C.-C. Tsai, and J. Yang. Stable deterministic multithreading through schedule memoization. In *proceedings of the 9th USENIX Conference on Operating Systems Design and Implementation (OSDI)*, 2010.

[33] H. Cui, J. Wu, J. Gallagher, H. Guo, and J. Yang. Efficient deterministic multithreading through schedule relaxation. In *proceedings of the Twenty-Third ACM Symposium on Operating Systems Principles (SOSP)*, 2011.

[34] H. Cui, J. Simsa, Y.-H. Lin, H. Li, B. Blum, X. Xu, J. Yang, G. A. Gibson, and R. E. Bryant. Parrot: a practical runtime for deterministic, stable, and reliable threads. In *proceedings of the Twenty-Fourth ACM Symposium on Operating Systems Principles (SOSP)*, 2013.

[35] J. Dean and S. Ghemawat. MapReduce: Simplified Data Processing on Large Clusters. In *proceedings of the 6th conference on Symposium on Operating Systems Design and Implementation (OSDI)*, 2004.

[36] A. Demers, T. Reps, and T. Teitelbaum. Incremental evaluation for attribute grammars with application to syntax-directed editors. In *proceedings of the 8th ACM SIGPLAN-SIGACT Symposium on Principles of Programming Languages (POPL)*, 1981.

[37] C. Demetrescu, I. Finocchi, and G. Italiano. *Handbook on Data Structures and Applications*, chapter 36: Dynamic Graphs. Dinesh Mehta and Sartaj Sahni (eds.), CRC Press Series, in Computer and Information Science, 2005.

[38] C. Demetrescu, I. Finocchi, and G. Italiano. *Handbook on Data Structures and Applications*, chapter 35: Dynamic Trees. Dinesh Mehta and Sartaj Sahni (eds.), CRC Press Series, in Computer and Information Science, 2005.

[39] J. Devietti, B. Lucia, L. Ceze, and M. Oskin. DMP: Deterministic Shared Memory Multiprocessing. In *proceedings of the 14th international conference on Architectural Support for Programming Languages and Operating Systems (ASPLOS)*, 2009.

[40] J. Devietti, J. Nelson, T. Bergan, L. Ceze, and D. Grossman. RCDC: A Relaxed Consistency Deterministic Computer. *proceedings of the 16th international conference on Architectural Support for Programming Languages and Operating Systems (ASPLOS)*, 2011.

[41] G. W. Dunlap, S. T. King, S. Cinar, M. A. Basrai, and P. M. Chen. ReVirt: Enabling Intrusion Analysis Through Virtual-machine Logging and Replay. *proceedings of the 5th symposium on Operating Systems Design and Implementation (OSDI)*, 2002.

[42] D. Eppstein, Z. Galil, and G. F. Italiano. Dynamic graph algorithms. In M. J. Atallah, editor, *Algorithms and Theory of Computation Handbook*, chapter 8. CRC Press, 1999.

[43] C. Flanagan and S. N. Freund. FastTrack: Efficient and Precise Dynamic Race Detection. In *proceedings of the 2009 ACM SIGPLAN conference on Programming Language Design and Implementation (PLDI)*, 2009.

[44] K. Gharachorloo, D. Lenoski, J. Laudon, P. Gibbons, A. Gupta, and J. Hennessy. Memory Consistency and Event Ordering in Scalable Shared-memory Multiprocessors. In *proceedings of the 17th Annual International Symposium on Computer Architecture (ISCA)*, 1990.

[45] L. Guibas. Modeling motion. In *Handbook of Discrete and Computational Geometry*. 2004.

[46] L. J. Guibas. Kinetic data structures: a state of the art report. In *proceedings of the third Workshop on the Algorithmic Foundations of Robotics (WAFR)*, 1998.

[47] P. K. Gunda, L. Ravindranath, C. A. Thekkath, Y. Yu, and L. Zhuang. Nectar: automatic management of data and computation in datacenters. In *proceedings of the 9th USENIX conference on Operating systems design and implementation (OSDI)*, 2010.

[48] M. Hammer, U. A. Acar, M. Rajagopalan, and A. Ghuloum. A proposal for parallel self-adjusting computation. In *proceedings of the 2007 workshop on Declarative Aspects of Multicore Programming (DAMP)*, 2007.

[49] M. A. Hammer, U. A. Acar, and Y. Chen. CEAL: a C-Based Language for Self-Adjusting Computation. In *proceedings of the 2009 ACM SIGPLAN conference on Programming Language Design and Implementation (PLDI)*, 2009.

[50] M. A. Hammer, K. Y. Phang, M. Hicks, and J. S. Foster. Adapton: Composable, demand-driven incremental computation. In *proceedings of the 35th ACM SIGPLAN Conference on Programming Language Design and Implementation (PLDI)*, 2014.

[51] A. Heydon, R. Levin, and Y. Yu. Caching Function Calls Using Precise Dependencies. In *proceedings of the ACM SIGPLAN 2000 conference on Programming Language Design and Implementation (PLDI)*, 2000.

[52] N. Honarmand and J. Torrellas. RelaxReplay: Record and Replay for Relaxed-consistency Multiprocessors. In *proceedings of the 19th International Conference on Architectural Support for Programming Languages and Operating Systems (ASPLOS)*, 2014.

[53] R. Hoover. *Incremental Graph Evaluation.* PhD thesis, Department of Computer Science, Cornell University, May 1987.

[54] D. R. Hower, P. Dudnik, M. D. Hill, and D. A. Wood. Calvin: Deterministic or not? free will to choose. In *proceedings of the 2011 IEEE 17th International Symposium on High Performance Computer Architecture (HPCA)*, 2011.

[55] M. Isard, M. Budiu, Y. Yu, A. Birrell, and D. Fetterly. Dryad: distributed data-parallel programs from sequential building blocks. In *proceedings of the 2nd ACM SIGOPS/EuroSys European Conference on Computer Systems (EuroSys)*, 2007.

[56] P. Keleher, A. L. Cox, S. Dwarkadas, and W. Zwaenepoel. Treadmarks: Distributed shared memory on standard workstations and operating systems. In *proceedings of the USENIX Winter 1994 Technical Conference on USENIX Winter 1994 Technical Conference (USENIX)*, 1994.

[57] O. Laadan, N. Viennot, and J. Nieh. Transparent, lightweight application execution replay on commodity multiprocessor operating systems. In *proceedings of the ACM SIGMETRICS*

international conference on Measurement and modeling of computer systems (SIGMETRICS), 2010.

[58] L. Lamport. How to make a correct multiprocess program execute correctly on a multiprocessor. *IEEE Transactions on Computers*, 1997.

[59] D. Lee, B. Wester, K. Veeraraghavan, S. Narayanasamy, P. M. Chen, and J. Flinn. Respec: Efficient Online Multiprocessor Replayvia Speculation and External Determinism. In *proceedings of the 15th edition of ASPLOS on Architectural Support for Programming Languages and Operating Systems (ASPLOS)*, 2010.

[60] R. Ley-Wild, M. Fluet, and U. A. Acar. Compiling Self-Adjusting Programs with Continuations. In *proceedings of the 13th ACM SIGPLAN International Conference on Functional programming (ICFP)*, 2008.

[61] R. Ley-Wild, U. A. Acar, and M. Fluet. A cost semantics for self-adjusting computation. In *proceedings of the 26th Annual ACM Symposium on Principles of Programming Languages (POPL)*, 2009.

[62] T. Liu and E. D. Berger. SHERIFF: Precise Detection and Automatic Mitigation of False Sharing. In *proceedings of the 2011 ACM International Conference on Object Oriented Programming Systems Languages and Applications (OOPSLA)*, 2011.

[63] T. Liu, C. Curtsinger, and E. D. Berger. Dthreads: Efficient Deterministic Multithreading. In *proceedings of the Twenty-Third ACM Symposium on Operating Systems Principles (SOSP)*, 2011.

[64] D. Logothetis, C. Olston, B. Reed, K. C. Webb, and K. Yocum. Stateful Bulk Processing for Incremental Analytics. In *proceedings of the 1st ACM Symposium on Cloud Computing (SoCC)*, 2010.

[65] F. Mattern. Virtual Time and Global States of Distributed Systems. In *Parallel and Distributed Algorithms*, 1989.

[66] A. Muthitacharoen, B. Chen, and D. Mazières. A Low-bandwidth Network File System. In *proceedings of the 18th ACM Symposium on Operating Systems Principles (SOSP)*, 2001.

[67] M. Olszewski, J. Ansel, and S. Amarasinghe. Kendo: Efficient Deterministic Multithreading in Software. In *proceedings of the 14th international conference on Architectural Support for Programming Languages and Operating Systems (ASPLOS)*, 2009.

[68] M. H. Overmars and J. van Leeuwen. Maintenance of configurations in the plane. *Journal of Computer and System Sciences*, 23:166–204, 1981.

[69] S. Park, Y. Zhou, W. Xiong, Z. Yin, R. Kaushik, K. H. Lee, and S. Lu. PRES: Probabilistic Replay with Execution Sketching on Multiprocessors. In *proceedings of the ACM SIGOPS 22nd Symposium on Operating Systems Principles (SOSP)*, 2009.

[70] L. Popa, M. Budiu, Y. Yu, and M. Isard. DryadInc: Reusing Work in Large-scale Computations. In *USENIX Workshop on Hot Topics in Cloud Computing (HotCloud)*, 2009.

[71] E. Pozniansky and A. Schuster. Efficient On-the-Fly Data Race Detection in Multithreaded C++ Programs. In *proceedings of the ninth ACM SIGPLAN symposium on Principles and Practice of Parallel Programming (PPoPP)*, 2003.

[72] W. Pugh. *Incremental Computation via Function Caching*. PhD thesis, Department of Computer Science, Cornell University, Aug. 1988.

[73] G. Ramalingam and T. Reps. A Categorized Bibliography on Incremental Computation. In *proceedings of the 20th ACM SIGPLAN-SIGACT symposium on Principles of Programming Languages (POPL)*, 1993.

[74] C. Ranger, R. Raghuraman, A. Penmetsa, G. Bradski, and C. Kozyrakis. Evaluating MapReduce for Multi-core and Multiprocessor Systems. In *proceedings of the 2007 IEEE 13th International Symposium on High Performance Computer Architecture (HPCA)*, 2007.

[75] M. Ronsse and K. De Bosschere. RecPlay: A Fully Integrated Practical Record/Replay System. *ACM Transactions on Computer Systems (TOCS)*, 1999.

[76] H.-W. Tseng and D. M. Tullsen. Data-Triggered Threads: Eliminating Redundant Computation. In *proceedings of 17th International Symposium on High Performance Computer Architecture (HPCA)*, 2011.

[77] H.-W. Tseng and D. M. Tullsen. Software Data-triggered Threads. In *proceedings of the ACM International Conference on Object Oriented Programming Systems Languages and Applications (OOPSLA)*, 2012.

[78] H.-W. Tseng and D. M. Tullsen. CDTT: Compiler-generated data-triggered threads. In *proceedings of 17th International Symposium on High Performance Computer Architecture (HPCA)*, 2014.

[79] K. Veeraraghavan, P. M. Chen, J. Flinn, and S. Narayanasamy. Detecting and Surviving Data Races Using Complementary Schedules. In *proceedings of the Twenty-Third ACM Symposium on Operating Systems Principles (SOSP)*, 2011.

[80] K. Veeraraghavan, D. Lee, B. Wester, J. Ouyang, P. M. Chen, J. Flinn, and S. Narayanasamy. DoublePlay: Parallelizing Sequential Logging and Replay. In *proceedings of the sixteenth international conference on Architectural support for programming languages and operating system (ASPLOS)*, 2011.

[81] N. Viennot, S. Nair, and J. Nieh. Transparent Mutable Replay for Multicore Debugging and Patch Validation. In *proceedings of the 18th International Conference on Architectural Support for Programming Languages and Operating Systems (ASPLOS)*, 2013.

[82] W. Xiong, S. Park, J. Zhang, Y. Zhou, and Z. Ma. Ad hoc Synchronization Considered Harmful. In *proceedings of the 9th USENIX conference on Operating Systems Design and Implementation (OSDI)*, 2010.

NumaGiC: a Garbage Collector for Big Data on Big NUMA Machines

Lokesh Gidra
LIP6-UPMC/INRIA
lokesh.gidra@lip6.fr

Gaël Thomas
SAMOVAR-Telecom SudParis
gael.thomas@telecom-sudparis.eu

Julien Sopena
LIP6-UPMC/INRIA
julien.sopena@lip6.fr

Marc Shapiro
LIP6-INRIA/UPMC
marc.shapiro@acm.org

Nhan Nguyen
Chalmers University of Technology
nhann@chalmers.se

Abstract

On contemporary cache-coherent Non-Uniform Memory Access (ccNUMA) architectures, applications with a large memory footprint suffer from the cost of the garbage collector (GC), because, as the GC scans the reference graph, it makes many remote memory accesses, saturating the interconnect between memory nodes. We address this problem with NumaGiC, a GC with a mostly-distributed design. In order to maximise memory access locality during collection, a GC thread avoids accessing a different memory node, instead notifying a remote GC thread with a message; nonetheless, NumaGiC avoids the drawbacks of a pure distributed design, which tends to decrease parallelism. We compare NumaGiC with Parallel Scavenge and NAPS on two different ccNUMA architectures running on the Hotspot Java Virtual Machine of OpenJDK 7. On Spark and Neo4j, two industry-strength analytics applications, with heap sizes ranging from 160 GB to 350 GB, and on SPECjbb2013 and SPECjbb2005, NumaGiC improves overall performance by up to 45% over NAPS (up to 94% over Parallel Scavenge), and increases the performance of the collector itself by up to 3.6× over NAPS (up to 5.4× over Parallel Scavenge).

Categories and Subject Descriptors D.4.2 [*Software*]: Garbage collection

General Terms Experimentation, Performance

Keywords Garbage collection; NUMA; multicore

ASPLOS '15, March 14 - 18 2015, Istanbul, Turkey.
Copyright © 2015 ACM 978-1-4503-2835-7/15/03... $15.00.
http://dx.doi.org/10.1145/2694344.2694361

1. Introduction

Data-analytics programs require large amounts of computing power and memory. When run on modern multicore computers with a cache-coherent Non-Uniform Memory Access (ccNUMA) architecture, they suffer from a high overhead during garbage collection (GC) caused by a bad memory access locality. A ccNUMA architecture consists of a network of nodes, each comprising several cores and a local memory bank. A ccNUMA architecture hides the distributed nature of the memory from the application. The application thus unknowingly creates *inter-node references* when it stores a reference to an object located on a given node into the memory of another node. In turn, when a GC thread traverses the object graph to identify live objects, it silently traverses inter-node references and thus processes objects on any memory node. Consequently, GC threads access remote memory often, which increases memory access latency, and causes a large network traffic that can saturate the network between the nodes.

Intuitively, to access only local memory, a GC thread that encounters a reference to a remote object might delegate the processing of that object to a GC thread running on the remote node. This design, unfortunately, degrades parallelism, because a GC thread remains idle when it does not have local objects to collect, waiting for another GC thread to reach some object located on its own node.

Based on this observation, we designed the NumaGiC collector to aim for memory access locality during the GC, without degrading GC parallelism. It features a *mostly-distributed* design, in which a GC thread can be in two modes. *Local mode* focuses on memory access locality and avoids remote object access. In this mode, when a GC thread finds a reference to an object located on a remote node, it notifies a GC thread on the remote node, which processes the object and its reachable subgraph (i.e., objects that it points to, and so on recursively) locally. A GC thread enters *work-stealing mode* when it runs out of local objects to process. Work-stealing mode focuses on parallelism and allows a GC thread to "steal" references to process from any other node, and to access such references itself, even if they are remote. A GC thread in work-stealing mode periodically re-enters local mode, in order to check whether some local reference has become available again, either sent by a remote thread, or discovered by scanning a stolen reference.

NumaGiC also includes a set of NUMA-friendly placement policies that prepare the heap for the mostly-distributed design. First, the policies aim at minimising the number of inter-node references. Because sending a reference is slightly more costly than remotely accessing a small object, sending a reference is only beneficial if, on average, the referenced object itself references many objects on its same node. In this case, the cost of sending the reference is amortised over the memory access locality of the receiving GC thread. Second, the policies aim to balance the amount of live objects across memory nodes, in order to equalise the work between GC threads. Indeed, if some nodes are underloaded, their GC threads quickly enter work-stealing mode and start accessing the overloaded nodes, which can potentially saturate their memory controller.

We implemented NumaGiC in the Hotspot Java Virtual Machine of OpenJDK 7. NumaGiC targets long-running computations that use large data sets, for which a throughput-oriented *stop-the-world* GC algorithm is suitable.[1] NumaGiC is based on Parallel Scavenge, the default throughput-oriented GC of Hotspot. Our experiments compare NumaGiC with (a slightly improved version of) Parallel Scavenge, and with an improved version of Parallel Scavenge designed for ccNUMA architectures called NAPS [10]. NAPS balances memory access among nodes and improves memory access locality for only newly-allocated objects, whereas NumaGiC also improves memory access locality for objects that survive collection and enforces memory access locality by using messages when GC threads have local memory to collect.

We evaluate NumaGiC against two widely-used big-data engines, Spark [23] and Neo4j [17], with Java heaps sized from 110 GB to 350 GB. We also evaluate two industry-standard benchmarks, SPECjbb2013 [25], and SPECjbb2005 [24], along with the DaCapo 9.12 and SPECjvm2008 benchmarks. We experiment both on a 48-core AMD Magny-Cours machine with 8 nodes and a total memory size of 256 GB, and on a 40-core Intel Xeon E7 hyper-threaded machine with two execution units per core, with 4 nodes and total memory size of 512 GB. Our evaluation shows that:

- On applications with large heap, NumaGiC always increases the overall performance of applications on the two machines. With heap size that provide the best possible application performance for the three evaluated GC, NumaGiC improves the overall performance of applications by up to 45% over NAPS, and by up to 94% over Parallel Scavenge. This result shows that a mostly distributed design increases substantially the performance of applications with large heap on ccNUMA machines, and that a mostly distributed design seems to improve performance independently of the architecture.
- On applications with large heap with the most efficient heap size for all the GC, NumaGiC increases collector throughput, *i.e.*, the number of live bytes processed per time unit, on the two machines by up to 3.6× and by up to 5.4×, compared to NAPS and Parallel Scavenge respectively.
- On applications with large heap, NumaGiC scales substantially better than NAPS, and Parallel Scavenge with increasing number of NUMA nodes. NumaGiC scales almost linearly in case of SPECjbb2005, and Spark. The only limiting factor in its scalability is the amount of inter-node shared objects, which depends on the application's execution behavior. The design of NumaGiC itself is scalable.
- On 33 applications from DaCapo 9.12 and SPECjbb2008 with smaller working set, NumaGiC improves substantially the performance of 7 applications by more than 5%, and only degrades the performance of a single application by more than 5% (by 8%). This result shows that a mostly distributed design is almost always beneficial and statistically beneficial for 20% of the applications with modest workload.

The paper is organized as follow. Section 2 presents Parallel Scavenge, the GC at the basis of NumaGiC. Section 3 presents the NUMA-friendly placement policies, and Section 4 the design of NumaGiC. Section 5 reports on our evaluation results and discusses their implications. Section 6 reviews related work, and Section 7 concludes the paper.

2. Background

A garbage collector (GC) observes the memory of some application process, called the mutator. Starting from some well-known roots, it records which objects are referenced, *scans* them for more references, and so on recursively. Reachable objects are *live*; unreachable ones are garbage and are deallocated.

Parallel Scavenge is the default GC of the Hotspot Java Virtual Machine, and forms the starting point for this work. Parallel Scavenge is a stop-the-world, parallel and generational collector [13]. This means that the application is suspended during a collection, that it spawns several parallel GC threads, and that it segregates objects into generations. Generations are justified by the observation that, in the common case, a young object becomes garbage more quickly than an older object [2, 14, 29].

[1] A stop-the-world GC algorithm suspends the application during collection, in order to avoid concurrent access to the heap by the application. A stop-the-world GC is opposed to a concurrent GC [13], which favours response time at the expense of throughput, because it requires fine-grain synchronisation between the application and the GC.

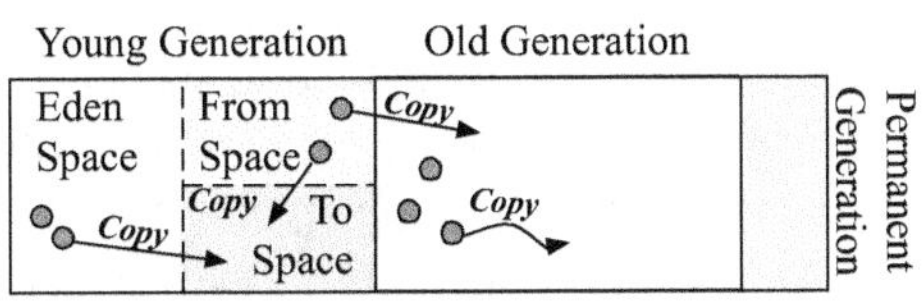

Figure 1. Memory Layout of Parallel Scavenge

Parallel Scavenge has three generations (see Figure 1): the *young generation* contains recently-allocated objects, the *old generation* contains older objects, and the *permanent generation* contains class definitions. Hereafter, we conflate the permanent with the old generation to simplify the presentation. Parallel Scavenge has two kinds of collections. A *young collection* collects only the young generation; a *full collection* collects both generations. Parallel Scavenge leverages the generational hypothesis by performing young collections more frequently than full collections.

In the remainder of this section, we describe the young and the full collectors, then discuss the parallelism of Parallel Scavenge, and finally discuss the memory placement of Parallel Scavenge.

2.1 Parallel Scavenge young collection

The Parallel Scavenge young collection is a copying algorithm. When it reaches a live object, it copies it elsewhere in order to compact the memory. This design fights fragmentation, and ensures that dead memory can be recycled in large chunks.

Parallel Scavenge promotes a young object to the old generation only after it has survived a few young collections. For this purpose, it divides the young generation into the so-called *eden space* and two *survivor spaces*, called *from-space* and *to-space*.

Parallel Scavenge allocates new objects in eden space. The from-space contains the young objects that have survived a few collections, and, before a collection, the to-space is empty.

Parallel Scavenge copies live objects of both the eden space and the from-space, either to the to-space or to the old generation, according to their age (see Figure 1). At the end of collection, the eden space and the from-space are empty and can be recycled, and to-space contains the surviving young objects. In the next cycle, the eden space again serves to allocate new objects, and the from- and to-spaces are swapped.

The roots for young collection are the global variables, the stacks of the mutator threads, and the old-to-young root objects, *i.e.*, the old-generation objects that reference objects in the young generation. Parallel Scavenge identifies the old-to-young root objects by instrumenting writes performed by the mutator. It divides the old generation into chunks called cards [21, 30]. Each card has a corresponding bit in a *card table*, indicating whether the card might contain a reference to the young generation. The GC traverses the card table, in order to identify the cards that potentially contain old-to-young root objects. Each time an old object is assigned with a reference towards the young generation, the Java Virtual Machine marks the corresponding card table entry "dirty," indicating the possible existence of a young-generation root.

2.2 Full collection

Full Collection re-uses many of the data structures and algorithms used by young collection. It uses a three-phase mark-compact algorithm, compacting the old generation by copying live objects to the beginning of the old generation memory area to avoid fragmentation. In the first phase, called the marking phase, the GC threads traverse the object graph in parallel and mark the live objects. In the second, summary phase, Parallel Scavenge calculates (sequentially) the destination address of the live objects; this mapping is organised in regions of 4 KB each. In the third, compacting phase, the GC threads process the regions in parallel and copy the live objects to the beginning of the old generation.

2.3 Parallelism in Parallel Scavenge

Parallel Scavenge uses a master-slave design. The master thread, called the VM Thread, queues some tasks, described next, in a single task queue. Then it starts the parallel phase, in which GC threads dequeue tasks and perform the corresponding work.

A **root task** records some root of the object graph. Root tasks are used both in the copying phase of the young collector and in the marking phase of the full collector. A GC thread that dequeues a root task traverses the object graph depth first. For this purpose, the thread maintains a so-called *pending queue* of references, initialized with the references indicated in the root task. When the thread dequeues a reference, if the referenced object was already processed, the GC thread skips it. Otherwise, it either copies (in the young collector) or marks (in the marking phase of the full collector) the object, and finally scans the object and appends the references it contains to its pending queue.[2] When the pending queue is empty, the root task is finished.

A **compacting task** is used by a GC thread to compact the heap during the compacting phase of the full collector, by copying the regions, according to the mapping computed during the summary phase. A GC thread copies the objects from (one or more) source regions to some empty destination region. The destination region may be originally empty, or may become empty because its objects have been copied elsewhere. This requires some synchronisation, which uses the pending queues. Initially, each GC thread adds to its pending queue a subset of the empty regions. For each destination region, the GC thread copies the corresponding objects from their source regions and updates the references contained in

[2] Note that the GC traverses each live reference exactly once, and hence, the number of reference accesses is equal to the number of references.

the destination region. When a source region becomes empty, it is added to the GC thread's pending queue, and so on recursively.

The **steal task** is the last task on the queue. When a GC thread reaches the steal task, this means that it has no other work to do, and should now steal references from randomly-chosen pending queues.

When, after several random steal attempts, the GC thread does not find any work, it synchronises with the other GC threads with a termination protocol. It increments a global counter, which counts the number of GC threads in the termination protocol, and waits for the other GC threads. While it waits, it regularly checks all the pending queues of all the other GC threads, and leaves the termination protocol by restarting the steal task if it finds work to perform.

2.4 Parallel Scavenge Baseline

The original Parallel Scavenge suffers from memory access imbalance on NUMA machines, which drastically degrades its performance [10]. Furthermore, it suffers from a synchronisation design flaw, unrelated to our study of memory placement [10]. Since it is a rather simple fix, and to ensure a fair comparison, we hereafter consider a slightly modified version of Parallel Scavenge, which we shall call Parallel Scavenge Baseline or PSB. Borrowing from NAPS [10], PSB corrects the synchronisation flaw, and uses an *interleaved* memory placement policy, in which pages are mapped from different physical nodes in round-robin. This ensures that memory is approximately uniformly allocated from all the nodes, and hence, memory access is expected to be uniformly and randomly distributed among all the nodes.

3. NUMA-friendly placement

Before turning to the GC algorithm itself, we present NUMA-friendly policies designed to optimise the memory placement for the mostly-distributed design. As stated in the introduction, since sending an inter-node reference is slightly more expensive than remotely accessing a small object, we aim to minimise the number of inter-node references, improving what we call the *spatial NUMA locality* property. Furthermore, also as explained in the introduction, *memory allocation balance* is important, to avoid saturating some memory nodes.

Placement occurs, either when the mutator first allocates an object, or when the GC copies an object to a new location. To be efficient, the placement decision should take less time than the benefit of improved memory placement. For instance, we found that the aggressive graph partitioning heuristics of Stanton and Kliot [26], although highly effective to minimise the number of inter-node references and to balance the memory allocation among the nodes, are much too costly for our purpose.

Therefore, we focus on simple policies that require only local information, are computed quickly, and have a small memory overhead. Placement may be somewhat suboptimal, but should remain satisfactory relative to the low computation overhead. In order to identify interesting policies, we first analyse the natural object graph topology created by several applications. Then, based on this analysis, we propose NUMA-friendly placement policies that leverage this topology.

3.1 Object graph analysis

In order to improve the spatial NUMA locality and the memory allocation balance, we first analyse the object graph of five applications, chosen for their diverse allocation patterns: Spark, a multi-threaded map-reduce engine [23]; Neo4j, an embedded, disk-based, fully transanctional Java persistence engine that manages graph data [17]; SPECjbb2013, a business logic service-side application benchmark that defines groups of threads with different behaviours [25]; SPECjbb2005, another business logic service-side application benchmark where all the threads have the same behaviour [24]; and H2, an in-memory database from the DaCapo 9.12 benchmark [4, 11].

We analyse the topology created by the applications in HotSpot 7 running 48 GC threads on an AMD Magny-Cours machine with 48 cores and eight memory nodes. We use a customised version of PSB, which ensures that the objects allocated by a mutator thread running on node i always stay on node i.[3] In this experiment, as in all the experiments presented in the paper, we let the Linux scheduler places the mutator threads on the cores. Table 1 reports the following metrics:

- The *heap size* that we set for the experiment.
- The *proportion of clustered references*, defined as the following ratio: the number of references between objects allocated by the mutator threads of the same node, divided by the total number of references. We report separately the proportion of clustered references between young objects, from old to young objects, and among all the objects. The first two are traversed during a young collection, while all the references are traversed during a full collection. In order to gather representative numbers, we ignore the first few collections to avoid warm-up effects, and thus measure the proportion of clustered references on a snapshot of memory taken during the 8th full collection for Spark, 5th for Neo4j, SPECjbb2005 and SPECjbb2013, and 3th for H2.
- The *thread allocation imbalance*, defined as the standard deviation over the average number of objects allocated by the mutator threads running on each node.

We observe that the proportion of clustered references is always high, especially between young objects and from old to young objects. Indeed, our experiment reports a proportion between 77% and 100% between young objects, between

[3] This version of PSB is exactly the pure distributed algorithm described in Section 5.5.

	Heap size	Proportion of clustered references			Thread allocation imbalance
		Young	Old-to-young	All	
Spark	32GB	0.99	0.91	0.53	0.10
Neo4j	32GB	0.99	0.72	0.27	0.21
SpecJBB2013	24GB	0.99	0.99	0.51	0.07
SpecJBB2005	4GB	1.00	0.18	0.55	0.09
H2	2GB	0.77	0.16	0.50	0.40

Table 1. Analysis of the object graph

16% and 99% from old to young objects and between 27% and 55% for the other references, whereas, if clustering were random, we would expect a proportion of clustered reference equal to $1/8 = 12.5\%$ with eight nodes. This shows that the applications considered have a natural tendency to cluster their objects.

Furthermore, we observe that memory allocation imbalance varies between the applications, from highly balanced for Spark, SPECjbb2013 and SPECjbb2005, to imbalanced for H2. This confirms the need for placement policies to counter-balance the latter case.

3.2 NUMA-friendly placement

We have designed our placement policies based on the above observations. We can leverage the observation that the mutator threads of the same node tend to naturally cluster the objects that they allocate to the objective of spatial NUMA locality: all we need to do is to ensure that an object allocated by a mutator thread is placed on the same node as the mutator thread.

In addition to improving locality for the GC, this memory placement policy also has the interesting side-effect of improving application locality, because a mutator thread tends to access mostly the objects that it has allocated itself.

We also observed an imbalanced allocation pattern in some applications. Therefore, always placing all objects allocated by a mutator thread on the same node would be detrimental to memory allocation balance. Therefore, we should also design policies to alleviate this imbalance, by migrating objects from overloaded memory nodes to underloaded memory nodes during collection.

With this in mind, we designed four different and complementary policies:

- *Node-Local Allocation* places the object allocated by a mutator thread on the same node where the mutator thread is running.
- The *Node-Local Root* policy ensures that the roots of a GC thread are chosen to be located mostly on its running node.
- During a young collection, *Node-Local Copy* policy copies a live object to the node where the GC thread is running.
- During the compacting phase of a full collection, the *Node-Local Compact* policy ensures that an object being compacted remains on the same node where it was previously located.

The first policy ensures that a mutator thread allocates to its own node initially. The other three avoid object migration, so that the object stays where it was allocated. The middle two avoid object migration during a young collection because a GC thread on node i mainly processes objects of node i and copies them on node i. The node-local compact policy simply prevents object migration during a full collection.

For applications with an imbalanced allocation pattern, the Node-Local Copy policy, in conjunction with stealing, also tends to re-balance the load. Consider the case where Node A hosts more objects than Node B. Consequently, processing on Node B will finish sooner than Node A. As presented in Section 2, rather than remaining idle, the GC threads on Node B will start "stealing" i.e., to process remaining objects of Node A. The Node-Local Copy policy ensures that GC threads on B will copy the objects to B, restoring the balance.

3.3 Implementation details

In order to be able to map addresses to nodes, we make use of the *fragmented spaces* of NAPS [10]. A fragmented space is partitioned into *logical segments*, where the virtual address range of each segment is physically allocated on a different node. In contrast to an interleaved space (which maps pages randomly from all nodes, see Section 2.4), a fragmented space allows a GC thread to retrieve the segment and NUMA location of an object from its address. The GC thread can also place an object onto a specific NUMA node by using a segment mapped to the desired node.

NAPS implemented fragmented space for the young generation, with the goal of memory allocation balance. We extend NAPS implementation to the old generation, by adding a per-segment compacting algorithm, which applies the Node-Local Compacting policy of not migrating objects between nodes. Beside the goal of enforcing the spatial NUMA-locality and the memory allocation balance, we have also optimised the memory access locality during the compacting phase by ensuring that a GC thread selects the regions of its node before stealing the regions of the other nodes.

In order to implement the Node-Local Root policy, we partition the card table into segments. Each segment of the card table corresponds to a segment of the old generation, and hence identifies old-to-young roots from a given node.

Also for the Node-Local Root policy, we ensure that a GC thread processes the stack of a mutator thread running on its node, which mainly contains references allocated by the mutator thread, thus allocated on the same node, thanks to the Node-Local Allocation policy.

4. NumaGiC

NumaGiC focuses on improving memory access locality without degrading parallelism of the GC. A GC thread normally runs in *local mode*, in which it collects its own node's memory only. It switches to *work-stealing mode* when parallelism degrades. In work-stealing mode, a GC thread can steal work from other threads, and is allowed to collect the memory of other nodes remotely.

We present the two modes and the conditions for switching between them.

4.1 Local mode

In local mode, a GC thread collects its local memory only. When processing a reference, the GC thread checks for the home node of the referenced object, *i.e.*, the node that hosts the physical memory mapped at the virtual address of the object. If the home-node is the node of the GC thread, then the GC thread processes[4] the object itself. Otherwise, it sends the reference to the home node of the object, and a GC thread attached to the remote home node will receive and process the reference. Checking the home-node of an object is fast, as it consists of looking up a virtual address in a map of segments of the fragmented spaces (see Section 3.3).

Moreover, when a GC thread idles in local mode, it may steal work from the pending queues (described in Section 2.3) of the other GC threads of its node, but not from remote nodes.

Communication infrastructure. Our initial design used a single channel per node, where other nodes would post messages; experience shows that this design suffers high contention between senders. Therefore, NumaGiC uses a communication channel per each pair of nodes, implemented with an array-based lock-free bounded queue [12].

Because multiple threads can send on the same queue, sending a message is synchronised thanks to an atomic compare-and-swap, a relatively costly operation. In order to mitigate this cost, references are buffered and sent in bulk. The evaluation of Section 5.4 shows that buffering 16 references for the full collections, and 128 references for young collections gives satisfactory performance.

A GC thread checks the receiving end of its message channels regularly, in order to receive messages: *(i)* when it starts to execute a GC task, and *(ii)* regularly while stealing from other threads of the same node.

4.2 Work-stealing mode

In work-stealing mode, a GC thread may steal from any node, and may access both local or remote memory. In work-stealing mode, a GC thread steals references from three groups of locations; when it finds a reference to steal in one of these groups, it continues to steal from the same group as long as possible, in order to avoid unsuccessful steal attempts. The first group consists of its own transmit buffers, cancelling the messages it sent that were not yet delivered. The second group consists of the receive side of other nodes' communication channels. The third group consists of the pending queues of other GC threads.

When a GC thread does not find references to steal, it waits for termination. Classically, asynchronous communication creates a termination problem [5]. For instance, even though a GC thread might observe that its pending queues and its receive channel are all empty, this does not suffice to terminate it, because a message might actually be in flight from another GC thread.

To solve this problem, a GC thread does not enter the termination protocol of the parallel phase (described in Section 2.3) unless it observes that all of the messages that it has sent have been delivered. For this purpose, before entering the termination protocol, it verifies that the remote receive side of every of its communication channels is empty, by reading remote memory.

After having observed that all its sent messages are received, a GC thread waits for termination, by incrementing a shared counter and regularly checking all termination.

4.3 Switching between local and work-stealing modes

A GC thread enters work-stealing mode when its does not find local work: when its local pending queue is empty, when its steal attempts from the pending queues of the GC threads of its node have failed, and when its receive channels are empty.

Once a GC thread is in work-stealing mode, it adapts to current conditions by regularly re-entering local mode. The rationale for this adaptive behaviour is twofold. First, local work can become available again if a stolen object or one of its reachable objects is local; in this case, it makes sense to switch back to the local mode, because the received reference will often open up a significant sub-graph, thanks to spatial NUMA locality. Second, re-entering local mode and back to work-stealing mode ensures that the GC thread will retry to steal from all the groups, regularly checking all sources of work again, especially its receive channels.

We tuned the frequency of re-entering local mode, finding that switching back to local-mode every 1024 stolen objects gives satisfactory performance in all our experiments.

5. Evaluation of NumaGiC

This section studies the performance of NumaGiC, using both standard benchmarks and widely-used, industrially-relevant applications. We first describe the hardware and software settings, followed by the applications used in the evaluation. Then, we study the impact of the policies presented in Section 3, and the impact of some design parameters and trade-offs on a small set of experiments. Finally, we undertake a full-scale evaluation of the impact of NumaGiC followed by an analysis of its scalability.

5.1 Hardware and software

We run our experiments with the Hotspot Java Virtual Machine of OpenJDK 7, on two different machines.

[4] Processing an object means copying it during young collection, and marking it live during full collection.

The first one, called *Amd48* hereafter, is a Magny-Cours machine with four AMD Opteron 6172 sockets, each consisting of two nodes. Each node has six cores (2.1 GHz clock rate) and 32 GB of RAM. In total there are 48 cores and 256 GB of RAM on eight nodes. The nodes are interconnected by HyperTransport 3.0 links, with a maximum distance of two hops. The system runs a Linux 3.9.7 64-bit kernel and gcc 4.6.1. NumaGiC is configured with 48 GC threads on Amd48.

The second machine, called *Intel80* hereafter, is a an Intel server with four Xeon E7-2860 processors, each consisting of a single node. Each node has 10 cores (2.27 GHz clock rate) and 128 GB of RAM. Each core carries two hyper threads. In total, there are 40 cores (80 hardware threads) and 512 GB RAM on four nodes. The nodes are interconnected by QuickPath Interconnect links, with a maximum distance of two hops. The system runs a Linux 3.8.0 64-bit kernel and gcc 4.7.2. NumaGiC is configured with 80 GC threads on Intel80.

5.2 Applications and Benchmarks

Our evaluation uses two big-data analytics engines, two industry-standard benchmarks, and two benchmark suites.

Spark Spark is an in-memory map-reduce engine for large-scale data processing [23]. We use Spark 0.9.0 to run a page-rank computation on a dataset consisting of a subset of a graph of 1.8 billion edges taken from the Friendster social network [8].

On Amd48, we use two configurations, one with 100 million edges, and the other with 1 billion edges. For the first one, we set the heap size to 32 GB. The computation triggers approximately 175 young and 15 full collections and lasts for roughly 22 minutes with PSB (Parallel Scavenge Baseline), which is sufficiently short to run a large number of experiments. This is also the configuration used for the evaluation of the memory-placement policies of Section 5.3. The second configuration is much more demanding; we run it with heap sizes increasing from 110 GB to 160 GB, in steps of 25 GB. On Intel80, we measure only the 1.8-billion edge configuration, with heap sizes ranging from 250 GB to 350 GB, in steps of 50 GB.

The database itself is stored on disk. Following the Spark developers' advice, we use the remaining RAM to mount an in-memory file system `tmpfs` for Spark's intermediate results. Thus, these experiments make use of all the available RAM. Furthermore, they run on all the cores of the machine.

Neo4j Neo4j is an embedded, disk-based, fully transactional Java persistence engine that manages graph data [17]. Neo4j caches nodes, relationships and properties in the Java heap, to accelerate computation. We implemented a driver program that uses Neo4j 2.1.2 as a library package, and queries the database for the shortest path between a given source node and 100,000 randomly-chosen destination nodes. We use the native shortest-path algorithm of Neo4j, and execute it in parallel using the fork/join infrastructure provided by the Java library. The database used for this experiment is also created from the Friendster dataset.

On Amd48, we use the first billion edges, and on Intel80, we use all the 1.8 billion edges. We run it with heap sizes ranging from 110 GB to 160 GB, in steps of 25 GB on Amd48, and from 250 GB to 350 GB, in steps of 50 GB, on Intel80. We follow the advice of the Neo4j developers, to leave the rest of the RAM for use by the file-system cache. This experiment also makes use of all the available RAM and all the cores.

SPECjbb2005 and SPECjbb2013 SPECjbb2005 and SPECjbb2013 are two business logic service-side application benchmarks [24, 25] that model supermarket companies. SPECjbb2005 only models the middle tier server, using a set of identical threads, each one modelling a warehouse; each warehouse runs in complete isolation. SPECjbb2013 models all the components of the company, using a larger number threads with different behaviours, interacting together.

For SPECjbb2005, we run a warm-up round of 30 seconds, then a measurement round of eight minutes. On Amd48 (resp. Intel80), we evaluate different heap sizes, from 4 GB to 8 GB, in steps of 2 GB (resp. from 8 GB to 12 GB, in steps of 2 GB). For SPECjbb2013, we let the benchmark compute the maximal workload that can be executed efficiently on the machines, which ensures that all mutator threads are working. On both Amd48 and Intel80, we evaluate different heap sizes, from 24 GB to 40 GB, in steps of 8 GB.

DaCapo 9.12 and SPECjvm2008 The DaCapo 9.12 and SPECjvm2008 benchmarks are widely used to measure the performance of Java virtual machines. They include 52 real applications with synthetic workloads; we retained all 33 that are multi-threaded.

For the DaCapo applications, we selected the largest workload. For the SPECjvm2008 applications, we have fixed the number of operations to 40 because this value ensures that all the mutator threads are working. We do not configure a specific heap size, instead, relying on Hotspot's default resizing policy. The experiments execute with one mutator thread and one GC thread per core.

The resulting heap sizes are the smallest of our evaluation and; therefore, we expect that the impact of GC on overall performance will be small. These benchmarks are also not representative of the big-data applications targeted by the NumaGiC design. Nonetheless, we include them in our evaluation, both for completeness, and to evaluate the performance impact of NumaGiC's multiple queues, which should be most apparent in such applications with a small memory footprint.

5.3 Evaluation of the policies

This section presents an evaluation of the placement policies discussed in Section 3.2. For this analysis, we focus on Spark with a 32 GB heap size running on the AMD Magny-Cours

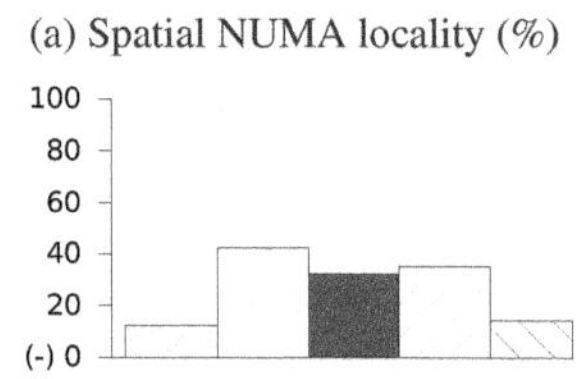

Experiment Name	Heap layout		Node-Local			
	Young	Old	Allocation	Copy	Compact	Root
PSB	Interleaved	Interleaved	No	No	No	No
PSB+Numa	Fragmented	Fragmented	Yes	Yes	Yes	Yes
PSB+Compact	Interleaved	Fragmented	No	Promotion*	Yes	No
PSB+CompRoot	Interleaved	Fragmented	No	Promotion*	Yes	Yes
NAPS	Fragmented	Interleaved	Yes	Yes	No	No

*: Only during promotion to the old generation.

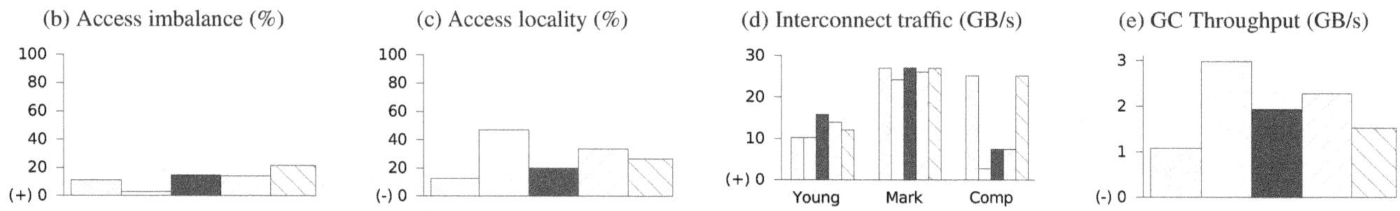

Figure 2. Evaluation of the NUMA-friendly placement policies. (+) = lower is better, (-) = higher is better.

with 48 cores and 8 nodes. The results are similar for the other evaluated applications and on both machines.

Figure 2 reports the following metrics from the experiment:

- *Spatial NUMA locality*: the ratio of number of local references (i.e., between objects on the same node) in the object graph to the total number of references. As for the graph analysis (see Section 3.1), we measure the Spatial NUMA locality on the snapshot of the object graph taken during the 8th full collection. Higher is better.
- *Memory access imbalance*: for each GC thread, we compute the standard deviation of the ratio of number of accesses to each node over the total number of accesses, and then report the average. Lower is better.
- *Memory access locality*: the ratio of local memory accesses (read or write) performed by the GC threads, over the total number of memory accesses. Higher is better.
- *Interconnect traffic*: the average number of GB/s transmitted on the interconnect by a node during collection. We report separately traffic during the young collections, during the marking phases of the full collections, and during the compacting phases of the full collections. Lower is better.
- *GC throughput*: the number of gigabytes of live data scanned per second by the collector. Higher is better.

To characterise the effect of each policy, we compare different variants. The baseline is PSB (see Section 2.4). As indicated in the table of the figure, PSB+Numa extends PSB with fragmented spaces and the four NUMA-friendly placement policies described in Section 3.2. We observe that the policies improves spatial NUMA locality, as the PSB+Numa algorithm increases the fraction of local references from 12% to 42% (see Figure 2.a). We also observe that memory access balance is slightly better with PSB+Numa than with PSB, with a standard deviation of 2.8% vs. 11%, which is already low (see Figure 2.b).

In the rest of this section, the variants PSB+Compact, PSB+CompRoot and NAPS [10] enable a finer-grain comparison. PSB+Compact turns on fragmented spaces only in the old generation, does Node-Local Compacting during a full collection, and does Node-Local Copy when promoting from young to old generation, but not when copying from young to young generation. PSB+CompRoot is the same as PSB+Compact, with the addition of Node-Local Root policy. NAPS uses fragmented spaces in the young generation only, and enables the Node-Local Allocation and Node-Local Copy policies when copying from the young to the young generation, but not when promoting from the young to the old generation.

Thanks to the rebalancing effect of the Node-Local Copy policy used in conjunction with stealing, we observe that memory access balance remains good in all the experiments, with a 20% standard deviation in the worst case (see Figure 2.b). Consequently, we focus only on spatial NUMA locality in what follows.

Spatial NUMA locality Observe that the Node-Local Compact policy, in conjunction with the Node-Local Copy policy during object promotion, yields the highest single improvement of spatial NUMA locality, from 12% with PSB to 32% with PSB+Compact (see Figure 2.a). When a GC thread promotes an object from the young to the old generation, the Node-Local Copy policy copies a root object and its reachable sub-graph to the node of the GC thread, thus avoiding remote references in the object graph. Thereafter, the Node-Local Compact policy preserves this placement during full collections by preventing object migration. We have measured that 75% of the references are between objects of the old generation. For this reason, improving spatial NUMA locality in the old generation has a large impact on the overall spatial NUMA locality, since it concerns a large part of the heap.

Comparing PSB+CompRoot with PSB+Compact, we observe that the Node-Local Root policy alone does not have a significant effect on spatial NUMA locality. In PSB+CompRoot, the young space is interleaved. Memory pages in the heap are allocated in round robin from every nodes, thus, old-to-young root references and young-young references are randomised between the nodes, exactly as in PSB+Compact.

Comparing PSB with NAPS, observe that the Node-Local Copy and Allocation policies alone do not have a significant effect on spatial NUMA locality. NAPS improves it inside the young generation, but old-to-young references are still random because the old space is interleaved. We have measured that only 6% of the references are inside the young generation in Spark; thus NAPS has only a marginal effect on spatial NUMA locality. NAPS uses these two policies, not to improve spatial NUMA locality, but only to improve memory access balance, because the Node-Local Copy policy, in conjunction with stealing, re-balances the load (as explained in Section 3.2).

Comparing PSB+Compact with PSB+Numa, observe that the Node-Local Copy and Allocation policies, when used in conjunction with the two other policies, improve spatial NUMA locality from 32% to 42%. In this case, old-to-young and young-to-old references, which concern 19% of the references, have a better spatial NUMA locality (roughly 50% of these references are local). This is because the conjunction of all the placement policies ensures that objects allocated by some application thread are allocated on its same node, and remain there when they are copied.

To summarise, this study shows that, individually, each of the policy does not have a drastic effect on spatial NUMA locality, but that, when they are used in conjunction, they multiply the spatial NUMA locality by 3.5×.

GC throughput improvements It is interesting to observe that our NUMA-friendly placement policies have the side-effect of improving GC throughput (Figure 2.e). This is because they also improve memory access locality (Figure 2.c).

Node-Local Compaction improves memory access locality, from 13% with PSB to 20% with PSB+Compact. As explained in Section 3.3, a GC thread first processes the regions of its node before stealing, which avoids many remote access during the compacting phase (Figure 2.c). This improved memory access locality drastically reduces interconnect traffic during the compacting phase (7.5 GB/s instead of 25.1 GB/s, see Figure 2.d).

Node-Local Root alone also improves memory access locality substantially, with 33% local access in PSB+CompRoot, compared to 20% for PSB+Compact (Figure 2.c). This is because a GC thread selects old-to-young root objects from its own node during a young collection. Moreover, when combined with the other policies, the Node-Local Copy and Node-Local Allocation policies ensure that a root object generally references objects on the same node. As a result, memory access locality improves substantially, from 33% with PSB+CompRoot, to 47% with PSB+Numa (Figure 2.c).

Overall, the improved memory access locality translates to better GC throughput, reaching 3.0 GB/s with PSB+Numa, compared to 1.0 GB/s for PSB (Figure 2.e).

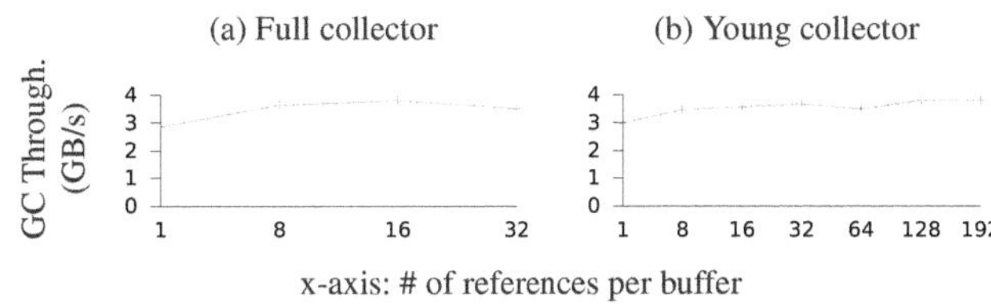

Figure 3. GC throughput of NumaGiC with varying transmit buffer sizes (higher is better).

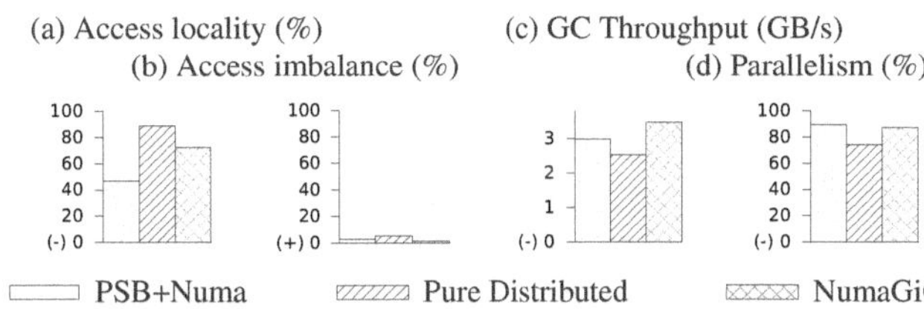

Figure 4. Memory access locality versus parallelism
(-) = higher is better, (+) = lower is better

5.4 Impact of transmit buffer size

One of the internal design parameters of NumaGiC is transmit buffer size (see Section 4.1); we study its impact on performance. For this experiment, we run Spark with the small workload on Amd48. Figure 3 reports the GC throughput of NumaGiC, i.e., the number of gigabytes of live data collected per second, with varying transmit buffer sizes. Figure 3.a varies the buffer size used in the full collector, and sets a fixed size of 128 references for the young collector. Figure 3.b varies the buffer size used by the young collector, and sets the full-collector's buffer size to 16 references.

We observe that performance increases quickly with buffer size. However, the increase ceases around 16 references (resp. 128) for the full (resp. young) collector. Experiments with other applications, not reported here, confirm that these values give good performance, on both Amd48 and on Intel80. Therefore, we retain these values in the rest of our experiments.

5.5 Memory access locality versus parallelism

As stated in the introduction, enforcing memory access locality can be detrimental to parallelism. To highlight this issue, we run Spark with the small workload on Amd48 with three different GC set-ups: PSB+Numa, which adds all the NUMA-friendly placement policies of Section 3.2 to Parallel Scavenge Baseline (PSB), Pure Distributed, a version of NumaGiC in which a GC thread always stay in local mode, and full NumaGiC.

Figure 4 reports three metrics defined in Section 5.3, the memory access locality (a), the memory access imbalance (b) and the GC throughput (c). It also reports the parallelism of the GC (d), defined as the fraction of time where GC threads are not idle. We consider idle time to be the time in the

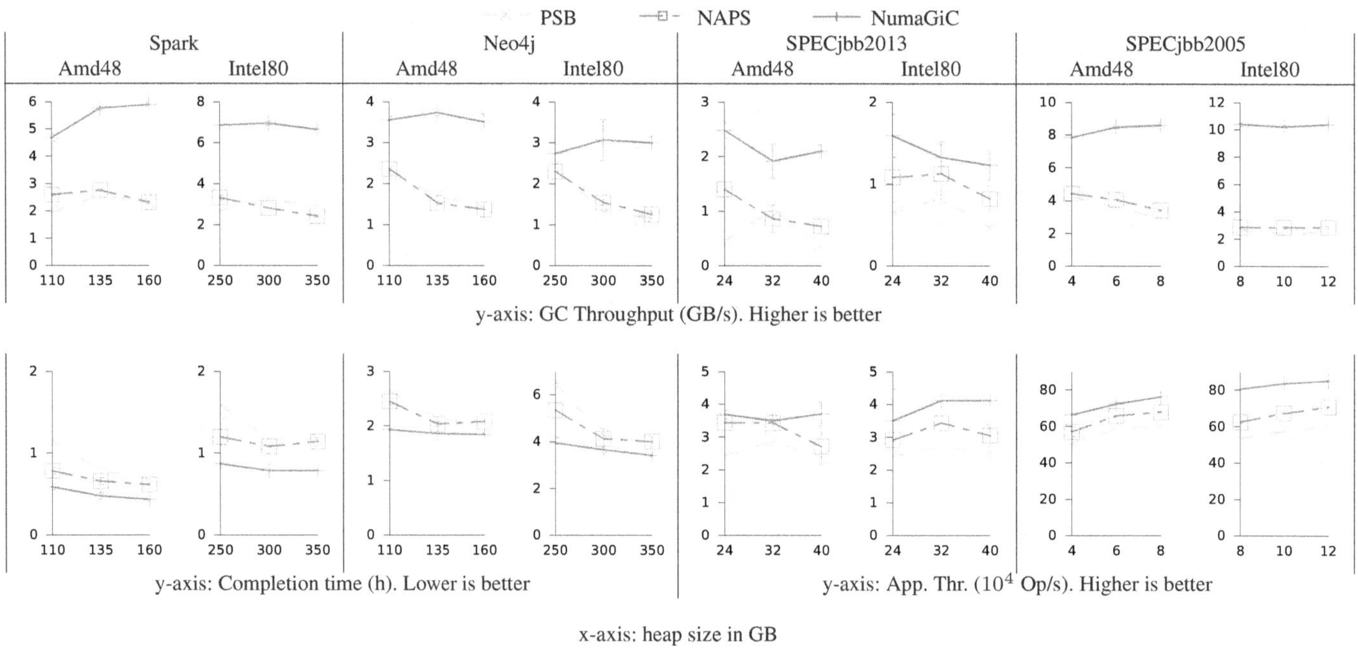

Figure 5. Evaluation of the applications with large heap.

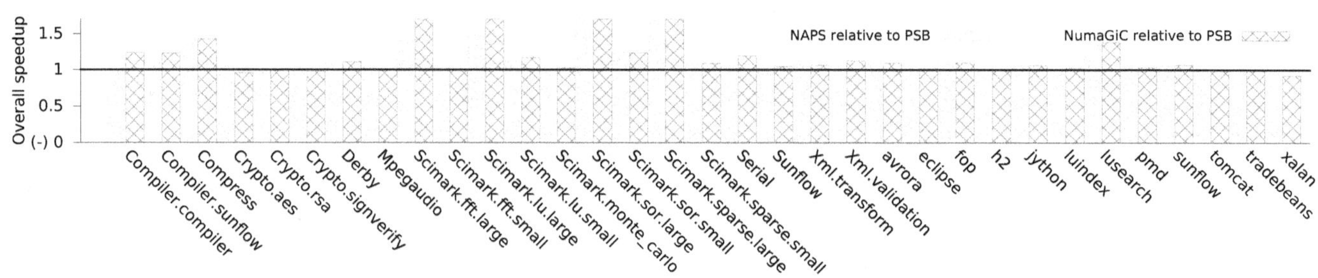

Figure 6. Evaluation of applications with small heap (DaCapo and SPECjvm2008). Higher is better.

termination protocol, *i.e.*, where it synchronises to terminate the parallel phase (see Section 2.3).

We can observe that memory access balance remains good with Pure Distributed (Figure 4.b). However, this observation is not significant. For example, memory allocation, and thus access, is imbalanced with H2, as shown in Table 1. Indeed, by construction, Pure Distributed algorithm does not migrate objects, and therefore, memory access balance by the GC is directly correlated to the allocation pattern of the mutator.

Moreover, for Spark, although Pure Distributed improves memory access locality substantially over PSB+Numa (Figure 4.a), throughput decreases, from 3.0 GB/s down to 2.5 GB/s (Figure 4.c). This is caused by degraded parallelism, because GC threads are idle 26% of the time in the Pure Distributed algorithm, against only 11% in PSB+Numa (Figure 4.d).

Analysing this problem, we observe a sort of a convoy effect, in which nodes take turns, working one after the other. Because the NUMA-friendly policies reinforce spatial NUMA locality, the object graph tends to structure itself into connected components, each one allocated on a single node, and linked to one another across nodes. We observe furthermore that the out-degree of object is small, 2.4 on average, and that the proportion of roots in the full object graph is around 0.008% (roughly 15,000 objects), also quite small. As a result, the number of connected components reached by the full collector at a given point in time tends to be relatively small, and sometimes even restricted to a subset of the nodes. In this case, some GC threads do not have any local work. Since, by design, the pure distributed algorithm prevents remote accesses, the GC threads remain idle, which degrades parallelism.

Observe that NumaGiC corrects this problem by providing the best of the PSB+Numa and the Pure Distributed algorithms. The parallelism of NumaGiC remains at the level of PSB+Numa (11% of idle time for PSB+Numa against 13% for NumaGiC, see Figure 4.d). At the same time, NumaGiC degrades memory access locality slightly, compared to Pure Distributed (from 88% to 72% of local accesses, see Figure 4.a), but it remains largely improved over PSB+Numa (47% of local accesses). Thanks to improved memory access locality GC throughput increases from 3 GB/s in PSB+Numa, to 3.5 GB/s in NumaGiC (Figure 4.c).

5.6 Performance analysis

This sections studies the impact of NumaGiC, both on GC performance (throughput and duration of the GC phase), and on overall performance (how end-to-end application performance is impacted by NumaGiC).

Figure 5 reports GC throughput and overall speedup of Spark (under large workload on Amd48), Neo4j, SPECjbb-2005 and SPECjbb2013 on Amd48 and Intel80. We report the average and standard deviation over 3 runs.

As explained earlier, we vary the heap size. We were unable to identify the minimal heap size for Spark and Neo4j because the runs last too long. For example, on Amd48, the computation of Neo4j lasts for 2h37 with PSB and a heap size of 110 GB, but does not complete even in 12 hours with a heap size of 100 GB. For this reason, for Spark and Neo4j, we use the smallest heap size that ensures that the application terminates in less than 8 hours.

Observe that NumaGiC always improves the GC throughput over NAPS, up to 2.9× on Amd48 and up to 3.6× on Intel80, which translates into an overall improvement (application + GC) up to 42% on Amd48 and up to 45% on Intel80. With heap sizes that provide the best overall performance for all the GC (160 GB on Amd48 and 350 GB on Intel80 for Spark and Neo4j, 8 GB and 12 GB for SPECjbb2005, 40 GB and 40 GB for SPECjbb2013), the overall improvement ranges between 12% and 42% on Amd48 and between 12% and 45% on Intel80.

Figure 6 reports the GC throughput and the speedup, in terms of completion time, of the DaCapo and SPECjvm2008 benchmarks on Amd48. Since these applications have small workloads, we expect the performance impact of GC to be modest. Nonetheless, observe that, compared to NAPS, NumaGiC improves the overall performance of seven of the applications by more than 5% (up to 32% for Scimark.fft.large), does not change it by more than 5% for 25 of them, and degrades performance by more than 5% in a single application (Crypto.AES, degraded by 8%). For this application, GC throughput actually improves, but, as we let Hotspot uses its default resizing policy, this modifies the heap resizing behaviour, causing the number of collections to double. In summary, even for small heaps, 20% of the applications see significant overall improvement thanks to the the better memory access locality of NumaGiC, and with the sole exception of Crypto.AES, NumaGiC never degrades performance relative to NAPS.

To summarise, big-data applications with a large heap benefit substantially from NumaGiC. It significantly improves garbage collector throughput, which translates into a significant overall application improvement. With small heap sizes, NumaGiC is either neutral (most cases), rarely degrades performance somewhat (one application), and improves overall performance in 20% of the evaluated applications. Furthermore, the fact that the improvements remain similar on two different hardware architectures tends to show that our mostly-distributed design is independent from a specific hardware design.

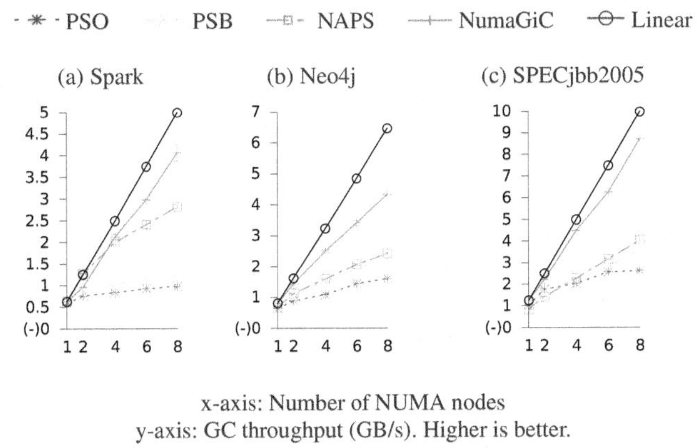

Figure 7. Scalability for three applications with large heap

5.7 Scalability

This section studies the scalability of the garbage collectors discussed in this paper, as the number of NUMA nodes increases. The experiments were conducted on Spark (40GB), Neo4j (32GB), and SPECjbb2005 (6GB). SPECjbb2013 is not included, as its performance exhibits a large standard deviation at low core count, and hence does not provide stable results.

Figure 7 shows the scalability of GC throughput of the original Parallel Scavenge distributed with Hotspot (PSO), our improved version of Parallel Scavenge (PSB), NAPS, and NumaGiC. For comparison, we also plot linear throughput relative to the 1-node performance of NumaGiC.

As shown in the figure, NumaGiC scales substantially better than all the other three GCs. NumaGiC scales almost linearly with SPECjbb2005, slightly less with Spark, and again less with Neo4j. This variation of scalability is directly related to the proportion of clustered objects of each application, as shown in Table 1. An application such as SPECjbb2005 has a high proportion of clustered objects, or in other words low inter-node sharing, which leads to higher scalability. In contrast, Neo4j has a lower proportion of clustered objects, hence lower scalability. In this case, more inter-node shared objects cause more inter-node messages in NumaGiC, which in turn degrades performance.

6. State of the Art

Our work is inspired by multi-kernels [3, 18] and clustered operating systems [22] for multi-core machines. These systems partition memory between cores or NUMA nodes, and communicate via messages. The partitioning avoids remote memory accesses and ensures memory access locality. Our starting point is similar: NumaGiC partitions a Java Virtual Machine's address space between nodes, and isolates nodes during collection, in order to avoid remote memory accesses. However, we showed in Section 5.5 that strict partitioning degrades parallelism, and hence performance. Therefore, we take a pragmatic approach; we relax the local access constraints to avoid leaving GC threads idle, and leverage remote access when beneficial to performance.

The best throughput-oriented stop-the-world GC in the standard HotSpot JVM is Parallel Scavenge, which scales poorly on large-scale multiprocessors [9]. An improved version of Parallel Scavenge called NAPS was proposed by Gidra et al. [10]. NAPS improves memory access balance on a ccNUMA machine. However, as our evaluation shows, the memory access locality of NAPS is poor. Thanks to its adaptive distributed design, NumaGiC has better memory access locality, which translates to a better performance.

Zhou and Demsky [31] designed a parallel NUMA-aware mark-and-compact collector on their proprietary Java Virtual Machine, targeting the TILE-Gx microprocessor family. Zhou and Demsky target relatively small heap sizes, between 1.5 GB and 4 GB, whereas we consider big-data applications with heap sizes of more than 150 GB. Similarly to NumaGiC, in their collector, each core collects its own local memory, and sends messages when it finds remote references. The study of Zhou and Demsky considers only a mark-and-compact algorithm, similar to the one used in the old generation of NumaGiC. In contrast, NumaGiC is a generational GC with two generations with multiple spaces, which complicates the design, especially at the boundary between the spaces. Moreover, Zhou and Demsky focus on the locality of the application and the GC. They do not consider balancing memory access among the nodes, but recent studies showed that unbalanced memory access has a dramatic impact [6, 10]. They do not consider improving spatial NUMA locality, whereas we observe that a distributed design is beneficial only if the number of remote references is low. Finally, although Zhou and Demsky state that restricting GC threads to accessing only local memory can degrade parallelism, they do not observe it in their evaluation, and thus do not propose a solution. Our own evaluation shows that this issue is central to performance.

Ogasawara [19] and Tikir and Hollingsworth [28] study how NUMA effects impact performance of the language runtime. They copy an object to the memory node where it is accessed the most. This aims to improve application locality, but does not address GC locality, as we have done with NumaGiC.

A widely-used technique to improve concurrency is the thread-local heap [1, 7, 16, 20, 27]. With this technique, when first allocated, an object is placed in a heap local to the creating mutator thread. Later, it migrates to a shared global heap only if it becomes referenced from the shared heap. This heap layout supports collecting a thread-local heap concurrently with the mutator threads on the other cores. The partitioned eden space in NumaGiC is similar because it allows a mutator thread to allocate its memory locally, but it has a radically different goal. However, our partitioned eden space could probably be used as a building block towards NUMA thread-local heaps collected currently.

In order to improve memory access balance and locality for native applications, some recent work proposes to migrate, or even to replicate, whole memory pages by observing the memory access pattern of the application at the operating system kernel level [6, 15]. NumaGiC does not use this technique, because, in order to avoid fragmentation, a copying GC continuously moves objects around in memory, obfuscating the memory access patterns observed by the operating system kernel.

7. Conclusion

We presented the rationale and the detailed design of NumaGiC, a mostly-distributed, adaptive GC for ccNUMA architectures. NumaGiC is designed for high throughput, to be used for long-running applications with a large memory footprint, typical of big-data computations.

NumaGiC's distributed design avoids the costly remote accesses of non-NUMA-aware GCs. However, NumaGiC pragmatically uses remote access when it is beneficial to performance, and switches between the local mode (avoiding remote access) and the work-stealing mode (maximising parallelism), according to the current workload. Thanks to this design, NumaGiC demonstrates high memory access locality without loss of parallelism, which translates to a drastic reduction of interconnect traffic, and to a substantial improvement of GC throughput, which translates to an overall speedup between 12% and 45% over NAPS on the two ccNUMA machines for applications with large heaps.

As future work, we plan to study a concurrent GC for ccNUMA architecture, where each node could collect its memory in isolation. Indeed, in applications where responsiveness is important, suspending the application for long GC pauses is not tolerable. These kinds of applications require a concurrent collector, which runs concurrently with the application. Because they need to synchronise at a fine grain with the mutator (to detect changes to the object graph), concurrent collectors are considerably more complex. HotSpot comes with a choice of collectors, including concurrent ones. We observe that they all suffer from poor locality, as they access remote memory nodes roughly 80% of the time, on the 48-core machine. The techniques used in this study to avoid remote access are most likely applicable to a concurrent collector as well. Indeed, they appear unrelated to the concurrent collector's synchronisation with application, since they concern mainly the mapping of the heap on the different nodes and the communication between the GC threads.

References

[1] T. A. Anderson. Optimizations in a private nursery-based garbage collector. In *ISMM '10*, pages 21–30. ACM, 2010.

[2] A. W. Appel. Simple generational garbage collection and fast allocation. *SP&E*, 19(2):171–183, 1989.

[3] A. Baumann, P. Barham, P.-E. Dagand, T. Harris, R. Isaacs, S. Peter, T. Roscoe, A. Schüpbach, and A. Singhania. The multikernel: a new OS architecture for scalable multicore systems. In *SOSP '09*, pages 29–44. ACM, 2009.

[4] S. M. Blackburn, R. Garner, C. Hoffmann, A. M. Khang, K. S. McKinley, R. Bentzur, A. Diwan, D. Feinberg, D. Frampton, S. Z. Guyer, M. Hirzel, A. Hosking, M. Jump, H. Lee, J. E. B. Moss, A. Phansalkar, D. Stefanović, T. VanDrunen, D. von Dincklage, and B. Wiedermann. The DaCapo benchmarks: Java benchmarking development and analysis. In *OOPSLA '06*, pages 169–190. ACM, 2006.

[5] K. M. Chandy and L. Lamport. Distributed snapshots: Determining global states of distributed systems. *TOCS*, 3(1):63–75, 1985.

[6] M. Dashti, A. Fedorova, J. Funston, F. Gaud, R. Lachaize, B. Lepers, V. Quema, and M. Roth. Traffic management: A holistic approach to memory placement on NUMA systems. In *ASPLOS '13*, pages 381–394. ACM, 2013.

[7] D. Doligez and X. Leroy. A concurrent, generational garbage collector for a multithreaded implementation of ml. In *POPL '93*, pages 113–123. ACM, 1993.

[8] Friendster. SNAP: network datasets: Friendster social network. `http://snap.stanford.edu/data/com-Friendster.html`, 2014.

[9] L. Gidra, G. Thomas, J. Sopena, and M. Shapiro. Assessing the scalability of garbage collectors on many cores. In *SOSP Workshop on Programming Languages and Operating Systems, PLOS '11*, pages 1–5. ACM, 2011.

[10] L. Gidra, G. Thomas, J. Sopena, and M. Shapiro. A study of the scalability of stop-the-world garbage collectors on multicores. In *ASPLOS '13*, pages 229–240. ACM, 2013.

[11] H2. H2 database engine. `http://www.h2database.com/`, 2014.

[12] M. Herlihy and N. Shavit. *The Art of Multiprocessor Programming*. Morgan Kaufmann, 2008.

[13] R. Jones, A. Hosking, and E. Moss. *The garbage collection handbook: the art of automatic memory management*. Chapman & Hall/CRC, 1st edition, 2011.

[14] H. Lieberman and C. Hewitt. A real-time garbage collector based on the lifetimes of objects. *CACM*, 26(6):419–429, 1983.

[15] LinuxMemPolicy. What is Linux memory policy? `http://www.kernel.org/doc/Documentation/vm/numa_memory_policy.txt`, 2014.

[16] S. Marlow and S. Peyton Jones. Multicore garbage collection with local heaps. In *ISMM '11*, pages 21–32. ACM, 2011.

[17] Neo4j. Neo4j – the world's leading graph database. `http://www.neo4j.org`, 2014.

[18] E. B. Nightingale, O. Hodson, R. McIlroy, C. Hawblitzel, and G. Hunt. Helios: heterogeneous multiprocessing with satellite kernels. In *SOSP '09*, pages 221–234. ACM, 2009.

[19] T. Ogasawara. NUMA-aware memory manager with dominant-thread-based copying GC. In *OOPSLA '09*, pages 377–390. ACM, 2009.

[20] K. Sivaramakrishnan, L. Ziarek, and S. Jagannathan. Eliminating read barriers through procrastination and cleanliness. In *ISMM '12*, pages 49–60. ACM, 2012.

[21] P. Sobalvarro. A lifetime-based garbage collector for LISP systems on general-purpose computers. Technical report, Cambridge, MA, USA, 1988.

[22] X. Song, H. Chen, R. Chen, Y. Wang, and B. Zang. A case for scaling applications to many-core with OS clustering. In *EuroSys '11*, pages 61–76. ACM, 2011.

[23] Spark. Apache Spark– lightning-fast cluster computing. `http://spark.apache.org`, 2014.

[24] SPECjbb2005. SPECjbb2005 home page. `http://www.spec.org/jbb2005/`, 2014.

[25] SPECjbb2013. SPECjbb2013 home page. `http://www.spec.org/jbb2013/`, 2014.

[26] I. Stanton and G. Kliot. Streaming graph partitioning for large distributed graphs. In *KDD '12*, pages 1222–1230. ACM, 2012.

[27] B. Steensgaard. Thread-specific heaps for multi-threaded programs. In *ISMM '00*, pages 18–24. ACM, 2000.

[28] M. M. Tikir and J. K. Hollingsworth. NUMA-aware Java heaps for server applications. In *IPDPS '05*, pages 108–117. IEEE Computer Society, 2005.

[29] D. Ungar. Generation scavenging: A non-disruptive high performance storage reclamation algorithm. In *SDE '84*, pages 157–167. ACM, 1984.

[30] P. R. Wilson and T. G. Moher. A "card-marking" scheme for controlling intergenerational references in generation-based garbage collection on stock hardware. *SIGPLAN Notice*, 24 (5):87–92, 1989.

[31] J. Zhou and B. Demsky. Memory management for many-core processors with software configurable locality policies. In *ISMM '12*, pages 3–14. ACM, 2012.

This research was supported in part by ANR (France) projects ConcoRDanT (ANR-10-BLAN 0208), Infra-JVM (ANR-11-INFR-008-01) and STREAMS (ANR-2010-SEGI-010-02), and by COST Action IC1001 Euro-TM.

FACADE: A Compiler and Runtime for (Almost) Object-Bounded Big Data Applications

Khanh Nguyen Kai Wang Yingyi Bu Lu Fang Jianfei Hu Guoqing Xu

University of California, Irvine

{khanhtn1, wangk7, yingyib, lfang3, jianfeih, guoqingx}@ics.uci.edu

Abstract

The past decade has witnessed the increasing demands on data-driven business intelligence that led to the proliferation of data-intensive applications. A managed object-oriented programming language such as Java is often the developer's choice for implementing such applications, due to its quick development cycle and rich community resource. While the use of such languages makes programming easier, their automated memory management comes at a cost. When the managed runtime meets Big Data, this cost is significantly magnified and becomes a scalability-prohibiting bottleneck.

This paper presents a novel compiler framework, called FACADE, that can generate highly-efficient data manipulation code by automatically transforming the *data path* of an existing Big Data application. The key treatment is that in the generated code, the number of runtime heap objects created for data types in each thread is (almost) *statically bounded*, leading to significantly reduced memory management cost and improved scalability. We have implemented FACADE and used it to transform 7 common applications on 3 real-world, already well-optimized Big Data frameworks: GraphChi, Hyracks, and GPS. Our experimental results are very positive: the generated programs have (1) achieved a 3%–48% execution time reduction and an up to 88× GC reduction; (2) consumed up to 50% less memory, and (3) scaled to much larger datasets.

Categories and Subject Descriptors D.3.4 [*Programming Languages*]: Processors—Code generation, compilers, memory management, optimization, run-time environments

General Terms Language, Measurements, Performance

ASPLOS '15, March 14–18, 2015, Istanbul, Turkey.

http://dx.doi.org/10.1145/2694344.2694345

Keywords Big Data applications, managed languages, memory management, performance optimization

1. Introduction

Modern computing has entered the era of Big Data. Developing systems that can *scale* to massive amounts of data is a key challenge faced by both researchers and practitioners. The mainstream approach to scalability is to enable distributed processing. As a result, existing platforms utilize large numbers of machines in clusters or in the cloud; data are partitioned among machines so that many processors can work simultaneously on a task. Typical parallel frameworks include, to name a few, FlumeJava [20], Giraph [9], GPS [58], Hive [61], Hadoop [10], Hyracks [16], Spark [74], Storm [63], and Pig [56].

However, all of these Big Data systems are written in managed languages (i.e., Java and Scala), which are known for their simple usage, easy memory management, and large community support. While these languages simplify development effort, their managed runtime has a high cost—often referred to as *runtime bloat* [53, 65, 67–71]—which cannot be amortized by increasing the number of data-processing machines in a cluster. Poor performance on each node reduces the scalability of the entire cluster: a large number of machines are needed to process a small dataset, resulting in excessive use of resources and increased communication overhead. This paper explores a new direction to scale Big Data systems, that is, how to effectively optimize the managed runtime of a data processing system to improve its performance and scalability on each machine.

1.1 Motivation

The managed runtime suffers from two major performance issues: excessive use of pointers and references leading to high space overhead (and thus low memory packing factors) as well as frequent GC runs preventing the main threads from making satisfactory progress. Comprehensive studies across many contemporary Big Data systems [18] confirm that these overheads lead to significantly reduced scalability—e.g., applications crash with `OutOfMemoryError`, although the size of the processed dataset is much smaller than the heap size—as well as exceedingly high memory management costs—e.g., the GC time accounts for up to 50% of the overall execution time. Despite the many optimizations [6, 7, 16, 19, 21, 23–25, 33, 38, 41, 45, 48, 49, 52, 54–57, 60, 61, 72, 73, 76] from various research communities, poor performance inherent with the managed runtime remains a serious problem that can devaluate these domain-specific optimization techniques.

Switching back to an unmanaged language such as C or C++ appears to be a reasonable choice. However, unmanaged languages are more error-prone; debugging memory problems in an unmanaged language is known to be a painful task, which can be further exacerbated by the many "Big Data" effects, such as distributed execution environment, extremely large numbers of data items, and long running time. Furthermore, since a great number of existing Big Data frameworks were already developed in a managed language (e.g., Java and Scala), it is unrealistic to re-implement them from scratch. The proposed work aims to solve this fundamental problem by developing a systematic optimization technique that can dramatically improve the performance of a wide variety of Java-based Big Data systems while still allowing the developers to enjoy all the benefits of a managed programming language.

1.2 Observations

Our first observation is that there exists a clear boundary between the *control path* and the *data path* in a Big Data system. The control path organizes tasks into pipelines and performs optimizations, while the data path represents and manipulates data. Although the data path creates most of the runtime objects, its implementation is rather simple and its code size is often small. For instance, in a typical Big Data application that runs on a shared-nothing cluster, a driver controls the pipeline execution on the master node, while each slave node runs data manipulation algorithms (e.g., hashing, sorting, or grouping) to manipulate data. The driver belongs to the control path that does not touch any data, while data manipulation functions belong to the data path that creates massive number of objects to represent and process data items.

Our second observation is that to develop a scalable system, the number of *data objects and their references in the heap* must *not* grow proportionally with the cardinality of the dataset. It is often harmless, however, to create objects in the control path, because their numbers are very small and independent of the size of the input. Our ultimate goal is, thus, to significantly reduce the object representations of data items so that they are not subject to the regular Java memory management. A straightforward way to achieve the goal is to modify a JVM to create a new (data) heap (in parallel with the original heap) and allocate all data objects in this heap. The GC does not scan the data heap, whose memory can be reclaimed either manually or by techniques such as region-based memory management [14, 29, 30, 32, 35, 37, 50]. While this approach appears promising, its implementation dictates a major re-design of the runtime system in a commercial JVM—a metacircular JVM such as Jikes RVM often does not support very large heaps—which makes it difficult to prototype and deploy in real-world settings.

1.3 Contributions

To improve practicality, this paper presents a *non-intrusive* technique, named FACADE, an alternative approach that aims to reduce the cost of the managed runtime by limiting the number of heap objects and references at the compiler level, without needing any JVM modification. FACADE contains a novel compiler framework—as well as its runtime support—that can *statically bound* the number of heap objects representing data items in each thread. This is achieved by breaking a long-held object-oriented programming principle: objects are used both to store data and to provide data manipulation interfaces.

FACADE advocates to separate data storage from data manipulation: data are stored in the off-heap, native memory (i.e., unbounded) while heap objects are created as *facades* only for control purposes such as function calls (i.e., bounded). As the program executes, a *many-to-one mapping* is maintained between arbitrarily many data items in native memory and a statically bounded set of facade objects in the heap. In other words, each facade keeps getting reused to represent data items. An iteration-based memory management mechanism is used to reclaim data items from native memory: data records allocated in one iteration are deallocated as a whole at the end of the iteration. The GC only scans the managed heap, which contains a very small number of control objects and facades.

To enforce this model, we develop a compiler that can transform an existing Big Data program into an (almost) object-bounded program: the number of heap objects created for a data type in one thread is bounded by certain source code properties (i.e., a compile-time constant). More formally, FACADE reduces the number of data objects from $O(s)$ to $O(t * n + p)$, where s represents the cardinality of the dataset, t is the number of threads, n is the number of data types, and p is the number of page objects used to store data. Details of these bounds can be found in §3.4.

In practice, the reduction is often in the scale of several orders of magnitude. As an example, for GraphChi [41], a single-machine graph processing system, FACADE has reduced the number of objects created for vertices and edges from $14,257,280,923$ to $1,363$. Although t and p cannot be bounded statically, they are usually very small, and hence the total number of objects is "almost" statically bounded. Since data items are no longer represented by heap objects, the space overhead due to headers and pointers are significantly reduced; furthermore, the managed heap becomes much smaller, resulting in reduced GC effort. For instance, the execution of the transformed page rank program in GraphChi with the *twitter-2010* graph [40] is 27% faster, consumes 28% less memory, and has 84% less GC time than the original program.

Why does* FACADE *operate at the right level? There exists a body of work that attempts to reduce the number of objects in a Java execution by employing different levels of techniques, ranging from programming guidelines [28] through static program analyses [15, 22, 26, 46, 59] to low-level systems support [66]. Despite the commendable efforts of these techniques, none of them are practical enough to improve performance for large-scale Big Data programs: sophisticated interprocedural static analyses (such as escape analysis [22] and object inlining [26]) cannot scale to highly framework-intensive codebases while purely systems-based techniques (such as Resurrector [66]) cannot scale to large heaps with billions of objects.

The design of FACADE crosses the layers of compiler and runtime system, exploiting native memory to represent data objects instead of using static analysis to eliminate them. Practicality is the main reason for this design. On one hand, the design enables our compiler to perform simple local (method[1]-based) code transformation, making it possible for FACADE to scale to a large codebase. On the other hand, the combination of code transformation and the leveraging of the native memory support from a commercial JVM eliminates the need to modify the JVM, enabling FACADE to scale to a very large heap.

The FACADE compiler is implemented in the Soot compiler framework [4, 64] and supports most of the Java 7 features. The user's effort is reasonably small: she only needs to (1) identify iterations, which are often very well-defined in Big Data frameworks, as well as (2) specify the data path by providing a list of Java classes to be transformed. FACADE automatically synthesizes data conversion functions for data types that flow across the boundary and inserts calls to these functions at appropriate program points to convert data formats. We have applied FACADE to 7 commonly-used applications on 3 real-world, already well-optimized Big Data frameworks: GraphChi, Hyracks, and GPS. Our experimental results demonstrate that (1) the transformation is very fast (e.g., less than 20 seconds), and (2) the generated code is much more efficient and scalable than the original code (e.g., runs up to 2× faster, consumes up to 2× less memory, and scales to much larger datasets).

2. The FACADE Execution Model

This section discusses the FACADE execution model and gives an overview of the proposed transformation technique.

2.1 Data Storage Based on Native Memory

We propose to store data records in native memory. Similarly to regular memory allocation, our data allocation operates at the page granularity. A memory page is a fixed-length contiguous block of memory in the off-heap native memory, obtained through a JVM's native support.

[1] We use terms "method" and "function" interchangeably.

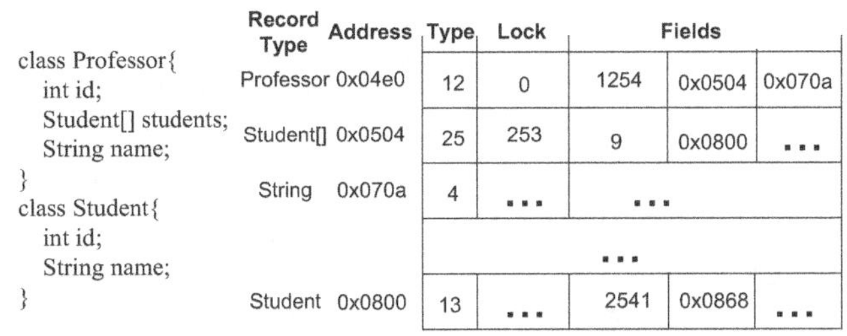

Figure 1. A data structure in regular Java and its corresponding data layout in a native page.

To provide a better memory management interface, each native page is wrapped into a Java object, with functions that can be inserted by the compiler to manipulate the page. Note that the number of page objects (i.e., p in $O(t * n + p)$) cannot be statically bounded in our system, as it depends on the amount of data to be processed. However, by controlling the size of each page and recycling pages, we often need only a small number of pages to process a large dataset. The scalability bottleneck of an object-oriented Big Data application lies in the creation of small data objects and data structures containing them; our system aims to bound their numbers.

From a regular Java program P, FACADE generates a new program P', in which the data contents of each instantiation of a data class are stored in a native memory page rather than in a heap object. To facilitate transformation, the way a data record is stored in a page is exactly the same as the way it was stored in an object.

Figure 1 shows the data layout for an example data structure in our page-based storage system. Each data record (which used to be represented by an object in P) starts with a 2-byte type ID, representing the type of the record. For example, the IDs for `Professor`, `Student[]`, `String`, and `Student` are 12, 25, 4, and 13, respectively. These types will be used to implement virtual method dispatch during the execution of P'. Type ID is followed by a 2-byte lock field, which stores the ID of a lock when the data record is used to synchronize a block of code. We find it sufficient to use 2 bytes to represent class IDs and lock IDs: the number of data classes is often much smaller than 2^{15}; so is the number of distinct locks needed. Details of the lock implementation and the concurrency support can be found in §3.4.

For an array record, the length of the array (4 bytes) is stored immediately after the lock ID. In the example, the number of student records in the array is 9. The actual data contents (originally stored in object fields) are stored subsequently. For instance, field `id` of the professor record contains an integer 1254; the fields `students` and `name` contain memory addresses `0x0504` and `0x070a`, respectively.

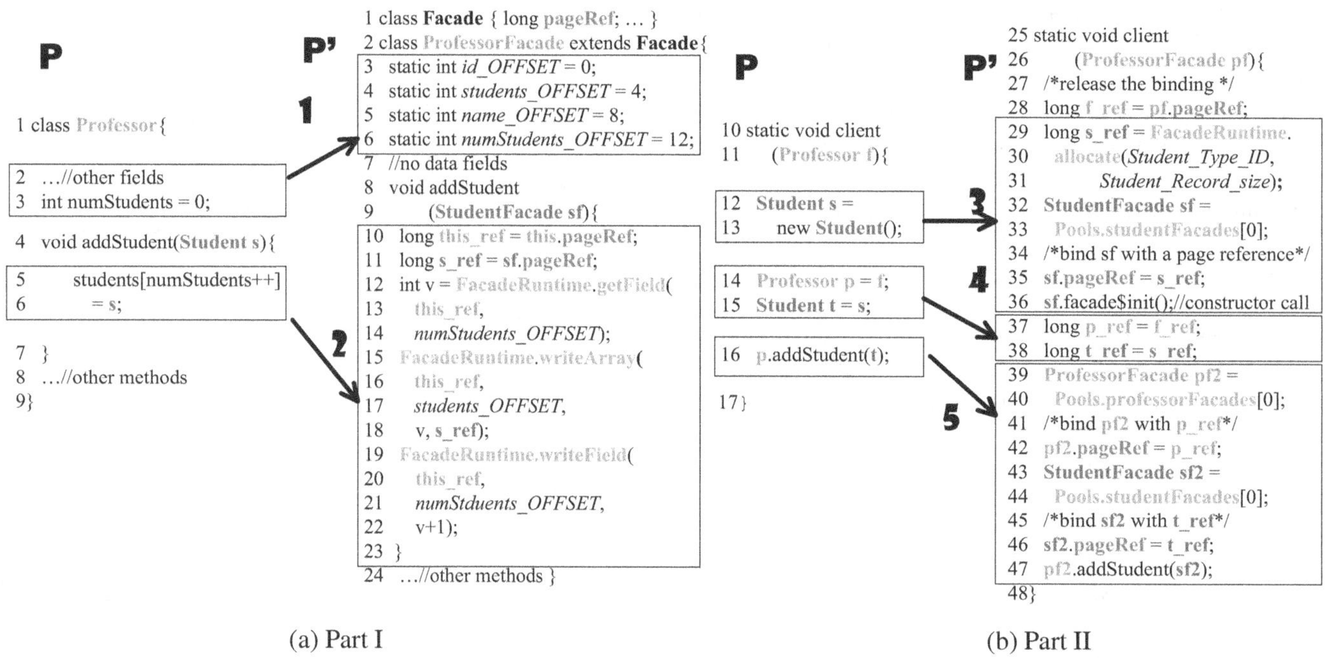

Figure 2. A transformation example.

2.2 Using Objects as Facades

We propose to create heap objects as *facades* for a data type, that is, they are used only for *control* purposes such as method calls, parameter passing, or dynamic type checks, but do *not* contain actual data. Figure 2 depicts an example with five transformations. Suppose all fields of the `Professor` class in Figure 1 are also in the `Professor` class in Figure 2 (a). For simplicity of illustration, we show the original, unoptimized version of the generated program, under the assumption that the program is single-threaded and free of virtual calls. We will discuss the support of these features later.

Figure 2 (a) shows the class transformation. For illustration, let us suppose both `Professor` and `Student` are data classes. For `Professor`, FACADE generates a facade class `ProfessorFacade`, containing all methods defined in `Professor`. `ProfessorFacade` extends class `Facade`, which has a field `pageRef` that records the page-based reference of a data record (such as `0x0504` in Figure 1). Setting a page reference to the field `pageRef` of a facade *binds* the data record with the facade, so that methods defined in the facade will be invoked to process this record. A reader can think of this field as the `this` reference in a regular Java program.

Transformation 1 `ProfessorFacade` does not contain any instance field; for each instance field f in `Professor`, `ProfessorFacade` contains a static field *f_Offset*, specifying the offset (in numbers of bytes) of f to the starting address of the data record. These offsets will be used to transform field accesses.

Transformation 2 For method `addStudent` in `Professor`, FACADE generates a new method with the same name in `ProfessorFacade`. First, its signature is changed in such a way that if a parameter has a data class type (e.g., `Student`) in P, it now has a facade type (e.g., `StudentFacade`) in P'. Since a facade does not contain actual data, the new facade parameter *sf* in P' is used only to pass the page reference of the data record that corresponds to the original parameter in P. The first task inside the generated method is to retrieve the page references (line 10 and 11 in P') from the receiver (i.e., `this`) and *sf*, and keeps them in two local variables *this_ref* and *s_ref*. Any subsequent statement that uses objects (pointed to by) `this` and s in P will be transformed to use the page references *this_ref* and *s_ref* in P', respectively. The field accesses at lines 5 and 6 in P are transformed to three separate calls to our library methods that read values from and write values to a page. Note that what is written into the array is the page reference *s_ref* pointing to a student record—all references to regular data objects in P are substituted by page references in P'.

Transformation 3 The allocation at lines 12–13 in P is transformed to lines 29–36 in P'. FACADE allocates space based on the student size by calling a library method `allocate`, which returns a page reference *s_ref*. Since the allocation in P involves a constructor call, we need to generate a new call in P'. The challenge is how to find a receiver (facade) object on which the call can be made. FACADE generates code to retrieve an available `StudentFacade` object from the pool (lines 32–33 in P') and bind it with the page reference *s_ref* (lines 35). In this case, the first facade in the pool is always available; the reason will be explained shortly. The constructor in P is converted to a regular method `facade$init` in P'. FACADE generates a call to `facade$init` on the retrieved facade object (line 36).

Transformation 4 Variable assignments (lines 14–15) in P are transformed into page reference assignments (lines 37–38) in P'.

Transformation 5 Similarly, a call to `addStudent` on the `Professor` object in P (line 16) is transformed to a call to the same method on the `ProfessorFacade` object in P' (line 47). However, before generating the call site at line 47, we have to emit additional code to prepare for (1) the receiver `ProfessorFacade` object *pf2* and (2) the parameter `StudentFacade` object *sf2*. This preparation can be done in a similar manner by requesting available facades from different pools and binding them with the corresponding references (lines 39–46).

2.3 Bounding the Number of Facades in Each Thread

Since a facade is used only to carry a page reference for a control task (e.g., parameter passing, value returning, etc.), the facade is available for reuse once the page reference it carries is loaded to a stack variable—from this point on, the page reference will be propagated and used. A key treatment here is that for a pair of instructions (e.g., s and t) that bind a facade with a page reference and release the binding, our compiler guarantees that t is the immediate successor of s on the data dependence graph. In other words, no instructions between s and t can read or write the facade object accessed by s or t. Examples of such instruction pairs include lines 42 and 10, and lines 46 and 11 in P' of Figure 2.

The facade is reusable immediately after instruction t to carry other page references. This treatment enables an important property in (each thread of) P': *for any control instruction that needs a facade of a data type, all facades in the pool for the type are available for use.* This explains why it is always safe to use the first facade of the pool at lines 33, 40, and 44. Data instructions that access the heap do not need facades because they have been transformed to access native memory using page references.

Clearly, the number of facades needed for a data type depends on the number of operands of this type needed in a control instruction. For example, if a call site in P requires n arguments of type `Student`, we need at least n `StudentFacade` objects in P' for parameter passing (e.g., `Pools.studentFacades[0]`, ..., `Pools.studentFacades[`n `- 1]`). Since a call instruction takes many more operands than other kinds of instructions, it is often the case that the number of facades for type `DFacade` in P' is bounded by the maximal number of arguments of type `D` required by a call in P. Based on this observation, we can inspect all call sites in P in a pre-transformation pass and compute a bound statically for each data type. The bound will be used to determine the size of the facade pool for the type (e.g., `Pools.studentFacades`) *statically*.

This property of P' distinguishes our approach from traditional object pooling, which often requires explicit (runtime) support for requesting/returning objects from/to the pool and does not provide any bound guarantee. A detailed discussion on how FACADE differs from object pooling can be found in § 5.

It is easy to see that at different points, different facades may be retrieved from the pool to carry the same page reference. For instance, in Figure 2 (b), although variable p (line 16) and parameter f (line 11) refer to the same object in P, their corresponding facades *pf* and *pf2* in P' may not be the same. In a single-threaded execution, this would not cause any inconsistency because page references determine data records and facades are used only to execute control flow. Multithreading will be discussed in §3.4.

2.4 Performance Benefits

P' has the following clear advantages over P. First, each data record has only a 4-byte "header" space (8 bytes for an array) in P' while the size of an object header is 12 bytes (16 bytes for an array) in P. This is due to the reduction of the lock space as well as the complete elimination of space used for GC. Second, all data records are stored in native pages and no longer subject to garbage collection. This can lead to an orders-of-magnitude reduction on the number of nodes and edges traversed by the GC. Third, native-memory-based data storage reduces the memory access cost. In addition, FACADE inlines all data records whose size can be statically determined, which improves data locality and reduces the cost of memory dereferences.

3. FACADE Design and Implementation

To use FACADE, a user needs to provide a list of data classes that form the data path of an application. Our compiler transforms the data path to page allocate objects representing data items without touching the control path. This handling enables the design of simple intraprocedural analysis and transformation as well as aggressive optimizations (such as type specialization), making it possible for FACADE to scale to large-scale framework-intensive systems. While our transformations can be formalized and their correctness can be proved, we describe them in plain language to make the paper accessible to a broad community of researchers and practitioners.

3.1 Our Assumptions

Based on the (user-provided) list of data classes, FACADE makes two important "closed-world" assumptions. The first one is a *reference-closed-world* assumption that requires all reference-typed fields declared in a data class to have data types. This is a valid assumption—there are two major kinds of data classes in a Big Data application: classes representing data tuples (e.g., graph nodes and edges) and those representing data manipulation functions, such as sorter, grouper, etc. Both kinds of classes rarely contain fields of non-data types. Java supports a collections framework and data structures in this framework can store both data objects and non-data objects. In FACADE, a collection (e.g., HashMap) is treated as a data type; a new type (e.g., HashMapFacade) is thus generated in the data path. The original type is still used in the control path. If FACADE detects a data object flows from the control path to the data path or a paged data record flows the other way around, it automatically synthesizes a *data conversion function* to convert data formats. Detailed discussion can be found in §3.5.

The second assumption is a *type-closed-world* assumption that requires that for a data class c, c's superclasses (except `java.lang.Object`, which is the root of the class hierarchy in Java) and subclasses must be data classes. This is also a valid assumption because a data class usually does not inherit a non-data class (and vice versa). The assumption makes it possible for us to determine the field layout of a data record in a page—fields declared in a superclass are stored before fields in a subclass and their offsets can all be statically computed. A special handling here is that we allow both a data class and a non-data class to implement the same Java interface (such as `Comparable`). Doing this will not create any page layout issue because an interface does not contain instance fields. FACADE checks these two assumptions before transformation and reports compilation errors upon violations. The developer needs to refactor the program to fix the violations.

3.2 Data Class Transformation

Class hierarchy transformation For each method m in a data class D, FACADE generates a new method m' in a facade class *DFacade* such that m and m' have the same name; for each parameter of a data class type T in m, m' has a corresponding parameter of a facade type *TFacade*. If D extends another data class E, this relationship is preserved by having *DFacade* extends *EFacade*. All static fields declared in D are also in *DFacade*; however, *DFacade* does not contain any instance field.

One challenge here is how to appropriately handle Java interfaces. If an interface I is implemented by both a data class C and a non-data class D, and the interface has a method that has a data-class type parameter, changing the signature of the method will create inconsistencies. In this case, we create a new interface *IFacade* with the modified method and make all facades *DFacade* implement *IFacade*. While traversing the class hierarchy to transform classes, FACADE generates a type ID for each transformed class. This type ID is actually used as a pointer that points to a facade pool corresponding to the type—upon a virtual dispatch, the type ID will be used to retrieve a facade of the appropriate type at run time.

Instruction transformation Instruction transformation is performed on the control flow graph (CFG) of a SSA-based intermediate representation (IR). The output of the transformation is a new CFG containing the same basic block structures but different instructions in each block. The transformations for different kinds of instructions are summarized in Table 1. Here we discuss only a few interesting cases. For a field write in (i.e., $a.f = b$ in case 3), if b has a data type but a does not (case 3.3), FACADE considers this write as an *interaction point* (IP), an operation at which data flows across the control-data boundary. FACADE synthesizes a data conversion function `long convertToB(B)` that converts data format from a paged data record back to a heap object (see §3.5). If a has a data type but b does not (case 3.4), FACADE generates a compilation error as our first assumption (that data types cannot reference non-data types) is violated. The developer needs to refactor the program to make it FACADE-transformable.

An IP may also be a load that reads a data object from a non-data object (case 4.3) or a method call that passes a data object into a method in the control path (case 6.3). At each IP, data conversion functions will be synthesized and invoked to convert data formats. Note that data conversion often occurs before the execution of the data path or after it is done. Hence, these data conversion functions would often not be executed many times and cause much overhead.

Resolving types In two cases, we need to emit a call to a method named `resolve` to resolve the runtime type corresponding to a page reference. First, when a virtual call $a.m(b, \ldots)$ is encountered (case 6.1), the type of the receiver variable a often cannot be statically determined. Hence, we generate a call `resolve`(a_ref), which uses the type ID of the record pointed to by a_ref to find a facade of the appropriate type. However, since this information can be obtained only at run time, it creates difficulties for the compiler to select a facade object as the receiver from the pool (i.e., what index i should be used to access `Pools.aFacades`[i]).

To solve the problem, we maintain a separate *receiver facade pool* for each data type. The pool contains only a single facade object; the `resolve` method always returns the facade from this pool, which is separated from the parameter pool. Note that we do not need to resolve the type of a parameter (say b), because b is not used as a receiver to call a method. We can simply obtain a facade from the parameter pool based on b's declared (static) type, and use it to carry b's page reference.

The second case in which we need a `resolve` is the handling of an `instanceof` type check, which is shown in case 7 of Table 1.

3.3 Computing Bounds

Before the transformation, FACADE inspects parameters of each method in the data path to compute a bound for each data type. This bound will be used as the length of the facade array (i.e., the parameter pool) for the type. Note that the bound computation is based merely on the static types of parameters. Although a parameter with a general type may receive an object of a specific type at run time, a facade of the

Instructions in P	*Conditions*	*Code generation in* P'
(1) Method prologue	(1.1) s is a parameter of data type in P	Create a variable s_ref for each facade parameter sf; emit instruction $s\_ref = sf.pageRef$; add $\langle s, s\_ref\rangle$ into the variable-reference table v
(2) $a = b$	(2.1) a has a data type	Look up table v to find the reference variable b_ref for b; emit instruction $a\_ref = b\_ref$; add $\langle a, a\_ref\rangle$ into v
	(2.2) Otherwise	Generate $a = b$
(3) $a.f = b$	(3.1) Both a and b have data types	Retrieve a_ref and b_ref from table v; emit a call `setField` (a_ref, f_Offset, b_ref)
	(3.2) None of them have a data type	Emit $a.f = b$
	(3.3) b has a data type, a doesn't (Interaction Point)	Synthesize a data conversion function $B\ covertToB(long)$; emit a call $a.f = convertToB(b\_ref)$
	(3.4) a has a data type, b doesn't	Assumption violation; generate a compilation error
(4) $b = a.f$	(4.1) Both a and b have data types	Retrieve a_ref from table v; emit a call b_ref = `getField` (a_ref, f_Offset); add $\langle b, b\_ref\rangle$ into v
	(4.2) None of them have a data type	Emit instruction $b = a.f$
	(4.3) a has a data type, b doesn't (Interaction Point)	Synthesize a data conversion function $long\ covertFromB(B)$; emit a call $b\_ref = convertFromB(a.f)$; add $\langle b, b\_ref\rangle$ into v
	(4.4) b has a data type but a doesn't	Assumption violation; generate a compilation error
(5) $return\ a$	(5.1) a has a data type	Retrieve a_ref from v; emit three instructions: $AFacade\ af = Pools.aFacades[0]$; $af.pageRef = a\_ref$; $return\ af$
	(5.2) Otherwise	Emit instruction $return\ a$
(6) $a.m(\ldots, b, \ldots)$	(6.1) Both a and b have data types; b is the i-th parameter that has type B	Retrieve a_ref and b_ref from table v; emit five instructions: $AFacade\ af = resolve(a\_ref)$; $BFacade\ bf = Pools.bFacades[i]$; $af.pageRef = a\_ref$; $bf.pageRef = b\_ref$; $af.m(\ldots, bf, \ldots)$
	(6.2) a has a data type, b doesn't	Emit the same instructions as (6.1), except the last call is $af.m(\ldots, b, \ldots)$
	(6.3) b has a data type, a doesn't (Interaction Point)	Synthesize function $B\ covertToB(long)$; emit a call $a.m(\ldots, covertToB(b\_ref), \ldots)$
	(6.4) None of them have a data type	Emit a call $a.m(\ldots, b, \ldots)$
(7) $boolean\ t = a$ $instanceof\ B$	(7.1) a has a data type and B is a data type	Retrieve a_ref from v; emit two instructions: $AFacade\ af = resolve(a\_ref)$; $t = af\ instanceof\ BFacade$
	(7.2) B is an array type	Emit $t = arrayTypeID(a) == ID(B)$
	(7.3) None of them have a data type	Emit $t = a\ instanceof\ B$

Table 1. A summary of code generation; suppose variables a and b have types A and B, respectively.

general type will be sufficient to carry the page reference of the data record (as discussed above) from a caller to a callee. Since we use a separate pool for receivers, the target method will always be executed appropriately. If the declared type of a parameter is an *abstract* type (such as interface) that cannot have concrete instances, we find an arbitrary (concrete) subtype c of this abstract type, and attribute the parameter to c when computing bounds. FACADE generates code to retrieve a facade from c's pool to pass the parameter.

Once the bound for each data type is calculated, FACADE generates the class `Pools` by allocating, for each type, an array as a field whose length is the bound of the type. The array will be used as the parameter pool for the type. FACADE generates an additional field in `Pools` that references its receiver pool (i.e., one single facade) for the type. Eventually, FACADE emits an `init` method in `Pools`, which will be invoked by our library to create facade instances and populate parameter pools.

3.4 Supporting Concurrency

Naïvely transforming a multi-threaded program may introduce concurrency bugs. For example, in P', two concurrent threads may simultaneously write different page references into the same facade object, leading to a data race. The problem can be easily solved by performing thread-local facade pooling: for each data type, the receiver pool and the regular pool are maintained for each thread. We implement this by associating one instance of class `Pools` with each thread;

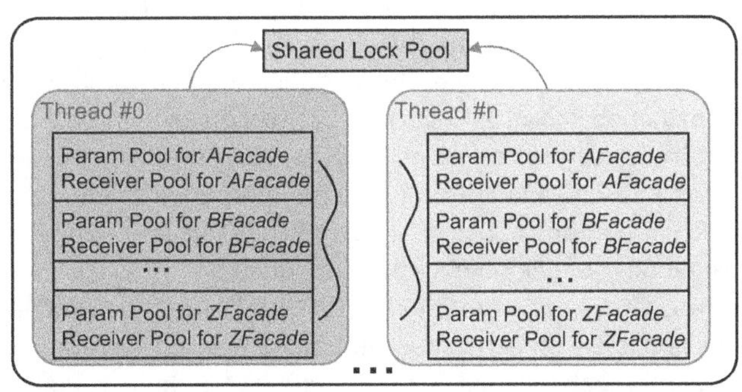

Figure 3. A graphical representation of threads and pools, where *AFacade*, *BFacade*, …, and *ZFacade* are facade types.

the `init` method (discussed in §3.3) is invoked upon the creation of the thread.

Both implicit and explicit locks are supported in Java. Explicit locking is automatically supported by FACADE: all `Lock` and `Thread` related classes are in the control path and not modified by FACADE. For implicit locking (i.e., the intrinsic lock in an object is used), we need to add additional support to guarantee the freedom of race conditions. One possible solution is as follows: for each object o that is used as a lock in a `synchronized` $(o)\{\ldots\}$ construct (i.e., which is translated to an `enterMonitor`(o) and an `exitMonitor`(o) instruction to protect the code in between), FACADE emits code to obtain a facade o' corresponding to o (if o has a data type) and then generates a new construct `synchronized` $(o')\{\ldots\}$. However, this handling may introduce data races—for two code regions protected by the same object in P, two different facades (and thus distinct locks) may be obtained in P' to protect them.

We solve the problem by implementing a special lock class and creating a new *lock pool* (shown in Figure 3) that is shared among threads; each object in the pool is an instance of the lock class. The lock pool maintains an atomic bit vector, each set bit of which indicates a lock being used. For each `enterMonitor`(o) instruction in P, FACADE generates code that first checks whether the lock field of the data record corresponding to o already contains a lock ID. If it does, we retrieve the lock from the pool using the ID; otherwise, our runtime consults the bit vector to find the first available lock (say l) in the pool, writes its index into the record, and flips the corresponding bit. We replace o with l in `enterMonitor` and `exitMonitor`, so that l will be used to protect the critical section instead.

Each lock has a field that keeps track of the number of threads currently blocking on the lock; it is incremented upon an `enterMonitor` and decremented upon an `exitMonitor`. If the number becomes zero at an `exitMonitor`, we return the lock to the pool, flip its corresponding bit, and zeroing out the lock space of the data record. Operations such as `wait` and `notify` will be performed on the lock object inside the block.

Worst-case object numbers in P and P' In P, each data item needs an object representation, and thus, the number of heap objects needed is $O(s)$, where s is the cardinality of the input dataset. In P', each thread has a facade pool for a data type. Since the number of facades needed for a data type is a compile-time constant, the total number of facades in the system is $O(t * n)$, where t and n are the numbers of threads and data types, respectively. Considering the additional objects created to represent native pages, the number of heap objects needed in P' is $O(t * n + p)$, where p is the number of native pages.

Note that the addition of the lock pool does not change this bound. The number of lock objects needed first depends on the number of synchronized blocks that can be concurrently executed (i.e., blocks protected by distinct locks), which is bounded by the number of threads t. Since intrinsic locks in Java are reentrant, the number of locks required in each thread also depends on the depth of nested synchronized blocks, which is bounded by the maximal depth of runtime call stack in a JVM, a compile-time constant. Hence, the number of lock objects is $O(t)$ and the total number of objects in the application is still $O(t * n + p)$.

3.5 Data Conversion Functions

For each IP that involves a data type D, FACADE automatically synthesizes a conversion function for D; this function will be used to convert the format of the data before it crosses the boundary. An IP can be either an *entry* point at which data flows from the control path into the data path or an *exit* point at which data flows in a reverse direction. For an entry point, a `long convertFromA(A)` method is generated for each involved data type A; the method reads each field in an object of A (using reflection) and writes the value into a page. Exit points are handled in a similar manner.

3.6 Memory Allocation and Page Management

The FACADE runtime system maintains a list of pages, each of which has a 32K space (i.e., a common practice in the database design [31]). To improve allocation performance, we classify pages into size classes (similarly to what a high-performance allocator would do for a regular program), each used to allocate objects that fall into a different size range. When allocating a data record on a page, we apply the following two allocation policies whenever possible: (1) continuous allocation requests get contiguous space (to maximize locality); (2) large arrays are allocated on empty pages: allocating them on non-empty pages may cause them to span multiple pages, therefore increasing access costs. Otherwise, we request memory from the first page on the list that has enough space for the record. To allow fast allocation for multithreading, we create a distinct *page manager* (that maintains separate size classes and pages) per thread so that different threads concurrently allocate data records on their thread-local pages.

The data path is *iteration-based*. We define an iteration to be a repeatedly executed block of code such that the lifetimes of data objects created in different executions of this block are completely disjoint. In a typical Big Data program, a dataset is often partitioned before being processed; different iterations of a data manipulation algorithm (e.g., sorting, hashing, or other computations) then process distinct partitions of the dataset. Hence, pages requested in one iteration of P' are released all at once when the iteration ends. Although different Big Data frameworks have different ways of implementing the iteration logic, there often exists a clear mark between different iterations, e.g., a call to start to begin an iteration and a call to flush to end it.

We rely on a user-provided pair of iteration-start and iteration-end calls to determine when to recycle pages. Our experience with a variety of applications shows that iterations are often very well defined and program points to place these calls can be easily found even by novices without much understanding of the program logic. For example, in GraphChi [41], a single-machine graph processing framework, iteration-start and iteration-end are the callbacks explicitly defined by the framework. Although we had zero knowledge about this framework, it took us only a few minutes to find these events. Note that iteration-based memory management is used only to deallocate data records and it is unsafe to use it to manage control objects. Those objects can cross multiple iterations and, hence, we leave them to the GC for memory reclamation.

In order to quickly recycle memory, we allow the developer to register *nested iterations*. If a user-specified iteration-start occurs in the middle of an already-running iteration, a *sub-iteration* starts; we create a new page manager, make it a child of the page manager for the current iteration, and start using it to allocate memory. The page manager for a thread is made a child of the manager for the iteration where the thread is created. Hence, each page manager has a pair $\langle iterationID, thread \rangle$ identifier and they form a tree structure at run time. When a (sub-)iteration finishes, we simply find its page manager m and recursively release pages controlled by the managers in the subtree rooted at m. Recycling can be done efficiently by creating a thread for each page manager and letting them reclaim memory concurrently.

Since each thread t is assigned a page manager upon its creation, the pair identifier for its default page manager is $\langle \perp, t \rangle$; $\perp$ represents the fact that no iteration has started yet. Data records that need to be created before any iteration starts (e.g., usually large arrays) are allocated by this default page manager and will not be deallocated until thread t terminates.

We have transformed all data classes in the JDK including various collection classes and array-based utility classes. Commonly-used native methods such as `System.arraycopy` and `Unsafe.compareAndSwap` are manually modeled. We have also implemented a set of optimization techniques, including (1) inlining of large arrays, primitive type wrappers (e.g., `Integer`), and objects that can be determined immutable statically; (2) static resolution of virtual calls based on a points-to analysis; and (3) use of a special "oversize" class to allocate large arrays whose size is bigger than 32K; pages on this class can be deallocated earlier when they are no longer needed (e.g., upon the resizing of a data structure). Details of these optimizations are omitted from this paper.

3.7 Correctness Argument

It is easy to see the correctness of the class transformation and the generation of data accessing instructions, because the data layout in a native memory page is the same as in a heap object. This subsection focuses on the following two aspects of correctness.

Facade usage correctness If a page reference is assigned to a facade that has not released another page reference, a problem would result. However, it is guaranteed that this situation will not occur because (1) a thread will never use a facade from another thread's pool and (2) for any index i in a facade pool p, the page reference field of $p[i]$ will never be written twice without a read of the field in between. The read will load the page reference onto the thread's stack and use it for the subsequent data accesses.

Memory management correctness Iteration-based memory management coverts dynamic memory reclamation to static reclamation and it is very difficult to make it correct for general objects in a scalable way. FACADE performs iteration-based deallocation only for data items in native memory. Data items allocated in one iteration represent the data partition processed in the iteration. These items will often not be needed when a different data partition is processed (in a different iteration). Since practicality is our central design goal, we choose not to perform any conservative static analysis (e.g., escape analysis [22]) to verify whether data items can escape. A real-world Big Data application is often *framework-intensive* and the heavy use of interfaces in the program code makes it extremely difficult for any interprocedural analysis to produce precise results. Instead, we simply assume that instances of the user-specified data classes can never escape the iteration boundary.

The memory management correctness thus relies on the user's correct specification of data classes. Admittedly, a considerable amount of user effort is needed to understand the program and perform specifications. §4 reports our own experiences with finding data classes for real-world programs that we have never studied.

4. Evaluation

The implementation of FACADE is based on the Soot Java compiler infrastructure and consists of approximately 40,000 lines of Java code. We selected 3 well-designed Big Data frameworks and used FACADE to transform their data paths. Our evaluation on 7 common data analytical applications on both single machines and clusters shows that, even for already well-optimized systems, FACADE can still improve their performance and scalability considerably.

4.1 GraphChi

Transformation GraphChi [41] is a high-performance graph analytical framework that has been well optimized for efficient processing of large graphs on a single machine. Since we had not had any previous experience with GraphChi, we started out by profiling instances of data types to understand the control and data path of the system. The profiling results show that `ChiVertex`, `ChiPointer`, and `VertexDegree` are the only three classes whose instances grow proportionally with the input data size. From these 3 classes, FACADE detected 18 *boundary classes* that interact with data classes but do not have many instances themselves. Boundary classes have both data and non-data fields. We allow the user to annotate data fields with Java pragmas so that FACADE can transform these classes and only page allocate their data fields.

With about 40-person-hour work (to understand data classes, profile their numbers, and annotate boundary classes for a system we had never studied before), FACADE transformed all of these classes (7753 Jimple instructions) in 10.3 seconds, at a speed of 752.7 instructions per second. Iterations and intervals are explicitly defined in GraphChi—it took us only a few minutes to add callbacks to define iterations and sub-iterations.

Test setup We tested the generated code and compared its performance with that of the original GraphChi code. The experiments were performed on a 4-core server with 4 Intel Xeon E5620 (2.40GHz) processors and 50GB of RAM, running Linux 2.6.32. We experimented extensively with two representative applications, page rank (PR) and connected components (CC). The graph used was the *twitter-2010* graph [40], consisting of 42M vertices and 1.5B edges.

We used the Java HotSpot(TM) 64-Bit Server VM (build 20.2-b06, mixed mode) to run all experiments. The state-of-the-art parallel generational GC was used for memory reclamation. This GC combines parallel Scavenge (i.e., copying) for the young generation and parallel Mark-Sweep-Compact for the old generation to quickly reclaim unreachable objects. GraphChi uses a parallel sliding windows algorithm that partitions data into shards. Since the number of shards has only little impact on performance (as reported in Figure 8(c) in [41] and also confirmed in our experiments), we fixed the number of shards to 20 in our experiments.

Performance GraphChi determines the amount of data to load and process (i.e., memory budget) in each iteration dynamically based on the maximum heap size. This is a very effective approach to reduce memory pressure and has been shown to be much more efficient than loading a fixed amount data per iteration. We ran P and P' with the same maximal heap size so that the same amount of data is loaded in each iteration (i.e., guaranteeing the same I/O time in both executions). Note that P' actually does not need a large heap because of the use of native memory. We tried various heap sizes and found that the smallest heap size for running P' was 2.5GB while P could not execute when the heap was smaller than 4GB.

Table 2 shows the detailed performance comparisons. Note that our performance numbers may look different from those reported in [41], because their experiments used SSD and a C++ version of GraphChi. In Table 2, P' outperforms P for all configurations. The performance improvements FACADE has achieved for PR and CC over *twitter-2010* are, respectively, **26.8%** and **5.8%**; larger gains were seen when we experimented with smaller graphs (discussed shortly). The generated program P' not only has much less

App	*ET(s)*	*UT(s)*	*LT(s)*	*GT(s)*	*PM(M)*
PR-8g	1540.8	675.5	786.6	317.1	8469.8
PR'-8g	**1180.7**	**515.3**	**584.8**	**50.2**	**6135.4**
PR-6g	1561.2	694.0	785.2	270.1	6566.5
PR'-6g	**1146.2**	**518.8**	**545.6**	**49.3**	**6152.6**
PR-4g	1663.7	761.6	811.5	380.7	**4448.7**
PR'-4g	**1159.2**	**499.2**	**580.0**	**50.6**	6127.4
CC-8g	2338.1	1051.2	722.7	218.5	8398.3
CC'-8g	**2207.8**	**984.3**	**661.0**	**50.3**	**6051.6**
CC-6g	2245.8	1005.4	698.2	179.5	6557.8
CC'-6g	**2143.4**	**951.6**	**628.2**	**49.3**	**6045.3**
CC-4g	2288.5	1029.8	713.7	197.4	**4427.4**
CC'-4g	**2120.9**	**932.7**	**630.4**	**50.6**	6057.0

Table 2. GraphChi performance comparisons on *twitter-2010*: reported are the total execution times (*ET*), engine update times (*UT*), data load times (*LT*), garbage collection times (*GT*), and peak memory consumptions (*PM*); each application has two runs (e.g., original run PR and facade run PR') under three different memory budgets (e.g., 8GB, 6GB, and 4GB); time and memory are measured in seconds and megabytes, respectively; *PM* is computed by calculating the maximum from a set of samples of JVM memory consumptions collected periodically from pmap; graph preprocessing time is not included; numbers that show better performance are highlighted.

GC time (i.e., an average 5.1× reduction); data load and engine update time has also been reduced primarily due to inlining and direct memory accesses.

For PR, the number of objects for its data classes has been reduced from $14,257,280,923$ to $1,000$ memory pages $+11*(16*2+1) = 1,363$—other than the main thread, GraphChi uses two thread pools, each containing 16 threads, and each thread has a pool of 11 facades—which leads to dramatically decreased GC effort. The cost of page creation and recycling is negligible: the time it took to create and recycle pages was less than 5 seconds during the execution of PR' with 5 major iterations and 159 sub-iterations.

For P, its memory consumption is bounded by the maximum heap size, while the memory usage for P' is quite stable across different memory budget configurations. This is because our heap contains only objects in control path, whose numbers are very small; the off-heap data storage is not subject to the GC and is only determined by the amount of data processed. For both P and P', their running time does not vary much as the memory budget changes. This is primarily due to the adaptive data loading algorithm used by GraphChi. For systems that do not have this design, significant time increase and the GC efforts can often be seen when the heap becomes smaller, and thus, further performance improvement can be expected from FACADE's optimization. Note that under a 4GB heap, P consumes less memory than P'. This is because the GC reclaims objects immediately after they become unreachable while FACADE

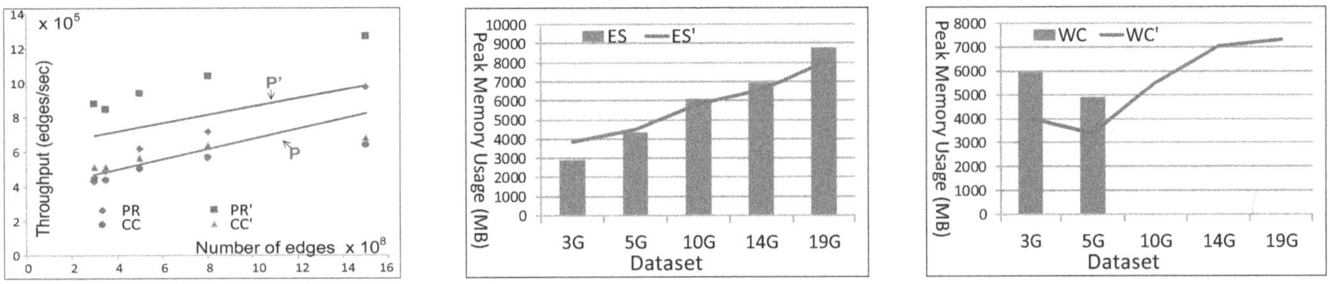

(a) (b) (c)

Figure 4. (a) **Computational throughput of GraphChi** on various graphs (X-axis is the number of edges); each trend-line is a least-squares fit to the average throughput of a program. (b) **Memory usage of external sort (ES) on Hyracks**. (c) **Memory usage of word count (WC) on Hyracks**.

Data	*ES*	*ES'*	*WC*	*WC'*
3GB	95.5	**89.3**	**48.9**	57.4
5GB	178.2	**167.1**	**72.5**	180.8
10GB	326.3	**302.5**	OME(683.1)	**1887.1**
14GB	459.0	**426.0**	OME(943.2)	**2693.0**
19GB	806.4	**607.5**	OME(772.4)	**3160.2**

Table 3. Hyracks performance comparisons on different datasets: reported are the total execution times of ES, ES', WC, and WC' measured in seconds; OME(n) means the program runs out of memory in n seconds.

allows dead data records to accumulate until the end of a (sub-)iteration (i.e., trades off space for time).

Scalability We measured scalability by computing *throughput*, the number of edges processed in a second. From the *twitter-2010* graph, we generated four smaller graphs with different sizes. We fed these graphs to PR and CC to obtain the scalability trends, which are shown in Figure 4 (a). An 8GB heap was used to run P and P'. For both versions, they scale very well with the increase of the data size. The generated program P' has higher throughput than P for all the graphs. In fact, for some of the smaller graphs, the performance difference between P and P' is even larger than what is reported in Table 2. For example, on a graph with 300M edges, PR' and CC' are **48%** and **17%** faster than PR and CC, respectively.

4.2 Hyracks

Hyracks [2, 16] is a data parallel platform that runs data-intensive jobs on a cluster of shared-nothing machines. It has been optimized manually to allow only byte buffers to store data and has been shown to have better scalability than object-based frameworks such as Hadoop. However, the user functions can still (and mostly likely will) use object-based data structures for data manipulation.

After FACADE transformed a significant portion of the high-level data manipulation functions in Hyracks, we evaluated performance and scalability with two commonly-used applications, word count (WC) and external sort (ES). It took us 10 person hours to find and annotate these user-defined operators; FACADE transformed the 8 (data and boundary) classes in 15 seconds, resulting in a speed of 990 instructions per second. Iterations are easy to identify: calls to iteration-start and iteration-end are placed at the beginning and the end of each Hyracks operator (i.e., one computation cycle), respectively.

Test setup We ran Hyracks on a 10-slave-node (c3.2x large) Amazon EC2 cluster. Each machine has 2 quad-core Intel Xeon E5-2680 v2 processors (2.80GHz) and 15G RAM, running Linux 3.10.35, with enhanced networking performance. The same JVM and GC were used in this experiment. We converted a subset of Yahoo!'s publicly available AltaVista Web Page Hyperlink Connectivity Graph dataset [5] into a set of plain text files as input data. The dataset was partitioned among the slaves in a round-robin manner. The two applications were executed as follows: we created a total of 80 concurrent workers across the cluster, each of which reads a local partition of the data. Both WC and ES have a MapReduce-style computation model: each worker computes a local result from its own data partition and writes the result into the Hadoop Distributed File System (HDFS) running on the cluster; after hash-based shuffling, a reduce phase is then started to compute the final results.

Unlike GraphChi that adaptively loads data into memory, Hyracks loads all data upfront before update starts. We ran both P and P' with an 8GB heap. When the heap is exhausted in P, JVM terminates immediately with out-of-memory errors. Naïvely comparing scalability would create unfairness for P, because P' uses much native memory. To enable a fair comparison, we disallowed the total memory consumption of P' (including both heap and native space) to go beyond 8GB. In other words, an execution of P' that consumes more than 8GB memory is considered as an "out-of-memory" failure.

Performance and scalability Table 3 shows a detailed running time comparison between P and P' on datasets of different sizes (which are all generated from the Yahoo! web graph data). P' outperforms P for all the inputs except the two smallest (3GB and 5GB) ones for WC. For these dataset, each machine processes a very small data partition (i.e., 300MB and 500MB). The GC effort for both P and P' is very small, and hence, the extra effort of pool accesses and page-based memory management performed in P' slows down the execution. However, as the size of the dataset increases, this effort can be easily offset from the large savings of GC costs. We can also observe that P' scales to much larger datasets than P. For example, WC fails in 683.1 seconds when processing 10GB, while WC' successfully finishes in 3160.2 seconds for the 19GB dataset. Although both ES and ES' can scale to 19GB, ES' is about **24.7%** faster than ES.

Figure 4 (b) and (c) show the memory usage comparisons for ES and WC, respectively. Each bar represents the memory consumption (in GB) of the original program P while a red line connects the memory consumptions of P' for different datasets. If P runs out of memory, its memory consumption is not shown. It is clear to see that P' has smaller memory footprint than P in almost all the cases. In addition, P' has achieved an overall 25× reduction in the GC time, with a maximum 88× (from 346.2 seconds to 3.9 seconds).

4.3 GPS

GPS [58] is a distributed graph processing system developed for scalable processing of large graphs. We profiled the execution and identified a total number of 4 (vertex- and graph-related) data classes whose instances grow proportionally with the data size. Starting from these classes, FACADE further detected 44 data classes and 13 boundary classes. After an approximate 30-person-hour effort of understanding these classes, FACADE transformed a total number of 61 classes (including 10691 Jimple instructions) in 9.7 seconds, yielding a 1102 instructions per second compilation speed.

We used three applications—page rank, k-means, and random walk—to evaluate performance. The same (Amazon EC2) cluster environment was used to run the experiments. Due to space limitations, here we only briefly describe our experimental results.

GPS is overall less scalable than GraphChi and Hyracks due to its object array-based representation of an input graph. However, its extensive use of primitive arrays, which is similar in spirit to what FACADE intends to achieve, leads to relatively small GC effort. For example, GC accounts for only 1–17% of the running time. The set of inputs we used includes the *twitter-2010* graph, the *LiveJournal* graph, and 5 synthetic supergraphs of *LiveJournal* (e.g., the largest supergraph has 120M vertices and 1.7B edges). Compared to the original implementation P, the generated version P' has achieved a 3–15.4% running time reduction, a 10–39.8% GC time reduction, as well as an up to 14.4% space reduction. P and P' have about the same running time on the smallest graph (with 4.8M vertices and 68M edges). However, for all the other graphs in the input set, clear performance improvements can be observed on P'.

4.4 Summary

Although we had never studied any of these frameworks before, we found that the majority of the manual effort was spent on profiling each system to understand the data path and setting up the execution environments. Once we identified an initial set of data classes, the effort to specify iterations and annotate boundary classes was almost negligible. It would have taken much less time had the developers of these frameworks used FACADE themselves.

5. Related Work

Optimizations of Big Data applications While there exists a large body of work on optimizing Big Data applications, these existing efforts focus on domain-specific optimizations, including, for example, data pipeline optimizations [7, 16, 19, 21, 33, 38, 41, 55, 73, 76], query optimizations [23, 25, 45, 52, 54, 56], and Map-Reduce-related optimizations [6, 24, 47, 57, 60, 61, 72]. Despite the commendable accomplishments of these optimizations, Big Data performance is fundamentally limited by memory inefficiencies inherent with the underlying programming systems. Zing [1] is a commercial system developed by Azul that can lower the latency for Java-based Big Data applications by making larger in-memory indexes. This paper attempts to solve this problem by limiting the number of objects used to represent data records, an approach that is orthogonal to, and will provide benefit for, all existing optimization techniques.

Region-based memory management Region-based memory management was first used in the implementations of functional languages [8, 62] such as Standard ML [35], and then was extended to Prolog [50], C [29, 30, 32, 37], and real-time Java [13, 17, 39]. More recently, some mark-region hybrid methods such as Immix [14] combine tracing GC with regions to improve GC performance for Java. Although our iteration-based memory management is similar in spirit to region-based memory management, the FACADE execution model is novel and necessary to reduce objects in Java applications without modifying a commercial JVM. There are many static analyses (such as region types [13, 17]) developed to support region-based memory management. Most of these analyses focus on the detection of region-allocatable objects, assuming that (1) a new programming model will be used to allocate them and (2) there already exists a modified runtime system (e.g., a new JVM) that supports region-based allocation. On the contrary, FACADE is a non-intrusive technique that compiles the program and allocates objects based on an existing JVM, without needing developers to write new programs as well as any JVM modification.

Reducing objects via program analysis Object inlining [26, 46] is a technique that statically inlines objects in a data structure into its root to reduce the number of pointers and headers. Free-Me [34] adds compiler-inserted frees to a GC-based system. Pool-based allocation proposed by Lattner et al. [42–44] uses a context-sensitive pointer analysis to identify objects that belong to a logical data structure and allocate them into the same pool to improve locality. Design patterns [28] such as `Singleton` and `FlyWeight` aim to reuse objects. However, these techniques have limited usefulness—even if we can reuse data objects across iterations, the number of heap objects in each iteration is not reduced and these objects still need to be traversed frequently by the GC.

Shuft et al. [59] propose a static technique that exploits *prolific types*—types that have large numbers of instances—to enable aggressive optimizations and fast garbage collection. Objects with prolific types are allocated in a prolific region, which is frequently scanned by GC (analogous to to a nursery in a generation collector); objects with non-prolific types are allocated in a regular region, which is less frequently scanned (analogous to an old generation). The insight is that the instances of prolific types are usually temporary and short-lived. FACADE is motivated by a completely opposite observation: data types have great numbers of objects, which are often long-lived; frequently scanning those objects can create prohibitively high GC overhead. Hence, we allocate data records in native memory without creating objects to represent them. Moreover, FACADE adopts a new execution model and does not require any profile.

Object pooling is a well-known technique for reducing the number of objects. For example, Java 7 supports the use of thread pools to save thread instances. Our facade pool differs from traditional object pooling in three important aspects. First, while they have the same goal of reducing objects, they achieve the goal in completely different ways: FACADE moves data objects out of the heap to native memory while object pooling recycles and reuses instances after they are no longer used by the program. Second, the facade pool has a bound; we provide a guarantee that the number of objects in the pool will not exceed the bound. On the contrary, object pooling does not provide any bound guarantee. In fact, it will hurt performance if most of the objects from the pool cannot be reused, because the pool will keep growing and take much memory. Finally, retrieving/returning facades from/to the pool is automatically done by the compiler while object pooling depends on the developer's insight—the developer has to know what objects have disjoint lifetimes and write code explicitly to recycle them.

Resource limits systems Starting with mechanisms as simple as the setrlimit system call, limits have long been supported by POSIX-style operating systems. Recent work such as resource containers [12] provides a hierarchical mechanism for enforcing limits on resources, especially the CPU. HiStar [75] organizes space usage into a hierarchy of containers with quotas. Any object not reachable from the root container is garbage collected. At the programming language level, a lot of work [11, 36] has gone towards resource limits for Java. FACADE can be thought of as a special resource limits system that statically bounds object usage for each thread. However, FACADE does not bound the general memory usage, which still grows with the size of dataset.

PADS, value types, and Rust Most of the existing efforts for language development focus on providing support for data representation (such as the PADS project [27, 51]), rather than improving performance for data processing. Expanded types in Eiffel and value types in C# are used to declare data with simple structures. Value types can be stack allocated or inlined into heap objects. While using value types to represent data items appears to be a promising idea, its effectiveness is actually rather limited. For example, if data items are stack allocated, they have limited scope and cannot easily flow across multiple functions. One the other hand, always inlining data items into heap objects can significantly increase memory consumption, especially when a data structure grows (e.g., resizing of a hash map) and two copies of the data structure are needed simultaneously.

Moreover, these data items are no longer amenable to iteration-based memory management—they cannot be released until their owner objects are reclaimed, leading to significant memory inefficiencies. Rust [3] is a systems programming language designed by Mozilla that allows developers to specify what memory gets managed by the GC and managed manually. While Rust may enable future development of scalable Big Data systems, the goal of FACADE is to transform a large number of existing programs written in Java without letting developers rewrite programs.

6. Conclusions

Growing datasets require efficiency on all levels of the processing stack. This paper targets the performance problem caused by excessive object creation in a managed Big Data system, and proposes a compiler and runtime FACADE that achieves high efficiency by performing a semantics-preserving transformation of the data path of a Big Data program to statically bound the number of heap objects representing data items. Our experimental results demonstrate that the generated programs are more (time and memory) efficient and scalable than their object-based counterparts.

Acknowledgments

We would like to thank Michael Bond, David Liu, Kathryn McKinley, Feng Qin, and Dacong Yan for their helpful comments on an early draft of the paper. We also thank the ASPLOS reviewers for their valuable and thorough comments. This material is based upon work supported by the National Science Foundation under grant CNS-1321179 and CCF-1409829, and by the Office of Naval Research under grant N00014-14-1-0549.

References

[1] Zing: Java for the real time business. `http://www.azulsystems.com/products/zing/whatisit`.

[2] Hyracks: A data parallel platform. `http://code.google.com/p/hyracks/`, 2014.

[3] The Rust programming language. `http://www.rust-lang.org/`, 2014.

[4] Soot framework. `http://www.sable.mcgill.ca/soot/`, 2014.

[5] Yahoo! webscope program. `http://webscope.sandbox.yahoo.com/`, 2014.

[6] F. N. Afrati and J. D. Ullman. Optimizing joins in a map-reduce environment. In *International Conference on Extending Database Technology (EDBT)*, pages 99–110, 2010.

[7] P. Agrawal, D. Kifer, and C. Olston. Scheduling shared scans of large data files. *Proc. VLDB Endow.*, 1(1):958–969, 2008.

[8] A. Aiken, M. Fähndrich, and R. Levien. Better static memory management: improving region-based analysis of higher-order languages. In *ACM SIGPLAN Conference on Programming Language Design and Implementation (PLDI)*, pages 174–185, 1995.

[9] Giraph: Open-source implementation of Pregel. `http://incubator.apache.org/giraph/`.

[10] Hadoop: Open-source implementation of MapReduce. `http://hadoop.apache.org`.

[11] G. Back and W. C. Hsieh. The KaffeOS Java Runtime System. *ACM Transactions on Programming Languages and Systems (TOPLAS)*, 27(4):583–630, 2005.

[12] G. Banga, P. Druschel, and J. C. Mogul. Resource containers: A new facility for resource management in server systems. In *USENIX Symposium on Operating Systems Design and Implementation (OSDI)*, pages 45–58, 1999.

[13] W. S. Beebee and M. C. Rinard. An implementation of scoped memory for real-time java. In *International Conference on Embedded Software (EMSOFT)*, pages 289–305, 2001.

[14] S. M. Blackburn and K. S. McKinley. Immix: a mark-region garbage collector with space efficiency, fast collection, and mutator performance. In *ACM SIGPLAN Conference on Programming Language Design and Implementation (PLDI)*, pages 22–32, 2008.

[15] B. Blanchet. Escape analysis for object-oriented languages. Applications to Java. In *ACM SIGPLAN International Conference on Object-Oriented Programming, Systems, Languages, and Applications (OOPSLA)*, pages 20–34, 1999.

[16] V. R. Borkar, M. J. Carey, R. Grover, N. Onose, and R. Vernica. Hyracks: A flexible and extensible foundation for data-intensive computing. In *International Conference on Data Engineering (ICDE)*, pages 1151–1162, 2011.

[17] C. Boyapati, A. Salcianu, W. Beebee, Jr., and M. Rinard. Ownership types for safe region-based memory management in real-time java. In *ACM SIGPLAN Conference on Programming Language Design and Implementation (PLDI)*, pages 324–337, 2003.

[18] Y. Bu, V. Borkar, G. Xu, and M. J. Carey. A bloat-aware design for big data applications. In *ACM SIGNPLAN International Symposium on Memory Management (ISMM)*, pages 119–130, 2013.

[19] R. Chaiken, B. Jenkins, P.-A. Larson, B. Ramsey, D. Shakib, S. Weaver, and J. Zhou. SCOPE: easy and efficient parallel processing of massive data sets. *Proc. VLDB Endow.*, 1(2):1265–1276, 2008.

[20] C. Chambers, A. Raniwala, F. Perry, S. Adams, R. R. Henry, R. Bradshaw, and N. Weizenbaum. FlumeJava: easy, efficient data-parallel pipelines. In *ACM SIGPLAN Conference on Programming Language Design and Implementation (PLDI)*, pages 363–375, 2010.

[21] C. Chambers, A. Raniwala, F. Perry, S. Adams, R. R. Henry, R. Bradshaw, and N. Weizenbaum. FlumeJava: easy, efficient data-parallel pipelines. In *ACM SIGPLAN Conference on Programming Language Design and Implementation (PLDI)*, pages 363–375, 2010.

[22] J. Choi, M. Gupta, M. Serrano, V. Sreedhar, and S. Midkiff. Escape analysis for Java. In *ACM SIGPLAN International Conference on Object-Oriented Programming, Systems, Languages, and Applications (OOPSLA)*, pages 1–19, 1999.

[23] T. Condie, N. Conway, P. Alvaro, J. M. Hellerstein, K. Elmeleegy, and R. Sears. Mapreduce online. In *USENIX Symposium on Networked Systems Design and Implementation (NSDI)*, pages 21–21, 2010.

[24] J. Dean and S. Ghemawat. Mapreduce: simplified data processing on large clusters. *Commun. ACM*, 51(1):107–113, 2008.

[25] J. Dittrich, J.-A. Quiané-Ruiz, A. Jindal, Y. Kargin, V. Setty, and J. Schad. Hadoop++: making a yellow elephant run like a cheetah (without it even noticing). *Proc. VLDB Endow.*, 3:515–529, 2010.

[26] J. Dolby and A. Chien. An automatic object inlining optimization and its evaluation. In *ACM SIGPLAN Conference on Programming Language Design and Implementation (PLDI)*, pages 345–357, 2000.

[27] K. Fisher, Y. Mandelbaum, and D. Walker. The next 700 data description languages. In *ACM SIGPLAN-SIGACT Symposium on Principles of Programming Languages (POPL)*, pages 2–15, 2006.

[28] E. Gamma, R. Helm, R. Johnson, and J. Vlissides. *Design Patterns: Elements of Reusable Object-Oriented Software*. Addison-Wesley, 1995.

[29] D. Gay and A. Aiken. Memory management with explicit regions. In *ACM SIGPLAN Conference on Programming Language Design and Implementation (PLDI)*, pages 313–323, 1998.

[30] D. Gay and A. Aiken. Language support for regions. In *ACM SIGPLAN Conference on Programming Language Design and Implementation (PLDI)*, pages 70–80, 2001.

[31] G. Graefe. Query evaluation techniques for large databases. *ACM Comput. Surv.*, 25(2):73–170, 1993.

[32] D. Grossman, G. Morrisett, T. Jim, M. Hicks, Y. Wang, and J. Cheney. Region-based memory management in cyclone. In *ACM SIGPLAN Conference on Programming Language Design and Implementation (PLDI)*, pages 282–293, 2002.

[33] Z. Guo, X. Fan, R. Chen, J. Zhang, H. Zhou, S. McDirmid, C. Liu, W. Lin, J. Zhou, and L. Zhou. Spotting code optimizations in data-parallel pipelines through periscope. In *USENIX Symposium on Operating Systems Design and Implementation (OSDI)*, pages 121–133, 2012.

[34] S. Z. Guyer, K. S. McKinley, and D. Frampton. Free-Me: a static analysis for automatic individual object reclamation. In *ACM SIGPLAN Conference on Programming Language Design and Implementation (PLDI)*, pages 364–375, 2006.

[35] N. Hallenberg, M. Elsman, and M. Tofte. Combining region inference and garbage collection. In *ACM SIGPLAN Conference on Programming Language Design and Implementation (PLDI)*, pages 141–152, 2002.

[36] C. Hawblitzel and T. von Eicken. Luna: A flexible Java protection system. In *USENIX Symposium on Operating Systems Design and Implementation (OSDI)*, pages 391–403, 2002.

[37] M. Hicks, G. Morrisett, D. Grossman, and T. Jim. Experience with safe manual memory-management in cyclone. In *ACM SIGNPLAN International Symposium on Memory Management (ISMM)*, pages 73–84, 2004.

[38] M. Isard, M. Budiu, Y. Yu, A. Birrell, and D. Fetterly. Dryad: distributed data-parallel programs from sequential building blocks. In *European Conference on Computer Systems (EuroSys)*, pages 59–72, 2007.

[39] S. Kowshik, D. Dhurjati, and V. Adve. Ensuring code safety without runtime checks for real-time control systems. In *International Conference on Architecture and Synthesis for Embedded Systems (CASES)*, pages 288–297, 2002.

[40] H. Kwak, C. Lee, H. Park, and S. Moon. What is twitter, a social network or a news media? In *International World Wide Web Conference (WWW)*, pages 591–600, 2010.

[41] A. Kyrola, G. Blelloch, and C. Guestrin. GraphChi: Large-Scale Graph Computation on Just a PC. In *USENIX Symposium on Operating Systems Design and Implementation (OSDI)*, pages 31–46, 2012.

[42] C. Lattner. *Macroscopic Data Structure Analysis and Optimization*. PhD thesis, University of Illinois at Urbana-Champaign, 2005.

[43] C. Lattner and V. Adve. Automatic pool allocation: improving performance by controlling data structure layout in the heap. In *ACM SIGPLAN Conference on Programming Language Design and Implementation (PLDI)*, pages 129–142, 2005.

[44] C. Lattner, A. Lenharth, and V. Adve. Making context-sensitive points-to analysis with heap cloning practical for the real world. In *ACM SIGPLAN Conference on Programming Language Design and Implementation (PLDI)*, pages 278–289, 2007.

[45] R. Lee, T. Luo, Y. Huai, F. Wang, Y. He, and X. Zhang. Ysmart: Yet another SQL-to-MapReduce translator. In *IEEE International Conference on Distributed Computing Systems (ICDCS)*, pages 25–36, 2011.

[46] O. Lhotak and L. Hendren. Run-time evaluation of opportunities for object inlining in Java. *Concurrency and Computation: Practice and Experience*, 17(5-6):515–537, 2005.

[47] J. Liu, N. Ravi, S. Chakradhar, and M. Kandemir. Panacea: Towards holistic optimization of MapReduce applications. In *International Symposium on Code Generation and Optimization (CGO)*, pages 33–43, 2012.

[48] Y. Low, J. Gonzalez, A. Kyrola, D. Bickson, C. Guestrin, and J. M. Hellerstein. GraphLab: A new parallel framework for machine learning. In *Conference on Uncertainty in Artificial Intelligence (UAI)*, pages 340–349, 2010.

[49] Y. Low, J. Gonzalez, A. Kyrola, D. Bickson, C. Guestrin, and J. M. Hellerstein. Distributed GraphLab: A framework for machine learning in the cloud. *Proc. VLDB Endow.*, 5(8):716–727, 2012.

[50] H. Makholm. A region-based memory manager for prolog. In *ACM SIGNPLAN International Symposium on Memory Management (ISMM)*, pages 25–34, 2000.

[51] Y. Mandelbaum, K. Fisher, D. Walker, M. F. Fernández, and A. Gleyzer. PADS/ML: a functional data description language. In *ACM SIGPLAN-SIGACT Symposium on Principles of Programming Languages (POPL)*, pages 77–83, 2007.

[52] D. G. Murray, M. Isard, and Y. Yu. Steno: automatic optimization of declarative queries. In *ACM SIGPLAN Conference on Programming Language Design and Implementation (PLDI)*, pages 121–131, 2011.

[53] K. Nguyen and G. Xu. Cachetor: Detecting cacheable data to remove bloat. In *ACM SIGSOFT International Symposium on the Foundations of Software Engineering (FSE)*, pages 268–278, 2013.

[54] T. Nykiel, M. Potamias, C. Mishra, G. Kollios, and N. Koudas. Mrshare: sharing across multiple queries in mapreduce. *Proc. VLDB Endow.*, 3(1-2):494–505, 2010.

[55] C. Olston, B. Reed, A. Silberstein, and U. Srivastava. Automatic optimization of parallel dataflow programs. In *USENIX USENIX Annual Technical Conference (ATC)*, pages 267–273, 2008.

[56] C. Olston, B. Reed, U. Srivastava, R. Kumar, and A. Tomkins. Pig latin: a not-so-foreign language for data processing. In *ACM SIGMOD International Conference on Management of Data (SIGMOD)*, pages 1099–1110, 2008.

[57] R. Pike, S. Dorward, R. Griesemer, and S. Quinlan. Interpreting the data: Parallel analysis with Sawzall. *Sci. Program.*, 13(4):277–298, 2005.

[58] S. Salihoglu and J. Widom. GPS: A graph processing system. In *Scientific and Statistical Database Management*, July 2013.

[59] Y. Shuf, M. Gupta, R. Bordawekar, and J. P. Singh. Exploiting prolific types for memory management and optimizations. In *ACM SIGPLAN-SIGACT Symposium on Principles of Programming Languages (POPL)*, pages 295–306, 2002.

[60] A. Thusoo, J. S. Sarma, N. Jain, Z. Shao, P. Chakka, S. Anthony, H. Liu, P. Wyckoff, and R. Murthy. Hive: a warehousing solution over a map-reduce framework. *Proc. VLDB Endow.*, 2(2):1626–1629, 2009.

[61] A. Thusoo, J. S. Sarma, N. Jain, Z. Shao, P. Chakka, N. Zhang, S. Antony, H. Liu, and R. Murthy. Hive - a petabyte scale data warehouse using hadoop. In *International Conference on Data Engineering (ICDE)*, pages 996–1005, 2010.

[62] M. Tofte and J.-P. Talpin. Implementation of the typed call-by-value lamda-calculus using a stack of regions. In *ACM*

SIGPLAN-SIGACT Symposium on Principles of Programming Languages (POPL), pages 188–201, 1994.

[63] Storm: dstributed and fault-tolerant realtime computation. `https://github.com/nathanmarz/storm`.

[64] R. Vallée-Rai, E. Gagnon, L. Hendren, P. Lam, P. Pominville, and V. Sundaresan. Optimizing Java bytecode using the Soot framework: Is it feasible? In *International Conference on Compiler Construction (CC)*, pages 18–34, 2000.

[65] G. Xu. Finding reusable data structures. In *ACM SIGPLAN International Conference on Object-Oriented Programming, Systems, Languages, and Applications (OOPSLA)*, pages 1017–1034, 2012.

[66] G. Xu. Resurrector: A tunable object lifetime profiling technique for optimizing real-world programs. In *ACM SIGPLAN International Conference on Object-Oriented Programming, Systems, Languages, and Applications (OOPSLA)*, pages 111–130, 2013.

[67] G. Xu, M. Arnold, N. Mitchell, A. Rountev, E. Schonberg, and G. Sevitsky. Finding low-utility data structures. In *ACM SIGPLAN Conference on Programming Language Design and Implementation (PLDI)*, pages 174–186, 2010.

[68] G. Xu, M. Arnold, N. Mitchell, A. Rountev, and G. Sevitsky. Go with the flow: Profiling copies to find runtime bloat. In *ACM SIGPLAN Conference on Programming Language Design and Implementation (PLDI)*, pages 419–430, 2009.

[69] G. Xu, N. Mitchell, M. Arnold, A. Rountev, and G. Sevitsky. Software bloat analysis: Finding, removing, and preventing performance problems in modern large-scale object-oriented applications. In *ACM SIGSOFT FSE/SDP Working Conference on the Future of Software Engineering Research (FoSER)*, pages 421–426, 2010.

[70] G. Xu and A. Rountev. Detecting inefficiently-used containers to avoid bloat. In *ACM SIGPLAN Conference on Programming Language Design and Implementation (PLDI)*, pages 160–173, 2010.

[71] G. Xu, D. Yan, and A. Rountev. Static detection of loop-invariant data structures. In *European Conference on Object-Oriented Programming (ECOOP)*, pages 738–763, 2012.

[72] H.-c. Yang, A. Dasdan, R.-L. Hsiao, and D. S. Parker. Map-reduce-merge: simplified relational data processing on large clusters. In *ACM SIGMOD International Conference on Management of Data (SIGMOD)*, pages 1029–1040, 2007.

[73] Y. Yu, M. Isard, D. Fetterly, M. Budiu, U. Erlingsson, P. K. Gunda, and J. Currey. DryadLINQ: a system for general-purpose distributed data-parallel computing using a high-level language. In *USENIX Symposium on Operating Systems Design and Implementation (OSDI)*, pages 1–14, 2008.

[74] M. Zaharia, M. Chowdhury, M. J. Franklin, S. Shenker, and I. Stoica. Spark: cluster computing with working sets. In *USENIX conference on Hot topics in cloud computing (HotCloud)*, page 10, Berkeley, CA, USA, 2010.

[75] N. Zeldovich, S. Boyd-Wickizer, E. Kohler, and D. Mazières. Making information flow explicit in histar. In *USENIX Symposium on Operating Systems Design and Implementation (OSDI)*, pages 263–278, 2006.

[76] J. Zhou, P.-Å. Larson, and R. Chaiken. Incorporating partitioning and parallel plans into the SCOPE optimizer. In *International Conference on Data Engineering (ICDE)*, pages 1060–1071, 2010.

Architectural Support for Dynamic Linking

Varun Agrawal, Abhiroop Dabral, Tapti Palit, Yongming Shen, Michael Ferdman
COMPAS
Stony Brook University

Abstract

All software in use today relies on libraries, including standard libraries (e.g., C, C++) and application-specific libraries (e.g., libxml, libpng). Most libraries are loaded in memory and dynamically linked when programs are launched, resolving symbol addresses across the applications and libraries. Dynamic linking has many benefits: It allows code to be reused between applications, conserves memory (because only one copy of a library is kept in memory for all the applications that share it), and allows libraries to be patched and updated without modifying programs, among numerous other benefits. However, these benefits come at the cost of performance. For every call made to a function in a dynamically linked library, a trampoline is used to read the function address from a lookup table and branch to the function, incurring memory load and branch operations. Static linking avoids this performance penalty, but loses all the benefits of dynamic linking. Given its myriad benefits, dynamic linking is the predominant choice today, despite the performance cost.

In this work, we propose a speculative hardware mechanism to optimize dynamic linking by avoiding executing the trampolines for library function calls, providing the benefits of dynamic linking with the performance of static linking. Speculatively skipping the memory load and branch operations of the library call trampolines improves performance by reducing the number of executed instructions and gains additional performance by reducing pressure on the instruction and data caches, TLBs, and branch predictors. Because the indirect targets of library call trampolines do not change during program execution, our speculative mechanism never misspeculates in practice. We evaluate our technique on real hardware with production software and observe up to 4% speedup using only 1.5KB of on-chip storage.

Categories and Subject Descriptors C.4 [**Performance of Systems**]: Performance of Systems—Design studies

Keywords Dynamic Linking; Hardware Memoization; Instruction Elision; Branch Prediction

ASPLOS '15, March 14 - 18 2015, Istanbul, Turkey
Copyright 2015 ACM 978-1-4503-2835-7/15/03…$15.00
http://dx.doi.org/10.1145/2694344.2694392

1 Introduction

All computer programs in use today rely on software libraries. Libraries can be linked dynamically, deferring much of the linking process to the launch of the program. Dynamically linked libraries offer numerous benefits over static linking: they allow code reuse between applications, conserve memory (because only one copy of a library is kept in memory for all applications that share it), allow libraries to be patched and updated without modifying programs, enable effective address space layout randomization for security [21], and many others. As a result, dynamic linking is the predominant choice in all systems today [7].

To facilitate dynamic linking of libraries, compiled programs include function call trampolines in their binaries. When a program is launched, the dynamic linker maps the libraries into the process address space and resolves external symbols in the program and between the libraries, populating the symbol addresses in a global lookup table. Subsequently, every call to a library function executes a trampoline that reads the corresponding function address from a lookup table and jumps to the target library function. The trampoline execution is an overhead of dynamic linking compared to static linking, increasing the number of instructions executed and adding pressure on the instruction cache and I-TLB for trampoline instructions, the data cache and D-TLB for storing addresses in lookup tables, and the branch predictor and branch target buffers.

Several techniques can mitigate the performance degradation associated with the overhead of dynamic linking. The entire penalty can be avoided by statically linking libraries. However, static linking loses the benefits of dynamic linking and is therefore not used in practice (the design of many complex applications does not even permit static linking). Hardware memoization techniques [8, 22] offer an alternative approach in which trampolines can be skipped by memoizing trampoline execution; however, these techniques lie on the critical path of instruction fetch. Some overheads of dynamic linking can be mitigated through profile-driven optimization [17] of data and instruction layout in memory [14], but these approaches are limited to improving the cache and TLB behavior; optimization does not eliminate trampolines or the branch predictor pressure they create.

We observe that much of the performance overhead of dynamic linking can be avoided. Entries in the dynamic linker lookup tables are updated only once, when each symbol is resolved, typically at the first execution of the corresponding library call. All subsequent invocations of the trampolines are unnecessary and serve only to create performance overheads. Noting this, we propose a lightweight hardware mechanism that leverages existing branch predictor structures to optimize the function calls in dynamically linked libraries by speculatively skipping trampoline execution, providing the performance of static linking while retaining the benefits of dynamic linking. Our technique does not affect the processor's critical path, as it uses the existing branch target buffers and branch predictor update mechanisms. The approach works on all dynamically linked library techniques that we are aware of, across architectures (e.g., ARM and x86) and modern operating systems (e.g., Linux, Windows, BSDs).

To demonstrate the effectiveness of our approach, we use software to model the effect of the proposed hardware technique on real server hardware running production software, using existing performance counters to demonstrate the reduced pressure on the various microarchitectural structures. For an Apache web server running the SPECweb 2009 workload, for example, approximately 1% of the executed instructions are in trampolines for library function calls. Skipping the execution of the trampolines reduces instruction cache misses, data cache misses, and branch mispredictions. As a result, Apache performance (request processing latency) improves by 4%.

The software technique we use to emulate our proposed hardware solution incorporates assumptions that prevent its use in production systems: our software loads all executable code (including libraries) in a contiguous 2GB of the address space to limit relative jump offsets, changes page permissions of executable code on demand, uses profiling to locate library function call sites, copies executable code pages after they are patched, and increases load time for applications. To make a software technique practical, the software and compiler toolchains need to change significantly and security implications must be addressed. Given these limitations, we advocate a lightweight hardware solution that works transparently on existing systems, without requiring software modifications. However, with sufficient ecosystem change, a software mechanism that leverages our observations may also become viable.

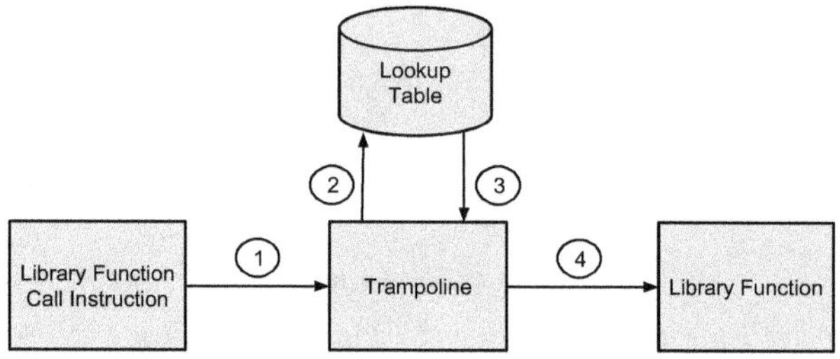

Figure 1. Library function call mechanism for dynamically-linked libraries.

2 Dynamic Linking

Dynamic linking is the predominant method of linking libraries in today's systems. In dynamic linking, external symbols used in a program and across libraries are pointed to small trampoline routines automatically inserted into the binaries by the compiler. The dynamic linker populates the corresponding symbol addresses into lookup tables referenced by the trampolines. When a program is launched, the dynamic linker maps the dynamically linked libraries into the application's memory space and allocates the corresponding lookup tables. Figure 1 shows the function call mechanism for dynamically linked libraries; every call to a library function jumps to a trampoline that reads the address of the target library function from a lookup table and then jumps to the function defined in the library's binary.

Figure 2 shows the instructions that are executed when calling the *printf* function in a dynamically linked library on x86 and ARM architectures with ELF binaries. The trampolines in these systems are defined in the procedure linkage table (PLT) sections. The trampoline for *printf* is called *printf@plt.* All the call/branch sites in the application and library binaries that call *printf* actually call the *printf@plt* trampoline. The trampoline comprises an x86 indirect *jmp* instruction (or two *add*s and a *branch* for ARM). The indi-

```
.text:      ...
            call    printf@plt
            ...
.plt:       ...
printf@plt:
            jmp     *(printf@got.plt)
            push    0x10
            jmp     .plt
            ...
.text:      ...
printf:     push    %rbp
            ...
            ret
```

(a) x86-64

```
.text:      ...
            bl      printf@plt
            ...
.plt:       ...
printf@plt:
            add     ...
            add     ...
            ldr     pc, [printf@got.plt]
            ...
.text:      ...
printf:     push    {fp,lr}
            ...
            pop     {fp,pc}
```

(b) ARM

Figure 2. Library function call examples for a dynamically-linked ELF executable.

rect branch instruction reads the global offset table (GOT) location *printf@got.plt* and branches to the address loaded from it. Resolution of function symbols is typically done in a lazy fashion. Initially, the dynamic linker populates all entries in the GOT to branch to the dynamic linker's own resolver function. Upon the first invocation of each library function, the resolver updates the GOT lookup table entry with the real library function's address, ensuring that subsequent executions of the trampoline find the address of *printf* when reading *printf@got.plt*.

Trampoline instructions are not densely packed in the PLT section. For each trampoline, several additional instructions follow the indirect branch. These additional instructions are used only on the first trampoline (resolver) execution to indicate to the resolver the name of the function being resolved. Moreover, compilers typically allocate PLT entries in the order in which the corresponding functions are defined in the source. Because only a small, random subset of available library functions are typically called by a program, the PLT sections are sparsely used and accesses to the PLT and GOT entries exhibit practically no spatial locality.

2.1 Benefits of Dynamic Linking

Dynamic linking is considered indispensable in the software and OS communities. The performance overheads are well worth the benefits, some of which we outline below.

Flexibility Dynamically linked libraries greatly enhance portability, particularly with *standard* libraries that provide a common system interface.

Dynamically linked libraries allow bug and security fixes to be incorporated systemwide by simply restarting applications with updated library binaries, without requiring modifications to each application.

With dynamically linked libraries, users can customize application execution by specifying which libraries to use and by selecting different implementations of specific functions from different libraries.

Memory conservation Libraries grow over time with the addition of new interfaces and functionality. Although most of the functions of any given library are not used by any single application that links against that library, the full library code must still be loaded in memory. Dynamic linking allows for a single read-only copy of the library binary to be mapped into all processes that need it, potentially saving gigabytes of memory on systems with large numbers of processes [19].

Security Shared libraries enable vital security measures, such as address space layout randomization [21]. The position-independent nature of dynamic libraries allows programs to randomly map shared libraries into application virtual address spaces. This means that the locations of program and library code change with each process invocation, limiting the ability of malicious users to mount attacks.

2.2 Penalties Incurred by Dynamic Linking

Dynamic linking incurs many penalties that reduce system performance. The source of these penalties is the trampolines; a trampoline is executed for every call to a library function, performing an extra memory load and an extra indirect branch. Complex applications that use many libraries (e.g., Apache, Memcached, MySQL and Firefox) frequently perform library calls from within the application and between shared libraries, resulting in significant overheads from trampoline execution and its side effects.

Instructions Calling library functions puts pressure on the instruction cache [20], as one cache line is occupied for each trampoline. On x86-64 systems using ELF binaries, trampolines are 16 bytes, allowing only four trampolines per 64-byte instruction cache line [9]. However, because the trampolines are sparsely spread throughout the PLT sections, an instruction cache line is effectively dedicated to each library call made by the application and each library. For example, if an application and four libraries against which it is linked frequently call *write*, five instruction cache lines are dedicated to the trampolines for this *write* library function (one in each PLT). The trampoline instructions put similar pressure on the instruction translation lookaside buffer (I-TLB).

Data working set Every trampoline performs a load operation that reads the library function pointer from the linker's lookup table. As in the instruction cache, the lookup tables (e.g., GOT) occupy data cache lines and data TLB entries. Although function pointers are more densely packed in memory than are the trampolines, storing eight pointers in each 64-byte cache line, the storage is similarly sparse and one cache line is needed for each library function called from the application and one for each calling library.

Branch prediction accuracy Branch predictor storage is extremely limited due to its critical nature; conflicts in the branch predictor structures lead to direction and target mispredictions, reducing system performance [15]. Statically linked function calls require one branch for their invocation; dynamically linked libraries require two branches for each library call—one to branch to the trampoline and a second one to branch to the actual function. Thus, dynamically linked libraries occupy two entries in the branch predictor tables and branch target buffers (BTB) per call, creating greater pressure on these structures. As a result, dynamic linking has an increased conflict rate and reduced accuracy compared to static linking.

Although the benefits of dynamic linking overshadow the penalties, the penalties are substantial, particularly in complex applications. The hardware technique we propose in this work ameliorates those penalties by skipping trampoline execution entirely, avoiding the allocation of instruction cache lines for trampolines, data cache lines for lookup tables, and branch predictor entries for trampoline branches. By reducing the number of executed instructions and consequently the pressure on these microarchitectural structures, our approach retains all the benefits of dynamic linking and achieves the performance of static linking.

2.3 Challenges of a Software Solution

In dynamic linking, library function addresses are unknown when a program's code is compiled, preventing the program binary from directly calling the target functions. This necessitates the use of trampolines, which read a resolved target address from the GOTPLT and branch to the appropriate location. A dynamic resolver, which executes on the first invocation of each library function, identifies the target address and installs it into the GOTPLT. Although it is functionally effective, this approach hampers performance because the trampoline remains in the call path of each subsequent library function invocation.

At first glance, it seems possible to create an alternative dynamic resolver that avoids trampoline overheads. Rather than dynamically populating the GOTPLT with the target function's address, the dynamic resolver could directly modify the instruction at the call site with the target address. Future executions of the same call site would then call the needed library function directly, avoiding the performance overheads associated with executing the trampoline. However, this naive approach presents a number of challenges.

First, although library functions called from the application binary are similar to functions called from other libraries, they would be affected differently by the naive software solution. Real systems load libraries above the heap and far from their call sites in the virtual address space. As a result, the distance between the target address and the call site is much more than 2GB. For example, the x86 ISA encodes relative call targets using an offset from the call site; the instruction encoding is limited to an offset of 2GB. As a result, either the ISA has to change to support larger offsets or the software, including the conventional process memory map, must change to allow dynamically linked libraries to be loaded between the text and heap sections.

Another challenge arises from unconventional tricks for calling functions, such as using a *jump* instead of a *call* instruction to invoke a function. In a conventional scenario, a dynamic resolver can examine the stack to determine the location of the call site to patch. However, when the unconventional approach is used, the stack does not contain the address to patch (the address of a jump), instead pointing to the address of the preceding call; patching this call instruction would result in incorrect execution. A software solution would therefore need to address this possibility; either additional mechanisms would have to be added to disassemble the call site pointed to by the stack to verify that it is the appropriate location to patch, or toolchain changes would have to be made to enable the compiler to communicate a list of valid patch sites to the resolver.

The software solution could also create enormous memory overheads. Dynamic linking uses a copy-on-write (COW) mechanism to share a single executable read-only copy of each library between all applications in the system. However, the libraries are mapped at a different address in each application's virtual address space. Further, when a process is forked, the executable code is shared by the parent and child processes. Patching the call sites both in the libraries (when they call other libraries) and in the application binary will have different effects based on whether child processes are forked before or after patching. Patching before fork will retain the COW property, retaining just one copy of each code page. However, patching after fork will force allocation of a new physical memory page for each process. Busy servers with thousands of processes and thousands of library function call sites could waste multiple gigabytes of RAM on these unnecessary page copies. Avoiding this memory overhead with a software solution would require patching all call sites before the fork, which precludes the traditional lazy resolver mechanisms and requires modifying the compiler toolchain to include lists of all library function call sites to patch.

Even if the memory overheads associated with lazy resolution in this scenario were acceptable, the software solution would still have significant performance implications because an application can have thousands of library functions (including library functions calling other libraries), a fraction of which are actually used. Lazy resolution supports fast application load times by resolving functions only when they are called for the first time, regardless of which call site triggers the resolution. Thus, a single library function will be resolved only once in the traditional dynamic linking approach. By contrast, the naive software solution to avoid dynamic linking overheads would need to perform binary patching for each call site, even if all call sites pointed to one library function. The software solution may therefore incur significant performance overheads, especially considering that for each call site patch, the OS must be involved to unprotect the code page and make it writable and the resolver must keep track of all patched call sites for the rare case of library unload.

Even if these implementation challenges could be overcome, the software approach introduces a number of security challenges. The benefits of address-space layout randomization would be eroded because shared libraries would have to be placed within 2GB from call sites. Additionally, because the loader must unprotect code pages to patch call sites, the system creates an opportunity for attackers to inject malicious code [2].

2.4 Similar Techniques

The mechanism of dynamic linking is a special case of a lookup table, in which the address of a function is looked up in a table (here, the PLT) and control flow jumps to that function address. We describe two related techniques that use lookup tables to change program control flow.

2.4.1 GNU Indirect Functions

New processors include specialized instructions that optimize particular computations. Many commonly used functions can benefit from these specialized instructions if they are available. In order to support different hardware, and thus allow access to these specialized instructions, libraries usually include several different implementations of a function, choosing the best implementation based on the hardware available when the application is loaded. The GNU linker provides a feature, called *ifunc*, which chooses from among the different candidate implementations using a resolver function that determines the hardware capabilities. Because the compiler is not aware of which function will be selected at load time, calls to *ifuncs* are made using the PLT in the same way that dynamically linked functions are called. Available in GNU libc since version 2.10, this mechanism is used extensively for common library routines (e.g., string manipulation functions) and is also available to software developers, who use it to incorporate platform-specific *ifunc* implementations directly in executable binaries.

2.4.2 C++ Virtual Functions

Declaring C++ member functions *virtual* allows objects to access them even if the object's pointer is passed as a pointer of the superclass. Virtual function addresses are dereferenced from the object's data structure, which then performs a direct call to the function address. This mechanism is similar to calls to dynamically linked functions, as both look up the target function in a table and then branch to it. However, the instruction sequence for address resolution and invocation of C++ virtual functions differ significantly from that of dynamic library calls.

3 Architectural Support for Dynamic Linking

Calls to functions in dynamically linked libraries occur with sufficiently high frequency to warrant hardware support in high-performance systems. In this work, we describe a speculative hardware mechanism to improve the performance of dynamic linking by skipping trampoline execution.

On an x86-64 system, trampolines comprise a complex indirect branch instruction that performs both load and branch operations. When a *call* instruction is fetched, the branch predictor provides the address of the trampoline in the PLT section. The trampoline virtual address is then translated to its physical address using the I-TLB and the trampoline instruction is fetched from the L1 instruction cache. The indirect branch instruction performs a load operation that uses the D-TLB to translate the GOT entry address and fetches the function pointer from the L1 data cache. Finally, the retrieved pointer is translated using the I-TLB to determine the address of the actual function.

Although the trampoline indirect branch instruction performs two expensive operations [13], the result of these instructions does not change after the first trampoline invocation (the pointer loaded from the GOT and the library function address do not change during program execution). The behavior of the proposed mechanism relies on this fact, skipping the trampolines whenever possible while maintaining an architectural state identical to the unmodified system.

3.1 Hardware Overview

Our mechanism uses existing hardware of the processor front end to trick instruction fetch into skipping the fetching of the trampoline (in turn, tricking the back end into skipping its execution). This is accomplished by storing the address of each library function in the BTB entry that would normally store the address of the trampoline corresponding to that function. The processor front end does not require any modifications to perform this operation, as the target address is set using the standard branch predictor feedback mechanism from the back end [24]. In the back end, the branch resolution and misprediction identification mechanism are modified to check whether the real branch target is the address of a trampoline; if it is, the processor treats the predicted address as correct if the predicted target matches the target of the trampoline's branch. To facilitate this comparison, a retire-time alternate BTB (ABTB) structure stores a mapping of trampoline addresses to library function addresses.

To ensure correctness in the rare event that the trampoline targets change, we use a bloom filter [1] to store the addresses of the GOT entries that represent trampoline targets corresponding to the entries in the ABTB. If an entry in the GOT is modified and the GOT entry hits in the bloom filter, then the target of the ABTB may be incorrect. In this case, we clear the entire ABTB table and rely on the standard branch misprediction logic to ensure correct execution (in practice, this happens only once per library call, at the start of a program's execution, making this overhead irrelevant).

Entries are added to ABTB and the bloom filter during the retire stage of the processor pipeline. We use the characteristic of a trampoline (call instruction followed by indirect branch instruction) to populate the ABTB and bloom filter. The ABTB and bloom filter entries are context specific and can be directly tied to the mechanisms and optimizations available for maintaining (or flushing) the BTB and TLB entries on context switch.

3.2 Speculative Trampoline Skip

Front end In the front end, we use the existing branch predictor mechanism to skip trampoline execution. When fetching a library function call instruction, the branch predictor provides the target of the call instruction. During normal execution, the target would be the function's trampoline; we change the branch prediction update mechanism to make the actual function address the target of the call instruction. The

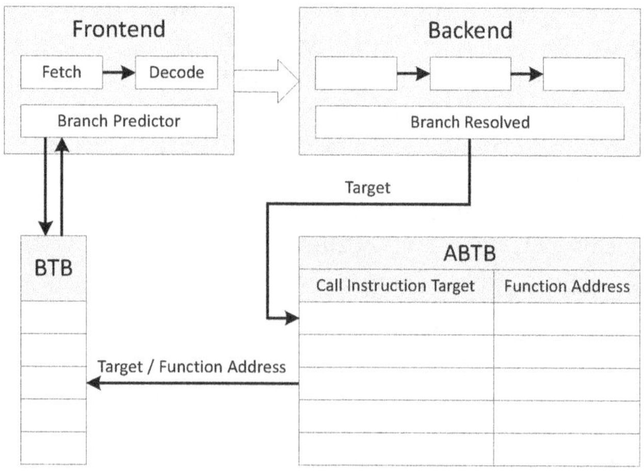

Figure 3. Speculative trampoline skip mechanism.

function address is read from a BTB entry that is indexed using the call instruction's program counter. The target is speculative; the branch predictor update mechanism corrects any mispredictions. Modifying the BTB entry in this way means the trampoline does not get executed, reducing the pressure on the instruction cache, data cache, I-TLB, and D-TLB, as well as on the BTB and branch predictor.

Back end In the back end, our hardware solution modifies the branch predictor update mechanism to use the target of the library call instruction and not the trampoline address. Branch prediction is speculative; the processor executes the instructions as they are fetched, whether the branch predictor provides the function address or the trampoline address. When the target of the call instruction is resolved, the branch predictor update mechanism tests whether the target was predicted correctly. If a misprediction is identified, the BTB entry is corrected. As long as the address in the GOT is not modified, the target of the trampoline does not change and the modified branch target prediction remains correct.

Figure 3 shows our hardware mechanism with an ABTB table. The ABTB maps the real target of the call instruction (the trampoline's address) to the target of the trampoline (the library function address). When the back end resolves the target of a branch instruction, the address is looked up in ABTB. If the target is not found in ABTB, the branch predictor operates without modification, updating the BTB with the real branch target. However, if the target matches an ABTB entry, the branch resolution mechanism uses the result of the ABTB lookup as the correct branch target.

Entries in ABTB are valid as long as the corresponding entries in the GOT section are not modified. A small bloom filter that contains the GOT addresses corresponding to the entries in ABTB is sufficient to detect when any GOT entry is updated. When the processor retires a store instruction to an address that hits in the bloom filter (or an invalidation for such an address is received from the coherence subsystem), all entries in ABTB and the bloom filter are cleared. At program startup, when GOT entries are initially populated, clearing the ABTB prevents the program from skipping the trampolines until the ABTB is populated with the correct final targets, at which point the addresses are never updated again in practice.

Populating the ABTB Library function calls have a distinguishing pattern: a call instruction is followed by an indirect branch. When a call instruction is retired, the resolved target of the call instruction is noted. On retiring the subsequent instruction, if that instruction is an indirect branch, the preceding call's target is used as the index into the ABTB and the target of the indirect branch instruction is used as the value. The bloom filter is updated with the source address from which the indirect branch's address is loaded. In all other cases, no new entries are added to the ABTB.

3.3 Handling Misspeculation

All speculative hardware mechanisms need to ensure that the processor recovers the correct execution state gracefully in case of misspeculation. In most cases, this recovery is expensive, as it requires flushing the pipeline to remove instructions following the misspeculation. In our proposed hardware, misspeculation happens when the result of the BTB doesn't match the result of a matching ABTB entry. There are four possible cases where this can happen:

Conflicts in BTB entries When there are conflicts in the BTB entries, the branch predictor mispredicts and the processor fetches the wrong instructions following the library function call. To recover from such misspeculation, the hardware mechanism described in Section 3.2 fetches instructions from the library function instead of its trampoline. Because the program binary is unmodified, conflicts in BTB are *not* significantly affected by our approach. In fact, skipping trampolines reduces pressure on the BTB, reducing the probability of conflicts occurring in the first place.

GOT entry of library function modified The address of a library function is resolved on the first call to that function from a given module (application or library). It is then stored in the GOT entry for the module corresponding to that function. On the first invocation of a call instruction, the branch predictor cannot predict correctly, so the first call always results in a branch misprediction. Once the function address is resolved and stored in the GOT, it remains unmodified for the life of the program (unless the module is unloaded, which does not occur in practice).

In our hardware, the second invocation of a call instruction to a library function will also mispredict, as the trampoline has never branched to the function before. This is also true in the base system, as the branch predictor can predict the call instruction target (trampoline) correctly, but cannot predict the trampoline target correctly. On subsequent invocations, however, the branch targets are correctly predicted both by the base system and by our proposed hardware. In summary, we do not introduce any branch mispredictions that were not present in the base system.

Missing ABTB entry after a hit in bloom filter As discussed in Section 3.2, all ABTB entries are removed if the address of a store operation hits in the bloom filter. Modification of function addresses after the first invocation is rare, and thus, entries in ABTB stabilize rapidly and do not get cleared in practice. However, when the ABTB is cleared, the system behaves in exactly the same way as a base system without hardware support for dynamic linking, hence incurring exactly the same number of misspeculations.

Missing ABTB entry after context switch In an OS context switch, the processor starts executing a different program having a different virtual to physical address mapping. Addresses in the ABTB are virtual and become invalid after a context switch in the same way that the TLB entries do. If, however, a mechanism is employed to retain TLB entries on a context switch (e.g., using address space IDs), the same mechanism applies to the ABTB, avoiding misspeculation.

3.4 Alternate Implementation

The mechanism we describe introduces no architecturally visible changes to the hardware. If, however, architecturally visible changes can be introduced, the hardware cost of the proposed technique can be reduced by avoiding the bloom filter and requiring the software to explicitly invalidate the ABTB. This process is analogous to architectures that do not enforce coherence between the instruction and data caches, requiring an explicit instruction cache flush when instructions in memory are updated [16].

4 Methodology

To measure the impact of our technique, we conduct experiments on a real system and mimic the behavior of the proposed hardware technique by modifying the dynamic linker software so that it changes the targets of call instructions from the trampoline routines to the function address. Although this approach enables us to measure the effects of the proposed hardware, it is functionally similar to static linking, in that it loses all of the benefits of dynamic linking. Removing or updating a library could result in dangling call instruction targets. Thus, this implementation, which is designed solely for the purpose of evaluation, doesn't support unloading or replacing libraries; on the other hand, the hardware we propose implicitly supports these operations.

4.1 Hardware

Our experiments were conducted on a Dell server with two Intel® Xeon® E5450 [11] CPUs and 32 GB of memory. The CPUs run at 3.0 GHz. L1 and L2 caches are private to each core and a 12MB L3 cache is shared among all cores. To avoid interference during measurement, we bind server and client processes on two different sets of cores.

Table 1. Software Versions

CentOS	6.5 x86-64
Linux Kernel	2.6.32-431.el6.x86_64
glibc	2.12.1
gcc	4.4.7
Intel® Pin®	x86 64 bit, Rev. 65163
Intel® VTune™ XE 2013	Update 17 (build 353306)

4.2 Software

The software configuration is shown in Table 1. We use Intel® VTune™ to measure L1D misses, L1I misses, DTLB misses, ITLB misses, and branch mispredictions.[1] Together, these measurements show how skipping library call trampolines affects the pressure on the various hardware components of the CPU. Performance counters are aggregated across all cores that run the processes under study.

4.3 Experimental Dynamic Linker

Intel® Pin® is used to collect library call information, identifying all library call sites and their corresponding trampoline targets after they are resolved during program execution. When a call instruction followed by an indirection branch instruction is observed, the pintool records the instruction addresses and the branch targets.

We modify the dynamic linker in glibc to support skipping library call trampolines. The modified dynamic linker uses the pintool output to determine the locations of the call sites and patches them directly in the text section. Every recorded "call and indirect branch" sequence is replaced with a call to the corresponding target. To achieve this goal, our modified linker removes application security restrictions by making the entire address space writable. To ensure consistent behavior across the various application runs (with and without the pintool, the base case and the experimental case), we disable address space randomization and use a custom allocator in glibc to load all libraries within the 32-bit reach of the patched call instructions in the original application and library binaries.

4.4 Workloads

We measure the performance of four applications in our experiment; three server applications and one desktop application. For server applications, we measure the Apache web server, Memcached, and MySQL. For the desktop application, we measure the Firefox web browser.

Apache web server We use Apache web server version 2.2.25 with the prefork MPM module. The PHP module is installed

1. The CPU has two performance counter registers. We use two counters per analysis run, one for the instruction count and one for the target metric. Multiplexing all counters within the same analysis run increases interference from VTune, especially when measuring DTLB misses.

as a shared library. To measure the server's performance, we use SPECweb 2009 1.20 [23] as the workload.

To measure performance, we instrument the Apache server to measure the latency of each request type from the arrival of the first packet of a request until the transmission of the last reply packet. To plot a smooth distribution curve of the measured latencies, we run the experiment for 10 hours at close to peak load. For every 10,000 requests, we observe 5 to 6 outlier measurements of significantly longer request latency caused by perturbations in the system (e.g., the performance counter interrupts). The outliers exist in both the base and experimental case and we omit them from the plots for clarity.

Memcached We use Memcached [6] version 1.4.15 with Libevent version 2.0.21. The client and dataset are taken from CloudSuite [4]. Parameters for Memcached are taken from the CloudSuite web site; we use a client with four threads and a target of 100,000 requests per second.

To measure performance, we instrument the Memcached server to measure the latency of the *get* and *set* requests. Due to the short execution duration of the requests, the timestamp counter register (RDTSC [10]) is used to collect timestamps without triggering system calls. We benchmark for one hour to get data for smooth and stable plots.

MySQL We use the TPC-C benchmark from OLTP-Bench [3] to measure the response time of the server for different request types. We present results only for the most popular requests types, *New Order* and *Payment.*

Firefox To measure desktop application performance, we use the official x86-64 Linux Firefox version 30.0 binary [5]. The Peacekeeper [18] browser benchmark suite runs an array of HTML5 and JavaScript performance tests that are representative of typical browser usage. We use the cumulative and individual scores for each test run to evaluate performance improvement with the proposed hardware.

5 Results

We evaluate the performance of an x86-64 processor running our workloads under a dynamic linker that emulates the proposed hardware by patching the binaries in memory to skip trampolines. Results show that our proposed hardware increases overall performance by eliminating the execution of expensive trampoline instructions and reducing pressure on the caches, TLBs, and branch predictor.

5.1 Opportunity

All programs use dynamically linked libraries; however, the extent to which each application depends on libraries is different. For our hardware approach to affect the performance of a program, the number of library function calls must be significant. In Table 2, we show the percentage of executed instructions that lie in a function trampoline. In a complex application like Apache, the number of library calls is much higher than in Memcached, which provides relatively simple functionality. The number of library calls in desktop applications such as Firefox is even lower, as execution is dominated by small computation kernels.

Table 2. Instructions in trampoline per kilo instruction

Workload	Trampoline Instructions (PKI)
Apache	12.23
Firefox	0.72
Memcached	1.75
MySQL	5.56

Table 3 shows the number of distinct trampolines accessed during the measurement period. Apache has a large number of trampolines, exercising many library calls across many libraries. Firefox uses an even larger number of distinct library calls, but they are exercised less frequently. On the other hand, even though Memcached has a higher frequency of library calls, there are only 33 distinct trampolines used, owing to the limited functionality of the server.

Table 3. Number of trampolines used by program execution

Workload	Distinct Trampoline Count
Apache	501
Firefox	2457
Memcached	33
MySQL	1611

We further break down the distinct trampolines by their relative execution frequency in Figure 4. The steep cutoffs visible for Apache and Memcached indicate that a very specific set of library calls was made for every request serviced, whereas the Firefox curve is much less steep, as the program accesses many different libraries to execute the diverse functionality exercised by the benchmark tests. For Memcached, the majority of library calls are made to fewer than 10 library functions.

5.2 Microarchitectural Benefits

In addition to the instructions executed within the library call trampolines, Section 2.2 discusses the additional microarchitectural penalties of dynamic linking. We use performance counters to measure the effect of our technique on the instruction cache, data cache, I-TLB, D-TLB, and branch prediction behavior. The results are presented in Table 4. As expected, the greatest impact on the microarchitecture is observed when running Apache, which makes the largest number of library calls to the largest number of library functions among the three workloads. Cache miss rates, TLB miss rates, and branch mispredictions drop across all workloads when trampolines are skipped. The improvements in Apache are so significant that the second-order performance impact of these microarchitectural

Table 4. Performance counters (values are per kilo instruction)

Performance Counter	Apache		Firefox		Memcached		MySQL	
	Base	Enhanced	Base	Enhanced	Base	Enhanced	Base	Enhanced
I-$ Misses	109.31	104.22	10.70	10.38	51.99	51.42	25.21	24.93
I-TLB Misses	1.78	1.18	0.87	0.79	0.03	0	2.41	2.36
D-$ Misses	7.96	7.56	2.66	2.67	12.25	12.16	8.48	8.46
D-TLB Misses	4.03	4.62	1.54	1.75	4.74	4.73	2.86	2.77
Branch Mispredictions	13.46	12.32	4.84	4.77	5.48	5.30	14.44	14.40

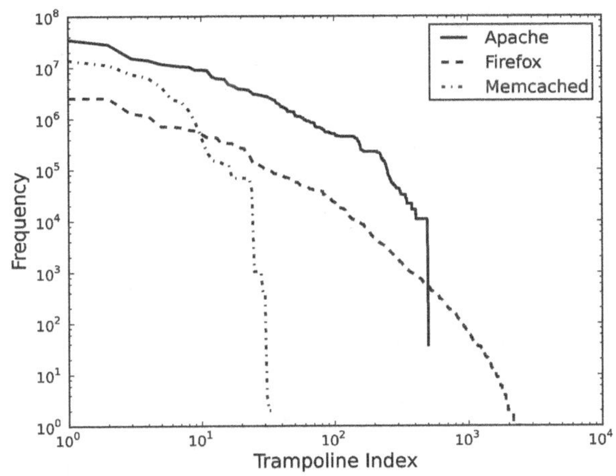

Figure 4. Frequency of trampolines.

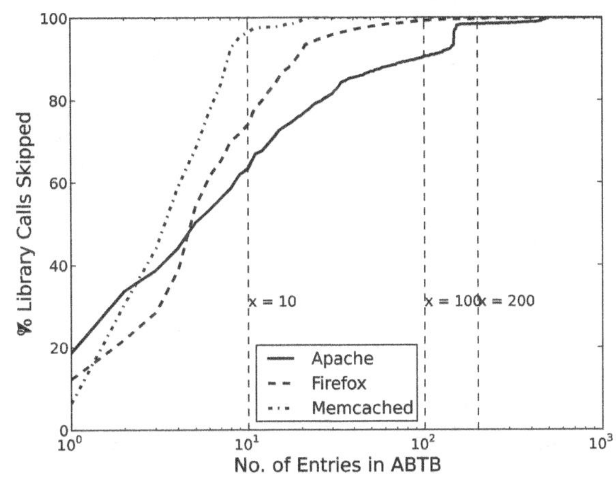

Figure 5. Percentage of library function call trampolines skipped for different sizes of ABTB.

improvements is actually greater than the first-order impact of skipping the trampoline instructions. In Memcached, although there are only a small number of distinct library function calls, skipping the trampolines is sufficient to eliminate all I-TLB conflict misses.

5.3 Hardware Cost

Every microarchitectural enhancement must be judged by the tradeoff between its benefit and its cost. Our experiments demonstrate the benefits of the proposed hardware support for dynamic linking, in terms of reducing the number of executed instructions and alleviating microarchitectural pressure. We now estimate the size of the ABTB needed to achieve these benefits.

Every entry in the ABTB consumes 12 bytes, six bytes for the call instruction's target and six bytes for the function address.[2] To estimate the required size of ABTB, we collect traces of our workloads and count the number of library call trampolines that can be skipped for different ABTB sizes. Figure 5 shows the distribution (number of entries in log scale) of the percentage of library call trampolines skipped for different sizes of the ABTB. We see that with just 16 entries (192 bytes), we can skip more than 75% of the trampolines in any of the three workloads. With a 256-entry ABTB, totaling less than 1.5KB, nearly all actively used trampolines can be skipped.[3]

Figure 5 provides an interesting additional insight into the instruction patterns of the workloads. A steep slope in the plot indicates that there is a repeating sequence of library functions that are called frequently. A small ABTB can skip all trampolines within that repeating sequence, as long as it is large enough to cover the full sequence. This implies the existence of ABTB "working sets" that can be used to reason about application behavior.

5.4 Performance

In Figure 6, we present the cumulative distribution function (CDF) of the percentage of requests served as a function of the response time for each request type in the SPECweb 2009 workload. We measure the response time of the server in microseconds; the CDF shows the fraction of requests served within the particular response time. When the Apache server runs without executing the trampolines (enhanced), the tail latencies are unaffected while the average response times are improved up to 4% over the base case.

2. x86-64 supports distinct virtual addresses up to 48 bits.

3. We do not consider additional savings made possible by offset encoding.

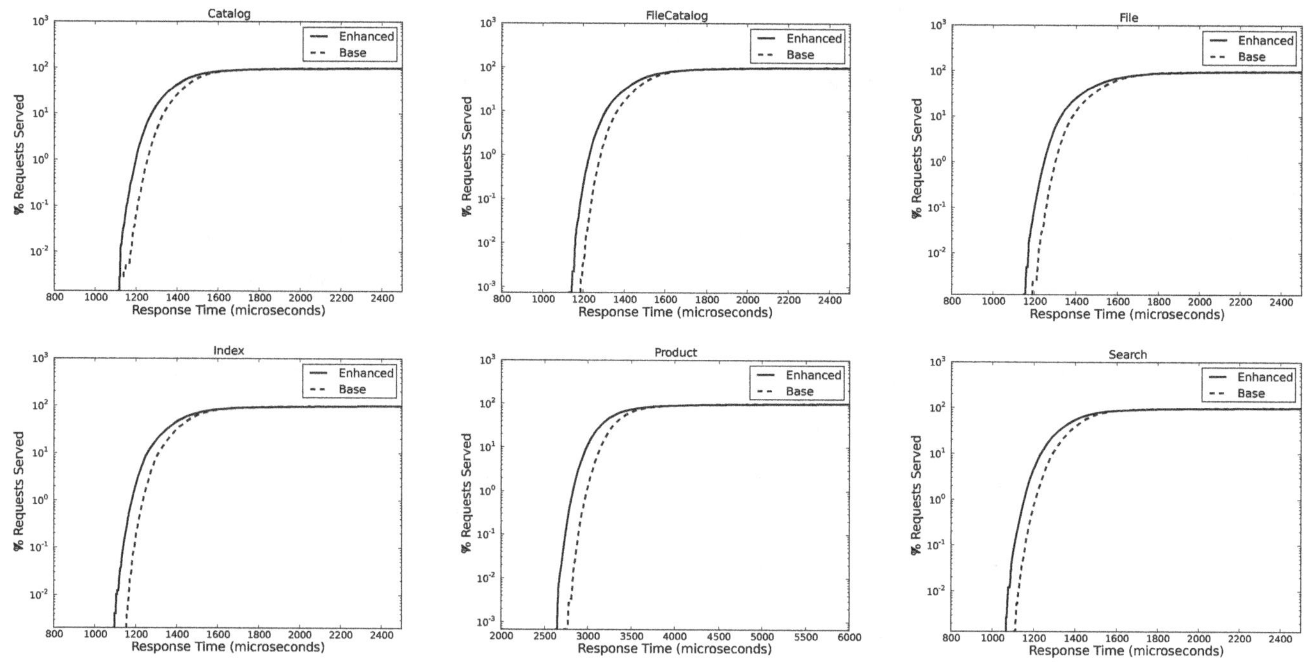

Figure 6. Cumulative distribution of the percentage of Apache requests served within the specified response time.

Table 5. Firefox Peacekeeper scores (higher is better)

Workload	Base	Enhanced
Rendering (fps)	49.31	50.64
HTML5 Canvas (fps)	37.47	37.94
Data (ops)	22,499	22,727
DOM operations (ops)	16,547	16,850
Text parsing (ops)	214,897	216,625

Table 5 presents Firefox web browser performance scores (higher is better). Performance improved for all workload categories included in the Peacekeeper benchmark. In rendering and DOM operations, the main tasks performed by web browsers in normal operation, we observed improvements of more than 2.7% and 1.8%, respectively. Text parsing performance improved by 0.8% due to the heavy use of string operations from shared libraries.

Figure 7 presents the performance improvement for Memcached under the proposed hardware technique. The two plots show histograms of request processing time for the Memcached GET and SET requests. Because the service experiences a wide range of request latencies, we plot the buckets within the largest peak, which accounts for the majority of requests (we omit other minor peaks for clarity, as they follow similar trends). For both request types, the peaks of the histograms for the enhanced version (skipping the trampolines) are shifted to the left, indicating an average reduction in request processing time.

Figure 8 shows the CDF of requests served vs. response time of the requests for MySQL. This data is summarized in

Table 6. Response Time of MySQL Requests in milliseconds (lower is better)

Requests	New Order		Payment	
	Base	**Enhanced**	**Base**	**Enhanced**
50%	43.5	43.0	17.9	17.7
75%	57.3	56.9	27.9	27.2
90%	72.8	72.3	37.2	35.9
95%	87.1	86.8	44.4	43.0

Table 6, which demonstrates that more time is required to serve a given percentage of requests in the base system than in the enhanced system.

5.5 Memory Savings

Multithreaded server software shares code pages across threads, allowing a software approach to patch the call instructions in shared pages with target addresses (in our test suite, Firefox, Memcached, and MySQL fall into this category). However, many server applications use the *prefork* model to serve requests. For example, the main Apache web server spawns child processes to handle requests, but does not itself perform any request processing. A software approach to patching code pages for prefork software precludes the OS copy-on-write mechanism, increasing memory consumption. Our hardware solution has no memory overheads in the prefork case, allowing code pages to remain unmodified and shared across processes.

If call site patching is applied to all processes in a system, the patched code pages in all libraries would be copied to each running process, resulting in memory overhead that

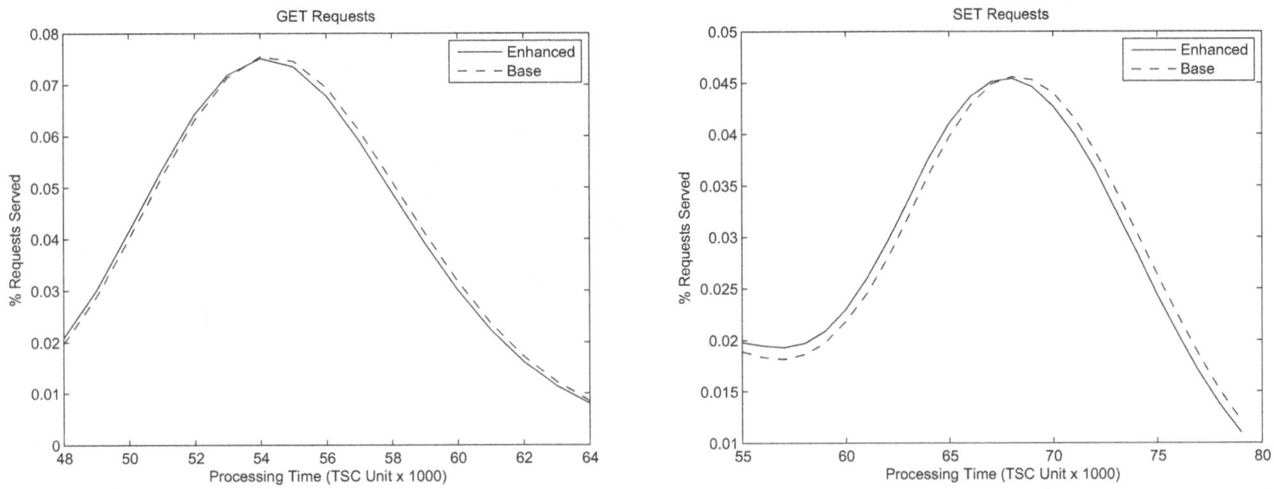

Figure 7. Histogram of Memcached requests served for a given request processing time.

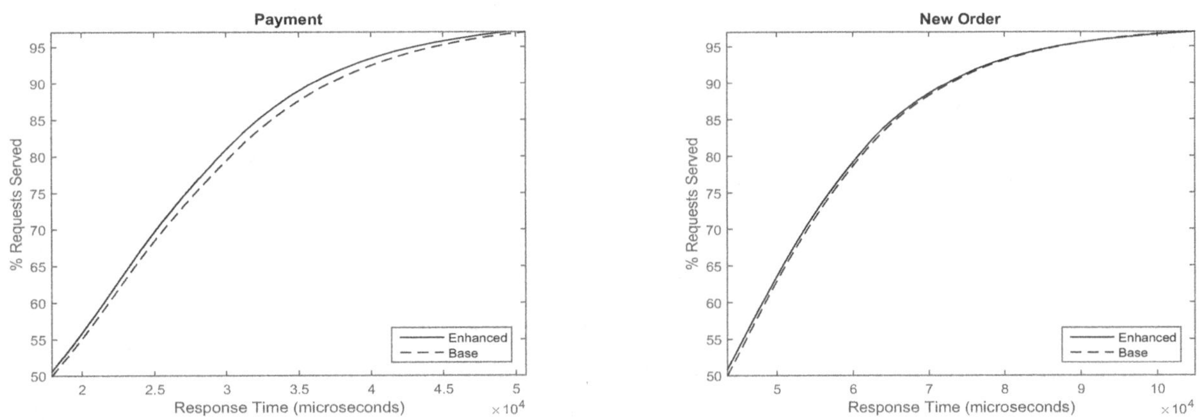

Figure 8. CDF of MySQL requests served within the specified response time.

can easily exceed multiple gigabytes. Even if patching is only applied to processes of the server application, significant overhead can still occur. For example, busy Apache servers have hundreds or even thousands of processes running concurrently. With dynamic patching (Apache binary, PHP, and supporting libraries) on the first invocation of each library call, approximately 280 code pages will be copied, resulting in 1.1MB of wasted memory for each process, or on the order of 0.5GB of RAM for a typical busy server.

6 Related Work

Sodani and Sohi proposed an instruction reuse technique to improve application performance by skipping the execution of instructions that repeat their work [22]. In their technique, a buffer stores the results of instructions indexed by the inputs of the instruction and its PC. During instruction fetch, inputs of an instruction are used in a lookup, skipping execution if a previous result is found. In a modern out-of-order processor, there can be more than 100 instructions in flight and the inputs of the fetched instruction are unavailable. Moreover, reading values from memory is expensive and is therefore not done by this technique. Thus, this approach cannot be used to skip dynamically linked library trampolines. Even if it is modified to consider memory inputs, simply fetching the trampoline instructions and performing the memory lookup would lose most of the microarchitectural benefits of the hardware we propose.

Huang and Lilja propose a hardware memoization technique that records the results of basic blocks and reuses entire blocks [8]. To store results, an entry needs to be large, supporting storage of multiple inputs and outputs. Library call trampolines are small basic blocks (one instruction on x86-64), making this technique excessively expensive for the benefits achieved. Moreover, both memoization techniques lie on the critical path of the instruction fetch and may impact the system's clock frequency [12], whereas the hardware support for dynamic linking that we propose operates primarily at retire time, off the critical path.

Kistler and Franz propose continuous optimization of programs using profile-guided optimization [14]. They propose load-time optimization to make use of as much information about the system as possible. Profiling helps restructure code and data in memory to increase the likelihood of cache hits. This approach can benefit dynamic linking by collocating frequently used PLT and GOT entries close to each other to reduce their footprint in the caches and TLBs. However, it does not reduce the number of instructions executed or the number of branch predictor and target buffer entries used, as the trampoline instructions must still be fetched and executed.

7 Conclusions

Although static linking yields higher performance, dynamic linking has become the predominant choice for integrating libraries into today's complex applications, due to its myriad benefits, from flexibility in development and deployment, to memory conservation across processes and system security. The software community has embraced dynamic linking, largely ignoring the costs that arise from the use of trampolines that perform function pointer table lookups and execute additional indirect branches.

In this work, we showed that a simple hardware mechanism, working in tandem with existing branch predictor structures, can improve performance by speculatively skipping trampoline execution. The mechanism relies on the fact that the lookup result and indirect branch target of the trampoline do not change after their first invocation. We evaluated our proposed hardware technique by emulating the behavior of the hardware on a real system, demonstrating that using only 1.5KB of storage, a retire-time (off critical path) mechanism can eliminate the overheads of dynamic linking, reducing instruction cache, data cache, I-TLB, D-TLB, BTB, and branch predictor pressure to achieve performance improvements of up to 4%.

8 References

[1] Burton H. Bloom. Space/time trade-offs in hash coding with allowable errors. *Commun. ACM*, 13(7):422–426, July 1970.

[2] Willem De Groef, Nick Nikiforakis, Yves Younan, and Frank Piessens. Jitsec: Just-in-time security for code injection attacks. In *Benelux Workshop on Information and System Security (WISSEC)*, 2010.

[3] Djellel Eddine Difallah, Andrew Pavlo, Carlo Curino, and Philippe Cudré-Mauroux. Oltp-bench: An extensible testbed for benchmarking relational databases. *PVLDB*, 7(4):277–288, 2013.

[4] Michael Ferdman, Almutaz Adileh, Onur Kocberber, Stavros Volos, Mohammad Alisafaee, Djordje Jevdjic, Cansu Kaynak, Adrian Daniel Popescu, Anastasia Ailamaki, and Babak Falsafi. Clearing the Clouds: A Study of Emerging Scale-out Workloads on Modern Hardware. In *17th International Conference on Architectural Support for Programming Languages and Operating Systems (ASPLOS)*, 2012. recognized as Best Paper by the program committee and recognized as Top Pick of 2013 by IEEE Micro.

[5] Firefox. https://www.mozilla.org/en-US/firefox/new/.

[6] Brad Fitzpatrick. Distributed caching with memcached. *Linux J.*, 2004(124):5–, August 2004.

[7] Michael Franz. Dynamic linking of software components. *Computer*, 30(3):74–81, March 1997.

[8] Jian Huang and David Lilja. Exploiting basic block value locality with block reuse. In *Proceedings of the 5th International Symposium on High Performance Computer Architecture*, HPCA '99, pages 106–, Washington, DC, USA, 1999. IEEE Computer Society.

[9] Intel Corporation. *extregistered 64 and IA-32 Architectures Optimization Reference Manual*. Intel, March 2009.

[10] Intel Corporation. *extregistered 64 and IA-32 Architectures Software Developer's Manual*. Intel, December 2009.

[11] Intel Xeon Processor E5450 (12M Cache, 3.00 GHz, 1333 MHz FSB). http://ark.intel.com/products/33083/Intel-Xeon-Processor-E5450-12M-Cache-3_00-GHz-1333-MHz-FSB.

[12] Daniel A. Jiménez. Reconsidering complex branch predictors. In *Proceedings of the 9th International Symposium on High-Performance Computer Architecture*, HPCA '03, pages 43–, Washington, DC, USA, 2003. IEEE Computer Society.

[13] Hyesoon Kim, José A. Joao, Onur Mutlu, Chang Joo Lee, Yale N. Patt, and Robert Cohn. Vpc prediction: Reducing the cost of indirect branches via hardware-based dynamic devirtualization. In *Proceedings of the 34th Annual International Symposium on Computer Architecture*, ISCA '07, pages 424–435, New York, NY, USA, 2007. ACM.

[14] Thomas Kistler and Michael Franz. Continuous program optimization: A case study. *ACM Trans. Program. Lang. Syst.*, 25(4):500–548, July 2003.

[15] Pierre Michaud, AndréSeznec, and Richard Uhlig. Trading conflict and capacity aliasing in conditional branch predictors. In *Proceedings of the 24th Annual International Symposium on Computer Architecture*, ISCA '97, pages 292–303, New York, NY, USA, 1997. ACM.

[16] S. Owicki and A. Agarwal. Evaluating the performance of software cache coherence. In *Proceedings of the Third International Conference on Architectural Support for Programming Languages and Operating Systems*, ASPLOS III, pages 230–242, New York, NY, USA, 1989. ACM.

[17] David A. Padua and Michael J. Wolfe. Advanced compiler optimizations for supercomputers. *Commun. ACM*, 29(12):1184–1201, December 1986.

[18] Peacekeeper - The universal Browser Test. http://peacekeeper.futuremark.com/.

[19] Donald E. Porter, Silas Boyd-Wickizer, Jon Howell, Reuben Olinsky, and Galen C. Hunt. Rethinking the library os from the top down. In *Proceedings of the Sixteenth International Conference on Architectural Support for Programming Languages and Operating Systems*, ASPLOS XVI, pages 291–304, New York, NY, USA, 2011. ACM.

[20] Parthasarathy Ranganathan, Kourosh Gharachorloo, Sarita V Adve, and Luiz Andre Barroso. Performance of database workloads on shared-memory systems with out-of-order processors. In *Proceedings of the 8th International Conference on Architectural Support for Programming Languages and Operating Systems*, October 1998.

[21] Hovav Shacham, Matthew Page, Ben Pfaff, Eu-Jin Goh, Nagendra Modadugu, and Dan Boneh. On the effectiveness of address-space randomization. In *Proceedings of the 11th ACM Conference on Computer and Communications Security*, CCS '04, pages 298–307, New York, NY, USA, 2004. ACM.

[22] Avinash Sodani and Gurindar S. Sohi. Dynamic instruction reuse. In *Proceedings of the 24th Annual International Symposium on Computer Architecture*, ISCA '97, pages 194–205, New York, NY, USA, 1997. ACM.

[23] SPEC - Standard Performance Evaluation Corporation. http://www.spec.org/.

[24] Tse-Yu Yeh and Yale N. Patt. Two-level adaptive training branch prediction. In *Proceedings of the 24th Annual International Symposium on Microarchitecture*, MICRO 24, pages 51–61, New York, NY, USA, 1991. ACM.

Author Index

www.ingramcontent.com/pod-product-compliance
Lightning Source LLC
LaVergne TN
LVHW080110011026
849160LV00013B/1061